The Bedford Anthology of
World Literature
The Modern World,
1650–The Present

Volume 2

Compact Edition

The Bedford Anthology of
World Literature

The Modern World,
1650–The Present

EDITED BY

Paul Davis
Gary Harrison
David M. Johnson
John F. Crawford

THE UNIVERSITY OF NEW MEXICO

BEDFORD / ST. MARTIN'S

Boston ◆ New York

For Bedford/St. Martin's

Developmental Editor: Caroline Thompson
Production Editor: Karen Stocz
Senior Production Supervisor: Nancy Myers
Marketing Manager: Adrienne Petsick
Editorial Assistant: Marisa Feinstein
Text Design: Anna Palchik and Jean Hammond
Cover Design: Donna Lee Dennison
Cover Art: Archibald J. Motley Jr., *Blues,* 1929, Chicago History Museum
Composition: TexTech International
Printing and Binding: Quebecor World Taunton

President: Joan E. Feinberg
Editorial Director: Denise B. Wydra
Editor in Chief: Karen S. Henry
Director of Marketing: Karen R. Soeltz
Director of Editing, Design, and Production: Marcia Cohen
Assistant Director of Editing, Design, and Production: Elise S. Kaiser
Managing Editor: Elizabeth M. Schaaf

Library of Congress Control Number: 2008925872

Manufactured in the United States of America.

3   2   1   0   9   8
f   e   d   c   b   a

For information, write: Bedford/St. Martin's, 75 Arlington Street, Boston, MA 02116
(617-399-4000)

ISBN-10: 0–312–44154–1
ISBN-13: 978–0–312–44154–8

Acknowledgments

Abé Kobo, "The Red Cocoon," translated by Lane Dunlop from *Late Chrysanthemum: 21 Stories from the Japanese* (San Francisco: North Point Press, 1986). Copyright © 1986 by Lane Dunlop. Reprinted with the permission of the translator.

Acknowledgments and copyrights are continued at the back of the book on pages 1819–22, which constitute an extension of the copyright page. It is a violation of the law to reproduce these selections by any means whatsoever without the written permission of the copyright holder.

PREFACE

๛ Our thinking about teaching world literature goes back to 1985, when we received a grant from the National Endowment of the Humanities to develop and team teach a new kind of course—one that integrated the rich literary traditions of Asia, India, the Arabic world, the Americas, and Europe. As year-long courses in world literature became more widely taught in the United States, and as the number and range of texts taught in these courses greatly increased, we developed *The Bedford Anthology of World Literature*, a six-volume collection designed to meet the challenges of taking—and teaching—the world literature course.

Now we have streamlined *The Bedford Anthology of World Literature* to address the need for a two-volume edition that can be used in both one- and two-semester courses. Basing our choices on reviews, expert advice, and our ongoing classroom experience, we provide a substantial and carefully balanced selection of Western and non-Western texts chronologically arranged in a compact, teachable format. We give special emphasis to the works most commonly taught in the survey course. By linking them to clusters of texts that represent themes that recur and resonate across cultures, we provide options for drawing connections among works and across traditions. A distinctive variety of pedagogical features gives students the help they need to understand individual works of literature, while extensive historical and background materials help them place the works in context. Throughout, a uniquely extensive illustration program brings the pedagogy into focus, and the literature and contextual materials to life.

AN ENTIRE WORLD OF LITERATURE

The Compact Edition offers **twenty-seven complete longer works with additional fiction, drama, poetry, letters, and essays** in the best available editions and translations. Complete works include Homer's *The Odyssey,* Sophocles' *Antigone, Beowulf,* Dante's *The Inferno,* and Shakespeare's *The Tempest* in Volume One; Molière's *Tartuffe,* Voltaire's *Candide,* Conrad's *Heart of Darkness,* Kafka's *The Metamorphosis,* and Achebe's *Things Fall Apart* in Volume Two. Even as we have reduced the number of texts for the two-volume format, we have nonetheless added some new works in order to respond to the ongoing revaluation and expansion of the canon as well as to better meet the pedagogical ends of world literature courses as they are being taught today. Among the additions to Volume One are new poems from Sappho and new excerpts from *The Aeneid,* Plato's *Republic,* Boethius's *The Consolation of Philosophy,* and Sir Thomas More's *Utopia.* In Volume Two we have added works including Immanuel Kant's "What is Enlightenment," selections from Frederick Douglass's *Narrative of the Life of Frederick Douglass,* and new poems by Friedrich Hölderlin, Alphonse Lamartine, and Rosalía de Castro; also, Guy du Maupassant's "Regret," Henrik Ibsen's *A Doll's House,* Jawaharlal Nehru's "Speech on the Granting of Indian Independence," and excerpts from André Breton's *The Surrealist Manifesto.*

In addition to a broad selection of literature, we provide **a variety of help for understanding the readings**. Our thorough, informative, and readable introductions and headnotes provide biographical and literary background for each author and text. Generous footnotes, marginal notes, critical quotations, and cross-references help students navigate this wealth of information. Phonetic pronunciation guides help with unfamiliar author, character, and place names. For help with literary and historical vocabulary, key terms throughout the text refer students to a comprehensive glossary at the end of each volume. Further Research bibliographies following headnotes and introductions list sources for students who want to read more critical, biographical, or historical information about an author or work.

Each volume is divided into two parts to avoid organizing literary history within a European period frame.

Osman Hamdy Bey, Excavation at Nippur, 1903
Mesopotamian cities were among the earliest urban centers in antiquity. With the invention of writing in Egypt and Mesopotamia sometime around 3300 B.C.E., rulers were able to oversee larger and larger administrative areas. One of the earliest uses of writing was in keeping track of the practical and myriad details of government, from taxes and birth and death records to business transactions. This extremely realistic painting shows the early twentieth-century excavation at Nippur, a major Mesopotamian city. (University of Pennsylvania Museum [Negative #58-6807])

The Ancient World

Beginnings - 100 C.E.

CHRONOLOGICAL STRUCTURE AND TEACHABLE ORGANIZATION

When we take into account the literary histories of Japan, China, India, the Arabic and Muslim world, Africa, and the Americas, a structure based upon traditional European periods, such as medieval and Renaissance, Enlightenment and Romanticism, becomes highly problematic. The literatures within the world's traditions developed within their own unique historical and cultural trajectories, and it is not really until the twentieth century—and even then not without caution—that we can speak of a modernism or postmodernism that reaches across the world's many borders. In light of these issues, we have arranged our texts chronologically throughout both volumes, while providing historical and cultural contexts in our general introductions and headnotes. We use a four-period model, dividing each volume into two parts, as follows.

The first part of Volume One focuses upon the ancient world, from the beginnings of literature to about 100 c.e., the second upon the medieval and Early Modern World through about 1650. Two **general introductions**, one for each part, provide historical and cultural contexts for the various literatures and traditions represented in the volume. We chose to end Volume One with the mid seventeenth-century because it marks that crucial moment when the histories of various regions and

Comparative timelines in each general introduction list what happened, where, and when in three overarching categories: history and politics; literature; and science, culture, and technology.

*B*ungling Doctor Faust's order to dispossess an aging rustic couple from their picturesque cottage in a linden grove, the devil Mephistopheles and his crew set fire to the place. In the ensuing inferno the innocent pair, Philemon and Baucis, their cottage, and their chapel—all signs of a vanishing agricultural world—are lost. A warden who has witnessed the fire from his tower encapsulates what it all means: "What once was a joy to see / After centuries is gone." In this scene from *Faust*, Part 2, the German writer Johann Wolfgang von Goethe characterizes the onset of modernity in Europe as the catastrophic collapse of an agrarian world cemented by feudal social ties and religious bonds. While that simple world was always something of an ideal, it is undeniable that accelerating socio-economic changes sweeping Europe in the period from 1650 to 1850 led to a transfer of power from a landed gentry to a commercial and manufacturing class whose center was the city, not the country. The forces of secularization, urbanization, and commercialization that promoted and accompanied

these changes—and which are still at work today—extended their transformative reach to other areas of the world, such as India, Africa, and the Americas, and led to new ways of thinking and feeling, new forms of art and literature, and new means of producing and disseminating printed materials, including literary works.

The eighteenth century is the last century of what historians call the Early Modern Period, extending from about 1500 to 1800, although sometimes extended fifty years in either direction. While historians of Europe usually emphasize a break between the eighteenth and nineteenth centuries, we must acknowledge that intellectual, cultural, and political transformations in Europe, much less the world, do not conveniently observe the temporal markers of the Roman calendar. Writers who exerted a profound influence upon the Enlightenment, for example, such as René Descartes (1596–1650), Jean-Baptiste Poquelin Molière (1622–1673), John Locke (1632–1704), and Isaac Newton (1642–1727), published their major works closer to 1650. Moreover, in Europe, the eighteenth century—typically described

COMPARATIVE TIMELINE FOR 1650–1850

Date	History and Politics	Literature	Science, Culture, and Technology
1650–1659	1641 Dutch begin trade with Japan.		
	1652 Dutch colonists found Cape Town in South Africa.		
	1657 Great Fire destroys Edo, Japan.		
	1658 Aurangzeb succeeds Shah Jahan as Mughal emperor in India.		
1660–1669	1660 Charles II; Restoration of Stuart monarchy in England		1660 Royal Society founded in London.
	1662 Kangxi (second emperor of Manchu dynasty) begins reign in China.	1664 Molière, *Tartuffe*	
	1666 Great Fire of London		1688 Margaret Cavendish, *The Grounds of Natural Philosophy*
	1669 Hinduism outlawed by Mughals in India; many Hindu temples destroyed.		
1670–1679		1670s Çelebi writes *Book of Travels*	
	1675–76 King Philip's War between American settlers and the Wampanoag		
	1675–78 Sikh rebellion against Mughal empire in India		
1680–1689	1680 Tsunayoshi becomes shogun in Japan. Ashanti (Asante) Kingdom founded in West Africa. Pueblo Revolt in New Mexico drives out Spanish.		1680 Anton van Leeuwenhoek discovers bacteria.

Date	History and Politics	Literature	Science, Culture, and Technology
1680–1689 (cont.)	1685 Louis XIV revokes Edict of Nantes; absolute monarchy in France. Kangxi opens Chinese ports to foreigners.		
			1687 Newton, *Mathematical Principles*
	1688 Glorious Revolution in England (James II deposed; William and Mary crowned)		1688 Genroku period in Japan; beginnings of kabuki theater
1690–1699			1690 Locke, *Two Treatises on Government* and *Essay Concerning Human Understanding*
		1691 Sor Juana, *Reply to Sor Filotea*	
1700–1709	1701–14 War of the Spanish Succession		
	1703 Peter I founds St. Petersburg in Russia.	1702 Bashō, *Narrow Road through the Backcountry*	1702 First daily newspaper published in London.
			1704 Newton, *Opticks*
	1707 Death of Mughal emperor Aurangzeb accelerates decline of Mughal empire in India.		1706 Excavations of Pompeii and Herculaneum begin.
	1709 Ienobu new shogun in Japan		1709 Invention of the piano

empires became the history of the world. While considerable contact among civilizations took place in the ancient world and medieval period, the oceanic voyages of developing European nation states in the fifteenth through the seventeenth centuries vastly expanded the networks of intercultural contact, commerce, and confrontation. We believe that Shakespeare's *The Tempest* serves as the best hinge upon which to hang the change of volumes, because the play thematizes the shift to a global history, announcing the end of an era even as it inaugurates an inquiry into the vexing contradictions of the brave new world of increasing globalization that will resound through the works we find throughout the second volume.

Volume Two similarly divides into two parts with their own general introductions, the first focusing upon the period from about 1650 to 1850, the second from 1850 to the present. Volume Two begins with Molière's *Tartuffe,* Pu Song-Ling's "The Mural," and Bashō's *Narrow Road through the Backcountry.* These late seventeenth-century works point in their distinctive ways and in their particular contexts to the early modernity of France, China, and Japan, and arise in periods of social, economic, and cultural transformation that will accelerate through the eighteenth, nineteenth, and twentieth centuries.

TEXTS IN CONTEXT

Within the overall chronological framework of this anthology, we have grouped certain selections to give teachers a flexible means of helping students make connections with unfamiliar and diverse texts. Based on our research and the advice of our reviewers, we have chosen twenty of the most commonly taught texts as **"Text in Context"** works and used them to anchor **"In the World"** sections — literary clusters that vastly expand the sampling of texts and the possibilities for dialogue between various countries and their cultural traditions.

Each "Text in Context" work is accompanied by additional illustrations or maps and is linked to an "In the World" section that groups various writings written around the world at about the same time on a related theme. Thus, ancient texts on the theme of "Heroes and Adventure" are linked to Homer's *The Odyssey;* medieval writings on "Courts and Codes of Rule" accompany Murasaki Shikibu's *The Tale of Genji;* and twentieth-century texts on themes of "War, Conflict, and Resistance" are related to T. S. Eliot's *The Waste Land.* "In the World" clusters emphasize social and historical contexts, helping students understand that the people across historical, cultural, and national divides have sought in similar but distinct ways to imagine and praise their gods, to codify their laws, to commemorate and celebrate their heroes and heroines, to come to terms with their political and social revolutions, and to articulate and grasp the meaning and complexity of their private loves, lives, and losses. We have kept the "In the World" sections distinct from the "Text in Context" works to provide more flexibility for teachers — key texts can be taught with related clusters or by themselves.

A second type of cluster that we call **"In the Tradition"** traces specific poetic traditions within and across cultures in order to highlight the development and

Each Text in Context *work is linked to an* In the World *section, a cluster of writings on a related theme that were written around the world near the time of the* Text in Context *work.*

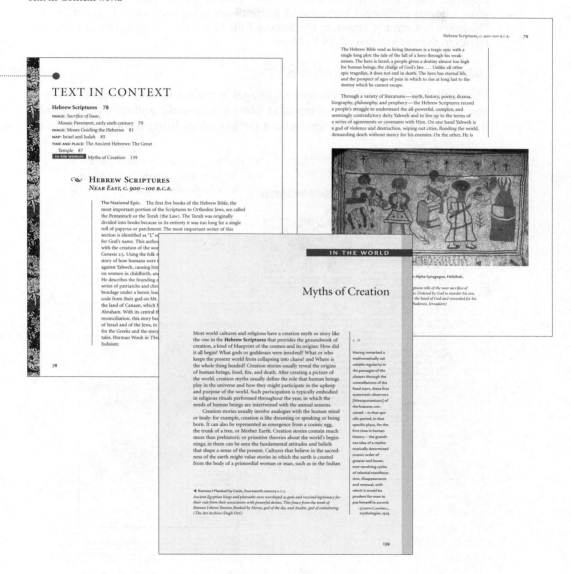

diversity of certain genres and forms. We include three of these "In the Tradition" sections in this edition: "Poets of the Tang Dynasty," "Andalusian and European Love Lyrics," and "The Romantic Lyric." These clusters help students imagine a conversation among a variety of writers around similar ideas and forms.

"Time and Place" boxes further orient students in the era and culture connected with the literature they're reading or help make thematic connections among events from different times and places. Thus, "Ancient Greece: The Origins of Greek Drama" gives students additional background for understanding the work of Sophocles, and "Nineteenth-Century America: The Seneca Falls Conference" highlights an event that relates to themes in Ibsen's *A Doll's House*.

UNPARALLELED VISUAL FEATURES

The anthology's superb collection of images is meant to help students relate to and understand literature that might at first seem spatially and temporally remote from their experience. **Maps** throughout the anthology bring students closer to the

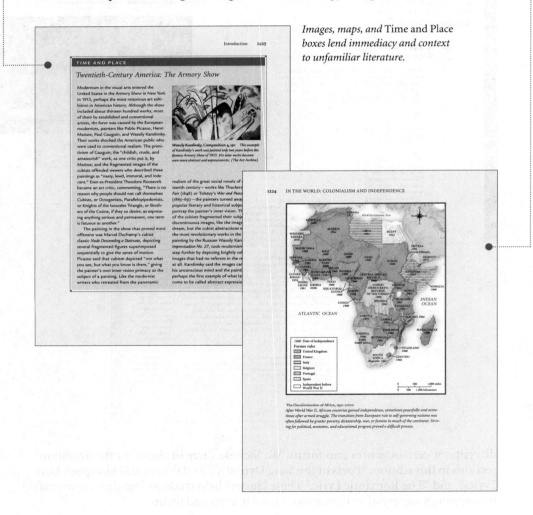

Images, maps, and Time and Place *boxes lend immediacy and context to unfamiliar literature.*

regions various literatures have come from, illustrating shifting national boundaries, industrial growth, the effects of conquest and colonialism, and the travels of Odysseus, Candide, Bashō, and Olaudah Equiano. **Illustrations**—art, photographs, cartoons, and cultural artifacts—offer perspectives on the context of literary works and their present-day relevance. Medieval images of Roland in the architecture of the Chartres Cathedral, twentieth-century performances of Shakespeare's *The Tempest* and Ibsen's *A Doll's House*, the ad Harriet Jacobs's owner ran for her capture and return, and a nineteenth-century Nigerian sculpture of a European missionary are just a few examples.

PRINT AND ONLINE ANCILLARIES

The instructor's manual, *Resources for Teaching* THE BEDFORD ANTHOLOGY OF WORLD LITERATURE, Compact Edition, provides additional information about the anthology's texts and authors; suggestions for discussion, research, and writing, both in the classroom and beyond; and suggestions for drawing additional connections among the various texts in the anthology. Lists of related print and media resources for each selection are also included. The manual concludes with advice for developing a world literature syllabus and sample syllabi.

Students using the free companion site at **bedfordstmartins.com/worldlit compact** will find additional historical background, quizzes, annotated research links, additional information about particular authors, and discussions of the enduring twenty-first century relevance of particular works. Web links throughout the anthology direct students to additional content on the free companion site.

Award-winning trade titles are available for packaging at significant savings. Add more value and choice to your students' learning experiences by packaging *The Bedford Anthology of World Literature*, Compact Edition, with any of a thousand titles from Farrar, Straus and Giroux; Picador; St. Martin's Press; and other Macmillan trade publishers—at discounts of up to 50 percent off the regular price. To learn more, contact your local Bedford/St. Martin's sales representative. To see a complete list of titles available for packaging, go to bedfordstmartins.com/tradeup.

The broad spectrum of literary texts, practical and accessible editorial apparatus, and teachable organization of the anthology offer teachers and students choices for navigating the familiar and unfamiliar territories of world literature. For some students, the excitement of discovery will lie in the exotic details of a foreign setting or in the music of a declaration of love, while others will delight in the broad panorama of history they construct when reading a variety of works from different traditions written around the same time. Others may find the contrast between cultures or historical eras to be the defining moment of discovery. Any number of possibilities exist for our students as they come into imaginative and critical contact with the people, places, and worlds that exist between the covers of *The Bedford Anthology of World Literature*, Compact Edition.

ACKNOWLEDGMENTS

This anthology and its predecessors began in a team-taught, multicultural "great books" course at the University of New Mexico, initially developed with a grant from the National Endowment for the Humanities. The grant gave us ample time to generate the curriculum for the course, and it also supported the luxury and challenge of team teaching. This anthology reflects the discussions of texts and teaching strategies that took place over many years among ourselves and colleagues who have participated with us in teaching the course—Cheryl Fresch, Virginia Hampton, Mary Rooks, Claire Waters, Richard K. Waters, Mary Bess Whidden, and most recently Feroza Jussawalla, Ron Shumaker, Birgit Schmidt-Rosemann, and Robin Runia. We especially want to thank our cherished colleague, co-teacher, and co-editor Patricia Clark Smith, whose creativity, camaraderie, and command of the world's literatures and languages are felt throughout these pages. Without her generous spirit and laughter, her insight and vision, her dedication to our students, and her love of life and teaching this anthology would not be what it is today. We also acknowledge Joseph B. Zavadil, who began our first anthology with us but died in the early stages of its development. Joe's wit, scholarship, and humanity also endures with us. Above all, we must thank the hundreds of students in our world literature classes over the last twenty years at the University of New Mexico. From their questions, challenges, suggestions, and ideas—and from their patience and curiosity—we have fashioned not only an anthology but a way of teaching world literature as a conversation in context—a way of teaching that we share here with our readers.

Reviewers from many colleges and universities helped shape the six books of *The Bedford Anthology of World Literature* (2004) with their advice and suggestions. We thank in particular a special group of reviewers who looked in depth at the manuscript for each of the six books, offering us targeted advice about the anthology's strengths and weaknesses:

Cora Agatucci, Central Oregon Community College; Michael Austin, Shepherd College; Maryam Barrie, Washtenaw Community College; John Bartle, Hamilton College; Jeffry Berry, Adrian College; Lois Bragg, Gallaudet University; Ron Carter, Rappahannock Community College; Robin Clouser, Ursinus College; Eugene R. Cunnar, New Mexico State University; Karen Dahr, Ellsworth Community College; Kristine Daines, Arizona State University; Sarah Dangelantonio, Franklin Pierce College; Jim Doan, Nova SE University; Melora Giardetti, Simpson College; Audley Hall, North West Arkansas Community College; Dean Hall, Kansas State University; Joris Heise, Sinclair Community College; Diane Long Hoeveler, Marquette University; Glenn Hopp, Howard Payne University; Mickey Jackson, Golden West College; Feroza Jussawalla, University of New Mexico; Linda Karch, Norwich University; David Karnos, Montana State University; William Laskowski, Jamestown College; Pat Lonchar, University of the Incarnate Word; Donald Mager, The Mott University; Judy B. McInnis, University of Delaware; Becky McLaughlin, University of South Alabama; Tony J. Morris, University of Indianapolis; Deborah Schlacks, University of Wisconsin; James Snowden, Cedarville University; David T. Stout, Luzerne

County Community College; Arline Thorn, West Virginia State College; Ann Volin, University of Kansas; Mary Wack, Washington State University; Jayne A. Widmayer, Boise State University; and William Woods, Wichita State University.

We are grateful to the perceptive instructors—more than two hundred of them—who responded to our questionnaire in the early stages of planning the Compact Edition. These teachers shared valuable information with us about their courses, their students, and what they wanted in a world literature anthology:

Allison Adair, Boston University; Kristelle Aherne, Masconomet High School; Donald Alban, Liberty University; William Allegrezza, Indiana University Northwest; Maurice Amen, Holy Cross College; Dustin Anderson, Florida State University; Janet Anderson, Clackamas Community College; Robert Anderson, Oakland University; Helen Andretta, York College–CUNY; Kit Andrews, Western Oregon University; Lauryn Angel-Cann, University of North Texas; Gabriel Arquilevich, Ventura College; Melvin Arrington, University of Mississippi; Clinton Atchley, Henderson State University; Carolyn Ayers, St. Mary's University of Minnesota; Alison Baker, California Polytechnic State University–Pomona; Anne Baker, North Carolina State University; Christopher Baker, Armstrong Atlantic State University; Kimberly Baker, Illinois Institute of Art; Robert Baker, Fairmont State College; David Barney, Palm Beach Community College South; Terry Barr, Presbyterian College; Bette-B Bauer, College of Saint Mary; Evelyn Beck, Piedmont Technical College; Daniel Bender, Pace University–Pleasantville; Lysbeth Benkert, Northern State University; Kate Benzel, University of Nebraska at Kearney; Eric Berlatsky, University of Maryland; Mark Bernheim, Miami University; Debra Berry, Community College of Southern Nevada; Stephan Bertman, Lawrence Technological University; Linda Best, Kean University; Michael Bibby, Shippensburg University of Pennsylvania; Suzanne Black, Southwest State University; Marlin Blaine, California State University–Fullerton; Laurel Bollinger, University of Alabama–Huntsville; Scott Boltwood, Emory and Henry College; Ashley Bonds, Copiah-Lincoln Community College; Shelly Borgstrom, Rogers State University; Lucia Bortoli, Ohio State University; Paul Brandt, Kent State University; Christopher Brooks, Wichita State University; Jennifer Browdy de Hernandez, State University of New York at Albany; Kevin Brown, Lee University; Jeb Butler, Boston College; Jeff Butler, University of Iowa; Pamela Butsch, Jefferson Community College Southwest; William Cain, Wellesley College; Juan Calle, Broward Community College North; Lynne Callender, Legacy High School; Mike Campbell, Yakima Valley Community College; Erskine Carter, Black Hawk Col-Quad Cities; Cindy Catherwood, Metropolitan Community College–South; Patricia Cearley, South Plains College; Iclal Cetin, State University of New York at Buffalo; Julie Chappell, Tarleton State University; Amy Chesbro, Washtenaw Community College; Barbara Christian, University of Alaska–Anchorage Kenai Peni; Holly Ciotti, Glendale High School; William Clemente, Peru State College; Jeff Cofer, Bellevue Community College; Barbara Cole, Sandhills Community College; Ernest Cole, University of Connecticut; Christine Colon, Wheaton College; Michael Colson, Allan Hancock College; Susan Comfort, Indiana University of Pennsylvania;

Helen Connell, Barry University; Randy Connor, Los Medanos College; Linda Conway, Howard College; Stephen Cooper, Troy State University; Deborah Core, Eastern Kentucky University; Judith Cortelloni, Lincoln College; Peter Cortland, Quinnipac University; Timothy Costello, Moorhead Area Schools; James Cotter, Mount St. Mary College; Robert Cox, Southeast Kentucky Community and Technical College–Middlesboro; James Crawford, Walters State Community College; Merilee Cunningham, University of Houston–Downtown; Rita Dandridge, Norfolk State University; Craig Davos, Smith College; Anne Dayton, Slippery Rock University of Pennsylvania; Laura Dearing, Jefferson Community College Southwest; Paula Del Fiore, Cranston High School West; Anna Dewart, Coastal Georgia Community College; Emily Dial-Driver, Rogers State University; Sheila Diecidue, University of South Florida; Martha Diede, Northwest College; S. Dobranski, Georgia State University; Mary Dockray-Miller, Lesley University; Brian Doherty, University of Texas; Virginia Doland, Biola University; Cecilia Donohue, Madonna University; Stephen Donohue, Rock Valley College; Maria Doyle, State University of West Georgia; Kendall Dunkelberg, Mississippi University for Women; Emily Dziuban, University of Tennessee–Knoxville; Mark Eaton, Azusa Pacific University; Marie Eckstrom, Rio Hondo College; George William Eggers, University of Connecticut; Sarah Eichelman, Walters State Community College; Juliene Empric, Eckerd College; Bruce Engle, Morehead State University; Carol Fadda-Conrey, Purdue University–Main Campus; Scott Failla, Barnard College; Carol-Ann Farkas, Massachusetts College of Pharmacy and Allied Health; Pamela Faulkner, Concord College; Donald Fay, Kennesaw State University; Maryanne Felter, Cayuga Community College; Jill Ferguson, Notra Dame de Namur University; Suzanne Ferriss, Nova Southeastern University; Lois Feuer, California State University–Dominguez Hills; Matthew Fike, Winthrop University; Hannah Fischthal, Saint John's University; Johanna Fisher, SUNY College at Buffalo; Christine Flanagan, University of the Sciences in Phildelphia; Agnes Fleck, College of Saint Scholastica; Erwin Ford, Albany State University; Robert Forman, Saint John's University; Michael Fournier, Georgia State University; Stephen Fox, Gallaudet University; Christina Francis, Arizona State University; Wanda Fries, Somerset Community College; Joanne Gabel, Reading Area Community College; Maria Galindo, Ocean County College; Paul Gallipeo, Adirondack Community College; Susan Gardner, La Sierra University; David Garlock, Baruch College CUNY; Margaret Geiger, Cuyahoga Community College–Eastern; Erin Geller, Halls High School; Nate Gordon, Kishwaukee College; Kevin Grauke, University of North Texas; Karen Gray, University of Louisville; David Greene, Adelphi University; Nicole Greene, Xavier University of Louisiana; Loren Gruber, Missouri Valley College; Rachel Habermehl, University of Minnesota–Crookston; Keith Hale, South Texas Community College; Dewey Hall, Mt. San Antonio College; Randolph Handel, Santa Fe Community College; Leigh Harbin, Angelo State University; Vasantha Harinath, North Central State College; William Harris, University of Texas at Brownsville; Betty Hart, University of Southern Indiana; Joetta Harty, George Washington University; Janis Haswell, Texas A&M University at Corpus Christi; Roberta Hawkins, Shorewood High School; Wilda Head, Central Baptist College; Kathy Heininge, University of California–Davis; Ed Higgins, George Fox University;

Barbara Hiles-Mesle, Graceland College; James Hirsh, Georgia State University; Nika Hoffman, Crossroads School for Arts and Sciences; Randall Holt, Columbia Gorge Community College; Rebecca Hooker, University of New Mexico; Brooke Hopkins, University of Utah; Elizabeth Huergo, Montgomery College–Rockville; Laurie Hughes, Richland Community College; Byan Hull, Portland Community College–Sylvania; Elizabeth Huston, Eastfield College; Richard Iadonisi, Grand Valley State University; Candice Jackson, Tougaloo College; Robert Jakubovic, Raymond Walters College; Elaine Kauvar, Baruch College CUNY; Anita Kerr, North Carolina State University; John Lux, Baruch College CUNY; Jamie Marchant, Auburn University; J. Eric Miller, Kennesaw State University; Deborah Preston, Georgia Perimeter College; Wylene Rholetter, Auburn University; Charles Riley, Baruch College CUNY; Mark Trevor Smith, Southwest Missouri State University; and Tami Whitney, Creighton University.

For help in shaping the Compact Edition, we thank the many reviewers who provided in-depth feedback on the table of contents, choice of translations, organization, and editorial apparatus: Christine Abbott, Como Coso Community College; Oty Agbajoh-Laoye, Monmouth University; Heidi E. Ajrami, Victoria College; Allison E. Alison, Southeastern Community College; Lemiya Almaas, University of Minnesota–Twin Cities; Donald F. Andrews, Chattanooga State Technical Community College; Frances B. Auld, University of South Florida; Diane S. Baird, Palm Beach Community College; J.T. Barbarese, Rutgers University–Camden; Mojgan Behmand, George Mason University; Marilyn Booth, University of Illinois–Urbana-Champaign; Arnold J. Bradford, Northern Virginia Community College; Julie Brannon, Jacksonville University; Caridad Caballero, University of Georgia; Farida (Farrah) M. Cato, University of Central Florida; Barbara Mather Cobb, Murray State University; Ruth M. Cook, Milligan College; Carole Creekmore, Georgia Perimeter College–South; Robert W. Croft, Gainesville College; Jason DePolo, North Carolina A&T State University; Dwonna Goldstone, Austin Peay State University; David R. Greene, Long Island University–C.W. Post; Michael Grimwood, North Carolina State University; Anna R. Holloway, Fort Valley State University; Melissa Jackson, Midland College; Lars R. Jones, Florida Institute of Technology; Rodney D. Keller, Brigham Young University–Idaho; Pam Kingsbury, University of North Alabama; Roger Lathbury, George Mason University; Dianna Laurent, Southeastern Louisiana University; Michael Mackey, Community College of Denver; J. Hunter Morgan, Glenville State College; John H. Morgan, Eastern Kentucky University; James Norton, Marian College; Keith R. Prendergast, Pensacola Junior College; Peter Quinn, Salem State College; Wylene Rholetter, Auburn University; Jennifer O. Rosti, Roanoke College; Mimosa Stephenson, University of Texas at Brownsville; Matthew Stewart, Boston University; Charles F. Warren, Salem State College; Sally Padgett Wheeler, Georgia Perimeter College–Rockdale.

Finally, we thank the fourteen members of our Editorial Advisory Board, who reviewed the table of contents and sections of the manuscript at multiple stages, providing valuable advice throughout this book's development.

Editorial Advisory Board

No anthology of this size comes into being without critical and supportive friends and advisors. Our thanks go to the Department of English at the University of New Mexico (UNM) and its chair, David Jones, who supported our work. Among our colleagues and associates, we particularly want to thank Helen Damico, Feroza Jussawalla, Mary Power, Carmen Nocentelli-Truett, and Ron Shumaker, as well as Paul Lauter, Manjeet Tangri, and Fidel Fajardo-Acosta. Robin Runia provided research and editorial assistance and drafted the "Time and Place" box on the Encyclopedia Project.

An anthology of this scope is an undertaking that calls for a courageous, imaginitive, and supportive publisher. Joan Feinberg, Denise Wydra, Karen Henry, Steve Scipione, and Alanya Harter at Bedford/St. Martin's possess these qualities; we especially appreciate their confidence in our ability to carry out this task. Kaitlin Hannon guided the project in its early stages, and Carrie Thompson stepped in to develop the manuscript and see it through to completion. Abby Bielagus and Marisa Feinstein assisted with numerous tasks, large and small. Martha Friedman and Connie Gardner served as photo researchers, and Jean Hammond and Anna Palchik fine-tuned the design. Adrienne Petsick enthusiastically developed and coordinated the marketing plan. We also owe special thanks to Karen Stocz for skillfully copyediting and guiding the manuscript through production, Elizabeth Schaaf for overseeing the production process, and Rebecca Merrill for producing the Web site.

Most of all, we thank our families, especially Mary Davis, Patricia Clark Smith, Marlys Harrison, and Mona Johnson, for their patience and encouragement.

Paul Davis
Gary Harrison
David M. Johnson
John F. Crawford

A NOTE ON TRANSLATION

As anthologies of world literature have included an increasing number of texts from around the world, the use of quality translations of these texts has become not only necessary, but a mark of excellence for a particular anthology. The necessity for reading texts in translation has brought a recognition that different versions of the same text vary in quality and accessibility—not just any rendition will do. Teachers now *request* certain translations of favorite literary works, such as the Christian Bible, Homer's *The Odyssey* or Dante's *Divine Comedy*. A translation might adequately communicate the literal meaning of the original work, but miss entirely its cultural background or the artistry of a passage—both of which support and enhance that meaning. At the other extreme is the impressionistic version that recreates the spirit of the original work, but deviates from its meaning, thereby misleading the reader. Every translator faces the dilemma of what Benedetto Croce has stated as the extremes—either "Faithful ugliness or faithless beauty."

Among the most important and most popular texts from the ancient world are Homer's epics and the Greek dramas; Robert Fitzgerald's translation of Homer's *The Odyssey* and Robert Fagles's excellent versions of Homer's *The Iliad,* Aeschylus' *Agamemnon,* and Sophocles' *Antigone* are faithful to the original Greek and uniquely accessible to the modern reader. In a similar fashion, Horace Gregory's translations of Catullus and Rolfe Humphries' translations of Ovid span the distance between ancient Rome and today. Despite the fact that the scholarship of the King James Version of the Bible needs to be updated, we use this version because it is considered the most literary translation in English. Not only do many readers of English grow up with the King James, its antiquated syntax and vocabulary resonate with a sense of the sacred, and are echoed throughout later literature in English. R. M. Liuzza has provided us with what is possibly the most accurate modern poetic translation of *Beowulf.*

The best translations do not merely duplicate a work but re-create it in a new idiom. Because of poetic elements such as rhyme, meter, stanzas, and figures of speech, translating poetry presents unique challenges. Stephen Spender and J. L. Gili's translations of Federico García Lorca are excellent, as are the translations by several hands of the poets of the Tang dynasty in China. We use several different translators for Ghalib's and Pablo Neruda's poems, providing the reader with different perspectives on one of the major poets of the nineteenth century and one of the most important poets of the twentieth century.

Translating from one culture to another adds an additional layer of complexity, be it philosophical or symbolic. For example, as one of the most important religious documents of ancient India, the Bhagavad Gita alludes continuously to the complexities of classical Hinduism; Barbara Stoler Miller offers a unique, interpretive bridge from this ancient text to a modern reader. She also provides us with a multi-voiced version of the Indian classic by Kalidasa, *Shakuntala and the Ring of Recollection,* which also invokes Hindu themes—particularly that of *dharma* or duty. In terms of symbolism, while "cherry blossom" in a line of poetry to American readers may suggest a particular spring bloom or flower of the fruit tree, to Japanese readers "cherry blossom" invokes a cultural tradition that, depending on context, may suggest ideas of purity, transience, delicacy, and even of self-sacrifice. Richard Bodner's translation of Bashō's *Narrow Road through the Backcountry* and Edward Seidensticker's translation of *The Tale of Genji* are both sensitive to such cultural nuance, and both translations do justice to the poetic and prose passages of each work.

Some translations are so excellent they become classics in their own right. This is true of David Magarshack's translation of Tolstoy's *The Death of Ivan Ilych,* his rendering of Chekhov's *The Cherry Orchard,* and Richard Wilbur's *Tartuffe.* Edith Grossman's subtle and sophisticated version of *Don Quixote* is one of the best modern translations of a world classic. J. A. Underwood's refreshingly updated version of *The Metamorphosis* demonstrates why Kafka remains one of the most influential and timely writers of the past century.

No translation can substitute for reading the world's classics in their original languages. Nonetheless, the art of translation in the modern age has reached such a high level of both accuracy and artistry that we now have access to a full range of translations of world literature in its variety and significance. *The Bedford Anthology of World Literature,* Compact Edition, offers what we believe are the most reliable and readable translations of the major works included here.

About the Editors

Paul Davis (Ph.D., University of Wisconsin), professor emeritus of English at the University of New Mexico, has been the recipient of several teaching awards and academic honors, including that of Master Teacher. He has taught courses since 1962 in composition, rhetoric, and nineteenth-century literature and has written and edited many scholarly books, including *The Penguin Dickens Companion* (1999), *Dickens A to Z* (1998), and *The Lives and Times of Ebenezer Scrooge* (1990). He has also written numerous scholarly and popular articles on solar energy and Victorian book illustration. His most recent book is *Critical Companion to Charles Dickens* (2007).

Gary Harrison (Ph.D., Stanford University), professor and director of graduate studies at the University of New Mexico, has won numerous fellowships and awards for scholarship and teaching. He has taught courses in world literature, British Romanticism, and literary theory at the University of New Mexico since 1987. Harrison's publications include a critical study on William Wordsworth, *Wordsworth's Vagrant Muse: Poetry, Poverty, and Power* (1994); as well as several articles on topics such as John Clare's poetry, Romanticism and ecology, nineteenth-century culture, and teaching world literature.

David M. Johnson (Ph.D., University of Connecticut), professor emeritus of English at the University of New Mexico, has taught courses in world literature, mythology, the Bible as literature, philosophy and literature, and creative writing since 1965. He has written, edited, and contributed to numerous scholarly books and collections of poetry, including *Fire in the Fields* (1996) and *Lord of the Dawn: The Legend of Quetzalcoatl* (1987). He has also published scholarly articles, poetry, and translations of Nahuatl myths. His most recent book of poetry is *Rebirth of Wonder: Poems of the Common Life* (University of New Mexico Press, 2007).

John F. Crawford (Ph.D., Columbia University; postdoctoral studies, Yale University), associate professor of English at the University of New Mexico, has taught medieval, world, and other literature courses since 1965 at a number of institutions, including California Institute of Technology and Hunter College and Herbert Lehmann College of CUNY. The publisher of West End Press, an independent literary press with 120 titles, Crawford has also edited *This Is About Vision: Interviews with Southwestern Writers* (1990) and written articles on multicultural literature of the Southwest.

Pronunciation Key

This key applies to the pronunciation guides that appear in the margins and before most selections in *The Bedford Anthology of World Literature,* Compact Edition. The syllable receiving the main stress is CAPITALIZED.

a	mat, alabaster, laugh	MAT, AL-uh-bas-tur, LAF
ah	mama, Americana, Congo	MAH-mah, uh-meh-rih-KAH-nuh, KAHNG-goh
ar	cartoon, Harvard	kar-TOON, HAR-vurd
aw	saw, raucous	SAW, RAW-kus
ay (or a)	may, Abraham, shake	MAY, AY-bruh-ham, SHAKE
b	bet	BET
ch	church, matchstick	CHURCH, MACH-stik
d	desk	DESK
e	Edward, melted	ED-wurd, MEL-tid
ee	meet, ream, petite	MEET, REEM, puh-TEET
eh	cherub, derriere	CHEH-rub, DEH-ree-ehr
f	final	FIGH-nul
g	got, giddy	GAHT, GIH-dee
h	happenstance	HAP-un-stans
i	mit, Ipswich, impression	MIT, IP-swich, im-PRESH-un
igh (or i)	eyesore, right, Anglophile	IGH-sore, RITE, ANG-gloh-file
ih	Philippines	FIH-luh-peenz
j	judgment	JUJ-mint
k	kitten	KIT-tun
l	light, allocate	LITE, AL-oh-kate
m	ramrod	RAM-rahd
n	ran	RAN
ng	rang, thinker	RANG, THING-ker
oh (or o)	open, owned, lonesome	OH-pun, OHND, LONE-sum
ong	wrong, bonkers	RONG, BONG-kurz
oo	moot, mute, super	MOOT, MYOOT, SOO-pur
ow	loud, dowager, how	LOWD, DOW-uh-jur, HOW
oy	boy, boil, oiler	BOY, BOYL, OY-lur
p	pet	PET
r	right, wretched	RITE, RECH-id
s	see, citizen	SEE, SIH-tuh-zun
sh	shingle	SHING-gul
t	test	TEST
th	thin	THIN
th	this, whether	*TH*IS, WEH-*th*ur
u	until, sumptuous, lovely	un-TIL, SUMP-choo-us, LUV-lee
uh	about, vacation, suddenly	uh-BOWT, vuh-KAY-shun, SUH-dun-lee
ur	fur, bird, term, beggar	FUR, BURD, TURM, BEG-ur
v	vacuum	VAK-yoo-um
w	western	WES-turn
y	yesterday	YES-tur-day
z	zero, loser	ZEE-roh, LOO-zur
zh	treasure	TREH-zhur

Where a name is given two pronunciations, usually the first is the most familiar pronunciation in English and the second is a more exact rendering of the native pronunciation.

In the pronunciations of French names, nasalized vowels are indicated by adding "ng" after the vowel.

Japanese words have no strong stress accent, so the syllables marked as stressed are so given only for the convenience of English speakers.

CONTENTS

❧ Seventeenth Century–Nineteenth Century, 1650–1850 3

✺ Nineteenth Century–Twenty-First Century, 1850–Present   *863*

The Bedford Anthology of
World Literature
The Modern World,
1650–The Present

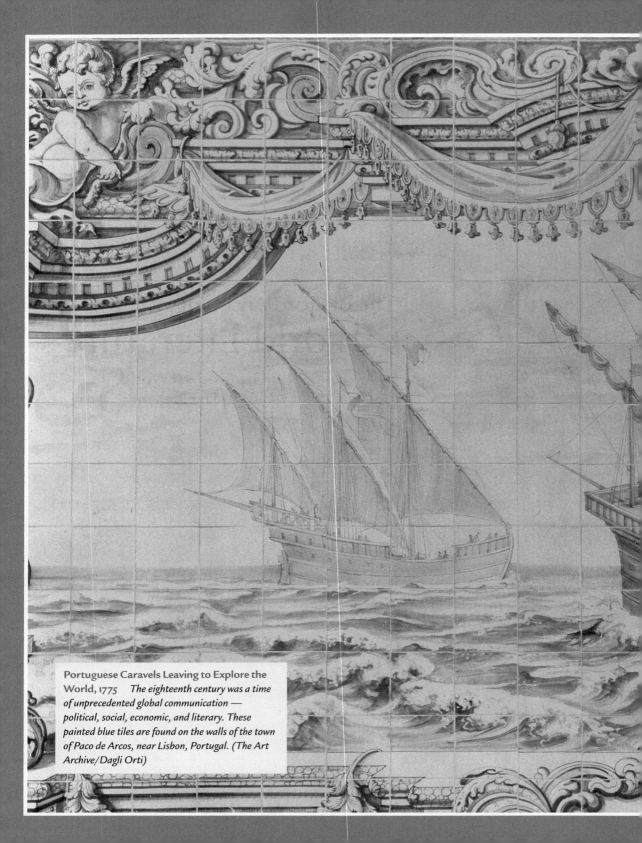

Portuguese Caravels Leaving to Explore the World, 1775 *The eighteenth century was a time of unprecedented global communication — political, social, economic, and literary. These painted blue tiles are found on the walls of the town of Paco de Arcos, near Lisbon, Portugal. (The Art Archive/Dagli Orti)*

Seventeenth Century –
Nineteenth Century

1650–1850

ungling Doctor Faust's order to dispossess an aging rustic couple from their picturesque cottage in a linden grove, the devil Mephistopheles and his crew set fire to the place. In the ensuing inferno the innocent pair, Philemon and Baucis, their cottage, and their chapel—all signs of a vanishing agricultural world—are lost. A warden who has witnessed the fire from his tower encapsulates what it all means: "What once was a joy to see / After centuries is gone." In this scene from *Faust,* Part 2, the German writer Johann Wolfgang von Goethe characterizes the onset of modernity in Europe as the catastrophic collapse of an agrarian world cemented by feudal social ties and religious bonds. While that simple world was always something of an ideal, it is undeniable that accelerating socio-economic changes sweeping Europe in the period from 1650 to 1850 led to a transfer of power from a landed gentry to a commercial and manufacturing class whose center was the city, not the country. The forces of secularization, urbanization, and commercialization that promoted and accompanied

COMPARATIVE TIMELINE FOR 1650–1850

Date	History and Politics	Literature	Science, Culture, and Technology
1650–1659	1641 Dutch begin trade with Japan.		
	1652 Dutch colonists found Cape Town in South Africa.		
	1657 Great Fire destroys Edo, Japan.		
	1658 Aurangzeb succeeds Shah Jahan as Mughal emperor in India.		
1660–1669	1660 Charles II; Restoration of Stuart monarchy in England		1660 Royal Society founded in London.
	1662 Kangxi (second emperor of Manchu dynasty) begins reign in China.	1664 Molière, *Tartuffe*	
	1666 Great Fire of London		1668 Margaret Cavendish, *The Grounds of Natural Philosophy*
	1669 Hinduism outlawed by Mughals in India; many Hindu temples destroyed.		
1670–1679		1670s Çelebi writes *Book of Travels*	
	1675–76 King Philip's War between American settlers and the Wampanoag		
	1675–78 Sikh rebellion against Mughal empire in India		
1680–1689	1680 Tsunayoshi becomes shogun in Japan. Ashanti (Asante) Kingdom founded in West Africa. Pueblo Revolt in New Mexico drives out Spanish.		1680 Anton van Leeuwenhoek discovers bacteria.

these changes—and which are still at work today—extended their transformative reach to other areas of the world, such as India, Africa, and the Americas, and led to new ways of thinking and feeling, new forms of art and literature, and new means of producing and disseminating printed materials, including literary works.

The eighteenth century is the last century of what historians call the Early Modern Period, extending from about 1500 to 1800, although sometimes extended fifty years in either direction. While historians of Europe usually emphasize a break between the eighteenth and nineteenth centuries, we must acknowledge that intellectual, cultural, and political transformations in Europe, much less the world, do not conveniently observe the temporal markers of the Roman calendar. Writers who exerted a profound influence upon the Enlightenment, for example, such as René Descartes (1596–1650), Jean-Baptiste Poquelin Molière (1622–1673), John Locke (1632–1704), and Isaac Newton (1642–1727), published their major works closer to 1650. Moreover, in Europe, the eighteenth century—typically described

Date	History and Politics	Literature	Science, Culture, and Technology
1680–1689 (cont.)	1685 Louis XIV revokes Edict of Nantes; absolute monarchy in France. Kangxi opens Chinese ports to foreigners.		1687 Newton, *Mathematical Principles*
	1688 Glorious Revolution in England (James II deposed; William and Mary crowned)		1688 Genroku period in Japan; beginnings of *kabuki* theater
1690–1699			1690 Locke, *Two Treatises on Government* and *Essay Concerning Human Understanding*
		1691 Sor Juana, *Reply to Sor Filotea*	
1700–1709	1701–14 War of the Spanish Succession		
		1702 Bashō, *Narrow Road through the Backcountry*	1702 First daily newspaper published in London.
	1703 Peter I founds St. Petersburg in Russia.		
			1704 Newton, *Opticks*
			1706 Excavations of Pompeii and Herculaneum begin.
	1707 Death of Mughal emperor Aurangzeb accelerates decline of Mughal empire in India.		
	1709 Ienobu new shogun in Japan		1709 Invention of the piano

as an "Age of Enlightenment" characterized by an emphasis upon reason, rationality, and sociability—does not abruptly give way at the turn of the century to its successor, "Romanticism," characterized by an emphasis upon feeling, imagination, and individualism. When, as we do here, we take into account the literary histories of Japan, China, India, the Arabic and Muslim world, Africa, and the Americas, the problems of periodization become even more acute, since each of these traditions developed within its own unique historical trajectory. In Japan, for example, Matsuo Bashō (1644–1694) and Ihara Saikaku (1642–1693) are writers associated with the Tokugawa era, a period stretching from 1600 to 1868. In China, Pu Song-Ling (1640–1715) and Cao Xueqin (c. 1715–1763) produced their fiction during the Qing dynasty that began in 1644 and, though enfeebled in the mid-nineteenth century, did not end until 1911. Similarly, in India, Ramprasad Sen (1718–1775) and Ghalib (1797–1869) wrote their poetry during the years of the Mughal empire that flourished from 1526 to 1857. Thus, some of the works included in the first half

Date	History and Politics	Literature	Science, Culture, and Technology
1710–1719			1710 Handel becomes music director to George I.
	1713 Peace of Utrecht; French domination of Europe ends. Treaty of Utrecht		1714 Fahrenheit invents mercury thermometer.
	1716 Yoshimune shogun in Japan		
1720–1729			1720 Mammoth *History of Japan* by Tokugawa Mitsukuni completed; Yoshimune lifts restrictions on study of Western thought in Japan.
	1723 Collapse of Safavid empire		
	1726 Treaty between British colonists and the Iroquois League against France	1726 Swift, *Gulliver's Travels*	
			1729 Bach, *St. Matthew Passion*
1730–1739		1733–34 Pope, *An Essay on Man*	
			1735 Linnaeus, *Systema Naturae*
	1736-94 Literary censorship in China		
			1739 Hume, *Treatise of Human Nature*

of this volume fall outside the boundaries of 1650 to 1850 proper. All of the works included, however, reflect the changes in relations among world civilizations that were taking place during this time, when for better or for worse intellectual, cultural, economic, and political exchange and contact among the regions of the world were expanding at an ever accelerating rate.

GLOBAL CONTACT, CONFLICT, AND EXCHANGE

During the fifteenth and sixteenth centuries, European voyages of discovery and conquest, as well as the expansion of the Ottoman empire, had established global networks of trade and cross-cultural exchange. Improvements in technology — especially in shipbuilding, navigation, and arms — extended the global reach of burgeoning nation-states, so that by the seventeenth century Portugal, Spain, and the Netherlands had established trading stations and colonies in sub-Saharan Africa, India, China, and the Americas. By the end of the eighteenth century,

Date	History and Politics	Literature	Science, Culture, and Technology
1740–1749	1740 Frederick the Great assumes control of Prussia; Maria Theresa head of Hapsburg empire		
	1745 Ieharu shogun in Japan		
			1748 Montesquieu, *Spirit of the Laws*
1750–1759			1751 Benjamin Franklin invents lightning rod.
			1751–72 Diderot, *Encyclopedia*
	1755 Lisbon earthquake kills 30,000 people.		
	1756–63 Seven Years' War; massacre of British in Black Hole of Calcutta		
	1757 Battle of Plassey in India; British defeat Mughal forces in Bengal.		
		1759 Voltaire, *Candide, or Optimism*	
1760–1769	1760 George III crowned king of England.		1760s–70s Color wood block printing in Japan begins to flourish with Harunobu and Utamoro.
	1762 Catherine II takes power in Russia.		
	1763 End of the Seven Years' War. Britain gains colonial territories from France and Spain, including Canada, Tobago, and Florida; Spain gets Louisiana from France.	1763 Montagu, *The Turkish Letters*	
	1765 The Stamp Act		

England and France had extended their reach into those areas, as well. Capital, goods, and commodities circulated around the world and began to transform economies and social habits throughout the world. Of course, one of the major trade activities from the sixteenth century through the mid-nineteenth century was the slave trade begun by Portugal, Spain, France, England, and Holland.

The slave trade had a traumatic impact on the societies of sub-Saharan Africa. Political upheavals along the Gold Coast of northwestern Africa occurred in the seventeenth and eighteenth centuries, at the peak of the Atlantic slave trade, as coastal entrepreneurs profited from the trade in human souls. This was a time of empire building in the Niger Delta, when such kingdoms as Benin, Dahomey, and Asante reached their zenith. It is estimated that between 1540 and 1807 as many as 4.5 to 6 million Africans were transported from their homelands to be used in the silver and gold mines of South America, the sugar plantations of the West Indies and Brazil, and the coffee and tobacco plantations of the United States.

Date	History and Politics	Literature	Science, Culture, and Technology
1760–1769 (cont.)	1766 Ali Bey becomes ruler of Egypt; proclaims independence of Turks.	1766 Pu Song-Ling, *Strange Stories from a Chinese Studio*	1767–69 Bougainville sails around the world.
			1769 James Watt patents steam engine.
1770–1779	1770 Captain James Cook lands at Australia.		1770 James Hargreaves patents spinning jenny.
	1773 The Tea Act leads to the Boston Tea Party.		1772–82 Editing of *The Complete Collection of Written Materials Divided into Four Categories (Siku Chuanshu)*, a collection of all printed works in China
	1774 British East India Company officer Warren Hastings becomes governor of India.		
	1775 First Maratha War in India	c. 1775 Ramprasad Sen poems	
	1775–83 American War of Independence		
	1776 Declaration of Independence		1776 Paine, *Common Sense*; Smith, *Wealth of Nations*
			1777 Haydn, C Major Symphony
1780–1789		1781–88 Rousseau, *Confessions*	1781 Kant, *Critique of Pure Reason*
	1783 Treaty of Paris; United States recognized as an independent nation.	1784 Smith, *Elegiac Sonnets*	1784 Kant, "What Is Enlightenment?"
			1785 Charles Wilkins publishes first European (English) translation of Bhagavad Gita.

This African diaspora transformed the demographic makeup of Africa, Europe, and the Americas and would have a profound and enduring impact on world history.

Cultural and economic exchange proliferated throughout the Arabic world and Asia as well. Istanbul was a major center of trade, and in the early eighteenth century Sultan Ahmed III inaugurated the so-called *Lale Devri* or "Tulip Age" (1718–1730), leading to an increased economic and cultural exchange with Europe, especially France, as well as to an increased diplomatic presence throughout Europe. Shifting balances of power and trade impacted the Ottoman, Safavid, and Mughal empires in the Middle East and India. In the seventeenth century the English, alongside the Dutch and French, had already established textile factories in India. After the Battle of Plassey in 1757, the English basically controlled Bengal and had laid the foundation for the expansion of their empire into the nineteenth century. Eventually pressures from Europe and Russia would

Date	History and Politics	Literature	Science, Culture, and Technology
1780–1789 (cont.)	1787 Sierra Leone founded by British colonists.		1787–88 Mozart, *Don Giovanni* and the last three symphonies
	1789 U.S. Constitution ratified; George Washington elected first U.S. president. Storming of the Bastille; Declaration of the Rights of Man and Citizen; French Revolution begins.	1789 Equiano, *The Interesting Narrative of the Life of Olaudah Equiano*	
1790–1799	1791 U.S. Bill of Rights ratified. Toussaint L'Ouverture leads slave revolt in Hispaniola (Haiti).		
	1792 French Republic founded by National Convention. Denmark prohibits slave trade.	1792 Wollstonecraft, *A Vindication of the Rights of Woman*	
	1793 Lord McCartney's mission to China to increase trade. Louis XVI beheaded.	1794 Blake, *Songs of Innocence* and *Songs of Experience*	1793 David, *The Murder of Marat*
			1795 Haydn completes the twelve London symphonies
		1796 Diderot, *Supplement to the Voyage of Bougainville*	1796 Jenner develops vaccine against smallpox.
	1798–1801 Napoleon invades Egypt.	1798 Wordsworth and Coleridge, *Lyrical Ballads*	1799 Rosetta Stone discovered in Egypt by Napoleon's troops; provides key to translating Egyptian hieroglyphics.
	1799 Napoleon becomes first consul of France.		

contribute to the decline and fall of the Mughals in India and the Ottomans throughout the Mediterranean in the mid-eighteenth and nineteenth centuries, respectively. Japan and China, which prospered in the eighteenth century, strictly regulated contact and trade with Europe. The Tokugawa government in Japan issued a series of seclusion policies in the 1630s that prohibited Japanese travel abroad and severely limited European access to Japan's ports. In 1757, the Chinese emperor Qianlong (1710–99) decreed that foreign traders could only land at Canton, and only between November and March. Nonetheless, European demand for tea, porcelains, furniture, and other commodities and goods grew during this period, and by the early nineteenth century pressure from the West eventually would lead to the collapse of the Tokugawa empire in Japan and the demise of the Qing dynasty in China. In sum, between 1650 and 1850 intercultural contact and exchange of various degrees of reciprocity linked the histories of nearly every geographic region of the world. By the eighteenth century, as historian J. M. Roberts puts it, the peoples of the globe had reached "the era of world history."

Date	History and Politics	Literature	Science, Culture, and Technology
1800–1809		1800 Novalis, *Hymns to the Night*	
	1802 British gain control over central India.		
	1803 Louisiana Purchase	1803 Abu Taleb, *The Travels of Mirza Abu Taleb Khan*	
	1804 Napoleon becomes emperor of France. Haitian independence declared.		1804 Beethoven, *Eroica Symphony*; David, *The Coronation of Napoleon Bonaparte*
	1807 Slave trade abolished throughout British empire.		1807 Fulton's *Clermont* navigates the Hudson River.
	1808 United States prohibits importation of slaves from Africa.	1808 Goethe, *Faust*, Part I	1808 Beethoven, *Symphony No. 5*
	1809 Ecuador gains independence from Spain.		1809 Lamarck, *Principles of Zoology*
1810–1819	1810 Height of Napoleon's power		1810 Goya, *The Disasters of War*
	1811 Luddites destroy factory machines in northern England.		1811 Stephenson, first locomotive
		1812 Byron, *Childe Harold's Pilgrimage*, Part I	1812 The Brothers Grimm, *Fairy Tales*
	1813 Simón Bolivar becomes dictator in Venezuela.		
	1814 Lord Hastings, governor of India, declares war on Gurkhas in Nepal.		
	1815 Battle of Waterloo		
			1816 Rossini, *The Barber of Seville*
		1817 Coleridge, *Sibylline Leaves*	

INTELLECTUAL AND SOCIAL CHANGE

Despite ongoing conflicts, the period between 1650 and 1850 saw relative peace and—especially for Europe, China, and Japan—prosperity. Rapid population growth led to the increasing importance of urban life. On the heels of increased commerce and manufacture, many parts of Europe and Japan saw the rise of an energetic and thriving middle class whose intellectual and moral values presented various challenges to the traditional social and political order. The boundaries between social groups became more permeable and the question of personal and social identity became more complex as wealthy merchant families united through marriage with the families of traditional landed aristocrats. Greater public access to education as well as cheaper methods of printing and papermaking helped to promote literacy in many parts of Europe, the United States, China, and Japan. Middle-class demand for entertainment and diversions led to the transformation of classical literary forms and the development of new ones.

Date	History and Politics		Literature		Science, Culture, and Technology	
1810–1819 (cont.)	1818	France abolishes slave trade. British defeat the Maratha Confederacy in India.	1818	Leopardi, "The Infinite"		
			1819	Keats, *Odes*	1819	Gericault, *The Raft of Medusa*
1820–1829			1820	Lamartine, *Poetic Meditations*	1820	Ampère discovers electrical current.
	1821	Greek war of independence begins. Napoleon dies.	1821	Manzoni, "The Fifth of May"	1821	First fossilized skeleton of a dinosaur discovered.
	1822	Brazil becomes independent of Portugal.			1822	Schubert, *Unfinished Symphony*
	1823	Mexico becomes a republic. Monroe Doctrine				
	1824	Slavery abolished in Central America.	1826	Hölderlin, *Lyrical Poems*	1825	Erie Canal finished.
			1827	Heine, *The Book of Songs*		
			1828	Leopardi, "To Sylvia" and "The Solitary Thrush"	1828	Nerval, translation of Goethe's *Faust*
	1829	Slavery abolished in Mexico.				
1830–1839	1830	Revolution in Paris; Louis Phillippe becomes king of France. Indian Removal Act; Native Americans relocated to west of the Mississippi. Belgium gains independence.			1830	Delacroix, *Liberty Guiding the People*
			1832	Goethe, *Faust*, Part II	1832	Horoshige, *Fifty-three Stages of the Tohaido*
					1833	Lyell, *Principles of Geology*; Hokusai, *Thirty-six Views of Mt. Fuji*
	1833	Slavery abolished in British colonies.				
					1834	Babbage invents principle of the computer.

In Europe—particularly in France and England—an intellectual revolution now known as the ENLIGHTENMENT shook the foundations of societies previously ruled by kings and the church. New faith in the powers of empirical science, rationalism, and philosophy to resolve social problems intensified the secularism that had taken shape during the Renaissance. In Japan, thinkers also promoted a shift from metaphysical speculation to pragmatism. NEO-CONFUCIANISTS debated the relative authority of the emperor and shogun (the hereditary military commander in feudal Japan), spurred on empirical methods of investigation and direct observation of natural phenomena, and advocated systematic programs of education. In China, philosophers such as Huang Zong-Xi (Huang Tsung-hsi, 1610–1695) and Wang Fu-chi (Wang Fu-chih, 1619–1692) took a more rigorous, scientific approach to the study of science, politics, history, and society than had previous generations.

Spurred on in part by the intellectual developments of the late seventeenth and eighteenth centuries, Europe and America entered a period of widespread revolution and reform aimed at toppling the vestiges of absolute monarchy and

Date	History and Politics	Literature	Science, Culture, and Technology
1830–1839 (cont.)	1836 The Alamo 1837 Victoria becomes queen of Great Britain.	1837 Pushkin, *The Bronze Horseman*	
			1838 Daguerre develops the daguerreotype photographic process.
	1839 Independent Republic of Natal founded by Boers. 1839–42 First Opium War between Britain and China; Chinese ports opened to British traders.		1839 Goodyear vulcanizes rubber.
1840–1849			1840 de Tocqueville, *Democracy in America*
	1841 Britain proclaims sovereignty over Hong Kong.	1843 Çelebi, *Book of Travels* published.	1843 Prescott, *History of the Conquest of Mexico*
	1844 Daniel O'Connell found guilty of conspiracy against British rule in Ireland. Dominican Republic becomes independent of Haiti.	1844 Droste-Hülshoff, *Poems* 1845 Douglass, *Narrative of the Life of Frederick Douglass, an American Slave*	1844 Turner, *Rain, Steam, and Speed*
	1846 First Sikh War ends; Treaty of Lahore. Polish revolt 1848 Revolt in Paris; Louis Napoleon elected president. Revolution in Vienna; Metternich resigns. Revolution in Berlin. Revolutions in Venice, Milan, Parma, and Rome. Czech revolt in Prague. Treaty of Guadalupe Hildago ends Mexican–U.S. War.	1846 Whittier, *Voices of Freedom*	1846 Smithsonian Institution founded. Howe invents sewing machine. Berlioz, *Damnation of Faust*

aristocratic privilege that had relied upon the church to support its hierarchical policies and structure. The American (1776) and French (1789) Revolutions, uprisings against monarchy inspired by Enlightenment rationalism, would in turn inspire revolutionary movements in Poland, Haiti, Venezuela, Mexico, and even Egypt in the early nineteenth century. At the same time, the Industrial Revolution, which began in the last third of the eighteenth century, transformed material conditions and increased opportunities for trade, emigration, and colonization, so that by the end of the nineteenth century industrial Europe controlled much of the world, and Westernization both threatened and attracted the nations of Asia and Africa.

NEW LITERARY FORMS

The development throughout the eighteenth and nineteenth centuries of a literate middle class, with greater leisure time and spending power, allowed a publishing industry and new literary forms to thrive. As the population grew and standards

Date	History and Politics	Literature	Science, Culture, and Technology
1840–1849 (cont.)	1849 Mazzini proclaims Rome a republic. Revolts in Dresden and Baden. British defeat Sikhs at Chillianwalla. Britain annexes the Punjab.		1849 California Gold Rush
1850–1859	1850 Outbreak of Anglo–Kaffir War		
	1850–64 Taiping Rebellion in China		
	1852 South African Republic (Transvaal) established.		
	1854 Commodore Perry negotiates first Japanese–American treaty.		
	1855 Crimean War	1855 Whitman, *Song of Myself*	
	1856 Britain annexes Oudh, India, and Natal.		
	1857 Peace of Paris ends Anglo–Persian War. Sepoy Rebellion against British rule		
	1858 Treaty of Tientsin ends Anglo–Chinese War.		
	1858–63 Mexican civil war; Maximilian named emperor.		
			1859 Gounod, *Faust*
1860–1869	1861–65 U.S. Civil War	1861 Jacobs, *Incidents in the Life of a Slave Girl*	
		1862 Douglass, "Emancipation Proclaimed"	
		1863 de Castro, *Galician Songs*	

of living rose, the urban life of the middle classes began to dominate the attention of writers. Aristocratic models of classical tragedy and romance gave way to plays and novels exploring questions that were of particular concern to the BOURGEOISIE: social fluidity, personal identity, public morality, and private feeling. In Europe, the NOVEL developed as a realistic form that dramatized the moral and social life of ordinary people. In Japan and China, where it had a longer tradition, fiction was adapted to reflect the lives of the townspeople and to portray realistically the social life among all ranks.

Middle-class readers also looked to literature for entertainment and instruction. Poets and playwrights turned away from the highly stylized diction and formal structures associated with aristocratic culture and classical conventions and began to use more colloquial language and more popular forms. The early Romantic poets in Europe revived and transformed popular forms such as the ballad, and they looked to folk tales and folk songs as sources of inspiration rooted in the lore and land of their local communities. The Romantic turn inward, the exploration of personal feelings and states of mind, led to the widespread interest in autobiographical or semiautobiographical works of fiction and nonfiction, the rise of lyric poetry, and an interest in the supernatural and fantastic. In the post-Napoleonic years, after 1815, a new cosmopolitanism and sense of nation building led Romantic writers to model their works upon exalted forms and verse styles, such as hymns and odes, for their lyric meditations and reflections.

Dramatists in Japan turned to the relatively new forms of KABUKI (live theater) and JORURI (puppet theater) to reflect urban life, while those in Europe used the stage to exercise the much-valued wit of urban culture and poke fun at country life. And writers benefited from the new popularity of a variety of prose genres during this period. Readers were drawn also to almanacs, essays, autobiographies, confessions, collections of letters, and conduct books—guides designed to help people improve their social status.

The increased contact among peoples from diverse parts of the world—both voluntary and involuntary—also had an impact on literature during this time. TRAVEL NARRATIVES, recounting the adventures of visitors to foreign countries as well as fictional accounts of travels that often satirized customs of the homeland, enjoyed enormous popularity. The slave trade led to a new genre known as the SLAVE NARRATIVE, an autobiographical account of a person's captivity, education, and emancipation. In America, CAPTIVITY NARRATIVES—first-person stories of women and men captured and released by American Indians—emerged as a subgenre. Literary production from 1650 to 1850 reflected the social, economic, and cultural shifts everywhere in the world: the expanding range of human experience, the greater status and prosperity of the middle classes, and the increasing cultural and ethnic diversity of a world continuing to expand.

EUROPE: ENLIGHTENMENT THROUGH ROMANTICISM

Throughout much of the seventeenth century, Europe was in turmoil, some of which spilled over into the eighteenth century. The Thirty Years' War (1618–1648) saw fighting and confusion in all of Europe and heightened religious factionalism. A series of attempts on the part of discontented nobles in England and members of the Parlement of Paris in France to limit the powers of the monarch resulted in the English Civil War (1642–1660) and the Fronde (1648–1653). These conflicts restricted royal power in England and strengthened it in France — leading to further revolutionary struggles at the end of the eighteenth century.

As Europeans extended their reach to almost all parts of the world and enriched their countries with goods and raw materials from the colonies, they fought among themselves to seize or secure precious trade routes or promising colonial holdings. The Seven Years' War (1756 to 1763) — in which Britain and Prussia joined forces against Austria, Russia, France, and Spain — is considered by some to be the first global war. Land and sea battles raged over who could finally claim ownership of British, French, and Spanish colonial holdings in India and North America. At the end of the war, France gave up its claims in India and Canada and the land east of the Mississippi River to Britain and the Louisiana Territory to Spain; Spain in turn gave up Florida to Britain. At the end of the Seven Years' War, Great Britain was in a position to become the leading colonial power in the world. Pressures for reform brought on by French intellectuals and the example of the American Revolution led to the bloody conclusion of the French Revolution. Beginning with the storming of the Bastille in 1789, the French people finally brought down Louis XVI, secured a share of power for the middle classes, and began to rebuild their society under the guiding lamp of Reason, literally idolized as a secular god.

The democratic revolutions of the late eighteenth and early nineteenth centuries were often bound up with (or soon followed by) nationalist movements. In the midst and wake of the Napoleonic Wars (1799–1815) many countries, including Poland, Italy, Spain, Greece, Mexico, and Venezuela, engaged in hard-fought struggles for independence and freedom that involved a nationalist self-fashioning. Out of these struggles came a new intellectual and cultural movement — Romanticism — that involved a recovery of local folk tales, a celebration of local histories and heroes, and a passionate attachment to local places, landscapes, and monuments. From this intellectual and historical ferment emerged a pantheon of heroes, many of whom pursued the contradictory goals of liberation and imperial conquest. While they fought for freedom and independence

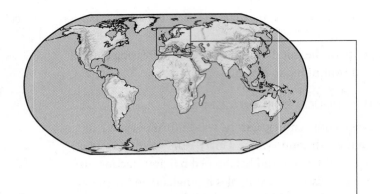

Europe in 1740

By 1740, Europe had achieved a kind of diplomatic equilibrium in which no one nation dominated. There were, however, certain divisions of power: Spain, the Dutch Republic, Poland-Lithuania, and Sweden had declined in might and influence, while Great Britain, Russia, Prussia, and Austria had become more powerful.

from the monarchs and feudal lords who had inherited power, or from imperial and foreign powers—such as the Austrian and Ottoman empires—they inspired nationalistic fervor as they consolidated smaller states into nations (for example, Italy and Germany) or, like Napoleon, pursued dreams of empire.

Enlightenment.   In the eighteenth century, ENLIGHTENMENT thinkers and philosophers—known in France as the *philosophes*—set out by means of reason and direct observation to discover the fundamental laws governing nature, humanity, and society. The *philosophes* believed that such discoveries would free the world from tyranny, violence, and instability. If, they reasoned, universal laws such as those discovered by English scientist Isaac Newton (1642–1727) governed the natural world, surely similar laws must govern human nature and social institutions. The delineation of such laws was the project of David Hume's *A Treatise of Human Nature* (1739–40), in which the Scottish philosopher attempted to "introduce the experimental method of reasoning into moral subjects." By discovering laws governing "moral subjects"—such as knowledge, belief, the passions, justice, and goodness—human beings could learn to live together more harmoniously and perhaps experience unlimited progress. While many *philosophes* had doubts about how far such progress could go, by the end of the eighteenth century the Marquis de Condorcet's *Sketch for a Historical Picture of the Progress of the Human Mind* (1793) claimed "that the perfectibility of man is truly indefinite; and that the progress of this perfectibility . . . has no other limit than the duration of the globe upon which nature has cast us."

The Slave Trade.   Ironically, the age named the Enlightenment was in at least one respect also an era of great blindness. Colonial expansion created a flood of new goods and materials in the trade networks, stimulating commerce and manufacturing. But since colonial trade focused mainly on labor-intensive crops such as sugar, tobacco, coffee, and cotton, many European fortunes were being built on the foundation of slavery. As we can see from the SLAVE NARRATIVE by Olaudah Equiano (1789) (p. 448), by the eighteenth century African traders from the kingdoms of Benin and Ife, among others, were selling Africans to Europeans in exchange for European goods. An estimated 4.5 to 6 million African men, women, and children were sold and sent to the Americas and the Caribbean, where they were put to work on plantations. When they died because of poor health or abuse, they were simply replaced by more men and women from Africa. Three times as many men, women, and children died from disease or mistreatment during the voyage from Africa to the colonies as actually arrived. Shackled together in rows so tight that they could hardly move, the captives suffered near starvation and dehydration; suicide was a powerful temptation. European empires were built in part on conflict within Africa, and resulted in political strife among and within African states and a seriously depleted population. The African diaspora would have a profound impact on world history and culture over the next two centuries, introducing elements of African culture to the rest of the world as well as leading to ethnic and racial tension.

Neoclassicism.   Eighteenth-century artists and writers in Europe, Japan, and China also began to direct their attention to the tastes and concerns of the increasingly literate and prosperous middle classes. As a result, new forms of music, art, and literature emerged. Throughout Europe the arts shifted their focus from the courts and country houses of the aristocracy to the salons and coffeehouses of the bourgeoisie. Writers during the first part of the eighteenth century—in what is known as NEOCLASSICAL literature—imitated classical models and placed emphasis on conventional form, public purpose, and urbane wit. Neoclassical refers to the classical tradition of Greco-Roman literature and mythology and an emphasis on classical values of decorum and wit (decorum signifies stylistic grace and the perfect balance between form and expression; wit denotes an inventiveness tempered by good judgment).

Just as Newton had discovered general laws and a grand order in the cosmos, so the Neoclassical poet wanted to discover the general laws of art. In the works of Augustan-age poets such as Horace and Virgil, Neoclassical writers found rules governing art that they believed were equivalent to natural laws. In drama, these rules were characterized by the "unities" of time, place, and action derived in part from Aristotle's *Poetics*. In contrast to the expansive plays of Shakespeare with their multiple subplots, Neoclassical dramatists such as Jean Racine (1639–1699) limited their heroic tragedies to a single action, place, and time. In accordance with the principles of decorum, writers developed an elevated and formal poetic diction suited for serious subjects often drawn from, and almost always alluding to, classical and biblical history and mythology. The great Neoclassical writers saw these rules as flexible rather than as prescriptions to follow to the letter. The one precept that all Neoclassical writers agreed on was taken from Horace, who had said that all art and literature should both please and instruct.

Cultures that value order and decorum tend to bring attention to their opposites—disorder and the grotesque—and beneath the polished surface of Neoclassical works the prince of misrule threatens to break out. There is always a hypocrite or rake—a seducer without scruples—as in Molière's *Tartuffe*, to threaten the delicate codes of propriety and decency; always a Yahoo—a savage man—as in Jonathan Swift's *Gulliver's Travels*, to disturb the all-too-perfect universe of the rational Houyhnhnms. One of the predominant forms of European literature in the eighteenth century was SATIRE, a gentle or biting critique of morals and manners that generally sought to instruct or to effect some kind of change in society. Satire appeared in all major genres, including drama, poetry, and prose. *Tartuffe* (p. 51) attacks the hypocrisy of the middle classes in France, as well as their complacent acceptance of rigid domestic roles. For Molière, his comic play aimed to "correct men's vices," by displaying them in exaggerated form. This principle of HYPERBOLE — blowing things out of proportion — is found in the satirical fiction of the era as well, represented here by Voltaire's *Candide* (p. 302) and Jonathan Swift's *Gulliver's Travels* (p. 232). *Candide,* which follows the episodic adventures of a naive young man of the same name, exploits the possibilities of the satirical tale, and uses Candide's misadventures to attack the pieties of European society. Similarly, *Gulliver's Travels* combines the formal features of the travel narrative with those of the satirical tale to ridicule what Swift saw as the hypocritical values, self-complacency, and vicious nature of the people of Britain. At the same time, he produces an immensely entertaining fantasy that anticipates modern science fiction.

By the mid-eighteenth century, the conventions of reason and tradition had grown somewhat stale, if not stifling, and the critical temperament of the early Enlightenment became infused instead with a spirit of feeling. Decorum and urbane wit had to make room for a growing taste for the expressive, the meditative, and the spontaneous. Practical guides to manners flourished in the popular press, as the increasing number of middle-class readers sought to elevate themselves both economically and socially. In addition to the satirical tale, the novel, and the autobiography, the TRAVEL NARRATIVE, or travelogue, was an immensely popular form of literature in the seventeenth and eighteenth centuries. These accounts of journeys to "exotic" lands often took the form of letters, as in Lady Mary Wortley Montagu's *Turkish Letters* (p. 168). Europeans also enjoyed reading fictional accounts of their own countries presumably seen through the eyes of a foreigner; Montesquieu's *Persian Letters* (1721) and Oliver Goldsmith's *The Citizen of the World* (1762) are two important such works. On occasion, European readers could see themselves through the lens of actual travelers, such as Mirza Abu Taleb Khan, who recorded his impressions of Europeans — primarily the Irish and the English — in his *Travels* (p. 179), translated into English in 1810.

The NOVEL, focusing primarily on the morals and manners of the middle classes, stands out as the preeminent literary form of the later eighteenth century, taking the place of the satirical tale. Increasingly, the European novel concerned itself with sentiment and feeling, as in Jean-Jacques Rousseau's *Julie, or The New Héloise* (1761) and *Émile* (1762). Rousseau led a revolution of feeling, shifting the emphasis of the Enlightenment from reason to emotion, especially private emotion. In the exploration of the private self recorded in his autobiography *Confessions* (p. 410), Rousseau converts the travel narrative's voyage to a new land of striking contrasts into an introspective, sentimental journey, discovering human nature itself. In *Confessions,* Rousseau conducts his experiments in the laboratory of his own heart, examining the "chain of the feelings" that he claims have marked the development of his being. Rousseau's writings reflected a growing shift toward feeling in the second half of the eighteenth century, and his writing exerted tremendous influence on European literature. *Confessions* anticipated the explosion of creativity and emphasis on imagination, feeling, and self-reflection that emerged during the ROMANTIC era of the early nineteenth century.

Romanticism.   Like the political revolutions in America, France, the Caribbean, Poland, and Spanish America, a revolution in philosophy and the arts sought to liberate its practitioners from the rules and conventions of earlier generations. The works of Jean-Jacques Rousseau, as we note above, inspired a turn from reason to feeling and imagination. Whereas the Enlightenment had heralded reason and empirical experimentation as the primary means to discover truth and as the key agents of change, ROMANTICS celebrated instead imagination and feeling as ways to truly connect with the world and oneself. Furthermore, for the Romantics, imagination and feeling were modes of truth that could free the mind from the imperial hold of the external world, the human heart from the restraints of social decorum, the citizen from the chains of political tyranny, and the artist from rules and convention.

Romantic poetry as a whole is characterized by its reaction against the conventions and rules of NEOCLASSICAL poetry and by its emphasis on the innate, the subjective, the emotional, and the ideal. Neoclassical poets of the eighteenth century held up a mirror to nature; Romantic poets illuminated nature with the light of the imagination. Nature serves not as a palette for the Romantic poet's paintbrush but as a companion spirit that guides the poet in the act of creation. The Romantic poet looks upon nature not so much as a source of external impressions but more as a creative power that helps to free unconscious resources and break down the boundaries between the self and the other, the inner and the outer. As in Italian poet Giacomo Leopardi's (1798–1837) "The Infinite" (p. 791) and German poet Novalis's (1772–1801) "Yearning for Death" (p. 773), these meditations are often also longings for the infinite, an elusive ideal, or an unattainable other. Thus,

WWW   For more information about the culture and context of Europe from 1650 to 1850, see bedfordstmartins.com/worldlitcompact.

many Romantic poems involve quests, similar to those of the medieval knight in search of the Holy Grail and Dante's journey toward Beatrice. Indeed, in the late eighteenth century the word *romantic* was associated with the medieval and the Gothic. Unlike the medieval knight, however, the hero of the Romantic quest enacts a self-conscious meditation on his failure to attain the object of his desire.

Despite their tendencies toward solitude and private reverie, Romantic poets, perhaps paradoxically, were deeply engaged with social issues and politics, particularly with the French Revolution. When the young English poet William Wordsworth (1770–1850) visited France in the first year of the Revolution, he found "The land all swarmed with passion" and the people "risen up/Fresh as the morning star." Many Romantic writers hoped that their poetry and philosophy would effect a similar transformation of society and its misguided values by transforming the consciousness of the individual. Thus, the most private reverie may resonate with social and historical aspiration and anticipate a world organized by principles of human sympathy and love rather than self-interest and greed. Nonetheless, as a response to the failure of the French Revolution to realize fully the democratic reforms it had promised, many Romantic poets, including Shelley, Leopardi, and the French poet Alphonse de Lamartine (1790–1869), qualified their sense of hope with at best a cautious skepticism, at worst a deep pessimism about the present and the future.

AMERICA: THE COLONIAL PERIOD TO EMANCIPATION

America in the seventeenth century was a place of religious, ethnic, and cultural diversity. People had come to the New World from all over Europe—from England, France, Italy, Germany, Sweden, Holland, and Belgium—for a variety of reasons. Some had fled persecution or run from their past; others were chasing their dreams. Still others, from another continent, had arrived in shackles.

While Boston was the center of Puritan culture, Philadelphia nurtured the Society of Friends, more commonly known as Quakers, who eschewed sacraments and ritual, turning to their "inner light" instead for spiritual guidance. Pennsylvania was also home to Mennonites, Baptists, Amish, Huguenots, and others who accepted the invitation of William Penn (1644–1718), the colony's founder, to enjoy complete religious tolerance. In New York and Maryland, Protestants settled alongside Catholics, Jews, and Anglicans; Anglicans settled throughout the colonies but particularly in the Carolinas, Maryland, and Virginia.

By the eighteenth century the increasingly heterogeneous colonies were becoming more unified by means of commerce and trade, the need for mutual protection, and the desire for cultural exchange. Moreover, population growth, manufactures, and trade had created thriving cities, such as Philadelphia and

Boston, that equaled those of Europe. Colleges began to appear. Harvard was founded in 1636, and by 1754, the College of William and Mary, Yale, and what would later be Princeton, Columbia, and the University of Pennsylvania (the first secular institution of higher learning) were established. Presses for books, newspapers, and pamphlets proliferated, also started by Puritans in the 1630s. With the circulation of newspapers, essays, and pamphlets written by and about the colonists, a sense of identity distinctive from that of the Old World began to take hold in the people of the thirteen colonies.

Early American Literature.   Although American poetry and drama made some fledgling advances during the seventeenth and eighteenth centuries, the great era of American poetry would not arrive until the nineteenth century. The earliest works of American literature were mainly diaries, letters, and journals describing voyages to the New World, explorations along its coasts or riverways, and journeys into its interior. During the colonial period, extensive histories appeared, such as John Smith's *The General History of Virginia* (1624), which described the land and the natives of these new places and recounted the plight of the colonists. Puritans wrote treatises and sermons on church doctrine, as well as spiritual autobiographies and philosophical reflections on religion and politics. These works influenced later autobiographical writings, including Mary Rowlandson's *Narrative of the Captivity and Restoration of Mrs. Mary Rowlandson,* one of the earliest CAPTIVITY NARRATIVES. Rowlandson interprets everything that happens to her as a sign of God's judgment and grace, exemplifying the Puritans' tendency to seek out evidence of salvation in their lives.

By the mid-eighteenth century the political ideas of European ENLIGHTENMENT philosophers such as John Locke (1632–1704) and the new science of Isaac Newton (1642–1727) had reached the colonies. In contrast to the Puritan view of the world, which emphasized human depravity and helplessness to change history, Enlightenment thinkers celebrated human potential to shape their world through reason and practical experimentation. The ideas of progress and human perfectibility as well as the appreciation of civil rights, social justice, and equality were a dramatic departure from Puritan theocratic views and served to boost the popularity of tolerance and government-by-consensus in the colonies. No American better represents the American Enlightenment than the community leader, inventor, and statesman Benjamin Franklin (1706–1790), whose life is a model of rational inquiry, experimentation, civic virtue, and humanitarianism.

Benjamin Franklin's earliest writings were satirical essays published in newspapers, which along with periodicals were flourishing by the 1750s. Franklin also wrote, edited, and published *Poor Richard's Almanack* (1733–1758), one of the most enduring of the ever-popular almanacs—eclectic compendiums of aphorisms, astronomical predictions, weather forecasts, and entertaining tidbits. Franklin's popular *Autobiography,* written between 1771 and 1788, but not published in full until 1868, offered a chronicle of his life as well as an exemplary guide to the frugal, pragmatic, and useful life of an enlightened citizen.

Thomas Paine's *Common Sense* (1776), which presented the case for American independence, became an important document in the revolutionary politics of America, Britain, and France. *The Federalist Papers,* a series of essays published in newspapers between October 1787 and April 1788, aimed to persuade skeptical readers of the need to ratify the Constitution. Written by Alexander Hamilton (1755–1804), James Madison (1751–1836), and John Jay (1745–1829), these essays have had a lasting influence on American politics and literary history. Of all the political documents from this period, none ranks higher perhaps than Thomas Jefferson's Declaration of Independence (p. 397), which exemplifies American Enlightenment thought. In a rhetorical style that embodies Jefferson's classical sense of balance and order, the Declaration catalogs American grievances against the English Crown while elucidating the idealistic principles of the new republic.

Toward Revolution and Independence.   After the Peace of Paris treaty ended the French and Indian War in 1763, Britain acquired the entire East Coast of North America as well as Canada and the Gulf Coast, to the mouth of the Mississippi. In the same year, in response to Pontiac's Rebellion—an armed effort by Great Lakes Indians to avert further encroachments on their territory and to reclaim their traditions—England issued the Proclamation of 1763, banning settlement west of the Appalachian Mountains, and the Stamp Act of 1765, imposing taxes on legal documents, newspapers, and licenses. Despite protests England continued to legislate restrictions and taxes, which led to more civil disturbances, culminating in the Boston Tea Party of 1773, when Americans dumped hundreds of pounds of tea into Boston Harbor. The power struggle between England and America had reached an impasse.

Approximately six months after the First Continental Congress met in Philadelphia to approve a Declaration of Rights and Grievances condemning England's trade policies, British troops squared off against a group of Massachusetts militia known as minutemen; on the morning of April 19, 1775, a shot was fired, leading to the first casualties of the American War of Independence. As fighting fanned

www   For more information about the culture and context of America from 1650 to 1850, see bedfordstmartins.com/worldlitcompact.

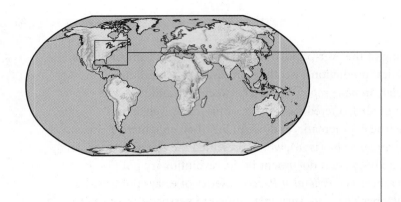

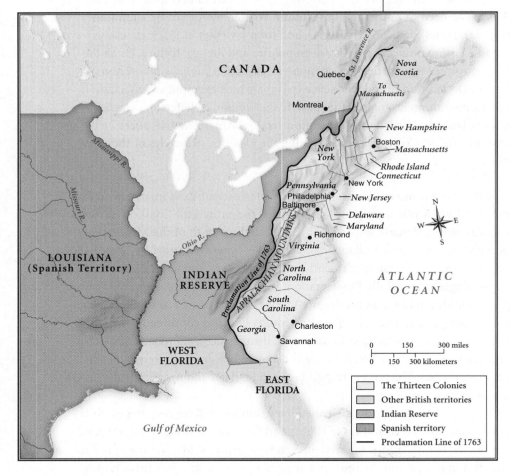

British North America, c. 1763

In 1763 Britain imposed the Proclamation Line, which prohibited white settlement to the west of the established thirteen colonies, in what was known as an Indian Reserve. Britain also decided to maintain a freestanding army to protect its interests in North America, which included Canada. These moves infuriated the American colonists, who wanted more autonomy, and helped sow the seeds of the American Revolution that began a little more than a decade later.

"The Bostonians in Distress"
After the Boston Tea Party, in which exasperated Bostonians threw English tea into Boston Harbor to protest rising taxes, England closed the port of Boston with the Boston Port Act of 1774. In this cartoon, Bostonians are incarcerated—cut off from food and supplies—and dependent on neighboring townspeople to provide for them. (The Art Archive)

out through the colonies, the Second Continental Congress convened in Philadelphia, beginning on May 10, 1775; within two months, delegates to the Congress signed the Declaration of Independence. It was July 4, 1776. For the next seven years England and the American colonies were at war, which ended with the Treaty of Paris, signed on September 3, 1783.

With independence from England secured, the American colonists began to forge a nation. The new Congress called for a Constitutional Convention for the purpose of building on the 1781 Articles of Confederation, which had set forth the colonies' first principles of union. The Convention delegates, including Benjamin Franklin and Thomas Jefferson (1743–1826), emerged with a signed document on September 17, 1787, and by June 1788 nine states had ratified the United States Constitution. The republican ideals of the Constitution—the division of government into branches, the independence of states, and equality—were unique to the eighteenth century. Later revolutionary movements elsewhere would use the Declaration of Independence and to some degree the Constitution as models for their own independence and governments.

Post-Revolutionary American Culture.   The U.S. Constitution was based on ideals promoted by the Enlightenment philosophers of France and England, and the former colonies were indebted to European military leaders, such as the French general Lafayette (1757–1834) and the Polish general Kosciusko (1746–1817), who had joined the upstarts' struggle out of a devotion to liberty. American writers of the post-revolutionary period were similarly indebted to Europeans. James Fenimore Cooper (1789–1851), author of what are known as the Leatherstocking Tales about the American frontier, was often called "the American Scott" because his works seemed to do for American history what Sir Walter Scott's had done for Scotland's. Nathaniel Hawthorne's (1804–1864) supernatural and symbolic stories about New England were compared with the works of European gothic and supernatural storytellers such as E. T. A. Hoffmann. Some literary historians would claim that America did not produce a distinctively American literature until Mark Twain published *Huckleberry Finn* in 1884, and at least one art historian has claimed that American painting did not achieve a uniquely American point of view until the work of Jackson Pollock in the 1930s and 1940s.

Whatever their stylistic indebtedness to European art and literature, however, American artists and writers did possess their own distinctly American subject matter. The physical presence of a frontier of wilderness provided Americans with a unique experience of mystery, beckoning, and challenge not available to European writers and artists, and much of the American art of the nineteenth century is imaginatively caught up in its existence. Also, the Puritan heritage of many early American writers, such as Hawthorne and Herman Melville (1819–1891), found expression in a biblically based mythology of the new nation. Perhaps the most authentically American voice prior to Mark Twain's was that of Walt Whitman (p. 845). His *Song of Myself* announces itself as a poem in the ROMANTIC vein, taking as its subject the poet himself. It is very different, however, from Wordsworth's autobiographical Romantic epic, *The Prelude* (written in 1805 but not published until 1850), which was subtitled "Growth of a Poet's Mind." In that work, Wordsworth writes of his personal, subjective experience; in *Song of Myself,* Whitman makes his personal experience the basis for a celebration of the richness and diversity of America. His song becomes America's song, and its catalogs of the country's landscape and people established Whitman's reputation abroad as "the poet of democracy." Standing on the Pacific coast, the poet marvelled at the breadth and size of America and at its non-Eurocentric perspective, in which a person could face west and look toward the East.

Slavery and Emancipation.   The other great struggle in nineteenth-century America was an internal one—the fight against slavery. European travelers to the United States were fond of pointing out the hypocrisy of the institution of slavery in a nation that boasted of its commitment to liberty. Although American opposition to slavery began as an attempt to realize the principles of the Declaration of Independence and the U.S. Constitution, the abolition movement also belonged to a worldwide effort. When the French revolutionaries declared the "rights of man," they encouraged people everywhere to consider the injustice of slavery. Toussaint-Louverture, the "black Napoleon" of the French colony of Haiti, where slaves far outnumbered European colonists, in 1791 led a revolt to free the slaves and secure independence for the island. In the nations liberated by Simón Bolívar in Latin America, new constitutions often included a provision prohibiting slavery. The movements to end slavery in the British colonies and the United States had their first successes in 1807 and 1808, when Britain and the United States stopped participating in the slave trade. Britain abolished slavery in its colonies in 1833; it took a war to prompt President Lincoln, the "Great Emancipator," to issue the Emancipation Proclamation in 1862. The Civil War (1861–65) was fought to abolish slavery, preserve the Union, and eliminate the feudal agricultural economy of the South that relied upon slavery and was thought to be an impediment to the industrial and economic development of the nation as a whole. Unlike most wars of liberation during the nineteenth century, the Civil War was started by the conservatives, the South. However, the war's outcomes—national unity, a free economy, and the expansion of democracy—were those sought by liberal movements elsewhere.

Literature of Emancipation.   Besides the works of abolitionist authors such as Harriet Beecher Stowe (1811–1896), whose *Uncle Tom's Cabin* (1852) is a classic of the antislavery movement, the literary legacy of slavery lies within the many SLAVE NARRATIVES—autobiographical stories telling of the captivity, escape, and ultimate freedom of slaves—and sorrow songs, or spirituals, produced in the nineteenth century. Using imagery that drew on everyday experience as well as the Bible to evoke the slaves' situation and express the meaning of freedom, these spirituals contain some of the most moving poetry of the century. Among the many American slave narratives, usually published with the aid of Northern abolitionists, are the autobiographies of Frederick Douglass (1817–1895) (p. 520), the activist, journalist, and public servant, and Harriet Jacobs (p. 499), who published her narrative under the pen name Linda Brent.

JAPAN: THE TOKUGAWA ERA

The period in Japan from 1603 to 1868 is known as the Tokugawa, or Edo, period, named after its first *shogun,* or military ruler, and the capital city. Like its European counterparts, Japan in the late seventeenth and early eighteenth centuries enjoyed a period of relative calm after a series of chaotic civil wars among rival *daimyo,* or feudal lords. Continuing the consolidation of power that had begun in the middle of the sixteenth century, in 1603 Tokugawa Ieyasu (r. 1603–1616) instituted a military government, the *shogunate,* which ruled Japan from the capital city Edo (now Tokyo) for the next two hundred years. Under the Tokugawa shogunate, the emperor was retained as a ceremonial figure, while the shogun and the officials of his central administration, the *bakufu,* were charged with the actual governance. Promoting neo-Confucianist doctrines that emphasized loyalty, duty, and filial piety, the Tokugawa rulers attempted to maintain a rigidly hierarchical society divided into four distinct groups—warriors (*samurai*), farmers, artisans, and merchants. Population growth, the rise of the urban middle classes, and the introduction of new trades and professions during this era, however, confounded the fourfold scheme.

East-West Relations.   Japan's direct trade and exchange of ideas with Westerners began when Portuguese merchants first arrived in 1543. Among other goods, the Europeans introduced gunpowder and firearms to the Japanese. Francis Xavier, a Jesuit missionary, arrived in Japan in 1549 and was followed by priests from other orders, including Franciscans, who joined in efforts to convert the Japanese to Christianity. By the time of the Tokugawa shogunate there were several hundred thousand Japanese Christians, particularly in the southern islands. Repeating similar mistakes that had been made in China, some of the missionaries, with the backing of the pope, destroyed Japanese idols and interfered with local politics. In reprisal, Tokugawa ordered the expulsion of all Christian missionaries in 1612. After a failed revolt by Christians on the island of Kyushu in 1637, Christianity was banned altogether and Japan effectively closed its doors to foreign trade. With the exception of some limited trade with Korea and China, after 1641 only the Dutch, under strict

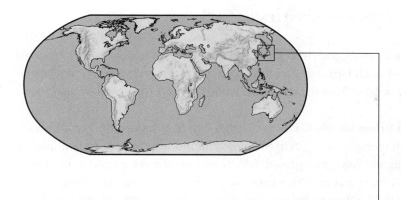

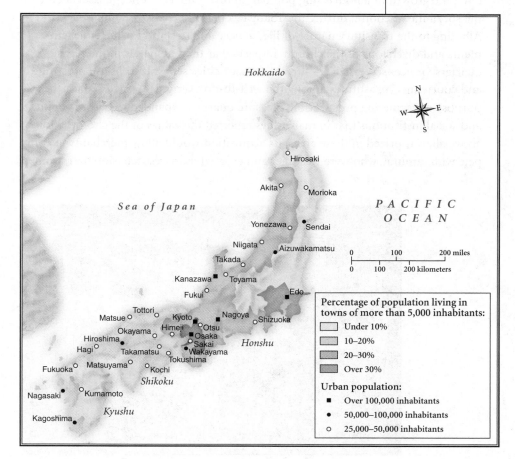

Population Density in Late Tokugawa Japan

In 1603, Tokugawa Ieyasu instituted a military government, the shogunate, which ruled Japan for the next two hundred years. This period was known as the Tokugawa or Edo period. As this map indicates, one notable change in Japanese society during this time was population growth, especially in the cities. A previously rigid social structure gave way to new trades, professions, and classes — the middle classes — and urban life changed dramatically.

regulations, exchanged goods with Japan, operating a small trading post in Nagasaki harbor; meanwhile all Japanese were forbidden to travel outside the country. Japan was effectively isolated from the rest of the world for more than two hundred years.

Growth of the Urban Middle Classes.   The growth of cities and the expansion of commerce and manufacturing exerted a powerful influence on society and the arts in Japan during the Tokugawa period. Edo, Kyoto, and Osaka, in particular, grew into thriving commercial centers, where *chonin,* or artisans and merchants, fostered the growth of a flourishing popular culture. One key concept associated with the social life of chonin during the Tokugawa period is *ukiyo,* or "floating world." Alluding to the transitory nature of life, *ukiyo* came to stand for the entertainments and diversions of the chonin, in particular their activities in the pleasure quarters, or licensed districts—areas of major cities set aside to house prostitutes and courtesans (prostitutes among the well-to-do). Originally enclosed for the purpose of regulating prostitution, pleasure quarters expanded to become cultural and social institutions that in many ways reflected the values of the chonin. Money, above all, was prized in these areas; its acquisition would allow merchants to compete with samurai, who were wealthier and enjoyed more respect. Moreover, women

Torii Kiyotada, *Middle Street of the Yoshiwara*, c. 1740. Hand-Colored Woodblock Print
Many Japanese woodblock prints of the eighteenth century portrayed the "floating world," the pleasure district in Edo (Tokyo), where the newly affluent bourgeoisie enjoyed the company of courtesans, storytellers, jesters, and other entertainers. (Art Institute of Chicago)

in the pleasure quarters achieved a level of independence and respect not possible under the strict doctrines of subordination ushered in by Tokugawa rulers. In the pleasure quarters, men enjoyed the attentions of beautiful and sometimes well-educated courtesans, who observed formal standards of etiquette.

This "floating world" of openly sexual relationships regulated by formal rituals of courtship and economic exchange was often in conflict with the world of family and social responsibility. Marriage at the time often had very little to do with romantic love. As among the upper classes in Europe, China, and India, marriages were often arranged by interested parents as a means to preserve or maintain social standing and economic power, especially among samurai and the wealthiest *chonin*. While some husbands and wives fell in love with each other, some did not, and a man with sufficient funds to both support his wife and finance a relationship with a courtesan had tacit license to do so. Women, however, were bound by marriage; a married woman who took a lover was subject by law to execution. As can be seen in the plays of Chikamatsu Monzaemon (1653–1742) and the fiction of Ihara Saikaku (1642–1693), complications stemming from a man's divided affections at home and in the floating world figures prominently in the writing of the Tokugawa era.

Neo-Confucianism.   Although BUDDHISM and the native Shintoism played a strong role in Japanese religious life, education and social practices in the Tokugawa era were based largely on neo-Confucianist principles. A school of thought associated with the Chinese philosopher Zhu Xi (Chu Hsi, 1130–1200) and developed in Japan by Fujiwara Seika (1561–1619) and Hayashi Razan (1583–1657), NEO-CONFUCIANISM appealed to the ruling shoguns because it suited their aim to promote social stability and hierarchical order. For many members of Japanese society, neo-Confucianism was beneficial because it spread literacy through the classes, and even among women. Unlike most of their European peers, Japanese women studied in public or private schools, but they lost some of their previous rights to inheritance, property, and divorce under the strict Tokugawan rules of subordination.

During the Tokugawa era, neo-Confucianism began to reflect a new worldview, one oriented in its "investigation of things"—a common phrase of the time—to an empirical observation of nature. In a spirit of inquiry very much like that of their contemporaries in Europe, philosophers such as Kaibara Ekken (1630–1714) and Baien Miura (1723–1789)—whose work is excerpted in the *In the World* section "Enlightenment and the Spirit of Inquiry"—argued that in order to find our place in nature, we need to escape from convention and habit and seek to discover the principles and laws that govern nature. Kaibara in particular helped to spread neo-Confucian ideas widely, writing several treatises addressed to the newly liter-ate classes and to women and children. Thus, the Tokugawa era witnessed a ren-aissance in philosophical thinking, the development of empirical studies, and the spread of education.

The Rise of Popular Literature.   Japanese literature and arts flourished during the seventeenth and eighteenth centuries as a result of the peace and economic stability of the Tokugawa period. Before this time, literature had been written by and for the elite—samurai and nobles. As such, it reflected the beliefs and culture of the upper classes; literature aimed at the common people was designed primar-ily to proclaim the values of the elite and particularly to reinforce loyalty and piety. Two phenomena of the sixteenth and seventeenth centuries began to change all that: the development of printing and the rise of the *chonin*. By the late six-teenth century, following the example of Jesuits who had used wood and copper type, Japan developed a relatively inexpensive form of woodblock printing. With this new method, various kinds of writing—as well as woodblock prints—could reach a wide audience. And when urban artisans and merchants began to do well in the commercial cities of Edo, Kyoto, and Osaka, they exerted a tremendous influence on the form and content of literature and the arts.

In poetry, too, significant changes took place in the Tokugawa era, particularly in the case of *haikai* master Matsuo Bashō (1644–1694) (p. 122), whose work would revolutionize Japanese poetry and Japanese taste. Bashō's artistic sensibility evolved from his studies of the Japanese and Chinese classics, but his work is remarkable for its innovation, especially in the art of *haibun*, a mixture of linked verse and prose in which Bashō describes his sojourns through the countryside to sacred shrines and other places far from the floating world of the cities. In the six-

Although mass education did not produce widespread literacy until well into the eighteenth century, in the late seventeenth century *chonin* demand for enter-tainment began to affect both drama and fiction. In a portion of the Tokugawa era known as the Genroku period (1688–1704; see Time and Place box, p. 124) writers such as dramatist Chikamatsu Monzaemon and fiction writer Ihara Saikaku began writing plays, short stories, and novels that reflected the lives and values of the middle classes. Whereas the courtly *Nō* dramas appealed to the elite tastes of samurai and aristocrats, two new forms of drama—KABUKI, or live drama, and JORURI, or puppet theater—increasingly took for their themes the lives of courte-sans, bankers, tradesmen, and artisans living in cities.

In poetry, too, significant changes took place in the Tokugawa era, particularly in the case of *haikai* master Matsuo Bashō (1644–1694) (p. 122), whose work would revolutionize Japanese poetry and Japanese taste. Bashō's artistic sensibility evolved from his studies of the Japanese and Chinese classics, but his work is remarkable for its innovation, especially in the art of *haibun*, a mixture of linked verse and prose in which Bashō describes his sojourns through the countryside to sacred shrines and other places far from the floating world of the cities. In the six-

WWW   For more information about the culture and context of Japan from 1650 to 1850, see bedfordstmartins.com/worldlitcompact.

teenth century haikai was a popular, satiric form of poetry; Bashō made it into a meditative, reflective form of personal expression.

CHINA: THE EARLY QING DYNASTY

Like Europe and Japan, China experienced a period of relative peace in the eighteenth century that had been preceded by a time of civil unrest. At the end of the Ming dynasty (1368–1644), general dissatisfaction among the people culminated in a revolt led by Li Zicheng (1604–1651), whose rebel army took the capital of Beijing (Peking) in 1644. Seizing the opportunity to intervene and take control of China themselves, the MANCHU, a people from what is now Manchuria, enlisted the help of some disgruntled Ming generals and set themselves up as rulers in Beijing. By 1683, when Emperor Kangxi (r. 1661–1722) seized Taiwan, Manchu rule had engulfed both north and south China. Thus was born the Qing (Ch'ing) or Manchu dynasty that endured until the October Revolution of 1911.

The Qing Dynasty.   After more than fifty years of severe repression at the onset of their reign, the Manchu eased their policies and replaced terror with strategic accommodation. Adopting the Chinese system of bureaucratic government, the Manchu inaugurated a period of peace and prosperity in China. Manchu soldiers, known as Bannermen, enforced Manchu policies and helped stabilize China's many miles of border while extending its boundaries. The Qing emperors increased trade with Europe and Russia and brokered a system of shared governance that enabled the Manchu to maintain the chief authority while including some Chinese, even in the highest ranks of government, and benefitting from the administrative expertise of the Chinese intelligentsia. In addition, the Manchu eventually won the favor of small farmers by promoting agriculture and keeping taxes low, at least through the mid-eighteenth century. The Manchu embraced the traditional CONFUCIAN principles of order, revived the Chinese system of civil service examinations, and patronized the arts, letters, and scholarship.

Confucianism and Literacy.   The Confucian doctrines espoused by Qing emperors emphasized hierarchy, filial piety, and loyalty. Like the so-called enlightened despots of Europe, Kangxi was not only an effective politician and leader but also a cultured individual—an amateur musician, a poet, and a calligrapher who displayed a keen interest in traditional Chinese history and culture. His respect for that culture and his desire to discourage potential dissent led him to push for rote memorization of the Confucian classics and imitation of classical poetic and aesthetic forms. Kangxi and later Manchu emperors promoted a high degree of literacy, some of which trickled down to the larger population. During this time,

Leng Mei, Lady
with Attendants
in a Garden, Early
Eighteenth Century.
Hanging Scroll
*(Courtesy of the
Museum of Fine Arts,
Boston. Reproduced
with permission.
© 2000 Museum of
Fine Arts, Boston.
All Rights Reserved.)*

along with their training in etiquette, calligraphy, and poetry, some women received at least an introduction to the Confucianist texts, which their brothers and male cousins studied intensively in order to pass the civil service examinations. The Manchu sponsored a number of extensive writing projects, including the translation of Chinese texts into Manchu, the writing of a detailed history of the Ming dynasty, and the production of a massive illustrated encyclopedia that covered astronomy, mathematics, geography, history, zoology, philosophy, literature, law, politics, and more. But above all these works stood *The Complete Collection of Written Materials Divided into Four Categories,* completed in 1782 after ten years by a group of 360 scholars and 15,000 copyists; this treatise on and compilation of all known materials in print or manuscript contained nearly 80,000 volumes, grouped into four categories: canonical, historical, philosophical, and literary. While this work was a valuable bibliographical resource, it was also used by Emperor Qianlong (r. 1736–96) to censor and destroy any texts that he believed were hostile to the Manchu.

East-West Contact.   By the eighteenth century China had had a long, if discontinuous, history of trading with the West. Often that trade was conducted through middlemen—Arabs, Turks, and Mongols—who controlled the lands linking the western Chinese border to the port towns of the Mediterranean. From at least the thirteenth century, expeditions like those of Marco Polo had reached China directly via land routes, and by 1514 the Portuguese had come by sea and set up limited trade with Canton. The Dutch arrived in 1624, establishing a trading center on the island of Taiwan (then called Formosa), and the English set up trade at Canton in 1699. The Chinese strictly regulated the activities of these European traders, who did a heavy business in Chinese silks, porcelain, and tea. In exchange the Chinese wanted only gold or silver, for they had no desire for European goods. When the British emissary Lord Macartney tried to increase Britain's access to China in 1793, Emperor Qianlong made clear the Chinese position: ". . . the virtue of the Celestial dynasty having spread far and wide, the kings of myriad nations come by land and sea with all sorts of precious things. Consequently there is nothing we lack, as your principal envoy and others have themselves observed. We have never set much store on strange or ingenious objects, nor do we need any more of your country's manufactures. . . ."

The Chinese were interested, however, in Western science, astronomy, and mathematics, so that scholars such as the Italian Jesuit Matteo Ricci (1552–1610) were not only tolerated but respected. The Jesuits helped the Chinese in cartography, translated treatises (for example, Galileo's writings on astronomy), and improved the design of firearms. These missionaries converted some two to three

Scholar and Attendant. Porcelain
*During the Qing dynasty, scholars were once again revered members of society. People of
literary accomplishment were portrayed in art with an air of tranquility and nobility.
(Laurie Platt Winfrey)*

hundred thousand Chinese to Christianity by the eighteenth century. Dominican
and Franciscan missionaries, however, condemned Confucianism and tried to force
strict Catholic ritual on already converted Christians. As a result, the Manchu
expelled all foreign missionaries in 1742. After 1757, when an imperial decree limited all foreign trade to Canton, the Qing dynasty, like the neighboring Tokugawa
government in Japan, maintained a policy of isolation and exclusion until the
British forced China to open its ports to foreigners in the nineteenth century.

By the end of the eighteenth century, the expense of maintaining China's long inland border had begun to sap the imperial budgetary reserves. This led to an increase in taxes on agriculture and peasants, precipitating the White Lotus Rebellion (1796–1804). Although this rebellion was eventually suppressed, the Qing dynasty was beginning to weaken in the face of governmental corruption, overspending, increased population, and, eventually, the aggressive actions of the British that culminated in the Opium War (1839–42). That war opened Chinese ports to the British and ultimately to large-scale foreign trade. Staving off foreign intervention and struggling with internal problems, the Qing dynasty managed to endure through the nineteenth century, finally collapsing with the October Revolution of 1911, led by followers of Sun Yat-sen (1866–1925), founder of the first Chinese republic and often called the father of modern China.

Chinese Literature.   As in Europe and Japan, China during the late Ming (1368–1644) and early Qing (1644–1911) dynasties witnessed a burgeoning of popular, or vernacular, literature (literature written in the spoken dialect rather than in the classical literary style), due in part to rising urban populations and the spread of literacy. Those who had previously relied on oral storytellers and classical plays for their entertainment were drawn to literary forms like the short story, the novel, and popular theater. Like their European and Japanese counterparts, Chinese writers moved toward realistic depictions of everyday life and therefore used a more colloquial style of writing. Some writers also left behind autobiographical writings or "records," such as Shen Fu's *Six Records of a Floating Life,* a touching memoir written in 1809.

While drama had always been popular in China and took many forms, ranging from variety plays to musical performances, in the late seventeenth century a new, highly elaborate drama emerged that was aimed primarily at elite, literate audiences. These so-called southern-style Chinese plays, unlike the short, four-act plays of the northern-style, or Yuan, play, sometimes comprised more than fifty scenes. Two of the most important are *The Peony Pavilion (Mu-dan ting)* by Tang Xian-zu and *The Peach Blossom Fan* by Kong Shang-ren. Also during the seventeenth and eighteenth centuries, some of China's greatest novels appeared, including *The Journey to the West,* also known as *Monkey (Xi-you ji,* 1592), and above all *The Story of the Stone (Shitouji),* also known as *The Dream of the Red Chamber (Hung lou meng).* *The Story of the Stone,* by Cao Xueqin and Gao E, is considered China's greatest novel, equivalent to Cervantes's *Don Quixote* and Tolstoy's *War and Peace* (1863–69). Centered on the declining fortunes of the affluent Jia clan, the novel presents a panoramic view of Chinese society in the early Qing dynasty.

Short fiction also flourished during this time, particularly VERNACULAR FICTION — stories that came from folklore and oral traditions. Three writers who devoted their lives to collecting and rewriting popular stories and folklore, and in some cases composing new works, were Feng Meng-long (1574–1646), Ling Meng-chu (1574–1646), and Pu Song-Ling (P'u Sung Ling; 1640–1715) (p. 116). Many of the collected stories are realistic tales of merchants and people living in the cities, though ghost stories and stories about court life were still popular. Pu Song-Ling's *Strange Stories from a Chinese Studio* (*Liao-zhai zhi-yi*, 1766) were written in the classical rather than vernacular style. They portray everyday life but often contain elements of the supernatural as well. "The Mural," included in this book (p. 119), emphasizes the fantastic and supernatural aspects of Pu Song-Ling's fiction.

As the Qing dynasty advanced, the morality implicit in Confucianist doctrines was strictly interpreted and enforced. From 1774 to 1794 a literary inquisition took place under the rule of Qianlong. Early works were censored and many writers were arrested for portraying the Manchus in an unflattering light. Overall more than ten thousand books were prohibited and over two thousand works destroyed. This massive censorship was just one of many signs of the government's weakness in the late eighteenth century, setting the stage for the decline and final collapse of the Qing dynasty over the next century. By the nineteenth century, China was on the verge of a European onslaught that would utterly transform its society. Writers would look back on the late Ming and early Qing periods as one of the greatest cultural and literary eras since the Tang dynasty (618–907), which had basked in the light of poets such as Li Bai (701–762) and Du Fu (712–770).

INDIA: THE MUGHAL EMPIRE

Beginning in the mid-sixteenth century, Mongol-Muslim conquerors, known by their Persian name as Mughals, seized parts of northwest India and began to establish an empire that by the seventeenth century encompassed a territory marked by Kabul in the northwest, Surat and Calicut on the Arabian Sea, and Calcutta on the Bay of Bengal. Reaching its apex under the rule of Akbar (r. 1556–1605), the Mughal empire endured through the eighteenth century, until India became tied to imperial Europe, particularly Great Britain.

Akbar, "the Great Mughal," instituted a program of religious tolerance, abolishing the hated poll tax on non-Muslims and allowing some Hindus to serve in court and hold government positions. His policies led to a period of stability, accompanied by a flowering of the arts and architecture. Akbar was succeeded at his death by the relatively ineffective Jahangir (r. 1605–1628) and then by Shah Jahan (r. 1628–1658), whose skills at expanding the empire were matched by his

www For more information about the culture and context of China and India from 1650 to 1850, see bedfordstmartins.com/worldlitcompact.

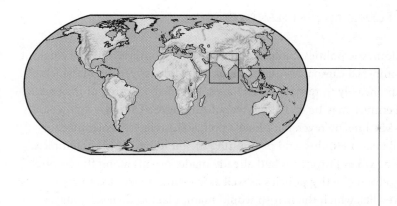

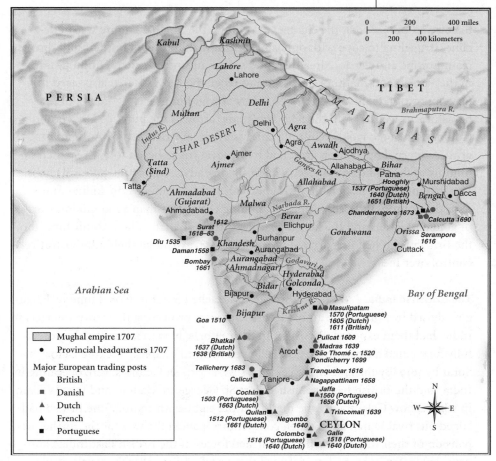

Mughal India, 1707

In the beginning of the eighteenth century, much of India was united under the Mughals, a group of Mongol-Muslim rulers who had descended from the north. India flourished under Mughal rule, its splendor rivaled only by the Ottoman and Chinese empires. The Taj Mahal was constructed under Mughal rulers, and many provinces of India were unified for the first time.

ineptitude in domestic politics. Building the Taj Mahal, in Agra, and carrying out the emperor's imperial campaigns almost bankrupted the government, which taxed agriculture heavily to recuperate its losses. But the beginning of the end of the Mughal empire may be laid at the feet of Aurangzeb (r. 1658–1707), who alienated non-Muslims by reversing Akbar's policies of religious tolerance, restoring the poll tax on Hindus, and prohibiting the building of Hindu temples. Enacted at a time when Europeans had already made inroads along the empire's coasts, Aurangzeb's restrictive policies as well as exorbitant taxes led to civil unrest and finally to revolts, which the British would manipulate to their advantage.

Revolt and Unrest.   In the eighteenth century, the Mughal empire was in decline, struggling to cope with opposition from within its own borders and threats from Europe and Persia. Already in the late seventeenth century, Hindu peasants in the Punjab and Mathura had begun to rebel; the Mughals had also faced military opposition from a Hindu force led by Shivaji Bhonsle (1627–1680), of Maharashtra, as well as from the Sikh *khalsa,* or "army of the pure," led by guru Gobind Rai (1666–1708). While Shivaji was eventually defeated by Aurangzeb's armies, internal opposition grew and many local rulers began to reassert their autonomy at the end of Aurangzeb's reign. Taking advantage of the political chaos, Persians under the leadership of Nadir Shah sacked Delhi in 1739, killing more than thirty thousand people and absconding with more than $200 million worth of gold and jewels and the fabled peacock throne of Shah Jahan. At this time, too, the British, who had first arrived at Surat in 1608, expanded their administrative control over India.

The British in India.   When the British first reached Surat in 1608, Emperor Jahangir, advised by Portuguese ambassadors who were protecting their own interests in India, had them expelled. Persistent in their efforts, however, the British successfully negotiated a treaty in 1613 that allowed them to establish a textile factory at Surat by 1619. By the end of the century, several British factories were operating in India, and the British had established Fort St. George, at Madras, and Fort William, in what is now Calcutta. By the middle of the eighteenth century, the British had edged out rival Dutch and French competitors, paving the way for the further expansion of their interests. When the armed forces of the British East India Company, led by Sir Robert Clive, defeated the *nawab* of Bengal at the Battle of Plassey in 1757, the British established firm control over Bengal. This turning point secured the future of British imperial power and led the way to British expansion and absolute control over India in the next several decades. Many Indians entered into the service of the British and some, such as Abu Taleb (1752–1806), an Indian

Lady Elijah Impey, Wife of the Chief Justice of Bengal, 1782
*This painting shows an eighteenth-century British drawing room in colonial India, filled
with Indians tending to the wife of a British ruler. (The Art Archive)*

Muslim from Oudh, traveled to the British Isles. Abu Taleb's *Travels,* excerpted in
this book (p. 179), records his impressions of British society.

In the nineteenth century the British would consolidate and extend their power
in India, gaining control of the whole Indian subcontinent through a series of
colonial wars and through taking advantage of the divisions in the region after the
collapse of the Mughal empire. During the first half of the century the British were
occupied with expelling the French from southern India, challenging the Russians
on the northern borders and in Afghanistan, defeating the HINDU Marathi forces
in central and northern India, and pushing out from their central power base in
Bengal to take over neighboring states and prevent incursions over the borders.
Until the 1830s, the British had taken largely an economic and legal interest in
India and made little attempt to impose European culture on the Indian people.
With the growing influence of evangelical Christians in the British government
after passage of the Reform Bill of 1832, however, missionaries were sent to India
and English was declared the medium of instruction in many Indian schools.
Along with the English language a new curriculum including English literature,
philosophy, and political and social theory was adopted for Indian schools. While

many Indians welcomed the opportunity to study and gain access to Western ideas and science, the imposition of Western culture also sparked resistance. The second half of the century saw a revival of interest in Hinduism, protests against the excesses of British colonialism, and the beginnings of an independence movement.

The Sepoy Rebellion.   Symbolically, the Sepoy Rebellion of 1857–58, in India often called the First War of Independence, was the century's defining event in Indian-British relations. The Sepoys, native troops in the British army, had over the years protested several times against their treatment by British officers. When some of their perquisites were cut and they were no longer exempted from foreign service—an assignment that violated some caste rules—the Sepoys were angered. Ordered to bite off the ends of cartridges that were lubricated with a mixture of cow and pig fat—offensive to both Hindus and Muslims—they took up arms. In a series of rebellions at Delhi, Lucknow, Peshawar, and several other sites across northern and central India, the Sepoys challenged the British. The disturbances lasted over a year, from May 1857 until July 1858. Although the military revolt never expanded into a broader national movement, the soldiers had considerable sympathy and covert support from conservative landowners and religious leaders who were distrustful of Westernization.

After a successful military campaign to put down the rebellion, the British pulled back from the liberalizing measures they had instituted before the uprising. They abandoned their attempts to abolish *suttee* (the ritual burning of widows on their husbands' funeral pyres), infanticide of unwanted daughters, and the traditional ban on widows remarrying. Traditional factions of Indian society who resisted Westernization were placated. The British also abolished the British East India Company, which had administered the colony for the British, and placed India under the direct rule of the crown. They reorganized the army, increasing the percentage of European troops and providing some opportunities for Indian troops to be promoted into positions of limited authority. They also opened up positions in the colonial administration to Indians and established a policy of limited consultation with them on political and legislative issues. These measures pleased the Westernized middle class, who had been disappointed by the British decision to abandon reform of the caste system and the marriage laws.

Indian Literature.   As was its religion, India's arts and literature during the Mughal period involved a rich mixture of Islamic, Persian, and Hindu influences. Mughal painting, which flourished under the patronage of Akbar, for example, combines Persian and Indian elements. Indian painters even adapted the halo from European images of saints and reinterpreted it in portraits of their emperors.

Indian Procession
This painting illustrates the prominence of the gods in eighteenth-century Indian life.
(Courtesy of the British Musuem)

The architecture of the time, one of the greatest achievements of the Mughal empire, reflects this multicultural synthesis. The most outstanding example is the Taj Mahal. Built under the reign of Shah Jahan as a tribute to the memory of his wife, Mumtaz Mahal, this spectacular mausoleum, one of the world's most beautiful buildings, was designed by Persian architects and built by Indian craftsmen and laborers; it incorporates Byzantine, Persian, and Hindu elements.

One key force in Indian literature during the Mughal period was the revival of devotional literature, or *bhakti*, which played a role in India's maintaining a distinctively Indian identity. Bhakti was also a movement, and like the Protestant revolt against Catholicism in Europe it emphasized a personal devotion and an ecstatic union with God and was in part directed against the more rigid orthodoxy of Hinduism and its priests. While some members of the lower castes in the Mughal era turned to Islam to escape the rigid hierarchy of Hinduism, others turned to Bhakti, which spread throughout India from the thirteenth to the eighteenth centuries. Bhakti poets wrote in the vernacular languages rather than Sanskrit, the language of Hindu classics. Poets such as Nanak (1469–1538), the founder of the Sikhs, and Tulsidas (1532–1623), the author of the great retelling of the story of Rama, *Ramcaritmanas,* wrote in Hindi; Jnanesvar (1275–1296), the author of commentaries on the Bhagavad Gita, wrote in Marathi; and Ramprasad Sen (1718–1775) wrote in Bengali (see p. 438). Bhakti writers composed hymns of praise to the god Vishnu and, less often, the god Shiva as well as to the Mother Goddess and Shiva's consort, or spouse, Shakti. These hymns were meant to be sung in a kind of dance performance known as *kirtan,* whereby a worshiper would experience an immediate communion with God. Hence these hymns typically display a passionate intensity and employ the language of love—emotional and sexual—to express the devotee's relation to the god or goddess, as in the poems of Ramprasad, whose work is excerpted here. A Bengali poet and Bhakti devotee of the fearsome goddess Kali, Ramprasad represents the culmination of the Bhakti tradition.

Among the greatest of the early or mid-nineteenth century poets was Mirza Asadullah Beg Khan, known as Ghalib (1797–1869). Writing in Urdu, a language close to Hindi, which contains elements of Persian and Arabic, Ghalib draws upon Persian literary forms, particularly the *qasidah,* poems of praise, like the western ode, and the *ghazal,* a rhymed lyric of three to seven couplets that may be compared to the sonnet. Living in Delhi and serving in the court of King Bahadur Shah Zafar, a rival poet, Ghalib witnessed the atrocities of the Sepoy Rebellion firsthand, and he condemned both sides for their lack of humanity and for turning the city of Delhi into a sea of blood. Reflecting in part on his disillusionment with the world around him, Ghalib's poetry often alludes elliptically to his personal experience with the conflict in his country and is characterized by an intense sense of longing and desire, ironically undercut by a sense of the impossibility of fruition. One of the nineteenth century's finest lyric poets, Ghalib is revered in northern India as the great master of the *ghazal.*

Ghalib's poetry responds to the turmoil of India in the late eighteenth and early nineteenth centuries as the Mughal empire was being drawn apart from internal conflicts, exacerbated, of course, by the increasingly tight British administrative and military grip of many parts of the country. Through British colonial schools, western literature and literary forms spread throughout the country, leading to some assimilation of western forms, as well as reactions against this ideological or cultural incursion upon native traditions. Nonetheless, Sanskrit literature, as well as Arabic and Persian literature, also exerted considerable influence upon Indian writers—particularly Islamic writers—giving rise to a variety of hybridized works that anticipates the writing of later nineteenth- and twentieth-century Indian literature.

JEAN-BAPTISTE POQUELIN MOLIÈRE
B. FRANCE, 1622–1673

The seventeenth century was a celebrated period in French drama that included the works of dramatists Corneille, Racine,[1] and Molière; it was comparable to the Elizabethan Age in England, which had Marlowe, Ben Jonson, and Shakespeare.[2] It was a time in France when the theater matured, with professional touring companies and public theaters, even though the actor's lifestyle was condemned by the clergy. The search by mathematicians for regularity in the cosmos was mirrored by the desire of kings and rulers for order and harmony. Artists, in turn, adopted orderly, **NEOCLASSICAL** standards for artistic expression and developed rules for judging works of art. The absolute standard for elegance and decorum in all phases of life was France's King Louis XIV;[3] his palace at Versailles and Paris itself became centers of culture similar to Rome under the Caesars. The court became the model for the upper classes, who sought to distance themselves from the lower classes and anything that could be considered vulgar. The possessions and behavior that distinguished the upper crust in the seventeenth century were essentially the same as those seen today: fine clothes and elegant manners, training in foreign languages, and a refined taste for art, food, and music.

Molière contributed to the new social order by writing "comedies of manners": plays that deal with the social conventions of gentlemen and gentlewomen in a sophisticated age. The slavish imitation of contemporary fashions by the middle class also became a handy target for comedy and **SATIRE**. We still use the words *fop* and *dandy*—taken from seventeenth-century drama—to describe the individual whose vanity yields to excesses. While to all appearances, science was making astonishing strides in discovering and describing a rational universe, human society, for all its hopes and pretensions, seemed to lag behind. It was easier to formulate a new law of physics than to eradicate a basic fault of human nature, such as greed. **Molière** used the full resources of French theater to expose the gap between the ideal and the real by creating comedies that poked fun at hypocrisy, greed, affectation, zealotry, and immoderation. Despite the pervasive influence of the Catholic Church on seventeenth-century France, Molière's plays are not concerned with the religious implications

Jean-Baptiste Poquelin Molière, Seventeenth Century. Watercolor *Molière as a young man. (Giraudon / Art Resource, N.Y.)*

moh-LYEHR

---

[1] **Corneille, Racine:** The French dramatist Pierre Corneille (1606–1684) is known for his tragedies. It is sometimes said that the production of his *El Cid* in 1636 was the beginning of the Neoclassical period of French theater. Jean Racine (1639–1699) became famous for plays such as *Phaedra* (1677).

[2] **Marlowe, Ben Jonson, and Shakespeare:** The life of the promising playwright Christopher Marlowe (1564–1593) was sadly cut short in a tavern brawl. Ben Jonson (1572–1637) wrote several masterpieces of satiric comedy, including *The Alchemist* (1610). William Shakespeare (1564–1616) is England's most famous dramatist, known for both comedies and tragedies.

[3] **Louis XIV:** Called the Sun King, Louis XIV reigned for an unusually long period in France, from 1643 to 1715, and set the standards for political and social behavior.

of imperfection but rather with the social consequences of immoderation and poor taste, when individuals fail to comply with the ideals of fairness, reasonableness, and common sense.

The Son of the Court Upholsterer.   Jean-Baptiste Poquelin was in line to inherit his father's position as *tapissier ordinaire du roi,* the king's upholsterer, and enjoy a comfortable life. He received a fine education at College de Clermont, a Jesuit college, and practiced law for a short time. In 1643 he drastically changed careers by becoming one of nine founders of an acting company in Paris, the *Illustre Théâtre.* Taking the stage name of Molière for the first time, he devoted the rest of his life to theater — writing, directing, staging, and producing plays. Although theater was popular with the general public, the acting profession itself was condemned by the clergy; in fact, an actor was automatically excommunicated by the church and denied Christian burial unless a renunciation of his chosen career was forthcoming before death.

Molière's new company was a total failure, at least financially; twice the playwright ended up in jail for debts. As a result, he retreated to the countryside where he learned the organizational nuts and bolts of successful theater by touring the back roads and provinces of France. For thirteen years he served an apprenticeship in the various practical and artistic responsibilities of a theatrical company. He also turned his attention from tragedies to comedies — his true calling.

In 1658 Molière returned to Paris, found favor with the court through Louis XIV's brother, "Monsieur," and had an indisputable hit with *The High-Brow Young Ladies (Les précieuses ridicules,* 1659). From then on he enjoyed huge success and the patronage of the king. The titles of his masterpieces constitute a list of the kinds of people he subjected to satire and ridicule. *School for Wives (L'ecole des femmes,* 1662) examines the insecurities of courtship. *Don Juan* (1665) picks up the theme of the playboy and explores intimate relationships. *The Misanthrope* (1666) exposes the shortsightedness of a self-righteous intellectual. *The Miser (L'avare,* 1668), as the title gives away, satirizes lust for money. *The Would-Be Gentleman (Le bourgeois gentilhomme,* 1670) turns on the aspiring middle classes, and *The Learned Ladies (Les femmes savantes,* 1672) attacks educated women. In his last play, *The Hypochondriac, (Le malade imaginaire,* 1673), Molière depicts a hypochondriac at the mercy of the medical profession, a subject that grew out of his personal experiences during the last years of his life. Molière weathered the uncertainties of live theater and the maintenance of an acting company by writing a large number of plays. One of his editors, René Bray, estimates that in a fourteen-year period, 1660–73, Molière wrote thirty-one plays. In all, his company performed ninety-three Molière plays.

Molière died in 1673, a few hours after having acted the title role in *The Hypochondriac.* Priests were not allowed to bring the last rites to him, so Molière did not have the opportunity to renounce his profession. He was denied a Christian burial until his widow and friends persuaded the king to intervene with the archbishop. Only then was one of France's

Molière is so great that he astonishes us afresh every time we read him. He is a man apart; his plays border on the tragic, and no one has the courage to try and imitate him.

—AUGUSTIN SAINTE-BEUVE, critic, 1914

greatest playwrights buried, after dark, in the Saint-Joseph Cemetery on February 21. One can only wonder how Molière would have staged such a convoluted scenario. Molière understood the potential role of theater in the transformation of society. In the preface to *Tartuffe*, he explains why he chose religious hypocrisy for ridicule in that play and why the instrument of satire is so effective:

> If the function of comedy is to correct men's vices, I do not see why any should be exempt. Such a condition in our society would be much more dangerous than the thing itself; and we have seen that the theater is admirably suited to provide correction. The most forceful lines of a serious moral statement are usually less powerful than those of satire; and nothing will reform most men better than the depiction of their faults. It is a vigorous blow to vices to expose them to public laughter.

The Elements of Comedy.   The first version of *Tartuffe*—the first three acts—was performed on May 12, 1664. The archbishop of Paris, Queen Mother Anne of Austria, and the Company of the Blessed Sacrament protested the play to Louis XIV; the play was banned, and Molière was censured. The extreme religious climate of the times is reflected by Pierre Roulé, vicar of St. Barthémy, who wrote that Molière was a "demon in flesh" and "should be burned at the stake as a foretaste of the fires of hell. . . ." The play was rewritten and performed on August 5, 1667, at the Palais-Royal. The president of Parliament brought in the police, and the play was stopped. The archbishop of Paris denounced this version from the pulpit and threatened spectators with excommunication. Although Molière petitioned Louis XIV for relief, the king had to steer politically between the religious zealots and Molière and his sympathizers. The third version of the play, the version we have today, was finally produced in 1669.

Molière's comedy relies upon stock characters, character types that appeared in other plays of the period: the foolish father who is an obstacle to his child's love life; the clever or impudent servant who interjects her witty opinions; the old lady with amusing eccentricities; the virtuous wife. The stock ending for a comedy is the happy marriage, which symbolizes the restoration of order to a society previously threatened by disorder. Molière uses a single character, Tartuffe, to embody the vice he wishes to ridicule—hypocrisy. The satire, as well as the humor, resides in the difference between appearance and reality, between the mask worn by Tartuffe and the man behind the mask. Tartuffe's manipulation of other characters in the play while wearing a mask represents a threat to society. The ultimate goal of the play itself is the unmasking of Tartuffe.

The character Tartuffe is a pious hypocrite who weasels his way into the household of a rather shallow, naive man named Orgon. Using religious flattery, Tartuffe eventually persuades Orgon to give him his daughter's hand, while making passes at Orgon's wife. The play becomes even more complicated and potentially damaging when Tartuffe replaces Orgon's son as the inheritor of Orgon's estate. Incredible as it seems, the

Molière said that comedy should "correct men's errors in the course of amusing them." This marks him as a satirist, one of that ancient breed who use art forms and public forums to attack correctable human faults with the lance of ridicule.

–DAVID RICHARD JONES

www For links to more information about Molière, a quiz on *Tartuffe*, and information about the 21st-century relevance of *Tartuffe*, see bedfordstmartins .com/worldlit compact.

church actually did place moral arbiters in people's homes to reform a family's practices, so Molière was cutting close to reality with his drama. Although Orgon seems decent enough, he is gullible and incapable of getting beneath the false masks worn by Tartuffe.

One of the persistent themes in this play is how private life with its passions and ambiguities can conflict with an orderly code of behavior in the public sphere. Marriage is a convenient arrangement for showing the discrepancies between public gestures and private needs, especially with the explosive power of sexuality. Although the women in the play clearly reveal the subordinate roles of women in French society of the time, two of them nevertheless have strong, intelligent roles to play. The servant Dorine not only provides humor with her outrageous tongue, she often articulates a sensible explanation for activities in the play. Orgon's wife, Elmire, is clever enough to ensnare Tartuffe in his own lust.

Underneath the laughter and wit in *Tartuffe* there is a persistent faith in common sense and the individual; with the unmasking of human foibles comes the person who, regardless of social rank, is able to sort out the excesses of human nature and pursue a path of moderation and caring companionship. It is Orgon's brother-in-law, **Cléante**, who consistently shows a common-sense point of view and an ethic of moderation; his rational commentaries reflect an **ENLIGHTENMENT** perspective, tying Molière to the conventional wisdom of his time:

klay-AHNT

> Ah, Brother, man's a strangely fashioned creature
> Who seldom is content to follow Nature,
> But recklessly pursues his inclination
> Beyond the narrow bounds of moderation,
> And often, by transgressing Reason's laws,
> Perverts a lofty aim or noble cause.

Early in the play, Orgon is incapable of appreciating the good sense behind Cléante's words, but through sad experiences and the timely intervention of the king at the end of the play, Orgon triumphs, and his daughter is promised to the appropriate suitor. Although the conclusion of the play indirectly raises questions about the patriarchal system that made Tartuffe's escapades possible, Orgon will "give **Valère**, whose love has proven so true, / The wedded happiness which is his due." Certainly the best ending for a comedy.

vah-LEHR

The attack on religious hypocrisy in *Tartuffe* (1664) ruffled the feathers of both clergy and laity, especially a secret society of Christian extremists called the Company of the Blessed Sacrament, a lay group whose task was to report private sins of the family to public authorities. The play was banned from public view by the king. In defending his play, Molière attributed the censorship to the very hypocrites he was satirizing and commented on them in the preface to the play's first printed edition (1669).

> This is a comedy about which a great deal of fuss has been made, and it has long been persecuted. The people it makes fun of have certainly shown [by keeping his play off the stage for nearly five

years] that they command more influence in France than any of
those I have been concerned with before. Noblemen, pretentious
women, cuckolds, and doctors have all submitted to being put on
the stage and pretended to be as amused as everyone else at the way
I portrayed them, but the hypocrites would not stand for a joke. . . .

Molière's defense is not completely without holes since there were those
who felt that his attacks on excessive or false piety might also blemish the
reputations of the truly pious. After rewriting the play twice in response
to criticism, Molière's third version of the play met with great success.

■ **FURTHER RESEARCH**

Biography
Mantzius, Karl. *Molière*. 1908.
Scott, Virginia. *Molière: A Theatrical Life*. 2000.
Walker, Hallam. *Molière*. 1990.

Historical Background
Knutson, Harold C. *The Triumph of Wit*. 1988.

Criticism
Gossman, Lionel. *Men and Masks: A Study of Molière*. 1963.
Hubert, J. D. *Molière and the Company of Intellect*. 1962.
Lewis, D. B. Wyndham. *Molière: The Comic Mask*. 1959.
Mander, Gertrude. *Molière*. 1973.

■ **PRONUNCIATION**

Cléante: klay-AHNT
Damis: dah-MEES
Flipote: flee-POTE
Molière: moh-LYEHR
Valère: vah-LEHR

Jean Michel le Jeune Moreau, *Scene from Molière's* **Tartuffe**
This scene illustrates the surreptitious behavior featured in Tartuffe.
(Snark / Art Resource, N.Y.)

❧ Tartuffe

Translated by Richard Wilbur

MME. PERNELLE, *Orgon's mother*
ORGON, *Elmire's husband*
ELMIRE, *Orgon's wife*
DAMIS, *Orgon's son, Elmire's stepson*
MARIANE, *Orgon's daughter, Elmire's*
   stepdaughter, in love with Valère
VALÈRE, *in love with Mariane*

CLÉANTE, *Orgon's brother-in-law*
TARTUFFE, *a hypocrite*
DORINE, *Mariane's lady's-maid*
M. LOYAL, *a bailiff*
A POLICE OFFICER
FLIPOTE, *Mme. Pernelle's maid*

THE SCENE THROUGHOUT: ORGON's *house in paris*

ACT I

Scene 1

MADAME PERNELLE:
   Come, come, Flipote; it's time I left this place.
ELMIRE:
   I can't keep up, you walk at such a pace.
MADAME PERNELLE:
   Don't trouble, child; no need to show me out.
   It's not your manners I'm concerned about.
ELMIRE:
   We merely pay you the respect we owe.
   But, Mother, why this hurry? Must you go?
MADAME PERNELLE:
   I must. This house appalls me. No one in it
   Will pay attention for a single minute.
   Children, I take my leave much vexed in spirit.
10   I offer good advice, but you won't hear it.
   You all break in and chatter on and on.
   It's like a madhouse with the keeper gone.
DORINE:
   If . . .
MADAME PERNELLE:
       Girl, you talk too much, and I'm afraid
   You're far too saucy for a lady's-maid.
   You push in everywhere and have your say.
DAMIS:
   But . . .
MADAME PERNELLE:
       You, boy, grow more foolish every day.
   To think my grandson should be such a dunce!

I've said a hundred times, if I've said it once,
That if you keep the course on which you've started,
20   You'll leave your worthy father broken-hearted.
MARIANE:
I think . . .
MADAME PERNELLE:
And you, his sister, seem so pure,
So shy, so innocent, and so demure.
But you know what they say about still waters.
I pity parents with secretive daughters.
ELMIRE:
Now, Mother . . .
MADAME PERNELLE:
And as for you, child, let me add
That your behavior is extremely bad,
And a poor example for these children, too.
Their dear, dead mother did far better than you.
You're much too free with money, and I'm distressed
30   To see you so elaborately dressed.
When it's one's husband that one aims to please,
One has no need of costly fripperies.
CLÉANTE:
Oh, Madame, really . . .
MADAME PERNELLE:
You are her brother, Sir,
And I respect and love you; yet if I were
My son, this lady's good and pious spouse,
I wouldn't make you welcome in my house.
You're full of worldly counsels which, I fear,
Aren't suitable for decent folk to hear.
I've spoken bluntly, Sir; but it behooves us
40   Not to mince words when righteous fervor moves us.
DAMIS:
Your man Tartuffe is full of holy speeches . . .
MADAME PERNELLE:
And practises precisely what he preaches.
He's a fine man, and should be listened to.
I will not hear him mocked by fools like you.
DAMIS:
Good God! Do you expect me to submit
To the tyranny of that carping hypocrite?
Must we forgo all joys and satisfactions
Because that bigot censures all our actions?
DORINE:
To hear him talk—and he talks all the time—

50   There's nothing one can do that's not a crime.
         He rails at everything, your dear Tartuffe.

MADAME PERNELLE:

         Whatever he reproves deserves reproof.
         He's out to save your souls, and all of you
         Must love him, as my son would have you do.

DAMIS:

         Ah no, Grandmother, I could never take
         To such a rascal, even for my father's sake.
         That's how I feel, and I shall not dissemble.
         His every action makes me seethe and tremble
         With helpless anger, and I have no doubt
60   That he and I will shortly have it out.

DORINE:

         Surely it is a shame and a disgrace
         To see this man usurp the master's place—
         To see this beggar who, when first he came,
         Had not a shoe or shoestring to his name
         So far forget himself that he behaves
         As if the house were his, and we his slaves.

MADAME PERNELLE:

         Well, mark my words, your souls would fare far better
         If you obeyed his precepts to the letter.

DORINE:

         You see him as a saint. I'm far less awed;
70   In fact, I see right through him. He's a fraud.

MADAME PERNELLE:

         Nonsense.

DORINE:

                 His man Laurent's the same, or worse;
         I'd not trust either with a penny purse.

MADAME PERNELLE:

         I can't say what his servant's morals may be;
         His own great goodness I can guarantee.
         You all regard him with distaste and fear
         Because he tells you what you're loath to hear,
         Condemns your sins, points out your moral flaws,
         And humbly strives to further Heaven's cause.

DORINE:

         If sin is all that bothers him, why is it
80   He's so upset when folk drop in to visit?
         Is Heaven so outraged by a social call
         That he must prophesy against us all?
         I'll tell you what I think: if you ask me,
         He's jealous of my mistress' company.

MADAME PERNELLE:
    Rubbish! [*to* ELMIRE] He's not alone, child, in complaining
    Of all your promiscuous entertaining.
    Why, the whole neighborhood's upset, I know,
    By all these carriages that come and go,
    With crowds of guests parading in and out
90   And noisy servants loitering about.
    In all of this, I'm sure there's nothing vicious;
    But why give people cause to be suspicious?
CLÉANTE:
    They need no cause; they'll talk in any case.
    Madam, this world would be a joyless place
    If, fearing what malicious tongues might say,
    We locked our doors and turned our friends away.
    And even if one did so dreary a thing,
    D'you think those tongues would cease their chattering?
    One can't fight slander; it's a losing battle;
100   Let us instead ignore their tittle-tattle.
    Let's strive to live by conscience's clear decrees,
    And let the gossips gossip as they please.
DORINE:
    If there is talk against us, I know the source:
    It's Daphne and her little husband, of course.
    Those who have greatest cause for guilt and shame
    Are quickest to besmirch a neighbor's name.
    When there's a chance for libel, they never miss it;
    When something can be made to seem illicit
    They're off at once to spread the joyous news,
110   Adding to fact what fantasies they choose.
    By talking up their neighbor's indiscretions
    They seek to camouflage their own transgressions,
    Hoping that others' innocent affairs
    Will lend a hue of innocence to theirs,
    Or that their own black guilt will come to seem
    Part of a general shady color-scheme.
MADAME PERNELLE:
    All that is quite irrelevant. I doubt
    That anyone's more virtuous and devout
    Than dear Orante; and I'm informed that she
120   Condemns your mode of life most vehemently.
DORINE:
    Oh, yes, she's strict, devout, and has no taint
    Of worldliness; in short, she seems a saint.
    But it was time which taught her that disguise;
    She's thus because she can't be otherwise.

So long as her attractions could enthrall,
She flounced and flirted and enjoyed it all,
But now that they're no longer what they were
She quits a world which fast is quitting her,
And wears a veil of virtue to conceal
130   Her bankrupt beauty and her lost appeal.
That's what becomes of old coquettes today:
Distressed when all their lovers fall away,
They see no recourse but to play the prude,
And so confer a style on solitude.
Thereafter, they're severe with everyone,
Condemning all our actions, pardoning none,
And claiming to be pure, austere, and zealous
When, if the truth were known, they're merely jealous,
And cannot bear to see another know
140   The pleasures time has forced them to forgo.

      MADAME PERNELLE [*initially to* ELMIRE]:
That sort of talk is what you like to hear,
Therefore you'd have us all keep still, my dear,
While Madam rattles on the livelong day.
Nevertheless, I mean to have my say.
I tell you that you're blest to have Tartuffe
Dwelling, as my son's guest, beneath this roof;
That Heaven has sent him to forestall its wrath
By leading you, once more, to the true path;
That all he reprehends is reprehensible,
150   And that you'd better heed him, and be sensible.
These visits, balls, and parties in which you revel
Are nothing but inventions of the Devil.
One never hears a word that's edifying:
Nothing but chaff and foolishness and lying,
As well as vicious gossip in which one's neighbor
Is cut to bits with epee, foil, and saber.
People of sense are driven half-insane
At such affairs, where noise and folly reign
And reputations perish thick and fast.
160   As a wise preacher said on Sunday last,
Parties are Towers of Babylon, because
The guests all babble on with never a pause;
And then he told a story which, I think . . .
[*To* CLÉANTE] I heard that laugh, Sir, and I saw that wink!
Go find your silly friends and laugh some more!
Enough; I'm going; don't show me to the door.
I leave this household much dismayed and vexed;
I cannot say when I shall see you next.

[*Slapping* FLIPOTE] Wake up, don't stand there gaping into space!
170   I'll slap some sense into that stupid face.
Move, move, you slut.

Scene 2

CLÉANTE:

                I think I'll stay behind;
I want no further pieces of her mind.
How that old lady . . .

DORINE:

                 Oh, what wouldn't she say
If she could hear you speak of her that way!
She'd thank you for the *lady,* but I'm sure
She'd find the *old* a little premature.

CLÉANTE:

My, what a scene she made, and what a din!
And how this man Tartuffe has taken her in!

DORINE:

Yes, but her son is even worse deceived;
10   His folly must be seen to be believed.
In the late troubles, he played an able part
And served his king with wise and loyal heart,
But he's quite lost his senses since he fell
Beneath Tartuffe's infatuating spell.
He calls him brother, and loves him as his life,
Preferring him to mother, child, or wife.
In him and him alone will he confide;
He's made him his confessor and his guide;
He pets and pampers him with love more tender
20   Than any pretty mistress could engender,
Gives him the place of honor when they dine,
Delights to see him gorging like a swine,
Stuffs him with dainties till his guts distend,
And when he belches, cries "God bless you, friend!"
In short, he's mad; he worships him; he dotes;
His deeds he marvels at, his words he quotes,
Thinking each act a miracle, each word
Oracular as those that Moses heard.
Tartuffe, much pleased to find so easy a victim,
30   Has in a hundred ways beguiled and tricked him,
Milked him of money, and with his permission
Established here a sort of Inquisition.
Even Laurent, his lackey, dares to give
Us arrogant advice on how to live;
He sermonizes us in thundering tones

And confiscates our ribbons and colognes.
Last week he tore a kerchief into pieces
Because he found it pressed in a *Life of Jesus:*
He said it was a sin to juxtapose
40   Unholy vanities and holy prose.

Scene 3

ELMIRE [*to* CLÉANTE]:
    You did well not to follow; she stood in the door
    And said *verbatim* all she'd said before.
    I saw my husband coming. I think I'd best
    Go upstairs now, and take a little rest.
CLÉANTE:
    I'll wait and greet him here; then I must go.
    I've really only time to say hello.
DAMIS:
    Sound him about my sister's wedding, please.
    I think Tartuffe's against it, and that he's
    Been urging Father to withdraw his blessing.
10   As you well know, I'd find that most distressing.
    Unless my sister and Valère can marry,
    My hopes to wed *his* sister will miscarry,
    And I'm determined . . .
DORINE:
                    He's coming.

Scene 4

ORGON:
                    Ah, Brother, good-day.
CLÉANTE:
    Well, welcome back. I'm sorry I can't stay.
    How was the country? Blooming, I trust, and green?
ORGON:
    Excuse me, Brother; just one moment.
    [*To* DORINE]   Dorine . . .
    [*To* CLÉANTE] To put my mind at rest, I always learn
    The household news the moment I return.
    [*To* DORINE] Has all been well, these two days I've been gone?
    How are the family? What's been going on?
DORINE:
    Your wife, two days ago, had a bad fever,
10   And a fierce headache which refused to leave her.
ORGON:
    Ah. And Tartuffe?

DORINE:
                              Tartuffe? Why, he's round and red,
Bursting with health, and excellently fed.
ORGON:
    Poor fellow!
DORINE:
                              That night, the mistress was unable
To take a single bite at the dinner-table.
Her headache-pains, she said, were simply hellish.
ORGON:
    Ah. And Tartuffe?
DORINE:
                              He ate his meal with relish,
And zealously devoured in her presence
A leg of mutton and a brace of pheasants.
ORGON:
    Poor fellow!
DORINE:
                              Well, the pains continued strong,
20   And so she tossed and tossed the whole night long,
Now icy-cold, now burning like a flame.
We sat beside her bed till morning came.
ORGON:
    Ah. And Tartuffe?
DORINE:
                              Why, having eaten, he rose
And sought his room, already in a doze,
Got into his warm bed, and snored away
In perfect peace until the break of day.
ORGON:
    Poor fellow!
DORINE:
                              After much ado, we talked her
Into dispatching someone for the doctor.
He bled her, and the fever quickly fell.
ORGON:
    Ah. And Tartuffe?
DORINE:
                              He bore it very well.
30   To keep his cheerfulness at any cost,
And make up for the blood *Madame* had lost,
He drank, at lunch, four beakers full of port.
ORGON:
    Poor fellow!

DORINE:
>   Both are doing well, in short.
> I'll go and tell *Madame* that you've expressed
> Keen sympathy and anxious interest.

Scene 5

CLÉANTE:
>   That girl was laughing in your face, and though
>   I've no wish to offend you, even so
>   I'm bound to say that she had some excuse.
>   How can you possibly be such a goose?
>   Are you so dazed by this man's hocus-pocus
>   That all the world, save him, is out of focus?
>   You've given him clothing, shelter, food, and care;
>   Why must you also . . .

ORGON:
>   Brother, stop right there.
>   You do not know the man of whom you speak.

CLÉANTE:
10   I grant you that. But my judgment's not so weak
>   That I can't tell, by his effect on others . . .

ORGON:
>   Ah, when you meet him, you two will be like brothers!
>   There's been no loftier soul since time began.
>   He is a man who . . . a man who . . . an excellent man.
>   To keep his precepts is to be reborn,
>   And view this dunghill of a world with scorn.
>   Yes, thanks to him I'm a changed man indeed.
>   Under his tutelage my soul's been freed
>   From earthly loves, and every human tie:
20   My mother, children, brother, and wife could die,
>   And I'd not feel a single moment's pain.

CLÉANTE:
>   That's a fine sentiment, Brother; most humane.

ORGON:
>   Oh, had you seen Tartuffe as I first knew him,
>   Your heart, like mine, would have surrendered to him.
>   He used to come into our church each day
>   And humbly kneel nearby, and start to pray.
>   He'd draw the eyes of everybody there
>   By the deep fervor of his heartfelt prayer;
>   He'd sigh and weep, and sometimes with a sound
30   Of rapture he would bend and kiss the ground;
>   And when I rose to go, he'd run before

To offer me holy-water at the door.
His serving-man, no less devout than he,
Informed me of his master's poverty;
I gave him gifts, but in his humbleness
He'd beg me every time to give him less.
"Oh, that's too much," he'd cry, "too much by twice!
I don't deserve it. The half, Sir, would suffice."
And when I wouldn't take it back, he'd share

40   Half of it with the poor, right then and there.
At length, Heaven prompted me to take him in
To dwell with us, and free our souls from sin.
He guides our lives, and to protect my honor
Stays by my wife, and keeps an eye upon her;
He tells me whom she sees, and all she does,
And seems more jealous than I ever was!
And how austere he is! Why, he can detect
A mortal sin where you would least suspect;
In smallest trifles, he's extremely strict.

50   Last week, his conscience was severely pricked
Because, while praying, he had caught a flea
And killed it, so he felt, too wrathfully.

CLÉANTE:
Good God, man! Have you lost your common sense—
Or is this all some joke at my expense?
How can you stand there and in all sobriety . . .

ORGON:
Brother, your language savors of impiety.
Too much free-thinking's made your faith unsteady,
And as I've warned you many times already,
'Twill get you into trouble before you're through.

CLÉANTE:
60   So I've been told before by dupes like you:
Being blind, you'd have all others blind as well;
The clear-eyed man you call an infidel,
And he who sees through humbug and pretense
Is charged, by you, with want of reverence.
Spare me your warnings, Brother; I have no fear
Of speaking out, for you and Heaven to hear,
Against affected zeal and pious knavery.
There's true and false in piety, as in bravery,
And just as those whose courage shines the most

70   In battle, are the least inclined to boast,
So those whose hearts are truly pure and lowly
Don't make a flashy show of being holy.
There's a vast difference, so it seems to me,

Between true piety and hypocrisy:
How do you fail to see it, may I ask?
Is not a face quite different from a mask?
Cannot sincerity and cunning art,
Reality and semblance, be told apart?
Are scarecrows just like men, and do you hold
80   That a false coin is just as good as gold?
Ah, Brother, man's a strangely fashioned creature
Who seldom is content to follow Nature,
But recklessly pursues his inclination
Beyond the narrow bounds of moderation,
And often, by transgressing Reason's laws,
Perverts a lofty aim or noble cause.
A passing observation, but it applies.

ORGON:

I see, dear Brother, that you're profoundly wise;
You harbor all the insight of the age.
90   You are our one clear mind, our only sage,
The era's oracle, its Cato too,
And all mankind are fools compared to you.

CLÉANTE:

Brother, I don't pretend to be a sage,
Nor have I all the wisdom of the age.
There's just one insight I would dare to claim:
I know that true and false are not the same;
And just as there is nothing I more revere
Than a soul whose faith is steadfast and sincere,
Nothing that I more cherish and admire
100   Than honest zeal and true religious fire,
So there is nothing that I find more base
Than specious piety's dishonest face—
Than these bold mountebanks, these histrios
Whose impious mummeries and hollow shows
Exploit our love of Heaven, and make a jest
Of all that men think holiest and best;
These calculating souls who offer prayers
Not to their Maker, but as public wares,
And seek to buy respect and reputation
110   With lifted eyes and sighs of exaltation;
These charlatans, I say, whose pilgrim souls
Proceed, by way of Heaven, toward earthly goals,
Who weep and pray and swindle and extort,
Who preach the monkish life, but haunt the court,
Who make their zeal the partner of their vice—
Such men are vengeful, sly, and cold as ice,

And when there is an enemy to defame
They cloak their spite in fair religion's name,
Their private spleen and malice being made
To seem a high and virtuous crusade,
Until, to mankind's reverent applause,
They crucify their foe in Heaven's cause.
Such knaves are all too common; yet, for the wise,
True piety isn't hard to recognize,
And, happily, these present times provide us
With bright examples to instruct and guide us.
Consider Ariston and Périandre;
Look at Oronte, Alcidamas, Clitandre;
Their virtue is acknowledged; who could doubt it?
But you won't hear them beat the drum about it.
They're never ostentatious, never vain,
And their religion's moderate and humane;
It's not their way to criticize and chide:
They think censoriousness a mark of pride,
And therefore, letting others preach and rave,
They show, by deeds, how Christians should behave.
They think no evil of their fellow man,
But judge of him as kindly as they can.
They don't intrigue and wangle and conspire;
To lead a good life is their one desire;
The sinner wakes no rancorous hate in them;
It is the sin alone which they condemn;
Nor do they try to show a fiercer zeal
For Heaven's cause than Heaven itself could feel.
These men I honor, these men I advocate
As models for us all to emulate.
Your man is not their sort at all, I fear:
And, while your praise of him is quite sincere,
I think that you've been dreadfully deluded.

ORGON:
Now then, dear Brother, is your speech concluded?

CLÉANTE:
Why, yes.

ORGON:
                    Your servant, Sir. [*He turns to go.*]

CLÉANTE:
                                No, Brother; wait.
There's one more matter. You agreed of late
That young Valère might have your daughter's hand.

ORGON:
I did.

CLÉANTE:
　　　　And set the date, I understand.

ORGON:
　　Quite so.

CLÉANTE:
　　　　You've now postponed it; is that true?

ORGON:
　　No doubt.

CLÉANTE:
　　　　The match no longer pleases you?

ORGON:
　　Who knows?

CLÉANTE:
　　　　D'you mean to go back on your word?

ORGON:
　　I won't say that.

CLÉANTE:
　　　　Has anything occurred
Which might entitle you to break your pledge?

ORGON:
　　Perhaps.

CLÉANTE:
160　　　Why must you hem, and haw, and hedge?
The boy asked me to sound you in this affair . . .

ORGON:
　　It's been a pleasure.

CLÉANTE:
　　　　But what shall I tell Valère?

ORGON:
　　Whatever you like.

CLÉANTE:
　　　　But what have you decided?
What are your plans?

ORGON:
　　　　I plan, Sir, to be guided
By Heaven's will.

CLÉANTE:
　　　　Come, Brother, don't talk rot.
You've given Valère your word; will you keep it, or not?

ORGON:
　　Good day.

CLÉANTE:
　　　　This looks like poor Valère's undoing;
I'll go and warn him that there's trouble brewing.

ACT II

Scene 1

ORGON:
     Mariane.

MARIANE:
          Yes, Father?

ORGON:
               A word with you; come here.

MARIANE:
     What are you looking for?

ORGON [*peering into a small closet*]:
                    Eavesdroppers, dear.
I'm making sure we shan't be overheard.
Someone in there could catch our every word.
Ah, good, we're safe. Now, Mariane, my child,
You're a sweet girl who's tractable and mild,
Whom I hold dear, and think most highly of.

MARIANE:
     I'm deeply grateful, Father, for your love.

ORGON:
     That's well said, Daughter; and you can repay me

10   If, in all things, you'll cheerfully obey me.

MARIANE:
     To please you, Sir, is what delights me best.

ORGON:
     Good, good. Now, what d'you think of Tartuffe, our guest?

MARIANE:
     I, Sir?

ORGON:
          Yes. Weigh your answer; think it through.

MARIANE:
     Oh, dear. I'll say whatever you wish me to.

ORGON:
     That's wisely said, my Daughter. Say of him, then,
That he's the very worthiest of men,
And that you're fond of him, and would rejoice
In being his wife, if that should be my choice.
Well?

MARIANE:
          What?

ORGON:
               What's that?

MARIANE:
                    I . . .

ORGON:

                      Well?

MARIANE:

                      Forgive me, pray.

ORGON:

    Did you not hear me?

MARIANE:

20   Of *whom,* Sir, must I say
That I am fond of him, and would rejoice
In being his wife, if that should be your choice?

ORGON:

    Why, of Tartuffe.

MARIANE:

               But, Father, that's false, you know.
Why would you have me say what isn't so?

ORGON:

    Because I am resolved it shall be true.
That it's my wish should be enough for you.

MARIANE:

    You can't mean, Father . . .

ORGON:

                 Yes, Tartuffe shall be
Allied by marriage to this family,
And he's to be your husband, is that clear?

30   It's a father's privilege . . .

Scene 2

ORGON [*to* DORINE]:

              What are you doing in here?
Is curiosity so fierce a passion
With you, that you must eavesdrop in this fashion?

DORINE:

    There's lately been a rumor going about—
Based on some hunch or chance remark, no doubt—
That you mean Mariane to wed Tartuffe.
I've laughed it off, of course, as just a spoof.

ORGON:

    You find it so incredible?

DORINE:

                  Yes, I do.
I won't accept that story, even from you.

ORGON:

10   Well, you'll believe it when the thing is done.

DORINE:
Yes, yes, of course. Go on and have your fun.

ORGON:
I've never been more serious in my life.

DORINE:
Ha!

ORGON:
Daughter, I mean it; you're to be his wife.

DORINE:
No, don't believe your father; it's all a hoax.

ORGON:
See here, young woman . . .

DORINE:
Come, Sir, no more jokes;
You can't fool us.

ORGON:
How dare you talk that way?

DORINE:
All right, then: we believe you, sad to say.
But how a man like you, who looks so wise
And wears a moustache of such splendid size,
Can be so foolish as to . . .

ORGON:
20   Silence, please!
My girl, you take too many liberties.
I'm master here, as you must not forget.

DORINE:
Do let's discuss this calmly; don't be upset.
You can't be serious, Sir, about this plan.
What should that bigot want with Mariane?
Praying and fasting ought to keep him busy.
And then, in terms of wealth and rank, what is he?
Why should a man of poverty like you
Pick out a beggar son-in-law?

ORGON:
That will do.

30 Speak of his poverty with reverence.
His is a pure and saintly indigence
Which far transcends all worldly pride and pelf.
He lost his fortune, as he says himself,
Because he cared for Heaven alone, and so
Was careless of his interests here below.
I mean to get him out of his present straits
And help him to recover his estates—

Which, in his part of the world, have no small fame.
Poor though he is, he's a gentleman just the same.

DORINE:

40   Yes, so he tells us; and, Sir, it seems to me
Such pride goes very ill with piety.
A man whose spirit spurns this dungy earth
Ought not to brag of lands and noble birth;
Such worldly arrogance will hardly square
With meek devotion and the life of prayer.
. . . But this reproach, I see, has drawn a blank;
Let's speak, then, of his person, not his rank.
Doesn't it seem to you a trifle grim
To give a girl like her to a man like him?

50   When two are so ill-suited, can't you see
What the sad consequence is bound to be?
A young girl's virtue is imperilled, Sir,
When such a marriage is imposed on her;
For if one's bridegroom isn't to one's taste,
It's hardly an inducement to be chaste,
And many a man with horns upon his brow
Has made his wife the thing that she is now.
It's hard to be a faithful wife, in short,
To certain husbands of a certain sort,

60   And he who gives his daughter to a man she hates
Must answer for her sins at Heaven's gates.
Think, Sir, before you play so risky a role.

ORGON:

This servant-girl presumes to save my soul!

DORINE:

You would do well to ponder what I've said.

ORGON:

Daughter, we'll disregard this dunderhead.
Just trust your father's judgment. Oh, I'm aware
That I once promised you to young Valère;
But now I hear he gambles, which greatly shocks me;
What's more, I've doubts about his orthodoxy.

70   His visits to church, I note, are very few.

DORINE:

Would you have him go at the same hours as you,
And kneel nearby, to be sure of being seen?

ORGON:

I can dispense with such remarks, Dorine.
[*To* MARIANE] Tartuffe, however, is sure of Heaven's blessing,
And that's the only treasure worth possessing.

This match will bring you joys beyond all measure;
Your cup will overflow with every pleasure;
You two will interchange your faithful loves
Like two sweet cherubs, or two turtle-doves.
80 No harsh word shall be heard, no frown be seen,
And he shall make you happy as a queen.

DORINE:
And she'll make him a cuckold, just wait and see.

ORGON:
What language!

DORINE:
                        Oh, he's a man of destiny;
He's *made* for horns, and what the stars demand
Your daughter's virtue surely can't withstand.

ORGON:
Don't interrupt me further. Why can't you learn
That certain things are none of your concern?

DORINE:
It's for your own sake that I interfere.
[*She repeatedly interrupts* ORGON *just as he is turning to speak
to his daughter.*]

ORGON:
Most kind of you. Now, hold your tongue, d'you hear?

DORINE:
If I didn't love you . . .

ORGON:
90   Spare me your affection.

DORINE:
I love you, Sir, in spite of your objection.

ORGON:
Blast!

DORINE:
                I can't bear, Sir, for your honor's sake,
To let you make this ludicrous mistake.

ORGON:
You mean to go on talking?

DORINE:
                        If I didn't protest
This sinful marriage, my conscience couldn't rest.

ORGON:
If you don't hold your tongue, you little shrew . . .

DORINE:
What, lost your temper? A pious man like you?

ORGON:
Yes! Yes! You talk and talk. I'm maddened by it.

Once and for all, I tell you to be quiet.

DORINE:

100   Well, I'll be quiet. But I'll be thinking hard.

ORGON:

Think all you like, but you had better guard
That saucy tongue of yours, or I'll . . .
[*Turning back to* MARIANE]   Now, child,
I've weighed this matter fully.

DORINE [*aside*]:

It drives me wild

That I can't speak.
[ORGON *turns his head, and she is silent.*]

ORGON:

Tartuffe is no young dandy,

But, still, his person . . .

DORINE [*aside*]:

Is as sweet as candy.

ORGON:

Is such that, even if you shouldn't care
For his other merits . . .
[*He turns and stands facing* DORINE, *arms crossed.*]

DORINE [*aside*]:

They'll make a lovely pair.

If I were she, no man would marry me
Against my inclination, and go scot-free.

110   He'd learn, before the wedding-day was over,
How readily a wife can find a lover.

ORGON [*to* DORINE]:

It seems you treat my orders as a joke.

DORINE:

Why, what's the matter? 'Twas not to you I spoke.

ORGON:

What *were* you doing?

DORINE:

Talking to myself, that's all.

ORGON:

Ah! [*aside*] One more bit of impudence and gall,
And I shall give her a good slap in the face.
[*He puts himself in position to slap her;* DORINE, *whenever he glances at her,
stands immobile and silent.*]
Daughter, you shall accept, and with good grace,
The husband I've selected . . . Your wedding-day . . .
[*To* DORINE] Why don't you talk to yourself?

DORINE:

I've nothing to say.

ORGON:
>Come, just one word.

DORINE:
>120   No thank you, Sir. I pass.

ORGON:
>Come, speak; I'm waiting.

DORINE:
>I'd not be such an ass.

ORGON [*turning to* MARIANE]:
>In short, dear Daughter, I mean to be obeyed,
>And you must bow to the sound choice I've made.

DORINE [*moving away*]:
>I'd not wed such a monster, even in jest.
>[ORGON *attempts to slap her, but misses.*]

ORGON:
>Daughter, that maid of yours is a thorough pest;
>She makes me sinfully annoyed and nettled.
>I can't speak further; my nerves are too unsettled.
>She's so upset me by her insolent talk,
>I'll calm myself by going for a walk.

Scene 3

DORINE [*returning*]:
>Well, have you lost your tongue, girl? Must I play
>Your part, and say the lines you ought to say?
>Faced with a fate so hideous and absurd,
>Can you not utter one dissenting word?

MARIANE:
>What good would it do? A father's power is great.

DORINE:
>Resist him now, or it will be too late.

MARIANE:
>But . . .

DORINE:
>Tell him one cannot love at a father's whim;
>That you shall marry for yourself, not him;
>That since it's you who are to be the bride,
>10   It's you, not he, who must be satisfied;
>And that if his Tartuffe is so sublime,
>He's free to marry him at any time.

MARIANE:
>I've bowed so long to Father's strict control,
>I couldn't oppose him now, to save my soul.

DORINE:
> Come, come, Mariane. Do listen to reason, won't you?
> Valère has asked your hand. Do you love him, or don't you?

MARIANE:
> Oh, how unjust of you! What can you mean
> By asking such a question, dear Dorine?
> You know the depth of my affection for him;
20 > I've told you a hundred times how I adore him.

DORINE:
> I don't believe in everything I hear;
> Who knows if your professions were sincere?

MARIANE:
> They were, Dorine, and you do me wrong to doubt it;
> Heaven knows that I've been all too frank about it.

DORINE:
> You love him, then?

MARIANE:
>   Oh, more than I can express.

DORINE:
> And he, I take it, cares for you no less?

MARIANE:
> I think so.

DORINE:
>   And you both, with equal fire,
> Burn to be married?

MARIANE:
>   That is our one desire.

DORINE:
> What of Tartuffe, then? What of your father's plan?

MARIANE:
30 > I'll kill myself, if I'm forced to wed that man.

DORINE:
> I hadn't thought of that recourse. How splendid!
> Just die, and all your troubles will be ended!
> A fine solution. Oh, it maddens me
> To hear you talk in that self-pitying key.

MARIANE:
> Dorine, how harsh you are! It's most unfair.
> You have no sympathy for my despair.

DORINE:
> I've none at all for people who talk drivel
> And, faced with difficulties, whine and snivel.

MARIANE:
> No doubt I'm timid, but it would be wrong . . .

DORINE:

40   True love requires a heart that's firm and strong.

MARIANE:

I'm strong in my affection for Valère,
But coping with my father is his affair.

DORINE:

But if your father's brain has grown so cracked
Over his dear Tartuffe that he can retract
His blessing, though your wedding-day was named,
It's surely not Valère who's to be blamed.

MARIANE:

If I defied my father, as you suggest,
Would it not seem unmaidenly, at best?
Shall I defend my love at the expense

50   Of brazenness and disobedience?
Shall I parade my heart's desires, and flaunt . . .

DORINE:

No, I ask nothing of you. Clearly you want
To be Madame Tartuffe, and I feel bound
Not to oppose a wish so very sound.
What right have I to criticize the match?
Indeed, my dear, the man is a brilliant catch.
Monsieur Tartuffe! Now, there's a man of weight!
Yes, yes, Monsieur Tartuffe, I'm bound to state,
Is quite a person; that's not to be denied;

60   'Twill be no little thing to be his bride.
The world already rings with his renown;
He's a great noble — in his native town;
His ears are red, he has a pink complexion,
And all in all, he'll suit you to perfection.

MARIANE:

Dear God!

DORINE:

Oh, how triumphant you will feel
At having caught a husband so ideal!

MARIANE:

Oh, do stop teasing, and use your cleverness
To get me out of this appalling mess.
Advise me, and I'll do whatever you say.

DORINE:

70   Ah no, a dutiful daughter must obey
Her father, even if he weds her to an ape.
You've a bright future; why struggle to escape?
Tartuffe will take you back where his family lives,
To a small town aswarm with relatives —

Uncles and cousins whom you'll be charmed to meet.
You'll be received at once by the elite,
Calling upon the bailiff's wife, no less—
Even, perhaps, upon the mayoress,
Who'll sit you down in the *best* kitchen chair.
80   Then, once a year, you'll dance at the village fair
To the drone of bagpipes—two of them, in fact—
And see a puppet-show, or an animal act.
Your husband . . .

MARIANE:
               Oh, you turn my blood to ice!
Stop torturing me, and give me your advice.

DORINE [*threatening to go*]:
Your servant, Madam.

MARIANE:
             Dorine, I beg of you . . .

DORINE:
No, you deserve it; this marriage must go through.

MARIANE:
Dorine!

DORINE:
     No.

MARIANE:
        Not Tartuffe! You know I think him . . .

DORINE:
Tartuffe's your cup of tea, and you shall drink him.

MARIANE:
I've always told you everything, and relied . . .

DORINE:
90   No. You deserve to be tartuffified.

MARIANE:
Well, since you mock me and refuse to care,
I'll henceforth seek my solace in despair:
Despair shall be my counsellor and friend,
And help me bring my sorrows to an end.
              [*She starts to leave.*]

DORINE:
There now, come back; my anger has subsided.
You do deserve some pity, I've decided.

MARIANE:
Dorine, if Father makes me undergo
This dreadful martyrdom, I'll die, I know.

DORINE:
Don't fret; it won't be difficult to discover
100   Some plan of action . . . But here's Valère, your lover.

Scene 4

VALÈRE:
Madame, I've just received some wondrous news
Regarding which I'd like to hear your views.

MARIANE:
What news?

VALÈRE:
You're marrying Tartuffe.

MARIANE:
I find
That Father does have such a match in mind.

VALÈRE:
Your father, Madam . . .

MARIANE:
. . . has just this minute said
That it's Tartuffe he wishes me to wed.

VALÈRE:
Can he be serious?

MARIANE:
Oh, indeed he can;
He's clearly set his heart upon the plan.

VALÈRE:
And what position do you propose to take, Madam?

MARIANE:
Why—I don't know.

VALÈRE:
For heaven's sake—
You don't know?

MARIANE:
No.

VALÈRE:
Well, well!

MARIANE:
Advise me, do.

VALÈRE:
Marry the man. That's my advice to you.

MARIANE:
That's your advice?

VALÈRE:
Yes.

MARIANE:
Truly?

VALÈRE:
Oh, absolutely.

You couldn't choose more wisely, more astutely.

MARIANE:

Thanks for this counsel; I'll follow it, of course.

VALÈRE:

Do, do; I'm sure 'twill cost you no remorse.

MARIANE:

To give it didn't cause your heart to break.

VALÈRE:

I gave it, Madam, only for your sake.

MARIANE:

And it's for your sake that I take it, Sir.

DORINE [*withdrawing to the rear of the stage*]:

20   Let's see which fool will prove the stubborner.

VALÈRE:

So! I am nothing to you, and it was flat
Deception when you . . .

MARIANE:

Please, enough of that.
You've told me plainly that I should agree
To wed the man my father's chosen for me,
And since you've designed to counsel me so wisely,
I promise, Sir, to do as you advise me.

VALÈRE:

Ah, no, 'twas not by me that you were swayed.
No, your decision was already made;
Though now, to save appearances, you protest

30   That you're betraying me at my behest.

MARIANE:

Just as you say.

VALÈRE:

Quite so. And I now see
That you were never truly in love with me.

MARIANE:

Alas, you're free to think so if you choose.

VALÈRE:

I choose to think so, and here's a bit of news:
You've spurned my hand, but I know where to turn
For kinder treatment, as you shall quickly learn.

MARIANE:

I'm sure you do. Your noble qualities
Inspire affection . . .

VALÈRE:

Forget my qualities, please.
They don't inspire you overmuch, I find.

40   But there's another lady I have in mind

Whose sweet and generous nature will not scorn
To compensate me for the loss I've borne.

MARIANE:

I'm no great loss, and I'm sure that you'll transfer
Your heart quite painlessly from me to her.

VALÈRE:

I'll do my best to take it in my stride.
The pain I feel at being cast aside
Time and forgetfulness may put an end to.
Or if I can't forget, I shall pretend to.
No self-respecting person is expected
50   To go on loving once he's been rejected.

MARIANE:

Now, that's a fine, high-minded sentiment.

VALÈRE:

One to which any sane man would assent.
Would you prefer it if I pined away
In hopeless passion till my dying day?
Am I to yield you to a rival's arms
And not console myself with other charms?

MARIANE:

Go then: console yourself; don't hesitate.
I wish you to; indeed, I cannot wait.

VALÈRE:

You wish me to?

MARIANE:

                    Yes.

VALÈRE:

                    That's the final straw.
60   Madam, farewell. Your wish shall be my law.
[*He starts to leave, and then returns: this repeatedly.*]

MARIANE:

Splendid.

VALÈRE [*coming back again*]:

          This breach, remember, is of your making;
It's you who've driven me to the step I'm taking.

MARIANE:

Of course.

VALÈRE [*coming back again*]:

          Remember, too, that I am merely
Following your example.

MARIANE:

                    I see that clearly.

VALÈRE:

Enough. I'll go and do your bidding, then.

MARIANE:
    Good.
VALÈRE [*coming back again*]:
        You shall never see my face again.
MARIANE:
    Excellent.
VALÈRE [*walking to the door, then turning about*]:
            Yes?
MARIANE:
            What?
VALÈRE:
            What's that? What did you say?
MARIANE:
    Nothing. You're dreaming.
VALÈRE:
                Ah. Well, I'm on my way.
    Farewell, *Madame*.
                [*He moves slowly away.*]
MARIANE:
            Farewell.
DORINE [*to* MARIANE]:
            If you ask me,
70   Both of you are as mad as mad can be.
    Do stop this nonsense, now. I've only let you
    Squabble so long to see where it would get you.
    Whoa there, Monsieur Valère!
    [*She goes and seizes* VALÈRE *by the arm; he makes a great show of resistance.*]
VALÈRE:
                What's this, Dorine?
DORINE:
    Come here.
VALÈRE:
        No, no, my heart's too full of spleen.
    Don't hold me back; her wish must be obeyed.
DORINE:
    Stop!
VALÈRE:
        It's too late now; my decision's made.
DORINE:
    Oh, pooh!
MARIANE [*aside*]:
        He hates the sight of me, that's plain.
    I'll go, and so deliver him from pain.
DORINE [*leaving* VALÈRE, *running after* MARIANE]:
    And now *you* run away! Come back.

MARIANE:

                                 No, no.

80   Nothing you say will keep me here. Let go!

VALÈRE [*aside*]:

    She cannot bear my presence, I perceive.

    To spare her further torment, I shall leave.

DORINE [*leaving* MARIANE, *running after* VALÈRE]:

    Again! You'll not escape, Sir; don't you try it.

    Come here, you two. Stop fussing, and be quiet.

    [*She takes* VALÈRE *by the hand, then* MARIANE, *and draws them together.*]

VALÈRE [*to* DORINE]:

    What do you want of me?

MARIANE [*to* DORINE]:

                        What is the point of this?

DORINE:

    We're going to have a little armistice.

    [*To* VALÈRE] Now weren't you silly to get so overheated?

VALÈRE:

    Didn't you see how badly I was treated?

DORINE [*to* MARIANE]:

    Aren't you a simpleton, to have lost your head?

MARIANE:

90   Didn't you hear the hateful things he said?

DORINE [*to* VALÈRE]:

    You're both great fools. Her sole desire, Valère,

    Is to be yours in marriage. To that I'll swear.

    [*To* MARIANE] He loves you only, and he wants no wife

    But you, Mariane. On that I'll stake my life.

MARIANE [*to* VALÈRE]:

    Then why you advised me so, I cannot see.

VALÈRE [*to* MARIANE]:

    On such a question, why ask advice of *me*?

DORINE:

    Oh, you're impossible. Give me your hands, you two.

    [*To* VALÈRE] Yours first.

VALÈRE [*giving* DORINE *his hand*]:

                    But why?

DORINE [*to* MARIANE]:

                    And now a hand from you.

MARIANE [*also giving* DORINE *her hand*]:

    What are you doing?

DORINE:

                There: a perfect fit.

100   You suit each other better than you'll admit.

    [VALÈRE *and* MARIANE *hold hands for some time without looking at each other.*]

VALÈRE [*turning toward* MARIANE]:

    Ah, come, don't be so haughty. Give a man

    A look of kindness, won't you, Mariane?

    [MARIANE *turns toward* VALÈRE *and smiles.*]

DORINE:

    I tell you, lovers are completely mad!

VALÈRE [*to* MARIANE]:

    Now come, confess that you were very bad

    To hurt my feelings as you did just now.

    I have a just complaint, you must allow.

MARIANE:

    You must allow that you were most unpleasant . . .

DORINE:

    Let's table that discussion for the present;

    Your father has a plan which must be stopped.

MARIANE:

110   Advise us, then; what means must we adopt?

DORINE:

    We'll use all manner of means, and all at once.

    [*To* MARIANE] Your father's addled; he's acting like a dunce.

    Therefore you'd better humor the old fossil.

    Pretend to yield to him, be sweet and docile,

    And then postpone, as often as necessary,

    The day on which you have agreed to marry.

    You'll thus gain time, and time will turn the trick.

    Sometimes, for instance, you'll be taken sick,

    And that will seem good reason for delay;

120   Or some bad omen will make you change the day—

    You'll dream of muddy water, or you'll pass

    A dead man's hearse, or break a looking-glass.

    If all else fails, no man can marry you

    Unless you take his ring and say "I do."

    But now, let's separate. If they should find

    Us talking here, our plot might be divined.

    [*To* VALÈRE] Go to your friends, and tell them what's occurred,

    And have them urge her father to keep his word.

    Meanwhile, we'll stir her brother into action,

130   And get Elmire, as well, to join our faction.

    Good-bye.

VALÈRE [*to* MARIANE]:

            Though each of us will do his best,

    It's your true heart on which my hopes shall rest.

MARIANE [*to* VALÈRE]:

    Regardless of what Father may decide,

    None but Valère shall claim me as his bride.

VALÈRE:
> Oh, how those words content me! Come what will . . .

DORINE:
> Oh, lovers, lovers! Their tongues are never still.
> Be off, now.

VALÈRE [*turning to go, then turning back*]:
>   One last word . . .

DORINE:
>   No time to chat:
> *You* leave by this door; and *you* leave by that.
> [DORINE *pushes them, by the shoulders, toward opposing doors.*]

ACT III

Scene 1

DAMIS:
> May lightning strike me even as I speak,
> May all men call me cowardly and weak,
> If any fear or scruple holds me back
> From settling things, at once, with that great quack!

DORINE:
> Now, don't give way to violent emotion.
> Your father's merely talked about this notion,
> And words and deeds are far from being one.
> Much that is talked about is left undone.

DAMIS:
> No, I must stop that scoundrel's machinations;
> 10 I'll go and tell him off; I'm out of patience.

DORINE:
> Do calm down and be practical. I had rather
> My mistress dealt with him—and with your father.
> She has some influence with Tartuffe, I've noted.
> He hangs upon her words, seems most devoted,
> And may, indeed, be smitten by her charm.
> Pray Heaven it's true! 'Twould do our cause no harm.
> She sent for him, just now, to sound him out
> On this affair you're so incensed about;
> She'll find out where he stands, and tell him, too,
> 20 What dreadful strife and trouble will ensue
> If he lends countenance to your father's plan.
> I couldn't get in to see him, but his man
> Says that he's almost finished with his prayers.
> Go, now. I'll catch him when he comes downstairs.

DAMIS:
> I want to hear this conference, and I will.

DORINE:
    No, they must be alone.
DAMIS:
                        Oh, I'll keep still.
DORINE:
    Not you. I know your temper. You'd start a brawl,
    And shout and stamp your foot and spoil it all.
    Go on.
DAMIS:
                I won't; I have a perfect right . . .
DORINE:
30   Lord, you're a nuisance! He's coming; get out of sight.
    [DAMIS *conceals himself in a closet at the rear of the stage.*]

Scene 2

TARTUFFE [*observing* DORINE, *and calling to his manservant offstage*]:
    Hang up my hair-shirt, put my scourge in place,
    And pray, Laurent, for Heaven's perpetual grace.
    I'm going to the prison now, to share
    My last two coins with the poor wretches there.
DORINE [*aside*]:
    Dear God, what affectation! What a fake!
TARTUFFE:
    You wished to see me?
DORINE:
                        Yes . . .
TARTUFFE [*taking a handkerchief from his pocket*]:
                                For mercy's sake,
    Please take this handkerchief, before you speak.
DORINE:
    What?
TARTUFFE:
            Cover that bosom, girl. The flesh is weak,
    And unclean thoughts are difficult to control.
10   Such sights as that can undermine the soul.
DORINE:
    Your soul, it seems, has very poor defenses,
    And flesh makes quite an impact on your senses.
    It's strange that you're so easily excited;
    My own desires are not so soon ignited,
    And if I saw you naked as a beast,
    Not all your hide would tempt me in the least.
TARTUFFE:
    Girl, speak more modestly; unless you do,
    I shall be forced to take my leave of you.

DORINE:

    Oh, no, it's I who must be on my way;

20   I've just one little message to convey.

    Madame is coming down, and begs you, Sir,

    To wait and have a word or two with her.

TARTUFFE:

    Gladly.

DORINE [*aside*]:

           That had a softening effect!

    I think my guess about him was correct.

TARTUFFE:

    Will she be long?

DORINE:

           No: that's her step I hear.

    Ah, here she is, and I shall disappear.

Scene 3

TARTUFFE:

    May Heaven, whose infinite goodness we adore,

    Preserve your body and soul forevermore,

    And bless your days, and answer thus the plea

    Of one who is its humblest votary.

ELMIRE:

    I thank you for that pious wish. But please,

    Do take a chair and let's be more at ease.

    [*They sit down.*]

TARTUFFE:

    I trust that you are once more well and strong?

ELMIRE:

    Oh, yes: the fever didn't last for long.

TARTUFFE:

    My prayers are too unworthy, I am sure,

10   To have gained from Heaven this most gracious cure;

    But lately, Madam, my every supplication

    Has had for object your recuperation.

ELMIRE:

    You shouldn't have troubled so. I don't deserve it.

TARTUFFE:

    Your health is priceless, Madam, and to preserve it

    I'd gladly give my own, in all sincerity.

ELMIRE:

    Sir, you outdo us all in Christian charity.

    You've been most kind. I count myself your debtor.

TARTUFFE:

    'Twas nothing, Madam. I long to serve you better.

ELMIRE:
> There's a private matter I'm anxious to discuss.
20 > I'm glad there's no one here to hinder us.

TARTUFFE:
> I too am glad; it floods my heart with bliss
> To find myself alone with you like this.
> For just this chance I've prayed with all my power—
> But prayed in vain, until this happy hour.

ELMIRE:
> This won't take long, Sir, and I hope you'll be
> Entirely frank and unconstrained with me.

TARTUFFE:
> Indeed, there's nothing I had rather do
> Than bare my inmost heart and soul to you.
> First, let me say that what remarks I've made
30 > About the constant visits you are paid
> Were prompted not by any mean emotion,
> But rather by a pure and deep devotion,
> A fervent zeal . . .

ELMIRE:
>   No need for explanation.
> Your sole concern, I'm sure, was my salvation.

TARTUFFE [*taking* ELMIRE's *hand and pressing her fingertips*]:
> Quite so; and such great fervor do I feel . . .

ELMIRE:
> Ooh! Please! You're pinching!

TARTUFFE:
>   'Twas from excess of zeal.
> I never meant to cause you pain, I swear.
> I'd rather . . .
> [*He places his hand on* ELMIRE's *knee.*]

ELMIRE:
>   What can your hand be doing there?

TARTUFFE:
> Feeling your gown; what soft, fine-woven stuff!

ELMIRE:
40 > Please, I'm extremely ticklish. That's enough.
> [*She draws her chair away;* TARTUFFE *pulls his after her.*]

TARTUFFE [*fondling the lace collar of her gown*]:
> My, my what lovely lacework on your dress!
> The workmanship's miraculous, no less.
> I've not seen anything to equal it.

ELMIRE:
> Yes, quite. But let's talk business for a bit.
> They say my husband means to break his word

And give his daughter to you, Sir. Had you heard?

TARTUFFE:

He did once mention it. But I confess
I dream of quite a different happiness.
It's elsewhere, Madam, that my eyes discern
50   The promise of that bliss for which I yearn.

ELMIRE:

I see: you care for nothing here below.

TARTUFFE

Ah, well—my heart's not made of stone, you know.

ELMIRE:

All your desires mount heavenward, I'm sure,
In scorn of all that's earthly and impure.

TARTUFFE:

A love of heavenly beauty does not preclude
A proper love for earthly pulchritude;
Our senses are quite rightly captivated
By perfect works our Maker has created.
Some glory clings to all that Heaven has made;
60   In you, all Heaven's marvels are displayed.
On that fair face, such beauties have been lavished,
The eyes are dazzled and the heart is ravished;
How could I look on you, O flawless creature,
And not adore the Author of all Nature,
Feeling a love both passionate and pure
For you, his triumph of self-portraiture?
At first, I trembled lest that love should be
A subtle snare that Hell had laid for me;
I vowed to flee the sight of you, eschewing
70   A rapture that might prove my soul's undoing;
But soon, fair being, I became aware
That my deep passion could be made to square
With rectitude, and with my bounden duty.
I thereupon surrendered to your beauty.
It is, I know, presumptuous on my part
To bring you this poor offering of my heart,
And it is not my merit, Heaven knows,
But your compassion on which my hopes repose.
You are my peace, my solace, my salvation;
80   On you depends my bliss—or desolation;
I bide your judgment and, as you think best,
I shall be either miserable or blest.

ELMIRE:

Your declaration is most gallant, Sir,
But don't you think it's out of character?

> You'd have done better to restrain your passion
> And think before you spoke in such a fashion.
> It ill becomes a pious man like you . . .

TARTUFFE:

> I may be pious, but I'm human too:
> With your celestial charms before his eyes,
90 > A man has not the power to be wise.
> I know such words sound strangely, coming from me,
> But I'm no angel, nor was meant to be,
> And if you blame my passion, you must needs
> Reproach as well the charms on which it feeds.
> Your loveliness I had no sooner seen
> Than you became my soul's unrivalled queen;
> Before your seraph glance, divinely sweet,
> My heart's defenses crumbled in defeat,
> And nothing fasting, prayer, or tears might do
100 > Could stay my spirit from adoring you.
> My eyes, my sighs have told you in the past
> What now my lips make bold to say at last,
> And if, in your great goodness, you will deign
> To look upon your slave, and ease his pain,—
> If, in compassion for my soul's distress,
> You'll stoop to comfort my unworthiness,
> I'll raise to you, in thanks for that sweet manna,
> An endless hymn, an infinite hosanna.
> With me, of course, there need be no anxiety,
110 > No fear of scandal or of notoriety.
> These young court gallants, whom all the ladies fancy,
> Are vain in speech, in action rash and chancy;
> When they succeed in love, the world soon knows it;
> No favor's granted them but they disclose it
> And by the looseness of their tongues profane
> The very altar where their hearts have lain.
> Men of my sort, however, love discreetly,
> And one may trust our reticence completely.
> My keen concern for my good name insures
120 > The absolute security of yours;
> In short, I offer you, my dear Elmire,
> Love without scandal, pleasure without fear.

ELMIRE:

> I've heard your well-turned speeches to the end,
> And what you urge I clearly apprehend.
> Aren't you afraid that I may take a notion
> To tell my husband of your warm devotion,
> And that, supposing he were duly told,

His feelings toward you might grow rather cold?

TARTUFFE:

I know, dear lady, that your exceeding charity

130   Will lead your heart to pardon my temerity;

That you'll excuse my violent affection

As human weakness, human imperfection;

And that—O fairest!—you will bear in mind

That I'm but flesh and blood, and am not blind.

ELMIRE:

Some women might do otherwise, perhaps,

But I shall be discreet about your lapse;

I'll tell my husband nothing of what's occurred

If, in return, you'll give your solemn word

To advocate as forcefully as you can

140   The marriage of Valère and Mariane,

Renouncing all desire to dispossess

Another of his rightful happiness,

And . . .

Scene 4

DAMIS [*emerging from the closet where he has been hiding*]:

No! We'll not hush up this vile affair;

I heard it all inside that closet there,

Where Heaven, in order to confound the pride

Of this great rascal, prompted me to hide.

Ah, now I have my long-awaited chance

To punish his deceit and arrogance,

And give my father clear and shocking proof

Of the black character of his dear Tartuffe.

ELMIRE:

Ah no, Damis; I'll be content if he

10   Will study to deserve my leniency.

I've promised silence—don't make me break my word;

To make a scandal would be too absurd.

Good wives laugh off such trifles, and forget them;

Why should they tell their husbands, and upset them?

DAMIS:

You have your reasons for taking such a course,

And I have reasons too, of equal force.

To spare him now would be insanely wrong.

I've swallowed my just wrath for far too long

And watched this insolent bigot bringing strife

20   And bitterness into our family life.

Too long he's meddled in my father's affairs,

Thwarting my marriage-hopes, and poor Valère's.
It's high time that my father was undeceived,
And now I've proof that can't be disbelieved—
Proof that was furnished me by Heaven above.
It's too good not to take advantage of.
This is my chance, and I deserve to lose it
If, for one moment, I hesitate to use it.

ELMIRE:

Damis . . .

DAMIS:

        No, I must do what I think right.
30   Madam, my heart is bursting with delight,
And, say whatever you will, I'll not consent
To lose the sweet revenge on which I'm bent.
I'll settle matters without more ado;
And here, most opportunely, is my cue.

Scene 5

DAMIS:

Father, I'm glad you've joined us. Let us advise you
Of some fresh news which doubtless will surprise you.
You've just now been repaid with interest
For all your loving-kindness to our guest.
He's proved his warm and grateful feelings toward you;
It's with a pair of horns he would reward you.
Yes, I surprised him with your wife, and heard
His whole adulterous offer, every word.
She, with her all too gentle disposition,
10   Would not have told you of his proposition;
But I shall not make terms with brazen lechery,
And feel that not to tell you would be treachery.

ELMIRE:

And I hold that one's husband's peace of mind
Should not be spoilt by tattle of this kind.
One's honor doesn't require it: to be proficient
In keeping men at bay is quite sufficient.
These are my sentiments, and I wish, Damis,
That you had heeded me and held your peace.

Scene 6

ORGON:

Can it be true, this dreadful thing I hear?

TARTUFFE:

Yes, Brother, I'm a wicked man, I fear:

A wretched sinner, all depraved and twisted,
The greatest villain that has ever existed.
My life's one heap of crimes, which grows each minute;
There's naught but foulness and corruption in it;
And I perceive that Heaven, outraged by me,
Has chosen this occasion to mortify me.
Charge me with any deed you wish to name;
10   I'll not defend myself, but take the blame.
Believe what you are told, and drive Tartuffe
Like some base criminal from beneath your roof;
Yes, drive me hence, and with a parting curse:
I shan't protest, for I deserve far worse.

ORGON [*to* DAMIS]:
Ah, you deceitful boy, how dare you try
To stain his purity with so foul a lie?

DAMIS:
What! Are you taken in by such a bluff?
Did you not hear . . . ?

ORGON:
                              Enough, you rogue, enough!

TARTUFFE:
Ah, Brother, let him speak: you're being unjust.
20   Believe his story; the boy deserves your trust.
Why, after all, should you have faith in me?
How can you know what I might do, or be?
Is it on my good actions that you base
Your favor? Do you trust my pious face?
Ah, no, don't be deceived by hollow shows;
I'm far, alas, from being what men suppose;
Though the world takes me for a man of worth,
I'm truly the most worthless man on earth.
[*To* DAMIS] Yes, my dear son, speak out now: call me the chief
30   Of sinners, a wretch, a murderer, a thief;
Load me with all the names men most abhor;
I'll not complain; I've earned them all, and more;
I'll kneel here while you pour them on my head
As a just punishment for the life I've led.

ORGON [*to* TARTUFFE]:
This is too much, dear Brother.
[*To* DAMIS]   Have you no heart?

DAMIS:
Are you so hoodwinked by this rascal's art . . . ?

ORGON:
Be still, you monster.
[*To* TARTUFFE]   Brother, I pray you, rise.
[*To* DAMIS] Villain!

DAMIS:
           But . . .

ORGON:
                   Silence!

DAMIS:
                          Can't you realize . . . ?

ORGON:
     Just one word more, and I'll tear you limb from limb.

TARTUFFE:
40   In God's name, Brother, don't be harsh with him.
     I'd rather far be tortured at the stake
     Than see him bear one scratch for my poor sake.

ORGON [*to* DAMIS]:
     Ingrate!

TARTUFFE:
           If I must beg you, on bended knee,
     To pardon him . . .

ORGON [*falling to his knees, addressing* TARTUFFE]:
                   Such goodness cannot be!
     [*To* DAMIS] Now, *there's* true charity!

DAMIS:
                       What, you . . . ?

ORGON:
                               Villain, be still!
     I know your motives; I know you wish him ill:
     Yes, all of you—wife, children, servants, all—
     Conspire against him and desire his fall,
     Employing every shameful trick you can
50   To alienate me from this saintly man.
     Ah, but the more you seek to drive him away,
     The more I'll do to keep him. Without delay,
     I'll spite this household and confound its pride
     By giving him my daughter as his bride.

DAMIS:
     You're going to force her to accept his hand?

ORGON:
     Yes, and this very night, d'you understand?
     I shall defy you all, and make it clear
     That I'm the one who gives the orders here.
     Come, wretch, kneel down and clasp his blessed feet,
60   And ask his pardon for your black deceit.

DAMIS:
     I ask that swindler's pardon? Why, I'd rather . . .

ORGON:
     So! You insult him, and defy your father!
     A stick! A stick! [*to* TARTUFFE] No, no—release me, do.

[*To* DAMIS] Out of my house this minute! Be off with you,
And never dare set foot in it again.

DAMIS:
Well, I shall go, but . . .

ORGON:
                              Well, go quickly, then.
I disinherit you; an empty purse
Is all you'll get from me — except my curse!

Scene 7

ORGON:
How he blasphemed your goodness! What a son!

TARTUFFE:
Forgive him, Lord, as I've already done.
[*To* ORGON] You can't know how it hurts when someone tries
To blacken me in my dear Brother's eyes.

ORGON:
Ahh!

TARTUFFE:
            The mere thought of such ingratitude
Plunges my soul into so dark a mood . . .
Such horror grips my heart . . . I gasp for breath,
And cannot speak, and feel myself near death.

ORGON [*He runs, in tears, to the door through which he has just driven his son.*]:
You blackguard! Why did I spare you? Why did I not

10   Break you in little pieces on the spot?
Compose yourself, and don't be hurt, dear friend.

TARTUFFE:
These scenes, these dreadful quarrels, have got to end.
I've much upset your household, and I perceive
That the best thing will be for me to leave.

ORGON:
What are you saying!

TARTUFFE:
                              They're all against me here;
They'd have you think me false and insincere.

ORGON:
Ah, what of that? Have I ceased believing in you?

TARTUFFE:
Their adverse talk will certainly continue,
And charges which you now repudiate

20   You may find credible at a later date.

ORGON:
No, Brother, never.

TARTUFFE:
Brother, a wife can sway
Her husband's mind in many a subtle way.

ORGON:
No, no.

TARTUFFE:
To leave at once is the solution;
Thus only can I end their persecution.

ORGON:
No, no, I'll not allow it; you shall remain.

TARTUFFE:
Ah, well; 'twill mean much martyrdom and pain,
But if you wish it . . .

ORGON:
Ah!

TARTUFFE:
Enough; so be it.
But one thing must be settled, as I see it.
For your dear honor, and for our friendship's sake,
30   There's one precaution I feel bound to take.
I shall avoid your wife, and keep away . . .

ORGON:
No, you shall not, whatever they may say.
It pleases me to vex them, and for spite
I'd have them see you with her day and night.
What's more, I'm going to drive them to despair
By making you my only son and heir;
This very day, I'll give to you alone
Clear deed and title to everything I own.
A dear, good friend and son-in-law-to-be
40   Is more than wife, or child, or kin to me.
Will you accept my offer, dearest son?

TARTUFFE:
In all things, let the will of Heaven be done.

ORGON:
Poor fellow! Come, we'll go draw up the deed.
Then let them burst with disappointed greed!

ACT IV

Scene 1

CLÉANTE:
Yes, all the town's discussing it, and truly,
Their comments do not flatter you unduly.

I'm glad we've met, Sir, and I'll give my view
Of this sad matter in a word or two.
As for who's guilty, that I shan't discuss;
Let's say it was Damis who caused the fuss;
Assuming, then, that you have been ill-used
By young Damis, and groundlessly accused,
Ought not a Christian to forgive, and ought
10   He not to stifle every vengeful thought?
Should you stand by and watch a father make
His only son an exile for your sake?
Again I tell you frankly, be advised:
The whole town, high and low, is scandalized;
This quarrel must be mended, and my advice is
Not to push matters to a further crisis.
No, sacrifice your wrath to God above,
And help Damis regain his father's love.

TARTUFFE:

Alas, for my part I should take great joy
20   In doing so. I've nothing against the boy.
I pardon all, I harbor no resentment;
To serve him would afford me much contentment.
But Heaven's interest will not have it so:
If he comes back, then I shall have to go.
After his conduct—so extreme, so vicious—
Our further intercourse would look suspicious.
God knows what people would think! Why, they'd describe
My goodness to him as a sort of bribe;
They'd say that out of guilt I made pretense
30   Of loving-kindness and benevolence—
That, fearing my accuser's tongue, I strove
To buy his silence with a show of love.

CLÉANTE:

Your reasoning is badly warped and stretched,
And these excuses, Sir, are most far-fetched.
Why put yourself in charge of Heaven's cause?
Does Heaven need our help to enforce its laws?
Leave vengeance to the Lord, Sir; while we live,
Our duty's not to punish, but forgive;
And what the Lord commands, we should obey
40   Without regard to what the world may say.
What! Shall the fear of being misunderstood
Prevent our doing what is right and good?
No, no; let's simply do what Heaven ordains,
And let no other thoughts perplex our brains.

TARTUFFE:

> Again, Sir, let me say that I've forgiven
> Damis, and thus obeyed the laws of Heaven;
> But I am not commanded by the Bible
> To live with one who smears my name with libel.

CLÉANTE:

> Were you commanded, Sir, to indulge the whim
50 > Of poor Orgon, and to encourage him
> In suddenly transferring to your name
> A large estate to which you have no claim?

TARTUFFE:

> 'Twould never occur to those who know me best
> To think I acted from self-interest.
> The treasures of this world I quite despise;
> Their specious glitter does not charm my eyes;
> And if I have resigned myself to taking
> The gift which my dear Brother insists on making,
> I do so only, as he well understands,
60 > Lest so much wealth fall into wicked hands,
> Lest those to whom it might descend in time
> Turn it to purposes of sin and crime,
> And not, as I shall do, make use of it
> For Heaven's glory and mankind's benefit.

CLÉANTE:

> Forget these trumped-up fears. Your argument
> Is one the rightful heir might well resent;
> It *is* a moral burden to inherit
> Such wealth, but give Damis a chance to bear it.
> And would it not be worse to be accused
70 > Of swindling, than to see that wealth misused?
> I'm shocked that you allowed Orgon to broach
> This matter, and that you feel no self-reproach;
> Does true religion teach that lawful heirs
> May freely be deprived of what is theirs?
> And if the Lord has told you in your heart
> That you and young Damis must dwell apart,
> Would it not be the decent thing to beat
> A generous and honorable retreat,
> Rather than let the son of the house be sent,
80 > For your convenience, into banishment?
> Sir, if you wish to prove the honesty
> Of your intentions . . .

TARTUFFE:

> Sir, it is half-past three.

I've certain pious duties to attend to,
And hope my prompt departure won't offend you.
CLÉANTE [*alone*]:
    Damn.

Scene 2

DORINE:
        Stay, Sir, and help Mariane, for Heaven's sake!
    She's suffering so, I fear her heart will break.
    Her father's plan to marry her off tonight
    Has put the poor child in a desperate plight.
    I hear him coming. Let's stand together, now,
    And see if we can't change his mind, somehow,
    About this match we all deplore and fear.

Scene 3

ORGON:
        Hah! Glad to find you all assembled here.
    [*To* MARIANE] This contract, child, contains your happiness,
    And what it says I think your heart can guess.
MARIANE [*falling to her knees*]:
        Sir, by that Heaven which sees me here distressed,
    And by whatever else can move your breast,
    Do not employ a father's power, I pray you,
    To crush my heart and force it to obey you,
    Nor by your harsh commands oppress me so
    That I'll begrudge the duty which I owe—
10 And do not so embitter and enslave me
    That I shall hate the very life you gave me.
    If my sweet hopes must perish, if you refuse
    To give me to the one I've dared to choose,
    Spare me at least—I beg you, I implore—
    The pain of wedding one whom I abhor;
    And do not, by a heartless use of force,
    Drive me to contemplate some desperate course.
ORGON [*feeling himself touched by her*]:
        Be firm, my soul. No human weakness, now.
MARIANE:
        I don't resent your love for him. Allow
20 Your heart free rein, Sir; give him your property,
    And if that's not enough, take mine from me;
    He's welcome to my money; take it, do,
    But don't, I pray, include my person too.
    Spare me, I beg you; and let me end the tale

Of my sad days behind a convent veil.

ORGON:

A convent! Hah! When crossed in their amours,
All lovesick girls have had the same thought as yours.
Get up! The more you loathe the man, and dread him,
The more ennobling it will be to wed him.
30　　Marry Tartuffe, and mortify your flesh!
Enough; don't start that whimpering afresh.

DORINE:

But why . . . ?

ORGON:

　　　　　Be still, there. Speak when you're spoken to.
Not one more bit of impudence out of you.

CLÉANTE:

If I may offer a word of counsel here . . .

ORGON:

Brother, in counseling you have no peer;
All your advice is forceful, sound, and clever;
I don't propose to follow it, however.

ELMIRE [*to* ORGON]:

I am amazed, and don't know what to say;
Your blindness simply takes my breath away.
40　　You are indeed bewitched, to take no warning
From our account of what occurred this morning.

ORGON:

Madam, I know a few plain facts, and one
Is that you're partial to my rascal son;
Hence, when he sought to make Tartuffe the victim
Of a base lie, you dared not contradict him.
Ah, but you underplayed your part, my pet;
You should have looked more angry, more upset.

ELMIRE:

When men make overtures, must we reply
With righteous anger and a battle-cry?
50　　Must we turn back their amorous advances
With sharp reproaches and with fiery glances?
Myself, I find such offers merely amusing,
And make no scenes and fusses in refusing;
My taste is for good-natured rectitude,
And I dislike the savage sort of prude
Who guards her virtue with her teeth and claws,
And tears men's eyes out for the slightest cause:
The Lord preserve me from such honor as that,
Which bites and scratches like an alley-cat!
60　　I've found that a polite and cool rebuff

Discourages a lover quite enough.

ORGON:
I know the facts, and I shall not be shaken.

ELMIRE:
I marvel at your power to be mistaken.
Would it, I wonder, carry weight with you
If I could *show* you that our tale was true?

ORGON:
Show me?

ELMIRE:
        Yes.

ORGON:
           Rot.

ELMIRE:
             Come, what if I found a way
To make you see the facts as plain as day?

ORGON:
Nonsense.

ELMIRE:
          Do answer me; don't be absurd.
I'm not now asking you to trust our word.
70 Suppose that from some hiding-place in here
You learned the whole sad truth by eye and ear—
What would you say of your good friend, after that?

ORGON:
Why, I'd say . . . nothing, by Jehoshaphat!
It can't be true.

ELMIRE:
          You've been too long deceived,
And I'm quite tired of being disbelieved.
Come now: let's put my statements to the test,
And you shall see the truth made manifest.

ORGON:
I'll take that challenge. Now do your uttermost.
We'll see how you make good your empty boast.

ELMIRE [*to* DORINE]:
Send him to me.

DORINE:
80   He's crafty; it may be hard
To catch the cunning scoundrel off his guard.

ELMIRE:
No, amorous men are gullible. Their conceit
So blinds them that they're never hard to cheat.
Have him come down. [*To* CLÉANTE *and* MARIANE] Please leave us,
    for a bit.

Scene 4

ELMIRE:
Pull up this table, and get under it.

ORGON:
What?

ELMIRE:
It's essential that you be well-hidden.

ORGON:
Why there?

ELMIRE:
Oh, Heavens! Just do as you are bidden.
I have my plans; we'll soon see how they fare.
Under the table, now; and once you're there,
Take care that you are neither seen nor heard.

ORGON:
Well, I'll indulge you, since I gave my word
To see you through this infantile charade.

ELMIRE:
Once it is over, you'll be glad we played.
[*To her husband, who is now under the table*] I'm going to act quite strangely,
10   now, and you
Must not be shocked at anything I do.
Whatever I may say, you must excuse
As part of that deceit I'm forced to use.
I shall employ sweet speeches in the task
Of making that impostor drop his mask;
I'll give encouragement to his bold desires,
And furnish fuel to his amorous fires.
Since it's for your sake, and for his destruction,
That I shall seem to yield to his seduction,
20   I'll gladly stop whenever you decide
That all your doubts are fully satisfied.
I'll count on you, as soon as you have seen
What sort of man he is, to intervene,
And not expose me to his odious lust
One moment longer than you feel you must.
Remember: you're to save me from my plight
Whenever . . . He's coming! Hush! Keep out of sight!

Scene 5

TARTUFFE:
You wish to have a word with me, I'm told.

ELMIRE:
Yes. I've a little secret to unfold.

Before I speak, however, it would be wise
To close that door, and look about for spies.
[TARTUFFE *goes to the door, closes it, and returns.*]
The very last thing that must happen now
Is a repetition of this morning's row.
I've never been so badly caught off guard.
Oh, how I feared for you! You saw how hard
I tried to make that troublesome Damis
10   Control his dreadful temper, and hold his peace.
In my confusion, I didn't have the sense
Simply to contradict his evidence;
But as it happened, that was for the best,
And all has worked out in our interest.
This storm has only bettered your position;
My husband doesn't have the least suspicion,
And now, in mockery of those who do,
He bids me be continually with you.
And that is why, quite fearless of reproof,
20   I now can be alone with my Tartuffe,
And why my heart—perhaps too quick to yield—
Feels free to let its passion be revealed.

TARTUFFE:
Madam, your words confuse me. Not long ago,
You spoke in quite a different style, you know.

ELMIRE:
Ah, Sir, if that refusal made you smart,
It's little that you know of woman's heart,
Or what that heart is trying to convey
When it resists in such a feeble way!
Always, at first, our modesty prevents
30   The frank avowal of tender sentiments;
However high the passion which inflames us,
Still, to confess its power somehow shames us.
Thus we reluct, at first, yet in a tone
Which tells you that our heart is overthrown,
That what our lips deny, our pulse confesses,
And that, in time, all noes will turn to yesses.
I fear my words are all too frank and free,
And a poor proof of woman's modesty;
But since I'm started, tell me, if you will—
40   Would I have tried to make Damis be still,
Would I have listened, calm and unoffended,
Until your lengthy offer of love was ended,
And been so very mild in my reaction,
Had your sweet words not given me satisfaction?

And when I tried to force you to undo
The marriage-plans my husband has in view,
What did my urgent pleading signify
If not that I admired you, and that I
Deplored the thought that someone else might own
50   Part of a heart I wished for mine alone?

TARTUFFE:
Madam, no happiness is so complete
As when, from lips we love, come words so sweet;
Their nectar floods my every sense, and drains
In honeyed rivulets through all my veins.
To please you is my joy, my only goal;
Your love is the restorer of my soul;
And yet I must beg leave, now, to confess
Some lingering doubts as to my happiness.
Might this not be a trick? Might not the catch
60   Be that you wish me to break off the match
With Mariane, and so have feigned to love me?
I shan't quite trust your fond opinion of me
Until the feelings you've expressed so sweetly
Are demonstrated somewhat more concretely,
And you have shown, by certain kind concessions,
That I may put my faith in your professions.

ELMIRE [*She coughs, to warn her husband.*]:
Why be in such a hurry? Must my heart
Exhaust its bounty at the very start?
To make that sweet admission cost me dear,
70   But you'll not be content, it would appear,
Unless my store of favors is disbursed
To the last farthing, and at the very first.

TARTUFFE:
The less we merit, the less we dare to hope,
And with our doubts, mere words can never cope.
We trust no promised bliss till we receive it;
Not till a joy is ours can we believe it.
I, who so little merit your esteem,
Can't credit this fulfillment of my dream,
And shan't believe it, Madam, until I savor
80   Some palpable assurance of your favor.

ELMIRE:
My, how tyrannical your love can be,
And how it flusters and perplexes me!
How furiously you take one's heart in hand,
And make your every wish a fierce command!
Come, must you hound and harry me to death?

Will you not give me time to catch my breath?
Can it be right to press me with such force,
Give me no quarter, show me no remorse,
And take advantage, by your stern insistence,
90   Of the fond feelings which weaken my resistance?

TARTUFFE:
Well, if you look with favor upon my love,
Why, then, begrudge me some clear proof thereof?

ELMIRE:
But how can I consent without offense
To Heaven, toward which you feel such reverence?

TARTUFFE:
If Heaven is all that holds you back, don't worry.
I can remove that hindrance in a hurry.
Nothing of that sort need obstruct our path.

ELMIRE:
Must one not be afraid of Heaven's wrath?

TARTUFFE:
Madam, forget such fears, and be my pupil,
100   And I shall teach you how to conquer scruple.
Some joys, it's true, are wrong in Heaven's eyes;
Yet Heaven is not averse to compromise;
There is a science, lately formulated,
Whereby one's conscience may be liberated,
And any wrongful act you care to mention
May be redeemed by purity of intention.
I'll teach you, Madam, the secrets of that science;
Meanwhile, just place on me your full reliance.
Assuage my keen desires, and feel no dread:
110   The sin, if any, shall be on my head.
[ELMIRE *coughs, this time more loudly.*]
You've a bad cough.

ELMIRE:
                                Yes, yes. It's bad indeed.

TARTUFFE [*producing a little paper bag*]:
A bit of licorice may be what you need.

ELMIRE:
No, I've a stubborn cold, it seems. I'm sure it
Will take much more than licorice to cure it.

TARTUFFE:
How aggravating.

ELMIRE:
                                Oh, more than I can say.

TARTUFFE:
If you're still troubled, think of things this way:

No one shall know our joys, save us alone,
And there's no evil till the act is known;
It's scandal, Madam, which makes it an offense,
120   And it's no sin to sin in confidence.
ELMIRE [*having coughed once more*]:
Well, clearly I must do as you require,
And yield to your importunate desire.
It is apparent, now, that nothing less
Will satisfy you, and so I acquiesce.
To go so far is much against my will;
I'm vexed that it should come to this; but still,
Since you are so determined on it, since you
Will not allow mere language to convince you,
And since you ask for concrete evidence, I
130   See nothing for it, now, but to comply.
If this is sinful, if I'm wrong to do it,
So much the worse for him who drove me to it.
The fault can surely not be charged to me.
TARTUFFE:
Madam, the fault is mine, if fault there be,
And . . .
ELMIRE:
                Open the door a little, and peek out;
I wouldn't want my husband poking about.
TARTUFFE:
Why worry about that man? Each day he grows
More gullible; one can lead him by the nose.
To find us here would fill him with delight,
140   And if he saw the worst, he'd doubt his sight.
ELMIRE:
Nevertheless, do step out for a minute
Into the hall, and see that no one's in it.

Scene 6

ORGON [*coming out from under the table*]:
That man's a perfect monster, I must admit!
I'm simply stunned. I can't get over it.
ELMIRE:
What, coming out so soon? How premature!
Get back in hiding, and wait until you're sure.
Stay till the end, and be convinced completely;
We mustn't stop till things are proved concretely.
ORGON:
Hell never harbored anything so vicious!

ELMIRE:
    Tut, don't be hasty. Try to be judicious.
    Wait, and be certain that there's no mistake.
10 No jumping to conclusions, for Heaven's sake!
    [*She places* ORGON *behind her, as* TARTUFFE *re-enters.*]

Scene 7

TARTUFFE [*not seeing* ORGON]:
    Madam, all things have worked out to perfection;
    I've given the neighboring rooms a full inspection;
    No one's about; and now I may at last . . .
ORGON [*intercepting him*]:
    Hold on, my passionate fellow, not so fast!
    I should advise a little more restraint.
    Well, so you thought you'd fool me, my dear saint!
    How soon you wearied of the saintly life—
    Wedding my daughter, and coveting my wife!
    I've long suspected you, and had a feeling
10 That soon I'd catch you at your double-dealing.
    Just now, you've given me evidence galore;
    It's quite enough; I have no wish for more.
ELMIRE [*to* TARTUFFE]:
    I'm sorry to have treated you so slyly,
    But circumstances forced me to be wily.
TARTUFFE:
    Brother, you can't think . . .
ORGON:
                           No more talk from you;
    Just leave this household, without more ado.
TARTUFFE:
    What I intended . . .
ORGON:
                       That seems fairly clear.
    Spare me your falsehoods and get out of here.
TARTUFFE:
    No, I'm the master, and you're the one to go!
20 This house belongs to me, I'll have you know,
    And I shall show you that you can't hurt *me*
    By this contemptible conspiracy,
    That those who cross me know not what they do,
    And that I've means to expose and punish you,
    Avenge offended Heaven, and make you grieve
    That ever you dared order me to leave.

Scene 8

ELMIRE:
What was the point of all that angry chatter?
ORGON:
Dear God, I'm worried. This is no laughing matter.
ELMIRE:
How so?
ORGON:
    I fear I understood his drift.
I'm much disturbed about that deed of gift.
ELMIRE:
You gave him . . . ?
ORGON:
      Yes, it's all been drawn and signed.
But one thing more is weighing on my mind.
ELMIRE:
What's that?
ORGON:
    I'll tell you; but first let's see if there's
A certain strong-box in his room upstairs.

ACT V

Scene 1

CLÉANTE:
Where are you going so fast?
ORGON:
      God knows!
CLÉANTE:
        Then wait;
Let's have a conference, and deliberate
On how this situation's to be met.
ORGON:
That strong-box has me utterly upset;
This is the worst of many, many shocks.
CLÉANTE:
Is there some fearful mystery in that box?
ORGON:
My poor friend Argas brought that box to me
With his own hands, in utmost secrecy;
'Twas on the very morning of his flight.
It's full of papers which, if they came to light,
Would ruin him—or such is my impression.

10

CLÉANTE:
    Then why did you let it out of your possession?

ORGON:
    Those papers vexed my conscience, and it seemed best
    To ask the counsel of my pious guest.
    The cunning scoundrel got me to agree
    To leave the strong-box in his custody,
    So that, in case of an investigation,
    I could employ a slight equivocation
    And swear I didn't have it, and thereby,
20   At no expense to conscience, tell a lie.

CLÉANTE:
    It looks to me as if you're out on a limb.
    Trusting him with that box, and offering him
    That deed of gift, were actions of a kind
    Which scarcely indicate a prudent mind.
    With two such weapons, he has the upper hand,
    And since you're vulnerable, as matters stand,
    You erred once more in bringing him to bay.
    You should have acted in some subtler way.

ORGON:
    Just think of it: behind that fervent face,
30   A heart so wicked, and a soul so base!
    I took him in, a hungry beggar, and then . . .
    Enough, by God! I'm through with pious men:
    Henceforth I'll hate the whole false brotherhood,
    And persecute them worse than Satan could.

CLÉANTE:
    Ah, there you go — extravagant as ever!
    Why can you not be rational? You never
    Manage to take the middle course, it seems,
    But jump, instead, between absurd extremes.
    You've recognized your recent grave mistake
40   In falling victim to a pious fake;
    Now, to correct that error, must you embrace
    An even greater error in its place,
    And judge our worthy neighbors as a whole
    By what you've learned of one corrupted soul?
    Come, just because one rascal made you swallow
    A show of zeal which turned out to be hollow,
    Shall you conclude that all men are deceivers,
    And that, today, there are no true believers?
    Let atheists make that foolish inference;
50   Learn to distinguish virtue from pretense,
    Be cautious in bestowing admiration,

And cultivate a sober moderation.
Don't humor fraud, but also don't asperse
True piety; the latter fault is worse,
And it is best to err, if err one must,
As you have done, upon the side of trust.

Scene 2

DAMIS:

Father, I hear that scoundrel's uttered threats
Against you; that he pridefully forgets
How, in his need, he was befriended by you,
And means to use your gifts to crucify you.

ORGON:

It's true, my boy. I'm too distressed for tears.

DAMIS:

Leave it to me, Sir; let me trim his ears.
Faced with such insolence, we must not waver.
I shall rejoice in doing you the favor
Of cutting short his life, and your distress.

CLÉANTE:

10   What a display of young hotheadedness!
Do learn to moderate your fits of rage.
In this just kingdom, this enlightened age,
One does not settle things by violence.

Scene 3

MADAME PERNELLE:

I hear strange tales of very strange events.

ORGON:

Yes, strange events which these two eyes beheld.
The man's ingratitude is unparalleled.
I save a wretched pauper from starvation,
House him, and treat him like a blood relation,
Shower him every day with my largesse,
Give him my daughter, and all that I possess;
And meanwhile the unconscionable knave
Tries to induce my wife to misbehave;

10   And not content with such extreme rascality,
Now threatens me with my own liberality,
And aims, by taking base advantage of
The gifts I gave him out of Christian love,
To drive me from my house, a ruined man,
And make me end a pauper, as he began.

DORINE:
    Poor fellow!

MADAME PERNELLE:
         No, my son, I'll never bring
    Myself to think him guilty of such a thing.

ORGON:
    How's that?

MADAME PERNELLE:
         The righteous always were maligned.

ORGON:
    Speak clearly, Mother. Say what's on your mind.

MADAME PERNELLE:
20   I mean that I can smell a rat, my dear.
    You know how everybody hates him, here.

ORGON:
    That has no bearing on the case at all.

MADAME PERNELLE:
    I told you a hundred times, when you were small,
    That virtue in this world is hated ever;
    Malicious men may die, but malice never.

ORGON:
    No doubt that's true, but how does it apply?

MADAME PERNELLE:
    They've turned you against him by a clever lie.

ORGON:
    I've told you, I was there and saw it done.

MADAME PERNELLE:
    Ah, slanderers will stop at nothing, Son.

ORGON:
30   Mother, I'll lose my temper . . . For the last time,
    I tell you I was witness to the crime.

MADAME PERNELLE:
    The tongues of spite are busy night and noon,
    And to their venom no man is immune.

ORGON:
    You're talking nonsense. Can't you realize
    I saw it; saw it; saw it with my eyes?
    Saw, do you understand me? Must I shout it
    Into your ears before you'll cease to doubt it?

MADAME PERNELLE:
    Appearances can deceive, my son. Dear me,
    We cannot always judge by what we see.

ORGON:
    Drat! Drat!

MADAME PERNELLE:
40   One often interprets things awry;

Good can seem evil to a suspicious eye.

ORGON:

Was I to see his pawing at Elmire
As an act of charity?

MADAME PERNELLE:

Till his guilt is clear,
A man deserves the benefit of the doubt.
You should have waited, to see how things turned out.

ORGON:

Great God in Heaven, what more proof did I need?
Was I to sit there, watching, until he'd . . .
You drive me to the brink of impropriety.

MADAME PERNELLE:

No, no, a man of such surpassing piety
50   Could not do such a thing. You cannot shake me.
I don't believe it, and you shall not make me.

ORGON:

You vex me so that, if you weren't my mother,
I'd say to you . . . some dreadful thing or other.

DORINE:

It's your turn now, Sir, not to be listened to;
You'd not trust us, and now she won't trust you.

CLÉANTE:

My friends, we're wasting time which should be spent
In facing up to our predicament.
I fear that scoundrel's threats weren't made in sport.

DAMIS:

Do you think he'd have the nerve to go to court?

ELMIRE:

60   I'm sure he won't: they'd find it all too crude
A case of swindling and ingratitude.

CLÉANTE:

Don't be too sure. He won't be at a loss
To give his claims a high and righteous gloss;
And clever rogues with far less valid cause
Have trapped their victims in a web of laws.
I say again that to antagonize
A man so strongly armed was most unwise.

ORGON:

I know it; but the man's appalling cheek
Outraged me so, I couldn't control my pique.

CLÉANTE:

70   I wish to Heaven that we could devise
Some truce between you, or some compromise.

ELMIRE:

If I had known what cards he held, I'd not

Have roused his anger by my little plot.
ORGON [*to* DORINE, *as* M. LOYAL *enters*]:
    What is that fellow looking for? Who is he?
    Go talk to him—and tell him that I'm busy.

Scene 4

MONSIEUR LOYAL:
    Good day, dear sister. Kindly let me see
    Your master.
DORINE:
                    He's involved with company,
    And cannot be disturbed just now, I fear.
MONSIEUR LOYAL:
    I hate to intrude; but what has brought me here
    Will not disturb your master, in any event.
    Indeed, my news will make him most content.
DORINE:
    Your name?
MONSIEUR LOYAL:
                    Just say that I bring greetings from
    Monsieur Tartuffe, on whose behalf I've come.
DORINE [*to* ORGON]:
    Sir, he's a very gracious man, and bears
10   A message from Tartuffe, which, he declares,
    Will make you most content.
CLÉANTE:
                    Upon my word,
    I think this man had best be seen, and heard.
ORGON:
    Perhaps he has some settlement to suggest.
    How shall I treat him? What manner would be best?
CLÉANTE:
    Control your anger, and if he should mention
    Some fair adjustment, give him your full attention.
MONSIEUR LOYAL:
    Good health to you, good Sir. May Heaven confound
    Your enemies, and may your joys abound.
ORGON [*aside, to* CLÉANTE]:
    A gentle salutation: it confirms
20   My guess that he is here to offer terms.
MONSIEUR LOYAL:
    I've always held your family most dear;
    I served your father, Sir, for many a year.
ORGON:
    Sir, I must ask your pardon; to my shame,

I cannot now recall your face or name.

MONSIEUR LOYAL:

Loyal's my name; I come from Normandy,
And I'm a bailiff, in all modesty.
For forty years, praise God, it's been my boast
To serve with honor in that vital post,
And I am here, Sir, if you will permit
30　The liberty, to serve you with this writ . . .

ORGON:

To—*what?*

MONSIEUR LOYAL:

　　　　Now, please, Sir, let us have no friction:
It's nothing but an order of eviction.
You are to move your goods and family out
And make way for new occupants, without
Deferment or delay, and give the keys . . .

ORGON:

I? Leave this house?

MONSIEUR LOYAL:

　　　　　Why yes, Sir, if you please.
This house, Sir, from the cellar to the roof,
Belongs now to the good Monsieur Tartuffe,
And he is lord and master of your estate
40　By virtue of a deed of present date,
Drawn in due form, with clearest legal phrasing . . .

DAMIS:

Your insolence is utterly amazing!

MONSIEUR LOYAL:

Young man, my business here is not with you,
But with your wise and temperate father, who,
Like every worthy citizen, stands in awe
Of justice, and would never obstruct the law.

ORGON:

But . . .

MONSIEUR LOYAL:

　　　　Not for a million, Sir, would you rebel
Against authority; I know that well.
You'll not make trouble, Sir, or interfere
50　With the execution of my duties here.

DAMIS:

Someone may execute a smart tattoo
On that black jacket of yours, before you're through.

MONSIEUR LOYAL:

Sir, bid your son be silent. I'd much regret
Having to mention such a nasty threat

Of violence, in writing my report.
DORINE [*aside*]:
    This man Loyal's a most disloyal sort!
MONSIEUR LOYAL:
    I love all men of upright character,
    And when I agreed to serve these papers, Sir,
    It was your feelings that I had in mind.
60   I couldn't bear to see the case assigned
    To someone else, who might esteem you less
    And so subject you to unpleasantness.
ORGON:
    What's more unpleasant than telling a man to leave
    His house and home?
MONSIEUR LOYAL:
                You'd like a short reprieve?
    If you desire it, Sir, I shall not press you,
    But wait until tomorrow to dispossess you.
    Splendid. I'll come and spend the night here, then,
    Most quietly, with half a score of men.
    For form's sake, you might bring me, just before
70   You go to bed, the keys to the front door.
    My men, I promise, will be on their best
    Behavior, and will not disturb your rest.
    But bright and early, Sir, you must be quick
    And move out all your furniture, every stick:
    The men I've chosen are both young and strong,
    And with their help it shouldn't take you long.
    In short, I'll make things pleasant and convenient,
    And since I'm being so extremely lenient,
    Please show me, Sir, a like consideration,
80   And give me your entire cooperation.
ORGON [*aside*]:
    I may be all but bankrupt, but I vow
    I'd give a hundred louis, here and now,
    Just for the pleasure of landing one good clout
    Right on the end of that complacent snout.
CLÉANTE:
    Careful; don't make things worse.
DAMIS:
                   My bootsole itches
    To give that beggar a good kick in the breeches.
DORINE:
    Monsieur Loyal, I'd love to hear the whack
    Of a stout stick across your fine broad back.

MONSIEUR LOYAL:

    Take care: a woman too may go to jail if

90   She uses threatening language to a bailiff.

CLÉANTE:

    Enough, enough, Sir. This must not go on.

    Give me that paper, please, and then begone.

MONSIEUR LOYAL:

    Well, *au revoir.* God give you all good cheer!

ORGON:

    May God confound you, and him who sent you here!

Scene 5

ORGON:

    Now, Mother, was I right or not? This writ

    Should change your notion of Tartuffe a bit.

    Do you perceive his villainy at last?

MADAME PERNELLE:

    I'm thunderstruck. I'm utterly aghast.

DORINE:

    Oh, come, be fair. You mustn't take offense

    At this new proof of his benevolence.

    He's acting out of selfless love, I know.

    Material things enslave the soul, and so

    He kindly has arranged your liberation

10   From all that might endanger your salvation.

ORGON:

    Will you not ever hold your tongue, you dunce?

CLÉANTE:

    Come, you must take some action, and at once.

ELMIRE:

    Go tell the world of the low trick he's tried.

    The deed of gift is surely nullified

    By such behavior, and public rage will not

    Permit the wretch to carry out his plot.

Scene 6

VALÈRE:

    Sir, though I hate to bring you more bad news,

    Such is the danger that I cannot choose.

    A friend who is extremely close to me

    And knows my interest in your family

    Has, for my sake, presumed to violate

    The secrecy that's due to things of state,

And sends me word that you are in a plight
From which your one salvation lies in flight.
That scoundrel who's imposed upon you so
Denounced you to the King an hour ago
And, as supporting evidence, displayed
The strong-box of a certain renegade
Whose secret papers, so he testified,
You had disloyally agreed to hide.
I don't know just what charges may be pressed,
But there's a warrant out for your arrest;
Tartuffe has been instructed, furthermore,
To guide the arresting officer to your door.

CLÉANTE:
He's clearly done this to facilitate
His seizure of your house and your estate.

ORGON:
That man, I must say, is a vicious beast!

VALÈRE:
Quick, Sir; you mustn't tarry in the least.
My carriage is outside, to take you hence;
This thousand louis should cover all expense.
Let's lose no time, or you shall be undone;
The sole defense, in this case, is to run.
I shall go with you all the way, and place you
In a safe refuge to which they'll never trace you.

ORGON:
Alas, dear boy, I wish that I could show you
My gratitude for everything I owe you.
But now is not the time; I pray the Lord
That I may live to give you your reward.
Farewell, my dears; be careful . . .

CLÉANTE:
Brother, hurry.
We shall take care of things; you needn't worry.

Scene 7

TARTUFFE:
Gently, Sir, gently; stay right where you are.
No need for haste; your lodging isn't far.
You're off to prison, by order of the Prince.

ORGON:
This is the crowning blow, you wretch; and since
It means my total ruin and defeat,
Your villainy is now at last complete.

TARTUFFE:

    You needn't try to provoke me; it's no use.

    Those who serve Heaven must expect abuse.

CLÉANTE:

    You are indeed most patient, sweet, and blameless.

DORINE:

10   How he exploits the name of Heaven! It's shameless.

TARTUFFE:

    Your taunts and mockeries are all for naught;

    To do my duty is my only thought.

MARIANE:

    Your love of duty is most meritorious,

    And what you've done is little short of glorious.

TARTUFFE:

    All deeds are glorious, Madam, which obey

    The sovereign prince who sent me here today.

ORGON:

    I rescued you when you were destitute;

    Have you forgotten that, you thankless brute?

TARTUFFE:

    No, no, I well remember everything;

20   But my first duty is to serve my King.

    That obligation is so paramount

    That other claims, beside it, do not count;

    And for it I would sacrifice my wife,

    My family, my friend, or my own life.

ELMIRE:

    Hypocrite!

DORINE:

             All that we most revere, he uses

    To cloak his plots and camouflage his ruses.

CLÉANTE:

    If it is true that you are animated

    By pure and loyal zeal, as you have stated,

    Why was this zeal not roused until you'd sought

30   To make Orgon a cuckold, and been caught?

    Why weren't you moved to give your evidence

    Until your outraged host had driven you hence?

    I shan't say that the gift of all his treasure

    Ought to have damped your zeal in any measure;

    But if he is a traitor, as you declare,

    How could you condescend to be his heir?

TARTUFFE [*to the* OFFICER]:

    Sir, spare me all this clamor; it's growing shrill.

    Please carry out your orders, if you will.

OFFICER:
    Yes, I've delayed too long, Sir. Thank you kindly.
40   You're just the proper person to remind me.
    Come, you are off to join the other boarders
    In the King's prison, according to his orders.

TARTUFFE:
    Who? I, Sir?

OFFICER:
          Yes.

TARTUFFE:
              To prison? This can't be true!

OFFICER:
    I owe an explanation, but not to you.
    [*To* ORGON] Sir, all is well; rest easy, and be grateful.
    We serve a Prince to whom all sham is hateful,
    A Prince who sees into our inmost hearts,
    And can't be fooled by any trickster's arts.
    His royal soul, though generous and human,
50   Views all things with discernment and acumen;
    His sovereign reason is not lightly swayed,
    And all his judgments are discreetly weighed.
    He honors righteous men of every kind,
    And yet his zeal for virtue is not blind,
    Nor does his love of piety numb his wits
    And make him tolerant of hypocrites.
    'Twas hardly likely that this man could cozen
    A King who's foiled such liars by the dozen.
    With one keen glance, the King perceived the whole
60   Perverseness and corruption of his soul,
    And thus high Heaven's justice was displayed:
    Betraying you, the rogue stood self-betrayed.
    The King soon recognized Tartuffe as one
    Notorious by another name, who'd done
    So many vicious crimes that one could fill
    Ten volumes with them, and be writing still.
    But to be brief: our sovereign was appalled
    By this man's treachery toward you, which he called
    The last, worst villainy of a vile career,
70   And bade me follow the impostor here
    To see how gross his impudence could be,
    And force him to restore your property.
    Your private papers, by the King's command,
    I hereby seize and give into your hand.
    The King, by royal order, invalidates
    The deed which gave this rascal your estates,

And pardons, furthermore, your grave offense
In harboring an exile's documents.
By these decrees, our Prince rewards you for
80   Your loyal deeds in the late civil war,
And shows how heartfelt is his satisfaction
In recompensing any worthy action,
How much he prizes merit, and how he makes
More of men's virtues than of their mistakes.

DORINE:
    Heaven be praised!

MADAME PERNELLE:
                        I breathe again, at last.

ELMIRE:
    We're safe.

MARIANE:
                I can't believe the danger's past.

ORGON [*to* TARTUFFE]:
    Well, traitor, now you see . . .

CLÉANTE:
                                    Ah, Brother, please,
    Let's not descend to such indigniaes.
    Leave the poor wretch to his unhappy fate,
90   And don't say anything to aggravate
    His present woes; but rather hope that he
    Will soon embrace an honest piety,
    And mend his ways, and by a true repentance
    Move our just King to moderate his sentence.
    Meanwhile, go kneel before your sovereign's throne
    And thank him for the mercies he has shown.

ORGON:
    Well said: let's go at once and, gladly kneeling,
    Express the gratitude which all are feeling.
    Then, when that first great duty has been done,
100   We'll turn with pleasure to a second one,
    And give Valère, whose love has proven so true,
    The wedded happiness which is his due.

PU SONG-LING (P'U SUNG LING)

B. CHINA, 1640–1715

poo-song-LING

Pu Song-Ling's short stories are as well known in China as are those of E. T. A. Hoffmann[1] in Germany and Edgar Allan Poe[2] in the United States. Like Hoffmann and Poe, Pu Song-Ling wrote about the strange and the fantastic; his stories concern ordinary people whose lives somehow come into contact with the supernatural in the form of ghosts, fox spirits, genii, and other uncanny beings. Moreover, like his European and American counterparts, Pu Song-Ling transformed the supernatural tale into a sophisticated art form. His classic collection of 431 tales, *Strange Stories from a Chinese Studio* (*Liao-zhai zhi-yi*, 1766), influenced the revival of the classical-language story in China and delighted readers. Though their elevated prose style makes them difficult even for Chinese readers, Pu Song-Ling's stories continue to be praised as classics and—reproduced in other forms and translated into modern Chinese and other languages— to appeal to a wide audience.

"Chill and Desolate as a Monastery."   Pu Song-Ling was born in 1640 in Shan-dong (Shantung) province. He lived during the early years of the **Qing** (Ch'ing) dynasty (1644–1911), a time of transition when many families of the gentry, including Pu Song-Ling's own, were disenfranchised, as power shifted hands to the new Manchu rulers. In a brief autobiographical record, Pu Song-Ling describes himself as thin and of poor health and says that his father's home was "chill and desolate as a monastery." Although he received a solid classical education and passed the first stage of his examinations, Pu Song-Ling failed the provincial civil service exam at least twice. Unable to gain access to a government position, he remained in his native province of Shan-dong, teaching, collecting tales, and writing. He worked for some time as a personal secretary and then as a private tutor to a prominent family, from 1672 to 1710.

ching

An ardent collector of classical and popular stories, Pu Song-Ling might be considered a folklorist who listened attentively to the tales circulating among the people of Shan-dong. Apparently he began writing early in life, but the first version of *Strange Tales* did not appear until 1679, when Pu Song-Ling was almost forty years old. The compendium first circulated in manuscript form only, for Pu Song-Ling could not afford to have it printed. Over the years he continued to add to and revise the tales; in the meantime he wrote a novel, three plays, poetry, and lyrics to be sung to popular tunes. In 1710, when Pu Song-Ling was seventy years old, he was given an official post as a senior licentiate because of his literary

www For more information about Pu Song-Ling and a quiz on "The Mural," see bedfordstmartins .com/worldlit compact.

---

[1] **E. T. A. Hoffmann** (1776–1822): German Romantic writer of supernatural and fantastic tales such as "The Sandman" and "The Mines of Falun," published in the early nineteenth century.

[2] **Edgar Allan Poe** (1809–1849): This nineteenth-century American writer produced classic suspense tales such as "The Fall of the House of Usher" and "The Telltale Heart."

Pu Song-Ling, Page
from *Liao-zhai zhi-yi*
(*University of
Wisconsin-Madison
Library*)

reputation. Pu Song-Ling died a short time later, in 1715; the final version of *Strange Tales* was published posthumously in 1766.

Short Fiction in the Early Qing.   The final century of the Ming dynasty[3] and the early years of the Qing dynasty, when Pu Song-Ling lived, coincided with an increase in the production of VERNACULAR FICTION. As with the rise of the European NOVEL, the popularity of vernacular fiction in China was partly the result of the prosperity of the urban middle classes, who were drawn to the short story, the novel, and popular theater as forms of diversion and entertainment. *Strange Stories from a Chinese Studio* (also translated as *Strange Tales* or *Uncanny Stories from a Scholar's Studio*) are portraits of everyday life, but ones in which the characters inevitably brush up against the supernatural in the form of ghosts, fox spirits, immortals, and other beings. Pu Song-Ling wrote his stories in a refined, "old style" prose that imitated classical styles dating back to the

---

[3]**Ming dynasty** (1368–1644): A blossoming of Chinese culture, the restoration of Confucianism, and an elevation of the arts, including porcelain, architecture, drama, and the novel, are characteristic of this period.

Western Han era (206 B.C.E.– 8 C.E.). When his collection was first printed, classical supernatural stories were accompanied by extensive annotations and critical commentaries.

Strange Stories from a Chinese Studio.   After committing overheard popular stories to memory, Pu Song-Ling would polish them into a new form. Of his own storytelling abilities, Pu Song-Ling wrote,

> My talents are not those of Kan Pao, elegant explorer of the records of the Gods; I am rather animated by the spirit of Su Tung-p'o,[4] who loved to hear men speak of the supernatural. I get people to commit what they tell me to writing, and subsequently I dress it up in the form of a story; and thus, in the lapse of time my friends from all quarters have supplied me with quantities of material, which, from my habit of collecting, has grown into a vast pile.

His self-assessment notwithstanding, Pu Song-Ling's reputation as a great writer rests not on his abilities as a listener and collector but on his fine prose styling by which he transformed the stories he heard into works of art. Indeed, while Chinese critics appreciate the wit and irony of Pu Song-Ling's stories, they single out for praise their elevated style. Pu Song-Ling was a meticulous artist who honed and polished his stories until they met all the formal requirements of classic Chinese prose style—simplicity, invention, innovation, and density of allusions. Unfortunately, the apparent simplicity of these tales in translation doesn't do justice to Pu Song-Ling's perfection of this complex prose form.

Whereas earlier Chinese tales of the supernatural take for granted a belief in spirits and magical powers, Pu Song-Ling's stories demonstrate a somewhat unique treatment of the otherworldly. In stories such as "The Wise Neighbor," spirits embody human attributes and interact with human characters in ways more "natural" than supernatural. Moreover, as Stephen Owen has noted, there is often an "undercurrent of whimsy and humor" when the ordinary characters recognize the appearance of the supernatural in their world. As Owen puts it, "At the very moment that the supernatural reveals itself in the ordinary world, . . . the strange has become ordinary."

"The Mural" takes its readers into a kind of dreamscape that confounds the divide between illusion and reality. Here Chu, the master of letters, gazes into a mural depicting heavenly maidens scattering flowers and becomes so mesmerized by one of the figures that he is transported into another world. Chu encounters a female apparition whose existence may be illusory. Yet the characters seem to be physically present in, or incorporated into, the world of the "illusion," further confusing the boundary between reality and imagination.

■ **FURTHER RESEARCH**

Biography

Giles, Herbert A. *A History of Chinese Literature.* 1901; rpt. 1967.
———, trans. *Strange Stories from a Chinese Studio.* 1925.

---

[4]**Kan Pao:** Fourth-century author of a thirty-volume work called *Supernatural Researches.* **Su Tung-p'o:** Poet and essayist from the tenth century.

Criticism

Chang, Chun-shu. *Redefining History: Ghosts, Spirits, and Human Society in Pëu Sung-ling's World, 1640–1715*. 1998.

Owen, Stephen, ed. Introduction to Pu Song-ling in *An Anthology of Chinese Literature: Beginnings to 1911*. 1996.

Zeitlin, Judith T. *Historian of the Strange: Pu Songling and the Chinese Classical Tale*. 1993.

■ **PRONUNCIATION**

Pao-chih: bow-JUR

Pu Song-Ling: poo-song-LING

Qing: ching

❧ The Mural

Translated by Denis C. Mair and Victor H. Mair

While staying in the capital, Meng Lung-t'an of Kiangsi and Master of Letters Chu once happened upon a monastery. Neither the shrine-hall nor the meditation room was very spacious, and only one old monk was found putting up within. Seeing the guests enter, the monk straightened up his clothes, went to greet them, and showed them around the place. An image of Zen Master Pao-chih[1] stood in the shrine-hall. On either side-wall were painted fine murals with lifelike human figures. The east wall depicted the Buddhist legend of "Heavenly Maidens Scattering Flowers." Among the figures was a young girl with flowing hair with a flower in her hand and a faint smile on her face. Her cherry-red lips were on the verge of moving, and the liquid pools of her eyes seemed to stir with wavelike glances. After gazing intently for some time, Chu's self-possession began to waver, and his thoughts grew so abstracted that he fell into a trance. His body went adrift as if floating on mist; suddenly he was inside the mural. Peak upon peak of palaces and pavilions made him feel as if he was beyond this earth. An old monk was preaching the Dharma[2] on a dais, around which stood a large crowd of viewers in robes with their right shoulders bared out of respect. Chu mingled in among them.

Before long, he felt someone tugging furtively at his sleeve. He turned to look, and there was the girl with flowing hair giving him a dazzling smile. She tripped abruptly away, and he lost no time following her along a winding walkway into a small chamber. Once there, he hesitated to approach any farther. When she turned her head and raised the flower with a beckoning motion, he went across to her in the quiet, deserted chamber. Swiftly he embraced her and, as she did not put up much resistance, they

---

[1] **Pao-chih:** Pao zhi; a legendary monk from the era of the Northern (386–581) and Southern (420–589) dynasties.

[2] **Dharma:** In Buddhism, the truth that reflects the moral law of the universe.

grew intimate. When it was over she told him not to make a sound and left, closing the door behind her. That night she came again. After two days of this, the girl's companions realized what was happening and searched together until they found the scholar.

"A little gentleman is already growing in your belly, but still you wear those flowing tresses, pretending to be a maiden," they said teasingly. Holding out hairpins and earrings, they pressured her to put her hair up in the coiled knot of a married woman, which she did in silent embarrassment. One of the girls said, "Sisters, let's not outstay our welcome." At this the group left all in a titter.

Looking at the soft, cloudlike chignon piled atop her head and her phoenix ringlets curved low before her ears, the scholar was more struck by her charms than when she had worn her hair long. Seeing that no one was around, he began to make free with her. His heart throbbed at her musky fragrance but, before they had quite finished their pleasure, the heavy tread of leather boots was heard. A clanking of chains and manacles was followed by clamorous, arguing voices. The girl got up in alarm. Peering out, they saw an officer dressed in armor, his face black as lacquer, with chains in one hand and a mace in the other. Standing around him were all the maidens. "Is this all of you?" asked the officer. "We're all here," they answered. "Report if any of you are concealing a man from the lower world. Don't bring trouble on yourselves." "We aren't," said the maidens in unison. The officer turned around and looked malevolently in the direction of the chamber, giving every appearance of an intention to search it. The girl's face turned pale as ashes in fear. "Quick, hide under the bed," she told Chu in panic. She opened a little door in the wall and was gone in an instant. Chu lay prostrate, hardly daring to take a little breath. Soon he heard the sound of boots stumping into, then back out of, the room. Before long, the din of voices gradually receded. He regained some composure, though the sound of passersby discussing the matter could be heard frequently outside the door. After cringing there for quite some time, he heard ringing in his ears and felt a burning ache in his eyes. Though the intensity of these sensations threatened to overwhelm him, there was no choice but to listen quietly for the girl's return. He was reduced to the point that he no longer recalled where he had been before coming here.

Just then his friend Meng Lung-t'an, who had been standing in the shrine-hall, found that Chu had disappeared in the blink of an eye. Perplexed, he asked the monk what had happened. "He has gone to hear a sermon on the Dharma," said the monk laughingly. "Where?" asked Meng. "Not far," was the answer. After a moment, the monk tapped on the wall with his finger and called, "Why do you tarry so long, my good patron?" Presently there appeared on the wall an image of Chu standing motionless with his head cocked to one side as if listening to something. "You have kept your traveling companion waiting a long time," called the monk again. Thereupon he drifted out of the mural and down to the floor. He stood woodenly, his mind like burned-out ashes, with eyes staring straight ahead and legs wobbling. Meng was terribly frightened, but in time calmed down enough to ask what had happened. It turned out that Chu had been hiding under the bed when he heard a thunderous knocking, so he came out of the room to listen for the source of the sound.

They looked at the girl holding the flower and saw, instead of flowing hair, a high coiled chignon on her head. Chu bowed down to the old monk in amazement and asked the reason for this. "Illusion is born in the mind. How can a poor mendicant like myself explain it?" laughed the monk. Chu was dispirited and cast down; Meng was shaken and confused. Together they walked down the shrine-hall steps and left.

The Chronicler of the Tales comments: "'Illusion is born in the mind.' These sound like the words of one who has found the truth. A wanton mind gives rise to visions of lustfulness. The mind dominated by lust gives rise to a state of fear. The Bodhisattva[3] made it possible for ignorant persons to attain realization for themselves. All the myriad transformations of illusion are nothing but the movements of the human mind itself. The old monk spoke in earnest solicitude, but regrettably there is no sign that the youth found enlightenment in his words and entered the mountains with hair unbound to seek the truth."

---

[3] **Bodhisattva:** A reference to Guanshiyin, who attained Buddhahood, but out of compassion returns to help those who are suffering.

TEXT IN CONTEXT

❧ MATSUO BASHŌ
B. JAPAN, 1644–1694

Bashō
*This portrait on
a scroll depicts an
elderly Bashō,
weathered from his
years of traveling.
[Itsuo Museum,
Osaka]*

In the last months of his life, Matsuo Bashō handed a poem to one of
his numerous students:

> Do not copy me—
> do not be like a cantaloupe
> cut into halves.

This advice was not easy to follow. Although Bashō did not invent
the short poetic form known today as haiku, he mastered the form by
broadening its emotional and thematic possibilities; in effect, Bashō's
became the standard by which all later haiku were measured. And to
serious admirers, Bashō is much more than an expert poet; long after
his death, he is regarded as a sage or a religious teacher. Bashō led a
simple, almost monastic life. He was often withdrawn from society
and available only to a few disciples and other poets. These characteristics earned him the title "saint of haiku."

Published eight years after his death, Bashō's most famous work,
Narrow Road through the Backcountry (Oku-no-hosomichi) could be
classified as travel literature, but it recounts journeys that are totally
different from those of travelers such as Lady Mary Wortley Montagu
or fictional travelers such as Candide and Lemuel Gulliver. Bashō's
journeys are best characterized as pilgrimages to natural and artificial
shrines, where he experiences the connections or relationships among
places, their histories, previous visitors, friends, and himself. Bashō uses
brief poems and carefully written prose to capture intimate moments
of coalescence. These passages are like a series of photographs in which

the camera points both outward and inward, bringing the two dimensions together—the poet in the place.

In *Narrow Road through the Backcountry,* Bashō shows his mastery of the poetic travel diary. Dating from the Heian period (794–1185), the travel diary or *haibun* developed into a sophisticated art form, wherein writers sought not to describe the places, people, and events they experienced but to give artistic shape to their journey and evoke a sense of the emotional resonance and philosophical significance.

In the earliest travel diaries such as *The Tosa Diary* (tenth century), *waka,* five-line poems consisting of thirty-one syllables (*mora*) distributed in a pattern of 5–7–5–7–7, were interspersed among prose passages. The master of *waka* was Saigyo (twelfth century), who wrote *waka* about the deep connection between humans and nature. Eventually, *renga,* or "linked verse," poetry was adapted in travel diaries. Developing from the thirteenth century, *renga* was a genre of collaborative poetry composed by two or more writers who alternated three- and two-line stanzas to form poetic sequences of up to one-hundred stanzas. The crucial opening verse, the *hokku* (5–7–5 syllables), was often composed so that it could stand alone—the origin of what today is called haiku.

Renga, which grew out of Japanese court culture, was characterized by elevated language, serious tone, and elegant style. By Bashō's time, the high seriousness of *renga* had given way to a new style of linked verse, *haikai no renga,* which brought a more playful tone and more commonplace subjects. *Haikai—hai* meaning "play"; *kai* meaning "friendly exchange"—was a kind of liberated *renga* featuring popular, even vulgar, topics and often containing fewer than the typical one-hundred stanzas common to *renga.* Under Bashō's influence, *haikai* found a middle ground between elegance and vulgarity, and the introductory *hokku* gained a kind of independent status that gave rise to the three-line *haiku,* which eventually replaced *haikai.* The combining of *haikai* and prose in travel diaries during the Tokugawa period (1603–1867) was called *haibun,* meaning *haikai* prose or *haikai* literature.

www For a quiz on *Narrow Road through the Backcountry,* see bedfordstmartins .com/worldlit compact.

Eighteenth-Century Japan: Genroku Period

Between 1688 and 1704 Japan experienced a cultural renaissance in literature and the arts, brought on in part by the power and wealth of the *chonin*, or merchant classes, whose secular values inspired a new aesthetic. Known as the Genroku period, this moment of cultural creativity was centered in the cities of Edo, Japan's capital; Kyoto; and Osaka, the premier commercial city. The cultural revival was marked by a turn toward popular forms that exploited new developments in woodblock printing and that plumbed the everyday lives of the artisans, merchants, bankers, courtesans, and actors who frequented the licensed districts, or pleasure quarters. During Genroku, the transitory pleasures of the "floating world" were a dominating influence. Painters, woodblock printers, dramatists, and fiction writers were eager to satisfy the tastes and reflect the values of the thriving townspeople. In painting, Ogata Korin (1658–1716) moved away from conventional, Chinese-inspired scenes and depicted the lives of *chonin*, as did the woodblock printer Utamoro (1754–1806). In drama, Chikamatsu Monzaemon (1653–1724) transformed the *joruri*, or popular puppet theater, becoming one of the first writers in the world to focus on the domestic and personal tragedies of common people. His *sewamono*, or domestic plays, often dramatized actual incidents that had taken place in Kyoto or Edo; like Goethe's immensely popular novel *The Sorrows of Young Werther* (1774), which set off a series of imitation suicides in late-eighteenth-century Germany, Chikamatsu's *shinju* plays were so widely influential that the government banned their performance in order to stem the growing number of imitation suicides in Japan. Ihara Saikaku (1642–1693) became the leading popular fiction writer of the time, using colloquial language to transform the Japanese novel into a realistic story that focused on the loves and lives of artisans and merchants. Matsuo Bashō (1644–1694) recast *haikai,* or linked verse, into personal expression, conveying a direct sense of nature and a spirit of reverie. Scholarship, too, blossomed during this time. Philosophers such as Ogyu Sorai (1666–1728) and Arai Hakuseki (1657–1725) redirected Japanese thought from metaphysics toward a more empirical study of philology, linguistics, history, ethics, and politics. Overall, the Genroku period was a reflection of the society that had emerged in the first century of the Tokugawa era, and it left a lasting mark on Japanese literature, culture, and sensibility.

H. Suzuki, Sprigging a Plum Tree, *c. 1755   This woodcut depicts two pleasure-seekers of the floating world of the Genroku period. (The Art Archive/ Eileen Tweedy)*

Choosing a Life of Poetry.   Matsuo **Bashō** was born in 1644 in the town of **Ueno**, southeast of Kyoto. The son of a minor samurai serving the ruling Todo family, Matsuo Munefusa, later known as Bashō, seemed destined to follow his father's footsteps. When he was nine, Bashō became an attendant to the Todo family, serving primarily as a companion to Yoshitada, the eleven-year-old heir. For nearly thirteen years, Bashō and Yoshitada were constant companions and friends, and as part of their training they studied linked verse under a local master. When Yoshitada died in 1666, Bashō, now twenty-three years old, broke away from his duties to the Todo family and went to Kyoto where he continued his studies of poetry, calligraphy, and the classics. When Bashō returned to his hometown of Ueno in 1671, he published an anthology of poetry entitled *The Seashell Game (Kai Oi)*. The next year he moved to Edo (Tokyo), a young, thriving city. Changing his pen name from Sobo to Tosei, Bashō became associated with Soin (1605–1682), a master poet, who taught him the importance of writing about ordinary life.

BAH-shoh
oo-EH-noh

Bashō's work began to appear in numerous anthologies, and disciples gathered around him. In 1680 they built him a house and presented him with a young Japanese banana tree, a *bashō,* which provided a name for his house and eventually a new pen name. Before Bashō, haiku were stiff and formalized, encumbered with rules. Bashō opened up new possibilities for the form, using simple images and making clear associations between the concrete and the abstract. Bashō advised his followers: "Do not seek to follow in the footsteps of the men of old; seek what they sought."

With the priest Buccho, Bashō studied Zen Buddhism,[1] which has its roots in **DAOISM** as well as traditional **BUDDHISM,** and his perception of the world began to change. Nobuyuki Yuasa translates Bashō's description of his new awareness: "What is important is to keep our mind high in the world of true understanding, and returning to the world of our daily experience to seek therein the truth of beauty. No matter what we may be doing at a given moment, we must not forget that it has a bearing upon our everlasting self which is poetry."

The Famous Frog Haiku.   In 1684, Bashō went on his first major journey, to a region southwest of Edo; his account of it, which included prose and poetry, was published as *The Record of a Weather-Exposed Skeleton.* After his return to Edo, his poems continued to be published

---

[1] **Zen Buddhism:** Originating in sixth-century China, its goals are self-realization and enlightenment. The ultimate goal is an indefinable moment of consciousness in which the contradictions caused by one's intellect are transcended in an experience of cosmic unity — a moment of enlightenment.

in anthologies; his most famous poem appeared in the collection *Frog Contest (Kawazu Awase)* in 1686.

> *Furu ike ya*
> *Kawazu tobikomu*
> *Mizu no oto*
>
> Ancient pond
> Frog jumps in—
>   Sound of water.

Although a technical definition of haiku stipulates a three-line stanza with alternating 5-7-5 syllables in the lines, it is not always possible to translate Japanese into English and retain the syllable count. The translation above has fewer syllables than the Japanese original; some translators even add more syllables and lines, adding articles and linking words to accommodate Western—English-speaking—readers. Such readers may be unfamiliar with the lean flashes of reality in haiku. The Japanese original is, however, a model haiku; the first line sets the scene in nature, and the last two lines suggest an instant insight or new perspective. On a first reading, the poet seems to be describing an objective scene with a simple literal meaning: One can imagine sitting by a pond in absolute quiet and then hearing the sound of a frog plopping into the water and perhaps seeing the ripples resonate outward in broad, ever-widening circles. But without stretching the situation at all, one can also easily make the connection between the pond and the poet's consciousness, and a moment when the sound of water resonates within the psyche, bringing a rich focus to the poet's attention, connecting the internal with the external. No philosophy, no psychology, just a brief look at a moment of connection.

His followers could find in him almost anything they sought—a town dandy, a youthful dreamer, a Buddhist recluse, a lonely wanderer, a nihilistic misanthrope, a happy humorist, an enlightened sage.

– MAKOTO UEDA, literary historian and scholar, 1970

On the Road Again.   Bashō's second major journey, in 1688, which followed the same route as his first, resulted in two works, *Records of a Travel-Worn Satchel* and *A Visit to Sarashina Village.* Through experience, Bashō was learning how to balance prose with poetry; his message was becoming clearer, as witnessed by a passage in *Records of a Travel-Worn Satchel:* "All who have achieved real excellence in any art, possess one thing in common, that is, a mind to obey nature, to be one with nature, throughout the four seasons of the year. Whatever such a mind sees is a flower, and whatever such a mind dreams of is the moon."

In *Narrow Road through the Backcountry,* Bashō records his third major journey, which was begun in the spring of 1689 and lasted more than two years. Before leaving Edo at the age of forty-five, he sold his house, suggesting that he did not expect to return. More than the previous two journeys, this one was a culminating pilgrimage and reflects his mature vision of the meaning of life. Back once again in Edo, he spent four years writing and revising the work, which was first published, posthumously, in 1702. In the spring of 1694, at the age of fifty, Bashō began his final journey to the south of Japan. En route, he became sick and died.

Narrow Road through the Backcountry.   Bashō's *Narrow Road through the Backcountry,* a great masterpiece of *haibun* and one of the most well-known works of Japanese literature, was begun after Bashō returned from his journey in 1689. Polishing his work until his death in 1689 (it was not published until 1702), Bashō drew upon and transformed the themes and styles of the earlier *haibun* into a high form of self-conscious literary art. Indeed, his journey, which follows in part the steps of the medieval monk–poet Saigyo (1118–1190), seems to have been inspired by the desire to commemorate the anniversary of that poet's death and to find inspiration from the places associated with

Bashō's Journeys, 1684–1689
Matsuo Bashō covered much of north-central Japan in his travels, which he documented in his famous haikai. This map covers his journey through the backcountry, 1689.

Saigyo. As Donald Keene has noted, "Bashō's main purpose seems to have been to renew his art by direct contact with sites that had inspired the poets of the past" — mountains, shrines, barrier gates, villages, rivers, and other places that were layered with literary, historical, and spiritual resonances.

In a mixture of biography and fiction, prose and poetry, Bashō describes visits to temples, historical shrines, poet friends, and intensely beautiful vistas. He passes through gates, climbs mountains, and looks at the moon. He is on a religious pilgrimage that is best described in Zen Buddhist terms. He is not looking for some kind of salvation but for moments of consciousness in which he closely identifies with the scene at hand in what might be called "mystical identification" with the outside world, the flow of reality.

At the outset of the pilgrimage, Bashō is nervous, filled with anxiety. Careful preparations have to be made. Travel was difficult at that time, even dangerous, and his destination was a relatively unexplored portion of Japan — a fine symbol of the areas of consciousness that he expects to open up and engage. Each passage through a barrier gate represents another stage in Bashō's quest. The experience of the first, the Shirakawa Barrier, is captured by Bashō's travel companion, Sora, who describes the change of clothes that was part of the rite of passage through the gate.

Many of the famous shrines on Bashō's itinerary, like the Islands of Matsushima, have been celebrated in other literary works, but it is characteristic of Bashō that, even at such sacred sites he often makes a direct connection with ordinary reality using ordinary, everyday objects and subjects.

> autumn frost
> all hands busy with
>   melons and eggplants

In Bashō's work, a simple or seemingly insignificant thing often becomes the lightning rod for a Zen experience. At the Tada Shrine, a samurai's helmet evokes several meanings of loss associated with past dynasties and wars. But the ultimate and final loss — death itself — is evoked by the chirp of a cricket under the helmet, suggesting the living person who once wore the helmet but now is dead.

> "such a tragic fate"
> the captain's helmet shelters
>   . . . just a cricket now

Making an Emotional Connection.   If Bashō can capture a moment of connection in a brief poem, then it is possible that his reader may

---

Bashō is said to have had more than two thousand students at the time of his death. If this number is debatable, there is no question about his position: Few Japanese poets have enjoyed so high and so lasting a reputation.

– MAKOTO UEDA

have a similar experience reading the poem. The poem does not appeal to the intellect; it does not explain in logical terms how the world is connected. Rather the poem speaks to the intuition or the imagination, which can immediately grasp the association.

Bashō is particularly famous for invoking a quality called *sabi* to link the lines and images of verses; *sabi* is an atmosphere of sadness and loneliness from the past that colors the present, as in the following:

> lonelier even
> than Suma Beach
> —this autumn shore
>
> in each wave
> a swirl of churning shells &
> broken clover bits

Pilgrimages were often not simply a matter of visiting a shrine, but visiting it at the right time of year or during a full moon. Toward the end of his journey, Bashō passes through the Uguisu Barrier, crosses a mountain pass, and arrives at an inn whose host advises him to take advantage of the moonlight at the Myōjin shrine at Kei. Bashō prepares the reader for the shrine in prose: "There seemed a certain unearthly air about the place in the night silence, with moonlight through the pines turning the white sand before the stone shrine to frost." In the past, an abbot had started a tradition of carrying sand into the shrine area for the comfort of worshipers; Bashō's haiku makes this connection.

> moon illumined—
> sand carrying pilgrims to
> sand-carrying shrine

The light of the moon reflecting on the sand is analogous to the poet's imagination or consciousness fully participating in the sacredness of that shrine, a kind of climax for Bashō's journey.

Bashō has had a continuing influence in Japan. Early in the twentieth century, when Japanese writers admired Western Romantic writers such as Wordsworth, Goethe, and Hoffmann,[2] they considered Bashō a Japanese Romantic. When French symbolist poets such as Baudelaire, Mallarmé, and Verlaine[3] became the vogue in Japan, Bashō was made a

---

[2] **Wordsworth, Goethe, and Hoffmann:** William Wordsworth (1770–1850) was an English Romantic poet who wrote intimately about nature. Goethe (1749–1832), one of the greatest of all German literary figures, wrote *Faust,* a poetic drama, and several novels, including *The Sorrows of Young Werther* (1774). E. T. A. Hoffmann (1776–1822) was a German writer and composer who described the fantastic depths of nature.

[3] **Baudelaire, Mallarmé, and Verlaine:** Charles Baudelaire (1821–1867), Stéphane Mallarmé (1842–1898), and Paul Verlaine (1844–1896) were French poets who sought exotic or eccentric moments in their poetry.

symbolist as well, with his deep appreciation for the connection of all things. Bashō and haiku were largely discovered at the turn of the century by Westerners. The exquisitely lean poem appealed particularly to British and American imagist poets such as Ezra Pound, Amy Lowell, and William Carlos Williams.[4] Today haiku is well known throughout the United States and Europe.

■ FURTHER RESEARCH

Biography
Yamamoto, Kenkichi. *Bashō*. 1957.
Makoto Ueda, *Matsuo Bashō*. 1970.

Historical Background
Blyth, R. H. *Zen in English Literature and Oriental Classics*. 1960.
Henderson, Harold G. *An Introduction to Haiku*. 1958.
Kato, Shuichi. *A History of Japanese Literature*. 1997.
Keene, Donald. *Anthology of Japanese Literature*. 1955.
Miner, Earl. *Japanese Linked Poetry: An Account with Translations of Renga and Haikai Sequences*. 1979.
Suzuki, D. T. *Zen and Japanese Culture*. 1970. See especially Chapter VII, "Zen and Haiku."

Criticism
Aitken, Robert. *A Zen Wave: Bashō's Haiku and Zen*. 1978; 2003.
Kerkham, Eleanor, ed. *Matsuo Bashō's Poetic Spaces: Exploring Haikai Intersections*. 2006.
Miner, Earl. *Naming Properties: Nominal References in Travel Writings by Bashō and Sora, Johnson and Boswell*. 1996.
Shirane, Haruo. *Traces of Dreams: Landscape, Cultural Memory, and the Poetry of Bashō*. 1998.
Ueda, Makoto. *Bashō and His Interpreters: Selected Hokku with Commentary*. 1995.

■ PRONUNCIATION

Bashō: BAH-shoh
Genroku: gen-ROH-koo
Hiraizumi: hee-right-ZOO-mee
Iizuka: ee-ee-ZOO-kah
Muro-No-Yashima: MOO-roh noh YAH-shi-mah
Myozenji: myoh-ZEN-jee
renga: RENG-gah
Ryushakuji: ryoo-shah-KOO-jee
Saigyo: SIGH-gyoh
Tsukinowa: tski-NOH-wah (tsoo-ki-NOH-wah)
Tsutsujigaoka: tsoots-jee-gah-OH-kah (tsoo-tsoo-jee-gah-OH-kah)
Ueno: oo-EH-noh
Yanaka: yah-NAH-kah
Yoichi: yoh-EE-chee

---

[4]**Ezra Pound, Amy Lowell, and William Carlos Williams:** Pound (1885–1972), Lowell (1874–1925), and Williams (1883–1963) were American poets who, in addition to writing longer poems, composed short, compact poems that are like photographic moments.

~ Narrow Road through the Backcountry

Translated by Richard Bodner

Sun and moon[1] are constant travelers, days and months without end, even across generations. Years, too, come and go with the seasons. And for those who float their lives away on ships or grow bent with age before horses carrying freight from place to place, home itself becomes the open road. Some famous wanderers even passed away while traveling. At some point, whenever it was, drifting clouds drew forth my own urge to wander. After roaming nearby seashores last fall, I returned to my riverside cottage just in time to sweep cobwebs away for the new year, when spring mists rising from rice fields woke my old longing to pass beyond the barrier-gate at Shirakawa into the far backcountry, and I could turn my mind to nothing but beckoning trails. As if possessed, I mended my trousers, tied a new cord to my hat, burned "*moxa*"[2] for leg strength, and dreamed of a full moon over Matsushima in the Pine Islands. Then I left my grass-topped hut for good, to stay at Sampu's guesthouse until setting out.

> from thatched cottage door
> into a new world turning
> at dolls' festival[3]

—opener of an eight-verse "front fold" (first page) of linked poetry[4] left on the post on my way out.

Under the Seedling Moon,[5] by then a pale thin thread still waning, we set out in the misty faint light of dawn, with distant Fuji summit and blooming cherry trees of Ueno and Yanaka barely visible. Would I ever see these again, I wondered? Friends who'd gathered the night before boarded the boat to come along as far as Senju

A note on the translation: The text reprinted here (dedicated to Robert Aitken, retired *roshi* of the Diamond Sangha, for a lifetime of "bringing Bashō across") is from Bodner's *Backcountry Trails: A Poet's Journey* (Dragon Mountain Translation Society, 2007), with notes specially adapted for this anthology.

---

[1] **Sun and moon:** An old expression for "days and months," as found in earlier poems.

[2] **"*moxa*":** Still in use, *moxa* is an herbal powder shaped into little cones or nodules, set on key "energy points," then lit and allowed to burn down for acupuncture-related effects.

[3] **dolls' festival:** When little girls bring all their favorite dolls out for a party, it's sometimes called "Girls' Festival" or "Peach Festival" (celebrated on the third day of the third month, more or less late April in Bashō's time, now observed March 3). Passed on to a family with a little girl, his cottage might indeed become "a house for dolls" (another reading), turning into a new world inside even as he turns into a new world beyond.

[4] **linked poetry:** Bashō is considered a great master in the art of *renga* (linked poetry), which includes various poetic forms—two of which (one with a hundred verses, one with fifty) have a first page (or "front fold") of eight links. No such *renga* from Bashō's departure or with this *hokku* (opening verse) is currently known.

[5] **Seedling Moon:** The third month in Bashō's lunar calendar. According to the Gregorian calendar, he left on May 16 (later than planned because of bad weather).

Landing. Here the great distance ahead swelled up in my heart. Such a dream of shifting images this world seems, yet how attached we get, I thought, a little misty.

> departing spring
> birds call — even fish eyes
>   cloud over

— my ink's first brushed words, starting a record of the journey while lingering on the path as if going nowhere. Then friends watched, until back beyond sight, only shadows.

This year, which would be 1689 (Genroku two), I got such a bug to go wandering to the far north and deep through the interior, I imagined frost settling in my hair *"under foreign snowy skies"* while enduring many hardships for eyes to behold places ears had heard of, returning alive perhaps only with good luck. Weighed down with such thoughts, I bent under my pack, like heavy-headed *kusa* grass.[6] I'd set out to travel light, with only what a body might easily carry for itself, but then added a cloak for night cold, cotton kimono, rainwear, things like brushes-&-ink, plus going away gifts hard to turn down or leave behind — a traveler's burden.

At the "Burning Birthroom Shrine" of Muro-No-Yashima my companion, Sora, said, "the deity here is the same Blossoming Princess as at Fuji, and the place named after her closed-in birthing chamber supposedly burst into flames with Lord Prince Hohodemi ("From Flames Arisen") then born out of the blaze, sure proof of a purely divine conception. So poetry about it usually includes smoke." Also, it's forbidden to eat *konoshiro* fish here, which smells like flesh when burned. This and other such tales are well known.[7]

Last night of the third moon, we stopped at Nikko's foot, where our inn keeper said, "I'm called Buddha Gozaemon[8] for my honesty, so make yourself completely at home and at ease." Had Buddha himself appeared in just such a humble form to aid travelers like us through this world of dust and ashes? Observed carefully, our host did seem utterly without cleverness, just "straightforward, simple-minded and down-to-earth," embodying such old ideals with integrity worthy of respect.

First day of the fourth moon, we paid our respects to Nikko itself, the Sunlit Mountain. Long ago, it was called *Ni-ko,* "twice wild." When Master Kukai started a temple here, he renamed it *Nik-ko,* slightly shifting characters to signify "sun" and "radiant light," as if seeing ahead a thousand years over the horizon to our enlightened time now — with blessings in all directions and all classes living in peace. Filled with such radiance, I set down my brush, nothing more to say, just

---

[6] **heavy-headed *kusa* grass:** A description also related to the roots of the place name "Soka."

[7] Bashō introduces both high and low folklore, first a traditional story of local Shinto mythology (in which a pregnant goddess's questioned virtue is proven pure when she gives birth in the midst of divine fire), then an associated tidbit about a kind of fish said to smell like a burning corpse when cooked.

[8] **Buddha Gozaemon:** Characters in the innkeeper's name relate to "protection," and "gate," though he earns his nickname from his down-to-earth homely quality. The passage sheds light on the ideal person described in the Confucian *Analects* — one without pretense, embodying the values of simplicity, sincerity, and integrity.

yes, how brilliant!
green leaves, young leaves
　　luminous within[9]

Blackhair Mountain (Kurokamiyama) was patched with snow and mist-drifts, so Sora wrote:

　crest shorn
　Blackhair Mountain changing
　　its covering, too.[10]

Sora, born Kawai Sogoro,[11] lived next door to *bashō* cottage,[12] almost eave to eave, and helped with wood and water chores in the *bashō's* shadow. Lured by the bright prospects of places like Matsushima and Kisakata, he offered to take on hardships of the road. On leaving, he shaved his head, put on a monk's black robes, and changed his name's "*So-go*"[13] characters slightly to read "Enlightening," so his words about "changing" went on resounding as we climbed more than a mile up to a waterfall leaping out from above a cave before plunging on down a hundred feet into a clear green pool ringed by countless rocks. Squeezed into the hollow behind the cascades, we peered out at Rearview Falls.

　still awhile behind
　waterfall's opening in
　　summer seclusion[14]

Starting across Nasu Moor to visit a Nasu District friend on our way toward a place called Blackwing (Kurobane), we tried a shortcut through fields towards a village not far off, but rain came on as dark approached, so we passed the night at a farmhouse. Setting off again in the morning, we saw a horse in a pasture with a man cutting hay nearby; still unsure of our way, we asked him for help with directions. Rough as his life seemed, he lacked not compassion. "Hmm, what can we do?" he replied. "These paths keep branching, with countless cross-trails, and bad luck for a traveler who doesn't know where he's heading, it's so easy to get lost. Better take my horse as far as he'll go. When he stops, just send him back." Two children ran along

---

[9] **luminous within**: Bashō gives land and language equal attention here, then focuses in on the light through translucent leaves — at once down-to-earth and spiritual, humble and elegant.

[10] *its covering, too*: They arrive at Blackhhair Mountain (Kurokamiyama) on the traditional day for changing into summer clothes. (Sora has also shaved his head in the manner of pilgrimage monks.)

[11] **Kawai Sogoro**: *Kawai* is his family name (presented first, in traditional Japanese style); *Sogoro* is his given name.

[12] *bashō* cottage: The *bashō* is an exotic kind of broadleafed plaintain. One planted as a yard-warming gift gave the cottage its nickname — the *bashō-an* (broadleaf hut) — and its resident the pen name by which he is most known.

[13] "*So-go*": Sora's name change is homonymic, as from "bear" to "bare"; no change when spoken, but a shift in meaning from how it's written.

[14] **summer seclusion**: Suggests a traditional summer training period for mountain monks, with concentrated meditation and perhaps "ascetic practices" (like dipping in icy pools or standing in waterfalls).

beside us awhile, one a little beauty named *Kasane*, like that maiden flower sometimes called "manifold pink," such a rare and charming name Sora wrote:

> *pretty Kasane,*
>   *a perfect character for—*
>   *"petal-folded pink"*

At the village, we attached a little something to the saddle and turned the horse back.

At Blackwing (Kurobane), a castle town, we called at the Deputy Chief's house, a
certain gentleman named Joboji, who seemed pleased with our surprise appearance.
We talked day and night, and with his younger brother, Tosui, and were then invited
to his house, too, and taken around to meet all the relatives. So days passed. One day
we skirted the town by the old "Dog-Shooting Grounds,"[15] then wove through
Nasu's famous bamboo thicket to Foxwoman Tamamo's tomb. From there we paid
our respects at the warrior god shrine dedicated to Hachiman, whose spirit Nasu's
own hero Yoichi invoked before piercing with his arrow the rising sun on a fan suspended from a ship far offshore during the battle of Yashima Bay.[16] I was more moved
returning to Tosui's house as dark deepened. Leaving next morning, we stopped at a
Shugen mountain monk training school nearby, invited to the practice hall to see
the founder's high-ridged wooden sandals on display.

> in summer foothills
> bowing before well-worn clogs
>   on the way out

Beyond Cloud Cliff Temple (Unganji), my meditation teacher Butcho[17] once
lived in a mountaintop shelter near which, he said, he'd written on a rock with burnt
pine long ago: *"barely a few feet high & wide, my thatched hut—in the way . . . but for
rain."*

To see what was left of it, we pointed our staffs to Unganji. Joined by a merry
and chattering group of youths, we reached the base of the mountain before we
knew it. Here the path thinned out and almost disappeared where pines and cedars
clustered with shadows far above the valley. Wet mosses oozed and dripped, and
even early summer air seemed chilled. At the end of Ten-Views Path, we stood a
moment by the bridge, then crossed over and passed through a gate. Searching for
traces of Butcho's retreat, we climbed the mountainside beyond and—yes, up
there!—we found a small hut perched on a stone ledge before a cave, just like

---

[15] **"Dog-Shooting Grounds":** Among the highlights of local history and folklore, the stadium where an old
sport (shooting dogs with blunt-tipped arrows) used to be practiced. Folklore claimed it helped train warriors
to deal with fox demons like "Fox-lady Tamamo" (of whom we hear more shortly).

[16] **Yashima Bay:** Depicts an event in the epic struggle between Heike and Genji clans, in 1185, when the district's
native hero Yoichi, a great archer, hit the sun painted on a fan suspended on a pole on a moving ship (with life
and death riding on the shot).

[17] **Butcho:** Guided Bashō in *zazen*, sitting meditation, and other aspects of Zen practice.

Myozenji's "Death's Gate Cave" or Fa Yun's "Rock-top's Stone Room."[18] Scrambling up, I scribbled spontaneously

> not a woodpecker—
> alone among summer trees
> his small quiet hut
>   —left on a post.

From Blackwing, I rode the Deputy Chief's horse toward the "Stifled-Life Stone" at Sessoseki; when the groom leading it asked for a poem, I was moved he cared.

> draw the horse on, sir—
> sideways across the field
> a cuckoo's call![19]

The famous killing stone[20] itself was in a dark little canyon in the mountain's shadow, where noxious hotsprings flow with stifling fumes—dead butterflies, moths, bees and the like so thickly layered, the sand beneath was barely visible.

Yes! *"Where clear spring water flows,"* that wonderful trembling willow Saigyo wrote of was still growing on a bank between rice fields near Ashino village. A local cultural official had repeatedly encouraged me to seek it out, so I'd long wondered about it, and here I was at last, in its actual shadow![21]

> a whole rice paddy
> was planted before leaving
> willow's welcome shade

Restless with anticipation, yet growing clearer and calmer day by day as we made our way towards it, we finally reached Shirakawa Checkpoint, and I, of course, recalled Kanemori's,[22] *"if I could only send word to the capital to tell of it . . ."* One of the Three Great Border Gates, or barriers, Shirakawa is a favorite of poets, with many offerings left behind in response, so Noin's[23] "autumn winds" whispered in my ear a line of crimson maple leaves lingering amidst the rich summer green of the actual branches, while through the pale white flowers of roadside shrubs other small white flowers pressed, white on white, like the snow reported by someone passing in

---

[18] **"Death's Gate Cave" . . . "Rock-top's Stone Room":** Two famous rustic meditation retreats where seeker sages sat for long periods, contemplating fundamental reality and the nature of original being.

[19] **cuckoo's call:** Bashō offers the groom a poem brushed across a paper strip made for this purpose. The last line, *hototogisu*, is the name for both the bird and its call, its sound said to be like "*hotototo*" (made only by this kind of Asian cuckoo).

[20] **killing stone:** Folklore claims the Fox-lady's soul, released from animal form, entered the "breath-sucking stone" and gave it its foul character.

[21] **shadow:** Saigyo had passed five hundred years earlier, yet his shadow remains, intertwined with the willow's.

[22] **Kanemori:** Poet who died in 990.

[23] **Noin:** Monk born around 987.

winter. Kiyosuke's[24] brush once pictured a man of long ago donning a formal black hat before crossing, so Sora offered:

> *little white flowers*
> *to cap the great crossing*
> *in style.*

We continued across Abiyoyo River with Aizu Peak to our left; Iwaki, Soma and Miharu villages off to the right; mountains dividing Hitachi and Shimotsuke beyond. With overcast sky, we passed Mirror Pond[25]—reflecting nothing.

At Suka River, a post town, a fellow named Tokyu invited us to stay for four or five days, asking right off what poetic responses famous Shirakawa had drawn forth. "Worn out in body and mind from the rigors of traveling, and my spirit so taken by the place itself, enriched with memories from earlier poets," I explained, "little new of my own came forth, just

> for inspiration
> rice-planting songs
> in the backcountry

—all that was drawn from my brush, since it would have been a shame to pass without at least a *single* poem." But then, with this for opener, second and third verses followed from others, and before we were done, we'd made three complete linked poetry sequences, more than a hundred stanzas[26] in all, together.

In an out-of-the-way part of town, a religious hermit[27] lived completely apart, in the shade of a great chestnut tree, and I thought of Saigyo's *"gathering horse chestnuts deep in the mountains,"* describing just such a life. Handed paper, I wrote: our sign for "chestnut" is actually composed of two characters, "west" over "tree," suggesting "western heaven" or "Pure Land Paradise."[28] So Master Gyogi Bosatsu[29] used only chestnut for his staff and the posts supporting his abode.

> few in this world
> notice—just under the eaves
> chestnut flowers there

About five leagues from Tokyu's house and past Hiwada Post, the Asaka Hills rise up near the road. Since it was around the famous *katsumi* iris time, and with lots of marshy meadow about, I asked and asked again about the flower. "Which is the

---

[24] **Kiyosuke:** Died around 1175.

[25] **Mirror Pond:** Can also be translated "Shadow Lake."

[26] **hundred stanzas:** From Bashō's humble opening verse about backcountry planting songs, more than a hundred links grew. The first of the three sequences, a *kasen* of 36 verses, survives.

[27] **religious hermit:** Using the *haikai* pen name *Rissai* (Chestnut), he welcomed a linked poetry party with Bashō.

[28] **"Pure Land Paradise":** Bashō seems to be suggesting something more like Hui Neng's "with pure mind/the Pure Land is/right here" (*Sixth Patriarch Sutra*), i.e., a present enlightenment not some far off "heaven of the west."

[29] **Gyogi Bosatsu:** Monk who helped build the Todai Temple and died in 749. Considered a "bodhisattva," one who pledges to keep at it until all sentient beings are liberated.

katsumi? Where can we find *katsumi*?" But no one seemed to know anything about it, so we went on searching, "*katsumi . . . katsumi*" on our lips till setting sun grazed the far ridge. Then we turned right at Nihonmatsu's Twin Pines, peered a moment into the Black Cave's mouth at Kurozuka,[30] and hurried on to Fukushima for the night.

On the following day we sought out Shinobu[31] village and asked about its famous letter-rubbing stone, which we found half buried at the base of a far hill. Some local youngsters came along and explained the stone used to be near the hill-top, but that farmers there got fed up with sightseers tearing their green grain up for dye, so shoved it over the cliff towards the valley below, where it landed—and remains—face down in the earth. So it might well be true.

> pressing seedlings in
> as hands of old once pressed stone
> shinobu's unseen face

At Tsukinowa, we took Moonarc ferry across to the post town of Rapids Over-look, from which Administrator Sato's old place was supposedly just a short way fur-ther on tucked in hills to the left. Asking as we went, we followed directions through Open Meadow (Sabano) by the village of Iizuka (Rice Mound), and finally to a place called Maruyama, or Roundtop, where some castle ruins remain. My eyes filled up at the old stones where the gate used to be, then overflowed at the family graves in the nearby temple grounds. I was especially moved by those two young widows who had ridden home in the fallen Sato sons' armor.[32] Accounts of their gallantry make one's sleeves wet with tears—yet here so much closer to home than that Tombstone of Tears[33] in China! After tea in the temple, we learned Benkei's prayer pack[34] and Yoshitsune's sword were among its treasures.

> prayer pack and sword
> displayed high up for Boys' Day
> a wind-sock carp[35]

—first day of rice-planting moon.

We stopped that night back in Iizuka, steamed in hotbaths, then found for lodg-ing just thin rice mats over bare dirt in a rundown place with no lamp, bedding down

---

[30] **Kurozuka:** A black cave supposedly home to a traveler-eating female demon.

[31] **Shinobu:** The same name is used for the place, the stone, and the plant leaves used to dye a cloth rubbed on the stone face to receive an impression (of one's "true love," as well as of any inscribed characters). With some-thing akin to the sense of "forget-me-not," it also suggests thinking of someone and recalling the past.

[32] **Sato sons' armor:** The sons died in service to Yoshitsune, hero betrayed by his brother (the shogun Yoritomo), around 1189 (five hundred years before Bashō takes Yoshitsune's route in reverse). The two Sato widows re-turned wearing their fallen husbands' armor (possibly so the aged and dying Sato mother might think her sons safe and victorious).

[33] **Tombstone of Tears:** A place in China, of which it was said that all who came there wept, and maybe the stone, too. (Wet sleeves may be considered an idiomatic expression for shedding tears.)

[34] **Benkei's . . . pack:** The "giant monk" Benkei, Yoshitsune's loyal sidekick, who died trying to protect his friend, carried a kind of portable chest with religious items.

[35] **wind-sock carp:** These are flown from poles in honor of the household sons on Boy's Day (fifth day of the fifth moon, now celebrated May 5).

by firepit light as thunder rumbled in and rain came down through leaks. With mosquitoes and fleas, and my old complaint[36] returning, I couldn't sleep. Finally, just when I thought I might pass out at last, the short darkness passed instead, and we were off again, dragging haggard night shadows.

With so far yet to go beyond the horizon, we hired horses up to Kori Post. My recurring ailment was still a problem, but I thought how a long pilgrimage involves detachment, letting the world go, life itself transient, a fleeting moment passing quickly away . . . even along this roadside maybe . . . thus one must accept as just so whatever fate holds. . . . Musing thus on the character of such yielding, my spirits gradually revived, until I found myself striding along without a care, just one foot after another, as if one here in this world and one already in the next — and so stumbled on beyond the Great Barrier Gate of Okido into the Da-te district.

Past castle towns like Abumizuri and Shirioshi, we entered Kasashima district and asked about Fujiwara Sanekata's[37] grave-mound. "See that little village, Minowa, with straw rain-thatch in those hills far off to the right? Beyond that is Kasashima itself, where the Road God's Shrine is and the memorial grass remains." But with Fifth Moon rains, the road looked so bad, and so washed out ourselves, we just gazed from afar. How well these names fit now — Minowa (Straw Raincoat) and Kasashima[38] (Umbrella Isle). So I brushed

> far Kasashima —
> Umbrella Island's where? down
> monsoon's muddy road

— and we stopped for the night at Iwanuma.

Wide-eyed with wonder before Takekuma's legendary Double Pines rising just as long ago from shared roots into two great branching trunks, I naturally thought of Noin's famous poem on his second visit,[39] *"no sign now of that twin pine there,"* after a new governor had cut it for a bridge across the Natori River. It's been reported cut down and regrown time and again over almost a thousand years. I can report it in fine shape now! As we left Edo, our friend Kyohaku had offered *"when late cherry blooms don't forget to stop at Takekuma's twin pine"* so now I replied,

> cherry blossom time
> here and now — this two-trunked pine
> — just three moons older[40]

---

[36] **my old complaint:** May have included some bowel difficulty, fever and chills, all especially hard on travelers.

[37] **Fujiwara Sanekata:** A poet and battle captain sent to Mutsu (Oku) as governor in 996 (some say exiled for being cantankerous). Folklore has him dying on the way (for not paying respects to the road god), but historians believe he got there and served awhile, dying in 998.

[38] **Kasashima:** A *kasa* is a combination rain-hat and umbrella, and *shima* an island, thus Umbrella Isle.

[39] **second visit:** The poet monk Noin, returning on the Oku Road in the eleventh century, wondered if *"a thousand years might have passed"* between coming and going, finding the tree gone.

[40] **three moons older:** Another famous poem on the Takekuma pine says, *"If you ask of it, locals talk of three moons,"* possibly a reference to how long since having been cut. Bashō's poem has roots of a thousand years and branches three moons back (when he and his friends had "split").

Crossing Natori River, we entered Sendai on Iris Festival eve, time to adorn eaves with "blue flags."[41] We found an inn for a few days and searched out an artist named Kaemon[42] for our guide. Said to be a spirited poet, he'd tracked down various obscure local places mentioned in old poems. With bush clovers thick on Miyagi Moor, scenery looked promising for fall. At Tamada, Yokono, and Tsutsujigaoka (Azalea Hill), white flowering horse-loco bushes[43] were at their peak.

Entering Underwood, an evergreen forest too thick for sunlight to penetrate, heavy dew brought up a famous old poem beginning, "*Attendants, your master's umbrella!*"[44] As sun declined we paid our respects at Yakushi temple, dedicated to a medicine Buddha known as "healer of souls," and at Tenjin Shrine, honoring a famous scholar priest, as well as other such places. As parting gifts, Kaemon gave us sketches of Matsushima and Shiogama, then, with an artist's inspired touch, added straw sandals whose cords had been dyed an iris blue.

> with such blue laces
> fresh irises seem to bloom
>   from our sandal tops

With Kaemon's sketches as guide, we soon found ourselves on the "*oku-no-hosomichi*"[45] itself, Oku's Backcountry Trail, that slender road winding inland between hills and by the source of a renowned reed-straw woven into many famous poems and braided into fine mats, its ten-strand sedge serving as traditional tribute to the Governor still.

Continuing on by old Fort Taga,[46] near Ichikawa village we came to a crossroads marking the Oku Trailhead with the famous Tsubo Stone—a moss-covered monument over six feet high and about three feet wide, just barely readable now by fingering grooves. After giving province and border distances in four directions, the crossroad stone's inscription added: "Fortress built 1st year of Jinki [724] by General Azuma-udo, sent north as regional commander . . . Repaired 6th year of Tempyo-hoji [762] by Lord Asakari, northeastern commander. Recorded 1st day of 12th moon in Shomu's reign."

Most places mentioned in old poetry can never be exactly located. Mountains crumble through time, landslides change river courses, floods wash out roads,

---

[41] **"blue flags"**: A kind of iris, associated with Boys' Day.

[42] **Kaemon**: A woodblock carver who also ran a *haikai* bookstore, he was happy to show his visitors poetry-related sights, including some mostly forgotten before he'd searched them out.

[43] **horse-loco bushes**: A danger to horses (cf. "loco weed").

[44] *umbrella*: The same rain-hat (*kasa*) as at *Kasashima,* here needed because of the thick dew (or rain caught up in the trees, falling again), according to the anonymous poet Bashō quotes from an eleventh-century anthology.

[45] **"*oku-no-hosomichi*"**: Oku's Narrow Road is both the name of the particular trail and the title of the work as a whole. The province name, Oku, has roots that suggest "backcountry" and "interior." The specific trail had a thousand years of history and poetry woven in by Bashō's time, though it's now known especially for his passage.

[46] **Fort Taga**: Stockade outpost from the 700s, mostly forgotten before an archeological project had unearthed the stone marker not long before Bashō's visit.

tombstones sink into earth, saplings replace great trees growing for generations; hardly anything remains where it was for long. Yet faced with this monument of nearly a thousand years, I felt so powerfully linked with the past and people of old, I forgot all the journey's difficulties and, in gratitude for such a road blessing, wept with joy.

After looking for the Sunk-In-Water Stone in Noda's Jewel River, and after a few other places commemorated in poetry, we reached Pine Mountain Spit (*Sue-no-Matsuyama*) and near Land's End its almost namesake temple—with identical characters but read in Chinese style.[47] All around between the pines were graves—so much for lovers' intimate vows to remain forever *"wings of a single bird"* or like *"twin trees eternally linked with intertwining branches,"*[48] yet come finally to this deep lonliness of merciless time, temple vesper bells at dusk settling on the Shiogama shore.

Early summer rain cleared some, and in faint moonlight Magaki Isle seemed so close, as little fishing boats came pulling toward shore together and, floating in with them, voices of men dividing the catch. Recalling lines about *"sad hands upon the net"* and *"the melancholy creak of mooring ropes"* deepened the feeling. A blind musician plucked his *biwa*[49] that night, chanting frontier ballads and Oku airs; neither warrior songs with martial rhythms, nor dance hall barrack tunes, but beyond-the-border melodies in a loud backcountry style, so near our pillows and so late, we couldn't sleep, moved by such traditions being kept up in such an out-of-the-way place.

In early morning we paid our respects at Shiogama's Myojin Shrine, its immense pillars and resplendently painted beams recently restored by the province governor. Flights of steep stone steps rise up where the road ends, and morning sun blazed on brilliant vermilion lacquered railings with such splendid brightness! Even in this remote backcountry are such priceless national treasures, and traditions for preserving them. Before the shrine, an old stone lantern bore on its metal lid the inscription: "given in 3rd year of Bunji [1187] by Izumi Saburo,"[50] a five hundred year old image shining still in our sight. Saburo was a brave soldier whose loyalty and filial devotion are respected to this day. As was well written, "Follow true virtue's way, the path of character and integrity, stick to right principles, and your light will shine through time."

With sun nearing its height, we hired a boat to Matsushima. After a short crossing, we landed on the beach at Ojima (Big Isle). As has often been observed, these Pine Islands are among the most beautiful places in our land of the rising sun, easily equal to Lake Dotei's Tung-ting in Hunan and Western Lake in Hangchow, reportedly among the best China has to offer. Here, open sea enters from the southeast so

---

[47] **Chinese style**: *Kanji* characters (ideographic symbols representing ideas rather than sounds) can be spoken or "read" in various ways, this one in the Chinese style instead of the vernacular Japanese. (Think of international road signs, numbers, or the "&" for analogies.)

[48] *wings . . . branches*: The Tang era Chinese poem is by Po Chui (Bo Juyi).

[49] *biwa*: A plaintive four-stringed lute.

[50] **Izumi Saburo**: Yoshitsune's loyal ally, betrayed by his brother. (He died at twenty-two, Yoshitsune about thirty.) The governor Masamune restored the shrine in Bashō's century.

a wide bay swells with each tide like the Sekko River in flood. Islands beyond counting rise from end to end, some steep with sharp heaven-piercing peaks; some low,
stretched out into the wave-surge and tide-swell; some bunched in twos and threes,
or layered one behind another like babes on mothers' backs; others, as if with islands
in their arms, suggesting the protective embrace of parents and grandparents.

The pines here are an intense green, with sea-sprayed branches and exquisitely
wind-twisted spines wound as if artfully trained, like a beautiful woman made a
touch more lovely still before her reflecting glass. Yet here the artist is a maker of
mountains, earth's original divine creation, and whose brush can fully mirror such?

Ojima, sometimes called Male Isle, is actually a peninsula still connected to the
mainland while curving far out into the sea. Near its tip, are the ruins of zen master
Ungo's[51] remote retreat and his *zazen* sitting meditation rock. Here and there among
the pines, secluded rustic huts shelter religious solitaries living silently within even
now, thin lines of smoke curling up from their humble fires of pine-needles, twigs
and cones. The serene tranquility of one such place especially touched my heart and,
though I did not know who lived there, its spirit drew me closer as the moon rose,
shimmering in the sea, too, transfixing all.

Back to the inlet for lodging, we found an inn and an upper-story room with
windows open wide to the sea. Resting this night on the journey, at one with gentle
wind and drifting clouds, our spirits soared with such beauty around us, Sora wrote:

>   at Matsushima
>   as if crane-winged
>   a nightbird's[52] song

Silent and wordless, I tried to sleep, but couldn't. When I was leaving my old hut for
the road, Sodo had given me a Chinese-style poem about Matsushima, and Hara
Anteki a *waka*[53] "*on pine-shored isles,*" so I undid my knapsack for them, along with
some verses by Sampu and Dakushi, all my companions that night.

On the eleventh we stopped at Zuigan Temple, its abbot thirty-second in succession since that Great Soul Makabe took Ch'an vows in T'ang era China, founding
this temple on his return. More recently, Dharma Master Ungo came and, thanks to
his efforts, renewed both its spirit and structure, promoting both understanding and
rebuilding. With its gold-leaf walls and gilded Buddhas shining, we might have been
in "enlightened paradise" itself. Yet I wondered where the rustic thatched retreat of
that holy sage Kenbutsu[54] might be.

On the twelfth, we started towards Hiraizumi (Peaceful Spring), with various
places memorialized in poetry supposed to be along our way—like Aneha's Big Sister

---

[51] **Ungo:** Zen master who died in 1658.

[52] *nightbird*: The same *hototogisu* heard crossing Nasu Moor.

[53] *waka*: May be thought of as a five-lined poetic form from which linked poetry grew (joining alternating links
of three and two lines). However many descriptions there were of Matsushima's beauty before, Bashō's is best
known now.

[54] **Kenbutsu:** A sage, visited by Saigyo at Ojima, who "gave the holy scrolls voice," chanting the Lotus Sutra in
particular many thousand times.

Pine and Odae's Cord-Cutting Bridge—but soon found ourselves on a nearly lifeless path instead, just tracks from occasional hunters and woodcutters, not knowing which way was which, having missed a turn somewhere, winding up at a harbor town called Ishi-no-Maki[55] (Rollingstones). Far across the water, crowded with hundreds of little coastal cargo boats plying the inlet, rose Goldbloom Mountain (Kinkazan), where from its deep mine *"gold flowers blossom,"* as a poet once wrote Emperor Shomu. In the village meanwhile, clustered houses jostled for space, with countless smoke-trails from cooking fires coiling up end to end. Here we were, without intending it, and, unable to find an inn with a room, we ended up in a pitiful shack for the night.

Setting off again at first light, we seemed to ramble awhile almost at random, in a maze of strange paths, then followed the Kitakami Riverbank without a break, catching just a few glimpses from afar of spots made famous by poems—Wet Sleeves Crossing, Obuchi Meadow, Reedflats of Mano. We slogged on around a long boggy marsh with spirits sinking, spending the night at a place called Toima, only reaching Hiraizumi finally the next day, a distance of seven or eight miles in all.

Hiraizumi's great gate stands in ruins a little ways before where Hidehira's[56] court had been. Passed as if in a sleep, the splendor of three generations of Fujiwaras now just an overgrown field, only Goldenbird Hill, once part of the palace garden park, retaining its form. Climbing up to High Fort overlook, Yoshitsune's last refuge, we spied Kitakami River winding through the plains far below, from Nambu to the south. Koromo River curves by Izumi Castle,[57] then joins Kitakami's greater stream directly beneath the overlook. Other ruins, like Yasuhira's fort beyond Koromo checkpoint, which had once guarded the approach south from Ezo tribesmen, remained beyond. But for all their power and loyal retainers who fought so bravely in this stronghold here, such glory is so fleeting that of their valiant effort only so much grass remains. Tu Fu's words seemed to drift and echo in the wind: *"with the country in ruins, yet mountains and rivers remain, and through castle rubble, spring returns grass to green again."*[58] Moist-eyed, we took off our hats and sat.

> just summer grass
> of warrior dreams remains
> the only trace

---

[55] **Ishi-no-Maki:** In Bashō's riff on tangled paths, the *"maki"* means "roll" (of silk, of scroll, or sea), "coil," or "wind up." Some may recognize the term from the *sushi* bar, for a roll wrapped in seaweed. Here it's a roll "of stones."

[56] **Hidehira:** Hiraizumi Castle was built by Fujiwara Kiyohira and maintained by the next two generations (Motohira and Hidehira); but then Hidehira's son Yasuhira proved disloyal, a betrayal that led to his downfall and Hiraizumi's destruction in 1189.

[57] **Izumi Castle:** Home of Izumi Saburo (who had donated the lantern at the Shiogama shrine), the one Hidehira son who remained loyal to Yoshitsune.

[58] *"with . . . to green again":* Bashō recalls one of China's most famous poems, by Tu Fu (Du Fu, 712–770); his response became one of Japan's most famous.

And Sora added:

> as snowflowers
> old Kanefusa's[59] white hair
>   seems to reappear

Both Chuson Temple halls, whose wonders we had heard of, were open. The Sutra Study Hall held images of the three generations of great Hiraizumi generals whose coffins rested in the Great Hall of Splendor[60] along with well-shaped Buddhas. The famous "seven gems" were absent, however, and its once-jeweled door was cracked. Once gold-leafed pillars spoke of hard times, frosts and snows. It would probably be completely gone by now, returned to grass and brush, but for renovated walls and a newly tiled roof offering some protection from wind and rain. So preserved, it continues, memories stretching a thousand years.

> summer rains
> once again passing over
>   'Enlightenment Hall'

With Nambu road so far off, we passed the night at Iwade village, then went on by Little Black Point and Water Island to Crying Babe Hotspring[61] and Shitomae Checkpoint, sometimes called "Passwater Crossing" since it's where Yoshitsune's newborn first pee'd when they were fleeing north across these mountains. Few travelers came this route, and the border-gate guard eyed us with some suspicion, only letting us through after a long wait. With dark overtaking us, we struggled up a steep mountain path, finding rough shelter finally at another guard's hut by the trail. For three days fierce winds and rain held us prisoner.

> with fleas and lice
> a horse passes — water
>   by my pillow

Our host said that high mountains with unclear trails stood between us and Dewa, so we better have a guide see us across. We hired a gigantic young fellow with a bent oak staff that looked alive and a great curved dagger at his belt. I feared we were heading for disaster, in great danger at least, following after. Then, as warned, mountains loomed high, with thick forest beyond a single bird's song, so deep and dark we might as well have been passing through at night. Wind blew dust *"in ragged shadow clouds"*[62] as we pushed through bamboo thickets and *shino* brush, forded streams, and stumbled over rocks across Notched Blade Pass until, sopping with cold sweat, we came to safer ground at last in the Mogami region. "Lucky to get here," our

---

[59] *Kanefusa*: Yoshitsune's loyal old retainer, who died so bravely and honorably here.

[60] **Great Hall of Splendor**: The "Shining Practice Place" or "Enlightenment Hall," built in 1124.

[61] **Crying Babe Hotpring**: The site where Yoshitsune's newborn first cried, with the family fleeing from those seeking to kill them. *Shitomae,* for related historical reasons explained in the text, means "urinating before," a theme Bashō will follow awhile.

[62] *"in ragged shadow clouds"*: Another snippet on the wind from Tu Fu (Du Fu).

guide said, dropping us off. "Usually it's not this easy. In fact, I've never brought anyone across before without at least *some* accident."—hearing which set hearts racing again.

At Obanazawa (Big Flower Valley), we stopped to see a fellow named Seifu,[63] a well-off brush flower merchant. From his frequent comings and goings between here and the capital, he knew what traveling was like and how travelers feel, so he urged us to stay several days to refresh ourselves from our hard trail, making us feel at home and providing various diversions.

> so warmly welcomed
> cool summer breezes with
> such rare ease

> out from under
> the silkworm shed
> a toad's voice

> eyebrow brushes
> powder to face
> the flower itself

And by Sora:

> *in rustic garb*
> *from olden days*
> *the silkworm keeper*

In Yamagata, the Ryushakuji mountain temple founded by abbot Jikaku[64] remains well taken care of in a serene secluded place steeped in peace and quiet. Urged to it by many, we back tracked from Obanazawa a ways off our route, arriving in the still light of late afternoon. Arranging space in the guesthouse, we set right off up the steep slope towards the shrine far above, between great boulders, one after another, past old-growth pines and cypresses, over ancient earth and by aged stone veiled with velvet smooth spots of soft green moss. On top, we found the sanctuary doors shut tight and no sound. Skirting the drop-off edge on all fours, we made our prostrations to the ground, heart and mind touched by such stillness.

> ... silence ...
> sinking in stone
> cicada sound

---

[63] **Seifu**: In contrast to the rugged wilderness of Notched Blade Pass, the travelers are put up in luxurious ease by a wealthy safflower merchant who also happens to be a well-known *haikai* poet and editor of three anthologies.

[64] **Jikaku** (792–862): Jikaku Daishi is the same Zen master who built the Zuigan temple visited earlier. Founder of the Tendai lineage of Buddhism, he combined local esoteric teachings with meditation training learned in China.

We waited for good weather to take a boat down the Mogami, at a place called Stoneyfield (Oishida), where seeds of an old-fashioned linked poetry had once been sown, taken root and kept on producing in later generations. With a heartfelt muse at play as through rustic reed flutes still, locals said, "we stumble along in the dark, lost between old style and new, uncertain of the way, in need of a guide." So we sat together and composed whatever inspiration drew forth as offering. Imagine — my humble poetic way watering blooms even here in far off Stoneyfield!

Mogamigawa, meanwhile, begins swelling in the far north of Michinoku and from the pathless interior beyond, reaching its fullness here in Yamagata before plunging through many perilous places further on, like Go-stones Rapids and Down the Falcon's Dive, before eventually dropping near Mount Itajiki to join the sea at Sakata. Sometimes used for rice and thus called "rice boats," our little craft seemed like just such a grain disappearing into foaming white cascades, swept downstream between sheer cliffs rising close up on both sides. In places deep forest foliage stretched over us, and under just such a green explosion of leaves, we swept past the "Immortals Hall" of *Sennin-do,* balanced in the air partly over the water at the land's edge. Filled with recent downpours, the strong current put our speck of boat in some peril time and again.

> heavy summer rains
> gathered swiftness surging down
> Mogamigawa[65]

Third day, sixth moon: we reached Featherblack Mountain (Hakuroyama) where a fellow named Zushi Sakichi introduced us to Master Egaku Ajari, acting abbot in charge, who welcomed us warmly, arranging board and lodging at the temple annex in Minamidani (South Valley). We gathered at the main temple hall the next day to make linked poetry together. I expressed my appreciation in the opening verse:

> how wonderful
> this snow blessed taste of air
> in South Valley

On the fifth, at Featherblack Mountain (Hakuroyama), we paid our respects at its first temple, a Gongen shrine founded by Master Nojo at an unknown time. Though the Book of Rites[66] mentions a shrine at "Ushu's Satoyama," that may well be from a scribe's mistaken copying of what was originally *Kuroyama* (*Black Mountain*), almost the same character. Since *U-shu* is an old way of saying the province name, perhaps its province indicator *shu* was dropped, then the alternative version "De-hwa" (Tribute-feather) shortened to make *Hwa-kuro-yama* (*Feather-Black-Mountain*). An old geography book claims the name "feather offering" comes

---

[65] **Mogamigawa:** Bashō stayed three days at Oishida (from July 14) because of rainy weather, giving all the more force to the Mogami, already one of the fastest rivers in Japan. The temple passed is associated with *shamanic* practices, and with Yoshitsune's mountain-monk ally.

[66] **Book of Rites:** The *Engi-shiki* is a collection of prayers, rules, and procedures dating from 927.

from the old practice of sending feathers from here to the capital as a kind of tax or tribute.[67]

Featherblack (*Hakuro*), Moon (*Gassan*) and Hotspring (*Yudono*) make up what's called the "Feather Offering Three Mountain Pilgrimage" (*Dewa Sangan*). The temple here, meanwhile, is related to Kanei temple in Buko near Edo, part of the Tendai lineage whose clear-moon insight-meditation energy goes on shining from mountaintop to mountaintop, temple to temple, mind to mind. So devotees cloistered here serve the mountain while encouraging each other's practice, to inspire timeless blessings for all.[68]

On the eighth we climbed Gassan (Moon), wrapped in monkly cotton hoods and scarves wound around with white linked paper-strips. Calling on all our inner strength, we followed mountain monks up and up through mist and cloud, patches of snow and ice, as if far enough to join our path with sun and moon's. Almost out of breath, our chilled bodies crossed through a last gateway between clouds — and then there we were at the summit, after sun had set and moon arisen. We spread *shino* grass for beds and clumped bamboo leaves for pillows to rest that night.

Rising at first light through drifting clouds, we started down at dawn towards the Yudono trail. Near the valley, we passed a famous swordsmith's forge, built on the bank of this sacred stream 500 years earlier by blade-master Gassan, who took his own name from the mountain. Tempering himself and each sword in these magical, purifying waters, he prepared mind and body for the task at hand, so his "moon" imprint on a blade signifies a true treasure. He must've drawn power from these waters as in China swordsmiths drew from what was called the Dragon Spring. Such deep dedication of Kanchiang and his wife Muyeh, for example, with the famous swords they forged together, reminds us what devotion any great work requires and what profound immersion in such a sincere approach can accomplish.

Reflecting thus while resting on a trailside rock, I noticed just then a small cherry tree barely three feet high, yet half in bloom so far out of season. Bringing spring back with its flowers opening out of a bed of late snow, its fragrance seemed all the more persistent for its difficulties of life on the mountain, as if "*plum blossom's scent in summer's heat*" had returned or Gyoson's "*wild cherry and zen solitude*" bloomed again here in what this tree had to teach. But from here, pilgrimage custom forbids description, so I put away my brush.[69]

Back at the temple guesthouse in South Valley, the abbot handed me paper strips, asking for my impressions of the three mountains.

---

[67] **tax or tribute:** Bashō offers a somewhat detailed hypothesis about how the ideographic characters might have shifted through time to help explain an otherwise unusual name.

[68] **blessings for all:** Again, two traditions flow into a single stream at the temple. One is Tendai with its focus on insight meditation, a transmission with many lessons from Ch'an schools in China. The other is a *yamabushi* (mountain priest) tradition emphasizing the land-spirit, divine power in the heart of nature, and ascetic practices far from secular society.

[69] **put away my brush:** Like the solitary who "sleeps by the river to purify his ears," Bashō leaves words behind (along with distinctions of subject and object, individual mind and great mind) to enter the unspoken-zone. As in Matsushima, however, he'll again be challenged to describe the indescribable, this time by the abbot in charge. How to describe the impact of the place without breaking the rule against description?

> morning's chill sharp as
> a three-day crescent fading
> over black mountain

> clouds swirl around peaks
> dissolving bit by bit into
> Moon Mountain

> unable to speak
> of Honorable Hotspring—
> here, feel my wet sleeve

while Sora added:

> *at Mount Hotspring*
> *on path of emptied pockets*
> *our tears left, too*[70]

From Hakuro, we were invited to samurai Nagayama Shigeyuki's house at Crane Hill (Tsuregaoka), a castle town, where we composed a *kasen*[71] of linked poetry together. Sakichi had come along this far and saw us off as we boarded a boat for Sakata and the home of a Dr. En'an, who writes in *haikai* under the pen-name Fugyoku.

> Steaming Mountain
> to Bay of Winds
> one cool evening

> blazing red sun
> into the sea plunging
> Mogami River, too

Our eyes had taken in such measureless beauty of rivers and mountains, land and sea, and still a small place in the heart quickened us on even further north toward Kisakata. From the harbor at Port Sakata we crossed a pass, then wound along a rocky shoreline, pressing on through dunes and across sandy beaches, more than three miles, arriving as sun sank. Sea-winds picked up bits of sand and rain gusts veiled Mount Chokai.[72] Suddenly it was so dark, and rain cast such a spell of gloom over all, we groped on as through an enchanted landscape in a fantasy, *"through shimmering veils of rain dreamily moving."*[73] We imagined it getting better

---

[70] *our tears left, too*: Sora's tears follow not only Bashō's example, but a trail where pilgrims shed coins and other currencies, emptying pockets according to custom (and where words were left behind).

[71] *kasen*: A form of *haikai no renga* (*haikai*-style linked poetry) with thirty-six stanzas, named for thirty-six legendary poets.

[72] Mount Chokai: A volcanic mountain sometimes called Dewa's Fuji, with old and new cones.

[73] *"through . . . rain dreamily moving"*: Bashō evokes echoes of a poem (by Su-Tung-p'o, 1036–1101), about drinking rice wine by the water as rain passes, comparing Lake Hsi to Queen Hsi-shih (*Xi Shi* in Pinyin; *Seishi* in Japanese), a legendary beauty.

when the storm cleared, at least hoped so, huddling in a fisherman's reed shed by the bay, waiting for weather to lift.

Next morning, with clear sky and brilliant, almost blinding sun, we set off in a small boat, pointing first towards Noin's Island to pay our respects at what had been the sage's refuge for three years, then across to the far shore in search of that ancient cherry tree whose reflection Saigyo had captured in a net of words — *"water's blossoms rowed over by the fisherman's boat"* — so that now the tree reminds us of the master poet's brush.

Near this shore was an imperial tomb, supposed to be the Empress Jingu's, at the Kanmanju temple, but I'd never heard of her coming or otherwise connected here, so who knows? At the temple, we stopped in the master's sitting room, and when hanging bamboo screens were raised, rolled section by section, beheld an unfolding panorama all around: Chokai Mountain "holding heaven up" to the south, and its reflection in water; to the east, a raised road-bed along the shore, stretching toward far-off Akita; Muyamuya Barrier blocking the way west; to the north, the sea where it enters and leaves its sheltered harbor at Shiogoshi Inlet through shallows at the tide's mouth.[74]

Kisakata was reminiscent of Matsushima,[75] but different, for where Matsushima seemed to smile with cheerful beauty, Kisakata seemed to frown and brood in its melancholy isolation, expressing a troubled spirit, perhaps, like a beautiful woman with a broken heart.

> in Kisa Bay rain —
> curled beautiful Seishi's soft
> mimosa silk sleep[76]

> wading cranes
> cooling off
> in the shallows

At the tideflats festival:

> *Kisakata, ah—*
> *what odd special tastes*
> *as feast for the spirit?*

(by Sora)

> *by a fisherman's shack*
> *taking the evening air*
> *on a driftwood door*

(by Taiji, a merchant from Mino)

---

[74] **Chokai Mountain . . . tide's mouth:** Note the economy of strokes with which the master's brush sweeps the 360-degree panorama as the bamboo screens are rolled up, one after another. (The visitors had sought a certain tomb, but found this lively "opening" instead.)

[75] **reminiscent of Matsushima:** Even on the map, Kisakata mirrors Matsushima, with reversed orientations.

[76] **mimosa silk sleep:** In Bashō's exquisitely musical poem, the bay in rain becomes *Seishi* again, the legendary beauty, a little dreamy in this weather, with drooping pink mimosa silk. (The word used means both a silky mimosa and "asleep.")

Noticing an osprey nest on a rock:

> *nest above the waves*
> *the rock-set bonds*
> *of an osprey pair*[77]

(by Sora)

We hung around for days on end at Sakata, watching clouds gathered over the far road. Our hearts ached when we heard how many miles we were still from the Kaga capital. We eventually crossed the Nizu border[78] into Echigo and finally on to the Ichiburi Barrier in Etchu, a hard nine-day stretch alternating heat and rain, and with my illness coming on again, unable to write.

> seventh moon festival—[79]
> even the night of the 6th
> a little odd

> wild Wild Sea
> & over Sado Island splashed
> . . . a river of stars

Today we made our way by some of the journey's most dangerous places,[80] like "Lost Children Gorge," "Parents Gone Drop-off," a rope bridge called "Dogs Turn Back," and another place aptly named "No-Horse Crossing." Utterly exhausted, we turned to our pillows almost as soon as we reached the border-town of Ichifuri.

Then we heard whispering voices of what sounded like probably two young women through paper-screen walls from the next room, and mingling in, an old man's voice. From what I could gather, they seemed to be pleasure-girls[81] from Nigata in Echizu on their way to Ise Shrine.[82] The man seemed to have come along

---

[77] *osprey pair*: Here at the northernmost point of the journey, Bashō offers us a wonderful sequence of linked poetry, two by him, then a chain of three he attributes to Sora and Taiji (of whom nothing more is known than what Bashō tells us).

[78] **Nizu border**: Starting out in 653 as a frontier outpost guarding the south against Ezo tribes, it was just a humble police checkpoint with a border guard's hut in Bashō's time.

[79] **seventh moon festival**: Celebrated the seventh day of the seventh moon (now displaced to July 7), the Tanabata festival included a "heavenly" love story about star-crossed lovers (represented by Vega and Altair) meeting once a year to exchange poems across the "river of stars" (the Milky Way), "as if across a bridge of birds," a reference continuing in the last line of the next verse (*ama-no-gawa*, heaven's river, Japanese name for the galaxy).

[80] **dangerous places**: There are many dangerous places along this stretch of coast where travelers must cross gorges, hug cliffs, or watch out for "sleeper waves," which sweep suddenly in to wash the unwary off their feet (sometimes even out to sea). Alternative renderings of the places mentioned might be: "Parents/Children Out of Mind," and "Horse Returns Alone."

[81] **pleasure-girls**: There's no exact cultural equivalent for the "play girls," who combine a spectrum of associations from old man's bimbo, hostess, and escort to courtesan and call girl. Bashō's are neither down-and-out prostitutes nor star geishas, however. Sora's account has no record of them, or of the poem he supposedly wrote down for Bashō, raising speculation the whole passage may have been created after for artistic purposes.

[82] **Ise Shrine**: The shrine, ceremonially rebuilt about every twenty years since 688, is a popular tourist destination among all classes (even with some reputation as a rendezvous spot for lovers). Bashō and Sora are on their way there, too, though not directly enough to serve as guides.

just this far, to the border, returning home the next day with letters they were writing and bits of spoken messages. Their whispered voices drifted into my sleep as dream-talk, as if from that old geisha's poem, *"where white waves curl and break in swirls of foam, we fallen children of the floating world, fisherwomen casting our nets to every chance, inconstant lover, pay for our past sins with each new day of shame. . . ."* With words floating in and merging with dreams, I drifted off.

But then as we were preparing to leave the next morning, these same women approached with misty eyes, and one said, "We are lost and helpless, not knowing the way. By virtue of your monkly robes, grant us your compassion, please, that with the boundless grace of Buddha's blessing, we may follow in your footsteps — at a discreet distance of course."

"I'm very sorry," I responded on setting out, "but we're not going straight anywhere, just stopping and detouring often off the main road. Plenty of folks will be going your way — you can follow any — and I'm sure that the goddess of boundless compassion will bring you safely across." But I carried sorrowful thoughts of them a long while.

> under one roof
> pleasure-girls sleeping also
>   bush-clovers and the moon

> (spoken to Sora, who wrote it down)

Some claim Kurobe River has "48 channels" flowing to the sea, and we certainly crossed countless streams and nameless watercourses on our way to Old Nago Bay. It wasn't *"flowering spring,"* of course, yet I wondered anyway about *"the waving wisterias of Tako"* even now in early fall, so I asked about the route, and was told, "Yes, worth a look, just a couple miles from here along the coast and then past that mountain over there — though you'll find only a few fishing shanties along the way, and probably not even that for lodging." So warned off, we continued directly on into Kaga province.

> winding seaside trails
> in & out drifting
>   the scent of rice

Across Snowflower Mountain (Unohanayama) and the Kurikara valley, we reached Kanazawa in mid seventh moon and met up with a writing friend named Kasho, a merchant traveling from Osaka, sharing our inn. A young local poet named Issho, widely known for his devotion to *haikai* and admired even beyond this region for his contributions to linked poetry, had died last winter, and his older brother was just then holding a memorial service.

> at the grave shaking
> mournful voices wail
>   autumn wind

Invited to a thatched hut after:

> autumn frost
> all hands busy with
>   melons and eggplants

And back on the way:

> red on red:
> unfeeling blazing sun uncaring
>   autumn wind

>   well named 'Little Pines'
> sweetly sighing wind through
>   clover & pampas grass

In Little Pines (Komatsu), we stopped at Tada Shrine and saw Sanemori's helmet and imperial armor of woven brocade. Presented to him as a Genji clan member by Lord Yoshitomo himself, it's said, they were obviously not for an ordinary soldier. The helmet was inlaid from eyebrow visor to earflaps with golden chrysanthemums interwoven with abstract scrollwork, with golden dragons flanking the crown and upwardly curving gilded horns. Shrine records preserved the story of Sanemori's death in battle and how Kiso Yoshinaka sent his lieutenant Higuchi Jiro here with these relics and a prayer.

>   "such a tragic fate"[83]
> the captain's helmet shelters
>   . . . just a cricket now

At Nata, a Kwannon temple dedicated to compassion is tucked in a fold of the foothills. With the White Mountains behind us, we reached it by turning left on the route to some hotbaths ahead. Emperor Kazan,[84] after retiring from the world, made a pilgrimage to thirty-three sacred temple sites before enshrining this image of Kwannon here, a perfect expression of mercy and caring. It's said he named this place "Na-ta" from the *Na* of Nachi and the *Ta* of Tanagumi, first and last of the thirty-three sites. The temple slope held many unusual rocks and a small reed-thatched retreat soulfully set on a stone ledge among old pines.

>   Whitestone Mountain
> bleached stones & paler still
>   — autumn wind

At Yamanaka, we soaked in hot baths supposed to be second in effects only to those at Ariake.

>   mountain bath
> pungent life-flower scent[85]
>   in rising steam

---

[83] **"such a tragic fate"**: This is a quote from someone seeing Sanemori's head on a pole, presented almost as if spoken by the cricket, whose "voice" reveals its hiding place.

[84] **Emperor Kazan** (968–1008): Kazan dedicated the place and image to Kwannon, goddess of compassion, an embodiment of mercy, grace, and caring.

[85] **life-flower scent**: From a kind of chrysanthemum, reputed to have health-giving properties.

Our host was a youngster named Kumenosuke, whose father had loved *haikai*[86] poetry. It's said the Kyoto poet Teishitsu came by here as a novice and was so outclassed he returned to Kyoto immediately to study with Master Teitoku, and that later, when he was well known and in demand as a poetry judge, he refused to take fees from local people here because of his early experience—this story long part of Yamanakan folklore. Meanwhile, Sora developed stomach troubles and hurried off to stay with relatives in Nagashima near Ise, offering this on leaving:

> *walking on and on*
> *dropping maybe buried by*
> *bush clovers covered*

With the pain of the one going and the emptiness of the one left behind, we were like wild ducks parting, each losing its partner in clouds, so I responded:

> now autumn dew
> washes from my hat the words
> "here travelers two"[87]

I stopped the next night at a Zen temple, Zenshoji, past the castle town of Daishoji, still in Kaga country. Sora had stayed here the night before, leaving behind:

> *all night long*
> *listening to autumn wind*
> *out back, the mountain*

"*Just one night, yet as if a thousand leagues apart,*"[88] I thought, awake in the same hall, listening to wind and mountain, too. Long before the sun, voices chanting sutras rose. When the gong sounded, I joined the gathering in the dining hall, then, thinking I should reach the Echizen district that day, was just hurrying off when young monks rushed down the steps after me with brush, paper and ink stone. Willows in the courtyard were losing foliage then, so I offered, as thanks:[89]

> sweeping the path
> in a rush on the way out
> scattering willow leaves

brushed quickly, my sandals already on and in motion.

---

[86] *haikai*: See glossary. At Yamanaka ("Mountain Hotbath"), the young host's late father had dramatically outdone a young visitor in a poetry contest, so the novice rushed off to study with a renowned teacher. After becoming famous himself, he attributed his later success to the impact of the "happy humiliation" suffered here, or so the story goes.

[87] "**here travelers two**": A favorite inscription for traveling companions. The dew is cousin to both clouds and tears.

[88] "*Just one . . . apart*": Bashō quotes an old Chinese poem about the pains of parting ("Clouds roam a thousand *li*. . . . Who knows my heart's sorrow?").

[89] **as thanks**: After a customarily silent breakfast, a guest might be expected to perform some small service, like sweeping the walkway, thus Bashō's brushed offering.

Past the Echizen border, I took a poled boat across Yoshizaki Inlet to Shiogoshi Pines, recalling: "*All night long storm-driven waves beat & break on the wind-blown shore—moonlight through Shiogoshi pines . . .*" Attributed to Saigyo,[90] this poem so perfectly expressed the spirit of the place, another line would be like a sixth finger, one too many.

An old acquaintance had become head priest of the Sky Dragon temple at Tenryuji, so I went by to renew our connection. Hokushi[91] had tagged along from Kanazawa. Not planning to come this far, yet reluctant to turn back, he ended up coming all the way, his keen eye noting many beautiful places with fine poems along the route. On parting, I gave him:

> a farewell scribbled
> quickly on my summer fan
> — & torn apart

Then I headed more than three miles further into the mountains to a zen temple founded by Dogen,[92] called Eihei-ji. Locating it so deep in the mountains and "*so far from the Capital*" was no accident, but the natural fruit of Dogen's deep attention.

With the castle town of Fukui not far away, I set out after supper. Arriving there as darkness fell, I had no idea which way to take to find my friend Tosai's house. An old samurai who had turned to poetry, Tosai visited me once in Edo, but so long ago—maybe ten years—I thought he'd probably be quite old now or even dead. But on asking, I was told he was still going strong, and given directions.

In a secluded lane off the beaten path, I came finally to a rustic little cottage entangled in gourd vines and moonflowers,[93] its door hidden by a cypress broom thicket and cockscomb left to run wild. This must be the place, I figured, and knocked at the door. A humble little woman, just right for the house, appeared, asking, "And where did you come from, Holy Reverend? I'm afraid the master of the house is out at so-and-so's—not too far away, so if you want him, you could check there." She seemed to be his wife, quite wonderful really, as if out of an old story. I followed her directions straightaway, tracked him down, and ended up staying two nights at their house before setting off.

Leaving in time to catch the harvest moon at Tsuruga Bay, Tosai tucked up his kimono in a funny way to come along "as a guidepost to point your route where paths branch. . . ." With White Mountains disappearing, Hina Peak came into view. Then we continued across Asamuzu Bridge, through the thickly seeded reed-heads of Tamae, past Bush Warbler Checkpoint, and over yet another "Hotspring Pass." By Flint Castle ruins, near Mount Return, I heard the first wild geese announcing autumn on their way south.

---

[90] **Saigyo:** The poem quoted may not be Saigyo's, after all, but one by Ren'nyo (1415–1499).

[91] **Hokushi:** Considered one of Bashō's closest students, he wrote down what Bashō said at Yamanaka, a record published in 1862.

[92] **Dogen** (1200–1253): Sometimes called "the Great Teacher," Dogen breathed life into a Zen tradition. His place is dedicated to spiritual progress, thus far from the capital (Kyoto, crowded with temples).

[93] **moonflowers:** *Yugao* in Japanese, the whole section overflows with echoes from the "*yugao*" chapter in *The Tale of Genji*.

Evening of the fourteenth, the night before full moon, we found lodging at an inn by Tsuruga Harbor. How bright the moonlight shone. "What will it be like tomorrow?!" I wondered aloud, and our inn-keeper replied, "Who knows? Weather's so changeable here, there's no telling what clouds might or might not be by then." So after warm rice wine, we set off together for the old Emperor Chuai's tomb, part of the Myojin memorial shrine in Hehi.

There seemed a certain unearthly air about the place wrapped in such night silence, with moonlight through the pines turning white sand to frost by the stone shrine. "Long ago," my host said, "the second abbot cut reed-grass, moved earth and rocks, drained a way through the marsh, and then hauled sand to ease the access for pilgrims. His example became a custom, continuing today, of bringing sand to what is now sometimes even called the "Sand-carrying Pilgrim's Shrine."[94]

> moon illumined—
> sand carrying pilgrims to
> sand-carrying shrine

And on the fifteenth, just as our host foretold it might, it rained.

> harvest moon?
> in these parts
> who knows?

On the sixteenth, the sky cleared back up. Interested in collecting some small colored shells, we sailed to Pink Beach at Iro,[95] a couple miles out. A prosperous poet called Tenya something-or-other[96] brought along well-stocked lunch baskets, bamboo sake flasks, and helpers for the crossing. With a smart tailwind, we were there in no time. Along the shore were just a few fishermen's shacks and a small weather-beaten Hokke sect temple, where we sat, savoring green tea and hot rice wine—and the overwhelming melancholy of the isolated shore at evening.

> lonelier even
> than Suma Beach
>   — this autumn shore

> in each wave
> a swirl of churning shells &
>   broken clover bits

I handed Tosai[97] the brush for a description of our time there, which we left at the temple.

---

[94] **"Sand-carrying Pilgrim's Shrine"**: Just as the "Yugao" (moonflower) was a key background element in the Fukui section, here the critical term is *Yugyo* (pilgrimage), used as a proper name for a sect of Buddhism, for the "sand-carriers" within that lineage, and for the devotion of practitioners.

[95] **Pink Beach at Iro**: This shore was famous for its many hued shells, including the pinkish *masuho,* a shellfish that "stains the tides," according to a poem by Saigyo.

[96] **Tenya something-or-other**: Presumably Tenya Gorozaemon, a shipper and *haikai* poet.

[97] **Tosai**: The "old samurai" Bashō had joined up with in Fukui. His account of the visit is reportedly still in the temple there.

My friend Rotsu, who'd joined us in Tsuruga harbor with horses, came with us to Mino and then to the walled castle town of Ogaki, where Sora showed up from Ise, and Etsujin galloped in, and we all gathered at Joko's house. Soon we were joined by Zensensi, plus Keiko and his sons, with other dear friends arriving day and night. All greeted me[98] with such joy and affection, it seemed as if I'd just returned from that far land of the Great Beyond, and so in a way perhaps I had.

But then, on the sixth day of the ninth or "Long" moon, not yet fully recovered from the fatigue of traveling, here I was stepping back in a boat again, setting off for the dedication rites at Ise. . . .

> *Futami clams*
> > *bound flesh and shells*
> > > *at parting—autumn, too*[99]

[Scribe's Epilog, by Soryu][100]

In Bashō's wonderful journey-book, the down to earth becomes eloquent and the light touch powerful, with radiant beauty and pure insight at each surprising turn of the trail, so one moment we rise up to applaud, the next stretch out, stirred to the core. Once I grabbed my coat, ready to take that road myself; then sat back down to draw all the more meaning from the heart-felt imagery of the master's way. What a mindful treasure-trove and deep reservoir of inspiration we find within! Bashō is like that divine weaver whose every knot in the net of creation is a shining *vajra* jewel. Yet even now frost gathers in his brows.

—Early summer, 1694.

by Soryu

---

[98] **All greeted me:** The men rushing in to welcome Bashō are all considered "members of Bashō's school." Rotsu was a wandering poet, Etsujin a merchant, Joko an ex-samurai monk and poetry judge, Zensensi a high-ranking local samurai (though the name also suggests zen teacher), Keiko and his three sons all government servants. Bashō arrived in Ogaki in early October (approaching the tail end of autumn), leaving again soon for the shrine at Ise back on the east coast.

[99] *autumn, too*: Bashō himself seems to have used this kind of unusual stagger for the last poem, one of the hardest to translate. Its term *futami* refers to Futami Bay, an inlet near Ise, famous for its clams, but with a variety of root meanings of its own also (e.g., shell-bodied, bound flesh, a jewel-inlaid box, something with two views . . .). The poem evokes the essence of parting, going separate ways: Bashō and his friends, the opening shells, the flesh from the shell—and autumn, too. It also suggests a kind of *joining*, however, being a perfect match for the "departing spring" poem he wrote on setting out. One may note that Bashō's first published book, more than twenty years earlier, was called *Seashell game* and involved comparing paired poems; and also that Saigyo had written a famous poem about girls collecting shells "on the Futami shore" for just such a seashell-matching game. (Perhaps all the poems and/or prose sections in Bashō's masterwork have such "matches," a game worth exploring.)

[100] **Scribe's Epilog, by Soryu:** Soryu was the scribe or calligrapher who prepared the final draft of "clean copy," presumably under Bashō's supervision, in 1694, five years after the original journey. Bashō had given his brushed trail the dedicated attention "any great work requires," a lesson learned from ancient blade-masters and small, late-blooming trees in mountains. The "oku no hosomichi" is not just an aesthetic work, but something like an inner trail that illuminates from within, as Soryu describes.

Travel and Cultural Encounter

p. 131

Matsuo Bashō's **Narrow Road through the Backcountry** has roots in the *nikki,* or poetic diaries, of the Heian period (794–1192) in Japan—in particular the *Tosa Diary* written by the influential poet and editor of the *Kokinshu* Ki no Tsurayuki. Written in the persona of a woman returning by sea and land from Tosa province to Kyoto and recounting her daily reflections, the *Tosa Diary* focuses less upon the journey itself and more upon the traveler's inner reflections—on grief, loss, and poetry. In the thirteenth and fourteenth centuries, the earliest forms of *haibun* emerged, such as the anonymously written *Journey along the Seacoast Road* and *A Journey East of the Barrier* as well as Abutsu's *Diary of the Waning Moon.* Like the medieval pilgrimage and travel narratives of Europeans, these diaries recount journeys to shrines, capital cities, and historical monuments, and record to various degrees the traveler's impressions about and responses to sights and scenes along the way. For Bashō, travel brings him into a closer unity with Japanese literary tradition and culture, and Japanese history and landscape. By contrast, many of the travel narratives included here from Turkey, Europe, and Muslim India focus upon initial impressions and descriptions of unfamiliar places, as well as upon dramatizing points of contact with cultural difference.

Evliya Çelebi, Lady Mary Wortley Montagu, and Mirzah Abu Taleb Khan, in particular, are moving far afield from their own countries, and their interest is in recounting the unique character of people and places unfamiliar to their readers. Taking advantage of improvements in means of transportation, expanded networks of communication, and increased knowledge of the world, seventeenth- and eighteenth-century travelers began to visit places

William Hodges, *View of Part of the City of Benares,* c. 1781. Wash and Ink over Pencil
*European travelers arriving at the port of Benares, a Hindu holy city on the banks of the
Ganges in India, observed beautiful architecture far different from that of their home
countries. (Yale Center for British Art, Paul Mellon Collection)*

once accessible only to the hardiest of adventurers. Nonetheless, tour-
ism was a long way from being the industry it is today, and most
people's desire to travel had to be satisfied vicariously, through reading. Thus, like the tales of pilgrimage and discovery from earlier centuries, the TRAVEL NARRATIVE allowed readers to venture into what
was for most of them *terra incognita*—unknown land, a place known
perhaps as little more than a name on a map or in a history book.

EUROPEAN TRAVELERS

European readers were fascinated with what they considered to be
exotic cultures. Inspired early in the century by the Galland translation of *Thousand and One Nights* (1704–17),[1] the European appetite
for the Orient virtually guaranteed the popularity of published
accounts—genuine and invented—of travels to China, India, and

---

[1]*Thousand and One Nights:* Also known as the *Arabian Nights;* a collection of Indian, Arabic, and Persian tales
dating from the ninth century C.E. (or earlier) to the fourteenth century. The stories include those of Sinbad
the Sailor, Ali Baba and the Forty Thieves, and Aladdin and his magic lamp.

loo-EE ahn-TWAHN
duh boo-gen-VEEL
duh-NEE dee-DROH,
p. 174
p. 168

the Middle East. These travel narratives appeared in many forms, from actual accounts of voyages such as those of James Cook[2] and **Louis Antoine de Bougainville,**[3] to philosophical treatises such as **Denis Diderot**'s *Supplement to the Voyage of Bougainville,* and to diaries and letters such as Lady Mary Wortley Montagu's *Turkish Letters.* Lady Mary's ***Turkish Letters*** provide a detailed and authentic account of her stay in Turkey, a place her readers would have considered representative of the mysterious East.

NON-EUROPEAN TRAVELERS

While Europeans were eager to read the latest stories from travelers to China, India, Africa, and the Islamic world, readers from those places were also eager to learn more about what we might call the mysterious West. From medieval times, some of the greatest world travelers came from the Islamic world, in part because of the injunction from the Qur'an (Koran) that every Muslim must undertake pilgrimage to Mecca at least once or twice in his or her lifetime. The Moroccan traveler Ibn Battuta (1304–1377), for example, has been called the Marco Polo of Islam, and his travels took him to North Africa, Egypt, Palestine, Syria, and even to India and China. In the seventeenth century, one of the world's great travelers was **Evliya Çelebi** from Istanbul. He traveled extensively throughout the far-reaching borders of the Ottoman empire, reaching places such as Austria, Iran, and Crete. His ***Book of Travels,*** written after he moved to Egypt in 1671, earned him a reputation as one of the Ottoman empire's greatest writers. A century later, another Muslim traveler, Mirza Abu Taleb Khan, set down his impressions of Europeans in his own *Travels.*

ev-lee-YAH
cheh-leh-BEE
p. 163

---

[2]**James Cook** (1728–1779): English sea captain who voyaged around the world in 1768, sailing to Australia, New Zealand, the Sandwich Islands, the West Coast of what is now the United States, and Hawaii, where he was killed.

[3]**Louis Antoine de Bougainville** (1729–1811): French naval officer and navigator who undertook a voyage from 1766 to 1769 that led him to the Falkland and Solomon Islands; he described this expedition in *Voyage around the World* (1771).

European Trade Patterns. c. 1740

Europe dominated world trade in the mid-eighteenth century. As indicated by the diagram "The Triangular Trade," Europe stood at the top of the pyramid-like structure of world trade patterns, exploiting other areas of the world to increase its own wealth. Following the flow of goods, raw materials, and slaves, travelers from many countries visited new places for purposes of military duty, business, and curiosity.

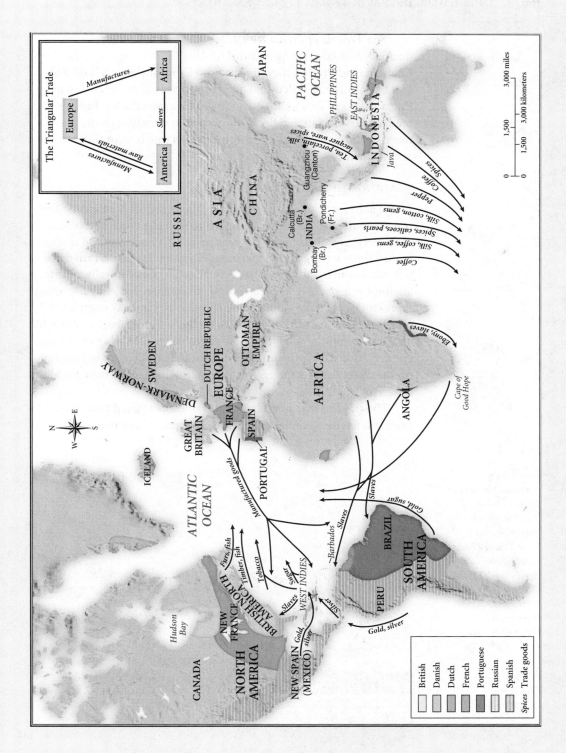

The Triangular Trade

Europe — Manufactures → Africa

Africa — Slaves → America

America — Raw materials → Europe

Europe — Manufactures → America

JAPAN

PACIFIC OCEAN

PHILIPPINES

EAST INDIES

INDONESIA

Tea, porcelain, silk, lacquer ware, spices

Guangzhou (Canton)

Java

Coffee

Spices

Pepper

Silk, cotton, gems

Pondicherry (Fr.)

Spices, calicoes, pearls

Silk, coffee, gems

Calcutta (Br.)

INDIA

Bombay (Br.)

Coffee

CHINA

ASIA

RUSSIA

3,000 miles

3,000 kilometers

1,500

1,500

0

0

DUTCH REPUBLIC

OTTOMAN EMPIRE

DENMARK-NORWAY

SWEDEN

EUROPE

FRANCE

SPAIN

GREAT BRITAIN

PORTUGAL

AFRICA

ANGOLA

Ebony slaves

Cape of Good Hope

ICELAND

ATLANTIC OCEAN

N E W S

Manufactured goods

Slaves

Slaves

Gold, sugar

Barbados

Slaves

BRAZIL

SOUTH AMERICA

PERU

Furs, fish

Timber, fish

Tobacco

Sugar

Slaves

WEST INDIES

Silver

Gold, silver

Gold, silver

CANADA

Hudson Bay

NEW FRANCE

BRITISH NORTH AMERICA

NORTH AMERICA

NEW SPAIN (MEXICO)

Gold, silver

British

Danish

Dutch

French

Portuguese

Russian

Spanish

Spices   Trade goods

159

p. 179

ah-Boo TAH-lib

The ***Travels of Mirza Abu Taleb Khan*** offers an extensive, detailed, and fascinating account of **Abu Taleb**'s trips to Ireland, England, and France, then on through Constantinople, Baghdad, and back home to Calcutta. During his nearly three-year stay in England, Abu Taleb painted a picture of Europe for his Indian readers. His narrative reflects on European customs, particularly those of the English, about whom he finds much to praise and blame.

READING THE TRAVEL NARRATIVE

Travel accounts raise many questions about the authenticity of the traveler-narrator, his or her ability to represent people and places accurately, as well as his or her reasons, both conscious and unconscious, for traveling and for writing. Although travel narratives may put two cultures into dialogue, they also contain culturally specific assumptions made by the narrator or the writer that sway his or her representations. Like Gulliver, the traveler may appear completely open to the new world in which he or she is immersed, but often he or she takes up the role of a knowledgeable mediator between two cultures, translating the unfamiliar into the familiar, or, depending on the effect desired, exaggerating the unfamiliar into the radically different.

The traveler carries certain culturally constructed predispositions, preferences, and often unconscious prejudices that may

After Johann Bernhard Fischer von Erlach, *The King of Siam's Residence,* Engraving, 1721 From *Entwurf einer historischen Architektur. (Private Collection / the Stapleton Collection / Bridgeman Art Library)*

distort his or her representations. Thus, writers who actually venture into the contact zones—points of connection between people normally separated by culture, history, geography, or race—may unintentionally or unavoidably misrepresent those they meet. These narratives are often subject to factual errors due to a failure to sympathize with the peoples or customs described. Such lapses may result in distortions and exaggerations, like those exploited satirically in Swift's *Gulliver's Travels.* Accounts of these contact zones raise questions not only about the places and peoples described but also about the writers and their own cultural assumptions and values.

■ PRONUNCIATION
Louis Antoine de Bougainville: loo-EE ahn-TWAHN duh boo-gen-VEEL
Denis Diderot: duh-NEE dee-DROH (DEE-duh-roh)
Evliya Çelebi: ev-lee-YAH cheh-leh-BEE
Abu Taleb: ah-BOO TAH-lib (AH-boo)

❧ EVLIYA ÇELEBI
B. TURKEY, 1611–C. 1684

One of the world's great travelers, Evliya Çelebi was born in Istanbul in 1611, the son of the wealthy Mehmet Zilli, the court goldsmith, and his wife, who was related to Melek Ahmed Pasha, a man who would eventually become the grand vizier. As he was growing up, Evliya learned his father's trade, but he also received a comprehensive education in the Islamic sciences and the Qur'an, becoming an accomplished singer of Qur'anic verses. When Evliya was twenty years old, the prophet Muhammad appeared to him in a dream and gave his blessing to Evliya's WANDERLUST. This blessing was soon to become relevant, for after completing his education at the palace school of Sultan Murat IV, Evliya entered into the service of various *pashas,* high-ranking officials, whose missions took him to the remotest boundaries of the Ottoman empire and beyond to Austria and Iran. Over his lifetime, Evliya traveled from Istanbul to the Caucasus Mountains, to Crimea and Crete, throughout Anatolia and to Syria, and to the Balkans. In 1655, he went to Vienna in the company of Kara Mehmed Pasha, who was making an embassy there; and in 1671 he took the pilgrimage to Mecca. After making the *HAJJ,* Evliya settled in Egypt, where he lived for the rest of his life.

In Egypt Evliya began writing his *Book of Travels,* working from copious notes that he had kept during his years of traveling, as well as drawing from other writings and from his memory. The manuscript he left behind was not published until 1843, when an Arabic version of selected passages appeared in print. This edition was followed by the first eight volumes published from 1896 to 1928 and the final two volumes from 1935 to 1938. The book's popularity in the Arabic world quickly rose, and Evliya is now considered one of the greatest of the Ottoman writers, valued for his detailed descriptions as well as for his exaggerated and fantastic accounts of people and events. Evliya's tendency to embellish his accounts is in good evidence in the passage presented here, in which he describes the thousand skills of the seventy-year-old Abdal Khan and the palace gardens at Bitlis, a city in the southeastern corner of what is now Turkey.

A note on the text: Evliya was in Bitlis on three separate occasions in 1655 and 1656. The translator and editor of the selections that follow, Robert Dankoff, has compiled these materials into a single volume for the series of partial editions of Evliya Çelebi's travels published by E. J. Brill and under the general editorship of Klaus Kreiser (1990). The notes to the text are based on the translator's (indicated in parentheses), with additions of the editors'.

Ottoman Court, Seventeenth Century
This Turkish manuscript shows Venetian ambassador Jacopo Soranzo being received at the Ottoman court in Constantinople for peace negotiations. (The Art Archive/Museo Correr Venice/Dagli Orti)

FROM

∽ The Book of Travels

Translated by Robert Dankoff

[THE COURT OF ABDAL KHAN, GOVERNOR OF BITLIS]

Abdal Khan's[1] thousand skills. Aside from being versed in alchemy and magic and several hundred occult philosophical sciences, he is—according to the Hadith,[2] "Science is two, the science of bodies, and the science of religions"—a master physician, next to whom the ancient physicians such as Galen and Hippocrates and Socrates and Philekos[3] are not even schoolboys; for they were reckoned physicians according to the men of their time, but this Khan is a master pulse-taker and blood-letter according to the nature of the sick and the weakly of the present age.

He even treated an eighty-year-old sick and weakly opium addict, who had turned into a wishbone, giving him decoctions and hot baths and cures beggaring description, so that this meager fellow found new life and became fresh and ruddy as a Tebkani apple within three days. He has, like Jesus, given life to some thousands of individuals such as this.

He is also an incomparable surgeon, and has set and wrapped many a man who has tumbled from his horse or fallen from his roof, so that the fellow was on his feet in seven days. He even has a kind of mummy-powder which, if ingested by an emaciated man, his slender waist fills out to Iskender's sash.

He is such a fine horseman that, when he mounts his swift steed, playing jereed or polo, or engaging in battle, he is like Rüstem of Zabulistan or Shaghad of Iran. [. . .]

We spent the ten-day halt in his palace with our lord the Pasha. Each day from dawn to dusk there was a constant stream of musicians and buffoons and acrobats, displaying their wares and receiving gifts from the Khan and the Pasha. Because of the Khan's reputation as patron of the arts and sciences, skilled men would come to him from every country, and if they were well-rounded and cultivated individuals, the Khan would give them gardened palaces and slavegirls and timars and dye works in order that he might keep them tied down in the valley of Bitlis and so acquire some of their skills. Thus the Khan became a second Cemshid, spending all his free time learning new skills. And thus the city of Bitlis was filled with skilled masters.

As for the master players on the shawm and the trumpet and the kettle drum and the cymbals in the Khan's band, their like is not to be found in the imperial workshop itself, let alone in that of a vizier. For he himself performs concerts (*pīşrev*) and is knowledgeable in the various musical sciences. And he has masters in his band who perform *küll-i külliyāt, zenc īr* in the twenty-four rhythmic cycles,

---

[1] *Abdal Khan:* The governor of the city of Bitlis (in what is now southeastern Turkey).

[2] **Hadith:** The traditional record or collection of sayings and deeds of Muhammad, second only in importance to the Qu'ran in Islamic tradition. The translator notes that "Evliya always cites this dubious Hadith when he mentions medicine."

[3] **Philekos:** Galen, Hippocrates, Socrates, Philekos.

shükūfe-zār, and *peshrevs* in the *ṣabā* mode and the *ẓarb-i fetiḥ* rhythmic cycle.[4] Each one is like Cemshid who invented the shawm. When they perform in the evening, or in the predawn when no one is stirring, they delight the listener.

The Khan's pleasure garden. On the harem side of this garden palace there is a garden as long and broad as the range of a bowshot. If the seas were ink and the trees were pens, and all the scribes gathered, they could not record a drop in the ocean or a mote in the sunlight of due description and praise of this garden. Suffice it to say that all the fruit-bearing trees are planted in rows, each one swaying with the zephyr breeze like beauties with girded loins. Aside from the fig, the sycamore, the banana, and the cypress, all varieties are present. In some nooks and crannies there are even lemon and orange saplings which are protected with felt coverings during the winter. There are also charming and lavish pleasure-domes, like so many castles of Khavarnak, each one difference in style from the others, and each the work of a master of a different land.

The pools and jets and fountains here are not to be found in Turkey. Each pool is surrounded by a mosaic floor of varicolored marble, like Indian-style mother-of-pearl and marquetry inlay. Streams of water as thick as a man's neck flow into the pools from the mouths of various demons, lions, and dragons; then pour down into the reticulated garden beds. There is also water springing up from jets. In certain cases, forty or fifty streams jet out of a single hole and mingle together like a beauty's tresses. The marvelous thing is that they all issue from one mouth. Some of the pleasure-domes have suspended glass and crystal bowls, which give a melancholy sound when the water jets strike them, while the larger ones channel the water so that it cascades like rain. Some of the jets have a wheel suspended above, which turns when the jet stream strikes. Others have a hollow ball the size of a watermelon, which turns and bobs in the air. In short, the master craftsmen of every land have created such wonders that the tongue cannot express.

There are beds with thousands of flowers of various sorts, including rose, hyacinth, sweet basil, violet, judas-tree, jonquil, *nebatī*(?), camel's neck, camphor-tree, peony, Roman musk, carnation, syringa, lily, iris, narcissus, cyclamen, jasmine, tulip, and hollyhock. Each bed is laid out differently, and they intoxicate with the scent of jonquils and other blossoms. As for the varieties of fruit trees, there are saplings from as far away as Isfahan, Tebriz, and Nakhshevan. Even though this garden was constructed only recently, when Sultan Murad IV saw it during the Revan campaign, he was astounded.

The Khan's artificial lake. Behind the aforementioned garden on the northern side there was a flowing spring called Ayn-i Taklaban. The Khan dammed up the lower part of the stream and made a sea-like lagoon. The dam is like the Wall of Iskender or the Wall of Magog, and myriad fishes swim in the lake. The Khan had caiques constructed and decked out, and he himself used to row alone, or else

---

[4] *küll-i . . .* cycle: These terms refer to different types of musical styles distinguished by different compound rhythms.

he would take his household out for excursions, thereby dissipating his longing for the sea.

One day, by God's wisdom, the women were not sitting properly in the caique and it capsized, leaving several slavegirls drowned. After that he gave up the sport, only occasionally going fishing. The lake is very deep. Once, when the flood waters were severe, one side of the dam broke and the rushing waters destroyed quite a few houses in the Taklaban quarter. When the Kurds cursed the Khan, wishing that he too would be ruined, he reconstructed all of their houses.

The garden bath. A delightful bath goes off the treasury room of the above-mentioned Khan's palace, and gives onto a dressing-room. It has gardens on three sides, and the dressing-room has windows overlooking the gardens, all with bronze and iron grating like Fakhri cut-outs, also shutters of Arab-style carved (wood), which the khans of Persia sent from Tebriz as gifts. The shutter carvings are filled in with raw black ambergris, and as the zephyr breeze strikes them from without, the men within enjoy the fragrance.

All four walls of this dressing-room are covered with varicolored porcelain tiles. And going all around the lofty dome and over the upper sills of the windows, in calligraphy written enchantingly on the tiles by the hand of Mehemmed Riza of Tebriz, is Fuzuli's[5] "Bath Kaside." [. . .]

In the very center of this dressing-room are fountains full of water shooting toward the dome from three hundred places. Its floor is paved with Egyptian-style varicolored marble. The jet in the center of the pool strikes the glass bowl at the peak of the dome and then rains down. All the servants here are lovely Circassian, Abkhazian and Georgian ghulams,[6] each outfitted with a jewelled belt worth a thousand piasters, adorned with daggers and knives, and walking about on clogs with inlaid mother-of-pearl, like so many peacocks of paradise. They give the bathers silk waist-wrappers and clogs like their own, and serve them respectfully.

When one enters the bath from the dressing-room, one finds oneself in a large domed room called the tepidarium *(şovukluk),* but the water of the pools and fountains in the middle of this room is all hot, and the walls are all covered with varicolored tiles. The floor here too is paved with marble mosaic "China-rose" while the sturdy enamel dome is brightened by porcelain tiles and ornamented with numerous chandeliers.

The next room is the caldarium *(ḥammām-i germā).* It is as though one entered a pool of light, for there is no sign of a wall rising on all sides to the lofty dome. Rather, this great round dome is perched on tall columns, and between the columns are windows of clear and polished rock crystal and Murano cut glass. When the sun strikes the windows, the inside of the bath become "light upon light."[7] In the garden of Irem outside these windows a thousand nightingales wail and cry, as the bathers within listen and watch them feed their chicks, and observe the flowering

---

[5] **Fuzuli** (1495–1556): A Turkish poet of the Ottoman empire; the poem mentioned is a famous ghazal of his.

[6] **ghulams:** Slaves.

[7] **"light upon light":** An allusion to the Qur'an 24:35. [Translator's note.]

trees and the singing birds' nests and the tall and brightly colored flowers arrayed on the ground.

In the middle of this bath is a large pool with jets spouting up on all sides, the jet in the center reaching as high as the bowl in the dome and then pouring down into the hot water. Ruby-colored petals of rose and carnation are floating in the pool and stick to the bathers' skin, imparting their perfume. Each cubicle has a two-jar sarcophagus bath. This room also is paved with marble that dazzles the eye, since it is inlaid with precious stones, like the eye of a bird: jade, turquoise, onyx, amber, fisheye, agate, *yemenī,* and garnets. And attached to the columns that are between the windows are wash basins of onyx, porphyry, *yerekān* stone, *ferah* stone, and Chinese porcelain, carved to such perfection that the marble cutters of today could not even strike a chisel at it. The craftsmen made the water flow out of the marble columns into the basins in a marvelous manner. All the spouts are gold and silver, the bowls as well, and the jet pipes are pure silver. The atmosphere is so delightful, one seems to be enjoying eternal life. As the fountain streams strike the various chandeliers and wheels and suspended crystal bowls, they turn in the air, which is also a rare sight. On the lower level (lit., skirts) of this dome are fine calligraphic inscriptions with verses relating to the bath. Lovely slaveboys, with silken indigo waistbands wrapped round their naked bodies, service the bathers with *fūtūnī* bathgloves and scented soaps. When they loosen their tresses, the distraught lover goes out of his mind. Some of them light censers and incense-burners with aloes and ambergris, so the bath is filled with fragrance.

In sum, the tongue falls short in describing this bath, or the grand palace, or the garden of Irem. For in the expenditure of filigree-work in these buildings, and in grace and elegance and cleanliness, it is a peerless bath of unique design whose like I have not seen in forty-one years of travel.

The master builder in each of his works brought forth such marvels of art that no former architect under the sun achieved such a construction. Only God knows what it cost to make such a wondrous mansion. Even Sultan Murad, during the Revan campaign, when he entered this bath and found the cold water flowing with rose-water, and the hot with steam; and in one cubicle five lovely male attendants with black tresses, and in another five fairy-graced and angel-faced virgin maiden attendants; — even he exclaimed with delight: "If only this bath were in *my* palace!" It is truly a wonderful and charming bath.

Among the important English travelers in the eighteenth century was Lady Mary Wortley Montagu. Lady Mary was born in 1689, the daughter of Evelyn Pierrepont, a wealthy Whig who eventually became marquess of Dorchester. As a teenager Mary taught herself Latin and read widely in the classics and the popular novels of her time. Known for her keen intelligence, wit, and conversation, she moved within an elite literary circle that featured some of the greatest English writers of the day, including Alexander Pope, against whom she wrote some pointed satirical poems. In 1712 she eloped with Edward Wortley Montagu, who became ambassador to the Turkish government four years later. In January 1716 Montagu and her husband departed for Turkey, where they stayed until May 1718. While in Turkey, she learned the native language and acquired some knowledge of Turkish literature; in addition, she sought out information about inoculation for smallpox and introduced the practice to England upon her return. During her time abroad, Montagu kept notes and wrote letters describing her experiences, which she later compiled into what is known as *The Turkish Letters,* not published until 1763, a year after her death in London at the age of seventy-four. Among others, the great English historian Edward Gibbon, author of *The History of the Decline and Fall of the Roman Empire* (1776–88), praised Montagu's *Turkish Letters* for their lively style and their erudition; in his words, "What fire, what ease, what knowledge of Europe and Asia!"

Unlike the fictional constructs in Montesquieu and Goldsmith, Montagu's *Turkish Letters* attempts as nearly as possible to account for the manners and customs she witnessed directly in Turkey. The letters give us a rare opportunity to see Turkish society from a European woman's point of view, in this case relatively untainted by the prejudices common to travel narratives about the East. Remarkably, Montagu records in the letters presented here first-hand impressions of a Turkish harem and a mosque, spaces usually forbidden to Western travelers. Acknowledging her limited understanding of the Ottoman culture, Montagu often avoids romanticizing or demeaning Turkish customs, as other European writers were wont to do; instead she conveys her admiration and respect for her hosts as well as her sympathy — as in the letter included here — for some of the women she meets.

We travellers are in very hard circumstances: If we say nothing but what has been said before us, we are dull, and we have observed nothing. If we tell any thing new, we are laughed at as fabulous and romantic, not allowing for the difference of ranks, which afford difference of company, more curiosity, or the changes of customs, that happen every twenty years in every country.

– LADY MARY
WORTLEY MONTAGU
The Turkish Letters

FROM

～ The Turkish Letters

To the Countess of ———— [Mar]

Pera of Constantinople, March 10, O.S. [1718]

. . . I went to see the Sultana Hafiteń,[1] favourite of the late Emperor Mustapha, who, you know, (or perhaps you don't know) was deposed by his brother, the reigning Sultan Achmet, and died a few weeks after, being poisoned, as it was generally believed. This lady was, immediately after his death, saluted with an absolute order to leave the seraglio, and choose herself a husband from the great men at the Porte.[2] I suppose you may imagine her overjoyed at this proposal. Quite contrary: These women, who are called, and esteem themselves, queens, look upon this liberty as the greatest disgrace and affront that can happen to them. She threw herself at the Sultan's feet, and begged him to poignard her, rather than use his brother's widow with that contempt. She represented to him, in agonies of sorrow, that she was privileged from this misfortune, by having brought five princes into the Ottoman family; but all the boys being dead, and only one girl surviving, this excuse was not received, and she [was] compelled to make her choice. She chose Bekir Effendi, then secretary of state, and above fourscore years old, to convince the world that she firmly intended to keep the vow she had made, of never suffering a second husband to approach her bed; and since she must honour some subject so far as to be called his wife, she would choose him as a mark of her gratitude, since it was he that had presented her at the age of ten years old, to her last lord. But she has never permitted him to pay her one visit; though it is now fifteen years she has been in his house, where she passes her time in uninterrupted mourning, with a constancy very little known in Christendom, especially in a widow of twenty-one, for she is now but thirty-six. She has no black eunuchs for her guard, her husband being obliged to respect her as a queen, and not inquire at all into what is done in her apartment, where I was led into a large room with a sofa the whole length of it, adorned with white marble pillars like a *ruelle*,[3] covered with pale blue figured velvet on a silver ground, with cushions of the same, where I was desired to repose till the Sultana appeared, who had contrived this manner of reception to avoid rising up at my entrance, though she made me an inclination of her head when I rose up to her. I was very glad to observe a lady that had been distinguished by the favour of an emperor, to whom beauties were every day presented from all parts of the world. But she did not seem to me to have ever been half so beautiful as the fair Fatima I saw at Adrianople; though she had the

---

[1] **Sultana Hafiteń:** Widow of Sultan Mustafa II, who ruled from 1695 to 1703. She later became the wife of the Grand Vizier, the chief authority in the Ottoman empire, second only to the sultan. [All notes are the editors'.]

[2] **the Porte:** The official name of the Turkish government, taken from the high gate at the entrance to the building housing the Grand Vizier's administrative offices.

[3] *ruelle:* A passageway or lane.

remains of a fine face, more decayed by sorrow than time. But her dress was some-thing so surprisingly rich, I cannot forbear describing it to you. She wore a vest called *donalma,* and which differs from a *caftán* by longer sleeves, and folding over at the bottom. It was of purple cloth, strait to her shape, and thick set, on each side, down to her feet, and round the sleeves, with pearls of the best water, of the same size as their buttons commonly are. You must not suppose I mean as large as those of my Lord———, but about the bigness of a pea; and to these buttons large loops of dia-monds, in the form of those gold loops so common upon birthday coats. This habit was tied, at the waist, with two large tassels of smaller pearl, and round the arms embroidered with large diamonds: Her shift fastened at the bottom with a great dia-mond, shaped like a lozenge; Her girdle as broad as the broadest English ribbon, entirely covered with diamonds. Round her neck she wore three chains, which reached to her knees: one of large pearl, at the bottom of which hung a fine coloured emerald, as big as a turkey-egg; another, consisting of two hundred emeralds, close joined together, of the most lively green, perfectly matched, every one as large as a half-crown piece, and as thick as three crown pieces; and another of small emeralds, perfectly round. But her earrings eclipsed all the rest. They were two diamonds, shaped exactly like pears, as large as a big hazel-nut. Round her *talpoche*[4] she had four strings of pearl, the whitest and most perfect in the world, at least enough to make four necklaces, every one as large as the Duchess of Marlborough's, and of the same size, fastened with two roses, consisting of a large ruby for the middle stone, and round them twenty drops of clean diamonds to each. Beside this, her head-dress was covered with bodkins of emeralds and diamonds. She wore large diamond bracelets, and had five rings on her fingers, all single diamonds, (except Mr. Pitt's[5]) the largest I ever saw in my life. It is for jewellers to compute the value of these things; but, according to the common estimation of jewels in our part of the world, her whole dress must be worth above a hundred thousand pounds sterling. This I am very sure of, that no European queen has half the quantity; and the empress's jewels, though very fine, would look very mean near hers.

She gave me a dinner of fifty dishes of meat, which (after their fashion) were placed on the table but one at a time, and was extremely tedious. But the magnifi-cence of her table answered very well to that of her dress. The knives were of gold, the hafts set with diamonds. But the piece of luxury that grieved my eyes was the tablecloth and napkins, which were all tiffany, embroidered with silks and gold, in the finest manner, in natural flowers. It was with the utmost regret that I made use of these costly napkins, as finely wrought as the finest handkerchiefs that ever came out of this country. You may be sure, that they were entirely spoiled before dinner was over. The sherbet (which is the liquor they drink at meals) was served in china bowls; but the covers and salvers massy gold. After dinner, water was brought in a gold basin, and towels of the same kind of the napkins, which I very unwillingly wiped my hands upon; and coffee was served in china, with gold *soucoupes.*[6]

---

[4] *talpoche:* A kind of bonnet with elongated sides.

[5] **Mr. Pitt:** William Pitt, Earl of Chatham (1708–1778), a powerful English statesman.

[6] *soucoupes:* Saucers.

The Sultana seemed in very good humour, and talked to me with the utmost civility. I did not omit this opportunity of learning all that I possibly could of the seraglio, which is so entirely unknown among us. She assured me, that the story of the Sultan's throwing a handkerchief is altogether fabulous; and the manner upon that occasion, no other but that he sends the *kyslár agá*,[7] to signify to the lady the honour he intends her. She is immediately complimented upon it by the others, and led to the bath, where she is perfumed and dressed in the most magnificent and becoming manner. The Emperor precedes his visit by a royal present, and then comes into her apartment: neither is there any such thing as her creeping in at the bed's foot. She said, that the first he made choice of was always after the first in rank, and not the mother of the eldest son, as other writers would make us believe. Sometimes the Sultan diverts himself in the company of all his ladies, who stand in a circle round him. And she confessed that they were ready to die with jealousy and envy of the happy she that he distinguished by any appearance of preference. But this seemed to me neither better nor worse than the circles in most courts, where the glance of the monarch is watched, and every smile waited for with impatience, and envied by those who cannot obtain it.

She never mentioned the Sultan[8] without tears in her eyes, yet she seemed very fond of the discourse. "My past happiness," said she, "appears a dream to me. Yet I cannot forget that I was beloved by the greatest and most lovely of mankind. I was chosen from all the rest, to make all his campaigns with him; I would not survive him, if I was not passionately fond of the princess my daughter. Yet all my tenderness for her was hardly enough to make me preserve my life. When I lost him, I passed a whole twelvemonth without seeing the light. Time has softened my despair; yet I now pass some days every week in tears, devoted to the memory of my Sultan."

There was no affectation in these words. It was easy to see she was in a deep melancholy, though her good humour made her willing to divert me.

She asked me to walk in her garden, and one of her slaves immediately brought her a *pellice*[9] of rich brocade lined with sables. I waited on her into the garden, which had nothing in it remarkable but the fountains; and from thence she shewed me all her apartments. In her bed-chamber her toilet was displayed, consisting of two looking-glasses, the frames covered with pearls, and her night *talpoche* set with bodkins of jewels, and near it three vests of fine sables, every one of which is, at least, worth a thousand dollars (two hundred pounds English money). I don't doubt these rich habits were purposely placed in sight, but they seemed negligently thrown on the sofa. When I took my leave of her, I was complimented with perfumes, as at the Grand Vizier's, and presented with a very fine embroidered handkerchief. Her slaves were to the number of thirty, besides ten little ones, the eldest not above seven years old. These were the most beautiful girls I ever saw, all richly dressed; and I observed that the Sultana took a great deal of pleasure in these lovely children, which is a vast expense; for there is not a handsome girl of that age to be bought under a hundred

---

[7] *kyslár agá:* The chief eunuch of the seraglio and key official of the court.

[8] the Sultan: Mustafa II, who died in 1703.

[9] *pellice:* A long cloak lined with fur.

pounds sterling. They wore little garlands of flowers, and their own hair, braided, which was all their head-dress; but their habits all of gold stuffs. These served her coffee, kneeling; brought water when she washed, &c. It is a great part of the business of the older slaves to take care of these girls, to learn them to embroider, and serve them as carefully as if they were children of the family.

Now, do I fancy that you imagine I have entertained you, all this while, with a relation that has, at least, received many embellishments from my hand? This is but too like (say you) the Arabian Tales: these embroidered napkins! and a jewel as large as a turkey's egg! — You forget, dear sister, those very tales were written by an author of this country, and (excepting the enchantments) are a real representation of the manners here. We travellers are in very hard circumstances: If we say nothing but what has been said before us, we are dull, and we have observed nothing. If we tell any thing new, we are laughed at as fabulous and romantic, not allowing for the difference of ranks, which afford difference of company, more curiosity, or the changes of customs, that happen every twenty years in every country. But people judge of travellers exactly with the same candour, good nature, and impartiality, they judge of their neighbours upon all occasions. For my part, if I live to return amongst you, I am so well acquainted with the morals of all my dear friends and acquaintance, that I am resolved to tell them nothing at all, to avoid the imputation (which their charity would certainly incline them to) of my telling too much. But I depend upon your knowing me enough to believe whatever I seriously assert for truth; though I give you leave to be surprised at an account so new to you.

But what would you say if I told you, that I have been in a harém, where the winter apartment was wainscoted with inlaid work of mother-of-pearl, ivory of different colours, and olive wood, exactly like the little boxes you have seen brought out of this country; and those rooms designed for summer, the walls all crusted with japan china, the roofs gilt, and the floors spread with the finest Persian carpets? Yet there is nothing more true; such is the palace of my lovely friend, the fair Fatima, whom I was acquainted with at Adrianople. I went to visit her yesterday; and, if possible, she appeared to me handsomer than before. She met me at the door of her chamber, and, giving me her hand with the best grace in the world — "You Christian ladies," said she, with a smile that made her as handsome as an angel, "have the reputation of inconstancy, and I did not expect, whatever goodness you expressed for me at Adrianople, that I should ever see you again. But I am now convinced that I have really the happiness of pleasing you; and, if you knew how I speak of you amongst our ladies, you would be assured that you do me justice if you think me your friend." She placed me in the corner of the sofa, and I spent the afternoon in her conversation, with the greatest pleasure in the world.

The Sultana Hafiteń is, what one would naturally expect to find a Turkish lady, willing to oblige, but not knowing how to go about it; and it is easy to see in her manner, that she has lived secluded from the world. But Fatima has all the politeness and good breeding of a court; with an air that inspires, at once, respect and tenderness; and now I understand her language, I find her wit as engaging as her beauty. She is very curious after the manners of other countries, and has not that partiality for her own, so common to little minds. A Greek that I carried with me, who had never seen her before, (nor could have been admitted now, if she had not been in my train,) shewed that surprise at her beauty and manner which is unavoidable at the first sight, and said to me in Italian, "This is no Turkish lady, she is certainly some Christian." Fatima guessed she spoke of her, and asked what she said. I would not have told, thinking she would have been no better pleased with the compliment than one of our court beauties to be told she had the air of a Turk; but the Greek lady told it her; and she smiled, saying, "It is not the first time I have heard so: My mother was a Poloneze, taken at the siege of Caminiec;[10] and my father used to rally me, saying, He believed his Christian wife had found some Christian gallant; for I had not the air of a Turkish girl." I assured her, that, if all the Turkish ladies were like her, it was absolutely necessary to confine them from public view, for the repose of mankind; and proceeded to tell her what a noise such a face as hers would make in London or Paris. "I can't believe you," replied she agreeably; "if beauty was so much valued in your country as you say, they would never have suffered you to leave it." Perhaps, dear sister, you laugh at my vanity in repeating this compliment; but I only do it as I think it very well turned, and give it you as an instance of the spirit of her conversation.

Her house was magnificently furnished, and very well fancied; her winter rooms being furnished with figured velvet on gold grounds, and those for summer with fine Indian quilting embroidered with gold. The houses of the great Turkish ladies are kept clean with as much nicety as those in Holland. This was situated in a high part of the town; and from the windows of her summer apartment we had the prospect of the sea, the islands, and the Asian mountains. . . .

---

[10]**Camieniec:** A chief town in the Russian district of Podolio, a part of the Ottoman empire since 1672; it had long been a site of fighting between Poles and Turks. Turkey lost Camieniec to Russia in 1795.

∾ DENIS DIDEROT
B. FRANCE, 1713–1784

Denis Diderot was born in 1713 in the Champagne region of France and educated in Jesuit schools; eventually he moved to Paris where he completed his Masters of Arts in 1732, after which he supported himself primarily by tutoring, translating, and writing. In 1751, Diderot, along with Jean d'Alembert, began a twenty-year project to complete the *Encyclopedia,* which aimed to tabulate and catalog all that was known in philosophy, science, the arts, and the trades. Diderot also wrote novels and philosophical treatises, including *Rameau's Nephew* (not published until 1823), *The Dream of d'Alembert* (1769), and the *Supplement to The Voyage of Bougainville* (completed in 1772 but not published until more than twenty years later).

Diderot began the *Supplement* as a review of Louis Antoine de Bougainville's *Voyage around the World* (1771), describing the French explorer's voyage made between 1766 and 1769. The first Frenchman to sail around the world, Bougainville described the expulsion of the Jesuits from Paraguay in 1768, an event he witnessed, and he refuted the popular view (stemming from accounts of Magellan's[1] visit to Patagonia) that the natives of Tierra del Fuego were giants. Like other European travelers to the South Seas, Bougainville described Tahiti as a kind of terrestrial paradise. In the European imagination, the people of the South Seas were thought to live an idyllic life of ease and sexual freedom, released by nature's bounty from the necessity for labor and happily imitating natural law in their social practices.

In the *Supplement,* Diderot blends the conventions of the TRAVEL NARRATIVE with those of philosophical dialogue, as he sets up a conversation between two unidentified Frenchmen, "A" and "B." They report the testimony of a Tahitian chieftain, who predicts the demise of his people and customs, as well as a dialogue between a French priest and a Tahitian named Orou. This conversation, part of which we include here, contrasts European customs and religious mores with those of Tahiti as a means of weighing the merits of natural law, as Diderot imagines it to be practiced among the islanders. The sexual freedom of the Tahitians starkly contrasts with the taboo-ridden practices of the Europeans, represented by the Almoner, whose natural desires come into conflict with the artificial laws of civil and religious authority. These laws, Diderot suggests, lead to hypocrisy, since European men and women still secretly follow the compelling urges of that greater force—natural law. Diderot's depiction of the European as a person tormented by the struggle between natural desires and artificial moral constraints in some ways anticipates Nietzsche's[2] analysis of morality and Freud's[3] conception of the conflict between the unconscious and the conscious.

Our selection begins just after one of the speakers has described the arrival of Bougainville's vessel in Tahiti, at which time the Tahitians put on a lavish "spectacle of hospitality" for their visitors. The unnamed priest has been invited into the home of Orou, where the dramatized conflict between natural and artificial man, represented by Orou and the Almoner, begins. As their conversation proceeds, the text invites questions about how much Diderot's text plays to the curiosity of his European readers, and how much to their philosophical interests.

A note on the translation: The translation by Jean Stewart and Jonathan Kemp reprinted here faithfully reproduces the dialogue between Orou and the Almoner. All notes are the editors'.

> Whether you burn or don't burn in your country doesn't matter to me. But you will not judge the morals of Europe by those of Tahiti, nor, consequently, the morals of Tahiti by those of Europe.
>
> – OROU TO THE ALMONER in Diderot's *Supplement to the Voyage of Bougainville*

---

[1]**Magellan:** Ferdinand Magellan (c. 1480–1521), Portuguese-born explorer and navigator who led the first voyage around the world, leaving from Spain in 1519 and reaching Patagonia, the Marianas, and the Philippines, where he was killed.

[2]**Nietzsche:** Friedrich Wilhelm Nietzsche (1844–1900), German philosopher known for his attack on the "slave morality" of Judaeo-Christian culture and his commentary on the condition of modern humanity; his works include *Thus Spake Zarathustra* (1883–91) and *Beyond Good and Evil* (1886).

[3]**Freud:** Sigmund Freud (1856–1939), Austrian psychiatrist and founder of the modern practice of psychoanalysis; his writings on dreams, the ego, the id, and the unconscious created a revolution in the understanding of human behavior.

FROM

~ Supplement to the Voyage of Bougainville

Translated by Jean Stewart and Jonathan Kemp

3. DISCUSSION BETWEEN THE ALMONER AND OROU

B: In the sharing of Bougainville's crew among the Tahitians, the almoner was allotted to Orou; they were about the same age, thirty-five to thirty-six. Orou had then only his wife and three daughters, called Asto, Palli, and Thia. They undressed the almoner, bathed his face, hands, and feet, and served him a wholesome and frugal meal. When he was about to go to bed, Orou, who had been absent with his family, reappeared, and presenting to him his wife and three daughters, all naked, said: "You have eaten, you are young and in good health; if you sleep alone you will sleep badly, for man needs a companion beside him at night. There is my wife, there are my daughters; choose the one who pleases you best. But if you wish to oblige me you will give preference to the youngest of my daughters, who has not yet had any children." The mother added: "Alas! But it's no good complaining about it; poor Thia! it is not her fault."

The almoner answered that his religion, his office, good morals, and decency would not allow him to accept these offers.

Orou replied: "I do not know what this thing is that you call 'religion'; but I can only think ill of it, since it prevents you from tasting an innocent pleasure to which nature, the sovereign mistress, invites us all; prevents you from giving existence to one of your own kind, from doing a service which a father, mother, and children all ask of you, from doing something for a host who has received you well, and from enriching a nation, by giving it one more citizen. I do not know what this thing is which you call your 'office' but your first duty is to be a man and to be grateful. I do not suggest that you should introduce into your country the ways of Orou, but Orou, your host and friend, begs you to lend yourself to the ways of Tahiti. Whether the ways of Tahiti are better or worse than yours is an easy question to decide. Has the land of your birth more people than it can feed? If so your ways are neither worse nor better than ours. But can it feed more than it has? Our ways are better than yours. As to the sense of decency which you offer as objection, I understand you; I agree that I was wrong, and I ask your pardon. I do not want you to injure your health; if you are tired, you must have rest; but I hope that you will not continue to sadden us. See the care you have made appear on all these faces; they fear lest you should have found blemishes on them which merit your disdain. But when it is only the pleasure of doing honour to one of my daughters, amidst her companions and sisters, and of doing a good action, won't that suffice you? Be generous!"

THE ALMONER: It's not that: they are all equally beautiful; but my religion! my office!

OROU: They are mine and I offer them to you; they are their own and they give themselves to you. Whatever may be the purity of conscience which the thing "religion" and the thing "office" prescribe, you can accept them without scruple. I am not abusing my authority at all; be sure that I know and respect the rights of the individual."

Here the truthful almoner agrees that Providence had never exposed him to such violent temptation. He was young, he became agitated and tormented; he turned his eyes away from the lovely suppliants, and then regarded them again; he raised his hands and eyes to the sky. Thia, the youngest, clasped his knees and said: "Stranger, do not distress my father and mother, do not afflict me. Honour me in the hut, among my own people; raise me to the rank of my sisters, who mock me. Asto, the eldest, already had three children; the second, Palli, has two; but Thia has none at all. Stranger, honest stranger, do not repulse me; make me a mother, make me a child that I can one day lead by the hand, by my side, here in Tahiti; who may be seen held at my breast in nine months' time; one of whom I shall be so proud and who will be part of my dowry when I go from my parents' hut to another's. I shall perhaps be more lucky with you than with our young Tahitians. If you will grant me this favour I shall never forget you; I shall bless you all my life. I shall write your name on my arm and on your son's; we shall pronounce it always with joy. And when you leave these shores, my good wishes will go with you on the seas till you reach your own land."

The candid almoner said that she clasped his knees, and gazed into his eyes so expressively and so touchingly; that she wept; that her father, mother, and sisters withdrew; that he remained alone with her, and that, still saying "my religion, my office," he found himself the next morning lying beside the young girl, who overwhelmed him with caresses, and who invited her parents and sisters, when they came to their bed in the morning, to join their gratitude to hers. Asto and Palli, who had withdrawn, returned bringing food, fruits and drink. They kissed their sister and made vows over her. They all ate together.

Then Orou, left alone with the almoner, said to him:

"I see that my daughter is well satisfied with you and I thank you. But would you teach me what is meant by this word 'religion' which you have repeated so many times and so sorrowfully?"

The almoner, after having mused a moment answered: "Who made your hut and the things which furnish it?"

OROU: I did.

THE ALMONER: Well then, we believe that this world and all that it contains is the work of a maker.

OROU: Has he feet, hands, and a head then?

THE ALMONER: No.

OROU: Where is his dwelling-place?

THE ALMONER: Everywhere.

OROU: Here too?

THE ALMONER: Here.

OROU: We have never seen him.

THE ALMONER: One doesn't see him.

OROU: That's an indifferent father, then! He must be old, for he will at least be as old as his work.

THE ALMONER: He does not age. He spoke to our ancestors, gave them laws, prescribed the manner in which he wished to be honoured; he ordered a certain behaviour as being good, and he forbade them certain other actions as being wicked.

OROU: I follow you; and one of the actions he forbade them, as wicked, was to lie with a woman or a girl? Why, then, did he make two sexes?

THE ALMONER: That they might unite; but with certain requisite conditions, after certain preliminary ceremonies in consequence of which the man belongs to the woman and only to her; and the woman belongs to the man, and only to him.

OROU: For their whole lives?

THE ALMONER: For the whole of their lives.

OROU: So that if it happened that a woman should lie with a man other than her husband, or a husband with another woman . . . but that couldn't happen. Since the maker is there and this displeases him, he will know how to prevent them doing it.

THE ALMONER: No; he lets them do it, and they sin against the law of God (for it is thus we call the great maker) against the law of the country; and they commit a crime.

OROU: I should be sorry to offend you by what I say, but if you would permit me, I would give you my opinion.

THE ALMONER: Speak.

OROU: I find these singular precepts opposed to nature and contrary to reason, made to multiply crimes and to plague at every moment this old maker, who has made everything, without help of hands, or head, or tools, who is everywhere and is not seen anywhere, who exists to-day and to-morrow and yet is not a day older, who commands and is not obeyed, who can prevent and yet does not do so. Contrary to nature because these precepts suppose that a free, thinking, and sentient being can be the property of a being like himself. On what is this law founded? Don't you see that in your country they have confused the thing which has neither consciousness nor thought, nor desire, nor will; which one picks up, puts down, keeps or exchanges, without injury to it, or without its complaining, have confused this with the thing which cannot be exchanged or acquired, which has liberty, will, desire, which can give or refuse itself for a moment or for ever, which laments and suffers, and which cannot become an article of commerce, without its character being forgotten and violence done to its nature; contrary to the general law of existence? In fact, nothing could appear to you more senseless than a precept which refuses to admit that change which is a part of us, which commands a constancy which cannot be found there and which violates the liberty of the male and female by chaining them for ever to each other; more senseless than a fidelity which limits the most capricious of enjoyments to one individual; than an oath of the immutability of two beings made of flesh; and all that in the face of a sky which never for a moment remains the same, in caverns which threaten destruction, below a rock which falls to powder, at the foot of a tree which cracks, on a stone which rocks? Believe me, you have made the condition of man worse than that of animals. I do not know what your great maker may be; but I rejoice that he has never spoken to our forefathers, and I wish that he may never speak to our children; for he might tell them the same foolishness, and they commit the folly of believing it. Yesterday, at supper, you mentioned "magistrates" and "priests," whose authority regulates your conduct; but, tell me, are they the masters of good and evil? Can they make what is just to be unjust, and unjust, just? Does it rest with them to attribute good to harmful actions, and evil to innocent or useful actions? You could not think it, for, at that rate, there would be neither true nor false, good nor bad, beautiful nor ugly; or at any rate only what pleased your great maker, your magistrates and your priests to pronounce so. And from one moment to another you would be obliged to change your ideas and your conduct. One day someone would tell you, on behalf of one of your three masters, to kill, and you would be obliged by your conscience to kill; another day, "steal," and you would have to steal; or "do not eat this fruit" and you would not dare to eat it; "I forbid you this vegetable or animal" and you would take care not to touch them. There is no good thing that could not be forbidden you, and no wickedness that you could not be ordered to do. And what would you be reduced to, if your three masters, disagreeing among themselves, should at once permit, enjoin, and forbid you the same thing, as I believe must often happen. Then, to please the priest you must become embroiled with the magistrate; to satisfy the magistrate you must displease the great maker; and to make yourself agreeable to the great maker you must renounce nature. And do you know what will happen then? You will neglect all of them, and you will be neither man, nor citizen, nor pious; you will be nothing; you will be out of favour with all the kinds of authorities, at odds even with yourself, tormented by your heart, persecuted by your enraged masters; and wretched as I saw you yesterday evening when I offered my wife and daughters to you, and you cried out, "But my religion, my office!"

Do you want to know what is good and what is bad in all times and in all places? Hold fast to the nature of things and of actions; to your relations with your fellows; to the influence of your conduct on your individual usefulness and the general good. You are mad if you believe that there is anything, high or low in the universe, which can add to or subtract from the laws of nature. Her eternal will is that good should be preferred to evil, and the general good to the individual good. You may ordain the opposite but you will not be obeyed. You will multiply the number of malefactors and the wretched by fear, punishment, and remorse. You will deprave consciences; you will corrupt minds. They will not know what to do or what to avoid. Disturbed in their state of innocence, at ease with crime, they will have lost their guiding star. . . .

MIRZA ABU TALEB KHAN
B. INDIA, 1752–?1806

Like the Chinese after the "Great Withdrawal" of 1433, Hindus in India were discouraged if not prohibited from traveling overseas. Unlike the Chinese, however, whose isolation resulted from a governmental edict, Hindus, especially those of the highest castes, restricted travel because they believed that contact with foreigners was unclean. Indian Muslims, however, such as Mirza Abu Taleb Khan, gave in to their desire to travel. Indeed, because all members of Islam are enjoined to undertake a pilgrimage to Mecca at least once in their lives, Muslims were accustomed to long journeys, often across strange lands.

As the British presence in and administrative control of India increased, curiosity about Britain intensified. Abu Taleb, born at Lucknow in 1752, is one of the first Indians to leave behind a narrative of his travels to England. He worked for some time as a government employee in Bengal and Oudh, and after being forced early into retirement, he joined the service of the British and moved to Calcutta. When it became clear he would not achieve the high post that he had hoped for, he accepted an invitation to travel to England.

Abu Taleb spent three years in England, where he was put on display to the king and queen and where he became a favorite with some English aristocrats who entertained him as "the Persian prince." His account of these years, *Travels of Mirza Abu Taleb Khan,* was written upon his return to Calcutta in 1803 and published in an English translation by Charles Stewart in 1810. It records what he found remarkable and different in England, gives us a sense of his attraction to life in high society, and shows his disdain of European religion and philosophy. While documenting the curious habits of the English and praising their technological advances and manufacturing abilities, he attacks their apparent greed and their want of religious feeling and humility. As he explains in his introductory remarks, he hopes that his account would both entertain his readers and provide them with some examples of useful English practices.

A note on the translation: This is the Charles Stewart translation, originally published in 1810. Thus the capitalization, punctuation, and spelling reflect those of early-nineteenth-century written English. All notes are the editors'.

It . . . occurred to him, that if he were to write all the circumstances of his journey through Europe, to describe the curiosities and wonders which he saw, and to give some account of the manners and customs of the various nations he visited, all of which are little known to Asiatics, it would afford a gratifying banquet to his countrymen.

– ABU TALEB, *Travels*

FROM

∾ Travels of Mirza Abu Taleb Khan

Translated by Charles Stewart

In the Name of the Most merciful God

INTRODUCTION

Glory be to God, the Lord of all worlds, who has conferred innumerable blessings on mankind, and accomplished all the laudable desires of his creatures. Praise be also to the Chosen of Mankind, the traveller over the whole expanse of the heavens, (Mohammed), and benedictions without end on his descendants and companions.

The wanderer over the face of the earth, Abu Taleb the son of Mohammed of Ispahan, begs leave to inform the curious in biography, that, owing to several adverse circumstances, finding it inconvenient to remain at home, he was compelled to undertake many tedious journeys; during which, he associated with men of all nations, and beheld various wonders, both by sea and by land.

It therefore occurred to him, that if he were to write all the circumstances of his journey through Europe, to describe the curiosities and wonders which he saw, and to give some account of the manners and customs of the various nations he visited, all of which are little known to Asiatics, it would afford a gratifying banquet to his countrymen.

He was also of opinion, that many of the customs, inventions, sciences, and ordinances of Europe, the good effects of which are apparent in those countries, might with great advantage [be] imitated by Mohammedans. . . .

A few weeks subsequent to my visit to Mr. Dundas,[1] I had the honour of being introduced to the King; and on the following day was presented to her most gracious Majesty Queen Charlotte. Both of these illustrious personages received me in the most condescending manner, and, after having honoured me with some conversation, commanded me to come frequently to court. After this introduction, I received invitations from all the Princess; and the Nobility vied with each other in their attention to me. Hospitality is one of the most esteemed virtues of the English; and I experienced it to such a degree, that I was seldom disengaged. In these parties I enjoyed every luxury my heart could desire. Their viands were delicious, and wines exquisite. The beauty of the women, and their grace in dancing, delighted my imagination; while the variety and melody of their music charmed all my senses.

I may perhaps be accused of personal vanity by saying, that my society was courted, and that my wit and repartees, with some *impromptu* applications of

---

[1]Before moving to London, Abu Taleb landed in Dublin where he spent several months among the Irish. **Henry Dundas** (1742–1811) was Member of Parliament for Midlothian and later for Edinburgh, Scotland; Dundas held various offices, including home secretary and secretary of war, in the ministry of William Pitt, then prime minister. **George III** (r. 1760–1820) was king of Great Britain; **Queen Charlotte** (1744–1818) was his wife. Abu Taleb had recently been a guest at Dundas's country estate at Wimbledon.

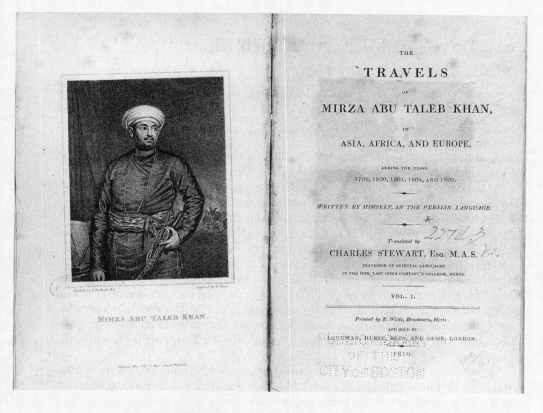

Portrait of Mirza Abu Taleb Khan and Frontispiece to *Travels of Mirza Abu Taleb Khan,* Vol. I., 1810

The English translation of Abu Taleb's Travels *was published in 1810, seven years after he completed the journey undertaken from 1799 to 1803. (Courtesy of the Trustees of the Boston Public Library)*

Oriental poetry, were the subject of conversation in the politest circles. I freely confess, that, during my residence in England, I was so exhilarated by the coolness of the climate and so devoid of all care, that I followed the advice of our immortal poet Hafiz,[2] and gave myself up to love and gaiety. . . .

When I first arrived in London, it had been my determination to have opened a Public Academy to be patronized by Government, for instructing such of the English as were destined to fill important situations in the East, in the Hindoostany, Persian, and Arabic languages. The plan I proposed was, that I should commence with a limited number of pupils, selected for the purpose, who were not to go abroad; but, each of these to instruct a number of others: thus as one candle may

---

[2]**Hafiz:** Shams al-Din Hafiz (c. 1320–90), a master of the *ghazal;* often considered to be the greatest lyric poet in the Persian language.

light a thousand, so I hoped to have spread the cultivation of the Persian language all over the kingdom. By these means I expected to have passed my time in England in a rational and advantageous manner; beneficial both to myself, and to the nation I came to visit. I therefore took an early opportunity of mentioning the subject to the Ministers of the Empire: but whether it was owing to their having too many other affairs to attend to, or that they did not give my plan that consideration which, from its obvious utility, it deserved, I met with no encouragement. What rendered their indifference on this subject very provoking, was: many individuals were so desirous of learning the Oriental languages, that they attended self-taught masters, ignorant of every principle of the science, and paid them half-a-guinea a lesson. . . .

Oxford is a very ancient city, and the most celebrated *Seat of Learning* of the Empire. All the public buildings are constructed of hewn stone, and much resemble in form some of the Hindoo temples. The streets are very wide and regular, and several of them are planted on each side with trees. In this place are assembled the most learned men of the nation, and students come here from all parts.

There are twenty-three different colleges, each containing an extensive library. In *one* of these libraries I saw nearly 10,000 Arabic and Persian manuscripts. The collective name of these twenty-three colleges is *The University,* meaning an assemblage of all the sciences. For the use of the University, a very magnificent *Observatory* has been erected, with much philosophical and astronomical skill. It contains a great variety of instruments, and some very large telescopes.

There is here, also, a large building for the sole use of anatomy. One of the Professors did me the favour to shew me every part of this edifice, and to explain many of the mysteries of this useful science, which afforded me very great satisfaction. In the hall, were suspended the skeletons not only of men, women, and children, but also of all species of animals. In another apartment was as exact representation of all the veins, arteries, and muscles of the human body, filled with red and yellow wax, minutely imitating Nature. The Professor particularly pointed out to me the great nerve, which, commencing at the head, runs down the back-bone, where it divides it into four great branches, one of which extends down each arm, and leg, to the ends of the fingers and toes. In another room were, preserved in spirits, several bodies of children, who had something peculiar in their conformation. One of these *lusus Nature*[3] had two heads and four feet, but only one body. The mother having died in the act of parturition, the womb, with the children, was cut out, and preserved entire. . . .

CHAPTER XIX

It now becomes an unpleasant, and perhaps ungrateful, part of my duty, by complying with the positive desire of Lady Spenser[4] and several other of my friends, to

---

[3]*lusus Nature*: *Lusus Naturae* is Latin for *a freak of nature.*

[4]Lady Spenser: Abu Taleb most likely refers to Lady Caroline Spencer (1743–1811), wife of George Spencer, (1739–1811), Fourth Duke of Marlborough, who lived at Blenheim.

mention those defects and vices which appeared to me to pervade the English character, but which, perhaps, only existed in my own imagination. If the hints I shall
give are not applicable, I hope they will be attributed to want of judgement, rather
than to malice or ingratitude: but if my suggestions are acknowledged to be correct,
I trust they (the English) will thank me for my candour, and endeavour to amend
their errors.

VERSE

He is your friend, who, like a mirror, exhibits all your defects:
Not he, who, like a comb, covers them over with the hairs of flattery.

As my experience and knowledge of the common people were chiefly acquired
in London, it may, and with great probability, be objected, that there are more
vicious people to be found in the capital than in all the rest of the empire.

The first and greatest defect I observed in the English, is their want of faith in religion, and their great inclination to philosophy (atheism). The effects of these principles, or rather want of principle, is very conspicuous in the lower orders of people,
who are totally devoid of honesty. They are, indeed, cautious how they transgress
against the laws, from fear of punishment; but whenever an opportunity offers of pur-
loining any thing without the risk of detection, they never pass it by. They are also ever
on the watch to appropriate to themselves the property of the rich, who, on this
account, are obliged constantly to keep their doors shut, and never to permit an unknown person to enter them. At present, owing to the vigilance of the magistrates, the
severity of the laws, and the honour of the superior classes of people, no very bad consequences are to be apprehended; but if ever such nefarious practices should become
prevalent, and should creep in among the higher classes, inevitable ruin must ensue.

The second defect, most conspicuous in the English character, is pride, or insolence. Puffed up with their power and good fortune for the last fifty years, they are
not apprehensive of adversity, and take no pains to avert it. Thus, when the people of
London, some time ago, assembled in mobs on account of the great increase of taxes
and high price of provisions, and were nearly in a state of insurrection,—although
the magistrates, by their vigilance in watching them, and by causing parties of soldiers to patrole the streets day and night, to disperse all persons whom they saw
assembling together, succeeded in quieting the disturbance,—yet no pains were
afterwards taken to eradicate the evil. Some of the men in power said, it had been
merely a plan of the artificers to obtain higher wages (an attempt frequently made by
the English tradesmen); others were of opinion that no remedy could be applied;
therefore no further notice was taken of the affair. All this, I say, betrays a blind confidence, which, instead of meeting the danger, and endeavouring to prevent it, waits
till the misfortune arrives, and then attempts to remedy it. Such was the case with
the late King of France,[5] who took no step to oppose the Revolution, till it was too

---

[5]**late King of France:** Louis XVI (r. 1774–1792), king of France during the French Revolution, imprisoned and
guillotined on January 21, 1793.

late. This self-confidence is to be found, more or less, in every Englishman: it how-ever differs much from the pride of the Indians and Persians.

Their third defect is a passion for acquiring money, and their attachment to worldly affairs. Although these bad qualities are not so reprehensible in them as in countries more subject to the vicissitudes of fortune, (because, in England, property is so well protected by the laws, that every person reaps the fruits of his industry, and, in his old age, enjoys the earnings or economy of his youth,) yet sordid and illiberal habits are generally found to accompany avarice and parsimony, and, conse-quently, render the possessor of them contemptible: on the contrary, generosity, if it does not launch into prodigality, but is guided by the hand of prudence, will render a man respected and esteemed.

The fourth of their frailities is a desire of ease, and a dislike to exertion: this, however, prevails only in a moderate degree, and bears no proportion to the apathy and indolence of the smokers of opium of Hindoostan and Constantinople; it only prevents them from perfecting themselves in science, and exerting themselves in the service of their friends, upon what they *choose* to call trivial occasions. I must, how-ever, remark, that friendship is much oftener cemented by acts of courtesy and good-nature, than by conferring permanent obligations; the opportunities of doing which can seldom occur, whereas the former happen daily. In London, I had some-times occasion to trouble my friends to interpret for me, in the adjustment of my accounts with my landlord and others; but, in every instance, I found that, rather than be at the trouble of stopping for five minutes longer, and saying a few words in my defence, they would yield to an unjust demand, and offer to pay the items I objected to at their own expence: at the same time, an aversion to the employment of interpreter or mediator was so conspicuous in their countenance, that, latterly, I desisted from troubling them. In this respect I found the French much more courte-ous; for if, in Paris, the master of an hotel attempted to impose on me, the gentlemen present always interfered, and compelled him to do me justice.

Upon a cursory observation of the conduct of gentlemen in London, you would suppose they had a vast deal of business to attend to; whereas nine out of ten, of those I was acquainted with at the west end of the town, had scarcely any thing to do. An hour or two immediately after breakfast may be allotted to business, but the rest of the day is devoted to visiting and pleasure. If a person calls on any of these gentle-men, it is more than probable he is told by the servant, his master is *not at home;* but this is merely an idle excuse, to avoid the visits of people, whose business they are either ignorant of, or do not wish to be troubled with. If the suppliant calls in the morning; and is by chance admitted to the master of the house, before he can tell half his story, he is informed, that it is now the hour of business, and a particular engagement in the city requires the gentleman's immediate attendance. If he calls later in the day, the gentleman is just going out to pay a visit of consequence, and therefore cannot be detained: but if the petitioner, unabashed by such checks, con-tinues to relate his narrative, he is set down as a brute, and never again permitted to enter the doors. In this instance, I again say that the French are greatly superior to the English; they are always courteous, and never betray those symptoms of impa-tience so conspicuous and reprehensible in the English character.

Their fifth defect is nearly allied to the former, and is termed irritability of temper. This passion often leads them to quarrel with their friends and acquaintances, without any substantial cause. Of the bad effects of this quality, strangers seldom have much reason to complain; but as society can only be supported by mutual forbearance, and sometimes shutting our eyes on the frailties or ignorance of our friends, it often causes animosities and disunion between the nearest relatives, and hurries the possessor into dilemmas whence he frequently finds it difficult to extricate himself.

The sixth defect of the English is their throwing away their time, in sleeping, eating, and dressing; for, besides the necessary ablutions, they every morning shave, and dress their hair; then, to accommodate themselves to the fashion, they put on twenty-five different articles of dress: all this, except shaving, is repeated before dinner, and the whole of these clothes are again to be taken off at night: so that not less than two complete hours can be allowed on this account. One hour is expended at breakfast; three hours at dinner; and the three following hours are devoted to tea, and the company of the ladies. Nine hours are given up to sleep: so that there remain just six hours, out of the twenty-four, for visiting and business. If they are reproached with this waste of time, they reply, "How is it to be avoided?" I answer them thus: "Curtail the number of your garments; render your dress simple; wear your beards; and give up less of your time to eating, drinking, and sleeping."

Their seventh defect is a luxurious manner of living, by which their wants are increased a hundred-fold. Observe their kitchens, filled with various utensils; their rooms, fitted up with costly furniture; their side-boards, covered with plate; their tables, loaded with expensive glass and china; their cellars, stocked with wines from every quarter of the world; their parks, abounding in game of various sorts; and their ponds, stored with fish. All these expences are incurred to pamper their appetites, which, from long indulgence, have gained such absolute sway over them, that a diminution of these luxuries would be considered, by many, as a serious misfortune. How unintelligible to them is the verse of one of their own Poets:

> Man wants but little here below,
> Nor wants that little long.

It is certain, that luxurious living generates many disorders, and is productive of various other bad consequences.

If the persons above alluded to will take the trouble of reading the history of the Arabians and Tartars, they will discover that both these nations acquired their extensive conquests, not by their numbers, nor by the superiority of their arms, which were merely bows and arrows, and swords: no, it was from the paucity of their wants: they were always prepared for action, and could subsist on the coarsest food. Their chiefs were content with the fare of their soldiers, and their personal expences were a mere trifle. Thus, when they took possession of an enemy's country they ever found the current revenue of it more than requisite for their simple but effective form of government; and, instead of raising the taxes on their new subjects, they frequently alleviated one half their burthen. The approach of their armies, therefore, instead of being dreaded, was wished for by the neighbouring people, and every facility given to their conquests. To this alone must be ascribed the rapidity with which they over-ran great part of the globe, in so short a period. . . .

The eighth defect of the English is vanity, and arrogance, respecting their acquirements in science, and a knowledge of foreign languages, for, as soon as one of them acquires the smallest insight into the principles of any science, or the rudiments of any foreign language, he immediately sits down and composes a work on the subject, and, by means of the Press, circulates books which have no more intrinsic worth than the toys bestowed on children, which serve to amuse the ignorant, but are of no use to the learned. This is not merely my own opinion, but was confirmed to me both by Greeks and Frenchmen, whose languages are cultivated in England with more ardour than any others. Such, however, is the infatuation of the English, that they give the author implicit credit for his profound knowledge, and purchase his books. Even those who are judges of the subject do not discountenance this measure, but contend, that a little knowledge is better than entire ignorance, and that perfection can only be acquired by degrees. This axiom I deny; for the portion of science and truth contained in many of their books is so small, that much time is thrown away in reading them: besides, erroneous opinions and bad habits are often contracted by the perusal of such works, which are more difficult to eradicate, than it is to implant correct ideas in a mind totally uncultivated.

Far be it from me to depreciate the transcendant abilities and angelic character of Sir William Jones;[6] but his Persian Grammar, having been written when he was a young man, and previous to his having acquired any experience in Hidoostan, is, in many places, very defective; and it is much to be regretted that his public avocations, and other studies, did not permit him to revise it, after he had been some years in India. Whenever I was applied to by any person for instruction in the Persian language who had previously studied this grammar, I found it much more difficult to correct the bad pronunciation he had acquired, and the errors he had adopted, than it was to instruct a person who had never before seen the Persian alphabet. Such books are now so numerous in London, that, in a short time, it will be difficult to discriminate or separate them from works of real value.

A ninth failing prevalent among the English is selfishness. They frequently endeavour to benefit themselves, without attending to the injury it may do to others: and when they seek their own advantage, they are more humble and submissive than appears to me proper; for after they have obtained their object, they are either ashamed of their former conduct, or dislike the continuance of it so much, that they frequently break off the connection. Others, restrained by a sense of propriety, still keep up the intercourse, and endeavour to make the person they have injured, or whom they have deceived by promises, forget the circumstance, by their flattering and courteous behavior. . . .

---

[6]Sir William Jones (1746–94): An English jurist and philologist who served for eleven years as a justice in Calcutta; with an expert knowledge of more than thirteen languages, he was one of the leading translators in England of Arabic, Persian, and Sanskrit literature, including poems from the Persian poet Hafiz and the *Shakuntula* by the Indian writer Kalidasa (fifth century C.E.).

The tenth vice of this nation is want of chastity; for under this head I not only include the reprehensible conduct of young women running away with their lovers, and others cohabiting with a man before marriage, but the great degree of licentiousness practised by numbers of both sexes in London; evinced by the multiplicity of public-houses and bagnios in every part of the town. I was credibly informed, that in the single parish of Mary-la-bonne,[7] which is only a sixth part of London, there reside sixty thousand courtezans; besides which, there is scarcely, a street in the metropolis where they are not to be found. The conduct of these women is rendered still more blameable, by their hiring lodgings in or frequenting streets which from their names ought only to be the abode of virtue and religion; for instance, "Paradise Street," "Modest Court," "St. James's Street," "St. Martin's Lane," and "St. Paul's Churchyard." The first of these is to be the residence of the righteous; the second implies virtue; and the others are named after the holy Apostles of the Blessed Messiah. Then there is Queen Anne Street, and Charlotte Street; the one named after the greatest, the other after the best, of Queens. I however think, that persons who let the lodgings are much more reprehensible than the unfortunate women themselves.

The eleventh vice of the English is extravagance, that is, living beyond their incomes by incurring useless expences, and keeping up unnecessary establishments. Some of these I have before alluded to, under the head of luxuries; but to those are now to be added the establishments of carriages, horses, and servants, two sets of which are frequently kept, one for the husband, the other for his wife. Much money is also lavished in London, on balls, masquerades, routs etc. Sometimes the sum of £1000 is thus expended in one night's entertainment. I have known gentlemen in the receipt of six or seven thousand pounds a year, who were so straitened by such inconsiderate expences, that if asked by a friend for the loan of *ten pounds,* could not comply with this trifling request. This spirit of extravagance appears daily to increase; and being imitated by merchants and tradesmen, must have the worst of consequences; for if these people find the profits of their trade not sufficient to support their expences, they will attempt to supply the deficiency by dishonest means, and at length take to highway robbery. It also encourages dissipation and profligacy in the lower classes, which tend to the subversion of all order and good government. . . .

Their twelfth defect is a contempt for the customs of other nations, and the preference they give to their own; although theirs, in fact, may be much inferior. I had a striking instance of this prejudice in the conduct of my fellow-passengers on board ship. Some of these, who were otherwise respectable characters, ridiculed the idea of my wearing trowsers, and a night dress, when I went to bed; and contended, that they slept much more at their ease by going to bed nearly naked. I replied, that I slept very comfortably; that mine was certainly the most decent mode; and that, in the event of any sudden accident happening, I could run on deck instantly, and, if requisite, jump into the boat in a minute; whilst they must either lose some time in dressing, or come out of their cabins in a very immodest manner. In answer to this, they said, such sudden accidents seldom occurred, but that if it did happen, they

---

[7]**Mary-la-bonne:** Marylebone is a district in north London.

would not hesitate to come on deck in their shirts only. This I give merely as a specimen of their obstinacy, and prejudice in favour of their own customs.

In London, I was frequently attacked on the apparent unreasonableness and childishness of some of the Mohammedan customs; but as, from my knowledge of the English character, I was convinced it would be folly to argue the point philosophically with them, I contended myself with parrying the subject. Thus, when they attempted to turn into ridicule the ceremonies used by the pilgrims on their arrival at Mecca, I asked them, why they supposed the ceremony of baptism, by a clergyman, requisite for the salvation of a child, who could not possibly be sensible what he was about. When they reproached us for eating with our hands; I replied, "There is by this mode no danger of cutting yourself or your neighbours; and it is an old and a true proverb, 'The nearer the bone, the sweeter the meat': but, exclusive of these advantages, a man's own hands are surely cleaner than the *feet of a baker's boy;* for it is well known, that half the bread in London is kneaded by the feet." By this mode of argument I, completely silenced all my adversaries, and frequently turned the laugh against them, when they expected to have refuted me and made me appear ridiculous.

Many of these vices, or defects, are not natural to the English; but have been ingrafted on them by prosperity and luxury; the bad consequences of which have not yet appeared; and, for two reasons, may not be conspicuous for some time. The first of these is the strength of constitution both of individuals and of the Government: for if a person of a strong constitution swallow a dose of poison, its deleterious effects are sometimes carried off by the power of the nerves; but if a weak person should take it, he would certainly fall a victim. The second reason is, that their neighbours are not exempt from these vices; nay, possess them in a greater proportion. Our poet Sady[8] has said,

> To the inhabitants of Paradise, Purgatory would seem a Hell:
> But to Sinners in Hell, Purgatory would be a Paradise.

From what I saw and heard of the complaints and dissatisfaction of the common people in England, I am convinced, if the French had succeeded in establishing a happy and quiet government, whereby the taxes could have been abolished, and the price of provisions reduced, the English would, of themselves, have followed their example, and united with them: for, even during the height of the war, many of the English imitated the fashions, follies, and vices of the French, to an absurd degree.

Few of the English have good sense or candour enough to acknowledge the prevalence and growth of these vices, or defects, among them; but, like the smokers of *beng* (hempseed) in Turkey, when told of the virtues of their ancestors, and their own present degeneracy, make themselves ready for battle, and say, "No nation was ever exempt from vices: the people and the governments you describe as possessing such angelic virtues were not a bit better than ourselves; and so long as we are not worse than our neighbours, no danger is to be apprehended." This reasoning is, however, false; for fire still retains its inflammable nature, whether it is summer or

---

[8]**Sady:** S'adi (c. 1219–91), one of the greatest of the Persian poets, known for his *Gulistan* (The Rose Garden).

winter; and the flame, though for a short time smothered by a heap of fuel thrown on it, breaks out in the sequel with the greatest violence. In like manner, vice will, sooner or later, cause destruction to its possessor.

CHAPTER XX

I fear, in the foregoing Chapter, I have fatigued my readers with a long detail of the vices, or defects of the English: I shall, therefore, now give some account of their virtues; but, lest I should be accused of flattery, will endeavour to avoid prolixity on this subject.

The first of the English virtues is a high sense of honour, especially among the better classes. This is the effect of a liberal education, and of the contempt with which those who do not possess it are regarded. . . .

Their second good quality is a reverence for every thing or person possessing superior excellence. This mode of thinking has this great advantage—it makes them emulous of acquiring the esteem of the world, and thus renders them better men. . . .

The third of their perfections is a dread of offending against the rules of propriety, or the laws of the realm: they are therefore generally content with their own situations, and very seldom attempt to exalt themselves by base or nefarious practices. By these means the establishments of Church and State are supported, and the bonds of society strengthened; for when men are ambitious of raising themselves from inferior to exalted situations, they attempt to overcome all obstacles; and though a few gain their object, the greater part are disappointed, and become, ever after, unhappy and discontended.

The fourth of their virtues is a strong desire to improve the situations of the common people, and an aversion to do any thing which can injure them. It may be said, that in so doing they are not perfectly disinterested; for that the benefits of many of these institutions and inventions revert to themselves. . . .

Their fifth good quality is so nearly allied to weakness, that by some worldly people it has been called such: I mean, an adherence to the rules of fashion. By this arbitrary law, the rich are obliged not only to alter the shape of their clothes every year, but also to change all the furniture of their houses. It would be thought quite derogatory to a person of taste, to have his drawing room fitted up in the same manner for two successive years. The advantage of this profusion is the encouragement it gives to ingenuity and manufacturers of every kind; and it enables the middling and lower classes of people to supply their wants at a cheap rate, by purchasing the old fashioned articles.

Their sixth excellence is a passion for mechanism, and their numerous contrivances for facilitating labour and industry.

Their seventh perfection is plainness of manners: and sincerity of disposition; the former is evinced in the colours of their clothes, which are generally of a dark hue, and exempt from all tawdriness; and the latter, by their open and manly conduct.

Their other good qualities are good natural sense and soundness of judgement, which induce them to prefer things that are useful to those that are brilliant; to which may be added, their perseverance in the acquirement of science, and the attainment of wealth and honours.

Their hospitality is also very praiseworthy, and their attention to their guests can nowhere be exceeded. They have an aversion to sit down to table *alone;* and from their liberal conduct on this subject, one would suppose the following verse had been written by an Englishman:

> May the food of the misanthrope be cast to the dogs!
> May he who eats alone be shortly eaten by the worms!

It is said, that all these virtues were formerly possessed in a greater degree by the English, and that the present race owe much of their fame and celebrity to their ancestors.

The English have very peculiar opinions on the subject of *perfection.* They insist, that it is merely an ideal quality, and depends entirely upon comparison; that mankind have risen, by degrees, from the state of savages to the exalted dignity of the great philosopher NEWTON:[9] but that, so far from having yet attained *perfection,* it is possible that, in future ages, philosophers will look with as much contempt on the acquirements of Newton, as we now do on the rude state of the arts among savages. If this axiom of theirs be correct, man has yet much to learn, and all his boasted knowledge is but vanity.

---

[9]**Newton:** Sir Isaac Newton (1642–1727), English physicist and mathematician known for his discovery and formulation of the laws of gravity and the development of calculus; his greatest work is the *Mathematical Principles of Natural Philosophy,* or *Principia Mathematica* (1687).

❧ SOR JUANA INÉS DE LA CRUZ
B. MEXICO, 1648–1695

WAH-nah ee-NEZ de la
KROOZ

fee-loh-TAY-ah

One of the most learned intellectuals of New Spain during the Colonial era, Sor **Juana Inés de la Cruz** has become widely recognized as one of her era's greatest writers. Sor Juana distinguished herself as a poet with a facility in many poetic forms, a dramatist of both sacred and secular plays, and a prose writer of treatises on theology and music. Her most famous treatise, the *Response to the Most Illustrious Poetess Sor **Filotea** de la Cruz* (1691), finds a place among such renowned testimonials to the love of learning as Ibn Sinna's (Avicenna) *Autobiography* (tenth century), Giovanni Pico della Mirandola's *On the Dignity of Man* (1486), and Niccolo Machiavelli's *Letter to Francesco Vettori* (1513). It also stands out as one of the most eloquent and erudite defenses of women's right to education, along with Mary Astell's *A Serious Proposal to the Ladies* (1694) and Mary Wollstonecraft's *Vindication of the Rights of Woman* (1792).[1] Sor Juana's reputation and her writing circulated throughout colonial Mexico and Spain, where she was known — both honorifically and problematically — as the "Tenth Muse of Mexico." Recently, interest in and acclaim for Sor Juana's writings in Spanish and in translation has undergone a dramatic renewal, in part because of her proto-feminist ideas on women's intellectual freedom and in part because of the enduring art of her poetry and drama.

Child Prodigy. Juana Inés Ramírez de Asbaje was born in San Miguel Nepantla, a small village southeast of Mexico City, in 1648. She was the child of Isabel Ramírez de Santillana, from Meixco, and Pedro Manuel de Abaje, from the Basque region of Spain. They lived on a small hacienda, where the young girl, having learned to read at the age of three, spent much of her time immersed in the books of her grandfather's library. As she tells us in her *Reply to Sor Filotea,* Sor Juana placed high demands upon herself as a scholar and subjected herself to a restricted diet in order to facilitate her learning. When she was about eight years old, she moved to Mexico City to live with her maternal aunt, María Ramírez, whose husband was a successful merchant. In Mexico City, Juana Inés impressed people with her precocious knowledge of diverse topics, and further demonstrated the tremendous intellectual abilities and ardent desire for learning that would endure throughout her life.

Attracting the attention of the court, Juana Inés soon became lady-in-waiting to the Vicereine Leonor Carreto, in the court of the Don

---

[1] **Ibn Sinna . . . Wollstonecraft:** Also Avicenna (980–1037); one of the most important Islamic philosophers of the Middle Ages, whose work attempted to reconcile Greek philosophy with the revelations of the Qur'an and the doctrines of the Hadith, the collected sayings of Muhammad. Giovanni Pico della Mirandola (1463–1494): Italian philosopher. Niccolò Machiavelli (1469–1527): Italian political thinker and author of *The Prince*. Mary Astell (1666–1731): English defender of women's education. Mary Wollstonecraft (1759–1797): One of the most important English feminist writers of the late eighteenth century (see p. 401).

Miguel Cabrera,
1695–1768, Sor Juana
Inés de la Cruz
The great writer of
New Spain is shown
here in her habit at a
writing desk with a
rosary in one hand
and a book in the
other. (The Art
Archive/National
History Museum
Mexico City/Dagli
Orti)

Antonio Sebastian Toledo, the Viceroy of New Spain in Mexico City. While there she wrote plays, occasional verse and panegyric poetry commemorating social and political events, and lyric poetry in the popular baroque style of the era. Although she would not completely sever her ties to the court for many years, in 1667 Sor Juana entered the Carmelite convent of San Jose; after two years she took vows in the Hieronomite order of the convent of Santa Paula, where she remained for the rest of her life. Sor Juana tells us she moved from the court to the convent, despite anticipated interruptions to her studies and intrusions upon "the peaceful silence of [her] books," because she thought the convent would best lead to her salvation. Scholars have suggested that as a lower-class intellectual woman of questionable birth (she was most likely an illegitimate child), outside of marriage the convent was the only option available to her.

Convent and Conflict.   Sor Juana continued her studies while in the convent, reaching into subjects normally outside the sphere of women's education, such as mathematics, logic, and classics. Among her acquaintances was Carlos Sigüenza y Góngora,[2] the leading humanist writer of New Spain

---

[2] **Carlos Sigüenza y Góngora** (1645–1700): Jesuit priest, scholar, newspaper editor, poet, geographer, astronomer, and statesman was the author of books on a variety of subjects; he wrote an elegy upon the death of Sor Juana.

during this time. With him she would likely have discussed matters of astronomy, geography, history, literature, and other topics, including their mutual interest in the language and culture of the indigenous peoples of Mexico. In 1680, Sor Juana befriended María Luisa, countess of Paredes and wife of the new Viceroy, Tomás Antonio de la Cerda, the Marquis de la Laguna. The new viceroy and vicereine encouraged and promoted Sor Juana's work, and when the vicereine returned to Spain in 1688, she helped to get Sor Juana's works published there. Many of Sor Juana's most passionate love lyrics were written for her friend and patroness María Luisa. As her literary and intellectual reputation grew, jealousy and envy led to increasing numbers of attacks upon her work. Among those who disapproved of her writing were the Jesuit priest Antonio Núñez de Miranda, her confessor, and the powerful archbishop Francisco Auguiar y Seijas.

KAR-tah ah-teh-nah-
GOH-ree-kal-kah

The attacks on Sor Juana and efforts to turn her away from writing gained momentum after the publication of Sor Juana's **Carta atenagórica**, "Letter worthy of Athena," in 1690. In this treatise, Sor Juana criticized an influential sermon delivered some forty years earlier by the Portuguese Jesuit priest and orator Antonio de Vieira. The topic of Vieira's sermon was Christ's *fineza*, his expression of love for man signified by washing the feet of his disciples. Sor Juana, taking up the position of the Church Fathers, argued that Christ's greatest *fineza* was in fact his withholding of such favors. Sor Juana had written her critique upon the request of a friend, probably Manuel Fernández de Santa Cruz, Bishop of Puebla, with the understanding that it would not be published. Nonetheless, the Bishop published her treatise, prefaced with his own letter written under the pseudonym of "Sor Filotea de la Cruz" attacking the *Carta's* theology, admonishing Sor Juana for her lack of humility, and ironically chastising her for paying too much attention to worldly rather than spiritual matters. After the publication of her famous *Reply to Sor Filotea* in 1691, Archbishop Siejas, among others, pressed for her to put down her books and pen. Although she wrote a few more poems before her death from the plague in 1694, Sor Juana sold off the books in her extraordinary library as well as her musical and scientific instruments, and she devoted the last years of life to caring for her sisters in the convent. There is some evidence that the strains of self-reproach evidenced in her *Reply* took a firm hold on her conscience; in the convent's register of 1694 she wrote, "Yo, la peor del mundo," —I, Sor Juana, the worst of the world.

The Poems.   Octavio Paz, the eminent Mexican critic, poet, and biographer of Sor Juana, has said that Sor Juana Inés de la Cruz is one of the top five lyric poets of the Spanish language. Sor Juana mastered the range of verse and dramatic forms of sixteenth- and seventeenth-century Spanish literature—known as the Golden Age of Spanish literature.[3] Sor Juana wrote more than twenty-five plays, including full-length sacramental dramas known as *autos,* short one-act plays called *loas,* and sacred comedies.

---

[3] **Golden Age of Spanish literature:** *Siglio de Oro,* the Spanish Golden Age was a period of great cultural and intellectual efflorescence beginning in the late sixteenth century and lasting through the end of the seventeenth century.

The Divine Narcissus, one of her finest *autos,* brilliantly uses the myth of Narcissus to retell allegorically the story of Christ's passion, death, and resurrection; the play's one-act *loa* dramatizes the synthesis of the Christian eucharist and the Aztec festival of the seeds. Thus, the play and its *loa* dramatize Sor Juana's belief in the possibility of reconciliation or synthesis between Christian and pagan ritual and myth. Sor Juana was also a master of the various verse forms circulating in her time, including sonnets, epigrams, romances, and *villancicos,* a form of ballad adapted for religious ceremony. She wrote celebratory poems for the viceregal court, as well as love poems in the style of Spanish lyric poets of the Golden Age such as Luis de Góngora (1561–1627) and Lope de Vega (1562–1635), to whom she has been compared. As with her plays, to her poems Sor Juana often brought Mexican themes and motifs, and in two poems she introduced multiple voicings by mixing Nahuatl and Spanish. Perhaps her most powerful poem, **El Sueño** (*The Dream*), is a highly allusive and complex philosophical meditation on the quest of a soul moving toward more perfect knowledge.

el SWEH-nyoh

Sor Juana's lyrics range from sharp-witted attacks on men's treatment of women to subtle explorations of the emotional extremities of love. In an era that admired the lavish display of highly self-conscious artistry—witty turns of phrase, unexpected metaphors and startling similes, tortuous logic, and rhetorical flourish—Sor Juana held her own among her contemporaries. The two sonnets printed here show affinities with the logical ingenuity and striking conceits—startling metaphors— associated in English poetry with John Donne, who, like Sor Juana, wrote secular love lyrics and devotional poetry. "Love, at First, Is Fashioned of Agitation" is also reminiscent of Shakespeare's sonnets; it invokes an atmosphere of tension and anatomizes love rather than describing the beaituies of the lover. In "The Rhetoric of Tears" Sor Juan creates a stunning conceit in the image of tears as the molten substance of her heart— a palpable testimony to the intensity of her love.

Reply to Sor Filotea.   A subtle display of her wit and learning, couched in a text outwardly testifying to her humility and subservience to the authority of the Church, the *Reply to Sor Filotea,* as it is sometimes called, demonstrates Sor Juana's mastery of language and rhetoric, as well as the breadth of her reading in scripture and theological texts. The autobiographical narrative underlying the *Reply* portrays Sor Juana as a gifted child with an insatiable desire to learn and to exercise her critical intelligence. From the first moment when, in her words, she was "illuminated by the light of reason" her "inclination toward letters has been so vehement, so overpowering, that not even the admonitions of others . . . not my own meditations . . . have been sufficient to cause me to forswear this natural impulse that God placed in me: . . ." Her "inclination," as she calls it, both a curse and a gift from Heaven, was so strong that even when cut off from books she was unable to temper the quick fire of her thoughts; a spinning top and the frying of an egg led her to reflections upon the physics of motion and the chemistry of liquids. As she claims that her studies of subjects as various as logic, rhetoric, physics, geometry, music, and architecture were to better prepare her to understand "the peak of Sacred Theology," she also adduces a host of women both pagan and Christian, such as Hyapatia of Alexandria, Aspasia of Miletus, Saint Paula, and Saint Catherine of Alexandria,[4] all of whom were renowned for their extraordinary learning and intelligence, some of whom were praised for their devotion to study and their writings. By implication, Sor Juana fashions herself as part of that venerable company. Nonetheless, soon after the *Reply to Sor Filotea* was published in 1691, Sor Juana put down her pen. Octavio Paz summed up the *Reply* this way: "A critical autobiography, a defense of her right to learn, and a confession of the limits of all human learning, this text announced her final submission." While some believe that last statement to be too strong, it is true that she wrote very little in the last few years of her life.

The *Reply to Sor Filotea* is less a defense of the *Carta atenagórica* than it is a defense of women's intellectual and educational rights, as well as an intellectual and spiritual autobiography of Sor Juana herself. The logical and rhetorical subtlety and sophistication of the *Reply* as well as its display of her learning—both secular and religious—provides ample evidence of Sor Juana's intelligence and mastery of her craft as a writer. The ambiguities of tone and diction, the unsettled balance between resignation and affirmation, and the constant shifting between secular and religious registers have led to many contradictory interpretations. The *Reply* has been seen as a work of literary self-fashioning and as an act of self-censure; a strategic attack upon patriarchal restrictions for women and a confession of guilt under those very terms; a calculated display of her brilliance and education and a vow of silence. Moreover, throughout the text Sor Juana shifts voices, as if playing many parts in a drama; a sense of contrition gives way to righteous indignation, a profession of ignorance to a celebration of erudite learning. Pride gives way to humility, confession to assertion, and then back again. Throughout, however, the *Reply* gives readers a sense of Sor Juana's life, her dedication to study, her vehement "inclination toward letters," and her diligence and devotion to the arts and sciences that may well have become, as she says, her means to salvation in the next life, but most certainly in this one.

■ FURTHER RESEARCH

Flynn, Gerard. *Sor Juana Inés de la Cruz.* 1971.
Kirk, Pamela. *Sor Juana Inés de la Cruz: Religion, Art, and Feminism.* 1998.
Luciani, Frederick. *Literary Self-Fashioning in Sor Juana Inés de la Cruz.* 2004.
Merrim, Stephanie. *Feminist Perspectives on Sor Juana Inés de la Cruz.* 1999.

---

[4] **Hyapatia of Alexandria** (C. 370–415 C.E.): Egyptian-born Neoplatonist philosopher, mathematician, and teacher. **Aspasia of Miletus** (fifth century B.C.E.): Consort of the Athenian leader Pericles (c. 495–429 B.C.E.) renowned for her skills in rhetoric and knowledge of philosophy. **Saint Paula** (347–404): A Roman widow who joined St. Jerome in the Holy Land, where she founded a nunnery and aided St. Jerome in his studies of Scripture. **Saint Catherine of Alexandria** (fourth century): A Christian martyr renowned for her keen intelligence and philosophical understanding.

———. *Early Modern Women's Writing and Sor Juana Inés de la Cruz.* 1999.

Paz, Octavio. *Sor Juana: Or, the Traps of Faith.* Trans. Margaret Sayers Peden. 1982; rpt. 1990.

■ **PRONUNCIATION**

Carta atenagórica: KAR-tah ah-teh-nah-GOH-ree-kah

El Sueño: el SWEH-nyoh

Filotea: fee-loh-TAY-ah

Juana Inés de la Cruz: WAH-nah ee-NEZ de la KROOZ

~ Love, at First, Is Fashioned of Agitation

Translated by S. G. Morley

Love, at first, is fashioned of agitation,
Ardors, anxiety, and wakeful hours;
By danger, risk, and fear it spreads its power,
And feeds on weeping and on supplication.

It learns from coolness and indifference,
Preserves its life beneath faithless veneers,
Until, with jealousy or with offense,
It extinguishes its fire in its tears.

Love's beginning, middle, and its end are these:
10   Then why, Alcino, does it so displease
That Celia, who once loved you, now should leave you?

Is that a cause for sorrow and remorse?
Alcino mine, no, love did not deceive you:
It merely ran its customary course.

~ The Rhetoric of Tears

Translated by Frank J. Warnke

Tonight, my dearest, when I spoke to thee,
I noted in thy bearing and thy face
That words of mine could not thy doubts erase,
Or prove I wanted thee my heart to see;

Then love, which my avowals came to prop,
Conquered, and the impossible occurred:
I fell to weeping tears which sorrow poured,
Which my melting heart distilled in copious drop.

No more reproaches, ah my love, forbear;
10 Let doubt not hold thee in tormenting bonds,
Nor let vile jealousy thy peace impair
With foolish shades, with vain and useless wounds,
Since thou hast seen and touched a liquid rare—
My molten heart caught up between thy hands.

∾ Response to Sor Filotea

Translated by Margaret Sayers Peden

My most illustrious *señora*, dear lady.[1] It has not been my will, my poor health, or my justifiable apprehension that for so many days delayed my response. How could I write, considering that at my very first step my clumsy pen encountered two obstructions in its path? The first (and, for me, the most uncompromising) is to know how to reply to your most learned, most prudent, most holy, and most loving letter. For I recall that when Saint Thomas, the Angelic Doctor of Scholasticism, was asked about his silence regarding his teacher Albertus Magnus, he replied that he had not spoken because he knew no words worthy of Albertus.[2] With so much greater reason, must not I too be silent? Not, like the Saint, out of humility, but because in reality I know nothing I can say that is worthy of you. The second obstruction is to know how to express my appreciation for a favor as unexpected as extreme, for having my scribblings printed, a gift so immeasurable as to surpass my most ambitious aspiration, my most fervent desire, which even as a person of reason never entered my thoughts. Yours was a kindness, finally, of such magnitude that words cannot express my gratitude, a kindness exceeding the bounds of appreciation,

---

[1] **dear lady:** Sor Filotea was the pseudonym adopted by Manuel Fernández de Santa Cruz, the Bishop of Puebla.
[2] **Saint Thomas . . . Albertus:** Thomas Aquinas (c. 1225–1274) was an eminent Catholic theologian and scholastic philosopher; author of the influential study of Christian doctrine known as the *Summa Theologica* (c. 1266). **Albertus Magnus** (c. 1206–1290): renowned theologian, philosopher and natural scientist; teacher of Aquinas.

A note on the translation: Margaret Sayers Peden's translation of the *Response to Sor Filotea* in this volume is the first translation of the work into the English language, originally commissioned by a small independent press, Lime Rock Press, Inc. of Salisbury, Connecticut. The translation appeared in 1982 in a limited edition volume entitled *A Woman of Genius*, illustrated with photographs by Gabriel North Seymour. The text is copyright 1982 by Lime Rock Press, Inc. and is reprinted here with permission.

as great as it was unexpected—which is as Quintilian[3] said: *aspirations engender minor glory; benefices,*[4] *major.* To such a degree as to impose silence on the receiver.

When the blessedly sterile—that she might miraculously become fecund—Mother of John the Baptist saw in her house such an extraordinary visitor as the Mother of the Word, her reason became clouded and her speech deserted her; and thus, in the place of thanks, she burst out with doubts and questions: *And whence is to me* [*that the mother of my Lord should come to me?*][5] And whence cometh such a thing to *me?* And so also it fell to Saul when he found himself the chosen, the anointed, King of Israel: *Am I not a son of Jemini, of the least tribe of Israel, and my kindred the last among all the families of the tribe of Benjamin? Why then hast thou spoken this word to me?*[6] And thus say I, most honorable lady. Why do I receive such favor? By chance, am I other than an humble nun, the lowliest creature of the world, the most unworthy to occupy your attention? "Wherefore then speakest thou so to me?" "And whence is this to me?"

Nor to the first obstruction do I have any response other than I am little worthy of your eyes; nor to the second, other than wonder, in the stead of thanks, saying that I am not capable of thanking you for the smallest part of that which I owe you. This is not pretended modesty, lady, but the simplest truth issuing from the depths of my heart, that when the letter which with propriety you called *Atenagórica*[7] reached my hands, in print, I burst into tears of confusion (withal, that tears do not come easily to me) because it seemed to me that your favor was but a remonstrance God made against the wrong I have committed, and that in the same way He corrects others with punishment He wishes to subject me with benefices, with this special favor for which I know myself to be His debtor as for an infinitude of others from His boundless kindness. I looked upon this favor as a particular way to shame and confound me, it being the most exquisite means of castigation, that of causing me, by my own intellect, to be the judge who pronounces sentence and who denounces my ingratitude. And thus, when here in my solitude I think on these things, I am wont to say: Blessed art Thou, oh Lord, for Thou hast not chosen to place in the hands of others my judgment, nor yet in mine, but hast reserved that to Thy own, and freed me from myself, and from the necessity to sit in judgment on myself, which judgment, forced from my own intellect, could be no less than condemnation, but Thou hast reserved me to Thy mercy, because Thou lovest me more than I can love myself.

---

[3] Quintilian: Marcus Fabius Quintilian (c. 35 to 100 c.e.) was a leading Roman rhetorician and orator; author of an influential textbook on rhetoric, the *Institutio Oratoria.*

[4] *benefices*: Beneficial or good works.

[5] *[that the . . . come to me]*: The passage refers to the meeting of Elizabeth, mother of John the Baptist, and Mary, mother of Jesus. See Luke 1:39–45.

[6] *Am I . . . word to me?* This is the reply of Saul, the first king of the Israelites, to Samuel, the prophet. See I Samuel 9:15–21.

[7] *Atenagórica*: This title refers to the *Carta atenagórica,* "Letter worthy of Athena," in which Sor Juana criticized the sermon of Father Vieyra. Athena was the Greek goddess of wisdom.

I beg you, lady, to forgive this digression to which I was drawn by the power of truth, and, if I am to confess all the truth, I shall confess that I cast about for some manner by which I might flee the difficulty of a reply, and was sorely tempted to take refuge in silence. But as silence is a negative thing, though it explains a great deal through the very stress of not explaining, we must assign some meaning to it that we may understand what the silence is intended to say, for if not, silence will say nothing, as that is its very office: *to say nothing.* The holy Chosen Vessel, Saint Paul, having been caught up into paradise, and having heard the arcane secrets of God, *heard secret words, which it is not granted to man to utter.*[8] He does not say what he heard, he says that he cannot say it. So that of things one cannot say, it is needful to say at least that they cannot be said, so that it may be understood that not speaking is not the same as having nothing to say, but rather being unable to express the many things there are to say. Saint John says that if all the marvels our Redeemer wrought "were written every one, the world itself, I think, would not be able to contain the books that should be written."[9] And Vieyra[10] says on this point that in this single phrase the Evangelist said more than in all else he wrote; and this same Lusitanian Phoenix speaks well (but when does he not speak well, even when it is not well he speak?) because in those words Saint John said everything left unsaid and expressed all that was left to be expressed. And thus I, lady, shall respond only that I do not know how to respond; I shall thank you in saying only that I am incapable of thanking you; and I shall say, through the indication of what I leave to silence, that it is only with the confidence of one who is favored and with the protection of one who is honorable that I presume to address your magnificence, and if this be folly, be forgiving of it, for folly may be good fortune, and in this manner I shall provide further occasion for your benignity and you will better shape my appreciation.

Because he was halting of speech, Moses thought himself unworthy to speak with Pharaoh, but after he found himself highly favored of God, and thus inspired, he not only spoke with God Almighty but dared ask the impossible: *shew me thy face.*[11] In this same manner, lady, and in view of how you favor me, I no longer see as impossible the obstructions I posed in the beginning: for who was it who had my letter printed unbeknownst to me? Who entitled it, who bore the cost, who honored it, it being so unworthy in itself, and in its author? What will such a person not do, not pardon? What would he fail to do, or fail to pardon? And thus, based on the supposition that I speak under the safe-conduct of your favor, and with the assurance of

---

[8] **The holy Chosen Vessel . . . to utter:** 2 Corinthians 12:4 and throughout 2 Corinthians 10–13; here St. Paul discusses the relative merits of humility and boasting——a passage highly pertinent to Sor Juana's purpose here.

[9] **Saint John says . . . should be written:** John 21:25.

[10] **Vieyra:** The Portuguese Jesuit Antonio Vieira (1608–1697) wrote the popular sermon on Christ's greatest gift (*fineza*) that Sor Juana challenged in the *Carta atenagórica.* She refers to him in the next sentence as the Lusitanian, that is, Portuguese, Phoenix. Sor Juana was known as the Mexican Phoenix.

[11] *shew me thy face*: In Exodus 33:12–23, Moses asks the Lord to show him His face or His ways, and the Lord responds that Moses may see His back, but not His face.

your benignity and with the knowledge that like a second Ahasuerus[12] you have offered to me to kiss the top of the golden scepter of your affection as a sign of conceding to me your benevolent license to speak and offer judgments in your exalted presence, I say to you that I have taken to heart your most holy admonition that I apply myself to the study of the Sacred Books, which, though it comes in the guise of counsel, will have for me the authority of a precept, but with the not insignificant consolation that even before your counsel I was disposed to obey your pastoral suggestion, as your direction, which may be inferred from the premise and arguments of my Letter. For I know well that your most sensible warning is not directed against it, but rather against those worldly matters of which I have written. And thus I had hoped with the Letter to make amends for any lack of application you may (with great reason) have inferred from others of my writings; and, speaking more particularly, I confess to you with all the candor of which you are deserving, and with the truth and clarity which are the natural custom in me, that my not having written often of sacred matters was not caused by disaffection or by want of application, but by the abundant fear and reverence due those Sacred Letters, knowing myself incapable of their comprehension and unworthy of their employment. Always resounding in my ears, with no little horror, I hear God's threat and prohibition to sinners like myself. *Why dost thou declare my justices, and take my covenant in thy mouth?*[13] This question, as well as the knowledge that even learned men are forbidden to read the Canticle of Canticles[14] until they have passed thirty years of age, or even Genesis—the latter for its obscurity, the former in order that the sweetness of those epithalamia not serve as occasion for imprudent youth to transmute their meaning into carnal emotion, as borne out by my exalted Father Saint Jerome,[15] who ordered that these be the last verses to be studied, and for the same reason: *And finally, one may read without peril the Song of Songs, for if it is read early one may suffer harm through not understanding those Epithalamia of the spiritual wedding which is expressed in carnal terms.* And Seneca[16] says: *In the early years the faith is dim.* For how then would I have dared take in my unworthy hands these verses, defying

---

[12] **Ahasuerus:** The king of Persia (often identified with Xerxes I [486–465 B.C.E.]). In the Book of Esther, Ahasuerus banished his first wife, Vashti, for disobedience and later fell in love with and made Esther his queen. Esther convinced Ahasuerus to execute Haman, his prime minister, in place of her cousin Mordecai, thus becoming known as a protector of the Jews. See Esther 5:2–3 and 8:4 where the king acknowledges his favor to Esther by extending his golden scepter.

[13] *Why dost . . . thy mouth?*: Psalms 50:16.

[14] **Canticle of Canticles:** Song of Songs, or, the Song of Solomon.

[15] **Father Saint Jerome** (c. 342–420): An early Church Father, theologian, and translator (from Greek and Hebrew into Latin) of the Vulgate Bible, the Latin version standard throughout the Middle Ages and the Renaissance. Sor Juana belonged to the Hieronymite Order, also known as the Order of St. Jerome. The quotation is from his Epistle 107, to the Roman matron Laeta, advising her on the education of her daughter known as Paula the Younger.

[16] **Seneca:** Lucius Annaeus Seneca (c. 4 B.C.E. to 63 C.E.), a Roman philosopher, dramatist, and senator; author of tragedies, dialogues, and letters on a wide variety of topics.

gender, age, and, above all, custom? And thus I confess that many times this fear has plucked my pen from my hand and has turned my thoughts back toward the very same reason from which they had wished to be born: which obstacle did not impinge upon profane matters, for a heresy against art is not punished by the Holy Office but by the judicious with derision, and by critics with censure, and censure, *just or unjust, is not to be feared,* as it does not forbid the taking of communion or hearing of mass, and offers me little or no cause for anxiety, because in the opinion of those who defame my art, I have neither the obligation to know nor the aptitude to triumph. If, then, I err, I suffer neither blame nor discredit: I suffer no blame, as I have no obligation; no discredit, as I have no possibility of triumphing — *and no one is obliged to do the impossible.* And, in truth, I have written nothing except when compelled and constrained, and then only to give pleasure to others; not alone without pleasure of my own, but with absolute repugnance, for I have never deemed myself one who has any worth in letters or the wit necessity demands of one who would write; and thus my customary response to those who press me, above all in sacred matters, is, what capacity of reason have I? what application? what resources? what rudimentary knowledge of such matters beyond that of the most superficial scholarly degrees? Leave these matters to those who understand them; I wish no quarrel with the Holy Office,[17] for I am ignorant, and I tremble that I may express some proposition that will cause offense or twist the true meaning of some scripture. I do not study to write, even less to teach — which in one like myself were unseemly pride — but only to the end that if I study, I will be ignorant of less. This is my response, and these are my feelings.

I have never written of my own choice, but at the urging of others, to whom with reason I might say, *You have compelled me.*[18] But one truth I shall not deny (first, because it is well-known to all, and second, because although it has not worked in my favor, God has granted me the mercy of loving truth above all else), which is that from the moment I was first illuminated by the light of reason, my inclination toward letters has been so vehement, so overpowering, that not even the admonitions of others — and I have suffered many — nor my own meditations — and they have not been few — have been sufficient to cause me to forswear this natural impulse that God placed in me: the Lord God knows why, and for what purpose. And He knows that I have prayed that He dim the light of my reason, leaving only that which is needed to keep His Law, for there are those who would say that all else is unwanted in a woman, and there are even those who would hold that such knowledge does injury. And my Holy Father knows too that as I have been unable to achieve this (my prayer has not been answered), I have sought to veil the light of my reason — along with my name — and to offer it up only to Him who bestowed it upon me, and He knows that none other was the cause for my entering into

---

[17] **Holy Office:** The Office of the Inquisition.

[18] *You have compelled me:* 2 Corinthians 12:11. The complete text broadens the implications: "I am become a fool in glorying; ye have compelled me: for I ought to have been commended of you: for in nothing am I behind the very chiefest apostles, though I be nothing."

Religion, notwithstanding that the spiritual exercises and company of a community were repugnant to the freedom and quiet I desired for my studious endeavors. And later, in that community, the Lord God knows—and, in the world, only the one who must know[19]—how diligently I sought to obscure my name, and how this was not permitted, saying it was temptation: and so it would have been. If it were in my power, lady, to repay you in some part what I owe you, it might be done by telling you this thing which has never before passed my lips, except to be spoken to the one who should hear it. It is my hope that by having opened wide to you the doors of my heart, by having made patent to you its most deeply-hidden secrets, you will deem my confidence not unworthy of the debt I owe to your most august person and to your most uncommon favors.

Continuing the narration of my inclinations, of which I wish to give you a thorough account, I will tell you that I was not yet three years old when my mother determined to send one of my elder sisters to learn to read at a school for girls we call the *Amigas.* Affection, and mischief, caused me to follow her, and when I observed how she was being taught her lessons I was so inflamed with the desire to know how to read, that deceiving—for so I knew it to be—the mistress, I told her that my mother had meant for me to have lessons too. She did not believe it, as it was little to be believed, but, to humor me, she acceded. I continued to go there, and she continued to teach me, but now, as experience had disabused her, with all seriousness; and I learned so quickly that before my mother knew of it I could already read, for my teacher had kept it from her in order to reveal the surprise and reap the reward at one and the same time. And I, you may be sure, kept the secret, fearing that I would be whipped for having acted without permission. The woman who taught me, may God bless and keep her, is still alive and can bear witness to all I say.

I also remember that in those days, my tastes being those common to that age, I abstained from eating cheese because I had heard that it made one slow of wits, for in me the desire for learning was stronger than the desire for eating—as powerful as that is in children. When later, being six or seven, and having learned how to read and write, along with all the other skills of needlework and household arts that girls learn, it came to my attention that in Mexico City there were Schools, and a University, in which one studied the sciences. The moment I heard this, I began to plague my mother with insistent and importunate pleas: she should dress me in boy's clothing and send me to Mexico City to live with relatives, to study and be tutored at the University. She would not permit it, and she was wise, but I assuaged my disappointment by reading the many and varied books belonging to my grandfather, and there were not enough punishments, nor reprimands, to prevent me from reading: so that when I came to the city many marveled, not so much at my natural wit, as at my memory, and at the amount of learning I had mastered at an age when many have scarcely learned to speak well.

I began to study Latin grammar—in all, I believe, I had no more than twenty lessons—and so intense was my concern that though among women (especially a

---

[19] **In the world . . . must know:** Her confessor at the time was Antonio Núñez de Miranda.

woman in the flower of her youth) the natural adornment of one's hair is held in such high esteem, I cut off mine to the breadth of some four to six fingers, measuring the place it had reached, and imposing upon myself the condition that if by the time it had again grown to that length I had not learned such and such a thing I had set for myself to learn while my hair was growing, I would again cut it off as punishment for being so slow-witted. And it did happen that my hair grew out and still I had not learned what I had set for myself—because my hair grew quickly and I learned slowly—and in fact I did cut it in punishment for such stupidity: for there seemed to me no cause for a head to be adorned with hair and naked of learning—which was the more desired embellishment. And so I entered the religious order, knowing that life there entailed certain conditions (I refer to superficial, and not fundamental, regards) most repugnant to my nature; but given the total antipathy I felt for marriage, I deemed convent life the least unsuitable and the most honorable I could elect if I were to insure my salvation. Working against that end, first (as, finally, the most important) was the matter of all the trivial aspects of my nature that nourished my pride, such as wishing to live alone, and wishing to have no obligatory occupation that would inhibit the freedom of my studies, nor the sounds of a community that would intrude upon the peaceful silence of my books. These desires caused me to falter some while in my decision, until certain learned persons enlightened me, explaining that they were temptation, and, with divine favor, I overcame them, and took upon myself the state which now so unworthily I hold. I believed that I was fleeing from myself, but—wretch that I am!—I brought with me my worst enemy, my inclination, which I do not know whether to consider a gift or a punishment from Heaven, for once dimmed and encumbered by the many activities common to Religion, that inclination exploded in me like gunpowder, proving how *privation is the source of appetite.*

I turned again (which is badly put, for I never ceased), I continued, then, in my studious endeavour (which for me was respite during those moments not occupied by my duties) of reading and more reading, of study and more study, with no teachers but my books. Thus I learned how difficult it is to study those soulless letters, lacking a human voice or the explication of a teacher. But I suffered this labor happily for my love of learning. Oh, had it only been for love of God, which were proper, how worthwhile it would have been! I strove mightily to elevate these studies, to dedicate them to His service, as the goal to which I aspired was to study Theology—it seeming to me debilitating for a Catholic not to know everything in this life of the Divine Mysteries that can be learned through natural means—and, being a nun and not a layperson, it was seemly that I profess my vows to learning through ecclesiastical channels; and especially, being a daughter of a Saint Jerome and a Saint Paula,[20] it was essential that such erudite parents not be shamed by a

---

[20] **Saint Paula** (c. 347–404 C.E.): A wealthy Roman widow who met St. Jerome at Rome in 382. In 385, following behind Jerome, she and her daughter Eustochium made a pilgrimage to the Holy Land and Egypt before settling in Bethlehem, where she founded a nunnery alongside the monastery founded by St. Jerome. There Paula mastered Hebrew and aided St. Jerome in his studies of Scripture, and serves here as another example of a learned woman. She is the grandmother of Paula the Younger (see note 15).

witless daughter. This is the argument I proposed to myself, and it seemed to me well-reasoned. It was, however (and this cannot be denied) merely glorification and approbation of my inclination, and enjoyment of it offered as justification.

And so I continued, as I have said, directing the course of my studies toward the peak of Sacred Theology, it seeming necessary to me, in order to scale those heights, to climb the steps of the human sciences and arts; for how could one undertake the study of the Queen of Sciences if first one had not come to know her servants? How, without Logic, could I be apprised of the general and specific way in which the Holy Scripture is written? How, without Rhetoric, could I understand its figures, its tropes, its locutions? How, without Physics, so many innate questions concerning the nature of animals, their sacrifices, wherein exist so many symbols, many already declared, many still to be discovered? How should I know whether Saul's being refreshed by the sound of David's harp was due to the virtue and natural power of Music, or to a transcendent power God wished to place in David?[21] How, without Arithmetic, could one understand the computations of the years, days, months, hours, those mysterious weeks communicated by Gabriel to Daniel,[22] and others for whose understanding one must know the nature, concordance, and properties of numbers? How, without Geometry,[23] could one measure the Holy Arc of the Covenant[24] and the Holy City of Jerusalem, whose mysterious measures are foursquare in all their dimensions, as well as the miraculous proportions of all their parts? How, without Architecture, could one know the great Temple of Solomon, of which God Himself was the Author who conceived the disposition and the design, and the Wise King but the overseer who executed it, of which temple there was no foundation without mystery, no column without symbolism, no cornice without allusion, no architrave without significance; and similarly others of its parts, of which the least fillet was never intended solely for the service and complement of Art, but as symbol of greater things? How, without great knowledge of the laws and parts of which History is comprised, could one understand historical Books? Or those recapitulations in which many times what happened first is seen in the narrated account to have happened later? How, without great learning in Canon and Civil Law, could one understand Legal Books? How, without great erudition, could one apprehend the secular histories of which the Holy Scripture makes mention, such as the many customs of the Gentiles, their many rites, their many ways of

---

[21] **How should I know . . . place in David?:** The music from David's harp drove out an evil spirit visited upon King Saul. See 1 Samuel 16:14–23.

[22] **Gabriel to Daniel:** In the Book of Daniel, the angel Gabriel appears several times to Daniel to interpret Daniel's visions, many of which involve arithmetical and chronological detail; see Daniel 9:21–27, for example.

[23] **Geometry:** Sor Juana's list of subjects that she must master to lead her toward the ultimate goal of "Sacred Theology" adapts and expands upon the medieval system of education divided into the trivium (grammar, rhetoric, and logic) and quadrivium (arithmetic, geometry, music, astronomy), the study of which, in Latin, prepared students to advance to the study of theology.

[24] **Holy Arc of the Covenant:** This sacred chest, adorned with gold and the figures of two cherubim, contains the stone tablets of the Ten Commandments; see Exodus 25:10–22.

speaking? How without the abundant laws and lessons of the Holy Fathers could one understand the obscure lesson of the Prophets? And without being expert in Music, how could one understand the exquisite precision of the musical proportions that grace so many Scriptures, particularly those in which Abraham beseeches God in defense of the Cities,[25] asking whether He would spare the place were there but fifty just men therein; and then Abraham reduced that number to five less than fifty, forty-five, which is a ninth, and is as Mi to Re; then to forty, which is a tone, and is as Re to Mi; from forty to thirty, which is a diatessaron, the interval of the perfect fourth; from thirty to twenty, which is the perfect fifth, and from twenty to ten, which is the octave, the diapason; and as there are no further harmonic proportions, made no further reductions. How might one understand this without Music? And there in the Book of Job, God says to Job: *Shalt thou be able to join together the shining stars the Pleiades, or canst thou stop the turning about of Arcturus? Canst thou bring forth the day star in its time and make the evening star to rise upon the children of the earth?*[26] Which message, without knowledge of Astrology, would be impossible to apprehend. And not only these noble sciences; there is no applied art that is not mentioned. And, finally, in consideration of the Book that comprises all books, and the Science in which all sciences are embraced, and for whose comprehension all sciences serve, and even after knowing them all (which we now see is not easy, nor even possible), there is one condition that takes precedence over all the rest, which is uninterrupted prayer and purity of life, that one may entreat of God that purgation of spirit and illumination of mind necessary for the understanding of such elevated matters: and if that be lacking, none of the aforesaid will have been of any purpose.

Of the Angelic Doctor Saint Thomas the Church affirms: *When reading the most difficult passages of the Holy Scripture, he joined fast with prayer. And he was wont to say to his companion Brother Reginald that all he knew derived not so much from study or his own labor as from the grace of God.* How then should I — so lacking in virtue and so poorly read — find courage to write? But as I had acquired the rudiments of learning, I continued to study ceaselessly divers subjects, having for none any particular inclination, but for all in general; and having studied some more than others was not owing to preference, but to the chance that more books on certain subjects had fallen into my hands, causing the election of them through no discretion of my own. And as I was not directed by preference, nor, forced by the need to fulfill certain scholarly requirements, constrained by time in the pursuit of any subject, I found myself free to study numerous topics at the same time, or to leave some for others; although in this scheme some order was observed, for some I deigned study and others diversion, and in the latter I found respite from the former. From which it follows that though I have studied many things I know nothing, as some have inhibited the learning of others. I speak specifically of the practical aspect of those arts that

---

[25] **Abraham beseeches God in defense of the Cities:** Abraham asks God whether or not He will spare Sodom from destruction on behalf of the righteous; see Genesis 18:23–33.

[26] *Shalt thou . . . children of the earth?*: Job 38:31–32.

allow practice, because it is clear that when the pen moves the compass must lie idle, and while the harp is played the organ is stilled, *et sic de caeteris.*[27] And because much practice is required of one who would acquire facility, none who divides his interest among various exercises may reach perfection. Whereas in the formal and theoretical arts the contrary is true, and I would hope to persuade all with my experience, which is that one need not inhibit the other, but, in fact, each may illuminate and open the way to others, by nature of their variations and their hidden links, which were placed in this universal chain by the wisdom of their Author in such a way that they conform and are joined together with admirable unity and harmony. This is the very chain the ancients believed did issue from the mouth of Jupiter, from which were suspended all things linked one with another, as is demonstrated by the Reverend Father Athanasius Kircher in his curious book, *De Magnate.*[28] All things issue from God, Who is at once the center and the circumference from which and in which all lines begin and end.

   I myself can affirm that what I have not understood in an author in one branch of knowledge I may understand in a second in a branch that seems remote from the first. And authors, in their elucidation, may suggest metaphorical examples in other arts: as when logicians say that to prove whether parts are equal, the mean is to the extremes as a determined measure to two equidistant bodies; or in stating how the argument of the logician moves, in the manner of a straight line, along the shortest route, while that of the rhetorician moves, as a curve, by the longest, but that both finally arrive at the same point. And similarly, as it is when they say that the Expositors are like an open hand, and the Scholastics like a closed fist. And thus it is no apology, nor do I offer it as such, to say that I have studied many subjects, seeing that each augments the other; but that I have not profited is the fault of my own ineptitude and the inadequacy of my intelligence, not the fault of the variety. But what may be offered as exoneration is that I undertook this great task without benefit of teacher, or fellow students with whom to confer and discuss, having for a master no other than a mute book, and for a colleague, an insentient inkwell; and in the stead of explication and exercise, many obstructions, not merely those of my religious obligations (for it is already known how useful and advantageous is the time employed in them), rather, all the attendant details of living in a community: how I might be reading, and those in the adjoining cell would wish to play their instruments, and sing; how I might be studying, and two servants who had quarreled would select me to judge their dispute; or how I might be writing, and a friend come to visit me, doing me no favor but with the best of will, at which time one must not only accept the inconvenience, but be grateful for the hurt. And such occurrences are the normal state of affairs, for as the times I set apart for study are those remaining after the ordinary duties of the community are

---

[27] *et sic de caeteris*: And so for other things.

[28] *De Magnate*: Athanasius Kircher (1602–1680), a seventeenth-century German Jesuit known for his great erudition and the vast scope of his knowledge ranging from Egyptology to the natural sciences. His *De Magnate,* or *Magnes* (1641), compiled what was known of magnetism and electricity in his time and describes a magnetic clock that he designed.

fulfilled, they are the same moments available to my sisters, in which they may come to interrupt my labor; and only those who have experience of such a community will know how true this is, and how it is only the strength of my vocation that allows me happiness; that, and the great love existing between me and my beloved sisters, for as love is union, it knows no extremes of distance.

With this I confess how interminable has been my labor; and how I am unable to say what I have with envy heard others state—that they have not been plagued by the thirst for knowledge: blessed are they. For me, not the knowing (for still I do not know), merely the desiring to know, has been such torment that I can say, as has my Father Saint Jerome (although not with his accomplishment) . . . *my conscience is witness to what effort I have expended, what difficulties I have suffered, how many times I have despaired, how often I have ceased my labors and turned to them again, driven by the hunger for knowledge; my conscience is witness, and that of those who have lived beside me.*[29] With the exception of the companions and witnesses (for I have been denied even this consolation), I can attest to the truth of these words. And to the fact that even so, my dark inclination has been so great that it has conquered all else!

It has been my fortune that, among other benefices, I owe to God a most tender and affable nature, and because of it my sisters (who being good women do not take note of my faults) hold me in great affection, and take pleasure in my company; and knowing this, and moved by the great love I hold for them—having greater reason than they—I enjoy even more *their* company. Thus I was wont in our rare idle moments to visit among them, offering them consolation and entertaining myself in their conversation. I could not help but note, however, that in these times I was neglecting my study, and I made a vow not to enter any cell unless obliged by obedience or charity; for without such a compelling constraint—the constraint of mere intention not being sufficient—my love would be more powerful than my will. I would (knowing well my frailty) make this vow for the period of a few weeks, or a month, and when that time had expired, I would allow myself a brief respite of a day or two before renewing it, using that time not so much for rest (for *not* studying has never been restful for me) as to assure that I not be deemed cold, remote, or ungrateful in the little-deserved affection of my dearest sisters.

In this practice one may recognize the strength of my inclination. I give thanks to God, Who willed that such an ungovernable force be turned toward letters and not to some other vice. From this it may also be inferred how obdurately against the current my poor studies have sailed (more accurately, have foundered). For still to be related is the most arduous of my difficulties—those mentioned until now, either compulsory or fortuitous, being merely tangential—and still unreported the more-directly aimed slings and arrows that have acted to impede and prevent the exercise of my study. Who would have doubted, having witnessed such general approbation, that I sailed before the wind across calm seas, amid the laurels of widespread

---

[29] *my conscience . . . beside me*: From St. Jerome, Letter to Rusticus (Letter 125).

acclaim. But our Lord God knows that it has not been so; He knows how from amongst the blossoms of this very acclaim emerged such a number of aroused vipers, hissing their emulation and their persecution, that one could not count them. But the most noxious, those who most deeply wounded me, have not been those who persecuted me with open loathing and malice, but rather those who in loving me and desiring my well-being (and who are deserving of God's blessing for their good intent) have mortified and tormented me more than those others with their abhorrence. "Such studies are not in conformity with sacred innocence; surely she will be lost; surely she will, by cause of her very perspicacity and acuity, grow heady at such exalted heights." How was I to endure? An uncommon sort of martyrdom in which I was both martyr and executioner.

And as for my (in me, twice hapless) facility in making verses, even though they be sacred verses, what sorrows have I not suffered? What sorrows not ceased to suffer? Be assured, lady, it is often that I have meditated on how one who distinguishes himself—or one on whom God chooses to confer distinction, for it is only He who may do so—is received as a common enemy, because it seems to some that he usurps the applause they deserve, or that he dams up the admiration to which they aspired, and so they persecute that person.

That politically barbaric law of Athens by which any person who excelled by cause of his natural gifts and virtues was exiled from his Republic in order that he not threaten the public freedom still endures, is still observed in our day, although not for the reasons held by the Athenians. Those reasons have been replaced by another, no less efficient though not as well founded, seeming, rather, a maxim more appropriate to that impious Machiavelli[30]—which is to abhor one who excels, because he deprives others of regard. And thus it happens, and thus it has always happened.

For if not, what was the cause of the rage and loathing the Pharisees directed against Christ, there being so many reasons to love Him? If we behold His presence, what is more to be loved than that Divine beauty? What more powerful to stir one's heart? For if ordinary human beauty holds sway over strength of will, and is able to subdue it with tender and enticing vehemence, what power would Divine beauty exert, with all its prerogatives and sovereign endowments? What might move, what affect, what not move and not affect, such incomprehensible beauty, that beauteous face through which, as through a polished crystal, were diffused the rays of Divinity? What would not be moved by that semblance which beyond incomparable human perfections revealed Divine illuminations? If the visage of Moses, merely from conversation with God, caused men to fear to come near him, how much finer must be the face of God-made-flesh?[31] And among other virtues, what more to be loved than

---

[30] **Machiavelli:** Niccolò Machiavelli (1469–1527), Italian statesman, historian, and political philosopher, wrote the controversial book *The Prince,* enumerating expedient measures by which a ruler should gain and secure power.

[31] **If the visage . . . God-made-flesh?:** Exodus 34:29–30.

that celestial modesty? That sweetness and kindness disseminating mercy in every movement? That profound humility and gentleness? Those words of eternal life and eternal wisdom? How therefore is it possible that such beauty did not stir their souls, that they did not follow after Him, enamored and enlightened?

The Holy Mother, my Mother Teresa,[32] says that when she beheld the beauty of Christ, never again was she inclined toward any human creature, for she saw nothing that was not ugliness compared to such beauty. How was it then that in men it engendered such contrary reactions? For although they were uncouth and vile and had no knowledge or appreciation of His perfections, not even as they might profit from them, how was it they were not moved by the many advantages of such benefices as He performed for them, healing the sick, resurrecting the dead, restoring those possessed of the devil? How was it they did not love Him? But God is witness that it was for these very acts they did not love Him, that they despised Him. As they themselves testified.

They gather together in their council and say: *What do we? for this man doth many miracles.*[33] Can this be cause? If they had said: here is an evil-doer, a transgressor of the law, a rabble-rouser who with deceit stirs up the populace, they would have lied—as they did indeed lie when they spoke these things. But there were more apposite reasons for effecting what they desired, which was to take His life; and to give as reason that he had performed wondrous deeds seems not befitting learned men, for such were the Pharisees. Thus it is that in the heat of passion learned men erupt with such irrelevancies; for we know it as truth that only for this reason was it determined that Christ should die. Oh, men, if men you may be called, being so like to brutes, what is the cause of so cruel a determination? Their only response is that "this man doth many miracles." May God forgive them. Then is performing signal deeds cause enough that one should die? This "he doth many miracles" evokes *the root of Jesse, who standeth for an ensign of the people,*[34] and that *and for a sign which shall be contradicted.*[35] He is a sign? Then He shall die. He excels? Then He shall suffer, for that is the reward for one who excels.

Often on the crest of temples are placed as adornment figures of the winds and of fame, and to defend them from the birds, they are covered with iron barbs; this appears to be in defense, but is in truth obligatory propriety: the figure thus elevated cannot avoid becoming the target of those barbs; there on high is found the animosity of the air, on high, the ferocity of the elements, on high is unleashed the anger of the thunderbolt, on high stands the target for slings and arrows. Oh unhappy eminence,

---

[32] **Mother Teresa:** Saint Teresa de Ávila (1515–1582), a Spanish Carmelite nun and reformer of the Carmelite Order; she wrote an autobiography and several mystical prose works. In 1970 she became the first woman to be named one of the Doctors of the Church.

[33] *for this man doth many miracles:* The Pharisees say this as they seek to thwart Christ's growing influence; see John 11:47–48.

[34] *the root . . . ensign of the people:* Isaiah 11:10.

[35] *a sign which shall be contradicted:* Luke 2:34.

exposed to such uncounted perils. Oh sign, become the target of envy and the butt of contradiction. Whatever eminence, whether that of dignity, nobility, riches, beauty, or science, must suffer this burden; but the eminence that undergoes the most severe attack is that of reason. First, because it is the most defenseless, for riches and power strike out against those who dare attack them; but not so reason, for while it is the greater it is more modest and long-suffering, and defends itself less. Second, as Gracian stated so eruditely, *favors in man's reason are favors in his nature.*[36] For no other cause except that the angel is superior in reason is the angel above man; for no other cause does man stand above the beast but by his reason; and thus, as no one wishes to be lower than another, neither does he confess that another is superior in reason, as reason is a consequence of being superior. One will abide, and will confess that another is nobler than he, that another is richer, more handsome, and even that he is more learned, but that another is richer in reason scarcely any will confess: *Rare is he who will concede genius.*[37] That is why the assault against this virtue works to such profit.

When the soldiers mocked, made entertainment and diversion of our Lord Jesus Christ, they brought Him a worn purple garment and a hollow reed, and a crown of thorns to crown Him King of Fools. But though the reed and the purple were an affront, they did not cause suffering. Why does only the crown give pain? Is it not enough that like the other emblems the crown was a symbol of ridicule and ignominy, as that was its intent? No. Because the sacred head of Christ and His divine intellect were the depository of wisdom, and the world is not satisfied for wisdom to be the object of mere ridicule, it must also be done injury and harm. A head that is a storehouse of wisdom can expect nothing but a crown of thorns. What garland may human wisdom expect when it is known what was bestowed on that divine wisdom? Roman pride crowned the many achievements of their Captains with many crowns: he who defended the city received the civic crown; he who fought his way into the hostile camp received the camp crown; he who scaled the wall, the mural; he who liberated a besieged city, or any army besieged either in the field or in their encampment, received the obsidional, the siege, crown; other feats were crowned with naval, ovation, or triumphal crowns, as described by Pliny and Aulus Gellius.[38] Observing so many and varied crowns, I debated as to which Christ's crown must have been, and determined that it was the siege crown, for (as well you know lady) that was the most honored crown and was called obsidional after *obsidio,* which means siege; which crown was made not from gold, or silver, but from the

---

[36] Gracian . . . *in his nature*: Baltasar Gracián (1601–1658), a Spanish Jesuit priest, scholar, and philosopher; his works include a collection of maxims entitled *The Art of Worldly Wisdom* (1647), from which the quote is taken, and a philosophical novel, *The Critic* (1651–57).

[37] *Rare is he who will concede genius*: Martial, *Epigrams* 8:18.

[38] **Pliny and Aulus Gellius:** Pliny the Younger (c. 63–c. 113 C.E.) was a Roman orator and author of *Letters* and other works; Aulus Gellius (c. 123–165 C.E.) wrote *Attic Nights,* a compendium of quotations from earlier Greek and Latin works.

leaves and grasses flourishing on the field where the feat was achieved. And as the heroic feat of Christ was to break the siege of the Prince of Darkness, who had laid siege to all the earth, as is told in the Book of Job, quoting Satan: *I have gone round about the earth, and walked through it,*[39] and as St. Peter says: *As a roaring lion, goeth about seeking whom he may devour.*[40] And our Master came and caused him to lift the siege: *Now shall the prince of this world be cast out.*[41] So the soldiers crowned Him not with gold or silver but with the natural fruit of the world, which was the field of battle—and which, after the curse *Thorns also and thistles shall it bring forth to thee,*[42] produced only thorns—and thus it was a most fitting crown for the courageous and wise Conqueror, with which His mother Synagogue crowned Him. And the daughters of Zion, weeping, came out to witness the sorrowful triumph, as they had come rejoicing for the triumph of Solomon, because the triumph of the wise is earned with sorrow and celebrated with weeping, which is the manner of the triumph of wisdom; and as Christ is the King of wisdom, He was the first to wear that crown; and as it was sanctified on His brow, it removed all fear and dread from those who are wise, for they know they need aspire to no other honor.

The Living Word, Life, wished to restore life to Lazarus, who was dead. His disciples did not know His purpose and they said to Him: *Rabbi, the Jews but now sought to stone thee; and goest thou thither again?*[43] And the Redeemer calmed their fear: *Are there not twelve hours of the day?*[44] It seems they feared because there had been those who wished to stone Him when He rebuked them, calling them thieves and not shepherds of sheep. And thus the disciples feared that if He returned to the same place—for even though rebukes be just, they are often badly received—He would be risking his life. But once having been disabused and having realized that He was setting forth to raise up Lazarus from the dead, what was it that caused Thomas, like Peter in the Garden, to say *Let us also go, that we may die with him?*[45] What say you, Sainted Apostle? The Lord does not go out to die; whence your misgiving? For Christ goes not to rebuke, but to work an act of mercy, and therefore they will do Him no harm. These same Jews could have assured you, for when He reproved those who wished to stone Him, *Many good works I have shewed you from my Father; for which of those works do you stone me?* they replied: *For a good work we stone thee not; but for blasphemy.*[46] And as they say they will not stone Him for doing good works, and now He goes to do a work so great as to raise up Lazarus from the dead, whence your misgiving? Why do you fear? Were it not better to say: let us go to

---

[39] *I have . . . walked through it*: Job 1:7.

[40] *As a . . . he may devour*: That is, Satan as a roaring lion; see 1 Peter 5:8.

[41] *Now shall . . . be cast out*: John 12:31.

[42] *Thorns . . . forth to thee*: Genesis 3:18.

[43] *Rabbi . . . thither again*: John 11:8.

[44] *Are . . . hours of the day*: John 11:9.

[45] *Let us . . . die with him?*: John 11:16.

[46] *For a . . . for blasphemy*: John 10:32–33.

gather the fruits of appreciation for the good work our Master is about to do; to see Him lauded and applauded for His benefice; to see men marvel at His miracle. Why speak words seemingly so alien to the circumstance as *Let us also go?* Ah, woe, the Saint feared as a prudent man and spoke as an Apostle. Does Christ not go to work a miracle? Why, what *greater* peril? It is less to be suffered that pride endure rebukes than envy witness miracles. In all the above, most honored lady, I do not wish to say (nor is such folly to be found in me) that I have been persecuted for my wisdom, but merely for my love of wisdom and letters, having achieved neither one nor the other.

At one time even the Prince of the Apostles was very far from wisdom, as is emphasized in that *But Peter followed afar off.*[47] Very distant from the laurels of a learned man is one so little in his judgment that he was *Not knowing what he said.*[48] And being questioned on his mastery of wisdom, he himself was witness that he had not achieved the first measure: *But he denied him, saying: Woman, I know him not.*[49] And what becomes of him? We find that having this reputation of ignorance, he did not enjoy its good fortune, but, rather, the affliction of being taken for wise. And why? There was no other motive but: *This man also was with him.*[50] He was fond of wisdom, it filled his heart, he followed after it, he prided himself as a pursuer and lover of wisdom; and although he followed from so *afar off* that he neither understood nor achieved it, his love for it was sufficient that he incur its torments. And there was present that soldier to cause him distress, and a certain maid-servant to cause him grief. I confess that I find myself very distant from the goals of wisdom, for all that I have desired to follow it, even from *afar off*. But in this I have been brought closer to the fire of persecution, to the crucible of torment, and to such lengths that they have asked that study be forbidden to me.

At one time this was achieved through the offices of a very saintly and ingenuous Abbess who believed that study was a thing of the Inquisition, who commanded me not to study. I obeyed her (the three some months her power to command endured) in that I did not take up a book; but that I study not at all is not within my power to achieve, and this I could not obey, for though I did not study in books, I studied all the things that God had wrought, reading in them, as in writing and in books, all the workings of the universe. I looked on nothing without reflexion; I heard nothing without meditation, even in the most minute and imperfect things; because as there is no creature, however lowly, in which one cannot recognize that *God made me,* there is none that does not astound reason, if properly meditated on. Thus, I reiterate, I saw and admired all things; so that even the very persons with whom I spoke, and the things they said, were cause for a thousand meditations. Whence the variety of genius and wit, being all of a single species? Which the

---

[47] *But Peter followed afar off:* Luke 22:54.

[48] *Not knowing what he said:* Luke 9:33.

[49] *I know him not:* Peter, after the Last Supper, denied that he knew Jesus, after a maid-servant identified him as one of the disciples; see Luke 22:55–60.

[50] *This man also was with him:* This is the maid's charge against Peter; see Luke 22:57.

temperaments and hidden qualities that occasioned such variety? If I saw a figure, I was forever combining the proportion of its lines and measuring it with my reason and reducing it to new proportions. Occasionally as I walked along the far wall of one of our dormitories (which is a most capacious room) I observed that though the lines of the two sides were parallel and the ceiling perfectly level, in my sight they were distorted, the lines seeming to incline toward one another, the ceiling seeming lower in the distance than in proximity: from which I inferred that *visual* lines run straight but not parallel, forming a pyramidal figure. I pondered whether this might not be the reason that caused the ancients to question whether the world were spherical. Because, although it so seems, this could be a deception of vision, suggesting concavities where possibly none existed.

This manner of reflection has always been my habit, and is quite beyond my will to control; on the contrary, I am wont to become vexed that my intellect makes me weary; and I believed that it was so with everyone, as well as making verses, until experience taught me otherwise; and it is so strong in me this nature, or custom, that I look at nothing without giving it further examination. Once in my presence two young girls were spinning a top and scarcely had I seen the motion and the figure described, when I began, out of this madness of mine, to meditate on the effortless *motus*[51] of the spherical form, and how the impulse persisted even when free and independent of its cause—for the top continued to dance even at some distance from the child's hand, which was the causal force. And not content with this, I had flour brought and sprinkled about, so that as the top danced one might learn whether these were perfect circles it described with its movement; and I found that they were not, but, rather, spiral lines that lost their circularity as the impetus declined. Other girls sat playing at spillikins[52] (surely the most frivolous game that children play); I walked closer to observe the figures they formed, and seeing that by chance three lay in a triangle, I set to joining one with another, recalling that this was said to be the form of the mysterious ring of Solomon,[53] in which he was able to see the distant splendor and images of the Holy Trinity, by virtue of which the ring worked such prodigies and marvels. And the same shape was said to form David's harp, and that is why Saul was refreshed at its sound; and harps today largely conserve that shape.

And what shall I tell you, lady, of the natural secrets I have discovered while cooking? I see that an egg holds together and fries in butter or in oil, but, on the contrary, in syrup shrivels into shreds; observe that to keep sugar in a liquid state one need only add a drop or two of water in which a quince or other bitter fruit has been soaked; observe that the yolk and the white of one egg are so dissimilar that each with sugar produces a result not obtainable with both together. I do not wish to weary you with such inconsequential matters, and make mention of them only to

---

[51] *motus*: Motion.   [52] spillikins: The game of pick-up sticks.

[53] ring of Solomon: Sor Juana may refer here to the legendary seal of Solomon, sometimes thought of as two intersecting triangles forming the Star of David.

give you full notice of my nature, for I believe they will be occasion for laughter. But, lady, as women, what wisdom may be ours if not the philosophies of the kitchen? Lupercio Leonardo[54] spoke well when he said: how well one may philosophize when preparing dinner. And I often say, when observing these trivial details: had Aristotle prepared victuals, he would have written more. And pursuing the manner of my cogitations, I tell you that this process is so continuous in me that I have no need for books. And on one occasion, when because of a grave upset of the stomach the physicians forbade me to study, I passed thus some days, but then I proposed that it would be less harmful if they allowed me books, because so vigorous and vehement were my cogitations that my spirit was consumed more greatly in a quarter of an hour than in four days' studying books. And thus they were persuaded to allow me to read. And moreover, lady, not even have my dreams been excluded from this ceaseless agitation of my imagination; indeed, in dreams it is wont to work more freely and less encumbered, collating with greater clarity and calm the gleanings of the day, arguing and making verses, of which I could offer you an extended catalogue, as well as of some arguments and inventions that I have better achieved sleeping than awake. I relinquish this subject in order not to tire you, for the above is sufficient to allow your discretion and acuity to penetrate perfectly and perceive my nature, as well as the beginnings, the methods, and the present state of my studies.

Even, lady, were these merits (and I see them celebrated as such in men), they would not have been so in me for I cannot but study. If they are fault, then, for the same reasons, I believe I have none. Nevertheless, I live always with so little confidence in myself that neither in my study, nor in any other thing, do I trust my judgment; and thus I remit the decision to your sovereign genius, submitting myself to whatever sentence you may bestow, without controversy, without reluctance, for I have wished here only to present you with a simple narration of my inclination toward letters.

I confess, too, that though it is true, as I have stated, that I had no need of books, it is nonetheless also true that they have been no little inspiration, in divine as in human letters. Because I find a Debbora[55] administering the law, both military and political, and governing a people among whom there were many learned men. I find a most wise Queen of Saba,[56] so learned that she dares to challenge with hard questions the wisdom of the greatest of all wise men, without being reprimanded for doing so, but, rather, as a consequence, to judge unbelievers. I see many and illustrious women; some blessed with the gift of prophecy, like Abigail; others of persuasion, like Esther;

---

[54] **Lupercio Leonardo:** Lupercio Leonardo de Argensola (1559–1613), Spanish poet and playwright, wrote moral poetry and satires. The quotation appears in the First Satire of Lupercio's brother Bernardo's *First Satire;* Bernardo Leonardo de Argensola (1562–1631) was also a poet, satirist, and historian.

[55] **Debbora:** Deborah, the prophetess and wife of Lapidoth, as judge and advisor assisted the Israelites in their struggle against the Canaanites; see Judges 4 and 5.

[56] **Queen of Saba:** The Queen of Sheba; after testing King Solomon's wisdom and finding him worthy, she lavished him with gifts; see 1 Kings 1:1–13 and 2 Chronicles 9:1–12.

others with pity, like Rahab; others with perseverance, like Anna,[57] the mother of Samuel; and an infinite number of others, with divers gifts and virtues.

If I again turn to the Gentiles, the first I encounter are the Sibyls,[58] those women chosen by God to prophesy the principal mysteries of our Faith, and with learned and elegant verses that surpass admiration. I see adored as a goddess of the sciences a woman like Minerva,[59] the daughter of the first Jupiter and mistress over all the wisdom of Athens. I see a Polla Argentaria, who helped Lucan, her husband, write his epic *Pharsalia*.[60] I see the daughter of the divine Tiresias,[61] more learned than her father. I see a Zenobia,[62] Queen of the Palmyrans, as wise as she was valiant. An Arete, most learned daughter of Aristippus.[63] A Nicostrata, framer of Latin verses and most erudite in Greek. An Aspasia of Miletus,[64] who taught philosophy and rhetoric, and who was a teacher of the philosopher Pericles. An Hypatia, who taught astrology, and studied many years in Alexandria. A Leontium,[65] a Greek woman, who questioned the philosopher Theophrastus, and convinced him. A Julia, a Corinna, a Cornelia;[66] and, finally, a great throng of women deserving to be named, some as Greeks, some as muses, some as seers; for all were nothing more than

[57] **Abigail; Esther; Rahab; Anna:** All four are strong women from the Hebrew Scriptures. Abigail (1 Samuel 25:2–35), a prophetess, saved her husband from King David's wrath by prophesying David's future; when her husband Nabal was struck down by God, she became David's wife. Esther (Esther 5–9), wife of King Ahasuerus, was known as the protector of the Jews (see note 12). Rahab (Joshua 2:1–7) was a prostitute from Jericho who harbored two spies sent into the city by Joshua. Anna (1 Samuel 1:1–20), is Hannah, the mother of the prophet Samuel.

[58] **Sibyls:** Female prophets of Greece and Rome, some of whom Sor Juana names in this passage.

[59] **Minerva:** Roman goddess of wisdom; Athena in Greek mythology.

[60] *Pharsalia*: Epic poem about the civil war between Julius Caesar and Pompey by the first-century C.E. Roman poet Marcus Annaeus Lucanus.

[61] **daughter of the divine Tiresias:** Manto is the daughter of the blind seer Tiresias, a prophet of Zeus associated with the city of Thebes.

[62] **Zenobia:** Also Xenobia, daughter of an Arab chieftain, ruled as Queen of Palmyra, an Arab kingdom, from 267 to 272, after the death of her husband King Septimius Odaenathus.

[63] **Aristippus** (c. 435–356 B.C.E.): Greek philosopher who believed that pleasure was the ultimate goal of life.

[64] **Nicostrata; Aspasia of Miletus:** Nicostrata, also known as Carmenta, was an Arcadian prophetess and legendary founder of the Roman alphabet. Aspasia (fifth century B.C.E.), moved from Miletus to Athens, where she became the consort of the Athenian leader Pericles (c. 495–429 B.C.E.) and was renowned for her skills in rhetoric, her knowledge of philosophy, and her sharp intellect.

[65] **Hypatia; Leontium:** Hypatia of Alexandria (c. 370–415 C.E.) was an Egyptian-born Neoplatonist, mathematician, and teacher; mob violence brought about her death, and she may have been targeted because of political jealousy or religious fear of her intelligence and teachings. Leontium (fourth to third centuries B.C.E.) was known as an intellectual and Epicurian who wrote a treatise against Theophratus (c. 370–c. 285 B.C.E.), the student of Aristotle and naturalist who presided over the Lyceum after Aristotle's death.

[66] **Julia; Corinna, Cornelia:** Julia Domna (c. 170–217 C.E.), also known as Julia the Philosopher, was married to Roman emperor Septimius Severus (r. 193–211). Corinna of Tanagra (fifth century B.C.E?) was a lyric poet from Boeotia. Cornelia (c. 190–100 B.C.E.), daughter of Scipio Africanus (235–183 B.C.E.), the hero who defeated Hannibal in the Second Punic War, and wife of Tiberius Sempronius Gracchus, was widely praised as an exemplary Roman matron and woman of letters. She took charge of the education of her children—among whom were the Gracchi, the military leader and senator Tiberius Gracchus (163–132 B.C.E.) and his brother, the Roman politician Gaius Gracchus (154–121 B.C.E.).

learned women, held, and celebrated—and venerated as well—as such by antiquity. Without mentioning an infinity of other women whose names fill books. For example, I find the Egyptian Catherine,[67] studying and influencing the wisdom of all the wise men of Egypt. I see a Gertrude[68] studying, writing, and teaching. And not to overlook examples close to home, I see my most holy mother Paula,[69] learned in Hebrew, Greek, and Latin, and most able in interpreting the Scriptures. And what greater praise than, having as her chronicler a Jeronimus Maximus,[70] that Saint scarcely found himself competent for his task, and says, with that weighty deliberation and energetic precision with which he so well expressed himself: "If all the members of my body were tongues, they still would not be sufficient to proclaim the wisdom and virtue of Paula." Similarly praiseworthy was the widow Blesilla; also, the illustrious virgin Eustochium,[71] both daughters of this same saint; especially the second, who, for her knowledge, was called the Prodigy of the World. The Roman Fabiola was most well-versed in the Holy Scripture. Proba Falconia,[72] a Roman woman, wrote elegant centos, containing verses from Virgil, about the mysteries of Our Holy Faith. It is well-known by all that Queen Isabella,[73] wife of the tenth Alfonso, wrote about astrology. Many others I do not list, out of the desire not merely to transcribe what others have said (a vice I have always abominated); and many are flourishing today, as witness Christina Alexandra,[74] Queen of Sweden, as learned as she is valiant and magnanimous, and the Most Honorable Ladies, the Duquesa of Aveyro[75] and the Condesa of Villaumbrosa.

The venerable Doctor Arce[76] (by his virtue and learning a worthy teacher of the Scriptures) in his scholarly *Bibliorum* raises this question: *Is it permissible for women*

---

[67] **Catherine:** Saint Catherine of Alexandria (fourth century) was renowned for her keen intelligence and philosophical understanding; like Sor Juana, Catherine is reported to have debated some of Alexandria's most learned men when she was just a teenager.

[68] **Gertrude:** Saint Gertrude the Great (1256–c. 1302), a Benedictine nun and mystic noted for her devotion to her studies and for her spiritual writings.

[69] **Paula:** Saint Paula (see note 20).

[70] **Jeronimus Maximus:** St. Jerome (see note 15).

[71] **Blesilla; Eustochium:** Both were daughters of St. Paula; after Blesilla's death in 384, Eustochium traveled with Saint Paula to the Holy Land, where she, her mother, and St. Jerome founded a hospice, monastery, and convent.

[72] **Fabiola; Proba Falconia:** Fabiola (d. 399?) was a Roman matron who joined the Church after the death of her second husband and eventually joined St. Paula and St. Jerome in the Holy Land. Proba Falconia or Faltonia Betitia Proba (fourth century C.E.) was a Roman matron who converted to Christianity and wrote the *Cento virgilianus,* a poem composed of "remixed" verses from Virgil recounting the stories of Genesis and Exodus and the life of Jesus.

[73] **Queen Isabella:** An obscure reference, because Violante of Aragon, not Isabella, was the wife of Alfonso X, Alfonso the Wise (1221–1284), also called Alfonso the Astronomer, who was known for his keen study in astronomy and cosmology. His mother was Isabella of Swabia.

[74] **Christina Alexandra:** Maria Christina Alexandra (1626–1689), queen of Sweden, received an unusually thorough education for a woman of her time and was a patron of the arts and sciences.

[75] **Duquesa of Aveyro:** Maria Guadalupe de Lencastre (1630–1715), the sixth Duchess of Aveiro, was a most generous benefactor to Jesuit missions throughout New Spain.

[76] **Doctor Arce:** Juan Díaz de Arce (1594–1653), a professor of theology and the author of a four-volume book on interpreting the Bible, from which Sor Juana quotes here.

to dedicate themselves to the study of the Holy Scriptures, and to their interpretation? and he offers as negative arguments the opinions of many saints, especially that of the Apostle: *Let women keep silence in the churches; for it is not permitted them to speak,* etc.[77] He later cites other opinions and, from the same Apostle, verses from his letter to Titus: *The aged women in like manner, in holy attire . . . teaching well,*[78] with interpretations by the Holy Fathers. Finally he resolves, with all prudence, that teaching publicly from a University chair, or preaching from the pulpit, is not permissible for women; but that to study, write, and teach privately not only is permissible, but most advantageous and useful. It is evident that this is not to be the case with all women, but with those to whom God may have granted special virtue and prudence, and who may be well advanced in learning, and having the essential talent and requisites for such a sacred calling. This view is indeed just, so much so that not only women, who are held to be so inept, but also men, who merely for being men believe they are wise, should be prohibited from interpreting the Sacred Word if they are not learned and virtuous and of gentle and well-inclined natures; that this is not so has been, I believe, at the root of so much sectarianism and so many heresies. For there are many who study but are ignorant, especially those who are in spirit arrogant, troubled, and proud, so eager for new interpretations of the Word (which itself rejects new interpretations) that merely for the sake of saying what no one else has said they speak a heresy, and even then are not content. Of these the Holy Spirit says: *For wisdom will not enter into a malicious soul.*[79] To such as these more harm results from knowing than from ignorance. A wise man has said: he who does not know Latin is not a complete fool, but he who knows it is well qualified to be. And I would add that a fool may reach perfection (if ignorance may tolerate perfection) by having studied his tittle of philosophy and theology and by having some learning of tongues, by which he may be a fool in many sciences and languages: a great fool cannot be contained solely in his mother tongue.

For such as these, I reiterate, study is harmful, because it is as if to place a sword in the hands of a madman; which, though a most noble instrument for defense, is in his hands his own death and that of many others. So were the Divine Scriptures in the possession of the evil Pelagius and the intractable Arius, of the evil Luther, and the other heresiarchs like our own Doctor (who was neither ours nor a doctor) Cazalla.[80] To these men, wisdom was harmful, although it is the greatest nourishment and the life of the soul; in the same way that in a stomach of sickly constitution

---

[77] *Let women . . . speak,* etc.: 1 Corinthians 14:34–35 commands women to be silent in church.

[78] *The aged . . . teaching well*: In the Epistle to Titus 2:3–5, St. Paul enjoins older women to teach their daughters to be sober, good, and chaste; to love their children; and to love and obey their husbands.

[79] *For wisdom . . . a malicious soul*: From one of the apocryphal books, Wisdom 1:4.

[80] **Pelagius, Arius, Luther, Cazalla:** All four are notorious heretics in the eyes of the Catholic church. Pelagius (fifth century) was a British monk who denied the doctrine of original sin. Arius (fourth century) was a theologian in Alexandria who taught that Christ was not co-eternal and co-equal with God the Father. Luther (1483–1546) was the German theologian who led the Protestant Reformation against the Catholic Church. Augustino Cazallo (1510–1559), a Spanish Lutheran, was burned at the stake by the Inquisition for his heretical teachings.

and adulterated complexion, the finer the nourishment it receives, the more arid, fermented, and perverse are the humors it produces; thus these evil men: the more they study, the worse opinions they engender, their reason being obstructed with the very substance meant to nourish it, and they study much and digest little, exceeding the limits of the vessel of their reason. Of which the Apostle says: *For I say, by the grace that is given me, to all that are among you, not to be more wise than it behoveth to be wise, but to be wise unto sobriety, and according as God hath divided to every one the measure of faith.*[81] And in truth, the Apostle did not direct these words to women, but to men; and that *keep silence* is intended not only for women, but for *all* incompetents. If I desire to know as much, or more, than Aristotle or Saint Augustine, and if I have not the aptitude of Saint Augustine or Aristotle, though I study more than either, not only will I not achieve learning, but I will weaken and dull the workings of my feeble reason with the disproportionateness of the goal.

Oh, that each of us—I, being ignorant, the first—should take the measure of our talents before we study or, more important, write with the covetous ambition to equal and even surpass others, how little spirit we should have for it, and how many errors we should avoid, and how many tortured intellects of which we have experience, we should have had no experience! And I place my own ignorance in the forefront of all these, for if I knew all I should, I would not write. And I protest that I do so only to obey you; and with such apprehension that you owe me more that I have taken up my pen in fear than you would have owed had I presented you more perfect works. But it is well that they go to your correction. Cross them out, tear them up, reprove me, and I shall appreciate that more than all the vain applause others may offer. *That just men shall correct me in mercy, and shall reprove me; but let not the oil of the sinner fatten my head.*[82]

And returning again to our Arce, I say that in affirmation of his opinion he cites the words of my father, Saint Jerome: *To Leta, Upon the Education of Her Daughter.* Where he says: *Accustom her tongue, still young, to the sweetness of the Psalms. Even the names through which little by little she will become accustomed to form her phrases should not be chosen by chance, but selected and repeated with care; the prophets must be included, of course, and the apostles, as well, and all the Patriarchs beginning with Adam and down to Matthew and Luke, so that as she practices other things she will be readying her memory for the future. Let your daily task be taken from the flower of the Scriptures.*[83] And if this Saint desired that a young girl scarcely beginning to talk be educated in this fashion, what would he desire for his nuns and his spiritual daughters? These beliefs are illustrated in the examples of the previously mentioned Eustochium and Fabiola, and Marcella, her sister, and Pacatula, and others whom the Saint honors in his epistles, exhorting them to this sacred exercise, as they are recognized in the epistle I cited, *Let your daily task . . .* , which is affirmation of and agreement with the aged women . . . *teaching well* of Saint Paul. My illustrious

---

[81] *For I say . . . of faith*: Romans 12:3.

[82] *That just . . . my head*: Psalm 141:5.

[83] *Accustom her . . . Scriptures*: St. Jerome, from Letter 107, the Epistle to Laeta.

Father's *Let your daily task* . . . makes clear that the teacher of the child is to be Leta herself, the child's mother.

Oh, how much injury might have been avoided in our land if our aged women had been learned, as was Leta, and had they known how to instruct as directed by Saint Paul and by my Father, Saint Jerome. And failing this, and because of the considerable idleness to which our poor women have been relegated, if a father desires to provide his daughters with more than ordinary learning, he is forced by necessity, and by the absence of wise elder women, to bring men to teach the skills of reading, writing, counting, the playing of musical instruments, and other accomplishments, from which no little harm results, as is experienced every day in doleful examples of perilous association, because through the immediacy of contact and the intimacy born from the passage of time, what one may never have thought possible is easily accomplished. For which reason many prefer to leave their daughters unpolished and uncultured rather than to expose them to such notorious peril as that of familiarity with men, which quandary could be prevented if there were learned elder women, as Saint Paul wished to see, and if the teaching were handed down from one to another, as is the custom with domestic crafts and all other traditional skills.

For what objection can there be that an older woman, learned in letters and in sacred conversation and customs, have in her charge the education of young girls? This would prevent these girls being lost either for lack of instruction or for hesitating to offer instruction through such dangerous means as male teachers, for even when there is no greater risk of indecency than to seat beside a modest woman (who still may blush when her own father looks directly at her) a strange man who treats her as if he were a member of the household and with the authority of an intimate, the modesty demanded in interchange with men and in conversation with them is sufficient reason that such an arrangement not be permitted. For I do not find that the custom of men teaching women is without its peril, lest it be in the severe tribunal of the confessional, or from the remote decency of the pulpit, or in the distant learning of books—never in the personal contact of immediacy. And the world knows this is true; and, notwithstanding, it is permitted solely from the want of learned elder women. Then is it not detrimental, the lack of such women? This question should be addressed by those who, bound to that *Let women keep silence in the church,* say that it is blasphemy for women to learn and teach, as if it were not the Apostle himself who said: *The aged women . . . teaching well.* As well as the fact that this prohibition touches upon historical fact as reported by Eusebius:[84] which is that in the early Church, women were charged with teaching the doctrine to one another in the temples and the sound of this teaching caused confusion as the Apostles were preaching and this is the reason they were ordered to be silent; and even today, while the homilist is preaching, one does not pray aloud.

Who will argue that for the comprehension of many Scriptures one must be familiar with the history, customs, ceremonies, proverbs, and even the manners of

---

[84] **Eusebius:** Eusebius of Caesaria (c. 260–c. 340), an early historian of the Church.

speaking of those times in which they were written, if one is to apprehend the references and allusions of more than a few passages of the Holy Word. *And rend your heart and not your garments.*[85] Is this not a reference to the ceremony in which Hebrews rent their garments as a sign of grief, as did the evil pontiff when he said that Christ had blasphemed? In many scriptures the Apostle writes of succour for widows; did they not refer to the customs of those times? Does not the example of the valiant woman, *Her husband is honourable in the gates,*[86] allude to the fact that the tribunals of the judges were at the gates of the cities? That *Dare terram Deo,* give of your land to God, did that not mean to make some votive offering? And did they not call the public sinners *hiemantes,*[87] those who endure the winter, because they made their penance in the open air instead of at a town gate as others did? And Christ's plaint to that Pharisee who had neither kissed him nor given him water for his feet, was that not because it was the Jews' usual custom to offer these acts of hospitality? And we find an infinite number of additional instances not only in the Divine Letters, but human as well, such as *adorate purpuram,* venerate the purple, which meant obey the King; *manumittere eum,* manumit them, alluding to the custom and ceremony of striking the slave with one's hand to signify his freedom. That *intonuit coelum,* heaven thundered, in Virgil, which alludes to the augury of thunder from the west, which was held to be good. Martial's *tu nunquam leporem edisti,* you never ate hare, has not only the wit of ambiguity in its *leporem,* but, as well, the allusion to the reputed propensity of hares [to bless with beauty those who dine on them].[88] That proverb *maleam legens, quae sunt domi obliviscere,* to sail along the shore of Malia is to forget what one has at home, alludes to the great peril of the promontory of Laconia.[89] That chaste matron's response to the unwanted suit of her pretender: "the hinge-pins shall not be oiled for my sake, nor shall the torches blaze," meaning that she did not want to marry, alluded to the ceremony of anointing the doorways with oils and lighting the nuptial torches in the wedding ceremony, as if now we would say, they shall not prepare the thirteen coins for my dowry, nor shall the priest invoke the blessing. And thus it is with many comments of Virgil and Homer and all the poets and orators. In addition, how many are the difficulties found even in the grammar of the Holy Scripture, such as writing a plural for a singular, or changing from the second to third persons, as in the Psalms, *Let him kiss me with the kiss of his mouth, for thy breasts are better than wine.*[90] Or placing adjectives in the genitive instead of the accusative, as in

---

[85] *And rend . . . garments:* Joel 2:13.

[86] *Her husband is . . . gates:* Proverbs 31:23.

[87] *hiemantes:* From Latin *hiems* for winter; as Sor Juana indicates, penitents had to stand outside the church and hence were exposed to the weather.

[88] **[to bless . . . dine on them]:** Martial *Epigrams* 5:29; the epigram plays upon the resemblance between Latin *leporum* (hare) and *lepor* (charm).

[89] **Malea, Laconia:** Cape Malea is a peninsula located at the southeastern extremity of the Peloponnese in Greece, a region known as Laconia or Lacedaemonia and the site of ancient Sparta; the Cape was notoriously dangerous to ships rounding the southern tip of the peninsula.

[90] *Let him . . . wine:* Song of Solomon 1:2.

Calicem salutaris accipiam, I will take the chalice of salvation.[91] Or to replace the feminine with the masculine, and, in contrast, to call any sin adultery.

All this demands more investigation than some believe, who strictly as grammarians, or, at most, employing the four principles of applied logic, attempt to interpret the Scriptures while clinging to that *Let the women keep silence in the church,* not knowing how it is to be interpreted. As well as that other verse, *Let the women learn in silence.*[92] For this latter scripture works more to women's favor than their disfavor, as it commands them to learn; and it is only natural that they must maintain silence while they learn. And it is also written, *Hear, oh Israel, and be silent.* Which addresses the entire congregation of men and women, commanding all to silence, because if one is to hear and learn, it is with good reason that he attend and be silent. And if it is not so, I would want these interpreters and expositors of Saint Paul to explain to me how they interpret that scripture, *Let the women keep silence in the church.* For either they must understand it to refer to the material church, that is the church of pulpits and cathedras, or to the spiritual, the community of the faithful, which is the Church. If they understand it to be the former, which, in my opinion, is its true interpretation, then we see that if in fact it is not permitted of women to read publicly in church, nor preach, why do they censure those who study privately? And if they understand the latter, and wish that the prohibition of the Apostle be applied transcendentally—that not even in private are women to be permitted to write or study—how are we to view the fact that the Church permitted a Gertrude, a Santa Teresa, a Saint Birgitta, the Nun of Agreda,[93] and so many others, to write? And if they say to me that these women were saints, they speak the truth; but this poses no obstacle to my argument. First, because Saint Paul's proposition is absolute, and encompasses all women not excepting saints, as Martha and Mary, Marcella, Mary mother of Jacob, and Salome,[94] all were in their time, and many other zealous women of the early Church. But we see, too, that the Church allows women who are not saints to write, for the Nun of Agreda and Sor María de la Antigua[95] are not canonized, yet their writings are circulated. And when Santa Teresa and the others were writing, they were not as yet canonized. In which case, Saint Paul's prohibition was directed solely to the public office of the pulpit, for if the Apostle had forbidden women to write, the Church would not have allowed it. Now I do not make so bold

---

[91] **chalice of salvation:** Psalm 116:13.

[92] *Let the women learn in silence*: 1 Timothy 2:11. In the First Epistle to Timothy, Chapter 2:11–15, St. Paul enjoins women to "learn in silence with all subjection," citing Eve's transgression at being deceived by the serpent as grounds for their subordination.

[93] **Gertrude, Santa Teresa, Saint Birgitta, the Nun of Agreda:** See notes 68 and 32 for Gertrude and Teresa. Saint Birgitta, also called Bridget (c. 1303–1373), founded the Order of Saint Savior in 1346; she wrote an account of her visions. Maria de Agreda (1602–1665) was a Spanish nun who recounted her revelations in *The Mystic City of God: A Divine History of the Mother of God* published posthumously in 1670.

[94] **Martha and Mary, Marcella, Mary mother of Jacob, Salome:** All but Marcella, who was one of the students of St. Jerome, are associated with the life of Jesus. For the sisters Martha and Mary, see Luke 10:38–52 and John 12:2–3; for Mary, mother of Jacob (or James) and Salome, see Mark 16:1.

[95] **Sor María de la Antigua:**(1544–1617): A Spanish nun and author.

as to teach—which in me would be excessively presumptuous—and as for writing, that requires a greater talent than mine, and serious reflection. As Saint Cyprian[96] says: *The things we write require most conscientious consideration.* I have desired to study that I might be ignorant of less; for (according to Saint Augustine)[97] some things are learned to be enacted and others only to be known: *We learn some things to know them, others, to do them.* Then, where is the offense to be found if even what is licit to women—which is to teach by writing—I do not perform, as I know that I am lacking in means following the counsel of Quintilian:[98] *Let each person learn not only from the precepts of others, but also let him reap counsel from his own nature.*

If the offense is to be found in the *Atenagórica* letter, was that letter anything other than the simple expression of my feeling, written with the implicit permission of our Holy Mother Church? For if the Church, in her most sacred authority, does not forbid it, why must others do so? That I proffered an opinion contrary to that of de Vieyra was audacious, but, as a Father, was it not audacious that he speak against the three Holy Fathers of the Church? My reason, such as it is, is it not as unfettered as his, as both issue from the same source? Is his opinion to be considered as a revelation, as a principle of the Holy Faith, that we must accept blindly? Furthermore, I maintained at all times the respect due such a virtuous man, a respect in which his defender was sadly wanting, ignoring the phrase of Titus Lucius:[99] *Respect is companion to the arts.* I did not touch a thread of the robes of the Society of Jesus; nor did I write for other than the consideration of the person who suggested that I write. And, according to Pliny,[100] *how different the condition of one who writes from that of one who merely speaks.* Had I believed the letter was to be published I would not have been so inattentive. If, as the censor says, the letter is heretical, why does he not denounce it? And with that he would be avenged, and I content, for, which is only seemly, I esteem more highly my reputation as a Catholic and obedient daughter of the Holy Mother Church than all the approbation due a learned woman. If the letter is rash, and he does well to criticize it, then laugh, even if with the laugh of the rabbit, for I have not asked that he approve; as I was free to dissent from de Vieyra, so will anyone be free to oppose my opinion.

But how I have strayed, lady. None of this pertains here, nor is it intended for your ears, but as I was discussing my accusers I remembered the words of one that recently have appeared, and, though my intent was to speak in general, my pen, unbidden, slipped, and began to respond in particular. And so, returning to our Arce, he says that he knew in this city two nuns: one in the Convent of the Regina,

---

[96] **Saint Cyprian:** Thascius Caecilius Cyprianus (d. 258 C.E.), Bishop of Carthage and Church Father.

[97] **Saint Augustine:** Aurelius Augustinus (354–430 C.E.), Bishop of Hippo and one of the Church Fathers, was a philosopher and theologian, whose works helped lay the foundation of Christian thought; author of *On Christian Doctrine, Confessions,* and *The City of God,* among other writings.

[98] **Quintilian:** Marcus Fabius Quintilianus (c. 35–95 C.E.), Roman rhetorician whose *Institutio Oratoria* (c. 95 C.E.), emphasizing the moral and intellectual education of the orator, is one of the classic works on rhetoric.

[99] **Titus Lucius:** An obscure reference; Tito Lucio in the original text.

[100] **Pliny:** See note 38.

who had so thoroughly committed the Breviary to memory that with the greatest promptitude and propriety she applied in her conversation its verses, psalms, and maxims of saintly homilies. The other, in the Convent of the Conception, was so accustomed to reading the Epistles of my Father Saint Jerome, and the Locutions of this Saint, that Arce says, *It seemed I was listening to Saint Jerome himself, speaking in Spanish.* And of this latter woman he says that after her death he learned that she had translated these Epistles into the Spanish language. What a pity that such talents could not have been employed in major studies with scientific principles. He does not give the name of either, although he offers these women as confirmation of his opinion, which is that not only is it licit, but most useful and essential for women to study the Holy Word, and even more essential for nuns; and that study is the very thing to which your wisdom exhorts me, and in which so many arguments concur.

Then if I turn my eyes to the oft-chastised faculty of making verses—which is in me so natural that I must discipline myself that even this letter not be written in that form—I might cite those lines, *All I wished to express took the form of verse.*[101] And seeing that so many condemn and criticize this ability, I have conscientiously sought to find what harm may be in it, and I have not found it, but, rather, I see verse acclaimed in the mouths of the Sibyls, sanctified in the pens of the Prophets, especially King David, of whom the exalted Expositor my beloved Father[102] says (explicating the measure of his metres): *in the manner of Horace and Pindar, now it hurries along in iambs, now it rings in alcaic, now swells in sapphic, then arrives in broken feet.* The greater part of the Holy Books are in metre, as is the Book of Moses; and those of Job (as Saint Isidore states in his *Etymologiae*)[103] are in heroic verse. Solomon wrote the Canticle of Canticles in verse; and Jeremiah, his *Lamentations*. And so, says Cassiodorus:[104] *All poetic expression had as its source the Holy Scriptures.* For not only does our Catholic Church not disdain verse, it employs verse in its hymns, and recites the lines of Saint Ambrose, Saint Thomas, Saint Isidore,[105] and others. Saint Bonaventure[106] was so taken with verse that he writes scarcely a page where it does

---

[101] *All I . . . form of verse*: From Roman poet Ovid's *Tristia*, Book 4, 10:24–26.

[102] **beloved Father**: Saint Jerome; in the quotation that follows he praises the poetry of Israel's legendary King David (tenth century B.C.E.), said to have composed some of the Psalms, to the lyric poetry of the Greek poet Pindar (522 to 443 B.C.E.) and the Roman poet Horace (65 to 8 B.C.E.).

[103] *Etymologiae*: An encyclopedic work by St. Isidore of Seville (c. 560–636), Archbishop of Seville, doctor of the Church, and author of books on history, theology, and natural history; *Etymologiae* (*Origins*) served in the Middle Ages as a repository of knowledge about Greek and Roman culture, history, philosophy, and natural science.

[104] **Cassiodorus**: Flavius Magnus Aurelius Cassiodorus (fifth to sixth centuries C.E.) was a Sicilian-born Roman statesman, scholar, collector of books and manuscripts, and later a monk, whose *Insitutiones* served as a guide for monastic scholarship and Biblical study.

[105] **Saint Ambrose, Saint Thomas, Saint Isidore**: Saint Ambrose (c. 340–397) was bishop of Milan and a doctor of the Church; Saint Thomas Aquinas (1221–1274), doctor of the Church and perhaps its greatest theologian, wrote the *Summa Theologica* analyzing Christian theology in terms of classical philosophy. For Saint Isidore, see note 103.

[106] **Saint Bonaventure**: Saint Bonaventure (1221–74), Italian-born doctor of the Church, was a Franciscan monk, authoring a biography of Saint Francis; he studied at the University of Paris and later became the cardinal and bishop of Albano.

not appear. It is readily apparent that Saint Paul had studied verse, for he quotes and translates verses of Aratus: *For in him we live, and move, and are.* And he quotes also that verse of Parmenides:[107] *The Cretans are always liars, evil beasts, slothful bellies.* Saint Gregory Nazianzen[108] argues in elegant verses the questions of matrimony and virginity. And, how should I tire? The Queen of Wisdom, Our Lady, with Her sacred lips, intoned the Canticle of the Magnificat;[109] and having brought forth this example, it would be offensive to add others that were profane, even those of the most serious and learned men, for this alone is more than sufficient confirmation; and even though Hebrew elegance could not be compressed into Latin measure, for which reason, although the sacred translator, more attentive to the importance of the meaning, omitted the verse, the Psalms retain the number and divisions of verses, and what harm is to be found in them? For misuse is not the blame of art, but rather of the evil teacher who perverts the arts, making of them the snare of the devil; and this occurs in all the arts and sciences.

And if the evil is attributed to the fact that a woman employs them, we have seen how many have done so in praiseworthy fashion; what then is the evil in my being a woman? I confess openly my own baseness and meanness, but I judge that no couplet of mine has been deemed indecent. Furthermore, I have never written of my own will, but under the pleas and injunctions of others; to such a degree that the only piece I remember having written for my own pleasure was a little trifle they called *El sueño*.[110] That letter, lady, which you so greatly honored, I wrote more with repugnance than any other emotion; both by reason of the fact that it treated sacred matters, for which (as I have stated) I hold such reverent awe, and because it seems to wish to impugn, a practice for which I have natural aversion; and I believe that had I foreseen the blessed destiny to which it was fated—for like a second Moses[111] I had set it adrift, naked, on the waters of the Nile of silence, where you, a princess, found and cherished it—I believe, I reiterate, that had I known, the very hands of which it was born would have drowned it, out of the fear that these clumsy scribblings from my ignorance appear before the light of your great wisdom; by which one knows the munificence of your kindness, for your goodwill applauds precisely what your reason must wish to reject. For as fate cast it before your doors, so exposed, so orphaned, that it fell to you even to give it a name, I must lament that

---

[107] **Aratus; Parmenides:** Saint Paul cites the Greek poet Aratus (third to second centuries B.C.E) in Acts 17:28; and the Greek philosopher and poet Parmenides (fifth to fourth centuries B.C.E.) in Titus 1:12.

[108] **Saint Gregory Nazianzen:** Gregory of Nazianzus (c. 325–389), doctor of the Church, became Bishop of Constantinople; in addition to publishing works on theology, earning him the nickname "Gregory the Theologian," he wrote several religious poems.

[109] **Canticle of the Magnificat:** Mary, mother of Jesus, uttered what is known as the Magnificat, when upon visiting Elisabeth, mother of John the Baptist; see Luke 1:46–55.

[110] ***El sueño*:** The title of Sor Juana's most important poem, an extended meditation upon the soul's flight to spiritual knowledge.

[111] **a second Moses:** The allusion is to the infant Moses, who had to be hidden away and eventually set adrift on the Nile River where he was found by the daughter of Pharaoh; see Exodus 2:1–6.

among other deformities it also bears the blemish of haste, both because of the unrelenting ill-health I suffer, and for the profusion of duties imposed on me by obedience, as well as the want of anyone to guide me in my writing and the need that it all come from my hand, and, finally, because the writing went against my nature and I wished only to keep my promise to one whom I could not disobey, I could not find the time to finish properly, and thus I failed to include whole treatises and many arguments that presented themselves to me, but which I omitted in order to put an end to the writing—many, that had I known the letter was to be printed, I would not have excluded, even if merely to satisfy some objections that have since arisen and which could have been refuted. But I shall not be so ill-mannered as to place such indecent objects before the purity of your eyes, for it is enough that my ignorance be an offense in your sight, without need of entrusting to it the effronteries of others. But if in their audacity these latter should wing their way to you (and they are of such little weight that this will happen) then you will command what I am to do; for, if it does not run contrary to your will, my defense shall be not to take up my pen, for I deem that one affront need not occasion another, if one recognizes the error in the very place it lies concealed. As my Father Saint Jerome says, *good discourse seeks not secret things;* and Saint Ambrose, *it is the nature of a guilty conscience to lie concealed.* Nor do I consider that I have been impugned, for one statute of the Law states: *An accusation will not endure unless nurtured by the person who brought it forth.* What *is* a matter to be weighed is the effort spent in copying the accusation. A strange madness, to expend more effort in denying acclaim than in earning it! I, lady, have chosen not to respond (although others did so without my knowledge); it suffices that I have seen certain treatises, among them, one so learned I send it to you so that reading it will compensate in part for the time you squandered on my writing. If, lady, you wish that I act contrary to what I have proposed here for your judgment and opinion, the merest indication of your desire will, as is seemly, countermand my inclination, which, as I have told you, is to be silent, for although Saint John Chrysostom[112] says, *those who slander must be refuted, and those who question, taught,* I know also that Saint Gregory[113] says, *It is no less a victory to tolerate enemies than to overcome them.* And that patience conquers by tolerating and triumphs by suffering. And if among the Roman Gentiles it was the custom when their captains were at the highest peak of glory—when returning triumphant from other nations, robed in purple and wreathed with laurel, crowned-but-conquered kings pulling their carriages in the stead of beasts, accompanied by the spoils of the riches of all the world, the conquering troops adorned with the insignia of their heroic feats, hearing the plaudits of the people who showered them with titles of honor and

---

[112] **Saint John Chrysostom** (c. 347–407 C.E.): A Syrian-born priest and theologian who eventually became Bishop of Constantinople; he was celebrated as a great public speaker, earning his reputation in part by speaking against abuses in the Church—hence his name Chrysostomos, which translates from the Greek to "golden mouthed."

[113] **Saint Gregory:** Gregory the Great (c. 540–604), a Doctor of the Church, exerted a powerful influence—as monk, abbot, author, and after 590 as pope—upon the reformation of Catholic principles and practices during his time.

renown such as Fathers of the Nation, Columns of the Empire, Walls of Rome, Shelter of the Republic, and other glorious names—a soldier went before these captains in this moment of the supreme apogee of glory and human happiness crying out in a loud voice to the conqueror (by his consent and order of the Senate): Behold how you are mortal; behold how you have this or that defect, not excepting the most shameful, as happened in the triumph of Caesar, when the vilest soldiers clamored in his ear: *Beware, Romans, for we bring you the bald adulterer.* Which was done so that in the midst of such honor the conquerers not be swelled up with pride, and that the ballast of these insults act as counterweight to the bellying sails of such approbation, and that the ship of good judgment not founder amidst the winds of acclamation. If this, I say, was the practice among Gentiles, who knew only the light of Natural Law, how much might we Catholics, under the injunction to love our enemies, achieve by tolerating them? And in my own behalf I can attest that calumny has often mortified me, but never harmed me, being that I hold as a great fool one who having occasion to receive credit suffers the difficulty and loses the credit, as it is with those who do not resign themselves to death, but, in the end, die anyway, their resistance not having prevented death, but merely deprived them of the credit of resignation and caused them to die badly when they might have died well. And thus, lady, I believe these experiences do more good than harm, and I hold as greater the jeopardy of applause to human weakness, as we are wont to appropriate praise that is not our own, and must be ever watchful, and carry graven on our hearts those words of the Apostle: *Or what hast thou that thou hast not received? And if thou hast received, why doest thou glory as if thou hadst not received it.*[114] so that these words serve as a shield to fend off the sharp barbs of commendations, which are as spears which when not attributed to God (whose they are), claim our lives and cause us to be thieves of God's honor and usurpers of the talents He bestowed on us and the gifts that He lent to us, for which we must give the most strict accounting. And thus, lady, I fear applause more than calumny, because the latter, with but the simple act of patience becomes gain, while the former requires many acts of reflection and humility and proper recognition so that it not become harm. And I know and recognize that it is by special favor of God that I know this, as it enables me in either instance to act in accord with the words of Saint Augustine: *One must believe neither the friend who praises nor the enemy who detracts.* Although, most often I squander God's favor, or vitiate with such defects and imperfections that I spoil what, being His, was good. And thus in what little of mine that has been printed, neither the use of my name, nor even consent for the printing, was given by my own counsel, but by the license of another who lies outside my domain, as was also true with the printing of the *Atenagórica* letter, and only a few *Exercises of the Incarnation* and *Offerings of the Sorrows*[115] were printed for public devotions with my pleasure but without my name;

---

[114] *Or what . . . not received it*: 1 Corinthians 4:7.

[115] *Exercises of the Incarnation, Offerings of the Sorrows*: Two of Sor Juana's devotional works published in her time.

of which I am sending some few copies that (if you so desire) you may distribute them among our sisters, the nuns of that holy community, as well as in that city. I send but one copy of the *Sorrows* because the others have been exhausted and I could find no other copy. I wrote them long ago, solely for the devotions of my sisters, and later they were spread abroad; and their contents are disproportionate as regards my unworthiness and my ignorance, and they profited that they touched on matters of our exalted Queen; for I cannot explain what it is that inflames the coldest heart when one refers to the Most Holy Mary. It is my only desire, esteemed lady, to remit to you works worthy of your virtue and wisdom; as the poet said:

> Though strength may falter, good will must be praised.
> In this, I believe, the gods will be content.[116]

If ever I write again, my scribbling will always find its way to the haven of your holy feet and the certainty of your correction, for I have no other jewel with which to pay you, and, in the lament of Seneca, he who has once bestowed benefices has committed himself to continue; and so you must be repaid out of your own munificence, for only in this way shall I with dignity be freed from debt and avoid that the words of that same Seneca[117] come to pass: *It is contemptible to be surpassed in benefices.* For in his gallantry the generous creditor gives to the poor debtor the means to satisfy his debt. So God gave His gift to a world unable to repay Him: He gave His son that He be offered a recompense worthy of Him.

If, most venerable lady, the tone of this letter may not have seemed right and proper, I ask forgiveness for its homely familiarity, and the less than seemly respect in which by treating you as a nun, one of my sisters, I have lost sight of the remoteness of your most illustrious person; which, had I seen you without your veil, would never have occurred; but you in all your prudence and mercy will supplement or amend the language, and if you find unsuitable the *Vos* of the address I have employed, believing that for the reverence I owe you, Your Reverence seemed little reverent, modify it in whatever manner seems appropriate to your due, for I have not dared exceed the limits of your custom, nor transgress the boundary of your modesty.

And hold me in your grace, and entreat for me divine grace, of which the Lord God grant you large measure, and keep you, as I pray Him, and am needful. From this convent of our Father Saint Jerome in Mexico City, the first day of the month of March of sixteen hundred and ninety-one. Allow me to kiss your hand, your most favored.

---

[116] **Though strength . . . will be content:** The lines are from Ovid's *Letters from the Black Sea*, 3, 4:79–80.

[117] **Seneca:** From Seneca's *On Benefits* 5:2.1; for Seneca, see note 16.

✆ JONATHAN SWIFT
B. IRELAND, 1667–1745

Satire was the most prominent literary genre of the European **ENLIGHT-ENMENT**, especially in France and England; its most powerful and notorious practitioner was the clergyman, political pamphleteer, poet, and prose stylist Jonathan Swift. Swift began demonstrating his genius for wit and biting satire in 1704 with the publication of *The Battle of the Books* and *A Tale of a Tub*. His masterpiece, *Gulliver's Travels* (1726), enjoyed immediate popularity and today is one of the most widely read books in the world. Modeled roughly on popular travel books and exploration narratives, *Gulliver's Travels* attacks the grossness, folly, and wickedness of human beings with stinging accuracy. The novel's realistic description of absurd events and imaginary societies anticipates science fiction and fantasy literature. Its vision of humanity, by turns hilarious, disgusting, and terrifying, has drawn charges of misanthropy and even madness. Readers who have only met *Gulliver's Travels* in abbreviated versions—as the story of a kindly traveler stranded in a Disneyesque land of miniature people and knee-high palaces—are often shocked by the actual text. Indeed, the physical and moral ugliness reflected in Swift's well-polished mirror leave no reader quite secure in his or her own virtue and dignity. Swift's satiric genius derives from his uncanny ability to provide entertainment and amusement even as he scolds and admonishes his readers.

Anglo-Irish Origins. Jonathan Swift was born in Dublin, Ireland, in 1667, the child of English parents. He was raised by his widowed mother, his father having died before he was born. Supported by his paternal uncle, Swift was educated at Kilkenny School and then at Trinity College, Dublin. Like many Anglo-Irish seeking to avoid the troubles in Ireland just after the Glorious Revolution of 1688,[1] Swift fled to England in 1689. There he joined the household of retired diplomat Sir William Temple, who introduced his new secretary into important intellectual and political circles. While at Temple's, Swift took orders in the Anglican Church, although this initially seems to have been a practical move rather than a response to a passionate calling. In other ways, he began to discover his real tastes, talents, and vocations. He read widely in politics, philosophy, and literature; he made friends with the leading wits, poets, and intellectuals of his day, among them Alexander Pope, John Gay, and Joseph Addison. He undertook the education of Temple's steward's young daughter Esther Johnson, who became his lifelong friend, perhaps his lover or even his wife, in a relationship whose nature remained a secret. The letters and poems between Swift and his "Stella" are testaments to their lifelong playful, loving devotion to each other.

www For links to more information about Swift, a quiz on *Gulliver's Travels,* and information about the 21st-century relevance of *Gulliver's Travels,* see bedford stmartins.com/ worldlitcompact.

---

[1] **Glorious Revolution of 1688:** Refers to the forced abdication in England of the Catholic king, James II, whose attempts to exercise royal authority over Parliament galvanized the largely Protestant nation against him.

Swift the Satirist.   In the 1690s, Swift began to come into his full powers as a writer, producing *The Battle of the Books* and *A Tale of a Tub,* both published in 1704. *The Battle of the Books* attacks corruption in educational and intellectual circles, defending classical writers against the moderns. In this satire, Swift describes the classical writers as modest bees who work earnestly to make honey and the beeswax used in candles, thus supplying civilization with both "sweetness and light." The modern writer, in contrast, is a bloated spider, utterly self-involved, spinning "nothing but dirt" out of his own entrails. *A Tale of a Tub* in part satirizes religious fanaticism from both Puritan and High Church extremes. Here, Swift depicts Christianity as a simple serviceable coat. High Church people, unable to value simplicity, decorate the garment with all sorts of gilded frippery and make faddish alterations until the garment becomes nearly unrecognizable; in their turn, rabid reformers angrily rip out the new seams and tear off all adornments, nearly destroying the fabric of the poor coat entirely. Rereading *A Tale of a Tub* as an old man, Swift exclaimed, "God, I had genius then!" It was clear from both of these early works that, like many satirists, Swift was ultimately a conservative; while he savagely critiques the status quo, he takes an equally acid view of radical attempts at reform and the waste and devastation they are likely to bring about.

Return to Ireland.   In 1699, Swift returned to Ireland as chaplain to the lord justice, although he still cherished hopes of a post back in England. Like most Anglo-Irish, Swift regarded it as a penance to live in what he called "wretched Dublin in miserable Ireland"; warmth, light, laughter, and civilization lay across the Irish Sea in England. From this point on, he seems to have become deeply committed to his double vocation as clergyman and writer. He served and defended the Anglican Church with fierce devotion and continued to write brilliant political and religious satires. In 1713 he was given the deanship at Dublin's St. Patrick's Cathedral. Once Britain's Tory government fell from power, weakening the influence of Swift's friends, he resigned himself to spending the remainder of his life in Ireland.

Despite his own feelings about living in Ireland, Swift won the enduring respect of Irish people for two brilliant satirical pieces. *The Drapier Letters* (1724) are written as if by a humble Dublin draper; the letters take aim at England's corrupt move to devalue Irish coinage when Ireland was already in a severe depression. Britain offered a reward for the name of the author of the anonymous *Letters,* but although Swift's authorship was widely known, no one betrayed him. *A Modest Proposal* (1729), a satire on the many cold-blooded or impractical "projects" devised by British outsiders to solve the woes of the Irish economy, was published five years later. In this outrageous satire, Swift's persona, a social scientist, recommends in a sweetly reasonable voice that the dual problems of Irish famine and Irish overpopulation could be solved by the simple expedient of breeding, raising, butchering, and eating Irish babies. In the end, he seems to suggest that he has been driven mad by the utter failure of the humane and rational solutions he has proposed in the past to the Irish and the English alike.

Death. Swift apparently suffered most of his life from Ménière's syndrome, the neurological condition marked by increasing deafness, vertigo, and nausea. His life darkened toward its end as the disease worsened. Esther Johnson, his beloved friend, died in 1728. By 1732, Swift's ailments caused him to resign his duties as dean, although he remained mentally sound. Gradually, old friends deserted him, and in 1742, after he suffered a paralytic stroke that left him mute, guardians were appointed to manage his affairs. He died in 1745. The epitaph Swift composed for himself in Latin was well translated by his countryman William Butler Yeats:

> Swift has sailed into his rest.
> Savage indignation there
> Cannot lacerate his breast.
> Imitate him if you dare,
> World-besotted traveller, he
> Served human liberty.

Gulliver's Travels, **Early Voyages.** *Travels into Several Remote Nations of the World* (1726), supposedly penned by "Lemuel Gulliver, first a surgeon and then a captain of several Ships," is Swift's greatest work, and it is one of the richest in the English language. Its surface is so simple and fascinating that children enjoy it; its depths are so complex that critics have been fighting about it ever since its appearance. Lemuel Gulliver (from *gull,* an easily duped person) is portrayed as a decent, occasionally resourceful fellow who, like Voltaire's Candide, is not terribly bright and is apt to accept uncritically what he's told. Gulliver undertakes four voyages in the course of the *Travels;* what follows here is a portion of the third trip and all of the fourth.

On Gulliver's first voyage, he is shipwrecked on the shores of the Lilliputians, who initially appear to be an enchantingly tiny and delicate people; their smallness in other regards—their overly dainty manners, their petty politics, and their narrow-mindedness—reveals itself, but only very gradually, to Gulliver, who will be accused by his Lilliputian enemies of such offenses as urinating in public (which he does in order to put out a raging fire in the palace) and of committing adultery with the six-inch-tall wife of the Lilliputian secretary of the treasury.

His second voyage lands Gulliver among the Brobdingnagians, giants whose blunt speech and physical grossness disgust him; Brobdingnagian warts and pimples appear the size of boulders to the fastidious Gulliver. But these giants prove to be as large-hearted and broad-minded as they are physically big. Gulliver finds himself in the awkward position of defending English government and European culture to their thoughtful king, who can only shake his head at the inhumane, petty, and wasteful practices he hears described.

The third voyage is largely a satire upon "projectors," or mock scientists, at the Grand Academy of Lagado, a spoof on the Royal Society of London. The theory-maddened projectors do not care that their social, linguistic, and scientific experiments are impractical or destructive; the experiment is all.

Swift haunts me; he is always just round the next corner.

—W. B. Yeats,
Introduction,
Words upon the Window-Pane, 1934

Who that has read Dean Swift's disgusting description of the Yahoos, and insipid one of Houyhnhnm with a philosophical eye, can avoid seeing the futility of degrading the passions, or making man rest in contentment?

—Mary Wollstonecraft, *A Vindication of the Rights of Woman,* 1792

Portrait of
Lemuel Gulliver
This engraving is
from the 1726 Motte
edition of Gulliver's
Travels. *(Courtesy*
of the Trustees of the
Boston Public
Library)

p. 302

Final Voyage.   The final voyage is the most troubling. It takes Gulliver to the country of the **Houyhnhnms,** supremely rational horses, and their nasty-tempered draft-animals, the human-looking Yahoos. The tempered judgment, orderly society, and well-mannered behavior of the Houyhnhnms contrast with the irrationality, social disorder, and contemptible behavior of the Yahoos. The stately form of the well-groomed Houyhnhnms, a sign of their superior stature, sets them apart from the disgusting, filthy, and unkempt Yahoos. Swift's depiction of the Yahoos as grotesque caricatures of human beings elicits an intellectual as well as a bodily response from his readers. Like Gulliver, while readers may admire the Houyhnhnms and see, at least at first, their temperate rationality as a model for human behavior, they cannot help but recognize their grosser, more vicious potentials in the Yahoos. Like Gulliver, readers may want to deny that resemblance, but the text, like the Houyhnhnm master who reminds Gulliver of his apparent kinship with the Yahoos, insists upon that identity.

Houyhnhnm society is arguably in some ways an improvement over European ones. Free as it is from all dissent, shock, excess, greed, pride, and grief, it is a sort of utopia, but like *Candide*'s Eldorado, it is not quite ideal, in that normal human beings would have a difficult time submitting to a lifetime of Houyhnhnmland's bland conformity. The upper-class equine citizens graze together in unending amiability, conversing about the virtues of friendship and benevolence. Their lives are supported by the work of their own Houyhnhnm servant-class. Those with white, sorrel, and gray coats are said to be "naturally" the inferiors of bay, black, and dapple-gray

Houyhnhnms, and everyone accepts the rules; there are no rebels here. The catch is that, for good or ill, human beings are not Houyhnhnms: They possess feelings as well as reason. If human beings are not Houyhnhnms, neither are they Yahoos, although they have the capacity to soar as high and sink as low as those two creatures. Some readers believe that the Yahoos are a reflection of Swift's own hatred of people. Swift admitted to hating "all nations, professions, and communities," but said that he loved individuals. What *Gulliver's Travels* would show, according to Swift, was that the being so-called "*animal rationale . . .* would only be *rationis capax*"; that is, human beings, often called the rational animal, seldom realize their capacity to reason. Nonetheless, Gulliver's contempt for others, including members of his own family and the generous Pedro de Mendez after his return home, leaves the question of Swift's own views open for discussion.

Houyhnhnms.   The Houyhnhnms cannot be read as simple allegorical figures for the good of human reason. The rigid order of their society, which includes discrimination within their own ranks as well as an utter abhorrence for and enslavement of the Yahoos, is not a model of the perfect society, as some readers may think.

Gulliver, always easily impressed, is totally won to the horses' way of life, and desperately disassociates himself from the Yahoos. His voice takes on a whinnying note and his gait is a modified trot, in imitation of his idols. Gulliver thinks of himself and the Houyhnhnms as Us, the Yahoos as Them. Exiled from the land, he embarks in a boat caulked with Yahoo tallow whose sails are fashioned from tanned Yahoo skins, and he troubles himself no more than the Houyhnhnms about Yahoo genocide. Later, he is disgusted by the very sight of the generous captain who rescues him, and once back home he is only by degrees able to bear the company of his own family, preferring to be with his carriage horses. Perhaps the final indictment is that people are capable of such mad egotism as Gulliver displays at the end, sitting smug and deluded in his darkened stable.

> I have ever hated all nations, professions, and communities, and all my love is toward individuals; for instance, I hate the tribe of lawyers, but I love Counsellor Such-a-one, Judge Such-a one; for so with physicians, . . . soldiers, English, Scotch, French, and the rest. But principally I hate and detest that animal called man, although I heartily love John, Peter, Thomas, and so forth.
>
> – Jonathan Swift, Letter to Alexander Pope, 1725

■ **FURTHER RESEARCH**

Biography
Ehrenpreis, Irvin. *The Personality of Jonathan Swift.* 1958.
——. *Swift: The Man, His Works, and the Age.* 1962.
Nokes, David. *Jonathan Swift, A Hypocrite Reversed: A Critical Biography.* 1985.

Criticism
Bloom, Harold, ed. *Jonathan Swift's* Gulliver's Travels. 1996.
Flynn, Carol Houlihan. *The Body in Swift and Defoe.* 1990.
Fox, Christopher. *The Cambridge Companion to Jonathan Swift.* 2003.
Palmeri, Frank, ed. *Critical Essays on Jonathan Swift.* 1993.
Rawson, Claude Julien, ed. *Swift: A Collection of Critical Essays.* 1994.
Wood, Nigel, ed. *Jonathan Swift.* 1999.
Zimmerman, Everett. *Swift's Narrative Satires: Author and Authority.* 1983.

■ **PRONUNCIATION**
Houyhnhnms: HWIN-ims

⟡ Gulliver's Travels

PART IV

A Voyage to the Country
of the Houyhnhnms[1]

CHAPTER 1. *The Author sets out as Captain of a ship. His men conspire against him, confine him a long time to his cabin, set him on shore in an unknown land. He travels up into the country. The* Yahoos, *a strange sort of animal, described. The Author meets two* Houyhnhnms.

I continued at home with my wife and children about five months in a very happy condition, if I could have learned the lesson of knowing when I was well. I left my poor wife big with child, and accepted an advantageous offer made me to be Captain of the *Adventurer,* a stout merchantman of 350 tons: for I understood navigation well, and being grown weary of a surgeon's employment at sea, which however I could exercise upon occasion, I took a skilful young man of that calling, one Robert Purefoy, into my ship. We set sail from Portsmouth upon the seventh day of September, 1710; on the fourteenth we met with Captain Pocock of Bristol, at Teneriffe,[2] who was going to the bay of Campechy,[3] to cut logwood. On the sixteenth, he was parted from us by a storm; I heard since my return, that his ship foundered, and none escaped but one cabin boy. He was an honest man, and a good sailor, but a little too positive in his own opinions, which was the cause of his destruction, as it hath been of several others. For if he had followed my advice, he might have been safe at home with his family at this time, as well as myself.

I had several men died in my ship of calentures,[4] so that I was forced to get recruits out of Barbadoes, and the Leeward Islands, where I touched by the direction of the merchants who employed me, which I had soon too much cause to repent: for I found afterwards that most of them had been buccaneers. I had fifty hands on board, and my orders were, that I should trade with the Indians in the South-Sea, and make what discoveries I could. These rogues whom I had picked up debauched my other men, and they all formed a conspiracy to seize the ship and secure me; which they did one morning, rushing into my cabin, and binding me hand and foot, threatening to throw me overboard, if I offered to stir. I told them, I was their prisoner, and would submit. This they made me swear to do, and then they unbound me, only fastening one of my legs with a chain near my bed, and placed a sentry at my door with his piece charged, who

---

[1] **Houyhnhnms:** The name is meant to sound like the neigh of a horse.

[2] **Teneriffe:** One of the Canary Islands.

[3] **Campechy:** In the Gulf of Mexico.

[4] **calentures:** A tropical fever.

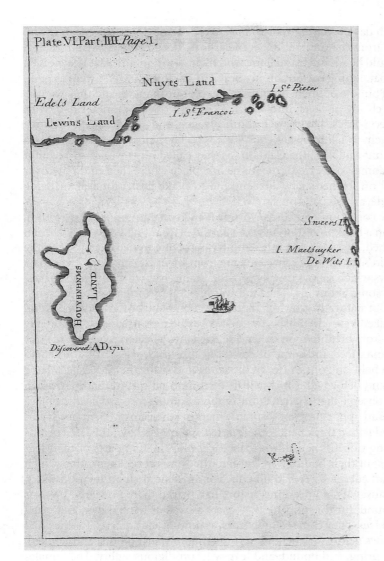

Plate VI.Part.IIII.*Page*.1.

Edels Land

Lewins Land

Nuyts Land

I.S! Francoi

I.S! Pieter

Sweers I.

I. Maelsuyker

De Wits I.

HOUYHNHNMS LAND

Discovered AD 1711

was commanded to shoot me dead, if I attempted my liberty. They sent me down victuals and drink, and took the government of the ship to themselves. Their design was to turn pirates, and plunder the Spaniards, which they could not do, till they got more men. But first they resolved to sell the goods in the ship, and then go to Madagascar for recruits, several among them having died since my confinement. They sailed many weeks, and traded with the Indians, but I knew not what course they took, being kept a close prisoner in my cabin, and expecting nothing less than to be murdered, as they often threatened me.

Upon the ninth day of May, 1711, one James Welch came down to my cabin; and said he had orders from the Captain to get me ashore. I expostulated with him, but in vain; neither would he so much as tell me who their new Captain was. They forced me into the longboat, letting me put on my best suit of clothes, which were as good as new, and a small bundle of linen, but no arms except my hanger; and they were so civil as not to search my pockets, into which I conveyed what money I had, with some other little necessaries. They rowed about a league, and then set me down on a strand. I desired them to tell me what country it was. They all swore, they knew no more than myself, but said, that the Captain (as they called him) was resolved, after they had sold the lading, to get rid of me in the first place where they could discover land. They pushed off immediately, advising me to make haste, for fear of being overtaken by the tide, and so bade me farewell.

In this desolate condition I advanced forward, and soon got upon firm ground, where I sat down on a bank to rest myself, and consider what I had best to do. When I was a little refreshed, I went up into the country, resolving to deliver myself to the first savages I should meet, and purchase my life from them by some bracelets, glass rings, and other toys which sailors usually provide themselves with in those voyages, and whereof I had some about me. The land was divided by long rows of trees, not regularly planted, but naturally growing; there was great plenty of grass, and several fields of oats. I walked very circumspectly for fear of being surprised, or suddenly shot with an arrow from behind or on either side. I fell into a beaten road, where I saw many tracks of human feet, and some of cows, but most of horses. At last I beheld several animals in a field, and one or two of the same kind sitting in trees. Their shape was very singular, and deformed, which a little discomposed me, so that I lay down behind a thicket to observe them better. Some of them coming forward near the place where I lay, gave me an opportunity of distinctly marking their form. Their heads and breasts were covered with a thick hair, some frizzled and others lank; they had beards like goats, and a long ridge of hair down their backs and the fore parts of their legs and feet, but the rest of their bodies were bare, so that I might see their skins, which were of a brown buff colour. They had no tails, nor any hair at all on their buttocks, except about the anus; which, I presume, nature had placed there to defend them as they sat on the ground; for this posture they used, as well as lying down, and often stood on their hind feet. They climbed high trees, as nimbly as a squirrel, for they had strong extended claws before and behind, terminating in sharp points, and hooked. They would often spring, and bound, and leap with prodigious agility. The females were not so large as the males; they had long lank hair on their heads, but none on their faces, nor any thing more than a sort of down on the rest of their bodies, except about the anus, and pudenda. Their dugs hung between their fore-feet, and often reached almost to the ground as they walked. The hair of both sexes was of several colours, brown, red, black, and yellow. Upon the whole, I never beheld in all my travels so disagreeable an animal, nor one against which I naturally conceived so strong an antipathy. So that thinking I had seen enough, full of contempt and aversion, I got up and pursued the beaten road, hoping it might direct me to the cabin of some Indian. I had not got far when I met one of these creatures full in my way, and coming up directly to me. The ugly monster, when he saw me, distorted several ways every feature of his visage, and stared as at an object he had never seen before; then approaching nearer, lifted up his fore-paw, whether out of curiosity or mischief, I could not tell. But I drew my hanger, and gave him a good blow with the flat side of it, for I durst not strike with the edge, fearing the inhabitants might be provoked against me, if they should come to know, that I had killed or maimed any of their cattle. When the beast felt the smart, he drew back, and roared so loud, that a herd of at least forty came flocking about me from the next field, howling and making odious faces; but I ran to the body of a tree, and leaning my back against it, kept them off by waving my hanger. Several of this cursed brood getting hold of the branches behind, leapt up into the tree, from whence they began to discharge their excrements on my head; however, I escaped pretty well, by sticking close to the stem of the tree, but was almost stifled with the filth, which fell about me on every side.

In the midst of this distress, I observed them all to run away on a sudden as fast as they could, at which I ventured to leave the tree, and pursue the road, wondering what it was that could put them into this fright. But looking on my left hand, I saw a horse walking softly in the field; which my persecutors having sooner discovered, was the cause of their flight. The horse started a little when he came near me, but soon recovering himself, looked full in my face with manifest tokens of wonder: he viewed my hands and feet, walking round me several times. I would have pursued my journey, but he placed himself directly in the way, yet looking with a very mild aspect, never offering the least violence. We stood gazing at each other for some time; at last I took the boldness to reach my hand towards his neck, with a design to stroke it, using the common style and whistle of jockeys when they are going to handle a strange horse. But this animal seeming to receive my civilities with disdain, shook his head, and bent his brows, softly raising up his right fore-foot to remove my hand. Then he neighed three or four times, but in so different a cadence, that I almost began to think he was speaking to himself in some language of his own.

While he and I were thus employed, another horse came up; who applying himself to the first in very formal manner, they gently struck each other's right hoof before, neighing several times by turns, and varying the sound, which seemed to be almost articulate. They went some paces off, as if it were to confer together, walking side by side, backward and forward, like persons deliberating upon some affair of weight, but often turning their eyes towards me, as it were to watch that I might not escape. I was amazed to see such actions and behaviour in brute beasts, and concluded with myself, that if the inhabitants of this country were endued with a proportionable degree of reason, they must needs be the wisest people upon earth. This thought gave me so much comfort, that I resolved to go forward until I could discover some house or village, or meet with any of the natives, leaving the two horses to discourse together as they pleased. But the first, who was a dapple gray, observing me to steal off, neighed after me in so expressive a tone, that I fancied myself to understand what he meant; whereupon I turned back, and came near him, to expect his farther commands: but concealing my fear as much as I could, for I began to be in some pain, how this adventure might terminate; and the reader will easily believe I did not much like my present situation.

The two horses came up close to me, looking with great earnestness upon my face and hands. The gray steed rubbed my hat all round with his right fore-hoof, and discomposed it so much that I was forced to adjust it better, by taking it off, and settling it again; whereat both he and his companion (who was a brown bay) appeared to be much surprised: The latter felt the lappet of my coat, and finding it to hang loose about me, they both looked with new signs of wonder. He stroked my right hand, seeming to admire the softness and colour; but he squeezed it so hard between his hoof and his pastern, that I was forced to roar; after which they both touched me with all possible tenderness. They were under great perplexity about my shoes and stockings, which they felt very often, neighing to each other, and using various gestures, not unlike those of a philosopher, when he would attempt to solve some new and difficult phenomenon.

Upon the whole, the behaviour of these animals was so orderly and rational, so acute and judicious, that I at last concluded, they must needs be magicians, who had thus metamorphosed themselves upon some design, and seeing a stranger in the way, were resolved to divert themselves with him; or perhaps were really amazed at the sight of a man so very different in habit, feature, and complexion from those who might probably live in so remote a climate. Upon the strength of this reasoning, I ventured to address them in the following manner: Gentlemen, if you be conjurers, as I have good cause to believe, you can understand any language; therefore I make bold to let your worships know, that I am a poor distressed English man, driven by his misfortunes upon your coast, and I entreat one of you, to let me ride upon his back, as if he were a real horse, to some house or village, where I can be relieved. In return of which favour, I will make you a present of this knife and bracelet (taking them out of my pocket). The two creatures stood silent while I spoke, seeming to listen with great attention; and when I had ended, they neighed frequently towards each other, as if they were engaged in serious conversation. I plainly observed, that their language expressed the passions very well, and the words might with little pains be resolved into an alphabet more easily than the Chinese.

I could frequently distinguish the word *Yahoo*, which was repeated by each of them several times; and although it was impossible for me to conjecture what it meant, yet while the two horses were busy in conversation, I endeavoured to practise this word upon my tongue; and as soon as they were silent, I boldly pronounced *Yahoo* in a loud voice, imitating, at the same time, as near as I could, the neighing of a horse; at which they were both visibly surprised, and the gray repeated the same word twice, as if he meant to teach me the right accent, wherein I spoke after him as well as I could, and found myself perceivably to improve every time, though very far from any degree of perfection. Then the bay tried me with a second word, much harder to be pronounced; but reducing it to the English orthography, may be spelt thus, *Houyhnhnm*. I did not succeed in this so well as the former, but after two or three farther trials, I had better fortune; and they both appeared amazed at my capacity.

After some further discourse, which I then conjectured might relate to me, the two friends took their leaves, with the same compliment of striking each other's hoof; and the gray made me signs that I should walk before him, wherein I thought it prudent to comply, till I could find a better director. When I offered to slacken my pace, he would cry *Hhuun, Hhuun;* I guessed his meaning, and gave him to understand, as well as I could, that I was weary, and not able to walk faster; upon which, he would stand a while to let me rest.

CHAPTER 2. *The Author conducted by a* Houyhnhnm *to his house. The house described. The Author's reception. The food of the* Houyhnhnms. *The Author in distress for want of meat, is at last relieved. His manner of feeding in this country.*

Having travelled about three miles, we came to a long kind of building, made of timber, stuck in the ground, and wattled across; the roof was low, and covered with straw. I now began to be a little comforted, and took out some toys, which travellers usually carry for presents to the savage Indians of America and other parts, in hopes the people of the house would be thereby encouraged to receive me kindly. The horse made me a sign to go in first; it was a large room with a smooth clay floor, and a rack and manger extending the whole length on one side. There were three nags, and two mares, not eating, but some of them sitting down upon their hams, which I very much wondered at; but wondered more to see the rest employed in domestic business. These seemed but ordinary cattle; however, this confirmed my first opinion, that a people who could so far civilise brute animals, must needs excel in wisdom all the nations of the world. The gray came in just after, and thereby prevented any ill treatment, which the others might have given me. He neighed to them several times in a style of authority, and received answers.

Beyond this room there were three others, reaching the length of the house, to which you passed through three doors, opposite to each other, in the manner of a vista; we went through the second room towards the third; here the gray walked in first, beckoning me to attend: I waited in the second room, and got ready my presents for the master and mistress of the house: They were two knives, three bracelets of false pearl, a small looking-glass, and a bead necklace. The horse neighed three or four times, and I waited to hear some answers in a human voice, but I heard no other returns, than in the same dialect, only one or two a little shriller than his. I began to think that this house must belong to some person of great note among them, because there appeared so much ceremony before I could gain admittance. But, that a man of quality should be served all by horses, was beyond my comprehension. I feared my brain was disturbed by my sufferings and misfortunes: I roused myself, and looked about me in the room where I was left alone; this was furnished like the first, only after a more elegant manner. I rubbed my eyes often, but the same objects still occurred. I pinched my arms and sides, to awake myself, hoping I might be in a dream. I then absolutely concluded, that all these appearances could be nothing else but necromancy and magic. But I had no time to pursue these reflections; for the gray horse came to the door, and made me a sign to follow him into the third room, where I saw a very comely mare, together with a colt and foal, sitting on their haunches, upon mats of straw, not unartfully made, and perfectly neat and clean.

The mare soon after my entrance, rose from her mat, and coming up close, after having nicely observed my hands and face, gave me a most contemptuous look; then turning to the horse, I heard the word *Yahoo* often repeated betwixt them; the meaning of which word I could not then comprehend, although it were the first I had learned to pronounce; but I was soon better informed, to my everlasting mortification: for the horse beckoning to me with his head, and repeating the word *Hhuun, Hhuun,* as he did upon the road, which I understood was to attend him, led me out into a kind of court, where was another building at some distance from the house. Here we entered, and I saw three of those detestable creatures, whom I first met after my landing, feeding upon roots, and the flesh of some animals, which I afterwards found to be that of asses and dogs, and now and then a cow dead by accident or disease. They were all tied by the neck with strong withes, fastened to a beam; they held their food between the claws of their fore-feet, and tore it with their teeth.

The master horse ordered a sorrel nag, one of his servants, to untie the largest of these animals, and take him into the yard. The beast and I were brought close together, and our countenances diligently compared, both by master and servant, who thereupon repeated several times the word *Yahoo*. My horror and astonishment are not to be described, when I observed, in this abominable animal, a perfect human figure: the face of it indeed was flat and broad, the nose depressed, the lips large, and the mouth wide. But these differences are common to all savage nations, where the lineaments of the countenance are distorted by the natives suffering their infants to lie grovelling on the earth, or by carrying them on their backs, nuzzling with their face against the mother's shoulders. The fore-feet of the *Yahoo* differed from my hands in nothing else but the length of the nails, the coarseness and brownness of the palms, and the hairiness on the backs. There was the same resemblance between our feet, with the same differences, which I knew very well, though the horses did not, because of my shoes and stockings; the same in every part of our bodies, except as to hairiness and colour, which I have already described.

The great difficulty that seemed to stick with the two horses, was, to see the rest of my body so very different from that of a *Yahoo*, for which I was obliged to my clothes, whereof they had no conception. The sorrel nag offered me a root, which he held (after their manner, as we shall describe in its proper place) between his hoof and pastern; I took it in my hand, and having smelt it, returned it to him again as civilly as I could. He brought out of the *Yahoo's* kennel a piece of ass's flesh, but it smelt so offensively that I turned from it with loathing: he then threw it to the *Yahoo*, by whom it was greedily devoured. He afterwards showed me a wisp of hay, and a fetlock full of oats; but I shook my head, to signify, that neither of these were food for me. And indeed, I now apprehended that I must absolutely starve, if I did not get to some of my own species; for as to those filthy *Yahoos*, although there were few greater lovers of mankind, at that time, than myself, yet I confess I never saw any sensitive being so detestable on all accounts; and the more I came near them, the more hateful they grew, while I stayed in that country. This the master horse observed by my behaviour, and therefore sent the *Yahoo* back to his kennel. He then put his fore-hoof to his mouth, at which I was much surprised, although he did it with ease, and with a motion that appeared perfectly natural, and made other signs to know what I would eat; but I could not return him such an answer as he was able to apprehend; and if he had understood me, I did not see how it was possible to contrive any way for finding myself nourishment. While we were thus engaged, I observed a cow passing by, whereupon I pointed to her, and expressed a desire to let me go and milk her. This had its effect; for he led me back into the house, and ordered a mare-servant to open a room, where a good store of milk lay in earthen and wooden vessels, after a very orderly and cleanly manner. She gave me a large bowl full, of which I drank very heartily, and found myself well refreshed.

About noon I saw coming towards the house a kind of vehicle, drawn like a sledge by four *Yahoos*. There was in it an old steed, who seemed to be of quality; he alighted with his hind-feet forward, having by accident got a hurt in his left fore-foot. He came to dine with our horse, who received him with great civility. They dined in the best room, and had oats boiled in milk for the second course, which the old horse eat warm, but the rest cold. Their mangers were placed circular in the middle of the room, and divided into several partitions, round which they sat on their haunches upon bosses of straw. In the middle was a large rack with angles answering to every partition of the manger; so that each horse and mare eat their own hay, and their own mash of oats and milk, with much decency and regularity. The behaviour of the young colt and foal appeared very modest, and that of the master and mistress extremely cheerful and complaisant to their guest. The gray ordered me to stand by him, and much discourse passed between him and his friend concerning me, as I found by the stranger's often looking on me, and the frequent repetition of the word *Yahoo*.

I happened to wear my gloves, which the master gray observing, seemed perplexed, discovering signs of wonder what I had done to my fore-feet; he put his hoof three or four times to them, as if he would signify, that I should reduce them to their former shape, which I presently did, pulling off both my gloves, and putting them into my pocket. This occasioned farther talk, and I saw the company was pleased with my behaviour, whereof I soon found the good effects. I was ordered to speak the few words I understood, and while they were at dinner, the master taught me the names for oats, milk, fire, water, and some others; which I could readily pronounce after him, having from my youth a great facility in learning languages.

When dinner was done, the master horse took me aside, and by signs and words made me understand the concern that he was in, that I had nothing to eat. Oats in their tongue are called *hlunnh*. This word I pronounced two or three times; for although I had refused them at first, yet upon second thoughts, I considered that I could contrive to make of them a kind of bread, which might be sufficient with milk to keep me alive, till I could make my escape to some other country, and to creatures of my own species. The horse immediately ordered a white mare-servant of his family to bring me a good quantity of oats in a sort of wooden tray. These I heated before the fire as well as I could, and rubbed them till the husks came off, which I made a shift to winnow from the grain; I ground and beat them between two stones, then took water, and made them into a paste or cake, which I toasted at the fire, and ate warm with milk. It was at first a very insipid diet, though common enough in many parts of Europe, but grew tolerable by time; and having been often reduced to hard fare in my life, this was not the first experiment I had made how easily nature is satisfied. And I cannot but observe, that I never had one hour's sickness, while I stayed in this island. 'Tis true, I sometimes made a shift to catch a rabbit, or bird, by springes[5] made of *Yahoos'* hairs, and I often gathered wholesome herbs, which I boiled, and eat as salads with my bread, and now and then, for a rarity, I made a little butter, and drank the

---

[5] **springes:** Snares.

whey. I was at first at a great loss for salt; but custom soon reconciled the want of it; and I am confident that the frequent use of salt among us is an effect of luxury, and was first introduced only as a provocative to drink; except where it is necessary for preserving of flesh in long voyages, or in places remote from great markets. For we observe no animal to be fond of it but man: and as to myself, when I left this country, it was a great while before I could endure the taste of it in anything that I eat.

This is enough to say upon the subject of my diet, wherewith other travellers fill their books, as if the readers were personally concerned whether we fared well or ill. However, it was necessary to mention this matter, lest the world should think it impossible that I could find sustenance for three years in such a country, and among such inhabitants.

When it grew towards evening, the master horse ordered a place for me to lodge in; it was but six yards from the house, and separated from the stable of the *Yahoos*. Here I got some straw, and covering myself with my own clothes, slept very sound. But I was in a short time better accommodated, as the reader shall know hereafter, when I come to treat more particularly about my way of living.

CHAPTER 3. *The Author studious to learn the language, the* Houyhnhnm *his master assists in teaching him. The language described. Several* Houyhnhnms *of quality come out of curiosity to see the Author. He gives his master a short account of his voyage.*

My principal endeavour was to learn the language, which my master (for so I shall henceforth call him), and his children, and every servant of his house, were desirous to teach me. For they looked upon it as a prodigy that a brute animal should discover such marks of a rational creature. I pointed to every thing, and enquired the name of it, which I wrote down in my journal-book when I was alone, and corrected my bad accent by desiring those of the family to pronounce it often. In this employment, a sorrel nag, one of the under servants, was very ready to assist me.

In speaking, they pronounce through the nose and throat, and their language approaches nearest to the High-Dutch, or German, of any I know in Europe; but is much more graceful and significant. The Emperor Charles V. made almost the same observation, when he said, that if he were to speak to his horse, it should be in High-Dutch.

The curiosity and impatience of my master were so great, that he spent many hours of his leisure to instruct me. He was convinced (as he afterwards told me) that I must be a *Yahoo,* but my teachableness, civility, and cleanliness, astonished him; which were qualities altogether so opposite to those animals. He was most perplexed about my clothes, reasoning sometimes with himself, whether they were a part of my body: for I never pulled them off till the family were asleep, and got them on before they waked in the morning. My master was eager to learn from whence I came, how I acquired those appearances of reason, which I discovered in all my actions, and to know my story from my own mouth, which he hoped he should soon do by the great proficiency I made in learning and pronouncing their words and sentences. To help my memory, I formed all I learned into the English alphabet, and writ the words down with the translations. This last, after some time, I ventured to do in my master's presence. It cost me much trouble to explain to him what I was doing; for the inhabitants have not the least idea of books or literature.

In about ten weeks time I was able to understand most of his questions, and in three months could give him some tolerable answers. He was extremely curious to know from what part of the country I came, and how I was taught to imitate a rational creature, because the *Yahoos* (whom he saw I exactly resembled in my head, hands, and face, that were only visible), with some appearance of cunning, and the strongest disposition to mischief, were observed to be the most unteachable of all brutes. I answered, that I came over the sea from a far place, with many others of my own kind, in a great hollow vessel made of the bodies of trees. That my companions forced me to land on this coast, and then left me to shift for myself. It was with some difficulty, and by the help of many signs, that I brought him to understand me. He replied, that I must needs be mistaken, or that I *said the thing which was not.* (For they have no word in their language to express lying or falsehood.) He knew it was impossible that there could be a country beyond the sea, or that a parcel of brutes could move a wooden vessel whither they pleased upon water. He was sure no *Houyhnhnm* alive could make such a vessel, nor would trust *Yahoos* to manage it.

The word *Houyhnhnm,* in their tongue, signifies a *horse,* and in its etymology, *the perfection of nature.* I told my master, that I was at a loss for expression, but would improve as fast as I could; and hoped in a short time I should be able to tell him wonders: he was pleased to direct his own mare, his colt and foal, and the servants of the family, to take all opportunities of instructing me, and every day for two or three hours, he was at the same pains himself. Several horses and mares of quality in the neighbourhood came often to our house upon the report spread of a wonderful *Yahoo,* that could speak like a *Houyhnhnm,* and seemed in his words and actions to discover some glimmerings of reason. These delighted to converse with me: they put many questions, and received such answers as I was able to return. By all these advantages, I made so great a progress, that in five months from my arrival I understood whatever was spoke, and could express myself tolerably well.

The *Houyhnhnms* who came to visit my master, out of a design of seeing and talking with me, could hardly believe me to be a right *Yahoo,* because my body had a different covering from others of my kind. They were astonished to observe me without the usual hair or skin, except on my head, face, and hands; but I discovered that secret to my master, upon an accident, which happened about a fortnight before.

I have already told the reader, that every night when the family were gone to bed, it was my custom to strip and cover myself with my clothes: it happened one morning early, that my master sent for me, by the sorrel nag, who was his valet; when he came, I was fast asleep, my clothes fallen off on one side, and my shirt above my waist. I awaked at the noise he made, and observed him to deliver his message in some disorder; after which he went to my master, and in a great fright gave him a very confused account of what he had seen. This I presently discovered; for going as soon as I was dressed, to pay my attendance upon his Honour, he asked me the meaning of what his servant had reported, that I was not the same thing when I slept as I appeared to be at other times; that his valet assured him, some part of me was white, some yellow, at least not so white, and some brown.

I had hitherto concealed the secret of my dress, in order to distinguish myself, as much as possible, from that cursed race of *Yahoos;* but now I found it in vain to do so any longer. Besides, I considered that my clothes and shoes would soon wear out, which already were in a declining condition, and must be supplied by some contrivance from the hides of *Yahoos* or other brutes; whereby the whole secret would be known. I therefore told my master, that in the country from whence I came, those of my kind always covered their bodies with the hairs of certain animals prepared by art, as well for decency as to avoid the inclemencies of air, both hot and cold; of which, as to my own person, I would give him immediate conviction, if he pleased to command me: only desiring his excuse, if I did not expose those parts that nature taught us to conceal. He said my discourse was all very strange, but especially the last part; for he could not understand why nature should teach us to conceal what nature had given. That neither himself nor family were ashamed of any parts of their bodies; but however I might do as I pleased. Whereupon, I first unbuttoned my coat, and pulled it off. I did the same with my waistcoat; I drew off my shoes, stockings, and breeches. I let my shirt down to my waist, and drew up the bottom, fastening it like a girdle about my middle to hide my nakedness.

My master observed the whole performance with great signs of curiosity and admiration. He took up all my clothes in his pastern, one piece after another, and examined them diligently; he then stroked my body very gently, and looked round me several times, after which he said, it was plain that I must be a perfect *Yahoo;* but that I differed very much from the rest of my species, in the softness, and whiteness, and smoothness of my skin, my want of hair in several parts of my body, the shape and shortness of my claws behind and before, and my affectation of walking continually on my two hinder feet. He desired to see no more, and gave me leave to put on my clothes again, for I was shuddering with cold.

I expressed my uneasiness at his giving me so often the appellation of *Yahoo,* an odious animal, for which I had so utter a hatred and contempt. I begged he would forbear applying that word to me, and take the same order in his family, and among his friends whom he suffered to see me. I requested likewise, that the secret of my having a false covering to my body might be known to none but himself, at least as long as my present clothing should last; for as to what the sorrel nag his valet had observed, his Honour might command him to conceal it.

All this my master very graciously consented to, and thus the secret was kept till my clothes began to wear out, which I was forced to supply by several contrivances, that shall hereafter be mentioned. In the meantime, he desired I would go on with my utmost diligence to learn their language, because he was more astonished at my capacity for speech and reason, than at the figure of my body, whether it were covered or no; adding, that he waited with some impatience to hear the wonders which I promised to tell him.

From thenceforward he doubled the pains he had been at to instruct me; he brought me into all company, and made them treat me with civility, because, as he told them, privately, this would put me into good humour, and make me more diverting.

Every day when I waited on him, beside the trouble he was at in teaching, he would ask me several questions concerning myself, which I answered as well as I could; and by these means he had already received some general ideas, though very imperfect. It would be tedious to relate the several steps by which I advanced to a more regular conversation: But the first account I gave of myself in any order and length, was to this purpose:

That I came from a very far country, as I already had attempted to tell him, with about fifty more of my own species; that we travelled upon the seas, in a great hollow vessel made of wood, and larger than his Honour's house. I described the ship to him in the best terms I could, and explained by the help of my handkerchief displayed, how it was driven forward by the wind. That upon a quarrel among us, I was set on shore on this coast, where I walked forward without knowing whither, till he delivered me from the persecution of those execrable *Yahoos.* He asked me, who made the ship, and how it was possible that the *Houyhnhnms* of my country would leave it to the management of brutes? My answer was, that I durst proceed no further in my relation, unless he would give me his word and honour that he would not be offended, and then I would tell him the wonders I had so often promised. He agreed; and I went on by assuring him, that the ship was made by creatures like myself, who in all the countries I had travelled, as well as in my own, were the only governing, rational animals; and that upon my arrival hither, I was as much astonished to see the *Houyhnhnms* act like rational beings, as he or his friends could be in finding some marks of reason in a creature he was pleased to call a *Yahoo,* to which I owned my resemblance in every part, but could not account for their degenerate and brutal nature. I said farther, that if good fortune ever restored me to my native country, to relate my travels hither, as I resolved to do, every body would believe that I *said the thing which was not;* that I invented the story out of my own head; and with all possible respect to himself, his family and friends, and under his promise of not being offended, our countrymen would hardly think it probable, that a *Houyhnhnm* should be the presiding creature of a nation, and a *Yahoo* the brute.

CHAPTER 4. *The* Houyhnhnms' *notion of truth and falsehood. The Author's discourse disapproved by his master. The Author gives a more particular account of himself, and the accidents of his voyage.*

My master heard me with great appearances of uneasiness in his countenance, because *doubting,* or *not believing,* are so little known in this country, that the inhabitants cannot tell how to behave themselves under such circumstances. And I remember in frequent discourses with my master concerning the nature of manhood, in other parts of the world, having occasion to talk of *lying* and *false representation,* it was with much difficulty that he comprehended what I meant, although he had otherwise a most acute judgment. For he argued thus: that the use of speech was to make us understand one another, and to receive information of facts; now if any one *said the thing which was not,* these ends were defeated; because I cannot properly be said to understand him; and I am so far from receiving information, that he leaves me worse than in ignorance, for I am led to believe a thing black when it is white, and short when it is long. And these were all the notions he had concerning that faculty of *lying,* so perfectly well understood, and so universally practised, among human creatures.

To return from this digression; when I asserted that the *Yahoos* were the only governing animals in my country, which my master said was altogether past his conception, he desired to know, whether we had *Houyhnhnms* among us, and what was their employment: I told him, we had great numbers, that in summer they grazed in the fields, and in winter were kept in houses, with hay and oats, where *Yahoo* servants were employed to rub their skins smooth, comb their manes, pick their feet, serve them with food, and make their beds. I understand you well, said my master, it is now very plain, from all you have spoken, that whatever share of reason the *Yahoos* pretend to, the *Houyhnhnms* are your masters; I heartily wish our *Yahoos* would be so tractable. I begged his Honour would please to excuse me from proceeding any farther, because I was very certain that the account he expected from me would be highly displeasing. But he insisted in commanding me to let him know the best and the worst: I told him, he should be obeyed. I owned, that the *Houyhnhnms* among us, whom we called horses, were the most generous and comely animals we had, that they excelled in strength and swiftness; and when they belonged to persons of quality, employed in travelling, racing, or drawing chariots, they were treated with much kindness and care, till they fell into diseases, or became foundered in the feet; and then they were sold, and used to all kind of drudgery till they died; after which their skins were stripped and sold for what they were worth, and their bodies left to be devoured by dogs and birds of prey. But the common race of horses had not so good fortune, being kept by farmers and carriers, and other mean people, who put them to greater labour, and fed them worse. I described, as well as I could, our way of riding, the shape and use of a bridle, a saddle, a spur, and a whip, of harness and wheels. I added, that we fastened plates of a certain hard substance called iron at the bottom of their feet, to preserve their hoofs from being broken by the stony ways on which we often travelled.

My master, after some expressions of great indignation, wondered how we dared to venture upon a *Houyhnhnm's* back, for he was sure, that the weakest servant in his house would be able to shake off the strongest *Yahoo,* or by lying down, and rolling on his back, squeeze the brute to death. I answered, that our horses were trained up from three or four years old to the several uses we intended them for; that if any of them proved intolerably vicious, they were employed for carriages; that they were severely beaten while they were young for any mischievous tricks; that the males, designed for common use of riding or draught, were generally castrated about two years after their birth, to take down their spirits, and make them more tame and gentle; that they were indeed sensible of rewards and punishments; but his Honour would please to consider, that they had not the least tincture of reason any more than the *Yahoos* in this country.

It put me to the pains of many circumlocutions to give my master a right idea of what I spoke; for their language doth not abound in variety of words, because their wants and passions are fewer than among us. But it is impossible to express his noble resentment at our savage treatment of the *Houyhnhnm* race, particularly after I had explained the manner and use of castrating horses among us, to hinder them from propagating their kind, and to render them more servile. He said, if it were possible there could be any country where *Yahoos* alone were endued with reason, they certainly must be the governing animal, because reason will in time always prevail against brutal strength. But, considering the frame of our bodies, and especially of mine, he thought no creature of equal bulk was so ill contrived, for employing that reason in the common offices of life; whereupon he desired to know whether those among whom I lived resembled me or the *Yahoos* of his country. I assured him, that I was as well shaped as most of my age; but the younger and the females were much more soft and tender, and the skins of the latter generally as white as milk. He said, I differed indeed from other *Yahoos,* being much more cleanly, and not altogether so deformed, but, in point of real advantage, he thought I differed for the worse. That my nails were of no use either to my fore or hinder-feet; as to my fore-feet, he could not properly call them by that name, for he never observed me to walk upon them; that they were too soft to bear the ground; that I generally went with them uncovered, neither was the covering I sometimes wore on them, of the same shape, or so strong as that on my feet behind. That I could not walk with any security, for if either of my hinder-feet slipped, I must inevitably fall. He then began to find fault with other parts of my body, the flatness of my face, the prominence of my nose, my eyes placed directly in front, so that I could not look on either side without turning my head: that I was not able to feed myself, without lifting one of my fore-feet to my mouth: and therefore nature had placed those joints to answer that necessity. He knew not what could be the use of those several clefts and divisions in my feet behind; these were too soft to bear the hardness and sharpness of stones without a covering made from the skin of some other brute; that my whole body wanted a fence against heat and cold, which I was forced to put on and off every day with tediousness and trouble. And lastly, that he observed every animal in this country naturally to abhor the *Yahoos,* whom the weaker avoided, and the stronger drove from them. So that supposing us to have the gift of reason, he could not see how it were possible to cure that natural antipathy which every creature discovered against us; nor consequently, how we could tame and render them serviceable. However, he would (as he said) debate the matter no farther, because he was more desirous to know my own story, the country where I was born, and the several actions and events of my life before I came hither.

I assured him, how extremely desirous I was that he should be satisfied on every point; but I doubted much, whether it would be possible for me to explain myself on several subjects whereof his Honour could have no conception, because I saw nothing in his country to which I could resemble them. That, however, I would do my best, and strive to express myself by similitudes, humbly desiring his assistance when I wanted proper words; which he was pleased to promise me.

I said, my birth was of honest parents in an island called England, which was remote from this country, as many days' journey as the strongest of his Honour's servants could travel in the annual course of the sun. That I was bred a surgeon, whose trade it is to cure wounds and hurts in the body, got by accident or violence; that my country was governed by a female man, whom we called a Queen. That I left it to get riches, whereby I might maintain myself and family when I should return. That, in my last voyage, I was commander of the ship, and had about fifty *Yahoos* under me, many of which died at sea, and I was forced to supply them by others picked out from several nations. That our ship was twice in danger of being sunk; the first time by a great storm, and the second, by striking against a rock. Here my master interposed, by asking me, how I could persuade strangers out of different countries to venture with me, after the losses I had sustained, and the hazards I had run. I said, they were fellows of desperate fortunes, forced to fly from the places of their birth, on account of their poverty or their crimes. Some were undone by lawsuits; others spent all they had in drinking, whoring, and gaming; others fled for treason; many for murder, theft, poisoning, robbery, perjury, forgery, coining false money, for committing rapes or sodomy, for flying from their colours, or deserting to the enemy, and most of them had broken prison; none of these durst return to their native countries for fear of being hanged, or of starving in a jail; and therefore were under the necessity of seeking a livelihood in other places.

During this discourse, my master was pleased to interrupt me several times; I had made use of many circumlocutions in describing to him the nature of the several crimes for which most of our crew had been forced to fly their country. This labour took up several days' conversation, before he was able to comprehend me. He was wholly at a loss to know what could be the use or necessity of practising those vices. To clear up which I endeavoured to give some ideas of the desire of power and riches, of the terrible effects of lust, intemperance, malice, and envy. All this I was forced to define and describe by putting of cases, and making of suppositions. After which, like one whose imagination was struck with something never seen or heard of before, he would lift up his eyes with amazement and indignation. Power, government, war, law, punishment, and a thousand other things had no terms, wherein that language could express them, which made the difficulty almost insuperable to give my master any conception of what I meant. But being of an excellent understanding, much improved by contemplation and converse, he at last arrived at a competent knowledge of what human nature in our parts of the world is capable to perform, and desired I would give him some particular account of that land which we call Europe, but especially of my own country.

CHAPTER 5. *The Author, at his master's commands, informs him of the state of* England. *The causes of war among the princes of* Europe. *The Author begins to explain the* English *constitution.*

The reader may please to observe, that the following extract of many conversations I had with my master, contains a summary of the most material points, which were discoursed at several times for above two years; his Honour often desiring fuller satisfaction as I farther improved in the *Houyhnhnm* tongue. I laid before him, as well as I could, the whole state of Europe; I discoursed of trade and manufactures, of arts and sciences; and the answers I gave to all the questions he made, as they arose upon several subjects, were a fund of conversation not to be exhausted. But I shall here only set down the substance of what passed between us concerning my own country, reducing it into order as well as I can, without any regard to time or other circumstances, while I strictly adhere to truth. My only concern is, that I shall hardly be able to do justice to my master's arguments and expressions, which must needs suffer by my want of capacity, as well as by a translation into our barbarous English.

In obedience, therefore, to his Honour's commands, I related to him the Revolution under the Prince of Orange; the long war with France entered into by the said prince, and renewed by his successor, the present Queen, wherein the greatest powers of Christendom were engaged, and which still continued: I computed at his request, that about a million of *Yahoos* might have been killed in the whole progress of it; and perhaps a hundred or more cities taken, and thrice as many ships burnt or sunk.[6]

He asked me what were the usual causes or motives that made one country go to war with another. I answered they were innumerable; but I should only mention a few of the chief. Sometimes the ambition of princes, who never think they have land or people enough to govern; sometimes the corruption of ministers, who engage their master in a war in order to stifle or divert the clamour of the subjects against their evil administration. Difference in opinions hath cost many millions of lives: for instance, whether flesh be bread, or bread be flesh; whether the juice of a certain berry be blood or wine; whether whistling be a vice or a virtue; whether it be better to kiss a post, or throw it into the fire; what is the best colour for a coat, whether black, white, red, or gray; and whether it should be long or short, narrow or wide, dirty or clean; with many more.[7] Neither are any wars so furious and bloody, or of so long continuance, as those occasioned by difference in opinion, especially if it be in things indifferent.

Sometimes the quarrel between two princes is to decide which of them shall dispossess a third of his dominions, where neither of them pretend to any right. Sometimes one prince quarrelleth with another, for fear the other should quarrel with him. Sometimes a war is entered upon, because the enemy is too strong, and sometimes because he is too weak. Sometimes our neighbours want the things which we have, or have the things which we want; and we both fight, till they take ours or give us theirs. It is a very justifiable cause of a war to invade a country after the people have been wasted by famine, destroyed by pestilence, or embroiled by factions among themselves. It is justifiable to enter into war against our nearest ally, when one of his towns lies convenient for us, or a territory of land, that would render our dominions round and complete. If a prince sends forces into a nation, where the people are poor and ignorant, he may lawfully put half of them to death, and make slaves of the rest, in order to civilize and reduce them from their barbarous way of living. It is a very kingly, honourable, and frequent practice, when one prince desires the assistance of another to secure him against an invasion, that the assistant, when he hath driven out the invader, should seize on the dominions himself, and kill, imprison, or banish the prince he came to relieve. Alliance by blood or marriage is a frequent cause of war between princes; and the nearer the kindred is, the greater is their disposition to quarrel: Poor nations are hungry, and rich nations are proud; and pride and hunger will ever be at variance. For these reasons, the trade of a

---

[6] Gulliver disingenuously describes to his master the "Glorious Revolution" of 1688 that ousted the English James II, and the War of the Spanish Succession, which occupied the decade between 1703 and 1713.

[7] Gulliver alludes to a number of religious doctrines and practices disputed hotly by Christians since the Reformation. He refers specifically here to transubstantiation (the Catholic belief that the bread and wine in Communion become the body and blood of Jesus Christ), to the use of crucifixes and music in worship, and to the wearing of ecclesiastical robes.

soldier is held the most honourable of all others; because a soldier is a *Yahoo* hired to kill in cold blood as many of his own species, who have never offended him, as possibly he can.

There is likewise a kind of beggarly princes in Europe, not able to make war by themselves, who hire out their troops to richer nations, for so much a day to each man; of which they keep three fourths to themselves, and it is the best part of their maintenance; such are those in Germany and other northern parts of Europe.

What you have told me (said my master), upon the subject of war, does indeed discover most admirably the effects of that reason you pretend to: however, it is happy that the shame is greater than the danger; and that nature hath left you utterly uncapable of doing much mischief.

For your mouths lying flat with your faces, you can hardly bite each other to any purpose, unless by consent. Then as to the claws upon your feet before and behind, they are so short and tender, that one of our *Yahoos* would drive a dozen of yours before him. And therefore in recounting the numbers of those who have been killed in battle, I cannot but think that you have *said the thing which is not.*

I could not forbear shaking my head, and smiling a little at his ignorance. And being no stranger to the art of war, I gave him a description of cannons, culverins, muskets, carabines, pistols, bullets, powder, swords, bayonets, battles, sieges, retreats, attacks, undermines, countermines, bombardments, sea fights; ships sunk with a thousand men, twenty thousand killed on each side; dying groans, limbs flying in the air, smoke, noise, confusion, trampling to death under horses' feet; flight, pursuit, victory; fields strewed with carcases left for food to dogs, and wolves, and birds of prey; plundering, stripping, ravishing, burning and destroying. And to set forth the valour of my own dear countrymen, I assured him, that I had seen them blow up a hundred enemies at once in a siege, and as many in a ship, and beheld the dead bodies come down in pieces from the clouds, to the great diversion of the spectators.

I was going on to more particulars, when my master commanded me silence. He said, whoever understood the nature of *Yahoos* might easily believe it possible for so vile an animal to be capable of every action I had named, if their strength and cunning equalled their malice. But as my discourse had increased his abhorrence of the whole species, so he found it gave him a disturbance in his mind, to which he was wholly a stranger before. He thought his ears being used to such abominable words, might by degrees admit them with less detestation. That although he hated the *Yahoos* of this country, yet he no more blamed them for their odious qualities, than he did a *gnnayh* (a bird of prey) for its cruelty, or a sharp stone for cutting his hoof. But when a creature pretending to reason could be capable of such enormities, he dreaded lest the corruption of that faculty might be worse than brutality itself. He seemed therefore confident, that instead of reason, we were only possessed of some quality fitted to increase our natural vices; as the reflection from a troubled stream returns the image of an ill-shapen body, not only larger, but more distorted.

He added, that he had heard too much upon the subject of war, both in this, and some former discourses. There was another point which a little perplexed him at present. I had informed him, that some of our crew left their country on account of being ruined by *Law;* that I had already explained the meaning of the word; but he was at a loss how it should come to pass, that the law which was intended for every man's preservation, should be any man's ruin. Therefore he desired to be farther satisfied what I meant by law, and the dispensers thereof, according to the present practice in my own country; because he thought nature and reason were sufficient guides for a reasonable animal, as we pretended to be, in showing us what we ought to do, and what to avoid.

I assured his Honour, that law was a science wherein I had not much conversed, further than by employing advocates, in vain, upon some injustices that had been done me; however, I would give him all the satisfaction I was able.

I said, there was a society of men among us, bred up from their youth in the art of proving by words multiplied for the purpose, that white is black, and black is white, according as they are paid. To this society all the rest of the people are slaves. For example, if my neighbour hath a mind to my cow, he hires a lawyer to prove that he ought to have my cow from me. I must then hire another to defend my right, it being against all rules of law that any man should be allowed to speak for himself. Now in this case, I, who am the right owner, lie under two great disadvantages. First, my lawyer, being practised almost from his cradle in defending falsehood, is quite out of his element when he would be an advocate for justice, which as an office unnatural, he always attempts with great awkwardness, if not with ill-will. The second disadvantage is, that my lawyer must proceed with great caution, or else he will be reprimanded by the judges, and abhorred by his brethren, as one that would lessen the practice of the law. And therefore I have but two methods to preserve my cow. The first is, to gain over my adversary's lawyer with a double fee; who will then betray his client, by insinuating that he hath justice on his side. The second way is for my lawyer to make my cause appear as unjust as he can, by allowing the cow to belong to my adversary; and this, if it be skilfully done, will certainly bespeak the favour of the bench.

Now, your Honour is to know, that these judges are persons appointed to decide all controversies of property, as well as for the trial of criminals, and picked out from the most dexterous lawyers, who are grown old or lazy, and having been biassed all their lives against truth and equity, are under such a fatal necessity of favouring fraud, perjury, and oppression, that I have known several of them refuse a large bribe from the side where justice lay, rather than injure the faculty,[8] by doing any thing unbecoming their nature or their office.

It is a maxim among these lawyers, that whatever hath been done before, may legally be done again: and therefore they take special care to record all the decisions formerly made against common justice, and the general reason of mankind. These, under the name of *precedents,* they produce as authorities, to justify the most iniquitous opinions; and the judges never fail of directing accordingly.

In pleading, they studiously avoid entering into the merits of the cause; but are loud, violent, and tedious in dwelling upon all circumstances which are not to the purpose. For instance, in the case already mentioned: they never desire to know

---

[8] **faculty:** Profession.

what claim or title my adversary hath to my cow; but whether the said cow were red or black; her horns long or short; whether the field I graze her in be round or square; whether she was milked at home or abroad; what diseases she is subject to, and the like; after which they consult precedents, adjourn the cause from time to time, and in ten, twenty, or thirty years, come to an issue.

It is likewise to be observed, that this society hath a peculiar cant and jargon of their own, that no other mortal can understand, and wherein all their laws are written, which they take special care to multiply; whereby they have wholly confounded the very essence of truth and falsehood, of right and wrong; so that it will take thirty years to decide whether the field left me by my ancestors for six generations belongs to me, or to a stranger three hundred miles off.

In the trial of persons accused for crimes against the state, the method is much more short and commendable: the judge first sends to sound the disposition of those in power, after which he can easily hang or save the criminal, strictly preserving all due forms of law.

Here my master interposing, said it was a pity, that creatures endowed with such prodigious abilities of mind as these lawyers, by the description I gave of them, must certainly be, were not rather encouraged to be instructors of others in wisdom and knowledge. In answer to which, I assured his Honour, that in all points out of their own trade, they were usually the most ignorant and stupid generation among us, the most despicable in common conversation, avowed enemies to all knowledge and learning, and equally disposed to pervert the general reason of mankind in every other subject of discourse, as in that of their own profession.

CHAPTER 6. *A continuation of the state of* England. *The character of a first or chief minister of state in* European *courts.*

My master was yet wholly at a loss to understand what motives could incite this race of lawyers to perplex, disquiet, and weary themselves, and engage in a confederacy of injustice, merely for the sake of injuring their fellow-animals; neither could he comprehend what I meant in saying they did it for hire. Whereupon I was at much pains to describe to him the use of money, the materials it was made of, and the value of the metals; that when a *Yahoo* had got a great store of this precious substance, he was able to purchase whatever he had a mind to; the finest clothing, the noblest houses, great tracts of land, the most costly meats and drinks, and have his choice of the most beautiful females. Therefore since money alone was able to perform all these feats, our *Yahoos* thought they could never have enough of it to spend or to save, as they found themselves inclined from their natural bent either to profusion or avarice. That the rich man enjoyed the fruit of the poor man's labour, and the latter were a thousand to one in proportion to the former. That the bulk of our people were forced to live miserably, by labouring every day for small wages to make a few live plentifully. I enlarged myself much on these and many other particulars to the same purpose; but his Honour was still to seek,[9] for he went upon a supposition that

---

[9] **still to seek:** Still did not understand.

all animals had a title to their share in the productions of the earth, and especially those who presided over the rest. Therefore he desired I would let him know, what these costly meats were, and how any of us happened to want them. Whereupon I enumerated as many sorts as came into my head, with the various methods of dressing them, which could not be done without sending vessels by sea to every part of the world, as well for liquors to drink, as for sauces, and innumerable other conveniences. I assured him, that this whole globe of earth must be at least three times gone round, before one of our better female *Yahoos* could get her breakfast, or a cup to put it in. He said, that must needs be a miserable country which cannot furnish food for its own inhabitants. But what he chiefly wondered at, was how such vast tracts of ground as I described should be wholly without fresh water, and the people put to the necessity of sending over the sea for drink. I replied, that England (the dear place of my nativity) was computed to produce three times the quantity of food, more than its inhabitants are able to consume, as well as liquors extracted from grain, or pressed out of the fruit of certain trees, which made excellent drink, and the same proportion in every other convenience of life. But, in order to feed the luxury and intemperance of the males, and the vanity of the females, we sent away the greatest part of our necessary things to other countries, from whence in return we brought the materials of diseases, folly, and vice, to spend among ourselves. Hence it follows of necessity, that vast numbers of our people are compelled to seek their livelihood by begging, robbing, stealing, cheating, pimping, forswearing, flattering, suborning, forging, gaming, lying, fawning, hectoring, voting, scribbling, star-gazing, poisoning, whoring, canting, libelling, free-thinking, and the like occupations: every one of which terms, I was at much pains to make him understand.

That wine was not imported among us from foreign countries, to supply the want of water or other drinks, but because it was a sort of liquid which made us merry, by putting us out of our senses; diverted all melancholy thoughts, begat wild extravagant imaginations in the brain, raised our hopes, and banished our fears, suspended every office of reason for a time, and deprived us of the use of our limbs, till we fell into a profound sleep; although it must be confessed, that we always awaked sick and dispirited, and that the use of this liquor filled us with diseases, which made our lives uncomfortable and short.

But beside all this, the bulk of our people supported themselves by furnishing the necessities or conveniences of life to the rich, and to each other. For instance, when I am at home and dressed as I ought to be, I carry on my body the workmanship of an hundred tradesmen; the building and furniture of my house employ as many more, and five times the number to adorn my wife.

I was going on to tell him of another sort of people, who get their livelihood by attending the sick, having upon some occasions informed his Honour that many of my crew had died of diseases. But here it was with the utmost difficulty, that I brought him to apprehend what I meant. He could easily conceive, that a *Houyhnhnm* grew weak and heavy a few days before his death, or by some accident might hurt a limb. But that nature, who works all things to perfection, should suffer any pains to breed in our bodies, he thought impossible, and desired to know the reason of so unaccountable an evil. I told him, we fed on a thousand things which operated contrary to each other; that we eat when we were not hungry, and drank without the provocation of thirst; that we sat whole nights drinking strong liquors without eating a bit, which disposed us to sloth, inflamed our bodies, and precipitated or prevented digestion. That prostitute female *Yahoos* acquired a certain malady, which bred rottenness in the bones of those who fell into their embraces; that this and many other diseases were propagated from father to son, so that great numbers came into the world with complicated maladies upon them; that it would be endless to give him a catalogue of all diseases incident to human bodies; for they would not be fewer than five or six hundred, spread over every limb and joint; in short, every part, external and intestine, having diseases appropriated to each. To remedy which, there was a sort of people bred up among us, in the profession or pretence of curing the sick. And because I had some skill in the faculty, I would in gratitude to his Honour, let him know the whole mystery and method by which they proceed.

Their fundamental is, that all diseases arise from repletion, from whence they conclude, that a great evacuation of the body is necessary, either through the natural passage, or upwards at the mouth. Their next business is, from herbs, minerals, gums, oils, shells, salts, juices, seaweed, excrements, barks of trees, serpents, toads, frogs, spiders, dead men's flesh and bones, birds, beasts, and fishes, to form a composition for smell and taste the most abominable, nauseous, and detestable, they can possibly contrive, which the stomach immediately rejects with loathing; and this they call a vomit; or else from the same store-house, with some other poisonous additions, they command us to take in at the orifice above or below (just as the physician then happens to be disposed) a medicine equally annoying and disgustful to the bowels; which relaxing the belly, drives down all before it, and this they call a purge, or a clyster. For nature (as the physicians allege) having intended the superior anterior orifice only for the intromission of solids and liquids, and the inferior posterior for ejection, these artists ingeniously considering that in all diseases nature is forced out of her seat, therefore to replace her in it, the body must be treated in a manner directly contrary, by interchanging the use of each orifice; forcing solids and liquids in at the anus, and making evacuations at the mouth.

But, besides real diseases, we are subject to many that are only imaginary, for which the physicians have invented imaginary cures; these have their several names, and so have the drugs that are proper for them, and with these our female *Yahoos* are always infested.

One great excellency in this tribe is their skill at prognostics, wherein they seldom fail; their predictions in real diseases, when they rise to any degree of malignity, generally portending death, which is always in their power, when recovery is not: and therefore, upon any unexpected signs of amendment, after they have pronounced their sentence, rather than be accused as false prophets, they know how to approve[10] their sagacity to the world by a seasonable dose.

They are likewise of special use to husbands and wives, who are grown weary of their mates; to eldest sons, to great ministers of state, and often to princes.

---

[10] **approve:** Prove.

I had formerly upon occasion discoursed with my master upon the nature of government in general, and particularly of our own excellent constitution, deservedly the wonder and envy of the whole world. But having here accidentally mentioned a minister of state, he commanded me some time after to inform him, what species of *Yahoo* I particularly meant by that appellation.

I told him, that a First or Chief Minister of State, who was the person I intended to describe, was a creature wholly exempt from joy and grief, love and hatred, pity and anger; at least made use of no other passions but a violent desire of wealth, power, and titles; that he applies his words to all uses, except to the indication of his mind; that he never tells a truth, but with an intent that you should take it for a lie; nor a lie, but with a design that you should take it for a truth; that those he speaks worst of behind their backs, are in the surest way of preferment; and whenever he begins to praise you to others or to yourself, you are from that day forlorn. The worst mark you can receive is a promise, especially when it is confirmed with an oath; after which every wise man retires, and gives over all hopes.

There are three methods by which a man may rise to be chief minister: the first is, by knowing how with prudence to dispose of a wife, a daughter, or a sister: the second, by betraying or undermining his predecessor: and the third is, by a furious zeal in public assemblies against the corruptions of the court. But a wise prince would rather choose to employ those who practise the last of these methods; because such zealots prove always the most obsequious and subservient to the will and passions of their master. That these ministers having all employments at their disposal, preserve themselves in power, by bribing the majority of a senate or great council; and at last, by an expedient called an Act of Indemnity[11] (whereof I described the nature to him) they secure themselves from after-reckonings, and retire from the public, laden with the spoils of the nation.

The palace of a chief minister is a seminary to breed up others in his own trade: the pages, lackeys, and porters, by imitating their master, become ministers of state in their several districts, and learn to excel in the three principal ingredients, of insolence, lying, and bribery. Accordingly, they have a subaltern court paid to them by persons of the best rank, and sometimes by the force of dexterity and impudence, arrive through several gradations to be successors to their lord.

He is usually governed by a decayed wench, or favourite footman, who are the tunnels through which all graces are conveyed, and may properly be called, in the last resort, the governors of the kingdom.

One day in discourse my master, having heard me mention the nobility of my country, was pleased to make me a compliment which I could not pretend to deserve: that he was sure I must have been born of some noble family, because I far exceeded in shape, colour, and cleanliness, all the *Yahoos* of his nation, although I seemed to fail in strength and agility, which must be imputed to my different way of living from those other brutes; and besides, I was not only endowed with the faculty of speech, but likewise with some rudiments of reason, to a degree, that with all his acquaintance I passed for a prodigy.

---

[11] **Act of Indemnity:** Legislation providing immunity to statesmen who have unknowingly violated a law.

He made me observe, that among the *Houyhnhnms,* the white, the sorrel, and the iron-gray, were not so exactly shaped as the bay, the dapple-gray, and the black; nor born with equal talents of the mind, or a capacity to improve them; and therefore continued always in the condition of servants, without ever aspiring to match out of their own race, which in that country would be reckoned monstrous and unnatural.

I made his Honour my most humble acknowledgments for the good opinion he was pleased to conceive of me; but assured him at the same time, that my birth was of the lower sort, having been born of plain honest parents, who were just able to give me a tolerable education; that nobility among us was altogether a different thing from the idea he had of it; that our young noblemen are bred from their childhood in idleness and luxury; that as soon as years will permit, they consume their vigour, and contract odious diseases among lewd females; and when their fortunes are almost ruined, they marry some woman of mean birth, disagreeable person, and unsound constitution, merely for the sake of money, whom they hate and despise. That the productions of such marriages are generally scrofulous, ricketty, or deformed children; by which means the family seldom continues above three generations, unless the wife takes care to provide a healthy father among her neighbours or domestics, in order to improve and continue the breed. That a weak diseased body, a meagre countenance, and sallow complexion, are the true marks of noble blood; and a healthy robust appearance is so disgraceful in a man of quality, that the world concludes his real father to have been a groom or a coachman. The imperfections of his mind run parallel with those of his body, being a composition of spleen, dullness, ignorance, caprice, sensuality, and pride.

Without the consent of this illustrious body, no law can be enacted, repealed, or altered; and these have the decision of all our possessions without appeal.

CHAPTER 7. *The Author's great love of his native country. His master's observations upon the constitution and administration of* England, *as described by the Author, with parallel cases and comparisons. His master's observations upon human nature.*

The reader may be disposed to wonder how I could prevail on myself to give so free a representation of my own species, among a race of mortals who are already too apt to conceive the vilest opinion of human kind, from that entire congruity betwixt me and their *Yahoos.* But I must freely confess, that the many virtues of those excellent quadrupeds placed in opposite view to human corruptions, had so far opened my eyes and enlarged my understanding, that I began to view the actions and passions of man in a very different light, and to think the honour of my own kind not worth managing; which, besides, it was impossible for me to do before a person of so acute a judgment as my master, who daily convinced me of a thousand faults in myself, whereof I had not the least perception before, and which with us would never be numbered even among human infirmities. I had likewise learned from his example an utter detestation of all falsehood or disguise; and truth appeared so amiable to me, that I determined upon sacrificing every thing to it.

Let me deal so candidly with the reader, as to confess, that there was yet a much stronger motive for the freedom I took in my representation of things. I had not been a year in this country, before I contracted such a love and veneration for the inhabitants, that I entered on a firm resolution never to return to human kind, but to pass the rest of my life among these admirable *Houyhnhnms* in the contemplation and practice of every virtue; where I could have no example or incitement to vice. But it was decreed by fortune, my perpetual enemy, that so great a felicity should not fall to my share. However, it is now some comfort to reflect, that in what I said of my countrymen, I extenuated their faults as much as I durst before so strict an examiner, and upon every article gave as favourable a turn as the matter would bear. For, indeed, who is there alive that will not be swayed by his bias and partiality to the place of his birth?

I have related the substance of several conversations I had with my master, during the greatest part of the time I had the honour to be in his service, but have indeed for brevity sake omitted much more than is here set down.

When I had answered all his questions, and his curiosity seemed to be fully satisfied; he sent for me one morning early, and commanding me to sit down at some distance (an honour which he had never before conferred upon me), he said, he had been very seriously considering my whole story, as far as it related both to myself and my country; that he looked upon us as a sort of animals to whose share, by what accident he could not conjecture, some small pittance of reason had fallen, whereof we made no other use than by its assistance to aggravate our natural corruptions, and to acquire new ones, which nature had not given us. That we disarmed ourselves of the few abilities she had bestowed, had been very successful in multiplying our original wants, and seemed to spend our whole lives in vain endeavours to supply them by our own inventions. That as to myself, was manifest I had neither the strength or agility of a common *Yahoo;* that I walked infirmly on my hinder feet; had found out a contrivance to make my claws of no use or defence, and to remove the hair from my chin, which was intended as a shelter from the sun and the weather. Lastly, that I could neither run with speed, nor climb trees like my brethren (as he called them) the *Yahoos* in this country.

That our institutions of government and law were plainly owing to our gross defects in reason, and by consequence, in virtue; because reason alone is sufficient to govern a rational creature; which was therefore a character we had no pretence to challenge, even from the account I had given of my own people; although he manifestly perceived, that in order to favour them, I had concealed many particulars, and often *said the thing which was not.*

He was the more confirmed in this opinion, because he observed, that as I agreed in every feature of my body with other *Yahoos,* except where it was to my real disadvantage in point of strength, speed and activity, the shortness of my claws, and some other particulars where nature had no part; so from the representation I had given him of our lives, our manners, and our actions, he found as near a resemblance in the disposition of our minds. He said the *Yahoos* were known to hate one another more than they did any different species of animals; and the reason usually assigned was the odiousness of their own shapes, which all could see in the rest, but not in themselves. He had therefore begun to think it not unwise in us to cover our bodies, and by that invention conceal many of our own deformities from each other, which would else be hardly supportable. But he now found he had been mistaken, and that the dissensions of those brutes in his country were owing to the same cause with ours, as I had described them. For if (said he), you throw among five *Yahoos* as much food as would be sufficient for fifty, they will, instead of eating peaceably, fall together by the ears, each single one impatient to have all to itself; and therefore a servant was usually employed to stand by while they were feeding abroad, and those kept at home were tied at a distance from each other: that if a cow died of age or accident, before a *Houyhnhnm* could secure it for his own *Yahoos,* those in the neighbourhood would come in herds to seize it, and then would ensue such a battle as I had described, with terrible wounds made by their claws on both sides, although they seldom were able to kill one another, for want of such convenient instruments of death as we had invented. At other times the like battles have been fought between the *Yahoos* of several neighbourhoods without any visible cause; those of one district watching all opportunities to surprise the next before they are prepared. But if they find their project hath miscarried, they return home, and, for want of enemies, engage in what I call a civil war among themselves.

That in some fields of his country, there are certain shining stones of several colours, whereof the *Yahoos* are violently fond, and when part of these stones is fixed in the earth, as it sometimes happeneth, they will dig with their claws for whole days to get them out, then carry them away, and hide them by heaps in their kennels; but still looking round with great caution, for fear their comrades should find out their treasure. My master said, he could never discover the reason of this unnatural appetite, or how these stones could be of any use to a *Yahoo;* but now he believed it might proceed from the same principle of avarice which I had ascribed to mankind: that he had once, by way of experiment, privately removed a heap of these stones from the place where one of his *Yahoos* had buried it: whereupon, the sordid animal missing his treasure, by his loud lamenting brought the whole herd to the place, there miserably howled, then fell to biting and tearing the rest, began to pine away, would neither eat, nor sleep, nor work, till he ordered a servant privately to convey the stones into the same hole, and hide them as before; which when his *Yahoo* had found, he presently recovered his spirits and good humour, but took good care to remove them to a better hiding place, and hath ever since been a very serviceable brute.

My master farther assured me, which I also observed myself, that in the fields where the shining stones abound, the fiercest and most frequent battles are fought, occasioned by perpetual inroads of the neighbouring *Yahoos.*

He said, it was common when two *Yahoos* discovered such a stone in a field, and were contending which of them should be the proprietor, a third would take the advantage, and carry it away from them both; which my master would needs contend to have some kind of resemblance with our suits at law; wherein I thought it for our credit not to undeceive him; since the decision he mentioned was much more equitable than many decrees among us; because the plaintiff and defendant there lost nothing beside the stone they contended for, whereas our courts of equity would never have dismissed the cause while either of them had any thing left.

My master continuing his discourse, said, there was nothing that rendered the *Yahoos* more odious than their undistinguishing appetite to devour every thing that came in their way, whether herbs, roots, berries, the corrupted flesh of animals, or all mingled together: and it was peculiar in their temper, that they were fonder of what they could get by rapine or stealth at a greater distance, than much better food provided for them at home. If their prey held out, they would eat till they were ready to burst, after which nature had pointed out to them a certain root that gave them a general evacuation.

There was also another kind of root very juicy, but somewhat rare and difficult to be found, which the *Yahoos* sought for with much eagerness, and would suck it with great delight; and it produced in them the same effects that wine hath upon us. It would make them sometimes hug, and sometimes tear one another; they would howl and grin, and chatter, and reel, and tumble, and then fall asleep in the mud.

I did indeed observe, that the *Yahoos* were the only animals in this country subject to any diseases; which, however, were much fewer than horses have among us, and contracted not by any ill treatment they meet with, but by the nastiness and greediness of that sordid brute. Neither has their language any more than a general appellation for those maladies, which is borrowed from the name of the beast, and called *Hnea-Yahoo,* or *Yahoo's evil,* and the cure prescribed is a mixture of their own dung and urine forcibly put down the *Yahoo's* throat. This I have since often known to have been taken with success, and do freely recommend it to my countrymen, for the public good, as an admirable specific against all diseases produced by repletion.

As to learning, government, arts, manufactures, and the like, my master confessed he could find little or no resemblance between the *Yahoos* of that country and those in ours. For he only meant to observe what parity there was in our natures. He had heard indeed some curious *Houyhnhnms* observe, that in most herds there was a sort of ruling *Yahoo* (as among us there is generally some leading or principal stag in a pack), who was always more deformed in body, and mischievous in disposition, than any of the rest. That this leader had usually a favourite as like himself as he could get, whose employment was to lick his master's feet and posteriors, and drive the female *Yahoos* to his kennel; for which he was now and then rewarded with a piece of ass's flesh. This favourite is hated by the whole herd, and therefore to protect himself, keeps always near the person of his leader. He usually continues in office till a worse can be found; but the very moment he is discarded, his successor, at the head of all the *Yahoos* in that district, young and old, male and female, come in a body, and discharge their excrements upon him from head to foot. But how far this might be applicable to our courts and favourites, and ministers of state, my master said I could best determine.

I durst make no return to this malicious insinuation, which debased human understanding below the sagacity of a common hound, who has judgment enough to distinguish and follow the cry of the ablest dog in the pack, without being ever mistaken.

My master told me, there were some qualities remarkable in the *Yahoos,* which he had not observed me to mention, or at least very slightly, in the accounts I had given him of human kind. He said, those animals, like other brutes, had their females in common; but in this they differed, that the she-*Yahoo* would admit the male while she was pregnant; and that the hes would quarrel and fight with the females as fiercely as with each other. Both which practices were such degrees of infamous brutality, that no other sensitive creature ever arrived at.

Another thing he wondered at in the *Yahoos,* was their strange disposition to nastiness and dirt, whereas there appears to be a natural love of cleanliness in all other animals. As to the two former accusations, I was glad to let them pass without any reply, because I had not a word to offer upon them in defence of my species, which otherwise I certainly had done from my own inclinations. But I could have easily vindicated human kind from the imputation of singularity upon the last article, if there had been any swine in that country (as unluckily for me there were not), which although it may be a sweeter quadruped than a *Yahoo,* cannot I humbly conceive in justice pretend to more cleanliness; and so his Honour himself must have owned, if he had seen their filthy way of feeding, and their custom of wallowing and sleeping in the mud.

My master likewise mentioned another quality which his servants had discovered in several *Yahoos,* and to him was wholly unaccountable. He said, a fancy would sometimes take a *Yahoo* to retire into a corner, to lie down and howl, and groan, and spurn away all that came near him, although he were young and fat, wanted neither food nor water; nor did the servants imagine what could possibly ail him. And the only remedy they found was to set him to hard work, after which he would infallibly come to himself. To this I was silent out of partiality to my own kind; yet here I could plainly discover the true seeds of spleen, which only seizeth on the lazy, the luxurious, and the rich; who, if they were forced to undergo the same regimen, I would undertake for the cure.

His Honour had further observed, that a female *Yahoo* would often stand behind a bank or bush, to gaze on the young males passing by, and then appear, and hide, using many antic gestures and grimaces, at which time it was observed, that she had a most offensive smell; and when any of the males advanced, would slowly retire, looking often back, and with a counterfeit show of fear, run off into some convenient place where she knew the male would follow her.

At other times if a female stranger came among them, three or four of her own sex would get about her, and stare and chatter, and grin, and smell her all over; and then turn off with gestures that seemed to express contempt and disdain.

Perhaps my master might refine a little in these speculations, which he had drawn from what he observed himself, or had been told him by others; however, I could not reflect without some amazement, and much sorrow, that the rudiments of lewdness, coquetry, censure, and scandal, should have place by instinct in womankind.

I expected every moment, that my master would accuse the *Yahoos* of those unnatural appetites in both sexes, so common among us. But nature, it seems, hath not been so expert a school-mistress; and these politer pleasures are entirely the productions of art and reason, on our side of the globe.

CHAPTER 8. *The Author relates several particulars of the* Yahoos. *The great virtues of the* Houyhnhnms. *The education and exercise of their youth. Their general assembly.*

As I ought to have understood human nature much better than I supposed it possible for my master to do, so it was easy to apply the character he gave of the *Yahoos* to myself and my countrymen; and I believed I could yet make farther discoveries from my own observation. I therefore often begged his favour to let me go among the herds of *Yahoos* in the neighbourhood, to which he always very graciously consented, being perfectly convinced that the hatred I bore those brutes would never suffer me to be corrupted by them; and his Honour ordered one of his servants, a strong sorrel nag, very honest and good-natured, to be my guard, without whose protection I durst not undertake such adventures. For I have already told the reader how much I was pestered by those odious animals upon my first arrival. And I afterwards failed very narrowly three or four times of falling into their clutches, when I happened to stray at any distance without my hanger. And I have reason to believe they had some imagination that I was of their own species, which I often assisted myself, by stripping up my sleeves, and showing my naked arms and breast in their sight, when my protector was with me. At which times they would approach as near as they durst, and imitate my actions after the manner of monkeys, but ever with great signs of hatred; as a tame jackdaw with cap and stockings is always persecuted by the wild ones, when he happens to be got among them.

They are prodigiously nimble from their infancy; however, I once caught a young male of three years old, and endeavoured by all marks of tenderness to make it quiet; but the little imp fell a squalling, and scratching, and biting with such violence, that I was forced to let it go; and it was high time, for a whole troop of old ones came about us at the noise, but finding the cub was safe (for away it ran), and my sorrel nag being by, they durst not venture near us. I observed the young animal's flesh to smell very rank, and the stink was somewhat between a weasel and a fox, but much more disagreeable. I forgot another circumstance (and perhaps I might have the reader's pardon if it were wholly omitted), that while I held the odious vermin in my hands, it voided its filthy excrements of a yellow liquid substance, all over my clothes; but by good fortune there was a small brook hard by, where I washed myself as clean as I could; although I durst not come into my master's presence, until I were sufficiently aired.

By what I could discover, the *Yahoos* appear to be the most unteachable of all animals, their capacities never reaching higher than to draw or carry burdens. Yet I am of opinion, this defect ariseth chiefly from a perverse, restive disposition. For they are cunning, malicious, treacherous, and revengeful. They are strong and hardy, but of a cowardly spirit, and by consequence, insolent, abject, and cruel. It is observed, that the red-haired of both sexes are more libidinous and mischievous than the rest, whom yet they much exceed in strength and activity.

The *Houyhnhnms* keep the *Yahoos* for present use in huts not far from the house; but the rest are sent abroad to certain fields, where they dig up roots, eat several kinds of herbs, and search about for carrion, or sometimes catch weasels and *luhimuhs* (a sort of wild rat), which they greedily devour. Nature hath taught them to dig deep holes with their nails on the side of a rising ground, wherein they lie by themselves; only the kennels of the females are larger, sufficient to hold two or three cubs.

They swim from their infancy like frogs, and are able to continue long under water, where they often take fish, which the females carry home to their young. And upon this occasion, I hope the reader will pardon my relating an odd adventure.

Being one day abroad with my protector the sorrel nag, and the weather exceeding hot, I entreated him to let me bathe in a river that was near. He consented, and I immediately stripped myself stark naked, and went down softly into the stream. It happened that a young female *Yahoo,* standing behind a bank, saw the whole proceeding, and inflamed by desire, as the nag and I conjectured, came running with all speed, and leaped into the water, within five yards of the place where I bathed. I was never in my life so terribly frighted; the nag was grazing at some distance, not suspecting any harm. She embraced me after a most fulsome manner; I roared as loud as I could, and the nag came galloping towards me, whereupon she quitted her grasp, with the utmost reluctancy, and leaped upon the opposite bank, where she stood gazing and howling all the time I was putting on my clothes.

This was matter of diversion to my master and his family, as well as of mortification to myself. For now I could no longer deny that I was a real *Yahoo* in every limb and feature, since the females had a natural propensity to me, as one of their own species. Neither was the hair of this brute of a red colour (which might have been some excuse for an appetite a little irregular), but black as a sloe, and her countenance did not make an appearance altogether so hideous as the rest of the kind; for, I think, she could not be above eleven years old.

Having lived three years in this country, the reader I suppose will expect, that I should, like other travellers, give him some account of the manners and customs of its inhabitants, which it was indeed my principal study to learn.

As these noble *Houyhnhnms* are endowed by nature with a general disposition to all virtues, and have no conceptions or ideas of what is evil in a rational creature, so their grand maxim is, to cultivate reason, and to be wholly governed by it. Neither is reason among them a point problematical as with us, where men can argue with plausibility on both sides of the question; but strikes you with immediate conviction; as it must needs do where it is not mingled, obscured, or discoloured by passion and interest. I remember it was with extreme difficulty that I could bring my master to understand the meaning of the word *opinion,* or how a point could be disputable; because reason taught us to affirm or deny only where we are certain; and beyond our knowledge we cannot do either. So that controversies, wranglings, disputes, and positiveness in false or dubious propositions, are evils unknown among the *Houyhnhnms.* In the like manner when I used to explain to him our several systems of natural philosophy, he would laugh that a creature pretending to reason, should value itself upon the knowledge of other people's conjectures, and in things, where that knowledge, if it were certain, could be of no use. Wherein he agreed entirely with the sentiments of Socrates, as Plato delivers them; which I mention as the highest honour I can do that prince of philosophers. I have often since reflected what destruction such a doctrine would make in the libraries of Europe; and how many paths to fame would be then shut up in the learned world.

Friendship and benevolence are the two principal virtues among the *Houyhnhnms;* and these not confined to particular objects, but universal to the whole race. For a stranger from the remotest part is equally treated with the nearest neighbour, and wherever he goes, looks upon himself as at home. They preserve decency and civility in the highest degrees, but are altogether ignorant of ceremony. They have no fondness for their colts or foals, but the care they take in educating them proceeds entirely from the dictates of reason. And I observed my master to show the same affection to his neighbour's issue that he had for his own. They will have it that nature teaches them to love the whole species, and it is reason only that maketh a distinction of persons, where there is a superior degree of virtue.

When the matron *Houyhnhnms* have produced one of each sex, they no longer accompany with their consorts, except they lose one of their issue by some casualty, which very seldom happens; but in such a case they meet again, or when the like accident befalls a person whose wife is past bearing, some other couple bestow him one of their own colts, and then go together again till the mother is pregnant. This caution is necessary to prevent the country from being overburthened with numbers. But the race of inferior *Houyhnhnms* bred up to be servants is not so strictly limited upon this article; these are allowed to produce three of each sex, to be domestics in the noble families.

In their marriages they are exactly careful to choose such colours as will not make any disagreeable mixture in the breed. Strength is chiefly valued in the male, and comeliness in the female; not upon the account of love, but to preserve the race from degenerating; for where a female happens to excel in strength, a consort is chosen with regard to comeliness. Courtship, love, presents, jointures, settlements, have no place in their thoughts; or terms whereby to express them in their language. The young couple meet and are joined, merely because it is the determination of their parents and friends: it is what they see done every day, and they look upon it as one of the necessary actions of a reasonable being. But the violation of marriage, or any other unchastity, was never heard of: and the married pair pass their lives with the same friendship, and mutual benevolence that they bear to all others of the same species, who come in their way; without jealousy, fondness, quarrelling, or discontent.

In educating the youth of both sexes, their method is admirable, and highly deserves our imitation. These are not suffered to taste a grain of oats, except upon certain days, till eighteen years old; nor milk, but very rarely; and in summer they graze two hours in the morning, and as many in the evening, which their parents likewise observe; but the servants are not allowed above half that time, and a great part of their grass is brought home, which they eat at the most convenient hours, when they can be best spared from work.

Temperance, industry, exercise, and cleanliness, are the lessons equally enjoined to the young ones of both sexes: and my master thought it monstrous in us to give the females a different kind of education from the males, except in some articles of domestic management; whereby as he truly observed, one half of our natives were good for nothing but bringing children into the world: and to trust the care of our children to such useless animals, he said, was yet a greater instance of brutality.

But the *Houyhnhnms* train up their youth to strength, speed, and hardiness, by exercising them in running races up and down steep hills, and over hard stony grounds; and when they are all in a sweat, they are ordered to leap over head and ears into a pond or a river. Four times a year the youth of a certain district meet to show their proficiency in running and leaping, and other feats of strength and agility; where the victor is rewarded with a song made in his or her praise. On this festival the servants drive a herd of *Yahoos* into the field, laden with hay, and oats, and milk, for a repast to the *Houyhnhnms;* after which, these brutes are immediately driven back again, for fear of being noisome to the assembly.

Every fourth year, at the vernal equinox, there is a representative council of the whole nation, which meets in a plain about twenty miles from our house, and continues about five or six days. Here they enquire into the state and condition of the several districts; whether they abound or be deficient in hay or oats, or cows or *Yahoos*. And wherever there is any want (which is but seldom), it is immediately supplied by unanimous consent and contribution. Here likewise the regulation of children is settled: as for instance, if a *Houyhnhnm* hath two males, he changeth one of them with another that hath two females; and when a child hath been lost by any casualty, where the mother is past breeding, it is determined what family in the district shall breed another to supply the loss.

CHAPTER 9. *A grand debate at the general assembly of the* Houyhnhnms, *and how it was determined. The learning of the* Houyhnhnms. *Their buildings. Their manner of burials. The defectiveness of their language.*

One of these grand assemblies was held in my time, about three months before my departure, whither my master went as the representative of our district. In this council was resumed their old debate, and indeed, the only debate which ever happened in that country; whereof my master after his return gave me a very particular account.

The question to be debated was, whether the *Yahoos* should be exterminated from the face of the earth. One of the members for the affirmative offered several arguments of great strength and weight, alleging, that as the *Yahoos* were the most filthy, noisome, and deformed animal which nature ever produced, so they were the most restive and indocible, mischievous and malicious: they would privately suck the teats of the *Houyhnhnms*' cows, kill and devour their cats, trample down their oats and grass, if they were not continually watched, and commit a thousand other extravagancies. He took notice of a general tradition, that *Yahoos* had not been always in that country; but, that many ages ago, two of these brutes appeared together upon a mountain; whether produced by the heat of the sun upon corrupted mud and slime, or from the ooze and froth of the sea, was never known. That these *Yahoos* engendered, and their brood in a short time grew so numerous as to over-run and infest the whole nation. That the *Houyhnhnms* to get rid of this evil, made a general hunting, and at last enclosed the whole herd; and destroying the elder, every *Houyhnhnm* kept two young ones in a kennel, and brought them to such a degree of tameness, as an animal so savage by nature can be capable of acquiring; using them for draught and carriage. That there seemed to be much truth in this tradition, and that those creatures could not be *Ylnhniamshy* (or *aborigines* of the land), because of the violent hatred the *Houyhnhnms,* as well as all other animals, bore them; which although their evil disposition sufficiently deserved, could never have arrived at so high a degree, if they had been aborigines, or else they would have long since been rooted out. That the inhabitants taking a fancy to use the service of the *Yahoos,* had very imprudently neglected to cultivate the breed of asses, which were a comely animal, easily kept, more tame and orderly, without any offensive smell, strong enough for labour, although they yield to the other in agility of body; and if their braying be no agreeable sound, it is far preferable to the horrible howlings of the *Yahoos.*

Several others declared their sentiments to the same purpose, when my master proposed an expedient to the assembly, whereof he had indeed borrowed the hint from me. He approved of the tradition mentioned by the honourable member, who spoke before, and affirmed, that the two *Yahoos* said to be first seen among them, had been driven thither over the sea; that coming to land, and being forsaken by their companions, they retired to the mountains, and degenerating by degrees, became in process of time, much more savage than those of their own species in the country from whence these two originals came. The reason of this assertion was, that he had now in his possession a certain wonderful *Yahoo* (meaning myself), which most of them had heard of, and many of them had seen. He then related to them, how he first found me; that my body was all covered with an artificial composure of the skins and hairs of other animals; that I spoke in a language of my own, and had thoroughly learned theirs: that I had related to him the accidents which brought me thither: that when he saw me without my covering, I was an exact *Yahoo* in every part, only of a whiter colour, less hairy, and with shorter claws. He added, how I had endeavoured to persuade him, that in my own and other countries the *Yahoos* acted as the governing, rational animal, and held the *Houyhnhnms* in servitude: that he observed in me all the qualities of a *Yahoo*, only a little more civilized by some tincture of reason, which however was in a degree as far inferior to the *Houyhnhnm* race, as the *Yahoos* of their country were to me: that, among other things, I mentioned a custom we had of castrating *Houyhnhnms* when they were young, in order to render them tame; that the operation was easy and safe; that it was no shame to learn wisdom from brutes, as industry is taught by the ant, and building by the swallow. (For so I translate the word *lyhannh*, although it be a much larger fowl.) That this invention might be practised upon the younger *Yahoos* here, which, besides rendering them tractable and fitter for use, would in an age put an end to the whole species without destroying life. That in the mean time the *Houyhnhnms* should be exhorted to cultivate the breed of asses, which, as they are in all respects more valuable brutes, so they have this advantage, to be fit for service at five years old, which the others are not till twelve.

This was all my master thought fit to tell me at that time, of what passed in the grand council. But he was pleased to conceal one particular, which related personally to myself, whereof I soon felt the unhappy effect, as the reader will know in its proper place, and from whence I date all the succeeding misfortunes of my life.

The *Houyhnhnms* have no letters, and consequently their knowledge is all traditional. But there happening few events of any moment among a people so well united, naturally disposed to every virtue, wholly governed by reason, and cut off from all commerce with other nations, the historical part is easily preserved without burthening their memories. I have already observed, that they are subject to no diseases, and therefore can have no need of physicians. However, they have excellent medicines composed of herbs, to cure accidental bruises and cuts in the pastern or frog of the foot by sharp stones, as well as other maims and hurts in the several parts of the body.

They calculate the year by the revolution of the sun and moon, but use no subdivision into weeks. They are well enough acquainted with the motions of those two luminaries, and understand the nature of eclipses; and this is the utmost progress of their astronomy.

In poetry they must be allowed to excel all other mortals; wherein the justness of their similes, and the minuteness, as well as exactness of their descriptions, are indeed inimitable. Their verses abound very much in both of these, and usually contain either some exalted notions of friendship and benevolence, or the praises of those who were victors in races, and other bodily exercises. Their buildings, although very rude and simple, are not inconvenient, but well contrived to defend them from all injuries of cold and heat. They have a kind of tree, which at forty years old loosens in the root, and falls with the first storm: It grows very straight, and being pointed like stakes with a sharp stone (for the *Houyhnhnms* know not the use of iron), they stick them erect in the ground about ten inches asunder, and then weave in oat-straw, or sometimes wattles betwixt them. The roof is made after the same manner, and so are the doors.

The *Houyhnhnms* use the hollow part between the pastern and the hoof of their fore-feet, as we do our hands, and this with greater dexterity than I could at first imagine. I have seen a white mare of our family thread a needle (which I lent her on purpose) with that joint. They milk their cows, reap their oats, and do all the work which requires hands, in the same manner. They have a kind of hard flints, which by grinding against other stones, they form into instruments, that serve instead of wedges, axes, and hammers. With tools made of these flints, they likewise cut their hay, and reap their oats, which there groweth naturally in several fields: The *Yahoos* draw home the sheaves in carriages, and the servants tread them in certain covered huts, to get out the grain, which is kept in stores. They make a rude kind of earthen and wooden vessels, and bake the former in the sun.

If they can avoid casualties, they die only of old age, and are buried in the obscurest places that can be found, their friends and relations expressing neither joy nor grief at their departure; nor does the dying person discover the least regret that he is leaving the world, any more than if he were upon returning home from a visit to one of his neighbours. I remember my master having once made an appointment with a friend and his family to come to his house upon some affair of importance; on the day fixed, the mistress and her two children came very late; she made two excuses, first for her husband, who, as she said, happened that very morning to *shnuwnh*. The word is strongly expressive in their language, but not easily rendered into English; it signifies, *to retire to his first mother.* Her excuse for not coming sooner was, that her husband dying late in the morning, she was a good while consulting her servants about a convenient place where his body should be laid; and I observed she behaved herself at our house as cheerfully as the rest. She died about three months after.

They live generally to seventy or seventy-five years, very seldom to fourscore: some weeks before their death they feel a gradual decay, but without pain. During this time they are much visited by their friends, because they cannot go abroad with their usual ease and satisfaction. However, about ten days before their death, which they seldom fail in computing, they return the visits that have been made them by those who are nearest in the neighbourhood, being carried in a convenient sledge drawn by *Yahoos;* which vehicle they use, not only upon this occasion, but when they grow old, upon long journeys, or when they are lamed by any accident. And therefore when the dying *Houyhnhnms* return those visits, they take a solemn leave of their friends, as if they were going to some remote part of the country, where they designed to pass the rest of their lives.

I know not whether it may be worth observing, that the *Houyhnhnms* have no word in their language to express any thing that is evil, except what they borrow from the deformities or ill qualities of the *Yahoos.* Thus they denote the folly of a servant, an omission of a child, a stone that cuts their feet, a continuance of foul or unseasonable weather, and the like, by adding to each the epithet of *Yahoo.* For instance, *Hhnm Yahoo, Whnaholm Yahoo, Ynlhmndwihlma Yahoo,* and an ill-contrived house *Ynholmhnmrohlnw Yahoo.*

I could with great pleasure enlarge further upon the manners and virtues of this excellent people; but intending in a short time to publish a volume by itself expressly upon that subject, I refer the reader thither. And in the mean time, proceed to relate my own sad catastrophe.

CHAPTER 10. *The Author's economy, and happy life among the* Houyhnhnms. *His great improvement in virtue, by conversing with them. Their conversations. The Author has notice given him by his master that he must depart from the country. He falls into a swoon for grief, but submits. He contrives and finishes a canoe, by the help of a fellow-servant, and puts to sea at a venture.*

I had settled my little economy to my own heart's content. My master had ordered a room to be made for me after their manner, about six yards from the house; the sides and floors of which I plastered with clay, and covered with rush-mats of my own contriving; I had beaten hemp, which there grows wild, and made of it a sort of ticking: this I filled with the feathers of several birds I had taken with springes made of *Yahoos'* hairs, and were excellent food. I had worked two chairs with my knife, the sorrel nag helping me in the grosser and more laborious part. When my clothes were worn to rags, I made myself others with the skins of rabbits, and of a certain beautiful animal about the same size, called *nnuhnoh,* the skin of which is covered with a fine down. Of these I likewise made very tolerable stockings. I soled my shoes with wood which I cut from a tree, and fitted to the upper leather, and when this was worn out, I supplied it with the skins of *Yahoos* dried in the sun. I often got honey out of hollow trees, which I mingled with water, or eat with my bread. No man could more verify the truth of these two maxims, *That nature is very easily satisfied;* and *That necessity is the mother of invention.* I enjoyed perfect health of body, and tranquillity of mind; I did not feel the treachery of inconstancy of a friend, nor the injuries of a secret or open enemy. I had no occasion of bribing, flattering or pimping, to procure the favour of any great man or of his minion. I wanted no fence against fraud or oppression; here was neither physician to destroy my body, nor lawyer to ruin my fortune; no informer to watch my words and actions, or forge accusations against me for hire: here were no gibers, censurers, backbiters, pickpockets, highwaymen, house-breakers, attorneys, bawds, buffoons, gamesters, politicians, wits, splenetics, tedious talkers, controvertists, ravishers, murderers, robbers, virtuosos; no leaders or followers of party and faction; no encouragers to vice, by seducement or examples; no dungeon, axes, gibbets, whipping-posts, or pillories; no cheating shopkeepers or mechanics; no pride, vanity, or affectation; no fops, bullies, drunkards, strolling whores, or poxes; no ranting, lewd, expensive wives; no stupid, proud pedants; no importunate, overbearing, quarrelsome, noisy, roaring, empty, conceited, swearing companions; no scoundrels, raised from the dust for the sake of their vices, or nobility thrown into it on account of their virtues; no lords, fiddlers, judges, or dancing-masters.

I had the favour of being admitted to several *Houyhnhnms,* who came to visit or dine with my master; where his Honour graciously suffered me to wait in the room, and listen to their discourse. Both he and his company would often descend to ask me questions, and receive my answers. I had also sometimes the honour of attending my master in his visits to others. I never presumed to speak, except in answer to a question; and then I did it with inward regret, because it was a loss of so much time for improving myself: but I was infinitely delighted with the station of an humble auditor in such conversations, where nothing passed but what was useful, expressed in the fewest and most significant words; where (as I have already said) the greatest decency was observed, without the least degree of ceremony; where no person spoke without being pleased himself, and pleasing his companions; where there was no interruption, tediousness, heat, or difference of sentiments. They have a notion, that when people are met together, a short silence doth much improve conversation: this I found to be true; for during those little intermissions of talk, new ideas would arise in their thoughts, which very much enlivened the discourse. Their subjects are generally on friendship and benevolence, or order and economy; sometimes upon the visible operations of nature, or ancient traditions; upon the bounds and limits of virtue; upon the unerring rules of reason, or upon some determinations to be taken at the next great assembly; and often upon the various excellencies of poetry. I may add, without vanity, that my presence often gave them sufficient matter for discourse, because it afforded my master an occasion of letting his friends into the history of me and my country, upon which they were all pleased to descant in a manner not very advantageous to human kind; and for that reason I shall not repeat what they said: only I may be allowed to observe, that his Honour, to my great admiration, appeared to understand the nature of *Yahoos* much better than myself. He went through all our vices and follies, and discovered many which I had never mentioned to him, by only supposing what qualities a *Yahoo* of their country, with a small proportion of reason, might be capable of exerting; and concluded, with too much probability, how vile as well as miserable such a creature must be.

I freely confess, that all the little knowledge I have of any value, was acquired by the lectures I received from my master, and from hearing the discourses of him and his friends; to which I should be prouder to listen, than to dictate to the greatest and wisest assembly in Europe. I admired the strength, comeliness, and speed of the inhabitants; and such a constellation of virtues in such amiable persons produced in me the highest veneration. At first, indeed, I did not feel that natural awe which the *Yahoos* and all other animals bear towards them; but it grew upon me by degrees, much sooner than I imagined, and was mingled with a respectful love and gratitude, that they would condescend to distinguish me from the rest of my species.

When I thought of my family, my friends, my countrymen, or human race in general, I considered them as they really were, *Yahoos* in shape and disposition, perhaps a little more civilized, and qualified with the gift of speech, but making no other use of reason, than to improve and multiply those vices, whereof their brethren in this country had only the share that nature allotted them. When I happened to behold the reflection of my own form in a lake or fountain, I turned away my face in horror and detestation of myself, and could better endure the sight of a common *Yahoo,* than of my own person. By conversing with the *Houyhnhnms,* and looking upon them with delight, I fell to imitate their gait and gesture, which is now grown into a habit, and my friends often tell me in a blunt way, that *I trot like a horse;* which, however, I take for a great compliment. Neither shall I disown, that in speaking I am apt to fall into the voice and manner of the *Houyhnhnms,* and hear myself ridiculed on that account without the least mortification.

In the midst of all this happiness, and when I looked upon myself to be fully settled for life, my master sent for me one morning a little earlier than his usual hour. I observed by his countenance that he was in some perplexity, and at a loss how to begin what he had to speak. After a short silence, he told me, he did not know how I would take what he was going to say; that in the last general assembly, when the affair of the *Yahoos* was entered upon, the representatives had taken offence at his keeping a *Yahoo* (meaning myself) in his family more like a *Houyhnhnm* than a brute animal. That he was known frequently to converse with me, as if he could receive some advantage or pleasure in my company; that such a practice was not agreeable to reason or nature, or a thing ever heard of before among them. The assembly did therefore exhort him, either to employ me like the rest of my species, or command me to swim back to the place from whence I came. That the first of these expedients was utterly rejected by all the *Houyhnhnms* who had ever seen me at his house or their own: for they alleged, that because I had some rudiments of reason, added to the natural pravity of those animals, it was to be feared, I might be able to seduce them into the woody and mountainous parts of the country, and bring them in troops by night to destroy the *Houyhnhnms'* cattle, as being naturally of the ravenous kind, and averse from labour.

My master added, that he was daily pressed by the *Houyhnhnms* of the neighbourhood to have the assembly's exhortation executed, which he could not put off much longer. He doubted it would be impossible for me to swim to another country, and therefore wished I would contrive some sort of vehicle resembling those I had described to him, that might carry me on the sea; in which work I should have the assistance of his own servants, as well as those of his neighbours. He concluded, that for his own part, he could have been content to keep me in his service as long as I lived; because he found I had cured myself of some bad habits and dispositions, by endeavouring, as far as my inferior nature was capable, to imitate the *Houyhnhnms.*

I should here observe to the reader, that a decree of the general assembly in this country is expressed by the word *hnheoayn,* which signifies an exhortation, as near as I can render it; for they have no conception how a rational creature can be compelled, but only advised, or exhorted; because no person can disobey reason, without giving up his claim to be a rational creature.

I was struck with the utmost grief and despair at my master's discourse; and being unable to support the agonies I was under, I fell into a swoon at his feet; when I came to myself, he told me, that he concluded I had been dead (for these people are subject to no such imbecilities of nature). I answered, in a faint voice, that death would have been too great an happiness; that although I could not blame the assembly's exhortation, or the urgency of his friends; yet, in my weak and corrupt judgment, I thought it might consist with reason to have been less rigorous. That I could not swim a league, and probably the nearest land to theirs might be distant above an hundred: that many materials, necessary for making a small vessel to carry me off, were wholly wanting in this country, which, however, I would attempt in obedience and gratitude to his Honour, although I concluded the thing to be impossible, and therefore looked on myself as already devoted to destruction. That the certain prospect of an unnatural death was the least of my evils: for, supposing I should escape with life by some strange adventure, how could I think with temper[12] of passing my days among *Yahoos,* and relapsing into my old corruptions, for want of examples to lead and keep me within the paths of virtue. That I knew too well upon what solid reasons all the determinations of the wise *Houyhnhnms* were founded, not to be shaken by arguments of mine, a miserable *Yahoo;* and therefore, after presenting him with my humble thanks for the offer of his servants' assistance in making a vessel, and desiring a reasonable time for so difficult a work, I told him I would endeavour to preserve a wretched being; and, if ever I returned to England, was not without hopes of being useful to my own species, by celebrating the praises of the renowned *Houyhnhnms,* and proposing their virtues to the imitation of mankind.

My master in a few words made me a very gracious reply, allowed me the space of two months to finish my boat; and ordered the sorrel nag, my fellow-servant (for so at this distance I may presume to call him) to follow my instructions, because I told my master, that his help would be sufficient, and I knew he had a tenderness for me.

In his company my first business was to go to that part of the coast where my rebellious crew had ordered me to be set on shore. I got upon a height, and looking on every side into the sea, fancied I saw a small island, towards the north-east: I took out my pocket-glass, and could then clearly distinguish it about five leagues off, as I computed; but it appeared to the sorrel nag to be only a blue cloud: for, as he had no conception of any country beside his own, so he could not be as expert in distinguishing remote objects at sea, as we who so much converse in that element.

After I had discovered this island, I considered no farther; but resolved it should, if possible, be the first place of my banishment, leaving the consequence to fortune.

---

[12] **with temper:** Calmly.

I returned home, and consulting with the sorrel nag, we went into a copse at some distance, where I with my knife, and he with a sharp flint fastened very artificially,[13] after their manner, to a wooden handle, cut down several oak wattles about the thickness of a walking-staff, and some larger pieces. But I shall not trouble the reader with a particular description of my own mechanics; let it suffice to say, that in six weeks time, with the help of the sorrel nag, who performed the parts that required most labour, I finished a sort of Indian canoe, but much larger, covering it with the skins of *Yahoos* well stitched together, with hempen threads of my own making. My sail was likewise composed of the skins of the same animal; but I made use of the youngest I could get, the older being too tough and thick; and I likewise provided myself with four paddles. I laid in a stock of boiled flesh, of rabbits and fowls, and took with me two vessels, one filled with milk, and the other with water.

I tried my canoe in a large pond near my master's house, and then corrected in it what was amiss; stopping all the chinks with *Yahoos'* tallow, till I found it staunch, and able to bear me, and my freight. And when it was as complete as I could possibly make it, I had it drawn on a carriage very gently by *Yahoos* to the seaside, under the conduct of the sorrel nag, and another servant.

When all was ready, and the day came for my departure, I took leave of my master and lady, and the whole family, my eyes flowing with tears, and my heart quite sunk with grief. But his Honour, out of curiosity, and, perhaps (if I may speak it without vanity) partly out of kindness, was determined to see me in my canoe, and got several of his neighbouring friends to accompany him. I was forced to wait above an hour for the tide, and then observing the wind very fortunately bearing towards the island, to which I intended to steer my course, I took a second leave of my master: but as I was going to prostrate myself to kiss his hoof, he did me the honour to raise it gently to my mouth. I am not ignorant how much I have been censured for mentioning this last particular. For my detractors are pleased to think it improbable, that so illustrious a person should descend to give so great a mark of distinction to a creature so inferior as I. Neither have I forgot, how apt some travellers are to boast of extraordinary favours they have received. But if these censurers were better acquainted with the noble and courteous disposition of the *Houyhnhnms,* they would soon change their opinion.

I paid my respects to the rest of the *Houyhnhnms* in his Honour's company; then getting into my canoe, I pushed off from shore.

CHAPTER 11. *The Author's dangerous voyage. He arrives at* New Holland, *hoping to settle there. Is wounded with an arrow by one of the natives. Is seized and carried by force into a* Portuguese *ship. The great civilities of the Captain. The Author arrives at* England.

I began this desperate voyage on February 15, 1714–15, at 9 o'clock in the morning. The wind was very favourable; however, I made use at first only of my paddles; but considering I should soon be weary, and that the wind might chop about, I ventured

---

[13] **artificially:** Cunningly.

to set up my little sail; and thus, with the help of the tide, I went at the rate of a league and a half an hour, as near as I could guess. My master and his friends continued on the shore, till I was almost out of sight; and I often heard the sorrel nag (who always loved me) crying out, *Hnuy illa nyha majah Yahoo,* Take care of thyself, gentle *Yahoo.*

My design was, if possible, to discover some small island uninhabited, yet sufficient by my labour to furnish me with the necessaries of life, which I would have thought a greater happiness than to be first minister in the politest court of Europe; so horrible was the idea I conceived of returning to live in the society and under the government of *Yahoos.* For in such a solitude as I desired, I could at least enjoy my own thoughts, and reflect with delight on the virtues of those inimitable *Houyhnhnms,* without any opportunity of degenerating into the vices and corruptions of my own species.

The reader may remember what I related when my crew conspired against me, and confined me to my cabin. How I continued there several weeks, without knowing what course we took; and when I was put ashore in the long boat, how the sailors told me with oaths, whether true or false, that they knew not in what part of the world we were. However, I did then believe us to be about ten degrees southward of the Cape of Good Hope, or about forty-five degrees southern latitude, as I gathered from some general words I overheard among them, being I supposed to the south-east in their intended voyage to Madagascar. And although this were little better than conjecture, yet I resolved to steer my course eastward, hoping to reach the south-west coast of New Holland, and perhaps some such island as I desired, lying westward of it. The wind was full west, and by six in the evening I computed I had gone eastward at least eighteen leagues, when I spied a very small island about half a league off, which I soon reached. It was nothing but a rock with one creek,[14] naturally arched by the force of tempests. Here I put in my canoe, and climbing up a part of the rock, I could plainly discover land to the east, extending from south to north. I lay all night in my canoe; and repeating my voyage early in the morning, I arrived in seven hours to the south-east point of New Holland. This confirmed me in the opinion I have long entertained, that the maps and charts place this country at least three degrees more to the east than it really is; which thought I communicated many years ago to my worthy friend Mr. Herman Moll, and gave him my reasons for it, although he hath rather chosen to follow other authors.

I saw no inhabitants in the place where I landed, and being unarmed, I was afraid of venturing far into the country. I found some shellfish on the shore, and eat them raw, not daring to kindle a fire, for fear of being discovered by the natives. I continued three days feeding on oysters and limpets, to save my own provisions; and I fortunately found a brook of excellent water, which gave me great relief.

On the fourth day, venturing out early a little too far, I saw twenty or thirty natives upon a height, not above five hundred yards from me. They were stark naked, men, women, and children round a fire, as I could discover by the smoke. One of them spied me, and gave notice to the rest; five of them advanced towards

---

[14] **creek:** Bay or sheltered cove.

me, leaving the women and children at the fire. I made what haste I could to the shore, and getting into my canoe, shoved off: the savages observing me retreat, ran after me; and before I could get far enough into the sea, discharged an arrow, which wounded me deeply on the inside of my left knee (I shall carry the mark to my grave). I apprehended the arrow might be poisoned, and paddling out of the reach of their darts (being a calm day), I made a shift to suck the wound, and dress it as well as I could.

I was at a loss what to do, for I durst not return to the same landing-place, but stood to the north, and was forced to paddle; for the wind, though very gentle, was against me, blowing north-west. As I was looking about for a secure landing-place, I saw a sail to the north-north-east, which appearing every minute more visible, I was in some doubt whether I should wait for them or no; but at last my detestation of the *Yahoo* race prevailed, and turning my canoe, I sailed and paddled together to the south, and got into the same creek from whence I set out in the morning, choosing rather to trust myself among these barbarians, than live with European *Yahoos.* I drew up my canoe as close as I could to the shore, and hid myself behind a stone by the little brook, which, as I have already said, was excellent water.

The ship came within half a league of this creek, and sent her long boat with vessels to take in fresh water (for the place it seems was very well known), but I did not observe it till the boat was almost on shore, and it was too late to seek another hiding-place. The seamen at their landing observed my canoe, and rummaging it all over, easily conjectured that the owner could not be far off. Four of them well armed searched every cranny and lurking-hole, till at last they found me flat on my face behind the stone. They gazed awhile in admiration at my strange uncouth dress; my coat made of skins, my wooden-soled shoes, and my furred stockings; from whence, however, they concluded I was not a native of the place, who all go naked. One of the seamen in Portuguese bid me rise, and asked who I was. I understood that language very well, and getting upon my feet, said, I was a poor *Yahoo,* banished from the *Houyhnhnms,* and desired they would please to let me depart. They admired to hear me answer them in their own tongue, and saw by my complexion I must be an European; but were at a loss to know what I meant by *Yahoos* and *Houyhnhnms,* and at the same time fell a laughing at my strange tone in speaking, which resembled the neighing of a horse. I trembled all the while betwixt fear and hatred. I again desired leave to depart, and was gently moving to my canoe; but they laid hold of me, desiring to know, what country I was of? whence I came? with many other questions. I told them, I was born in England, from whence I came about five years ago, and then their country and ours were at peace. I therefore hoped they would not treat me as an enemy, since I meant them no harm, but was a poor *Yahoo,* seeking some desolate place where to pass the remainder of his unfortunate life.

When they began to talk, I thought I never heard or saw any thing so unnatural; for it appeared to me as monstrous as if a dog or a cow should speak in England, or a *Yahoo* in *Houyhnhnm-land.* The honest Portuguese were equally amazed at my strange dress, and the odd manner of delivering my words, which however they understood very well. They spoke to me with great humanity, and said they were sure their Captain would carry me *gratis* to Lisbon, from whence I might return to my own country; that two of the seamen would go back to the ship, inform the Captain of what they had seen, and receive his orders; in the mean time, unless I would give my solemn oath not to fly, they would secure me by force. I thought it best to comply with their proposal. They were very curious to know my story, but I gave them very little satisfaction; and they all conjectured that my misfortunes had impaired my reason. In two hours the boat, which went loaden with vessels of water, returned with the Captain's command to fetch me on board. I fell on my knees to preserve my liberty; but all was in vain, and the men having tied me with cords, heaved me into the boat, from whence I was taken into the ship, and from thence into the Captain's cabin.

His name was Pedro de Mendez; he was a very courteous and generous person; he entreated me to give some account of myself, and desired to know what I would eat or drink; said, I should be used as well as himself, and spoke so many obliging things, that I wondered to find such civilities from a *Yahoo*. However, I remained silent and sullen; I was ready to faint at the very smell of him and his men. At last I desired something to eat out of my own canoe; but he ordered me a chicken and some excellent wine, and then directed that I should be put to bed in a very clean cabin. I would not undress myself, but lay on the bed-clothes, and in half an hour stole out, when I thought the crew was at dinner, and getting to the side of the ship was going to leap into the sea, and swim for my life, rather than continue among *Yahoos*. But one of the seamen prevented me, and having informed the Captain, I was chained to my cabin.

After dinner Don Pedro came to me, and desired to know my reason for so desperate an attempt; assured me he only meant to do me all the service he was able; and spoke so very movingly, that at last I descended to treat him like an animal which had some little portion of reason. I gave him a very short relation of my voyage; of the conspiracy against me by my own men; of the country where they set me on shore, and of my three years' residence there. All which he looked upon as if it were a dream or a vision; whereat I took great offence; for I had quite forgot the faculty of lying, so peculiar to *Yahoos* in all countries where they preside, and, consequently the disposition of suspecting truth in others of their own species. I asked him, whether it were the custom in his country to *say the thing that was not?* I assured him I had almost forgot what he meant by falsehood, and if I had lived a thousand years in *Houyhnhnm-land,* I should never have heard a lie from the meanest servant; that I was altogether indifferent whether he believed me or no; but however, in return for his favours, I would give so much allowance to the corruption of his nature, as to answer any objection he would please to make, and then he might easily discover the truth.

The Captain, a wise man, after many endeavours to catch me tripping in some part of my story, at last began to have a better opinion of my veracity. But he added, that since I professed so inviolable an attachment to truth, I must give him my word of honour to bear him company in this voyage, without attempting any thing against my life, or else he would continue me a prisoner till we arrived at Lisbon. I gave him the promise he required; but at the same time protested that I would suffer the greatest hardships rather than return to live among *Yahoos*.

Our voyage passed without any considerable accident. In gratitude to the Captain I sometimes sat with him at his earnest request, and strove to conceal my antipathy to human kind, although it often broke out, which he suffered to pass without observation. But the greatest part of the day, I confined myself to my cabin, to avoid seeing any of the crew. The Captain had often entreated me to strip myself of my savage dress, and offered to lend me the best suit of clothes he had. This I would not be prevailed on to accept, abhorring to cover myself with any thing that had been on the back of a *Yahoo.* I only desired he would lend me two clean shirts, which having been washed since he wore them, I believed would not so much defile me. These I changed every second day, and washed them myself.

We arrived at Lisbon, Nov. 5, 1715. At our landing the Captain forced me to cover myself with his cloak, to prevent the rabble from crowding about me. I was conveyed to his own house, and at my earnest request, he led me up to the highest room backwards.[15] I conjured him to conceal from all persons what I had told him of the *Houyhnhnms,* because the least hint of such a story would not only draw numbers of people to see me, but probably put me in danger of being imprisoned, or burnt by the Inquisition. The Captain persuaded me to accept a suit of clothes newly made; but I would not suffer the tailor to take my measure; however, Don Pedro being almost my size, they fitted me well enough. He accoutred me with other necessaries all new, which I aired for twenty-four hours before I would use them.

The Captain had no wife, nor above three servants, none of which were suffered to attend at meals, and his whole deportment was so obliging, added to very good *human* understanding, that I really began to tolerate his company. He gained so far upon me, that I ventured to look out of the back window. By degrees I was brought into another room, from whence I peeped into the street, but drew my head back in a fright. In a week's time he seduced me down to the door. I found my terror gradually lessened, but my hatred and contempt seemed to increase. I was at last bold enough to walk the street in his company, but kept my nose well stopped with rue, or sometimes with tobacco.

In ten days, Don Pedro, to whom I had given some account of my domestic affairs, put it upon me as a matter of honour and conscience, that I ought to return to my native country, and live at home with my wife and children. He told me, there was an English ship in the port just ready to sail, and he would furnish me with all things necessary. It would be tedious to repeat his arguments, and my contradictions. He said it was altogether impossible to find such a solitary island as I desired to live in; but I might command in my own house, and pass my time in a manner as recluse as I pleased.

I complied at last, finding I could not do better. I left Lisbon the 24th day of November, in an English merchantman, but who was the master I never inquired. Don Pedro accompanied me to the ship, and lent me twenty pounds. He took kind leave of me, and embraced me at parting, which I bore as well as I could. During this last voyage I had no commerce with the master or any of his men; but pretending I was sick, kept close in my cabin. On the fifth of December, 1715, we cast anchor in

---

[15]**highest . . . backwards:** To the rear of the house, away from the street.

the Downs about nine in the morning, and at three in the afternoon I got safe to my house at Rotherhith.

My wife and family received me with great surprise and joy, because they concluded me certainly dead; but I must freely confess the sight of them filled me only with hatred, disgust, and contempt, and the more by reflecting on the near alliance I had to them. For, although since my unfortunate exile from the *Houyhnhnm* country, I had compelled myself to tolerate the sight of *Yahoos,* and to converse with Don Pedro de Mendez; yet my memory and imagination were perpetually filled with the virtues and ideas of those exalted *Houyhnhnms.* And when I began to consider, that by copulating with one of the *Yahoo* species I had become a parent of more, it struck me with the utmost shame, confusion, and horror.

As soon as I entered the house, my wife took me in her arms, and kissed me; at which, having not been used to the touch of that odious animal for so many years, I fell in a swoon for almost an hour. At the time I am writing it is five years since my last return to England: during the first year, I could not endure my wife or children in my presence, the very smell of them was intolerable; much less could I suffer them to eat in the same room. To this hour they dare not presume to touch my bread, or drink out of the same cup, neither was I ever able to let one of them take me by the hand. The first money I laid out was to buy two young stone-horses,[16] which I keep in a good stable, and next to them the groom is my greatest favourite; for I feel my spirits revived by the smell he contracts in the stable. My horses understand me tolerably well; I converse with them at least four hours every day. They are strangers to bridle or saddle; they live in great amity with me, and friendship to each other.

CHAPTER 12. *The Author's veracity. His design in publishing this work. His censure of those travellers who swerve from the truth. The Author clears himself from any sinister ends in writing. An objection answered. The method of planting colonies. His native country commended. The right of the Crown to those countries described by the Author, is justified. The difficulty of conquering them. The Author takes his last leave of the reader; proposeth his manner of living for the future, gives good advice, and concludes.*

Thus, gentle reader, I have given thee a faithful history of my travels for sixteen years and above seven months; wherein I have not been so studious of ornament as truth. I could perhaps like others have astonished thee with strange improbable tales; but I rather chose to relate plain matter of fact in the simplest manner and style; because my principal design was to inform, and not to amuse thee.

It is easy for us who travel into remote countries, which are seldom visited by Englishmen or other Europeans, to form descriptions of wonderful animals both at sea and land. Whereas a traveller's chief aim should be to make men wiser and better, and to improve their minds by the bad as well as good example of what they deliver concerning foreign places.

I could heartily wish a law was enacted, that every traveller, before he were permitted to publish his voyages, should be obliged to make oath before the Lord High

---

[16] **stone-horses:** Stallions.

Chancellor that all he intended to print was absolutely true to the best of his knowledge; for then the world would no longer be deceived as it usually is, while some writers, to make their works pass the better upon the public, impose the grossest falsities on the unwary reader. I have perused several books of travels with great delight in my younger days; but having since gone over most parts of the globe, and been able to contradict many fabulous accounts from my own observation, it hath given me a great disgust against this part of reading, and some indignation to see the credulity of mankind so impudently abused. Therefore since my acquaintance were pleased to think my poor endeavours might not be unacceptable to my country, I imposed on myself as a maxim, never to be swerved from, that I would *strictly adhere to truth;* neither indeed can I be ever under the least temptation to vary from it, while I retain in my mind the lectures and example of my noble master, and the other illustrious *Houyhnhnms,* of whom I had so long the honour to be an humble hearer.

> *Nec si miserum Fortuna Sinonem*
> *Finxit, vanum etiam, mendacemque improba finget.*[17]

I know very well how little reputation is to be got by writings which require neither genius nor learning, nor indeed any other talent, except a good memory, or an exact journal. I know likewise, that writers of travels, like dictionary-makers, are sunk into oblivion by the weight and bulk of those who come after, and therefore lie uppermost. And it is highly probable, that such travellers who shall hereafter visit the countries described in this work of mine, may, by detecting my errors (if there be any), and adding many new discoveries of their own, justle me out of vogue, and stand in my place, making the world forget that I was ever an author. This indeed would be too great a mortification if I wrote for fame: But, as my sole intention was the PUBLIC GOOD, I cannot be altogether disappointed. For who can read of the virtues I have mentioned in the glorious *Houyhnhnms,* without being ashamed of his own vices, when he considers himself as the reasoning, governing animal of his country? I shall say nothing of those remote nations where *Yahoos* preside; amongst which the least corrupted are the *Brobdingnagians,* whose wise maxims in morality and government it would be our happiness to observe. But I forbear descanting farther, and rather leave the judicious reader to his own remarks and applications.

I am not a little pleased that this work of mine can possibly meet with no censurers: for what objections can be made against a writer who relates only plain facts that happened in such distant countries, where we have not the least interest with respect either to trade or negotiations? I have carefully avoided every fault with which common writers of travels are often too justly charged. Besides, I meddle not the least with any party, but write without passion, prejudice, or ill-will against any man or number of men whatsoever. I write for the noblest end, to inform and

---

[17] *Nec . . . finget:* Virgil, *Aeneid* 2, 79–80: ". . . fate may have made Sinon miserable, but she will never be able to make him into a liar." Sinon was the Greek who persuaded the Trojans to admit the wooden horse through their gates, and he was very much a liar; Gulliver ironically and unwittingly quotes these lines to attest to his own reliability.

instruct mankind, over whom I may, without breach of modesty, pretend to some superiority, from the advantages I received by conversing so long among the most accomplished *Houyhnhnms.* I write without any view towards profit or praise. I never suffer a word to pass that may look like reflection, or possibly give the least offence even to those who are most ready to take it. So that I hope I may with justice pronounce myself an author perfectly blameless, against whom the tribes of answerers, considerers, observers, reflecters, detecters, remarkers, will never be able to find matter for exercising their talents.

I confess, it was whispered to me, that I was bound in duty as a subject of England, to have given in a memorial to a Secretary of State, at my first coming over; because, whatever lands are discovered by a subject, belong to the Crown. But I doubt whether our conquests in the countries I treat of, would be as easy as those of Ferdinando Cortez over the naked Americans. The *Lilliputians* I think, are hardly worth the charge of a fleet and army to reduce them; and I question whether it might be prudent or safe to attempt the *Brobdingnagians;* or whether an English army would be much at their ease with the Flying Island over their heads. The *Houyhnhnms,* indeed, appear not to be so well prepared for war, a science to which they are perfect strangers, and especially against missive weapons. However, supposing myself to be a minister of state, I could never give my advice for invading them. Their prudence, unanimity, unacquaintedness with fear, and their love of their country, would amply supply all defects in the military art. Imagine twenty thousand of them breaking into the midst of an European army, confounding the ranks, overturning the carriages, battering the warriors' faces into mummy[18] by terrible yerks[19] from their hinder hoofs; for they would well deserve the character given to Augustus: *Recalcitrat undique tutus.*[20] But instead of proposals for conquering that magnanimous nation, I rather wish they were in a capacity or disposition to send a sufficient number of their inhabitants for civilizing Europe, by teaching us the first principles of honour, justice, truth, temperance, public spirit, fortitude, chastity, friendship, benevolence, and fidelity. The names of all which virtues are still retained among us in most languages and are to be met with in modern as well as ancient authors; which I am able to assert from my own small reading.

But I had another reason which made me less forward to enlarge his Majesty's dominions by my discoveries. To say the truth, I had conceived a few scruples with relation to the distributive justice of princes upon these occasions. For instance, a crew of pirates are driven by a storm they know not whither; at length a boy discovers land from the topmast; they go on shore to rob and plunder; they see an harmless people, are entertained with kindness, they give the country a new name, they take formal possession of it for their king, they set up a rotten plank or a stone for a memorial, they murder two or three dozen of the natives, bring away a couple more by force for a sample, return home, and get their pardon. Here commences a new dominion

---

[18] **into mummy:** Into powder; the modern equivalent would be "into a pulp."

[19] **yerks:** Kicks.

[20] *Recalcitrat . . . tutus:* Horace, *Satires* 2:1:20; "He kicks backward, guarding himself at every point."

acquired with a title by *divine right*. Ships are sent with the first opportunity; the natives driven out or destroyed, their princes tortured to discover their gold; a free licence given to all acts of inhumanity and lust, the earth reeking with the blood of its inhabitants: and this execrable crew of butchers employed in so pious an expedition, is a *modern colony* sent to convert and civilize an idolatrous and barbarous people.

But this description, I confess, doth by no means affect the British nation, who may be an example to the whole world for their wisdom, care, and justice in planting colonies; their liberal endowments for the advancement of religion and learning; their choice of devout and able pastors to propagate Christianity; their caution in stocking their provinces with people of sober lives and conversations from this the mother kingdom; their strict regard to the distribution of justice, in supplying the civil administration through all their colonies with officers of the greatest abilities, utter strangers to corruption; and to crown all, by sending the most vigilant and virtuous governors, who have no other views than the happiness of the people over whom they preside, and the honour of the King their master.

But, as those countries which I have described do not appear to have any desire of being conquered, and enslaved, murdered or driven out by colonies; nor abound either in gold, silver, sugar, or tobacco; I did humbly conceive, they were by no means proper objects of our zeal, our valour, or our interest. However, if those whom it more concerns think fit to be of another opinion, I am ready to depose, when I shall be lawfully called, that no European did ever visit these countries before me. I mean, if the inhabitants ought to be believed; unless a dispute may arise about the two *Yahoos,* said to have been seen many ages ago on a mountain in *Houyhnhnm-land.*

But, as to the formality of taking possession in my Sovereign's name, it never came once into my thoughts; and if it had, yet as my affairs then stood, I should perhaps in point of prudence and self-preservation, have put it off to a better opportunity.

Having thus answered the only objection that can ever be raised against me as a traveller, I here take a final leave of all my courteous readers, and return to enjoy my own speculations in my little garden at Redriff, to apply those excellent lessons of virtue which I learned among the *Houyhnhnms;* to instruct the *Yahoos* of my own family as far as I shall find them docible animals; to behold my figure often in a glass, and thus if possible habituate myself by time to tolerate the sight of a human creature: to lament the brutality of *Houyhnhnms* in my own country, but always treat their persons with respect, for the sake of my noble master, his family, his friends, and the whole *Houyhnhnm* race, whom these of ours have the honour to resemble in all their lineaments, however their intellectuals came to degenerate.

I began last week to permit my wife to sit at dinner with me, at the farthest end of a long table; and to answer (but with the utmost brevity) the few questions I asked her. Yet the smell of a *Yahoo* continuing very offensive, I always keep my nose well stopped with rue, lavender, or tobacco leaves. And although it be hard for a man late in life to remove old habits, I am not altogether out of hopes in some time to suffer a neighbour *Yahoo* in my company, without the apprehensions I am yet under of his teeth or his claws.

My reconcilement to the *Yahoo*-kind in general might not be so difficult, if they would be content with those vices and follies only which nature hath entitled them to. I am not in the least provoked at the sight of a lawyer, a pickpocket, a colonel, a fool, a lord, a gamester, a politician, a whore-master, a physician, an evidence, a suborner, an attorney, a traitor, or the like; this is all according to the due course of things: but when I behold a lump of deformity, and diseases both in body and mind, smitten with *pride,* it immediately breaks all the measures of my patience; neither shall I be ever able to comprehend how such an animal and such a vice could tally together. The wise and virtuous *Houyhnhnms,* who abound in all excellencies that can adorn a rational creature, have no name for this vice in their language, which hath no terms to express any thing that is evil, except those whereby they describe the detestable qualities of their *Yahoos,* among which they were not able to distinguish this of pride, for want of thoroughly understanding human nature, as it showeth itself in other countries, where that animal presides. But I, who had more experience, could plainly observe some rudiments of it among the wild *Yahoos.*

But the *Houyhnhnms,* who live under the government of reason, are no more proud of the good qualities they possess, than I should be for not wanting a leg or an arm, which no man in his wits would boast of, although he must be miserable without them. I dwell the longer upon this subject from the desire I have to make the society of an English *Yahoo* by any means not insupportable; and therefore I here entreat those who have any tincture of this absurd vice, that they will not presume to come in my sight.

ᴕᴥ ALEXANDER POPE
B. ENGLAND, 1688–1744

By 1737, the English poet Alexander Pope, physically impaired from childhood and nearing fifty, was already arranging and collating his poetry and his vast correspondence for final editions, as though he sensed his life were nearing its end. (He would, in fact, die at fifty-six.) In the midst of worsening physical ailments and the somber task of readying his work for posterity, Pope presented the Prince of Wales, with whom he had maintained a wary friendship, a puppy from his Great Dane Bounce's new litter, together with a collar engraved with a couplet:[1]

I am his Highness' Dog at Kew;
Pray tell me Sir, whose Dog are you?

Minor verse, to be sure, but in a number of ways it embodies Pope's work and times. Pope's poetry grows out of and flourishes within an intensely

---

[1] **couplet:** A two-line, rhymed stanza. Pope was the master of the **heroic couplet,** an iambic-pentameter stanza that completes its thought within the closed two-line form, as in this example from *An Essay on Man:*

Through worlds unnumber'd though the God be known,
'Tis ours to trace him only in our own.

gossipy and self-conscious aristocratic society. The couplet is designed to be read and reacted to by people fawning over the royal puppy, their reactions observed by others in the know. The couplet itself is very economical, small enough to fit upon a dog collar, packing into its neat repetition of the word *dog* much comment about those who fawn, those who follow, and those who are owned. Pope is matchless for his compressed subtlety, his ability to manipulate sound to convey thought. And finally, there is the darkness just beneath the surface of the playful gesture. Dogs are said to have pure hearts and to remain loyal even toward abusive owners. How many people had compromised their morality and judgment in the Prince's court in return for a good dinner or some privilege?

Avatar of a New Augustan Age.   In his own time, Pope was mocked and despised for his work, his opinions, and his body, which was cruelly misshapen and weakened by tuberculosis of the spine. But he was also regarded as *the* poet among poets, *the* heir of the spirit of Western European poetry, *the* British writer against whom others must be measured. Physical deformities were fair game for satirists in Pope's day, and vicious caricatures of the dwarfed and hunchbacked poet showed Pope's head grotesquely topping the body of a spider or a monkey. At the same time, it became fashionable to paint and sculpt him nobly posed in the company of Homer, Virgil, Dante, Chaucer, Petrarch, and other forebears of the grand tradition of European literature.

The ancestors whose traditions Pope most consciously sought to make new in his own Augustan Age[2] were Roman classical authors. Horace[3] is his model for the *Moral Essays,* where in easy, colloquial language he takes on the excesses and shortcomings of women, or landscape gardeners, or the moneyed aristocracy. Lucretius's[4] *De rerum natura* inspired Pope and his contemporaries to present complex philosophical ideas in verse, as Pope does in his *Essay on Man.* Above all, the epic poets, chiefly Homer and Virgil, echo constantly in Pope's poetry. His thorough knowledge of their poetry's scope and music becomes transmuted in his brilliant MOCK EPICS[5] *The Rape of the Lock* (1712, 1714) and *The Dunciad* (1742), where contemporary people's mundane affairs are depicted surrounded by epic panoply partly to underscore their tawdriness. The pedantic scholar Colley Cibber,[6] the principal butt of *The Dunciad,*

www For links to more information about Pope and the 21st-century relevance of *An Essay on Man,* see bedfordstmartins .com/worldlit compact.

---

[2] **Augustan Age:** Associated with the first half of the eighteenth century and with British Neoclassicism, the Augustan Age was named after the period when Augustus (63 B.C.E.–14 C.E.) ruled the Roman Empire and many of the great Latin poets, especially Horace and Virgil, flourished.

[3] **Horace** (65 B.C.E.–8 B.C.E.): Greatest of the Latin lyric poets of the Augustan Age in Rome.

[4] **Lucretius** (C. 99 B.C.E.–C. 55 B.C.E.): Latin poet who argued for a materialistic worldview in his philosophical poem *De rerum natura (On the Nature of Things).*

[5] MOCK EPIC: A form that parodies the epic by treating a trivial subject in an elevated style, employing such conventions of the form as the plea to a muse for inspiration, an extended simile, a heroic epithet, or descriptive title added to a person's name.

[6] **Colley Cibber** (1671–1757): English dramatist and actor-manager, appointed poet laureate of England in 1730.

builds a ceremonial bonfire of the writings he has been unable to sell in honor of the goddess Dulness, but just in time she stops him from burning these treasures and whisks him off to her sordid palace amid the flea-markets of London in order to proclaim him her own dear heir. Other goddesses and their favorites from classical epics come to mind—Thetis and Achilles, Athene and Odysseus, Venus and Aeneas[7]—but with a mocking difference. Pope was celebrated not only for his technical mastery of rhyme and rhythm and his ability to catch the particular satiric spirit of the times: He also gave his contemporaries confidence that this new Augustan Age was indeed an extension of a great classical tradition that valued sense, treasured knowledge, and ridiculed folly.

A Catholic Outsider.   Pope was born in 1688 into a well-do-to Catholic linen merchant's family in London, which was a fiercely anti-Catholic city. In 1711 the Pope family moved to a small farm in Windsor Forest, some thirty miles from London, where other Catholic families sought relief from persecution. Pope's passion for country scenes and gardening began here in this gentle landscape. Fragile health limited his experience of both the natural world and school; his tubercular, hunched spine halted his growth at four feet six inches, and he was racked by fierce headaches and respiratory problems all his life. But the little boy's mind was remarkable. He avidly read English, French, and Latin poetry, and his father encouraged him to write verses of his own.

Pope's Catholicism barred him from the universities, but he was determined to venture beyond his household. In 1705 he gained a ready education by walking boldly into Will's Coffeehouse in London, where the famous writers of the older generation still gathered. Pope struck the old guard as an odd country bumpkin, but they recognized his genius, and by 1709 he had published his first poems, imitations of Virgil's *Eclogues.*

Literary Successes in London.   In 1711 the audacious newcomer brought out his *Essay on Criticism,* a long poem in which he dispensed literary criticism and wickedly satirized a number of his elders along the way. At twenty-three Pope was already famous and controversial, and in the next few years, between 1712 and 1714, he produced *The Rape of the Lock,* his brilliant mock-heroic account of a feud among society men and women. In that same year, Pope made a new set of extraordinary friends, mostly Tory and literary, whom he would keep for life, among them **Jonathan Swift** and John Gay.[8] Together they devised the character of a droning pedant named Martinus Scriblerus, for whom they invented a vast body of memoirs and correspondence. Swift and Pope especially spurred each other's genius, but the circle of friends, many of whom held

---

In Pope I cannot read
a line
But with a sigh I wish
it mine;
When he can in one
couplet fix
More sense than I
can do in six,
It gives me such a
jealous fit,
I cry, "Pox take him
and his wit!"

– JONATHAN SWIFT,
"Verses on the Death
of Dr. Swift," 1739

p. 227

---

[7] **Thetis . . . Aeneas:** The hero of the classical epic was usually supported and protected by a goddess, who was often his mother. In Homer's *Iliad,* Thetis protects her son Achilles, as Venus does her son Aeneas in Virgil's *Aeneid.* Although Athene is not Odysseus's mother, she acts as his guardian in the *Iliad* and the *Odyssey.*

[8] **John Gay** (1685–1732): The English playwright and poet best known for *The Beggar's Opera* (1728).

political offices, was scattered when Queen Anne died in 1714 and the Tory government fell.

Country Life in Twickenham.   Pope next translated Homer's *The Iliad* into English, a five-year project. In 1719, a year after his father's death, he and his mother moved to a villa at Twickenham, on whose five acres he would exercise his passion for landscape gardening. He built a rustic grotto and outfitted it with a system of lamps and mirrors, enabling him

Marcellus Laroon the Younger, *A Concert at Montagu House,* **1735. Pencil, Ink, and Wash**

This drawing portrays a gathering in an aristocratic English home during Pope's time. (The Courtauld Institute Gallery, Somerset House, London)

to project on small surfaces, in tiny "moving images," the river traffic on the Thames, much as he captured the social world of England in the miniature frame of the heroic couplet. At Twickenham he entertained company, including a number of strong and intellectual women such as Martha Blount, with whom he had an enduring friendship.

The Dunciad and Later Life.   After his early and fast-paced start, the years between 1719 and 1728 were a sort of hiatus in Pope's career, largely filled with editing Shakespeare, translating the classics, and landscape gardening. But in 1728 came the *The Dunciad,* a dark mock epic in which

Pope took on not merely *dunces,* his personal literary enemies, but everything that embodied for him the petty corruption, shoddy art, and slipping standards that might quietly erode an entire culture. In 1743 an edition of the revised poem, complete with full names of the dunces whom it satirized, was offered to the public. Although Pope's poetry now turned increasingly to moral and philosophical subjects such as those in *An Essay on Man,* Pope never stopped writing SATIRE; *The Dunciad,* in particular, kept appearing in ever more elaborate editions, and Pope remained a prolific writer to the end. He died of asthma on May 30, 1744, after receiving the last rites of the church.

An Essay on Man.   Dedicated to Henry St. John, Lord Bolingbroke, *An Essay on Man* was published anonymously in 1733–34, a time when his satires such as *The Dunciad* had made Pope many enemies who would have immediately attacked the poem had they known it was from his hand. In the poem, Pope set out to "vindicate the ways of God to man" and to show the order and design of nature and the universe. That aim was not unlike Milton's in *Paradise Lost,* to which Pope alludes in Epistle 1; but Pope, while drawing upon Greco-Roman philosophy, Christian theology, and Newtonian science, presents a more secular philosophical system than Milton's. The four "epistles" of *An Essay on Man* embark upon a philosophical survey of "the nature and state of man" in four aspects: with respect to the universe, to man himself, to society, and to happiness. The poem was conceived as part of a much larger, unfinished project, *Moral Essays,* wherein Pope hoped to elaborate a complete system of ethics. Four other poems of that grand project were completed before Pope's death and are now known collectively as the *Epistles to Several Persons.* In the course of exploring the condition, relation, and purpose of human beings in the world, *An Essay on Man* attempts to set morals and manners in order by reminding human beings of their proper place in the order of things.

Where the *Essay on Criticism* reconciles taste and poetics with the laws of nature, *An Essay on Man* describes a rational, hierarchical arrangement of everything in creation. Each plant, animal, and inanimate thing occupies its intended place, and all are linked in a grand system of interdependence that benefits the whole. Pope's poem adduces the concept of the "great chain of being," an idea of a hierarchically ordered universe that goes back as far as Plato and Aristotle. Important to this idea is that the beings occupying each link of the chain observe the laws providentially defined for their particular category. For most sentient beings, denied the luxury of free will, functioning within these parameters presents no problem at all, for without free will their destinies follow the laws of nature by necessity. Human beings, however, because of their free will, continually transgress those parameters, thereby disturbing the order of things. This principle applies not just to the natural order but to the social, and even aesthetic, order. As Pope had cautioned critics as early as the *Essay on Criticism* (1711), "Nature to all things fixed the limits fit, / And wisely curbed proud man's pretending wit."

Epistles 1 and 2 of *An Essay on Man* suggest that human beings are wont to forget their place in the world, overstep their limits, and succumb to excesses—in reason or in passion. Such propensity to err by dint of free will defines the human lot. Rather than give in to error, however, the poems suggest that humans must strive to make a virtue of their capacity to err: they must act with self-consciousness and good judgment to temper and control, but not stifle, this capacity. Emphasizing the purposive interconnectedness of the world, Epistle 3 underscores the partiality of human knowledge in contrast to God's wisdom. Thus, human claims to knowledge and pride in human achievements should be made in moderation. In the words of Epistle 2, human beings are "darkly wise, and rudely great: With too much knowledge for the Sceptic side, / With too much weakness for the Stoic's pride." In the spirit of Enlightenment thought, Pope's *Essay on Man* advises that as humans learn to cope with the contending forces that drive and divide family, community, and society, they must focus their glass upon those things within reach: "Know then thyself, presume not God to scan; The proper study of Mankind is Man."

■ **FURTHER RESEARCH**

Biography
Mack, Maynard. *Alexander Pope: A Life.* 1985.

Criticism
Broich, Ulrich. *The Eighteenth-Century Mock-Heroic Poem.* 1990.
Brown, Laura. *Alexander Pope.* 1985.
Knellwolf, Christa. *A Contradiction Still: Representations of Women in the Poetry of Alexander Pope.* 1998.
Rogers, Pat. *Introduction to Pope.* 1975.
Rousseau, G. S., ed. *Twentieth-Century Interpretations of* The Rape of the Lock: *A Collection of Critical Essays.* 1969.
Solomon, Harry M. *The Rape of the Text: Reading and Misreading Pope's* Essay on Man. 1993.

∾ An Essay on Man

To Henry St. John, Lord Bolingbroke

EPISTLE 1

Of the Nature and State of Man with respect to the Universe

Awake, my St. John![1] leave all meaner things
To low ambition, and the pride of kings.
Let us (since life can little more supply
Than just to look about us and to die)
Expatiate free° o'er all this scene of man;   roam freely

---

[1] **St. John:** Henry St. John, Viscount Bolingbroke (1678–1751), Pope's friend who is admonished here for not keeping his part of the deal to write a companion set of philosophical reflections in prose.

A mighty maze! but not without a plan;
A wild, where weeds and flowers promiscuous shoot,
Or garden, tempting with forbidden fruit.
Together let us beat this ample field,
10 Try what the open, what the covert yield;
The latent tracts, the giddy heights, explore
Of all who blindly creep, or sightless soar;
Eye Nature's walks, shoot folly as it flies,
And catch the manners living as they rise;
Laugh where we must, be candid where we can;
But vindicate the ways of God to man.[2]

    1. Say first, of God above, or man below,
What can we reason, but from what we know?
Of man, what see we but his station here,
20 From which to reason, or to which refer?
Through worlds unnumbered though the God be known,
'Tis ours to trace him only in our own.
He, who through vast immensity can pierce,
See worlds on worlds compose one universe,
Observe how system into system runs,
What other planets circle other suns,
What varied being peoples every star,
May tell why Heaven has made us as we are.
But of this frame the bearings, and the ties,
30 The strong connections, nice dependencies,
Gradations just, has thy pervading soul
Looked through? or can a part contain the whole?
    Is the great chain,[3] that draws all to agree,
And drawn supports, upheld by God, or thee?

    2. Presumptuous man! the reason wouldst thou find,
Why formed so weak, so little, and so blind?
First, if thou canst, the harder reason guess,
Why formed no weaker, blinder, and no less!
Ask of thy mother earth, why oaks are made
40 Taller or stronger than the weeds they shade?
Or ask of yonder argent fields above,
Why Jove's satellites are less than Jove?

---

[2] **But vindicate . . . to man:** An allusion to John Milton's *Paradise Lost* 1:26, where Milton declares the purpose of his epic is to "justify the ways of God to men."

[3] **the great chain:** The Great Chain of Being, the popular medieval and Renaissance concept that all things and beings in the universe are ordered in a graduated hierarchy with the basest elements, like lead, at the bottom, and God at the top; human beings occupied the center of this seamless continuum.

Of systems possible, if 'tis confessed
That Wisdom Infinite must form the best,
Where all must full or not coherent be,
And all that rises, rise in due degree;
Then, in the scale of reasoning life, 'tis plain,
There must be, somewhere, such a rank as man:
And all the question (wrangle e'er so long)
50 Is only this, if God has placed him wrong?
   Respecting man, whatever wrong we call,
May, must be right, as relative to all.
In human works, though labored on with pain,
A thousand movements scarce one purpose gain;
In God's, one single can its end produce;
Yet serves to second too some other use.
So man, who here seems principal alone,
Perhaps acts second to some sphere unknown,
Touches some wheel, or verges to some goal;
60 'Tis but a part we see, and not a whole.
   When the proud steed shall know why man restrains
His fiery course, or drives him o'er the plains;
When the dull ox, why now he breaks the clod,
Is now a victim, and now Egypt's god:
Then shall man's pride and dullness comprehend
His actions', passions', being's use and end;
Why doing, suffering, checked, impelled; and why
This hour a slave, the next a deity.
   Then say not man's imperfect, Heaven in fault;
70 Say rather, man's as perfect as he ought;
His knowledge measured to his state and place,
His time a moment, and a point his space.
If to be perfect in a certain sphere,
What matter, soon or late, or here or there?
The blest today is as completely so,
As who began a thousand years ago.

   3. Heaven from all creatures hides the book of Fate,
All but the page prescribed, their present state:
From brutes what men, from men what spirits know:
80 Or who could suffer being here below?
The lamb thy riot dooms to bleed today,
Had he thy reason, would he skip and play?
Pleased to the last, he crops the flowery food,
And licks the hand just raised to shed his blood.
O blindness to the future! kindly given,
That each may fill the circle marked by Heaven:

Who sees with equal eye, as God of all,
A hero perish, or a sparrow fall,
Atoms or systems° into ruin hurled,   solar systems
90 And now a bubble burst, and now a world.
      Hope humbly then; with trembling pinions soar;
Wait the great teacher Death, and God adore!
What future bliss, he gives not thee to know,
But gives that hope to be thy blessing now.
Hope springs eternal in the human breast:
Man never is, but always to be blest:
The soul, uneasy and confined from home,
Rests and expatiates in a life to come.
      Lo! the poor Indian, whose untutored mind
100 Sees God in clouds, or hears him in the wind;
His soul proud Science never taught to stray
Far as the solar walk, or milky way;
Yet simple Nature to his hope has given,
Behind the cloud-topped hill, an humbler heaven;
Some safer world in depth of woods embraced,
Some happier island in the watery waste,
Where slaves once more their native land behold,
No fiends torment, no Christians thirst for gold!
To be, contents his natural desire,
110 He asks no angel's wing, no seraph's fire;
But thinks, admitted to that equal sky,
His faithful dog shall bear him company.

      4. Go, wiser thou! and, in thy scale of sense,
Weigh thy opinion against Providence;
Call imperfection what thou fancy'st such,
Say, here he gives too little, there too much;
Destroy all creatures for thy sport or gust,°   taste
Yet cry, if man's unhappy, God's unjust;
If man alone engross not Heaven's high care,
120 Alone made perfect here, immortal there:
Snatch from his hand the balance and the rod,
Rejudge his justice, be the God of God!
      In pride, in reasoning pride, our error lies;
All quit their sphere, and rush into the skies.
Pride still is aiming at the blest abodes,
Men would be angels, angels would be gods.
Aspiring to be gods, if angels fell,
Aspiring to be angels, men rebel:
And who but wishes to invert the laws
130 Of order, sins against the Eternal Cause.

5. Ask for what end the heavenly bodies shine,
Earth for whose use? Pride answers, "'Tis for mine:
For me kind Nature wakes her genial power,
Suckles each herb, and spreads out every flower;
Annual for me, the grape, the rose renew
The juice nectareous, and the balmy dew;
For me, the mine a thousand treasures brings;
For me, health gushes from a thousand springs;
Seas roll to waft me, suns to light me rise;
140 My footstool earth, my canopy the skies."
     But errs not Nature from this gracious end,
From burning suns when livid deaths descend,
When earthquakes swallow, or when tempests sweep
Towns to one grave, whole nations to the deep?
"No," 'tis replied, "the first Almighty Cause
Acts not by partial, but by general laws;
The exceptions few; some change since all began,
And what created perfect?" — Why then man?
If the great end be human happiness,
150 Then Nature deviates; and can man do less?
As much that end a constant course requires
Of showers and sunshine, as of man's desires;
As much eternal springs and cloudless skies,
As men forever temperate, calm, and wise.
If plagues or earthquakes break not Heaven's design,
Why then a Borgia, or a Catiline?[4]
Who knows but he whose hand the lightning forms,
Who heaves old ocean, and who wings the storms,
Pours fierce ambition in a Caesar's mind,
160 Or turns young Ammon[5] loose to scourge mankind?
From pride, from pride, our very reasoning springs;
Account for moral, as for natural things:
Why charge we Heaven in those, in these acquit?
In both, to reason right is to submit.
     Better for us, perhaps, it might appear,
Were there all harmony, all virtue here;

---

[4] **Borgia, Catiline:** Cesare Borgia (1476–1507), son of Pope Alexander VI; Renaissance Italian prince who was, with other members of his powerful family, notorious for ruthless opportunism, greed, cruelty, and treachery. Lucius Sergius Catiline (c. 108–62 B.C.E.) was an ambitious and treacherous conspirator against the Roman state.

[5] **Ammon:** Alexander the Great (356–323 B.C.E.), king of Macedon, student of Aristotle, and powerful general who extended his empire by subduing Greece, defeating the Persians, and pushing all the way to Egypt, where he founded the city Alexandria, and to India, where his armies refused to push farther.

That never air or ocean felt the wind;
That never passion discomposed the mind:
But ALL subsists by elemental strife;
170 And passions are the elements of life.
The general ORDER, since the whole began,
Is kept in Nature, and is kept in man.

      6. What would this man? Now upward will he soar,
And little less than angel, would be more;
Now looking downwards, just as grieved appears
To want the strength of bulls, the fur of bears.
Made for his use all creatures if he call,
Say what their use, had he the powers of all?
Nature to these, without profusion, kind,
180 The proper organs, proper powers assigned;
Each seeming want compènsated of course,
Here with degrees of swiftness, there of force;
All in exact proportion to the state;
Nothing to add, and nothing to abate.
Each beast, each insect, happy in its own;
Is Heaven unkind to man, and man alone?
Shall he alone, whom rational we call,
Be pleased with nothing, if not blessed with all?
      The bliss of man (could pride that blessing find)
190 Is not to act or think beyond mankind;
No powers of body or of soul to share,
But what his nature and his state can bear.
Why has not man a microscopic eye?
For this plain reason, man is not a fly.
Say what the use, were finer optics given,
To inspect a mite, not comprehend the heaven?
Or touch, if tremblingly alive all o'er,
To smart and agonize at every pore?
Or quick effluvia⁶ darting through the brain,
200 Die of a rose in aromatic pain?
If nature thundered in his opening ears,
And stunned him with the music of the spheres,
How would he wish that Heaven had left him still
The whispering zephyr, and the purling rill?
Who finds not Providence all good and wise,
Alike in what it gives, and what denies?

---

⁶ **effluvia:** Streams of particles that were thought to convey sensory impressions to the brain.

7. Far as creation's ample range extends,
The scale of sensual,° mental powers ascends: sensory
Mark how it mounts, to man's imperial race,
210   From the green myriads in the peopled grass:
What modes of sight betwixt each wide extreme,
The mole's dim curtain, and the lynx's beam:
Of smell, the headlong lioness between,
And hound sagacious on the tainted green:[7]
Of hearing, from the life that fills the flood,
To that which warbles through the vernal wood:
The spider's touch, how exquisitely fine!
Feels at each thread, and lives along the line:
In the nice° bee, what sense so subtly true   discriminating
220   From poisonous herbs extracts the healing dew:
How instinct varies in the groveling swine,
Compared, half-reasoning elephant, with thine!
'Twixt that, and reason, what a nice barrier,
Forever separate, yet forever near!
Remembrance and reflection how allied;
What thin partitions sense from thought divide:
And middle natures, how they long to join,
Yet never pass the insuperable line!
Without this just gradation, could they be
230   Subjected, these to those, or all to thee?
The powers of all subdued by thee alone,
Is not thy reason all these powers in one?

8. See, through this air, this ocean, and this earth,
All matter quick, and bursting into birth.
Above, how high progressive life may go!
Around, how wide! how deep extend below!
Vast Chain of Being! which from God began,
Natures ethereal, human, angel, man,
Beast, bird, fish, insect, what no eye can see,
240   No glass can reach! from Infinite to thee,
From thee to nothing. — On superior powers
Were we to press, inferior might on ours:
Or in the full creation leave a void,
Where, one step broken, the great scale's destroyed:
From Nature's chain whatever link you strike,
Tenth or ten thousandth, breaks the chain alike.

---

[7] Of smell . . . green: The lioness, who has a poor sense of smell, rushes headlong at her quarry, unlike the hound whose acute sense of smell enables it to track its prey.

And, if each system in gradation roll
Alike essential to the amazing whole,
The least confusion but in one, not all
250   That system only, but the whole must fall.
Let earth unbalanced from her orbit fly,
Planets and suns run lawless through the sky,
Let ruling angels from their spheres be hurled,
Being on being wrecked, and world on world,
Heaven's whole foundations to their center nod,
And Nature tremble to the throne of God:
All this dread ORDER break — for whom? for thee?
Vile worm! — oh, madness, pride, impiety!

9. What if the foot, ordained the dust to tread,
260   Or hand, to toil, aspired to be the head?
What if the head, the eye, or ear repined
To serve mere engines to the ruling Mind?[8]
Just as absurd, to mourn the tasks or pains,
The great directing mind of all ordains.
All are but parts one stupendous whole,
Whose body Nature is, and God the soul;
That, changed through all, and yet in all the same,
Great in the earth, as in the ethereal frame,
Warms in the sun, refreshes in the breeze,
270   Glows in the stars, and blossoms in the trees,
Lives through all life, extends through all extent,
Spreads undivided, operates unspent,
Breathes in our soul, informs our mortal part,
As full, as perfect, in a hair as heart;
As full, as perfect, in vile man that mourns,
As the rapt seraph that adores and burns;
To him no high, no low, no great, no small;
He fills, he bounds, connects, and equals° all.   makes equal

10. Cease then, nor order imperfection name:
280   Our proper bliss depends on what we blame.
Know thy own point: this kind, this due degree
Of blindness, weakness, Heaven bestows on thee.
Submit — In this, or any other sphere,
Secure to be as blest as thou canst bear:
Safe in the hand of one disposing Power,
Or in the natal, or the mortal hour.

---

[8] **What if . . . Mind?:** Allusion to 1 Corinthians 12:14–26.

All Nature is but art, unknown to thee;
All chance, direction, which thou canst not see;
All discord, harmony not understood;
290   All partial evil, universal good:
And, spite of pride, in erring reason's spite,
One truth is clear: Whatever is, is RIGHT.

FROM EPISTLE 2

Of the Nature and State of Man, with respect
to Himself, as an Individual

Know then thyself, presume not God to scan;
The proper study of Mankind is Man.
Plac'd on this isthmus of a middle state,
A being darkly wise, and rudely great:
With too much knowledge for the Sceptic side,
With too much weakness for the Stoic's pride,
He hangs between; in doubt to act, or rest,
In doubt to deem himself a God, or Beast;
In doubt his Mind or Body to prefer,
10   Born but to die, and reas'ning but to err;
Alike in ignorance, his reason such,
Whether he thinks too little, or too much:
Chaos of Thought and Passion, all confus'd;
Still by himself abus'd, or disabus'd;
Created half to rise, and half to fall;
Great lord of all things, yet a prey to all;
Sole judge of Truth, in endless Error hurl'd:
The glory, jest, and riddle of the world!
    Go, wond'rous creature! mount where Science guides,
20   Go, measure earth, weigh air, and state the tides;
Instruct the planets in what orbs to run,
Correct old Time, and regulate the Sun;
Go, soar with Plato to th' empyreal sphere,[9]
To the first good, first perfect, and first fair;
Or tread the mazy round his follow'rs trod,
And quitting sense call imitating God;
As Eastern priests in giddy circles run,

---

[9] **Go, soar . . . empyreal sphere:** Pope suggests here that transcendental realm of the perfect Forms or Ideas described by Greek philosopher Plato (c. 427–347 B.C.E.) was located in the remotest sphere of the Ptolemaic universe, which put the earth at the center of the universe, surrounded by nine spheres and the empyrean, the realm of the angels and God.

And turn their heads to imitate the Sun.
Go, teach Eternal Wisdom how to rule—
30 Then drop into thyself, and be a fool!
     Superior beings, when of late they saw
A mortal Man unfold all Nature's law,
Admir'd such wisdom in an earthly shape,
And shew'd a Newton[10] as we shew an Ape.
     Could he, whose rules the rapid Comet bind,
Describe or fix one movement of his Mind?
Who saw its fires here rise, and there descend,
Explain his own beginning, or his end?
Alas what wonder! Man's superior part
40 Uncheck'd may rise, and climb from art to art:
But when his own great work is but begun,
What Reason weaves, by Passion is undone.
     Trace Science then, with Modesty thy guide;
First strip off all her equipage of Pride,
Deduct what is but Vanity, or Dress,
Or Learning's Luxury, or Idleness;
Or tricks to shew the stretch of human brain,
Mere curious pleasure, or ingenious pain:
Expunge the whole, or lop th' excrescent parts
50 Of all, our Vices have created Arts:
Then see how little the remaining sum,
Which serv'd the past, and must the times to come!
     2. Two Principles in human nature reign;
Self-love, to urge, and Reason, to restrain;
Not this a good, nor that a bad we call,
Each works its end, to move or govern all:
And to their proper operation still,
Ascribe all Good; to their improper, Ill.
     Self-love, the spring of motion, acts° the soul;   activates
60 Reason's comparing balance rules the whole.
Man, but for that, no action could attend,
And, but for this, were active to no end;
Fix'd like a plant on his peculiar spot,
To draw nutrition, propagate, and rot;
Or, meteor-like, flame lawless thro' the void,
Destroying others, by himself destroy'd.
     Most strength the moving principle requires;
Active its task, it prompts, impels, inspires.

---

[10] **Newton:** Sir Isaac Newton (1642–1727), English physicist, mathematician, and scientist whose *Mathematical Principles of Natural Philosophy,* known as the *Principia* (1687), was considered in Pope's time to be the greatest example of human genius and scientific achievement.

Sedate and quiet the comparing lies,
70 Form'd but to check, delib'rate, and advise.
Self-love still stronger, as its objects nigh;
Reason's at distance, and in prospect lie:
That sees immediate good by present sense;
Reason, the future and the consequence.
Thicker than arguments, temptations throng,
At best more watchful this, but that more strong.
The action of the stronger to suspend
Reason still use, to Reason still attend:
Attention, habit and experience gains,
80 Each strengthens Reason, and Self-love restrains.
        Let subtle schoolmen teach these friends to fight,
More studious to divide than to unite,
And Grace and Virtue, Sense and Reason split,
With all the rash dexterity of Wit:
Wits, just like fools, at war about a Name,
Have full as oft no meaning, or the same.
Self-love and Reason to one end aspire,
Pain their aversion, Pleasure their desire;
But greedy that is object would devour,
90 This taste the honey, and not wound the flow'r:
Pleasure, or wrong or rightly understood,
Our greatest evil, or our greatest good. . . .

FROM EPISTLE 3

Of the Nature and State of Man
with respect to Society

Here then we rest: "The Universal Cause
Acts to one end, but acts by various laws."
In all the madness of superfluous health,
The trim of pride, the impudence of wealth,
Let this great truth be present night and day;
But most be present, if we preach or pray.

     1. Look round our World; behold the chain of Love
Combining all below and all above.
See plastic Nature working to this end,
10 The single atoms each to other tend,
Attract, attracted to, the next in place
Formed and impelled its neighbour to embrace.
See Matter next, with various life endued,
Press to one centre still, the general Good.

See dying vegetables life sustain,
See life dissolving vegetate again:
All forms that perish other forms supply,
(By turns we catch the vital breath, and die)
Like bubbles on the sea of Matter born,
20 They rise, they break, and to that sea return.
Nothing is foreign: Parts relate to whole;
One all-extending, all-preserving Soul
Connects each being, greatest with the least;
Made Beast in aid of Man, and Man of Beast;
All served, all serving: nothing stands alone;
The chain holds on, and where it ends, unknown.
      Has God, thou fool! worked solely for thy good,
Thy joy, thy pastime, thy attire, thy food?
Who for thy table feeds the wanton fawn,
30 For him as kindly spread the flowery lawn:
Is it for thee the lark ascends and sings?
Joy tunes his voice, joy elevates his wings.
Is it for thee the linnet pours his throat?
Loves of his own and raptures swell the note.
The bounding steed you pompously bestride,
Shares with his lord the pleasure and the pride.
Is thine alone the seed that strews the plain?
The birds of heaven shall vindicate their grain.
Thine the full harvest of the golden year?
40 Part pays, and justly, the deserving steer:
The hog, that ploughs not nor obeys thy call,
Lives on the labours of this lord of all.
      Know, Nature's children all divide her care;
The fur that warms a monarch, warmed a bear.
While Man exclaims, "See all things for my use!"
"See man for mine!" replies a pampered goose:
And just as short of reason He must fall,
Who thinks all made for one, not one for all.

TEXT IN CONTEXT

❧ FRANÇOIS-MARIE AROUET DE VOLTAIRE
B. FRANCE, 1694–1778

Catherine Lusurier,
Portrait of Voltaire,
1718. Oil on Canvas
*Voltaire as a young
man. (Réunion des
Musées Nationaux /
Art Resource, NY)*

During the **FRENCH REVOLUTION**, more than ten years after his death, Voltaire's bones were transported to Paris in a hearse inscribed "Poet, philosopher, historian, he gave wings to the human intelligence; he prepared us for freedom." More than any other single person of the eighteenth century, Voltaire epitomizes in the breadth of his intellectual endeavors the Age of Enlightenment, which put its faith in human reason and a rational universe, championed human rights, and believed that reason could chart a commonsense path for improving the human condition. Voltaire was not an originator of ideas, but he took hold of the liberal precepts of his time — such as John Locke's[1] theories on equality and human rights, Isaac Newton's[2] natural philosophy, and English deism — and became the propagandist for these ideas in France and eventually throughout Europe. For more than sixty years he was an outspoken critic of French society and for most of his life he was a refugee from his own country.

The Young Rebel.   The facts of Voltaire's life are a testimony to his life-long desire to put ideas into action as well as to the power of his foes, who tried to silence his extraordinary voice. Voltaire was born François-Marie Arouet to a prosperous bourgeois family. He was introduced at an early

---

[1] **John Locke** (1632–1704): Influential English philosopher. In *Essay Concerning Human Understanding* (1690), he proposed that the human mind at birth is a *tabula rasa,* or blank slate, that experience fills up. (see p. 381)

[2] **Isaac Newton** (1642–1727): Brilliant English mathematician and physicist who formulated the laws of gravity and motion, thereby describing the physical workings of the cosmos and presenting it as a finely tuned machine.

age to DEISM by his godfather, the Abbé de Châteauneuf. Deism was the belief that a rational deity created the world and left the running of it to natural laws, much as a watchmaker makes a watch to run on its own. Voltaire embraced deism his entire life, and it formed the basis of his unending attacks on Christianity. He was given a solid classical education at a famous Jesuit school, College Louis-le-Grand. While in his teens he steered away from his father's law profession and instead became involved with various social factions in Paris, where he wrote libelous poems for which he was briefly jailed and then exiled from France. At twenty-three he adopted the pen name of "Voltaire," the exact meaning of which is unknown. His first serious literary efforts were in the theater; his play *Oedipe* (1718)[3] was a financial success. In it the main culprit is God, who becomes responsible for the crimes of Oedipus and Jocasta. A popular epic poem, *Le Henriade,* celebrated Henry IV[4] as a champion of religious tolerance in the sixteenth century.

In 1725, Voltaire's life took a sharp turn. He was insulted by the chevalier de Rohan; Voltaire returned the insult and was beaten up by Rohan's hired thugs, in full view of aristocrats whom Voltaire had previously thought of as friends. He challenged Rohan to a duel, but on the appointed day he was arrested, jailed, and exiled to England for almost three years, from 1726 to 1729. He was so impressed by English tolerance in the areas of religion and speech that he learned to speak and read English and became friends with **Alexander Pope**, **Jonathan Swift**, and the English dramatist William Congreve (1670–1729). Voltaire gained access to the English court by way of Sir Robert Walpole, an important English statesman, and Lord Bolingbroke, a friend of writers and a gentleman philosopher. Voltaire also became acquainted with the writings and ideas of Shakespeare, Bacon,[5] Locke, and Newton, and with the English parliamentary system.

Based on his experiences in England, he wrote *Philosophical Letters (Lettres philosophiques);* an English version was published in 1733 and a French edition in 1734. While complimenting English ways, it indirectly criticized the abuses of French institutions. The book was condemned in France, copies of it were burned, and a warrant was issued for Voltaire's arrest. This time, Voltaire was prepared for the attack; financially secure,

www   For links to more information about Voltaire, a quiz on *Candide,* and information about the 21st-century relevance of *Candide,* see bedford stmartins.com/worldlitcompact.

pp. 278, 227

---

[3] *Oedipe:* The ancient myth of a king who killed his father and married his mother was first dramatized in ancient Greece by Sophocles (496–406 B.C.E.) in *Oedipus the King.*

[4] **Henry IV:** During a period of heavy religious persecution, Henry IV of France (1589–1610) issued the Edict of Nantes, which granted Protestants—especially the Huguenots—freedom of worship.

[5] **Bacon:** English philosopher Francis Bacon (1561–1626) introduced empiricism—experiment and observation—to scientific thought.

he took up residence with Emilie de Breteuil, Marquise du Châtelet, at the château of Cirey, situated in the independent duchy of Lorraine. At this refuge, Voltaire wrote plays and essays, experimented with physics in a laboratory, and supported the development of iron foundries. His book on the philosophy of history, *Essay on the Manners and the Spirit of Nations* (1756), stretched the domain of history to include prebiblical and Asian civilizations. He wrote a blizzard of essays and pamphlets attacking the corruption of his era and often published them under various pen names. His lucid writing style and biting wit, however, readily identified him.

Diplomatic and Religious Difficulties.   For several years, Frederick the Great of Prussia had been trying to entice Voltaire to his court in Potsdam, where he was creating a royal environment for art and ideas. Voltaire at last joined him, but this alliance of two extremely headstrong

Jean-Honoré
Fragonard,
The Love Letter, 1770.
Oil on Canvas
This eighteenth-century portrait illustrates the vanity of French society in Voltaire's time. (The Metropolitan Museum of Art, The Jules Bache Collection, 1949. All rights reserved, the Metropolitan Museum of Art)

men was doomed. Voltaire was not cut from diplomatic cloth and soon was embroiled in intrigues and social power plays. The finale came when Maupertuis, the president of the Academy of Berlin, had the philosopher König dismissed from the academy. Frederick backed Maupertuis and Voltaire took König's side, eventually publishing a lampoon of Maupertuis, *Diatribe of Doctor Akaia* (1752). Apparently, Voltaire obtained permission to publish this work by deceiving Frederick about the documents he was actually signing. Frederick burned the work and had Voltaire arrested.

Having been denied a residence in France, Voltaire at sixty years of age bought a country house on the border between Geneva and France. At this house called *Les Délices* (The Delights), along with his mistress, Madame Denis, and his niece, he established his own literary "court," along with a private theater where his plays were performed. Geneva, however, had a ban against theater of any kind, and again Voltaire's freedoms were threatened. He persuaded a friend, Jean Le Rond d'Alembert, to criticize Geneva's prohibition in the *Encyclopedia;* **Jean-Jacques Rousseau**, the most famous citizen of Geneva, answered this article and Voltaire in his important *Letter to d'Alembert* (1758), which defended Geneva's ban.

p. 407

Voltaire again had to move, and he bought Ferney, a large estate just inside the border of France but fronting on Lake Geneva. As the patriarch of Ferney, he experimented with a model agricultural community. During this time he also developed a stone quarry and built factories for manufacturing tiles, stockings, watches, and leather goods. He started schools and promoted fair wages and equitable taxes, and he actively defended victims of civil injustice. In one case, he rescued a young noblewoman from a convent and established her in his household, nicknaming her "Belle et Bonne" ("beautiful and good"). He eventually matched her with the marquis of Villette. And all the while he played host to the most illustrious scientists, philosophers, and artists of his time.

By 1760 his reputation as an opponent of Christianity had become almost legendary. In a letter to Voltaire, Denis Diderot addressed him as his "sublime, honorable and dear Anti-Christ." Voltaire's *Philosophical Dictionary* (1764) was a culminating diatribe against conventional religion and a delineation of his own brand of deism. Under the heading "Religion," Voltaire discusses a deity who is a product of Copernicus and Newton, not the Bible. The *Philosophical Dictionary* was immediately condemned and burned by both Protestant and Catholic authorities. In February 1778, after an absence of twenty-eight years, Voltaire returned to Paris, where he was celebrated by the Académie Française, local and foreign dignitaries, and crowds of chanting Parisians. When he died ten weeks later, on May 30, he was denied burial by Christian authorities but was secretly interred at the abbey of Scellières in Champagne.

Candide.   Voltaire's literary output amounted to more than one hundred thirty-five volumes in a modern French edition. He wrote dozens of plays and novels, and his several histories focused on important political figures. But it is his philosophical tales, especially *Zadig* (1748) and *Candide* (1759), that have brought him the greatest fame since the eighteenth century. Voltaire writes *didactic* fiction; that is, he is always interested in teaching, in using his plot and characters to develop arguments about contemporary issues. He is not concerned with creating well-rounded characters. And he is less interested in the aesthetics of fiction than in the clarity of intellectual discussion. Generally, his technique is to express his opinions through various characters from history or mythology; a character might represent a particular philosophy. His plots using Asian characters and settings are mirrors continually reflecting back on Europe or France.

Candide, whose very name suggests openness, is a naive optimist who has been educated by an impractical philosopher, Pangloss, whose name indicates a simplification of all experience. With his belief that all is for the best in the best of all possible worlds, Pangloss represents the ivory tower philosopher whose theories are radically disconnected from reality. In Chapter 5, Candide, wounded from the Lisbon earthquake, urgently begs for some wine and oil. Deaf to his request, Pangloss speculates: "This concussion of the earth is no new thing . . . the city of Lima in South America, experienced the same last year; the same cause, the same effects; there is certainly a vein of sulphur all the way underground from Lima to Lisbon." Meanwhile, Candide faints.

Voltaire's Pangloss suggests the German mathematician and philosopher Gottfried Wilhelm Leibniz (1646–1716), who claimed that this world is the best of all possible worlds. Because the universe was created by a God whose plans are perfect, the universe must be perfect, too, Leibniz argued. It has been suggested that Voltaire is also satirizing Christian Wolff (1679–1754), another German mathematician and philosopher who expressed the optimism and confidence of the age in a book titled *Reasonable Thoughts on God, the World, and the Soul of Man, Also on Things in General.* In fact, Voltaire is ridiculing any simplistic explanation for the complexities of experience, any universal principle that is applied unquestioningly to every situation. In particular he satirizes any religious belief that accounts for human disasters such as the Lisbon earthquake by reference to an ultimate good or a beneficent Providence. Although evil might be justified as some form of good or a mystery in God's ultimate plan, Voltaire prefers to link evil to human choice and weakness. The Lisbon earthquake of 1755 produced hardship that optimists had difficulty explaining away: The innocent suffered in hospitals, in homes, and on the streets. In all his works, Voltaire's real enemy is complacency, any attitude or theory that seems content with the present state of affairs. No particular Christian denomination, whether Protestant or Catholic, is safe from Voltaire's scorn.

In one adventure after another, Candide is exposed to the treachery and immorality, the greed and lust just below the surface of political officials, military commanders, and religious professionals. This wide range of experiences and the work's short chapters keep *Candide* entertaining and engaging. In Candide's search for situations that would confound Pangloss's philosophy, he finally meets Martin, a thoroughgoing pessimist. Steering a philosophical course between the two extremes, Candide arrives in Constantinople and is rejoined by his former comrades, including his beloved Lady **Cunégonde**. Candide's adjustments to all the changes in their respective lives leads to conclusions about living the simple life. He proposes a practical, modest realism; the importance of work is alluded to in the enigmatic dictum that ends the work: "We must cultivate our garden."

koo-nay-GOHND

■ **FURTHER RESEARCH**

Biography
Besterman, Theodore. *Voltaire.* 1976.
Brailsford, Henry N. *Voltaire.* 1935.
Wade, Ira O. *The Intellectual Development of Voltaire.* 1969.

Intellectual History
Keener, F. M. *The Chain of Being.* 1983.

Criticism
Cullter, M., ed. *The Enlightenment and the Comic Mode.* 1990.
Gay, Peter. *Candide.* 1963.
————. *Voltaire's Politics: The Poet as Realist.* 1959.
Wade, Ira O. *Voltaire and* Candide: *A Study in the Fusion of History, Art, and Philosophy.* 1959.

■ **PRONUNCIATION**

Cunégonde: koo-nay-GOHND
Giroflèe: zhee-roh-FLAY
Oreillons: oh-ray-YAWNG
Voltaire: vohl-TEHR

❧ Candide, or Optimism

Translated from the German of Dr. Ralph. With the Additions Found in the Doctor's Pocket When He Died at Minden in the Year of Our Lord 1759

Translated by Daniel Gordon

CHAPTER 1

How Candide was brought up in a fine castle, and how he was driven out of it

In the land of Westphalia,[1] in the castle of the Baron of Thunder-ten-tronckh, lived a youth endowed by nature with the gentlest of characters. His face was the mirror of his soul. His judgment was quite sound, his mind simple as could be; this is the reason, I think, that he was named Candide. The old servants of the house suspected that he was the son of the Baron's sister and of a good and honorable gentleman of the region whom that lady refused to marry because he could prove only seventy-one generations[2] of noble lineage, the rest of his family tree having been lost in the shadows of time.

The Baron was one of the most powerful lords in Westphalia because his castle had a gate and windows. His reception hall was even decorated with a piece of tapestry. The barnyard dogs formed a hunting pack when the need arose; the stable boys doubled as his attendants in the chase; the village vicar was his archpriest. They all called him My Lord, and they always laughed at his jokes.

The Baroness, who weighed around three hundred and fifty pounds, was widely admired for that reason, and bestowed favors on visitors with a discretion that made her even more eminent. Her daughter Cunégonde,[3] aged seventeen, was rosy-cheeked, fresh, plump, and appetizing. The Baron's son seemed to be the equal of his father in every way. The tutor Pangloss[4] was the oracle of the household, and little Candide absorbed his lessons with all the good faith of his age and character.

Pangloss taught metaphysico-theologico-cosmolo-boobology.[5] He proved admirably that there is no effect without a cause and that, in this best of all possible

---

[1] **Westphalia:** A region in northwestern Germany. The fictional translator, Doctor Ralph, supposedly died there at the battle of Minden during the Seven Years' War (1756–63). "Thunder-ten-tronckh" is Voltaire's parodic name for the estate.

[2] **seventy-one generations:** The number, amounting to two thousand years of uninterrupted nobility, is meant to be ridiculously high.

[3] **Cunégonde:** From Queen Kunigunda, the wife of Holy Roman Emperor Henry II (973–1024). She proved her fidelity by walking barefoot and blindfolded over hot irons; hence, her name adds to Voltaire's irony.

[4] **Pangloss:** "All tongue" (from Greek).

[5] **cosmolo-boobology:** Voltaire uses "cosmolo-nigologie," containing the hidden French word *nigaud,* meaning simpleton; the translator uses "boob" to convey the same meaning in English.

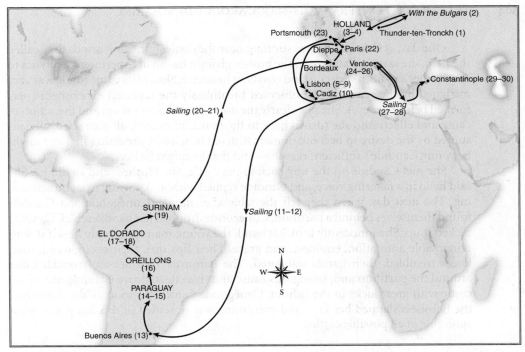

Candide's Travels

Numbers in parentheses indicate chapters of the text.

worlds,[6] the Baron's castle was the finest of all castles, and his wife the best of all possible Baronesses.

"It has been proven," he used to say, "that things cannot be other than what they are, for since everything is made for an end, everything is necessarily for the best end. Observe that noses were made to wear spectacles, hence we have spectacles. Legs are patently devised to be breeched, and so we have breeches. Stones were made to be quarried and to build castles with; hence My Lord has a fine castle. The greatest Baron of the province must have the finest residence. And since pigs were made to be eaten, we eat pork all year round. Therefore, those who have affirmed that all is well talk nonsense; they ought to have said that all is for the best."[7]

Candide listened attentively and believed innocently; for he found Miss Cunégonde extremely beautiful, though he never dared to tell her so. He concluded that after the happiness of being born Baron of Thunder-ten-tronckh, the second degree of happiness was to be Miss Cunégonde, the third was to see her every day, and the fourth was to listen to Master Pangloss, the greatest philosopher in the province and consequently in the whole world.

---

[6] **best . . . worlds:** An allusion to the belief of the German philosopher Leibniz (1646–1716), who argued that in creating the world, God had made "the most perfect of all possible states or governments."

[7] **for the best:** Voltaire here parodies the so-called argument from design, promoted by Leibniz and others, that suggests everything in the world is here for a specific purpose.

One day, as Cunégonde was strolling near the castle in the tiny woods they called the Park, she saw Dr. Pangloss in the bushes giving a lesson in experimental physics to her mother's maid, a very cute and obedient brunette. Now Miss Cunégonde was very intrigued by the sciences. She observed breathlessly the repeated experiments performed before her eyes. She saw clearly the doctor's sufficient reason and the action of cause and effect. And she turned back to the house all excited, all distracted, all consumed by the desire to become more instructed in science, dreaming that she might be young Candide's sufficient reason—and that he might be hers.

She met Candide on the way back to the castle. She blushed, and so did he. She said hello in a faltering voice, and Candide replied without knowing what he was saying. The next day, when they left the table after dinner, Cunégonde and Candide found themselves behind a partition. Cunégonde dropped her handkerchief, Candide picked it up. She innocently took his hand, the young man innocently kissed it with remarkable animation, emotion, and grace. Their lips met, their eyes glowed, their knees trembled, their hands wandered. The Baron of Thunder-ten-tronckh came around the partition and, seeing this cause and this effect, drove Candide out of the castle with great kicks in the behind. Cunégonde fainted. As soon as she recovered, the Baroness slapped her face, and everything was unsettled in this finest and most agreeable of all possible castles.

Chapter 2

What became of Candide among the Bulgars[8]

Expelled from earthly paradise, Candide walked for a long time without knowing where he was going, weeping, raising his eyes to heaven, and looking back frequently toward the finest of castles which contained the most lovely of baron's daughters. He lay down to sleep, without supper, in the furrow of a plowed field. The snow came down in large flakes. The next day, chilled to the bone, Candide dragged himself toward the nearest town, called Waldberghoff-trarbk-dikdorff. Penniless and dying of hunger and exhaustion, he came to a sad halt at the door of an inn. Two men dressed in blue[9] noticed him.

"Comrade," said one of them, "there is a well-built lad, and he is the right height too."

They approached Candide and politely invited him to dinner.

"Gentlemen," Candide answered with charming modesty, "you honor me greatly, but I lack the means to pay my share."

"But sir!" said one of the blues, "we never make people pay who have your looks and merit. Aren't you five feet ten inches tall?"

---

[8] *Bulgars:* The Prussian troops of Frederick the Great, king of Prussia from 1740 to 1786. Because it resembles in sound the French *bougre* (English "bugger"), the word suggests pederasty or sodomy.

[9] **dressed in blue:** Prussian recruiting officers wore blue and selected men for various regiments according to their size.

"Yes, gentlemen, that's my height," he said with a bow.

"Then, sir, kindly be seated. We will not only pay for your dinner, but we will never let a man like you fall short of money. Men are created only in order to help each other."

"You're right," said Candide. "That's what Dr. Pangloss always told me, and I see clearly that everything is for the best."

They urged him to accept a little money. He took it and offered to sign a promissory note, but they would not hear of it, and they all sat down to eat.

"Don't you have a tender love for your . . ."

"Oh yes!" Candide answered. "I have a tender love for Miss Cunégonde."

"No," one of the men stated, "we want to know if you have a tender love for the King of the Bulgars."

"Not at all," he said, "since I've never met him."

"What? He is the most charming of kings, and we must drink to his health."

"All right, I'll be happy to, gentlemen!" And he drank.

"That's enough," they said. "You are now the pillar, the upholder, the defender, the hero of the Bulgars. Your fortune is made, and your glory assured."

Immediately they put irons on his feet and led him to the regiment. He had to turn right, turn left, order arms, load arms, aim, fire, and do it all in double time. At the end he got thirty strokes of the rod. The next day, he did the drill a little less badly and got only twenty. The third day he got only ten, and was regarded by his comrades as a prodigy.

Candide, completely bewildered, did not yet discern very clearly how he was a hero. One fine spring day he took it into his head to go for a walk. He kept going forward, believing that humans, just like animals, had the right to use their legs as they wished.[10] He had barely gone five miles, when four other heroes, all over six feet, caught up with him, tied him, and threw him in a dungeon. In accordance with due process, he was asked which he preferred: to be thrashed thirty-six times by the entire regiment, or to receive twelve bullets in the brain all at once. He protested that human will is free and that he desired neither alternative; but he was forced to choose. Making use of the divine *liberty* that still remained to him, he elected to run the gauntlet thirty-six times. Two times he did so. The regiment was made up of two thousand men. That made four thousand strokes of the rod, which laid bare every muscle and nerve from his neck to his behind. As they were preparing for the third run, Candide, unable to go on, requested them to be kind enough to smash in his head.

The request was granted. They blindfolded him and told him to kneel. At that moment the King of the Bulgars arrived on the scene and inquired about the victim's crime. Now the King was a genius and understood from what he was told that Candide was a young metaphysician, utterly ignorant about the things of this world, and he pardoned him with a generosity that will be praised in all newspapers and in all ages. A worthy surgeon cured Candide in three weeks with the ointments prescribed

---

[10] **to use . . . they wished:** This episode alludes to the case of an actual deserter, whom Voltaire helped to free from prison. Leibniz's doctrine of free will was thought to promote desertion.

by Dioscorides.[11] He already had a little skin and was able to walk when the King of the Bulgars joined battle with the King of the Abars.[12]

CHAPTER 3

How Candide escaped from the Bulgars,
and what became of him

Nothing was so splendid, so brisk, so brilliant, and so well-ordered as these two armies. The trumpets, fifes, oboes, drums, and cannons produced such a harmony as was never heard in hell. First the cannons laid low about six thousand men on each side; then the musketry removed from the best of worlds around nine or ten thousand scoundrels who were festering on its surface. The bayonet was also the sufficient reason for the death of several thousand men. The total must have been about thirty thousand souls. Candide, trembling like a philosopher, hid himself as best he could while this heroic butchery took place.

Finally, while each king was having his forces celebrate victory with a *Te Deum*,[13] Candide decided to theorize about causes and effects somewhere else. Making his way through heaps of the dead and dying, he came to a nearby village; it had been reduced to ashes. This was an Abar village that the Bulgars had burned in accordance with international law. Here, old men riddled with wounds looked on as life departed from their wives whose throats had been slit and whose children still clung to their blood-soaked breasts. There, young girls who had been disemboweled after they had satisfied the natural needs of various heroes, heaved their last sighs. Others, half-burned, screamed for someone to hasten their deaths. Brains were spattered over the ground amidst severed arms and legs.

Candide fled full speed to another village. This one belonged to the Bulgars, and the Abar heroes had treated it in the same manner. Forging onward through ruins and treading upon twitching limbs, Candide at last arrived outside the theater of war, carrying a few provisions in his knapsack and never forgetting Miss Cunégonde. His supplies ran out when he was in Holland; but having heard that everyone in this country was rich and that the people there were Christians, he had no doubt that he would be treated as well as he had been in the Baron's castle before he had been driven from it on account of the lovely eyes of Miss Cunégonde.

He requested alms of several grave individuals. They all replied that if he continued to beg he would be shut up in a house of correction to teach him how to behave.

Then he approached a man who had just finished giving a lecture on the topic of charity for a whole hour to a large assembly. The orator looked askance at him and said:

"What are you doing here? Are you here for the good cause?"

---

[11] **Dioscorides:** Greek physician from the first century C.E. who wrote a treatise on medicines.

[12] **King of the Abars:** The Abars, a semibarbaric Scythian tribe, here refers to the French who fought against the Prussians during the Seven Years' War (1756–63).

[13] ***Te Deum:*** A Latin hymn celebrating victory.

"There is no effect without a cause," Candide answered modestly. "Everything is linked by necessity and arranged for the best. I had to be driven from Miss Cunégonde; I had to run the gauntlet; and I have to beg for my bread until I can earn it. None of this could have been otherwise."

"My friend," said the orator, "do you believe the Pope is the Antichrist?"

"I never heard anyone say so," answered Candide, "but whether he is or not, I have no bread."

"And you do not deserve to eat any," said the other. "Go away, you scoundrel, you wretch, and never show your face here again!"

The orator's wife, having watched from a window above, and seeing a man who was not sure the Pope was the Antichrist, poured on his head a pot full of————. Oh Heavens! The zeal of pious women knows no bounds!

A man who had never been baptized, a good Anabaptist[14] named Jacques, saw the cruel and ignominious treatment inflicted on one of his fellows, a two-legged creature without feathers and with a soul. He took Candide home, washed him, gave him bread and beer, presented him with two florins, and even volunteered to teach him how to work in his Dutch factory, which specialized in the production of authentic Persian rugs. Candide was ready to kiss the man's feet and exclaimed:

"Dr. Pangloss was certainly right to tell me that all is for the best in this world. I am infinitely more touched by your extreme generosity than by the harshness of that gentleman in the black coat and his wife."

The next day, on a walk, he met a beggar all covered with sores, his eyes dull as death, the end of his nose rotting, mouth twisted, teeth black, a raspy voice, tortured by a violent cough, and spitting out a tooth with every spasm.

CHAPTER 4

*How Candide met his old philosophy teacher,
Dr. Pangloss, and what ensued*

Candide, touched by horror and even more by compassion, gave this dreadful beggar the two florins he had received from Jacques, the worthy Anabaptist. The phantom stared at him, burst into tears, and threw his arms around his neck. Candide recoiled in terror.

"Alas," said one wretch to the other, "don't you recognize your dear Pangloss any more?"

"Can it be so? You, my dear master! You, in this horrible state! What misfortune has befallen you? Why are you no longer in the finest of castles? What has become of Miss Cunégonde, that pearl of young ladies, that masterpiece of nature?"

"I cannot go on," said Pangloss.

---

[14]**Anabaptist:** A number of liberal religious groups were called Anabaptists in sixteenth-century Europe. They were persecuted for their beliefs in such things as adult baptism. Holland granted Anabaptists asylum, and Voltaire respected their ideas and lifestyle. Jacques demonstrates their compassion for humans: two-footed, rational beings without feathers, according to Plato's definition.

Candide promptly led him to the Anabaptist's stable, where he gave him a morsel of bread, and when Pangloss had recovered:

"Well," said he, "Cunégonde?"

"She is dead," replied Pangloss.

Candide fainted at this word. His friend revived him with some old vinegar that happened to be in the stable. Candide opened his eyes.

"Cunégonde is dead! Ah, best of worlds, where are you now? But what illness did she die of? Did it stem from seeing me violently kicked out of her father's fine castle?"

"No," said Pangloss. "She was disemboweled by Bulgar soldiers after being raped until she was unconscious. They smashed in the head of the Baron when he tried to defend her; the Baroness was hacked to pieces; and my poor pupil was treated exactly the same as his sister.[15] As for the castle, not one stone was left standing upright. Not a single barn, sheep, duck, or tree is left. But we have avenged ourselves in full, for the Abars did the same thing to a nearby estate that belonged to a Bulgar lord."

At this account Candide fainted again, but after he came back to his senses and expressed his sorrow, he inquired about the cause and effect, the sufficient reason, which had reduced Pangloss to such a pitiful state.

"Alas," said he, "it is love; love, the consoler of the human race, the guardian of the universe, the soul of all sensitive beings, tender love."

"Alas," said Candide, "I have known this love, this ruler of hearts, this soul of our soul: It never got me anything except one kiss and twenty kicks in the ass. And why did this beautiful cause produce in you such a disgusting effect?"

Pangloss answered in these terms:

"Oh my dear Candide! You knew Paquette, our venerable Baron's pretty maid. In her arms I tasted the delights of paradise, which have produced the hellish torments from which I now suffer. She had the disease before me, and she may well be dead by now. Paquette received this present from a very learned Franciscan monk, who was able to trace it back to its primary source. For it came to him from an old countess, who got it from a cavalry captain, who owed it to a marquise, who had it from a page, who caught it from a Jesuit, who during his novitiate received it directly from a ship-mate of Christopher Columbus.[16] As for myself, I shall not give it to anyone, for I am dying."

"Oh Pangloss!" exclaimed Candide, "What a strange genealogy! Isn't the devil at the root of it all?"

"Not at all," the great man replied. "It was an indispensable element of the best of worlds, a necessary ingredient. For had Columbus not caught this disease on an American island, this disease which poisons the source of reproduction, which often prevents reproduction entirely, and which is clearly opposed to the great purpose of nature—then we would have neither chocolate nor cochineal. It must also be noted that until now, this malady, like theological conflict, is limited to the European

---

[15] **same as his sister:** Voltaire associates homosexuality with Cunégonde's brother here and elsewhere in the text.

[16] **For it came . . . Christopher Columbus:** Syphilis spread to Europe from the Americas.

continent. The Turks, Indians, Persians, Chinese, Siamese, and Japanese are not yet acquainted with it. But the principle of sufficient reason will bring it to them as well, in due course of time. Meanwhile, it is making amazing progress among us, especially in those vast armies composed of decent, well-bred scholarship boys, who shape the destiny of nations. You can be sure that when thirty thousand men fight a pitched battle against an equal number of troops, there are about twenty thousand syphilitics on each side."

"Very impressive," said Candide, "but we must get you cured."

"How can I be?" said Pangloss. "I am penniless, my friend, and nowhere on earth can you be bled or get an enema for free."

This last remark made up Candide's mind. He proceeded to throw himself at the feet of his charitable Anabaptist Jacques and painted such a moving picture of his friend's condition that the good man immediately took in Dr. Pangloss and paid for his treatment. In the cure Pangloss lost only one eye and one ear. He could write well and knew arithmetic perfectly. The Anabaptist Jacques made him his bookkeeper. Two months later he was obliged to go to Lisbon on business, and he took his two philosophers with him on the boat. Pangloss explained to him how everything was for the best. Jacques was not convinced.

"Surely," he said, "humankind has corrupted its nature a little, for people were not born wolves, yet they have become wolves. God did not give them heavy cannon or bayonets, yet they have invented them to destroy each other. I could also refer to bankruptcies, and the system of justice that confiscates a bankrupt man's property just to prevent the creditors from getting it."

"All that is indispensable," replied the one-eyed doctor. "Private misfortunes work for the general good, so the more private misfortunes there are, the more all is well."

While he was theorizing, the sky clouded over, the winds rushed in from the four corners of the globe, and the ship was assailed by a terrible storm just as the port of Lisbon came into view.

CHAPTER 5

Storm, shipwreck, earthquake, and what happened to
Dr. Pangloss, Candide, and Jacques the Anabaptist

Half the passengers, weakened and nearly dying from the indescribable agony that the rolling of a ship inflicts on the nerves and humors of a body shaken in different directions, were not even strong enough to recognize how great the danger was. The other half were shrieking and praying. The sails were in shreds, the masts in pieces, the hull split open. Everybody worked who could, but no one cooperated and no one commanded. The Anabaptist was trying to help on the upper deck. A panicked sailor struck him violently and laid him out flat, but his own blow threw him off balance and he fell headfirst over the side. He caught on to part of the broken mast and remained hanging there. The good Jacques got up and ran to his aid, helping him to climb back up; but in the process he was thrown into the sea, right in front of the sailor, who let him drown without even condescending to look at him. Candide rushed over and saw his benefactor appear on the surface for an instant before sinking forever into the deep. He wanted to dive into the sea after him, but the philosopher Pangloss stopped him by demonstrating that the Lisbon harbor was designed expressly for this Anabaptist to drown in. While he was perfecting his logical proof, the ship broke into two and everyone perished except for Pangloss, Candide, and that brutal sailor who had drowned the virtuous Anabaptist. The rogue swam with ease to the shore, while Pangloss and Candide drifted there on a plank.

When they had recovered, they walked toward Lisbon. They still had a little money, with which they hoped to avert hunger after escaping from the storm.

They had scarcely set foot in the city, still mourning the death of their benefactor, when they felt the ground tremble beneath them. The sea boiled up in the port and snapped the ships lying at anchor. Whirlwinds of flame and ashes bellowed through the streets and public squares. Houses crumbled. The roofs collapsed onto their foundations, and then the foundations themselves disintegrated. Thirty thousand inhabitants of every age and sex were crushed in the ruins.[17]

Swearing and whistling, the sailor remarked, "I can get something out of this."

"What can be the sufficient reason for this phenomenon?" asked Pangloss.

"It's the end of the world!" cried Candide.

The sailor jumped into the wreckage without hesitation. He defied death in the search for money, found what he was looking for, seized it, got drunk and, after sobering up a bit, coupled with the first available girl whose favors he could buy, on the ruins of destroyed houses and amid the dead and dying. Pangloss, however, began to tug on his sleeve.

"My friend," he said, "this is not good form. You are ignoring the principles of universal reason; this is not the time or the place."

"By the blood of Christ," said the other, "I am a sailor and was born in Batavia. I have trampled on the cross[18] four times to make my four voyages to Japan — you are knocking on the wrong door here with your universal reason!"

Some falling stones had wounded Candide. He lay flat on the street, covered with debris, calling out to Pangloss, "Alas! Bring me a little wine and oil; I'm dying."

"This earthquake is not a unique phenomenon," Pangloss replied. "The city of Lima in South America experienced the same shocks in South America last year. Same causes, same effects — there must be a vein of sulphur running underground from Lima to Lisbon."

"That's highly probable," said Candide, "but for God's sake, a little oil and wine."

"What do you mean, probable?" retorted the philosopher. "I maintain that the thing is a logical necessity."

---

[17] **crushed . . . ruins:** A devastating earthquake struck Lisbon on November 1, 1755, killing up to forty thousand people. Voltaire saw the earthquake as evidence that there is no benevolent design in God's providence.

[18] **Batavia . . . cross:** Batavia was the Dutch name for Djakarta, in Java, the city from which they controlled their East Asian trade. Japan had closed its ports to foreigners in 1639, exempting only the Dutch, with restrictions. Stamping on the crucifix was rumored to be required of the Dutch traders, but this was never Japanese policy.

Candide lost consciousness, and then Pangloss brought him some water from a nearby fountain.

The next day, as they wandered through the rubble, they found some food, which partially restored their strength. Then they fell to work with those who were aiding the survivors. Some of the citizens whom they rescued organized a dinner that was as nice as could be expected in such a disaster. The meal was sad, it is true; the guests watered their bread with their tears. Pangloss, however, consoled them with his assurances that things could not be otherwise.

"For," he said, "all this is for the best, for if there is a volcano in Lisbon, it could not be anywhere else. For it is impossible that something be where it is not. For all is well."

A little dark man, a spy of the Inquisition[19] who was seated next to Pangloss, politely spoke up: "Apparently the gentleman does not believe in original sin, for if everything is for the best, then the fall of man and the punishment for sin never took place."

"I very humbly request Your Excellency's pardon," Pangloss responded even more politely. "For the fall of man and the curse that came with it were necessary components of the best of all possible worlds."

"So the gentleman does not believe in free will?" said the spy.

"Excuse me, Your Excellency," said Pangloss, "but freedom can be reconciled with absolute necessity, for it was necessary for us to be endowed with freedom; for, after all, a determined will . . ."

Pangloss was in the middle of his sentence when the spy nodded to the armed attendant who was then pouring him a glass of port wine, otherwise known as Oporto.

CHAPTER 6

How they made a fine auto-da-fé to prevent earthquakes,
and how Candide was whipped

When this earthquake, which had destroyed three-quarters of Lisbon, came to an end, the wise men of the land could think of no more effective way of avoiding total ruin than to give the people a fine auto-da-fé.[20] The faculty of the University of Coimbra had concluded that the spectacle of roasting several persons over a slow fire in a ceremonious fashion is an infallible secret for preventing the earth from quaking. They had therefore seized a man from the Basque province who had been convicted of marrying the godmother of his godchild, and two Portuguese men, who when eating a chicken, had removed the bacon seasoning.[21]

---

[19] **spy of the Inquisition:** An undercover agent of the Inquisition. The Papal Inquisition of the sixteenth century, sponsored by the Roman Catholic Church, dealt with Protestantism; the Spanish Inquisition, lasting from the fifteenth through the nineteenth centuries, sought to identify and punish heretics, especially Jews and Muslims who continued to practice their beliefs, despite claiming conversion to Christianity.

[20] **auto-da-fé:** Literally, an "act of faith"; a public ceremony announcing and carrying out the judgment of the Inquisition. Such an incident had taken place in Lisbon on June 20, 1756.

[21] **Basque . . . bacon seasoning:** By marrying his child's godmother, the man from the Basque province would have broken laws against "spiritual incest"; the Portuguese are suspected of being Jews.

After dinner, Dr. Pangloss and his disciple Candide were also arrested, the first for saying what he said, the second for listening with an air of approval. They were led separately to some extremely cool rooms in which no one was ever bothered by the sun. A week later they were both dressed in yellow robes and their heads were adorned with paper caps.[22] Candide's cap and robe were painted with inverted flames and with devils without tails or claws, whereas Pangloss's devils had claws and tails and his flames were right side up. Thus attired, they marched in procession and heard a very touching sermon, followed by charming penitential music. Candide was whipped in cadence with the chant; the man from the Basque province and the two who avoided the bacon were burned; and Pangloss was hanged, though it was not the customary form of execution. The same day the earth shook again[23] with a terrible uproar.

Stunned, stupefied, frantic, bleeding, trembling, Candide thought to himself, "If this is the best of all possible worlds, what are the others like? I can reconcile myself to this beating because I already got one from the Bulgars. But oh, my dear Pangloss! The greatest of all philosophers, was it necessary to see you hanged, without knowing why? Oh, my dear Anabaptist! The best of men, was it necessary for you to drown in the port? Oh! Miss Cunégonde, the pearl of young ladies, was it necessary that your belly be split open?"

Candide left the scene of punishment, barely able to stand, having been lectured, lacerated, absolved, and blessed. But an old woman approached and said, "My son, take courage, follow me."

CHAPTER 7

How an old woman took care of Candide,
and how he regained what he had loved

Candide did not take courage, but he followed the old woman into a shack. She gave him a jar of ointment for his wounds and left him food and drink. She showed him to a tidy little bed, with a suit of clothing beside it.

"Eat, drink, sleep," said she, "and may Our Lady of Atocha, My Lord Saint Anthony of Padua, and My Lord Saint James of Compostela take care of you! I will return tomorrow."

Candide, still overwhelmed by all he had seen, all he had suffered, and even more by the old woman's charity, tried to kiss her hand.

"It is not my hand you should kiss," said the old woman. "I will return tomorrow. Use the ointment, eat, and sleep."

---

[22] **yellow robes . . . caps:** A long yellow cape and a cone-shaped hat were the ceremonial dress of the Inquisition's prisoners.

[23] **earth shook again:** A second earthquake struck Lisbon on December 20, 1755.

Despite his many sufferings, Candide did eat and sleep. The next morning the old woman brought him breakfast, examined his back, and treated it herself with another ointment. Afterwards she brought him lunch, and in the evening, supper. The following day she performed the same ceremonies.

"Who are you?" Candide kept asking. "Who made you so kind? How can I ever repay you?"

The good woman never answered. She came back in the evening, this time without supper.

"Come with me," she said, "and don't say a word."

She took him by the arm and they walked together into the country for a quarter mile. They arrived at an isolated house, surrounded by gardens and ponds. The old woman knocked on a small door. It opened, and she escorted Candide up a concealed staircase, into a gilded chamber, and onto a brocaded couch. Then she closed the door and disappeared. Candide thought he was hallucinating. His life, which had been a nightmare, now seemed like a pleasant dream.

The old woman soon reappeared. With great difficulty she supported a trembling young lady, with a splendid figure, sparkling with jewels, and covered by a veil.

"Remove this veil," said the old woman to Candide.

The young man stepped forward and lifted it with a timid hand. What a moment! What a surprise! He thought he perceived Miss Cunégonde—and he did, for it was she. He grew faint, speech failed him, he fell at her feet. Cunégonde collapsed on the sofa. The old woman plied them with spirits; they came to their senses and spoke to each other. First came broken words, then simultaneous questions and answers, sighs, tears, and moans. The old lady urged them to be more quiet, and left them alone.

"What! It's really you," said Candide. "You are alive! I've found you again in Portugal! Then you were not raped? They didn't slice open your belly as the philosopher Pangloss claimed?"

"It did happen," said the lovely Cunégonde, "but one doesn't always die from those two accidents."

"But your father and mother, murdered?"

"Too true," said Cunégonde crying.

"And your brother?"

"Also killed."

"And why are you in Portugal? How did you know I was here? In what mysterious way did you arrange to bring me here?"

"I will tell you everything," replied the lady, "but first you must tell me everything that has happened to you since the innocent kiss you gave me and the violent kicks you received."

Candide obeyed her with deep respect, and though he was still in shock, his voice weak and trembling, and his spine still aching, he related in simple words everything he had suffered since their parting. Cunégonde raised her eyes to heaven. She wept at the death of the good Anabaptist and of Pangloss; after which she spoke in these terms to Candide, who did not miss a word, and who consumed her with his eyes.

CHAPTER 8

Cunégonde's story

"I was sleeping soundly in my bed when heaven chose to send the Bulgars to our fine castle of Thunder-ten-tronckh. They butchered my father and brother and cut my mother to pieces. A large Bulgar, well over six feet tall, seeing that I had fainted at this spectacle, began to rape me; this brought me to and I regained my senses. I shrieked, I struggled, I bit, I scratched, I tried to tear the eyes out of that big Bulgar—not knowing that everything happening then in my father's castle was part of military custom. The brute stabbed me in the belly on the left side, where I still have a scar."

"Alas! I hope to see that," said the simple Candide.

"You will," said Cunégonde, "but let me go on."

"Please go on," said Candide.

She took up the thread of her story: "A Bulgar captain came by. He saw me, all covered in blood, as well as the soldier who was too busy to salute him. Enraged by the brute's lack of respect for his rank, the captain killed him while he was still on top of my body. Then he had my wound dressed and took me to his quarters as a prisoner of war. I laundered the few shirts he had, I did his cooking. I have to admit, he found me attractive, and I won't deny that he was a handsome man, with soft, white skin. But he had no intellect, no philosophy; it was clear that he had not been raised by Dr. Pangloss. Three months later, he had lost all his money and grown sick of me, so he sold me to Don Issachar, a Jew who traded in Holland and Portugal and who had a passionate taste for women. This Jew took a great liking to my person, but he never conquered it. I resisted him better than I did the Bulgar soldier. A lady of honor may be raped once, but it strengthens her virtue for the future. In order to tame me, the Jew brought me to this country house. I always used to think there was nothing on earth so beautiful as the castle of Thunder-ten-tronckh. I have that illusion no longer.

"The Grand Inquisitor noticed me one day at mass. He ogled me and sent me a message that he had to speak to me about secret affairs. I was escorted to his palace, where I informed him of my high birth. He pointed out how much it was beneath my rank to belong to an Israelite. His agents suggested to Don Issachar to cede me to His Lordship. But Don Issachar, who is the court banker and a man of prestige, flatly refused. The Inquisitor threatened him with an auto-da-fé. Finally, my Jew, intimidated, made a deal whereby the house and I belong to them jointly: The Jew would get Mondays, Wednesdays, and the Sabbath, and the Inquisitor all other days of the week. The contract has lasted six months, though not without quarrels, because they have never been able to decide if the night between Saturday and Sunday belongs to the old Sabbath or the new.[24] As for me, I've resisted them both so far, and I think that's why their love for me has been so strong.

"Finally, to ward off the scourge of earthquakes and to intimidate Issachar, the Inquisitor decided to celebrate an auto-da-fé. He honored me with an invitation. I had

---

[24] **old Sabbath or the new:** That is, the Hebrew Bible of the Jews, or the New Testament of the Christians.

a very good seat and they served refreshments to the ladies between the mass and the execution. I was truly gripped by horror when I saw them burn the two Jews and that upright fellow from the Basque country who had married his godchild's godmother. But imagine my surprise, my terror, my agitation, when I saw, in a yellow robe and underneath a paper cap, a form resembling Pangloss! I rubbed my eyes, I peered closely, I saw him hanged, I fainted. I had scarcely recovered my senses when I saw you, stripped down naked. This was the height of my horror, consternation, pain, and despair. I will tell you, in truth, that your skin is even whiter, and more delightfully tinted with pink, than that of my Bulgar captain. This sight redoubled all the emotions that were crushing me, devouring me. I cried out, I tried to say, 'Stop, barbarians!' but my voice failed and my cries would have been futile. After you had been thoroughly whipped, I began to think: 'How can it be that the gentle Candide and the wise Pangloss have come to Lisbon, one to receive a hundred lashes, the other to be hanged by order of the Inquisitor whose mistress I am? Pangloss deceived me cruelly when he taught me that everything is for the best in this world.'

"Frantic and exhausted, half out of my mind and half on the verge of expiring from weakness, my head was filled with images of my murdered father, mother, and brother; of the insolence of my vile Bulgar soldier and the slashing he inflicted on me; of my servitude as a cook to my Bulgar captain; of my vile Don Issacher and my abominable Inquisitor; of the hanging of Dr. Pangloss and the solemn hymn of penitence sung while they whipped you; and above all, of the kiss I once gave you behind a partition, the day I saw you for the last time. I praised God for bringing you back to me after so many ordeals. I asked my old servant to take care of you and to bring you here as soon as she could. She has done the job well. I have tasted the indescribable pleasure of seeing you, hearing you, speaking to you again. But you must be burning with hunger. My desire is strong. Let us begin with supper."

So they sat down to table together, and after supper they installed themselves on that lovely couch that was already mentioned. There they were, when Señor Don Issachar, one of the masters of the house, arrived. It was the Sabbath day. He had come to enjoy his rights and to profess his tender love.

CHAPTER 9

What happened to Cunégonde, Candide,
the Grand Inquisitor, and a Jew

This Issachar was the most hot-tempered Hebrew seen in Israel since the Babylonian captivity.

"What!" he said. "You Christian bitch, you are not satisfied with the Inquisitor? I have to share you with this scoundrel too?"

With these words he unsheathed a long dagger that he always carried with him, and supposing his adversary to be defenseless, flung himself at Candide. But our good Westphalian had gotten a fine sword from the old woman along with the suit of clothes. Though his character was gentle, he drew his sword and laid the Israelite out cold and stiff on the floor, at the feet of the beautiful Cunégonde.

"Holy Virgin!" she cried. "What are we going to do now? A man killed in my house! If the police come, we're finished."

"If Pangloss had not been hanged," said Candide, "he would offer us good advice in this emergency, for he was a great philosopher. In his absence, let's consult the old woman."

She was a prudent woman and was about to give her opinion when another little door opened. It was one o'clock in the morning, the beginning of Sunday. This day belonged to the Inquisitor. He came in and saw the whipped Candide with a sword in his hand, a dead man on the floor, Cunégonde in panic, and the old woman advising them.

This is what went on at that instant in Candide's mind, and how he theorized: "If this holy man calls for help, he will infallibly have me burned, and perhaps Cunégonde too; he has caused me to be whipped brutally; he is my rival; I have killed once already; there is no time to hesitate."

This reflection was swift and clear. Without giving the Inquisitor time to recover from his surprise, he ran his sword through his body, and cast him beside the Jew.

"You've done it again," said Cunégonde. "We're beyond salvation now; we're excommunicated, our last hour has come. How have you managed, you who are so gentle, to kill a Jew and a prelate in two minutes?"

"My fair lady," answered Candide, "when a man is in love, inflamed by jealousy, and whipped by the Inquisition, he is no longer himself."

The old woman spoke up at that moment: "There are three Andalusian horses in the stable, with saddles and bridles. Let the brave Candide prepare them. My Lady has some diamonds and gold coins. Let us mount quickly—though I can sit on only one buttock—and ride to Cadiz. The weather is ideal, and it is a great pleasure to travel in the cool of the night."

Candide immediately saddled the three horses. The three of them covered thirty miles at one stretch. While they were getting away, the officers of the Holy Brotherhood[25] arrived at the house. They buried the Inquisitor in a fine church, and threw Issachar in the public dump.

Candide, Cunégonde, and the old woman were already at an inn in the little town of Avacena in the middle of the Sierra-Morena mountains, and they spoke as follows.

CHAPTER 10

How Candide, Cunégonde, and the
old woman arrived at Cadiz in distress,
and how they set sail

"Who could have stolen my gold and my diamonds?" exclaimed Cunégonde, weeping. "What are we going to live on now? What are we going to do? Where can I find Inquisitors and Jews who will give me more?"

---

[25] **Holy Brotherhood:** A semireligious Spanish order that had police powers.

"Alas," said the old woman, "I strongly suspect a venerable Franciscan who slept at the same inn with us yesterday at Badajoz. God forgive me if my judgment is rash, but he came into our chamber twice, and he left the inn long before we did."

"Alas," said Candide, "the wise Pangloss often proved to me that the goods of the earth are common to all men, that everyone has an equal right to them. By this logic, the Franciscan should have left us enough to finish our journey. Didn't he leave you anything at all, my lovely Cunégonde?"

"Not a cent," said she.

"What is our plan?" Candide asked.

"We must sell one of the horses," said the old woman. "I will ride on the horse's rump behind my lady—though I can sit on only one buttock—and we will travel to Cadiz."

There was a Benedectine prior staying in the same inn. He bought the horse at a low price. Candide, Cunégonde, and the old woman passed through Lucena, Chillas, and Lebrixa, and finally reached Cadiz. A fleet was being fitted out there, and troops were being assembled to teach a lesson to the Jesuit fathers in Paraguay. The Jesuits had been accused of inciting one of the tribes near the town of Sacramento[26] to revolt against the kings of Spain and Portugal. Candide, having served in the Bulgar army, performed a Bulgar drill in front of the general of the little army with such grace, speed, skill, pride, and agility that he was put in charge of a company of infantry. He was a captain now. He embarked with Miss Cunégonde, the old woman, two valets, and the two Andalusian horses that had belonged to the Grand Inquisitor of Portugal.

Throughout the crossing, they theorized at length about the philosophy of poor Pangloss.

"We are heading for a different world," said Candide. "I am sure that over there all is well, because I have to admit that where we come from, there are grounds for complaining about how things are, both physically and morally."

"I love you with all my heart," Cunégonde told him, "but my soul is still terrified by what I have seen and endured."

"All will be well," Candide replied. "The sea of this New World is superior to the sea of our Europe; it is calmer, with steadier winds. I am certain the New World is the best of all possible universes."

"May God grant that it be so," said Cunégonde. "But my universe has been so terribly unhappy that my heart is nearly closed to the possibility of hope."

"The two of you are complaining," the old woman said to them. "Alas! You have never seen misfortunes like mine."

Cunégonde almost burst out laughing. She found it amusing that the good woman claimed to be more unhappy than herself.

"Alas!" she said. "My dear woman, unless you have been raped by two Bulgars, been stabbed in the belly twice, seen two of your castles demolished, witnessed the

---

[26] **Sacramento:** Colonia del Sacramento, in Paraguay. The Jesuits, who began their rebellion against Spain and Portugal in 1750, were expelled from Paraguay in 1769.

murder of two mothers and fathers, and watched two of your lovers being whipped in an auto-da-fé, I don't see how you can outdo me. Besides, I was born to be a baroness, with seventy-two generations of nobility, and I was forced to be a cook."

"Madame," replied the old woman, "you know nothing of my birth, and if I showed you my behind, you would speak differently and suspend your judgment."

These remarks aroused intense curiosity in the minds of Cunégonde and Candide. The old woman spoke to them in these terms.

CHAPTER 11
The old woman's story

"My eyes were not always crusty and bloodshot, my nose did not always touch my chin, and I was not always a servant. I am the daughter of Pope Urban X and the Princess of Palestrina.[27] I lived until the age of fourteen in a palace so luxurious that all the castles of your German barons would not have served as stables. Any one of my dresses was worth more than all the treasures of Westphalia. I was growing in beauty, elegance, and accomplishment in the midst of pleasures, honors, and the highest hopes. I was beginning to inspire love. My bosom was forming, and what a bosom! White, firm, sculptured like the ancient statue of Venus. And what eyes! What lashes! What black brows! What flames blazed in my irises and sparkled brighter than the stars, as the local poets used to tell me. The women who dressed and undressed me fell into ecstasies when they beheld me from the front and from the rear, and any man would have desired to be in their place.

"I was betrothed to the ruling prince of Massa-Carrara. What a prince! As attractive as I, filled with sweetness and delight, with a brilliant wit and burning passion. I loved him as one always loves for the first time, with adoration and frenzy. The wedding was at hand. The pomp and splendor were unprecedented. It was an endless series of feasts, equestrian tournaments, comic operas, and all Italy honored me with sonnets of which not a single one was any good.

"I was on the verge of bliss, when an old marquise who had been my prince's mistress invited him for a cup of cocoa. He died in less than two hours, in horrible convulsions. But that was only a trifle. My mother, stricken with grief, though less than I, wished to escape from this tragic scene for a while. She had a very fine estate near Gaeta.[28] Our transport was a papal galley ship, gilded like the altar of St. Peter's in Rome. Suddenly a pirate ship from Salé swept down and boarded us. Our soldiers defended themselves like true soldiers of the Pope: They all kneeled down, threw aside their arms, and begged the pirates for absolution *in articulo mortis*.[29]

---

[27] **Pope . . . Palestrina:** The following note is allegedly by Voltaire: "Note the author's extreme discretion! So far there has been no pope named Urban X; he is afraid to ascribe a bastard daughter to a known pope. What circumspection! What delicacy of conscience!" Palestrina is a town in the province of Rome, Italy.

[28] **Gaeta:** An Italian port town north of Naples.

[29] *in articulo mortis:* At the point of death.

"The pirates immediately stripped them naked as monkeys, along with my mother, our ladies-in-waiting, and myself. The speed with which those gentlemen can undress people is amazing. But what surprised me even more was that they inserted their fingers in all of us, in a place where we women usually admit only the nozzle of an enema. This ceremony seemed quite bizarre to me; but that is how one sees everything foreign when one has never been abroad. I soon learned that they wished to see if we had diamonds hidden there. It is an age-old custom among the civilized people who patrol the seas. I also learned that the pious Knights of Malta always observe this ceremony when they capture Turkish men and women. It's a rule of international law that has never been broken.

"I will not tell you how hard it is for a young princess to be dragged off to Morocco as a slave with her mother. You can imagine everything we had to endure in the pirate ship. My mother was still beautiful; our ladies-in-waiting and even our ordinary servants had more charm than could be found in all of Africa. As for me, I was ravishing, I was beauty and grace made flesh, and I was a virgin. But not for long. The flower I had reserved for the handsome prince of Massa-Carrara was plucked by the pirate captain. He was an abominable Negro who thought he was bestowing great favors on me. The Princess of Palestrina and I certainly had to be very strong to withstand everything we went through up to our arrival in Morocco. But we can skip the details; these things are so common that they are not worth describing.

"Morocco was swimming in blood when we arrived. Fifty sons of the Emperor Muley Ismael[30] each had his own faction, which produced fifty civil wars of blacks against blacks, blacks against browns, browns against browns, mulattoes against mulattoes. There was constant slaughter throughout the empire.

"Scarcely had we landed when some blacks of a faction hostile to my pirate came on the scene to take away the booty. We were, after the diamonds and gold, his most precious possessions. The fight that took place before my eyes was worse than anything you ever see in your European climates. The peoples of the North do not have hot blood. Their lust for women is not as strong as it is in Africa. It is as if Europeans have milk in their veins, while vitriol and fire flow through the veins of the inhabitants of Mount Atlas and the countries nearby. They fought to possess us with the fury of the lions, tigers, and vipers of their land. A Moor snatched my mother by the right arm, my captain's lieutenant held her by the left. Another Moorish soldier took her by one leg, one of our pirates clung to the other. Nearly all our women were quickly pulled in this way by four soldiers. My captain shielded me behind him. Brandishing his scimitar, he killed everyone who stood up to his rage. At last I saw all our women, and then my mother, ripped and sliced and massacred by the monsters who were fighting over them. The other hostages, the pirates who had captured them, the soldiers, sailors, blacks, browns, whites, mulattoes, and finally my captain—all were killed, and I myself lay dying on a heap of corpses. As everyone knows, scenes like this were occurring for more than seven hundred and fifty miles around, without anyone failing to observe the five daily prayers prescribed by Mohammed.

---

[30] **Muley Ismael:** A sultan of Morocco who died in 1727, leaving his kingdom in disarray.

"I freed myself with great difficulty from that tangled mob of bleeding cadavers and I crawled under a large orange tree on the bank of a nearby stream. There I collapsed from fear, exhaustion, horror, despair, and hunger. Soon my weary mind surrendered to an oblivion that was more of a frightful blackout than a pleasant repose. I was in that state of weakness and insensibility, between life and death, when I felt the pressure of something wriggling on my body. I opened my eyes and saw a white man with a handsome face who was moaning and whispering, '*O che sciagura d'essere senza coglioni!*'[31]

CHAPTER 12

Continuation of the old woman's story

"Astonished and delighted to hear my native tongue, and equally surprised by the words this man was uttering, I replied that there were worse misfortunes than the one he was complaining of. I gave him a brief account of my own horrors, and fainted again. He carried me to a nearby house, put me to bed, fed me, waited on me, comforted me, flattered me, and told me he had never seen anything as beautiful as I, and that he had never so much regretted the loss of what no one could ever give back to him.

"'I was born in Naples,' he told me, 'where they castrate two or three thousand children every year. Some die as a result, others acquire the ability to sing more beautifully than women, still others go on to rule states. In my case, the operation was a great success, and I became a musician in the chapel of the Princess of Palestrina.'

"'Of my mother!' I cried out.

"'Of your mother?' he exclaimed, while bursting into tears. 'Why—are you that little princess I brought up to the age of six, and who even then promised to be as gorgeous as you are now?'

"'Yes, I am. My mother is four hundred paces away, cut into four pieces, under a pile of corpses. . . .'

"I told him everything that happened to me, and he in turn told me of his adventures. He had been sent to the King of Morocco by a Christian power to conclude a treaty: The King was supposed to receive gunpowder, cannons, and ships and use these to exterminate the commerce of other Christian powers.

"'My mission is accomplished,' said the worthy eunuch. 'I am setting sail to Ceuta, and I shall bring you back to Italy. But *che sciagura d'essere senza coglioni!*'

"I thanked him with tears of gratitude and pity; and instead of bringing me to Italy, he transported me to Algiers and sold me to the Dey of that province. Hardly had the sale taken place, when the plague, which was sweeping over Africa, Asia, and Europe, broke out violently in Algiers. You have seen earthquakes, but tell me, young lady, have you ever had the plague?"

"Never," replied the Baron's daughter.

"If you had been afflicted with it," the old woman went on, "you would admit that it is much worse than an earthquake. It is very widespread in Africa, and I was

---

[31] *'O che . . . coglioni!':* "O, what a misfortune to be without testicles!"

struck by it. Imagine the situation of a pope's daughter, only fifteen years old, who in the space of three months had undergone poverty and slavery, had been raped almost every day, had seen her mother cut in four pieces, had endured hunger and war, and now faced death from the plague in Algiers. As it turned out, I survived, but my eunuch, the Dey, and nearly the whole harem of Algiers, perished.

"When the first ravages of this ghastly plague were over, the Dey's slaves were sold off. A merchant purchased me and brought me to Tunis. He sold me to another merchant, who sold me once more in Tripoli. From Tripoli I was resold to Alexandria, from Alexandria to Smyrna, from Smyrna to Constantinople. In the end I belonged to an Aga of the Janissaries, who was shortly sent off to defend Azov[32] against the attacking Russians.

"The Aga, a very gallant man, took his whole harem with him, and lodged us in a little fort on the shore of the Sea of Azov, guarded by two black eunuchs and twenty soldiers. Our side killed a prodigious number of Russians, but they repaid us with interest. The settlement at Azov was put to fire and sword, and neither women nor children were spared. The last place left was our little fort. The enemy tried to starve us out. The twenty Janissaries had sworn never to surrender. When they became famished, they were obliged to eat our two eunuchs, for fear of breaking their oath. A few days later they resolved to eat the women.

"We had with us a very pious and compassionate imam,[33] who preached a fine sermon, persuading them not to kill us altogether. 'Just cut off one buttock from each of these ladies,' he said, 'and you will dine well. If you need more, you can have the same fare in a few days. You will please heaven with such a charitable deed, and you will be saved from this calamity.'

"He was very eloquent and persuaded them. They performed the horrible operation on us. The imam rubbed us with the same balm that they put on children who have just been circumcised. We were all nearly dead.

"Scarcely had the Janissaries finished the meal we had furnished them, when more Russians arrived in flat-bottomed boats; not a single Janissary escaped alive. The Russians paid no attention to our condition. But there are French doctors everywhere, and one of them, who was very clever, took care of us. He cured us, and I will remember to the end of my life that when my wounds were healed, he made advances to me. Besides that, he told us all to take comfort. He assured us that such things usually happened in sieges and that it was one of the rules of war.

"As soon as my companions and I could walk, we were sent off to Moscow. I fell to the lot of a Boyar,[34] who made me his gardener and gave me twenty lashes per day. But when this noble was broken on the wheel two years later, along with thirty or so other Boyars, over a little intrigue at the royal court, I took advantage of the incident.

---

[32] **Azov:** Town near the mouth of the river Don in Crimea; it was attacked by Russian forces led by Peter the Great in 1695–96. The janissaries, "janizaries," were the elite forces of the Ottoman Turks.

[33] **imam:** A Muslim holy man.

[34] **Boyar:** A high-ranking Russian aristocrat; a group of boyars unsuccessfully tried to overthrow Peter the Great (r. 1682–1725) in 1798.

I fled. I traversed the whole of Russia. For a long time I was a barmaid in Riga, then in Rostock, Wismar, Leipzig, Cassel, Utrecht, Leyden, the Hague, and Rotterdam. I have grown old in misery and infamy, with only half a behind, and never forgetting that I was the daughter of a Pope.

"I considered suicide a hundred times, but I still loved life. That ridiculous preference is perhaps one of our most tragic instincts. For what could be more stupid than this: to seek to carry forever a weight that we always feel like casting to the ground? To view our existence with horror, and to cling tightly to our existence? To caress the snake that devours us, until it has consumed our heart?

"In the countries that fate made me traverse, and in the inns where I worked, I have seen vast numbers of people who detested their own lives; but I have seen only twelve who voluntarily brought an end to their suffering—three Negroes, four Englishmen, four Genevans, and a German professor named Robek.[35] I ended up becoming a servant to the Jew, Don Issachar. He assigned me to you, my lovely Lady. I have attached myself to your destiny, and I have been more concerned with your fortune than my own. I would never have spoken about my sufferings had you not provoked me a bit, and were it not the custom on ships to pass the time with stories. In short, My Lady, I have some experience, I know the world. I propose that you amuse yourselves by asking each passenger to tell you his story, and if you find a single one who has not frequently cursed his own life, who has not often told himself that he was the unhappiest of men, then throw me into the sea headfirst."

CHAPTER 13

How Candide was forced to part from the lovely Cunégonde
and the old woman

After hearing the old woman's story, the lovely Cunégonde showed her all the courtesy due to a person of her rank and merit. She accepted the old woman's proposal too, and got all the passengers, one by one, to recount their life stories. She and Candide had to admit that the old woman was right.

"It's too bad," said Candide, "that the wise Pangloss was hanged, contrary to custom, in an auto-da-fé. He would say admirable things about the physical and moral evil that cover land and sea, and I would now be independent enough to make a few respectful objections."

As each passenger was telling his story, the vessel sailed on. They landed at Buenos Aires. Cunégonde, Captain Candide, and the old woman proceeded to the home of Governor Don Fernando d'Ibaraa y Figueora y Mascarenes y Lampourdos y Souza. This lord had the pride appropriate to a man with so many names. He addressed people with the most noble disdain, tilting his nose so high in the air, raising his voice so mercilessly, adopting so imperious a tone, affecting so haughty a bearing, that everyone who met him wanted to beat him up. He loved women with a

---

[35] **Robek:** Johan Robeck (1678–1739), an advocate of suicide, who killed himself by drowning.

frenzy, and Cunégonde seemed to him the most beautiful creature he had ever seen. The first thing he did was to ask if she were the Captain's wife. His manner of asking the question alarmed Candide. He did not dare say she was his wife, because in fact she was not. He did not dare say she was his sister, because she was not that either; and even though this diplomatic lie was once very fashionable among the ancients[36] and can still be useful to the moderns, his soul was too pure to foresake the truth.

"Miss Cunégonde," he said, "will soon honor me by becoming my wife, and we humbly beseech Your Excellency to perform the ceremony."

Don Fernando d'Ibaraa y Figueora y Mascarenes y Lampourdos y Souza stroked his mustache, and with a spiteful smile ordered Captain Candide to go off and inspect his troops. Candide obeyed, while the Governor remained with Miss Cunégonde. He declared his passion and vowed he would marry her the next day, in the presence of the Catholic Church or in any other manner that would please her loveliness. Cunégonde requested fifteen minutes to gather her thoughts, to consult the old woman, and to make a decision.

The old woman said to Cunégonde, "My Lady, you have seventy-two generations of nobility, and not a penny. You now have a chance to be the wife of a man who is the greatest lord in South America and who has a very handsome mustache. Is this a time for you to pretend to be absolutely faithful? You were raped by the Bulgars. A Jew and an Inquisitor enjoyed your favors. Suffering bestows privileges. If I were in your place, I assure you, I would have no qualms about marrying the Governor and securing the welfare of Captain Candide."

While the old woman was speaking with all the prudence that comes from age and experience, a little ship was seen entering the port carrying a Spanish magistrate and police officers. This is what happened.

The old woman had been quite right earlier when she suspected that it was a long-sleeved Franciscan who had stolen Cunégonde's gold and jewels in the town of Badajoz when she and Candide were in flight. The monk had tried to sell some of the gems to a jeweler, but the merchant recognized them as belonging to the Grand Inquisitor. The Franciscan, prior to his hanging, confessed that he had stolen them. He described the persons he had robbed and the route they were taking. It was already known that Cunégonde and Candide had fled. They were traced to Cadiz. A ship was sent to pursue them without delay. This vessel was now in the port of Buenos Aires. A rumor spread that a magistrate was coming ashore to prosecute the murderers of the Grand Inquisitor. The prudent old woman instantly recognized what had to be done.

"You cannot escape," she told Cunégonde, "but you have nothing to fear. You are not the one who killed the Inquisitor, and besides, the Governor loves you and will not tolerate anyone who mistreats you. Stay here."

She then sped off to Candide. "Run away," she said, "or you will be burned within an hour."

---

[36] **among the ancients:** Voltaire refers to the story of Abraham and Sarah in Genesis 12 and of Isaac and Rebecca in Genesis 26.

There was not a moment to lose — but how to part from Cunégonde, and where to hide?

Chapter 14

How Candide and Cacambo were received by the Jesuits in Paraguay

Candide had brought with him from Cadiz a valet of the kind often found on the coasts of Spain and in the colonies. He was one quarter Spanish, the child of a half-breed father in Tucuman.[37] He had been a choir boy, a sacristan, a sailor, a monk, a salesman, a soldier, and a lackey. His name was Cacambo, and he was very attached to his master because his master was a very good man. He saddled the two Andalusian horses as fast as possible.

"Let's go, Master, let's follow the old woman's advice. Let's get out of here and run for it without looking back."

Candide shed tears. "Oh, my darling Cunégonde! Why must I abandon you now, when the Governor is about to marry us? Cunégonde, so far from home, what will become of you?"

"She'll manage on her own," said Cacambo. "Women always find ways to keep themselves afloat; God sees to it; let's move."

"Where are you taking me? Where are we going? What will we do without Cunégonde?" asked Candide.

"By St. James of Compostela," said Cacambo, "you were going to make war against the Jesuits; let's go make war *for* them! I know the roads, I'll take you to their kingdom. They'll be pleased to have a captain who can move like a Bulgar. You'll become fabulously wealthy. If a man doesn't get his due in one world, he can always get it in another. It's a great pleasure to see and do new things."

"So you've been in Paraguay before?" asked Candide.

"I certainly have," said Cacambo. "I was a cook at the College of the Assumption, and I know the government of the *Padres*[38] as well as I know the streets of Cadiz. Their government is marvellous. The kingdom is already more than seven hundred and fifty miles across. It is divided into thirty provinces. The *Padres* have everything, the people nothing. It's a masterpiece of reason and justice. Personally, I can't think of anything as heavenly as the *Padres*. Over here they make war against the kings of Spain and Portugal, and in Europe they hear the confessions of the same kings. Here they kill Spaniards, and in Madrid they send them to heaven. I love it. Let's get going. You're going to be the happiest of men. What pleasure the *Padres* will feel when they learn that a Captain is coming who knows how to move like a Bulgar!"

As soon as they approached the first border post, Cacambo told the advance guards that a captain wished to speak to the Commander. Word was sent back to the rear guards, and a Paraguayan officer ran to inform the Commander. Candide and

---

[37] **Tucuman:** An Argentinian province northwest of Buenos Aires.

[38] *Padres:* The Jesuit fathers.

Cacambo were first disarmed, and their Andalusian horses were confiscated. The two strangers were escorted through two files of soldiers, at the end of which was the Commander, with a three-cornered hat on his head, a tucked-up gown, a sword at his side, and a short pike in his hand. He made a sign, and immediately twenty-four soldiers surrounded the two newcomers. A sergeant told them that they would have to wait, that the Commander could not speak to them and that the Reverend Provincial Father did not allow any Spaniard to parley except in his presence, or to remain in the country for more than three hours.

"And where is the Reverend Provincial Father?" asked Cacambo.

"He is inspecting the troops, after having said Mass," answered the sergeant, "and you will not be allowed to kiss his spurs until three hours from now."

"But," Cacambo said, "the Captain and I are dying of hunger, and he's not Spanish at all, he's German. Couldn't we have something for breakfast while we wait for His Reverence?"

The sergeant promptly went to report this speech to the Commander.

"God be praised!" said this Lord. "Since he is a German, I can speak to him. Bring him to my arbor."

Candide was immediately led into a shady retreat adorned with a pretty colonnade in green and golden marble and with trellises containing parrots, hummingbirds of different kinds, guinea fowl, and every other sort of rare bird. An excellent meal was prepared in gold vessels, and while the Paraguayans were eating corn out of wooden bowls in the open fields, under the blazing sun, the Commander entered the arbor.

He was a very handsome young man, with a round face, fair skin, red cheeks, arched eyebrows, bright eyes, pink ears, and vermillion lips; he had a proud bearing, but it was not the pride of a Spaniard or a Jesuit. The confiscated weapons were restored to Candide and Cacambo, as were the two Andalusian horses. Cacambo fed them oats beside the arbor, keeping a close eye on them, for fear of a new assault.

Candide first kissed the hem of the Commander's robe, then they sat down to eat.

"So, you are German," said the Jesuit in that language.

"Yes, Reverend Father," said Candide.

As they uttered these words, each looked at the other with extreme surprise, and with barely controlled emotion.

"And what part of Germany are you from?" asked the Jesuit.

"From the rotten Province of Westphalia," said Candide. "I was born in the castle of Thunder-ten-tronckh."

"Oh heaven! Is it possible!" exclaimed the Commander.

"What a miracle!" cried Candide.

"Can it be you?" said the Commander.

"This is not possible," said Candide.

They both fell over backwards; they embraced; they shed streams of tears.

"What! Is it really you, my Reverend Father? You, the brother of the lovely Cunégonde! You, who were killed by the Bulgars! You, the son of My Lord the Baron! You, a Jesuit in Paraguay! I have to admit, the world is a very strange place. Oh Pangloss! Pangloss! How happy you would be if you had not been hanged!"

The Commander dismissed the Negro slaves and the Paraguayans who were serving drinks in goblets of rock crystal. He thanked God and St. Ignatius a thousand times. He clasped Candide in his arms; their faces were bathed in tears.

"You're going to be even more surprised, more moved, more beside yourself," said Candide, "when I tell you that your sister, Miss Cunégonde, whom you thought was disemboweled, is in good health."

"Where?"

"In this area, with the Governor of Buenos Aires. I was supposed to help him fight you."

Every word they spoke during their long conversation revealed a new wonder. Their souls leapt from their tongues, drew in meaning through their ears, and sparkled brilliantly in their eyes. As they were Germans, they drank for a long time while they waited for the Reverend Provincial Father; and the Commander spoke to Candide as follows.

CHAPTER 15

How Candide killed the brother
of his beloved Cunégonde

"The horrible day when I saw my mother and father killed, and my sister raped, will remain in my memory forever. When the Bulgars withdrew, my adorable sister was nowhere to be found. A cart was loaded with my mother, my father, myself, two serving girls, and three little boys whose throats had been slit. We were to be buried in a Jesuit chapel five miles from the castle of my ancestors. A Jesuit sprinkled holy water on us; it was horribly salty, and a few drops of it got into my eyes. The priest noticed a slight movement of my eyelid. He placed his hand on my heart and felt it beating. I was treated, and three weeks later, I was in good shape again.

"You know, my dear Candide, I was a very pretty boy; I became even more so; and the Reverend Father Croust,[39] superior of the abbey, conceived a very tender friendship for me. He dressed me in the gown of a novice, and soon after that I was sent to Rome. The Father General needed a fresh set of young German Jesuit recruits. The rulers of Paraguay take in as few Spanish Jesuits as they can. They prefer foreigners because they think they can control them better. The Reverend Father General judged me fit to labor in this vineyard. We set out, a Pole, a Tyrolean, and I. Upon arrival, I was honored with the position of subdeacon and lieutenant. Today I am a colonel and a priest. We will give an energetic reception to the King of Spain's troops. I guarantee you they will be excommunicated and defeated. Providence has sent you here to help us. But is it true that my beloved sister Cunégonde is in the region, with the Governor of Buenos Aires?"

Candide assured him by swearing that nothing was more true. They began to shed tears all over again.

---

[39] **Father Croust:** A French Jesuit priest who had quarreled with Voltaire in 1754; Voltaire insinuates here that Croust is a pederast.

The Baron embraced Candide repeatedly, calling him his brother, his savior.

"Ah! My dear Candide," he said, "perhaps we can enter the city as conquerors and liberate my sister Cunégonde."

"I certainly hope so," said Candide, "because I was planning to marry her, and still am."

"You insolent swine!" replied the Baron. "You would have the impudence to marry my sister, who has seventy-two generations of nobility! I find it highly offensive that you dare to mention such an impossible plan to me."

Candide, petrified by this speech, answered him, "My Reverend Father, all the generations in the world make no difference. I rescued your sister from the arms of a Jew and an Inquisitor. She owes me a great deal, she wants to marry me. Dr. Pangloss always taught me that men are equal, and I am certainly going to marry her."

"We shall see about that, you scoundrel," said the Jesuit Baron Thunder-ten-tronckh, and in that instant he dealt him a great blow across the face with the flat side of his sword. Candide rapidly drew his own and thrust it into the Jesuit Baron's stomach, right up to the hilt. But when he drew out the steaming weapon, he began to weep.

"Alas, my God!" he said. "I've killed my old master, my friend, my brother-in-law. I'm the kindest man in the world, and here I've already killed three men — and two of them were priests."

Cacambo, who was standing guard at the gate to the arbor, ran in.

"There's nothing left to do but to make them pay dearly for our lives," his master told him. "They'll surely come into the arbor now; we must die with sword in hand."

Cacambo, who had seen the likes of this many times before, did not lose his head. He took the Jesuit robe that the Baron was wearing, put it on Candide, gave him the dead man's cornered hat, and had him mount his horse. All this was done in the twinkling of an eye.

"Let's gallop, Master. Everyone will take you for a Jesuit on a field mission, and we'll cross the border before they can come after us."

He was already charging ahead as he spoke, and then he cried out in Spanish, "Make way, make way for the Reverend Father Colonel!"

CHAPTER 16

What happened to the two travelers with two girls, two monkeys, and the savages called Oreillons

Candide and his valet had crossed the frontier, and still no one back at camp knew about the German Jesuit's death. The astute Cacambo had taken care to fill his saddlebag with bread, chocolate, ham, fruit, and some bottles of wine. With their Andalusian horses they plunged into an unknown land where they found no roads. Finally, a beautiful meadow, interlaced with streams, appeared before them. Our two travelers freed their horses to graze. Cacambo advised his master to eat, and he began to set the example.

"How do you expect me to eat ham," said Candide, "when I just killed the son of My Lord the Baron and find myself condemned never to see the lovely Cunégonde again? What's the use of prolonging my miserable days, if I have to endure them far away from her, in remorse and despair? And what will the *Journal de Trévoux*[40] say?"

While speaking in this way, he did not fail to eat. The sun began to set. The two wanderers heard some faint cries that seemed to proceed from women. They could not tell if these were cries of pain or joy, but they jumped to their feet with that anxiety and alarm that everything arouses in an unknown country.

The sounds came from two girls, completely nude, who were running spryly along the edge of the meadow, while two monkeys pursued them, snapping at their buttocks. Candide was moved by pity. The Bulgars had taught him how to shoot, and he was able to knock a nut off a bush without stirring the leaves. He raised his double-barreled musket from Spain, fired, and killed the two monkeys.

"God be praised, my dear Cacambo. I've rescued these two poor creatures from a great danger. If I committed a sin in killing an Inquisitor and a Jesuit, I've now redeemed myself by saving the lives of two girls. Perhaps these two young ladies are of noble birth, and my deed will bring us great rewards in this land."

He was going to say more, but his tongue became paralyzed when he saw the girls tenderly embrace the two monkeys, burst into tears over their bodies, and fill the air with cries of intense grief.

"I didn't expect them to be so forgiving," he said, after a long pause, to Cacambo, who replied: "That was a brilliant thing to do, Sir! You just killed the young ladies' lovers."

"Their lovers! Is that possible? You must be joking. What evidence do you have?"

"My dear Master," responded Cacambo, "you're always surprised by everything. Why do you find it so bizarre that in some countries monkeys obtain the favors of the ladies? They are a quarter human, just as I am a quarter Spanish."

"Alas!" said Candide. "I do recall hearing Dr. Pangloss say that such things used to happen, that these mixtures engendered pans, fauns, and satyrs, and that many of the heroes of ancient times saw them. But I thought that was all a fable."

"Now you should be convinced that it's the truth," said Cacambo, "and you can see how this truth is still practiced by people who have not been educated. But I'm afraid these ladies are going to make big trouble for us."

These solid reflections persuaded Candide to leave the meadow and plunge into a forest. He dined there with Cacambo, and the two of them, after cursing the Inquisitor of Portugal, the Governor of Buenos Aires, and the Baron, fell asleep on the moss. When they woke up, they noticed that they could not move; the reason was that during the night the native Oreillons,[41] to whom the two ladies had denounced

---

[40] *Journal de Trévoux:* A Jesuit journal that launched several attacks upon Voltaire.

[41] **Oreillons:** The French word Voltaire uses to translate the Spanish *Orejones,* meaning "big-eared." Voltaire got the word *orejones* from a history of Peru by Garcilaso de Vega, upon which he based much of his description of South America.

them, had tied them down with cords made of bark. They were surrounded by about fifty Oreillons, completely nude, armed with arrows, clubs, and stone axes. Some were bringing a huge cauldron to boil; others were preparing spits; and all of them were chanting: "It's a Jesuit, it's a Jesuit; here's our revenge and here's a good meal; let's eat Jesuit, let's eat Jesuit."

"Dear Master, I warned you," Cacambo blurted out sadly, "that these two girls would bring us trouble."

Candide, seeing the cauldron and the spits, exclaimed, "We're definitely going to be roasted or boiled. Ah! What would Dr. Pangloss say, if he knew what the pure state of nature is really like? All is well they say; but I confess it's harsh to have lost Miss Cunégonde and to be skewered by Oreillons."

Cacambo never lost his head. "Don't give up hope yet," he said to the cheerless Candide. "I know a bit of the lingo of tribes like this; I'm going to speak to them."

"Remember to explain to them," added Candide, "that it's the height of inhumanity to cook human beings, and that it's not very Christian either."

"Gentlemen," said Cacambo, "you intend to eat a Jesuit today; that is appropriate; nothing is more just than to treat one's enemies in this way. Indeed, natural law teaches us to kill our neighbor, and that is how everyone behaves the whole world over. If we Europeans do not exercise our right to eat others, it is because we have other ingredients for a good meal. But you do not have the same resources. It certainly makes more sense to eat your enemies than to abandon the fruits of victory to crows and ravens. But gentlemen, you do not wish to eat your friends. You think you are going to put a Jesuit on the spit, but it is your defender, the enemy of your enemies, whom you are going to roast. As for myself, I was born in your country; this gentleman whom you see is my master; and far from being a Jesuit, he just killed a Jesuit! He is wearing the plunder, and that is the source of your mistake. To verify what I am telling you, take his robe, bring it to the first outpost of the kingdom of the *Padres*. Learn for yourselves if my master has not killed a Jesuit officer. It will not take long; you can always eat us later if you find that I have lied to you. But if I have spoken the truth, you are too familiar with the principles of international justice, morality, and law not to spare our lives."

The Oreillons found this speech very reasonable. They commissioned two leaders to determine the truth with haste. The two deputies carried out their mission with precision and soon came back with the good news. The Oreillons untied their two prisoners, made all kinds of apologies, offered them girls, gave them refreshments, and escorted them up to the boundary of their state, shouting joyfully, "He's not a Jesuit, he's not a Jesuit!"

Candide could not stop admiring the cause of his deliverance. "What a people!" he kept saying. "What men! What morals! If I hadn't been lucky enough to stick a sword through the body of Miss Cunégonde's brother, I would have been eaten without mercy. But it turns out the pure state of nature is good, because I only had to show these people I wasn't a Jesuit, and they treated me with enormous kindness."

CHAPTER 17

Arrival of Candide and his valet in the country
of Eldorado,[42] *and what they saw there*

When they were at the Oreillons' border, Cacambo said to Candide, "You see, this hemisphere is no better than the other. Listen, let's take the shortest route back to Europe."

"How can we?" said Candide. "And where would we go? If I go back to my country, the Bulgars and Abars are slaughtering everyone. If I return to Portugal, I'll be burned. If we stay here, we run the risk of being put on a spit. And how can I bring myself to leave the part of the world where Miss Cunégonde lives?"

"Let's head for Cayenne," said Cacambo. "There we can find some Frenchmen who travel all over the world. They'll be able to help. Perhaps God will have pity on us."

It was not easy to get to Cayenne. They had a good idea, more or less, of the direction to take; but everywhere mountains, rivers, cliffs, bandits, and savages blocked their way. Their horses died of fatigue; their provisions were used up; they lived on wild fruits for a whole month. At last they found themselves by a little river, fringed with coconut trees, which nourished their lives and hopes.

Cacambo, whose advice was always as good as the old woman's, said to Candide: "We can't go any further, we've walked enough. I see an empty canoe on the shore. Let's fill it with coconuts, jump into this little bark, and drift with the current. A river always leads to some inhabited place. If we don't find something we like, we'll at least find something new."

"Let's go," said Candide, "and may Providence guide us."

They drifted for several miles between banks that were sometimes fertile, sometimes barren, sometimes level, sometimes steep. The river grew steadily broader, and eventually vanished under a vault of terrifying rocks that soared into the sky. The two travelers had the boldness to abandon themselves to the currents below this vault. The river narrowed at this point and carried them along with horrifying speed and noise. After twenty-four hours, they saw daylight again, but their canoe broke apart against the reefs. They had to crawl from rock to rock for three miles. Finally, they discovered a vast horizon trimmed by unscalable mountains. The lowlands were cultivated for pleasure as well as profit. Everywhere the useful was combined with the pleasing. The roads were covered, or rather embellished, with elegantly shaped carriages made from a shiny material, carrying men and women of extraordinary beauty, drawn swiftly by large red sheep that surpassed in speed the finest horses of Andalusia, Tetuan, and Mequinez.

"Here at last," said Candide, "is a country that is better than Westphalia."

He and Cacambo stepped into the first village they encountered. Some of the village children, covered with bits of golden brocade, were playing quoits near the village gate. Our two men from the other world watched them with interest. Their

---

[42] *Eldorado:* El Dorado, the legendary land or city of gold said to be somewhere in Central or South America; it was named after the fabled chieftain El Dorado, whose name means "the gilded one."

quoits were rather large rounded objects, yellow, red, and green, which sparkled brilliantly. Out of curiosity the travelers picked some up: gold, emeralds, rubies, of which the smallest would have been the greatest ornament of the Mogul's throne.

"No doubt about it," said Cacambo, "these youngsters playing quoits are the children of the King of this land."

Just then the village schoolteacher appeared to call the children back to school.

"There," said Candide, "is the tutor to the royal family."

The little beggars promptly stopped playing, leaving their quoits on the ground, along with their other playthings. Candide picked them up, ran after the instructor, and humbly presented them to him, using signs to tell him that the royal children had forgotten their gold and precious stones. The village schoolteacher smiled and threw them to the ground, looked briefly at Candide's face with surprise, and went on his way.

The travelers did not fail to keep the gold, rubies, and emeralds.

"Where are we?" exclaimed Candide. "The children of kings must be well educated here because they are taught to despise gold and jewels."

Cacambo was as surprised as Candide. Next they arrived at the first house in the village. It was built like a European palace. A throng of people crowded around the door, and even more were inside. A delightful music was audible, and a delicious odor of cooking filled the air. Cacambo walked up to the door and heard them speaking Peruvian. It was his mother tongue, for everyone knows that Cacambo was born in Tucuman, in a village where Peruvian was the only language.

"I'll act as your interpreter," he said to Candide. "Let's enter, this is an inn."

Two waiters and two waitresses, dressed in gold cloth, with their hair bound up in ribbons, invited them to be seated at the common dining table. They served four tureens of soup, each garnished with two parrots, a boiled condor weighing two hundred pounds, two savory roasted monkeys, three hundred round-billed hummingbirds on one platter, and six hundred straight-billed hummingbirds on another, exquisite stews, delicious pastries; and everything served on platters of a sort of rock crystal. The waiters and waitresses poured several liqueurs made from sugar cane. The guests were mostly merchants and coachmen, all extremely polite, who asked Cacambo a few questions with unintrusive discretion, and answered his own questions with the utmost clarity.

When the meal was over, Cacambo, like Candide, thought he was paying his bill amply by dropping on the table two of those large pieces of gold he had picked up. The host and hostess burst out laughing and slapped their knees for a long time. Finally, they became serious.

"Gentlemen," said the host, "we can easily see that you are foreigners; we are not accustomed to seeing any around here. Forgive us for laughing when you offered to pay us with stones from our highways. You obviously have none of our currency, but you do not need it to dine here. All inns established for the convenience of trade are paid for by the Government. You have dined poorly here because this is a poor village; but everywhere else you'll be given the reception you deserve."

Cacambo explained to Candide all of the host's remarks, and Candide heard them with the same wonder and amazement that his friend Cacambo showed in translating them.

"What is this country," they asked each other, "unknown to the rest of the world, and where the whole arrangement of Nature is so different from our own?"

"This is probably the country where all is well," Candide observed, "for it is absolutely necessary that one such country exist. And in spite of what Dr. Pangloss used to say, I often observed that everything was for the worst in Westphalia."

CHAPTER 18

What they saw in the land of Eldorado

Cacambo expressed his curiosity to his host, and the host said to him, "I am a very ignorant man, and am content to be so; but we do have an old gentleman, retired from the royal court, who is the most learned person in the kingdom, and the most communicative."

Without delay he brought Cacambo to the old man's house. Candide was merely the supporting actor now and accompanied his valet. They went into a very simple home, for the door was only silver, and the interior paneling merely gold, though designed with so much taste that the richest paneling could not surpass it. The lobby floor, it is true, was encrusted only with rubies and emeralds, but the harmonious pattern in which everything was arranged compensated for this extreme simplicity.

The old man received the two foreigners on a sofa stuffed with hummingbird feathers. He offered them liqueurs in diamond vases; after which he satisfied their curiosity in these terms.

"I am a hundred and seventy-two years old, and my late father, who was Master of the Royal Stables, told me about the astounding revolutions in Peru that he had witnessed. The kingdom we are in is the original homeland of the Incas, who unwisely left it to go out and make foreign conquests, and who ended up being destroyed by the Spanish.

"More wisdom was shown by some princes who remained here in their native land. They commanded, with the nation's consent, that no inhabitant of our little kingdom would ever leave it; and this rule has preserved our innocence and our happiness. The Spanish have some vague knowledge of this country, which they call *El Dorado,* and an English lord named Raleigh[43] even came close to it about a hundred years ago. But since we are surrounded by impassable mountains and precipices, we have so far been safe from the greed of European nations, which have an incredible passion for the stones and mud of our land and would murder every one of us to get some."

The conversation continued for a long time. It turned on the form of government, the morals, the women, the public entertainments, the arts. Finally, Candide, who always had a taste for metaphysics, inquired through Cacambo if the country had a religion.

The old man blushed slightly.

---

[43] **Raleigh:** Sir Walter Raleigh (1554–1618), English explorer and writer whose *Discovery of Guiana* (1596), describing his exploration of the Orinoco River valley in 1595, helped to promote the legend of El Dorado.

"How could you ever think we did not? Do you take us for ungrateful wretches?"

Cacambo humbly asked what the religion of Eldorado was. The old man blushed again.

"Is there more than one religion?" he said. "We have, I believe, the same religion as everyone else. We worship God from morning to night."

"Do you worship just one God?" asked Cacambo, who continued to translate Candide's uncertainties.

"I see no reason," said the old man, "to believe in two, three, or four. I must say that people from your world ask very odd questions."

Candide did not tire of interrogating the good old man through Cacambo. He wanted to know how one prayed to God in Eldorado.

"We do not pray at all," said the good and respectable sage; "we have nothing to ask him for; he has given us everything we need, and we thank him constantly."

Candide was curious to see the priests. He asked where they were. The kindly old-timer smiled.

"My friends," said he, "we are all priests. The King and all the heads of families solemnly chant the psalms of thanksgiving every morning, and five or six thousand citizens sing along with them."

"What! You have no monks who lecture, debate, govern, conspire, and burn people who don't agree with them?"

"We would be crazy if we did," said the old man. "Everyone here has the same beliefs, and we do not understand what your monks are for."

Candide was in ecstasy at these remarks, and said to himself, "This is very different from Westphalia and the Baron's chateau. If our friend Pangloss had seen Eldorado, he would have stopped asserting that the castle of Thunder-ten-tronckh was the best thing on earth. Travel is certainly instructive."

After this long conversation, the kindly old-timer had a carriage harnessed with six sheep and had twelve of his servants take the two travelers to the court.

"Forgive me," he said to them, "if my age deprives me of the honor of accompanying you. The King will give you a reception that will not disappoint you, and I am sure you will excuse us for any customs that happen to displease you."

Candide and Cacambo climbed into the carriage. The six sheep flew off, and in less than four hours they arrived at the royal palace, located on the edge of the capital city. The portal was two hundred and twenty feet high and a hundred wide. It is impossible to describe the materials it was made of, but it was obvious that it was vastly superior to those stones and sand we call gold and jewels.

Twenty beautiful girls of the palace guard met Candide and Cacambo as they descended from the carriage, escorted them to the baths, and dressed them in robes spun from hummingbird down. Then the Grand Lords and Ladies of the Crown walked them to His Majesty's apartment, passing between two lines of a thousand musicians each, as was the custom. As they approached the throne room, Cacambo asked a Grand Officer how they were supposed to show respect for His Majesty. By falling on their knees or flat on their stomachs? By putting their hands on their heads or behind their backs? By licking the dust off the floor? In short, what was the ceremony?

"The custom," said the Grand Officer, "is to embrace the King and kiss him on both cheeks."

Candide and Cacambo hugged His Majesty, who received them with the utmost grace and politely invited them to have supper with him later. In the meantime, they were shown the city: the public buildings rising to the clouds; the open markets decorated with countless columns; the fountains of clear water, the fountains of rose water, and the fountains of liqueurs made from sugar cane, which flowed continuously in great public squares that were paved with a kind of precious stone that gave off the scent of cloves and cinnamon. Candide asked to see the law courts; they told him that none existed and that trials never occurred. He inquired whether they had prisons, and the answer was no. What surprised him even more, and gave him the most pleasure, was the Palace of Science, in which he visited a gallery, two thousand paces long, filled with instruments for mathematics and physics.

After spending the whole afternoon touring about one-thousandth of the city, they returned to the Palace. Candide sat down to supper with His Majesty, his valet Cacambo, and several ladies. Never did they taste better food, and never did they encounter a more urbane host than His Majesty. Cacambo explained the King's witticisms to Candide, and they were witty even in translation. Of all the astonishing things Candide saw and heard, this was by no means the least astonishing.

They spent a month in this retreat. Candide never stopped saying to Cacambo: "It's true, my friend, and I'll repeat it: The castle where I was born doesn't compare to the land we're in now. But still, Miss Cunégonde isn't here, and you probably have a mistress yourself somewhere in Europe. If we stay here, we'll just be like everyone else, whereas if we return to our world, even with only twelve sheep loaded with stones from Eldorado, we'll be richer than all the kings put together. We won't have to be afraid of inquisitors, and we'll easily be able to rescue Miss Cunégonde."

This speech pleased Cacambo. People so much like to roam around, and then show off at home and brag about what they have seen in their travels, that the two happy men resolved to be happy no longer, and to ask His Majesty for permission to leave.

"You are doing a foolish thing," the King said to them. "I know that my country is insignificant, but when one is tolerably well off somewhere one ought to remain there. I certainly have no right to confine foreigners; such tyranny is inconsistent with our customs and with our laws. All men are free. You may leave at will, but the way out is very difficult. It is impossible to go against the swift currents which miraculously brought you here and which flow through the vaults of rock. The mountains surrounding my entire realm are ten thousand feet high and as straight as walls. Each one is more than twenty-five miles wide, and the only way down the other side is over vertical cliffs. Since you are absolutely determined to leave, however, I will order the Royal Engineers to design something that can transport you comfortably. When you have been conveyed to the other side of the mountains, no one will be able to accompany you beyond; for my subjects have sworn never to leave this retreat, and they are too wise to break their vows. But ask me for anything else you desire."

"We ask of Your Majesty," said Cacambo, "only a few sheep loaded with provisions, and some of the stones and mud of your country."

The King laughed. "I do not comprehend," he said, "the taste you Europeans have for our yellow mud; but take as much as you want, and may it bring you well-being."

He promptly gave orders to his engineers to make a machine to hoist these two extraordinary men out of the kingdom. Three thousand expert physicists worked on it; it was ready in two weeks and cost no more than twenty million pounds sterling in the local currency. Candide and Cacambo were placed in the machine. There were two large red sheep, saddled and bridled, for them to ride after they traversed the mountains, as well as twenty pack sheep loaded with provisions, thirty carrying gifts of the country's most curious items, and fifty loaded with gold, precious stones, and diamonds. The king tenderly embraced the two vagabonds.

It was a wonderful spectacle to see their departure and the ingenious way in which they and their sheep were hauled over the mountains. The physicists took leave of them after setting them down safely, and Candide's only aim and desire now was to present his sheep to Miss Cunégonde.

"We have enough to pay off the Governor of Buenos Aires," he said, "if Miss Cunégonde can be purchased. Let's head for Cayenne,[44] let's set sail, and we will see what kingdom we can buy."

CHAPTER 19

What happened to them in Surinam, and how Candide became acquainted with Martin

The first day was quite pleasant for our two travelers. They were encouraged by the idea that they possessed more treasure than all of Asia, Europe, and Africa combined. Candide was elated, and carved the name of Cunégonde on trees. On the second day, two of their sheep sank into a swamp and were buried with their cargo; two other sheep died of fatigue a few days after that; seven or eight perished of hunger in a desert; others fell off some cliffs a few days later. Finally, after a hundred days of travel, they had only two sheep left.

Candide said to Cacambo, "My friend, you see how the riches of this world are ephemeral; nothing is solid but virtue and the happiness of seeing Miss Cunégonde again."

"I agree," said Cacambo, "but we still have two sheep with more treasure than the King of Spain will ever have, and I see in the distance a city that I suspect is Surinam, which belongs to the Dutch. We are at the end of our troubles and the beginning of our happiness."

As they approached the town they saw a Negro stretched out on the ground, wearing only a pair of blue linen trunks that were half torn away. The poor man was missing his left leg and right hand.

"Oh my God!" Candide said to him in Dutch. "What are you doing in this horrible condition, my friend?"

---

[44] **Cayenne:** Small island off the coast of Guiana, colonized by the French in 1635. Surinam, where Candide goes next, was a Dutch colony in Guiana just north of Cayenne.

"I'm waiting for my master, Mr. Vanderdendur,[45] the famous merchant," replied the Negro.

"Was it Mr. Vanderdendur," asked Candide, "who treated you this way?"

"Yes, sir," said the Negro, "it's normal. They give us one pair of linen trunks twice a year as our only clothing. When we work in the sugar mills and catch our fingers in the grinder, they cut off our hand. When we try to escape, they cut off our leg. I've had both punishments. It is at this price that you eat sugar in Europe. Yet, when my mother sold me for ten Patagonian crowns on the coast of Guinea, she said to me, 'My dear child, pray to our charms, worship them forever, they will bring you happiness. You have the honor of becoming a slave to our Masters, the whites, and by doing so, you are making your parents rich.' Alas, I don't know if they became rich, but I certainly didn't. Dogs, monkeys, and parrots are a thousand times less miserable than we are. The Dutch sorcerers who converted me tell me every Sunday that we are all children of Adam, whites and blacks. I'm no genealogist, but if these preachers are right, we're all cousins. Now you have to admit that you can't treat your relatives more horribly than this."

"Oh Pangloss!" exclaimed Candide. "You had no idea this abomination existed. That does it; I have to renounce your optimism after all."

"What's optimism?" asked Cacambo.

"Alas!" said Candide, "it's the mania for insisting that all is well when one is suffering."

And he shed tears as he looked at the Negro. He was still crying when he entered Surinam.

The first thing he did was to inquire whether there was a ship in the harbor that could sail to Buenos Aires. The person they asked happened to be a Spanish captain who offered to make an honest deal with them and arranged to meet them later at an inn. Candide and the trusty Cacambo went to wait for him with their two sheep.

Candide, who wore his heart on his sleeve, told the Spaniard about all his adventures, and revealed that he wished to carry off Miss Cunégonde.

"The last thing I would do is take you to Buenos Aires," said the Captain. "I would be hanged, and so would you. The lovely Cunégonde is His Lordship's favorite mistress."

This was a lightning bolt for Candide. He wept for a long time. Finally, he drew Cacambo aside.

"Here's what you must do, my dear friend. Each of us has in his pockets five or six million worth of diamonds. You're more clever than I am. Go get Miss Cunégonde in Buenos Aires. If the Governor makes any trouble, give him a million. If he doesn't give in to that, offer him two. You never killed an inquisitor, they won't be suspicious of you. I'll fit out another boat and go to Venice and wait for you. It's a free country where you don't have to be afraid of Bulgars or Abars or Jews or inquisitors."

---

[45] **Mr. Vanderdendur:** Some readers suggest this name alludes to a Dutch bookseller named VanDuren who had quarreled with Voltaire.

Cacambo approved of this wise resolution. He was in distress at having to sepa-rate from such a good master, who had become his intimate friend. But the pleasure of being useful to him outweighed the pain of leaving him. They embraced and shed tears. Candide urged him not to forget the old woman. Cacambo left the very next day. He was a very fine man, that Cacambo.

Candide stayed on in Surinam, waiting until another Captain could take him to Italy with the two sheep he had left. He hired servants and bought everything he needed for a long voyage. Finally, Mr. Vanderdendur, proprietor of a big ship, came to introduce himself.

"How much do you want," Candide asked this man, "to take me straight to Venice, me, my men, my baggage, and those two sheep?"

The owner suggested ten thousand piastres. Candide immediately accepted.

"Ho ho," said the prudent Vanderdendur to himself, "this foreigner gives up ten thousand piastres in a second! He must be very rich."

Then, returning a moment later, he declared that he could not embark for less than twenty thousand.

"All right, you shall be paid," said Candide.

"Hey," the merchant said under his breath, "this man gives twenty thousand piastres as easily as he gives ten."

He came back again and said that he could not transport him to Venice for less than thirty thousand piastres.

"Then you will get thirty thousand," Candide replied.

"Ah ha," the Dutch merchant said to himself again, "thirty thousand piastres mean nothing to this man. Without any doubt, the two sheep are carrying immense treasures. Let us leave it as it stands. We will collect our thirty thousand piastres first, and then we will see."

Candide sold two little diamonds, the smaller of which was worth more than all the money the merchant demanded. He paid in advance. The two sheep were loaded on board. Candide followed on a small boat in order to join the ship in the harbor. The merchant seized the moment, raised the sail, and cut loose with a favorable wind. Candide, bewildered and stupefied, soon lost sight of him.

"Alas!" he cried out. "There's a trick worthy of the Old World."

He returned to shore, sunk in misery, for after all he had lost enough to make the fortune of twenty monarchs. He rushed to the house of a Dutch judge, and since he was a bit excited, he knocked rudely on the door. He entered, related his adven-ture, and shouted a bit louder than was necessary. The judge began by fining him ten thousand piastres for the noise he had made. Then he listened patiently, promised to review the case as soon as the merchant returned, and charged him another ten thousand piastres for the consultation.

These measures completed Candide's despair. He had, it is true, experienced other misfortunes a thousand times more painful, but the heartless character of the judge, and of the man who robbed him, amplified his bitterness and plunged him into a black melancholy. The viciousness of men appeared to him in all its ugliness, and he fed exclusively on thoughts of gloom. Finally, when a French ship was about to leave for Bordeaux, he took a cabin at a fair price, and since he no longer had any sheep laden with diamonds to bring with him, he announced in town that he would pay the fare, board, and two thousand piastres to any honest man who wished to make the voyage with him, on condition that this man should be the most disgusted with his lot and the most miserable in the province.

A throng of applicants appeared that an entire fleet could not have held. Candide wished to select the most promising candidates; he picked out about twenty persons who seemed sociable enough and all claimed to be the most qualified. He assembled them in his inn and gave them supper, on condition that each one swear to tell his story faithfully. He would choose the one who seemed to deserve the most pity and to have the strongest claim to being unhappy with his lot; the others would receive some smaller reward.

The session lasted until four in the morning. As he listened to all their adventures, Candide remembered what the old woman had told him on the way to Buenos Aires, and the wager she had made that there was no one on board who had not experienced great misfortunes. He thought of Pangloss at each tale he heard.

"That Pangloss," he said, "would be hard put to defend his system now. I wish he were here. Obviously, if all is well, it's in Eldorado and not in the rest of the world."

Finally, he decided in favor of a poor scholar who had worked in the bookstores of Amsterdam for ten years. He came to the conclusion that there was no profession on earth with which a man could be more disgusted.

This scholar, who was in fact a decent man, had been robbed by his wife, beaten by his son, and abandoned by his daughter, who had eloped with a Portuguese. He had just been deprived of the little job that barely supported him, and the preachers of Surinam were persecuting him because they took him to be a Socinian.[46] In truth, the others were at least as unfortunate as he, but Candide hoped that the scholar would relieve his boredom during the voyage. All his other rivals thought that Candide was doing them a great injustice, but he appeased them by giving them a hundred piastres each.

CHAPTER 20

What happened to Candide and Martin at sea

The old scholar, whose name was Martin, thus set out for Bordeaux with Candide. They had both seen much, and suffered much; and even if the ship had been scheduled to sail from Surinam to Japan by the Cape of Good Hope, they would have had enough material to discuss moral and physical evil throughout the entire voyage.

Yet, Candide had one great advantage over Martin: He still hoped to see Miss Cunégonde again, while Martin had nothing to hope for. Besides, he still had some gold and diamonds. Even though he had lost a hundred big red sheep packed with

---

[46]**Socinian:** Socinianism was a religious movement stemming from the work of Laelius Socinus, a sixteenth-century Polish theologian, who praised the power of reason and challenged the Christian mysteries such as the Trinity and the virgin birth.

the greatest treasures of the earth, and even though he was still tormented by the Dutch merchant's trickery, when he thought about what he still had in his pockets, and when he spoke of Cunégonde, especially after a good meal, he still leaned toward the system of Pangloss.

"But you, Mister Martin," said he to the scholar, "what do you think of all this? What's your conception of moral and physical evil?"

"Sir," replied Martin, "my priests accused me of being a Socinian; but the truth is that I am a Manichean."[47]

"You're joking," said Candide, "there are no more Manicheans in the world."

"There's myself," said Martin. "I don't know what to do about it, but I can't think any other way."

"The Devil must be inside your body," said Candide.

"He's so involved in the affairs of this world," said Martin, "that he may well be in my body and everywhere else too. But I confess that when I survey this globe, or rather this tiny ball, I think that God has abandoned it all to some evil being— except of course Eldorado. Very rarely have I seen a town that did not wish for the destruction of the next town, or a family that did not seek to exterminate some other family. Everywhere the weak hate the powerful in whose presence they slither, and the strong look after the weak like sheep to be fleeced and slaughtered. A million assassins in uniform, roaming from one end of Europe to the other, murder and pillage with discipline in order to earn their daily bread, and no profession confers more honor. And in those towns that seem to enjoy peace and where the arts flourish, the jealousies, cares, and anxieties that devour men are greater than the scourges suffered by a besieged city. Secret distress is much worse than public misfortune. In short, I've seen enough, and suffered enough, to be a Manichean."

"Yet there's some good," replied Candide.

"That may be," said Martin, "but I never saw it."

In the middle of this discussion, they heard the sound of cannon growing louder at every moment. Every one reached for his spyglass and saw two ships fighting about three miles away. The wind brought them both so close to the French ship that they had the pleasure of watching the fight in comfort. Finally one of the two ships assaulted the other with a broadside so low and accurate that it sank toward the bottom. Candide and Martin clearly discerned about a hundred men on the deck of the sinking vessel; they all raised their hands to heaven and wailed in terror. A moment later they were all swallowed up.

"Well," said Martin, "that's how men treat each other."

"It's true," said Candide, "there's something diabolical in this affair."

As he uttered these words he made out something bright red swimming toward the ship. They launched a lifeboat to see what it could be: It was one of his sheep. Candide's joy at regaining his one sheep was greater than his grief when he had lost a hundred of them packed with big diamonds from Eldorado.

---

[47] **Manichean:** The Manicheans, followers of the Persian sage Mani (third century C.E.), believed that life was a struggle between the active forces of light and darkness.

The French Captain soon discovered that the Captain of the attacking ship was Spanish and that the Captain of the submerged ship was a Dutch pirate; it was, in fact, the same who had robbed Candide. The immense riches stolen by that scoundrel were buried with him in the sea, and only one of the sheep survived.

"You see," Candide said to Martin, "sometimes crime is punished. That villainous Dutch merchant got the fate he deserved."

"Yes," said Martin, "but was it necessary for the ship's passengers to perish as well? God punished the deceiver, the Devil drowned the others."

Meanwhile the French and Spanish vessels continued on their way, and Candide continued his conversations with Martin. They debated for two weeks in a row, and at the end of this period they were no more advanced than on the first day. Nevertheless, they were talking, communicating ideas, and consoling one another. Candide caressed his sheep.

"Since I have found you again, I may well find Miss Cunégonde again too."

CHAPTER 21

How Candide and Martin theorized as they approached the coast of France

At last they sighted the coast of France.

"Have you been in France before, Mister Martin?" asked Candide.

"Yes," said Martin, "I have traversed many of the provinces. There are some where half the inhabitants are insane, some where the people are not to be trusted, some where they are quite gentle and rather ignorant, and others where they act like dandies all the time; and in all of them the principal occupation is lovemaking, the second is slandering, and the third is saying stupid things."

"But Mister Martin, have you ever seen Paris?"

"Yes, I have seen Paris. It has people in all of the above categories. It's a chaos, it's a mob in which everyone is seeking pleasure and in which almost no one finds it, at least so far as I could see. I did not stay there long. When I arrived I was robbed of all I had by pickpockets at the Saint Germain fair. I was arrested myself as a thief and did a week in prison, and after that I became a printer's proofreader in order to earn enough to return to Holland on foot. I met the low-life of scribblers, the low-life of conspirators, and the low-life of convulsionaries.[48] They say there are some very polite people in that city; I wish it were true."

"As for me, I'm not at all curious to see France," said Candide. "You can easily understand that when someone has spent a month in Eldorado, nothing else on earth is appealing any more, except Miss Cunégonde. I am going to wait for her in Venice. We will cross France to get to Italy. Will you join me?"

---

[48] **convulsionaries:** The Jansenists, a conservative sect of arch-Catholics who followed the teachings of Cornelis Jansen (1585–1638), the bishop of Ypres. Their doctrines and public displays of spiritual ecstasy were denounced by the papal authorities and created much controversy in eighteenth-century France.

"Very gladly," Martin said. "They say that Venice is a good place only for the Venetian nobles but that they also receive foreigners well when they have a lot of money. I don't have any, but you do; I will follow you anywhere."

"By the way," said Candide, "do you think that the earth was originally a sea, as it states in that fat book[49] belonging to the ship's Captain?"

"I believe nothing of the sort," said Martin, "any more than all the other pipe dreams that people have been selling recently."

"But then for what purpose was the earth formed?" asked Candide.

"To drive us crazy," replied Martin.

"Aren't you amazed," Candide went on, "by the story I told you about those two girls who were in love with the monkeys in the land of the Oreillons?"

"Not at all," Martin said, "I see nothing bizarre in that passion. I have seen so many extraordinary things that nothing is extraordinary any more."

"Do you think," Candide asked, "that men have always massacred each other as they do today, and that they have always been liars, cheaters, traitors, ingrates, brigands, weaklings, deserters, cowards, enviers, gluttons, drunks, misers, profiteers, predators, slanderers, perverts, fanatics, hypocrites, and morons?"

"Do you think," Martin said, "that hawks have always eaten pigeons when they found any?"

"Yes, of course," said Candide.

"Well," said Martin, "if hawks have always had the same character, why do you expect that men have changed theirs?"

"Oh!" said Candide, "that's very different, for free will. . . ."

As they were theorizing, they arrived in Bordeaux.

CHAPTER 22

What happened to Candide and Martin in France

Candide stopped in Bordeaux only as long as it took to sell a few stones from Eldorado and to hire a fine carriage with two seats, for he could no longer do without his philosopher, Martin. He was very upset, however, that he had to leave his sheep. He left it with the Bordeaux Academy of Sciences, which organized its annual essay competition around the question of why this sheep's wool was red. The prize was awarded to a scholar from the North,[50] who proved by A plus B minus C divided by Z that the sheep had to be red, and that it would die of the sheep-pox.

Meanwhile, all the travelers Candide met in the inns along the road said to him, "We are going to Paris!" This general eagerness finally made him want to see the capital; it was not far off the route to Venice anyway.

---

[49] fat book: The Bible, which describes the earth as having been covered in water (Genesis 1.6–7).

[50] scholar from the North: Maupertuis Le Lapon, a mathematician who tried to prove the existence of God with mathematical proofs.

He entered through the Faubourg Saint-Marceau[51] and thought he was in the ugliest village of Westphalia.

Scarcely was Candide in his hotel when he was struck by a mild illness caused by his fatigue. As he had an enormous diamond on his finger, and people had noticed a prodigiously heavy trunk among his belongings, he immediately had at his bedside two doctors whom he had not summoned, several intimate friends who would not leave him, and two pious women who kept his soup warm.

Martin said, "I remember being sick too during my first trip to Paris. I was a very poor man, so I had no friends, no pious ladies, no doctors, and I got better."

However, with the aid of medicines and bloodlettings, Candide's illness grew serious. A parish priest came and sweetly asked for a note payable to the bearer in the next world.[52] Candide would have nothing to do with it. The pious ladies assured him it was the latest fashion. Candide answered that he was not a fashionable man. Martin wanted to throw the priest out the window. The cleric swore that he would never grant Candide a proper burial. Martin swore that he would properly bury the cleric if he kept on bothering them. The quarrel heated up. Martin took him by the shoulders and rudely threw him out, creating a great scandal that was duly noted in a police report.

Candide recovered, and throughout his convalescence he had very good company for supper. They played cards for high stakes. Candide was surprised that he never got any aces, and Martin was not surprised at all.

Among those who bestowed upon him the city's favors was a little Perigordian Abbé, one of those fellows on the move who is always alert, obliging, assertive, flattering, solicitous, and who lies in wait for foreigners passing through, offering to tell them about the town's scandals and to obtain pleasures for them at any price. This man first took Candide and Martin to the theater. They were performing a new tragedy. Candide was seated next to some highbrow critics. That did not prevent him from weeping at the perfectly acted scenes. One of the theorizers beside him said during the intermission:

"It is highly improper of you to weep. That actress is very bad, the actor playing opposite her is worse, and the play is even worse than the actors. The author does not know a word of Arabic, yet the scene takes place in Arabia. Moreover, he does not believe in innate ideas.[53] Tomorrow I will bring you twenty pamphlets against him."

"Sir, how many plays do you have in France?" Candide asked the Abbé.

"Five or six thousand," replied the Abbé.

"That's a lot," said Candide. "How many of them are good?"

---

[51] **Faubourg Saint-Marceau:** A notoriously rough-and-tumble district in Paris during Voltaire's time.

[52] **note . . . next world:** A *billet de confession,* or certificate of confession, that in Voltaire's time was needed to obtain the last rites from a priest and to be buried in consecrated ground.

[53] **innate ideas:** According to the French philosopher René Descartes (1596–1650), we are born with some ideas already in our minds. Many philosophers refuted this notion, including the English philosopher John Locke (1632–1704).

"Fifteen or sixteen," answered the other.

"That's a lot," said Martin.

Candide was very pleased by an actress who played Queen Elizabeth in a rather dull tragedy[54] that is still performed from time to time.

"I like that actress a lot," he said to Martin. "She resembles Miss Cunégonde. I would like to pay her my respects."

The Perigordian Abbé volunteered to take him to her house. Candide, raised in Germany, asked what the etiquette was and how one treated the Queen of England in France.

"It depends," said the Abbé. "In the provinces you take them to a hotel. In Paris, you show them more respect if they are attractive, and then you throw them into the public dump when they are dead."[55]

"Queens in the public dump!" said Candide.

"Yes, that's how it is," said Martin. "The Abbé is right. I was in Paris when Miss Monime[56] passed, as they say, from this life to the next. They refused to give her what these people call 'the rites of burial,' in other words, the right to rot with all the beggars of the neighborhood in a sordid cemetery. Her troupe buried her all alone at the corner of the Rue de Bourgogne; it must have caused her extreme pain, for she always had a noble mind."

"That was very impolite," said Candide.

"What do you expect?" said Martin. "These people are made that way. Imagine every possible contradiction, every possible inconsistency; you will find it in the government, in the courts, in the churches, in the plays of this odd nation."

"Is it true that people in Paris always laugh?" asked Candide.

"Yes," said the Abbé, "but they are furious at the same time; for here people complain about everything with great bursts of laughter; they even laugh while committing the most detestable crimes."

"Who was that fat pig," asked Candide, "who said so many nasty things about the play that made me weep, and about the actors who gave me so much pleasure?"

"He is an illness in human form," replied the Abbé, "who makes a living by saying nasty things about every play and every book. He hates anyone who becomes popular, just as eunuchs hate anyone who makes love. He is one of those serpents of the literary world who feed on filth and poison; he is a folliculator."

"What do you mean by *folliculator*?" asked Candide.

"A scribbler of worthless folios, a Fréron,"[57] said the Abbé.

---

[54] **dull tragedy:** *Le Comte d'Essex (The Earl of Essex)* by Thomas Corneille (1625–1709), the younger brother of the renowned playwright Pierre Corneille (1606–1684).

[55] **public dump . . . dead:** Actors and actresses could not be buried in consecrated ground, a policy against which Voltaire argued throughout his career.

[56] **Miss Monime:** A character in the play *Mithridate* by Jean Racine (1639–1699); here, Voltaire uses the name to refer to Adrienne Lecouvrer (1690–1730), a popular actress whose death led Voltaire to write a poem protesting the church's burial policy for actors and actresses.

[57] **Fréron:** A journalist who had criticized Voltaire's plays.

Candide, Martin, and the Perigordian had this discussion on the stairway, as they watched the crowd file out of the theater.

"Even though I'm very impatient to see Miss Cunégonde again," said Candide, "I would still like to have supper with Miss Clairon,[58] for she seemed admirable to me."

The Abbé was not in a position to approach Miss Clairon, who received only good company.

"She is already engaged this evening," he said, "but I will have the honor of introducing you to another lady of distinction, and there you will come to know Paris as if you had been here over four years."

Candide was naturally curious and let himself be taken to the lady's home in the middle of the Faubourg Saint-Honoré. A group was busy playing faro[59] there; twelve sad punters each had a small series of cards that plainly registered their bad luck. A deep silence reigned, the punters' faces were white, the banker's look was anxious, and the lady of the house, seated beside the pitiless banker, observed with the eyes of a lynx every doubling of the stakes, every multiple bet, which the players signified by bending their cards. She exposed cheaters strictly but politely, without anger, for fear of losing her clients. The Lady went by the name of the Marquise de Parolignac.[60] Her fifteen-year-old daughter sat with the punters and winked at her mother to reveal the tricks these poor men were playing to repair the cruelties of chance. The Perigordian Abbé, Candide, and Martin entered. No one stood up, greeted them, or looked at them. Everyone was profoundly occupied with his cards.

"The Baroness of Thunder-ten-tronckh was more civil," thought Candide.

The Abbé, however, whispered in the ear of the Marquise. She stood up halfway and honored Candide with a gracious smile and Martin with a noble nod of the head. She arranged for Candide to sit and play cards. He lost fifty thousand francs in two rounds. Afterwards they had a very gay supper, and everyone was surprised that Candide was not disturbed by his loss. The lackeys said to each other, in their lackey language, "He must be some English Milord."

The supper was like most suppers in Paris: first silence; then a buzz of indistinguishable words; then jokes, insipid for the most part; inaccurate news; bad theory; a little politics, and a lot of slander. They even discussed new books.

"Has anyone seen," asked the Perigordian Abbé, "the novel by Monsieur Gauchat, Doctor of Theology?"[61]

"Yes," answered one of the guests, "but I could not finish it. We have a mass of trivial writings, but all of them put together do not match the triviality of Gauchat, Doctor of Theology. I am so nauseated by this multitude of detestable books that are swamping us that I have taken to playing faro."

---

[58] **Miss Clairon:** Claire Leris (1723–1803), a popular actress who performed in several of Voltaire's plays.

[59] **faro:** A popular card game in the eighteenth century, in which the players, called punters, place bets against the dealer, known as the banker.

[60] **Marquise de Parolignac:** In faro, to *parole* means to double the bet, an illegal move; hence, the lady is a cardsharp.

[61] **Gauchat . . . Theology:** One of Voltaire's critics.

"And the *Miscellaneous Essays* of Archdeacon T——,[62] what do you think of them?" asked the Abbé.

"Oh!" said Madame de Parolignac, "that deadly bore! How fervently he says what everyone already knows! How heavily he discusses what is not worth the slightest notice! How he appropriates without wit the wit of others! How he spoils what he steals! How he disgusts me! But he will disgust me no more; after reading a few pages of the Archdeacon, I am through."

Seated at the table was a man of learning and taste who supported what the Marquise said. Next they discussed tragedies. The Lady asked why tragedies that were unreadable were sometimes performed on the stage. The man of taste explained very clearly that a play could be popular and worthless at the same time. With just a few words he proved that it was not enough to bring in one or two of those situations found in novels and that always seduce the audience. Rather, the writer had to be original without being bizarre; to be sublime, and always natural; to know the human heart and make it speak; to be a great poet without letting any character in the play appear to be a poet; to know the language perfectly, speak it purely, with a flowing harmony, and make it rhyme without ever straining the sense.

"Whoever does not observe each of these rules," he added, "can write one or two tragedies that receive applause at the theater, but he will never take a place among the ranks of good writers. There are very few good tragedies. Some are merely idylls in well-written and well-rhymed dialogues; others are political theories that put you to sleep, or endless declamations that repulse you; still others are the reveries of fanatics in a barbarous style, filled with disconnected notions, long orations to the gods—because the author has no idea how to communicate with men—false maxims, and pompous commonplaces."

Candide listened attentively to this speech and formed a great opinion of the speaker. Since the Marquise had taken care to seat him next to her, he leaned toward her and took the liberty of asking her who that man was who spoke so well.

"He is a scholar," said the Lady, "who does not play faro and whom the Abbé sometimes brings here for supper. He has a thorough knowledge of tragedies and books. He wrote a tragedy that was hissed in the theater and one book which no one has ever seen outside of his publisher's shop, except the copy that he presented to me."

"What a great man!" said Candide. "He is another Pangloss."

Then, turning toward him, he said, "Sir, no doubt you think that everything is for the best in the physical and moral worlds and that nothing could be otherwise than it is?"

"I, sir?" the scholar replied. "I think nothing of the sort. I find that we are wholly off course, that no one knows his station or his duties, what he is doing or should be doing, and that except during supper, when people are relatively gay and accommodating, the rest of the time is spent in trivial quarrels: Jansenists against Molinists,[63]

---

[62] **Archdeacon T——**: Trublet, another of Voltaire's critics.

[63] **Molinists:** Followers of Luis de Molina (1535–1600), the Molinists were Jesuits who opposed the Jansenists (see note 48) in questions about the role of will and grace in attaining salvation.

men of parlement against men of the Church, men of letters against men of letters, courtiers against courtiers, financiers against the people, wives against their husbands, relatives against relatives: It is an eternal war."

Candide answered, "I've seen worse, but a wise man, who later had the misfortune to be hanged, taught me that such things are admirable: They are shadows in a beautiful picture."

"Your hanged teacher was mocking the world," said Martin. "Those shadows are horrible stains."

"It's men who make the stains," said Candide, "and they can't avoid it."

"Then it isn't their fault," said Martin.

Most of the card players, who grasped none of this exchange, were drinking. Martin continued to theorize with the scholars, and Candide recited part of his adventures to the Lady of the house.

After supper, the Marquise brought Candide into her boudoir and sat him down on a sofa.

"Well," she said, "are you still passionately in love with Miss Cunégonde of Thunder-ten-tronckh?"

"Yes, Madame," replied Candide.

The Marquise responded with a tender smile, "You answered me like a young man from Westphalia. A Frenchman would have said, 'It is true that I loved Miss Cunégonde, but when I see you, Madame, I fear that I am no longer in love with her.'"

"Alas! Madame," said Candide, "I will answer any way you want."

"Your passion for her," said the Marquise, "began when you picked up her handkerchief; I want you to pick up my garter."

"With all my heart," said Candide, and he picked it up.

"But I would like you to put it back on me," and Candide did so.

"Look at what a foreigner you are," said the Lady. "I sometimes force my Parisian lovers to languish for two weeks, but I am giving myself to you on the first night, because one should always bestow the favors of one's country on a young man from Westphalia."

The beauty had observed two enormous diamonds on the fingers of her young visitor, and she praised them so unselfishly that they passed from Candide's fingers to hers.

While returning home with his Perigordian Abbé, Candide felt some remorse at having been unfaithful to Miss Cunégonde. The Abbé took part in his sorrow. He had got only a small share of the fifty thousand francs Candide had lost in the card game, and of the value of the two diamonds that had been half given away by him and half extorted from him. His scheme was to profit, as much as possible, from any advantages that his association with Candide could provide. He spoke to him a great deal about Cunégonde, and Candide told him that he would certainly ask the lovely Lady to forgive him for his infidelity when he saw her again in Venice.

The Perigordian multiplied his compliments and favors, and took a tender interest in everything Candide said, everything he did, everything he wanted to do.

"So you have a rendez-vous in Venice, sir?" he asked.

"Yes, Abbé," said Candide; "I absolutely must go find Miss Cunégonde."

Then, carried away by the pleasure of talking about his loved one, he recounted, as was his habit, part of his adventures with that illustrious Lady from Westphalia.

"I suppose," said the Abbé, "that Miss Cunégonde is highly cultivated and writes charming letters."

"I never got any from her," said Candide. "Remember that when I was driven from the castle because of my love for her, I couldn't write to her. Then soon afterward, I learned she was dead. Then I found her again. Then I lost her. And now I've sent a messenger to her, six thousand miles away, and I'm waiting for his return."

The Abbé listened attentively, and then appeared to be lost in thought. He soon took leave of the two foreigners after embracing them affectionately. The next day, when Candide awoke, he received a letter composed as follows:

"Sir, my very dear lover, for a week I have been ill in this city. I know that you are here. I would fly into your arms if I could move. I heard that you had passed through Bordeaux. I left the faithful Cacambo and the old woman there; they will soon follow me. The Governor of Buenos Aires got everything from me he wanted, but I still have your heart. Come, the sight of you will bring me back to life, or make me die of pleasure."

This charming, unexpected letter filled Candide with inexpressible joy, and the illness of his dear Cunégonde struck him with grief. Torn between these two sentiments, he took his gold and diamonds and drove with Martin to the hotel where Miss Cunégonde was staying. He went in, trembling with emotion, on the verge of sobbing, his heart pounding. He tried to draw apart the bed curtains; he wanted more light.

"You mustn't do that," said the maid. "Light will kill her," and she abruptly closed the curtain.

"My dear Cunégonde," said Candide, weeping, "how are you feeling? If you can't see me, talk to me at least."

"She cannot speak," said the maid.

But she drew out from the bed a plump hand, which Candide watered with tears for a long time, before filling it with diamonds. He also left a sack of gold on the armchair. In the midst of his raptures a police officer arrived, followed by the Perigordian Abbé and a squad of soldiers.

"Are these the foreigners under suspicion?" shouted the officer.

He immediately had them under guard, and ordered his henchmen to drag them to prison.

"This isn't the way they treated foreigners in Eldorado," said Candide.

"I'm more of a Manichean than ever," said Martin.

"But sir, where are you taking us?" said Candide.

"To a dungeon," said the officer.

Martin, who had regained his composure, figured out that the Lady claiming to be Cunégonde was a fraud, the Perigordian Abbé a fraud who had seized the chance to exploit Candide's innocence, and the police officer another fraud who could easily be bought off.

Rather than expose himself to the judicial process, Candide, enlightened by his advisor, and still eager to see the real Cunégonde, presented the officer with three little diamonds worth about three thousand pistoles each.

"Ah sir!" said the man with the ivory baton, "even if you committed every crime imaginable, you're still the best man in the world. Three diamonds! Worth three thousand pistoles each! Sir! I would rather die than take you to jail. They are arresting all foreigners now, but leave everything to me. I have a brother at Dieppe, in Normandy. I'll take you there, and if you have a little diamond for him, he'll take care of you, just like me."

"And why are they arresting all foreigners?" asked Candide.

The Perigordian Abbé spoke up and said, "It's because a beggar from the region of Atrebatum[64] fell under the influence of foolish ideas, and they were enough to inspire him to attempt a parricide, not like the one of May, 1610, but like the one of December, 1594, and like so many others attempted in other years, in other months, and by other beggars inspired by foolish ideas."

The officer then explained what it was all about.

"Oh, the monsters!" exclaimed Candide. "What! Such atrocities in a nation that dances and sings! Let me out of this country where monkeys attack tigers. I lived among bears in my country. Only in Eldorado did I live with human beings. In the name of God, officer, take me to Venice, where I am supposed to meet Miss Cunégonde."

"I can only take you to Lower Normandy," said the enforcer.

And he immediately removed the chains, announced that he had made a mistake, dismissed his men, and brought Candide and Martin to Dieppe, where he left them in the hands of his brother. There was a little Dutch ship in the harbor. The Norman, with the help of three other diamonds, developed into the most helpful of men and conducted Candide and his retinue onto the vessel bound for Portsmouth in England. It was not en route to Venice, but Candide felt that he had escaped from hell, and he confidently expected to resume the direction to Venice at the first opportunity.

CHAPTER 23

How Candide and Martin came to the shores of England, and what they saw there

"Oh, Pangloss! Pangloss! Oh, Martin! Martin! Oh, my darling Cunégonde! What is this world we live in?" cried Candide on the Dutch ship.

"Something insane, something abominable," replied Martin.

"You've lived in England. Are they as insane there as in France?"

"It's just a different kind of insanity," said Martin. "You know that these two countries have been at war[65] over a few acres of snow in Canada, and that they are spending more on this lovely war than all of Canada is worth. As for whether there are more people in one country than another who ought to be put away, my limited

---

[64] **Atrebatum:** Artois, a district that was home to Robert François Damiens, who tried to assassinate King Louis XV in 1757. December 1594 and May 1610 are the dates of two attempts on the life of King Henry IV (Henry of Navarre) of France; the second was successful.

[65] **war:** The war between France and England over Canada, which did not end until the Peace of Paris in 1763.

intellect cannot say. I can only tell you that, in general, the people we are going to see are very melancholy."

As they were chatting, they arrived at Portsmouth. A large crowd of people covered the shore, looking out intently at a rather stout man[66] who was on his knees, blindfolded, on the deck of a naval ship. Four soldiers stationed in front of this man peacefully fired three bullets each into his brain; and the entire crowd went away extremely satisfied.

"What's this all about?" asked Candide, "and what evil demon is exercising his empire everywhere?"

He asked about the identity of the large man who was just ceremoniously murdered.

"He's an Admiral," was the answer.

"And why kill this Admiral?"

"It's because," came the answer, "he didn't kill enough people. He was engaged in a battle with a French Admiral and was later judged to have kept too great a distance from the enemy."

"But," said Candide, "the French Admiral was as far from the English Admiral as the latter was from the former."

"That's incontestable," was the response. "But in this country they think it's good to kill an Admiral from time to time, to encourage the others."

Candide was so stunned and shocked by what he saw and heard that he would not even set foot on land. He made a deal with the Dutch Captain (though the Captain could have robbed him like the one in Surinam) to take him to Venice without delay.

The Captain was ready two days later. They sailed along the coast of France. They passed within sight of Lisbon, and Candide shuddered. They entered the Straits of Gibraltar and the Mediterranean. At last they landed in Venice.

"God be praised," said Candide, embracing Martin. "This is where I will see the lovely Cunégonde again. I trust Cacambo as much as myself. All is well, all goes well, all is proceeding as best as it can."

CHAPTER 24

About Paquette and Brother Giroflée

As soon as he was in Venice, he looked for Cacambo in all the inns, all the cafés, and among all the ladies of pleasure, without finding him. He sent messengers every day to investigate every arriving boat, great and small: no news of Cacambo.

"What!" he said to Martin. "I've had time to go from Surinam to Bordeaux, from Bordeaux to Paris, from Paris to Dieppe, from Dieppe to Portsmouth, to sail along the coast of Portugal and Spain, to cross the entire Mediterranean, to spend several months in Venice—and the lovely Cunégonde still hasn't arrived! All I've encountered in her place is one pretentious strumpet and one Perigordian Abbé!

---

[66] **stout man:** The British admiral John Byng, who was executed on March 17, 1757, after being defeated by the French fleet; Voltaire had tried to stop the execution.

Cunégonde is surely dead, and there is nothing left for me to do but die. Oh! It would have been better to stay in the paradise of Eldorado than to return to this accursed Europe. How right you are, my dear Martin! All is but illusion and catastrophe."

He fell into a black melancholy and attended none of the fashionable operas and entertainments of the carnival season. None of the ladies tempted him in the least.

Martin said to him: "You are really very naive if you think a half-breed valet, with five or six million in his pocket, is going to track down your mistress at the other end of the world and bring her to you in Venice. If he finds her, he'll take her for himself. If he doesn't find her, he'll take someone else. I advise you to forget about your valet Cacambo and your mistress Cunégonde."

Martin was not very comforting. Candide's melancholy grew worse, and Martin never stopped proving to him that there was little virtue and little happiness in the world, except perhaps in Eldorado, where nobody can go.

While they were discussing this important matter and waiting for Cunégonde, Candide noticed a young Theatine[67] monk in the Piazza San Marco, arm in arm with a girl. The monk looked fresh, plump, and vigorous; his eyes were brilliant, his manner confident, his head erect, his step proud. The girl was very pretty and she was singing. She gazed lovingly at him, and from time to time pinched his chubby cheeks.

"You'll at least admit," said Candide, "that those two are happy. Until now I've found nothing but miserable people throughout the inhabitable world, except Eldorado; but that girl and that monk, I'll bet they're very happy creatures."

"I'll bet they're not," said Martin.

"All we need to do is invite them to dinner," said Candide, "and we'll see if I'm wrong."

He immediately approached them, paid his respects, and invited them back to his inn to eat macaroni, Lombardy partridges, and caviar, and to drink wines from Montepulciano, Vesuvius, Cyprus, and Samos. The young lady blushed, the monk accepted the offer, and the girl followed, looking at Candide with surprised and confused eyes, which were dimmed by an occasional tear.

Scarcely had she entered Candide's room when she said, "What! Master Candide does not recognize Paquette!"

At these words, Candide, who had not looked at her closely until then, because he was preoccupied with Cunégonde, said, "Alas! my poor child, so it's you, you who put Dr. Pangloss in the fine shape in which I saw him?"

"Alas! sir, I'm the one," said Paquette. "I see you know all about it. I heard about the terrible suffering inflicted on the household of the Baroness and on the fair Cunégonde. I swear to you, my fate has been no less unhappy. I was a pure and innocent girl when you saw me last. A Franciscan who was my confessor seduced me with ease. The consequences were horrible. I was forced to leave the castle shortly

---

[67] **Theatine:** A Catholic religious order founded in 1524 by several monks, including Giovanni Pietro Carafa, who became Pope Paul IV; maintaining a strict vow of poverty, the order aimed to restore a sense of moral rigor and virtue to the church.

after the Baron had driven you out with great kicks in the behind. If a famous doctor hadn't taken pity on me, I would have died. For some time, as an expression of gratitude, I was this doctor's mistress. His wife was insanely jealous and used to beat me every day without mercy; she was a Fury. The doctor was the ugliest man alive, and I the unhappiest of all creatures, constantly beaten on account of a man I did not love.

"You understand, Sir, how dangerous it is for a nagging woman to be a doctor's wife. One day, enraged by his wife's complaints, he gave her some medicine for a slight cold; it was so effective that she died two hours later in horrible convulsions. Her relatives started criminal proceedings; he fled, and I was the one put in prison. My innocence would never have saved me if I had not been rather pretty. The judge set me free, on condition that he become the doctor's successor. I was soon replaced by another woman, driven away without any support, and obliged to continue that shameful profession which you men think is so pleasant but which is a miserable abyss for us. I came to Venice to exercise the profession. Oh! Sir, if only you could imagine what it's like to be obliged to caress equally an old merchant, a lawyer, a monk, a gondolier, an Abbé; to be exposed to every kind of insult and outrage; to be frequently reduced to borrowing a skirt so that some disgusting man can have the pleasure of lifting it; to be robbed by one man of what you've earned from another; to be blackmailed by officers of the law; and to have no future in view except an atrocious old age, a hospital, and the public dump—if you could imagine all this, you'd conclude that I am one of the most miserable creatures on earth."

Paquette thus opened her heart to the good Candide in a private room, in the presence of Martin, who said to Candide, "You see, I've already won half the bet."

Brother Giroflée[68] had remained in the dining room and was having a drink while he waited for dinner.

"But," said Candide to Paquette, "you looked so gay, so happy, when I saw you; you were singing, you were caressing the monk with spontaneous affection; you seemed as happy then as you now claim to be miserable."

"Oh, Sir!" replied Paquette, "that's precisely one of the agonies of this profession. Yesterday I was robbed and beaten by an officer, and today I must appear to be in good spirits in order to give pleasure to a monk."

Candide did not wish to hear any more. He admitted that Martin was right. They sat down to eat with Paquette and the Theatine. The meal was quite amusing, and by the end, they were talking freely.

"Father," said Candide to the monk, "you seem to be enjoying a life that the whole world would envy. The flower of health blooms in your face; your features radiate with joy; you have a very pretty girl for recreation, and you seem content with your lot as a Theatine."

"Upon my word, Sir, I would like to see every Theatine at the bottom of the sea. A hundred times I have been tempted to set fire to the monastery and to run off and become a Turk. When I was fifteen my parents forced me to put on this detestable robe

---

[68] **Giroflée:** His name means "gillyflower"; *Paquette* means "daisy."

so they could leave more property to my accursed older brother, God confound him! Jealousy, discord, and rage fill the monastery. It is true that with a few bad sermons I bring in some money, half of which the Prior steals from me, half of which I use to procure women. But when I return to the monastery at night, I am ready to smash my head against the walls of the dormitory—and all the brothers feel the same."

Turning to Candide with his usual coolness, Martin said, "Well, haven't I won the whole bet?"

Candide gave two thousand piastres to Paquette and a thousand to brother Giroflée.

"I assure you," he said, "with that they will be happy."

"I know you're wrong," said Martin. "With those piastres you may even make them more unhappy than they ever were."

"Perhaps so," said Candide, "but one thing comforts me. I am learning that we often encounter people again whom we never thought we could find. It's quite possible that, having found my red sheep and Paquette again, I will also come across Cunégonde."

"If you do, I hope she makes you happy," said Martin, "but I strongly doubt she will."

"You're a hard man," said Candide.

"It's because I've lived," said Martin.

"But look at those gondoliers," said Candide. "Aren't they singing all day long?"

"You don't see them at home, with their wives and bratty children," said Martin.

"The Doge[69] has his troubles, the gondoliers have theirs. It's true that on the whole, the fate of a gondolier is preferable to that of a Doge, but I think the difference is so small that it's not worth examining."

"People talk," said Candide, "about a Senator Pococurante,[70] who lives in the fine palace on the Brenta and who generously receives foreigners. They claim he's a man who has never known sorrow."

"I'd like to see such a rare specimen," said Martin.

Candide promptly sent word to ask Lord Pococurante's permission to see him the next day.

CHAPTER 25

A visit to Lord Pococurante, nobleman of Venice

Candide and Martin took a gondola down the Brenta and arrived at the noble Pococurante's palace. The gardens were ordered harmoniously and adorned with beautiful marble statues, and the palace itself was an architectural splendor. The master of the house, a man of sixty, and very wealthy, greeted his two curious visitors politely but with very little warmth, which disappointed Candide and impressed Martin.

---

[69] **Doge:** Chief magistrate of the republic of Venice.

[70] **Pococurante:** The name means "small care."

First, two pretty and neatly attired girls served them cocoa whipped to a froth. Candide could not resist praising their beauty, grace, and dexterity.

"They are quite amusing creatures," said Senator Pococurante. "I sometimes take them to bed with me, for I am very tired of the ladies in town, their coquetries, their jealousies, their quarrels, their moods, their pettiness, their vanity, their foolishness, as well as the sonnets you have to compose or commission for them. But now these two girls are beginning to bore me too."

After the meal, Candide strolled through a long gallery and was surprised by the beauty of the paintings. He asked which master had painted the first two.

"They are by Raphael," said the Senator. "I bought them out of vanity at a high price a few years ago. People say they are the finest in Italy, but they do not give me any pleasure. The colors are too dark, the figures are not rounded enough and do not stand out enough, the draperies do not look like real cloth at all. In short, in spite of what they say, I do not consider them to be true imitations of Nature. I only like a painting when I think I am seeing Nature itself, but there are no paintings of this kind. I possess many paintings, but I do not look at them any more."

Pococurante had a concerto performed as they waited for dinner. Candide found the music delicious.

"That noise," said Pococurante, "may be amusing for a half hour, but if it goes on longer it tires everybody, though no one dares to admit it. The music of today is merely an art of performing difficult pieces, and what is merely difficult cannot be pleasing for very long.

"Perhaps I would like opera better, had they not discovered the formula for making it a revolting freak show. I have nothing against those who wish to see bad tragedies set to music, where the scenes are crudely written to introduce two or three ridiculous songs that show off an actress's windpipe. I have nothing against those who are willing or able to swoon with pleasure when a eunuch twitters the role of Caesar or Cato and struts awkwardly around the stage. But as for myself, I have long given up these trifles, which are now considered the glory of Italy, and for which Sovereigns pay so extravagantly."

Candide argued a little, but with discretion. Martin was entirely of the Senator's opinion.

They sat down to dine, and after an excellent dinner, they went into the library. Candide, seeing a superbly bound volume of Homer, complimented the most illustrious Lord on his good taste.

"Here," he said, "is a book that used to be a delight to the great Pangloss, the best philosopher in Germany."

"It has no such effect on me," said Pococurante coldly. "I was once under the delusion that reading gave me pleasure. But that endless series of battles that are all alike, those gods who are always intervening without doing anything decisive, that Helen who is the cause of the war and who hardly plays a role in the story, that Troy which is forever besieged and never captured—all of this bores me to death. I have had opportunities to ask scholars if reading it bores them as much as it does me. All the sincere ones confessed that the book puts them to sleep but added that one must always have it in one's library as a monument to antiquity, like those rusty coins that cannot be spent."

"Your Excellency doesn't have the same opinion of Virgil?" said Candide.

"I grant," said Pococurante, "that the second, fourth, and sixth books of his *Aeneid* are excellent. But as for the pious Aeneas, the strong Cloanthes, the trusty Achates, the little Ascanius, the idiotic King Latinus, the bourgeois Amata, the insipid Lavinia, I can imagine nothing more cold or unpleasant. I prefer Tasso and the fantasy stories of Ariosto."

"Dare I ask, Sir," said Candide, "if you do not take pleasure in reading Horace?"

"Some of his maxims," said Pococurante, "can be of use to a man of the world, and since they are compressed into energetic verse, they easily become engraved in the memory. But I care very little about his journey to Brundisium, or his description of a bad dinner, or the quarrel between two ruffians, one named something like Pupilus, whose words, he says, *were full of pus,* and the other whose words *were like vinegar.*[71] I can read only with extreme disgust his coarse verses against old women and witches, and I do not see what merit there can be in telling his friend Maecenas that if the latter places him in the ranks of lyric poets, he will strike the stars with his sublime forehead. Fools admire everything in an author who has a good reputation. I read only for myself; I like only what I can use."

Candide, who had been brought up never to judge anything for himself, was astonished by what he heard. Martin found Pococurante's way of thinking quite reasonable.

"Oh, here is Cicero," said Candide. "This great man — I can't imagine that you tire of reading him?"

"I never read him," replied the Venetian. "What does it matter to me if he defended Rabirius and Cluentius? I have enough lawsuits of my own to deal with. I was more inclined to appreciate his philosophical works, but when I saw that he doubted everything, I concluded that I already knew as much as he, and that I did not need anyone's help to become ignorant."

"Ah, here are eighty volumes of the proceedings of a scientific academy," exclaimed Martin. "There may be some good things in there."

"There would be," said Pococurante, "if any of the authors of this hotchpotch had invented even a new way of producing pins. But there is nothing in these books except vain theoretical systems, and not a single useful thing."

"Look at all those plays over there!" said Candide. "In Italian, Spanish, French!"

"Yes," said the Senator, "there are three thousand, and not three dozen good ones. As for those collections of sermons, which as a whole are not worth one page of Seneca, and all those thick volumes of theology, you may be sure that neither I, nor anybody else, ever opens them."

Martin noticed some shelves loaded with English books.

"I suppose," he said, "that a republican would derive pleasure from most of these books written in defense of freedom."

"Yes," said Pococurante, "it is noble to write what one thinks; it is the privilege of humankind. Throughout Italy people write only what they do not think. The

---

[71] *pus . . . vinegar:* Voltaire here alludes to Horace's *Satires* 1.7, which Pococurante is garbling.

inhabitants of the land of the Caesars and Antonines do not dare to have a single idea without the permission of a Dominican. I would support the liberty that inspires English writers, if only selfishness and the spirit of faction did not corrupt all that is good in that precious freedom."

Candide, noticing a volume of Milton, asked him if he did not regard this author as a great man.

"Who?" said Pococurante. "This barbarian who writes a long commentary on the first chapter of Genesis in ten books of harsh verse? This crude imitator of the Greeks who disfigures the Creation and who, even though the Scriptures represent the Eternal Being producing the universe with His words, has the Messiah pull out a big compass from a heavenly closet in order to design His work? Am I supposed to admire a man who spoils Tasso's images of Hell and the Devil? who disguises Lucifer sometimes as a toad, sometimes as a pygmy? who has him give the same speech a hundred times and makes him argue about theology? who takes so seriously Ariosto's comical story about the invention of firearms that he makes the demons shoot cannons in Heaven? Neither I nor anyone else in Italy could draw pleasure from such pitiful absurdities. The marriage of Sin and Death, and the snakes to which Sin gives birth, make any man vomit who has the slightest sense of good taste. And his long description of a hospital can be interesting only to gravediggers. This obscure, bizarre, and disgusting poem was despised when it was published; today I simply treat it as it was treated in the author's country by his contemporaries. Furthermore, I say what I think, and whether or not others agree matters very little to me."

Candide was distressed by these remarks. He respected Homer, and he liked Milton a bit.

"Alas!" he whispered to Martin, "I'm afraid this man may have an imperious contempt for our German poets."

"There's no harm in that," said Martin.

"Oh, what a superior man," Candide hissed. "What a great genius is this Pococurante! Nothing can please him."

After they had reviewed all the books in this manner, they went down into the garden. Candide praised the abundance of beauty.

"I know of nothing in such bad taste," said the Master. "We have nothing here but trifles; tomorrow I am going to redesign it on a nobler plan."

When the two curious travelers had taken leave of His Excellency, Candide said to Martin, "Well, you must admit that we just saw the happiest of men, for he is above everything he possesses."

"Don't you see," said Martin, "that he is disgusted with everything he possesses? Plato said a long time ago that the best stomachs are not those which refuse all food."

"But," said Candide, "isn't there joy in criticizing everything, in perceiving faults where other people think they see beauties?"

"That's to say," replied Martin, "that there is joy in having no joy?"

"Oh well!" said Candide. "So the only happy person in the world will be myself, when I see Miss Cunégonde again."

"It's always a good thing to hope," said Martin.

Yet the days flowed by, and then the weeks. Cacambo did not appear, and Candide was so immersed in his own sorrow that he did not even wonder why Paquette and Brother Giroflée had never returned to thank him.

CHAPTER 26

*How Candide and Martin had supper
with six foreigners, and who they were*

One evening when Candide, accompanied by Martin, was about to sit down to eat with the foreigners who were lodging in the same hotel, a man whose face was the color of soot came up behind him, took him by the arm, and said, "Be ready to leave with us, do not fail."

Candide turned and saw Cacambo. Nothing but the sight of Cunégonde could have surprised and pleased him more. He nearly went mad with joy. He embraced his dear friend.

"Cunégonde must surely be here. Where is she? Take me to her, let me die of joy with her."

"Cunégonde isn't here," said Cacambo, "she's in Constantinople."

"Good heavens! In Constantinople! But even if she were in China, I'd leave in a second; let's go!"

"We'll leave after supper," replied Cacambo. "I can't tell you more. I'm a slave. My Master awaits me, I must wait on him. Don't say a word. Eat and be ready."

Candide, his heart pounding, his mind in turmoil, torn between joy and sorrow, delighted to see his faithful agent again and astonished to find him a slave, and filled with the thought of finding his mistress again, sat down with Martin, who was observing these events coolly, and with six foreigners who had come to spend the carnival season in Venice.

Cacambo, who was pouring the drinks for one of these foreigners, leaned toward his Master near the end of the meal and said, "Sire, Your Majesty may leave when he wishes; the ship is ready."

Having said these words, he walked away. The astonished guests looked at each other without uttering a single word. Then another servant approached his Master and said, "Sire, Your Majesty's carriage is in Padua and the boat is ready."

The Master gestured and the servant left. The other guests looked at each other again, and their mutual surprise redoubled. A third valet likewise approached a third foreigner and said, "Sire, I assure you, Your Majesty should not stay here any longer. I will prepare everything." And he promptly disappeared.

By now Candide and Martin were sure it was a carnival masquerade.

A fourth servant said to the fourth Master, "Your Majesty may depart when he wishes," and left like the others. The fifth valet said the same thing to a fifth Master. But the sixth valet spoke differently to the sixth foreigner, who was seated next to Candide: "I swear, Sire, they will not give any more credit to Your Majesty, or to me; we could easily be locked up tonight, you and I. I am going to take care of my own affairs. Farewell."

With all the servants gone, the six foreigners, Candide, and Martin remained in deep silence. Finally Candide broke through it.

"Gentlemen," said he, "this is a remarkable jest. Why are you all behaving like royalty? I assure you that neither I nor Martin is a King."

It was Cacambo's master who spoke up gravely, saying in Italian, "I am not jesting. My name is Achmet III.[72] I was the Grand Sultan for many years; I dethroned my brother; my nephew dethroned me; my viziers had their throats cut; I am permitted to finish out my life in my old harem; my nephew, the current Grand Sultan, Mahmoud, allows me to travel; and I have come to spend the carnival season in Venice."

The young man next to Achmet spoke next, "My name is Ivan; I was Emperor of all the Russias; I was dethroned as an infant; my mother and father were locked up; I was reared in jail; I sometimes get permission to travel, in the company of guards; and I have come to spend the carnival season in Venice."

The third said, "I am Charles Edward, King of England; my father ceded me his rights to the kingdom; I struggled to maintain them; the hearts of eight hundred of my supporters were ripped out and thrown in their faces; I was put in prison; I am going to Rome to visit the King, my father, who was dethroned like me and my grandfather; and I have come to spend the carnival season in Venice."

The fourth then spoke up: "I am the King of the Poles; the fortunes of war deprived me of my hereditary states; my father experienced the same reversal; I resign myself to Providence like Sultan Achmet, Emperor Ivan, and King Charles Edward, may they be granted long lives; and I have come to spend the carnival season in Venice."

The fifth said: "I am also King of the Poles; I lost my kingdom twice; but Providence has given me another state, where I have done more good than all of the Kings of the Sarmatians were able to do on the banks of the Vistula; I too resign myself to Providence; and I have come to spend the carnival season in Venice."

It remained for the sixth monarch to speak.

"Gentlemen," said he, "I am not as great a Master as you are, but even so, I too was once a King. I am Theodore; I was elected King of Corsica; I used to be called 'Your Majesty,' and now I am lucky if I am called 'Sir'; I used to mint new coins, and now I am penniless; I used to have two secretaries of state and now I do not even have a valet; I used to sit on a throne and I ended up lying for years on straw in a London prison. I fear I will be treated the same here, though I have come, like Your Majesties, to spend the carnival season in Venice."

The five other Kings listened to this speech with noble compassion. Each gave King Theodore twenty sequins to obtain suits and shirts. Candide presented him with a diamond worth two thousand sequins.

"Who is this ordinary citizen," said the five Kings, "who is in a position to give a hundred times more than any of us, and who voluntarily gives it?"

---

[72] **Achmet III:** This ruler and the others named are all drawn from history and were either deposed early or defeated. Achmet III of Turkey lived from 1673 to 1736; Ivan VI of Russia, from 1740 to 1764; Charles Edward Stuart (Bonnie Prince Charlie) of England and Scotland, from 1720 to 1788; Augustus III of Poland, from 1697 to 1763; Stanislas Leczinski of Poland, from 1677 to 1766; and Thedore von Neuhof, briefly king of Corsica, from 1690 to 1756.

Just as they were leaving the table, there arrived at the same hotel four other Serene Highnesses who had also lost their states through the fortunes of war, and who had come to spend the rest of the carnival season in Venice. But Candide took no notice of these newcomers. His only concern was to go find his dear Cunégonde in Constantinople.

<h2 style="text-align:center">CHAPTER 27</h2>

Candide's voyage to Constantinople

Faithful Cacambo had convinced the Turkish captain who was taking Sultan Achmet to Constantinople to admit Candide and Martin on board. The two of them embarked after prostrating themselves before His Miserable Highness. On the way, Candide said to Martin:

"We had supper with six dethroned Kings, and I even gave alms to one of them. Perhaps there are many other Princes even more unfortunate. As for me, I've only lost a hundred sheep, and I am flying into the arms of Cunégonde. My dear Martin, once again Pangloss was right: all is well."

"I wish it were so," said Martin.

"But," said Candide, "that was an extraordinary adventure we just had in Venice. No one before ever saw six dethroned Kings dining together in an inn or even heard of such a thing."

"It is no more extraordinary," said Martin, "than most of the things that have happened to us. It is very common for Kings to be dethroned. And as for the honor we had to dine with them, that is a trifle unworthy of our attention. What does it matter with whom you have supper, as long as you eat well?"

Scarcely was Candide on the ship than he embraced his old valet, his friend Cacambo.

"Well, what is Cunégonde doing?" he asked him. "Is she still a marvel of beauty? Does she still love me? Is she in good health? Surely you have bought a palace in Constantinople for her?"

"My dear master," answered Cacambo, "Cunégonde is scrubbing dishes on the shores of the Propontis for a Prince who has very few dishes. She's a slave in the household of a former Sovereign named Ragotski.[73] He is in exile and the Grand Turk supports him with three crowns a day. But what is even worse, she has lost her beauty and become horribly ugly."

"Ah! beautiful or ugly," said Candide, "I am an honorable man, and I am bound to love her forever. But how was she reduced to such an abject condition when I gave you five or six million?"

"All right," said Cacambo, "I had to give two million to Señor Don Fernando d'Ibaraa y Figueora y Mascarenes y Lampourdos y Souza, Governor of Buenos Aires, for permission to take back Miss Cunégonde. Then a pirate gallantly stole the

---

[73] **Ragotski:** Francis Leopold Rakoczy (1676–1735), Hungarian king of Transylvania from 1704 to 1711, who went into Turkey in exile after refusing to accept defeat at the hands of the Austrians.

rest. This pirate brought us to Cape Matapan, Melos, Nicaria, Samos, Petra, to the Dardanelles, Marmora, and Scutari. Cunégonde and the old woman are servants with that Prince I was telling you about, and I am a slave of the dethroned Sultan."

"What a horrifying series of calamities!" said Candide. "Yet, after all, I still have some diamonds. I will easily rescue Miss Cunégonde. What a pity that she's become so ugly."

Then turning toward Martin, he asked: "Which of us do you think is the most to be pitied, Emperor Achmet, Emperor Ivan, King Charles Edward, or me?"

"I have no idea," said Martin. "I would have to be inside your hearts to know."

"Ah!" said Candide. "If Pangloss were here, he would know, and he would tell us what to think."

"I don't know," said Martin, "what kind of scales your Pangloss had for weighing the miseries of humankind, and for appraising their pains. The one thing I take for granted is that there are millions of people on earth who are a hundred times more to be pitied than King Charles Edward, Emperor Ivan, and Sultan Achmet."

"That may well be true," said Candide.

In a few days they arrived in the Bosporus. Candide began by purchasing Cacambo's liberation at a high price. Then, without wasting any time, he flung himself and his companions into a galley ship to go search for Cunégonde on the shores of Propontis, however ugly she might be.

Among the crew condemned to the galleys were two convicts who were rowing very badly, and upon whose bare shoulders the Levantine[74] Captain occasionally applied a few lashes of a bullwhip. Naturally intrigued, Candide looked at them more closely than the other convicts and moved toward them with pity. Some features of their disfigured faces struck him as having a slight resemblance to Pangloss and that unfortunate Jesuit, that Baron, that brother of Miss Cunégonde. This image moved and saddened him. He looked at them again more closely.

"Truly," he said to Cacambo, "if I hadn't seen the hanging of Dr. Pangloss, and if I hadn't had the misfortune of killing the Baron, I would swear that they are rowing in this galley."

At the words "Baron" and "Pangloss," the two convicts let out a loud cry, stopped rowing, and dropped their oars. The Levantine Captain rushed over with the whip and redoubled his strokes.

"Stop, stop, Sir," cried Candide. "I will give you as much money as you want."

"What! It's Candide!" cried one of the convicts.

"What! It's Candide!" cried the other.

"Is this a dream?" said Candide. "Am I awake? Am I really on this ship? Is that the Baron whom I killed? Is that Dr. Pangloss whom I saw hanged?"

"It is, it is!" they replied.

"What! Is that the great philosopher?" said Martin.

"Now, Mr. Levantine Captain," said Candide, "how much money do you want for the ransom of the gentleman from Thunder-ten-tronckh, one of the leading Barons of the Empire, and Mr. Pangloss, the most profound metaphysician of Germany?"

---

[74] **Levantine:** From the Levant, the lands bordering the eastern Mediterranean Sea.

"Dog of a Christian," answered the Levantine captain, "since these two dogs of Christian slaves are Barons and metaphysicians, which is obviously a great honor in your country, you will give me fifty thousand sequins for them."

"You shall have them, Sir. Take me in a flash back to Constantinople, and you will be paid on the spot. No, take me first to Lady Cunégonde."

But after Candide's first offer, the Levantine Captain had already turned the prow toward the city, and the oars began to move faster than a bird's wings cleave the air.

Candide embraced the Baron and Pangloss a hundred times. "How is it that I didn't kill you, my dear Baron? And my dear Pangloss, how is it that you're alive after being hanged? And why are you both on the Turkish galleys?"

"Is it really true that my dear sister is in this country?" asked the Baron.

"Yes," replied Cacambo.

"At last I have found my dear Candide," cried Pangloss.

Candide introduced them to Martin and Cacambo. Everyone embraced, everyone spoke at the same time. The galley ship flew swiftly, and soon they were in the port. They summoned a Jew, who paid fifty thousand sequins for one of Candide's rings worth a hundred thousand, and who swore by Abraham that he could not offer more. Candide immediately paid the ransom for the Baron and Pangloss. The latter threw himself at his liberator's feet and bathed them with tears; the former thanked him with a nod and promised to pay back the money at the first opportunity.

"But is it really possible that my sister is in Turkey?" he asked.

"Nothing is more possible," Cacambo answered, "because she is scrubbing dishes for a Transylvanian prince."

They promptly summoned two Jews. Candide sold two more diamonds, and they all set out in another galley ship to rescue Miss Cunégonde.

CHAPTER 28

What happened to Candide, Cunégonde, Pangloss, Martin, etc.

"Forgive me once again," said Candide to the Baron. "Forgive me, my Reverend Father, for having run you through with a thrust of my sword."

"Forget about it," said the Baron. "I was a bit too hasty, I admit. But since you want to know how fortune brought me to the galleys, I will tell you. After my wound was cured by an apothecary, who was a brother in the Jesuit college, I was captured in a Spanish raid, abducted, and imprisoned in Buenos Aires just at the time my sister left. I asked permission to return to Rome to work in the Father General's office. Instead, I was sent to Constantinople to be the chaplain in the French ambassador's office. One evening, scarcely a week after I took up my new position, I met a young, good-looking page in the Sultan's court. It was hot. The young man wished to have a bath, and I took the opportunity to have one too. I did not know that it was a capital crime for a Christian to be found naked with a young Muslim. A cadi sentenced me to be beaten a hundred times with a cane on the soles of the feet, and condemned me to the galleys. I do not think there has ever been a more horrible miscarriage of justice. But I would like to know why my sister is in the kitchen of a Transylvanian Sovereign who is in exile among the Turks."

"And you, my dear Pangloss," said Candide, "how is it that I am able to see you again?"

"It is true," said Pangloss, "that you saw me hanged. Of course, I was supposed to be burned, but you will recall that it began to rain heavily when they were preparing to cook me. The storm was so violent that they lost hope of kindling the fire. They hanged me because they could do no better. A surgeon purchased my corpse, brought me home, dissected me. First he made a cross-shaped incision from my navel up and out to my collarbones. Never had a man been hanged more poorly than I had been. The Executioner for High Affairs of the Holy Inquisition, a subdeacon, really knew how to burn people with style, but he was not accustomed to hanging them. The rope was wet and did not slip smoothly; it became knotted; in short, I was still breathing. The cross-shaped incision released such a great cry from inside me that my surgeon fell over backward. Thinking that he was dissecting the Devil, he ran out, in mortal terror, falling down the staircase as he left. His wife rushed in from a nearby room when she heard the commotion. She saw me lying on the table with my cross-shaped incision. Even more frightened than her husband, she fled and stumbled over him as she left. When they had calmed down a bit, I heard her say to him, 'My dear, whatever led you to dissect a heretic? Don't you know, the Devil is always in the bodies of those people? I am going to get a priest to exorcise him right away.'

"I shuddered at these words, and I gathered whatever strength I still had left to call out, 'Take pity on me!' Finally the Portuguese barber took courage. He sewed up my skin. His wife even took care of me. I was on my feet in two weeks. The barber found me a job as lackey to a Knight of Malta who was headed for Venice. But my Master had no money to pay me, so I began to work for a Venetian merchant, and I accompanied him to Constantinople.

"One day I had an impulse to go into a mosque. It was empty except for an old imam and a very pretty young worshipper saying her prayers. Her bosom was completely uncovered, and between her breasts was a lovely bouquet of tulips, roses, anemones, buttercups, hyacinths, and primroses. She dropped her bouquet. I picked it up and I put it back in place with meticulous care. I took so much time replacing it that the imam became angry, and when he saw that I was a Christian he called for help. They brought me before the cadi, who sentenced me to a hundred strokes with a cane on the soles of the feet, and condemned me to the galleys. I was chained up in the very same galley ship and behind the same oar as the Baron. In that galley there were also four young men from Marseilles, five Neapolitan priests, and two monks from Corfu, who told us that similar things occurred every day. The Baron claims that he has endured greater injustice than I. I argue, however, that it is more lawful to replace a bouquet of flowers on a young woman's bosom than to be naked with a young male page. We were debating the question constantly and receiving twenty lashes of the bullwhip per day, when the chain of events of this universe led you to our galley in order to ransom us."

"Well, my dear Pangloss," Candide said, "when you were being hanged, dissected, beaten black and blue, and when you were rowing in the galleys, did you still think that everything is for the best in this world?"

"I still hold to my original opinion," replied Pangloss. "For after all, I am a philosopher, and it is not appropriate for me to take back my word. Leibniz is never mistaken. Moreover, preestablished harmony is the finest aspect of the universe, along with the plenum and subtle matter."[75]

CHAPTER 29

How Candide found Cunégonde
and the old woman again

While Candide, the Baron, Pangloss, Martin, and Cacambo were reciting their adventures, theorizing about contingent and noncontingent events in the universe, and having debates about cause and effect, moral and physical evil, free will and determinism, and the consolations available to a galley slave in Turkey, they landed on the shore of the Propontis and came to the house of the Transylvanian Prince. The first thing they saw was Cunégonde and the old woman hanging towels on a line to dry.

The Baron turned pale at this sight. Candide, the tender lover, seeing his beautiful Cunégonde's swarthy complexion, bloodshot eyes, withered bosom, wrinkled cheeks, and peeling red skin, recoiled three paces in horror, then approached her out of respect for decency. She embraced Candide and her brother. They embraced the old woman, and Candide paid the ransom for her and Cunégonde.

There was a little farm in the area. The old woman suggested to Candide that they settle into it until the destiny of the group improved. Cunégonde did not know she had become ugly; no one told her. She reminded Candide of his promise in so firm a tone that the good Candide dared not refuse her. He thus informed the Baron of their intention to marry.

"I will never accept," said the Baron, "such baseness from her, and such insolence from you. I will not allow myself to be disgraced in this way. It would prevent my sister's children from entering the noble orders in Germany.[76] No, never will my sister marry anyone but a Baron of the Empire."

Cunégonde threw herself at his feet and bathed them with tears. He was inflexible.

"You stubborn idiot," said Candide, "I rescued you from the galleys, I paid for your ransom and freed your sister. She was washing dishes here, and she's ugly. I have the generosity to make her my wife and you still protest against it. I would kill you again if I gave in to my anger."

"You may kill me again," said the Baron, "but you will never marry my sister while I am alive."

---

[75] **plenum and subtle matter:** These terms come from Leibniz's theories and signify the matter that fills space (*plenum*) and the spiritual entities of the universe (subtle matter, or *materia subtilis*), including mind, soul, and spirit.

[76] **noble orders in Germany:** Assemblies of knights.

<h2 style="text-align:center">CHAPTER 30</h2>

Conclusion

In his heart, Candide had no desire to marry Cunégonde. But the Baron's extreme arrogance made him resolve to conclude the marriage, and Cunégonde pressed him so strongly that he could not take back his word. He consulted Pangloss, Martin, and the trusty Cacambo. Pangloss wrote a fine treatise in which he proved that the Baron had no legal rights over his sister and that, in accordance with all the laws of the Empire, she could marry Candide by the left hand.[77] Martin was in favor of throwing the Baron into the sea. Cacambo suggested they send him back to the Levantine Captain to serve his full term on the galleys, and then send him to the Father General in Rome on the first available ship. This idea was received very favorably. The old woman approved of it. They kept it secret from the Baron's sister. The plan was executed at a modest expense, and they had the pleasure of snaring a Jesuit and punishing the pride of a German baron at the same time.

It is quite natural to imagine that after so many disasters, Candide, now married to his mistress and living with the philosopher Pangloss, the philosopher Martin, the prudent Cacambo, and the old woman, and having also saved many diamonds from the land of the ancient Incas, must have enjoyed the most agreeable life in the world. But he was so cheated by the Jews that he soon found himself with nothing more than the little farm. His wife, growing uglier every day, became shrewish and intolerable. The old woman was infirm and even nastier than Cunégonde. Cacambo, who labored in the garden and traveled to Constantinople to sell vegetables, was worn out with toil and cursed his fate. Pangloss was in despair because he was not a star in some German university. As for Martin, fully persuaded that people are equally wretched everywhere, he bore life with patience.

Candide, Martin, and Pangloss sometimes debated metaphysical and moral issues. From the windows of the farm they often saw ships loaded with effendis, pashas, and cadis being exiled to Lemnos, Mytilene, and Erzerum. They saw other cadis, pashas, and effendis take the place of the exiles, and suffer exile in their turn. They saw heads being neatly impaled for presentation at the Sublime Port.[78] These spectacles intensified their arguments, and when they were not debating, the boredom was so excessive that the old woman dared one day to say to them:

"I'd like to know which is worse — to be raped a hundred times by Negro pirates, to have a buttock cut off, to run the gauntlet among the Bulgars, to be whipped and hanged in an auto-da-fé, to be dissected, to row on the galleys, in short, to experience every misfortune we have known — or to stay here without anything to do?"

"That's a deep question," said Candide.

These remarks gave birth to new reflections, and it was Martin who concluded that human beings are destined to live in either convulsive anxiety or lethargic boredom.

---

[77] **marry . . . left hand:** A morganatic marriage in which the member of the lower rank gives up any rights to the rank or property of the other.

[78] **Sublime Port:** The main gate of the sultan's palace.

Candide did not accept this, but he offered no alternative. Pangloss admitted that he had always suffered horribly, but having once affirmed that everything in the world functioned marvellously, he kept affirming it, and never believed it.

One event especially served to confirm Martin in his dreadful principles, to make Candide hesitate more than ever before, and to embarrass Pangloss. It was the arrival at their farm of Paquette and Brother Giroflée, in the most extreme misery. They had quickly wasted their three thousand piastres; they had parted; come back together; quarreled; been put in prison; escaped; and in the end Brother Giroflée had become a Turk. Paquette practiced her trade throughout, and never earned anything.

"I was right," said Martin to Candide, "that your gifts would soon be squandered and would only make them more miserable. You were rolling in millions of piastres, you and Cacambo, and you were no happier than Brother Giroflée and Paquette."

"Ah! Ah!" said Pangloss to Paquette. "Heaven has brought you back to us, my poor child! Do you realize that you cost me the tip of my nose, an eye, and an ear? Look at you! Oh! What a world!"

This new adventure led them to philosophize more than ever.

There lived in the region a very famous dervish[79] who was reputed to be the best philosopher in Turkey. They went to consult him. Pangloss spoke for everyone: "Master, we have come to ask you to tell us why such a strange animal as man was ever created."

"Why meddle in that?" said the dervish. "Is it any business of yours?"

"But Reverend Father," said Candide, "there is a horrible amount of evil in the world."

"What difference does it make," said the dervish, "if there is good or evil? When His Highness sends a ship to Egypt, does he worry about whether or not the mice are comfortable on board?"

"Then what is to be done?" said Pangloss.

"Keep silent," said the dervish.

"It was my humble expectation," said Pangloss, "that I could theorize a bit with you about effects and causes, the best of possible worlds, the origin of evil, the nature of the soul, and preestablished harmony."

At these words the dervish slammed the door in their faces.

During this conversation, news was spreading that the mufti and two viziers of the divan[80] had been strangled in Constantinople, and that many of their friends had been impaled. This catastrophe created a great uproar everywhere, for a few hours. Pangloss, Candide, and Martin, on their way back to the little farm, met a kindly old man, enjoying the fresh air by his door under a grove of orange trees. Pangloss, who was as curious as he was philosophical, asked him the name of the mufti who had just been strangled.

"I have no idea," replied the kindly old man, "and I have never known the name of any mufti or any vizier. I am entirely ignorant of the matter you refer to. I assume

---

[79] **dervish:** Member of an Islamic religious order.

[80] **viziers of the divan:** Advisors to the sultan; a mufti is an Islamic interpreter of the religious law.

that in general those who meddle in public affairs perish, sometimes miserably, and that they deserve it. But I never think about what people are doing in Constantinople. I am content to sell them the fruits of the garden that I cultivate."

Having said these words, he invited the foreigners into his home. His two daughters and two sons served them several kinds of sherbet which they had made themselves, Turkish cream flavored with candied citron, oranges, lemons, limes, pineapples, pistachios, and mocha coffee unadulterated by the bad coffee of Batavia and the West Indies. Afterwards the kindly old Muslim's daughters sprinkled perfume on the beards of Candide, Pangloss, and Martin.

"You must possess," said Candide to the Turk, "a vast and magnificent estate?"

"I only have twenty acres," replied the Turk. "I cultivate them with my children. Work keeps away three great evils: boredom, vice, and indigence."

While returning to his farm, Candide reflected deeply on the Turk's words. He said to Pangloss and Martin, "That kindly old man seems to have made a better life than the six kings we had the honor of eating supper with."

"Power and glory," said Pangloss, "are very dangerous, as all the philosophers tell us. For indeed, Eglon, King of the Moabites, was assassinated by Ehud; Absalom was hanged by his hair and pierced with three spears; King Nadab, son of Jeroboam, was killed by Baasha; King Elah by Zimri; Ahaziah by Jehu; Athaliah by Jehoiada; Kings Jehoiakim, Jeconiah, and Zedekiah became slaves. You know how Croesus perished, and Astyages, Darius, Dionysius of Syracuse, Pyrrhus, Perseus, Hannibal, Jugurtha, Ariovistus, Caesar, Pompey, Nero, Otho, Vitellius, Domitian, Richard II of England, Edward II, Henry IV, Richard III, Mary Stuart, Charles I, the three Henrys of France, the Emperor Henry IV. You know. . . ."

"I know," said Candide, "that we must cultivate our garden."

"You are right," said Pangloss, "for when man was placed in the Garden of Eden, he was placed there *ut operaretur eum*,[81] in order to work on it, which proves that humankind was not made for rest."

"Let us work without theorizing," said Martin. "That is the only way to make life bearable."

The little society entered into this laudable plan. Each began to exercise his talents. The little bit of earth became productive. Cunégonde was undeniably very ugly, but she baked excellent pastries. Paquette embroidered. The old woman took care of the linen. No one failed to contribute, not even Brother Giroflée. He was a very good carpenter and even became a sociable fellow.

And sometimes Pangloss would say to Candide, "All events are linked together in the best of all possible worlds. For after all, if you had not been driven from a fine castle with great kicks in the behind for loving Miss Cunégonde, if you had not been seized by the Inquisition, if you had not crossed South America on foot, if you had not thrust a sword into the Baron, if you had not lost your sheep from the good country of Eldorado, you would not be here eating candied citrons and pistachios."

"That is well said," replied Candide, "but we must cultivate our garden."

---

[81] *ut operaretur eum:* Latin for "so that he should work it."

Enlightenment and the Spirit of Inquiry

p. 302

Voltaire's **Candide,** a relentless attack on human illusions, rigid dogma, and institutional cruelty of all kinds, reflects the late-seventeenth- and eighteenth-century spirit of inquiry in Europe that encouraged people to question their cultural assumptions and their accepted place in the world. Confident in their ability to discern the laws of nature and of human society, ENLIGHTENMENT thinkers—called the *philosophes* in France—were determined to shrug off conventional ways of thinking in order to see the world anew as well as to dismantle old institutions and design new ones along better models. In contrast to Voltaire's Pangloss, who believes that this is the best of all possible worlds, the *philosophes* thought that society was ready for a major overhaul. By using reason, empirical investigation, and mechanical ingenuity, they hoped to overcome superstition, prejudice, and the abuses of religion and politics. Faith in the power of reason to effect change brought with it a strong sense of hope that—through education, reflection, and the application of new ideas and inventions— human beings might progress to a state of near perfection.

DARING TO KNOW

p. 390

In "**What Is the Enlightenment?**" (1784), the great German philosopher Immanuel Kant (1724–1804) defines enlightenment as "man's release from his self-incurred minority," by which he means release from his fear to exercise his reason and judgment independently.

▶ Ascent of the Montgolfier Brothers' Hot-Air Balloon, 1783
This color engraving depicts the Montgolfier brothers' famous balloon flight before an audience of the royal family at Versailles. (The Bridgeman Art Library International Ltd.)

The Engine to Raise Water by Fire, 1747. Engraving *A diagram of Newcomen's steam engine for* Universal Magazine. *(Private collection / Bridgeman Art Library)*

In the Horatian motto *sapere aude*—"dare to know"—Kant and others found the principle upon which Western philosophy hinged in the eighteenth century: Dare to reason independently and question authority.

ruh-NAY day-KART

p. 381

p. 376

This revolution in man's thinking was driven, in part, by the earlier advances of philosophers such as **René Descartes** (1596–1650) and **John Locke** (1632–1704) and astronomers and natural philosophers (scientists) such as Nicolas Copernicus (1473–1543), Galileo Galilei (1564–1642), and Sir Isaac Newton (1642–1727). Impatient with the limits, contradictions, and abstractions of conventional logic and mathematics, Descartes set out to reduce the principles of analysis to some basic laws. In *Discourse on Method* (1637) his first rule would be "to accept nothing as true which I did not clearly recognize to be so: that is to say, carefully to avoid precipitation and prejudice in judgments. . . ." From that deceptively simple premise, Descartes arrived at what is known as the *Cogito,* from *cogito ergo sum*—"I think, therefore I am." Though we cannot doubt the

François Nicolas Martinet, *Jean-Pierre Blanchard's Flying Machine.* Eighteenth-Century Color Lithograph *Scientists of the eighteenth century became fascinated with theories of flight; some theories were more fantastic than others. (Musée de l'Air et de l'Espace, Le Bourget, France / Lautes-Giraudon-Bridgeman Art Library)*

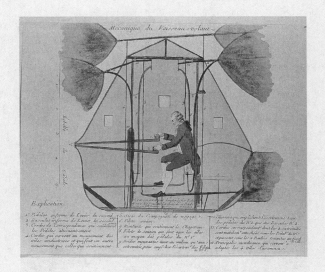

existence of mind *(res cogitans),* Descartes declared, we can doubt the existence of matter *(res extensa);* hence, the mind must be radically different from matter—a concept known as Cartesian dualism. Eventually concluding that a benevolent God does exist, Descartes's philosophy provides reasonable assurance that the material world is not an illusion and that we can be confident in our observations and sense-knowledge of it. Descartes' "method of doubt" would become a key element of Enlightenment thinking, which was underscored by Newton's discovery of what were believed to be the fundamental laws governing motion, gravity, and light. Newton's notion that we could "derive the rest of the phenomena of Nature by . . . reasoning from mechanical principles" became another important premise for Enlightenment thinkers and bolstered the view that nature, including human nature, was a machine governed by universal principles. The idea that God was a great craftsman who had assembled the universe and set it in motion spurred empirical experimentation and intellectual inquiry, for it was believed that if human beings could discover the fundamental principles that kept the great machine in motion they could achieve mastery over it and take charge of their own history.

The works of these philosophers, along with those of other thinkers, gave rise to the notion best expressed by Alexander Pope's ***Essay on Man***, Epistle 1, that "All Nature is but Art, unknown to thee." That is, all nature is governed by orderly and ultimately discernible laws somewhat beyond the ken of ordinary perceptions and

From these forces, by other propositions which are also mathematical, I deduce the motions of the planets, the comets, the moon, and the sea. I wish we could derive the rest of the phenomena of Nature by the same kind of reasoning from mechanical principles. . . .

– ISAAC NEWTON, Preface to *Mathematical Principles of Natural Philosophy*, 1686

p. 284

Guiguet, Benjamin Franklin Conducting His Lightning Experiments, *1752 This is a French artist's engraving of the famous story of Franklin's experiments with electricity. Franklin is said to have tied a key to a kite to see if lightning — electricity — would strike the key. (Mary Evans Picture Library)*

understanding. Enlightenment thinkers believed that through careful and fresh reasoning and observation, man could eventually understand the fundamental laws of nature and human nature and use that knowledge to make the world more just and humane. Hence, the spirit of inquiry in science went hand in hand with the spirit of social, political, and religious reform.

After the middle of the century, American politician-philosopher Thomas Jefferson (1743–1826) and English writer-reformer Mary Wollstonecraft (1759–1797), among others, embodied the spirit of Enlightenment as political and social reform as they set out to defend the rights of citizens and women, respectively. In Jefferson's view, the foundation for independence lies in "self-evident" truths about human equality and the rights to life, liberty, and the pursuit of happiness. Jefferson's ideas were rooted in the political philosophy of the English philosopher John Locke (1632–1704), who advanced the idea that citizens and government should form a social contract in which individual life, health, liberty, and property should be protected; for Locke, in the most extreme cases, revolutions might be necessary to safeguard those liberties. Jefferson's Declaration of Independence advances Locke's ideas and substitutes the "pursuit of happiness" for Locke's "inalienable right of property." Following the logic of Jefferson's arguments for individual liberties, as well as those of Jean Jacques Rousseau (1712–1778) and the French Declaration of the Rights of Man and Citizen (1789), which stated the principles of the French Revolution, Mary Wollstonecraft argued in her *Vindication of the Rights of Woman* (1792) that women should have the same freedoms and opportunities for participatory citizenship, including voting, that men have. In that work, she anatomized the condition of women in England and called for an end to the abuses in domestic, social, and political life that women endured. In the celebrated Age of Reason, emphasizing liberty and independence, women had been left out of the picture. In the Enlightenment spirit that informs its arguments, *A Vindication* addresses wide-reaching injustice in society, for both men and women. It criticizes the moral turpitude and idleness of the aristocracy; exposes the institution of hereditary property as an instrument that perpetuates unmerited social and economic privilege; and advocates that friendship based upon reason, understanding, and affection replace passion as the basis for relationships between men and women. Above all, it advocates that women be granted dignity and respect for their intellectual potential and accomplishments.

p. 403

TIME AND PLACE

Eighteenth-Century France: The Encyclopedia Project

In 1751, Denis Diderot and Jean Le Rond d'Alembert published the first volume of *Encyclopédie, ou Dictionnaire raisonné des sciences, des arts et des métiers (Encyclopedia, or Methodical Dictionary of the Sciences, Arts, and Trades)* in France. This collaborative project aimed to record all new knowledge produced since the Renaissance and to serve as a medium for the promotion of Enlightenment ideals. More than twenty-one editors — including leading philosophers such as Voltaire, Rousseau, Montesquieu, D'Holbach, and Turgot —

compiled more than 71,800 entries and more than 3,000 illustrations.

In his *Preliminary Discourse to the Encyclopedia,* d'Alembert describes its indebtedness to the work of English philosophers Francis Bacon and John Locke. Both d'Alembert and Diderot embraced Locke's position that all knowledge is grounded in sensory perception and experience. From Bacon, they took the notion that empirical knowledge may be divided into the general categories of history, philosophy, and poetry correlated to the

Eighteenth-Century France: The Encyclopedia Project *continued*

Denis Diderot writing the Encyclopedia, *nineteenth-century engraving. (The Art Archive/Private Collection/Dagli Orti)*

human faculties of memory, reason, and imagination. The *Encyclopedia*'s system of classification and its ranking of the branches of knowledge is based on these three categories, serving as a means to help readers navigate the text as well as to understand the connections among the various alphabetical entries. In part due to Locke and Bacon's influence, Diderot and d'Alembert devoted much attention to the latest discoveries in the natural sciences, mathematics, medicine, mechanics, and technology; many entries were lavishly illustrated, allowing readers to see the machinery that was transforming their world.

Articles on religion and government met with heavy criticism. The editors believed that empirical analysis and critical reason could liberate men from religious and political superstition, intolerance, and persecution; thus, many entries advocate religious tolerance, political reform, and economic and educational equality. Because the *Encyclopedia* openly questioned the foundations of French political and religious authority—denying, for example, the immortality of the soul and denouncing that belief as superstition—many political officials and religious leaders called for the suppression or censorship of the *Encyclopedia*. Others condemned the editors as political revolutionaries or demanded that they be excommunicated from the church. In 1752 the first two volumes were suppressed by the King's Council, and in 1759 further sales and printing of the *Encyclopedia* were again banned. Nonetheless, supported by powerful authorities favorable to the project, Diderot continued work on the final volumes. To his dismay, Diderot learned that his publisher, André François Le Breton, fearing reprisals from the authorities, had silently edited or deleted sections he thought were too politically dangerous. In the end, supported at first by private subscription, the *Encyclopedia* proved an economic and intellectual success. In 1772, the *Encyclopedia*'s seventeen volumes of text and eleven volumes of illustrations were completed. Today it remains a defining monument of the French Enlightenment and a powerful testament to the spirit of inquiry and reform that swept Europe and the Americas in the eighteenth and early nineteenth centuries.

Farming in Four Seasons: Irrigation Pump for Lifting Water, 1625–50
The Edo, or Tokugawa, period in Japan saw many technical advancements, such as the development of the irrigation pump, which allowed for speedier farming and in turn yielded more food. (Freer Gallery of Art, Smithsonian Institution, Washington, D.C.: Purchase, F1981.30)

TOKUGAWAN NEO-CONFUCIANISM

In Japan, beginning in the late seventeenth century, Hayashi Razan (1583–1657), also known as Doshun, exerted a powerful influence upon neo-Confucianist doctrines in Japan. NEO-CONFUCIANISM, a blend of CONFUCIANISM, BUDDHISM, and DAOISM, stemmed from the teachings of the Chinese philosopher Zhu Xi (Chu Hsi; 1130–1200). Zhu Xi's particular blend of metaphysics, ethics, and politics as adapted by Doshun was well suited to the Tokugawa-era shoguns, who benefited from a society guided by principles that emphasized orderly participation in the world. In the study of metaphysics, Doshun, following Zhu Xi, contemplated the fundamental motive force behind all things, or *li.* Later Japanese neo-Confucians, including **Kaibara Ekken** (1630–1714), author of *Grave Doubts,* and **Baien Miura** (1723–1789), who wrote *Discourse on Metaphysics* and other treatises, transformed the study of *li* into a systematic analysis of nature, society, and economics, moving Japanese neo-Confucianism toward an empirical science. As can be seen in ***Reply to Taga Bokkei*** included here, Baien, best known perhaps for his work in economics, questions the widespread dependence on orthodox principles, insisting that the way to true understanding requires freeing the mind from the pieties and accepted wisdom of the past and opening up to a direct investigation of nature and humanity, much as the Enlightenment thinkers in Europe were proposing.

■ **PRONUNCIATION**

Baien Miura: BAH-yen mee-OO-rah
René Descartes: ruh-NAY day-CART
Kaibara Ekken: kigh-BAH-rah EK-ken

kigh-BAH rah EK-ken

BAH-yen mee-OO-rah

p. 385

∾ René Descartes
b. France, 1596–1650

French philosopher, mathematician, and scientist René Descartes is, along with Francis Bacon, one of the founders of modern thought. If Bacon is the father of empiricism and experimental science, Descartes is the father of rationalism and theoretical science. He set out to create a single, mathematically based method for all the sciences and in doing so developed the systematic practice of "methodical doubt" or "Cartesian skepticism." He describes this process in his two most important philosophic treatises, *Discourse on Method* (1637) and *Meditations* (1642). The passage from *Discourse on Method* that follows is an account of the reve-

René Descartes,
Descartes' Universe,
1668
*Descartes' drawing
shows how matter
that fills the universe
is collected in vortices,
with a star at the
center of each. Some
vortices have orbiting
planets. The path of a
comet is shown by the
wavy line beginning
at N and moving
upwards. (Copyright
Image Select / Art
Resource, NY)*

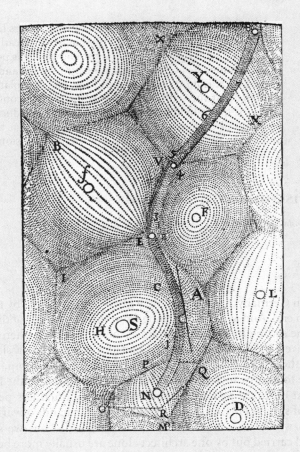

latory moment when Descartes discovered this method and its fundamental truth. It occurred when he was in the Bavarian army during the winter of 1619–1620; on one particularly cold day spent meditating in a warm room, he claims that he completed half his philosophy. In his meditations Descartes began by doubting the existence of all things and all the convictions he held about the world, seeking out any conviction that resisted such skepticism. He discovered that he could doubt everything except that he was doubting. By this process of elimination he arrived at his fundamental truth, *cogito ergo sum,* "I think, therefore I am."

By locating the source of truth in the mind or the self rather than in the external world or a divine being, Descartes changed the direction of Western thought. Instead of looking to past learning as a repository of truth, as his Renaissance predecessors had done, Descartes regarded works of the past as compilations of error. He sought truth in the mind alone. Intuition, "clear and distinct" ideas that could not be doubted, such as his *cogito ergo sum,* became the starting points from which he deduced other truths. He summarized this position in one of his twenty-one *Rules for the Direction of the Mind:* "In the subjects we propose to investigate, our inquiries should be directed, not to what others have thought, nor to what we ourselves conjecture, but to what we can clearly and perspicuously behold and with certainty deduce; for knowledge is not won in any other way." Although he began by retreating into the self and relying on his own powers of reasoning, Descartes did not end in isolation or solipsism— thinking that the self is the only reality. On the contrary, from the certainty of his individualistic starting point, he deduced the existence of God and of a material reality, and he believed that through good sense and reason others would arrive at the same conclusions.

∽ Discourse on Method

Translated by Elizabeth S. Haldane and G. R. T. Ross

FROM

PART 2

I was then in Germany, to which country I had been attracted by the wars which are not yet at an end. And as I was returning from the coronation of the Emperor to join the army, the setting in of winter detained me in a quarter where, since I found no society to divert me, while fortunately I had also no cares or passions to trouble me, I remained the whole day shut up alone in a stove-heated room, where I had complete leisure to occupy myself with my own thoughts. One of the first of the considerations that occurred to me was that there is very often less perfection in works composed of several portions, and carried out by the hands of various masters, than in those on which one individual alone has worked. Thus we see that buildings planned and carried out by one architect alone are usually more beautiful and better proportioned than those which many have tried to put in order and improve, making use of old walls which were built with other ends in view. In the same way also, those ancient cities which, originally mere villages, have become in the process of time great towns, are usually badly constructed in comparison with those which are regularly laid out on a plain by a surveyor who is free to follow his own ideas. Even though, considering their buildings each one apart, there is often as much or more display of skill in the one case than in the other, the former have large buildings and small buildings indiscriminately placed together, thus rendering the streets crooked and irregular, so that it might be said that it was chance rather than the will of men guided by reason that led to such an arrangement. And if we consider that this happens despite the fact that from all time there have been certain officials who have had the special duty of looking after the buildings of private individuals in order that they may be public ornaments, we shall understand how difficult it is to bring about much that is satisfactory in operating only upon the works of others. Thus I imagined that those people who were once half-savage, and who have become civilized only by slow degrees, merely forming their laws as the disagreeable necessities of their crimes and quarrels constrained them, could not succeed in establishing so good a system of government as those who, from the time they first came together as communities, carried into effect the constitution laid down by some prudent legislator. Thus it is quite certain that the constitution of the true Religion whose ordinances are of God alone is incomparably better regulated than any other. And, to come down to human affairs, I believe that if Sparta was very flourishing in former times, this was not because of the excellence of each and every one of its laws, seeing that many were very strange and even contrary to good morals, but because, being drawn up by one individual, they all tended towards the same end. And similarly I thought that the sciences found in books—in those at least whose reasonings are only probable and which have no demonstrations, composed as they are of the gradually accumulated opinions of many different individuals—do not approach so near to the truth as the simple reasoning which a man of common sense can quite naturally carry out respecting the things which come immediately before him. Again I thought that since we have all been children before being men, and since it has for long fallen to us to be governed by our appetites and by our teachers (who often enough contradicted one another, and none of whom perhaps counselled us always for the best), it is almost impossible that our judgments should be so excellent or solid as they should have been had we had complete use of our reason since our birth, and had we been guided by its means alone.

It is true that we do not find that all the houses in a town are rased to the ground for the sole reason that the town is to be rebuilt in another fashion, with streets made more beautiful; but at the same time we see that many people cause their own houses to be knocked down in order to rebuild them, and that sometimes they are forced so to do where there is danger of the houses falling of themselves, and when the foundations are not secure. From such examples I argued to myself that there was no plausibility in the claim of any private individual to reform a state by altering everything, and by overturning it throughout, in order to set it right again. Nor is it likewise probable that the whole body of the Sciences, or the order of teaching established by the Schools, should be reformed. But as regards all the opinions which up to this time I had embraced, I thought I could not do better than endeavour once for all to sweep them completely away, so that they might later on be replaced, either by others which were better, or by the same, when I had made them conform to the uniformity of a rational scheme. And I firmly believed that by this means I should succeed in directing my life much better than if I had only built on old foundations, and relied on principles of which I allowed myself to be in youth persuaded without having inquired into their truth. . . .

. . . My design has never extended beyond trying to reform my own opinion and to build on a foundation which is entirely my own. If my work has given me a certain satisfaction, so that I here present to you a draft of it, I do not do so because I wish to advise anybody to imitate it. Those to whom God has been most beneficent in the bestowal of His graces will perhaps form designs which are more elevated; but I fear much that this particular one will seem too venturesome for many. The simple resolve to strip oneself of all opinions and beliefs formerly received is not to be regarded as an example that each man should follow, and the world may be said to be mainly composed of two classes of minds neither of which could prudently adopt it. There are those who, believing themselves to be cleverer than they are, cannot restrain themselves from being precipitate in judgment and have not sufficient patience to arrange their thoughts in proper order; hence, once a man of this description had taken the liberty of doubting the principles he formerly accepted, and had deviated from the beaten track, he would never be able to maintain the path which must be followed to reach the appointed end more quickly, and he would hence remain wandering astray all through his life. Secondly, there are those who having reason or modesty enough to judge that they are less capable of distinguishing truth from falsehood than some others from whom instruction might be obtained, are right in contenting themselves with following the opinions of these others rather than in searching better ones for themselves . . .

Among the different branches of Philosophy, I had in my younger days to a certain extent studied Logic; and in those of Mathematics, Geometrical Analysis, and Algebra — three arts or sciences which seemed as though they ought to contribute something to the design I had in view. But in examining them I observed in respect to Logic that the syllogisms and the greater part of the other teaching served better in explaining to others those things that one knows (or like the art of Lully, in enabling one to speak without judgment of those things of which one is ignorant) than in learning what is new. And although in reality Logic contains many precepts which are very true and very good, there are at the same time mingled with them so many others which are hurtful or superfluous, that it is almost as difficult to separate the two as to draw a Diana or a Minerva out of a block of marble which is not yet roughly hewn. And as to the Analysis of the ancients and the Algebra of the moderns, besides the fact that they embrace only matters the most abstract, such as appear to have no actual use, the former is always so restricted to the consideration of symbols that it cannot exercise the Understanding without greatly fatiguing the Imagination; and in the latter one is so subjected to certain rules and formulas that the result is the construction of an art which is confused and obscure, and which embarrasses the mind, instead of a science which contributes to its cultivation. This made me feel that some other Method must be found, which, comprising the advantages of the three, is yet exempt from their faults. And as a multiplicity of laws often furnishes excuses for evil-doing, and as a State is hence much better ruled when, having but very few laws, these are most strictly observed; so, instead of the great number of precepts of which Logic is composed, I believed that I should find the four which I shall state quite sufficient, provided that I adhered to a firm and constant resolve never on any single occasion to fail in their observance.

The first of these was to accept nothing as true which I did not clearly recognise to be so: that is to say, carefully to avoid precipitation and prejudice in judgments, and to accept in them nothing more than what was presented to my mind so clearly and distinctly that I could have no occasion to doubt it.

The second was to divide up each of the difficulties which I examined into as many parts as possible, and as seemed requisite in order that it might be resolved in the best manner possible.

The third was to carry on my reflections in due order, commencing with objects that were the most simple and easy to understand, in order to rise little by little, or by degrees, to knowledge of the most complex, assuming an order, even if a fictitious one, among those which do not follow a natural sequence relatively to one another.

The last was in all cases to make enumerations so complete and reviews so general that I should be certain of having omitted nothing. . . .

I can venture to say that the exact observation of the few precepts which I had chosen gave me so much facility in sifting out all the questions embraced in these two sciences [Geometry and Algebra], that in the two or three months which I employed in examining them—commencing with the most simple and general, and making each truth that I discovered a rule for helping me to find others—not only did I arrive at the solution of many questions which I had hitherto regarded as most difficult, but, towards the end, it seemed to me that I was able to determine in the case of those of which I was still ignorant, by what means, and in how far, it was possible to solve them. In this I might perhaps appear to you to be very vain if you did not remember that having but one truth to discover in respect to each matter, whoever succeeds in finding it knows in its regard as much as can be known. It is the same as with a child, for instance, who has been instructed in Arithmetic and has made an addition according to the rule prescribed; he may be sure of having found as regards the sum of figures given to him all that the human mind can know. For, in conclusion, the Method which teaches us to follow the true order and enumerate exactly every term in the matter under investigation contains everything which gives certainty to the rules of Arithmetic.

But what pleased me most in this Method was that I was certain by its means of exercising my reason in all things, if not perfectly, at least as well as was in my power. And besides this, I felt in making use of it that my mind gradually accustomed itself to conceive of its objects more accurately and distinctly; and not having restricted this Method to any particular matter, I promised myself to apply it as usefully to the difficulties of other sciences as I had done to those of Algebra. Not that on this account I dared undertake to examine just at once all those that might present themselves; for that would itself have been contrary to the order which the Method prescribes. But having noticed that the knowledge of these difficulties must be dependent on principles derived from Philosophy in which I yet found nothing to be certain, I thought that it was requisite above all to try to establish certainty in it. I considered also that since this endeavour is the most important in all the world, and that in which precipitation and prejudice were most to be feared, I should not try to grapple with it till I had attained to a much riper age than that of three and twenty, which was the age I had reached. I thought, too, that I should first of all employ much time in preparing myself for the work by eradicating from my mind all the wrong opinions which I had up to this time accepted, and accumulating a variety of experiences fitted later on to afford matter for my reasonings, and by ever exercising myself in the Method which I had prescribed, in order more and more to fortify myself in the power of using it. . . .

FROM

PART 4

I do not know that I ought to tell you of the first meditations there made by me, for they are so metaphysical and so unusual that they may perhaps not be acceptable to everyone. And yet at the same time, in order that one may judge whether the foundations which I have laid are sufficiently secure, I find myself constrained in some measure to refer to them. For a long time I had remarked that it is sometimes requisite in common life to follow opinions which one knows to be most uncertain, exactly as though they were indisputable, as has been said above. But because in this case I wished to give myself entirely to the search after Truth, I thought that it was necessary for me to take an apparently opposite course, and to reject as absolutely false everything as to which I could imagine the least ground of doubt, in order to see if afterwards there remained anything in my belief that was entirely certain. Thus, because our senses sometimes deceive us, I wished to suppose that nothing is just as they cause us to imagine it to be; and because there are men who deceive themselves in their reasoning and fall into paralogisms, even concerning the simplest matters of geometry, and judging that I was as subject to error as was any other, I rejected as false all the reasons formerly accepted by me as demonstrations. And since all the same thoughts and conceptions which we have while awake may also come to us in sleep, without any of them being at that time true, I resolved to assume that everything that ever entered into my mind was no more true than the illusions of my dreams. But immediately afterwards I noticed that whilst I thus wished to think all things false, it was absolutely essential that the "I" who thought this should be some[thing], and remarking that this truth *I think, therefore I am* was so certain and so assured that all the most extravagant suppositions brought forward by the sceptics were incapable of shaking it, I came to the conclusion that I could receive it without scruple as the first principle of the Philosophy for which I was seeking.

And then, examining attentively that which I was, I saw that I could conceive that I had no body, and that there was no world nor place where I might be; but yet that I could not for all that conceive that I was not. On the contrary, I saw from the very fact that I thought of doubting the truth of other things, it very evidently and certainly followed that I was; on the other hand if I had only ceased from thinking, even if all the rest of what I had ever imagined had really existed, I should have no reason for thinking that I had existed. From that I knew that I was a substance the whole essence or nature of which is to think, and that for its existence there is no need of any place, nor does it depend on any material thing; so that this "me," that is to say, the soul by which I am what I am, is entirely distinct from body, and is even more easy to know than is the latter; and even if body were not, the soul would not cease to be what it is.

After this I considered generally what in a proposition is requisite in order to be true and certain; for since I had just discovered one which I knew to be such, I thought that I ought also to know in what this certainty consisted. And having remarked that there was nothing at all in the statement *I think, therefore I am* which assures me of having thereby made a true assertion, excepting that I see very clearly that to think it is necessary to be, I came to the conclusion that I might assume, as a general rule, that the things which we conceive very clearly and distinctly are all true—remembering, however, that there is some difficulty in ascertaining which are those that we distinctly conceive.

JOHN LOCKE
B. ENGLAND, 1632–1704

John Locke was born in 1632 in Somerset, England. After being tutored by his father, Locke attended Westminster School for formal training and in 1652 began studies at Christ Church, Oxford. Influenced at Oxford by Robert Boyle, the leading chemist of the time, Locke gained familiarity with the experimental method, the scientific method of employing ideas, methods, or materials that have not been tried before. After graduating from Oxford in 1656, Locke served as a tutor, a physician, and a personal representative for Anthony Ashley Cooper, first earl of Shaftesbury, making contacts with scientists, physicians, and politicians in England and in France. After the death of Cooper in 1683 and fearing reprisals for his liberal views during the turbulent period before the Glorious Revolution of 1688, Locke left England for Holland, where he worked on *Essay Concerning Human Understanding* and *Two Treatises on Government*. Upon his return he continued writing and served as commissioner with the Board of Trade and Plantations from 1697 to 1700. He died on October 28, 1704.

Locke's *Two Treatises on Government*, published in 1690, was to have a profound influence on political theory in the eighteenth century and prepared the way for the acceptance of the principles at the core of the American and French Revolutions. The first *Treatise* attacked the idea of divine right, under which kings traced their authority to God's appointment. The second *Treatise*, excerpted here, laid the foundation for the theory of natural rights. In a state of nature, all men — and Locke's use of that term refers to just men, not women — are free and equal. That state of nature guarantees men the basic rights of life, liberty, health, and property, so long as a man's actions do not infringe upon the rights of another. In a state of nature, however, some people inevitably do infringe upon another's natural rights. Hence, man enters into a civil society through what Locke calls a social contract, in which he gives up some of his freedoms in order to guarantee the preservation of as many natural rights as possible. The ruler must enforce that guarantee, and the ruler must havethe full consent of the people. If a ruler fails in that task, the people have the right to depose him (or her). Thus, Locke justified the deposition of the Stuarts and the bringing in, as he puts it, of "our great restorer, the present King William." Locke could not have foreseen, nor would he have approved of, the revolutions of the next century that his theories helped inspire.

A note on the text: The excerpt from Locke's *Second Treatise on Government* is based on the 1690 edition of the text. Spelling, punctuation, and capitalization have been normalized for contemporary readers.

> . . . [Man] is willing to join in society with others who are already united, or have a mind to unite for the mutual preservation of their lives, liberties, and estates, which I call by the general name — property.
> – JOHN LOCKE,
> *The Second Treatise on Government*

FROM

❧ The Second Treatise on Government

OF THE STATE OF NATURE

To understand political power aright and derive it from its original, we must consider what estate all men are naturally in, and that is a state of perfect freedom to order their actions, and dispose of their possessions and persons as they think fit, within the bounds of the law of nature, without asking leave or depending upon the will of any other man.

A state also of equality, wherein all the power and jurisdiction is reciprocal, no one having more than another, there being nothing more evident than that creatures of the same species and rank, promiscuously born to all the same advantages of nature and the use of the same faculties, should also be equal one amongst another, without subordination or subjection, unless the lord and master of them all should, by any manifest declaration of his will, set one above another and confer on him, by an evident and clear appointment, an undoubted right to dominion and sovereignty. . . .

But though this be a state of liberty, yet it is not a state of license; though man in that state have an uncontrollable liberty to dispose of his person or possessions, yet he has not liberty to destroy himself, or so much as any creature in his possession, but where some nobler use than its bare preservation calls for it. The state of nature has a law of nature to govern it, which obliges every one; and reason, which is that law, teaches all mankind who will but consult it, that being all equal and independent, no one ought to harm another in his life, health, liberty, or possessions. For men being all the workmanship of one omnipotent and infinitely wise Maker—all the servants of one sovereign Master, sent into the world by His order and about His business—they are His property, whose workmanship they are, made to last during His, not one another's pleasure. And, being furnished with like faculties, sharing all in one community of nature, there cannot be supposed any such subordination among us that may authorize us to destroy one another, as if we were made for one another's uses, as the inferior ranks of creatures are for ours. Every one as he is bound to preserve himself, and not to quit his station willfully, so by the like reason, when his own preservation comes not in competition, ought he as much as he can to preserve the rest of mankind, and not unless it be to do justice on an offender, take away or impair the life or what tends to be the preservation of the life, the liberty, health, limb, or goods of another. . . .

OF THE BEGINNINGS OF POLITICAL SOCIETIES

Men, being, as has been said, by nature all free, equal, and independent, no one can be put out of this estate and subjected to the political power of another without his own consent. The only way whereby anyone divests himself of his natural liberty and puts on the bonds of civil society is by agreeing with other men to join and unite into a community for their comfortable, safe, and peaceable living one amongst another, in a secure enjoyment of their properties, and a greater security against any that are not of it. This any number of men may do, because it injures not the freedom of the rest; they are left as they were in the liberty of the state of nature. When any number of men have so consented to make one community or government, they are thereby presently incorporated and make one body politic, wherein the majority have a right to act and conclude the rest. . . .

And thus every man, by consenting with others to make one body politic under one government, puts himself under an obligation to every one of that society to submit to the determination of the majority and to be concluded by it; or else this original compact whereby he with others incorporates into one society, would signify nothing. . . .

For if the consent of the majority shall not, in reason, be received as the act of the whole and conclude every individual, nothing but the consent of every individual can make anything to be the act of the whole: but such a consent is next to impossible ever to be had. . . .

OF THE ENDS OF POLITICAL SOCIETY AND GOVERNMENT

If man in the state of nature be so free as has been said, if he be absolute lord of his own person and possessions, equal to the greatest and subject to nobody, why will he part with his freedom? Why will he give up this empire and subject himself to the dominion and control of any other power? To which it is obvious to answer, that though in the state of nature he hath such a right, yet the enjoyment of it is very uncertain and constantly exposed to the invasion of others; for all being kings as much as he, every man his equal, and the greater part no strict observers of equity and justice, the enjoyment of the property he has in this state is very unsafe, very insecure. This makes him willing to quit this condition which, however free, is full of fears and continual dangers; and it is not without reason that he seeks out and is willing to join in society with others who are already united, or have a mind to unite for the mutual preservation of their lives, liberties, and estates, which I call by the general name—property.

The great and chief end, therefore, of men uniting into commonwealths, and putting themselves under government, is the preservation of their property; to which in the state of nature there are many things wanting.

First, there wants an established, settled, known law, received and allowed by common consent to be the standard of right and wrong, and the common measure to decide all controversies between them. For though the law of nature be plain and intelligible to all rational creatures, yet men, being biased by their interest, as well as ignorant for want of study of it, are not apt to allow of it as a law binding to them in the application of it to their particular cases.

Secondly, in the state of nature there wants a known and indifferent judge, with authority to determine all differences according to the established law. For every one in that state, being both judge and executioner of the law of nature, men being partial to themselves, passion and revenge is very apt to carry them too far, and with too much heat in their own cases, as well as negligence and unconcernedness, make them too remiss in other men's.

Thirdly, in the state of nature there often wants power to back and support the sentence when right and to give it due execution. They who by any injustice offend will seldom fail where they are able by force to make good their injustice. Such resistance many times makes the punishment dangerous and frequently destructive to those who attempt it.

Thus mankind, notwithstanding all the privileges of the state of nature, being but in an ill condition while they remain in it, are quickly driven into society. Hence it comes to pass that we seldom find any number of men live any time together in this state. The inconveniences that they are therein exposed to by the irregular and uncertain exercise of the power every man has of punishing the transgressions of others, make them take sanctuary under the established laws of government, and therein seek the preservation of their property. It is this makes them so willingly give up every one his single power of punishing to be exercised by such alone as shall be appointed to it amongst them, and by such rules as the community, or those authorized by them to that purpose, shall agree on. And in this we have the original right and rise of both the legislative and executive power as well as of the governments and societies themselves. . . .

But though men when they enter into society give up the equality, liberty, and executive power they had in the state of nature into the hands of the society, to be so far disposed of by the legislative as the good of the society shall require, yet it being only with an intention in every one the better to preserve himself, his liberty and property (for no rational creature can be supposed to change his condition with an intention to be worse), the power of the society or legislative constituted by them can never be supposed to extend farther than the common good, but is obliged to secure every one's property by providing against those three defects above mentioned that made the state of nature so unsafe and uneasy. And so, whoever has the legislative or supreme power of any commonwealth, is bound to govern by established standing laws, promulgated and known to the people, and not by extemporary decrees; by indifferent and upright judges, who are to decide controversies by those laws; and to employ the force of the community at home only in the execution of such laws, or abroad to prevent or redress foreign injuries and secure the community from inroads and invasion. And all this to be directed to no other end, but the peace, safety, and public good of the people.

∽ BAIEN MIURA
B. JAPAN, 1723–1789

> Baien Miura was born in 1723 on Kyushu, the southernmost island of Japan. By the time he was eighteen, he had come into contact with Western science and befriended Asada Goryu (1734–1799), the greatest contemporary mathematician and astronomer in Japan. Baien, later a physician like his father, mastered the Chinese classics and eventually extended his reputation as a philosopher throughout Japanese intellectual circles. Philosopher, economist, moralist, poet, mathematician, astronomer, and physician, he exemplified the spirit of rationalism and inquiry of his time

in his homeland. Like those of his European peers, Baien's studies and writings encompassed metaphysics, ethics, and economics. Indeed, his work *The Origin of Price* was known in Europe because his economic views were similar to those of Adam Smith, who promoted free trade and limited government influence on the economy. And like Benjamin Franklin in America, Baien was interested in practical matters; he devised a system of cooperative savings for his village. Baien died in 1789, just a year before the Act of Prohibition outlawed opposition to NEO-CONFUCIAN orthodoxy, whose ideas Baien had pushed to the limit of acceptability.

While scholars of Japanese philosophy caution against easy comparisons between Baien and the European ENLIGHTENMENT thinkers, his philosophy, like theirs, marks a significant departure from and questioning of traditional thinking. In Japan at that time, tradition meant the Confucian system of Zhu Xi, which the Tokugawa shogunate had vigorously promoted during Baien's lifetime. In the selection that follows, from "Reply to Taga Bokkei," Baien, somewhat like Descartes, argues that we must slough off the old skin of conventional learning, free ourselves from attachments to habitual understanding, and begin to see and study phenomena objectively and with no preconceptions. Baien's opinion of book learning as a guide to truth can be seen in a letter he wrote to Asada Goryu, in which he reflects on a sunset:

> I thought of the scene that had stirred me with joy and wonder. It was made up of real things, true enough, but it was at the same time far from being real. And I thought of the sayings of those philosophers and scholars whose writings are so bulky that oxen perspire pulling them and libraries are full to overflowing with them. Are they not inspired by so many evening scenes from pavilions which aroused and delighted the sense of these philosophers?

Baien advises us to rid ourselves of our assumptions and dive into the world: "In order to know objects, man must . . . put his own interests aside and enter into the world of objects; only in that way can his intellect hope to comprehend Heaven-and-earth and understand all things." Baien hoped to inspire his contemporaries to adopt a new, empirical way of investigating life.

A note on the translation: This is the Rosemary Mercer translation of Baien's scientific work. All notes are the editors'.

> If we approach each thing with an unbiased mind, then we shall see that all these things, the rising and setting of the sun and moon, the constant changes of generation and decay, the eyes by which we see, the ears by which we hear, the limbs by which we move, the very mind itself which thinks these things, cannot have a single explanation.
>
> – BAIEN MIURA, "Reply to Taga Bokki"

FROM

❧ Reply to Taga Bokkei

Translated by Rosemary Mercer

1. You ask me the meaning of "static form and dynamic flux" *(konron utsubotsu),* and indeed, as heaven-and-earth is the house of man, scholars should make heaven-and-earth the first object of their study.

It is true that since the introduction of Western science the calendrical studies of astronomy, geography, and the motions of the heavenly bodies have been studied with more and more precision, but that is all there is to it. To my knowledge not one scholar has had a deep knowledge of the *jōri*[1] of heaven and earth. Throughout the whole wide world and the infinity of ages past, countless people have pondered over heaven and earth. Heaven and earth are not concealed, but before us day and night, so how is it that no-one has seen them clearly?

1.1 It is simply because from the moment we are born we unwittingly accustom ourselves to what we see, hear, and touch, confining ourselves by habits of thought, and we do not come to doubt or question things. These attachments are the fixations of mind that Buddhists call *"jikke."*[2] If they are not removed, the function of the mind is impeded.

Ananda[3] had received enlightenment, but because he had been a monkey in his previous life, he retained the *jikke* of a monkey. That is a good allegory, for insofar as human beings analyse and speculate about phenomena with human minds, it is difficult for us to give up our human prejudices. Past and present thinkers alike have been affected by these attachments, they have painted the manifold things of heaven and earth with their human colours. It is not easy to open our eyes wide and see with far-sightedness.

Let us consider these attachments. Because human beings walk with their feet, and grasp things with their hands, attachments of thought could lead people to believe that the motions of heaven and creations of nature also require feet and hands. It could even force them to think that snakes which have no feet, and fish which have no hands, are deficient or handicapped.

Without feet, heaven turns day and night; without hands, natural creation makes flowers bloom, provides us with children, and brings forth fish and birds. If indeed we are so confined within ourselves, celestial revolutions and natural creations should be objects of great curiosity. Although our curiosity should be aroused about certain things, no-one questions them, because we see them before us from morning to evening, passing them by with total unconcern.

When one looks at a thing as the thing it is, heaven-and-earth alone is one object, water and fire are each single objects, and plants, trees, fish, and animals, as well as human beings, are each independent objects. Ourselves and others alike are each objects.

Being human we see things in relation to ourselves, a habit that we cannot readily abandon when we look at other things. It is a human habit to think of things and see things always in human terms. Look at a children's picture book about a rat's wedding, or at a book about goblins. The rats are not treated as rats in the form that we have always known them, they are made into human beings in every detail. The bridegroom wears ceremonial robes with a pair of swords, the bride wears a

---

[1] *jōri*: Sometimes translated as "natural law"; it means something like the essential nature of things, or the structure of reality. In Baien's work, *jōri* often means the way we grasp reality, how it appears to us.

[2] *"jikke"*: A Buddhist concept of the customary habits of thought that stem from or perpetuate illusions or unexamined assumptions about the world.

[3] Ananda: Or *Anan* in Japanese — one of the favorite disciples of the Buddha.

gown with a long veil and rides in a palanquin borne by footmen and soldiers, all in imitation of a human wedding. Again, when we look at a book about goblins, we find no pictures of umbrellas changed into tea mills, or brooms changed into buckets, instead we see goblins with eyes, noses, hands, and feet, everything is changed into human form. A picture of Nirvana[4] shows the dragon lord dressed exactly in human clothes, and to indicate his dragon form a helmet is drawn on his head.

When people in such a state of mind speculate about heaven and earth they believe there to be a great lord in the heavens. Upon the solid earth they believe that there are gods of wind, thunder, and suchlike, portrayed as hideous in appearance, but moving around on feet, and working with their hands. Wind is stored in a bag, and thunder is sounded from a great drum. If there were really such a bag, how would it have come to be there in the first place? If there were really a great drum, what skin could have been stretched across it? If one were to go on like this, the heavens would not be able to turn without feet, nor could natural creation work without hands.

Furthermore, to take a simple example, animals are all male or female, but plants have no sex. It is the way of animals that they require both male and female to reproduce, and it is the way of plants that they flourish despite the absence of sexes. If we were to think of other things in terms of ourselves, how could we ever understand their *ri*?[5]

To use another allegory, it is as though fire had a mind and thought about water, wondering "How does water burn things, how does it dry them?" thinking always in terms of its own attributes, never being aware of those it lacks. Conversely, if water also had a mind, when it thought about fire it might think about fire in terms of what it lacks itself. The utmost powers of the intellect and the exertions of a lifetime could be of little benefit under such conditions.

In accordance with the maxim from *I Ching*,[6] "Strive to progress by small steps," I shall tell you a simple story.

Once upon a time there was a mikado who heard of a beautiful wisteria in Sakai and had it transplanted to his palace garden. One night a beautiful maiden appeared to him in a dream, chanting mournfully "I must return to the beloved wisteria groves of Sakai." He awoke from the dream believing that the flowers were grieving for their homeland, and had the wisteria sent back.

---

[4] **Nirvana:** In Buddhism and Hinduism, the state of eternal bliss that occurs when the soul is finally liberated from the cycle of death and rebirth.

[5] *ri:* In the neo-Confucian thought of twelfth-century Chinese philosopher Zhu Xi (1130–1200), *ri* (the Japanese term), the fundamental, transcendental principle, works in tandem with *ki,* the physical force that governs all things. By Baien's time, Kaibara Ekken (1630–1714) had rejected this dualistic philosophy and argued in favor of a single principle, *seiri* or *ri,* as the natural law governing the universe.

[6] *I Ching:* The *Yi Jing,* known in English as *The Book of Changes,* is essentially a manual that describes an intricate system of divination based on different combinations of hexagrams, consisting of varied patterns of broken *(yin)* and solid *(yang)* lines. The book was produced over several centuries, dating back as far as the eleventh century B.C.E., accumulating commentaries and explanations over time, up through Confucius (551–479 B.C.E.), who added his "Ten Wings" to the work.

There are numerous such stories. Nevertheless, plants have no minds, and are not the figures that appear in dreams. It is the human heart that grieves for the homeland it has left, or sighs for days gone by. It is the movement of the human heart that attributes feelings to flowers, and composes lyrics about the commonplace. Wisteria flowers do not do these things. When we transfer our feelings to flowers which are innocent of them, we make flowers human too.

From ancient times, even the most outstanding thinkers have suffered such an affliction. Confined in a human world they have not been able to detach themselves from mankind, their sight has been obstructed, their thoughts have been fixed by habit and their minds have not been prepared to question things. If our minds are not ready to doubt or question, we could quite easily end our days in a state of stupor.

Nevertheless, it should not be said that there is nothing which makes people wonder. When they experience thunder or earthquakes, they all shake their heads and wonder what might be happening. But when I watch them do this, I wonder *why* they wonder about thunder and earthquakes. People wonder why the earth shakes, without enquiring how things are when it does not shake, or they marvel when it thunders, without enquiring how things are when there is no thunder. Doesn't this seem foolish? From the innocent moment of birth, it is inevitable that we should form habits of thought from what we see, hear, and touch, but people think they understand these things because they are familiar with them.

When I ask a person why a stone falls to the ground when it is released from my hand, he says "because it is heavy, everyone knows this." But he does not understand this thing he says he knows. He does not realise that he is speaking from habit, and to all intents he may as well be speaking in a drunken stupor.

For it is not strange things that should arouse our curiosity, but everyday things like the falling stone. That is what Confucius[7] means when he asks how we can expect to understand death when we do not understand life. People wonder what will happen to them when they die, yet they do not know how to conduct their present lives. As the saying goes, we cannot cross the next river before we have crossed this one. But people persist in worrying about the next crossing, ignoring the crossing straight before them. It is a mystery to me why they do this. Surely, before wondering whether a stone might speak we should wonder how it is that we ourselves should speak, before wondering whether a dead tree might flower, we should find out why it is that a living tree should flower.

If we approach each thing with an unbiased mind, then we shall see that all these things, the rising and setting of the sun and moon, the constant changes of generation and decay, the eyes by which we see, the ears by which we hear, the limbs by which we move, the very mind itself which thinks these things, cannot have a single

---

[7] **Confucius:** Kongfuzi (c. 551–479 B.C.E.), Chinese philosopher thought to be the source of *Analects,* a collection of aphorisms and dialogues recorded by his disciples. His teachings led to the founding of Confucianism, one of the most important moral and religious systems of thought in China and Japan, particularly as it was modified by later commentators.

explanation. When we ask about them, people answer simply that this is how things must be, and leave it at that: eyes "must" see, ears "must" hear, heavy objects "must" sink, light objects "must" float, these things are "common knowledge." By this token we should say simply that thunder roars because it must and earthquakes shake because they must. If a dead tree were to bloom it would be because it must bloom, if a stone were to speak it would be because it must speak.

Now someone who has read a little might tell us that thunder is the conflict of yin and yang,[8] but if we were to ask him what yin and yang are he would not know. In this respect the learned man is no better than the fool.

So when we try to understand heaven and earth, we begin by wondering about thunder or earthquakes, and heaven and earth become one vast area of doubt. A wild animal will hide when it is about to strike, a vulture will fold its wings when it is about to attack, so we ourselves should pause to reflect thoroughly before undertaking these enquiries. When a bow is drawn, the further the arrow hand is pulled back from the bow, the further the arrow will travel. He who has many doubts achieves understanding, he who has no doubts is like the man who shoots an arrow without drawing the bowstring well back.

People do not understand heaven and earth because they are confined to the familiar, they hold fast to their habits of thought. This means that if we are to see heaven and earth with insight, our first task is to query familiar everyday things, to regard everything we come across as an object of curiosity, and to acknowledge that we who are doubting and thinking are merely human, with human habits. . . .

If we were to rely entirely on books for knowledge, believing this knowledge to be thorough — as though the lords of creation themselves had spoken to us and things could not possibly be otherwise — we should still be relying on human habits of thought, there would be no escape.

Thus I may visit schools and speak to the masters, and because when I question them I find that they share my own ideas and attitudes, I call them educated and well informed. I ponder the relics of the past, and study the geography of distant lands, how far away they are to west or east, and a hundred other such things. For noting things beyond what I see and hear directly, and confirming other people's discoveries, books are indeed important. Nevertheless, heaven and earth are neither old nor new, ancient nor modern, they are always constant and unchanging. The fire in my fireplace is the same fire that is ten thousand miles away, the water in my bowl was the same water a thousand ages ago. Since this is so, if we try to understand heaven and earth, and to understand this fire and this water, we must first apply ourselves to the unchanging. When we consult the books beside us, we should reject anything contrary to our findings, and accept only what does agree. . . .

---

[8] **yin and yang:** A pair of interdynamic opposites derived from a dualistic system of ancient Chinese philosophy; symbolically representing the sun and the moon, *yang* is positive, active, and strong, while *yin* is negative, passive, and weak; an excess of one or the other in any aspect of life and consciousness is to be avoided.

ᘓ IMMANUEL KANT
B. PRUSSIA, 1724–1804

> A lifelong resident of Königsberg, Prussia, Immanuel Kant (1724–1804) is one of the most important philosophers of eighteenth-century Europe. The author of *The Critique of Pure Reason* (1781), *The Critique of Practical Reason* (1788), and *The Critique of Judgment* (1790) — three works that inaugurated what has been called a "Copernican Revolution in philosophy" — Kant questioned what we can know, how we know it, and how we make aesthetic and moral judgments. In these ground-breaking meditations, Kant asks what are the conditions of possibility that exist in the mind — the subject — that enable us to know? His answer, the grounds of a critical idealism, is that preexisting faculties in the mind shape our knowledge, our very apprehension, of the world. For Kant, the mind orders and classifies experience in terms of fundamental and innate categories, including space, time, quantity, quality, and modality. In contrast to empirical philosophers such as John Locke, for whom the world shaped the mind, for Kant, "The understanding is itself the lawgiver of nature." That is, the knowing subject, not the known object, is the foundation of truth. As he says, in *The Critique of Pure Reason,* the "understanding has rules which I must presuppose as being in me prior to objects being given me." Kant's transcendental idealism, which asserts the priority and even universality of the subject, exerted a powerful influence on subsequent European philosophy and became the basis for German Romantic theory and poetics.
>
> Kant's essay "What Is Enlightenment?" emphasizes the value of intellectual freedom and argues that, while one must follow the dictates and laws currently in place, one should exercise his or her judgment and reason in a public discourse aimed at transforming those laws and bringing about a more just society.

ᘓ What Is Enlightenment?

Translated by Mary J. Gregor

Enlightenment is the human being's emergence from his self-incurred minority.[1] *Minority* is inability to make use of one's own understanding without direction from another. This minority is *self-incurred* when its cause lies not in lack of understanding but in lack of resolution and courage to use it without direction from another.

---

[1] *minority:* The legal status of not being able to speak for oneself. [All notes are the editors'.]

Sapere aude![2] Have courage to make use of your *own* understanding! is thus the motto of enlightenment.

It is because of laziness and cowardice that so great a part of humankind, after nature has long since emancipated them from other people's direction (*naturaliter maiorennes*),[3] nevertheless gladly remains minors for life, and that it becomes so easy for others to set themselves up as their guardians. It is so comfortable to be a minor! If I have a book that understands for me, a spiritual advisor who has a conscience for me, a doctor who decides upon a regimen for me, and so forth, I need not trouble myself at all. I need not think, if only I can pay; others will readily undertake the irksome business for me. That by far the greatest part of humankind (including the entire fair sex) should hold the step toward majority to be not only troublesome but also highly dangerous will soon be seen to by those guardians who have kindly taken it upon themselves to supervise them; after they have made their domesticated animals dumb and carefully prevented these placid creatures from daring to take a single step without the walking cart in which they have confined them, they then show them the danger that threatens them if they try to walk alone. Now this danger is not in fact so great, for by a few falls they would eventually learn to walk; but an example of this kind makes them timid and usually frightens them away from any further attempt.

Thus it is difficult for any single individual to extricate himself from the minority that has become almost nature to him. He has even grown fond of it and is really unable for the time being to make use of his own understanding, because he was never allowed to make the attempt. Precepts and formulas, those mechanical instruments of a rational use, or rather misuse, of his natural endowments, are the ball and chain of an everlasting minority. And anyone who did throw them off would still make only an uncertain leap over even the narrowest ditch, since he would not be accustomed to free movement of this kind. Hence there are only a few who have succeeded, by their own cultivation of their spirit, in extricating themselves from minority and yet walking confidently.

But that a public should enlighten itself is more possible; indeed this is almost inevitable, if only it is left its freedom. For there will always be a few independent thinkers, even among the established guardians of the great masses, who, after having themselves cast off the yoke of minority, will disseminate the spirit of a rational valuing of one's own worth and of the calling of each individual to think for himself. What should be noted here is that the public, which was previously put under this yoke by the guardians, may subsequently itself compel them to remain under it, if the public is suitably stirred up by some of its guardians who are themselves incapable of any enlightenment; so harmful is it to implant prejudices, because they finally take their revenge on the very people who, or whose predecessors, were their authors. Thus a public can achieve enlightenment only slowly. A revolution may well bring about a falling off of personal despotism and of avaricious or tyrannical

---

[2] *Sapere aude!:* "Dare to know." Horace: Epistles 1.2.40.

[3] *naturaliter maiorennes:* Latin for "those who come of age by dint of nature."

oppression, but never a true reform in one's way of thinking; instead new prejudices will serve just as well as old ones to harness the great unthinking masses.

For this enlightenment, however, nothing is required but *freedom,* and indeed the least harmful of anything that could even be called freedom: namely, freedom to make *public use* of one's reason in all matters. But I hear from all sides the cry: *Do not argue!* The officer says: Do not argue but drill! The tax official: Do not argue but pay! The clergyman: Do not argue but believe! (Only one ruler[4] in the world says: *Argue* as much as you will and about whatever you will, *but obey!*) Everywhere there are restrictions on freedom. But what sort of restriction hinders enlightenment, and what sort does not hinder but instead promotes it? — I reply: The *public* use of one's reason must always be free, and it alone can bring about enlightenment among human beings; the *private use* of one's reason may, however, often be very narrowly restricted without this particularly hindering the progress of enlightenment. But by the public use of one's own reason I understand that use which someone makes of it *as a scholar* before the entire public of the *world of readers.* What I call the private use of reason is that which one may make of it in a certain *civil* post or office with which he is entrusted. Now, for many affairs conducted in the interest of a commonwealth a certain mechanism is necessary, by means of which some members of the commonwealth must behave merely passively, so as to be directed by the government, through an artful unanimity, to public ends (or at least prevented from destroying such ends). Here it is, certainly, impermissible to argue; instead, one must obey. But insofar as this part of the machine also regards himself as a member of a whole commonwealth, even of the society of citizens of the world, and so in his capacity of a scholar who by his writings addresses a public in the proper sense of the word, he can certainly argue without thereby harming the affairs assigned to him in part as a passive member. Thus it would be ruinous if an officer, receiving an order from his superiors, wanted while on duty to engage openly in subtle reasoning about its appropriateness or utility; he must obey. But he cannot fairly be prevented, as a scholar, from making remarks about errors in the military service and from putting these before his public for appraisal. A citizen cannot refuse to pay the taxes imposed upon him; an impertinent censure of such levies when he is to pay them may even be punished as a scandal (which could occasion general insubordination). But the same citizen does not act against the duty of a citizen when, as a scholar, he publicly expresses his thoughts about the inappropriateness or even injustice of such decrees. So too, a clergyman is bound to deliver his discourse to the pupils in his catechism class and to his congregation in accordance with the creed of the church he serves, for he was employed by it on that condition. But as a scholar he has complete freedom and is even called upon to communicate to the public all his carefully examined and well-intentioned thoughts about what is erroneous in that creed and his suggestions for a better arrangement of the religious and ecclesiastical body. And there is nothing in this that could be laid as a burden on his conscience. For what he teaches in consequence of his office as carrying out the business of the church, he represents as something with

---

[4] **one ruler:** The "enlightened monarch" Frederick the Great, King of Prussia from 1740 to 1786.

respect to which he does not have free power to teach as he thinks best, but which he is appointed to deliver as prescribed and in the name of another. He will say: Our church teaches this or that; here are the arguments it uses. He then extracts all practical uses for his congregation from precepts to which he would not himself subscribe with full conviction but which he can nevertheless undertake to deliver because it is still not altogether impossible that truth may lie concealed in them, and in any case there is at least nothing contradictory to inner religion present in them. For if he believed he had found the latter in them, he could not in conscience hold his office; he would have to resign from it. Thus the use that an appointed teacher makes of his reason before his congregation is merely a *private use;* for a congregation, however large a gathering it may be, is still only a domestic gathering; and with respect to it he, as a priest, is not and cannot be free, since he is carrying out another's commission. On the other hand as a scholar, who by his writings speaks to the public in the strict sense, that is, the world—hence a clergyman in the *public use* of his reason—he enjoys an unrestricted freedom to make use of his own reason and to speak in his own person. For that the guardians of the people (in spiritual matters) should themselves be minors is an absurdity that amounts to the perpetuation of absurdities.

But should not a society of clergymen, such as an ecclesiastical synod or a venerable classis[5] (as it calls itself among the Dutch), be authorized to bind itself by oath to a certain unalterable creed, in order to carry on an unceasing guardianship over each of its members and by means of them over the people, and even to perpetuate this? I say that this is quite impossible. Such a contract, concluded to keep all further enlightenment away from the human race forever, is absolutely null and void, even if it were ratified by the supreme power, by imperial diets and by the most solemn peace treaties. One age cannot bind itself and conspire to put the following one into such a condition that it would be impossible for it to enlarge its cognitions (especially in such urgent matters) and to purify them of errors, and generally to make further progress in enlightenment. This would be a crime against human nature, whose original vocation lies precisely in such progress; and succeeding generations are therefore perfectly authorized to reject such decisions as unauthorized and made sacrilegiously. The touchstone of whatever can be decided upon as law for a people lies in the question: whether a people could impose such a law upon itself. Now this might indeed be possible for a determinate short time, in expectation as it were of a better one, in order to introduce a certain order; during that time each citizen, particularly a clergyman, would be left free, in his capacity as a scholar, to make his remarks publicly, that is, through writings, about defects in the present institution; meanwhile, the order introduced would last until public insight into the nature of these things had become so widespread and confirmed that by the union of their voices (even if not all of them) it could submit a proposal to the crown, to take under its protection those congregations that have, perhaps in accordance with their concepts of better insight, agreed to an altered religious institution, but without hindering those that wanted to acquiesce in

---

[5] classis: The presbytery, an assembly of clergymen, elders, and theologians that functions as a governing body in the Presbyterian church.

the old one. But it is absolutely impermissible to agree, even for a single lifetime, to a permanent religious constitution not to be doubted publicly by anyone and thereby, as it were, to nullify a period of time in the progress of humanity toward improvement and make it fruitless and hence detrimental to posterity. One can indeed, for his own person and even then only for some time, postpone enlightenment in what it is incumbent upon him to know; but to renounce enlightenment, whether for his own person or even more so for posterity, is to violate the sacred right of humanity and trample it underfoot. But what a people may never decide upon for itself, a monarch may still less decide upon for a people; for his legislative authority rests precisely on this, that he unites in his will the collective will of the people. As long as he sees to it that any true or supposed improvement is consistent with civil order, he can for the rest leave it to his subjects to do what they find it necessary to do for the sake of their salvation; that is no concern of his, but it is indeed his concern to prevent any one of them from forcibly hindering others from working to the best of their ability to determine and promote their salvation. It even infringes upon his majesty if he meddles in these affairs by honoring with governmental inspection the writings in which his subjects attempt to clarify their insight, as well as if he does this from his own supreme insight, in which case he exposes himself to the reproach *Caesar non est supra grammaticos,*[6] but much more so if he demeans his supreme authority so far as to support the spiritual despotism of a few tyrants within his state against the rest of his subjects.

If it is now asked whether we at present live in an *enlightened* age, the answer is: No, but we do live in an *age of enlightenment.* As matters now stand, a good deal more is required for people on the whole to be in the position, or even able to be put into the position, of using their own understanding confidently and well in religious matters, without another's guidance. But we do have distinct intimations that the field is now being opened for them to work freely in this direction and that the hindrances to universal enlightenment or to humankind's emergence from its self-incurred minority are gradually becoming fewer. In this regard this age is the age of enlightenment or the century of Frederick.[7]

A prince who does not find it beneath himself to say that he considers it his *duty* not to prescribe anything to human beings in religious matters but to leave them complete freedom, who thus even declines the arrogant name of *tolerance,* is himself enlightened and deserves to be praised by a grateful world and by posterity as the one who first released the human race from minority, at least from the side of government, and left each free to make use of his own reason in all matters of conscience. Under him, venerable clergymen, notwithstanding their official duties, may in their capacity as scholars freely and publicly lay before the world for examination their judgments and insights deviating here and there from the creed adopted, and still more may any other who is not restricted by any official duties. This spirit of freedom is also spreading abroad, even where it has to struggle with external obstacles of a government which misunderstands itself. For it shines as an example to such a government that in

---

[6] *Caesar non est supra grammaticos:* "Caesar is not above the grammarians."

[7] **Frederick:** Frederick the Great; see note 4.

freedom there is not the least cause for anxiety about public concord and the unity of the commonwealth. People gradually work their way out of barbarism of their own accord if only one does not intentionally contrive to keep them in it.

I have put the main point of enlightenment, of people's emergence from their self-incurred minority, chiefly in *matters of religion* because our rulers have no interest in playing guardian over their subjects with respect to the arts and sciences and also because that minority, being the most harmful, is also the most disgraceful of all. But the frame of mind of a head of state who favors the first goes still further and sees that even with respect to his *legislation* there is no danger in allowing his subjects to make *public* use of their own reason and to publish to the world their thoughts about a better way of formulating it, even with candid criticism of that already given; we have a shining example of this, in which no monarch has yet surpassed the one whom we honor.

But only one who, himself enlightened, is not afraid of phantoms, but at the same time has a well-disciplined and numerous army ready to guarantee public peace, can say what a free state may not dare to say: *Argue as much as you will and about what you will; only obey!* Here a strange, unexpected course is revealed in human affairs, as happens elsewhere too if it is considered in the large, where almost everything is paradoxical. A greater degree of civil freedom seems advantageous to a people's freedom of *spirit* and nevertheless puts up insurmountable barriers to it; a lesser degree of the former, on the other hand, provides a space for the latter to expand to its full capacity. Thus when nature has unwrapped, from under this hard shell, the seed for which she cares most tenderly, namely the propensity and calling to *think* freely, the latter gradually works back upon the mentality of the people (which thereby gradually becomes capable of *freedom* in acting) and eventually even upon the principles of *government,* which finds it profitable to itself to treat the human being, *who is now more than a machine,* in keeping with his dignity.

Königsberg in Prussia, 30th September, 1784

☙ THOMAS JEFFERSON
B. UNITED STATES, 1743–1826

Thomas Jefferson was a man of enormous intellectual ability and tremendous breadth whose interests ranged from the theoretical to the practical. At various times during his lifetime he was a scientist, an architect, a philosopher, a statesman, a farmer, a politician. Jefferson was also a product of his age; as much as any American of his time, he embodied the optimistic spirit of the Enlightenment. He believed in the common sense of individuals and thought that citizens could best govern themselves, provided they had access to free education and support of democratic institutions. He wrote treatises on political theory, scientific agriculture, and

Thomas Jefferson
A Philosopher a Patriote and a Friend
Dessine par son Ami Tadee Kosciusko
Et Grave par M.ʳ Sobolewicz.

Thaddeus Kosciusko, *Portrait of Thomas Jefferson.* Aquatint Kosciusko, a Polish general who offered his services to the American Revolution, here portrays Jefferson in the style of a classical Greek philosopher, looking to the heavens and wearing a wreath on his head. The inscription below his portrait reads, "A Philosopher a Patriot and a Friend." (The Pierpont Morgan Library/Art Resource, NY)

Again and again Jefferson urged that the people be educated and informed through a broad common-school system and a free press. Although he had small faith in the power of republics to resist corruption and decay, he hoped that mass education would stem this degenerative process.

— RICHARD HOFSTADTER, 1948

Anglo-Saxon grammar, and he designed his beautiful home at Monticello and the halls of the University of Virginia.

Jefferson became governor of Virginia in 1779 and founded the University of Virginia in 1819. Before his political career was finished he succeeded Benjamin Franklin[1] as a minister to France (1785), served as the first U.S. Secretary of State (1790–93), the second vice-president of the United States (1797–1801), and its third president (1801–09). His one book, *Notes on the State of Virginia* (1782), is a compendium of personal and scientific observations about Virginia's landscape and people as well as observations on slavery, race, environment, and revolution. Jefferson is best remembered, however, for the Declaration of Independence (1776), a document of stunning rhetorical power and clarity.

In the spring of 1776, as the war with England heated up and Thomas Paine's[2] pamphlet, *Common Sense,* was preaching the politics of

---

[1] Benjamin Franklin (1706–1790): Scientist, publisher, and inventor who served the United States as a diplomat in Great Britain and France.

[2] Thomas Paine (1737–1809): Libertarian English writer who worked for the American colonies during the American Revolution.

independence, the Second Continental Congress appointed a committee of five to draft a formal declaration of independence. Although the committee as a whole generated the ideas and Franklin and John Adams[3] edited the work, Jefferson was largely responsible for the first version of the document. It was written in the tradition of the English Bill of Rights (1689), which defines the limits of the monarchy and enumerates certain inviolable political and civil rights of the English citizenry. It was not simply a declaration of independence; it was a succinct philosophical statement defending the principles by which such an act of separation might take place, justifying the American Revolution. The document is organized in three parts: a statement of the rational basis for having and supporting government; a detailed description of the abuses of the English government; and a logical, inevitable conclusion that independence is right and necessary. The Declaration of Independence is a splendid example of a philosophical manifesto put into practice as a basis for a Constitution and new form of democratic government. Jefferson died on the fiftieth anniversary of its signing, July 4, 1826.

> His attachment to those of his friends whom he could make useful to himself was thoroughgoing and exemplary.
>
> – JOHN QUINCY ADAMS, Diary, 1836

∾ Declaration of Independence

IN CONGRESS, JULY 4, 1776

The Unanimous Declaration of the Thirteen United States of America

When in the Course of human events, it becomes necessary for one people to dissolve the political bands which have connected them with another, and to assume among the Powers of the earth, the separate and equal station to which the Laws of Nature and of Nature's God entitle them, a decent respect to the opinions of mankind requires that they should declare the causes which impel them to the separation.

We hold these truths to be self-evident, that all men are created equal, that they are endowed by their Creator with certain unalienable Rights, that among these are Life, Liberty and the pursuit of Happiness. That to secure these rights, Governments are instituted among Men, deriving their just powers from the consent of the governed. That whenever any Form of Government becomes destructive of these ends, it is the Right of the People to alter or to abolish it, and to institute a new Government, laying its foundation on such principles and organizing its powers in such form, as to them shall seem most likely to effect their Safety and Happiness. Prudence, indeed, will dictate that Governments long established should not be changed for light and transient causes; and accordingly all experience hath shown, that mankind are more disposed to suffer, while evils are sufferable, than to right

---

[3] John Adams (1735–1826): Delegate to the Second Continental Congress and member of the committee responsible for drafting the Declaration of Independence. He became the second president of the United States (1797–1801).

themselves by abolishing the forms to which they are accustomed. But when a long train of abuses and usurpations, pursuing invariably the same Object evinces a design to reduce them under absolute Despotism, it is their right, it is their duty, to throw off such Government, and to provide new Guards for their future security. — Such has been the patient sufferance of these Colonies; and such is now the necessity which constrains them to alter their former Systems of Government. The history of the present King of Great Britain is a history of repeated injuries and usurpations, all having in direct object the establishment of an absolute Tyranny over these States. To prove this, let Facts be submitted to a candid world.

He has refused his Assent to Laws, the most wholesome and necessary for the public good.

He has forbidden his Governors to pass Laws of immediate and pressing importance, unless suspended in their operation till his Assent should be obtained; and when so suspended, he has utterly neglected to attend to them.

He has refused to pass other laws for the accommodation of large districts of people, unless those people would relinquish the right of Representation in the Legislature, a right inestimable to them and formidable to tyrants only.

He has called together legislative bodies at places unusual, uncomfortable, and distant from the depository of their Public Records, for the sole purpose of fatiguing them into compliance with his measures.

He has dissolved Representative Houses repeatedly, for opposing with manly firmness his invasions on the rights of the people.

He has refused for a long time, after such dissolutions, to cause others to be elected; whereby the Legislative Powers, incapable of Annihilation, have returned to the People at large for their exercise; the State remaining in the mean time exposed to all the dangers of invasion from without, and convulsions within.

He has endeavoured to prevent the population of these States; for that purpose obstructing the Laws for Naturalization of Foreigners; refusing to pass others to encourage their migration hither, and raising the conditions of new Appropriations of Lands.

He has obstructed the Administration of Justice, by refusing his Assent to Laws for establishing Judiciary Powers.

He has made Judges dependent on his Will alone, for the tenure of their offices, and the amount and payment of their salaries.

He has erected a multitude of New Offices, and sent hither swarms of Officers to harass our People, and eat out their substance.

He has kept among us, in times of peace, Standing Armies without the Consent of our legislature.

He has affected to render the Military independent of and superior to the Civil Power.

He has combined with others to subject us to a jurisdiction foreign to our constitution, and unacknowledged by our laws; giving his Assent to their acts of pretended Legislation:

For quartering large bodies of armed troops among us:

William Stone, Engraving of the Declaration of Independence, 1823

(Courtesy of the National Archives)

For protecting them, by a mock Trial, from Punishment for any Murders which they should commit on the Inhabitants of these States:

For cutting off our Trade with all parts of the world:

For imposing taxes on us without our Consent:

For depriving us in many cases, of the benefits of Trial by Jury:

For transporting us beyond Seas to be tried for pretended offences:

For abolishing the free System of English Laws in a neighbouring Province, establishing therein an Arbitrary government, and enlarging its Boundaries so as to render it at once an example and fit instrument for introducing the same absolute rule into these Colonies:

For taking away our Charters, abolishing our most valuable Laws, and altering fundamentally the Forms of our Governments:

For suspending our own Legislatures, and declaring themselves invested with Power to legislate for us in all cases whatsoever.

He has abdicated Government here, by declaring us out of his Protection and waging War against us.

He has plundered our seas, ravaged our Coasts, burnt our towns, and destroyed the lives of our people.

He is at this time transporting large armies of foreign mercenaries to compleat the works of death, desolation and tyranny, already begun with circumstances of Cruelty & perfidy scarcely parallel'd in the most barbarous ages, and totally unworthy the Head of a civilized nation.

He has constrained our fellow Citizens taken Captive on the High Seas to bear Arms against their Country, to become the executioners of their friends and Brethren, or to fall themselves by their Hands.

He has excited domestic insurrections amongst us, and has endeavoured to bring on the inhabitants of our frontiers, the merciless Indian Savages, whose known rule of warfare, is an undistinguished destruction of all ages, sexes and conditions.

In every stage of these Oppressions We have Petitioned for Redress in the most humble terms: Our repeated Petitions have been answered only by repeated injury. A Prince, whose character is thus marked by every act which may define a Tyrant, is unfit to be the ruler of a free People.

Nor have We been wanting in attention to our British brethren. We have warned them from time to time of attempts by their legislature to extend an unwarrantable jurisdiction over us. We have reminded them of the circumstances of our emigration and settlement here. We have appealed to their native justice and magnanimity, and we have conjured them by the ties of our common kindred to disavow these usurpations, which, would inevitably interrupt our connections and correspondence. They too have been deaf to the voice of justice and of consanguinity. We must, therefore, acquiesce in the necessity, which denounces our Separation, and hold them, as we hold the rest of mankind, Enemies in War, in Peace Friends.

We, therefore, the Representatives of the united States of America, in General Congress, Assembled, appealing to the Supreme Judge of the world for the rectitude of our intentions, do, in the Name, and by Authority of the good People of these Colonies, solemnly publish and declare, That these United Colonies are, and of

Right ought to be Free and Independent States, that they are Absolved from all Allegiance to the British Crown, and that all political connection between them and the State of Great Britain, is and ought to be totally dissolved; and that as Free and Independent States, they have full Power to levy War, conclude Peace, contract Alliances, establish Commerce, and to do all other Acts and Things which Independent States may of right do. And for the support of this Declaration, with a firm reliance on the Protection of Divine Providence, we mutually pledge to each other our Lives, our Fortunes and our sacred Honor.

✸ MARY WOLLSTONECRAFT
B. *ENGLAND, 1759–1797*

Mary Wollstonecraft was born in 1759 in London, where she received a formal education and was called on to help support her family, whose modest fortunes her father had lost. After nursing her dying mother, at the age of nineteen Wollstonecraft founded a school for girls in Islington and then another in Newington Green, where Dr. Richard Price encouraged the inquisitive and intelligent woman to read the works of the ENLIGHTENMENT philosophers. After unhappy relationships with the painter Henry Fuseli and the American entrepreneur and gambler Gilbert Imlay, Wollstonecraft eventually married William Godwin, the most respected radical philosopher of the time and author of the important *Enquiry Concerning Political Justice* (1793). In addition to treatises on women's rights, Wollstonecraft wrote books on the French Revolution, education, and travel as well as two novels. She died in September 1797, about ten days after giving birth to Mary Wollstonecraft Godwin, later Mary Shelley, the author of *Frankenstein*.

Wollstonecraft's first work, *Thoughts on the Education of Daughters* (1786), promoting an enlightened view of education for women, paved the way for *A Vindication of the Rights of Woman* (1792), a full-blown critique of education for women and a defense of women's rights. Although the way had been partially prepared in England by Mary Astell's *Some Reflections upon Marriage* (1700) and Catherine Macaulay's *Letters on Education* (1790), Wollstonecraft's treatise pointed more directly to the blatant injustice of the present "false system of education" for women, particularly the kind of education advocated in Jean Jacques Rousseau's *Émile*. Wollstonecraft attacks Rousseau's ideal woman, Sophy, arguing that she is a model for no more than a man's plaything—trained in superficial conversation, shallow thinking, and frivolous accomplishments. For Wollstonecraft, Sophy symbolizes a false ideal of woman subordinated to wrong-headed social conventions and education that makes women into "alluring objects for the moment"—toys for the amusement and titillation of men. Such women not only become subordinate to and dependent on men for their economic and social standing, but they are prevented from

> Let woman share the rights and she will emulate the virtues of man; for she must grow more perfect when emancipated, or justify the authority that chains such a weak being to her duty.
>
> – MARY WOLLSTONECRAFT, *A Vindication of the Rights of Woman*

John Opie, *Mary Wollstonecraft,* c. 1790–91
This portrait was painted when Wollstonecraft was thirty-one or thirty-two years old. (Tate Gallery, London/Art Resource)

developing into capable and contributing citizens. Cultivated as ornamental objects, women cannot form rational friendships with or earn the respect of their husbands, who, as a result, turn to affairs with younger women when their wives lose their "charms." Wollstonecraft asserts that women must receive an education that will prepare them to build marriages based not on subordination and passion, as Rousseau would have it, but on equal partnership and levelheaded friendship with men.

A Vindication of the Rights of Woman elicited a strong reaction from many conservative writers, who attacked Wollstonecraft's character and free thinking. After her untimely death, her husband added fuel to this fire by publishing, rather naively, a candid biography of her life, *Memoirs of the Author of "A Vindication of the Rights of Woman."* Eventually Wollstonecraft found sympathetic readers among the budding feminist writers of the nineteenth century, including the English writers Mary Hays and Mary Ann Evans (George Eliot), and the American feminists Lucretia Mott and Elizabeth Cady Stanton, who organized the first women's rights convention in Seneca Falls, New York, in 1848 (see p. 1063).

A note on the text: Wollstonecraft's spelling and punctuation have been modernized. All notes are the editors' unless otherwise indicated.

FROM

ಬ A Vindication of the Rights of Woman

INTRODUCTION TO THE FIRST EDITION

After considering the historic page, and viewing the living world with anxious solicitude, the most melancholy emotions of sorrowful indignation have depressed my spirits, and I have sighed when obliged to confess, that either nature has made a great difference between man and man, or that the civilization which has hitherto taken place in the world has been very partial. I have turned over various books written on the subject of education, and patiently observed the conduct of parents and the management of schools; but what has been the result?—a profound conviction that the neglected education of my fellow-creatures is the grand source of the misery I deplore; and that women, in particular, are rendered weak and wretched by a variety of concurring causes, originating from one hasty conclusion. The conduct and manners of women, in fact, evidently prove that their minds are not in a healthy state; for, like the flowers which are planted in too rich a soil, strength and usefulness are sacrificed to beauty; and the flaunting leaves, after having pleased a fastidious eye, fade, disregarded on the stalk, long before the season when they ought to have arrived at maturity. One cause of this barren blooming I attribute to a false system of education, gathered from the books written on this subject by men who, considering females rather as women than human creatures, have been more anxious to make them alluring mistresses than affectionate wives and rational mothers; and the understanding of the sex has been so bubbled by this specious homage, that the civilized women of the present century, with a few exceptions, are only anxious to inspire love, when they ought to cherish a nobler ambition, and by their abilities and virtues exact respect.

In a treatise, therefore, on female rights and manners, the works which have been particularly written for their improvement must not be overlooked; especially when it is asserted, in direct terms, that the minds of women are enfeebled by false refinement; that the books of instruction, written by men of genius, have had the same tendency as more frivolous productions; and that, in the true style of Mahometanism, they are treated as a kind of subordinate beings, and not as a part of the human species, when improveable reason is allowed to be the dignified distinction which raises men above the brute creation, and puts a natural sceptre in a feeble hand.

Yet, because I am a woman, I would not lead my readers to suppose that I mean violently to agitate the contested question respecting the quality or inferiority of the sex; but as the subject lies in my way, and I cannot pass it over without subjecting the main tendency of my reasoning to misconstruction, I shall stop a moment to deliver, in a few words, my opinion. In the government of the physical world it is observable that the female in point of strength is, in general, inferior to the male. This is the law of nature; and it does not appear to be suspended or abrogated in favour of woman. A degree of physical superiority cannot, therefore, be denied—and it is a noble prerogative! But not content with this natural pre-eminence, men endeavour to sink us still lower, merely to render us alluring objects for a moment; and women, intoxicated by the adoration which men, under the influence of their senses, pay them, do not seek to obtain a durable interest in their hearts, or to become the friends of the fellow creatures who find amusement in their society.

I am aware of an obvious inference: — from every quarter have I heard exclamations against masculine women; but where are they to be found? If by this appellation men mean to inveigh against their ardour in hunting, shooting, and gaming, I shall most cordially join in the cry; but if it be against the imitation of manly virtues, or, more properly speaking, the attainment of those talents and virtues, the exercise of which ennobles the human character, and which raise females in the scale of animal being, when they are comprehensively termed mankind; — all those who view them with a philosophic eye must, I should think, wish with me, that they may every day grow more and more masculine.

This discussion naturally divides the subject. I shall first consider women in the grand light of human creatures, who, in common with men, are placed on this earth to unfold their faculties; and afterwards I shall more particularly point out their peculiar designation.

I wish also to steer clear of an error which many respectable writers have fallen into; for the instruction which has hitherto been addressed to women, has rather been applicable to *ladies,* if the little indirect advice, that is scattered through Sandford and Merton,[1] be excepted; but, addressing my sex in a firmer tone, I pay particular attention to those in the middle class, because they appear to be in the most natural state. Perhaps the seeds of false refinement, immorality, and vanity, have ever been shed by the great. Weak, artificial beings, raised above the common wants and affections of their race, in a premature unnatural manner, undermine the very foundation of virtue, and spread corruption through the whole mass of society! As a class of mankind they have the strongest claim to pity; the education of the rich tends to render them vain and helpless, and the unfolding mind is not strengthened by the practice of those duties which dignify the human character. They only live to amuse themselves, and by the same law which in nature invariably produces certain effects, they soon only afford barren amusement.

But as I purpose taking a separate view of the different ranks of society, and of the moral character of women, in each, this hint is, for the present, sufficient; and I have only alluded to the subject, because it appears to me to be the very essence of an introduction to give a cursory account of the contents of the work it introduces.

My own sex, I hope, will excuse me, if I treat them like rational creatures, instead of flattering their *fascinating* graces, and viewing them as if they were in a state of perpetual childhood, unable to stand alone. I earnestly wish to point out in what true dignity and human happiness consists — I wish to persuade women to endeavour to acquire strength, both of mind and body, and to convince them that the soft

---

[1] **Sandford and Merton:** *The History of Sandford and Merton* (1783–89), a popular children's book by Thomas Day.

phrases, susceptibility of heart, delicacy of sentiment, and refinement of taste, are almost synonymous with epithets of weakness, and that those beings who are only the objects of pity and that kind of love, which has been termed its sister, will soon become objects of contempt.

Dismissing, then, those pretty feminine phrases, which the men condescendingly use to soften our slavish dependence, and despising that weak elegancy of mind, exquisite sensibility, and sweet docility of manners, supposed to be the sexual characteristics of the weaker vessel, I wish to show that elegance is inferior to virtue, that the first object of laudable ambition is to obtain a character as a human being, regardless of the distinction of sex; and that secondary views should be brought to this simple touchstone.

This is a rough sketch of my plan; and should I express my conviction with the energetic emotions that I feel whenever I think of the subject, the dictates of experience and reflection will be felt by some of my readers. Animated by this important object, I shall disdain to cull my phrases or polish my style;—I aim at being useful, and sincerity will render me unaffected; for, wishing rather to persuade by the force of my arguments, than dazzle by the elegance of my language, I shall not waste my time in rounding periods, or in fabricating the turgid bombast of artificial feelings, which, coming from the head, never reach the heart. I shall be employed about things, not words! and, anxious to render my sex more respectable members of society, I shall try to avoid that flowery diction which has slided from essays into novels, and from novels into familiar letters and conversation.

These pretty superlatives, dropping glibly from the tongue, vitiate the taste, and create a kind of sickly delicacy that turns away from simple unadorned truth; and a deluge of false sentiments and overstretched feelings, stifling the natural emotions of the heart, render the domestic pleasures insipid, that ought to sweeten the exercise of those severe duties, which educate a rational and immortal being for a nobler field of action.

The education of women has, of late, been more attended to than formerly; yet they are still reckoned a frivolous sex, and ridiculed or pitied by the writers who endeavour by satire or instruction to improve them. It is acknowledged that they spend many of the first years of their lives in acquiring a smattering of accomplishments; meanwhile strength of body and mind are sacrificed to libertine notions of beauty, to the desire of establishing themselves,—the only way women can rise in the world,—by marriage. And this desire making mere animals of them, when they marry they act as such children may be expected to act:—they dress; they paint, and nickname God's creatures. Surely these weak beings are only fit for a seraglio!—Can they be expected to govern a family with judgment, or take care of the poor babes whom they bring into the world?

If then it can be fairly deduced from the present conduct of the sex, from the prevalent fondness for pleasure which takes place of ambition and those nobler passions that open and enlarge the soul; that the instruction which women have hitherto received has only tended with the constitution of civil society, to render them insignificant objects of desire—mere propagators of fools!—if it can be proved that in aiming to accomplish them, without cultivating their understandings, they are taken out of their sphere of duties, and made ridiculous and useless when the short-lived bloom of beauty is over,[2] I presume that *rational* men will excuse me for endeavouring to persuade them to become more masculine and respectable.

Indeed the word *masculine* is only a bugbear: there is little reason to fear that women will acquire too much courage or fortitude; for their apparent inferiority with respect to bodily strength, must render them, in some degree, dependent on men in the various relations of life; but why should it be increased by prejudices that give a sex to virtue, and confound simple truths with sensual reveries?

Women are, in fact, so much degraded by mistaken notions of female excellence, that I do not mean to add a paradox when I assert, that this artificial weakness produces a propensity to tyrannize, and gives birth to cunning, the natural opponent of strength, which leads them to play off those contemptible infantine airs that undermine esteem even whilst they excite desire. Let men become more chaste and modest, and if women do not grow wiser in the same ratio, it will be clear that they have weaker understandings. It seems scarcely necessary to say, that I now speak of the sex in general. Many individuals have more sense than their male relatives; and, as nothing preponderates where there is a constant struggle for an equilibrium, without it has naturally more gravity, some women govern their husbands without degrading themselves, because intellect will always govern.

---

[2] A lively writer, I cannot recollect his name, asks what business women turned of forty have to do in the world? [Wollstonecraft's note.]

∞ JEAN-JACQUES ROUSSEAU
B. FRANCE, 1712–1778

Often considered a precursor to and certainly one of the greatest influences on the European Romantic movement, Jean-Jacques Rousseau rediscovered (if not reinvented) the inner life for an era otherwise occupied with external accomplishments and achievements. While other philosophers sought to promote, through the corrosive acid of SATIRE, a more humane and just society that acted in accordance with the tenets of reason, Rousseau found the seat of humanity and justice in the record of his own life, in the history of the growth of his own reason and feelings. The *Confessions,* written between 1765 and 1770 but published posthumously from 1781 to 1788, records Rousseau's tortuous journey into the depths of his being, his pilgrimage to the childhood origins of the self. For Lord Byron,[1] the great English Romantic poet, Rousseau was the "apostle of affliction" who "threw / Enchantment over passion, and from woe / Wrung overwhelming eloquence" (*Childe Harold* III, Canto 77). In recording these thoughts about sentiment and feeling, Rousseau exerted an influence on Western thought that still informs our discussions of art, literature, politics, society, and human nature.

Separation from Family. Rousseau was born in Geneva in 1712, the son of Isaac Rousseau, a watchmaker who was exiled when Jean-Jacques was ten years old, and Susanne Bernard, who died a few days after the boy's birth. His father introduced Jean-Jacques at a young age to the contemporary novels his mother had left behind and then to the classics, and to this reading Rousseau attributes the birth of his intensity of feeling. Upon Isaac's exile, father and son were separated, and Jean-Jacques moved in with his uncle, who set him up as an engraver's apprentice. After three unhappy years, in March 1728 the young man rather impulsively left Geneva, beginning a brief period of vagabondage through Europe, taking up jobs ranging from footman to tutor.

Citizen of Geneva. Ending up eventually in Turin, Rousseau converted to Catholicism and moved in with thirty-year-old Madame de Warens, with whom he lived at Chambery and at her country house at Les Charmettes until 1742. During these years Rousseau continued his self-education, keeping extensive notes on a wide range of subjects, including science, mathematics, astronomy, and music. In 1742 Rousseau left for Paris, where he received the patronage of Madame Dupin, among others; fell in love with Thérèse Levasseur (among others), a laundress whom he would eventually marry; met Denis Diderot and Jean Le Rond d'Alembert, the editors of the

Maurice-Quentin de La Tour, Detail from *Portrait of Jean-Jacques Rousseau.* Pastel *A portrait of the philosopher as a young man. (Giraudon / Art Resource, NY)*

www For links to more information about Rousseau, a quiz on *Confessions,* and information about the 21st-century relevance of *Confessions,* see bedfordstmartins .com/worldlit compact.

---

[1] **Lord Byron:** George Gordon, Lord Byron (1788–1824), celebrated English Romantic poet, known for his creation of the Byronic hero, a gloomy, self-tormented outcast whose heroic desire and defiance of authority give him a dubious freedom (see pp. 722, 759).

Encyclopedia; and took up his writing in great earnest. In 1750, at the age of thirty-eight, he earned a prize from the Academy of Dijon for his *Discourse on the Sciences and Arts* and began making a name for himself as a writer of plays and operas, especially *The Village Soothsayer,* performed first in 1752. Two years later, while visiting Geneva, Rousseau converted back to Protestantism. Over the next decade, the "Citizen of Geneva," as Rousseau sometimes called himself, penned a succession of important philosophical treatises, works of criticism, and fiction, including *Discourse on Inequality* (1755), *Julie, or the New Heloise* (1761), *The Social Contract* (1762), and *Émile* (1762). In *Letter to d'Alembert on Plays* (1758), an important work that would set Rousseau apart from Voltaire and other *philosophes,* Rousseau rejected Voltaire's plan to bring a theater to Geneva. Defending the prohibition of theaters in Geneva, he argued that drama corrupts its audiences and wastes money.

But by 1762, Rousseau had written *Émile* and *The Social Contract,* pitting himself against the authorities. His demand in these works for individual liberties, his indictment of government and European civilization for inevitably corrupting the innate goodness of human beings, and his ideas for political reform exceeded the tolerance of those in power. On June 9, 1762, the Parlement of Paris issued a warrant for Rousseau's arrest, and ten days later the Advisory Council of Geneva banned and burned both books.

Exile.   Rousseau's flight from Paris only began a pattern of persecution and expulsion that took him across Europe — from Motiers, a territory in Prussia, to the Isle of Saint-Pierre; back to Paris, where he assumed various aliases; to England on the invitation of the philosopher David Hume; and finally back to Paris, where he was allowed to remain from 1770 until his death in 1778, even though the order for his arrest was not rescinded. In his last years he wrote the moving and troubled *Reveries of a Solitary Walker* (1782), in which he attempts to vindicate his life and work to posterity. This work records the isolation and alienation brought on by years of persecution and hostile criticism.

Rousseau's *Julie* "changed the ways in which people thought and felt and acted."

– MAURICE CRANSTON, *The Noble Savage: Jean-Jacques Rousseau,* 1991

Society and Feeling.   *Discourse on Inequality* and *Discourse on Political Economy,* both published in 1755, as well as *The Social Contract,* focus on the place of the individual in society and the means by which corrupt systems of government, education, and culture erode the basic goodness of human beings. In the novels *Julie, or the New Heloise* and *Émile* Rousseau again addresses the corruption of human beings by government and civilization, emphasizing the role that nature and feeling play in the development of the self. In his novels, as in his other writings, he upholds the virtues of childhood innocence, contemplative communication with nature, and the perfectibility of society. Rousseau's ideas became a part of and some would say inaugurated European **ROMANTICISM**, and many European writers of the early nineteenth century followed in Rousseau's footsteps, setting off along an inner path in search of a self that could transcend or escape the effects of social conditioning and acculturation.

The *Confessions*.   A revolutionary work of self-reflection and self-invention, *Confessions* covers Rousseau's life through 1766, when he went to England to begin working on his autobiography in earnest. Although he completed the manuscript in 1770, *Confessions* was not published until after his death in 1778. The work appeared in two parts: Books 1 through 6 in 1781; Books 7 through 12 in 1788. The first chapter from *Confessions* is characteristic of the whole in its unabashed revelation of intimate details, its bold claims to honesty, if not accuracy, and its not always successful negotiation between narcissism and humility. This last feature of the work often presents difficulties for some readers, who, unconvinced by Rousseau's claims, find him mired in self-pity and even arrogance. Full disclosure of one's personal life, however, always invites such criticism, and even Benjamin Franklin's *Autobiography,* in which Franklin avoids discussing the intimate details of his personal life, often walks a fine line between self-invention and self-revelation, vanity and sincerity. Certainly Rousseau's autobiography anticipates, perhaps even initiates, the movement toward the self-conscious display of emotion and the confessional mode of Romantic and post-Romantic European writing of the next two centuries. The *Confessions* parades before its readers a succession of errors, misfortunes, and misdeeds. Ironically, perhaps, Rousseau presents these faults to show that he is at heart a man of virtue and sensitivity, that truth and goodness are woven into the very fabric of his being. So far as the actual details of incidents in his life go, Rousseau admits to imprecision; but he argues that he cares more to present a record of his feelings than an account of events.

Although some note a certain disingenuousness in the autobiography, Rousseau's *Confessions* introduced to the Age of Enlightenment "the man of feeling," a person who attempts to bring the mind into balance with the heart through self-reflection, acts of compassion, and an appreciation of the delicate interplay of emotion involved in human relationships. Yet, like other Enlightenment writers who satirize the affectation and hypocrisy of their age, Rousseau distinguishes between true feeling and artificial manners. A key concept in his work is *amour propre,* or the love of social approval. Governed by *amour propre,* he says, a person loses touch with his or her true self, for his or her actions and manners are oriented toward winning the approval and respect of others. Thus, marking a transition between the Enlightenment and the age of Romanticism, Rousseau seeks in *Confessions* and other writings to achieve a kind of transparency of the self, to express the true rather than the false self. *Confessions* in particular purports to be the "artless" record of the life and feelings of a man who was essentially honest and innately good, despite the faults and errors that clutter the course of his life. In this regard, Rousseau's autobiography may be usefully compared to St. Augustine's;[2] but whereas Augustine attributes his essential goodness and salvation to the grace of God, Rousseau finds the source of his goodness in human nature itself.

> The real object of my *Confessions* is, to contribute to an accurate knowledge of my inner being in all the different situations of my life.
>
> – ROUSSEAU, *Confessions*

---

[2] **St. Augustine** (354–430 C.E.): The Bishop of Hippo, who became one of the most influential theologians of the Christian church through his writings, the spiritual autobiography *Confessions* (397–400) and *The City of God* (412–26). (See Augustine, Volume 1.)

■ **FURTHER RESEARCH**

Biography

Cranston, Maurice. *The Noble Savage: Jean-Jacques Rousseau.* 1991.
——. *The Solitary Self: Jean-Jacques Rousseau in Exile and Adversity.* 1997.
Guéhenno, Jean. *Jean-Jacques.* 1948–52.
Winwar, Frances. *Jean-Jacques Rousseau: Conscience of an Era.* 1983.

Criticism

France, Peter. *Rousseau,* Confessions. 1987.
Kavanaugh, Thomas M. *Writing the Truth: Authority and Desire in the Works of Rousseau.* 1987.
Kelly, Christopher. *Rousseau's Exemplary Life: The* Confessions *as Political Philosophy.* 1987.
——. *Rousseau as Author: Consecrating One's Life to Truth.* 2003.
Shklar, Judith. *Men and Citizens: A Study of Rousseau's Social Theory.* 1969.
Starobinski, Jean. *Jean-Jacques Rousseau: Transparency and Obstruction.* 1971; trans. 1988.
Williams, Huntington. *Rousseau and Romantic Autobiography.* 1983.

■ **PRONUNCIATION**

Bossey: baw-SEE
Ducommun: doo-kom-OON
Goton: goh-TOHNG
Lambercier: lahm-behr-SYAY
Masseron: mahs-ROHNG
Jean-Jacques Rousseau: zhawng-zhahk roo-SOH
Verrat: veh-RAH
de Vulson: duh vool-SOHNG

FROM

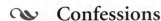

Confessions

Translator anonymous

BOOK 1

[1712–1719]

I am commencing an undertaking, hitherto without precedent, and which will never find an imitator. I desire to set before my fellows the likeness of a man in all the truth of nature, and that man will be myself.

Myself alone! I know the feelings of my heart, and I know men. I am not made like any of those I have seen; I venture to believe that I am not made like any of those who are in existence. If I am not better, at least I am different. Whether Nature has acted rightly or wrongly in destroying the mould in which she cast me, can only be decided after I have been read.

Let the trumpet of the Day of Judgment sound when it will, I will present myself before the Sovereign Judge with this book in my hand. I will say boldly: "This is what

I have done, what I have thought, what I was. I have told the good and the bad with equal frankness. I have neither omitted anything bad, nor interpolated anything good. If I have occasionally made use of some immaterial embellishments, this has only been in order to fill a gap caused by lack of memory. I may have assumed the truth of that which I knew might have been true, never of that which I knew to be false. I have shown myself as I was: mean and contemptible, good, highminded and sublime, according as I was one or the other. I have unveiled my inmost self even as Thou hast seen it, O Eternal Being. Gather round me the countless host of my fellow-men; let them hear my confessions, lament for my unworthiness, and blush for my imperfections. Then let each of them in turn reveal, with the same frankness, the secrets of his heart at the foot of the Throne, and say, if he dare, '*I was better than that man!*'"

I was born at Geneva, in the year 1712, and was the son of Isaac Rousseau and Susanne Bernard, citizens. The distribution of a very moderate inheritance amongst fifteen children had reduced my father's portion almost to nothing; and his only means of livelihood was his trade of watchmaker, in which he was really very clever. My mother, a daughter of the Protestant minister Bernard, was better off. She was clever and beautiful, and my father had found difficulty in obtaining her hand. Their affection for each other had commenced almost as soon as they were born. When only eight years old, they walked every evening upon the Treille;[1] at ten, they were inseparable. Sympathy and union of soul strengthened in them the feeling produced by intimacy. Both, naturally full of tender sensibility, only waited for the moment when they should find the same disposition in another—or, rather, this moment waited for them, and each abandoned his heart to the first which opened to receive it. Destiny, which appeared to oppose their passion, only encouraged it. The young lover, unable to obtain possession of his mistress, was consumed by grief. She advised him to travel, and endeavour to forget her. He travelled, but without result, and returned more in love than ever. He found her whom he loved still faithful and true. After this trial of affection, nothing was left for them but to love each other all their lives. This they swore to do, and Heaven blessed their oath.

Gabriel Bernard, my mother's brother, fell in love with one of my father's sisters, who only consented to accept the hand of the brother, on condition that her own brother married the sister. Love arranged everything, and the two marriages took place on the same day. Thus my uncle became the husband of my aunt, and their children were doubly my first cousins. At the end of a year, a child was born to both, after which they were again obliged to separate.

My uncle Bernard was an engineer. He took service in the Empire and in Hungary, under Prince Eugène.[2] He distinguished himself at the siege and battle of Belgrade. My father, after the birth of my only brother, set out for Constantinople, whither he was summoned to undertake the post of watchmaker to the Sultan. During his

---

[1] **Treille:** A popular walk or promenade in Geneva.

[2] **Empire . . . Eugène:** The Austrian empire; Eugène was an Austrian general who served in the wars against Turkey.

absence, my mother's beauty, intellect, and talents gained for her the devotion of numerous admirers. M. de la Closure, the French Resident, was one of the most eager to offer his. His passion must have been great, for, thirty years later, I saw him greatly affected when speaking to me of her. To enable her to resist such advances, my mother had more than her virtue: she loved her husband tenderly. She pressed him to return; he left all, and returned. I was the unhappy fruit of this return. Ten months later I was born, a weak and ailing child; I cost my mother her life, and my birth was the first of my misfortunes.

I have never heard how my father bore this loss, but I know that he was inconsolable. He believed that he saw his wife again in me, without being able to forget that it was I who had robbed him of her; he never embraced me without my perceiving, by his sighs and the convulsive manner in which he clasped me to his breast, that a bitter regret was mingled with his caresses, which were on that account only the more tender. When he said to me, "Jean Jacques, let us talk of your mother," I used to answer, "Well, then, my father, we will weep!" — and this word alone was sufficient to move him to tears. "Ah!" said he, with a sigh, "give her back to me, console me for her loss, fill the void which she has left in my soul. Should I love you as I do, if you were only my son?" Forty years after he had lost her, he died in the arms of a second wife, but the name of the first was on his lips and her image at the bottom of his heart.

Such were the authors of my existence. Of all the gifts which Heaven had bestowed upon them, a sensitive heart is the only one they bequeathed to me; it had been the source of their happiness, but for me it proved the source of all the misfortunes of my life.

I was brought into the world in an almost dying condition; little hope was entertained of saving my life. I carried within me the germs of a complaint which the course of time has strengthened, and which at times allows me a respite only to make me suffer more cruelly in another manner. One of my father's sisters, an amiable and virtuous young woman, took such care of me that she saved my life. At this moment, while I am writing, she is still alive, at the age of eighty, nursing a husband younger than herself, but exhausted by excessive drinking. Dear aunt,[3] I forgive you for having preserved my life; and I deeply regret that, at the end of your days, I am unable to repay the tender care which you lavished upon me at the beginning of my own. My dear old nurse Jacqueline is also still alive, healthy and robust. The hands which opened my eyes at my birth will be able to close them for me at my death.

I felt before I thought: This is the common lot of humanity. I experienced it more than others. I do not know what I did until I was five or six years old. I do not know how I learned to read; I only remember my earliest reading, and the effect it had upon me; from that time I date my uninterrupted self-consciousness. My mother had left some romances behind her, which my father and I began to read after supper. At first it was only a question of practising me in reading by the aid of amusing books; but soon the interest became so lively, that we used to read in turns

---

[3] **aunt:** Madame Gonçeru, to whom Rousseau paid a small stipend.

without stopping, and spent whole nights in this occupation. We were unable to leave off until the volume was finished. Sometimes, my father, hearing the swallows begin to twitter in the early morning, would say, quite ashamed, "Let us go to bed; I am more of a child than yourself."

In a short time I acquired, by this dangerous method, not only extreme facility in reading and understanding what I read, but a knowledge of the passions that was unique in a child of my age. I had no idea of things in themselves, although all the feelings of actual life were already known to me. I had conceived nothing, but felt everything. These confused emotions which I felt one after the other, certainly did not warp the reasoning powers which I did not as yet possess; but they shaped them in me of a peculiar stamp, and gave me odd and romantic notions of human life, of which experience and reflection have never been able wholly to cure me.

[1719–1723]

The romances came to an end in the summer of 1719. The following winter brought us something different. My mother's library being exhausted, we had recourse to the share of her father's which had fallen to us. Luckily, there were some good books in it; in fact, it could hardly have been otherwise, for the library had been collected by a minister, who was even a learned man according to the fashion of the day, and was at the same time a man of taste and intellect. The "History of the Empire and the Church," by Le Sueur; Bossuet's "Treatise upon Universal History"; Plutarch's "Lives of Famous Men"; Nani's "History of Venice"; Ovid's "Metamorphoses"; La Bruyère; Fontenelle's "Worlds"; his "Dialogues of the Dead"; and some volumes of Molière — all these were brought over into my father's room, and I read to him out of them while he worked. I conceived a taste for them that was rare and perhaps unique at my age. Plutarch, especially, became my favourite author. The pleasure I took in reading him over and over again cured me a little of my taste for romance, and I soon preferred Agesilaus, Brutus, and Aristides to Orondates, Artamenes, and Juba.[4] This interesting reading, and the conversations between my father and myself to which it gave rise, formed in me the free and republican spirit, the proud and indomitable character unable to endure slavery or servitude, which has tormented me throughout my life in situations the least fitted to afford it scope. Unceasingly occupied with thoughts of Rome and Athens, living as it were amongst their great men, myself by birth the citizen of a republic and the son of a father whose patriotism was his strongest passion, I was fired by his example; I believed myself a Greek or a Roman; I lost my identity in that of the individual whose life I was reading; the recitals of the qualities of endurance and intrepidity which arrested my attention made my eyes glisten and strengthened my voice. One day, while I was relating the history of Scaevola[5] at

---

[4] **Agesilaus . . . Juba:** Agesilaus, Brutus, and Aristides appear in Plutarch's *Lives* (c. 100 C.E.); the last three are heroes from popular romances.

[5] **Scaevola:** The legendary Roman hero; when about to be executed for attempting to kill the Etruscan chief Lars Porsena, who was attacking Rome, Scaevola (which means "left-handed") held his right hand in fire to show his determination. The chief was so impressed that he withdrew his forces from Rome.

table, those present were alarmed to see me come forward and hold my hand over a chafing-dish, to illustrate his action.

I had a brother seven years older than myself, who was learning my father's trade. The excessive affection which was lavished upon myself caused him to be somewhat neglected, which treatment I cannot approve of. His education felt the consequences of this neglect. He took to evil courses before he was old enough to be a regular profligate. He was put with another master, from whom he was continually running away, as he had done from home. I hardly ever saw him; I can scarcely say that I knew him; but I never ceased to love him tenderly, and he loved me as much as a vagabond can love anything. I remember that, on one occasion, when my father was chastising him harshly and in anger, I threw myself impetuously between them and embraced him closely. In this manner I covered his body with mine, and received the blows which were aimed at him; I so obstinately maintained my position that at last my father was obliged to leave off, being either disarmed by my cries and tears, or afraid of hurting me more than him. At last, my brother turned out so badly that he ran away and disappeared altogether. Sometime afterwards we heard that he was in Germany. He never once wrote to us. From that time nothing more has been heard of him, and thus I have remained an only son.

If this poor boy was carelessly brought up, this was not the case with his brother; the children of kings could not be more carefully looked after than I was during my early years—worshipped by all around me, and, which is far less common, treated as a beloved, never as a spoiled child. Till I left my father's house, I was never once allowed to run about the streets by myself with the other children; in my case no one ever had to satisfy or check any of those fantastic whims which are attributed to Nature, but are all in reality the result of education. I had the faults of my age: I was a chatterbox, a glutton, and, sometimes, a liar. I would have stolen fruits, bonbons, or eatables; but I have never found pleasure in doing harm or damage, in accusing others, or in tormenting poor dumb animals. I remember, however, that I once made water in a saucepan belonging to one of our neighbours, Madame Clot, while she was at church. I declare that, even now, the recollection of this makes me laugh, because Madame Clot, a good woman in other respects, was the most confirmed old grumbler I have ever known. Such is the brief and true story of all my childish offences.

How could I become wicked, when I had nothing but examples of gentleness before my eyes, and none around me but the best people in the world? My father, my aunt, my nurse, my relations, our friends, our neighbours, all who surrounded me, did not, it is true, obey me, but they loved me; and I loved them in return. My wishes were so little excited and so little opposed, that it did not occur to me to have any. I can swear that, until I served under a master, I never knew what a fancy was. Except during the time I spent in reading or writing in my father's company, or when my nurse took me for a walk, I was always with my aunt, sitting or standing by her side, watching her at her embroidery or listening to her singing; and I was content. Her cheerfulness, her gentleness, and her pleasant face have stamped so deep and lively an impression on my mind that I can still see her manner, look, and attitude; I remember her affectionate language: I could describe what clothes she wore and how her head was dressed, not forgetting the two little curls of black hair on her temples, which she wore in accordance with the fashion of the time.

I am convinced that it is to her I owe the taste, or rather passion, for music, which only became fully developed in me a long time afterwards. She knew a prodigious number of tunes and songs which she used to sing in a very thin, gentle voice. This excellent woman's cheerfulness of soul banished dreaminess and melancholy from herself and all around her. The attraction which her singing possessed for me was so great, that not only have several of her songs always remained in my memory, but even now, when I have lost her, and as I grew older, many of them, totally forgotten since the days of my childhood, return to my mind with inexpressible charm. Would anyone believe that I, an old dotard, eaten up by cares and troubles, sometimes find myself weeping like a child, when I mumble one of those little airs in a voice already broken and trembling? One of them, especially, has come back to me completely, as far as the tune is concerned; the second half of the words, however, has obstinately resisted all my efforts to recall it, although I have an indistinct recollection of the rhymes. Here is the beginning, and all that I can remember of the rest:

> Tircis, I dare not listen
> To your pipe
> Under the elm;
> For already in our village
> People have begun to talk.
>
> . . . to engage
> . . . with a shepherd
> . . . without danger
> And always the thorn is with the rose.[6]

I ask, where is the affecting charm which my heart finds in this song? it is a whim, which I am quite unable to understand; but, be that as it may, it is absolutely impossible for me to sing it through without being interrupted by my tears. I have intended, times without number, to write to Paris to make inquiries concerning the remainder of the words, in case anyone should happen to know them; but I am almost certain that the pleasure which I feel in recalling the air would partly disappear, if it should be proved that others besides my poor aunt Susan have sung it.

Such were my earliest emotions on my entry into life; thus began to form or display itself in me that heart at once so proud and tender, that character so effeminate but yet indomitable, which, ever wavering between timidity and courage, weakness and self-control, has throughout my life made me inconsistent, and has caused abstinence and enjoyment, pleasure and prudence equally to elude my grasp.

This course of education was interrupted by an accident, the consequences of which have exercised an influence upon the remainder of my life. My father had a quarrel with a captain in the French army, named Gautier, who was connected with some of the members of the Common Council. This Gautier, a cowardly and insolent

---

[6] Rousseau's text deliberately leaves out the sixth line of this popular song: "It is dangerous for a heart."

fellow (whose nose happened to bleed during the affray), in order to avenge himself, accused my father of having drawn his sword within the city walls. My father, whom they wanted to send to prison, persisted that, in accordance with the law, the accuser ought to be imprisoned as well as himself. Being unable to have his way in this, he preferred to quit Geneva and expatriate himself for the rest of his life, than to give way on a point in which honour and liberty appeared to him to be compromised.

I remained under the care of my uncle Bernard, who was at the time employed upon the fortifications of Geneva. His eldest daughter was dead, but he had a son of the same age as myself. We were sent together to Bossey,[7] to board with the Protestant minister Lambercier, in order to learn, together with Latin, all the sorry trash which is included under the name of education.

Two years spent in the village in some degree softened my Roman roughness and made me a child again. At Geneva, where no tasks were imposed upon me, I loved reading and study, which were almost my only amusements; at Bossey, my tasks made me love the games which formed a break in them. The country was so new to me, that my enjoyment of it never palled. I conceived so lively an affection for it, that it has never since died out. The remembrance of the happy days I have spent there filled me with regretful longing for its pleasures, at all periods of my life, until the day which has brought me back to it. M. Lambercier was a very intelligent person, who, without neglecting our education, never imposed excessive tasks upon us. The fact that, in spite of my dislike of restraint, I have never recalled my hours of study with any feeling of disgust—and also that, even if I did not learn much from him, I learnt without difficulty what I did learn and never forgot it—is sufficient proof that his system of instruction was a good one.

The simplicity of this country life was of inestimable value to me, in that it opened my heart to friendship. Up to that time I had only known lofty but imaginary sentiments. The habit of living peacefully together with my cousin Bernard drew us together in tender bonds of union. In a short time, my feelings towards him became more affectionate than those with which I had regarded my brother, and they have never been effaced. He was a tall, lanky, weakly boy, as gentle in disposition as he was feeble in body, who never abused the preference which was shown to him in the house as the son of my guardian. Our tasks, our amusements, our tastes were the same: we were alone, we were of the same age, each of us needed a companion: separation was to us, in a manner, annihilation. Although we had few opportunities of proving our mutual attachment, it was very great; not only were we unable to live an instant apart, but we did not imagine it possible that we could ever be separated. Being, both of us, ready to yield to tenderness, and docile, provided compulsion was not used, we always agreed in everything. If, in the presence of those who looked after us, he had some advantage over me in consequence of the favour with which they regarded him, when we were alone I had an advantage over him which restored the equilibrium. When we were saying our lessons, I prompted him if he hesitated; when I had finished my exercise, I helped him with his; and in our amusements, my

---

[7] **Bossey:** A village three miles from Geneva.

more active mind always led the way. In short, our two characters harmonised so well, and the friendship which united us was so sincere, that, in the five years and more, during which, whether at Bossey or Geneva, we were almost inseparable, although I confess that we often fought, it was never necessary to separate us, none of our quarrels ever lasted longer than a quarter of an hour, and neither of us ever made any accusation against the other. These observations are, if you will, childish, but they furnish an example which, since the time that there have been children, is perhaps unique.

The life which I led at Bossey suited me so well that, had it only lasted longer, it would have completely decided my character. Tender, affectionate, and gentle feelings formed its foundation. I believe that no individual of our species was naturally more free from vanity than myself. I raised myself by fits and starts to lofty flights, but immediately fell down again into my natural languor. My liveliest desire was to be loved by all who came near me. I was of a gentle disposition; my cousin and our guardians were the same. During two whole years I was neither the witness nor the victim of any violent feeling. Everything nourished in my heart those tendencies which it received from Nature. I knew no higher happiness than to see all the world satisfied with me and with everything. I shall never forget how, if I happened to hesitate when saying my catechism in church, nothing troubled me more than to observe signs of restlessness and dissatisfaction on Mademoiselle Lambercier's face. That alone troubled me more than the disgrace of failing in public, which, nevertheless, affected me greatly: for, although little susceptible to praise, I felt shame keenly; and I may say here that the thought of Mademoiselle's reproaches caused me less uneasiness than the fear of offending her.

When it was necessary, however, neither she nor her brother were wanting in severity; but, since this severity was nearly always just, and never passionate, it pained me without making me insubordinate. Failure to please grieved me more than punishment, and signs of dissatisfaction hurt me more than corporal chastisement. It is somewhat embarrassing to explain myself more clearly, but, nevertheless, I must do so. How differently would one deal with youth, if one could more clearly see the remote effects of the usual method of treatment, which is employed always without discrimination, frequently without discretion! The important lesson which may be drawn from an example as common as it is fatal makes me decide to mention it.

As Mademoiselle Lambercier had the affection of a mother for us, she also exercised the authority of one, and sometimes carried it so far as to inflict upon us the punishment of children when we had deserved it. For some time she was content with threats, and this threat of a punishment that was quite new to me appeared very terrible; but, after it had been carried out, I found the reality less terrible than the expectation; and, what was still more strange, this chastisement made me still more devoted to her who had inflicted it. It needed all the strength of this devotion and all my natural docility to keep myself from doing something which would have deservedly brought upon me a repetition of it; for I had found in the pain, even in the disgrace, a mixture of sensuality which had left me less afraid than desirous of experiencing it again from the same hand. No doubt some precocious sexual instinct was mingled with this feeling, for the same chastisement inflicted by her brother would not have seemed to me at all pleasant. But, considering his disposition, there was little cause to fear the substitution; and if I kept myself from deserving punishment, it was solely for fear of displeasing Mademoiselle Lambercier; for, so great is the power exercised over me by kindness, even by that which is due to the senses, that it has always controlled the latter in my heart.

The repetition of the offence, which I avoided without being afraid of it, occurred without any fault of mine, that is to say, of my will, and I may say that I profited by it without any qualm of conscience. But this second time was also the last; for Mademoiselle Lambercier, who had no doubt noticed something which convinced her that the punishment did not have the desired effect, declared that it tired her too much, and that she would abandon it. Until then we had slept in her room, sometimes even in her bed during the winter. Two days afterwards we were put to sleep in another room, and from that time I had the honour, which I would gladly have dispensed with, of being treated by her as a big boy.

Who would believe that this childish punishment, inflicted upon me when only eight years old by a young woman of thirty, disposed of my tastes, my desires, my passions, and my own self for the remainder of my life, and that in a manner exactly contrary to that which should have been the natural result? When my feelings were once inflamed, my desires so went astray that, limited to what I had already felt, they did not trouble themselves to look for anything else. In spite of my hot blood, which has been inflamed with sensuality almost from my birth, I kept myself free from every taint until the age when the coldest and most sluggish temperaments begin to develop. In torments for a long time, without knowing why, I devoured with burning glances all the pretty women I met; my imagination unceasingly recalled them to me, only to make use of them in my own fashion, and to make of them so many Mlles. Lambercier.

Even after I had reached years of maturity, this curious taste, always abiding with me and carried to depravity and even frenzy, preserved my morality, which it might naturally have been expected to destroy. If ever a bringing-up was chaste and modest, assuredly mine was. My three aunts were not only models of propriety, but reserved to a degree which has long since been unknown amongst women. My father, a man of pleasure, but a gallant of the old school, never said a word, even in the presence of women whom he loved more than others, which would have brought a blush to a maiden's cheek; and the respect due to children has never been so much insisted upon as in my family and in my presence. In this respect I found M. Lambercier equally careful; and an excellent servant was dismissed for having used a somewhat too free expression in our presence. Until I was a young man, I not only had no distinct idea of the union of the sexes, but the confused notion which I had regarding it never presented itself to me except in a hateful and disgusting form. For common prostitutes I felt a loathing which has never been effaced: the sight of a profligate always filled me with contempt, even with affright. My horror of debauchery became thus pronounced ever since the day when, walking to Little Sacconex[8] by a hollow way, I saw on both sides holes in the ground, where I was told

---

[8] Little Sacconex: A village near Geneva.

that these creatures carried on their intercourse. The thought of the one always brought back to my mind the copulation of dogs, and the bare recollection was sufficient to disgust me.

This tendency of my bringing-up, in itself adapted to delay the first outbreaks of an inflammable temperament, was assisted, as I have already said, by the direction which the first indications of sensuality took in my case. Only busying my imagination with what I had actually felt, in spite of most uncomfortable effervescence of blood, I only knew how to turn my desires in the direction of that kind of pleasure with which I was acquainted, without ever going as far as that which had been made hateful to me, and which, without my having the least suspicion of it, was so closely related to the other. In my foolish fancies, in my erotic frenzies, in the extravagant acts to which they sometimes led me, I had recourse in my imagination to the assistance of the other sex, without ever thinking that it was serviceable for any purpose than that for which I was burning to make use of it.

In this manner, then, in spite of an ardent, lascivious, and precocious temperament, I passed the age of puberty without desiring, even without knowing of any other sensual pleasures than those of which Mademoiselle Lambercier had most innocently given me the idea; and when, in course of time, I became a man, that which should have destroyed me again preserved me. My old childish taste, instead of disappearing, became so associated with the other, that I could never banish it from the desires kindled by my senses; and this madness, joined to my natural shyness, has always made me very unenterprising with women, for want of courage to say all or power to do all. The kind of enjoyment, of which the other was only for me the final consummation, could neither be appropriated by him who longed for it, nor guessed by her who was able to bestow it. Thus I have spent my life in idle longing, without saying a word, in the presence of those whom I loved most. Too bashful to declare my taste, I at least satisfied it in situations which had reference to it and kept up the idea of it. To lie at the feet of an imperious mistress, to obey her commands, to ask her forgiveness—this was for me a sweet enjoyment; and, the more my lively imagination heated my blood, the more I presented the appearance of a bashful lover. It may be easily imagined that this manner of making love does not lead to very speedy results, and is not very dangerous to the virtue of those who are its object. For this reason I have rarely possessed, but have none the less enjoyed myself in my own way—that is to say, in imagination. Thus it has happened that my senses, in harmony with my timid disposition and my romantic spirit, have kept my sentiments pure and my morals blameless, owing to the very tastes which, combined with a little more impudence, might have plunged me into the most brutal sensuality.

I have taken the first and most difficult step in the dark and dirty labyrinth of my confessions. It is easier to admit that which is criminal than that which is ridiculous and makes a man feel ashamed. Henceforth I am sure of myself; after having ventured to say so much, I can shrink from nothing. One may judge what such confessions have cost me, from the fact that, during the whole course of my life, I have never dared to declare my folly to those whom I loved with the frenzy of a passion which deprived me of sight and hearing, which robbed me of my senses and caused me to tremble all over with a convulsive movement. I have never brought myself, even when on most intimate terms, to ask women to grant me the only favour of all which was wanting. This never happened to me but once — in my childhood, with a girl of my own age; even then, it was she who first proposed it.

While thus going back to the first traces of my inner life, I find elements which sometimes appear incompatible, and yet have united in order to produce with vigour a simple and uniform effect; and I find others which, although apparently the same, have formed combinations so different, owing to the co-operation of certain circumstances, that one would never imagine that these elements were in any way connected. Who, for instance, would believe that one of the most powerful movements of my soul was tempered in the same spring from which a stream of sensuality and effeminacy has entered my blood? Without leaving the subject of which I have just spoken, I shall produce by means of it a very different impression.

One day I was learning my lesson by myself in the room next to the kitchen. The servant had put Mademoiselle Lambercier's combs in front of the fire-place to dry. When she came back to fetch them, she found one with a whole row of teeth broken. Who was to blame for the damage? No one except myself had entered the room. On being questioned, I denied that I had touched the comb. M. and Mademoiselle Lambercier both began to admonish, to press, and to threaten me; I obstinately persisted in my denial; but the evidence was too strong, and outweighed all my protestations, although it was the first time that I had been found to lie so boldly. The matter was regarded as serious, as in fact it deserved to be. The mischievousness, the falsehood, the obstinacy appeared equally deserving of punishment; but this time it was not by Mademoiselle Lambercier that chastisement was inflicted. My uncle Bernard was written to, and he came. My poor cousin was accused of another equally grave offence; we were involved in the same punishment. It was terrible. Had they wished to look for the remedy in the evil itself and to deaden for ever my depraved senses, they could not have set to work better, and for a long time my senses left me undisturbed.

They could not draw from me the desired confession. Although I was several times brought up before them and reduced to a pitiable condition, I remained unshaken. I would have endured death, and made up my mind to do so. Force was obliged to yield to the diabolical obstinacy of a child — as they called my firmness. At last I emerged from this cruel trial, utterly broken, but triumphant.

It is now nearly fifty years since this incident took place, and I have no fear of being punished again for the same thing. Well, then, I declare in the sight of heaven that I was innocent of the offence, that I neither broke nor touched the comb, that I never went near the fire-place, and had never even thought of doing so. It would be useless to ask me how the damage was done: I do not know, and I cannot understand; all that I know for certain is, that I had nothing to do with it.

Imagine a child, shy and obedient in ordinary life, but fiery, proud, and unruly in his passions: a child who had always been led by the voice of reason and always treated with gentleness, justice, and consideration, who had not even a notion of injustice, and who for the first time becomes acquainted with so terrible an example of it on the part of the very people whom he most loves and respects! What an upset of ideas! what a disturbance of feelings! what revolution in his heart, in his brain, in the whole of his little intellectual and moral being! Imagine all this, I say, if possible.

As for myself, I feel incapable of disentangling and following up the least trace of what then took place within me.

I had not yet sense enough to feel how much appearances were against me, and to put myself in the place of the others. I kept to my own place, and all that I felt was the harshness of a frightful punishment for an offence which I had not committed. The bodily pain, although severe, I felt but little: all I felt was indignation, rage, despair. My cousin, whose case was almost the same, and who had been punished for an involuntary mistake as if it had been a premeditated act, following my example, flew into a rage, and worked himself up to the same pitch of excitement as myself. Both in the same bed, we embraced each other with convulsive transports: we felt suffocated; and when at length our young hearts, somewhat relieved, were able to vent their wrath, we sat upright in bed and began to shout, times without number, with all our might: *Carnifex! carnifex! carnifex!*[9]

While I write these words, I feel that my pulse beats faster; those moments will always be present to me though I should live a hundred thousand years. That first feeling of violence and injustice has remained so deeply graven on my soul, that all the ideas connected with it bring back to me my first emotion; and this feeling, which, in its origin, had reference only to myself, has become so strong in itself and so completely detached from all personal interest, that, when I see or hear of any act of injustice—whoever is the victim of it, and wherever it is committed—my heart kindles with rage, as if the effect of it recoiled upon myself. When I read of the cruelties of a ferocious tyrant, the crafty atrocities of a rascally priest, I would gladly set out to plunge a dagger into the heart of such wretches, although I had to die for it a hundred times. I have often put myself in a perspiration, pursuing or stoning a cock, a cow, a dog, or any animal which I saw tormenting another merely because it felt itself the stronger. This impulse may be natural to me, and I believe that it is; but the profound impression left upon me by the first injustice I suffered was too long and too strongly connected with it, not to have greatly strengthened it.

With the above incident the tranquillity of my childish life was over. From that moment I ceased to enjoy a pure happiness, and even at the present day I feel that the recollection of the charms of my childhood ceases there. We remained a few months longer at Bossey. We were there, as the first man is represented to us—still in the earthly paradise, but we no longer enjoyed it; in appearance our condition was the same, in reality it was quite a different manner of existence. Attachment, respect, intimacy, and confidence no longer united pupils and guides: we no longer regarded them as gods, who were able to read in our hearts; we became less ashamed of doing wrong and more afraid of being accused; we began to dissemble, to be insubordinate, to lie. All the vices of our age corrupted our innocence and threw a veil of ugliness over our amusements. Even the country lost in our eyes that charm of gentleness and simplicity which goes to the heart. It appeared to us lonely and sombre: it seemed as it were covered with a veil which concealed its beauties from our eyes. We ceased to cultivate our little gardens, our plants, our flowers. We no longer scratched up the

---

[9] *Carnifex:* Executioner or torturer (Latin).

ground gently, or cried with joy when we saw the seed which we had sown beginning to sprout. We were disgusted with the life, and others were disgusted with us; my uncle took us away, and we separated from M. and Mademoiselle Lambercier, having had enough of each other, and feeling but little regret at the separation.

Nearly thirty years have passed since I left Bossey, without my recalling to mind my stay there with any connected and pleasurable recollections; but, now that I have passed the prime of life and am approaching old age, I feel these same recollections springing up again while others disappear; they stamp themselves upon my memory with features, the charm and strength of which increase daily, as if, feeling life already slipping away, I were endeavouring to grasp it again by its commencement. The most trifling incidents of that time please me, simply because they belong to that period. I remember all the details of place, persons, and time. I see the maid or the manservant busy in the room, a swallow darting through the window, a fly settling on my hand while I was saying my lesson: I see the whole arrangement of the room in which we used to live; M. Lambercier's study on the right, a copperplate engraving of all the Popes, a barometer, a large almanack hanging on the wall, the raspberry bushes which, growing in a garden situated on very high ground facing the back of the house, shaded the window and sometimes forced their way through it. I am quite aware that the reader does not want to know all this; but I am bound to tell him. Why have I not the courage to relate to him in like manner all the trifling anecdotes of that happy time, which still make me tremble with joy when I recall them? Five or six in particular—but let us make a bargain. I will let you off five, but I wish to tell you one, only one, provided that you will permit me to tell it in as much detail as possible, in order to prolong my enjoyment.

If I only had your pleasure in view, I might choose the story of Mademoiselle Lambercier's backside, which, owing to an unfortunate somersault at the bottom of the meadow, was exhibited in full view to the King of Sardinia, who happened to be passing by; but that of the walnut-tree on the terrace is more amusing for me who took an active part in it, whereas I was merely a spectator of the somersault; besides, I declare that I found absolutely nothing to laugh at in an accident which, although comic in itself, alarmed me for the safety of a person whom I loved as a mother and, perhaps, even more.

Now, O curious readers of the important history of the walnut-tree on the terrace, listen to the horrible tragedy, and keep from shuddering if you can!

Outside the gate of the court, on the left of the entrance, there was a terrace, where we often went to sit in the afternoon. As it was entirely unprotected from the sun, M. Lambercier had a walnut-tree planted there. The process of planting was carried out with the greatest solemnity. The two boarders were its godfathers; and, while the hole was being filled up, we each of us held the tree with one hand and sang songs of triumph. In order to water it, a kind of basin was made round the foot. Every day, eager spectators of this watering, my cousin and I became more strongly convinced, as was natural, that it was a finer thing to plant a tree on a terrace than a flag upon a breach, and we resolved to win this glory for ourselves without sharing it with anyone.

With this object, we proceeded to cut a slip from a young willow, and planted it on the terrace, at a distance of about eight or ten feet from the august walnut-tree. We did not forget to dig a similar trench round our tree; the difficulty was how to fill it, for the water came from some distance, and we were not allowed to run and fetch it. However, it was absolutely necessary to have some for our willow. For a few days, we had recourse to all kinds of devices to get some, and we succeeded so well that we saw it bud and put forth little leaves, the growth of which we measured every hour, convinced that, although not yet a foot high, it would soon afford us a shade.

As our tree so completely claimed our attention that we were quite incapable of attending to or learning anything else, and were in a sort of delirium: as our guardians, not knowing what was the matter with us, kept a tighter hand upon us, we saw the fatal moment approaching when we should be without water, and were inconsolable at the thought of seeing our tree perish from drought. At length necessity, the mother of invention, suggested to us how to save ourselves from grief and the tree from certain death; this was, to make a channel underground, which should secretly conduct part of the water intended for the walnut-tree to our willow. This undertaking was at first unsuccessful, in spite of the eagerness with which it was carried out. We had made the incline so clumsily that the water did not run at all. The earth fell in and stopped up the channel; the entrance was filled with mud; everything went wrong. But nothing disheartened us: *Labor omnia vincit improbus.*[10] We dug our basin deeper, in order to allow the water to run; we cut some bottoms of boxes into small narrow planks, some of which were laid flat, one after the other, and others set up on both sides of these at an angle, thus forming a triangular canal for our conduit. At the entrance we stuck small pieces of wood, some little distance apart, which, forming a kind of grating or lattice-work, kept back the mud and stones, without stopping the passage of the water. We carefully covered our work with well-trodden earth; and when all was ready, we awaited, in the greatest excitement of hope and fear, the time of watering. After centuries of waiting, the hour at length arrived; M. Lambercier came as usual to assist at the operation, during which we both kept behind him, in order to conceal our tree, to which very luckily he turned his back.

No sooner had the first pail of water been poured out, than we saw some of it running into our basin. At this sight, our prudence deserted us: we began to utter cries of joy which made M. Lambercier turn round; this was a pity, for he took great delight in seeing how good the soil of the walnut-tree was, and how greedily it absorbed the water. Astonished at seeing it distribute itself into two basins, he cried out in his turn, looked, perceived the trick, ordered a pickaxe to be brought, and, with one blow, broke off two or three pieces from our planks; then, crying loudly, "An aqueduct, an aqueduct!" he dealt merciless blows in every direction, each of which went straight to our hearts. In a moment planks, conduit, basin, willow, everything was destroyed and uprooted, without his having uttered a single word, during this terrible work of destruction, except the exclamation which he incessantly repeated. "An aqueduct!" he cried, while demolishing everything, "an aqueduct, an aqueduct!"

---

[10] *Labor . . . improbus:* "Tenacious work overcomes all difficulties." (Virgil, *Georgics* I)

It will naturally be imagined that the adventure turned out badly for the little architects: that would be a mistake: it was all over. M. Lambercier never uttered a single word of reproach, or looked upon us with displeasure, and said nothing more about it; shortly afterwards, we even heard him laughing loudly with his sister, for his laughter could be heard a long way off; and what was still more astonishing, when the first fright was over, we ourselves were not much troubled about the matter. We planted another tree somewhere else, and often reminded ourselves of the disaster that overtook the first, by repeating with emphasis, "An aqueduct, an aqueduct!" Hitherto I had had intermittent attacks of pride, when I was Aristides or Brutus; then it was that I felt the first well-defined promptings of vanity. To have been able to construct an aqueduct with our own hands, to have put a cutting in competition with a large tree, appeared to me the height of glory. At ten years of age I was a better judge on this point than Cæsar at thirty.

The thought of this walnut-tree and the little history connected with it has remained so vivid in my memory, or returned to it, that one of the plans which gave me the greatest pleasure, on my journey to Geneva, in 1754, was to go to Bossey and revisit the memorials of my boyish amusements, above all, the dear walnut-tree, which by that time must have been a third of a century old; but I was so continually occupied, so little my own master, that I could never find the moment to afford myself this satisfaction. There is little prospect of the opportunity ever occurring again; yet the wish has not disappeared with the hope; and I am almost certain that, if ever I should return to those beloved spots and find my dear walnut-tree still alive, I should water it with my tears.

After my return to Geneva, I lived for two or three years[11] with my uncle, waiting until my friends had decided what was to be done with me. As he intended his own son to be an engineer, he made him learn a little drawing and taught him the elements of Euclid.[12] I learned these subjects together with him, and acquired a taste for them, especially for drawing. In the meantime, it was debated whether I should be a watchmaker, an attorney, or a minister. My own preference was for the last, for preaching seemed to me to be a very fine thing; but the small income from my mother's property, which had to be divided between my brother and myself, was not sufficient to allow me to prosecute my studies. As, considering my age at that time, there was no immediate need to decide, I remained for the present with my uncle, making little use of my time and, in addition, as was only fair, paying a tolerably large sum for my board. My uncle, a man of pleasure like my father, was unable, like him, to tie himself down to his duties, and troubled himself little enough about us. My aunt was somewhat of a pietist, and preferred to sing psalms rather than attend to our education. We were allowed almost absolute freedom, which we never abused. Always inseparable, we were quite contented with our own society; and, having no temptation to make companions of the street boys of our own age, we learned

---

[11] **two . . . years:** Rousseau actually lived with his uncle for less than a year; this is only one of the many details in the autobiography that is inaccurate.

[12] **Euclid:** Third-century Greek mathematician, whose *Elements* established many of the principles of geometry.

none of the dissolute habits into which idleness might have led us. I am even wrong in saying that we were idle, for we were never less so in our lives; and the most fortunate thing was, that all the ways of amusing ourselves, with which we successively became infatuated, kept us together busy in the house, without our being even tempted to go out into the street. We made cages, flutes, shuttlecocks, drums, houses, squirts, and cross-bows. We spoilt my good old grandfather's tools in trying to make watches as he did. We had a special taste for wasting paper, drawing, painting in water-colours, illuminating, and spoiling colours. An Italian showman, named Gamba-Corta, came to Geneva; we went to see him once and never wanted to go again. But he had a marionette-show, and we proceeded to make marionettes; his marionettes played comedies and we composed comedies for ours. For want of a squeaker, we imitated Punch's voice in our throat, in order to play the charming comedies, which our poor and kind relations had the patience to sit and listen to. But, my uncle Bernard having one day read aloud in the family circle a very fine sermon which he had composed himself, we abandoned comedy and began to write sermons. These details are not very interesting, I confess, but they show how exceedingly well-conducted our early education must have been, seeing that we, almost masters of our time and ourselves at so tender an age, were so little tempted to abuse our opportunities. We had so little need of making companions, that we even neglected the chances of doing so. When we went for a walk, we looked at their amusements as we passed by without the slightest desire, or even the idea of taking part in them. Our friendship so completely filled our hearts, that it was enough for us to be together to make the simplest amusements a delight.

Being thus inseparable, we began to attract attention: the more so as, my cousin being very tall while I was very short, we made an oddly-assorted couple. His long, slim figure, his little face like a boiled apple, his gentle manner, and his slovenly walk excited the children's ridicule. In the *patois* of the district he was nicknamed Barna Bredanna,[13] and, directly we went out, we heard nothing but "Barna Bredanna!" all round us. He endured it more quietly than I did: I lost my temper and wanted to fight. This was just what the little rascals desired. I fought and was beaten. My poor cousin helped me as well as he could; but he was weak, and a single blow of the fist knocked him down. Then I became furious. However, although I received blows in abundance, I was not the real object of attack, but Barna Bredanna; but my obstinate anger made matters so much worse, that, in future, we only ventured to go out during school-hours, for fear of being hooted and followed.

Behold me already a redresser of wrongs! In order to be a regular Paladin[14] I only wanted a lady; I had two. From time to time I went to see my father at Nyon, a little town in the Vaud country, where he had settled. He was very much liked, and his son felt the effects of his popularity. During the short time I stayed with him, friends vied with each other in making me welcome. A certain Madame de Vulson, especially, bestowed a thousand caresses upon me, and, to crown all, her daughter

---

[13] **Barna Bredanna:** A "bridled donkey."

[14] **Paladin:** A chivalric hero from the twelfth-century *Song of Roland*.

took me for her lover. It is easy to understand the meaning of a lover eleven years old for a girl of twenty-two. But all these roguish young women are so ready to put little puppets in front in order to hide larger ones, or to tempt them with the idea of an amusement which they know how to render attractive! As for myself, I saw no incongruity between us and took the matter seriously; I abandoned myself with all my heart, or rather with all my head—for it was only in that part of me that I was in love, although madly—and my transports, excitement, and frenzy produced scenes enough to make anyone split his sides with laughing.

I am acquainted with two very distinct and very real kinds of love, which have scarcely anything in common, although both are very fervent, and which both differ from tender friendship. The whole course of my life has been divided between these two kinds of love, essentially so different, and I have even felt them both at the same time; for instance, at the time of which I am speaking, while I took possession of Mademoiselle de Vulson so openly and so tyrannically that I could not endure that any man should approach her, I had several meetings, brief but lively, with a certain little Mademoiselle Goton, in which she deigned to play the schoolmistress, and that was all; but this all, which was really all for me, seemed to me the height of happiness; and, already feeling the value of the mystery, although I only knew how to make use of it as a child, I paid Mademoiselle de Vulson, who had scarcely any suspicion of it, in the same coin, for the assiduity with which she made use of me to conceal other amours. But, to my great regret, my secret was discovered, or not so well kept on the part of my little schoolmistress as on my own; we were soon separated; and, some time afterwards, on my return to Geneva, while passing through Coutance, I heard some little girls cry, in an undertone, "Goton tic-tac Rousseau!"[15]

This little Mademoiselle Goton was really a singular person. Without being pretty, she had a face which was not easy to forget, and which I still recall to mind, often too tenderly for an old fool. Neither her form, nor her manner, nor, above all, her eyes were in keeping with her age. She had a proud and commanding air, which suited her part admirably, and which in fact had suggested the first idea of it to us. But the oddest thing about her was a mixture of impudence and reserve which it was difficult to comprehend. She took the greatest liberties with me, but never allowed me to take any with her. She treated me just like a child, which makes me believe, either that she was no longer one herself, or that, on the contrary, she was still childish enough to see nothing but an amusement in the danger to which she exposed herself.

I belonged entirely, so to say, to each of these two persons, and so completely, that, when I was with one, I never thought of the other. In other respects, there was not the slightest similarity between the feelings with which they inspired me. I could have spent all my life with Mademoiselle de Vulson, without ever thinking of leaving her; but, when I approached her, my joy was tranquil and free from emotion. I loved her above all in fashionable society; the witty sallies, railleries, and even the petty

---

[15] **Coutance:** A district in Geneva where Rousseau's family lived after 1718; **tic-tac:** Goton is in love with, or comes to blows with, Rousseau.

jealousies attracted and interested me; I felt a pride and glory in the marks of preference she bestowed upon me in the presence of grown-up rivals whom she appeared
to treat with disdain. I was tormented, but I loved the torment. The applause,
encouragement, and laughter warmed and inspired me. I had fits of passion and
broke out into audacious sallies. In society, I was transported with love; in a *tête-à-
tête* I should have been constrained, cold, perhaps wearied. However, I felt a real tenderness for her; I suffered when she was ill; I would have given my own health to
restore her own, and, observe! I knew very well from experience the meaning of illness and health. When absent from her, I thought of her and missed her; when I was
by her side, her caresses reached my heart—not my senses. I was intimate with her
with impunity; my imagination demanded no more than she granted; yet I could
not have endured to see her do even as much for others. I loved her as a brother, but
I was as jealous of her as a lover.

I should have been as jealous of Mademoiselle Goton as a Turk, a madman, or a
tiger, if I had once imagined that she could accord the same treatment to another as
to myself; for even that was a favour which I had to ask on my knees. I approached
Mademoiselle de Vulson with lively pleasure, but without emotion; whereas, if I only
saw Mademoiselle Goton, I saw nothing else, all my senses were bewildered. With
the former I was familiar without familiarity; while on the contrary, in the presence
of the latter, I was as bashful as I was excited, even in the midst of our greatest famil-
iarities. I believe that, if I had remained with her long, I should have died; the throb-
bings of my heart would have suffocated me. I was equally afraid of displeasing
either; but I was more attentive to the one and more obedient to the other. Nothing
in the world would have made me annoy Mademoiselle de Vulson; but if Mademoiselle Goton had ordered me to throw myself into the flames, I believe I should have
obeyed her immediately.

My amour, or rather my meetings, with the latter, continued only for a short
time—happily for both of us. Although my relations with Mademoiselle de Vulson
had not the same danger, they were not without their catastrophe, after they had
lasted a little longer. The end of all such connections should always be somewhat
romantic, and furnish occasion for exclamations of sorrow. Although my connection with Mademoiselle de Vulson was less lively, it was perhaps closer. We never separated without tears, and it is remarkable into what an overwhelming void I felt
myself plunged as soon as I had left her. I could speak and think of nothing but her;
my regret was genuine and lively; but I believe that, at bottom, this heroic regret was
not felt altogether for her, and that, without my perceiving it, the amusements, of
which she was the centre, played their part in it. To moderate the pangs of absence,
we wrote letters to each other, pathetic enough to melt the heart of a stone. At last I
triumphed; she could endure it no longer, and came to Geneva to see me. This time
my head was completely turned; I was drunk and mad during the two days she
remained. When she left I wanted to throw myself in the water after her, and the air
resounded with my screams. Eight days afterwards she sent me some bonbons and
gloves, which I should have considered a great compliment, if I had not learnt at the
same time that she was married, and that the visit with which she had been pleased
to honour me was really made in order to buy her wedding-dress. I will not attempt

to describe my fury; it may be imagined. In my noble rage I swore that I would never see the faithless one again, being unable to imagine a more terrible punishment for her. She did not, however, die of it; for, twenty years afterwards, when on a visit to my father, while rowing with him on the lake, I asked who the ladies were whom I saw in a boat not far from ours. "What!" said my father with a smile, "does not your heart tell you? it is your old love, Mademoiselle de Vulson that was, now Madame Cristin." I started at the almost forgotten name, but I told the boatmen to change their course. Although I had a fine opportunity of avenging myself at that moment, I did not think it worth while to perjure myself and to renew a quarrel, twenty years old, with a woman of forty.

[1723–1728]

Thus the most valuable time of my boyhood was wasted in follies, before my future career had been decided upon. After long deliberation as to the bent of my natural inclination, a profession was determined upon for which I had the least taste; I was put with M. Masseron, the town clerk, in order to learn, under his tuition, the useful trade of a *fee-grabber*.[16] This nickname was extremely distasteful to me; the hope of gaining a number of crowns in a somewhat sordid business by no means flattered my pride; the occupation itself appeared to me wearisome and unendurable; the constant application, the feeling of servitude completed my dislike, and I never entered the office without a feeling of horror, which daily increased in intensity. M. Masseron, on his part, was ill-satisfied with me, and treated me with contempt; he continually reproached me with my dullness and stupidity, dinning into my ears every day that my uncle had told him that I knew something, whereas, in reality, I knew nothing; that he had promised him a sharp lad, and had given him a jackass. At last I was dismissed from the office in disgrace as being utterly incapable, and M. Masseron's clerks declared that I was good for nothing except to handle a file.

My calling being thus settled, I was apprenticed, not, however, to a watchmaker, but to an engraver. The contempt with which I had been treated by M. Masseron had made me very humble, and I obeyed without a murmur. My new master, M. Ducommun, was a rough and violent young man, who in a short time succeeded in tarnishing all the brightness of my childhood, stupefying my loving and lively nature, and reducing me, in mind as well as in position, to a real state of apprenticeship. My Latin, my antiquities, my history, were all for a long time forgotten; I did not even remember that there had ever been any Romans in the world. My father, when I went to see him, no longer found in me his idol; for the ladies I was no longer the gallant Jean Jacques; and I felt so certain myself that the Lamberciers would not have recognised their pupil in me, that I was ashamed to pay them a visit, and have never seen them since. The vilest tastes, the lowest street-blackguardism took the place of my simple amusements and effaced even the remembrance of them. I must, in spite of a most upright training, have had a great propensity to degenerate; for the

---

[16] *fee-grabber:* A lawyer.

change took place with great rapidity, without the least trouble, and never did so precocious a Cæsar so rapidly become a Laridon.[17]

The trade in itself was not disagreeable to me; I had a decided taste for drawing; the handling of a graving-tool amused me; and as the claims upon the skill of a watchmaker's engraver were limited, I hoped to attain perfection. I should, perhaps, have done so, had not my master's brutality and excessive restraint disgusted me with my work. I stole some of my working hours to devote to similar occupations, but which had for me the charm of freedom. I engraved medals for an order of knighthood for myself and my companions. My master surprised me at this contraband occupation, and gave me a sound thrashing, declaring that I was training for a coiner, because our medals bore the arms of the Republic. I can swear that I had no idea at all of bad, and only a very faint one of good, money. I knew better how the Roman *As*[18] was made than our three-sou pieces.

My master's tyranny at length made the work, of which I should have been very fond, altogether unbearable, and filled me with vices which I should otherwise have hated, such as lying, idleness, and thieving. The recollection of the alteration produced in me by that period of my life has taught me, better than anything else, the difference between filial dependence and abject servitude. Naturally shy and timid, no fault was more foreign to my disposition than impudence; but I had enjoyed an honourable liberty, which hitherto had only been gradually restrained, and at length disappeared altogether. I was bold with my father, unrestrained with M. Lambercier, and modest with my uncle; I became timid with my master, and from that moment I was a lost child. Accustomed to perfect equality in my intercourse with my superiors, knowing no pleasure which was not within my reach, seeing no dish of which I could not have a share, having no desire which I could not have openly expressed, and carrying my heart upon my lips—it is easy to judge what I was bound to become, in a house in which I did not venture to open my mouth, where I was obliged to leave the table before the meal was half over, and the room as soon as I had nothing more to do there; where, incessantly fettered to my work, I saw only objects of enjoyment for others and of privation for myself; where the sight of the liberty enjoyed by my master and companions increased the weight of my servitude; where, in disputes about matters as to which I was best informed, I did not venture to open my mouth; where, in short, everything that I saw became for my heart an object of longing, simply because I was deprived of all. From that time my ease of manner, my gaiety, the happy expressions which, in former times, when I had done something wrong, had gained me immunity from punishment—all were gone. I cannot help laughing when I remember how, one evening, at my father's house, having been sent to bed without any supper for some piece of roguery, I passed through the kitchen with my melancholy piece of bread, and, seeing the joint turning on the spit, sniffed at it. All the household was standing round the hearth, and, in passing, I was obliged to say good-night to everybody. When I had gone the round, I winked at the joint, which

---

[17] **Laridon**: A degenerate dog, from La Fontaine's *Fables* (1668 f.).

[18] *As*: A Roman unit of monetary measure.

looked so nice and smelt so good, and could not help bowing to it as well, and saying in a mournful voice, "Good-night, roast beef!" This naive sally amused them so much that they made me stop to supper. Perhaps it might have had the same effect with my master, but I am sure that it would never have occurred to me, and that I should not have had the courage, to say it in his presence.

In this manner I learnt to covet in silence, to dissemble, to lie, and, lastly, to steal — an idea which, up to that time, had never even entered my mind, and of which since then I have never been able to cure myself completely. Covetousness and weakness always lead in that direction. This explains why all servants are rogues, and why all apprentices ought to be; but the latter, in a peaceful state of equality, where all that they see is within their reach, lose, as they grow up, this disgraceful propensity. Not having had the same advantages, I have not been able to reap the same benefits.

It is nearly always good, but badly-directed principles, that make a child take the first step towards evil. In spite of continual privations and temptations, I had been more than a year with my master without being able to make up my mind to take anything, even eatables. My first theft was a matter of obliging some one else, but it opened the door to others, the motive of which was not so praiseworthy.

My master had a journeyman, named M. Verrat, whose house was in the neighbourhood, and had a garden some way off which produced very fine asparagus. M. Verrat, who was not too well supplied with money, conceived the idea of stealing some of his mother's young asparagus and selling it in order to provide himself with two or three good breakfasts. As he was unwilling to run the risk himself, and was not very active, he selected me for the expedition. After some preliminary cajoleries, which the more easily succeeded with me as I did not see their aim, he proposed it to me as an idea that had struck him on the spur of the moment. I strongly opposed it; he persisted. I have never been able to resist flattery: I gave in. I went every morning to gather a crop of the finest asparagus, and carried it to the Molard, where some good woman, who saw that I had just stolen it, told me so to my face in order to get it cheaper. In my fright I took whatever she chose to offer me, and took it to Verrat. The amount was immediately converted into a breakfast, of which I was the purveyor, and which he shared with another companion; I myself was quite satisfied with a few scraps, and never even touched their wine.

This little arrangement continued several days, without its even occurring to me to rob the robber, and to levy my tithe of the proceeds of M. Verrat's asparagus. I performed my part in the transaction with the greatest loyalty; my only motive was to please him who prompted me to carry it out. And yet, if I had been caught, what blows, abuse, and cruel treatment should I have had to endure, while the wretch, who would have been sure to give me the lie, would have been believed on his word, and I should have suffered double punishment for having had the impudence to accuse him, seeing that he was a journeyman, while I was only an apprentice! So true it is that, in every condition of life, the strong man who is guilty saves himself at the expense of the innocent who is weak.

In this manner I learned that stealing was not so terrible a thing as I had imagined, and I soon knew how to make such good use of my discovery, that nothing I desired, if it was within my reach, was safe from me. I was not absolutely ill-fed, and abstinence was only rendered difficult to me from seeing that my master observed it so ill himself. The custom of sending young people from the table when the most appetising dishes are brought on appears to me admirably adapted to make them gluttons as well as thieves. In a short time I became both the one and the other; and, as a rule, I came off very well; occasionally, when I was caught, very badly.

I shudder, and at the same time laugh, when I remember an apple-hunt which cost me dear. These apples were at the bottom of a store-room, which was lighted from the kitchen by means of a high grating. One day, when I was alone in the house, I climbed upon the kneading-trough, in order to look at the precious fruit in the garden of the Hesperides,[19] which was out of my reach. I went to fetch the spit to see if I could touch the apples; it was too short. To make it longer, I tied on to it another little spit which was used for small game, for my master was very fond of sport. I thrust several times without success; at last, to my great delight, I felt that I had secured an apple. I pulled very gently; the apple was close to the grating; I was ready to catch hold of it. But who can describe my grief, when I found that it was too large to pass through the bars? How many expedients I tried, to get it through! I had to find supports to keep the spit in its place, a knife long enough to divide the apple, a lath to hold it up. At last I managed to divide it, and hoped to be able to pull the pieces towards me one after the other; but no sooner were they separated than they both fell into the store-room. Compassionate reader, share my affliction!

I by no means lost courage; but I had lost considerable time. I was afraid of being surprised. I put off a more lucky attempt till the following day, and returned to my work as quietly as if I had done nothing, without thinking of the two tell-tale witnesses in the store-room.

The next day, finding the opportunity favourable, I made a fresh attempt. I climbed upon my stool, lengthened the spit, adjusted it, and was ready to make a lunge . . . but, unfortunately, the dragon was not asleep; all at once the door of the store-room opened, my master came out, folded his arms, looked at me, and said, "Courage!" . . . the pen falls from my hand.

In consequence of continuous ill-treatment I soon became less sensitive to it, and regarded it as a kind of compensation for theft, which gave me the right to continue the latter. Instead of looking back and considering the punishment, I looked forward and thought of revenge. I considered that, if I were beaten as a rogue, I was entitled to behave like one. I found that stealing and a flogging went together, and constituted a sort of bargain, and that, if I performed my part, I could safely leave my master to carry out his own. With this idea, I began to steal more quietly than before. I said to myself: "What will be the result? I shall be flogged. Never mind; I am made to be flogged."

I am fond of eating, but am not greedy; I am sensual, but not a gourmand; too many other tastes prevent that. I have never troubled myself about my food except when my heart has been unoccupied: and that has so seldom been the case during my life that I have scarcely had time to think about dainties. For this reason I did

---

[19] **Hesperides:** In Greek mythology, the nymphs who guarded a tree of golden apples.

not long confine my thievish propensities to eatables, but soon extended them to everything which tempted me; and, if I did not become a regular thief, it was because I have never been much tempted by money. Leading out of the common workshop was a private room belonging to my master, the door of which I found means to open and shut without being noticed. There I laid under contribution his best tools, drawings, proofs—in fact, everything which attracted me and which he purposely kept out of my reach. At bottom, these thefts were quite innocent, being only committed to serve him; but I was transported with joy at having these trifles in my power; I thought that I was robbing him of his talent together with its productions. Besides, I found boxes containing gold and silver filings, little trinkets, valuables, and coins. When I had four or five sous in my pocket, I thought I was rich; and yet, far from touching anything of what I found there, I do not even remember that I ever cast longing eyes upon it. I looked upon it with more affright than pleasure. I believe that this horror of stealing money and valuables was in great part the result of my bringing-up. With it were combined secret thoughts of disgrace, prison, punishment, and the gallows, which would have made me shudder if I had been tempted; whereas my tricks only appeared to me in the light of pieces of mischief, and in fact were nothing else. They could lead to nothing but a sound flogging from my master, and I prepared myself for that beforehand.

But, I repeat, I never felt sufficient longing to need to control myself; I had nothing to contend with. A single sheet of fine drawing-paper tempted me more than money enough to buy a ream of it. This singularity is connected with one of the peculiarities of my character; it has exercised such great influence upon my conduct that it is worth while to explain it.

I am a man of very strong passions, and, while I am stirred by them, nothing can equal my impetuosity; I forget all discretion, all feelings of respect, fear, and decency; I am cynical, impudent, violent, and fearless; no feeling of shame keeps me back, no danger frightens me; with the exception of the single object which occupies my thoughts, the universe is nothing to me. But all this lasts only for a moment, and the following moment plunges me into complete annihilation. In my calmer moments I am indolence and timidity itself; everything frightens and discourages me; a fly, buzzing past, alarms me; a word which I have to say, a gesture which I have to make, terrifies my idleness; fear and shame overpower me to such an extent that I would gladly hide myself from the sight of my fellow-creatures. If I have to act, I do not know what to do; if I have to speak, I do not know what to say; if anyone looks at me, I am put out of countenance. When I am strongly moved I sometimes know how to find the right words, but in ordinary conversation I can find absolutely nothing, and my condition is unbearable for the simple reason that I am obliged to speak.

Add to this, that none of my prevailing tastes centre in things that can be bought. I want nothing but unadulterated pleasures, and money poisons all. For instance, I am fond of the pleasures of the table; but, as I cannot endure either the constraint of good society or the drunkenness of the tavern, I can only enjoy them with a friend; alone, I cannot do so, for my imagination then occupies itself with other things, and eating affords me no pleasure. If my heated blood longs for women, my excited heart longs still more for affection. Women who could be bought for money would lose for me all their charms; I even doubt whether it would be in me to make use of them. I find it the same with all pleasures within my reach; unless they cost me nothing, I find them insipid. I only love those enjoyments which belong to no one but the first man who knows how to enjoy them.

Money has never appeared to me as valuable as it is generally considered. More than that, it has never even appeared to me particularly convenient. It is good for nothing in itself; it has to be changed before it can be enjoyed; one is obliged to buy, to bargain, to be often cheated, to pay dearly, to be badly served. I should like something which is good in quality; with my money I am sure to get it bad. If I pay a high price for a fresh egg, it is stale; for a nice piece of fruit, it is unripe; for a girl, she is spoilt. I am fond of good wine, but where am I to get it? At a wine merchant's? Whatever I do, he is sure to poison me. If I really wish to be well served, what trouble and embarrassment it entails! I must have friends, correspondents, give commissions, write, go backwards and forwards, wait, and in the end be often deceived! What trouble with my money! my fear of it is greater than my fondness for good wine.

Times without number, during my apprenticeship and afterwards, I have gone out with the intention of buying some delicacy. Coming to a pastrycook's shop, I notice some women at the counter; I think I can already see them laughing amongst themselves at the little glutton. I go to a fruiterer's; I eye the fine pears; their smell tempts me. Two or three young people close by me look at me; a man who knows me is standing in front of his shop; I see a girl approaching in the distance: is it the housemaid? My short-sightedness causes all kinds of illusions. I take all the passers-by for acquaintances; everywhere I am intimidated, restrained by some obstacle; my desire increases with my shame, and at last I return home like a fool, consumed with longing, having in my pocket the means of satisfying it, and yet not having had the courage to buy anything.

I should enter into the most insipid details if, in relating how my money was spent by myself or others, I were to describe the embarrassment, the shame, the repugnance, the inconvenience, the annoyances of all kinds which I have always experienced. In proportion as the reader, following the course of my life, becomes acquainted with my real temperament, he will understand all this, without my taking the trouble to tell him.

This being understood, it will be easy to comprehend one of my apparent inconsistencies—the union of an almost sordid avarice with the greatest contempt for money. It is a piece of furniture in which I find so little convenience, that it never enters my mind to long for it when I have not got it, and that, when I have got it, I keep it for a long time without spending it, for want of knowing how to make use of it in a way to please myself; but if a convenient and agreeable opportunity presents itself, I make such good use of it that my purse is empty before I know it. Besides this, one need not expect to find in me that curious characteristic of misers—that of spending for the sake of ostentation; on the contrary, I spend in secret for the sake of enjoyment; far from glorying in my expenditure, I conceal it. I feel so strongly that money is of no use to me, that I am almost ashamed to have any, still more to make use of it. If I had ever had an income sufficient to live comfortably upon, I am certain that I should never have been tempted to be a miser. I should have spent it all, without attempting to increase it; but my precarious circumstances make me careful. I worship freedom; I abhor restraint, trouble, dependence. As long as the money in my purse lasts, it assures my independence; it relieves me of the trouble of finding expedients to replenish it, a necessity which always inspired me with dread; but the fear of seeing it exhausted makes me hoard it carefully. The money which a man possesses is the instrument of freedom; that which we eagerly pursue is the instrument of slavery. Therefore I hold fast to that which I have, and desire nothing.

My disinterestedness is, therefore, nothing but idleness; the pleasure of possession is not worth the trouble of acquisition. In like manner, my extravagance is nothing but idleness; when the opportunity of spending agreeably presents itself, it cannot be too profitably employed. Money tempts me less than things, because between money and the possession of the desired object there is always an intermediary, whereas between the thing itself and the enjoyment of it there is none. If I see the thing, it tempts me; if I only see the means of gaining possession of it, it does not. For this reason I have committed thefts, and even now I sometimes pilfer trifles which tempt me, and which I prefer to take rather than to ask for; but neither when a child nor a grown-up man do I ever remember to have robbed anyone of a farthing, except on one occasion, fifteen years ago, when I stole seven *livres* ten *sous*. The incident is worth recording, for it contains a most extraordinary mixture of folly and impudence, which I should have found difficulty in believing if it concerned anyone but myself.

It took place at Paris. I was walking with M. de Franceuil in the Palais-Royal about five o'clock. He pulled out his watch, looked at it, and said: "Let us go to the Opera." I agreed; we went. He took two tickets for the amphitheatre, gave me one, and went on in front with the other. I followed him; he went in. Entering after him, I found the door blocked. I looked, and seeing everybody standing up, thought it would be easy to lose myself in the crowd, or at any rate to make M. de Franceuil believe that I had lost myself. I went out, took back my check, then my money, and went off, without thinking that as soon as I had reached the door everybody had taken their seats, and that M. de Franceuil clearly saw that I was no longer there.

As nothing was ever more foreign to my disposition than such behaviour, I mention it in order to show that there are moments of semi-delirium during which men must not be judged by their actions. I did not exactly want to steal the money, I wanted to steal the employment of it; the less of a theft it was, the greater its disgracefulness.

I should never finish these details if I were to follow all the paths along which, during my apprenticeship, I descended from the sublimity of heroism to the depths of worthlessness. And yet, although I adopted the vices of my position, I could not altogether acquire a taste for them. I wearied of the amusements of my companions; and when excessive restraint had rendered work unendurable to me, I grew tired of everything. This renewed my taste for reading, which I had for some time lost. This reading, for which I stole time from my work, became a new offence which brought new punishment upon me. The taste for it, provoked by constraint, became a passion, and soon a regular madness. La Tribu, a well-known lender of books, provided me with all kinds of literature. Good or bad, all were alike to me; I had no choice, and read everything with equal avidity. I read at the work-table, I read on my errands,

I read in the wardrobe, and forgot myself for hours together; my head became giddy with reading; I could do nothing else. My master watched me, surprised me, beat me, took away my books. How many volumes were torn, burnt, and thrown out of the window! how many works were left in odd volumes in La Tribu's stock! When I had no more money to pay her, I gave her my shirts, neckties, and clothes; my three sous of pocket-money were regularly taken to her every Sunday.

Well, then, I shall be told, money had become necessary to me. That is true; but it was not until my passion for reading had deprived me of all activity. Completely devoted to my new hobby, I did nothing but read, and no longer stole. Here again is one of my characteristic peculiarities. In the midst of a certain attachment to any manner of life, a mere trifle distracts me, alters me, rivets my attention, and finally becomes a passion. Then everything is forgotten; I no longer think of anything except the new object which engrosses my attention. My heart beat with impatience to turn over the leaves of the new book which I had in my pocket; I pulled it out as soon as I was alone, and thought no more of rummaging my master's work-room. I can hardly believe that I should have stolen even if I had had more expensive tastes. Limited to the present, it was not in my way to make preparations in this manner for the future. La Tribu gave me credit, the payments on account were small, and, as soon as I had my book in my pocket, I forgot everything else. The money which came to me honestly passed in the same manner into the hands of this woman; and, when she pressed me, nothing was easier to dispose of than my own property. It required too much foresight to steal in advance, and I was not even tempted to steal in order to pay.

In consequence of quarrels, blows, and secret and ill-chosen reading, my disposition became savage and taciturn; my mind became altogether perverted, and I lived like a misanthrope. However, if my good taste did not keep me from silly and insipid books, my good fortune preserved me from such as were filthy and licentious; not that La Tribu, a woman in all respects most accommodating, would have made any scruple about lending them to me; but, in order to increase their importance, she always mentioned them to me with an air of mystery which had just the effect of making me refuse them, as much from disgust as from shame; and chance aided my modest disposition so well, that I was more than thirty years old before I set eyes upon any of those dangerous books which a fine lady finds inconvenient because they can only be read with one hand.

In less than a year I exhausted La Tribu's little stock, and want of occupation, during my spare time, became painful to me. I had been cured of my childish and knavish propensities by my passion for reading, and even by the books I read, which, although ill-chosen and frequently bad, filled my heart with nobler sentiments than those with which my sphere of life had inspired me. Disgusted with everything that was within my reach, and feeling that everything which might have tempted me was too far removed from me, I saw nothing possible which might have flattered my heart. My excited senses had long clamoured for an enjoyment, the object of which I could not even imagine. I was as far removed from actual enjoyment as if I had been sexless; and, already fully developed and sensitive, I sometimes thought of my crazes, but saw nothing beyond them. In this strange situation, my restless imagination entered upon an occupation which saved me from myself and calmed my growing sensuality. This consisted in feeding myself upon the situations which had interested me in the course of my reading, in recalling them, in varying them, in combining them, in making them so truly my own that I became one of the persons who filled my imagination, and always saw myself in the situations most agreeable to my taste; and that, finally, the fictitious state in which I succeeded in putting myself made me forget my actual state with which I was so dissatisfied. This love of imaginary objects, and the readiness with which I occupied myself with them, ended by disgusting me with everything around me, and decided that liking for solitude which has never left me. In the sequel we shall see more than once the curious effects of this disposition, apparently so gloomy and misanthropic, but which is really due to a too affectionate, too loving, and too tender heart, which, being unable to find any in existence resembling it, is obliged to nourish itself with fancies. For the present, it is sufficient for me to have defined the origin and first cause of a propensity which has modified all my passions, and which, restraining them by means of themselves, has always made me slow to act, owing to my excessive impetuosity in desire.

In this manner I reached my sixteenth year, restless, dissatisfied with myself and everything, without any of the tastes of my condition of life, without any of the pleasures of my age, consumed by desires of the object of which I was ignorant, weeping without any cause for tears, sighing without knowing why—in short, tenderly caressing my chimeras, since I saw nothing around me which counterbalanced them. On Sundays, my fellow-apprentices came to fetch me after service to go and amuse myself with them. I would gladly have escaped from them if I had been able; but, once engaged in their amusements, I became more excited and went further than any of them; it was as difficult to set me going as to stop me. Such was always my disposition. During our walks outside the city I always went further than any of them without thinking about my return, unless others thought of it for me. Twice I was caught: the gates were shut before I could get back. The next day I was treated as may be imagined; the second time I was promised such a reception if it ever happened again, that I resolved not to run the risk of it; yet this third time, so dreaded, came to pass. My watchfulness was rendered useless by a confounded Captain Minutoli, who always shut the gate at which he was on guard half-an-hour before the others. I was returning with two companions. About half a league from the city I heard the retreat sounded: I doubled my pace: I heard the tattoo[20] beat, and ran with all my might. I arrived out of breath and bathed in perspiration; my heart beat; from a distance I saw the soldiers at their posts; I rushed up and cried out with a voice half-choked. It was too late! Twenty paces from the outposts, I saw the first bridge raised. I shuddered when I saw those terrible horns rising in the air—a sinister and fatal omen of the destiny which that moment was opening for me.

In the first violence of my grief I threw myself on the *glacis*[21] and bit the ground. My companions, laughing at their misfortune, immediately made up their minds what to do. I did the same, but my resolution was different from theirs. On the spot I swore never to return to my master; and the next morning, when they entered the

---

[20] **tattoo:** A signal, sounded before taps, to call soldiers to their barracks for the night.

[21] *glacis:* The slope in front of the city walls.

city after the gates were opened, I said good-bye to them for ever, only begging them secretly to inform my cousin Bernard of the resolution I had taken, and of the place where he might be able to see me once more.

After I had entered upon my apprenticeship I saw less of him. For some time we used to meet on Sunday, but gradually each of us adopted other habits, and we saw one another less frequently. I am convinced that his mother had much to do with this change. He was a child of the upper city; I, a poor apprentice, was only a child of Saint-Gervais.[22] In spite of our relationship, there was no longer any equality between us; it was derogatory to him to associate with me. However, relations were not entirely broken off between us, and, as he was a good-natured lad, he sometimes followed the dictates of his heart instead of his mother's instructions. When he was informed of my resolution, he hastened to me, not to try and dissuade me from it or to share it, but to lessen the inconveniences of my flight by some small presents, since my own resources could not take me very far. Amongst other things he gave me a small sword, which had taken my fancy exceedingly, and which I carried as far as Turin, where necessity obliged me to dispose of it, and where, as the saying is, I passed it through my body. The more I have since reflected upon the manner in which he behaved towards me at this critical moment, the more I have felt convinced that he followed the instructions of his mother, and perhaps of his father; for it is inconceivable that, left to himself, he would not have made some effort to keep me back, or would not have been tempted to follow; but, no! he rather encouraged me in my plan than tried to dissuade me; and, when he saw me quite determined, he left me without shedding many tears. We have never corresponded or seen each other since. It is a pity: his character was essentially good; we were made to love each other.

Before I abandon myself to the fatality of my lot, allow me to turn my eyes for a moment upon the destiny which, in the nature of things, would have awaited me if I had fallen into the hands of a better master. Nothing was more suitable to my disposition or better adapted to make me happy than the quiet and obscure lot of a respectable artisan, especially of a certain class such as that of the engravers of Geneva. Such a position, sufficiently lucrative to afford a comfortable livelihood, but not sufficiently so to lead to fortune, would have limited my ambition for the rest of my days, and, leaving me an honourable leisure to cultivate modest tastes, would have confined me within my own sphere, without offering me the means of getting out of it. My imaginative powers were rich enough to beautify all callings with their chimeras, and strong enough to transport me, so to speak, at will from one to another; so it would have been immaterial to me in what position I actually found myself. It could not have been so far from the place where I was to my first castle in the air, that I could not have taken up my abode there without any difficulty. From this alone it followed that the simplest vocation, that which involved the least trouble and anxiety, that which allowed the greatest mental freedom, was the one which suited me best: and that was exactly my own. I should have passed a peaceful and

---

[22] **He . . . Saint-Gervais:** Bernard lived in the more fashionable part of Geneva; Rousseau lived in the Saint-Gervais, the poorer part.

quiet life, such as my disposition required, in the bosom of my religion, my country, my family, and my friends, in the monotony of a profession that suited my taste, and in a society after my own heart. I should have been a good Christian, a good citizen, a good father of a family, a good friend, a good workman, a good man in every relation of life. I should have loved my position in life, perhaps honoured it; and, having spent a life—simple, indeed, and obscure, but calm and serene—I should have died peacefully in the bosom of my family. Though, doubtless, soon forgotten, I should at least have been regretted as long as anyone remembered me.

Instead of that—what picture am I going to draw? Let us not anticipate the sorrows of my life; I shall occupy my readers more than enough with this melancholy subject.

∾ RAMPRASAD SEN
B. INDIA, 1718–1775

BAHK-tee

SHAHK-tee; KAH-lee

RAHM-pruh-sahd

The intensely religious village life of India produced not only storytellers— whose primary purpose was transmitting the stories of gods, goddesses, heroes, and heroines—but also poets who expressed ordinary people's spiritual longing for God. Emotional worship or surrender to God in Hinduism is called *bhakti*. Bhakti became a religious movement in India during the religious reforms of the eighth, ninth, and tenth centuries. A particular version of bhakti was devoted to feminine divinity; in India there had been a long history of worshiping the great goddess **Shakti**[1] — also known as **Kali** and Durga—but a resurgence of her worship, led by the poet **Ramprasad** Sen, took place in Bengal[2] during the eighteenth century. Like medieval Christian poets devoted to the Virgin Mother, Bengal poets of this time favored the feminine dimension of God, which seemed to invite a personal relationship, an opportunity for conversation, and expressions of sadness and longing.

www For more information about Ramprasad, see bedfordstmartins .com/worldlit compact.

Ramprasad's simple lyricism and familiar images touched a broad range of listeners; his songs appealed to scholars and peasants alike. His poetic skills influenced succeeding generations of Indian poets. Rabindranath Tagore, the most famous Bengali writer of the late nineteenth century, composed Kali songs even though he was not a worshiper of Kali himself; he merged the goddess's image with nationalistic devotion.

---

[1] **Shakti:** Shakti is the collective name for the consort of Shiva who has several names. **Shakti** is the feminine dynamic energy by which God creates, preserves, and dissolves the world. **Kali** is usually portrayed as terrifying: blue-black, three-eyed, and four-armed, with a necklace of human heads and a girdle of severed hands. **Durga**, "the unfathomable one," is one of the oldest versions of the Great Mother: fair complexioned and riding a lion, she releases humans from rebirth with her touch.

[2] **Bengal:** A region in the northeast Indian peninsula, now divided between India and Bangladesh.

An androgynous, naked Shiva is attended by Parvati, his spouse, who offers him liquid refreshment. The bull represents Shiva; the lion, Parvati; and the elephant-headed creature is Ganesha, a popular Hindu god. (Courtesy of the British Museum)

Poet and Legend. Ramprasad Sen was born in Kumarhatta, now Halishar, about twenty-five miles from Calcutta. His father, Ramram Sen, was of the Vaidyas caste—that of physicians. Ramprasad had a minimal education and was versed in Sanskrit, Persian, and Hindi as well as Bengali. As a young man he got a job in Calcutta as a clerk with an estate manager, Valulachandra Ghosal. Rather than paying attention to the accounts, Ramprasad wrote poetry. When his employer discovered the way Ramprasad was spending his time he was angry, but Ghosal was sympathetic to the young man's yearnings to serve Kali and provided him

These [Ramprasad's poems] have gone to the heart of a people as few poets' work has done. Such songs as the exquisite "This day will surely pass, Mother, this day will pass," I have heard from coolies on the road or workers in the paddy fields; I have heard it by broad rivers at sunset, when the parrots were flying to roost and the village folk thronging from marketing to the ferry. . . .

– critic EDWARD THOMPSON, 1923

with a pension and an introduction to the court of the Raja of Krishnagar. Here Ramprasad rose to the position of "Entertainer of Poets."

Ramprasad became famous during his lifetime, and there are numerous legends about his encounters with Kali and her demands on him. His poems, which were first passed down orally, have been collected in several volumes. *Vidyasundar,* which was composed in the 1760s or 1770s, is an extended poem about how the Raja of Kanchi's son won the hand of the Raja of Burdwan's daughter. *Kalikirttan* is a collection of songs or hymns to Kali. The poems in *Krishnakirttan* are devoted to Krishna.

Ramprasad died in 1775. One legend says that he died with a Kali song on his lips, beseeching her to save him, and that indeed he slipped away from the endless cycle of reincarnations into Brahman.[3] In another version, Ramprasad followed an image of Kali into the Ganges River while reciting poems to her and drowned. He was regarded a saint.

Background for Bengali Songs to Kali.   In most world religions there are at least two significant paths followed by most practitioners: the path of legalism and the path of mysticism. The first is a matter of believing certain doctrines, following prescribed rules or laws, and performing certain rituals interpreted and led by a priest, minister, rabbi, or imam. The second is one of direct, personal experience of the sacred and involves various techniques for achieving mystical union with the divine without the mediation of a priest or institution. In the history of Hinduism, Brahmanism[4] represents the orthodox path of legalism: The Brahman priest, who masters the appropriate ceremonies or rituals, serves as an intercessor between the worshiper and god. The mystical cults in India are grouped under the name *bhakti,* a Sanskrit word meaning the path of total surrender to god as a means of achieving salvation. A guru, rather than a priest, serves as a bhakti guide. For both the orthodox and the bhakti the goal is the same: Salvation is *moksha,* the release from *samsara*—the cycle of life, death, and rebirth—in order to be unified with God.

Since the tenth century of Indian history, Hinduism had primarily centered around the worship of two deities: Vishnu—in his manifestations, or avatars, as Rama and Krishna—and Shiva.[5] In Hinduism, worshipers are also often devoted to the consort of a deity; when the goddess is recognized as the energy or power behind existence, she is known as Shakti. Ramprasad's particular kind of bhakti worship was directed at Shiva's consort, **Shakti** or the Great Mother. The rituals and meditative practices describing the Shakti pathway are contained in sacred texts called Tantra; Shaktism is also called Tantrism. A particular branch of tantric worship involves sexual practices that are said to lead to a mystical union with Shakti.

---

[3] **Brahman:** In Hinduism, the Absolute Reality which transcends all thought, all names, and definitions. There is no equivalent concept in religions that feature a personal god.

[4] **Brahmanism:** Brahmanism recognizes the creator Brahma and the priestly class of Brahmans who administer the appropriate Hindu rituals.

[5] **Vishnu . . . Shiva:** Manifestations of Brahman, the Absolute or Ultimate Being. They form a trinity with Brahma, the creator, who has little ceremonial or cult importance.

As a couple, Shiva represents transcendent power and Kali immanent or manifested power. Kali is usually represented as dancing or in sexual union with Shiva. Sri Ramakrishna (1836–1886), a famous mystic from the nineteenth century, described one of his visions of Kali in a way that described her two aspects coming together. He saw a beautiful woman emerge from the Ganges and approach a grove of trees where he was meditating. The woman gave birth to a beautiful baby, and she gently nursed it. After a while she suddenly changed into a horrible monster. She took the infant in her ugly jaws and crushed it. She chewed it, swallowed it, and then returned to the Ganges and disappeared into the water. Sri Ramakrishna's vision exemplifies the idea of Kali as a totality that reconciles creation and dissolution.

Ramprasad's Kali Songs.   To somebody living in the West, writing love songs to the terrible and ferocious Kali might seem strange, yet Kali embraces many aspects of life. For Ramprasad, Kali ultimately represented release from the endless sufferings of mortality. In his poems, Ramprasad uses standard bhakti themes: Kali's neglect of her devotee, her carelessness, her preoccupation with wild dancing and her habit of standing on Shiva; the poet complains about her and threatens to give up on her. Kali's role as a goddess in the universe parallels the role she plays in Ramprasad's poetry and life.

Because Ramprasad's poems were initially passed down orally, multiple versions of the same poem arose, a challenge for any translator. Furthermore, these Kali songs were usually written in simple, colloquial Bengali, which demands a colloquial American English translation in order to communicate the voice of the poems. Kali is often addressed as "Mother" in the songs, suggesting the personal relationship of a child to its mother, or the feelings of the individual toward the greater, cosmic reality. In "It's This Hope in Hope," Ramprasad laments being lured into this world by Kali and fooled by the world's appearance of sweetness. Ramprasad's sense of play is evident in "The Dark Mother Is Flying a Kite," although the metaphor of kite-flying ultimately takes on a serious dimension.

In "Kali, Why Are You Naked Again?" the poet evokes the popular image of Kali standing on the body of Shiva and gently chides her about her nudity. Part of the poignant attraction of a Kali song comes from the contrast between the playful tenderness of the poet and the horrifying power of the goddess. As in a personal relationship, the poet expresses disappointment, threatens to break off contact, pinpoints the mother's neglect. But in "Now Cry Kali and Take the Plunge!" the poet challenges himself to dive into the sea of consciousness and confesses his shortcomings and failures. "Why Should I Go to Kashi?" is an important statement about the bhakti spiritual path; Ramprasad makes it clear that he does not personally subscribe to the path of pilgrimage and sacrificial offerings, the brand of Hinduism associated with Brahmanism. In "What's More to Fear around This Place?" Ramprasad gives Shiva a role but concludes with an image of Kali as a tree bearing the fruits of release and immortality. With his clear, down-to-earth, accessible images, Ramprasad established a tone for Kali songs that was imitated by generations of writers after him.

The peasants and the *pandits* enjoy his songs equally. They draw solace from them in the hour of despair and even at the moment of death. The dying man brought to the banks of the Ganges asks his companions to sing Ramprasadi songs.

– critic SUKUMAR SEN, 1971

■ **FURTHER RESEARCH**

Cultural Background

Dutt, Romesh Chunder. *Cultural Heritage of Bengal.* 1962.

Kinsley, David R. *The Sword and the Flute: Kali and Krnsa, Dark Visions of the Terrible and the Sublime in Hindu Mythology.* 1975.

McDaniel, June. *The Madness of the Saints: Ecstatic Religion in Bengal.* 1989.

Mookerjee, Ajit. *Kali: The Feminine Force.* 1988.

Criticism

McLean, Malcolm. *Devoted to the Goddess: The Life and Work of Ramprasad.* 1998.

Sen, Ramprasad. *Grace and Mercy in Her Wild Hair: Selected Poems to the Mother Goddess.* 1982. (See the introduction by Leonard Nathan and Clinton Seely.)

Sen, Sukumar. *History of Bengali Literature.* 1971.

Thompson, Edward J., and Arthur Marshman Spencer. *Bengali Religious Lyrics, Sakta.* 1923.

■ **PRONUNCIATION**

bhakti: BAHK-tee
Kali: KAH-lee
Ramprasad: RAHM-pruh-sahd
Shakti: SHAK-tee

∾ It's This Hope in Hope

This and the following five poems translated by Leonard Nathan and Clinton Seely

It's this hope in hope, this happening again
To be in the world, this being over and over,
The bee's blunder when it goes for
The painted version of the lotus.

You've given me bitter leaves,
Swearing they were sweet, and my old
Sweet tooth has cost me a whole day
Spitting the bitterness out.

Mother, You lured me into this world,
You said: "Let's play," only to cheat
My hope out of its hope with Your playing.

Ramprasad says:[1] In this game
The end was a foregone conclusion.
Now, at dusk, take up Your child
In Your arms and go home.

---

[1] **Ramprasad says:** It is common for Ramprasad to use his own name in these oral poems, as a way to identify the poet. Doing so also allows him to enter the poem as an identifiable voice.

∾ The Dark Mother Is Flying a Kite

The dark Mother
Is flying a kite
In the world's fairground.

O, Mind, see—you are up there
In the gusts of hope,
Payed out on the string of illusion,
Your frame strung together
Skeleton and pulse stuck on.

But the Maker overdid it,
Giving the kite too much ego[1]
In the building,
Toughening the string with glue
And powdered glass.[2]

So Mother, if out of a thousand kites
You lose one or two,
Laugh and clap.

Prasad° says: that kite is going to take off   short for *Ramprasad*
In the southern breeze,
And on the other shore
Of this ocean of lives
It will dive fast to its freedom.

---

[1] **ego:** Ramprasad refers to his "Mind," meaning that part of him that is subject to delusion and false hope, akin to the term *psyche*. The translators add to the concept by saying "too much ego" in the third stanza, choosing a word associated with Sigmund Freud that Ramprasad would not have used.

[2] **powdered glass:** Kite strings are coated with glue and powdered glass for the purpose of cutting down another flyer's kite.

❧ Kali, Why Are You Naked Again?

Kali, why are You naked again?
Good grief, haven't You any shame?

Mother, don't You have clothes?
Where is the pride of a king's daughter?

And, Mother, is this some family duty—
This standing on the chest of Your man?

You're naked, He's naked,
You hang around the burning grounds.[1]

O, Mother, we are dying of shame.
10   Now put on Your woman's clothes.

Mother, Your necklace gleams,
Those human heads shine at Your throat.

Prasad says: Even Shiva fears You
When You're like this.

---

[1] **burning grounds:** The places where bodies are cremated, the place where Shiva and Kali cut away all unnecessary, egotistical elements from the human psyche.

～ Now Cry Kali and Take the Plunge!

Now cry Kali and take the plunge!
O, my Mind, dive into this sea,
This heart which has yet to be sounded.
There are gems down there that two or three dives
Aren't going to get. Now, hold your breath
And jump! Kick down to where She sits[1]
Deep in the wise waters, a great pearl.
You can do it, all it takes
Is overwhelming love and the memory
Of Shiva's good words.[2]

Down there the Six Passions cruise
Like crocodiles snapping at anything
That moves, so cover yourself with knowledge
Like turmeric[3] smeared on the skin —
The odor will keep them off.
I tell you there's a world of wealth
In that water.

Ramprasad says: Dive in
And you're going to come up with a fortune.

---

[1] **She sits:** A reference to Kali's residence at the bottom of consciousness or at the base of the spinal column, in the lowest *chakra*. The six chakras are centers of energy stretching from the base of the spinal column to the top of the head.

[2] **Shiva's good words:** Shiva is the speaker in the tantric texts.

[3] **turmeric:** A yellow plant of the ginger family; smeared on the body, it is believed to ward off crocodiles. Turmeric may also refer to adopting the yellow robes of the ascetic to help ward off the passions.

∾   Why Should I Go to Kashi?

Why should I go to Kashi?[1]
At Her feet you'll find it all—
Gaya,[2] the Ganges, Kashi.
Meditating in my lotus heart[3]
I float on blissful waters.
Her feet are red lotuses
Crammed with shrines
And Her name spoken
Consumes evil like a fire
10   In a pile of dry cotton.
If there is no head to worry,
You can't have a headache.

Everytime I hear about Gaya,
The offerings there, the good deeds
Recited, I laugh. I know Shiva
Has said that dying at Kashi saves.
But I know too that salvation
Always follows worship around
Like a slave, and what's this salvation
20   If it swallows the saved like water
In water? Sugar I love
But haven't the slightest desire
To merge with sugar.

Ramprasad says with amazement:
Grace and mercy in Her wild hair—
Think of that
And all good things[4] are yours.

---

[1] **Kashi:** Kashi is Benares, the residence of Shiva, and one of the most sacred sites along the Ganges.

[2] **Gaya:** A place of pilgrimage in northeastern India, the site of Gautama Buddha's enlightenment.

[3] **lotus heart:** The fourth chakra, the center of mystical powers.

[4] **good things:** There are four good things to get from life: 1. (*dharma*) lawful order, sacred duty, and moral virtue; 2. (*artha*) power and success; 3. (*kama*) love and pleasure; and 4. (*moksha*) release from delusion and the limitations of existence.

ꙮ What's More to Fear around This Place?

What's more to fear
Around this place?

My body is Tara's[1] field
In which the God of Gods
Like a good farmer
Sows His seed with a great *mantra.*[2]

Around this body, faith
Is set like a fence
With patience for posts.

10   With Shiva watching
What can the thieves of time
Hope to do?

He oversees the Six Oxen
Driving them out of the barn.

He mows the grass of sin
With the honed blade of Kali's name.

Love rains down
And Devotion night and day.

Prasad says: On Kali's tree
20   Goodness, wealth, love and release
Can be had for the picking.

---

[1] **Tara:** Another name for Kali; this is not — on the surface at least — the popular Tara of Tibetan Buddhism.

[2] *mantra:* A sacred utterance, often used for meditation.

TEXT IN CONTEXT

ꙮ OLAUDAH EQUIANO
B. AFRICA, 1745–1797

oh-LOW-dah
eh-kwee-AH-noh

About two years before the publication of the misadventures of Voltaire's ill-fated hero Candide, a ten-year-old African was kidnapped from his home in Essaka, in what is now Nigeria. An innocent like Candide, this young man was taken into slavery and eventually sold to traders on the Atlantic coast, where he would embark on a very real journey into misfortune, oppression, and despair. His eloquent tale of betrayal, enslavement, hardship, and finally emancipation, *The Interesting Narrative of the Life of* **Olaudah Equiano,** was published in London in 1789. Although a few slaves had told their stories in print before—most notably Ignatius Sancho[1] and Ottobah Cugoano[2]— *Equiano's Travels,* as it is often called, marks a crucial moment in the development of a significant new literary genre, the SLAVE NARRATIVE. Reflecting its author's spiritual and intellectual resolution and framing the incidents of his life as a slave in a deeply felt humanitarianism, this story would inspire over the next century such works as Frederick Douglass's ***Narrative of the Life of Frederick Douglass*** (1845) and Harriet Jacobs's ***Incidents in the Life of a Slave Girl*** (1861).

p. 522
p. 501

---

[1] **Ignatius Sancho** (1729–1780): Writer of the African diaspora who was born aboard a slave ship and educated in the household of the Duchess of Montagu; he became an art critic and grocer, and corresponded with several important figures in England. His *Letters of the Late Ignatius Sancho* appeared in 1782.

[2] **Ottobah Cugoano** (1757?–early nineteenth century): African writer who, like Equiano, was captured from the western coast of Africa and sold into slavery.

Ibo Life.   Equiano's "round unvarnished tale," as it was called in an early review, begins with a brief description of his birth in 1745. His father, he tells us, was one of the chief elders, the Embrenche, of his community, and as a child Equiano was blessed with good omens. In the first chapter of his book, Equiano describes the society, religious beliefs, and customs of the **Ibo** people with whom he spent his childhood. Within each village, a council of elders settled matters that affected the community and mediated disputes between parties. Nonetheless, a village assembly, which was open to all except the *osu* or slaves, ensured that members of the village had a voice in the decision-making process. As can be seen in Chinua Achebe's ***Things Fall Apart***, which describes the Ibo traditions more than a century after Equiano's death, the Ibo also were organized along a complex system of age-group, kinship, and ritual ties. In the eighteenth century, they had an intricate network of trade among themselves and with their neighbors to the south who inhabited the city-states in the Niger delta region. Among the "commodities" traded were human beings, and when he was about eleven, Equiano was kidnapped by a raiding party and eventually taken to the Atlantic coast to be sold into slavery.

EE-boh

p. 1604

Portrait of Olaudah Equiano, 1789
This engraving appeared in the first publication of The Interesting Narrative of the Life of Olaudah Equiano. *Note that Equiano is holding a Bible opened to Acts, Chapters IV and V. (Courtesy of the American Antiquarian Society, Worcester, Mass.)*

www   For links to more information about Olaudah Equiano and quizzes on *The Interesting Narrative,* see bedford stmartins.com/ worldlitcompact.

Slavery.   Equiano's story up to this point is fairly typical of the thousands of men, women, and children who were kidnapped by rival tribes or parties of raiders and exchanged for rifles, textiles, tobacco, iron, brass, and other items. Sometimes, as in Equiano's case, the captured would pass through a number of hands on their forced journey to the coastal towns along the Gold Coast or in the Niger delta, where they were held in forts until sold to European slave traders. From there they were packed into the infamous "slavers," the crowded ships that would take them to the West Indies or the United States. In his narrative, Equiano describes the horrible conditions aboard the slave ship, the anxieties and sorrows he suffered upon being moved from place to place and being separated from his sister. He was taken to Barbados, then to Virginia, and sold to a plantation owner. Within a few months he was sold again to Michael Henry Pascal, a British naval captain, with whom Equiano sailed to England, Holland, and North America, where his ship engaged in battles during the Seven Years' War. Through Pascal, Equiano learned to read and write, and he was treated with kindness and with some measure of respect by Pascal's relatives, the Guerins, in London. In 1763 Pascal sold Equiano to Captain James Doran, who took him to the West Indies, where he finally ended up the property of Robert King, a Quaker merchant.

Freedom.   Equiano notes early on that the name Olaudah means "fortunate one," and although his life would suggest the opposite, he reminds readers who haven't seen the horrors of the slave trade that, by comparison with most Africans taken into slavery, he can only

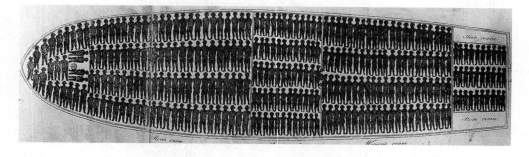

Slave Ship

Along with slave narratives, abolitionists circulated illustrations of the horrendous conditions aboard slave ships. (Courtesy of the American Antiquarian Society, Worcester, Mass.)

consider himself "as a particular favorite of Heaven." Working for King, Equiano managed to save enough money to buy his freedom on July 11, 1766. He writes: "Before night, I, who had been a slave in the morning, trembling at the will of another, was become my own master, and completely free." Nonetheless, partly because he felt a debt of gratitude, Equiano remained in King's service as an able-bodied sailor for another year. On July 26, 1767, Equiano left for London, where he worked for a while as a hairdresser and bolstered his education before returning to the life he had come to know as a seafarer and small trader. Signing on with several ships in various capacities, Equiano traveled widely during this time throughout the Mediterranean as well as to Central America, the West Indies, and the Arctic. He traveled with Constantine John Phipps, who led a dangerous expedition by way of the Arctic in search of a northeast passage to India. That voyage had a profound influence on Equiano's life; the ships were for some time trapped in frozen waters, and Equiano once nearly drowned during an attempt to drag the boats free from the ice. The experience, he writes, "made a lasting impression on my mind, and by the grace of God proved afterwards a mercy to me; it caused me to reflect deeply on my eternal state, and to seek the Lord with full purpose of heart ere it was too late."

Conversion.   Equiano's conversion marks an important turning point in his autobiography and aligns the narrative with spiritual autobiographies such as Augustine's *Confessions* and slave narratives such as Frederick Douglass's, texts in which conversion to Christianity is a climactic moment in the plot. Equiano's conversion experience is fraught with doubt and uncertainty, troubled dreams and feelings of guilt, leading ultimately to a vision on October 6, 1774, of Jesus on the cross. In the months leading up to his conversion and in the months it takes to unfold, Equiano studies the Bible carefully, puzzling over key passages and seeking advice from others. Often he pauses over the discrepancy between Christian teachings and slavery, shocked by the hypocrisy of those who preach the former and practice the latter. He also notes similarities between Christian and especially Hebrew practices and the customs of the Ibo.

Once convinced of the authenticity of his spiritual transformation and well studied in the Bible, Equiano joined the Methodist Church and became something of an evangelist, sparring over doctrine with a Catholic priest in Cadiz and preaching to the Mosquito Indians during his voyage to Central America in 1776. After establishing his residence

Equiano's *Narrative* is so richly structured that it became the prototype of the nineteenth-century slave narrative.

– HENRY LOUIS GATES JR., *The Classic Slave Narratives,* 1987

Surely this traffic
cannot be good,
which spreads like a
pestilence, and taints
what it touches!
which violates that
first natural right of
mankind, equality
and independency,
and gives one man a
dominion over his
fellows which God
could never intend!

   – OLAUDAH EQUIANO,
    Interesting Narrative

in London, Equiano grew into an active leader in the abolitionist and
antislavery movement and worked for a while as the commissary of
stores and provisions for the Sierra Leone project, an effort to resettle
displaced Africans in Sierra Leone. In 1787 he founded the Sons of
Africa, an abolitionist group, and in 1790 he submitted a petition to Parliament advocating the abolition of slavery. In 1792, Equiano married
Susanna Cullen, with whom he had two daughters, Anna Maria and
Johanna. In 1796, a few months after the birth of their second daughter,
Susanna died, followed by Equiano on March 31, 1797. Anna Maria survived her father by only a few months, leaving behind only Johanna,
who inherited £950 from the family estate in 1816 when she turned
twenty-one; after that, nothing more is known of her.

Work.   First published in 1789, *The Interesting Narrative of the Life of
Olaudah Equiano, or Gustavus Vassa the African* was enormously popular
in England and the United States, with eight English and one American
edition printed by 1794. By 1797 the work had been translated into Dutch,
Russian, and French. As a work of autobiography, moral exhortation, and
social criticism, Equiano's book greatly enhanced the growing antislavery
movement in England that eventually led to the abolition in that country
of the slave trade in 1807 and the emancipation of slaves in the British
colonies in 1833–34. But Equiano's narrative also came under attack, with
charges of fraud raised against the text's accuracy, the author's identity,
and the story's very authenticity. In the preface to a sixth edition, Equiano
answers these charges, labeling them "invidious falsehoods." The authenticity of slave narratives was questioned often in England and the United
States. Following Equiano's example, both Frederick Douglass and Harriet
Jacobs added to their titles the phrase, "Written by Himself" or "Written
by Herself," in anticipation of such doubts.

    While important as a social text, *The Life of Olaudah Equiano* is
also a significant literary achievement that exerted a powerful influence
on subsequent slave narratives and generations of Anglo-African and
African American writers, including some present-day authors. As critic
Henry Louis Gates Jr. observes in *The Classic Slave Narratives,* "Equiano's
Narrative is so richly structured that it became the prototype of the
nineteenth-century slave narrative." Gates points to a key structural
feature of the slave narrative, a weaving together of plots in which the
passage from slavery to emancipation follows from or is accompanied
by a transition from oral culture to written culture and a surrendering
to spiritual, Christian redemption. Rhetorically moving and vividly
descriptive, Equiano's *Life* personalizes what for most readers are
remote horrors, even as it presents Equiano himself as an exemplary

Nineteenth-Century Americas: The Haitian Revolution

In 1789, the year of the French Revolution and the year when Equiano's *Narrative* was published, St. Domingue, now Haiti, was France's most prosperous colony. It produced two-fifths of the world's sugar and half the world's coffee, and it accounted for forty percent of French overseas trade. Its population of more than half a million included about 25,000 white colonists, an equal number of free citizens of mixed descent, or *gens de couleur* as they were known, and more than 500,000 slaves of African descent. The struggle for liberty, fraternity, and equality in France was translated into a slave rebellion in this colonial context.

Francois-Dominique Toussaint-Louverture Declaring the Constitution of the Republic of Haiti, July 1, 1801. Toussaint-Louverture, the "black Napolean," is shown here with Haiti's constitution in hand. The presence of God and the bishop in this engraving is an expression of the divine source and inspiration of the document. (The Bridgeman Art Library)

In the wake of the violence in France, white small holders (*petits blancs* who worked small farms) and large plantation owners (*grands blancs*) in St. Domingue marshaled their slaves into fighting forces and struggled against each other for political control of the colony. However, when the French National Assembly granted political rights to propertied *gens de couleur* in 1790, the whites banded together to prevent racial equality, and the political struggle turned into a racial war. Slaves originally mobilized to fight for their white masters chose to fight for their own emancipation. Pierre-Dominique Toussaint-Louverture became governor general of the colony in 1797, and led the slaves to defeat one opponent after another — the white plantation owners and small holders, invading forces of Spanish and English troops, and Napoleon's army of 44,000, led by the emperor's brother-in-law, General Charles Victor Emmanuel Leclerc. Toussaint-Louverture was captured by trickery during the Napoleonic campaign and imprisoned in France, where he died in captivity. His successor Jean-Jacques Dessalines declared the colony's independence on January 1, 1804.

Although France managed to hold on to its other Caribbean colonies, the Haitian Revolution redefined the aims of the French Revolution for the Western Hemisphere. It spurred on antislavery movements that led to the abolition of the slave trade and eventually slavery itself in the British and French colonies. It also encouraged abolitionists in the United States and linked emancipation with the causes of freedom and democracy in the West. Convinced that the example of Haiti would bring about more revolutions, slaveholders throughout the Americas developed what historian Anthony Maingot has called a "terrified consciousness."

figure who embodies the ENLIGHTENMENT ideals of ingenuity, stoic fortitude, and compassion for others.

p. 302

p. 232

As a travelogue, moral critique, and adventure story, *The Life of Olaudah Equiano* shares features with **Candide** and even with Swift's **Gulliver's Travels**. Yet in Equiano's odyssey, the hardships and oppression are not fiction but reality.

■ FURTHER RESEARCH

Biography
Walvin, James. *An African's Life: The Life and Times of Olaudah Equiano, 1745–1797.* 1998.

Background
Acholonu, Catherine Obianuju. *The Igbo Roots of Olaudah Equiano.* 1989.
Davis, Charles T., and Henry Louis Gates Jr. *The Slave's Narrative.* 1985.
Edwards, Paul. *Black Writers in England, 1760–1890.* 1991.
Gates, Henry Louis, Jr. *The Classic Slave Narratives.* 1987.

Criticism
Allison, Robert, ed. Introduction. *The Interesting Narrative of the Life of Olaudah Equiano, Written by Himself.* 1995.
Costanzo, Angelo. *Surprising Narrative: Olaudah Equiano and the Beginnings of Black Autobiography.* 1987.
Edwards, Paul, ed. Introduction. *The Life of Olaudah Equiano.* 1988.
Gates, Henry Louis, Jr., and William L. Andrews, eds. *Pioneers of the Black Atlantic: Five Slave Narratives from the Enlightenment, 1772–1815.* 1998.
Sandiford, Keith. *Measuring the Moment: Strategies of Protest in Eighteenth-Century Afro-English Writing.* 1988.

■ PRONUNCIATION

Olaudah Equiano: oh-LOW-dah eh-kwee-AH-noh
Ibo: EE-boh

∾ The Interesting Narrative of the Life of Olaudah Equiano

FROM **CHAPTER 1**

[Equiano's Igbo Roots]

I believe it is difficult for those who publish their own memoirs to escape the imputation of vanity; nor is this the only disadvantage under which they labor: it is also their misfortune that what is uncommon is rarely, if ever, believed, and what is obvious we are apt to turn from with disgust, and to charge the writer with impertinence. People generally think those memoirs only worthy to be read or remembered which abound in great or striking events, those, in short, which in a high degree excite either admiration or pity; all others they consign to contempt and oblivion. It is therefore, I confess, not a little hazardous in a private and obscure individual, and a stranger too, thus to solicit the indulgent attention of the public, especially when I own I offer here the history of neither a saint, a hero, nor a tyrant. I believe there are few events in my life which have not happened to many; it is true the incidents of it are numerous, and, did I consider myself an European, I might say my sufferings were great; but when I compare my lot with that of most of my countrymen, I regard myself as a *particular favorite of heaven,* and acknowledge the mercies of Providence in every occurrence of my life. If, then, the following narrative does not appear sufficiently interesting to engage general attention, let my motive be some excuse for its publication. I am not so foolishly vain as to expect from it either immortality or literary reputation. If it affords any satisfaction to my numerous friends, at whose request it has been written, or in the smallest degree promotes the interests of humanity, the ends for which it was undertaken will be fully attained, and every wish of my heart gratified. Let it therefore be remembered, that, in wishing to avoid censure, I do not aspire to praise.

That part of Africa, known by the name of Guinea, to which the trade for slaves is carried on, extends along the coast above 3400 miles, from Senegal to Angola, and includes a variety of kingdoms. Of these the most considerable is the kingdom of Benin,[1] both as to extent and wealth, the richness and cultivation of the soil, the power of its king, and the number and warlike disposition of the inhabitants. It is situated nearly under the line,[2] and extends along the coast about 170 miles, but runs back into the interior part of Africa to a distance hitherto, I believe, unexplored by

---

A note on the text: The text reprinted here is from Robert Allison's edition of *The Interesting Narrative* (Boston: Bedford/St. Martin's, 1995). All notes, unless otherwise indicated, are taken or adapted from those of Allison.

[1] **Benin:** The kingdom of Benin, with its capital in the city of Benin, extended from the Niger delta to the city of Lagos.

[2] **the line:** The equator.

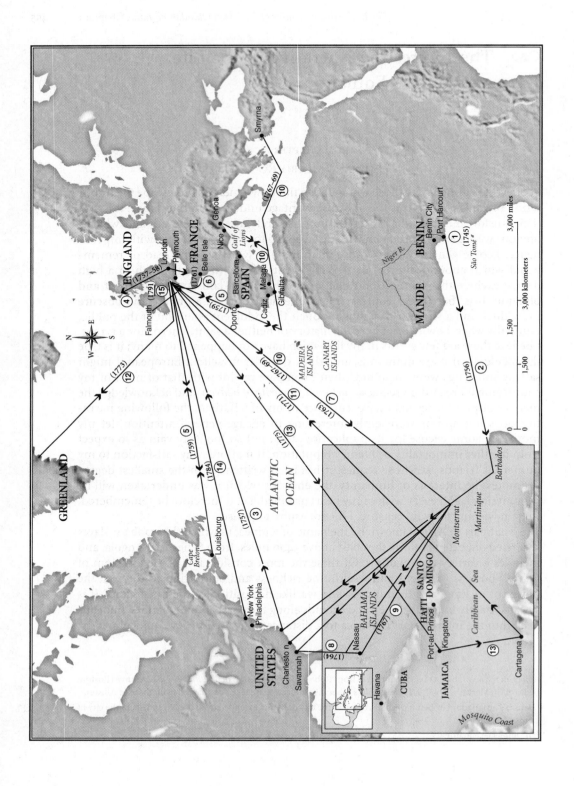

GREENLAND

ENGLAND
London
Plymouth
Falmouth (1791)
④ (1757–58)
⑮

FRANCE
Belle Isle
(1761) ⑥
⑤ (1759)
Oporto
SPAIN
Barcelona
Cadiz Malaga
Gibraltar

Genoa
Nice
Gulf of Lions
⑩

Smyrna
⑩ (1767–69)

BENIN
MANDE
Benin City
Port Harcourt
① (1745)
② (1756)
Niger R.
São Tomé

UNITED
STATES
Cape
Breton
Louisbourg
New York
Philadelphia
Charleston
Savannah

(1773) ⑫
⑤ (1759)
(1784) ⑭
(1757) ③

ATLANTIC
OCEAN

⑩ (1767–69) ⑩
⑪ (1771)
⑬ (1775)
⑦ (1763)

MADEIRA
ISLANDS
CANARY
ISLANDS

Barbados
Montserrat
Martinique
Caribbean Sea
Cartagena ⑬

⑧ (1764)
Nassau
BAHAMA
ISLANDS
(1767) ⑨
HAITI SANTO
DOMINGO
Port-au-Prince
Kingston
JAMAICA

CUBA
Havana
Mosquito Coast

3,000 miles
3,000 kilometers
1,500
1,500
0
0

N
E
W
S

Compass rose

◀ The Voyages of Olaudah Equiano

Equiano spent ten years as a slave on trade ships that made their way back and forth across the Atlantic. His extraordinary travels continued after he gained his freedom, as he voyaged to the West Indies, continental Europe, Turkey, and Ireland.

KEY	The Voyages of Olaudah Equiano*	
1.	1745	Born into Ibo tribe in Essaka, a village in Benin (now Nigeria).
2.	1756	Kidnapped and boarded on a slave ship; taken to Barbados, then to Virginia.
3.	1757	Bought by Michael Henry Pascal, a British naval officer, who names Equiano Gustavus Vassa and takes him to England.
4.	1757–58	Serves in British navy. Travels to Holland, Scotland, Orkneys, and the coast of France.
5.	1759	Sets out for Mediterranean and arrives at Gibraltar; sails to Barcelona through the Gulf of Lyons.
6.	1761	Nearly shipwrecked while headed toward Belle Isle.
7.	1763	Sold in England; sent to Montserrat and sold to Robert King.
8.	1764	Works on trading voyages between West Indies and mainland American colonies. Obtains freedom on July 11, 1766.
9.	1767	Shipwrecked in Bahamas. Retreats to New Providence (Nassau), then to Georgia, then back to Martinique and Montserrat.
10.	1767–69	Sails to London, continues on to Nice, Leghorn, Villa Franca, the Archipelago Islands, Turkey, and Genoa. Converts to Christianity.
11.	1771	Travels to West Indies — Madeira, Barbados, Grenada, Nevis, and Jamaica.
12.	1773	Sails for Arctic seeking a northeast passage to India; explores Greenland.
13.	1775	Admitted to Communion in Westminster Church, London. Voyages to Mosquito Coast (Nicaragua) with Dr. Irving to establish a plantation; returns to England.
14.	1784	Sails for New York.
15.	1791	Gives talks in Ireland.

* Double arrows indicate journey and return. Numerals indicate chapters of the text.

any traveller, and seems only terminated at length by the empire of Abyssinia, near 1500 miles from its beginning. This kingdom is divided into many provinces or districts, in one of the most remote and fertile of which, I was born, in the year 1745, situated in a charming fruitful vale, named Essaka. The distance of this province from the capital of Benin and the sea coast must be very considerable, for I had never heard of white men or Europeans, nor of the sea; and our subjection to the king of Benin was little more than nominal, for every transaction of the government, as far as my slender observation extended, was conducted by the chief or elders of the place. The manners and government of a people who have little commerce with other countries are generally very simple, and the history of what passes in one family or village may serve as a specimen of the whole nation.

My father was one of those elders or chiefs I have spoken of, and was styled Embrenche, a term, as I remember, importing the highest distinction, and signifying in our language a *mark* of grandeur. This mark is conferred on the person entitled to it, by cutting the skin across at the top of the forehead, and drawing it down to the eyebrows; and while it is in this situation applying a warm hand, and rubbing it until it shrinks up into a thick *weal* across the lower part of the forehead.[3] Most of the judges and senators were thus marked; my father had long borne it; I had seen it conferred on one of my brothers, and I also was *destined* to receive it by my parents. Those Embrenche, or chief men, decided disputes and punished crimes, for which purpose they always assembled together. The proceedings were generally short, and in most cases the law of retaliation prevailed. [. . .]

As we live in a country where nature is prodigal of her favors, our wants are few and easily supplied; of course we have few manufactures. They consist for the most part of calicoes, earthen ware, ornaments, and instruments of war and husbandry. But these make no part of our commerce, the principal articles of which, as I have observed, are provisions. In such a state, money is of little use; however, we have some small pieces of coin, if I may call them such. They are made something like an anchor, but I do not remember either their value or denomination. We have also markets, at which I have been frequently with my mother. These are sometimes visited by stout mahogany-colored men from the south-west of us: we call them *Oye-Eboe*,[4] which term signifies red men living at a distance. They generally bring us fire-arms, gun-powder, hats, beads, and dried fish. The last we esteemed a great rarity, as our waters were only brooks and springs. These articles they barter with us for odoriferous woods and earth, and our salt of wood ashes. They always carry slaves through our land; but the strictest account is exacted of their manner of procuring them before they are suffered to pass. Sometimes, indeed, we sold slaves to them, but they were only prisoners of war, or such among us as had been convicted of kidnapping, or adultery, and some other crimes, which we esteemed heinous. This practice of kidnapping induces me to think, that, notwithstanding all our strictness, their principal business among us was to trepan our people. I remember too, they carried great sacks along with them, which not long after, I had an opportunity of fatally seeing applied to that infamous purpose.

Our land is uncommonly rich and fruitful, and produces all kinds of vegetables in great abundance. We have plenty of Indian corn, and vast quantities of cotton and tobacco. Our pineapples grow without culture; they are about the size of the largest sugar-loaf, and finely flavored. We have also spices of different kinds, particularly pepper, and a variety of delicious fruits which I have never seen in Europe, together with gums of various kinds, and honey in abundance. All our industry is exerted to improve these blessings of nature. Agriculture is our chief employment; and everyone, even the children and women, are engaged in it. Thus we are all habituated to

---

[3] *weal . . . forehead:* The Ibo phrase *igbu ichi* refers to this scarring of the face, and *mgburichi*, which Equiano renders as *Embrenche*, means "men who bear such scars." Both derive from *ichi*, "to crown." (Catherine Obianuju Acholonu, *The Igbo Roots of Olaudah Equiano: An Anthropological Research.* [Owerri, Nigeria: Afa Publications, 1989], 10–12, 29–30.)

[4] *Oye-Eboe: Oyibo* is "light-colored person." Acholonu suggests that these may have been Aro people, a mahogany-colored people from south of Isseke. Those from Arochukwu were involved in the slave trade, exchanging their captives for guns, gunpowder, and other European goods. (Acholonu, *Igbo Roots,* 14)

labor from our earliest years. Everyone contributes something to the common stock; and, as we are unacquainted with idleness, we have no beggars. The benefits of such a mode of living are obvious. The West India planters prefer the slaves of Benin or Eboe[5] to those of any other part of Guinea, for their hardiness, intelligence, integrity, and zeal. Those benefits are felt by us in the general healthiness of the people, and in their vigor and activity; I might have added, too, in their comeliness. Deformity is indeed unknown amongst us, I mean that of shape. Numbers of the natives of Eboe now in London might be brought in support of this assertion: for, in regard to complexion, ideas of beauty are wholly relative. I remember while in Africa to have seen three Negro children who were tawny, and another quite white, who were universally regarded by myself, and the natives in general, as far as related to their complexions, as deformed. Our women, too, were, in my eye at least, uncommonly graceful, alert, and modest to a degree of bashfulness; nor do I remember to have heard of an instance of incontinence amongst them before marriage. They are also remarkably cheerful. Indeed, cheerfulness and affability are two of the leading characteristics of our nation.

Our tillage is exercised in a large plain or common, some hour's walk from our dwellings, and all the neighbors resort thither in a body. They use no beasts of husbandry; and their only instruments are hoes, axes, shovels, and beaks, or pointed iron, to dig with. Sometimes we are visited by locusts, which come in large clouds, so as to darken the air, and destroy our harvest. This, however, happens rarely, but when it does, a famine is produced by it. I remember an instance or two wherein this happened. This common is often the theatre of war; and therefore when our people go out to till their land, they not only go in a body, but generally take their arms with them for fear of a surprise; and when they apprehend an invasion, they guard the avenues to their dwellings, by driving sticks into the ground, which are so sharp at one end as to pierce the foot, and are generally dipt in poison. From what I can recollect of these battles, they appear to have been irruptions of one little state or district on the other, to obtain prisoners or booty. Perhaps they were incited to this by those traders who brought the European goods I mentioned, amongst us. Such a mode of obtaining slaves in Africa is common; and I believe more are procured this way, and by kidnapping, than any other.[6] When a trader wants slaves, he applies to a chief for them, and tempts him with his wares. It is not extraordinary, if on this occasion he yields to the temptation with as little firmness, and accepts the price of his fellow creature's liberty, with as little reluctance as the enlightened merchant. Accordingly he falls on his neighbors, and a desperate battle ensues. If he prevails and takes prisoners, he gratifies his avarice by selling them; but, if his party be vanquished, and he falls into the hands of the enemy, he is put to death; for, as he has been known to foment their quarrels, it is thought dangerous to let him survive, and no ransom can save him, though all other prisoners may be redeemed. We have fire-arms, bows and

---

[5] **Eboe:** Ibo or Igbo.

[6] See Benezet's "Account of Guinea," throughout. [Equiano's note.] Anthony Benezet (1713–1784), a Philadelphia Quaker, wrote *Some Historical Account of Guinea: Its situation, produce, and the general disposition of its inhabitants with an inquiry into the rise and progress of the Slave Trade . . .* (1771) and other antislavery tracts.

arrows, broad two-edged swords and javelins; we have shields also which cover a man from head to foot. All are taught the use of these weapons; even our women are warriors, and march boldly out to fight along with the men. Our whole district is a kind of militia: on a certain signal given, such as the firing of a gun at night, they all rise in arms and rush upon their enemy. It is perhaps something remarkable, that when our people march to the field a red flag or banner is borne before them.

I was once a witness to a battle in our common. We had been all at work in it one day as usual, when our people were suddenly attacked. I climbed a tree at some distance, from which I beheld the fight. There were many women as well as men on both sides; among others my mother was there, and armed with a broad sword. After fighting for a considerable time with great fury, and many had been killed, our people obtained the victory, and took their enemy's Chief a prisoner. He was carried off in great triumph, and, though he offered a large ransom for his life, he was put to death. A virgin of note among our enemies had been slain in the battle, and her arm was exposed in our marketplace, where our trophies were always exhibited. The spoils were divided according to the merit of the warriors. Those prisoners which were not sold or redeemed, we kept as slaves; but how different was their condition from that of the slaves in the West Indies! With us, they do no more work than other members of the community, even their master; their food, clothing, and lodging were nearly the same as theirs (except that they were not permitted to eat with those who were free-born); and there was scarce any other difference between them, than a superior degree of importance which the head of a family possesses in our state, and that authority which, as such, he exercises over every part of his household. Some of these slaves have even slaves under them as their own property, and for their own use.

As to religion, the natives believe that there is one Creator of all things, and that he lives in the sun, and is girted round with a belt; that he may never eat or drink, but, according to some, he smokes a pipe, which is our own favorite luxury. They believe he governs events, especially our deaths or captivity; but, as for the doctrine of eternity, I do not remember to have ever heard of it; some, however, believe in the transmigration of souls in a certain degree. Those spirits which were not transmigrated, such as their dear friends or relations, they believe always attend them, and guard them from the bad spirits or their foes. For this reason they always, before eating, as I have observed, put some small portion of the meat, and pour some of their drink, on the ground for them; and they often make oblations of the blood of beasts or fowls at their graves. I was very fond of my mother, and almost constantly with her. When she went to make these oblations at her mother's tomb, which was a kind of small solitary thatched house, I sometimes attended her. There she made her libations, and spent most of the night in cries and lamentations. I have been often extremely terrified on these occasions. The loneliness of the place, the darkness of the night, and the ceremony of libation, naturally awful and gloomy, were heightened by my mother's lamentations; and these concurring with the doleful cries of birds, by which these places were frequented, gave an inexpressible terror to the scene.

We compute the year from the day on which the sun crosses the line, and on its setting that evening, there is a general shout throughout the land; at least, I can speak from my own knowledge, throughout our vicinity. The people at the same time make a great noise with rattles, not unlike the basket rattles used by children here, though much larger, and hold up their hands to heaven for a blessing. It is then the greatest offerings are made; and those children whom our wise men foretell will be fortunate are then presented to different people. I remember many used to come to see me, and I was carried about to others for that purpose. They have many offerings, particularly at full moons; generally two, at harvest, before the fruits are taken out of the ground; and when any young animals are killed, sometimes they offer up part of them as a sacrifice. These offerings, when made by one of the heads of a family, serve for the whole. I remember we often had them at my father's and my uncle's, and their families have been present. Some of our offerings are eaten with bitter herbs. We had a saying among us to anyone of a cross temper, "That if they were to be eaten, they should be eaten with bitter herbs."

We practised circumcision like the Jews, and made offerings and feasts on that occasion, in the same manner as they did. Like them also, our children were named from some event, some circumstance, or fancied foreboding, at the time of their birth. I was named *Olaudah,*[7] which in our language signifies vicissitude, or fortunate; also, one favored, and having a loud voice and well spoken. I remember we never polluted the name of the object of our adoration; on the contrary, it was always mentioned with the greatest reverence; and we were totally unacquainted with swearing, and all those terms of abuse and reproach which find their way so readily and copiously into the language of more civilized people. The only expressions of that kind I remember were, "May you rot, or may you swell, or may a beast take you." [. . .]

FROM **CHAPTER 2**

[CAPTIVITY AND SLAVERY; THE SLAVE SHIP]

I hope the reader will not think I have trespassed on his patience in introducing myself to him with some account of the manners and customs of my country. They had been implanted in me with great care, and made an impression on my mind, which time could not erase, and which all the adversity and variety of fortune I have since experienced, served only to rivet and record: for, whether the love of one's country be real or imaginary, or a lesson of reason, or an instinct of nature, I still look back with pleasure on the first scenes of my life, though that pleasure has been for the most part mingled with sorrow.

I have already acquainted the reader with the time and place of my birth. My father, besides many slaves, had a numerous family, of which seven lived to grow up,

---

[7] *Olaudah: Ola,* or ring, is a symbol of good fortune to the Ibo. *Ude* means "pleasing sound." (Acholonu, *Igbo Roots,* 42–43)

including myself and sister, who was the only daughter. As I was the youngest of the sons, I became, of course, the greatest favorite with my mother, and was always with her; and she used to take particular pains to form my mind.[8] I was trained up from my earliest years in the art of war: my daily exercise was shooting and throwing javelins, and my mother adorned me with emblems, after the manner of our greatest warriors. In this way I grew up till I had turned the age of eleven, when an end was put to my happiness in the following manner: Generally, when the grown people in the neighborhood were gone far in the fields to labor, the children assembled together in some of the neighboring premises to play; and commonly some of us used to get up a tree to look out for any assailant, or kidnapper, that might come upon us — for they sometimes took those opportunities of our parents' absence, to attack and carry off as many as they could seize. One day as I was watching at the top of a tree in our yard, I saw one of those people come into the yard of our next neighbor but one, to kidnap, there being many stout young people in it. Immediately on this I gave the alarm of the rogue, and he was surrounded by the stoutest of them, who entangled him with cords, so that he could not escape, till some of the grown people came and secured him. But, alas! ere long it was my fate to be thus attacked, and to be carried off, when none of the grown people were nigh.

One day, when all our people were gone out to their works as usual, and only I and my dear sister were left to mind the house, two men and a woman got over our walls, and in a moment seized us both, and, without giving us time to cry out, or make resistance, they stopped our mouths, and ran off with us into the nearest wood. Here they tied our hands, and continued to carry us as far as they could, till night came on, when we reached a small house, where the robbers halted for refreshment, and spent the night. We were then unbound, but were unable to take any food; and, being quite overpowered by fatigue and grief, our only relief was some sleep, which allayed our misfortune for a short time. The next morning we left the house, and continued travelling all the day. For a long time we had kept the woods, but at last we came into a road which I believed I knew. I had now some hopes of being delivered; for we had advanced but a little way before I discovered some people at a distance, on which I began to cry out for their assistance; but my cries had no other effect than to make them tie me faster and stop my mouth, and then they put me into a large sack. They also stopped my sister's mouth, and tied her hands; and in this manner we proceeded till we were out of sight of these people. When we went to rest the following night, they offered us some victuals, but we refused it; and the only comfort we had was in being in one another's arms all that night, and bathing each other with our tears. But alas! we were soon deprived of even the small comfort of weeping together.

The next day proved a day of greater sorrow than I had yet experienced; for my sister and I were then separated, while we lay clasped in each other's arms. It was in vain that we besought them not to part us; she was torn from me, and immediately carried away, while I was left in a state of distraction not to be described. I cried and

---

[8] **My father . . . form my mind:** Acholonu identifies Equiano's father as Ichie Ekwealuo, born about 1700, and his mother as Nwansoro, from the village of Uli. (Acholonu, *Igbo Roots,* 42–43)

grieved continually; and for several days did not eat anything but what they forced into my mouth. At length, after many days' travelling, during which I had often changed masters, I got into the hands of a chieftain, in a very pleasant country. This man had two wives and some children, and they all used me extremely well, and did all they could do to comfort me; particularly the first wife, who was something like my mother. Although I was a great many days' journey from my father's house, yet these people spoke exactly the same language with us. This first master of mine, as I may call him, was a smith, and my principal employment was working his bellows, which were the same kind as I had seen in my vicinity. They were in some respects not unlike the stoves here in gentlemen's kitchens, and were covered over with leather; and in the middle of that leather a stick was fixed, and a person stood up, and worked it in the same manner as is done to pump water out of a cask with a hand pump. I believe it was gold he worked, for it was of a lovely bright yellow color, and was worn by the women on their wrists and ankles.

I was there I suppose about a month, and they at last used to trust me some little distance from the house. This liberty I used in embracing every opportunity to inquire the way to my own home; and I also sometimes, for the same purpose, went with the maidens, in the cool of the evenings, to bring pitchers of water from the springs for the use of the house. I had also remarked where the sun rose in the morning, and set in the evening, as I had travelled along; and I had observed that my father's house was towards the rising of the sun. I therefore determined to seize the first opportunity of making my escape, and to shape my course for that quarter; for I was quite oppressed and weighed down by grief after my mother and friends; and my love of liberty, ever great, was strengthened by the mortifying circumstance of not daring to eat with the free-born children, although I was mostly their companion.

While I was projecting my escape, one day an unlucky event happened, which quite disconcerted my plan, and put an end to my hopes. I used to be sometimes employed in assisting an elderly slave to cook and take care of the poultry; and one morning, while I was feeding some chickens, I happened to toss a small pebble at one of them, which hit it on the middle, and directly killed it. The old slave, having soon after missed the chicken, inquired after it; and on my relating the accident (for I told her the truth, for my mother would never suffer me to tell a lie), she flew into a violent passion, and threatened that I should suffer for it; and, my master being out, she immediately went and told her mistress what I had done. This alarmed me very much, and I expected an instant flogging, which to me was uncommonly dreadful, for I had seldom been beaten at home. I therefore resolved to fly; and accordingly I ran into a thicket that was hard by, and hid myself in the bushes. Soon afterwards my mistress and the slave returned, and, not seeing me, they searched all the house, but not finding me, and I not making answer when they called to me, they thought I had run away, and the whole neighborhood was raised in the pursuit of me.

In that part of the country, as in ours, the houses and villages were skirted with woods, or shrubberies, and the bushes were so thick that a man could readily conceal himself in them, so as to elude the strictest search. The neighbors continued the whole day looking for me, and several times many of them came within a few yards of the place where I lay hid. I expected every moment, when I heard a rustling among the trees, to be found out, and punished by my master; but they never discovered me, though they were often so near that I even heard their conjectures as they were looking about for me; and I now learned from them that any attempts to return home would be hopeless. Most of them supposed I had fled towards home; but the distance was so great, and the way so intricate, that they thought I could never reach it, and that I should be lost in the woods. When I heard this I was seized with a violent panic, and abandoned myself to despair. Night, too, began to approach, and aggravated all my fears. I had before entertained hopes of getting home, and had determined when it should be dark to make the attempt; but I was now convinced it was fruitless, and began to consider that, if possibly I could escape all other animals, I could not those of the human kind; and that, not knowing the way, I must perish in the woods. Thus was I like the hunted deer—

———— Every leaf and every whisp'ring breath,
Convey'd a foe, and every foe a death.

I heard frequent rustlings among the leaves, and being pretty sure they were snakes, I expected every instant to be stung by them. This increased my anguish, and the horror of my situation became now quite insupportable. I at length quitted the thicket, very faint and hungry, for I had not eaten or drank anything all the day, and crept to my master's kitchen, from whence I set out at first, which was an open shed, and laid myself down in the ashes with an anxious wish for death, to relieve me from all my pains. I was scarcely awake in the morning, when the old woman slave, who was the first up, came to light the fire, and saw me in the fireplace. She was very much surprised to see me, and could scarcely believe her own eyes. She now promised to intercede for me, and went for her master, who soon after came, and, having slightly reprimanded me, ordered me to be taken care of, and not ill treated.

Soon after this, my master's only daughter, and child by his first wife, sickened and died, which affected him so much that for sometime he was almost frantic, and really would have killed himself, had he not been watched and prevented. However, in a short time afterwards he recovered, and I was again sold. I was now carried to the left of the sun's rising, through many dreary wastes and dismal woods, amidst the hideous roarings of wild beasts. The people I was sold to used to carry me very often, when I was tired, either on their shoulders or on their backs. I saw many convenient well-built sheds along the road, at proper distances, to accommodate the merchants and travellers, who lay in those buildings along with their wives, who often accompany them; and they always go well armed.

From the time I left my own nation, I always found somebody that understood me till I came to the sea coast. The languages of different nations did not totally differ, nor were they so copious as those of the Europeans, particularly the English. They were therefore easily learned; and, while I was journeying thus through Africa, I acquired two or three different tongues. In this manner I had been travelling for a considerable time, when, one evening, to my great surprise, whom should I see brought to the house where I was but my dear sister! As soon as she saw me, she gave a loud shriek, and ran into my arms—I was quite overpowered; neither of us could speak, but, for a considerable time, clung to each other in mutual embraces, unable to do anything but weep. Our meeting affected all who saw us; and, indeed, I must acknowledge, in honor of those sable destroyers of human rights, that I never met with any ill treatment, or saw any offered to their slaves, except tying them, when necessary, to keep them from running away.

When these people knew we were brother and sister, they indulged us to be together; and the man, to whom I supposed we belonged, lay with us, he in the middle, while she and I held one another by the hands across his breast all night; and thus for a while we forgot our misfortunes, in the joy of being together; but even this small comfort was soon to have an end; for scarcely had the fatal morning appeared when she was again torn from me forever! I was now more miserable, if possible, than before. The small relief which her presence gave me from pain, was gone, and the wretchedness of my situation was redoubled by my anxiety after her fate, and my apprehensions lest her sufferings should be greater than mine, when I could not be with her to alleviate them. Yes, thou dear partner of all my childish sports! thou sharer of my joys and sorrows! happy should I have ever esteemed myself to encounter every misery for you and to procure your freedom by the sacrifice of my own. Though you were early forced from my arms, your image has been always riveted in my heart, from which neither time nor fortune have been able to remove it; so that, while the thoughts of your sufferings have damped my prosperity, they have mingled with adversity and increased its bitterness. To that Heaven which protects the weak from the strong, I commit the care of your innocence and virtues, if they have not already received their full reward, and if your youth and delicacy have not long since fallen victims to the violence of the African trader, the pestilential stench of a Guinea ship, the seasoning in the European colonies, or the lash and lust of a brutal and unrelenting overseer.

I did not long remain after my sister. I was again sold, and carried through a number of places, till after travelling a considerable time, I came to a town called Tinmah, in the most beautiful country I had yet seen in Africa.[9] It was extremely rich, and there were many rivulets which flowed through it, and supplied a large pond in the centre of the town, where the people washed. Here I saw for the first time cocoanuts, which I thought superior to any nuts I had ever tasted before; and the trees, which were loaded, were also interspersed among the houses, which had commodious shades adjoining, and were in the same manner as ours, the insides being neatly plastered and whitewashed. Here I also saw and tasted for the first time, sugar-cane. Their money consisted of little white shells, the size of the finger nail. I was sold here for one hundred and seventy-two of them, by a merchant who lived and brought me there.

I had been about two or three days at his house, when a wealthy widow, a neighbor of his, came there one evening, and brought with her an only son, a young gentleman about my own age and size. Here they saw me; and, having taken a fancy to me, I was bought of the merchant, and went home with them. Her house and

---

[9]**Tinmah . . . Africa:** Possibly Utuma, Utu Etim, or Tinan, villages on the border between Ibo and Ibibio. (Acholonu, *Igbo Roots,* 7–9)

premises were situated close to one of those rivulets I have mentioned, and were the finest I ever saw in Africa: they were very extensive, and she had a number of slaves to attend her. The next day I was washed and perfumed, and when meal time came, I was led into the presence of my mistress, and ate and drank before her with her son. This filled me with astonishment; and I could scarce help expressing my surprise that the young gentleman should suffer me, who was bound, to eat with him who was free; and not only so, but that he would not at any time either eat or drink till I had taken first, because I was the eldest, which was agreeable to our custom. Indeed, every thing here, and all their treatment of me, made me forget that I was a slave. The language of these people resembled ours so nearly, that we understood each other perfectly. They had also the very same customs as we. There were likewise slaves daily to attend us, while my young master and I, with other boys, sported with our darts and bows and arrows, as I had been used to do at home. In this resemblance to my former happy state, I passed about two months; and I now began to think I was to be adopted into the family, and was beginning to be reconciled to my situation, and to forget by degrees my misfortunes, when all at once the delusion vanished; for, without the least previous knowledge, one morning early, while my dear master and companion was still asleep, I was awakened out of my reverie to fresh sorrow, and hurried away even amongst the uncircumcised.

Thus, at the very moment I dreamed of the greatest happiness, I found myself most miserable; and it seemed as if fortune wished to give me this taste of joy only to render the reverse more poignant. The change I now experienced was as painful as it was sudden and unexpected. It was a change indeed, from a state of bliss to a scene which is inexpressible by me, as it discovered to me an element I had never before beheld, and till then had no idea of, and wherein such instances of hardship and cruelty continually occurred, as I can never reflect on but with horror.

All the nations and people I had hitherto passed through, resembled our own in their manners, customs, and language; but I came at length to a country, the inhabitants of which differed from us in all those particulars. I was very much struck with this difference, especially when I came among a people who did not circumcise, and ate without washing their hands. They cooked also in iron pots, and had European cutlasses and cross bows, which were unknown to us, and fought with their fists among themselves. Their women were not so modest as ours, for they ate, and drank, and slept with their men. But above all, I was amazed to see no sacrifices or offerings among them. In some of those places the people ornamented themselves with scars, and likewise filed their teeth very sharp. They wanted sometimes to ornament me in the same manner, but I would not suffer them; hoping that I might some time be among a people who did not thus disfigure themselves, as I thought they did. At last I came to the banks of a large river which was covered with canoes, in which the people appeared to live with their household utensils, and provisions of all kinds. I was beyond measure astonished at this, as I had never before seen any water larger than a pond or a rivulet; and my surprise was mingled with no small fear when I was put into one of these canoes, and we began to paddle and move along the river. We continued going on thus till night, and when we came to land, and made fires on the banks, each family by themselves; some dragged their canoes on shore, others stayed and cooked in theirs, and laid in them all night. Those on the land had mats, of which they made tents, some in the shape of little houses; in these we slept; and after the morning meal, we embarked again and proceeded as before. I was often very much astonished to see some of the women, as well as the men, jump into the water, dive to the bottom, come up again, and swim about.

Thus I continued to travel, sometimes by land, sometimes by water, through different countries and various nations, till, at the end of six or seven months after I had been kidnapped, I arrived at the sea coast. [. . .]

The first object which saluted my eyes when I arrived on the coast, was the sea, and a slave ship, which was then riding at anchor, and waiting for its cargo. These filled me with astonishment, which was soon converted into terror, when I was carried on board. I was immediately handled, and tossed up to see if I were sound, by some of the crew; and I was now persuaded that I had gotten into a world of bad spirits, and that they were going to kill me. Their complexions, too, differing so much from ours, their long hair, and the language they spoke (which was very different from any I had ever heard), united to confirm me in this belief. Indeed, such were the horrors of my views and fears at the moment, that, if ten thousand worlds had been my own, I would have freely parted with them all to have exchanged my condition with that of the meanest slave in my own country. When I looked round the ship too, and saw a large furnance of copper boiling, and a multitude of black people of every description chained together, every one of their countenances expressing dejection and sorrow, I no longer doubted of my fate; and, quite overpowered with horror and anguish, I fell motionless on the deck and fainted. When I recovered a little, I found some black people about me, who I believed were some of those who had brought me on board, and had been receiving their pay; they talked to me in order to cheer me, but all in vain. I asked them if we were not to be eaten by those white men with horrible looks, red faces, and long hair. They told me I was not, and one of the crew brought me a small portion of spirituous liquor in a wine glass; but being afraid of him, I would not take it out of his hand. One of the blacks therefore took it from him and gave it to me, and I took a little down my palate, which, instead of reviving me, as they thought it would, threw me into the greatest consternation at the strange feeling it produced, having never tasted any such liquor before. Soon after this, the blacks who brought me on board went off, and left me abandoned to despair.

I now saw myself deprived of all chance of returning to my native country, or even the least glimpse of hope of gaining the shore, which I now considered as friendly; and I even wished for my former slavery in preference to my present situation, which was filled with horrors of every kind, still heightened by my ignorance of what I was to undergo. I was not long suffered to indulge my grief; I was soon put down under the decks, and there I received such a salutation in my nostrils as I had never experienced in my life: so that, with the loathsomeness of the stench, and crying together, I became so sick and low that I was not able to eat, nor had I the least desire to taste anything. I now wished for the last friend, death, to relieve me; but soon, to my grief, two of the white men offered me eatables; and, on my refusing to eat, one of them held me fast by the hands, and laid me across, I think, the windlass, and tied my feet, while the other flogged me severely. I had never experienced anything of this kind before, and, although not being used to the water, I naturally feared that element the first time I saw it, yet, nevertheless, could I have got over the nettings, I would have jumped over the side, but I could not; and besides, the crew used to watch us very closely who were not chained down to the decks, lest we should leap into the water; and I have seen some of these poor African prisoners most severely cut, for attempting to do so, and hourly whipped for not eating. This indeed was often the case with myself.

In a little time after, amongst the poor chained men, I found some of my own nation, which in a small degree gave ease to my mind. I inquired of these what was to be done with us? They gave me to understand, we were to be carried to these white people's country to work for them. I then was a little revived, and thought, if it were no worse than working, my situation was not so desperate; but still I feared I should be put to death, the white people looked and acted, as I thought, in so savage a manner; for I had never seen among any people such instances of brutal cruelty; and this not only shown towards us blacks, but also to some of the whites themselves. One white man in particular I saw, when we were permitted to be on deck, flogged so unmercifully with a large rope near the foremast, that he died in consequence of it; and they tossed him over the side as they would have done a brute. This made me fear these people the more; and I expected nothing less than to be treated in the same manner. I could not help expressing my fears and apprehensions to some of my countrymen; I asked them if these people had no country, but lived in this hollow place (the ship)? They told me they did not, but came from a distant one. "Then," said I, "how comes it in all our country we never heard of them?" They told me because they lived so very far off. I then asked where were their women? had they any like themselves? I was told they had. "And why," said I, "do we not see them?" They answered, because they were left behind. I asked how the vessel could go? They told me they could not tell; but that there was cloth put upon the masts by the help of the ropes I saw, and then the vessel went on; and the white men had some spell or magic they put in the water when they liked, in order to stop the vessel. I was exceedingly amazed at this account, and really thought they were spirits. I therefore wished much to be from amongst them, for I expected they would sacrifice me; but my wishes were vain—for we were so quartered that it was impossible for any of us to make our escape.

While we stayed on the coast I was mostly on deck; and one day, to my great astonishment, I saw one of these vessels coming in with the sails up. As soon as the whites saw it, they gave a great shout, at which we were amazed; and the more so, as the vessel appeared larger by approaching nearer. At last, she came to an anchor in my sight, and when the anchor was let go, I and my countrymen who saw it, were lost in astonishment to observe the vessel stop—and were now convinced it was done by magic. Soon after this the other ship got her boats out, and they came on board of us, and the people of both ships seemed very glad to see each other. Several of the strangers also shook hands with us black people, and made motions with their hands, signifying I suppose, we were to go to their country, but we did not understand them.

At last, when the ship we were in, had got in all her cargo, they made ready with many fearful noises, and we were all put under deck, so that we could not see how they managed the vessel. But this disappointment was the least of my sorrow. The stench of the hold while we were on the coast was so intolerably loathsome, that it was dangerous to remain there for any time, and some of us had been permitted to stay on the deck for the fresh air; but now that the whole ship's cargo were confined together, it became absolutely pestilential. The closeness of the place, and the heat of the climate, added to the number in the ship, which was so crowded that each had scarcely room to turn himself, almost suffocated us. This produced copious perspirations, so that the air soon became unfit for respiration, from a variety of loathsome smells, and brought on a sickness among the slaves, of which many died— thus falling victims to the improvident avarice, as I may call it, of their purchasers. This wretched situation was again aggravated by the galling of the chains, now became insupportable, and the filth of the necessary tubs, into which the children often fell, and were almost suffocated. The shrieks of the women, and the groans of the dying, rendered the whole a scene of horror almost inconceivable. Happily perhaps, for myself, I was soon reduced so low here that it was thought necessary to keep me almost always on deck; and from my extreme youth I was not put in fetters. In this situation I expected every hour to share the fate of my companions, some of whom were almost daily brought upon deck at the point of death, which I began to hope would soon put an end to my miseries. Often did I think many of the inhabitants of the deep much more happy than myself. I envied them the freedom they enjoyed, and as often wished I could change my condition for theirs. Every circumstance I met with, served only to render my state more painful, and heightened my apprehensions, and my opinion of the cruelty of the whites.

One day they had taken a number of fishes; and when they had killed and satisfied themselves with as many as they thought fit, to our astonishment who were on deck, rather than give any of them to us to eat, as we expected, they tossed the remaining fish into the sea again, although we begged and prayed for some as well as we could, but in vain; and some of my countrymen, being pressed by hunger, took an opportunity, when they thought no one saw them, of trying to get a little privately; but they were discovered, and the attempt procured them some very severe floggings.

One day, when we had a smooth sea and moderate wind, two of my wearied countrymen who were chained together (I was near them at the time), preferring death to such a life of misery, somehow made through the nettings and jumped into the sea; immediately, another quite dejected fellow, who, on account of his illness, was suffered to be out of irons, also followed their example; and I believe many more would very soon have done the same, if they had not been prevented by the ship's crew, who were instantly alarmed. Those of us that were the most active, were in a moment put down under the deck; and there was such a noise and confusion amongst the people of the ship as I never heard before, to stop her, and get the boat out to go after the slaves. However, two of the wretches were drowned, but they got the other, and afterwards flogged him unmercifully, for thus attempting to prefer death to slavery. In this manner we continued to undergo more hardships than I can now relate, hardships which are inseparable from this accursed trade. Many a time we were near suffocation from the want of fresh air, which we were often without for whole days together. This, and the stench of the necessary tubs, carried off many.

During our passage, I first saw flying fishes, which surprised me very much; they used frequently to fly across the ship, and many of them fell on the deck. I also now first saw the use of the quadrant; I had often with astonishment seen the mariners make observations with it, and I could not think what it meant. They at last took notice of my surprise; and one of them, willing to increase it, as well as to gratify my curiosity, made me one day look through it. The clouds appeared to me to be land, which disappeared as they passed along. This heightened my wonder; and I was now more persuaded than ever, that I was in another world, and that every thing about me was magic.

At last we came in sight of the island of Barbadoes, at which the whites on board gave a great shout, and made many signs of joy to us. We did not know what to think of this; but as the vessel drew nearer, we plainly saw the harbor, and other ships of different kinds and sizes, and we soon anchored amongst them, off Bridgetown. Many merchants and planters now came on board, though it was in the evening. They put us in separate parcels, and examined us attentively. They also made us jump, and pointed to the land, signifying we were to go there. We thought by this, we should be eaten by these ugly men, as they appeared to us; and, when soon after we were all put down under the deck again, there was much dread and trembling among us, and nothing but bitter cries to be heard all the night from these apprehensions, insomuch, that at last the white people got some old slaves from the land to pacify us. They told us we were not to be eaten, but to work, and were soon to go on land, where we should see many of our country people. This report eased us much. And sure enough, soon after we were landed, there came to us Africans of all languages.

We were conducted immediately to the merchant's yard, where we were all pent up together, like so many sheep in a fold, without regard to sex or age. As every object was new to me, everything I saw filled me with surprise. What struck me first, was, that the houses were built with bricks and stories, and in every other respect different from those I had seen in Africa; but I was still more astonished on seeing people on horseback. I did not know what this could mean; and, indeed, I thought these people were full of nothing but magical arts. While I was in this astonishment, one of my fellow prisoners spoke to a countryman of his, about the horses, who said they were the same kind they had in their country. I understood them, though they were from a distant part of Africa; and I thought it odd I had not seen any horses there; but afterwards, when I came to converse with different Africans, I found they had many horses amongst them, and much larger than those I then saw.

We were not many days in the merchant's custody, before we were sold after their usual manner, which is this: On a signal given (as the beat of a drum), the buyers rush at once into the yard where the slaves are confined, and make choice of that parcel they like best. The noise and clamor with which this is attended, and the eagerness visible in the countenances of the buyers, serve not a little to increase the apprehension of terrified Africans, who may well be supposed to consider them as the ministers of that destruction to which they think themselves devoted. In this manner, without scruple, are relations and friends separated, most of them never to see each other again.

I remember, in the vessel in which I was brought over, in the men's apartment, there were several brothers, who, in the sale, were sold in different lots; and it was very moving on this occasion, to see and hear their cries at parting. O, ye nominal Christians! might not an African ask you—Learned you this from your God, who says unto you, Do unto all men as you would men should do unto you? Is it not enough that we are torn from our country and friends, to toil for your luxury and lust of gain? Must every tender feeling be likewise sacrificed to your avarice? Are the dearest friends and relations, now rendered more dear by their separation from their kindred, still to be parted from each other, and thus prevented from cheering the gloom of slavery, with the small comfort of being together, and mingling their sufferings and sorrows? Why are parents to lose their children, brothers their sisters, or husbands their wives? Surely, this is a new refinement in cruelty, which, while it has no advantage to atone for it, thus aggravates distress, and adds fresh horrors even to the wretchedness of slavery.

FROM CHAPTER 3
[SOLD TO CAPTAIN PASCAL; A NEW NAME]

I now totally lost the small remains of comfort I had enjoyed in conversing with my countrymen; the women too, who used to wash and take care of me were all gone different ways, and I never saw one of them afterwards.

I stayed in this island for a few days, I believe it could not be above a fortnight, when I, and some few more slaves that were not saleable amongst the rest, from very much fretting, were shipped off in a sloop for North America. On the passage we were better treated than when we were coming from Africa, and we had plenty of rice and fat pork. We were landed up a river a good way from the sea, about Virginia county, where we saw few or none of our native Africans, and not one soul who could talk to me. I was a few weeks weeding grass and gathering stones in a plantation; and at last all my companions were distributed different ways, and only myself was left. I was now exceedingly miserable, and thought myself worse off than any of the rest of my companions, for they could talk to each other, but I had no person to speak to that I could understand. In this state, I was constantly grieving and pining, and wishing for death rather than anything else.

While I was in this plantation, the gentleman, to whom I suppose the estate belonged, being unwell, I was one day sent for to his dwelling-house to fan him; when I came into the room where he was I was very much affrighted at some things I saw, and the more so as I had seen a black woman slave as I came through the house, who was cooking the dinner, and the poor creature was cruelly loaded with various kinds of iron machines; she had one particularly on her head, which locked her mouth so fast that she could scarcely speak; and could not eat nor drink. I was much astonished and shocked at this contrivance, which I afterwards learned was called the iron muzzle. Soon after I had a fan put in my hand, to fan the gentleman while he slept; and so I did indeed with great fear. While he was fast asleep I indulged myself a great deal in looking about the room, which to me appeared very fine and curious.

The first object that engaged my attention was a watch which hung on the chimney, and was going. I was quite surprised at the noise it made, and was afraid it would tell the gentleman anything I might do amiss; and when I immediately after observed a picture hanging in the room, which appeared constantly to look at me, I was still more affrighted, having never seen such things as these before. At one time I thought it was something relative to magic; and not seeing it move I thought it might be some way the whites had to keep their great men when they died, and offer them libations as we used to do our friendly spirits. In this state of anxiety I remained till my master awoke, when I was dismissed out of the room, to my no small satisfaction and relief; for I thought that these people were all made up of wonders.

In this place I was called Jacob; but on board the *African Snow,* I was called Michael. I had been some time in this miserable, forlorn, and much dejected state, without having anyone to talk to, which made my life a burden, when the kind and unknown hand of the Creator (who in every deed leads the blind in a way they know not) now began to appear, to my comfort; for one day the captain of a merchant ship, called the *Industrious Bee,* came on some business to my master's house. This gentleman, whose name was Michael Henry Pascal, was a lieutenant in the Royal Navy, but now commanded this trading ship, which was somewhere in the confines of the county many miles off. While he was at my master's house, it happened that he saw me, and liked me so well that he made a purchase of me. I think I have often heard him say he gave thirty or forty pounds sterling for me; but I do not remember which. However, he meant me for a present to some of his friends in England: and as I was sent accordingly from the house of my then master (one Mr. Campbell) to the place where the ship lay; I was conducted on horseback by an elderly black man (a mode of travelling which appeared very odd to me). When I arrived I was carried on board a fine large ship, loaded with tobacco, &c., and just ready to sail for England.

I now thought my condition much mended; I had sails to lie on, and plenty of good victuals to eat; and everybody on board used me very kindly, quite contrary to what I had seen of any white people before; I therefore began to think that they were not all of the same disposition. A few days after I was on board we sailed for England. I was still at a loss to conjecture my destiny. By this time, however, I could smatter a little imperfect English; and I wanted to know as well as I could where we were going. Some of the people of the ship used to tell me they were going to carry me back to my own country, and this made me very happy. I was quite rejoiced at the idea of going back, and thought if I could get home what wonders I should have to tell. But I was reserved for another fate, and was soon undeceived when we came within sight of the English coast.

While I was on board this ship, my captain and master named me *Gustavus Vassa.*[10] I at that time began to understand him a little, and refused to be called so,

[10] *Gustavus Vassa:* Gustavus Ericksson Vasa (1496–1560), a Swedish nobleman, led a successful revolt against Danish rule in the 1520s; as Gustavus I, he ruled Sweden from 1523 to 1560. At the time of Equiano's capture, Henry Brooke's *Gustavus Vasa, the Deliverer of His Country* was a popular English play.

and told him as well as I could that I would be called Jacob; but he said I should not, and still called me Gustavus: and when I refused to answer to my new name, which I at first did, it gained me many a cuff; so at length I submitted, and by which I have been known ever since.

The ship had a very long passage; and on that account we had very short allowance of provisions. Towards the last, we had only one pound and a half of bread per week, and about the same quantity of meat, and one quart of water a day. We spoke with only one vessel the whole time we were at sea, and but once we caught a few fishes. In our extremities the captain and people told me in jest they would kill and eat me; but I thought them in earnest, and was depressed beyond measure, expecting every moment to be my last. While I was in this situation, one evening they caught, with a good deal of trouble, a large shark, and got it on board. This gladdened my poor heart exceedingly, as I thought it would serve the people to eat instead of their eating me; but very soon, to my astonishment, they cut off a small part of the tail, and tossed the rest over the side. This renewed my consternation; and I did not know what to think of these white people, though I very much feared they would kill and eat me.

There was on board the ship a young lad who had never been at sea before, about four or five years older than myself: his name was Richard Baker. He was a native of America, had received an excellent education, and was of a most amiable temper. Soon after I went on board, he showed me a great deal of partiality and attention, and in return I grew extremely fond of him. We at length became inseparable; and, for the space of two years, he was of very great use to me, and was my constant companion and instructor. Although this dear youth had many slaves of his own, yet he and I have gone through many sufferings together on shipboard; and we have many nights lain in each other's bosoms when we were in great distress. Thus such a friendship was cemented between us as we cherished till his death, which, to my very great sorrow, happened in the year 1759, when he was up the Archipelago, on board his Majesty's ship the *Preston:* an event which I have never ceased to regret, as I lost at once a kind interpreter, an agreeable companion, and a faithful friend; who, at the age of fifteen, discovered a mind superior to prejudice; and who was not ashamed to notice, to associate with, and to be the friend and instructor of one who was ignorant, a stranger, of a different complexion, and a slave! [. . .]

FROM **CHAPTER 4**

[Baptism and the Desire for Freedom]

It was now between two and three years since I first came to England, a great part of which I had spent at sea; so that I became inured to that service, and began to consider myself as happily situated, for my master treated me always extremely well; and my attachment and gratitude to him were very great. From the various scenes I had beheld on shipboard, I soon grew a stranger to terror of every kind, and was, in that respect at least, almost an Englishman. I have often reflected with surprise that I never felt half the alarm at any of the numerous dangers I have been in, that I was filled with at the first sight of the Europeans, and at every act of theirs, even the most trifling, when I first came among them, and for some time afterwards. That fear, however, which was the effect of my ignorance, wore away as I began to know them. I could now speak English tolerably well, and I perfectly understood everything that was said. I not only felt myself quite easy with these new countrymen, but relished their society and manners. I no longer looked upon them as spirits, but as men superior to us; and therefore I had the stronger desire to resemble them, to imbibe their spirit, and imitate their manners. I therefore embraced every occasion of improvement, and every new thing that I observed I treasured up in my memory. I had long wished to be able to read and write; and for this purpose I took every opportunity to gain instruction, but had made as yet very little progress. However, when I went to London with my master, I had soon an opportunity of improving myself, which I gladly embraced. Shortly after my arrival, he sent me to wait upon the Miss Guerins, who had treated me with much kindness when I was there before; and they sent me to school.

While I was attending these ladies, their servants told me I could not go to Heaven unless I was baptized. This made me very uneasy, for I had now some faint idea of a future state: accordingly I communicated my anxiety to the eldest Miss Guerin, with whom I was become a favorite, and pressed her to have me baptized; when to my great joy, she told me I should. She had formerly asked my master to let me be baptized, but he had refused. However she now insisted on it; and he being under some obligation to her brother, complied with her request. So I was baptized in St. Margaret's church, Westminster, in February 1759, by my present name. The clergyman at the same time, gave me a book, called *A Guide to the Indians*, written by the Bishop of Sodor and Man.[11] On this occasion, Miss Guerin did me the honor to stand as god-mother, and afterwards gave me a treat.

I used to attend these ladies about the town, in which service I was extremely happy; as I had thus many opportunities of seeing London, which I desired of all things. I was sometimes, however, with my master at his rendezvous house, which was at the foot of Westminster bridge. Here I used to enjoy myself in playing about the bridge stairs, and often in the waterman's wherries,[12] with other boys. On one of these occasions there was another boy with me in a wherry, and we went out into the current of the river; while we were there, two more stout boys came to us in another wherry, and abusing us for taking the boat, desired me to get into the other wherry-boat. Accordingly, I went to get out of the wherry I was in, but just as I had got one of my feet into the other boat, the boys shoved it off, so that I fell into the Thames; and, not being able to swim, I should unavoidably have been drowned, but for the assistance of some watermen who providentially came to my relief. [. . .]

After our ship was fitted out again for service, in September she went to Guernsey, where I was very glad to see my old hostess, who was now a widow, and my former little charming companion, her daughter. I spent some time here very happily with them, till October, when we had orders to repair to Portsmouth. We

---

[11] **Bishop of Sodor and Man:** Thomas Wilson (1697–1755); wrote *The Knowledge and Practice of Christianity Made Easy for the Meanest Mental Capacities; or, an Essay towards an Instruction for the Indains* in the form of a dialogue between an Indian and a Christian (London: 1740).

[12] **wherries:** Long, light rowboats.

parted from each other with a great deal of affection; and I promised to return soon, and see them again, not knowing what all powerful fate had determined for me. Our ship having arrived at Portsmouth, we went into the harbor, and remained there till the latter end of November, when we heard great talk about a peace; and, to our very great joy, in the beginning of December we had orders to go up to London with our ship, to be paid off. We received this news with loud huzzas, and every other demonstration of gladness; and nothing but mirth was to be seen throughout every part of the ship. I too was not without my share of the general joy on this occasion.

I thought now of nothing but being freed, and working for myself, and thereby getting money to enable me to get a good education; for I always had a great desire to be able at least to read and write; and while I was on ship-board, I had endeavored to improve myself in both. While I was in the *Etna,* particularly, the captain's clerk taught me to write, and gave me a smattering of arithmetic, as far as the rule of three. There was also one Daniel Queen, about forty years of age, a man very well educated, who messed with me on board this ship, and he likewise dressed and attended the captain. Fortunately this man soon became very much attached to me, and took very great pains to instruct me in many things. He taught me to shave and dress hair a little, and also to read in the Bible, explaining many passages to me, which I did not comprehend. I was wonderfully surprised to see the laws and rules of my own country written almost exactly here; a circumstance which I believe tended to impress our manners and customs more deeply on my memory. I used to tell him of this resemblance, and many a time we have sat up the whole night together at this employment. In short, he was like a father to me, and some even used to call me after his name; they also styled me the black Christian. Indeed, I almost loved him with the affection of a son. Many things I have denied myself that he might have them; and when I used to play at marbles, or any other game, and won a few half-pence, or got any little money, which I sometimes did, for shaving anyone, I used to buy him a little sugar or tobacco, as far as my stock of money would go. He used to say, that he and I never should part; and that when our ship was paid off, as I was as free as himself, or any other man on board, he would instruct me in his business, by which I might gain a good livelihood.

This gave me new life and spirits; and my heart burned within me, while I thought the time long till I obtained my freedom. For though my master had not promised it to me, yet, besides the assurances I had received, that he had no right to detain me, he always treated me with the greatest kindness, and reposed in me an unbounded confidence; he even paid attention to my morals, and would never suffer me to deceive him, or tell lies, of which he used to tell me the consequences; and that if I did so, God would not love me. So that, from all this tenderness, I had never once supposed, in all my dreams of freedom, that he would think of detaining me any longer than I wished.

In pursuance of our orders, we sailed from Portsmouth for the Thames, and arrived at Deptford the 10th of December, where we cast anchor just as it was high water. The ship was up about half an hour, when my master ordered the barge to be manned; and all in an instant, without having before given me the least reason to suspect anything of the matter, he forced me into the barge, saying, I was going to

leave him, but he would take care I should not. I was so struck with the unexpectedness of this proceeding, that for some time I did not make a reply, only I made an
offer to go for my books and chest of clothes, but he swore I should not move out
of his sight, and if I did, he would cut my throat, at the same time taking his hanger.
I began, however, to collect myself, and plucking up courage, I told him I was free,
and he could not by law serve me so. But this only enraged him the more: and he
continued to swear, and said he would soon let me know whether he would or not,
and at that instant sprung himself into the barge from the ship, to the astonishment
and sorrow of all on board.

   The tide, rather unluckily for me, had just turned downward, so that we quickly
fell down the river along with it, till we came among some outward-bound West
Indiamen; for he was resolved to put me on board the first vessel he could get to
receive me. The boat's crew, who pulled against their will, became quite faint, different times, and would have gone ashore, but he would not let them. Some of them
strove then to cheer me, and told me he could not sell me, and that they would stand
by me, which revived me a little, and I still entertained hopes; for, as they pulled
along, he asked some vessels to receive me, but they would not. But, just as we had
got a little below Gravesend, we came alongside of a ship which was going away the
next tide for the West Indies. Her name was the *Charming Sally*, Captain James
Doran, and my master went on board, and agreed with him for me; and in a little
time I was sent for into the cabin.

   When I came there, Captain Doran asked me if I knew him. I answered that I did
not. "Then," said he, "you are now my slave." I told him my master could not sell me to
him, nor to anyone else. "Why," said he, "did not your master buy you?" I confessed he
did. "But I have served him," said I, "many years, and he has taken all my wages and
prize-money, for I had only got one six pence during the war; besides this I have been
baptized, and by the laws of the land no man has a right to sell me." And I added that
I had heard a lawyer and others at different times tell my master so. They both then
said that those people who told me so, were not my friends; but I replied, "It was very
extraordinary that other people did not know the law as well as they."

   Upon this Captain Doran said I talked too much English; and if I did not behave
myself well, and be quiet, he had a method on board to make me. I was too well convinced of his power over me to doubt what he said; and my former sufferings in the
slave-ship presenting themselves to my mind, the recollection of them made me
shudder. However, before I retired I told them that, as I could not get any right
among men here, I hoped I should hereafter in Heaven; and I immediately left the
cabin, filled with resentment and sorrow. The only coat I had with me my master
took away with him, and said, "If your prize money had been £10,000, I had a right
to it all, and would have taken it."

   I had about nine guineas, which, during my long sea-faring life, I had scraped
together from trifling perquisites and little ventures; and I hid it at that instant, lest
my master should take that from me likewise, still hoping that by some means or
other I should make my escape to the shore; and indeed some of my old shipmates
told me not to despair, for they would get me back again; and that, as soon as they
could get their pay, they would immediately come to Portsmouth to me, where the
ship was going. But, alas! all my hopes were baffled, and the hour of my deliverance

was yet far off. My master, having soon concluded his bargain with the captain, came out of the cabin, and he and his people got into the boat and put off. I followed them with aching eyes as long as I could, and when they were out of sight I threw myself on the deck, with a heart ready to burst with sorrow and anguish.

FROM CHAPTER 5

[SOLD TO ROBERT KING; THE HORRORS OF THE WEST INDIES]

However, the next morning, the 30th of December, the wind being brisk and easterly, the *Eolus* frigate, which was to escort the convoy, made a signal for sailing. All the ships then got up their anchors; and, before any of my friends had an opportunity to come off to my relief, to my inexpressible anguish, our ship had got under way. What tumultuous emotions agitated my soul when the convoy got under sail, and I a prisoner on board, now without hope! I kept my swimming eyes upon the land in a state of unutterable grief; not knowing what to do, and despairing how to help myself. While my mind was in this situation, the fleet sailed on, and in one day's time I lost sight of the wished-for land. In the first expression of my grief I reproached my fate, and wished I had never been born. I was ready to curse the tide that bore us, the gale that wafted my prison, and even the ship that conducted us; and I called on death to relieve me from the horrors I felt and dreaded, that I might be in that place

> Where slaves are free, and men oppress no more.
> Fool that I was, inur'd so long to pain,
> To trust to hope, or dream of joy again.
> . . . .
> Now dragg'd once more beyond the western main,
> To groan beneath some dastard planter's chain;
> Where my poor countrymen in bondage wait
> The long enfranchisement of a ling'ring fate.
> Hard ling'ring fate! while, ere the dawn of day,
> Rous'd by the lash they go their cheerless way;
> And as their souls with shame and anguish burn,
> Salute with groans unwelcome morn's return;
> And, chiding ev'ry hour the slow pac'd sun,
> Pursue their toils till all his race is run.
> No eye to mark their suff'rings with a tear,
> No friend to comfort, and no hope to cheer;
> Then, like the dull unpity'd brutes, repair
> To stalls as wretched, and as coarse a fare;
> Thank heaven one day of misery was o'er,
> Then sink to sleep, and wish to wake no more.[13]

---

[13] "The Dying Negro" [by Thomas Day], a poem originally published in 1773. Perhaps it may not be deemed impertinent here to add, that this elegant and pathetic little poem was occasioned, as appears by the advertisement prefixed to it, by the following incident. "A black, who, a few days before had run away from his master, and got himself christened, with intent to marry a white woman, his fellow-servant, being taken and sent on board a ship in the Thames, took an opportunity of shooting himself through the head." [Equiano's note.]

The turbulence of my emotions, however, naturally gave way to calmer thoughts, and I soon perceived what fate had decreed no mortal on earth could prevent. The convoy sailed on without any accident, with a pleasant gale and smooth sea, for six weeks, till February, when one morning the *Eolus* ran down a brig, one of the convoy, and she instantly went down, and was engulfed in the dark recesses of the ocean. The convoy was immediately thrown into great confusion till it was day-light; and the *Eolus* was illumined with lights, to prevent any further mischief. On the 13th of February, 1763, from the mast-head, we descried our destined island, Montserrat; and soon after I beheld those

> Regions of sorrow, doleful shades, where peace
> And rest can rarely dwell. Hope never comes
> That comes to all, but torture without end
> Still urges.[14]

At the sight of this land of bondage, a fresh horror ran through all my frame, and chilled me to the heart. My former slavery now rose in dreadful review to my mind, and displayed nothing but misery, stripes, and chains; and, in the first paroxysm of my grief, I called upon God's thunder, and his avenging power, to direct the stroke of death to me, rather than permit me to become a slave, and be sold from lord to lord.

In this state of my mind our ship came to anchor, and soon after discharged her cargo. I now knew what it was to work hard; I was made to help unload and load the ship. And, to comfort me in my distress in that time, two of the sailors robbed me of all my money, and ran away from the ship. I had been so long used to a European climate, that at first I felt the scorching West India sun very painful, while the dashing surf would toss the boat and the people in it, frequently above high water mark. Sometimes our limbs were broken with this, or even attended with instant death, and I was day by day mangled and torn.

About the middle of May, when the ship was got ready to sail for England, I all the time believing that fate's blackest clouds were gathering over my head, and expecting their bursting would mix me with the dead, Captain Doran sent for me ashore one morning, and I was told by the messenger that my fate was then determined. With trembling steps and fluttering heart, I came to the captain, and found with him one Mr. Robert King, a Quaker, and the first merchant in the place. The captain then told me my former master had sent me there to be sold; but that he had desired him to get me the best master he could, as he told him I was a very deserving boy, which Captain Doran said he found to be true; and if he were to stay in the West Indies, he would be glad to keep me himself; but he could not venture to take me to London, for he was very sure that when I came there I would leave him. I at that instant burst out a crying, and begged much of him to take me to England with him, but all to no purpose. He told me he had got me the very best master in the whole island, with whom I should be as happy as if I were in England, and for that reason he chose to let him have me, though he could sell me to his own brother-in-law for a great deal more money than what he got from this gentleman. Mr. King, my new

---

[14]**Regions . . . Still urges:** John Milton, *Paradise Lost,* 1:65–68.

master, then made a reply, and said the reason he had bought me was on account of my good character; and as he had not the least doubt of my good behavior, I should be very well off with him. He also told me he did not live in the West Indies, but at Philadelphia, where he was going soon; and, as I understood something of the rules of arithmetic, when we got there he would put me to school, and fit me for a clerk.

This conversation relieved my mind a little, and I left those gentlemen considerably more at ease in myself than when I came to them; and I was very thankful to Captain Doran, and even to my old master, for the character they had given me: a character which I afterwards found of infinite service to me. I went on board again, and took leave of all my ship-mates, and the next day the ship sailed. When she weighed anchor, I went to the waterside and looked at her with a very wishful and aching heart, and followed her with my eyes until she was totally out of sight. I was so bowed down with grief, that I could not hold up my head for many months; and if my new master had not been kind to me, I believe I should have died under it at last. And, indeed, I soon found that he fully deserved the good character which Captain Doran gave me of him, for he possessed a most amiable disposition and temper, and was very charitable and humane. If any of his slaves behaved amiss he did not beat or use them ill, but parted with them. This made them afraid of disobliging him; and as he treated his slaves better than any other man on the island, so he was better and more faithfully served by them in return. By this kind treatment I did at last endeavor to compose myself; and with fortitude, though moneyless, determined to face whatever fate had decreed for me. Mr. King soon asked me what I could do; and at the same time said he did not mean to treat me as a common slave. I told him I knew something of seamanship, and could shave and dress hair pretty well; and I could refine wines, which I had learned on shipboard, where I had often done it; and that I could write, and understood arithmetic tolerably well, as far as the Rule of Three. He then asked me if I knew anything of gauging, and, on my answering that I did not, he said one of his clerks should teach me to gauge.

Mr. King dealt in all manner of merchandise, and kept from one to six clerks. He loaded many vessels in a year; particularly to Philadelphia, where he was born; and was connected with a great mercantile house in that city. He had, besides, many vessels and droggers,[15] of different sizes, which used to go about the island; and others, to collect rum, sugar, and other goods. I understood pulling and managing those boats very well; and this hard work, which was the first that he set me to, in the sugar seasons used to be my constant employment. I have rowed the boat, and slaved at the oars, from one hour to sixteen in the twenty-four, during which I had fifteen pence sterling per day to live on, though sometimes only ten pence.

However, this was considerably more than was allowed to other slaves that used to work often with me, and belonged to other gentlemen on the island. Those poor souls had never more than nine pence per day, and seldom more than six pence, from their masters or owners, though they earned them three or four pistareens.[16]

---

[15] **droggers:** Droghers, or slow, clumsy boats.

[16] **pistareens:** These pistareens are of the value of a shilling. [Equiano's note.]

For it is a common practice in the West Indies for men to purchase slaves, though they have not plantations themselves, in order to let them out to planters and merchants at so much a piece by the day, and they give what allowance they choose out of this product of their daily work to their slaves for subsistence; this allowance is often very scanty. My master often gave the owners of the slaves two and a half of these pieces per day, and found the poor fellows in victuals himself, because he thought their owners did not feed them well enough according to the work they did.

The slaves used to like this very well; and, as they knew my master to be a man of feeling, they were always glad to work for him, in preference to any other gentleman; some of whom, after they had been paid for these poor people's labors, would not give them their allowance out of it. Many times have I even seen these unfortunate wretches beaten for asking for their pay; and often severely flogged by their owners if they did not bring them their daily or weekly money exactly to the time; though the poor creatures were obliged to wait on the gentlemen they had worked for, sometimes more than half the day before they could get their pay; and this generally on Sundays, when they wanted the time for themselves. In particular, I knew a countryman of mine who once did not bring the weekly money directly that it was earned; and, though he brought it the same day to his master, yet he was staked to the ground for his pretended negligence, and was just going to receive a hundred lashes, but for a gentleman who begged him off with fifty. [. . .]

I had the good fortune to please my master in every department in which he employed me; and there was scarcely any part of his business, or household affairs, in which I was not occasionally engaged. I often supplied the place of a clerk, in receiving and delivering cargoes to the ships, in tending stores, and delivering goods. And besides this, I used to shave and dress my master when convenient, and take care of his horse; and when it was necessary, which was very often, I worked likewise on board of different vessels of his. By these means I became very useful to my master, and saved him, as he used to acknowledge, above a hundred pounds a year. Nor did he scruple to say I was of more advantage to him than any of his clerks; though their usual wages in the West Indies are from sixty to a hundred pounds current a year.

I have sometimes heard it asserted that a Negro cannot earn his master the first cost; but nothing can be further from the truth. I suppose nine-tenths of the mechanics throughout the West Indies are Negro slaves; and I well know the coopers[17] among them earn two dollars a day, the carpenters the same, and oftentimes more; as also the masons, smiths, and fishermen, &c. and I have known many slaves whose masters would not take a thousand pounds current for them. But surely this assertion refutes itself; for, if it be true, why do the planters and merchants pay such a price for slaves? And, above all, why do those who make this assertion exclaim the most loudly against the abolition of the slave trade? So much are men blinded, and to such inconsistent arguments are they driven by mistaken interest! I grant, indeed, that slaves are sometimes, by half-feeding, half-clothing, over-working, and stripes,

---

[17] **coopers:** Barrel makers.

reduced so low, that they are turned out as unfit for service, and left to perish in the woods, or expire on a dung-hill.

My master was several times offered by different gentlemen one hundred guineas for me, but he always told them he would not sell me, to my great joy. And I used to double my diligence and care, for fear of getting into the hands of those men who did not allow a valuable slave the common support of life. Many of them even used to find fault with my master for feeding his slaves so well as he did, although I often went hungry, and an Englishman might think my fare very indifferent; but he used to tell them he always would do it, because the slaves thereby looked better and did more work.

While I was thus employed by my master, I was often a witness to cruelties of every kind, which were exercised on my unhappy fellow slaves. I used frequently to have different cargoes of new Negroes in my care for sale; and it was almost a constant practice with our clerks, and other whites, to commit violent depredations on the chastity of the female slaves; and these I was, though with reluctance, obliged to submit to at all times, being unable to help them. When we have had some of these slaves on board my master's vessels, to carry them to other islands, or to America, I have known our mates to commit these acts most shamefully, to the disgrace, not of Christians only, but of men. I have even known them to gratify their brutal passion with females not ten years old; and these abominations, some of them practised to such scandalous excess, that one of our captains discharged the mate and others on that account. And yet in Montserrat I have seen a Negro man staked to the ground, and cut most shockingly, and then his ears cut off bit by bit, because he had been connected with a white woman who was a common prostitute; as if it were no crime in the whites to rob an innocent African girl of her virtue, but most heinous in a black man only to gratify a passion of nature, where the temptation was offered by one of a different color, though the most abandoned woman of her species.

One Mr. D—— told me that he had sold 41,000 Negroes, and that he once cut off a Negro man's leg for running away. I asked him if the man had died in the operation, how he, as a Christian, could answer for the horrid act before God? and he told me, answering was a thing of another world, what he thought and did were policy. I told him that the Christian doctrine taught us to do unto others as we would that others should do unto us. He then said that his scheme had the desired effect— it cured that man and some others of running away.

Another Negro man was half hanged, and then burnt, for attempting to poison a cruel overseer. Thus by repeated cruelties, are the wretched first urged to despair, and then murdered, because they still retain so much of human nature about them as to wish to put an end to their misery, and retaliate on their tyrants! These overseers are indeed for the most part persons of the worst character of any denomination of men in the West Indies. Unfortunately, many humane gentlemen, by not residing on their estates, are obliged to leave the management of them in the hands of these human butchers, who cut and mangle the slaves in a shocking manner on the most trifling occasions, and altogether treat them in every respect like brutes. They pay no regard to the situation of pregnant women, nor the least attention to the lodging of the field Negroes. Their huts, which ought to be well covered, and the place dry where they take their little repose, are often open sheds, built in damp places; so that when the poor creatures return tired from the toils of the field, they contract many disorders, from being exposed to the damp air in this uncomfortable state, while they are heated, and their pores are open. This neglect certainly conspires with many others to cause a decrease in the births as well as in the lives of the grown Negroes.

I can quote many instances of gentlemen who reside on their estates in the West Indies, and then the scene is quite changed; the Negroes are treated with lenity and proper care, by which their lives are prolonged, and their masters profited. To the honor of humanity, I knew several gentlemen who managed their estates in this manner, and they found that benevolence was their true interest. And, among many I could mention in several of the islands, I knew one in Monserrat[18] whose slaves looked remarkably well, and never needed any fresh supplies of Negroes; and there are many other estates, especially in Barbadoes, which, from such judicious treatment, need no fresh stock of Negroes at any time. I have the honor of knowing a most worthy and humane gentleman, who is a native of Barbadoes, and has estates there.[19] This gentleman has written a treatise on the usage of his own slaves. He allows them two hours of refreshment at mid-day, and many other indulgencies and comforts, particularly in their lodging; and, besides this, he raises more provisions on his estate than they can destroy; so that by these attentions he saves the lives of his Negroes, and keeps them healthy, and as happy as the condition of slavery can admit. I myself, as shall appear in the sequel, managed an estate, where, by those attentions, the Negroes were uncommonly cheerful and healthy, and did more work by half than by the common mode of treatment they usually do. For want, therefore, of such care and attention to the poor Negroes, and otherwise oppressed as they are, it is no wonder that the decrease should require 20,000 new Negroes annually to fill up the vacant places of the dead.

Even in Barbadoes, notwithstanding those humane exceptions which I have mentioned, and others I am acquainted with, which justly make it quoted as a place where slaves meet with the best treatment, and need fewest recruits of any in the West Indies, yet this island requires 1,000 Negroes annually to keep up the original stock, which is only 80,000. So that the whole term of a Negro's life may be said to be there but sixteen years![20] And yet the climate here in every respect is the same as that from which they are taken, except in being more wholesome. Do the British colonies decrease in this manner? And yet what prodigious difference is there between an English and West India climate?

While I was in Montserrat I knew a Negro man, named Emanuel Sankey, who endeavored to escape from his miserable bondage, by concealing himself on board of a London ship: but fate did not favor the poor oppressed man; for, being discovered when the vessel was under sail, he was delivered up again to his master. This

---

[18] **Monserrat:** Mr. Dubury, and many others, Montserrat. [Equiano's note.]

[19] **gentleman . . . estates there:** Sir Phillip Gibbes, Baronet, Barbadoes. [Equiano's note.]

[20] **but sixteen years!:** Benezet's "Account of Guinea," p. 16. [Equiano's note.]

Christian master immediately pinned the wretch down to the ground at each wrist and ankle, and then took some sticks of sealing wax, and lighted them, and dropped it all over his back. There was another master who was noted for cruelty; and I believe he had not a slave but what had been cut, and had pieces fairly taken out of the flesh. And after they had been punished thus, he used to make them get into a long wooden box or case he had for that purpose, in which he shut them up during pleasure. It was just about the height and breadth of a man; and the poor wretches had no room, when in the case, to move.

It was very common in several of the islands, particularly in St. Kitts, for the slaves to be branded with the initial letters of their master's name; and a load of heavy iron hooks hung about their necks. Indeed on the most trifling occasions they were loaded with chains; and often instruments of torture were added. The iron muzzle, thumb-screws, &c., are so well known as not to need a description, and were sometimes applied for the slightest faults. I have seen a Negro beaten till some of his bones were broken, for only letting a pot boil over. Is it surprising that usage like this should drive the poor creatures to despair, and make them seek a refuge in death from those evils which render their lives intolerable? — while,

> With shudd'ring horror pale, and eyes aghast,
> They view their lamentable lot, and find
> No rest![21]

This they frequently do. A Negro man, on board a vessel of my master, while I belonged to her, having been put in irons for some trifling misdemeanor, and kept in that state for some days, being weary of life, took an opportunity of jumping over-board into the sea; however, he was picked up without being drowned. Another, whose life was also a burden to him, resolved to starve himself to death, and refused to eat any victuals. This procured him a severe flogging; and he also, on the first occasion which offered, jumped overboard at Charleston, but was saved.

Nor is there any greater regard shown to the little property than there is to the persons and lives of the Negroes. I have already related an instance or two of partic-ular oppression out of many which I have witnessed; but the following is frequent in all the islands. The wretched field slaves, after toiling all the day for an unfeeling owner, who gives them but little victuals, steal sometimes a few moments from rest or refreshment to gather some small portion of grass, according as their time will admit. This they commonly tie up in a parcel; either a bit's worth (six pence) or half a bit's worth, and bring it to town, or to the market, to sell. Nothing is more common than for the white people on this occasion to take the grass from them without pay-ing for it; and not only so, but too often also, to my knowledge, our clerks, and many others, at the same time have committed acts of violence on the poor, wretched, and helpless females; whom I have seen for hours stand crying to no purpose, and get no redress or pay of any kind. Is not this one common and crying sin enough to bring down God's judgment on the islands? He tells us the oppressor and the oppressed

---

[21] **With shudd'ring . . . No rest!:** John Milton, *Paradise Lost,* 2: 616–18.

are both in his hands; and if these are not the poor, the broken-hearted, the blind, the captive, the bruised, which our Saviour speaks of, who are they? [. . .]

I have often seen slaves, particularly those who were meagre, in different islands, put into scales and weighed, and then sold from three pence to six pence or nine pence a pound. My master, however, whose humanity was shocked at this mode, used to sell such by the lump. And at or after a sale, it was not uncommon to see Negroes taken from their wives, wives taken from their husbands, and children from their parents, and sent off to other islands, and wherever else their merciless lords choose; and probably never more during life see each other! Oftentimes my heart has bled at these partings, when the friends of the departed have been at the water-side, and with sighs and tears, have kept their eyes fixed on the vessel, till it went out of sight.

A poor Creole Negro, I knew well, who, after having been often thus transported from island to island, at last resided in Montserrat. This man used to tell me many melancholy tales of himself. Generally, after he had done working for his master, he used to employ his few leisure moments to go a fishing. When he had caught any fish, his master would frequently take them from him without paying him; and at other times some other white people would serve him in the same manner. One day he said to me, very movingly, "Sometimes when a white man take away my fish, I go to my maser, and he get me my right; and when my maser by strength take away my fishes, what me must do? I can't go to any body to be righted; then," said the poor man, looking up above, "I must look up to God Mighty in the top for right." This artless tale moved me much, and I could not help feeling the just cause Moses had in redressing his brother against the Egyptian.[22] I exhorted the man to look up still to the God on the top, since there was no redress below. Though I little thought then that I myself should more than once experience such imposition, and need the same exhortation hereafter, in my own transactions in the islands, and that even this poor man and I should some time after suffer together in the same manner, as shall be related hereafter.

Nor was such usage as this confined to particular places or individuals, for in all the different islands in which I have been (and I have visited no less than fifteen) the treatment of the slaves was nearly the same; so nearly, indeed, that the history of an island, or even a plantation, with a few such exceptions as I have mentioned, might serve for a history of the whole. Such a tendency has the slave trade to debauch men's minds, and harden them to every feeling of humanity! For I will not suppose that the dealers in slaves are born worse than other men — No; such is the fatality of this mistaken avarice that it corrupts the milk of human kindness and turns it into gall. And, had the pursuits of those men been different, they might have been as generous, as tender-hearted and just, as they are unfeeling, rapacious, and cruel. Surely this traffic cannot be good, which spreads like a pestilence, and taints what it touches! which violates that first natural right of mankind, equality and independency, and gives one man a dominion over his fellows which God could never intend! For it raises the owner to a state as far above man as it depresses the slave below it; and, with all the

---

[22] **Moses . . . Egyptian:** See Exodus 2:11–12.

presumption of human pride, sets a distinction between them, immeasurable in extent, and endless in duration! Yet how mistaken is the avarice even of the planters. Are slaves more useful by being thus humbled to the condition of brutes than they would be if suffered to enjoy the privileges of men? The freedom which diffuses health and prosperity throughout Britain answers you — No. When you make men slaves, you deprive them of half their virtue; you set them, in your own conduct, an example of fraud, rapine, and cruelty, and compel them to live with you in a state of war; and yet you complain that they are not honest or faithful! You stupify them with stripes, and think it necessary to keep them in a state of ignorance. And yet you assert that they are incapable of learning; that their minds are such a barren soil or moor that culture would be lost on them; and that they come from a climate where nature, though prodigal of her bounties in a degree unknown to yourselves, has left man alone scant and unfinished, and incapable of enjoying the treasures she has poured out for him! An assertion at once impious and absurd. Why do you use those instruments of torture? Are they fit to be applied by one rational being to another? And are ye not struck with shame and mortification, to see the partakers of your nature reduced so low? But, above all, are there no dangers attending this mode of treatment? Are you not hourly in dread of an insurrection? Nor would it be surprising; for when

> —————No peace is given
> To us enslav'd, but custody severe,
> And stripes and arbitrary punishment
> Inflicted — What peace can we return?
> But to our power, hostility and hate;
> Untam'd reluctance, and revenge, though slow.
> Yet ever plotting how the conqueror least
> May reap his conquest, and may least rejoice
> In doing what we most in suffering feel.[23]

But by changing your conduct, and treating your slaves as men, every cause of fear would be banished. They would be faithful, honest, intelligent, and vigorous; and peace, prosperity, and happiness would attend you.

FROM CHAPTER 7
[FREEDOM]

We set sail once more for Montserrat, and arrived there safe, but much out of humor with our friend the silversmith. When we had unladen the vessel, and I had sold my venture, finding myself master of about forty-seven pounds—I consulted my true friend, the captain, how I should proceed in offering my master the money for my freedom. He told me to come on a certain morning, when he and my master would be at breakfast together. Accordingly, on that morning I went, and met the captain there, as he had appointed. When I went in I made my obeisance to my master, and

---

[23] **No peace . . . feel:** Milton, *Paradise Lost,* 2: 332–40.

with my money in my hand, and many fears in my heart, I prayed him to be as good as his offer to me, when he was pleased to promise me my freedom as soon as I could purchase it. This speech seemed to confound him, he began to recoil, and my heart that instant sunk within me. "What," said he, "give you your freedom? Why, where did you get the money? Have you got forty pounds sterling?" "Yes, sir," I answered. "How did you get it?" replied he. I told him, very honestly. The captain then said he knew I got the money honestly, and with much industry, and that I was particularly careful. On which my master replied, I got money much faster than he did; and said he would not have made me the promise he did if he had thought I should have got the money so soon. "Come, come," said my worthy captain, clapping my master on the back, "Come, Robert (which was his name), I think you must let him have his freedom; you have laid your money out very well; you have received a very good interest for it all this time, and here is now the principal at last. I know Gustavus has earned you more than a hundred a year, and he will save you money, as he will not leave you. Come, Robert, take the money."

My master then said he would not be worse than his promise; and, taking the money, told me to go to the Secretary at the Register Office, and get my manumission drawn up. These words of my master were like a voice from heaven to me. In an instant all my trepidation was turned into unutterable bliss; and I most reverently bowed myself with gratitude, unable to express my feelings, but by the overflowing of my eyes, and a heart replete with thanks to God, while my true and worthy friend, the captain, congratulated us both with a peculiar degree of heart-felt pleasure. As soon as the first transports of my joy were over, and that I had expressed my thanks to these my worthy friends, in the best manner I was able, I rose with a heart full of affection and reverence, and left the room, in order to obey my master's joyful mandate of going to the Register Office. As I was leaving the house I called to mind the words of the Psalmist, in the 126th Psalm,[24] and like him, "I glorified God in my heart, in whom I trusted." These words had been impressed on my mind from the very day I was forced from Deptford to the present hour, and I now saw them, as I thought, fulfilled and verified. My imagination was all rapture as I flew to the Register Office; and, in this respect, like the apostle Peter[25] (whose deliverance from prison was so sudden and extraordinary that he thought he was in a vision), I could scarcely believe I was awake. Heavens! who could do justice to my feelings at this moment! Not conquering heroes themselves, in the midst of a triumph—Not the tender mother who has just regained her long lost infant, and presses it to her heart—Not the weary hungry mariner, at the sight of the desired friendly port—Not the lover, when he once more embraces his beloved mistress, after she has been ravished from his arms! All within my breast was tumult, wildness, and delirium! My feet scarcely touched the ground, for they were winged with joy; and, like Elijah, as he rose to Heaven, they "were with lightning sped as I went on." Everyone I met I told of my happiness, and blazed about the virtue of my amiable master and captain.

---

[24] **126th Psalm:** "Thanksgiving for Return from Captivity."

[25] **Peter:** Acts 12:9. [Equiano's note.]

When I got to the office and acquainted the Register with my errand, he congratulated me on the occasion, and told me he would draw up my manumission for half price, which was a guinea. I thanked him for his kindness; and, having received it, and paid him, I hastened to my master to get him to sign it, that I might be fully released. Accordingly he signed the manumission that day; so that, before night, I, who had been a slave in the morning, trembling at the will of another, was become my own master, and completely free. I thought this was the happiest day I had ever experienced; and my joy was still heightened by the blessings and prayers of many of the sable race, particularly the aged, to whom my heart had ever been attached with reverence.

As the form of my manumission has something peculiar in it, and expresses the absolute power and dominion one man claims over his fellow, I shall beg leave to present it before my readers at full length.

MONTSERRAT.

To all men unto whom these presents shall come: I, Robert King, of the parish of St. Anthony, in the said island, merchant, send greeting: Know ye, that I the aforesaid Robert King, for and in consideration of the sum of seventy pounds current money of the said island, to me in hand paid, and to the intent that a Negro man-slave, named Gustavus Vassa, shall and may become free, having manumitted, emancipated, enfranchised, and set free, and by these presents do manumit, emancipate, enfranchise, and set free, the aforesaid Negro man-slave, named Gustavus Vassa, for ever; hereby giving, granting, and releasing unto him, the said Gustavus Vassa, all right, title, dominion, sovereignty, and property, which, as lord and master over the aforesaid Gustavus Vassa, I had, or now have, or by any means whatsoever I may or can hereafter possibly have over him the aforesaid Negro, for ever. In witness whereof, I the above said Robert King have unto these presents set my hand and seal this tenth day of July, in the year of our Lord one thousand seven hundred and sixty-six.

ROBERT KING

Signed, sealed, and delivered in the presence of Terry Legay, Montserrat. Registered the within manumission at full length, this eleventh day of July 1766, in liber. D.

TERRY LEGAY, Register

In short, the fair as well as the black people immediately styled me by a new appellation, to me the most desirable in the world, which was freeman; and at the dances I gave, my Georgia super-fine blue clothes made no indifferent appearance, as I thought. Some of the sable females, who formerly stood aloof, now began to relax and appear less coy; but my heart was still fixed on London, where I hoped to be ere long. So that my worthy captain and his owner, my late master, finding that the bent of my mind was towards London, said to me, "We hope you won't leave us, but that you will still be with the vessels." Here gratitude bowed me down; and none but the generous mind can judge of my feelings, struggling between inclination and duty. However, notwithstanding my wish to be in London, I obediently answered my benefactors, that I would go in the vessel, and not leave them; and from that day I was entered on board as an able-bodied sailor, at thirty-six shillings per month, besides what perquisites I could make.

My intention was to make a voyage or two, entirely to please these my honored patrons; but I determined that the year following, if it pleased God, I would see Old England once more, and surprise my old master, Captain Pascal, who was hourly in my mind; for I still loved him, notwithstanding his usage of me, and pleased myself with thinking what he would say, when he saw what the Lord had done for me in so short a time, instead of being, as he might perhaps suppose, under the cruel yoke of some planter. With these kind of reveries I used often to entertain myself, and shorten the time till my return; and now, being as in my original free African state, I embarked on board the *Nancy,* after having got all things ready for our voyage. In this state of serenity, we sailed for St. Eustatius; and having smooth seas and calm weather, we soon arrived there. After taking our cargo on board, we proceeded to Savannah, in Georgia, in August, 1766. While we were there, as usual, I used to go for the cargo up the rivers in boats; and on this business have been frequently beset by alligators, which were very numerous on that coast; and shot many of them when they have been near getting into our boats, which we have with great difficulty sometimes prevented, and have been very much frightened at them. I have seen a young one sold in Georgia alive for six pence. [. . .]

FROM CHAPTER 9

[LONDON; SELF IMPROVEMENT]

[. . .] We had a most prosperous voyage, and, at the end of seven weeks, arrived at Cherry Garden[26] stairs. Thus were my longing eyes once more gratified with the sight of London, after having been absent from it above four years. I immediately received my wages, and I never had earned seven guineas so quick in my life before; I had thirty-seven guineas in all, when I got cleared from the ship. I now entered upon a scene quite new to me, but full of hope. In this situation my first thoughts were to look out for some of my former friends, and amongst the first of those were the Miss Guerins. As soon, therefore, as I had regaled myself I went in quest of those kind ladies, whom I was very impatient to see; and with some difficulty and perseverance, I found them at May's-hill, Greenwich. They were most agreeably surprised to see me, and I quite overjoyed at meeting with them. I told them my history, at which they expressed great wonder, and freely acknowledged it did their cousin, Captain Pascal, no honor. He then visited there frequently; and I met him four or five days after in Greenwich park.

When he saw me he appeared a good deal surprised, and asked me how I came back? I answered, "In a ship." To which he replied dryly, "I suppose you did not walk back to London on the water." As I saw, by his manner, that he did not seem to be sorry for his behavior to me, and that I had not much reason to expect any favor

---

[26] **Cherry Garden:** A pier on the Thames in London.

from him, I told him that he had used me very ill, after I had been such a faithful servant to him for so many years; on which, without saying any more, he turned about and went away. A few days after this I met Capt. Pascal at Miss Guerin's house, and asked him for my prize money. He said there was none due to me; for, if my prize money had been £10,000 he had a right to it all. I told him I was informed otherwise: on which he bade me defiance; and in a bantering tone, desired me to commence a law-suit against him for it: "There are lawyers enough," said he, "that will take the cause in hand, and you had better try it." I told him then that I would try it, which enraged him very much; however, out of regard to the ladies, I remained still, and never made any farther demand of my right.

Some time afterwards these friendly ladies asked me what I meant to do with myself, and how they could assist me. I thanked them, and said, if they pleased, I would be their servant; but if not, I had thirty-seven guineas, which would support me for some time, I would be much obliged to them to recommend me to some person who would teach me a business whereby I might earn my living. They answered me very politely, that they were sorry it did not suit them to take me as their servant, and asked me what business I should like to learn? I said, hair dressing. They then promised to assist me in this; and soon after they recommended me to a gentleman, whom I had known before, one Capt. O'Hara, who treated me with much kindness, and procured me a master, a hair dresser, in Coventry court Haymarket, with whom he placed me. I was with this man from September till the February following. In that time we had a neighbor in the same court who taught the French horn. He used to blow it so well that I was charmed with it, and agreed with him to teach me to blow it. Accordingly he took me in hand, and began to instruct me, and I soon learned all the three parts. I took great delight in blowing on this instrument, the evenings being long; and besides that I was fond of it, I did not like to be idle, and it filled up my vacant hours innocently. At this time also I agreed with the Rev. Mr. Gregory, who lived in the same court, where he kept an academy and an evening school, to improve me in arithmetic. This he did as far as barter and alligation; so that all the time I was there I was entirely employed.

In February 1768 I hired myself to Dr. Charles Irving, in Pallmall, so celebrated for his successful experiments in making sea water fresh; and here I had plenty of hair dressing to improve my hand. This gentleman was an excellent master; he was exceedingly kind and good tempered; and allowed me in the evenings to attend my schools, which I esteemed a great blessing; therefore I thanked God and him for it, and used all my diligence to improve the opportunity. This diligence and attention recommended me to the notice and care of my three preceptors, who, on their parts, bestowed a great deal of pains in my instruction, and besides, were all very kind to me. My wages, however, which were by two-thirds less than ever I had in my life (for I had only £12 per annum), I soon found would not be sufficient to defray this extraordinary expense of masters, and my own necessary expenses; my old thirty-seven guineas had by this time worn all away to one. I thought it best, therefore, to try the sea again in quest of more money, as I had been bred to it, and had hitherto found the profession of it successful. I had also a very great desire to see Turkey, and

I now determined to gratify it. Accordingly, in the month of May, 1768, I told the doctor my wish to go to sea again, to which he made no opposition; and we parted on friendly terms. [. . .]

FROM **CHAPTER 10**

[CONVERSION]

[. . .] During this time I was out of employ, nor was I likely to get a situation suitable for me, which obliged me to go once more to sea. I engaged as steward of a ship called the *Hope,* Captain Richard Strange, bound from London to Cadiz in Spain. In a short time after I was on board, I heard the name of God much blasphemed, and I feared greatly lest I should catch the horrible infection. I thought if I sinned again after having life and death set evidently before me, I should certainly go to hell. My mind was uncommonly chagrined, and I murmured much at God's providential dealings with me, and was discontented with the commandments, that I could not be saved by what I had done; I hated all things, and wished I had never been born; confusion seized me, and I wished to be annihilated.

One day I was standing on the very edge of the stern of the ship, thinking to drown myself; but this scripture was instantly impressed on my mind—"That no murderer hath eternal life abiding in him" (I John 3:15). Then I paused and thought myself the unhappiest man living. Again I was convinced that the Lord was better to me than I deserved, and I was better off in the world than many. After this I began to fear death; I fretted, mourned, and prayed, till I became a burden to others, but more so to myself. At length I concluded to beg my bread on shore rather than go again to sea amongst a people who feared not God, and I entreated the captain three different times to discharge me; he would not, but each time gave me greater and greater encouragement to continue with him, and all on board shewed me very great civility: notwithstanding all this I was unwilling to embark again. At last some of my religious friends advised me, by saying it was my lawful calling, consequently it was my duty to obey, and that God was not confined to place, &c., &c. particularly Mr. G———S———, the governor of Tothil-fields, Bridewell, who pitied my case, and read the eleventh chapter of the Hebrews to me, with exhortations. He prayed for me, and I believed that he prevailed on my behalf, as my burden was then greatly removed, and I found a heartfelt resignation to the will of God. The good man gave me a pocket Bible and Alleine's *Alarm to the Unconverted.* We parted, and the next day I went on board again. We sailed for Spain, and I found favor with the captain. It was the fourth of the month of September when we sailed from London; we had a delightful voyage to Cadiz, where we arrived the twenty-third of the same month. The place is strong, commands a fine prospect, and is very rich. The Spanish galleons frequent that port, and some arrived whilst we were there. I had many opportunities of reading the scriptures. I wrestled hard with God in fervent prayer, who had declared in his word that he would hear the groanings and deep sighs of the poor in spirit. I found this verified to my utter astonishment and comfort in the following manner.

On the morning of the 6th of October (I pray you to attend), all that day, I thought I should either see or hear something supernatural. I had a secret impulse on my mind of something that was to take place, which drove me continually for that time to a throne of grace. It pleased God to enable me to wrestle with him, as Jacob did: I prayed that if sudden death were to happen, and I perished, it might be at Christ's feet.

In the evening of the same day, as I was reading and meditating on the fourth chapter of Acts, twelfth verse,[27] under the solemn apprehensions of eternity, and reflecting on my past actions, I began to think I had lived a moral life, and that I had a proper ground to believe I had an interest in the divine favor; but still meditating on the subject, not knowing whether salvation was to be had partly for our own good deeds or solely as the sovereign gift of God; in this deep consternation the Lord was pleased to break in upon my soul with his bright beams of heavenly light; and in an instant, as it were, removing the veil, and letting light into a dark place, I saw clearly with an eye of faith, the crucified Saviour bleeding on the cross on mount Calvary; the scriptures became an unsealed book; I saw myself a condemned criminal under the law, which came with its full force to my conscience, and when "the commandment came sin revived, and I died." I saw the Lord Jesus Christ in his humiliation, loaded and bearing my reproach, sin, and shame. I then clearly perceived that by the deeds of the law no flesh living could be justified. I was then convinced that by the first Adam sin came, and by the second Adam (the Lord Jesus Christ) all that are saved must be made alive. It was given me at that time to know what it was to be born again (John 3:5). I saw the eighth chapter to the Romans, and the doctrines of God's decrees, verified agreeable to his eternal, everlasting, and unchangeable purposes. The word of God was sweet to my taste, yea, sweeter than honey and the honeycomb. Christ was revealed to my soul as the chiefest among ten thousand. These heavenly moments were really as life to the dead, and what John calls an earnest of the Spirit.[28] This was indeed unspeakable, and I firmly believe undeniable by many.

Now every leading providential circumstance that happened to me, from the day I was taken from my parents to that hour, was then in my view, as if it had but just then occurred. I was sensible of the invisible hand of God, which guided and protected me, when in truth I knew it not: still the Lord pursued me, although I slighted and disregarded it; this mercy melted me down. When I considered my poor wretched state I wept, seeing what a great debtor I was to sovereign free grace. Now the Ethiopian was willing to be saved by Jesus Christ, the sinner's only surety, and also to rely on none other person or thing for salvation. Self was obnoxious, and good works he had none, for it is God that worketh in us both to will and to do.

Oh! the amazing things of that hour can never be told—it was joy in the Holy Ghost! I felt an astonishing change; the burden of sin, the gaping jaws of hell, and the fears of death, that weighed me down before, now lost their horror; indeed I thought death would now be the best earthly friend I ever had. Such were my grief and joy as

---

[27] **Acts, twelfth verse:** "And there is salvation in no one else, for there is no other name under heaven given among men by which we must be saved."

[28] **earnest of the Spirit:** John 16:13, 14, &c. [Equiano's note.]

I believe are seldom experienced. I was bathed in tears, and said, What am I that God should thus look on me, the vilest of sinners? I felt a deep concern for my mother and friends, which occasioned me to pray with fresh ardor; and in the abyss of thought, I viewed the unconverted people of the world in a very awful state, being without God and without hope.

It pleased God to pour out on me the spirit of prayer and the grace of supplication, so that in loud acclamations I was enabled to praise and glorify his most holy name. When I got out of the cabin, and told some of the people what the Lord had done for me, alas! who could understand me or believe my report! None but to whom the arm of the Lord was revealed. I became a barbarian to them in talking of the love of Christ: his name was to me as ointment poured forth, indeed it was sweet to my soul, but to them a rock of offense. I thought my case singular, and every hour a day until I came to London, for I much longed to be with some to whom I could tell of the wonders of God's love towards me, and join in prayer to him whom my soul loved and thirsted after. I had uncommon commotions within, such as few can tell aught about.

Now the Bible was my only companion and comfort; I prized it much, with many thanks to God that I could read it for myself, and was not left to be tossed about or led by man's devices and notions. The worth of a soul cannot be told. May the Lord give the reader an understanding in this. Whenever I looked in the Bible I saw things new, and many texts were immediately applied to me with great comfort, for I knew that to me was the word of salvation sent. Sure I was that the Spirit which indited the word opened my heart to receive the truth of it as it is in Jesus—that the same Spirit enabled me to act in faith upon the promises that were precious to me, and enabled me to believe to the salvation of my soul. By free grace I was persuaded that I had a part in the first resurrection, and was enlightened with the "light of the living" (Job 33:30). I wished for a man of God with whom I might converse: my soul was like the chariots of Amminadib (Canticles 6:12). . . .

During this period we remained at Cadiz until our ship got laden. We sailed about the fourth of November; and, having a good passage, we arrived in London the month following, to my comfort, with heartfelt gratitude to God for his rich and unspeakable mercies. [. . .]

FROM CHAPTER 12
[CONCLUSION]

Such were the various scenes which I was a witness to, and the fortune I experienced until the year 1777. Since that period, my life has been more uniform, and the incidents of it fewer, than in any other equal number of years preceding; I therefore hasten to the conclusion of a narrative which I fear the reader may think already sufficiently tedious.

I had suffered so many impositions in my commercial transactions in different parts of the world, that I became heartily disgusted with the sea-faring life, and was determined not to return to it, at least for some time. I therefore once more engaged in service shortly after my return, and continued for the most part in this situation until 1784. [. . .]

[. . .] Since the first publication of my *Narrative*, I have been in a great variety of scenes in many parts of Great Britain, Ireland, and Scotland, an account of which might not improperly be added here;[29] but this would swell the volume too much, I shall only observe in general, that in May 1791, I sailed from Liverpool to Dublin, where I was very kindly received, and from thence to Cork, and then travelled over many counties in Ireland. I was everywhere exceedingly well treated, by persons of all ranks. I found the people extremely hospitable, particularly in Belfast, where I took my passage on board of a vessel for Clyde, on the 29th of January, and arrived at Greenock on the 30th. Soon after I returned to London, where I found persons of note from Holland and Germany, who requested me to go there; and I was glad to hear that an edition of my *Narrative* had been printed in both places, also in New York. I remained in London till I heard the debate in the House of Commons on the slave trade, April the 2d and 3d. I then went to Soham in Cambridgeshire, and was married on the 7th of April to Miss Cullen, daughter of James and Ann Cullen, late of Ely.[30]

I have only therefore to request the reader's indulgence and conclude. I am far from the vanity of thinking there is any merit in this narrative: I hope censure will be suspended, when it is considered that it was written by one who was as unwilling as unable to adorn the plainness of truth by the coloring of imagination. My life and fortune have been extremely checkered, and my adventures various. Nay even those I have related are considerably abridged. If any incident in this little work should appear uninteresting and trifling to most readers, I can only say, as my excuse for mentioning it, that almost every event of my life made an impression on my mind, and influenced my conduct. I early accustomed myself to look at the hand of God in the minutest occurrence, and to learn from it a lesson of morality and religion; and in this light every circumstance I have related was to me of importance. After all, what makes any event important, unless by its observation we become better and wiser, and learn "to do justly, to love mercy, and to walk humbly before God"? To those who are possessed of this spirit, there is scarcely any book or incident so trifling that does not afford some profit, while to others the experience of ages seems of no use; and even to pour out to them the treasures of wisdom is throwing the jewels of instruction away.

THE END

---

[29] **added here:** *Viz.* Some curious adventures beneath the earth, in a river in Manchester, and a most astonishing one under the Peak of Derbyshire—and in September 1792, I went 90 fathoms down St. Anthony's Colliery, at Newcastle, under the river Tyne some hundreds of yards on Durham side. [Equiano's note.]

[30] **married . . . Ely:** See *Gentleman's Magazine* for April 1792, *Literary and Biographical Magazine,* and *British Review* for May 1792, and the *Edinburgh Historical Register* or *Monthly Intelligencer* for April 1792. [Equiano's note.]

Slave Narratives and Emancipation

p. 448

pp. 499, 520

The slave narrative originated in the eighteenth century with works by Ignatius Sancho, Ottobah Cugoana, and **Olaudah Equiano**, but it gained momentum and fully developed as a literary genre in the United States during the first half of the nineteenth century in the hands of such writers as **Harriet A. Jacobs** and **Frederick Douglass**. Slave narratives were an important and influential component of the broader Emancipation movement in Britain and the United States. Accounts of the cruelty, injustice, and despair endured by slaves—as well as their hope, strength, and sometimes emancipation—these narratives combined autobiography, moral exhortation, and social criticism to draw attention to the plight of slaves and to indict the hypocrisy of slavery in nations founded upon doctrines of independence and the rights of man. Drawing upon the philosophical and political ideas that had led to the American and French revolutions of the previous century, the Emancipation movement aimed not only to abolish slavery and free the slaves but to extend to former slaves the economic, political, and legal rights from which they had been excluded.

After years of agitation, Britain and the United States withdrew from the transatlantic slave trade in 1807 and 1808, respectively. In 1834, Britain abolished slavery in its West Indian colonies, and shortly thereafter Denmark, Sweden, France, Holland, Spain, and Portugal followed suit. On January 1, 1863, President Abraham Lincoln issued the "Emancipation Proclamation," freeing slaves in the United States. Frederick Douglass, the African American activist, abolitionist, and former slave celebrated the Proclamation in his

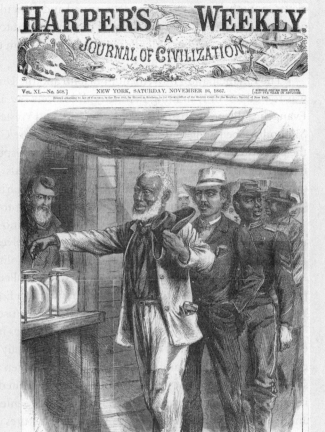

Cover of *Harper's Weekly*, "The First Vote," 1867*Soon after slavery was outlawed, a series of constitutional amendments granted African Americans the right to vote. Although many whites in the South used intimidation, even murder, to protest this advancement, African Americans still exercised their newfound right. (Schomburg Center for Research in Black Culture, New York Public Library)*

"Emancipation Proclaimed" as "the most important of any to which the President of the United States has ever signed his name." Two years later, on December 6, 1865, the American congress ratified the Thirteenth Amendment to the Constitution, abolishing slavery as a legal institution in the United States. The last country in the Americas to abolish slavery was Brazil in 1888. Emancipation from slavery, celebrated in the **African American folk songs** included in this section, did not immediately translate into equality and freedom for former slaves. The joy and hope that came with the Emancipation Proclamation was quashed as the freed slaves encountered "the wrath of our infuriated masters," as Frederick Douglass put it. The freed

p. 540

p. 544

Northerners know
nothing at all about
slavery. They think it
is perpetual bondage
only. They have no
conception of the
depth of *degradation*
involved in that
word, SLAVERY.

– A WOMAN OF
NORTH CAROLINA,
quoted on the title
page of the first
edition of *Incidents*

p. 726

slaves, nonetheless, set out on a determined and difficult project to acquire property, education, jobs, and money needed to found a life for their children and grandchildren far different from the one they had known.

The Emancipation movement in Britain and the United States was rooted not only in Enlightenment philosophy but also in Evangelical Protestantism. Quakers, Baptists, and Wesleyan Methodists, believing in the equality of all men before God and in the individual's free will to choose divine grace, were especially tireless in working to end slavery. Lincoln, though not a zealous abolitionist, grounded his belief in emancipation in a concept of spiritual freedom. "This is a world of compensation," he wrote in a letter to H. L. Pierce, "and he who would be no slave must consent to have no slave. Those who deny freedom to others deserve it not for themselves, and, under a just God, cannot long retain it." One of the ways abolitionists in America and Europe promoted their cause was by collecting and publishing slave narratives, such as those of Olaudah Equiano and Harriet Jacobs, whose story was published under the pseudonym "Linda Brent." The real people behind these narratives insist on their own identity through acts of open rebellion or carefully masked defiance against racism and oppression. They were often joined and supported by prominent white abolitionists in the United States and in England, such as Harriet Beecher Stowe,[1] **John Greenleaf Whittier**, and Lydia Maria Child,[2] who helped to sponsor lectures and publications by former slaves who had escaped to the North. But as Frederick Douglass, author of the best known of all slave narratives would remark in 1855, the free person, however sympathetic, "cannot see things in the same light with the slave, because he does not, and cannot, look from the same point from which the slave does."

FEATURES OF THE SLAVE NARRATIVE

The slave narratives produced in the United States—more than six thousand existing book-length narratives, Works Progress Administration interviews, and occasional essays, it has been estimated—vary

---

[1] **Harriet Beecher Stowe** (1811–96): Novelist and abolitionist author of the popular and controversial *Uncle Tom's Cabin* (1851).

[2] **Lydia Maria Child** (1802–80): Novelist, social critic, abolitionist, and feminist; author of *The Frugal Housewife* (1829), *The Mother's Book* (1831), and several historical novels about life in New England.

In de Lan' o' Cotton, 1899
Freed slaves in the South had scant employment prospects; many, like those seen in this photograph, continued to work on cotton plantations. (Library of Congress)

greatly. But as James Olney and other scholars have pointed out, these texts share certain features of form and structure. For example, the authors often give accounts of how they learned to read and write and of the crucial role literacy plays in resisting slavery; they often include descriptions of slave auctions and feature an account of one spectacularly brutal master or overseer. Most have a story to tell about one particularly strong and resolute slave who resists white authority, and most remark on how avowedly Christian slaveholders are worse than the ones who aren't especially religious. All these elements can be found in Jacobs's *Incidents in the Life of a Slave Girl*, as can two others whose significance may easily escape contemporary readers. First, slave narratives were always printed with testimonials and portraits as well as other prefatory material attesting to the author's existence and truthfulness; second, with astonishing consistency, the narratives' opening sentences begin, "I was born. . . ." Such features in the published narratives served to

p. 501

combat charges that the books and stories were mere abolitionist propaganda, heavily doctored or in fact authored by white zealots. The testimonials, portraits, and especially the ability to put into writing the words *I was born* were ways for the author to insist upon his or her very existence as a human being, a man or a woman capable of thought, feeling, and speech.

AFRICAN AMERICAN FOLK SONGS

The themes of the slave narratives—the injustice of slavery, the suffering it brought to those it held captive, and the desire for escape and freedom—appear also in the African American folk songs or spirituals. These songs of the southern slaves are now recognized as some of America's greatest music. In his *Narrative,* Frederick Douglass writes that some of these songs told a profound, but often veiled, "tale of woe"; other songs insist upon the power of hope and the promise of deliverance. In 1903, W. E. B. Du Bois[3] wrote that these "Sorrow Songs," as he called them, "articulate the message of the slave to the world," and he claimed that they are "the sole American music, . . . the most beautiful expression of human experience from this side of the seas." Combining African and American elements, most spirituals date from the eighteenth century and the first half of the nineteenth century and were passed down orally from one generation to the next. After the Civil War, the songs were written down and performed by groups such as the Fisk Jubilee Singers, from Nashville, Tennessee, who in 1871 were the first choral group to include spirituals in a concert program. The response they received was so positive that soon they and similar choral groups were performing spirituals throughout the United States and abroad.

■ **FURTHER RESEARCH**

General Criticism
Baker, Houston A., Jr. *Blues, Ideology, and Afro-American Literature.* 1987.
Davis, Charles T., and Henry Louis Gates Jr. Introduction to *The Slave's Narrative.* 1991.

Frederick Douglass
Huggins, Nathan Irvin. *Slave and Citizen: The Life of Frederick Douglass.* 1980.
McFeely, William S. *Frederick Douglass.* 1991.

---

[3] **W. E. B. Du Bois** (1868–1963): Harvard educated African American scholar, professor, and writer, Du Bois was one of the founders of the National Association for the Advancement of Colored People (NAACP) and the author of several books including *The Souls of Black Folk* (1903), in which his essay "The Sorrow Songs" appears.

Harriet Jacobs

Johnson, Yvonne. *The Voices of African American Women: The Use of Narrative and Authorial Voice in the Works of Harriet Jacobs, Zora Neale Hurston, and Alike Walker.* 1998.

Yellin, Jean Fagin. *Harriet Jacobs: A Life.* 2005.

Yellin, Jean Fagin., ed. *Incidents in the Life of a Slave Girl.* 1987.

African American Folk Songs

Dixon, Christa K. *Negro Spirituals: From Bible to Folk Song.* 1976.

DuBois, W. E. B. "The Sorrow Songs." *The Souls of Black Folk.* 1903.

Johnson, James Weldon. "O Black and Unknown Bards." 1930.

Johnson, James Weldon, and J. Rosamond Johnson. *The Book of American Negro Spirituals.* 1925.

——. *The Second Book of Negro Spirituals.* 1926.

Lovell, John, Jr. *Black Song: The Forge and the Flame.* 1972.

Thurman, Howard. *Deep River.* 1945.

❧ Harriet A. Jacobs (Linda Brent)
b. United States, c. 1813–1897

Harriet Jacobs was born into slavery in about 1813 in Edenton, North Carolina. She was orphaned early; her maternal grandmother, Molly Horniblow ("Aunt Martha"), was a freedwoman who made her living as a baker. When Jacobs was eleven, her first mistress died, and she was bequeathed to the three-year-old daughter of Dr. James Norcom ("Dr. Flint"). Norcom soon began a dogged campaign of sexual harassment against Jacobs. Despite Flint's threats and entreaties, she resisted or evaded all his attempts at seduction and rape. When he forbade her to marry the African American freedman whom she loved, she took for her lover another influential white man, the young lawyer Samuel Tredwell Sawyer ("Mr. Sands"), by whom she bore two children, Joseph and Louisa Matilda. She explains the psychology that prompts her to accept the sympathetic Sawyer, but she acknowledges that the relationship is "sinful." In 1835, Dr. Norcom punished Jacobs for continuing to refuse him by exiling her to his plantation, where slaves were treated more brutally than in town; next, he threatened to bring her children to the plantation and make them suffer particularly hard enslavement. Jacobs reasoned that if she were to disappear, Norcom would find her motherless children a mere burden and might sell them to an agent secretly representing their white father, whom she hoped would then free them.

For nearly seven years, while most people believed her dead or fled to the North, Jacobs hid in a cramped crawl space in the attic of her grandmother's house, afraid to reveal her presence even to her own children. Sawyer was indeed able to purchase Joseph and Louisa Matilda, but he never got around to the crucial legal matter of setting them free. Jacobs at last escaped by boat in 1842 to New York City, where she worked as a

www For more information about Jacobs and a quiz on *Incidents in the Life of a Slave Girl,* see bedfordstmartins.com/worldlitcompact.

Advertisement for
Capture of Harriet
Jacobs, July 4, 1835
Placed on Indepen-
dence Day, this ad
was submitted by
James Norcom,
Harriet Jacobs's
master. After she fled
Norcom's plantation,
Jacobs spent seven
years hiding in the
crawl space of her
grandmother's attic
before escaping to the
North. (Courtesy of
the North Carolina
Office of Archives and
History)

$100 REWARD

WILL be given for the apprehension and
delivery of my Servant Girl HAR-
RIET. She is a light mulatto, 21 years of
age, about 5 feet 4 inches high, of a thick
and corpulent habit, having on her head a
thick covering of black hair that curls naturally, but which can be easily combed
straight. She speaks easily and fluently, and
has an agreeable carriage and address. Being
a good seamstress, she has been accustomed
to dress well, has a variety of very fine
clothes, made in the prevailing fashion, and
will probably appear, if abroad, tricked out
in gay and fashionable finery. As this girl
absconded from the plantation of my son
without any known cause or provocation, it
is probable she designs to transport herself
to the North.

The above reward, with all reasonable
charges, will be given for apprehending her,
or securing her in any prison or jail within
the U. States.

All persons are hereby forewarned against
harboring or entertaining her, or being in
any way instrumental in her escape, under
the most rigorous penalties of the law.

JAMES NORCOM.

Edenton, N. C. June 30   tf2w

nursemaid for the family of the editor Nathaniel Parker Willis.[1] There, she met Frederick Douglass, the most prominent writer and orator who had escaped slavery, and Amy Post[2] and Lydia Maria Child, writers active in the causes of abolition and women's rights. There, too, she was at last reunited with her children. Her son Joseph became a sailor, a livelihood that kept him out of slavery's reach, but Jacobs and Louisa Matilda were traced to New York by the vengeful Norcom and his adult daughter. The Norcoms threatened to reclaim Jacobs and her daughter until Willis's wife purchased Jacobs and set her free.

Jacobs's friends urged her to tell her story, but for some time she held back because of the pain and shame of revealing the sexual history so central to that telling. (It is worthwhile to remember that more than 140 years later, it is still hard for women and men to speak about histories of rape and childhood sexual abuse.) Above all, Jacobs feared her daughter Louisa Matilda's reaction to her story, especially because Jacobs's grand-mother, who was supportive in all else, had condemned Jacobs for

---

[1] **Nathaniel Parker Willis** (1806–1867): American poet, travel writer, playwright, magazine editor, and critic.

[2] **Amy Post** (1802–1889): Quaker abolitionist and feminist.

becoming Sawyer's lover and getting pregnant by him. Finally Jacobs agreed to write her autobiography, hoping that she might galvanize women to oppose the evils of slavery. With some help from editor Lydia Maria Child—whose work on the text was demonstrably that of an editor, not a ghostwriter—Jacobs brought out *Incidents in the Life of a Slave Girl* in 1861. Once Louisa Matilda knew the story, she embraced her mother along with her history, rejoicing in Jacobs's courage.

After the Civil War, Jacobs did relief work for freed slaves in the South and raised money for that cause in England. Toward the latter part of her life, she ran a boardinghouse in Cambridge, Massachusetts; she died in 1897. Louisa Matilda Jacobs continued her mother's work in relief and civil rights.

> With Frederick Douglass's account of his life, [*Incidents in the Life of a Slave Girl*] is one of the two archetypes in the genre of the slave narrative.
>
> – JEAN FAGAN YELLIN, for her edition of the book, 1987

∾ Incidents in the Life of a Slave Girl

CHAPTER 1. CHILDHOOD

I was born a slave; but I never knew it till six years of happy childhood had passed away. My father was a carpenter, and considered so intelligent and skillful in his trade, that, when buildings out of the common line were to be erected, he was sent for from long distances, to be head workman. On condition of paying his mistress two hundred dollars a year, and supporting himself, he was allowed to work at his trade, and manage his own affairs. His strongest wish was to purchase his children; but, though he several times offered his hard earnings for that purpose, he never succeeded. In complexion my parents were a light shade of brownish yellow, and were termed mulattoes. They lived together in a comfortable home; and, though we were all slaves, I was so fondly shielded that I never dreamed I was a piece of merchandise, trusted to them for safe keeping, and liable to be demanded of them at any moment. I had one brother, William, who was two years younger than myself—a bright, affectionate child. I had also a great treasure in my maternal grandmother, who was a remarkable woman in many respects. She was the daughter of a planter in South Carolina, who, at his death, left her mother and his three children free, with money to go to St. Augustine, where they had relatives. It was during the Revolutionary War; and they were captured on their passage, carried back, and sold to different purchasers. Such was the story my grandmother used to tell me; but I do not remember all the particulars. She was a little girl when she was captured and sold to the keeper of a large hotel. I have often heard her tell how hard she fared during childhood. But as she grew older she evinced so much intelligence, and was so faithful, that her master and mistress could not help seeing it was for their interest to take care of such a valuable piece of property. She became an indispensable personage in the household, officiating in all capacities, from cook and wet nurse to seamstress. She was much praised for her cooking; and her nice crackers became so famous in

the neighborhood that many people were desirous of obtaining them. In consequence of numerous requests of this kind, she asked permission of her mistress to
bake crackers at night, after all the household work was done; and she obtained leave
to do it, provided she would clothe herself and her children from the profits. Upon
these terms, after working hard all day for her mistress, she began her midnight bak-
ings, assisted by her two oldest children. The business proved profitable; and each
year she laid by a little, which was saved for a fund to purchase her children. Her
master died, and the property was divided among his heirs. The widow had her
dower in the hotel, which she continued to keep open. My grandmother remained in
her service as a slave; but her children were divided among her master's children. As
she had five, Benjamin, the youngest one, was sold, in order that each heir might
have an equal portion of dollars and cents. There was so little difference in our ages
that he seemed more like my brother than my uncle. He was a bright, handsome lad,
nearly white; for he inherited the complexion my grandmother had derived from
Anglo-Saxon ancestors. Though only ten years old, seven hundred and twenty dollars were paid for him. His sale was a terrible blow to my grandmother; but she was
naturally hopeful, and she went to work with renewed energy, trusting in time to be
able to purchase some of her children. She had laid up three hundred dollars, which
her mistress one day begged as a loan, promising to pay her soon. The reader probably knows that no promise or writing given to a slave is legally binding; for, according to Southern laws, a slave, *being* property, can *hold* no property. When my
grandmother lent her hard earnings to her mistress, she trusted solely to her honor.
The honor of a slaveholder to a slave!

To this good grandmother I was indebted for many comforts. My brother Willie
and I often received portions of the crackers, cakes, and preserves she made to sell;
and after we ceased to be children we were indebted to her for many more important
services.

Such were the unusually fortunate circumstances of my early childhood. When I
was six years old, my mother died; and then, for the first time, I learned, by the talk
around me, that I was a slave. My mother's mistress was the daughter of my grandmother's mistress. She was the foster sister of my mother; they were both nourished
at my grandmother's breast. In fact, my mother had been weaned at three months
old, that the babe of the mistress might obtain sufficient food. They played together
as children; and, when they became women, my mother was a most faithful servant
to her whiter foster sister. On her death-bed her mistress promised that her children
should never suffer for any thing; and during her lifetime she kept her word. They all
spoke kindly of my dead mother, who had been a slave merely in name, but in nature
was noble and womanly. I grieved for her, and my young mind was troubled with the
thought who would now take care of me and my little brother. I was told that my
home was now to be with her mistress; and I found it a happy one. No toilsome or
disagreeable duties were imposed upon me. My mistress was so kind to me that I was
always glad to do her bidding, and proud to labor for her as much as my young years
would permit. I would sit by her side for hours, sewing diligently, with a heart as free
from care as that of any free-born white child. When she thought I was tired, she
would send me out to run and jump; and away I bounded, to gather berries or
flowers to decorate her room. Those were happy days—too happy to last. The slave

child had no thought for the morrow; but there came that blight, which too surely waits on every human being born to be a chattel.

When I was nearly twelve years old, my kind mistress sickened and died. As I saw the cheek grow paler, and the eye more glassy, how earnestly I prayed in my heart that she might live! I loved her; for she had been almost like a mother to me. My prayers were not answered. She died, and they buried her in the little churchyard, where, day after day, my tears fell upon her grave.

I was sent to spend a week with my grandmother. I was now old enough to begin to think of the future; and again and again I asked myself what they would do with me. I felt sure I should never find another mistress so kind as the one who was gone. She had promised my dying mother that her children should never suffer for any thing; and when I remembered that, and recalled her many proofs of attachment to me, I could not help having some hopes that she had left me free. My friends were almost certain it would be so. They thought she would be sure to do it, on account of my mother's love and faithful service. But, alas! we all know that the memory of a faithful slave does not avail much to save her children from the auction block.

After a brief period of suspense, the will of my mistress was read, and we learned that she had bequeathed me to her sister's daughter, a child of five years old. So vanished our hopes. My mistress had taught me the precepts of God's Word: "Thou shalt love thy neighbor as thyself." "Whatsoever ye would that men should do unto you, do ye even so unto them." But I was her slave, and I suppose she did not recognize me as her neighbor. I would give much to blot out from my memory that one great wrong. As a child, I loved my mistress; and, looking back on the happy days I spent with her, I try to think with less bitterness of this act of injustice. While I was with her, she taught me to read and spell; and for this privilege, which so rarely falls to the lot of a slave, I bless her memory.

She possessed but few slaves; and at her death those were all distributed among her relatives.[1] Five of them were my grandmother's children, and had shared the same milk that nourished her mother's children. Notwithstanding my grandmother's long and faithful service to her owners, not one of her children escaped the auction block. These God-breathing machines are no more, in the sight of their masters, than the cotton they plant, or the horses they tend.

from CHAPTER 2. THE NEW MASTER AND MISTRESS

Dr. Flint, a physician in the neighborhood, had married the sister of my mistress, and I was now the property of their little daughter. It was not without murmuring that I prepared for my new home; and what added to my unhappiness, was the fact that my brother William was purchased by the same family. My father, by his nature, as well as by the habit of transacting business as a skillful mechanic, had more of the feelings of a freeman than is common among slaves. My brother was a spirited boy; and being brought up under such influences, he early detested the name of master and mistress. One day, when his father and his mistress had happened to call him at

---

[1] **among her relatives:** Jacobs was taken into the household of Dr. James Norcomb, the "Dr. Flint" of the text; he was married to Jacobs's first mistress's sister.

the same time, he hesitated between the two; being perplexed to know which had the strongest claim upon his obedience. He finally concluded to go to his mistress. When my father reproved him for it, he said, "You both called me, and I didn't know which I ought to go to first."

[. . .] When I had been in the family a few weeks, one of the plantation slaves was brought to town, by order of his master. It was near night when he arrived, and Dr. Flint ordered him to be taken to the work house, and tied up to the joist, so that his feet would just escape the ground. In that situation he was to wait till the doctor had taken his tea. I shall never forget that night. Never before, in my life, had I heard hundreds of blows fall, in succession, on a human being. His piteous groans, and his "O, pray don't, massa," rang in my ear for months afterwards. There were many conjectures as to the cause of this terrible punishment. Some said master accused him of stealing corn; others said the slave had quarrelled with his wife, in presence of the overseer, and had accused his master of being the father of her child. They were both black, and the child was very fair.

I went into the work house next morning, and saw the cowhide still wet with blood, and the boards all covered with gore. The poor man lived, and continued to quarrel with his wife. A few months afterwards Dr. Flint handed them both over to a slavetrader. The guilty man put their value into his pocket, and had the satisfaction of knowing that they were out of sight and hearing. When the mother was delivered into the trader's hands, she said, "You *promised* to treat me well." To which he replied, "You have let your tongue run too far; damn you!" She had forgotten that it was a crime for a slave to tell who was the father of her child.

From others than the master persecution also comes in such cases. I once saw a young slave girl dying soon after the birth of a child nearly white. In her agony she cried out, "O Lord, come and take me!" Her mistress stood by, and mocked at her like an incarnate fiend. "You suffer, do you?" she exclaimed. "I am glad of it. You deserve it all, and more too."

The girl's mother said, "The baby is dead, thank God; and I hope my poor child will soon be in heaven, too."

"Heaven!" retorted the mistress. "There is no such place for the like of her and her bastard."

The poor mother turned away, sobbing. Her dying daughter called her, feebly, and as she bent over her, I heard her say, "Don't grieve so, mother; God knows all about it; and he will have mercy upon me."

Her sufferings, afterwards, became so intense, that her mistress felt unable to stay; but when she left the room, the scornful smile was still on her lips. Seven children called her mother. The poor black woman had but the one child, whose eyes she saw closing in death, while she thanked God for taking her away from the greater bitterness of life.

from Chapter 5. The Trials of Girlhood

During the first years of my service in Dr. Flint's family, I was accustomed to share some indulgences with the children of my mistress. Though this seemed to me no more than right, I was grateful for it, and tried to merit the kindness by the faithful discharge of my duties. But I now entered on my fifteenth year—a sad epoch in the life of a slave girl. My master began to whisper foul words in my ear. Young as I was, I could not remain ignorant of their import. I tried to treat them with indifference or contempt. The master's age, my extreme youth, and the fear that his conduct would be reported to my grandmother, made him bear this treatment for many months. He was a crafty man, and resorted to many means to accomplish his purposes. Sometimes he had stormy, terrific ways, that made his victims tremble; sometimes he assumed a gentleness that he thought must surely subdue. Of the two, I preferred his stormy moods, although they left me trembling. He tried his utmost to corrupt the pure principles my grandmother had instilled. He peopled my young mind with unclean images, such as only a vile monster could think of. I turned from him with disgust and hatred. But he was my master. I was compelled to live under the same roof with him—where I saw a man forty years my senior daily violating the most sacred commandments of nature. He told me I was his property; that I must be subject to his will in all things. My soul revolted against the mean tyranny. But where could I turn for protection? No matter whether the slave girl be as black as ebony or as fair as her mistress. In either case, there is no shadow of law to protect her from insult, from violence, or even from death; all these are inflicted by fiends who bear the shape of men. The mistress, who ought to protect the helpless victim, has no other feelings towards her but those of jealousy and rage. The degradation, the wrongs, the vices, that grow out of slavery, are more than I can describe. They are greater than you would willingly believe. Surely, if you credited one half the truths that are told you concerning the helpless millions suffering in this cruel bondage, you at the north would not help to tighten the yoke. You surely would refuse to do for the master, on your own soil, the mean and cruel work which trained bloodhounds and the lowest class of whites do for him at the south.

Every where the years bring to all enough of sin and sorrow; but in slavery the very dawn of life is darkened by these shadows. Even the little child, who is accustomed to wait on her mistress and her children, will learn, before she is twelve years old, why it is that her mistress hates such and such a one among the slaves. Perhaps the child's own mother is among those hated ones. She listens to violent outbreaks of jealous passion, and cannot help understanding what is the cause. She will become prematurely knowing in evil things. Soon she will learn to tremble when she hears her master's footfall. She will be compelled to realize that she is no longer a child. If God has bestowed beauty upon her, it will prove her greatest curse. That which commands admiration in the white woman only hastens the degradation of the female slave. I know that some are too much brutalized by slavery to feel the humiliation of their position; but many slaves feel it most acutely, and shrink from the memory of it. I cannot tell how much I suffered in the presence of these wrongs, nor how I am still pained by the retrospect. My master met me at every turn, reminding me that I belonged to him, and swearing by heaven and earth that he would compel me to submit to him. If I went out for a breath of fresh air, after a day of unwearied toil, his footsteps dogged me. If I knelt by my mother's grave, his dark shadow fell on me even there. The light heart which nature had given me became heavy with sad forebodings. The other slaves in my master's house noticed the change. Many of them pitied me; but none dared to ask the cause. They had no need to inquire. They knew too well the guilty practices under that roof; and they were aware that to speak of them was an offence that never went unpunished. [. . .]

CHAPTER 6. THE JEALOUS MISTRESS

I would ten thousand times rather that my children should be the half-starved paupers of Ireland than to be the most pampered among the slaves of America. I would rather drudge out my life on a cotton plantation, till the grave opened to give me rest, than to live with an unprincipled master and a jealous mistress. The felon's home in a penitentiary is preferable. He may repent, and turn from the error of his ways, and so find peace; but it is not so with a favorite slave. She is not allowed to have any pride of character. It is deemed a crime in her to wish to be virtuous.

Mrs. Flint possessed the key to her husband's character before I was born. She might have used this knowledge to counsel and to screen the young and the innocent among her slaves; but for them she had no sympathy. They were the objects of her constant suspicion and malevolence. She watched her husband with unceasing vigilance; but he was well practised in means to evade it. What he could not find opportunity to say in words he manifested in signs. He invented more than were ever thought of in a deaf and dumb asylum. I let them pass, as if I did not understand what he meant; and many were the curses and threats bestowed on me for my stupidity. One day he caught me teaching myself to write. He frowned, as if he was not well pleased; but I suppose he came to the conclusion that such an accomplishment might help to advance his favorite scheme. Before long, notes were often slipped into my hand. I would return them, saying, "I can't read them, sir." "Can't you?" he replied; "then I must read them to you." He always finished the reading by asking, "Do you understand?" Sometimes he would complain of the heat of the tea room, and order his supper to be placed on a small table in the piazza. He would seat himself there with a well-satisfied smile, and tell me to stand by and brush away the flies. He would eat very slowly, pausing between the mouthfuls. These intervals were employed in describing the happiness I was so foolishly throwing away, and in threatening me with the penalty that finally awaited my stubborn disobedience. He boasted much of the forbearance he had exercised towards me, and reminded me that there was a limit to his patience. When I succeeded in avoiding opportunities for him to talk to me at home, I was ordered to come to his office, to do some errand. When there, I was obliged to stand and listen to such language as he saw fit to address to me. Sometimes I so openly expressed my contempt for him that he would become violently enraged, and I wondered why he did not strike me. Circumstanced as he was, he probably thought it was better policy to be forbearing. But the state of things grew worse and worse daily. In desperation I told him that I must and would apply to my grandmother for protection. He threatened me with death, and worse than death, if I made any complaint to her. Strange to say, I did not despair. I was naturally of a buoyant disposition, and always I had a hope of somehow getting out of his clutches. Like many a poor, simple slave before me, I trusted that some threads of joy would yet be woven into my dark destiny.

I had entered my sixteenth year, and every day it became more apparent that my presence was intolerable to Mrs. Flint. Angry words frequently passed between her and her husband. He had never punished me himself, and he would not allow any body else to punish me. In that respect, she was never satisfied; but, in her angry moods, no terms were too vile for her to bestow upon me. Yet I, whom she detested so bitterly, had far more pity for her than he had, whose duty it was to make her life happy. I never wronged her, or wished to wrong her; and one word of kindness from her would have brought me to her feet.

After repeated quarrels between the doctor and his wife, he announced his intention to take his youngest daughter, then four years old, to sleep in his apartment. It was necessary that a servant should sleep in the same room, to be on hand if the child stirred. I was selected for that office, and informed for what purpose that arrangement had been made. By managing to keep within sight of people, as much as possible, during the day time, I had hitherto succeeded in eluding my master, though a razor was often held to my throat to force me to change this line of policy. At night I slept by the side of my great aunt, where I felt safe. He was too prudent to come into her room. She was an old woman, and had been in the family many years. Moreover, as a married man, and a professional man, he deemed it necessary to save appearances in some degree. But he resolved to remove the obstacle in the way of his scheme; and he thought he had planned it so that he should evade suspicion. He was well aware how much I prized my refuge by the side of my old aunt, and he determined to dispossess me of it. The first night the doctor had the little child in his room alone. The next morning, I was ordered to take my station as nurse the following night. A kind Providence interposed in my favor. During the day Mrs. Flint heard of this new arrangement, and a storm followed. I rejoiced to hear it rage.

After a while my mistress sent for me to come to her room. Her first question was, "Did you know you were to sleep in the doctor's room?"

"Yes, ma'am."

"Who told you?"

"My master."

"Will you answer truly all the questions I ask?"

"Yes, ma'am."

"Tell me, then, as you hope to be forgiven, are you innocent of what I have accused you?"

"I am."

She handed me a Bible, and said, "Lay your hand on your heart, kiss this holy book, and swear before God that you tell me the truth."

I took the oath she required, and I did it with a clear conscience.

"You have taken God's holy word to testify your innocence," said she. "If you have deceived me, beware! Now take this stool, sit down, look me directly in the face, and tell me all that has passed between your master and you."

I did as she ordered. As I went on with my account her color changed frequently, she wept, and sometimes groaned. She spoke in tones so sad, that I was touched by her grief. The tears came to my eyes; but I was soon convinced that her emotions arose from anger and wounded pride. She felt that her marriage vows were desecrated, her dignity insulted; but she had no compassion for the poor victim of her husband's perfidy. She pitied herself as a martyr; but she was incapable of feeling for the condition of shame and misery in which her unfortunate, helpless slave was placed.

Yet perhaps she had some touch of feeling for me; for when the conference was ended, she spoke kindly, and promised to protect me. I should have been much comforted by this assurance if I could have had confidence in it; but my experiences in slavery had filled me with distrust. She was not a very refined woman, and had not much control over her passions. I was an object of her jealousy, and, consequently, of her hatred; and I knew I could not expect kindness or confidence from her under the circumstances in which I was placed. I could not blame her. Slaveholders' wives feel as other women would under similar circumstances. The fire of her temper kindled from small sparks, and now the flame became so intense that the doctor was obliged to give up his intended arrangement.

I knew I had ignited the torch, and I expected to suffer for it afterwards; but I felt too thankful to my mistress for the timely aid she rendered me to care much about that. She now took me to sleep in a room adjoining her own. There I was an object of her especial care, though not of her especial comfort, for she spent many a sleepless night to watch over me. Sometimes I woke up, and found her bending over me. At other times she whispered in my ear, as though it was her husband who was speaking to me, and listened to hear what I would answer. If she startled me, on such occasions, she would glide stealthily away; and the next morning she would tell me I had been talking in my sleep, and ask who I was talking to. At last, I began to be fearful for my life. It had been often threatened; and you can imagine, better than I can describe, what an unpleasant sensation it must produce to wake up in the dead of night and find a jealous woman bending over you. Terrible as this experience was, I had fears that it would give place to one more terrible.

My mistress grew weary of her vigils; they did not prove satisfactory. She changed her tactics. She now tried the trick of accusing my master of crime, in my presence, and gave my name as the author of the accusation. To my utter astonishment, he replied, "I don't believe it: but if she did acknowledge it, you tortured her into exposing me." Tortured into exposing him! Truly, Satan had no difficulty in distinguishing the color of his soul! I understood his object in making this false representation. It was to show me that I gained nothing by seeking the protection of my mistress; that the power was still all in his own hands. I pitied Mrs. Flint. She was a second wife, many years the junior of her husband; and the hoary-headed miscreant was enough to try the patience of a wiser and better woman. She was completely foiled, and knew not how to proceed. She would gladly have had me flogged for my supposed false oath; but, as I have already stated, the doctor never allowed any one to whip me. The old sinner was politic. The application of the lash might have led to remarks that would have exposed him in the eyes of his children and grandchildren. How often did I rejoice that I lived in a town where all the inhabitants knew each other! If I had been on a remote plantation, or lost among the multitude of a crowded city, I should not be a living woman at this day.

The secrets of slavery are concealed like those of the Inquisition. My master was, to my knowledge, the father of eleven slaves. But did the mothers dare to tell who was the father of their children? Did the other slaves dare to allude to it, except in whispers among themselves? No, indeed! They knew too well the terrible consequences.

My grandmother could not avoid seeing things which excited her suspicions. She was uneasy about me, and tried various ways to buy me; but the neverchanging answer was always repeated: "Linda does not belong to *me*. She is my daughter's property, and I have no legal right to sell her." The conscientious man! He was too scrupulous to *sell* me; but he had no scruples whatever about committing a much greater wrong against the helpless young girl placed under his guardianship, as his daughter's property. Sometimes my persecutor would ask me whether I would like to be sold. I told him I would rather be sold to any body than to lead such a life as I did. On such occasions he would assume the air of a very injured individual, and reproach me for my ingratitude. "Did I not take you into the house, and make you the companion of my own children?" he would say. "Have I ever treated you like a negro? I have never allowed you to be punished, not even to please your mistress. And this is the recompense I get, you ungrateful girl!" I answered that he had reasons of his own for screening me from punishment, and that the course he pursued made my mistress hate me and persecute me. If I wept, he would say, "Poor child! Don't cry! don't cry! I will make peace for you with your mistress. Only let me arrange matters in my own way. Poor, foolish girl! you don't know what is for your own good. I would cherish you. I would make a lady of you. Now go, and think of all I have promised you."

I did think of it.

Reader, I draw no imaginary pictures of southern homes. I am telling you the plain truth. Yet when victims make their escape from this wild beast of Slavery, northerners consent to act the part of bloodhounds, and hunt the poor fugitive back into his den, "full of dead men's bones, and all uncleanness." Nay, more, they are not only willing, but proud, to give their daughters in marriage to slaveholders. The poor girls have romantic notions of a sunny clime, and of the flowering vines that all the year round shade a happy home. To what disappointments are they destined! The young wife soon learns that the husband in whose hands she has placed her happiness pays no regard to his marriage vows. Children of every shade of complexion play with her own fair babies, and too well she knows that they are born unto him of his own household. Jealousy and hatred enter the flowery home, and it is ravaged of its loveliness.

Southern women often marry a man knowing that he is the father of many little slaves. They do not trouble themselves about it. They regard such children as property, as marketable as the pigs on the plantation, and it is seldom that they do not make them aware of this by passing them into the slavetrader's hands as soon as possible, and thus getting them out of their sight. I am glad to say there are some honorable exceptions.

I have myself known two southern wives who exhorted their husbands to free those slaves towards whom they stood in a "parental relation;" and their request was granted. These husbands blushed before the superior nobleness of their wives' natures. Though they had only counselled them to do that which it was their duty to do, it commanded their respect, and rendered their conduct more exemplary. Concealment was at an end, and confidence took the place of distrust.

Though this bad institution deadens the moral sense, even in white women, to a fearful extent, it is not altogether extinct. I have heard southern ladies say of Mr. Such a one, "He not only thinks it no disgrace to be the father of those little niggers, but he is not ashamed to call himself their master. I declare, such things ought not to be tolerated in any decent society!"

CHAPTER 10. A PERILOUS PASSAGE IN THE SLAVE GIRL'S LIFE

After my lover[2] went away, Dr. Flint contrived a new plan. He seemed to have an idea that my fear of my mistress was his greatest obstacle. In the blandest tones, he told me that he was going to build a small house for me, in a secluded place, four miles away from the town. I shuddered; but I was constrained to listen, while he talked of his intention to give me a home of my own, and to make a lady of me. Hitherto, I had escaped my dreaded fate, by being in the midst of people. My grandmother had already had high words with my master about me. She had told him pretty plainly what she thought of his character, and there was considerable gossip in the neighborhood about our affairs, to which the open-mouthed jealousy of Mrs. Flint contributed not a little. When my master said he was going to build a house for me, and that he could do it with little trouble and expense, I was in hopes something would happen to frustrate his scheme; but I soon heard that the house was actually begun. I vowed before my Maker that I would never enter it. I had rather toil on the plantation from dawn till dark; I had rather live and die in jail, than drag on, from day to day, through such a living death. I was determined that the master, whom I so hated and loathed, who had blighted the prospects of my youth, and made my life a desert, should not, after my long struggle with him, succeed at last in trampling his victim under his feet. I would do any thing, every thing, for the sake of defeating him. What *could* I do? I thought and thought, till I became desperate, and made a plunge into the abyss.

And now, reader, I come to a period in my unhappy life, which I would gladly forget if I could. The remembrance fills me with sorrow and shame. It pains me to tell you of it; but I have promised to tell you the truth, and I will do it honestly, let it cost me what it may. I will not try to screen myself behind the plea of compulsion from a master; for it was not so. Neither can I plead ignorance or thoughtlessness. For years, my master had done his utmost to pollute my mind with foul images, and to destroy the pure principles inculcated by my grandmother, and the good mistress of my childhood. The influences of slavery had had the same effect on me that they had on other young girls; they had made me prematurely knowing, concerning the evil ways of the world. I knew what I did, and I did it with deliberate calculation.

---

[2]**my lover:** Jacobs had fallen in love with a free-born black carpenter who wanted to buy her freedom and marry her; Dr. Flint interfered and would not agree to the proposal, and the carpenter left for Savannah, Georgia.

But, O, ye happy women, whose purity has been sheltered from childhood, who have been free to choose the objects of your affection, whose homes are protected by law, do not judge the poor desolate slave girl too severely! If slavery had been abolished, I, also, could have married the man of my choice; I could have had a home shielded by the laws; and I should have been spared the painful task of confessing what I am now about to relate; but all my prospects had been blighted by slavery. I wanted to keep myself pure; and, under the most adverse circumstances, I tried hard to preserve my self-respect; but I was struggling alone in the powerful grasp of the demon Slavery; and the monster proved too strong for me. I felt as if I was forsaken by God and man; as if all my efforts must be frustrated; and I became reckless in my despair.

I have told you that Dr. Flint's persecutions and his wife's jealousy had given rise to some gossip in the neighborhood. Among others, it chanced that a white unmarried gentleman had obtained some knowledge of the circumstances in which I was placed. He knew my grandmother, and often spoke to me in the street. He became interested for me, and asked questions about my master, which I answered in part. He expressed a great deal of sympathy, and a wish to aid me. He constantly sought opportunities to see me, and wrote to me frequently. I was a poor slave girl, only fifteen years old.

So much attention from a superior person was, of course, flattering; for human nature is the same in all. I also felt grateful for his sympathy, and encouraged by his kind words. It seemed to me a great thing to have such a friend. By degrees, a more tender feeling crept into my heart. He was an educated and eloquent gentleman; too eloquent, alas, for the poor slave girl who trusted in him. Of course I saw whither all this was tending. I knew the impassable gulf between us; but to be an object of interest to a man who is not married, and who is not her master, is agreeable to the pride and feelings of a slave, if her miserable situation has left her any pride or sentiment. It seems less degrading to give one's self, than to submit to compulsion. There is something akin to freedom in having a lover who has no control over you, except that which he gains by kindness and attachment. A master may treat you as rudely as he pleases, and you dare not speak; moreover, the wrong does not seem so great with an unmarried man, as with one who has a wife to be made unhappy. There may be sophistry in all this; but the condition of a slave confuses all principles of morality, and, in fact, renders the practice of them impossible.

When I found that my master had actually begun to build the lonely cottage, other feelings mixed with those I have described. Revenge, and calculations of interest, were added to flattered vanity and sincere gratitude for kindness. I knew nothing would enrage Dr. Flint so much as to know that I favored another; and it was something to triumph over my tyrant even in that small way. I thought he would revenge himself by selling me, and I was sure my friend, Mr. Sands,[3] would buy me. He was a man of more generosity and feeling than my master, and I thought my freedom could be easily obtained from him. The crisis of my fate now came so near that I was

---

[3] **Mr. Sands:** Samuel Tredwell Sawyer (1800–1865), a white attorney; Jacobs had two children with him— Joseph and Louisa—called in her narrative Benny and Ellen.

desperate. I shuddered to think of being the mother of children that should be owned by my old tyrant. I knew that as soon as a new fancy took him, his victims were sold far off to get rid of them; especially if they had children. I had seen several women sold, with his babies at the breast. He never allowed his offspring by slaves to remain long in sight of himself and his wife. Of a man who was not my master I could ask to have my children well supported; and in this case, I felt confident I should obtain the boon. I also felt quite sure that they would be made free. With all these thoughts revolving in my mind, and seeing no other way of escaping the doom I so much dreaded, I made a headlong plunge. Pity me, and pardon me, O virtuous reader! You never knew what it is to be a slave; to be entirely unprotected by law or custom; to have the laws reduce you to the condition of a chattel, entirely subject to the will of another. You never exhausted your ingenuity in avoiding the snares, and eluding the power of a hated tyrant; you never shuddered at the sound of his foot-steps, and trembled within hearing of his voice. I know I did wrong. No one can feel it more sensibly than I do. The painful and humiliating memory will haunt me to my dying day. Still, in looking back, calmly, on the events of my life, I feel that the slave woman ought not to be judged by the same standard as others.

The months passed on. I had many unhappy hours. I secretly mourned over the sorrow I was bringing on my grandmother, who had so tried to shield me from harm. I knew that I was the greatest comfort of her old age, and that it was a source of pride to her that I had not degraded myself, like most of the slaves. I wanted to confess to her that I was no longer worthy of her love; but I could not utter the dreaded words.

As for Dr. Flint, I had a feeling of satisfaction and triumph in the thought of telling *him.* From time to time he told me of his intended arrangements, and I was silent. At last, he came and told me the cottage was completed, and ordered me to go to it. I told him I would never enter it. He said, "I have heard enough of such talk as that. You shall go, if you are carried by force; and you shall remain there."

I replied, "I will never go there. In a few months I shall be a mother."

He stood and looked at me in dumb amazement, and left the house without a word. I thought I should be happy in my triumph over him. But now that the truth was out, and my relatives would hear of it, I felt wretched. Humble as were their cir-cumstances, they had pride in my good character. Now, how could I look them in the face? My self-respect was gone! I had resolved that I would be virtuous, though I was a slave. I had said, "Let the storm beat! I will brave it till I die." And now, how humil-iated I felt!

I went to my grandmother. My lips moved to make confession, but the words stuck in my throat. I sat down in the shade of a tree at her door and began to sew. I think she saw something unusual was the matter with me. The mother of slaves is very watchful. She knows there is no security for her children. After they have entered their teens she lives in daily expectation of trouble. This leads to many ques-tions. If the girl is of a sensitive nature, timidity keeps her from answering truthfully, and this well-meant course has a tendency to drive her from maternal counsels. Presently, in came my mistress, like a mad woman, and accused me concerning her husband. My grandmother, whose suspicions had been previously awakened, believed what she said. She exclaimed, "O Linda! has it come to this? I had rather see you dead than to see you as you now are. You are a disgrace to your dead mother."

She tore from my fingers my mother's wedding ring and her silver thimble. "Go away!" she exclaimed, "and never come to my house, again." Her reproaches fell so hot and heavy, that they left me no chance to answer. Bitter tears, such as the eyes never shed but once, were my only answer. I rose from my seat, but fell back again, sobbing. She did not speak to me; but the tears were running down her furrowed cheeks, and they scorched me like fire. She had always been so kind to me! *So* kind! How I longed to throw myself at her feet, and tell her all the truth! But she had ordered me to go, and never to come there again. After a few minutes, I mustered strength, and started to obey her. With what feelings did I now close that little gate, which I used to open with such an eager hand in my childhood! It closed upon me with a sound I never heard before.

Where could I go? I was afraid to return to my master's. I walked on recklessly, not caring where I went, or what would become of me. When I had gone four or five miles, fatigue compelled me to stop. I sat down on the stump of an old tree. The stars were shining through the boughs above me. How they mocked me, with their bright, calm light! The hours passed by, and as I sat there alone a chilliness and deadly sickness came over me. I sank on the ground. My mind was full of horrid thoughts. I prayed to die; but the prayer was not answered. At last, with great effort I roused myself, and walked some distance further, to the house of a woman who had been a friend of my mother. When I told her why I was there, she spoke soothingly to me; but I could not be comforted. I thought I could bear my shame if I could only be reconciled to my grandmother. I longed to open my heart to her. I thought if she could know the real state of the case, and all I had been bearing for years, she would perhaps judge me less harshly. My friend advised me to send for her. I did so; but days of agonizing suspense passed before she came. Had she utterly forsaken me? No. She came at last. I knelt before her, and told her the things that had poisoned my life; how long I had been persecuted; that I saw no way of escape; and in an hour of extremity I had become desperate. She listened in silence. I told her I would bear any thing and do any thing, if in time I had hopes of obtaining her forgiveness. I begged of her to pity me, for my dead mother's sake. And she did pity me. She did not say, "I forgive you;" but she looked at me lovingly, with her eyes full of tears. She laid her old hand gently on my head, and murmured, "Poor child! Poor child!"

FROM CHAPTER 21. THE LOOPHOLE OF RETREAT[4]

A small shed had been added to my grandmother's house years ago. Some boards were laid across the joists at the top, and between these boards and the roof was a very small garret, never occupied by any thing but rats and mice. It was a pent roof, covered with nothing but shingles, according to the southern custom for such

---

[4] In the missing chapters Dr. Flint has continued his persecution of Jacobs. When she resists his overtures, he punishes her by sending her to his plantation, separating her from her two young children. Eventually, Jacobs escapes from the plantation and hides in a storeroom provided by a sympathetic white woman. Flint, frustrated and angry from his unsuccessful search for Jacobs, sells her children and her brother to a slave trader, but by a ruse they are in turn purchased by their white but unacknowledged father, Mr. Sands. When Flint is about to discover Jacobs's hiding place, she escapes, and goes into hiding in her grandmother's house.

buildings. The garret was only nine feet long and seven wide. The highest part was three feet high, and sloped down abruptly to the loose board floor. There was no admission for either light or air. My uncle Phillip, who was a carpenter, had very skillfully made a concealed trap-door, which communicated with the storeroom. He had been doing this while I was waiting in the swamp. The storeroom opened upon a piazza. To this hole I was conveyed as soon as I entered the house. The air was stifling; the darkness total. A bed had been spread on the floor. I could sleep quite comfortably on one side; but the slope was so sudden that I could not turn on the other without hitting the roof. The rats and mice ran over my bed; but I was weary, and I slept such sleep as the wretched may, when a tempest has passed over them. Morning came. I knew it only by the noises I heard; for in my small den day and night were all the same. I suffered for air even more than for light. But I was not comfortless. I heard the voices of my children. There was joy and there was sadness in the sound. It made my tears flow. How I longed to speak to them! I was eager to look on their faces; but there was no hole, no crack, through which I could peep. This continued darkness was oppressive. It seemed horrible to sit or lie in a cramped position day after day, without one gleam of light. Yet I would have chosen this, rather than my lot as a slave, though white people considered it an easy one; and it was so compared with the fate of others. I was never cruelly over-worked; I was never lacerated with the whip from head to foot; I was never so beaten and bruised that I could not turn from one side to the other; I never had my heel-strings cut to prevent my running away; I was never chained to a log and forced to drag it about, while I toiled in the fields from morning till night; I was never branded with hot iron, or torn by bloodhounds. On the contrary, I had always been kindly treated, and tenderly cared for, until I came into the hands of Dr. Flint. I had never wished for freedom till then. But though my life in slavery was comparatively devoid of hardships, God pity the woman who is compelled to lead such a life!

My food was passed up to me through the trap-door my uncle had contrived; and my grandmother, my uncle Phillip, and aunt Nancy would seize such opportunities as they could, to mount up there and chat with me at the opening. But of course this was not safe in the daytime. It must all be done in darkness. It was impossible for me to move in an erect position, but I crawled about my den for exercise. One day I hit my head against something, and found it was a gimlet.[5] My uncle had left it sticking there when he made the trap-door. I was as rejoiced as Robinson Crusoe could have been at finding such a treasure. It put a lucky thought into my head. I said to myself, "Now I will have some light. Now I will see my children." I did not dare to begin my work during the daytime, for fear of attracting attention. But I groped round; and having found the side next the street, where I could frequently see my children, I stuck the gimlet in and waited for evening. I bored three rows of holes, one above another; then I bored out the interstices between. I thus succeeded in making one hole about an inch long and an inch broad. I sat by it till late into the night, to enjoy the little whiff of air that floated in. In the morning I watched for my children. The first person I saw in the street was Dr. Flint. I had a shuddering,

---

[5] gimlet: A small hand tool for boring holes.

superstitious feeling that it was a bad omen. Several familiar faces passed by. At last I heard the merry laugh of children, and presently two sweet little faces were looking up at me, as though they knew I was there, and were conscious of the joy they imparted. How I longed to *tell* them I was there!

My condition was now a little improved. But for weeks I was tormented by hundreds of little red insects, fine as a needle's point, that pierced through my skin, and produced an intolerable burning. The good grandmother gave me herb teas and cooling medicines, and finally I got rid of them. The heat of my den was intense, for nothing but thin shingles protected me from the scorching summer's sun. But I had my consolations. Through my peeping-hole I could watch the children, and when they were near enough, I could hear their talk. [. . .]

Autumn came, with a pleasant abatement of heat. My eyes had become accustomed to the dim light, and by holding my book or work in a certain position near the aperture I contrived to read and sew. That was a great relief to the tedious monotony of my life. But when winter came, the cold penetrated through the thin shingle roof, and I was dreadfully chilled. The winters there are not so long, or so severe, as in northern latitudes; but the houses are not built to shelter from cold, and my little den was peculiarly comfortless. The kind grandmother brought me bedclothes and warm drinks. Often I was obliged to lie in bed all day to keep comfortable; but with all my precautions, my shoulders and feet were frostbitten. O, those long, gloomy days, with no object for my eye to rest upon, and no thoughts to occupy my mind, except the dreary past and the uncertain future! I was thankful when there came a day sufficiently mild for me to wrap myself up and sit at the loophole to watch the passers by. Southerners have the habit of stopping and talking in the streets, and I heard many conversations not intended to meet my ears. I heard slave-hunters planning how to catch some poor fugitive. Several times I heard allusions to Dr. Flint, myself, and the history of my children, who, perhaps, were playing near the gate. One would say, "I wouldn't move my little finger to catch her, as old Flint's property." Another would say, "I'll catch *any* nigger for the reward. A man ought to have what belongs to him, if he *is* a damned brute." The opinion was often expressed that I was in the Free States. Very rarely did any one suggest that I might be in the vicinity. Had the least suspicion rested on my grandmother's house, it would have been burned to the ground. But it was the last place they thought of. Yet there was no place, where slavery existed, that could have afforded me so good a place of concealment. [. . .]

from Chapter 23. Still in Prison

When spring returned, and I took in the little patch of green the aperture commanded, I asked myself how many more summers and winters I must be condemned to spend thus. I longed to draw in a plentiful draught of fresh air, to stretch my cramped limbs, to have room to stand erect, to feel the earth under my feet again. My relatives were constantly on the lookout for a chance of escape; but none offered that seemed practicable, and even tolerably safe. The hot summer came again, and made the turpentine drop from the thin roof over my head.

During the long nights I was restless for want of air, and I had no room to toss and turn. There was but one compensation; the atmosphere was so stifled that even mosquitos would not condescend to buzz in it. With all my detestation of Dr. Flint, I could hardly wish him a worse punishment, either in this world or that which is to come, than to suffer what I suffered in one single summer. Yet the laws allowed *him* to be out in the free air, while I, guiltless of crime, was pent up here, as the only means of avoiding the cruelties the laws allowed him to inflict upon me! I don't know what kept life within me. Again and again, I thought I should die before long; but I saw the leaves of another autumn whirl through the air, and felt the touch of another winter. In summer the most terrible thunder storms were acceptable, for the rain came through the roof, and I rolled up my bed that it might cool the hot boards under it. Later in the season, storms sometimes wet my clothes through and through, and that was not comfortable when the air grew chilly. Moderate storms I could keep out by filling the chinks with oakum.

But uncomfortable as my situation was, I had glimpses of things out of doors, which made me thankful for my wretched hiding-place. [. . .]

I suffered much more during the second winter than I did during the first. My limbs were benumbed by inaction, and the cold filled them with cramp. I had a very painful sensation of coldness in my head; even my face and tongue stiffened, and I lost the power of speech. Of course it was impossible, under the circumstances, to summon any physician. My brother William came and did all he could for me. Uncle Phillip also watched tenderly over me; and poor grandmother crept up and down to inquire whether there were any signs of returning life. I was restored to consciousness by the dashing of cold water in my face, and found myself leaning against my brother's arm, while he bent over me with streaming eyes. He afterwards told me he thought I was dying, for I had been in an unconscious state sixteen hours. I next became delirious, and was in great danger of betraying myself and my friends. To prevent this, they stupefied me with drugs. I remained in bed six weeks, weary in body and sick at heart. How to get medical advice was the question. William finally went to a Thompsonian[6] doctor, and described himself as having all my pains and aches. He returned with herbs, roots, and ointment. He was especially charged to rub on the ointment by a fire; but how could a fire be made in my little den? Charcoal in a furnace was tried, but there was no outlet for the gas, and it nearly cost me my life. Afterwards coals, already kindled, were brought up in an iron pan, and placed on bricks. I was so weak, and it was so long since I had enjoyed the warmth of a fire, that those few coals actually made me weep. I think the medicines did me some good; but my recovery was very slow. Dark thoughts passed through my mind as I lay there day after day. I tried to be thankful for my little cell, dismal as it was, and even to love it, as part of the price I had paid for the redemption of my children. Sometimes I thought God was a compassionate Father, who would forgive my sins for the sake of my sufferings. At other times, it seemed to me there was no justice or mercy in the divine government. I asked why the

---

[6]**Thompsonian:** Named after Samuel Thompson (1763–1843), a doctor who attempted to cure disease by raising the internal body temperature.

curse of slavery was permitted to exist, and why I had been so persecuted and wronged from youth upward. These things took the shape of mystery, which is to this day not so clear to my soul as I trust it will be hereafter. [. . .]

FROM Chapter 29. Preparations for Escape

I hardly expect that the reader will credit me, when I affirm that I lived in that little dismal hole, almost deprived of light and air, and with no space to move my limbs, for nearly seven years.[7] But it is a fact; and to me a sad one, even now; for my body still suffers from the effects of that long imprisonment, to say nothing of my soul. Members of my family, now living in New York and Boston, can testify to the truth of what I say. [. . .]

And now I must go back a few months in my story. I have stated that the first of January was the time for selling slaves, or leasing them out to new masters. If time were counted by heart-throbs, the poor slaves might reckon years of suffering during that festival so joyous to the free. On the New Year's day preceding my aunt's death, one of my friends, named Fanny, was to be sold at auction, to pay her master's debts. My thoughts were with her during all the day, and at night I anxiously inquired what had been her fate. I was told that she had been sold to one master, and her four little girls to another master, far distant; that she had escaped from her purchaser, and was not to be found. Her mother was the old Aggie I have spoken of. She lived in a small tenement belonging to my grandmother, and built on the same lot with her own house. Her dwelling was searched and watched, and that brought the patrols so near me that I was obliged to keep very close in my den. The hunters were somehow eluded; and not long afterwards Benny accidentally caught sight of Fanny in her mother's hut. He told his grandmother, who charged him never to speak of it, explaining to him the frightful consequences; and he never betrayed the trust. Aggie little dreamed that my grandmother knew where her daughter was concealed, and that the stooping form of her old neighbor was bending under a similar burden of anxiety and fear; but these dangerous secrets deepened the sympathy between the two old persecuted mothers.

My friend Fanny and I remained many weeks hidden within call of each other; but she was unconscious of the fact. I longed to have her share my den, which seemed a more secure retreat than her own; but I had brought so much trouble on my grandmother, that it seemed wrong to ask her to incur greater risks. My restlessness increased. I had lived too long in bodily pain and anguish of spirit. Always I was in dread that by some accident, or some contrivance, slavery would succeed in snatching my children from me. This thought drove me nearly frantic, and I determined to steer for the North Star[8] at all hazards. At this crisis, Providence opened an unexpected way for me to escape. My friend Peter came one evening, and asked to speak with me. "Your day has come, Linda," said he. "I have found a chance for you

---

[7] **seven years:** Jacobs lived in her grandmother's attic crawl space from August 1835 to June 1842.

[8] **North Star:** Runaway slaves, who often traveled by night, were guided by this star.

to go to the Free States. You have a fortnight to decide." The news seemed too good to be true; but Peter explained his arrangements, and told me all that was necessary was for me to say I would go. I was going to answer him with a joyful yes, when the thought of Benny came to my mind. I told him the temptation was exceedingly strong, but I was terribly afraid of Dr. Flint's alleged power over my child, and that I could not go and leave him behind. Peter remonstrated earnestly. He said such a good chance might never occur again; that Benny was free, and could be sent to me; and that for the sake of my children's welfare I ought not to hesitate a moment. I told him I would consult with Uncle Phillip. My uncle rejoiced in the plan, and bade me go by all means. He promised, if his life was spared, that he would either bring or send my son to me as soon as I reached a place of safety. I resolved to go, but thought nothing had better be said to my grandmother till very near the time of departure. But my uncle thought she would feel it more keenly if I left her so suddenly. "I will reason with her," said he, "and convince her how necessary it is, not only for your sake, but for hers also. You cannot be blind to the fact that she is sinking under her burdens." I was not blind to it. I knew that my concealment was an ever-present source of anxiety, and that the older she grew the more nervously fearful she was of discovery. My uncle talked with her, and finally succeeded in persuading her that it was absolutely necessary for me to seize the chance so unexpectedly offered.

The anticipation of being a free woman proved almost too much for my weak frame. The excitement stimulated me, and at the same time bewildered me. I made busy preparations for my journey, and for my son to follow me. I resolved to have an interview with him before I went, that I might give him cautions and advice, and tell him how anxiously I should be waiting for him at the north. Grandmother stole up to me as often as possible to whisper words of counsel. She insisted upon my writing to Dr. Flint, as soon as I arrived in the Free States, and asking him to sell me to her. She said she would sacrifice her house, and all she had in the world, for the sake of having me safe with my children in any part of the world. If she could only live to know *that* she could die in peace. I promised the dear old faithful friend that I would write to her as soon as I arrived, and put the letter in a safe way to reach her; but in my own mind I resolved that not another cent of her hard earnings should be spent to pay rapacious slaveholders for what they called their property. And even if I had not been unwilling to buy what I had already a right to possess, common humanity would have prevented me from accepting the generous offer, at the expense of turning my aged relative out of house and home, when she was trembling on the brink of the grave.

I was to escape in a vessel; but I forbear to mention any further particulars. I was in readiness, but the vessel was unexpectedly detained several days. [. . .]

I made all my arrangements to go on board as soon as it was dusk. The intervening time I resolved to spend with my son. I had not spoken to him for seven years, though I had been under the same roof, and seen him every day, when I was well enough to sit at the loophole. I did not dare to venture beyond the storeroom; so they brought him there, and locked us up together, in a place concealed from the piazza door. It was an agitating interview for both of us. After we had talked and wept together for a little while, he said, "Mother, I'm glad you're going away. I wish I could go with you. I knew you was here; and I have been *so* afraid they would come and catch you!"

I was greatly surprised, and asked him how he had found it out.

He replied, "I was standing under the eaves, one day, before Ellen[9] went away, and I heard somebody cough up over the wood shed. I don't know what made me think it was you, but I did think so. I missed Ellen, the night before she went away; and grandmother brought her back into the room in the night; and I thought maybe she'd been to see *you,* before she went, for I heard grandmother whisper to her, 'Now go to sleep; and remember never to tell.'"

I asked him if he ever mentioned his suspicions to his sister. He said he never did; but after he heard the cough, if he saw her playing with other children on that side of the house, he always tried to coax her round to the other side, for fear they would hear me cough, too. He said he had kept a close lookout for Dr. Flint, and if he saw him speak to a constable, or a patrol, he always told grandmother. I now recollected that I had seen him manifest uneasiness, when people were on that side of the house, and I had at the time been puzzled to conjecture a motive for his actions. Such prudence may seem extraordinary in a boy of twelve years, but slaves, being surrounded by mysteries, deceptions, and dangers, early learn to be suspicious and watchful, and prematurely cautious and cunning. He had never asked a question of grandmother, or Uncle Phillip, and I had often heard him chime in with other children, when they spoke of my being at the north.

I told him I was now really going to the Free States, and if he was a good, honest boy, and a loving child to his dear old grandmother, the Lord would bless him, and bring him to me, and we and Ellen would live together. He began to tell me that grandmother had not eaten any thing all day. While he was speaking, the door was unlocked, and she came in with a small bag of money, which she wanted me to take. I begged her to keep a part of it, at least, to pay for Benny's being sent to the north; but she insisted, while her tears were falling fast, that I should take the whole. "You may be sick among strangers," she said, "and they would send you to the poorhouse to die." Ah, that good grandmother!

For the last time I went up to my nook. Its desolate appearance no longer chilled me, for the light of hope had risen in my soul. Yet, even with the blessed prospect of freedom before me, I felt very sad at leaving forever that old homestead, where I had been sheltered so long by the dear old grandmother; where I had dreamed my first young dream of love; and where, after that had faded away, my children came to twine themselves so closely round my desolate heart. As the hour approached for me to leave, I again descended to the storeroom. My grandmother and Benny were there. She took me by the hand, and said, "Linda, let us pray." We knelt down together, with my child pressed to my heart, and my other arm round the faithful, loving old friend I was about to leave forever. On no other occasion has it ever been

---

[9] **Ellen:** Jacobs's daughter Louisa; she had been sent to the north by her white father, Samuel Tredwell Sawyer (Mr. Sands in the text), to protect her from the machinations of Dr. Norcomb (Dr. Flint), who still claimed her as his property.

my lot to listen to so fervent a supplication for mercy and protection. It thrilled through my heart, and inspired me with trust in God.

Peter was waiting for me in the street. I was soon by his side, faint in body, but strong of purpose. I did not look back upon the old place, though I felt that I should never see it again.

FROM CHAPTER 30. NORTHWARD BOUND

[. . .] Ten days after we left land we were approaching Philadelphia. The captain said we should arrive there in the night, but he thought we had better wait till morning, and go on shore in broad daylight, as the best way to avoid suspicion.

I replied, "You know best. But will you stay on board and protect us?"

He saw that I was suspicious, and he said he was sorry, now that he had brought us to the end of our voyage, to find I had so little confidence in him. Ah, if he had ever been a slave he would have known how difficult it was to trust a white man. He assured us that we might sleep through the night without fear; that he would take care we were not left unprotected. Be it said to the honor of this captain, Southerner as he was, that if Fanny and I had been white ladies, and our passage lawfully engaged, he could not have treated us more respectfully. My intelligent friend, Peter, had rightly estimated the character of the man to whose honor he had intrusted us.

The next morning I was on deck as soon as the day dawned. I called Fanny to see the sun rise, for the first time in our lives, on free soil; for such I *then* believed it to be. We watched the reddening sky, and saw the great orb come up slowly out of the water, as it seemed. Soon the waves began to sparkle, and every thing caught the beautiful glow. Before us lay the city of strangers. We looked at each other, and the eyes of both were moistened with tears. We had escaped from slavery, and we supposed ourselves to be safe from the hunters. But we were alone in the world, and we had left dear ties behind us; ties cruelly sundered by the demon Slavery.

❧ FREDERICK DOUGLASS
B. UNITED STATES, 1818?–95

The son of Harriet Bailey, a slave working as a field hand, and a white father he never knew, Frederick Augustus Bailey Douglass was born on a farm in Tuckahoe, Maryland, near the coast. He spent his earliest years away from his mother on the plantation of a man called Colonel Lloyd. Although his mother was allowed to visit him a few times, he never got to know her or to learn anything about his father, who was rumored to be his mother's master. After his mother's death, when he was seven years old, Fred Douglass, as he was called, was moved to Baltimore, where he worked as a servant for Hugh Auld, a shipbuilder, whose wife began to teach him to read and write. When Mr. Auld forbade the lessons, Douglass realized that a key to keeping a man a slave was to keep him ignorant, and from this moment he recognized that literacy was a cornerstone of freedom. He spent seven years in Baltimore, enlisting when he could the help of white boys he met while running errands to help him learn to read. In a book titled *The Columbian Orator,* a popular collection of essays, dialogues, and speeches which Douglass managed to smuggle with him on his ventures, he began to explore and to articulate philosophically the idea of emancipation and rehearsed several arguments against slavery adduced in one of the dialogues in the text.

In 1832, Douglass left Baltimore to live in St. Michael's, Maryland, with a new master, Thomas Auld, whose cruelty starkly contrasted what Douglass had experienced in Baltimore. Here — while contracted out for a year to Mr. Covey, a man notorious for his cruelty — Douglass achieved a small triumph by successfully and physically thwarting one of Covey's attempts to beat him. Douglass escaped violent repercussions, he believes, only because Covey, who had a reputation as a "well-trained negro-breaker and slave driver" feared losing his reputation if word that he had been cowed by Douglass got out. In January 1834, Douglass left Covey for Mr. Freeland, where he was much better treated and where he continued his self-education. The next year, he was caught planning his first attempt at escape. To Douglass's surprise, Captain Auld returned him to Baltimore where Hugh Auld, the Captain's brother, employed him as an apprentice shipbuilder, but he was not free. On September 3, 1838, Douglass fled via train and steamboat to New York and quickly settled in New Bedford, Massachusetts, where he was joined by Anna Murray, his fiancée, a free black woman from Baltimore who had helped him in his escape.

In New Bedford, Douglass continued his education and eventually began to give speeches for the Anti Slavery Society. Celebrated for his eloquence and delivery, he began a new career as orator and writer. In 1845 he published the first edition of his autobiography, *Narrative of the Life of Frederick Douglass, an American Slave. Written by Himself* (1845). Immediately popular both in the United States and overseas, the book went through three other expanded and revised editions in 1855, 1881, and 1892. Fearing reprisals after the publication of his work, Douglass embarked for Great Britain where he joined his friend and fellow abolitionist William Lloyd Garrison (1805–1879) on a lecture tour before returning to the United States in March of 1847. Friends in England raised money to purchase Douglass's freedom, and when he returned he moved to Rochester, New York, where in 1848 he launched *The North Star,* an antislavery newspaper. Douglass became a tireless advocate of emancipation and the rights of women. "Emancipation Proclaimed," his observations on the Emancipation Proclamation and President Lincoln, are taken from the October 1862 issue of a magazine he published, *Douglass' Monthly.* In his later years, Douglass served as an advisor to President Lincoln during the Civil War, helped to campaign for the ratification of the Thirteenth and Fifteenth Amendments, and received several government positions. About a year after the death of his wife Anna in August 1882, Douglass married Helen Pitts, a white woman involved in the women's suffrage movement. He died of a heart attack in 1895.

Portrait of Frederick Douglass, 1856
This photograph was taken of the abolitionist and statesman Frederick Douglass about seven years before Lincoln signed the Emancipation Proclamation, which freed all U.S. slaves. (National Portrait Gallery/Art Resource)

∾ The Narrative of the Life of Frederick Douglass

CHAPTER I

[CHILDHOOD]

I was born in Tuckahoe, near Hillsborough, and about twelve miles from Easton, in Talbot county, Maryland. I have no accurate knowledge of my age, never having seen any authentic record containing it. By far the larger part of the slaves know as little of their ages as horses know of theirs, and it is the wish of most masters within my knowledge to keep their slaves thus ignorant. I do not remember to have ever met a slave who could tell of his birthday. They seldom come nearer to it than planting-time, harvest-time, cherry-time, spring-time, or fall-time. A want of information concerning my own was a source of unhappiness to me even during childhood. The white children could tell their ages. I could not tell why I ought to be deprived of the same privilege. I was not allowed to make any inquiries of my master concerning it. He deemed all such inquiries on the part of a slave improper and impertinent, and evidence of a restless spirit. The nearest estimate I can give makes me now between twenty-seven and twenty-eight years of age. I come to this, from hearing my master say, some time during 1835, I was about seventeen years old.

My mother was named Harriet Bailey. She was the daughter of Isaac and Betsey Bailey, both colored, and quite dark. My mother was of a darker complexion than either my grandmother or grandfather.

My father was a white man. He was admitted to be such by all I ever heard speak of my parentage. The opinion was also whispered that my master was my father; but of the correctness of this opinion, I know nothing; the means of knowing was withheld from me. My mother and I were separated when I was but an infant—before I knew her as my mother. It is a common custom, in the part of Maryland from which I ran away, to part children from their mothers at a very early age. Frequently, before the child has reached its twelfth month, its mother is taken from it, and hired out on some farm a considerable distance off, and the child is placed under the care of an old woman, too old for field labor. For what this separation is done, I do not know, unless it be to hinder the development of the child's affection toward its mother, and to blunt and destroy the natural affection of the mother for the child. This is the inevitable result.

I never saw my mother, to know her as such, more than four or five times in my life; and each of these times was very short in duration, and at night. She was hired by a Mr. Stewart, who lived about twelve miles from my home. She made her journeys to see me in the night, travelling the whole distance on foot, after the performance of her day's work. She was a field hand, and a whipping is the penalty of not being in the field at sunrise, unless a slave has special permission from his or her master to the contrary—a permission which they seldom get, and one that gives to him that gives it the proud name of being a kind master. I do not recollect of ever seeing my mother by the light of day. She was with me in the night. She would lie down with me, and get me to sleep, but long before I waked she was gone. Very little communication ever took place between us. Death soon ended what little we could have while she lived, and with it her hardships and suffering. She died when I was about seven years old, on one of my master's farms, near Lee's Mill. I was not allowed to be present during her illness, at her death, or burial. She was gone long before I knew any thing about it. Never having enjoyed, to any considerable extent, her soothing presence, her tender and watchful care, I received the tidings of her death with much the same emotions I should have probably felt at the death of a stranger.

Called thus suddenly away, she left me without the slightest intimation of who my father was. The whisper that my master was my father, may or may not be true; and, true or false, it is of but little consequence to my purpose whilst the face remains, in all its glaring odiousness, that slaveholders have ordained, and by law established, that the children of slave women shall in all cases follow the condition of their mothers; and this is done too obviously to administer to their own lusts, and make gratification of their wicked desires profitable as well as pleasurable; for by this cunning arrangement, the slaveholder, in cases not a few, sustains to his slaves the double relation of master and father.

I know of such cases; and it is worthy of remark that such slaves invariably suffer greater hardships, and have more to contend with, than others. They are, in the first place, a constant offence to their mistress. She is ever disposed to find fault with them; they can seldom do any thing to please her; she is never better pleased than when she sees them under the lash, especially when she suspects her husband of showing to his mulatto children favors which he withholds from his black slaves. The master is frequently compelled to sell this class of his slaves, out of deference to the feelings of his white wife; and, cruel as the deed may strike any one to be, for a man to sell his own children to human flesh-mongers, it is often the dictate of humanity for him to do so; for, unless he does this, he must not only whip them himself, but must stand by and see one white son tie up his brother, of but few shades darker complexion than himself, and ply the gory lash to his naked back; and if he lisp one word of disapproval, it is set down to his parental partiality, and only makes a bad matter worse, both for himself and the slave whom he would protect and defend.

Every year brings with it multitudes of this class of slaves. It was doubtless in consequence of a knowledge of this fact, that one great statesman of the south predicted the downfall of slavery by the inevitable laws of population. Whether this prophecy is ever fulfilled or not, it is nevertheless plain that a very different-looking class of people are springing up at the south, and are now held in slavery, from those originally brought to this country from Africa; and if their increase will do no other good, it will do away the force of the argument, that God cursed Ham,[1] and

---

[1] **God cursed Ham:** Ham, the son of Noah, was the father of Canaan; Noah cursed his grandson by pronouncing that he would be the "servant of servants." This curse, misapplied to Ham, thought to be the father of black peoples in Africa, was cited to justify slavery by its apologists in the eighteenth and nineteenth centuries. See Genesis 9:18–27 and 10:6–15.

therefore American slavery is right. If the lineal descendants of Ham are alone to be scripturally enslaved, it is certain that slavery at the south must soon become unscriptural; for thousands are ushered into the world, annually, who, like myself, owe their existence to white fathers, and those fathers most frequently their own masters.

I have had two masters. My first master's name was Anthony. I do not remember his first name. He was generally called Captain Anthony—a title which, I presume, he acquired by sailing a craft on the Chesapeake Bay. He was not considered a rich slaveholder. He owned two or three farms, and about thirty slaves. His farms and slaves were under the care of an overseer. The overseer's name was Plummer. Mr. Plummer was a miserable drunkard, a profane swearer, and a savage monster. He always went armed with a cowskin and a heavy cudgel. I have known him to cut and slash the women's heads so horribly, that even master would be enraged at his cruelty, and would threaten to whip him if he did not mind himself. Master, however, was not a humane slaveholder. It required extraordinary barbarity on the part of an overseer to affect him. He was a cruel man, hardened by a long life of slaveholding. He would at times seem to take great pleasure in whipping a slave. I have often been awakened at the dawn of day by the most heart-rending shrieks of an own aunt of mine, whom he used to tie up to a joist, and whip upon her naked back till she was literally covered with blood. No words, no tears, no prayers, from his gory victim, seemed to move his iron heart from its bloody purpose. The louder she screamed, the harder he whipped; and where the blood ran fastest, there he whipped longest. He would whip her to make her scream, and whip her to make her hush; and not until overcome by fatigue, would he cease to swing the blood-dotted cowskin. I remember the first time I ever witnessed this horrible exhibition. I was quite a child, but I well remember it. I never shall forget it whilst I remember any thing. It was the first of a long series of such outrages, of which I was doomed to be a witness and a participant. It struck me with awful force. It was the blood-stained gate, the entrance to the hell of slavery, through which I was about to pass. It was a most terrible spectacle. I wish I could commit to paper the feelings with which I beheld it.

This occurrence took place very soon after I went to live with my old master, and under the following circumstances. Aunt Hester went out one night,—where or for what I do not know,—and happened to be absent when my master desired her presence. He had ordered her not to go out evenings, and warned her that she must never let him catch her in company with a young man, who was paying attention to her, belonging to Colonel Lloyd. The young man's name was Ned Roberts, generally called Lloyd's Ned. Why master was so careful of her, may be safely left to conjecture. She was a woman of noble form, and of graceful proportions, having very few equals, and fewer superiors, in personal appearance, among the colored or white women of our neighborhood.

Aunt Hester had not only disobeyed his orders in going out, but had been found in company with Lloyd's Ned; which circumstance, I found, from what he said while whipping her, was the chief offence. Had he been a man of pure morals himself, he might have been thought interested in protecting the innocence of my aunt; but those who knew him will not suspect him of any such virtue. Before he commenced whipping Aunt Hester, he took her into the kitchen, and stripped her from neck to waist, leaving her neck, shoulders, and back, entirely naked. He then told her to cross her hands, calling her at the same time a d——d b——h. After crossing her hands, he tied them with a strong rope, and led her to a stool under a large hook in the joist, put in for the purpose. He made her get upon the stool, and tied her hands to the hook. She now stood fair for his infernal purpose. Her arms were stretched up at their full length, so that she stood upon the ends of her toes. He then said to her, "Now, you d——d b——h, I'll learn you how to disobey my orders!" and after rolling up his sleeves, he commenced to lay on the heavy cowskin, and soon the warm, red blood (amid heart-rending shrieks from her, and horrid oaths from him) came dripping to the floor. I was so terrified and horror-stricken at the sight, that I hid myself in a closet, and dared not venture out till long after the bloody transaction was over. I expected it would be my turn next. It was all new to me. I had never seen any thing like it before. I had always lived with my grandmother on the outskirts of the plantation, where she was put to raise the children of the younger women. I had therefore been, until now, out of the way of the bloody scenes that often occurred on the plantation.

FROM CHAPTER II
[GREAT HOUSE FARM]

My master's family consisted of two sons, Andrew and Richard; one daughter, Lucretia, and her husband, Captain Thomas Auld. They lived in one house, upon the home plantation of Colonel Edward Lloyd. My master was Colonel Lloyd's clerk and superintendent. He was what might be called the overseers of the overseers. I spent two years of childhood on this plantation in my old master's family. It was here that I witnessed the bloody transaction recorded in the first chapter; and as I received my first impressions of slavery on this plantation, I will give some description of it, and of slavery as it there existed. The plantation is about twelve miles north of Easton, in Talbot county, and is situated on the border of Miles River. The principal products raised upon it were tobacco, corn, and wheat. These were raised in great abundance; so that, with the products of this and the other farms belonging to him, he was able to keep in almost constant employment a large sloop, in carrying them to market at Baltimore. This sloop was named Sally Lloyd, in honor of one of the colonel's daughters. My master's son-in-law, Captain Auld, was master of the vessel; she was otherwise manned by the colonel's own slaves. Their names were Peter, Isaac, Rich, and Jake. These were esteemed very highly by the other slaves, and looked upon as the privileged ones of the plantation; for it was no small affair, in the eyes of the slaves, to be allowed to see Baltimore. [. . .]

The home plantation of Colonel Lloyd wore the appearance of a country village. All the mechanical operations for all the farms were performed here. The shoemaking and mending, the blacksmithing, cartwrighting, coopering, weaving, and grain-grinding, were all performed by the slaves on the home plantation. The whole place wore a business-like aspect very unlike the neighboring farms. The number of houses, too, conspired to give it advantage over the neighboring farms. It was called by the slaves the *Great House Farm*. Few privileges were esteemed higher, by the slaves of the out-farms, than that of being selected to do errands at the Great House Farm. It was associated in their minds with greatness. A representative could not be prouder of his election to a seat in the American Congress, than a slave on one of the out-farms would be of his election to do errands at the Great House Farm. They regarded it as evidence of great confidence reposed in them by their overseers; and it was on this account, as well as a constant desire to be out of the field from under the driver's lash, that they esteemed it a high privilege, one worth careful living for. He was called the smartest and most trusty fellow, who had this honor conferred upon him the most frequently. The competitors for this office sought as diligently to please their overseers, as the office-seekers in the political parties seek to please and deceive the people. The same traits of character might be seen in Colonel Lloyd's slaves, as are seen in the slaves of the political parties.

The slaves selected to go to the Great House Farm, for the monthly allowance for themselves and their fellow-slaves, were peculiarly enthusiastic. While on their way, they would make the dense old woods, for miles around, reverberate with their wild songs, revealing at once the highest joy and the deepest sadness. They would compose and sing as they went along, consulting neither time nor tune. The thought that came up, came out—if not in the word, in the sound;—and as frequently in the one as in the other. They would sometimes sing the most pathetic sentiment in the most rapturous tone, and the most rapturous sentiment in the most pathetic tone. Into all of their songs they would manage to weave something of the Great House Farm. Especially would they do this, when leaving home. They would then sing most exultingly the following words:—

> "I am going away to the Great House Farm!
> O, yea! O, yea! O!"

This they would sing, as a chorus, to words which to many would seem unmeaning jargon, but which, nevertheless, were full of meaning to themselves. I have sometimes thought that the mere hearing of those songs would do more to impress some minds with the horrible character of slavery, than the reading of whole volumes of philosophy on the subject could do.

I did not, when a slave, understand the deep meaning of those rude and apparently incoherent songs. I was myself within the circle; so that I neither saw nor heard as those without might see and hear. They told a tale of woe which was then altogether beyond my feeble comprehension; they were tones loud, long, and deep; they breathed the prayer and complaint of souls boiling over with the bitterest anguish. Every tone was a testimony against slavery, and a prayer to God for deliverance from chains. The hearing of those wild notes always depressed my spirit, and filled me with ineffable sadness. I have frequently found myself in tears while hearing them. The mere recurrence to those songs, even now, afflicts me; and while I am writing these lines, an expression of feeling has already found its way down my cheek. To those songs I trace my first glimmering conception of the dehumanizing character of slavery. I can never get rid of that conception. Those songs still follow me, to deepen my hatred of slavery, and quicken my sympathies for my brethren in bonds. If any one wishes to be impressed with the soul-killing effects of slavery, let him go to Colonel Lloyd's plantation, and, on allowance-day, place himself in the deep pine woods, and there let him, in silence, analyze the sounds that shall pass through the chambers of his soul,—and if he is not thus impressed, it will only be because "there is no flesh in his obdurate heart."

I have often been utterly astonished, since I came to the north, to find persons who could speak of the singing, among slaves, as evidence of their contentment and happiness. It is impossible to conceive of a greater mistake. Slaves sing most when they are most unhappy. The songs of the slave represent the sorrows of his heart; and he is relieved by them, only as an aching heart is relieved by its tears. At least, such is my experience. I have often sung to drown my sorrow, but seldom to express my happiness. Crying for joy, and singing for joy, were alike uncommon to me while in the jaws of slavery. The singing of a man cast away upon a desolate island might be as appropriately considered as evidence of contentment and happiness, as the singing of a slave; the songs of the one and of the other are prompted by the same emotion.

FROM CHAPTER V

[MOVE TO BALTIMORE]

[. . .] I was probably between seven and eight years old when I left Colonel Lloyd's plantation. I left it with joy. I shall never forget the ecstasy with which I received the intelligence that my old master (Anthony) had determined to let me go to Baltimore, to live with Mr. Hugh Auld, brother to my old master's son-in-law, Captain Thomas Auld. I received this information about three days before my departure. They were three of the happiest days I ever enjoyed. I spent the most part of all these three days in the creek, washing off the plantation scurf, and preparing myself for my departure.[. . .]

I look upon my departure from Colonel Lloyd's plantation as one of the most interesting events of my life. It is possible, and even quite probable, that but for the mere circumstance of being removed from that plantation to Baltimore, I should have to-day, instead of being here seated by my own table, in the enjoyment of freedom and the happiness of home, writing this Narrative, been confined in the galling chains of slavery. Going to live at Baltimore laid the foundation, and opened the gateway, to all my subsequent prosperity. I have ever regarded it as the first plain manifestation of that kind providence which has ever since attended me, and marked my life with so many favors. I regarded the selection of myself as being somewhat remarkable. There were a number of slave children that might have been sent from the plantation to Baltimore. There were those younger, those older, and those of the same age. I was chosen from among them all, and was the first, last, and only choice.

I may be deemed superstitious, and even egotistical, in regarding this event as a special interposition of divine Providence in my favor. But I should be false to the earliest sentiments of my soul, if I suppressed the opinion. I prefer to be true to myself, even at the hazard of incurring the ridicule of others, rather than to be false, and incur my own abhorrence. From my earliest recollection, I date the entertainment of a deep conviction that slavery would not always be able to hold me within its foul embrace; and in the darkest hours of my career in slavery, this living word of faith and spirit of hope departed not from me, but remained like ministering angels to cheer me through the gloom. This good spirit was from God, and to him I offer thanksgiving and praise.

FROM CHAPTER VI

[LEARNING TO READ AND WRITE]

[. . .] Very soon after I went to live with Mr. and Mrs. Auld, she very kindly commenced to teach me the A, B, C. After I had learned this, she assisted me in learning to spell words of three or four letters. Just at this point of my progress, Mr. Auld found out what was going on, and at once forbade Mrs. Auld to instruct me further, telling her, among other things, that it was unlawful, as well as unsafe, to teach a slave to read. To use his own words, further, he said, "If you give a nigger an inch, he will take an ell. A nigger should know nothing but to obey his mater — to do as he is told to do. Learning would *spoil* the best nigger in the world. Now," said he, "if you teach that nigger (speaking of myself) how to read, there would be no keeping him. It would forever unfit him to be a slave. He would at once become unmanageable, and of no value to his master. As to himself, it could do him no good, but a great deal of harm. It would make him discontented and unhappy." These words sank deep into my heart, stirred up sentiments within that lay slumbering, and called into existence an entirely new train of thought. It was a new and special revelation, explaining dark and mysterious things, with which my youthful understanding had struggled, but struggled in vain. I now understood what had been to me a most perplexing difficulty — to wit, the white man's power to enslave the black man. It was a grand achievement, and I prized it highly. From that moment, I understood the pathway from slavery to freedom. It was just what I wanted, and I got it at a time when I the least expected it. Whilst I was saddened by the thought of losing the aid of my kind mistress, I was gladdened by the invaluable instruction which, by the merest accident, I had gained from my master. Though conscious of the difficulty of learning without a teacher, I set out with high hope, and a fixed purpose, at whatever cost of trouble, to learn how to read. The very decided manner with which he spoke, and strove to impress his wife with the evil consequences of giving me instruction, served to convince me that he was deeply sensible of the truths he was uttering. It gave me the best assurance that I might rely with the utmost confidence on the results which, he said, would flow from teaching me to read. What he most dreaded, that I most desired. What he most loved, that I most hated. That which to him was a great evil, to be carefully shunned, was to me a great good, to be diligently sought; and the argument which he so warmly urged, against my learning to read, only served to inspire me with a desire and determination to learn. In learning to read, I owe almost as much to the bitter opposition of my master, as to the kindly aid of my mistress. I acknowledge the benefit of both. [. . .]

CHAPTER VII
[LITERACY]

I lived in Master Hugh's family about seven years. During this time, I succeeded in learning to read and write. In accomplishing this, I was compelled to resort to various stratagems. I had no regular teacher. My mistress, who had kindly commenced to instruct me, had, in compliance with the advice and direction of her husband, not only ceased to instruct, but had set her face against my being instructed by any one else. It is due, however, to my mistress to say of her, that she did not adopt this course of treatment immediately. She at first lacked the depravity indispensable to shutting me up in mental darkness. It was at least necessary for her to have some training in the exercise of irresponsible power, to make her equal to the task of treating me as though I were a brute.

My mistress was, as I have said, a kind and tender-hearted woman; and in the simplicity of her soul she commenced, when I first went to live with her, to treat me as she supposed one human being ought to treat another. In entering upon the duties of a slaveholder, she did not seem to perceive that I sustained to her the relation of a mere chattel, and that for her to treat me as a human being was not only wrong, but dangerously so. Slavery proved as injurious to her as it did to me. When I went there, she was a pious, warm, and tenderhearted woman. There was no sorrow or suffering for which she had not a tear. She had bread for the hungry, clothes for the naked, and comfort for every mourner that came within her reach. Slavery soon proved its ability to divest her of these heavenly qualities. Under its influence, the tender heart became stone, and the lamblike disposition gave way to one of tiger-like fierceness. The first step in her downward course was in her ceasing to instruct me. She now commenced to practise her husband's precepts. She finally became even more violent in her opposition than her husband himself. She was not satisfied with simply doing as well as he had commanded; she seemed anxious to do better. Nothing seemed to make her more angry than to see me with a newspaper. She seemed to think that here lay the danger. I have had her rush at me with a face made all up of fury, and snatch from me a newspaper, in a manner that fully revealed her apprehension. She was an apt woman; and a little experience soon demonstrated, to her satisfaction, that education and slavery were incompatible with each other.

From this time I was most narrowly watched. If I was in a separate room any considerable length of time, I was sure to be suspected of having a book, and was at once called to give an account of myself. All this, however, was too late. The first step had been taken. Mistress, in teaching me the alphabet, had given me the *inch*, and no precaution could prevent me from taking the *ell*.

The plan which I adopted, and the one by which I was most successful, was that of making friends of all the little white boys whom I met in the street. As many of these as I could, I converted into teachers. With their kindly aid, obtained at different times and in different places, I finally succeeded in learning to read. When I was sent of errands, I always took my book with me, and by going one part of my errand quickly, I found time to get a lesson before my return. I used also to carry bread with me, enough of which was always in the house, and to which I was always welcome;

for I was much better off in this regard than many of the poor white children in our neighborhood. This bread I used to bestow upon the hungry little urchins, who, in return, would give me that more valuable bread of knowledge. I am strongly tempted to give the names of two or three of those little boys, as a testimonial of the gratitude and affection I bear them; but prudence forbids;—not that it would injure me, but it might embarrass them; for it is almost an unpardonable offence to teach slaves to read in this Christian country. It is enough to say of the dear little fellows, that they lived on Philpot Street, very near Durgin and Bailey's shipyard. I used to talk this matter of slavery over with them. I would sometimes say to them, I wished I could be as free as they would be when they got to be men. "You will be free as soon as you are twenty-one, *but I am a slave for life!* Have not I as good a right to be free as you have?" These words used to trouble them; they would express for me the liveliest sympathy, and console me with the hope that something would occur by which I might be free.

I was now about twelve years old, and the thought of being *a slave for life* began to bear heavily upon my heart. Just about this time, I got hold of a book entitled "The Columbian orator."[2] Every opportunity I got, I used to read this book. Among much of other interesting matter, I found in it a dialogue between a master and his slave. The slave was represented as having run away from his master three times. The dialogue represented the conversation which took place between them, when the slave was retaken the third time. In this dialogue, the whole argument in behalf of slavery was brought forward by the master, all of which was disposed of by the slave. The slave was made to say some very smart as well as impressive things in reply to his master—things which had the desired though unexpected effect; for the conversation resulted in the voluntary emancipation of the slave on the part of the master.

In the same book, I met with one of Sheridan's[3] mighty speeches on and in behalf of Catholic emancipation. These were choice documents to me. I read them over and over again with unabated interest. They gave tongue to interesting thoughts of my own soul, which had frequently flashed through my mind, and died away for want of utterance. The moral which I gained from the dialogue was the power of truth over the conscience of even a slaveholder. What I got from Sheridan was a bold denunciation of slavery, and a powerful vindication of human rights. The reading of these documents enabled me to utter my thoughts, and to meet the arguments brought forward to sustain slavery; but while they relieved me of one difficulty, they brought on another even more painful than the one of which I was relieved. The more I read, the more I was led to abhor and detest my enslavers. I could regard them in no other light than a band of successful robbers, who had left their homes, and gone to Africa, and stolen us from our homes, and in a strange land reduced us to slavery. I loathed them as being the meanest as well as the most wicked

---

[2] **"The Columbian orator":** *The Columbian Orator* (1797) by Caleb Bingham (1757–1817) was a popular anthology of speeches, dialogues, and essays used as a textbook on oratory.

[3] **Sheridan:** Thomas Sheridan (1719–1788), Irish educator and orator who wrote several books on public speaking.

of men. As I read and contemplated the subject, behold! that very discontentment which Master Hugh had predicted would follow my learning to read had already come, to torment and sting my soul to unutterable anguish. As I writhed under it, I would at times feel that learning to read had been a curse rather than a blessing. It had given me a view of my wretched condition, without the remedy. I opened my eyes to the horrible pit, but to no ladder upon which to get out. In moments of agony, I envied my fellow-slaves for their stupidity. I have often wished myself a beast. I preferred the condition of the meanest reptile to my own. Any thing, no matter what, to get rid of thinking! It was this everlasting thinking of my condition that tormented me. There was no getting rid of it. It was pressed upon me by every object within sight or hearing, animate or inanimate. The silver trump of freedom had roused my soul to eternal wakefulness. Freedom now appeared, to disappear no more forever. It was heard in every sound, and seen in every thing. It was ever present to torment me with a sense of my wretched condition. I saw nothing without seeing it, I heard nothing without hearing it, and felt nothing without feeling it. It looked from every star, it smiled in every calm, breathed in every wind, and moved in every storm.

I often found myself regretting my own existence, and wishing myself dead; and but for the hope of being free, I have no doubt but that I should have killed myself, or done something for which I should have been killed. While in this state of mind, I was eager to hear any one speak of slavery. I was a ready listener. Every little while, I could hear something about the abolitionists. It was some time before I found what the word meant. It was always used in such connections as to make it an interesting word to me. If a slave ran away and succeeded in getting clear, or if a slave killed his master, set fire to a barn, or did any thing very wrong in the mind of a slaveholder, it was spoken of as the fruit of *abolition.* Hearing the word in this connection very often, I set about learning what it meant. The dictionary afforded me little or no help. I found it was "the act of abolishing;" but then I did not know what was to be abolished. Here I was perplexed. I did not dare to ask any one about its meaning, for I was satisfied that it was something they wanted me to know very little about. After a patient waiting, I got one of our city papers, containing an account of the number of petitions from the north, praying for the abolition of slavery in the District of Columbia, and of the slave trade between the States. From this time I understood the words *abolition* and *abolitionist,* and always drew near when that word was spoken, expecting to hear something of importance to myself and fellow-slaves. The light broke in upon me by degrees. I went one day down on the wharf of Mr. Waters; and seeing two Irishmen unloading a scow of stone, I went, unasked, and helped them. When we had finished, one of them came to me and asked me if I were a slave. I told him I was. He asked, "Are ye a slave for life?" I told him that I was. The good Irishman seemed to be deeply affected by the statement. He said to the other that it was a pity so fine a little fellow as myself should be a slave for life. He said it was a shame to hold me. They both advised me to run away to the north; that I should find friends there, and that I should be free. I pretended not to be interested in what they said, and treated them as if I did not understand them; for I feared they might be treacherous.

White men have been known to encourage slaves to escape, and then, to get the reward, catch them and return them to their masters. I was afraid that these seemingly good men might use me so; but I nevertheless remembered their advice, and from that time I resolved to run away. I looked forward to a time at which it would be safe for me to escape. I was too young to think of doing so immediately; besides, I wished to learn how to write, as I might have occasion to write my own pass. I consoled myself with the hope that I should one day find a good chance. Meanwhile, I would learn to write.

The idea as to how I might learn to write was suggested to me by being in Durgin and Bailey's ship-yard, and frequently seeing the ship carpenters, after hewing, and getting a piece of timber ready for use, write on the timber the name of that part of the ship for which it was intended. When a piece of timber was intended for the larboard side, it would be marked thus—"L." When a piece was for the starboard side, it would be marked thus—"S." A piece for the larboard side forward, would be marked thus—"L. F." When a piece was for starboard side forward, it would be marked thus—"S. F." For larboard aft, it would be marked thus—"L. A." For starboard aft, it would be marked thus—"S. A." I soon learned the names of these letters, and for what they were intended when placed upon a piece of timber in the shipyard. I immediately commenced copying them, and in a short time was able to make the four letters named. After that, when I met with any boy who I knew could write, I would tell him I could write as well as he. The next word would be, "I don't believe you. Let me see you try it." I would then make the letters which I had been so fortunate as to learn, and ask him to beat that. In this way I got a good many lessons in writing, which it is quite possible I should never have gotten in any other way. During this time, my copy-book was the board fence, brick wall, and pavement; my pen and ink was a lump of chalk. With these, I learned mainly how to write. I then commenced and continued copying the Italics in Webster's Spelling Book, until I could make them all without looking at the book. By this time, my little Master Thomas had gone to school, and learned how to write, and had written over a number of copy-books. These had been brought home, and shown to some of our near neighbors, and then laid aside. My mistress used to go to class meeting at the Wilk Street meeting-house every Monday afternoon, and leave me to take care of the house. When left thus, I used to spend the time in writing in the spaces left in Master Thomas's copy-book, copying what he had written. I continued to do this until I could write a hand very similar to that of Master Thomas. Thus, after a long, tedious effort for years, I finally succeeded in learning how to write.

FROM CHAPTER X

[ATTEMPTED ESCAPE]

[. . .] At the close of the year 1834, Mr. Freeland again hired me of my master, for the year 1835. But, by this time, I began to want to live *upon free land* as well as *with Freeland;* and I was no longer content, therefore, to live with him or any other slaveholder. I began, with the commencement of the year, to prepare myself for a final struggle, which should decide my fate one way or the other. My tendency was upward. I was fast approaching manhood, and year after year had passed, and I was still a slave. These thoughts roused me—I must do something. I therefore resolved that 1835 should not pass without witnessing an attempt, on my part, to secure my liberty. But I was not willing to cherish this determination alone. My fellow-slaves were dear to me. I was anxious to have them participate with me in this, my life-giving determination. I therefore, though with great prudence, commenced early to ascertain their views and feelings in regard to their condition, and to imbue their minds with thoughts of freedom. I bent myself to devising ways and means for our escape, and meanwhile strove, on all fitting occasions, to impress them with the gross fraud and inhumanity of slavery. I went first to Henry, next to John, then to the others. I found, in them all, warm hearts and noble spirits. They were ready to hear, and ready to act when a feasible plan should be proposed. This was what I wanted. I talked to them of our want of manhood, if we submitted to our enslavement without at least one noble effort to be free. We met often, and consulted frequently, and told our hopes and fears, recounted the difficulties, real and imagined, which we should be called on to meet. At times we were almost disposed to give up, and try to content ourselves with our wretched lot; at others, we were firm and unbending in our determination to go. Whenever we suggested any plan, there was shrinking—the odds were fearful. Our path was beset with the greatest obstacles; and if we succeeded in gaining the end of it, our right to be free was yet questionable—we were yet liable to be returned to bondage. We could see no spot, this side of the ocean, where we could be free. We knew nothing about Canada. Our knowledge of the north did not extend farther than New York; and to go there, and be forever harassed with the frightful liability of being returned to slavery—with the certainty of being treated tenfold worse than before—the thought was truly a horrible one, and one which it was not easy to overcome. The case sometimes stood thus: At every gate through which we were to pass, we saw a watchman—at every ferry a guard—on every bridge a sentinel—and in every wood a patrol. We were hemmed in upon every side. Here were the difficulties, real or imagined—the good to be sought, and the evil to be shunned. On the one hand, there stood slavery, a stern reality, glaring frightfully upon us,—its robes already crimsoned with the blood of millions, and even now feasting itself greedily upon our own flesh. On the other hand, away back in the dim distance, under the flickering light of the north star, behind some craggy hill or snow-covered mountain, stood a doubtful freedom—half frozen—beckoning us to come and share its hospitality. This in itself was sometimes enough to stagger us; but when we permitted ourselves to survey the road, we were frequently appalled. Upon either side we saw grim death, assuming the most horrid shapes. Now it was starvation, causing us to eat our own flesh;—now we were contending with the waves, and were drowned;—now we were overtaken, and torn to pieces by the fangs of the terrible bloodhound. We were stung by scorpions, chased by wild beasts, bitten by snakes, and finally, after having nearly reached the desired spot,—after swimming rivers, encountering wild beasts, sleeping in the woods, suffering hunger and nakedness, — we were overtaken by our pursuers, and, in our resistance, we were shot dead upon the spot! I say, this picture sometimes appalled us, and made us

> "rather bear those ills we had,
> Than fly to others, that we knew not of."[4]

In coming to a fixed determination to run away, we did more than Patrick Henry, when he resolved upon liberty or death. With us it was a doubtful liberty at most, and almost certain death if we failed. For my part, I should prefer death to hopeless bondage.

Sandy, one of our number, gave up the notion, but still encouraged us. Our company then consisted of Henry Harris, John Harris, Henry Bailey, Charles Roberts, and myself. Henry Bailey was my uncle, and belonged to my master. Charles married my aunt; he belonged to my master's father-in-law, Mr. William Hamilton.

The plan we finally concluded upon was, to get a large canoe belonging to Mr. Hamilton, and upon the Saturday night previous to Easter holidays, paddle directly up the Chesapeake Bay. On our arrival at the head of the bay, a distance of seventy or eighty miles from where we lived, it was our purpose to turn our canoe adrift, and follow the guidance of the north star till we got beyond the limits of Maryland. Our reason for taking the water route was, that we were less liable to be suspected as runaways; we hoped to be regarded as fishermen; whereas, if we should take the land route, we should be subjected to interruptions of almost every kind. Any one having a white face, and being so disposed, could stop us, and subject us to examination.

The week before our intended start, I wrote several protections, one for each of us. As well as I can remember, they were in the following words, to wit: —

> "This is to certify that I, the undersigned, have given the bearer, my servant, full liberty to go to Baltimore, and spend the Easter holidays. Written with mine own hand, &c., 1835.
>
> "WILLIAM HAMILTON,
> "Near St. Michael's, in Talbot county, Maryland."

We were not going to Baltimore; but, in going up the bay, we went toward Baltimore, and these protections were only intended to protect us while on the bay.

As the time drew near for our departure, our anxiety became more and more intense. It was truly a matter of life and death with us. The strength of our determination was about to be fully tested. At this time, I was very active in explaining every difficulty, removing every doubt, dispelling every fear, and inspiring all with the firmness indispensable to success in our undertaking; assuring them that half was gained the instant we made the move; we had talked long enough; we were now ready to move; if not now, we never should be; and if we did not intend to move now, we had as well fold our arms, sit down, and acknowledge ourselves fit only to be slaves. This, none of us were prepared to acknowledge. Every man stood firm; and at our last meeting, we pledged ourselves afresh, in the most solemn manner, that, at

---

[4] "rather . . . not of": Lines adapted from William Shakespeare's *Hamlet* 3.1.81–2.

the time appointed, we would certainly start in pursuit of freedom. This was in the middle of the week, at the end of which we were to be off. We went, as usual, to our several fields of labor, but with bosoms highly agitated with thoughts of our truly hazardous undertaking. We tried to conceal our feelings as much as possible; and I think we succeeded very well.

After a painful waiting, the Saturday morning, whose night was to witness our departure, came. I hailed it with joy, bring what of sadness it might. Friday night was a sleepless one for me. I probably felt more anxious than the rest, because I was, by common consent, at the head of the whole affair. The responsibility of success or failure lay heavily upon me. The glory of the one, and the confusion of the other, were alike mine. The first two hours of that morning were such as I never experienced before, and hope never to again. Early in the morning; we went, as usual, to the field. We were spreading manure; and all at once, while thus engaged, I was overwhelmed with an indescribable feeling, in the fulness of which I turned to Sandy, who was near by, and said, "We are betrayed!" "Well," said he, "that thought has this moment struck me." We said no more. I was never more certain of any thing.[5]

FROM CHAPTER XI

[FREEDOM]

I now come to that part of my life during which I planned, and finally succeeded in making, my escape from slavery. But before narrating any of the peculiar circumstances, I deem it proper to make known my intention not to state all the facts connected with the transaction. My reasons for pursuing this course may be understood from the following: First, were I to give a minute statement of all the facts, it is not only possible, but quite probable, that others would thereby be involved in the most embarrassing difficulties. Secondly, such a statement would most undoubtedly induce greater vigilance on the part of slaveholders than has existed heretofore among them; which would, of course, be the means of guarding a door whereby some dear brother bondman might escape his galling chains. I deeply regret the necessity that impels me to suppress any thing of importance connected with my experience in slavery. It would afford me great pleasure indeed, as well as materially add to the interest of my narrative, were I at liberty to gratify a curiosity, which I know exists in the minds of many, by an accurate statement of all the facts pertaining to my most fortunate escape. But I must deprive myself of this pleasure, and the curious of the gratification which such a statement would afford. I would allow myself to suffer under the greatest imputations which evil-minded men might suggest, rather than exculpate myself, and thereby run the hazard of closing the slightest avenue by which a brother slave might clear himself of the chains and fetters of slavery. [. . .]

---

[5] **more certain of any thing:** Their plan having been revealed, Douglass and his friends were arrested. Captain Auld took Douglass from jail and returned him to Baltimore, where Hugh Auld hired him out as a caulker in a shipyard.

In the early part of the year 1838, I became quite restless. I could see no reason why I should, at the end of each week, pour the reward of my toil into the purse of my master. When I carried to him my weekly wages, he would, after counting the money, look me in the face with a robber-like fierceness, and ask, "Is this all?" He was satisfied with nothing less than the last cent. He would, however, when I made him six dollars, sometimes give me six cents, to encourage me. It had the opposite effect. I regarded it as a sort of admission of my right to the whole. The fact that he gave me any part of my wages was proof, to my mind, that he believed me entitled to the whole of them. I always felt worse for having received any thing; for I feared that the giving me a few cents would ease his conscience, and make him feel himself to be a pretty honorable sort of robber. My discontent grew upon me. I was ever on the look-out for means of escape; and, finding no direct means, I determined to try to hire my time, with a view of getting money with which to make my escape. In the spring of 1838, when Master Thomas came to Baltimore to purchase his spring goods, I got an opportunity, and applied to him to allow me to hire my time. He unhesitatingly refused my request, and told me this was another stratagem by which to escape. He told me I could go nowhere but that he could get me; and that, in the event of my running away, he should spare no pains in his efforts to catch me. He exhorted me to content myself, and be obedient. He told me, if I would be happy, I must lay out no plans for the future. He said, if I behaved myself properly, he would take care of me. Indeed, he advised me to complete thoughtlessness of the future, and taught me to depend solely upon him for happiness. He seemed to see fully the pressing necessity of setting aside my intellectual nature, in order to contentment in slavery. But in spite of him, and even in spite of myself, I continued to think, and to think about the injustice of my enslavement, and the means of escape.

About two months after this, I applied to Master Hugh for the privilege of hiring my time. He was not acquainted with the fact that I had applied to Master Thomas, and had been refused. He too, at first, seemed disposed to refuse; but, after some reflection, he granted me the privilege, and proposed the following terms: I was to be allowed all my time, make all contracts with those for whom I worked, and find my own employment; and, in return for this liberty, I was to pay him three dollars at the end of each week; find myself in calking tools, and in board and clothing. My board was two dollars and a half per week. This, with the wear and tear of clothing and calking tools, made my regular expenses about six dollars per week. This amount I was compelled to make up, or relinquish the privilege of hiring my time. Rain or shine, work or no work, at the end of each week the money must be forthcoming, or I must give up my privilege. This arrangement, it will be perceived, was decidedly in my master's favor. It relieved him of all need of looking after me. His money was sure. He received all the benefits of slaveholding without its evils; while I endured all the evils of a slave, and suffered all the care and anxiety of a freeman. I found it a hard bargain. But, hard as it was, I thought it better than the old mode of getting along. It was a step towards freedom to be allowed to bear the responsibilities of a freeman, and I was determined to hold on upon it. I bent myself to the work of making money. I was ready to work at night as well as day, and by the most untiring perseverance and industry, I made enough to meet my expenses, and lay up a little money every week. I went on thus from May till August. Master Hugh then refused to allow me to hire my time longer. The ground for his refusal was a failure on my part, one Saturday night, to pay him for my week's time. [. . .] I thought the matter over during the next day, Sunday, and finally resolved upon the third day of September, as the day upon which I would make a second attempt to secure my freedom. I now had three weeks during which to prepare for my journey. Early on Monday morning, before Master Hugh had time to make any engagement for me, I went out and got employment of Mr. Butler, at his shipyard near the drawbridge, upon what is called the City Block, thus making it unnecessary for him to seek employment for me. At the end of the week, I brought him between eight and nine dollars. He seemed very well pleased, and asked me why I did not do the same the week before. He little knew what my plans were. My object in working steadily was to remove any suspicion he might entertain of my intent to run away; and in this I succeeded admirably. I suppose he thought I was never better satisfied with my condition than at the very time during which I was planning my escape. The second week passed, and again I carried him my full wages; and so well pleased was he, that he gave me twenty-five cents, (quite a large sum for a slaveholder to give a slave,) and bade me to make a good use of it. I told him I would.

Things went on without very smoothly indeed, but within there was trouble. It is impossible for me to describe my feelings as the time of my contemplated start drew near. I had a number of warm-hearted friends in Baltimore,—friends that I loved almost as I did my life,—and the thought of being separated from them forever was painful beyond expression. It is my opinion that thousands would escape from slavery, who now remain, but for the strong cords of affection that bind them to their friends. The thought of leaving my friends was decidedly the most painful thought with which I had to contend. The love of them was my tender point, and shook my decision more than all things else. Besides the pain of separation, the dread and apprehension of a failure exceeded what I had experienced at my first attempt. The appalling defeat I then sustained returned to torment me. I felt assured that, if I failed in this attempt, my case would be a hopeless one—it would seal my fate as a slave forever. I could not hope to get off with any thing less than the severest punishment, and being placed beyond the means of escape. It required no very vivid imagination to depict the most frightful scenes through which I should have to pass, in case I failed. The wretchedness of slavery, and the blessedness of freedom, were perpetually before me. It was life and death with me. But I remained firm, and, according to my resolution, on the third day of September, 1838, I left my chains, and succeeded in reaching New York without the slightest interruption of any kind. How I did so,—what means I adopted,—what direction I travelled, and by what mode of conveyance,—I must leave unexplained, for the reasons before mentioned.

I have been frequently asked how I felt when I found myself in a free State. I have never been able to answer the question with any satisfaction to myself. It was a moment of the highest excitement I ever experienced. I suppose I felt as one may imagine the unarmed mariner to feel when he is rescued by a friendly man-of-war from the pursuit of a pirate. In writing to a dear friend, immediately after my arrival at New York, I said I felt like one who had escaped a den of hungry lions. This state of mind, however, very soon subsided; and I was again seized with a feeling of great insecurity and loneliness. I was yet liable to be taken back, and subjected to all the tortures of slavery. This in itself was enough to damp the ardor of my enthusiasm. But the loneliness overcame me. There I was in the midst of thousands, and yet a perfect stranger; without home and without friends, in the midst of thousands of my own brethren—children of a common Father, and yet I dared not to unfold to any one of them my sad condition. I was afraid to speak to any one for fear of speaking to the wrong one, and thereby falling into the hands of money-loving kidnappers, whose business it was to lie in wait for the panting fugitive, as the ferocious beasts of the forest lie in wait for their prey. The motto which I adopted when I started from slavery was this—"Trust no man!" I saw in every white man an enemy, and in almost every colored man cause for distrust. It was a most painful situation; and, to understand it, one must needs experience it, or imagine himself in similar circumstances. Let him be a fugitive slave in a strange land—a land given up to be the hunting-ground for slaveholders—whose inhabitants are legalized kidnappers—where he is every moment subjected to the terrible liability of being seized upon by his fellow-men, as the hideous crocodile seizes upon his prey!— I say, let him place himself in my situation—without home or friends—without money or credit—wanting shelter, and no one to give it—wanting bread, and no money to buy it,—and at the same time let him feel that he is pursued by merciless men-hunters, and in total darkness as to what to do, where to go, or where to stay,—perfectly helpless both as to the means of defence and means of escape,—in the midst of plenty, yet suffering the terrible gnawings of hunger,—in the midst of houses, yet having no home,—among fellowmen, yet feeling as if in the midst of wild beasts, whose greediness to swallow up the trembling and half-famished fugitive is only equalled by that with which the monsters of the deep swallow up the helpless fish upon which they subsist,—I say, let him be placed in this most trying situation,—the situation in which I was placed,—then, and not till then, will he fully appreciate the hardships of, and know how to sympathize with, the toil-worn and whip-scarred fugitive slave.

Thank Heaven, I remained but a short time in this distressed situation. I was relieved from it by the humane hand of Mr. DAVID RUGGLES, whose vigilance, kindness, and perseverance, I shall never forget. I am glad of an opportunity to express, as far as words can, the love and gratitude I bear him. Mr. Ruggles is now afflicted with blindness, and is himself in need of the same kind offices which he was once so forward in the performance of toward others. I had been in New York but a few days, when Mr. Ruggles sought me out, and very kindly took me to his boarding-house at the corner of Church and Lespenard Streets. Mr. Ruggles was then very deeply engaged in the memorable *Darg* case, as well as attending to a number of other fugitive slaves, devising ways and means for their successful escape; and, though watched and hemmed in on almost every side, he seemed to be more than a match for his enemies.

Very soon after I went to Mr. Ruggles, he wished to know of me where I wanted to go; as he deemed it unsafe for me to remain in New York. I told him I was a calker, and should like to go where I could get work. I thought of going to Canada; but he decided against it, and in favor of my going to New Bedford, thinking I should be able to get work there at my trade. At this time, Anna,[6] my intended wife, came on; for I wrote to her immediately after my arrival at New York, (notwithstanding my homeless, houseless, and helpless condition,) informing her of my successful flight, and wishing her to come on forthwith. In a few days after her arrival, Mr. Ruggles called in the Rev. J. W. C. Pennington, who, in the presence of Mr. Ruggles, Mrs. Michaels, and two or three others, performed the marriage ceremony, and gave us a certificate, of which the following is an exact copy:—

"This may certify, that I joined together in holy matrimony Frederick Johnson[7] and Anna Murray, as man and wife, in the presence of Mr. David Ruggles and Mrs. Michaels.

"JAMES W. C. PENNINGTON.

"*New York, Sept.* 15, 1838."

Upon receiving this certificate, and a five-dollar bill from Mr. Ruggles, I shouldered one part of our baggage, and Anna took up the other, and we set out forthwith to take passage on board of the steamboat John W. Richmond for Newport, on our way to New Bedford. Mr. Ruggles gave me a letter to a Mr. Shaw in Newport, and told me, in case my money did not serve me to New Bedford, to stop in Newport and obtain further assistance; but upon our arrival at Newport, we were so anxious to get to a place of safety, that, notwithstanding we lacked the necessary money to pay our fare, we decided to take seats in the stage, and promise to pay when we got to New Bedford. We were encouraged to do this by two excellent gentlemen, residents of New Bedford, whose names I afterward ascertained to be Joseph Ricketson and William C. Taber. They seemed at once to understand our circumstances, and gave us such assurance of their friendliness as put us fully at ease in their presence. It was good indeed to meet with such friends, at such a time. Upon reaching New Bedford, we were directed to the house of Mr. Nathan Johnson, by whom we were kindly received, and hospitably provided for. Both Mr. and Mrs. Johnson took a deep and lively interest in our welfare. They proved themselves quite worthy of the name of abolitionists. When the stage-driver found us unable to pay our fare, he held on upon our baggage as security for the debt. I had but to mention the fact to Mr. Johnson, and he forthwith advanced the money.

We now began to feel a degree of safety, and to prepare ourselves for the duties and responsibilities of a life of freedom. On the morning after our arrival at New Bedford, while at the breakfast-table, the question arose as to what name I should be called by. The name given me by my mother was, "Frederick Augustus Washington

---

[6] **Anna:** She was free. [Douglass's note.] Anna Murray, a free-woman, whom Douglass met in Baltimore; they had five children.

[7] **Frederick Johnson:** I had changed my name from Frederick *Bailey* to that of Johnson. [Douglass's note.]

Bailey." I, however, had dispensed with the two middle names long before I left Maryland, so that I was generally known by the name of "Frederick Bailey." I started from Baltimore bearing the name of "Stanley." When I got to New York, I again changed my name to "Frederick Johnson," and thought that would be the last change. But when I got to New Bedford, I found it necessary again to change my name. The reason of this necessity was, that there were so many Johnsons in New Bedford, it was already quite difficult to distinguish between them. I gave Mr. Johnson the privilege of choosing me a name, but told him he must not take from me the name of "Frederick." I must hold on to that, to preserve a sense of my identity. Mr. Johnson had just been reading the "Lady of the Lake,"[8] and at once suggested that my name be "Douglass." From that time until now I have been called "Frederick Douglass;" and as I am more widely known by that name than by either of the others, I shall continue to use it as my own. [. . .]

∾ Emancipation Proclaimed

Common sense, the necessities of the war, to say nothing of the dictation of justice and humanity have at last prevailed. We shout for joy that we live to record this righteous decree. *Abraham Lincoln,* President of the United States, Commander-in-Chief of the army and navy, in his own peculiar, cautious, forbearing, and hesitating way, slow, but we hope sure, has, while the loyal heart was near breaking with despair, proclaimed and declared: *"That on the First of January, in the Year of Our Lord One Thousand, Eight Hundred and Sixty-three, All Persons Held as Slaves Within Any State or Any Designated Part of a State, The People Whereof Shall Then be in Rebellion Against the United States, Shall be Thenceforward and Forever Free."* "Free forever" oh! long enslaved millions, whose cries have so vexed the air and sky, suffer on a few more days in sorrow, the hour of your deliverance draws nigh! Oh! Ye millions of free and loyal men who have earnestly sought to free your bleeding country from the dreadful ravages of revolution and anarchy, lift up now your voices with joy and thanksgiving for with freedom to the slave will come peace and safety to your country. President Lincoln has embraced in this proclamation the law of Congress passed more than six months ago, prohibiting the employment of any part of the army and naval forces of the United States, to return fugitive slaves to their masters, commanded all officers of the army and navy to respect and obey its provisions. He has still further declared his intention to urge upon the Legislature of all the slave

---

[8] **"Lady of the Lake":** (1810) A highly popular narrative poem by Sir Walter Scott (1771–1832), based on the clash between King James V and the Douglas clan of Scotland.

States not in rebellion the immediate or gradual abolishment of slavery. But read the proclamation for it is the most important of any to which the President of the United States has ever signed his name.

Opinions will widely differ as to the practical effect of this measure upon the war. All that class at the North who have not lost their affection for slavery will regard the measure as the very worst that could be devised, and as likely to lead to endless mischief. All their plans for the future have been projected with a view to a reconstruction of the American Government upon the basis of compromise between slaveholding and non-slaveholding States. The thought of a country unified in sentiments, objects, and ideas, has not entered into their political calculations, and hence this newly declared policy of the Government, which contemplates one glorious homogeneous people, doing away at a blow with the whole class of compromisers and corrupters, will meet their stern opposition. Will that opposition prevail? Will it lead the President to reconsider and retract? Not a word of it. Abraham Lincoln may be slow, Abraham Lincoln may desire peace even at the price of leaving our terrible national sore untouched, to fester on for generations, but Abraham Lincoln is not the man to reconsider, retract, and contradict words and purposes solemnly proclaimed over his official signature.

The careful, and we think, the slothful deliberation which he has observed in reaching this obvious policy, is a guarantee against retraction. But even if the temper and spirit of the President himself were other than what they are, events greater than the President, events which have slowly wrung this proclamation from him may be relied on to carry him forward in the same direction. To look back now would only load him with heavier evils, while diminishing his ability, for overcoming those with which he now has to contend. To recall his proclamation would only increase rebel pride, rebel sense of power and would be hailed as a direct admission of weakness on the part of the Federal Government, while it would cause heaviness of heart and depression of national enthusiasm all over the loyal North and West. No, Abraham Lincoln will take no step backward. His word has gone out over the country and the world, giving joy and gladness to the friends of freedom and progress wherever those words are read, and he will stand by them, and carry them out to the letter. If he has taught us to confide in nothing else, he has taught us to confide in his word. The want of Constitutional power, the want of military power, the tendency of the measure to intensify Southern hate, and to exasperate the rebels, the tendency to drive from him all that class of Democrats at the North, whose loyalty has been conditioned on his restoring the union as it was, slavery and all, have all been considered, and he has taken his ground notwithstanding. The President doubtless saw, as we see, that it is not more absurd to talk about restoring the union, without hurting slavery, than restoring the union without hurting the rebels. As to exasperating the South, there can be no more in the cup than the cup will hold, and that was full already. The whole situation having been carefully scanned, before Mr. Lincoln could be made to budge an inch, he will now stand his ground. Border State influence, and the influence of half-loyal men, have been exerted and have done their worst. The end of these two influences is implied in this proclamation. Hereafter, the inspiration as well as the men and the money for carrying on the war will come from the North, and not from half-loyal border States.

The effect of this paper upon the disposition of Europe will be great and increasing. It changes the character of the war in European eyes and gives it an important principle as an object, instead of national pride and interest. It recognizes and declares the real nature of the contest, and places the North on the side of justice and civilization, and the rebels on the side of robbery and barbarism. It will disarm all purpose on the part of European Government to intervene in favor of the rebels and thus cast off at a blow one source of rebel power. All through the war thus far, the rebel ambassadors in foreign countries have been able to silence all expression of sympathy with the North as to slavery. With much more than a show of truth, they said that the Federal Government, no more than the Confederate Government, contemplated the abolition of slavery.

But will not this measure be frowned upon by our officers and men in the field? We have heard of many thousands who have resolved that they will throw up their commissions and lay down their arms, just so soon as they are required to carry on a war against slavery. Making all allowances for exaggeration there are doubtless far too many of this sort in the loyal army. Putting this kind of loyalty and patriotism to the test, will be one of the best collateral effects of the measure. Any man who leaves the field on such a ground will be an argument in favor of the proclamation, and will prove that his heart has been more with slavery than with his country. Let the army be cleansed from all such proslavery vermin, and its health and strength will be greatly improved. But there can be no reason to fear the loss of many officers or men by resignation or desertion. We have no doubt that the measure was brought to the attention of most of our leading Generals, and blind as some of them have seemed to be in the earlier part of the war, most of them have seen enough to convince them that there can be no end to this war that does not end slavery. At any rate, we may hope that for every pro-slavery man that shall start from the ranks of our loyal army, there will be two anti-slavery men to fill up the vacancy, and in this war one truly devoted to the cause of Emancipation is worth two of the opposite sort.

Whether slavery will be abolished in the manner now proposed by President Lincoln, depends of course upon two conditions, the first specified and the second implied. The first is that the slave States shall be in rebellion on and after the first day of January 1863 and the second is we must have the ability to put down that rebellion. About the first there can be very little doubt. The South is thoroughly in earnest and confident. It has staked everything upon the rebellion. Its experience thus far in the field has rather increased its hopes of final success than diminished them. Its armies now hold us at bay at all points, and the war is confined to the border States slave and free. If Richmond were in our hands and Virginia at our mercy, the vast regions beyond would still remain to be subdued. But the rebels confront us on the Potomac, the Ohio, and the Mississippi. Kentucky, Maryland, Missouri, and Virginia are in debate on the battlefields and their people are divided by the line which separates treason from loyalty. In short we are yet, after eighteen months of war, confined to the outer margin of the rebellion. We have scarcely more than touched the surface of the terrible evil. It has been raising large quantities of food during the past summer. While the masters have been fighting abroad, the slaves have been busy working at home to supply them with the means of continuing the struggle. They will not down at the bidding of this Proclamation, but may be safely relied upon till January and long after January. A month or two will put an end to general fighting for the winter. When the leaves fall we shall hear again of bad roads, winter quarters, and spring campaigns. The South which has thus far withstood our arms will not fall at once before our pens. All fears for the abolition of slavery arising from this apprehension may be dismissed. Whoever, therefore, lives to see the first day of next January, should Abraham Lincoln be then alive and President of the United States, may confidently look in the morning papers for the final proclamation, granting freedom, and freedom forever, to all slaves within the rebel States. On the next point nothing need be said. We have full power to put down the rebellion. Unless one man is more than a match for four, unless the South breeds braver and better men than the North, unless slavery is more precious than liberty, unless a just cause kindles a feebler enthusiasm than a wicked and villainous one, the men of the loyal States will put down this rebellion and slavery, and all the sooner will they put down that rebellion by coupling slavery with that object. Tenderness towards slavery has been the loyal weakness during the war. Fighting the slaveholders with one hand and holding the slaves with the other, has been fairly tried and has failed. We have now inaugurated a wiser and better policy, a policy which is better for the loyal cause than an hundred thousand armed men. The Star Spangled Banner is now the harbinger of Liberty and the millions in bondage, inured to hardships, accustomed to toil, ready to suffer, ready to fight, to dare and to die, will rally under that banner wherever they see it gloriously unfolded to the breeze. Now let the Government go forward in its mission of Liberty as the only condition of peace and union, by weeding out the army and navy of all such officers as the late Col. Miles, whose sympathies are now known to have been with the rebels. Let only the men who assent heartily to the wisdom and the justice of the anti-slavery policy of the Government be lifted into command; let the black man have an arm as well as a heart in this war, and the tide of battle which has thus far only waved backward and forward, will steadily set in our favor. The rebellion suppressed, slavery abolished, and America will, higher than ever, sit as a queen among the nations of the earth.

Now for the work. During the interval between now and next January, let every friend of the long enslaved bondman do his utmost in swelling the tide of anti-slavery sentiment, by writing, speaking, money, and example. Let our aim be to make the North a unit in favor of the President's policy, and see to it that our voices and votes, shall forever extinguish that latent and malignant sentiment at the North, which has from the first cheered on the rebels in their atrocious crimes against the union, and has systematically sought to paralyze the national arm in striking down the slave-holding rebellion. We are ready for this service or any other, in this, we trust the last struggle with the monster slavery.

AFRICAN AMERICAN FOLK SONGS
UNITED STATES, EIGHTEENTH–EARLY NINETEENTH CENTURIES

African American Folk Songs, or spirituals, were called the "Sorrow Songs" by the great African American scholar and writer W. E. B. Du Bois (1868–1963). A hybrid form, these spirituals combine elements of African and American traditions, as well as allusions to African and Christian religions. Most spirituals are based on biblical stories or Christian hymns. The slaves' relationship with Christianity, however, was problematic, for Christianity was the religion of the slave masters. Howard Thurman, an African American theologian, suggests that some of the power of spirituals derives from this paradoxical connection. In *Deep River*, his study of spirituals, he remarks:

> When the master gave the slave his (the master's) God, for a long time it meant that it was difficult to disentangle religious experience from slavery sanction. . . . By some amazing but vastly creative spiritual insight the slave undertook the redemption of a religion that the master had profaned in his midst.

Spirituals sometimes made a clear distinction between those who professed to be Christians and those who really were. The Christianity of the spirituals is grounded in personal experience, not in theological doctrines. Praying consoles the singer who "feel[s] like a motherless chile" in a spiritual that prefigures the blues. Spirituals often give personal testimony of the ways in which the liberating Bible stories affect the singer.

Slave Quarters, Hermitage Plantation, outside Savannah, GA, 1900
Typically, slave houses lacked windowpanes and provided only the most basic shelter. (Library of Congress)

The great themes of the slaves' Christianity and their spirituals are freedom and deliverance. The stories of Moses leading the Israelites out of bondage and crossing over the river Jordan into the Promised Land and of Jesus' death and resurrection were sung as tales of deliverance from the trials of this life. The mention of freedom in spirituals was often a coded message about escape. In spirituals such as "Go Down, Moses," Egypt stood for the institution of slavery, and the journey to the Promised Land represented the Underground Railroad and freedom in the North. Harriet Tubman (c. 1820–1913), who led many slaves to freedom on the Underground Railroad, was nicknamed "Moses," who led the Israelites out of slavery in Egypt. She used "Go Down, Moses" as a code to rally those slaves who sought to escape. "Follow the Drinkin' Gourd" even provided a kind of map to slaves who would use the Big Dipper to guide them northward at night.

The spiritual "Hold On!" links biblical stories of Noah and Mary to an agricultural metaphor — plowing a field, which was work familiar to almost every slave. By the end of the song, the straight furrow has become the straight path to heaven and, by implication, the road to the "promised land" of the North. This spiritual "work song," its rhythms and repetitions attuned to the rhythms of physical work, foreshadows such post-slavery work songs as "John Henry," which described the superhuman effort of a pile driver on the railroad, who gave his life to prove that he was stronger than the new mechanical steam drill.

> The sole American music, . . . the most beautiful expression of human experience from this side of the seas.
>
> – W. E. B. Du Bois on "The Sorrow Songs"

∾ Go Down, Moses[1]

Go down, Moses,
Way down in Egypt land,
Tell ol' Pharaoh,
Let my people go!

1.

When Israel was in Egypt's land,
　　Let my people go.
Oppressed so hard they could not stand,
　　Let my people go.

2.

Thus said the Lord, bold Moses said, . . .
If not I'll smite your firstborn dead. . . .

---

[1] *"Go Down, Moses"*: This spiritual is based on the account of Moses leading the Hebrews out of slavery in Egypt in Exodus, chapters 1–15.

3.

No more shall they in bondage toil; . . .
Let them come out with Egypt's spoil. . . .

4.

When Israel out of Egypt came . . .
And left the proud oppressive land, . . .

5.

O, 'twas a dark and dismal night . . .
When Moses led the Israelites. . . .

6.

'Twas good ole Moses and Aaron, too, . . .
'Twas they that led the armies through. . . .

7.

The Lord told Moses what to do . . .
To lead the children of Israel through. . . .

8.

O come along, Moses, you'll not get lost; . . .
Stretch out your rod and come across. . . .

9.

As Israel stood by the water side, . . .
At the command of God it did divide. . . .

10.

When they had reached the other shore . . .
They sang a song of triumph o'er. . . .

11.

Pharaoh said he would go across, . . .
But Pharaoh and his host were lost. . . .

12.

O, Moses, the cloud shall cleave the way, . . .
A fire by night, a shade by day. . . .

13.

You'll not get lost in the wilderness . . .
With a lighted candle in your breast. . . .

14.

Jordan shall stand up like a wall, . . .
And the walls of Jericho shall fall. . . .

15.

Your foes shall not before you stand, . . .
And you'll possess fair Canaan's land. . . .

16.

'Twas just about at harvest time . . .
When Joshua led his host divine. . . .

17.

O let us all from bondage flee . . .
And let us all in Christ be free. . . .

18.

We need not always weep and moan . . .
And wear these slavery chains forlorn. . . .

19.

This world's a wilderness of woe; . . .
O, let us on to Canaan go. . . .

20.

What a beautiful morning that will be . . .
When time breaks up in eternity. . . .

21.

O brethren, brethren, you'd better be engaged, . . .
For the devil he's out on a big rampage. . . .

22.

The devil he thought he had me fast, . . .
But I thought I'd break his chains at last. . . .

23.

O take yer shoes from off your feet . . .
And walk into the golden street. . . .

24.

I'll tell you what I likes de best: . . .
It is the shouting Methodist. . . .

25.

I do believe without a doubt . . .
That a Christian has the right to shout. . . .

◐ Deep River[1]

Deep river, my home is over Jordan,
Deep river, Lord, I want to cross over into campground.
Lord, I want to cross over into campground,
Lord, I want to cross over into campground.

Oh, chillun, Oh, don't you want to go to that gospel feast,
That promised land, that land where all is peace?
Walk into heaven, and take my seat,
And cast my crown at Jesus' feet,[2]
Lord, I want to cross over into campground.

---

[1] *"Deep River":* The deep river in this spiritual is on one level the river Jordan, the river of passage for the Israelites in Exodus and later the river in which Jesus is baptized. On a figurative level it is the river that divides this life from the next, and perhaps in a more concrete but masked reference, the Ohio River, which divided the North from the South.

[2] *And cast . . . feet:* An allusion to Revelation 4:10–11: "The four and twenty elders fall down before him that sat on the throne, and worship him that liveth for ever and ever, and cast down their crowns before the throne, saying, Thou art worthy, O Lord, to receive glory and honor and power."

10 Deep river, my home is over Jordan,
Deep river, Lord, I want to cross over into campground.
Lord, I want to cross over into campground,
Lord, I want to cross over into campground,

∾ Follow the Drinkin' Gourd[1]

Follow the drinkin' gourd!
Follow the drinkin' gourd!
For the old man is a-waitin' for to carry you to freedom
If you follow the drinkin' gourd

When the sun comes up & the first quail calls / Follow . . .
For the old man is a-waitin' for to carry you . . . / Follow . . .

The river bank will make a mighty good road
The dead trees will show you the way
Left foot, peg foot, travelin' on . . . / Follow . . .

10 The river ends between two hills / Follow . . .
There's another river on the other side . . . / Follow . . .

∾ Sometimes I Feel Like a Motherless Chile

1.

Sometimes I feel like a motherless chile,
Sometimes I feel like a motherless chile,
Sometimes I feel like a motherless chile,
Far, far away from home,
A long, long ways from home.

Then I get down on my knees an' pray.
Get down on my knees an' pray.

2.

Sometimes I feel like I'm almost gone,
Sometimes I feel like I'm almost gone,
Sometimes I feel like I'm almost gone,

---

[1] *"Follow the Drinkin' Gourd":* The "gourd" in this song is the Big Dipper, a guide to the North Star that pointed the way to freedom in the North or in Canada for escaping slaves traveling at night.

Far, far away from home,
A long, long ways from home.

Then I get down on my knees an' pray,
Get down on my knees an' pray.

❧ Hold On!

Keep your hand on-a dat plow!
Hold on!
Hold on! Hold on!
Keep your hand right on-a dat plow!
Hold on!

1.

Noah, Noah, lemme come in,
Doors all fastened an de winders pinned.
Keep your hand on-a dat plow!
Noah said, You done lost yo' track,
Can't plow straight an' keep a-lookin' back.

2.

Sister Mary had a gold chain;
Every link was my Jesus' name.
Keep your hand on-a dat plow!
Keep on plowin' an' don't you tire;
Every row goes hi'er an' hi'er.

3.

Ef you wanner git to Heben
I'll tell you how:
Keep your hand right on-a dat plow!
Ef dat plow stays in-a your hand,
Land you straight in de Promise' Land.

∽ John Henry[1]

John Henry was a little baby
Sittin' on his papa's knee
He picked up a hammer & a little piece of steel
Said "Hammer's gonna be the death of me, Lord, Lord!
Hammer's gonna be the death of me"

The captain said to John Henry
"Gonna bring that steam drill 'round
Gonna bring that steam drill out on the job
Gonna whop that steel on down Lord, Lord / Whop . . ."

10   John Henry told his captain
"A man ain't nothin' but a man
But before I let your steam drill beat me down
I'd die with a hammer in my hand . . ."

John Henry said to his shaker
"Shaker, why don't you sing?
I'm throwin' 30 lbs. from my hips on down
Just listen to that cold steel ring . . ."

John Henry said to his Shaker
"Shaker, you'd better pray
20   'Cause if I miss that little piece of steel
Tomorrow be your buryin' day!"

The Shaker said to John Henry
"I think this mountain's cavin' in!"
John Henry said to his Shaker, "Man
That ain't nothin' but my hammer suckin' wind!"

---

[1] *"John Henry":* This familiar folk song, a Negro work song from the post-slavery period, is said to be based on a real event that took place in the Swannanoa Tunnel in West Virginia in the 1870s. In the song, John Henry becomes a mythic figure—like Paul Bunyan or Lincoln—symbolizing human strength that resists the power of the machine.

The man that invented the steam drill
Thought he was mighty fine
But John Henry made 15 ft.
The steam drill only made nine . . .

30   John Henry hammered in the mountain
His hammer was striking fire
But he worked so hard, he broke his poor heart
He laid down his hammer & he died . . .

John Henry had a little woman
Her name was Polly Ann
John Henry took sick & went to his bed
Polly Ann drove steel like a man . . .

John Henry had a little baby
You could hold him in the palm of your hand
40   The last words I heard that poor boy say
"My daddy was a steel-driving man . . ."

They took John Henry to the graveyard
And they buried him in the sand
And every locomotive comes a-roaring by
Says "There lies a steel-driving man . . ."

Well every Monday morning
When the bluebirds begin to sing
You can hear John Henry a mile or more
You can hear John Henry's hammer ring . . .

TEXT IN CONTEXT

∾ JOHANN WOLFGANG VON GOETHE
B. GERMANY, 1749–1832

Goethe's lifetime, from 1749 to 1832, spanned a turbulent era marked
by ground-shaking events such as the American and French revolutions, the Napoleonic Wars, and the wars of independence in South
America. Such a time called for, and seemed to inspire, men and
women of titanic ambition, talent, and achievement not only in the
arts of politics and war but in music and literature as well. Among
those of his era, Goethe ranks easily among such remarkable contemporaries as Thomas Jefferson, Napoleon Bonaparte, Simón Bolívar,
and Ludwig von Beethoven; and like them, he has left his name on his
era, sometimes called the "Goethezeit"—the age of Goethe. Poet, playwright, autobiographer, novelist, critic, and journalist, Goethe seemed
to try his hand at nearly every literary form. And he was a painter,
theater manager, statesman, bureaucrat, educational theorist, and
scientist as well—a "Renaissance man."[1] Goethe's masterwork, the
long dramatic poem *Faust,* the story of another Renaissance man,
is the defining work of German literature in the nineteenth century.
In *The Romantic School,* Heinrich Heine remarked that "the German
people is itself that learned Doctor Faust. It is itself that spiritualist
who finally through his intellect has grasped the inadequacy of the

YOH-hahn
VOHLF-gahng
fon GAY-tuh

---

[1] **"Renaissance man":** A term used to describe a person who is accomplished in many disciplines, especially
in both the sciences and the arts, like such multidimensional persons from the European Renaissance as
Leonardo Da Vinci.

intellect and demands material pleasures and restores to the flesh its rights."

Sturm und Drang.   Born in Frankfurt into an affluent bourgeois family, Goethe had a happy childhood before going off to the University of Leipzig when he was sixteen. There he published his first volumes of poetry, but he left for health reasons before completing his degree. In 1770 he went to the University of Strasbourg to study law, where he met Johann Gottfried Herder,[2] the critic and philosopher who was the formative influence on the **Sturm und Drang** (Storm and Stress) movement, a German literary movement of the 1770s that sought to overthrow the cult of rationalism by emphasizing feeling, imagination, and natural simplicity. Among the leading figures of the Sturm und Drang, sometimes seen as the first wave of Romanticism in Germany, were Herder, Friedrich Schiller,[3] and Goethe himself. Influenced by Herder, Goethe wrote *Götz von Berlichingen* (1773), the first major literary work of the movement, and *The Sorrows of Young Werther* (*Die Leiden des Jungen Werther*) (1774), its major work. The story of a sensitive young man driven to suicide by his alienation from the conventional world, his emotional absolutism, and his frustrated passion for a country girl, *Werther* was an immediate sensation. Goethe, who had written the novel as a critique of the excesses to which unbridled sensibility could lead, was somewhat taken aback by the phenomenal reception of the novel, and its eponymous anti-hero became an unlikely role model for melancholy young men hoping to display their own delicacy of taste, passion, and sensibility. Werther's blue coat and yellow waistcoat became the fashion, and a rash of suicides occurred in the wake of the novel's popularity, similar to those that followed Chikamatsu's *shinju* plays in Japan.[4] The Scottish writer Thomas Carlyle (1795–1881) said that Goethe's book caught the spirit of the age and gave expression to "the nameless unrest and longing discontent which was then agitating every bosom."

SHTOORM oont
DRAHNG

---

[2] **Johann Gottfried Herder** (1744–1803): German folklorist, critic, and translator; a primitivist who believed that nature was best comprehended through the senses and feelings rather than through reason.

[3] **Friedrich Schiller** (1759–1805): German dramatist whose idealistic dramas promoting freedom were the most popular plays on the nineteenth-century German stage. The best known of his nine plays are *The Robbers* (1781); *Mary Stuart* (1801), about Mary of Scotland; and *The Maid of Orleans* (1802), about Joan of Arc.

[4] **Chikamatsu's . . . Japan:** Chikamatsu Monzaemon's (1653–1724) play *The Love Suicides at Amijima* (1721) was such a popular work that the Japanese government took steps to curb the number of suicides in its wake.

Johann Heinrich
Wilhelm Tischbein,
*Goethe in the
Campagna*, 1787
*This portrait of
Goethe as a young
man, with his coat
draped dramatically
around his body,
evokes his Romantic
sensibilities. (Art
Resource)*

Return to Classical Ideals.   In 1775 Goethe moved to **Weimar**, where   VIGH-mar
he spent most of the rest of his life working as Minister of State for the
reigning duke, Charles Augustus, while continuing to write and carry
out scientific investigations. The poems of his early years in Weimar
modify the extreme emotionalism of his Sturm und Drang works to
reveal a growing objectivity. Nature becomes less a projection of the
author's moods than something existing in its own right. This more
classical bent in Goethe's work was encouraged by his visit to Italy
in 1786–87. The works from this Italian period, especially *Iphigenie in
Tauris* (1787) and *Roman Elegies* (1788–89), celebrate classical ideals
and humanity's power to free itself from the delusions of its own
consciousness.

In the 1790s Goethe, like nearly all Europeans of the time, was
caught up in the French Revolution and its aftermath. He accompanied
Augustus on a disastrous military campaign in France in 1792. Out of
these experiences, Goethe wrote several books: the war dramas *Hermann
and Dorothea* (1797) and *The Natural Daughter* (1804), and his most
important work during this period, *Wilhelm Meister's Apprenticeship*
(*Wilhelm Meister's Lehrjahr*) (1796), a Bildungsroman—a novel devoted
to describing the learning process, or the "apprenticeship," of a young
person learning about life. Goethe had worked on the novel for several
years, and it might be said to describe his own learning process during
his first two decades in Weimar.

Collaboration with Schiller.   Among Goethe's most productive years   The whole will always
were those at the turn of the century when he collaborated with   remain a fragment.
Friedrich Schiller. From 1794 until Schiller's death in 1805, the two   – GOETHE on *Faust*

pp. 736, 799

writers formed a friendship and literary collaboration similar to that of **William Wordsworth** and **Samuel Taylor Coleridge** in England. Although nearly opposites in poetic temperament and intellectual disposition—Goethe, oriented toward the real; Schiller, toward the ideal—the two writers found their differences complementary, at least most of the time. Together they mutually reinforced each other's work in what became a high point in the literary careers of both men. The poetic vision they elaborated through their correspondence and in essays they composed for *Die Horen* (The Horae), a literary journal founded by Schiller, is known as Weimar Classicism, named after the Duchy of Weimar where they lived. Weimar classicism sought to articulate an aesthetics of wholeness and balance, modeled not upon the urbane polish of the Augustan poets of Rome (as in NEOCLASSICISM) but upon the spontaneous creativity of ancient Greek poets and Shakespeare—poets whom they closely identified with the creative power inherent in raw and unmediated nature. The aim of this aesthetic was to bring human beings—writers and readers—into balance with their innermost drives and to integrate our proclivity for abstract reflection with embodied experience. In reconciling or integrating the ideal with the real, the thinking subject with the natural object, poetry could have the effect of bringing harmony not just to the individual but to society as a whole. One can see in the struggle between the real and the ideal an anticipation of the conflicts that drive Faust from the mastery of abstract and arcane knowledge to the leap into concrete experience—from the word to the deed.

Late Works.   At the time of Schiller's death, Goethe was recognized not only as a representative of Weimar Classicism but—somewhat reluctantly—as the embodiment of German Romanticism that had been developing very systematically and self-consciously at nearby Jena where August Wilhelm and Friedrich Schlegel, among others, were outlining a Romantic poetics in the pages of their journal *The Athenaeum*. The complicated balance between Romantic and Classic in Goethe's work (as well as the complications of defining precisely those two terms) continues to be a topic of debate among scholars of Romanticism. Suffice it to say that despite his overt opposition to what he considered the excesses of Romanticism as it was being defined in Germany at the time (mysticism, solipsism, nationalism, and medievalism, among others), Goethe's later work shares many of its tendencies—a keen interest in the psychological exploration of the self, a celebration of the creative power of the human imagination, a deep feeling for nature as a ground and source of being, and a sense of the possibilities for poetry in the broadest sense to transform consciousness and society.

After Schiller's death, Goethe published the psychological novel *Elective Affinities* (*Die Wahlverwandschaften*) (1809), which explores the night side of human relationships. Goethe also continued his scientific work, publishing in 1805–10 his most important scientific papers, *Theory of Color.* In the later years of his life, Goethe became interested in non-Western literature, developing an ideal of a **Weltliteratur** (world literature), works that transcended national differences to advance a universal civilization. His own poems in *Divan of West and East* (*West-Östlichen Diwan*) (1819) were inspired by Persian poetry and attempt to marry East and West. By the last decade of his life, Goethe had become a reigning, but not uncontroversial, sage, and Weimar a place of pilgrimage for writers, artists, and intellectuals from all over Europe.

VELT-li-tuh-rah-toor

Faust, an Autobiographical Work.   Goethe worked on *Faust* throughout his life. *Urfaust,* an early version of the poem that was not published during Goethe's lifetime, was probably written in the early 1780s. The first published version, *Faust, a Fragment,* appeared in 1790 and the completed *Faust, Part I* in 1808. *Faust, Part II,* which Goethe worked on in the last years of his life, was published after his death in 1832. In the play's final verses, he challenges his readers to make sense of it: "Our play is rather like the whole life of man / We make a start, we make an end — / But make a whole of it? Well, do so if you can."

Goethe's challenge defines one of the central critical issues presented by *Faust:* whether or not it can be read as a unified and coherent work of art. Because it was written at different periods throughout Goethe's life, many commentators have read it as an autobiographical poem telling of Goethe's intellectual and creative growth. Like Goethe, Faust is a **RENAISSANCE** man. Restless and dissatisfied with the limitations of his human situation, he seeks greater knowledge and experience. The two warring souls within him may characterize two competing aspects of Goethe's character: his rational, scientific side, and his intuitive, poetic side. The two aspects of human nature represented by **Mephistopheles** and Faust, worldly cynicism and optimistic striving, may also reveal crucial contradictions in Goethe's own character.

meh-fis-TAH-fuh-leez

Faust as Everyman.   But Faust is also a representative of the time, a kind of Everyman at the brink of modernity and embodying in his own mind and experience the contradictions and upheavals of the period. The original folk stories of the Faust legend emerged in the late

Henry Moses, *Faust and Mephistopheles in the Witches Cave,* 1820
This English engraving depicts the "Witch's Kitchen" section of Faust, Part I. *Note how the engraver includes imagery from the text: the monkeys playing with the globe, the hearth, the forms in the steam, and the "bizarre paraphernalia of witchcraft." (Courtesy of the Trustees of the Boston Public Library)*

Middle Ages as a way of articulating the change from the church-dominated hierarchical consciousness of the Middle Ages to the humanism of the Renaissance. The struggle between these competing points of view can be seen in Christopher Marlowe's version of the story, *The Tragical History of Doctor Faustus* (c. 1592). Goethe's *Faust* reflects a similar transition, from pre-revolutionary, aristocratic, religious, and mercantile Europe to a post-revolutionary, democratic, secular, and industrial world.

By basing his drama on a folk story, Goethe exemplifies the Sturm und Drang and Romantic interest in the primitive, for in the simple stories of the people, writers like Herder and Wordsworth thought they could get beneath the veneer of civilization and get at the true nature of things. But Goethe significantly transformed the original folk story. *Faust* is no longer the story of the contest between good and evil or between the power of the church and the individual. Goethe's *Faust* explores instead alternative worldviews, different aspects of Faust's consciousness. When he rejects *word* and *mind* as adequate translations

Voilá un homme!
(There is a man!)
– NAPOLEON on Goethe

for the beginning of the Gospel of St. John and substitutes instead, "In the beginning was the Deed," Faust bespeaks the division within himself and the choice that Mephistopheles will offer him. Rejecting *mind,* Faust turns his back on his past, on his role as an Enlightenment scholar. Affirming the *Deed,* he chooses experience and action, to become a man of the world, of the body rather than the mind, of the parts of himself that he has previously ignored. From this perspective, Mephistopheles is not so much a separate character or a representation of evil as he is a projection of Faust's consciousness, a representative of one of the "two souls" that reside within Faust's breast. The poem pits Mephistopheles' cynicism and despair against Faust's optimism; it explores the interplay between the physical and spiritual, the human and divine.

Mephistopheles does not offer Faust a chance to break rules or to challenge authority but rather a chance to explore another reality. Rather than mind, he offers body; rather than idea, he offers experience. But the immersion in experience is dangerous; acting in the moment, from emotional spontaneity rather than rational consideration, can have tragic consequences. Valentine's death, for example, is an unforeseen result of Faust's affair with Margaret. Unthinking action inevitably leads to errors. And Faust's search for the fullest expression of his nature leads to tragic errors that result in the destruction of Margaret, her family, and Baucis and Philemon. If Mephistopheles is not a representative of evil in Goethe's poem, Faust is not an unqualified representative of good. In both aspects of his character, the divided Faust is caught in ambiguities and paradoxes.

Nineteenth-century readers tended to see *Faust* as a drama of a man redeemed by striving, for in spite of his mistakes Faust never ceases searching for the good. He is never satisfied with the limitations of the experiences that Mephistopheles offers him. These early critics often pointed to the last act in Part II, where Faust drains a marsh to develop a construction project, as an indication that he has transcended his selfishness and redeemed his earlier errors by engaging in altruistic service to humankind. Modern readers, less enamored of grand development projects and less willing to affirm action for its own sake, have not been so easily convinced that Faust has grown. After all, they point out, Baucis and Philemon are sacrificed so that Faust's project can proceed. The ending of the play, then, is problematic. Is it tragic or comic? Is Faust redeemed, or is the end a cosmic mockery? Stuart Atkins suggests these paradoxical ambiguities when he describes *Faust* as "the drama of a man destroyed by the larger force than himself which is life and yet enjoying triumph in inevitable defeat."

www For more information about Goethe, quizzes on *Faust,* and information about the 21st-century relevance of *Faust,* see bedford stmartins.com/ worldlitcompact.

■ **FURTHER RESEARCH**

Biography

Boyle, Nicholas. *Goethe: The Poet and the Age.* 2 vols. 1991, 2000.
Fairley, Barker. *A Study of Goethe.* 1947.
Hatfield, Henry. *Goethe: A Critical Introduction.* 1963.
Reed, Terence. *Goethe.* 1984.
Williams, John R. *The Life of Goethe: A Critical Biography.* 1998.

Criticism

Arndt, W. and Cyrus Hamlin, eds. *Faust.* 2000. A critical edition that includes
     background materials and critical essays on the play.
Atkins, Stuart. *Goethe's* Faust: *A Literary Analysis.* 1964.
Brown, Jane K. Faust: *Theater of the World.* 1992.
———. *Goethe's* Faust: *The German Tragedy.* 1986.
Mason, Eudo C. *Goethe's* Faust: *Its Genesis and Purport.* 1967.

Other Versions of the Faust Story

Mann, Thomas. *Doktor Faustus.* 1947. A satire of Hitler's Third Reich.
Marlowe, Christopher. *Doctor Faustus.* 1592–93. (Book 3)

■ **PRONUNCIATION**

Altmayer: AHLT-mire
Auerbach: OW-ur-bahk
Euphorion: yoo-FORE-ee-on
Johann Wolfgang Von Goethe: YOH-hahn VOHLF-gahng fon GAY-tuh
Mephistopheles: meh-fis-TAH-fuh-leez
Proktophantasmist: prahk-toh-fan-TAZ-mist
Sturm und Drang: SHTOORM oont DRAHNG
Wagner: VAHG-nur
Walpurgisnacht: vahl-POOR-gis-nahkt
Weimar: VIGH-mar
Weltliteratur: VELT-li-tuh-rah-toor

Faust

Translated by Charles E. Passage

CHARACTERS IN THE PROLOGUE IN HEAVEN

THE LORD
RAPHAEL
GABRIEL

MICHAEL
MEPHISTOPHELES

CHARACTERS IN THE TRAGEDY

FAUST
MEPHISTOPHELES
WAGNER, *a student*
LIESCHEN
MARGARET (*also* GRETCHEN)
MARTHA, MARGARET's *neighbor*
VALENTINE, MARGARET's *brother*
OLD PEASANT

A STUDENT
ELIZABETH, *an acquaintance of* MARGARET
WITCHES, *old and young;*
     WIZARDS; WILL-O'-THE-WISP;
     PROKTOPHANTASMIST; THE BEAUTY;
     SERVIBILIS; MONKEYS; SPIRITS; ANIMALS;
     APPRENTICES; COUNTRY-FOLK; CITIZENS;
     BEGGAR; STUDENTS; *etc.*

CHARACTERS IN PART II

FAUST	LEMURS
MEPHISTOPHELES *in various guises*	*The* FOUR GRAY WOMEN: WANT, GUILT,
ARIEL	CARE, DISTRESS
BAUCIS	A PENITENT
PHILEMON	DOCTOR MARIANUS
A TRAVELER	CHORUS OF ANGELS *and* PENITENTS *and*
THE THREE MIGHTY MEN	*various Heavenly characters*
LYNCEUS	

PROLOGUE IN HEAVEN[1]

RAPHAEL:

> The sun sings as it sang of old
> With brother spheres in rival sound,
> In thundrous motion onward rolled
> Completing its appointed round.
> The angels draw strength from the sight,
> Though fathom it no angel may;
> The great works of surpassing might
250　> Are grand as on Creation day.

GABRIEL:

> And swift beyond conception flies
> The turning earth, now dark, now bright,
> With clarity of paradise
> Succeeding deep and dreadful night;
> The sea in foam from its broad source
> Against the base of cliffs is hurled,
> And down the sphere's eternal course
> Both cliff and sea are onward whirled.

MICHAEL:

> And storms a roaring battle wage
260　> From sea to land, from land to sea,
> And forge a chain amid their rage,
> A chain of utmost potency.
> There blazing lightning-flashes sear
> The path for bursting thunder's way—
> And yet thy heralds, Lord, revere
> The mild procession of thy day.

ALL THREE:

> The angels draw strength from the sight,
> Though fathom it no angel may;
> The great works of surpassing might
270　> Are grand as on Creation day.

---

[1] The "Dedication" and the "Prologue in the Theater" that precede this section have been omitted.

MEPHISTOPHELES:

Since you, O Lord, approach again and see
These people here and ask us how we do,
And since you used to like my company,
Behold me also here among this crew.
Excuse me, I can not be eloquent,
Not even if I'm scorned by all your staff;
My grand style would provoke your merriment
If you had not forgotten how to laugh.
Of suns and worlds there's nothing I can say;
280   How men torment themselves is what I see.
The little earth-god stays the same perpetually
And still is just as odd as on Creation day.
He would be better off at least
If you had not endowed him with the heavens' light;
He terms it Reason and exerts the right
To be more brute than any beast.
He seems like — craving pardon of Your Grace —
One of the spindle-shank grasshopper race
That flit around and as they hop
290   Sing out their ancient ditty where they stop.
He should stay in the grass where he has sung!
He sticks his nose in every pile of dung.

THE LORD:

Is there no more that you could add?
Is finding fault all you can do?
Is nothing on earth ever right with you?

MEPHISTOPHELES:

No, Lord! I find things there, as always, downright bad.
The human race in all its woes I so deplore
I hate to plague the poor things any more.

THE LORD:

Do you know Faust?

MEPHISTOPHELES:

               The Doctor?

THE LORD: And my servant.

MEPHISTOPHELES:

300   He serves you in a curious way, I think.
Not earthly is the poor fool's food and drink.
An inner ferment drives him far
And he is half aware that he is mad;
From heaven he demands the fairest star,
From earth all peaks of pleasure to be had,
And nothing near and nothing far
Will calm his troubled heart or make it glad.

THE LORD:

> Though now he serves me but confusedly,
> I soon shall guide him on toward what is clear.
310   The gardener knows, when green comes to the tree,
> That flowers and fruit will deck the coming year.

MEPHISTOPHELES:

> What will you bet you lose him if you give
> Me your permission now to steer
> Him gently down my path instead?

THE LORD:

> As long as he on earth may live,
> To you such shall not be gainsaid.
> Man errs as long as he can strive.

MEPHISTOPHELES:

> Thank you for that; for with the dead
> I never hankered much to be.
320   It is the plump, fresh cheeks that mean the most to me.
> I'm out to corpses calling at my house;
> I play the way the cat does with the mouse.

THE LORD:

> Good, then! The matter is agreed!
> Divert this spirit from his primal source,
> And if you can ensnare him, lead
> Him with you on your downward course;
> And stand abashed when you have to confess:
> A good man harried in his dark distraction
> Can still perceive the ways of righteousness.

MEPHISTOPHELES:

330   All right! It won't be any long transaction.
> I have no fears at all for my bet's sake.
> And once I've won, let it be understood
> You will admit my triumph as you should.
> Dust shall he eat, and call it good,
> Just like my aunt,[2] the celebrated snake.

THE LORD:

> There too feel wholly free to try;
> Toward your kind I have borne no hate.
> Of all the spirits that deny,
> The scoffer burdens me with slightest weight.
340   Man's activeness can all too easily go slack,
> He loves to be in ease unqualified;
> Hence I set a companion at his side

---

[2] aunt: Usually translated "cousin," an allusion to Satan.

To goad him like a devil from the back.
     But you, true sons of gods, may you
Rejoice in beauty that is full and true!
May that which is evolving and alive
Encompass you in bonds that Love has wrought;
And what exists in wavering semblance, strive
To fix in final permanence of thought.

[*The heavens close, the* ARCHANGELS *disperse.*]

MEPHISTOPHELES:

350   From time to time I like to see the Boss,
And with him like to keep things on the level.
It's really nice in one of such high class
To be so decent with the very Devil.

FROM THE FIRST PART OF THE TRAGEDY

NIGHT

FAUST *restless in his chair at his desk in a narrow and high-vaulted Gothic room.*
FAUST:
I've read, alas! through philosophy,
Medicine and jurisprudence too,
And, to my grief, theology
With ardent labor studied through.
And here I stand with all my lore,
Poor fool, no wiser than before!

360   I'm Master, I'm Doctor, and with my reading
These ten years now I have been leading
My scholars on wild-goose hunts, out
And in, cross-lots, and round about—
To find that nothing can be known!
This burns my very marrow and bone.
I'm shrewder, it's true, than all the tribes
Of Doctors and Masters and priests and scribes;
Neither doubts nor scruples now can daunt me,
Neither hell nor devils now can haunt me—

370   But by the same token I lose all delight.
I don't pretend to know anything aright,
I don't pretend to have in mind
Things I could teach to improve mankind.
Nor have I lands nor treasure hoards,
Nor honors and splendors the world affords;
No dog would want to live this way!
And so I've yielded to magic's sway,
To see if spirits' force and speech
Might not bring many a mystery in reach;

380   So I no longer need to go
On saying things that I don't know;
So I may learn the things that hold
The world together at its core,
So I may potencies and seeds behold,
And trade in empty words no more.
      O if, full moon, you did but shine
Your last upon this pain of mine,
Whom I have watched ascending bright
Here at my desk in mid of night;
390   Then over books and papers here,
Sad friend, you would come into view.
Ah, could I on some mountain height
Rove beneath your mellow light,
Drift on with spirits round mountain caves,
Waft over meadows your dim light laves,
And, clear of learning's fumes, renew
Myself in baths of healing dew!
      Am I still in this prison stall?
Accursed, musty hole-in-the-wall,
400   Where the very light of heaven strains
But dully through the painted panes!
      By these enormous book-piles bounded
Which dust bedecks and worms devour,
Which are by sooty charts surrounded
Up to the vaultings where they tower;
With jars shelved round me, and retorts,
With instruments packed in and jammed,
Ancestral junk together crammed—
Such is your world! A world of sorts!
410   Do you still wonder why your heart
Is choked with fear within your breast?
Why nameless pain checks every start
Toward life and leaves you so oppressed?
Instead of Nature's living sphere
Wherein God placed mankind of old,
Brute skeletons surround you here
And dead men's bones and smoke and mold.
      Flee! Up! And out into the land!
Does not this mystic book indeed,
420   From Nostradamus'[3] very hand,
Give all the guidance that you need?

---

[3] **Nostradamus:** French astrologer and physician Michel de Notredame (1503–1566).

Then you will recognize the courses
Of stars; within you will unfold,
At Nature's prompting, your soul's forces
As spirits speech with spirits hold.
In vain this arid brooding here
The sacred signs to clarify —
You spirits who are hovering near,
If you can hear me, give reply!

[*He opens the book and glimpses the sign of the macrocosm.*]

430 Ha! Suddenly what rapture at this view
Goes rushing through my senses once again!
I feel a youthful joy of life course new
And ardent through my every nerve and vein.
Was it a god who wrote these signs whereby
My inward tempest-rage is stilled
And my poor heart with joy is filled
And with a mystic impulse high
The powers of Nature all around me are revealed?
Am I a god? I feel so light!

440 In these pure signs I see the whole
Of operative Nature spread before my soul.
Now what the wise man says I understand aright:
"The spirit world is not locked off from thee;
Thy heart is dead, thy mind's bolt drawn!
Up, scholar, and bathe cheerfully
Thy earthly breast in rosy dawn!"

[*He contemplates the sign.*]

How all things interweave to form the Whole,
Each in another finds its life and goal!
How each of heaven's powers soars and descends

450 And each to each the golden buckets lends;
On fragrant-blessed wings
From heaven piercing to earth's core
Till all the cosmos sweetly rings!
  O what a sight! — A sight, but nothing more!
Where can I grasp you, Nature without end?
You breasts, where? Source of all our lives,[4]
On which both heaven and earth depend,
Toward you my withered heart so strives —
You flow, you swell, and must I thirst in vain?

---

[4]**You . . . lives:** The image is that of a mother-earth goddess, perhaps like the ancient Diana of Ephesus, who was represented with innumerable breasts that gave suck to all creatures.

[Impatiently he turns pages of the book and glimpses the sign of the Earth Spirit.]

460   How differently I am affected by this sign!
You, Spirit of the Earth, are nearer me,
I feel more potent energy,
I feel aglow as with new wine.
I feel the strength to brave the world, to go
And shoulder earthly weal and earthly woe,
To wrestle with the tempests there,
In shipwreck's grinding crash not to despair.
Clouds gather over me —
The moon conceals its light —
470   The lamp has vanished!
Mists rise! — Red lightnings dart and flash
About my head — Down from
The vaulted roof cold horror blows
And seizes me!
Spirit implored, I feel you hovering near.
Reveal yourself!
O how my heart is rent with fear!
With new emotion
My senses riot in wild commotion!
480   My heart surrenders to you utterly!
You must! You must! though it cost life to me!

[He seizes the book and mystically pronounces the sign of the Spirit. A reddish flame flashes. The spirit appears in the flame.]

SPIRIT:
    Who calls me?

FAUST [*cowering*]:
            Ghastly shape!

SPIRIT:
                    With might
You have compelled me to appear,
You have long sucked about my sphere,
Now —

FAUST:
      No! I cannot bear the sight!

SPIRIT:
    You begged so breathlessly to bring me near
To hear my voice and see my face as well;
I bow before your strong compulsive spell,
And here I am! — What childish fear
490   Besets you, superman! Where is the soul that cried?
Where is the heart that made and bore a world inside
Itself and sought amid its gleeful pride
To be with spirits equal and allied?

> Where are you, Faust, whose voice called out to me,
> Who forced yourself on me so urgently?
> Are you the one who, having felt my breath,
> Now tremble to your being's depth,
> A terrified and cringing worm?

FAUST:

> Shall I give way before you, thing of flame?
500 > I am your equal. Faust is my name!

SPIRIT:

> In tides of life, in action's storm
> *I* surge as a wave,
> Swaying ceaselessly;
> Birth and the grave,
> An endless sea,
> A changeful flowing,
> A life all glowing:
> I work in the hum of the loom of time
> Weaving the living raiment of godhead sublime.

FAUST:

510 > O you who roam the world from end to end,
> Restless Spirit, I feel so close to you!

SPIRIT:

> You are like the spirit you comprehend,
> Not me!

[Disappears.]

FAUST [*overwhelmed*]:

> Not you?
> Whom then?
> I, image of the godhead!
> Not even rank with you!

[A knock.]

> God's death! I know who's there — my famulus[5] —
> This puts an end to my great joy!
520 > To think that dry-bones should destroy
> The fullness of these visions thus!

[Enter WAGNER *in a dressing gown and nightcap, a lamp in his hand.* FAUST *turns around impatiently.]*

WAGNER:

> Excuse me! I heard you declaiming;
> It surely was a Grecian tragedy?
> There I would like some more proficiency,

---

[5] **famulus:** A graduate assistant to a professor.

Today it gets so much acclaiming.
I've sometimes heard it said a preacher
Could profit with an actor for a teacher.

FAUST:

Yes, if the preacher is an actor too,
As may on some occasions be the case.

WAGNER:

530   Oh, cooped up in one's museum all year through
And hardly seeing folks except on holidays,
Hardly by telescope, how can one find
Persuasive skills wherewith to guide mankind?

FAUST:

Unless you feel it you will not succeed;
Unless up from your soul it wells
And all your listeners' hearts compels
By utmost satisfaction of a need,
You'll always fail. With paste and glue,
By grinding others' feasts for hash,
540   By blowing your small flame up too
Above your paltry pile of ash,
High praise you'll get in apes' and children's sight,
If that's what suits your hankering—
But heart with heart you never will unite
If from your heart it does not spring.

WAGNER:

Delivery makes the speaker's real success,
And that's just where I feel my backwardness.

FAUST:

Try for an honest win! Why rail
Like any bell-loud fool there is?
550   Good sense and reason will prevail
Without a lot of artifice.
If you have serious things to say,
Why hunt for words out of your way?
Your flashy speeches on which you have pinned
The frilly cutouts of men's artistry
Are unrefreshing as the misty wind
That sighs through withered leaves autumnally!

WAGNER:

Oh Lord! How long is art,
How short our life! And ever
560   Amid my work and critical endeavor
Despair besets my head and heart.
How difficult the means are to come by
That get one back up to the source,

And then before one finishes mid-course,
Poor devil, one must up and die.

FAUST:

Is that the sacred font, a parchment roll,
From which a drink will sate your thirst forever?
Refreshment will delight you never
Unless it surges up from your own soul.

WAGNER:

570　But what delight there is in pages
That lead us to the spirit of the ages!
In seeing how before us wise men thought
And how far glorious progress has been brought.

FAUST:

O yes, up to the furthest star!
My friend, the eras and past ages are
For us a book with seven seals.[6]
What you the spirit of the ages call
Is only those men's spirits after all
Held as a mirror that reveals
580　The times. They're often just a source of gloom!
You take one look at them and run away.
A trash can and a littered storage room,
At best a plot for some heroic play
With excellent pragmatic saws
That come resoundingly from puppets' jaws.

WAGNER:

But then the world! The mind and heart of man!
To learn about those things is our whole aim.

FAUST:

Yes, call it learning if you can!
But who dares call a child by its right name?
590　The few who such things ever learned,
Who foolishly their brimming hearts unsealed
And to the mob their feelings and their thoughts revealed,
Were in all ages crucified or burned.
But it is late into the night, my friend,
We must break off now for the present.

WAGNER:

I would have liked to stay awake and spend
The time in talk so learned and so pleasant.
But since tomorrow will be Easter Day,
I'll ask some further questions if I may.

----

[6] **book . . . seals:** See Revelation 5:1.

600 I have industriously pursued my studying;
I know a lot, but would like to know everything.

[*Exit.*]

FAUST [*alone*]:
Why hope does not abandon all such brains
That cling forever to such shallow stuff!
They dig for treasure and are glad enough
To turn up angleworms for all their pains!
    May such a human voice presume to speak
Where spirits closed around me in full ranks?
And yet for this one time I give you thanks,
Of all earth's sons the poorest and most weak.
610 You pulled me back from the despair and panic
That threatened to destroy my very mind.
That vision loomed so vast and so titanic
That I felt dwarfed and of the dwarfish kind.
    I, image of the godhead, who supposed
Myself so near eternal verity,
Who reveled in celestial clarity,
My earthly substance quite deposed,
I, more than cherub, whose free strength presumed
To flow through Nature's veins, myself creating,
620 Thereby in godlike life participating,
How I must pay for my expostulating!
There by a word of thunder I was consumed!
    Your equal I dare not pretend to be;
If I had power to make you come to me,
I did not have the power to make you stay.
In that brief moment's ecstasy
I felt so small and yet so great;
You thrust me backwards cruelly
To my uncertain human fate.
630 Who will instruct me? What must I not do?
Should I give every impulse play?
Alas, our very actions, like our sorrows too,
Build obstacles in our life's way.
    On the most glorious things mind can conceive
Things strange and ever stranger force intrusion;
Once we the good things of this world achieve,
We term the better things cheat and delusion.
The noble feelings that conferred our life
Are paralyzed amid our earthly strife.
640   If Fantasy once soared through endless space
And hopefully aspired to the sublime,
She is content now with a little place

When joys have foundered in the gulf of time.
Deep down within the heart Care builds her nest
And causing hidden pain she broods,
And brooding restlessly she troubles joy and rest;
Assuming ever different masks and moods,
She may appear as house and home, as child, as wife,
As poison, dagger, flood, or fire;
650   You dread what never does transpire,
And what you never lose you grieve for all your life.
        I am not like the gods! Too sharp I feel that thrust!
I am more like the worm that burrows in the dust,
That living there and finding sustenance
Is crushed beneath a passing foot by chance.
        Is all of this not dust that these walls hold
Upon their hundred shelves oppressing me?
The rubbish which with nonsense thousandfold
Confines me in this world of moths distressfully?
660   Should I find *here* the things I need?
When in perhaps a thousand books I read
That men have been tormented everywhere,
Though one may have been happy here and there?—
What is your grinning message, hollow skull,
But that your brain, like mine, once sought the day
In all its lightness, but amid the twilight dull,
Lusting for truth, went miserably astray?
And all you instruments make fun of me
With wheel and cog and drum and block:
670   I stood before the door, you should have been the key;
Your wards are intricate but do not turn the lock.
Mysterious in broad daylight,
Nature's veil can not be filched by you,
And what she keeps back from your prying spirit's sight
You will not wrest from her by lever or by screw.
You old contrivances unused by me,
You served my father's needs, hence here you stay.
You, ancient scroll, have blackened steadily
As long as dull lamps on this desk have smoked away.
680   Better if I had squandered my small estate
Than sweat and by that little be oppressed!
Whatever you inherit from your late
Forebears, see that it is possessed.
Things unused are a burden of great weight;
The hour can use what it alone creates, at best.
        But why does my gaze fix on that spot over there?
Is that small bottle then a magnet to my eyes?

Why is all suddenly so bright and fair
As when in a dark wood clear moonlight round us lies?
690   Rare phial, I salute you as I draw
You down with reverence and with awe.
In you I honor human skill and art.
You essence of all lovely slumber-flowers,
You extract of all subtle deadly powers,
Unto your master now your grace impart!
I see you, and my suffering is eased,
I clasp you, and my strugglings have ceased,
The flood tide of my spirit ebbs away.
To open seas I am shown forth by signs,
700 Before my feet the mirror-water shines,
And I am lured to new shores by new day.
      A fiery chariot comes on airy pinions
Down toward me! I feel ready now and free
To rise by new paths unto aether's wide dominions,
To newer spheres of pure activity.
This higher life! This godlike ecstasy!
And you, but now a worm, have you acquired such worth?
Yes, only turn your back decisively
Upon the lovely sun of earth!
710 By your presumptuous will, fling wide the portals
Past which each man would rather slink away.
Now is the time to prove by deeds that mortals
Yield not to gods in dignity's array:
To shrink not back from that dark cavern where
Imagination sees itself to torment damned,
To press on toward that thoroughfare
Around whose narrow mouth all hell is spanned:
To take that step with cheer, to force egress—
Though at the risk of passing into nothingness.
720   Come down, you glass of crystal purity,
Come forth out of your ancient case to me
Who have not thought of you these many years.
You used to gleam amid my father's feasts
And used to gladden earnest guests
As you were passed from hand to hand with cheers.
Your gorgeous braid of pictures deftly twined,
The drinker's pledge to tell of them in rhyme
And drain your hollow rondure at one time,
These bring back many youthful nights to mind;
730 I shall not this time pass you to a neighbor,
To prove my wit upon your art I shall not labor;
Here is a juice that makes one drunk with no delay.

Its brownish liquid streams and fills your hollow.
This final drink which now shall follow,
Which I prepared and which I choose to swallow,
Be it a festive high salute to coming day!

[He lifts the glass to his lips.]
[A peal of bells and choral song.]
CHORUS OF ANGELS:
    Christ is arisen!
    Joy to the mortal
    Whom the pernicious
740   Lingering, inherited
    Dearths encompassed.

FAUST:
    What bright clear tone, what whirring drone profound
    Makes me put this glass from my lips away?
    Do you deep bells already sound
    The solemn first hour of the Easter Day?
    Do you choirs sing the song that once such comfort gave
    When angels sang it by the darkness of a grave
    Assuring a new covenant that day?

CHORUS OF WOMEN:
    With spices enbalmed
750   Here we had carried Him,
    We, His devoted,
    Here we had buried Him;
    With winding cloths
    Cleanly we wrapped Him;
    But, alas, we find
    Christ is not here.

CHORUS OF ANGELS:
    Christ is arisen!
    Blessed the loving
    Who stood the troubling,
760   Stood the healing,
    Chastening test.

FAUST:
    Why seek here in the dust for me,
    You heavenly tones so mighty and so mild?
    Ring out around where gentle souls may be.
    I hear your tidings but I lack for faith,
    And Miracle is Faith's most favored child.
    As high as to those spheres I dare not soar
    Whence sound these tidings of great joy;
    Yet by these sounds, familiar since I was a boy,
770   I now am summoned back to life once more.

Once there would downward rush to me the kiss
Of heavenly love in solemn Sabbath hour;
Then plenitude of bell tones rang with mystic power
And prayer had the intensity of bliss;
Past comprehension sweet, a yearning
Drove me to wander field and forest where
Amid a thousand hot tears burning
I felt a world arise which was most fair.
The merry games of youth are summoned by that song,
780   And free delight of springtime festival;
And by that memory with childlike feeling strong
I am kept from this final step of all.
Sing on, sweet songs, in that celestial strain!
A teardrop falls, the earth has me again!

CHORUS OF DISCIPLES:
    If from the dead
    He has ascended,
    Living, sublime,
    Glorious on high,
    If He in His growth
790   Nears creative joy,
    We, alas, are still here
    On the bosom of earth.
    He has left His own
    Behind here to languish,
    Master, we mourn
    Thy happiness.

CHORUS OF ANGELS:
    Christ is arisen
    From the womb of decay;
    Bonds that imprison
800   You, rend gladsome away!
    For you as you praise Him,
    Proving your love,
    Fraternally sharing,
    Preaching and faring,
    Rapture proclaiming,
    For you the Master is near,
    For you He is here.

OUTSIDE THE CITY GATE

All sorts of people coming out for a walk.
SEVERAL APPRENTICES:
    But why go up the hill?

OTHERS:
> We're going to the Hunting Lodge up there.

THE FIRST ONES:
810
> We'd rather walk out to the Mill.

ONE APPRENTICE:
> I'd suggest you go to the Reservoir.

THE SECOND:
> It's not a pleasant walk, you know.

OTHERS:
> How about you?

A THIRD:
> I'll go where the others go.

A FOURTH:
> Come on to Burgdorf! There you're sure to find good cheer,
> The prettiest girls and also first-rate beer,
> And the best fights you'll ever face.

A FIFTH:
> You glutton, do you itch to go
> For your third drubbing in a row?
> I have a horror of that place.

SERVING GIRL:
820
> No, no! I'm going back now, if you please.

ANOTHER:
> We'll surely find him standing by those poplar trees.

THE FIRST GIRL:
> For me that's no great lucky chance;
> He'll walk at your side and he'll dance
> With none but you upon the lea.
> What good will your fun be to me?

THE OTHER GIRL:
> He won't be there alone today; he said
> He'd bring along the curlyhead.

SCHOLAR:
> Damn! How those lusty wenches hit their stride!
> Brother, come on! We'll walk it at their side.
830
> Strong beer, tobacco with a bite,
> A girl decked in her best, just suit my appetite.

GIRL OF THE MIDDLE CLASS:
> Just see those handsome boys! It certainly
> Is just a shame and a disgrace;
> They could enjoy the very best society,
> And after serving girls they chase.

SECOND SCHOLAR [*to the* FIRST]:
> Don't go so fast! Behind us are two more,
> Both very nicely dressed;
> One is my neighbor from next door

In whom I take an interest.
840 They walk demurely, but you'll see
How they will overtake us finally.

THE FIRST:
No, Brother, I don't like things in my way.
Quick! Let's not lose these wildfowl on our chase.
The hand that wields the broom on Saturday
On Sunday will provide the best embrace.

CITIZEN:
No, this new burgomaster, I don't care for him,
And now he's in, he daily gets more grim.
And for the city, what's he done?
Don't things get worse from day to day?
850 More rules than ever to obey,
And taxes worse than any yet, bar none.

BEGGAR [*sings*]:
Kind gentlemen and ladies fair,
So rosy-cheeked and gay of dress,
Be good enough to hear my prayer,
Relieve my want and my distress.
Let me not vainly tune my lay.
Glad is the giver and only he.
Now that all men keep holiday,
Be there a harvest day for me.

ANOTHER CITIZEN:
860 There's nothing better for Sunday or a holiday
Than talk about war and war's alarms,
When off in Turkey people up in arms
Are battling in a far-off fray.
You sip your glass, stand by the window side,
And down the river watch the painted vessels glide,
Then come home in the evening all at ease,
Blessing peace and the times of peace.

THIRD CITIZEN:
Yes, neighbor, that's the way I like it too:
Let them beat out each other's brains,
870 Turn everything up wrong-end-to,
So long as here at home our good old way remains.

OLD WOMAN [*to the* MIDDLE-CLASS GIRLS]:
Heyday! How smart! My young and pretty crew!
Now who could help but fall for you? —
But don't act quite so proud. You'll do!
And what you're after, I could help you to.

MIDDLE-CLASS GIRL:
Come, Agatha! I don't want to be seen
In public with such witches. It's quite true

My future lover last Saint Andrew's E'en
In flesh and blood she let me view[7] —

THE OTHER GIRL:

880   She showed me mine too in her crystal glass,
A soldier type, with dashing friends behind him;
I look for him in every one I pass
And yet I just don't seem to find him.

SOLDIERS:

Castles and towers,
Ramparts so high,
Girls of disdainful
Scorn-casting eye,
I'd like to win!
Keen is the contest,
890   Grand is the pay!
        We'll let the trumpets
Sound out the call,
Whether to joy
Or to downfall.
There's an assault!
That is the life!
Maidens and castles
Surrender in strife.
Keen is the contest,
900   Grand is the pay!
And then the soldiers
Go marching away.

[*Enter* FAUST *and* WAGNER.]

FAUST:

From ice are released the streams and brooks
At springtime's lovely, life-giving gaze;
Now hope smiles green down valley ways;
Old Winter feebly flees to nooks
Of rugged hills, and as he hies
Casts backward from him in his flight
Impotent showers of gritty ice
910   In streaks over meadows newly green.
But the sun permits of nothing white,
Everything is growth and striving,
All things are in colors reviving,

---

[7] My . . . view: On November 30 Saint Andrew, the patron saint of the unmarried, offers visions of future lovers and spouses.

And lack of flowers in the countryside
By gay-clad humans is supplied.
Turn and from these heights look down
And backwards yonder toward the town.
From the hollow, gloomy gate
Streams a throng in motley array.

920   All want to sun themselves today.
The Lord's resurrection they celebrate
For they are themselves new risen from tombs:
From squalid houses' dingy rooms,
From tradesman's and apprentice' chains,
From crushing streets and choking lanes,
From roof's and gable's oppressive mass,
From their churches' everlasting night,
They are all brought forth into the light.
See now, just see how swiftly they pass

930   And scatter to fields' and gardens' grass
And how so many merry boats
The river's length and breadth there floats,
How almost sinking with its load
That last barque pushes from the quay.
From even the hillside's distant road
Bright costumes glimmer colorfully.
Sounds of village mirth arise,
Here is the people's true paradise.
Both great and small send up a cheer:

940   "Here I am human, I can *be* human here!"
WAGNER:
Doctor, to take a walk with you
Is an honor and a gain, of course,
But come here alone, that I'd never do,
Because I am a foe of all things coarse.
This fiddling, shouting, bowling, I detest
And all that with it goes along;
They rage as if by fiends possessed
And call it pleasure, call it song!

[*Peasants under the linden tree. Dance and song.*]
The shepherd for the dance got dressed

950   In wreath and bows and fancy vest,
And bravely did he show.
Beneath the linden lass and lad
Were dancing round and round like mad.
Juchhe! Juchhe!
Juchheisa! Heisa! He!

So went the fiddlebow.
    In through the crowd he pushed in haste
And jostled one girl in the waist
All with his sharp elbow.
960   The buxom lass, she turned her head,
"Well, that was stupid, now!" she said.
Juchhe! Juchhe!
Juchheisa! Heisa! He!
"Don't be so rude, fine fellow!"
    The ring spun round with all its might,
They danced to left, they danced to right,
And see the coattails go!
And they got red, and they got warm,
And breathless waited arm in arm,
970   Juchhe! Juchhe!
Juchheisa! Heisa! He!
A hip against an elbow.
    "Don't be so free! How many a maid
Has been betrothed and been betrayed
By carrying on just so!"
And yet he coaxed her to one side,
And from the linden far and wide
Juchhe! Juchhe!
Juchheisa! Heisa! He!
980   Rang shout and fiddlebow.

OLD PEASANT:

Doctor, it's really nice of you
Not to shun our mirth today,
And such a learnèd master too,
To mingle with the folk this way.
Therefore accept our finest stein
Filled with cool drink and let me first
Present it with this wish of mine:
May it not only quench your thirst—
May all its count of drops be added to
990   The sum of days that are allotted you.

FAUST:

I take the cooling drink you offer me
And wish you thanks and all prosperity.

[*The people gather around in a circle.*]

OLD PEASANT:

Indeed it was most kind of you
On this glad day to come here thus,
For in the evil days gone by

You proved a friend to all of us.
Many a man is here alive
Because your father in the past
Saved him from raging fever's fury
1000 When he had stemmed the plague at last.
And as a young man you went too
Among the houses of the pest;
Many a corpse they carried out
But you came healthy from the test.
You bore up under trials severe;
The Helper yonder helped the helper here.

ALL:

Good health attend the proven man,
Long may he help, as help he can!

FAUST:

Bow to Him yonder who provides
1010 His help and teaches help besides.

[*He walks on with* WAGNER.]

WAGNER:

What feelings must be yours, O noble man,
Before the veneration of this crowd!
O fortunate indeed is one who can
So profit from the gifts with which he is endowed!
The fathers show you to their sons,
Each asks and pushes in and runs,
The fiddle stops, the dancer waits,
They stand in rows where you pass by,
And all their caps go flying high:
1020 A little more and they would bend the knee
As if there passed the Venerabile.

FAUST:

Only a few steps more now up to yonder stone
And we shall rest from our long walk. Up there
I often used to sit and brood alone
And rack myself with fasting and with prayer.
Then rich in hope, in faith secure,
By wringing of hands, by tears and sighs,
I sought the plague's end to assure
By forcing the Lord of the skies.
1030 Praise sounds like mockery on the people's part.
If you could only read within my heart
How little father and son
Were worthy of the fame they won!
My father was a man of honor but obscure

Who over Nature and her holy spheres would brood
In his own way and with capricious mood,
Though wholly upright, to be sure.
With other adepts of the art he locked
Himself in his black kitchen and from lists
1040 Of endless recipes sought to concoct
A blend of the antagonists.[8]
There a Red Lion — a wooer to aspire —
Was in a warm bath with the Lily wed,
And both were then tormented over open fire
From one into the other bridal bed.
If the Young Queen was then espied
In rainbow hues within the flask,
There was our medicine; the patients died,
And "Who got well?" none thought to ask.
1050 Thus we with hellish tonics wrought more ills
Among these valleys and these hills,
And raged more fiercely, than the pest.
I gave the poison out to thousands with my hand;
They withered, and I have to stand
And hear the ruthless killers blessed.

WAGNER:
How can such things make you downcast?
Has not a good man done sufficient
In being conscientious and proficient
At skills transmitted from the past?
1060 If you respect your father in your youth,
You will receive his fund of knowledge whole;
If as a man you swell the store of truth,
Your son can then achieve a higher goal.

FAUST:
O happy he who still can hope
To rise out of the sea of errors here!
What one most needs to know exceeds his scope,
And what one knows is useless and unclear.
But let us not spoil hours that are so fair
With these dark melancholy thoughts of mine!
1070 See how beneath the sunset air
The green-girt cottages all shine.
The sun moves on, the day has spent its force,

---

[8] Using actual sixteenth-century terms, Goethe describes the manufacture of "the Philosopher's Stone" in an alchemist's laboratory ("black kitchen").

Yonder it speeds, new day eliciting.
O that I am swept upward on no wing
To follow it forever in its course!
Then I would see by deathless evening rays
The silent world beneath my feet,
All valleys calmed, all mountaintops ablaze,
And silver brooks with golden rivers meet.
1080 No mountains then would block my godlike flight
For all the chasms gashed across their ways;
And soon the sea with its warmed bays
Would open to my wondering sight.
But now the goddess seems to sink down finally;
But a new impulse wakes in me,
I hasten forth to drink her everlasting light,
With day in front of me and at my back the night,
With waves down under me and over me the sky.
A glorious dream, dreamed while the day declined.
1090 Alas, that to the pinions of the mind
No wing corporeal is joined as their ally.
And yet inborn in all our race
Is impulse upward, forward, and along,
When overhead and lost in azure space
The lark pours forth its trilling song,
When over jagged pine tree heights
The full-spread eagle wheels its flights,
And when across the seas and plains
Onward press the homing cranes.

WAGNER:
1100 I have had moody hours of my own,
But such an impulse I have never known.
The spectacle of woods and fields soon cloys,
I'll never envy birds their pinionage;
But how we *are* borne on by mental joys
From book to book, from page to page!
How sweet and fair the winter nights become,
A blessed life glows warm in every limb,
And oh! if one unrolls a noble parchment tome,
The whole of heaven then comes down to him.

FAUST:
1110 By one impulse alone are you possessed,
O may you never know the other!
Two souls abide, alas, within my breast,
And each one seeks for riddance from the other.
The one clings with a dogged love and lust

With clutching parts unto this present world,
The other surges fiercely from the dust
Unto sublime ancestral fields.
If there are spirits in the air
Between the earth and heaven holding sway,
Descend out of your golden fragrance there
And to new life of many hues sweep me away!
Yes, if a magic mantle were but mine,
And if to far-off lands it bore me,
Not for all costly raiment placed before me
Would I exchange it; kings' cloaks I would decline!

1120

WAGNER:
Do not invoke that well-known troop
That stream above us in the murky air,
Who from all quarters down on mankind swoop
And bring the thousand perils they prepare.
With whetted spirit fangs down from the north
They pitch upon you with their arrowy tongues;
Out of the morning's east they issue forth
To prey with parching breath upon your lungs;
And if the south up from the desert drives
Those which heap fire on fire upon your brain,
The west brings on the swarm that first revives
Then drowns you as it drowns the field and plain.
They listen eagerly, on mischief bent,
And to deceive us, willingly comply,
They often pose as being heaven sent
And lisp like angels when they lie.
But let us go. The world has all turned grey,
The air is chill, mist closes out the day.
With nightfall one enjoys a room. —
Why do you stand and stare with wondering gaze?
What so arrests you out there in the gloom?

1130

1140

FAUST:
Do you see that black dog that through the stubble strays?

WAGNER:
He looks quite unremarkable to me.

FAUST:
Look close! What do you take the beast to be?

WAGNER:
A poodle, searching with his natural bent
And snuffing for his master's scent.

1150

FAUST:
Do you see how he spirals round us, snail-
shell-wise, and ever closer on our trail?

And if I'm not mistaken, he lays welts
Of fire behind him in his wake.

WAGNER:
    I see a plain black poodle, nothing else;
    Your eyes must be the cause of some mistake.

FAUST:
    I seem to see deft snares of magic laid
    For future bondage round our feet somehow.

WAGNER:
1160   I see him run about uncertain and afraid
    Because he sees two strangers, not his master now.

FAUST:
    The circle narrows, he is near!

WAGNER:
    You see! It's just a dog, no phantom here.
    He growls, he doubts, lies belly-flat and all,
    And wags his tail. All doggish protocol.

FAUST:
    Come here! Come join our company!

WAGNER:
    He's just a foolish pup. You see?
    You stop, and he will wait for you,
    You speak to him, and he'll jump up on you,
1170   Lose something, and he'll fetch it quick,
    Or go in water for a stick.

FAUST:
    You must be right, I see there's not a trace
    Of spirits. It's his training he displays.

WAGNER:
    A sage himself will often find
    He likes a dog that's trained to mind.
    Yes, he deserves your favor totally,
    A model scholar of the students, he.

[*They go in through the city gate.*]

STUDY ROOM

FAUST *entering with the poodle.*
FAUST:
    From field and meadow I withdraw
    Which deepest darkness now bedecks,
1180   With holy and foreboding awe
    The better soul within us wakes.
    Asleep now are my wild desires,
    My vehement activity;

The love of mankind now aspires,
The love of God aspires in me.
     Be quiet, poodle! Why should you romp and rove?
What are you snuffing there at the sill?
Go and lie down behind the stove,
I'll give you my best pillow if you're still.

1190   Out there on the hill-road back to town
You amused us by running and frisking your best;
Now accept your keep from me; lie down
And be a welcome and quiet guest.
     Ah, when in our close cell by night
The lamp burns with a friendly cheer,
Then deep within us all grows bright
And hearts that know themselves grow clear.
Reason begins once more to speak
And hope begins to bloom again,

1200   The brooks of life we yearn to seek
And to life's source, ah! to attain.
     Stop growling, poodle! With the sacred tones that rise
And now my total soul embrace,
Your animal noise is out of place.
We are accustomed to having men despise
What they do not understand;
The good and the beautiful they misprize,
Finding it cumbersome, they scowl and growl;
Must a dog, like men, set up a howl?

1210   But alas! with the best of will I feel no more
Contentment welling up from my heart's core.
Why must the stream so soon run dry
And we again here thirsting lie?
These things experiences familiarize.
But this lack can find compensation,
The supernatural we learn to prize,
And then we long for revelation,
Which nowhere burns more nobly or more bright
Than here in the New Testament. Tonight

1220   An impulse urges me to reach
Out for this basic text and with sincere
Emotion make its holy meaning clear
Within my own beloved German speech.

[*He opens a volume and sets about it.*]
    It says: "In the beginning was the *Word*."[9]
    Already I am stuck! And who will help afford?

---

[9] "In . . . *Word*.": John 1:1.

Mere word I cannot possibly so prize,
I must translate it otherwise.
Now if the Spirit lends me proper light,
"In the beginning was the *Mind*" would be more nearly right.
1230 Consider that first line with care,
The pen must not be overhasty there!
Can it be mind that makes and shapes all things?
It should read: "In the beginning was the *Power*."
But even as I write down this word too,
Something warns me that it will not do.
Now suddenly the Spirit prompts me in my need,
I confidently write: "In the beginning was the *Deed!*"
     If I'm to share this room with you,
Poodle, that howling must be curbed.
1240 And stop that barking too!
I cannot be disturbed
By one who raises such a din.
One of us must give in
And leave this cell we're in.
I hate to drive you out of here,
But the door is open, the way is clear.
But what is this I see?
Can such things happen naturally?
Is this reality or fraud?
1250 My poodle grows both long and broad!
He rises up with might;
No dog's shape this! This can't be right!
What phantom have I harbored thus?
He's like a hippopotamus
With fiery eyes and ghastly teeth.
O, I see what's beneath!
For such a mongrel of hell
The Key of Solomon works well.[10]

SPIRITS [*in the corridor*]:
Captive inside there is one of us,
1260 Stay out here, follow him none of us.
Like a fox in an iron snare
A lynx of hell is cornered in there.
But take heed!
Hover to, hover fro,
Above, below,
And pretty soon he'll be freed.

---

[10] Key of Solomon: *Solomon's Key,* or the *Clavicula Salomonis,* was a standard book used by magicians in the Middle Ages. It gave the rules for controlling spirits.

If you can help him in aught
Don't leave him caught.
Many a turn he has done
1270   Helping us every one.

FAUST:

To deal with the beast before
Me, I'll use the spell of the four:[11]
    Salamander shall kindle,
Undine shall coil,
Sylph shall dwindle;
Kobold shall toil.
    Lacking the lore
Of the elements four,
Not knowing aright
1280   Their use and might,
None shall be lord
Of the spirit horde.
    Vanish in flame,
Salamander!
Together rush and stream,
Undine!
In meteor glory gleam,
Sylph!
Bring help to the house,
1290   Incubus! Incubus!
Step forth and make an ending! Thus!
    None of the four
Lurks in the beast.
He lies and grins at me as before,
I have not harmed him in the least.
You'll hear me tell
A stronger spell.
    Do you, fellow, live
As hell's fugitive?
1300   See this sign[12] now
To which they bow,
The black hordes of hell!
    With hair abristle he starts to swell.
    Forfeiter of bliss,
Can you read this?

---

[11] **the spell of the four:** The spirits of the four elements: Fire, Water, Air, and Earth.

[12] **this sign:** The sign INRI or JNRJ, abbreviation for "Jesus the Nazarene, King of the Jews" (*Jesus Nazarenus Rex Judaeorum*), which Pilate had inscribed on the cross that held the body of Jesus at the crucifixion (John 19:19). Faust apparently holds a crucifix over the shape-shifting spirit-beast.

The never-created
Of name unstated,
Diffused through all heavens' expanse,
Transpierced by the infamous lance?
1310   Back of the stove he flees from my spells,
There like an elephant he swells,
He fills the room entire,
He melts like a mist of sleet.
Rise ceilingwards no higher!
Fall down at your master's feet.
You see that mine is no idle threat.
With sacred flame I will scorch you yet.
Await not the might
Of the triply burning light![13]
1320   Await not the sight
Of my arts in their fullest measure!

[*As the mist falls away,* MEPHISTOPHELES *steps forth from behind the stove, dressed as a traveling scholar.*]

MEPHISTOPHELES:
Why all the fuss? What is the gentleman's pleasure?

FAUST:
So this was what was in the cur!
A traveling scholar? That's the best joke I've heard yet.

MEPHISTOPHELES:
I salute you, learned Sir.
You had me in a mighty sweat.

FAUST:
What is your name?

MEPHISTOPHELES:
For one so disesteeming
The word, the question seems so small to me,
And for a man disdainful of all seeming,
1330   Who searches only for reality.

FAUST:
With gentlemen like you, their nature is deduced
Quite often from the name that's used,
As all too patently applies
When you are named Corrupter, Liar, God of Flies.[14]
All right, who are you then?

---

[13] **triply . . . light!:** The "sign" of the Trinity.

[14] **Corrupter . . . Flies:** The "Baal-Zebub the god of Ekron" of II Kings 1:2, usually etymologized as "the god of flies" or "the fly-god."

MEPHISTOPHELES:
>   Part of that Force which would
> Do evil ever yet forever works the good.

FAUST:
> What sense is there beneath that riddling guise?

MEPHISTOPHELES:
> I am the Spirit that constantly denies!
> And rightly so; for everything that's ever brought
> To life deserves to come to naught.
> Better if nothing ever came to be.
> Thus all that you call sin, you see,
> And havoc — evil, in short — is meant
> To be my proper element.

FAUST:
> You call yourself a part, yet stand quite whole before me there?

MEPHISTOPHELES:
> It is the modest truth that I declare.
> Now folly's little microcosm, man,
> Boasts *himself* whole as often as he can. . . .
> I am part of the part which once was absolute,
> Part of the Darkness which gave birth to Light,
> The haughty Light, which now seeks to dispute
> The ancient rank and range of Mother Night,
> But unsuccessfully, because, try as it will,
> It is stuck fast to bodies still.
> It streams from bodies, bodies it makes fair,
> A body hinders its progression; thus I hope
> It won't be long before its scope
> Will in the bodies' ruination share.

FAUST:
> I see your fine objectives now!
> Wholesale annihilation fails somehow,
> So you go at it one by one.

MEPHISTOPHELES:
> I don't get far, when all is said and done.
> The thing opposed to Nothingness,
> This stupid earth, this Somethingness,
> For all that I have undertaken
> Against it, still remains unshaken;
> In spite of tempest, earthquake, flood, and flame
> The earth and ocean calmly stay the same.
> And as for that damned stuff, the brood of beasts and man,
> With them there's nothing I can do.
> To think how many I have buried too!
> Fresh blood runs in their veins just as it always ran.

Line numbers: 1340, 1350, 1360, 1370

And so it goes. Sometimes I could despair!
In earth, in water, and in air
A thousand growing things unfold,
In dryness, wetness, warmth, and cold!
Had I not specially reserved the flame,
I wouldn't have a thing in my own name.

FAUST:

So you shake your cold devil's fist
1380   Clenched in futile rage malign,
So you the endless Power resist,
The creative, living, and benign!
Some other goal had best be sought,
Chaos' own fantastic son!

MEPHISTOPHELES:

We really shall give this some thought
And talk about it more anon.
Right now, however, might I go?

FAUST:

Why you should ask, I don't quite see.
Now that we've made acquaintance, though,
1390   Come any time to visit me.
Here is the window, there the doors,
The chimney too is practical.

MEPHISTOPHELES:

Must I confess? To leave this room of yours
There is a trifling obstacle.
The witch's foot[15] there on the sill—

FAUST:

The pentagram distresses you?
But tell me now, O son of hell,
If that prevents you, how did you get through?
Could such a spirit be so blind?

MEPHISTOPHELES:

1400   Observe it carefully. It's ill designed.
One point there, facing outward as it were,
Is just a bit disjoined, you see.

FAUST:

Now what a lucky chance for me!
And so you are my prisoner?
And all by merest accident!

MEPHISTOPHELES:

The poodle did not notice when in he went.

---

[15] **witch's foot:** Another term for the pentagram, a symbol made up of interlocking triangles to form a five-pointed star used to ward off evil spirits.

Things now take on a different shape:
The Devil's caught and can't escape.

FAUST:

But why not use the window to withdraw?

MEPHISTOPHELES:

1410 With devils and with spirits it's a law:
Where they slipped in, they must go out.
The first is up to us, the second leaves no doubt:
There we are slaves.

FAUST:

So hell has its own law?
I find that good, because a pact could then
Perhaps be worked out with you gentlemen?

MEPHISTOPHELES:

What once is promised, you will revel in,
No skimping and no spreading thin.
But such things can't be done so fast,
We'll speak of that when next we meet.
1420 And now I beg you first and last
To let me make my fair retreat.

FAUST:

Just for a single moment yet remain
And tell me of some pleasant news.

MEPHISTOPHELES:

No, let me go now! I'll come back again,
Then you can ask me all you choose.

FAUST:

I never had a plan so bold
As capturing you. You walked into the snare.
Whoever holds the Devil, let him hold!
A second time he will not have him there.

MEPHISTOPHELES:

1430 I am quite ready, if you choose,
To keep you company and stay,
But on condition that I use
My worthy skills to while the time away.

FAUST:

I'd like to see them, so feel free,
Just so the skills work pleasantly.

MEPHISTOPHELES:

Your senses will, my friend, gain more
In this hour than you've known before
In one whole year's monotony.
And what my dainty spirits sing you,
1440 The lovely images they bring you

Will be no empty magic play.
Your sense of smell shall be delighted,
Your sense of taste shall be excited,
And feelings will sweep you away.
No preparation shall we need;
We are assembled, so proceed!

SPIRITS:

Vanish, you gloomy
Vaultings above!
Lovelier hue
1450   Of aether's blue
Be shed in here!
O might the darkling
Clouds melt for once!
Stars begin sparkling;
Mellower suns
Shine now in here.
Sons of the air,
Of beauty rare,
Hover thronging,
1460   Wafting in light.
Ardent longing
Follows their flight.
Raiment in strands
Shed as streamer bands
Cover the lands,
Cover the groves
Where lovers vow,
Lost in reverie,
Lifelong loves.
1470   Arbors on arbors!
Lush greenery!
Masses of grapes
Tumble from vines
Into presses and vats,
Gush now as brooks
Of foaming wines,
Trickle as rills
Through gorges that wind,
Leaving the hills
1480   Far behind,
Widening to lakes
Around the abundance
Of verdant heights.
And then the birds

Drink delight,
Fly to the sun,
Fly to the bright
Islands that gleam
Drifting and glittering
1490   Upon the stream;
There we hear choirs
Of jubilant throngs,
See them on meadows,
At dances and songs,
Disporting free
In festivity;
Climbing, some,
Over the peaks,
Skimming, some,
1500   Over the lakes,
Still others fly;
All toward the high
Joy of existence,
All toward the distance
Of loving stars.

MEPHISTOPHELES:
He is asleep. Well done, my dainty, airy youngsters!
You lulled him loyally, my songsters!
I am much in your debt for such a concert.
You are not yet the man to hold the Devil fast!
1510   Around him your sweet dream illusions cast
And steep him in a sea of fancy;
But now I need a rat's tooth to divest
This threshold of its necromancy.
No lengthy incantation will be needed,
Here comes one rustling up, and my word will be heeded.
The Master of the rats and mice,
Of bedbugs, flies, and frogs and lice,
Commands you boldly to appear
And gnaw this carven threshold clear
1520   Where he has daubed a jot of oil —
Ah, there you scamper up to toil!
Get right to work! I'm hemmed in by the wedge
That's right there on the outer edge.
Just one more bite and then it's done. —
Now, till we meet again, Faustus, dream on!

FAUST [*waking*]:
Have I been once again betrayed?
The spirit throng has fled so utterly

That I but dreamed the Devil came and stayed
And that a poodle got away from me?

STUDY ROOM (II)

FAUST:

1530   A knock? Come in! Who now comes bothering me?

MEPHISTOPHELES:

         It's I.

FAUST:

              Come in!

MEPHISTOPHELES:

                    A third call there must be.

FAUST:

         Come in, then!

MEPHISTOPHELES:

                    That's the way I like to hear you.
         We shall, I trust, get on quite well,
         For I have come here to dispel
         Your moods, and as a noble squire be near you,
         Clad all in scarlet and gold braid,
         With my short cape of stiff silk made,
         A rooster feather on my hat,
         A long sharp rapier at my side,

1540   And I advise you to provide
         Yourself a costume just like that,
         So you, untrammeled and set free,
         Can find out just what life can be.

FAUST:

         No matter what might be my own attire,
         I would feel life cramped anyway.
         I am too old merely to play,
         Too young to be without desire.
         What can the world give me? Renounce,
         Renounce shalt thou, thou shalt renounce!

1550   That is the everlasting song
         Dinned in our ears throughout the course
         Of all our lives, which all life long
         Each hour sings until it's hoarse.
         Mornings I wake with horror and could weep
         Hot tears at seeing the new sun
         Which will not grant me in its sweep
         Fulfillment of a single wish, not one,
         Which mars anticipated joys
         Themselves with willful captiousness

1560   And with a thousand petty frets destroys

My eager heart's creativeness.
At nightfall I must lie down ill at ease
Upon my couch of misery where
There will be neither rest nor peace,
Wild dreams will terrify me even there.
The god that in my heart abides
Can stir my soul's profoundest springs;
He over all my energies presides
But cannot alter outward things.

1570   Existence is a weight by which I am oppressed,
With death desired, life something to detest.

MEPHISTOPHELES:
And yet Death never is a wholly welcome guest.

FAUST:
O happy he around whose brow Death winds
The blood-stained wreath in victory's radiance,
Or he whom in a girl's embrace Death finds
After the hectic whirling of the dance!
O, had I in my exultation sunk
Down dead before the lofty Spirit's power!

MEPHISTOPHELES:
And yet a brownish potion was not drunk
1580   By someone on a certain midnight hour.

FAUST:
Spying, it seems, amuses you.

MEPHISTOPHELES:
I dare
Not claim omniscience, but of much I am aware.

FAUST:
If from that harrowing confusion
A sweet familiar tone drew me away,
Belied me with a child's profusion
Of memories from a former day,
I now curse everything that holds the soul
Enchanted by the lures of sorcery
And charms it in this dreary hole
1590   By sweet illusion and duplicity!
Cursed be the lofty self-opinion
With which the mind itself deludes!
Cursed be phenomena's dominion
Which on our senses so intrudes!
Cursed be the cheating dream obsessions
With name and fame that have us so beguiled!
Cursed be what we have deemed possessions:
Servant and plow, and wife and child!

Cursed be old Mammon when with treasure
1600   He lures to deeds adventurous
Or when for idleness and pleasure
He spreads the pillows soft for us!
Cursed be the nectar of the grape!
Cursed be love at its happiest!
And cursed be hope! And cursed be faith!
And cursed be patience more than all the rest!

CHORUS OF SPIRITS [*invisible*]:
Woe! Woe!
You have destroyed
The beauteous world
1610   With mighty fist;
It crumbles, it collapses!
A demigod has shattered it!
We carry
The fragments to the void,
We grieve
For beauty so destroyed.
More mightily,
Son of earth,
More splendidly
1620   Bring it to birth,
Rebuild it in the heart of you!
Begin a new
Life course
With senses clear,
And may new songs
Hail it with cheer!

MEPHISTOPHELES:
These are the minions
From my dominions.
Precociously wise,
1630   Deeds and desires they now advise.
Out of solitude
Where senses and saps are glued,
To the wide world's view
They lure and summon you.
    Cease toying with your sorrow then,
Which tears your life as vulture-talons tear;
The worst of company makes you aware
You are a man with other men.
This does not indicate
1640   That you're to run with the pack;
I am not one of the great,

But if you want a track
Through life together with me,
I'll adapt myself quite willingly
To be yours right here and now.
I am your fellow,
If it suits you, to the grave,
I am your servant and your slave.

FAUST:
And what am I supposed to do for you?

MEPHISTOPHELES:
1650   There's lots of time before that's due.

FAUST:
No, no! The Devil is an egoist
And does not willingly assist
Another just for God's sake. I insist
You make all your conditions clear;
Such a slave is one to fear.

MEPHISTOPHELES:
I'll bind myself to be your servant *here*
And at your beck and call wait tirelessly,
If when there in the *yonder* we appear
You will perform the same for me.

FAUST:
1660   The yonder is of small concern.
Once you have smashed this world to pieces,
The other one may come to be in turn.
It is out of this earth that my joy springs
And this sun shines upon my sufferings;
Once free of them, this trouble ceases;
Then come what may and as time brings.
About all that I do not wish to hear,
Whether in future there is hate and love
And whether in that yonder sphere
1670   There is a new beneath and new above.

MEPHISTOPHELES:
In this mood you dare venture it. Just make
The compact, and I then will undertake
To turn my skills to joy. I'll give you more
Than any man has ever seen before.

FAUST:
Poor, sorry Devil, what could you deliver?
Was human mind in lofty aspiration ever
Comprehended by the likes of you?
Do you have food that does not satisfy? Or do
You have red gold that will run through

1680   The hand like quicksilver and away?
     A game that none may win who play?
     A girl who in my very arms
     Will pledge love to my neighbor with her eyes?
     Or honor with its godlike charms
     Which like a shooting star flashes and dies?
     Show me the fruit that rots right on the tree,
     And trees that every day leaf out anew!

MEPHISTOPHELES:
     Such a demand does not daunt me,
     Such treasures I can furnish you.
1690   But still the time will come around, good friend,
     When we shall want to relish things in peace.

FAUST:
     If ever I lie down upon a bed of ease,
     Then let that be my final end!
     If you can cozen me with lies
     Into a self-complacency,
     Or can beguile with pleasures you devise,
     Let that day be the last for me!
     This bet I offer!

MEPHISTOPHELES:
         Done!

FAUST:
         And I agree:
     If I to any moment say:
1700   Linger on! You are so fair!
     Put me in fetters straightaway,
     Then I can die for all I care!
     Then toll bells for my funeral,
     Then of your service you are free,
     The clock may stop, the clock hand fall,
     And time be past and done for me!

MEPHISTOPHELES:
     Consider well, we shall remember this.

FAUST:
     And that would be quite right of you.
     I have committed no presumptuousness.
1710   I am a slave no matter what I do,
     Yours or another's, we may dismiss.

MEPHISTOPHELES:
     I will begin right with your doctoral feast
     And be your slave this very day.
     For life and death's sake, though, just one thing, if I may:
     Just write a line or two at least.

FAUST:

You ask for written forms, you pedant? Can
You never have known man, or known the word of man?
Is it not enough that by the word I gave
The die of all my days is finally cast?
1720 Does not the world down all its rivers rave,
And should a promise hold me fast?
But this illusion in our hearts is set
And who has ever wanted to uproot it yet?
Happy the man whose heart is true and pure,
No sacrifice he makes will he regret!
A parchment, though, with seal and signature,
That is a ghost at which all people shy.
The word is dead before the ink is dry
And wax and leather hold the mastery.
1730 What, evil spirit, do you want from me?
Bronze, marble, parchment, paper? And then
Am I to write with stylus, chisel, or a pen?
The choice is yours and wholly free.

MEPHISTOPHELES:

Why carry on so heatedly
And force your eloquence so high?
Just any little scrap will do;
You sign it with a drop of blood.

FAUST:

If that is satisfactory to you,
We'll let it stand at that absurdity.

MEPHISTOPHELES:

1740 Blood is a juice of very special kind.

FAUST:

I'll honor this pact, you need not be afraid!
The aim of all my strength and mind
Will be to keep this promise I have made.
I puffed myself up far too grand;
In your class I deserve to be.
The mighty Spirit spurned me and
Nature locks herself from me.
The thread of thought is snapped off short,
Knowledge I loathe of every sort.
1750 Let us now sate our ardent passion
In depths of sensuality!
Let miracles of every fashion
Be brought in veils of mystery!
Let us plunge in the flood of time and chance,
Into the tide of circumstance!

Let grief and gratification,
Success and frustration
Spell one another as they can;
Restless doing is the only way for man.

MEPHISTOPHELES:

1760 There is no goal or limit set.
Snatch tidbits as impulse prompts you to,
Take on the wing whatever you can get!
And may you digest what pleases you.
Just help yourself and don't be coy.

FAUST:

But I tell you there is no talk of joy.
I vow myself to frenzy, agonies of gratification,
Enamored hatred, quickening frustration.
Cured of the will to knowledge now, my mind
And heart shall be closed to no sorrow any more

1770 And all that is the lot of human kind
I want to feel down to my senses' core,
Grasp with my mind their worst things and their best,
Heap all their joys and troubles on my breast,
And thus my self to their selves' limits to extend,
And like them perish foundering at the end.

MEPHISTOPHELES:

Believe me, many a thousand year
I've chewed this rugged food, and I well know
That from the cradle to the bier
No man digests this ancient sourdough.

1780 This whole, believe the likes of us,
For deity alone was made.
He dwells in timeless radiance glorious,
Us he has relegated to the shade,
You, day and night alone can aid.

FAUST:

But I am set on it.

MEPHISTOPHELES:

                    Easy said!
There's just one thing that could go wrong:
Time is short and art is long;
You could, I think, be taught and led.
Choose a poet for your associate,

1790 Let the gentleman's thoughts have their free bent
To heap upon your reverend pate
All noble qualities he can invent:
The lion's nobility,
The fleetness of the hind,

The fiery blood of Italy,
The Northman's steadfast mind.
Have him for you the secret find
Of magnanimity and guile combined,
Then make you fall in love by plan
1800   While youthful passions are in flame.
I'd like myself to meet just such a man,
I'd give him "Sir Microcosm" for a name.

FAUST:

What am I then, if seeking to attain
That toward which all my senses strain,
The crown of mankind, is in vain?

MEPHISTOPHELES:

You're after all — just what you are.
Wear wigs of a million ringlets as you will,
Put ell-thick soles beneath your feet, and still
You will remain just what you are.

FAUST:

1810   I feel that I have fruitlessly amassed
All treasures of the human mind,
And now when I sit down at last
No fresh strength wells within my heart, I find;
I'm not one hair's breadth taller nor one whit
Closer to the infinite.

MEPHISTOPHELES:

These matters, my good Sir, you see
Much in the ordinary light;
We must proceed more cleverly
Before life's joys have taken flight.
1820   What the Devil! You've got hands and feet,
You've got a head, you've got a prat;
Are all the things that I find sweet
Less mine for all of that?
If I can buy six stallions, can
I not call their strength also mine?
I race along and am a proper man
As if their four-and-twenty legs were mine.
Come on, then! Let this brooding be!
And off into the world with me!
1830   I tell you, any speculative fellow
Is like a beast led round and round
By demons on a heath all dry and yellow
When on all sides lies good green pasture ground.

FAUST:

But how do we begin?

MEPHISTOPHELES:

                First we will get away.
What kind of dungeon is this anyway?
What kind of life do you lead if
You bore yourself and bore the youngsters stiff?
Leave that to Neighbor Sleek-and-Slow.
Why go on threshing straw? There is no doubt

1840 The best things that you know
You dare not tell the boys about.
I hear one now out in the hall.

FAUST:

I simply cannot see him now.

MEPHISTOPHELES:

The poor lad has been waiting, after all,
And must not go uncomforted somehow.
Come, lend your cap and gown to me;
The mask will suit me admirably.

[*He changes clothes.*]

Just trust my wits and I'll succeed.
A quarter of an hour is all I need.

1850 Meanwhile get ready for your travels with all speed.

                                    [*Exit* FAUST.]

MEPHISTOPHELES [*in* FAUST's *long gown*]:

Scorn reason and the lore of mind,
Supremest powers of mankind,
Just let the Prince of Lies endow
Your strength with his illusions now
And I will have you unconditionally—
Fate has conferred on him a mind
That urges ever onward with incontinency,
Whose eager striving is of such a kind
That early joys are overleaped and left behind.

1860 I'll drag him through wild life at last,
Through shallow insipidity,
I'll make him wriggle, stultify, stick fast,
And in his insatiety
His greedy lips will find that food and drink float past.
He will vainly beg refreshment on the way.
Had his lot not been with the Devil cast,
He would go to the Devil anyway.

[*Enter a* STUDENT.]

STUDENT:

I've been here just a short time, Sir,
And come to you with deference

1870 To meet a man, and see and hear,
Of whom all speak with reverence.

MEPHISTOPHELES:
I must approve your courtesy.
A man like other men you see.
Have you inquired around elsewhere?

STUDENT:
Take me, I entreat you, in your care.
I come with fresh blood, spirits high,
And money in tolerable supply.
My mother was loath to have me go,
But I would like to learn and know.

MEPHISTOPHELES:
1880 Then this is just the place to come.

STUDENT:
Frankly, I'd rather be back home.
I feel confined within these walls,
I'm ill at ease amid these halls,
The space is cramped, you never see
Green country or a single tree.
And in these rooms with benches lined
I lose my hearing, sight, and mind.

MEPHISTOPHELES:
It all depends on habit. Right at first
The infant will not take its mother's breast,
1890 But then it finds relief from thirst
And soon it feeds away with zest.
So you to Wisdom's breast will turn
And every day more strongly yearn.

STUDENT:
I'll hang upon her neck with all affection
If you will set me in the right direction.

MEPHISTOPHELES:
First tell me, before we go on,
What course have you decided on?

STUDENT:
I want to be quite erudite;
I'd like to comprehend aright
1900 What all there is on earth, in heaven as well,
In science and in nature too.

MEPHISTOPHELES:
You're on the right track, I can tell;
Just see that nothing distracts you.

STUDENT:
With body and soul it shall be done.

But to be frank, I would like in some ways
A little freedom and some fun
On pleasant summer holidays.

MEPHISTOPHELES:

Make good use of your time, so fast it flies.
You'll gain time if you just will organize.

1910   And so, dear friend, I would advise
First off *collegium logicum*.°   a course in logic
There you will get your mind well braced
In Spanish boots[16] so tightly laced
That it will henceforth toe the taut
And cautiously marked line of thought
And not go will-o'-the-wisping out
And in, across, and round about.
They will spend days on teaching you
About how things you used to do —

1920   Like eating, drinking — just like that,
Need One! Two! Three! for getting at.
For with thought-manufactures
It's like a weaver's masterpiece:
A thousand threads one treadle plies,
The shuttles dart back to and fro,
Unseen the threads together flow,
A thousand knots one movement ties;
Then comes the philosopher to have his say
And proves things have to be this way:

1930   The first being so, the second so,
The third and fourth are so-and-so;
If first and second were absent, neither
Would third and fourth be present either.
All scholars find this very clever,
None have turned weavers yet, however.
Whoever wants to know and write about
A living thing, first drives the spirit out;
He has the parts then in his grasp,
But gone is the spirit's holding-clasp.

1940   *Encheiresin naturae*[17] chemists call it now,
Mocking themselves, they know not how.

STUDENT:

I don't just get all you imply.

---

[16] **Spanish boots:** An instrument of torture consisting of metal boots that were screwed tighter and tighter.

[17] *Encheiresin naturae:* "Nature's hand-hold," the term of J. R. Spielmann, an eighteenth-century chemist, for the power that holds biological components together in a living organism.

MEPHISTOPHELES:

    It will go better by and by,
    Once you have all these things principified
    And properly classified.

STUDENT:

    I feel as dazed by all you've said
    As if a mill wheel spun inside my head.

MEPHISTOPHELES:

    Above all else you next must turn
    To metaphysics. See that you learn
1950   Profoundly and with might and main
    What does not fit the human brain.
    For what fits in — or misfits — grand
    Resounding phrases are on hand.
    But this semester most of all
    Keep schedule, be punctual.
    You'll have five classes every day;
    Be in there on the stroke of the bell.
    See that you are prepared as well,
    With paragraphs worked up in such a way
1960   That you can see with just a look
    There's nothing said but what is in the book;
    And take your notes with dedication
    As if the Holy Ghost gave the dictation!

STUDENT:

    No second time need I be told,
    I see its usefulness all right;
    What one gets down in black and white
    One can take home and feel consoled.

MEPHISTOPHELES:

    But name your field of concentration!

STUDENT:

    I don't feel law is just the thing for me.

MEPHISTOPHELES:

1970   I cannot blame you there especially,
    Well do I know the law school situation.
    Laws are perpetrated like disease
    Hereditary in some families;
    From generation to generation they are bred
    And furtively from place to place they spread.
    Sense turns to nonsense, wise works to a mire.
    Woe that you are a grandson and born late!
    About the legal right that is innate
    In man, they do not so much as inquire.

STUDENT:

1980   You make my own aversion still more great.
    He whom you teach is fortunate.
    I'd almost take theology, in a way.

MEPHISTOPHELES:

    I wouldn't want to lead you astray.
    That branch of learning, once you do begin it,
    It's so hard to avoid the path of sin,
    There's so much hidden poison lurking in it
    And you can hardly tell this from the medicine.
    Again it's best to follow only one man there
    And by that master's statements swear.

1990   Cling hard and fast to words, in sum;
    Then through sure portals you will come
    To Certainty's own templed home.

STUDENT:

    But words must have ideas too behind them.

MEPHISTOPHELES:

    Quite so! But just don't fret too much to no avail,
    Because just when ideas fail
    Words will crop up, and timely you will find them.
    With words you can most excellently dispute,
    Words can a system constitute,
    In words you can put faith and not be shaken,

2000   And from a word not one iota can be taken.

STUDENT:

    Forgive me for so importuning you,
    But I must trouble you again.
    Would you say just a telling word or two
    About the course in medicine?
    Three years is a short time, and O my God!
    The field itself is far too broad.
    With just a little hint alone
    One feels it would not seem so great.

MEPHISTOPHELES [*aside*]:

    I've had enough of this dry tone,

2010   I've got to play the Devil straight.

[*aloud*]

    The gist of medicine is grasped with ease;
    You study through the great world and the small
    To let it go on after all
    As God may please.
    In vain you'll go a-roving scientifically,
    There each learns only what he can;

But one who grasps the moment, he
Is truly the right man.
You've got a good build on the whole,

2020   And you won't lack for impudence;
If you just have self-confidence
You'll have the trust of many a soul.
And learn to manage women, of that make sure;
For all their endless Ah!'s and Oh!'s
And thousand woes
Depend on one point only for their cure,
And if you're halfway decent about that,
You'll have them all under your hat.
First, by a title win their confidence

2030   That your skills many skills transcend,
Then you can finger every little thing and be
Welcome where others wait for years on end.
Know how to take her little pulse, and grasp her
With slyly passionate glances while you clasp her
Around her trim and slender waist
To see how tightly she is laced.

STUDENT:
Now that's more like it! The where and how I see!

MEPHISTOPHELES:
Grey, my dear friend, is all of theory,
And verdant is life's golden tree.

STUDENT:

2040   I swear it's all just like a dream to me.
Might I come back another time to sound
Your wisdom to its depths profound?

MEPHISTOPHELES:
I'll gladly do anything I may.

STUDENT:
It's just impossible to go away
Unless you take my album here and sign.
Would you do me the honor of a line?

MEPHISTOPHELES:
With pleasure.

[*He writes and gives the album back.*]
STUDENT [*reads*]:
Eritis sicut Deus, scientes bonum et malum.[18]

[*He respectfully closes the book and takes his leave.*]

---

[18] *Eritis . . . malum:* "Ye shall be as gods, knowing good and evil" (Genesis 3:5); Satan's temptation to Eve in the Garden of Eden.

MEPHISTOPHELES:

    Just follow that old saying and my cousin, the snake,

2050   And you will surely tremble for your God's-likeness' sake!

[*Reenter* FAUST.]

FAUST:

    And where do we go now?

MEPHISTOPHELES:

                    The choice is up to you.

    We'll see the small world first, and then the great one too.

    What joy, what profit will be yours

    As you sail glibly through this course!

FAUST:

    But with this long beard on my face

    I lack for easy social grace.

    This bold attempt will never work with me,

    I never could get on in company,

    In front of others I feel small and harassed,

2060   I'll be continually embarrassed.

MEPHISTOPHELES:

    Good friend, all that is needed, time will give.

    Once you have confidence, you will know how to live.

FAUST:

    How do we travel, though, and get about?

    Do you have servants, coach and pair?

MEPHISTOPHELES:

    All we need do is spread this mantle out

    And it will take us through the air.

    But see that on this daring flight

    Beginning now you travel light.

    A little fire gas I will now prepare

2070   Will lift us to the upper air,

    And if we're light, we'll go up fast from here.

    Congratulations on your new career!

    [. . .]

WITCH'S KITCHEN[19]

A large cauldron stands over the fire on a low hearth. Amid the steam rising from it various forms are seen. A MONKEY *sits by the kettle skimming it and watching that it does not boil over. The* HE-MONKEY *sits nearby with the young ones, warming himself. Walls and ceiling are hung with the most bizarre paraphernalia of witchcraft.*

---

[19] Scene V, "Auerbach's Cellar in Leipzig," in which Mephistopheles astounds some drunken students by drawing wine from a table, has been omitted.

FAUST:

    I am revolted by this crazy witchery;
    I shall be cured, you guarantee,
    In this stark raving rookery?
2340   Must I seek counsel from an aged crone?
    And will her filthy cookery
    Take thirty years off from my flesh and bone?
    Alas for me if you can nothing better find!
    Already hope has vanished, I despair.
    Has neither Nature nor a wholesome mind
    Devised a balm to cure me anywhere?

MEPHISTOPHELES:

    Ah, now, my friend, you're talking sense once more.
    There is a natural way to make you young again,
    But that is in another book, and on that score
2350   It forms a curious chapter even then.

FAUST:

    I want to hear it.

MEPHISTOPHELES:

                  Good! A way without recourse
    To money, medicine, or sorcery:
    Straight to the fields direct your course
    And start to dig immediately;
    There keep yourself and keep your mind
    Within a circle close confined,
    Eat only unadulterated food,
    Live with the beasts as beast, and count it good
    To strew the harvest field with your own dung;
2360   There is no better way, believe me,
    Up to age eighty to stay young.

FAUST:

    I am not used to that, nor could I ever stand
    To take a shovel in my hand.
    For me that narrow life would never do.

MEPHISTOPHELES:

    Well, then it's to the witch for you.

FAUST:

    But why just this old hag? What makes
    You say that *you* can't brew the cup?

MEPHISTOPHELES:

    A pretty pastime that! I could put up
    A thousand bridges in the time it takes.
2370   This work needs skill and knowledge, it is true,
    But it requires some patience too.
    A quiet mind may work for years on end

But time alone achieves the potent blend.
And as for what there may be to it,
There's many an odd ingredient.
The Devil taught her how to brew it,
But by himself the Devil cannot do it.

[*catching sight of the* ANIMALS]
    Ah, see the cute breed by the fire!
    That is the maid, that is the squire.

[*to* THE ANIMALS]
2380   Where is the lady of the house?
THE ANIMALS:
    Out of the house
    On a carouse
    Up chimney and away.
MEPHISTOPHELES:
    How long does she rampage today?
THE ANIMALS:
    Until we get our paws warm, anyway.
MEPHISTOPHELES [*to* FAUST]:
    How do you like these cunning creatures?
FAUST:
    Repulsive to the nth degree.
MEPHISTOPHELES:
    No, discourse such as this one features
    Is just the kind that most entrances me.

[*to the* ANIMALS]
2390   Now, you accursed puppets you,
    Why are you paddling in that broth, pray tell?
THE ANIMALS:
    We're cooking up some beggars' stew.
MEPHISTOPHELES:
    You'll have a good big clientele.
THE HE-MONKEY [*coming over and fawning on* MEPHISTOPHELES]:
    O roll the dice
    And make me nice
    And rich with gains!
    My lot is bad,
    But if I had
    Some money, I'd have brains.
MEPHISTOPHELES:
2400   How happy would this monkey be
    If he could play the lottery!

[*Meanwhile the young monkeys have been playing with a large globe and now roll it forward.*]

THE HE-MONKEY:
>   That is the world;
>   Spun and twirled,
>   It never ceases;
>   It rings like glass,
>   But hollow, alas,
>   It breaks to pieces.
>   Here it gleams bright,
>   And here more bright,
2410
>   Alive am I.
>   Dear son, I say
>   Keep far away,
>   For you must die.
>   It's made of clay,
>   And splinters fly.

MEPHISTOPHELES:
>   And why the sieve?

THE HE-MONKEY [*takes it down*]:
>   I'd know you if
>   You were a thief.[20]

[*He runs to the* SHE-MONKEY *and has her look through it.*]
>   Look through the sieve:
2420
>   You see the thief
>   And name him not?

MEPHISTOPHELES [*going over to the fire*]:
>   And why the pot?

THE HE-MONKEY AND THE SHE-MONKEY:
>   The silly sot!
>   Not know the pot,
>   Not know the kettle?

MEPHISTOPHELES:
>   Uncivil beast!

THE HE-MONKEY:
>   Here, take the whisk
>   And sit on the settle.

[*He has* MEPHISTOPHELES *sit down.*]

FAUST [*has all this time been standing in front of a mirror, now going up to it, now
    stepping back away from it*]:
>   What do I see with form divine
2430
>   Upon this magic mirror shine?
>   O Love, lend me the swiftest of your pinions
>   And take me off to her dominions!

---

[20]why . . . thief: Thieves were supposed to be recognizable as such when viewed through a sieve.

Unless I stand right here in this one place
And do not venture to go near,
I see her misted only and unclear —
A woman of the utmost grace!
Can any woman be so fair?
In this recumbent body do I face
The essence of all heavens here?

2440   Is there on earth the like of it?

MEPHISTOPHELES:

It's natural, if a god will six whole days expend
And then himself shout bravo! in the end,
That something smart must come of it.
Go right ahead and gaze your fill;
Just such a sweetheart I can well provide,
And lucky is the man who will
Then take her with him as his bride.

[FAUST *keeps right on looking into the mirror.* MEPHISTOPHELES *sprawls on the settle and toys with the whisk as he goes on speaking.*]

I sit here like a king upon his throne,
I hold a scepter, and I lack a crown alone.

[*The* ANIMALS, *who have been going through all kinds of odd motions helter-skelter, bring* MEPHISTOPHELES *a crown amid loud cries.*]

THE ANIMALS:

2450   O just be so good
As with sweat and blood
To glue this crown and lime it.

[*They handle the crown clumsily and break it in two pieces, then hop around with the pieces.*]

Now it is done!
We talk, look, and run,
We listen and rhyme it —

FAUST [*toward the mirror*]:

I'm going crazy here, I feel!

MEPHISTOPHELES [*pointing to the* ANIMALS]:

My own head now almost begins to reel.

THE ANIMALS:

If we have luck
And don't get stuck

2460   We'll make sense yet!

FAUST [*as before*]:

My heart is catching fire within!
Let's get away from here, and fast!

MEPHISTOPHELES [*in his previous posture*]:

This much you'll have to grant at least:
As poets they are genuine.

[*The kettle, which the* SHE-MONKEY *has left unwatched, begins to boil over. A great flame flashes up the chimney. Down through the flame comes the* WITCH *with hideous screams.*]

THE WITCH:

  Ow! Ow! Ow! Ow!
  Damnable brute! Accursed sow!
  Neglect the kettle, scorch your mate!
  Accursed beast!

[*catching sight of* FAUST *and* MEPHISTOPHELES]

  What have we here?
2470 Who are you here?
  What do you want?
  Who has sneaked in?
  Flames and groans
  Consume your bones!

[*She dips the skimmer into the kettle and scoops flames at* FAUST, MEPHISTOPHELES, *and the* ANIMALS. *The* ANIMALS *whimper.*]

MEPHISTOPHELES [*reverses the whisk he is holding and goes smashing the glasses and pots*]:

  Crash! And smash!
  There goes your trash!
  Your glassware's done!
  It's all in fun,
  I'm only beating time,
2480 Carrion, to your rhyme.

[*as the* WITCH *falls back in fury and horror*]

  You recognize me, Bone-bag? Skeleton?
  You know your master and your lord?
  What keeps me now from going on
  To pulverize you and your monkey horde!
  For my red coat you have such small respect?
  My rooster feather you don't recognize?
  Is my face hidden? Or do you expect
  I'll state my name and enterprise?

THE WITCH:

  O Sir, forgive this rude salute from me!
2490 And yet no horse hoof do I see;
  And then where is your raven pair?

MEPHISTOPHELES:

  This time I'll let you get away with it.
  It has been quite some while, I will admit,
  Since last we met. And to be fair,
  The culture that has licked the world up slick
  Has even with the Devil turned the trick.
  The northern phantom is no longer to be found;

Where will you see horns, tail, or claws around?
As for the foot, which I can't do without,
2500 It would work me much social harm, I fear;
And so, like many a young man, I've gone about
With padded calves this many a long year.

THE WITCH [*dancing*]:
I'll lose my mind for jubilation
To see Squire Satan back in circulation!

MEPHISTOPHELES:
Woman, I forbid that appellation!

THE WITCH:
Why? What harm has it ever done?

MEPHISTOPHELES:
It's long since passed to fable books and vanished.
Yet people are no better off. The Evil One
They're rid of, but their evils are not banished.
2510 Just call me Baron, that will do.
I am a cavalier like any cavalier.
You do not doubt my noble blood, and you
Can see the coat of arms that I wear here.

[*He makes an indecent gesture.*]

THE WITCH [*laughing immoderately*]:
Ha! Ha! Just like you, that I'll swear!
Oh you're a rogue, just as you always were!

MEPHISTOPHELES [*to* FAUST]:
Learn this, my friend! This is the way
To handle witches any day.

THE WITCH:
Now, gentlemen, how can I be of use?

MEPHISTOPHELES:
A good glass of the well-known juice,
2520 But of your oldest, is what I'm after;
It's years that put the powers in those brews.

THE WITCH:
Why, sure! Here is a bottle on my shelf
From which I sometimes take a nip myself
And which no longer has a trace of stink.
I'll gladly pour you out a little glass.

[*softly*]
But if this man here unprepared should drink,
You know he'll die before two hours pass.

MEPHISTOPHELES:
He's a good friend, and I mean things to thrive with him;
Give him the best your kitchen offers, serve him well.

2530   So draw your circle, speak your spell,
       And fill his cup right to the brim.

[*With bizarre gestures the* WITCH *describes a circle and places strange things inside it. Meanwhile the glasses begin to ring and the kettle to boom and make music. Finally she fetches a great book and disposes the monkeys within the circle to serve her as a lectern and to hold torches. She beckons* FAUST *to come to her.*]

FAUST [*to* MEPHISTOPHELES]:
       Now tell me, what is all this leading to?
       These frantic motions and this wild ado
       And all of this disgusting stuff
       I've known and hated long enough.

MEPHISTOPHELES:
       On, nonsense! It's just for the fun of it!
       And don't be such a prig! As a physician,
       She needs to hocus-pocus just a bit
       So that the juice can work on your condition.

[*He gets* FAUST *into the circle.*]

THE WITCH [*begins to declaim with great bombast out of a book*]:
2540   This must ye ken!
       From one take ten;
       Skip two; and then
       Even up three,
       And rich you'll be.
       Leave out the four.
       From five and six,
       Thus says the witch,
       Make seven and eight,
       And all is straight.
2550   And nine is one,
       And ten is none.
       This is the witch's one-times-one!

FAUST:
       I think the hag's in fever and delirium.

MEPHISTOPHELES:
       Oh, there is lots more still to come.
       As I well know, the whole book's in that vein.
       I've wasted much time going through its pages,
       For total paradox will still remain
       A mystery alike to fools and sages.
       My friend, the art is old and new.
2560   For ages it has been the thing to do,
       By Three and One, and One and Three,
       To broadcast error in guise of verity.
       And so they teach and jabber unperturbed;

With fools, though, who is going to bother?
Man has a way of thinking, when he hears a word,
That certainly behind it lies some thought or other.
THE WITCH [*continues*]:
   The lofty force
   Of wisdom's source
   Is from the whole world hidden.
2570   Once give up thinking,
   And in a twinkling
   It's granted you unbidden.
FAUST:
What nonsense is she spouting now before us?
My head is going to split before too long.
I feel as if I'm listening to a chorus
Of fools a hundred thousand strong.
MEPHISTOPHELES:
Enough, O worthy Sibyl! Pray, no more!
Bring on your potion now, and pour
A goblet quickly to the brim;
2580 My friend is safe, your drink won't injure him.
He is a man of many titles,
And many a dram has warmed his vitals.

[*With many ceremonies the* WITCH *pours out the drink in a goblet. As* FAUST *raises it to his mouth a little flame arises.*]
Just drink it down. Go on! You'll love
The way it makes your heart soar higher.
What! With the Devil hand-in-glove
And boggle at a little fire?

[*The* WITCH *dissolves the circle.* FAUST *steps forth.*]
Come right on out! You must not rest.
THE WITCH:
And may the dram do you much good!
MEPHISTOPHELES [*to the* WITCH]:
If you have any favor to request,
2590 Just tell me on Walpurgis,[21] if you would.
THE WITCH:
Here is a spell; say it occasionally
And you'll see strange results without a doubt.
MEPHISTOPHELES [*to* FAUST]:
Just come along, entrust yourself to me.
You must perspire now necessarily

---

[21]**Walpurgis:** The Bloksberg, highest peak of the Harz Mountains, was the traditional scene of devils' orgies on St. Walpurga's Night, April 30.

    To get the force to penetrate both in and out.
    I'll teach you later all the joys of indolence,
    And soon to your heart's pleasure you'll commence
    To feel how Cupid rises up and hops about.

FAUST:
    Just one more quick look in the mirror there!
2600   That womanly form was O! So fair!

MEPHISTOPHELES:
    No, no! For soon, alive before you here
    The paragon of women shall appear.

[*aside*]
    With that drink in you, you will find
    All women Helens to your mind.

A STREET

FAUST:
    Fair lady, may I be so free
    As to offer my arm and company?

MARGARET:
    I'm neither a lady nor fair, and may
    Go unescorted on my way.

[*She disengages herself and goes on.*]
FAUST:
    By heaven, but that child is sweet!
2610   Like none I ever chanced to meet.
    So virtuous and modest, yes,
    But with a touch of spunkiness.
    Her lips so red, her cheek so bright,
    I never shall forget the sight.
    The shy way she cast down her eye
    Has pressed itself deep in my heart;
    And then the quick and short reply,
    That was the most delightful part!

[*Enter* MEPHISTOPHELES.]
    You must get me that girl, you hear?

MEPHISTOPHELES:
2620   Which one?

FAUST:
              She just went by me here.

MEPHISTOPHELES:
    That one? She just came from the priest,
    He absolved her from her sins and all;
    I stole up near the confessional.
    She's just a simple little thing,

Went to confession just for nothing.
On such as she I have no hold.

FAUST:

And yet she's past fourteen years old.

MEPHISTOPHELES:

Why, you talk just like Jack the Rake
Who wants all flowers to bloom for his sake

2630   And fancies that no honor is,
Or favor, but the picking's his.
It doesn't always work that way.

FAUST:

Dear Master Laudable, I say
Don't bother me with your legality!
And I am telling you outright,
Unless that creature of delight
Lies in my arms this very night,
At midnight we part company.

MEPHISTOPHELES:

Remember there are limits! I

2640   Need fourteen days at least to try
And find an opportunity.

FAUST:

Had I but seven hours clear,
I wouldn't need the Devil near
To lead that girl astray for me.

MEPHISTOPHELES:

You're talking like a Frenchman. Wait!
And don't be put out or annoyed:
What good's a thing too soon enjoyed?
The pleasure is not half so great
As when you first parade the doll

2650   Through every sort of folderol
And knead and pat and shape her well,
The way that all French novels tell.

FAUST:

I've appetite enough without it.

MEPHISTOPHELES:

With no more joking now about it:
I'm telling you that pretty child
Will not be hurriedly beguiled.
There's nothing to be gained by force;
To cunning we must have recourse.

FAUST:

Get me some of that angel's attire!

2660   Lead me to her place of rest!

> Get me the kerchief from her breast,
> A garter for my love's desire!

MEPHISTOPHELES:
> Just so you see that I do heed
> Your pain and serve your every need,
> We shall not waste a single minute.
> I'll take you to her room and put you in it.

FAUST:
> And shall I see her? have her?

MEPHISTOPHELES:
>   No!
> She'll be at a neighbor's when we go.
> And all alone there you can dwell
2670
> Upon the fragrance of her cell
> And hope for future joys as well.

FAUST:
> Can we go now?

MEPHISTOPHELES:
>   It's too soon yet.

FAUST:
> Get me a gift for her, and don't forget.

> *[Exit.]*

MEPHISTOPHELES:
> What! Gifts so soon! That's fine! He'll be right in his glory!
> I know a lot of pretty places
> Where there are buried treasure cases;
> I must go through my inventory!

> *[Exit.]*

EVENING

A small, neat room. MARGARET *braiding her hair and doing it up.*

MARGARET:
> I'd give a good deal if I knew
> Who was that gentleman today!
2680
> He had a very gallant way
> And comes of noble lineage too.
> That much I could read from his face —
> Or he'd not be so bold in the first place.

> *[Exit.]*

[Enter FAUST *and* MEPHISTOPHELES.*]*

MEPHISTOPHELES:
> Come on! But softly. In you go!

FAUST *[after a silence]*:
> I beg you, leave me here alone.

MEPHISTOPHELES [*peering about*]:
 Not every girl's this neat, you know?

              [*Exit.*]

FAUST [*looking all around*]:
 Welcome, lovely twilight gloom
 That hovers in this sacred room!
 Seize on my heart, sweet love pangs who
2690 Both live and languish on hope's own dew.
 How everything here is imbued
 With stillness, order, and content!
 Here in this poverty, what plenitude!
 Here in this prison, what ravishment!

[*He throws himself into the leather armchair beside the bed.*]
 O you who have both joy and sorrow known
 From times gone by, clasp me too in your arms!
 How often at this patriarchal throne
 Children have gathered round about in swarms!
 Perhaps my sweetheart, plump-cheeked, used to stand
2700 Here grateful for a Christmas present and
 Devoutly kiss her grandsire's withered hand.
 I feel your spirit, maiden, playing
 About me, breathing order, plenitude,
 And every day in mother-fashion saying
 The cloth upon the table must be fresh renewed
 And underfoot clean sand be strewed.
 Dear hand! so godlike! In it lies
 What turns a cottage to a paradise.
 And here!

[*He lifts the bed curtains.*]
    What chill of rapture seizes me!
2710 Here I could linger on for hours.
 Here, Nature, you with your creative powers
 From light dreams brought the angel forth to be;
 Here lay the child, her bosom warm
 With life; here tenderly there grew
 With pure and sacred help from you
 The godlike image of her form.
   And you? What purpose brought you here?
 How I am touched with shame sincere!
 What do you want? Why is your heart so sore?
2720 O sorry Faust! I know you now no more.
   Does magic haze surround me everywhere?
 I pressed for pleasure with no least delay,
 And in a love dream here I melt away!

Are we the toys of every breath of air?
    If she this moment now were to come by,
What punishment your impudence would meet!
The loud-mouth lummox — O how small! — would lie
Dissolved in shame before her feet.

[*Enter* MEPHISTOPHELES.]

MEPHISTOPHELES:
    Quick now! I see her at the gate.

FAUST:

2730   Away! And never to come back!

MEPHISTOPHELES:
    Here is a casket of some weight,
I took it elsewhere from a rack.
Just put it in her clothespress there,
It'll make her head swim, that I'll swear.
I put some little baubles in it
To bait another bauble and win it.
A girl's a girl and play is play.

FAUST:
    I wonder . . . should I?

MEPHISTOPHELES:
               You delay?
You wouldn't maybe want to keep the baubles?

2740   In that case I advise Your Lust
To save my pretty daytime, just
Don't bother me with further troubles.
You are not miserly, I trust!
I scratch my head, I rub my hands —

[*He puts the casket in the clothespress and pushes the lock shut again.*]
    Off and away now!
To get that lovely child to play now
Into your heart's desires and plans.
And you stand all
Poised to proceed to lecture hall,

2750   And as if in the flesh, and grey,
Physics and Metaphysics led the way.
Come on!

                                    [*Exeunt.*]

[*Enter* MARGARET *with a lamp.*]

MARGARET:
    It's close in here, there is no air.

[*She opens the window.*]
    And yet it's not so warm out there.
I feel so odd, I can't say how —
I do wish Mother would come home now.

I'm chilled all over, and shivering!
I'm such a foolish, timid thing!

[*She begins to sing as she undresses.*]
    There was a king of Thule
2760 True even to the grave,
To whom a golden goblet
His dying mistress gave.
    Naught did he hold more dear,
He drained it every feast;
And from his eye a tear
Welled each time as he ceased.
    When life was nearly done,
His towns he totaled up,
Begrudged his heir not one,
2770 But did not give the cup.
    There with his vassals all
At royal board sat he
In high ancestral hall
Of his castle by the sea.
    The old toper then stood up,
Quaffed off his last life-glow,
And flung the sacred cup
Down to the flood below.
    He saw it fall, and drink,
2780 And sink deep in the sea;
Then did his eyelids sink,
And no drop more drank he.

[*She opens the clothespress to put her clothes away and catches sight of the jewel casket.*]
How did this pretty casket get in here?
I locked the press, I'm sure. How queer!
What can it have inside it? Can it be
That someone left it as security
For money Mother has provided?
Here on a ribbon hangs a little key—
I think I'll have a look inside it!
2790 What's this? O Lord in heaven! See!
I've never seen the like in all my days!
A noble lady with such jewelry
Could walk with pride on holidays.
I wonder how this chain would look on me?
Such glorious things! Whose could they be?

[*She puts it on and steps up to the mirror.*]
If just these earrings could be mine!
One looks so different in them right away.
What good does beauty do, young thing? It may

Be very well to wonder at,
2800   But people let it go at that;
They praise you half in pity.
Gold serves all ends,
On gold depends
Everything. Ah, we poor!

PROMENADE

FAUST *pacing up and down in thought.* MEPHISTOPHELES *comes to him.*
MEPHISTOPHELES:
Now by the element of hell! By love refused!
I wish I knew a stronger oath that could be used!
FAUST:
What's this? What's griping you so badly?
I've never seen a face the like of this!
MEPHISTOPHELES:
Why, I'd surrender to the Devil gladly
2810   If I were not the Devil as it is!
FAUST:
Have you gone off your head? I grant
It suits you, though, to rave and rant.
MEPHISTOPHELES:
Just think, those jewels for Gretchen that I got,
Some priest has made off with the lot! —
Her mother got to see the things,
Off went her dire imaginings;
That woman's got some sense of smell,
She has prayerbook-sniffing on the brain,
A whiff of any item, and she can tell
2820   Whether the thing is sacred or profane.
That jewelry she spotted in a minute
As having no great blessing in it.
"My child," she cried, "ill-gotten good
Ensnares the soul, consumes the blood.
Before Our Lady we will lay it,
With heaven's manna she'll repay it."[22]
Margretlein pulled a pouty face,
Called it a gift horse, and in any case
She thought he wasn't godless, he
2830   Who sneaked it in so cleverly.
The mother had a priest drop by;
No sooner did he the trick espy
Than his eyes lit up with what he saw.
"This shows an upright mind," quoth he,

---

[22] "heaven's . . . it": Revelation 2:17: "To him that overcometh will I give to eat of the hidden manna."

"Self-conquest gains us victory.
The church has a good healthy maw,
She's swallowed up whole countries, still
She never yet has eaten her fill.
The church, dear ladies, alone has health
2840   For digestion of ill-gotten wealth."

FAUST:

That's nothing but the usual game,
A king and a Jew can do the same.

MEPHISTOPHELES:

Then up he scooped brooch, chain, and rings
As if they were just trivial things
With no more thanks, if's, and's, or but's
Than if they were a bag of nuts,
Promised them celestial reward—
All edified, they thanked him for it.

FAUST:

And Gretchen?

MEPHISTOPHELES:

Sits lost now in concern,
2850   Not knowing yet which way to turn;
Thinks day and night about the gems,
But more of him from whom the present stems.

FAUST:

I hate to see the dear girl worry.
Get her a new set in a hurry.
The first one wasn't too much anyway.

MEPHISTOPHELES:

My gentleman finds this mere child's play.

FAUST:

And here's the way I want it. Go
Make friends there with that neighbor. Show
You're not a devil made of sugar water,
2860   Get those new gems and have them brought her.

MEPHISTOPHELES:

Sir, I obey with all my heart.

[*Exit* FAUST.]

This fool in love will huff and puff
The sun and moon and stars apart
To get his sweetheart pastime stuff.

[*Exit.*]

THE NEIGHBOR'S HOUSE

MARTHA *alone.*

MARTHA:

Now God forgive my husband, he

Has not done the right thing by me.
Way off into the world he's gone,
And leaves me on the straw alone.
Yet he surely had no cause on my part,

2870   God knows I loved him with all my heart.

[*She weeps.*]
He could be dead!—If I just knew for sure!
Or had a statement with a signature!

[*Enter* MARGARET.]
MARGARET:
Dame Martha!
MARTHA:
                          What is it, Gretelchen?
MARGARET:
My knees are sinking under me.
I've found one in my press again,
Another casket, of ebony,
And this time it's a gorgeous set
Far richer than the first one yet.
MARTHA:

2880   This time you mustn't tell your mother,
Off it would go to church just like the other.
MARGARET:
O look at them! Just see! Just see!
MARTHA [*putting them on her*]:
You *are* a lucky creature!
MARGARET:
                                    Unfortunately
In church or on the street I do not dare
Be seen in them, or anywhere.
MARTHA:
You just come over frequently,
Put on the jewels in secret here,
Walk by the mirror an hour or so in privacy,
And we'll enjoy them, never fear.
There'll come a chance, a holiday, before we're done,

2890   Where you can show them to the people one by one,
A necklace first, pearl ear-drops next; your mother
Won't notice it, or we'll make up some thing or other.
MARGARET:
But who could bring both caskets here?
There's something not quite right…

[*A knock.*]
                                          Oh, dear!
Could that be Mother coming here?

MARTHA [*looking through the blinds*]:
> It's a strange gentleman—Come in!

[MEPHISTOPHELES *steps in.*]
MEPHISTOPHELES:
> I'm so free as to step right in,
> The ladies must excuse my liberty.

[*Steps back respectfully before* MARGARET.]
> I wish to see Dame Martha Schwerdtlein, if I may.
MARTHA:
2900
> Right here! What might the gentleman have to say?
MEPHISTOPHELES [*aside to her*]:
> I know you now, that is enough for me.
> You have distinguished company.
> Forgive my freedom, I shall then
> Return this afternoon again.
MARTHA [*aloud*]:
> Child, think of it! The gentleman takes
> You for some lady! For mercy's sakes!
MARGARET:
> I'm just a poor young girl; I find
> The gentleman is far too kind.
> These gems do not belong to me.
MEPHISTOPHELES:
2910
> Oh, it's not just the jewelry.
> She has a quick glance, and a way!
> I am delighted I may stay.
MARTHA:
> What is your errand then? I'm very—
MEPHISTOPHELES:
> I wish my tidings were more merry.
> I trust you will not make me rue this meeting:
> Your husband is dead and sends you greeting.
MARTHA:
> He's dead! That faithful heart! Oh, my!
> My husband's dead! Oh! I shall die!
MARGARET:
> Dear lady, Oh! Do not despair!
MEPHISTOPHELES:
2920
> Now listen to the sad affair.
MARGARET:
> I hope I never, never love.
> Such loss as this I would die of.
MEPHISTOPHELES:
> Glad must have sad, sad must have glad, as always.

MARTHA:
>O tell me all about his dying!

MEPHISTOPHELES:
>At Padua, by Saint Anthony's
>They buried him, and he is lying
>In ground well sanctified and blest
>At cool and everlasting rest.

MARTHA:
>And there is nothing else you bring?

MEPHISTOPHELES:
2930
>Yes, one request and solemn enterprise:
>Three hundred Masses for him you should have them sing.
>My pockets are quite empty otherwise.

MARTHA:
>What, not a luck-piece, or a trinket such
>As any journeyman deep in his pack would hoard
>As a remembrance token stored
>And sooner starve or beg than use it!

MEPHISTOPHELES:
>Madam, it grieves me very much;
>Indeed he did not waste his money or lose it.
>And much did he his failings then deplore,
2940
>Yes, and complained of his hard luck still more.

MARGARET:
>To think that human fortunes so miscarry!
>Many's the Requiem I'll pray for him, I'm sure.

MEPHISTOPHELES:
>Ah, you deserve now very soon to marry,
>A child of such a kindly nature.

MARGARET:
>It's not yet time for that. Oh, no!

MEPHISTOPHELES:
>If not a husband, then meanwhile a beau.
>It's one of heaven's greatest graces
>To hold so dear a thing in one's embraces.

MARGARET:
>It's not the custom here for one.

MEPHISTOPHELES:
2950
>Custom or not, it still is done.

MARTHA:
>But tell me more!

MEPHISTOPHELES:
>   I stood at his bedside —
>Half-rotten straw it was and little more
>Than horse manure; but in good Christian style he died,

Yet found he had still further items on his score.
"How I detest myself!" he cried with dying breath,
"For having left my business and my wife!
Ah, that remembrance is my death.
If she would just forgive me in this life!" —

MARTHA [*weeping*]:
    The good man! I long since forgave.

MEPHISTOPHELES:
2960   "God knows, though, she was more to blame than I."

MARTHA:
    It's a lie! And he with one foot in the grave!

MEPHISTOPHELES:
    Oh, he was talking through his hat
    There at the end, if I am half a judge.
    "I had no time to sit and yawn," he said,
    "First children and then earning children's bread,
    Bread in the widest sense, at that,
    And could not even eat my share in peace."

MARTHA:
    Did he forget my love, how I would drudge
    Both day and night and never cease?

MEPHISTOPHELES:
2970   No, he remembered that all right.
    "As I put out from Malta," he went on,
    "I prayed for wife and children fervently;
    Then heaven too disposed things favorably
    So our ship took a Turkish galleon
    With treasure for the great Sultan aboard.
    Then bravery came in for reward
    And I got, as was only fair,
    My own well calculated share."

MARTHA:
    What! Where? Do you suppose he buried it?

MEPHISTOPHELES:
2980   Who knows where the four winds have carried it?
    A pretty girl took him in tow when he
    Was roaming Naples there without a friend;
    She showed him so much love and loyalty
    He bore the marks right to his blessed end.

MARTHA:
    The rogue! He robbed his children like a thief!
    And all that misery and grief
    Could not prevent the shameful life he led.

MEPHISTOPHELES:
    But that, you see, is why he's dead.

Were I in your place now, you know,
2990   I'd mourn him for a decent year and then
Be casting round meanwhile to find another beau.

MARTHA:
Oh Lord, the kind my first man was,
I'll never in this world find such again.
There never was a fonder fool than mine.
Only, he liked the roving life too much,
And foreign women, and foreign wine,
And then, of course, those devilish dice.

MEPHISTOPHELES:
Well, well, it could have worked out fine
If he had only taken such
3000   Good care on his part to be nice.
I swear on those terms it is true
I would myself exchange rings with you.

MARTHA:
Oh, the gentleman has such joking ways!

MEPHISTOPHELES [*aside*]:
It's time for me to be pushing onward!
She'd hold the very Devil to his word.

[*to* GRETCHEN]
How are things with your heart these days?

MARGARET:
What do you mean, Sir?

MEPHISTOPHELES [*aside*]:
                     O you innocents!
Ladies, farewell!

MARGARET:
            Farewell.

MARTHA:
                   One word yet! What I crave is
Some little piece of evidence
3010   Of when and how my sweetheart died and where his grave is.
I've always been a friend of orderliness,
I'd like to read his death note in the weekly press.

MEPHISTOPHELES:
Good woman, what two witnesses report
Will stand as truth in any court.
I have a friend, quite serious,
I'll bring him to the judge with us.
I'll go and get him.

MARTHA:
              Do that! Do!

MEPHISTOPHELES:
      This lady will be with you too?
      A splendid lad, much traveled. He

3020 Shows ladies every courtesy.

MARGARET:
      The gentleman would make me blush for shame.

MEPHISTOPHELES:
      Before no earthly king that one could name.

MARTHA:
      Out in the garden to the rear
      This afternoon we'll expect both of you here.

A STREET

FAUST:
      How is it? Will it work? Will it succeed?

MEPHISTOPHELES:
      Ah, bravo! I find you aflame indeed.
      Gretchen is yours now pretty soon.
      You meet at neighbor Martha's house this afternoon.
      The woman is expressly made

3030 To work the pimp and gypsy trade!

FAUST:
      Good!

MEPHISTOPHELES:
                  Ah, but something is required of us.

FAUST:
      One good turn deserves another.

MEPHISTOPHELES:
      We will depose some testimony or other
      To say her husband's bones are to be found
      In Padua in consecrated ground.

FAUST:
      Fine! First we'll need to do some journey-going.

MEPHISTOPHELES:
      Sancta simplicitas! For that we need not fuss.
      Just testify, and never mind the knowing.

FAUST:
      Think of a better plan, or nothing doing.

MEPHISTOPHELES:
3040 O saintly man! and sanctimonious!
      False witness then you never bore
      In all your length of life before?
      Have you not with great power given definition
      Of God, the world, and all the world's condition,

Of man, man's heart, man's mind, and what is more,
With brazen brow and with no lack of breath?
And when you come right down to it,
You knew as much about them, you'll admit,
As you know of this Mister Schwerdtlein's death!

FAUST:

3050   You are a liar and a sophist too.

MEPHISTOPHELES:

Or would be, if I didn't know a thing or two.
Tomorrow will you not deceive
Poor Gretchen and then make her believe
The vows of soul-felt love you swear?

FAUST:

And from my heart.

MEPHISTOPHELES:

                    All good and fair!
Then comes eternal faith, and love still higher,
Then comes the super-almighty desire—
Will that be heartfelt too, I inquire?

FAUST:

Stop there! It will!—If I have feeling,
3060   And for this feeling, for this reeling
Seek a name, and finding none,
With all my senses through the wide world run,
And clutch at words supreme, and claim
That boundless, boundless is the flame
That burns me, infinite and never done,
Is that a devilish, lying game?

MEPHISTOPHELES:

I still am right!

FAUST:

                    Mark this and heed it,
And spare me further waste of throat and lung:
To win an argument takes no more than a tongue,
3070   That's all that's needed.
But come, this chatter fills me with disgust,
For you are right, primarily because I must.

A GARDEN

MARGARET *on* FAUST'*s arm,* MARTHA *with* MEPHISTOPHELES, *strolling up and down.*

MARGARET:

I feel, Sir, you are only sparing me
And shaming me by condescending so.
A traveler, from charity,

Will often take things as they go.
I realize my conversation can
Not possibly amuse such an experienced man.

FAUST:
3080
One glance of yours, one word delights me more
Than all of this world's wisdom-store.

[*He kisses her hand.*]

MARGARET:
How can you kiss it? It must seem to you
So coarse, so rough a hand to kiss.
What kinds of tasks have I not had to do!
You do not know how strict my mother is.

[*They pass on.*]

MARTHA:
And so, Sir, you are traveling constantly?

MEPHISTOPHELES:
Business and duty keep us on our way.
Many a place one leaves regretfully,
But then one simply cannot stay.

MARTHA:
It may well do while in one's prime
3090
To rove about the world as a rolling stone,
But then comes the unhappy time,
And dragging to the grave, a bachelor, alone,
Was never good for anyone.

MEPHISTOPHELES:
Ah, such with horror I anticipate.

MARTHA:
Then act, dear Sir, before it is too late.

[*They pass on.*]

MARGARET:
But out of sight is out of mind!
Your courtesy comes naturally;
But you have friends in quantity
Who are more clever than my kind.

FAUST:
3100
Dear girl, believe me, clever in that sense
Means usually a close self-interest.

MARGARET:
Really?

FAUST:
To think simplicity and innocence
Are unaware their sacred way is best,

That lowliness and sweet humility
Are bounteous Nature's highest gifts—

MARGARET:
Think only for a moment's time of me,
I shall have time enough to think of you.

FAUST:
Then you are much alone?

MARGARET:
Yes, our house is a little one,
3110   And yet it must be tended to.
We have no maid, hence I must cook and sweep and knit
And sew, and do the errands early and late;
And then my mother is a bit
Too strict and strait.
And yet she has no need to scrimp and save this way;
We could live better far than others, you might say;
My father left a sizeable estate,
A house and garden past the city gate.
But I have rather quiet days of late.
3120   My brother is a soldier,
My little sister died;
The child did sometimes leave me with my patience tried,
And yet I'd gladly have the trouble back again,
She was so dear to me.

FAUST:
An angel, if like you.

MARGARET:
I brought her up; she dearly loved me too.
She was born following my father's death.
Mother we thought at her last breath,
She was so miserable, but then
She slowly, slowly got her strength again.
3130   It was impossible for her to nurse
The little mite herself, of course,
And so I raised her all alone
On milk and water; she became my own.
In my arms, in my lap she smiled,
Wriggled, and grew up to be a child.

FAUST:
You must have known the purest happiness.

MARGARET:
But many trying hours nonetheless.
At night her little cradle used to stand
Beside my bed, and she had but to stir
3140   And I was there at hand,

Sometimes to feed her, sometimes to comfort her,
Sometimes when she would not be still, to rise
And pace the floor with her to soothe her cries,
And yet be at the washtub early, do
The marketing and tend the hearth fire too,
And every morrow like today.
One's spirits are not always cheerful, Sir, that way;
Yet food is relished better, as is rest.

[*They pass on.*]

MARTHA:
    Poor women! They are badly off indeed,
3150   A bachelor is hard to change, they say.

MEPHISTOPHELES:
    Someone like you is all that I would need
    To set me on a better way.

MARTHA:
    But is there no one, Sir, that you have found?
    Speak frankly, is your heart in no wise bound?

MEPHISTOPHELES:
    The proverb says: A wife and one's own household
    Are worth their weight in pearls and gold.

MARTHA:
    But I mean, have you felt no inclination?

MEPHISTOPHELES:
    I have met everywhere with much consideration.

MARTHA:
    But has your heart in no case been impressed?

MEPHISTOPHELES:
3160   With ladies one must not presume to jest.

MARTHA:
    Oh, you misunderstand me!

MEPHISTOPHELES:
                        What a shame! I find
    I understand — that you are very kind.

[*They pass on.*]

FAUST:
    And so you did, my angel, recognize
    Me in the garden here at the first look?

MARGARET:
    Did you not see how I cast down my eyes?

FAUST:
    And you forgive the liberty I took
    And all my impudence before
    When you had just left the cathedral door?

MARGARET:
   I was confused, the experience was all new.
3170   No one could say bad things of me.
   Ah, thought I, could he possibly
   Have noted something brazen or bold in you?
   He seemed to think here was a girl he could
   Treat in just any way he would.
   I must confess that then I hardly knew
   What soon began to argue in your favor;
   But I was angry with myself, however,
   For not becoming angrier with you.
FAUST:
   My darling!
MARGARET:
          Wait!

[*She picks a star flower and plucks the petals off it one by one.*]
FAUST:
          What is it? A bouquet?
MARGARET:
3180   No, just a game.
FAUST:
          What?
MARGARET:
          You'd laugh at me if I should say.

[*She murmurs something as she goes on plucking.*]
FAUST:
   What are you murmuring?
MARGARET [*half aloud*]:
          He loves me—loves me not.
FAUST:
   You lovely creature of the skies!
MARGARET [*continuing*]:
   Loves me—not—loves me—not—

[*with delight as she reaches the last petal*]
   He loves me!
FAUST:
          Yes, my child! And let this language of
   The flowers be your oracle. He loves you!
   Do you know what that means? He loves you!

[*He takes both her hands.*]
MARGARET:
   I'm trembling!

FAUST:

      O do not tremble! Let this glance

      And let this pressure of my hands

3190   Say what is inexpressible:

      To yield oneself entirely and to feel

      A rapture that must be everlasting!

      Eternal! — Its end would be despair.

      No! Without end! Without end!

[MARGARET *presses his hands, disengages herself, and runs off. He stands in thought for a moment, then follows her.*]

MARTHA [*coming along*]:

      It's getting dark.

MEPHISTOPHELES:

                  We must be on our way.

MARTHA:

      I'd ask you gentlemen to stay,

      But this is such a wicked neighborhood.

      It seems that no one has a thing to do

      Or put his mind to

3200   But watch his neighbor's every move and stir.

      No matter what one does, there's always talk.

      What of our couple?

MEPHISTOPHELES:

                  They've flown up the arbor walk.

      The wanton butterflies!

MARTHA:

                He seems to take to her.

MEPHISTOPHELES:

      And she to him. Such is the world's old way.

A SUMMER HOUSE

MARGARET *comes running in, hides behind the door, puts her finger to her lips, and peeps through the crack.*

MARGARET:

      He's coming!

[FAUST *comes along.*]

FAUST:

                Little rogue, to tease me so!

      I'll catch you!

[*He kisses her.*]

MARGARET [*embracing him and returning his kiss*]:

      From my heart I love you so!

[MEPHISTOPHELES *knocks.*]

FAUST [*stamping his foot*]:
    Who's there?

MEPHISTOPHELES:
                 A friend!

FAUST:
                    A beast!

MEPHISTOPHELES:
                       It's time for us to go.

[MARTHA *comes along.*]

MARTHA:
    Yes, it is late, Sir.

FAUST:
                May I not escort you, though?

MARGARET:
    My mother would — farewell!

FAUST:
                     Ah, must I leave you then?

3210   Farewell!

MARTHA:
        Adieu!

MARGARET:
           But soon to meet again!

                        [*Exeunt* FAUST *and* MEPHISTOPHELES.]

    Dear Lord! What things and things there can
    Come to the mind of such a man!
    I stand abashed, and for the life of me
    Cannot do other than agree.
    A simple child, I cannot see
    Whatever it is he finds in me.

                                  [*Exit.*]

FOREST AND CAVERN

FAUST:
    Spirit sublime, thou gavest me, gavest me all
    For which I asked. Thou didst not turn in vain
    Thy countenance upon me in the fire.
3220   Thou gavest me glorious Nature for my kingdom,
    And power to feel it and enjoy it. No
    Cold, marveling observation didst thou grant me,
    Deep vision to her very heart thou hast
    Vouchsafed, as into the heart of a friend.
    Thou dost conduct the ranks of living creatures
    Before me and teachest me to know my brethren
    In quiet bush, in air, and in the water.
    And when the storm in forest roars and snarls,

And the giant fir comes crashing down, and, falling,
3230   Crushes its neighbor boughs and neighbor stems,
And hills make hollow thunder of its fall,
Then dost thou guide me to safe caverns, showest
Me then unto myself, and my own bosom's
Profound and secret wonders are revealed.
And when before my sight the pure moon rises
And casts its mellow comfort, then from crags
And rain-sprent bushes there come drifting toward me
The silvery forms from ages now gone by,
Allaying meditation's austere pleasure.
3240   That no perfection is to man allotted,
I now perceive. Along with this delight
That brings me near and nearer to the gods,
Thou gavest me this companion whom I can
No longer do without, however he
Degrades me to myself or insolently
Turns thy gifts by a breath to nothingness.
Officiously he fans a frantic fire
Within my bosom for that lovely girl.
Thus from desire I stagger to enjoyment
3250   And in enjoyment languish for desire.

[*Enter* MEPHISTOPHELES.]

MEPHISTOPHELES:
Won't you have had enough of this life presently?
How can it in the long run do for you?
All well and good to try it out and see,
But then go on to something new!

FAUST:
I do wish you had more to do
Than pester me on a good day.

MEPHISTOPHELES:
All right, then, I won't bother you.
You dare not mean that anyway.
In you, friend, gruff, uncivil, and annoyed,
3260   There's nothing much to lose, indeed.
The whole day long you keep my time employed!
But from my master's nose it's hard to read
What pleases him and what one should avoid.

FAUST:
Now there is just the proper tone!
He wants my thanks for having been annoying.

MEPHISTOPHELES:
What kind of life would you now be enjoying,

Poor son of earth, without the help I've shown?
But I have long since cured you anyhow
From gibberish your imagination talked,
3270   And if it weren't for me you would have walked
Right off this earthly globe by now.
Why should you mope around and stare
Owl-like at cave and rocky lair?
Why suck up food from soggy moss and trickling stone
Just like a toad all, all alone?
A fine sweet pastime! That stick-in-the-mud
Professor still is in your blood.

FAUST:

Can you conceive the fresh vitality
This wilderness existence gives to me?
3280   But if you could conceive it, yes,
You would be devil enough to block my happiness.

MEPHISTOPHELES:

A superterrestrial delight!
To lie around on dewy hills at night,
Clasp earth and heaven to you in a rapture,
Inflate yourself to deity's great size,
Delve to earth's core by impulse of surmise,
All six days' creation in your own heart capture,
In pride of power enjoy I know not what,
In ecstasy blend with the All there on the spot,
3290   The son of earth dissolved in vision,
And then the lofty intuition —

[*with a gesture*]

To end — just how, I must not mention.

FAUST:

O vile!

MEPHISTOPHELES:

That does not please you much; meanwhile
You have the right to speak your moral "Vile!"
Before chaste ears one must not talk about
What chaste hearts cannot do without.
All right: occasional pleasure of a lie
To yourself, is something I will not deny;
But you won't last long in that vein.
3300   Soon you will be elsewhere attracted,
Or if it goes too long, distracted
To madness or to anguished pain.
Enough of this! Your sweetheart sits there in her room,
Around her everything is gloom.

You never leave her thoughts, and she
Loves you just overwhelmingly.
Passion came to flood first on your part,
As melting snow will send a brooklet running high;
You poured all that into her heart,
3310   And now your brook is running dry.
It seems to me, instead of playing king
In woodland wilds, so great a lord
Might help the childish little thing
And give her loving some reward.
Time hangs upon her like a pall,
She stands by the window, watches the clouds along
And past the ancient city wall.
"If I were a little bird!" so goes her song
Half the night and all day long.
3320   Sometimes cheerful, mostly sad and of
No further power of tears,
Then calm again, so it appears,
And always in love.

FAUST:
    Serpent! Serpent!

MEPHISTOPHELES [*aside*]:
    Admit I've got you there!

FAUST:
    Infamous being! Begone! And do not dare
    So much as speak that lovely creature's name!
    Do not arouse desire in me to where
    Half-maddened senses burst in open flame!

MEPHISTOPHELES:
3330   What, then? She thinks you fled from her,
    And more or less that's just what did occur.

FAUST:
    I am near her, and even if I were
    Afar, I could not lose her or forget;
    The very body of the Lord, when her
    Lips touch it, rouses envy and regret.

MEPHISTOPHELES:
    My friend, I've often envied you indeed
    The twin roes[23] that among the lilies feed.

FAUST:
    Pander, begone!

---

[23] **the twin roes:** An allusion to the Song of Solomon, 4:5: "Thy two breasts are like two young roes that are twins, which feed among the lilies."

MEPHISTOPHELES:

        Fine! I laugh while you rail.

The God that created girls and boys

3340   Saw that the noblest power He enjoys

Was seeing that occasion should not fail.

Come on, then! What a shame this is!

You're going to your sweetheart's room

And not off to your doom.

FAUST:

What if I do find heaven in her arms?

What if in her embrace my spirit warms?

Do I not still feel her distress?

Am I not still the fugitive, the homeless,

The monster without rest or purpose sweeping

3350   Like a cataract from crag to crag and leaping

In frenzy of desire to the abyss?

While at one side, she, with her childlike mind,

Dwells in a cottage on the Alpine slope

With all her quiet life confined

Within her small world's narrow scope.

And I, the God-detested,

Had not enough, but wrested

The crag away and scattered

Its ruins as they shattered

3360   To undermine her and her peace as well!

The victim you demanded, fiend of hell!

Help, Devil, make this time of anguish brief!

Let it be soon if it must be!

Let her fate crash in ruins over me,

Together let us come to grief.

MEPHISTOPHELES:

Ah, now it seethes again and glows!

Go in and comfort her, you lout!

A head like yours beholds the close

Of doom as soon as he sees no way out.

3370   Hurrah for men that bravely dare!

You're half bedeviled anyway;

There's nothing sillier in the world, I say,

Than being a devil in despair.

GRETCHEN'S ROOM

GRETCHEN *at her spinning wheel, alone.*

GRETCHEN:

My peace is gone,

My heart is sore,
I'll find it never
And nevermore.
      When he does not come
I live in a tomb,
3380   The world is all
Bitter as gall.
      O, my poor head
Is quite distraught,
And my poor mind
Is overwrought.
      My peace is gone,
My heart is sore,
I'll find it never
And nevermore.
3390   I look from my window
Only to greet him,
I leave the house
Only to meet him.
      His noble gait
And form and guise,
The smile of his mouth,
The spell of his eyes,
      The magic in
Those words of his,
3400   The clasp of his hand,
And oh! — his kiss.
      My peace is gone,
My heart is sore,
I'll find it never
And nevermore.
      My bosom aches
To feel him near,
Oh, could I clasp
And hold him here
3410   And kiss and kiss him
Whom I so cherish,
Beneath his kisses
I would perish!

MARTHA'S GARDEN

MARGARET:
      Promise me, Henry!
FAUST:
                  If I can!

MARGARET:
    About religion, what do you feel now, say?
    You are a good, warmhearted man,
    And yet I fear you're not inclined that way.

FAUST:
    Leave that, my child! That I love you, you feel;
    For those I love, my flesh and blood I'd give,
3420   And no one's church or feelings would I steal.

MARGARET:
    But that is not enough! One must believe!

FAUST:
    Must one?

MARGARET:
            O, if I had some influence!
    You do not even revere the sacraments.

FAUST:
    I do revere them.

MARGARET:
             But without desire.
    It's long since you have gone to Mass or to confession.
    Do you believe in God?

FAUST:
             My darling, who can say:
    I believe in God?
    Ask priest or sage you may,
    And their replies seem odd
3430   Mockings of the asker.

MARGARET:
            Then you do not believe?

FAUST:
    My answer, dear one, do not misconceive!
    Who can name
    Him, or proclaim:
    I believe in Him?
    Who is so cold
    As to make bold
    To say: I do not believe in Him?
    The all-embracing,
    The all-sustaining,
3440   Does He not hold and sustain
    You, me, Himself?
    Does heaven not arch high above us?
    Does earth not lie firm here below?
    And do not everlasting stars
    Rise with a kindly glance?

Do I not gaze into your eyes,
And do not all things crowd
Into your head and heart,
Working in eternal mystery
3450   Invisibly visible at your side?
Let these things fill your heart, vast as they are,
And when you are entirely happy in that feeling,
Then call it what you will:
Heart, Fortune, Love, or God!
I have no name for it.
Feeling is everything,
Names are sound and smoke
Obscuring heaven's glow.

MARGARET:
That is all very good and fair;
3460   The priest says much the same, although
He used a different wording as he spoke.

FAUST:
It is said everywhere
By all hearts underneath the sky of day,
Each heart in its own way;
So why not I in mine?

MARGARET:
It sounds all right when you express it so;
There's something not quite right about it, though;
You have no Christianity.

FAUST:
Dear child!

MARGARET:
It has this long time troubled me
3470   To find you keep the company you do.

FAUST:
How so?

MARGARET:
The person whom you have with you,
In my profoundest being I abhor,
And nothing in my life before
So cut me to the heart
As this man's face when he came near.

FAUST:
My darling, have no fear.

MARGARET:
His presence roils my blood, yet for my part,
People otherwise win my heart;
Much as I yearn to have you near,

3480   This person inspires in me a secret fear,
And if I take him for a scoundrel too,
God forgive me for the wrong I do!

FAUST:
Such queer fish also have to be.

MARGARET:
To live with him would never do for me!
Let him but so much as appear,
He looks about with such a sneer
And half enraged;
Nothing can keep his sympathy engaged;
Upon his brow it's written clear

3490   That he can hold no person dear.
In your embrace I feel so free,
So warm, so yielded utterly;
His presence chokes me, chills me through and through.

FAUST:
O you intuitive angel, you!

MARGARET:
This so overwhelms me, that when
He joins us, be it where it may,
It seems that I no longer love you then.
With him there, I could never pray.
This eats my very heart; and you,

3500   Henry, must feel the same thing too.

FAUST:
This is a matter of antipathy.

MARGARET:
I must be going.

FAUST:
                    O, when will it be
That I may for a little hour rest
In your embrace in quiet, breast to breast?

MARGARET:
If I but slept alone, this very night
I'd leave the door unbolted, you realize,
But Mother's sleep is always light,
And if she took us by surprise,
I would die on the spot, I think.

FAUST:
3510   There is no need for that, my dear!
Here is a little phial. A mere
Three drops into her drink
Will shroud up Nature in deep sleep.

MARGARET:
> What will I not do for your sake?
> It will not harm her, though, to take?

FAUST:
> Would I propose it, Love, if that were so?

MARGARET:
> I look at you, dear man, and do not know
> What so compels me to your will;
> Already I have done so much for you
> That there is little left for me to do.

3520

> [*Exit.*]

[*Enter* MEPHISTOPHELES.]

MEPHISTOPHELES:
> The little monkey's gone?

FAUST:
> You spied again?

MEPHISTOPHELES:
> I could
> Not help but hear it word for word:
> Professor had his catechism heard;
> I hope it does you lots of good.
> Girls have a way of wanting to find out
> Whether a man's conventionally devout.
> They think: he gave in there, he'll truckle to us, no doubt.

FAUST:
> You, monster, do not realize
> How this good loyal soul can be
> So full of faith and trust —
> Which things alone suffice
> To make her bliss — and worry holily
> For fear she must look on her best beloved as lost.

3530

MEPHISTOPHELES:
> You supersensual sensual wooer,
> A girl has got you on a puppet wire.

FAUST:
> You misbegotten thing of filth and fire!

MEPHISTOPHELES:
> She's mighty clever too at physiognomy:
> When I am present, she feels — how, she's not just sure,
> My mask bodes meaning at a hidden level;
> She thinks beyond a doubt I'm a "Genie,"
> And possibly the very Devil.
> Tonight, then — ?

3540

FAUST:
> What is that to you?

MEPHISTOPHELES:
>I have my pleasure in it too!

AT THE WELL

GRETCHEN *and* LIESCHEN *with pitchers.*

LIESCHEN:
>About Barbie, I suppose you've heard?

GRETCHEN:
>I get out very little. Not a word.

LIESCHEN:
>Why, Sibyl was telling me today.
>She's finally gone down Fools' Way.
>That's what grand airs will do!

GRETCHEN:
>   How so?

LIESCHEN:
>   It stinks!
>She's feeding two now when she eats and drinks.

GRETCHEN:
3550   Ah!

LIESCHEN:
>   Serves her right! And long enough
>She hung around that fellow. All that stuff!
>It was walk and jaunt
>Out to the village and dancing haunt,
>And everywhere she had to shine,
>Always treating her to pastry and wine;
>She got to think her good looks were so fine
>She lost her self-respect and nothing would do
>But she accepted presents from him too.
>It was kiss and cuddle, and pretty soon
3560   The flower that she had was gone.

GRETCHEN:
>O the poor thing!

LIESCHEN:
>   Is it pity that you feel!
>When our kind sat at the spinning wheel
>And our mothers wouldn't let us out at night,
>There she was with her lover at sweet delight
>Down on the bench in the dark entryway
>With never an hour too long for such play.
>So let her go now with head bowed down
>And do church penance in a sinner's gown!

GRETCHEN:
>But surely he'll take her as his wife!

LIESCHEN:

3570   He'd be a fool! A chipper lad
        Finds fun is elsewhere to be had.
        Besides, he's gone.

GRETCHEN:

                    O, that's not fair!

LIESCHEN:

        If she gets him, she'll find it bad.
        The boys will rip her wreath, and what's more,
        They'll strew chopped straw around her door!²⁴

                                        [*Exit.*]

GRETCHEN [*walking home*]:

        How firmly I could once inveigh
        When any young girl went astray!
        For others' sins I could not find
        Words enough to speak my mind!

3580   Black as it was, blacker it had to be,
        And still it wasn't black enough for me.
        I thanked my stars and was so game,
        And now I stand exposed to shame!
        Yet all that led me to this pass
        Was so good, and so dear, alas!

ZWINGER²⁵

In a niche of the wall a statue of the Mater dolorosa²⁶ *with jugs of flowers in front of it.*
GRETCHEN [*puts fresh flowers in the jugs*]:

        O deign
        Amid your pain
        To look in mercy on my grief
            With sword thrust through

3590   The heart of you,
        You gaze up to your Son in death.
            To Him on high
        You breathe your sigh
        For His and your distressful grief.
            Who knows

---

²⁴ strew . . . door!: A traditional way of punishing promiscuous girls.

²⁵ Zwinger: An untranslatable term for the open space between the last houses of a town and the inside of the city walls, sometimes the open space between two parallel city walls. Gretchen has sought the most out-of-the-way spot in the city for her private devotions.

²⁶ *Mater dolorosa:* A statue of Mary, the mother of Jesus, in an attitude of grief as she beholds the crucifixion; in accordance with Luke 2:35 her visible heart is pierced with a sword. The text that follows freely adapts the famous thirteenth-century hymn *Stabat mater dolorosa.*

What throes
Wrack me, flesh and bone?
What makes my poor heart sick with fear
And what it is I plead for here,
3600   Only you know, you alone!
            No matter where I go,
I know such woe, such woe
Here within my breast!
I am not quite alone,
Alas! I weep, I moan,
My heart is so distressed.
            The flowerpots at my window
Had only tears for dew
When early in the morning
3610   I picked these flowers for you.
            When bright into my room
The early sun had come,
Upon my bed in gloom
I sat, with sorrow numb.
            Help! Rescue me from shame and death!
O deign
Amid your pain
To look in mercy on my grief!

NIGHT

The street in front of GRETCHEN's *door.* VALENTINE, *a soldier,* GRETCHEN's *brother.*
VALENTINE:
        When I used to be in a merry crowd
3620   Where many a fellow liked to boast,
And lads in praise of girls grew loud
And to their fairest raised a toast
And drowned praise in glasses' overflow,
Then, braced on my elbows, I
Would sit with calm assurance by
And listen to their braggadocio;
Then I would stroke my beard and smile
And take my brimming glass in hand
And say: "To each his own! Meanwhile
3630   Where is there one in all the land
To hold a candle or compare
With my sister Gretel anywhere?"
Clink! Clank! the round of glasses went;
"He's right!" some shouted in assent,
"The glory of her sex!" cried some,

And all the braggarts sat there dumb.
But now!—I could tear my hair and crawl
Right up the side of the smooth wall!—
Now every rascal that comes near
3640   Can twit me with a jibe or sneer!
With every chance word dropped I sweat
Like one who has not paid a debt.
I'd knock the whole lot down if I
Could only tell them that they lie.
        What have we here? Who's sneaking along?
There are two of them, if I'm not wrong.
If he's the one, I'll grab his hide,
He won't get out of here alive!

[*Enter* FAUST *and* MEPHISTOPHELES.]

FAUST:

How from the window of that sacristy
3650   The vigil lamp casts forth its flickering light
Sidewise faint and fainter down the night,
And darkness closes around totally.
So in my heart the darkness reigns.

MEPHISTOPHELES:

And I feel like a cat with loving-pains
That sneaks up fire escapes and crawls
And slinks along the sides of walls;
I feel so cozy at it, and so right,
With a bit of thievery, a bit of rutting to it.
Through all my limbs I feel an ache for
3660   The glorious Walpurgis Night.
Day after tomorrow brings us to it;
Then one knows what he stays awake for.

FAUST:

Will it come to the top, that treasure
I see glimmering over there?

MEPHISTOPHELES:

You very soon will have the pleasure
Of lifting the pot to upper air.
Just recently I took a squint:
It's full of ducats shiny from the mint.

FAUST:

Not a jewel, not a ring
3670   To add to others of my girl's?

MEPHISTOPHELES:

I do believe I saw a string
Of something that looked much like pearls.

FAUST:
> That's good. I really hate to go
> Without a gift to take with me.

MEPHISTOPHELES:
> You needn't fuss and trouble so
> About enjoying something free.
> But now that all the stars are in the sky,
> You'll hear a real art work from me:
> I'll sing her a moral lullaby
3680
> To befool her the more certainly.

[*He sings to the zither.*]
> What dost thou here
> With dawn so near,
> O Katie dear,
> Outside your sweetheart's door?
> Maiden, beware
> Of entering there
> Lest forth you fare
> A maiden nevermore.
>   Maidens, take heed!
3690
> Once do the deed,
> And all you need
> Is: Good night, you poor things!
> If you're in love,
> To no thief give
> The thing you have
> Except with wedding rings.

VALENTINE [*steps forward*]:
> Who is it you're luring? By the Element!
> You accursed rat-catcher, you!
> To the Devil first with the instrument!
3700
> Then to the Devil with the singer too!

MEPHISTOPHELES:
> The zither's smashed, there's nothing left of it.

VALENTINE:
> And next there is a skull to split!

MEPHISTOPHELES [*to* FAUST]:
> Don't flinch, Professor, and don't fluster!
> Come close in by me, and don't tarry.
> Quick! Whip out your feather duster!
> Just thrust away and I will parry.

VALENTINE:
> Then parry this!

MEPHISTOPHELES:
>   Why not?

VALENTINE:

> This too!

MEPHISTOPHELES:

> Of course!

VALENTINE:

> I think the Devil fights in you!
> What's this? My hand is going lame.

MEPHISTOPHELES [*to* FAUST]:

3710
> Thrust home!

VALENTINE [*falls*]:

> O!

MEPHISTOPHELES:

> There, the lummox is quite tame.
> Come on! It's time for us to disappear.
> Soon they will raise a murderous hue and cry.
> With the police I always can get by,
> But of the court of blood I stand in fear.

MARTHA [*at the window*]:

> Come out! Come out!

GRETCHEN [*at the window*]:

> Bring out a light!

MARTHA [*as before*]:

> They swear and scuffle, shout and fight.

PEOPLE:

> Here's one already dead!

MARTHA [*coming out*]:

> Where are the murderers? Have they fled?

GRETCHEN [*coming out*]:

> Who's lying here?

PEOPLE:

> Your mother's son.

GRETCHEN:

3720
> Almighty God! I am undone!

VALENTINE:

> I'm dying! That's a tale
> Soon told and sooner done.
> Why do you women stand and wail?
> Come close and hear me, everyone!

[*They all gather around him.*]

> My Gretchen, see! too young you are
> And not yet wise enough by far,
> You do not manage right.
> In confidence I'll tell you more:
> You have turned out to be a whore,
3730
> And being one, be one outright.

GRETCHEN:
> My brother! God! What do you mean?

VALENTINE:
> Leave our Lord God out of this farce. What's done
> Is done, alas! and cannot be undone.
> And what comes next will soon be seen.
> You started secretly with one,
> It won't be long till others come,
> And when a dozen more have had you,
> The whole town will have had you too.
> > When shame is born, she first appears

3740
> Stealthily amid the world
> And with the veil of darkness furled
> About her head and ears.
> First one would gladly slay her outright.
> But as she grows and waxes bold,
> She walks quite naked in the daylight,
> But is no fairer to behold.
> The uglier her visage grows,
> The more by open day she goes.
> > The time already I foresee

3750
> When all the decent citizenry
> Will from you, harlot, turn away
> As from a plague corpse in their way.
> Your heart will sink within you when
> They look you in the eye! No more
> Golden chains will you wear then!
> Or stand by the altar in church as before!
> No more in collars of fine lace
> Will you come proudly to the dancing place!
> Off to a dismal corner you will slouch

3760
> Where the beggars and the cripples crouch.[27]
> And even though God may forgive,
> Accursed here on earth you still will live.

MARTHA:
> Commend your soul to God! Will you
> Take blasphemy upon you too?

VALENTINE:
> If I could reach your withered skin and bone,
> You shameless, pandering, old crone,
> I do believe that I could win
> Full pardon for my every sin!

---

[27] No more . . . crouch: As Goethe had observingly read, a Frankfurt police ordinance of the fifteenth century forbade promiscuous women to wear jewelry, silk, satin, or damask, and denied them the use of a pew in church. This latter requirement would force them to remain at the rear with the "beggars and the cripples."

GRETCHEN:
    My brother! What pain of hell for me!

VALENTINE:
3770   I tell you, let your weeping be!
    When you gave up your honor, you gave
    The fiercest heart-stab I could know.
    Now through the sleep of death I go
    To God, a soldier true and brave.

                    [*Dies.*]

CATHEDRAL

Service, organ, and choir. GRETCHEN *among many people. An* EVIL SPIRIT *behind* GRETCHEN.

EVIL SPIRIT:
    How different, Gretchen, it was
    When still full of innocence
    You approached this altar,
    From your little dog-eared prayer book
    Murmuring prayers,
    Half childish play,
3780   Half God in heart!
    Gretchen!
    Where are your thoughts?
    Within your heart
    What deed of crime?
    Do you pray for your mother's soul that slept
    Away unto the long, long pain because of you?
    Whose blood is on your doorstep?
    —And underneath your heart
    Does not a new life quicken,
3790   Tormenting itself and you
    With its premonitory presence?

GRETCHEN:
    Alas! Alas!
    If I could be rid of the thoughts
    That rush this way and that way
    Despite my will!

CHOIR:
    Dies irae, dies illa
    solvet saeclum in favilla.[28]

---

[28] *Dies . . . favilla:* The opening of the greatest of medieval hymns, the *Dies irae,* composed before 1250, proba-bly by Thomas of Celano, and used in masses of the dead: "The day of wrath, that day / Shall dissolve the world in fire." Through nineteen three-line stanzas the hymn describes the end of the world and the Last Judgment.

[*The organ sounds.*]

EVIL SPIRIT:

      Wrath seizes you!

3800   The trumpet sounds!

      The graves shudder!

      And your heart

      From ashen rest,

      For flames of torment

      Once more reconstituted,

      Quakes forth.

GRETCHEN:

      If I were out of here!

      I feel as if the organ were

      Stifling my breath,

3810   As if the choir dissolved

      My inmost heart.

CHOIR:

      Judex ergo cum sedebit,

      quidquid latet adparebit,

      nil inultum remanebit.[29]

GRETCHEN:

      I cannot breathe!

      The pillars of the wall

      Imprison me!

      The vaulted roof

      Crushes me! — Air!

EVIL SPIRIT:

3820   Concealment! Sin and shame

      Are not concealed.

      Air? Light?

      Woe to you!

CHOIR:

      Quid sum miser tunc dicturus?

      Quem patronum rogaturus?

      Cum vix justus sit securus.[30]

EVIL SPIRIT:

      The clarified avert

      Their countenances from you.

      The pure shudder to reach

---

[29]*Judex . . . remanebit:* "Therefore when the Judge shall sit, / Whatever is hidden shall appear, / Nothing shall remain unavenged."

[30]*Quid . . . securus:* "What shall I, wretched, say? / What patron shall I call upon? / When scarcely the just man is safe."

3830   Out hands to you.
    Woe!

CHOIR:

    Quid sum miser tunc dicturus?

GRETCHEN:

    Neighbor! Your smelling-bottle!

[*She falls in a faint.*]

WALPURGIS NIGHT

The Harz Mountains. Vicinity of Schierke and Elend.[31]

MEPHISTOPHELES:

    Now don't you long for broomstick-transportation?
    I'd like the toughest he-goat there can be.
    We're far yet, by this route, from destination.

FAUST:

    Since my legs still are holding out so sturdily,
    This knotty stick will do for me.
    Why take a short cut anyway?
3840   Slinking through this labyrinth of alleys,
    Then climbing cliffs above these valleys
    Where streams plunge down in everlasting spray,
    Such is the spice of pleasure on this way!
    Springtime over birches weaves its spell,
    It's sensed already by the very pine;
    Why should it not affect our limbs as well?

MEPHISTOPHELES:

    There's no such feeling in these limbs of mine!
    Within me all is winter's chill;
    On my path I'd prefer the frost and snow.
3850   How drearily the reddish moon's disc, still
    Not full, is rising with belated glow
    And giving such bad light that any step now
    Will have us bumping into rock or tree!
    I'll call a will-o'-the-wisp,[32] if you'll allow.

---

[31] *Harz . . . Elend:* Saint Walpurgis (Walpurga, Walburga, Valburg, d. 780) was a niece of Saint Boniface and herself a missionary to Germany. By coincidence, her church calendar day, April 30, fell together with the pagan festivals on the eve of May Day, the end of winter and the beginning of summer. Under the Christian dispensation, those festivals, like the Halloween festivals (Oct. 31) at the end of summer and the beginning of winter, passed into folklore as devils' orgies. Folklore further localized those orgies on the Brocken, the highest peak of the Harz Mountains in central Germany. From the village of Elend a two- or three-hour walk leads past the village of Schierke to a desolate plateau and finally to the top of the Brocken.

[32] will-o'-the-wisp: (*ignus fatuus,* Jack-o'-Lantern) A conglomeration of phosphorescent gas from decayed vegetation in swamps. By night it resembles an eerily swaying lantern.

I see one burning merrily.
Hey, there, my friend! May I request your flare?
Why flash for nothing over there?
Just be so good and light our way up here.

WILL-O'-THE-WISP:

I hope sheer awe will give me mastery
3860   Over my natural instability;
Most commonly we go a zigzag career.

MEPHISTOPHELES:

Ho, ho! It's man you want to imitate!
Now in the Devil's name, go straight!
Or else I'll blow your flicker-life right out.

WILL-O'-THE-WISP:

You are the master here beyond a doubt,
And so I'll do my best to serve you nicely.
Remember, though! The mountain is magic-mad tonight,
And if you want a will-o'-the-wisp to lend you light
You mustn't take these matters too precisely.

[FAUST, MEPHISTOPHELES, WILL-O'-THE-WISP *in alternating song.*]
3870   Having entered, as it seems,
Realms of magic and of dreams,
Guide us well so that we may
Get along our upward way
Through the vast and empty waste.
        Tree after tree, with what mad haste
They rush past us as we go,
See the boulders bending low,
And the rocks of long-nosed sort,
How they snore and how they snort.
3880   Athwart the turf, the stones athwart,
Brook and brooklet speeds along.
Is it rustling? Is it song?
Do I hear love's sweet lament
Singing of days from heaven sent?
What we hope and what we love!
And the echo is retold
Like a tale from times of old.
        To-whit! To-whoo! it sounds away,
Screech owl, plover, and the jay;
3890   Have all these stayed wide awake?
Are those efts amid the brake?
Long of haunch and thick of paunch!
And the roots that wind and coil
Snakelike out of stone and soil
Knot the bonds of wondrous snares,

Scare us, take us unawares;
Out of tough and living gnarls
Polyp arms reach out in snarls
For the traveler's foot. Mice scurry
3900   Thousand-colored by drove and flurry
Through the moss and through the heather!
And the fireflies in ascent
Densely swarm and swirl together,
Escort to bewilderment.
      Have we stopped or are we trying
To continue onward flying?
Everything is whirling by,
Rocks and trees are making faces,
Wandering lights in many places
3910   Bloat and bulge and multiply.

MEPHISTOPHELES:

Grab my cloak-end and hold tight.
Here's a sort of medium height
Which for our amazement shows
How Mammon in the mountain glows.

FAUST:

How oddly in the valley bottoms gleams
A dull glow like the break of day,
And even in the chasm's deepest seams
It probes and gropes its searching way.
There steam puffs forth, there vapor twines,
3920   Here through the mist the splendor shines,
Now dwindling to a slender thread,
Now gushing like a fountainhead.
It fans out in a hundred veins
A long stretch of the valley run,
Then where the narrow pass constrains
Its course, it merges into one.
There sparks are gusting high and higher
Like golden sand strewn on the night.
Look! There along its entire height
3930   The cliff-face kindles into fire.

MEPHISTOPHELES:

Has not Sir Mammon done some fine contriving
To illuminate his palace hall?
You're lucky to have seen it all.
But now I scent the boisterous guests arriving.

FAUST:

How the wind's bride rides the air!
How she beats my back with cuff and blow!

MEPHISTOPHELES:

> Grab on to this cliff's ancient ribs with care
> Or she will hurl you to the chasm far below.
> A mist has thickened the night.

3940

> Hark! Through the forests, what a crashing!
> The startled owls fly up in fright.
> Hark! The splitting and the smashing
> Of pillars in the greenwood hall!
> Boughs strain and snap and fall.
> The tree trunks' mighty moaning!
> The tree roots' creaking and groaning!
> In fearful entanglement they all
> Go tumbling to their crushing fall,
> And through the wreckage-littered hollows

3950

> The hissing wind howls and wallows.
> Do you hear voices there on high?
> In the distance, or nearby?
> Yes, the mountain all along
> Is bathed in frenzied magic song.

WITCHES [*in chorus*]:

> The witches to the Brocken ride,
> The stubble is yellow, the corn is green.
> There with great crowds up every side,
> Seated on high, Lord Urian° is seen.   the Devil
> And on they go over stock and stone,

3960

> The he-goat st——s from the f——ts of the crone.[33]

A VOICE:

> Old Baubo[34] by herself comes now,
> Riding on a farrow sow.

CHORUS:

> Pay honor where honor is due!
> Dame Baubo, up and on with you!
> A mother astride a husky sow,
> The whole witch crew can follow now.

A VOICE:

> Which way did *you* come?

A VOICE:

> By Ilsenstein crest.
> And I took a peep in an owlet's nest:
> What eyes she made at me!

---

[33] "The he-goat stinks from the farts of the crone."

[34] **Old Baubo:** In Greek mythology, an obscene and bestial nurse of Demeter.

A VOICE:

O go to hell!

3970   Why must you drive so hard!

A VOICE:

    She skinned me alive,

    I'll never survive!

WITCHES [*chorus*]:

    The way is broad, the way is long,

    O what a mad and crazy throng!

    The broomstick scratches, the pitchfork pokes,

    The mother bursts open, the infant chokes.

WITCHMASTERS [*semi-chorus*]:

    We creep along like a snail in his house,

    The women are always up ahead.

    For traveling to the Devil's house,

3980   Women are a thousand steps ahead.

THE OTHER HALF:

    Why, that's no cause for sorry faces!

    Women need the thousand paces;

    But let them hurry all they can,

    One jump is all it takes a man.

A VOICE [*above*]:

    Come on along from Felsensee there, you!

VOICES [*from below*]:

    We'd like to make the top there too.

    We wash and are as clean as clean can be,

    And still the same sterility.

BOTH CHORUSES:

    The wind has died, the star has fled,

3990   The dull moon hides, and in its stead

    The whizzings of our magic choir

    Strike forth a thousand sparks of fire.

A VOICE [*from below*]:

    Wait! Wait! Or I'll get left!

A VOICE [*from above*]:

    Who's calling from that rocky cleft?

A VOICE [*from below*]:

    Take me with you! Take me with you!

    Three hundred years I have been climbing

    And still can't make the top, I find.

    I'd like to be with my own kind.

BOTH CHORUSES:

    A broom or stick will carry you,

4000   A pitchfork or a he-goat too;

    Whoever cannot fly today

    Is lost forever, you might say.

HALF-WITCH [*below*]:

> Here all these years I've minced along;
> How did the others get so far ahead?
> I have no peace at home, and yet
> Can't get in here where I belong.

CHORUS OF WITCHES:

> The salve puts courage in a hag,
> A sail is made from any rag,
> For a ship any trough will do;
4010 > None flies unless today he flew.

BOTH CHORUSES:

> And when the topmost peak we round
> Just coast along and graze the ground,
> So far and wide the heath will be
> Hid by your swarm of witchery.

[*They alight.*]

MEPHISTOPHELES:

> They push and shove, they bustle and gab,
> They hiss and swirl, they hustle and blab!
> They glow, shed sparks, and stink and burn!
> The very witches' element!
> Hold tight to me, or we'll be swept apart in turn.
4020 > Where are you?

FAUST:

> Here!

MEPHISTOPHELES:

> What? Swept so far so soon?
> I must invoke my house-right and call the tune.
> Squire Voland° comes! Give ground, sweet rabble, ground!   the Devil
> Grab on to me, Professor! In one bound
> We'll give this mob the slip quite easily;
> It's too mad even for the likes of me.
> There's something shining with a very special flare
> Down in those bushes. Curiosity
> Impels me. Come! We'll drop in there.

FAUST:

> You Spirit of Contradiction! Be my guiding light!
4030 > I think it was a move that made good sense:
> We travel to the Brocken on Walpurgis Night
> To isolate ourselves up here by preference.

MEPHISTOPHELES:

> Just see the jolly fires! Why here
> A club has gathered for good cheer.
> In little circles one is not alone.

FAUST:

I'd rather be up there, I own.
I see the glow and twisting smoke.
The crowd streams toward the Evil One;
There many a riddle must be undone.

MEPHISTOPHELES:

4040
And many a riddle also spun.
But let the great world revel away,
Here where it's quiet we shall stay.
It is a usage long since instituted
That in the great world little worlds are constituted.
I see young witches naked and bare,
And old ones clothed more prudently;
For my sake, show them courtesy,
The effort is small, the jest is rare.
I hear some tuning up of instruments.
4050
Damned whine and drone! One must get used to it.
Come on! Come on! Now there's no help for it,
I'll go in first and prepare your entrance,
And you will owe me for another work of mine.
This is no little space, you must admit, my friend.
Look, and your eye can hardly see the end.
A hundred bonfires burn there in a line;
There's dancing, chatting, cooking, drinking, making love;
What better things than these can you think of?

FAUST:

In which of your roles will you now appear,
4060
Magician or Devil, to introduce me here?

MEPHISTOPHELES:

Most commonly I go incognito,
But on such gala days one lets one's Orders show.
I have no Garter to distinguish me,
But here the cloven hoof is held in dignity.
You see that snail that's creeping toward us there
Its feelers have already spied
My presence somehow in the air;
I couldn't hide here even if I tried.
Come on! We'll stroll along from fire to fire,
4070
I'll be the wooer and you can be the squire.

[*to some people who are sitting around some dying embers*]
Old gentlemen, what are you doing here?
I'd praise you if I found you in the midst of cheer
Surrounded by the noise and youthful riot;
Alone at home we get our fill of quiet.

GENERAL:
> Who can put any faith in nations,
> Do for them all you may have done?
> With women and with populations
> Youth is always number one.

PRIME MINISTER:
> They're too far off the right course now today,
> 4080   I still stick with the men of old;
> For frankly, when we had our way,
> That was the actual Age of Gold.

PARVENU:
> We weren't so stupid either, you'll allow,
> And often did what we should not;
> But everything is topsy-turvy now
> Just when we'd like to keep the things we've got.

AUTHOR:
> Where can you read a publication
> With even a modicum of sense?
> As for the younger generation,
> 4090   They are the height of impudence.

MEPHISTOPHELES [*who suddenly looks very old*]:
> I feel men ripe for doomsday, now my legs
> Are climbing Witches' Hill in their last climb;
> And since my cask is running dregs,
> The world is also running out of time.

HUCKSTER WITCH:
> O Sirs, don't pass me by this way!
> Don't miss this opportunity!
> Just give my wares some scrutiny,
> All sorts of things are on display.
> Across the earth you will not find
> 4100   A booth like this; no item here, not one
> But what has good sound mischief done
> At some time to the world and human kind.
> No dagger here but what has dripped with gore,
> No cup but what has served to pour
> Consuming poison in some healthy frame,
> No jewel but what has misled to her shame
> Some lovely girl, no sword but of the kind
> That stabbed an adversary from behind.

MEPHISTOPHELES:
> Cousin, you're out of date in times like these.
> 4110   What's done is past, what's past is done.
> Get in a stock of novelties!
> With us it's novelties or none.

FAUST:

    If I don't lose my mind! But I declare

    This really is what I would call a fair!

MEPHISTOPHELES:

    The whole mad rout is pushing on above;

    You're being shoved, though you may think you shove.

FAUST:

    Now who is that?

MEPHISTOPHELES:

            Observe her with some care,

    For that is Lilith.[35]

FAUST:

          Who?

MEPHISTOPHELES:

           Adam's first wife.

    Beware of her resplendent hair,

4120   The one adornment that she glories in,

    Once she entraps a young man in that snare,

    She won't so quickly let him out again.

FAUST:

    That old witch with the young one sitting there,

    They've kicked their heels around, that pair!

MEPHISTOPHELES:

    No rest for them today. Ah! They're beginning

    Another dance. Come on! Let's get into the swing.

FAUST [*dancing with the* YOUNG WITCH]:

    A lovely dream once came to me;

    In it I saw an apple tree,

    Two lovely apples shone upon it,

4130   They charmed me so, I climbed up on it.

THE BEAUTY:

    Apples always were your craze

    From Paradise to present days.

    I feel joy fill me through and through

    To think my garden bears them too.

MEPHISTOPHELES [*with the* OLD WITCH]:

    A dismal dream once came to me;

    In it I saw a cloven tree,

    It had a black, almighty hole;

    Yet black as it was, it charmed my soul.

---

[35] Lilith: In Hebrew folklore, Adam's first wife, before Eve, in Genesis 1; she refused to be subordinate to Adam and retreated to the Red Sea where she haunted lonely places and attacked children.

THE OLD WITCH:

    I proffer now my best salute
4140   To the Knight with the Horse's Hoof!
    So if your cork will do, go to it,
    Unless large bung won't let you do it.

PROKTOPHANTASMIST:[36]

    Accursed mob! This is presumptuous!
    Was it not long since proved to you
    Ghosts do not have the same feet humans do?
    And here you dance just like the rest of us!

THE BEAUTY [*dancing*]:

    And what does *he* want at our ball?

FAUST [*dancing*]:

    Oh, he turns up just anywhere at all.
    What others dance, he must evaluate.
4150   If there's a step about which he can't prate,
    It's just as if the step had not occurred.
    It bothers him the most when we go forward.
    If you would run in circles round about
    The way he does in his old mill,
    He'd call it good and sing its praises still,
    Especially if his opinion were sought out.

PROKTOPHANTASMIST:

    But you're still here! Oh! This is insolent!
    Begone! Why, we brought in Enlightenment!
    This Devil's pack, with them all rules are flouted.
4160   We are so clever, yet there is no doubt about it:
    There's still a ghost at Tegel. How long have I swept
    Illusions out, and still I find they're kept.

THE BEAUTY:

    Then go away and let us have the field.

PROKTOPHANTASMIST:

    I tell you spirits to your faces
    I will not stand for any traces
    Of spirit despotism I can't wield.

[*The dancing goes on.*]

    I just can't win today, no matter what I do.
    But I can always take a trip;
    And I still hope, before I'm done, to slip
4170   One over on the devils and the writers too.

---

[36] Proktophantasmist: This character is a parody of Friedrich Nicolai (1733–1811), an aging rationalist and leader of the Berlin Enlightenment who had written a parody of Goethe's novel, *The Sorrows of Young Werther.*

MEPHISTOPHELES:

>Down in the nearest puddle he will plump,
>That is the best assuagement he can find;
>If leeches feast upon his rump,
>He will be cured of ghosts and his own mind.

[*to* FAUST, *who has left the dance*]

>Why do you leave that pretty girl
>Who in the dance so sweetly sang?

FAUST:

>Because a little red mouse sprang
>Out of her mouth while she was singing.

MEPHISTOPHELES:

>What's wrong with that? The mouse was still not grey.
>Why raise such questions and be bringing
>Them to a trysting hour anyway?

FAUST:

>Then I saw—

MEPHISTOPHELES:

>   What?

FAUST:

>   Mephisto, do you see
>A pale girl standing over there alone?
>She drags herself but slowly from the place
>And seems to move with shackled feet.
>I must confess she has the sweet
>Look of my kindly Gretchen's face.

MEPHISTOPHELES:

>Let that be! That bodes well for no one.
>It is a magic image, lifeless, an eidolon.
>Encounters with such are not good;
>The fixed stare freezes human blood
>And one is turned almost to stone—
>You've heard of the Medusa,[37] I suppose.

FAUST:

>Indeed, a corpse's eyes are those,
>Unshut by loving hand. That is the breast
>That Gretchen offered for my rest,
>That is the dear, sweet body I have known.

4180

4190

---

[37] **the Medusa:** Greek mythological figure whose hair was made of serpents; turned men into stone by looking at them. She was slain by Perseus, who cut off her head.

MEPHISTOPHELES:
> You easily misguided fool, that's magic art.
> She looks to every man like his own sweetheart.

FAUST:
> 4200   What suffering! And what delight!
> My eyes can not shift from that sight.
> How oddly round that lovely throat there lies
> A single band of scarlet thread
> No broader than a knife has bled.

MEPHISTOPHELES:
> Quite right! And I can see it likewise.
> Beneath her arm she also carries that same head
> Since Perseus cut it off for her.
> And you crave for illusion still!
> Come, let us climb that little hill,
> 4210   The Prater[38] is no merrier,
> And if I haven't been misled,
> I actually see a theater.
> What's being given?

SERVIBILIS:
>   A minute yet before it starts.
> A new play, last of seven in a row;
> That is the number given in these parts.
> A dilettant made up the show,
> And dilettanti take the parts.
> Forgive me, Sirs, if I now disappear;
> I just delight in running up the curtain.

MEPHISTOPHELES:
> 4220   I'm glad to find you on the Blocksberg here,
> It's just where you belong, that's certain.

ARIEL:
> If mind or Nature gave you wings
>   And any wing discloses,
> Follow where my leading brings
>   You to the Hill of Roses.

ORCHESTRA [*pianissimo*]:
> Gauze of mist and cloud-bank's edge
>   Are touched with streaks of dawn.
> Breeze in branch and wind in sedge,
>   And everything is gone.
> [. . .]

---

[38] **The Prater:** Famous park in Vienna.

GLOOMY DAY, A FIELD[39]

FAUST: In misery! Desperate! Long wandering pitifully upon the earth and now in prison! Locked up as a wrongdoer for ghastly torments in a jail, that lovely, unfortunate creature! To come to this! To this!—Perfidious, worthless Spirit, and this you kept from me!—Stand there, yes, stand there! Roll those devilish eyes furiously in your head! Stand and defy me with your unbearable presence! In prison! In irrevocable misery! Delivered over to evil spirits and to judging, heartless humanity! And meanwhile you lull me with insipid dissipations, conceal her increasing misery from me, and let her go helpless to destruction!

MEPHISTOPHELES: She is not the first.

FAUST: Cur! Monster of abomination!—Turn him, Infinite Spirit, turn the worm back into his canine form, the way he used to like to trot along in front of me often in time of night, and roll at the feet of the harmless traveler, and cling to the shoulders of one who fell. Turn him back into his favorite shape, so he can crawl on his belly in the sand up to me and I can kick him, the reprobate!—Not the first!—Grief! Grief beyond the grasp of any human soul, that more than one creature has sunk to the depths of such misery, that the first did not atone for the guilt of all the others in her writhing and deathly agony before the eyes of Eternal Forgiveness! It grinds through my marrow and my life, the misery of this one alone; you grin complacently over the fate of thousands!

MEPHISTOPHELES: Now we are once again at the limit of our wits, where the minds of you mortals go overboard. Why do you make common cause with us if you can't go through with it? You want to fly and are not proof to dizziness? Did we force ourselves on you, or you on us?

FAUST: Do not bare your ravening fangs at me that way! I loathe it!—Great and glorious Spirit who didst deign to appear to me, who knowest my heart and my soul, why dost thou forge me together with this infamous associate who gloats on harm and revels in destruction?

MEPHISTOPHELES: Are you through?

FAUST: Save her! Or woe to you! The ghastliest of curses upon you unto millennia!

MEPHISTOPHELES: I cannot loose the avenger's bonds, nor open his locks.—Save her!—Who was it plunged her into ruin? I or you? [FAUST *gazes wildly about.*] So you reach for thunderbolts? Lucky they were not given to you miserable mortals! To pulverize an innocent person in his path is the way of the tyrant, in order to relieve his feelings.

FAUST: Take me there! She shall be free!

MEPHISTOPHELES: And the risk you run? Remember: blood-guilt from your hand still lies upon the city. Over the place where the slain man fell hover avenging spirits in wait for the returning murderer.

---

[39] Scene 22, "Walpurgis-Night's Dream," a puzzling scene seldom included in dramatic productions of *Faust*, has been omitted.

FAUST: This yet from you? A world of murder and death upon you, monster! Take me there, I say, and set her free!

MEPHISTOPHELES: I will take you, and what I *can* do: hear! Do I have all power in heaven and on earth? The jailer's senses I will becloud, *you* get possession of his keys and lead her out yourself with your human hand. I will stand watch! The magic horses are ready, I will carry you away. This much I can do.

FAUST: Up and away!

NIGHT, OPEN COUNTRY

FAUST, MEPHISTOPHELES, *rushing on black horses.*

FAUST:
  What are they doing yonder on Gallows Rock?

MEPHISTOPHELES:
4400 I don't know what they're brewing or doing.

FAUST:
  They soar and swoop, bending and stooping.

MEPHISTOPHELES:
  A crew of witches.

FAUST:
  They strew and bless.

MEPHISTOPHELES:
  On past! On past!

DUNGEON

FAUST *in front of a little iron door, with a bunch of keys and a lamp.*
FAUST:
  A horror long unfamiliar over me crawls,
  Grief seizes me, grief common to human kind.
  She is imprisoned in these clammy walls,
  Her crime a fond illusion of the mind.
  You shrink back from her door
4410 Afraid to see her once more!
  On! Delay brings Death up from behind.

[*He seizes the lock.*]
[*Singing is heard from inside.*]
  My mother, the whore,
  She murdered me!
  My father, the rogue,
  He has eaten me!
  Little sister has laid
  My bones away
  In a place of cool, cool shade.
  And I am turned into a woodland bird;
4420 Fly away! Fly away!

FAUST [*unlocking the door*]:
>   She does not dream her lover can thus hear
>   Her clanking chains, her rustling straw so near.

[*He enters.*]

MARGARET [*cowering on her pallet*]:
>   They're coming. O how bitter it is to die!

FAUST [*softly*]:
>   Be still! Be still! I come to set you free.

MARGARET [*throwing herself at his feet*]:
>   If you are human, feel my misery.

FAUST:
>   You'll wake the jailer with your cry!

[*He takes hold of the chains to unlock them.*]

MARGARET [*on her knees*]:
>   Who was it, headsman, who could give
>   You so much power!
>   You take me at the midnight hour.
4430
>   Have pity on me, let me live!
>   Is tomorrow morning not time enough?

[*She stands up.*]

>   Am I not still so young, so young!
>   To die so soon!
>   And I was beautiful, and that was my undoing.
>   My friend was near, now he is near no more.
>   My wreath lies torn, the flowers scattered that I wore.
>   O do not seize me so violently!
>   What have I done to you? O pity me!
>   Let me not in vain implore,
4440
>   I never saw you in my life before!

FAUST:
>   Will I survive such misery!

MARGARET:
>   I am now wholly in your might.
>   First let me nurse my child again.
>   I fondled it all through the night;
>   They took it from me just to cause me pain,
>   And now they say that I have slain
>   My child. Now I shall never more be glad.
>   And they sing songs about me! How can they be
>   So wicked! So runs an ancient story, but who bade
4450
>   Them make that tale fit me!

FAUST [*falling on his knees*]:
>   A lover at your feet implores
>   You to come forth out of these woeful doors.

MARGARET [*kneels with him*]:
    O let us kneel and call upon the saints in prayer!
    Look! Underneath that stair,
    Beneath that threshold there,
    Hell seethes! Beneath the floor
    The Evil One
    Makes ghastly noise
    Of tumult and uproar!

FAUST [*loudly*]:
4460   Gretchen! Gretchen!

MARGARET [*attentively*]:
    That was my beloved's voice!

[*She jumps up. Her chains fall off.*]
    Where is he? I heard him calling me.
    No one can stop me. I am free!
    To his arms I will fly,
    And at his heart I'll lie!
    Gretchen, he called! He stood there at that door.
    And through the howling din of hell's uproar,
    Through the wrath of devils' mocking noise
    I recognized that sweet, that loving voice.

FAUST:
4470   I *am* here!

MARGARET:
           You! O say that once again!

[*embracing him*]
    It *is* he! Where is anguish now, or pain?
    Where is my prison's agony?
    You come to set me free!
    And I am saved! —
    There is the street once more where I
    That first time saw you passing by.
    There is the cheerful garden too
    With Martha and me waiting for you.

FAUST [*trying to lead her away*]:
    Come with me! Come with me!

MARGARET:
               O tarry!
4480   I gladly tarry where you tarry.

[*caressing him*]
FAUST:
    Hurry!
    Unless you hurry,
    It will cost us a bitter price.

MARGARET:
>What! Can you no longer kiss?
>So briefly gone, so soon returned,
>My friend, and kissing all unlearned?
>Why am I frightened with such strange alarms,
>When from your words, your glances, overwhelmingly
>I once felt all of heaven in your arms,
4490
>When you would kiss as though to stifle me?
>Kiss me now, or
>I will kiss you!

[*She embraces him.*]
>Alas! your lips are cold,
>And dumb.
>What has become
>Of your loving?
>Who has robbed me of it?

[*She turns away from him.*]
FAUST:
>Come! Follow me! My darling, be bold!
>I'll love you with a passion thousandfold,
4500
>Only come with me! That's all I'd have you do!
MARGARET [*turning toward him*]:
>But is it you? But is it really you?
FAUST:
>It is! But come with me!
MARGARET:
>   You loose my chain,
>And take me back into your arms again.
>How is it that you do not shrink from me? —
>Do you know who it is, my friend, you're setting free?
FAUST:
>Come! Come! Deep night will soon be done.
MARGARET:
>I sent my mother to her death,
>I drowned my child — the one
>Born to both you and me — yes, to you too.
4510
>It *is* you! I can not believe it yet.
>Give me your hand! It is no dream!
>Your dear hand! — O! But it is wet!
>Wipe it off. But still I seem
>To see blood on it.
>My God! What have you done!
>Put up your sword,
>That much I ask!

FAUST:

O let the past be past and done
Or you will be my death.

MARGARET:

4520   No, you must stay alive!
The graves I will describe for you,
And you must see to them
This coming morning;
The best spot give to my mother,
And next to her my brother;
Bury me off a little way,
But not too far away;
And the babe at my right breast.
No one else will lie by me! —

4530   To nestle at your side so lovingly,
That was a rapture sweet and blest!
But for me that will never come again.
It seems as if I had to force my way to you,
As if you spurned me away from you;
Yet it is you, and your look is so winsome.

FAUST:

If you feel it is I, then come!

MARGARET:

Out there?

FAUST:

To freedom.

MARGARET:

If the grave is there,
If Death is waiting, come!

4540   From there to my eternal bed
But not one step beyond —
You go? O Henry, if I could go too!

FAUST:

You can! If you but will! There is the door.

MARGARET:

I cannot go! For me hope is no more.
What good is flight? They only hunt me down.
It is so wretched to have to beg,
And with an evil conscience too!
It is so wretched to wander far from home,
And they would catch me anyway!

FAUST:

4550   I will stay with you.

MARGARET:

O quick! O quick!

Save your poor child.
Go up the path
That skirts the brook
And across the bridge
To the woods beyond,
Left, where the plank is
In the pond.
Catch it quick!

4560   It tries to rise,
It struggles still!
Save it! Save it!

FAUST:
Control yourself!
One step, and you are free!

MARGARET:
If only we were past the hill!
There sits my mother on a stone,
And I am cold with dread!
There sits my mother on a stone
And shakes her head.

4570   She does not beckon, does not nod, her head sinks lower,
She slept so long, she wakes no more.
She slept so we might love.
O those were happy times!

FAUST:
If all things fail that I can say,
Then I must carry you away.

MARGARET:
No, let me go! I will not suffer violence!
Let go the hand that murderously holds me so fast!
I did all things to please you in the past.

FAUST:
The day shows grey. My love! My love!

MARGARET:
4580   Yes, daylight penetrates. The final day.
It was to be my wedding day.
Tell no one you have been with Gretchen.
Alas! rough hands
Have ripped the wreath I wore.
And we shall meet once more,
But not at the dance.
The crowd wells forth, it swells and grows
And overflows
The streets, the square;

4590   The staff is broken, the death knell fills the air.[40]
    How I am seized and bound!
    I am already at the block.
    The neck of every living soul around
    Foresenses the ax blade and its shock.
    The crowd is silent as a tomb.

FAUST:
    Would I were never born!

[MEPHISTOPHELES *appears outside.*]

MEPHISTOPHELES:
    Up! Or it is your doom.
    Useless dallying! Shilly-shallying!
    My horses shudder outside the door,[41]
4600   It is the break of day.

MARGARET:
    What rises out of the floor?
    He! He! Send him away!
    What does he want in this sacred place?[42]
    He comes for me!

FAUST:
                 You shall live!

MARGARET:
    Judgment of God! Myself to Thee I give!

MEPHISTOPHELES [*to* FAUST]:
    Come on! Come on! Or I'll leave you here with her.

MARGARET:
    Father, I am Thine! Deliver me!
    You angels! Sacred hosts, descend!
    Guard me about, protect me and defend!
4610   Henry! I shudder to behold you.

MEPHISTOPHELES:
    She is condemned!

A VOICE [*from above*]:
               Is saved!

MEPHISTOPHELES [*to* FAUST]:
                   Hither to me!

---

[40] staff . . . air: The judge broke a wand as a way to symbolize a death sentence.

[41] My . . . door: They are magic horses of the night and cannot bear the light of day.

[42] sacred place: A condemned person's place of confinement was inaccessible to evil spirits; that Mephistopheles dares intrude is a sign of his desperation lest he lose Faust.

[*disappears with* FAUST.]

A VOICE [*from within, dying away*]:
　　Henry! Henry!

FROM THE SECOND PART OF THE TRAGEDY

Act One

PLEASANT REGION

FAUST *reclining on flowery greensward, restless, trying to sleep. Twilight. A ring of spirits hovering and flitting, graceful tiny forms.*

ARIEL[43] [*song accompanied by Aeolian harps*]:
　　When the blossoms of the spring
　　Float as rain down to the earth,
　　When green fields are shimmering
　　For all who are of this world's birth,
　　Elfins of high spirit race
　　Haste to help where help they can;
　　Be he holy, be he base,
4620　　They grieve for the grieving man.
　　　　You airy hoverers where this head now lies,
　　Reveal yourselves in noble elfin guise,
　　Assuage the frantic turmoil of his soul,
　　Withdraw the fiery bitter arrows of remorse,
　　From horror lived through, purge and make him whole.
　　　　Four are the watches of night's course,
　　Be prompt to keep them gladly and in full.
　　First, on cool pillows let his head be laid,
　　Then bathe him in the Lethe of the dew;
4630　　Lithe shall his strained and stiffened limbs be made
　　And rest deliver him to day, all new.
　　Perform the fairest elfin rite,
　　Restore him to the holy light.

CHORUS [*singly, by twos, and in combination, alternately and together*]:
　　When the air lies warm and calm
　　Over green-hemmed field and dale,
　　Twilight wafts a fragrant balm,
　　Wafts sweet mists in veil on veil,
　　Whispers softly of sweet peace,
　　Rocks the heart to childlike rest,
4640　　Grants this weary man's eyes ease,
　　Shuts the portals of the west.
　　　　Night has come with total dark,

---

[43] Ariel and the Elves symbolize the curative powers of Nature.

Holily star moves to star,
Sovereign fire and feeble spark
Glitters near and glows afar,
Glitters here lake-mirrored, glows
High up in the clear of night;
Sealing joy in deep repose,
Reigns the moon in fullest light.
4650   Now these hours are snuffed out,
Pain and joy have died away;
Health is certain; banish doubt,
Put your trust in coming day.
Green dawn valleys, hills are pillows
Fluffed for shadowed rest and sweet,
Harvestwards in silver billows
Sway and surge the tides of wheat.
         Wish on wishes to obtain,
Look to skies all bright aloft.
4660   Lightest fetters still restrain,
Sleep is seed coat: sluff it off!
Though the many shrink and waver,
Do not tarry to make bold;
All things tend in that man's favor
Who perceives and takes swift hold.

[*Tremendous tumult proclaims the approach of the sun.*]
ARIEL:
Hark! the horal tempest nears!
Sounding but to spirit ears
Where the newborn day appears.
Cliff gates, rasping, open; under
4670   Phoebus' chariot wheels rolls thunder;
What mighty din the daylight brings!
Drumrolls pounding, trumpets sounding,
Eyesight-dazzling, ear-astounding,
Unheard be such unheard things.[44]
Into headed flowers dart!
Lie there still in deepest part,
Under leaves, in clefts of rock:
Deafness comes of such a shock!

FAUST:
Life's pulse, renewed in vigor, throbs to greet
4680   Aethereal dawning of the gentle light.

---

[44] Cliff . . . things: Because such sounds ("sounding but to spirit ears") would, if received by physical ears,
drive the hearer to madness, if not annihilate him.

New-quickened, Earth, thou breathest at my feet,
Thou who wert also constant through the night;
Already thou conferrest joy once more
And rousest resolution of great might
To strive for highest being evermore.
    In shimmering dawn revealed the world now lies,
The thousand voices of the forest soar,
A radiance streams in glory from the skies
Though mists in valleys still are drifted deep,
4690 And branches fresh with life emerge and rise
From fragrant glens where they were drowned in sleep;
By dull depths yielded up, hue clears on hue
Where pearls from glistening bloom and petal weep,
And paradise emerges to my view.
    Lift up your eyes! — Each giant mountain height
Proclaims the solemnest of hours anew.
They soonest catch the everlasting light
Which will thereafter unto us descend.
Now down the Alpine lawns steep-sloping, bright
4700 New radiance and clarity extend
And step by step their last objectives gain.
The sun comes forth! But when I that way tend,
I am struck blind, I turn aside in pain.
    So is it with our yearning hopes that tried
And finally their utmost wish attain
When portals of fulfillment open wide.
And now as those eternal depths upraise
Flame so tremendous, we stand terrified;
We sought to set the torch of life ablaze
4710 And find ourselves engulfed in seas of fire!
Is it great love, or hate, whose burning gaze
Strikes now a mighty grief, now vast desire,
Till we turn backwards to the earth and run
And veil ourselves in youth's soft cloud attire?
    Behind me only be the shining sun!
The cataract that through the cleft rock roars
To ever mounting rapture has me won;
From plunge to plunge it overflows and pours
Itself in thousands and uncounted streams
4720 While high in air mist-veil on mist-veil soars.
But O how glorious through the storm there gleams
The changeless, ever changeful rainbow bent,
Sometimes distinct, sometimes with shattered beams,
Dispensing showers of cool and fragrant scent.
Man's effort is there mirrored in that strife.

Reflect and by reflection comprehend:
There in that rainbow's radiance *is* our life.[45]
[. . .]

Act Five[46]

OPEN COUNTRY

A TRAVELER:

Those dark lindens, well I know them,
Standing in their strength of age;
Once again I pass below them
After such long pilgrimage.
Here, then, is the place at last;
That same cottage sheltered me,
On those dunes I once was cast
11050   By the tempest-ridden sea.
I should like to bless my hosts,
Such a kindly, sturdy pair,
Who were old then on these coasts,
All too old still to be there.
What good folk they used to be!
Shall I knock? Call out? — Good greeting!
If your hospitality
Still brings good to strangers meeting.

BAUCIS [*a little old woman, very ancient*]:

Welcome, comer, softly speak,
11060   Do not break my husband's rest;
From his sleep the old man, weak,
Draws brief waking's rapid zest.

TRAVELER:

Tell me, Mother, is it you
Who once saved the young man's life?
To whom now fresh thanks are due,
Both to husband and to wife?

---

[45] **Behind me . . . our life:** The complex thought may be paraphrased: Humankind is no match for the sun; its vital force is more appropriately symbolized by the cataract that rushes onward because its nature is to rush onward; human achievement is a by-product like the rainbow, sometimes realized in full, more often realized only in segments of its shattered arch.

[46] After a series of symbolic adventures, including a marriage to Helen of Troy, a visit to the underworld realm of the Mothers, and the experience of a new classical golden age, Faust, now an old man of 100 years, has reached the final days of his life. Yet he is still an active man, as the development project he undertakes in this act indicates.

Are you Baucis, who to my
Half-dead lips new life once gave?

[*The husband appears.*]
You Philemon, who saved my
11070　Drowning treasure from the wave?
By the flames of your quick fire,
By your bell's sweet silver sound,
That adventure grim and dire
Safe conclusion from you found.
　　Let me step down here a way,
Gazing on the boundless sea;
Let me kneel and let me pray,
For my heart oppresses me.

[*He walks forward on the dune.*]
PHILEMON [*to* BAUCIS]:
Hurry now to set the table
11080　Underneath the garden trees.
Let him go, he is not able
To believe what his eye sees.

[*standing next to the* TRAVELER]
That by which you were mistreated,
Wave on wild wave foaming, lies—
See you!—as a garden treated,
As a scene from Paradise.
Aging, I was not on hand
To be helpful as before;
While my strength waned, waves were banned
11090　Far out from the former shore.
Clever lords set daring wights
Dredging ditches, damming, diking,
Curbing ocean's sovereign rights,
Ruling it to their own liking.
Field on field, see! green and sweet,
Meadow, garden, forest, town.—
Come, however, come and eat,
For the sun will soon be down.—
Sails loom there against the west
11100　Seeking port and safe repair;
Like the birds, they know their nest,
For the harbor now is there.
Thus at furthest range of sight
Lies the blue fringe of the main,

All the rest to left and right
Is a thickly peopled plain.

[*In the garden. The three at table.*]
BAUCIS:
    You are silent? do not eat
    Though your lips are starved for food?
PHILEMON:
    He is marveling at the feat;
11110   Tell him how those matters stood.
BAUCIS:
    As for marvels, this was one!
    Even now it troubles me;
    For the whole affair was done
    Not as rightful things should be.
PHILEMON:
    Should the Emperor be to blame
    If he let him have this shore?
    Did a herald not proclaim
    That with trumpets at our door?
    Near our dunes they first were seen;
11120   Swiftly tents and shacks appeared.
    But amid the verdant green
    Soon a palace was upreared.
BAUCIS:
    Daytimes, noisy varlets might
    Vainly hack and delve away;
    Where the flamelets swarmed by night
    Stood a dike the following day.
    Human sacrifices bled,
    Nighttime heard them shriek and wail,
    Seawards rolled the tides of red,
11130   Morning saw a new canal.
    Godless is he, and he still
    Wants our cottage, wants our trees,
    As a swaggering neighbor, will
    Have us as dependencies.
PHILEMON:
    Yet he offered us a fine
    Homestead on the new-made land.
BAUCIS:
    Trust no bottom dredged from brine,
    On your headland make your stand!
PHILEMON:
    To our chapel come away

11140　　Final sunlight to behold,
　　　　Let us sound the bells and pray
　　　　Kneeling to the God of old.

PALACE

Spacious ornamental garden; a large, straight canal. FAUST *in extreme old age, walking and meditating.*

LYNCEUS THE TOWER WARDEN [*through a speaking-trumpet*]:
　　　　The sun sinks down, the final ships
　　　　Are moving briskly into port.
　　　　One mighty barque makes for the slips
　　　　On the canal close by your court.
　　　　The colored ensigns flutter faster,
　　　　The sturdy masts stand tall and straight,
　　　　The boatman hails you as his master,
11150　　And Fortune hails you as most great.

[*The little bell rings out on the dune.*]
FAUST [*starting up*]:
　　　　Accursed bell! In profanation,
　　　　Like spiteful shot it wounds my ear;
　　　　Before me lies my vast creation,
　　　　Vexation dogs me at the rear;
　　　　The envious sound reminds me still
　　　　Complete possession is not mine,
　　　　The brown hut on the linden hill,
　　　　The moldering church is still not mine.
　　　　If I desired its coolness, I
11160　　Would seek its alien shade with fear,
　　　　A thorn to my foot, a thorn to my eye.
　　　　Would I were far away from here!
TOWER WARDEN [*as above*]:
　　　　How gaily comes the boat with sails
　　　　Before the gentle evening gales.
　　　　How swift its course looms up with hoard
　　　　Of boxes, bales, and chests aboard.

[*A splendid ship richly and colorfully laden with produce of foreign climes.* MEPHISTOPHELES. *The* THREE MIGHTY MEN.]
CHORUS:
　　　　And so we land,
　　　　And so we meet.
　　　　Our master and
11170　　Our lord we greet.

[*They disembark; the wares are brought ashore.*]
MEPHISTOPHELES:

So we have proved ourselves, content
If we our master's praises earn.
We had but two ships when we went
But now have twenty on return.
The mighty things that we have wrought
Show by the cargo we have brought.
Free ocean is mind's liberation:
Who there cares for deliberation!
What counts is sudden grasp and grip

11180   To catch a fish or catch a ship,
And once you have control of three,
A fourth is hooked quite easily;
The fifth is in a sorry plight
For you have might and therefore right.
"What" is the question, never "How."
If I don't mix up stern and bow,
Then business, war, and piracy
Are an unsevered trinity.

THE THREE MIGHTY MEN:

No thanks we get!

11190   We get no thanks!
Our master thinks
Our cargo stinks.
He makes a face,
He takes no pleasure
For all we bring
Him royal treasure.

MEPHISTOPHELES:

Expect no more.
What do you care?
After all,

11200   You got your share.

THE MEN:

That was only
In sport. Now we
Demand to share
Equally.

MEPHISTOPHELES:

First arrange
In hall on hall
These costly items
One and all.
Once he sees

11210
The precious sight,
Once he reckons
Costs aright,
He won't skimp
You in the least,
He'll give the fleet
Feast on feast.
The gay birds come with morning's tide
And for them I can best provide.

[*The cargo is removed.*]
MEPHISTOPHELES [*to* FAUST]:
With solemn brow, with somber glance
11220
You take these noble gifts of Chance;
Your wisdom has been glorified,
The shore and ocean are allied,
In swift career from shore the sea
Accepts your vessels willingly;
Admit that now your arm extends
From here to earth's extremest ends.
Here it began, on this spot stood
The very first poor shack of wood;
A little ditch was scraped in loam
11230
Where now the oar leaps swift with foam.
Your own high thought, your servers' toil
Have won the prize from sea and soil.
From here . . .

FAUST:
            O be that "here" accursed!
It's just the thing I mind the worst.
I must tell you as my ally
I cannot bear it, I am maimed
In heart, blow after blow, thereby,
And telling you, I am ashamed.
Those old folks up there ought to move,
11240
I'd like those lindens for my seat;
Those few trees not my own disprove
My worldwide claims and spell defeat.
There for the prospect I would now
Build scaffolding from bough to bough
And open vistas looking on
All the things that I have done,
And have in one view all combined
This masterpiece of human mind,
With shrewd sense spurring active feats

11250   Throughout far nations' dwelling seats.
      This is the torment of the rack,
In wealth perceiving what we lack.
The sound of bells, the lindens' bloom
Give me the sense of church and tomb;
The will that nothing could withstand
Is broken here upon this sand.
What can I do about it? Tell
Me! I am frantic from that bell.

MEPHISTOPHELES:
Such nuisance cannot help but gall
11260   You, that is only natural.
Who would deny it? Far and near
That jangling grates on every ear.
And that damned ding-dong-diddle, why!
It shrouds the cheerful evening sky,
It butts in on your every turn
From baby-bath to funeral urn,
As if between the ding and dong
Life were a mere dream all along.

FAUST:
Resistance, stubborn selfishness
11270   Can spoil the lordliest success,
Until in angry pain one must
Grow tired at last of being just.

MEPHISTOPHELES:
Why should you fuss about things here
When colonizing's your career?

FAUST:
Then go and get them off my path! —
You know the pretty homestead where
I mean to move the aged pair.

MEPHISTOPHELES:
We'll move them out to their new ground
Before there's time to look around.
11280   For any violence that's done
A pretty place will soon atone.

[*He gives a shrill whistle.*]
[*Enter the* THREE MIGHTY MEN.]
Come! Do as your lord bids you do.
Tomorrow he will feast the crew.

THE THREE:
The old man met us with a slight.
A nice feast is no more than right.

[*Exeunt.*]

MEPHISTOPHELES [*ad spectatores*]:
    What happed of old now haps anew:
    For there was Naboth's vineyard too. (I Kings 21)[47]

DEEP NIGHT

LYNCEUS THE TOWER WARDEN [*on the watchtower, singing*]:
    For sight I was born,
    For viewing was set;
11290   To watchtower sworn,
    I love the world yet.
    I gaze out afar,
    I see what is near,
    The moon and the star,
    The forest and deer.
    Thus splendors of ages
    On all sides I view;
    As I found them all good,
    So I find myself too.
11300   You fortunate eyes,
    For all you have seen,
    Whatever it was,
    It still was so fine!

[*A pause.*]
        Not alone for my delight
    Am I stationed here so high;
    In the darkness of the night
    Monstrous horror strikes my eye!
    I see sparks that dart and blow
    Through the linden trees' twin night,
11310   Strong and stronger twists the glow
    As the wind's draft fans it bright.
    Hah! the cottage is on fire!
    Walls that moist and mossy stand;
    Speedy rescue they require
    And no rescue is at hand.
    Oh! those kindly aged folk,
    Always careful with their fire,
    Now are victims of the smoke
    In disaster dread and dire!
11320   Flames flame up, red stands the shape

---

[47] What . . . too: See I Kings 21. When Naboth refused to sell his vineyard to King Ahab, Queen Jezebel had Naboth arrested and killed.

Of that black and mossy shell;
If those good folk could escape
From that wildly burning hell!
Tongues of lightning lightly leap,
Through the leaves and branches sweep;
Withered boughs, they flare and burn,
Falling with a sudden blaze.
Must my eyes so much discern?
Alas for my far-sighted gaze!

11330   Now the chapel goes down crashing,
Crushed by weight of limb and bough,
Pointed flames go writhing, flashing
To the highest treetops now.
Scarlet burns each hollow tree
To the very roots at last.

[*A long pause. Song.*]
What was once a joy to see
After centuries has passed.

FAUST [*on the balcony, toward the dunes*]:
Above me what a whimpering dirge.
The word is here, the sound is late;

11340   My warder wails; my deep thoughts urge
That this deed was precipitate.
But if the lindens have been wrecked
And left as charred stumps hideously,
A lookout I shall soon erect
To face out toward infinity.
I also see the new house where
In peace the aged couple stays,
Who, sensing my kind wish and care,
Will now enjoy their latter days.

MEPHISTOPHELES AND THE THREE [*below*]:

11350   We come at a good rapid trot,
But go off well, the thing did not.
We rapped, we knocked, we rapped again,
And still they would not let us in.
We battered and we knocked away,
The rotten door fell in and lay;
We shouted out in threat and call
But found they heard us not at all.
As happens in such cases, they
Just would not hear, would not obey;

11360   We had no time to waste or spare
And soon we cleared them out of there.

The couple's sufferings were slight,
And all they did was die of fright.
A stranger there put up a show
Of force and had to be laid low.
Amid the brief course of the match
Some scattered coals got in the thatch,
And now the fire is blazing free
To the cremation of all three.

FAUST:

11370   To all my words then you were deaf!
I wanted an exchange, not theft.
Upon this ruthless action be
My curse! Share in it equally!

CHORUS:

The ancient saying still makes sense:
Bow willingly to violence;
But if you bravely make resistance,
Risk house and home — and your existence.

                                                  [*Exeunt.*]

FAUST [*on the balcony*]:

The stars conceal their gaze and shining,
The fire sinks smoldering and declining;
11380   A faint gust fans it fitfully
And wafts its smoke and scent to me.
Too rashly bidden, too rashly done! —
What glides so spectrally toward me?

MIDNIGHT

Enter FOUR GREY WOMEN.

THE FIRST:

My name is Want.

THE SECOND:

                           My name is Guilt.

THE THIRD:

My name is Care.

THE FOURTH:

                        My name is Distress.

THREE [*together*]:

The door is fast-bolted, we cannot get in,
The owner is wealthy, we'll never get in.

WANT:

Here I turn to shadow.

GUILT:

                       Here I have no place.

DISTRESS:
 From me is averted the much-pampered face.
CARE:
11390 You sisters, you can not and may not get in,
 But Care through the keyhole will make her way in.

              [CARE *disappears.*]

WANT:
 O sisters, grey sisters, away let us glide.
GUILT:
 I'll be your ally and walk close at your side.
DISTRESS:
 And close on your footsteps will follow Distress.
THE THREE:
 Hard rides now the cloud, disappears now the star,
 From behind, from behind, from afar, from afar
 There comes now our brother, and his name is — Death.

              [*Exeunt.*]

FAUST [*in the palace*]:
 Four I saw come, but only three go hence,
 And of their speech I could not catch the sense.
11400 "Distress" I heard, and like caught breath
 A gloomy rhyme-word followed — "Death."
 It sounded hollow, hushed with ghostly fear.
 I've still not fought my way into the clear.
 If I could sweep my path from magic free
 And quite unlearn the spells of sorcery,
 If I could face you, Nature, as a man,
 It then would be worth while to be a man.
  Such was I once, before I cursed to doom
 Both myself and the world in that dark room.
11410 The air so teems with monsters ghostly shaped
 That no one knows how they can be escaped.
 If *one* day laughs amid sweet reason's light,
 Dreams weave us round with cobwebs that same night.
 If vernal fields make our glad hearts beat faster,
 A bird croaks; and what does he croak? Disaster.
 Ensnared by superstition soon and late,
 It works and shows itself and hints our fate,
 And daunted we stand helpless in the gloom.
  The door creaks, yet no one comes in the room.
[*shaken*]
11420 Is someone here?
CARE:
      Well may you ask. I am.

FAUST:
And you, who are you then?

CARE:
But here I am.

FAUST:
Go back, then!

CARE:
I am in my proper station.

FAUST [*angered at first, then appeased; to himself*]:
Then watch yourself and speak no incantation.

CARE:
If no ear for me were found,
In the heart I still would sound.
In my ever changeful guise
Fearful force I exercise,
On the highroad, on the sea
Bearing you dread company,
11430   Ever found though sought for never,
Cursed and yet cajoled forever.
But have you never yet known Care?

FAUST:
I have but raced on through the world;
I seized on every pleasure by the hair;
What did not satisfy, I let go by,
And what eluded me, I let it be.
I have but craved, accomplished my delight,
Then wished anew, and so with main and might
Stormed through my life; first grandly and with passion,
11440   But now more wisely, in more prudent fashion.
I know enough about the world of men,
The prospect yonder is beyond our ken;
A fool is he who that way blinks his eyes
And fancies kindred beings in the skies.
Let him stand firm here and here look around:
This world is not mute if the man is sound.
Why need he stray off to eternity!
What he knows here is certainty.
So let him walk along his earthly day:
11450   If spirits haunt him, let him go his way,
Find joy and torment in his forward stride,
And at each moment be unsatisfied.

CARE:
One whom I can once possess
Finds the whole world profitless;

Eternal gloom descends and lies,
For him suns neither set nor rise;
With external senses whole,
Darkness dwells within his soul,
On the earth there is no treasure
11460   He can grasp or own with pleasure,
He starves in plenty, and for him
Weal and woe become mere whim;
Be it bliss or be it sorrow,
He postpones it till the morrow;
Living in the future ever,
He succeeds in no endeavor.

FAUST:
Stop! You will not succeed with me!
I will not hear such folly. Hence!
Hearing this evil litany
11470   Could addle wisest men's good sense.

CARE:
Whether he should go or stay,
His decision seeps away;
At broad highways' midmost he
Gropes by half-steps hesitantly.
He gets deep and deeper lost,
Sees all things as purpose-crossed,
Burdening himself and others,
Breathing deeply as he smothers,
Neither dead nor yet alive,
11480   Succumb he can't, nor yet survive.
Galling "O, I should!" combined
With his painful "Never mind . . . ,"
Liberated and suppressed,
Semi-sleeping with no rest,
He is fixed in place and groomed
For the hell to which he's doomed.

FAUST:
Unholy specters! Thus you have betrayed
The race of humans time and time again,
And out of days of mere indifference made
11490   A filthy snarl and tangled net of pain.
From demons one can scarcely be quite free,
Not to be broken are the spirit ties,
And yet your power, great as it may be,
O Care, I will not recognize.

CARE:
Then feel it now, as I behind
Me leave my curse and turn from you.

Since human beings all their lives are blind,
Now, Faustus, be you just so too!

[*She breathes upon him. Exit.*]

FAUST [*blinded*]:

The night seems deep and deeper to be sinking,
11500   Bright light still shines within myself alone.
I hasten to enact what I am thinking;
No will imposes save the master's own.
Up, servers, from your couches, every man,
And gladly see the boldness of my plan!
Take up your tools, swing shovel now and spade!
Bring instantly to flower the lands surveyed.
Strict ordering and swift diligence
Will yield the fairest recompense.
In this great task one mind commands
11510   Sufficiently a thousand hands.

GREAT FORECOURT OF THE PALACE

Torches.

MEPHISTOPHELES [*as Foreman leading the way*]:

This way! This way! Come on! Come on!
You shambling lemur batches,[48]
You semi-natures made of bone
And frazzled sinew patches.

LEMURS [*in chorus*]:

We come at call, we are on hand,
And as we heard by half,
There is, they say, a spacious land
That we're supposed to have.
Sharp-pointed stakes, here's your supply,
11520   Here is the measuring chain;
The summons was for us, but why,
Quite slips our minds again.

MEPHISTOPHELES:

No fussing now for elegance,
Just go by your own measurements;
The tallest should lie down upon the ground,
The rest can lift the sod up all around.
Just sink the longish trench four-sided
With which our forebears were provided.
Out of the palace to the narrow home,
11530   That is the sorry end to which we come.

---

[48] **shambling . . . batches:** Roman spirits of the unrighteous dead, represented as skeletons held together by their funeral wrappings.

LEMURS [*digging and making droll gestures*]:
　　When I was young and lived and loved,
　　Methought that was full sweet,
　　When frolic rang and mirth was loud
　　There I would stir my feet.
　　　　Now spiteful Age has struck at me
　　And hit me with his crutch;
　　I stumbled on a yawning grave—
　　Why must they open such!

FAUST [*coming from the palace and groping his way by the doorposts*]:
　　O how this clang of spades delights my soul!
11540　　These are the many who perform my toil
　　And reconcile the earth with its own soil
　　And for the waves set up a goal
　　And gird tight limits round the sea.

MEPHISTOPHELES [*aside*]:
　　And yet all your activity
　　Serves us, with dam and dike creation;
　　For Neptune the great water devil
　　You are preparing one big revel.
　　You all are lost in every wise—
　　The elements are our allies,
11550　　And things head for annihilation.

FAUST:
　　Foreman!

MEPHISTOPHELES:
　　　　Here!

FAUST:
　　　　　　By any means you may,
　　Get workmen here by throngs and hordes,
　　Incite with strictness and rewards,
　　Entice them, urge them, give them pay!
　　I want to have reports each day of how
　　The trench proceeds that we are starting now.

MEPHISTOPHELES [*half-aloud*]:
　　They talked no trench when last they gave
　　Reports to me, but of a grave.

FAUST:
　　A swamp there by the mountain lies,
11560　　Infecting everything attained;
　　If that foul pool could once be drained,
　　The feat would outstrip every prize.
　　For many millions I shall open spaces
　　Where they, not safe but active-free, have dwelling places.
　　Verdant the fields and fruitful; man and beast

Alike upon that newest earth well pleased,
Shall settle soon the mighty strength of hill
Raised by a bold and busy people's will,
And here inside, a land like Paradise.
11570 Then let the outer flood to dike's rim rise,
And as it eats and seeks to crush by force,
The common will will rush to stem its course.
To this opinion I am given wholly
And this is wisdom's final say:
Freedom and life belong to that man solely
Who must reconquer them each day.
Thus child and man and old man will live here
Beset by peril year on busy year.
Such in their multitudes I hope to see
11580 On free soil standing with a people free.
Then to that moment I could say:
Linger on, you are so fair!
Nor can the traces of my earthly day
In many aeons pass away. —
Foresensing all the rapture of that dream,
This present moment gives me joy supreme.

[FAUST *sinks back; the* LEMURS *take hold of him and lay him down on the ground.*]
MEPHISTOPHELES:
No joy could sate him, no bliss could satisfy,
He chased his changeful vision to the last;
This final moment, paltry, void, and dry,
11590 The poor wretch wants to hold it fast.
Time masters him who could withstand
My power, the old man lies here on the sand.
The clock has stopped—
CHORUS:
Has stopped. As death-still as the midnight.
The clock hand falls.
MEPHISTOPHELES:
It falls. And "it is finished."[49]
CHORUS:
And all is over.
MEPHISTOPHELES:
Over! Stupid word!
Does it make sense?
Over, and sheerest naught, total indifference!

---

[49] "it is finished": A parody of Christ's last words on the Cross. (John 19:30)

All this creating comes to what?
To make things as if they were not.
11600 "A thing is over now!" What does that mean?
The same as if the thing had never been,
Yet circles round and round as if it *were*.
Eternal Emptiness I still prefer.

BURIAL

LEMUR [*solo*]:

O, who so badly built this house
With shovel and with spade?

LEMURS [*chorus*]:

For you, mute guest in hempen shroud,
It's far too finely made.

LEMUR [*solo*]:

And who so badly decked the hall?
Of tables, chairs, not any?

LEMURS [*chorus*]

11610 The lease was short-termed. After all,
Believers are so many.

MEPHISTOPHELES:

Here lies the body; if the spirit strays,
I'll soon confront it with that blood-signed scroll—
They have so many methods nowadays
To cheat the Devil of a soul.
Our old way seems to give offense,
Our new way they do not condone;
Once I'd have done it all alone,
Where now I have to have assistants.
11620 We're badly off on every score.
Old rights, time-honored ways of yore—
There's nothing left that you can trust.
Time was, a soul rode up the final gasp;
Then as with quickest mouse I'd make a thrust
And whoops! there she would be tight in my grasp.
Now they hang back, won't leave the dismal place,
Inside the filthy corpse they tarry late;
The elements in mutual hate
Expel them finally by sheer disgrace.
11630 And if I fret for days and hours now,
There still are questions of When? Where? and How?
Old Death has lost his rapid strength; about
The very Whether? there has long been doubt.
On dead-stiff limbs I've doted often, then
A false alarm and off they walked again.

[Fantastic and imperious conjuring gestures.]
    Come on, then! On the double! All of you
    Lords of the straight, lords of the crooked horn,
    Chips off the ancient block, you devils born,
    And bring the jaws of hell up with you too.
11640   For hell has many, many sets of jaws,
    By different ranks and standings it devours,
    But we won't haggle over rules and laws
    From now on in this final game of ours.

[The hideous jaws of hell open on the left.]
    The eyeteeth gape; up from the vaulted pit
    There seethes a tide of flame in raging flow,
    And through the steam-clouds in the back of it
    I see the fiery city all aglow.
    The red tide breaks in surges to the very teeth,
    The damned swim, hoping rescue, up the bath;
11650   But the hyena champs them back beneath
    And they retrace in pain their burning path.
    There's much more off in nooks you may perceive,
    The scariest things jammed in the tightest space!
    It's good to scare the sinners: they believe
    It's only an imaginary place.

[to the FAT DEVILS *with short, straight horns]*
    You paunchy rascals with the cheeks that burn,
    All fattened up on brimstone, how you glow!
    Short dumpy things with necks that cannot turn,
    Watch for a gleam of phosphor here below:
11660   That will be Soul, or Psyche with the wings;[50]
    Once they're pulled off, she's just a nasty worm;
    I'll set my seal on her, then off she slings
    Down to the whirlwind and the fiery storm!
       Those nether regions watch with care,
    You lard-guts! Duty bids you so.
    For if she deigns to dwell down there
    We do not just exactly know.
    The navel's where she likes to hide—
    Watch there, she might whisk past you to one side.

[to the LEAN DEVILS *with long, crooked horns]*
11670   You fancy bucks, you giant fuglemen,
    Keep sawing air, don't stop from first to last.
    With arms and sharp claws spread, be ready when

---

[50] **Psyche . . . wings:** *Psyche,* the Greek word for *soul,* represented as a butterfly.

The fluttering thing on fleeing wing comes past.
She surely must find her old house a bore;
Then too, the "genius"[51] also wants to soar.

[*Glory from above, on the right*]
THE HEAVENLY HOST:
Follow, you envoys
Of celestial joys
In unhurried flight:
Sinners forgiving,
11680   Dust to make living;
Down from above
Tokens of love
To all creatures giving
In hovering flight.

MEPHISTOPHELES:
Discords I hear and mawkish whimpering
Coming from topside with unwelcome light.
It's that half-boy-half-maiden simpering
In which a canting taste takes such delight.
In our depravity, you know, we meant
11690   And planned destruction for the human race;
The most disgraceful thing we could invent
Would, in *their* worship, be in place.
        Just see the minions mince and charm!
They've snitched a lot of souls in just this wise
By turning our own weapons to our harm;
They're devils too, though in disguise.
To lose out now would mean eternal shame;
Up to that grave, then, and cling fast to same!

CHORUS OF ANGELS [*strewing roses*]:
Refulgence of roses
11700   Fragrance expending!
Tremulous, swaying,
Life-force conveying,
Branchlet-bewisped
Buds now unclasped,
Bloom fullest and best.
        Springtime arise,
Crimson and green;
Bring Paradise
To him at his rest.

---

[51] **"genius"**: The spirit that inhabits the human body.

MEPHISTOPHELES [*to the* SATANS]:

11710   Why do you duck and wince? Is that hell's play?
        Stand firm and let them strew away.
        Back to your stations, gawks, and stay!
        They fancy they are going to snow
        Hot devils under with their posy show.
        Your breath will melt and shrivel that away.
        Now blow, you puff-cheeks! There! Enough! Enough!
        You've bleached and blanched them with your huff and puff. —
        Don't blow so lustily, shut snout and nose!
        O, now you've overblown your blows.
11720   You must learn when to stop! When will you learn!
        They're shriveled, but they're going to scorch and burn!
        As bright and poisonous flames they're drifting near!
        Stand firm against them, crowd together here!
        All courage vanishes, strength ebbs away.
        The devils scent strange fires' caressing play.

ANGELS [*chorus*]:

        Blossoms of joy,
        Flames of high gladness,
        Love they expend,
        Bliss they portend,
11730   Heart as it may:
        Truth in their words,
        Clear aetherwards
        Eternal hordes,
        Limitless day!

MEPHISTOPHELES:

        O curses on this ninny band!
        Upon their heads the Satans stand.
        The louts turn cartwheels down the path
        And plop ass-backwards into hell.
        Take comfort from your well deserved hot bath!
11740   *I'm* staying on here for a spell. —

[*knocking aside the drifting roses*]

        Will-o'-the-wisps, begone! Shine as you will,
        Once caught, you're little turds of jelly still.
        Why flutter so? Just go away! And quick!
        Like pitch and sulphur to my neck they stick!

ANGELS [*chorus*]:

        What you may not possess
        You must abjure;
        What gives your heart distress
        You must not endure.

If it crowds in by force,

11750   We must take valiant course.

Love only lovers

Brings to the door.

MEPHISTOPHELES:

My head and liver burn, my heart is rent.

A super-devilish element!

Worse stinging far than hell's own fire. ——

That's why you lift laments so dire,

Unhappy lovers, who forever crane

Your necks to look at loved ones who disdain.

    Me too! But what makes my head that way tend?

11760   Am I not sworn to fight them to the end?

I used to find them such a hateful sight.

Has something alien pierced me through and through?

I love to have these darling boys in view.

What keeps me now from cursing them tonight?

If *I* am gulled at this late date,

Who will then as "the Fool" be styled?

These handsome rascals that I hate

Seem just too lovely, and I am beguiled. ——

    Now pretty lads, come tell me true:

11770   Are you too not of Lucifer's family?

You're just so nice, I'd like a kiss from you,

I feel you're just the thing for me.

It comes so cozily, so naturally,

As if we'd met a thousand times before,

So kitten-sly and raffishly;

With every glance you charm me more and more.

Come closer, grant me just one glance!

ANGELS:

But why do you fall back when we advance?

We move up closer; meet us if you can.

[*The* ANGELS, *moving about, come to occupy the entire space.*]

MEPHISTOPHELES [*who is forced into the proscenium*]:

11780   You call *us* spirits damned, but you

Are the real witch-masters tried and true,

For you seduce both maid and man. ——

O cursed adventure! Do you claim

This is the element of love?

My entire body is aflame,

I hardly feel the burning from above. ——

You hover to and fro; come down and stir

Your lovely limbs in ways a trifle worldlier.

11790
>Your seriousness is most becoming for a while,
>But just for once I'd like to see you smile;
>That would give me a pleasure unsurpassed.
>I mean the kind of looks that lovers cast.
>A flicker of the lips, and there we'll have it.
>I like you best, there, lad so slim and tall,
>But clergy-looks don't go with you at all.
>Give me a glance that's just the least bit avid.
>Then, too, you could more decent-nakedly appear;
>Those flowing robes are all too morals-emphasizing—
>They turn their backs—a glimpse now from the rear!—

11800
>The little monkeys are so appetizing!

CHORUS OF ANGELS:
>Turn, flames of love,
>Toward clarity;
>Be the self-damned saved
>By verity;
>Self-redeemed be they
>From evil's sway,
>Blessed to be
>In the totality.

MEPHISTOPHELES [*getting control of himself*]:
>What is this!—I am raw with sores all round,

11810
>A very Job, shocked at the state he's in
>And yet triumphant as he looks within
>Himself and trusts himself and his own kin;
>My noble devil parts are safe and sound,
>The love infection breaks out through the skin.
>Now that the cursed flames are out, I call
>Down curses, as you well deserve, on one and all!

CHORUS OF ANGELS:
>Sacred ardors!
>Whom you surround
>Has full life found

11820
>With the good, in bliss.
>Ascend up allied
>And praises wreathe,
>In air purified
>The spirit may breathe!

[*They ascend, bearing with them* FAUST'*s immortal part.*]
MEPHISTOPHELES [*looking about*]:
>What's this?—Now where can they have gone?
>You juveniles have caught me by surprise
>And off to heaven with the booty flown.

So that's why they were nibbling at this grave!
They've made off with my great and unique prize,
11830   The soul which he to me once pledged and gave,
They've smuggled it away, that's what they've done.
     To whom can I go for redress?
Who will get me my well-earned right?
You have been fooled in your old days. Confess,
However, you deserve your sorry plight.
I have outrageously mismanaged,
A mighty outlay—shamefully!—is lost,
Absurd amour and common lust have managed
To catch the canny Devil to his cost.
1840   But if the one of wise experience got
Himself involved in that mad, childish game,
Still, slight the folly was most surely not
Which caught him at the last and overcame.

MOUNTAIN GORGES

Forest, cliff, wilderness. Holy anchorites,[52] *disposed up the mountainside, stationed in the ravines.*

CHORUS AND ECHO:
   Woodlands, they falter toward it,
Cliffsides, they weigh against it,
Root-snarls, they clutch into it,
Tree dense to tree up along it.
Waves in a foaming welter,
Nethermost cave yields shelter.
11850   Lions in silence rove
Friendly and tame around,
Reverencing holy ground,
Love's holy treasure-trove.
PATER ECSTATICUS[53] [*floating up and down*]:
   Ecstasy's ceaseless fire,
Love's bond of hot desire,
Seething heart of pain,
Foaming joy divine.
Arrows, transfix me!
Lances, enforce me!

---

[52] *Holy anchorites:* Hermits of the early Christian centuries who withdrew into the wilderness to devote their entire existence to the adoration of God. Goethe here makes them symbols of intense aspiration utterly possessed by love.

[53] *Pater Ecstaticus:* The title given to Saint Anthony; this spirit is mystical with a longing for the infinite.

11860   Cudgels, batter me!
   Lightning bolts, shatter me!
   So the All may utterly
   Abolish the Nullity,
   Gleam the fixed star above,
   Essence of endless love.

PATER PROFUNDUS[54] [*lower region*]:
   As rocky chasms here beneath
   On deeper chasms base their thrusts,
   As countless brooklets, shining, seethe
   In downward leaps and foaming gusts,
11870   As upward to the air above
   The tall tree in its power strains,
   Just so, it is almighty Love
   That forms all things and all sustains.
      There is a roaring all around
   As if woods were billows under gales,
   And yet there falls with gracious sound
   The wealth of waters to the vales,
   As if bound to bring moisture there;
   The lightning flash of flaming dart
11880   That struck to purify the air
   And purge infection from its heart—
      All are Love's messengers proclaiming
   Creation's ceaseless workings multifold.
   May my soul also know such flaming,
   Where spirit, now perplexed and cold,
   In gross net of the senses caught,
   Is riveted in chains that smart.
   O God! Assuage and calm my thought,
   Illuminate my needy heart!

PATER SERAPHICUS[55] [*middle region*]:
11890   What cloud of dawning at this minute
   Parts the pine trees' floating hair?
   Do I guess what lives within it?
   Here is a youthful spirit choir.

CHORUS OF BLESSED BOYS:[56]
   Tell us, Father, where we wander,
   Tell us, kind man, who we are.

---

[54] **Pater Profundus:** The title of St. Bernard of Clairvaux; a spirit of the lower region (profundus), this spirit is earthy and sense-bound.

[55] **Pater Seraphicus:** The title of St. Francis of Assisi; this spirit is self-denying and concerned for others.

[56] **Chorus . . . boys:** The souls of the infant dead.

Happy are we, and so tender
Is the life that we all bear.

PATER SERAPHICUS:

Children, you were midnight-born[57]
Sense and spirit half attained;
11900 From your parents you were torn,
For the angels you were gained.
One who loves, before your faces
You feel present; draw, then, near;
Rugged earthways left no traces
On you as you now appear.
Come you down, and with the loan
Of my earthly-bounded eyes,
Using them as if your own,
View the land that round you lies.

[He takes them into himself.]
11910 These are trees; these, cliffsides jutting;
That, a waterfall that plunges,
By its awesome down-course cutting
Short the steep path as it lunges.

BLESSED BOYS [*from within*]:

This is mighty to behold,
But a place in which to grieve,
Chills us with a terror cold.
Good man, kind man, let us leave.

PATER SERAPHICUS:

Rise to higher spheres; mature
Unobserved by any eyes,
11920 As, in ways forever pure,
God's own presence fortifies.
For throughout free air above
Spirits taste no other food
Than revelation of eternal Love
Which nurtures to beatitude.

CHORUS OF BLESSED BOYS [*circling about the highest peaks*]:

Gladly entwine
Hands in a ring,
With feelings divine
Dance and sing.
11930 Trust in the lore
Divinely told,

---

[57] **midnight-born:** Children born at midnight were thought to have little chance of living.

Him you adore
You shall behold.

ANGELS [*soaring in the higher atmosphere, bearing the immortal part of* FAUST]:
Delivered is he now from ill,
Whom we a spirit deemed:
"Who strives forever with a will,
By us can be redeemed."
And if in him the higher Love
Has had a share, to meet him

11940   Will come the blessed host above
And warmly greet him.

THE YOUNGER ANGELS:
Loving-holy penitents,
By the roses that they rained,
Helped us to the triumph gained
In this task of eminence,
Helped to win this treasured soul.
Demons yielded from their goal,
Devils at our onslaught fled.
Spirits felt Love's pain instead

11950   Of their usual hellish anguish;
Bitter pangs could even vanquish
The arch-Satan's self. Exult!
Joyous is the high result!

THE MORE PERFECTED ANGELS:
Earth remnants still arrest us,
Hard to endure;
Were he made of asbestos,
He is not pure.[58]
When once strong spirit force
Subsumes man's elements,

11960   No angels can divorce
The quintessence
Of dual self made one;
The two parts allied
Eternal Love alone
Can then divide.

THE YOUNGER ANGELS:
Misted at rocky height
Spirits appear
Moving closer in sight

---

[58] **Were he . . . pure:** Although asbestos is an unburnable material, it is nonetheless material and thus not spiritual.

As they haste along.
11970   The cloudlets grow more clear,
I see a lively throng
Of blessed boys,
From earth's oppression free,
Joined in a ring,
Glad with the joys
Of spheres so beauteously
Decked with new spring.
With these let him begin,
And, rising with them, win
11980   Perfection gradually.

THE BLESSED BOYS:
With joy we receive
Him in pupa stage;
In him we achieve
Angelic pledge.
Unravel the cocoon strands
Around him rife.
Great he already stands
With holy life.

DOCTOR MARIANUS[59] [*in the highest, purest cell*]:
The prospect here is free,
11990   The mind uplifting.
There ladies move past me
Upward drifting.
The Glorious One beneath
Her starry wreath
In splendor there is seen,
All Heaven's Queen.

[*enraptured*]
Highest mistress of the world,
Admit me, in this blue
Tent of heaven here unfurled,
12000   To thy mystery's view.
What earnestly and tenderly
Stirs men's hearts, approve,
And all things they bring to thee
In holy joy of love.
Courage fights invincibly
Till thou bidd'st it cease,

---

[59] **Doctor Marianus:** A teacher of the cult of the Virgin Mary.

Ardor mellows suddenly
As thou givest peace.
Virgin pure in fairest sense,
12010 Mother, of all honor worth,
Queen in eminence,
Of gods the peer by birth.
    Around her densely
gather clouds,
Penitents
In gentle crowds
About her knees,
Bright aether breathing,
Mercy beseeching.
12020   To thee, inviolate,
It is not denied
That the easily misled
Should in thee confide.
    In their weakness swept away,
Hard they are to save;
Who of his own power may
Wrest chains from lust's slave?
Whose foot will not fail him fast
On the slippery path?
12030 Who is not deceived at last
By a cozening breath?

[*The* MATER GLORIOSA *soars forth.*]
CHORUS OF FEMALE PENITENTS:
    Thou soarest on high
To eternal realms.
O hear our cry!
Peerless art thou,
Merciful art thou!
MAGNA PECCATRIX (St. Luke 7:36):[60]
    By the love which at the feet
Of thy transfigured Son God-born
Shed tears as though of balsam sweet
12040 Despite the Pharisee's high scorn;
By the alabaster ointment box
Shedding fragrance down on Him,
By the hair and flowing locks
Which then dried each sacred limb —

---

[60] **Magna Peccatrix:** The "greatly sinful woman" who washed Jesus' feet at the house of the Pharisee.

MULIER SAMARITANA (St. John 4):[61]
    By the well whereto were driven
    Abram's herds, and by the well-dips
    Whence a cooling drink was given
    To the Saviour's thirsting lips;
    By the spring of purity
12050   Which from thence outpours and flows
    Ever clear and copiously
    As through all the worlds it goes—

MARIA AEGYPTIACA[62] [*Acta Sanctorum*]:
    By the consecrated tomb
    Where the Lord was laid of yore,
    By the arm that beckoned doom,
    Thrusting me back from the door;
    By the forty-year repentance
    That I lived in desert waste,
    By the blessed farewell sentence
12060   That upon the sand I traced—

ALL THREE:
    Thou who never dost deny
    Help to those whose sins are great,
    And eternally on high
    Dost repentance elevate,
    Grant to this good soul as well,
    Who did only once transgress,
    Hardly knowing that she fell—
    Grant remission limitless.

UNA POENITENTIUM, ONCE NAMED GRETCHEN [*nestling close*]:
    Deign, O deign,
12070   Amid thy reign
    In radiance,
    To look in mercy on my joy.
    My once beloved,
    No more troubled,
    Joins me in joy.

BLESSED BOYS [*drawing near in a circling movement*]:
    So soon he has outgrown us
    In might of limb;
    Reward will soon be shown us
    For care of him.

---

[61] **Mulier Samaritana:** The "woman of Samaria" who drew water for Jesus to drink.

[62] **Maria Aegyptiaca:** Mary of Egypt was forbidden to enter the Church of the Holy Sepulchre in Jerusalem and did penance in the desert for forty-eight years.

12080   Too little time we sojourned
    For life to reach us,
    But those things he has learned,
    And he will teach us.

A PENITENT, ONCE NAMED GRETCHEN:
    Amid the noble choir of Heaven
    He hardly knows that self of his,
    He guesses not the new life given,
    Yet of the holy host he is.
    See how he wrests himself out free
    Of his integument of earth,
12090   How in ethereal raiment he
    Shows youthful vigor in new birth.
    Vouchsafe to me to be his guide,
    His eyes still dazzle with new day.

MATER GLORIOSA:
    Rise, and in higher spheres abide;
    He will sense you and find the way.

DOCTOR MARIANUS [*prostrate on his face, in adoration*]:
    Gaze upward to that saving glance;
    Toward beatitude,
    Gentle penitents, advance,
    Be changed with gratitude.
12100   Let every better sense be keen
    To do thee service duly;
    Virgin, Mother, and our Queen,
    Goddess, help us truly.

CHORUS MYSTICUS:
    All transitory
    Things represent;
    Inadequates here
    Become event,
    Ineffables here,
    Accomplishment;
12110   The Eternal-Feminine
    Draws us onward.[63]

---

[63] **All . . . onward:** These lines can be interpreted as follows: All transitory things are — as in Plato's doctrine — imperfect reflections of divine realities. Humankind's utmost striving while on earth is necessary, but it requires the complement of heavenly assistance. Transition from earthly form into eternal form is accomplished, but no words are adequate to describe it. The Eternal-Feminine is the unfailing inspiration, the moving force giving impetus in earthly life as in the life hereafter to strive from lesser stages upward toward infinite perfection. That perfection is Love; in Dante's final line of the *Paradiso,* "the Love that moves the sun and the other stars."

Faust and the Romantic Hero

The American and French revolutions of 1776 and 1789 promised to fulfill—even to exceed—the hope of the *philosophes,* which was to establish a political order founded upon civil rights and social justice, religious toleration and civility that would promote human progress toward perfection. With those revolutions new political ideas stirred up by philosophers such as John Locke and Jean Jacques Rousseau seemed to have come to life in the theater of world history. If July 4, 1776, gave rise to a new nation, it also inaugurated a series of political revolutions in France, the Caribbean, Poland, and South America, where Enlightenment philosophy and Romantic ideals spawned a new generation of revolutionary heroes, such as George Washington in America; Toussaint Louverture in Haiti; Tadeusz Kosciuszko in Poland; Simón Bolívar in Venezuela; and, above all Napoleon Bonaparte in France. Such men embodied the Romantic hero, a man who by dint of genius, talent, and uncompromising will seemed able to overcome any obstacle to challenge and change the world.

Among the heroes for the new age, Napoleon was paradigmatic. For his advocates and adversaries alike, Napoleon was for better or for worse a modern Prometheus, the Greek Titan who stole fire from Zeus to bring human beings art, science, and craftsmanship. Like the defiant Titan, the Romantic hero rebelled against authoritarian injustice and sought to benefit humanity, although he was often

▶ Jacques-Louis David, *Napoleon at St. Bernhard.* Painting
Napoleon embodied the heroic ideals of the early nineteenth century, and paintings such as this depiccted him as a noble, confident warrior. (Kunsthistorisches Museum)

BONAPARTE

pp. 560, 719

p. 724

caught between those two roles. In Napoleon's case, those roles became reversed. His steadfast dedication to his innate gifts and talents took him from relatively humble beginnings in Corsica to the highest pinnacles of society and power. In his guise as a self-made man of genius and action, Napoleon, man and myth, seemed to embody the spirit of inexorable action celebrated in Goethe's *Faust*. Works such as Alessandro Manzoni's "**The Fifth of May**," Lord Byron's *Childe Harold*, and Ludwig von Beethoven's *Eroica* symphony (originally dedicated to Napoleon) attributed to Napoleon the restlessness, tempestuousness, and epic grandeur that characterizes Goethe's *Faust* and the very spirit of the age. Yet in 1804 when Napoleon crowned himself emperor in an ostentatious ceremony reminiscent of the coronation of the Roman emperor Caesar, it became clear to many that Napoleon's ambition to be Master of Europe undermined his promise as a revolutionary liberator. Defying Europe's monarchs, the Promethean Napoleon had now become a Zeus-like tyrant in his own right. For Romantic writers, Napoleon became emblematic of the failed overreacher, a fallen Titan who had succumbed to his own Faustian desire.

In arts and ideology, the nineteenth century would become what one twentieth-century critic characterized as "a century of hero-worship." And even if sometimes the search failed to turn up a hero, or turned up an anti-hero, the belief in heroes and the ongoing watch for them would, as Thomas Carlyle asserted in *On Heroes, Hero-Worship, and The Heroic in History* (1841), save the century from destruction: "For myself in these days, I seem to see in this indestructibility of Hero-worship the everlasting adamant lower than which the confused wreck of revolutionary things cannot fall. . . . That man, in some sense or other, worships Heroes; that we all of us reverence and must ever reverence Great Men: this is, to me, the living rock amid all rushings-down whatsoever;—the one fixed point in modern revolutionary history."

FAUST, THE DIVIDED ROMANTIC HERO

Both rebel and ruler, the ROMANTIC HERO lives in contradiction. As a revolutionary, he is an outsider, even an outlaw, who challenges the divine and social order of things. His isolation, however, involves him in a contradiction, for it cuts him off from those he hopes to

TIME AND PLACE

Nineteenth-Century Europe: The Eroica Symphony

Like many of his contemporaries, Ludwig von Beethoven (1770–1827) held a vexed and ambivalent opinion of Napoleon Bonaparte. The story of Beethoven's Third Symphony, the *Eroica,* points to the contradictory positions Europe took as it sought to comprehend and evaluate the young general turned emperor.

In the 1790s, when Napoleon inherited the title of "modern Prometheus" from Benjamin Franklin in the European imagination, Beethoven associated Napoleon with Prometheus, as we can see from the compositional links between his score for Salvatore Vigano's 1800 ballet, *Creatures of Prometheus,* and *Eroica,* which was written with Bonaparte in mind and was at first dedicated to him. Vigano's native Italy had a vexed relationship with Napoleon, whose defeat of Austria could help Italy form a republic, but whose imperialist designs threatened only to replace one foreign power with another. In his "Buonaparte Liberatore" (1797), Italian poet Ugo Foscolo celebrated Napoleon as the liberator of Italy, but after Bonaparte ceded part of Venice to the Austrians in the 1797 Treaty of Campo Formio, Foscolo retracted his praise and criticized Napoleon in his novel *The Last Letters of Jacopo Ortis.* Vigano and Beethoven shared in the early enthusiasm for Napoleon who, as First Consul, was widely praised as a liberator and a republican bearing the spirit of Enlightenment and revolution. Some biographers and critics believe that when Beethoven used the *Prometheus* finale in the fourth movement of the *Eroica,* he did so fully conscious of the association between Napoleon and Prometheus, who appears in the ballet as creator and benefactor of humanity, as the bringer of arts and culture.

Jacques Louis David, detail of The Coronation of Napoleon Bonaparte, 1804   *Having declared himself Emperor, Napoleon crowns his wife Josephine as Empress of France. (The Art Archive/Musée du Louvre Paris/Dagli Orti)*

Moreover, when Beethoven began sketching ideas for the *Eroica* Symphony in 1802, he was also at work on the E-flat Piano Variations, Opus 35, which he called the "Prometheus" Variations. Prometheus and Napoleon seem to be very much connected in Beethoven's mind.

Of course, Beethoven famously flew into a fit of indignant rage when he learned of the May 18, 1804 decree that the French Republic would allow Napoleon to declare himself emperor. The coronation took place on December 2, 1804. Reportedly, crying out that Napoleon was nothing more than an ordinary mortal, sharing the general sense of betrayal,

Nineteenth-Century Europe: The Eroica *Symphony* continued

Beethoven angrily blotted out the dedication to Bonaparte on the title page of the *Eroica* — a scene depicted in Bernard Rose's 1994 film *Immortal Beloved,* starring Gary Oldman as Beethoven. By the time the score for *Eroica* was published in 1806, Beethoven had suppressed all evidence that the symphony was in any way connected to Napoleon. As Beethoven's biographer Norman Solomon and others observe, the title page to Beethoven's own score of the symphony shows the line "Intitulata Bonaparte" crossed out, but retains in Beethoven's own hand the line *Geschrieben auf Bonaparte* — "written about Bonaparte." Only when it was published in October 1806, did the "Sinfonia Grande" acquire the title *Eroica,* with the subtitle "composed to celebrate the memory of a great man." Like Goethe, Byron, Manzoni, Stendahl, and many others who praised the otherwise corrupt Napoleon as the "genius of action," Beethoven's anger with Napoleon did not mean disillusionment with the republican or heroic values that Bonaparte once represented for the composer's generation. Nor did Beethoven's revocation of the dedication to Napoleon signal the end of his fascination with the man, whose talent, genius, and energy mirrored Beethoven's own. Like Napoleon, Beethoven was notorious for his own uncompromising will, virtuoso talent, genius, and passionate intensity, and the Third, and especially the Ninth Symphony, Beethoven's most Napoleonic work, earned a reputation for Beethoven nearly as controversial and provocative as Napoleon's. Like the general turned emperor, Beethoven became a figure whom none could ignore and whose career continues to spellbind both his admirers and his critics.

zah-ruh-THOOS-truh

p. 730
p. 968

lead. **Zarathustra**, Nietzsche's prophet of the Superman in *Thus Spoke Zarathustra* (1883–84), is spurned by the people to whom he preaches in the marketplace. Dostoevsky's Christ in "**The Grand Inquisitor**" demands too much when he calls for mankind to sacrifice comfort and security and choose freedom instead. These heroes cannot be both above the world and in the world at the same time. Faust is also caught in this Romantic contradiction. He describes himself as a divided man: "Two souls abide, alas, within my breast," he laments, "And each one seeks for riddance from the other." On one hand he yearns for supernatural knowledge and on the other he desires to be immersed in worldly experience. By mastering medicine, law, science, and theology, he isolates himself from the rest of mankind, and by seeking forbidden knowledge he becomes an intellectual outlaw yet also hopes to participate in the common human experience. **Gerard de Nerval** (1808–1855) in his "Observations on Goethe's Faust" characterizes Faust's situation when he observes "his is all the grandeur and strength of the human race, his is also all its weaknesses." Goethe's version of the Faust story does not emphasize

zhuh-RAR duh
nur-VAHL

Faust's heresy, and it does not end with the hero condemned to hell. Faust's desire to know and experience everything, his "striving," is his great virtue and the source of his ultimate redemption. But it is also his "tragedy" in that it leads to the death and suffering of Margaret and her family; even his redemptive final project to reclaim the marshes and develop housing for common people makes martyrs of Baucis and Philemon. The play forces one to consider the costs of heroism and progress and to recognize the tragic dimensions of experience.

NAPOLEON

If Faust is the great literary hero, then Napoleon is the defining historical hero of the century, receiving high praise and blame from many writers. A man of immense ambition, Napoleon was the most admired and feared military commander of his time. He conquered an empire that stretched across Europe, from the Iberian peninsula to the Russian border, and even reached into parts of North Africa. An outsider and upstart from Corsica, a rebel from "the people," Napoleon fit the ROMANTIC model of the hero who would oppose the old regime and institute governmental reforms to bring order and progress to France and the continent. Even his enemies revered him as a master of military strategy and as the ruler who rescued the French Revolution from the anarchy of the Reign of Terror. Yet in the end Napoleon's promise was blighted by his imperial designs, and the other nations of Europe eventually banded together to defeat and exile him, making him an international outlaw. He ended his days alone on St. Helena Island in the South Atlantic, where he died in 1821, but lived on in the imagination of such nineteenth-century writers as Lord Byron, **Stendhal**, and Tolstoy.[1]

Byron's Napoleon, like Faust, is a man of extremes and contradictions, a hero who rejects human limitations and "aspire[s]/ Beyond the fitting medium of desire." In Childe Harold's ruminations on Napoleon, Byron transforms the emperor into a **BYRONIC HERO**, a type of literary outlaw he popularized in poems celebrating such

> For myself in these days, I seem to see in this indestructibility of Hero-worship the everlasting adamant lower than which the confused wreck of revolutionary things cannot fall. . . . That man, in some sense or other, worships Heroes; that we all of us reverence and must ever reverence Great Men; this is, to me, the living rock amid all rushings-down whatsoever, — the one fixed point in modern revolutionary history.
>
> – THOMAS CARLYLE, *Heroes and Hero-Worship*

sten-DAWL

---

[1] **Stendhal:** The pen name of French novelist Marie Henri Beyle (1783–1842), a soldier in Napoleon's army during the Italian campaign in 1800 and again during the Russian campaign in 1812. He treats Napoleon as a heroic figure in his novel *The Red and the Black* (1831). **Leo Tolstoy** (1828–1910): Russian novelist (p. 983) who studies Napoleon's "heroism" in *War and Peace* (1865–69), his novel about Napoleon's Russian campaign.

"mixt and extreme" figures as Cain and Don Juan. Byron's Napoleon assumes a godlike role and scornfully looks down on mankind. A restless, "unquiet" spirit, he is both the conqueror and the captive of those who elevate and ultimately humiliate him, simultaneously heroic leader and outlaw.

too-SEHNG
loo-vehr-TOOR

Touissant-Louverture.   Pierre-Dominique **Toussaint-Louverture**, leader of a slave rebellion in Haiti in the 1790s and self-proclaimed ruler of the island in 1801, was often called "the black Napoleon." His skills as a military strategist and government administrator, as well as his ultimate fate—dying in exile in a French prison in 1803—link his life story with that of the revolutionary emperor. Both were "upstarts" who had risen to positions of power. As a former slave who liberated his country from slavery, Toussaint-Louverture assumed especially heroic stature in the eyes of the abolitionists who sought to end slavery in the Caribbean and the southern United States. **John Greenleaf Whittier**, perhaps the most influential poet among the American abolitionists, celebrated Toussaint-Louverture as a martyred hero of the movement. In his poem "Toussaint L'Ouverture," from his *Voices of Freedom* collection (1846), he describes the rebel general as he leads the slaves to freedom, declaring "The yoke is spurned, the chain is broken; / . . . No more the mocking White shall rest / His foot upon the Negro's breast." Whittier ends the poem celebrating "one of earth's great spirits."

p. 726

ARGUING ABOUT HEROISM

The celebration of heroes such as Toussaint-Louverture and Napoleon in the literature and art of the nineteenth century was part of a larger discussion about the nature and consequences of heroism. While Carlyle worshipped heroes as the saviors of the time, the Faustian figures in nineteenth-century literature often descended into self-destructive obsessions and madness. Mary Shelley's Victor Frankenstein dies pursuing the monster he created; Herman Melville's Captain Ahab in *Moby-Dick* (1851) is destroyed by the white whale; Ibsen's Halvard Solness in *Master Builder* (1892) falls from the grandiose tower he has constructed. And in *War and Peace* (1865–69), a novel about Napoleon's Russian campaign and the century's most sustained treatment of the subject of heroism, Tolstoy set out to prove that great men do not determine history. The real heroes of that novel are the Russian peasants, the

I want a hero.
– BYRON, *Don Juan*

Japanese Samurai Armor
Samurai lived by a very strict code and, accordingly, wore ornate, specially designed armor. (Art Resource)

anonymous instruments of the historical forces that ultimately defeat the arrogant strong man.

To the dominant bourgeoisie of the later nineteenth century, the heroic virtues of the old aristocracy had become suspect. Strength, nobility, and military prowess had been devalued, and more domestic qualities like thrift, honesty, and industry gained stature. Friedrich **Nietzsche**, however, writing at the end of the century, attacked these newer virtues, calling them "slave morality." In a wishful prophesy Nietzsche predicted the arrival of a race of Supermen who would reject such Christian virtues and adopt a harsh and ruthless heroic ethic in their place.

REVIVING THE WAY OF THE SAMURAI

Nineteenth-century Japanese society was, in many ways, even more constrained with rules and conventions than was Europe's. By the end of the century, however, Japan had been opened to the West and its traditions were changing. **Inazo Nitobé**'s characterization of the Japanese in terms of **Bushido**, the traditional code of the samurai, both recalls the heroic virtues of the warrior class and suggests the ways in which they were altered by the bourgeois culture of the time. Nitobé, a Japanese Christian, relates samurai virtues to Western ethics and softens them with the Christian ideals of love and compassion. Nitobé has been contrasted with Nietzsche — while Nietzsche rejects Christian virtues for the Supermen of his future society, Nitobé calls on those values to soften the warrior culture he celebrates.

■ **PRONUNCIATION**

Bushido: boo-shee-DOH
Gerard de Nerval: zhuh-RAR duh nur-VAHL
Nietzsche: NEE-chuh (NEE-chee)
Stendhal: sten-DAWL
Toussaint-Louverture: too-SEHNG loo-vehr-TOOR
Zarathustra: zah-ruh-THOOS-truh

NEE-chuh (NEE-chee)

p. 732
boo-shee-DOH

❧ ALESSANDRO MANZONI
B. ITALY, 1785–1873

Alessandro Manzoni was born in Milan in 1785 to Pietro Manzoni and Giulia Beccaria. His maternal grandfather was Cesare Beccaria, political theorist and prison reformer who wrote the ground-breaking *On Crimes and Punishments* (1764). His parents separated in 1792, and after a troubled, sometimes dissipated youth, in 1808 Manzoni married Henriette Blondel, a Swiss Calvinist from Geneva. Shortly after the marriage, Manzoni and his wife underwent a spiritual conversion and joined the Catholic Church, to which Manzoni devoted himself studiously. Renouncing Voltaire and the critical Enlightenment tradition, Manzoni divided his time between devotional prayer and writing. Although he had begun writing poetry when he was about fifteen years old and had published some poetry when he was in his early twenties, it was not until after his conversion that Manzoni's considerable literary talents were recognized. While much of his work focused upon religious themes, as in *Inni Sacri* (*Sacred Hymns*, 1812–15), Manzoni also wrote on secular, patriotic themes, celebrating the liberation of Italy and the formation of an Italian republic. His first major success was the verse drama *Il conte di Carmagnola* (*The Story of Carmagnola*, 1820), which won him the praise of Goethe. By that time, some Italian writers were self-consciously writing under the name of *romantismo*, and Manzoni numbered himself among these Romantic writers. In 1821, the death of Napoleon inspired Manzoni to compose *Il cinque maggio* ("The Fifth of May"), one of many poems written to commemorate Napoleon. In 1821 he also began his most famous work, *I promessi sposi* (*The Betrothed*), which remains one of the great historical novels of the nineteenth century, and he continued writing plays, including *Adelchi* (1822), as well as poetry and prose. *The Betrothed* was published in 1827 to immediate praise, but Manzoni constantly revised the novel until a final edition came out in 1840. Manzoni lived another thirty-three years, studying and writing on Italian history and language, dying at the age of eighty-eight in 1873. "The Fifth of May," which captures the mixture of praise and blame, respect and disappointment evoked by Napoleon, is often considered one of the greatest of Italian lyrics of the nineteenth century.

❧ The Fifth of May

Translated by Joseph Tusiani

He's dead. Just as his body,
his breathing ended, lay
oblivious, immobile,
bereft of its great day,
so at this news mankind
lies thunderstruck and stunned,

musing upon the final
hour of the man of fate,
unsure if a new, mortal
10   footprint will soon or late
appear within our midst,
treading his sanguine dust.

My poet's fancy saw him
bright on a throne one day;
but when through varied fortune
he fell, and rose, and lay,
I did not blend my song
With thousands of the throng.

Virgin to servile homage
20   and cowardly offense,
roused by the sudden setting
of all that light immense,
now on his urn I cast
a paean that may last.

From Pyramids to Alps, from
the Tagus to the Rhine,
he bade the lightning follow
his more resplendent sign:
From Don to Scylla, he
30   Thundered from sea to sea.

True glory? Let the future
its hard pronouncement give:
we bow to his Creator,
Who did more deeply leave
in one man's life and death
the imprint of His breath.

The restlessness and tempest
of a most daring plan,
the sureness of a kingdom
40   that bends a tameless man
(he grabs it, to attain
what hope had deemed insane):

all he experienced — after
the peril glory's height,

retreat and then new triumph,
the throne, the exile's plight:
twice trodden in the mud
and twice adored as God.

He named himself: two centuries
50 fighting each other still,
looked up to him, submissive,
heeding as fate his will:
commanding quietude,
between them, judge, he stood.

And then he vanished, ending
his days on a brief shore—
a sign of boundless envy
and pity still at war,
of unabated hate
60 and love defying fate.

As on a shipwrecked seaman
the whirling waves weigh deep,
the waves above whose summit
he could until now keep
his glance, eager to gain
a distant land in vain:

so on that soul the burden
of recollections fell.
How oft to future ages
70 he wished his life to tell,
but, as his fingers shook,
he closed his endless book!

How often in the silent
death of a dismal day,
his arms inertly folded,
his gaze without its ray,
he stood within the blast
of his remembered past!

Again he saw the mobile
80 tents, the assaulted meads,
the lightning of the squadrons,
the rushing waves of steeds,

the signal for advance,
the fast obedience.

Maybe by all this torment
his peaceless soul was driven,
ah, to despair; but quickly
a valid hand from heaven
lifted him, kind and fair,
90   to a more healthy air.

Along hope's flowered meadows
it taught him then to go
towards everlasting prairies
where higher prizes glow,
where glory that was bright
is silent dark of night.

Deathless and beauteous, balmy
Faith, used to victories!
Write this down, too: be joyous,
100   for never did a prouder
grandeur stoop down to see
the shame of Calvary.

You, all malicious murmur
ban from his poor remains:
that God Who strikes and comforts,
Who weakens and sustains,
near the forsaken pall
came down to rest and call.

❧ GEORGE GORDON, LORD BYRON
B. ENGLAND, 1788–1824

The most notorious of the English **ROMANTIC** poets, Lord Byron was viewed in his own time, particularly in Europe, as the model Romantic bard. The heroes of his poems—Childe Harold, Manfred, Don Juan, and others—became versions of the "**BYRONIC HERO**," a moody and restless wanderer, haunted by an unnamed guilt in his mysterious past. Byron himself, in his own time, was assumed to be the source for these tormented figures. His life does provide much to support that hypothesis. A nobleman who assumed his title at age ten, he dissipated much of his inheritance in riotous living; carried on a scandalous affair with his half-sister, Augusta Leigh; separated from his wife, Annabella Milbanke, after a year of marriage; and fathered an illegitimate child by poet Percy Bysshe Shelley's wife's sister, Claire Clairmont. Serving a brief stint in the House of Lords, Byron was committed to liberal causes; he was also a devoted friend and a generous master to his dependents. He cultivated his reputation as a kind of hero, fashioning himself as a world traveler, swimming across the Hellespont, the strait between the European and Asian parts of Turkey, and fighting for Greek independence from the Turks. In the latter cause Byron died, at only 36 years of age.

    Childe Harold's Pilgrimage (1812, 1816, 1818), a narrative based on Byron's own travels throughout Europe, was an overnight sensation. After the first cantos appeared in 1812, Byron claimed he "awoke one morning and found myself famous." The melancholy, worldly, and cosmopolitan traveler Childe Harold, who narrates the poem, gives a Byronic cast to the places and people he meets. Even Napoleon, in the excerpt that follows, takes on the contradictory characteristics of the Byronic hero. Published in 1816, this part of *Childe Harold* was written after Napoleon's defeat at the Battle of Waterloo in 1815, after which Napoleon was forced into exile on the island of St. Helena in the South Atlantic.

Traveler Gazing over the Mist
This painting by German artist Caspar David Friedrich (1774–1840) depicts the Romantic archetype of a solitary man contemplating a vastness. (Hamburger Kunstahlle)

∾ Childe Harold's Pilgrimage

CANTO 3

Napoleon

36.

> There sunk the greatest, nor the worst of men,
> Whose spirit antithetically mixt
> One moment of the mightiest, and again
> On little objects with like firmness fixt,
> Extreme in all things! hadst thou been betwixt,
> Thy throne had still been thine, or never been;
> For daring made thy rise as fall: thou seek'st
> Even now to re-assume the imperial mien,
> And shake again the world, the Thunderer of the scene!

37.

> Conqueror and captive of the earth art thou!
> She trembles at thee still, and thy wild name
> Was ne'er more bruited in men's minds than now
> That thou art nothing, save the jest of Fame,
> Who wooed thee once, thy vassal, and became
> The flatterer of thy fierceness, till thou wert
> A god unto thyself; nor less the same
> To the astounded kingdoms all inert,
> Who deem'd thee for a time whate'er thou didst assert.

38.

> Oh, more or less than man — in high or low,
> Battling with nations, flying from the field;
> Now making monarchs' necks thy footstool, now
> More than thy meanest soldier taught to yield;
> An empire thou couldst crush, command, rebuild,
> But govern not thy pettiest passion, nor,
> However deeply in men's spirits skill'd,
> Look through thine own, nor curb the lust of war,
> Nor learn that tempted Fate will leave the loftiest star.

39.

> Yet well thy soul hath brook'd the turning tide
> With that untaught innate philosophy,
> Which, be it wisdom, coldness, or deep pride,

Is gall and wormwood to an enemy.
When the whole host of hatred stood hard by,
To watch and mock thee shrinking, thou hast smiled
With a sedate and all-enduring eye;—
When Fortune fled her spoil'd and favourite child,
He stood unbowed beneath the ills upon him piled.

40.

Sager than in thy fortunes; for in them
Ambition steel'd thee on too far to show
That just habitual scorn which could contemn
Men and their thoughts; 'twas wise to feel, not so
To wear it ever on thy lip and brow,
And spurn the instruments thou wert to use
Till they were turn'd unto thine overthrow:
'Tis but a worthless world to win or lose;
So hath it proved to thee, and all such lot who choose.

41.

If, like a tower upon a headlong rock,
Thou hadst been made to stand or fall alone,
Such scorn of man had help'd to brave the shock;
But men's thoughts were the steps which paved thy throne,
Their admiration thy best weapon shone;
The part of Philip's son° was thine, not then   Alexander the Great
(Unless aside thy purple had been thrown)
Like stern Diogenes[1] to mock at men;
For sceptred cynics earth were far too wide a den.

42.

But quiet to quick bosoms is a hell,
And *there* hath been thy bane; there is a fire
And motion of the soul which will not dwell
In its own narrow being, but aspire
Beyond the fitting medium of desire;
And, but once kindled, quenchless evermore,
Preys upon high adventure, nor can tire
Of aught but rest; a fever at the core,
Fatal to him who bears, to all who ever bore.

43.

This makes the madmen who have made men mad
By their contagion; Conquerors and Kings,

---

[1] **Diogenes** (c. 412–323 B.C.E.): Greek Cynic philosopher. His philosophy so impressed Alexander that the ruler declared, "If I were not Alexander, I should wish to be Diogenes."

Founders of sects and systems, to whom add
Sophists, Bards, Statesmen, all unquiet things
Which stir too strongly the soul's secret springs,
And are themselves the fools to those they fool;
Envied, yet how unenviable! what stings
Are theirs! One breast laid open were a school
Which would unteach mankind the lust to shine or rule:

44.

Their breath is agitation, and their life
A storm whereon they ride, to sink at last,
And yet so nurs'd and bigotted to strife,
That should their days, surviving perils past,
Melt to calm twilight, they feel overcast
With sorrow and supineness, and so die;
Even as a flame unfed, which runs to waste
With its own flickering, or a sword laid by
Which eats into itself, and rusts ingloriously.

45.

He who ascends to mountain-tops, shall find
The loftiest peaks most wrapt in clouds and snow;
He who surpasses or subdues mankind,
Must look down on the hate of those below.
Though high *above* the sun of glory glow,
And far *beneath* the earth and ocean spread,
Round him are icy rocks, and loudly blow
Contending tempests on his naked head,
And thus reward the toils which to those summits led.

∾ JOHN GREENLEAF WHITTIER
B. UNITED STATES, 1807–1892

And men shall learn
to speak of thee
As one of earth's
great spirits
– WHITTIER, of
Toussaint-
Louverture

One of the most popular American poets of his time, Whittier was often linked with Henry Wadsworth Longfellow as a poet for all seasons. A Quaker with deep religious and social convictions, Whittier gave up a career as a journalist to work toward the abolition of slavery. Much of his literary work, particularly in the middle years of his life, was devoted to promoting the abolitionist cause. "Toussaint L'Ouverture," the poem from which the passage that follows is taken, was written in 1846 for the volume *Songs of Freedom* and celebrates the life and martyrdom of Toussaint-Louverture.

FROM

◌ Toussaint L'Ouverture

Sleep calmly in thy dungeon-tomb,
    Beneath Besançon's[1] alien sky,
Dark Haytien! — for the time shall come,
Yea, even now is nigh, —
When, everywhere, thy name shall be
Redeemed from *color's infamy;*
220 And men shall learn to speak of thee
As one of earth's great spirits, born
In servitude, and nursed in scorn,
Casting aside the weary weight
And fetters of its low estate,
In that strong majesty of soul
    Which knows no color, tongue, or clime, —
Which still hath spurned the base control
    Of tyrants through all time!
Far other hands than mine may wreath
230 The laurel round the brow of death,
And speak thy praise as one whose word
A thousand fiery spirits stirred, —
Who crushed his foeman as a worm, —
Whose step on human hearts fell firm: —
Be mine the better task to find
A tribute for thy lofty mind,
Amidst whose gloomy vengeance shone
Some milder virtues all thine own, —
Some gleams of feeling, pure and warm,
240 Like sunshine on a sky of storm, —
Proofs that the Negro's heart retains
Some nobleness amidst its chains, —
That kindness to the wronged is never
Without its excellent reward, —
Holy to human-kind, and ever
Acceptable to God.

---

[1] Besançon: City in east-central France where Toussaint-Louverture was imprisoned and buried.

❧ FRIEDRICH NIETZSCHE
B. GERMANY, 1844–1900

Friedrich Nietzsche is one of the most controversial and influential nineteenth-century philosophers. Born in Germany, the son of a Lutheran minister, Nietzsche went to the universities of Bonn and Leipzig before becoming, in 1869, a professor of classical philology at the University of Basel in Switzerland, a post he held for ten years. In his early works, *The Birth of Tragedy from the Spirit of Music* (1872) and *Untimely Meditations* (1873–76), Nietzsche wrote, in part, as an apostle of the composer Richard Wagner. But he broke with Wagner at the end of the decade and, after resigning from the university, went on in the 1880s to write the works on which his reputation is based: *The Gay Science* (1882), *Thus Spoke Zarathustra* (1883–84), *Beyond Good and Evil* (1886), and *The Genealogy of Morals* (1887). In 1889 he suffered a mental breakdown and was largely incapacitated during the last decade of his life.

An evolutionary thinker, Nietzsche replaced the Darwinian struggle for existence with a struggle for power. His ideal was the SUPERMAN (*Übermensch*), a superior man who unites the Dionysian (passion) and the Apollonian (reason), creatively employing both to become a higher type of human being. Such fulfillment, Nietzsche thought, was thwarted by both ENLIGHTENMENT rationalism, which encouraged conformity, and Christianity, which promoted weakness and failure. The Superman, by contrast, celebrated the passions and the body as well as the mind, affirming this world and the present moment rather than otherworldly consolation, thus taking responsibility for his own freedom and destiny. The passage from *The Gay Science* describes the new age that Nietzsche envisages and the men who will prepare the way for the Superman. The selection from *Thus Spoke Zarathustra* picks up after Zarathustra has spent ten years in the wilderness and has returned to society as a prophet, bringing news of the Superman and seeking the men who will prepare the way for him. He will discover, however, that those in the marketplace are not ready to hear his message. Nietzsche's use of literary forms to communicate philosophical ideas was a practice adopted by such later philosophers as Sartre and Camus, who developed their philosophical statements in novels and plays. The influence of Nietzsche's ideas on twentieth-century writers, especially the EXISTENTIALISTS, was profound.

A note on the translation: Walter Kauffmann avoids the biblical rhetoric often used by Nietzsche's translators. His strategy reduces the shock effect of Nietzsche's assertions and gives the ideas more direct statement. Consistent with this strategy, he renders the concept by which Nietzsche is best known as *overman* rather than *superman*.

Zoroaster or Zarathustra Educating His People *This illustration comes from a series of late-nineteenth-century collectors' cards found in French bouillon-cube containers. Zoroaster, or Zarathustra, was an ancient figure who preached a dualistic, good-versus-evil, apocalyptic philosophy. The religion he founded, Zoroastrianism, represented for Nietzsche a more authentic religion than Christianity. (Art Archive)*

FROM

∾ The Gay Science

Translated by Walter Kaufmann

[283]

Preparatory men. I welcome all signs that a more manly, a warlike, age is about to begin, an age which, above all, will give honor to valor once again. For this age shall prepare the way for one yet higher, and it shall gather the strength which this higher age will need one day—this age which is to carry heroism into the pursuit of knowledge and *wage wars* for the sake of thoughts and their consequences. To this end we now need many preparatory valorous men who cannot leap into being out of nothing—any more than out of the sand and slime of our present civilization and metropolitanism: men who are bent on seeking for that aspect in all things which must be *overcome;* men characterized by cheerfulness, patience, unpretentiousness, and contempt for all great vanities, as well as by magnanimity in victory and forbearance regarding the small vanities of the vanquished; men possessed of keen and free judgment concerning all victors and the share of chance in every victory and every fame; men who have their own festivals, their own weekdays, their own periods of mourning, who are accustomed to command with assurance and are no less ready to obey when necessary, in both cases equally proud and serving their own cause; men who are in greater danger, more fruitful, and happier! For, believe me, the secret of the greatest fruitfulness and the greatest enjoyment of existence is: to *live dangerously!* Build your cities under Vesuvius![1] Send your ships into uncharted seas! Live at war with your peers and yourselves! Be robbers and conquerors, as long as you cannot be rulers and owners, you lovers of knowledge! Soon the age will be past when you could be satisfied to live like shy deer, hidden in the woods! At long last the pursuit of knowledge will reach out for its due: it will want to *rule* and *own,* and you with it!

FROM

∾ Thus Spoke Zarathustra: First Part

Translated by Walter Kaufmann

3

[THE SUPERMAN]

When Zarathustra came into the next town, which lies on the edge of the forest, he found many people gathered together in the market place; for it had been promised that there would be a tightrope walker. And Zarathustra spoke thus to the people:

"*I teach you the overman.* Man is something that shall be overcome. What have you done to overcome him?

---

[1] **Vesuvius:** Volcano near Naples in Italy; an eruption of Vesuvius buried the city of Pompeii in 79 B.C.E.

"All beings so far have created something beyond themselves; and do you want to be the ebb of this great flood and even go back to the beasts rather than overcome man? What is the ape to man? A laughingstock or a painful embarrassment. And man shall be just that for the overman: a laughingstock or a painful embarrassment. You have made your way from worm to man, and much in you is still worm. Once you were apes, and even now, too, man is more ape than any ape.

"Whoever is the wisest among you is also a mere conflict and cross between plant and ghost. But do I bid you become ghosts or plants?

"Behold, I teach you the overman. The overman is the meaning of the earth. Let your will say: the overman *shall be* the meaning of the earth! I beseech you, my brothers, *remain faithful to the earth,* and do not believe those who speak to you of otherworldly hopes! Poison-mixers are they, whether they know it or not. Despisers of life are they, decaying and poisoned themselves, of whom the earth is weary: so let them go.

"Once the sin against God was the greatest sin; but God died, and these sinners died with him. To sin against the earth is now the most dreadful thing, and to esteem the entrails of the unknowable higher than the meaning of the earth.

"Once the soul looked contemptuously upon the body, and then this contempt was the highest: she wanted the body meager, ghastly, and starved. Thus she hoped to escape it and the earth. Oh, this soul herself was still meager, ghastly, and starved: and cruelty was the lust of this soul. But you, too, my brothers, tell me: what does your body proclaim of your soul? Is not your soul poverty and filth and wretched contentment?

"Verily, a polluted stream is man. One must be a sea to be able to receive a polluted stream without becoming unclean. Behold, I teach you the overman: he is this sea; in him your great contempt can go under.

"What is the greatest experience you can have? It is the hour of the great contempt. The hour in which your happiness, too, arouses your disgust, and even your reason and your virtue.

"The hour when you say, 'What matters my happiness? It is poverty and filth and wretched contentment. But my happiness ought to justify existence itself.'

"The hour when you say, 'What matters my reason? Does it crave knowledge as the lion his food? It is poverty and filth and wretched contentment.'

"The hour when you say, 'What matters my virtue? As yet it has not made me rage. How weary I am of my good and my evil! All that is poverty and filth and wretched contentment.'

"The hour when you say, 'What matters my justice? I do not see that I am flames and fuel. But the just are flames and fuel.'

"The hour when you say, 'What matters my pity? Is not pity the cross on which he is nailed who loves man? But my pity is no crucifixion.'

"Have you yet spoken thus? Have you yet cried thus? Oh, that I might have heard you cry thus!

'Not your sin but your thrift cries to heaven; your meanness even in your sin cries to heaven.

"Where is the lightning to lick you with its tongue? Where is the frenzy with which you should be inoculated?

"Behold, I teach you the overman: he is this lightning, he is this frenzy."

When Zarathustra had spoken thus, one of the people cried: "Now we have heard enough about the tightrope walker; now let us see him too!" And all the people laughed at Zarathustra. But the tightrope walker, believing that the word concerned him, began his performance.

❧ INAZO NITOBÉ

B. JAPAN, 1862–1933

A Soldier in Full
Armour, Nineteenth
Century
*Depictions of samurai
often focused on their
stylish armor and
their proud warrior's
disposition. (National
Trust Photographic
Library/John
Hammond)*

Professor, internationalist, and interpreter of Japan to the West, Inazo Nitobé drew on his extensive knowledge of Western literature and philosophy to explain — by contrast and comparison — his native culture. Educated at the Sapporo Agricultural School and the University of Tokyo, with graduate study done at Johns Hopkins University and the University of Halle, in Germany, where he received his Ph.D. in 1890, Nitobé began his professional career as a professor of agricultural economics. When illness forced him to resign in 1897 and to come to America, he wrote his best-known work, *Bushido: The Soul of Japan* (1899), in English to explain the Japanese psyche to the West. Nitobé used *Bushido* — the traditional ethical system of the SAMURAI, which taught rectitude, benevolence, honor, loyalty, and self-control as its primary virtues — to structure his account of the Japanese mind. Even though feudalism had been officially abolished in Nitobé's native country, many of its qualities remained in Japanese culture. There was, in fact, a revived interest in Bushido as modernization took place, and the classic work on the subject, *Hagakare (Bushido, the Way of the Samarai)* by Tsunetomo Yamamoto (1659–1719), which had been underground for two centuries, was published for the first time for the general reader in 1906. Nitobé, in the final chapter of his book, explains the contemporary appeal of Bushido as a counter to Western materialism. However, he recognized that the age of military heroism was past and, as a Japanese Christian, he believed that Japan would integrate the virtues of Bushido with Christian individualism.

FROM

❧ Bushido: The Soul of Japan

Principalities and powers are arrayed against the Precepts of Knighthood. Already, as Veblen[1] says, "the decay of the ceremonial code — or, as it is otherwise called, the vulgarization of life — among the industrial classes proper, has become one of the chief enormities of latter-day civilization in the eyes of all persons of delicate sensibilities." . . .

---

[1] Veblen: Thornstein Veblen (1857–1929), American economist and social scientist.

The state built upon the rock of Honour and fortified by the same — shall we call it the *Ehrenstaat,*[2] or, after the manner of Carlyle, the Heroarchy? — is fast falling into the hands of quibbling lawyers and gibbering politicians armed with logic-chopping engines of war. The words which a great thinker used in speaking of Theresa and Antigone may aptly be repeated of the samurai, that "the medium in which their ardent deeds took shape is forever gone."[3]

Alas for knightly virtues! alas for samurai pride! Morality ushered into the world with the sound of bugles and drums, is destined to fade away as "the captains and the kings depart."

If history can teach us anything, the state built on martial virtues — be it a city like Sparta or an Empire like Rome — can never make on earth a "continuing city." Universal and natural as is the fighting instinct in man, fruitful as it has proved to be of noble sentiments and manly virtues, it does not comprehend the whole man. Beneath the instinct to fight there lurks a diviner instinct — to love. We have seen that Shintoism, Mencius, and Wan Yang Ming,[4] have all clearly taught it; but Bushido and all other militant types of ethics, engrossed, doubtless, with questions of immediate practical need, too often forgot duly to emphasize this fact. Life has grown larger in these latter times. Callings nobler and broader than a warrior's claim our attention today. With an enlarged view of life, with the growth of democracy, with better knowledge of other peoples and nations, the Confucian idea of benevolence — dare I also add the Buddhist idea of pity? — will expand into the Christian conception of love. Men have become more than subjects, having grown to the estate of citizens; nay, they are more than citizens — being men. Though war clouds hang heavy upon our horizon, we will believe that the wings of the angel of peace can disperse them. The history of the world confirms the prophecy that "the meek shall inherit the earth."[5] A nation that sells its birthright of peace, and backslides from the front rank of industrialism into the file of filibusterism, makes a poor bargain indeed!

When the conditions of society are so changed that they have become not only adverse but hostile to Bushido, it is time for it to prepare for an honourable burial. It is just as difficult to point out when chivalry dies, as to determine the exact time of its inception. Dr. Miller says that chivalry was formally abolished in the year 1559, when Henry II. of France was slain in a tournament. With us, the edict formally abolishing feudalism in 1871 was the signal to toll the knell of Bushido. The edict, issued five years later, prohibiting the wearing of swords, rang out the old, "the unbought grace of life, the cheap defence of nations, the nurse of manly sentiment and heroic enterprise," it rang in the new age of "sophisters, economists, and calculators."

---

[2] *Ehrenstaat:* A German term coined by Nitobé, meaning the country of honor.

[3] **"the medium . . . forever gone":** Nitobé does not identify the thinker he is quoting here.

[4] **Shintoism . . . Ming:** Shintoism is the traditional religion of Japan; Mencius (c. 371–288 B.C.E.) was a classical Confucian philosopher (Volume 1); Wan Yang Ming (1472–1529) was a Chinese philosopher and reformer of neo-Confucianism.

[5] **"the meek . . . earth":** Matthew 5:5.

It has been said that Japan won her late war with China by means of Murata guns and Krupp cannon; it has been said the victory was the work of a modern school-system; but these are less than half-truths. Does ever a piano, be it of the choicest workmanship of Ehrbar or Steinway burst forth into the Rhapsodies of Liszt or the Sonatas of Beethoven, without a master's hand? Or, if guns win battles, why did not Louis Napoleon beat the Prussians with his *Mitrailleuse*,[6] or the Spaniards with their Mausers the Filipinos, whose arms were no better than the old-fashioned Remingtons? Needless to repeat what has grown a trite saying, — that it is the spirit that quickeneth, without which the best of implements profiteth but little. The most improved guns and cannon do not shoot of their own accord; the most modern educational system does not make a coward a hero. No! What won the battles on the Yalu, in Corea and Manchuria,[7] were the ghosts of our fathers, guiding our hands and beating in our hearts. They are not dead, those ghosts, the spirits of our warlike ancestors. To those who have eyes to see, they are clearly visible. Scratch a Japanese of the most advanced ideas, and he will show a samurai. The great inheritance of honour, of valour, and of all martial virtues is, as Professor Cramb[8] very fitly expresses it, "but ours on trust, the fief inalienable of the dead and of the generations to come," and the summons of the present is to guard this heritage, nor to bate one jot of the ancient spirit; the summons of the future will be so to widen its scope to apply it in all walks and relations of life.

It has been predicted — and predictions have been corroborated by the events of the last half-century — that the moral system of Feudal Japan, like its castles and its armouries, will crumble into dust, and new ethics rise phoenix-like to lead New Japan in her path of progress. Desirable and probable as the fulfilment of such a prophecy is, we must not forget that a phoenix rises only from its own ashes, and that it is not a bird of passage, neither does it fly on pinions borrowed from other birds. "The Kingdom of God is within you."[9] It does not come rolling down the mountains, however lofty; it does not come sailing across the seas, however broad. "God has granted," says the Koran, "to every people a prophet in its own tongue." The seeds of the Kingdom, as vouched for and apprehended by the Japanese mind, blossomed in Bushido. Now its days are closing—sad to say, before its full fruition—and we turn in every direction for other sources of sweetness and light, of strength and comfort, but among them there is as yet nothing found to take its place. The profit-and-loss philosophy of utilitarians and materialists finds favour among logic-choppers with half a soul. The only other ethical system which is powerful enough to cope with utilitarianism and materialism is Christianity, in comparison with which Bushido, it must be confessed, is like "a dimly burning wick" which the

---

[6] *Mitrailleuse:* Machine guns.

[7] Yalu . . . Manchuria: In the China-Japanese War of 1894–95, Japan claimed victory after pushing China out of Korea and gaining temporary control of the Yalu River dividing Korea from Manchuria.

[8] Professor Cramb: John A. Cramb (1862–1913), British historian who advocated a policy of military strength.

[9] "The Kingdom . . . you": Luke 17:21.

Messiah was proclaimed not to quench, but to fan into a flame. Like His Hebrew precursors, the prophets—notably Isaiah, Jeremiah, Amos, and Habakkuk—Bushido laid particular stress on the moral conduct of rulers and public men and of nations, whereas the ethics of Christ, which deal almost solely with individuals and His personal followers, will find more and more practical application as individualism, in its capacity of a moral factor, grows in potency. The domineering, self-assertive, so-called master-morality of Nietzsche, itself akin in some respects to Bushido, is, if I am not greatly mistaken, a passing phase or temporary reaction against what he terms, by morbid distortion, the humble, self-denying slave-morality of the Nazarene.

Christianity and materialism (including utilitarianism)—or will the future reduce them to still more archaic forms of Hebraism and Hellenism?—will divide the world between them. Lesser systems of morals will ally themselves to either side for their preservation. On which side will Bushido enlist? Having no set dogma or formula to defend, it can afford to disappear as an entity; like the cherry blossom, it is willing to die at the first gust of the morning breeze. But a total extinction will never be its lot. Who can say that stoicism[10] is dead? It is dead as a system; but it is alive as a virtue: its energy and vitality are still felt through many channels of life—in the philosophy of Western nations, in the jurisprudence of all the civilized world. Nay, wherever man struggles to raise himself above himself, wherever his spirit masters his flesh by his own exertions, there we see the immortal discipline of Zeno at work.

Bushido as an independent code of ethics may vanish, but its power will not perish from the earth; its schools of martial prowess or civic honour may be demolished, but its light and its glory will long survive their ruins. Like its symbolic flower, after it is blown to the four winds, it will still bless mankind with the perfume with which it will enrich life. Ages after, when its customaries will have been buried and its very name forgotten, its fragrance will come floating in the air as from a far-off, unseen hill, "the wayside gaze beyond";—then in the beautiful language of the Quaker poet,[11]

> "The traveller owns the grateful sense
> Of sweetness near, he knows not whence,
> And, pausing, takes with forehead bare
> The benediction of the air."

---

[10] **stoicism:** Philosophical school of classical Greece and Rome, founded by Zeno of Citium (c. 334–c. 262 B.C.E.), that taught the virtues of endurance, virtuous living, and self-reliance.

[11] **Quaker poet:** American poet John Greenleaf Whittier (1807–1892); the passage is from his "Snow-bound: A Winter Idyl."

WILLIAM WORDSWORTH
B. ENGLAND, 1770–1850

William Wordsworth
Befitting his role as Romantic poet, Wordsworth here appears withdrawn and deep in thought, his head resting in his hand. (Corbis)

Few poets embody the **ROMANTIC** spirit of the age in England so much as William Wordsworth. Although he completed most of his great poetry between 1793 and 1807, Wordsworth continued writing until his death in 1850. Spanning the period from the **FRENCH REVOLUTION** until well into the **VICTORIAN** era, Wordsworth's poetic output, like Goethe's, offers a unique record of the transformations in political and poetic sentiment in the nineteenth century. A self-conscious reformer in his youth, Wordsworth supported the early stages of the French Revolution, hoping that it would inspire England to take steps toward political reform. That spirit of reform carried over into his early poetry, in which he rejected elaborate poetic diction and the stale personifications of neoclassical poetry, using instead the plain language of everyday speech in poems that focused on the feelings and dignity of common people. For many literary historians, 1798, the year in which Wordsworth and Samuel Taylor Coleridge published *Lyrical Ballads,* stands as the inaugural year of Romantic poetry in England. In Wordsworth's middle and later years, his enthusiasm for political reform began to wane, but he continued to write important and innovative poetry, and eventually became England's poet laureate. Though younger poets, notably Lord Byron, Percy Bysshe Shelley, and Robert Browning,[1] berated Wordsworth for his political conservatism, he had ardent supporters throughout the nineteenth and twentieth centuries and undoubtedly remains one of the most influential British poets from the nineteenth century.

Early Childhood.   William Wordsworth was born April 7, 1770, in the small Cumberland village of Cockermouth near the English Lake District. The son of a lawyer who managed the vast estates of the Earl of Lonsdale, Wordsworth at first enjoyed a pleasant childhood along the banks of River Derwent. When he was seven years old, however, his mother died and the family, including his three brothers and his sister, Dorothy, went to live among different relatives. William went with his brother Richard to Hawkshead, Lancashire, to live with Anne Tyson while they attended grammar school. During these formative days, which he remembers fondly in his great work *The Prelude* (1805 and 1850), Wordsworth spent much of his free time roaming the surrounding countryside and hills.

---

[1] **Lord Byron** (1788–1824): English Romantic poet most widely known throughout Europe, satirized Wordsworth and other Lake School poets in *English Bards and Scotch Reviewers* (1809) and in *Don Juan* (1819–24). **Percy Bysshe Shelley** (1792–1822): Author of *Prometheus Unbound* (1820) and *Adonais* (1821), among many other poems, criticized Wordsworth in his sonnet "To Wordsworth" (1816). **Robert Browning** (1812–1889): Master of the dramatic monologue and author of *The Ring and the Book* (1868–69), among many other poems, lamented Wordsworth's political shift to the right in "The Lost Leader" (1845).

Cambridge and France.   Wordsworth's father died in 1783, and although he had left an estate of nearly 5,000 pounds claimed against the Earl of Lonsdale, the Earl withheld payment, leaving the Wordsworth children dependent on their uncles. In 1787, Wordsworth entered St. John's College, Cambridge, taking a minimal interest in his courses while pursuing a broad range of independent reading in the classics, Italian, and contemporary English literature. Leaving Cambridge in January 1791, Wordsworth took a degree without distinction and disappointed his uncles' hopes that he would take a position in the church. The summer before taking his degree, Wordsworth had traveled to France and toured on foot through the Swiss and Italian Alps with his friend Robert Jones. France in the summer of 1790 was in a ferment of revolutionary hope and fear; as Wordsworth writes in *The Prelude,* Book 9, "The land all swarmed with passion" and the people were "risen up / Fresh as the morning star." The Revolution had begun a year before with the storming of the Bastille on July 14, 1789, and sympathizers with the revolutionary principles saw in France the possibility for the overthrow of absolutism. A new age and spirit was being born; Book 10 of *The Prelude* expresses Wordsworth's sense of hope in those early years of the Revolution: "Bliss was it in that dawn to be alive."

Wordsworth returned to France in 1791 when a more somber mood hung over the Revolution. With Louis XVI under house arrest and division within the National Assembly, Paris was in confusion. Although Wordsworth was not in France during the executions of Louis and Marie Antoinette in January and October 1793, respectively, Wordsworth felt from England the shock that jarred all of Europe at the Reign of Terror that followed shortly thereafter. During the Reign of Terror—a series of trials and summary executions aimed at quelling anti-republican sentiment and eliminating traitors—more than 2,600 people were executed in fifteen months. In the words of Wordsworth's *Prelude,* Book 10, it was "A woeful time for them whose hopes did still / Outlast the shock." Although some European intellectuals continued to support the Revolution even through the shadow of the guillotine, seeing violence as an unfortunate but necessary stage of radical transformation, the Reign of Terror largely tempered or extinguished altogether the hopes that before had been so profound. In *Ode: Intimations of Immortality,* Wordsworth uses the form of the ODE to focus on the theme of loss of innocence. The speaker's struggle to find "abundant recompense" from that loss serves as a metaphor for the struggle of many Europeans whose vision of an egalitarian society gave way to disenchantment in the violent wake of the Revolution.

Grasmere.   During the turbulent years of the Revolution, Wordsworth was in England, taking walking tours, drifting in and out of London's radical circles (which included William Godwin and Mary Wollstonecraft), visiting his friends and family, and finally setting up a home with his sister Dorothy Wordsworth, first at Racedown in 1795, later at Alfoxden in 1798, and finally at Grasmere in the heart of the English Lake District in 1799 after a brief trip to Germany. In 1797, while at Racedown, Wordsworth began his famous friendship and collaboration with Samuel Taylor Coleridge. In 1798, Wordsworth and Coleridge published *Lyrical*

www For links to more information about Wordsworth, a quiz on his poetry, and information about his 21st-century relevance, see bedfordstmartins .com/worldlit compact.

Wordsworth, together with Blake, is the last of a giant race of poets to whom the moderns are as indebted as the neoclassical poets to their Renaissance predecessors.
– GEOFFREY HARTMAN, 1975

Ballads; "Lines Composed a Few Miles above Tintern Abbey," included in the selection that follows, was published as the final poem in that collection. During the trip to Germany from September through April 1799, Wordsworth, somewhat disillusioned and disoriented in unfamiliar surroundings and enduring a bitterly cold winter, wrote some of his most enigmatic lyrics known as the "Lucy" poems. Many critics have been drawn by the indeterminacies of "A Slumber Did My Spirit Seal," a haunting and open-ended meditation on death and loss that Coleridge characterized as a "sublime epitaph."

"Tintern Abbey" and the later *Ode: Intimations of Immortality* (composed between 1802 and 1804) are more highly stylized than most of the poems in *Lyrical Ballads,* but both demonstrate Wordsworth's intense interest in exploring the relationships between feeling and consciousness, mind and nature, the past and present. In their philosophical musing and their displaced grappling with the great concerns of the Revolution, "Tintern Abbey" and *Ode* mark the beginning and end of one of Wordsworth's most productive phases, 1798 to 1805. He continued to write poetry—including what some think to be his greatest work, the fourteen-book *Prelude*—for almost another forty years. Having established a home at Grasmere with his wife, Mary Hutchinson, and his sister, Wordsworth set up a thriving poetic "cottage industry." Between 1798 and 1850, he published several volumes of poetry, including *Poems in Two Volumes* in 1807, *The Excursion* in 1814, and *Yarrow Revisited, and Other Poems* in 1835. Wordsworth took part in the sonnet revival of the early nineteenth century, and he later published a collection of his verse in that form in *The Sonnets of William Wordsworth* (1838). What some think of as his greatest work, *The Prelude,* an epic-length autobiographical poem begun in 1798 and heavily revised over the course of the next forty years, was not published until after his death on April 23, 1850.

The 1807 *Poems in Two Volumes* included "The world is too much with us" and "Composed upon Westminster Bridge, September 3, 1802," two among a number of meditative and stately sonnets written around the time Wordsworth and his sister took the opportunity of the Treaty of Amiens (March 27, 1802) and traveled to France to settle matters with his former lover, Annette Vallon, whom he had met on his first trip to France in 1791, and their now ten-year old daughter. The first sonnet attests to Wordsworth's belief that commerce and industry, urbanization and the trivial preoccupations of modern life divert our attention from the truth and beauty of nature, an anchor and refuge of the soul. In the Preface to *Lyrical Ballads* that accompanied the second edition in 1800, Wordsworth had written that "a multitude of causes, unknown to former times, are now acting with a combined force to blunt the discriminating powers of the mind, and, unfitting it for all voluntary exertion, to reduce it to a state of almost savage torpor"; the poem expresses a deep and emphatic sense of the consequent loss of connection to the natural world. In the second sonnet, Wordsworth describes the beauty of London, captured in a tranquil moment at daybreak; the poem frames London, still and stately, in the language of natural beauty—as if London itself was the gathering place of field, sun, and sky.

Tintern Abbey, 1869
This ruined cathedral in the Wye River valley locates in part the setting of "Lines Composed a Few Miles above Tintern Abbey." (Library of Congress)

Nature and Philosophy.   Often erroneously called a "nature poet" (in the sense of a poet who merely describes the natural world and the land-scape), Wordsworth primarily writes of the relationship between mind and nature, what he sees as the reciprocal interaction between nature and human consciousness. Looking forward to a long philosophical poem that he and Coleridge had projected as his life's goal, Wordsworth delin-eated what turned out to be the subject matter for almost all of his poems, and especially *The Prelude*. In the "Prospectus to *The Recluse*," Wordsworth dismisses the typical mythological subject matter of epic poems and turns his attention instead to "the Mind of Man — /My haunt, and the main region of my song." What he hopes to show in the course of this work is

> How exquisitely the individual Mind
> (And the progressive powers perhaps no less
> Of the whole species) to the external World
> Is fitted: — and how exquisitely, too —
> Theme this but little heard of among men
> The external World is fitted to the Mind.

The primary experience of nature, in both its beautiful and terrify-ing aspects, Wordsworth believes, is vitally important for sustaining and invigorating the spiritual strength and creative power of human beings through later times of trial, loss, and confinement in places that offer less inspiration. The sustenance that these moments of contact with nature offer, however, depends on a reciprocating power — rendered variously as a "wise passiveness" and an "auxiliar light" — from the heart and mind of the person encountering nature. These moments of intensive and reflexive experience become for Wordsworth "spots of time" with a "fruc-tifying virtue," a dialogue that generates in the individual the power to awaken new feelings from memories at a later time.

■ FURTHER RESEARCH

Biography
Gill, Stephen. *William Wordsworth: A Life.* 1990.

Criticism
Campbell, Patrick, ed. *Wordsworth and Coleridge: Lyrical Ballads: Critical Perspectives.* 1991.
Cronin, Richard, ed. *1798: The Year of the Lyrical Ballads.* 1998.
Glen, Heather. *Vision and Disenchantment: Blake's Songs and Wordsworth's Lyrical Ballads.* 1983.
Hartman, Geoffrey H. *Wordsworth's Poetry, 1787–1814.* 1964.
Jacobus, Mary. *Tradition and Experiment in Wordsworth's Lyrical Ballads.* 1976.
Parrish, Stephen Maxfield. *The Art of the Lyrical Ballads.* 1973.

FROM

～ Lyrical Ballads

Expostulation and Reply

"Why William, on that old grey stone,
Thus for the length of half a day,
Why William, sit you thus alone,
And dream your time away?

"Where are your books? that light bequeath'd
To beings else forlorn and blind!
Up! Up! and drink the spirit breath'd
From dead men to their kind.

"You look round on your mother earth,
10 As if she for no purpose bore you;
As if you were her first-born birth,
And none had lived before you!"

One morning thus, by Esthwaite lake,
When life was sweet I knew not why,
To me my good friend Matthew spake,
And thus I made reply.

"The eye it cannot chuse but see,
We cannot bid the ear be still;
Our bodies feel, where'er they be,
20 Against, or with our will.

"Nor less I deem that there are powers,
Which of themselves our minds impress,
That we can feed this mind of ours,
In a wise passiveness.

"Think you, mid all this mighty sum
Of things for ever speaking,
That nothing of itself will come,
But we must still be seeking?

"—Then ask not wherefore, here, alone,
30 Conversing as I may,
I sit upon this old grey stone,
And dream my time away."

The Tables Turned

An Evening Scene, on the Same Subject

Up! up! my friend, and clear your looks,
Why all this toil and trouble?
Up! up! my friend, and quit your books,
Or surely you'll grow double.

The sun above the mountain's head,
A freshening lustre mellow,
Through all the long green fields has spread,
His first sweet evening yellow.

Books! 'tis a dull and endless strife,
10   Come, hear the woodland linnet,
How sweet his music; on my life
There's more of wisdom in it.

And hark! how blithe the throstle sings!
And he is no mean preacher;
Come forth into the light of things,
Let Nature be your teacher.

She has a world of ready wealth,
Our minds and hearts to bless —
Spontaneous wisdom breathed by health,
20   Truth breathed by cheerfulness.

One impulse from a vernal wood
May teach you more of man;
Of moral evil and of good,
Than all the sages can.

Sweet is the lore which nature brings;
Our meddling intellect
Misshapes the beauteous forms of things;
— We murder to dissect.

Enough of science and of art;
30   Close up these barren leaves;
Come forth, and bring with you a heart
That watches and receives.

Lines Composed a Few Miles above Tintern Abbey[1]

Five years have past; five summers, with the length
Of five long winters! and again I hear
These waters,[2] rolling from their mountain-springs
With a soft inland murmur. — Once again
Do I behold these steep and lofty cliffs,
That on a wild secluded scene impress
Thoughts of more deep seclusion; and connect
The landscape with the quiet of the sky.
The day is come when I again repose
10 Here, under this dark sycamore, and view
These plots of cottage-ground, these orchard-tufts,
Which at this season, with their unripe fruits,
Are clad in one green hue, and lose themselves
'Mid groves and copses. Once again I see
These hedge-rows, hardly hedge-rows, little lines
Of sportive wood run wild: these pastoral farms,
Green to the very door; and wreaths of smoke
Sent up, in silence, from among the trees!
With some uncertain notice, as might seem
20 Of vagrant dwellers in the houseless woods,
Or of some Hermit's cave, where by his fire
The Hermit sits alone.
                These beauteous forms,
Through a long absence, have not been to me
As is a landscape to a blind man's eye:
But oft, in lonely rooms, and 'mid the din
Of towns and cities, I have owed to them
In hours of weariness, sensations sweet,
Felt in the blood, and felt along the heart;
And passing even into my purer mind,
30 With tranquil restoration: — feelings too
Of unremembered pleasure: such, perhaps,
As have no slight or trivial influence
On that best portion of a good man's life,
His little, nameless, unremembered, acts
Of kindness and of love. Nor less, I trust,
To them I may have owed another gift,
Of aspect more sublime; that blessed mood,

---

[1] **Tintern Abbey:** Then as now, a ruined monastery in Monmouthshire.
[2] **These waters:** The Wye, a river that runs through Wales and western England.

In which the burden of the mystery,
In which the heavy and the weary weight
40 Of all this unintelligible world,
Is lightened:—that serene and blessed mood,
In which the affections gently lead us on,—
Until, the breath of this corporeal frame
And even the motion of our human blood
Almost suspended, we are laid asleep
In body, and become a living soul:
While with an eye made quiet by the power
Of harmony, and the deep power of joy,
We see into the life of things.
                                      If this
50 Be but a vain belief, yet, oh! how oft—
In darkness and amid the many shapes
Of joyless daylight; when the fretful stir
Unprofitable, and the fever of the world,
Have hung upon the beatings of my heart—
How oft, in spirit, have I turned to thee,
O sylvan Wye! thou wanderer through the woods,
How often has my spirit turned to thee!

        And now, with gleams of half-extinguished thought,
With many recognitions dim and faint,
60 And somewhat of a sad perplexity,
The picture of the mind revives again:
While here I stand, not only with the sense
Of present pleasure, but with pleasing thoughts
That in this moment there is life and food
For future years. And so I dare to hope,
Though changed, no doubt, from what I was when first
I came among these hills; when like a roe
I bounded o'er the mountains, by the sides
Of the deep rivers, and the lonely streams,
70 Wherever nature led: more like a man
Flying from something that he dreads, than one
Who sought the thing he loved. For nature then
(The coarser pleasures of my boyish days,
And their glad animal movements all gone by)
To me was all in all.—I cannot paint
What then I was. The sounding cataract
Haunted me like a passion: the tall rock,
The mountain, and the deep and gloomy wood,
Their colours and their forms, were then to me

80 An appetite; a feeling and a love,
    That had no need of a remoter charm,
    By thought supplied, nor any interest
    Unborrowed from the eye. — That time is past,
    And all its aching joys are now no more,
    And all its dizzy raptures. Not for this
    Faint I, nor mourn nor murmur; other gifts
    Have followed; for such loss, I would believe,
    Abundant recompense. For I have learned
    To look on nature, not as in the hour
90 Of thoughtless youth; but hearing oftentimes
    The still, sad music of humanity,
    Nor harsh nor grating, though of ample power
    To chasten and subdue. And I have felt
    A presence that disturbs me with the joy
    Of elevated thoughts; a sense sublime
    Of something far more deeply interfused,
    Whose dwelling is the light of setting suns,
    And the round ocean and the living air,
    And the blue sky, and in the mind of man:
100 A motion and a spirit, that impels
    All thinking things, all objects of all thought,
    And rolls through all things. Therefore am I still
    A lover of the meadows and the woods,
    And mountains; and of all that we behold
    From this green earth; of all the mighty world
    Of eye, and ear, — both what they half create,
    And what perceive; well pleased to recognize
    In nature and the language of the sense,
    The anchor of my purest thoughts, the nurse,
110 The guide, the guardian of my heart, and soul
    Of all my moral being.
                       Nor perchance,
    If I were not thus taught, should I the more
    Suffer my genial[3] spirits to decay:
    For thou art with me here upon the banks
    Of this fair river; thou my dearest Friend,[4]
    My dear, dear Friend; and in thy voice I catch
    The language of my former heart, and read

---

[3] **genial:** Creative and generative of both imaginative works and social feeling.

[4] **my dearest Friend:** Dorothy Wordsworth, the poet's sister.

My former pleasures in the shooting lights
Of thy wild eyes. Oh! yet a little while
120 May I behold in thee what I was once,
My dear, dear Sister! and this prayer I make,
Knowing that Nature never did betray
The heart that loved her; 'tis her privilege,
Through all the years of this our life, to lead
From joy to joy: for she can so inform
The mind that is within us, so impress
With quietness and beauty, and so feed
With lofty thoughts, that neither evil tongues,
Rash judgements, nor the sneers of selfish men,
130 Nor greetings where no kindness is, nor all
The dreary intercourse of daily life,
Shall e'er prevail against us, or disturb
Our cheerful faith, that all which we behold
Is full of blessings. Therefore let the moon
Shine on thee in thy solitary walk;
And let the misty mountain-winds be free
To blow against thee: and, in after years,
When these wild ecstasies shall be matured
Into a sober pleasure; when thy mind
140 Shall be a mansion for all lovely forms,
Thy memory be as a dwelling-place
For all sweet sounds and harmonies; oh! then,
If solitude, or fear, or pain, or grief,
Should be thy portion, with what healing thoughts
Of tender joy wilt thou remember me,
And these my exhortations! Nor, perchance —
If I should be where I no more can hear
Thy voice, nor catch from thy wild eyes these gleams
Of past existence — wilt thou then forget
150 That on the banks of this delightful stream
We stood together; and that I, so long
A worshipper of Nature, hither came
Unwearied in that service: rather say
With warmer love — oh! with far deeper zeal
Of holier love. Nor wilt thou then forget,
That after many wanderings, many years
Of absence, these steep woods and lofty cliffs,
And this green pastoral landscape, were to me
More dear, both for themselves and for thy sake!

❧ A slumber did my spirit seal

A slumber did my spirit seal;
    I had no human fears:
She seemed a thing that could not feel
    The touch of earthly years.

No motion has she now, no force;
    She neither hears nor sees;
Rolled round in earth's diurnal course,
    With rocks, and stones, and trees.

❧ The world is too much with us

The world is too much with us; late and soon,
Getting and spending, we lay waste our powers:
Little we see in Nature that is ours;
We have given our hearts away, a sordid boon!
This Sea that bares her bosom to the moon,
The winds that will be howling at all hours,
And are up-gathered now like sleeping flowers;
For this, for everything, we are out of tune;
It moves us not. — Great God! I'd rather be
10 A Pagan suckled in a creed outworn;
So might I, standing on this pleasant lea,
Have glimpses that would make me less forlorn;
Have sight of Proteus rising from the sea;
Or hear old Triton blow his wreathèd horn.

❧ Composed upon Westminster Bridge, September 3, 1802

Earth has not anything to show more fair:
Dull would he be of soul who could pass by
A sight so touching in its majesty;
This City now doth, like a garment, wear
The beauty of the morning; silent, bare,
Ships, towers, domes, theatres, and temples lie
Open unto the fields, and to the sky;
All bright and glittering in the smokeless air.

Never did sun more beautifully steep
10 In his first splendour, valley, rock, or hill;
Ne'er saw I, never felt, a calm so deep!
The river glideth at his own sweet will:
Dear God! the very houses seem asleep;
And all that mighty heart is lying still!

❧ Ode: Intimations of Immortality

The Child is Father of the Man;
And I could wish my days to be
Bound each to each by natural piety.[1]

1.

There was a time when meadow, grove, and stream,
The earth, and every common sight,
    To me did seem
      Apparelled in celestial light,
The glory and the freshness of a dream.
It is not now as it hath been of yore;—
    Turn wheresoe'er I may,
      By night or day,
The things which I have seen I now can see no more.

2.

10   The Rainbow comes and goes,
      And lovely is the Rose;
      The Moon doth with delight
Look round her when the heavens are bare;
      Waters on a starry night
      Are beautiful and fair;
    The sunshine is a glorious birth;
    But yet I know, where'er I go,
That there hath past away a glory from the earth.

3.

Now, while the birds thus sing a joyous song,
20   And while the young lambs bound
      As to the tabor's sound,

---

[1] These are the final lines from an earlier poem, "My Heart Leaps Up."

To me alone there came a thought of grief:
A timely utterance gave that thought relief,
      And I again am strong:
The cataracts blow their trumpets from the steep;
No more shall grief of mine the season wrong;
I hear the Echoes through the mountains throng,
The Winds come to me from the fields of sleep,
      And all the earth is gay;
30   Land and sea
     Give themselves up to jollity,
      And with the heart of May
Doth every Beast keep holiday;—
      Thou Child of Joy,
Shout round me, let me hear thy shouts, thou happy Shepherd-boy!

4.

Ye blessèd Creatures, I have heard the call
     Ye to each other make; I see
The heavens laugh with you in your jubilee;
     My heart is at your festival,
40   My head hath its coronal,
The fulness of your bliss, I feel—I feel it all.
      Oh evil day! if I were sullen
      While Earth herself is adorning,
        This sweet May-morning,
     And the Children are culling
        On every side,
     In a thousand valleys far and wide,
     Fresh flowers: while the sun shines warm,
And the Babe leaps up on his Mother's arm:—
50   I hear, I hear, with joy I hear!
     —But there's a Tree, of many, one,
A single Field which I have looked upon,
Both of them speak of something that is gone:
      The Pansy at my feet
      Doth the same tale repeat:
Whither is fled the visionary gleam?
Where is it now, the glory and the dream?

5.

Our birth is but a sleep and a forgetting:
The Soul that rises with us, our life's Star,
60   Hath had elsewhere its setting,
      And cometh from afar:

Not in entire forgetfulness,
And not in utter nakedness,
But trailing clouds of glory do we come
From God, who is our home:
Heaven lies about us in our infancy!
Shades of the prison-house begin to close
Upon the growing Boy,
But He
70 Beholds the light, and whence it flows,
He sees it in his joy;
The Youth, who daily farther from the east
Must travel, still is Nature's Priest,
And by the vision splendid
Is on his way attended;
At length the Man perceives it die away,
And fade into the light of common day.

6.

Earth fills her lap with pleasures of her own;
Yearnings she hath in her own natural kind,
80 And, even with something of a Mother's mind,
And no unworthy aim,
The homely Nurse doth all she can
To make her Foster-child, her Inmate Man,
Forget the glories he hath known,
And that imperial palace whence he came.

7.

Behold the Child among his new-born blisses,
A six years' Darling of a pigmy size!
See, where 'mid work of his own hand he lies,
Fretted by sallies of his mother's kisses,
90 With light upon him from his father's eyes!
See, at his feet, some little plan or chart,
Some fragment from his dream of human life,
Shaped by himself with newly-learnèd art;
A wedding or a festival,
A mourning or a funeral;
And this hath now his heart,
And unto this he frames his song:
Then will he fit his tongue
To dialogues of business, love, or strife;
100 But it will not be long
Ere this be thrown aside,

And with new joy and pride
The little Actor cons another part;
Filling from time to time his "humorous stage"[2]
With all the Persons, down to palsied Age,
That Life brings with her in her equipage;
    As if his whole vocation
    Were endless imitation.

8.

Thou, whose exterior semblance doth belie
110   Thy Soul's immensity;
Thou best Philosopher, who yet dost keep
Thy heritage, thou Eye among the blind,
That, deaf and silent, read'st the eternal deep,
Haunted for ever by the eternal mind,—
    Mighty Prophet! Seer blest!
    On whom those truths do rest,
Which we are toiling all our lives to find,
In darkness lost, the darkness of the grave;
Thou, over whom thy Immortality
120 Broods like the Day, a Master o'er a Slave,
A Presence which is not to be put by;
Thou little Child, yet glorious in the might
Of heaven-born freedom on thy being's height,
Why with such earnest pains dost thou provoke
The years to bring the inevitable yoke,
Thus blindly with thy blessedness at strife?
Full soon thy Soul shall have her earthly freight,
And custom lie upon thee with a weight,
Heavy as frost, and deep almost as life!

9.

130   O joy! that in our embers
    Is something that doth live,
    That nature yet remembers
    What was so fugitive!
The thought of our past years in me doth breed
Perpetual benediction: not indeed
For that which is most worthy to be blest;
Delight and liberty, the simple creed

---

[2] **"humorous stage"**: From a sonnet dedicated to Fulke Greville in Elizabethan poet Samuel Daniel's *Musophilus* (1599).

Of Childhood, whether busy or at rest,
With new-fledged hope still fluttering in his breast: —
140   Not for these I raise
         The song of thanks and praise;
      But for those obstinate questionings
      Of sense and outward things,
      Fallings from us, vanishings;
      Blank misgivings of a Creature
Moving about in worlds not realized,
High instincts before which our mortal Nature
Did tremble like a guilty Thing surprised:
         But for those first affections,
150   Those shadowy recollections,
      Which, be they what they may,
Are yet the fountain light of all our day,
Are yet a master light of all our seeing;
      Uphold us, cherish, and have power to make
Our noisy years seem moments in the being
Of the eternal Silence: truths that wake,
         To perish never;
Which neither listlessness, nor mad endeavour,
         Nor Man nor Boy,
160 Nor all that is at enmity with joy,
Can utterly abolish or destroy!
         Hence in a season of calm weather
         Though inland far we be,
Our Souls have sight of that immortal sea
         Which brought us hither,
         Can in a moment travel thither,
And see the Children sport upon the shore,
And hear the mighty waters rolling evermore.

10.

Then sing, ye Birds, sing, sing a joyous song!
170   And let the young Lambs bound
         As to the tabor's sound!
We in thought will join your throng,
         Ye that pipe and ye that play,
         Ye that through your hearts today
         Feel the gladness of the May!
What though the radiance which was once so bright
Be now for ever taken from my sight,
         Though nothing can bring back the hour
Of splendour in the grass, of glory in the flower;

180   We will grieve not, rather find
        Strength in what remains behind;
        In the primal sympathy
        Which having been must ever be;
        In the soothing thoughts that spring
        Out of human suffering;
        In the faith that looks through death,
    In years that bring the philosophic mind.

11.

    And O, ye Fountains, Meadows, Hills, and Groves,
    Forebode not any severing of our loves!
190 Yet in my heart of hearts I feel your might;
    I only have relinquished one delight
    To live beneath your more habitual sway.
    I love the Brooks which down their channels fret,
    Even more than when I tripped lightly as they;
    The innocent brightness of a new-born Day
            Is lovely yet;
    The Clouds that gather round the setting sun
    Do take a sober colouring from an eye
    That hath kept watch o'er man's mortality;
200 Another race hath been, and other palms are won.
    Thanks to the human heart by which we live,
    Thanks to its tenderness, its joys, and fears,
    To me the meanest flower that blows can give
    Thoughts that do often lie too deep for tears.

The Romantic Lyric

During the late eighteenth century, the American and French revolutions rocked both sides of the Atlantic, and this age witnessed the great personalities of leaders such as Napoleon Bonaparte, Frederick the Great of Prussia, Catherine the Great of Russia, and Mary Theresa[1] of the Hapsburg empire. Just prior to or contemporary with this political ferment came the earliest stirrings of Romanticism in the novels and essays of Jean Jacques Rousseau in France; the essays, novels, poetry, and plays of Johann Gottfried Herder, Friedrich Schiller, and Johann Wolfgang von Goethe[2] during the *Sturm und Drang* in Germany; and the novels of Samuel Richardson, Laurence Sterne, and Henry MacKenzie[3] in the Age of Sensibility in England. Following Rousseau's *The New Heloise* (1761) and *Émile*

[1] **Napoleon Bonaparte, Frederick the Great, Catherine the Great, Maria Theresa: Bonaparte** (1769–1821) rose from relatively humble origins to become the leader of the French army during the French Revolution and eventually became the ruler of France, as first consul and then as emperor. **Frederick II of Prussia** (1712–1786) and **Catherine II of Russia** (1729–1796) were known as "enlightened monarchs" because of their support (albeit qualified) of Enlightenment ideas and their patronage of the arts and education. Although unsympathetic with the Enlightenment, **Maria Theresa** (1717–1780), the Hapsburg empress, initiated many reforms that benefited Austria and helped to unify the Hapsburg empire.

[2] **Johann Gottfried Herder, Friedrich Schiller, Johann Wolfgang von Goethe:** The German writers **Herder** (1744–1803) and **Schiller** (1759–1805) were leading figures of the *Sturm und Drang* (Storm and Stress) movement in the arts and culture in late eighteenth-century Germany, which emphasized individualism and high passion. Both Herder and Schiller influenced **Goethe** (1749–1832), the greatest German writer of the nineteenth century (see p. 553).

[3] **Samuel Richardson, Laurence Sterne, Henry MacKenzie:** English novelist **Richardson** (1689–1761), the author of *Pamela, or Virtue Rewarded* (1740); Irish novelist **Sterne** (1713–1768), author of *Tristram Shandy* (1759–1767) and *A Sentimental Journey through France and Italy* (1768); and Scottish novelist **Mackenzie** (1745–1831), author of *The Man of Feeling* (1771), are leading figures in the development of the sentimental novel, usually featuring a virtuous but vulnerable young woman of delicate feeling whose honor is besieged by a rakish "gentleman" of dubious character.

(1762), Goethe's first major literary work, *The Sorrows of Young Werther* (1774), reflected the new emphasis on feeling, imagination, and natural simplicity. Although Goethe intended the novel as a critique of the excesses of sensibility, enthusiastic readers both in and outside of Germany made a hero out of Goethe's delicate and emotionally volatile Werther. This unexpected response, known as *Wertherkrankheit* (Werther disease), shows that Europe was not only ready for but eager to promote the shift in consciousness that was taking place at the end of the eighteenth century, a shift that would emphasize the uncertain and sometimes chaotic states of passion, feeling, and experience—sensuous and sensual—above reason and order.

By the beginning of the nineteenth century, Romanticism was in full swing in Germany and in England, with France, Spain, and Russia to follow within the next two decades. Romantic poetry and poetics were marked above all by the inward turn of the poet, whose subjective meditations and reveries were linked to reflections upon the creative powers of the human imagination. Drawing inspiration from the creative and dynamic forces of nature, the Romantic writers revitalized interest in the natural world, and many of them sought out remote or solitary places as refuge from society and as sites for meditation and reflection. For the Romantics, imagination took the place of reason as the mode of inquiry into the worlds of mind and matter. This is not to say that Romantic writers and theorists threw rationality out the door altogether, displacing reason with feeling. English poets **William Wordsworth** and **Samuel Taylor Coleridge**, for example, believed that no one who had not thought deeply and felt strongly could be a true poet; **John Keats** famously praised Wordsworth's ability to "think into the human heart." Moreover, if Romanticism posits a return to nature as a desirable goal, that return usually does not imply a nostalgic return to a natural state of primitive or childhood innocence. Rather, Romantic poets and theorists generally recognize that the original state of innocence and unity with nature can never be recovered, yet they find value and a sense of power in the creative attempt to achieve some compensatory state of mind or being—what Wordsworth calls "abundant recompense" in "**Lines Composed a Few Miles above Tintern Abbey.**" Thus, for many Romantics, the separation from nature was a cause for qualified joy, because from that separation—a version of

> . . . if Poetry comes not as naturally as the Leaves to a tree it had better not come at all. . . ."
>
> – KEATS, Letter to John Taylor, 1818

pp. 736, 799

p. 778

p. 743

p. 791

the fortunate fall[4]—human beings discovered their freedom and their destiny. The Romantic ideally sought to realize their inner human nature without reference to outside or conventional authority. Yet, that process of self-discovery and self-invention, as Giacomo Leopardi captures in "**The Infinite**," was destined never to be completed; poised always at the threshold of resolution, foundering at the edge of sea or horizon, the impossible Romantic quest could only lead to an endless chain of desire. Hence, many Romantic lyric poems embody a powerful and palpable sense of longing for an unrealizable ideal—beauty, truth, social harmony, self-fulfillment. The Spanish poet Gustavo Adolfo Bécquer (1836–1870) captures the spirit of this endless quest in "Nameless Spirit," when he writes "I live with the formless / life of idea."

LYRIC POETRY

In lyric poetry the Romantics found a suitable medium for exploring inner states of feeling, shaping a sense of the philosophical ideal. Romantic lyrics usually involve a meditation by the speaker upon some poignant moment of personal experience leading to philosophical insight or speculation. More often than not, these meditations involve the speaker in relation to some aspect of nature—either as setting or as kindred power—or of poetry as an instrument for approaching beauty, truth, the ideal. The Romantic lyric ranges over a variety of topics but nearly always centers upon the speaker's emotional response to the issues raised in the poem. Lyric poetry in the Romantic era thus emphasized the expression of subjective reflections upon and feelings about such questions as the relationship between mind and nature, poetry and art, love and loss, transience and immortality, solitude and companionship, suffering and joy, despair and hope. While it is tempting (and often accurate) to attribute the feelings expressed in lyric poetry to the poet herself or himself, lyric poets often use their poetry to explore states of emotion and feeling not necessarily their own. By inventing a persona stricken with grief, inflamed by desire, or overwhelmed by the beauty or sublimity of nature, lyric poets hoped to plumb the depth and range of inner

. . . Blake's great value as a personal influence in English literature is that he is so outstanding an example of a precious quality of mental independence.

– NORTHROP FRYE, critic, 1947

---

[4] **the fortunate fall:** The *felix culpa*, or fortunate fall, posited that the sin of Adam and Eve was a necessary, and hence beneficial, error because it led to the coming of Christ and his forgiveness that would leave to salvation.

experience. In some cases, particularly with writers such as **Charlotte Smith** and **Lord Byron** in England, poets capitalized upon creating a semifictional persona in their lyrics—a surrogate self whose experiences, thoughts, and feelings were not necessarily identical to their own. The gap between the real and the fictional self presented in the poetry allured and also challenged their readers, who were forced to negotiate the boundaries between the real and fictional selves.

pp. 760, 722

The impossibility of ever completing the Romantic quest for self-realization or attaining the ideal (for possibility is infinite) led many Romantic lyric poets to a deep sense of despair, disillusionment, and a longing for death. The world constructed by art and poetry became for some a place preferable to life, yet poets like Keats in "**Ode on a Grecian Urn**" recognized the limits of that world as an aesthetic construct—a "cold Pastoral." Seeking to transcend the limitations of the world, some poets find themselves, as in Keats's "**Ode to a Nightingale**," "half in love with easeful Death." Leopardi's celebrated elegy "**To Sylvia**" asks if disappointment and loss are the necessary consequences, in the human world, of hope and love. He portrays Sylvia as a kind of Fate leading him to death: "from afar you pointed me the way / To coldest death and the stark sepulcher." In "**Yearning for Death**," Part 6 of *Hymns to the Night,* Novalis describes death as "a bursting forth" and "glad departure."

p. 782

p. 779
p. 791

p. 773

Romantic lyrics often figure life as a death—or, conversely, death as life. In Wordsworth's "**Ode: Intimations of Immortality**," for example, birth is but an end of our immortal spiritual existence, so that death leads back to our true identity, our true nature as an incorporeal being. In some poets, such as Byron, Heine, Lamartine, and Leopardi, the frustration at human limitations leads to a kind of *contemptus mundi,* a contempt for the world or, more precisely, contempt for the bourgeois world of getting and spending. Hence the familiar trope of the Romantic poet as solitary, an exile or outsider of either delicate sensibility or titanic passion. Charlotte Smith's *Elegiac Sonnets* construct the poet as such a figure, framed in a finer tone, as Keats would put it, than her fellow human beings.

p. 748

FORMS OF ROMANTIC LYRIC

Lyric poetry does not designate a poetic structure or form, so much as a type of subjective, expressive poetry. Thus, as these selections demonstrate, the Romantic lyric takes a variety of forms—from

Keats . . . saw life as a process in which no fixed order, no clear "balance of good and evil," was discernible. For him life was a mystery, a mist, a chaos in which pleasure and pain were inextricably entangled.
– ANNE MELLOR,
English Romantic Irony

songs and ballads, to sonnets and hymns, odes and elegies. The apparent simplicity of romantic songs (in German: *lieder*) and ballads deserves special attention, because poets such as William Blake and Heinrich Heine subvert the simple surface of such verse with powerful irony that calls into question the values apparently celebrated in the poems. Blake's "**The Chimney Sweeper**" from *Songs of Innocence,* for example, invites us to question exploitation of children in London whose dreams of a better life after death blind them to the injustice of their immediate circumstances—an exploitation made clear in the same poem from *Songs of Experience.*

p. 764

Although Romanticism is often seen as a revolt against the rigidity of poetic forms and poetic diction common to early-eighteenth-century, Neoclassical poetry, Romantic poets—and even those of the early generations—turned to a variety of classical and conventional forms, in part to express the high seriousness of their project. Epic hexameter verse, Miltonic blank verse, hymns, odes,[5] as well as other conventional forms found in Romantic lyric poetry, signal the purpose and seriousness of many romantic lyrics. Hymns and odes signal the strong affiliation between secular and religious feeling in Romanticism—and in the ode, the strong connections many Romantic poets had for Greece, in particular. The use of such exalted forms of verse point to the Romantic poets' sense of the sublime purpose—albeit often in condensed, intense short poems—of their work.

■ **FURTHER RESEARCH**

Cranston, Maurice. *The Romantic Movement.* 1994.
Ferber, Michael, ed. *A Companion to European Romanticism.* 2005.
Hosek, Chaviva, and Patricia Parker, eds. *Lyric Poetry: Beyond the New Criticism.* 1985.
Nemoianu, Virgil. *The Taming of Romanticism.* 1984.
Porter, Roy, and Mikulás Teich, eds. *Romanticism in National Context.* 1988.
Roe, Nicholas, ed. *Romanticism: An Oxford Guide.* 2005.

---

[5] **hexameter; blank verse; hymns; odes:** Hexameter, a line of six metrical feet, was the standard verse form for Greek and Latin epic poetry. Blank verse, unrhymed lines of five metrical feet (pentameter), was used by English poet John Milton (1608–1674) for his epic *Paradise Lost* (1667, 1684). Hymns are lyric poems or songs traditionally written to convey religious feeling or to commemorate religious rituals or events; and odes are lyric poems written to express dignified praise or to commemorate secular—such as historical, political, or athletic—events.

TIME AND PLACE

Nineteenth-Century Europe: The Death of Lord Byron

In 1821, Greeks set out to free themselves from four hundred years of Turkish rule. Their struggle rallied liberals throughout Europe, who were happy to see the cause of liberty spreading to the country that had invented the idea of democracy. Committees were formed to support Greece and idealistic young men journeyed south to join the battle. Lord Byron, who had come to love Greece during his travels there in 1809–10, was placed on the London Greek Committee, even though scandal over his sexual escapades had driven him from England into self-imposed exile in Italy.

In 1823 Byron took an active part in the battle. He mustered a small force, outfitted them in elaborately plumed "Homeric helmets," and in July set sail for Greece. Besides soldiers, he also had money from the London committee as well as several thousand pounds of his own in tow. He stopped for a few months in the Ionian Isles deliberating how best to support the cause of Greek independence without just joining one of the bickering factions. In December Byron made it past the Turkish naval blockade and landed at Missolonghi, a town on the south central coast of Greece.

His role in Missolonghi, however, was more banker and diplomat than general. The troops he mustered fell into disarray, and Byron never had a chance to lead them in battle. His time was taken up responding to requests for money, administering support from abroad, and fighting off illness. The climate at Missolonghi was unhealthful. Swamps encircled the town and the winter weather was damp and rainy. In mid February, Byron suffered an attack of fever.

His doctors counseled him to leave, but he insisted "it is proper that I should remain in Greece; and it were better to die doing something than nothing." In mid April, after a chilling ride in a rain storm, Byron fell into a fever and, weakened by the treatment of his doctors who bled him with leeches, died within a week.

Although he did not die in battle, he nevertheless became a hero, a symbol of the Romantic spirit of liberty and independence. A member of the London Greek Committee told him, "Your present endeavor is certainly the most glorious ever undertaken by man." His death was commemorated by memorial services in nearly every town in Greece and Byron's statue dominates the Garden of Heroes at Missolonghi. Scandal had denied him a place of burial in the Poet's Corner in Westminster Abbey. He was buried in his family's vault at the parish church in Nottinghamshire.

Lodovico Liparini, **Lord Byron Swearing Oath on Tomb of Marcos Batzaris.** *Batzaris was the leader of the Greek war of independence. He had corresponded with Byron, who took over his army. (The Art Archive/Civiche Raccolte Museo L. Bailo Treviso/Dagli Orti)*

CHARLOTTE SMITH
B. ENGLAND, 1749–1806

After the death of her mother, four-year-old Charlotte Turner was taken from the pleasant countryside estate where she was born in 1749 and moved to London, where she was raised by her aunt, and from where she made frequent visit to the Sussex Downs. When she was fifteen, her opportunistic father, Nicholas Turner, remarried for money, and Charlotte was essentially forced out of the household by her hateful stepmother—a figure that shows up in her later novels. Charlotte's disastrous marriage to the wealthy but reckless Benjamin Smith in 1765 led to misfortune, sorrow, and eventually separation. The couple had twelve children, including three who died in early childhood and a daughter, Augusta, who died at the age of twenty in 1794. Having squandered much of the fortune he inherited from his merchant father, Benjamin Smith, accompanied by his wife, was sent to debtor's prison in 1783. From that low point, Charlotte wrote and in the next year published her *Elegiac Sonnets* (1784), a highly successful collection of melancholy poems that, along with William Lisle Bowles's *Fourteen Sonnets* (1789), set off a revival in England of the sonnet as a major lyric form. In the sonnets, two of which are included here, Smith adopts a melancholy persona whose sorrowful lamentations and observations of suffering reflect her own but also reach to include those of others. A few of her sonnets, for example, are written in the voice of Werther, the tragic hero of sensibility or man of feeling in Goethe's *The Sorrows of Young Werther.* Many of the sonnets blur the boundary between Smith's real life and feelings and that of the speaker. In her own time she was both praised and criticized for putting her private life on public display in her works and for her sympathies for the French Revolution and radical political reform in England. Nonetheless, the feeling for the natural world (supplemented by a serious study of botany), the melancholy voice and the delicate sensibility and compassion displayed in her work touched a nerve with the reading public and influenced later writers, including William Wordsworth and John Keats. With the profits from sales of the first edition of *Elegiac Sonnets,* Charlotte secured the release of her family from debtor's prison and found her calling as a writer. By the end of the 1780s, she had established herself as a popular writer of novels, children's books, and longer poems. Her later works include the novels *Desmond* (1792), *The Old Manor House* (1793), and *The Young Philosopher* (1798), and two stunning longer blank-verse poems *The Emigrants* (1793) and *Beachy Head* (1807).

✍ Written in the Church-Yard at Middleton in Sussex[1]

Press'd by the Moon, mute arbitress of tides,
 While the loud equinox its power combines,
 The sea no more its swelling surge confines,
But o'er the shrinking land sublimely rides.
The wild blast, rising from the Western cave,
 Drives the huge billows from their heaving bed;
 Tears from their grassy tombs the village dead,
And breaks the silent sabbath of the grave!
With shells and sea-weed mingled, on the shore
10 Lo! their bones whiten in the frequent wave;
 But vain to them the winds and waters rave;
They hear the warring elements no more:
While I am doom'd — by life's long storm opprest,
To gaze with envy on their gloomy rest.

---

[1] Middleton is a village on the margin of the sea, in Sussex, containing only two or three houses. There were formerly several acres of ground between its small church and the sea, which now, by its continual encroachments, approaches within a few feet of this half [-] ruined and humble edifice. The wall, which once surrounded the churchyard, is entirely swept away, many of the graves broken up, and the remains of bodies interred washed into the sea: whence human bones are found among the sand and shingles on the shore. [Smith's note.]

✍ The Sea View[1]

The upland shepherd, as reclined he lies
 On the soft turf that clothes the mountain brow,
Marks the bright sea-line mingling with the skies;
 Or from his course celestial, sinking slow,
 The summer-sun in purple radiance low,
Blaze on the western waters; the wide scene
 Magnificent, and tranquil, seems to spread
Even o'er the rustic's breast a joy serene,
When, like dark plague-spots by the Demons shed,
10 Charged deep with death, upon the waves, far seen,
 Move the war-freighted ships; and fierce and red,
 Flash their destructive fire. — The mangled dead
And dying victims then pollute the flood.
Ah! thus man spoils Heaven's glorious works with blood!

---

[1] "'Tis delicate felicity that shrinks / when rocking winds are loud." Walpole. [Smith's note.]

WILLIAM BLAKE
B. ENGLAND, 1757–1827

Perhaps no writer of the early nineteenth century represents the revolt against the empirical philosophy of the Enlightenment more than the English poet, printmaker, and visionary William Blake. The son of a hosier, Blake was born in London on November 28, 1757, and grew up in London, where very early he displayed a talent for drawing and a proclivity for mystical visions. In 1782 Blake married Catherine Boucher, who assisted him in his work as a commercial engraver; seven years later he finished *Songs of Innocence*. Blake's masterful irony disturbs the apparently pleasant and joyful surfaces of *Songs of Innocence*, enabling us to construct a more troubled account of what takes place in each poem. By 1794 Blake had added the companion poems comprising *Songs of Experience*, which treat the same topics from a more openly critical perspective. Although some critics equate Blake's innocence with childhood and experience with adulthood, these two categories more accurately represent, in Blake's terms, "two contrary states of the human soul," for either perspective is available to the human consciousness at any age. Blake continued to apply his fullest energies to his longer prophetic works, including *Jerusalem* and *The Four Zoas*, even after the dismal failure of an exhibition of his work in 1809. In his later years Blake turned primarily to painting and drawing, completing superb illustrations for the works of Virgil and Dante and for the Book of Job. He died on August 12, 1827, reportedly singing with joy.

FROM

Songs of Innocence

INTRODUCTION

Piping down the valleys wild
Piping songs of pleasant glee
On a cloud I saw a child.
And he laughing said to me.

Pipe a song about a Lamb;
So I piped with merry chear,
Piper pipe that song again—
So I piped, he wept to hear.

Drop thy pipe thy happy pipe
10 Sing thy songs of happy chear,

So I sung the same again
While he wept with joy to hear

Piper sit thee down and write
In a book that all may read—
So he vanish'd from my sight.
And I pluck'd a hollow reed.

And I made a rural pen,
And I stain'd the water clear,
And I wrote my happy songs
20 Every child may joy to hear

THE LAMB

Little Lamb who made thee
Dost thou know who made thee
Gave thee life & bid thee feed.
By the stream & o'er the mead;

William Blake,
"The Lamb," 1794
(*Art Resource*)

Gave thee clothing of delight,
Softest clothing wooly bright;
Gave thee such a tender voice,
Making all the vales rejoice!
        Little Lamb who made thee
10   Dost thou know who made thee

        Little Lamb I'll tell thee,
        Little Lamb I'll tell thee!
He is called by thy name,
For he calls himself a Lamb:
He is meek & he is mild,
He became a little child:
I a child & thou a lamb,
We are called by his name.
        Little Lamb God bless thee.
20   Little Lamb God bless thee.

THE CHIMNEY SWEEPER

When my mother died I was very young,
And my father sold me while yet my tongue,
Could scarcely cry weep weep weep weep.
So your chimneys I sweep & in soot I sleep.

Theres little Tom Dacre, who cried when his head
That curl'd like a lambs back, was shav'd, so I said.
Hush Tom never mind it, for when your head's bare,
You know that the soot cannot spoil your white hair.

And so he was quiet, & that very night,
10 As Tom was a sleeping he had such a sight,
That thousands of sweepers Dick, Joe Ned & Jack
Were all of them lock'd up in coffins of black

And by came an Angel who had a bright key,
And he open'd the coffins & set them all free.
Then down a green plain leaping laughing they run
And wash in a river and shine in the Sun.

Then naked & white, all their bags left behind,
They rise upon clouds, and sport in the wind.
And the Angel told Tom if he'd be a good boy,
20 He'd have God for his father & never want joy.

And so Tom awoke and we rose in the dark
And got with our bags & our brushes to work.
Tho' the morning was cold, Tom was happy & warm,
So if all do their duty, they need not fear harm.

HOLY THURSDAY

Twas on a Holy Thursday[1] their innocent faces clean
The children walking two & two in red & blue & green
Grey headed beadles walkd before with wands as white as snow
Till into the high dome of Pauls[2] they like Thames[3] waters flow

O what a multitude they seemd these flowers of London town
Seated in companies they sit with radiance all their own
The hum of multitudes was there but multitudes of lambs
Thousands of little boys & girls raising their innocent hands

Now like a mighty wind they raise to heaven the voice of song
10 Or like harmonious thunderings the seats of heaven among
Beneath them sit the aged men wise guardians[4] of the poor
Then cherish pity, lest you drive an angel from your door

FROM

℘ Songs of Experience

INTRODUCTION

Hear the voice of the Bard!
Who Present, Past, & Future sees
Whose ears have heard,
The Holy Word,
That walk'd among the ancient trees.

Calling the lapsed Soul
And weeping in the evening dew;

---

[1] **Holy Thursday:** Normally designates Ascension Day, the fortieth day after Easter. The annual charity-school services, to which this poem refers, were held on the first Thursday in May, unless that day fell on Ascension Day.

[2] **Pauls:** St. Paul's Cathedral in London.

[3] **Thames:** River that runs through London.

[4] **wise guardians:** The overseers or governors of the charity schools.

That might controll,
The starry pole;
10 And fallen fallen light renew!

O Earth O Earth return!
Arise from out the dewy grass;
Night is worn,
And the morn
Rises from the slumberous mass.

Turn away no more:
Why wilt thou turn away
The starry floor
The watry shore
20 Is giv'n thee till the break of day.

EARTH'S ANSWER

Earth rais'd up her head,
From the darkness dread & drear.
Her light fled:
Stony dread!
And her locks cover'd with grey despair.

Prison'd on watry shore
Starry Jealousy does keep my den
Cold and hoar
Weeping o'er
10 I hear the Father of the ancient men

Selfish father of men
Cruel jealous selfish fear
Can delight
Chain'd in night
The virgins of youth and morning bear.

Does spring hide its joy
When buds and blossoms grow?
Does the sower?
Sow by night?
20 Or the plowman in darkness plow?

Break this heavy chain,
That does freeze my bones around

Selfish! vain,
Eternal bane!
That free Love with bondage bound.

HOLY THURSDAY

Is this a holy thing to see,
In a rich and fruitful land,
Babes reducd to misery,
Fed with cold and usurous hand?

Is that trembling cry a song?
Can it be a song of joy?
And so many children poor?
It is a land of poverty!

And their sun does never shine.
10   And their fields are bleak & bare.
And their ways are fill'd with thorns.
It is eternal winter there.

For where-e'er the sun does shine,
And where-e'er the rain does fall:
Babe can never hunger there,
Nor poverty the mind appall.

THE CHIMNEY SWEEPER

A little black thing among the snow:
Crying weep, weep, in notes of woe!
Where are thy father & mother? say?
They are both gone up to the church to pray.

Because I was happy upon the heath,
And smil'd among the winters snow:
They clothed me in the clothes of death,
And taught me to sing the notes of woe.

And because I am happy, & dance & sing,
10   They think they have done me no injury:
And are gone to praise God & his Priest & King
Who make up a heaven of our misery.

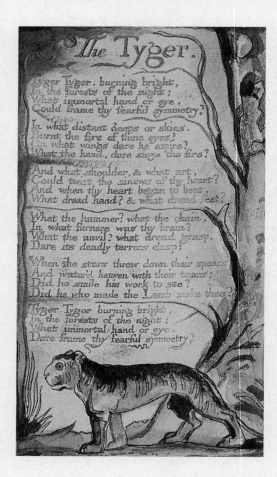

THE TYGER

Tyger Tyger, burning bright,
In the forests of the night;
What immortal hand or eye,
Could frame thy fearful symmetry?

In what distant deeps or skies
Burnt the fire of thine eyes!
On what wings dare he aspire?
What the hand, dare sieze the fire?

And what shoulder, & what art,
10 Could twist the sinews of thy heart?

And when thy heart began to beat,
What dread hand? & what dread feet?

What the hammer? what the chain,
In what furnace was thy brain?
What the anvil? what dread grasp,
Dare its deadly terrors clasp?

When the stars threw down their spears
And water'd heaven with their tears:
Did he smile his work to see?
20 Did he who made the Lamb make thee?

Tyger, Tyger burning bright,
In the forests of the night:
What immortal hand or eye,
Dare frame thy fearful symmetry?

LONDON

I wander thro' each charter'd[5] street,
Near where the charter'd Thames does flow.
And mark in every face I meet
Marks of weakness, marks of woe.

In every cry of every Man,
In every Infants cry of fear,
In every voice: in every ban,
The mind-forg'd manacles I hear

How the Chimney-sweepers cry
10 Every blackning Church appalls,
And the hapless Soldiers sigh,
Runs in blood down Palace walls

But most thro' midnight streets I hear
How the youthful Harlots curse
Blasts the new-born Infants tear
And blights with plagues the Marriage hearse

---

[5] London's charters granted certain liberties and privileges to its citizens and also demarcated the rights of property.

Friedrich Hölderlin was born in Lauffen am Neckar, in southwestern Germany, on March 20, 1770. Hölderlin lost both his father and stepfather as a child; nonetheless, his mother saw to his education, and at eighteen he entered the theological seminary at the University of Tübingen. There he became friends with the young Georg Wilhelm Friedrich Hegel and Friedrich Wilhelm von Schelling, two of Germany's most important idealist philosophers. A supporter of the French Revolution, by 1793 when he graduated from Tübingen, Hölderlin had abandoned his plan for a career in the church and worked as a tutor, first in Gotha and then in Frankfurt. He fell in love with Susette Gontard, a married woman who was the model for Diotima, the idealized heroine of his epistolary novel *Hyperion* (1797–99). Publicly denounced by Susette's husband Jakob Gontard, a wealthy Frankfurt banker, Hölderlin found himself in embarrassed and difficult circumstances. Supported by his mother and by Friedrich Schiller, whom he had met in Jena, where he lived from 1794–1800, Hölderlin continued writing, completing *Hyperion;* working on *The Death of Empedocles* (1798), an unfinished drama; and writing poetry. In 1802, partly in reaction to news of Susette's death, the poet suffered a serious fit of the mental illness that would soon debilitate him. After he recovered, over the next four years, Hölderlin wrote many of the lyrics for which he is celebrated. A devoted Hellenist who immersed himself in the study of Greek lyric poetry, particularly the works of the Greek lyric poet Pindar (518?–c. 438 B.C.E.), Hölderlin wrote in a unique style that does not so much bridge as collapse the serenity and poise of classical style upon the high intensity of Romantic feeling. "The Half of Life" captures in concise, epigrammatic lines and images the belatedness associated with Romantic sensibility, whereas "Hyperion's Song of Fate" succinctly articulates the restlessness and homelessness of the spirit in the world. After experiencing a productive period from 1802 to 1806, Hölderlin suffered another breakdown that led to a brief period of confinement at Tübingen, after which he spent the rest of his life under the care of Ernst Zimmer, a sympathetic carpenter who took the poet into his home, where he died thirty-six years later in 1843. His *Lyrical Poems* was published in 1826; his *Complete Works* in 1846.

The Half of Life

Translated by Christopher Middleton

With yellow pears the country,
Brimming with wild roses,
Hangs into the lake,
You gracious swans,
And drunk with kisses
Your heads you dip
Into the holy lucid water.

Where, ah where shall I find,
When winter comes, the flowers,
10 And where the sunshine
And shadows of the earth?
Walls stand
Speechless and cold, in the wind
The weathervanes clatter.

Hyperion's[1] Song of Fate

Translated by Christopher Middleton

You walk up there in the light
    On floors like velvet, blissful spirits.
        Shining winds divine
            Touch you lightly
                As a harper touches holy
                    Strings with her fingers.

Fateless as babes asleep
    They breathe, the celestials.
        Chastely kept
10   In a simple bud,
                For them the spirit
                    Flowers eternal,
                        And in bliss their eyes
                            Gaze in eternal
                                Calm clarity.

---

[1] **Hyperion:** In Greek mythology, a Titan sun god who was the father of Eos, the dawn; Helius, the sun; and Selene, the moon.

But to us it is given
   To find no resting place,
     We faint, we fall,
      Suffering, human,
20   Blindly from one
        To the next moment
         Like water flung
          From rock to rock down
           Long years into uncertainty.

NOVALIS (GEORG FRIEDRICH PHILIPP, BARON VON HARDENBERG)
B. GERMANY, 1772–1801

Georg Friedrich Philipp, Baron von Hardenberg, known as Novalis—a name he took from "de Novali," which his ancestors had used—was born in 1772 in the Harz mountain region of Germany. Raised in a Lutheran family who embraced Pietism, a movement emphasizing personal devotion to God, Novalis eventually attended university at Jena, Leipzig, and Wittenberg, taking a law degree in 1794. Jena, one of the founding centers of German Romanticism, was then home to such pre-eminent German thinkers such as Friedrich Schiller, Gottfried Herder, F. W. J. Schelling, and Friedrich and August Wilhelm Schlegel. Like his father, Novalis eventually worked in the directorate of the saltworks; his keen interest in mining and geology led him to formal studies at the Mining Academy of Freiberg. A key event in his life was the death of his young fiancée, Sophie von Kühn, in 1797. By 1798 Novalis was publishing poems in the *Athenaeum*, the foremost literary journal of early German Romanticism, which in 1800 published Novalis's celebrated *Hymns to the Night*, an innovative cycle of six meditations upon night and death. Mixing prose and verse, these powerful professions of faith turn upside down the conventional hierarchy that privileges day over night. Novalis portrays night as a mysterious presence that permeates our very being, as the ultimate source of visionary insight, and as an embodiment of our true destiny. While many of his Romantic contemporaries in Germany, such as Hölderlin, looked to Greece for their poetic forms and inspiration, Novalis turned to the Middle Ages and the Christian mystical tradition. In *Christianity or Europe*, written in 1799 but not published until 1826, Novalis gave Germany an idealized vision of its medieval Christian past. "Yearning for Death," Part 6 of the *Hymns to the Night*, captures Novalis's nostalgia for the nobility of spirit he found in the middle ages, as well as his sense that death, as a kind of rebirth, leads us to our true homeland. Only a few months after the publication of *Hymns to the Night*, Novalis died of tuberculosis, the same disease that had taken the life of Sophie and that would claim the life of the twenty-four-year-old English poet John Keats nearly two decades later. Among Novalis's other important works is the incomplete novel *Heinrich von Ofterdingen*, celebrated for its recurrent symbol of the "blue flower," a symbol of an object of desire, which became a symbol for German Romanticism as a whole.

FROM

∾ Hymns to the Night

Translated by Charles E. Passage

YEARNING FOR DEATH

Down now into the dark earth's womb,
From Light's domain away!
Wild rage of grief and pangs of gloom
Mark glad departure's day.
In narrow barque[1] we swiftly ply
To land along the shores of sky.

Praised be the everlasting Night,
Praised be eternal slumber!
Day's heat has withered us, and blight
10 Of sorrows without number.
For alien lands we no more yearn,
To our Father's house we would return.

In this world what can us betide
Our love and constancy?
When old things have been put aside
What use can new things be?
O! lonely stands and all undone
Whoever loves the times foregone.

The times foregone, when in bright dance
20 High spirits flamed, and when
The Father's hand and countenance
Were still in mankind's ken,
And nobly, simply, many bore
The lofty image that he bore.

---

[1] **barque:** A small sailboat.

The times foregone, when full-bloom-blowing
Primaeval races throve,
And children toward God's kingdom going
For death and torment strove;
And when, though life and pleasure spoke,
30   Yet many hearts, for loving, broke.

Those times, when God himself revealed
Himself with youthful ardor,
And with love's strength his sweet life sealed
In young death as a martyr,
Refusing not the smart and pain,
That it might be our dearer gain.

We see them now, with anxious yearning,
Shrouded in dark of night;
In temporal life our hot thirst's burning
40   Will not be slaked outright;
Unto our homeland we must go
That we that holy time may know.

What holds up our return? To rest
Our loved ones are long laid.
At their graves closes our lives' quest,
Sad are we and afraid.
There is no more for us to seek,
The heart is sated, the world is bleak.

A mystic shudder, sweet, unbounded,
50   Now courses through our marrow;
Methinks from the far distance sounded
An echo of our sorrow.
Perhaps our loved ones likewise longing
Have wafted us this sigh of longing.

Down to the sweet bride[2] come away,
To Jesus whom we love!
Good cheer! The evening dawn shows gray
On them who grieve and love.
Dream bursts our bonds and sinks us free
60   To our Father's arms eternally.

---

[2] sweet bride: Jesus.

ALPHONSE DE LAMARTINE
B. FRANCE, 1790–1869

Alphonse de Lamartine was born in October 1790 into an aristocratic, Roman Catholic family in Mâcon, France. He was educated at home and at schools in Lyons and Belley, becoming an avid reader of German, French, and classical literature. In the years 1811–1812, Lamartine traveled through Italy, returning to France briefly before leaving again for Switzerland and Aix-les-Bains, in the Savoy region of France. When Napoleon was defeated at Waterloo, the Royalist Lamartine returned to Paris and served for a while in the body guard for Louis XVIII (1755–1824), the restored Bourbon monarch in France. In October 1816 he fell in love with Julie Charles, a married woman whom he met at a spa on Lake Bourget near Aix-les-Bains; anticipating her death from tuberculosis and the end of the relationship, Lamartine wrote "The Lake," a moving elegy that hauntingly recalls his meeting with Madame Charles, who died in December 1817. Although semiautobiographical, the poem becomes a timeless elegy for universal loss, and the speaker's plaintive apostrophes to nature, bidding it to preserve the memory of his love, perhaps do less to affirm nature's power to hold on to the delicate memory than to confirm the certainty of transience and loss. "The Lake" was published in 1820, in *Poetic Meditations,* a collection of elegiac lyrics that some see as the inauguration of Romanticism in France. Unlike many of the poets of his era, Lamartine had a political career, serving first as a diplomat in Naples and Florence, during which time he continued to write, publishing *New Poetic Meditations* in 1823 and the *Last Canto of Childe Harold,* a tribute to Lord Byron, two years later. After a period that included an extended trip to Palestine and Turkey, Lamartine returned to France and became a celebrated politician. Although his father had been a Royalist imprisoned during the Revolution, Lamartine had acquired more liberal views, and he became one of the leaders of provisional government after the 1848 Revolution in France. Failing to get elected as president in 1848, Lamartine took a downard turn, and he ended his life in straitened circumstances, writing histories and essays and relying upon government support. He died on February 28, 1869; among his other notable works are the *Poetic and Religious Harmonies* (1830), a collection of poems; *Voyage to the Orient* (1835), a travel narrative; *Jocelyn* (1837), a narrative poem; and *History of the Girondins* (1847).

The Lake

Translated by Andrea Moorhead

And thus, forever driven towards new shores,
Swept into eternal night without return,
Will we never, for even one day, drop anchor
    On time's vast ocean?

O lake! Only a year has now gone by,
And to these dear waves she would have seen again,
Look! I'm returning alone to sit on the very rock
    Where you last saw her rest!

Then as now, you rumbled under these great rocks;
10 Then as now, you broke against their torn flanks;
The wind hurling the foam from your waves
    Onto her adored feet.

One evening, you recall? We drifted in silence;
Far off on the water and under the stars hearing
Only the rhythmic sound of oars striking
    Your melodious waves.

Suddenly strains unknown on earth
Echoed from the enchanted shore;
The water paid heed, and the voice so dear
20   To me spoke these words:

"O time, suspend your flight! and you, blessed hours,
    Suspend your swift passage.
Allow us to savor the fleeting delights
    Of our most happy days!

So many wretched people beseech you:
    Flow, flow quickly for them;
Take away the cares devouring them;
    Overlook the happy.

But I ask in vain for just a few more moments,
30   Time escaping me flees;
While I beg the night: 'Slow down,' already
    It fades into the dawn.

Then let us love, let us love! And the fleeting hours
    Let us hasten to enjoy.
We have no port, time itself has no shore;
    It glides by, and we pass away."

Jealous time, will these moments of such intoxication,
Love flooding us with overwhelming bliss,
Fly past us with the same speed
40   As dark and painful days?

What! will we not keep at least the trace of them?
What! They are gone forever? Totally lost?
This time that gave them and is obliterating them,
    Will it never return them to us?

Eternity, nothingness, past, somber abysses,
What are you doing with the days you swallow up?
Speak: will you ever give back the sublime bliss
    You stole from us?

O lake! silent rocks! shaded grottoes! dark forest!
50 You whom time can spare or even rejuvenate,
Preserve, noble nature, preserve from this night
    At least the memory!

May it live in your peace, may it be in your storms,
Beautiful lake, and in the light of your glad slopes,
And in these tall dark firs and in these savage rocks,
    Overhanging your waves.

May it be in the trembling zephyr passing by,
In the endless sounds that carry from shore to shore
In the silver faced star[1] that whitens your surface
60   With its softened brilliance.

May the moaning wind and sighing reed,
May the delicate scent of your fragrant breeze,
May everything that we hear and see and breathe,
    Awaken the memory of—their love!

---

[1] silver faced star: The moon.

JOHN KEATS

B. ENGLAND, 1795–1821

Portrait of John
Keats, after a
painting by
W. Hilton.
*Keats lived to be only
26, when he died of
tuberculosis. This
portrait evokes his
inquisitive nature.*
(Corbis)

www For links to
more information
about Keats and
his 21st-century
relevance, see
bedfordstmartins
.com/worldlit
compact.

During his life of twenty-six years, John Keats produced a body of lyrics, odes, and narrative poems that have placed him among the highest ranks of Romantic poets. Born in London in 1795, the son of a stablemaster, John was educated at Enfield school in London, where his literary interests were encouraged by Charles Cowden Clarke, who became a lifelong mentor for Keats. After his mother's death of tuberculosis in 1810 (he had lost his father to a riding accident in 1804), Keats was taken out of school and for four years was apprenticed to the surgeon Thomas Hammond. In 1815 he became a surgeon's assistant at Guy's Hospital, but within a year, encouraged by Leigh Hunt, editor of *The Examiner,* and a circle of reform-minded writers who would eventually be known as the "Cockney School," Keats gave up his medical studies for poetry. His first book of poems published in 1817 included "On First Looking into Chapman's Homer" and "Sleep and Poetry," two works that revealed his talent and declared his devotion to the study and writing of poetry. The next year, Keats published *Endymion,* which received some particularly rancorous reviews from conservative reviewers, and he took his brother Tom, dying of tuberculosis, under his wing. Undaunted by the negative criticism, Keats stood tenaciously by his plan to become a great poet, and the year 1819 confirmed those aspirations. In that year, Keats wrote the great poems of his career, among which are included some of the finest poems in English: "The Eve of St. Agnes," "La Belle Dame sans Merci: A Ballad," the six magnificent odes, "Lamia," and a number of fine sonnets. Keats's poetry was acclaimed for its vivid detail, sonorous musicality, and sensuous imagery. The dramatic movement of Keats's "Ode to a Nightingale" enacts Keats's belief that the poet has no identity in the sense that poetry in part results from the poet's capacity for sympathetic identification with another. The Nightingale here represents an ideal, and the annihilation of the poet's bodily senses in his identification with the bird as symbol enables him to experience, albeit momentarily, a world of beauty from which he inevitably must be separated. In "Ode on a Grecian Urn," the poet's imagination similarly overflows with activity when his senses are suspended in a moment of reverie or contemplation; here the "unheard melodies" are sweeter than heard ones, just as the poet's imaginative response to the static figures painted on the vase bring them to life. The poem is a testament to the power of art and imagination. In February 1820, Keats coughed up blood and soon realized that he had tuberculosis. Advised to go to a warmer climate for the winter, Keats moved to Italy where he died in Rome on February 23, 1821.

᧽   On First Looking into Chapman's Homer

Much have I travell'd in the realms of gold,[1]
    And many goodly states and kingdoms seen;
    Round many western islands have I been
Which bards in fealty to Apollo[2] hold.
Oft of one wide expanse had I been told
    That deep-brow'd Homer ruled as his demesne;
    Yet did I never breathe its pure serene
Till I heard Chapman speak out loud and bold:
Then felt I like some watcher of the skies
10   When a new planet swims into his ken;[3]
Or like stout Cortez[4] when with eagle eyes
    He star'd at the Pacific — and all his men
Look'd at each other with a wild surmise —
    Silent, upon a peak in Darien.[5]

---

[1] **realms of gold:** Douglas Bush links this phrase to Apollo's "Western halls of gold," though they possibly allude to El Dorado, the legendary city of gold; some critics have suggested Keats may also be referring to the gilded pages of bound books.
[2] **Apollo:** The god of poetry and inspiration in Greek mythology.
[3] **new planet . . . ken:** Most likely alludes to the discovery of Uranus by the astronomer F. W. Herschel in 1781.
[4] **Cortez:** Keats here mistakes Hernando Cortez (1485–1547) for Balboa (1475–1517), who actually reached the Pacific when crossing through Panama in 1513.
[5] **Darien:** A mountain range in eastern Panama; Keats uses the word to mean Panama itself.

᧽   Ode to a Nightingale

1.

My heart aches, and a drowsy numbness pains
    My sense, as though of hemlock I had drunk,
Or emptied some dull opiate to the drains
    One minute past, and Lethe-wards[1] had sunk:
'Tis not through envy of thy happy lot,
    But being too happy in thine happiness, —
        That thou, light-wingéd Dryad° of the trees,   *wood nymph*
        In some melodious plot

---

[1] **Lethe-wards:** Lethe is the river of forgetfulness in Greek mythology.

Of beechen green, and shadows numberless,
10   Singest of summer in full-throated ease.

2.

O, for a draught of vintage! that hath been
          Cool'd a long age in the deep-delvéd earth,
Tasting of Flora and the country green,
          Dance, and Provençal song, and sunburnt mirth!
O for a beaker full of the warm South,
          Full of the true, the blushful Hippocrene,[2]
                    With beaded bubbles winking at the brim,
                              And purple-stainéd mouth;
          That I might drink, and leave the world unseen,
20   And with thee fade away into the forest dim:

3.

Fade far away, dissolve, and quite forget
          What thou among the leaves hast never known,
The weariness, the fever, and the fret
          Here, where men sit and hear each other groan;
Where palsy shakes a few, sad, last gray hairs,
          Where youth grows pale, and spectre-thin, and dies;
                    Where but to think is to be full of sorrow
                              And leaden-eyed despairs,
          Where Beauty cannot keep her lustrous eyes,
30   Or new Love pine at them beyond to-morrow.

4.

Away! away! for I will fly to thee,
          Not charioted by Bacchus and his pards,°   leopards
But on the viewless wings of Poesy,
          Though the dull brain perplexes and retards:
Already with thee! tender is the night,
          And haply° the Queen-Moon is on her throne,   perhaps
                    Cluster'd around by all her starry Fays;°   fairies
                              But here there is no light,
          Save what from heaven is with the breezes blown
40   Through verdurous glooms and winding mossy ways.

---

[2] **Hippocrene:** Fountain of the Muses on Mt. Helicon in Greece.

5.

I cannot see what flowers are at my feet,
    Nor what soft incense hangs upon the boughs,
But, in embalméd darkness, guess each sweet
    Wherewith the seasonable month endows
The grass, the thicket, and the fruit-tree wild;
    White hawthorn, and the pastoral eglantine;
        Fast fading violets cover'd up in leaves;
            And mid-May's eldest child,
    The coming musk-rose, full of dewy wine,
50   The murmurous haunt of flies on summer eves.

6.

Darkling° I listen; and, for many a time   *in the dark*
    I have been half in love with easeful Death,
Call'd him soft names in many a muséd rhyme,
    To take into the air my quiet breath;
Now more than ever seems it rich to die,
    To cease upon the midnight with no pain,
        While thou art pouring forth thy soul abroad
            In such an ecstasy!
    Still wouldst thou sing, and I have ears in vain —
60   To thy high requiem become a sod.

7.

Thou wast not born for death, immortal Bird!
    No hungry generations tread thee down;
The voice I hear this passing night was heard
    In ancient days by emperor and clown:
Perhaps the self-same song that found a path
    Through the sad heart of Ruth,[3] when, sick for home,
    She stood in tears amid the alien corn;
        The same that oft-times hath
Charm'd magic casements, opening on the foam
70   Of perilous seas, in faery lands forlorn.

8.

Forlorn! the very word is like a bell
    To toll me back from thee to my sole self!

---

[3] **Ruth:** The widowed exile from Moab in the Book of Ruth, who chooses to remain loyal to her mother-in-law and go to Bethlehem, giving up her homeland and joining the people of Judah.

Adieu! the fancy cannot cheat so well
    As she is fam'd to do, deceiving elf.
Adieu! adieu! thy plaintive anthem fades
    Past the near meadows, over the still stream,
        Up the hill-side; and now 'tis buried deep
        In the next valley-glades:
    Was it a vision, or a waking dream?
80   Fled is that music: — Do I wake or sleep?

➷ Ode on a Grecian Urn

1.

Thou still unravish'd bride of quietness,
    Thou foster-child of silence and slow time,
Sylvan historian, who canst thus express
    A flowery tale more sweetly than our rhyme:
What leaf-fring'd legend haunts about thy shape
    Of deities or mortals, or of both,
        In Tempe or the dales of Arcady?[1]
    What men or gods are these? What maidens loth?
What mad pursuit? What struggle to escape?
10   What pipes and timbrels?° What wild ecstasy?   tambourines

2.

Heard melodies are sweet, but those unheard
    Are sweeter; therefore, ye soft pipes, play on;
Not to the sensual ear, but, more endear'd,
    Pipe to the spirit ditties of no tone:
Fair youth, beneath the trees, thou canst not leave
    Thy song, nor ever can those trees be bare;
        Bold lover, never, never canst thou kiss,
Though winning near the goal — yet, do not grieve;
    She cannot fade, though thou hast not thy bliss,
20   For ever wilt thou love, and she be fair!

---

[1] **Tempe:** A lovely valley in Greece near Mount Olympus;   **Arcady:** Region in the Peloponnese, here symbolizing rural beauty.

3.

Ah, happy, happy boughs! that cannot shed
    Your leaves, nor ever bid the spring adieu;
And, happy melodist, unweariéd,
    For ever piping songs for ever new:
More happy love! more happy, happy love!
    For ever warm and still to be enjoy'd,
        For ever panting, and for ever young;
All breathing human passion far above,
    That leaves a heart high-sorrowful and cloy'd,
30   A burning forehead, and a parching tongue.

4.

Who are these coming to the sacrifice?
    To what green altar, O mysterious priest,
Lead'st thou that heifer lowing at the skies,
    And all her silken flanks with garlands drest?
What little town by river or sea shore,
    Or mountain-built with peaceful citadel,
        Is emptied of this folk, this pious morn?
And, little town, thy streets for evermore
    Will silent be; and not a soul to tell
40   Why thou art desolate, can e'er return.

5.

O Attic[2] shape! Fair attitude! with brede°   pattern
    Of marble men and maidens overwrought,
With forest branches and the trodden weed;
    Thou, silent form, dost tease us out of thought
As doth eternity: Cold pastoral!
    When old age shall this generation waste,
        Thou shalt remain, in midst of other woe
Than ours, a friend to man, to whom thou say'st,
"Beauty is truth, truth beauty,"[3] — that is all
50   Ye know on earth, and all ye need to know.

---

[2] **Attic:** Attica, the region in Greece where Athens is located.

[3] **"Beauty . . . beauty":** The first published version of this poem, appearing in *Annals of the Fine Arts,* does not have this phrase in quotation marks; the second version, published in *Lamia, Isabella, The Eve of St. Agnes, and Other Poems* (1820), which Keats saw into press, does. The last two lines of this poem have presented a textual and critical problem for scholars and critics.

ANNETTE VON DROSTE-HÜLSHOFF

B. GERMANY, 1797–1848

One of the most important German women writers of the nineteenth century, Annette von Droste-Hülshoff was born in January 1797 in Westphalia to an aristocratic Roman Catholic family. She was raised in their castle, Schloss Hülshoff, until the death of her father in 1825. As a child she suffered from chronic illness. At Burg Hülshoff, she received a superb private education from tutors. Although she made several journeys to Bonn and other cities where she made some long-term and important connections with literary circles (including the brothers Grimm), she lived a relatively cloistered life. She never married, remaining with her family at Schloss Hülshoff; then at Rüschaus, where her mother moved after her father's death; and finally at Meersburg. Because of the limits imposed upon her, Droste-Hülshoff is sometimes compared to Emily Dickinson, who led a similarly cloistered life and who also found in poetry a means to broaden her world and express feelings of resistance and independence. Although Droste-Hülshoff began writing early in life, profound disappointment with a hopeless love triangle in 1820 led her to write in earnest. In that year, she began writing some of the religious poems for *The Spiritual Year,* which did not appear in print until after her death. A key event in her life was meeting Levin Schücking, a young writer whom she fell in love with in 1837. A year later she published her first collection, *Poems* (1838). Spurred on by Schücking, with whom Droste-Hülshoff was coauthoring a book on her beloved Westphalia, she began writing the Romantic lyrics on nature, disappointment, and love that were published in *Poems* (1844). In poems such as "On the Tower," a meditation upon her loneliness, we see her strong affinity to the countryside of Westphalia as well as her desire for making a larger connection to place and to community — something that would have been made more probable, she indicates, were she not a woman. In addition to her poetry, Droste-Hülshoff wrote a celebrated novel, *The Jew's Beech* (1842), about the murder of a Jew in her native Westphalia, as well as dramatic fragments and works of prose — including the sketches of Westphalia. She died in 1848 at the Schloss Meersburg.

On the Tower

Translated by Ruth Angress

I stand on the tower's high balcony,
The shrieking starling streaks by.
And like a maenad I let the storm
Rumple and tear at my hair.
Oh my wild comrade and crazy boy,
I long to embrace you and match

My strength against yours, two steps from the edge
And wrestle with you to the death.

And as I look down at the beach, the waves
10 Are like hunting dogs at play,
Foaming and bellowing they rave,
And up leaps the glistening spray.
How gladly I'd jump to be among
That raging pack of hounds
And follow through the coral woods
The walrus with merry sound.

And further I see a pennant blow
Bold as a battle banner.
And the prow of the ship goes up and down,
20 As I watch from my airy rampart.
Oh, I want to stand in that fighting ship
And grasp the steering wheel
And over the spitting, hissing deep
Glide as the seagull will.

If I were a hunter, out in the wild,
If I were a bit of a soldier,
If I were at least and simply a man,
Then Heaven would counsel and hold me.
But now I must sit like a good little girl,
30 Sweet, delicate and fair.
And I have to hide to let the wind
Blow freely through my hair.

∽ In the Grass

Translated by James Edward Tobin

Refreshing rest, ecstatic dream,
Sweet scent of herbs suffusing grass,
Deep, deep, wild-rushing stream;
When sky absorbs the clouds that pass,
When dancing laughter reels around
Your head like fluttering Mayflowers,
When gay notes drift across the ground,
Lime blossoms falling on a grave in showers—

Then all the ghosts within your breast
10   (Dead love, dead pleasure, and dead time)
Stir gently, gently, as in quest
Of breath, stiffly, as a masked mime
Gropes sight beyond closed eyelashes;
Then all this wealth, abandoned, binned
As rubbish, sings hidden splashes
Of timid sound, like bells fingered by wind.

Hours, you are briefer than the kiss
Of sunbeam lips on saddened sea,
Than the cry of autumn birds is,
20   Dropped like pearls of melody,
Than sun-bright sparkle on the shell
The scuttling beetle wears for shield,
Than hand clasp broken by farewell,
A thinning warmth its lonely, final yield.

Despite this, Heaven, grant to me
One gift: for every bird's bright voice
A spirit matching the blue, free,
Limitless sky which is its choice;
For every weakened ray of light
30   My hem line's iridescent gleam;
For every hand my clasp, warm, tight;
For every joy the seedling of a dream.

❧ HEINRICH HEINE
B. GERMANY, 1797–1856

Freedom is a new
religion, the religion
of our age.
    – HEINRICH HEINE

The son of German-Jewish drape merchants, Heinrich Heine was born in
1797 in Düsseldorf, Germany. Heine began his literary career during his
university years at Bonn, Göttingen, and Berlin, publishing poetry in
magazines and bringing out a small collection, *Poems by H. Heine*, in 1821.
After receiving a law degree in 1825, Heine traveled throughout Germany,
England, France, and Italy, writing some prose pieces—including *The
Harz Journey*—as well as poetry. The poems that appeared in *Tragedies
with a Lyrical Intermezzo* (1823), *Travel Pictures* (1826–27), and *The Book
of Songs* (1827) invoke Romantic themes, such as the struggle between
the ideal and real, the sorrows of unrequited love, and the longing for

self-annihilation, but Heine treats these themes with a degree of irony that questions their validity. After the Revolution of 1830, in May 1831, Heine moved permanently to Paris, a place more amenable to his liberal ideals than the politically conservative and nationalistic Germany. The publication of three important essays on French and German culture soon followed: *French Affairs* (1832), *The Romantic School* (1833–35), and *Concerning the History of Religion and Philosophy in Germany* (1834–35). *The Romantic School* traces the origins of German Romanticism to Medieval Catholicism and critically describes the idealistic character of German Romanticism. In 1844 appeared *New Poems,* in which the ironic tone of the early work deepens and the Romantic themes often give way to overtly political poems, such as "The Silesian Weavers." Not long after the publication of *New Poems,* Heine fell ill, and from 1848 until his death in February 1856 he was confined to what he called his "mattress grave." Though bedridden, before his death Heine published two major publications that confirmed his reputation as one of Germany's greatest poets, a master of technique and self-conscious irony—*Romanzero* (1851) and *Poems of 1853 and 1854* (1854).

Portrait of Heinrich Heine. Engraving *Heine was known for his youthful looks and well-kept appearance. (Bibliothèque Nationale, Paris)*

A Spruce is standing lonely

Translated by Gary Harrison

A spruce is standing lonely
Far north on a barren height.
Sleepy; and white blanketed
Enclosed in snow and ice.

He dreams of a distant palm,
Far off in an Orient place,
Lonely and silently mourning
On a burning rock-cliff face.

The Minnesingers

Translated by Louis Untermeyer

Come the minnesingers, raising
    Dust and laughter and lament.
Here's a contest that's amazing;
    Here's a curious tournament.

Wild and ever restless Fancy
    Is the minnesinger's horse,

Art his shield, the Word his lance; he
    Bears them lightly round the course.

Many women pleased and pleasant,
10   Smile and drop a flower down;
But the right one's never present
    With the rightful laurel-crown.

Other fighters nimbly canter
    To the lists, care-free and whole;
But we minnesingers enter
    With a death-wound in our soul.

And the one who wrings the inmost
    Song-blood from his burning breast,
He's the victor; he shall win most
20   Praise and smiles and all the rest.

The Silesian Weavers[1]

Translated by Aaron Kramer

In gloomy eyes there wells no tear.
Grinding their teeth, they are sitting here:
Germany, your shroud's on our loom;
And in it we weave the threefold doom.
    We're weaving; we're weaving.

Doomed be the God who was deaf to our prayer
In winter's cold and hunger's despair.
All in vain we hoped and bided;
He only mocked us, hoaxed, derided—
10   We're weaving; we're weaving.

---

[1] *The Silesian Weavers:* Published in Karl Marx's *Forward!* in 1844, this poem commemorates the June 1844 revolt of the destitute weavers from Peterswaldau in Silesia, then part of Prussia, against their employers. The rebellion was quickly and brutally suppressed by Prussian troops. Heine's poem was a rallying point for German workers for many years. One of the earliest German workers' revolts, this action by the weavers contributed to the growing dissension that culminated in the revolutions that swept Europe in 1848, which limited the powers of the Prussian king to which the poem refers, Friedrich Wilhelm IV.

Doomed be the king, the rich man's king,
Who would not be moved by our suffering,
Who tore the last coin out of our hands,
And let us be shot by his bloodthirsty bands—
    We're weaving; we're weaving.

Doomed be the fatherland, false name,
Where nothing thrives but disgrace and shame,
Where flowers are crushed before they unfold,
Where the worm is quickened by rot and mold—
20   We're weaving; we're weaving.

The loom is creaking, the shuttle flies;
Nor night nor day do we close our eyes.
Old Germany, your shroud's on our loom,
And in it we weave the threefold doom;
    We're weaving; we're weaving.

❧ The Asra[1]

Translated by Ernst Feise

Daily went the Sultan's beauteous
Daughter walking for her pleasure
In the evening at the fountain
Where the splashing waters whiten.

Daily stood the youthful bondsman
In the evening at the fountain
Where the splashing waters whiten,
Daily he grew pale and paler.

Then one evening stepped the princess
10 Up to him with sudden questions:
"You must tell me what your name is,
What your country is, your kinfolk."

---

[1] ***The Asra:*** The story on which this poem is based appears in *On Love* by the French writer Stendhal, the author of *The Red and the Black* (1830). The poem, written in the ballad form, describes the hopeless love of a member of the Asra, a legendary tribe of slaves who are doomed to die when they fall in love. The impossibility of the love between the slave and the Sultan's daughter is underscored not only by the curse upon the Asra, but by the class difference between the bondsman (slave) and the princess.

And the bondsman said: "Mohamet
Is my name, I am from Yemen,
And my kinsmen are the Asra,
They who die when love befalls them."

GIACOMO LEOPARDI
B. *ITALY, 1798–1837*

Giacomo Leopardi was born June 29, 1798, into an aristocratic family in Recanati, an Italian village near Ancona. The family had fallen into difficult circumstances, in part due to his father's gambling habits, and Leopardi's mother focused her attentions on rescuing the family's finances, setting up a regime of discipline and frugality in the household. Chronically ill but gifted with an ardent curiosity and capacious intelligence, Leopardi found refuge from the apparent indifference of his mother in the books of his father's extensive library. At first under the guidance of tutors, whose abilities he quickly outstripped, Leopardi virtually taught himself Latin, Greek, Hebrew, and several modern European languages and acquired a prodigious knowledge of classical and modern literature, rhetoric, and philosophy. The cost he paid for his assiduous studies was high: his ailments only intensified as he grew older, and eventually he suffered from curvature of the spine and near blindness. As a teenager he wrote scholarly treatises, translations, essays, and poems—many on patriotic and historical themes. In 1817 he began writing *Zibaldone* (*A Miscellany*), containing his thoughts, apothegms, and philological and philosophical ideas; by the time of its completion in 1832, it ran to over four thousand pages. Family circumstances and his physical condition led him to the cosmic pessimism that characterizes the philosophy of *Zibaldone.* Paradoxically, this pessimism drives the appreciation of the beauty of nature and art that he expresses in his poetry. As in "The Infinite" (1818), one of his idylls, and "To Sylvia" (1828), one of his finest elegies, the possibility that beauty, truth, and nature may offer some consolation seems continually undermined by the disappointment and bitterness of life itself. "The Solitary Thrush" (1828) shows the poet unfavorably comparing his lot to the bird's solitary existence. Unlike the bird, the poet is filled with self-conscious bitterness and regret, and can find no comfort in memories of the past or empty promises of the future. Not until he was twenty-four years old did Leopardi finally escape from the home he saw as a prison and the town he saw as a provincial backwater—first to Rome and then to other cities, including Milan, Florence, Pisa, and eventually to Naples, where he succumbed to cholera during the epidemic of 1837. Among the works he left behind are several philosophical treatises, *Moral Notebooks, Thoughts,* and *Zibaldone,* as well as the *Canti,* his collected poems of 1831 and 1835. Some literary historians consider Leopardi to be one of Italy's greatest poets, second only to Dante and Petrarch.

ᴥ The Infinite

Translated by Ottavio M. Casale

This lonely hill has always been so dear
To me, and dear the hedge which hides away
The reaches of the sky. But sitting here
And wondering, I fashion in my mind
The endless spaces far beyond, the more
Than human silences, and deepest peace;
So that the heart is on the edge of fear.
And when I hear the wind come blowing through
The trees, I pit its voice against that boundless
10 Silence and summon up eternity,
And the dead seasons, and the present one,
Alive with all its sound. And thus it is
In this immensity my thought is drowned:
And sweet to me the foundering in this sea.

ᴥ To Sylvia

Translated by Ottavio M. Casale

Sylvia. Do you remember still
The moments of your mortal lifetime here,
When such a loveliness
Shone in the elusive laughter of your eyes,
And you, contemplative and gay, climbed toward
The summit of your youth?

The tranquil chambers held,
The paths re-echoed, your perpetual song,
When at your woman's tasks
10 You sat, content to concentrate upon

The future beckoning within your mind.
It was the fragrant May,
And thus you passed your time.

    I often used to leave
The dear, belabored pages which consumed
So much of me and of my youth, and from
Ancestral balconies
Would lean to hear the music of your voice,
Your fingers humming through
20 The intricacies of the weaving work.
And I would gaze upon
The blue surrounding sky,
The paths and gardens golden in the sun,
And there the far-off sea, and here the mountain.
No human tongue can tell
What I felt then within my brimming heart.

    What tendernesses then,
What hopes, what hearts were ours, O Sylvia mine!
How large a thing seemed life, and destiny!
30 When I recall those bright anticipations,
Bitterness invades,
And I turn once again to mourn my lot.
O Nature, Nature, why
Do you not keep the promises you gave?
Why trick the children so?

    Before the winter struck the summer grass,
You died, my gentle girl,
Besieged by hidden illness and possessed.
You never saw the flowering of your years.
40 Your heart was never melted by the praise
Of your dark hair, your shy,
Enamoured eyes. Nor did you with your friends
Conspire on holidays to talk of love.

    The expectation failed
As soon for me, and fate denied my youth.
Ah how gone by, gone by,
You dear companion of my dawning time,
The hope that I lament!
Is this the world we knew? And these the joys
50 The love, the labors, happenings we shared?
And this the destiny

Of human beings? My poor one, when
The truth rose up, you fell,
And from afar you pointed me the way
To coldest death and the stark sepulchre.

The Solitary Thrush

Translated by Eamon Grennan

Perched on top of that old tower,
You sing as long as daylight lasts,
The sweet sound of you winding
Round and round the valley.
Spring shimmers
In the air, comes with a green rush
Through the open fields, is a sight
To soften any heart. You can hear
Sheep bleating, bellowing cattle,
10 While the other birds swoop and wheel
Cheerily round the wide blue sky,
Having the time of their lives together.
Like an outsider, lost in thought,
You are looking on at it all:
Neither companions nor wild flights
Fire your heart; games like these
Mean nothing to you. You sing,
And in singing spend the best
Part of your life and the passing year.

20 Ah, how these habits of mine
Are just like yours! Whatever the reason,
I haven't time for the light heart and laughter
Belonging to youth, nor any time
For you, youth's own companion, love,
Which later brings many a bitter sigh.
In truth I'm a fugitive from it all
And, still young, I all but live
The life of a hermit, a stranger even
In the place I was born.
30 This day already dwindling into dusk
Is a feast in these parts. You can hear
The bells ring round a clear sky

And a far-off thunder of guns
Booming and booming from farm to farm.

All dressed up in their Sunday best,
The young who live around here
Leave their houses and stroll the roads,
Looking and looked at, joy in their hearts.
Alone in this remote corner,
40 I walk out all by myself,
Putting off pleasure, postponing play:
And gazing about at the radiant air
I'm struck by how the sinking sun
After a day as perfect as this one
Melts among the distant hills,
And seems to say
That blessed youth itself is fading.

Solitary little singer, when you
Reach the evening of those days
50 Which the stars have numbered for you,
You'll not grieve, surely,
For the life you've led, since even
The slightest twist of your will
Is nature's way. But to me,
If I fail to escape
Loathsome old age —
When these eyes will mean nothing
To any other heart, the world be nothing
But a blank to them,
60 Each day more desolate, every day
Darker than the one before — what then
Will this longing for solitude
Seem like to me? What then
Will these years, or even I myself,
Seem to have been? Alas,
I'll be sick with regret, and over and over,
But inconsolable, looking back.

ROSALÍA DE CASTRO
B. GALICIA (SPAIN), 1837–1885

Rosalía de Castro was born February 24, 1837, in Santiago de Compostela, the Galician capital. The illegitimate child of a priest, de Castro was raised by her mother's family, rejoining her mother in 1852 when she was fifteen years old. Although she did not receive a formal education, she began writing poetry in her native Galician, a language related to Portuguese. In 1857, de Castro went to Madrid where she published her first book of poems. In Madrid she reconnected with Manuel Murguía, a Galician historian, journalist, and collector of folktales, whom she had known when he was in Santiago de Compostela. They were married the next year and eventually had seven children. Murguía and de Castro became leading figures in what is known as the *Rexurdimento,* "the rebirth," of Galician language as a medium for serious literary expression. After the heyday of the Galician-Portuguese troubadours in the thirteenth and fourteenth centuries, a long hiatus known as the *Seculos Escuros,* the Dark Ages, set in, and Galician was marginalized as a literary language until the nineteenth century revival. De Castro's *Galician Songs* (1863) is one of the major publications of the *Rexurdimento,* for the poems of that volume—all written in Galician—celebrate the countryside and folklore of her native land. In addition to a few works of short fiction, de Castro published two other major volumes of poetry, *Follas novas* (in Galician, 1880) and *On the Banks of the Sar* (in Castilian Spanish, 1884). These last two volumes are marked by a sense of belatedness and melancholy, in part because many of the poems were written when she was suffering from cancer, of which she died in July 1885. "The ailing woman felt her forces ebb" serves as a kind of epitaph, as well as a poem witnessing the pain she must have suffered from her disease. However, as we see in "A glowworm scatters flashes through the moss" and especially in "I tend a Beautiful Plant" and "It is Said Plants Cannot Speak," a sense of qualified hope and even resilience emerges from some of her poems. Rosalía de Castro is considered to be one of the greatest of all Galician poets, and every May 17 the publication of her *Galician Songs* is celebrated in festivities known as Galician Literature Day.

I Tend a Beautiful Plant

Translated by Lou Charnon-Deutsch

I tend a beautiful plant
    that loves and seeks the shade
    like the orphaned soul that searches
disheartened, lovesick and alone,
and there, where the light of day

never reaches except between shady
myrtle branches, or the dark pane
    of a narrow window,
she flourishes, so fresh and sweet-smelling,
and she becomes ever more radiant and luxuriant,
10   but when a ray of sun caresses her leaves
she languishes and withers and dies.

✢ It Is Said Plants Cannot Speak

Translated by Lou Charnon-Deutsch

It is said plants cannot speak, nor
        springs nor birds
nor the waves with their murmurs, nor
    the stars with light.
So they say, but it is not so, for whenever
    I pass by
they whisper about me and exclaim:
                                "There
    goes that madwoman, dreaming again
of her eternal springtime of life and of
10   field;
she stares at the frost-covered fields with
    trembling and fear
knowing that soon, very soon, she will
    also be gray."
    "My hair is streaked with gray, like the
        frost on the meadows,
yet, incurable somnambulant, I continue
    to dream
of the eternal springtime of life, though I
20   see it fading,
and the perennial freshness of the field
    and soul
though the field is already harvested,
and the soul reduced to ashes."
    Oh, stars and springs and flowers,
        mock not my dreams!
Without them, how could I admire you,
    nay, how could I live?"

A glowworm scatters flashes through the moss

Translated by S. Griswold Morley

A glowworm scatters flashes through the moss;
A star gleams in its high remote domain.
Abyss above, and in the depths abyss:
What things come to an end and what remain?
    Man's thought—we call it science!—peers and pries
Into the soundless dark. But it is vain:
When all is done, we still are ignorant
Of what things reach an end, and what remain.

    Kneeling before an image rudely carved,
10 I sink my spirit in the Infinite,
And—is it impious?—I vacillate
And tremble, questioning Heaven and Hell of it.
    What are we? What is death ? Only the bell,
From its exalted station echoing, speaks
An answer to my wailing, and a flood
Of burning tears flows down my shrunken cheeks.
    What horrible agony! Thou, only Thou,
O God, canst see and understand me now.

    Is it true Thou see'st my sorrow? Then, O Lord,
20 Have mercy on me, and to my eyes restore
The blessèd blindfold. Give me back the faith
That I have lost. Never permit me more
To wander orphaned, my support destroyed:
On earth, through desert wastes of life;
Thereafter, in a plain of endless void.

    The bell still tolls,—and still the lips are mute,
        The features give no sign.
He lets my humbled heart remain engulfed
In darkness,—He, the Redeemer, the divine.
30 Silence is with me yet; only beneath
        A somber arch of stone
Beyond the vacant nave, softly resounds
The mystic accent of an organ-tone.

    All, all is ended—perhaps—except my sorrow,
        That two-edged blade;

All ended, save the doubt that tosses us
From a black shade into a blacker shade.

    The world is empty, Heaven untenanted,
My soul is sick, and trodden in the dust
40 The holy altar where I used to breathe
My simple vows of ecstasy and trust.

    My Deity, shattered in a thousand bits,
Has fallen to chasms where I cannot see.
I rush to seek Him, and my groping meets
A solitary vast vacuity.

    When lo! from their lofty marble niches,
Angels gazed down in sorrow; and in my ears
Murmured a gentle voice: "Unhappy soul,
    Take hope; pour out thy tears
50 Before the feet of the Most High;
But well remember this: No insolent cry
    To Heaven makes its way
From one whose heart adores material things,
Who makes an idol out of Adam's clay."

∾ The ailing women felt her forces ebb

Translated by S. Griswold Morley

    The ailing woman felt her forces ebb
With summer, and knew her time was imminent.
      "In autumn I shall die,"
She thought, half-melancholy, half-content,
"And I shall feel the leaves, that will be dead
Like me, drop on the grave in which I lie."

    Not even Death would do her so much pleasure.
      Cruel to her he too,
In winter spared her life, and when anew
10 The earth was being born in blossoming,
Slew her by inches to the joyous hymns
      Of fair and merry spring!

❧ SAMUEL TAYLOR COLERIDGE
B. ENGLAND, 1772–1834

Samuel Taylor Coleridge had one of the most lively and fertile minds of his generation. Like Goethe and Goethe's Faust, Coleridge took all of human knowledge for his inquiry, including the classics, history, religion, philosophy, music, art, theology, and literary criticism. Providing the intellectual bridge between GERMAN ROMANTICISM and the England of his day, Coleridge developed key ideas concerning the godlike role of the artist, the centrality of the creative imagination, the fundamental structure of reality, and the mythic connection between consciousness and nature. His search for a comprehensive system that would unite the individual with nature led to the idea that the mind does not simply "collect" sensations and reflect upon them, but that it also actively, creatively, shapes perception. Although we do not entirely create our realities, we certainly qualify and formulate our sensations, and this kind of mental activity was integral to Coleridge's conviction that art, in its broadest function, "is the mediatress between, and reconciler of, nature and man."

Henry Meyer, *Portrait of Samuel Taylor Coleridge.* Engraving. Drawing by Charles Robert Leslie *Portrait of Coleridge as a young man.* (The Bridgeman Art Library)

Experiments during Coleridge's Early Years. Born October 21, 1772, Coleridge was the son of a clergyman and schoolmaster who died when Coleridge was nine. Shortly thereafter Coleridge was sent to Christ's Hospital in London, where he received a classical education and dabbled in metaphysics, theology, and social satire. After a year at Jesus College, Cambridge, he enlisted in the Light Dragoons, a cavalry unit, under the name of Silas Tompkin Comberbach, but he was ill-suited for military life and returned to Cambridge. In 1794 he met the poet Robert Southey (1774–1843), and together they made plans to establish a utopian society called a Pantisocracy, in which everyone would share power and be equal, on the banks of the Susquehanna River in America. Coleridge agreed to marry Sarah Fricker as part of the scheme to populate the colony. When the Pantisocracy plans fell through, Coleridge nevertheless married Sarah in 1795, after having left Cambridge without a degree. Following the birth of their first son, David Hartley—named after Coleridge's favorite philosopher[1] at the time—they moved to a cottage at Nether Stowey.

In 1797 a close friendship arose between Coleridge and William Wordsworth that would significantly change their personal and professional lives. Coleridge's admiration for Wordsworth was initially unqualified: "Wordsworth is a very great man, the only man to whom *at all times* and *in all modes of excellence* I feel myself inferior." Their long conversations and periods of creativity led to the publication of *Lyrical Ballads* in 1798, a book that changed the course of English literature and ushered in an era of imaginative genius that would later be called Romanticism. In that same year, an annuity of 150 pounds from Josiah and Tom Wedgwood—

www For links to more information about Coleridge and quizzes on his poetry, see bedford stmartins.com/worldlitcompact.

---

[1] **David Hartley** (1705–1757): The founder of Associationist psychology.

Max Beerbohm,
*Samuel Taylor
Coleridge, Table
Talking,* 1904
*Coleridge's
conversations were
known for their
brilliance and
charm—they were
recorded and
published—but this
engraving, meant
ironically, shows
Coleridge literally
boring his audience
to sleep.* (The
Bridgeman Art
Library)

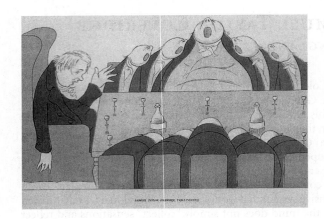

p. 390

from a family famous for pottery—allowed Coleridge to concentrate on his writing. Coleridge wrote his best poems and, in fact, most of his poems during the period of 1798 to 1802. In September 1798, Wordsworth and his sister, Dorothy, journeyed with Coleridge to Germany, where Coleridge's study of German philosophy, especially **Immanuel Kant**, profoundly influenced his ideas about nature and the imagination.

The Damaged Archangel.   Soon after returning to England in July 1799, Coleridge fell in love with Sara Hutchinson, the sister of William Wordsworth's soon to be wife, Mary Hutchinson. Incompatible with his wife, who was pregnant with their son Derwent at the time, Coleridge thought of Sara Hutchinson as his soul mate and agonized over his dilemma. These circumstances aggravated Coleridge's physical constitution. Laudanum, a derivative of opium, was prescribed for Coleridge's poor health, particularly for the painful attacks of rheumatism he suffered. During the winter of 1800 to 1801 Coleridge became convinced that he had a debilitating addiction to opium, which he was taking in heavy doses. This recognition contributed to periods of depression and Coleridge's own uncertainty about his worth as a person, a writer, and a thinker. A journey to Malta and other parts of Europe in 1804 was designed as a rest cure for his mind and body. Coleridge returned to England, however, even more addicted to opium, estranged from his wife, and plagued by financial problems.

Coleridge's mental and physical health led to his tendency to leave written works unfinished. His friend Charles Lamb called him a "damaged archangel," and he and other friends doubted that Coleridge lived up to his grand potential. Nevertheless, the quantity and variety of his writing, including notebooks and marginalia, is impressive. Because of financial need in 1808, he gave a series of public lectures on poetry and drama that he would continue for the next few years. His lectures on Shakespeare are particularly important for their insights into Shakespeare's characters. Coleridge also wrote for newspapers, and his periodical, *The*

A poet's heart and intellect should be *combined,* intimately combined and unified with the great appearances of nature and not merely held in solution and loose mixture with them. . . .

  – S. T. Coleridge to
Sotheby, 1802

Friend, lasted for more than a year. A play, *Remorse,* was successfully produced in 1813. Finally in 1816, relief came to Coleridge in the person of James Gillman, a Highgate doctor who took Coleridge into his home and looked after his health by controlling his addiction. There Coleridge spent the last eighteen years of his life actively writing plays and essays devoted to religious and social subjects. His most important piece of prose, *Biographia Literaria,* a mixture of autobiography, criticism, and philosophy, was published in 1817. Even his conversations, known for their brilliance and charm, were recorded and published. Americans Ralph Waldo Emerson and James Fenimore Cooper[2] made the pilgrimage to England to talk with him. Percy Shelley, a younger Romantic poet, said, "Coleridge is a cloud-circled meteor of the air, a hooded eagle among blinking owls."

Writing the Mysteries of Life.   In *Biographia Literaria,* Coleridge describes the plan for *Lyrical Ballads:* Wordsworth was to write poems that would "give the charm of novelty to things of every day" and direct the mind "to the loveliness and the wonders of the world before us." Coleridge would choose "persons and characters supernatural" for poems that would contain "a semblance of truth sufficient to procure for these shadows of imagination that willing suspension of disbelief for the moment, which constitutes poetic faith." The original edition of *Lyrical Ballads* began with Coleridge's "Rime of the Ancyent Marinere," as it was then titled, and concluded with Wordsworth's "Tintern Abbey."

"The Ancient Mariner."   "The Rime of the Ancyent Marinere," originally written as an imitation of a medieval Germanic ballad complete with archaic diction, dumbfounded its earliest readers. Wordsworth believed the archaisms and the general incomprehensibility of the poem ruined the sales of *Lyrical Ballads,* and he called for Coleridge to make revisions before the second edition was published in 1800. Coleridge did revise the poem several times, publishing in his collection *Sybilline Leaves* (1817) the version, with marginal glosses added, that most readers know and that we reprint here. Wordsworth's complaints notwithstanding, "The Rime of the Ancient Mariner," as it was retitled, is largely responsible for Coleridge's poetic fame, along with two other poems of the supernatural, "Kubla Khan" and "Christabel," which are unfinished. These poems reveal the poet's interest in exotic travelogues and the mysterious, supernatural world of the Gothic.[3]

Coleridge gleaned some of the details in this poem from accounts of voyages around Cape Horn and in the Pacific; his descriptions of

> Coleridge . . . may be regarded as the leading English representative of the European reactions against the eighteenth century. . . . There was at this time a new spirit afloat, a sense that there were spiritual needs, and unseen realities, which had been unrecognized in the religious, ethical, political and aesthetic teachings of the immediate past. The new demand was for an interpretation of the whole range of human experience which should be richer, more deeply satisfying, than the old, dry, superficial rationalism.
>
> – Basil Willey, 1966

---

[2] **Ralph Waldo Emerson and James Fenimore Cooper: Emerson** (1803–1882) was a philosopher and poet with interests similar to Coleridge's; Emerson was associated with Transcendentalism, a nineteenth-century movement in American thought. **Cooper** (1789–1851) became famous for his frontier novels, such as *The Last of the Mohicans* (1826).

[3] **Gothic:** The Gothic movement of the nineteenth century is known for its exploration of horror, mystery, and the supernatural as well as its transgression of moral boundaries.

phosphorescence at night and other travel details ring strikingly true. The poem draws on the traditions of Ahasuarus, the Wandering Jew,[4] and the Flying Dutchman[5]—the man who after committing a sin must wander the earth and tell his story to others, presumably to save them from a similar fate. It is not farfetched to see in the ancient mariner's solitary lifestyle Coleridge's own propensity for wandering and solitude. In fact, the major images of the poem—sea, calm, wind, murder, bird, sailing, snakes—are metaphors for inner states of the mind or psyche, so that the poem can be read as both a literal voyage and an allegory of the mind or soul.

When writer and critic Anna Barbauld accused the poem of having no moral, Coleridge replied that he thought the poem had too much of a moral and concluded: "It ought to have had no more moral than the Arabian Nights' tale of the merchant's sitting down to eat dates by the side of a well, and throwing the shells aside, and lo! a genie starts up, and says he *must* kill the aforesaid merchant, *because* one of the date shells had, it seems, put out the eye of the genie's son." (*Table Talk*)

"Kubla Khan."   Coleridge claimed that he composed "Kubla Khan," named for the grandson of Genghis Khan,[6] in an opium dream that was interrupted by a visitor, an explanation that has caused a great deal of controversy. The first two-thirds of the poem have elements of fantastical writing: an exotic location, dreamlike imagery with sexual overtones, an elusive situation, and lush sound patterns. The symbolism of the "deep romantic chasm" is not only mysterious and erotic but also connotes danger with the "Ancestral voices prophesying war!"

A concern with nature shows up in many of Coleridge's poems, but a higher priority is given to the inner life, the nature of introspection, the formative importance of the imagination, and the sinuous motion of moods and dreams—much of which we would now call psychology. Like other Romantics such as E. T. A. Hoffmann and Novalis, Coleridge explored the shadowy valleys of faith and despair, lofty creation and cataclysmic destruction.

> Coleridge is a cloud-circled meteor of the air, a hooded eagle among blinking owls.
>
> – PERCY SHELLEY

■ **FURTHER RESEARCH**

Biography

Ashton, Rosemary. *The Life of Samuel Taylor Coleridge: A Critical Biography.* 1996.
Davidson, Graham. *Coleridge's Career.* 1990.
Holmes, Richard. *Coleridge: Early Visions.* 1989.
Roe, Nicholas. *Wordsworth and Coleridge: The Radical Years.* 1988.

---

[4] **Ahasuarus, the Wandering Jew:** Many legends down through the ages revolve around a person who rejected Jesus on the last day of his life and was doomed to wander the earth in penance until Judgment Day. He is called the Wandering Jew; one of his names is Ahasuarus.

[5] **the Flying Dutchman:** The legend of the Flying Dutchman is a variant of the guilt and penance motif; the name refers to the captain of a ship who is guilty of a curse or vow and must captain his ship crewed by dead men until doomsday.

[6] **Genghis Khan:** (1162?–1227) Great Mongol conqueror of central Asia.

Criticism

Bate, Walter Jackson. *Coleridge*. 1968.
Beer, John. *Coleridge's Poetic Intelligence*. 1975.
Campbell, P., ed. *Wordsworth and Coleridge: Lyrical Ballads: Critical Perspectives*. 1991.
Lowes, John Livingston. *The Road to Xanadu*. 1927.

∾   The Rime of the Ancient Mariner

IN SEVEN PARTS

Facile credo, plures esse Naturas invisibiles quam visibles in rerum universitate. Sed horum omnium familiam quis nobis enarrabit? et gradus et cognationes et discrimina et singulorum munera? Quid agunt? quae loca habitant? Harum rerum notitiam semper ambivit ingenium humanum, nunquam attigit. Juvat, interea, non diffiteor, quandoque in animo, tanquam in tabulâ, majoris et melioris mundi imaginem contemplari: ne mens assuefacta hodiernae vitae minutiis se contrahat nimis, et tota subsidat in pusillas cogitationes. Sed veritati interea invigilandum est, modusque servandus, ut certa ab incertis, diem a nocte, distinguamus.
         —T. BURNET, ARCHAEOL. PHIL. p. 68.[1]

ARGUMENT

How a Ship having passed the Line was driven by storms to the cold Country towards the South Pole; and how from thence she made her course to the tropical Latitude of the Great Pacific Ocean; and of the strange things that befell; and in what manner the Ancyent Marinere came back to his own Country.

PART 1

It is an ancient Mariner,
And he stoppeth one of three.
"By thy long gray beard and glittering eye,
Now wherefore stopp'st thou me?

"The Bridegroom's doors are opened wide,
And I am next of kin,

An ancient Mariner meeteth three Gallants bidden to a wedding-feast, and detaineth one.

---

[1] **Latin epigraph:** "I readily believe that there are more invisible than visible Natures in the universe. But who will explain for us the family of all these beings, and the ranks and relations and distinguishing features and functions of each? What do they do? What places do they inhabit? The human mind has always sought the knowledge of these things, but never attained it. Meanwhile I do not deny that it is helpful sometimes to contemplate in the mind, as on a tablet, the image of a greater and better world, lest the intellect, habituated to the petty things of daily life, narrow itself and sink wholly into trivial thoughts. But at the same time we must be watchful for the truth and keep a sense of proportion, so that we may distinguish the certain from the uncertain, day from night." [Thomas Burnet, 1692]

The guests are met, the feast is set:
May'st hear the merry din."

He holds him with his skinny hand;
10   "There was a ship," quoth he.
"Hold off! unhand me, gray-beard loon!"
Eftsoons° his hand dropt he.

at once

He holds him with his glittering eye—
The Wedding-Guest stood still,
And listens like a three years' child.
The Mariner hath his will.

The Wedding-Guest is spellbound by the eye of the old seafaring man and constrained to hear his tale.

The Wedding-Guest sat on a stone:
He cannot choose but hear;
And thus spake on that ancient man,
20   The bright-eyed Mariner.

"The ship was cheered, the harbor cleared,
Merrily did we drop
Below the kirk,° below the hill,
Below the light-house top.

church

"The sun came up upon the left,
Out of the sea came he!
And he shone bright, and on the right
Went down into the sea.

The Mariner tells how the ship sailed southward with a good wind and fair weather, till it reached the Line.

"Higher and higher every day,
30   Till over the mast at noon²—"
The Wedding-Guest here beat his breast,
For he heard the loud bassoon.

The bride hath paced into the hall,
Red as a rose is she;
Nodding their heads before her goes
The merry minstrelsy.

The Wedding-Guest heareth the bridal music; but the Mariner continueth his tale.

The Wedding-Guest he beat his breast,
Yet he cannot choose but hear;
And thus spake on that ancient man,
40   The bright-eyed Mariner.

---

²**over the mast at noon:** The sun is straight up at noon at the equator.

"And now the Storm-blast came, and he
Was tyrannous and strong:
He struck with his o'ertaking wings,
And chased us south along.

"With sloping masts and dipping prow,
As who pursued with yell and blow
Still treads the shadow of his foe,
And forward bends his head,
The ship drove fast, loud roared the blast,
50   And southward aye we fled.

"And now there came both mist and snow,
And it grew wondrous cold:
And ice, mast-high, came floating by,
As green as emerald.

"And through the drifts the snowy clifts
Did send a dismal sheen:
Nor shapes of men nor beasts we ken—
The ice was all between.

"The ice was here, the ice was there,
60   The ice was all around:
It cracked and growled, and roared and howled,
Like noises in a swound!°

swoon

"At length did cross an Albatross,
Through the fog it came;
As if it had been a Christian soul,
We hailed it in God's name.

"It ate the food it ne'er had eat,
And round and round it flew.
The ice did split with a thunder-fit;
70   The helmsman steered us through!

"And a good south wind sprung up behind;
The Albatross did follow,
And every day, for food or play,
Came to the mariners' hollo!

"In mist or cloud, on mast or shroud,
It perched for vespers nine;
Whiles all the night, through fog-smoke white,
Glimmered the white moon-shine."

"God save thee, ancient Mariner!
80   From the fiends, that plague thee thus! —
Why look'st thou so?" — "With my cross-bow
I shot the Albatross!"

The ancient Mariner inhospitably killeth the pious bird of good omen.

PART 2

"The Sun now rose upon the right:[3]
Out of the sea came he,
Still hid in mist, and on the left
Went down into the sea.

"And the good south wind still blew behind,
But no sweet bird did follow,
Nor any day for food or play
90   Came to the mariners' hollo!

"And I had done a hellish thing,
And it would work 'em woe:
For all averred, I had killed the bird
That made the breeze to blow.
Ah, wretch! said they, the bird to slay,
That made the breeze to blow!

His shipmates cry out against the ancient Mariner, for killing the bird of good luck.

"Nor dim nor red, like God's own head,
The glorious Sun uprist:
Then all averred, I had killed the bird
100 That brought the fog and mist.
Twas right, said they, such birds to slay,
That bring the fog and mist.

But when the fog cleared off they justify the same, and thus make themselves accomplices in the crime.

"The fair breeze blew, the white foam flew,
The furrow followed free;
We were the first that ever burst
Into that silent sea.

The fair breeze continues; the ship enters the Pacific Ocean, and sails northward, even till it reaches the Line.

"Down dropt the breeze, the sails dropt down,
Twas sad as sad could be;
And we did speak only to break
110 The silence of the sea!

The ship hath been suddenly becalmed.

"All in a hot and copper sky,
The bloody Sun, at noon,

---

[3] **Sun . . . right:** Having rounded Cape Horn, the ship heads north with the sunrise on the right side.

Right up above the mast did stand,
No bigger than the Moon.

"Day after day, day after day,
We stuck, nor breath nor motion;
As idle as a painted ship
Upon a painted ocean.

"Water, water, everywhere,
120 And all the boards did shrink;
Water, water, everywhere,
Nor any drop to drink.

And the Albatross begins to be avenged.

"The very deep did rot: O Christ!
That ever this should be!
Yea, slimy things did crawl with legs
Upon the slimy sea.

"About, about, in reel and rout
The death-fires[4] danced at night;
The water, like a witch's oils,
130 Burnt green, and blue and white.

A Spirit had followed them; one of the invisible inhabitants of this planet, neither departed souls nor angels; concerning whom the learned Jew, Josephus, and the Platonic Constantinopolitan, Michael Psellus, may be consulted.

"And some in dreams assured were
Of the Spirit that plagued us so;
Nine fathom deep he had followed us
From the land of mist and snow.

They are very numerous, and there is no climate or element without one or more.

"And every tongue, through utter drought,
Was withered at the root;
We could not speak, no more than if
We had been choked with soot.

"Ah! well-a-day! what evil looks
140 Had I from old and young!
Instead of the cross, the Albatross
About my neck was hung.

The shipmates, in their sore distress, would fain throw the whole guilt on the ancient Mariner: in sign whereof they hang the dead sea-bird round his neck.

---

[4] **death-fires:** The corposant, or St. Elmo's fire, on the ship's rigging.

PART 3

"There passed a weary time. Each throat
Was parched, and glazed each eye.
A weary time! a weary time!
How glazed each weary eye,
When looking westward, I beheld
A something in the sky.

The ancient Mariner beholdeth a sign in the element afar off.

"At first it seemed a little speck,
150   And then it seemed a mist;
It moved and moved, and took at last
A certain shape, I wist.°   knew

"A speck, a mist, a shape, I wist!
And still it neared and neared:
As if it dodged a water-sprite,
It plunged and tacked and veered.

"With throats unslaked, with black lips baked,
We could nor laugh nor wail;
Through utter drought all dumb we stood!
160   I bit my arm, I sucked the blood,
And cried, A sail! a sail!

At its nearer approach, it seemeth him to be a ship; and at a dear ransom he freeth his speech from the bonds of thirst.

"With throats unslaked, with black lips baked,
Agape they heard me call:
Gramercy!⁵ they for joy did grin,
And all at once their breath drew in,
As they were drinking all.

A flash of joy;

"See! see! (I cried) she tacks no more!
Hither to work us weal°   benefit
Without a breeze, without a tide,
170   She steadies with upright keel!

And horror follows. For can it be a ship that comes onward without wind or tide?

"The western wave was all aflame,
The day was well nigh done!
Almost upon the western wave
Rested the broad bright Sun;
When that strange shape drove suddenly
Betwixt us and the Sun.

---

⁵ **Gramercy!**: French *grand-merci*, "great thanks."

"And straight the Sun was flecked with bars,
(Heaven's Mother send us grace!)
As if through a dungeon-grate he peered
180 With broad and burning face.

"Alas! (thought I, and my heart beat loud)
How fast she nears and nears!
Are those her sails that glance in the Sun,
Like restless gossameres?[6]

"Are those her ribs through which the Sun
Did peer, as through a grate?
And is that Woman all her crew?
Is that a Death? and are there two?
Is Death that woman's mate?

And its ribs are seen as bars on the face of the setting Sun. The Specter-Woman and her Deathmate, and no other on board the skeleton-ship.

190 "Her lips were red, her looks were free,
Her locks were yellow as gold:
Her skin was as white as leprosy,
The Night-mare Life-in-Death was she,
Who thicks man's blood with cold.

Like vessel, like crew!

"The naked hulk alongside came,
And the twain were casting dice;
'The game is done! I've won! I've won!'
Quoth she, and whistles thrice.

Death and Life-in-Death have diced for the ship's crew, and she (the latter) winneth the ancient Mariner.

"The Sun's rim dips; the stars rush out:
200 At one stride comes the dark;
With far-heard whisper, o'er the sea,
Off shot the specter-bark.

No twilight within the courts of the Sun.

"We listened and looked sideways up!
Fear at my heart, as at a cup,
My life-blood seemed to sip!
The stars were dim, and thick the night,
The steersman's face by his lamp gleamed white;
From the sails the dew did drip —
Till clomb above the eastern bar
210 The hornéd Moon, with one bright star
Within the nether tip.

At the rising of the Moon,

"One after one, by the star-dogged Moon,
Too quick for groan or sigh,

One after another,

---

[6] **gossameres:** A film of cobwebs.

Each turned his face with a ghastly pang,
And cursed me with his eye.

"Four times fifty living men,
(And I heard nor sigh nor groan)
With heavy thump, a lifeless lump
They dropt down one by one.

His shipmates drop down dead.

220   "The souls did from their bodies fly—
They fled to bliss or woe!
And every soul, it passed me by
Like the whizz of my cross-bow!"

But Life-in-Death begins her work on the ancient Mariner.

PART 4

"I fear thee, ancient Mariner!
I fear thy skinny hand!
And thou art long, and lank, and brown,
As is the ribbed sea-sand.

The Wedding-Guest feareth that a Spirit is talking to him;

"I fear thee and thy glittering eye,
And thy skinny hand, so brown."—
230   "Fear not, fear not, thou Wedding-Guest!
This body dropt not down.

But the ancient Mariner assureth him of his bodily life, and proceedeth to relate his horrible penance.

"Alone, alone, all, all alone,
Alone on a wide, wide sea!
And never a saint took pity on
My soul in agony.

"The many men, so beautiful!
And they all dead did lie:
And a thousand thousand slimy things
Lived on; and so did I.

He despiseth the creatures of the calm.

240   "I looked upon the rotting sea,
And drew my eyes away;
I looked upon the rotting deck,
And there the dead men lay.

And envieth that they should live, and so many lie dead.

"I looked to heaven, and tried to pray;
But or ever a prayer had gusht,
A wicked whisper came, and made
My heart as dry as dust.

"I closed my lids, and kept them close,
And the balls like pulses beat;
250 For the sky and the sea, and the sea and the sky
Lay like a load on my weary eye,
And the dead were at my feet.

"The cold sweat melted from their limbs,
Nor rot nor reek did they:
The look with which they looked on me
Had never passed away.

But the curse liveth for him in
the eye of the dead men.

"An orphan's curse would drag to hell
A spirit from on high;
But oh! more horrible than that
260 Is a curse in a dead man's eye!
Seven days, seven nights, I saw that curse,
And yet I could not die.

"The moving Moon went up the sky,
And nowhere did abide:
Softly she was going up,
And a star or two beside —

In his loneliness and fixedness
he yearneth towards the
journeying Moon, and the stars
that still sojourn, yet still move
onward; and everywhere the
blue sky belongs to them, and is
their appointed rest, and their
native country and their own
natural homes, which they enter
unannounced, as lords that are
certainly expected, and yet there
is a silent joy at their arrival.

"Her beams bemocked the sultry main,
Like April hoar-frost spread;
But where the ship's huge shadow lay,
270 The charméd water burnt alway
A still and awful red.

"Beyond the shadow of the ship,
I watched the water-snakes:
They moved in tracks of shining white,
And when they reared, the elfish light
Fell off in hoary flakes.

By the light of the Moon he
beholdeth God's creatures of the
great calm.

"Within the shadow of the ship
I watched their rich attire:
Blue, glossy green, and velvet black,
280 They coiled and swam; and every track
Was a flash of golden fire.

"O happy living things! no tongue
Their beauty might declare:
A spring of love gushed from my heart,
And I blessed them unaware;

Their beauty and their
happiness.

He blesseth them in his heart.

Sure my kind saint took pity on me,
And I blessed them unaware.

"The selfsame moment I could pray;   *The spell begins to break.*
And from my neck so free
290   The Albatross fell off, and sank
Like lead into the sea."

PART 5

"Oh sleep! it is a gentle thing,
Beloved from pole to pole!
To Mary Queen the praise be given!
She sent the gentle sleep from Heaven,
That slid into my soul.

"The silly° buckets on the deck,   unused   *By grace of the holy Mother, the*
That had so long remained,   *ancient Mariner is refreshed*
I dreamt that they were filled with dew;   *with rain.*
300   And when I awoke, it rained.

"My lips were wet, my throat was cold,
My garments all were dank;
Sure I had drunken in my dreams,
And still my body drank.

"I moved, and could not feel my limbs:
I was so light—almost
I thought that I had died in sleep,
And was a blessed ghost.

"And soon I heard a roaring wind: *He heareth sounds and seeth*
310   It did not come anear;   *strange sights and commotions*
But with its sound it shook the sails,   *in the sky and the elements.*
That were so thin and sere.

"The upper air burst into life!
And a hundred fire-flags sheen,[7]
To and fro they were hurried about!
And to and fro, and in and out,
The wan stars danced between.

---

[7] **sheen:** Shone; these are the Southern Lights.

"And the coming wind did roar more loud,
And the sails did sigh like sedge;
320 And the rain poured down from one black cloud;
The Moon was at its edge.

"The thick black cloud was cleft, and still
The Moon was at its side:
Like waters shot from some high crag,
The lightning fell with never a jag,
A river steep and wide.

"The loud wind never reached the ship,
Yet now the ship moved on!
Beneath the lightning and the Moon
330 The dead men gave a groan.

The bodies of the ship's crew are inspired, and the ship moves on;

"They groaned, they stirred, they all uprose,
Nor spake, nor moved their eyes;
It had been strange, even in a dream,
To have seen those dead men rise.

"The helmsman steered, the ship moved on;
Yet never a breeze up blew;
The mariners all 'gan work the ropes,
Where they were wont to do;
They raised their limbs like lifeless tools —
340 We were a ghastly crew.

"The body of my brother's son
Stood by me, knee to knee:
The body and I pulled at one rope,
But he said nought to me."

"I fear thee, ancient Mariner!"
"Be calm, thou Wedding-Guest!
'Twas not those souls that fled in pain,
Which to their corses° came again,   corpses
But a troop of spirits blest:

But not by the souls of the men, nor by demons of earth or middle air, but by a blessed troop of angelic spirits, sent down by the invocation of the guardian saint.

350 "For when it dawned — they dropped their arms,
And clustered round the mast;
Sweet sounds rose slowly through their mouths,
And from their bodies passed.

"Around, around, flew each sweet sound,
Then darted to the Sun;
Slowly the sounds came back again,
Now mixed, now one by one.

"Sometimes a-dropping from the sky
I heard the skylark sing;
360   Sometimes all little birds that are,
How they seemed to fill the sea and air
With their sweet jargoning!°   warbling

"And now 'twas like all instruments,
Now like a lonely flute;
And now it is an angel's song,
That makes the heavens be mute.

"It ceased; yet still the sails made on
A pleasant noise till noon,
A noise like of a hidden brook
370   In the leafy month of June,
That to the sleeping woods all night
Singeth a quiet tune.

"Till noon we quietly sailed on,
Yet never a breeze did breathe:
Slowly and smoothly went the ship,
Moved onward from beneath.

"Under the keel nine fathom deep,   *The lonesome Spirit from the*
From the land of mist and snow,   *south pole carries on the ship as*
The Spirit slid: and it was he   *far as the Line, in obedience to*
                                         the angelic troop, but still
380   That made the ship to go.   *requireth vengeance.*
The sails at noon left off their tune,
And the ship stood still also.

"The Sun, right up above the mast,
Had fixed her to the ocean:
But in a minute she 'gan stir,
With a short uneasy motion—
Backwards and forwards half her length
With a short uneasy motion.

"Then like a pawing horse let go,
390   She made a sudden bound:

It flung the blood into my head,
And I fell down in a swound.

"How long in that same fit I lay,
I have not[8] to declare;
But ere my living life returned,
I heard, and in my soul discerned,
Two voices in the air.

"'Is it he?' quoth one, 'Is this the man?
By Him who died on cross,
400 With his cruel bow he laid full low
The harmless Albatross.

"'The Spirit who bideth by himself
In the land of mist and snow,
He loved the bird that loved the man
Who shot him with his bow.'

"The other was a softer voice,
As soft as honey-dew:
Quoth he, 'The man hath penance done,
And penance more will do.'"

The Polar Spirit's fellow demons, the invisible inhabitants of the element, take part in his wrong; and two of them relate, one to the other that penance long and heavy for the ancient Mariner hath been accorded to the Polar Spirit, who returneth southward.

PART 6

FIRST VOICE

410 "'But tell me, tell me! speak again,
Thy soft response renewing—
What makes that ship drive on so fast?
What is the ocean doing?'

SECOND VOICE

"'Still as a slave before his lord,
The ocean hath no blast;
His great bright eye most silently
Up to the Moon is cast—

"'If he may know which way to go;
For she guides him smooth or grim.

---

[8] **I have not:** That is, "I do not know."

420 See, brother, see! how graciously
She looketh down on him.'

FIRST VOICE

" 'But why drives on that ship so fast,
Without or wave or wind?'

SECOND VOICE

" 'The air is cut away before,
And closes from behind.'
" 'Fly, brother, fly! more high, more high!
Or we shall be belated:
For slow and slow that ship will go,
When the Mariner's trance is abated.'

The Mariner hath been cast into a trance; for the angelic power causeth the vessel to drive northward faster than human life could endure.

430 "I woke, and we were sailing on
As in a gentle weather:
'Twas night, calm night, the moon was high;
The dead men stood together.

The supernatural motion is retarded; the Mariner awakes, and his penance begins anew.

"All stood together on the deck,
For a charnel-dungeon fitter:
All fixed on me their stony eyes,
That in the Moon did glitter.

"The pang, the curse, with which they died,
Had never passed away:
440 I could not draw my eyes from theirs,
Nor turn them up to pray.

"And now this spell was snapt: once more
I viewed the ocean green,
And looked far forth, yet little saw
Of what had else been seen—

The curse is finally expiated.

"Like one, that on a lonesome road
Doth walk in fear and dread,
And having once turned round, walks on,
And turns no more his head;
450 Because he knows, a frightful fiend
Doth close behind him tread.

"But soon there breathed a wind on me,
Nor sound nor motion made:

Its path was not upon the sea,
In ripple or in shade.

"It raised my hair, it fanned my cheek
Like a meadow-gale of spring—
It mingled strangely with my fears,
Yet it felt like a welcoming.

460 "Swiftly, swiftly flew the ship,
Yet she sailed softly too:
Sweetly, sweetly blew the breeze—
On me alone it blew.

"Oh! dream of joy! is this indeed
The light-house top I see?
Is this the hill? is this the kirk?
Is this mine own countree?

And the ancient Mariner
beholdeth his native country.

"We drifted o'er the harbor-bar,
And I with sobs did pray—
470 O let me be awake, my God!
Or let me sleep alway.

"The harbor-bay was clear as glass,
So smoothly it was strewn!
And on the bay the moonlight lay,
And the shadow of the Moon.

"The rock shone bright, the kirk no less,
That stands above the rock:
The moonlight steeped in silentness
The steady weathercock.

480 "And the bay was white with silent light
Till, rising from the same,
Full many shapes, that shadows were,
In crimson colors came.

The angelic spirits leave the
dead bodies,

"A little distance from the prow
Those crimson shadows were:
I turned my eyes upon the deck—
Oh, Christ! what saw I there!

"Each corse lay flat, lifeless and flat,
And, by the holy rood!°   cross

490 A man all light, a seraph-man,[9]
On every corse there stood.

"This seraph-band, each waved his hand,
It was a heavenly sight!
They stood as signals to the land,
Each one a lovely light;

*And appear in their own forms
of light.*

"This seraph-band, each waved his hand,
No voice did they impart—
No voice; but oh! the silence sank
Like music on my heart.

500 "But soon I heard the dash of oars,
I heard the Pilot's cheer;
My head was turned perforce away,
And I saw a boat appear.

"The Pilot and the Pilot's boy,
I heard them coming fast:
Dear Lord in Heaven! it was a joy
The dead men could not blast.

"I saw a third—I heard his voice:
It is the Hermit good!
510 He singeth loud his godly hymns
That he makes in the wood.
He'll shrieve my soul, he'll wash away
The Albatross's blood."

PART 7

"This Hermit good lives in that wood
Which slopes down to the sea.
How loudly his sweet voice he rears!
He loves to talk with marineres
That come from a far countree.

The Hermit of the wood,

"He kneels at morn, and noon, and eve—
520 He hath a cushion plump:
It is the moss that wholly hides
The rotted old oak-stump.

---

[9] **Seraph-man:** The highest rank of angels.

"The skiff-boat neared: I heard them talk,
'Why, this is strange, I trow!
Where are those lights so many and fair,
That signal made but now?'

"'Strange, by my faith!' the Hermit said —
'And they answered not our cheer!
The planks looked warped! and see those sails,
530 How thin they are and sere!
I never saw aught like to them,
Unless perchance it were

*Approacheth the ship with
wonder.*

"'Brown skeletons of leaves that lag
My forest-brook along;
When the ivy-tod° is heavy with snow,
And the owlet whoops to the wolf below,
That eats the she-wolf's young.'

clump

"'Dear Lord! it hath a fiendish look —
(The Pilot made reply)
540 I am a-feared' — 'Push on, push on!'
Said the Hermit cheerily.

"The boat came closer to the ship,
But I nor spake nor stirred;
The boat came close beneath the ship,
And straight a sound was heard.

"Under the water it rumbled on,
Still louder and more dread:
It reached the ship, it split the bay;
The ship went down like lead.

The ship suddenly sinketh.

550 "Stunned by that loud and dreadful sound,
Which sky and ocean smote,
Like one that hath been seven days drowned
My body lay afloat;
But swift as dreams, myself I found
Within the Pilot's boat.

*The ancient Mariner is saved in
the Pilot's boat.*

"Upon the whirl, where sank the ship,
The boat spun round and round;
And all was still, save that the hill
Was telling of the sound.

560   "I moved my lips — the Pilot shrieked
     And fell down in a fit;
     The holy Hermit raised his eyes,
     And prayed where he did sit.

     "I took the oars: the Pilot's boy,
     Who now doth crazy go,
     Laughed loud and long, and all the while
     His eyes went to and fro.
     'Ha! ha!' quoth he, 'full plain I see,
     The Devil knows how to row.'

570   "And now, all in my own countree,
     I stood on the firm land!
     The Hermit stepped forth from the boat,
     And scarcely he could stand.

     "'O shrieve me, shrieve me, holy man!'
     The Hermit crossed his brow.
     'Say quick,' quoth he, 'I bid thee say —
     What manner of man art thou?'

The ancient Mariner earnestly entreateth the Hermit to shrieve him; and the penance of life falls on him.

     "Forthwith this frame of mine was wrenched
     With a woful agony,
580   Which forced me to begin my tale;
     And then it left me free.

     "Since then, at an uncertain hour,
     That agony returns;
     And till my ghastly tale is told,
     This heart within me burns.

And ever and anon throughout his future life an agony constraineth him to travel from land to land.

     "I pass, like night, from land to land;
     I have strange power of speech;
     That moment that his face I see,
     I know the man that must hear me:
590   To him my tale I teach.

     "What loud uproar bursts from that door!
     The wedding-guests are there:
     But in the garden-bower the bride
     And bride-maids singing are:
     And hark the little vesper bell,
     Which biddeth me to prayer!

"O Wedding-Guest! this soul hath been
Alone on a wide, wide sea:
So lonely 'twas, that God himself
600 Scarce seeméd there to be.

"Oh sweeter than the marriage-feast,
'Tis sweeter far to me,
To walk together to the kirk
With a goodly company! —

"To walk together to the kirk,
And all together pray,
While each to his great Father bends,
Old men, and babes, and loving friends,
And youths and maidens gay!

610 "Farewell, farewell! but this I tell   *And to teach by his own*
To thee, thou Wedding-Guest!   *example love and reverence to*
He prayeth well, who loveth well   *all things that God made and*
Both man and bird and beast.   *loveth.*

"He prayeth best, who loveth best
All things both great and small;
For the dear God who loveth us,
He made and loveth all."

The Mariner, whose eye is bright,
Whose beard with age is hoar,
620 Is gone: and now the Wedding-Guest
Turned from the bridegroom's door.

He went like one that hath been stunned,
And is of sense forlorn:
A sadder and a wiser man,
He rose the morrow morn.

～ Kubla Khan

In Xanadu did Kubla Khan[1]
A stately pleasure-dome decree:
Where Alph,[2] the sacred river, ran
Through caverns measureless to man
Down to a sunless sea.
So twice five miles of fertile ground
With walls and towers were girdled round:
And here were gardens bright with sinuous rills,
Where blossomed many an incense-bearing tree;
10 And here were forests ancient as the hills,
Enfolding sunny spots of greenery.

But oh! that deep romantic chasm which slanted
Down the green hill athwart a cedarn cover!
A savage place! as holy and enchanted
As e'er beneath a waning moon was haunted
By woman wailing for her demon-lover!
And from this chasm, with ceaseless turmoil seething,
As if this earth in fast thick pants were breathing,
A mighty fountain momently was forced;
20 Amid whose swift half-intermitted burst
Huge fragments vaulted like rebounding hail,
Or chaffy grain beneath the thresher's flail:
And 'mid these dancing rocks at once and ever
It flung up momently the sacred river.
Five miles meandering with a mazy motion
Through wood and dale the sacred river ran,
Then reached the caverns measureless to man,
And sank in tumult to a lifeless ocean:
And 'mid this tumult Kubla heard from far
30 Ancestral voices prophesying war!
    The shadow of the dome of pleasure
    Floated midway on the waves;
    Where was heard the mingled measure
    From the fountain and the caves.
It was a miracle of rare device,
A sunny pleasure-dome with caves of ice!

---

[1] **Kubla Khan:** Mongol emperor (1215?–1294).

[2] **Alph:** Perhaps the Alpheus River, but certainly a primordial river.

A damsel with a dulcimer
In a vision once I saw:
It was an Abyssinian maid,
40 And on her dulcimer she played,
Singing of Mount Abora.
Could I revive within me,
Her symphony and song,
To such a deep delight 'twould win me,
That with music loud and long,
I would build that dome in air,
That sunny dome! those caves of ice!
And all who heard should see them there,
And all should cry, Beware! Beware!
50 His flashing eyes, his floating hair!
Weave a circle round him thrice,
And close your eyes with holy dread,
For he on honey-dew hath fed,
And drunk the milk of Paradise.

❧ GHALIB (MIRZA ASADULLAH BEG KHAN)
B. INDIA, 1797–1869

Mirza Asadullah Beg Khan, known by his pen name of **Ghalib**, is the foremost poet of the URDU language, a hybrid tongue derived from a combination of Indian dialects and Persian. In some ways, Urdu reflects the cultural and religious synthesis of the Mughal empire in its heyday, during the sixteenth and seventeenth centuries, when under the emperors Akbar, Shah Jahan, and Aurangzeb[1] the Indo-Muslim culture flourished, producing such poets as Tulsidas (1532–1623) and such monuments as the Taj Mahal (completed in 1653). By Ghalib's time, the Mughal empire was in decline, in part from internal conflicts, but especially from changes stemming from the European, particularly British, presence in India. After the Battle of Plassey in which British forces defeated the army of *nawab*[2] Siraj-ud-daula in 1757, England strengthened its power in Bengal and eventually over greater India. By the time of Ghalib's birth in 1797,

MEER-zah
ah-sah-doo-LAH
BEG KAHN, GAH-leeb

---

[1] **Akbar . . . Aurangzeb:** Mughal emperors of India from 1556 to 1605, 1628 to 1658, and 1658 to 1707, respectively. Akbar, known for his just rule, extended the empire; Shah Jahan oversaw the flourishing of culture, including the building of the Taj Mahal; Aurangzeb, after imprisoning his father, further extended the empire's boundaries, but by implementing persecution of the Hindus and Sikhs ultimately weakened his authority over the Indian population.

[2] *nawab:* A provincial ruler in India under the Moghul empire.

the British East India Company—the arm of British political authority in India—exerted considerable influence over the remnants of Mughal power in Delhi, where Ghalib lived. In the course of Ghalib's lifetime, the British extended their political, economic, and cultural control throughout India, claiming ownership rights to lands and titles, and taking charge of the country's administration, economy, and communications. Thus, Ghalib witnessed the unraveling of India and the increasing influence, for both better and worse, of the British colonial government. A social and psychological record of India's transformations is registered in Ghalib's finely crafted letters, diaries, and poetry.

Early Life.   Ghalib was born in Agra in December 1797 or January 1798 into a wealthy Muslim family with Turkish roots. His father, an army officer, died before Ghalib was five years old, so Ghalib was raised in the household of his wealthy maternal grand-uncle. Around 1810, at age thirteen, Ghalib was married to the daughter of an aristocratic family, and by 1812 he was settled in Delhi, the capital of the declining Mughal empire. Ghalib continued his education in Delhi and began to refine his poetic style. As in China, young men of the ruling classes were expected to achieve a mastery of poetry; Ghalib studied Persian literature, history, and religion with Mulla Abdussamad Harmuzd, an Iranian tutor and scholar who sometimes appears in Ghalib's poetry as a voice addressing the poet's critics. Though Ghalib indicates that he preferred youthful diversions, such as playing chess and flying kites, to his studies, he must have excelled at his literary training, for some scholars suggest that many of his major works in Urdu were completed by 1816, when he would have been nineteen years old; others suggest his productive years of writing in Urdu came when he was in his early twenties. Whatever the case, Ghalib compiled a collection of his Urdu poems when he was twenty-four, after which he wrote primarily in Persian until 1847, when as a member of the court of Bahadur Shah Zafar (Bahadur Shah II; r. 1837–1857), the last Mughal emperor, he again wrote in Urdu.

A Troubled Time.   In his twenties Ghalib encountered financial difficulties when family infighting interrupted his pension. In 1831, in his early thirties, he lost a six-year-long lawsuit over his inheritance from his guardian uncle and began what was to become a lifelong nuisance of intermittently filing petitions to the British government to secure a pension. Not until 1847, when he entered the court of Bahadur Shah II at Delhi, did he regain financial security. Ghalib was appointed to write the official history of the Mughal empire, and he resumed writing poetry—panegyric verse, or eulogy, and **ghazals**—and prose in Urdu, a language he had abandoned in his work for some time except to correct the several editions of his poetry issued between 1821 and 1847. After the 1854 death of Ghalib's archrival Zauk, the emperor's tutor in poetry, Ghalib took over that position and completed the first volume of his history of the Mughals. The planned second volume, never completed, was interrupted by the Indian (Sepoy) Mutiny of 1857. Brought on by widespread resentment against British political and cultural policies—land annexation,

gah-ZAHL

conscription of Indian men, and insensitivity to Muslim and Hindu customs—the revolt began in May at Meerut, just thirty miles north of Delhi. As a small liberating army, the Sepoys (Indian police) from Meerut advanced to Delhi to liberate Ghalib's patron, Emperor Bahadur Shah II. In succeeding months, the revolt spread to sites beyond Delhi; it lacked unity and direction, however, and was quickly and ruthlessly suppressed. In September 1857 the British deposed Bahadur Shah II, who went into exile in Burma. With the execution of the former emperor's two sons, the Mughal dynasty came to an end. Disenchanted by the atrocities he had witnessed from both sides during the rebellion, Ghalib left an account of the revolt, critical of both the Indian resistance and the British forces, in his diary of 1857 known as *Bouquet of Flowers (Dast-Ambooh).*

Although Ghalib had been impressed with the results of British influence during a two-year stay, in 1828 and 1829, at the port town of Calcutta, a center of British power, the British response to the rebellion gave him deep pause. At least two of his friends who had survived the interrogations and executions in Delhi had had their libraries destroyed. Ghalib himself was left destitute and had to sell off some of his household goods to get by. Eventually obtaining a small allowance from the nawab of Rampur as well as a pension from the new government, Ghalib remained in Delhi as many other Delhians went into exile in the north. He published a collection of letters, *Ud-i-Hindi,* in 1868; written in Urdu, these letters along with his memoir constitute fine examples of Urdu prose style. Ghalib died on February 15, 1869, leaving a legacy of great love poems, or *ghazals,* in the tradition of Hafiz, Rumi, and Kabir.[3]

Ghalib
The great Urdu poet Mirza Asadullah Beg Khan, or Ghalib, wrote his poetry as India came under the influence of Britain, bearing witness to great change in his lifetime. (Diodia Picture Library)

The *Ghazal.* While his prose works and letters are remembered for their elegance, Ghalib is most revered for his mastery of the Urdu *ghazal.* The *ghazal* developed from seventh-century Arabic poetry and became a popular poetic form in Persian, Turkish, and eventually Urdu, in which language poets like Ghalib explored the form's full potential. The *ghazal* is a form of lyric poetry composed of three to seven couplets (Ghalib often used five), rhymed *aa ba ca da,* and so on. This rhyme scheme, known as **qafiyah**, is strictly followed. Many classical *ghazals* introduce what is called the **radif**, a word or phrase repeated at the end of each couplet in the series, further challenging the poet's skills. The strength of the *ghazal* lies in the couplet, or **shi'r.** Each couplet stands alone as a highly condensed and stylized thematic unit that invokes traditional motifs and figures. Each *shi'r* in a *ghazal* may be a self-contained unit that need not flow logically into the next. The *ghazal* in Urdu poetry was thought of as a string of pearls, each *shi'r* contributing to the mood and general sense of the whole, but not, as in the English or Italian sonnet, following a thematic logic. Given the independent character of each *shi'r* in the series,

kah-FEE-yah
RAH-deef

SHEER

---

[3] **Hafiz . . . Kabir:** Hafiz and Rumi were two of the greatest Persian poets from the fourteenth and thirteenth centuries, respectively; Kabir was a great fourteenth-century poet from India who wrote in Hindi. All three are associated with Sufism, a religious strand woven from Muslim and Hindu forms of mysticism, which stresses the longing for an ecstatic union with God.

Sufi poets, when they use the words "wine" and "the tavern," mean the state of the soul, but when Ghalib uses these words, he means wine and taverns.

– SUNIL DUTTA, "Ghalib and His Work," 1999

the ghazal is comparable to the Japanese *renga,* whose links among various haiku are often indirect and tonal rather than linear and logical.

The *ghazal* typically offers a reflection on spiritual and secular love, most often from the point of view of a disappointed lover longing after an unattainable object of desire. In this regard, the *ghazal* is similar to European love poetry, particularly the Renaissance love sonnet and the Romantic lyric. As in those traditions, the *ghazal* expresses the seemingly hopeless but ardent desire of a lover faced with the impossibility of ever grasping the elusive beloved. Moreover, the image of the beloved blurs the boundaries between corporeal and spiritual love; as a metaphor for a spiritual object, the beloved always threatens, or promises, to indicate an embodied worldly one. Drawing on traditional imagery dating back to the *ghazal*'s origins in Persian and Arabic poetry, the poet focuses on settings such as the desert, the garden, and the drinking party, and calls on conventional symbols such as the candle, the nightingale, and the rose. These latter images symbolize the illuminated or enflamed spirit, the lover, or the beloved. A common motif involves a nightingale away seeking its lover in a garden while its nest is being destroyed by worldly forces—the quest for the ideal leading to the neglect of the everyday.

Ghalib's *Ghazals*.   Written from the heart of a fading empire in the throes of colonial conflict, Ghalib's poetry registers the power of a poet and a poetic tradition to endure and adapt as they respond to the pressures, promises, desires, and disappointments that accompany cultural, social, and economic upheaval. While invoking the conventional motifs and themes associated with the *ghazal,* Ghalib, like other virtuoso poets, transforms them into something more. In his hands, the form becomes a distinctive utterance reflecting his personal response to the unsettled conditions of his private and public life: the stress of financial uncertainty, the loss of social status, the desire to embrace life intensely, and a deep sorrow at the collapse of the Mughal empire. Ghalib's *ghazals* are sometimes intensely private and melancholy; at other times they seem oriented toward public expression and they approach satire. More often, the two realms collapse into each other so that the public becomes private and vice versa.

Although Ghalib found life itself a thing worth cherishing, he was keenly aware of, and deeply experienced in, its myriad disappointments and cruelties. In contrast to Sufi poets like Hafiz, whose poetry aspires toward a mystical effacement of the self, Ghalib's poetry embraces the world with an intensity that insinuates a broad range of experience and a desire for fulfillment in the present. Sunil Dutta puts it simply: "One could say that in thought and intellect, Ghalib resembles Rumi and Hafiz, but the emotion of his poems goes in a different direction from the Sufis. Ghalib has great spiritual intensity, but it comes with a worldliness of the sort we associate with Shakespeare more than with Wordsworth or Herbert."[4] Throughout Ghalib's *ghazals* there is a genuine sense of despair, of

---

[4]**Herbert:** George Herbert (1593–1633), an Anglican priest and English metaphysical poet whose verse emphasizes spiritual devotion and a longing for God.

powers lost, of the futility of human endeavors, and of his own failures. Simultaneously, however, his poetry registers an equally intense sense of striving that is often figured as a manifestation of divine power, as in "Why didn't I shrink in the blaze of that face?" Ghalib's poetry is about the embodiment of spirituality, and part of that embodiment is the language of the verse itself, its rhythm and music. Although the sound of the original Urdu is lost in translation, the success of Ghalib's language is confirmed by the sustained power of his verse, which even today is widely memorized and recited by Urdu speakers in India.

www For links to more information about Ghalib and a quiz on his work, see bedford stmartins.com/ worldlitcompact.

■ FURTHER RESEARCH

Biography
Prigarina, Natalia. *Mirza Ghalib: A Creative Biography*. Trans. M. Osama Faruqi. 2000.
Russell, Ralph, and Khurshidul Islam. *Ghalib: Life and Letters*. 1969.

Translations and Editions
Ahmad, Aijaz. *Ghazals of Ghalib*. 1971.
Bly, Robert, and Sunil Dutta. *The Lightning Should Have Fallen on Ghalib: Selected Poems of Ghalib*. 1999.
Russell, Ralph, ed. *The Oxford India Ghalibi: Life, Letters, and Ghazals*. 2003.

Criticism
Jafri, Sardar, and Qurratulain Hyder. *Ghalib and His Poetry*. 1970.
Russell, Ralph, and Khurshidul Islam. *Three Mughal Poets*. 1968.
Sadiq, Muhammad. *A History of Urdu Literature*. 1984.

■ PRONUNCIATION

Ghalib (Mirza Asadullah Beg Khan): GAH-leeb (MEER-zah ah-sah-doo-LAH BEG KAHN)
ghazal: gah-ZAHL
qafiyah: kah-FEE-yah
radif: RAH-deef
sh'ir: SHEER
srivilas: sree-VEE-lus, shree-VEE-lus
Vaishnava: VIGH-shnuh-vuh

❧ The drop dies in the river

Translated by W. S. Merwin

The drop dies in the river
of its joy
pain goes so far it cures itself

in the spring after the heavy rain the cloud
disappears
that was nothing but tears

in the spring the mirror turns green[1]
holding a miracle
Change the shining wind

10   the rose led us to our eyes

let whatever is be open

---

[1] **mirror turns green:** Refers to making mirrors by applying a green polish to the back surface; in the heavy humidity of spring winds, the face of such mirrors would sometimes turn green. The image suggests the transformative powers of invisible natural forces.

∾ Why didn't I shrink in the blaze of that face?

Translated by Adrienne Rich

Why didn't I shrink in the blaze of that face?[1]
I flare up, apprehending the gaze that returned that vision unblinded.

Out in the world they call me a disciple of fire
because the words of my grief fall like a shower of sparks.

Many have fallen in love with the slim neck of the decanter;
seeing you walk, the wave of the wine trembles with envy.

We and the poems we make get bought and sold together;
but we knew all along for whom they were intended.

The lightning-stroke of the vision was meant for us, not for Sinai;
10   the wine should be poured for him who possesses the goblet.

---

[1] **the blaze of that face:** As becomes apparent in line 9, this poem alludes to the story of Moses, to whom God reveals Himself on Mt. Sinai in the form of a flash of burning light, a story that appears in both the Bible and the Qur'an (Koran).

ꙮ Is it you, O God

Translated by Adrienne Rich

Is it you, O God, whose coming begins to amaze me?
The mirror has turned to a six-tiered ground of waiting.

Every crowded speck of dust has become a whole mist of longing;
if this world is a net, the entire desert is its prey.

The dew has polished the sheen of the flowering branch.
The nights of spring are finished, nightingale.

Don't go unveiled into that valley of Majnoon:[1]
every grain of sand there is an atom of desire.

Nightingale, give me a bundle of sticks for building:
10   I hear the thunder of the first days of our spring.

---

[1] **Majnoon:** Majnoon, whose name means "insane," is a legendary lover of Leyla, both of whom are celebrated in ancient Arabic and Turkish poetry; their love might be compared with that of the legendary Italian lovers Paulo and Francesca or to that of the pilgrim Dante and his Beatrice in Dante's *Divine Comedy*.

ꙮ It is a long time since my love stayed with me here

Translated by W. S. Merwin

It is a long time since my love stayed with me here
And the sparkling goblet lit up our evening together.

Again my complaining breath comes hot, showering sparks.
It is a long time since we saw the night filled with flares.

Again the old enemies, heart and eye, come together
Pining for chances to see her, to brood upon her.

Again I long for her to appear on her balcony,
the wind veiling her face in her black hair.

Again the heart yearns for free days and nights, as before,
10   to think of nothing and no one but her.

∾ There are a thousand desires like this

Translated by W. S. Merwin

There are a thousand desires like this, each needing a lifetime.
Of my wishes, many were gratified, but far from enough.

We have heard of Adam driven from paradise.
My fall from grace was far worse, when I left where you live.

At this time they couple my name with drunkenness.
One more age has dawned that needs Jamshed's cup.[1]

Each time we expected sympathy for our failings
the blade of disaster fell, and we were found near death.

Oh preacher, for God's sake do not raise the Kaa'ba's curtain.[2]
10   It may hide one more idol in which there can be no belief.

---

[1] **Jamshed's cup:** Jamshed was a legendary Persian king who could see the future in a magic cup.
[2] **Kaa'ba's curtain:** Kaa'ba was the most important shrine of Islam, a small building housing the Black Stone at the Great Mosque in Mecca. Before Islam, the Kaa'ba was a site of pagan worship.

∾ Don't Skimp with Me Today

Translated by Robert Bly with Sunil Dutta

For tomorrow's sake, don't skimp with me on wine today.
A stingy portion implies a suspicion of heaven's abundance.

The horse of life is galloping; we'll never know the stopping place.
Our hands are not touching the reins, nor our feet the stirrups.

I keep a certain distance from the reality of things.
It's the same distance between me and utter confusion.

The scene, the one looking, and the ability to see are all the same.
If that is so, why am I confused about what is in front of me?

The greatness of a river depends on its magnificent face.
10 If we break it into bubbles and drops and waves, we are lost.

She is not free from her ways to increase her beauty.
The mirror she sees is on the inside of her veil.

What we think is obvious is so far beyond our comprehension.
We are still dreaming even when we dream we are awake.

From the smell of my friend's friend I get the smell of my friend.
Listen, Ghalib, you are busy worshiping God's friend.

∾ A Lamp in a Strong Wind

Translated by Robert Bly with Sunil Dutta

My wailing—oh inventor of torture—is just a mode of petition.
It's really a request for more torture, and not a complaint.

Even though my house is destroyed, I recognize the value of open space.
In the deliciousness of the desert I forget about home.

To the wise, a storm of difficulty may be a school.
The slaps of waves resemble the slaps of a master.

Things have gone so far that she doesn't even say hello.
If I complain to God, she knows my complaints have no effect.

Why are the roses and the tulips losing their elegant colors?
10   Maybe they recognize they are lamps in the path of a strong wind.

In the street where you live I see the splendor of Paradise.
But Paradise is not as crowded as your street.

Ghalib, which mouth are you using when you complain of your exile?
Have you forgotten the unkindness of people in your own city?

❧ ALEXANDER PUSHKIN
B. RUSSIA, 1799–1837

ah-lik-SAHN-dur
POOSH-kin

on-YAY-gin
p. 722

The three great Romantic writers in Russia during the early nineteenth century were Nikolai Gogol, Mikhail Lermontov,[1] and **Alexander Pushkin**. Pushkin holds the place in Russian literature that Shakespeare and Goethe occupy in the literature of their countries. Because of its formal and stylistic diversity, range, and innovation, like Shakespeare's and Goethe's, Pushkin's work does not easily fall into a single category. Indeed, his greatest work, *Eugene **Onegin***, a novel written in verse and modeled on **Byron's** *Don Juan*, combines features of the Romantic lyric but looks forward to the shift toward Realism in its depiction of character and its straightforward plot. *Onegin,* like Pushkin's other works, celebrates in true Romantic form the genius and independence of the "natural man" who does not hesitate to challenge conventional authority and power.

Early Life. Alexander Sergeyevich Pushkin was born in Moscow in 1799; his father was a minor writer and his mother the granddaughter of an Ethiopian slave in the court of Peter the Great who eventually became a landowner and a general. Pushkin was proud of both his boyar ancestry—the aristocratic class below the ruling princes at the time—on his father's side and his African ancestry on his mother's, and he honored the latter in *The Negro of Peter the Great,* a novel that remained incomplete at his death in 1837. Trained at home to read and speak French, as most aristocratic children were in early-nineteenth-century Russia, Pushkin in his youth wrote poetry in French rather than his native Russian. Eventually he attended the lycée at Tsarskoe Selo, a highly selective and elite school that specialized in turning the sons of aristocrats into soldiers and civil servants. While at school, Pushkin wrote poetry, a comic play, a novel, and a short story—in Russian now—exercising early his talent to explore, master, and even parody the dominant forms of literature.

> [Pushkin's] preoccupation with Peter the Great and his epoch made him the progenitor of a Russian national mythology that shaped the historical discourse of generations of Russian writers and intellectuals.
>
> – SVETLANA EVDOKIMOVA, historian, 1999

Exile and Poetry. Steeped in the ENLIGHTENMENT tradition of political and social thought that was standard fare at the lycée, Pushkin graduated in 1817 and took a position with the Foreign Office in St. Petersburg. Two poems that he wrote during this early period, "Freedom" (1817) and "The Village" (1819), show Pushkin's flirtation with revolutionary ideas— especially sympathy for the plight of serfs, a qualified attack on Tsar Alexander's despotism, and a more general (and less threatening) love of freedom. This dalliance, however, along with his membership in a revolutionary group called The Green Lamp, ultimately led to his exile in the south, in Ekaterinoslav, under charges of circulating seditious literature.

---

[1]**Nikolai Gogol, Mikhail Lermontov:** Nikolai Vasilyevich **Gogol** (1809–1852), Russian fiction writer whose most important novel is *Dead Souls* (1842); Mikhail Yurevich **Lermontov** (1814–1841), Russian poet and novelist who like Pushkin was an admirer of Lord Byron; his most famous novel is *A Hero of Our Time* (1840).

Pushkin was taken in by the Raevsky family, who introduced him to the work of Byron. During the early 1820s, Pushkin, who was now with General Raevsky in Kishinev and eventually Odessa, on the Black Sea, found himself in a rich cultural ferment of Romanian, Greek, Jewish, Armenian, and even Gypsy traditions. In Odessa there were many Greek refugees in exile from their country, now under the domination of the Ottoman Empire. Like Byron and Shelley in England, Pushkin grew sympathetic to the revolt of the Greeks against the occupying Ottomans. Indeed, Byron's work became increasingly important to Pushkin as he finished some of the most important poems of his southern cycle—*The Prisoner of the Caucasus* (1822), *The Fountain of Bakhchisarai* (1823), and *The Gipsies* (1824)—and began writing *Eugene Onegin*. With the publication of these narrative poems, Pushkin's genius was immediately recognized. The free form and rebel heroes of the poems, their interest in "natural man," and their disenchantment with authoritarian rule clearly set Pushkin among the great Romantics of his age.

Orest Admamovic Kiprenski, *Portrait of Pushkin.* *(Art Resource)*

Pardon and Patronage.   In 1824, after a disagreement with the governor, Pushkin was again exiled, this time to his mother's estate at Mikhailovskoye, where he continued to work on *Eugene Onegin* and completed a second masterpiece, *Boris Godunov* (1825), a tragedy written in verse. Consistent with Pushkin's opposition to French classicism and his quest for freer form, *Boris Godunov* rejects the strict "unities" of French classical tragedy[2] in favor of a Shakespearean openness. Because of the unconventional form, the play, like Byron's *Manfred*, remained popular as a closet drama but was not produced until 1870. In 1825, following Tsar Alexander's death and the **DECEMBRIST REVOLT**, Pushkin met with the new tsar, Nicholas, who extended both a pardon and patronage to Pushkin. Pushkin thought his work would now be free from censorship, but Nicholas objected to portions of *Boris Godunov*. In 1831, Pushkin married Natalia Goncharov, whose love of court society and flirtatiousness led six years later to Pushkin's death in a duel with one of her suitors, a French émigré named Baron d'Anthes.

Eugene Onegin.   Begun in 1823 and published in chapter form through 1830, this work, like Byron's *Don Juan,* grew by accretion. It is the story of the love between a young man who has left St. Petersburg to live on the estate of his uncle and the young Tatyana, the daughter of a nearby family. The episodes of *Onegin* often leave the two main characters aside to pursue other—some might say digressive—themes and scenes, including stories about minor characters, descriptions of places, and observations on literature. In these stanzas, the verse novel offers a detailed panorama of Russian culture in the early nineteenth century, including the politics of the Decembrist Revolt and the influence of European literature on early Russian Romanticism.

www   For links to more information about Pushkin and a quiz on *The Bronze Horseman,* see bedfordstmartins .com/worldlit compact.

---

[2] **the unities:** In French Neoclassical criticism, critics argued that playwrights must observe the unities of time, place, and action: the events depicted on stage should not exceed a period of 24 hours, they should be limited to one place, and they should all center around a single action, with little or no digression into subplots.

yiv-GYAY-nee

The Little Plays.   During the 1830s, Pushkin began publishing a series of "little plays," dramatic narrative poems that treat important cultural moments or ideas. *The Stone Guest* retells the story of Don Juan, and *Mozart and Salieri* depicts Salieri's[3] fabled jealousy of Mozart, a theme revived in our time by Peter Shaffer's *Amadeus.* Pushkin identifies Mozart's work with spontaneity and genius, in contrast to the studied craftsmanship of Salieri's work, which cannot reach the same creative heights and so frustrates the otherwise competent musician. In addition, Pushkin wrote during the 1830s a number of short stories and novellas, including *The Queen of Spades* (1834) and *The Captain's Daughter* (1836), the latter of which returns to a historical event, the Pugachev rebellion, for a story that objectively depicts the land-owning classes in the nineteenth century.

The Bronze Horseman (completed in 1833 and published in 1837), included here, is one of Pushkin's literary treatments of Tsar Peter the Great, the horseman of the bronze statue. The story takes place during the great flood of St. Petersburg in 1824 and poignantly sets up a contrast between Peter's greatness and the incidents in the life of the petty clerk **Yevgeni**. Pushkin praises the building of St. Petersburg, the work and vision of Tsar Peter, in response to those who questioned the wisdom of building on such a desolate site constantly threatened by the sea. In the poem, the destructive potential of the sea suggests a severe historical necessity that threatens to desolate the works of human creativity and craft. Once for Pushkin an image of freedom, as it is in Byron's poetry, the sea here becomes a predatory beast that feeds upon the city.

The Bronze Horseman.   In this narrative poem, Yevgeni, a prototype of the ubiquitous clerks that one finds in Gogol and Dostoevsky, loses all that he loves in the flood. In his bitter disappointment, he castigates Peter, the city's founder, by scorning the statue of the Bronze Horseman, which seems to come to life and chase him through the city. Yevgeni's vision of ruin contrasts with Peter's vision for the city as he studies the bleak Baltic coastland upon which he, Faust-like, wants to found a city to mark both his own greatness and the greatness of his nation. Peter's reclamation of the barren land stands as a heroic act of imagination and power. But the triumph of human creativity over natural forces ultimately fails, and Yevgeni and others like him must bear the burden of Peter's lack of total mastery. The opposition between Yevgeni and Peter also has a political dimension, for it roused early critics to see the poem as an opposition between the individual and the state—hence the original censorship imposed by Tsar Nicholas. Critics disagree over which character represents the hero: Peter or Yevgeni. Is Peter a creative genius who defies natural desolation and realizes his vision in the building of the city, or is he a despot whose overreaching ambition leads to the desolation of the small people like Yevgeni? Is Yevgeni simply the common person outdone by greater human, political, and natural powers, or is he a hero who despite

---

[3] **Salieri:** Antonio Salieri (1750–1825), Italian-born composer and music teacher whose pupils included the great Romantic composers Ludwig von Beethoven (1770–1827) and Franz Schubert (1797–1828).

John H. Clark, *View of the Palace of Peter the Great and the Senate House at St. Petersburg,* 1815. Etching
This majestic statue in St. Petersburg of Peter the Great atop his horse, also known as the Bronze Horseman, was the inspiration for the Pushkin poem of the same name. (The Bridgeman Art Library)

his weakness challenges these powers, a spokesperson for the oppressed masses whose helpless defiance nonetheless foreshadows a revolution?

■ **FURTHER RESEARCH**

Biography
Binyon, T. J. *Pushkin: A Biography.* 2003.
Feinstein, Elaine. *Pushkin: A Biography.* 1999.
Sandler, Stephanie. *Distant Pleasures.* 1989.
Troyat, Henry. *Pushkin.* 1936; rpt. 1971.

Criticism
Arndt, Walter. *Pushkin Threefold: Narrative, Lyric, Polemic and Ribald Verse.* 1972.
Bethea, David M., ed. *Pushkin Today.* 1993.
Briggs, A. D. P. *Alexander Pushkin: A Critical Study.* 1983.
Evdokimova, Svetlana. *Pushkin's Historical Imagination.* 1999.
Lednicki, Waclaw. *Pushkin's* Bronze Horseman: *The Story of a Masterpiece.* 1955.
Sandler, Stephanie. *Commemorating Pushkin: Russia's Myth of a National Poet.* 2004.

■ **PRONUNCIATION**

Neva: NYEH-vuh
Onegin: on-YAY-gin
Alexander Pushkin: ah-lik-SAHN-dur POOSH-kin
Yevgeni: yiv-GYAY-nee

∿ The Bronze Horseman

Translated by D. M. Thomas

A TALE OF ST. PETERSBURG

Introduction

On a shore washed by desolate waves, *he*[1] stood,
Full of high thoughts, and gazed into the distance.
The broad river rushed before him; a wretched skiff
Sped on it in solitude. Here and there,
Like black specks on the mossy, marshy banks,
Were huts, the shelter of the hapless Finn;
And forest, never visited by rays
Of the mist-shrouded sun, rustled all round.

And he thought: From here we will outface the Swede;
10 To spite our haughty neighbour I shall found
A city here.[2] By nature we are fated
To cut a window through to Europe,
To stand with a firm foothold on the sea.
Ships of every flag, on waves unknown
To them, will come to visit us, and we
Shall revel in the open sea.

A hundred years have passed, and the young city,
The grace and wonder of the northern lands,
Out of the gloom of forests and the mud
20 Of marshes splendidly has risen; where once
The Finnish fisherman, the sad stepson
Of nature, standing alone on the low banks,
Cast into unknown waters his worn net,
Now huge harmonious palaces and towers
Crowd on the bustling banks; ships in their throngs
Speed from all ends of the earth to the rich quays;
The Neva[3] is clad in granite; bridges hang

---

[1] *he:* Peter I, the Great (1672–1725), tsar of Russia from 1682 to 1725, who led the Westernization of Russia, often by stern measures.

[2] With the aid of Italian and French architects, in 1703 Peter began to construct St. Petersburg, or Petrograd; the new city was a monument to Peter's plans for Westernizing Russia and a symbol of strength against longtime foes, including Sweden, just across the Baltic.

[3] **The Neva:** The river that runs through St. Petersburg into the Baltic; the poem is based on the devastating flood of 1824 when the Neva overflowed its banks.

Poised over her waters; her islands are covered
With dark-green gardens, and before the younger
30 Capital, ancient Moscow has grown pale,
Like a widow in purple before a new empress.

I love you, Peter's creation, I love your stern
Harmonious look, the Neva's majestic flow,
Her granite banks, the iron tracery
Of your railings, the transparent twilight and
The moonless glitter of your pensive nights,
When in my room I write or read without
A lamp, and slumbering masses of deserted
Streets shine clearly, and the Admiralty spire
40 Is luminous, and, without letting in
The dark of night to golden skies, one dawn
Hastens to relieve another, granting
A mere half-hour to night. I love
The motionless air and frost of your harsh winter,
The sledges coursing along the solid Neva,
Girls' faces brighter than roses, and the sparkle
And noise and sound of voices at the balls,
And, at the hour of the bachelor's feast, the hiss
Of foaming goblets and the pale-blue flame
50 Of punch. I love the warlike energy
Of Mars' Field,[4] the uniform beauty of the troops
Of infantry and of the horses, tattered
Remnants of those victorious banners in array
Harmoniously swaying, the gleam of those
Bronze helmets, shot through in battle. O martial
Capital,[5] I love the smoke and thunder
Of your fortress, when the empress of the north
Presents a son to the royal house, or when
Russia celebrates another victory
60 Over the foe, or when the Neva, breaking
Her blue ice, bears it to the seas, exulting,
Scenting spring days.

Flaunt your beauty, Peter's
City, and stand unshakeable like Russia,
So that even the conquered elements may make
Their peace with you; let the Finnish waves

---

[4] **Mars' Field:** The parade grounds in St. Petersburg.

[5] **Capital:** St. Petersburg was capital of Russia from 1712 to 1914, when the capital moved to Moscow.

Forget their enmity and ancient bondage,
And let them not disturb with empty spite
Peter's eternal sleep!

      There was a dreadful time — the memory of it
70 Is still fresh . . . I will begin my narrative
Of it for you, my friends. My tale will be sad.

1.

November over darkened Petrograd.
With a roar of waves splashing against the edges
Of her shapely bounds, the Neva tossed
Like a sick man in his restless bed.
It was already late and dark; against
The window angrily the rain was beating,
And the wind blew, howling sadly. At that time
Came young Yevgeni home, from friends . . . We'll call
80 Our hero by this name. It's pleasant, and
Has long been congenial to my pen.
We do not need his surname, though perhaps
In times gone by it shone, under the pen
Of Karamzin,[6] rang forth in our native legends;
But now it is forgotten by the world
And fame. Our hero lives in Kolomna,[7] works
Somewhere, avoids the paths of the famous, mourns
Neither dead relatives nor the forgotten past.

      And so, having come home, Yevgeni tossed
90 His cloak aside, undressed, lay down. But for
A long time could not fall asleep, disturbed
By divers thoughts. What did he think about?
About the fact that he was poor, by toil
Would have to earn honour and independence;
That God might have granted him more brains and money;
That there are lazy devils, after all,
For whom life is so easy! That he had been
A clerk for two years; he also thought the weather
Was not becoming any calmer; that
100 The river was still rising; as like as not,

---

[6] **Karamzin:** Nikolai Mikhailovich Karamzin (1766–1825), Russian writer and historian, author of the *History of the Russian State* (1818–24).

[7] **Kolomna:** At the time, an outlying suburb of Petersburg.

The bridges on the Neva had been raised,
And for two or three days he would be cut off
From Parasha. At that point Yevgeni sighed
From his heart, and fell to dreaming like a poet.
        "Get married? Me? Why not! It would be hard,
Of course; but then, I'm young and healthy, ready
To toil day and night; somehow or other
I'll fix myself a humble, simple shelter
Where Parasha and I can live in quiet.
110 After a year or two I'll get a job,
And Parasha will bring up our children . . . Then
We shall begin to live, and thus we'll go
Hand in hand to the grave, and our grandchildren
Will bury us . . ."

        Thus he dreamed. And he felt sad that night,
And wished the wind would not howl gloomily,
The rain not beat so angrily at the window . . .

        At last he closed his sleepy eyes. And now
The foul night thins, and the pale day draws on . . .
The dreadful day!

120   All night the Neva rushed
Towards the sea against the storm, unable
To overcome the madness of the winds . . .
She could no longer carry on the struggle . . .
By morning, throngs of people on her banks
Admired the spray, the mountains and the foam
Of maddened waters. But harried by the gale
Out of the gulf, the Neva turned back, angry,
Turbulent, and swamped the islands. The weather
Raged more fiercely, Neva swelled up and roared,
130 Bubbling like a cauldron; suddenly
Hurled herself on the city like a beast.
Everything ran before her, everything
Suddenly became deserted—suddenly
The waters flowed into the cellars underground,
The canals surged up to the railings,
And Petropolis floated up, like Triton,[8]
Plunged to the waist in water.

---

[8]**Triton:** A sea god, son of the chief god of the sea, Poseidon, and Amphitrite, a sea goddess; Triton calmed the waters by sounding a conch shell.

Siege! Assault! The sly waves climb like thieves
Through the windows. Scudding boats smash the panes
140 With their sterns. Hawkers' trays, fragments of huts,
Beams, roofs, the wares of thrifty trading,
The chattels of pale poverty, bridges swept
Away by the storm, coffins from the buried
Cemetery—all float along the streets!

The people gaze upon the wrath of God
And await their doom. Alas! All's swept away:
Shelter and food—where shall they find them?

In that dread year the late Tsar in his glory
Still ruled Russia. He came out on to the balcony,
150 Sad, troubled, and said: "Tsars cannot master
The divine elements." He sat down and with thoughtful
Sorrowful eyes gazed on the dire disaster:
The squares like lakes; broad rivers of streets
Pouring into them. The palace a sad island.
The Tsar spoke—from end to end of the city,
Along streets near and far, a dangerous journey
Through the storm waters, generals set off
To save the people, drowning in their homes.

There, in Peter's square, where in the corner
160 A new house towers, where over the lofty porch
Two guardian lions stand like living creatures
With upraised paw—there sat, astride the marble
Beast, hatless, his arms crossed tightly,
Motionless and fearfully pale, Yevgeni.
He was afraid, poor fellow, not for himself.
He did not hear the greedy billow rise,
Lapping his soles; he did not feel the rain
Lashing his face, nor the wind, wildly howling,
Tear his hat from his head. His desperate gaze
170 Was fixed on one distant point. Like mountains,
There the waves rose up from the seething depths,
And raged, there the storm howled, there wreckage
Rushed to and fro . . . God, God! There—
Alas!—so close to the waves, almost by the gulf
Itself, is an unpainted fence and a willow
And a small ramshackle house: there they live,
A widow and her daughter, Parasha, his dream . . .
Or is all this a dream? Is all our life
Nothing but an empty dream, heaven's jest?

180   And he, as though bewitched, as if riveted
To the marble, cannot get down! Around him
Is water and nothing else! And, his back turned
To him, in unshakeable eminence, over
The angry river, the turbulent Neva, stands
The Image, with outstretched arm, on his bronze horse.

2.

    But now, satiated with destruction, wearied
By her insolent violence, the Neva drew back,
Revelling in the chaos she had caused,
And carelessly abandoning her booty.
190 Thus a marauder, bursting into a village with
His savage band, smashes, slashes, shatters,
And robs; shrieks, gnashing of teeth, violence,
Oaths, panic, howls! And weighed down by their plunder,
Fearing pursuit, exhausted, the robbers leave
For home, dropping their plunder on the way.

    The water fell, the roadway was visible,
And my Yevgeni, in hope and fear and grief,
Hastened with sinking heart to the scarcely abated
River. But full of their victory the waves
200 Still seethed angrily, as though beneath them
Fires were smouldering; foam still covered them,
And heavily the Neva breathed, like a horse
Galloping home from battle. Yevgeni looks:
He sees a boat; he runs towards his find;
Shouts to the ferryman — and for ten kopecks
The carefree ferryman rows him across the billows.

    And long the experienced oarsman struggled with
The stormy waves, and all the time the skiff
Was on the point of plunging with its rash crew
210 To the depths, between the ranges of the waves
— And at last he reached the bank.
                 The wretched man
Runs down a familiar street to familiar places.
He gazes, and can recognize nothing.
A dreadful vision! All is piled up before him:
This has been hurled down, that has been torn away;
The little houses have become twisted, others
Have completely collapsed, others have been shifted
By the waves; all around, as on a battlefield,

Corpses are strewn. Yevgeni rushes headlong,
220 Remembering nothing, exhausted by torments,
To the place where fate awaits him with unknown tidings,
As with a sealed letter. And now he is
Already rushing through the suburb, and here
Is the bay, and close by is the house . . .
What is this? . . .
                    He stopped. Went back and turned.
Looked . . . walked forward . . . looked again.
Here is the place where their house stood;
Here is the willow. There were gates here — swept
Away, evidently. But where is the house?
230 And, full of gloomy anxiety, he walks, he walks
Around, talks loudly to himself — and then,
Striking his forehead with his hand, he laughed.

        Darkness fell upon the city, shaking
With terror; long its people did not sleep,
But talked among themselves of the past day.

        Dawn's light shone over the pale capital
And found no trace of the disaster; loss
Was covered by a purple cloak. And life
Resumed its customary order. People
240 Walked coldly, impassively, along cleared streets.
Government officials, leaving their night's shelter,
Went to their jobs. The indomitable tradesman
Opened his cellar looted by the Neva,
Hoping to make good his loss at his neighbour's expense.
Boats were being hauled away from courtyards.

        Already Count Khvostov,[9] beloved of heaven,
Was singing the disaster of Neva's banks
In his immortal verses.

                    But my poor, poor
Yevgeni! . . . Alas! his confused mind could not endure
250 The shocks he had suffered. His ears still heard
The boom of Neva and the winds. Silently
He wandered round, filled with dreadful thoughts.
Some sort of dream tormented him. A week,
A month, went by — still he did not go home.

---

[9] **Count Khvostov:** A minor poet and contemporary of Pushkin.

When the time ran out, his landlord leased
His abandoned nook to a poor poet. Yevgeni
Did not come to collect his belongings. He grew
A stranger to the world. All day he wandered
On foot, and slept at night on the embankment;
260 He fed on scraps handed to him through windows.
Tattered and mouldy grew his shabby clothes.
Children threw stones at him. Often the whips
Of coachmen lashed him, for he could not find his way;
It seemed he noticed nothing, deafened by
An inner turmoil. And so he dragged out his life,
Neither beast nor man, neither this nor that,
Not of the living world nor of the dead . . .

      Once he was sleeping on the Neva banks.
The days of summer were declining towards autumn.
270 A sickly wind was breathing. The sullen wave
Splashed against the embankment, reproachfully
Grumbling and beating against the smooth steps,
Like a petitioner at the door of judges
Who keep turning him away. The poor wretch woke.
It was dark: rain dripped, the wind howled gloomily;
A distant watchman traded cries with it.
      Yevgeni started up; recalled his nightmare;
Hastily he set off wandering, until
He suddenly stopped — and slowly began to cast
280 His eyes around, with wild fear on his face.
He found himself at the foot of the pillars of
The great house. Over the porch the lions stood
On guard, like living creatures, with their paws
Upraised; and eminently dark and high
Above the railed-in rock, with arm outstretched,
The Image, mounted on his horse of bronze.
      Yevgeni shuddered. Terribly his thoughts
Grew clear in him. He recognized the place
Where the flood played, where greedy waves had pressed,
290 Rioting round him angrily, and the lions,
And the square, and him who motionlessly
Held aloft his bronze head in the darkness,
Him by whose fateful will the city had
Been founded on the sea . . . How terrible
He was in the surrounding murk! What thought
Was on his brow, what strength was hidden in him!
And in that steed what fire! Where do you gallop,
Proud steed, and where will you plant your hoofs?
O mighty master of fate! was it not thus,

300 Towering on the precipice's brink,
You reared up Russia with your iron curb?

The poor madman walked around the pedestal
Of the Image, and brought wild looks to bear
On the countenance of the lord of half the world.
His breast contracted, his brow was pressed against
The cold railings, his eyes were sealed by mist,
Flames ran through his heart, his blood boiled.
Sombrely he stood before the statue;
His teeth clenched, his hands tightened, trembling
310 With wrath, possessed by a dark power, he whispered:
"All right then, wonder-worker, just you wait!"
And suddenly set off running at breakneck speed.
It seemed to him that the face of the dead Tsar,
Momentarily flaring up with rage,
Was slowly turning . . . Across the empty square
He runs, and hears behind him — like the rumble
Of thunder — the clash and clangor of hoofs
Heavily galloping over the shaking square.
And lit by the pale moonlight, stretching out
320 His hand aloft, the Bronze Horseman rushes
After him on his ponderously galloping mount;
And all night long, wherever the madman ran,
The Bronze Horseman followed with a ringing clatter.

And from that time, whenever his wanderings took him
Into that square, confusion appeared on his face.
Hastily he would press his hand to his heart,
As though to ease its torment, he would doff
His tattered cap, he would not raise his troubled
Eyes, and would go on by some roundabout way.

330 A small island can be seen off-shore. Sometimes
A fisherman out late will moor there with
His net and cook his meagre supper. Or
Some civil servant, boating on a Sunday,
Will pay a visit to the barren island.
No grass grows, not a blade. The flood, in sport,
Had driven a ramshackle little house there.
Above the water it had taken root
Like a black bush. Last spring a wooden barge
Carried away the wreckage. By the threshold
340 They found my madman, and on that very spot
For the love of God they buried his cold corpse.

WALT WHITMAN
B. UNITED STATES, 1819–1892

Walt Whitman has had a tremendous influence on American poetry, both in form and content. He attempted to create a truly indigenous American poetry, one that would match in rhythm and image the unique and incredible variety and breadth of the American landscape and the American people. He was a poet of the new American democracy, of people who were largely absent from the European tradition of poetry: the working classes, women, slaves, prostitutes, felons, adventurers. He was a poet of great empathy, excluding no one and nothing from his vast range of subjects. As Whitman says himself again and again, he is the poet of both the beautiful and the plain, the body and the soul; and his sexual honesty and refusal to feel ashamed of the body was a slap in the face to VICTORIAN prudishness. Although Whitman is thought of as an American original, his influences included contemporary literature. He was especially affected by Ralph Waldo Emerson's TRANSCENDENTALISM as well as by an eclectic range of beliefs that located divinity within humans as well as outside of them. He trusted intuition, revered nature, and respected the common man. Whitman celebrated nationalism and was part of the ongoing search for an American identity separate from European culture and classical Greek and Roman influences. As he told one of his disciples, "Everything comes out of the dirt — everything comes out of the people . . . not university people . . . people, people, just people." Whitman worked at projecting a hearty and public persona in his poetry; by the end of his life, his face was emblazoned on cigar boxes, and a Whitman fan club in England venerated a lock of his hair and a stuffed canary that had once been his pet.

Gabriel Harnson, Daguerreotype of Walt Whitman, c. 1853. *Whitman at middle age had a certain ruggedness about him that suggested a wise and well-traveled man. (Oscar Lion Collection, Rare Book Division, Humanities and Social Sciences Library, New York Public Library)*

A Born Observer.   Whitman was born at West Hills, on Long Island, on May 31, 1819, the second of eight children of a loving mother and the father for whom he was named. The elder Walt, according to his son, was "mean, angered, unjust," an alcoholic who had trouble making ends meet. Whitman's best legacy from his father was political; Thomas Paine[1] was a family hero, and the Whitmans supported liberal and feminist causes. When Whitman was four, his father abandoned farming and turned to building or buying houses and quickly selling them; the family moved almost yearly. Whitman left school at twelve for a string of jobs as a printer's devil (an apprentice), teacher, house builder, and newspaper editor. Above all, like other great naturalists and poets, the young Whitman was a born voyeur, loafer, and eavesdropper, a friendly spy taking note of nesting birds, seasonal weeds, and molting snakes, and a hanger-out registering the sights, sounds, and smells of working people's lives. He gave voice to some of his ideas about democracy and America at this time in editorials for the Brooklyn *Eagle*.

www   For links to more information about Whitman, see bedfordstmartins .com/worldlit compact.

---

[1] **Thomas Paine** (1737–1809): American revolutionary patriot and liberal thinker.

A trip in 1848 opened his eyes to the vastness and wonder of the American landscape and the possibilities of the frontier; he went down the Ohio and Mississippi rivers to New Orleans, back north again to Chicago, then east by way of the Great Lakes and the Hudson River.

Whitman's early writings, such as his sentimental novel *Franklin Evans: Or, The Inebriate,* showed little promise. But the imaginative soil out of which *Leaves of Grass* came to flower in 1855 was, as Whitman said, "plowed and manured" well before he began to write that astonishing work. In 1855, he published the book at his own expense. It contained twelve poems and a preface that made plain that Whitman knew he was doing something important and daring. It would remain his chief work, and throughout his life he continually enlarged, revised, rearranged, and lovingly tended to it, adding to it out of all he experienced.

The Effects of the Civil War.   In 1861, when his brother George suffered a mild wound in the Civil War at Fredericksburg, Virginia, Whitman traveled to Washington to take care of him and there found a second true vocation as a nurse, an unpaid "wound dresser" tending the injured and soothing the dying. Eventually, Whitman found a clerkship in the Indian Bureau in the Department of Interior to support himself. He fetched candy, pickles, and tobacco for the patients, played word games with them, or just listened to them talk of war and home.

The Good Gray Poet.   Sightings of President Lincoln in the streets of the capital moved Whitman profoundly. Although the two never met, tradition has it that Lincoln admired *Leaves of Grass* and on seeing Whitman in a crowd remarked, "He looks like a man." At Lincoln's death in 1865, Whitman wrote "When Lilacs Last in the Dooryard Bloomed," one of the great elegiac poems of Western literature. After the war, he was forced out of his job when the Secretary of the Interior came across a copy of *Leaves of Grass* and charged the poet with obscenity; friends rallied, and William D. O'Connor wrote a passionate defense of Whitman in a pamphlet entitled *The Good Gray Poet,* a name Whitman retained. Whitman was even appointed to a clerkship in the Attorney General's office. In 1871 he published the fifth edition of *Leaves of Grass* as well as *Democratic Vistas,* a plea to Americans to beware of materialism and to seek instead a visionary, spiritual, and cultural democracy, a theme echoed in his poem, "Passage to India." "Passage to India" is an extended poem that celebrates two major engineering feats: the joining of the Union Pacific and the Central Pacific railroads in Utah on May 10, 1869, and the completion of the Suez Canal in 1869. For Whitman, these events mean more than a physical connection between East and West, they symbolize a spiritual relationship with India and the East and the opportunity to connect with and learn from the wisdom of that part of the world.

Since contracting malaria during his stint as a nurse, Whitman's health had been poor. In 1873 he had a stroke and returned north to New Jersey to recuperate at his brother George's house; his mother died soon after. Still, he continued to revise and rearrange *Leaves,* and his fame grew to cult status in the United States and Europe. In 1879, this poet who had imaginatively cataloged the North American continent at last saw for himself the American West, as far as the Rockies: ". . . wonders, revelations I wouldn't have missed for my life . . . the Prairie States, the real America," he reported. Whitman died in Camden, New Jersey, on March 26, 1892.

An American Poet and *Leaves of Grass*. The 1855 edition of *Leaves of Grass* got almost no critical notice except for anonymous reviews by its author. But Ralph Waldo Emerson wrote, "I greet you at the beginning of a great career, which must yet have had a long foreground somewhere, for such a start." Without asking permission, Whitman used Emerson's letter to promote his book; Emerson didn't seem to mind, but the literary establishment thought this self-promotion confirmed Whitman's vulgarity. For the frontispiece to the book Whitman chose an engraving of himself lounging in an open-necked shirt like "one of the roughs," the plain working men he admired and to whom he sought to give voice.

During his years of editing, carpentering, and writing formulaic fiction, Whitman was also tirelessly reading—Shakespeare, the Bible, Greek and Roman literature, the English Romantic poets, and the Bhagavad Gita[2] and other Asian texts. From his contemporaries he mainly gauged how he did *not* want to write: He would avoid "rippling" cadences, elaborate "poetical images," a "tedious and affected" voice. Music—folk songs and spirituals, grand opera and oratorios—enraptured him. From opera especially he learned the techniques of antiphony (responsive chanting), long, flexible, narrative lines, and setting off powerful lyric sections in the manner of arias, or solos. He was casting aside conventional poetic forms, trying instead to catch the rhythms of "the grand American expression" in what is now called free verse, "brawny enough and limber and fun enough" to match any poetry.

Song of Myself. *Song of Myself,* a poem of several sections within *Leaves of Grass,* is Whitman's epic. Its hero is not a warrior like Homer's Odysseus in *The Odyssey* nor a wandering soul like Dante's Medieval pilgrim in *The Divine Comedy.* Whitman's "Me Myself" is both spirit and body, "hankering, gross, mystical, nude," a self that contains all creation and has empathetic connections to dinosaurs, runaway slaves, Bowery prostitutes, opera singers, longshoremen, alligators snoozing on riverbanks, and the remotest of stars. Thus, Whitman's "I" expands into a "we" of great diversity. The popular section six introduces grass as a metaphor to connect with various objects and with human beings. An important theme is struck in section twenty-one when Whitman says, "I am the poet of the Body and I am the poet of the Soul." He breaks through Victorian prudery and celebrates the sacredness and beauty of the physical body. Body and soul merge in section forty-eight. The poet's sympathies

"I greet you at the beginning of a great career, which yet must have had a long foreground somewhere, for such a start. I rubbed my eyes a little, to see if this sunbeam were no illusion; but the solid sense of the book is a sober certainty."

– RALPH WALDO EMERSON, about the first edition of *Leaves of Grass* in a letter to Whitman, 1855

---

[2] **Bhagavad Gita** (first century C.E.): Ancient Hindu wisdom text that deals with the spiritual tools necessary for survival.

Whitman did for poetry what Miguel de Cervantes did for the novel, Bertolt Brecht did for theater, and Pablo Picasso did for painting: he redefined the rules. In terms of style and subject matter most twentieth century poets in the United States — and many throughout the world — are his grandchildren.

– JOEL L. SWERDLOW, "America's Poet: Walt Whitman," *National Geographic,* December 1994

extend to animals in section thirty-two. The epic, like Whitman's whole body of poetry, is characterized by small vignettes or sketches as well as by long lists or catalogs. An honesty and calm attitude toward death are found in section forty-nine. Section fifty shows Whitman's prescience about living beyond his mortality through his writing.

Whitman's self in *Song of Myself* is uniquely American and democratic — one that "mutter[s] the word En Masse." His heroic act is to apprehend and pass on the revelation of the democracy of creation, a vision available to all. And yet he is not special, he is no miracle, except in the way all things, even the ants and the "heap'd stones, elder, mullein, and pokeweed" are miracles. Whitman assures the reader in the haunting last lines of *Song of Myself* that he is hanging out, loafing somewhere, encouraging the reader's own journey to discover universal democracy:

Failing to fetch me at first keep encouraged,
Missing me one place search another,
I stop somewhere waiting for you.

Facing West from California's Shores. "Facing West from California's Shores" extends Whitman's vision westward as he searches for the "house of maternity," the cultural cradle of civilization that gave rise to migrations to the West and became the basis for the great variety of peoples and beliefs in the United States. With a very enlightened perspective for his times, Whitman pays tribute to the religious influence of India as well as other parts of Asia. The questions that conclude the poem suggest that Whitman is uncertain whether he has been able to link the world to his American experience.

One measure of Walt Whitman is the praise he receives from other writers, past and present, and how he revealed to them their own creativity and self-worth. With his writing's free rhythms and open structure, his sexual directness, his colloquial vocabulary, and his democratic inclusion of all peoples in his poetry, he has empowered generations of readers.

■ **FURTHER RESEARCH**

Biography
Allen, Gay Wilson. *The Solitary Singer: A Critical Biography of Walt Whitman.* 1955; rpt. 1985.
Loving, Jerome. *Walt Whitman: The Song of Himself.* 1999.
Reynolds, David S. *Walt Whitman.* 2004.

History and Criticism
Erkilla, Betsy. *Whitman the Political Poet.* 1989.
Killingsworth, M. Jimmie. *Whitman's Poetry of the Body: Sexuality, Politics, and the Text.* 1989.
Maslan, Mark. *Whitman Possessed: Poetry, Sexuality, and Popular Authority.* 2001.
Reynolds, David S. *Beneath the American Renaissance: The Subversive Imagination in the Age of Emerson and Melville.* 1988.
——— . *Walt Whitman's America: A Cultural Biography.* 1995.
Thomas, M. Wynn. *The Lunar Light of Whitman's Poetry.* 1987.

FROM

ↄ   # Song of Myself

1.

I Celebrate myself, and sing myself,
And what I assume you shall assume,
For every atom belonging to me as good belongs to you.

I loafe and invite my soul,
I lean and loafe at my ease observing a spear of summer grass.

My tongue, every atom of my blood, form'd from this soil, this air,
Born here of parents born here from parents the same, and their parents the same,
I, now thirty-seven years old in perfect health begin,
Hoping to cease not till death.

10 Creeds and schools in abeyance,
Retiring back a while suffced at what they are, but never forgotten,
I harbor for good or bad, I permit to speak at every hazard,
Nature without check with original energy.

2.

Houses and rooms are full of perfumes, the shelves are crowded with perfumes,
I breathe the fragrance myself and know it and like it,
The distillation would intoxicate me also, but I shall not let it.

The atmosphere is not a perfume, it has no taste of the distillation, it is odorless,
It is for my mouth forever, I am in love with it,
I will go to the bank by the wood and become undisguised and naked,
I am mad for it to be in contact with me.

The smoke of my own breath,
Echoes, ripples, buzz'd whispers, love-root, silk-thread, crotch and vine,
10 My respiration and inspiration, the beating of my heart, the passing of blood and
       air through my lungs,
The sniff of green leaves and dry leaves, and of the shore and dark-color'd searocks,
       and of hay in the barn,
The sound of the belch'd words of my voice loos'd to the eddies of the wind,
A few light kisses, a few embraces, a reaching around of arms,
The play of shine and shade on the trees as the supple boughs wag,
The delight alone or in the rush of the streets, or along the fields and hill-sides,
The feeling of health, the full-noon trill, the song of me rising from bed and
       meeting the sun.

Have you reckon'd a thousand acres much? have you reckon'd the earth much?
Have you practis'd so long to learn to read?
Have you felt so proud to get at the meaning of poems?

20 Stop this day and night with me and you shall possess the origin of all poems,
You shall possess the good of the earth and sun, (there are millions of suns left,)
You shall no longer take things at second or third hand, nor look through the eyes
     of the dead, nor feed on the spectres in books,
You shall not look through my eyes either, nor take things from me,
You shall listen to all sides and filter them from your self.

5.

I believe in you my soul, the other I am must not abase itself to you,
And you must not be abased to the other.

Loafe with me on the grass, loose the stop from your throat,
Not words, not music or rhyme I want, not custom or lecture, not even the best,
Only the lull I like, the hum of your valvèd voice.

I mind how once we lay such a transparent summer morning,
How you settled your head athwart my hips and gently turn'd over upon me,
And parted the shirt from my bosom-bone, and plunged your tongue to my bare-
     stript heart,
And reach'd till you felt my beard, and reach'd till you held my feet.

10 Swiftly arose and spread around me the peace and knowledge that pass all the
     argument of the earth,
And I know that the hand of God is the promise of my own,
And I know that the spirit of God is the brother of my own,
And that all the men ever born are also my brothers, and the women my sisters and
     lovers,
And that a kelson[1] of the creation is love,
And limitless are leaves stiff or drooping in the fields,
And brown ants in the little wells beneath them,
And mossy scabs of the worm fence, heap'd stones, elder, mullein and pokeweed.

6.

A child said *What is the grass?* fetching it to me with full hands;
How could I answer the child? I do not know what it is any more than he.
I guess it must be the flag of my disposition, out of hopeful green stuff woven.

---

[1] **kelson:** The superstructure of a ship's keel.

Or I guess it is the handkerchief of the Lord,
A scented gift and remembrancer designedly dropt,
Bearing the owner's name someway in the corners, that we may see and remark, and
    say *Whose?*

Or I guess the grass is itself a child, the produced babe of the vegetation.

Or I guess it is a uniform hieroglyphic,
And it means, Sprouting alike in broad zones and narrow zones,
10 Growing among black folks as among white,
Kanuck,[2] Tuckahoe,[3] Congressman, Cuff,[4] I give them the same, I receive them the
    same.

And now it seems to me the beautiful uncut hair of graves.

Tenderly will I use you curling grass,
It may be you transpire from the breasts of young men,
It may be if I had known them I would have loved them,
It may be you are from old people, or from offspring taken soon out of their
    mothers' laps,
And here you are the mothers' laps.

This grass is very dark to be from the white heads of old mothers,
Darker than the colorless beards of old men,
20 Dark to come from under the faint red roofs of mouths.
O I perceive after all so many uttering tongues,
And I perceive they do not come from the roofs of mouths for nothing.

I wish I could translate the hints about the dead young men and women,
And the hints about old men and mothers, and the offspring taken soon out of their
    laps.

What do you think has become of the young and old men?
And what do you think has become of the women and children?

They are alive and well somewhere,
The smallest sprout shows there is really no death,
And if ever there was it led forward life, and does not wait at the end to arrest it,
30 And ceas'd the moment life appear'd.
All goes onward and outward, nothing collapses,
And to die is different from what any one supposed, and luckier.

---

[2] **Kanuck:** French Canadian.

[3] **Tuckahoe:** Resident of tidewater Virginia.

[4] **Cuff:** African American.

16.

I am of old and young, of the foolish as much as the wise,
Regardless of others, ever regardful of others,
Maternal as well as paternal, a child as well as a man,
Stuff'd with the stuff that is coarse and stuff'd with the stuff that is fine,
One of the Nation of many nations, the smallest the same and the largest the same,
A Southerner soon as a Northerner, a planter nonchalant and hospitable down by
    the Oconee I live,
A Yankee bound my own way ready for trade, my joints the limberest joints on
    earth and the sternest joints on earth,
A Kentuckian walking the vale of the Elkhorn in my deer-skin leggings, a
    Louisianian or Georgian,
A boatman over lakes or bays or along coasts, a Hoosier, Badger, Buckeye;[5]

10 At home on Kanadian snow-shoes or up in the bush, or with fishermen off
    Newfoundland,
At home in the fleet of ice-boats, sailing with the rest and tacking,
At home on the hills of Vermont or in the woods of Maine, or the Texan ranch,
Comrade of Californians, comrade of free North-Westerners, (loving their big
    proportions,)
Comrade of raftsmen and coalmen, comrade of all who shake hands and welcome
    to drink and meat,
A learner with the simplest, a teacher of the thoughtfulest,
A novice beginning yet experient of myriads of seasons,
Of every hue and caste am I, of every rank and religion,
A farmer, mechanic, artist, gentleman, sailor, Quaker,
Prisoner, fancy-man, rowdy, lawyer, physician, priest,
20 I resist any thing better than my own diversity,
Breathe the air but leave plenty after me,
And am not stuck up, and am in my place.

(The moth and the fish-eggs are in their place,
The bright suns I see and the dark suns I cannot see are in their place,
The palpable is in its place and the impalpable is in its place.)

17.

These are really the thoughts of all men in all ages and lands, they are not original
    with me,
If they are not yours as much as mine they are nothing, or next to nothing,
If they are not the riddle and the untying of the riddle they are nothing,
If they are not just as close as they are distant they are nothing.

---

[5] **Hoosier . . . Buckeye:** Nicknames, respectively, for natives of Indiana, Wisconsin, and Ohio.

This is the grass that grows wherever the land is and the water is,
This the common air that bathes the globe.

21.

I am the poet of the Body and I am the poet of the Soul,
The pleasures of heaven are with me and the pains of hell are with me,
The first I graft and increase upon myself, the latter I translate into a new tongue.

I am the poet of the woman the same as the man,
And I say it is as great to be a woman as to be a man,
And I say there is nothing greater than the mother of men.

I chant the chant of dilation or pride,
We have had ducking and deprecating about enough,
I show that size is only development.

10   Have you outstript the rest? are you the President?
It is a trifle, they will more than arrive there every one, and still pass on.

I am he that walks with the tender and growing night,
I call to the earth and sea half-held by the night.

Press close bare-bosom'd night—press close magnetic nourishing night!
Night of south winds—night of the large few stars!
Still nodding night—mad naked summer night.

Smile O voluptuous cool-breath'd earth!
Earth of the slumbering and liquid trees!
Earth of departed sunset—earth of the mountains misty-topt!
20   Earth of the vitreous pour of the full moon just tinged with blue!
Earth of shine and dark mottling the tide of the river!
Earth of the limpid gray of clouds brighter and clearer for my sake!
Far-swooping elbow'd earth—rich apple-blossom'd earth!
Smile, for your lover comes.

Prodigal, you have given me love,—therefore I to you give love!
O unspeakable passionate love.

24.

Walt Whitman, a kosmos, of Manhattan the son,
Turbulent, fleshy, sensual, eating, drinking and breeding,
No sentimentalist, no stander above men and women or apart from them,
No more modest than immodest.

Unscrew the locks from the doors!
Unscrew the doors themselves from their jambs!

Whoever degrades another degrades me,
And whatever is done or said returns at last to me.

Through me the afflatus surging and surging, through me the current and index.

10   I speak the pass-word primeval, I give the sign of democracy,
By God! I will accept nothing which all cannot have their counterpart of on the
    same terms.
Through me many long dumb voices,
Voices of the interminable generations of prisoners and slaves,
Voices of the diseas'd and despairing and of thieves and dwarfs,
Voices of cycles of preparation and accretion,
And of the threads that connect the stars, and of wombs and of the father-stuff,
And of the rights of them the others are down upon,
Of the deform'd, trivial, flat, foolish, despised,
Fog in the air, beetles rolling balls of dung.

20   Through me forbidden voices,
Voices of sexes and lusts, voices veil'd and I remove the veil,
Voices indecent by me clarified and transfigur'd.

I do not press my fingers across my mouth,
I keep as delicate around the bowels as around the head and heart,
Copulation is no more rank to me than death is.

I believe in the flesh and the appetites,
Seeing, hearing, feeling, are miracles, and each part and tag of me is a miracle.

Divine am I inside and out, and I make holy whatever I touch or am touch'd from,
The scent of these arm-pits aroma finer than prayer,
30   This head more than churches, bibles, and all the creeds.

If I worship one thing more than another it shall be the spread of my own body, or
    any part of it,
Translucent mould of me it shall be you!
Shaded ledges and rests it shall be you!
Firm masculine colter[6] it shall be you!
Whatever goes to the tilth of me it shall be you!
You my rich blood! your milky stream pale strippings of my life!

---

[6] **colter:** The cutting edge of a plow; metaphorically, the penis.

Breast that presses against other breasts it shall be you!
My brain it shall be your occult convolutions!
Root of wash'd sweet-flag! timorous pond-snipe! nest of guarded duplicate eggs! it
    shall be you!
40 Mix'd tussled hay of head, beard, brawn, it shall be you!
Trickling sap of maple, fibre of manly wheat, it shall be you!
Sun so generous it shall be you!
Vapors lighting and shading my face it shall be you!
You sweaty brooks and dews it shall be you!
Winds whose soft-tickling genitals rub against me it shall be you!
Broad muscular fields, branches of live oak, loving lounger in my winding paths, it
    shall be you!
Hands I have taken, face I have kiss'd, mortal I have ever touch'd, it shall be you.

I dote on myself, there is that lot of me and all so luscious,
Each moment and whatever happens thrills me with joy,
50 I cannot tell how my ankles bend, nor whence the cause of my faintest wish,
Nor the cause of the friendship I emit, nor the cause of the friendship I take again.

That I walk up my stoop, I pause to consider if it really be,
A morning-glory at my window satisfies me more than the metaphysics of books.

To behold the day-break!
The little light fades the immense and diaphanous shadows,
The air tastes good to my palate.

Hefts of the moving world at innocent gambols silently rising freshly exuding,
Scooting obliquely high and low.

Something I cannot see puts upward libidinous prongs,
60 Seas of bright juice suffuse heaven.

The earth by the sky staid with, the daily close of their junction,
The heav'd challenge from the east that moment over my head,
The mocking taunt. See then whether you shall be master!

31.

I believe a leaf of grass is no less than the journey-work of the stars,
And the pismire is equally perfect, and a grain of sand, and the egg of the wren,
And the tree-toad is a chef-d'œuvre for the highest,
And the running blackberry would adorn the parlors of heaven,
And the narrowest hinge in my hand puts to scorn all machinery,
And the cow crunching with depress'd head surpasses any statue,
And a mouse is miracle enough to stagger sextillions of infidels.

I find I incorporate gneiss, coal, long-threaded moss, fruits, grains, esculent roots,
And am stucco'd with quadrupeds and birds all over,
10 And have distanced what is behind me for good reasons,
But call any thing back again when I desire it.

In vain the speeding or shyness,
In vain the plutonic rocks send their old heat against my approach,
In vain the mastodon retreats beneath its own powder'd bones,
In vain objects stand leagues off and assume manifold shapes,
In vain the ocean settling in hollows and the great monsters lying low,
In vain the buzzard houses herself with the sky,
In vain the snake slides through the creepers and logs,
In vain the elk takes to the inner passes of the woods,
20 In vain the razor-bill'd auk sails far north to Labrador,
I follow quickly, I ascend to the nest in the fissure of the cliff.

32.

I think I could turn and live with animals, they are so placid and self-contain'd,
I stand and look at them long and long.

They do not sweat and whine about their condition,
They do not lie awake in the dark and weep for their sins,
They do not make me sick discussing their duty to God,
Not one is dissatisfied, not one is demented with the mania of owning things,
Not one kneels to another, nor to his kind that lived thousands of years ago,
Not one is respectable or unhappy over the whole earth.

So they show their relations to me and I accept them,
10 They bring me tokens of myself, they evince them plainly in their possession.

I wonder where they get those tokens,
Did I pass that way huge times ago and negligently drop them?

Myself moving forward then and now and forever,
Gathering and showing more always and with velocity,
Infinite and omnigenous, and the like of these among them,
Not too exclusive toward the reachers of my remembrancers,

Picking out here one that I love, and now go with him on brotherly terms.

A gigantic beauty of a stallion, fresh and responsive to my caresses,
Head high in the forehead, wide between the ears,
20 Limbs glossy and supple, tail dusting the ground,
Eyes full of sparkling wickedness, ears finely cut, flexibly moving.

His nostrils dilate as my heels embrace him,
His well-built limbs tremble with pleasure as we race around and return.

I but use you a minute, then I resign you, stallion,
Why do I need your paces when I myself out-gallop them?
Even as I stand or sit passing faster than you.

48.

I have said that the soul is not more than the body,
And I have said that the body is not more than the soul,
And nothing, not God, is greater to one than one's self is,
And whoever walks a furlong without sympathy walks to his own funeral drest in
    his shroud,
And I or you pocketless of a dime may purchase the pick of the earth,
And to glance with an eye or show a bean in its pod confounds the learning of all
    times,
And there is no trade or employment but the young man following it may become a
    hero,
And there is no object so soft but it makes a hub for the wheel'd universe,
And I say to any man or woman, Let your soul stand cool and composed before a
    million universes.

10   And I say to mankind, Be not curious about God,
For I who am curious about each am not curious about God,
(No array of terms can say how much I am at peace about God and about death.)

I hear and behold God in every object, yet understand God not in the least,
Nor do I understand who there can be more wonderful than myself.

Why should I wish to see God better than this day?
I see something of God each hour of the twenty-four, and each moment then,
In the faces of men and women I see God, and in my own face in the glass,
I find letters from God dropt in the street, and every one is sign'd by God's name,
And I leave them where they are, for I know that wheresoe'er I go,
20   Others will punctually come for ever and ever.

49.

And as to you Death, and you bitter hug of mortality, it is idle to try to alarm me.

To his work without flinching the accoucheur[7] comes,
I see the elder-hand pressing receiving supporting,

---

[7] **accoucheur:** A midwife or obstetrician.

I recline by the sills of the exquisite flexible doors,
And mark the outlet, and mark the relief and escape.

And as to you Corpse I think you are good manure, but that does not offend me,
I smell the white roses sweet-scented and growing,
I reach to the leafy lips, I reach to the polish'd breasts of melons.

And as to you Life I reckon you are the leavings of many deaths,
10   (No doubt I have died myself ten thousand times before.)

I hear you whispering there O stars of heaven,
O suns—O grass of graves—O perpetual transfers and promotions,
If you do not say any thing how can I say any thing?

Of the turbid pool that lies in the autumn forest,
Of the moon that descends the steeps of the soughing twilight,
Toss, sparkles of day and dusk—toss on the black stems that decay in the muck,
Toss to the moaning gibberish of the dry limbs.

I ascend from the moon, I ascend from the night,
I perceive that the ghastly glimmer is noonday sunbeams reflected,
20   And debouch to the steady and central from the offspring great or small.

50.

There is that in me—I do not know what it is—but I know it is in me.

Wrench'd and sweaty—calm and cool then my body becomes,
I sleep—I sleep long.

I do not know it—it is without name—it is a word unsaid,
It is not in any dictionary, utterance, symbol.

Something it swings on more than the earth I swing on,
To it the creation is the friend whose embracing awakes me.
Perhaps I might tell more. Outlines! I plead for my brothers and sisters.
Do you see O my brothers and sisters?
10   It is not chaos or death—it is form, union, plan—it is eternal life—it is
        Happiness.

51.

The past and present wilt—I have fill'd them, emptied them,
And proceed to fill my next fold of the future.

Listener up there! what have you to confide to me?
Look in my face while I snuff the sidle of evening,
(Talk honestly, no one else hears you, and I stay only a minute longer.)

Do I contradict myself?
Very well then I contradict myself,
(I am large, I contain multitudes.)

I concentrate toward them that are nigh, I wait on the door-slab.

10 Who has done his day's work? who will soonest be through with his supper?
Who wishes to walk with me?

Will you speak before I am gone? will you prove already too late?

52.

The spotted hawk swoops by and accuses me, he complains of my gab and my
   loitering.

I too am not a bit tamed, I too am untranslatable,
I sound my barbaric yawp over the roofs of the world.

The last scud of day holds back for me,
It flings my likeness after the rest and true as any on the shadow'd wilds,
It coaxes me to the vapor and the dusk.

I depart as air, I shake my white locks at the runaway sun,
I effuse my flesh in eddies, and drift it in lacy jags.

I bequeath myself to the dirt to grow from the grass I love,
10 If you want me again look for me under your boot-soles.

You will hardly know who I am or what I mean,
But I shall be good health to you nevertheless,
And filter and fibre your blood.

Failing to fetch me at first keep encouraged,
Missing me one place search another,
I stop somewhere waiting for you.

❧ Facing West from California's Shores

Facing west from California's shores,
Inquiring, tireless, seeking what is yet unfound,
I, a child, very old, over waves, towards the house of maternity, the land of
    migrations, look afar,
Look off the shores of my Western sea, the circle almost circled;
For starting westward from Hindustan, from the vales of Kashmere,
From Asia, from the north, from the God, the sage, and the hero,
From the south, from the flowery peninsulas and the spice islands,
Long having wander'd since, round the earth having wander'd,
Now I face home again, very pleas'd and joyous,
10 (But where is what I started for so long ago?
and why is it yet unfound?)

Yamakawa Shuko, *Three Sisters,* Taishō Period
Rapid industrialization and urbanization
in the late nineteenth century led to
transformations in society and culture
throughout the twentieth century. This image
from the Taishō Period in Japan (1912–1926),
a time of rapid change, juxtaposes the
traditional and the modern. (Honolulu
Academy of Arts Purchase, Beatrice Watson
Parrent Fund, 2002 [11822.1])

The literature of the last century and a half is a record of the increasing globalization of culture. Joseph Conrad's *Heart of Darkness* can be seen as emblematic of the period. Conrad, born Jósef Teodor Konrad Korzeniowski in 1857, left his native Poland when he was seventeen to work on a French ship. He later sailed on English ships and became a British citizen. Fluent in both French and English, he eventually settled in England and before he was forty published the first of his many novels in English, *Almayer's Folly* (1895), a story set in the Maylay Peninsula in Southeast Asia. Most of his novels take place outside England—in Asia, Africa, eastern Europe, and Latin America. Today Conrad would probably be described as a "hybrid" writer, one whose life and work bring together more than one culture, one of many writers who represents an emerging global perspective. From Herman Melville and Gustave Flaubert, who were inspired by their travels in exotic lands, to Salman Rushdie and Edwidge Danticat, who left their homelands to enter another culture, the literature of 1850 to the present depicts the experience of crossing cultures. Indeed, separating literatures into

COMPARATIVE TIMELINE FOR 1850–THE PRESENT

Date	History and Politics	Literature	Science, Culture, and Technology
		1847 Marx and Engels, *The Communist Manifesto*	1848 Seneca Falls Conference
1850–1859	1854 Commodore Perry negotiates first Japanese-American treaty. Republican party formed in United States.		
		1856 Melville, "Bartleby the Scrivener"	
	1857 Sepoy Rebellion against British rule	1857 Baudelaire, *Les fleurs du mal*	
	1859 Franco-Austrian War	1859 Darwin, *The Origin of Species*	1859 First oil well drilled at Titusville, Pa.
1860–1869	1861 Emancipation of the serfs in Russia. U.S. Civil War begins.	1861 Jacobs, *Incidents in the Life of a Slave Girl*	1861 Pasteurization introduced following Pasteur's work on microorganisms.
	1862 Bismarck becomes Prussian prime minister.		
	1863 Emancipation Proclamation		1863 Joseph Lister introduces antiseptic surgery. Manet, *Olympia*
	1865 End of U.S. Civil War; Lincoln assassinated.	1865 Dickens, *Our Mutual Friend*	1865 Mendel develops laws of genetic inheritance.

national categories makes less and less sense and becomes increasingly difficult. The period has witnessed the emergence of a world literature.

TOWARD A GLOBAL CULTURE

The Modern Period began with Europe dominating the rest of the world. Controlling nearly four-fifths of the land surface of the earth, the West imagined itself as the force of peace and progress. A second wave of industrialization introduced electricity, chemicals, and oil; it especially transformed transportation and communications, making possible the automobile, the telephone, the radio, and the airplane. Science had achieved the status of a religion. Even nations like China that had previously resisted Westernization sought the benefits of science and industry.

By the time the twentieth century concluded, Europe had been displaced from its former centrality by an emerging global culture. Two world wars and numerous lesser wars changed the maps and turned what had been virtually a European monologue into a conversation among many old and new nation-states throughout

Date	History and Politics	Literature	Science, Culture, and Technology
	1867 Tokugawa shogunate ends in Japan, replaced by Meiji emperor.	1867 Zola, *Thérèse Raquin*	1867 Nobel manufactures dynamite.
	1868 Revolution in Spain		1868 Brahms, *German Requiem*
1870–1879	1869 Opening of Suez Canal		
	1870 Franco-Prussian War		
	1871 Germany unified under Prussian emperor.		1871 Stanley meets Livingstone.
			1872 Whistler, *The Artist's Mother*
	1873 Republic proclaimed in Spain. Famine in Bengal		1873 Japan adopts European calendar.
			1874 First impressionist exhibition, Paris
			1875 Bizet, *Carmen* Schliemann, *Troy and Its Remains*
		1876 Rassundari Devi, *Amar Jiban*	
	1877 Satsuma Revolt in Japan suppressed.	1877 Flaubert, "A Simple Heart"	1876 Wagner's *Ring Cycle* first performed.
	1878 Russia defeats the Ottoman empire.		
	1879 British-Zulu War	1879 Ibsen, *A Doll's House*	1879 Edison develops incandescent lamp.

the world. The gas attacks of World War I, the scientific experimentation of the Nazis during the Holocaust, and the atomic bombs that ended World War II had undermined the belief that science brought only progress and prosperity. New sciences, such as psychology, anthropology, and sociology, sought to understand the sources of irrationality, violence, and brutality. As they explored the human psyche, psychologists and anthropologists realized that savage impulses were not limited to "primitive" peoples. Eventually the simple dichotomy of "primitive" and "civilized" lost its validity.

In the colonial era that extended through the first half of the twentieth century, industrialized nations exploited their colonies as sources of raw materials and as markets for manufactured goods. Although they claimed to be bringing European enlightenment to benighted parts of the globe, imperialists were really engaged in what Conrad's Marlow calls a "squeeze." They grabbed ivory, rubber, and oil but had little interest in the cultural productions of "savage" peoples. A cultural exchange began nevertheless. According to legend, some Japanese ceramics came to the West wrapped in the woodblock prints that inspired

Date	History and Politics	Literature	Science, Culture, and Technology
1880–1889		1880 Dostoevsky, *The Brothers Karamazov*	1880 Rodin, *The Thinker*
		1882 Nietzsche, *The Gay Science*	
		1883 Nietzsche, *Thus Spoke Zarathustra*	
	1885 Congo becomes personal possession of Leopold II of Belgium.		1885 Benz develops prototype of automobile.
	1886 First Indian National Congress	1886 Tolstoy, *The Death of Ivan Ilych*	1886 Statue of Liberty dedicated.
			1888 Eastman develops hand camera.
			1889 Eiffel Tower
1890–1899	1890 First general election in Japan Battle at Wounded Knee	1890 Dickinson, *Poems* (published posthumously) Williams, *An Open Letter to His Serene Majesty Leopold II*	
	1891 Famine in Russia		1891 Kinescope movie camera invented by Thomas Edison.
			1892 Diesel patents heavy oil engine. Monet paints Rouen Cathedral.

artists such as Vincent Van Gogh and James Whistler. African tribal art caught the attention of European modernist painters, especially Pablo Picasso. Hindu gurus from India and Zen masters from Japan promoted their spiritual disciplines in the West. In the first sixty-five years of the twentieth century, only two writers from outside Euro-American cultures had won the Nobel Prize for literature: Rabindranath Tagore of India in 1913 and Gabriela Mistral of Chile in 1945. In the past forty years, however, twelve writers from Africa, Asia, the Middle East, and Latin America have been awarded the prize. Like the world music movement that has put Ladysmith Black Mambazo on the American charts and made the Beatles big in Asia, the "world literature movement" begun in the middle of the last century has made literature global.

Nationalism in literature was replaced by cross-culturalism. Joseph Conrad, who migrated from Poland to France and then England at the beginning of the twentieth century to become an English novelist, would prove to be one of the first of the century's world citizens. His successors include Vladimir Nabokov and Aleksandr Solzhenitsyn, an émigré and an exile, respectively, who came from Russia to the

Date	History and Politics	Literature	Science, Culture, and Technology
	1895 Sino-Japanese War ends in defeat of Chinese.	1895 Pardo Bazán, "The Revolver" Ichiyo, "The Thirteenth Night"	1895 Röntgen discovers X-rays. First motion picture
			1896 Nobel endows Nobel prizes.
	1899 Boer War	1899 Nitobé, *Bushido: The Soul of Japan* Kipling, "The White Man's Burden"	
1990–1909	1901 Death of Queen Victoria	1900 Freud, *Interpretation of Dreams*	1900 Planck develops quantum theory.
	1901 Commonwealth of Australia formed.		1901 Marconi broadcasts radio signals.
	1902 Anglo-Japanese Treaty recognizes independence of Korea and China.	1902 Conrad, *Heart of Darkness*	1902 Gauguin, *Riders to the Sea*
	1903 British complete conquest of Nigeria.	1903 W. E. B. DuBois, *The Souls of Black Folk*	1903 Wright brothers' first flight.
		1904 Chekhov, *The Cherry Orchard* Akiko, "I Beg You, Brother, Do Not Die"	1904 Weber, *The Protestant Ethic and the Spirit of Capitalism* Puccini, *Madame Butterfly*
		1902 Twain, *King Leopold's Soliloquy*	
	1905 Sinn Fein Party founded in Dublin. Russo-Japanese War ends with Japanese victory. Revolution in Russia; tsar establishes a national assembly. Partition of Bengal		1905 Einstein, special theory of relativity German expressionist movement

United States; Derek Walcott, Claude McKay, Michelle Cliff, and V. S. Naipaul, who all migrated from the West Indies to the United States or Britain; Aimé Césaire from Martinique and Samuel Beckett from Ireland, who both went to Paris; and James Baldwin from the United States, who spent many years in Paris and North Africa. Some of these migrants were driven into exile by political oppression, censorship, or poor economic conditions, but all were part of the increasing globalization of culture.

In addition to being globalized, literature also became diversified. Many formerly unheard voices joined the cultural conversation, especially women and members of ethnic and cultural minorities. New American literatures of ethnic subcultures, such as Chicano and Native American literature, developed themes of cultural pride and allegories of cultural history and mythology that recall the nationalistic literatures of Europe and America in the nineteenth century. They are part of a worldwide postcolonial movement through which many former colonies are constructing national identities. As industrialization has brought global culture to nearly every landscape on earth, an appreciation of the differences between cultures and individuals has also awakened.

Date	History and Politics	Literature	Science, Culture, and Technology
		1907 Kipling awarded Nobel Prize.	1907 Cubist exhibition in Paris
			1909 Peary reaches North Pole.
1910–1919	1910 Union of South Africa established. Japan annexes Korea. China abolishes slavery.		1911 Matisse, *Red Studio*
			1912 Titanic disaster.
	1913 Balkan War	1913 Tagore awarded Nobel Prize.	1913 Stravinsky, *The Rite of Spring* The Armory Show
	1914 World War I begins.		1914 Ford pioneers the assembly line.
		1915 Kafka, *The Metamorphosis* Eliot, "The Love Song of J. Alfred Prufrock"	1915 Einstein, general theory of relativity Sanger indicted for *Family Limitation* Griffith, *Birth of a Nation*
		1916 Tagore, *Broken Ties*	
	1916 Easter Rebellion of Irish nationalists against British rule		
	1917 United States enters World War I.	1918 Lu Xun, "A Madman's Diary" Death of Wilfred Owen	
	1918 World War I armistice signed.		
	1919 Treaty of Versailles British kill 400 Indian protestors at Amritsar. Prohibition amendment ratified.		1919 First transatlantic flight Bauhaus founded by Walter Gropius.

SCIENCE, INDUSTRY, AND URBANIZATION

In the second half of the nineteenth century the Enlightenment faith in the power of science was augmented by the important discoveries of scientists such as French biologist Louis Pasteur (1822–1895), who developed the germ theory of disease; Russian chemist Dmitri Mendeleyev (1834–1907), who formulated the periodic table of the elements; and British physicist Michael Faraday (1791–1867), who discovered the theoretical foundations of electricity. The scientific method was extended to areas of study that are now considered the province of the social sciences: economics, politics, anthropology, and sociology. With each new application of scientific study, the conviction grew that nature was an orderly system of laws and that mankind, by discovering those laws, could control the natural world.

The power of science became visible in the achievements of the Industrial Revolution. In 1851, Britain celebrated its industrial might in the Crystal Palace Exhibition, displaying the multitude of industrial products that defined its economic power. Other nations followed Britain's example, and by the end of the nineteenth century, the United States, Japan, and all of the European nations

Date	History and Politics	Literature	Science, Culture, and Technology
1920–1929	1920 League of Nations established. Irish independence Gandhi emerges as leader of Indian independence movement.		
	1921 First Indian parliament	1921 Hughes, "The Negro Speaks of Rivers"	
	1922 League of Nations mandates establish European protectorates in the Middle East. Soviet Union forms. Irish Free State established.	1922 Eliot, *The Waste Land* McKay, *Harlem Shadows*	1922 Tomb of Tutankhamen discovered.
		1923 Yeats awarded Nobel Prize.	1923 LeCorbusier, *Towards a New Architecture*
		1924 Breton, *The Surrealist Manifesto*	
	1925 Hitler, *Mein Kampf,* vol. 1	1925 Cullen, "Heritage"	1925 Scopes trial
			1927 Lindbergh's flight across the atlantic
	1928 Stalin takes over leadership of Soviet Union.	1928 Yeats, *The Tower*	1928 Gershwin, *An American in Paris* Fleming discovers penicillin.
	1929 Stock market crash; beginning of Great Depression	1929 Woolf, *A Room of One's Own*	1929 O'Keefe, *Black Flower and Blue Larkspur*

except Russia had become industrialized and urbanized. Even in Russia, as Anton Chekhov's (1860–1904) (p. 1247) *The Cherry Orchard* (1904) makes clear, the old feudal society was a thing of the past.

With industry came urbanization. Workers were lured from the countryside to join the growing urban proletariat, the working class, in quickly built boomtowns with few public services, poor sanitation, and crowded housing. Disease was rampant in these new cities. Industrial workers, whose wages were set by the forces of competition, had no protection against unemployment or brutal working conditions. Men, women, and children worked long hours—sometimes as many as fourteen a day, six days a week. With few safety measures to protect workers from the machines, industrial accidents were common. Removed from nature at work, crammed into crowded tenements at home, and reduced to cogs in the industrial machine, these human beings seemed to be creatures from a new age, mere animals caught in a daily struggle for survival.

The rapid transformation brought about by industrialization may be nowhere more apparent than in Japan. In 1854 when Commodore Perry opened Japanese ports to trade with the West, ending the 350-year isolation of Japan under the Tokugawa shoguns, Japan began a rapid process of industrialization

Date	History and Politics	Literature	Science, Culture, and Technology
1930–1939	1930 Gandhi leads march against British salt monopoly.		
	1931 Japan invades Manchuria.		1931 Empire State Building
	1932 F. D. Roosevelt elected; New Deal begins.		1932 Earhart first woman to fly solo across the Atlantic.
	1933 Repeal of Prohibition Hitler becomes German chancellor, granted dictatorial powers.	1934 Lorca, "Lament for Ignacio Sanchez Mejías"	
		1935 Neruda, "Ode with a Lament"	
	1936 Mussolini and Hitler proclaim Rome-Berlin axis. Spanish civil war Chiang Kai-shek declares war on Japan.		
	1937 French suppress rebellion in Morocco. Japan invades China.	1937 Rao, *Kanthapura*	1937 Picasso, *Guernica*
	1939 World War II	1939 Césaire, *Notebook of a Return to the Native Land* Neruda, "Hymn and Return"	
1940–1949	1941 Japan attacks Pearl Harbor; U.S. enters war.	1942 Camus, *The Myth of Sisyphus and Other Essays*	1942 Fermi splits the atom.

East River Bridge (Brooklyn Bridge), 1870

The Brooklyn Bridge was one of the great American technological marvels of the nineteenth century. Comprising thousands of steel suspension cables, the elegant bridge connecting Brooklyn and downtown Manhattan was a bold representation of America's economic and industrial growth. (Library of Congress)

Date	History and Politics	Literature	Science, Culture, and Technology
	1944 D Day, June 6	1943 Neruda, "Sexual Water"	
	1945 Germany surrenders; V-E Day, May 8 United States drops atomic bombs on Hiroshima and Nagasaki; Japan surrenders. Arab League founded. United Nations founded.	1945 Senghor, *Shadow Songs*	
	1946 Nuremberg Tribunal		
	1947 Indian independence U.N. develops plan for partitioning Palestine. Truman Doctrine, offering support for countries opposing communism.	1947 Nehru, "Speech on the Granting of Indian Independence"	
	1948 Gandhi assassinated. War in Palestine between Arabs and Jews; founding of Israel.	1948 T. S. Eliot awarded Nobel Prize.	1948 Bell Labs develops transistor. Pollock, *Composition No. 1*
	1949 NATO established. People's Republic of China proclaimed by Mao Zedong. Apartheid introduced in South Africa.		

and urbanization. Opposed to treaties with the West, a number of clan leaders, who called themselves the Satcho Hito group, overthrew the Tokugawa in a brief but bloody rebellion in the 1860s, took control of the government, and led the Japanese into the modern world through the so-called Meiji Restoration. The Meiji leaders appealed to Japanese conservatism by characterizing their revolution as one that sought to restore the emperor, who took the name of Meiji, to a position of honor. Meiji leaders moved the imperial palace from its peripheral location in Kyoto to Edo (now Tokyo), the center of political power. Their policies, however, were not conservative. They encouraged a careful exchange of ideas and technology with the West, announcing in the charter of 1868 that "knowledge shall be sought from all the world and thus shall the foundation of the Imperial polity be strengthened," and they sent scientists and engineers to be educated in the West.

The emperor became the symbolic representative of the nationalistic fervor that gripped the modernizing nation. Loyalty to the emperor, the development of industry, and the modernization of the military enabled Japan to defeat first China in 1894 and then Russia, which was trying to gain territory in Manchuria and Korea, in 1905. After these victories, Western leaders recognized Japan as a major world power. Many writers of the period dealt with the psychological dislocations that resulted from the nation's sudden move to modernization. Inazo Nitobé (1862–1932) ascribed the samurai's difficulties to the differences between the feudal code and the ethics of the business world. Westernization, or modernization—terms that were nearly synonymous at the time—prompted

www   For more information about culture and context in the nineteenth century, see bedfordstmartins.com/worldlitcompact.

Date	History and Politics	Literature	Science, Culture, and Technology
1950–1959	1950 Korean War	1950 Abé Kobo, "The Red Cocoon" Neruda, "The United Fruit Co."	
	1951 End of Allied occupation in Japan		
	1952 First hydrogen bomb exploded by United States. Eisenhower elected president. Mau Mau Rebellion in Kenya Laos gains independence from France.		1953 Crick and Watson model structure of DNA. Beauvoir, *The Second Sex*
	1954 Senator McCarthy censured by Senate. France surrenders to Vietminh; Vietnam divided at 17th parallel.		1954 *Brown vs. Board of Education* desegregates public schools.

Kobaysgu Kiyochika, Scene from the Sino-Japanese War in Korea. Woodblock engraving
This graphic scene from the late nineteenth century shows a very different Japan from that of a century before. After Commodore Perry's arrival in 1853, Japan opened its doors to the West and to its Asian neighbors. Its industry and military developed quickly, and Japan was encouraged to expand its borders, first engaging in the Sino-Japanese War with China over the Korean peninsula. (The Bridgeman Art Library)

Date	History and Politics	Literature	Science, Culture, and Technology
1955	Communist countries in eastern Europe form Warsaw Pact.		1955 Montgomery bus boycott.
1956	Suez crisis; Nasser nationalizes the Suez Canal. Soviet invasion of Hungary. Islamic Republic of Pakistan declared.	1957 Camus, *Exile and the Kingdom* Camus awarded Nobel Prize.	1957 Launch of *Sputnik* Bernstein, *West Side Story*
1958	Egypt and Syria form the United Arab Republic.	1958 Beckett, *Krapp's Last Tape* Achebe, *Things Fall Apart*	1958 Beatnik movement Elvis Presley, "Heartbreak Hotel"
1959	Cuban revolution Chinese suppress rebellion in Tibet; Dalai Lama flees Homelands established in South Africa.		

a nostalgic interest in *Bushido*, the ethical code of samurai. Inazo Nitobé's (1862–1932) best-selling book, *Bushido: The Soul of Japan* (1899), went through numerous editions in the first two decades of the twentieth century.

COLONIAL EXPANSION

As the industrial nations sought to expand their markets and secure sources of raw materials, they established colonies in less developed parts of the world, especially in Asia and Africa. Gradually, they set themselves up as the colonial owners or managers of much of the rest of the globe; by 1900 the imperial nations controlled more than four-fifths of the world's land surface. Western-made maps of Asia and Africa were colored to identify their absentee owners. Britain, the most successful of the colonial powers, circled the globe in British red with an empire on which the sun never set.

While imperial powers exploited the economic and human resources of colonized countries and undermined those societies' traditional cultures, they also bestowed the mixed blessings of new Western institutions, ideas, and material goods on their colonies. In India, the jewel in Britain's imperial crown, the urban middle class benefited from the inexpensive textiles imported from British factories, but these manufactured fabrics put many Indian hand-loom weavers out of work. The middle class also gained access to Western education. In Bengal and other Indian provinces, young writers inspired by the English Romantic poets they had studied in British colonial schools created a new Indian poetry written in Bengali and other vernacular languages. As the British colonial administration brought together the disparate Indian states, these new vernacular literatures contributed to a growing nationalism. Ironically, the liberal political ideas of British

Date	History and Politics	Literature	Science, Culture, and Technology
1960–1969	1960 Eichmann found guilty. Seventeen nations win independence from European powers. Sharpeville; 69 black demonstrators killed in South Africa.		
	1961 Bay of Pigs invasion Berlin Wall erected.		1961 Gagarin first man in space. Beatles perform in Liverpool; Bob Dylan debuts in New York.
	1962 Cuban missile crisis Algerian independence American combat troops sent to Vietnam.	1962 Borges, "The Garden of the Forking Paths" Neruda, "Poet's Obligation"	1962 Carson, *Silent Spring*

Calcutta c. 1900

*By the nineteenth century the British would consolidate and extend their power across
most of India. Along with the English language, a curriculum including English
literature, philosophy, and political and social theory was introduced into Indian schools.
Although the British held deep economic and legal interests in India, severe poverty still
reigned in much of the subcontinent. Scenes such as the one pictured here were common,
with large groups of people bathing or performing religious rituals in the dirty waters of
the Ganges. (Getty Images)*

Date	History and Politics	Literature	Science, Culture, and Technology
	1963 JFK assassinated.	1963 Mahfouz, "Zaabalawi" Akhmatova, *Requiem*	1963 Pop art
	1964 China tests atomic bomb.		
	1965 Vietnam War escalates; U.S. begins bombing campaign. War between India and Pakistan.		1965 Malcolm X shot.
	1966 Cultural Revolution in China.	1966 Sachs awarded Nobel Prize.	
	1967 Six-Day War between Israel and Arab nations		1967 Barnard performs first heart transplant.

philosophers that were part of the standard colonial curriculum helped to shape the Indian independence movement that began late in the nineteenth century.

The more progressive forces that formed the Congress Movement in the 1880s — the real beginning of the campaign for Indian independence — came from the Westernized middle class. The inspiration for the Congress Movement came from leaders like the Hindu Ram Mohun Roy (1772–1833), who sought to reform Hindu polytheism and unite Hindu and Christian ideas. This reforming impulse, promoted by several prominent teachers and leaders during the century, reached its quintessential expression in the Tagore family. Debendranath Tagore (1817–1905), a follower of Ram Mohun Roy, took over leadership of the movement after Roy's death; he sought to return Hinduism to monotheism, founded schools, and promoted the cause of national liberation. Among his fourteen children were poets, artists, and intellectuals, most notably Rabindranath (1861–1941), the central figure in the BENGALI RENAISSANCE, which sought to create a national literature in the Bengali language that would be both Indian and "modern."

Date	History and Politics	Literature	Science, Culture, and Technology
	1968 Martin Luther King Jr. and Robert Kennedy assassinated. Prague Spring Student uprisings in France and West Germany		
	1969 Yasir Arafat elected chairman of the PLO. Sectarian violence in Northern Ireland	1969 Beckett awarded Nobel Prize.	1969 Armstrong and Aldrin first men on the moon.
1970–1979	1971 East Pakistan declares independence; Bangladesh founded.	1971 Neruda awarded Nobel Prize.	1971 Hoff invents computer chip.
	1972 Nixon visits China.	1972 Márquez, "A Very Old Man with Enormous Wings"	
	1973 Arab states attack Israel and are defeated. OPEC cartel triples oil prices. U.S. troops leave Vietnam.		
	1974 Watergate scandal; Nixon resigns.		
	1975 War in Lebanon Franco dies; Juan Carlos becomes king of Spain.	1975 Achebe, "An Image of Africa"	
	1976 Deaths of Chinese leaders Mao Zedong and Zhou Enlai. Soweto protests in South Africa.		1976 Haley, *Roots* Wosniak and Jobs develop the personal computer.

Although Western ideas were assimilated to some degree in many non-Western countries, there was nonetheless a deep distrust of Western thought and in particular of scientific materialism. Confronting the onslaught of Western culture, many Asian writers looked for ways to adopt the material benefits of technology without giving up their spiritual and cultural traditions. Indian writer Rabindranath Tagore suggested that an appropriate cultural exchange between equals would be for the West to trade science to the East in return for Eastern spiritual knowledge. In the colonial relationship, however, the exchange was unequal. Along with Western material goods, the East also took in Western missionaries, teachers, and literary models. The Bengali writers were often linked to British authors; Tagore was sometimes called the Shelley of India. Among his colleagues in the movement, poet Madhusudan Datta (1834–1873) was known as the Milton of India, and novelist Bankim Chandra Chatterjee (1838–1894), the Scott of Bengal. Another important writer of the time, playwright Girish Chandra Ghose (1844–1922), seems to have escaped without a Western epithet. Tagore and

Date	History and Politics	Literature	Science, Culture, and Technology
	1977 President Sadat of Egypt visits Jerusalem.		1978 Birth of first test-tube baby
	1979 Israel and Egypt sign peace treaty at Camp David. Ayatollah Khomeini establishes Islamic republic in Iran. Soviet Union invades Afghanistan. Saddam Hussein becomes president of Iraq.		
1980–1989	1980–1988 Iraq-Iran War	1981 Brooks, "To the Diaspora"	1981 AIDS first recognized as a disease
	1981 Sadat assassinated.		
		1982 Márquez awarded Nobel Prize.	1982 Lin, Vietnam Veterans Memorial
	1984 Indira Gandhi assassinated.	1984 Rifaat, "My World of the Unknown"	
	1986 Space shuttle *Challenger* explodes. Chernobyl nuclear accident in the Ukraine	1987 Walcott, *The Arkansas Testament*	
	1988 Soviet Union begins withdrawing troops from Afghanistan.	1988 Rushdie, *The Satanic Verses* Mahfouz awarded Nobel Prize.	
	1989 End of Communist regimes in Eastern Europe Berlin Wall torn down. Tiananmen Square demonstrators shot.	1989 Bei Dao exiled from China.	

his colleagues celebrated Indian values and traditions within Western literary forms, like the novel and short story, incorporating some Western ideas, especially the UTILITARIAN philosophies of Jeremy Bentham and John Stuart Mill, but the "Indian" side of their work was sometimes lost in translation.

REALISM

By 1850 the Industrial Revolution had transformed Europe into a collection of industrial and urban nations. The writers of the second half of the nineteenth century, broadly described as realists, abandoned the romantic hope of restoring the "green and pleasant land" of a pastoral past. They sought instead to portray as accurately as they could the commonplace life around them. They found little cause for optimism in the world produced by industrialization as they focused their work on the "unnatural" life in the cities where money defined relationships between people and repetitive work reduced laborers to machines. As a literary subject this urban proletariat lacked the appealing persona and the folk wisdom of the

Date	History and Politics	Literature	Science, Culture, and Technology
1990–1999	1990 East and West Germany are reunited. Iraq invades Kuwait. Nelson Mandela released from prison.	1990 O'Brien, *The Things They Carried*	1990 Hubble space telescope placed in orbit.
	1991 Iraq defeated by U.S.-led coalition. Warsaw Pact dissolved. Gorbachev resigns as Soviet premier; USSR ceases to exist.		
	1992 Canada, Mexico, and United States form the North American Free Trade Association (NAFTA). Hindu extremists demolish Ayodhya mosque in India. Islamic rebels capture Kabul and overthrow communist government.	1992 Walcott awarded Nobel Prize.	
	1993 Czech and Slovak republics established as separate countries.		
	1994 Nelson Mandela becomes president of South Africa. Palestinian Authority takes control of Gaza Strip. Zapatista uprising in Mexico.	1994 Rushdie, "The Courter"	1994 World Wide Web created.

rural peasants who had been celebrated by the Romantics. The industrial workers were characterized by the Realists as victims of material and spiritual oppression.

The Realists saw the urban middle classes, with their self-serving materialism and vulgar display of wealth, as soulless. They were "Philistines," said Matthew Arnold (1822–1888), uncultured and ignorant of art and intellectual thought; Gustave Flaubert (1821–1880), speaking for many writers, asserted, "Hatred of the Bourgeois is the beginning of wisdom." Lacking subjects for idealization, realists attempted instead to describe as accurately as they could the common-place life around them. Novelists Charles Dickens (1812–1870) (p. 1037) in England, Emilia Pardo Bazán (1852–1921) (p. 1120) in Spain, and Émile Zola (1840–1902) (p. 1054) in France visited factories and slums and exposed the social problems created by industrialization in *Hard Times, The Women Orator,* and *Germinal,* respectively. The Romantics had idealized human beings as creatures defined by their desire for freedom. The Realists, like Fyodor Dostoevsky's (1821–1881) (p. 963) cynical Grand Inquisitor, were convinced that the great mass of humanity would trade freedom for bread.

Date	History and Politics	Literature	Science, Culture, and Technology
	1995 Israeli prime minister Yitzhak Rabin assassinated. Bosnian war Uprising in Russian province of Chechnya Terrorist bombing of federal building in Oklahoma City	1995 Danticat, *Krik? Krak!* 1996 Szymborska awarded Nobel Prize.	
	1997 Hong Kong returned to China.		1997 Sheep cloned in Britain. Gehry, Guggenheim Museum in Bilbao, Spain
2000–The Present	1999 War in Kosovo 2001 Terrorist attacks on World Trade Center in New York City and Pentagon in Washington, D.C. U.S.-led invasion of Afghanistan		2000 Human genome deciphered.
	2003 Darfur conflict begins in Sudan. U.S.-led invasion of Iraq		2002 Scientists confirm presence of water on Mars.
		2006 Bei Dao invited to return to China.	

The Industrial Revolution changed the literary marketplace. The steam printing press, invented in 1810, made it possible to produce large quantities of inexpensive magazines and books, which were sold to a growing reading public. Besides books of instruction and religious tracts — two of the most popular genres at the time — novels were being published by the many new publishing houses and read by a growing number of literate readers. This new audience included large numbers of women, who were particularly interested in reading works by and about women. Among the major European novelists of the period were George Eliot (1819–1880) in England; George Sand (1804–1876) in France; Emilia Pardo Bazán in Spain; and Harriet Beecher Stowe (1811–1896) in the United States. Many of the period's most important novels, even those written by men, have female protagonists — among them Flaubert's *Madame Bovary* (1857), Leo Tolstoy's (1828–1910) *Anna Karenina* (1877), and Eliot's *Middlemarch* (1872). Women's lives especially interested realist novelists, because most avenues for heroic public action were closed to women; women were confined to the sphere of the commonplace and the everyday. In this book, Realist literature about women is represented by Flaubert's "A Simple Heart" (1877) (p. 941), the biography of a servant woman; Emilia Pardo Bazán's "The Revolver" (1895) (p. 1122), a story about a husband's psychological oppression of his wife; Henrik Ibsen's (1828–1906) *A Doll's House* (1879) (p. 1065), a controversial social drama about a woman who abandons her husband and children to seek fulfillment on her own; and Higuchi Ichiyo's (1872–1896) "The Thirteenth Night" (1895) (p. 1126), a story about a Japanese housewife who contemplates as similar rebellion. Ibsen, the Norwegian father of Realist drama, devoted so many of his plays to exploring women's issues that he was honored by a feminist organization.

Science in the nineteenth century seemed to have material explanations for everything, and when Charles Darwin's (1809–1882) (p. 1029) evolutionary theory, first published in 1859 in *The Origin of Species,* reduced humans to animals and explained creation as a random process, many were ready to accept German philosopher Friedrich Nietzsche's (1844–1900) assertion that "God is dead." Lacking belief in an orderly universe, the Realists simply tried to describe ordinary people and everyday things objectively, without suggesting that they were part of a larger design or had any deep spiritual meaning. Flaubert, in "A Simple Heart" (p. 941), seems to be mocking the search for such significance when he makes Félicité's holy spirit a bedraggled parrot. The NATURALISTS, writers such as Émile Zola in France and Theodore Dreiser (1871–1945) in America, went one Darwinian step further than the Realists: Life is not simply ordinary and trivial, they suggested, it is physically determined; and human beings, like the rest of the animal creation, are driven by biological needs and instinctual desires.

In spite of their cynicism and apparent objectivity, Realists often affirmed, sometimes inadvertently, the importance of feeling and the power of imagination. The Realist in Flaubert looked on such provincial characters as Felicité and Madame Bovary with ironic disdain, but in a Romantic gesture, he was so drawn to identify with the latter that he exclaimed, "I am Madame Bovary." Tolstoy's Ivan Ilych, for all his shallowness and petty materialism, when faced with death accepts his common humanity; as he does, he elicits our sympathy. Srivlas, in Rabindranath Tagore's *Broken Ties* (p. 1293), in spite of his western materialism, is drawn to Satish's Indian spirituality. While an awareness of loss and the presence of death had tempered the idealism of the Romantics, the cold objectivity of the Realists was often softened by their recognition of the universality of the human condition.

WORLD WAR I AND ITS AFTERMATH

The competition among European nations for control of disputed territories in eastern Europe and for sources of raw materials and new markets in Asia and Africa reached an impasse in the first decade of the twentieth century, when German expansionism threatened to engulf the rest of Europe. France, Russia, and Britain went to war to contain Germany and its allies, Austria and Italy. After the German strategy to defeat the French quickly and move on to other fronts failed, the war settled into a long and brutal siege in which millions of young men from all the European nations perished. Soldiers died hideous deaths in the massive trench warfare of World War I (1914–1918) — by gassing, shelling, and aerial bombardment — and more troops of more nationalities were slaughtered under grimmer conditions than in any previous war. The conflict ground to a stalemate in western Europe in 1917. America belatedly entered the war in 1917, and the fresh American troops made enough of a difference that Germany surrendered by November 1918.

Although the war was fought with the expectation that it would produce lasting peace, it had just the opposite effect. The Treaty of Versailles (1919), which ended the war, reconfigured the map of Europe in ways that would soon antagonize both Germany and Russia, and it punished Germany with ruinous demands for reparations. In little more than a decade, the Germans, financially broken and restless for more *lebensraum* (living space), embraced an even more virulent nationalism — fascist National Socialism, or Nazism — and instigated a new war.

Although the protagonists in World War I were the major European powers, the war reached far beyond the borders of Europe. By choosing to side with Germany, the Ottoman empire, which had ruled the Middle East, southeastern Europe, and north Africa from its capital in Turkey since 1299, was brought to its final collapse. The resulting power vacuum allowed Turkish nationalists under the leadership of Mustapha Kemal Ataturk (1881–1938) to establish a secular republic. The new League of Nations placed other Ottoman lands in the Middle East under either French or British administration, a resolution that created many of the inequities and tensions in that region that still plague the world nearly a century later. The British and French roles in the Middle East differed from those that Britain and France had played in colonial Africa, for now they were administrators, not rulers. Nevertheless, the Europeans' interference in Middle Eastern affairs was often resented and led to such confrontations as the Suez crisis between Egypt and Britain in 1956. In other parts of the world, European nations had recruited their colonial subjects to fight in the First World War. After the war, German colonies went to the victors: African colonies, for example, were divided among Britain, France, and Belgium; Japan was even able to seize some of the remote German possessions in the Pacific.

Russia had entered World War I in 1914 ill prepared for battle. Russian industry was not capable of supplying the army that was under the personal charge of Tsar Nicholas II (1868–1918). Long-standing discontent with the autocratic tsar was intensified by his incompetence as a military commander and by the bungling of his generals. After two million Russian soldiers were killed in the first two years of the war and an economic crisis and food shortages wracked the homeland, Russia lost the will to continue fighting abroad. Nicholas was forced to abdicate early in 1917, and the country plunged into civil war. Loosely organized "White," or Menshevik, forces pursued a vague program of social democracy while "Red," or Bolshevik, forces sought to institute a COMMUNIST government in what would later be known as the Russian or Communist Revolution. Under the leadership of Vladimir Ulianov Lenin (1870–1924), the Bolsheviks' Red Army won out by 1921, but the industrial and agricultural sectors of the Russian economy had been devastated. The first item on Lenin's postrevolution agenda was to rebuild Russia economically, a program that was cut short by his death in 1924. The subsequent struggle for power among the leaders of the politburo, the policy-making and executive arm of the Communist Party, led to the dictatorship of Josef Stalin (1879–1953), who consolidated his position by 1928 and ruled the nation for the next quarter century.

Many Western intellectuals saw the Great Depression that followed the stock market crash of 1929 as proof of Karl Marx's prediction of the collapse of capitalism. Although Karl Marx (1818–1883), the economist who developed communist theory, had asserted that communist revolutions would take place in the most advanced capitalist countries, Russia, the one existing communist state, had been the least industrialized of the European nations, and its brand of communism in fact emphasized dictatorship at the expense of the proletariat. In spite of its short-comings, however, Russia was an alternative to the ruthless capitalist economies that seemed to produce wealth for the few and unemployment and misery for the many. The Great Depression did not bring any of the more advanced European countries to revolution, but it did encourage the growth of communist and socialist parties, on the left, and a reactionary nationalism, on the right, in the form of FASCISM. Fascists took power in Nazi Germany, the Italy of Benito Mussolini (1883–1945), the Spain of Francisco Franco (1892–1975), and the China of Chiang Kai-shek (1887–1975). Communism characterized itself as the movement that opposed fascism and transcended national interests to represent the international working class; in the eyes of many, it became the international alternative to nationalistic fascism.

As part of his international vision Lenin had encouraged the development of communist movements in many nonindustrial countries, particularly in colonial or formerly colonial countries in North Africa, the Middle East, and Asia. By allying themselves with the nationalistic and independence movements in those countries, communists appealed to people who resented colonial exploitation and wished to modernize without being Westernized. This strategy was most successful in China, where the Communists joined forces with the nationalist revolution led by Sun Yat-sen (1866–1925) and his successor Chiang Kai-shek. When Chiang Kai-shek later tried to suppress the Communists, he inspired revolutionary opposition led by Mao Zedong (1893–1976) that eventually defeated the Nationalists and in 1949 established the People's Republic of China.

MODERNISM

The first two decades of the twentieth century could be called the twilight of the ENLIGHTENMENT, the last time people held comforting beliefs in science and progress. The shock of the First World War shattered that faith and thrust the times into intellectual, cultural, and political crises. The following lines from "The Second Coming," written in 1920 by William Butler Yeats (1865–1939), one of Europe's most visionary poets, capture the spirit of the age that witnessed the Russian Revolution, the horrors of World War I, and the collapse of accepted truths in science, religion, and politics:

> Things fall apart, the center cannot hold;
> Mere anarchy is loosed upon the world,
> The blood-dimmed tide is loosed, and everywhere
> The ceremony of innocence is drowned;
> The best lack all conviction, while the worst
> Are full of passionate intensity.

Oswald Spengler (1880–1936) in *Decline of the West* (1918) asserted that the West had lived out its allotted cycle of glory, citing World War I as a point of no return in the downward spiral to final desolation. Since Europe had not suffered a widespread war for nearly a century, even the memories of earlier conflicts were distant. The young men who fought in the trenches had been nursed on comfortable pieties about God, country, and bravery, and had not even matured before they became the "lost generation," so called because so many had been wiped out on the battlefields or disillusioned by the destruction of the Great War. The wartime poets, many of whom died in combat, articulated the trauma of their war experience. The traditionalism of the verse forms of Wilfred Owen (1893–1918) (p. 1485) is undermined by the subject matter of trench warfare and gas attacks, which turns the madness of war into surreal nightmare. The death and destruction wrought by the war seemed to confirm Friedrich Nietzsche, who in the preceding century had declared: "God is dead."

The Waste Land (1922) (p. 1458) by T. S. Eliot (1888–1965), probably the classic description of modernist malaise, imagines modern urban society as a sterile, materialistic wasteland in which the search for meaning is filled with detours and dead ends. The poem pieces together realistic vignettes of banal urban life with fragments of great literary works from the past, shards of a broken and forgotten tradition. Communication between individuals is faulty or nonexistent, sexual relations mechanical and alienating. Although the end of the poem suggests potential sources of healing, *The Waste Land*, like much modernist writing from the first half of the twentieth century, is less concerned with a cure than with describing the societal sickness.

The chief diagnostician of the diseased modern psyche was Viennese physician Sigmund Freud (1856–1939) (p. 1429), who described human beings in very different terms from those of the Enlightenment scientists. Instead of rational creatures who by seeking their own self-interests served the best interests of all, human beings, according to Freud, were driven by stifled desires and unconscious drives. Freud developed a scientific theory to explain the role of dreams, secret desires, personal history, and sexuality in defining the individual and to account for how modern urban society frustrates and forces suppression of those desires, causing neuroses. Freud developed psychoanalysis to enable individuals to overcome neuroses by becoming more aware of their suppressed inner life. Freud's ideas spurred an interest in consciousness, the role of sexuality in forming the individual, and the ways in which the perceiver affects his or her perceptions of the external world. Visual artists turned away from painting the exterior world to expressing on canvas their own interior visions. Sometimes this change in perspective produced pictures that distorted or transformed reality, as in the work of cubist painter Pablo Picasso (1881–1973). Other artists, known as abstract expressionists, or action painters, made no attempt to relate the images on their canvases to any exterior reality.

"Primitive" cultures, in which, Freud thought, natural impulses and instinctive drives were more openly expressed, became the focus of much scholarship. One of the early classics in the new fields of comparative religion and anthropology was *The Golden Bough* (1890) by Sir James Frazer (1854–1941). A broad survey of myth and ritual, this work was intended to defend the truth of Christianity against pagan religions, but it actually provided a rich symbolic tapestry for reevaluating the archetypal roots of Christianity and its resemblance to pagan religions. The similarities between "primitive" and modern cultures that Frazer brought to light appeared to argue against the myth of progress, especially when modern secularism was seen to be shallow and materialistic in comparison with the mythology of tribal or traditional societies. Bronislaw Malinowski (1884–1942), one of the first anthropologists to study native people in the field, challenged the nineteenth-century contention that myth represented prelogical or prescientific thinking and a rudimentary stage of civilization. By implication, Malinowski questioned any simplistic application of the idea of progress or lack of progress to native cultures.

Some of the new social scientists found universal "deep structures" beneath the superficial differences among cultures. Carl Gustav Jung (1875–1961) believed that social codes governing religious, social, and cultural practices were not particular to certain cultures or historical periods but universal and timeless. In myth, literature, art, and religious symbolism, Jung found what he called "ARCHETYPES," or age-old symbols, such as the Quest, the Great Mother, and the Wise Man, that suggested that human beings in diverse times and cultures shared a common spiritual and psychic makeup.

The new focus on the perceiver and on consciousness prompted a growing uncertainty about the physical world and the nature of reality. After progressing in the nineteenth century to a place where they could explain nearly all material phenomena, the physical sciences were transformed in the twentieth century by quantum physics and the theory of relativity. The complex theories of such scientists as Max Planck (1858–1947), Albert Einstein (1879–1955), Niels Bohr (1885–1962), and Werner Heisenberg (1901–1976) constituted a paradigm shift that revised the Newtonian worldview in place since the seventeenth century. Einstein's theory of relativity modified the customary three-dimensional view of things, adding time as a necessary fourth dimension in any physical description of an object. In 1927,

Werner Heisenberg's experiments with electrons led to his "uncertainty principle," which implied that scientists could not describe reality exactly because they could not simultaneously observe both the position and velocity of an electron. The work of these scientists paved the way for the discovery of a fascinating subatomic world that, to paraphrase Yeats's "The Second Coming," would eventually "vex the world to nightmare" with the nuclear bomb.

The general uncertainty about the nature of reality along with the alienation and fragmentation that followed the war produced feverish cultural activity as artists and writers sought new expressions for the unfamiliar world they confronted. AVANT-GARDE movements in art, music, and literature abounded, giving some credence to the insight of Mexican poet Octavio Paz (1914–1998) that "Modernity is a sort of creative self-destruction." Artists, musicians, and writers seemed to be trying to outpace the dizzying technological changes with artistic experimentation. In 1909 the Italian writer Filippo Marinetti (1876–1944) launched futurism, which strove to capture in the arts the aggressive and iconoclastic spirit of the new science and the rapidity of industrial and technological change. Other avant-garde schools, such as fauvism, expressionism, cubism, vorticism, and surrealism, challenged materialism, tepid conservatism, and the timid conformity of the bourgeoisie in social and cultural life.

Artists such as the French postimpressionist Paul Cézanne (1839–1906), the Russian Wassily Kandinsky (1866–1944), and Pablo Picasso took painting toward a complex, geometrical display of surfaces. In their creations, objects and figures were fragmented and distorted through multiple planes crisscrossing the canvas. American painter Jackson Pollock (1912–1956) went a step further, dripping paint on his canvases and making their subject the act of painting itself. In music, Viennese composer Arnold Schoenberg (1874–1951) and Russian composer Igor Stravinsky (1882–1971) challenged harmonic and melodic conventions by introducing atonality and polytonality. Atonality abandoned the concept of key; polytonality allowed the composer to intermix keys at will. Both approaches resulted in a strange new music that replaced harmony with dissonance and discord. When Stravinsky's ballet *The Rite of Spring* opened in Paris in 1913, shocked patrons rioted. The distortion in these artists' works reflected the feel of early-twentieth-century Europe, which seemed to be spinning out of control.

Like the war that engendered it, MODERNISM began in Europe but its effects were global. As Western science and technology spread to many non-Western countries and as Western-educated artists and intellectuals carried modernism back to their native countries, experimentation in the arts and literature shaped movements in India, Japan, and many Latin American countries. Indian artists

like Amrita Shergil (1913–1941) and Jamini Roy (1887–1972) melded Indian traditions with those of European modernism in their paintings. The fiction of Japanese novelist Tanizaki Junichiro (1886–1965) attempted to reconcile Western ideas,
particularly those of Freud, with Japanese tradition. Even such anticolonial revolutionaries as Aimé Césaire (1913–2008) from Martinique and Léopold Senghor
(1906–2001) from Senegal were profoundly influenced by European modernism.

MODERNIST LITERATURE

In his poem "September 1913," Yeats lashed out at the Dublin middle classes whose
obtuseness prevented a collection of impressionist paintings from being acquired
by the city:

> What need you, being come to sense,
> But fumble in a greasy till
> And add the halfpence to the pence
> And prayer to shivering prayer, until
> You have dried the marrow from the bone?

Yeats's countryman James Joyce (1882–1941) also found fault with the Irish middle
class in *Dubliners* (1914) and *A Portrait of the Artist as a Young Man* (1916) before
shocking the sensibilities of the whole of Europe with the more experimental and
sexually explicit *Ulysses* (1922). Italian playwright Luigi Pirandello (1867–1936) did
away with the conventions of realistic theater in his experimental play *Six Characters in Search of an Author* (1921); at its premier performance in Rome, Pirandello
had to be protected from offended audience members. The German novelist Franz
Kafka (1883–1924) characterized modern life as a nightmare of bureaucratic
anonymity that reduced his protagonists to paranoia. English novelist and poet
D. H. Lawrence (1885–1930) featured sexually explicit themes and unabashedly
sensual characters. Futurism, expressionism, and cubism found kindred spirits in
such writers as Ezra Pound (1885–1972), Gottfried Benn (1886–1956), and Gertrude
Stein (1874–1946), all of whom experimented with form, narrative structure, and
language.

   Twentieth-century novelists turned from social realism to psychological
exploration, using first-person narration to tell stories that were more about their
narrators than about the stories they told. In Japan, novelists such as Shimazaki
Toson (1872–1943) developed a whole new genre known as the "I-Novel"
(*shishosetsu*), autobiographical and confessional stories told in the first person.
When modernists did employ a third-person voice, it was not that of the omnis-
cient narrator of nineteenth-century fiction; this new point of view was limited to
a single consciousness. Inheritors of nineteenth-century ROMANTICISM like Yeats

and Russian poet Anna Akhmatova (1889–1966) (p. 000) used the first person even when writing about the momentous events of their time. Yeats writes of his personal involvement in the struggle for Irish independence and Akhmatova speaks directly of her suffering under Stalin's oppressive regime.

Many modernists attempted to mirror the era's changes in consciousness with nonlinear patterns of language. Imagist poets T. S. Eliot and Ezra Pound juxtaposed associated images in their work to convey a nondiscursive inner reality. Spanish poet Federico García Lorca (1898–1936) funneled folk and surrealist influences to picture the world of dreams in disconnected, evocative images. Joyce's *Finnegans Wake* (1939) carried experimentation with language to its logical conclusion, inventing words by assembling familiar sounds into strange and ambiguous new combinations.

The most important innovations in fiction were those of Joyce, Marcel Proust (1871–1922), and Virginia Woolf (1882–1941) (p. 1365), who experimented with ways to represent consciousness in prose. In his monumental sequence of novels *Remembrance of Things Past* (*A la recherche du temps perdu,* 1913–1927), Proust explored the role of time and memory in shaping one's awareness of the world. Joyce and Woolf tried to replicate the "STREAM OF CONSCIOUSNESS"; in flowing, unpunctuated sentences that merged memory and present awareness and followed an associative logic, these writers evoked the inner life of their characters.

The modernists' experimentation with form, obscure personal symbolism, unfamiliar or invented language, and bleak subject matter alienated many readers. Often these writers were communicating with only a small cultural elite. Modernists often made the artist himself the subject of a work, as in Joyce's *Portrait of the Artist as a Young Man* and Thomas Mann's (1875–1955) *Death in Venice* (1912). The artist appears in these works as an exiled, isolated, and alienated figure cut off from the common people.

WORLD WAR II AND BEYOND

Very soon after 1918 it became clear that the forces that had started the First World War were preparing for another confrontation. Competition among colonial powers, ultranationalism, the rise of dictators, and the stresses of a worldwide depression brought Europe and the rest of the world to the brink of explosion in the late 1930s. Two contradictory versions of Western civilization opposed each other. Fascists presented themselves as preservers or restorers of a pure European culture that would reverse the decline of the West. Their opponents saw Fascists as achieving order only by destroying the free democratic institutions that were the West's finest achievement. With the rise of fascism, many people were drawn to the Marxian conclusion that revolution was the inevitable result of the divide between capitalists and the working classes. Dismayed by the failure of capitalist governments to put a stop to Hitler, Mussolini, and Franco, people were drawn into affiliations with the communist parties and other leftist movements that formed a diverse and committed Popular Front opposed to fascism. That opposition was dramatically and tragically expressed in the Spanish civil war (1936–1939), in which international brigades of idealistic leftists volunteered to fight beside the Spanish Republicans in an unsuccessful effort to preserve the democratic second Spanish Republic against the coalition of conservative and Fascist forces under General Franco.

No one was prepared for the scope of World War II. The war reached beyond Europe into China, Japan, and colonial possessions of the European powers in Africa and Asia. Nor was anyone ready for the extent of the devastation, the leveling of whole cities by aerial bombardment and the civilian genocide of the

Aftermath of Hiroshima
The scene of devastation in Hiroshima after August 6, 1945. (The Art Archive)

Holocaust. The massive suffering, the torture, and the deaths of millions of Jews, Gypsies, homosexuals, and others whom the Nazis deemed unfit to live was beyond comprehension. These atrocities were carried out with a deliberate and scientific efficiency that applied the principles of industrial organization and technological productivity to the business of mass murder. And the dropping of atomic bombs on Hiroshima and Nagasaki by the United States at the end of the war raised unsettling ethical and technological questions. Would atomic energy restore belief in science and progress or had it simply given humanity the power to create Armageddon?

In some ways, World War II fulfilled its stated mission: "to save the world for democracy." Not only were democratic governments established in the defeated countries — Germany, Italy, and Japan — but the war also forced democratic changes in the victorious nations as well, such as the decline of the class system in Britain and a move toward racial integration in the United States. The war also gave impetus to independence movements throughout the colonized world. Before World War II there was one independent country in Africa — Liberia; by the beginning of the twenty-first century, there were no remaining African colonies. World War II was the twentieth century's pivotal event. Its consequences and the issues it raised but did not settle, such as the realignment of the Middle East, are still shaping the world's experience today.

Europe, Asia, parts of Africa, and the Middle East awoke from World War II as from a nightmare of devastation and suffering. Although some writers looked on the war as a prelude to the apocalypse, the biblical end of the world, others, especially in Europe and Japan, saw in the rubble an opportunity to rebuild a society now rid, they thought, of narrow nationalism, militarism, and expansionist designs. In the face of sometimes seemingly insurmountable obstacles and despite devastating setbacks, since World War II many nations took steps toward improving relations and understanding among the various countries and cultures of the world. The United Nations was founded in 1945 to mediate conflicts between member nations, to provide economic and technological assistance to countries in need, and to promote cooperation and cultural understanding. Fifty countries joined the four "sponsoring" nations — Britain, China, the Soviet Union, and the United States — to sign the original U.N. charter, and by 1960 another fifty had added their names to the document.

Despite the hope for world peace, the first decade after the war witnessed many regional conflicts, some of which, like the Greek civil war (1946–1949), the Chinese Communist revolution (1945–1949), and the Korean War (1950–1953), threatened to erupt into large-scale confrontations. Even as the peace agreements were being signed at Yalta in 1945, the frost of the cold war between the West and the Soviet Union was crystallizing. Treaties essentially had divided the world into Western and communist blocs, best symbolized perhaps by Germany, which was split into West and East. Both sides attempted to enlarge their spheres of influence, the West in the NATO alliance, the Soviet Union in the Warsaw Pact with its Eastern European satellite states. Both sides also sought to enlist the allegiance of countries in the Third World. Conflicts on the fringes, in Korea, for example, and Cuba, threatened to turn the cold war hot. When the Soviet Union announced in 1953 that it had developed a hydrogen bomb to match that of the United States, the standoff took on a more menacing aspect.

Europe and Japan lost most of their remaining colonies in Africa and Asia in the two decades following World War II. Often, as in the case of India and Pakistan, North and South Vietnam, Indonesia, and various African states, including South Africa, the collapse of colonialism introduced a turbulent period of civil, religious, and nationalist strife. The independence movements in these regions also marked a renewal of interest in traditional cultural practices, folklore, religion, and native languages. In Africa, for example, writers such as Jomo Kenyatta (1893–1978) and Ngugi Wa Thiong'o (b. 1938) of Kenya, Chinua Achebe (b. 1930) and Wole Soyinka (b. 1934) of Nigeria, and Alex La Guma (1925–1985) and Lewis Nkosi (b. 1936) of South Africa adapted traditional forms of oral storytelling to European narrative to celebrate African identity and articulate unique aspects of the African experience.

The colonial struggle in Indochina—Laos, Cambodia, and Vietnam—had far-reaching implications for the United States. Ho Chi Minh (1890–1969), who had lived in China, Moscow, and Paris, led the nationalist Vietminh against the French, who gave up their colonial holdings in Vietnam after a major defeat at Dien Bien Phu in 1954. Vietnam was then divided into two parts, North and South. The revolutionary nationalist leader Ho Chi Minh ruled the North while Diem Ngo Dinh (1901–1963), supported by the United States, was the official leader of the South. Diem's regime was unpopular, and a succession of coup attempts against him ultimately led to direct U.S. military intervention in 1964; America feared that a Communist takeover in South Vietnam would lead to further revolutions in the region. Arguably the United States's most unpopular war, the Vietnam War polarized public opinion throughout the country, especially after heavy U.S. losses during the Tet offensive of January 1968, which prompted massive antiwar demonstrations in both the United States and Europe. The antiwar and civil rights movements in the United States and the independence efforts around the world fomented a global struggle for basic human rights.

When the Berlin Wall came down in 1989, at least symbolically ending the cold war, some claimed that "the end of history" had been reached, for the separation of the world into three entities—the Free World, the Communist World, and the Third World—no longer stood. Every country had become a member of a single global community, a participant in an expanding free market connected to one network of communications. The arrogance of the assumption that the only significant differences in the world had been those between the capitalist West and the communist East was compounded in the notion that once those oppositions disappeared, the world had become homogenous. Some Asian observers of the world scene have described the almost continuous wars on their continent since World War II, wars that often involved Western interference, as World War III. In the wake of the cold war, many countries remained suspicious of modernization and Westernization, resisted the economic exploitation of poor by rich nations, and viewed globalization as American subjugation of the rest of the world. Nevertheless, in the sixty years since the Second World War, advances in communications and transportation have brought the world closer together and laid the foundations for a global community. The cultural history and literature of the period can be characterized from two different perspectives: postcolonialism and postmodernism.

POSTCOLONIALISM

The term POSTCOLONIALISM is sometimes used to describe the period following World War II; viewed from the point of view of colonized peoples, the struggle against colonialism is *the* important movement of the second half of the twentieth century. Although agitation to end colonial occupation had been organized in some countries, such as India, for example, as early as the late nineteenth century, it was not until after World War II that most independence movements came to successful fruition. Led by Mahatma Gandhi (1869–1948), India gained independence in 1947. In the years that followed, independence movements and wars of liberation challenged colonialism throughout Asia and Africa. Although some colonial possessions remained intact at the end of the century—the Falkland Islands (Britain), the Canary Islands (Spain), New Caledonia (France), and Puerto Rico (United States) to name a few—the age of colonialism ended almost completely with the twentieth century.

The struggle to break the hold of colonial domination sometimes turned into civil war, as competing factions sought to control the destiny of a newly independent nation. In some cases, colonizers had created a single territory out of smaller tribal areas; when the colonial masters left, there was no longer an enforcer to hold disparate groups together and no natives prepared to take over the job of governing. In other places, governmental and social institutions had been well established and natives trained for leadership positions, but this native elite was often distrusted as being agents of the colonial culture that had been overthrown.

Educated and independent direction often came from writers, scholars, and intellectuals. Many writers, such as Nigerian poet Christopher Okibo (1932–1967) and Cape Verdean poet Amilcar Cabral (1924–1973), died while engaged in the struggle for independence. Frantz Fanon (1925–1961), a psychiatrist from Martinique who practiced in Algeria before joining the Algerian revolutionaries, wrote insightful social analyses of colonialism and passionate polemics against colonizers in *Black Skin, White Masks* (1952) and *The Wretched of the Earth* (1961). Writers who did not actively fight, like Indian novelist Raja Rao (1909–2006) (p. 1241), who lived in an ashram and supported Gandhi's movement, wrote of the battle for independence. Writers and intellectuals who led independence movements or fought in revolutionary armies often took the lead in recovering or inventing an identity for their new nations after independence was gained. Aimé Césaire (1913–2008) (p. 1714), a poet from Martinique, attacked colonialism in his *Discourse on Colonialism* (1950) and fought for independence in the French Chamber of Deputies. Léopold Senghor (1906–2001) (p. 1711), another poet, served as president of Senegal from 1960 to 1981. Postcolonial writers employed the tools of folklore, mythology, and realism inherited from the nineteenth-century European Romantics and **REALISTS** to construct that cultural history and identity for their homelands. Their Realist novels create what critic Frederic Jameson has called a "national allegory," stories that tell a myth of a nation through accounts of individual lives.

In the postcolonial context, however, the project of literary nation-building raises troubling questions. Can formerly colonized peoples retrieve their precolonial culture, or have they been forever changed by their engagement with the colonizers and cut off from the past by a hiatus often lasting several generations? Can the indigenous elements in a culture be distinguished from colonial accretions? Writers that had no precolonial written language worry that they can write only in the European languages learned in colonial schools, the "languages of the oppressors." By doing so, do they prolong the oppression and use a language ill-suited to express their culture's unique view of the world?

POSTMODERNISM

In its simplest sense, the controversial term POSTMODERNISM refers to the period after the modernist period, roughly from World War II to the present. "Postcolonials" viewed the same period from the perspective of formerly colonized peoples. *Postmodern* describes the period from the perspective of the former colonizers. World War II, with its massive bombing of civilian populations, the genocidal destruction of the Holocaust, and the dropping of the atomic bomb magnified the horrors of the First World War and deepened postwar despair. T. S. Eliot had tried to piece together the fragments of Western culture after World War I; writers and artists after the Second World War, like the poets included in *In the World: War, Conflict, and Resistance* (p. 1473), wondered whether there were any fragments left. If the modernists were disillusioned and sought vainly for meaning, many post-modernists began with the assumption that there was no meaning to search for.

Postwar despair was formulated into a philosophy by the French EXISTENTIAL-ISTS. Led by Jean-Paul Sartre (1905–1980), whose ideas were shaped by his experiences fighting in the French resistance movement during the war, the existentialists did not simply abandon the pieties of patriotism and honor. They called into question all the essential Truths of the Western tradition. Asserting that "existence precedes essence," they considered any attempt to find meaning beyond an individual's experience — in God, for example, in a national ideal, or in a concept of human nature — a form of "bad faith." One could not use Christianity or patriotism as justification for one's choices. Faced with radical isolation and the lack of any inherent meaning in the world, a condition the existentialists — especially Albert Camus (1913–1960) — referred to as "the absurd," the existential individual had to take total responsibility for his or her actions, for his or her existence. By doing so, individuals defined themselves. By rejecting the concept of essences, or established truths, existentialists established one of the tenets of postmodernism: that there are no essential truths.

The existentialists' rejection of established ideas was a prelude to the spurning of many institutions prompted by the antiwar and civil rights movements of the late 1960s. A worldwide quest for greater human rights challenged such institutions as the family, public schools, the university, police departments, and civil administrations. In May 1968, police moved in on rioting students at the Sorbonne, France's most prestigious university, setting off months of often violent protests. In what German-born philosopher Herbert Marcuse (1898–1979) called the "Great Refusal," students aimed to topple the elitist hierarchy of the university, to make the curriculum reflect more accurately the social and political realities of the time, and to provide greater access to education for minorities and the poor. A new generation of French intellectuals, including Jacques Lacan (1901–1981), Michel Foucault (1926–1984), Jean-François Lyotard (1924–1998), and Jacques Derrida (1930–2004), subverted such Establishment values as humanism and the priority of the individual; they repudiated the materialism and conservatism that, in their view, limited power and prestige to a privileged few. These writers continue to exert a significant influence among postmodern intellectuals, many of whom began their higher education during or just after the Vietnam era in the 1970s.

Postmodernists replaced essentialism (truths) with pluralism and seriousness with playfulness. Jean-François Lyotard reformulated the existential rejection of essences, calling it "incredulity toward metanarratives" (stories that explain an underlying truth). There is no one story, no eternal truth, no one set of laws that explains the world, Lyotard said. Rather, there are many narratives. Like other post-modern theorists, Lyotard could trace his intellectual ancestry back to Ferdinand de Saussure, whose linguistic theory described language not as a way of represent-ing an external reality but as an arbitrary system of signs (words) that derive their meaning from the network of relationships within a language. Rejecting the high seriousness that characterizes discussions of the "big ideas" or the great books of the Western tradition, Lyotard employed the metaphor of "language games" to describe the way humanity's many stories relate to one another. Modernists often took art very seriously, but postmodernists indulge in artistic playfulness and parody. They mix genres, make paintings of soup cans, wrap buildings in massive curtains, record sounds in the street as a substitute for music. Unlike modernist architects who implemented the maxim that "form follows function" by attempting to reduce a building to its simplest functional components, postmodern architects mix styles, add unnecessary and playful decoration, and include stairways and doors that lead nowhere.

Postmodernists also "decenter" or "deconstruct" traditional notions. Jacques Derrida, whose work also builds on the linguistic theories of Saussure, calls essen-tial ideas, or metanarratives, "centers." According to Derrida, centers are related to their opposites, the "others" that are "marginalized" in relation to them. For example, male marginalizes female, white marginalizes black, West marginalizes East, mind marginalizes body, speech marginalizes writing. Postmodernists "decenter" such pairs, opening up a free play between opposites and allowing the marginalized other, temporarily at least, to play a central role. Such decentering challenges established authority. "Man is no longer to be the measure of all things, the center of the universe," concludes Leonard Meyer, writing of "the end of the Renaissance" in 1963. Even the authority of the author is passé; for postmodernists, the formerly marginalized reader determines the meaning of a text.

Postmodernists also decentered traditional notions of character. For Jacques Lacan, the self is inevitably alienated since the "I" it uses to describe itself makes the self an object, an other. By decentering character, postmodernists also chal-lenged traditional notions of plot, which depicts a character's growth through a causative series of actions.

Although manipulating the center and the margin can be seen as a kind of game, it also, of course, has serious political and social implications. By equating knowledge and power, philosopher Michel Foucault showed how some schools of thought become accepted and others rejected and how people construct a worldview and an understanding of themselves by adopting the terms of the dominant discourses around them. His analysis of prisons and mental institutions explores how those institutions are socially constructed and suggests ways in which different ideas about criminality or mental illness could change the world. Telling the world from the perspective of the repressed and marginalized has opened contemporary thought to many formerly ignored points of view — for example, those of women and of racial and cultural minorities.

Modernists assumed that some works of art were more serious and hence more valuable than others. Works of high culture — classical music or abstract expressionist painting, for example — were significant; popular songs or the illustrations of Norman Rockwell (1894–1978) were not. Postmodernists reject such hierarchical distinctions; there are simply many texts, many discourses, many pictures. Meaning is not inherent in the work, but is supplied by the reader, the listener, the viewer. In a culture where everything becomes a commodity and value is established in the marketplace, postmodernists make no distinction between fine and popular art, for all art is bought and sold. In the postmodern world, multiplicity rules. Distinctions between high and low, past and present, reality and illusion, serious and frivolous make little sense when everything is on the Internet. National borders are crossed with a keystroke. There are as many versions of reality as there are perspectives.

POSTMODERN AND POSTCOLONIAL LITERATURE

Modernism did not suddenly disappear after World War II. The aestheticism, experimentation, and engagement with interior reality that dominated literature in the first half of the twentieth century was continued in the work of later writers and incorporated into many postmodern works. The inventions in Argentinean writer Jorge Luis Borges's (1899–1986) (p. 1533) labyrinthine short stories and in Abé Kobo's (1924–1993) "The Red Cocoon" (p. 1442) are descended, for example, from the bizarre worlds in the stories of Franz Kafka. But after World War II, modernism became international, comprising as many voices from the margins as from the white, male, European "center."

In Joseph Conrad's (1857–1924) *Heart of Darkness* (1902) (p. 1159), Conrad and his narrator, Marlow, are clearly appalled by the excesses of the colonizers, though neither is able to view the Congo through African eyes. *Heart of Darkness* is not so much about Africa as it is about Marlow and his demonic alter-ego, Kurtz, and the journey the novella chronicles is on one level a look into the divided psyche of the colonizers. Nigerian novelist Chinua Achebe (b. 1930) directly critiques Conrad's book in "An Image of Africa," (p. 1722) and in his own novel *Things Fall Apart*

(1958) (p. 1604), he implicitly attacks the stereotypical objectification of Africans in *Heart of Darkness* by individualizing his own hero, Okonkwo, and describing the richness of his culture. In doing so, he challenges European racism while offering Africans an image of their cultural identity.

Such postcolonial cultural construction is a recent example of what European Romantics did in the nineteenth century, when they collected folklore and wrote novels to articulate an identity for the emerging nations of Europe, in what could be called the first wave of postcolonial literature. The writers of the Bengali Renaissance—Rabindranath Tagore (1861–1941) and others—based poems on Bengali folk songs and wrote fiction that explored the conflict between their Indian and British heritages. Writers of the Irish Renaissance, from the 1890s to the 1920s, active in the political struggle to free Ireland from British rule, wrote about their native culture. Yeats uses Irish mythology and history in his poems as a way of establishing a distinct cultural identity for the Irish and thus justify Ireland's independence from Britain. The Irish Renaissance, in turn, strongly influenced writers of the Harlem Renaissance of the 1920s and 1930s, who sought to establish a black culture with African roots and its own distinctive music, art, and literature. For the first generation of postcolonial African writers, such as Léopold Senghor of Senegal or Wole Soyinka (b. 1934) of Nigeria, the writers of the Harlem Renaissance—especially Claude McKay (1889–1948) and Langston Hughes (1902–1967)—were defining figures who had pioneered a black literature. This history is traced in some of the selections in *In the World: Images of Africa* (p. 1694).

To rebuild cultures undermined by colonialism, writers sometimes recovered, sometimes invented a history and mythology for their people. In poems like "The Lake Isle of Innisfree" and "Who Goes with Fergus?" Yeats creates an idealized Irish rural landscape and mythology that contrasts with the urban rationalism of Great Britain. Achebe places Okonkwo in a culture of stories and ritual practices that defines his difference from the Europeans and presages his confusion when caught between African and European influences. In recording Okonkwo's cultural heritage, Achebe confirms its reality and, by extension, its equality with European culture.

Nations that emerged from colonialism faced a dual challenge: to discover or create their own independent identity and to establish themselves amid a globalizing world. Increasingly, twentieth-century writers from all nations were becoming international citizens who melded their particular national identity with a global outlook. As writers moved from one nation to another, they became world citizens with what Salman Rushdie (b. 1947) calls "imaginary homelands," and their perspective changed from postcolonial to postmodernist.

Nearly all the postcolonial writers of the second half of the twentieth century decentered the Western version of things by making formerly nameless natives into living persons. In his search for Zaabalawi, for example, Naguib Mahfouz's (b. 1911) narrator gives Cairo a history, a spiritual center, and a mystery independent of Western orientalism. Postcolonial decentering combines with postmodern playfulness in "The Courter" (p. 1763), by Anglo-Indian Salman Rushdie. He dramatizes the relations between the margin and the center, using wordplay, puns, parody, allusions, serendipitous happenings, and bizarre surprises to facilitate the free play between them. Rushdie's adolescent hero is pulled between his Indian heritage and the lure of Western popular culture.

Language games become the subject as well as a technique in such stories as Borges's "The Garden of Forking Paths" (p. 1536). Borges challenges traditional ideas about character and plot by imagining a world where everything is possible and where different aspects of characters emerge in alternating plots. There is no "metacharacter"—one who determines the possibilities of the story.

Established categories for postmodern authors do not make much sense. Rushdie, for example, was born in India and educated in England; he worked in Pakistan, eventually claimed British citizenship, and now lives in New York. He has written novels reflecting each of these changing geographical identities, and he calls himself an "English writer" and a "translated man." He might be best described as a world writer. Mexican novelist Carlos Fuentes describes his situation in terms that hold true for many of his contemporaries. "I don't see myself as a nationalist writer at all," he commented. "I don't believe in nationalism in literature. Especially today, I think literature is an international event." Even when contemporary writers treat their native culture, they often do so with a broad audience in mind. Chinua Achebe, for example, was aware that he was writing about tribal culture in his native Nigeria for readers who would include many non-Nigerians. Indeed, in the essay "An Image of Africa," he implies that one important goal of his novel is to make Africans real to European and American readers by decentering their perspective on Africa. In similar ways, Alifa Rifaat (b. 1930) (p. 1746), and Edwidge Danticat (b. 1969) (p. 1779) reestablish point of view by writing as women and former marginalized subjects. Perhaps no writer has taken the notion of decentering further than Abé Kobo, who in "The Red Cocoon" writes from the point of view of a cocoon.

www   For more information about culture and context in the nineteenth and twentieth centuries, see bedfordstmartins.com/worldlitcompact.

HERMAN MELVILLE
B. UNITED STATES, 1819–1891

In the span of the six years from 1850 to 1855, in a decade characterized by F. O. Matthiewson as the American Renaissance, Emerson published *Representative Men* (1850), Thoreau, *Walden* (1854), Hawthorne, *The Scarlet Letter* (1850) and *The House of Seven Gables* (1851), Harriet Beecher Stowe, *Uncle Tom's Cabin* (1852), and Whitman, *Leaves of Grass* (1855). It's hard to find any six-year period with a richer trove of literary treasures. And that is without counting what may arguably be the most important American literary work of the time, Herman Melville's *Moby Dick,* published in 1851, when Melville was only thirty-two years old. This formidable work, with its encyclopedic treatment of whaling and its philosophic engagement with the big questions of life, seems to be the work of a much older writer. Thoroughly American in its ambitious and brash philosophizing, *Moby Dick* may come closer than any other work of American literature to the elusive status of the "great American novel." It is at the same time one of the monuments of world literature, transcending its origins as an adventure story by an American sailor to become one of the great philosophic novels of the nineteenth century, along with Dostoevsky's *The Brothers Karamazov* (1879–80), Tolstoy's *War and Peace* (1866–69), and Dickens's *Little Dorrit* (1855).

Melville's Childhood. Although he was descended from prominent colonial American families, Herman Melville was not a child of privilege. His father, a dry goods merchant, died bankrupt when Herman was twelve, and his mother took him, his elder brother, **Gansevoort**, and six younger children to Albany where the family could live more cheaply than in New York City. There Herman began a series of occupations by working six days a week as a clerk in the New York State Bank. In his teens he went on to clerk in his brother's store, take care of his uncle's farm, teach at a district school, and earn a certificate in surveying and engineering. He also attended school for short periods during these years and began writing, submitting short articles to Albany-area newspapers.

Education on a Whaleboat. In 1839, when he was twenty, Melville began his real education when he signed on as a hired boy on the *St. Lawrence* and sailed to Liverpool, a trip he later wrote about in *Redburn, His First Voyage* (1849). When he returned to the States, he briefly tried teaching again and took an exploratory trip west to look over opportunities there before returning to seafaring. In 1841 he joined the crew of the whaler *Acushnet* bound for the Pacific. During the next four years, on a series of voyages and stopovers in the Pacific, he gathered the experiences that he would later draw on in much of his literary work. He could claim, as Ishmael, the narrator of *Moby Dick,* does, that "a whale-ship was my Yale College and my Harvard." He stayed with the *Acushnet* for eighteen months before jumping ship in the Marquesas Islands, curious to

Herman Melville in Headshoulders Photo, c. 1870s to 1880s
Melville in middle age. (Bettman/ Corbis)

GAHNS-vohrt

uh-KUSH-net

confirm the natives' notoriety for cannibalism and sexual license. His first novel, *Typee: A Peep at Polynesian Life* (1846), was based on the several weeks he spent on those islands. Shipping out on an Australian whaler, he was briefly imprisoned in Tahiti with other members of the crew for failing to carry out shipboard duties. He lingered in Tahiti and spent time in Hawaii between other voyages before enlisting in the American navy, where he was assigned to the frigate *United States* and a fourteen-month voyage to Boston.

Early Work.   From his experiences during these seafaring years, Melville created nearly all his fiction. After *Typee* (1846), Melville wrote **Omoo**: *A Narrative of Adventures in the South Seas* (1847), which tells of his voyage to Tahiti and his imprisonment there. *Redburn* is an account of his first voyage to Liverpool, and *White Jacket* (1850) is about his time aboard the *United States*. These early works earned Melville a reputation as a travel writer and a novelist of the sea, but he had larger ambitions. In 1849 he had written *Mardi*, which turned sea travel into political and religious allegory, an experiment that did not sit well with his readers. Nevertheless, Melville turned again to allegory in 1851 in his masterpiece, *Moby Dick*, a novel that uses the genre of a seagoing adventure story to tell an allegorical and symbolic tale about a young man's search for the meaning of life and community.

Melville and Hawthorne.   Melville's maturation from a travel writer to a great symbolic novelist owed something to his relationship with Nathaniel Hawthorne. After he married in 1847, Melville moved to a farm outside Pittsfield, Masssachusetts, near the home of Hawthorne. Hawthorne at the time was America's premier novelist, an artist whom Melville described as the "American Shakespeare" and to whom he would dedicate *Moby Dick*. For Melville, his mentor's works were models of philosophical novels that treated serious themes, such as the relation of good and evil, symbolically. Hawthorne found in Melville an honest searcher for whom the great philosophical issues were open and troubling questions. "He can neither believe, nor be comfortable in his unbelief," Hawthorne wrote of Melville in *Notebooks*; "If he were a religious man, he would be one of the most truly religious and reverential; he has a very high and noble nature, and better worth of immortality than most of us."

Moby Dick.   Melville first adopted a symbolic method in his works in the late 1840s. The method reached its peak in *Moby Dick*—a story of the whaling ship *Pequod*, the maniacal Captain Ahab, and the captain's obsessive search for a great white whale. With a crew recruited from all corners of the earth, Ahab searches across the immensity of the Pacific Ocean for the whale that will ultimately destroy him, his ship, and all the members of his crew except for Ishmael, the one survivor who lives to tell the story. The novel is both a compendium of information about whales and whaling and a work of symbolic imagery that reminds the reader that this is much more than an adventure story: Ahab's artificial leg,

oh-MOO

www   For more information about Melville and a quiz on "Bartleby the Scrivener," see bedfordstmartins .com/worldlit compact.

made from the ivory of a whale's jawbone; a crew of cannibals and Pacific Islanders who perform strange pagan rites; a harpoon tempered in the blood of the pagan harpooners; a coffin that serves as a sea chest. The overriding central symbol, Moby Dick, the name Ahab gives to the white whale, comprises the contradictory possibilities of the human search for meaning and the inevitable frustration of that quest: The white whale

p. 1386
p. 1580

embodies both good and evil, God and meaninglessness, creation and destruction.

Moby Dick was not enthusiastically received when it first appeared, and writing it may have taken more out of Melville than even he knew. After 1851 his productivity declined and he was troubled by periods of depression and despair. The best of his later works were *The Confidence Man* (1857), a satire of American attitudes and morals set on a Mississippi riverboat, *The Piazza Tales* (1856), a collection of short stories that included "Bartleby," and the posthumously published novella *Billy Budd* (1924). In the mid-1860s, troubled by the lack of acceptance for his work and in need of money, Melville largely gave up writing and took a job as a customs inspector that he held for nineteen years.

Bartleby.   Melville's first published short story, "Bartleby the Scrivener," first appeared anonymously in *Putnam's Magazine* in 1853. Written after *Moby Dick*, the story is about a writer, a scrivener, who faces a psychological "wall" and "prefers" not to write. Melville's own psychological despair upon completing *Moby Dick* and learning that his readers failed to comprehend or accept the work became the material out of which he fashioned this parable of the enigmatic scrivener and his employer. If "Bartleby" is an autobiographical narrative, it is one told not with self-pity but with a gallows humor that turns the Dead Letter Office into a literary graveyard and the Tombs into Bartleby's Westminster Abbey.[1]

Whatever its sources in Melville's own life, "Bartleby" has a symbolic richness comparable to that of *Moby Dick*. Commentators have found in it a satiric commentary on the superficiality of American life, an attack on lawyers, a story of class struggle, a critique of materialistic capitalism, an affirmation of the civil disobedience and passive resistance advocated by Thoreau and Gandhi, a biography of a saintlike Christ figure, a clinical study of a madman, and a story that prefigures the work of **Franz Kafka** and **Albert Camus** in the twentieth century. There is some truth to each of these interpretations and to others too numerous to catalog here.

Melville first published "Bartleby" anonymously, and his technique in the story seems designed to maintain his anonymity. By telling the story through the lawyer, Melville hides his own intentions. Through point of view, Melville manages to conceal himself and his attitude toward the story and to render the narrator as enigmatic as Bartleby. Clearly "Bartleby," like *Moby Dick,* is a work intended, as Keats says of his mysterious Grecian urn, to "tease us out of thought" by eluding easy classification or interpretation. In the end Bartleby remains uniquely himself, an unforgettable character whose "I would prefer not to" becomes as lodged in our consciousness as Scrooge's "Bah, humbug" in Dickens's *Christmas Carol.* Bartleby contradicts conventional expectations: His negativity makes him visible and his passivity makes him heroic.

---

[1] **Westminster Abbey:** A cathedral in London where the famous and distinguished are buried.

■ **FURTHER RESEARCH**

Biography
Hardwick, Elizabeth. *Herman Melville.* 2000.
Howard, Leon. *Herman Melville: A Biography.* 1951.
Parker, Hershel. *Herman Melville: A Biography.* 1996.
Robertson-Lorant, Laurie. *Melville: A Biography.* 1996.

Criticism
Bryant, John. *A Companion to Melville Studies.* 1986.
Delbanco, Andrew. *Melville: His World and Work.* 2005.
Fredricks, Nancy. *Melville's Art of Democracy.* 1995.
Inge, M. Thomas, ed. *Bartleby the Inscrutable: A Collection of Commentary on Herman
    Melville's Tale "Bartleby the Scrivener."* 1979.
McCall, Dan. *The Silence of Bartleby.* 1989.
Vincent, Howard P., ed. "Bartleby the Scrivener: *The Melville Annual / A Symposium.*"
    1965.

■ **PRONUNCIATION**

Acushnet: uh-KUSH-net
Gansevoort: GANS-vohrt
Omoo: oh-MOO

✎ Bartleby the Scrivener

I am a rather elderly man. The nature of my avocations, for the last thirty years, has brought me into more than ordinary contact with what would seem an interesting and somewhat singular set of men, of whom, as yet, nothing, that I know of, has ever been written — I mean, the law-copyists, or scriveners. I have known very many of them, professionally and privately, and, if I pleased, could relate divers histories, at which good-natured gentlemen might smile, and sentimental souls might weep. But I waive the biographies of all other scriveners, for a few passages in the life of Bartleby, who was a scrivener, the strangest I ever saw, or heard of. While, of other law-copyists, I might write the complete life, of Bartleby nothing of that sort can be done. I believe that no materials exist for a full and satisfactory biography of this man. It is an irreparable loss to literature. Bartleby was one of those beings of whom nothing is ascertainable, except from the original sources, and, in his case, those are very small. What my own astonished eyes saw of Bartleby, *that* is all I know of him, except, indeed, one vague report, which will appear in the sequel.

Ere introducing the scrivener, as he first appeared to me, it is fit I make some mention of myself, my *employés,* my business, my chambers, and general surroundings; because some such description is indispensable to an adequate understanding of the chief character about to be presented. Imprimis:[1] I am a man who, from his

---

[1] **Imprimis:** In the first place.

youth upwards, has been filled with a profound conviction that the easiest way of life is the best. Hence, though I belong to a profession proverbially energetic and nervous, even to turbulence, at times, yet nothing of that sort have I ever suffered to invade my peace. I am one of those unambitious lawyers who never addresses a jury, or in any way draw down public applause; but, in the cool tranquillity of a snug retreat, do a snug business among rich men's bonds, and mortgages, and title-deeds. All who know me, consider me an eminently *safe* man. The late John Jacob Astor,[2] a personage little given to poetic enthusiasm, had no hesitation in pronouncing my first grand point to be prudence; my next, method. I do not speak it in vanity, but simply record the fact, that I was not unemployed in my profession by the late John Jacob Astor; a name which, I admit, I love to repeat; for it hath a rounded and orbicular sound to it, and rings like unto bullion. I will freely add, that I was not insensible to the late John Jacob Astor's good opinion.

Some time prior to the period at which this little history begins, my avocations had been largely increased. The good old office, now extinct in the State of New York, of a Master in Chancery, had been conferred upon me. It was not a very arduous office, but very pleasantly remunerative. I seldom lose my temper; much more seldom indulge in dangerous indignation at wrongs and outrages; but I must be permitted to be rash here and declare, that I consider the sudden and violent abrogation of the office of Master in Chancery,[3] by the new Constitution, as a — — premature act; inasmuch as I had counted upon a lifelease of the profits, whereas I only received those of a few short years. But this is by the way.

My chambers were up stairs, at No. — Wall Street. At one end, they looked upon the white wall of the interior of a spacious skylight shaft, penetrating the building from top to bottom.

This view might have been considered rather tame than otherwise, deficient in what landscape painters call "life." But, if so, the view from the other end of my chambers offered, at least, a contrast, if nothing more. In that direction, my windows commanded an unobstructed view of a lofty brick wall, black by age and everlasting shade; which wall required no spyglass to bring out its lurking beauties, but, for the benefit of all near-sighted spectators, was pushed up to within ten feet of my window-panes. Owing to the great height of the surrounding buildings, and my chambers being on the second floor, the interval between this wall and mine not a little resembled a huge square cistern.

At the period just preceding the advent of Bartleby, I had two persons as copyists in my employment, and a promising lad as an office-boy. First, Turkey; second, Nippers; third, Ginger Nut. These may seem names, the like of which are not usually found in the Directory. In truth, they were nicknames, mutually conferred upon each other by my three clerks, and were deemed expressive of their respective persons or

---

[2]**John Jacob Astor** (1768–1848): Businessman who made a fortune in the fur trade and was the wealthiest landlord in New York City in 1848.

[3] **Master in Chancery:** When the new constitution abolished the position of Master of Chancery, the narrator lost a sinecure—an undemanding salaried job—that had guaranteed him a steady income.

characters. Turkey was a short, pursy Englishman, of about my own age—that is, somewhere not far from sixty. In the morning, one might say, his face was of a fine florid hue, but after twelve o'clock, meridian—his dinner hour—it blazed like a grate full of Christmas coals; and continued blazing—but, as it were, with a gradual wane—till six o'clock, P.M., or thereabouts; after which, I saw no more of the proprietor of the face, which, gaining its meridian with the sun, seemed to set with it, to rise, culminate, and decline the following day, with the like regularity and undiminished glory. There are many singular coincidences I have known in the course of my life, not the least among which was the fact, that, exactly when Turkey displayed his fullest beams from his red and radiant countenance, just then, too, at that critical moment, began the daily period when I considered his business capacities as seriously disturbed for the remainder of the twenty-four hours. Not that he was absolutely idle, or averse to business then; far from it. The difficulty was, he was apt to be altogether too energetic. There was a strange, inflamed, flurried, flighty recklessness of activity about him. He would be incautious in dipping his pen into his inkstand. All his blots upon my documents were dropped there after twelve o'clock, meridian. Indeed, not only would he be reckless, and sadly given to making blots in the afternoon, but, some days, he went further, and was rather noisy. At such times, too, his face flamed with augmented blazonry, as if cannel coal had been heaped on anthracite. He made an unpleasant racket with his chair; spilled his sand-box; in mending his pens, impatiently split them all to pieces, and threw them on the floor in a sudden passion; stood up, and leaned over his table, boxing his papers about in a most indecorous manner, very sad to behold in an elderly man like him. Nevertheless, as he was in many ways a most valuable person to me, and all the time before twelve o'clock meridian, was the quickest, steadiest creature, too, accomplishing a great deal of work in a style not easily to be matched—for these reasons, I was willing to overlook his eccentricities, though, indeed, occasionally, I remonstrated with him. I did this very gently, however, because, though the civilest, nay, the blandest and most reverential of men in the morning, yet, in the afternoon, he was disposed, upon provocation, to be slightly rash with his tongue—in fact, insolent. Now, valuing his morning services as I did, and resolved not to lose them—yet, at the same time, made uncomfortable by his inflamed way after twelve o'clock—and being a man of peace, unwilling by my admonitions to call forth unseemly retorts from him, I took upon me, one Saturday noon (he was always worse on Saturdays) to hint to him, very kindly, that, perhaps, now that he was growing old, it might be well to abridge his labors; in short, he need not come to my chambers after twelve o'clock, but, dinner over, had best go home to his lodgings, and rest himself till teatime. But no; he insisted upon his afternoon devotions. His countenance became intolerably fervid, as he oratorically assured me—gesticulating with a long ruler at the other end of the room—that if his services in the morning were useful, how indispensable, then, in the afternoon?

   "With submission, sir," said Turkey, on this occasion, "I consider myself your right-hand man. In the morning I but marshal and deploy my columns; but in the afternoon I put myself at their head, and gallantly charge the foe, thus"—and he made a violent thrust with the ruler.

   "But the blots, Turkey," intimated I.

"True; but, with submission, sir, behold these hairs! I am getting old. Surely, sir, a blot or two of a warm afternoon is not to be severely urged against gray hairs. Old age—even if it blot the page—is honorable. With submission, sir, we *both* are getting old."

This appeal to my fellow feeling was hardly to be resisted. At all events, I saw that go he would not. So, I made up my mind to let him stay, resolving, nevertheless, to see to it that, during the afternoon, he had to do with my less important papers.

Nippers, the second on my list, was a whiskered, sallow, and upon the whole, rather piratical-looking young man, of about five and twenty. I always deemed him the victim of two evil powers—ambition and indigestion. The ambition was evinced by a certain impatience of the duties of a mere copyist, an unwarrantable usurpation of strictly professional affairs, such as the original drawing up of legal documents. The indigestion seemed betokened in an occasional nervous testiness and grinning irritability, causing the teeth to audibly grind together over mistakes committed in copying; unnecessary maledictions, hissed, rather than spoken, in the heat of business; and especially by a continual discontent with the height of the table where he worked. Though of a very ingenious, mechanical turn, Nippers could never get this table to suit him. He put chips under it, blocks of various sorts, bits of pasteboard, and at last went so far as to attempt an exquisite adjustment, by final pieces of folded blotting paper. But no invention would answer. If, for the sake of easing his back, he brought the table lid at a sharp angle well up towards his chin, and wrote there like a man using the steep roof of a Dutch house for his desk, then he declared that it stopped the circulation in his arms. If now he lowered the table to his waistbands, and stooped over it in writing, then there was a sore aching in his back. In short, the truth of the matter was, Nippers knew not what he wanted. Or, if he wanted anything, it was to be rid of a scrivener's table altogether. Among the manifestations of his diseased ambition was a fondness he had for receiving visits from certain ambiguous-looking fellows in seedy coats, whom he called his clients. Indeed, I was aware that not only was he, at times, considerable of a ward politician, but he occasionally did a little business at the Justices' courts, and was not unknown on the steps of the Tombs.[4] I have good reason to believe, however, that one individual who called upon him at my chambers, and who, with a grand air, he insisted was his client, was no other than a dun, and the alleged title deed, a bill. But, with all his failings, and the annoyances he caused me, Nippers, like his compatriot Turkey, was a very useful man to me; wrote a neat, swift hand; and, when he chose, was not deficient in a gentlemanly sort of deportment. Added to this, he always dressed in a gentlemanly sort of way; and so, incidentally, reflected credit upon my chambers. Whereas, with respect to Turkey, I had much ado to keep him from being a reproach to me. His clothes were apt to look oily, and smell of eating houses. He wore his pantaloons very loose and baggy in summer. His coats were execrable; his hat not to be handled. But while the hat was a thing of indifference to me, inasmuch as his natural civility and deference, as a dependent Englishman, always led him to doff it the

---

[4] **the Tombs:** The maximum security prison in New York City.

moment he entered the room, yet his coat was another matter. Concerning his coats, I reasoned with him; but with no effect. The truth was, I suppose, that a man with so small an income could not afford to sport such a lustrous face and a lustrous coat at one and the same time. As Nippers once observed, Turkey's money went chiefly for red ink. One winter day, I presented Turkey with a highly respectable-looking coat of my own — a padded gray coat, of a most comfortable warmth, and which buttoned straight up from the knee to the neck. I thought Turkey would appreciate the favor, and abate his rashness and obstreperousness of afternoons. But no; I verily believe that buttoning himself up in so downy and blanketlike a coat had a pernicious effect upon him — upon the same principle that too much oats are bad for horses. In fact, precisely as a rash, restive horse is said to feel his oats, so Turkey felt his coat. It made him insolent. He was a man whom prosperity harmed.

Though, concerning the self-indulgent habits of Turkey, I had my own private surmises, yet, touching Nippers, I was well persuaded that, whatever might be his faults in other respects, he was, at least, a temperate young man. But, indeed, nature herself seemed to have been his vintner, and, at his birth, charged him so thoroughly with an irritable, brandylike disposition, that all subsequent potations were needless. When I consider how, amid the stillness of my chambers, Nippers would sometimes impatiently rise from his seat, and stooping over his table, spread his arms wide apart, seize the whole desk, and move it, and jerk it, with a grim, grinding motion on the floor, as if the table were a perverse voluntary agent and vexing him, I plainly perceive that, for Nippers, brandy and water were altogether superfluous.

It was fortunate for me that, owing to its peculiar cause — indigestion — the irritability and consequent nervousness of Nippers were mainly observable in the morning, while in the afternoon he was comparatively mild. So that, Turkey's paroxysms only coming on about twelve o'clock, I never had to do with their eccentricities at one time. Their fits relieved each other, like guards. When Nippers's was on, Turkey's was off; and *vice versa*. This was a good natural arrangement, under the circumstances.

Ginger Nut, the third on my list, was a lad some twelve years old. His father was a carman, ambitious of seeing his son on the bench instead of a cart, before he died. So he sent him to my office, as student at law, errand boy, cleaner, and sweeper, at the rate of one dollar a week. He had a little desk to himself; but he did not use it much. Upon inspection, the drawer exhibited a great array of the shells of various sorts of nuts. Indeed, to this quick-witted youth, the whole noble science of the law was contained in a nutshell. Not the least among the employments of Ginger Nut, as well as one which he discharged with the most alacrity, was his duty as cake and apple purveyor for Turkey and Nippers. Copying law-papers being proverbially a dry, husky sort of business, my two scriveners were fain to moisten their mouths very often with Spitzenbergs,[5] to be had at the numerous stalls nigh the Custom House and Post Office. Also, they sent Ginger Nut very frequently for that peculiar cake — small, flat, round, and very spicy — after which he had been named by them. Of a

---

[5] **Spitzenbergs:** A variety of apple.

cold morning, when business was but dull, Turkey would gobble up scores of these cakes, as if they were mere wafers—indeed, they sell them at the rate of six or eight for a penny—the scrape of his pen blending with the crunching of the crisp particles in his mouth. Rashest of all the fiery afternoon blunders and flurried rashnesses of Turkey was his once moistening a ginger cake between his lips and clapping it onto a mortgage for a seal. I came within an ace of dismissing him then. But he mollified me by making an oriental bow, and saying—

"With submission, sir, it was generous of me to find you in stationery on my own account."

Now my original business—that of a conveyancer and title hunter, and drawer-up of recondite documents of all sorts—was considerably increased by receiving the master's office. There was now great work for scriveners. Not only must I push the clerks already with me, but I must have additional help.

In answer to my advertisement, a motionless young man one morning stood upon my office threshold, the door being open, for it was summer. I can see that figure now—pallidly neat, pitiably respectable, incurably forlorn! It was Bartleby.

After a few words touching his qualifications, I engaged him, glad to have among my corps of copyists a man of so singularly sedate an aspect, which I thought might operate beneficially upon the flighty temper of Turkey, and the fiery one of Nippers.

I should have stated before that ground-glass folding doors divided my premises into two parts, one of which was occupied by my scriveners, the other by myself. According to my humor, I threw open these doors, or closed them. I resolved to assign Bartleby a corner by the folding doors, but on my side of them, so as to have this quiet man within easy call, in case any trifling thing was to be done. I placed his desk close up to a small side window in that part of the room, a window which originally had afforded a lateral view of certain grimy backyards and bricks, but which, owing to subsequent erections, commanded at present no view at all, though it gave some light. Within three feet of the panes was a wall, and the light came down from far above, between two lofty buildings, as from a very small opening in a dome. Still further to a satisfactory arrangement, I procured a high green folding screen, which might entirely isolate Bartleby from my sight, though not remove him from my voice. And thus, in a manner, privacy and society were conjoined.

At first, Bartleby did an extraordinary quantity of writing. As if long famishing for something to copy, he seemed to gorge himself on my documents. There was no pause for digestion. He ran a day and night line, copying by sunlight and by candle-light. I should have been quite delighted with his application, had he been cheerfully industrious. But he wrote on silently, palely, mechanically.

It is, of course, an indispensable part of a scrivener's business to verify the accuracy of his copy, word by word. Where there are two or more scriveners in an office, they assist each other in this examination, one reading from the copy, the other holding the original. It is a very dull, wearisome, and lethargic affair. I can readily imagine that, to some sanguine temperaments, it would be altogether intolerable. For example, I cannot credit that the mettlesome poet, Byron, would have contentedly sat down with Bartleby to examine a law document of, say five hundred pages, closely written in a crimpy hand.

Now and then, in the haste of business, it had been my habit to assist in comparing some brief document myself, calling Turkey or Nippers for this purpose. One object I had, in placing Bartleby so handy to me behind the screen, was to avail myself of his services on such trivial occasions. It was on the third day, I think, of his being with me, and before any necessity had arisen for having his own writing examined, that, being much hurried to complete a small affair I had in hand, I abruptly called to Bartleby. In my haste and natural expectancy of instant compliance, I sat with my head bent over the original on my desk, and my right hand sideways, and somewhat nervously extended with the copy, so that, immediately upon emerging from his retreat, Bartleby might snatch it and proceed to business without the least delay.

In this very attitude did I sit when I called to him, rapidly stating what it was I wanted him to do—namely, to examine a small paper with me. Imagine my surprise, nay, my consternation, when, without moving from his privacy, Bartleby, in a singularly mild, firm voice, replied, "I would prefer not to."

I sat awhile in perfect silence, rallying my stunned faculties. Immediately it occurred to me that my ears had deceived me, or Bartleby had entirely misunderstood my meaning. I repeated my request in the clearest tone I could assume; but in quite as clear a one came the previous reply, "I would prefer not to."

"Prefer not to," echoed I, rising in high excitement, and crossing the room with a stride. "What do you mean? Are you moonstruck? I want you to help me compare this sheet here—take it," and I thrust it towards him.

"I would prefer not to," said he.

I looked at him steadfastly. His face was leanly composed; his gray eye dimly calm. Not a wrinkle of agitation rippled him. Had there been the least uneasiness, anger, impatience, or impertinence in his manner; in other words, had there been anything ordinarily human about him, doubtless I should have violently dismissed him from the premises. But as it was, I should have as soon thought of turning my pale plaster-of-paris bust of Cicero[6] out of doors. I stood gazing at him awhile, as he went on with his own writing, and then reseated myself at my desk. This is very strange, thought I. What had one best do? But my business hurried me. I concluded to forget the matter for the present, reserving it for my future leisure. So calling Nippers from the other room, the paper was speedily examined.

A few days after this, Bartleby concluded four lengthy documents, being quadruplicates of a week's testimony taken before me in my High Court of Chancery. It became necessary to examine them. It was an important suit, and great accuracy was imperative. Having all things arranged, I called Turkey, Nippers, and Ginger Nut from the next room, meaning to place the four copies in the hands of my four clerks, while I should read from the original. Accordingly, Turkey, Nippers, and Ginger Nut had taken their seats in a row, each with his document in his hand, when I called to Bartleby to join this interesting group.

"Bartleby! quick, I am waiting."

---

[6]**Cicero:** Marcus Tullius Cicero (106–43 B.C.E.), Roman orator and legal philosopher; hence a figure of symbolic importance to a lawyer.

I heard a slow scrape of his chair legs on the uncarpeted floor, and soon he appeared standing at the entrance of his hermitage.

"What is wanted?" said he, mildly.

"The copies, the copies," said I, hurriedly. "We are going to examine them. There—" and I held towards him the fourth quadruplicate.

"I would prefer not to," he said, and gently disappeared behind the screen.

For a few moments I was turned into a pillar of salt,[7] standing at the head of my seated column of clerks. Recovering myself, I advanced towards the screen, and demanded the reason for such extraordinary conduct.

"*Why* do you refuse?"

"I would prefer not to."

With any other man I should have flown outright into a dreadful passion, scorned all further words, and thrust him ignominiously from my presence. But there was something about Bartleby that not only strangely disarmed me, but in a wonderful manner, touched and disconcerted me. I began to reason with him.

"These are your own copies we are about to examine. It is labor saving to you, because one examination will answer for your four papers. It is common usage. Every copyist is bound to help examine his copy. Is it not so? Will you not speak? Answer!"

"I prefer not to," he replied in a flutelike tone. It seemed to me that, while I had been addressing him, he carefully revolved every statement that I made; fully comprehended the meaning; could not gainsay the irresistible conclusion; but, at the same time, some paramount consideration prevailed with him to reply as he did.

"You are decided, then, not to comply with my request—a request made according to common usage and common sense?"

He briefly gave me to understand, that on that point my judgment was sound. Yes: His decision was irreversible.

It is not seldom the case that, when a man is browbeaten in some unprecedented and violently unreasonable way, he begins to stagger in his own plainest faith. He begins, as it were, vaguely to surmise that, wonderful as it may be, all the justice and all the reason is on the other side. Accordingly, if any disinterested persons are present, he turns to them for some reinforcement of his own faltering mind.

"Turkey," said I, "what do you think of this? Am I not right?"

"With submission, sir," said Turkey, in his blandest tone, "I think that you are."

"Nippers," said I, "what do *you* think of it?"

"I think I should kick him out of the office."

(The reader, of nice perceptions, will here perceive that, it being morning, Turkey's answer is couched in polite and tranquil terms, but Nippers's replies in ill-tempered ones. Or, to repeat a previous sentence, Nippers's ugly mood was on duty, and Turkey's off.)

"Ginger Nut," said I, willing to enlist the smallest suffrage in my behalf, "what do *you* think of it?"

---

[7] **turned . . . salt:** The punishment meted out to Lot's wife for looking back (Genesis 19:26).

"I think, sir, he's a little *loony,*" replied Ginger Nut, with a grin.

"You hear what they say," said I, turning towards the screen, "come forth and do your duty."

But he vouchsafed no reply. I pondered a moment in sore perplexity. But once more business hurried me. I determined again to postpone the consideration of this dilemma to my future leisure. With a little trouble we made out to examine the papers without Bartleby, though at every page or two Turkey deferentially dropped his opinion, that this proceeding was quite out of the common; while Nippers, twitching in his chair with a dyspeptic nervousness, ground out, between his set teeth, occasional hissing maledictions against the stubborn oaf behind the screen. And for his (Nippers's) part, this was the first and the last time he would do another man's business without pay.

Meanwhile Bartleby sat in his hermitage, oblivious to everything but his own peculiar business there.

Some days passed, the scrivener being employed upon another lengthy work. His late remarkable conduct led me to regard his ways narrowly. I observed that he never went to dinner; indeed, that he never went anywhere. As yet I had never, of my personal knowledge, known him to be outside of my office. He was a perpetual sentry in the corner. At about eleven o'clock though, in the morning, I noticed that Ginger Nut would advance toward the opening in Bartleby's screen, as if silently beckoned thither by a gesture invisible to me where I sat. The boy would then leave the office, jingling a few pence, and reappear with a handful of ginger nuts, which he delivered in the hermitage, receiving two of the cakes for his trouble.

He lives, then, on ginger nuts, thought I; never eats a dinner, properly speaking; he must be a vegetarian, then; but no; he never eats even vegetables; he eats nothing but ginger nuts. My mind then ran on in reveries concerning the probable effects upon the human constitution of living entirely on ginger nuts. Ginger nuts are so called, because they contain ginger as one of their peculiar constituents, and the final flavoring one. Now, what was ginger? A hot, spicy thing. Was Bartleby hot and spicy? Not at all. Ginger, then, had no effect upon Bartleby. Probably he preferred it should have none.

Nothing so aggravates an earnest person as a passive resistance. If the individual so resisted be of a not inhumane temper, and the resisting one perfectly harmless in his passivity, then, in the better mood of the former, he will endeavor charitably to construe to his imagination what proves impossible to be solved by his judgment. Even so, for the most part, I regarded Bartleby and his ways. Poor fellow! thought I, he means no mischief; it is plain he intends no insolence; his aspect sufficiently evinces that his eccentricities are involuntary. He is useful to me. I can get along with him. If I turn him away, the chances are he will fall in with some less indulgent employer, and then he will be rudely treated, and perhaps driven forth miserably to starve. Yes. Here I can cheaply purchase a delicious self-approval. To befriend Bartleby; to humor him in his strange willfulness, will cost me little or nothing, while I lay up in my soul what will eventually prove a sweet morsel for my conscience. But this mood was not invariable with me. The passiveness of Bartleby sometimes irritated me. I felt strangely goaded on to encounter him in new opposition—to elicit some angry spark from him answerable to my own. But, indeed, I might as well have essayed to strike fire with my knuckles against a bit of Windsor soap. But one afternoon the evil impulse in me mastered me, and the following little scene ensued:

"Bartleby," said I, "when those papers are all copied, I will compare them with you."

"I would prefer not to."

"How? Surely you do not mean to persist in that mulish vagary?"

No answer.

I threw open the folding doors nearby, and, turning upon Turkey and Nippers, exclaimed:

"Bartleby a second time says he won't examine his papers. What do you think of it, Turkey?"

It was afternoon, be it remembered. Turkey sat glowing like a brass boiler; his bald head steaming; his hands reeling among his blotted papers.

"Think of it?" roared Turkey; "I think I'll just step behind his screen, and black his eyes for him!"

So saying, Turkey rose to his feet and threw his arms into a pugilistic position. He was hurrying away to make good his promise, when I detained him, alarmed at the effect of incautiously rousing Turkey's combativeness after dinner.

"Sit down, Turkey," said I, "and hear what Nippers has to say. What do you think of it, Nippers? Would I not be justified in immediately dismissing Bartleby?"

"Excuse me, that is for you to decide, sir. I think his conduct quite unusual, and, indeed, unjust, as regards Turkey and myself. But it may only be a passing whim."

"Ah," exclaimed I, "you have strangely changed your mind, then—you speak very gently of him now."

"All beer," cried Turkey; "gentleness is effects of beer—Nippers and I dined together today. You see how gentle *I* am, sir. Shall I go and black his eyes?"

"You refer to Bartleby, I suppose. No, not today, Turkey," I replied; "pray, put up your fists."

I closed the doors, and again advanced towards Bartleby. I felt additional incentives tempting me to my face. I burned to be rebelled against again. I remembered that Bartleby never left the office.

"Bartleby," said I, "Ginger Nut is away; just step around to the Post Office, won't you?" (it was but a three minutes' walk) "and see if there is anything for me."

"I would prefer not to."

"You *will* not?"

"I *prefer* not."

I staggered to my desk, and sat there in a deep study. My blind inveteracy returned. Was there any other thing in which I could procure myself to be ignominiously repulsed by this lean, penniless wight?—my hired clerk? What added thing is there, perfectly reasonable, that he will be sure to refuse to do?

"Bartleby!"

No answer.

"Bartleby," in a louder tone.

No answer.

"Bartleby," I roared.

Like a very ghost, agreeably to the laws of magical invocation, at the third summons, he appeared at the entrance of his hermitage.

"Go to the next room, and tell Nipper to come to me."

"I prefer not to," he respectfully and slowly said, and mildly disappeared.

"Very good, Bartleby," said I, in a quiet sort of serenely-severe, self-possessed tone, intimating the unalterable purpose of some terrible retribution very close at hand. At the moment I half intended something of the kind. But upon the whole, as it was drawing towards my dinner hour, I thought it best to put on my hat and walk home for the day, suffering much from perplexity and distress of mind.

Shall I acknowledge it? The conclusion of this whole business was, that it soon became a fixed fact of my chambers, that a pale young scrivener, by the name of Bartleby, had a desk there; that he copied for me at the usual rate of four cents a folio (one hundred words); but he was permanently exempt from examining the work done by him, that duty being transferred to Turkey and Nippers, out of compliment, doubtless, to their superior acuteness; moreover, said Bartleby was never, on any account, to be dispatched on the most trivial errand of any sort; and that even if entreated to take upon him such a matter, it was generally understood that he would "prefer not to"—in other words, that he would refuse point-blank.

As days passed on, I became considerably reconciled to Bartleby. His steadiness, his freedom from all dissipation, his incessant industry (except when he chose to throw himself into a standing revery behind his screen), his great stillness, his unalterableness of demeanor under all circumstances, made him a valuable acquisition. One prime thing was this—*he was always there*—first in the morning, continually through the day, and the last at night. I had a singular confidence in his honesty. I felt my most precious papers perfectly safe in his hands. Sometimes, to be sure, I could not, for the very soul of me, avoid falling into sudden spasmodic passions with him. For it was exceeding difficult to bear in mind all the time those strange peculiarities, privileges, and unheard-of exemptions, forming the tacit stipulations on Bartleby's part under which he remained in my office. Now and then, in the eagerness of dispatching pressing business, I would inadvertently summon Bartleby, in a short, rapid tone, to put his finger, say, on the incipient tie of a bit of red tape with which I was about compressing some papers. Of course, from behind the screen the usual answer, "I prefer not to," was sure to come; and then, how could a human creature, with the common infirmities of our nature, refrain from bitterly exclaiming upon such perverseness—such unreasonableness. However, every added repulse of this sort which I received only tended to lessen the probability of my repeating the inadvertence.

Here it must be said that according to the custom of most legal gentlemen occupying chambers in densely populated law buildings, there were several keys to my door. One was kept by a woman residing in the attic, which person weekly scrubbed and daily swept and dusted my apartments. Another was kept by Turkey for convenience' sake. The third I sometimes carried in my own pocket. The fourth I knew not who had.

Now, one Sunday morning I happened to go to Trinity Church, to hear a celebrated preacher, and finding myself rather early on the ground I thought I would walk around to my chambers for a while. Luckily I had my key with me; but upon applying it to the lock, I found it resisted by something inserted from the inside. Quite surprised, I called out; when to my consternation a key was turned from within; and thrusting his lean visage at me, and holding the door ajar, the apparition of Bartleby appeared, in his shirt sleeves, and otherwise in a strangely tattered *déshabillé*, saying quietly that he was sorry, but he was deeply engaged just then, and — preferred not admitting me at present. In a brief word or two, he moreover added, that perhaps I had better walk around the block two or three times, and by that time he would probably have concluded his affairs.

Now, the utterly unsurmised appearance of Bartleby, tenanting my law chambers of a Sunday morning, with his cadaverously gentlemanly nonchalance, yet withal firm and self-possessed, had such a strange effect upon me, that incontinently I slunk away from my own door, and did as desired. But not without sundry twinges of impotent rebellion against the mild effrontery of this unaccountable scrivener. Indeed, it was his wonderful mildness chiefly, which not only disarmed me, but unmanned me, as it were. For I consider that one, for the time, is somehow unmanned when he tranquilly permits his hired clerk to dictate to him, and order him away from his own premises. Furthermore, I was full of uneasiness as to what Bartleby could possibly be doing in my office in his shirt sleeves, and in an otherwise dismantled condition of a Sunday morning. Was anything amiss going on? Nay, that was out of the question. It was not to be thought of for a moment that Bartleby was an immoral person. But what could he be doing there? — copying? Nay again, whatever might be his eccentricities, Bartleby was an eminently decorous person. He would be the last man to sit down to his desk in any state approaching to nudity. Besides, it was Sunday; and there was something about Bartleby that forbade the supposition that he would by any secular occupation violate the proprieties of the day.

Nevertheless, my mind was not pacified; and full of a restless curiosity, at last I returned to the door. Without hindrance I inserted my key, opened it, and entered. Bartleby was not to be seen. I looked round anxiously, peeped behind his screen; but it was very plain that he was gone. Upon more closely examining the place, I surmised that for an indefinite period Bartleby must have eaten, dressed, and slept in my office, and that, too, without plate, mirror, or bed. The cushioned seat of a rickety old sofa in one corner bore the faint impress of a lean, reclining form. Rolled away under his desk, I found a blanket; under the empty grate, a blacking box and brush; on a chair, a tin basin, with soap and a ragged towel; in a newspaper a few crumbs of ginger nuts and a morsel of cheese. Yes, thought I, it is evident enough that Bartleby has been making his home here, keeping bachelor's hall all by himself. Immediately then the thought came sweeping across me, what miserable friendlessness and loneliness are here revealed! His poverty is great; but his solitude, how horrible! Think of it. Of a Sunday, Wall Street is deserted as Petra;[8] and every night of every day it is an emptiness. This building, too, which of weekdays hums with industry and life, at nightfall echoes with sheer vacancy, and all through Sunday is forlorn. And here Bartleby

---

[8] **Petra:** An ancient city in Jordan discovered in 1812 after having been deserted for centuries.

makes his home; sole spectator of a solitude which he has seen all populous — a sort of innocent and transformed Marius[9] brooding among the ruins of Carthage!

For the first time in my life a feeling of overpowering stinging melancholy seized me. Before, I had never experienced aught but a not-unpleasing sadness. The bond of a common humanity now drew me irresistibly to gloom. A fraternal melancholy! For both I and Bartleby were sons of Adam. I remembered the bright silks and sparkling faces I had seen that day, in gala trim, swanlike sailing down the Mississippi of Broadway; and I contrasted them with the pallid copyist, and thought to myself, Ah, happiness courts the light, so we deem the world is gay; but misery hides aloof, so we deem that misery there is none. These sad fancyings — chimeras, doubtless, of a sick and silly brain — led on to other and more special thoughts, concerning the eccentricities of Bartleby. Presentiments of strange discoveries hovered round me. The scrivener's pale form appeared to me laid out, among uncaring strangers, in its shivering winding sheet.

Suddenly I was attracted by Bartleby's closed desk, the key in open sight left in the lock.

I mean no mischief, seek the gratification of no heartless curiosity, thought I; besides, the desk is mine, and it contents, too, so I will make bold to look within. Everything was methodically arranged, the papers smoothly placed. The pigeon holes were deep, and removing the files of documents, I groped into their recesses. Presently I felt something there, and dragged it out. It was an old bandanna handkerchief, heavy and knotted. I opened it, and saw it was a savings bank.

I now recalled all the quiet mysteries which I had noted in the man. I remembered that he never spoke but to answer; that, though at intervals he had considerable time to himself, yet I had never seen him reading — no, not even a newspaper; that for long periods he would stand looking out, at his pale window behind the screen, upon the dead brick wall; I was quite sure he never visited any refectory or eating house; while his pale face clearly indicated that he never drank beer like Turkey, or tea and coffee even, like other men; that he never went anywhere in particular that I could learn; never went out for a walk, unless, indeed, that was the case at present; that he had declined telling who he was, or whence he came, or whether he had any relatives in the world; that though so thin and pale, he never complained of ill health. And more than all, I remembered a certain unconscious air of pallid — how shall I call it? — of pallid haughtiness, say, or rather an austere reserve about him, which had positively awed me into my tame compliance with his eccentricities, when I had feared to ask him to do the slightest incidental thing for me, even though I might know, from his long-continued motionlessness, that behind his screen he must be standing in one of those dead-wall reveries of his.

Recovering all these things, and coupling them with the recently discovered fact that he made my office his constant abiding place and home, and not forgetful of his morbid moodiness; revolving all these things, a prudential feeling began to steal over

---

[9] **Marius:** Caius Marius (157–86 B.C.E.), a Plebian who fought in Africa and became a general in the Roman army; he later quarreled with the rulers in Rome and was exiled.

me. My first emotions had been those of pure melancholy and sincerest pity; but just in proportion as the forlornness of Bartleby grew and grew to my imagination, did that same melancholy merge into fear, that pity into repulsion. So true it is, and so terrible, too, that up to a certain point the thought or sight of misery enlists our best affections; but, in certain special cases, beyond that point it does not. They err who would assert that invariably this is owing to the inherent selfishness of the human heart. It rather proceeds from a certain hopelessness of remedying excessive and organic ill. To a sensitive being, pity is not seldom pain. And when at last it is perceived that such pity cannot lead to effectual succor, common sense bids the soul be rid of it. What I saw that morning persuaded me that the scrivener was the victim of innate and incurable disorder. I might give alms to his body; but his body did not pain him; it was his soul that suffered, and his soul I could not reach.

I did not accomplish the purpose of going to Trinity Church that morning. Somehow, the things I had seen disqualified me for the time from churchgoing. I walked homeward, thinking what I would do with Bartleby. Finally, I resolved upon this—I would put certain calm questions to him the next morning, touching his history, etc., and if he declined to answer them openly and unreservedly (and I supposed he would prefer not), then to give him a twenty dollar bill over and above whatever I might owe him, and tell him his services were no longer required; but that if in any other way I could assist him, I would be happy to do so, especially if he desired to return to his native place, wherever that might be, I would willingly help to defray the expenses. Moreover, if, after reaching home, he found himself at any time in want of aid, a letter from him would be sure of a reply.

The next morning came.

"Bartleby," said I, gently calling to him behind his screen.

No reply.

"Bartleby," said I, in a still gentler tone, "come here; I am not going to ask you to do anything you would prefer not to do—I simply wish to speak to you."

Upon this he noiselessly slid into view.

"Will you tell me, Bartleby, where you were born?"

"I would prefer not to."

"Will you tell me *anything* about yourself?"

"I would prefer not to."

"But what reasonable objection can you have to speak to me? I feel friendly towards you."

He did not look at me while I spoke, but kept his glance fixed upon my bust of Cicero, which, as I then sat, was directly behind me, some six inches above my head.

"What is your answer, Bartleby," said I, after waiting a considerable time for a reply, during which his countenance remained immovable, only there was the faintest conceivable tremor of the white attenuated mouth.

"At present I prefer to give no answer," he said, and retired into his hermitage.

It was rather weak in me I confess, but his manner, on this occasion, nettled me. Not only did there seem to lurk in it a certain calm disdain, but his perverseness seemed ungrateful, considering the undeniable good usage and indulgence he had received from me.

Again I sat ruminating what I should do. Mortified as I was at his behavior, and resolved as I had been to dismiss him when I entered my office, nevertheless I strangely felt something superstitious knocking at my heart, and forbidding me to carry out my purpose, and denouncing me for a villain if I dared to breathe one bitter word against this forlornest of mankind. At last, familiarly drawing my chair behind his screen, I sat down and said: "Bartleby, never mind, then, about revealing your history; but let me entreat you, as a friend, to comply as far as may be with the usages of this office. Say now, you will help to examine papers tomorrow or next day: In short, say now, that in a day or two you will begin to be a little reasonable:—Say so, Bartleby."

"At present I would prefer not to be a little reasonable," was his mildly cadaverous reply.

Just then the folding doors opened, and Nippers approached. He seemed suffering from an unusually bad night's rest, induced by severer indigestion than common. He overheard those final words of Bartleby.

"*Prefer not,* eh?" gritted Nippers—"I'd *prefer* him, if I were you, sir," addressing me—"I'd *prefer* him; I'd give him preferences, the stubborn mule! What is it, sir, pray, that he *prefers* not to do now?"

Bartleby moved not a limb.

"Mr. Nippers," said I, "I'd prefer that you would withdraw for the present."

Somehow, of late, I had got into the way of involuntarily using this word "prefer" upon all sorts of not exactly suitable occasions. And I trembled to think that my contact with the scrivener had already and seriously affected me in a mental way. And what further and deeper aberration might it not yet produce? This apprehension had not been without efficacy in determining me to summary measures.

As Nippers, looking very sour and sulky, was departing, Turkey blandly and deferentially approached.

"With submission, sir," said he, "yesterday I was thinking about Bartleby here, and I think that if he would but prefer to take a quart of good ale every day, it would do much towards mending him, and enabling him to assist in examining his papers."

"So you have got the word, too," said I, slightly excited.

"With submission, what word, sir," asked Turkey, respectfully crowding himself into the contracted space behind the screen, and by so doing, making me jostle the scrivener. "What word, sir?"

"I would prefer to be left alone here," said Bartleby, as if offended at being mobbed in his privacy.

"*That's* the word, Turkey," said I—"*that's* it."

"Oh, *prefer?* oh yes—queer word. I never use it myself. But, sir, as I was saying, if he would but prefer—"

"Turkey," interrupted I, "you will please withdraw."

"Oh certainly, sir, if you prefer that I should."

As he opened the folding door to retire, Nippers at his desk caught a glimpse of me, and asked whether I would prefer to have a certain paper copied on blue paper or white. He did not in the least roguishly accent the word prefer. It was plain that it involuntarily rolled from his tongue. I thought to myself, surely I must get rid of a demented man, who already has in some degree turned the tongues, if not the heads of myself and clerks. But I thought it prudent not to break the dismission at once.

The next day I noticed that Bartleby did nothing but stand at his window in his dead-wall revery. Upon asking him why he did not write, he said that he had decided upon doing no more writing.

"Why, how now? what next?" exclaimed I, "do no more writing?"

"No more."

"And what is the reason?"

"Do you not see the reason for yourself," he indifferently replied.

I looked steadfastly at him, and perceived that his eyes looked dull and glazed. Instantly it occurred to me, that his unexampled diligence in copying by his dim window for the first few weeks of his stay with me might have temporarily impaired his vision.

I was touched. I said something in condolence with him. I hinted that of course he did wisely in abstaining from writing for a while; and urged him to embrace that opportunity of taking wholesome exercise in the open air. This, however, he did not do. A few days after this, my other clerks being absent, and being in a great hurry to dispatch certain letters by the mail, I thought that, having nothing else earthly to do, Bartleby would surely be less inflexible than usual, and carry these letters to the post office. But he blankly declined. So, much to my inconvenience, I went myself.

Still added days went by. Whether Bartleby's eyes improved or not, I could not say. To all appearance I thought they did. But when I asked him if they did, he vouchsafed no answer. At all events, he would do no copying. At last, in reply to my urgings, he informed me that he had permanently given up copying.

"What!" exclaimed I; "suppose your eyes should get entirely well—better than ever before—would you not copy then?"

"I have given up copying," he answered, and slid aside.

He remained as ever, a fixture in my chamber. Nay—if that were possible—he became still more of a fixture than before. What was to be done? He would do nothing in the office; why should he stay there? In plain fact, he had now become a millstone to me, not only useless as a necklace, but afflictive to bear. Yet I was sorry for him. I speak less than truth when I say that, on his own account, he occasioned me uneasiness. If he would but have named a single relative or friend, I would instantly have written, and urged their taking the poor fellow away to some convenient retreat. But he seemed alone, absolutely alone in the universe. A bit of wreck in the mid-Atlantic. At length, necessities connected with my business tyrannized over all other considerations. Decently as I could, I told Bartleby that in six days' time he must unconditionally leave the office. I warned him to take measures, in the interval, for procuring some other abode. I offered to assist him in his endeavor, if he himself would but take the first step towards a removal. "And when you finally quit me, Bartleby," added I, "I shall see that you go not away entirely unprovided. Six days from this hour, remember."

At the expiration of that period, I peeped behind the screen, and lo! Bartleby was there.

I buttoned up my coat, balanced myself; advanced slowly towards him, touched his shoulder, and said, "The time has come; you must quit this place; I am sorry for you; here is money; but you must go."

"I would prefer not," he replied, with his back still towards me.

"You *must*."

He remained silent.

Now I had an unbounded confidence in this man's common honesty. He had frequently restored to me sixpences and shillings carelessly dropped upon the floor, for I am apt to be very reckless in such shirt-button affairs. The proceeding, then, which followed will not be deemed extraordinary.

"Bartleby," said I, "I owe you twelve dollars on account; here are thirty-two; the odd twenty are yours—Will you take it?" and I handed the bills towards him.

But he made no motion.

"I will leave them here, then," putting them under a weight on the table. Then taking my hat and cane and going to the door, I tranquilly turned and added— "After you have removed your things from these offices, Bartleby, you will of course lock the door—since everyone is now gone for the day but you—and if you please, slip your key underneath the mat, so that I may have it in the morning. I shall not see you again; so good-bye to you. If, hereafter, in your new place of abode, I can be of any service to you, do not fail to advise me by letter. Good-bye, Bartleby, and fare you well."

But he answered not a word; like the last column of some ruined temple, he remained standing mute and solitary in the middle of the otherwise deserted room.

As I walked home in a pensive mood, my vanity got the better of my pity. I could not but highly plume myself on my masterly management in getting rid of Bartleby. Masterly I call it, and such it must appear to any dispassionate thinker. The beauty of my procedure seemed to consist in its perfect quietness. There was no vulgar bullying, no bravado of any sort, no choleric hectoring, and striding to and fro across the apartment, jerking out vehement commands for Bartleby to bundle himself off with his beggarly traps. Nothing of the kind. Without loudly bidding Bartleby depart— as an inferior genius might have done—I *assumed* the ground that depart he must; and upon that assumption built all I had to say. The more I thought over my procedure, the more I was charmed with it. Nevertheless, next morning, upon awakening, I had my doubts—I had somehow slept off the fumes of vanity. One of the coolest and wisest hours a man has, is just after he awakes in the morning. My procedure seemed as sagacious as ever—but only in theory. How it would prove in practice— there was the rub. It was truly a beautiful thought to have assumed Bartleby's departure; but, after all, that assumption was simply my own, and none of Bartleby's. The great point was, not whether I had assumed that he would quit me, but whether he would prefer so to do. He was more a man of preferences than assumptions.

After breakfast, I walked downtown, arguing the probabilities *pro* and *con*. One moment I thought it would prove a miserable failure, and Bartleby would be found all alive at my office as usual; the next moment it seemed certain that I should find his chair empty. And so I kept veering about. At the corner of Broadway and Canal Street, I saw quite an excited group of people standing in earnest conversation.

"I'll take odds he doesn't," said a voice as I passed.

"Doesn't go?—done!" said I; "put up your money."

I was instinctively putting my hand in my pocket to produce my own, when I remembered that this was an election day. The words I had overheard bore no reference to Bartleby, but to the success or nonsuccess of some candidate for the mayoralty. In my intent frame of mind, I had, as it were, imagined that all Broadway shared in my excitement, and were debating the same question with me. I passed on, very thankful that the uproar of the street screened my momentary absentmindedness.

As I had intended, I was earlier than usual at my office door. I stood listening for a moment. All was still. He must be gone. I tried the knob. The door was locked. Yes, my procedure had worked to a charm; he indeed must be vanished. Yet a certain melancholy mixed with this; I was almost sorry for my brilliant success. I was fumbling under the doormat for the key, which Bartleby was to have left there for me, when accidentally my knee knocked against a panel, producing a summoning sound, and in response a voice came to me from within—"Not yet; I am occupied."

It was Bartleby.

I was thunderstruck. For an instant I stood like the man who, pipe in mouth, was killed one cloudless afternoon long ago in Virginia, by summer lightning; at his own warm open window he was killed, and remained leaning out there upon the dreamy afternoon, till some one touched him, when he fell.

"Not gone!" I murmured at last. But again obeying that wondrous ascendancy which the inscrutable scrivener had over me, and from which ascendancy, for all my chafing, I could not completely escape, I slowly went downstairs and out into the street, and while walking round the block, considered what I should next do in this unheard-of perplexity. Turn the man out by an actual thrusting I could not; to drive him away by calling him hard names would not do; calling in the police was an unpleasant idea; and yet, permit him to enjoy his cadaverous triumph over me— this, too, I could not think of. What was to be done? or, if nothing could be done, was there anything further that I could *assume* in the matter? Yes, as before I had prospectively assumed that Bartleby would depart, so now I might retrospectively assume that departed he was. In the legitimate carrying out of this assumption, I might enter my office in a great hurry, and pretending not to see Bartleby at all, walk straight against him as if he were air. Such a proceeding would in a singular degree have the appearance of a home-thrust. It was hardly possible that Bartleby could withstand such an application of the doctrine of assumptions. But upon second thoughts the success of the plan seemed rather dubious. I resolved to argue the matter over with him again.

"Bartleby," said I, entering the office, with a quietly severe expression, "I am seriously displeased. I am pained, Bartleby, I had thought better of you. I had imagined you of such a gentlemanly organization, that in any delicate dilemma a slight hint would suffice—in short, an assumption. But it appears I am deceived. Why," I added, unaffectedly starting, "you have not even touched that money yet," pointing to it, just where I had left it the evening previous.

He answered nothing.

"Will you, or will you not, quit me?" I now demanded in a sudden passion, advancing close to him.

"I would prefer *not* to quit you," he replied, gently emphasizing the *not*.

"What earthly right have you to stay here? Do you pay any rent? Do you pay my taxes? Or is this property yours?"

He answered nothing.

"Are you ready to go on and write now? Are your eyes recovered? Could you copy a small paper for me this morning? or help examine a few lines? or step round to the post office? In a word, will you do anything at all, to give a coloring to your refusal to depart the premises?"

He silently retired into his hermitage.

I was now in such a state of nervous resentment that I thought it but prudent to check myself at present from further demonstration. Bartleby and I were alone. I remembered the tragedy of the unfortunate Adams and the still more unfortunate Colt[10] in the solitary office of the latter; and how poor Colt, being dreadfully incensed by Adams, and imprudently permitting himself to get wildly excited, was at unawares hurried into his fatal act—an act which certainly no man could possibly deplore more than the actor himself. Often it had occurred to me in my ponderings upon the subject, that had that altercation taken place in the public street, or at a private residence, it would not have terminated as it did. It was the circumstance of being alone in a solitary office, upstairs, of a building entirely unhallowed by humanizing domestic associations—an uncarpeted office, doubtless, of a dusty, haggard sort of appearance—this it must have been, which greatly helped to enhance the irritable desperation of the hapless Colt.

But when this old Adam of resentment rose in me and tempted me concerning Bartleby, I grappled him and threw him. How? Why, simply by recalling the divine injunction: "A new commandment give I unto you, that ye love one another."[11] Yes, this it was that saved me. Aside from higher considerations, charity often operates as a vastly wise and prudent principle—a great safeguard to its possessor. Men have committed murder for jealousy's sake, and anger's sake, and hatred's sake, and selfishness' sake, and spiritual pride's sake; but no man, that ever I heard of, ever committed a diabolical murder for sweet charity's sake. Mere self-interest, then, if no better motive can be enlisted, should, especially with high-tempered men, prompt all beings to charity and philanthropy. At any rate, upon the occasion in question, I strove to drown my exasperated feelings towards the scrivener by benevolently construing his conduct. Poor fellow, poor fellow! thought I, he don't mean anything; and besides, he has seen hard times, and ought to be indulged.

---

[10] **tragedy . . . Colt:** In a notorious crime of 1842 John C. Colt, who was writing a textbook on bookkeeping, murdered his printer, Samuel Adams, when he became enraged about an overcharge in the printer's bill. After killing Adams with an axe in his office, Colt put the body in a trunk and shipped it to New Orleans. It was discovered en route and Colt was arrested and condemned to be hanged. Colt committed suicide a half hour before his scheduled execution.

[11] **"A new . . . one another":** Jesus' injunction to his disciples (John 13:34).

I endeavored, also, immediately to occupy myself, and at the same time to comfort my despondency. I tried to fancy, that in the course of the morning, at such time as might prove agreeable to him, Bartleby, of his own free accord, would emerge from his hermitage and take up some decided line of march in the direction of the door. But no. Half-past twelve o'clock came; Turkey began to glow in the face, overturn his inkstand, and become generally obstreperous; Nippers abated down into quietude and courtesy; Ginger Nut munched his noon apple; and Bartleby remained standing at his window in one of his profoundest dead-wall reveries. Will it be credited? Ought I to acknowledge it? That afternoon I left the office without saying one further word to him.

Some days now passed, during which, at leisure intervals, I looked a little into "Edwards on the Will" and "Priestley on Necessity."[12] Under the circumstances, those books induced a salutary feeling. Gradually I slid into the persuasion that these troubles of mine, touching the scrivener, had been all predestined from eternity, and Bartleby was billeted upon me for some mysterious purpose of an all-wise Providence, which it was not for a mere mortal like me to fathom. Yes, Bartleby, stay there behind your screen, thought I; I shall persecute you no more; you are harmless and noiseless as any of these old chairs; in short, I never feel so private as when I know you are here. At last I see it, I feel it; I penetrate to the predestinated purpose of my life. I am content. Others may have loftier parts to enact; but my mission in this world, Bartleby, is to furnish you with office-room for such period as you may see fit to remain.

I believe that this wise and blessed frame of mind would have continued with me, had it not been for the unsolicited and uncharitable remarks obtruded upon me by my professional friends who visited the rooms. But thus it often is, that the constant friction of illiberal minds wears out at last the best resolves of the more generous. Though to be sure, when I reflected upon it, it was not strange that people entering my office should be struck by the peculiar aspect of the unaccountable Bartleby, and so be tempted to throw out some sinister observations concerning him. Sometimes an attorney, having business with me, and calling at my office, and finding no one but the scrivener there, would undertake to obtain some sort of precise information from him touching my whereabouts; but without heeding his idle talk, Bartleby would remain standing immovable in the middle of the room. So after contemplating him in that position for a time, the attorney would depart, no wiser than he came.

Also, when a reference was going on, and the room full of lawyers and witnesses, and business driving fast, some deeply occupied legal gentleman present, seeing Bartleby wholly unemployed, would request him to run round to his (the legal gentleman's) office and fetch some papers for him. Thereupon, Bartleby would tranquilly decline, and yet remain idle as before. Then the lawyer would give a great stare, and turn to me. And what could I say? At last I was made aware that all through the

---

[12] **"Edwards . . . Necessity":** Jonathan Edwards (1703–1758) was a Puritan cleric whose *Freedom of the Will* (1754) reconciled human will with predestination; Joseph Priestley (1733–1804) was an English scientist and Unitarian theologian whose doctrine of necessity was based on natural determinism.

circle of my professional acquaintance, a whisper of wonder was running round, having reference to the strange creature I kept at my office. This worried me very much. And as the idea came upon me of his possibly turning out a long-lived man, and keep occupying my chambers, and denying my authority; and perplexing my visitors; and scandalizing my professional reputation; and casting a general gloom over the premises; keeping soul and body together to the last upon his savings (for doubtless he spent but half a dime a day), and in the end perhaps outlive me, and claim possession of my office by right of his perpetual occupancy: As all these dark anticipations crowded upon me more and more, and my friends continually intruded their relentless remarks upon the apparition in my room; a great change was wrought in me. I resolved to gather all my faculties together, and forever rid me of this intolerable incubus.

Ere revolving any complicated project, however, adapted to this end, I first simply suggested to Bartleby the propriety of his permanent departure. In a calm and serious tone, I commended the idea to his careful and mature consideration. But, having taken three days to meditate upon it, he apprised me, that his original determination remained the same; in short, that he still preferred to abide with me.

What shall I do? I now said to myself, buttoning up my coat to the last button. What shall I do? what ought I to do? what does conscience say I *should* do with this man, or, rather, ghost? Rid myself of him, I must; go, he shall. But how? You will not thrust him, the poor, pale, passive mortal—you will not thrust such a helpless creature out of your door? you will not dishonor yourself by such cruelty? No, I will not, I cannot do that. Rather would I let him live and die here, and then mason up his remains in the wall. What, then, will you do? For all your coaxing, he will not budge. Bribes he leaves under your own paperweight on your table; in short, it is quite plain that he prefers to cling to you.

Then something severe, something unusual must be done. What! surely you will not have him collared by a constable, and commit his innocent pallor to the common jail? And upon what ground could you procure such a thing to be done?—a vagrant, is he? What! he a vagrant, a wanderer, who refuses to budge? It is because he will *not* be a vagrant, then, that you seek to count him *as* a vagrant. That is too absurd. No visible means of support: there I have him. Wrong again: for indubitably he *does* support himself, and that is the only unanswerable proof that any man can show of his possessing the means so to do. No more, then. Since he will not quit me, I must quit him. I will change my offices; I will move elsewhere, and give him fair notice, that if I find him on my new premises I will then proceed against him as a common trespasser.

Acting accordingly, next day I thus addressed him: "I find these chambers too far from the City Hall; the air is unwholesome. In a word, I propose to remove my offices next week, and shall no longer require your services. I tell you this now, in order that you may seek another place."

He made no reply; and nothing more was said.

On the appointed day I engaged carts and men, proceeded to my chambers, and, having but little furniture, everything was removed in a few hours. Throughout, the scrivener remained standing behind the screen, which I directed to be removed the last thing. It was withdrawn; and, being folded up like a huge folio, left him the motionless occupant of a naked room. I stood in the entry watching him a moment, while something from within me upbraided me.

I reentered, with my hand in my pocket—and—and my heart in my mouth.

"Good-bye, Bartleby; I am going—good-bye, and God some way bless you; and take that," slipping something in his hand. But it dropped upon the floor, and then—strange to say—I tore myself from him whom I had so longed to be rid of.

Established in my new quarters, for a day or two I kept the door locked, and started at every footfall in the passages. When I returned to my rooms, after any little absence, I would pause at the threshold for an instant, and attentively listen, ere applying my key. But these fears were needless. Bartleby never came nigh me.

I thought all was going well, when a perturbed-looking stranger visited me, inquiring whether I was the person who had recently occupied rooms at No. — Wall Street.

Full of forebodings, I replied that I was.

"Then, sir," said the stranger, who proved a lawyer, "you are responsible for the man you left there. He refuses to do any copying; he refuses to do anything; he says he prefers not to; and he refuses to quit the premises."

"I am very sorry, sir," said I, with assumed tranquillity, but an inward tremor, "but, really, the man you allude to is nothing to me—he is no relation or apprentice of mine, that you should hold me responsible for him."

"In mercy's name, who is he?"

"I certainly cannot inform you. I know nothing about him. Formerly I employed him as a copyist; but he has done nothing for me now for some time past."

"I shall settle him, then—good morning, sir."

Several days passed, and I heard nothing more and, though I often felt a charitable prompting to call at the place and see poor Bartleby, yet a certain squeamishness, of I know not what, withheld me.

All is over with him, by this time, thought I, at last, when, through another week, no further intelligence reached me. But, coming to my room the day after, I found several persons waiting at my door in a high state of nervous excitement.

"That's the man—here he comes," cried the foremost one, whom I recognized as the lawyer who had previously called upon me alone.

"You must take him away, sir, at once," cried a portly person among them, advancing upon me, and whom I knew to be the landlord of No. — Wall Street. "These gentlemen, my tenants, cannot stand it any longer; Mr. B——," pointing to the lawyer, "has turned him out of his room, and he now persists in haunting the building generally, sitting upon the banisters of the stairs by day, and sleeping in the entry by night. Everybody is concerned; clients are leaving the offices; some fears are entertained of a mob; something you must do, and that without delay."

Aghast at this torrent, I fell back before it, and would fain have locked myself in my new quarters. In vain I persisted that Bartleby was nothing to me—no more than to anyone else. In vain—I was the last person known to have anything to do with him, and they held me to the terrible account. Fearful, then, of being exposed in the papers (as one person present obscurely threatened), I considered the matter, and, at length, said, that if the lawyer would give me a confidential interview with the scrivener, in his (the lawyer's) own room, I would, that afternoon, strive my best to rid them of the nuisance they complained of.

Going upstairs to my old haunt, there was Bartleby silently sitting upon the banister at the landing.

"What are you doing here, Bartleby?" said I.

"Sitting upon the banister," he mildly replied.

I motioned him into the lawyer's room, who then left us.

"Bartleby," said I, "are you aware that you are the cause of great tribulation to me, by persisting in occupying the entry after being dismissed from the office?"

No answer.

"Now one of two things must take place. Either you must do something, or something must be done to you. Now what sort of business would you like to engage in? Would you like to reengage in copying for someone?"

"No; I would prefer not to make any change."

"Would you like a clerkship in a dry-goods store?"

"There is too much confinement about that. No, I would not like a clerkship; but I am not particular."

"Too much confinement," I cried, "why, you keep yourself confined all the time!"

"I would prefer not to take a clerkship," he rejoined, as if to settle that little item at once.

"How would a bartender's business suit you? There is no trying of the eyesight in that."

"I would not like it at all; though as I said before, I am not particular."

His unwonted wordiness inspirited me. I returned to the charge.

"Well, then, would you like to travel through the country collecting bills for the merchants? That would improve your health."

"No, I would prefer to be doing something else."

"How, then, would going as a companion to Europe, to entertain some young gentleman with your conversation — how would that suit you?"

"Not at all. It does not strike me that there is anything definite about that. I like to be stationary. But I am not particular."

"Stationary you shall be, then," I cried, now losing all patience, and, for the first time in all my exasperating connection with him, fairly flying into a passion. "If you do not go away from these premises before night, I shall feel bound — indeed, I *am* bound — to — to — to quit the premises myself!" I rather absurdly concluded, knowing not with what possible threat to try to frighten his immobility into compliance. Despairing of all further efforts, I was precipitately leaving him, when a final thought occurred to me — one which had not been wholly unindulged before.

"Bartleby," said I, in the kindest tone I could assume under such exciting circumstances, "will you go home with me now — not to my office, but my dwelling — and remain there till we can conclude upon some convenient arrangement for you at our leisure? Come, let us start now, right away."

"No: at present I would prefer not to make any change at all."

I answered nothing; but, effectually dodging everyone by the suddenness and rapidity of my flight, rushed from the building, ran up Wall Street towards Broadway, and, jumping into the first omnibus, was soon removed from pursuit. As soon as tranquillity returned, I distinctly perceived that I had now done all that I possibly could, both in respect to the demands of the landlord and his tenants, and with regard to my own desire and sense of duty, to benefit Bartleby, and shield him from rude persecution. I now strove to be entirely carefree and quiescent; and my conscience justified me in the attempt; though, indeed, it was not so successful as I could have wished. So fearful was I of being again hunted out by the incensed landlord and his exasperated tenants, that, surrendering my business to Nippers, for a few days, I drove about the upper part of the town and through the suburbs, in my rockaway;[13] crossed over to Jersey City and Hoboken, and paid fugitive visits to Manhattanville and Astoria. In fact, I almost lived in my rockaway for the time.

When again I entered my office, lo, a note from the landlord lay upon the desk. I opened it with trembling hands. It informed me that the writer had sent to the police, and had Bartleby removed to the Tombs as a vagrant. Moreover, since I knew more about him than anyone else, he wished me to appear at that place, and make a suitable statement of the facts. These tidings had a conflicting effect upon me. At first I was indignant; but, at last, almost approved. The landlord's energetic, summary disposition, had led him to adopt a procedure which I do not think I would have decided upon myself; and yet, as a last resort, under such peculiar circumstances, it seemed the only plan.

As I afterwards learned, the poor scrivener, when told that he must be conducted to the Tombs, offered not the slightest obstacle, but, in his pale, unmoving way, silently acquiesced.

Some of the compassionate and curious bystanders joined the party; and headed by one of the constables arm in arm with Bartleby, the silent procession filed its way through all the noise, and heat, and joy of the roaring thoroughfares at noon.

The same day I received the note, I went to the Tombs, or, to speak more properly, the Halls of Justice. Seeking the right officer, I stated the purpose of my call, and was informed that the individual I described was, indeed, within. I then assured the functionary that Bartleby was a perfectly honest man, and greatly to be compassionated, however unaccountably eccentric. I narrated all I knew, and closed by suggesting the idea of letting him remain in as indulgent confinement as possible, till something less harsh might be done—though, indeed, I hardly knew what. At all events, if nothing else could be decided upon, the almshouse must receive him. I then begged to have an interview.

Being under no disgraceful charge, and quite serene and harmless in all his ways, they had permitted him freely to wander about the prison, and, especially, in the inclosed grass-platted yards thereof. And so I found him there, standing all alone in the quietest of the yards, his face towards a high wall, while all around, from the narrow slits of the jail windows, I thought I saw peering out upon him the eyes of murderers and thieves.

"Bartleby!"

---

[13] **rockaway:** A four-wheeled carriage.

"I know you," he said, without looking round — "and I want nothing to say to you."

"It was not I that brought you here, Bartleby," said I, keenly pained at his implied suspicion. "And to you, this should not be so vile a place. Nothing reproachful attaches to you by being here. And see, it is not so sad a place as one might think. Look, there is the sky, and here is the grass."

"I know where I am," he replied, but would say nothing more, and so I left him.

As I entered the corridor again, a broad meatlike man, in an apron, accosted me, and, jerking his thumb over his shoulder, said — "Is that your friend?"

"Yes."

"Does he want to starve? If he does, let him live on the prison fare, that's all."

"Who are you?" asked I, not knowing what to make of such an unofficially speaking person in such a place.

"I am the grub-man. Such gentlemen as have friends here, hire me to provide them with something good to eat."

"Is this so?" said I, turning to the turnkey.

He said it was.

"Well, then," said I, slipping some silver into the grub-man's hands (for so they called him), "I want you to give particular attention to my friend there; let him have the best dinner you can get. And you must be as polite to him as possible."

"Introduce me, will you?" said the grub-man, looking at me with an expression which seemed to say he was all impatience for an opportunity to give a specimen of his breeding.

Thinking it would prove of benefit to the scrivener, I acquiesced; and, asking the grub-man his name, went up with him to Bartleby.

"Bartleby, this is a friend; you will find him very useful to you."

"Your sarvant, sir, your sarvant," said the grub-man, making a low salutation behind his apron. "Hope you find it pleasant here, sir; nice grounds — cool apartments — hope you'll stay with us some time — try to make it agreeable. What will you have for dinner today?"

"I prefer not to dine today," said Bartleby, turning away. "It would disagree with me; I am unused to dinners." So saying, he slowly moved to the other side of the inclosure, and took up a position fronting the dead wall.

"How's this?" said the grub-man, addressing me with a stare of astonishment. "He's odd, ain't he?"

"I think he is a little deranged," said I, sadly.

"Deranged? deranged, is it? Well, now, upon my word, I thought that friend of yourn was a gentleman forger; they are always pale and genteel-like, them forgers. I can't help pity 'em — can't help it, sir. Did you know Monroe Edwards?" he added, touchingly, and paused. Then, laying his hand piteously on my shoulder, sighed, "He died of consumption at Sing-Sing.[14] So you weren't acquainted with Monroe?"

---

[14] **Sing-Sing:** Site of the New York State penitentiary.

"No, I was never socially acquainted with any forgers. But I cannot stop longer. Look to my friend yonder. You will not lose by it. I will see you again."

Some few days after this, I again obtained admission to the Tombs, and went through the corridors in quest of Bartleby; but without finding him.

"I saw him coming from his cell not long ago," said a turnkey, "maybe he's gone to loiter in the yards."

So I went in that direction.

"Are you looking for the silent man?" said another turnkey, passing me. "Yonder he lies — sleeping in the yard there. 'Tis not twenty minutes since I saw him lie down."

The yard was entirely quiet. It was not accessible to the common prisoners. The surrounding walls, of amazing thickness, kept off all sounds behind them. The Egyptian character of the masonry weighed upon me with its gloom. But a soft imprisoned turf grew underfoot. The heart of the eternal pyramids, it seemed, wherein, by some strange magic, through the clefts, grass seed, dropped by birds, had sprung.

Strangely huddled at the base of the wall, his knees drawn up, and lying on his side, his head touching the cold stones, I saw the wasted Bartleby. But nothing stirred. I paused; then went close up to him; stooped over, and saw that his dim eyes were open; otherwise he seemed profoundly sleeping. Something prompted me to touch him. I felt his hand, when a tingling shiver ran up my arm and down my spine to my feet.

The round face of the grub-man peered upon me now. "His dinner is ready. Won't he dine today, either? Or does he live without dining?"

"Lives without dining," said I, and closed the eyes.

"Eh! — He's asleep, ain't he?"

"With kings and counselors," murmured I.

There would seem little need for proceeding further in this history. Imagination will readily supply the meager recital of poor Bartleby's interment. But, ere parting with the reader, let me say, that if this little narrative has sufficiently interested him, to awaken curiosity as to who Bartleby was, and what manner of life he led prior to the present narrator's making his acquaintance, I can only reply, that in such curiosity I fully share, but am wholly unable to gratify it. Yet here I hardly know whether I should divulge one little item of rumor, which came to my ear a few months after the scrivener's decease. Upon what basis it rested, I could never ascertain; and hence, how true it is I cannot now tell. But, inasmuch as this vague report has not been without a certain suggestive interest to me, however sad, it may prove the same with some others; and so I will briefly mention it. The report was this: that Bartleby had been a subordinate clerk in the Dead Letter Office at Washington, from which he had been suddenly removed by a change in the administration. When I think over this rumor, hardly can I express the emotions which seize me. Dead letters! does it not sound like dead men? Conceive a man by nature and misfortune prone to a pallid hopelessness, can any business seem more fitted to heighten it than that of continually handling these dead letters, and assorting them for the flames? For by the cartload they are annually burned. Sometimes from out the folded paper the pale clerk takes a ring—the finger it was meant for, perhaps, molders in the grave; a bank note sent in swiftest charity—he whom it would relieve, nor eats nor hungers any more; pardon for those who died despairing; hope for those who died unhoping; good tidings for those who died stifled by unrelieved calamities. On errands of life, these letters speed to death.

Ah, Bartleby! Ah, humanity!

ॐ CHARLES BAUDELAIRE
B. FRANCE, 1821–1867

One of the most important and influential French poets of the nineteenth century, **Charles Baudelaire** took the poetry of his country in a new direction. Like the German poet **Heinrich Heine** (1797–1856), Baudelaire rejected many of the tenets of the ROMANTIC school and cultivated a more impersonal, critically distanced voice in his work. While not completely abandoning the idealism of his Romantic predecessors and contemporaries, Baudelaire embraced the brute realities of life in poetry that is as concrete as it is shocking. Baudelaire believed that human beings were naturally wicked, inevitably drawn to and fascinated with crime and deviance; his poetry confronts readers as hypocrites and presents them with sometimes repugnant spectacles of the beauty inherent in things conventionally deemed perverse, horrible, and repulsive. Beauty itself, as he writes in "Hymn to Beauty," partakes of both the "infernal and the divine," and it bestows upon us both "kindnesses and crimes." Although Baudelaire's honest exploration of taboo subjects subjected him and his work to public condemnation, the poet's grasp of what he called the "primeval perversity of man" marked a change in literary sensibility in nineteenth-century Europe, pointing to the MODERNISM of the next century. The dynamic tension between the ideal and the real in Baudelaire's poetry, his conscientious craftsmanship, and his engagement with the most sordid details of human life exerted a profound influence on late nineteenth-century and modernist poetry in Europe and beyond, including that of T. S. Eliot (1888–1965), Paul Valéry (1871–1945), and Rainer Maria Rilke (1875–1926). In the words of French symbolist poet Paul Verlaine (1844–1896), "the profound originality of Charles Baudelaire is to represent powerfully and essentially modern man. . . ."

SHARL boh-duh-LARE
p. 786

**Studio of Goupil,
Charles Baudelaire,
Photograph**
*Baudelaire's
confrontational
poetry finds beauty in
things conventionally
deemed perverse,
horrible, and
repulsive. (Corbis)*

The School Years.   Charles Baudelaire was born in Paris in 1821 into a family of respectable means. His father, François Baudelaire, died in 1825, after which Charles was raised by his mother, Caroline Defayis, and stepfather, Jacques Aupick, a military officer whom the boy deeply resented. In 1832, after moving to Lyons with his family, Baudelaire attended school at Collège de Lyon, and later, after returning to Paris in 1836, at Lycée

www For links to more information about Baudelaire, see bedfordstmartins .com/worldlit compact.

Louis-le-Grand, where he developed a keen interest in modern literature. Despite winning several academic prizes, while at lycée Baudelaire began to develop the deep sense of boredom, or ENNUI, that later became a major theme in his poetry. Having been expelled from the lycée for his troublesome behavior, Baudelaire took his *baccalauréat* examinations at another school, the Collège Saint Louis, in 1839 and was faced with choosing a career. Against his stepfather's wishes, the young Baudelaire plunged into a life of literature and art in the Latin Quarter, at that time a student ghetto of cheap lodgings, cafés, bars, and brothels. Here Baudelaire devoured the new literature that was coming out, absorbed himself in the new art, and, when not carousing, wrote poetry.

The Latin Quarter.   In 1841, two years after he took his examinations, Baudelaire's mother and General Aupick put him on a ship bound for Calcutta as a means to reform his bad behavior. The twenty-year-old Baudelaire was not happy to be away from his friends and he returned to France on another vessel, having refused to reboard his ship when it reached Saint-Denis de la Réunion, off the coast of Madagascar in the Indian Ocean. Returning to his unconventional life and now determined more than ever to be a writer, Baudelaire immersed himself in the bars and cafés of the Latin Quarter, where he began writing some of the poems that would appear in his most important work, *The Flowers of Evil* (*Les fleurs du mal,* 1857). He also began his relationship with Jeanne Duval, a Creole woman with whom he lived on and off for many years and who is the "black Venus" of his poems. Upon turning twenty-one in 1842 Baudelaire received a tightly restricted inheritance from his father and began frequenting art galleries and museums. Baudelaire's *Salons* (1845, 1846, and 1859) and his essays on the paintings of Eugène Delacroix and Constantin Guys, among others, represent a formidable body of art criticism. In the midst of the Revolution of 1848, Baudelaire discovered the works of Edgar Allan Poe, with whom he strongly identified and whose formalist poetic principles Baudelaire found strikingly similar to his own. Baudelaire at the time was known in literary and artistic circles as an art critic and obscure poet. With his translations of Poe, appearing from 1856 to 1865, he began to catch the attention of the broader public.

> But with Baudelaire, French poetry at length passes beyond our frontiers. It is read throughout the world; it takes its place as the charac- teristic poetry of modernity; it encour- ages imitation, it enriches countless minds.
>
> – PAUL VALÉRY, poet and critic, 1924

Poet of Evil.   The appearance in June 1857 of *The Flowers of Evil,* the first collection of Baudelaire's poetry, earned him almost immediate notoriety; the book was immediately condemned by reviewers and French officials, who ordered the book seized on the grounds that it offended public and religious morals. Like Gustave Flaubert, who had been acquitted earlier in the year on charges of obscenity for *Madame Bovary,* Baudelaire was brought to trial, in August 1857. Although he was acquitted on charges of blasphemy, he had to pay a fine for violating public morality and leave out six poems from all subsequent editions of the book. In 1862 Baudelaire published twenty prose poems that formed the basis of a posthumously published collection of fifty such poems called *Paris Spleen.* In that same year he suffered a stroke that he rightly interpreted as a portent of his

Jean Beraud, *Boulevard des Capuchines and the Théâtre du Vaudeville in 1889.* **Painting**
Baudelaire sought to help his readers transcend what he called spleen *— the restless malaise affecting modern life. His experience of that life was Paris, with its bourgeois lifestyle and busy street life. (Giraudon/Art Resource)*

death. From 1864 to March 1866, suffering from poor health and living in poverty, Baudelaire gave a few lectures in Belgium and in 1865 arranged to publish a new collection titled *The Waifs of Charles Baudelaire,* which contained some new poems as well as the ones that had been banned in France. In June 1866, after suffering a debilitating stroke two months before, Baudelaire returned to Paris, where he died on August 31, 1867.

Ennui.   Edgar Allan Poe's rejection of the role of inspiration in poetic composition and his focus on deliberate craftsmanship appealed to Baudelaire, who spoke of his own writing as a "travail," a labor. Although Baudelaire shared in the Romantic poets' quest for beauty, he believed that it would be found not in airy flights of the imagination but, paradoxically, in the midst of the most revolting realities. He dismissed the Romantic idea of nature as a ground of human goodness and purity, believing that nature—human nature, in particular—is composed of more evil than good; as he puts it in *The Painter of Modern Life,* "Evil happens without effort, naturally; Good is always the product of some art." A poet of the city rather than of the country, Baudelaire believed that carefully wrought works of art, not solitary Romantic reveries in the countryside, would liberate human beings from the melancholic inertia

> Baudelaire is indeed the greatest exemplar in *modern* poetry in any language, for his verse and language is the nearest thing to a complete renovation that we have experienced. But his renovation of an attitude towards life is no less radical and no less important.
>
> – T. S. ELIOT

that he called *ennui*. For Baudelaire, ennui—profound boredom and apathy associated with blindly following custom and convention—was the worst crime of all.

Flowers of Evil to *Paris Spleen*.   Baudelaire's poetry places the real and the ideal in a tense balance, projecting the ideal of perfection onto a future just out of reach while immersing the reader in the repetition of human imperfection. Baudelaire's work anticipates that of the SYMBOLIST school of poets, a group that included Stéphane Mallarmé (1842–1898), Paul Verlaine (1844–1896), Arthur Rimbaud (1854–1891), and Jules Laforgue (1860–1887). The Symbolists sought to create a language imitating the qualities of music by freeing poetry from the conventional structures and forms of versification (verse-writing) adhered to by their predecessors. By means of symbols—signs or images that serve as points of convergence— Symbolists hoped to evoke a sense of the beautiful and of unity among all things. For these poets, the symbol, like music, should remain elusive and ambiguous; as a means of evading or denying the referential function of language, the symbol evokes language's mystery. Some of Baudelaire's poems, particularly "Correspondences," place special emphasis on symbols. Nevertheless, even as Baudelaire approaches the infinite and the beautiful—often figured by the Symbolists as the *azure,* the deep blue of the open sky—he draws the reader to horrific details of the real.

In *The Flowers of Evil*, Baudelaire's first collection of poetry, published in 1857, the pursuit of the ideal involves a deliberately shocking embrace of what conventional society deems unsavory, even repulsive. Baudelaire divided the poems in this work into five thematic sections: Spleen and the Ideal, Flowers of Evil, Revolt, Wine, and Death. The first edition contained one hundred poems, plus "To the Reader," a prefatory poem set apart from the rest that serves as an overture to the volume. In "To the Reader," Baudelaire declares himself the poet of evil and promises to hold up a mirror to what hypocrites refuse to confront. In stark, sensuous detail, as in "Carrion," which describes a decaying corpse, Baudelaire pushes toward the extreme limits of human experience. *The Flowers of Evil* explores the sordid and the grotesque partly to shock its readers and partly to move them to find beauty in the ugliness of their everyday lives. In a collection of prose poems written in the last two decades of his life, *Paris Spleen* (1862), Baudelaire softens the imagery and tone of his work while still addressing the distemper of modern urban life. In prose poems that strive for the effect of music, Baudelaire captures the despair as well as the pleasure of melancholy and solitude as the solitary poet moves among crowds of strangers in the city. In these poems, perhaps even more than in *The Flowers of Evil*, Baudelaire foretells of the experience of alienation that writers of the early twentieth century would elaborate on.

■ **FURTHER RESEARCH**

Biography
Pichois, Claude. *Baudelaire.* 1989.
Starkie, Enid. *Baudelaire.* 1953.

Criticism

Bloom, Harold, ed. *Charles Baudelaire*. 1987.
Evans, Margery A. *Baudelaire and Intertextuality: Poetry at the Crossroads*. 1993.
Hyslop, Lois Boe. *Charles Baudelaire Revisited*. 1992.
Lloyd, Rosemary. *Baudelaire's World*. 2002.
Peyre, Henry, ed. *Baudelaire: A Collection of Critical Essays*. 1962.
Porter, Laurence M. *The Crisis of French Symbolism*. 1990.

■ **PRONUNCIATION**

Charles Baudelaire: SHARL boh-duh-LARE

∾ To the Reader

Translated by Stanley Kunitz

Ignorance, error, cupidity, and sin
Possess our souls and exercise our flesh;
Habitually we cultivate remorse
As beggars entertain and nurse their lice.

Our sins are stubborn. Cowards when contrite
We overpay confession with our pains,
And when we're back again in human mire
Vile tears, we think, will wash away our stains.

Thrice-potent Satan in our cursèd bed
10 Lulls us to sleep, our spirit overkissed,
Until the precious metal of our will
Is vaporized—that cunning alchemist!

Who but the Devil pulls our waking-strings!
Abominations lure us to their side;
Each day we take another step to hell,
Descending through the stench, unhorrified.

Like an exhausted rake who mouths and chews
The martyrized breast of an old withered whore
We steal, in passing, whatever joys we can,
20 Squeezing the driest orange all the more.

Packed in our brains incestuous as worms
Our demons celebrate in drunken gangs,
And when we breathe, that hollow rasp is Death
Sliding invisibly down into our lungs.

If the dull canvas of our wretched life
Is unembellished with such pretty ware
As knives or poison, pyromania, rape,
It is because our soul's too weak to dare!

But in this den of jackals, monkeys, curs,
30   Scorpions, buzzards, snakes, — this paradise
Of filthy beasts that screech, howl, grovel, grunt —
In this menagerie of mankind's vice

There's one supremely hideous and impure!
Soft-spoken, not the type to cause a scene,
He'd willingly make rubble of the earth
And swallow up creation in a yawn.

I mean *Ennui!* who in his hookah-dreams
Produces hangmen and real tears together.
How well you know this fastidious monster, reader,
40   —Hypocrite reader, you — my double! my brother!

∾ The Albatross

Translated by Richard Wilbur

Often, for pastime, mariners will ensnare
The albatross, that vast sea-bird who sweeps
On high companionable pinion where
Their vessel glides upon the bitter deeps.

Torn from his native space, this captive king
Flounders upon the deck in stricken pride,
And pitiably lets his great white wing
Drag like a heavy paddle at his side.

This rider of winds, how awkward he is, and weak!
10   How droll he seems, who lately was all grace!
A sailor pokes a pipestem into his beak;
Another, hobbling, mocks his trammeled pace.

The Poet is like this monarch of the clouds,
Familiar of storms, of stars, and of all high things;
Exiled on earth amidst its hooting crowds,
He cannot walk, borne down by his giant wings.

ᘓ   Correspondences

Translated by Richard Wilbur

Nature is a temple whose living colonnades
Breathe forth a mystic speech in fitful sighs;
Man wanders among symbols in those glades
Where all things watch him with familiar eyes.

Like dwindling echoes gathered far away
Into a deep and thronging unison
Huge as the night or as the light of day,
All scents and sounds and colors meet as one.

Perfumes there are as sweet as the oboe's sound,
10 Green as the prairies, fresh as a child's caress,
    —And there are others, rich, corrupt, profound

And of an infinite pervasiveness,
Like myrrh, or musk, or amber, that excite
The ecstasies of sense, the soul's delight.

ᘓ   Hymn to Beauty

Translated by Dorothy Martin

From heaven or hell, O Beauty, come you hence?
Out from your gaze, infernal and divine,
Pours blended evil and beneficence,
And therefore men have likened you to wine.

Sunset and dawn within your eyes are fair;
Stormlike you scatter perfume into space;
Your kiss, a philtre from an amphora rare,
Charms boys to courage and makes heroes base.

Whence come you, from what spheres, or inky deeps,
10 With careless hand joy and distress to strew?
Fate, like a dog at heel, behind you creeps;
You govern all things here, and naught you rue.

You walk upon the dead with scornful glances,
Among your gems Horror is not least fair;

Murder, the dearest of your baubles, dances
Upon your haughty breast with amorous air.

Mothlike around your flame the transient, turning,
Crackles and flames and cries, "Ah, heavenly doom!"
The quivering lover o'er his mistress yearning
20 Is but a dying man who woos his tomb.

From heaven or the abyss? Let questioning be,
O artless monster wreaking endless pain,
So that your smile and glance throw wide to me
An infinite that I have loved in vain.

From Satan or from God? Holy or vile?
Let questioning rest. O soft-eyed sprite, my queen,
O rhythm, perfume, light — so you beguile
Time from his slothfulness, the world from spleen.

❧ Carrion

Translated by Richard Howard

Remember, my soul, the thing we saw
    that lovely summer day?
On a pile of stones where the path turned off
    the hideous carrion —

legs in the air, like a whore — displayed
    indifferent to the last,
a belly slick with lethal sweat
    and swollen with foul gas.

the sun lit up that rottenness
10   as though to roast it through,
restoring to Nature a hundredfold
    what she had here made one.

And heaven watched the splendid corpse
    like a flower open wide —
you nearly fainted dead away
    at the perfume it gave off.

Flies kept humming over the guts
 from which a gleaming clot
of maggots poured to finish off
20 what scraps of flesh remained.

The tide of trembling vermin sank,
 then bubbled up afresh
as if the carcass, drawing breath,
 by *their* lives lived again

and made a curious music there —
 like running water, or wind,
or the rattle of chaff the winnower
 loosens in his fan.

Shapeless — nothing was left but a dream
30 the artist had sketched in,
forgotten, and only later on
 finished from memory.

Behind the rocks an anxious bitch
 eyed us reproachfully,
waiting for the chance to resume
 her interrupted feast.

— Yet you will come to this offence,
 this horrible decay,
you, the light of my life, the sun
40 and moon and stars of my love!

Yes, you will come to this, my queen,
 after the sacraments,
when you rot underground among
 the bones already there.

But as their kisses eat you up,
 my Beauty, tell the worms
I've kept the sacred essence, saved
 the form of my rotted loves!

GUSTAVE FLAUBERT
B. FRANCE, 1821–1880

ҩ

goo-STAHV floh-BARE

Perhaps more than any other writer of the nineteenth century, **Gustave Flaubert** can be described as the exemplar of REALISM. *Madame Bovary* (1856), his masterwork, models the objective narrative technique and commonplace subject matter of the Realists, and Flaubert's statements about writing articulate the basic concepts of Realist literary theory. Realists worldwide—from Guy de Maupassant and Émile Zola in France to Henry James in America and Ivan Turgenev[1] in Russia—modeled their work on Flaubert's and took instruction from his principles for writing fiction. He was, in Henry James's phrase, the "novelist's novelist." Vladimir Nabokov[2] summarized Flaubert's achievement in the following terms:

> Ponder most carefully the following fact: a master of Flaubert's artistic power manages to transform what he has conceived as a sordid world inhabited by frauds and philistines and mediocrities and brutes and wayward ladies into one of the most perfect pieces of fiction known, and this he achieves by bringing all the parts into harmony, by the inner force of style, by all such devices of form as the counterpoint of transition from one theme to another, of fore-shadowing and echoes.

As a stylist Flaubert has been particularly influential on later writers.

www For links to more information about Flaubert and a quiz on "A Simple Heart," see bedford stmartins.com/ worldlitcompact.

An Uneventful Life. Born into a medical family in Rouen in 1821, Flaubert claimed that his clinical powers of observation were the result of having a "doctor's eye." He saw the provincial life of his native Normandy as diseased, afflicted by stultifying conventionality. As a schoolboy he compiled lists of *idées reçues,* or received ideas, to mock the banality of bourgeois life, and for relief from provincial tedium, he began writing exotic romantic stories, including *The Memoirs of a Fool,* written at age sixteen, recounting his secret love for an older married woman. He escaped Normandy by going to Paris to study law, but after failing his examinations and suffering a nervous breakdown he withdrew from the university and returned home in 1846. Although he took occasional trips to Paris and traveled to Greece, North Africa, and the Middle East, Flaubert spent the rest of his uneventful life on the family estate in Normandy, living with his mother and niece, and writing. He devoted

---

[1] **Maupassant . . . Turgenev:** Leading Realist novelists of the late nineteenth century. **Guy de Maupassant** (1850–1893), French writer of short stories and sometimes novelist, see p. 1048; **Henry James** (1843–1916), American novelist and critic best known for *The Portrait of a Lady* (1881); **Émile Zola** (1840–1902), French novelist, leader of the Naturalists, and author of many novels, including *Nana* (1880) and *Germinal* (1885), see p. 1054; **Ivan Turgenev** (1818–1883), Russian novelist, dramatist, and short-story writer; author of *Fathers and Sons* (1861) and other works.

[2] **Vladimir Nabokov** (1899–1977): Russian American novelist best known for *Lolita* (1955).

himself to his art, laboring several years over each of his books as he searched for just the right word or detail to develop a story. He never married.

Realism and Objectivity.   Flaubert's first work was the extravagant early narrative *The Temptation of St. Anthony,* the manuscript of which a friend advised him to burn, suggesting that he try instead to write a more "down to earth" novel based on an actual case. The actual case he had in mind was that of a local doctor's wife who had deceived her husband. Convinced, Flaubert began writing *Madame Bovary,* his first published novel. Writing the novel took five years and forced its author into very disciplined habits of composition. Flaubert strove to attain complete objectivity in the presentation of his story, eliminating all commentary by the author and hiding his attitude toward the characters and their story. "The author, in his work," he wrote, "must be like God in the Universe, present everywhere and visible nowhere." Although he was contemptuous of the bourgeois provincialism of his characters and of Emma Bovary's romantic delusions, Flaubert attempted to enter sympathetically into her world and to record the story of her adulteries with absolute objectivity. He measured his success as an artist by his capacity to enter "at every moment into skins which are antipathetic to me." He claimed victory in this struggle when he asserted, "I am Madame Bovary." As his heroine he could be everywhere in his novel, yet visible nowhere.

Le Seul Mot Juste.   Flaubert sought absolute economy of expression and precise concreteness for his novel, with each detail contributing to a unity of tone. He wanted his style to be "as rhythmical as verse and as precise as the language of science." The subject matter of the story, he believed, was not important. The important thing was to choose *le seul mot juste*—the one right word. "The only truth in this world," Flaubert asserted, "is in the well-made sentence." But many of Flaubert's contemporary readers were unimpressed by the stylistic merit of the novel and believed that the subject matter was in fact important. They were outraged by Emma's adulteries. After the novel appeared in 1856, the French government brought charges against the author for "outraging public morals and religion." At trial Flaubert narrowly escaped conviction, and in the process he gained public notoriety.

Romantic Indulgence and Realist Restraint.   Flaubert's achievements as a Realist were not easily come by, for his Romantic impulses were strong. Unlike **Charles Dickens** and **Fyodor Dostoevsky**, who infused their realistic depiction of urban life with a personal, Romantic mythology within a single work, Flaubert satisfied his dual inclinations in separate works, alternating between writing excessive and indulgent romances and carefully controlled realistic novels.

In his next novel, *Salammbô* (1863), Flaubert returned to Romantic excesses. A historical novel that takes place in ancient Carthage, it indulges in lush orientalism, describing the unrestrained indulgences of its Eastern

J. Lemot, *Gustave Flaubert Dissecting Madame Bovary,* Parodie, 1869
Flaubert strove for economy of expression and absolute concreteness in his work, in which he aimed to be "as precise as the language of science." Depicted here as a surgeon dissecting his patient, Flaubert is satirized for being overly clinical in his writing. (The Bridgeman Art Library)

pp. 1037, 963

Flaubert, the "novelist's novelist."
– HENRY JAMES

setting in extravagant language. *A Sentimental Education* (1869) was a return to the Realist style of *Madame Bovary.* An account of the passion of its young hero, Frederic Moreau, for an older woman, the novel is set against a very detailed historical account of the period preceding the coup d'état of 1851 when Louis Napoleon dissolved the Second Republic and declared the Second Empire. Flaubert had reworked this novel several times, beginning it many years earlier in *The Memoirs of a Fool.* Similarly, his Romantic next book, *The Temptation of St. Anthony* (1874), was one that he had rewritten at different stages of his life. His changing religious views can be traced in its various versions, from early antireligious nihilism to a later respect for religion in the final published version.

A Realistic Saint's Life.   Flaubert's last published collection, *Three Tales* (1877), reveals both sides of the author's character in its sharply contrasting stories: "A Simple Heart," "The Legend of St. Julian Hospitaller," and "Herodias." As different as these three stories are from one another, they are all, like *The Temptation of St. Anthony,* saints' lives — biographies of saints, a genre especially popular in the Middle Ages. "A Simple Heart," closest to *Madame Bovary* in subject matter and technique, shows Flaubert's ability to sympathize with his provincial characters and to understand their lives from the inside. **Félicité**'s life, unlike Emma Bovary's, is not sordid; rather, it is a triumph of the commonplace, a simple life that achieves saintly dignity.

fay-lee-see-TAY

"A Simple Heart" follows many of the conventions of the traditional saint's tale, which typically included accounts of the conversion, temptation, miracles, and death — often by martyrdom — of saints. The course of Félicité's life structures the story, which begins with her childhood and ends with her beatific death. It is also a realistic story. Writing of Normandy, where he lived nearly all his life, Flaubert describes in precise detail the small provincial town of **Pont-l'Évêque** and the surrounding countryside. In this drab, grey world of sculleries and provincial dullness, Félicité's parrot is an exotic bit of color that gives an absurd dimension to the meaning of her life. The literary model of the saint's life is an implied Romantic contrast with the seeming triviality and absurdity of Félicité's life. Flaubert's identification with his character is what closes the gap between the ideal and the absurd. It is this gap — between ideal perfection and imperfect reality — and writers' encounters with it in their experience that informed the idealism of the early Romantics and the Realism of their successors.

pong lay-VEK

■ **FURTHER RESEARCH**

Biography
Brown, Frederic K. *Flaubert: A Biography.* 2006.
Sartre, Jean-Paul. *The Family Idiot: Gustave Flaubert.* Tr. Carol Cosman. 1981.

Criticism
Brombert, Victor. *The Novels of Flaubert.* 1966.
Cortland, Peter. *A Reader's Guide to Flaubert.* 1968.
Culler, Jonathan. *Flaubert: The Uses of Uncertainty.* 1974.

Giraud, Raymond, ed. *Flaubert: A Collection of Critical Essays*. 1964.
Israel-Pelletier, Aimée. *Flaubert's Straight and Suspect Saints: The Unity of* Trois Contes.
    1991. Includes a chapter on "A Simple Heart."
Schor, Naomi, and Henry F. Majewski. *Flaubert and Postmodernism*. 1984. Includes
    two essays on the novellas.

Related Works
Barnes, Julian. *Flaubert's Parrot*. 1984. A contemporary novel based on Flaubert's
    life and the themes of "A Simple Heart."

■ **PRONUNCIATION**

Félicité: fay-lee-see-TAY
Gustave Flaubert: goo-STAHV floh-BARE
Pont-l'Évêque: pong lay-VEK

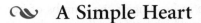 A Simple Heart

Translated by Arthur McDowall

1

Madame Aubain's servant Félicité was the envy of the ladies of Pont-l'Évêque[1] for half a century.

She received a hundred francs a year. For that she was cook and general servant, and did the sewing, washing, and ironing; she could bridle a horse, fatten poultry, and churn butter—and she remained faithful to her mistress, unamiable as the latter was.

Mme. Aubain had married a gay bachelor without money who died at the beginning of 1809, leaving her with two small children and a quantity of debts. She then sold all her property except the farms of Toucques and Geffosses, which brought in five thousand francs a year at most, and left her house in Saint-Melaine for a less expensive one that had belonged to her family and was situated behind the market.

This house had a slate roof and stood between an alley and a lane that went down to the river. There was an unevenness in the levels of the rooms which made you stumble. A narrow hall divided the kitchen from the "parlour" where Mme. Aubain spent her day, sitting in a wicker easy chair by the window. Against the panels, which were painted white, was a row of eight mahogany chairs. On an old piano under the barometer a heap of wooden and cardboard boxes rose like a pyramid. A stuffed armchair stood on either side of the Louis-Quinze chimney-piece, which was in yellow marble with a clock in the middle of it modelled like a temple of Vesta.[2] The whole room was a little musty, as the floor was lower than the garden.

---

[1] **Pont-l'Évêque:** A village in Normandy.

[2] **Vesta:** The Roman goddess of the hearth.

The first floor began with "Madame's" room: very large, with a pale-flowered wall-paper and a portrait of "Monsieur" as a dandy of the period. It led to a smaller room, where there were two children's cots without mattresses. Next came the drawing-room, which was always shut up and full of furniture covered with sheets. Then there was a corridor leading to a study. The shelves of a large bookcase were respectably lined with books and papers, and its three wings surrounded a broad writing-table in darkwood. The two panels at the end of the room were covered with pen-drawings, water-colour landscapes, and engravings by Audran,[3] all relics of better days and vanished splendour. Félicité's room on the top floor got its light from a dormer-window, which looked over the meadows.

She rose at daybreak to be in time for Mass, and worked till evening without stopping. Then, when dinner was over, the plates and dishes in order, and the door shut fast, she thrust the log under the ashes and went to sleep in front of the hearth with her rosary in her hand. Félicité was the stubbornest of all bargainers; and as for cleanness, the polish on her saucepans was the despair of other servants. Thrifty in all things, she ate slowly, gathering off the table in her fingers the crumbs of her loaf—a twelve-pound loaf expressly baked for her, which lasted for three weeks.

At all times of year she wore a print handkerchief fastened with a pin behind, a bonnet that covered her hair, grey stockings, a red skirt, and a bibbed apron—such as hospital nurses wear—over her jacket.

Her face was thin and her voice sharp. At twenty-five she looked like forty. From fifty onwards she seemed of no particular age; and with her silence, straight figure, and precise movements she was like a woman made of wood, and going by clockwork.

2

She had had her love-story like another.

Her father, a mason, had been killed by falling off some scaffolding. Then her mother died, her sisters scattered, and a farmer took her in and employed her, while she was still quite little, to herd the cows at pasture. She shivered in rags and would lie flat on the ground to drink water from the ponds; she was beaten for nothing, and finally turned out for the theft of thirty sous which she did not steal. She went to another farm, where she became dairy-maid; and as she was liked by her employers her companions were jealous of her.

One evening in August (she was then eighteen) they took her to the assembly at Colleville. She was dazed and stupefied in an instant by the noise of the fiddlers, the lights in the trees, the gay medley of dresses, the lace, the gold crosses, and the throng of people jigging all together. While she kept shyly apart a young man with a well-to-do air, who was leaning on the shaft of a cart and smoking his pipe, came up to ask her to dance. He treated her to cider, coffee, and cake, and bought her a silk handkerchief; and then, imagining she had guessed his meaning, offered to see her home.

---

[3] **Audran:** Gérard Audran (1640–1703) made engravings of famous paintings for use in home decoration.

At the edge of a field of oats he pushed her roughly down. She was frightened and began to cry out; and he went off.

One evening later she was on the Beaumont road. A big hay-wagon was moving slowly along; she wanted to get in front of it, and as she brushed past the wheels she recognized Theodore. He greeted her quite calmly, saying she must excuse it all because it was "the fault of the drink." She could not think of any answer and wanted to run away.

He began at once to talk about the harvest and the worthies of the commune, for his father had left Colleville for the farm at Les Écots, so that now he and she were neighbours. "Ah!" she said. He added that they thought of settling him in life. Well, he was in no hurry; he was waiting for a wife to his fancy. She dropped her head; and then he asked her if she thought of marrying. She answered with a smile that it was mean to make fun of her.

"But I am not, I swear!"—and he passed his left hand round her waist. She walked in the support of his embrace; their steps grew slower. The wind was soft, the stars glittered, the huge wagon-load of hay swayed in front of them, and dust rose from the dragging steps of the four horses. Then, without a word of command, they turned to the right. He clasped her once more in his arms, and she disappeared into the shadow.

The week after Theodore secured some assignations with her.

They met at the end of farmyards, behind a wall, or under a solitary tree. She was not innocent as young ladies are—she had learned knowledge from the animals—but her reason and the instinct of her honour would not let her fall. Her resistance exasperated Theodore's passion; so much so that to satisfy it—or perhaps quite artlessly,—he made her an offer of marriage. She was in doubt whether to trust him, but he swore great oaths of fidelity.

Soon he confessed to something troublesome; the year before his parents had bought him a substitute for the army, but any day he might be taken again, and the idea of serving was a terror to him. Félicité took this cowardice of his as a sign of affection, and it redoubled hers. She stole away at night to see him, and when she reached their meeting-place Theodore racked her with his anxieties and urgings.

At last he declared that he would go himself to the prefecture for information, and would tell her the result on the following Sunday, between eleven and midnight.

When the moment came she sped towards her lover. Instead of him she found one of his friends.

He told her that she would not see Theodore any more. To ensure himself against conscription he had married an old woman, Madame Lehoussais, of Toucques, who was very rich.

There was an uncontrollable burst of grief. She threw herself on the ground, screamed, called to the God of mercy, and moaned by herself in the fields till daylight came. Then she came back to the farm and announced that she was going to leave; and at the end of the month she received her wages, tied all her small belongings with a handkerchief, and went to Pont-l'Évêque.

In front of the inn there she made inquiries of a woman in a widow's cap, who, as it happened, was just looking for a cook. The girl did not know much, but her willingness seemed so great and her demands so small that Mme. Aubain ended by saying:

"Very well, then, I will take you."

A quarter of an hour afterwards Félicité was installed in her house.

She lived there at first in a tremble, as it were, at "the style of the house" and the memory of "Monsieur" floating over it all. Paul and Virginie, the first aged seven and the other hardly four, seemed to her beings of a precious substance; she carried them on her back like a horse; it was a sorrow to her that Mme. Aubain would not let her kiss them every minute. And yet she was happy there. Her grief had melted in the pleasantness of things all round.

Every Thursday regular visitors came in for a game of boston,[4] and Félicité got the cards and foot-warmers ready beforehand. They arrived punctually at eight and left before the stroke of eleven.

On Monday mornings the dealer who lodged in the covered passage spread out all his old iron on the ground. Then a hum of voices began to fill the town, mingled with the neighing of horses, bleating of lambs, grunting of pigs, and the sharp rattle of carts along the street. About noon, when the market was at its height, you might see a tall, hook-nosed old countryman with his cap pushed back making his appearance at the door. It was Robelin, the farmer of Geffosses. A little later came Liébard, the farmer from Toucques — short, red, and corpulent — in a grey jacket and gaiters shod with spurs.

Both had poultry or cheese to offer their landlord. Félicité was invariably a match for their cunning, and they went away filled with respect for her.

At vague intervals Mme. Aubain had a visit from the Marquis de Gremanville, one of her uncles, who had ruined himself by debauchery and now lived at Falaise on his last remaining morsel of land. He invariably came at the luncheon hour, with a dreadful poodle whose paws left all the furniture in a mess. In spite of efforts to show his breeding, which he carried to the point of raising his hat every time he mentioned "my late father," habit was too strong for him; he poured himself out glass after glass and fired off improper remarks. Félicité edged him politely out of the house — "You have had enough, Monsieur de Gremanville! Another time!" — and she shut the door on him.

She opened it with pleasure to M. Bourais, who had been a lawyer. His baldness, his white stock, frilled shirt, and roomy brown coat, his way of rounding the arm as he took snuff—his whole person, in fact, created that disturbance of mind which overtakes us at the sight of extraordinary men.

As he looked after the property of "Madame" he remained shut up with her for hours in "Monsieur's" study, though all the time he was afraid of compromising himself. He respected the magistracy immensely, and had some pretensions to Latin.

---

[4] **boston:** Card game similar to whist, named after the birthplace of the American Revolution, to which the technical terms in the game refer.

To combine instruction and amusement he gave the children a geography book made up of a series of prints. They represented scenes in different parts of the world: cannibals with feathers on their heads, a monkey carrying off a young lady, Bedouins in the desert, the harpooning of a whale, and so on. Paul explained these engravings to Félicité; and that, in fact, was the whole of her literary education. The children's education was undertaken by Guyot, a poor creature employed at the town hall, who was famous for his beautiful hand and sharpened his penknife on his boots.

When the weather was bright the household set off early for a day at Geffosses Farm.

Its courtyard is on a slope, with the farmhouse in the middle, and the sea looks like a grey streak in the distance.

Félicité brought slices of cold meat out of her basket, and they breakfasted in a room adjoining the dairy. It was the only surviving fragment of a country house which was now no more. The wallpaper hung in tatters, and quivered in the draughts. Mme. Aubain sat with bowed head, overcome by her memories; the children became afraid to speak. "Why don't you play, then?" she would say, and off they went.

Paul climbed into the barn, caught birds, played at ducks and drakes over the pond, or hammered with his stick on the big casks which boomed like drums. Virginie fed the rabbits or dashed off to pick cornflowers, her quick legs showing their embroidered little drawers.

One autumn evening they went home by the fields. The moon was in its first quarter, lighting part of the sky; and mist floated like a scarf over the windings of the Toucques. Cattle, lying out in the middle of the grass, looked quietly at the four people as they passed. In the third meadow some of them got up and made a halfcircle in front of the walkers. "There's nothing to be afraid of," said Félicité, as she stroked the nearest on the back with a kind of crooning song; he wheeled round and the others did the same. But when they crossed the next pasture there was a formidable bellow. It was a bull, hidden by the mist. Mme. Aubain was about to run. "No! no! don't go so fast!" They mended their pace, however, and heard a loud breathing behind them which came nearer. His hoofs thudded on the meadow grass like hammers; why, he was galloping now! Félicité turned round, and tore up clods of earth with both hands and threw them in his eyes. He lowered his muzzle, waved his horns, and quivered with fury, bellowing terribly. Mme. Aubain, now at the end of the pasture with her two little ones, was looking wildly for a place to get over the high bank. Félicité was retreating, still with her face to the bull, keeping up a shower of clods which blinded him, and crying all the time, "Be quick! be quick!"

Mme. Aubain went down into the ditch, pushed Virginie first and then Paul, fell several times as she tried to climb the bank, and managed it at last by dint of courage.

The bull had driven Félicité to bay against a rail-fence; his slaver was streaming into her face; another second, and he would have gored her. She had just time to slip between two of the rails, and the big animal stopped short in amazement.

This adventure was talked of at Pont-l'Évêque for many a year. Félicité did not pride herself on it in the least, not having the barest suspicion that she had done anything heroic.

Virginie was the sole object of her thoughts, for the child developed a nervous complaint as a result of her fright, and M. Poupart, the doctor, advised sea-bathing at Trouville. It was not a frequented place then. Mme. Aubain collected information, consulted Bourais, and made preparations as though for a long journey.

Her luggage started a day in advance, in Liébard's cart. The next day he brought round two horses, one of which had a lady's saddle with a velvet back to it, while a cloak was rolled up to make a kind of seat on the crupper of the other. Mme. Aubain rode on that, behind the farmer. Félicité took charge of Virginie, and Paul mounted M. Lechaptois' donkey, lent on condition that great care was taken of it.

The road was so bad that its five miles took two hours. The horses sank in the mud up to their pasterns, and their haunches jerked abruptly in the effort to get out; or else they stumbled in the ruts, and at other moments had to jump. In some places Liébard's mare came suddenly to a halt. He waited patiently until she went on again, talking about the people who had properties along the road, and adding moral reflections to their history. So it was that as they were in the middle of Toucques, and passed under some windows bowered with nasturtiums, he shrugged his shoulders and said: "There's a Mme. Lehoussais lives there; instead of taking a young man she . . ." Félicité did not hear the rest; the horses were trotting and the donkey galloping: They all turned down a bypath; a gate swung open and two boys appeared; and the party dismounted in front of a manure-heap at the very threshold of the farmhouse door.

When Mme. Liébard saw her mistress she gave lavish signs of joy. She served her a luncheon with a sirloin of beef, tripe, black-pudding, a fricassee of chicken, sparkling cider, a fruit tart, and brandied plums; seasoning it all with compliments to Madame, who seemed in better health; Mademoiselle, who was "splendid" now; and Monsieur Paul, who had "filled out" wonderfully. Nor did she forget their deceased grandparents, whom the Liébards had known, as they had been in the service of the family for several generations. The farm, like them, had the stamp of antiquity. The beams on the ceiling were worm-eaten, the walls blackened with smoke, and the window-panes grey with dust. There was an oak dresser laden with every sort of useful article—jugs, plates, pewter bowls, wolf-traps, and sheep-shears; and a huge syringe made the children laugh. There was not a tree in the three court-yards without mushrooms growing at the bottom of it or a tuft of mistletoe on its boughs. Several of them had been thrown down by the wind. They had taken root again at the middle; and all were bending under their wealth of apples. The thatched roofs, like brown velvet and of varying thickness, withstood the heaviest squalls. The cart-shed, however, was falling into ruin. Mme. Aubain said she would see about it, and ordered the animals to be saddled again.

It was another half-hour before they reached Trouville. The little caravan dismounted to pass Écores—it was an overhanging cliff with boats below it—and three minutes later they were at the end of the quay and entered the courtyard of the Golden Lamb, kept by good Mme. David.

From the first days of their stay Virginie began to feel less weak, thanks to the change of air and the effect of the sea-baths. These, for want of a bathing-dress, she took in her chemise; and her nurse dressed her afterwards in a coastguard's cabin which was used by the bathers.

In the afternoons they took the donkey and went off beyond the Black Rocks, in the direction of Hennequeville. The path climbed at first through ground with dells in it like the green sward of a park, and then reached a plateau where grass fields and arable lay side by side. Hollies rose stiffly out of the briary tangle at the edge of the road; and here and there a great withered tree made zigzags in the blue air with its branches.

They nearly always rested in a meadow, with Deauville on their left, Havre on their right, and the open sea in front. It glittered in the sunshine, smooth as a mirror and so quiet that its murmur was scarcely to be heard; sparrows chirped in hiding and the immense sky arched over it all. Mme. Aubain sat doing her needlework; Virginie plaited rushes by her side; Félicité pulled up lavender, and Paul was bored and anxious to start home.

Other days they crossed the Toucques in a boat and looked for shells. When the tide went out sea-urchins, starfish, and jelly-fish were left exposed; and the children ran in pursuit of the foam-flakes which scudded in the wind. The sleepy waves broke on the sand and unrolled all along the beach; it stretched away out of sight, bounded on the land-side by the dunes which parted it from the Marsh, a wide meadow shaped like an arena. As they came home that way, Trouville, on the hill-slope in the background, grew bigger at every step, and its miscellaneous throng of houses seemed to break into a gay disorder.

On days when it was too hot they did not leave their room. From the dazzling brilliance outside light fell in streaks between the laths of the blinds. There were no sounds in the village; and on the pavement below not a soul. This silence round them deepened the quietness of things. In the distance, where men were caulking, there was a tap of hammers as they plugged the hulls, and a sluggish breeze wafted up the smell of tar.

The chief amusement was the return of the fishing-boats. They began to tack as soon as they had passed the buoys. The sails came down on two of the three masts; and they drew on with the foresail swelling like a balloon, glided through the splash of the waves, and when they had reached the middle of the harbour suddenly dropped anchor. Then the boats drew up against the quay. The sailors threw quivering fish over the side; a row of carts was waiting, and women in cotton bonnets darted out to take the baskets and give their men a kiss.

One of them came up to Félicité one day, and she entered the lodgings a little later in a state of delight. She had found a sister again—and then Nastasie Barette, "wife of Leroux," appeared, holding an infant at her breast and another child with her right hand, while on her left was a little cabin boy with his hands on his hips and a cap over his ear.

After a quarter of an hour Mme. Aubain sent them off; but they were always to be found hanging about the kitchen, or encountered in the course of a walk. The husband never appeared.

Félicité was seized with affection for them. She bought them a blanket, some shirts, and a stove; it was clear that they were making a good thing out of her. Mme. Aubain was annoyed by this weakness of hers, and she did not like the liberties taken by the nephew, who said "thee" and "thou" to Paul. So as Virginie was coughing and the fine weather gone, she returned to Pont-l'Évêque.

There M. Bourais enlightened her on the choice of a boys' school. The one at Caen was reputed to be the best, and Paul was sent to it. He said his good-byes bravely, content enough at going to live in a house where he would have companions.

Mme. Aubain resigned herself to her son's absence as a thing that had to be. Virginie thought about it less and less. Félicité missed the noise he made. But she found an occupation to distract her; from Christmas onward she took the little girl to catechism every day.

<h1 style="text-align:center">3</h1>

After making a genuflexion at the door she walked up between the double rows of chairs under the lofty nave, opened Mme. Aubain's pew, sat down, and began to look about her. The choir stalls were filled with the boys on the right and the girls on the left, and the curé stood by the lectern. On a painted window in the apse the Holy Ghost looked down upon the Virgin. Another window showed her on her knees before the child Jesus, and a group carved in wood behind the altar-shrine represented St. Michael overthrowing the dragon.

The priest began with a sketch of sacred history. The Garden, the Flood, the Tower of Babel, cities in flames, dying nations, and overturned idols passed like a dream before her eyes; and the dizzying vision left her with reverence for the Most High and fear of his wrath. Then she wept at the story of the Passion. Why had they crucified Him, when He loved the children, fed the multitudes, healed the blind, and had willed, in His meekness, to be born among the poor, on the dung-heap of a stable? The sowings, harvests, wine-presses, all the familiar things that the Gospel speaks of, were a part of her life. They had been made holy by God's passing; and she loved the lambs more tenderly for her love of the Lamb, and the doves because of the Holy Ghost.

She found it hard to imagine Him in person, for He was not merely a bird, but a flame as well, and a breath at other times. It may be His light, she thought, which flits at night about the edge of the marshes, His breathing which drives on the clouds, His voice which gives harmony to the bells; and she would sit rapt in adoration, enjoying the cool walls and the quiet of the church.

Of doctrines she understood nothing—did not even try to understand. The curé discoursed, the children repeated their lesson, and finally she went to sleep, waking up with a start when their wooden shoes clattered on the flagstones as they went away.

It was thus that Félicité, whose religious education had been neglected in her youth, learned the catechism by dint of hearing it; and from that time she copied all Virginie's observances, fasting as she did and confessing with her. On Corpus Christi Day they made a festal altar together.

The first communion loomed distractingly ahead. She fussed over the shoes, the rosary, the book and gloves; and how she trembled as she helped Virginie's mother to dress her!

All through the mass she was racked with anxiety. She could not see one side of the choir because of M. Bourais but straight in front of her was the flock of maidens, with white crowns above their hanging veils, making the impression of a field of snow; and she knew her dear child at a distance by her dainty neck and thoughtful air. The bell tinkled. The heads bowed, and there was silence. As the organ pealed, singers and congregation took up the "Agnus Dei";[5] then the procession of the boys began, and after them the girls rose. Step by step, with their hands joined in prayer, they went towards the lighted altar, knelt on the first step, received the sacrament in turn, and came back in the same order to their places. When Virginie's turn came Félicité leaned forward to see her; and with the imaginativeness of deep and tender feeling it seemed to her that she actually was the child; Virginie's face became hers, she was dressed in her clothes, it was her heart beating in her breast. As the moment came to open her mouth she closed her eyes and nearly fainted.

She appeared early in the sacristy next morning for Monsieur the curé to give her the communion. She took it with devotion, but it did not give her the same exquisite delight.

Mme. Aubain wanted to make her daughter into an accomplished person; and as Guyot could not teach her music or English she decided to place her in the Ursu- line Convent at Honfleur as a boarder. The child made no objection. Félicité sighed and thought that Madame lacked feeling. Then she reflected that her mistress might be right; matters of this kind were beyond her.

So one day an old spring-van drew up at the door, and out of it stepped a nun to fetch the young lady. Félicité hoisted the luggage on to the top, admonished the driver, and put six pots of preserves, a dozen pears, and a bunch of violets under the seat.

At the last moment Virginie broke into a fit of sobbing; she threw her arms round her mother, who kissed her on the forehead, saying over and over "Come, be brave! be brave!" The step was raised, and the carriage drove off.

Then Mme. Aubain's strength gave way; and in the evening all her friends—the Lormeau family, Mme. Lechaptois, the Rochefeuille ladies, M. de Houppeville, and Bourais—came in to console her.

To be without her daughter was very painful for her at first. But she heard from Virginie three times a week, wrote to her on the other days, walked in the garden, and so filled up the empty hours.

From sheer habit Félicité went into Virginie's room in the mornings and gazed at the walls. It was boredom to her not to have to comb the child's hair now, lace up her boots, tuck her into bed—and not to see her charming face perpetually and hold her hand when they went out together. In this idle condition she tried making lace. But her fingers were too heavy and broke the threads; she could not attend to anything, she had lost her sleep, and was, in her own words, "destroyed."

To "divert herself" she asked leave to have visits from her nephew Victor.

He arrived on Sundays after mass, rosy-cheeked, bare-chested, with the scent of the country he had walked through still about him. She laid her table promptly and they had lunch, sitting opposite each other. She ate as little as possible herself to save

---

[5] "Agnus Dei": A prayer to Christ, addressed to the "Lamb of God."

expense, but stuffed him with food so generous that at last he went to sleep. At the first stroke of vespers she woke him up, brushed his trousers, fastened his tie, and went to church, leaning on his arm with maternal pride.

Victor was always instructed by his parents to get something out of her—a packet of moist sugar, it might be, a cake of soap, spirits, or even money at times. He brought his things for her to mend and she took over the task, only too glad to have a reason for making him come back.

In August his father took him off on a coasting voyage. It was holiday time, and she was consoled by the arrival of the children. Paul, however, was getting selfish, and Virginie was too old to be called "thou" any longer; this put a constraint and barrier between them.

Victor went to Morlaix, Dunkirk, and Brighton in succession and made Félicité a present on his return from each voyage. It was a box made of shells the first time, a coffee cup the next, and on the third occasion a large gingerbread man. Victor was growing handsome. He was well made, had a hint of a moustache, good honest eyes, and a small leather hat pushed backwards like a pilot's. He entertained her by telling stories embroidered with nautical terms.

On a Monday, July 14, 1819 (she never forgot the date), he told her that he had signed on for the big voyage and next night but one he would take the Honfleur boat and join his schooner, which was to weigh anchor from Havre before long. Perhaps he would be gone two years.

The prospect of this long absence threw Félicité into deep distress; one more good-bye she must have, and on the Wednesday evening, when Madame's dinner was finished, she put on her clogs and made short work of the twelve miles between Pont-l'Évêque and Honfleur.

When she arrived in front of the Calvary she took the turn to the right instead of the left, got lost in the timber-yards, and retraced her steps; some people to whom she spoke advised her to be quick. She went all round the harbour basin, full of ships, and knocked against hawsers; then the ground fell away, lights flashed across each other, and she thought her wits had left her, for she saw horses up in the sky.

Others were neighing by the quay-side, frightened at the sea. They were lifted by a tackle and deposited in a boat, where passengers jostled each other among cider casks, cheese baskets, and sacks of grain; fowls could be heard clucking, the captain swore; and a cabin-boy stood leaning over the bows, indifferent to it all. Félicité, who had not recognized him, called "Victor!" and he raised his head; all at once, as she was darting forwards, the gangway was drawn back.

The Honfleur packet, women singing as they hauled it, passed out of harbour. Its framework creaked and the heavy waves whipped its bows. The canvas had swung round, no one could be seen on board now, and on the moon-silvered sea the boat made a black speck which paled gradually, dipped, and vanished.

As Félicité passed by the Calvary she had a wish to commend to God what she cherished most, and she stood there praying a long time with her face bathed in tears and her eyes towards the clouds. The town was asleep, coastguards were walking to and fro; and water poured without cessation through the holes in the sluice, with the noise of a torrent. The clocks struck two.

The convent parlour would not be open before day. If Félicité were late Madame would most certainly be annoyed; and in spite of her desire to kiss the other child she turned home. The maids at the inn were waking up as she came in to Pont-l'Évêque.

So the poor slip of a boy was going to toss for months and months at sea! She had not been frightened by his previous voyages. From England or Brittany you came back safe enough; but America, the colonies, the islands—these were lost in a dim region at the other end of the world.

Félicité's thoughts from that moment ran entirely on her nephew. On sunny days she was harassed by the idea of thirst; when there was a storm she was afraid of the lightning on his account. As she listened to the wind growling in the chimney or carrying off the slates she pictured him lashed by that same tempest, at the top of a shattered mast, with his body thrown backwards under a sheet of foam; or else (with a reminiscence of the illustrated geography) he was being eaten by savages, captured in a wood by monkeys, or dying on a desert shore. And never did she mention her anxieties.

Mme. Aubain had anxieties of her own, about her daughter. The good sisters found her an affectionate but delicate child. The slightest emotion unnerved her. She had to give up the piano.

Her mother stipulated for regular letters from the convent. She lost patience one morning when the postman did not come, and walked to and fro in the parlour from her armchair to the window. It was really amazing; not a word for four days!

To console Mme. Aubain by her own example Félicité remarked:

"As for me, Madame, it's six months since I heard . . ."

"From whom, pray?"

"Why . . . from my nephew," the servant answered gently.

"Oh! your nephew!" And Mme. Aubain resumed her walk with a shrug of the shoulders, as much as to say: "I was not thinking of him! And what is more, it's absurd! A scamp of a cabin-boy—what does he matter? . . . whereas my daughter . . . why, just think!"

Félicité, though she had been brought up on harshness, felt indignant with Madame—and then forgot. It seemed the simplest thing in the world to her to lose one's head over the little girl. For her the two children were equally important; a bond in her heart made them one, and their destinies must be the same.

She heard from the chemist that Victor's ship had arrived at Havana. He had read this piece of news in a gazette.

Cigars—they made her imagine Havana as a place where no one does anything but smoke, and there was Victor moving among the negroes in a cloud of tobacco. Could you, she wondered, "in case you needed," return by land? What was the distance from Pont-l'Évêque? She questioned M. Bourais to find out.

He reached for his atlas and began explaining the longitudes; Félicité's consternation provoked a fine pedantic smile. Finally he marked with his pencil a black, imperceptible point in the indentations of an oval spot, and said as he did so, "Here it is." She bent over the map; the maze of coloured lines wearied her eyes without conveying anything; and on an invitation from Bourais to tell him her difficulty she begged him to show her the house where Victor was living. Bourais threw up his arms, sneezed, and laughed immensely: a simplicity like hers was a positive joy. And Félicité did not understand the reason; how could she when she expected, very likely, to see the actual image of her nephew—so stunted was her mind!

A fortnight afterwards Liébard came into the kitchen at market-time as usual and handed her a letter from her brother-in-law. As neither of them could read she took it to her mistress.

Mme. Aubain, who was counting the stitches in her knitting, put the work down by her side, broke the seal of the letter, started, and said in a low voice, with a look of meaning:

"It is bad news . . . that they have to tell you. Your nephew . . ."

He was dead. The letter said no more.

Félicité fell on to a chair, leaning her head against the wainscot; and she closed her eyelids, which suddenly flushed pink. Then with bent forehead, hands hanging, and fixed eyes, she said at intervals:

"Poor little lad! poor little lad!"

Liébard watched her and heaved sighs. Mme. Aubain trembled a little.

She suggested that Félicité should go to see her sister at Trouville. Félicité answered by a gesture that she had no need.

There was a silence. The worthy Liébard thought it was time for them to withdraw.

Then Félicité said:

"They don't care, not they!"

Her head dropped again; and she took up mechanically, from time to time, the long needles on her work-table.

Women passed in the yard with a barrow of dripping linen.

As she saw them through the window-panes she remembered her washing; she had put it to soak the day before, to-day she must wring it out; and she left the room.

Her plank and tub were at the edge of the Toucques. She threw a pile of linen on the bank, rolled up her sleeves, and taking her wooden beater dealt lusty blows whose sound carried to the neighbouring gardens. The meadows were empty, the river stirred in the wind; and down below long grasses wavered, like the hair of corpses floating in the water. She kept her grief down and was very brave until the evening; but once in her room she surrendered to it utterly, lying stretched on the mattress with her face in the pillow and her hands clenched against her temples.

Much later she heard, from the captain himself, the circumstances of Victor's end. They had bled him too much at the hospital for yellow fever. Four doctors held him at once. He had died instantly, and the chief had said:

"Bah! there goes another!"

His parents had always been brutal to him. She preferred not to see them again; and they made no advances, either because they forgot her or from the callousness of the wretchedly poor.

Virginie began to grow weaker.

Tightness in her chest, coughing, continual fever, and veinings on her cheekbones betrayed some deep-seated complaint. M. Poupart had advised a stay in

Provence. Mme. Aubain determined on it, would have brought her daughter home at once but for the climate of Pont-l'Évêque.

She made an arrangement with a job-master, and he drove her to the convent every Tuesday. There is a terrace in the garden, with a view over the Seine. Virginie took walks there over the fallen vine-leaves, on her mother's arm. A shaft of sunlight through the clouds made her blink sometimes, as she gazed at the sails in the distance and the whole horizon from the castle of Tancarville to the light-houses at Havre. Afterwards they rested in the arbour. Her mother had secured a little cask of excellent Malaga; and Virginie, laughing at the idea of getting tipsy, drank a thimble full of it, no more.

Her strength came back visibly. The autumn glided gently away. Félicité reassured Mme. Aubain. But one evening, when she had been out on a commission in the neighbourhood, she found M. Poupart's gig at the door. He was in the hall, and Mme. Aubain was tying her bonnet.

"Give me my foot-warmer, purse, gloves! Quicker, come!"

Virginie had inflammation of the lungs; perhaps it was hopeless.

"Not yet!" said the doctor, and they both got into the carriage under whirling flakes of snow. Night was coming on and it was very cold.

Félicité rushed into the church to light a taper. Then she ran after the gig, came up with it in an hour, and jumped lightly in behind. As she hung on by the fringes a thought came into her mind: "The courtyard has not been shut up; supposing burglars got in!" And she jumped down.

At dawn next day she presented herself at the doctor's. He had come in and started for the country again. Then she waited in the inn, thinking that a letter would come by some hand or other. Finally, when it was twilight, she took the Lisieux coach.

The convent was at the end of a steep lane. When she was about half-way up it she heard strange sounds—a death-bell tolling. "It is for someone else," thought Félicité, and she pulled the knocker violently.

After some minutes there was a sound of trailing slippers, the door opened ajar, and a nun appeared.

The good sister, with an air of compunction, said that "she had just passed away." On the instant the bell of St. Leonard's tolled twice as fast.

Félicité went up to the second floor.

From the doorway she saw Virginie stretched on her back, with her hands joined, her mouth open, and head thrown back under a black crucifix that leaned towards her, between curtains that hung stiffly, less pale than was her face. Mme. Aubain, at the foot of the bed which she clasped with her arms, was choking with sobs of agony. The mother superior stood on the right. Three candlesticks on the chest of drawers made spots of red, and the mist came whitely through the windows. Nuns came and took Mme. Aubain away.

For two nights Félicité never left the dead child. She repeated the same prayers, sprinkled holy water over the sheets, came and sat down again, and watched her. At the end of the first vigil she noticed that the face had grown yellow, the lips turned blue, the nose was sharper, and the eyes sunk in. She kissed them several times, and would not have been immensely surprised if Virginie had opened them again; to minds like hers the supernatural is quite simple. She made the girl's toilette, wrapped her in her shroud, lifted her down into her bier, put a garland on her head, and spread out her hair. It was fair, and extraordinarily long for her age. Félicité cut off a big lock and slipped half of it into her bosom, determined that she should never part with it.

The body was brought back to Pont-l'Évêque, as Mme. Aubain intended; she followed the hearse in a closed carriage.

It took another three-quarters of an hour after the mass to reach the cemetery. Paul walked in front, sobbing. M. Bourais was behind, and then came the chief residents, the women shrouded in black mantles, and Félicité. She thought of her nephew; and because she had not been able to pay these honours to him her grief was doubled, as though the one were being buried with the other.

Mme. Aubain's despair was boundless. It was against God that she first rebelled, thinking it unjust of Him to have taken her daughter from her—she had never done evil and her conscience was so clear! Ah, no!—she ought to have taken Virginie off to the south. Other doctors would have saved her. She accused herself now, wanted to join her child, and broke into cries of distress in the middle of her dreams. One dream haunted her above all. Her husband, dressed as a sailor, was returning from a long voyage, and shedding tears he told her that he had been ordered to take Virginie away. Then they consulted how to hide her somewhere.

She came in once from the garden quite upset. A moment ago—and she pointed out the place—the father and daughter had appeared to her, standing side by side, and they did nothing, but they looked at her.

For several months after this she stayed inertly in her room. Félicité lectured her gently; she must live for her son's sake, and for the other, in remembrance of "her."

"Her?" answered Mme. Aubain, as though she were just waking up. "Ah, yes! . . . yes! . . . You do not forget her!" This was an allusion to the cemetery, where she was strictly forbidden to go.

Félicité went there every day.

Precisely at four she skirted the houses, climbed the hill, opened the gate, and came to Virginie's grave. It was a little column of pink marble with a stone underneath and a garden plot enclosed by chains. The beds were hidden under a coverlet of flowers. She watered their leaves, freshened the gravel, and knelt down to break up the earth better. When Mme. Aubain was able to come there she felt a relief and a sort of consolation.

Then years slipped away, one like another, and their only episodes were the great festivals as they recurred—Easter, the Assumption, All Saints' Day. Household occurrences marked dates that were referred to afterwards. In 1825, for instance, two glaziers white-washed the hall; in 1827 a piece of the roof fell into the courtyard and nearly killed a man. In the summer of 1828 it was Madame's turn to offer the consecrated bread; Bourais, about this time, mysteriously absented himself; and one by one the old acquaintances passed away: Guyot, Liébard, Mme. Lechaptois, Robelin, and Uncle Gremanville, who had been paralysed for a long time.

One night the driver of the mail-coach announced the Revolution of July[6] in Pont-l'Évêque. A new sub-prefect was appointed a few days later—Baron de Larsonnière, who had been consul in America, and brought with him, besides his wife, a sister-in-law and three young ladies, already growing up. They were to be seen about on their lawn, in loose blouses, and they had a negro and a parrot. They paid a call on Mme. Aubain which she did not fail to return. The moment they were seen in the distance Félicité ran to let her mistress know. But only one thing could really move her feelings—the letters from her son.

He was swallowed up in a tavern life and could follow no career. She paid his debts, he made new ones; and the sighs that Mme. Aubain uttered as she sat knitting by the window reached Félicité at her spinning-wheel in the kitchen.

They took walks together along the espaliered wall, always talking of Virginie and wondering if such and such a thing would have pleased her and what, on some occasion, she would have been likely to say.

All her small belongings filled a cupboard in the two-bedded room. Mme. Aubain inspected them as seldom as she could. One summer day she made up her mind to it—and some moths flew out of the wardrobe.

Virginie's dresses were in a row underneath a shelf, on which there were three dolls, some hoops, a set of toy pots and pans, and the basin that she used. They took out her petticoats as well, and the stockings and handkerchiefs, and laid them out on the two beds before folding them up again. The sunshine lit up these poor things, bringing out their stains and the creases made by the body's movements. The air was warm and blue, a blackbird warbled, life seemed bathed in a deep sweetness. They found a little plush hat with thick, chestnut-coloured pile; but it was eaten all over by moths. Félicité begged it for her own. Their eyes met fixedly and filled with tears; at last the mistress opened her arms, the servant threw herself into them, and they embraced each other, satisfying their grief in a kiss that made them equal.

It was the first time in their lives, Mme. Aubain's nature not being expansive. Félicité was as grateful as though she had received a favour, and cherished her mistress from that moment with the devotion of an animal and a religious worship.

The kindness of her heart unfolded.

When she heard the drums of a marching regiment in the street she posted herself at the door with a pitcher of cider and asked the soldiers to drink. She nursed cholera patients and protected the Polish refugees;[7] one of these even declared that he wished to marry her. They quarrelled, however; for when she came back from the Angelus one morning she found that he had got into her kitchen and made himself a vinegar salad which he was quietly eating.

After the Poles came father Colmiche, an old man who was supposed to have committed atrocities in '93.[8] He lived by the side of the river in the ruins of a pigsty.

---

[6] **Revolution of July:** In 1830 the Bourbons were expelled and Louis Philippe became king of France.

[7] **Polish refugees:** After Russia suppressed the Polish uprisings in 1831, many Polish refugees came to France.

[8] **atrocities in '93:** The Reign of Terror during the French Revolution began in 1793.

The little boys watched him through the cracks in the wall, and threw pebbles at him which fell on the pallet where he lay constantly shaken by a catarrh; his hair was very long, his eyes inflamed, and there was a tumour on his arm bigger than his head. She got him some linen and tried to clean up his miserable hole; her dream was to establish him in the bake-house, without letting him annoy Madame. When the tumour burst she dressed it every day; sometimes she brought him cake, and would put him in the sunshine on a truss of straw. The poor old man, slobbering and trembling, thanked her in his worn-out voice, was terrified that he might lose her, and stretched out his hands when he saw her go away. He died; and she had a mass said for the repose of his soul.

That very day a great happiness befell her; just at dinner-time appeared Mme. de Larsonnière's negro, carrying the parrot in its cage, with perch, chain, and padlock. A note from the baroness informed Mme. Aubain that her husband had been raised to a prefecture and they were starting that evening; she begged her to accept the bird as a memento and mark of her regard.

For a long time he had absorbed Félicité's imagination, because he came from America; and that name reminded her of Victor, so much so that she made inquiries of the negro. She had once gone so far as to say "How Madame would enjoy having him!"

The negro repeated the remark to his mistress; and as she could not take the bird away with her she chose this way of getting rid of him.

4

His name was Loulou. His body was green and the tips of his wings rose-pink; his forehead was blue and his throat golden.

But he had the tiresome habits of biting his perch, tearing out his feathers, sprinkling his dirt about, and spattering the water of his tub. He annoyed Mme. Aubain, and she gave him to Félicité for good.

She endeavoured to train him; soon he could repeat "Nice boy! Your servant, sir! Good morning, Marie!" He was placed by the side of the door, and astonished several people by not answering to the name Jacquot, for all parrots are called Jacquot. People compared him to a turkey and a log of wood, and stabbed Félicité to the heart each time. Strange obstinacy on Loulou's part!—directly you looked at him he refused to speak.

None the less he was eager for society; for on Sundays, while the Rochefeuille ladies, M. de Houppeville, and new familiars—Onfroy the apothecary, Monsieur Varin, and Captain Mathieu—were playing their game of cards, he beat the windows with his wings and threw himself about so frantically that they could not hear each other speak.

Bourais' face, undoubtedly, struck him as extremely droll. Directly he saw it he began to laugh—and laugh with all his might. His peals rang through the courtyard and were repeated by the echo; the neighbours came to their windows and laughed too; while M. Bourais, gliding along under the wall to escape the parrot's eye, and hiding his profile with his hat, got to the river and then entered by the garden gate. There was a lack of tenderness in the looks which he darted at the bird.

Loulou had been slapped by the butcher-boy for making so free as to plunge his head into his basket; and since then he was always trying to nip him through his shirt. Fabu threatened to wring his neck, although he was not cruel, for all his tattooed arms and large whiskers. Far from it; he really rather liked the parrot, and in a jovial humour even wanted to teach him to swear. Félicité, who was alarmed by such proceedings, put the bird in the kitchen. His little chain was taken off and he roamed about the house.

His way of going downstairs was to lean on each step with the curve of his beak, raise the right foot, and then the left; and Félicité was afraid that these gymnastics brought on fits of giddiness. He fell ill and could not talk or eat any longer. There was a growth under his tongue, such as fowls have sometimes. She cured him by tearing the pellicle off with her finger-nails. Mr. Paul was thoughtless enough one day to blow some cigar smoke into his nostrils, and another time when Mme. Lormeau was teasing him with the end of her umbrella he snapped at the ferrule. Finally he got lost.

Félicité had put him on the grass to refresh him, and gone away for a minute, and when she came back—no sign of the parrot! She began by looking for him in the shrubs, by the waterside, and over the roofs, without listening to her mistress's cries of "Take care, do! You are out of your wits!" Then she investigated all the gardens in Pont-l'Évêque, and stopped the passers-by. "You don't ever happen to have seen my parrot, by any chance, do you?" And she gave a description of the parrot to those who did not know him. Suddenly, behind the mills at the foot of the hill she thought she could make out something green that fluttered. But on the top of the hill there was nothing. A hawker assured her that he had come across the parrot just before, at Saint-Melaine, in Mère Simon's shop. She rushed there; they had no idea of what she meant. At last she came home exhausted, with her slippers in shreds and despair in her soul; and as she was sitting in the middle of the garden-seat at Madame's side, telling the whole story of her efforts, a light weight dropped on to her shoulder—it was Loulou! What on earth had he been doing? Taking a walk in the neighbourhood, perhaps!

She had some trouble in recovering from this, or rather never did recover. As the result of a chill she had an attack of quinsy,[9] and soon afterwards an earache. Three years later she was deaf; and she spoke very loud, even in church. Though Félicité's sins might have been published in every corner of the diocese without dishonour to her or scandal to anybody, his Reverence the priest thought it right now to hear her confession in the sacristy only.

Imaginary noises in the head completed her upset. Her mistress often said to her, "Heavens! how stupid you are!" "Yes, Madame," she replied, and looked about for something.

Her little circle of ideas grew still narrower; the peal of church-bells and the lowing of cattle ceased to exist for her. All living beings moved as silently as ghosts. One sound only reached her ears now—the parrot's voice.

---

[9] **quinsy:** Tonsillitis.

Loulou, as though to amuse her, reproduced the click-clack of the turn-spit, the shrill call of a man selling fish, and the noise of the saw in the joiner's house opposite; when the bell rang he imitated Mme. Aubain's "Félicité! the door! the door!"

They carried on conversations, he endlessly reciting the three phrases in his repertory, to which she replied with words that were just as disconnected but uttered what was in her heart. Loulou was almost a son and a lover to her in her isolated state. He climbed up her fingers, nibbled at her lips, and clung to her kerchief; and when she bent her forehead and shook her head gently to and fro, as nurses do, the great wings of her bonnet and the bird's wings quivered together.

When the clouds massed and the thunder rumbled Loulou broke into cries, perhaps remembering the downpours in his native forests. The streaming rain made him absolutely mad; he fluttered wildly about, dashing up to the ceiling, upset everything, and went out through the window to dabble in the garden; but he was back quickly to perch on one of the fire-dogs[10] and hopped about to dry himself, exhibiting his tail and his beak in turn.

One morning in the terrible winter of 1837 she had put him in front of the fireplace because of the cold. She found him dead, in the middle of his cage: head downwards, with his claws in the wires. He had died from congestion, no doubt. But Félicité thought he had been poisoned with parsley, and though there was no proof of any kind her suspicions inclined to Fabu.

She wept so piteously that her mistress said to her, "Well, then, have him stuffed!"

She asked advice from the chemist, who had always been kind to the parrot. He wrote to Havre, and a person called Fellacher undertook the business. But as parcels sometimes got lost in the coach she decided to take the parrot as far as Honfleur herself.

Along the sides of the road were leafless apple-trees, one after the other. Ice covered the ditches. Dogs barked about the farms; and Félicité, with her hands under her cloak, her little black sabots[11] and her basket, walked briskly in the middle of the road.

She crossed the forest, passed High Oak, and reached St. Gatien.

A cloud of dust rose behind her, and in it a mail-coach, carried away by the steep hill, rushed down at full gallop like a hurricane. Seeing this woman who would not get out of the way, the driver stood up in front and the postilion shouted too. He could not hold in his four horses, which increased their pace, and the two leaders were grazing her when he threw them to one side with a jerk of the reins. But he was wild with rage, and lifting his arm as he passed at full speed, gave her such a lash from waist to neck with his big whip that she fell on her back.

Her first act, when she recovered consciousness, was to open her basket. Loulou was happily none the worse. She felt a burn in her right cheek, and when she put her hands against it they were red; the blood was flowing.

---

[10] **fire-dogs:** Andirons.

[11] **sabots:** Wooden shoes.

She sat down on a heap of stones and bound up her face with her handkerchief. Then she ate a crust of bread which she had put in the basket as a precaution, and found a consolation for her wound in gazing at the bird.

When she reached the crest of Ecquemauville she saw the Honfleur lights sparkling in the night sky like a company of stars; beyond, the sea stretched dimly. Then a faintness overtook her and she stopped; her wretched childhood, the disillusion of her first love, her nephew's going away, and Virginie's death all came back to her at once like the waves of an oncoming tide, rose to her throat, and choked her.

Afterwards, at the boat, she made a point of speaking to the captain, begging him to take care of the parcel, though she did not tell him what was in it.

Fellacher kept the parrot a long time. He was always promising it for the following week. After six months he announced that a packing-case had started, and then nothing more was heard of it. It really seemed as though Loulou was never coming back. "Ah, they have stolen him!" she thought.

He arrived at last, and looked superb. There he was, erect upon a branch which screwed into a mahogany socket, with a foot in the air and his head on one side, biting a nut which the bird-stuffer — with a taste for impressiveness — had gilded.

Félicité shut him up in her room. It was a place to which few people were admitted, and held so many religious objects and miscellaneous things that it looked like a chapel and bazaar in one.

A big cupboard impeded you as you opened the door. Opposite the window commanding the garden a little round one looked into the court; there was a table by the folding-bed with a water-jug, two combs, and a cube of blue soap in a chipped plate. On the walls hung rosaries, medals, several benign Virgins, and a holy water vessel made out of cocoa-nut; on the chest of drawers, which was covered with a cloth like an altar, was the shell box that Victor had given her, and after that a watering-can, a toy-balloon, exercise-books, the illustrated geography, and a pair of young lady's boots; and, fastened by its ribbons to the nail of the looking-glass, hung the little plush hat! Félicité carried observances of this kind so far as to keep one of Monsieur's frock-coats. All the old rubbish which Mme. Aubain did not want any longer she laid hands on for her room. That was why there were artificial flowers along the edge of the chest of drawers and a portrait of the Comte d'Artois[12] in the little window recess.

With the aid of a bracket Loulou was established over the chimney, which jutted into the room. Every morning when she woke up she saw him there in the dawning light, and recalled old days and the smallest details of insignificant acts in a deep quietness which knew no pain.

Holding, as she did, no communication with anyone, Félicité lived as insensibly as if she were walking in her sleep. The Corpus Christi processions roused her to life again. Then she went round begging mats and candlesticks from the neighbours to decorate the altar they put up in the street.

---

[12] **Comte d'Artois:** Title of Charles X (1757–1836), the last of the Bourbon kings. He ruled between 1824 and 1830 and died in 1836 in exile.

In church she was always gazing at the Holy Ghost in the window, and observed that there was something of the parrot in him. The likeness was still clearer, she thought, on a crude colour-print representing the baptism of Our Lord. With his purple wings and emerald body he was the very image of Loulou.

She bought him, and hung him up instead of the Comte d'Artois, so that she could see them both together in one glance. They were linked in her thoughts; and the parrot was consecrated by his association with the Holy Ghost, which became more vivid to her eye and more intelligible. The Father could not have chosen to express Himself through a dove, for such creatures cannot speak; it must have been one of Loulou's ancestors, surely. And though Félicité looked at the picture while she said her prayers she swerved a little from time to time towards the parrot.

She wanted to join the Ladies of the Virgin, but Mme. Aubain dissuaded her.

And then a great event loomed up before them — Paul's marriage.

He had been a solicitor's clerk to begin with, and then tried business, the Customs, the Inland Revenue, and made efforts, even, to get into the Rivers and Forests. By an inspiration from heaven he had suddenly, at thirty-six, discovered his real line — the Registrar's Office. And there he showed such marked capacity that an inspector had offered him his daughter's hand and promised him his influence.

So Paul, grown serious, brought the lady to see his mother.

She sniffed at the ways of Pont-l'Évêque, gave herself great airs, and wounded Félicité's feelings. Mme. Aubain was relieved at her departure.

The week after came news of M. Bourais' death in an inn in Lower Brittany. The rumour of suicide was confirmed, and doubts arose as to his honesty. Mme. Aubain studied his accounts, and soon found out the whole tale of his misdoings — embezzled arrears, secret sales of wood, forged receipts, etc. Besides that he had an illegitimate child, and "relations with a person at Dozulé."

These shameful facts distressed her greatly. In March 1853 she was seized with a pain in the chest; her tongue seemed to be covered with film, and leeches did not ease the difficult breathing. On the ninth evening of her illness she died, just at seventy-two.

She passed as being younger, owing to the bands of brown hair which framed her pale, pock-marked face. There were few friends to regret her, for she had a stiffness of manner which kept people at a distance.

But Félicité mourned for her as one seldom mourns for a master. It upset her ideas and seemed contrary to the order of things, impossible and monstrous, that Madame should die before her.

Ten days afterwards, which was the time it took to hurry there from Besançon, the heirs arrived. The daughter-in-law ransacked the drawers, chose some furniture, and sold the rest; and then they went back to their registering.

Madame's armchair, her small round table, her foot-warmer, and the eight chairs were gone! Yellow patches in the middle of the panels showed where the engravings had hung. They had carried off the two little beds and the mattresses, and all Virginie's belongings had disappeared from the cupboard. Félicité went from floor to floor dazed with sorrow.

The next day there was a notice on the door, and the apothecary shouted in her ear that the house was for sale.

She tottered, and was obliged to sit down. What distressed her most of all was to give up her room, so suitable as it was for poor Loulou. She enveloped him with a look of anguish when she was imploring the Holy Ghost, and formed the idolatrous habit of kneeling in front of the parrot to say her prayers. Sometimes the sun shone in at the attic window and caught his glass eye, and a great luminous ray shot out of it and put her in an ecstasy.

She had a pension of three hundred and eighty francs a year which her mistress had left her. The garden gave her a supply of vegetables. As for clothes, she had enough to last her to the end of her days, and she economized in candles by going to bed at dusk.

She hardly ever went out, as she did not like passing the dealer's shop, where some of the old furniture was exposed for sale. Since her fit of giddiness she dragged one leg; and as her strength was failing Mère Simon, whose grocery business had collapsed, came every morning to split the wood and pump water for her.

Her eyes grew feeble. The shutters ceased to be thrown open. Years and years passed, and the house was neither let nor sold.

Félicité never asked for repairs because she was afraid of being sent away. The boards on the roof rotted; her bolster was wet for a whole winter. After Easter she spat blood.

Then Mère Simon called in a doctor. Félicité wanted to know what was the matter with her. But she was too deaf to hear, and the only word which reached her was "pneumonia." It was a word she knew, and she answered softly "Ah! like Madame," thinking it natural that she should follow her mistress.

The time for the festal shrines[13] was coming near. The first one was always at the bottom of the hill, the second in front of the post-office, and the third towards the middle of the street. There was some rivalry in the matter of this one, and the women of the parish ended by choosing Mme. Aubain's courtyard.

The hard breathing and fever increased. Félicité was vexed at doing nothing for the altar. If only she could at least have put something there! Then she thought of the parrot. The neighbours objected that it would not be decent. But the priest gave her permission, which so intensely delighted her that she begged him to accept Loulou, her sole possession, when she died.

From Tuesday to Saturday, the eve of the festival, she coughed more often. By the evening her face had shrivelled, her lips stuck to her gums, and she had vomitings; and at twilight next morning, feeling herself very low, she sent for a priest.

Three kindly women were round her during the extreme unction. Then she announced that she must speak to Fabu. He arrived in his Sunday clothes, by no means at his ease in the funereal atmosphere.

---

[13] **time . . . shrines:** At the festival for the local saint's day, a procession would march through a series of shrines.

"Forgive me," she said, with an effort to stretch out her arm; "I thought it was you who had killed him."

What did she mean by such stories? She suspected him of murder—a man like him! He waxed indignant, and was on the point of making a row.

"There," said the women, "she is no longer in her senses, you can see it well enough!"

Félicité spoke to shadows of her own from time to time. The women went away, and Mère Simon had breakfast. A little later she took Loulou and brought him close to Félicité with the words:

"Come, now, say good-bye to him!"

Loulou was not a corpse, but the worms devoured him; one of his wings was broken, and the tow was coming out of his stomach. But she was blind now; she kissed him on the forehead and kept him close against her cheek. Mère Simon took him back from her to put him on the altar.

5

Summer scents came up from the meadows; flies buzzed; the sun made the river glitter and heated the slates. Mère Simon came back into the room and fell softly asleep.

She woke at the noise of bells; the people were coming out from vespers. Félicité's delirium subsided. She thought of the procession and saw it as if she had been there.

All the school children, the church-singers, and the firemen walked on the pavement, while in the middle of the road the verger armed with his hallebard and the beadle with a large cross advanced in front. Then came the schoolmaster, with an eye on the boys, and the sister, anxious about her little girls; three of the daintiest, with angelic curls, scattered rose-petals in the air; the deacon controlled the band with outstretched arms; and two censer-bearers turned back at every step towards the Holy Sacrament, which was borne by Monsieur the curé, wearing his beautiful chasuble, under a canopy of dark-red velvet held up by four churchwardens. A crowd of people pressed behind, between the white cloths covering the house walls, and they reached the bottom of the hill.

A cold sweat moistened Félicité's temples. Mère Simon sponged her with a piece of linen, saying to herself that one day she would have to go that way.

The hum of the crowd increased, was very loud for an instant and then went further away.

A fusillade shook the window-panes. It was the postilions saluting the monstrance.[14] Félicité rolled her eyes and said as audibly as she could: "Does he look well?" The parrot was weighing on her mind.

Her agony began. A death-rattle that grew more and more convulsed made her sides heave. Bubbles of froth came at the corners of her mouth and her whole body trembled.

---

[14] **monstrance:** The container for the consecrated host.

Soon the booming of the ophicleides,[15] the high voices of the children, and the deep voices of the men were distinguishable. At intervals all was silent, and the tread of feet, deadened by the flowers they walked on, sounded like a flock pattering on grass.

The clergy appeared in the courtyard. Mère Simon clambered on to a chair to reach the attic window, and so looked down straight upon the shrine. Green garlands hung over the altar, which was decked with a flounce of English lace. In the middle was a small frame with relics in it; there were two orange-trees at the corners, and all along stood silver candlesticks and china vases, with sunflowers, lilies, peonies, foxgloves, and tufts of hortensia. This heap of blazing colour slanted from the level of the altar to the carpet which went on over the pavement; and some rare objects caught the eye. There was a silver-gilt sugar-basin with a crown of violets; pendants of Alençon stone glittered on the moss, and two Chinese screens displayed their landscapes. Loulou was hidden under roses, and showed nothing but his blue forehead, like a plaque of lapis lazuli.

The churchwardens, singers, and children took their places round the three sides of the court. The priest went slowly up the steps, and placed his great, radiant golden sun[16] upon the lace. Everyone knelt down. There was a deep silence; and the censers glided to and fro on the full swing of their chains.

An azure vapour rose up into Félicité's room. Her nostrils met it; she inhaled it sensuously, mystically; and then closed her eyes. Her lips smiled. The beats of her heart lessened one by one, vaguer each time and softer, as a fountain sinks, an echo disappears; and when she sighed her last breath she thought she saw an opening in the heavens, and a gigantic parrot hovering above her head.

⚘ FYODOR DOSTOEVSKY
B. RUSSIA, 1821–1881

Like other writers of Russia's Golden Age of Literature, Dostoevsky was concerned about the challenges his divided homeland was facing: some intellectuals and artists felt that Russia, with its remote geographical location, was out of the political and social mainstream of Europe. It was lagging behind the technical and democratic times, they thought, and should hasten the process of Westernization. The progressive winds blowing over Russia carried with them socialist ideas about atheism, revolution, and social progress. After his experiences with liberal political movements as a young man, Dostoevsky began to question whether human beings were essentially rational and could act reasonably according

---

[15] **ophicleides:** A deep-toned brass wind instrument.

[16] **golden sun:** The monstrance.

to an ideology or if there was a dark force within them shaping behavior. In his characters he examined the boundaries of reason and the shadowy side of human consciousness. Eventually he embraced orthodox ideas about sin, penance, and forgiveness, and sided with populist, or Slavophile,[1] ideas about peasants and nationalism, Christianity, and Russia's destiny. Because of his honest and detailed depictions of Russian life, Dostoevsky is usually classified as a Realist, along with Honoré de Balzac, Gustave Flaubert (p. 938), George Eliot, Charles Dickens (p. 1037), and Leo Tolstoy (p. 983), but this label is too limiting for his genius.

FYOH-dore
mik-AIL-oh-vitch
duh-stah-YEV-skee

The Young Radical. Fyodor Mikhailovich Dostoevsky was born October 30, 1821, in Moscow. His father was a doctor at a public hospital for the poor, where the family lived. This setting provided an early introduction to pain and suffering for the young Fyodor. His mother was sickly and died when he was sixteen. That same year he was enrolled at the Military Engineer's school in St. Petersburg. En route to the school he saw a government courier beat his coachman with his fists. "This revolting scene remained in my memory for the rest of my life," he wrote in 1876. During his five years of study in St. Petersburg his primary interest was literature.

Fyodor's retired father, who had had a reputation for brutality, was murdered by the peasants on his small estate while his son was away. Dostoevsky resigned his military commission in 1844, and, with some inherited money from his father, devoted himself to writing. The result was the publication of *Poor Folk* in 1846, which portrayed the lives of the lower classes. It was a big success, especially with Vissarion Grigoryevich Belinsky (1811–1848), the most important critic of the time and a champion of literary Realism and Western culture. Dostoevsky immediately became a part of the young Russian literary set with utopian, revolutionary schemes.

www For links to more information about Dostoevsky and a quiz on *The Brothers Karamazov,* see bedford stmartins.com/ worldlitcompact.

In reaction to the **REVOLUTION OF 1848** in France and out of fear that the winds of reform might make their way to Russia, Tsar Nicholas I had socialists, including Dostoevsky, rounded up and arrested in Moscow in 1849. They were tried and sentenced to death. In a prearranged sadistic plot devised to scare the young intellectuals, they were led blindfolded before a firing squad, and at the very last moment a reprieve was granted. Not surprisingly, Dostoevsky never forgot that moment either. He spent the next four years in penal servitude in Siberia. Released in 1854, he was assigned as a common soldier to a town on the Mongolian border where he married the consumptive widow of a customs official, a disastrous marriage that lasted until her death in 1864.

---

[1] **Slavophile:** Someone who admires Slavs, the dominant Russian ethnicity; in nineteenth-century Russia this term meant someone who believed in the national traditions of Russia and felt that Russia had the one true religion, and someone who felt destined to export Russian teachings and to establish the kingdom of God on earth.

A Change of Mind and Heart. While in prison, Dostoevsky underwent a profound conversion, replacing the progressive, revolutionary ideas of his youth with a more orthodox belief in the potential in human nature for evil, the cleansing benefits of suffering, the redemptive power of love, and a faith in the prophetic mission of the Russian peasant. He also experienced the first of the epileptic seizures that would haunt him the rest of his life. After nearly ten years of exile in Siberia, which is described in *The House of the Dead* (1862), Dostoevsky was finally permitted to return to European Russia and arrived in St. Petersburg in 1859. Three years after his first wife died and following a stormy affair, he married his stenographer, Anna Gregorievna Snitkin. They fled to Europe to avoid creditors, but eventually his wife brought some semblance of order and stability to his life. Dostoevsky's money problems resulted from his brother's debts and his own debilitating gambling; meanwhile he was writing some of the finest novels of the Western world, such as *Crime and Punishment* (1866) and *The Idiot* (1868). During the last ten years of his life he enjoyed comparatively easy circumstances along with popularity and respect. *A Raw Youth* was published in 1875, and from 1876 to 1880 he wrote *The Diary of a Writer,* a monthly journal. The climax of his writing career was a novel he had worked on for years, *The Brothers Karamazov* (1880), which was a huge success. Less than a year after its publication Dostoevsky died, on January 28, 1881.

Perov Vasilij, *Portrait of Fyodor Dostoevsky* *Dostoevsky's inquisitive and serious nature is evident in this painting. (Art Resource)*

Ideas of Flesh and Blood. Dostoevsky's novels are like laboratories where the major ideas of Europeans in the second half of the nineteenth century are dissected. The ideas are not examined abstractly as, say, in a philosophical treatise, but are embodied in flesh and blood individuals— that is, as lived ideas. Critic Nicholas Berdyaev writes that ideas for Dostoevsky "are fiery billows, never frozen categories . . . they are the destiny of living being, its burning motive-power." Typically, characters in Dostoevsky's major novels are in crisis, usually because of a crime or an immoral act they've committed. Rarely are his characters seen in the context of ordinary, everyday situations, the humdrum of work or play, complacency or habit—such as we might find in **Anton Chekhov**'s short stories. Dostoevsky tends to place his protagonists in margins between freedom and captivity, love and hate, crime and forgiveness, sin and salvation, life and death. Through these intense conflicts Dostoevsky bypasses mundane concerns in order to explore the ultimate questions of existence. Even though his own inner conflicts and spiritual odyssey became the basis for a number of his fictional heroes, it would be a mistake to read Dostoevsky's novels as solely autobiographical.

p. 1247

The Major Novels. In 1864 Dostoevsky used a vulgar persona to chastise Russian intellectuals in the short novel *Notes from Underground,* which initiated the period of his major novels and exhibits some of his favorite literary techniques. The title has also been translated as *Voices from Under the Floorboards,* suggesting that "underground" refers to not only a political or social position but a psychological or emotional space as well. In it a man with a wounded ego explores his own inner darkness in a tortured confessional monologue while indicting simplistic theories of social progress and the overzealous application of science to human beings. *Notes* was followed by *Crime and Punishment* in 1866, a novel that on one level is a psychological detective story in which an intelligent but desperate student murders a despicable old moneylender in order to steal enough money to continue his education. For much of the book the student, Raskolnikov, plays cat and mouse with Inspector Porfiry and his own conscience. Interwoven with the realistic, grim portraits of poor, disenfranchised urban life is the idea that, through the suffering it causes him, Raskolnikov's crime provides the occasion for his own redemption as assisted by Sonia, a saintly prostitute. In *The Idiot* (1868), Dostoevsky projects the spiritual insights of his own epileptic experiences onto his hero, Prince Myshkin, a fascinating mixture of goodness and innocence. *The Possessed* (1871) is a direct attack on the youthful revolutionaries who would use political philosophies from the West to reform Russia; indirectly Dostoevsky was answering Ivan Turgenev (1818–1883), whose sympathies appeared to be with the Westernizers in *Fathers and Sons* (1861). Although Dostoevsky's characters often get caught up in debating contemporary issues, it is usually the internal, psychological debate, the conflict of consciousness or conscience, that interests Dostoevsky.

 The Brothers Karamazov, from which the selected passage, "The Grand Inquisitor," is taken, is a story of parricide. In a strangely modern family configuration, father Karamazov has one son by his first wife, two sons by his second wife, and one illegitimate son by a simpleminded peasant. The boys' mothers die and the sons are raised by relatives so that the father can pursue his crude, hedonistic ways. They grow up to be very different in personality and interests but nevertheless representative of the diverse, conflicting parts of Dostoevsky himself and contemporary society. Dmitri is passionate and tempestuous like his father. Alyosha is both innocent and saintly. The illegitimate Smerdyakov is degenerate, an epileptic who eventually kills his father. Ivan is the intellectual, torn between doubt and faith, hope and nihilism, reflecting most directly Dostoevsky's own inner division. Ivan struggles with the idea of a loving God who could permit extensive suffering on earth, especially that of innocent children. All the brothers in their own ways live life passionately.

"The Grand Inquisitor."   Ivan recites "The Grand Inquisitor" to Alyosha, a work he calls his "poem in prose." The setting for Ivan's prose poem is Seville, Spain, at the height of the Inquisition in the sixteenth century, when the Roman Catholic hierarchy attempted to purge heretics and Protestant sympathizers from the church. In the poem Jesus has finally returned to earth to heal and comfort his people after fifteen centuries. He is immediately arrested and isolated by the Grand Inquisitor. In a persuasive and moving monologue, the Inquisitor explains to Jesus why the church as an institution had to betray his original mission and enslave people by exploiting "miracle, mystery, and authority." According to the Inquisitor, the masses were incapable of handling the freedom intended by Jesus and were willing to exchange it for bread and the illusion of freedom. The Inquisitor vacillates between powerful apologist for institutional cynicism and lonely, disillusioned atheist. In a perfect response to the Inquisitor's degradation, Jesus kisses him on the lips and departs.

Following "The Grand Inquisitor" in the novel is a discussion with Father Zossima, a true holy man who acts as a foil to the Inquisitor. Father Zossima preaches unconditional love for our fallen world: "Love all God's creation, the whole and every grain of sand in it. Love every leaf, every ray of God's light. Love the animals, love the plants, love everything. If you love everything, you will perceive the divine mystery in things. Once you perceive it, you will begin to comprehend it better every day. And you will come at last to love the whole world with an all-embracing love." In contrast to Father Zossima, the Inquisitor represents the corruption of the spirit through institutional authority.

Dostoevsky did not intend Ivan's prose poem to be a series of answers that prescribe a course of action. As a literary gem, it is meant to raise questions and stimulate multiple interpretations. Part of Dostoevsky's genius was that he went beyond the usual boundaries of nineteenth-century consciousness and called into question the institutions and programs of Western culture, exposing a spiritual wasteland that would plague the sensibilities of modern writers.

■ **FURTHER RESEARCH**

Biography
Magarshack, David. *Dostoevsky*. 1963.
Terras, F. M. *Dostoevsky: Life, Work, and Criticism*. 1984.

Historical Background
Mirsky, Dmitri. *History of Russian Literature*. 1963.

Criticism
Amoia, Alba della Fazia. *Fyodor Dostoevsky*. 1993.
Berdyaev, Nicholas. *Dostoevsky: An Interpretation*. 1957.
Ivanov, Vyacheslav. *Freedom and the Tragic Life: A Study in Dostoevsky*. 1952.
Jones, Malcolm, and Garth M. Terry, eds. *New Essays on Dostoevsky*. 1983.
Simmons, Ernest J. *Dostoevsky: The Making of a Novelist*. 1950.
Wellek, Rene, ed. *Dostoevsky: A Collection of Critical Essays*. 1962.

■ **PRONUNCIATION**
Fyodor Mikhailovich Dostoevsky: FYOH-dore mik-AIL-oh-vitch duh-stah-YEV-skee

On the furthest horizon Dostoevsky has lit beacons of such radiant brilliance that they seem to us not terrestrial fires, but stars in heaven; but he, all the while, is at our sides, guiding their rays into our breasts. . . . Inexorably he stands before us, with his penetrating, enigmatic gaze, the sombre and keen-eyed guide through the labyrinth of our souls, simultaneously guiding and spying upon us.

– VYACHESLAV IVANOV, critic, 1960

FROM

∽ The Brothers Karamazov

Translated by Constance Garnett

THE GRAND INQUISITOR

"*. . . Do you know, Alyosha—don't laugh! I made a poem about a year ago. If you can waste another ten minutes on me, I'll tell it to you.*"

"*You wrote a poem?*"

"*Oh, no, I didn't write it,*" laughed Ivan, "*and I've never written two lines of poetry in my life. But I made up this poem in prose and I remembered it. I was carried away when I made it up. You will be my first reader—that is, listener. Why should an author forego even one listener?*" smiled Ivan. "*Shall I tell it to you?*"

"*I am all attention,*" said Alyosha.

"*My poem is called 'The Grand Inquisitor'; it's a ridiculous thing, but I want to tell it to you.*"

"Even this must have a preface—that is, a literary preface," laughed Ivan, "and I am a poor hand at making one. You see, my action takes place in the sixteenth century, and at that time, as you probably learnt at school, it was customary in poetry to bring down heavenly powers on earth. Not to speak of Dante, in France clerks, as well as the monks in the monasteries, used to give regular performances in which the Madonna, the saints, the angels, Christ, and God Himself were brought on the stage. In those days it was done in all simplicity. In Victor Hugo's 'Notre Dame de Paris' an edifying and gratuitous spectacle was provided for the people in the Hotel de Ville of Paris in the reign of Louis XI in honor of the birth of the dauphin. It was called *Le bon jugement de la très sainte et gracieuse Vierge Marie,*[1] and she appears herself on the stage and pronounces her *bon jugement.* Similar plays, chiefly from the Old Testament, were occasionally performed in Moscow, too, up to the times of Peter the Great. But besides plays there were all sorts of legends and ballads scattered about the world, in which the saints and angels and all the powers of Heaven took part when required. In our monasteries the monks busied themselves in translating, copying, and even composing such poems—and even under the Tatars. There is, for instance, one such poem (of course, from the Greek), 'The Wanderings of Our Lady Through Hell,' with descriptions as bold as Dante's. Our Lady visits Hell, and the Archangel Michael leads her through the torments. She sees the sinners and their punishment. There she sees among others one noteworthy set of sinners in a burning lake; some of them sink to the bottom of the lake so that they can't swim out, and

---

A note on the translation: The translation of "The Grand Inquisitor" by Constance Garnett, first published as a part of *The Brothers Karamazov* in 1912, quickly became the standard translation of this work. All footnotes are the editors'.

---

[1] *Le bon . . . Marie:* The good judgment of the saintly and gracious Virgin Mary.

'these God forgets'—an expression of extraordinary depth and force. And so Our Lady, shocked and weeping, falls before the throne of God and begs for mercy for all in Hell—for all she has seen there, and indiscriminately. Her conversation with God is immensely interesting. She beseeches Him, she will not desist, and when God points to the hands and feet of her Son, nailed to the Cross, and asks, 'How can I forgive His tormentors?' she bids all the saints, all the martyrs, all the angels and archangels to fall down with her and pray for mercy on all without distinction. It ends by her winning from God a respite of suffering every year from Good Friday till Trinity day, and the sinners at once raise a cry of thankfulness from Hell, chanting, 'Thou art just, O Lord, in this judgment.' Well, my poem would have been of that kind if it had appeared at that time. He comes on the scene in my poem, but He says nothing, only appears and passes on. Fifteen centuries have passed since He promised to come in His glory, fifteen centuries since His prophet wrote, 'Behold, I come quickly';[2] 'Of that day and that hour knoweth no man, neither the Son, but the Father,'[3] as He Himself predicted on earth. But humanity awaits him with the same faith and with the same love. Oh, with greater faith, for it is fifteen centuries since man has ceased to see signs from Heaven.

> No signs from Heaven come today
> To add to what the heart doth say.

There was nothing left but faith in what the heart doth say. It is true there were many miracles in those days. There were saints who performed miraculous cures; some holy people, according to their biographies, were visited by the Queen of Heaven herself. But the devil did not slumber, and doubts were already arising among men of the truth of these miracles. And just then there appeared in the north of Germany a terrible new heresy. 'A huge star like to a torch' (that is, to a church) 'fell on the sources of the waters and they became bitter.' These heretics began blasphemously denying miracles. But those who remained faithful were all the more ardent in their faith. The tears of humanity rose up to Him as before, awaiting His coming, loved Him, hoped for Him, yearned to suffer and die for Him as before. And so many ages mankind had prayed with faith and fervor, 'O Lord our God, hasten Thy coming,' so many ages called upon Him, that in His infinite mercy He deigned to come down to His servants. Before that day He had come down, He had visited some holy men, martyrs, and hermits, as is written in their 'Lives.' Among us, Tyutchev,[4] with absolute faith in the truth of his words, bore witness that

> Bearing the Cross, in slavish dress,
> Weary and worn, the Heavenly King
> Our mother, Russia, came to bless,
> And through our land went wandering.

And that certainly was so, I assure you.

---

[2] **"Behold . . . quickly":** Revelations 22:7.

[3] **"Of . . . Father":** Mark 13:32.

[4] **Tyutchev** (1803–1873): A Russian poet.

"And behold, He deigned to appear for a moment to the people, to the tortured, suffering people, sunk in iniquity, but loving Him like children. My story is laid in Spain, in Seville, in the most terrible time of the Inquisition, when fires were lighted every day to the glory of God, and 'in the splendid *auto da fé*[5] the wicked heretics were burnt.' Oh, of course, this was not the coming in which He will appear according to His promise at the end of time in all His heavenly glory, and which will be sudden 'as lightning flashing from east to west.'[6] No, He visited His children only for a moment, and there where the flames were crackling round the heretics. In His infinite mercy He came once more among men in that human shape in which He walked among men for three years fifteen centuries ago. He came down to the 'hot pavement' of the southern town in which on the day before almost a hundred heretics had, *ad majorem gloriam Dei,*[7] been burnt by the cardinal, the Grand Inquisitor, in a magnificent *auto da fé,* in the presence of the king, the court, the knights, the cardinals, the most charming ladies of the court, and the whole population of Seville.

"He came softly, unobserved, and yet, strange to say, every one recognized Him. That might be one of the best passages in the poem. I mean, why they recognized Him. The people are irresistibly drawn to Him, they surround Him, they flock about Him, follow Him. He moves silently in their midst with a gentle smile of infinite compassion. The sun of love burns in His heart, light and power shine from His eyes, and their radiance, shed on the people, stirs their hearts with responsive love. He holds out His hands to them, blesses them, and a healing virtue comes from contact with Him, even with His garments. An old man in the crowd, blind from childhood, cries out, 'O Lord, heal me and I shall see Thee!' and, as it were, scales fall from his eyes and the blind man sees Him. The crowd weeps and kisses the earth under His feet. Children throw flowers before Him, sing, and cry hosannah. 'It is He — it is He!' all repeat. 'It must be He, it can be no one but Him!' He stops at the steps of the Seville cathedral at the moment when the weeping mourners are bringing in a little open white coffin. In it lies a child of seven, the only daughter of a prominent citizen. The dead child lies hidden in flowers. 'He will raise your child,' the crowd shouts to the weeping mother. The priest, coming to meet the coffin, looks perplexed and frowns, but the mother of the dead child throws herself at His feet with a wail. 'If it is Thou, raise my child!' she cries, holding out her hands to Him. The procession halts, the coffin is laid on the steps at His feet. He looks with compassion, and His lips once more softly pronounce, 'Maiden, arise!'[8] and the maiden arises. The little girl sits up in the coffin and looks round, smiling with wide-open wondering eyes, holding a bunch of white roses they had put in her hand.

"There are cries, sobs, confusion among the people, and at that moment the cardinal himself, the Grand Inquisitor, passes by the cathedral. He is an old man, almost ninety, tall and erect, with a withered face and sunken eyes, in which there is still a

---

[5] *auto da fé:* Literally, "act of faith"; indicates the burning of a heretic.
[6] **"as . . . west":** Matthew 24:27.
[7] *ad . . . Dei:* "For the greater glory of God," the Jesuits' motto.
[8] **"Maiden, arise!":** Mark 5:41.

gleam of light. He is not dressed in his gorgeous cardinal's robes, as he was the day before, when he was burning the enemies of the Roman Church—at that moment he was wearing his coarse, old, monk's cassock. At a distance behind him come his gloomy assistants and slaves and the 'holy guard.' He stops at the sight of the crowd and watches it from a distance. He sees everything; he sees them set the coffin down at His feet, sees the child rise up, and his face darkens. He knits his thick grey brows and his eyes gleam with a sinister fire. He holds out his finger and bids the guards take Him. And such is his power, so completely are the people cowed into submission and trembling obedience to him, that the crowd immediately makes way for the guards, and in the midst of deathlike silence they lay hands on Him and lead Him away. The crowd instantly bows down to the earth, like one man, before the old inquisitor. He blesses the people in silence and passes on. The guards lead their prisoner to the close, gloomy, vaulted prison in the ancient palace of the Holy Inquisition and shut Him in it. The day passes and is followed by the dark, burning 'breathless' night of Seville. The air is 'fragrant with laurel and lemon.' In the pitch darkness the iron door of the prison is suddenly opened and the Grand Inquisitor himself comes in with a light in his hand. He is alone; the door is closed at once behind him. He stands in the doorway and for a minute or two gazes into His face. At last he goes up slowly, sets the light on the table and speaks.

"'Is it Thou? Thou?' but receiving no answer, he adds at once, 'Don't answer, be silent. What canst Thou say, indeed? I know too well what Thou wouldst say. And Thou hast no right to add anything to what Thou hadst said of old. Why, then, art Thou come to hinder us? For Thou hast come to hinder us, and Thou knowest that. But dost Thou know what will be tomorrow? I know not who Thou art and care not to know whether it is Thou or only a semblance of Him, but tomorrow I shall condemn Thee and burn Thee at the stake as the worst of heretics. And the very people who have today kissed Thy feet, tomorrow at the faintest sign from me will rush to heap up the embers of Thy fire. Knowest Thou that? Yes, maybe Thou knowest it,' he added with thoughtful penetration, never for a moment taking his eyes off the Prisoner."

"I don't quite understand, Ivan. What does it mean?" Alyosha, who had been listening in silence, said with a smile. "Is it simply a wild fantasy, or a mistake on the part of the old man—some impossible *quid pro quo*?"[9]

"Take it as the last," said Ivan, laughing, "if you are so corrupted by modern realism and can't stand anything fantastic. If you like it to be a case of mistaken identity, let it be so. It is true," he went on, laughing, "the old man was ninety, and he might well be crazy over his set idea. He might have been struck by the appearance of the Prisoner. It might, in fact, be simply his ravings, the delusion of an old man of ninety, overexcited by the *auto da fé* of a hundred heretics the day before. But does it matter to us after all whether it was a mistake of identity or a wild fantasy? All that matters is that the old man should speak out, should speak openly of what he has thought in silence for ninety years."

"And the Prisoner too is silent? Does He look at him and not say a word?"

---

[9] *quid pro quo:* Misunderstanding.

"That's inevitable in any case," Ivan laughed again. "The old man has told Him He hasn't the right to add anything to what He has said of old. One may say it is the most fundamental feature of Roman Catholicism, in my opinion at least. 'All has been given by Thee to the Pope,' they say, 'and all, therefore, is still in the Pope's hands, and there is no need for Thee to come now at all. Thou must not meddle for the time, at least.' That's how they speak and write, too—the Jesuits, at any rate. I have read it myself in the works of their theologians. 'Hast Thou the right to reveal to us one of the mysteries of that world from which Thou hast come?' my old man asks Him, and answers the question for Him. 'No, Thou has not; that Thou mayest not add to what has been said of old, and mayest not take from men the freedom which Thou didst exalt when Thou wast on earth. Whatsoever Thou revealest anew will encroach on men's freedom of faith; for it will be manifest as a miracle, and the freedom of their faith was dearer to Thee than anything in those days fifteen hundred years ago. Didst Thou not often say then, "I will make you free"?[10] But now Thou hast seen these "free" men,' the old man adds suddenly, with a pensive smile. 'Yes, we've paid dearly for it,' he goes on, looking sternly at Him, 'but at last we have completed that work in Thy name. For fifteen centuries we have been wrestling with Thy freedom, but now it is ended and over for good. Dost Thou not believe that it's over for good? Thou lookest meekly at me and deignest not even to be wroth with me. But let me tell Thee that now, today, people are more persuaded than ever that they have perfect freedom, yet they have brought their freedom to us and laid it humbly at our feet. But that has been our doing. Was this what Thou didst? Was this Thy freedom?'"

"I don't understand again," Alyosha broke in. "Is he ironical, is he jesting?"

"Not a bit of it! He claims it as a merit for himself and his Church that at last they have vanquished freedom and have done so to make men happy. 'For now' (he is speaking of the Inquisition, of course) 'for the first time it has become possible to think of the happiness of men. Man was created a rebel; and how can rebels be happy? Thou wast warned,' he says to Him. 'Thou hast had no lack of admonitions, and warnings, but Thou didst not listen to those warnings; Thou didst reject the only way by which men might be made happy. But, fortunately, departing Thou didst hand on the work to us. Thou hast promised, Thou hast established by Thy word, Thou hast given to us the right to bind and to unbind, and now, of course, Thou canst not think of taking it away. Why, then, hast Thou come to hinder us?'"

"And what's the meaning of 'no lack of admonitions and warnings'?" asked Alyosha.

"Why, that's the chief part of what the old man must say.

"'The wise and dread Spirit, the spirit of self-destruction and nonexistence,' the old man goes on, 'the great spirit talked with Thee in the wilderness, and we are told in the books that he "tempted" Thee.[11] Is that so? And could anything truer be said than what he revealed to Thee in three questions and what Thou didst reject, and

---

[10] "I . . . free": For example, John 8:36.

[11] he "tempted" Thee: The story of Satan's temptation of Jesus is told in Matthew 4:1–11 and in Luke 4:1–13.

what in the books is called "the temptation"? And yet if there has ever been on earth a real stupendous miracle, it took place on that day, on the day of the three temptations. The statement of those three questions was itself the miracle. If it were possible to imagine simply for the sake of argument that those three questions of the dread spirit had perished utterly from the books, and that we had to restore them and to invent them anew, and to do so had gathered together all the wise men of the earth — rulers, chief priests, learned men, philosophers, poets — and had set them the task to invent three questions, such as would not only fit the occasion, but express in three words, three human phrases, the whole future history of the world and of humanity — dost Thou believe that all the wisdom of the earth united could have invented anything in depth and force equal to the three questions which were actually put to Thee then by the wise and mighty spirit in the wilderness? From those questions alone, from the miracle of their statement, we can see that we have here to do not with the fleeting human intelligence, but with the absolute and eternal. For in those three questions the whole subsequent history of mankind is, as it were, brought together into one whole, and foretold, and in them are united all the unsolved historical contradictions of human nature. At the time it could not be so clear, since the future was unknown; but now that fifteen hundred years have passed, we see that everything in those three questions was so justly divined and foretold, and has been so truly fulfilled, that nothing can be added to them or taken from them.

"'Judge Thyself who was right — Thou or he who questioned Thee then? Remember the first question; its meaning, in other words, was this: "Thou wouldst go into the world, and art going with empty hands, with some promise of freedom which men in their simplicity and their natural unruliness cannot even understand, which they fear and dread — for nothing has ever been more insupportable for a man and a human society than freedom. But seest Thou these stones in this parched and barren wilderness? Turn them into bread, and mankind will run after Thee like a flock of sheep, grateful and obedient, though forever trembling, lest Thou withdraw Thy hand and deny them Thy bread." But Thou wouldst not deprive man of freedom and didst reject the offer, thinking, what is that freedom worth, if obedience is bought with bread? Thou didst reply that man lives not by bread alone. But dost Thou know that for the sake of that earthly bread the spirit of the earth will rise up against Thee and will strive with Thee and overcome Thee, and all will follow him, crying, "Who can compare with this beast? He has given us fire from heaven!"[12] Dost Thou know that the ages will pass, and humanity will proclaim by the lips of their sages that there is no crime, and therefore no sin; there is only hunger? "Feed men, and then ask of them virtue!" that's what they'll write on the banner which they will raise against Thee, and with which they will destroy Thy temple. Where Thy temple stood will rise a new building; the terrible tower of Babel[13] will be built again, and though, like the one of old, it will not be finished, yet Thou mightest have prevented that new tower and have cut short the sufferings of men for a thousand years; for

---

[12] "Who can . . . heaven.": Revelations, 13:4, 13.

[13] **tower of Babel**: Genesis 11.

they will come back to us after a thousand years of agony with their tower. They will seek us again, hidden underground in the catacombs, for we shall be again persecuted and tortured. They will find us and cry to us, "Feed us, for those who have promised us fire from heaven haven't given it!" And then we shall finish building their tower, for he finishes the building who feeds them. And we alone shall feed them in Thy name, declaring falsely that it is in Thy name. Oh, never, never can they feed themselves without us! No science will give them bread so long as they remain free. In the end they will lay their freedom at our feet, and say to us, "Make us your slaves, but feed us." They will understand themselves, at last, that freedom and bread enough for all are inconceivable together, for never, never will they be able to share between them! They will be convinced, too, that they can never be free, for they are weak, vicious, worthless, and rebellious. Thou didst promise them the bread of Heaven, but, I repeat again, can it compare with earthly bread in the eyes of the weak, ever-sinful, and ignoble race of man? And if for the sake of the bread of Heaven thousands and tens of thousands shall follow Thee, what is to become of the millions and tens of thousands of millions of creatures who will not have the strength to forego the earthly bread for the sake of the heavenly? Or dost Thou care only for the tens of thousands of the great and strong, while the millions, numerous as the sands of the sea, who are weak but love Thee, must exist only for the sake of the great and strong? No, we care for the weak, too. They are sinful and rebellious, but in the end they too will become obedient. They will marvel at us and look on us as gods, because we are ready to endure the freedom which they have found so dreadful and to rule over them — so awful it will seem to them to be free. But we shall tell them that we are Thy servants and rule them in Thy name. We shall deceive them again, for we will not let Thee come to us again. That deception will be our suffering, for we shall be forced to lie.

"'This is the significance of the first question in the wilderness, and this is what Thou hast rejected for the sake of that freedom which Thou hast exalted above everything. Yet in this question lies hidden the great secret of this world. Choosing "bread," Thou wouldst have satisfied the universal and everlasting craving of humanity — to find someone to worship. So long as man remains free he strives for nothing so incessantly and so painfully as to find someone to worship. But man seeks to worship what is established beyond dispute, so that all men would agree at once to worship it. For these pitiful creatures are concerned not only to find what one or the other can worship, but to find something that all would believe in and worship; what is essential is that all may be *together* in it. This craving for *community* of worship is the chief misery of every man individually and of all humanity from the beginning of time. For the sake of common worship they've slain each other with the sword. They have set up gods and challenged one another, "Put away your gods and come and worship ours, or we will kill you and your gods!" And so it will be to the end of the world, even when gods disappear from the earth; they will fall down before idols just the same. Thou didst know, Thou couldst not but have known, this fundamental secret of human nature, but Thou didst reject the one infallible banner which was offered Thee to make all men bow down to Thee alone — the banner of earthly bread; and Thou hast rejected it for the sake of freedom and the bread of Heaven. Behold what Thou didst further. And all again in the name of freedom! I tell Thee that man is tormented by no greater anxiety than to find someone quickly to whom he can hand over the gift of freedom with which the ill-fated creature is born. But only one who can appease their conscience can take over their freedom. In bread there was offered Thee an invincible banner; give bread, and man will worship Thee, for nothing is more certain than bread. But if someone else gains possession of his conscience — oh! then he will cast away Thy bread and follow after him who has ensnared his conscience. In that Thou wast right. For the secret of man's being is not only to live but to have something to live for. Without a stable conception of the object of life, man would not consent to go on living, and would rather destroy himself than remain on earth, though he had bread in abundance. That is true. But what happened? Instead of taking men's freedom from them, Thou didst make it greater than ever! Didst Thou forget that man prefers peace, and even death, to freedom of choice in the knowledge of good and evil? Nothing is more seductive for man than his freedom of conscience, but nothing is a greater cause of suffering. And behold, instead of giving a firm foundation for setting the conscience of man at rest forever, Thou didst choose all that is exceptional, vague, and enigmatic; Thou didst choose what was utterly beyond the strength of men, acting as though Thou didst not love them at all — Thou who didst come to give Thy life for them! Instead of taking possession of man's freedom, Thou didst increase it, and burdened the spiritual kingdom of mankind with its sufferings forever. Thou didst desire man's free love, that he should follow Thee freely, enticed and taken captive by Thee. In place of the rigid, ancient law, man must hereafter with free heart decide for himself what is good and what is evil, having only Thy image before him as his guide. But didst Thou not know he would at last reject even Thy image and Thy truth, if he is weighed down with the fearful burden of free choice? They will cry aloud at last that the truth is not in Thee, for they could not have been left in greater confusion and suffering than Thou hast caused, laying upon them so many cares and unanswerable problems.

"'So that, in truth, Thou didst Thyself lay the foundation for the destruction of Thy kingdom, and no one is more to blame for it. Yet what was offered Thee? There are three powers, three powers alone, able to conquer and to hold captive forever the conscience of these impotent rebels for their happiness — those forces are miracle, mystery, and authority. Thou hast rejected all three and hast set the example for doing so. When the wise and dread spirit set Thee on the pinnacle of the temple and said to Thee, "If Thou wouldst know whether Thou art the Son of God then cast Thyself down, for it is written: the angels shall hold him up lest he fall and bruise himself, and Thou shalt know then whether Thou art the Son of God and shalt prove then how great is Thy faith in Thy Father." But Thou didst refuse and wouldst not cast Thyself down. Oh! of course, Thou didst proudly and well like God; but the weak, unruly race of men, are they gods? Oh, Thou didst know then that in taking one step, in making one movement to cast Thyself down, Thou wouldst be tempting God and have lost all Thy faith in Him, and wouldst have been dashed to pieces against that earth which Thou didst come to save. And the wise spirit that tempted Thee would have rejoiced. But I ask again, are there many like Thee? And couldst

Thou believe for one moment that men, too, could face such a temptation? Is the nature of men such that they can reject miracle, and at the great moments of their life, the moments of their deepest, most agonizing spiritual difficulties, cling only to the free verdict of the heart? Oh, Thou didst know that Thy deed would be recorded in books, would be handed down to remote times and the utmost ends of the earth, and Thou didst hope that man, following Thee, would cling to God and not ask for a miracle. But Thou didst not know that when man rejects miracle he rejects God too; for man seeks not so much God as the miraculous. And as man cannot bear to be without the miraculous, he will create new miracles of his own for himself, and will worship deeds of sorcery and witchcraft, though he might be a hundred times over a rebel, heretic, and infidel. Thou didst not come down from the Cross when they shouted to Thee, mocking and reviling Thee, "Come down from the Cross and we will believe that Thou art He."[14] Thou didst not come down, for again Thou wouldst not enslave man by a miracle, and didst crave faith given freely, not based on miracle. Thou didst crave for free love and not the base raptures of the slave before the might that has overawed him forever. But Thou didst think too highly of men therein, for they are slaves, of course, though rebellious by nature. Look round and judge; fifteen centuries have passed; look upon them. Whom hast Thou raised up to Thyself? I swear, man is weaker and baser by nature than Thou hast believed him! Can he, can he do what Thou didst? By showing him so much respect, Thou didst, as it were, cease to feel for him, for Thou didst ask far too much from him — Thou who hast loved him more than Thyself! Respecting him less, Thou wouldst have asked less of him. That would have been more like love, for his burden would have been lighter. He is weak and vile. What though he is everywhere now rebelling against our power, and proud of his rebellion? It is the pride of a child and a schoolboy. They are little children rioting and barring out the teacher at school. But their childish delight will end; it will cost them dear. They will cast down temples and drench the earth with blood. But they will see at last, the foolish children, that, though they are rebels, they are impotent rebels, unable to keep up their own rebellion. Bathed in their foolish tears, they will recognize at last that He who created them rebels must have meant to mock at them. They will say this in despair, and their utterance will be a blasphemy which will make them more unhappy still, for man's nature cannot bear blasphemy, and in the end alway avengeit on itself. And so unrest, confusion, and unhappiness — that is the present lot of man after Thou didst bear so much for their freedom! Thy great prophet tells in vision and in image that he saw all those who took part in the first resurrection and that there were of each tribe twelve thousand. But if there were so many of them, they must have been not men but gods. They had borne Thy cross, they had endured scores of years in the barren, hungry wilderness, living upon locusts and roots — and Thou mayest indeed point with pride at those children of freedom, of free love, of free and splendid sacrifice for Thy name. But remember that they were only some thousands; and what of the rest? And how are the other weak ones to blame, because they could not endure what the strong have endured? How is

---

[14] "Come . . . He": Mark 15:32.

the weak soul to blame that it is unable to receive such terrible gifts? Canst Thou have simply come to the elect and for the elect? But if so, it is a mystery and we cannot understand it. And if it is a mystery, we too have a right to preach a mystery, and to teach them that it's not the free judgment of their hearts, not love, that matters, but a mystery which they must follow blindly, even against their conscience. So we have done. We have corrected Thy work and have founded it upon *miracle, mystery,* and *authority.* And men rejoiced that they were again led like sheep, and that the terrible gift that had brought them such suffering was, at last, lifted from their hearts. Were we right teaching them this? Speak! Did we not love mankind, so meekly acknowledging their feebleness, lovingly lightening their burden, and permitting their weak nature even sin with our sanction? Why hast Thou come now to hinder us? And why dost Thou look silently and searchingly at me with Thy mild eyes? Be angry. I don't want Thy love, for I love Thee not. And what use is it for me to hide anything from Thee? Don't I know to Whom I am speaking? All that I can say is known to Thee already. And is it for me to conceal from Thee our mystery? Perhaps it is Thy will to hear it from my lips. Listen, then. We are not working with Thee, but with *him*—that is our mystery. It's long—eight centuries—since we have been on *his* side and not on Thine. Just eight centuries ago, we took from him what Thou didst reject with scorn, that last gift he offered Thee, showing Thee all the kingdoms of the earth.[15] We took from him Rome and the sword of Cæsar, and proclaimed ourselves sole rulers of the earth, though hitherto we have not been able to complete our work. But whose fault is that? Oh, the work is only beginning, but it has begun. It has long to await completion and the earth has yet much to suffer, but we shall triumph and shall be Cæsars, and then we shall plan the universal happiness of man. But Thou mightest have taken even the sword of Cæsar. Why didst Thou reject that last gift? Hadst Thou accepted that last counsel of the mighty spirit, Thou wouldst have accomplished all that man seeks on earth—that is, someone to worship, someone to keep his conscience, and some means of uniting all in one unanimous and harmonious ant heap, for the craving for universal unity is the third and last anguish of men. Mankind as a whole has always striven to organize a universal state. There have been many great nations with great histories, but the more highly they were developed the more unhappy they were, for they felt more acutely than other people the craving for world-wide union. The great conquerors, Timours and Genghis Khans,[16] whirled like hurricanes over the face of the earth, striving to subdue its people, and they too were but the unconscious expression of the same craving for universal unity. Hadst Thou taken the world and Cæsar's purple, Thou wouldst have founded the universal state and have given universal peace. For who can rule men if not he who holds their conscience and their bread in his hands? We have taken the sword of Cæsar, and in taking it, of course, have rejected Thee and followed *him.* Oh,

---

[15] **that last gift . . . earth:** In 401, Pope Innocent I claimed authority over the Roman Church, establishing an institution competitive with the Roman Empire.

[16] **Timours . . . Khans:** Timour, or Timur (c. 1336–1405), and Genghis Khan (c. 1167–1227) were Mongol conquerors.

ages are yet to come of the confusion of free thought, of their science and cannibalism. For having begun to build their tower of Babel without us, they will end, of course, with cannibalism. But then the beast will crawl to us and lick our feet and spatter them with tears of blood. And we shall sit upon the beast and raise the cup, and on it will be written, "Mystery." But then, and only then, the reign of peace and happiness will come for men. Thou art proud of Thine elect, but Thou hast only the elect, while we give rest to all. And besides, how many of those elect, those mighty ones who could become elect, have grown weary waiting for Thee, and have transferred and will transfer the powers of their spirit and the warmth of their heart to the other camp, and end by raising their *free* banner against Thee. Thou didst Thyself lift up that banner. But with us all will be happy and will no more rebel, nor destroy one another as under Thy freedom. Oh, we shall persuade them that they will only become free when they renounce their freedom to us and submit to us. And shall we be right or shall we be lying? They will be convinced that we are right, for they will remember the horrors of slavery and confusion to which Thy freedom brought them. Freedom, free thought and science, will lead them into such straits and will bring them face to face with such marvels and insoluble mysteries that some of them, the fierce and rebellious, will destroy themselves; others, rebellious but weak, will destroy one another, while the rest, weak and unhappy, will crawl fawning to our feet and whine to us: "Yes, you were right, you alone possess His mystery, and we come back to you, save us from ourselves!"

"'Receiving bread from us, they will see clearly that we take the bread made by their hands from them, to give it to them, without any miracle. They will see that we do not change the stones to bread, but in truth they will be more thankful for taking it from our hands than for the bread itself! For they will remember only too well that in old days, without our help, even the bread they made turned to stones in their hands, while since they have come back to us, the very stones have turned to bread in their hands. Too, too well they know the value of complete submission! And until men know that, they will be unhappy. Who is most to blame for their not knowing it, speak? Who scattered the flock and sent it astray on unknown paths? But the flock will come together again and will submit once more, and then it will be once for all. Then we shall give them the quiet humble happiness of weak creatures such as they are by nature. Oh, we shall persuade them at last not to be proud, for Thou didst lift them up and thereby taught them to be proud. We shall show them that they are weak, that they are only pitiful children, but that childlike happiness is the sweetest of all. They will become timid and will look to us and huddle close to us in fear, as chicks to the hen. They will marvel at us and will be awe-stricken before us, and will be proud at our being so powerful and clever, that we have been able to subdue such a turbulent flock of thousands of millions. They will tremble impotently before our wrath, their minds will grow fearful, they will be quick to shed tears like women and children, but they will be just as ready at a sign from us to pass to laughter and rejoicing, to happy mirth and childish song. Yes, we shall set them to work, but in their leisure hours we shall make their life like a child's game, with children's songs and innocent dance. Oh, we shall allow them even sin; they are weak and helpless, and they will love us like children because we allow them to sin. We shall tell them that every sin will be expiated, if it is done with our permission, that we allow them to sin because we love them, and the punishment for these sins we take upon ourselves. And we shall take it upon ourselves, and they will adore us as their saviors who have taken on themselves their sins before God. And they will have no secrets from us. We shall allow or forbid them to live with their wives and mistresses, to have or not to have children—according to whether they have been obedient or disobedient—and they will submit to us gladly and cheerfully. The most painful secrets of their conscience, all, all they will bring to us, and we shall have an answer for all. And they will be glad to believe our answer, for it will save them from the great anxiety and terrible agony they endure at present in making a free decision for themselves. And all will be happy, all the millions of creatures, except the hundred thousand who rule over them. For only we, we who guard the mystery, shall be unhappy. There will be thousands of millions of happy babes, and a hundred thousand sufferers who have taken upon themselves the curse of the knowledge of good and evil. Peacefully they will die, peacefully they will expire in Thy name, and beyond the grave they will find nothing but death. But we shall keep the secret, and for their happiness we shall allure them with the reward of heaven and eternity. Though if there were anything in the other world, it certainly would not be for such as they. It is prophesied that Thou wilt come again in victory, Thou wilt come with Thy chosen, the proud and strong, but we will say that they have only saved themselves, but we have saved all. We are told that the harlot who sits upon the beast, and holds in her hands the *mystery,* shall be put to shame, that the weak will rise up again, and will rend her royal purple and will strip naked her loathsome body.[17] But then I will stand up and point out to Thee the thousand millions of happy children who have known no sin. And we who have taken their sins upon us for their happiness will stand up before Thee and say: "Judge us if Thou canst and darest." Know that I fear Thee not. Know that I too have been in the wilderness, I too have lived on roots and locusts, I too prized the freedom with which Thou hast blessed men, and I too was striving to stand among Thy elect, among the strong and powerful, thirsting "to make up the number." But I awakened and would not serve madness. I turned back and joined the ranks of those *who have corrected Thy work.* I left the proud and went back to the humble, for the happiness of the humble. What I say to Thee will come to pass, and our dominion will be built up. I repeat, tomorrow Thou shalt see that obedient flock who at a sign from me will hasten to heap up the hot cinders about the pile on which I shall burn Thee for coming to hinder us. For if anyone has ever deserved our fires, it is Thou. Tomorrow I shall burn Thee. *Dixi.*'"[18]

Ivan stopped. He was carried away as he talked and spoke with excitement; when he had finished, he suddenly smiled.

Alyosha had listened in silence; toward the end he was greatly moved and seemed several times on the point of interrupting, but restrained himself. Now his words came with a rush.

---

[17] **the harlot . . . body:** The Whore of Babylon in Revelation 17.

[18] *Dixi:* The closing word for a religious pronouncement, meaning "I have spoken."

"But . . . that's absurd!" he cried, flushing. "Your poem is in praise of Jesus, not in blame of Him—as you meant it to be. And who will believe you about freedom? Is that the way to understand it? That's not the idea of it in the Orthodox Church . . . That's Rome, and not even the whole of Rome, it's false—those are the worst of the Catholics, the Inquisitors, the Jesuits! . . . And there could not be such a fantastic creature as your Inquisitor. What are these sins of mankind they take on themselves? Who are these keepers of the mystery who have taken some curse upon themselves for the happiness of mankind? When have they been seen? We know the Jesuits, they are spoken ill of, but surely they are not what you describe? They are not that at all, not at all. . . . They are simply the Romish army for the earthly sovereignty of the world in the future, with the Pontiff of Rome for Emperor . . . that's their ideal, but there's no sort of mystery or lofty melancholy about it. . . . It's simple lust of power, of filthy earthly gain, of domination—something like a universal serfdom with them as masters—that's all they stand for. They don't even believe in God, perhaps. Your suffering inquisitor is a mere fantasy."

"Stay, stay," laughed Ivan, "how hot you are! A fantasy you say, let it be so! Of course it's a fantasy. But allow me to say: Do you really think that the Roman Catholic movement of the last centuries is actually nothing but the lust of power, of filthy earthly gain? Is that Father Païssy's teaching?"

"No, no, on the contrary, Father Païssy did once say something the same as you . . . but of course it's not the same, not a bit the same," Alyosha hastily corrected himself.

"A precious admission, in spite of your 'not a bit the same.' I ask you why your Jesuits and inquisitors have united simply for vile material gain? Why can there not be among them one martyr oppressed by great sorrow and loving humanity? You see, only suppose that there was one such man among all those who desire nothing but filthy material gain—if there's only one like my old inquisitor, who had himself eaten roots in the desert and made frenzied efforts to subdue his flesh to make himself free and perfect. But yet all his life he loved humanity, and suddenly his eyes were opened, and he saw that it is no great moral blessedness to attain perfection and freedom, if at the same time one gains the conviction that billions of God's creatures have been created as a mockery, that they will never be capable of using their freedom, that these poor rebels can never turn into giants to complete the tower, that it was not for such geese that the great idealist dreamt his dream of harmony. Seeing all that, he turned back and joined—the clever people. Surely that could have happened?"

"Joined whom, what clever people?" cried Alyosha, completely carried away. "They have no such great cleverness and no mysteries and secrets. . . . Perhaps nothing but atheism, that's all their secret. Your inquisitor does not believe in God, that's his secret!"

"What if it is so! At last you have guessed it. It's perfectly true that that's the whole secret, but isn't that suffering, at least for a man like that, who has wasted his whole life in the desert and yet could not shake off his incurable love of humanity? In his old age he reached the clear conviction that nothing but the advice of the great dread spirit could build up any tolerable sort of life for the feeble, unruly, 'incomplete, empirical creatures created in jest.' And so, convinced of this, he sees that he must follow the counsel of the wise spirit, the dread spirit of death and destruction, and therefore accept lying and deception, and lead men consciously to death and destruction, and yet deceive them all the way so that they may not notice where they are being led, that the poor, blind creatures may at least on the way think themselves happy. And note, the deception is in the name of Him in Whose ideal the old man had so fervently believed all his life long. Is not that tragic? And if only one such stood at the head of the whole army 'filled with the lust of power only for the sake of filthy gain' — would not one such be enough to make a tragedy? More than that, one such standing at the head is enough to create the actual leading idea of the Roman Church with all its armies and Jesuits, its highest idea. I tell you frankly that I firmly believe that there has always been such a man among those who stood at the head of the movement. Who knows, there may have been some such even among the Roman Popes. Who knows, perhaps the spirit of that accursed old man who loves mankind so obstinately in his own way is to be found even now in a whole multitude of such old men, existing not by chance but by agreement, as a secret league formed long ago for the guarding of the mystery, to guard it from the weak and the unhappy, so as to make them happy. No doubt it is so, and so it must be indeed. I fancy that even among the Masons there's something of the same mystery at the bottom, and that that's why the Catholics so detest the Masons as their rivals breaking up the unity of the idea, while it is so essential that there should be one flock and one shepherd. . . . But from the way I defend my idea I might be an author impatient of your criticism. Enough of it."

"You are perhaps a Mason yourself!" broke suddenly from Alyosha. "You don't believe in God," he added, speaking this time very sorrowfully. He fancied besides that his brother was looking at him ironically. "How does your poem end?" he asked, suddenly looking down. "Or was it the end?"

"I meant it to end like this: When the Inquisitor ceased speaking, he waited some time for his Prisoner to answer him. His silence weighed down upon him. He saw the Prisoner had listened intently all the time, looking gently in his face and evidently not wishing to reply. The old man longed for Him to say something, however bitter and terrible. But He suddenly approached the old man in silence and softly kissed him on his bloodless, aged lips. That was all his answer. The old man shuddered. His lips moved. He went to the door, opened it, and said to him: 'Go, and come no more. . . . Come not at all, never, never!' And he let him out into the dark alleys of the town. The Prisoner went away."

"And the old man?"

"The kiss glows in his heart, but the old man adheres to his idea."

"And you with him, you too?" cried Alyosha, mournfully.

Ivan laughed.

"Why, it's all nonsense, Alyosha. It's only a senseless poem of a senseless student, who could never write two lines of verse. Why do you take it so seriously? Surely you don't suppose I am going straight off to the Jesuits, to join the men who are correcting His work? Good Lord, it's no business of mine. I told you, all I want is to live on to thirty, and then . . . dash the cup to the ground!"

"But the little sticky leaves, and the precious tombs, and the blue sky, and the woman you love! How will you live, how will you love them?" Alyosha cried sorrowfully. "With such a hell in your heart and your head, how can you? No, that's just what you are going away for, to join them . . . if not, you will kill yourself, you can't endure it!"

"There is a strength to endure everything," Ivan said with a cold smile.

"What strength?"

"The strength of the Karamazovs—the strength of the Karamazov baseness."

"To sink into debauchery, to stifle your soul with corruption, yes?"

"Possibly even that . . . only perhaps till I am thirty I shall escape it, and then—"

"How will you escape it? By what will you escape it? That's impossible with your ideas."

"In the Karamazov way, again."

" 'Everything is lawful,' you mean? Everything is lawful, is that it?"

Ivan scowled, and all at once turned strangely pale.

"Ah, you've caught up yesterday's phrase, which so offended Miüsov—and which Dmitri pounced upon so naïvely and paraphrased!" he smiled queerly. "Yes, if you like, 'everything is lawful' since the word has been said. I won't deny it. And Mitya's version isn't bad."

Alyosha looked at him in silence.

"I thought that going away from here I have you at least," Ivan said suddenly, with unexpected feeling; "but now I see that there is no place for me even in your heart, my dear hermit. The formula, 'all is lawful,' I won't renounce—will you renounce me for that, yes?"

Alyosha got up, went to him, and softly kissed him on the lips.

"That's plagiarism," cried Ivan, highly delighted. "You stole that from my poem. Thank you, though. Get up, Alyosha, it's time we were going, both of us."

They went out, but stopped when they reached the entrance of the restaurant.

"Listen, Alyosha," Ivan began in a resolute voice, "if I am really able to care for the sticky little leaves, I shall only love them remembering you. It's enough for me that you are somewhere here, and I shan't lose my desire for life yet. Is that enough for you? Take it as a declaration of love if you like. And now you go to the right and I to the left. And it's enough, do you hear—enough! I mean even if I don't go away tomorrow (I think I certainly shall go) and we meet again, don't say a word more on these subjects. I beg that particularly. And about Dmitri, too, I ask you especially never speak to me again," he added, with sudden irritation; "it's all exhausted, it has all been said over and over again, hasn't it? And I'll make you one promise in return for it. When, at thirty, I want to 'dash the cup to the ground,' wherever I may be I'll come to have one more talk with you, even though it were from America—you may be sure of that. I'll come on purpose. It will be very interesting to have a look at you, to see what you'll be by that time. It's rather a solemn promise, you see. And we really may be parting for seven years or ten. Come, go now to your Pater Seraphicus, he is dying. If he dies without you, you will be angry with me for having kept you. Goodbye, kiss me once more; that's right, now go."

TEXT IN CONTEXT

∽ LEO TOLSTOY
B. RUSSIA, 1828–1910

Leo Tolstoy was the most famous Russian of his time. With the publication of two grand novels, *War and Peace* (1862–69) and *Anna Karenina* (1877), Tolstoy held a place of elevated importance in European literary circles, but he gained worldwide fame when he turned his attention to the political and spiritual issues of his day, writing nonfiction books and pamphlets that criticized the Russian Tsarist regime and charted a new spirituality for his followers. During the last years of Tolstoy's life, people came from all over the world to visit him at his country estate. Like Dostoevsky, Tolstoy rejected the Western materialism and secularism that appeared to be a byproduct of modern science, believing that Russia's salvation lay in a reformation of Christian values. It is deceptive, however, to characterize Tolstoy as a great novelist who turned into a moralist. His whole life was a struggle between the body and the spirit, between reason and faith. As a Romantic, he celebrated the lives and simple values of peasants, people who lived close to the earth and close to their hearts. In contrast, his aristocratic background seemed hollow and hypocritical. Nevertheless, he was attracted to the benefits of the city, to books and literate conversation, as well as to the decadent pleasures provided by urban life. As Tolstoy tried to reconcile his life with his art, he reflected a larger nineteenth-century dichotomy between rational **ENLIGHTENMENT** ideals, which could transform society, and the fresh vision of **ROMANTICISM**, which could inflame the imagination of individuals, promote the irrational, and reject society.

The Aristocrat with Peasant Sympathies.   Tolstoy was born on August 28, 1828, to Count Nikolaj Tolstoy and his wife, the former Princess

LEE-oh TOLE-stoy

Count Leo Tolstoy, c. 1880
This photograph of Tolstoy at age fifty-two was taken soon after he had completed Anna Karenina. *(Library of Congress)*

www   For links to more information about Tolstoy, a quiz on *The Death of Ivan Ilych,* and the 21st-century relevance of *Ivan Ilych,* see bedfordstmartins .com/worldlit compact.

Volkonsky, on the large country estate of Yasnaya Polyana, some 120 miles south of Moscow. The deaths of his mother when he was two, his father when he was nine, and a guardian aunt when he was thirteen left Tolstoy on his own at an early age. Later, with his primary attention on wine, women, and gambling, Tolstoy failed several courses at the University of Kazan, where he studied Asian languages and law. He left the university in 1847 without a degree and returned to Yasnaya Polyana, where he tried to improve the living conditions of the serfs on his family's estate. Frustrated by the suspicion of the peasants concerning making changes, Leo and his brother Nikolai journeyed to Caucasus, in Southern Russia, where Leo joined the army in 1851. Fighting first against Muslims and then against the French and English in the CRIMEAN WAR (1853–56), Tolstoy turned his experiences into *Sevastopol Sketches* (1855), which along with an earlier work, *Childhood* (1852), brought him national recognition.

Two Epic Novels.   Uneasy with literary society in Russia, Tolstoy visited Europe, where he became convinced that Westernization would not solve his homeland's problems. He returned to Russia and continued writing at Yasnaya Polyana, establishing a progressive school there for the children of his illiterate workers. At age thirty-four he married Sofia, the eighteen-year-old, high-strung daughter of a court doctor. During the early years of his marriage, from 1863 to 1869, he wrote the monumental *War and Peace.* Focusing on the invasion of Russia by Napoleon in 1812, it is the panoramic, epic-like sweep of this work, its vibrant world of characters and settings, that establish it as one of the greatest novels ever written.

When Sofia insisted that they winter in Moscow, Leo became a census taker and for the first time confronted the appalling poverty and degradation of the poor working classes in Moscow's slums—men, women, and children who were being ground down by a kind of slave labor in the factories. Tolstoy's own luxurious lifestyle deeply troubled his conscience, and he was determined to simplify his way of life. He cut wood, swept floors, and plowed fields. He made his own leather boots, wore a peasant blouse and trousers, and went barefoot in the summer. He drank a brew of barley and acorns rather than coffee and set to work writing *Anna Karenina* (1875–77). In this novel of contemporary manners, Anna and Vronsky's illicit love is successful initially in defying the conventional codes of marriage, but the power of social mores eventually crushes it.

A Spiritual Crisis.   After completing *Anna Karenina,* Tolstoy was exhausted; he suffered a profound psychological and moral crisis

Tolstoy working the fields, engraving, 1889
Tolstoy's deep sympathy for the poor working classes led him to renounce a luxurious lifestyle. (Art Archive)

concerning the futility of material success and the relentless movement of time toward death. He was rich and famous, but he questioned the value of his greatest novels. His autobiography, *A Confession* (1879), written in the tradition of both St. Augustine's[1] and Rousseau's[2] *Confessions,* describes this crisis of faith and includes a poignant fable about a traveler on the steppes who is attacked by a furious wild beast: "To save himself the traveler gets into a waterless well; but at the bottom of it he sees a dragon with jaws wide open to devour him. The unhappy man dares not get out for fear of the wild beast, and dares not descend for fear of the dragon, so he catches hold of the branch of a wild plant growing in a crevice of the well. His arms grow tired, and he feels that he must soon perish . . . he sees two mice, one black and one white, gradually making their way round the stem of the wild plant on which he is hanging, nibbling it through. The plant will soon give way and break off, and he will fall into the jaws of the dragon . . . still hanging, he looks around him, and, finding some drops of honey on the leaves of the wild plant, he stretches out his tongue and licks them." The beast

---

[1] **St. Augustine** (354–430): An influential Catholic theologian from Hippo, North Africa, who wrote *Confessions* (c. 401) to tell the story of his conversion (see volume 1).

[2] **Rousseau** (1812–1878): A French writer who wrote his *Confessions* (published 1781–88) to illustrate the importance of the individual and the self's particular genius (see p. 407).

of time pursues mortals into the dragon of death, while day and night eat away at man's hold on life.

According to the fable, death should compel us to savor the drops of honey available in the present moment, but Tolstoy's experience with death brought despair. In addition to the family he lost as a young boy, death had claimed his brother, his son Petya, who died in 1873, and his beloved Aunt Toinette, who died the following year. Tolstoy turned to religion: He studied the Scriptures and the history of Christianity. He wrestled with the concept of God. He emulated the piety of Russian peasants and took to visiting monasteries, the most notable of which is the Optina Monastery, made famous by Dostoevsky in *The Brothers Karamazov*. The New Testament's Sermon on the Mount and especially Matthew 5:39 — "Do not resist evil" — became Tolstoy's program for moral and spiritual reform. He was attracted by the Beatitudes, the idea of dispossession of goods, pacifism, and strict self-control. Tolstoy's daring, courageous experiment was to take Jesus' Sermon on the Mount seriously and actually try to live by it. By stripping Christianity free of institutions, priesthood, and ritual, Tolstoy hoped to re-create a basic, moral Christianity that he hoped would liberate Russians from a corrupt religion controlled by the bureaucracy of the church.

Tolstoy's Mission of Nonviolence.   After *Anna Karenina* and his moral crisis of 1878, Tolstoy was no longer interested in literature as art, only in literature as message. Writing fiction was less important to him than producing a series of books and pamphlets explaining his own version of Jesus' teachings. *What I Believe* (1883) examines Jesus' pacifism, his instructions to resist not evil with evil, to turn the other cheek, and to love one's enemies. *What Then Must We Do* (1884) looks at the plight of the impoverished classes in Moscow, deplores the evils of money, and prescribes a return to the land. In *The Kingdom of God Is Within You* (1894), Tolstoy expresses his opposition to religious ritual and the abuses of church power. His particular form of Christian anarchy is summed up in five commandments: Do not be angry at anyone; Do not commit adultery; Do not swear any oaths; Do not repay evil with evil; Love your enemies and be good to both enemies and friends. Tolstoy also expressed his beliefs in works of fiction, including several short stories and one rather propagandistic novel, *The Resurrection* (1900), in which Prince Nekhludov comes to terms with the consequences of his promiscuity and the burdens of wealth through a spiritual resurrection.

Tolstoy's war on Orthodoxy led to his excommunication from the Russian Church in 1901. But outside Russia his reputation grew.

Christians, Jews, Muslims, and BUDDHISTS from all over the world came
to Yasnaya Polyana to sit at his feet. Mahatma Gandhi (1869–1948), who
became internationally famous for using the principles of nonviolence
to liberate India from Great Britain in 1947, first came to know Tolstoy
through *The Kingdom of God Is Within You,* and the two men corresponded. In both South Africa and India, Gandhi used Tolstoy's
principles to mount campaigns of civil disobedience against unjust
laws. Although his doctrine of nonviolence did not appeal to Russian
Marxists, Tolstoy's ideas helped shape the twentieth-century practices
of not only Gandhi but also civil rights leader Martin Luther King Jr.
(1929–1968) and Dorothy Day (1897–1980), the founder of the Catholic
Worker movement in New York City. For his part, Tolstoy admired the
transcendental writings of Emerson and Thoreau[3] in America, and he
looked to such European novelists and essayists as **Goethe, Dickens,**
and Montaigne[4] for inspiration. He was familiar with Buddhist
writings; the Qur'an, the sacred scriptures of Islam; and the Daoism
(Taoism) of Chinese philosopher Laozi (Lao Tzu).

pp. 553, 1037

    Because Tolstoy not only wrote about the moral principles of the
"good life," but earnestly attempted to incorporate his teachings into
daily living while also admitting his failures and shortcomings, he
gained world credibility, popularity, and a large personal following.
But life at home was neither easy nor tranquil with this secular saint.
Tolstoy's wife, Sofia, became increasingly jealous of his fame, and when
he threatened to give up his financial holdings and distribute them to
the poor, Sofia protested on behalf of herself and their thirteen children. On November 8, 1910, deeply troubled by his failure to live up to
his own ideals, Tolstoy wrote Sofia a farewell letter and secretly departed
Yasnaya Polyana. Falling ill on a train, he spent his final days in a station
master's house at Astapovo. Sofia did not see her husband of forty-eight
years until after he had slipped into a coma. He died on November 20.

Tolstoy's Development as a Writer.   Tolstoy's most famous work,
War and Peace, is a long, historical novel about the invasion of Russia
by Napoleon's army in 1812. Scholars have criticized Tolstoy's portrait of
Napoleon and the author's fatalistic theory of history, wherein events
are determined by Providence or Destiny. Within the vast panorama of
history, heroes and empires emerge and disappear, but the values of

---

[3] **Emerson and Thoreau: Ralph Waldo Emerson** (1803–1882) was an American philosopher who drew attention to the sacredness of nature. **Henry David Thoreau** (1817–1862) was a naturalist who wrote about the spirit
of nature and believed that wilderness was important for urban America.

[4] **Montaigne:** Michel Montaigne (1533–1592) was the French father of the modern essay.

love, marriage, and family endure. In the novel, epic battle scenes and military heroes are juxtaposed with scenes of social life in Moscow and St. Petersburg. And the heart of the novel is its detailed evocation of Russian life, which, episode after episode, builds into a coherent picture of a nineteenth-century world. For the hero, Pierre Bezukhov, the search for self-respect leads finally to the comfort of domestic values; in the end love, marriage, and family are the real victors.

Tolstoy's other monumental work, *Anna Karenina,* is a novel centered on social mores. Although at first Anna and Vronsky exhibit courage and magnitude in their illicit love affair, they are ultimately incapable of preserving their relationship in the face of social disapproval. The once-radiant Anna becomes wretchedly unhappy and tragically ends her life in suicide. Since the writing of *Anna Karenina,* there have been radical changes surrounding sexuality, marriage, and divorce that may make Anna's dilemma seem less immediate and intense than it was in Tolstoy's day. Tolstoy's own representative in the novel is Levin, who finds meaning in useful work. Tolstoy later repudiated his two magnificent classics in *What Is Art?* (1897), condemning art for art's sake. In their abundant, realistic detail those novels are aligned with works by nineteenth-century Realists such as French novelist **Gustave Flaubert**, but the mature Tolstoy questioned whether detail and in-depth portraits of characters obscured the message of his writings.

p. 938

The Death of Ivan Ilych.   Like Rousseau in France and Thoreau in the United States, Tolstoy came to believe that personal salvation lay in a simple, natural life lived apart from the destructive influences of cities. The corruption inherent in the values of urban officialdom is aptly illustrated by the following selection, *The Death of Ivan Ilych* (1886), which belongs to the second major period of Tolstoy's life when, after his spiritual crisis, he focused on reconciling life, literature, and morality. The story's plot is simple and straightforward; as indicated by its title, there is no suspense about the outcome. Ivan Ilych is a judge, a public official, who is making his way up the social and institutional ladder when one day he has a minor accident while fixing a curtain and his life is radically turned around. As he grows weaker, slowly dying, he experiences all the loneliness and isolation that he has sown in the bureaucratic handling of his clientele as well as his own family. At the very end, he experiences a transformation that allows him to let go of his wasted life.

Critic Vladimir Lakshin summed up Tolstoy's place among Russia's literary masters: "We like Chekhov, admire Dostoevsky, love Pushkin, but Tolstoy? As a combination artist, philosopher, public figure, and human being, he is *neobychny* [unparalleled; incomparable]."

■ **FURTHER RESEARCH**

Biography

Simmons, Ernest J. *Leo Tolstoy*. 1946.

Troyat, Henri. *Tolstoy*. 1967.

Wilson, A. N. *Tolstoy*. 1988.

Criticism

Bilbajons, Rimvydas. *Tolstoy's Aesthetics and His Art*. 1991.

Christian, R. F. *Tolstoy: A Critical Introduction*. 1969.

Greenwood, E. B. *Tolstoy: The Comprehensive Vision*. 1975.

Matlaw, Ralph. *Tolstoy: A Collection of Critical Essays*. 1967.

Rahv, Philip. *Image and Idea*. 1949. Contains an individual chapter on *The Death of Ivan Ilych*.

■ **PRONUNCIATION**

Leo Tolstoy: LEE-oh TOLE-stoy

Fëdor Vasilievich: FYOH-dore vah-SEE-lyi-vich

Peter Ivanovich: PEE-tur ee-VAH-nuh-vich

Praskovya Fëdorovna Golovina: prah-SKOH-vyah FYOH-duh-ruv-nah guh-lah-VYEEN-ah

Ivan Egorovich Shebek: ee-VAHN yi-GOH-ruh-vich SHEH-bek

Schwartz: SHVARTS

Gerasim: gi-RAH-seem

Ilya Epimovich Golovin: ee-LYAH yeh-PEE-muh-vich guh-lah-VEEN

Leshchetitsky: leesh-chee-TIT-skee, lyee-shyee-TIT-skee

Vladimir Ivanovich: vlah-DEE-mere ee-VAH-nuh-vich

Dmitri Ivanovich Petrishchev: DMEE-tree ee-VAH-nuh-vich pee-TREESH-chef

Adrienne Lecouvreur: ah-dree-EN luh-koov-RUR

∾ The Death of Ivan Ilych

Translated by David Magarshack

I

During an interval in the Melvinski trial in the large building of the Law Courts, the members and public prosecutor met in Ivan Egorovich Shebek's private room, where the conversation turned on the celebrated Krasovski case. Fëdor Vasilievich warmly maintained that it was not subject to their jurisdiction, Ivan Egorovich maintained the contrary, while Peter Ivanovich, not having entered into the discussion at the start, took no part in it but looked through the *Gazette* which had just been handed in.

"Gentlemen," he said, "Ivan Ilych has died!"

"You don't say so!"

"Here, read it yourself," replied Peter Ivanovich, handing Fëdor Vasilievich the paper still damp from the press. Surrounded by a black border were the words:

"Praskovya Fëdorovna Golovina, with profound sorrow, informs relatives and friends of the demise of her beloved husband Ivan Ilych Golovin, Member of the Court of Justice, which occurred on February the 4th of this year 1882. The funeral will take place on Friday at one o'clock in the afternoon."

Ivan Ilych had been a colleague of the gentlemen present and was liked by them all. He had been ill for some weeks with an illness said to be incurable. His post had been kept open for him, but there had been conjectures that in case of his death Alexeev might receive his appointment, and that either Vinnikov or Shtabel would succeed Alexeev. So on receiving the news of Ivan Ilych's death the first thought of each of the gentlemen in that private room was of the changes and promotions it might occasion among themselves or their acquaintances.

"I shall be sure to get Shtabel's place or Vinnikov's," thought Fëdor Vasilievich. "I was promised that long ago, and the promotion means an extra eight hundred rubles a year for me besides the allowance."

"Now I must apply for my brother-in-law's transfer from Kaluga," thought Peter Ivanovich. "My wife will be very glad, and then she won't be able to say that I never do anything for her relations."

"I thought he would never leave his bed again," said Peter Ivanovich aloud. "It's very sad."

"But what really was the matter with him?"

"The doctors couldn't say—at least they could, but each of them said something different. When last I saw him I thought he was getting better."

"And I haven't been to see him since the holidays. I always meant to go."

"Had he any property?"

"I think his wife had a little—but something quite trifling."

"We shall have to go to see her, but they live so terribly far away."

"Far away from you, you mean. Everything's far away from your place."

"You see, he never can forgive my living on the other side of the river," said Peter Ivanovich, smiling at Shebek. Then, still talking of the distances between different parts of the city, they returned to the Court.

Besides considerations as to the possible transfers and promotions likely to result from Ivan Ilych's death, the mere fact of the death of a near acquaintance aroused, as usual, in all who heard of it the complacent feeling that, "it is he who is dead and not I."

Each one thought or felt, "Well, he's dead but I'm alive!" But the more intimate of Ivan Ilych's acquaintances, his so-called friends, could not help thinking also that they would now have to fulfil the very tiresome demands of propriety by attending the funeral service and paying a visit of condolence to the widow.

Fëdor Vasilievich and Peter Ivanovich had been his nearest acquaintances. Peter Ivanovich had studied law with Ivan Ilych and had considered himself to be under obligations to him.

Having told his wife at dinner-time of Ivan Ilych's death and of his conjecture that it might be possible to get her brother transferred to their circuit, Peter Ivanovich sacrificed his usual nap, put on his evening clothes, and drove to Ivan Ilych's house.

At the entrance stood a carriage and two cabs.[1] Leaning against the wall in the hall downstairs near the cloak-stand was a coffin-lid covered with cloth of gold, ornamented with gold cord and tassels, that had been polished up with metal powder. Two ladies in black were taking off their fur cloaks. Peter Ivanovich recognized one of them as Ivan Ilych's sister, but the other was a stranger to him. His colleague Schwartz was just coming downstairs, but on seeing Peter Ivanovich enter he stopped and winked at him, as if to say: "Ivan Ilych has made a mess of things—not like you and me."

Schwartz's face with his Piccadilly whiskers[2] and his slim figure in evening dress, had as usual an air of elegant solemnity which contrasted with the playfulness of his character and had a special piquancy here, or so it seemed to Peter Ivanovich.

Peter Ivanovich allowed the ladies to precede him and slowly followed them upstairs. Schwartz did not come down but remained where he was, and Peter Ivanovich understood that he wanted to arrange where they should play bridge that evening. The ladies went upstairs to the widow's room, and Schwartz with seriously compressed lips but a playful look in his eyes, indicated by a twist of his eyebrows the room to the right where the body lay.

Peter Ivanovich, like everyone else on such occasions, entered feeling uncertain what he would have to do. All he knew was that at such times it is always safe to cross oneself. But he was not quite sure whether one should make obeisances while doing so. He therefore adopted a middle course. On entering the room he began crossing himself and made a slight movement resembling a bow. At the same time, as far as the motion of his head and arm allowed, he surveyed the room. Two young men— apparently nephews, one of whom was a high-school pupil—were leaving the room, crossing themselves as they did so. An old woman was standing motionless, and a lady with strangely arched eyebrows was saying something to her in a whisper. A vigorous, resolute Church Reader, in a frock-coat, was reading something in a loud voice with an expression that precluded any contradiction. The butler's assistant, Gerasim, stepping lightly in front of Peter Ivanovich, was strewing something on the floor. Noticing this, Peter Ivanovich was immediately aware of a faint odour of a decomposing body.

The last time he had called on Ivan Ilych, Peter Ivanovich had seen Gerasim in the study. Ivan Ilych had been particularly fond of him and he was performing the duty of a sick nurse.

Peter Ivanovich continued to make the sign of the cross slightly inclining his head in an intermediate direction between the coffin, the Reader, and the icons on the table in a corner of the room. Afterwards, when it seemed to him that this movement of his arm in crossing himself had gone on too long, he stopped and began to look at the corpse.

The dead man lay, as dead men always lie, in a specially heavy way, his rigid limbs sunk in the soft cushions of the coffin, with the head forever bowed on the

---

[1] **cabs:** Horse-drawn cabs.

[2] **Piccadilly whiskers:** Side whiskers.

pillow. His yellow waxen brow with bald patches over his sunken temples was thrust up in the way peculiar to the dead, the protruding nose seeming to press on the upper lip. He was much changed and had grown even thinner since Peter Ivanovich had last seen him, but, as is always the case with the dead, his face was handsomer and above all more dignified than when he was alive. The expression on the face said that what was necessary had been accomplished, and accomplished rightly. Besides this there was in that expression a reproach and a warning to the living. This warning seemed to Peter Ivanovich out of place, or at least not applicable to him. He felt a certain discomfort and so he hurriedly crossed himself once more and turned and went out of the door—too hurriedly and too regardless of propriety, as he himself was aware.

Schwartz was waiting for him in the adjoining room with legs spread wide apart and both hands toying with his top-hat behind his back. The mere sight of that playful, well-groomed, and elegant figure refreshed Peter Ivanovich. He felt that Schwartz was above all these happenings and would not surrender to any depressing influences. His very look said that this incident of a church service for Ivan Ilych could not be a sufficient reason for infringing the order of the session—in other words, that it would certainly not prevent his unwrapping a new pack of cards and shuffling them that evening while a footman placed four fresh candles on the table: in fact, that there was no reason for supposing that this incident would hinder their spending the evening agreeably. Indeed he said this in a whisper as Peter Ivanovich passed him, proposing that they should meet for a game at Fëdor Vasilievich's. But apparently Peter Ivanovich was not destined to play bridge that evening. Praskovya Fëdorovna (a short, fat woman who despite all efforts to the contrary had continued to broaden steadily from her shoulders downwards and who had the same extraordinarily arched eyebrows as the lady who had been standing by the coffin), dressed all in black, her head covered with lace, came out of her own room with some other ladies, conducted them to the room where the dead body lay, and said: "The service will begin immediately. Please go in."

Schwartz, making an indefinite bow, stood still, evidently neither accepting nor declining this invitation. Praskovya Fëdorovna, recognizing Peter Ivanovich, sighed, went close up to him, took his hand, and said: "I know you were a true friend to Ivan Ilych . . ." and looked at him awaiting some suitable response. And Peter Ivanovich knew that, just as it had been the right thing to cross himself in that room, so what he had to do here was to press her hand, sigh, and say, "Believe me. . . ." So he did all this and as he did it felt that the desired result had been achieved: that both he and she were touched.

"Come with me. I want to speak to you before it begins," said the widow. "Give me your arm."

Peter Ivanovich gave her his arm and they went to the inner rooms, passing Schwartz, who winked at Peter Ivanovich compassionately.

"That does for our bridge! Don't object if we find another player. Perhaps you can cut in when you do escape," said his playful look.

Peter Ivanovich sighed still more deeply and despondently, and Praskovya Fëdorovna pressed his arm gratefully. When they reached the drawing-room, upholstered in pink cretonne and lighted by a dim lamp, they sat down at the table—she on a sofa and Peter Ivanovich on a low pouffe, the springs of which yielded spasmodically under his weight. Praskovya Fëdorovna had been on the point of warning him to take another seat, but felt that such a warning was out of keeping with her present condition and so changed her mind. As he sat down on the pouffe Peter Ivanovich recalled how Ivan Ilych had arranged this room and had consulted him regarding this pink cretonne with green leaves. The whole room was full of furniture and knick-knacks, and on her way to the sofa the lace of the widow's black shawl caught on the carved edge of the table. Peter Ivanovich rose to detach it, and the springs of the pouffe, relieved of his weight, rose also and gave him a push. The widow began detaching her shawl herself, and Peter Ivanovich again sat down, suppressing the rebellious springs of the pouffe under him. But the widow had not quite freed herself and Peter Ivanovich got up again, and again the pouffe rebelled and even creaked. When this was all over she took out a clean cambric handkerchief and began to weep. The episode with the shawl and the struggle with the pouffe had cooled Peter Ivanovich's emotions and he sat there with a sullen look on his face. This awkward situation was interrupted by Sokolov, Ivan Ilych's butler, who came to report that the plot in the cemetery that Praskovya Fëdorovna had chosen would cost two hundred rubles. She stopped weeping and, looking at Peter Ivanovich with the air of a victim, remarked in French that it was very hard for her. Peter Ivanovich made a silent gesture signifying his full conviction that it must indeed be so.

"Please smoke," she said in a magnanimous yet crushed voice, and turned to discuss with Sokolov the price of the plot for the grave.

Peter Ivanovich while lighting his cigarette heard her inquiring very circumstantially into the prices of different plots in the cemetery and finally decide which she would take. When that was done she gave instructions about engaging the choir. Sokolov then left the room.

"I look after everything myself," she told Peter Ivanovich, shifting the albums that lay on the table; and noticing that the table was endangered by his cigarette-ash, she immediately passed him an ash-tray, saying as she did so: "I consider it an affectation to say that my grief prevents my attending to practical affairs. On the contrary, if anything can—I won't say console me, but—distract me, it is seeing to everything concerning him." She again took out her handkerchief as if preparing to cry, but suddenly, as if mastering her feeling, she shook herself and began to speak calmly. "But there is something I want to talk to you about."

Peter Ivanovich bowed, keeping control of the springs of the pouffe, which immediately began quivering under him.

"He suffered terribly the last few days."

"Did he?" said Peter Ivanovich.

"Oh, terribly! He screamed unceasingly, not for minutes but for hours. For the last three days he screamed incessantly. It was unendurable. I cannot understand how I bore it; you could hear him three rooms off. Oh, what I have suffered!"

"Is it possible that he was conscious all that time?" asked Peter Ivanovich.

"Yes," she whispered. "To the last moment. He took leave of us a quarter of an hour before he died, and asked us to take Volodya away."

The thought of the sufferings of this man he had known so intimately, first as a merry little boy, then as a school-mate, and later as a grown-up colleague, suddenly struck Peter Ivanovich with horror, despite an unpleasant consciousness of his own and this woman's dissimulation. He again saw that brow, and that nose pressing down on the lip, and felt afraid for himself.

"Three days of frightful suffering and then death! Why, that might suddenly, at any time, happen to me," he thought, and for a moment felt terrified. But—he did not himself know how—the customary reflection at once occurred to him that this had happened to Ivan Ilych and not to him, and that it should not and could not happen to him, and that to think that it could would be yielding to depression which he ought not to do, as Schwartz's expression plainly showed. After which reflection Peter Ivanovich felt reassured, and began to ask with interest about the details of Ivan Ilych's death, as though death was an accident natural to Ivan Ilych but certainly not to himself.

After many details of the really dreadful physical sufferings Ivan Ilych had endured (which details he learnt only from the effect those sufferings had produced on Praskovya Fëdorovna's nerves) the widow apparently found it necessary to get to business.

"Oh, Peter Ivanovich, how hard it is! How terribly, terribly hard!" and she again began to weep.

Peter Ivanovich sighed and waited for her to finish blowing her nose. When she had done so he said, "Believe me . . ." and she again began talking and brought out what was evidently her chief concern with him—namely, to question him as to how she could obtain a grant of money from the government on the occasion of her husband's death. She made it appear that she was asking Peter Ivanovich's advice about her pension, but he soon saw that she already knew about that to the minutest detail, more even than he did himself. She knew how much could be got out of the government in consequence of her husband's death, but wanted to find out whether she could not possibly extract something more. Peter Ivanovich tried to think of some means of doing so, but after reflecting for a while and, out of propriety, condemning the government for its niggardliness, he said he thought that nothing more could be got. Then she sighed and evidently began to devise means of getting rid of her visitor. Noticing this, he put out his cigarette, rose, pressed her hand, and went out into the anteroom.

In the dining-room where the clock stood that Ivan Ilych had liked so much and had bought at an antique shop, Peter Ivanovich met a priest and a few acquaintances who had come to attend the service, and he recognized Ivan Ilych's daughter, a handsome young woman. She was in black and her slim figure appeared slimmer than ever. She had a gloomy, determined, almost angry expression, and bowed to Peter Ivanovich as though he were in some way to blame. Behind her, with the same offended look, stood a wealthy young man, an examining magistrate, whom Peter Ivanovich also knew and who was her fiancé, as he had heard. He bowed mournfully to them and was about to pass into the death-chamber, when from under the stairs appeared the figure of Ivan Ilych's schoolboy son, who was extremely like his father.

He seemed a little Ivan Ilych, such as Peter Ivanovich remembered when they studied law together. His tear-stained eyes had in them the look that is seen in the eyes of boys of thirteen or fourteen who are not pure-minded. When he saw Peter Ivanovich he scowled morosely and shamefacedly. Peter Ivanovich nodded to him and entered the death-chamber. The service began: candles, groans, incense, tears, and sobs. Peter Ivanovich stood looking gloomily down at his feet. He did not look once at the dead man, did not yield to any depressing influence, and was one of the first to leave the room. There was no one in the anteroom, but Gerasim darted out of the dead man's room, rummaged with his strong hands among the fur coats to find Peter Ivanovich's and helped him on with it.

"Well, friend Gerasim," said Peter Ivanovich, so as to say something. "It's a sad affair, isn't it?"

"It's God's will. We shall all come to it some day," said Gerasim, displaying his teeth—the even, white teeth of a healthy peasant—and, like a man in the thick of urgent work, he briskly opened the front door, called the coachman, helped Peter Ivanovich into the sledge, and sprang back to the porch as if in readiness for what he had to do next.

Peter Ivanovich found the fresh air particularly pleasant after the smell of incense, the dead body, and carbolic acid.

"Where to, sir?" asked the coachman.

"It's not too late even now. . . . I'll call round on Fëdor Vasilievich."

He accordingly drove there and found them just finishing the first rubber, so that it was quite convenient for him to cut in.

II

Ivan Ilych's life had been most simple and most ordinary and therefore most terrible.

He had been a member of the Court of Justice, and died at the age of forty-five. His father had been an official who after serving in various ministries and departments in Petersburg had made the sort of career which brings men to positions from which by reason of their long service they cannot be dismissed, though they are obviously unfit to hold any responsible position, and for whom therefore posts are specially created, which though fictitious carry salaries of from six to ten thousand rubles that are not fictitious, and in receipt of which they live on to a great age.

Such was the Privy Councillor and superfluous member of various superfluous institutions, Ilya Epimovich Golovin.

He had three sons, of whom Ivan Ilych was the second. The eldest son was following in his father's footsteps only in another department, and was already approaching that stage in the service at which a similar sinecure would be reached. The third son was a failure. He had ruined his prospects in a number of positions and was now serving in the railway department. His father and brothers, and still more their wives, not merely disliked meeting him, but avoided remembering his existence unless compelled to do so. His sister had married Baron Greff, a Petersburg official of her father's type. Ivan Ilych was *le phénix de la famille*[3] as people said. He was neither as cold and formal as his elder brother nor as wild as the younger, but was a happy mean between them—an intelligent, polished, lively, and agreeable man. He had studied with his younger brother at the School of Law, but the latter had failed to complete the course and was expelled when he was in the fifth class. Ivan Ilych finished the course well. Even when he was at the School of Law he was just what he remained for the rest of his life: a capable, cheerful, good-natured, and sociable man, though strict in the fulfillment of what he considered to be his duty: and he considered his duty to be what was so considered by those in authority. Neither as a boy nor as a man was he a toady, but from early youth was by nature attracted to people of high station as a fly is drawn to the light, assimilating their ways and views of life and establishing friendly relations with them. All the enthusiasms of childhood and youth passed without leaving much trace on him; he succumbed to sensuality, to vanity, and latterly among the highest classes to liberalism, but always within limits which his instinct unfailingly indicated to him as correct.

At school he had done things which had formerly seemed to him very horrid and made him feel disgusted with himself when he did them; but when later on he saw that such actions were done by people of good position and that they did not regard them as wrong, he was able not exactly to regard them as right, but to forget about them entirely or not be at all troubled at remembering them.

Having graduated from the School of Law and qualified for the tenth rank of the civil service, and having received money from his father for his equipment, Ivan Ilych ordered himself clothes at Scharmer's, the fashionable tailor, hung a medallion inscribed *respice finem*[4] on his watch-chain, took leave of his professor and the prince who was patron of the school, had a farewell dinner with his comrades at Donon's first-class restaurant, and with his new and fashionable portmanteau, linen, clothes, shaving and other toilet appliances, and a travelling rug, all purchased at the best shops, he set off for one of the provinces where, through his father's influence, he had been attached to the Governor as an official for special service.

In the province Ivan Ilych soon arranged as easy and agreeable a position for himself as he had had at the School of Law. He performed his official tasks, made his career, and at the same time amused himself pleasantly and decorously. Occasionally he paid official visits to country districts, where he behaved with dignity both to his superiors and inferiors, and performed the duties entrusted to him, which related chiefly to the sectarians,[5] with an exactness and incorruptible honesty of which he could not but feel proud.

In official matters, despite his youth and taste for frivolous gaiety, he was exceedingly reserved, punctilious, and even severe; but in society he was often amusing and witty, and always good-natured, correct in his manner, and *bon enfant*,[6] as

---

[3] *le . . . famille:* French for "the phoenix of the family"; that is, a prodigy.

[4] *respice finem:* Latin for "regard the end."

[5] sectarians: The Old Believers, a sect that broke away from the Russian Orthodox Church in the seventeenth century; members were subject to numerous legal restrictions.

[6] *bon enfant:* French for "good child."

the governor and his wife—with whom he was like one of the family—used to say of him.

In the province he had an affair with a lady who made advances to the elegant young lawyer, and there was also a milliner; and there were carousals with aides-de-camp who visited the district, and after-supper visits to a certain outlying street of doubtful reputation; and there was too some obsequiousness to his chief and even to his chief's wife, but all this was done with such a tone of good breeding that no hard names could be applied to it. It all came under the heading of the French saying: *"Il faut que jeunesse se passe."*[7] It was all done with clean hands, in clean linen, with French phrases, and above all among people of the best society and consequently with the approval of people of rank.

So Ivan Ilych served for five years and then came a change in his official life. The new and reformed judicial institutions were introduced, and new men were needed. Ivan Ilych became such a new man. He was offered the post of examining magistrate, and he accepted it though the post was in another province and obliged him to give up the connexions he had formed and to make new ones. His friends met to give him a send-off; they had a group-photograph taken and presented him with a silver cigarette-case, and he set off to his new post.

As examining magistrate Ivan Ilych was just as *comme il faut*[8] and decorous a man, inspiring general respect and capable of separating his official duties from his private life, as he had been when acting as an official on special service. His duties now as examining magistrate were far more interesting and attractive than before. In his former position it had been pleasant to wear an undress uniform made by Scharmer, and to pass through the crowd of petitioners and officials who were timorously awaiting an audience with the governor, and who envied him as with free and easy gait he went straight into his chief's private room to have a cup of tea and a cigarette with him. But not many people had then been directly dependent on him—only police officials and the sectarians when he went on special missions—and he liked to treat them politely, almost as comrades, as if he were letting them feel that he who had the power to crush them was treating them in this simple, friendly way. There were then but few such people. But now, as an examining magistrate, Ivan Ilych felt that everyone without exception, even the most important and self-satisfied, was in his power, and that he need only write a few words on a sheet of paper with a certain heading, and this or that important, self-satisfied person would be brought before him in the role of an accused person or a witness, and if he did not choose to allow him to sit down, would have to stand before him and answer his questions. Ivan Ilych never abused his power; he tried on the contrary to soften its expression, but the consciousness of it and of the possibility of softening its effect, supplied the chief interest and attraction of his office. In his work itself, especially in his examinations, he very soon acquired a method of eliminating all considerations irrelevant to the legal aspect of the case, and reducing even the most complicated case to a form in which it would be presented on paper only in its externals,

---

[7] *"Il faut . . . passe":* French for "Youth must have its way."

[8] *comme il faut:* French for "as it should be."

completely excluding his personal opinion of the matter, while above all observing every prescribed formality. The work was new and Ivan Ilych was one of the first men to apply the new Code of 1864.[9]

On taking up the post of examining magistrate in a new town, he made new acquaintances and connexions, placed himself on a new footing, and assumed a somewhat different tone. He took up an attitude of rather dignified aloofness towards the provincial authorities, but picked out the best circle of legal gentlemen and wealthy gentry living in the town and assumed a tone of slight dissatisfaction with the government, of moderate liberalism, and of enlightened citizenship. At the same time, without at all altering the elegance of his toilet, he ceased shaving his chin and allowed his beard to grow as it pleased.

Ivan Ilych settled down very pleasantly in this new town. The society there, which inclined towards opposition to the Governor, was friendly, his salary was larger, and he began to play *vint* [a form of bridge], which he found added not a little to the pleasure of life, for he had a capacity for cards, played good-humouredly, and calculated rapidly and astutely, so that he usually won.

After living there for two years he met his future wife, Praskovya Fёdorovna Mikhel, who was the most attractive, clever, and brilliant girl of the set in which he moved, and among other amusements and relaxations from his labours as examining magistrate, Ivan Ilych established light and playful relations with her.

While he had been an official on special service he had been accustomed to dance, but now as an examining magistrate it was exceptional for him to do so. If he danced now, he did it as if to show that though he served under the reformed order of things, and had reached the fifth official rank, yet when it came to dancing he could do it better than most people. So at the end of an evening he sometimes danced with Praskovya Fёdorovna, and it was chiefly during these dances that he captivated her. She fell in love with him. Ivan Ilych had at first no definite intention of marrying, but when the girl fell in love with him he said to himself: "Really, why shouldn't I marry?"

Praskovya Fёdorovna came of a good family, was not bad looking, and had some little property. Ivan Ilych might have aspired to a more brilliant match, but even this was good. He had his salary, and she, he hoped, would have an equal income. She was well connected, and was a sweet, pretty, and thoroughly correct young woman. To say that Ivan Ilych married because he fell in love with Praskovya Fёdorovna and found that she sympathized with his views of life would be as incorrect as to say that he married because his social circle approved of the match. He was swayed by both these considerations: the marriage gave him personal satisfaction, and at the same time it was considered the right thing by the most highly placed of his associates.

So Ivan Ilych got married.

The preparations for marriage and the beginning of married life, with its conjugal caresses, the new furniture, new crockery, and new linen, were very pleasant until his wife became pregnant—so that Ivan Ilych had begun to think that marriage

---

[9] **Code of 1864:** After the emancipation of the serfs in 1861, the entire Russian legal system was reformed in 1864.

would not impair the easy, agreeable, gay, and always decorous character of his life, approved of by society and regarded by himself as natural, but would even improve it. But from the first months of his wife's pregnancy, something new, unpleasant, depressing, and unseemly, and from which there was no way of escape, unexpectedly showed itself.

His wife, without any reason—*de gaieté de cœur*[10] as Ivan Ilych expressed it to himself—began to disturb the pleasure and propriety of their life. She began to be jealous without any cause, expected him to devote his whole attention to her, found fault with everything, and made coarse and ill-mannered scenes.

At first Ivan Ilych hoped to escape from the unpleasantness of this state of affairs by the same easy and decorous relation to life that had served him heretofore: he tried to ignore his wife's disagreeable moods, continued to live in his usual easy and pleasant way, invited friends to his house for a game of cards, and also tried going out to his club or spending his evenings with friends. But one day his wife began upbraiding him so vigorously, using such coarse words, and continued to abuse him every time he did not fulfill her demands, so resolutely and with such evident determination not to give way till he submitted—that is, till he stayed at home and was bored just as she was—that he became alarmed. He now realized that matrimony—at any rate with Praskovya Fëdorovna—was not always conducive to the pleasures and amenities of life, but on the contrary often infringed both comfort and propriety, and that he must therefore entrench himself against such infringement. And Ivan Ilych began to seek for means of doing so. His official duties were the one thing that imposed upon Praskovya Fëdorovna, and by means of his official work and the duties attached to it he began struggling with his wife to secure his own independence.

With the birth of their child, the attempts to feed it and the various failures in doing so, and with the real and imaginary illnesses of mother and child, in which Ivan Ilych's sympathy was demanded but about which he understood nothing, the need of securing for himself an existence outside his family life became still more imperative.

As his wife grew more irritable and exacting and Ivan Ilych transferred the centre of gravity of his life more and more to his official work, so did he grow to like his work better and became more ambitious than before.

Very soon, within a year of his wedding, Ivan Ilych had realized that marriage, though it may add some comforts to life, is in fact a very intricate and difficult affair towards which in order to perform one's duty, that is, to lead a decorous life approved of by society, one must adopt a definite attitude just as towards one's official duties.

And Ivan Ilych evolved such an attitude towards married life. He only required of it those conveniences—dinner at home, housewife, and bed—which it could give him, and above all that propriety of external forms required by public opinion. For the rest he looked for light-hearted pleasure and propriety, and was very thankful when he found them, but if he met with antagonism and querulousness he at

---

[10] *de gaieté de cœur:* Literally, French for "out of gaiety of heart"; arbitrarily.

once retired into his separate fenced-off world of official duties, where he found satisfaction.

Ivan Ilych was esteemed a good official, and after three years was made Assistant Public Prosecutor. His new duties, their importance, the possibility of indicting and imprisoning anyone he chose, the publicity his speeches received, and the success he had in all these things, made his work still more attractive.

More children came. His wife became more and more querulous and ill-tempered, but the attitude Ivan Ilych had adopted towards his home life rendered him almost impervious to her grumbling.

After seven years' service in that town he was transferred to another province as Public Prosecutor. They moved, but were short of money and his wife did not like the place they moved to. Though the salary was higher the cost of living was greater, besides which two of their children died and family life became still more unpleasant for him.

Praskovya Fëdorovna blamed her husband for every inconvenience they encountered in their new home. Most of the conversations between husband and wife, especially as to the children's education, led to topics which recalled former disputes, and those disputes were apt to flare up again at any moment. There remained only those rare periods of amorousness which still came to them at times but did not last long. These were islets at which they anchored for a while and then again set out upon that ocean of veiled hostility which showed itself in their aloofness from one another. This aloofness might have grieved Ivan Ilych had he considered that it ought not to exist, but he now regarded the position as normal, and even made it the goal at which he aimed in family life. His aim was to free himself more and more from those unpleasantnesses and to give them a semblance of harmlessness and propriety. He attained this by spending less and less time with his family, and when obliged to be at home he tried to safeguard his position by the presence of outsiders. The chief thing however was that he had his official duties. The whole interest of his life now centred in the official world and that interest absorbed him. The consciousness of his power, being able to ruin anybody he wished to ruin, the importance, even the external dignity of his entry into court, or meetings with his subordinates, his success with superiors and inferiors, and above all his masterly handling of cases, of which he was conscious—all this gave him pleasure and filled his life, together with chats with his colleagues, dinners, and bridge. So that on the whole Ivan Ilych's life continued to flow as he considered it should do—pleasantly and properly.

So things continued for another seven years. His eldest daughter was already sixteen, another child had died, and only one son was left, a schoolboy and a subject of dissension. Ivan Ilych wanted to put him in the School of Law, but to spite him Praskovya Fëdorovna entered him at the High School. The daughter had been educated at home and had turned out well: the boy did not learn badly either.

III

So Ivan Ilych lived for seventeen years after his marriage. He was already a Public Prosecutor of long standing, and had declined several proposed transfers while awaiting a more desirable post, when an unanticipated and unpleasant occurrence quite upset the peaceful course of his life. He was expecting to be offered the post of presiding judge in a University town, but Happe somehow came to the front and obtained the appointment instead. Ivan Ilych became irritable, reproached Happe, and quarrelled both with him and with his immediate superiors — who became colder to him and again passed him over when other appointments were made.

This was in 1880, the hardest year of Ivan Ilych's life. It was then that it became evident on the one hand that his salary was insufficient for them to live on, and on the other that he had been forgotten, and not only this, but that what was for him the greatest and most cruel injustice appeared to others a quite ordinary occurrence. Even his father did not consider it his duty to help him. Ivan Ilych felt himself abandoned by everyone, and that they regarded his position with a salary of 3,500 rubles as quite normal and even fortunate. He alone knew that with the consciousness of the injustices done him, with his wife's incessant nagging, and with the debts he had contracted by living beyond his means, his position was far from normal.

In order to save money that summer he obtained leave of absence and went with his wife to live in the country at her brother's place.

In the country, without his work, he experienced *ennui* for the first time in his life, and not only *ennui* but intolerable depression, and he decided that it was impossible to go on living like that, and that it was necessary to take energetic measures.

Having passed a sleepless night pacing up and down the veranda, he decided to go to Petersburg and bestir himself, in order to punish those who had failed to appreciate him and to get transferred to another ministry.

Next day, despite many protests from his wife and her brother, he started for Petersburg with the sole object of obtaining a post with a salary of five thousand rubles a year. He was no longer bent on any particular department, or tendency, or kind of activity. All he now wanted was an appointment to another post with a salary of five thousand rubles, either in the administration, in the banks, with the railways, in one of the Empress Marya's Institutions,[11] or even in the customs — but it had to carry with it a salary of five thousand rubles and be in a ministry other than that in which they had failed to appreciate him.

And this quest of Ivan Ilych's was crowned with remarkable and unexpected success. At Kursk an acquaintance of his, F. I. Ilyin, got into the first-class carriage, sat down beside Ivan Ilych, and told him of a telegram just received by the Governor of Kursk announcing that a change was about to take place in the ministry: Peter Ivanovich was to be superseded by Ivan Semënovich.

The proposed change, apart from its significance for Russia, had a special significance for Ivan Ilych, because by bringing forward a new man, Peter Petrovich, and consequently his friend Zachar Ivanovich, it was highly favourable for Ivan Ilych, since Zachar Ivanovich was a friend and colleague of his.

In Moscow this news was confirmed, and on reaching Petersburg Ivan Ilych found Zachar Ivanovich and received a definite promise of an appointment in his former department of Justice.

A week later he telegraphed to his wife: "Zachar in Miller's place. I shall receive appointment on presentation of report."

---

[11] **Empress Marya's Institutions:** Charitable institutions founded by the Empress Marya, wife of Paul I.

Thanks to this change of personnel, Ivan Ilych had unexpectedly obtained an appointment in his former ministry which placed him two stages above his former colleagues besides giving him five thousand rubles salary and three thousand five hundred rubles for expenses connected with his removal. All his ill humour towards his former enemies and the whole department vanished, and Ivan Ilych was completely happy.

He returned to the country more cheerful and contented than he had been for a long time. Praskovya Fëdorovna also cheered up and a truce was arranged between them. Ivan Ilych told of how he had been fêted by everybody in Petersburg, how all those who had been his enemies were put to shame and now fawned on him, how envious they were of his appointment, and how much everybody in Petersburg had liked him.

Praskovya Fëdorovna listened to all this and appeared to believe it. She did not contradict anything, but only made plans for their life in the town to which they were going. Ivan Ilych saw with delight that these plans were his plans, that he and his wife agreed, and that, after a stumble, his life was regaining its due and natural character of pleasant lightheartedness and decorum.

Ivan Ilych had come back for a short time only, for he had to take up his new duties on the 10th of September. Moreover, he needed time to settle into the new place, to move all his belongings from the province, and to buy and order many additional things: in a word, to make such arrangements as he had resolved on, which were almost exactly what Praskovya Fëdorovna too had decided on.

Now that everything had happened so fortunately, and that he and his wife were at one in their aims and moreover saw so little of one another, they got on together better than they had done since the first years of marriage. Ivan Ilych had thought of taking his family away with him at once, but the insistence of his wife's brother and her sister-in-law, who had suddenly become particularly amiable and friendly to him and his family, induced him to depart alone.

So he departed, and the cheerful state of mind induced by his success and by the harmony between his wife and himself, the one intensifying the other, did not leave him. He found a delightful house, just the thing both he and his wife had dreamt of. Spacious, lofty reception rooms in the old style, a convenient and dignified study, rooms for his wife and daughter, a study for his son — it might have been specially built for them. Ivan Ilych himself superintended the arrangements, chose the wallpapers, supplemented the furniture (preferably with antiques which he considered particularly *comme il faut*), and supervised the upholstering. Everything progressed and progressed and approached the ideal he had set himself: even when things were only half completed they exceeded his expectations. He saw what a refined and elegant character, free from vulgarity, it would all have when it was ready. On falling asleep he pictured to himself how the reception-room would look. Looking at the yet unfinished drawing-room he could see the fireplace, the screen, the what-not, the little chairs dotted here and there, the dishes and plates on the walls, and the bronzes, as they would be when everything was in place. He was pleased by the thought of how his wife and daughter, who shared his taste in this matter, would be impressed by it. They were certainly not expecting as much. He had been particularly successful in finding, and buying cheaply, antiques which gave a particularly aristocratic character to the whole place. But in his letters he intentionally understated everything in order to be able to surprise them. All this so absorbed him that his new duties—though he liked his official work—interested him less than he had expected. Sometimes he even had moments of absent-mindedness during the Court Sessions, and would consider whether he should have straight or curved cornices for his curtains. He was so interested in it all that he often did things himself, rearranging the furniture, or rehanging the curtains. Once when mounting a step-ladder to show the upholsterer, who did not understand, how he wanted the hangings draped, he made a false step and slipped, but being a strong and agile man he clung on and only knocked his side against the knob of the window frame. The bruised place was painful but the pain soon passed, and he felt particularly bright and well just then. He wrote: "I feel fifteen years younger." He thought he would have everything ready by September, but it dragged on till mid-October. But the result was charming not only in his eyes but to everyone who saw it.

In reality it was just what is usually seen in the houses of people of moderate means who want to appear rich, and therefore succeed only in resembling others like themselves: there were damasks, dark wood, plants, rugs, and dull and polished bronzes—all the things people of a certain class have in order to resemble other people of that class. His house was so like the others that it would never have been noticed, but to him it all seemed to be quite exceptional. He was very happy when he met his family at the station and brought them to the newly furnished house all lit up, where a footman in a white tie opened the door into the hall decorated with plants, and when they went on into the drawing-room, and the study uttering exclamations of delight. He conducted them everywhere, drank in their praises eagerly, and beamed with pleasure. At tea that evening, when Praskovya Fëdorovna among other things asked him about his fall, he laughed and showed them how he had gone flying and had frightened the upholsterer.

"It's a good thing I'm a bit of an athlete. Another man might have been killed, but I merely knocked myself, just here; it hurts when it's touched, but it's passing off already—it's only a bruise."

So they began living in their new home—in which, as always happens, when they got thoroughly settled in they found they were just one room short—and with the increased income, which as always was just a little (some five hundred rubles) too little, but it was all very nice.

Things went particularly well at first, before everything was finally arranged and while something had still to be done: this thing bought, that thing ordered, another thing moved, and something else adjusted. Though there were some disputes between husband and wife, they were both so well satisfied and had so much to do that it all passed off without any serious quarrels. When nothing was left to arrange it became rather dull and something seemed to be lacking, but they were then making acquaintances, forming habits, and life was growing fuller.

Ivan Ilych spent his mornings at the law court and came home to dinner, and at first he was generally in a good humour, though he occasionally became irritable just on account of his house. (Every spot on the tablecloth or the upholstery, and every broken window-blind string, irritated him. He had devoted so much trouble to arranging it all that every disturbance of it distressed him.) But on the whole his life ran its course as he believed life should do: easily, pleasantly, and decorously.

He got up at nine, drank his coffee, read the paper, and then put on his undress uniform and went to the law courts. There the harness in which he worked had already been stretched to fit him and he donned it without a hitch: petitioners, inquiries at the chancery, the chancery itself, and the sittings public and administrative. In all this the thing was to exclude everything fresh and vital, which always disturbs the regular course of official business, and to admit only official relations with people, and then only on official grounds. A man would come, for instance, wanting some information. Ivan Ilych, as one in whose sphere the matter did not lie, would have nothing to do with him: but if the man had some business with him in his official capacity, something that could be expressed on officially stamped paper, he would do everything, positively everything he could within the limits of such relations, and in doing so would maintain the semblance of friendly human relations, that is, would observe the courtesies of life. As soon as the official relations ended, so did everything else. Ivan Ilych possessed this capacity to separate his real life from the official side of affairs and not mix the two, in the highest degree, and by long practice and natural aptitude had brought it to such a pitch that sometimes, in the manner of a virtuoso, he would even allow himself to let the human and official relations mingle. He let himself do this just because he felt that he could at any time he chose resume the strictly official attitude again and drop the human relation. And he did it all easily, pleasantly, correctly, and even artistically. In the intervals between the sessions he smoked, drank tea, chatted a little about politics, a little about general topics, a little about cards, but most of all about official appointments. Tired, but with the feelings of a virtuoso — one of the first violins who has played his part in an orchestra with precision — he would return home to find that his wife and daughter had been out paying calls, or had a visitor, and that his son had been to school, had done his homework with his tutor, and was duly learning what is taught at High Schools. Everything was as it should be. After dinner, if they had no visitors, Ivan Ilych sometimes read a book that was being much discussed at the time, and in the evening settled down to work, that is, read official papers, compared the depositions of witnesses, and noted paragraphs of the Code applying to them. This was neither dull nor amusing. It was dull when he might have been playing bridge, but if no bridge was available it was at any rate better than doing nothing or sitting with his wife. Ivan Ilych's chief pleasure was giving little dinners to which he invited men and women of good social position, and just as his drawing-room resembled all other drawing-rooms so did his enjoyable little parties resemble all other such parties.

Once they even gave a dance. Ivan Ilych enjoyed it and everything went off well, except that it led to a violent quarrel with his wife about the cakes and sweets. Praskovya Fëdorovna had made her own plans, but Ivan Ilych insisted on getting everything from an expensive confectioner and ordered too many cakes, and the quarrel occurred because some of those cakes were left over and the confectioner's bill came to forty-five rubles. It was a great and disagreeable quarrel. Praskovya

Fëdorovna called him "a fool and an imbecile," and he clutched at his head and made angry allusions to divorce.

But the dance itself had been enjoyable. The best people were there, and Ivan Ilych had danced with Princess Trufonova, a sister of the distinguished founder of the Society "Bear my Burden."

The pleasures connected with his work were pleasures of ambition; his social pleasures were those of vanity; but Ivan Ilych's greatest pleasure was playing bridge. He acknowledged that whatever disagreeable incident happened in his life, the pleasure that beamed like a ray of light above everything else was to sit down to bridge with good players, not noisy partners, and of course to four-handed bridge (with five players it was annoying to have to stand out, though one pretended not to mind), to play a clever and serious game (when the cards allowed it) and then to have supper and drink a glass of wine. After a game of bridge, especially if he had won a little (to win a large sum was unpleasant), Ivan Ilych went to bed in specially good humour.

So they lived. They formed a circle of acquaintances among the best people and were visited by people of importance and by young folk. In their views as to their acquaintances, husband, wife, and daughter were entirely agreed, and tacitly and unanimously kept at arm's length and shook off the various shabby friends and relations who, with much show of affection, gushed into the drawing-room with its Japanese plates on the walls. Soon these shabby friends ceased to obtrude themselves and only the best people remained in the Golovins' set.

Young men made up to Lisa, and Petrishchev, an examining magistrate and Dmitri Ivanovich Petrishchev's son and sole heir, began to be so attentive to her that Ivan Ilych had already spoken to Praskovya Fëdorovna about it, and considered whether they should not arrange a party for them, or get up some private theatricals.

So they lived, and all went well, without change, and life flowed pleasantly.

IV

They were all in good health. It could not be called ill health if Ivan Ilych sometimes said that he had a queer taste in his mouth and felt some discomfort in his left side.

But this discomfort increased and, though not exactly painful, grew into a sense of pressure in his side accompanied by ill humour. And his irritability became worse and worse and began to mar the agreeable, easy, and correct life that had established itself in the Golovin family. Quarrels between husband and wife became more and more frequent, and soon the ease and amenity disappeared and even the decorum was barely maintained. Scenes again became frequent, and very few of those islets remained on which husband and wife could meet without an explosion. Praskovya Fëdorovna now had good reason to say that her husband's temper was trying. With characteristic exaggeration she said he had always had a dreadful temper, and that it had needed all her good nature to put up with it for twenty years. It was true that now the quarrels were started by him. His bursts of temper always came just before dinner, often just as he began to eat his soup. Sometimes he noticed that a plate or dish was chipped, or the food was not right, or his son put his elbow on the table, or his daughter's hair was not done as he liked it, and for all this he blamed Praskovya Fëdorovna. At first she retorted and said disagreeable things to him, but once or twice he fell into such a rage at the beginning of dinner that she realized it was due to some physical derangement brought on by taking food, and so she restrained herself and did not answer, but only hurried to get the dinner over. She regarded this self-restraint as highly praiseworthy. Having come to the conclusion that her husband had a dreadful temper and made her life miserable, she began to feel sorry for herself, and the more she pitied herself the more she hated her husband. She began to wish he would die; yet she did not want him to die because then his salary would cease. And this irritated her against him still more. She considered herself dreadfully unhappy just because not even his death could save her, and though she concealed her exasperation, that hidden exasperation of hers increased his irritation also.

After one scene in which Ivan Ilych had been particularly unfair and after which he had said in explanation that he certainly was irritable but that it was due to his not being well, she said that if he was ill it should be attended to, and insisted on his going to see a celebrated doctor.

He went. Everything took place as he had expected and as it always does. There was the usual waiting and the important air assumed by the doctor, with which he was so familiar (resembling that which he himself assumed in court), and the sounding and listening, and the questions which called for answers that were fore-gone conclusions and were evidently unnecessary, and the look of importance which implied that "if only you put yourself in our hands we will arrange everything—we know indubitably how it has to be done, always in the same way for everybody alike." It was all just as it was in the law courts. The doctor put on just the same air towards him as he himself put on towards an accused person.

The doctor said that so-and-so indicated that there was so-and-so inside the patient, but if the investigation of so-and-so did not confirm this, then he must assume that and that. If he assumed that and that, then . . . and so on. To Ivan Ilych only one question was important: was his case serious or not? But the doctor ignored that inappropriate question. From his point of view it was not the one under consideration; the real question was to decide between a floating kidney, chronic catarrh, or appendicitis. It was not a question of Ivan Ilych's life or death, but one between a floating kidney and appendicitis. And that question the doctor solved brilliantly, as it seemed to Ivan Ilych, in favour of the appendix, with the reservation that should an examination of the urine give fresh indications the matter would be reconsidered. All this was just what Ivan Ilych had himself brilliantly accomplished a thousand times in dealing with men on trial. The doctor summed up just as brilliantly, looking over his spectacles triumphantly and even gaily at the accused. From the doctor's summing up Ivan Ilych concluded that things were bad, but that for the doctor, and perhaps for everybody else, it was a matter of indifference, though for him it was bad. And this conclusion struck him painfully, arousing in him a great feeling of pity for himself and of bitterness towards the doctor's indifference to a matter of such importance.

He said nothing of this, but rose, placed the doctor's fee on the table, and remarked with a sigh: "We sick people probably often put inappropriate questions. But tell me, in general, is this complaint dangerous, or not? . . ."

The doctor looked at him sternly over his spectacles with one eye, as if to say: "Prisoner, if you will not keep to the questions put to you, I shall be obliged to have you removed from the court."

"I have already told you what I consider necessary and proper. The analysis may show something more." And the doctor bowed.

Ivan Ilych went out slowly, seated himself disconsolately in his sledge, and drove home. All the way home he was going over what the doctor had said, trying to translate those complicated, obscure, scientific phrases into plain language and find in them an answer to the question: "Is my condition bad? Is it very bad? Or is there as yet nothing much wrong?" And it seemed to him that the meaning of what the doctor had said was that it was very bad. Everything in the streets seemed depressing. The cabmen, the houses, the passers-by, and the shops, were dismal. His ache, this dull gnawing ache that never ceased for a moment, seemed to have acquired a new and more serious significance from the doctor's dubious remarks. Ivan Ilych now watched it with a new and oppressive feeling.

He reached home and began to tell his wife about it. She listened, but in the middle of his account his daughter came in with her hat on, ready to go out with her mother. She sat down reluctantly to listen to this tedious story, but could not stand it long, and her mother too did not hear him to the end.

"Well, I am very glad," she said. "Mind now to take your medicine regularly. Give me the prescription and I'll send Gerasim to the chemist's." And she went to get ready to go out.

While she was in the room Ivan Ilych had hardly taken time to breathe, but he sighed deeply when she left it.

"Well," he thought, "perhaps it isn't so bad after all."

He began taking his medicine and following the doctor's directions, which had been altered after the examination of the urine. But then it happened that there was a contradiction between the indications drawn from the examination of the urine and the symptoms that showed themselves. It turned out that what was happening differed from what the doctor had told him, and that he had either forgotten, or blundered, or hidden something from him. He could not, however, be blamed for that, and Ivan Ilych still obeyed his orders implicitly and at first derived some comfort from doing so.

From the time of his visit to the doctor, Ivan Ilych's chief occupation was the exact fulfillment of the doctor's instructions regarding hygiene and the taking of medicine, and the observation of his pain and his excretions. His chief interests came to be people's ailments and people's health. When sickness, deaths, or recoveries were mentioned in his presence, especially when the illness resembled his own, he listened with agitation which he tried to hide, asked questions, and applied what he heard to his own case.

The pain did not grow less, but Ivan Ilych made efforts to force himself to think that he was better. And he could do this so long as nothing agitated him. But as soon as he had any unpleasantness with his wife, any lack of success in his official work, or held bad cards at bridge, he was at once acutely sensible of his disease. He had formerly borne such mischances, hoping soon to adjust what was wrong, to master it and attain success, or make a grand slam. But now every mischance upset him and plunged him into despair. He would say to himself: "There now, just as I was beginning to get better and the medicine had begun to take effect, comes this accursed misfortune, or unpleasantness. . . ." And he was furious with the mishap, or with the people who were causing the unpleasantness and killing him, for he felt that this fury was killing him but could not restrain it. One would have thought that it should have been clear to him that this exasperation with circumstances and people aggravated his illness, and that he ought therefore to ignore unpleasant occurrences. But he drew the very opposite conclusion; he said that he needed peace, and he watched for everything that might disturb it and became irritable at the slightest infringement of it. His condition was rendered worse by the fact that he read medical books and consulted doctors. The progress of his disease was so grad-ual that he could deceive himself when comparing one day with another — the difference was so slight. But when he consulted the doctors it seemed to him that he was getting worse, and even very rapidly. Yet despite this he was continually con-sulting them.

That month he went to see another celebrity, who told him almost the same as the first had done but put his questions rather differently, and the interview with this celebrity only increased Ivan Ilych's doubts and fears. A friend of a friend of his, a very good doctor, diagnosed his illness again quite differently from the others, and though he predicted recovery, his questions and suppositions bewildered Ivan Ilych still more and increased his doubts. A homeopathist diagnosed the disease in yet another way, and prescribed medicine which Ivan Ilych took secretly for a week. But after a week, not feeling any improvement and having lost confidence both in the former doctor's treatment and in this one's, he became still more despondent. One day a lady acquaintance mentioned a cure effected by a wonder-working icon. Ivan Ilych caught himself listening attentively and beginning to believe that it had occurred. This incident alarmed him. "Has my mind really weakened to such an extent?" he asked himself. "Nonsense! It's all rubbish. I mustn't give way to nervous fears but having chosen a doctor must keep strictly to his treatment. That is what I will do. Now it's all settled. I won't think about it, but will follow the treatment seri-ously till summer, and then we shall see. From now there must be no more of this wavering!" This was easy to say but impossible to carry out. The pain in his side oppressed him and seemed to grow worse and more incessant, while the taste in his mouth grew stranger and stranger. It seemed to him that his breath had a disgusting smell, and he was conscious of a loss of appetite and strength. There was no deceiv-ing himself: something terrible, new, and more important than anything before in his life, was taking place within him of which he alone was aware. Those about him did not understand or would not understand it, but thought everything in the world was going on as usual. That tormented Ivan Ilych more than anything. He saw that his household, especially his wife and daughter who were in a perfect whirl of visiting, did not understand anything of it and were annoyed that he was so depressed and so exacting, as if he were to blame for it. Though they tried to disguise it he saw that he was an obstacle in their path, and that his wife had adopted a definite line in regard to his illness and kept to it regardless of anything he said or did. Her attitude was this: "You know," she would say to her friends, "Ivan Ilych can't do as other people do, and keep to the treatment prescribed for him. One day he'll take his drops and keep strictly to his diet and go to bed in good time, but the next day unless I watch him he'll suddenly forget his medicine, eat sturgeon—which is forbidden—and sit up playing cards till one o'clock in the morning."

"Oh, come, when was that?" Ivan Ilych would ask in vexation. "Only once at Peter Ivanovich's."

"And yesterday with Shebek."

"Well, even if I hadn't stayed up, this pain would have kept me awake."

"Be that as it may you'll never get well like that, but will always make us wretched."

Praskovya Fëdorovna's attitude to Ivan Ilych's illness, as she expressed it both to others and to him, was that it was his own fault and was another of the annoyances he caused her. Ivan Ilych felt that this opinion escaped her involuntarily—but that did not make it easier for him.

At the law courts too, Ivan Ilych noticed, or thought he noticed, a strange attitude towards himself. It sometimes seemed to him that people were watching him inquisitively as a man whose place might soon be vacant. Then again, his friends would suddenly begin to chaff him in a friendly way about his low spirits, as if the awful, horrible, and unheard-of thing that was going on within him, incessantly gnawing at him and irresistibly drawing him away, was a very agreeable subject for jests. Schwartz in particular irritated him by his jocularity, vivacity, and *savoir-faire*, which reminded him of what he himself had been ten years ago.

Friends came to make up a set and they sat down to cards. They dealt, bending the new cards to soften them, and he sorted the diamonds in his hand and found he had seven. His partner said "No trumps" and supported him with two diamonds. What more could be wished for? It ought to be jolly and lively. They would make a grand slam. But suddenly Ivan Ilych was conscious of that gnawing pain, that taste in his mouth, and it seemed ridiculous that in such circumstances he should be pleased to make a grand slam.

He looked at his partner Mikhail Mikhaylovich, who rapped the table with his strong hand and instead of snatching up the tricks pushed the cards courteously and indulgently towards Ivan Ilych that he might have the pleasure of gathering them up without the trouble of stretching out his hand for them. "Does he think I am too weak to stretch out my arm?" thought Ivan Ilych, and forgetting what he was doing he over-trumped his partner, missing the grand slam by three tricks. And what was most awful of all was that he saw how upset Mikhail Mikhaylovich was about it but did not himself care. And it was dreadful to realize why he did not care.

They all saw that he was suffering, and said: "We can stop if you are tired. Take a rest." Lie down? No, he was not at all tired, and he finished the rubber. All were gloomy and silent. Ivan Ilych felt that he had diffused this gloom over them and could not dispel it. They had supper and went away, and Ivan Ilych was left alone with the consciousness that his life was poisoned and was poisoning the lives of others, and that this poison did not weaken but penetrated more and more deeply into his whole being.

With this consciousness, and with physical pain besides the terror, he must go to bed, often to lie awake the greater part of the night. Next morning he had to get up again, dress, go to the law courts, speak, and write; or if he did not go out, spend at home those twenty-four hours a day each of which was a torture. And he had to live thus all alone on the brink of an abyss, with no one who understood or pitied him.

V

So one month passed and then another. Just before the New Year his brother-in-law came to town and stayed at their house. Ivan Ilych was at the law courts and Praskovya Fëdorovna had gone shopping. When Ivan Ilych came home and entered his study he found his brother-in-law there—a healthy, florid man—unpacking his portmanteau himself. He raised his head on hearing Ivan Ilych's footsteps and looked up at him for a moment without a word. That stare told Ivan Ilych everything. His brother-in-law opened his mouth to utter an exclamation of surprise but checked himself, and that action confirmed it all.

"I have changed, eh?"

"Yes, there is a change."

And after that, try as he would to get his brother-in-law to return to the subject of his looks, the latter would say nothing about it. Praskovya Fëdorovna came home and her brother went out to her. Ivan Ilych locked the door and began to examine himself in the glass, first full face, then in profile. He took up a portrait of himself taken with his wife, and compared it with what he saw in the glass. The change in him was immense. Then he bared his arms to the elbow, looked at them, drew the sleeves down again, sat down on an ottoman, and grew blacker than night.

"No, no, this won't do!" he said to himself, and jumped up, went to the table, took up some law papers and began to read them, but could not continue. He unlocked the door and went into the reception-room, The door leading to the drawing-room was shut. He approached it on tiptoe and listened.

"No, you are exaggerating!" Praskovya Fëdorovna was saying.

"Exaggerating! Don't you see it? Why, he's a dead man! Look at his eyes—there's no light in them. But what is it that is wrong with him?"

"No one knows. Nikolaevich [that was another doctor] said something, but I don't know what. And Leshchetitsky [this was the celebrated specialist] said quite the contrary . . ."

Ivan Ilych walked away, went to his own room, lay down, and began musing: "The kidney, a floating kidney." He recalled all the doctors had told him of how it detached itself and swayed about. And by an effort of imagination he tried to catch that kidney and arrest it and support it. So little was needed for this, it seemed to him. "No, I'll go to see Peter Ivanovich again." [That was the friend whose friend was a doctor.] He rang, ordered the carriage, and got ready to go.

"Where are you going, Jean?"[12] asked his wife, with a specially sad and exceptionally kind look.

This exceptionally kind look irritated him. He looked morosely at her.

"I must go to see Peter Ivanovich."

He went to see Peter Ivanovich, and together they went to see his friend, the doctor. He was in, and Ivan Ilych had a long talk with him.

Reviewing the anatomical and physiological details of what in the doctor's opinion was going on inside him, he understood it all.

There was something, a small thing, in the vermiform appendix. It might all come right. Only stimulate the energy of one organ and check the activity of another, then absorption would take place and everything would come right. He got home rather late for dinner, ate his dinner, and conversed cheerfully, but could not for a long time bring himself to go back to work in his room. At last, however, he went to his study and did what was necessary, but the consciousness that he had put something aside — an important, intimate matter which he would revert to when his work was done — never left him. When he had finished his work he remembered that this intimate matter was the thought of his vermiform appendix. But he did not give himself up to it, and went to the drawing-room for tea. There were callers there, including the examining magistrate who was a desirable match for his daughter, and they were conversing, playing the piano, and singing. Ivan Ilych, as Praskovya Fëdorovna remarked, spent that evening more cheerfully than usual, but he never for a moment forgot that he had postponed the important matter of the appendix. At eleven o'clock he said good-night and went to his bedroom. Since his illness he had slept alone in a small room next to his study. He undressed and took up a novel by Zola,[13] but instead of reading it he fell into thought, and in his imagination that desired improvement in the vermiform appendix occurred. There was the absorption and evacuation and the re-establishment of normal activity. "Yes, that's it!" he said to himself. "One need only assist nature, that's all." He remembered his medicine, rose, took it, and lay down on his back watching for the beneficent action of the medicine and for it to lessen the pain. "I need only take it regularly and avoid all injurious influences. I am already feeling better, much better." He began touching his side: it was not painful to the touch. "There, I really don't feel it. It's much better already." He put out the light and turned on his side. . . . "The appendix is getting better, absorption is occurring." Suddenly he felt the old, familiar, dull, gnawing pain, stubborn and serious. There was the same familiar loathsome taste in his mouth. His heart sank and he felt dazed. "My God! My God!" he muttered. "Again, again! and it will never cease." And suddenly the matter presented itself in a quite different aspect. "Vermiform appendix! Kidney!" he said to himself. "It's not a question of appendix or kidney, but of life and . . . death. Yes, life was there and now it is going, going and I cannot stop it. Yes. Why deceive myself? Isn't it obvious to everyone but me that I'm dying, and that it's only a question of weeks, days . . . it may happen this moment. There was light and now there is darkness. I was here and now

---

[12] **"Jean"**: French version of Ivan.

[13] **Zola**: Émile Zola (1840–1902), a French novelist criticized by Tolstoy for his crude, naturalistic writing.

I'm going there! Where?" A chill came over him, his breathing ceased, and he felt only the throbbing of his heart.

"When I am not, what will there be? There will be nothing. Then where shall I be when I am no more? Can this be dying? No, I don't want to!" He jumped up and tried to light the candle, felt for it with trembling hands, dropped candle and candlestick on the floor, and fell back on his pillow.

"What's the use? It makes no difference," he said to himself, staring with wide-open eyes into the darkness. "Death. Yes, death. And none of them know or wish to know it, and they have no pity for me. Now they are playing." (He heard through the door the distant sound of a song and its accompaniment.) "It's all the same to them, but they will die too! Fools! I first, and they later, but it will be the same for them. And now they are merry . . . the beasts!"

Anger choked him and he was agonizingly, unbearably miserable. "It is impossible that all men have been doomed to suffer this awful horror!" He raised himself.

"Something must be wrong. I must calm myself—must think it all over from the beginning." And he again began thinking. "Yes, the beginning of my illness: I knocked my side, but I was still quite well that day and the next. It hurt a little, then rather more. I saw the doctors, then followed despondency and anguish, more doctors, and I drew nearer to the abyss. My strength grew less and I kept coming nearer and nearer, and now I have wasted away and there is no light in my eyes. I think of the appendix—but this is death! I think of mending the appendix, and all the while here is death! Can it really be death?" Again terror seized him and he gasped for breath. He leant down and began feeling for the matches, pressing with his elbow on the stand beside the bed. It was in his way and hurt him, he grew furious with it, pressed on it still harder, and upset it. Breathless and in despair he fell on his back, expecting death to come immediately.

Meanwhile the visitors were leaving. Praskovya Fëdorovna was seeing them off. She heard something fall and came in.

"What has happened?"

"Nothing. I knocked it over accidentally."

She went out and returned with a candle. He lay there panting heavily, like a man who has run a thousand yards, and stared upwards at her with a fixed look.

"What is it, Jean?"

"No . . . o . . . thing. I upset it." ("Why speak of it? She won't understand," he thought.)

And in truth she did not understand. She picked up the stand, lit his candle, and hurried away to see another visitor off. When she came back he still lay on his back, looking upwards.

"What is it? Do you feel worse?"

"Yes."

She shook her head and sat down.

"Do you know, Jean, I think we must ask Leshchetitsky to come and see you here."

This meant calling in the famous specialist, regardless of expense. He smiled malignantly and said "No." She remained a little longer and then went up to him and kissed his forehead.

While she was kissing him he hated her from the bottom of his soul and with difficulty refrained from pushing her away.

"Good-night. Please God you'll sleep."

"Yes."

VI

Ivan Ilych saw that he was dying, and he was in continual despair.

In the depth of his heart he knew he was dying, but not only was he not accustomed to the thought, he simply did not and could not grasp it.

The syllogism he had learnt from Kiezewetter's Logic:[14] "Caius is a man, men are mortal, therefore Caius is mortal," had always seemed to him correct as applied to Caius, but certainly not as applied to himself. That Caius—man in the abstract—was mortal, was perfectly correct, but he was not Caius, not an abstract man, but a creature quite, quite separate from all others. He had been little Vanya, with a mamma and a papa, with Mitya and Volodya, with the toys, a coachman and a nurse, afterwards with Katenka and with all the joys, griefs, and delights of childhood, boyhood, and youth. What did Caius know of the smell of that striped leather ball Vanya had been so fond of? Had Caius kissed his mother's hand like that, and did the silk of her dress rustle so for Caius? Had he rioted like that at school when the pastry was bad? Had Caius been in love like that? Could Caius preside at a session as he did? "Caius really was mortal, and it was right for him to die; but for me, little Vanya, Ivan Ilych, with all my thoughts and emotions, it's altogether a different matter. It cannot be that I ought to die. That would be too terrible."

Such was his feeling.

"If I had to die like Caius I should have known it was so. An inner voice would have told me so, but there was nothing of the sort in me and I and all my friends felt that our case was quite different from that of Caius. And now here it is!" he said to himself. "It can't be. It's impossible! But here it is. How is this? How is one to understand it?"

He could not understand it, and tried to drive this false, incorrect, morbid thought away and to replace it by other proper and healthy thoughts. But that thought, and not the thought only but the reality itself, seemed to come and confront him.

And to replace that thought he called up a succession of others, hoping to find in them some support. He tried to get back into the former current of thoughts that had once screened the thought of death from him. But strange to say, all that had formerly shut off, hidden, and destroyed, his consciousness of death, no longer had that effect. Ivan Ilych now spent most of his time in attempting to re-establish that old current. He would say to himself: "I will take up my duties again—after all I used to live by them." And banishing all doubts he would go to the law courts, enter into conversation with his colleagues, and sit carelessly as was his wont, scanning the crowd with a thoughtful look and leaning both his emaciated arms on the arms of

---

[14] **Kiezewetter's Logic:** Karl Kiezewetter(1706–1819) wrote a popular textbook, *Outline of Logic* (1796).

his oak chair; bending over as usual to a colleague and drawing his papers nearer he would interchange whispers with him, and then suddenly raising his eyes and sitting erect would pronounce certain words and open the proceedings. But suddenly in the midst of those proceedings the pain in his side, regardless of the stage the proceedings had reached, would begin its own gnawing work. Ivan Ilych would turn his attention to it and try to drive the thought of it away, but without success. *It* would come and stand before him and look at him, and he would be petrified and the light would die out of his eyes, and he would again begin asking himself whether *It* alone was true. And his colleagues and subordinates would see with surprise and distress that he, the brilliant and subtle judge, was becoming confused and making mistakes. He would shake himself, try to pull himself together, manage somehow to bring the sitting to a close, and return home with the sorrowful consciousness that his judicial labours could not as formerly hide from him what he wanted them to hide, and could not deliver him from *It*. And what was worst of all was that *It* drew his attention to itself not in order to make him take some action but only that he should look at *It*, look it straight in the face: look at it and without doing anything, suffer inexpressibly.

And to save himself from this condition Ivan Ilych looked for consolations—new screens—and new screens were found and for a while seemed to save him, but then they immediately fell to pieces or rather became transparent, as if *It* penetrated them and nothing could veil *It*.

In these latter days he would go into the drawing-room he had arranged—that drawing-room where he had fallen and for the sake of which (how bitterly ridiculous it seemed) he had sacrificed his life—for he knew that his illness originated with that knock. He would enter and see that something had scratched the polished table. He would look for the cause of this and find that it was the bronze ornamentation of an album, that had got bent. He would take up the expensive album which he had lovingly arranged, and feel vexed with his daughter and her friends for their untidiness—for the album was torn here and there and some of the photographs turned upside down. He would put it carefully in order and bend the ornamentation back into position. Then it would occur to him to place all those things in another corner of the room, near the plants. He could call the footman, but his daughter or wife would come to help him. They would not agree, and his wife would contradict him, and he would dispute and grow angry. But that was all right, for then he did not think about *It*. *It* was invisible.

But then, when he was moving something himself, his wife would say: "Let the servants do it. You will hurt yourself again." And suddenly *It* would flash through the screen and he would see it. It was just a flash, and he hoped it would disappear, but he would involuntarily pay attention to his side. "It sits there as before, gnawing just the same!" And he could no longer forget *It*, but could distinctly see it looking at him from behind the flowers. "What is it all for?"

"It really is so! I lost my life over that curtain as I might have done when storming a fort. Is that possible? How terrible and how stupid. It can't be true! It can't, but it is."

He would go to his study, lie down, and again be alone with *It:* face to face with *It.* And nothing could be done with *It* except to look at it and shudder.

VII

How it happened it is impossible to say because it came about step by step, unnoticed, but in the third month of Ivan Ilych's illness, his wife, his daughter, his son, his acquaintances, the doctors, the servants, and above all he himself, were aware that the whole interest he had for other people was whether he would soon vacate his place, and at last release the living from the discomfort caused by his presence and be himself released from his sufferings.

He slept less and less. He was given opium and hypodermic injections of morphine, but this did not relieve him. The dull depression he experienced in a somnolent condition at first gave him a little relief, but only as something new; afterwards it became as distressing as the pain itself or even more so.

Special foods were prepared for him by the doctors' orders, but all those foods became increasingly distasteful and disgusting to him.

For his excretions also special arrangements had to be made, and this was a torment to him every time—a torment from the uncleanliness, the unseemliness, and the smell, and from knowing that another person had to take part in it.

But just through this most unpleasant matter, Ivan Ilych obtained comfort. Gerasim, the butler's young assistant, always came in to carry the things out. Gerasim was a clean, fresh peasant lad, grown stout on town food and always cheerful and bright. At first the sight of him, in his clean Russian peasant costume, engaged in that disgusting task embarrassed Ivan Ilych.

Once when he got up from the commode too weak to draw up his trousers, he dropped into a soft armchair and looked with horror at his bare, enfeebled thighs with the muscles so sharply marked on them.

Gerasim with a firm light tread, his heavy boots emitting a pleasant smell of tar and fresh winter air, came in wearing a clean Hessian apron, the sleeves of his print shirt tucked up over his strong bare young arms; and refraining from looking at his sick master out of consideration for his feelings, and restraining the joy of life that beamed from his face, he went up to the commode.

"Gerasim!" said Ivan Ilych in a weak voice.

Gerasim started, evidently afraid he might have committed some blunder, and with a rapid movement turned his fresh, kind, simple young face which just showed the first downy signs of a beard.

"Yes, sir?"

"That must be very unpleasant for you. You must forgive me. I am helpless."

"Oh, why, sir," and Gerasim's eyes beamed and he showed his glistening white teeth, "what's a little trouble? It's a case of illness with you, sir."

And his deft strong hands did their accustomed task, and he went out of the room stepping lightly. Five minutes later he as lightly returned.

Ivan Ilych was still sitting in the same position in the armchair.

"Gerasim," he said when the latter had replaced the freshly-washed utensil. "Please come here and help me." Gerasim went up to him. "Lift me up. It is hard for me to get up, and I have sent Dmitri away."

Gerasim went up to him, grasped his master with his strong arms deftly but gently, in the same way that he stepped — lifted him, supported him with one hand, and with the other drew up his trousers and would have set him down again, but Ivan Ilych asked to be led to the sofa. Gerasim, without an effort and without apparent pressure, led him, almost lifting him, to the sofa and placed him on it.

"Thank you. How easily and well you do it all!"

Gerasim smiled again and turned to leave the room. But Ivan Ilych felt his presence such a comfort that he did not want to let him go.

"One thing more, please move up that chair. No, the other one — under my feet. It is easier for me when my feet are raised."

Gerasim brought the chair, set it down gently in place, and raised Ivan Ilych's legs on to it. It seemed to Ivan Ilych that he felt better while Gerasim was holding up his legs.

"It's better when my legs are higher," he said. "Place that cushion under them."

Gerasim did so. He again lifted the legs and placed them, and again Ivan Ilych felt better while Gerasim held his legs. When he set them down Ivan Ilych fancied he felt worse.

"Gerasim," he said. "Are you busy now?"

"Not at all, sir," said Gerasim, who had learnt from the townsfolk how to speak to gentlefolk.

"What have you still to do?"

"What have I to do? I've done everything except chopping the logs for tomorrow."

"Then hold my legs up a bit higher, can you?"

"Of course I can. Why not?" And Gerasim raised his master's legs higher and Ivan Ilych thought that in that position he did not feel any pain at all.

"And how about the logs?"

"Don't trouble about that, sir. There's plenty of time."

Ivan Ilych told Gerasim to sit down and hold his legs, and began to talk to him. And strange to say it seemed to him that he felt better while Gerasim held his legs up.

After that Ivan Ilych would sometimes call Gerasim and get him to hold his legs on his shoulders, and he liked talking to him. Gerasim did it all easily, willingly, simply, and with a good nature that touched Ivan Ilych. Health, strength, and vitality in other people were offensive to him, but Gerasim's strength and vitality did not mortify but soothed him.

What tormented Ivan Ilych most was the deception, the lie, which for some reason they all accepted, that he was not dying but was simply ill, and that he only need keep quiet and undergo a treatment and then something very good would result. He however knew that do what they would nothing would come of it, only still more agonizing suffering and death. This deception tortured him — their not wishing to admit what they all knew and what he knew, but wanting to lie to him concerning his terrible condition, and wishing and forcing him to participate in that lie. Those lies — lies enacted over him on the eve of his death and destined to degrade this awful, solemn act to the level of their visitings, their curtains, their sturgeon for dinner—were a terrible agony for Ivan Ilych. And strangely enough, many times when they were going through their antics over him he had been within a hair-breadth of calling out to them: "Stop lying! You know and I know that I am dying. Then at least stop lying about it!" But he had never had the spirit to do it. The awful, terrible act of his dying was, he could see, reduced by those about him to the level of a casual, unpleasant, and almost indecorous incident (as if someone entered a draw-ing-room diffusing an unpleasant odour) and this was done by that very decorum which he had served all his life long. He saw that no one felt for him, because no one even wished to grasp his position. Only Gerasim recognized it and pitied him. And so Ivan Ilych felt at ease only with him. He felt comforted when Gerasim supported his legs (sometimes all night long) and refused to go to bed, saying: "Don't you worry, Ivan Ilych. I'll get sleep enough later on," or when he suddenly became famil-iar and exclaimed: "If you weren't sick it would be another matter, but as it is, why should I grudge a little trouble?" Gerasim alone did not lie; everything showed that he alone understood the facts of the case and did not consider it necessary to dis-guise them, but simply felt sorry for his emaciated and enfeebled master. Once when Ivan Ilych was sending him away he even said straight out: "We shall all of us die, so why should I grudge a little trouble?"—expressing the fact that he did not think his work burdensome, because he was doing it for a dying man and hoped someone would do the same for him when his time came.

Apart from this lying, or because of it, what most tormented Ivan Ilych was that no one pitied him as he wished to be pitied. At certain moments after prolonged suf-fering he wished most of all (though he would have been ashamed to confess it) for someone to pity him as a sick child is pitied. He longed to be petted and comforted. He knew he was an important functionary, that he had a beard turning grey, and that therefore what he longed for was impossible, but still he longed for it. And in Gerasim's attitude towards him there was something akin to what he wished for, and so that attitude comforted him. Ivan Ilych wanted to weep, wanted to be petted and cried over, and then his colleague Shebek would come, and instead of weeping and being petted, Ivan Ilych would assume a serious, severe, and profound air, and by force of habit would express his opinion on a decision of the Court of Cassation and would stubbornly insist on that view. This falsity around him and within him did more than anything else to poison his last days.

VIII

It was morning. He knew it was morning because Gerasim had gone, and Peter the footman had come and put out the candles, drawn back one of the curtains, and begun quietly to tidy up. Whether it was morning or evening, Friday or Sunday, made no difference, it was all just the same: the gnawing, unmitigated, agonizing pain, never ceasing for an instant, the consciousness of life inexorably waning but not yet extinguished, the approach of that ever dreaded and hateful Death which was the only reality, and always the same falsity. What were days, weeks, hours, in such a case?

"Will you have some tea, sir?"

"He wants things to be regular, and wishes the gentlefolk to drink tea in the morning," thought Ivan Ilych, and only said "No."

"Wouldn't you like to move onto the sofa, sir?"

"He wants to tidy up the room, and I'm in the way. I am uncleanliness and disorder," he thought, and said only:

"No, leave me alone."

The man went on bustling about. Ivan Ilych stretched out his hand. Peter came up, ready to help.

"What is it, sir?"

"My watch."

Peter took the watch which was close at hand and gave it to his master.

"Half-past eight. Are they up?"

"No, sir, except Vladimir Ivanich" (the son) "who has gone to school. Praskovya Fëdorovna ordered me to wake her if you asked for her. Shall I do so?"

"No, there's no need to." "Perhaps I'd better have some tea," he thought, and added aloud: "Yes, bring me some tea."

Peter went to the door, but Ivan Ilych dreaded being left alone. "How can I keep him here? Oh yes, my medicine." "Peter, give me my medicine." "Why not? Perhaps it may still do me some good." He took a spoonful and swallowed it. "No, it won't help. It's all tomfoolery, all deception," he decided as soon as he became aware of the familiar, sickly, hopeless taste. "No, I can't believe in it any longer. But the pain, why this pain? If it would only cease just for a moment!" And he moaned. Peter turned towards him. "It's all right. Go and fetch me some tea."

Peter went out. Left alone Ivan Ilych groaned not so much with pain, terrible though that was, as from mental anguish. Always and for ever the same, always these endless days and nights. If only it would come quicker! If only *what* would come quicker? Death, darkness? . . . No, no! Anything rather than death!

When Peter returned with the tea on a tray, Ivan Ilych stared at him for a time in perplexity, not realizing who and what he was. Peter was disconcerted by that look and his embarrassment brought Ivan Ilych to himself.

"Oh, tea! All right, put it down. Only help me to wash and put on a clean shirt."

And Ivan Ilych began to wash. With pauses for rest, he washed his hands and then his face, cleaned his teeth, brushed his hair, and looked in the glass. He was terrified by what he saw, especially by the limp way in which his hair clung to his pallid forehead.

While his shirt was being changed he knew that he would be still more frightened at the sight of his body, so he avoided looking at it. Finally he was ready. He drew on a dressing-gown, wrapped himself in a plaid, and sat down in the armchair to take his tea. For a moment he felt refreshed, but as soon as he began to drink the tea he was again aware of the same taste, and the pain also returned. He finished it with an effort, and then lay down stretching out his legs, and dismissed Peter.

Always the same. Now a spark of hope flashes up, then a sea of despair rages, and always pain; always pain, always despair, and always the same. When alone he had a dreadful and distressing desire to call someone, but he knew beforehand that with others present it would be still worse. "Another dose of morphine—to lose consciousness. I will tell him, the doctor, that he must think of something else. It's impossible, impossible, to go on like this."

An hour and another pass like that. But now there is a ring at the door bell. Perhaps it's the doctor? It is. He comes in fresh, hearty, plump, and cheerful, with that look on his face that seems to say: "There now, you're in a panic about something, but we'll arrange it all for you directly!" The doctor knows this expression is out of place here, but he has put it on once for all and can't take it off—like a man who has put on a frock-coat in the morning to pay a round of calls.

The doctor rubs his hands vigorously and reassuringly.

"Brr! How cold it is! There's such a sharp frost; just let me warm myself!" he says, as if it were only a matter of waiting till he was warm, and then he would put everything right.

"Well now, how are you?"

Ivan Ilych feels that the doctor would like to say: "Well, how are our affairs?" but that even he feels that this would not do, and says instead: "What sort of a night have you had?"

Ivan Ilych looks at him as much as to say: "Are you really never ashamed of lying?" But the doctor does not wish to understand this question, and Ivan Ilych says: "Just as terrible as ever. The pain never leaves me and never subsides. If only something . . ."

"Yes, you sick people are always like that. . . . There, now I think I am warm enough. Even Praskovya Fëdorovna, who is so particular, could find no fault with my temperature. Well, now I can say good-morning," and the doctor presses his patient's hand.

Then, dropping his former playfulness, he begins with a most serious face to examine the patient, feeling his pulse and taking his temperature, and then begins the sounding and auscultation.

Ivan Ilych knows quite well and definitely that all this is nonsense and pure deception, but when the doctor, getting down on his knee, leans over him, putting his ear first higher then lower, and performs various gymnastic movements over him with a significant expression on his face, Ivan Ilych submits to it all as he used to submit to the speeches of the lawyers, though he knew very well that they were all lying and why they were lying.

The doctor, kneeling on the sofa, is still sounding him when Praskovya Fëdorovna's silk dress rustles at the door and she is heard scolding Peter for not having let her know of the doctor's arrival.

She comes in, kisses her husband, and at once proceeds to prove that she has been up a long time already, and only owing to a misunderstanding failed to be there when the doctor arrived.

Ivan Ilych looks at her, scans her all over, sets against her the whiteness and plumpness and cleanness of her hands and neck, the gloss of her hair, and the sparkle of her vivacious eyes. He hates her with his whole soul. And the thrill of hatred he feels for her makes him suffer from her touch.

Her attitude towards him and his disease is still the same. Just as the doctor had adopted a certain relation to his patient which he could not abandon, so had she formed one towards him—that he was not doing something he ought to do and was himself to blame, and that she reproached him lovingly for this—and she could not now change that attitude.

"You see he doesn't listen to me and doesn't take his medicine at the proper time. And above all he lies in a position that is no doubt bad for him—with his legs up."

She described how he made Gerasim hold his legs up.

The doctor smiled with a contemptuous affability that said: "What's to be done? These sick people do have foolish fancies of that kind, but we must forgive them."

When the examination was over the doctor looked at his watch, and then Praskovya Fëdorovna announced to Ivan Ilych that it was of course as he pleased, but she had sent today for a celebrated specialist who would examine him and have a consultation with Michael Danilovich (their regular doctor).

"Please don't raise any objections. I am doing this for my own sake," she said ironically, letting it be felt that she was doing it all for his sake and only said this to leave him no right to refuse. He remained silent, knitting his brows. He felt that he was so surrounded and involved in a mesh of falsity that it was hard to unravel anything.

Everything she did for him was entirely for her own sake, and she told him she was doing for herself what she actually was doing for herself, as if that was so incredible that he must understand the opposite.

At half-past eleven the celebrated specialist arrived. Again the sounding began and the significant conversations in his presence and in another room, about the kidneys and the appendix, and the questions and answers, with such an air of importance that again, instead of the real question of life and death which now alone confronted him, the question arose of the kidney and appendix which were not behaving as they ought to and would now be attacked by Michael Danilovich and the specialist and forced to amend their ways.

The celebrated specialist took leave of him with a serious though not hopeless look, and in reply to the timid question Ivan Ilych, with eyes glistening with fear and hope, put to him as to whether there was a chance of recovery, said that he could not vouch for it but there was a possibility. The look of hope with which Ivan Ilych watched the doctor out was so pathetic that Praskovya Fëdorovna, seeing it, even wept as she left the room to hand the doctor his fee.

The gleam of hope kindled by the doctor's encouragement did not last long. The same room, the same pictures, curtains, wall-paper, medicine bottles, were all there, and the same aching suffering body, and Ivan Ilych began to moan. They gave him a subcutaneous injection and he sank into oblivion.

It was twilight when he came to. They brought him his dinner and he swallowed some beef tea with difficulty, and then everything was the same again and night was coming on.

After dinner, at seven o'clock, Praskovya Fëdorovna came into the room in evening dress, her full bosom pushed up by her corset, and with traces of powder on her face. She had reminded him in the morning that they were going to the theatre. Sarah Bernhardt[15] was visiting the town and they had a box, which he had insisted

---

[15] Sarah Bernhardt (1844–1923): A popular French actress.

on their taking. Now he had forgotten about it and her toilet offended him, but he concealed his vexation when he remembered that he had himself insisted on their securing a box and going because it would be an instructive and aesthetic pleasure for the children.

Praskovya Fëdorovna came in, self-satisfied but yet with a rather guilty air. She sat down and asked how he was, but, as he saw, only for the sake of asking and not in order to learn about it, knowing that there was nothing to learn — and then went on to what she really wanted to say: that she would not on any account have gone but that the box had been taken and Helen and their daughter were going, as well as Petrishchev (the examining magistrate, their daughter's fiancé) and that it was out of the question to let them go alone; but that she would have much preferred to sit with him for a while; and he must be sure to follow the doctor's orders while she was away.

"Oh, and Fëdor Petrovich" (the fiancé) "would like to come in. May he? And Lisa?"

"All right."

Their daughter came in in full evening dress, her fresh young flesh exposed (making a show of that very flesh which in his own case caused so much suffering), strong, healthy, evidently in love, and impatient with illness, suffering, and death, because they interfered with her happiness.

Fëdor Petrovich came in too, in evening dress, his hair curled *à la Capoul*,[16] a tight stiff collar round his long sinewy neck, an enormous white shirt-front and narrow black trousers tightly stretched over his strong thighs. He had one white glove tightly drawn on, and was holding his opera hat in his hand.

Following him the schoolboy crept in unnoticed, in a new uniform, poor little fellow, and wearing gloves. Terribly dark shadows showed under his eyes, the meaning of which Ivan Ilych knew well.

His son had always seemed pathetic to him, and now it was dreadful to see the boy's frightened look of pity. It seemed to Ivan Ilych that Vasya was the only one besides Gerasim who understood and pitied him.

They all sat down and again asked how he was. A silence followed. Lisa asked her mother about the opera-glasses, and there was an altercation between mother and daughter as to who had taken them and where they had been put. This occasioned some unpleasantness.

Fëdor Petrovich inquired of Ivan Ilych whether he had ever seen Sarah Bernhardt. Ivan Ilych did not at first catch the question, but then replied: "No, have you seen her before?"

"Yes, in *Adrienne Lecouvreur*."[17]

Praskovya Fëdorovna mentioned some rôles in which Sarah Bernhardt was particularly good. Her daughter disagreed. Conversation sprang up as to the elegance and realism of her acting — the sort of conversation that is always repeated and is always the same.

---

[16] *à la Capoul*: "according to Capoul," a French style of curling hair.

[17] *"Adrienne Lecouvreur"*: A play by Eugène Scribe (1791–1861), a commercial playwright disliked by Tolstoy.

In the midst of the conversation Fëdor Petrovich glanced at Ivan Ilych and became silent. The others also looked at him and grew silent. Ivan Ilych was staring with glittering eyes straight before him, evidently indignant with them. This had to be rectified, but it was impossible to do so. The silence had to be broken, but for a time no one dared to break it and they all became afraid that the conventional deception would suddenly become obvious and the truth become plain to all. Lisa was the first to pluck up courage and break that silence, but by trying to hide what everybody was feeling, she betrayed it.

"Well, if we are going it's time to start," she said, looking at her watch, a present from her father, and with a faint and significant smile at Fëdor Petrovich relating to something known only to them. She got up with a rustle of her dress.

They all rose, said good-night, and went away.

When they had gone it seemed to Ivan Ilych that he felt better; the falsity had gone with them. But the pain remained—that same pain and that same fear that made everything monotonously alike, nothing harder and nothing easier. Everything was worse.

Again minute followed minute and hour followed hour. Everything remained the same and there was no cessation. And the inevitable end of it all became more and more terrible.

"Yes, send Gerasim here," he replied to a question Peter asked.

IX

His wife returned late at night. She came in on tiptoe, but he heard her, opened his eyes, and made haste to close them again. She wished to send Gerasim away and to sit with him herself, but he opened his eyes and said: "No, go away."

"Are you in great pain?"

"Always the same."

"Take some opium."

He agreed and took some. She went away.

Till about three in the morning he was in a state of stupefied misery. It seemed to him that he and his pain were being thrust into a narrow, deep black sack, but though they were pushed further and further in they could not be pushed to the bottom. And this, terrible enough in itself, was accompanied by suffering. He was frightened yet wanted to fall though the sack, he struggled but yet co-operated. And suddenly he broke through, fell, and regained consciousness. Gerasim was sitting at the foot of the bed dozing quietly and patiently, while he himself lay with his emaciated stockinged legs resting on Gerasim's shoulders; the same shaded candle was there and the same unceasing pain.

"Go away, Gerasim," he whispered.

"It's all right, sir. I'll stay a while."

"No. Go away."

He removed his legs from Gerasim's shoulders, turned sideways onto his arm, and felt sorry for himself. He only waited till Gerasim had gone into the next room and then restrained himself no longer but wept like a child. He wept on account of his helplessness, his terrible loneliness, the cruelty of man, the cruelty of God, and the absence of God.

"Why hast Thou done all this? Why hast Thou brought me here? Why, why dost Thou torment me so terribly?"

He did not expect an answer and yet wept because there was no answer and could be none. The pain again grew more acute, but he did not stir and did not call. He said to himself: "Go on! Strike me! But what is it for? What have I done to Thee? What is it for?"

Then he grew quiet and not only ceased weeping but even held his breath and became all attention. It was as though he were listening not to an audible voice but to the voice of his soul, to the current of thoughts arising within him.

"What is it you want?" was the first clear conception capable of expression in words, that he heard.

"What do you want? What do you want?" he repeated to himself.

"What do I want? To live and not to suffer," he answered.

And again he listened with such concentrated attention that even his pain did not distract him.

"To live? How?" asked his inner voice.

"Why, to live as I used to — well and pleasantly."

"As you lived before, well and pleasantly?" the voice repeated.

And in imagination he began to recall the best moments of his pleasant life. But strange to say none of those best moments of his pleasant life now seemed at all what they had then seemed — none of them except the first recollections of childhood. There, in childhood, there had been something really pleasant with which it would be possible to live if it could return. But the child who had experienced that happiness existed no longer, it was like a reminiscence of somebody else.

As soon as the period began which had produced the present Ivan Ilych, all that had then seemed joys now melted before his sight and turned into something trivial and often nasty.

And the further he departed from childhood and the nearer he came to the present the more worthless and doubtful were the joys. This began with the School of Law. A little that was really good was still found there — there was light-heartedness, friendship, and hope. But in the upper classes there had already been fewer of such good moments. Then during the first years of his official career, when he was in the service of the Governor, some pleasant moments again occurred: They were the memories of love for a woman. Then all became confused and there was still less of what was good; later on again there was still less that was good, and the further he went the less there was. His marriage, a mere accident, then the disenchantment that followed it, his wife's bad breath and the sensuality and hypocrisy: then that deadly official life and those preoccupations about money, a year of it, and two, and ten, and twenty, and always the same thing. And the longer it lasted the more deadly it became. "It is as if I had been going downhill while I imagined I was going up. And that is really what it was. I was going up in public opinion, but to the same extent life was ebbing away from me. And now it is all done and there is only death."

"Then what does it mean? Why? It can't be that life is so senseless and horrible. But if it really has been so horrible and senseless, why must I die and die in agony? There is something wrong!"

"Maybe I did not live as I ought to have done," it suddenly occurred to him. "But how could that be, when I did everything properly?" he replied, and immediately dismissed from his mind this, the sole solution of all the riddles of life and death, as something quite impossible.

"Then what do you want now? To live? Live how? Live as you lived in the law courts when the usher proclaimed 'The judge is coming!' The judge is coming, the judge!" he repeated to himself. "Here he is, the judge. But I am not guilty!" he exclaimed angrily. "What is it for?" And he ceased crying, but turning his face to the wall continued to ponder on the same question: Why, and for what purpose, is there all this horror? But however much he pondered he found no answer. And whenever the thought occurred to him, as it often did, that it all resulted from his not having lived as he ought to have done, he at once recalled the correctness of his whole life and dismissed so strange an idea.

X

Another fortnight passed. Ivan Ilych now no longer left his sofa. He would not lie in bed but lay on the sofa, facing the wall nearly all the time. He suffered ever the same unceasing agonies and in his loneliness pondered always on the same insoluble question: "What is this? Can it be that it is Death?" and the inner voice answered: "Yes, it is Death."

"Why these sufferings?" And the voice answered, "For no reason — they just are so." Beyond and besides this there was nothing.

From the very beginning of his illness, ever since he had first been to see the doctor, Ivan Ilych's life had been divided between two contrary and alternating moods: now it was despair and the expectation of this uncomprehended and terrible death, and now hope and an intently interested observation of the functioning of his organs. Now before his eyes there was only a kidney or an intestine that temporarily evaded its duty, and now only that incomprehensible and dreadful death from which it was impossible to escape.

These two states of mind had alternated from the very beginning of his illness, but the further it progressed the more doubtful and fantastic became the conception of the kidney, and the more real the sense of impending death.

He had but to call to mind what he had been three months before and what he was now, to call to mind with what regularity he had been going downhill, for every possibility of hope to be shattered.

Latterly during that loneliness in which he found himself as he lay facing the back of the sofa, a loneliness in the midst of a populous town and surrounded by numerous acquaintances and relations but that yet could not have been more complete anywhere — either at the bottom of the sea or under the earth — during that terrible loneliness Ivan Ilych had lived only in memories of the past. Pictures of his past rose before him one after another. They always began with what was nearest in time and then went back to what was most remote — to his childhood — and rested there. If he thought of the stewed prunes that had been offered him that day, his mind went back to the raw shrivelled French plums of his childhood, their peculiar flavour and the flow of saliva when he sucked their stones, and along with the memory of that taste came a whole series of memories of those days: his nurse, his brother, and their toys. "No, I mustn't think of that. . . . It is too painful," Ivan Ilych said to himself, and brought himself back to the present — to the button on the back of the sofa and the creases in its morocco. "Morocco is expensive, but it does not wear well: there had been a quarrel about it. It was a different kind of quarrel and a different kind of morocco that time when we tore father's portfolio and were punished, and mamma brought us some tarts. . . ." And again his thoughts dwelt on his childhood, and again it was painful and he tried to banish them and fix his mind on something else.

Then again together with that chain of memories another series passed through his mind — of how his illness had progressed and grown worse. There also the further back he looked the more life there had been. There had been more of what was good in life and more of life itself. The two merged together. "Just as the pain went on getting worse and worse, so my life grew worse and worse," he thought. "There is one bright spot there at the back, at the beginning of life, and afterwards all becomes blacker and blacker and proceeds more and more rapidly — in inverse ratio to the square of the distance from death," thought Ivan Ilych. And the example of a stone falling downwards with increasing velocity entered his mind. Life, a series of increasing sufferings, flies further and further towards its end — the most terrible suffering. "I am flying. . . ." He shuddered, shifted himself, and tried to resist, but was already aware that resistance was impossible, and again with eyes weary of gazing but unable to cease seeing what was before them, he stared at the back of the sofa and waited — awaiting that dreadful fall and shock and destruction.

"Resistance is impossible!" he said to himself. "If I could only understand what it is all for! But that too is impossible. An explanation would be possible if it could be said that I have not lived as I ought to. But it is impossible to say that," and he remembered all the legality, correctitude, and propriety of his life. "That at any rate can certainly not be admitted," he thought, and his lips smiled ironically as if someone could see that smile and be taken in by it. "There is no explanation! Agony, death . . . What for?"

XI

Another two weeks went by in this way and during that fortnight an event occurred that Ivan Ilych and his wife had desired. Petrishchev formally proposed. It happened in the evening. The next day Praskovya Fëdorovna came into her husband's room considering how best to inform him of it, but that very night there had been a fresh change for the worse in his condition. She found him still lying on the sofa but in a different position. He lay on his back, groaning and staring fixedly straight in front of him.

She began to remind him of his medicines, but he turned his eyes towards her with such a look that she did not finish what she was saying; so great an animosity, to her in particular, did that look express.

"For Christ's sake let me die in peace!" he said.

She would have gone away, but just then their daughter came in and went up to say good morning. He looked at her as he had done at his wife, and in reply to her inquiry about his health said dryly that he would soon free them all of himself. They were both silent and after sitting with him for a while went away.

"Is it our fault?" Lisa said to her mother. "It's as if we were to blame! I am sorry for papa, but why should we be tortured?"

The doctor came at his usual time. Ivan Ilych answered "Yes" and "No," never taking his angry eyes from him, and at last said: "You know you can do nothing for me, so leave me alone."

"We can ease your sufferings."

"You can't even do that. Let me be."

The doctor went into the drawing-room and told Praskovya Fëdorovna that the case was very serious and that the only resource left was opium to allay her husband's sufferings, which must be terrible.

It was true, as the doctor said, that Ivan Ilych's physical sufferings were terrible, but worse than the physical sufferings were his mental sufferings, which were his chief torture.

His mental sufferings were due to the fact that that night, as he looked at Gerasim's sleepy, good-natured face with its prominent cheek-bones, the question suddenly occurred to him: "What if my whole life has really been wrong?"

It occurred to him that what had appeared perfectly impossible before, namely that he had not spent his life as he should have done, might after all be true. It occurred to him that his scarcely perceptible attempts to struggle against what was considered good by the most highly placed people, those scarcely noticeable impulses which he had immediately suppressed, might have been the real thing, and all the rest false. And his professional duties and the whole arrangement of his life and of his family, and all his social and official interests, might all have been false. He tried to defend all those things to himself and suddenly felt the weakness of what he was defending. There was nothing to defend.

"But if that is so," he said to himself, "and I am leaving this life with the consciousness that I have lost all that was given me and it is impossible to rectify it—what then?"

He lay on his back and began to pass his life in review in quite a new way. In the morning when he saw first his footman, then his wife, then his daughter, and then the doctor, their every word and movement confirmed to him the awful truth that had been revealed to him during the night. In them he saw himself—all that for which he had lived—and saw clearly that it was not real at all, but a terrible and huge deception which had hidden both life and death. This consciousness intensified his physical suffering tenfold. He groaned and tossed about, and pulled at his clothing which choked and stifled him. And he hated them on that account.

He was given a large dose of opium and became unconscious, but at noon his sufferings began again. He drove everybody away and tossed from side to side.

His wife came to him and said:

"Jean, my dear, do this for me. It can't do any harm and often helps. Healthy people often do it."

He opened his eyes wide.

"What? Take communion? Why? It's unnecessary! However . . ."

She began to cry.

"Yes, do, my dear. I'll send for our priest. He is such a nice man."

"All right. Very well," he muttered.

When the priest came and heard his confession, Ivan Ilych was softened and seemed to feel a relief from his doubts and consequently from his sufferings, and for a moment there came a ray of hope. He again began to think of the vermiform appendix and the possibility of correcting it. He received the sacrament with tears in his eyes.

When they laid him down again afterwards he felt a moment's ease, and the hope that he might live awoke in him again. He began to think of the operation that had been suggested to him. "To live! I want to live!" he said to himself.

His wife came in to congratulate him after his communion, and when uttering the usual conventional words she added:

"You feel better, don't you?"

Without looking at her he said "Yes."

Her dress, her figure, the expression of her face, the tone of her voice, all revealed the same thing. "This is wrong, it is not as it should be. All you have lived for and still live for is falsehood and deception, hiding life and death from you." And as soon as he admitted that thought, his hatred and his agonizing physical suffering again sprang up, and with that suffering a consciousness of the unavoidable, approaching end. And to this was added a new sensation of grinding shooting pain and a feeling of suffocation.

The expression of his face when he uttered that "yes" was dreadful. Having uttered it, he looked her straight in the eyes, turned on his face with a rapidity extraordinary in his weak state and shouted:

"Go away! Go away and leave me alone!"

XII

From that moment the screaming began that continued for three days, and was so terrible that one could not hear it through two closed doors without horror. At the moment he answered his wife he realized that he was lost, that there was no return, that the end had come, the very end, and his doubts were still unsolved and remained doubts.

"Oh! Oh! Oh!" he cried in various intonations. He had begun by screaming "I won't!" and continued screaming on the letter O.

For three whole days, during which time did not exist for him, he struggled in that black sack into which he was being thrust by an invisible, resistless force. He struggled as a man condemned to death struggles in the hands of the executioner, knowing that he cannot save himself. And every moment he felt that despite all his efforts he was drawing nearer and nearer to what terrified him. He felt that his agony was due to his being thrust into that black hole and still more to his not being able to get right into it. He was hindered from getting into it by his conviction that his life had been a good one. That very justification of his life held him fast and prevented his moving forward, and it caused him most torment of all.

Suddenly some force struck him in the chest and side, making it still harder to breathe, and he fell through the hole and there at the bottom was a light. What had happened to him was like the sensation one sometimes experiences in a railway carriage when one thinks one is going backwards while one is really going forwards and suddenly becomes aware of the real direction.

"Yes, it was all not the right thing," he said to himself, "but that's no matter. It can be done. But what *is* the right thing?" he asked himself, and suddenly grew quiet.

This occurred at the end of the third day, two hours before his death. Just then his schoolboy son had crept softly in and gone up to the bedside. The dying man was still screaming desperately and waving his arms. His hand fell on the boy's head, and the boy caught it, pressed it to his lips, and began to cry.

At that very moment Ivan Ilych fell through and caught sight of the light, and it was revealed to him that though his life had not been what it should have been, this could still be rectified. He asked himself, "What *is* the right thing?" and grew still, listening. Then he felt that someone was kissing his hand. He opened his eyes, looked at his son, and felt sorry for him. His wife came up to him and he glanced at her. She was gazing at him open-mouthed, with undried tears on her nose and cheek and a despairing look on her face. He felt sorry for her too.

"Yes, I am making them wretched," he thought. "They are sorry, but it will be better for them when I die." He wished to say this but had not the strength to utter it. "Besides, why speak? I must act," he thought. With a look at his wife he indicated his son and said: "Take him away . . . sorry for him . . . sorry for you too. . . ." He tried to add, "forgive me," but said "forgo" and waved his hand, knowing that He whose understanding mattered would understand.

And suddenly it grew clear to him that what had been oppressing him and would not leave him was all dropping away at once from two sides, from ten sides, and from all sides. He was sorry for them, he must act so as not to hurt them: release them and free himself from these sufferings. "How good and how simple!" he thought. "And the pain?" he asked himself. "What has become of it? Where are you, pain?"

He turned his attention to it.

"Yes, here it is. Well, what of it? Let the pain be."

"And death . . . where is it?"

He sought his former accustomed fear of death and did not find it. "Where is it? What death?" There was no fear because there was no death.

In place of death there was light.

"So that's what it is!" he suddenly exclaimed aloud. "What joy!"

To him all this happened in a single instant, and the meaning of that instant did not change. For those present his agony continued for another two hours. Something rattled in his throat, his emaciated body twitched, then the gasping and rattle became less and less frequent.

"It is finished!" said someone near him.

He heard these words and repeated them in his soul.

"Death is finished," he said to himself. "It is no more!"

He drew in a breath, stopped in the midst of a sigh, stretched out, and died.

TIME AND PLACE

Nineteenth-Century Europe: Darwin's Origin of Species

Like many members of the Victorian middle class, Tolstoy's Ivan Ilych is unsettled by unconventional thinking and behavior. Perhaps the single most unsettling work published in the nineteenth century was Charles Darwin's *On the Origin of Species by Means of Natural Selection, or the Preservation of Favoured Races in the Struggle for Life* (1859). In 1858, when Darwin learned that his fellow scientist Alfred Russel Wallace (1823–1913) was about to publish a theory similar to the one he had been working on for over twenty years, he rushed to complete his magnum opus. *Origin of Species,* published a year later, described the mechanisms of evolution, the struggle for existence and natural selection, and developed an overarching theory that connected many fields of study.

The *Origin* aggravated a controversy that had been building for much of the century: the conflict between science and religion. "Religion," the evolutionary English philosopher Herbert Spencer asserted, "has been impelled by science to give up one after another of its dogmas." The two cutting-edge sciences of the nineteenth century, geology and biology, were in the vanguard of the assault. Geologists sought to separate geological theory from the Bible and to establish nature as the sole source of truths about the history of the earth. Charles Lyell, Darwin's friend and mentor, argued that changes in the earth's past were caused, not by divine intervention through catastrophes like Noah's flood, but by the same natural processes that operated in the present. Biologists attributed the extinction of some species and the emergence of others to natural rather than divine causes. Darwin brought together many of these ideas and integrated them into a coherent theory of the natural mechanisms by which life evolved: He became the representative of science and its challenges to religion.

The theory of evolution particularly challenged three Christian doctrines of creation. Evolution's account of the slow, continual modifications to biological species and its confirmation of the geologist's history of the earth discredited the Bible-based calendar that dated creation to about 4000 B.C.E. Evolution also challenged the creation narrative in Genesis, which describes all species being created at one time; Darwin contended that creation is an ongoing process, a continuous struggle out of which the surviving species emerge like victors in a battle. Finally, the idea that humans had evolved from lower forms challenged the notion of the "special creation" of mankind by God. That man should be a younger cousin of the ape was probably the idea most offensive to the church and its adherents.

Many poets and artists also objected to Darwin's universe. Alfred, Lord Tennyson, in

Nineteenth-Century Europe: Darwin's Origin of Species *continued*

his poem *In Memoriam,* despaired that the
evolutionists had replaced Nature's peaceable
kingdom with "Nature, red in tooth and
claw." Tolstoy wrote to his children that "the
views you have acquired about Darwinism,
evolution, and the struggle for existence
won't explain to you the meaning of your life
and won't give you guidance in your actions."
Edgar Allan Poe lamented that science was
substituting for the beauties of the imagination "dull realities." Later in the century,
however, these dull realities would show up in
the novels of the Realists, who consciously
tried to depict faithfully the physical world
around them.

Although Darwin's work created controversy when it originally appeared and is still
resisted in some quarters, it changed the way
we see the world. His ideas were accepted
quickly in the natural sciences and exerted a
broad influence in the social sciences as well.
By the end of the nineteenth century, evolutionary theories abounded to explain economic, social, political, and even religious
development.

Darwin ridiculed *Some of Darwin's critics were so
distressed by his theory of evolution that they parodied
him by depicting him as a monkey, or at least as a man
willing to equate monkeys with people. (Hulton/
Archive)*

Society and Its Discontents

In **The Death of Ivan Ilych** Tolstoy describes the life, career, and death of a nineteenth-century everyman. Ivan Ilych, whose Russian name resembles the American name "John Doe," is a judge and civil servant who has devoted himself to professional advancement, social climbing, and decorum. Ivan is obsessed with success and doing the proper thing. This superficial value system brings him external rewards, but it does not provide him with inner satisfaction. His marriage is unhappy, he is subject to occasional bouts of depression, and he is totally unprepared to deal with his own death. In stages ranging from boredom to depression, anger, self-pity, despair, and finally, acceptance, he becomes aware of the seriousness of his condition. Facing death alone, he realizes that the values that have guided him have made his life an "awful loneliness" based on lies and "the absence of God."

p. 989

Many of Tolstoy's contemporaries agreed that their time was a godless and superficial one. Artists and writers in particular found themselves at odds with the middle-class culture around them, which they considered diseased and vacuous. Their works depict their perceptions of the era's malady and their expressions of social alienation.

THE SOCIAL DISEASE

Ivan Ilych's ailment might be equated with the nineteenth century's disease. Signs of material progress were ubiquitous: trains that quadrupled the speed of travel; factories that produced all manner of goods and made them available to vast numbers of people; growing cities that offered new economic, educational, and

> An individual in the bourgeois state of development while honest, industrious, and virtuous, is also not unapt to be a miracle of timid and shortsighted selfishness.
>
> – THEODORE ROOSEVELT, *Century Magazine*, 1886

Edvard Munch,
The Scream, 1893
In this lithograph based on his famous painting The Scream, *Munch gives a stark rendering of despair — what Ivan Ilych might have called "an awful loneliness." (Art Resource)*

p. 1037
oh-noh-RAY de
bahl-ZAHK

cultural opportunities; overseas possessions supplying the new European economy with raw materials and foreign markets. Nevertheless, this material progress was attended by a haunting sense of loss. Peasants boarded the railways en route to a new beginning in the industrialized cities, leaving behind deserted rural villages. The celebrations of rural life in the poems of the early ROMANTICS were often odes to a disappearing way of life. The urban novelists of midcentury, **Charles Dickens** in England, for example, and **Honoré de Balzac**[1] in France, reminded readers of the lost rural life by its very absence in their work. Epitomized by "materialistic" Darwinism, the scientific worldview that drove the Industrial Revolution displaced long-established traditions and beliefs and seemed to confirm Nietzsche's proposition that God was dead. Tolstoy was just one of

---

[1] **Honoré de Balzac** (1799–1850): French novelist who wrote about life in Paris, especially in his series of novels entitled *The Human Comedy*.

Hetton Colliery

By the middle of the nineteenth century, signs of material progress in the industrializing world were abundant. Collieries—coal mines and processing plants—were established over much of northern Britain. Thick, black smoke and a generally dreary appearance marked mining towns as symbols of the grittier aspects of the Industrial Revolution. (The Art Archive)

many writers who considered the century itself diseased. In "The Scholar Gypsy" (1853), Matthew Arnold[2] refers to the "strange disease of modern life," a spiritual condition physically visible in the smoky cities, rampant with crowding, poverty, and illness. Karl

---

[2] **Matthew Arnold** (1822–1888): English poet, critic, and essayist; "The Scholar Gypsy" laments a lost time "when wits were fresh and clear."

Marx argued in *Capital* (1867) that physical and psychological illnesses of the time were an inevitable result of the division of labor inherent in the capitalist factory system. Dickens generalized Marx's analysis in *Little Dorrit* (1855), ascribing the mysterious "complaint" of the financier Merdle to greed and to a social system that reduced all human relationships to monetary exchanges.

THE DOMINANCE OF THE BOURGEOISIE

boor-zhwah-ZEE

The economic and social changes in Europe brought about by the Industrial and French Revolutions of the late eighteenth century established the urban middle class, or the BOURGEOISIE, as the economically and politically dominant group in society. These powerful merchants and factory owners had displaced the landed feudal aristocracy and created a new value system. Devoted to making money, enforcing rules of social decorum, and reordering society to guarantee its position and power, the bourgeoisie tended to measure everything materialistically. Individual success was counted in monetary terms, and social progress was monitored by the gross national product. The arts were also commercialized; with the end of the patronage system, in which writers and artists had been supported by wealthy arts enthusiasts, artists instead had to sell their work and live off the profits. Sales figures became measures of artistic merit. Even religion was reduced to the bottom line. Calvinistic Protestantism, the predominant religion of the new middle class, equated material success with spiritual providence.

Most poets, novelists, and painters maintained an uneasy relationship with the middle-class audience that supported their work. Charles Dickens, the most successful English writer of the century, was often considered a spokesman for the domestic virtues celebrated by the bourgeoisie. Nevertheless, he satirized superficial materialism in the character of Mr. Podsnap in *Our Mutual Friend* (1865), and analyzed the spiritual vacuity of middle-class culture in many of his other novels. In nearly all of his works he also attacked the neglect and exploitation of the poor by the institutions of bourgeois society.

CLASS STRUGGLE

p. 1039

Karl Marx and **Friedrich Engels**, MATERIALISTS who saw history as an economically determined series of class struggles, characterized their time as one caught in a struggle between the bourgeoisie and the remnants of the old FEUDAL ARISTOCRACY, which the bourgeoisie had dislodged from power. But the factory owners were also in conflict with the rising industrial PROLETARIAT, the workers who sold their labor to the employers for an hourly wage and operated the machines. These workers would ultimately defeat their employers, Marx and Engels contended. Their classic treatise concerning these class struggles is entitled *The Communist Manifesto* (1848).

ACKNOWLEDGING THE DISEASE

Like Tolstoy, **Guy de Maupassant**, Flaubert's protégé as a Realist and the master of the short-story form, wrote of the disease of the bourgeoisie. Maupassant diagnoses Monsieur Savel's excessive concern for propriety in "**Regret**" as a form of clinical depression. Savel has withdrawn from life and discovers too late, when he nears death, that his timidity has denied him the woman he secretly loves and the possibility of a fuller life. Like Ivan Ilych, Savel, when he confronts the presence of his own death, realizes the lack of fulfillment in his life.

GEE de moh-pah-SAWNG

p. 1049

SHOCKING THE BOURGEOISIE

Gustave Flaubert, the son of a physician, who scrutinized provincial middle-class life in *Madame Bovary* (1856) and other works, wrote in a letter: "Hatred of the Bourgeois is the beginning of virtue. But for me the term 'bourgeois' includes the bourgeois in overalls as well as the bourgeois who wears a frock coat. It is we, and we alone—that is the educated—who are the People, or, more accurately, the tradition of Humanity." Nineteenth-century artists had a love–hate relationship with their society and their times.

p. 938

Both Friedrich Nietzsche and **Émile Zola** scandalized their middle-class readers with works that challenged conventional ideas. **Nietzsche's** evolutionary philosophy envisioned a new race of Supermen who would reject Christian virtues as elements of a "slave morality" and adopt instead a harsh and ruthless ethic in their place. In the passage from **The Gay Science** (1882) he explains his controversial conclusion that "God is dead." Zola's fascination with natural sciences led him to a literary aesthetic based on an

eh-MEEL zoh-LAH

NEE-chuh

p. 1053

p. 1055

teh-REZ ra-KANG

evolutionary perspective, the theory of NATURALISM. In the passage from the **Preface to the Second Edition of *Thérèse Raquin*,** Zola defends his novel from critics who attacked its morality. He explains that his characters are creatures determined by physical laws, animals reacting instinctively to the physical and hereditary forces that work on them.

THE SAMURAI AND THE BOURGEOISIE

[The bourgeois] prefers comfort to pleasure, convenience to liberty, and a pleasant temperature to that deathly inner consuming fire.
– HERMANN HESSE, *Steppenwolf,* 1927

In Japan, a rising bourgeoisie struggled with an entrenched feudalism for more than two centuries. The Tokugawa SHOGUNATE that ruled from the early seventeenth century until 1868 had isolated Japan from the West in an attempt to curtail the power of the growing class of merchants and traders. A thriving bourgeois culture developed in the cities nevertheless, especially in Kyoto and in the capitol, Edo (Tokyo). The bourgeois arts, notably KABUKI, popular theater, and the woodcuts known as UKIYO-E, "pictures of the floating world," challenged the conventional arts of Japan's feudal aristocracy, such as the Nō drama and classical painting. Unlike the puritanical European middle class, the Japanese bourgeoisie openly celebrated the attractions of the floating world, the name given to the pleasure quarters of cities. Importing Western culture and ideas, however, was forbidden; those guilty of advocating contact with the West were subject to imprisonment.

After Commodore Perry's trade mission forced the opening of Japan to the West in 1854, the shogunate, a form of military government, rapidly lost power. The Constitution of 1868 established a government grounded in civil rights and promoted contact with the rest of the world. Although the Japanese were especially anxious to study Western science and to develop their nation industrially, they wanted somehow to preserve their traditional cultural and ethical values. The ethics that many Japanese affirmed were those of BUSHIDO, the "way of the samurai" in traditional Japanese feudalism. **Inazo Nitobé**'s 1899 best-seller, *Bushido: The Soul of Japan,* described Japanese culture in terms of the virtues of the samurai for Western audiences. In the passage from this work included in this section, Nitobé compares the samurai concept of honor and the Western utilitarian concept of honesty.

p. 1056

■ PRONUNCIATION

bourgeoisie: boor-zhwah-ZEE
Émile Zola: eh-MEEL zoh-LAH
Guy de Maupassant: GEE de moh-pah-SAWNG
Honoré de Balzac: oh-noh-RAY de bahl-ZAHK
Nietzsche: NEE-chuh (NEE-chee)
Thérèse Raquin: teh-REZ ra-KANG
ukiyo-e: OO-kee-yoh EH

❧ CHARLES DICKENS
B. ENGLAND, 1812–1870

The most important English novelist of the nineteenth century, Charles Dickens was a close observer of his times who provided a panorama of English society during the middle years of the century in his work. "Podsnappery" comes from Dickens's last completed novel, *Our Mutual Friend* (1865), which dissects and analyzes English society. Podsnap is the consummate bourgeois, an insurance agent whose self-satisfaction, xenophobia, and complacency model the attitudes of the ascendant middle class.

> He never could make out why everybody was not quite satisfied, and he felt conscious that he set a brilliant social example in being particularly well satisfied with most things, and, above all other things, with himself.
>
> – CHARLES DICKENS, *Our Mutual Friend*

Marcus Stone, *Podsnappery*, 1864

This engraving from Our Mutual Friend *depicts the society of bourgeois luminaries who share Podsnap's view of the world. (Courtesy of the Trustees of the Boston Public Library)*

FROM

∾ Our Mutual Friend

CHAPTER XI

Podsnappery

Mr. Podsnap was well to do, and stood very high in Mr. Podsnap's opinion. Beginning with a good inheritance, he had married a good inheritance, and had thriven exceedingly in the Marine Insurance way, and was quite satisfied. He never could make out why everybody was not quite satisfied, and he felt conscious that he set a brilliant social example in being particularly well satisfied with most things, and, above all other things, with himself.

Thus happily acquainted with his own merit and importance, Mr. Podsnap settled that whatever he put behind him he put out of existence. There was a dignified conclusiveness — not to add a grand convenience — in this way of getting rid of disagreeables, which had done much towards establishing Mr. Podsnap in his lofty place in Mr. Podsnap's satisfaction. "I don't want to know about it; I don't choose to discuss it; I don't admit it!" Mr. Podsnap had even acquired a peculiar flourish of his right arm in often clearing the world of its most difficult problems, by sweeping them behind him (and consequently sheer away) with those words and a flushed face. For they affronted him.

Mr. Podsnap's world was not a very large world, morally; no, nor even geographically: seeing that although his business was sustained upon commerce with other countries, he considered other countries, with that important reservation, a mistake, and of their manners and customs would conclusively observe, "Not English!," when, Presto! with a flourish of the arm, and a flush of the face, they were swept away. Elsewise, the world got up at eight, shaved close at a quarter-past, breakfasted at nine, went to the City[1] at ten, came home at half-past five, and dined at seven. Mr. Podsnap's notions of the Arts in their integrity might have been stated thus. Literature; large print, respectively descriptive of getting up at eight, shaving close at a quarter-past, breakfasting at nine, going to the City at ten, coming home at half-past five, and dining at seven. Painting and Sculpture; models and portraits representing Professors of getting up at eight, shaving close at a quarter-past, breakfasting at nine, going to the City at ten, coming home at half-past five, and dining at seven. Music; a respectable performance (without variations) on stringed and wind instruments, sedately expressive of getting up at eight, shaving close at a quarter-past, breakfasting at nine, going to the City at ten, coming home at half-past five, and dining at seven. Nothing else to be permitted to those same vagrants the Arts, on pain of excommunication. Nothing else To Be — anywhere!

---

[1] the City: The business district in London.

As a so eminently respectable man, Mr. Podsnap was sensible of its being required of him to take Providence under his protection. Consequently he always knew exactly what Providence meant. Inferior and less respectable men might fall short of that mark, but Mr. Podsnap was always up to it. And it was very remarkable (and must have been very comfortable) that what Providence meant, was invariably what Mr. Podsnap meant.

These may be said to have been the articles of a faith and school which the present chapter takes the liberty of calling, after its representative man, Podsnappery. They were confined within close bounds, as Mr. Podsnap's own head was confined by his shirt-collar; and they were enunciated with a sounding pomp that smacked of the creaking of Mr. Podsnap's own boots.

◐ KARL MARX
B. GERMANY, 1818–1883

◐ FRIEDRICH ENGELS
B. GERMANY, 1820–1895

Portrait of Karl Marx, April 1882, Algiers
This is the last known photograph of the political philosopher. (CORBIS)

"The philosophers have only *interpreted* the world; the point is to *change* it." Karl Marx, a doctor of philosophy from the University of Berlin, spent his lifetime studying the causes of human oppression and designing a social system called communism that he believed would put an end to it.

Marx was born in Prussia in 1818. After receiving his doctorate in 1841, he became editor of *Rheinische Zeitung,* a radical newspaper in Cologne. He met Friedrich Engels there, and married Jenny von Westphalen; both remained Marx's lifelong companions. He collaborated with Engels on *The German Ideology* in 1845 and 1846 and on *The Communist Manifesto* in 1848. Over the next twenty years, supported in part by Engels, Marx wrote his great work, *Capital.* He published the first volume in 1867, and Engels published the remaining two in 1885 and 1894, after Marx's death.

The Communist Manifesto, commissioned by the Communist League in London in 1847, is noteworthy for its tone. Part I announces the arrival of the world revolutionary movement. It portrays humankind as divided throughout history into opposing social classes, that have been narrowed down to two in the modern era: the bourgeoisie (the owners of the means of production) and the proletariat (those who must sell their labor in order to survive). It explains the dynamic of the Industrial Revolution. And it claims that the bourgeois revolution has gone out of control, until "what the bourgeoisie . . . produces, above all, is its own grave-diggers."

Friedrich Engels, Photograph
Engels was a German Socialist and the coauthor of The Communist Manifesto. *(Underwood & Underwood/CORBIS)*

Part II, not included here, responds to concerns that the communists would abolish not only private property but also the family, education, marriage, national boundaries, and other "eternal truths," such as morality and religion. One by one, Engels demonstrates that these seemingly universal phenomena have a bourgeois character. Then he lists the measures the proletariat will take to bring about social justice once it comes to power. These include the abolition of private property, a graduated income tax, the centralization of credit, and equality of labor. The English translation by Samuel Moore done in 1888 was edited by Engels and published in London.

FROM

The Communist Manifesto

Translated by Samuel Moore

I. BOURGEOIS AND PROLETARIANS[1]

The history of all hitherto existing society is the history of class struggles.

Freeman and slave, patrician and plebeian, lord and serf, guild-master and journeyman, in a word, oppressor and oppressed, stood in constant opposition to one another, carried on an uninterrupted, now hidden, now open fight, a fight that each time ended, either in a revolutionary re-constitution of society at large, or in the common ruin of the contending classes.

In the earlier epochs of history, we find almost everywhere a complicated arrangement of society into various orders, a manifold gradation of social rank. In ancient Rome we have patricians, knights, plebeians, slaves; in the Middle Ages, feudal lords, vassals, guild-masters, journeymen, apprentices, serfs; in almost all of these classes, again, subordinate gradations.

The modern bourgeois society that has sprouted from the ruins of feudal society has not done away with class antagonisms. It has but established new classes, new conditions of oppression, new forms of struggle in place of the old ones.

Our epoch, the epoch of the bourgeoisie, possesses, however, this distinctive feature: It has simplified the class antagonisms: Society as a whole is more and more splitting up into two great hostile camps, into two great classes directly facing each other: Bourgeoisie and Proletariat.

From the serfs of the Middle Ages sprang the chartered burghers of the earliest towns. From these burgesses the first elements of the bourgeoisie were developed.

---

[1] **Bourgeois . . . Proletarians:** "By bourgeoisie is meant the class of modern Capitalists, owners of the means of social production and employers of wage-labour. By proletariat, the class of modern wage-labourers who, having no means of production of their own, are reduced to selling their labour-power in order to live." [Engels, 1888]

The discovery of America, the rounding of the Cape, opened up fresh ground for the rising bourgeoisie. The East-Indian and Chinese markets, the colonisation of America, trade with the colonies, the increase in the means of exchange and in commodities generally, gave to commerce, to navigation, to industry, an impulse never before known, and thereby, to the revolutionary element in the tottering feudal society, a rapid development.

The feudal system of industry, under which industrial production was monopolised by closed guilds, now no longer sufficed for the growing wants of the new markets. The manufacturing system took its place. The guild-masters were pushed on one side by the manufacturing middle class; division of labour between the different corporate guilds vanished in the face of division of labour in each single workshop.

Meantime the markets kept ever growing, the demand ever rising. Even manufacture no longer sufficed. Thereupon, steam and machinery revolutionised industrial production. The place of manufacture was taken by the giant, Modern Industry, the place of the industrial middle class, by industrial millionaires, the leaders of whole industrial armies, the modern bourgeois.

Modern industry has established the world-market, for which the discovery of America paved the way. This market has given an immense development to commerce, to navigation, to communication by land. This development has, in its turn, reacted on the extension of industry; and in proportion as industry, commerce, navigation, railways extended, in the same proportion the bourgeoisie developed, increased its capital, and pushed into the background every class handed down from the Middle Ages.

We see, therefore, how the modern bourgeoisie is itself the product of a long course of development, of a series of revolutions in the modes of production and of exchange.

Each step in the development of the bourgeoisie was accompanied by a corresponding political advance of that class. An oppressed class under the sway of the feudal nobility, an armed and self-governing association in the mediaeval commune; here independent urban republic (as in Italy and Germany), there taxable "third estate" of the monarchy (as in France), afterwards, in the period of manufacture proper, serving either the semi-feudal or the absolute monarchy as a counterpoise against the nobility, and, in fact, corner-stone of the great monarchies in general, the bourgeoisie has at last, since the establishment of Modern Industry and of the world-market, conquered for itself, in the modern representative State, exclusive political sway. The executive of the modern State is but a committee for managing the common affairs of the whole bourgeoisie.

The bourgeoisie, historically, has played a most revolutionary part.

The bourgeoisie, wherever it has got the upper hand, has put an end to all feudal, patriarchal, idyllic relations. It has pitilessly torn asunder the motley feudal ties that bound man to his "natural superiors," and has left remaining no other nexus between man and man than naked self-interest, than callous "cash payment." It has drowned the most heavenly ecstasies of religious fervour, of chivalrous enthusiasm, of philistine sentimentalism, in the icy water of egotistical calculation. It has resolved personal worth into exchange value, and in place of the numberless indefeasible chartered freedoms, has set up that single, unconscionable freedom—Free Trade. In one word, for exploitation, veiled by religious and political illusions, it has substituted naked, shameless, direct, brutal exploitation.

The bourgeoisie has stripped of its halo every occupation hitherto honoured and looked up to with reverent awe. It has converted the physician, the lawyer, the priest, the poet, the man of science, into its paid wage-labourers.

The bourgeoisie has torn away from the family its sentimental veil, and has reduced the family relation to a mere money relation.

The bourgeoisie has disclosed how it came to pass that the brutal display of vigour in the Middle Ages, which Reactionists so much admire, found its fitting complement in the most slothful indolence. It has been the first to show what man's activity can bring about. It has accomplished wonders far surpassing Egyptian pyramids, Roman aqueducts, and Gothic cathedrals; it has conducted expeditions that put in the shade all former Exoduses of nations and crusades.

The bourgeoisie cannot exist without constantly revolutionising the instruments of production, and thereby the relations of production, and with them the whole relations of society. Conservation of the old modes of production in unaltered form, was, on the contrary, the first condition of existence for all earlier industrial classes. Constant revolutionising of production, uninterrupted disturbance of all social conditions, everlasting uncertainty and agitation distinguish the bourgeois epoch from all earlier ones. All fixed, fast-frozen relations, with their train of ancient and venerable prejudices and opinions, are swept away, all new-formed ones become antiquated before they can ossify. All that is solid melts into air, all that is holy is profaned, and man is at last compelled to face with sober senses, his real conditions of life, and his relations with his kind.

The need of a constantly expanding market for its product chases the bourgeoisie over the whole surface of the globe. It must nestle everywhere, settle everywhere, establish connexions everywhere.

The bourgeoisie has through its exploitation of the world-market given a cosmopolitan character to production and consumption in every country. To the great chagrin of Reactionists, it has drawn from under the feet of industry the national ground on which it stood. All old-established national industries have been destroyed or are daily being destroyed. They are dislodged by new industries, whose introduction becomes a life and death question for all civilised nations, by industries that no longer work up indigenous raw material, but raw material drawn from the remotest zones; industries whose products are consumed, not only at home, but in every quarter of the globe. In place of the old wants, satisfied by the productions of the country, we find new wants, requiring for their satisfaction the products of distant lands and climes. In place of the old local and national seclusion and self-sufficiency, we have intercourse in every direction, universal inter-dependence of nations. And as in material, so also in intellectual production. The intellectual creations of individual nations become common property. National one-sidedness and narrow-mindedness become more and more impossible, and from the numerous national and local literatures, there arises a world literature.

The bourgeoisie, by the rapid improvement of all instruments of production, by the immensely facilitated means of communication, draws all, even the most barbarian, nations into civilisation. The cheap prices of its commodities are the heavy artillery with which it batters down all Chinese walls, with which it forces the barbarians' intensely obstinate hatred of foreigners to capitulate. It compels all nations, on pain of extinction, to adopt the bourgeois mode of production; it compels them to introduce what it calls civilisation into their midst, *i.e.,* to become bourgeois themselves. In one word, it creates a world after its own image.

The bourgeoisie has subjected the country to the rule of the towns. It has created enormous cities, has greatly increased the urban population as compared with the rural, and has thus rescued a considerable part of the population from the idiocy of rural life. Just as it has made the country dependent on the towns, so it has made barbarian and semi-barbarian countries dependent on the civilised ones, nations of peasants on nations of bourgeois, the East on the West.

The bourgeoisie keeps more and more doing away with the scattered state of the population, of the means of production, and of property. It has agglomerated population, centralised means of production, and has concentrated property in a few hands. The necessary consequence of this was political centralisation. Independent, or but loosely connected provinces, with separate interests, laws, governments and systems of taxation, became lumped together into one nation, with one government, one code of laws, one national class-interest, one frontier and one customs-tariff.

The bourgeoisie, during its rule of scarce one hundred years, has created more massive and more colossal productive forces than have all preceding generations together. Subjection of Nature's forces to man, machinery, application of chemistry to industry and agriculture, steam-navigation, railways, electric telegraphs, clearing of whole continents for cultivation, canalisation of rivers, whole populations conjured out of the ground—what earlier century had even a presentiment that such productive forces slumbered in the lap of social labour?

We see then: The means of production and of exchange, on whose foundation the bourgeoisie built itself up, were generated in feudal society. At a certain stage in the development of these means of production and of exchange, the conditions under which feudal society produced and exchanged, the feudal organisation of agriculture and manufacturing industry, in one word, the feudal relations of property became no longer compatible with the already developed productive forces; they became so many fetters. They had to be burst asunder; they were burst asunder.

Into their place stepped free competition, accompanied by a social and political constitution adapted to it, and by the economical and political sway of the bourgeois class.

A similar movement is going on before our own eyes. Modern bourgeois society with its relations of production, of exchange and of property, a society that has conjured up such gigantic means of production and of exchange, is like the sorcerer, who is no longer able to control the powers of the nether world whom he has called up by his spells. For many a decade past the history of industry and commerce is but the history of the revolt of modern productive forces against modern conditions of production, against the property relations that are the conditions for the existence of the bourgeoisie and of its rule. It is enough to mention the commercial crises that by their periodical return put on its trial, each time more threateningly, the existence of the entire bourgeois society. In these crises a great part not only of the existing products, but also of the previously created productive forces, are periodically destroyed. In these crises there breaks out an epidemic that, in all earlier epochs, would have seemed an absurdity — the epidemic of over-production. Society suddenly finds itself put back into a state of momentary barbarism; it appears as if a famine, a universal war of devastation had cut off the supply of every means of subsistence; industry and commerce seem to be destroyed; and why? Because there is too much civilisation, too much means of subsistence, too much industry, too much commerce. The productive forces at the disposal of society no longer tend to further the development of the conditions of bourgeois property; on the contrary, they have become too powerful for these conditions, by which they are fettered, and so soon as they overcome these fetters, they bring disorder into the whole of bourgeois society, endanger the existence of bourgeois property. The conditions of bourgeois society are too narrow to comprise the wealth created by them. And how does the bourgeoisie get over these crises? On the one hand by enforced destruction of a mass of productive forces; on the other, by the conquest of new markets, and by the more thorough exploitation of the old ones. That is to say, by paving the way for more extensive and more destructive crises, and by diminishing the means whereby crises are prevented.

The weapons with which the bourgeoisie felled feudalism to the ground are now turned against the bourgeoisie itself.

But not only has the bourgeoisie forged the weapons that bring death to itself; it has also called into existence the men who are to wield those weapons — the modern working class — the proletarians.

In proportion as the bourgeoisie, *i.e.,* capital, is developed, in the same proportion is the proletariat, the modern working class, developed — a class of labourers, who live only so long as they find work, and who find work only so long as their labour increases capital. These labourers, who must sell themselves piece-meal, are a commodity, like every other article of commerce, and are consequently exposed to all the vicissitudes of competition, to all the fluctuations of the market.

Owing to the extensive use of machinery and to division of labour, the work of the proletarians has lost all individual character, and consequently, all charm for the workman. He becomes an appendage of the machine, and it is only the most simple, most monotonous, and most easily acquired knack, that is required of him. Hence, the cost of production of a workman is restricted, almost entirely, to the means of subsistence that he requires for his maintenance, and for the propagation of his race: But the price of a commodity, and therefore also of labour, is equal to its cost of production. In proportion, therefore, as the repulsiveness of the work increases, the wage decreases. Nay more, in proportion as the use of machinery and division of labour increases, in the same proportion the burden of toil also increases, whether by prolongation of the working hours, by increase of the work exacted in a given time or by increased speed of the machinery, etc.

Modern industry has converted the little workshop of the patriarchal master into the great factory of the industrial capitalist. Masses of labourers, crowded into the factory, are organised like soldiers. As privates of the industrial army they are placed under the command of a perfect hierarchy of officers and sergeants. Not only are they slaves of the bourgeois class, and of the bourgeois State; they are daily and hourly enslaved by the machine, by the over-looker, and, above all, by the individual bourgeois manufacturer himself. The more openly this despotism proclaims gain to be its end and aim, the more petty, the more hateful, and the more embittering it is.

The less the skill and exertion of strength implied in manual labour, in other words, the more modern industry becomes developed, the more is the labour of men superseded by that of women. Differences of age and sex have no longer any distinctive social validity for the working class. All are instruments of labour, more or less expensive to use, according to their age and sex.

No sooner is the exploitation of the labourer by the manufacturer, so far, at an end, that he receives his wages in cash, than he is set upon by the other portions of the bourgeoisie, the landlord, the shopkeeper, the pawnbroker, etc.

The lower strata of the middle class—the small tradespeople, shopkeepers, and retired tradesmen generally, the handicraftsmen and peasants—all these sink gradually into the proletariat, partly because their diminutive capital does not suffice for the scale on which Modern Industry is carried on, and is swamped in the competition with the large capitalists, partly because their specialised skill is rendered worthless by new methods of production. Thus the proletariat is recruited from all classes of the population.

The proletariat goes through various stages of development. With its birth begins its struggle with the bourgeoisie. At first the contest is carried on by individual labourers, then by the workpeople of a factory, then by the operatives of one trade, in one locality, against the individual bourgeois who directly exploits them. They direct their attacks not against the bourgeois conditions of production, but against the instruments of production themselves; they destroy imported wares that compete with their labour, they smash to pieces machinery, they set factories ablaze, they seek to restore by force the vanished status of the workman of the Middle Ages.

At this stage the labourers still form an incoherent mass scattered over the whole country, and broken up by their mutual competition. If anywhere they unite to form more compact bodies, this is not yet the consequence of their own active union, but of the union of the bourgeoisie, which class, in order to attain its own political ends, is compelled to set the whole proletariat in motion, and is moreover yet, for a time, able to do so. At this stage, therefore, the proletarians do not fight their enemies, but the enemies of their enemies, the remnants of absolute monarchy, the landowners, the non-industrial bourgeois, the petty bourgeoisie. Thus the whole historical movement is concentrated in the hands of the bourgeoisie; every victory so obtained is a victory for the bourgeoisie.

But with the development of industry the proletariat not only increases in number; it becomes concentrated in greater masses, its strength grows, and it feels that strength more. The various interests and conditions of life within the ranks of the proletariat are more and more equalised, in proportion as machinery obliterates all distinctions of labour, and nearly everywhere reduces wages to the same low level. The growing competition among the bourgeois, and the resulting commercial crises, make the wages of the workers ever more fluctuating. The unceasing improvement of machinery, ever more rapidly developing, makes their livelihood more and more precarious; the collisions between individual workmen and individual bourgeois take more and more the character of collisions between two classes. Thereupon the workers begin to form combinations (Trades Unions) against the bourgeois; they club together in order to keep up the rate of wages; they found permanent associations in order to make provision beforehand for these occasional revolts. Here and there the contest breaks out into riots.

Now and then the workers are victorious, but only for a time. The real fruit of their battles lies, not in the immediate result, but in the ever-expanding union of the workers. This union is helped on by the improved means of communication that are created by modern industry and that place the workers of different localities in contact with one another. It was just this contact that was needed to centralise the numerous local struggles, all of the same character, into one national struggle between classes. But every class struggle is a political struggle. And that union, to attain which the burghers of the Middle Ages, with their miserable highways, required centuries, the modern proletarians, thanks to railways, achieve in a few years.

This organisation of the proletarians into a class, and consequently into a political party, is continually being upset again by the competition between the workers themselves. But it ever rises up again, stronger, firmer, mightier. It compels legislative recognition of particular interests of the workers, by taking advantage of the divisions among the bourgeoisie itself. Thus the ten-hours' bill in England was carried.

Altogether collisions between the classes of the old society further, in many ways, the course of development of the proletariat. The bourgeoisie finds itself involved in a constant battle. At first with the aristocracy; later on, with those portions of the bourgeoisie itself, whose interests have become antagonistic to the progress of industry; at all times, with the bourgeoisie of foreign countries. In all these battles it sees itself compelled to appeal to the proletariat, to ask for its help, and thus, to drag it into the political arena. The bourgeoisie itself, therefore, supplies the proletariat with its own elements of political and general education, in other words, it furnishes the proletariat with weapons for fighting the bourgeoisie.

Further, as we have already seen, entire sections of the ruling classes are, by the advance of industry, precipitated into the proletariat, or are at least threatened in their conditions of existence. These also supply the proletariat with fresh elements of enlightenment and progress.

Finally, in times when the class struggle nears the decisive hour, the process of dissolution going on within the ruling class, in fact within the whole range of society, assumes such a violent, glaring character, that a small section of the ruling class cuts itself adrift, and joins the revolutionary class, the class that holds the future in its hands. Just as, therefore, at an earlier period, a section of the nobility went over to the bourgeoisie, so now a portion of the bourgeoisie goes over to the proletariat, and in particular, a portion of the bourgeois ideologists, who have raised themselves to the level of comprehending theoretically the historical movement as a whole.

Of all the classes that stand face to face with the bourgeoisie today, the proletariat alone is a really revolutionary class. The other classes decay and finally disappear in the face of Modern Industry; the proletariat is its special and essential product.

The lower middle class, the small manufacturer, the shopkeeper, the artisan, the peasant, all these fight against the bourgeoisie, to save from extinction their existence as fractions of the middle class. They are therefore not revolutionary, but conservative. Nay more, they are reactionary, for they try to roll back the wheel of history. If by chance they are revolutionary, they are so only in view of their impending transfer into the proletariat, they thus defend not their present, but their future interests, they desert their own standpoint to place themselves at that of the proletariat.

The "dangerous class,"[2] the social scum, that passively rotting mass thrown off by the lowest layers of old society, may, here and there, be swept into the movement by a proletarian revolution; its conditions of life, however, prepare it far more for the part of a bribed tool of reactionary intrigue.

In the conditions of the proletariat, those of old society at large are already virtually swamped. The proletarian is without property; his relation to his wife and children has no longer anything in common with the bourgeois family-relations; modern industrial labour, modern subjection to capital, the same in England as in France, in America as in Germany, has stripped him of every trace of national character. Law, morality, religion, are to him so many bourgeois prejudices, behind which lurk in ambush just as many bourgeois interests.

All the preceding classes that got the upper hand, sought to fortify their already acquired status by subjecting society at large to their conditions of appropriation. The proletarians cannot become masters of the productive forces of society, except by abolishing their own previous mode of appropriation, and thereby also every other previous mode of appropriation. They have nothing of their own to secure and to fortify; their mission is to destroy all previous securities for, and insurances of, individual property.

All previous historical movements were movements of minorities, or in the interests of minorities. The proletarian movement is the self-conscious, independent movement of the immense majority, in the interests of the immense majority. The proletariat, the lowest stratum of our present society, cannot stir, cannot raise itself up, without the whole superincumbent strata of official society being sprung into the air.

Though not in substance, yet in form, the struggle of the proletariat with the bourgeoisie is at first a national struggle. The proletariat of each country must, of course, first of all settle matters with its own bourgeoisie.

In depicting the most general phases of the development of the proletariat, we traced the more or less veiled civil war, raging within existing society, up to the point where that war breaks out into open revolution, and where the violent overthrow of the bourgeoisie lays the foundation for the sway of the proletariat.

Hitherto, every form of society has been based, as we have already seen, on the antagonism of oppressing and oppressed classes. But in order to oppress a class, certain conditions must be assured to it under which it can, at least, continue its slavish

---

[2] **The "dangerous class":** The German name for this underclass is *Lumpenproletariat*.

existence. The serf, in the period of serfdom, raised himself to membership in the commune, just as the petty bourgeois, under the yoke of feudal absolutism, managed to develop into a bourgeois. The modern labourer, on the contrary, instead of rising with the progress of industry, sinks deeper and deeper below the conditions of existence of his own class. He becomes a pauper, and pauperism develops more rapidly than population and wealth. And here it becomes evident, that the bourgeoisie is unfit any longer to be the ruling class in society, and to impose its conditions of existence upon society as an over-riding law. It is unfit to rule because it is incompetent to assure an existence to its slave within his slavery, because it cannot help letting him sink into such a state, that it has to feed him, instead of being fed by him. Society can no longer live under this bourgeoisie, in other words, its existence is no longer compatible with society.

The essential condition for the existence, and for the sway of the bourgeois class, is the formation and augmentation of capital; the condition for capital is wage-labour. Wage-labour rests exclusively on competition between the labourers. The advance of industry, whose involuntary promoter is the bourgeoisie, replaces the isolation of the labourers, due to competition, by their revolutionary combination, due to association. The development of Modern Industry, therefore, cuts from under its feet the very foundation on which the bourgeoisie produces and appropriates products. What the bourgeoisie, therefore, produces, above all, is its own grave-diggers. Its fall and the victory of the proletariat are equally inevitable.

❧ GUY DE MAUPASSANT
B. FRANCE, 1850–1893

Guy de Maupassant is remembered as the master of the short story, the writer most imitated by later practitioners of the form. In a life shortened by syphilis that brought him to madness and paralysis in his last years, Maupassant in only one productive decade (1880–1890) produced three hundred stories, six novels, and several plays. As a protégé of Gustave Flaubert, a friend of his family, Guy de Maupassant adopted Flaubert's realism, careful craftsmanship, close observation of life, and objectivity as a writer. Although he has often been characterized as a writer of surprise endings, the surprise in Maupassant's stories arises from his close observation of his subjects rather than rhetorical trickery, for he took as one of his writer's credos the advice he received from Flaubert: "There is a part of everything which is unexplored, because we are accustomed to using our eyes only in association with the memory of what people before us have thought of the thing we are looking at. Even the smallest thing has something in it which is unknown. We must find it."

∾ Regret

Translated by Roger Colet

Monsieur Savel, who was known in Mantes as "Old Savel," had just got up. It was raining. It was a sad autumn day; the leaves were falling. They were falling slowly in the rain, like rain of another kind, heavier and slower. Monsieur Savel was not in good spirits. He went from the fireplace to the window and from the window to the fireplace. Life had its dreary days. For him all its days would be dreary now, for he was sixty-two years old. He was alone in the world, an old bachelor, with nobody to share his life. How sad it was to die like that, all alone, without the comfort afforded by affection and devotion!

He thought about his barren, empty existence. He thought of the distant past, the past of his childhood, life at home with his parents; then school, the holidays, the period of his law studies in Paris. Then his father's illness and death.

He had come home to live with his mother. They had lived together very quietly, the young man and the old woman, wanting nothing more. She had died too. How sad a thing life was!

He had remained alone. And now it would soon be his turn to die. He would disappear, and it would be all over. There would be no Monsieur Paul Savel left on earth. What a dreadful thing to happen! Other people would live, would love, would laugh. Yes, they would enjoy themselves while he no longer existed! How strange it was that people could laugh, enjoy themselves, be merry and gay, when faced with the perpetual inevitability of death! If death were only a probability one could still entertain some hope; but no, it was inevitable, as inevitable as night after day.

It wouldn't be so terrible if only he had led a full life — if he had had adventures, exquisite pleasures, success or satisfaction of some sort or other. But he had had nothing. He had never done anything but get up, eat at the same hours, and go to bed again. And like that he had reached the age of sixty-two. He had not even got married, as other men did. Why not? Yes, why hadn't he got married? He could have done, for he was quite well off. Was it the opportunity which had been lacking? Perhaps. But then, that sort of opportunity had to be created. He was apathetic, that was the trouble. Apathy had been his great weakness, his failing, his vice. Some people spoiled their lives through apathy. It was so difficult for certain temperaments to get out of bed, to bustle about, to speak to people, to study problems.

He had never been loved. No woman had ever slept in his arms in the complete abandon of love. He knew nothing of the delicious anguish of waiting for a woman, the heavenly quivering of a hand clasped in his, the ecstasy of triumphant passion.

What superhuman happiness must fill the heart when two pairs of lips meet for the first time, when the embrace of four arms make a single creature, a supremely happy creature, of two creatures madly in love with each other!

Monsieur Savel had sat down in his dressing-gown, with his feet on the fender.

Admittedly his life had been a failure, an absolute failure. All the same, he had been in love. He had loved a woman secretly, painfully and apathetically, as he did everything else. Yes, he had loved his old friend Madame Sandres, the wife of his old companion Sandres. Oh, if only he had known her as a girl! But he had met her too late: she was already married. If she hadn't been, he would have proposed to her without the slightest doubt. Even so, he had loved her constantly, from the first day they had met.

He remembered how excited he had been every time he had seen her, how sad he had been every time he had left her, and the nights he had been unable to go to sleep for thinking of her.

In the morning he always woke up a little less in love with her than the night before. Why was that?

How pretty she had been in the old days, a dainty blonde, curly-haired and bubbling over with laughter! Sandres wasn't the man she ought to have married. Now she was fifty-eight. She seemed to be happy enough. Oh, if only she had loved him in the old days, if only she had loved him! And why shouldn't she have loved him, Savel, since he had been fond of her, Madame Sandres?

If only she had guessed his feelings! Hadn't she ever guessed anything, seen anything, understood anything? What would she have thought if she had? If he had spoken up, what would she have replied?

Savel asked himself a thousand other questions. He reviewed the whole of his life, trying to recapture a host of details.

He recalled all the long evenings spent playing cards at Sandres's house, when his friend's wife was young and charming.

He recalled things she had said to him, intonations her voice used to take on, silent little smiles which meant so much.

He recalled the walks the three of them had taken along the banks of the Seine and the picnics they had had on Sundays, for Sandres worked during the week at the sub-prefecture. And suddenly the distinct recollection came to him of an afternoon spent with her in a little wood by the river.

They had set out in the morning, taking their provisions with them wrapped in packets. It was a bright spring day, one of those days which make you feel quite light-headed. Everything smells good, everything seems happy, and the birds sing more gaily and dart about more swiftly. They had lunched on the grass under the willows, close to the water flowing lazily in the sunshine. The air was balmy, full of the smell of rising sap, and they breathed it in with delight. How good it was to be alive that day!

After lunch Sandres had stretched out on his back and gone to sleep. "The best nap I've ever had," he said when he woke up.

Madame Sandres had taken Savel's arm and the two of them had gone off along the river bank.

She leaned on his arm, laughing and saying: "I'm drunk, my dear, absolutely drunk."

He looked at her, his heart beating wildly. He felt himself turning pale, and was terrified that his eyes might be too bold, that the trembling of his hand might reveal his secret.

She had made herself a crown of leaves and water lilies, and had asked him: "Do you like me like this?"

As he made no reply — for he could think of nothing to say and felt more like falling on his knees — she had burst out laughing with a sort of irritated laughter, saying: "You big booby! You might at least say something!"

He felt close to tears, but he still couldn't find a single word to say.

All this came back to him now, as vividly as on the day it had happened. Why, he wondered, had she said to him: "You big booby! You might at least say something"?

And he recalled how tenderly she had leaned on his arm. Passing under a bent tree, he had felt her ear against his cheek, and he had drawn back abruptly, for fear that she should think this contact was deliberate.

When he had said: "Isn't it time we went back?" she had darted a strange glance at him. Yes, she had definitely looked at him in a peculiar way. It hadn't struck him at the time, but now he remembered it clearly.

"Just as you like. If you're feeling tired, let's go back." And he had replied: "It isn't that I'm feeling tired, but Sandres may be awake now."

With a shrug of her shoulders she had said: "If you're afraid my husband is awake, that's different. Let's go back."

On the way back she remained silent and no longer leaned on his arm. Why?

He hadn't asked himself this question before. Now he had the impression he could glimpse something he had never understood before.

Was it possible?

Monsieur Savel felt himself blush and stood up, feeling as overwhelmed as if, thirty years before, he had heard Madame Sandres tell him: "I love you."

Was it possible? The suspicion which had just dawned upon him was sheer torture. Was it possible that he hadn't noticed, that he hadn't guessed?

Oh, if that was true, if he had come so close to such happiness without grasping it!

He said to himself: "I must find out! I can't remain in this state of doubt! I must find out!"

And he got dressed hurriedly, throwing on his clothes. He thought to himself: "I'm sixty-two and she's fifty-eight; there's no reason why I shouldn't ask her that."

And he went out.

The Sandres house was on the other side of the street, practically opposite his own. He went over to it and banged the knocker. The little maid opened the door.

She was astonished to see him so early in the day.

"You here already, Monsieur Savel?" she said. "Has there been an accident?"

"No, my girl," Savel replied. "But go and tell your mistress that I would like to speak to her straight away."

"The fact is, Madame is making her pear jam for the winter and she's busy over the stove, so she isn't dressed, you see."

"Yes, but tell her it's about something very important."

The little maid went off and Savel started pacing nervously up and down the drawing-room. Yet he didn't feel at all embarrassed. He was going to ask her his question as naturally as he would have asked her for a recipe. After all, he was sixty-two years old . . .

The door opened; she appeared. She was now a stout, round woman with full cheeks and a loud laugh. She came in holding her hands away from her body, with her sleeves rolled up and her bare arms sticky with a sugary juice. She asked anxiously: "What's the matter? You aren't ill, are you?"

"No, my dear friend," he replied; "but I want to ask you about something very important to me which is tormenting me. Will you promise to answer me frankly?"

She smiled.

"I always speak frankly. Go on."

"Well, the fact is, I've loved you since the first day I met you. Did you ever suspect?"

She burst out laughing and replied with something of her old intonation: "You big booby! I knew from the very first day!"

Savel started trembling, and stammered: "You knew? . . . But then . . ."

He fell silent.

"Then what?" she asked.

He went on: "Then . . . what did you think? . . . What . . . what . . . what would you have replied?"

She laughed louder than ever. Drops of juice ran down her fingers and fell on to the floor.

"What would I have replied? But you didn't ask me anything. It wasn't for me to make a declaration."

Then he took a step towards her.

"Tell me," he said, "tell me. . . . Do you remember the day Sandres went to sleep on the grass after lunch . . . and we walked together as far as that bend in the river. . . ."

He waited. She had stopped laughing and was looking him straight in the eyes.

"Yes, I remember it all right."

Trembling slightly, he went on: "Well . . . that day . . . if I had been . . . if I had been enterprising . . . what would you have done?"

She started smiling like a woman who has no regrets, and replied frankly in a voice tinged with irony: "I would have yielded, my dear."

Then she turned on her heels and went back to her jam.

Savel left the house utterly crushed, as if some disaster had just befallen him. He walked straight ahead towards the river, striding through the rain without thinking where he was going. When he reached the river he turned right and followed the bank. He walked for a long time, as if urged on by some instinct. His clothes were running with water and his hat, as limp and shapeless as a wet rag, was dripping like a roof. He walked on and on, straight ahead. And at last he came to the place where they had lunched on that distant day which he found so painful to remember.

Then he sat down under the leafless trees, and wept.

FRIEDRICH NIETZSCHE
b. GERMANY, 1844–1900

Friedrich Nietzsche still provokes controversy and unsettles those who hold conventional ideas. This selection from *The Gay Science* (1882) explains his controversial conclusion that "God is dead," a casualty of the human evolution to a higher form of being. Only the Madman, who is ahead of his time, seems to be aware of the implications of God's demise.

For more information about Nietzsche, see page 728.

> The secret of the greatest fruitfulness and the greatest enjoyment of existence is: to *live dangerously!*
>
> – *The Gay Science*, 283

FROM

The Gay Science

Translated by Walter Kaufmann

THE MADMAN

Have you not heard of that madman who lit a lantern in the bright morning hours, ran to the market place, and cried incessantly, "I seek God! I seek God!" As many of those who do not believe in God were standing around just then, he provoked much laughter. Why, did he get lost? said one. Did he lose his way like a child? said another. Or is he hiding? Is he afraid of us? Has he gone on a voyage? or emigrated? Thus they yelled and laughed. The madman jumped into their midst and pierced them with his glances.

"Whither is God" he cried. "I shall tell you. *We have killed him*—you and I. All of us are his murderers. But how have we done this? How were we able to drink up the sea? Who gave us the sponge to wipe away the entire horizon? What did we do when we unchained this earth from its sun? Whither is it moving now? Whither are we moving now? Away from all suns? Are we not plunging continually? Backward, sideward, forward, in all directions? Is there any up or down left? Are we not straying as through an infinite nothing? Do we not feel the breath of empty space? Has it not become colder? Is not night and more night coming on all the while? Must not lanterns be lit in the morning? Do we not hear anything yet of the noise of the gravediggers who are burying God? Do we not smell anything yet of God's decomposition? Gods too decompose. God is dead. God remains dead. And we have killed him. How shall we, the murderers of all murderers, comfort ourselves? What was holiest and most powerful of all that the world has yet owned has bled to death under our knives. Who will wipe this blood off us? What water is there for us to clean ourselves? What festivals of atonement, what sacred games shall we have to invent?

Is not the greatness of this deed too great for us? Must not we ourselves become gods simply to seem worthy of it? There has never been a greater deed; and whoever will be born after us — for the sake of this deed he will be part of a higher history than all history hitherto."

Here the madman fell silent and looked again at his listeners; and they too were silent and stared at him in astonishment. At last he threw his lantern on the ground, and it broke and went out. "I come too early," he said then; "my time has not come yet. This tremendous event is still on its way, still wandering — it has not yet reached the ears of man. Lightning and thunder require time, the light of the stars requires time, deeds require time even after they are done, before they can be seen and heard. This deed is still more distant from them than the most distant stars — *and yet they have done it themselves.*"

It has been related further that on that same day the madman entered divers churches and there sang his *requiem aeternam deo.*[1] Led out and called to account, he is said to have replied each time, "What are these churches now if they are not the tombs and sepulchers of God?"

---

[1] *requiem aeternam deo:* Funeral hymn for the everlasting God.

ÉMILE ZOLA
B. FRANCE, 1840–1902

I hope that by now it is becoming clear that my object has been first and foremost a scientific one. . . . I simply applied to two living bodies the analytical method that surgeons apply to corpses.

– ZOLA, from *Thérèse Raquin*

French novelist, critic, and founder of the **NATURALIST** movement, Émile Zola applied the principles of scientific determinism to literature. In his *Rougon-Macquart* cycle of twenty novels (1871–1893), subtitled "The Natural and Social History of a Family Under the Second Empire," Zola performed a dissection of French society. His controversial work, which viewed human beings as creatures whose biological heredity determined their character, was often attacked as immoral or perverse. *Thérèse Raquin* (1867), an early novel, was the first in which Zola put his "experimental" — the term meant something like "empirical" — theory into practice. In the Preface to the second edition excerpted here, Zola explains his intent to those who he claims completely misunderstood the novel when it originally appeared.

Thérèse Raquin

Translated by Leonard Tancock

FROM

PREFACE TO THE SECOND EDITION

I was simple enough to suppose that this novel could do without a preface. Being accustomed to express my thoughts quite clearly and to stress even the minutest details of what I write, I hoped to be understood and judged without preliminary explanations. It seems I was mistaken.

The critics greeted this book with a churlish and horrified outcry. Certain virtuous people, in newspapers no less virtuous, made a grimace of disgust as they picked it up with the tongs to throw it into the fire. Even the minor literary reviews, the ones that retail nightly the tittle-tattle from alcoves and private rooms, held their noses and talked of filth and stench. I am not complaining about this reception; on the contrary I am delighted to observe that my colleagues have such maidenly susceptibilities. Obviously my work is the property of my judges and they can find it nauseating without my having any right to object, but what I do complain of is that not one of the modest journalists who blushed when they read *Thérèse Raquin* seems to have understood the novel. If they had, they might perhaps have blushed still more, but at any rate I should at the present moment be enjoying the deep satisfaction of having disgusted them for the right reason. Nothing is more annoying than hearing worthy people shouting about depravity when you know within yourself that they are doing so without any idea what they are shouting about.

So I am obliged to introduce my own work to my judges. I will do so in a few lines, simply to forestall any future misunderstanding.

In *Thérèse Raquin* my aim has been to study temperaments and not characters. That is the whole point of the book. I have chosen people completely dominated by their nerves and blood, without free will, drawn into each action of their lives by the inexorable laws of their physical nature. Thérèse and Laurent are human animals, nothing more. I have endeavoured to follow these animals through the devious working of their passions, the compulsion of their instincts, and the mental unbalance resulting from a nervous crisis. The sexual adventures of my hero and heroine are the satisfaction of a need, the murder they commit a consequence of their adultery, a consequence they accept just as wolves accept the slaughter of sheep. And finally, what I have had to call their remorse really amounts to a simple organic disorder, a revolt of the nervous system when strained to breaking-point. There is a complete absence of soul, I freely admit, since that is how I meant it to be.

I hope that by now it is becoming clear that my object has been first and foremost a scientific one. When my two characters, Thérèse and Laurent, were created, I set myself certain problems and solved them for the interest of the thing. I tried to explain the mysterious attraction that can spring up between two different temperaments, and I demonstrated the deep-seated disturbances of a sanguine nature brought into contact with a nervous one. If the novel is read with care, it will be seen that each chapter is a study of a curious physiological case. In a word, I had only one desire: given a highly-sexed man and an unsatisfied woman, to uncover the animal side of them and see that alone, then throw them together in a violent drama and note down with scrupulous care the sensations and actions of these creatures. I simply applied to two living bodies the analytical method that surgeons apply to corpses. . . .

❧ INAZO NITOBÉ
B. JAPAN, 1862–1933

> Inazo Nitobé's *Bushido: The Soul of Japan* (1899) sought to reveal the Japanese psyche to the West. In the passage excerpted here, Nitobé explains why the samurai have great difficulty adapting to middle-class ways by showing the antagonism between their traditional feudal ethics and the Western values of the marketplace. The text is from the 1905 Tokyo edition of *Bushido*.
>
> For more on Inazo Nitobé, see page 732.

FROM

❧ Bushido: The Soul of Japan

Those who are well acquainted with our history will remember that only a few years after our treaty ports were opened to foreign trade, feudalism was abolished,[1] and when with it the samurai's fiefs were taken and bonds issued to them in compensation, they were given liberty to invest them in mercantile transactions. Now you may ask, "Why could they not bring their much boasted veracity into their new business relations and so reform the old abuses?" Those who had eyes to see could not weep enough, those who had hearts to feel could not sympathize enough, with the fate of many a noble and honest samurai who signally and irrevocably failed in his new and unfamiliar field of trade and industry, through sheer lack of shrewdness in coping with his artful plebeian rival. When we know that eighty percent of the business houses fail in so industrial a country as America, is it any wonder that scarcely one among a hundred samurai who went into trade could succeed in his new vocation?

---

[1] **feudalism was abolished:** In 1871 the new constitutional government of Japan abolished feudalism and offered payments to former samurai to help them take up a new way of life.

It will be long before it will be recognized how many fortunes were wrecked in the attempt to apply Bushido ethics to business methods; but it was soon patent to every observing mind that the ways of wealth were not the ways of honor. In what respects, then, were they different?

Of the three incentives to Veracity that Lecky[2] enumerates, viz: the industrial, the political, and the philosophical, the first was altogether lacking in Bushido. As to the second, it could develop little in a political community under a feudal system. It is in its philosophical, and as Lecky says, in its highest aspect, that Honesty attained elevated rank in our catalogue of virtues. With all my sincere regard for the high commercial integrity of the Anglo-Saxon race, when I ask for the ultimate ground, I am told that "Honesty is the best policy," that it *pays* to be honest. Is not this virtue, then, its own reward? If it is followed because it brings in more cash than falsehood, I am afraid Bushido would rather indulge in lies!

If Bushido rejects a doctrine of *quid pro quo* rewards, the shrewder tradesman will readily accept it. Lecky has very truly remarked that Veracity owes its growth largely to commerce and manufacture; as Nietzsche puts it, "Honesty is the youngest of virtues"—in other words, it is the foster-child of industry, of modern industry. Without this mother, Veracity was like a blue-blood orphan whom only the most cultivated mind could adopt and nourish. Such minds were general among the samurai, but, for want of a more democratic and utilitarian foster-mother, the tender child failed to thrive.

---

[2] **Lecky:** William Lecky (1838–1903), liberal British historian known for *History of the Rise and Influence of the Spirit of Rationalism in Europe* (1865) and *History of England in the Eighteenth Century* (1878–90). Lecky challenged the notion that ethical behavior is the result of the influence of religion, arguing instead that it was the result of rational self-interest.

TEXT IN CONTEXT

HENRIK IBSEN
B. NORWAY, 1828–1906

HEN-rik IB-sin

Recalling his childhood in Skien, a logging village in rural Norway, **Henrik Ibsen** described the view from the window of his room as "only buildings, nothing green." And the structures that he particularly remembered — the church, the jail with its pillory, and the madhouse — may have been the models for the institutions that constrain and oppress the characters in his great social dramas, plays that dissect the institutions of Europe in the late nineteenth century.

Often called the "father of the modern drama," Ibsen is best known for realistic plays such as *A Doll's House* (1879), *An Enemy of the People* (1882), and *Hedda Gabler* (1890). These plays explore the ways in which bourgeois values and social conventions deny individuals opportunities for growth and fulfillment. Very different from the romantic comedies and melodramas that were the standard theatrical fare at the time, Ibsen's plays often shocked nineteenth-century audiences, who went to the theater to be amused. But the productions moved other playwrights and changed the course of drama, influencing especially such modern dramatists as George Bernard Shaw in England and Eugene O'Neill and Arthur Miller[1] in the United States — heirs to a dramatic tradition Shaw called "IBSENISM."

> More than any one man, it is he [Ibsen] who had made us "our world," that is to say, "our modernity."
>
> – EZRA POUND

---

[1] **Shaw . . . Miller: George Bernard Shaw** (1856–1950), Anglo-Irish playwright, critic, and social commentator, author of numerous plays, including *The Devil's Disciple* (1897), *Major Barbara* (1905), and *Man and Superman* (1905). **Eugene O'Neill** (1888–1953), American Playwright, author of *Ah, Wilderness!* (1933), *Long Day's Journey into Night* (1956), and many other plays. **Arthur Miller** (1915–2005), American playwright best known for *Death of a Salesman* (1949) and *The Crucible* (1953).

Early Poverty and Apprenticeship in the Theater.   Born the son
of a prosperous businessman in Skien in 1828, Ibsen learned early the
precariousness of bourgeois respectability. When he was nine, his
father's business failed and the family was cast into poverty and forced to
move ignominiously out of town. At fifteen, he left home to become
a druggist's apprentice at Grimstad, a small town fifty miles from his
home. There he spent six years and fathered an illegitimate child—a
buried secret in Ibsen's life much like those that show up in many of his
plays. He moved to Christiania (now Oslo) in 1850 with hopes of
entering the university, but he failed part of the entrance examinations
and went to work in a theater instead. And it was in the theater—as
producer, director, and writer—that Ibsen would spend the next
fourteen years learning his true craft.

Escape to Southern Europe.   In 1864 Ibsen fled the literal darkness
and bourgeois oppression of Norway to take up residence in Italy and
Germany, where he lived for the next twenty-seven years, returning to
Norway only twice for brief vacations before ultimately going back to his
native country. In Italy and Germany he wrote his great social dramas,
or "problem plays," beginning in 1877 with *The Pillars of Society,* which
stripped the veil of hypocrisy from community leaders to expose the rot
underneath. That play was followed by the scandalous *A Doll's House*
(1879) and *Ghosts* (1881). All three plays present the pillars of village
life—the church, marriage, and family—as oppressive and hypocritical
institutions. In these plays the characters are haunted by repressed
secrets that threaten to destroy them. *The Wild Duck* (1884), *An Enemy
of the People* (1882), and *Rosmersholm* (1882) are studies of characters
who are afraid to tell the truth. The human psychological dimension
becomes increasingly important for Ibsen, especially in such later plays
as *The Lady from the Sea* (1888), *Hedda Gabler* (1890), and *The Master
Builder* (1892), which explore the effects on women of their subordinate
role in society and men's aggressive dominance. In nearly all of Ibsen's
social plays one finds a hero or heroine constrained by social
institutions—the church, marriage, and middle-class respectability.
These characters are not simply victims of social forces, however; through
bad choices, mistakes, and personal weaknesses they suppress guilty
secrets or tell lies and contribute to creating their difficulties. The plays
almost always center on a moment of crisis when a secret or lie is revealed
and the hero or heroine must choose how to meet the revelation.

   Ibsen returned to Norway in 1891 and spent the last fifteen years
of his life in Christiania, where he died in 1906. Appropriately for a
playwright who was often at odds with society, his dying word was
tvertimod, meaning "on the contrary."

Henrik Ibsen, c. 1900
*This photograph
shows off Ibsen's
trademark full white
beard. (Austrian
Archives/Corbis)*

www For links to
more information
about Ibsen,
see bedford
stmartins.com/
worldlitcompact.

Mythological and Symbolic Plays.   Although best known for his
realistic social dramas, Ibsen was also a writer of symbol and mythology.
Much of his early work was devoted to historical and mythological
subjects, culminating in *Brand* (1865) and *Peer Gynt* (1867), two dramatic
poems that through Nordic folklore comment indirectly on contemporary Norway. In his plays of the late 1890s, such as *John Gabriel Borkman*
(1896) and *When We Dead Awaken* (1899), Ibsen turned to a more
symbolic and visionary style. In these less realistic works Ibsen can be
considered father to such modern symbolic dramatists as William Butler
Yeats and Tennessee Williams.[2]

In composing his plays, Ibsen employed the stylistic conventions of
the **WELL-MADE PLAY**: a single, central situation carefully constructed to
build to a climactic crisis, unity of time and place, and realistic dialogue
and stage settings. Ibsen's middle-class audiences could believe they were
observing their own lives or the lives of people like themselves when
watching one of his dramas. In his choice of subject matter, in the tragic
seriousness of many of the situations he explored, however, Ibsen broke
the mold of the well-made play. He also strayed from convention in his
treatment of female characters.

Ibsen's Feminism.   Many of Ibsen's unforgettable characters are
women whose marriages deny them opportunities for personal growth.
In *Ghosts*, for example, Mrs. Alving brings about her own unhappiness
and her son's destruction by maintaining a front of respectability to hide
the truth about her syphilitic husband and the corruption in her
marriage. In *Hedda Gabler*, probably Ibsen's most complex study of a
female protagonist, he explores the destructive impulses of his heroine.
Hedda, displaced from her aristocratic origins and trapped in a
bourgeois marriage to an academic, turns to manipulating others.
Incapable of any affirming, creative acts, Hedda destroys others and
herself. Her suicide at the end of the play shocked and unsettled Ibsen's
middle-class audience.

Honored by a Norwegian feminist society at the end of his life for
his treatment of women's issues, Ibsen commented, with a touch of his
characteristic contrariness, "I must disclaim the honor of consciously
working for women's rights. . . . To me it has been a question of human
rights." Even though Ibsen may not have written with a feminist agenda,

---

[2]Yeats . . . Williams: **William Butler Yeats** (1865–1939), Irish poet and playwright who drew on Irish mythology, folklore, and Japanese *Nō* drama to shape his symbolic poems; see p. 1341. **Tennessee Williams** (1914–1983),
American playwright best known for *The Glass Menagerie* (1945) and *A Streetcar Named Desire* (1947).

Claire Bloom as Nora in *A Doll's House*

Claire Bloom starred in Patrick Garland's 1971 stage production of A Doll's House *for the Playhouse Theatre in New York and reprised the role for Garland's 1973 film adaptation, co-starring Anthony Hopkins as Torvald. (SOPHIE BAKER/ ArenaPAL)*

he took his female characters seriously. The moral issues they faced were just as significant as those confronted by his male characters.

A Doll's House.   One of Ibsen's earliest social dramas, *A Doll's House* does not end tragically as some of his later plays do, but its critique of bourgeois marriage is just as telling. Ibsen worked within the conventions of the "well-made play." The plays of Augustin Eugène Scribe (1791–1861) established the rule for the well-made play. These "drawing-room comedies" were typically constructed around a single situation that built, scene by scene, to a climactic revelation. The situation usually involved a misunderstanding, a secret, or a suppressed document that, when discovered, prompted a reversal and a dénouement. The dialogue was colloquial and realistic, and the subject matter commonplace and trivial. The action in *A Doll's House* is focused in time and place, occurring over three days and taking place within the confines of the Helmers' living room. The plot turns melodramatically on the letter that reveals Nora's secret, but the issues raised by the play are far more serious than the inconsequential misunderstandings in popular comedies; and

A Doll's House, Ghosts, and *Hedda Gabler* provided resonant theatrical images that participated in the cultural redefinition of women's place in European society.

– CHARLES R. LYONS, critic, 1991

Janet McTeer as Nora
and Owen Teale as
Torvald, 1997
*Janet McTeer and
Owen Teale starred in
the Belasco Theater
production of* A Doll's
House, *directed by
Anthony Page in New
York in 1997. (Sara
Krulwich/ the* New
York Times/*Redux)*

the ending, instead of restoring the Helmers' marriage and affirming accepted domestic virtues, shocked its nineteenth-century audience by reversing their conventional expectations.

Ibsen underscores the irony in his reversal of convention by setting the play at Christmas, the domestic holiday when families gather and family histories come to light. Nora and Torvald must confront their past, but unlike Scrooge in Charles Dickens's *A Christmas Carol,* who is changed by doing so, the Helmers remain unchanged and unable to resolve the contradictions in their incompatible marriage. Torvald cannot compromise his desire to advance at the bank and Nora admits that she cannot remain in so confining a marriage.

Critics have sometimes been bothered by the apparent inconsistency in the character of Nora, wondering whether the domestic butterfly of the first act could turn into the courageous rebel of the last. But Nora is not really a different person at the end of the play; she simply hid her independence and courage earlier. Her "transformation" is more of a revelation, which Ibsen develops in rich detail. The differences between Nora and Mrs. Linde, the facts of her personal history, and the

Nineteenth-Century America: The Seneca Falls Conference

Although Ibsen was evasive about the political and social implications of his plays, *A Doll's House* was viewed from the time of its first performance as a play about women's rights. Even today it is performed as one of the classics of FEMINISM, a movement in Europe that had its roots in the work of such writers as Mary Wollstonecraft in the late eighteenth century.

The feminist movement in the United States had its symbolic beginning in 1848, the year of revolution throughout Europe and also the year in which Karl Marx and Friedrich Engels published *The Communist Manifesto*. Appropriately, the movement began as a result of the broader nineteenth-century movement for the emancipation of slaves when Elizabeth Cady Stanton (1815–1902) and Lucretia Mott (1793–1880) were denied an opportunity to address the World Anti-slavery Convention in London because they were women, even though they were official delegates to the meeting. In response they convened a conference on women's rights in Seneca Falls, New York, on July 19, 1848, and drafted a *Declaration of Sentiments and Resolutions* for adoption by the group.

Echoing the Declaration of Independence, their document asserted that "all men and women are created equal" and cataloged "the repeated injuries and usurpations on the part of man toward woman" that constitute "the history of mankind." By denying her the right to vote, limiting her property rights, casting her as a morally irresponsible being, excluding her from colleges, good jobs, and the ministry, men had reduced women to

Elizabeth Cady Stanton, 1856   Elizabeth Cady Stanton is pictured here with her daughter, Harriet, just a few years after the Seneca Falls Conference. (Library of Congress 3A49096U)

second-class dependency. The document ended with a series of resolutions, dedicating the signers to "the zealous and untiring efforts of both men and women . . . for securing to woman an equal participation with men in the various trades, professions, and commerce" and, above all, the "sacred right to the elective franchise."

The Seneca Falls Conference attracted 240 delegates to the meeting, including forty men. Among the delegates was Frederick Douglass, a leader in the movement to abolish slavery. Although the effort to gain women's rights was from its inception allied

Nineteenth-Century America: The Seneca Falls Conference *continued*

to the anti-slavery movement, women were excluded from the Fourteenth Amendment to the Constitution, which granted the right to vote to former male slaves in 1868.

In many countries the movement to abolish slavery led to the movement for women's rights, and agitation for women's suffrage was worldwide by the second half of the nineteenth century. By the time of the first world war, women in four nations had been granted the right to vote: New Zealand (1893), Australia (1902), Finland (1906), and Norway (1913). Elizabeth Cady Stanton and Lucretia Mott did not live to see the realization of their dream. After women's participation in the war effort softened resistance to women's suffrage, the Nineteenth Amendment to the Constitution finally granted American women the right to vote in 1920.

contrast between her courage and Torvald's conventionality show us that she is not changed in a single night like Scrooge, but is, at the end, simply acting consistently with the person she has always been. Ibsen's dramatic skill in using the characters Mrs. Linde and Krogstad as foils to draw out the hidden sides of Nora and Torvald prepares us for the inevitability of the ending.

A Doll's House shocked its original audiences. When the play opened in London critics attacked it as "a morbid and unwholesome play." A leading actress in the German production refused to perform the original ending and insisted that Ibsen write an alternative in which Nora stays with her husband and children. Although Ibsen complied with the actress's demand, he called the revised ending "a barbaric outrage." Yet in spite of their disapproval, audiences all over Europe crowded into performances of Ibsen's realistic play. A printed version, published before the premier performance in Copenhagen in 1879, sold out its first edition before the play opened three weeks later. Although they were outraged by Nora's exit, they were drawn to the theaters, for they saw in the Helmers middle-class people like themselves.

■ **FURTHER RESEARCH**

Biography
Ferguson, Robert. *Ibsen: A New Biography.* 1996.
Meyer, Michael. *Ibsen: A Biography.* 1971.

Criticism
Bryan, George B. *An Ibsen Companion.* 1984.
Downs, Brian. *Ibsen: The Intellectual Background.* 1948; *A Study of Six Plays by Ibsen.* 1950.
Hardwick, Elizabeth. *Seduction and Betrayal.* 1974.
Johnston, Brian. *The Ibsen Cycle: The Design of the Plays from* Pillars of Society *to* When We Dead Awaken. 1992.
McFarlane, James. *The Cambridge Companion to Ibsen.* 1994.
Shaw, George Bernard. *The Quintessence of Ibsenism.* 1891.

Templeton, Joan. *Ibsen's Women*. 1997.
Thomas, David. *Henrik Ibsen*. 1983.

On *A Doll's House*
Durbach, Errol. A Doll's House: *Ibsen's Myth of Transformation*. 1991.
Mitchell, Hayley R., ed. *Readings on* A Doll's House. 1999. A collection of critical
    essays on the play.

■ **PRONUNCIATION**
Henrik Ibsen: HEN-rik IB-sin

∾ A Doll's House

Translated by William Archer

ACT 1

CHARACTERS

TORVALD HELMER	THE HELMERS' THREE CHILDREN
NORA, *his wife*	ANNA, *their nurse*
DOCTOR RANK	A MAID-SERVANT (ELLEN)
MRS. LINDE	A PORTER
NILS KROGSTAD	

The action passes in Helmer's house (a flat) in Christiania.

A room, comfortably and tastefully, but not expensively, furnished. In the back, on the right, a door leads to the hall; on the left another door leads to Helmer's study. Between the two doors a pianoforte. In the middle of the left wall a door, and nearer the front a window. Near the window a round table with armchairs and a small sofa. In the right wall, somewhat to the back, a door, and against the same wall, further forward, a procelain stove; in front of it a couple of armchairs and a rocking chair. Between the stove and the side-door a small table. Engravings on the walls. A what-not with china and bric-à-brac. A small bookcase filled with handsomely bound books. Carpet. A fire in the stove. It is a winter day.

    A bell rings in the hall outside. Presently the outer door of the flat is heard to open. Then Nora enters, humming gaily. She is in outdoor dress, and carries several parcels, which she lays on the right-hand table. She leaves the door into the hall open, and a Porter is seen outside, carrying a Christmas tree and a basket, which he gives to the Maid-servant who has opened the door.

NORA: Hide the Christmas tree carefully, Ellen; the children must on no account see it before this evening, when it's lighted up. [*To the Porter, taking out her purse.*] How much?
PORTER: Fifty öre.[1]
NORA: There is a crown. No, keep the change.

---

[1] **Fifty öre:** Half a crown (krone), equivalent to a few dollars.

[*The Porter thanks her and goes. Nora shuts the door. She continues smiling in quiet glee as she takes off her outdoor things. Taking from her pocket a bag of macaroons, she eats one or two. Then she goes on tip-toe to her husband's door and listens.*]

NORA: Yes; he is at home.

[*She begins humming again, crossing to the table on the right.*]

HELMER: [*In his room.*] Is that my lark twittering there?

NORA: [*Busy opening some of her parcels.*] Yes, it is.

HELMER: Is it the squirrel frisking around?

NORA: Yes!

HELMER: When did the squirrel get home?

NORA: Just this minute. [*Hides the bag of macaroons in her pocket and wipes her mouth.*] Come here, Torvald, and see what I've been buying.

HELMER: Don't interrupt me. [*A little later he opens the door and looks in, pen in hand.*] Buying, did you say? What! All that? Has my little spendthrift been making the money fly again?

NORA: Why, Torvald, surely we can afford to launch out a little now. It's the first Christmas we haven't had to pinch.

HELMER: Come come; we can't afford to squander money.

NORA: Oh yes, Torvald, do let us squander a little, now—just the least little bit! You know you'll soon be earning heaps of money.

HELMER: Yes, from New Year's Day. But there's a whole quarter before my first salary is due.

NORA: Never mind; we can borrow in the meantime.

HELMER: Nora! [*He goes up to her and takes her playfully by the ear.*] Still my little featherbrain! Supposing I borrowed a thousand crowns today, and you made ducks and drakes of them during Christmas week, and then on New Year's Eve a tile blew off the roof and knocked my brains out—

NORA: [*Laying her hand on his mouth.*] Hush! How can you talk so horridly?

HELMER: But supposing it were to happen—what then?

NORA: If anything so dreadful happened, it would be all the same to me whether I was in debt or not.

HELMER: But what about the creditors?

NORA: They! Who cares for them? They're only strangers.

HELMER: Nora, Nora! What a woman you are! But seriously, Nora, you know my principles on these points. No debts! No borrowing! Home life ceases to be free and beautiful as soon as it is founded on borrowing and debt. We two have held out bravely till now, and we are not going to give in at the last.

NORA: [*Going to the fireplace.*] Very well—as you please, Torvald.

HELMER: [*Following her.*] Come come; my little lark mustn't droop her wings like that. What? Is my squirrel in the sulks? [*Takes out his purse.*] Nora, what do you think I have here?

NORA: [*Turning round quickly.*] Money!

HELMER: There! [*Gives her some notes.*] Of course I know all sorts of things are wanted at Christmas.

NORA: [*Counting.*] Ten, twenty, thirty, forty. Oh, thank you, thank you, Torvald! This will go a long way.

HELMER: I should hope so.

NORA: Yes, indeed; a long way! But come here, and let me show you all I've been buying. And so cheap! Look, here's a new suit for Ivar, and a little sword. Here are a horse and a trumpet for Bob. And here are a doll and a cradle for Emmy. They're only common; but they're good enough for her to pull to pieces. And dress-stuffs and kerchiefs for the servants. I ought to have got something better for old Anna.

HELMER: And what's in that other parcel?

NORA: [*Crying out.*] No, Torvald, you're not to see that until this evening!

HELMER: Oh! — Ah! — But now tell me, you little spendthrift, have you thought of anything for yourself?

NORA: For myself! Oh, I don't want anything.

HELMER: Nonsense! Just tell me something sensible you would like to have.

NORA: No, really I don't know of anything —— Well, listen, Torvald ——

HELMER: Well?

NORA: [*Playing with his coat-buttons, without looking him in the face.*] If you really want to give me some—thing, you might, you know — you might ——

HELMER: Well? Out with it!

NORA: [*Quickly.*] You might give me money, Torvald. Only just what you think you can spare; then I can buy something with it later on.

HELMER: But, Nora ——

NORA: Oh, please do, dear Torvald, please do! I should hang the money in lovely gilt paper on the Christmas tree. Wouldn't that be fun?

HELMER: What do they call the birds that are always making the money fly?

NORA: Yes, I know — spendthrifts, of course. But please do as I ask you, Torvald. Then I shall have time to think what I want most. Isn't that very sensible, now?

HELMER: [*Smiling.*] Certainly; that is to say, if you really kept the money I gave you, and really spent it on something for yourself. But it all goes in housekeeping, and for all manner of useless things, and then I have to pay up again.

NORA: But, Torvald ——

HELMER: Can you deny it, Nora dear? [*He puts his arm round her.*] It's a sweet little lark, but it gets through a lot of money. No one would believe how much it costs a man to keep such a little bird as you.

NORA: For shame! How can you say so? Why, I save as much as ever I can.

HELMER: [*Laughing.*] Very true — as much as you can — but that's precisely nothing.

NORA: [*Hums and smiles with covert glee.*] H'm! If you only knew, Torvald, what expenses we larks and squirrels have.

HELMER: You're a strange little being! Just like your father — always on the lookout for all the money you can lay your hands on; but the moment you have it, it seems to slip through your fingers; you never know what becomes of it. Well, one must take you as you are. It's in the blood. Yes, Nora, that sort of thing is hereditary.

NORA: I wish I had inherited many of papa's qualities.

HELMER: And I don't wish you anything but just what you are — my own, sweet little songbird. But I say — it strikes me you look so — so — what shall I call it? — so suspicious to-day——

NORA: Do I?

HELMER: You do, indeed. Look me full in the face.

NORA: [*Looking at him.*] Well?

HELMER: [*Threatening with his finger.*] Hasn't the little sweet-tooth been playing pranks today?

NORA: No; how can you think such a thing!

HELMER: Didn't she just look in at the confectioner's?

NORA: No, Torvald; really——

HELMER: Not to sip a little jelly?

NORA: No; certainly not.

HELMER: Hasn't she even nibbled a macaroon or two?

NORA: No, Torvald, indeed, indeed!

HELMER: Well, well, well; of course I'm only joking.

NORA: [*Goes to the table on the right.*] I shouldn't think of doing what you disapprove of.

HELMER: No, I'm sure of that; and, besides, you've given me your word—— [*Going towards her.*] Well, keep your little Christmas secrets to yourself, Nora darling. The Christmas tree will bring them all to light, I daresay.

NORA: Have you remembered to invite Doctor Rank?

HELMER: No. But it's not necessary; he'll come as a matter of course. Besides, I shall ask him when he looks in today. I've ordered some capital wine. Nora, you can't think how I look forward to this evening.

NORA: And I too. How the children will enjoy themselves, Torvald!

HELMER: Ah, it's glorious to feel that one has an assured position and ample means. Isn't it delightful to think of?

NORA: Oh, it's wonderful!

HELMER: Do you remember last Christmas? For three whole weeks beforehand you shut yourself up every evening till long past midnight to make flowers for the Christmas tree, and all sorts of other marvels that were to have astonished us. I was never so bored in my life.

NORA: I didn't bore myself at all.

HELMER: [*Smiling.*] But it came to little enough in the end, Nora.

NORA: Oh, are you going to tease me about that again? How could I help the cat getting in and pulling it all to pieces?

HELMER: To be sure you couldn't, my poor little Nora. You did your best to give us all pleasure, and that's the main point. But, all the same, it's a good thing the hard times are over.

NORA: Oh, isn't it wonderful?

HELMER: Now I needn't sit here boring myself all alone; and you needn't tire your blessed eyes and your delicate little fingers——

NORA: [*Clapping her hands.*] No, I needn't, need I, Torvald? Oh, how wonderful it is to think of? [*Takes his arm.*] And now I'll tell you how I think we ought to manage, Torvald. As soon as Christmas is over—— [*The hall-door bell rings.*]

Oh, there's a ring! [*Arranging the room.*] That's somebody come to call. How tiresome!

HELMER: I'm "not at home" to callers; remember that.

ELLEN: [*In the doorway.*] A lady to see you, ma'am.

NORA: Show her in.

ELLEN: [*To Helmer.*] And the doctor has just come, sir.

HELMER: Has he gone into my study?

ELLEN: Yes, sir.

[*Helmer goes into his study. Ellen ushers in Mrs. Linde, in travelling costume, and goes out, closing the door.*]

MRS. LINDE: [*Embarrassed and hesitating.*] How do you do, Nora?

NORA: [*Doubtfully.*] How do you do?

MRS. LINDE: I see you don't recognize me.

NORA: No, I don't think—oh yes!—I believe—— [*Suddenly brightening.*] What, Christina! Is it really you?

MRS. LINDE: Yes; really I!

NORA: Christina! And to think I didn't know you! But how could I—— [*More softly.*] How changed you are, Christina!

MRS. LINDE: Yes, no doubt. In nine or ten years——

NORA: Is it really so long since we met? Yes, so it is. Oh, the last eight years have been a happy time, I can tell you. And now you have come to town? All that long journey in midwinter! How brave of you!

MRS. LINDE: I arrived by this morning's steamer.

NORA: To have a merry Christmas, of course. Oh, how delightful! Yes, we will have a merry Christmas. Do take your things off. Aren't you frozen? [*Helping her.*] There; now we'll sit cosily by the fire. No, you take the armchair; I shall sit in this rocking chair. [*Seizes her hands.*] Yes, now I can see the dear old face again. It was only at the first glance—— But you're a little paler, Christina—and perhaps a little thinner.

MRS. LINDE: And much, much older, Nora.

NORA: Yes, perhaps a little older—not much—ever so little. [*She suddenly checks herself; seriously.*] Oh, what a thoughtless wretch I am! Here I sit chattering on, and—— Dear, dear Christina, can you forgive me!

MRS. LINDE: What do you mean, Nora?

NORA: [*Softly.*] Poor Christina! I forgot: you are a widow.

MRS. LINDE: Yes; my husband died three years ago.

NORA: I know, I know; I saw it in the papers. Oh, believe me, Christina, I did mean to write to you; but I kept putting it off, and something always came in the way.

MRS. LINDE: I can quite understand that, Nora dear.

NORA: No, Christina; it was horrid of me. Oh, you poor darling! how much you must have gone through!—And he left you nothing?

MRS. LINDE: Nothing.

NORA: And no children?

MRS. LINDE: None.

NORA: Nothing, nothing at all?

MRS. LINDE: Not even a sorrow or a longing to dwell upon.

NORA: [*Looking at her incredulously.*] My dear Christina, how is that possible?

MRS. LINDE: [*Smiling sadly and stroking her hair.*] Oh, it happens so sometimes, Nora.

NORA: So utterly alone! How dreadful that must be! I have three of the loveliest children. I can't show them to you just now; they're out with their nurse. But now you must tell me everything.

MRS. LINDE: No, no; I want you to tell me——

NORA: No, you must begin; I won't be egotistical today. Today I'll think only of you. Oh! but I must tell you one thing——perhaps you've heard of our great stroke of fortune?

MRS. LINDE: No. What is it?

NORA: Only think! my husband has been made manager of the Joint Stock Bank.

MRS. LINDE: Your husband! Oh, how fortunate!

NORA: Yes; isn't it? A lawyer's position is so uncertain, you see, especially when he won't touch any business that's the least bit—shady, as of course Torvald never would; and there I quite agree with him. Oh! you can imagine how glad we are. He is to enter on his new position at the New Year, and then he'll have a large salary, and percentages. In the future we shall be able to live quite differently— just as we please, in fact. Oh, Christina, I feel so lighthearted and happy! It's delightful to have lots of money, and no need to worry about things, isn't it?

MRS. LINDE: Yes; at any rate it must be delightful to have what you need.

NORA: No, not only what you need, but heaps of money—heaps!

MRS. LINDE: [*Smiling.*] Nora, Nora, haven't you learned reason yet? In our schooldays you were a shocking little spendthrift.

NORA: [*Quietly smiling.*] Yes; that's what Torvald says I am still. [*Holding up her forefinger.*] But "Nora, Nora" is not so silly as you all think. Oh! I haven't had the chance to be much of a spendthrift. We have both had to work.

MRS. LINDE: You too?

NORA: Yes, light fancy work: crochet, and embroidery, and things of that sort; [*Carelessly.*] and other work too. You know, of course, that Torvald left the Government service when we were married. He had little chance of promotion, and of course he required to make more money. But in the first year after our marriage he overworked himself terribly. He had to undertake all sorts of extra work, you know, and to slave early and late. He couldn't stand it, and fell dangerously ill. Then the doctors declared he must go to the South.

MRS. LINDE: You spent a whole year in Italy, didn't you?

NORA: Yes, we did. It wasn't easy to manage, I can tell you. It was just after Ivar's birth. But of course we had to go. Oh, it was a wonderful, delicious journey! And it saved Torvald's life. But it cost a frightful lot of money, Christina.

MRS. LINDE: So I should think.

NORA: Twelve hundred dollars! Four thousand eight hundred crowns![2] Isn't that a lot of money?

---

[2] **crowns:** The dollar was the old unit of currency in Norway. The crown was substituted for it shortly before the date of this play. [Translator's note.]

MRS. LINDE: How lucky you had the money to spend.

NORA: We got it from father, you must know.

MRS. LINDE: Ah, I see. He died just about that time, didn't he?

NORA: Yes, Christina, just then. And only think! I couldn't go and nurse him! I was expecting little Ivar's birth daily; and then I had my poor sick Torvald to attend to. Dear, kind old father! I never saw him again, Christina. Oh! that's the hardest thing I have had to bear since my marriage.

MRS. LINDE: I know how fond you were of him. But then you went to Italy?

NORA: Yes; you see, we had the money, and the doctors said we must lose no time. We started a month later.

MRS. LINDE: And your husband came back completely cured.

NORA: Sound as a bell.

MRS. LINDE: But — the doctor?

NORA: What do you mean?

MRS. LINDE: I thought as I came in your servant announced the doctor——

NORA: Oh, yes; Doctor Rank. But he doesn't come professionally. He is our best friend, and never lets a day pass without looking in. No, Torvald hasn't had an hour's illness since that time. And the children are so healthy and well, and so am I. [*Jumps up and claps her hands.*] Oh, Christina, Christina, what a wonderful thing it is to live and to be happy!—Oh, but it's really too horrid of me! Here am I talking about nothing but my own concerns. [*Seats herself upon a footstool close to Christina, and lays her arms on her friend's lap.*] Oh, don't be angry with me! Now tell me, is it really true that you didn't love your husband? What made you marry him, then?

MRS. LINDE: My mother was still alive, you see, bedridden and helpless; and then I had my two younger brothers to think of. I didn't think it would be right for me to refuse him.

NORA: Perhaps it wouldn't have been. I suppose he was rich then?

MRS. LINDE: Very well off, I believe. But his business was uncertain. It fell to pieces at his death, and there was nothing left.

NORA: And then—?

MRS. LINDE: Then I had to fight my way by keeping a shop, a little school, anything I could turn my hand to. The last three years have been one long struggle for me. But now it is over, Nora. My poor mother no longer needs me; she is at rest. And the boys are in business, and can look after themselves.

NORA: How free your life must feel!

MRS. LINDE: No, Nora; only inexpressibly empty. No one to live for! [*Stands up restlessly.*] That's why I could not bear to stay any longer in that out-of-the way corner. Here it must be easier to find some-thing to take one up—to occupy one's thoughts. If I could only get some settled employment—some office work.

NORA: But, Christina, that's such drudgery, and you look worn out already. It would be ever so much better for you to go to some watering place and rest.

MRS. LINDE: [*Going to the window.*] I have no father to give me the money, Nora.

NORA: [*Rising.*] Oh, don't be vexed with me.

MRS. LINDE: [*Going to her.*] My dear Nora, don't you be vexed with me. The worst of a position like mine is that it makes one so bitter. You have no one to work for, yet you have to be always on the strain. You must live; and so you become selfish. When I heard of the happy change in your fortunes—can you believe it?—I was glad for my own sake more than for yours.

NORA: How do you mean? Ah, I see! You think Torvald can perhaps do something for you.

MRS. LINDE: Yes; I thought so.

NORA: And so he shall, Christina. Just you leave it all to me. I shall lead up to it beautifully!—I shall think of some delightful plan to put him in a good humor! Oh, I should so love to help you.

MRS. LINDE: How good of you, Nora, to stand by me so warmly! Doubly good in you, who know so little of the troubles and burdens of life.

NORA: I? I know so little of——?

MRS. LINDE: [*Smiling.*] Oh, well—a little fancy work, and so forth.—You're a child, Nora.

NORA: [*Tosses her head and paces the room.*] Oh, come, you mustn't be so patronizing!

MRS. LINDE: No?

NORA: You're like the rest. You all think I'm fit for nothing really serious——

MRS. LINDE: Well, well——

NORA: You think I've had no troubles in this weary world.

MRS. LINDE: My dear Nora, you've just told me all your troubles.

NORA: Pooh—those trifles! [*Softly.*] I haven't told you the great thing.

MRS. LINDE: The great thing? What do you mean?

NORA: I know you look down upon me, Christina; but you have no right to. You are proud of having worked so hard and so long for your mother.

MRS. LINDE: I am sure I don't look down upon any one; but it's true I am both proud and glad when I remember that I was able to keep my mother's last days free from care.

NORA: And you're proud to think of what you have done for your brothers, too.

MRS. LINDE: Have I not the right to be?

NORA: Yes indeed. But now let me tell you, Christina—I, too, have something to be proud and glad of.

MRS. LINDE: I don't doubt it. But what do you mean?

NORA: Hush! Not so loud. Only think, if Torvald were to hear! He mustn't—not for worlds! No one must know about it, Christina—no one but you.

MRS. LINDE: Why, what can it be?

NORA: Come over here. [*Draws her down beside her on the sofa.*] Yes, Christina—I, too, have something to be proud and glad of. I saved Torvald's life.

MRS. LINDE: Saved his life? How?

NORA: I told you about our going to Italy. Torvald would have died but for that.

MRS. LINDE: Well—and your father gave you the money.

NORA: [*Smiling.*] Yes, so Torvald and every one believes; but——

MRS. LINDE: But——?

NORA: Papa didn't give us one penny. It was *I* that found the money.

MRS. LINDE: You? All that money?

NORA: Twelve hundred dollars. Four thousand eight hundred crowns. What do you say to that?

MRS. LINDE: My dear Nora, how did you manage it? Did you win it in the lottery?

NORA: [*Contemptuously.*] In the lottery? Pooh! Any one could have done that!

MRS. LINDE: Then wherever did you get it from?

NORA: [*Hums and smiles mysteriously.*] H'm; tra-la-la-la.

MRS. LINDE: Of course you couldn't borrow it.

NORA: No? Why not?

MRS. LINDE: Why, a wife can't borrow without her husband's consent.

NORA: [*Tossing her head.*] Oh! when the wife has some idea of business, and knows how to set about things——

MRS. LINDE: But, Nora, I don't understand——

NORA: Well, you needn't. I never said I borrowed the money. There are many ways I may have got it. [*Throws herself back on the sofa.*] I may have got it from some admirer. When one is so—attractive as I am——

MRS. LINDE: You're too silly, Nora.

NORA: Now I'm sure you're dying of curiosity, Christina——

MRS. LINDE: Listen to me, Nora dear: haven't you been a little rash?

NORA: [*Sitting upright again.*] Is it rash to save one's husband's life?

MRS. LINDE: I think it was rash of you, without his knowledge——

NORA: But it would have been fatal for him to know! Can't you understand that? He wasn't even to suspect how ill he was. The doctors came to me privately and told me his life was in danger—that nothing could save him but a winter in the South. Do you think I didn't try diplomacy first? I told him how I longed to have a trip abroad, like other young wives; I wept and prayed; I said he ought to think of my condition, and not to thwart me; and then I hinted that he could borrow the money. But then, Christina, he got almost angry. He said I was frivolous, and that it was his duty as a husband not to yield to my whims and fancies—so he called them. Very well, thought I, but saved you must be; and then I found the way to do it.

MRS. LINDE: And did your husband never learn from your father that the money was not from him?

NORA: No; never. Papa died at that very time. I meant to have told him all about it, and begged him to say nothing. But he was so ill—unhappily, it wasn't necessary.

MRS. LINDE: And you have never confessed to your husband?

NORA: Good heavens! What can you be thinking of? Tell him, when he has such a loathing of debt! And besides—how painful and humiliating it would be for Torvald, with his manly self-respect, to know that he owed anything to me! It would utterly upset the relation between us; our beautiful, happy home would never again be what it is.

MRS. LINDE: Will you never tell him?

NORA: [*Thoughtfully, half-smiling.*] Yes, some time perhaps—many, many years hence, when I'm—not so pretty. You mustn't laugh at me! Of course I mean when Torvald is not so much in love with me as he is now; when it doesn't amuse him any longer to see me dancing about, and dressing up and acting. Then it might be well to have something in reserve. [*Breaking off.*] Nonsense! nonsense! That time will never come. Now, what do you say to my grand secret, Christina? Am I fit for nothing now? You may believe it has cost me a lot of anxiety. It has been no joke to meet my engagements punctually. You must know, Christina, that in business there are things called installments, and quarterly interest, that are terribly hard to provide for. So I've had to pinch a little here and there, wherever I could. I couldn't save much out of the housekeeping, for of course Torvald had to live well. And I couldn't let the children go about badly dressed; all I got for them, I spent on them, the blessed darlings!

MRS. LINDE: Poor, Nora! So it had to come out of your own pocket money.

NORA: Yes, of couse. After all, the whole thing was my doing. When Torvald gave me money for clothes, and so on, I never spent more than half of it; I always bought the simplest and cheapest things. It's a mercy that everything suits me so well— Torvald never had any suspicions. But it was often very hard, Christina dear. For it's nice to be beautifully dressed—now, isn't it?

MRS. LINDE: Indeed it is.

NORA: Well, and besides that, I made money in other ways. Last winter I was so lucky—I got a heap of copying to do. I shut myself up every evening and wrote far into the night. Oh, sometimes I was so tired, so tired. And yet it was splendid to work in that way and earn money. I almost felt as if I was a man.

MRS. LINDE: Then how much have you been able to pay off?

NORA: Well, I can't precisely say. It's difficult to keep that sort of business clear. I only know that I've paid everything I could scrape together. Sometimes I really didn't know where to turn. [*Smiles.*] Then I used to sit here and pretend that a rich old gentleman was in love with me——

MRS. LINDE: What! What gentleman?

NORA: Oh, nobody!—that he was dead now, and that when his will was opened, there stood in large letters: "Pay over at once everything of which I die possessed to that charming person, Mrs. Nora Helmer."

MRS. LINDE: But, my dear Nora—what gentleman do you mean?

NORA: Oh dear, can't you understand? There wasn't any old gentleman: it was only what I used to dream when I was at my wits' end for money. But it doesn't matter now—the tiresome old creature may stay where he is for me. I care nothing for him or his will; for now my troubles are over. [*Springing up.*] Oh, Christina, how glorious it is to think of! Free from all anxiety! Free, quite free. To be able to play and romp about with the children; to have things tasteful and pretty in the house, exactly as Torvald likes it! And then the spring will soon be here, with the great blue sky. Perhaps then we shall have a little holiday. Perhaps I shall see the sea again. Oh, what a wonderful thing it is to live and to be happy! [*The hall door bell rings.*]

MRS. LINDE: [*Rising.*] There's a ring. Perhaps I had better go.

NORA: No; do stay. No one will come here. It's sure to be some one for Torvald.

ELLEN: [*In the doorway.*] If you please, ma'am, there's a gentleman to speak to Mr. Helmer.

NORA: Who is the gentleman?

KROGSTAD: [*In the doorway.*] It is I, Mrs. Helmer.

[*Mrs. Linde starts and turns away to the window.*]

NORA: [*Goes a step towards him, anxiously, speaking low.*] You? What is it? What do you want with my husband?

KROGSTAD: Bank business—in a way. I hold a small post in the Joint Stock Bank, and your husband is to be our new chief, I hear.

NORA: Then it is——?

KROGSTAD: Only tiresome business, Mrs. Helmer; nothing more.

NORA: Then will you please go to his study.

[*Krogstad goes. She bows indifferently while she closes the door into the hall. Then she goes to the stove and looks to the fire.*]

MRS. LINDE: Nora—who was that man?

NORA: A Mr. Krogstad—a lawyer.

MRS. LINDE: Then it was really he?

NORA: Do you know him?

MRS. LINDE: I used to know him—many years ago. He was in a lawyer's office in our town.

NORA: Yes, so he was.

MRS. LINDE: How he has changed!

NORA: I believe his marriage was unhappy.

MRS. LINDE: And he is a widower now?

NORA: With a lot of children. There! Now it will burn up.

[*She closes the stove, and pushes the rocking chair a little aside.*]

MRS. LINDE: His business is not of the most creditable, they say?

NORA: Isn't it? I daresay not. I don't know. But don't let us think of business—it's so tiresome.

[*Dr. Rank comes out of Helmer's room.*]

RANK: [*Still in the doorway.*] No, no; I'm in your way. I shall go and have a chat with your wife. [*Shuts the door and sees Mrs. Linde.*] Oh, I beg your pardon. I'm in the way here too.

NORA: No, not in the least. [*Introduces them.*] Doctor Rank—Mrs. Linde.

RANK: Oh, indeed; I've often heard Mrs. Linde's name; I think I passed you on the stairs as I came up.

MRS. LINDE: Yes; I go so very slowly. Stairs try me so much.

RANK: Ah—you are not very strong?

MRS. LINDE: Only overworked.

RANK: Nothing more? Then no doubt you've come to town to find rest in a round of dissipation?

MRS. LINDE: I have come to look for employment.

RANK: Is that an approved remedy for overwork?

MRS. LINDE: One must live, Doctor Rank.

RANK: Yes, that seems to be the general opinion.

NORA: Come, Doctor Rank — you want to live yourself.

RANK: To be sure I do. However wretched I may be, I want to drag on as long as possible. All my patients, too, have the same mania. And it's the same with people whose complaint is moral. At this very moment Helmer is talking to just such a moral incurable——

MRS. LINDE: [*Softly.*] Ah!

NORA: Whom do you mean?

RANK: Oh, a fellow named Krogstad, a man you know nothing about — corrupt to the very core of his character. But even he began by announcing, as a matter of vast importance, that he must live.

NORA: Indeed? And what did he want with Torvald?

RANK: I haven't an idea; I only gathered that it was some bank business.

NORA: I didn't know that Krog — that this Mr. Krogstad had anything to do with the Bank?

RANK: Yes. He has got some sort of place there. [*To Mrs. Linde.*] I don't know whether, in your part of the country, you have people who go grubbing and sniffing around in search of moral rottenness — and then, when they have found a "case," don't rest till they have got their man into some good position, where they can keep a watch upon him. Men with a clean bill of health they leave out in the cold.

MRS. LINDE: Well, I suppose the — delicate characters require most care.

RANK: [*Shrugs his shoulders.*] There we have it! It's that notion that makes society a hospital.

[*Nora, deep in her own thoughts, breaks into half-stifled laughter and claps her hands.*]

RANK: Why do you laugh at that? Have you any idea what "society" is?

NORA: What do I care for your tiresome society? I was laughing at something else — something excessively amusing. Tell me, Doctor Rank, are all the employees at the Bank dependent on Torvald now?

RANK: Is that what strikes you as excessively amusing?

NORA: [*Smiles and hums.*] Never mind, never mind! [*Walks about the room.*] Yes, it is funny to think that we — that Torvald has such power over so many people. [*Takes the bag from her pocket.*] Doctor Rank, will you have a macaroon?

RANK: What! — macaroons! I thought they were contraband here.

NORA: Yes; but Christina brought me these.

MRS. LINDE: What! I——?

NORA: Oh, well! Don't be frightened. You couldn't possibly know that Torvald had forbidden them. The fact is, he's afraid of me spoiling my teeth. But, oh bother, just for once! — That's for you, Doctor Rank! [*Puts a macaroon into his mouth.*]

And you too, Christina. And I'll have one while we're about it — only a tiny one, or at most two. [*Walks about again.*] Oh dear, I am happy! There's only one thing in the world I really want.

RANK: Well; what's that?

NORA: There's something I should so like to say — in Torvald's hearing.

RANK: Then why don't you say it?

NORA: Because I daren't, it's so ugly.

MRS. LINDE: Ugly?

RANK: In that case you'd better not. But to us you might —— What is it you would so like to say in Helmer's hearing?

NORA: I should so love to say "Damn it all!"

RANK: Are you out of your mind?

MRS. LINDE: Good gracious, Nora ——!

RANK: Say it — there he is!

NORA: [*Hides the macaroons.*] Hush — sh — sh

[*Helmer comes out of his room, hat in hand with his overcoat on his arm.*]

NORA: [*Going to him.*] Well, Torvald dear, have you got rid of him?

HELMER: Yes; he has just gone.

NORA: Let me introduce you — this is Christina, who has come to town ——

HELMER: Christina? Pardon me, I don't know ——

NORA: Mrs. Linde, Torvald dear — Christina Linde.

HELMER: [*To Mrs. Linde.*] Indeed! A school friend of my wife's, no doubt?

MRS. LINDE: Yes; we knew each other as girls.

NORA: And only think! She has taken this long journey on purpose to speak to you.

HELMER: To speak to me!

MRS. LINDE: Well, not quite ——

NORA: You see, Christina is tremendously clever at office work, and she's so anxious to work under a first-rate man of business in order to learn still more ——

HELMER: [*To Mrs. Linde.*] Very sensible indeed.

NORA: And when she heard you were appointed manager — it was telegraphed, you know — she started off at once, and —— Torvald, dear, for my sake, you must do something for Christina. Now can't you?

HELMER: It's not impossible. I presume Mrs. Linde is a widow?

MRS. LINDE: Yes.

HELMER: And you have already had some experience of business?

MRS. LINDE: A good deal.

HELMER: Well, then, it's very likely I may be able to find a place for you.

NORA: [*Clapping her hands.*] There now! There now!

HELMER: You have come at a fortunate moment, Mrs. Linde.

MRS. LINDE: Oh, how can I thank you ——?

HELMER: [*Smiling.*] There is no occasion. [*Puts on his overcoat.*] But for the present you must excuse me ——

RANK: Wait; I am going with you.

[*Fetches his fur coat from the hall and warms it at the fire.*]

NORA: Don't be long, Torvald dear.

HELMER: Only an hour; not more.

NORA: Are you going too, Christina?

MRS. LINDE: [*Putting on her walking things.*] Yes; I must set about looking for lodgings.

HELMER: Then perhaps we can go together?

NORA: [*Helping her.*] What a pity we haven't a spare room for you; but it's impossible ——

MRS. LINDE: I shouldn't think of troubling you. Good-bye, dear Nora, and thank you for all your kindness.

NORA: Good-bye for the present. Of course you'll come back this evening. And you, too, Doctor Rank. What! If you're well enough? Of course you'll be well enough. Only wrap up warmly. [*They go out, talking, into the hall. Outside on the stairs are heard children's voices.*] There they are! There they are! [*She runs to the outer door and opens it. The nurse, ANNA, enters the hall with the children.*] Come in! Come in! [*Stoops down and kisses the children.*] Oh, my sweet darlings! Do you see them, Christina? Aren't they lovely?

RANK: Don't let us stand here chattering in the draught.

HELMER: Come, Mrs. Linde; only mothers can stand such a temperature.

[*Dr. Rank, Helmer, and Mrs. Linde go down the stairs; Anna enters the room with the children; Nora also, shutting the door.*]

NORA: How fresh and bright you look! And what red cheeks you've got! Like apples and roses. [*The children chatter to her during what follows.*] Have you had great fun? That's splendid! Oh, really! You've been giving Emmy and Bob a ride on your sledge!—both at once, only think! Why, you're quite a man, Ivar. Oh, give her to me a little, Anna. My sweet little dolly! [*Takes the smallest from the nurse and dances with her.*] Yes, yes; mother will dance with Bob too. What! Did you have a game of snowballs? Oh, I wish I'd been there. No; leave them, Anna; I'll take their things off. Oh, yes, let me do it; it's such fun. Go to the nursery; you look frozen. You'll find some hot coffee on the stove.

[*The Nurse goes into the room on the left. Nora takes off the children's things and throws them down anywhere, while the children talk all together.*]

Really! A big dog ran after you? But he didn't bite you? No; dogs don't bite dear little dolly children. Don't peep into those parcels, Ivar. What is it? Wouldn't you like to know? Take care—it'll bite! What? Shall we have a game? What shall we play at? Hide-and-seek? Yes, let's play hide-and-seek. Bob shall hide first. Am I to? Yes, let me hide first.

[*She and the children play, with laughter and shouting, in the room and the adjacent one to the right. At last Nora hides under the table; the children come rushing in, look for her, but cannot find her, hear her half-choked laughter, rush to the table, lift up the cover and see her. Loud shouts. She creeps out, as though to frighten them. Fresh shouts. Meanwhile there has been a* knock at the door leading into the hall. No one has heard it. Now the door is half opened and* *Krogstad appears. He waits a little; the game is renewed.*]

KROGSTAD: I beg your pardon, Mrs. Helmer——

NORA: [*With a suppressed cry, turns round and half jumps up.*] Ah! What do you want?

KROGSTAD: Excuse me; the outer door was ajar—somebody must have forgotten to shut it——

NORA: [*Standing up.*] My husband is not at home, Mr. Krogstad.

KROGSTAD: I know it.

NORA: Then what do you want here?

KROGSTAD: To say a few words to you.

NORA: To me? [*To the children, softly.*] Go in to Anna. What? No, the strange man won't hurt mamma. When he's gone we'll go on playing. [*She leads the children into the left-hand room, and shuts the door behind them. Uneasy, in suspense.*] It is to me you wish to speak?

KROGSTAD: Yes, to you.

NORA: Today? But it's not the first yet——

KROGSTAD: No, today is Christmas Eve. It will depend upon yourself whether you have a merry Christmas.

NORA: What do you want? I'm not ready today——

KROGSTAD: Never mind that just now. I have come about another matter. You have a minute to spare?

NORA: Oh, yes, I suppose so; although——

KROGSTAD: Good. I was sitting in the restaurant opposite, and I saw your husband go down the street——

NORA: Well?

KROGSTAD: ——with a lady.

NORA: What then?

KROGSTAD: May I ask if the lady was a Mrs. Linde?

NORA: Yes.

KROGSTAD: Who has just come to town?

NORA: Yes. Today.

KROGSTAD: I believe she is an intimate friend of yours.

NORA: Certainly. But I don't understand——

KROGSTAD: I used to know her too.

NORA: I know you did.

KROGSTAD: Ah! You know all about it. I thought as much. Now, frankly, is Mrs. Linde to have a place in the Bank?

NORA: How dare you catechize me in this way, Mr. Krogstad—you, a subordinate of my husband's? But since you ask, you shall know. Yes, Mrs. Linde is to be employed. And it is I who recommended her, Mr. Krogstad. Now you know.

KROGSTAD: Then my guess was right.

NORA: [*Walking up and down.*] You see one has a wee bit of influence, after all. It doesn't follow because one's only a woman——When people are in a subordinate position, Mr. Krogstad, they ought really to be careful how they offend anybody who—h'm——

KROGSTAD: —— who has influence?

NORA: Exactly.

KROGSTAD: [*Taking another tone.*] Mrs. Helmer, will you have the kindness to employ your influence on my behalf?

NORA: What? How do you mean?

KROGSTAD: Will you be so good as to see that I retain my subordinate position in the Bank?

NORA: What do you mean? Who wants to take it from you?

KROGSTAD: Oh, you needn't pretend ignorance. I can very well understand that it cannot be pleasant for your friend to meet me; and I can also understand now for whose sake I am to be hounded out.

NORA: But I assure you——

KROGSTAD: Come come now, once for all: there is time yet, and I advise you to use your influence to prevent it.

NORA: But, Mr. Krogstad, I have no influence—absolutely none.

KROGSTAD: None? I thought you said a moment ago——

NORA: Of course not in that sense. I! How can you imagine that I should have any such influence over my husband?

KROGSTAD: Oh, I know your husband from our college days. I don't think he is any more inflexible than other husbands.

NORA: If you talk disrespectfully of my husband, I must request you to leave the house.

KROGSTAD: You are bold, madam.

NORA: I am afraid of you no longer. When New Year's Day is over, I shall soon be out of the whole business.

KROGSTAD: [*Controlling himself.*] Listen to me, Mrs. Helmer. If need be, I shall fight as though for my life to keep my little place in the Bank.

NORA: Yes, so it seems.

KROGSTAD: It's not only for the salary: that is what I care least about. It's something else—— Well, I had better make a clean breast of it. Of course you know, like every one else, that some years ago I—got into trouble.

NORA: I think I've heard something of the sort.

KROGSTAD: The matter never came into court; but from that moment all paths were barred to me. Then I took up the business you know about. I had to turn my hand to something; and I don't think I've been one of the worst. But now I must get clear of it all. My sons are growing up; for their sake I must try to recover my character as well as I can. This place in the Bank was the first step; and now your husband wants to kick me off the ladder, back into the mire.

NORA: But I assure you, Mr. Krogstad, I haven't the least power to help you.

KROGSTAD: That is because you have not the will; but I can compel you.

NORA: You won't tell my husband that I owe you money?

KROGSTAD: H'm; suppose I were to?

NORA: It would be shameful of you. [*With tears in her voice.*] The secret that is my joy and my pride—that he should learn it in such an ugly, coarse way—and from you. It would involve me in all sorts of unpleasantness——

KROGSTAD: Only unpleasantness

NORA: [*Hotly.*] But just do it. It's you that will come off worst, for then my husband will see what a bad man you are, and then you certainly won't keep your place.

KROGSTAD: I asked whether it was only domestic unpleasantness you feared?

NORA: If my husband gets to know about it, he will of course pay you off at once, and then we shall have nothing more to do with you.

KROGSTAD: [*Coming a pace nearer.*] Listen, Mrs. Helmer: either your memory is defective, or you don't know much about business. I must make the position a little clearer to you.

NORA: How so?

KROGSTAD: When your husband was ill, you came to me to borrow twelve hundred dollars.

NORA: I knew of nobody else.

KROGSTAD: I promised to find you the money——

NORA: And you did find it.

KROGSTAD: I promised to find you the money, on certain conditions. You were so much taken up at the time about your husband's illness, and so eager to have the wherewithal for your journey, that you probably did not give much thought to the details. Allow me to remind you of them. I promised to find you the amount in exchange for a note of hand, which I drew up.

NORA: Yes, and I signed it.

KROGSTAD: Quite right. But then I added a few lines, making your father security for the debt. Your father was to sign this.

NORA: Was to——? He did sign it!

KROGSTAD: I had left the date blank. That is to say, your father was himself to date his signature. Do you recollect that?

NORA: Yes, I believe——

KROGSTAD: Then I gave you the paper to send to your father, by post. Is not that so?

NORA: Yes.

KROGSTAD: And of course you did so at once; for within five or six days you brought me back the document with your father's signature; and I handed you the money.

NORA: Well? Have I not made my payments punctually?

KROGSTAD: Fairly—yes. But to return to the point: You were in great trouble at the time, Mrs. Helmer.

NORA: I was indeed!

KROGSTAD: Your father was very ill, I believe?

NORA: He was on his deathbed.

KROGSTAD: And died soon after?

NORA: Yes.

KROGSTAD: Tell me, Mrs. Helmer: do you happen to recollect the day of his death? The day of the month, I mean?

NORA: Father died on the 29th of September.

KROGSTAD: Quite correct. I have made inquiries. And here comes in the remarkable point— [*Produces a paper.*] which I cannot explain.

NORA: What remarkable point? I don't know——

KROGSTAD: The remarkable point, madam, that your father signed this paper three days after his death!

NORA: What! I don't understand——

KROGSTAD: Your father died on the 29th of September. But look here: he has dated his signature October 2nd! Is not that remarkable, Mrs. Helmer? [*NORA is silent*] Can you explain it? [*NORA continues silent.*] It is noteworthy, too, that the words "October 2nd" and the year are not in your father's handwriting, but in one which I believe I know. Well, this may be explained; your father may have forgotten to date his signature, and somebody may have added the date at random, before the fact of your father's death was known. There is nothing wrong in that. Everything depends on the signature. Of course it is genuine, Mrs. Helmer? It was really your father himself who wrote his name here?

NORA: [*After a short silence, throws her head back and looks defiantly at him.*] No, it was not. *I* wrote father's name.

KROGSTAD: Ah!——Are you aware, madam, that that is a dangerous admission?

NORA: How so? You will soon get your money.

KROGSTAD: May I ask you one more question? Why did you not send the paper to your father

NORA: It was impossible. Father was ill. If I had asked him for his signature, I should have had to tell him why I wanted the money; but he was so ill I really could not tell him that my husband's life was in danger. It was impossible.

KROGSTAD: Then it would have been better to have given up your tour.

NORA: No, I couldn't do that; my husband's life depended on that journey. I couldn't give it up.

KROGSTAD: And did it never occur to you that you were playing me false?

NORA: That was nothing to me. I didn't care in the least about you. I couldn't endure you for all the cruel difficulties you made, although you knew how ill my husband was.

KROGSTAD: Mrs. Helmer, you evidently do not realise what you have been guilty of. But I can assure you it was nothing more and nothing worse that made me an outcast from society.

NORA: You! You want me to believe that you did a brave thing to save your wife's life?

KROGSTAD: The law takes no account of motives.

NORA: Then it must be a very bad law.

KROGSTAD: Bad or not, if I produce this document in court, you will be condemned according to law.

NORA: I don't believe that. Do you mean to tell me that a daughter has no right to spare her dying father trouble and anxiety?——that a wife has no right to save her husband's life? I don't know much about the law, but I'm sure you'll find, somewhere or another, that that is allowed. And you don't know that——you, a lawyer! You must be a bad one, Mr. Krogstad.

KROGSTAD: Possibly. But business——such business as ours——I do understand. You believe that? Very well; now do as you please. But this I may tell you, that if I am flung into the gutter a second time, you shall keep me company.

[*Bows and goes out through hall.*]

NORA: [*Stands a while thinking, then tosses her head.*] Oh nonsense! He wants to frighten me. I'm not so foolish as that. [*Begins folding the children's clothes. Pauses.*] But——? No, it's impossible! Why, I did it for love!

CHILDREN: [*At the door, left.*] Mamma, the strange man has gone now.

NORA: Yes, yes, I know. But don't tell any one about the strange man. Do you hear? Not even papa!

CHILDREN: No, mamma; and now will you play with us again?

NORA: No, no; not now.

CHILDREN: Oh, do, mamma; you know you promised.

NORA: Yes, but I can't just now. Run to the nursery; I have so much to do. Run along, run along, and be good, my darlings! [*She pushes them gently into the inner room, and closes the door behind them. Sits on the sofa, embroiders a few stitches, but soon pauses.*] No! [*Throws down the work, rises, goes to the hall door and calls out.*] Ellen, bring in the Christmas tree! [*Goes to table, left, and opens the drawer; again pauses.*] No, its quite impossible!

ELLEN: [*With Christmas tree.*] Where shall I stand it, ma'am?

NORA: There, in the middle of the room.

ELLEN: Shall I bring in anything else?

NORA: No, thank you, I have all I want.

[*Ellen, having put down the tree, goes out.*]

NORA: [*Busy dressing the tree.*] There must be a candle here—and flowers there.— That horrible man! Nonsense, nonsense! there's nothing to be afraid of. The Christmas tree shall be beautiful. I'll do everything to please you, Torvald; I'll sing and dance, and——

[*Enter Helmer by the hall door, with a bundle of documents.*]

NORA: Oh. You're back already?

HELMER: Yes. Has anybody been here.

NORA: Here? No.

HELMER: That's odd. I saw Krogstad come out of the house.

NORA: Did you? Oh, yes, by-the-bye, he was here for a minute.

HELMER: Nora, I can see by your manner that he has been begging you to put in a good word for him.

NORA: Yes.

HELMER: And you were to do it as if of your own accord? You were to say nothing to me of his having been here. Didn't he suggest that too?

NORA: Yes, Torvald; but——

HELMER: Nora, Nora! And you could condescend to that! To speak to such a man, to make him a promise! And then to tell me an untruth about it!

NORA: An untruth!

HELMER: Didn't you say that nobody had been here? [*Threatens with his finger.*] My little bird must never do that again! A songbird must sing clear and true; no false notes. [*Puts his arm round her.*] That's so, isn't it? Yes, I was sure of it. [*Lets her go.*] And now we'll say no more about it. [*Sits down before the fire.*] Oh, how cozy and quiet it is here! [*Glances into his documents.*]

NORA: [*Busy with the tree, after a short silence.*] Torvald!

HELMER: Yes.

NORA: I'm looking forward so much to the Stenborgs' fancy ball the day after tomorrow.

HELMER: And I'm on tenterhooks to see what surprise you have in store for me.

NORA: Oh, it's too tiresome!

HELMER: What is?

NORA: I can't think of anything good. Everything seems so foolish and meaningless.

HELMER: Has little Nora made that discovery?

NORA: [*Behind his chair, with her arms on the back.*] Are you very busy, Torvald?

HELMER: Well——

NORA: What papers are those?

HELMER: Bank business.

NORA: Already!

HELMER: I have got the retiring manager to let me make some necessary changes in the staff and the organization. I can do this during Christmas week. I want to have everything straight by the New Year.

NORA: Then that's why that poor Krogstad——

HELMER: H'm.

NORA: [*Still leaning over the chair back and slowly stroking his hair.*] If you hadn't been so very busy, I should have asked you a great, great favor, Torvald.

HELMER: What can it be? Out with it.

NORA: Nobody has such perfect taste as you; and I should so love to look well at the fancy ball. Torvald, dear, couldn't you take me in hand, and settle what I'm to be, and arrange my costume for me?

HELMER: Aha! So my willful little woman is at a loss, and making signals of distress.

NORA: Yes, please, Torvald. I can't get on without your help.

HELMER: Well, well, I'll think it over, and we'll soon hit upon something.

NORA: Oh, how good that is of you! [*Goes to the tree again; pause.*] How well the red flowers show.——Tell me, was it anything so very dreadful this Krogstad got into trouble about?

HELMER: Forgery, that's all. Don't you know what that means?

NORA: Mayn't he have been driven to it by need?

HELMER: Yes; or, like so many others, he may have done it in pure heedlessness. I am not so hard-hearted as to condemn a man absolutely for a single fault.

NORA: No, surely not, Torvald!

HELMER: Many a man can retrieve his character, if he owns his crime and takes the punishment.

NORA: Punishment——?

HELMER: But Krogstad didn't do that. He evaded the law by means of tricks and subterfuges; and that is what has morally ruined him.

NORA: Do you think that——?

HELMER: Just think how a man with a thing of that sort on his conscience must be always lying and canting and shamming. Think of the mask he must wear even towards those who stand nearest him—towards his own wife and children. The effect on the children—that's the most terrible part of it, Nora.

NORA: Why?

HELMER: Because in such an atmosphere of lies home life is poisoned and contaminated in every fiber. Every breath the children draw contains some germ of evil.

NORA: [*Closer behind him.*] Are you sure of that?

HELMER: As a lawyer, my dear, I have seen it often enough. Nearly all cases of early corruption may be traced to lying mothers.

NORA: Why—mothers?

HELMER: It generally comes from the mother's side; but of course the father's influence may act in the same way. Every lawyer knows it too well. And here has this Krogstad been poisoning his own children for years past by a life of lies and hypocrisy—that is why I call him morally ruined. [*Holds out both hands to her.*] So my sweet little Nora must promise not to plead his cause. Shake hands upon it. Come, come, what's this? Give me your hand. That's right. Then it's a bargain. I assure you it would have been impossible for me to work with him. It gives me a positive sense of physical discomfort to come in contact with such people.

[*Nora draws her hand away, and moves to the other side of the Christmas tree.*]

NORA: How warm it is here. And I have so much to do.

HELMER: [*Rises and gathers up his papers.*] Yes, and I must try to get some of these papers looked through before dinner. And I shall think over your costume too. Perhaps I may even find something to hang in gilt paper on the Christmas tree. [*Lays his hand on her head.*] My precious little songbird!

[*He goes into his room and shuts the door.*]

NORA: [*Softly, after a pause.*] It can't be. It's impossible. It must be impossible!

ANNA: [*At the door; left.*] The little ones are begging so prettily to come to mamma.

NORA: No, no, no; don't let them come to me! Keep them with you, Anna.

ANNA: Very well, ma'am. [*Shuts the door.*]

NORA: [*Pale with terror.*] Corrupt my children!—Poison my home! [*Short pause. She throws back her head.*] It's not true! It can never, never be true!

ACT 2

The same room. In the corner, beside the piano, stands the Christmas tree, stripped, and with the candles burnt out. Nora's outdoor things lie on the sofa.

Nora, alone, is walking about restlessly. At last she stops by the sofa, and takes up her cloak.

NORA: [*Dropping the cloak.*] There's somebody coming! [*Goes to the hall door and listens.*] Nobody; of course nobody will come today, Christmas day; nor tomorrow either. But perhaps—— [*Opens the door and looks out.*]—No, nothing in the letter box; quite empty. [*Comes forward.*] Stuff and nonsense! Of course he won't really do anything. Such a thing couldn't happen. It's impossible! Why, I have three little children.

[*Anna enters from the left, with a large cardboard box.*]

ANNA: I've found the box with the fancy dress at last.

NORA: Thanks; put it down on the table.

ANNA: [*Does so.*] But I'm afraid it's very much out of order.

NORA: Oh, I wish I could tear it into a hundred thousand pieces!

ANNA: Oh, no. It can easily be put to rights — just a little patience.

NORA: I shall go and get Mrs. Linde to help me.

ANNA: Going out again? In such weather as this! You'll catch cold, ma'am, and be ill.

NORA: Worse things might happen. — What are the children doing?

ANNA: They're playing with, their Christmas presents, poor little dears; but ——

NORA: Do they often ask for me?

ANNA: You see they've been so used to having their mamma with them.

NORA: Yes; but, Anna, I can't have them so much with me in future.

ANNA: Well, little children get used to anything.

NORA: Do you think they do? Do you believe they would forget their mother if she went quite away?

ANNA: Gracious me! Quite away?

NORA: Tell me, Anna — I've so often wondered about it — how could you bring yourself to give your child up to strangers?

ANNA: I had to when I came to nurse my little Miss Nora.

NORA: But how could you make up your mind to it?

ANNA: When I had the chance of such a good place? A poor girl who's been in trouble must take what comes. That wicked man did nothing for me.

NORA: But your daughter must have forgotten you.

ANNA: Oh, no, ma'am, that she hasn't. She wrote to me both when she was confirmed and when she was married.

NORA: [*Embracing her.*] Dear old Anna — you were a good mother to me when I was little.

ANNA: My poor little Nora had no mother but me.

NORA: And if my little ones had nobody else, I'm sure you would —— Nonsense, nonsense! [*Opens the box.*] Go in to the children. Now I must —— You'll see how lovely I shall be tomorrow.

ANNA: I'm sure there will be no one at the ball so lovely as my Miss Nora.

[*She goes into the room on the left.*]

NORA: [*Takes the costume out of the box, but soon throws it down again.*] Oh, if I dared go out. If only nobody would come. If only nothing would happen here in the meantime. Rubbish; nobody is coming. Only not to think. What a delicious muff! Beautiful gloves, beautiful gloves! To forget — to forget! One, two, three, four, five, six — [*With a scream.*] Ah, there they come.

[*Goes towards the door, then stands irresolute. Mrs. Linde enters from the hall, where she has taken off her things.*]

NORA: Oh, it's you, Christina. There's nobody else there? I'm so glad you have come.

MRS. LINDE: I hear you called at my lodgings.

NORA: Yes, I was just passing. There's something you must help me with. Let us sit here on the sofa—so. Tomorrow evening there's to be a fancy ball at Consul Stenborg's overhead, and Torvald wants me to appear as a Neapolitan fishergirl, and dance the tarantella; I learned it at Capri.

MRS. LINDE: I see—quite a performance.

NORA: Yes, Torvald wishes it. Look, this is the costume; Torvald had it made for me in Italy. But now it's all so torn, I don't know——

MRS. LINDE: Oh, we shall soon set that to rights. It's only the trimming that has come loose here and there. Have you a needle and thread? Ah, here's the very thing.

NORA: Oh, how kind of you.

MRS. LINDE: [*Sewing.*] So you're to be in costume tomorrow, Nora? I'll tell you what—I shall come in for a moment to see you in all your glory. But I've quite forgotten to thank you for the pleasant evening yesterday.

NORA: [*Rises and walks across the room.*] Oh, yesterday, it didn't seem so pleasant as usual.—You should have come to town a little sooner, Christina.—Torvald has certainly the art of making home bright and beautiful.

MRS. LINDE: You too, I should think, or you wouldn't be your father's daughter. But tell me—is Doctor Rank always so depressed as he was last evening?

NORA: No, yesterday it was particularly noticeable. You see, he suffers from a dreadful illness. He has spinal consumption, poor fellow. They say his father was a horrible man, who kept mistresses and all sorts of things—so the son has been sickly from his childhood, you understand.

MRS. LINDE: [*Lets her sewing fall into her lap.*] Why, my darling Nora, how do you come to know such things?

NORA: [*Moving about the room.*] Oh, when one has three children, one sometimes has visits from women who are half—half doctors—and they talk of one thing and another.

MRS. LINDE: [*Goes on serving; a short pause.*] Does Doctor Rank come here every day?

NORA: Every day of his life. He has been Torvald's most intimate friend from boyhood, and he's a good friend of mine too. Doctor Rank is quite one of the family.

MRS. LINDE: But tell me—is he quite sincere? I mean, isn't he rather given to flattering people?

NORA: No, quite the contrary. Why should you think so?

MRS. LINDE: When you introduced us yesterday he said he had often heard my name; but I noticed afterwards that your husband had no notion who I was. How could Doctor Rank——

NORA: He was quite right, Christina. You see, Torvald loves me so indescribably, he wants to have me all to himself, as he says. When we were first married he was almost jealous if I even mentioned any of my old friends at home; so naturally I gave up doing it. But I often talk of the old times to Doctor Rank, for he likes to hear about them.

MRS. LINDE: Listen to me, Nora! You are still a child in many ways. I am older than you, and have had more experience. I'll tell you something? You ought to get clear of all this with Dr. Rank.

NORA: Get clear of what?

MRS. LINDE: The whole affair, I should say. You were talking yesterday of a rich admirer who was to find you money——

NORA: Yes, one who never existed, worse luck. What then?

MRS. LINDE: Has Doctor Rank money?

NORA: Yes, he has.

MRS. LINDE: And nobody to provide for?

NORA: Nobody. But——?

MRS. LINDE: And he comes here every day?

NORA: Yes, I told you so.

MRS. LINDE: I should have thought he would have had better taste.

NORA: I don't understand you a bit.

MRS. LINDE: Don't pretend, Nora. Do you suppose I can't guess who lent you the twelve hundred dollars?

NORA: Are you out of your senses? How can you think such a thing? A friend who comes here every day! Why, the position would be unbearable!

MRS. LINDE: Then it really is not he?

NORA: No, I assure you. It never for a moment occurred to me——Besides, at that time he had nothing to lend; he came into his property afterwards.

MRS. LINDE: Well, I believe that was lucky for you, Nora dear.

NORA: No, really, it would never have struck me to ask Dr. Rank——And yet, I'm certain that if I did——

MRS. LINDE: But of course you never would.

NORA: Of course not. It's inconceivable that it should ever be necessary. But I'm quite sure that if I spoke to Doctor Rank——

MRS. LINDE: Behind your husband's back?

NORA: I must get clear of the other thing; that's behind his back too. I must get clear of that.

MRS. LINDE: Yes, yes, I told you so yesterday; but——

NORA: [*Walking up and down.*] A man can manage these things much better than a woman.

MRS. LINDE: One's own husband, yes.

NORA: Nonsense. [*Stands still.*] When everything is paid, one gets back the paper.

MRS. LINDE: Of course.

NORA: And can tear it into a hundred thousand pieces, and burn it up, the nasty, filthy thing!

MRS. LINDE: [*Looks at her fixedly, lays down her work, and rises slowly.*] Nora, you are hiding something from me.

NORA: Can you see it in my face?

MRS. LINDE: Something has happened since yesterday morning. Nora, what is it?

NORA: [*Going towards her.*] Christina——! [*Listens.*] Hush! There's Torvald coming home. Do you mind going into the nursery for the present? Torvald can't bear to see dressmaking going on. Get Anna to help you.

MRS. LINDE: [*Gathers some of the things together.*] Very well; but I shan't go away until you have told me all about it.

[*She goes out to the left, as Helmer enters from the hall.*]

NORA: [*Runs to meet him.*] Oh, how I've been longing for you to come, Torvald dear!

HELMER: Was that the dressmaker —?

NORA: No, Christina. She's helping me with my costume. You'll see how nice I shall look.

HELMER: Yes, wasn't that a happy thought of mine?

NORA: Splendid! But isn't it good of me, too, to have given in to you about the tarantella?

HELMER: [*Takes her under the chin.*] Good of you! To give in to your own husband? Well well, you little madcap, I know you don't mean it. But I won't disturb you. I daresay you want to be "trying on."

NORA: And you are going to work, I suppose?

HELMER: Yes. [*Shows her a bundle of papers.*] Look here. I've just come from the Bank —— [*Goes towards his room.*]

NORA: Torvald.

HELMER: [*Stopping.*] Yes?

NORA: If your little squirrel, were to beg you for something so prettily ——

HELMER: Well?

NORA: Would you do it?

HELMER: I must know first what it is.

NORA: The squirrel would skip about and play all sorts of tricks if you would only be nice and kind.

HELMER: Come, then, out with it.

NORA: Your lark would twitter from morning till night ——

HELMER: Oh, that she does in any case.

NORA: I'll be an elf and dance in the moonlight for you, Torvald.

HELMER: Nora — you can't mean what you were hinting at this morning?

NORA: [*Coming nearer.*] Yes, Torvald, I beg and implore you!

HELMER: Have you really the courage to begin that again?

NORA: Yes, yes; for my sake, you must let Krogstad keep his place in the Bank.

HELMER: My dear Nora, it's his place I intend for Mrs. Linde.

NORA: Yes, that's so good of you. But instead of Krogstad, you could dismiss some other clerk.

HELMER: Why, this is incredible obstinacy! Because you have thoughtlessly promised to put in a word for him, I am to ——!

NORA: It's not that, Torvald. It's for your own sake. This man writes for the most scurrilous newspapers; you said so yourself. He can do you, no end of harm. I'm so terribly afraid of him ——

HELMER: Ah, I understand; it's old recollections that are frightening you.

NORA: What do you mean?

HELMER: Of course you're thinking of your father.

NORA: Yes — yes, of course. Only think of the shameful slanders wicked people used to write about father. I believe they would have got him dismissed if you hadn't been sent to look into the thing, and been kind to him, and helped him.

HELMER: My little Nora, between your father and me there is all the difference in the world. Your father was not altogether unimpeachable. I am; and I hope to remain so.

NORA: Oh, no one knows what wicked men may hit upon. We could live so quietly and happily now, in our cozy, peaceful home, you and I and the children, Torvald! That's why I beg and implore you——

HELMER: And it is just by pleading his cause that you make it impossible for me to keep him. It's already known at the Bank that I intend to dismiss Krogstad. If it were now reported that the new manager let himself be turned round his wife's little finger——

NORA: What then?

HELMER: Oh, nothing, so long as a willful woman can have her way——! I am to make myself a laughing stock to the whole staff, and set people saying that I am open to all sorts of outside influence? Take my word for it, I should soon feel the consequences. And besides— there is one thing that makes Krogstad impossible for me to work with——

NORA: What thing?

HELMER: I could perhaps have overlooked his moral failings at a pinch——

NORA: Yes, couldn't you, Torvald?

HELMER: And I hear he is good at his work. But the fact is, he was a college chum of mine—there was one of those rash friendships between us that one so often repents of later. I may as well confess it at once—he calls me by my Christian name; and he is tactless enough to do it even when others are present. He delights in putting on airs of familiarity— Torvald here, Torvald there! I assure you it's most painful to me. He would make my position at the Bank perfectly unendurable.

NORA: Torvald, surely you're not serious?

HELMER: No? Why not?

NORA: That's such a petty reason.

HELMER: What! Petty! Do you consider me petty!

NORA: No, on the contrary, Torvald dear; and that's just why——

HELMER: Never mind; you call my motives petty; then I must be petty too. Petty! Very well!— Now we'll put an end to this, once for all. [*Goes to the door into the hall and calls.*] Ellen!

NORA: What do you want?

HELMER: [*Searching among his papers.*] To settle the thing. [*Ellen enters.*] Here; take this letter; give it to a messenger. See that he takes it at once. The address is on it. Here's the money.

ELLEN: Very well, sir. [*Goes with the letter.*]

HELMER: [*Putting his papers together.*] There, Madam Obstinacy.

NORA: [*Breathless.*] Torvald—what was in the letter?

HELMER: Krogstad's dismissal.

NORA: Call it back again, Torvald! There's still time. Oh, Torvald, call it back again! For my sake, for your own, for the children's sake! Do you hear, Torvald? Do it! You don't know what that letter may bring upon us all.

HELMER: Too late.

NORA: Yes, too late.

HELMER: My dear Nora, I forgive your anxiety, though it's anything but flattering to me. Why should you suppose that *I* would be afraid of a wretched scribbler's spite? But I forgive you all the same, for it's a proof of your great love for me. [*Takes her in his arms.*] That's as it should be, my own dear Nora. Let what will happen—when it comes to the pinch, I shall have strength and courage enough. You shall see: my shoulders are broad enough to bear the whole burden.

NORA: [*Terror-struck.*] What do you mean by that?

HELMER: The whole burden, I say——

NORA: [*With decision.*] That you shall never, never do!

HELMER: Very well; then we'll share it, Nora, as man and wife. That is how it should be. [*Petting her.*] Are you satisfied now? Come, come, come, don't look like a scared dove. It's all nothing—foolish fancies.—Now you ought to play the tarantella through and practice with the tambourine. I shall sit in my inner room and shut both doors, so that I shall hear nothing. You can make as much noise as you please. [*Turns round in doorway.*] And when Rank comes, just tell him where I'm to be found.

[*He nods to her, and goes with his papers into his room, closing the door.*]

NORA: [*Bewildered with terror, stands as though rooted to the ground, and whispers.*] He would do it. Yes, he would do it. He would do it, in spite of all the world.— No, never that, never, never! Anything rather than that! Oh, for some way of escape! What shall I do——! [*Hall bell rings.*] Doctor Rank——!—Anything, anything, rather than——!

[*Nora draws her hands over her face, pulls herself together, goes to the door and opens it. Rank stands outside hanging up his fur coat. During what follows it begins to grow dark.*]

NORA: Good afternoon, Doctor Rank. I knew you by your ring. But you mustn't go to Torvald now. I believe he's busy.

RANK: And you? [*Enters and closes the door.*]

NORA: Oh, you know very well, I have always time for you.

RANK: Thank you. I shall avail myself of your kindness as long as I can.

NORA: What do you mean? As long as you can?

RANK: Yes. Does that frighten you?

NORA: I think it's an odd expression. Do you expect anything to happen?

RANK: Something I have long been prepared for; but I didn't think it would come so soon.

NORA: [*Catching at his arm.*] What have you discovered? Doctor Rank, you must tell me!

RANK: [*Sitting down by the stove.*] I am running down hill. There's no help for it.

NORA: [*Draws a long breath of relief.*] It's you——?

RANK: Who else should it be?—Why lie to one's self? I am the most wretched of all my patients, Mrs. Helmer. In these last days I have been auditing my life account—bankrupt! Perhaps before a month is over, I shall lie rotting in the churchyard.

NORA: Oh! What an ugly way to talk.

RANK: The thing itself is so confoundedly ugly, you see. But the worst of it is, so many other ugly things have to be gone through first. There is only one last investigation to be made, and when that is over I shall know pretty certainly when the breakup will begin. There's one thing I want to say to you: Helmer's delicate nature shrinks so from all that is horrible: I will not have him in my sickroom——

NORA: But, Doctor Rank——

RANK: I won't have him, I say——not on any account. I shall lock my door against him.——As soon as I am quite certain of the worst, I shall send you my visiting card with a black cross on it; and then you will know that the final horror has begun.

NORA: Why, you're perfectly unreasonable today; and I did so want you to be in a really good humor.

RANK: With death staring me in the face?——And to suffer thus for another's sin! Where's the justice of it? And in one way or another you can trace in every family some such inexorable retribution——

NORA: [*Stopping her ears.*] Nonsense, nonsense! Now cheer up!

RANK: Well, after all, the whole thing's only worth laughing at. My poor innocent spine must do penance for my father's wild oats.

NORA: [*At table, left.*] I suppose he was too fond of asparagus and Strasbourg pâté, wasn't he?

RANK: Yes; and truffles.

NORA: Yes, truffles, to be sure. And oysters, I believe?

RANK: Yes, oysters; oysters, of course.

NORA: And then all the port and champagne! It's sad that all these good things should attack the spine.

RANK: Especially when the luckless spine attacked never had any good of them.

NORA: Ah, yes, that's the worst of it.

RANK: [*Looks at her searchingly.*] H'm——

NORA: [*A moment later.*] Why did you smile?

RANK: No; it was you that laughed.

NORA: No; it was you that smiled, Dr. Rank.

RANK: [*Standing up.*] I see you're deeper than I thought.

NORA: I'm in such a crazy mood today.

RANK: So it seems.

NORA: [*With her hands on his shoulders.*] Dear, dear Doctor Rank, death shall not take you away from Torvald and me.

RANK: Oh, you'll easily get over the loss. The absent are soon forgotten.

NORA: [*Looks at him anxiously.*] Do you think so?

RANK: People make fresh ties, and then——

NORA: Who make fresh ties?

RANK: You and Helmer will, when I am gone. You yourself are taking time by the forelock, it seems to me. What was that Mrs. Linde doing here yesterday?

NORA: Oh!——you're surely not jealous of poor Christina?

RANK: Yes, I am. She will be my successor in this house. When I am out of the way, this woman will perhaps——

NORA: Hush! Not so loud! She's in there.

RANK: Today as well? You see!

NORA: Only to put my costume in order—dear me, how unreasonable you are! [*Sits on sofa.*] Now do be good, Doctor Rank! Tomorrow you shall see how beautifully I shall dance; and then you may fancy that I'm doing it all to please you—and of course Torvald as well. [*Takes various things out of box.*] Doctor Rank, sit down here, and I'll show you something.

RANK: [*Sitting.*] What is it?

NORA: Look here. Look!

RANK: Silk stockings.

NORA: Flesh-colored. Aren't they lovely? It's so dark here now; but tomorrow——No, no, no; you must only look at the feet. Oh, well, I suppose you may look at the rest too.

RANK: H'm——

NORA: What are you looking so critical about? Do you think they won't fit me?

RANK: I can't possibly give any competent opinion on that point.

NORA: [*Looking at him a moment.*] For shame! [*Hits him lightly on the ear with the stockings.*] Take that. [*Rolls them up again.*]

RANK: And what other wonders am I to see?

NORA: You sha'n't see anything more; for you don't behave nicely.

[*She hums a little and searches among the things.*]

RANK: [*After a short silence.*] When I sit here gossiping with you, I can't imagine—I simply cannot conceive—what would have become of me if I had never entered this house.

NORA: [*Smiling.*] Yes, I think you do feel at home with us.

RANK: [*More softly—looking straight before him.*] And now to have to leave it all——

NORA: Nonsense. You sha'n't leave us.

RANK: [*In the same tone.*] And not to be able to leave behind the slightest token of gratitude; scarcely even a passing regret—nothing but an empty place, that can be filled by the first comer.

NORA: And if I were to ask you for——? No——

RANK: For what?

NORA: For a great proof of your friendship.

RANK: Yes—yes?

NORA: I mean—for a very, very great service——

RANK: Would you really, for once, make me so happy?

NORA: Oh, you don't know what it is.

RANK: Then tell me.

NORA: No, I really can't, Doctor Rank. It's far, far too much—not only a service, but help and advice besides——

RANK: So much the better. I can't think what you can mean. But go on. Don't you trust me?

NORA: As I trust no one else. I know you are my best and truest friend. So I will tell you. Well then, Doctor Rank, there is something you must help me to prevent.

You know how deeply, how wonderfully Torvald loves me; he wouldn't hesitate a moment to give his very life for my sake.

RANK: [*Bending towards her.*] Nora—do you think he is the only one who——?

NORA: [*With a slight start.*] Who——?

RANK: Who would gladly give his life for you?

NORA: [*Sadly.*] Oh!

RANK: I have sworn that you shall know it before I—go. I shall never find a better opportunity.—Yes, Nora, now I have told you; and now you know that you can trust me as you can no one else.

NORA: [*Standing up; simply and calmly.*] Let me pass, please.

RANK: [*Makes way for her, but remains sitting.*] Nora——

NORA: [*In the doorway.*] Ellen, bring the lamp. [*Crosses to the stove.*] Oh dear, Doctor Rank, that was too bad of you.

RANK: [*Rising.*] That I have loved you as deeply as—any one else? Was that too bad of me?

NORA: No, but that you should have told me so. It was so unnecessary——

RANK: What do you mean? Did you know——?

[*Ellen enters with the lamp; sets it on the table and goes out again.*]

RANK: Nora—Mrs. Helmer—I ask you, did you know?

NORA: Oh, how can I tell what I knew or didn't know? I really can't say——How could you be so clumsy, Doctor Rank? It was all so nice!

RANK: Well, at any rate, you know now that I am at your service, body and soul. And now, go on.

NORA: [*Looking at him.*] Go on—now?

RANK: I beg you to tell me what you want.

NORA: I can tell you nothing now.

RANK: Yes, yes! You mustn't punish me in that way. Let me do for you whatever a man can.

NORA: You can do nothing for me now.——Besides, I really want no help. You shall see it was only my fancy. Yes, it must be so. Of course! [*Sits in the rocking chair, looks at him and smiles.*] You are a nice person, Doctor Rank! Aren't you ashamed of yourself, now that the lamp is on the table?

RANK: No; not exactly. But perhaps I ought to go—for ever.

NORA: No, indeed you mustn't. Of course you must come and go as you've always done. You know very well that Torvald can't do without you.

RANK: Yes, but you?

NORA: Oh, you know I always like to have you here.

RANK: That is just what led me astray. You are a riddle to me. It has often seemed to me as if you liked being with me almost as much as being with Helmer.

NORA: Yes; don't you see? There are people one loves, and others one likes to talk to.

RANK: Yes—there's something in that.

NORA: When I was a girl, of course I loved papa best. But it always delighted me to steal into the servants' room. In the first place they never lectured me, and in the second it was such fun to hear them talk.

RANK: Ah, I see; then it's their place I have taken?

NORA: [*Jumps up and hurries towards him.*] Oh, my dear Doctor Rank, I don't mean that. But you understand, with Torvald it's the same as with papa——

[*Ellen enters from the hall.*]

ELLEN: Please, ma'am—— [*Whispers to Nora, and gives her a card.*]

NORA: [*Glancing at card.*] Ah! [*Puts it in her pocket.*]

RANK: Anything wrong?

NORA: No, no, not in the least. It's only — it's my new costume——

RANK: Your costume! Why, it's there.

NORA: Oh, that one, yes. But this is another that—I have ordered it—Torvald mustn't know——

RANK: Aha! So that's the great secret.

NORA: Yes, of course. Please go to him; he's in the inner room. Do keep him while I——

RANK: Don't be alarmed; he sha'n't escape. [*Goes into Helmer's room.*]

NORA: [*To Ellen.*] Is he waiting in the kitchen?

ELLEN: Yes, he came up the back stair——

NORA: Didn't you tell him I was engaged?

ELLEN: Yes, but it was no use.

NORA: He won't go away?

ELLEN: No, ma'am, not until he has spoken to you.

NORA: Then let him come in; but quietly. And, Ellen—say nothing about it; it's a surprise for my husband.

ELLEN: Oh, yes, ma'am, I understand. [*She goes out.*]

NORA: It is coming! The dreadful thing is coming, after all. No, no, no, it can never be; it shall not!

[*She goes to Helmer's door and slips the bolt. Ellen opens the hall door for Krogstad, and shuts it after him. He wears a travelling-coat, high boots, and a fur cap.*]

NORA: [*Goes towards him.*] Speak softly; my husband is at home.

KROGSTAD: All right. That's nothing to me.

NORA: What do you want?

KROGSTAD: A little information.

NORA: Be quick, then. What is it?

KROGSTAD: You know I have got my dismissal.

NORA: I couldn't prevent it, Mr. Krogstad. I fought for you to the last, but it was of no use.

KROGSTAD: Does your husband care for you so little? He knows what I can bring upon you, and yet he dares——

NORA: How could you think I should tell him?

KROGSTAD: Well, as a matter of fact, I didn't think it. It wasn't like my friend Torvald Helmer to show so much courage——

NORA: Mr. Krogstad, be good enough to speak respectfully of my husband.

KROGSTAD: Certainly, with all due respect. But since you are so anxious to keep the matter secret, I suppose you are a little clearer than yesterday as to what you have done.

NORA: Clearer than you could ever make me.

KROGSTAD: Yes, such a bad lawyer as I——

NORA: What is it you want?

KROGSTAD: Only to see how you are getting on, Mrs. Helmer. I've been thinking about you all day. Even a mere moneylender, a gutter journalist, a—in short, a creature like me—has a little bit of what people call feeling.

NORA: Then show it; think of my little children.

KROGSTAD: Did you and your husband think of mine? But enough of that. I only wanted to tell you that you needn't take this matter too seriously. I shall not lodge any information, for the present.

NORA: No, surely not. I knew you wouldn't.

KROGSTAD: The whole thing can be settled quite amicably. Nobody need know. It can remain among us three.

NORA: My husband must never know.

KROGSTAD: How can you prevent it? Can you pay off the balance?

NORA: No, not at once.

KROGSTAD: Or have you any means of raising the money in the next few days?

NORA: None—that I will make use of.

KROGSTAD: And if you had, it would not help you now. If you offered me ever so much money down, you should not get back your I.O.U.

NORA: Tell me what you want to do with it.

KROGSTAD: I only want to keep it—to have it in my possession. No outsider shall hear anything of it. So, if you have any desperate scheme in your head——

NORA: What if I have?

KROGSTAD: If you should think of leaving your husband and children——

NORA: What if I do?

KROGSTAD: Or if you should think of—something worse——

NORA: How do you know that?

KROGSTAD: Put all that out of your head.

NORA: How did you know what I had in my mind?

KROGSTAD: Most of us think of that at first. I thought of it, too; but I hadn't the courage——

NORA: [*Tonelessly.*] Nor I.

KROGSTAD: [*Relieved.*] No, one hasn't. You haven't the courage either, have you?

NORA: I haven't, I haven't.

KROGSTAD: Besides, it would be very foolish.—Just one domestic storm, and it's all over. I have a letter in my pocket for your husband——

NORA: Telling him everything?

KROGSTAD: Sparing you as much as possible.

NORA: [*Quickly.*] He must never read that letter. Tear it up. I will manage to get the money somehow——

KROGSTAD: Pardon me, Mrs. Helmer, but I believe I told you——

NORA: Oh, I'm not talking about the money I owe you. Tell me how much you demand from my husband—I will get it.

KROGSTAD: I demand no money from your husband.

NORA: What do you demand then?

KROGSTAD: I will tell you. I want to regain my footing in the world. I want to rise; and your husband shall help me to do it. For the last eighteen months my record has been spotless; I have been in bitter need all the time; but I was content to fight my way up, step by step. Now, I've been thrust down again, and I will not be satisfied with merely being reinstated as a matter of grace. I want to rise, I tell you. I must get into the Bank again, in a higher position than before. Your husband shall create a place on purpose for me——

NORA: He will never do that!

KROGSTAD: He will do it; I know him—he won't dare to show fight! And when he and I are together there, you shall soon see! Before a year is out I shall be the manager's right hand. It won't be Torvald Helmer, but Nils Krogstad, that manages the Joint Stock Bank.

NORA: That shall never be.

KROGSTAD: Perhaps you will——?

NORA: Now I have the courage for it.

KROGSTAD: Oh, you don't frighten me! A sensitive, petted creature like you——

NORA: You shall see, you shall see!

KROGSTAD: Under the ice, perhaps? Down into the cold, black water? And next spring to come up again, ugly, hairless, unrecognizable——

NORA: You can't terrify me.

KROGSTAD: Nor you me. People don't do that sort of thing, Mrs. Helmer. And, after all, what would be the use of it? I have your husband in my pocket, all the same.

NORA: Afterwards? When I am no longer——?

KROGSTAD: You forget, your reputation remains in my hands! [*Nora stands speechless and looks at him.*] Well, now you are prepared. Do nothing foolish. As soon as Helmer has received my letter, I shall expect to hear from him. And remember that it is your husband himself who has forced me back again into such paths. That I will never forgive him. Good-bye, Mrs. Helmer.

[*Goes out through the hall. Nora hurries to the door, opens it a little, and listens.*]

NORA: He's going. He's not putting the letter into the box. No, no, it would be impossible! [*Opens the door further and further.*] What's that. He's standing still; not going down stairs. Has he changed his mind? Is he——? [*A letter falls into the box. Krogstad's footsteps are heard gradually receding down the stair. Nora utters a suppressed shriek, and rushes forward towards the sofa-table; pause.*] In the letter box! [*Slips shrinkingly up to the hall door.*] There it lies.—Torvald, Torvald—now we are lost!

[*Mrs. Linde enters from the left with the costume.*]

MRS. LINDE: There, I think it's all right now. Shall we just try it on?

NORA: [*Hoarsely and softly.*] Christina, come here.

MRS. LINDE: [*Throws dorm the dress on the sofa.*] What's the matter? You look quite distracted.

NORA: Come here. Do you see that letter? There, see — through the glass of the letter box.

MRS. LINDE: Yes, yes, I see it.

NORA: That letter is from Krogstad——

MRS. LINDE: Nora — it was Krogstad who lent you the money?

NORA: Yes; and now Torvald will know everything.

MRS. LINDE: Believe me, Nora, it's the best thing for both of you.

NORA: You don't know all yet. I have forged a name——

MRS. LINDE: Good heavens!

NORA: Now, listen to me, Christina; you shall bear me witness——

MRS. LINDE: How "witness"? What am I to——?

NORA: If I should go out of my mind — it might easily happen——

MRS. LINDE: Nora!

NORA: Or if anything else should happen to me — so that I couldn't be here——!

MRS. LINDE: Nora, Nora, you're quite beside yourself!

NORA: In case any one wanted to take it all upon himself — the whole blame — you understand——

MRS. LINDE: Yes, yes; but how can you think——?

NORA: You shall bear witness that it's not true, Christina. I'm not out of my mind at all; I know quite well what I'm saying; and I tell you nobody else knew anything about it; I did the whole thing, I myself. Remember that.

MRS. LINDE: I shall remember. But I don't understand what you mean——

NORA: Oh, how should you? It's the miracle coming to pass.

MRS. LINDE: The miracle?

NORA: Yes, the miracle. But it's so terrible, Christina; it mustn't happen for all the world.

MRS. LINDE: I shall go straight to Krogstad and talk to him.

NORA: Don't; he'll do you some harm.

MRS. LINDE: Once he would have done anything for me.

NORA: He?

MRS. LINDE: Where does he live?

NORA: Oh, how can I tell——? Yes—— [*Feels in her pocket.*] Here's his card. But the letter, the letter——!

HELMER: [*Knocking outside.*] Nora!

NORA: [*Shrieks in terror.*] Oh, what is it? What do you want?

HELMER: Well, well, don't be frightened. We're not coming in; you've bolted the door. Are you trying on your dress?

NORA: Yes, yes, I'm trying it on. It suits me so well, Torvald.

MRS. LINDE: [*Who has read the card.*] Why, he lives close by here.

NORA: Yes, but it's no use now. We are lost. The letter is there in the box.

MRS. LINDE: And your husband has the key?

NORA: Always.

MRS. LINDE: Krogstad must demand his letter back, unread. He must find some pretext——

NORA: But this is the very time when Torvald generally——

MRS. LINDE: Prevent him. Keep him occupied. I shall come back as quickly as I can.

[*She goes out hastily by the hall door.*]

NORA: [*Opens Helmer's door and peeps in.*] Torvald!

HELMER: Well, may one come into one's own room again at last? Come, Rank, we'll have a look—— [*In the doorway.*] But how's this?

NORA: What, Torvald dear?

HELMER: Rank led me to expect a grand transformation.

RANK: [*In the doorway.*] So I understood. I suppose I was mistaken.

NORA: No, no one shall see me in my glory till tomorrow evening.

HELMER: Why, Nora dear, you look so tired. Have you been practicing too hard?

NORA: No, I haven't practiced at all yet.

HELMER: But you'll have to——

NORA: Oh yes, I must, I must! But, Torvald, I can't get on at all without your help. I've forgotten everything.

HELMER: Oh, we shall soon freshen it up again.

NORA: Yes, do help me, Torvald. You must promise me——Oh, I'm so nervous about it. Before so many people——This evening you must give yourself up entirely to me. You mustn't do a stroke of work; you musn't even touch a pen. Do promise, Torvald dear!

HELMER: I promise. All this evening I shall be your slave. Little helpless thing——! But, by-the-bye, I must just—— [*Going to hall door.*]

NORA: What do you want there?

HELMER: Only to see if there are any letters.

NORA: No, no, don't do that, Torvald.

HELMER: Why not?

NORA: Torvald, I beg you not to. There are none there.

HELMER: Let me just see. [*Is going.*]

[*Nora, at the piano, plays the first bars of the tarantella.*]

HELMER: [*At the door, stops.*] Aha!

NORA: I can't dance tomorrow if I don't rehearse with you first.

HELMER: [*Going to her.*] Are you really so nervous, dear Nora?

NORA: Yes, dreadfully! Let me rehearse at once. We have time before dinner. Oh, do sit down and play for me, Torvald dear; direct me and put me right, as you used to do.

HELMER: With all the pleasure in life, since you wish it. [*Sits at piano.*]

[*Nora snatches the tambourine out of the box, and hurriedly drapes herself in a long parti-colored shawl; then, with a bound, stands in the middle of the floor.*]

NORA: Now play for me! Now I'll dance!

[*Helmer plays and Nora dances. Rank stands at the piano behind Helmer and looks on.*]

HELMER: [*Playing.*] Slower! Slower!

NORA: Can't do it slower!

HELMER: Not so violently, Nora.

NORA: I must! I must!

HELMER: [*Stops.*] No, no, Nora—that will never do.

NORA: [*Laughs and swings her tambourine.*] Didn't I tell you so!

RANK: Let me play for her.

HELMER: [*Rising.*] Yes, do—then I can direct her better.

[*Rank sits down to the piano and plays; Nora dances more and more wildly. Helmer stands by the stove and addresses frequent corrections to her; she seems not to hear. Her hair breaks loose, and falls over her shoulders. She does not notice it, but goes on dancing. Mrs. Linde enters and stands spellbound in the doorway.*]

MRS. LINDE: Ah——!

NORA: [*Dancing.*] We're having such fun here Christina!

HELMER: Why, Nora dear, you're dancing as if it were a matter of life and death.

NORA: So it is.

HELMER: Rank, stop! This is the merest madness. Stop, I say!

[*Rank stops playing, and Nora comes to a sudden standstill.*]

HELMER: [*Going towards her.*] I couldn't have believed it. You've positively forgotten all I taught you.

NORA: [*Throws the tambourine away.*] You see for yourself.

HELMER: You really do want teaching.

NORA: Yes, you see how much I need it. You must practice with me up to the last moment. Will you promise me, Torvald?

HELMER: Certainly, certainly.

NORA: Neither today nor tomorrow must you think of anything but me. You mustn't open a single letter—mustn't look at the letter box.

HELMER: Ah, you're still afraid of that man——

NORA: Oh yes, yes, I am.

HELMER: Nora, I can see it in your face—there's a letter from him in the box.

NORA: I don't know, I believe so. But you're not to read anything now; nothing ugly must come between us until all is over.

RANK: [*Softly, to Helmer.*] You mustn't contradict her.

HELMER: [*Putting his arm around her.*] The child shall have her own way. But tomorrow night, when the dance is over——

NORA: Then you shall be free.

[*Ellen appears in the doorway, right.*]

ELLEN: Dinner is on the table, ma'am.

NORA: We'll have some champagne, Ellen.

ELLEN: Yes, ma'am. [*Goes out.*]

HELMER: Dear me! Quite a banquet.

NORA: Yes, and we'll keep it up till morning. [*Calling out.*] And macaroons, Ellen—plenty—just this once.

HELMER: [*Seizing her hand.*] Come, come, don't let us have this wild excitement! Be my own little lark again.

NORA: Oh yes, I will. But now go into the dining room; and you too, Doctor Rank. Christina, you must help me to do up my hair.

RANK: [*Softly, as they go.*] There's nothing in the wind? Nothing—I mean——?

HELMER: Oh no, nothing of the kind. It's merely this babyish anxiety I was telling you about.

[*They go out to the right.*]

NORA: Well?

MRS. LINDE: He's gone out of town.

NORA: I saw it in your face.

MRS. LINDE: He comes back tomorrow evening. I left a note for him.

NORA: You shouldn't have done that. Things must take their course. After all, there's something glorious in waiting for the miracle.

MRS. LINDE: What is it you're waiting for?

NORA: Oh, you can't understand. Go to them in the dining room; I shall come in a moment.

[*Mrs. Linde goes into the dining room. Nora stands for a moment as though collecting her thoughts; then looks at her watch.*]

NORA: Five. Seven hours till midnight. Then twenty-four hours till the next midnight. Then the tarantella will be over. Twenty-four and seven? Thirty-one hours to live.

[*Helmer appears at the door, right.*]

HELMER: What has become of my little lark?

NORA: [*Runs to him with open arms.*] Here she is!

ACT 3

The same room. The table, with the chairs around it, in the middle. A lighted lamp on the table. The door to the hall stands open. Dance music is heard from the floor above.

Mrs. Linde sits by the table and absently turns the pages of a book. She tries to read, but seems unable to fix her attention; she frequently listens and looks anxiously towards the hall door.

MRS. LINDE: [*Looks at her watch.*] Not here yet; and the time is nearly up. If only he hasn't——[*Listens again.*] Ah, there he is. [*She goes into the hall and cautiously opens the outer door; soft footsteps are heard on the stairs; she whispers.*] Come in; there is no one here.

KROGSTAD: [*In the doorway.*] I found a note from you at my house. What does it mean?

MRS. LINDE: I must speak to you.

KROGSTAD: Indeed? And in this house?

MRS. LINDE: I could not see you at my rooms. They have no separate entrance. Come in; we are quite alone. The servants are asleep, and the Helmers are at the ball upstairs.

KROGSTAD: [*Coming into the room.*] Ah! So the Helmers are dancing this evening? Really?

MRS. LINDE: Yes. Why not?

KROGSTAD: Quite right. Why not?

MRS. LINDE: And now let us talk a little.

KROGSTAD: Have we two anything to say to each other?

MRS. LINDE: A great deal.

KROGSTAD: I should not have thought so.

MRS. LINDE: Because you have never really understood me.

KROGSTAD: What was there to understand? The most natural thing in the world — a heartless woman throws a man over when a better match offers.

MRS. LINDE: Do you really think me so heartless? Do you think I broke with you lightly?

KROGSTAD: Did you not?

MRS. LINDE: Do you really think so?

KROGSTAD: If not, why did you write me that letter?

MRS. LINDE: Was it not best? Since I had to break with you, was it not right that I should try to put an end to all that you felt for me?

KROGSTAD: [*Clenching his hands together.*] So that was it? And all this — for the sake of money!

MRS. LINDE: You ought not to forget that I had a helpless mother and two little brothers. We could not wait for you, Nils, as your prospects then stood.

KROGSTAD: Perhaps not; but you had no right to cast me off for the sake of others, whoever the others might be.

MRS. LINDE: I don't know. I have often asked myself whether I had the right.

KROGSTAD: [*More softly.*] When I had lost you, I seemed to have no firm ground left under my feet. Look at me now. I am a shipwrecked man clinging to a spar.

MRS. LINDE: Rescue may be at hand.

KROGSTAD: It was at hand; but then you came and stood in the way.

MRS. LINDE: Without my knowledge, Nils. I did not know till today that it was you I was to replace in the Bank.

KROGSTAD: Well, I take your word for it. But now that you do know, do you mean to give way?

MRS. LINDE: No, for that would not help you in the least.

KROGSTAD: Oh, help, help ——! I should do it whether or no.

MRS. LINDE: I have learned prudence. Life and bitter necessity have schooled me.

KROGSTAD: And life has taught me not to trust fine speeches.

MRS. LINDE: Then life has taught you a very sensible thing. But deeds you will trust?

KROGSTAD: What do you mean?

MRS. LINDE: You said you were a shipwrecked man, clinging to a spar.

KROGSTAD: I have good reason to say so.

MRS. LINDE: I too am shipwrecked, and clinging to a spar. I have no one to mourn for, no one to care for.

KROGSTAD: You made your own choice.

MRS. LINDE: No choice was left me.

KROGSTAD: Well, what then?

MRS. LINDE: Nils, how if we two shipwrecked people could join hands?

KROGSTAD: What!

MRS. LINDE: Two on a raft have a better chance than if each clings to a separate spar.

KROGSTAD: Christina!

MRS. LINDE: What do you think brought me to town?

KROGSTAD: Had you any thought of me?

MRS. LINDE: I must have work or I can't bear to live. All my life, as long as I can remember, I have worked; work has been my one great joy. Now I stand quite alone in the world, aimless and forlorn. There is no happiness in working for one's self. Nils, give me somebody and something to work for.

KROGSTAD: I cannot believe in all this. It is simply a woman's romantic craving for self-sacrifice.

MRS. LINDE: Have you ever found me romantic?

KROGSTAD: Would you really——? Tell me: do you know all my past?

MRS. LINDE: Yes.

KROGSTAD: And do you know what people say of me?

MRS. LINDE: Did you not say just now that with me you could have been another man?

KROGSTAD: I am sure of it.

MRS. LINDE: Is it too late?

KROGSTAD: Christina, do you know what you are doing? Yes, you do; I see it in your face. Have you the courage then——?

MRS. LINDE: I need some one to be a mother to, and your children need a mother. You need me, and I—I need you. Nils, I believe in your better self. With you I fear nothing.

KROGSTAD: [*Seizing her hands.*] Thank you—thank you, Christina. Now I shall, make others see me as you do. — Ah, I forgot——

MRS. LINDE: [*Listening.*] Hush! The tarantella! Go! Go!

KROGSTAD: Why? What is it?

MRS. LINDE: Don't you hear the dancing overhead? As soon as that is over they will be here.

KROGSTAD: Oh yes, I shall go. Nothing will come of this, after all. Of course, you don't know the step I have taken against the Helmers.

MRS. LINDE: Yes, Nils, I do know.

KROGSTAD: And yet you have the courage to——?

MRS. LINDE: I know to what lengths despair can drive a man.

KROGSTAD: Oh, if I could only undo it!

MRS. LINDE: You could. Your letter is still in the box.

KROGSTAD: Are you sure?

MRS. LINDE: Yes; but——

KROGSTAD: [*Looking to her searchingly.*] Is that what it all means? You want to save your friend at any price. Say it out—is that your idea?

MRS. LINDE: Nils, a woman who has once sold herself for the sake of others, does not do so again.

KROGSTAD: I shall demand my letter back again.

MRS. LINDE: No, no.

KROGSTAD: Yes, of course. I shall wait till Helmer comes; I shall tell him to give it back to me — that it's only about my dismissal — that I don't want it read ——

MRS. LINDE: No, Nils, you must not recall the letter.

KROGSTAD: But tell me, wasn't that just why you got me to come here?

MRS. LINDE: Yes, in my first alarm. But a day has passed since then, and in that day I have seen incredible things in this house. Helmer must know everything; there must be an end to this unhappy secret. These two must come to a full understanding. They must have done with all these shifts and subterfuges.

KROGSTAD: Very well, if you like to risk it. But one thing I can do, and at once ——

MRS. LINDE: [*Listening.*] Make haste! Go, go! The dance is over; we're not safe another moment.

KROGSTAD: I shall wait for you in the street.

MRS. LINDE: Yes, do; you must see me home.

KROGSTAD: I never was so happy in all my life!

[*Krogstad goes out by the outer door. The door between the room and the hall remains open.*]

MRS. LINDE: [*Arranging the room and getting her outdoor things together.*] What a change! What a change! To have some one to work for, to live for; a home to make happy! Well, it shall not be my fault if I fail. — I wish they would come. — [*Listens.*] Ah, here they are! I must get my things on.

[*Takes bonnet and cloak. Helmer's and Nora's voices are heard outside, a key is turned in the lock, and Helmer drags Nora almost by force into the hall. She wears the Italian costume with a large black shawl over it. He is in evening dress and wears a black domino,[3] open.*]

NORA: [*Struggling with him in the doorway.*] No, no, no! I won't go in! I want to go upstairs again; I don't want to leave so early!

HELMER: But, my dearest girl ——!

NORA: Oh, please, please, Torvald, I beseech you — only one hour more!

HELMER: Not one minute more, Nora dear; you know what we agreed. Come, come in; you're catching cold here.

[*He leads her gently into the room in spite of her resistance.*]

MRS. LINDE: Good evening.

NORA: Christina!

HELMER: What, Mrs. Linde! You here so late?

MRS. LINDE: Yes, I ought to apologize. I did so want to see Nora in her costume.

NORA: Have you been sitting here waiting for me?

MRS. LINDE: Yes; unfortunately I came too late. You had gone upstairs already, and I felt I couldn't go away without seeing you.

HELMER: [*Taking Nora's shawl off.*] Well then, just look at her! I assure you she's worth it. Isn't she lovely, Mrs. Linde?

MRS. LINDE: Yes, I must say ——

HELMER: Isn't she exquisite? Every one said so. But she's dreadfully obstinate, dear little creature. What's to be done with her? Just think, I had almost to force her away.

---

[3] *domino:* A hooded cap with an eye mask worn to masquerades.

NORA: Oh, Torvald, you'll be sorry some day that you didn't let me stay, if only for one half-hour more.

HELMER: There! You hear her, Mrs. Linde? She dances her tarantella with wild applause, and well she deserved it, I must say—though there was, perhaps, a little too much nature in her rendering of the idea—more than was, strictly speaking, artistic. But never mind—the point is, she made a great success, a tremendous success. Was I to let her remain after that—to weaken the impression? Not if I know it. I took my sweet little Capri girl—my capricious little Capri girl, I might say—under my arm; a rapid turn round the room, a curtsey to all sides, and—as they say in novels—the lovely apparition vanished! An exit should always be effective, Mrs. Linde; but I can't get Nora to see it. By Jove! it's warm here. [*Throws his domino on a chair and opens the door to his room.*] What! No light there? Oh, of course. Excuse me——[*Goes in and lights candles.*]

NORA: [*Whispers breathlessly.*] Well?

MRS. LINDE: [*Softly.*] I've spoken to him.

NORA: And——?

MRS. LINDE: Nora—you must tell your husband everything——

NORA: [*Tonelessly.*] I knew it!

MRS. LINDE: You have nothing to fear from Krogstad; but you must speak out.

NORA: I shall not speak?

MRS. LINDE: Then the letter will.

NORA: Thank you, Christina. Now I know what I have to do. Hush——!

HELMER: [*Coming back.*] Well, Mrs. Linde, have you admired her?

MRS. LINDE: Yes; and now I must say good night.

HELMER: What, already? Does this knitting belong to you?

MRS. LINDE: [*Takes it.*] Yes, thanks; I was nearly forgetting it.

HELMER: Then you do knit?

MRS. LINDE: Yes.

HELMER: Do you know, you ought to embroider instead?

MRS. LINDE: Indeed! Why?

HELMER: Because it's so much prettier. Look now! You hold the embroidery in the left hand, so, and then work the needle with the right hand, in a long, graceful curve—don't you?

MRS. LINDE: Yes, I suppose so.

HELMER: But knitting is always ugly. Just look—your arms close to your sides, and the needles going up and down—there's something Chinese about it.—They really gave us splendid champagne tonight.

MRS. LINDE: Well, good night, Nora, and don't be obstinate any more.

HELMER: Well said, Mrs. Linde!

MRS. LINDE: Good night, Mr. Helmer.

HELMER: [*Accompanying her to the door.*] Good night, good night; I hope you'll get safely home. I should be glad to—but you have such a short way to go. Good night, good night. [*She goes; Helmer shuts the door after her and comes forward again.*] At last we've got rid of her: she's a terrible bore.

NORA: Aren't you very tired, Torvald?

HELMER: No, not in the least.

NORA: Nor sleepy?

HELMER: Not a bit. I feel particularly lively. But you? You do look tired and sleepy.

NORA: Yes, very tired. I shall soon sleep now.

HELMER: There, you see. I was right after all not to let you stay longer.

NORA: Oh, everything you do is right.

HELMER: [*Kissing her forehead.*] Now my lark is speaking like a reasonable being. Did you notice how jolly Rank was this evening?

NORA: Indeed? Was he? I had no chance of speaking to him.

HELMER: Nor I, much; but I haven't seen him in such good spirits for a long time. [*Looks at Nora a little, then comes nearer her.*] It's splendid to be back in our own home, to be quite alone together!—Oh, you enchanting creature!

NORA: Don't look at me in that way, Torvald.

HELMER: I am not to look at my dearest treasure?—at all the loveliness that is mine, mine only, wholly and entirely mine?

NORA: [*Goes to the other side of the table.*] You mustn't say these things to me this evening.

HELMER: [*Following.*] I see you have the tarantella still in your blood—and that makes you all the more enticing. Listen! the other people are going now. [*More softly.*] Nora—soon the whole house will be still.

NORA: Yes, I hope so.

HELMER: Yes, don't you, Nora darling? When we are among strangers, do you know why I speak so little to you, and keep so far away, and only steal a glance at you now and then—do you know why I do it? Because I am fancying that we love each other in secret, that I am secretly betrothed to you, and that no one dreams that there is anything between us.

NORA: Yes, yes, yes. I know all your thoughts are with me.

HELMER: And then, when the time comes to go, and I put the shawl about your smooth, soft shoulders, and this glorious neck of yours, I imagine you are my bride, that our marriage is just over, that I am bringing you for the first time to my home—that I am alone with you for the first time—quite alone with you, in your trembling loveliness! All this evening I have been longing for you, and you only. When I watched you swaying and whirling in the tarantella—my blood boiled—I could endure it no longer; and that's why I made you come home with me so early——

NORA: Go now, Torvald! Go away from me. I won't have all this.

HELMER: What do you mean? Ah, I see you're teasing me, little Nora! Won't—won't! Am I not your husband——? [*A knock at the outer door.*]

NORA: [*Starts.*] Did you hear——?

HELMER: [*Going towards the hall.*] Who's there?

RANK: [*Outside.*] It is I; may I come in for a moment?

HELMER: [*In a low tone, annoyed.*] Oh! what can he want just now? [*Aloud.*] Wait a moment. [*Opens door.*] Come, it's nice of you to look in.

RANK: I thought I heard your voice, and that put it into my head. [*Looks round.*] Ah, this dear old place! How cozy you two are here!

HELMER: You seemed to find it pleasant enough upstairs, too.

RANK: Exceedingly. Why not? Why shouldn't one take one's share of everything in this world? All one can, at least, and as long as one can. The wine was splendid ——

HELMER: Especially the champagne.

RANK: Did you notice it? It's incredible the quantity I contrived to get down.

NORA: Torvald drank plenty of champagne, too.

RANK: Did he?

NORA: Yes, and it always puts him in such spirits.

RANK: Well, why shouldn't one have a jolly evening after a well-spent day?

HELMER: Well spent! Well, I haven't much to boast of in that respect.

RANK: [*Slapping him on the shoulder.*] But I have, don't you see?

NORA: I suppose you have been engaged in a scientific investigation, Doctor Rank?

RANK: Quite right.

HELMER: Bless me! Little Nora talking about scientific investigations!

NORA: Am I to congratulate you on the result?

RANK: By all means.

NORA: It was good then?

RANK: The best possible, both for doctor and patient — certainty.

NORA: [*Quickly and searchingly.*] Certainty?

RANK: Absolute certainty. Wasn't I right to enjoy myself after that?

NORA: Yes, quite right, Doctor Rank.

HELMER: And so say I, provided you don't have to pay for it tomorrow.

RANK: Well, in this life nothing is to be had for nothing.

NORA: Doctor Rank — I'm sure you are very fond of masquerades?

RANK: Yes, when there are plenty of amusing disguises ——

NORA: Tell me, what shall we two be at our next masquerade?

HELMER: Little featherbrain! Thinking of your next already!

RANK: We two? I'll tell you. You must go as a good fairy.

HELMER: Ah, but what costume would indicate that?

RANK: She has simply to wear her everyday dress.

HELMER: Capital! But don't you know what you will be yourself?

RANK: Yes, my dear friend, I am perfectly clear upon that point.

HELMER: Well?

RANK: At the next masquerade I shall be invisible.

HELMER: What a comical idea!

RANK: There's a big black hat — haven't you heard of the invisible hat? It comes down all over you, and then no one can see you.

HELMER: [*With a suppressed smile.*] No, you're right there.

RANK: But I'm quite forgetting what I came for. Helmer, give me a cigar — one of the dark Havanas.

HELMER: With the greatest pleasure. [*Hands cigar case.*]

RANK: [*Takes one and cuts the end off.*] Thank you.

NORA: [*Striking a wax match.*] Let me give you a light.

RANK: A thousand thanks.

[*She holds the match. He lights his cigar at it.*]

RANK: And now, good-bye!

HELMER: Good-bye, good-bye, my dear fellow.

NORA: Sleep well, Doctor Rank.

RANK: Thanks for the wish.

NORA: Wish me the same.

RANK: You? Very well, since you ask me—Sleep well. And thanks for the light. [*He nods to them both and goes out.*]

HELMER: [*In an undertone.*] He's been drinking a good deal.

NORA: [*Absently.*] I daresay. [*Helmer takes his bunch of keys from his pocket and goes into the hall.*] Torvald, what are you doing there?

HELMER: I must empty the letter box; it's quite full; there will be no room for the newspapers tomorrow morning.

NORA: Are you going to work tonight?

HELMER: You know very well I am not. —Why, how is this? Someone has been at the lock.

NORA: The lock——?

HELMER: I'm sure of it. What does it mean? I can't think that the servants——? Here's a broken hair pin. Nora, it's one of yours.

NORA: [*Quickly.*] It must have been the children——

HELMER: Then you must break them of such tricks. —There! At last I've got it open. [*Takes contents out and calls into the kitchen.*] Ellen!—Ellen, just put the hall door lamp out.

[*He returns with letters in his hand, and shuts the inner door.*]

HELMER: Just see how they've accumulated. [*Turning them over.*] Why, what's this?

NORA: [*At the window.*] The letter! Oh no, no, Torvald!

HELMER: Two visiting cards—from Rank.

NORA: From Doctor Rank?

HELMER: [*Looking at them.*] Doctor Rank. They were on the top. He must just have put them in.

NORA: Is there anything on them?

HELMER: There's a black cross over the name. Look at it. What an unpleasant idea! It looks just as if he were announcing his own death.

NORA: So he is.

HELMER: What! Do you know anything? Has he told you anything?

NORA: Yes. These cards mean that he has taken his last leave of us. He is going to shut himself up and die.

HELMER: Poor fellow! Of course I knew we couldn't hope to keep him long. But so soon——! And to go and creep into his lair like a wounded animal——.

NORA: When we must go, it is best to go silently Don't you think so, Torvald?

HELMER: [*Walking up and down.*] He had so grown into our lives, I can't realize that he is gone. He and his sufferings and his loneliness formed a sort of cloudy background to the sunshine of our happiness. —Well, perhaps it's best as it is— at any rate for him. [*Stands still.*] And perhaps for us too, Nora. Now we two are thrown entirely upon each other. [*Takes her in his arms.*] My darling wife! I feel as if I could never hold you close enough. Do you know, Nora, I often wish some danger might threaten you, that I might risk body and soul, and everything, everything, for your dear sake.

NORA: [*Tears herself from him and says firmly.*] Now you shall read your letters, Torvald.

HELMER: No, no; not tonight. I want to be with you, my sweet wife.

NORA: With the thought of your dying friend——?

HELMER: You are right. This has shaken us both. Unloveliness has come between us—thoughts of death and decay. We must seek to cast them off. Till then—we will remain apart.

NORA: [*Her arms round his neck.*] Torvald! Good night! good night!

HELMER: [*Kissing her forehead.*] Good night, my little songbird. Sleep well, Nora. Now I shall go and read my letters.

[*He goes with the letters in his hand into his room and shuts the door.*]

NORA: [*With wild eyes, gropes about her, seizes Helmer's domino, throws it round her, and whispers quickly, hoarsely, and brokenly.*] Never to see him again. Never, never, never. [*Throws her shawl over her head.*] Never to see the children again. Never, never.—Oh that black, icy water! Oh that bottomless——! If it were only over! Now he has it; he's reading it. Oh, no, no, no, not yet. Torvald, good-bye——! Good-bye, my little ones——!

[*She is rushing out by the hall; at the same moment Helmer flings his door open, and stands there with an open letter in his hand.*]

HELMER: Nora!

NORA: [*Shrieks.*] Ah——!

HELMER: What is this? Do you know what is in this letter?

NORA: Yes, I know. Let me go! Let me pass!

HELMER: [*Holds her back.*] Where do you want to go?

NORA: [*Tries to break away from him.*] You shall not save me, Torvald.

HELMER: [*Falling back.*] True! Is what he writes true? No, no, it is impossible that this can be true.

NORA: It is true. I have loved you beyond all else in the world.

HELMER: Pshaw—no silly evasions!

NORA: [*A step nearer him.*] Torvald——!

HELMER: Wretched woman—what have you done!

NORA: Let me go—you shall not save me! You shall not take my guilt upon yourself!

HELMER: I don't want any melodramatic airs. [*Locks the outer door.*] Here you shall stay and give an account of yourself. Do you understand what you have done? Answer! Do you understand it?

NORA: [*Looks at him fixedly, and says with a stiffening expression.*] Yes; now I begin fully to understand it.

HELMER: [*Walking up and down.*] Oh! what an awful awakening! During all these eight years—she who was my pride and my joy—a hypocrite, a liar—worse, worse—a criminal. Oh, the unfathomable hideousness of it all! Ugh! Ugh!

[*Nora says nothing, and continues to look fixedly at him.*]

HELMER: I ought to have known how it would be. I ought to have foreseen it. All your father's want of principle — be silent! — all your father's want of principle you have inherited — no religion, no morality, no sense of duty. How I am punished for screening him! I did it for your sake; and you reward me like this.

NORA: Yes — like this.

HELMER: You have destroyed my whole happiness. You have ruined my future. Oh, it's frightful to think of! I am in the power of a scoundrel; he can do whatever he pleases with me, demand whatever he chooses; he can domineer over me as much as he likes, and I must submit. And all this disaster and ruin is brought upon me by an unprincipled woman!

NORA: When I am out of the world, you will be free.

HELMER: Oh, no fine phrases. Your father, too, was always ready with them. What good would it do me, if you were "out of the world," as you say? No good whatever! He can publish the story all the same; I might even be suspected of collusion. People will think I was at the bottom of it all and egged you on. And for all this I have you to thank — you whom I have done nothing but pet and spoil during our whole married life. Do you understand now what you have done to me?

NORA: [*With cold calmness.*] Yes.

HELMER: The thing is so incredible, I can't grasp it. But we must come to an understanding. Take that shawl off. Take it off, I say! I must try to pacify him in one way or another — the matter must be hushed up, cost what it may. — As for you and me, we must make no outward change in our way of life — no outward change, you understand. Of course, you will continue to live here. But the children cannot be left in your care. I dare not trust them to you. — Oh, to have to say this to one I have loved so tenderly — whom I still——! But that must be a thing of the past. Henceforward there can be no question of happiness, but merely of saving the ruins, the shreds, the show—— [*A ring; Helmer starts.*] What's that? So late! Can it be the worst? Can he——? Hide yourself, Nora; say you are ill.

[*Nora stands motionless. Helmer goes to the door and opens it.*]

ELLEN: [*Half dressed, in the hall.*] Here is a letter for you, ma'am.

HELMER: Give it to me. [*Seizes the letter and shuts the door.*] Yes, from him. You shall not have it. I shall read it.

NORA: Read it!

HELMER: [*By the lamp.*] I have hardly the courage to. We may both be lost, both you and I. Ah! I must know. [*Hastily tears the letter open; reads a few lines, looks at an enclosure; with a cry of joy.*] Nora! [*Nora looks inquiringly at him.*]

HELMER: Nora! — Oh! I must read it again. — Yes, yes, it is so. I am saved! Nora, I am saved!

NORA: And I?

HELMER: You too, of course; we are both saved, both of us. Look here — he sends you back your promissory note. He writes that he regrets and apologizes that a happy turn in his life —— Oh, what matter what he writes. We are saved, Nora!

No one can harm you. Oh, Nora, Nora——; but first to get rid of this hateful thing. I'll just see —— [*Glances at the I.O.U.*] No, I will not look at it; the whole thing shall be nothing but a dream to me. [*Tears the I.O.U. and both letters in pieces. Throws them into the fire and watches them burn.*] There! it's gone!—He said that ever since Christmas Eve——Oh, Nora, they must have been three terrible days for you!

NORA: I have fought a hard fight for the last three days.

HELMER: And, in your agony you saw no other outlet but—— No; we won't think of that horror. We will only rejoice and repeat—it's over, all over! Don't you hear, Nora? You don't seem able to grasp it. Yes, it's over. What is this set look on your face? Oh, my poor Nora, I understand; you cannot believe that I have forgiven you. But I have, Nora; I swear it. I have forgiven everything. I know that what you did was all for love of me.

NORA: That is true.

HELMER: You loved me as a wife should love her husband. It was only the means that, in your inexperience, you misjudged. But do you think I love you the less because you cannot do without guidance? No, no. Only lean on me; I will counsel you, and guide you. I should be no true man if this very womanly helplessness did not make you doubly dear in my eyes. You mustn't dwell upon the hard things I said in my first moment of terror, when the world seemed to be tumbling about my ears. I have forgiven you, Nora—I swear I have forgiven you.

NORA: I thank you for your forgiveness. [*Goes out, to the right.*]

HELMER: No, stay——! [*Looking through the doorway.*] What are you going to do?

NORA: [*Inside.*] To take off my masquerade dress.

HELMER: [*In the doorway.*] Yes, do, dear. Try to calm down, and recover your balance, my scared little songbird. You may rest secure. I have broad wings to shield you. [*Walking up and down near the door.*] Oh, how lovely—how cozy our home is, Nora! Here you are safe; here I can shelter you like a hunted dove whom I have saved from the claws of the hawk. I shall soon bring your poor beating heart to rest; believe me, Nora, very soon. Tomorrow all this will seem quite different— everything will be as before. I shall not need to tell you again that I forgive you; you will feel for yourself that it is true. How could you think I could find it in my heart to drive you away, or even so much as to reproach you? Oh, you don't know a true man's heart, Nora. There is something indescribably sweet and soothing to a man in having forgiven his wife—honestly forgiven her, from the bottom of his heart. She becomes his property in a double sense. She is as though born again; she has become, so to speak, at once his wife and his child. That is what you shall henceforth be to me, my bewildered, helpless darling. Don't be troubled about anything, Nora; only open your heart to me, and I will be both will and conscience to you. [*Nora enters in everyday dress.*] Why, what's this? Not gone to bed? You have changed your dress?

NORA: Yes, Torvald; now I have changed my dress.

HELMER: But why now, so late——?

NORA: I shall not sleep tonight.

HELMER: But, Nora dear——

NORA: [*Looking at her watch.*] It's not so late yet. Sit down, Torvald; you and I have much to say to each other. [*She sits at one side of the table.*]

HELMER: Nora—what does this mean? Your cold, set face——

NORA: Sit down. It will take some time. I have much to talk over with you.

[*Helmer sits at the other side of the table.*]

HELMER: You alarm me, Nora. I don't understand you.

NORA: No, that is just it. You don't understand me; and I have never understood you—till tonight. No, don't interrupt. Only listen to what I say.—We must come to a final settlement, Torvald.

HELMER: How do you mean?

NORA: [*After a short silence.*] Does not one thing strike you as we sit here?

HELMER: What should strike me?

NORA: We have been married eight years. Does it not strike you that this is the first time we two, you and I, man and wife, have talked together seriously?

HELMER: Seriously! What do you call seriously?

NORA: During eight whole years, and more—ever since the day we first met—we have never exchanged one serious word about serious things.

HELMER: Was I always to trouble you with the cares you could not help me to bear?

NORA: I am not talking of cares. I say that we have never yet set ourselves seriously to get to the bottom of anything.

HELMER: Why, my dearest Nora, what have you to do with serious things?

NORA: There we have it! You have never understood me.—I have had great injustice done me, Torvald; first by father, and then by you.

HELMER: What! By your father and me?—By us, who have loved you more than all the world?

NORA: [*Shaking her head.*] You have never loved me. You only thought it amusing to be in love with me.

HELMER: Why, Nora, what a thing to say!

NORA: Yes, it is so, Torvald. While I was at home with father, he used to tell me all his opinions, and I held the same opinions. If I had others I said nothing about them, because he wouldn't have liked it. He used to call me his doll-child, and played with me as I played with my dolls. Then I came to live in your house——

HELMER: What an expression to use about our marriage!

NORA: [*Undisturbed.*] I mean I passed from father's hands into yours. You arranged everything according to your taste; and, I got the same tastes as you; or I pretended to—I don't know which—both ways, perhaps; sometimes one and sometimes the other. When I look back on it now, I seem to have been living here like a beggar, from hand to mouth. I lived by performing tricks for you, Torvald. But you would have it so. You and father have done me a great wrong. It is your fault that my life has come to nothing.

HELMER: Why, Nora, how unreasonable and ungrateful you are! Have you not been happy here?

NORA: No, never. I thought I was; but I never was.

HELMER: Not—not happy!

NORA: No; only merry. And you have always been so kind to me. But our house has been nothing but a playroom. Here I have been your doll-wife, just as at home I used to be papa's doll-child. And the children, in their turn, have been my dolls. I thought it fun when you played with me, just as the children did when I played with them. That has been our marriage, Torvald.

HELMER: There is some truth in what you say, exaggerated and overstrained though it be. But henceforth it shall be different. Playtime is over; now comes the time for education.

NORA: Whose education? Mine, or the children's?

HELMER: Both, my dear Nora.

NORA: Oh, Torvald, you are not the man to teach me to be a fit wife for you.

HELMER: And you can say that?

NORA: And I — how have I prepared myself to educate the children?

HELMER: Nora!

NORA: Did you not say yourself, a few minutes ago, you dared not trust them to me?

HELMER: In the excitement of the moment! Why should you dwell upon that?

NORA: No — you were perfectly right. That problem is beyond me. There is another to be solved first — I must try to educate myself. You are not the man to help me in that. I must set about it alone. And that is why I am leaving you.

HELMER: [*Jumping up.*] What — do you mean to say——?

NORA: I must stand quite alone if I am ever to know myself and my surroundings; so I cannot stay with you.

HELMER: Nora! Nora!

NORA: I am going at once. I daresay Christina will take me in for tonight——

HELMER: You are mad! I shall not allow it! I forbid it!

NORA: It is of no use your forbidding me anything now. I shall take with me what belongs to me. From you I will accept nothing, either now or afterwards.

HELMER: What madness this is!

NORA: Tomorrow I shall go home — I mean to what was my home. It will be easier for me to find some opening there.

HELMER: Oh, in your blind inexperience——

NORA: I must try to gain experience, Torvald.

HELMER: To forsake your home, your husband, and your children! And you don't consider what the world will say.

NORA: I can pay no heed to that. I only know that I must do it.

HELMER: This is monstrous! Can you forsake your holiest duties in this way?

NORA: What do you consider my holiest duties?

HELMER: Do I need to tell you that? Your duties to your husband and your children.

NORA: I have other duties equally sacred.

HELMER: Impossible! What duties do you mean?

NORA: My duties towards myself.

HELMER: Before all else you are a wife and a mother.

NORA: That I no longer believe. I believe that before all else I am a human being, just as much as you are — or at least that I should try to become one. I know that most people agree with you, Torvald, and that they say so in books. But henceforth I can't be satisfied with what most people say, and what is in books. I must think things out for myself, and try to get clear about them.

HELMER: Are you not clear about your place in your own home? Have you not an infallible guide in questions like these? Have you not religion?

NORA: Oh, Torvald, I don't really know what religion is.

HELMER: What do you mean?

NORA: I know nothing but what Pastor Hansen told me when I was confirmed. He explained that religion was this and that. When I get away from all this and stand alone, I will look into that matter too. I will see whether what he taught me is right, or, at any rate, whether it is right for me.

HELMER: Oh, this is unheard of! And from so young a woman! But if religion cannot keep you right, let me appeal to your conscience — for I suppose you have some moral feeling? Or, answer me: perhaps you have none?

NORA: Well, Torvald, it's not easy to say. I really don't know — I am all at sea about these things. I only know that I think quite differently from you about them. I hear, too, that the laws are different from what I thought; but I can't believe that they can be right. It appears that a woman has no right to spare her dying father, or to save her husband's life! I don't believe that.

HELMER: You talk like a child. You don't understand the society in which you live.

NORA: No, I do not. But now I shall try to learn. I must make up my mind which is right — society or I.

HELMER: Nora, you are ill; you are feverish; I almost think you are out of your senses.

NORA: I have never felt so much clearness and certainty as tonight.

HELMER: You are clear and certain enough to forsake husband and children?

NORA: Yes, I am.

HELMER: Then there is only one explanation possible.

NORA: What is that?

HELMER: You no longer love me.

NORA: No; that is just it.

HELMER: Nora! — Can you say so!

NORA: Oh, I'm so sorry, Torvald; for you've always been so kind to me. But I can't help it. I do not love you any longer.

HELMER: [*Mastering himself with difficulty.*] Are you clear and certain on this point too?

NORA: Yes, quite. That is why I will not stay here any longer.

HELMER: And can you also make clear to me how I have forfeited your love?

NORA: Yes, I can. It was this evening, when the miracle did not happen; for then I saw you were not the man I had imagined.

HELMER: Explain yourself more clearly; I don't understand.

NORA: I have waited so patiently all these eight years; for of course I saw clearly enough that miracles don't happen every day. When this crushing blow threatened me, I said to myself so confidently, "Now comes the miracle!" When Krogstad's letter lay in the box, it never for a moment occurred to me that you would think of submitting to that man's conditions. I was convinced that you would say to him, "Make it known to all the world"; and that then ——

HELMER: Well? When I had given my own wife's name up to disgrace and shame——?

NORA: Then I firmly believed that you would come forward, take everything upon yourself, and say, "I am the guilty one."

HELMER: Nora——!

NORA: You mean I would never have accepted such a sacrifice? No, certainly not. But what would my assertions have been worth in opposition to yours?—That was the miracle that I hoped for and dreaded. And it was to hinder that that I wanted to die.

HELMER: I would gladly work for you day and night, Nora—bear sorrow and want for your sake. But no man sacrifices his honor, even for one he loves.

NORA: Millions of women have done so.

HELMER: Oh, you think and talk like a silly child.

NORA: Very likely. But you neither think nor talk like the man I can share my life with. When your terror was over—not for what threatened me, but for yourself—when there was nothing more to fear—then it seemed to you as though nothing had happened. I was your lark again, your doll, just as before— whom you would take twice as much care of in future, because she was so weak and fragile. [*Stands up.*] Torvald—in that moment it burst upon me that I had been living here these eight years with a strange man, and had borne him three children.—Oh, I can't bear to think of it! I could tear myself to pieces!

HELMER: [*Sadly.*] I see it, I see it; an abyss has opened between us.—But, Nora, can it never be filled up?

NORA: As I now am, I am no wife for you.

HELMER: I have strength to become another man.

NORA: Perhaps—when your doll is taken away from you.

HELMER: To part—to part from you! No, Nora, no; I can't grasp the thought.

NORA: [*Going into room on the right.*] The more reason for the thing to happen.

[*She comes back with outdoor things and a small travelling bag, which she places on a chair.*]

HELMER: Nora, Nora, not now! Wait till tomorrow.

NORA: [*Putting on cloak.*] I can't spend the night in a strange man's house.

HELMER: But can we not live here, as brother and sister——?

NORA: [*Fastening her hat.*] You know very well that wouldn't last long. [*Puts on the shawl.*] Good-bye, Torvald. No, I won't go to the children. I know they are in better hands than mine. As I now am, I can be nothing to them.

HELMER: But some time, Nora—sometime——?

NORA: How can I tell? I have no idea what will become of me.

HELMER: But you are my wife, now and always!

NORA: Listen, Torvald—when a wife leaves her husband's house, as I am doing, I have heard that in the eyes of the law he is free from all duties towards her. At any rate, I release you from all duties. You must not feel yourself bound, any more than I shall. There must be perfect freedom on both sides. There, I give you back your ring. Give me mine.

HELMER: That too?

NORA: That too.

HELMER: Here it is.

NORA: Very well. Now it is all over. I lay the keys here. The servants know about everything in the house—better than I do. Tomorrow, when I have started, Christina will come to pack up the things I brought with me from home. I will have them sent after me.

HELMER: All over! all over! Nora, will you never think of me again?

NORA: Oh, I shall often think of you, and the children, and this house.

HELMER: May I write to you, Nora?

NORA: No—never. You must not.

HELMER: But I must send you——

NORA: Nothing, nothing.

HELMER: I must help you if you need it.

NORA: No, I say. I take nothing from strangers.

HELMER: Nora—can I never be more than a stranger to you?

NORA: [*Taking her travelling bag.*] Oh, Torvald, then the miracle of miracles would have to happen——

HELMER: What is the miracle of miracles?

NORA: Both of us would have to change so that—— Oh, Torvald, I no longer believe in miracles.

HELMER: But *I* will believe. Tell me! We must so change that——?

NORA: That communion between us shall be a marriage. Good-bye. [*She goes out by the hall door.*]

HELMER: [*Sinks into a chair by the door with his face in his hands.*] Nora! Nora! [*He looks round and rises.*] Empty. She is gone. [*A hope springs up in him.*] Ah! The miracle of miracles——?!

[*From below is heard the reverberation of a heavy door closing.*]

The Emancipation of Women

In classical Rome, *emancipation* was a term used to denote a father setting his son free from his authority; by the nineteenth century, the term had come to mean freeing men, women, and children from slavery, an institution described by its defenders as paternal. The emancipation, or abolition, movement begun in the late eighteenth century at about the same time as the French and American revolutions, became one of the defining movements of the 1800s, which might be called the century of emancipation. Emancipation was central to much of the philosophical, economic, and political thought of the period.

The forces of urbanization and industrialization that led to the decline of slavery also undermined traditional roles for women. As women entered the industrial workforce and were educated for positions outside the home, they challenged their traditional subordination to men. The concept of emancipation spread from the abolition of slavery to the feminist movement in which women sought to free themselves from the suffocating domesticity that defined women's roles in the mid-Victorian era. The watershed year for American feminists was 1848, when a convention held in Seneca Falls, New York, led by Elizabeth Cady Stanton and Lucretia Mott, adopted a series of resolutions modeled on the Declaration of Independence that amounted to a manifesto of the women's rights movement. By the last two decades of the century the movement had fostered a generation of women who questioned patriarchal authority and sought equal property rights as well as the right to vote.

> Could we have foreseen, when we called that convention, the ridicule, persecution, and misrepresentation that the demand for woman's political, religious, and social equality would involve; the long, weary years of waiting and hoping without success; I fear we should not have had the courage and conscience to begin such a protracted struggle, nor the faith and hope to continue the work.
>
> —ELIZABETH CADY STANTON, letter to Lucretia Mott, July 19, 1876

Women are supposed to be very calm generally: but women feel just as men feel; they need exercise for their faculties and a field for their efforts as much as their brothers do; they suffer from too rigid a restraint, too absolute a stagnation, precisely as men would suffer; and it is narrow-minded in their more privileged fellow-creatures to say that they ought to confine themselves to making puddings and knitting stockings, to playing on the piano and embroidering bags. It is thoughtless to condemn them, or laugh at them, if they seek to do more or learn more than custom has pronounced necessary for their sex.

—CHARLOTTE BRONTË,
Jane Eyre, 1847

Eugène Delacroix, *July 28th 1830, Liberty Leading the People*. Oil on canvas
On July 28, 1830, the revolution in France replaced the reactionary King Charles X with Louis Philippe, the "Citizen King." Although Louis Philippe was thought to bring liberty to France, he, too, ended up abdicating, during the revolution of February 1848. Nevertheless, this painting, celebrating the revolutionary ideals of liberty and freedom as well as the date Louis Philippe took power, stands as a worldwide symbol of emancipation from tyranny. (Art Resource)

Although Ibsen denied any feminist intent in writing *A Doll's House* (p. 1065), Nora's rejection of her domestic dependency expresses a growing awareness among women at the time. By refusing to play any longer the hypocritical role that Charles Dickens described in *David Copperfield* as "the child wife," Nora turns her back on her unequal marriage and seeks an independent life. She is a precursor to the figure of the "New Woman" who emerged in literature at the turn of the twentieth century in figures like Sue Bridehead in Thomas Hardy's *Jude the Obscure* (1895) and George Bernard Shaw's Vivie in *Mrs. Warren's Profession* (1894). These educated and financially independent women rejected domesticity, dressed and acted unconventionally, and demanded sexual freedom and an equal voice in public affairs.

THE FEMINIST CONTEXT

Although many of the works portraying the New Woman were written by male authors, some of them expressing their uneasiness with the changing gender roles of the time, many women writers also reflected the era's growing awareness of the situation of Western women and their desire to be free from oppression. As the commercial marketplace for literature expanded opportunities for writers to earn a living by their work, many women addressed women's issues, writing especially for the growing number of women readers. Among the important women writers who wrote about such topics were Charlotte Brontë (1816–1855) and George Eliot (Mary Ann Evans, 1819–1880) in England; George Sand (Amandine Aurore Dupin, 1804–1876) in France; Harriet Beecher Stowe (1811–1896) in the United States; and Emilia Pardo Bazán (1852–1921) in Spain, whose ironic treatment of the violent inequality in marriage is succinctly developed in "**The Revolver.**"

A similar consciousness was emerging in non-Western societies, as indicated in works by **Higuchi Ichiyo** and Rassundari Devi. Ichiyo's "**The Thirteenth Night**" echoes *A Doll's House* as it recounts

p. 1122

hee-GOO-chee
ee-chee-YOH

p. 1126

"Franchise for females," "Pray clear the way for these A-Persons," *Punch*, March 30, 1867. Engraving
This satirical drawing criticizes women's voting rights and John Stuart Mill (center), a highly influential thinker and writer on the issue of personal freedom. Mill is making way for women to vote, as angered men look on. (Mary Evans Picture Library)

its heroine's struggle to decide whether to leave her marriage. Her painful decision to return to her husband contrasts with Nora's decision to leave, but the family and cultural context in which she lives explains her choice.

uh-MAR jee-BAHN

p. 1138

ruh-soon-DAH-ree

DAY-vee

In her autobiography, *Amar Jiban,* **Rassundari Devi** describes the experience of being a child bride in traditional Indian village culture. Married at twelve to a stranger, Devi is separated from her family and assigned an unfamiliar role in a new household. Though not composed as a political polemic, *Amar Jiban* has many themes in common with other emancipation literature of the nineteenth century: the confining cultural restraints that make her a virtual prisoner in her husband's household, her sense of isolation and abandonment, her desire to read and write. Devi's diary thus became a document in the cause of the emancipation of women.

■ **PRONUNCIATION**

Amar Jiban: uh-MAR jee-BAHN
Higuchi Ichiyo: hee-GOO-chee ee-chee-YOH
Jūsan'ya: joo-sahn-YAH
Nitsuko: NEE-tsoo-koh
Oseki: oh-SHE-kee
Palanquin: puh-LANG-kwin
Potajia: poh-tah-JAH
Ramdia: rahm-DEE-uh
Rassundari Devi: ruh-soon-DAH-ree DAY-vee
Roku: ROH-koo
Ryusenji: ryoo-SEN-jee

✎ EMILIA PARDO BAZÁN
B. SPAIN, 1852–1921

www   For more information about Pardo Bazán and a quiz on her work, see bedford stmartins.com/ worldlitcompact.

Emilia Pardo Bazán is Spain's foremost woman novelist. Time has blunted the controversial edge of some of her intellectual positions and softened the scandal that some of her writings created when they first appeared. She is now recognized as one of the masters of Realist fiction, especially the short story, in which, as Walter Pattison points out, "there is no other Spaniard who is her equal." Besides nineteen novels, Pardo Bazán wrote twenty-one novellas, several important works of literary criticism, and nearly six hundred short stories. Aside from her feminism, she was politically conservative and did not believe that democracy could solve Spain's problems. She died in 1921.

An outspoken advocate for more opportunities for women, Pardo Bazán campaigned unsuccessfully to gain entry for herself and other women writers into the Royal Academy and successfully to be appointed a professor at the University of Madrid. She rejected the nearly universal assumption in Spain that the only role for women was marriage, and she had little respect for women whose lives were defined by that institution. Their "uselessness and intolerable insipidity," she asserted in *The Test* (*La prueba,* 1890) with characteristic bluntness, "was the combined product of a dull life, lack of education, narrowness of views, and frivolity." Many of her novels and stories were concerned with the situation of women in nineteenth-century society. She blamed Spain's sexist institutions for denying women educational opportunities and recognition for their achievements, but she also found fault with women who acquiesced in their own oppression.

Many of Pardo Bazán's short stories explore the psychological issues treated in her later novels and are surprisingly modern. Taking French Realist writer **Guy de Maupassant** (1850–1893), whom she considered "the master of short story writers," as her mentor, Pardo Bazán sought to match his "impeccable execution, the simplicity of his recourses, his mastery of composition, and the sobriety of his style." She wanted to achieve similar succinctness and focus, using a single subject and creating a single effect, and she often used the device so frequent in Maupassant of the surprise ending. In "The Pearls," for example, a story that recalls Maupassant's "The Necklace," a husband gives his wife expensive pearls only to find them at the apartment of his best friend, with whom his wife has had an assignation. The irony and corrosive cynicism in many of Pardo Bazán's stories also call to mind Maupassant.

Pardo Bazán also sought objectivity in her technique. Her stories are often told by a peripheral character within the tale who effaces the author as narrator. Pardo Bazán is thus also able to add a layer of irony to the stories: The older woman in "The Revolver," for example, can observe the young widow and provide information that enables the reader to assess the reliability of her account. First published in 1895, this story is one of Pardo Bazán's many feminist works.

The translation of "The Revolver" by Angel Flores done for a bilingual collection of Spanish stories was a rare translation of Pardo Bazán's work at the time it was published in 1960. Recent interest in women's writing has prompted the publication of two volumes of her stories in English translation since 1990.

In the short story there is no other Spaniard who is her equal.

–WALTER PATTISON, *Emilia Pardo Bazán,* 1971

p. 1048

❧ The Revolver

Translated by Angel Flores

In a burst of confidence, one of those provoked by the familiarity and companionship of bathing resorts, the woman suffering from heart trouble told me about her illness, with all the details of chokings, violent palpitations, dizziness, fainting spells, and collapses, in which one sees the final hour approach. . . . As she spoke, I looked her over carefully. She was a woman of about thirty-five or thirty-six, maimed by suffering; at least I thought so, but, on closer scrutiny, I began to suspect that there was something more than the physical in her ruin. As a matter of fact, she spoke and expressed herself like someone who had suffered a good deal, and I know that the ills of the body, when not of imminent gravity, are usually not enough to produce such a wasting away, such extreme dejection. And, noting how the broad leaves of the plane tree, touched with carmine by the artistic hand of autumn, fell to the ground majestically and lay stretched out like severed hands, I remarked, in order to gain her confidence, on the passing of all life, the melancholy of the transitoriness of everything . . .

"Nothing is anything," she answered, understanding at once that not curiosity but compassion was beckoning at the gates of her spirit. "Nothing is anything . . . unless we ourselves convert that nothing into something. Would to God we could see everything, always, with the slight but sad emotion produced in us by the fall of this foliage on the sand."

The sickly flush of her cheeks deepened, and then I realized that she had probably been very beautiful, although her beauty was effaced and gone, like the colors of a fine picture over which is passed cotton saturated with alcohol. Her blond, silky hair showed traces of ash, premature gray hair. Her features had withered away; her complexion especially revealed those disturbances of the blood which are slow poisonings, decompositions of the organism. Her soft blue eyes, veined with black, must have once been attractive, but now they were disfigured by something worse than age; a kind of aberration, which at certain moments lent them the glitter of madness.

We grew silent: but my way of contemplating her expressed my pity so plainly that she, sighing for a chance to unburden her heavy heart, made up her mind, and stopping from time to time to breathe and regain her strength, she told me the strange story.

"When I married, I was very much in love. . . . My husband was, compared to me, advanced in years; he was bordering on forty, and I was only nineteen. My temperament was gay and lively; I retained a child-like disposition, and when he was not home I would devote my time to singing, playing the piano, chatting and laughing with girl-friends who came to see me and envied me my happiness, my brilliant marriage, my devoted husband, and my brilliant social position.

"This lasted a year—the wonderful year of the honeymoon. The following spring, on our wedding anniversary, I began to notice that Reinaldo's disposition was changing. He was often in a gloomy mood, and, without my knowing the cause, he spoke to me harshly, and had outbursts of anger. But it was not long before I understood the origins of his transformation: Reinaldo had conceived a violent, irrational jealousy, a jealousy without object or cause, which, for that very reason, was doubly cruel and difficult to cure.

"If we went out together, he was watchful lest people stare at me or tell me, in passing, one of those silly things people say to young women; if he went out alone, he was suspicious of what I was doing in the house, and of the people who came to see me; if I went out alone, his suspicions and suppositions were even more defamatory. . . .

"If I proposed, pleadingly, that we stay home together, he was watchful of my saddened expression, of my supposed boredom, of my work, of an instant when, passing in front of the window, I happened to look outside. . . . He was watchful, above all, when he noticed that my birdlike disposition, my good, child-like humor, had disappeared, and that on many afternoons, when I turned on the lights, he found my skin shining with the damp, ardent trace of tears. Deprived of my innocent amusements, now separated from my friends and relatives, and from my own family, because Reinaldo interpreted as treacherous artifices the desire to communicate and look at faces other than his, I often wept, and did not respond to Reinaldo's transports of passion with the sweet abandonment of earlier times.

"One day, after one of the usual bitter scenes, my husband said:

"'Flora, I may be a madman, but I am not a fool. I have alienated your love, and although perhaps you would not have thought of deceiving me, in the future, without being able to remedy it, you would. Now I shall never again be your beloved. The swallows that have left do not return. But because, unfortunately, I love you more each day, and love you without peace, with eagerness and fever, I wish to point out that I have thought of a way which will prevent questions, quarrels, or tears between us—and once and for all you will know what our future will be.'

"Speaking thus, he took me by the arm and led me toward the bedroom.

"I went trembling; cruel presentiments froze me. Reinaldo opened the drawer of the small inlaid cabinet where he kept tobacco, a watch, and handkerchiefs, and showed me a large revolver, a sinister weapon.

"'Here,' he said, 'is your guarantee that in the future your life will be peaceful and pleasant. I shall never again demand an accounting of how you spend your time, or of your friends, or of your amusements. You are free, free as the air. But the day I see something that wounds me to the quick . . . that day, I swear by my mother! Without complaints or scenes, or the slightest sign that I am displeased, oh no, not that! I will get up quietly at night, take the weapon, put it to your temple, and you will wake up in eternity. Now you have been warned. . . . '

"As for me, I was in a daze, unconscious. It was necessary to send for the doctor, inasmuch as the fainting spell lasted. When I recovered consciousness and remembered, the convulsion took place. I must point out that I have a mortal fear of firearms; a younger brother of mine died of an accidental shot. My eyes, staring wildly, would not leave the drawer of the cabinet that held the revolver.

"I could not doubt, from Reinaldo's tone and the look on his face, that he was prepared to carry out his threat, and knowing also how easily his imagination grew confused, I began to consider myself as dead. As a matter of fact, Reinaldo kept his promise, and left me complete mistress of myself, without directing the slightest censure my way, or showing, even by a look, that he was opposed to any of my wishes or disapproved of my actions; but this itself frightened me, because it indicated the strength and tyranny of a resolute will . . . and, victim of a terror which every day grew more profound, I remained motionless, not daring to take a step. I would always see the steely reflection of the gun barrel.

"At night, insomnia kept my eyes open and I imagined I felt the metallic cold of a steel circle on my temple; or if I got to sleep, I woke up startled with palpitations that made my heart seem to leap from my breast, because I dreamed that an awful report was ripping apart the bones of my skull and blowing my brains out, dashing them against the wall. . . . And this lasted four years, four years without a single peaceful moment, when I never took a step without fearing that that step might give rise to tragedy."

"And how did that horrible situation end?" I asked, in order to bring her story to a close, because I saw her gasping for breath.

"It ended . . . with Reinaldo, who was thrown by a horse, and had some internal injury, being killed on the spot.

"Then, and only then, I knew that I still loved him, and I mourned him quite sincerely, although he was my executioner, and a systematic one at that!"

"And did you pick up the revolver to throw it out the window?"

"You'll see," she murmured. "Something rather extraordinary happened. I sent Reinaldo's manservant to remove the revolver from my room, because in my dreams I continued to see the shot and feel the chill on my temple. . . . And after he carried out the order, the manservant came to tell me: 'Señora, there was no cause for alarm. . . . This revolver wasn't loaded.'

"'It wasn't loaded?'

"'No, Señora; and it looks to me as though it never was. . . . As a matter of fact, the poor master never got around to buying the cartridges. Why, I would even ask him at times if he wanted me to go to the gunsmith's and get them, but he didn't answer, and then he never spoke of the matter again.'

"And so," added the sufferer from heart disease, "an unloaded revolver shot me, not in the head, but in the center of my heart, and believe me when I tell you that, in spite of digitalis and baths and all the remedies, the bullet is unsparing. . . . "

✺ HIGUCHI ICHIYO (HIGUCHI NITSUKO)
B. JAPAN, 1872–1896

www For links to more information about Ichiyo and a quiz on "The Thirteenth Night," see bedford stmartins.com/ worldlitcompact.

The biography of Higuchi Ichiyo has all the elements of the mythic tale of the Romantic writer struggling in abject poverty to survive and to continue writing. The tale often ends with the writer's great work being discovered only after he or she has died. Ichiyo's story has a somewhat happier ending. Her talents were widely recognized in the final year of her life, but she died at the age of twenty-four from tuberculosis. Although she was writing at a time when many of the younger Japanese writers were excited by new ideas entering Japan from the West and were imitating European Realists like Flaubert and Zola, Ichiyo, educated in the Japanese and Chinese classics, drew instead on Asian sources. She is one of the important REALISTS of the late nineteenth century, and the realism of her stories has a distinctly Japanese character.

Ichiyo was born Higuchi **Nitsuko** in 1872, the fifth child and second daughter of an ambitious peasant farmer who managed to buy his way into the SAMURAI class in 1867, at the time when Japan was Westernizing and doing away with traditional class distinctions. He sent his bookish daughter to a private finishing school for girls that emphasized poetry writing and the study of literary classics. When Nitsuko was seventeen, her father died, leaving the three women of the household to support themselves. Nitsuko set out to learn how to write fiction, hoping that she could earn money as an author. Her first story, "Flowers and Dusk" ("*Yamizakura*"), was published in 1892. For this publication, following Japanese custom, Nitsuko took the literary name Higuchi Ichiyo, a common practice among Japanese writers, who are often referred to by their pen name alone. In the next two years, Ichiyo published several more stories, relatively plotless mood pieces about unrequited love, loneliness, and isolation.

The major change in her work came with her family's move to **Ryusenji,** the slums. There the streets and alleys were crowded with people on the fringes of society searching for ways to survive. The conventional ROMANTICISM of the early tales gave way to stories about the children of the streets, prostitutes, and the poor grubbing for money. The deaths of family members, financial hardship, and Ichiyo's experience in Ryusenji inspired a realism that tapped into the pain of her own struggle and melded with her training in classical poetry. The result can be called poetic Realism.

When she died, Ichiyo left behind several thousand poems — mostly from her school days — several literary essays, twenty-one short stories, and a multivolume diary. Her reputation rests on four or five of the stories and on the diary she wrote throughout her life, particularly the last five years. Her training as a poet had honed her skills at evoking mood and place, qualities ever present in her fiction. "The Thirteenth Night" ("*Jusan'ya*"), published in 1895, treats its realistic subject matter — the pain of **Oseki**'s abusive marriage and **Roku**'s struggle to survive — in the poetic context of a moon-viewing ceremony. The ironic use of both Realist and Romantic modes evokes the disillusionment that both characters experience as they recall their childhood dreams and return to the struggles of their adult lives. Ichiyo's inspiration was wholly Japanese. Had she lived longer, the promise of these early works would surely have flowered, earning her a place beside the other women who so importantly shaped the course of Japanese fiction — **Sei Shonagon** and Lady **Murasaki**.[1]

NEE-tsoo-koh

ryoo-SEN-jee

joo-sahn-YAH
oh-SHE-kee
ROH-koo

SAY shoh-NAH-gone
moor-rah-SAH-kee

---

[1] **Sei Shonagon** (c. 966–c. 1017): *The Pillow Book of Sei Shonagon,* a diary of Sei's observations and fascinations, is the earliest example of autobiographical fiction and is one of the great works of Japanese literature; *The Tale of Genji* by Murasaki Shikibu (978–1015), or **Lady Murasaki**, has been called the first great novel in world literature.

∾ The Thirteenth Night (Jūsan'ya)

Translated by Robert Lyons Danly

Ordinarily, Oseki rode in a handsome black rickshaw, and, when her parents heard the sound of it approaching their gate, they would run out to greet her. Tonight however, she had hired a rickshaw on the street corner. She paid the driver, sent him away, and stood dejectedly at the door to her parents' house.

Inside, she could hear her father talking in the same loud voice as always. "You could say I'm one of the lucky ones. We have good children. Never a speck of trouble when they were growing up. People are always praising them. And we've never wanted for a thing, have we? Don't think I'm not thankful."

He would be talking to her mother, then. It gave Oseki pause. How was she going to broach the question of divorce when they were so happy, so unaware of things? What a sermon there would be! She was a mother herself, and it wasn't easy, God knows, leaving little Tarō behind. It was a bit late now to be bringing her parents such startling news. The last thing she wanted was to destroy their happiness, as if it were so many bubbles on a stream. For a moment, she felt the urge to go back without saying anything. She could go on just as before—mother to Tarō, wife to Isamu—and her parents could go on boasting of a son-in-law with an imperial appointment. So long as she was careful, nothing would have to change. The little gifts of food they liked, the spending money now and then, all the filial courtesies would continue. But if she had her way and went through with the divorce, it would be the end of everything. Tarō would be miserable with a stepmother. In a single instant, her parents would lose the only reason they had to hold their heads high. There was no telling what people would think of her. And her brother's future—any basis for his success in life—would be swept away by her selfishness and her caprice. Perhaps she *should* go back home to her husband. No! She couldn't. He was inhuman, and she trembled at the thought of him and reeled against the lattice at the gate.

Inside they heard the noise. "Who's there?" her father called out. "Some urchin at the wrong house, I suppose."

But the sound outside turned to laughter. "Papa, it's me." It was a lovely voice.

"Who is it?" Her father pushed back the sliding door. "Oseki! What are you doing here? And without a rickshaw, or your maid? Hurry up—come in. What a surprise! No, we certainly weren't expecting you. Don't bother about the door, I'll get it. Let's go into the other room. We can see the moon from there. Here, use a cushion. No, no, use a cushion, the mats are dirty. I told the landlord, but he says we have to wait till the matting people can get around to making new ones. Don't be so polite with us—you'll get dirty if you don't take a cushion. Well, well, it's awfully late for you to be visiting. Is everyone all right?"

Her father treated her with the usual courtesy, and it made Oseki feel uncomfortable. She disliked it when they deferred to her as the wife of someone important.

"Yes, everyone's fine, in spite of the weather." There, she had managed to bring her emotions under control. "I'm sorry for not coming sooner. How are you?"

"I've been fine. Not so much as a sneeze. Your mother has one of her fainting spells now and then, but it's nothing to speak of. If she lies down for a few hours, it goes away." From his hearty laugh, she could tell he was in good health.

"I don't see Inosuke. Has he gone out somewhere? Still studying hard?"

"He's just left for night school. He's had a promotion, Oseki, thanks to you," her mother said ebulliently as she served the tea. "His supervisor is quite fond of him. Everything seems to be going well. It's thanks to our having Harada Isamu for a son-in-law, of course. Not a day goes by we don't acknowledge it. Ino isn't very good with words, and I know that when he sees Isamu, he probably doesn't express his gratitude as fully as he might. You know about these things, Oseki. I hope you'll let Isamu know how grateful we are to him, and always do your best to make him happy. See to it that he keeps on taking an interest in Ino. How is Tarō in this weather? This change in the seasons! I could do without it. Is he still up to his old tricks? You should have brought him with you tonight. Grandpa and I would have liked to see him."

"I thought I would, but he goes to bed so early. He was already asleep when I left. He really is full of the dickens, and he never listens to reason. When I go out, he wants to go too. He follows me around the house and keeps a good eye on me. He's a handful, all right! I don't know what makes him that way."

She felt overcome with remorse at the thought of the little son she had abandoned. In her resolve to find a new life, she had left him sleeping in his bed. He would probably be awake by now, and calling for her, giving the maids no end of trouble. No treats would placate him tonight. His nursemaid and the housekeeper would end up threatening to wash their hands of him and feed him to the devil if he didn't behave himself. "The poor thing!" she wanted to cry out. But seeing her parents in such a happy mood, she held her tongue. Instead, she took several puffs on her pipe, coughing into her sleeve to hide her tears.

"By the old calendar, it's the thirteenth night.[1] You may think I'm old-fashioned," her mother said, "but I made some dumplings to offer to the moon, like the old moon-viewing parties. I know you like them. I thought I'd have Inosuke bring you some. But you know how self-conscious he is, he didn't want to have any part of it. So I didn't send you any on the fifteenth, and then I didn't think I ought to start in now.[2] Still, I did want you to have some—it's like a dream, that you've come tonight. It's as if you read my mind! You must have all kinds of good things to eat at home, Oseki, but it's not often you can have your mother's cooking, is it? Let's see you eat some beans and chestnuts—you used to like them so when you were little. Tonight you can forget you're a married woman. Be your old self, don't worry about your manners.

"You know, your father and I are always talking about your success. What an extraordinary match you've made, how wonderful it is, the circles you move in, how impressive you are. But I'm sure it's not easy being the wife of someone as important

---

[1] **thirteenth night:** By the old lunar calendar, it was the thirteenth night of the ninth month. On this night, along with the night of the fifteenth of the eighth month, moon-viewing parties were held, and delicacies, including special dumplings, were offered to friends and to the moon. [Translator.]

[2] It was considered bad form to offer the dumplings on only one of the two moon-viewing dates. [Translator.]

as Isamu. Why, it's hard just to have people under you—maids to manage, guests to entertain. Not to mention the problem of coming from a poor family like ours. I'll bet you have to be on your toes all the time to make a good impression. Your father and I are well aware of all this. That's why we don't want to make a nuisance of ourselves, much as we would like to see more of you and little Tarō. Sometimes, you know, we pass in front of your gate, in our cotton clothes and carrying our old umbrellas, and we look up at the bamboo blinds on the second floor and wonder to ourselves what you're doing. Then we walk on by. If only your own family were a little better off, you wouldn't have to be so ashamed of us. With all your other problems, if your father and mother were from a higher station, it would be one less thing for you to worry about . . . But what good does it do to talk like this? I can't even send over any dumplings for moon-viewing without being ashamed of the box. I know how you must feel."

Delighted as she was with her daughter's visit, all too quickly the woman had recalled anew how seldom these occasions were, how little freedom she had to see her own daughter.

"I really am an undutiful child," Oseki said, as if to allay her mother's regrets about their humble station. "I may look grand dressed up in soft silks and riding in a private rickshaw, but I can't even help my own parents. I've only helped myself. I'd be much happier doing piecework and living at home with you."

"Don't be a fool!" her father said. "You should never talk that way. What married woman supports her parents? When you were here, you were our daughter. But you're married now, you're the wife of Harada Isamu. Your only responsibility is to Isamu—to make him happy and to manage his household. It's a big job, to be sure, but it was your fate to marry a man who's somebody, Oseki. You have to take the bad with the good. Women are always complaining. Your mother is the same way. What a nuisance it is. She's been irritable all day, just because she couldn't give you any of her dumplings. She's made such a fuss over those dumplings, you'd better eat them up and put her mind at ease . . . Good, aren't they?"

When her father made a joke of things, how could Oseki introduce what she had come to talk about? Dutifully, she began to eat the chestnuts and soybeans her mother had prepared.

In the seven years she had been married, Oseki had never called on them at night. For her to come alone and without a gift was completely unprecedented. Somehow, too, she did not seem quite as well dressed as usual. In their joy at seeing her, at first her parents failed to detect any difference. But she had brought not one word of greeting from their son-in-law, her smile seemed forced. It appeared that something was troubling her.

Her father glanced at the clock on the desk. "Say, it's almost ten. Is it all right for you to stay the night? If you're going back, you'd better be off pretty soon." As he watched Oseki, he tried to fathom what was on his daughter's mind.

There was no more time for pleasantries, and she looked him in the eye. "Papa, actually, I've come to ask you something. Please hear me out." Stiffly, she bowed before him. A tear trickled down her cheek. She was about to reveal now the layers of sorrow she had been keeping to herself.

Disconcerted, her father leaned forward. "What is it?"

"I came here tonight vowing never to return to Isamu. He knows nothing about it. When I put Tarō to bed, I knew I would never see him again. He won't let anyone else take care of him, but I tricked him. I waited for him to fall asleep, and then, as he dreamt, I crept away like an evil spirit. Papa! Mama! Please put yourself in my place! Until today, I've never mentioned our relations to anyone. I've had second thoughts a hundred times, a thousand times, but now my mind's made up, for once and for all. I can't go on another day like this. I must leave Isamu. Please help me. I'll take on any kind of work. I'll do anything to help Inosuke. I just want to live life alone." She burst into sobs and bit her sleeve to try to hold them back. It seemed as if the black bamboo pattern on her robe would turn purple from her tears.

"What happened?" her mother and father asked, drawing closer to Oseki.

"I haven't said anything until now, but if you could see us together for half a day, you'd understand. The only time Isamu talks to me is when he has something for me to do. And even then, he's always hostile. In the morning when he wakes up and I ask him how he slept, he turns the other way and makes a point of showing his indifference. 'The garden is doing well,' he'll say, or something like that. This alone would suffice to make me angry, but he is my husband, so I hold my temper. I've never argued with him. He starts in at me at the breakfast table, and it never stops. In front of the maids even he complains how I can't do anything right, how ill-bred I am. If that were all, I could endure it, but he never lets up. He slights me for my lack of learning. You should hear him dismiss me as 'a woman without any education.' Nobody ever said I went to school with the nobility. I admit I can't hold my own in a discussion of flower arranging or the tea ceremony or poetry or art with the wives of his friends. But if it embarrasses him so much, why doesn't he let me take some proper lessons? He doesn't have to announce publicly how lowborn I am, so that my own maids stare at me!

"You know, for the first six months or so after we were married, he was always at my side, doing everything he could for me. But as soon as Tarō was born—it's frightening how much a man can change! After that, I felt as if I'd been thrown into a dark valley, and I haven't seen the sunlight since. At first I thought he must be teasing. But then I began to understand: he had tired of me, and that was that. He bullies and bullies me in the hope that eventually I'll run away or ask for a divorce.

"Even if he were making a fool of himself over some geisha or keeping a mistress, I would control my jealousy . . . I hear rumors from the maids, but that's the way men are. When a man works as hard as Isamu, you have to expect he'll want to play sometimes. When he goes out, I lay out his clothes carefully, to please him. But no matter how hard I try, nothing I do satisfies him. The reason he doesn't spend more time at home, he says, is because I do everything so badly. I can't even seem to hold my chopsticks to suit him. If he would just tell me what it is he doesn't like, it wouldn't be so bad, but all he ever says is how boring I am, how worthless. He sneers and says he can never have a conversation with me because I don't understand anything, and that, as far as he's concerned, I'm just a wet nurse for Tarō! He's a monster, not a husband. He doesn't come right out and tell me to go away. I'm such a coward, and so attached to Tarō, that I listen to his complaints and never speak up.

Then he calls me a slug and says how can he care for anyone with so little spirit or self-respect? On the other hand, if I do stand up for myself in the slightest, then he *will* tell me to go. Mama, it means nothing to me to leave him. He's a great man in name only, and I won't have a moment's regret at being divorced.

"But when I think of Tarō, who can't possibly understand any of this, left with only one parent, that's when my resolve weakens, and I go on apologizing for myself and trying to humor Isamu, and trembling at the least little thing. That's how I've lived until today—quietly enduring everything. How unlucky I've been!" In pouring out her sorrows to them, Oseki had already said much more than she had intended.

Her parents looked at each other in amazement. "We never dreamt things were like this between you."

For a while no one spoke.

Like any mother, she was partial to her children, and, the more she had listened to Oseki, the more distressed her mother felt. "I don't know what your father thinks but, in the first place, we didn't ask Isamu to marry you. What gall he has, complaining about your schooling, or your family's position! Perhaps he's already forgotten how things were, but *I* haven't. You were seventeen and it was New Year's when he first saw you. It was the seventh day of January, in the morning. I remember it very clearly. The pine boughs were still up on the gate. We lived in the old house then, in Sarugakuchō. You were playing badminton out in front with the little girl next door. She hit the shuttlecock into Isamu's carriage as it was passing by, and you went running after him to fetch it. Oh, he was taken with you the minute he saw you. Those go-betweens of his began arriving fast and furious. He had his heart set on you. I don't know how many times we refused. Why, we told him over and over again that our social standing was no match for his, that you were still a child, that you hadn't had the proper training yet—that, given our circumstances, we could hardly arrange for a big wedding. But he wouldn't hear of it. No, no. He had no parents, he said, so there wouldn't be any in-laws making demands to worry about. It was his choice alone, and, as far as he was concerned, no need to fret about social status or anything of the kind. As for training in the polite accomplishments, he said you could take lessons after you were married. He was so persuasive in his arguments. What care he said he'd lavish on you! We never asked him for it, but he even provided funds for your trousseau. You really were the girl of his dreams.

"The reason we don't visit you more often," her mother went on, "is certainly not because we're intimidated by Isamu's standing. You're not his mistress, after all. You're his lawful wife. He begged us for your hand. We have nothing to be embarrassed about on that account. Still, he is so successful. We live a simpler life. We're not about to start hanging onto the coattails of our son-in-law. I couldn't stand to have people think of us that way. It's not out of false pride that we want to be correct in our relations with Isamu. That's why we haven't called on you as often as we would have liked.

"How stupid of us! When he treats you like some foundling! How arrogant he is! He has no right to grumble that you're not cultivated. Oseki, if you don't protest when he criticizes you, it will only get worse. It will become a habit, this abuse of his.

First of all, he shouldn't say such things in front of the maids. When a wife's authority is questioned, before you know it, none of the servants will even listen to her. And in front of Tarō! What will happen if he starts to lose respect for you? I think you should speak your mind. If Isamu won't listen, walk out. Tell him you have a family of your own to turn to. I think you've made a terrible mistake in keeping quiet until now. You're too well-mannered. He's taken advantage of that. It makes me sick, just hearing about this. There's no reason to take any more from him. I don't care what our 'status' is—you *do* have a father and mother, and a brother, even if he is still young. Why should you have to suffer like this? Isn't that so, Papa? I'd like to see Isamu once and tell him a thing or two!" In her wrath the woman had lost all perspective.

For some time, Oseki's father had been listening with arms folded and eyes closed. "Now, Mother, don't say anything rash. Hearing all this for the first time, I've been trying to think what we should do. I know Oseki wouldn't say these things without a good reason. It's plain how you've suffered. Does Isamu know you're here tonight? Was there a new flare-up?" He spoke to his daughter in measured tones. "Has he mentioned a divorce yet?"

"Isamu hasn't been home since the day before yesterday," Oseki said. "But that doesn't mean anything. Sometimes he stays away for five or six days. Before he left, he got angry with me for the way I'd laid out his clothes. I apologized profusely, but he wouldn't listen. He ripped the kimono off and flung it on the floor and changed into a suit, one he took out himself. He yelled at me as he went out. 'There couldn't be another man as unhappy as I am,' he said, 'with a woman like you for a wife!' Why is he like this to me? Three hundred and sixty-five days a year, he says almost nothing. Then, on the rare occasions when he does speak, it's to heap abuse upon me. In the face of all this, do you think I want to go on being the wife of Harada Isamu? How can I go on being Tarō's mother? How can I go on wiping the tears away year after year in secret? I don't understand why I should have to suffer so. I've finally made up my mind to forget him, and my child, too.

"You know, when I think back to the days before I was married, I have no unpleasant memories. But the way I feel now, miserable enough to abandon innocent little Tarō as he lies sleeping, I know I can't go on living with Isamu. 'A child grows up even without his parents,' they say. He might be better off without such an unfortunate mother. A stepmother or a mistress—someone who gets along with Isamu—might do Tarō more good than I can. His father might grow to like the boy. In the long run, it's for his own benefit. After tonight, I'll never set foot in Isamu's house again." She spoke bravely, but her voice quavered. It was not so easy to cast off the affection she had for her child.

"Well, no one can say you're being unreasonable," her father sighed. "I'm sure it's been hard on you. It sounds like a dreadful marriage." For a long time he studied Oseki's appearance. Almost without a father's recognizing it, his daughter had become the perfect matron: the proper hairdo fastened with a gold circlet, the black crepe jacket, it was all very tasteful. How could he watch her throw these things away? How could he let her change into a work coat, with her sleeves tied up and her hair pulled back, the better to take in washing or to tackle the scrubbing? And there was Tarō to think of. A moment's anger could dismantle a hundred years of good fortune, and she would then be the butt of ridicule. Once she went back to being the daughter of Saitō Kazue, all the laughter and tears in the world could never reinstate her as the mother of Harada Tarō. She might well have no fondness for her husband, but forgetting her child would not be so easy. After they were separated, she would find herself yearning for him more and more. She would come to long for those days when she endured the ordeal for the sake of being with Tarō. It was Oseki's misfortune to have been born so beautiful, and to have married above herself.

When he thought about her hardships, the man's pity for his daughter doubled. "Oseki, you may think I'm heartless, that I don't understand your situation. But I'm not saying any of this to scold you: when people come from different backgrounds, it's only natural their ways of thinking aren't always going to be the same. I'm sure you're doing your best to please Isamu. But that doesn't mean everything is fine and dandy—not in his eyes, anyway. Isamu is a smart man. He knows what's what. I don't think he means to be unreasonable with you. It's often the case, though: men who are hardworking and admired by the world can sometimes be very selfish. Away from home they hide their swollen heads. With their families they let their hair down; they take out all the discontent they bring home from the office. It must be terribly hard on you to be the target of all Isamu's grievances.

"On the other hand, your responsibilities as the wife of a man like Isamu are of another kind altogether. You're not married to someone in the ward office, you know—some fellow who lights the fire underneath the kettle for you and goes off to work every day with lunch box tied to his waist. You can't compare Isamu's place in society with an ordinary office worker's. Even if he is fussy and a little difficult sometimes, it's still a wife's duty to humor her husband. You can never tell, but I'd be surprised if there are many wives who enjoy completely happy relations with their husbands. If you think you're the only one in a bind like this, Oseki, it'll only embitter you. Fact is, it's a burden many people have to bear. What with the difference in your backgrounds, it's natural you'd meet with more suffering than a wife whose husband comes from the same class.

"Your mother talks big, but remember: the fine salary your brother is making is all thanks to Isamu. They say the light a parent sheds on his child is sevenfold.[3] In that case, the benefits we've received from Isamu must be tenfold! His way of helping out is to do things behind the scenes, but we're indebted to him nonetheless. It's trying for you, Oseki, I know. Think what your marriage means to us, though, and to Inosuke, and to Tarō. If you've been able to put up with things this long, surely you can continue. And how do you know a divorce is the answer? Isamu would have custody of Tarō, and you'd be my daughter again. Once the bonds are cut, there's no

---

[3] the light . . . sevenfold: "Nana hikari dokoro ka tō hikari mo shite" in the original, which alludes to the saying, "Oya no hikari wa nana hikari": The light (i.e., favors and influence) of one's parents is sevenfold. [Translator.]

going back—even for a glimpse of little Tarō. If you're going to cry over spilt milk, you might as well do your crying as the wife of Harada. All right? Wouldn't that be better, Oseki? Get hold of yourself and go home tonight as if nothing had happened. Go on being just as careful as you have been. Even if you don't tell us anything more after this, we'll know now, we'll all understand how you feel. We'll share your tears with you." As he urged his daughter to bow to the inevitable, he too wiped a tear from his eyes.

Sobbing, Oseki gave in to his advice. "It was selfish of me to think of a divorce. You're right. If I couldn't see Tarō, there'd be no point in living. I might flee my present sorrows, but what kind of future would I have? If I could think of myself as already dead, that would solve everything . . . Then Tarō would have both his parents with him. It was a foolish idea I had, and I've troubled you with the whole unpleasant business. From tonight I will consider myself dead—a spirit who watches over Tarō. That way I can bear Isamu's cruelty for a hundred years to come. You've convinced me, Papa. Don't worry. I won't mention any of this again." No sooner had she wiped her eyes than fresh tears came.

"Poor child!" her mother sobbed.

At that moment even the bright moon looked disconsolate. Even the wild grasses in the vase, picked by her brother Inosuke from the thicket along the back bank, swayed as if to offer their sympathy.

Her parents' house was at the foot of Shinzaka in Ueno,[4] on the road toward Surugadai. It was a shady, secluded spot. But tonight the moon shone brilliantly, and on the main street it was as light as midday. Her parents were not patrons of any of the rickshaw stations; from their window they hailed a rickshawman as he went by.

"Well, then, if you agree, Oseki, I think you'd better be off. Going out without permission while your husband's away, you'll have a lot of explaining to do. It's getting late. It won't take long by rickshaw, though. We'll come soon and talk about things. But tonight you'd best get back." Her father led her by the hand as if to drag her out. The pity he felt for Oseki did not preclude his desire to see the matter settled quietly.

Oseki was resigned to her fate. "That's the end of it, this talk. I'm going home. I'm still Harada's wife. Isamu mustn't know about tonight. Inosuke still has the backing of an important man. Don't worry. As long as you are all happy, I won't have any regrets. I won't do anything rash, so please, you mustn't worry. From now on, I'll consider myself Isamu's property. I'll do whatever he says. Well, I'd better go. Say hello to Inosuke when he comes home. Take care of yourselves. The next time, I'll come with happy news." It was apparent in the way she rose to leave that Oseki had no choice in all of this.

Taking her purse, with what little money she had, Oseki's mother went out to the rickshaw driver. "How much is it to Surugadai?"

---

[4] **Ueno:** District on the northern edge of Tokyo, a commercial center for the merchant and artisan classes. Surugadai was a shopping area to the south.

"No, Mother. I'll pay. Thank you anyway." Her voice was subdued as she touched her sleeve to her face to brush a tear. Quietly, she passed through the front door and stepped into the rickshaw.

Inside the house, her father coughed to clear his voice, and, from the sound of it, he too was crying.

The faint cry of crickets sounded mournful in the moonglow and the autumn wind. No sooner had they reached Ueno than Oseki was given a start.

"I'm sorry," the man said, abruptly putting down the poles of the rickshaw. "I can't take you any farther. I won't charge you anything."

Oseki was astonished. "What? What am I supposed to do? I'm in a hurry. I'll pay you extra, please try. I'm not going to find another rickshaw in a lonely place like this, now, am I? Come on, do stop grumbling and take me home." She trembled slightly as she implored him.

"I'm not asking you to pay double. I'm asking you to let me stop. Please get out. I can't take you any farther. I'm too tired."

"Are you sick? What's the matter?" She began to raise her voice. "You can't just drop me here and say you're tired."

"Forgive me. I'm too tired, really." He held the lantern in his hand and stepped aside from the poles of the rickshaw.

"What a selfish man you are! All right, I won't ask you to take me all the way, just to where I can find another rickshaw. I'll pay you — at least go as far as Hirokōji." She spoke in a soft voice to cajole him.

"Well, you are a young lady. I suppose it wouldn't be very nice of me to leave you here, in this forsaken spot. It was wrong of me. All right, let's go. I'll take you there. I must have scared you."

When he picked up the lantern to be off, he did not seem so rough, and Oseki breathed a sigh of relief. Feeling safe in his charge, she looked into the man's face. He was twenty-five or -six, of dark complexion and a wiry build. He was not very tall. Wait — that face now turned away from her in the moonlight! She knew it! His name was on the tip of her tongue, but she hesitated to utter it.

"Is it you?" she asked before she knew what she was saying.

"Hm?" Surprised, he turned around to look at her.

"Goodness! It *is* you. Surely you haven't forgotten me, have you?" She slipped down from the rickshaw, never taking her eyes from him.

"Saitō Oseki? I'm ashamed for you to see me like this. How could I have known it was you — without eyes in the back of my head? I should have recognized you from your voice. I guess I've gotten pretty stupid," he said, avoiding her look.

Oseki studied him from head to toe. "No, no. If we had met walking in the street, I wouldn't have recognized you. Until just now I thought you were a stranger, only a rickshawman. Why should you have recognized me? Forgive *me*. How long have you been doing this? You're not overworking yourself, are you? You look frail. I heard somewhere that your aunt closed the shop in Ogawamachi and moved to the countryside. I'm not the person I used to be, either. Things get in the way of what we want," she sighed. "I haven't been able to visit you or even write you a letter. Where are you living now? How is your wife? Do you have children? Now and then I go to see the shops in Ogawamachi.[5] The old store looks the same as always. It's the same tobacco shop, only it's called the Notoya now. Whenever I go by, I look at it and think to myself, 'That's where Kōsaka Roku lived when we were children.' Remember how we used to sneak a smoke on the way to school? What little know-it-alls we were! I've always wondered where you'd gone, what you were doing now. Anyone as gentle as you would be having a hard time of it. I worried about you. When I go home to see my parents, I ask if anyone's heard what became of you. It's been five years since I moved away from Sarugakuchō, and all that time I've never heard a thing. How I've missed you!" She seemed to have forgotten that she was a married woman as she deluged him with her questions.

"I'm ashamed how low I've fallen," he said as he took his towel and wiped the sweat from his forehead. "I don't even have a place I can call home any more. I sleep upstairs in a cheap inn in Asakusa[6] run by a man named Murata. Some days I spend the whole day there, doing nothing. Some days, like tonight, I work until late pulling the rickshaw. Then when I get tired of it, I loaf again: my life's just going up in smoke. I heard that you were still as beautiful as ever, Oseki, and that you were someone's wife now. I always hoped that, by some slim chance, I'd see you again and we'd be able to talk once more. My life isn't worth anything, I didn't think it mattered what happened to me—but if I hadn't gone on living, I couldn't have met you tonight. Gosh, I'm glad you recognized me! Thank you, Oseki." He looked down at the ground.

There were tears in her eyes as Oseki tried to console him. "You're not the only one to suffer in this sad world . . . Tell me something about your wife."

"You probably knew her. She was the daughter of the Sugitas, kitty-corner from us. The one people were always complimenting for her fair skin and her pretty figure. Well, I was leading a bad life—out carousing, never coming home—which one of my pig-headed relatives mistook for proof that I ought to get married. Mother put her glasses on and began looking for candidates and soon settled on the Sugita girl. She kept pestering me, so I finally gave in. We were married just about the time I heard that you were expecting. And then, a year later, people were congratulating us. But you don't think a few baby's toys were enough to make me change my ways, do you? People think that with a pretty wife a man will stop playing around, and with a child he'll become more serious. But it wouldn't have mattered what beauty of a wife I had. Ono no Komachi, Lady Hsi Shih, Princess Sotoori[7] herself dancing before my eyes—my bad habits wouldn't have changed. Why should a little thing that reeks of its mother's milk inspire some sort of religious awakening in a man? I fooled around

---

[5] **Ogawamachi:** An area of small shops south of Ueno.

[6] **Asakusa:** A district in northeastern Tokyo; formerly the pleasure quarters for the old Edo.

[7] **Ono . . . Sotoori:** All three women were legendary beauties. Komachi was the great poetess of the early Heian period, who was ranked by Ki no Tsurayuki as one of the Six Poetic Geniuses. Hsi Shih (Sei Shi in Japanese) was the beloved of a Chinese warlord in the Chou dynasty, who offered her to a rival who defeated him in battle. The rival thereupon became so enamoured of Hsi Shih that he neglected his state and let it fall to ruin. Sotoori-hime was a consort to Emperor Ingyō (376–453). [Translator.]

to my heart's content and drank myself silly. I neglected my family, I had no use for work. It got to the point where I didn't have a chopstick to my name. That was three years ago. My mother went to live with my sister, who had gone to the provinces to marry. My wife took the baby and returned to her folks. We haven't had a thing to do with each other since. The baby was a girl, anyway, so I never missed her much. I heard she died late last year of typhoid. Girls are precocious, though—I bet she didn't die without remembering her papa. If she'd lived, she would have been five this year. I don't know why I'm telling you all this—it's not really very interesting."

A smile played across his somber face. "If I'd known it was you, Oseki, I wouldn't have been so gruff tonight. Come on, get in and I'll take you home. I must have given you a good scare. You know, I'm not much of a rickshawman, even. I don't get any thrill out of clutching these poles, I'll tell you that. What does a fellow like me have to look forward to? Making a living like a horse, like some ox! You think I'm happy when I get a few coins? You think a little wine's going to drive my sorrows away? I'm really fed up with it. Who cares if I have a passenger? When I'm tired, that's it! I don't go any farther. Pretty selfish and disgusting, aren't I? Well, come on, get in."

"What! Do you think I could ride now that I know who you are? It was different when I didn't know it was you. But I will ask you to walk with me as far as Hirokōji. *Please.* I'm afraid to stay here alone. We can talk along the way." Oseki held up the bottom of her kimono as she walked. The clatter of her lacquered sandals rang despondently against the cobblestones.

Of all her friends, he was the one she had never quite forgotten: Kōsaka's boy at the tobacco stall in Ogawamachi, where everything was always ship-shape. Now his skin was dark and he looked pretty shabby, but in the old days he had cut a different figure, in his fine matched cottons and his snappy apron. What a charmer he was then! So friendly and grown-up. He was just a boy, but the store did better under him than it had when his father was alive. Everyone thought so highly of him, he was so intelligent. He had certainly changed . . . After her engagement was announced, as she remembered it, he had become another person, wild and dissipated. The decline was so extraordinary, it seemed as if some evil spirit had taken hold of him. That's what people said. And tonight he looked it. It was pitiful . . . She would never have dreamt that Kōsaka Roku would end up living in a cheap rooming house.

He had been in love with her once, and, from the time she was twelve until she was seventeen, they saw each other every day. She used to imagine it would be like to sit behind the counter of the tobacco shop, reading the paper and waiting on customers. But then a stranger came along and asked her to marry him. Her parents pressed her, how could she defy them? She had always hoped to marry Roku, though he had never made any overtures, it was true. In the end, her parents persuaded her, and she told herself that her dreams of helping Roku run the shop were only that— the dreams of a schoolgirl, puppy love. She put him out of her mind and resigned herself to marrying Harada. It had not been easy; until the last moment, there were tears in Oseki's eyes for Kōsaka Roku. He must have yearned for her, too. Perhaps she was even the cause of his ruin. How repellent he must find it to see her tonight, looking smug and matronly. She was not as happy and contented as she might look, she wanted to tell him. She turned to him, wondering what he was thinking, but his face was blank, and he did not appear to be rejoicing in this rare encounter.

They came out into Hirokōji. Here Oseki would be able to find a rickshaw. She took some money from her purse and gently wrapped it in chrysanthemum paper. "Forgive me, Roku, for being rude," she said, offering it to him. "Please buy yourself some paper handkerchiefs or something. I haven't seen you in so long—there are so many things I'd like to say. It's hard to put them into words . . . Take good care of yourself, Roku, so your mother doesn't worry. I'll pray for you. I want to see the old Roku I used to know, with that fine shop again. Good-by."

He took the paper from her. "I shouldn't accept this. But since it's from you, I will. As a keepsake. I hate to say good-by to you, Oseki. It's been like a dream, seeing you again. Well, I'll be going too, then. It's lonely on the road late at night, isn't it?"

He started off with the empty rickshaw behind him, and when he had gone a little way he turned back to look at her. He was heading east; she would be going south. The branches of the willow trees trailed beside her in the moonlight as she walked, dispirited, along the main road. One living on the second floor of Murata's boardinghouse; the other, the wife of the great Harada: each knew his share of sadness in life.

❧ RASSUNDARI DEVI
B. INDIA, C. 1810–?

Rassundari Devi's *Amar Jiban* (*My Life*, 1876) was the first autobiography to be published in Bengali. Born in the village of Potajia at the beginning of the nineteenth century and raised by her mother after her father's death, Rassundari, following Indian custom, was married at age twelve and sent to live in her husband's family home. In the following excerpt, she describes this traumatic episode; in later sections, she details the drudgery of her life as a housekeeper and a mother and tells of how she secretly taught herself to read and write, accomplishments that enable her to compose her autobiography as she nears the end of her life. Though Rassundari wrote without an ideological agenda, her story is an important text in the emancipation literature of the nineteenth century.

Our selections are translated by Tanika Sarkar, lecturer in history at the Jawaharlal Nehru University in Delhi and author of *Words To Win: The Making of Amar Jiban: A Modern Autobiography* (1987).

> If I am asked to describe my state of mind, I would say that it was very much like the sacrificial goat being dragged to the altar, the same hopeless situation, the same agonized screams.
>
> —RASSUNDARI DEVI

FROM

❧ Amar Jiban (My Life)

Translated by Tanika Sarkar

THE THIRD COMPOSITION

. . . The news made me very happy indeed. I would be married. There would be music, I would hear the women ululating. How exciting that would be! Yet I felt scared at the same time. I cannot express the apprehensions that came to my mind. Meanwhile the various things necessary for the ceremony began to arrive. Relatives and guests began pouring in. I was scared to death by all this. I did not talk to anyone and spent most of the time weeping. Everybody did their best to reassure me. They embraced me, but the unspoken agony in my mind did not lift.

Later on I was cheered up by the ornaments, the red wedding sari, and the wedding music. I forgot my earlier worries and went about laughing and watching the elaborate preparations. My happiness knew no bounds. When everything was over the next day, I heard people asking my mother, "Are they leaving today?" I thought they were referring to the guests. Then the music started. There was an air of festivity. The guests must be leaving now, I thought. It made me happy and I went about following my mother. Presently everybody assembled inside the house. Some looked happy, but others were in tears. That made me feel really frightened. Then my brother, aunts, uncles, and my mother all took me in their arms by turn as they burst into tears. Their tears made me so sad that I began to cry too. I knew mother was going to hand me over to the other family. I tightened my hold on her and pleaded, "Don't give me over to them, Mother!" That made everybody present even more upset. They broke down and tried to say nice words to console me. My mother took me in her arms and said, "You are a good girl, you understand everything, don't you? God is with us, you needn't be afraid. You are going to come back to us in a few days' time. Every girl has to go to her in-laws' house. Nobody else cries like this. There is no reason to be so upset. Please calm down and talk to me." But I was trembling all over with fear. I was quite unable to speak. Somehow I managed to say through my tears: "Are you sure that God will go with me?" Mother promptly reassured me that he most certainly would. "He will be with you all the time, so stop crying now." But in spite of her soothing words my apprehensions kept growing and I could not check my tears.

With great effort they took me away from my mother. I still feel sad when I think of the state of mind I was in and the agony I was going through. As a matter of fact it is indeed a sad thing to leave one's parents, settle in some other place, and live under other people. A place where your parents are no longer your own. But such is the will of God, so it is praiseworthy.

I clung to whomever came to pick me up and went on weeping incessantly. Everyone, old and young, was moved to tears. Eventually they managed to put me

---

[1] **palanquin:** A litter carried on the shoulders of two or four bearers.

into a palanquin,[1] which was not the one intended for me. No sooner was I seated inside than the bearers started marching off. With none of my near ones close by I sank into a deep depression. Since there was no way out, I started praying through my tears: "Please be with me, God." If I am asked to describe my state of mind, I would say that it was very much like the sacrificial goat being dragged to the altar, the same hopeless situation, the same agonized screams. I could see none of my relatives near me. I was miserable, and in tears I kept calling for my mother. I also prayed with all my heart as Mother had told me to. If you ever feel afraid, think of God, she had said.

All these thoughts went through my mind as I sat weeping. Very soon I felt too parched to cry.

THE FOURTH COMPOSITION

Unable to cry any more I fell into deep sleep. I had no idea what happened after that and where I was taken.

When I woke up the next morning I found myself on a boat with none of my relations near me. All the people who came and talked were strangers. I thought of my mother and other members of the family, the affectionate neighbors, my playmates. Where were they now and where was I? So I started to weep once again. My heart felt as if it would break. All the people in the boat tried to console me. But that increased my misery because their kind words reminded me of the affection of my own people. Tears streamed down endlessly — I just couldn't stop them. I cried till I was out of breath. Besides the boat ride was a new experience and it made me feel sick. All I could do in my desperation was to think of God, and I did that, though the predominant emotion I felt was fear. But Mother had said, speak the name of God if you are afraid. So I just kept on repeating my prayers.

Only God will understand the predicament I was in — nobody else can have any idea. Even now I remember those days. The caged bird, the fish caught in the net.

Since it was the will of God, however, it was no use feeling sorry for myself. I am only writing about what I felt at the time. I do not know how other girls feel. Perhaps they do not feel as miserable as I did. Actually there are no obvious reasons for my sadness but the tears came constantly because I had to leave my own people.

People put birds in cages for their own amusement. Well, I was like a caged bird. And I would have to remain in this cage for life. I would never be freed. We spent a few more days on the boat. Then I heard people say that we were about to reach home. For one moment I thought they meant my home. It gave rise to mixed emotions and also to fear. God only knows what went through my mind. All I could do was cry — I spent all my days and nights crying. Strange are the ways of God! Your laws are so wonderful! You have taken me from my dear mother and from others I love so much and have brought me to this distant place. That night we landed. We arrived at their house and saw different people taking part in all sorts of merrymaking. But none of them was from my part of the country. I did not know a single one of them. I began to weep again. I was so upset that the stream of tears did not cease. Everybody tried to assure me that this was my home — that all these people and everything that I saw was mine — and that I had no reason to cry. From now on I would have to live here and look after the house. There was no reason to be upset. But even as they spoke, my longing increased because I knew I wouldn't be able to see my family. Sorrow engulfed me like a raging forest fire. Those who have had such experiences perhaps know how useless words seem in times of sorrow. If somebody loses her son, is it wise to rebuke her? Or ask her not to lament, saying he must have been an enemy in an earlier birth: "He was not your son really. He wouldn't have left you if he had been so. He was a plunderer — don't ever utter his name. . . ."

The Fifth Composition

My day used to begin very early — and there was no respite from housework till long past midnight. I could not rest, even for a moment. But thanks to the grace of God I did everything in a spirit of duty. No work seemed too tiring. Because God wished it, I managed to gradually finish all the household tasks. I was only fourteen then. Around this time, the idea that I should learn how to read books entered my mind. But unfortunately girls were not supposed to read in those days. "What is the world coming to?" they used to say. "To think that women will be doing the work of men! Never heard of it before. In this new age even this has come to be true! These days women are becoming famous and men seem good for nothing. Such strange things never happened before. There was even a woman ruler on the throne. Who knows what other changes are in store for us! The way things are going, a decent man will very soon lose his caste. Pretty soon the womenfolk will get together and study books."

When I overheard these conversations I used to feel really scared. I had never dared to tell anyone about my desires — but now I became afraid that they might come to know what was on my mind. I dared not look at a page with written letters on it, in case they attributed it to my desire for learning. But I prayed constantly to God. I said, "Please, God, help me learn, so that I can read religious books. Dear God, friend of the poor, I invoke your name only for this." I used to say, "God, you have brought me so far from my village Potajia — a journey of three days and three nights to Ramdia. You have made me leave my friends and my relations and have brought me to this faraway place. And now, this village of Ramdia has become my home. How strange that is! When I did not know how to do any housework, even the slightest attempt would please my mother. She used to praise me before the others. Look at me now. I am no longer free. I have learned to work for others. And there is so much I should do. These people have become very dear to me. . . ." All these thoughts raced through my mind and I would shed tears, hiding my face in the sari that was drawn over my head. Nobody knew of my sorrow. How could they know, for my face lay hidden. "Only you knew because you are my father, my God, the heart of my heart, the life of my life, the very cream of kindness. I float in your kindness all the time. You have been with me through good days and bad days. You know all that I have experienced; I cannot keep anything back from you. . . ."

EMILY DICKINSON

B. UNITED STATES, 1830–1886

Stylistically, Emily Dickinson's poems may not have had much influence on succeeding generations of writers; it is hard to name a single poet whose poems look or sound like Dickinson's crafted miniatures. Still, her legacy has been vast in that she has taught writers audacity. The female voices that speak in Emily Dickinson's poems are daring, subversive, and uncompromising; they weigh old assumptions and find them wanting, speak of desires deemed improper by society, defy convention, and invite cataclysm. Dickinson's work reminds us that the Romantic hero, the person who tests the limits of God's and society's tolerance, who always thirsts for something beyond, who experiences suicidal despair and shattering joy, can be a woman writing in an upstairs bedroom.

www For more information about Dickinson and a quiz on her poems, see bedford stmartins.com/ worldlitcompact.

A Secluded Life.   In some ways, we know a fair amount about Emily Dickinson. But we know little of her inner life except that it was intense. We do not know the name or even the sex of the person to whom in the early 1860s she wrote a series of anguished and openly erotic love letters, nor do we know whether those letters were ever sent. And we do not know why, after a rather lively childhood and adolescence, she sought a more and more secluded life.

Dickinson was born on December 10, 1830, in Amherst, Massachusetts, a beautiful village in the Berkshire hills whose vigorous intellectual life centered around Amherst College, for which her father and later her brother Austin served as treasurer. The Dickinson children were in awe all their lives of their stern but affectionate father, and Dickinson was exceptionally close to her brother, Austin, and her sister, Lavinia. Dickinson herself had an excellent education at Amherst Academy, and later, a single year at Mount Holyoke Female Seminary. Dickinson's was not the typical watered-down "female curriculum" of her day; her basic knowledge of botany, astronomy, physics, theology, and other subjects is evident throughout her poems. At Mount Holyoke, Dickinson revealed her independent turn of mind. When Mary Lyon, the revered founder, asked the assembled students to rise if they hoped to become Christians, only Dickinson remained seated. As is abundantly evident from her poems, Dickinson balked at conventional pieties and at easy answers to theological questions.

The beginning of Dickinson's gradual withdrawal from society can probably be dated from her leaving Mount Holyoke. As many have pointed out, her isolation may have been strategic. The amount of housework, child care, and social obligation visited upon even an unmarried daughter in a large family allowed little time for poetry. Later in her life, in the upstairs bedroom where she did most of her writing, Dickinson once pantomimed for her niece the act of locking herself in her room, saying "It's just a turn—and freedom, Mattie!"

Worldly Contact.   After Dickinson's departure from Mount Holyoke, she made a few trips with her family. In 1855, she visited Washington and Philadelphia with her father, then serving a term in Congress. In Philadelphia she met the married minister Charles Wadsworth, perhaps the person to whom, in the late 1850s and early 1860s, she addressed the "Master letters," painful expressions of hopeless longing that may never have been mailed.

Dickinson had written poems from adolescence on, but in the early 1860s — the time of the emotional crises hinted at in the Master letters — her creativity burgeoned. In 1862, in response to an essay by Thomas Wentworth Higginson in *The Atlantic Monthly* giving advice to young would-be writers, Dickinson sent him four poems, asking him in an unsigned letter to tell her whether he thought they "breathed"; she penciled her name lightly on a card, which she enclosed in a separate envelope. Higginson was too conventional to appreciate fully Dickinson's work — he often objected to the unorthodoxy of her grammar and vocabulary — but he was a generous lifelong mentor. Her childhood friend Helen Hunt Jackson (1830–1885), author of the popular romance *Ramona,* also respected Dickinson's work and kept urging her to publish, but her pleas were largely in vain. Dickinson cringed at the way her few published poems were altered and regularized by editors, and her reluctance to have her work tampered with may partially explain why she didn't send more of it out into the world. Certainly, even those closest to her did not guess how prolifically she wrote. At times during the 1860s, Dickinson seems to have written one or more poems a day.

Last Years.   Death was never far from any nineteenth-century household, but particular deaths were especially painful for Dickinson — several young men she had known died during the Civil War; her father, in 1874; her favorite nephew, Gilbert, in 1883; her beloved friend Judge Otis Lord, the following year. Not only death, but the slow process of dying, was a very present reality for Dickinson. Her mother, no brilliant intellectual but a pleasant and nurturing woman when she was well, became essentially an invalid in 1855, and until her death in 1882 the responsibility of nursing her fell mostly to Emily and Lavinia, the unmarried daughters.

In 1882, Dickinson's adored elder brother Austin embarked on a passionate, adulterous affair with Mabel Loomis Todd, the artistic young wife of an Amherst professor, a relationship that would endure until Austin's death in 1895. The lovers did not seek to divorce their partners, although everyone in both families knew what was going on, and the affair seems to have been an open secret throughout the scandalized community. Emily and Lavinia, at whose house the lovers often trysted, were apparently caught in the crossfire of family loyalties, but neither sister recorded a word about the situation.

In her last years, Dickinson saw no one face-to-face except certain family members and household servants, allowing her rare guests to sit in an adjacent room and speak to her through a door left slightly ajar. She died on May 15, 1886, of Bright's disease, a chronic inflammation of the kidneys. Shortly afterward, Lavinia discovered nearly eighteen hundred poems in various drawers and initially gave them to Austin's wife, Susan, with the thought that Susan might oversee their publication. Two years later, when Susan had made no effort to do so, Lavinia took the poems back and gave them to Dickinson's old mentor, Higginson, and Mabel Loomis Todd, herself something of a poet. The two jointly oversaw two small editions of selected poems in 1890 and 1891; in 1896, Todd brought out a third selection. These editions did exactly what Dickinson had disapproved of previously with their smoothing-out and normalizing of her distinctive voice. Thomas Johnson's edition of 1955, nearly seventy years after Dickinson's death, was the first to attempt to reproduce the poems as Dickinson had recorded them.

The Poet's Voice.   Dickinson once claimed to Higginson that her major influences were Keats,[1] the Brownings,[2] and the Bible; elsewhere, she would name Shakespeare and her lexicon as the books she depended on. She disavowed knowing her greatest poetic contemporary, Walt Whitman, whose work she had been told was "disgraceful." But the style of her verse was shaped by very homely influences indeed — principally, the "common meter" of hymn books. Her poems were also influenced by valentines and memorial verses for the dead, both avidly written and collected by genteel Amherst residents.

With these conventional pieces for reading material and music, Emily Dickinson somehow forged her extraordinary poems, the more extraordinary because the revolutionary things they say occur within such everyday structures. In hymn meter, she wonders whether God is not playing a game of hide-and-seek with his children, one that might end, horribly, with the major player having gone away, leaving people staring at their deaths into a nothingness; she takes the supposedly comforting phrase "the Lord giveth, and the Lord taketh away" and pushes it to its logical extreme, envisioning a God who is at once a stingy banker, a sneaky burglar, and overall a father to whose capricious principles of spiritual economy we are subjected as he gives us people to love and then snatches them away. Elsewhere, she envisions ecstatic erotic unions with a figure who may be a mortal lover, a version of Christ, or both; in either case, these are poems that defy and demand more and harder answers than churches or preachers may provide. Dickinson prefers painful truth, however discouraging, to anything less. Her eye for natural subjects is matchless; like Whitman, she is able to see beyond the usual pretty

---

[1] **Keats** (1795–1821): John Keats, the most symbolic of the English Romantic poets; his work suggested ways of handling symbolism to Dickinson. See p. 778.

[2] **the Brownings:** Robert Browning (1812–1889) and his wife, Elizabeth Barrett Browning (1806–1861), two renowned British Victorian poets who married in 1846 and moved to Florence, Italy. Elizabeth was an invalid most of her life due to a youthful riding accident. Their precarious relationship and passionate poetry made them popular favorites in both England and America.

subject. Her poems deal with rats, frogs, snakes, and bats as well as blue-birds, and she looks steadily at nature's darker side.

Perhaps most compelling of all is Dickinson's exploration of female power and powerlessness. She unflinchingly records a dream in which a flaccid worm she'd thoughtlessly let stay in her bedroom turns into a menacing male snake "ringed with power"; she pictures a spirited girl child who inwardly thwarts all adult efforts to repress her; she envisions standing in relation to some master, whether God or a human lover, as a gun to its owner, with its explosive power to kill directed at fellow female creatures. In a poem that for many modern readers seems to evoke experience of repeated sexual abuse, Dickinson asserts that a woman's life amounts to brief moments of feverish freedom bracketed by long periods of helpless oppression.

In addressing such subjects Dickinson defied nineteenth-century theology, patriarchy, and the ideal of the woman as "the angel in the house." Coming from a woman in small-town New England in the nineteenth century, that was heroism indeed.

■ **FURTHER RESEARCH**

Editions
Johnson, Thomas H., ed. *The Poems of Emily Dickinson*. 3 vols. 1951, 1955.
Johnson, Thomas H., and Theodora Ward, eds. *The Letters of Emily Dickinson*. 3 vols. 1958.

Biography
Sewall, Richard. *The Life of Emily Dickinson*. 2 vols. 1974.

Criticism
Dobson, J. *Dickinson and the Strategies of Reticence: The Woman Writer in Nineteenth Century America*. 1989.
Farr, Judith. *The Passion of Emily Dickinson*. 1992.
Ferlazzo, Paul J., ed. *Critical Essays on Emily Dickinson*. 1984.
Howe, Susan. *My Emily Dickinson*. 1985.
Juhasz, Suzanne, ed. *Feminist Critics Read Emily Dickinson*. 1983.
Smith, Martha Nell. *Rowing in Eden: Rereading Emily Dickinson*. 1992.

❧ I know that He exists

I know that He exists.
Somewhere — in Silence —
He has hid his rare life
From our gross eyes.

'Tis an instant's play.
'Tis a fond Ambush —
Just to make Bliss
Earn her own surprise!

But—should the play
10 Prove piercing earnest—
Should the glee—glaze—
In Death's—stiff—stare—

Would not the fun
Look too expensive!
Would not the jest—
Have crawled too far!

I never lost as much but twice

I never lost as much but twice,
And that was in the sod.
Twice have I stood a beggar
Before the door of God!

Angels—twice descending
Reimbursed my store—
Burglar! Banker—Father!
I am poor once more!

A narrow Fellow in the Grass

A narrow Fellow in the Grass
Occasionally rides—
You may have met Him—did you not
His notice sudden is—
The Grass divides as with a Comb—
A spotted shaft is seen—
And then it closes at your feet
And opens further on—

He likes a Boggy Acre
10 A Floor too cool for Corn—
Yet when a Boy, and Barefoot—
I more than once at Noon
Have passed, I thought, a Whip lash
Unbraiding in the Sun
When stooping to secure it
It wrinkled, and was gone—

Several of Nature's People
I know, and they know me—
I feel for them a transport
20   Of cordiality—

But never met this Fellow
Attended, or alone
Without a tighter breathing
And Zero at the Bone—

❧   Split the Lark—and you'll find the Music—

Split the Lark—and you'll find the Music—
Bulb after Bulb, in Silver rolled—
Scantily dealt to the Summer Morning
Saved for your Ear when Lutes be old.

Loose the Flood—you shall find it patent—
Gush after Gush, reserved for you—
Scarlet Experiment! Sceptic Thomas![1]
Now, do you doubt that your Bird was true?

---

[1] **Sceptic Thomas:** "Doubting Thomas," the disciple who declared he would not believe Jesus had risen unless he could place his fingers in Jesus' wounds; see John 20:24–29.

❧   Safe in their Alabaster Chambers—

Safe in their Alabaster Chambers—
Untouched by Morning
And untouched by Noon—
Sleep the meek members of the Resurrection—
Rafter of satin,
And Roof of stone.

Light laughs the breeze
In her Castle above them—
Babbles the Bee in a stolid Ear,
10   Pipe the Sweet Birds in ignorant cadence—
Ah, what sagacity perished here!

❧ I died for Beauty — but was scarce

I died for Beauty — but was scarce
Adjusted in the Tomb
When One who died for Truth, was lain
In an adjoining Room —

He questioned softly "Why I failed"?
"For Beauty", I replied —
"And I — for Truth — Themself are One —
We Brethren, are", He said —

And so, as Kinsmen, met a Night —
10 We talked between the Rooms —
Until the Moss had reached our lips —
And covered up — our names —

❧ The Brain — is wider than the Sky —

The Brain — is wider than the Sky —
For — put them side by side —
The one the other will contain
With ease — and You — beside —

The Brain is deeper than the sea —
For — hold them — Blue to Blue —
The one the other will absorb —
As Sponges — Buckets — do —

The Brain is just the weight of God —
10 For — Heft them — Pound for Pound —
And they will differ — if they do —
As Syllable from Sound —

❧ I dwell in Possibility —

I dwell in Possibility —
A fairer House than Prose —
More numerous of Windows —
Superior — for Doors —

Of Chambers as the Cedars—
Impregnable of Eye—
And for an Everlasting Roof
The Gambrels[1] of the Sky—

Of Visitors—the fairest—
10 For Occupation—This—
The spreading wide my narrow Hands
To gather Paradise—

---

[1] **The Gambrels:** Slopes, as in the large, arched gable roofs.

I like to see it lap the Miles—

I like to see it lap the Miles—
And lick the Valleys up—
And stop to feed itself at Tanks—
And then—prodigious step

Around a Pile of Mountains—
And supercilious peer
In Shanties—by the sides of Roads—
And then a Quarry pare

To fit its Ribs
10 And crawl between
Complaining all the while
In horrid—hooting stanza—
Then chase itself down Hill—

And neigh like Boanerges[1]—
Then—punctual as a Star
Stop—docile and omnipotent
At its own stable door—

---

[1] **Boanerges:** A thunderous preacher.

❧ I heard a Fly buzz—when I died—

I heard a Fly buzz—when I died—
The Stillness in the Room
Was like the Stillness in the Air—
Between the Heaves of Storm—

The Eyes around—had wrung them dry—
And Breaths were gathering firm
For that last Onset—when the King
Be witnessed—in the Room—

I willed my Keepsakes—Signed away
10 What portion of me be
Assignable—and then it was
There interposed a Fly—

With Blue—uncertain stumbling Buzz—
Between the light—and me—
And then the Windows failed—and then
I could not see to see—

❧ In Winter in my Room

In Winter in my Room
I came upon a Worm—
Pink, lank and warm—
But as he was a worm
And worms presume
Not quite with him at home—
Secured him by a string
To something neighboring
And went along.

10 A Trifle afterward
A thing occurred
I'd not believe it if I heard
But state with creeping blood—
A snake with mottles rare
Surveyed my chamber floor
In feature as the worm before
But ringed with power—

The very string with which
I tied him — too
20 When he was mean and new
That string was there —

I shrank — "How fair you are"!
Propitiation's claw —
"Afraid," he hissed
"Of me"?
"No cordiality" —
He fathomed me —
Then to a Rhythm *Slim*
Secreted in his Form
30 As Patterns swim
Projected him.

That time I flew
Both eyes his way
Lest he pursue
Nor ever ceased to run
Till in a distant Town
Towns on from mine
I set me down
This was a dream.

∾   They shut me up in Prose —

They shut me up in Prose —
As when a little Girl
They put me in the Closet —
Because they liked me "still" —
Still! Could themself have peeped —
And seen my Brain — go round —
They might as wise have lodged a Bird
For Treason — in the Pound —
Himself has but to will
10 And easy as a Star
Abolish his Captivity —
And laugh — No more have I —

❧ Much Madness is divinest Sense—

Much Madness is divinest Sense—
To a discerning Eye—
Much Sense—the starkest Madness—
'Tis the Majority
In this, as All, prevail—
Assent—and you are sane—
Demur—you're straightway dangerous—
And handled with a Chain—

❧ I like a look of Agony

I like a look of Agony,
Because I know it's true—
Men do not sham Convulsion,
Nor simulate, a Throe—

The Eyes glaze once—and that is Death—
Impossible to feign
The Beads upon the Forehead
By homely Anguish strung.

❧ Wild Nights—Wild Nights!

Wild Nights—Wild Nights!
Were I with thee
Wild Nights should be
Our luxury!
Futile—the Winds—
To a Heart in port—
Done with the Compass—
Done with the Chart!

Rowing in Eden—
10 Ah, the Sea!
Might I but moor—Tonight—
In Thee!

❧   My Life had stood—a Loaded Gun—

My Life had stood—a Loaded Gun—
In Corners—till a Day
The Owner passed—identified—
And carried Me away—

And now We roam in Sovereign Woods—
And now We hunt the Doe—
And every time I speak for Him—
The Mountains straight reply—

And do I smile, such cordial light
10   Upon the Valley glow—
It is as a Vesuvian[1] face
Had let its pleasure through—

And when at Night—Our good Day done—
I guard My Master's Head—
'Tis better than the Eider-Duck's
Deep Pillow—to have shared—

To foe of His—I'm deadly foe—
None stir the second time—
On whom I lay a Yellow Eye—
20   Or an emphatic Thumb—

Though I than He—may longer live
He longer must—than I—
For I have but the power to kill,
Without—the power to die—

---

[1] **Vesuvian:** From Mount Vesuvius, in Italy; volcanic.

❧   The Soul has Bandaged moments—

The Soul has Bandaged moments—
When too appalled to stir—
She feels some ghastly Fright come up
And stop to look at her—

Salute her—with long fingers—
Caress her freezing hair—
Sip, Goblin, from the very lips
The Lover—hovered—o'er—
Unworthy, that a thought so mean
10 Accost a Theme—so—fair—

The soul has moments of Escape—
When bursting all the doors—
She dances like a Bomb, abroad,
And swings upon the Hours,

As do the Bee—delirious borne—
Long Dungeoned from his Rose—
Touch Liberty—then know no more,
But Noon, and Paradise—

The Soul's retaken moments—
20 When, Felon led along,
With shackles on the plumed feet,
And staples, in the Song,

The Horror welcomes her, again,
These, are not brayed of Tongue—

∾ Success is counted sweetest

Success is counted sweetest
By those who ne'er succeed.
To comprehend a nectar
Requires sorest need.

Not one of all the purple Host
Who took the Flag today
Can tell the definition
So clear of Victory

As he defeated—dying—
10 On whose forbidden ear
The distant strains of triumph
Burst agonized and clear!

TEXT IN CONTEXT

∾ JOSEPH CONRAD
B. POLAND, 1857–1924

**Portrait of Conrad,
c. 1911
*(Hulton/Archive)***

Joseph Conrad's life and work cross cultural boundaries, making him representative of many writers of the twentieth century. Born a Pole in Russian-occupied Poland, Conrad went on to become a French merchant-seaman and then an English seaman and citizen. When he began writing he composed in English, his third language after Polish and French. Although he was a proud British citizen and a Polish nationalist, he was in a broad sense a European: a man whose political identity transcended any single national definition. Conrad's experience as a sailor in many parts of the world further broadened his identity, making him a kind of world citizen. Like most of his novels, *Heart of Darkness* (1902) is rooted in Conrad's own experience, but in this work his personal story is objectified to become the narrator Marlow's story, a story about storytelling itself and about the cultural experience of Europeans in Africa, a story that German writer Thomas Mann is reported to have said "prophetically inaugurated the twentieth century."

A Polish Nobleman Cased in British Tar.   Conrad was born **Jósef Teodor Konrad Walecz Korzeniowski** in 1857 in **Berdyczew** in Russian-occupied Polish Ukraine. His father, Apollo, a writer and translator of French and English literature, was a Polish nationalist. His participation in revolutionary activities led to the family being exiled to the far north of Russia when Conrad was four. The physical hardships of the exile led to his mother's death when he was seven and to his father's death just a few years later. So Conrad, an imaginative and sensitive child, was raised from age eleven by an uncle, **Tadeusz Bobrowski**. Although he grew up far from the sea, the boy dreamed of a life as a sailor, and when

YOO-zef tay-OH-dore
KOHN-rahd
VAH-wench
koh-zheh-NYAWF-skee;
bare-DIH-chef

tah-DAY-oosh
boh-BRAWF-skee

he was sixteen he convinced his uncle to allow him to seek a seagoing career. He joined the French merchant service, became involved in gunrunning and an intense love affair, and attempted suicide. At twenty Conrad switched to the English merchant service, and for the next twenty years he worked his way up from seaman to mate and master. His voyages took him to many other parts of the world, including the East and West Indies, Asia, Africa, and South America. When he left the merchant service in 1894 he was fluent in three languages, a British citizen with multinational work experience, and a European with a knowledge of cultures throughout the world.

Novelist of the Sea.   Conrad's second career—as an English novelist—began in 1895 with the publication of *Almayer's Folly* and lasted until his death in 1924. During that period Conrad wrote thirteen novels, two books of memoirs, and twenty-eight short stories. He established friendships with a large number of British and American writers of the time, including H. G. Wells, Rudyard Kipling, W. H. Hudson, John Galsworthy, Henry James, Stephen Crane, and Ford Madox Ford, with whom he collaborated on three books. Many of his novels and stories take place on ships isolated at sea, as do *Typhoon* (1902), *The Nigger of the "Narcissus"* (1898), and *The Secret Sharer* (1912). Others are set in exotic locations Conrad visited as a sailor: the Malay Peninsula in *An Outcast of the Islands* (1896) and *Lord Jim* (1900), a South Sea island in *Victory* (1915), and a South American mining town in *Nostromo* (1904). Conrad often studied the failure of Europeans to maintain their personal and cultural ideals in these exotic and alien places. His novels with European settings, such as *The Secret Agent* (1907), describing the activities of anarchist provocateurs in London, and *Under Western Eyes* (1911), about revolutionaries challenging Russian despotism, also treat failures of idealism. For this recurrent theme of lost or corrupted idealism, Conrad has been described as a deeply pessimistic writer. But in spite of their shortcomings his heroes are often engaging and sympathetic figures who have an idealistic belief in themselves and who follow a romantic desire for freedom. It may be that all Conrad's novels hearken back to his childhood experience as the son of a Polish nationalist who died for ideals that failed to become political realities because of the weaknesses of human beings and the complexities and imbalances of political relationships.

Although he is usually described as a novelist of the sea, Conrad used the sea and exotic settings symbolically to write about the human situation and the human spirit. In the preface to *Nigger of the "Narcissus,"* he said of its shipboard setting: "The problem . . . is not a problem of the sea, it is merely a problem that has arisen on board a ship where

> [Conrad] seems to write books about the sea, the Malay archipelago and the Congo, but he is really writing about the desperate, convoluted, hopeless heart of man.
>
> – Anthony Burgess, writer, 1979

the conditions of complete isolation from all land entanglements make it stand out with particular force and colouring."

Conrad in Africa.   *Heart of Darkness* is based on Conrad's 1890 journey up the Congo River. Like his narrator, Marlow, Conrad was hired by a Belgian trading company to captain a steamship on the Congo, but when he arrived in Africa he found that the ship he was hired to pilot had sunk. Conrad was left to spend most of his time as a mate on another vessel, taking over as captain only briefly when the regular master was incapacitated. The journey upriver entailed bringing out the body of a trader, a man named Klein who had died at a trading post deep in the interior of Africa. In *Heart of Darkness,* Conrad spoke of his own experience in the Congo as a transforming one: "Before the Congo," he wrote, "I was just a mere animal." Shortly after returning from that trip, he gave up the sea and turned to storytelling as his profession. In retelling his African experiences in *Heart of Darkness,* Conrad transformed his personal history into myth.

Marlow's journey into the heart of Africa becomes a journey into the human spirit. Ostensibly it is an account of the truth about Kurtz, a man whose talents and achievements earned him regard as an "extraordinary" human being—a model of European enlightenment. But when Marlow arrives at Kurtz's camp, he discovers that in the depths of his being Kurtz is "a horror." Marlow also makes discoveries about himself and about his "kinship" with Kurtz.

Conrad and Marlow.   In many ways *Heart of Darkness* is as much about Marlow and storytelling as it is about Africa or Kurtz or ivory. As in much modern literature, the truth here is not in the tale but in the teller. The initial description of Marlow's method of storytelling, which opens the novel, is also a blueprint for Conrad's narrative technique: "The yarns of seamen have a direct simplicity, the whole meaning of which lies within the shell of a cracked nut. But Marlow was not typical . . . and to him the meaning of an episode was not inside like a kernel but outside, enveloping the tale which brought it out only as a glow brings out a haze, in the likeness of one of these misty halos that sometimes are made visible by the spectral illumination of moonshine." Although Marlow is never explicit about what he learns from his experiences, his psychological kinship with Kurtz, or why he lies to Kurtz's intended, his account raises questions about how and why he was able to survive his journey and about the ways he differs from Kurtz and the other Europeans. Did he prevail through superior understanding or greater strength of will or moral character, or was it because he had a more repressed personality than the others? To what degree did he avoid complicity with Kurtz and the other colonizers? How much of what he tells us can we believe? What might he be trying to hide or repress that would make his account, at least to some extent, unreliable? What knowledge is he trying to pass on to those aboard the *Nellie*? There are hints but no definitive answers to these questions in the story.

Conrad and Colonialism.   Part of the "shell" that envelops Marlow's story is his critique of European colonialism. When Marlow compares Africa in the nineteenth century to England at the time of the Romans, he implies that his story is about colonialism and greed, about what he calls "the squeeze." Marlow's descriptions of the ivory trade and the European presence in Africa are solidly based on historical fact. In 1890, the Congo was in effect the personal domain of King Leopold II of Belgium, who promoted the commercial exploitation of the Congo's

Two Youths from the Congo
King Leopold of Belgium was notorious for his troops' ruthless treatment of Africans. Here, two boys bear the injury of contact with Belgian colonial soldiers. The boy on the left lost his hands to gangrene after soldiers bound him too tightly. The boy on the right had his hand cut off. (Courtesy of Anti-Slavery International, London)

resources and the virtual enslavement of its native people. Historical accounts confirm that there is no exaggeration in the excesses described by Marlow. He is clearly appalled by what he finds in Africa: the mistreatment of natives, the venality and hypocrisy of the Europeans, the colossal corruption at the inner station. He also suggests that these shortcomings are not unique to colonizers in Africa, but rather are deep drives of the human character and will manifest themselves if allowed unrestrained expression. In Kurtz, Marlow sees a monstrous reflection of himself. He is, at least in part, horrified by what he sees.

CHIN-wah
ah-CHAY-bay

Nigerian novelist **Chinua Achebe** has attacked this "European" story as an example of literary colonialism and European racism. *Heart of Darkness* is not about Africa, Achebe argues, for Conrad's Africa has no reality and the natives no individuality, no names. For Conrad, Marlow, and Europeans, he says, Africa and Africans are "other"—objects against which the Europeans define their own individuality. As critical as they may be of the abuses of the ivory trade, they, too, are exploiting Africa to reconstruct a European civilization by contrasting it with both black and white savagery in Africa. Achebe delivered his attack in a 1975 speech, "**An Image of Africa,**" at the University of Massachusetts long after Conrad's death—testimony to the enduring currency of Conrad's story and to the centrality of the questions it raises.

p. 1722

A Story about European Culture.   Marlow's experience is enlightening as well as horrifying. He has gained wisdom from his time in Africa, as his pose in the last scene as a meditating Buddha suggests. But he has acquired more than personal wisdom. Like epic heroes who journey to the underworld to gain the knowledge that will enable them to found nations, Marlow has traveled to Africa to recover what Europe—the "whited sepulchre"—has lost, repressed, or forgotten. In gaining that knowledge, Marlow's personal story becomes a cultural story, a modern epic about a deadened and wasted culture seeking to recover the vital heart of its humanity. His mission has been a dangerous and spiritually expensive one, and it is unclear how successful he was and whether what he gained was worth the horror.

My task which I am trying to achieve is, by the power of the written word, to make you hear, to make you feel — it is, before all, to make you *see*.

– JOSEPH CONRAD, Preface to *The Nigger of the "Narcissus"*

■ **FURTHER RESEARCH**

Biography
Baines, Jocelyn. *Joseph Conrad: A Critical Biography.* 1960.
Karl, Frederick. *Joseph Conrad: The Three Lives.* 1979.

Criticism
Adelman, Gary. *Heart of Darkness: Search for the Unconscious.* 1987.
Firchow, Peter Edgerly. *Envisioning Africa: Racism and Imperialism in Conrad's* Heart of Darkness. 2000.

Guerard, Albert. *Conrad the Novelist.* 1958.

Karl, Frederick. *A Reader's Guide to Joseph Conrad.* 1997.

Kimbrough, Robert, ed. Heart of Darkness: *An Authoritative Text, Backgrounds and Sources, Criticism.* 1988.

Lee, R. F. *Conrad's Colonialism.* 1969.

Murfin, Ross C., ed. *Joseph Conrad,* Heart of Darkness. *A Case Study in Contemporary Criticism.* 1989.

Page, Norman. *A Conrad Companion.* 1985.

■ **PRONUNCIATION**

Chinua Achebe: CHIN-wah ah-CHAY-bay

Berdyczew: bare-DIH-chef

Tadeusz Bobrowski: tah-DAY-oosh boh-BRAWF-skee

Jósef Teodor Konrad Walecz Korzeniowski: YOO-zef tay-OH-dore KOHN-rahd VAH-wench koh-zheh-NYAWF-skee

Nostromo: nah-STROH-moh

www For more information about Conrad and a quiz on *Heart of Darkness,* see bedford stmartins.com/ worldlitcompact.

∾ Heart of Darkness

1

The *Nellie,* a cruising yawl, swung to her anchor without a flutter of the sails, and was at rest. The flood had made, the wind was nearly calm, and being bound down the river, the only thing for it was to come to and wait for the turn of the tide.

The sea-reach of the Thames stretched before us like the beginning of an interminable waterway. In the offing[1] the sea and the sky were welded together without a joint, and in the luminous space the tanned sails of the barges drifting up with the tide seemed to stand still in red clusters of canvas sharply peaked, with gleams of varnished sprits. A haze rested on the low shores that ran out to sea in vanishing flatness. The air was dark above Gravesend, and farther back still seemed condensed into a mournful gloom, brooding motionless over the biggest, and the greatest, town on earth.

The Director of Companies was our captain and our host. We four affectionately watched his back as he stood in the bows looking to seaward. On the whole river there was nothing that looked half so nautical. He resembled a pilot, which to a seaman is trustworthiness personified. It was difficult to realize his work was not out there in the luminous estuary, but behind him, within the brooding gloom.

Between us there was, as I have already said somewhere, the bond of the sea. Besides holding our hearts together through long periods of separation, it had the effect of making us tolerant of each other's yarns—and even convictions. The Lawyer—the best of old fellows—had, because of his many years and many virtues, the only cushion on deck, and was lying on the only rug. The Accountant had brought out already a box of dominoes, and was toying architecturally with the bones. Marlow sat cross-legged right aft, leaning against the mizzen-mast. He had sunken cheeks, a

---

[1] offing: The horizon.

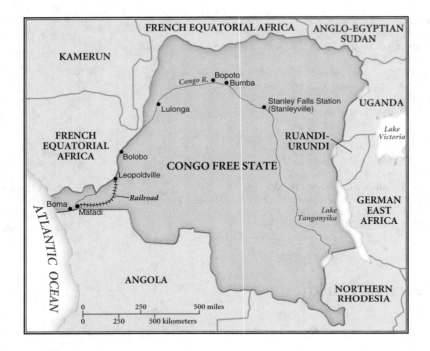

Congo Free State, 1890

The Congo of Conrad's time was, in fact, not a free state. A conference of European states in 1876 had assigned it to King Leopold II of Belgium as his personal property. Under Leopold's brutal rule, which lasted until his death in 1908, the people of the Congo were subjected to atrocities and forced labor. When Conrad journeyed through the Congo in 1890, many Congolese were virtual slaves under the harsh discipline of Leopold's officials.

yellow complexion, a straight back, an ascetic aspect, and, with his arms dropped, the palms of hands outwards, resembled an idol. The director, satisfied the anchor had good hold, made his way aft and sat down amongst us. We exchanged a few words lazily. Afterwards there was silence on board the yacht. For some reason or other we did not begin that game of dominoes. We felt meditative, and fit for nothing but placid staring. The day was ending in a serenity of still and exquisite brilliance. The water shone pacifically; the sky, without a speck, was a benign immensity of unstained light; the very mist on the Essex marshes was like a gauzy and radiant fabric, hung from the wooded rises inland, and draping the low shores in diaphanous folds. Only the gloom to the west, brooding over the upper reaches, became more sombre every minute, as if angered by the approach of the sun.

And at last, in its curved and imperceptible fall, the sun sank low, and from glowing white changed to a dull red without rays and without heat, as if about to go out suddenly, stricken to death by the touch of that gloom brooding over a crowd of men.

Forthwith a change came over the waters, and the serenity became less brilliant but more profound. The old river in its broad reach rested unruffled at the decline of day, after ages of good service done to the race that peopled its banks, spread out in the tranquil dignity of a waterway leading to the uttermost ends of the earth. We looked at the venerable stream not in the vivid flush of a short day that comes and departs for ever, but in the august light of abiding memories. And indeed nothing is easier for a man who has, as the phrase goes, "followed the sea" with reverence and affection, than to evoke the great spirit of the past upon the lower reaches of the Thames. The tidal current runs to and fro in its unceasing service, crowded with memories of men and ships it had borne to the rest of home or to the battles of the sea. It had known and served all the men of whom the nation is proud, from Sir Francis Drake to Sir John Franklin,[2] knights all, titled and untitled—the great knights-errant of the sea. It had borne all the ships whose names are like jewels flashing in the night of time, from the *Golden Hind* returning with her round flanks full of treasure, to be visited by the Queen's Highness and thus pass out of the gigantic tale, to the *Erebus* and *Terror,* bound on other conquests—and that never returned. It had known the ships and the men. They had sailed from Deptford, from Greenwich, from Erith—the adventurers and the settlers; kings' ships and the ships of men on 'Change;[3] captains, admirals, the dark "interlopers" of the Eastern trade, and the commissioned "generals" of East India fleets. Hunters for gold or pursuers of fame, they all had gone out on that stream, bearing the sword, and often the torch, messengers of the might within the land, bearers of a spark from the sacred fire. What greatness had not floated on the ebb of that river into the mystery of an unknown earth! . . . The dreams of men, the seed of commonwealths, the germs of empires.

The sun set; the dusk fell on the stream, and lights began to appear along the shore. The Chapman lighthouse, a three-legged thing erect on a mud-flat, shone strongly. Lights of ships moved in the fairway—a great stir of lights going up and going down. And farther west on the upper reaches the place of the monstrous town was still marked ominously on the sky, a brooding gloom in sunshine, a lurid glare under the stars.

"And this also," said Marlow suddenly, "has been one of the dark places of the earth."

He was the only man of us who still "followed the sea." The worst that could be said of him was that he did not represent his class. He was a seaman, but he was a wanderer, too, while most seamen lead, if one may so express it, a sedentary life. Their minds are of the stay-at-home order, and their home is always with them—the ship; and so is their country—the sea. One ship is very much like another, and the sea is always the same. In the immutability of their surroundings the foreign shores, the foreign faces, the changing immensity of life, glide past, veiled not by a sense of mystery but by a slightly disdainful ignorance; for there is nothing mysterious to a seaman unless it be the sea itself, which is the mistress of his existence and as inscrutable as Destiny. For the rest, after his hours of work, a casual stroll or a casual spree on shore suffices to unfold for him the secret of a whole continent, and generally he finds the secret not worth knowing. The yarns of seamen have a direct simplicity, the whole meaning of which lies within the shell of a cracked nut. But Marlow was not typical

---

[2] **Drake . . . Franklin:** Drake circumnavigated the globe from 1577 to 1580 on the *Golden Hind.* Franklin sought the Northwest Passage from 1845 to 1847 on the *Erebus* and the *Terror.*

[3] **'Change:** The Exchange, the British financial market.

(if his propensity to spin yarns be excepted), and to him the meaning of an episode was not inside like a kernel but outside, enveloping the tale which brought it out only as a glow brings out a haze, in the likeness of one of these misty halos that sometimes are made visible by the spectral illumination of moonshine.

His remark did not seem at all surprising. It was just like Marlow. It was accepted in silence. No one took the trouble to grunt even; and presently he said, very slow—

"I was thinking of very old times, when the Romans first came here, nineteen hundred years ago—the other day. . . . Light came out of this river since—you say Knights? Yes; but it is like a running blaze on a plain, like a flash of lightning in the clouds. We live in the flicker—may it last as long as the old earth keeps rolling! But darkness was here yesterday. Imagine the feelings of a commander of a fine—what d'ye call 'em?—trireme in the Mediterranean, ordered suddenly to the north; run overland across the Gauls in a hurry; put in charge of one of these craft the legionaries—a wonderful lot of handy men they must have been, too—used to build, apparently by the hundred, in a month or two, if we may believe what we read. Imagine him here—the very end of the world, a sea the colour of lead, a sky the colour of smoke, a kind of ship about as rigid as a concertina—and going up this river with stores, or orders, or what you like. Sand-banks, marshes, forests, savages,—precious little to eat fit for a civilized man, nothing but Thames water to drink. No Falernian[4] wine here, no going ashore. Here and there a military camp lost in a wilderness, like a needle in a bundle of hay—cold, fog, tempests, disease, exile, and death,—death skulking in the air, in the water, in the bush. They must have been dying like flies here. Oh, yes—he did it. Did it very well, too, no doubt, and without thinking much about it either, except afterwards to brag of what he had gone through in his time, perhaps. They were men enough to face the darkness. And perhaps he was cheered by keeping his eye on a chance of promotion to the fleet at Ravenna by and by, if he had good friends in Rome and survived the awful climate. Or think of a decent young citizen in a toga—perhaps too much dice, you know—coming out here in the train of some prefect, or tax-gatherer, or trader even, to mend his fortunes. Land in a swamp, march through the woods, and in some inland post feel the savagery, the utter savagery, had closed round him,—all that mysterious life of the wilderness that stirs in the forest, in the jungles, in the hearts of wild men. There's no initiation either into such mysteries. He has to live in the midst of the incomprehensible, which is also detestable. And it has a fascination, too, that goes to work upon him. The fascination of the abomination—you know, imagine the growing regrets, the longing to escape, the powerless disgust, the surrender, the hate."

He paused.

"Mind," he began again, lifting one arm from the elbow, the palm of the hand outwards, so that, with his legs folded before him, he had the pose of a Buddha preaching in European clothes and without a lotus-flower—"Mind, none of us would feel exactly like this. What saves us is efficiency—the devotion to efficiency. But these chaps were not much account, really. They were no colonists; their

---

[4] **Falernian:** A fine vintage wine.

administration was merely a squeeze, and nothing more, I suspect. They were conquerors, and for that you want only brute force—nothing to boast of, when you have it, since your strength is just an accident arising from the weakness of others. They grabbed what they could get for the sake of what was to be got. It was just robbery with violence, aggravated murder on a great scale, and men going at it blind—as is very proper for those who tackle a darkness. The conquest of the earth, which mostly means the taking it away from those who have a different complexion or slightly flatter noses than ourselves, is not a pretty thing when you look into it too much. What redeems it is the idea only. An idea at the back of it; not a sentimental pretence but an idea; and an unselfish belief in the idea—something you can set up, and bow down before, and offer a sacrifice to. . . ."

He broke off. Flames glided in the river, small green flames, red flames, white flames, pursuing, overtaking, joining, crossing each other—then separating slowly or hastily. The traffic of the great city went on in the deepening night upon the sleepless river. We looked on, waiting patiently—there was nothing else to do till the end of the flood; but it was only after a long silence, when he said, in a hesitating voice, "I suppose you fellows remember I did once turn fresh-water sailor for a bit," that we knew we were fated, before the ebb began to run, to hear about one of Marlow's inconclusive experiences.

"I don't want to bother you much with what happened to me personally," he began, showing in this remark the weakness of many tellers of tales who seem so often unaware of what their audience would best like to hear; "yet to understand the effect of it on me you ought to know how I got out there, what I saw, how I went up that river to the place where I first met the poor chap. It was the farthest point of navigation and the culminating point of my experience. It seemed somehow to throw a kind of light on everything about me—and into my thoughts. It was sombre enough, too—and pitiful—not extraordinary in any way—not very clear either. No, not very clear. And yet it seemed to throw a kind of light.

"I had then, as you remember, just returned to London after a lot of Indian Ocean, Pacific, China Seas—a regular dose of the East—six years or so, and I was loafing about, hindering you fellows in your work and invading your homes, just as though I had got a heavenly mission to civilize you. It was very fine for a time, but after a bit I did get tired of resting. Then I began to look for a ship—I should think the hardest work on earth. But the ships wouldn't even look at me. And I got tired of that game, too.

"Now when I was a little chap I had a passion for maps. I would look for hours at South America, or Africa, or Australia, and lose myself in all the glories of exploration. At that time there were many blank spaces on the earth, and when I saw one that looked particularly inviting on a map (but they all look that) I would put my finger on it and say, When I grow up I will go there. The North Pole was one of these places, I remember. Well, I haven't been there yet, and shall not try now. The glamour's off. Other places were scattered about the Equator, and in every sort of latitude all over the two hemispheres. I have been in some of them, and . . . well, we won't talk about that. But there was one yet—the biggest, the most blank, so to speak—that I had a hankering after.

"True, by this time it was not a blank space any more. It had got filled since my boyhood with rivers and lakes and names. It had ceased to be a blank space of delightful mystery—a white patch for a boy to dream gloriously over. It had become a place of darkness. But there was in it one river especially, a mighty big river, that you could see on the map, resembling an immense snake uncoiled, with its head in the sea, its body at rest curving afar over a vast country, and its tail lost in the depths of the land. And as I looked at the map of it in a shop-window, it fascinated me as a snake would a bird—a silly little bird. Then I remembered there was a big concern, a Company for trade on that river. Dash it all! I thought to myself, they can't trade without using some kind of craft on that lot of fresh water—steamboats! Why shouldn't I try to get charge of one? I went on along Fleet Street, but could not shake off the idea. The snake had charmed me.

"You understand it was a Continental concern, that Trading society; but I have a lot of relations living on the Continent, because it's cheap and not so nasty as it looks, they say.

"I am sorry to own I began to worry them. This was already a fresh departure for me. I was not used to get things that way, you know. I always went my own road and on my own legs where I had a mind to go. I wouldn't have believed it of myself; but, then—you see—I felt somehow I must get there by hook or by crook. So I worried them. The men said 'My dear fellow,' and did nothing. Then—would you believe it?—I tried the women. I, Charlie Marlow, set the women to work—to get a job. Heavens! Well, you see, the notion drove me. I had an aunt, a dear enthusiastic soul. She wrote: 'It will be delightful. I am ready to do anything, anything for you. It is a glorious idea. I know the wife of a very high personage in the Administration, and also a man who has lots of influence with,' etc., etc. She was determined to make no end of fuss to get me appointed skipper of a river steamboat, if such was my fancy.

"I got my appointment—of course; and I got it very quick. It appears the Company had received news that one of their captains had been killed in a scuffle with the natives. This was my chance, and it made me the more anxious to go. It was only months and months afterwards, when I made the attempt to recover what was left of the body, that I heard the original quarrel arose from a misunderstanding about some hens. Yes, two black hens. Fresleven—that was the fellow's name, a Dane—thought himself wronged somehow in the bargain, so he went ashore and started to hammer the chief of the village with a stick. Oh, it didn't surprise me in the least to hear this, and at the same time to be told that Fresleven was the gentlest, quietest creature that ever walked on two legs. No doubt he was; but he had been a couple of years already out there engaged in the noble cause, you know, and he probably felt the need at last of asserting his self-respect in some way. Therefore he whacked the old nigger mercilessly, while a big crowd of his people watched him, thunderstruck, till some man—I was told the chief's son—in desperation at hearing the old chap yell, made a tentative jab with a spear at the white man—and of course it went quite easy between the shoulder-blades. Then the whole population cleared into the forest, expecting all kinds of calamities to happen, while, on the other hand, the steamer Fresleven commanded left also in a bad panic, in charge of the engineer, I believe. Afterwards nobody seemed to trouble much about Fresleven's remains, till I got out and stepped into his shoes. I couldn't let it rest, though; but when an opportunity offered at last to meet my predecessor, the grass growing through his ribs was tall enough to hide his bones. They were all there. The supernatural being had not been touched after he fell. And the village was deserted, the huts gaped black, rotting, all askew within the fallen enclosures. A calamity had come to it, sure enough. The people had vanished. Mad terror had scattered them, men, women, and children, through the bush, and they had never returned. What became of the hens I don't know either. I should think the cause of progress got them, anyhow. However, through this glorious affair I got my appointment, before I had fairly begun to hope for it.

"I flew around like mad to get ready, and before forty-eight hours I was crossing the Channel to show myself to my employers, and sign the contract. In a very few hours I arrived in a city[5] that always makes me think of a whited sepulchre.[6] Prejudice no doubt. I had no difficulty in finding the Company's offices. It was the biggest thing in the town, and everybody I met was full of it. They were going to run an over-sea empire, and make no end of coin by trade.

"A narrow and deserted street in deep shadow, high houses, innumerable windows with venetian blinds, a dead silence, grass sprouting between the stones, imposing carriage archways right and left, immense double doors standing ponderously ajar. I slipped through one of these cracks, went up a swept and ungarnished staircase, as arid as a desert, and opened the first door I came to. Two women, one fat and the other slim, sat on straw-bottomed chairs, knitting black wool. The slim one got up and walked straight at me—still knitting with down-cast eyes—and only just as I began to think of getting out of her way, as you would for a somnambulist, stood still, and looked up. Her dress was as plain as an umbrella-cover, and she turned round without a word and preceded me into a waiting-room. I gave my name, and looked about. Deal[7] table in the middle, plain chairs all round the walls, on one end a large shining map, marked with all the colours of a rainbow. There was a vast amount of red—good to see at any time, because one knows that some real work is done in there, a deuce of a lot of blue, a little green, smears of orange, and, on the East Coast, a purple patch, to show where the jolly pioneers of progress drink the jolly lager-beer. However, I wasn't going into any of these. I was going into the yellow. Dead in the centre. And the river was there—fascinating—deadly—like a snake. Ough! A door opened, a white-haired secretarial head, but wearing a compassionate expression, appeared, and a skinny forefinger beckoned me into the sanctuary. Its light was dim, and a heavy writing-desk squatted in the middle. From behind that structure came out an impression of pale plumpness in a frock-coat. The great man himself. He was five feet six, I should judge, and had his grip on the handle-end of ever so many millions. He shook hands, I fancy, murmured vaguely, was satisfied with my French. *Bon voyage.*

"In about forty-five seconds I found myself again in the waiting-room with the compassionate secretary, who, full of desolation and sympathy, made me sign some

---

[5] **a city:** The capital of Belgium. Between 1885 and 1908, when it became a Belgian colony, the Congo—now the Democratic Republic of the Congo—was owned by King Leopold II of Belgium.

[6] **whited sepulchre:** Jesus compared the hypocritical Pharisees to whited sepulchres, or tombs, which "outwardly appear beautiful, but inwardly are full of dead men's bones." See Matthew 23:27.

[7] **Deal:** Pine.

document. I believe I undertook amongst other things not to disclose any trade secrets. Well, I am not going to.

"I began to feel slightly uneasy. You know I am not used to such ceremonies, and there was something ominous in the atmosphere. It was just as though I had been let into some conspiracy—I don't know—something not quite right; and I was glad to get out. In the outer room the two women knitted black wool feverishly. People were arriving, and the younger one was walking back and forth introducing them. The old one sat on her chair. Her flat cloth slippers were propped up on a foot-warmer, and a cat reposed on her lap. She wore a starched white affair on her head, had a wart on one cheek, and silver-rimmed spectacles hung on the tip of her nose. She glanced at me above the glasses. The swift and indifferent placidity of that look troubled me. Two youths with foolish and cheery countenances were being piloted over, and she threw at them the same quick glance of unconcerned wisdom. She seemed to know all about them and about me, too. An eerie feeling came over me. She seemed uncanny and fateful. Often far away there I thought of these two, guarding the door of Darkness, knitting black wool as for a warm pall, one introducing, introducing continuously to the unknown, the other scrutinizing the cheery and foolish faces with unconcerned old eyes. *Ave!* Old knitter of black wool. *Morituri te salutant.*[8] Not many of those she looked at ever saw her again—not half, by a long way.

"There was yet a visit to the doctor. 'A simple formality,' assured me the secretary, with an air of taking an immense part in all my sorrows. Accordingly a young chap wearing his hat over the left eyebrow, some clerk I suppose,—there must have been clerks in the business, though the house was as still as a house in a city of the dead—came from somewhere upstairs, and led me forth. He was shabby and careless, with ink-stains on the sleeves of his jacket, and his cravat was large and billowy, under a chin shaped like the toe of an old boot. It was a little too early for the doctor, so I proposed a drink, and thereupon he developed a vein of joviality. As we sat over our vermuths he glorified the Company's business, and by and by I expressed casually my surprise at him not going out there. He became very cool and collected all at once. 'I am not such a fool as I look, quoth Plato to his disciples,' he said sententiously, emptied his glass with great resolution, and we rose.

"The old doctor felt my pulse, evidently thinking of something else the while. 'Good, good for there,' he mumbled, and then with a certain eagerness asked me whether I would let him measure my head. Rather surprised, I said Yes, when he produced a thing like calipers and got the dimensions back and front and every way, taking notes carefully. He was an unshaven little man in a threadbare coat like a gaberdine, with his feet in slippers, and I thought him a harmless fool. 'I always ask leave, in the interests of science, to measure the crania of those going out there,' he said. 'And when they come back, too?' I asked. 'Oh, I never see them,' he remarked; 'and, moreover, the changes take place inside, you know.' He smiled, as if at some quiet joke. 'So you are going out there. Famous. Interesting, too.' He gave me a searching glance, and made another note. 'Ever any madness in your family?' he

---

[8] *Ave . . . salutant:* "Hail! Those who are about to die salute you." This was the gladiators' salute to the Roman emperor in the Colosseum.

asked, in a matter-of-fact tone. I felt very annoyed. 'Is that question in the interests of science, too?' 'It would be,' he said, without taking notice of my irritation, 'interesting for science to watch the mental changes of individuals, on the spot, but . . .' 'Are you an alienist?'[9] I interrupted. 'Every doctor should be—a little,' answered that original, imperturbably. 'I have a little theory which you Messieurs who go out there must help me to prove. This is my share in the advantages my country shall reap from the possession of such a magnificent dependency. The mere wealth I leave to others. Pardon my questions, but you are the first Englishman coming under my observation . . .' I hastened to assure him I was not in the least typical. 'If I were,' said I, 'I wouldn't be talking like this with you.' 'What you say is rather profound, and probably erroneous,' he said, with a laugh. 'Avoid irritation more than exposure to the sun. Adieu. How do you English say, eh? Good-bye. Ah! Good-bye. Adieu. In the tropics one must before everything keep calm.' . . . He lifted a warning forefinger. . . . '*Du calme, du calme. Adieu.*'

"One thing more remained to do—say good-bye to my excellent aunt. I found her triumphant. I had a cup of tea—the last decent cup of tea for many days—and in a room that most soothingly looked just as you would expect a lady's drawing-room to look, we had a long quiet chat by the fireside. In the course of these confidences it became quite plain to me I had been represented to the wife of the high dignitary, and goodness knows to how many more people besides, as an exceptional and gifted creature—a piece of good fortune for the Company—a man you don't get hold of every day. Good heavens! and I was going to take charge of a two-penny-half-penny river-steamboat with a penny whistle attached! It appeared, however, I was also one of the Workers, with a capital—you know. Something like an emissary of light, something like a lower sort of apostle. There had been a lot of such rot let loose in print and talk just about that time, and the excellent woman, living right in the rush of all that humbug, got carried off her feet. She talked about 'weaning those ignorant millions from their horrid ways,' till, upon my word, she made me quite uncomfortable. I ventured to hint that the Company was run for profit.

"'You forget, dear Charlie, that the labourer is worthy of his hire,'[10] she said, brightly. It's queer how out of touch with truth women are. They live in a world of their own, and there has never been anything like it, and never can be. It is too beautiful altogether, and if they were to set it up it would go to pieces before the first sunset. Some confounded fact we men have been living contentedly with ever since the day of creation would start up and knock the whole thing over.

"After this I got embraced, told to wear flannel, be sure to write often, and so on—and I left. In the street—I don't know why—a queer feeling came to me that I was an impostor. Odd thing that I, who used to clear out for any part of the world at twenty-four hours' notice, with less thought than most men give to the crossing of a street, had a moment—I won't say of hesitation, but of startled pause, before this commonplace affair. The best way I can explain it to you is by saying that, for a

---

[9] **alienist:** A psychiatrist.

[10] **the labourer . . . his hire:** See Luke 10:7.

second or two, I felt as though, instead of going to the centre of a continent, I were about to set off for the centre of the earth.

"I left in a French steamer, and she called in every blamed port they have out there, for, as far as I could see, the sole purpose of landing soldiers and custom-house officers. I watched the coast. Watching a coast as it slips by the ship is like thinking about an enigma. There it is before you — smiling, frowning, inviting, grand, mean, insipid, or savage, and always mute with an air of whispering, Come and find out. This one was almost featureless, as if still in the making, with an aspect of monotonous grimness. The edge of a colossal jungle, so dark-green as to be almost black, fringed with white surf, ran straight, like a ruled line, far, far away along a blue sea whose glitter was blurred by a creeping mist. The sun was fierce, the land seemed to glisten and drip with steam. Here and there grayish-whitish specks showed up clustered inside the white surf, with a flag flying above them perhaps. Settlements some centuries old, and still no bigger than pinheads on the untouched expanse of their background. We pounded along, stopped, landed soldiers; went on, landed custom-house clerks to levy toll in what looked like a God-forsaken wilderness, with a tin shed and a flag-pole lost in it; landed more soldiers — to take care of the custom-house clerks, presumably. Some, I heard, got drowned in the surf; but whether they did or not, nobody seemed particularly to care. They were just flung out there, and on we went. Every day the coast looked the same, as though we had not moved; but we passed various places — trading places — with names like Gran' Bassam, Little Popo; names that seemed to belong to some sordid farce acted in front of a sinister back-cloth. The idleness of a passenger, my isolation amongst all these men with whom I had no point of contact, the oily and languid sea, the uniform sombreness of the coast, seemed to keep me away from the truth of things, within the toil of a mournful and senseless delusion. The voice of the surf heard now and then was a positive pleasure, like the speech of a brother. It was something natural, that had its reason, that had a meaning. Now and then a boat from the shore gave one a momentary contact with reality. It was paddled by black fellows. You could see from afar the white of their eyeballs glistening. They shouted, sang; their bodies streamed with perspiration; they had faces like grotesque masks — these chaps; but they had bone, muscle, a wild vitality, an intense energy of movement, that was as natural and true as the surf along their coast. They wanted no excuse for being there. They were a great comfort to look at. For a time I would feel I belonged still to a world of straightforward facts; but the feeling would not last long. Something would turn up to scare it away. Once, I remember, we came upon a man-of-war anchored off the coast. There wasn't even a shed there, and she was shelling the bush. It appears the French had one of their wars going on thereabouts. Her ensign dropped limp like a rag; the muzzles of the long six-inch guns stuck out all over the low hull; the greasy, slimy swell swung her up lazily and let her down, swaying her thin masts. In the empty immensity of earth, sky, and water, there she was, incomprehensible, firing into a continent. Pop, would go one of the six-inch guns; a small flame would dart and vanish, a little white smoke would disappear, a tiny projectile would give a feeble screech — and nothing happened. Nothing could happen. There was a touch of insanity in the proceeding, a sense of lugubrious drollery in the sight; and it was not dissipated by somebody on board assuring me earnestly there was a camp of natives — he called them enemies! — hidden out of sight somewhere.

"We gave her her letters (I heard the men in that lonely ship were dying of fever at the rate of three a day) and went on. We called at some more places with farcical names, where the merry dance of death and trade goes on in a still and earthy atmosphere as of an overheated catacomb; all along the formless coast bordered by dangerous surf, as if Nature herself had tried to ward off intruders; in and out of rivers, streams of death in life, whose banks were rotting into mud, whose waters, thickened into slime, invaded the contorted mangroves,[11] that seemed to writhe at us in the extremity of an impotent despair. Nowhere did we stop long enough to get a particularized impression, but the general sense of vague and oppressive wonder grew upon me. It was like a weary pilgrimage amongst hints for nightmares.

"It was upward of thirty days before I saw the mouth of the big river. We anchored off the seat of the government. But my work would not begin till some two hundred miles farther on. So as soon as I could I made a start for a place thirty miles higher up.

"I had my passage on a little sea-going steamer. Her captain was a Swede, and knowing me for a seaman, invited me on the bridge. He was a young man, lean, fair, and morose, with lanky hair and a shuffling gait. As we left the miserable little wharf, he tossed his head contemptuously at the shore. 'Been living there?' he asked. I said, 'Yes.' 'Fine lot these government chaps — are they not?' he went on, speaking English with great precision and considerable bitterness. 'It is funny what some people will do for a few francs a month. I wonder what becomes of that kind when it goes up country?' I said to him I expected to see that soon. 'So-o-o!' he exclaimed. He shuffled athwart, keeping one eye ahead vigilantly. 'Don't be too sure,' he continued. 'The other day I took up a man who hanged himself on the road. He was a Swede, too.' 'Hanged himself! Why, in God's name?' I cried. He kept on looking out watchfully. 'Who knows? The sun too much for him, or the country perhaps.'

"At last we opened a reach. A rocky cliff appeared, mounds of turned-up earth by the shore, houses on a hill, others with iron roofs, amongst a waste of excavations, or hanging to the declivity. A continuous noise of the rapids above hovered over this scene of inhabited devastation. A lot of people, mostly black and naked, moved about like ants. A jetty projected into the river. A blinding sunlight drowned all this at times in a sudden recrudescence of glare. 'There's your Company's station,' said the Swede, pointing to three wooden barrack-like structures on the rocky slope. 'I will send your things up. Four boxes did you say? So. Farewell.'

"I came upon a boiler wallowing in the grass, then found a path leading up the hill. It turned aside for the boulders, and also for an undersized railway-truck lying there on its back with its wheels in the air. One was off. The thing looked as dead as the carcass of some animal. I came upon more pieces of decaying machinery, a stack of rusty rails. To the left a clump of trees made a shady spot, where dark things seemed to stir feebly. I blinked, the path was steep. A horn tooted to the right, and

---

[11] **mangroves:** Tropical maritime trees.

I saw the black people run. A heavy and dull detonation shook the ground, a puff of smoke came out of the cliff, and that was all. No change appeared on the face of the rock. They were building a railway. The cliff was not in the way or anything; but this objectless blasting was all the work going on.

"A slight clinking behind me made me turn my head. Six black men advanced in a file, toiling up the path. They walked erect and slow, balancing small baskets full of earth on their heads, and the clink kept time with their footsteps. Black rags were wound round their loins, and the short ends behind waggled to and fro like tails. I could see every rib, the joints of their limbs were like knots in a rope; each had an iron collar on his neck, and all were connected together with a chain whose bights[12] swung between them, rhythmically clinking. Another report from the cliff made me think suddenly of that ship of war I had seen firing into a continent. It was the same kind of ominous voice; but these men could by no stretch of imagination be called enemies. They were called criminals, and the outraged law, like the bursting shells, had come to them, an insoluble mystery from the sea. All their meagre breasts panted together, the violently dilated nostrils quivered, the eyes stared stonily up-hill. They passed me within six inches, without a glance, with that complete, death-like indifference of unhappy savages. Behind this raw matter one of the reclaimed, the product of the new forces at work, strolled despondently, carrying a rifle by its middle. He had a uniform jacket with one button off, and seeing a white man on the path, hoisted his weapon to his shoulder with alacrity. This was simple prudence, white men being so much alike at a distance that he could not tell who I might be. He was speedily reassured, and with a large, white, rascally grin, and a glance at his charge, seemed to take me into partnership in his exalted trust. After all, I also was a part of the great cause of these high and just proceedings.

"Instead of going up, I turned and descended to the left. My idea was to let that chain-gang get out of sight before I climbed the hill. You know I am not particularly tender; I've had to strike and to fend off. I've had to resist and to attack sometimes—that's only one way of resisting—without counting the exact cost, according to the demands of such sort of life as I had blundered into. I've seen the devil of violence, and the devil of greed, and the devil of hot desire; but, by all the stars! these were strong, lusty, red-eyed devils, that swayed and drove men—men, I tell you. But as I stood on this hillside, I foresaw that in the blinding sunshine of that land I would become acquainted with a flabby, pretending, weak-eyed devil of a rapacious and pitiless folly. How insidious he could be, too, I was only to find out several months later and a thousand miles farther. For a moment I stood appalled, as though by a warning. Finally I descended the hill, obliquely, towards the trees I had seen.

"I avoided a vast artificial hole somebody had been digging on the slope, the purpose of which I found it impossible to divine. It wasn't a quarry or a sandpit, anyhow. It was just a hole. It might have been connected with the philanthropic desire of giving the criminals something to do. I don't know. Then I nearly fell into a

---

[12] **bights:** Slack sections.

very narrow ravine, almost no more than a scar in the hillside. I discovered that a lot of imported drainage-pipes for the settlement had been tumbled in there. There wasn't one that was not broken. It was a wanton smash-up. At last I got under the trees. My purpose was to stroll into the shade for a moment; but no sooner within than it seemed to me I had stepped into the gloomy circle of some Inferno. The rapids were near, and an uninterrupted, uniform, headlong, rushing noise filled the mournful stillness of the grove, where not a breath stirred, not a leaf moved, with a mysterious sound — as though the tearing pace of the launched earth had suddenly become audible.

"Black shapes crouched, lay, sat between the trees leaning against the trunks, clinging to the earth, half coming out, half effaced within the dim light, in all the attitudes of pain, abandonment, and despair. Another mine on the cliff went off, followed by a slight shudder of the soil under my feet. The work was going on. The work! And this was the place where some of the helpers had withdrawn to die.

"They were dying slowly — it was very clear. They were not enemies, they were not criminals, they were nothing earthly now, — nothing but black shadows of disease and starvation, lying confusedly in the greenish gloom. Brought from all the recesses of the coast in all the legality of time contracts, lost in uncongenial surroundings, fed on unfamiliar food, they sickened, became inefficient, and were then allowed to crawl away and rest. These moribund shapes were free as air — and nearly as thin. I began to distinguish the gleam of the eyes under the trees. Then, glancing down, I saw a face near my hand. The black bones reclined at full length with one shoulder against the tree, and slowly the eyelids rose and the sunken eyes looked up at me, enormous and vacant, a kind of blind, white flicker in the depths of the orbs, which died out slowly. The man seemed young — almost a boy — but you know with them it's hard to tell. I found nothing else to do but to offer him one of my good Swede's ship's biscuits I had in my pocket. The fingers closed slowly on it and held — there was no other movement and no other glance. He had tied a bit of white worsted round his neck — Why? Where did he get it? Was it a badge — an ornament — a charm — a propitiatory act? Was there any idea at all connected with it? It looked startling round his black neck, this bit of white thread from beyond the seas.

"Near the same tree two more bundles of acute angles sat with their legs drawn up. One, with his chin propped on his knees, stared at nothing, in an intolerable and appalling manner: his brother phantom rested its forehead, as if overcome with a great weariness; and all about others were scattered in every pose of contorted collapse, as in some picture of a massacre or a pestilence. While I stood horror-struck, one of these creatures rose to his hands and knees, and went off on all-fours towards the river to drink. He lapped out of his hand, then sat up in the sunlight, crossing his shins in front of him, and after a time let his woolly head fall on his breastbone.

"I didn't want any more loitering in the shade, and I made haste towards the station. When near the buildings I met a white man, in such an unexpected elegance of get-up that in the first moment I took him for a sort of vision. I saw a high starched collar, white cuffs, a light alpaca jacket, snowy trousers, a clean necktie, and varnished boots. No hat. Hair parted, brushed, oiled, under a green-lined parasol held in a big white hand. He was amazing, and had a penholder behind his ear.

"I shook hands with this miracle, and I learned he was the Company's chief accountant, and that all the book-keeping was done at this station. He had come out for a moment, he said, 'to get a breath of fresh air.' The expression sounded wonderfully odd, with its suggestion of sedentary desk-life. I wouldn't have mentioned the fellow to you at all, only it was from his lips that I first heard the name of the man who is so indissolubly connected with the memories of that time. Moreover, I respected the fellow. Yes; I respected his collars, his vast cuffs, his brushed hair. His appearance was certainly that of a hairdresser's dummy; but in the great demoralization of the land he kept up his appearance. That's backbone. His starched collars and got-up shirt-fronts were achievements of character. He had been out nearly three years; and, later, I could not help asking him how he managed to sport such linen. He had just the faintest blush, and said modestly, 'I've been teaching one of the native women about the station. It was difficult. She had a distaste for the work.' Thus this man had verily accomplished something. And he was devoted to his books, which were in apple-pie order.

"Everything else in the station was in a muddle, — heads, things, buildings. Strings of dusty niggers with splay feet arrived and departed; a stream of manufactured goods, rubbishy cottons, beads, and brass-wire set into the depths of darkness, and in return came a precious trickle of ivory.

"I had to wait in the station for ten days—an eternity. I lived in a hut in the yard, but to be out of the chaos I would sometimes get into the accountant's office. It was built of horizontal planks, and so badly put together that, as he bent over his high desk, he was barred from neck to heels with narrow strips of sunlight. There was no need to open the big shutter to see. It was hot there, too; big flies buzzed fiendishly, and did not sting, but stabbed. I sat generally on the floor, while, of faultless appearance (and even slightly scented), perching on a high stool, he wrote, he wrote. Sometimes he stood up for exercise. When a truckle-bed with a sick man (some invalid agent from up-country) was put in there, he exhibited a gentle annoyance. 'The groans of this sick person,' he said, 'distract my attention. And without that it is extremely difficult to guard against clerical errors in this climate.'

"One day he remarked, without lifting his head, 'In the interior you will no doubt meet Mr. Kurtz.' On my asking who Mr. Kurtz was, he said he was a first-class agent; and seeing my disappointment at this information, he added slowly, laying down his pen, 'He is a very remarkable person.' Further questions elicited from him that Mr. Kurtz was at present in charge of a trading post, a very important one, in the true ivory-country, at 'the very bottom of there. Sends in as much ivory as all the others put together . . .' He began to write again. The sick man was too ill to groan. The flies buzzed in a great peace.

"Suddenly there was a growing murmur of voices and a great tramping of feet. A caravan had come in. A violent babble of uncouth sounds burst out on the other side of the planks. All the carriers were speaking together, and in the midst of the uproar the lamentable voice of the chief agent was heard 'giving it up' tearfully for the twentieth time that day. . . . He rose slowly. 'What a frightful row,' he said. He crossed the room gently to look at the sick man, and returning, said to me, 'He does not hear.'

'What! Dead?' I asked, startled. 'No, not yet,' he answered, with great composure. Then, alluding with a toss of the head to the tumult in the station-yard, 'When one has got to make correct entries, one comes to hate those savages—hate them to the death.' He remained thoughtful for a moment. 'When you see Mr. Kurtz,' he went on, 'tell him from me that everything here'—he glanced at the desk—'is very satisfactory. I don't like to write to him—with those messengers of ours you never know who may get hold of your letter—at that Central Station.' He stared at me for a moment with his mild, bulging eyes. 'Oh, he will go far, very far,' he began again. 'He will be somebody in the Administration before long. They, above—the Council in Europe, you know—mean him to be.'

"He turned to his work. The noise outside had ceased, and presently in going out I stopped at the door. In the steady buzz of flies the homeward-bound agent was lying flushed and insensible; the other, bent over his books, was making correct entries of perfectly correct transactions; and fifty feet below the doorstep I could see the still tree-tops of the grove of death.

"Next day I left that station at last, with a caravan of sixty men, for a two-hundred-mile tramp.

"No use telling you much about that. Paths, paths, everywhere; a stamped-in network of paths spreading over the empty land, through long grass, through burnt grass, through thickets, down and up chilly ravines, up and down stony hills ablaze with heat; and a solitude, a solitude, nobody, not a hut. The population had cleared out a long time ago. Well, if a lot of mysterious niggers armed with all kinds of fearful weapons suddenly took to travelling on the road between Deal and Gravesend, catching the yokels right and left to carry heavy loads for them, I fancy every farm and cottage thereabouts would get empty very soon. Only here the dwellings were gone, too. Still I passed through several abandoned villages. There's something pathetically childish in the ruins of grass walls. Day after day, with the stamp and shuffle of sixty pair of bare feet behind me, each pair under a 60-lb. load. Camp, cook, sleep, strike camp, march. Now and then a carrier dead in harness, at rest in the long grass near the path, with an empty water-gourd and his long staff lying by his side. A great silence around and above. Perhaps on some quiet night the tremor of far-off drums, sinking, swelling, a tremor vast, faint; a sound weird, appealing, suggestive, and wild—and perhaps with as profound a meaning as the sound of bells in a Christian country. Once a white man in an unbuttoned uniform, camping on the path with an armed escort of lank Zanzibaris, very hospitable and festive—not to say drunk. Was looking after the upkeep of the road he declared. Can't say I saw any road or any upkeep, unless the body of a middle-aged negro, with a bullet-hole in the forehead, upon which I absolutely stumbled three miles farther on, may be considered as a permanent improvement. I had a white companion, too, not a bad chap, but rather too fleshy and with the exasperating habit of fainting on the hot hillsides, miles away from the least bit of shade and water. Annoying, you know, to hold your own coat like a parasol over a man's head while he is coming-to. I couldn't help asking him once what he meant by coming there at all. 'To make money, of course. What do you think?' he said, scornfully. Then he got fever, and had to be carried in a hammock slung under a pole. As he weighed sixteen stone[13] I had no end of rows with the carriers. They jibbed,[14] ran away, sneaked off with their loads in the night—quite a mutiny. So, one evening, I made a speech in English with gestures, not one of which was lost to the sixty pairs of eyes before me, and the next morning I started the hammock off in front all right. An hour afterwards I came upon the whole concern wrecked in a bush—man, hammock, groans, blankets, horrors. The heavy pole had skinned his poor nose. He was very anxious for me to kill somebody, but there wasn't the shadow of a carrier near. I remembered the old doctor—'It would be interesting for science to watch the mental changes of individuals, on the spot.' I felt I was becoming scientifically interesting. However, all that is to no purpose. On the fifteenth day I came in sight of the big river again, and hobbled into the Central Station. It was on a back water surrounded by scrub and forest, with a pretty border of smelly mud on one side, and on the three others enclosed by a crazy fence of rushes. A neglected gap was all the gate it had, and the first glance at the place was enough to let you see the flabby devil was running that show. White men with long staves in their hands appeared languidly from amongst the buildings, strolling up to take a look at me, and then retired out of sight somewhere. One of them, a stout, excitable chap with black moustaches, informed me with great volubility and many disgressions, as soon as I told him who I was, that my steamer was at the bottom of the river. I was thunderstruck. What, how, why? Oh, it was 'all right.' The 'manager himself' was there. All quite correct. 'Everybody had behaved splendidly! splendidly!'—'you must,' he said in agitation, 'go and see the general manager at once. He is waiting!'

"I did not see the real significance of that wreck at once. I fancy I see it now, but I am not sure—not at all. Certainly the affair was too stupid—when I think of it—to be altogether natural. Still . . . But at the moment it presented itself simply as a confounded nuisance. The steamer was sunk. They had started two days before in a sudden hurry up the river with the manager on board, in charge of some volunteer skipper, and before they had been out three hours they tore the bottom out of her on stones, and she sank near the south bank. I asked myself what I was to do there, now my boat was lost. As a matter of fact, I had plenty to do in fishing my command out of the river. I had to set about it the very next day. That, and the repairs when I brought the pieces to the station, took some months.

"My first interview with the manager was curious. He did not ask me to sit down after my twenty-mile walk that morning. He was commonplace in complexion, in feature, in manners, and in voice. He was of middle size and of ordinary build. His eyes, of the usual blue, were perhaps remarkably cold, and he certainly could make his glance fall on one as trenchant and heavy as an axe. But even at these times the rest of his person seemed to disclaim the intention. Otherwise there was only an indefinable, faint expression of his lips, something stealthy—a smile—not a smile—I remember it, but I can't explain. It was unconscious, this smile was,

---

[13] **stone:** A British unit of weight equal to 14 pounds. Sixteen stone equals 224 pounds.
[14] **jibbed:** Balked.

though just after he had said something it got intensified for an instant. It came at the end of his speeches like a seal applied on the words to make the meaning of the commonest phrase appear absolutely inscrutable. He was a common trader, from his youth up employed in these parts—nothing more. He was obeyed, yet he inspired neither love nor fear, nor even respect. He inspired uneasiness. That was it! Uneasiness. Not a definite mistrust—just uneasiness—nothing more. You have no idea how effective such a . . . a . . . faculty can be. He had no genius for organizing, for initiative, or for order even. That was evident in such things as the deplorable state of the station. He had no learning, and no intelligence. His position had come to him—why? Perhaps because he was never ill . . . He had served three terms of three years out there . . . Because triumphant health in the general rout of constitutions is a kind of power in itself. When he went home on leave he rioted on a large scale—pompously. Jack[15] ashore—with a difference—in externals only. This one could gather from his casual talk. He originated nothing, he could keep the routine going—that's all. But he was great. He was great by this little thing that it was impossible to tell what could control such a man. He never gave that secret away. Perhaps there was nothing within him. Such a suspicion made one pause—for out there there were no external checks. Once when various tropical diseases had laid low almost every 'agent' in the station, he was heard to say, 'Men who come out here should have no entrails.' He sealed the utterance with that smile of his, as though it had been a door opening into a darkness he had in his keeping. You fancied you had seen things—but the seal was on. When annoyed at meal-times by the constant quarrels of the white men about precedence, he ordered an immense round table to be made, for which a special house had to be built. This was the station's mess-room. Where he sat was the first place—the rest were nowhere. One felt this to be his unalterable conviction. He was neither civil nor uncivil. He was quiet. He allowed his 'boy'—an overfed young negro from the coast—to treat the white men, under his very eyes, with provoking insolence.

"He began to speak as soon as he saw me. I had been very long on the road. He could not wait. Had to start without me. The up-river stations had to be relieved. There had been so many delays already that he did not know who was dead and who was alive, and how they got on—and so on, and so on. He paid no attention to my explanations, and, playing with a stick of sealing-wax, repeated several times that the situation was 'very grave, very grave.' There were rumours that a very important station was in jeopardy, and its chief, Mr. Kurtz, was ill. Hoped it was not true. Mr. Kurtz was . . . I felt weary and irritable. Hang Kurtz, I thought. I interrupted him by saying I had heard of Mr. Kurtz on the coast. 'Ah! So they talk of him down there,' he murmured to himself. Then he began again, assuring me Mr. Kurtz was the best agent he had, an exceptional man, of the greatest importance to the Company; therefore I could understand his anxiety. He was, he said, 'very, very uneasy.' Certainly he fidgeted on his chair a good deal, exclaimed, 'Ah, Mr. Kurtz!' broke the stick of sealing-wax and seemed dumfounded by the accident. Next thing he wanted to

---

[15]**Jack:** Jack Tar; a sailor.

know 'how long it would take to' . . . I interrupted him again. Being hungry, you know, and kept on my feet too, I was getting savage. 'How can I tell?' I said. 'I haven't even seen the wreck yet—some months, no doubt.' All this talk seemed to me so futile. 'Some months,' he said. 'Well, let us say three months before we can make a start. Yes. That ought to do the affair.' I flung out of his hut (he lived all alone in a clay hut with a sort of verandah) muttering to myself my opinion of him. He was a chattering idiot. Afterwards I took it back when it was borne in upon me startlingly with what extreme nicety he had estimated the time requisite for the 'affair.'

"I went to work the next day, turning, so to speak, my back on that station. In that way only it seemed to me I could keep my hold on the redeeming facts of life. Still, one must look about sometimes; and then I saw this station, these men strolling aimlessly about in the sunshine of the yard. I asked myself sometimes what it all meant. They wandered here and there with their absurd long staves in their hands, like a lot of faithless pilgrims bewitched inside a rotten fence. The word 'ivory' rang in the air, was whispered, was sighed. You would think they were praying to it. A taint of imbecile rapacity blew through it all, like a whiff from some corpse. By Jove! I've never seen anything so unreal in my life. And outside, the silent wilderness surrounding this cleared speck on the earth struck me as something great and invincible, like evil or truth, waiting patiently for the passing away of this fantastic invasion.

"Oh, these months! Well, never mind. Various things happened. One evening a grass shed full of calico, cotton prints, beads, and I don't know what else, burst into a blaze so suddenly that you would have thought the earth had opened to let an avenging fire consume all that trash. I was smoking my pipe quietly by my dismantled steamer, and saw them all cutting capers in the light, with their arms lifted high, when the stout man with moustaches came tearing down to the river, a tin pail in his hand, assured me that everybody was 'behaving splendidly, splendidly,' dipped about a quart of water and tore back again. I noticed there was a hole in the bottom of his pail.

"I strolled up. There was no hurry. You see the thing had gone off like a box of matches. It had been hopeless from the very first. The flame had leaped high, driven everybody back, lighted up everything—and collapsed. The shed was already a heap of embers glowing fiercely. A nigger was being beaten near by. They said he had caused the fire in some way; be that as it may, he was screeching most horribly. I saw him, later, for several days, sitting in a bit of shade looking very sick and trying to recover himself: afterwards he arose and went out—and the wilderness without a sound took him into its bosom again. As I approached the glow from the dark I found myself at the back of two men, talking. I heard the name of Kurtz pronounced, then the words, 'take advantage of this unfortunate accident.' One of the men was the manager. I wished him a good evening. 'Did you ever see anything like it—eh? it is incredible,' he said, and walked off. The other man remained. He was a first-class agent, young, gentlemanly, a bit reserved, with a forked little beard and a hooked nose. He was stand-offish with the other agents, and they on their side said he was the manager's spy upon them. As to me, I had hardly ever spoken to him before. We got into talk, and by and by we strolled away from the hissing ruins. Then he asked me to his room, which was in the main building of the station. He struck a match, and I perceived that this young aristocrat had not only a silver-mounted dressing-case but also a whole candle all to himself. Just at that time the manager was the only man supposed to have any right to candles. Native mats covered the clay walls; a collection of spears, assegais,[16] shields, knives was hung up in trophies. The business entrusted to this fellow was the making of bricks — so I had been informed; but there wasn't a fragment of a brick anywhere in the station, and he had been there more than a year — waiting. It seems he could not make bricks without something, I don't know what — straw maybe. Anyways, it could not be found there, and as it was not likely to be sent from Europe, it did not appear clear to me what he was waiting for. An act of special creation perhaps.[17] However, they were all waiting — all the six-teen or twenty pilgrims of them — for something; and upon my word it did not seem an uncongenial occupation, from the way they took it, though the only thing that ever came to them was disease — as far as I could see. They beguiled the time by backbiting and intriguing against each other in a foolish kind of way. There was an air of plotting about that station, but nothing came of it, of course. It was as unreal as everything else — as the philanthropic pretence of the whole concern, as their talk, as their government, as their show of work. The only real feeling was a desire to get appointed to a trading-post where ivory was to be had, so that they could earn percentages. They intrigued and slandered and hated each other only on that account, — but as to effectually lifting a little finger — oh, no. By heavens! there is something after all in the world allowing one man to steal a horse while another must not look at a halter. Steal a horse straight out. Very well. He has done it. Perhaps he can ride. But there is a way of looking at a halter that would provoke the most charitable of saints into a kick.

"I had no idea why he wanted to be sociable, but as we chatted in there it sud-denly occurred to me the fellow was trying to get at something — in fact, pumping me. He alluded constantly to Europe, to the people I was supposed to know there — putting leading questions as to my acquaintances in the sepulchral city, and so on. His little eyes glittered like mica discs — with curiosity — though he tried to keep up a bit of superciliousness. At first I was astonished, but very soon I became awfully curious to see what he would find out from me. I couldn't possibly imagine what I had in me to make it worth his while. It was very pretty to see how he baffled himself, for in truth my body was full only of chills, and my head had nothing in it but that wretched steamboat business. It was evident he took me for a perfectly shameless prevaricator. At last he got angry, and, to conceal a movement of furious annoyance, he yawned. I rose. Then I noticed a small sketch in oils, on a panel, representing a woman, draped and blindfolded, carrying a lighted torch. The background was sombre — almost black. The movement of the woman was stately, and the effect of the torch-light on the face was sinister.

---

[16] **assegais:** Javelins.

[17] **An act . . . perhaps:** Special creation was the belief, challenged by the evolutionists, that God created each species individually.

"It arrested me, and he stood by civilly, holding an empty half-pint champagne bottle (medical comforts) with the candle stuck in it. To my question he said Mr. Kurtz had painted this—in this very station more than a year ago—while waiting for means to go to his trading-post. 'Tell me, pray,' said I, 'who is this Mr. Kurtz?'

"'The chief of the Inner Station,' he answered in a short tone, looking away. 'Much obliged,' I said, laughing. 'And you are the brickmaker of the Central Station. Everyone knows that.' He was silent for a while. 'He is a prodigy,' he said at last. 'He is an emissary of pity, and science, and progress, and devil knows what else. We want,' he began to declaim suddenly, 'for the guidance of the cause intrusted to us by Europe, so to speak, higher intelligence, wide sympathies, a singleness of purpose.' 'Who says that?' I asked. 'Lots of them,' he replied. 'Some even write that; and so *he* comes here, a special being, as you ought to know.' 'Why ought I to know?' I interrupted, really surprised. He paid no attention. 'Yes. To-day he is chief of the best station, next year he will be assistant-manager, two years more and . . . but I daresay you know what he will be in two years' time. You are of the new gang—the gang of virtue. The same people who sent him specially also recommended you. Oh, don't say no. I've my own eyes to trust.' Light dawned upon me. My dear aunt's influential acquaintances were producing an unexpected effect upon that young man. I nearly burst into a laugh. 'Do you read the Company's confidential correspondence?' I asked. He hadn't a word to say. It was great fun. 'When Mr. Kurtz,' I continued, severely, 'is General Manager, you won't have the opportunity.'

"He blew the candle out suddenly, and we went outside. The moon had risen. Black figures strolled about listlessly, pouring water on the glow, whence proceeded a sound of hissing; steam ascended in the moonlight, the beaten nigger groaned somewhere. 'What a row the brute makes!' said the indefatigable man with the moustaches, appearing near us. 'Serve him right. Transgression—punishment—bang! Pitiless, pitiless. That's the only way. This will prevent all conflagrations for the future. I was just telling the manager . . .' He noticed my companion, and became crestfallen all at once. 'Not in bed yet,' he said, with a kind of servile heartiness; 'it's so natural. Ha! Danger—agitation.' He vanished. I went on to the river-side, and the other followed me. I heard a scathing murmur at my ear, 'Heap of muffs—go to.' The pilgrims could be seen in knots gesticulating, discussing. Several had still their staves in their hands. I verily believe they took these sticks to bed with them. Beyond the fence the forest stood up spectrally in the moonlight, and through the dim stir, through the faint sounds of that lamentable courtyard, the silence of the land went home to one's very heart—its mystery, its greatness, the amazing reality of its concealed life. The hurt nigger moaned feebly somewhere near by, and then fetched a deep sigh that made me mend my pace away from there. I felt a hand introducing itself under my arm. 'My dear sir,' said the fellow, 'I don't want to be misunderstood, and especially by you, who will see Mr. Kurtz long before I can have that pleasure. I wouldn't like him to get a false idea of my disposition. . . .'

"I let him run on, this papier-mâché Mephistopheles, and it seemed to me that if I tried I could poke my forefinger through him, and would find nothing inside but a little loose dirt, maybe. He, don't you see, had been planning to be assistant-manager by and by under the present man, and I could see that the coming of that Kurtz had upset them both not a little. He talked precipitately, and I did not try to stop him. I had my shoulders against the wreck of my steamer, hauled up on the slope like a carcass of some big river animal. The smell of mud, of primeval mud, by Jove! was in my nostrils, the high stillness of primeval forest was before my eyes; there were shiny patches on the black creek. The moon had spread over everything a thin layer of silver — over the rank grass, over the mud, upon the wall of matted vegetation standing higher than the wall of a temple, over the great river I could see through a sombre gap glittering, glittering, as it flowed broadly by without a murmur. All this was great, expectant, mute, while the man jabbered about himself. I wondered whether the stillness on the face of the immensity looking at us two were meant as an appeal or as a menace. What were we who had strayed in here? Could we handle that dumb thing, or would it handle us? I felt how big, how confoundedly big, was that thing that couldn't talk, and perhaps was deaf as well. What was in there? I could see a little ivory coming out from there, and I had heard Mr. Kurtz was in there. I had heard enough about it, too — God knows! Yet somehow it didn't bring any image with it — no more than if I had been told an angel or a fiend was in there. I believed it in the same way one of you might believe there are inhabitants in the planet Mars. I knew once a Scotch sailmaker who was certain, dead sure, there were people in Mars. If you asked him for some idea how they looked and behaved, he would get shy and mutter something about 'walking on all-fours.' If you as much as smiled, he would — though a man of sixty — offer to fight you. I would not have gone so far as to fight for Kurtz, but I went for him near enough to a lie. You know I hate, detest, and can't bear a lie, not because I am straighter than the rest of us, but simply because it appalls me. There is a taint of death, a flavour of mortality in lies — which is exactly what I hate and detest in the world — what I want to forget. It makes me miserable and sick, like biting something rotten would do. Temperament, I suppose. Well, I went near enough to it by letting the young fool there believe anything he liked to imagine as to my influence in Europe. I became in an instant as much of a pretence as the rest of the bewitched pilgrims. This simply because I had a notion it somehow would be of help to that Kurtz whom at the time I did not see — you understand. He was just a word for me. I did not see the man in the name any more than you do. Do you see him? Do you see the story? Do you see anything? It seems to me I am trying to tell you a dream — making a vain attempt, because no relation of a dream can convey the dream-sensation, that commingling of absurdity, surprise, and bewilderment in a tremor of struggling revolt, that notion of being captured by the incredible which is of the very essence of dreams. . . ."

He was silent for a while.

". . . No, it is impossible; it is impossible to convey the life-sensation of any given epoch of one's existence — that which makes its truth, its meaning — its subtle and penetrating essence. It is impossible. We live as we dream — alone. . . ."

He paused again as if reflecting, then added —

"Of course in this you fellows see more than I could then. You see me, whom you know. . . ."

It had become so pitch dark that we listeners could hardly see one another. For a long time already he, sitting apart, had been no more to us than a voice. There was not a word from anybody. The others might have been asleep, but I was awake. I listened, I listened on the watch for the sentence, for the word, that would give me the clue to the faint uneasiness inspired by this narrative that seemed to shape itself without human lips in the heavy night-air of the river.

"... Yes—I let him run on," Marlow began again, "and think what he pleased about the powers that were behind me. I did! And there was nothing behind me! There was nothing but that wretched, old, mangled steamboat I was leaning against, while he talked fluently about 'the necessity for every man to get on.' 'And when one comes out here, you conceive, it is not to gaze at the moon.' Mr. Kurtz was a 'universal genius,' but even a genius would find it easier to work with 'adequate tools— intelligent men.' He did not make bricks—why, there was a physical impossibility in the way—as I was well aware; and if he did secretarial work for the manager, it was because 'no sensible man rejects wantonly the confidence of his superiors.' Did I see it? I saw it. What more did I want? What I really wanted was rivets, by heaven! Rivets. To get on with the work—to stop the hole. Rivets I wanted. There were cases of them down at the coast—cases—piled up—burst—split! You kicked a loose rivet at every second step in that station yard on the hillside. Rivets had rolled into the grove of death. You could fill your pockets with rivets for the trouble of stooping down—and there wasn't one rivet to be found where it was wanted. We had plates that would do, but nothing to fasten them with. And every week the messenger, a lone negro, letter-bag on shoulder and staff in hand, left our station for the coast. And several times a week a coast caravan came in with trade goods—ghastly glazed calico that made you shudder only to look at it, glass beads value about a penny a quart, confounded spotted cotton handkerchiefs. And no rivets. Three carriers could have brought all that was wanted to set that steamboat afloat.

"He was becoming confidential now, but I fancy my unresponsive attitude must have exasperated him at last, for he judged it necessary to inform me he feared neither God nor devil, let alone any mere man. I said I could see that very well, but what I wanted was a certain quantity of rivets—and rivets were what really Mr. Kurtz wanted, if he had only known it. Now letters went to the coast every week. . . . 'My dear sir,' he cried, 'I write from dictation.' I demanded rivets. There was a way—for an intelligent man. He changed his manner; became very cold, and suddenly began to talk about a hippopotamus; wondered whether sleeping on board the steamer (I stuck to my salvage night and day) I wasn't disturbed. There was an old hippo that had the bad habit of getting out on the bank and roaming at night over the station grounds. The pilgrims used to turn out in a body and empty every rifle they could lay hands on at him. Some even had sat up o' nights for him. All this energy was wasted, though. 'That animal has a charmed life,' he said; 'but you can say this only of brutes in this country. No man—you apprehend me?—no man here bears a charmed life.' He stood there for a moment in the moonlight with his delicate hooked nose set a little askew, and his mica eyes glittering without a wink, then, with a curt Good-night, he strode off. I could see he was disturbed and considerably puzzled, which made me feel more hopeful than I had been for days. It was a great comfort to turn from that chap to my influential friend, the battered, twisted, ruined, tin-pot steamboat. I clambered on board. She rang under my feet like an empty Huntley & Palmer biscuit-tin kicked along a gutter; she was nothing so solid in make, and rather less pretty in shape, but I had expended enough hard work on her to make me love her. No influential friend would have served me better. She had given me a chance to come out a bit—to find out what I could do. No, I don't like work. I had rather laze about and think of all the fine things that can be done. I don't like work—no man does—but I like what is in the work,—the chance to find yourself. Your own reality—for yourself, not for others—what no other man can ever know. They can only see the mere show, and never can tell what it really means.

"I was not surprised to see somebody sitting aft, on the deck, with his legs dangling over the mud. You see I rather chummed with the few mechanics there were in that station, whom the other pilgrims naturally despised—on account of their imperfect manners, I suppose. This was the foreman—a boiler-maker by trade—a good worker. He was a lank, bony, yellow-faced man, with big intense eyes. His aspect was worried, and his head was as bald as the palm of my hand; but his hair in falling seemed to have stuck to his chin, and had prospered in the new locality, for his beard hung down to his waist. He was a widower with six young children (he had left them in charge of a sister of his to come out there), and the passion of his life was pigeon-flying. He was an enthusiast and a connoisseur. He would rave about pigeons. After work hours he used sometimes to come over from his hut for a talk about his children and his pigeons; at work, when he had to crawl in the mud under the bottom of the steamboat, he would tie up that beard of his in a kind of white serviette[18] he brought for the purpose. It had loops to go over his ears. In the evening he could be seen squatted on the bank rinsing that wrapper in the creek with great care, then spreading it solemnly on a bush to dry.

"I slapped him on the back and shouted, 'We shall have rivets!' He scrambled to his feet exclaiming, 'No! Rivets!' as though he couldn't believe his ears. Then in a low voice, 'You . . . eh?' I don't know why we behaved like lunatics. I put my finger to the side of my nose and nodded mysteriously. 'Good for you!' he cried, snapped his fingers above his head, lifting one foot. I tried a jig. We capered on the iron deck. A frightful clatter came out of that hulk, and the virgin forest on the other bank of the creek sent it back in a thundering roll upon the sleeping station. It must have made some of the pilgrims sit up in their hovels. A dark figure obscured the lighted doorway of the manager's hut, vanished, then, a second or so after, the doorway itself vanished, too. We stopped, and the silence driven away by the stamping of our feet flowed back again from the recesses of the land. The great wall of vegetation, an exuberant and entangled mass of trunks, branches, leaves, boughs, festoons, motionless in the moonlight, was like a rioting invasion of soundless life, a rolling wave of plants, piled up, crested, ready to topple over the creek, to sweep every little man of us out of his little existence. And it moved not. A deadened burst of mighty splashes and snorts reached us from afar, as though an ichthyosaurus had been taking a bath of glitter in the great river. 'After all,' said the boiler-maker in a reasonable tone, 'why

---

[18] **serviette:** A napkin.

shouldn't we get the rivets?' Why not, indeed! I did not know of any reason why we shouldn't. 'They'll come in three weeks,' I said, confidently.

"But they didn't. Instead of rivets there came an invasion, an infliction, a visitation. It came in sections during the next three weeks, each section headed by a donkey carrying a white man in new clothes and tan shoes, bowing from that elevation right and left to the impressed pilgrims. A quarrelsome band of footsore sulky niggers trod on the heels of the donkey; a lot of tents, camp-stools, tin boxes, white cases, brown bales would be shot down in the courtyard, and the air of mystery would deepen a little over the muddle of the station. Five such instalments came, with their absurd air of disorderly flight with the loot of innumerable outfit shops and provision stores, that, one would think, they were lugging, after a raid, into the wilderness for equitable division. It was an inextricable mess of things decent in themselves but that human folly made look like the spoils of thieving.

"This devoted band called itself the Eldorado Exploring Expedition, and I believe they were sworn to secrecy. Their talk, however, was the talk of sordid buccaneers: it was reckless without hardihood, greedy without audacity, and cruel without courage; there was not an atom of foresight or of serious intention in the whole batch of them, and they did not seem aware these things are wanted for the work of the world. To tear treasure out of the bowels of the land was their desire, with no more moral purpose at the back of it than there is in burglars breaking into a safe. Who paid the expenses of the noble enterprise I don't know; but the uncle of our manager was leader of that lot.

"In exterior he resembled a butcher in a poor neighbourhood, and his eyes had a look of sleepy cunning. He carried his fat paunch with ostentation on his short legs, and during the time his gang infested the station spoke to no one but his nephew. You could see these two roaming about all day long with their heads close together in an everlasting confab.

"I had given up worrying myself about the rivets. One's capacity for that kind of folly is more limited than you would suppose. I said Hang!—and let things slide. I had plenty of time for meditation, and now and then I would give some thought to Kurtz. I wasn't very interested in him. No. Still, I was curious to see whether this man, who had come out equipped with moral ideas of some sort, would climb to the top after all and how he would set about his work when there."

2

"One evening as I was lying flat on the deck of my steamboat, I heard voices approaching—and there were the nephew and the uncle strolling along the bank. I laid my head on my arm again, and had nearly lost myself in a doze, when somebody said in my ear, as it were: 'I am as harmless as a little child, but I don't like to be dictated to. Am I the manager—or am I not? I was ordered to send him there. It's incredible.' . . . I became aware that the two were standing on the shore alongside the forepart of the steamboat, just below my head. I did not move; it did not occur to me to move: I was sleepy. 'It *is* unpleasant,' grunted the uncle. 'He has asked the Administration to be sent there,' said the other, 'with the idea of showing what he could do; and I was instructed accordingly. Look at the influence that man must have. Is it not frightful?' They both agreed it was frightful, then made several bizarre remarks: 'Make rain and fine weather—one man—the Council—by the nose'— bits of absurd sentences that got the better of my drowsiness, so that I had pretty near the whole of my wits about me when the uncle said, 'The climate may do away with this difficulty for you. Is he alone there?' 'Yes,' answered the manager; 'he sent his assistant down the river with a note to me in these terms: "Clear this poor devil out of the country, and don't bother sending more of that sort. I had rather be alone than have the kind of men you can dispose of with me." It was more than a year ago. Can you imagine such impudence!' 'Anything since then?' asked the other, hoarsely. 'Ivory,' jerked the nephew; 'lots of it—prime sort—lots—most annoying, from him.' 'And with that?' questioned the heavy rumble. 'Invoice,' was the reply fired out, so to speak. Then silence. They had been talking about Kurtz.

"I was broad awake by this time, but, lying perfectly at ease, remained still, having no inducement to change my position. 'How did that ivory come all this way?' growled the elder man, who seemed very vexed. The other explained that it had come with a fleet of canoes in charge of an English half-caste clerk Kurtz had with him; that Kurtz had apparently intended to return himself, the station being by that time bare of goods and stores, but after coming three hundred miles, had suddenly decided to go back, which he started to do alone in a small dugout with four paddlers, leaving the half-caste to continue down the river with the ivory. The two fellows there seemed astounded at anybody attempting such a thing. They were at a loss for an adequate motive. As to me, I seemed to see Kurtz for the first time. It was a distinct glimpse: the dugout, four paddling savages, and the lone white man turning his back suddenly on the headquarters, on relief, on thoughts of home— perhaps; setting his face towards the depths of the wilderness, towards his empty and desolate station. I did not know the motive. Perhaps he was just simply a fine fellow who stuck to his work for its own sake. His name, you understand, had not been pronounced once. He was 'that man.' The half-caste, who, as far as I could see, had conducted a difficult trip with great prudence and pluck, was invariably alluded to as 'that scoundrel.' The 'scoundrel' had reported that the 'man' had been very ill—had recovered imperfectly. . . . The two below me moved away then a few paces, and strolled back and forth at some little distance. I heard: 'Military post—doctor— two hundred miles—quite alone now—unavoidable delays—nine months—no news—strange rumours.' They approached again, just as the manager was saying, 'No one, as far as I know, unless a species of wandering trader—a pestilential fellow, snapping ivory from the natives.' Who was it they were talking about now? I gathered in snatches that this was some man supposed to be in Kurtz's district, and of whom the manager did not approve. 'We will not be free from unfair competition till one of these fellows is hanged for an example,' he said. 'Certainly,' grunted the other; 'get him hanged! Why not? Anything—anything can be done in this country. That's what I say; nobody here, you understand, *here,* can endanger your position. And why? You stand the climate—you outlast them all. The danger is in Europe; but there before I left I took care to——' They moved off and whispered, then their voices rose again. 'The extraordinary series of delays is not my fault. I did my best.'

The fat man sighed. 'Very sad.' 'And the pestiferous absurdity of his talk,' continued the other; 'he bothered me enough when he was here. "Each station should be like a beacon on the road towards better things, a centre for trade of course, but also for humanizing, improving, instructing." Conceive you—that ass! And he wants to be manager! No, it's—' Here he got choked by excessive indignation, and I lifted my head the least bit. I was surprised to see how near they were—right under me. I could have spat upon their hats. They were looking on the ground, absorbed in thought. The manager was switching his leg with a slender twig: his sagacious relative lifted his head. 'You have been well since you came out this time?' he asked. The other gave a start. 'Who? I? Oh! Like a charm—like a charm. But the rest—oh, my goodness! All sick. They die so quick, too, that I haven't the time to send them out of the country—it's incredible!' 'H'm. Just so,' grunted the uncle. 'Ah! my boy, trust to this—I say, trust to this.' I saw him extend his short flipper of an arm for a gesture that took in the forest, the creek, the mud, the river,—seemed to beckon with a dishonouring flourish before the sunlit face of the land a treacherous appeal to the lurking death, to the hidden evil, to the profound darkness of its heart. It was so startling that I leaped to my feet and looked back at the edge of the forest, as though I had expected an answer of some sort to that black display of confidence. You know the foolish notions that come to one sometimes. The high stillness confronted these two figures with its ominous patience, waiting for the passing away of a fantastic invasion.

"They swore aloud together—out of sheer fright, I believe—then pretending not to know anything of my existence, turned back to the station. The sun was low; and leaning forward side by side, they seemed to be tugging painfully uphill their two ridiculous shadows of unequal length, that trailed behind them slowly over the tall grass without bending a single blade.

"In a few days the Eldorado Expedition went into the patient wilderness, that closed upon it as the sea closes over a diver. Long afterwards the news came that all the donkeys were dead. I know nothing as to the fate of the less valuable animals. They, no doubt, like the rest of us, found what they deserved. I did not inquire. I was then rather excited at the prospect of meeting Kurtz very soon. When I say very soon I mean it comparatively. It was just two months from the day we left the creek when we came to the bank below Kurtz's station.

"Going up that river was like travelling back to the earliest beginnings of the world, when vegetation rioted on the earth and the big trees were kings. An empty stream, a great silence, an impenetrable forest. The air was warm, thick, heavy, sluggish. There was no joy in the brilliance of sunshine. The long stretches of the waterway ran on, deserted, into the gloom of overshadowed distances. On silvery sandbanks hippos and alligators sunned themselves side by side. The broadening waters flowed through a mob of wooded islands; you lost your way on that river as you would in a desert, and butted all day long against shoals, trying to find the channel, till you thought yourself bewitched and cut off for ever from everything you had known once—somewhere—far away—in another existence perhaps. There were moments when one's past came back to one, as it will sometimes when you have not a moment to spare to yourself; but it came in the shape of an unrestful and noisy dream, remembered with wonder amongst the overwhelming realities of this strange world of plants, and water, and silence. And this stillness of life did not in the least resemble a peace. It was the stillness of an implacable force brooding over an inscrutable intention. It looked at you with a vengeful aspect. I got used to it afterwards; I did not see it any more; I had no time. I had to keep guessing at the channel; I had to discern, mostly by inspiration, the signs of hidden banks; I watched for sunken stones; I was learning to clap my teeth smartly before my heart flew out, when I shaved by a fluke some infernal sly old snag that would have ripped the life out of the tin-pot steamboat and drowned all the pilgrims; I had to keep a look-out for the signs of dead wood we could cut up in the night for next day's steaming. When you have to attend to things of that sort, to the mere incidents of the surface, the reality—the reality, I tell you—fades. The inner truth is hidden—luckily, luckily. But I felt it all the same; I felt often its mysterious stillness watching me at my monkey tricks, just as it watches you fellows performing on your respective tightropes for—what is it? half-a-crown a tumble——"

"Try to be civil, Marlow," growled a voice, and I knew there was at least one listener awake besides myself.

"I beg your pardon. I forgot the heartache which makes up the rest of the price. And indeed what does the price matter, if the trick be well done? You do your tricks very well. And I didn't do badly either, since I managed not to sink that steamboat on my first trip. It's a wonder to me yet. Imagine a blindfolded man set to drive a van over a bad road. I sweated and shivered over that business considerably, I can tell you. After all, for a seaman, to scrape the bottom of the thing that's supposed to float all the time under his care is the unpardonable sin. No one may know of it, but you never forget the thump—eh? A blow on the very heart. You remember it, you dream of it, you wake up at night and think of it—years after—and go hot and cold all over. I don't pretend to say that steamboat floated all the time. More than once she had to wade for a bit, with twenty cannibals splashing around and pushing. We had enlisted some of these chaps on the way for a crew. Fine fellows—cannibals—in their place. They were men one could work with, and I am grateful to them. And, after all, they did not eat each other before my face: they had brought along a provision of hippo-meat which went rotten, and made the mystery of the wilderness stink in my nostrils. Phoo! I can sniff it now. I had the manager on board and three or four pilgrims with their staves—all complete. Sometimes we came upon a station close by the bank, clinging to the skirts of the unknown, and the white men rushing out of a tumble-down hovel, with great gestures of joy and surprise and welcome, seemed very strange—had the appearance of being held there captive by a spell. The word ivory would ring in the air for a while—and on we went again into the silence, along empty reaches, round the still bends, between the high walls of our winding way, reverberating in hollow claps the ponderous beat of the stern-wheel. Trees, trees, millions of trees, massive, immense, running up high; and at their foot, hugging the bank against the stream, crept the little begrimed steamboat, like a sluggish beetle crawling on the floor of a lofty portico. It made you feel very small, very lost, and yet it was not altogether depressing, that feeling. After all, if you were small, the grimy beetle crawled on—which was just what you wanted it to do. Where the pilgrims

imagined it crawled to I don't know. To some place where they expected to get something, I bet! For me it crawled towards Kurtz—exclusively; but when the steam-
pipes started leaking we crawled very slow. The reaches opened before us and closed
behind, as if the forest had stepped leisurely across the water to bar the way for our
return. We penetrated deeper and deeper into the heart of darkness. It was very quiet
there. At night sometimes the roll of drums behind the curtain of trees would run up
the river and remain sustained faintly, as if hovering in the air high over our heads,
till the first break of day. Whether it meant war, peace, or prayer we could not tell.
The dawns were heralded by the descent of a chill stillness; the wood-cutters slept,
their fires burned low; the snapping of a twig would make you start. We were wanderers on a prehistoric earth, on an earth that wore the aspect of an unknown planet.
We could have fancied ourselves the first of men taking possession of an accursed
inheritance, to be subdued at the cost of profound anguish and of excessive toil. But
suddenly, as we struggled round a bend, there would be a glimpse of rush walls, of
peaked grass-roofs, a burst of yells, a whirl of black limbs, a mass of hands clapping,
of feet stamping, of bodies swaying, of eyes rolling, under the droop of heavy and
motionless foliage. The steamer toiled along slowly on the edge of a black and
incomprehensible frenzy. The prehistoric man was cursing us, praying to us, welcoming us—who could tell? We were cut off from the comprehension of our surroundings; we glided past like phantoms, wondering and secretly appalled, as sane
men would be before an enthusiastic outbreak in a madhouse. We could not understand because we were too far and could not remember, because we were travelling
in the night of first ages, of those ages that are gone, leaving hardly a sign—and no
memories.

"The earth seemed unearthly. We are accustomed to look upon the shackled
form of a conquered monster, but there—there you could look at a thing monstrous
and free. It was unearthly, and the men were——No, they were not inhuman. Well,
you know, that was the worst of it—this suspicion of their not being inhuman. It
would come slowly to one. They howled and leaped, and spun, and made horrid
faces; but what thrilled you was just the thought of their humanity—like yours—
the thought of your remote kinship with this wild and passionate uproar. Ugly. Yes, it
was ugly enough; but if you were man enough you would admit to yourself that
there was in you just the faintest trace of a response to the terrible frankness of that
noise, a dim suspicion of there being a meaning in it which you—you so remote
from the night of first ages—could comprehend. And why not? The mind of man is
capable of anything—because everything is in it, all the past as well as all the future.
What was there after all? Joy, fear, sorrow, devotion, valour, rage—who can tell?—
but truth—truth stripped of its cloak of time. Let the fool gape and shudder—the
man knows, and can look on without a wink. But he must at least be as much of a
man as these on the shore. He must meet that truth with his own true stuff—with
his own inborn strength. Principles won't do. Acquisitions, clothes, pretty rags—
rags that would fly off at the first good shake. No; you want a deliberate belief.
An appeal to me in this fiendish row—is there? Very well; I hear; I admit, but I have
a voice, too, and for good or evil mine is the speech that cannot be silenced. Of
course, a fool, what with sheer fright and fine sentiments, is always safe. Who's that

grunting? You wonder I didn't go ashore for a howl and a dance? Well, no—I didn't. Fine sentiments, you say? Fine sentiments, be hanged! I had no time. I had to mess about with white-lead and strips of woollen blanket helping to put bandages on those leaky steam-pipes—I tell you. I had to watch the steering, and circumvent those snags, and get the tin-pot along by hook or by crook. There was surface-truth enough in these things to save a wiser man. And between whiles I had to look after the savage who was fireman. He was an improved specimen; he could fire up a vertical boiler. He was there below me, and, upon my word, to look at him was as edifying as seeing a dog in a parody of breeches and a feather hat, walking on his hind-legs. A few months of training had done for that really fine chap. He squinted at the steam-gauge and at the water-gauge with an evident effort of intrepidity—and he had filed teeth, too, the poor devil, and the wool of his pate shaved into queer patterns, and three ornamental scars on each of his cheeks. He ought to have been clapping his hands and stamping his feet on the bank, instead of which he was hard at work, a thrall to strange witchcraft, full of improving knowledge. He was useful because he had been instructed; and what he knew was this—that should the water in that transparent thing disappear, the evil spirit inside the boiler would get angry through the greatness of his thirst, and take a terrible vengeance. So he sweated and fired up and watched the glass fearfully (with an impromptu charm, made of rags, tied to his arm, and a piece of polished bone, as big as a watch, stuck flat-ways through his lower lip), while the wooded banks slipped past us slowly, the short noise was left behind, the interminable miles of silence—and we crept on, towards Kurtz. But the snags were thick, the water was treacherous and shallow, the boiler seemed indeed to have a sulky devil in it, and thus neither that fireman nor I had any time to peer into our creepy thoughts.

"Some fifty miles below the Inner Station we came upon a hut of reeds, an inclined and melancholy pole, with the unrecognizable tatters of what had been a flag of some sort flying from it, and a neatly stacked wood-pile. This was unexpected. We came to the bank, and on the stack of firewood found a flat piece of board with some faded pencil-writing on it. When deciphered it said: 'Wood for you. Hurry up. Approach cautiously.' There was a signature, but it was illegible—not Kurtz—a much longer word. 'Hurry up.' Where? Up the river? 'Approach cautiously.' We had not done so. But the warning could not have been meant for the place where it could be only found after approach. Something was wrong above. But what—and how much? That was the question. We commented adversely upon the imbecility of that telegraphic style. The bush around said nothing, and would not let us look very far, either. A torn curtain of red twill hung in the doorway of the hut, and flapped sadly in our faces. The dwelling was dismantled; but we could see a white man had lived there not very long ago. There remained a rude table—a plank on two posts; a heap of rubbish reposed in a dark corner, and by the door I picked up a book. It had lost its covers, and the pages had been thumbed into a state of extremely dirty softness; but the back had been lovingly stitched afresh with white cotton thread, which looked clean yet. It was an extraordinary find. Its title was, *An Inquiry into some Points of Seamanship*, by a man Towser, Towson—some such name—Master in his Majesty's Navy. The matter looked dreary reading enough, with illustrative diagrams and repulsive tables of figures, and the copy was sixty years old. I handled this amazing antiquity with the greatest possible tenderness, lest it should dissolve in my hands. Within, Towson or Towser was inquiring earnestly into the breaking strain of ships' chains and tackle, and other such matters. Not a very enthralling book; but at the first glance you could see there a singleness of intention, an honest concern for the right way of going to work, which made these humble pages, thought out so many years ago, luminous with another than a professional light. The simple old sailor, with his talk of chains and purchases,[19] made me forget the jungle and the pilgrims in a delicious sensation of having come upon something unmistakably real. Such a book being there was wonderful enough; but still more astounding were the notes pencilled in the margin, and plainly referring to the text. I couldn't believe my eyes! They were in cipher! Yes, it looked like cipher. Fancy a man lugging with him a book of that description into this nowhere and studying it—and making notes—in cipher at that! It was an extravagant mystery.

"I had been dimly aware for some time of a worrying noise, and when I lifted my eyes I saw the wood-pile was gone, and the manager, aided by all the pilgrims, was shouting at me from the river-side. I slipped the book into my pocket. I assure you to leave off reading was like tearing myself away from the shelter of an old and solid friendship.

"I started the lame engine ahead. 'It must be this miserable trader—this intruder,' exclaimed the manager, looking back malevolently at the place we had left. 'He must be English,' I said. 'It will not save him from getting into trouble if he is not careful,' muttered the manager darkly. I observed with assumed innocence that no man was safe from trouble in this world.

"The current was more rapid now, the steamer seemed at her last gasp, the stern-wheel flopped languidly, and I caught myself listening on tiptoe for the next beat of the boat, for in sober truth I expected the wretched thing to give up every moment. It was like watching the last flickers of a life. But still we crawled. Sometimes I would pick out a tree a little way ahead to measure our progress towards Kurtz by, but I lost it invariably before we got abreast. To keep the eyes so long on one thing was too much for human patience. The manager displayed a beautiful resignation. I fretted and fumed and took to arguing with myself whether or no I would talk openly with Kurtz; but before I could come to any conclusion it occurred to me that my speech or my silence, indeed any action of mine, would be a mere futility. What did it matter what any one knew or ignored? What did it matter who was manager? One gets sometimes such a flash of insight. The essentials of this affair lay deep under the surface, beyond my reach, and beyond my power of meddling.

"Towards the evening of the second day we judged ourselves about eight miles from Kurtz's station. I wanted to push on; but the manager looked grave, and told me the navigation up there was so dangerous that it would be advisable, the sun being very low already, to wait where we were till next morning. Moreover, he pointed out that if the warning to approach cautiously were to be followed, we must

---

[19] **purchases:** Tackles or levers or similar mechanical devices.

approach in daylight—not at dusk, or in the dark. This was sensible enough. Eight miles meant nearly three hours' steaming for us, and I could also see suspicious ripples at the upper end of the reach. Nevertheless, I was annoyed beyond expression at the delay, and most unreasonably, too, since one night more could not matter much after so many months. As we had plenty of wood, and caution was the word, I brought up in the middle of the stream. The reach was narrow, straight, with high sides like a railway cutting. The dusk came gliding into it long before the sun had set. The current ran smooth and swift, but a dumb immobility sat on the banks. The living trees, lashed together by the creepers and every living bush of the undergrowth, might have been changed into stone, even to the slenderest twig, to the lightest leaf. It was not sleep—it seemed unnatural, like a state of trance. Not the faintest sound of any kind could be heard. You looked on amazed, and began to suspect yourself of being deaf—then the night came suddenly, and struck you blind as well. About three in the morning some large fish leaped, and the loud splash made me jump as though a gun had been fired. When the sun rose there was a white fog, very warm and clammy, and more blinding than the night. It did not shift or drive; it was just there, standing all round you like something solid. At eight or nine, perhaps, it lifted as a shutter lifts. We had a glimpse of the towering multitude of trees, of the immense matted jungle, with the blazing little ball of the sun hanging over it—all perfectly still—and then the white shutter came down again, smoothly, as if sliding in greased grooves. I ordered the chain, which we had begun to heave in, to be paid out again. Before it stopped running with a muffled rattle, a cry, a very loud cry, as of infinite desolation, soared slowly in the opaque air. It ceased. A complaining clamour, modulated in savage discords, filled our ears. The sheer unexpectedness of it made my hair stir under my cap. I don't know how it struck the others: to me it seemed as though the mist itself had screamed, so suddenly, and apparently from all sides at once, did this tumultuous and mournful uproar arise. It culminated in a hurried outbreak of almost intolerably excessive shrieking, which stopped short, leaving us stiffened in a variety of silly attitudes, and obstinately listening to the nearly as appalling and excessive silence. 'Good God! What is the meaning——' stammered at my elbow one of the pilgrims,—a little fat man, with sandy hair and red whiskers, who wore side-spring boots, and pink pyjamas tucked into his socks. Two others remained open-mouthed a whole minute, then dashed into the little cabin, to rush out incontinently and stand darting scared glances, with Winchesters at 'ready' in their hands. What we could see was just the steamer we were on, her outlines blurred as though she had been on the point of dissolving, and a misty strip of water, perhaps two feet broad, around her—and that was all. The rest of the world was nowhere, as far as our eyes and ears were concerned. Just nowhere. Gone, disappeared; swept off without leaving a whisper or a shadow behind.

"I went forward, and ordered the chain to be hauled in short, so as to be ready to trip the anchor and move the steamboat at once if necessary. 'Will they attack?' whispered an awed voice. 'We will be all butchered in this fog,' murmured another. The faces twitched with the strain, the hands trembled slightly, the eyes forgot to wink. It was very curious to see the contrast of expressions of the white men and of the black fellows of our crew, who were as much strangers to that part of the river as we, though their homes were only eight hundred miles away. The whites, of course greatly discomposed, had besides a curious look of being painfully shocked by such an outrageous row. The others had an alert, naturally interested expression; but their faces were essentially quiet, even those of the one or two who grinned as they hauled at the chain. Several exchanged short, grunting phrases, which seemed to settle the matter to their satisfaction. Their headman, a young, broad-chested black, severely draped in dark-blue fringed cloths, with fierce nostrils and his hair all done up art-fully in oily ringlets, stood near me. 'Aha!' I said, just for good fellowship's sake. 'Catch 'im,' he snapped, with a bloodshot widening of his eyes and a flash of sharp teeth—'catch 'im. Give 'im to us.' 'To you, eh?' I asked; 'what would you do with them?' 'Eat 'im!' he said, curtly, and, leaning his elbow on the rail, looked out into the fog in a dignified and profoundly pensive attitude. I would no doubt have been properly horrified, had it not occurred to me that he and his chaps must be very hungry: that they must have been growing increasingly hungry for at least this month past. They had been engaged for six months (I don't think a single one of them had any clear idea of time, as we at the end of countless ages have. They still belonged to the beginnings of time—had no inherited experience to teach them as it were), and of course, as long as there was a piece of paper written over in accor-dance with some farcical law or other made down the river, it didn't enter anybody's head to trouble how they would live. Certainly they had brought with them some rotten hippo-meat, which couldn't have lasted very long, anyway, even if the pil-grims hadn't, in the midst of a shocking hullabaloo, thrown a considerable quantity of it overboard. It looked like a high-handed proceeding; but it was really a case of legitimate self-defence. You can't breathe dead hippo waking, sleeping, and eating, and at the same time keep your precarious grip on existence. Besides that, they had given them every week three pieces of brass wire, each about nine inches long; and the theory was they were to buy their provisions with that currency in river-side vil-lages. You can see how *that* worked. There were either no villages, or the people were hostile, or the director, who like the rest of us fed out of tins, with an occasional old he-goat thrown in, didn't want to stop the steamer for some more or less recondite reason. So, unless they swallowed the wire itself, or made loops of it to snare the fishes with, I don't see what good their extravagant salary could be to them. I must say it was paid with a regularity worthy of a large and honourable trading company. For the rest, the only thing to eat—though it didn't look eatable in the least—I saw in their possession was a few lumps of some stuff like half-cooked dough, of a dirty lavender colour, they kept wrapped in leaves, and now and then swallowed a piece of, but so small that it seemed done more for the looks of the thing than for any seri-ous purpose of sustenance. Why in the name of all the gnawing devils of hunger they didn't go for us—they were thirty to five—and have a good tuck-in[20] for once, amazes me now when I think of it. They were big powerful men, with not much capacity to weigh the consequences, with courage, with strength, even yet, though their skins were no longer glossy and their muscles no longer hard. And I saw that

---

[20] **tuck-in:** A hearty meal.

something restraining, one of those human secrets that baffle probability, had come into play there. I looked at them with a swift quickening of interest — not because it occurred to me I might be eaten by them before very long, though I own to you that just then I perceived — in a new light, as it were — how unwholesome the pilgrims looked, and I hoped, yes I positively hoped, that my aspect was not so — what shall I say? — so — unappetizing: a touch of fantastic vanity which fitted well with the dream-sensation that pervaded all my days at that time. Perhaps I had a little fever, too. One can't live with one's finger everlastingly on one's pulse. I had often 'a little fever,' or a little touch of other things — the playful paw-strokes of the wilderness, the preliminary trifling before the more serious onslaught which came in due course. Yes; I looked at them as you would on any human being, with a curiosity of their impulses, motives, capacities, weaknesses, when brought to the test of an inexorable physical necessity. Restraint! What possible restraint? Was it superstition, disgust, patience, fear — or some kind of primitive honour? No fear can stand up to hunger, no patience can wear it out, disgust simply does not exist where hunger is; and as to superstition, beliefs, and what you may call principles, they are less than chaff in a breeze. Don't you know the devilry of lingering starvation, its exasperating torment, its black thoughts, its sombre and brooding ferocity? Well, I do. It takes a man all his inborn strength to fight hunger properly. It's really easier to face bereavement, dishonour, and the perdition of one's soul — than this kind of prolonged hunger. Sad, but true. And these chaps, too, had no earthly reason for any kind of scruple. Restraint! I would just as soon have expected restraint from a hyena prowling amongst the corpses of a battlefield. But there was the fact facing me — the fact dazzling, to be seen, like the foam on the depths of the sea, like a ripple on an unfathomable enigma, a mystery greater — when I thought of it — than the curious, inexplicable note of desperate grief in this savage clamour that had swept by us on the river-bank, behind the blind whiteness of the fog.

"Two pilgrims were quarrelling in hurried whispers as to which bank. 'Left.' 'No, no; how can you? Right, right, of course.' 'It is very serious,' said the manager's voice behind me; 'I would be desolated if anything should happen to Mr. Kurtz before we came up.' I looked at him, and had not the slightest doubt he was sincere. He was just the kind of man who would wish to preserve appearances. That was his restraint. But when he muttered something about going on at once, I did not even take the trouble to answer him. I knew, and he knew, that it was impossible. Were we to let go our hold of the bottom, we would be absolutely in the air — in space. We wouldn't be able to tell where we were going to — whether up or down stream, or across — till we fetched against one bank or the other, — and then we wouldn't know at first which it was. Of course I made no move. I had no mind for a smash-up. You couldn't imagine a more deadly place for a shipwreck. Whether drowned at once or not, we were sure to perish speedily in one way or another. 'I authorize you to take all the risks,' he said, after a short silence. 'I refuse to take any,' I said, shortly; which was just the answer he expected, though its tone might have surprised him. 'Well, I must defer to your judgment. You are captain,' he said, with marked civility. I turned my shoulder to him in sign of my appreciation, and looked into the fog. How long would it last? It was the most hopeless look-out. The approach to this Kurtz grubbing for ivory in the wretched bush was beset by as many dangers as though he had been an enchanted princess sleeping in a fabulous castle. 'Will they attack, do you think?' asked the manager, in a confidential tone.

"I did not think they would attack, for several obvious reasons. The thick fog was one. If they left the bank in their canoes they would get lost in it, as we would be if we attempted to move. Still, I had also judged the jungle of both banks quite impenetrable—and yet eyes were in it, eyes that had seen us. The river-side bushes were certainly very thick; but the undergrowth behind was evidently penetrable. However, during the short lift I had seen no canoes anywhere in the reach—certainly not abreast of the steamer. But what made the idea of attack inconceivable to me was the nature of the noise—of the cries we had heard. They had not the fierce character boding immediate hostile intention. Unexpected, wild, and violent as they had been, they had given me an irresistible impression of sorrow. The glimpse of the steamboat had for some reason filled those savages with unrestrained grief. The danger, if any, I expounded, was from our proximity to a great human passion let loose. Even extreme grief may ultimately vent itself in violence—but more generally takes the form of apathy. . . .

"You should have seen the pilgrims stare! They had no heart to grin, or even to revile me: but I believe they thought me gone mad—with fright, maybe. I delivered a regular lecture. My dear boys, it was no good bothering. Keep a look-out? Well, you may guess I watched the fog for the signs of lifting as a cat watches a mouse; but for anything else our eyes were of no more use to us than if we had been buried miles deep in a heap of cotton-wool. It felt like it, too—choking, warm, stifling. Besides, all I said, though it sounded extravagant, was absolutely true to fact. What we afterwards alluded to as an attack was really an attempt at repulse. The action was very far from being aggressive—it was not even defensive, in the usual sense: it was undertaken under the stress of desperation, and in its essence was purely protective.

"It developed itself, I should say, two hours after the fog lifted, and its commencement was at a spot, roughly speaking, about a mile and a half below Kurtz's station. We had just floundered and flopped round a bend, when I saw an islet, a mere grassy hummock of bright green, in the middle of the stream. It was the only thing of the kind; but as we opened the reach more, I perceived it was the head of a long sandbank, or rather of a chain of shallow patches stretching down the middle of the river. They were discoloured, just awash, and the whole lot was seen just under the water, exactly as a man's backbone is seen running down the middle of his back under the skin. Now, as far as I did see, I could go to the right or to the left of this. I didn't know either channel, of course. The banks looked pretty well alike, the depth appeared the same; but as I had been informed the station was on the west side, I naturally headed for the western passage.

"No sooner had we fairly entered it than I became aware it was much narrower than I had supposed. To the left of us there was the long uninterrupted shoal, and to the right a high, steep bank heavily overgrown with bushes. Above the bush the trees stood in serried ranks. The twigs overhung the current thickly, and from distance to distance a large limb of some tree projected rigidly over the stream. It was then well on in the afternoon, the face of the forest was gloomy, and a broad strip of shadow had already fallen on the water. In this shadow we steamed up—very slowly, as you may imagine. I sheered her well inshore—the water being deepest near the bank, as the sounding-pole informed me.

"One of my hungry and forbearing friends was sounding in the bows just below me. This steamboat was exactly like a decked scow. On the deck, there were two little teak-wood houses, with doors and windows. The boiler was in the fore-end, and the machinery right astern. Over the whole there was a light roof, supported on stanchions. The funnel projected through that roof, and in front of the funnel a small cabin built of light planks served for a pilot-house. It contained a couch, two camp-stools, a loaded Martini-Henry[21] leaning in one corner, a tiny table, and the steering-wheel. It had a wide door in front and a broad shutter at each side. All these were always thrown open, of course. I spent my days perched up there on the extreme fore-end of that roof, before the door. At night I slept, or tried to, on the couch. An athletic black belonging to some coast tribe, and educated by my poor predecessor, was the helmsman. He sported a pair of brass earrings, wore a blue cloth wrapper from the waist to the ankles, and thought all the world of himself. He was the most unstable kind of fool I had ever seen. He steered with no end of a swagger while you were by; but if he lost sight of you, he became instantly the prey of an abject funk, and would let that cripple of a steamboat get the upper hand of him in a minute.

"I was looking down at the sounding-pole, and feeling much annoyed to see at each try a little more of it stick out of that river, when I saw my poleman give up the business suddenly, and stretch himself flat on the deck, without even taking the trouble to haul his pole in. He kept hold on it though, and it trailed in the water. At the same time the fireman, whom I could also see below me, sat down abruptly before his furnace and ducked his head. I was amazed. Then I had to look at the river mighty quick, because there was a snag in the fairway. Sticks, little sticks, were flying about—thick: they were whizzing before my nose, dropping below me, striking behind me against my pilot-house. All this time the river, the shore, the woods, were very quiet—perfectly quiet. I could only hear the heavy splashing thump of the stern-wheel and the patter of these things. We cleared the snag clumsily. Arrows, by Jove! We were being shot at! I stepped in quickly to close the shutter on the land-side. That fool-helmsman, his hands on the spokes, was lifting his knees high, stamping his feet, champing his mouth, like a reined-in horse. Confound him! And we were staggering within ten feet of the bank. I had to lean right out to swing the heavy shutter, and I saw a face amongst the leaves on the level with my own, looking at me very fierce and steady; and then suddenly, as though a veil had been removed from my eyes, I made out, deep in the tangled gloom, naked breasts, arms, legs, glaring eyes,—the bush was swarming with human limbs in movement, glistening, of bronze colour. The twigs shook, swayed, and rustled, the arrows flew out of them, and then the shutter came to. 'Steer her straight,' I said to the helmsman. He held his head rigid, face forward; but his eyes rolled, he kept on lifting and setting down his feet gently, his mouth foamed a little. 'Keep quiet!' I said in a fury. I might just as well

---

[21] **Martini-Henry:** A powerful rifle.

have ordered a tree not to sway in the wind. I darted out. Below me there was a great scuffle of feet on the iron deck; confused exclamations; a voice screamed, 'Can you turn back?' I caught sight of a V-shaped ripple on the water ahead. What? Another snag! A fusillade burst out under my feet. The pilgrims had opened with their Winchesters, and were simply squirting lead into that bush. A deuce of a lot of smoke came up and drove slowly forward. I swore at it. Now I couldn't see the ripple or the snag either. I stood in the doorway, peering, and the arrows came in swarms. They might have been poisoned, but they looked as though they wouldn't kill a cat. The bush began to howl. Our wood-cutters raised a warlike whoop; the report of a rifle just at my back deafened me. I glanced over my shoulder, and the pilot-house was yet full of noise and smoke when I made a dash at the wheel. The fool-nigger had dropped everything, to throw the shutter open and let off that Martini-Henry. He stood before the wide opening, glaring, and I yelled at him to come back, while I straightened the sudden twist out of that steamboat. There was no room to turn even if I had wanted to, the snag was somewhere very near ahead in that confounded smoke, there was no time to lose, so I just crowded her into the bank — right into the bank, where I knew the water was deep.

"We tore slowly along the overhanging bushes in a whirl of broken twigs and flying leaves. The fusillade below stopped short, as I had foreseen it would when the squirts got empty. I threw my head back to a glinting whizz that traversed the pilot-house, in at one shutter-hole and out at the other. Looking past that mad helmsman, who was shaking the empty rifle and yelling at the shore, I saw vague forms of men running bent double, leaping, gliding, distinct, incomplete, evanescent. Something big appeared in the air before the shutter, the rifle went overboard, and the man stepped back swiftly, looked at me over his shoulder in an extraordinary, profound, familiar manner, and fell upon my feet. The side of his head hit the wheel twice, and the end of what appeared a long cane clattered round and knocked over a little camp-stool. It looked as though after wrenching that thing from somebody ashore he had lost his balance in the effort. The thin smoke had blown away, we were clear of the snag, and looking ahead I could see that in another hundred yards or so I would be free to sheer off, away from the bank; but my feet felt so very warm and wet that I had to look down. The man had rolled on his back and stared straight up at me; both his hands clutched that cane. It was the shaft of a spear that, either thrown or lunged through the opening, had caught him in the side just below the ribs; the blade had gone in out of sight, after making a frightful gash; my shoes were full; a pool of blood lay very still, gleaming dark-red under the wheel; his eyes shone with an amazing lustre. The fusillade burst out again. He looked at me anxiously, gripping the spear like something precious, with an air of being afraid I would try to take it away from him. I had to make an effort to free my eyes from his gaze and attend to the steering. With one hand I felt above my head for the line of the steam whistle, and jerked out screech after screech hurriedly. The tumult of angry and warlike yells was checked instantly, and then from the depths of the woods went out such a tremulous and prolonged wail of mournful fear and utter despair as may be imagined to follow the flight of the last hope from the earth. There was a great commotion in the bush; the shower of arrows stopped, a few dropping shots rang out sharply — then silence, in which the languid beat of the stern-wheel came plainly to my ears. I put the helm hard a-starboard at the moment when the pilgrim in pink pyjamas, very hot and agitated, appeared in the doorway. 'The manager sends me——' he began in an official tone, and stopped short. 'Good God!' he said, glaring at the wounded man.

"We two whites stood over him, and his lustrous and inquiring glance enveloped us both. I declare it looked as though he would presently put to us some question in an understandable language; but he died without uttering a sound, without moving a limb, without twitching a muscle. Only in the very last moment, as though in response to some sign we could not see, to some whisper we could not hear, he frowned heavily, and that frown gave to his black death-mask an inconceivably sombre, brooding, and menacing expression. The lustre of inquiring glance faded swiftly into vacant glassiness. 'Can you steer?' I asked the agent eagerly. He looked very dubious; but I made a grab at his arm, and he understood at once I meant him to steer whether or no. To tell you the truth, I was morbidly anxious to change my shoes and socks. 'He is dead,' murmured the fellow, immensely impressed. 'No doubt about it,' said I, tugging like mad at the shoe-laces. 'And by the way, I suppose Mr. Kurtz is dead as well by this time.'

"For the moment that was the dominant thought. There was a sense of extreme disappointment, as though I had found out I had been striving after something altogether without a substance. I couldn't have been more disgusted if I had travelled all this way for the sole purpose of talking with Mr. Kurtz. Talking with . . . I flung one shoe overboard, and became aware that that was exactly what I had been looking forward to—a talk with Kurtz. I made the strange discovery that I had never imagined him as doing, you know, but as discoursing. I didn't say to myself, 'Now I will never see him,' or 'Now I will never shake him by the hand,' but, 'now I will never hear him.' The man presented himself as a voice. Not of course that I did not connect him with some sort of action. Hadn't I been told in all the tones of jealousy and admiration that he had collected, bartered, swindled, or stolen more ivory than all the other agents together? That was not the point. The point was in his being a gifted creature, and that of all his gifts the one that stood out preëminently, that carried with it a sense of real presence, was his ability to talk, his words—the gift of expression, the bewildering, the illuminating, the most exalted and the most contemptible, the pulsating stream of light, or the deceitful flow from the heart of an impenetrable darkness.

"The other shoe went flying unto the devil-god of that river. I thought, By Jove! it's all over. We are too late; he has vanished—the gift has vanished, by means of some spear, arrow, or club. I will never hear that chap speak after all,—and my sorrow had a startling extravagance of emotion, even such as I had noticed in the howling sorrow of these savages in the bush. I couldn't have felt more of lonely desolation somehow, had I been robbed of a belief or had missed my destiny in life. . . . Why do you sigh in this beastly way, somebody? Absurd? Well, absurd. Good Lord! mustn't a man ever——Here, give me some tobacco." . . .

There was a pause of profound stillness, then a match flared, and Marlow's lean face appeared, worn, hollow, with downward folds and dropped eyelids, with an aspect of concentrated attention; and as he took vigorous draws at his pipe, it seemed to retreat and advance out of the night in the regular flicker of the tiny flame. The match went out.

"Absurd!" he cried. "This is the worst of trying to tell. . . . Here you all are, each moored with two good addresses, like a hulk with two anchors, a butcher round one corner, a policeman round another, excellent appetites, and temperature normal—you hear—normal from year's end to year's end. And you say, Absurd! Absurd be—exploded! Absurd! My dear boys, what can you expect from a man who out of sheer nervousness had just flung overboard a pair of new shoes! Now I think of it, it is amazing I did not shed tears. I am, upon the whole, proud of my fortitude. I was cut to the quick at the idea of having lost the inestimable privilege of listening to the gifted Kurtz. Of course I was wrong. The privilege was waiting for me. Oh, yes, I heard more than enough. And I was right, too. A voice. He was very little more than a voice. And I heard—him—it—this voice—other voices—all of them were so little more than voices—and the memory of that time itself lingers around me, impalpable, like a dying vibration of one immense jabber, silly, atrocious, sordid, savage, or simply mean, without any kind of sense. Voices, voices—even the girl her-self—now——"

He was silent for a long time.

"I laid the ghost of his gifts at last with a lie," he began, suddenly. "Girl! What? Did I mention a girl? Oh, she is out of it—completely. They—the women I mean—are out of it—should be out of it. We must help them to stay in that beautiful world of their own, lest ours gets worse. Oh, she had to be out of it. You should have heard the disinterred body of Mr. Kurtz saying, 'My Intended.' You would have perceived directly then how completely she was out of it. And the lofty frontal bone of Mr. Kurtz! They say the hair goes on growing sometimes, but this—ah—specimen, was impressively bald. The wilderness had patted him on the head, and, behold, it was like a ball—an ivory ball; it had caressed him, and—lo!—he had withered; it had taken him, loved him, embraced him, got into his veins, consumed his flesh, and sealed his soul to its own by the inconceivable ceremonies of some devilish initia-tion. He was its spoiled and pampered favourite. Ivory? I should think so. Heaps of it, stacks of it. The old mud shanty was bursting with it. You would think there was not a single tusk left either above or below the ground in the whole country. 'Mostly fossil,' the manager had remarked, disparagingly. It was no more fossil than I am; but they call it fossil when it is dug up. It appears these niggers do bury the tusks some-times—but evidently they couldn't bury this parcel deep enough to save the gifted Mr. Kurtz from his fate. We filled the steamboat with it, and had to pile a lot on the deck. Thus he could see and enjoy as long as he could see, because the appreciation of this favour had remained with him to the last. You should have heard him say, 'My ivory.' Oh, yes, I heard him. 'My Intended, my ivory, my station, my river, my——' everything belonged to him. It made me hold my breath in expectation of hearing the wilderness burst into a prodigious peal of laughter that would shake the fixed stars in their places. Everything belonged to him—but that was a trifle. The thing was to know what he belonged to, how many powers of darkness claimed him for their own. That was the reflection that made you creepy all over. It was impossible—it was not good for one either—trying to imagine. He had taken a high seat amongst the devils of the land—I mean literally. You can't understand. How could you?—with solid pavement under your feet, surrounded by kind neighbours ready to cheer you or to fall on you, stepping delicately between the butcher and the policeman, in the holy terror of scandal and gallows and lunatic asylums—how can you imagine what particular region of the first ages a man's untrammelled feet may take him into by the way of solitude—utter solitude without a policeman—by the way of silence—utter silence, where no warning voice of a kind neighbour can be heard whispering of public opinion? These little things make all the great difference. When they are gone you must fall back upon your own innate strength, upon your own capacity for faithfulness. Of course you may be too much of a fool to go wrong—too dull even to know you are being assaulted by the powers of darkness. I take it, no fool ever made a bargain for his soul with the devil: the fool is too much of a fool, or the devil too much of a devil—I don't know which. Or you may be such a thunderingly exalted creature as to be altogether deaf and blind to anything but heavenly sights and sounds. Then the earth for you is only a standing place—and whether to be like this is your loss or your gain I won't pretend to say. But most of us are neither one nor the other. The earth for us is a place to live in, where we must put up with sights, with sounds, with smells, too, by Jove!—breathe dead hippo, so to speak, and not be contaminated. And there, don't you see? your strength comes in, the faith in your ability for the digging of unostentatious holes to bury the stuff in—your power of devotion, not to yourself, but to an obscure, back-breaking business. And that's difficult enough. Mind, I am not trying to excuse or even explain—I am trying to account to myself for—for—Mr. Kurtz—for the shade of Mr. Kurtz. This initiated wraith from the back of Nowhere honoured me with its amazing confidence before it vanished altogether. This was because it could speak English to me. The original Kurtz had been educated partly in England, and—as he was good enough to say himself—his sympathies were in the right place. His mother was half-English, his father was half-French. All Europe contributed to the making of Kurtz; and by and by I learned that, most appropriately, the International Society for the Suppression of Savage Customs had intrusted him with the making of a report, for its future guidance. And he had written it, too. I've seen it. I've read it. It was eloquent, vibrating with eloquence, but too high-strung, I think. Seventeen pages of close writing he had found time for! But this must have been before his—let us say—nerves, went wrong, and caused him to preside at certain midnight dances ending with unspeakable rites, which—as far as I reluctantly gathered from what I heard at various times—were offered up to him—do you understand?—to Mr. Kurtz himself. But it was a beautiful piece of writing. The opening paragraph, however, in the light of later information, strikes me now as ominous. He began with the argument that we whites, from the point of development we had arrived at, 'must necessarily appear to them [savages] in the nature of supernatural beings—we approach them with the might as of a deity,' and so on, and so on. 'By the simple exercise of our will we can exert a power for good practically unbounded,' etc. etc. From that point he soared and took me with him. The peroration was magnificent, though difficult to remember, you know. It gave me the notion of an exotic Immensity ruled by an august Benevolence. It made me tingle with enthusiasm. This was the unbounded power of eloquence—of words—of burning noble words. There were no practical hints to interrupt the magic current of phrases, unless a kind of note at the foot of the last page, scrawled evidently much later, in an unsteady hand, may be regarded as the exposition of a method. It was very simple, and at the end of that moving appeal to every altruistic sentiment it blazed at you, luminous and terrifying, like a flash of lightning in a serene sky: 'Exterminate all the brutes!' The curious part was that he had apparently forgotten all about that valuable postscriptum, because, later on, when he in a sense came to himself, he repeatedly entreated me to take good care of 'my pamphlet' (he called it), as it was sure to have in the future a good influence upon his career. I had full information about all these things, and, besides, as it turned out, I was to have the care of his memory. I've done enough for it to give me the indisputable right to lay it, if I choose, for an everlasting rest in the dust-bin of progress, amongst all the sweepings and, figuratively speaking, all the dead cats of civilization. But then, you see, I can't choose. He won't be forgotten. Whatever he was, he was not common. He had the power to charm or frighten rudimentary souls into an aggravated witch-dance in his honour; he could also fill the small souls of the pilgrims with bitter misgivings: he had one devoted friend at least, and he had conquered one soul in the world that was neither rudimentary nor tainted with self-seeking. No; I can't forget him, though I am not prepared to affirm the fellow was exactly worth the life we lost in getting to him. I missed my late helmsman awfully,—I missed him even while his body was still lying in the pilot-house. Perhaps you will think it passing strange this regret for a savage who was no more account than a grain of sand in a black Sahara. Well, don't you see, he had done something, he had steered; for months I had him at my back—a help—an instrument. It was a kind of partnership. He steered for me—I had to look after him, I worried about his deficiencies, and thus a subtle bond had been created, of which I only became aware when it was suddenly broken. And the intimate profundity of that look he gave me when he received his hurt remains to this day in my memory—like a claim of distant kinship affirmed in a supreme moment.

"Poor fool! If he had only left that shutter alone. He had no restraint, no restraint—just like Kurtz—a tree swayed by the wind. As soon as I had put on a dry pair of slippers, I dragged him out, after first jerking the spear out of his side, which operation I confess I performed with my eyes shut tight. His heels leaped together over the little door-step; his shoulders were pressed to my breast; I hugged him from behind desperately. Oh! he was heavy, heavy; heavier than any man on earth, I should imagine. Then without more ado I tipped him overboard. The current snatched him as though he had been a wisp of grass, and I saw the body roll over twice before I lost sight of it for ever. All the pilgrims and the manager were then congregated on the awning-deck about the pilot-house, chattering at each other like a flock of excited magpies, and there was a scandalized murmur at my heartless promptitude. What they wanted to keep that body hanging about for I can't guess. Embalm it, maybe. But I had also heard another, and a very ominous, murmur on the deck below. My friends the wood-cutters were likewise scandalized, and with a better show of reason—though I admit that the reason itself was quite inadmissible. Oh, quite! I had made up my mind that if my late helmsman was to be eaten, the fishes alone should have him. He had been a very second-rate helmsman while alive, but now he was dead he might have become a first-class temptation, and possibly cause some startling trouble. Besides, I was anxious to take the wheel, the man in pink pyjamas showing himself a hopeless duffer at the business.

"This I did directly the simple funeral was over. We were going half-speed, keeping right in the middle of the stream, and I listened to the talk about me. They had given up Kurtz, they had given up the station; Kurtz was dead, and the station had been burnt—and so on—and so on. The red-haired pilgrim was beside himself with the thought that at least this poor Kurtz had been properly avenged. 'Say! We must have made a glorious slaughter of them in the bush. Eh? What do you think? Say?' He positively danced, the bloodthirsty little gingery[22] beggar. And he had nearly fainted when he saw the wounded man! I could not help saying, 'You made a glorious lot of smoke, anyhow.' I had seen, from the way the tops of the bushes rustled and flew, that almost all the shots had gone too high. You can't hit anything unless you take aim and fire from the shoulder; but these chaps fired from the hip with their eyes shut. The retreat, I maintained—and I was right—was caused by the screeching of the steam-whistle. Upon this they forgot Kurtz, and began to howl at me with indignant protests.

"The manager stood by the wheel murmuring confidentially about the necessity of getting well away down the river before dark at all events, when I saw in the distance a clearing on the river-side and the outlines of some sort of building. 'What's this?' I asked. He clapped his hands in wonder. 'The station!' he cried. I edged in at once, still going half-speed.

"Through my glasses I saw the slope of a hill interspersed with rare trees and perfectly free from undergrowth. A long decaying building on the summit was half buried in the high grass; the large holes in the peaked roof gaped black from afar; the jungle and the woods made a background. There was no enclosure or fence of any kind; but there had been one apparently, for near the house half-a-dozen slim posts remained in a row, roughly trimmed, and with their upper ends ornamented with round carved balls. The rails, or whatever there had been between, had disappeared. Of course the forest surrounded all that. The river-bank was clear, and on the water-side I saw a white man under a hat like a cart-wheel beckoning persistently with his whole arm. Examining the edge of the forest above and below, I was almost certain I could see movements—human forms gliding here and there. I steamed past prudently, then stopped the engines and let her drift down. The man on the shore began to shout, urging us to land. 'We have been attacked,' screamed the manager. 'I know—I know. It's all right,' yelled back the other, as cheerful as you please. 'Come along. It's all right. I am glad.'

"His aspect reminded me of something I had seen—something funny I had seen somewhere. As I manoeuvred to get alongside, I was asking myself, 'What does this fellow look like?' Suddenly I got it. He looked like a harlequin. His clothes had been made of some stuff that was brown holland[23] probably, but it was covered with

---

[22] **gingery:** Redheaded.

[23] **holland:** Unbleached cotton or linen.

patches all over, with bright patches, blue, red, and yellow—patches on the back, patches on the front, patches on elbows, on knees; coloured binding around his jacket, scarlet edging at the bottom of his trousers; and the sunshine made him look extremely gay and wonderfully neat withal, because you could see how beautifully all this patching had been done. A beardless, boyish face, very fair, no features to speak of, nose peeling, little blue eyes, smiles and frowns chasing each other over that open countenance like sunshine and shadow on a wind-swept plain. 'Look out, captain!' he cried; 'there's a snag lodged in here last night.' What! Another snag? I confess I swore shamefully. I had nearly holed my cripple, to finish off that charming trip. The harlequin on the bank turned his little pug-nose up to me. 'You English?' he asked, all smiles. 'Are you?' I shouted from the wheel. The smiles vanished, and he shook his head as if sorry for my disappointment. Then he brightened up. 'Never mind!' he cried, encouragingly. 'Are we in time?' I asked. 'He is up there,' he replied, with a toss of the head up the hill, and becoming gloomy all of a sudden. His face was like the autumn sky, overcast one moment and bright the next.

"When the manager, escorted by the pilgrims, all of them armed to the teeth, had gone to the house this chap came on board. 'I say, I don't like this. These natives are in the bush,' I said. He assured me earnestly it was all right. 'They are simple people,' he added; 'well, I am glad you came. It took me all my time to keep them off.' 'But you said it was all right,' I cried. 'Oh, they meant no harm,' he said; and as I stared he corrected himself, 'Not exactly.' Then vivaciously, 'My faith, your pilot-house wants a clean-up!' In the next breath he advised me to keep enough steam on the boiler to blow the whistle in case of any trouble. 'One good screech will do more for you than all your rifles. They are simple people,' he repeated. He rattled away at such a rate he quite overwhelmed me. He seemed to be trying to make up for lots of silence, and actually hinted, laughing, that such was the case. 'Don't you talk with Mr. Kurtz?' I said. 'You don't talk with that man—you listen to him,' he exclaimed with severe exaltation. 'But now——' He waved his arm, and in the twinkling of an eye was in the uttermost depths of despondency. In a moment he came up again with a jump, possessed himself of both my hands, shook them continuously, while he gabbled: 'Brother sailor . . . honour . . . pleasure . . . delight . . . introduce myself . . . Russian . . . son of an arch-priest . . . Government of Tambov . . . What? Tobacco! English tobacco; the excellent English tobacco! Now, that's brotherly. Smoke? Where's a sailor that does not smoke?'

"The pipe soothed him, and gradually I made out he had run away from school, had gone to sea in a Russian ship; ran away again; served some time in English ships; was now reconciled with the arch-priest. He made a point of that. 'But when one is young one must see things, gather experience, ideas; enlarge the mind.' 'Here!' I interrupted. 'You can never tell! Here I met Mr. Kurtz,' he said, youthfully solemn and reproachful. I held my tongue after that. It appears he had persuaded a Dutch trading-house on the coast to fit him out with stores and goods, and had started for the interior with a light heart, and no more idea of what would happen to him than a baby. He had been wandering about that river for nearly two years alone, cut off from everybody and everything. 'I am not so young as I look. I am twenty-five,' he said. 'At first old Van Shuyten would tell me to go to the devil,' he narrated with keen enjoyment; 'but I stuck to him, and talked and talked, till at last he got afraid I would talk the hind-leg off his favourite dog, so he gave me some cheap things and a few guns, and told me he hoped he would never see my face again. Good old Dutchman, Van Shuyten. I've sent him one small lot of ivory a year ago, so that he can't call me a little thief when I get back. I hope he got it. And for the rest I don't care. I had some wood stacked for you. That was my old house. Did you see?'

"I gave him Towson's book. He made as though he would kiss me, but restrained himself. 'The only book I had left, and I thought I had lost it,' he said, looking at it ecstatically. 'So many accidents happen to a man going about alone, you know. Canoes get upset sometimes—and sometimes you've got to clear out so quick when the people get angry.' He thumbed the pages. 'You made notes in Russian?' I asked. He nodded. 'I thought they were written in cipher,' I said. He laughed, then became serious. 'I had lots of trouble to keep these people off,' he said. 'Did they want to kill you?' I asked. 'Oh, no!' he cried, and checked himself. 'Why did they attack us?' I pursued. He hesitated, then said shamefacedly, 'They don't want him to go.' 'Don't they?' I said, curiously. He nodded a nod full of mystery and wisdom. 'I tell you,' he cried, 'this man has enlarged my mind.' He opened his arms wide, staring at me with his little blue eyes that were perfectly round."

3

"I looked at him, lost in astonishment. There he was before me, in motley, as though he had absconded from a troupe of mimes, enthusiastic, fabulous. His very existence was improbable, inexplicable, and altogether bewildering. He was an insoluble problem. It was inconceivable how he had existed, how he had succeeded in getting so far, how he had managed to remain—why he did not instantly disappear. 'I went a little farther,' he said, 'then still a little farther—till I had gone so far that I don't know how I'll ever get back. Never mind. Plenty time. I can manage. You take Kurtz away quick—quick—I tell you.' The glamour of youth enveloped his particoloured rags, his destitution, his loneliness, the essential desolation of his futile wanderings. For months—for years—his life hadn't been worth a day's purchase; and there he was gallantly, thoughtlessly alive, to all appearance indestructible solely by the virtue of his few years and of his unreflecting audacity. I was seduced into something like admiration—like envy. Glamour urged him on, glamour kept him unscathed. He surely wanted nothing from the wilderness but space to breathe in and to push on through. His need was to exist, and to move onwards at the greatest possible risk, and with a maximum of privation. If the absolutely pure, uncalculating, unpractical spirit of adventure had ever ruled a human being, it ruled this be-patched youth. I almost envied him the possession of this modest and clear flame. It seemed to have consumed all thought of self so completely, that even while he was talking to you, you forgot that it was he—the man before your eyes—who had gone through these things. I did not envy him his devotion to Kurtz, though. He had not meditated over it. It came to him, and he accepted it with a sort of eager fatalism. I must say that to me it appeared about the most dangerous thing in every way he had come upon so far.

"They had come together unavoidably, like two ships becalmed near each other, and lay rubbing sides at last. I suppose Kurtz wanted an audience, because on a certain occasion, when encamped in the forest, they had talked all night, or more probably Kurtz had talked. 'We talked of everything,' he said, quite transported at the recollection. 'I forgot there was such a thing as sleep. The night did not seem to last an hour. Everything! Everything! . . . Of love too.' 'Ah, he talked to you of love!' I said, much amused. 'It isn't what you think,' he cried, almost passionately. 'It was in general. He made me see things — things.'

"He threw his arms up. We were on deck at the time, and the headman of my wood-cutters, lounging near by, turned upon him his heavy and glittering eyes. I looked around, and I don't know why, but I assure you that never, never before, did this land, this river, this jungle, the very arch of this blazing sky, appear to me so hopeless and so dark, so impenetrable to human thought, so pitiless to human weakness. 'And, ever since, you have been with him, of course?' I said.

"On the contrary. It appears their intercourse had been very much broken by various causes. He had, as he informed me proudly, managed to nurse Kurtz through two illnesses (he alluded to it as you would to some risky feat), but as a rule Kurtz wandered alone, far in the depths of the forest. 'Very often coming to this station, I had to wait days and days before he would turn up,' he said. 'Ah, it was worth waiting for! — sometimes.' 'What was he doing? exploring or what?' I asked. 'Oh, yes, of course'; he had discovered lots of villages, a lake, too — he did not know exactly in what direction; it was dangerous to inquire too much — but mostly his expeditions had been for ivory. 'But he had no goods to trade with by that time,' I objected. 'There's a good lot of cartridges left even yet,' he answered, looking away. 'To speak plainly, he raided the country,' I said. He nodded. 'Not alone, surely!' He muttered something about the villages round that lake. 'Kurtz got the tribe to follow him, did he?' I suggested. He fidgeted a little. 'They adored him,' he said. The tone of these words was so extraordinary that I looked at him searchingly. It was curious to see his mingled eagerness and reluctance to speak of Kurtz. The man filled his life, occupied his thoughts, swayed his emotions. 'What can you expect?' he burst out; 'he came to them with thunder and lightning, you know — and they had never seen anything like it — and very terrible. He could be very terrible. You can't judge Mr. Kurtz as you would an ordinary man. No, no, no! Now — just to give you an idea — I don't mind telling you, he wanted to shoot me, too, one day — but I don't judge him.' 'Shoot you!' I cried. 'What for?' 'Well, I had a small lot of ivory the chief of that village near my house gave me. You see I used to shoot game for them. Well, he wanted it, and wouldn't hear reason. He declared he would shoot me unless I gave him the ivory and then cleared out of the country, because he could do so, and had a fancy for it, and there was nothing on earth to prevent him killing whom he jolly well pleased. And it was true, too. I gave him the ivory. What did I care! But I didn't clear out. No, no. I couldn't leave him. I had to be careful, of course, till we got friendly again for a time. He had his second illness then. Afterwards I had to keep out of the way; but I didn't mind. He was living for the most part in those villages on the lake. When he came down to the river, sometimes he would take to me, and sometimes it was better for me to be careful. This man suffered too much. He hated all this, and somehow he couldn't get away. When I had a chance I begged him to try and leave while there was time; I offered to go back with him. And he would say yes, and then he would remain; go off on another ivory hunt; disappear for weeks; forget himself amongst these people—forget himself—you know.' 'Why! he's mad,' I said. He protested indignantly. Mr. Kurtz couldn't be mad. If I had heard him talk, only two days ago, I wouldn't dare hint at such a thing. . . . I had taken up my binoculars while we talked, and was looking at the shore, sweeping the limit of the forest at each side and at the back of the house. The consciousness of there being people in that bush, so silent, so quiet—as silent and quiet as the ruined house on the hill—made me uneasy. There was no sign on the face of nature of this amazing tale that was not so much told as suggested to me in desolate exclamations, completed by shrugs, in interrupted phrases, in hints ending in deep sighs. The woods were unmoved, like a mask— heavy, like the closed door of a prison—they looked with their air of hidden knowl- edge, of patient expectation, of unapproachable silence. The Russian was explaining to me that it was only lately that Mr. Kurtz had come down to the river, bringing along with him all the fighting men of that lake tribe. He had been absent for several months—getting himself adored, I suppose—and had come down unexpectedly, with the intention to all appearance of making a raid either across the river or down stream. Evidently the appetite for more ivory had got the better of the—what shall I say?—less material aspirations. However he had got much worse suddenly. 'I heard he was lying helpless, and so I came up—took my chance,' said the Russian. 'Oh, he is bad, very bad.' I directed my glass to the house. There were no signs of life, but there was the ruined roof, the long mud wall peeping above the grass, with three little square window-holes, no two of the same size; all this brought within reach of my hand, as it were. And then I made a brusque movement, and one of the remain- ing posts of that vanished fence leaped up in the field of my glass. You remember I told you I had been struck at the distance by certain attempts at ornamentation, rather remarkable in the ruinous aspect of the place. Now I had suddenly a nearer view, and its first result was to make me throw my head back as if before a blow. Then I went carefully from post to post with my glass, and I saw my mistake. These round knobs were not ornamental but symbolic; they were expressive and puzzling, striking and disturbing—food for thought and also for vultures if there had been any looking down from the sky; but at all events for such ants as were industrious enough to ascend the pole. They would have been even more impressive, those heads on the stakes, if their faces had not been turned to the house. Only one, the first I had made out, was facing my way. I was not so shocked as you may think. The start back I had given was really nothing but a movement of surprise. I had expected to see a knob of wood there, you know. I returned deliberately to the first I had seen—and there it was, black, dried, sunken, with closed eyelids,—a head that seemed to sleep at the top of that pole, and with the shrunken dry lips showing a narrow white line of the teeth, was smiling, too, smiling continuously at some endless and jocose dream of that eternal slumber.

"I am not disclosing any trade secrets. In fact, the manager said afterwards that Mr. Kurtz's methods had ruined the district. I have no opinion on that point, but I want you clearly to understand that there was nothing exactly profitable in these heads being there. They only showed that Mr. Kurtz lacked restraint in the gratification of his various lusts, that there was something wanting in him—some small matter which, when the pressing need arose, could not be found under his magnificent eloquence. Whether he knew of this deficiency himself I can't say. I think the knowledge came to him at last—only at the very last. But the wilderness had found him out early, and had taken on him a terrible vengeance for the fantastic invasion. I think it had whispered to him things about himself which he did not know, things of which he had no conception till he took counsel with this great solitude—and the whisper had proved irresistibly fascinating. It echoed loudly within him because he was hollow at the core. . . . I put down the glass, and the head that had appeared near enough to be spoken to seemed at once to have leaped away from me into inaccessible distance.

"The admirer of Mr. Kurtz was a bit crestfallen. In a hurried, indistinct voice he began to assure me he had not dared to take these—say, symbols—down. He was not afraid of the natives; they would not stir till Mr. Kurtz gave the word. His ascendancy was extraordinary. The camps of these people surrounded the place, and the chiefs came every day to see him. They would crawl. . . . 'I don't want to know anything of the ceremonies used when approaching Mr. Kurtz,' I shouted. Curious, this feeling that came over me that such details would be more intolerable than those heads drying on the stakes under Mr. Kurtz's windows. After all, that was only a savage sight, while I seemed at one bound to have been transported into some lightless region of subtle horrors, where pure, uncomplicated savagery was a positive relief, being something that had a right to exist—obviously—in the sunshine. The young man looked at me with surprise. I suppose it did not occur to him that Mr. Kurtz was no idol of mine. He forgot I hadn't heard any of these splendid monologues on, what was it? on love, justice, conduct of life—or what not. If it had come to crawling before Mr. Kurtz, he crawled as much as the veriest savage of them all. I had no idea of the conditions, he said: these heads were the heads of rebels. I shocked him excessively by laughing. Rebels! What would be the next definition I was to hear? There had been enemies, criminals, workers—and these were rebels. Those rebellious heads looked very subdued to me on their sticks. 'You don't know how such a life tries a man like Kurtz,' cried Kurtz's last disciple. 'Well, and you?' I said. 'I! I! I am a simple man. I have no great thoughts. I want nothing from anybody. How can you compare me to . . . ?' His feelings were too much for speech, and suddenly he broke down. 'I don't understand,' he groaned. 'I've been doing my best to keep him alive, and that's enough. I had no hand in all this. I have no abilities. There hasn't been a drop of medicine or a mouthful of invalid food for months here. He was shamefully abandoned. A man like this, with such ideas. Shamefully! Shamefully! I—I—haven't slept for the last ten nights . . .'

"His voice lost itself in the calm of the evening. The long shadows of the forest had slipped downhill while we talked, had gone far beyond the ruined hovel, beyond the symbolic row of stakes. All this was in the gloom, while we down there were yet in the sunshine, and the stretch of the river abreast of the clearing glittered in a still and dazzling splendour, with a murky and overshadowed bend above and below. Not a living soul was seen on the shore. The bushes did not rustle.

"Suddenly round the corner of the house a group of men appeared, as though they had come up from the ground. They waded waist-deep in the grass, in a compact body, bearing an improvised stretcher in their midst. Instantly, in the emptiness of the landscape, a cry arose whose shrillness pierced the still air like a sharp arrow flying straight to the very heart of the land; and, as if by enchantment, streams of human beings — of naked human beings — with spears in their hands, with bows, with shields, with wild glances and savage movements, were poured into the clearing by the dark-faced and pensive forest. The bushes shook, the grass swayed for a time, and then everything stood still in attentive immobility.

" 'Now, if he does not say the right thing to them we are all done for,' said the Russian at my elbow. The knot of men with the stretcher had stopped, too, halfway to the steamer, as if petrified. I saw the man on the stretcher sit up, lank and with an uplifted arm, above the shoulders of the bearers. 'Let us hope that the man who can talk so well of love in general will find some particular reason to spare us this time,' I said. I resented bitterly the absurd danger of our situation, as if to be at the mercy of that atrocious phantom had been a dishonouring necessity. I could not hear a sound, but through my glasses I saw the thin arm extended commandingly, the lower jaw moving, the eyes of that apparition shining darkly far in its bony head that nodded with grotesque jerks. Kurtz — Kurtz — that means short in German — don't it? Well, the name was as true as everything else in his life — and death. He looked at least seven feet long. His covering had fallen off, and his body emerged from it pitiful and appalling as from a winding-sheet. I could see the cage of his ribs all astir, the bones of his arm waving. It was as though an animated image of death carved out of old ivory had been shaking its hand with menaces at a motionless crowd of men made of dark and glittering bronze. I saw him open his mouth wide — it gave him a weirdly voracious aspect, as though he had wanted to swallow all the air, all the earth, all the men before him. A deep voice reached me faintly. He must have been shouting. He fell back suddenly. The stretcher shook as the bearers staggered forward again, and almost at the same time I noticed that the crowd of savages was vanishing without any perceptible movement of retreat, as if the forest that had ejected these beings so suddenly had drawn them in again as the breath is drawn in a long aspiration.

"Some of the pilgrims behind the stretcher carried his arms — two shot-guns, a heavy rifle, and a light revolver-carbine — the thunderbolts of that pitiful Jupiter. The manager bent over him murmuring as he walked beside his head. They laid him down in one of the little cabins — just a room for a bedplace and a camp-stool or two, you know. We had brought his belated correspondence, and a lot of torn envelopes and open letters littered his bed. His hand roamed feebly amongst these papers. I was struck by the fire of his eyes and the composed languor of his expression. It was not so much the exhaustion of disease. He did not seem in pain. This shadow looked satiated and calm, as though for the moment it had had its fill of all the emotions.

"He rustled one of the letters, and looking straight in my face said, 'I am glad.' Somebody had been writing to him about me. These special recommendations were turning up again. The volume of tone he emitted without effort, almost without the trouble of moving his lips, amazed me. A voice! a voice! It was grave, profound, vibrating, while the man did not seem capable of a whisper. However, he had enough strength in him—factitious no doubt—to very nearly make an end of us, as you shall hear directly.

"The manager appeared silently in the doorway; I stepped out at once and he drew the curtain after me. The Russian, eyed curiously by the pilgrims, was staring at the shore. I followed the direction of his glance.

"Dark human shapes could be made out in the distance, flitting indistinctly against the gloomy border of the forest, and near the river two bronze figures, leaning on tall spears, stood in the sunlight under fantastic head-dresses of spotted skins, warlike and still in statuesque repose. And from right to left along the lighted shore moved a wild and gorgeous apparition of a woman.

"She walked with measured steps, draped in striped and fringed cloths, treading the earth proudly, with a slight jingle and flash of barbarous ornaments. She carried her head high; her hair was done in the shape of a helmet; she had brass leggings to the knee, brass wire gauntlets to the elbow, a crimson spot on her tawny cheek, innumerable necklaces of glass beads on her neck; bizarre things, charms, gifts of witch-men, that hung about her, glittered and trembled at every step. She must have had the value of several elephant tusks upon her. She was savage and superb, wild-eyed and magnificent; there was something ominous and stately in her deliberate progress. And in the hush that had fallen suddenly upon the whole sorrowful land, the immense wilderness, the colossal body of the fecund and mysterious life seemed to look at her, pensive, as though it had been looking at the image of its own tenebrous and passionate soul.

"She came abreast of the steamer, stood still, and faced us. Her long shadow fell to the water's edge. Her face had a tragic and fierce aspect of wild sorrow and of dumb pain mingled with the fear of some struggling, half-shaped resolve. She stood looking at us without a stir, and like the wilderness itself, with an air of brooding over an inscrutable purpose. A whole minute passed, and then she made a step forward. There was a low jingle, a glint of yellow metal, a sway of fringed draperies, and she stopped as if her heart had failed her. The young fellow by my side growled. The pilgrims murmured at my back. She looked at us all as if her life had depended upon the unswerving steadiness of her glance. Suddenly she opened her bared arms and threw them up rigid above her head, as though in an uncontrollable desire to touch the sky, and at the same time the swift shadows darted out on the earth, swept around on the river, gathering the steamer into a shadowy embrace. A formidable silence hung over the scene.

"She turned away slowly, walked on, following the bank, and passed into the bushes to the left. Once only her eyes gleamed back at us in the dusk of the thickets before she disappeared.

"'If she had offered to come aboard I really think I would have tried to shoot her,' said the man of patches, nervously. 'I have been risking my life every day for the last fortnight to keep her out of the house. She got in one day and kicked up a row about those miserable rags I picked up in the storeroom to mend my clothes with. I wasn't decent. At least it must have been that, for she talked like a fury to Kurtz for an hour, pointing at me now and then. I don't understand the dialect of this tribe. Luckily for me, I fancy Kurtz felt too ill that day to care, or there would have been mischief. I don't understand. . . . No—it's too much for me. Ah, well, it's all over now.'

"At this moment I heard Kurtz's deep voice behind the curtain: 'Save me!—save the ivory, you mean. Don't tell me. Save *me*! Why, I've had to save you. You are interrupting my plans now. Sick! Sick! Not so sick as you would like to believe. Never mind. I'll carry my ideas out yet—I will return. I'll show you what can be done. You with your little peddling notions—you are interfering with me. I will return. I. . . .'

"The manager came out. He did me the honour to take me under the arm and lead me aside. 'He is very low, very low,' he said. He considered it necessary to sigh, but neglected to be consistently sorrowful. 'We have done all we could for him— haven't we? But there is no disguising the fact, Mr. Kurtz has done more harm than good to the Company. He did not see the time was not ripe for vigorous action. Cautiously, cautiously—that's my principle. We must be cautious yet. The district is closed to us for a time. Deplorable! Upon the whole, the trade will suffer. I don't deny there is a remarkable quantity of ivory—mostly fossil. We must save it, at all events—but look how precarious the position is—and why? Because the method is unsound.' 'Do you,' said I, looking at the shore, 'call it "unsound method"?' 'Without doubt,' he exclaimed, hotly. 'Don't you?' . . . 'No method at all,' I murmured after a while. 'Exactly,' he exulted. 'I anticipated this. Shows a complete want of judgment. It is my duty to point it out in the proper quarter.' 'Oh,' said I, 'that fellow—what's his name?—the brickmaker, will make a readable report for you.' He appeared confounded for a moment. It seemed to me I had never breathed an atmosphere so vile, and I turned mentally to Kurtz for relief—positively for relief. 'Nevertheless I think Mr. Kurtz is a remarkable man,' I said with emphasis. He started, dropped on me a cold heavy glance, said very quietly, 'He *was*,' and turned his back on me. My hour of favour was over; I found myself lumped along with Kurtz as a partisan of methods for which the time was not ripe: I was unsound! Ah! but it was something to have at least a choice of nightmares.

"I had turned to the wilderness really, not to Mr. Kurtz, who, I was ready to admit, was as good as buried. And for a moment it seemed to me as if I also were buried in a vast grave full of unspeakable secrets. I felt an intolerable weight oppressing my breast, the smell of the damp earth, the unseen presence of victorious corruption, the darkness of an impenetrable night. . . . The Russian tapped me on the shoulder. I heard him mumbling and stammering something about 'brother seaman—couldn't conceal—knowledge of matters that would affect Mr. Kurtz's reputation.' I waited. For him evidently Mr. Kurtz was not in his grave; I suspect that for him Mr. Kurtz was one of the immortals. 'Well!' said I at last, 'speak out. As it happens, I am Mr. Kurtz's friend—in a way.'

"He stated with a good deal of formality that had we not been 'of the same profession,' he would have kept the matter to himself without regard to consequences. 'He suspected there was an active ill will towards him on the part of these white men that——' 'You are right,' I said, remembering a certain conversation I had overheard. 'The manager thinks you ought to be hanged.' He showed a concern at this intelligence which amused me at first. 'I had better get out of the way quietly,' he said, earnestly. 'I can do no more for Kurtz now, and they would soon find some excuse. What's to stop them? There's a military post three hundred miles from here.' 'Well, upon my word,' said I, 'perhaps you had better go if you have any friends amongst the savages near by.' 'Plenty,' he said. 'They are simple people—and I want nothing, you know.' He stood biting his lip, then: 'I don't want any harm to happen to these whites here, but of course I was thinking of Mr. Kurtz's reputation—but you are a brother seaman and——' 'All right,' said I, after a time. 'Mr. Kurtz's reputation is safe with me.' I did not know how truly I spoke.

"He informed me, lowering his voice, that it was Kurtz who had ordered the attack to be made on the steamer. 'He hated sometimes the idea of being taken away—and then again. . . . But I don't understand these matters. I am a simple man. He thought it would scare you away—that you would give it up, thinking him dead. I could not stop him. Oh, I had an awful time of it this last month.' 'Very well,' I said. 'He is all right now.' 'Ye-e-es,' he muttered, not very convinced apparently. 'Thanks,' said I; 'I shall keep my eyes open.' 'But quiet—eh?' he urged, anxiously. 'It would be awful for his reputation if anybody here——' I promised a complete discretion with great gravity. 'I have a canoe and three black fellows waiting not very far. I am off. Could you give me a few Martini-Henry cartridges?' I could, and did, with proper secrecy. He helped himself, with a wink at me, to a handful of my tobacco. 'Between sailors—you know—good English tobacco.' At the door of the pilot-house he turned round—'I say, haven't you a pair of shoes you could spare?' He raised one leg. 'Look.' The soles were tied with knotted strings sandal-wise under his bare feet. I rooted out an old pair, at which he looked with admiration before tucking it under his left arm. One of his pockets (bright red) was bulging with cartridges, from the other (dark blue) peeped 'Towson's Inquiry,' etc., etc. He seemed to think himself excellently well equipped for a renewed encounter with the wilderness. 'Ah! I'll never, never meet such a man again. You ought to have heard him recite poetry—his own, too, it was, he told me. Poetry!' He rolled his eyes at the recollection of these delights. 'Oh, he enlarged my mind!' 'Good-bye,' said I. He shook hands and vanished in the night. Sometimes I ask myself whether I had ever really seen him—whether it was possible to meet such a phenomenon! . . .

"When I woke up shortly after midnight his warning came to my mind with its hint of danger that seemed, in the starred darkness, real enough to make me get up for the purpose of having a look round. On the hill a big fire burned, illuminating fitfully a crooked corner of the station-house. One of the agents with a picket[24] of a few of our blacks, armed for the purpose, was keeping guard over the ivory; but deep within the forest, red gleams that wavered, that seemed to sink and rise from the ground amongst confused columnar shapes of intense blackness, showed the exact position of the camp where Mr. Kurtz's adorers were keeping their uneasy vigil. The monotonous beating of a big drum filled the air with muffled shocks and a lingering vibration. A steady droning sound of many men chanting each to himself

---

[24]**picket:** A band of sentries.

some weird incantation came out from the black, flat wall of the woods as the humming of bees comes out of a hive, and had a strange narcotic effect upon my half-awake senses. I believe I dozed off leaning over the rail, till an abrupt burst of yells, an overwhelming outbreak of a pent-up and mysterious frenzy, woke me up in a bewildered wonder. It was cut short all at once, and the low droning went on with an effect of audible and soothing silence. I glanced casually into the little cabin. A light was burning within, but Mr. Kurtz was not there.

"I think I would have raised an outcry if I had believed my eyes. But I didn't believe them at first—the thing seemed so impossible. The fact is I was completely unnerved by a sheer blank fright, pure abstract terror, unconnected with any distinct shape of physical danger. What made this emotion so overpowering was—how shall I define it?—the moral shock I received, as if something altogether monstrous, intolerable to thought and odious to the soul, had been thrust upon me unexpectedly. This lasted of course the merest fraction of a second, and then the usual sense of commonplace, deadly danger, the possibility of a sudden onslaught and massacre, or something of the kind, which I saw impending, was positively welcome and composing. It pacified me, in fact, so much, that I did not raise an alarm.

"There was an agent buttoned up inside an ulster[25] and sleeping on a chair on deck within three feet of me. The yells had not awakened him; he snored very slightly; I left him to his slumbers and leaped ashore. I did not betray Mr. Kurtz—it was ordered I should never betray him—it was written I should be loyal to the nightmare of my choice. I was anxious to deal with this shadow by myself alone,— and to this day I don't know why I was so jealous of sharing with any one the peculiar blackness of that experience.

"As soon as I got on the bank I saw a trail—a broad trail through the grass. I remember the exultation with which I said to myself, 'He can't walk—he is crawling on all-fours—I've got him.' The grass was wet with dew. I strode rapidly with clenched fists. I fancy I had some vague notion of falling upon him and giving him a drubbing. I don't know. I had some imbecile thoughts. The knitting old woman with the cat obtruded herself upon my memory as a most improper person to be sitting at the other end of such an affair. I saw a row of pilgrims squirting lead in the air out of Winchesters held to the hip. I thought I would never get back to the steamer, and imagined myself living alone and unarmed in the woods to an advanced age. Such silly things—you know. And I remember I confounded the beat of the drum with the beating of my heart, and was pleased at its calm regularity.

"I kept to the track though—then stopped to listen. The night was very clear; a dark blue space, sparkling with dew and starlight, in which black things stood very still. I thought I could see a kind of motion ahead of me. I was strangely cocksure of everything that night. I actually left the track and ran in a wide semicircle (I verily believe chuckling to myself) so as to get in front of that stir, of that motion I had seen—if indeed I had seen anything. I was circumventing Kurtz as though it had been a boyish game.

---

[25]**ulster:** A long overcoat.

"I came upon him, and, if he had not heard me coming, I would have fallen over him, too, but he got up in time. He rose, unsteady, long, pale, indistinct, like a vapour exhaled by the earth, and swayed slightly, misty and silent before me; while at my back the fires loomed between the trees, and the murmur of many voices issued from the forest. I had cut him off cleverly; but when actually confronting him I seemed to come to my senses, I saw the danger in its right proportion. It was by no means over yet. Suppose he began to shout? Though he could hardly stand, there was still plenty of vigour in his voice. 'Go away—hide yourself,' he said, in that profound tone. It was very awful. I glanced back. We were within thirty yards from the nearest fire. A black figure stood up, strode on long black legs, waving long black arms, across the glow. It had horns—antelope horns, I think—on its head. Some sorcerer, some witch-man, no doubt: it looked fiend-like enough. 'Do you know what you are doing?' I whispered. 'Perfectly,' he answered, raising his voice for that single word: it sounded to me far off and yet loud, like a hail through a speaking-trumpet. If he makes a row we are lost, I thought to myself. This clearly was not a case for fisticuffs, even apart from the very natural aversion I had to beat that Shadow—this wandering and tormented thing. 'You will be lost,' I said—'utterly lost.' One gets sometimes such a flash of inspiration, you know. I did say the right thing, though indeed he could not have been more irretrievably lost than he was at this very moment, when the foundations of our intimacy were being laid—to endure—to endure—even to the end—even beyond.

"'I had immense plans,' he muttered irresolutely. 'Yes,' said I; 'but if you try to shout I'll smash your head with——' There was not a stick or stone near. 'I will throttle you for good,' I corrected myself. 'I was on the threshold of great things,' he pleaded, in a voice of longing, with a wistfulness of tone that made my blood run cold. 'And now for this stupid scoundrel——' 'Your success in Europe is assured in any case,' I affirmed, steadily. I did not want to have the throttling of him, you understand—and indeed it would have been very little use for any practical purpose. I tried to break the spell—the heavy, mute spell of the wilderness—that seemed to draw him to its pitiless breast by the awakening of forgotten and brutal instincts, by the memory of gratified and monstrous passions. This alone, I was convinced, had driven him out to the edge of the forest, to the bush, towards the gleam of fires, the throb of drums, the drone of weird incantations; this alone had beguiled his unlawful soul beyond the bounds of permitted aspirations. And, don't you see, the terror of the position was not in being knocked on the head—though I had a very lively sense of that danger, too—but in this, that I had to deal with a being to whom I could not appeal in the name of anything high or low. I had, even like the niggers, to invoke him—himself—his own exalted and incredible degradation. There was nothing either above or below him, and I knew it. He had kicked himself loose of the earth. Confound the man! he had kicked the very earth to pieces. He was alone, and I before him did not know whether I stood on the ground or floated in the air. I've been telling you what we said—repeating the phrases we pronounced—but what's the good? They were common everyday words—the familiar, vague sounds exchanged on every waking day of life. But what of that? They had behind them, to my mind, the terrific suggestiveness of words heard in dreams, of phrases spoken in nightmares. Soul! If anybody had ever struggled with a soul, I am the man. And I wasn't arguing with a lunatic either. Believe me or not, his intelligence was perfectly clear—concentrated, it is true, upon himself with horrible intensity, yet clear; and therein was my only chance—barring, of course, the killing him there and then, which wasn't so good, on account of unavoidable noise. But his soul was mad. Being alone in the wilderness, it had looked within itself, and, by heavens! I tell you, it had gone mad. I had—for my sins, I suppose—to go through the ordeal of looking into it myself. No eloquence could have been so withering to one's belief in mankind as his final burst of sincerity. He struggled with himself, too. I saw it—I heard it. I saw the inconceivable mystery of a soul that knew no restraint, no faith, and no fear, yet struggling blindly with itself. I kept my head pretty well; but when I had him at last stretched on the couch, I wiped my forehead, while my legs shook under me as though I had carried half a ton on my back down that hill. And yet I had only supported him, his bony arm clasped round my neck—and he was not much heavier than a child.

"When next day we left at noon, the crowd, of whose presence behind the curtain of trees I had been acutely conscious all the time, flowed out of the woods again, filled the clearing, covered the slope with a mass of naked, breathing, quivering, bronze bodies. I steamed up a bit, then swung downstream, and two thousand eyes followed the evolutions of the splashing, thumping, fierce river-demon beating the water with its terrible tail and breathing black smoke into the air. In front of the first rank, along the river, three men, plastered with bright red earth from head to foot, strutted to and fro restlessly. When we came abreast again, they faced the river, stamped their feet, nodded their horned heads, swayed their scarlet bodies; they shook towards the fierce river-demon a bunch of black feathers, a mangy skin with a pendent tail—something that looked like a dried gourd; they shouted periodically together strings of amazing words that resembled no sounds of human language; and the deep murmurs of the crowd, interrupted suddenly, were like the responses of some satanic litany.

"We had carried Kurtz into the pilot-house: there was more air there. Lying on the couch, he stared through the open shutter. There was an eddy in the mass of human bodies, and the woman with helmeted head and tawny cheeks rushed out to the very brink of the stream. She put out her hands, shouted something, and all that wild mob took up the shout in a roaring chorus of articulated, rapid, breathless utterance.

"'Do you understand this?' I asked.

"He kept on looking out past me with fiery, longing eyes, with a mingled expression of wistfulness and hate. He made no answer, but I saw a smile, a smile of indefinable meaning, appear on his colourless lips that a moment after twitched convulsively. 'Do I not?' he said slowly, gasping, as if the words had been torn out of him by a supernatural power.

"I pulled the string of the whistle, and I did this because I saw the pilgrims on deck getting out their rifles with an air of anticipating a jolly lark. At the sudden screech there was a movement of abject terror through that wedged mass of bodies. 'Don't! don't you frighten them away,' cried someone on deck disconsolately. I pulled the string time after time. They broke and ran, they leaped, they crouched, they swerved, they dodged the flying terror of the sound. The three red chaps had fallen flat, face down on the shore, as though they had been shot dead. Only the barbarous and superb woman did not so much as flinch, and stretched tragically her bare arms after us over the sombre and glittering river.

"And then that imbecile crowd down on the deck started their little fun, and I could see nothing more for smoke.

"The brown current ran swiftly out of the heart of darkness, bearing us down towards the sea with twice the speed of our upward progress; and Kurtz's life was running swiftly, too, ebbing, ebbing out of his heart into the sea of inexorable time. The manager was very placid, he had no vital anxieties now, he took us both in with a comprehensive and satisfied glance: the 'affair' had come off as well as could be wished. I saw the time approaching when I would be left alone of the party of 'unsound method.' The pilgrims looked upon me with disfavour. I was, so to speak, numbered with the dead. It is strange how I accepted this unforeseen partnership, this choice of nightmares forced upon me in the tenebrous land invaded by these mean and greedy phantoms.

"Kurtz discoursed. A voice! a voice! It rang deep to the very last. It survived his strength to hide in the magnificent folds of eloquence the barren darkness of his heart. Oh, he struggled! he struggled! The wastes of his weary brain were haunted by shadowy images now — images of wealth and fame revolving obsequiously round his unextinguishable gift of noble and lofty expression. My Intended, my station, my career, my ideas — these were the subjects for the occasional utterances of elevated sentiments. The shade of the original Kurtz frequented the bedside of the hollow sham, whose fate it was to be buried presently in the mould of primeval earth. But both the diabolic love and the unearthly hate of the mysteries it had penetrated fought for the possession of that soul satiated with primitive emotions, avid of lying fame, of sham distinction, of all the appearances of success and power.

"Sometimes he was contemptibly childish. He desired to have kings meet him at railway-stations on his return from some ghastly Nowhere, where he intended to accomplish great things. 'You show them you have in you something that is really profitable, and then there will be no limits to the recognition of your ability,' he would say. 'Of course you must take care of the motives — right motives — always.' The long reaches that were like one and the same reach, monotonous bends that were exactly alike, slipped past the steamer with their multitude of secular[26] trees looking patiently after this grimy fragment of another world, the forerunner of change, of conquest, of trade, of massacres, of blessings. I looked ahead — piloting. 'Close the shutter,' said Kurtz suddenly one day; 'I can't bear to look at this.' I did so. There was a silence. 'Oh, but I will wring your heart yet!' he cried at the invisible wilderness.

"We broke down — as I had expected — and had to lie up for repairs at the head of an island. This delay was the first thing that shook Kurtz's confidence. One morning he gave me a packet of papers and a photograph — the lot tied together with a

---

[26] **secular:** Lasting from century to century.

shoe-string. 'Keep this for me,' he said. 'This noxious fool' (meaning the manager) 'is capable of prying into my boxes when I am not looking.' In the afternoon I saw him. He was lying on his back with closed eyes, and I withdrew quietly, but I heard him mutter, 'Live rightly, die, die . . .' I listened. There was nothing more. Was he rehearsing some speech in his sleep, or was it a fragment of a phrase from some newspaper article? He had been writing for the papers and meant to do so again, 'for the furthering of my ideas. It's a duty.'

"His was an impenetrable darkness. I looked at him as you peer down at a man who is lying at the bottom of a precipice where the sun never shines. But I had not much time to give him, because I was helping the engine-driver to take to pieces the leaky cylinders, to straighten a bent connecting-rod, and in other such matters. I lived in an infernal mess of rust, filings, nuts, bolts, spanners, hammers, ratchet-drills—things I abominate, because I don't get on with them. I tended the little forge we fortunately had aboard; I toiled wearily in a wretched scrap-heap—unless I had the shakes too bad to stand.

"One evening coming in with a candle I was startled to hear him say a little tremulously, 'I am lying here in the dark waiting for death.' The light was within a foot of his eyes. I forced myself to murmur, 'Oh, nonsense!' and stood over him as if transfixed.

"Anything approaching the change that came over his features I have never seen before, and hope never to see again. Oh, I wasn't touched. I was fascinated. It was as though a veil had been rent. I saw on that ivory face the expression of sombre pride, of ruthless power, of craven terror—of an intense and hopeless despair. Did he live his life again in every detail of desire, temptation, and surrender during that supreme moment of complete knowledge? He cried in a whisper at some image, at some vision—he cried out twice, a cry that was no more than a breath—

"'The horror! The horror!'

"I blew the candle out and left the cabin. The pilgrims were dining in the mess-room, and I took my place opposite the manager, who lifted his eyes to give me a questioning glance, which I successfully ignored. He leaned back, serene, with that peculiar smile of his sealing the unexpressed depths of his meanness. A continuous shower of small flies streamed upon the lamp, upon the cloth, upon our hands and faces. Suddenly the manager's boy put his insolent black head in the doorway, and said in a tone of scathing contempt—

"'Mistah Kurtz—he dead.'

"All the pilgrims rushed out to see. I remained, and went on with my dinner. I believe I was considered brutally callous. However, I did not eat much. There was a lamp in there—light, don't you know—and outside it was so beastly, beastly dark. I went no more near the remarkable man who had pronounced a judgment upon the adventures of his soul on this earth. The voice was gone. What else had been there? But I am of course aware that next day the pilgrims buried something in a muddy hole.

"And then they very nearly buried me.

"However, as you see, I did not go to join Kurtz there and then. I did not. I remained to dream the nightmare out to the end, and to show my loyalty to Kurtz once more. Destiny. My destiny! Droll thing life is—that mysterious arrangement of merciless logic for a futile purpose. The most you can hope from it is some knowledge of yourself—that comes too late—a crop of unextinguishable regrets. I have wrestled with death. It is the most unexciting contest you can imagine. It takes place in an impalpable grayness, with nothing underfoot, with nothing around, without spectators, without clamour, without glory, without the great desire of victory, without the great fear of defeat, in a sickly atmosphere of tepid scepticism, without much belief in your own right, and still less in that of your adversary. If such is the form of ultimate wisdom, then life is a greater riddle than some of us think it to be. I was within a hair's breadth of the last opportunity for pronouncement, and I found with humiliation that probably I would have nothing to say. This is the reason why I affirm that Kurtz was a remarkable man. He had something to say. He said it. Since I had peeped over the edge myself, I understand better the meaning of his stare, that could not see the flame of the candle, but was wide enough to embrace the whole universe, piercing enough to penetrate all the hearts that beat in the darkness. He had summed up—he had judged. 'The horror!' He was a remarkable man. After all, this was the expression of some sort of belief; it had candour, it had conviction, it had a vibrating note of revolt in its whisper, it had the appalling face of a glimpsed truth—the strange commingling of desire and hate. And it is not my own extremity I remember best—a vision of grayness without form filled with physical pain, and a careless contempt for the evanescence of all things—even of this pain itself. No! It is his extremity that I seem to have lived through. True, he had made that last stride, he had stepped over the edge, while I had been permitted to draw back my hesitating foot. And perhaps in this is the whole difference; perhaps all the wisdom, and all truth, and all sincerity, are just compressed into that inappreciable moment of time in which we step over the threshold of the invisible. Perhaps! I like to think my summing-up would not have been a word of careless contempt. Better his cry—much better. It was an affirmation, a moral victory paid for by innumerable defeats, by abominable terrors, by abominable satisfactions. But it was a victory! That is why I have remained loyal to Kurtz to the last, and even beyond, when a long time after I heard once more, not his own voice, but the echo of his magnificent eloquence thrown to me from a soul as translucently pure as a cliff of crystal.

"No, they did not bury me, though there is a period of time which I remember mistily, with a shuddering wonder, like a passage through some inconceivable world that had no hope in it and no desire. I found myself back in the sepulchral city resenting the sight of people hurrying through the streets to filch a little money from each other, to devour their infamous cookery, to gulp their unwholesome beer, to dream their insignificant and silly dreams. They trespassed upon my thoughts. They were intruders whose knowledge of life was to me an irritating pretence, because I felt so sure they could not possibly know the things I knew. Their bearing, which was simply the bearing of commonplace individuals going about their business in the assurance of perfect safety, was offensive to me like the outrageous flauntings of folly in the face of a danger it is unable to comprehend. I had no particular desire to enlighten them, but I had some difficulty in restraining myself from laughing in their faces, so full of stupid importance. I daresay I was not very well at that time. I tottered about the streets—there were various affairs to settle—grinning bitterly at perfectly respectable persons. I admit my behaviour was inexcusable, but then my temperature was seldom normal in these days. My dear aunt's endeavours to 'nurse up my strength' seemed altogether beside the mark. It was not my strength that wanted nursing, it was my imagination that wanted soothing. I kept the bundle of papers given me by Kurtz, not knowing exactly what to do with it. His mother had died lately, watched over, as I was told, by his Intended. A clean-shaved man, with an official manner and wearing gold-rimmed spectacles, called on me one day and made inquiries, at first circuitous, afterwards suavely pressing, about what he was pleased to denominate certain 'documents.' I was not surprised, because I had had two rows with the manager on the subject out there. I had refused to give up the smallest scrap out of that package, and I took the same attitude with the spectacled man. He became darkly menacing at last, and with much heat argued that the Company had the right to every bit of information about its 'territories.' And said he, 'Mr. Kurtz's knowledge of unexplored regions must have been necessarily extensive and peculiar—owing to his great abilities and to the deplorable circumstances in which he had been placed: therefore——' I assured him Mr. Kurtz's knowledge, however extensive, did not bear upon the problems of commerce or administration. He invoked then the name of science. 'It would be an incalculable loss if,' etc., etc. I offered him the report on the 'Suppression of Savage Customs,' with the postscriptum torn off. He took it up eagerly, but ended by sniffing at it with an air of contempt. 'This is not what we had a right to expect,' he remarked. 'Expect nothing else,' I said. 'There are only private letters.' He withdrew upon some threat of legal proceedings, and I saw him no more; but another fellow, calling himself Kurtz's cousin, appeared two days later, and was anxious to hear all the details about his dear relative's last moments. Incidentally he gave me to understand that Kurtz had been essentially a great musician. 'There was the making of an immense success,' said the man, who was an organist, I believe, with lank gray hair flowing over a greasy coat-collar. I had no reason to doubt his statement; and to this day I am unable to say what was Kurtz's profession, whether he ever had any—which was the greatest of his talents. I had taken him for a painter who wrote for the papers, or else for a journalist who could paint—but even the cousin (who took snuff during the interview) could not tell me what he had been—exactly. He was a universal genius—on that point I agreed with the old chap, who thereupon blew his nose noisily into a large cotton handkerchief and withdrew in senile agitation, bearing off some family letters and memoranda without importance. Ultimately a journalist anxious to know something of the fate of his 'dear colleague' turned up. This visitor informed me Kurtz's proper sphere ought to have been politics 'on the popular side.' He had furry straight eyebrows, bristly hair cropped short, an eye-glass on a broad ribbon, and, becoming expansive, confessed his opinion that Kurtz really couldn't write a bit—'but heavens! how that man could talk. He electrified large meetings. He had faith—don't you see?—he had the faith. He could get himself to believe anything—anything. He would have been a splendid leader of an extreme party.' 'What party?' I asked. 'Any party,' answered the other. 'He was an—an—extremist.' Did I not think so? I assented. Did I know, he asked, with a sudden flash of curiosity, 'what it was that had induced him to go out there?' 'Yes,' said I, and forthwith handed him the famous Report for publication, if he thought fit. He glanced through it hurriedly, mumbling all the time, judged 'it would do,' and took himself off with this plunder.

"Thus I was left at last with a slim packet of letters and the girl's portrait. She struck me as beautiful—I mean she had a beautiful expression. I know that the sunlight can be made to lie, too, yet one felt that no manipulation of light and pose could have conveyed the delicate shade of truthfulness upon those features. She seemed ready to listen without mental reservation, without suspicion, without a thought for herself. I concluded I would go and give her back her portrait and those letters myself. Curiosity? Yes; and also some other feeling perhaps. All that had been Kurtz's had passed out of my hands: his soul, his body, his station, his plans, his ivory, his career. There remained only his memory and his Intended—and I wanted to give that up, too, to the past, in a way—to surrender personally all that remained of him with me to that oblivion which is the last word of our common fate. I don't defend myself. I had no clear perception of what it was I really wanted. Perhaps it was an impulse of unconscious loyalty, or the fulfilment of one of those ironic necessities that lurk in the facts of human existence. I don't know. I can't tell. But I went.

"I thought his memory was like the other memories of the dead that accumulate in every man's life—a vague impress on the brain of shadows that had fallen on it in their swift and final passage; but before the high and ponderous door, between the tall houses of a street as still and decorous as a well-kept alley in a cemetery, I had a vision of him on the stretcher, opening his mouth voraciously, as if to devour all the earth with all its mankind. He lived then before me; he lived as much as he had ever lived—a shadow insatiable of splendid appearances, of frightful realities; a shadow darker than the shadow of the night, and draped nobly in the folds of a gorgeous eloquence. The vision seemed to enter the house with me—the stretcher, the phantombearers, the wild crowd of obedient worshippers, the gloom of the forests, the glitter of the reach between the murky bends, the beat of the drum, regular and muffled like the beating of a heart—the heart of a conquering darkness. It was a moment of triumph for the wilderness, an invading and vengeful rush which, it seemed to me, I would have to keep back alone for the salvation of another soul. And the memory of what I had heard him say afar there, with the horned shapes stirring at my back, in the glow of fires, within the patient woods, those broken phrases came back to me, were heard again in their ominous and terrifying simplicity. I remembered his abject pleading, his abject threats, the colossal scale of his vile desires, the meanness, the torment, the tempestuous anguish of his soul. And later on I seemed to see his collected languid manner, when he said one day, 'This lot of ivory now is really mine. The Company did not pay for it. I collected it myself at a very great personal risk. I am afraid they will try to claim it as theirs though. H'm. It is a difficult case. What do you think I ought to do—resist? Eh? I want no more than justice.' . . . He wanted no more than justice—no more than justice. I rang the bell before a mahogany door on the first floor, and while I waited he seemed to stare at me out of the glassy panel— stare with that wide and immense stare embracing, condemning, loathing all the universe. I seemed to hear the whispered cry, 'The horror! The horror!'

"The dusk was falling. I had to wait in a lofty drawing-room with three long windows from floor to ceiling that were like three luminous and bedraped columns.

The bent gilt legs and backs of the furniture shone in indistinct curves. The tall marble fireplace had a cold and monumental whiteness. A grand piano stood massively in a corner; with dark gleams on the flat surfaces like a sombre and polished sarcophagus. A high door opened—closed. I rose.

"She came forward, all in black, with a pale head, floating towards me in the dusk. She was in mourning. It was more than a year since his death, more than a year since the news came; she seemed as though she would remember and mourn for ever. She took both my hands in hers and murmured, 'I had heard you were coming.' I noticed she was not very young—I mean not girlish. She had a mature capacity for fidelity, for belief, for suffering. The room seemed to have grown darker, as if all the sad light of the cloudy evening had taken refuge on her forehead. This fair hair, this pale visage, this pure brow, seemed surrounded by an ashy halo from which the dark eyes looked out at me. Their glance was guileless, profound, confident, and trustful. She carried her sorrowful head as though she were proud of that sorrow, as though she would say, I—I alone know how to mourn for him as he deserves. But while we were still shaking hands, such a look of awful desolation came upon her face that I perceived she was one of those creatures that are not the playthings of Time. For her he had died only yesterday. And, by Jove! the impression was so powerful that for me, too, he seemed to have died only yesterday—nay, this very minute. I saw her and him in the same instant of time—his death and her sorrow—I saw her sorrow in the very moment of his death. Do you understand? I saw them together—I heard them together. She had said, with a deep catch of the breath, 'I have survived' while my strained ears seemed to hear distinctly, mingled with her tone of despairing regret, the summing up whisper of his eternal condemnation. I asked myself what I was doing there, with a sensation of panic in my heart as though I had blundered into a place of cruel and absurd mysteries not fit for a human being to behold. She motioned me to a chair. We sat down. I laid the packet gently on the little table, and she put her hand over it. . . . 'You knew him well,' she murmured, after a moment of mourning silence.

"'Intimacy grows quickly out there,' I said. 'I knew him as well as it is possible for one man to know another.'

"'And you admired him,' she said. 'It was impossible to know him and not to admire him. Was it?'

"'He was a remarkable man,' I said, unsteadily. Then before the appealing fixity of her gaze, that seemed to watch for more words on my lips, I went on, 'It was impossible not to——'

"'Love him,' she finished eagerly, silencing me into an appalled dumbness. 'How true! how true! But when you think that no one knew him so well as I! I had all his noble confidence. I knew him best.'

"'You knew him best,' I repeated. And perhaps she did. But with every word spoken the room was growing darker, and only her forehead, smooth and white, remained illumined by the unextinguishable light of belief and love.

"'You were his friend,' she went on. 'His friend,' she repeated, a little louder. 'You must have been, if he had given you this, and sent you to me. I feel I can speak to you—and oh! I must speak. I want you—you who have heard his last words— to know I have been worthy of him. . . . It is not pride. . . . Yes! I am proud to know

I understood him better than any one on earth—he told me so himself. And since his mother died I have had no one—no one—to—to——'

"I listened. The darkness deepened. I was not even sure whether he had given me the right bundle. I rather suspect he wanted me to take care of another batch of his papers which, after his death, I saw the manager examining under the lamp. And the girl talked, easing her pain in the certitude of my sympathy; she talked as thirsty men drink. I had heard that her engagement with Kurtz had been disapproved by her people. He wasn't rich enough or something. And indeed I don't know whether he had not been a pauper all his life. He had given me some reason to infer that it was his impatience of comparative poverty that drove him out there.

" '. . . Who was not his friend who had heard him speak once?' she was saying. 'He drew men towards him by what was best in them.' She looked at me with intensity. 'It is the gift of the great,' she went on, and the sound of her low voice seemed to have the accompaniment of all the other sounds, full of mystery, desolation, and sorrow, I had ever heard—the ripple of the river, the soughing of the trees swayed by the wind, the murmurs of the crowds, the faint ring of incomprehensible words cried from afar, the whisper of a voice speaking from beyond the threshold of an eternal darkness. 'But you have heard him! You know!' she cried.

" 'Yes, I know,' I said with something like despair in my heart, but bowing my head before the faith that was in her, before that great and saving illusion that shone with an unearthly glow in the darkness, in the triumphant darkness from which I could not have defended her—from which I could not even defend myself.

" 'What a loss to me—to us!'—she corrected herself with beautiful generosity; then added in a murmur, 'To the world.' By the last gleams of twilight I could see the glitter of her eyes, full of tears—of tears that would not fall.

" 'I have been very happy—very fortunate—very proud,' she went on. 'Too fortunate. Too happy for a little while. And now I am unhappy for—for life.'

"She stood up; her fair hair seemed to catch all the remaining light in a glimmer of gold. I rose, too.

" 'And of all this,' she went on, mournfully, 'of all his promise, and of all his greatness, of his generous mind, of his noble heart, nothing remains—nothing but a memory. You and I——'

" 'We shall always remember him,' I said, hastily.

" 'No!' she cried. 'It is impossible that all this should be lost—that such a life should be sacrificed to leave nothing—but sorrow. You know what vast plans he had. I knew of them, too—I could not perhaps understand—but others knew of them. Something must remain. His words, at least, have not died.'

" 'His words will remain,' I said.

" 'And his example,' she whispered to herself. 'Men looked up to him—his goodness shone in every act. His example——'

" 'True,' I said; 'his example, too. Yes, his example. I forgot that.'

" 'But I do not. I cannot—I cannot believe—not yet. I cannot believe that I shall never see him again, that nobody will see him again, never, never, never.'

"She put out her arms as if after a retreating figure, stretching them back and with clasped pale hands across the fading and narrow sheen of the window. Never see him! I saw him clearly enough then. I shall see this eloquent phantom as long as I live, and I shall see her, too, a tragic and familiar Shade, resembling in this gesture another one, tragic also, and bedecked with powerless charms, stretching bare brown arms over the glitter of the infernal stream, the stream of darkness. She said suddenly very low, 'He died as he lived.'

"'His end,' said I, with dull anger stirring in me, 'was in every way worthy of his life.'

"'And I was not with him,' she murmured. My anger subsided before a feeling of infinite pity.

"'Everything that could be done——' I mumbled.

"'Ah, but I believed in him more than any one on earth—more than his own mother, more than—himself. He needed me! Me! I would have treasured every sigh, every word, every sign, every glance.'

"I felt like a chill grip on my chest. 'Don't,' I said, in a muffled voice.

"'Forgive me. I—I—have mourned so long in silence—in silence. . . . You were with him—to the last? I think of his loneliness. Nobody near to understand him as I would have understood. Perhaps no one to hear. . . .'

"'To the very end,' I said, shakily. 'I heard his very last words. . . .' I stopped in a fright.

"'Repeat them,' she murmured in a heart-broken tone. 'I want—I want—something—something—to—to live with.'

"I was on the point of crying at her, 'Don't you hear them?' The dusk was repeating them in a persistent whisper all around us, in a whisper that seemed to swell menacingly like the first whisper of a rising wind. 'The horror! the horror!'

"'His last word—to live with,' she insisted. 'Don't you understand I loved him—I loved him—I loved him!'

"I pulled myself together and spoke slowly.

"'The last word he pronounced was—your name.'

"I heard a light sigh and then my heart stood still, stopped dead short by an exulting and terrible cry, by the cry of inconceivable triumph and of unspeakable pain. 'I knew it—I was sure!' . . . She knew. She was sure. I heard her weeping; she had hidden her face in her hands. It seemed to me that the house would collapse before I could escape, that the heavens would fall upon my head. But nothing happened. The heavens do not fall for such a trifle. Would they have fallen, I wonder, if I had rendered Kurtz that justice which was his due? Hadn't he said he wanted only justice? But I couldn't. I could not tell her. It would have been too dark—too dark altogether. . . ."

Marlow ceased, and sat apart, indistinct and silent, in the pose of a meditating Buddha. Nobody moved for a time. "We have lost the first of the ebb," said the Director, suddenly. I raised my head. The offing was barred by a black bank of clouds, and the tranquil waterway leading to the uttermost ends of the earth flowed sombre under an overcast sky—seemed to lead into the heart of an immense darkness.

Colonialism and Independence

p. 1159

Colonialism was one of the defining issues of the twentieth century, which began with most of Asia and Africa under the sway of European nations. In 1800, European powers controlled about 35 percent of the globe. The competition among them to gain additional colonies gathered momentum over the next hundred years until, by 1914, Europe—led by Britain, France, Holland, and Portugal—could claim approximately 85 percent of the earth's surface. European domination of large areas of Asia, Africa, and Latin America continued until after World War II, when colonies worldwide fought to gain their independence and a new age of "decolonization" or "postcolonialism" was ushered in. At the time it was written, *Heart of Darkness* (1902) was one of several literary attacks on the excesses of European colonialism.

"THE WHITE MAN'S BURDEN"

The primary impetus behind the acquisition of colonies, called at the time "the great game," was, of course, economic. An increasing population in Europe and a lack of enough agricultural land fueled the colonial enterprise. By 1870, for example, England could no

The wealth of a common global culture will . . . be expressed in the particularities of our different languages and cultures very much like a universal garden of many-coloured flowers.

– NGUGI, "Creating Space . . . " in *Moving the Centre* 24

▶ L'Africa É il Continente di Domani (Africa Is the Continent of Tomorrow).
Poster, Late 1930s
This piece of propaganda was created during Mussolini's Fascist regime in Italy. The Fascists, seeking to extend their reach by colonizing more of Africa (Italy had claimed Somalia in 1889), followed Great Britain, Germany, Portugal, Spain, and Belgium in acquiring parts of the continent. This poster was created to drum up public support for the campaign. (The Art Archive/Imperial War Museum)

Eng. Lit., my sister,
was more than a
cruel joke —
it was the heart
of alien conquest.

— FELIX MNTHALI

longer grow enough food to feed itself. Less developed countries and regions in Asia, Africa, and the Caribbean were exploited for cheap labor, raw materials used for manufactures in European factories, and land. On maps made by European cartographers, large areas of Asia and Africa appeared as "blank spaces," as Marlow says in *Heart of Darkness;* Europeans did not recognize the presence or the property rights of indigenous peoples, and these white spaces were colored in only when a European nation colonized an area.

Colonial conquest was justified in terms of the benefits it bestowed on the colonized. Along with economic development, the white man said he was bringing civilization and Christianity to unenlightened regions of the world. Furthermore, this was a mission, "the white man's burden," as it was referred to at the time, but as **Rudyard Kipling** claims in his poem of that title (1899), the job was often a thankless one. And there was always the danger of being engulfed like Kurtz in *Heart of Darkness* by the supposed darkness one had set out to enlighten.

p. 1228

COLONIALISM IN THE CONGO

The Free State of the Congo was one of the most cruel colonial enterprises of the late nineteenth century. In 1876 Leopold II of Belgium, a nation less than fifty years old with no overseas possessions, called a conference of the European powers to consider Africa and "to open to civilization the only part of our globe where Christianity has not penetrated and to pierce the darkness which envelops the entire population." Leopold's ulterior motive was to acquire a colony for himself, and in 1884 he convinced a Berlin conference to grant him nearly a million square miles in Central Africa to be known as the Congo Free State. By promising to allow open economic access and trade to all European powers, Leopold was given virtually absolute control over the territory, which he ruled—but never visited—until his death in 1908. Although his stated aims were humanitarian, his rule was despotic. His agents extracted ivory and rubber from the Congo using deception and violence and did almost nothing to bring enlightenment and civilization. George Washington Williams, an African American journalist and historian, was the first to expose Leopold's fraud and the cruelties he imposed on the Congolese people in *An Open Letter,* a missive addressed to

p. 1231

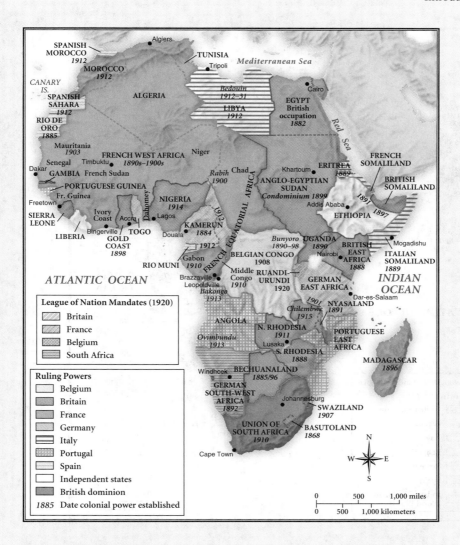

The Colonization of Africa, 1880–1939

From the late nineteenth century until the eve of World War II, most of Africa was divided up among seven European powers. The only independent states were Ethiopia and Liberia. After World War I, the newly formed League of Nations distributed Germany's African colonies to other countries, who were to govern them as "mandates," in preparation for eventual independence. Britain received German East Africa and Togo, South Africa was given German South-West Africa, while Kamerun (Cameroon) went to France and Ruandi-Urundi (Rwanda-Burundi) was assigned to Belgium.

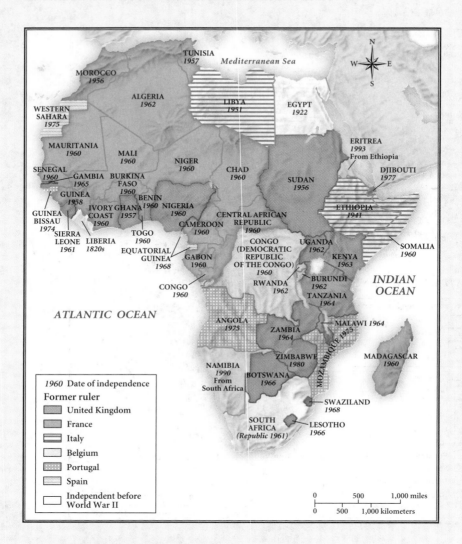

The Decolonization of Africa, 1951–2000

After World War II, African countries gained independence, sometimes peacefully and sometimes after armed struggle. The transition from European rule to self-governing nations was often followed by greater poverty, dictatorship, war, or famine in much of the continent. Striving for political, economic, and educational progress proved a difficult process.

the king and published in 1890. Leopold managed to discredit Williams and cover up his own crimes until the turn of the century, when a journalistic onslaught, especially from Britain and America, confirmed Williams's allegations. *Heart of Darkness* and Mark Twain's satiric essay ***King Leopold's Soliloquy*** (1905) were part of this storm of criticism.

p. 1238

COLONIZATION AND DECOLONIZATION IN INDIA

The "jewel in the crown" of the British Empire was India. The British had initiated trading ventures there in the early seventeenth century, but they did not consolidate their rule on the subcontinent until the first half of the nineteenth century. By 1867, when Queen Victoria was named Empress of India, the British had established political, educational, and social institutions as well as an economic network. Although there was periodic resistance to British rule, most notably in the Sepoy Rebellion in 1857, the Indians accommodated themselves to their colonial status, attending British schools, adopting British customs, using the English language, and serving in the Civil Service.

British rule in India brought together a myriad of separate states and provided a common language that transcended the many native tongues and facilitated communication with Europe. It also enabled a transition from an agrarian feudalism to more centralized and open social and governmental institutions, so that British colonialism has sometimes been characterized as a benign influence in India. The Indians themselves are often more ambivalent about the British contributions to their heritage. Many Indian writers willingly write in English and find their identity enriched by their cultural hybridity. **Raja Rao**, in the 1938 preface to his novel *Kanthapura,* expresses a somewhat more tentative attitude when he accepts the necessity of writing in English, acknowledging British influence as an important though complicating part of his identity.

p. 1241

British rule did not resolve all the conflicts within India, especially those between the majority Hindu and minority Muslim populations. Britain tried to settle the differences between these two groups by a partition of the country in 1905, but Hindu resistance forced revocation of the partition a few years later. Part of a growing nationalist movement, the resistance, led by the Hindu Congress Party, grew into a sustained campaign for independence. Its inspirational leader was Mahatma Gandhi, who organized mass demonstrations, strikes, and economic boycotts that finally forced the British to grant independence in 1947. Although Gandhi's message emphasized nonviolence, the differences between Hindus and Muslims sparked violent confrontations between the two groups and led to the division of the country into two — Hindu-majority India and the new Muslim nation of Pakistan — as part of the independence agreement. Ironically, the agreement, the long-sought goal of the Congress Party, also led to Gandhi's assassination by a fanatical Hindu nationalist who thought that Gandhi had conceded too much to the Muslims in negotiating its terms.

p. 1242

Coming just after the conclusion of World War II, the war that signaled the end of European colonialism, Indian independence can stand symbolically for the beginning of decolonization. The speech delivered by **Jawaharlal Nehru** on the eve of independence, August 14, 1947, is as familiar to Indians as Lincoln's Gettysburg Address and Martin Luther King Jr.'s speech at the March on Washington in 1963 are to Americans. In the decades following the war, many of the colonies of Britain, France, Holland, and other European countries were liberated — most dramatically, perhaps, India and Pakistan, Algeria, and Indonesia. At the same time, the civil rights movement emerged in the United States, a movement that Martin Luther King Jr., among others, connected with worldwide decolonization. By 1990 forty-nine new African nations had been formed and most of the European colonies in Asia had become independent countries. Writers from these new nations, often active participants in the struggles for independence, have emerged as participants in a world literature movement that now includes voices from many formerly silent peoples.

Twentieth-Century India: The Partition of Bengal

Although Calcutta had long been the administrative center of British rule in 1900 it was also the intellectual and cultural capital of Bengal, the region in eastern India constituting what are now the Indian states of West Bengal, Bihar, and Orissa as well as the nation of Bangladesh. With a population of more than 85 million, Bengal became increasingly difficult for the British to govern, so in 1905 Lord Curzon, viceroy of India, convinced the administration in London to partition Bengal into two parts. The struggle over the Partition illustrates some of the difficulties of colonial rule and foreshadowed the independence movement to come.

The Partition divided Bengal into Western Bengal (population 42 million Hindus, 9 million Muslims), and Eastern Bengal and Assam (population 18 million Muslims, 12 million Hindus). Some Muslims supported the plan because it created a separate district in which there would be a Muslim majority, but the National Congress, the predominantly Hindu party founded in 1885 to promote Indian nationalism, was committed to a policy of national unity. Not only did it oppose British "communalism"—drawing political divisions along religious lines—but it also supported a "one India" policy as a way of getting beyond the patchwork of states governed by princes and provincial rulers, maharajas and nawabs, into which India had fragmented. Indian liberals considered the Partition another example of a British colonial policy to divide and rule.

Those against the Partition responded with demonstrations, a boycott of British manufactured goods, and a campaign to buy Indian-made textiles. Some extremists carried out a terror campaign and assassinated some

Lord Curzon, viceroy of India, 1898–1905. (The Art Archive/Culver Pictures)

colonial officials. The resistance convinced the British to revoke the Partition in 1909 and to make some political reforms, creating more opportunities for Indian participation in government and recognizing some Muslim majority areas. The British also supported the founding of the All India Muslim League in 1906, an organization comparable to the predominantly Hindu National Congress.

The Partition and the response to it had a lasting impact. The movement to make and buy Indian textiles and the boycott of British goods were techniques later employed by Gandhi's nonviolent movement for independence. And the principle of division according to a region's religion would guide the partition of India and Pakistan in 1947, a decision that remains controversial today.

❧ RUDYARD KIPLING
B. INDIA, 1865–1936

> Though many of Kipling's works, particularly his short stories and novels, demonstrate an understanding and appreciation of the Indian people and their culture, in other works, like the poem "The White Man's Burden" (1899), Kipling sounds like a jingoistic imperialist. The poem's unquestioned assumption of European superiority expresses the attitude that promoted colonialism in the first place and excused its excesses, an attitude nearly universal among nineteenth-century Europeans, even those critical of colonial enterprise.

❧ The White Man's Burden

Take up the White Man's burden –
    Send forth the best ye breed –
Go, bind your sons to exile
    To serve your captives' need;
To wait, in heavy harness,
    On fluttered folk and wild –
Your new-caught sullen peoples,
    Half devil and half child.

Take up the White Man's burden –
10   In patience to abide,
To veil the threat of terror
    And check the show of pride;
By open speech and simple,
    An hundred times made plain,
To seek another's profit
    And work another's gain.

Take up the White Man's burden –
    The savage wars of peace –
Fill full the mouth of Famine,
20   And bid the sickness cease;
And when your goal is nearest
    (The end for others sought)

The Rhodes Colossus. Drawing *Cecil Rhodes was prime minister of the Cape Colony, in what is now South Africa, from 1890 to 1897. Here pictured as a giant straddling and taking the measure of the continent of Africa, he dreamed of expanding the British Empire "from the Cape to Cairo." (Hulton/Archive)*

Watch sloth and heathen folly
    Bring all your hope to nought.

Take up the White Man's burden –
    No iron rule of kings,
But toil of serf and sweeper –
    The tale of common things.
The ports ye shall not enter,
    The roads ye shall not tread,
Go, make them with your living
    And mark them with your dead.

Take up the White Man's burden,
    And reap his old reward –
The blame of those ye better
    The hate of those ye guard –

30

The cry of hosts ye humour
    (Ah, slowly?) toward the light: –
"Why brought ye us from bondage,
40   Our loved Egyptian night?"[1]

Take up the White Man's burden –
    Ye dare not stoop to less –
Nor call too loud on Freedom
    To cloak your weariness.
By all ye will or whisper,
    By all ye leave or do,
The silent sullen peoples
    Shall weigh your God and you.

Take up the White Man's burden!
50   Have done with childish days –
The lightly-proffered laurel,
    The easy ungrudged praise:
Comes now, to search your manhood
    Through all the thankless years,
Cold, edged with dear-bought wisdom,
    The judgment of your peers.

---

[1] **"Why . . . Egyptian night?":** When things got hard in the wilderness, the Israelites blamed Moses and Aaron for their troubles; see Exodus 16:23.

GEORGE WASHINGTON WILLIAMS
B. UNITED STATES, 1849–1891

Lawyer, clergyman, journalist, and historian, George Washington Williams is best known for *History of the Negro Race in America from* 1619 to 1880, a work that prompted W. E. B. Du Bois to call him "the greatest historian of the race." After interviewing Leopold II in 1889, Williams described the king as "one of the noblest sovereigns in the world; an emperor whose highest ambition is to serve the cause of Christian civilization." However, his subsequent experience in the Congo would change his mind about the sovereign. He arranged to visit the colony in 1890 to gather material for a book and to evaluate the feasibility of sending skilled black American artisans there to help in the Congo's development. During his six months there, he became increasingly disenchanted with Leopold and his colony. Williams's *An Open Letter,* written from Stanley Falls, was the first published attack on Leopold's project. Williams makes nearly all the same points that would be raised in the journalistic onslaught several years later. *An Open Letter,* published as a pamphlet in Europe and America in 1890, prompted much controversy. Leopold sought to discredit Williams by revealing that the journalist had exaggerated or misrepresented some of his educational credentials and his achievements as a soldier in the Civil War. Although these revelations silenced the critics of the Congo Free State for several years, later investigators confirmed all that Williams had to say about the Congo.

A note on the spelling: Though an American, Williams uses British spellings here. At the time, it was common to use British phrases and spellings in order to appear cultured.

> Against the deceit, fraud, robberies, arson, murder, slave-raiding, and general policy of cruelty of your Majesty's Government to the natives, stands their record of unexampled patience, long-suffering and forgiving spirit, which put the boasted civilization and professed religion of your Majesty's Government to the blush.
>
> – GEORGE WASHINGTON WILLIAMS, *An Open Letter*

FROM

An Open Letter to His Serene Majesty Leopold II

Good and Great Friend,

I have the honour to submit for your Majesty's consideration some reflections respecting the Independant State of Congo, based upon a careful study and inspection of the country and character of the personal Government you have established upon the African Continent.

In order that you may know the truth, the whole truth, and nothing but the truth, I implore your most gracious permission to address you without restraint, and with

French and German Administrators Agreeing on New Franco-German Boundary Lines in Lobaye Marshes, Congo. *Le Petit journal,* 1913. Engraving

European administrators presumed to delineate borders where previously none had existed, creating African nations that did not reflect the tribal make-up of the land. (The Art Archive/Bibliothèque Municipale Dijon/ Dagli Orti)

the frankness of a man who feels that he has a duty to perform to *History, Humanity, Civilization* and to the *Supreme Being,* who is himself the "King of Kings." . . .

In your personal letter to the President of the Republic of the United States of America, bearing date of August 1st, 1885, you said that the possessions of the International Association of the Congo will hereafter form the Independent State of the Congo. "I have at the same time the honour to inform you and the Government of the Republic of the United States of America that, authorised by the Belgian Legislative Chambers to become the Chief of the new State, I have taken, in accord with the Association, the title of Sovereign of the Independent State of Congo." Thus you assumed the headship of the State of Congo, and at once organised a personal Government. You have named its officers, created its laws, furnished its finances, and every act of the Government has been clothed with the majesty of your authority.

On the 25th of February 1884, a gentleman, who has sustained an intimate relation to your Majesty for many years, and who then wrote as expressing your sentiments, addressed a letter to the United States in which the following language occurs: — "It may be safely asserted that no barbarous people have ever so readily adopted the fostering care of benevolent enterprise, as have the tribes of the Congo, and never was there a more honest and practical effort made to increase their knowledge and secure their welfare." The letter, from which the above is an excerpt, was written for the purpose of securing the friendly action of the Committee on Foreign

Relations, which had under consideration a Senate Resolution in which the United States recognised the flag of the "Association Internationale du Congo" as the flag of a friendly Government. The letter was influential, because it was supposed to contain the truth respecting the natives, and the programme, not only of the Association, but of the new State, its legitimate successor, and of your Majesty.

When I arrived in the Congo, I naturally sought for the results of the brilliant programme: — *"fostering care," "benevolent enterprise,"* an *"honest and practical effort"* to increase the knowledge of the natives *"and secure their welfare."* I had never been able to conceive of Europeans, establishing a government in a tropical country, without building a hospital; and yet from the mouth of the Congo River to its headwaters, here at the seventh cataract, a distance of 1,448 miles, there is not a solitary hospital for Europeans, and only three sheds for sick Africans in the service of the State, not fit to be occupied by a horse. Sick sailors frequently die on board their vessels at Banana Point; and if it were not for the humanity of the Dutch Trading Company at that place — who have often opened their private hospital to the sick of other countries — many more might die. There is not a single chaplain in the employ of your Majesty's Government to console the sick or bury the dead. Your white men sicken and die in their quarters or on the caravan road, and seldom have Christian burial. With few exceptions, the surgeons of your Majesty's government have been gentlemen of professional ability, devoted to duty, but usually left with few medical stores and no quarters in which to treat their patients. The African soldiers and labourers of your Majesty's Government fare worse than the whites, because they have poorer quarters, quite as bad as those of the natives; and in the sheds, called hospitals, they languish upon a bed of bamboo poles without blankets, pillows or any food different from that served to them when well, rice and fish.

I was anxious to see to what extent the natives had *"adopted the fostering care"* of your Majesty's *"benevolent enterprise"* (?), and I was doomed to bitter disappointment. Instead of the natives of the Congo "adopting the fostering care" of your Majesty's Government, they everywhere complain that their land has been taken from them by force; that the Government is cruel and arbitrary, and declare that they neither love nor respect t[h]e Government and its flag. Your Majesty's Government has sequestered their land, burned their towns, stolen their property, enslaved their women and children, and committed other crimes too numerous to mention in detail. It is natural that they everywhere shrink from *"the fostering care"* your Majesty's Government so eagerly proffers them.

There has been, to my absolute knowledge, no *"honest and practical effort made to increase their knowledge and secure their welfare."* Your Majesty's Government has never spent one franc for educational purposes, nor institu[t]ed any practical system of industrialism. Indeed the most unpractical measures have been adopted *against* the natives in nearly every respect; and in the capital of your Majesty's Government at Boma there is not a native employed. The labour system is radically unpractical; the soldiers and labourers of your Majesty's Government are very largely imported from Zanzibar at a cost of £10 *per capita,* and from Sierre Leone, Liberia, Accra and Lagos at from £1 to £1/10. — *per capita.* These recruits are transported under circumstances more cruel than cattle in European countries. They eat their rice twice a day by the use of their fingers; they often thirst for water when the season is dry; they are exposed to the heat and rain, and sleep upon the damp and filthy decks of the vessels often so closely crowded as to lie in human ordure. And, of course, many die.

Upon the arrival of the survivors in the Congo they are set to work as labourers at one shilling a day; as soldiers they are promised sixteen shillings per month, in English money, but are usually paid off in cheap handkerchiefs and poisonous gin. The cruel and unjust treatment to which these people are subjected breaks the spirits of many of them, makes them distrust and despise your Majesty's Government. They are enemies, not patriots. . . .

From these general observations I wish now to pass to specific charges against your Majesty's Government.

FIRST. — Your Majesty's Government is deficient in the moral, military and financial strength, necessary to govern a territory of 1,508,000 square miles, 7,251 miles of navigation, and 31,694 square miles of lake surface. In the Lower Congo River there is but one post, in the cataract region one. From Leopoldville to N'Gombe, a distance of more than three hundred miles, there is not a single soldier or civilian. Not one out of every twenty State-officials know the language of the natives, although they are constantly issuing laws, difficult even for Europeans, and expect the natives to comprehend and obey them. Cruelties of the most astounding character are practised by the natives, such as burying slaves alive in the grave of a dead chief, cutting off the heads of captured warriors in native combats, and no effort is put forth by your Majesty's Government to prevent them. Between eight hundred and one thousand slaves are sold to be eaten by the natives of the Congo State annually; and slave raids, accomplished by the most cruel and murderous agencies, are carried on within the territorial limits of your Majesty's Government which is impotent. There are only 2,300 soldiers in the Congo.

SECOND. — Your Majesty's Government has established nearly fifty posts, consisting of from two to eight mercenary slave-soldiers from the East Coast. There is no white commissioned officer at these posts; they are in charge of the black Zanzibar soldiers, and the State expects them not only to sustain themselves, but to raid enough to feed the garrisons where the white men are stationed. These piratical, buccaneering posts compel the natives to furnish them with fish, goats, fowls, and vegetables at the mouths of their muskets; and whenever the natives refuse to feed these vampires, they report to the main station and white officers come with an expeditionary force and burn away the homes of the natives. These black soldiers, many of whom are slaves, exercise the power of life and death. They are ignorant and cruel, *because* they do not comprehend the natives; they are imposed upon them by the State. They make no report as to the number of robberies they commit, or the number of lives they take; they are only required to subsist upon the natives and thus relieve your Majesty's Government of the cost of feeding them. They are the greatest curse the country suffers now. . . .

FOURTH. — The Courts of your Majesty's Government are abortive, unjust, partial and delinquent. I have personally witnessed and examined their clumsy operations. The laws printed and circulated in Europe "for the protection of the blacks" in the Congo, are a dead letter and a fraud. I have heard an officer of the Belgian Army pleading the cause of a white man of low degree who had been guilty of beating and stabbing a black man, and urging race distinctions and prejudices as good and sufficient reasons why his client should be adjudged innocent. . . .

FIFTH. — Your Majesty's Government is excessively cruel to its prisoners, condemning them, for the slightest offences, to the chain gang, the like of which cannot be seen in any other Government in the civilised or uncivilised world. Often these ox-chains eat into the necks of the prisoners and produce sores about which the flies circle, aggravating the running wound; so the prisoner is constantly worried. These poor creatures are frequently beaten with a dried piece of hippopotamus skin, called a "chicote,"[1] and usually the blood flows at every stroke when well laid on. But the cruelties visited upon soldiers and workmen are not to be compared with the sufferings of the poor natives who, upon the slightest pretext, are thrust into the wretched prisons here in the Upper River. . . .

SIXTH. — Women are imported into your Majesty's Government for immoral purposes. They are introduced by two methods, viz., black men are dispatched to the Portuguese coast where they engage these women as mistresses of white men, who pay to the procurer a monthly sum. The other method is by capturing native women and condemning them to seven years' servitude for some imaginary crime against the State with which the villages of these women are charged. The State then hires these women out to the highest bidder, the officers having the first choice and then the men. Whenever children are born of such relations, the State maintains that the woman being its property the child belongs to it also. . . . There is only one post that I know of where there is not to be found children of the civil and military officers of your Majesty's Government abandoned to degradation; white men bringing their own flesh and blood under the lash of a most cruel master, the State of Congo.

SEVENTH. — Your Majesty's Government is engaged in trade and commerce, competing with the organised trade companies of Belgium, England, France, Portugal and Holland. It taxes all trading companies and exempts its own goods from export-duty, and makes many of its officers ivory-traders, with the promise of a liberal commission upon all they can buy or get for the State. State soldiers patrol many villages forbidding the natives to trade with any person but a State official, and when the natives refuse to accept the price of the State, their goods are seized by the Government that promised them "protection." When natives have persisted in trading with the trade-companies the State has punished their independence by burning the villages in the vicinity of the trading houses and driving the natives away. . . .

NINTH. — Your Majesty's Government has been, and is now, guilty of waging unjust and cruel wars against natives, with the hope of securing slaves and women, to minister to the behests of the officers of your Government. In such slave-hunting raids one village is armed by the State against the other, and the force thus secured is incorporated with the regular troops. I have no adequate terms with which to depict to your Majesty the brutal acts of your soldiers upon such raids as these. The soldiers who open the combat are usually the bloodthirsty cannibalistic Bangalas, who give

---

[1] **"chicote"**: A whip made of raw, sun-dried hippopotamus hide.

no quarter to the aged grandmother or nursing child at the breast of its mother. There are instances in which they have brought the heads of their victims to their white officers on the expeditionary steamers, and afterwards eaten the bodies of slain children. In one war two Belgian Army officers saw, from the deck of their steamer, a native in a canoe some distance away. He was not a combatant and was ignorant of the conflict in progress upon the shore, some distance away. The officers made a wager of £5 that they could hit the native with their rifles. Three shots were fired and the native fell dead, pierced through the head, and the trade canoe was transformed into a funeral barge and floated silently down the river.

In another war, waged without just cause, the Belgian Army officer in command of your Majesty's forces placed the men in two or three lines on the steamers and instructed them to commence firing when the whistles blew. The steamers approached the fated town, and, as was usual with them, the people came to the shore to look at the boats and sell different articles of food. There was a large crowd of men, women and children, laughing, talking and exposing their goods for sale. At once the shrill whistles of the steamers were heard, the soldiers levelled their guns and fired, and the people fell dead, and wounded, and groaning, and pleading for mercy. Many prisoners were made, and among them four comely looking young women. And now ensued a most revolting scene: your Majesty's officers quarreling over the selection of these women. The commander of this murderous expedition, with his garments stained with innocent blood, declared, that his rank entitled him to the first choice! Under the direction of this same officer the prisoners were reduced to servitude, and I saw them working upon the plantation of one of the stations of the State.

TENTH. — Your Majesty's Government is engaged in the slave-trade, wholesale and retail. It buys and sells and steals slaves. Your Majesty's Government gives £3 per head for able-bodied slaves for military service. Officers at the chief stations get the men and receive the money when they are transferred to the State; but there are some middle-men who only get from twenty to twenty-five francs per head. Three hundred and sixteen slaves were sent down the river recently, and others are to follow. These poor natives are sent hundreds of miles away from their villages, to serve among other natives whose language they do not know. When these men run away a reward of 1,000 N'taka is offered. Not long ago such a re-captured slave was given one hundred "chikote" each day until he died. Three hundred N'taka-brassrod is the price the State pays for a slave, when bought from a native. The labour force at the stations of your Majesty's Government in the Upper River is composed of slaves of all ages and both sexes. . . .

CONCLUSIONS

Against the deceit, fraud, robberies, arson, murder, slave-raiding, and general policy of cruelty of your Majesty's Government to the natives, stands their record of unexampled patience, long-suffering and forgiving spirit, which put the boasted civilisation and professed religion of your Majesty's Government to the blush. During thirteen years only one white man has lost his life by the hands of the natives, and only two white men have been killed in the Congo. Major Barttelot was shot by a Zanzibar soldier, and the captain of a Belgian trading-boat was the victim of his own rash and unjust treatment of a native chief.

All the crimes perpetrated in the Congo have been done in *your* name, and *you* must answer at the bar of Public Sentiment for the misgovernment of a people, whose lives and fortunes were entrusted to you by the august Conference of Berlin, 1884–1885. I now appeal to the Powers, which committed this infant State to your Majesty's charge, and to the great States which gave it international being; and whose majestic law you have scorned and trampled upon, to call and create an International Commission to investigate the charges herein preferred in the name of Humanity, Commerce, Constitutional Government and Christian Civilisation. . . .

I appeal to the Belgian people and to their Constitutional Government, so proud of its traditions, replete with the song and story of its champions of human liberty, and so jealous of its present position in the sisterhood of European States,—to cleanse itself from the imputation of the crimes with which your Majesty's personal State of Congo is polluted.

I appeal to Anti-Slavery Societies in all parts of Christendom, to Philanthropists, Christians, Statesmen, and to the great mass of people everywhere, to call upon the Governments of Europe, to hasten the close of the tragedy your Majesty's unlimited Monarchy is enacting in the Congo.

I appeal to our Heavenly Father, whose service is perfect love, in witness of the purity of my motives and the integrity of my aims; and to history and mankind I appeal for the demonstration and vindication of the truthfulness of the charges I have herein briefly outlined.

And all this upon the word of honour of a gentleman, I subscribe myself your Majesty's humble and obedient servant.

GEO. W. WILLIAMS.
Stanley Falls, Central Africa,
July 18th, 1890.

❧ MARK TWAIN (SAMUEL CLEMENS)
B. UNITED STATES, 1835–1910

The great American humorist Mark Twain, known for his novels *Tom Sawyer* (1876) and *Huckleberry Finn* (1883), also wrote travel narratives, journalistic essays, and occasional satires. He was especially active in the anti-imperialist cause, announcing after the Spanish-American War, in which the United States acquired Puerto Rico, the Philippines, and Guam: "I am an anti-imperialist. I am opposed to having the eagle put its talons on any other land." In 1901 Twain became a vice-president of the Congo Reform Association, and the next year he composed *King Leopold's*

Soliloquy (1902). Written in the last decade of Twain's life, *Soliloquy* is an example of the kind of true "slanders" that his Leopold complains about. By casting his satire in the voice of the king, Twain exposes Leopold's duplicity, as he exults in the way he has tricked the Americans; his arrogance, as he asserts that a king should be above criticism; and his hypocrisy, as he spouts religious sentiments while shedding the blood of the Congolese.

FROM

∾ King Leopold's Soliloquy

[*Throws down pamphlets which he has been reading. Excitedly combs his flowing spread of whiskers with his fingers; pounds the table with his fists; lets off brisk volleys of unsanctified language at brief intervals, repentantly drooping his head, between volleys, and kissing the Louis XI crucifix hanging from his neck, accompanying the kisses with mumbled apologies; presently rises, flushed and perspiring, and walks the floor, gesticulating*]

—— ——!!—— ——!! If I had them by the throat! [*Hastily kisses the crucifix, and mumbles*] In these twenty years I have spent millions to keep the press of the two hemispheres quiet, and still these leaks keep on occurring. I have spent other millions on religion and art, and what do I get for it? Nothing. Not a compliment. These generosities are studiedly ignored, in print. In print I get nothing but slanders—and slanders again—and still slanders, and slanders on top of slanders! Grant them true, what of it? They are slanders all the same, when uttered against a king.

Miscreants—they are telling *everything!* Oh, everything: how I went pilgriming among the Powers in tears, with my mouth full of Bible and my pelt oozing piety at every pore, and implored them to place the vast and rich and populous Congo Free State in trust in my hands as their agent, so that I might root out slavery and stop the slave raids, and lift up those twenty-five millions of gentle and harmless blacks out of darkness into light, the light of our blessed Redeemer, the light that streams from his holy Word, the light that makes glorious our noble civilization—lift them up and dry their tears and fill their bruised hearts with joy and gratitude—lift them up and make them comprehend that they were no longer outcasts and forsaken, but our very brothers in Christ; how America and thirteen great European states wept in sympathy with me, and were persuaded; how their representatives met in convention in Berlin and made me Head Foreman and Superintendent of the Congo State, and drafted out my powers and limitations, carefully guarding the persons and liberties and properties of the natives against hurt and harm; forbidding whisky traffic and gun traffic; providing courts of justice; making commerce free and fetterless to the merchants and traders of all nations, and welcoming and safe-guarding all missionaries of all creeds and denominations. They have told how I planned and prepared my establishment and selected my horde of officials—"pals" and "pimps" of mine, "unspeakable Belgians" every one—and hoisted my flag, and "took in" a President of the United States, and got him to be the first to recognize it and salute it. Oh, well, let them blackguard me if they like; it is a deep satisfaction to me to remember that I was a shade too smart for that nation that thinks itself so smart. Yes, I certainly did bunco a Yankee—as those people phrase it. Pirate flag? Let them call it so—perhaps it is. All the same, *they were the first to salute it.*

These meddlesome American missionaries! these frank British consuls! these blabbing Belgian-born traitor officials!—those tiresome parrots are always talking, always telling. They have told how for twenty years I have ruled the Congo State not as a trustee of the Powers, an agent, a subordinate, a foreman, but as a sovereign—sovereign over a fruitful domain four times as large as the German Empire—sovereign absolute, irresponsible, above all law; trampling the Berlin-made Congo charter under foot; barring out all foreign traders but myself; restricting commerce to myself, through concessionaires who are my creatures and confederates; seizing and holding the State as my personal property, the whole of its vast revenues as my private "swag"—mine, solely mine—claiming and holding its millions of people as my private property, my serfs, my slaves; their labor mine, with or without wage; the food they raise not their property but mine; the rubber, the ivory, and all the other riches of the land mine—mine solely—and gathered for me by the men, the women, and the little children under compulsion of lash and bullet, fire, starvation, mutilation, and the halter.

These pests!—it is as I say, they have kept back nothing! They have revealed these and yet other details which shame should have kept them silent about, since they were exposures of a king, a sacred personage and immune from reproach, by right of his selection and appointment to his great office by God himself; a king whose acts cannot be criticized without blasphemy, since God has observed them from the beginning and has manifested no dissatisfaction with them, nor shown disapproval of them, nor hampered nor interrupted them in any way. By this sign I recognize his approval of what I have done; his cordial and glad approval, I am sure I may say. Blest, crowned, beatified with this great reward, this golden reward, this unspeakably precious reward, why should I care for men's cursings and revilings of me? [*With a sudden outburst of feeling*] May they roast a million æons in— [*Catches his breath and effusively kisses the crucifix; sorrowfully murmurs, "I shall get myself damned yet, with these indiscretions of speech."*]

Yes, they go on telling everything, these chatterers! They tell how I levy incredibly burdensome taxes upon the natives—taxes which are a pure theft; taxes which they must satisfy by gathering rubber under hard and constantly harder conditions, and by raising and furnishing food supplies gratis—and it all comes out that, when they fall short of their tasks through hunger, sickness, despair, and ceaseless and exhausting labor without rest, and forsake their homes and flee to the woods to escape punishment, my black soldiers, drawn from unfriendly tribes, and instigated and directed by my Belgians, hunt them down and butcher them and burn their villages—reserving some of the girls. They tell it all: how I am wiping a nation of friendless creatures out of existence by every form of murder, for my private pocket's sake. But they never say, although they know it, that I have labored in the cause of religion at the same time and all the time, and have sent missionaries there (of a "convenient stripe," as they phrase it), to teach them the error of their ways and bring them to Him who is all mercy and love, and who is the sleepless guardian and friend of all who suffer. They tell only what is against me, they will not tell what is in my favor.

They tell how England required of me a Commission of Inquiry into Congo atrocities, and how, to quiet that meddling country, with its disagreeable Congo Reform Association, made up of earls and bishops and John Morleys and university grandees and other dudes, more interested in other people's business than in their own, I appointed it. Did it stop their mouths? No, they merely pointed out that it was a commission composed wholly of my "Congo butchers," "the very men whose acts were to be inquired into." They said it was equivalent to appointing a commission of wolves to inquire into depredations committed upon a sheepfold. *Nothing* can satisfy a cursed Englishman!

And are the fault-finders frank with my private character? They could not be more so if I were a plebeian, a peasant, a mechanic. They remind the world that from the earliest days my house has been chapel and brothel combined, and both industries working full time; that I practised cruelties upon my queen and my daughters, and supplemented them with daily shame and humiliations; that, when my queen lay in the happy refuge of her coffin, and a daughter implored me on her knees to let her look for the last time upon her mother's face, I refused; and that, three years ago, not being satisfied with the stolen spoils of a whole alien nation, I robbed my own child of her property and appeared by proxy in court, a spectacle to the civilized world, to defend the act and complete the crime. It is as I have said: They are unfair, unjust; they will resurrect and give new currency to such things as those, or to any other things that count against me, but they will not mention any act of mine that is in my favor. I have spent more money on art than any other monarch of my time, and they know it. Do they speak of it, do they tell about it? No, they do not. They prefer to work up what they call "ghastly statistics" into offensive kindergarten object lessons, whose purpose is to make sentimental people shudder, and prejudice them against me. They remark that "if the innocent blood shed in the Congo State by King Leopold were put in buckets and the buckets placed side by side, the line would stretch two thousand miles; if the skeletons of his ten millions of starved and butchered dead could rise up and march in single file, it would take them seven months and four days to pass a given point; if compacted together in a body, they would occupy more ground than St. Louis covers, World's Fair and all; if they should all clap their bony hands at once, the grisly crash would be heard at a distance of—" Damnation, it makes me tired! And they do similar miracles with the money I have distilled from that blood and put into my pocket. They pile it into Egyptian pyramids; they carpet Saharas with it; they spread it across the sky, and the shadow it casts makes twilight in the earth. And the tears I have caused, the hearts I have broken—oh, nothing can persuade them to let *them* alone!

RAJA RAO
B. INDIA, 1909–2006

Novelist Raja Rao, a Brahman from south India educated in Muslim schools, took part in the Indian independence movement and spent several years in a Gandhian ashram. (Brahmans are Hindus of the highest social caste.) He also spent long periods of his life in Europe and America, studying in France for most of the 1930s and teaching at the University of Texas from 1965 to 1983. His novel *The Serpent and the Rope* (1960) is the story of a search for spiritual truth in Europe and India. *Kanthapura* (1938), the novel whose foreword is reprinted here, describes Gandhi's nonviolent resistance to the British Raj in the context of a small Indian village. Rao briefly addresses two of the central issues facing Indian and other postcolonial writers: the use of the language of the colonial masters and its adequacy to convey the language and culture of an Indian village.

ꢀ Foreword to *Kanthapura*

There is no village in India, however mean, that has not a rich *sthala-purana,* or legendary history, of its own. Some god or godlike hero has passed by the village — Rama[1] might have rested under this pipal-tree, Sita[2] might have dried her clothes, after her bath, on this yellow stone, or the Mahatma[3] himself, on one of his many pilgrimages through the country, might have slept in this hut, the low one, by the village gate. In this way the past mingles with the present, and the gods mingle with men to make the repertory of your grandmother always bright. One such story from the contemporary annals of a village I have tried to tell.

The telling has not been easy. One has to convey in a language that is not one's own the spirit that is one's own. One has to convey the various shades and omissions of a certain thought-movement that looks maltreated in an alien language. I use the word "alien," yet English is not really an alien language to us. It is the language of our intellectual make-up—like Sanskrit or Persian was before—but not of our emotional make-up. We are all instinctively bilingual, many of us writing in our own

---

[1] **Rama:** An incarnation of Vishnu, one of the three central Hindu gods.

[2] **Sita:** Or Shiva, one of the gods in the central triad of Hinduism along with Brahma and Vishnu.

[3] **the Mahatma:** Hindu title of respect for a man of spirituality and high-mindedness; *the* Mahatma is Mohandas Gandhi; the appellation was first bestowed on him by Rabindranath Tagore.

language and in English. We cannot write like the English. We should not. We cannot write only as Indians. We have grown to look at the large world as part of us. Our method of expression therefore has to be a dialect which will some day prove to be as distinctive and colorful as the Irish or the American. Time alone will justify it.

After language the next problem is that of style. The tempo of Indian life must be infused into our English expression, even as the tempo of American or Irish life has gone into the making of theirs. We, in India, think quickly, we talk quickly, and when we move we move quickly. There must be something in the sun of India that makes us rush and tumble and run on. And our paths are paths interminable. The *Mahabharata* has 214,778 verses and the *Ramayana* 48,000. The *Puranas* are endless and innumerable.[4] We have neither punctuation nor the treacherous "ats" and "ons" to bother us—we tell one interminable tale. Episode follows episode, and when our thoughts stop our breath stops, and we move on to another thought. This was and still is the ordinary style of our storytelling. I have tried to follow it myself in this story.

It may have been told of an evening, when as the dusk falls, and through the sudden quiet, lights leap up in house after house, and stretching her bedding on the veranda, a grandmother might have told you, newcomer, the sad tale of her village.

---

[4] *Mahabharata . . . innumerable: Mahabharata* and *Ramayana* are the two great ancient Indian epics (see Book 1). *Puranas* are ancient poetic texts written between the fourth century B.C.E. and 1000 C.E. on metaphysical, mythical, and historical subjects for a popular audience.

༄ Jawaharlal Nehru
b. India, 1889–1964

Jawaharlal Nehru was, with Mahatma Gandhi, his mentor, one of the leaders of the National Congress Party in India that fought a nonviolent campaign for independence from Britain during the first half of the twentieth century. If Gandhi was the movement's spiritual guru and guide, Nehru was its political leader. He was the natural choice in 1947 as the independent nation's first prime minister, a position he held until his death in 1964. As leader he advocated women's rights, secularism, and India's non-aligned status in world affairs; he promoted industrialization as well as agrarian and land reform. A charismatic orator, Nehru's speech on the eve of Independence Day, August 15, 1947, is one of the classic documents of modern India, its "Gettysburg Address."

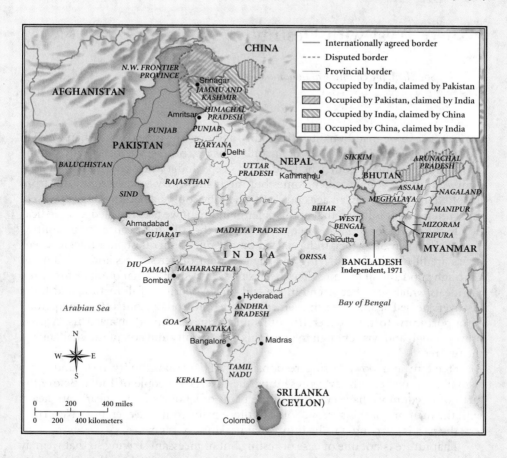

The Partition of India, 1947

Led by Mahatma Gandhi, the Indian independence movement realized its goal in 1947, winning independence from the United Kingdom. The mainly Muslim western provinces and Bengal became Pakistan, the rest remained India. Bengal was known as East Pakistan until a civil war in 1971 between West and East Pakistan resulted in the latter's independence and new name, Bangladesh. Ownership of the territory of Kashmir, which lies north of India and northeast of Pakistan, is still disputed.

∾ A Tryst with Destiny

Speech on the Granting of Indian Independence, August 14, 1947

I

Long years ago we made a tryst with destiny, and now the time comes when we shall redeem our pledge, not wholly or in full measure, but very substantially. At the stroke of the midnight hour, when the world sleeps, India will awake to life and freedom. A moment comes, which comes but rarely in history, when we step out from the old to the new, when an age ends, and when the soul of a nation, long supressed, finds utterance. It is fitting that at this solemn moment we take the pledge of dedication to the service of India and her people and to the still larger cause of humanity.

At the dawn of history India started on her unending quest, and trackless centuries are filled with her striving and the grandeur of her success and her failures. Through good and ill fortune alike she has never lost sight of that quest or forgotten the ideals which gave her strength. We end today a period of ill fortune and India discovers herself again. The achievement we celebrate today is but a step, an opening of opportunity, to the greater triumphs and achievements that await us. Are we brave enough and wise enough to grasp this opportunity and accept the challenge of the future?

Freedom and power bring responsibility. The responsibility rests upon this Assembly, a sovereign body representing the sovereign people of India. Before the birth of freedom we have endured all the pains of labour and our hearts are heavy with the memory of this sorrow. Some of those pains continue even now. Nevertheless, the past is over and it is the future that beckons to us now.

That future is not one of ease or resting but of incessant striving so that we may fulfil the pledges we have so often taken and the one we shall take today. The service of India means the service of the millions who suffer. It means the ending of poverty and ignorance and disease and inequality of opportunity. The ambition of the greatest man of our generation[1] has been to wipe every tear from every eye. That may be beyond us, but as long as there are tears and suffering, so long our work will not be over.

And so we have to labour and to work, and work hard, to give reality to our dreams. Those dreams are for India, but they are also for the world, for all the nations and peoples are too closely knit together today for any one of them to imagine that it can live apart. Peace has been said to be indivisible; so is freedom, so is prosperity now, and so also is disaster in this One World that can no longer be split into isolated fragments.

---

[1] **greatest man of our generation:** Mahatma K. Gandhi (1869–1948), the leader of the Indian independence movement.

To the people of India, whose representatives we are, we make an appeal to join us with faith and confidence in this great adventure. This is no time for petty and destructive criticism, no time for ill-will or blaming others. We have to build the noble mansion of free India where all her children may dwell.

II

The appointed day has come—the day appointed by destiny—and India stands forth again, after long slumber and struggle, awake, vital, free and independent. The past clings on to us still in some measure and we have to do much before we redeem the pledges we have so often taken. Yet the turning-point is past, and history begins anew for us, the history which we shall live and act and others will write about.

It is a fateful moment for us in India, for all Asia and for the world. A new star rises, the star of freedom in the East, a new hope comes into being, a vision long cherished materializes. May the star never set and that hope never be betrayed!

We rejoice in that freedom, even though clouds surround us, and many of our people are sorrowstricken and difficult problems encompass us. But freedom brings responsibilities and burdens and we have to face them in the spirit of a free and disciplined people.

On this day our first thoughts go to the architect of this freedom, the Father of our Nation,[2] who, embodying the old spirit of India, held aloft the torch of freedom and lighted up the darkness that surrounded us. We have often been unworthy followers of his and have strayed from his message, but not only we but succeeding generations will remember this message and bear the imprint in their hearts of this great son of India, magnificent in his faith and strength and courage and humility. We shall never allow that torch of freedom to be blown out, however high the wind or stormy the tempest.

Our next thoughts must be of the unknown volunteers and soldiers of freedom who, without praise or reward, have served India even unto death.

We think also of our brothers and sisters who have been cut off from us by political boundaries and who unhappily cannot share at present in the freedom that has come. They are of us and will remain of us whatever may happen, and we shall be sharers in their good [or] ill fortune alike.

The future beckons to us. Whither do we go and what shall be our endeavour? To bring freedom and opportunity to the common man, to the peasants and workers of India; to fight and end poverty and ignorance and disease; to build up a prosperous, democratic and progressive nation, and to create social, economic and political institutions which will ensure justice and fullness of life to every man and woman.

We have hard work ahead. There is no resting for any one of us till we redeem our pledge in full, till we make all the people of India what destiny intended them to be. We are citizens of a great country on the verge of bold advance, and we have to

---

[2] **Father of our Nation:** Gandhi.

live up to that high standard. All of us, to whatever religion we may belong, are equally the children of India with equal rights, privileges and obligations. We cannot encourage communalism or narrow-mindedness, for no nation can be great whose people are narrow in thought or in action.

To the nations and peoples of the world we send greetings and pledge ourselves to cooperate with them in furthering peace, freedom and democracy.

And to India, our much-loved motherland, the ancient, the eternal and the ever-new, we pay our reverent homage and we bind ourselves afresh to her service.

ANTON CHEKHOV
B. RUSSIA, 1860–1904

With highly refined writing skills, **Anton Chekhov** redefined both the drama and the short fiction of the nineteenth century and prepared both genres for the times ahead. In a letter to A. S. Suvorin, the editor of a Moscow newspaper, it is clear that Chekhov is charting a totally different course from the psychological treatments of Dostoevsky's novels or the epic landscapes of Tolstoy's *War and Peace,* a path down which generations of modern writers would follow the master. The correspondence contains a concise characterization of REALISM: "I think that it is not for writers to solve such questions as the existence of God, pessimism, etc. The writer's function is only to describe by whom, how, and under what conditions the questions of God and pessimism were discussed. The artist must be only an impartial witness of his characters and what they said, not their judge." In both his plays and his short stories, Chekhov wrote about ordinary people in ordinary situations, but the simplicity of his style is deceptive. In the small details, in the nuances of attitude and gesture, lie his genius for invoking, in all their beauty and sentiment, the profound ambiguities and complexities of human life. Chekhov was able to capture a uniquely "modern" consciousness: Self-knowledge is uncertain, and communication between individuals is always problematic and ambiguous. Missed communication is frequent in a rapidly changing society. Chekhov's writings reflect the uncertainty of ordinary life and the loss of faith in traditional beliefs at the end of the nineteenth century.

From Poverty to Short Stories.   Anton Pavlovich Chekhov was born at Taganrog on January 17, 1860. He attended a Greek preparatory school and later the Taganrog secondary school. His childhood was a time of poverty and beatings. Much later, in a letter to his close friend and publisher, Alexei Suvorin, Chekhov bitingly observed: "I acquired my belief in progress when still a child; I could not help believing in it, because the difference between the period when they flogged me and the period when they stopped flogging me was enormous." In 1879, three years after his father's grocery went bankrupt and the family relocated to Moscow to escape creditors, Anton enrolled in medical school and began to sell humorous, anecdotal, satiric stories to help support his family. During a visit to St. Petersburg in 1885, a year after receiving his medical degree, Chekhov discovered that he was famous. While still a student he had published almost 300 stories in the popular magazines of St. Petersburg and Moscow, and in 1886 *Motley Stories* was published, his first major collection. Chekhov was twenty-six years old. He described his writing technique: "I do not remember working more than a day on *any single* story of mine . . . I wrote my stories as reporters write their news about fires: mechanically, half-consciously, without worrying about either the reader or themselves." He would write 300 more short stories the following year.

AHN-tone CHEK-uf

www For more information about Chekhov and a quiz on *The Cherry Orchard,* see bedford stmartins.com/ worldlitcompact.

Chekhov Reading One of His Works

Chekhov is said to have written up to 300 stories in one year, often writing more than one a day. In this photograph he is reading to a group of attentive fans. (Art Resource)

The young author wrote and wrote and wrote, learning a style that would be a trademark in many of his stories.

Setting New Standards in Both Fiction and Drama.   In 1888, when Chekhov won the Pushkin Prize for the short story "The Steppe," his fiction attracted the attention of Dmitri Grigorovich, an important novelist of the 1840s. Grigorovich introduced Chekhov to Alexei Suvorin, who would publish many of Chekhov's most famous stories in his newspaper, *Novoe Vremya* (*New Times*). Suvorin even created a special literary supplement in the newspaper for Chekhov's work. Memorable short stories from that time are "Ward Number Six" and "A Lady with a Dog" and the novella, "The Duel." In 1887, Chekhov's first play, *Ivanov,* was produced in Moscow, launching his career. Thus Chekhov broke ground in two major literary forms and set standards of excellence for all writers who followed.

Nevertheless, Chekhov led the rather ordinary life of a Russian doctor of the late nineteenth century, with the exception of a strenuous trip he made in 1890 through Siberia to the penal colony on the island of Sakhalin. Chekhov made the trip on Tolstoy's suggestion and later described the inhumane conditions of the prisoners in *The Island of Sakhalin* (1894). In 1892 he purchased an estate fifty miles south of Moscow in the village of Melikhova, where he lived with his parents and spent his time writing, caring for patients, and contributing to local service projects. Chekhov

They are plays written on the simplest themes which in themselves are not interesting. But they are permeated by the eternal and he who feels this quality in them perceives that they are written for all eternity.

– CONSTANTINE STANISLAVSKY, *My Life in Art*

had contracted tuberculosis when he was twenty-three, and in 1897, when his health began to fail, he was forced to sell the Melikhova estate and move to a warmer climate. He spent the rest of his life in Yalta, where he wrote some of his best plays and cultivated strong friendships with Tolstoy and Maxim Gorky.[1]

Chekhov's Most Famous Plays.   Chekhov's best dramas were written in the 1890s and early 1900s for the Moscow Art Theatre, which was directed by Constantine Stanislavsky, one of the geniuses of modern theatre. In addition to *The Cherry Orchard* (1904), the plays of this period include *The Seagull* (1896), *Uncle Vanya* (1899), and *The Three Sisters* (1901). In 1901 Chekhov married an actress from the Moscow Art Theatre, Olga Leonardovna Knipper, and during the happy years of that union he wrote *The Cherry Orchard,* his masterpiece about the passing of the old order and the rise of the middle class. This play was produced on Chekhov's birthday, January 17, 1904. As it was also the twenty-fifth anniversary of his literary career, a grand celebration was planned for opening night. Nemirovich-Danchenko, the codirector of the theatre, paid the final tribute of the evening by saying to the playwright: "Our theatre is so much indebted to your talent, to your tender heart and pure soul, that you have every right to say 'This is my theatre.'" Chekhov died six months later, in Germany on July 2, 1904, at the Badenweiler spa in the Black Forest.

Themes and Artistry.   Although "The Beggar" and "The Bet" seem to bear the imprint of Tolstoy's nonviolent philosophy, Chekhov's stories and plays are rarely ideological in the sense that they can be neatly packaged by a moral or easily reduced to a philosophical statement. Chekhov's responses to the limited, often shallow perspectives of his characters do not reflect a particular political philosophy. Quick to deflate the arrogant and the pretentious, Chekhov was equally harsh with the crudities of life lived close to the soil.

It is often said that Chekhov's plays do not have a plot, and that this absence defines his approach to realism. Chekhov said that he wanted to show life as it is lived by ordinary people: "A play should be written in which people arrive, go away, have dinner, talk about the weather, and play cards. Life must be exactly as it is, and people as they are—not on stilts. . . . Let everything on the stage be just as complicated, and at the same time just as simple as it is in life."

Chekhov is a master stylist, able to evoke a whole scene or a character with just a few poignant details. He creates atmosphere and mood seemingly effortlessly, ranging over both urban and rural life. In a letter to his brother he talks about the use of suggestive detail to paint a scene: "You

> It seems to me that in the presence of Anton Pavlovich [Chekhov] everyone felt an unconscious desire to be simpler, more truthful, more himself, and I had many opportunities of observing how people threw off their attire of grand bookish phrases, fashionable expressions, and all the rest of the cheap trifles with which Russians in their anxiety to appear Europeans, adorn themselves. . . .
>
> – MAXIM GORKY

---

[1] Maxim Gorky (1868–1936): Russian novelist and playwright who was a political radical with deep sympathies for the lower classes. *The Lower Depths* is his best-known play outside of Russia. His nonfiction *Reminiscences* provides portraits of Tolstoy, Chekhov, and other contemporaries.

have to choose small details in describing nature, grouping them in such a way that if you close your eyes after reading it, you can picture the whole thing. For example, you'll get a picture of a moonlit night if you write that on the dam of the mill a piece of broken bottle flashed like a bright star and the black shadow of a dog or a wolf rolled by like a ball. . . ."

Chekhov's later work focuses on people's isolation, their inability to communicate with one another, and the oppressive boredom that grinds away at a person's vitality — the themes of his three masterpieces as well as of his first play, *Ivanov*. One of the later works, *Uncle Vanya* (1899), set in a country manor, is about disillusionment and fraud; nevertheless the devotion of Uncle Vanya and his niece, Sonia, brings some solace. *The Three Sisters* (1901), another play with very little action, explores the disappointments of love and the failure of three women to return to Moscow from the provinces. One of the sisters prophesies that "within another twenty-four or thirty years, everyone will work! Everyone!" an indictment of the leisure classes present in all of Chekhov's plays.

The Cherry Orchard. This play in three acts is subtitled a comedy and concerns the rather purposeless existence of an ineffectual upper-class family unable to save its estate from a debtor's auction. Chekhov's major contribution to theatre may have been showing how drama is as much embedded in the internal struggles of characters as it is in outward action. Through the disposition of a bankrupt estate in *The Cherry Orchard* he depicts people trapped in their personalities and circumstances, incapable of either decisive action or expression of their true feelings.

The restrained drama of Chekhov's plays seldom reaches the scale of tragedy but more often than not touches on sentiment and comedy. People make mistakes and suffer, but in the background is Chekhov's abiding faith in the quiet dignity of love and work, a life of simplicity and diligence. Maxim Gorky observed, "I have never known a man feel the importance of work as the foundation of all culture, so deeply, and for such varied reasons, as did Chekhov. . . . He loved to build, plant gardens, ornament the earth; he felt the poetry of labor. . . . Full of plans for the building of his house in Autka, he used to say: 'If every man did all he could on the piece of earth belonging to him, how beautiful would this world be!'"

■ **FURTHER RESEARCH**

Biography
Hingley, Ronald. *Chekhov: A Biographical and Critical Study.* 1966.
Simmons, Ernest J. *Chekhov: A Biography.* 1962. Probably the best biography.

Criticism
Gilman, Richard. *Chekhov's Plays: An Opening into Eternity.* 1995.
Hahn, Beverly. *Chekhov: A Study of Major Stories and Plays.* 1977.
Jackson, R. L. *Chekhov: A Collection of Critical Essays.* 1967. Contains various
    perspectives on Chekhov's life and work.

Matlaw, Ralph E., ed. *Anton Chekhov's Short Stories: Texts of the Stories, Backgrounds, Criticism.* 1975. This Norton Critical Edition provides excellent translations of the major short stories and helpful background information.

Rayfield, Donald. *Understanding Chekhov.* 1999.

Wellek, Rene, and N. D. Wellek. *Chekhov: New Perspectives.* 1984. A collection of contemporary criticism.

■ **PRONUNCIATION**

Yermolay Alexeyevich Lopakhin: yeer-moh-LIGH ah-lik-SYAY-yeh-vich lah-PAH-shin
Lyubov Andreyevna: lyoo-BOHF ahn-DRAY-yev-nah
Anton Chekhov: AHN-tone CHEK-uf
Simon Panteleyevich: see-MYONE pahn-tyeh-LYAY-eh-vich
Simeonov-Pishchik: YOH-nawf PEESH-chif
Peter (Pyotr) Sergeyevich Trofimov: PYOH-tur sir-GYAY-yeh-vich trah-FEE-muf

ॐ The Cherry Orchard

Translated by David Magarshack

CHARACTERS

LYUBOV (LYUBA) ANDREYEVNA RANEVSKY, *a landowner*
ANYA, *her daughter, aged seventeen*
VARYA, *her adopted daughter, aged twenty-four*
LEONID ANDREYEVICH GAYEV, *Mrs. Ranevsky's brother*
YERMOLAY ALEXEYEVICH LOPAKHIN, *a businessman*
PETER (PYOTR) SERGEYEVICH TROFIMOV, *a student*

BORIS BORISOVICH SIMEONOV-PISHCHIK, *a landowner*
CHARLOTTE IVANOVNA, *a governess*
SIMON PANTELEYEVICH YEPIKHODOV, *a clerk*
DUNYASHA, *a maid*
FIRS, *a manservant, aged eighty-seven*
YASHA, *a young manservant*
A HIKER
A STATIONMASTER
A POST OFFICE CLERK
GUESTS *and* SERVANTS

The action takes place on MRS. RANEVSKY's *estate.*

ACT ONE

A room which is still known as the nursery. One of the doors leads to Anya's room. Daybreak; the sun will be rising soon. It is May. The cherry trees are in blossom, but it is cold in the orchard. Morning frost. The windows of the room are shut.

Enter Dunyasha, carrying a candle, and Lopakhin with a book in his hand.

LOPAKHIN: The train's arrived, thank goodness. What's the time?

DUNYASHA: Nearly two o'clock, sir. [*Blows out the candle.*] It's light already.

LOPAKHIN: How late was the train? Two hours at least. [*Yawns and stretches.*] What a damn fool I am! Came here specially to meet them at the station and fell asleep.... Sat down in a chair and dropped off. What a nuisance! Why didn't you wake me?

DUNYASHA: I thought you'd gone, sir. [*Listens.*] I think they're coming.

LOPAKHIN [*listening*]: No. . . . I should have been there to help them with the luggage and so on. [*Pause.*] Mrs. Ranevsky's been abroad for five years. I wonder what she's like now. . . . She's such a nice person. Simple, easy-going. I remember when I was a lad of fifteen, my late father—he used to keep a shop in the village—punched me in the face and made my nose bleed. We'd gone into the yard to fetch something, and he was drunk. Mrs. Ranevsky—I remember it as if it happened yesterday, she was such a young girl then and so slim—took me to the washstand in this very room, the nursery. "Don't cry, little peasant," she said, "it won't matter by the time you're wed." [*Pause.*] Little peasant . . . It's quite true my father was a peasant, but here I am wearing a white waistcoat and brown shoes. A dirty peasant in a fashionable shop. . . . Except, of course, that I'm a rich man now, rolling in money. But, come to think of it, I'm a plain peasant still. . . . [*Turns the pages of his book.*] Been reading this book and haven't understood a word. Fell asleep reading it.

Pause.

DUNYASHA: The dogs have been awake all night; they know their masters are coming.

LOPAKHIN: What's the matter, Dunyasha? Why are you in such a state?

DUNYASHA: My hands are shaking. I think I'm going to faint.

LOPAKHIN: A little too refined, aren't you, Dunyasha? Quite the young lady. Dress, hair. It won't do, you know. Remember your place!

Enter Yepikhodov with a bunch of flowers; he wears a jacket and brightly polished high-boots which squeak loudly; on coming in, he drops the flowers.

YEPIKHODOV [*picking up the flowers*]: The gardener sent these. Said to put them in the dining room. [*Hands the flowers to* DUNYASHA.]

LOPAKHIN: Bring me some kvass[1] while you're about it.

DUNYASHA: Yes, sir. [*Goes out.*]

YEPIKHODOV: Thirty degrees, morning frost, and the cherry trees in full bloom. Can't say I think much of our climate, sir. [*Sighs.*] Our climate isn't particularly accommodating, is it, sir? Not when you want it to be, anyway. And another thing. The other day I bought myself this pair of boots, and believe me, sir, they squeak so terribly that it's more than a man can endure. Do you happen to know of something I could grease them with?

LOPAKHIN: Go away. You make me tired.

YEPIKHODOV: Every day, sir, I'm overtaken by some calamity. Not that I mind. I'm used to it. I just smile. [DUNYASHA *comes in and hands* LOPAKHIN *the kvass.*] I'll be off. [*Bumps into a chair and knocks it over.*] There you are, sir. [*Triumphantly.*] You see, sir, pardon the expression, this sort of circumstance . . . I mean to say . . . Remarkable! Quite remarkable! [*Goes out.*]

DUNYASHA: I simply must tell you, sir: Yepikhodov has proposed to me.

LOPAKHIN: Oh?

---

[1] **kvass**: Russian beer.

DUNYASHA: I really don't know what to do, sir. He's ever such a quiet fellow, except that sometimes he starts talking and you can't understand a word he says. It sounds all right and it's ever so moving, only you can't make head or tail of it. I like him a little, I think. I'm not sure though. He's madly in love with me. He's such an unlucky fellow, sir. Every day something happens to him. Everyone teases him about it. They've nicknamed him Twenty-two Calamities.

LOPAKHIN [*listens*]: I think I can hear them coming.

DUNYASHA: They're coming! Goodness, I don't know what's the matter with me. I've gone cold all over.

LOPAKHIN: Yes, they are coming all right. Let's go and meet them. Will she recognize me? We haven't seen each other for five years.

DUNYASHA [*agitated*]: I'm going to faint. Oh dear, I'm going to faint!

Two carriages can be heard driving up to the house. Lopakhin and Dunyasha go out quickly. The stage is empty. People can be heard making a noise in the adjoining rooms. Firs, who has been to meet Mrs. Ranevsky at the station, walks across the stage hurriedly, leaning on a stick. He wears an old-fashioned livery coat and a top hat; he keeps muttering to himself, but it is impossible to make out a single word. The noise offstage becomes louder. A voice is heard: "Let's go through here." Mrs. Ranevsky, Anya, and Charlotte, with a lap dog on a little chain, all wearing traveling clothes, Varya, wearing an overcoat and a head scarf, Gayev, Simeonov-Pishchik, Lopakhin, Dunyasha, carrying a bundle and an umbrella, and other servants with luggage walk across the stage.

ANYA: Let's go through here. Remember this room, Mother?

MRS. RANEVSKY [*joyfully, through tears*]: The nursery!

VARYA: It's so cold. My hands are quite numb. [*To* MRS. RANEVSKY] Your rooms, the white one and the mauve one, are just as you left them, Mother dear.

MRS. RANEVSKY: The nursery! My dear, my beautiful room! I used to sleep here when I was a little girl. [*Cries.*] I feel like a little girl again now. [*Kisses her brother and* VARYA, *and then her brother again.*] Varya is the same as ever. Looks like a nun. And I also recognized Dunyasha. [*Kisses* DUNYASHA.]

GAYEV: The train was two hours late. How do you like that? What a way to run a railway!

CHARLOTTE [*To* PISHCHIK]: My dog also eats nuts.

PISHCHIK [*surprised*]: Good Lord!

All, except Anya and Dunyasha, go out.

DUNYASHA: We thought you'd never come. [*Helps* ANYA *off with her coat and hat.*]

ANYA: I haven't slept for four nights on our journey. Now I'm chilled right through.

DUNYASHA: You left before Easter. It was snowing and freezing then. It's different now, isn't it? Darling Anya! [*Laughs and kisses her.*] I've missed you so much, my darling, my precious! Oh, I must tell you at once! I can't keep it to myself a minute longer. . . .

ANYA [*apathetically*]: What is it this time?

DUNYASHA: Our clerk, Yepikhodov, proposed to me after Easter.

ANYA: Always the same. [*Tidying her hair.*] I've lost all my hairpins. [*She is so tired, she can hardly stand.*]

DUNYASHA: I don't know what to think. He loves me so much, so much!

ANYA [*tenderly, looking through the door into her room*]: My own room, my own windows, just as if I'd never been away! I'm home again! As soon as I get up in the morning, I'll run out into the orchard. . . . Oh, if only I could sleep. I didn't sleep all the way back, I was so worried.

DUNYASHA: Mr. Trofimov arrived the day before yesterday.

ANYA [*joyfully*]: Peter!

DUNYASHA: He's asleep in the bathhouse. He's been living there. Afraid of being a nuisance, he says. [*Glancing at her watch.*] I really ought to wake him, except that Miss Varya told me not to. "Don't you dare wake him!" she said.

Varya comes in with a bunch of keys at her waist.

VARYA: Dunyasha, coffee quick! Mother's asking for some.

DUNYASHA: I won't be a minute! [*Goes out.*]

VARYA: Well, thank goodness you're all back. You're home again, my darling. [*Caressing her.*] My darling is home again! My sweet child is home again.

ANYA: I've had such an awful time!

VARYA: I can imagine it.

ANYA: I left before Easter. It was terribly cold then. All the way Charlotte kept talking and doing her conjuring tricks. Why did you force Charlotte on me?

VARYA: But you couldn't have gone alone, darling, could you? You're only seventeen!

ANYA: In Paris it was also cold and snowing. My French is awful. I found Mother living on the fourth floor. When I got there, she had some French visitors, a few ladies and an old Catholic priest with a book. The place was full of tobacco smoke and terribly uncomfortable. Suddenly I felt sorry for Mother, so sorry that I took her head in my arms, held it tightly, and couldn't let go. Afterwards Mother was very sweet to me. She was crying all the time.

VARYA [*through tears*]: Don't go on, Anya. Please don't.

ANYA: She'd already sold her villa near Mentone. She had nothing left. Nothing! I hadn't any money, either. There was hardly enough for the journey. Mother just won't understand! We had dinner at the station and she would order the most expensive things and tip the waiters a ruble each. Charlotte was just the same. Yasha, too, demanded to be given the same kind of food. It was simply awful! You see, Yasha is Mother's manservant. We've brought him back with us.

VARYA: Yes, I've seen the scoundrel.

ANYA: Well, what's been happening? Have you paid the interest on the mortgage?

VARYA: Heavens, no!

ANYA: Dear, oh dear . . .

VARYA: The estate will be up for sale in August.

ANYA: Oh dear!

LOPAKHIN [*puts his head through the door and bleats*]: Bah-h-h! [*Goes out.*]

VARYA [*through tears*]: Oh, I'd like to hit him! [*Shakes her fist.*]

ANYA [*gently embracing* VARYA]: Varya, has he proposed to you? [VARYA *shakes her head.*] But he loves you. Why don't you two come to an understanding? What are you waiting for?

VARYA: I don't think anything will come of it. He's so busy. He can't be bothered with me. Why, he doesn't even notice me. I wish I'd never known him. I can't stand the sight of him. Everyone's talking about our wedding, everyone's congratulating me, while there's really nothing in it. It's all so unreal. Like a dream. [*In a different tone of voice.*] You've got a new brooch. Like a bee, isn't it?

ANYA [*sadly*]: Yes, Mother bought it. [*Goes to her room, talking quite happily, like a child.*] You know, I went up in a balloon in Paris!

VARYA: My darling's home again! My dearest one's home again! [DUNYASHA *has come back with a coffeepot and is making coffee;* VARYA *is standing at the door of* ANYA's *room.*] All day long, darling, I'm busy about the house, and all the time I'm dreaming, dreaming. If only we could find a rich husband for you! My mind would be at rest then. I'd go into a convent and later on a pilgrimage to Kiev . . . to Moscow. Just keep going from one holy place to another. On and on. . . . Wonderful!

ANYA: The birds are singing in the orchard. What's the time?

VARYA: It's past two. It's time you were asleep, darling. [*Goes into* ANYA's *room.*] Wonderful!

Enter Yasha with a traveling rug and a small bag.

YASHA [*crossing the stage, in an affected genteel voice*]: May I be permitted to go through here?

DUNYASHA: I can hardly recognize you, Yasha. You've changed so much abroad.

YASHA: Hmmm . . . And who are you, may I ask?

DUNYASHA: When you left, I was no bigger than this. [*Shows her height from the floor with her hand.*] I'm Dunyasha, Fyodor Kozoedov's daughter. Don't you remember me?

YASHA: Mmmm . . . Juicy little cucumber! [*Looks round, then puts his arms around her; she utters a little scream and drops a saucer.* YASHA *goes out hurriedly.*]

VARYA [*in the doorway, crossly*]: What's going on there?

DUNYASHA [*in tears*]: I've broken a saucer.

VARYA: That's lucky.

ANYA [*coming out of her room*]: Mother must be told Peter's here.

VARYA: I gave orders not to wake him.

ANYA [*pensively*]: Father died six years ago. A month after that our brother, Grisha, was drowned in the river. Such a pretty little boy. He was only seven. Mother took it badly. She went away, went away never to come back. [*Shudders.*] Peter Trofimov was Grisha's tutor. He might remind her . . .

Firs comes in, wearing a jacket and a white waistcoat.

FIRS [*walks up to the coffeepot anxiously*]: Madam will have her coffee here. [*Puts on white gloves.*] Is the coffee ready? [*Sternly, to* DUNYASHA.] You there! Where's the cream?

DUNYASHA: Oh dear! [*Goes out quickly.*]

FIRS [*fussing round the coffeepot*]: The nincompoop! [*Muttering to himself.*] She's come from Paris. . . . Master used to go to Paris. . . . Aye, by coach. . . . [*Laughs.*]

VARYA: What are you talking about, Firs?

FIRS: Sorry, what did you say? [*Joyfully.*] Madam is home again! Home at last! I can die happy now. [*Weeps with joy.*]

Enter Mrs. Ranevsky, Gayev, and Simeonov-Pishchik, the last one wearing a Russian long-waisted coat of expensive cloth and wide trousers. As he enters, Gayev moves his arms and body as if he were playing billiards.

MRS. RANEVSKY: How does it go now? Let me think. Pot the red in the corner. Double into the middle pocket.

GAYEV: And straight into the corner! A long time ago, Lyuba, you and I slept in this room. Now I'm fifty-one. . . . Funny, isn't it!

LOPAKHIN: Aye, time flies.

GAYEV: I beg your pardon?

LOPAKHIN: "Time flies," I said.

GAYEV: The place reeks of patchouli.²

ANYA: I'm off to bed. Good night, Mother. [*Kisses her mother.*]

MRS. RANEVSKY: My sweet little darling! [*Kisses her hands.*] You're glad to be home, aren't you? I still can't believe it.

ANYA: Good night, Uncle.

GAYEV [*kissing her face and hands*]: God bless you. You're so like your mother! [*To his sister*] You were just like her at that age, Lyuba.

Anya shakes hands with Lopakhin and Pishchik. Goes out and shuts the door behind her.

MRS. RANEVSKY: She's terribly tired.

PISHCHIK: It was a long journey.

VARYA [*to* LOPAKHIN *and* PISHCHIK]: Well, gentlemen, it's past two o'clock. You mustn't outstay your welcome, must you?

MRS. RANEVSKY [*laughs*]: You're just the same, Varya. [*Draws* VARYA *to her and kisses her.*] Let me have my coffee first and then we'll all go. [FIRS *puts a little cushion under her feet.*] Thank you, Firs dear. I've got used to having coffee. I drink it day and night. Thank you, Firs, thank you, my dear old man. [*Kisses* FIRS.]

VARYA: I'd better make sure they've brought all the things in. [*Goes out.*]

MRS. RANEVSKY: Is it really me sitting here? [*Laughs.*] I feel like jumping about, waving my arms. [*Covers her face with her hands.*] And what if it's all a dream? God knows, I love my country. I love it dearly. I couldn't look out of the train for crying. [*Through tears.*] But, I suppose I'd better have my coffee. Thank you, Firs, thank you, dear old man. I'm so glad you're still alive.

FIRS: The day before yesterday . . .

GAYEV: He's a little deaf.

LOPAKHIN: At five o'clock I've got to leave for Kharkov. What a nuisance! I wish I could have had a good look at you, a good talk with you. You're still as magnificent as ever. . . .

PISHCHIK [*breathing heavily*]: Lovelier, I'd say. Dressed in the latest Paris fashion. If only I were twenty years younger—ho-ho-ho!

---

² **patchouli:** East Indian perfume.

LOPAKHIN: This brother of yours says that I'm an ignorant oaf, a tightfisted peasant, but I don't mind. Let him talk. All I want is that you should believe in me as you used to, that you should look at me as you used to with those wonderful eyes of yours. Merciful heavens! My father was a serf of your father and your grandfather, but you, you alone, did so much for me in the past that I forgot everything, and I love you just as if you were my own flesh and blood, more than my own flesh and blood.

MRS. RANEVSKY: I can't sit still, I can't. . . . [*Jumps up and walks about the room in great agitation.*] This happiness is more than I can bear. Laugh at me if you like. I'm making such a fool of myself. Oh, my darling little bookcase . . . [*Kisses the bookcase.*] My sweet little table . . .

GAYEV: You know, of course, that Nanny died here while you were away.

MRS. RANEVSKY [*sits down and drinks her coffee*]: Yes, God rest her soul. They wrote to tell me about it.

GAYEV: Anastasy, too, is dead. Boss-eyed Peter left me for another job. He's with the Police Superintendent in town now. [*Takes a box of fruit drops out of his pocket and sucks one.*]

PISHCHIK: My daughter Dashenka — er — wishes to be remembered to you.

LOPAKHIN: I'd like to say something very nice and cheerful to you. [*Glances at his watch.*] I shall have to be going in a moment and there isn't much time to talk. As you know, your cherry orchard's being sold to pay your debts. The auction is on the twenty-second of August. But there's no need to worry, my dear. You can sleep soundly. There's a way out. Here's my plan. Listen carefully, please. Your estate is only about twelve miles from town, and the railway is not very far away. Now, all you have to do is break up your cherry orchard and the land along the river into building plots and lease them out for country cottages. You'll then have an income of at least twenty-five thousand a year.

GAYEV: I'm sorry, but what utter nonsense!

MRS. RANEVSKY: I don't quite follow you, Lopakhin.

LOPAKHIN: You'll be able to charge your tenants at least twenty-five rubles a year for a plot of about three acres. I bet you anything that if you advertise now, there won't be a single plot left by the autumn. They will all be snapped up. In fact, I congratulate you. You are saved. The site is magnificent and the river is deep enough for bathing. Of course, the place will have to be cleared, tidied up. . . . I mean, all the old buildings will have to be pulled down, including, I'm sorry to say, this house, but it isn't any use to anybody any more, is it? The old cherry orchard will have to be cut down.

MRS. RANEVSKY: Cut down? My dear man, I'm very sorry but I don't think you know what you're talking about. If there's anything of interest, anything quite remarkable, in fact, in the whole county, it's our cherry orchard.

LOPAKHIN: The only remarkable thing about this orchard is that it's very large. It only produces a crop every other year, and even then you don't know what to do with the cherries. Nobody wants to buy them.

GAYEV: Why, you'll find our orchard mentioned in the encyclopedia.

LOPAKHIN [*glancing at his watch*]: If we can't think of anything and if we can't come to any decision, it won't be only your cherry orchard but your whole estate that will be sold at auction on the twenty-second of August. Make up your mind. I tell you, there is no other way. Take my word for it. There isn't.

FIRS: In the old days, forty or fifty years ago, the cherries used to be dried, preserved, made into jam, and sometimes———

GAYEV: Do shut up, Firs.

FIRS: ———and sometimes cartloads of dried cherries were sent to Moscow and Kharkov. Fetched a lot of money, they did. Soft and juicy, those cherries were. Sweet and such a lovely smell . . . They knew the recipe then. . . .

MRS. RANEVSKY: And where's the recipe now?

FIRS: Forgotten. No one remembers it.

PISHCHIK [*to* MRS. RANEVSKY]: What was it like in Paris? Eh? Eat any frogs?

MRS. RANEVSKY: I ate crocodiles.

PISHCHIK: Good Lord!

LOPAKHIN: Till recently there were only the gentry and the peasants in the country. Now we have holiday-makers. All our towns, even the smallest, are surrounded by country cottages. I shouldn't be surprised if in twenty years the holiday-maker multiplies enormously. All your holiday-maker does now is drink tea on the veranda, but it's quite in the cards that if he becomes the owner of three acres of land, he'll do a bit of farming on the side, and then your cherry orchard will become a happy, prosperous, thriving place.

GAYEV [*indignantly*]: What nonsense!

Enter Varya and Yasha.

VARYA: I've got two telegrams in here for you, Mother dear. [*Picks out a key and unlocks the old-fashioned bookcase with a jingling noise.*] Here they are.

MRS. RANEVSKY: They're from Paris. [*Tears the telegrams up without reading them.*] I've finished with Paris.

GAYEV: Do you know how old this bookcase is, Lyuba? Last week I pulled out the bottom drawer and saw some figures burned into it. This bookcase was made exactly a hundred years ago. What do you think of that? Eh? We ought really to celebrate its centenary. An inanimate object, but say what you like, it's a bookcase after all.

PISHCHIK [*amazed*]: A hundred years! Good Lord!

GAYEV: Yes, indeed. It's quite something. [*Feeling round the bookcase with his hands.*] Dear, highly esteemed bookcase, I salute you. For over a hundred years you have devoted yourself to the glorious ideals of goodness and justice. Throughout the hundred years your silent appeal to fruitful work has never faltered. It sustained [*through tears*] in several generations of our family, their courage and faith in a better future and fostered in us the ideals of goodness and social consciousness.

Pause.

LOPAKHIN: Aye. . . .

MRS. RANEVSKY: You haven't changed a bit, have you, darling Leonid?

GAYEV [*slightly embarrassed*]: Off the right into a corner! Pot into the middle pocket!

LOPAKHIN [*glancing at his watch*]: Well, afraid it's time I was off.

YASHA [*handing* MRS. RANEVSKY *her medicine*]: Your pills, ma'am.

PISHCHIK: Never take any medicines, dear lady. I don't suppose they'll do you much harm, but they won't do you any good either. Here, let me have 'em, my dear lady. [*Takes the box of pills from her, pours the pills into the palm of his hand, blows on them, puts them all into his mouth, and washes them down with kvass.*] There!

MRS. RANEVSKY [*alarmed*]: You're mad!

PISHCHIK: Swallowed the lot.

LOPAKHIN: The glutton!

All laugh.

FIRS: He was here at Easter, the gentleman was. Ate half a bucketful of pickled cucumbers, he did. . . . [*Mutters.*]

MRS. RANEVSKY: What is he saying?

VARYA: He's been muttering like that for the last three years. We've got used to it.

YASHA: Old age!

Charlotte, in a white dress, very thin and tightly laced, a lorgnette dangling from her belt, crosses the stage.

LOPAKHIN: I'm sorry, Miss Charlotte, I haven't had the chance of saying how-do-you-do to you. [*Tries to kiss her hand.*]

CHARLOTTE [*snatching her hand away*]: If I let you kiss my hand, you'll want to kiss my elbow, then my shoulder . . .

LOPAKHIN: It's not my lucky day. [*They all laugh.*] My dear Charlotte, show us a trick, please.

MRS. RANEVSKY: Yes, do show us a trick, Charlotte.

CHARLOTTE: I won't. I'm off to bed. [*Goes out.*]

LOPAKHIN: We'll meet again in three weeks. [*Kisses* MRS. RANEVSKY'*s hand.*] Good-bye for now. I must go. [*To* GAYEV.] So long. [*Embraces* PISHCHIK.] So long. [*Shakes hands with* VARYA *and then with* FIRS *and* YASHA.] I wish I didn't have to go. [*To* MRS. RANEVSKY.] Let me know if you make up your mind about the country cottages. If you decide to go ahead, I'll get you a loan of fifty thousand or more. Think it over seriously.

VARYA [*angrily*]: For goodness' sake, go!

LOPAKHIN: I'm going, I'm going. . . . [*Goes out.*]

GAYEV: The oaf! However, I'm sorry. Varya's going to marry him, isn't she? He's Varya's intended.

VARYA: Don't say things you'll be sorry for, Uncle.

MRS. RANEVSKY: But why not, Varya? I should be only too glad. He's a good man.

PISHCHIK: A most admirable fellow, to tell the truth. My Dashenka — er — also says that — er — says all sorts of things. [*Drops off and snores, but wakes up immediately.*] By the way, my dear lady, you will lend me two hundred and forty rubles, won't you? Must pay the interest on the mortgage tomorrow.

VARYA [*terrified*]: We have no money; we haven't!

MRS. RANEVSKY: We really haven't any, you know.

PISHCHIK: Have a good look around — you're sure to find it. [*Laughs.*] I never lose hope. Sometimes I think it's all over with me, I'm done for, then — hey presto — they build a railway over my land and pay me for it. Something's bound to turn up, if not today, then tomorrow. I'm certain of it. Dashenka might win two hundred thousand. She's got a ticket in the lottery, you know.

MRS. RANEVSKY: Well, I've finished my coffee. Now to bed.

FIRS [*brushing* GAYEV's *clothes admonishingly*]: Put the wrong trousers on again, sir. What am I to do with you?

VARYA [*in a low voice*]: Anya's asleep. [*Opens a window quietly.*] The sun has risen. It's no longer cold. Look, Mother dear. What lovely trees! Heavens, what wonderful air! The starlings are singing.

GAYEV [*opens another window*]: The orchard's all white. Lyuba, you haven't forgotten, have you? The long avenue there—it runs on and on, straight as an arrow. It gleams on moonlit nights. Remember? You haven't forgotten, have you?

MRS. RANEVSKY [*looking through the window at the orchard*]: Oh, my childhood, oh, my innocence! I slept in this nursery. I used to look out at the orchard from here. Every morning happiness used to wake with me. The orchard was just the same in those days. Nothing has changed. [*Laughs happily.*] White, all white! Oh, my orchard! After the dark, rainy autumn and the cold winter, you're young again, full of happiness; the heavenly angels haven't forsaken you. If only this heavy load could be lifted from my heart; if only I could forget my past!

GAYEV: Well, and now they're going to sell the orchard to pay our debts. Funny, isn't it?

MRS. RANEVSKY: Look! Mother's walking in the orchard in . . . a white dress! [*Laughs happily.*] It *is* Mother!

GAYEV: Where?

VARYA: Really, Mother dear, what are you saying?

MRS. RANEVSKY: There's no one there. I just imagined it. Over there, on the right, near the turning to the summer house, a little white tree's leaning over. It looks like a woman. [*Enter* TROFIMOV. *He is dressed in a shabby student's uniform and wears glasses.*] What an amazing orchard! Masses of white blossom. A blue sky . . .

TROFIMOV: I say, Mrs. Ranevsky . . . [*She looks round at him.*] I've just come to say hello. I'll go at once. [*Kisses her hand warmly.*] I was told to wait till morning, but I—I couldn't, I couldn't.

Mrs. Ranevsky gazes at him in bewilderment.

VARYA [*through tears*]: This is Peter Trofimov.

TROFIMOV: Peter Trofimov. Your son Grisha's old tutor. I haven't changed so much, have I?

Mrs. Ranevsky embraces him and weeps quietly.

GAYEV [*embarrassed*]: There, there, Lyuba.

VARYA [*cries*]: I did tell you to wait till tomorrow, didn't I, Peter?

MRS. RANEVSKY: Grisha, my . . . little boy. Grisha . . . my son.

VARYA: It can't be helped, Mother. It was God's will.

TROFIMOV [*gently, through tears*]: Now, now . . .

MRS. RANEVSKY [*weeping quietly*]: My little boy died, drowned. Why? Why, my friend? [*More quietly.*] Anya's asleep in there and here I am shouting, making a noise. . . . Well, Peter? You're not as good-looking as you were, are you? Why not? Why have you aged so much?

TROFIMOV: A peasant woman in a railway carriage called me "a moth-eaten gentleman."

MRS. RANEVSKY: You were only a boy then. A charming young student. Now you're growing thin on top, you wear glasses. . . . You're not still a student, are you? [*Walks toward the door.*]

TROFIMOV: I expect I shall be an eternal student.

MRS. RANEVSKY [*kisses her brother and then* VARYA]: Well, go to bed now. You, Leonid, have aged too.

PISHCHIK [*following her*]: So, we're off to bed now, are we? Oh dear, my gout! I think I'd better stay the night here. Now, what about letting me have the—er—two hundred and forty rubles tomorrow morning, dear lady? Early tomorrow morning. . . .

GAYEV: He does keep on, doesn't he?

PISHCHIK: Two hundred and forty rubles—to pay the interest on the mortgage.

MRS. RANEVSKY: But I haven't any money, my dear man.

PISHCHIK: I'll pay you back, dear lady. Such a trifling sum.

MRS. RANEVSKY: Oh, all right. Leonid will let you have it. Let him have it, Leonid.

GAYEV: Let him have it? The hell I will.

MRS. RANEVSKY: What else can we do? Let him have it, please. He needs it. He'll pay it back.

Mrs. Ranevsky, Trofimov, Pishchik, and Firs go out. Gayev, Varya, and Yasha remain.

GAYEV: My sister hasn't got out of the habit of throwing money about. [*To* YASHA.] Out of my way, fellow. You reek of the hen house.

YASHA [*grins*]: And you, sir, are the same as ever.

GAYEV: I beg your pardon? [*To* VARYA.] What did he say?

VARYA [*to* YASHA]: Your mother's come from the village. She's been sitting in the servants' quarters since yesterday. She wants to see you.

YASHA: Oh, bother her!

VARYA: You shameless bounder!

YASHA: I don't care. She could have come tomorrow, couldn't she? [*Goes out.*]

VARYA: Dear Mother is just the same as ever. Hasn't changed a bit. If you let her, she'd give away everything.

GAYEV: I suppose so. [*Pause.*] When a lot of remedies are suggested for an illness, it means that the illness is incurable. I've been thinking, racking my brains; I've got all sorts of remedies, lots of them, which, of course, means that I haven't got one. It would be marvelous if somebody left us some money. It would be marvelous if we found a very rich husband for Anya. It would be marvelous if one of us went to Yaroslavl to try our luck with our great-aunt, the Countess. She's very rich, you know. Very rich.

VARYA [*crying*]: If only God would help us.

GAYEV: Don't howl! Our aunt is very rich, but she doesn't like us. First, because my sister married a lawyer and not a nobleman. . . . [ANYA *appears in the doorway.*]

She did not marry a nobleman, and she has not been leading an exactly blameless life, has she? She's a good, kind, nice person. I love her very much. But, however much you try to make allowances for her, you have to admit that she is an immoral woman. You can sense it in every movement she makes.

VARYA [*in a whisper*]: Anya's standing in the doorway.

GAYEV: I beg your pardon? [*Pause.*] Funny thing, there's something in my right eye. Can't see properly. On Thursday, too, in the district court . . .

Anya comes in.

VARYA: Why aren't you asleep, Anya?

ANYA: I can't sleep, I can't.

GAYEV: My little darling! [*Kisses* ANYA's *face and hands.*] My dear child! [*Through tears.*] You're not my niece, you're my angel. You're everything to me. Believe me. Do believe me.

ANYA: I believe you, Uncle. Everyone loves you, everyone respects you, but, dear Uncle, you shouldn't talk so much. What were you saying just now about Mother, about your own sister? What did you say it for?

GAYEV: Well, yes, yes. [*He takes her hand and covers his face with it.*] You're quite right. It was dreadful. Dear God, dear God, help me! That speech I made to the bookcase today—it was so silly. The moment I finished it, I realized how silly it was.

VARYA: It's quite true, Uncle dear. You oughtn't to talk so much. Just don't talk, that's all.

ANYA: If you stopped talking, you'd feel much happier yourself.

GAYEV: Not another word. [*Kisses* ANYA's *and* VARYA's *hands.*] Not another word. Now to business. Last Thursday I was at the county court, and, well—er—I met a lot of people there, and we started talking about this and that, and—er—it would seem that we might manage to raise some money on a promissory note and pay the interest to the bank.

VARYA: Oh, if only God would help us!

GAYEV: I shall be there again on Tuesday, and I'll have another talk. [*To* VARYA.] For goodness' sake, don't howl! [*To* ANYA.] Your mother will have a talk with Lopakhin. I'm sure he won't refuse her. After you've had your rest, you'll go to Yaroslavl to see your great-aunt, the Countess. That's how we shall tackle the problem from three different sides, and I'm sure we'll get it settled. The interest we shall pay. Of that I'm quite sure. [*Puts a fruit drop in his mouth.*] I give you my word of honor, I swear by anything you like, the estate will not be sold! [*Excitedly.*] Why, I'll stake my life on it! Here's my hand; call me a rotten scoundrel if I allow the auction to take place. I stake my life on it!

ANYA [*has regained her composure; she looks happy*]: You're so good, Uncle dear! So clever! [*Embraces him.*] I'm no longer worried now. Not a bit worried. I'm happy.

Enter Firs.

FIRS [*reproachfully*]: Have you no fear of God, sir? When are you going to bed?

GAYEV: Presently, presently. Go away, Firs. Never mind, I'll undress myself this time. Well, children, bye-bye now. More about it tomorrow. Now you must go to bed. [*Kisses* ANYA *and* VARYA.] I'm a man of the eighties. People don't think much of that time, but let me tell you, I've suffered a great deal for my convictions during my life. It's not for nothing that the peasants love me. You have to know your peasant, you have to know how to ———

ANYA: There you go again, Uncle.

VARYA: Please, Uncle dear, don't talk so much.

FIRS [*angrily*]: Sir!

GAYEV: I'm coming, I'm coming. You two go to bed. Off two cushions into the middle. Pot the white!

Gayev goes out, Firs shuffling off after him.

ANYA: I'm not worried any longer now. I don't feel like going to Yaroslavl. I don't like my great-aunt, but I'm no longer worried. I ought to thank Uncle for that. [*Sits down.*]

VARYA: I ought to go to bed, and I shall be going in a moment. I must tell you first that something unpleasant happened here while you were away. You know, of course, that only a few old servants live in the old servants' quarters: Yefimushka, Polia, Evstigney, and, well, also Karp. They had been letting some tramps sleep there, but I didn't say anything about it. Then I heard that they were telling everybody that I'd given orders for them to be fed on nothing but dried peas. I'm supposed to be a miser, you see. It was all that Evstigney's doing. Well, I said to myself, if that's how it is, you just wait! So I sent for Evstigney. [*Yawns.*] He comes. "What do you mean," I said, "Evstigney, you silly old fool?" [*Looks at* ANYA.] Darling! [*Pause.*] Asleep . . . [*Takes* ANYA *by the arm.*] Come to bed, dear. . . . Come on! [*Leads her by the arm.*] My darling's fallen asleep. Come along. [*They go out. A shepherd's pipe is heard playing from far away on the other side of the orchard.* TROFIMOV *walks across the stage and, catching sight of* VARYA *and* ANYA, *stops.*] Shh! She's asleep, asleep. Come along, my sweet.

ANYA [*softly, half asleep*]: I'm so tired. . . . I keep hearing harness bells. Uncle . . . dear . . . Mother and Uncle . . .

VARYA: Come on, my sweet, come on. . . .

They go into Anya's room.

TROFIMOV [*deeply moved*]: My sun! My spring!

Curtain.

ACT TWO

Open country. A small tumbledown wayside chapel. Near it, a well, some large stones, which look like old gravestones, and an old bench. A road can be seen leading to Gayev's estate. On one side, a row of tall dark poplars; it is there that the cherry orchard begins. In the distance, some telegraph poles, and far, far away on the horizon, the outlines of a large town that is visible only in very fine, clear weather. The sun is about to set. Charlotte, Yasha, and Dunyasha are sitting on the bench; Yepikhodov is standing nearby and is playing a guitar; they all sit sunk in thought. Charlotte wears a man's old peaked hat; she has taken a shotgun from her shoulder and is adjusting the buckle on the strap.

CHARLOTTE [*pensively*]: I haven't a proper passport, I don't know how old I am, and I can't help thinking that I'm still a young girl. When I was a little girl, my father and mother used to travel the fairs and give performances — very good ones. I used to do the *salto mortale*³ and all sorts of other tricks. When Father and Mother died, a German lady adopted me and began educating me. Very well. I grew up and became a governess, but where I came from and who I am, I do not know. Who my parents were, I do not know either. They may not even have been married. I don't know. [*Takes a cucumber out of her pocket and starts eating it.*] I don't know anything. [*Pause.*] I'm longing to talk to someone, but there is no one to talk to. I haven't anyone. . . .

YEPIKHODOV [*plays his guitar and sings*]: "What care I for the world and its bustle? What care I for my friends and my foes?" . . . Nice to play a mandolin.

DUNYASHA: It's a guitar, not a mandolin. [*She looks at herself in a hand mirror and powders her face.*]

YEPIKHODOV: To a madman in love, it's a mandolin. [*Sings softly.*] "If only my heart was warmed by the fire of love requited."

Yasha joins in.

CHARLOTTE: How terribly these people sing! Ugh! Like hyenas.

DUNYASHA [*to* YASHA]: All the same, you're ever so lucky to have been abroad.

YASHA: Why, of course. Can't help agreeing with you there. [*Yawns, then lights a cigar.*]

YEPIKHODOV: Stands to reason. Abroad, everything's in excellent complexion. Been like that for ages.

YASHA: Naturally.

YEPIKHODOV: I'm a man of some education, I read all sorts of remarkable books, but what I simply can't understand is where it's all leading to. I mean, what do I really want — to live or to shoot myself? In any case, I always carry a revolver. Here it is. [*Shows them his revolver.*]

CHARLOTTE: That's done. Now I can go. [*Puts the shotgun over her shoulder.*] You're a very clever man, Yepikhodov. You frighten me to death. Women must be madly in love with you. Brrr! [*Walking away.*] These clever people are all so stupid. I've no one to talk to. Always alone, alone, I've no one, and who I am and what I am for is a mystery. [*Walks off slowly.*]

YEPIKHODOV: Strictly speaking, and apart from all other considerations, what I ought to say about myself, among other things, is that Fate treats me without mercy, like a storm a small boat. Even supposing I'm mistaken, why in that case should I wake up this morning and suddenly find a spider of quite enormous dimensions on my chest? As big as that. [*Uses both hands to show the spider's*

³ *salto mortale:* Italian for "leap of death"; here, a standing somersault.

size.] Or again, I pick up a jug of kvass and there's something quite outrageously indecent in it, like a cockroach. [*Pause.*] Have you ever read Buckle's *History of Civilization?*[4] [*Pause.*] May I have a word or two with you, Dunyasha?

DUNYASHA: Oh, all right. What is it?

YEPIKHODOV: I'd be very much obliged if you'd let me speak to you in private. [*Sighs.*]

DUNYASHA [*embarrassed*]: All right, only first bring me my cape, please. It's hanging near the wardrobe. It's so damp here.

YEPIKHODOV: Very well, I'll fetch it. . . . Now I know what to do with my revolver. [*Picks up his guitar and goes out strumming it.*]

YASHA: Twenty-two Calamities! A stupid fellow, between you and me. [*Yawns.*]

DUNYASHA: I hope to goodness he won't shoot himself. [*Pause.*] I'm ever so nervous. I can't help being worried all the time. I was taken into service when I was a little girl, and now I can't live like a peasant any more. See my hands? They're ever so white, as white as a young lady's. I've become so nervous, so sensitive, so like a lady. I'm afraid of everything. I'm simply terrified. So if you deceived me, Yasha, I don't know what would happen to my nerves.

YASHA [*kisses her*]: Little cucumber! Mind you, I expect every girl to be respectable. What I dislike most is for a girl to misbehave herself.

DUNYASHA: I've fallen passionately in love with you, Yasha. You're so educated. You can talk about anything.

Pause.

YASHA [*yawning*]: You see, in my opinion, if a girl is in love with somebody, it means she's immoral. [*Pause.*] It is so pleasant to smoke a cigar in the open air. [*Listens.*] Someone's coming. It's them. . . . [DUNYASHA *embraces him impulsively.*] Please go home and look as if you've been down to the river for a swim. Take that path or they'll think I had arranged to meet you here. Can't stand that sort of thing.

DUNYASHA [*coughing quietly*]: Your cigar has given me an awful headache. [*Goes out.*]

Yasha remains sitting near the chapel. Enter Mrs. Ranevsky, Gayev, and Lopakhin.

LOPAKHIN: You must make up your minds once and for all. There's not much time left. After all, it's quite a simple matter. Do you agree to lease your land for country cottages or don't you? Answer me in one word: yes or no. Just one word.

MRS. RANEVSKY: Who's been smoking such horrible cigars here? [*Sits down.*]

GAYEV: Now that they've built the railway, things are much more convenient. [*Sits down.*] We've been to town for lunch — pot the red in the middle! I really should have gone in to have a game first.

MRS. RANEVSKY: There's plenty of time.

LOPAKHIN: Just one word. [*Imploringly.*] Please give me your answer!

GAYEV [*yawns*]: I beg your pardon?

---

[4] *History of Civilization:* Henry Thomas Buckle's *History of Civilization in England* (1857–61), considered a very enlightened and progressive work in Chekhov's time.

MRS. RANEVSKY [*looking in her purse*]: Yesterday I had a lot of money, but I've hardly any left today. My poor Varya! Tries to economize by feeding everybody on milk soup and the old servants in the kitchen on peas, and I'm just throwing money about stupidly. [*Drops her purse, scattering some gold coins.*] Goodness gracious, all over the place! [*She looks annoyed.*]

YASHA: Allow me to pick 'em up, madam. It won't take a minute. [*Starts picking up the coins.*]

MRS. RANEVSKY: Thank you, Yasha. Why on earth did I go out to lunch? That disgusting restaurant of yours with its stupid band, and those tablecloths smelling of soap. Why did you have to drink so much, Leonid? Or eat so much? Or talk so much? You did talk a lot again in the restaurant today and all to no purpose. About the seventies and the decadents[5] . . . And who to? Talking about the decadents to waiters!

LOPAKHIN: Aye. . . .

GAYEV [*waving his arm*]: I'm incorrigible, that's clear. [*Irritably to* YASHA.] What are you hanging around here for?

YASHA [*laughs*]: I can't hear your voice without laughing, sir.

GAYEV [*to his sister*]: Either he or I.

MRS. RANEVSKY: Go away, Yasha. Run along.

YASHA [*returning the purse to* MRS. RANEVSKY]: At once, madam. [*Is hardly able to suppress his laughter.*] This very minute. [*Goes out.*]

LOPAKHIN: The rich merchant Deriganov is thinking of buying your estate. I'm told he's coming to the auction himself.

MRS. RANEVSKY: Where did you hear that?

LOPAKHIN: That's what they're saying in town.

GAYEV: Our Yaroslavl great-aunt has promised to send us money, but when and how much we do not know.

LOPAKHIN: How much will she send? A hundred thousand? Two hundred?

MRS. RANEVSKY: Well, I hardly think so. Ten or fifteen thousand at most. We must be thankful for that.

LOPAKHIN: I'm sorry, but such improvident people as you, such peculiar, unbusinesslike people, I've never met in my life! You're told in plain language that your estate's going to be sold, and you don't seem to understand.

MRS. RANEVSKY: But what are we to do? Tell us, please.

LOPAKHIN: I tell you every day. Every day I go on repeating the same thing over and over again. You must let out the cherry orchard and the land for country cottages, and you must do it now, as quickly as possible. The auction is on top of you! Try to understand! The moment you decide to let your land, you'll be able to raise as much money as you like, and you'll be saved.

MRS. RANEVSKY: Country cottages, holiday-makers — I'm sorry, but it's so vulgar.

GAYEV: I'm of your opinion entirely.

---

[5] **decadents:** Late-nineteenth-century artists who explored the dark and macabre side of human experience.

LOPAKHIN: I shall burst into tears or scream or have a fit. I can't stand it. You've worn me out! [*To* GAYEV.] You're a silly old woman!

GAYEV: I beg your pardon?

LOPAKHIN: A silly old woman! [*He gets up to go.*]

MRS. RANEVSKY [*in dismay*]: No, don't go. Please stay. I beg you. Perhaps we'll think of something.

LOPAKHIN: What is there to think of?

MRS. RANEVSKY: Please don't go. I beg you. Somehow I feel so much more cheerful with you here. [*Pause.*] I keep expecting something to happen, as though the house was going to collapse on top of us.

GAYEV [*deep in thought*]: Cannon off the cushion. Pot into the middle pocket. . . .

MRS. RANEVSKY: I'm afraid we've sinned too much ———

LOPAKHIN: You sinned!

GAYEV [*putting a fruit drop into his mouth*]: They say I squandered my entire fortune on fruit drops. [*Laughs.*]

MRS. RANEVSKY: Oh, my sins! . . . I've always thrown money about aimlessly, like a madwoman. Why, I even married a man who did nothing but pile up debts. My husband died of champagne. He drank like a fish. Then, worse luck, I fell in love with someone, had an affair with him, and it was just at that time—it was my first punishment, a blow that nearly killed me—that my boy was drowned in the river here. I went abroad, never to come back, never to see that river again. I shut my eyes and ran, beside myself, and *he* followed me—pitilessly, brutally. I bought a villa near Mentone because *he* had fallen ill. For the next three years I knew no rest, nursing him day and night. He wore me out. Everything inside me went dead. Then, last year, I had to sell the villa to pay my debts. I left for Paris, where he robbed me, deserted me, and went to live with another woman. I tried to poison myself. Oh, it was all so stupid, so shaming. . . . It was then that I suddenly felt an urge to go back to Russia, to my homeland, to my daughter. [*Dries her eyes.*] Lord, O Lord, be merciful! Forgive me my sins! Don't punish me any more! [*Takes a telegram from her pocket.*] I received this telegram from Paris today. He asks me to forgive him. He implores me to go back. [*Tears up the telegram.*] What's that? Music? [*Listens intently.*]

GAYEV: That's our famous Jewish band. Remember? Four fiddles, a flute, and a double bass.

MRS. RANEVSKY: Does it still exist? We ought to arrange a party and have them over to the house.

LOPAKHIN [*listening*]: I don't hear anything. [*Sings quietly.*] "And the Germans, if you pay 'em, will turn a Russian into a Frenchman." [*Laughs.*] I saw an excellent play at the theatre last night. It was very amusing.

MRS. RANEVSKY: I don't suppose it was amusing at all. You shouldn't be watching plays, but should be watching yourselves more often. What dull lives you live. What nonsense you talk.

LOPAKHIN: Perfectly true. Let's admit quite frankly that the life we lead is utterly stupid. [*Pause.*] My father was a peasant, an idiot. He understood nothing. He taught me nothing. He just beat me when he was drunk and always with a stick.

As a matter of fact, I'm just as big a blockhead and an idiot myself. I never learnt anything, and my handwriting is so abominable that I'm ashamed to let people see it.

MRS. RANEVSKY: You ought to get married, my friend.

LOPAKHIN: Yes. That's true.

MRS. RANEVSKY: Married to our Varya. She's a nice girl.

LOPAKHIN: Aye. . . .

MRS. RANEVSKY: Her father was a peasant too. She's a hard-working girl, and she loves you. That's the important thing. Why, you've been fond of her for a long time yourself.

LOPAKHIN: Very well. I've no objection. She's a good girl.

Pause.

GAYEV: I've been offered a job in a bank. Six thousand a year. Have you heard, Lyuba?

MRS. RANEVSKY: You in a bank! You'd better stay where you are.

Firs comes in carrying an overcoat.

FIRS [*to* GAYEV]: Please put it on, sir. It's damp out here.

GAYEV [*putting on the overcoat*]: You're a damned nuisance, my dear fellow.

FIRS: Come along, sir. Don't be difficult. . . . This morning, too, you went off without saying a word. [*Looks him over.*]

MRS. RANEVSKY: How you've aged, Firs!

FIRS: What's that, ma'am?

LOPAKHIN: Your mistress says you've aged a lot.

FIRS: I've been alive a long time. They were trying to marry me off before your dad was born. . . . [*Laughs.*] When freedom came,[6] I was already chief valet. I refused to accept freedom and stayed on with my master. [*Pause.*] I well remember how glad everyone was, but what they were glad about, they did not know themselves.

LOPAKHIN: It wasn't such a bad life before, was it? At least, they flogged you.

FIRS [*not hearing him*]: I should say so. The peasants stuck to their masters and the masters to their peasants. Now everybody does what he likes. You can't understand nothing.

GAYEV: Shut up, Firs. I have to go to town tomorrow. I've been promised an introduction to a general who might lend us some money on a promissory note.

LOPAKHIN: Nothing will come of it. You won't pay the interest, either. You may be sure of that.

MRS. RANEVSKY: Oh, he's just imagining things. There aren't any generals.

Enter Trofimov, Anya, and Varya.

GAYEV: Here they are at last.

ANYA: There's Mother.

---

[6]**When freedom came:** Tsar Alexander emancipated the serfs in 1861.

MRS. RANEVSKY [*affectionately*]: Come here, come here, my dears. [*Embracing* ANYA *and* VARYA.] If you only knew how much I love you both. Sit down beside me. That's right.

All sit down.

LOPAKHIN: Our eternal student is always walking about with the young ladies.

TROFIMOV: Mind your own business.

LOPAKHIN: He's nearly fifty and he's still a student.

TROFIMOV: Do drop your idiotic jokes.

LOPAKHIN: Why are you so angry, you funny fellow?

TROFIMOV: Well, stop pestering me.

LOPAKHIN [*laughs*]: Tell me, what do you think of me?

TROFIMOV: Simply this: You're a rich man and you'll soon be a millionaire. Now, just as a beast of prey devours everything in its path and so helps to preserve the balance of nature, so you, too, perform a similar function.

They all laugh.

VARYA: You'd better tell us about the planets, Peter.

MRS. RANEVSKY: No, let's carry on with what we were talking about yesterday.

TROFIMOV: What was that?

GAYEV: Pride.

TROFIMOV: We talked a lot yesterday, but we didn't arrive at any conclusion. As you see it, there's something mystical about the proud man. You may be right for all I know. But try to look at it simply, without being too clever. What sort of pride is it, is there any sense in it, if, physiologically, man is far from perfect? If, in fact, he is, in the vast majority of cases, coarse, stupid, and profoundly unhappy? It's time we stopped admiring ourselves. All we must do is—work!

GAYEV: We're going to die all the same.

TROFIMOV: Who knows? And what do you mean by "we're going to die"? A man may possess a hundred senses. When he dies, he loses only the five we know. The other ninety-five live on.

MRS. RANEVSKY: How clever you are, Peter!

LOPAKHIN [*ironically*]: Oh, frightfully!

TROFIMOV: Mankind marches on, perfecting its powers. Everything that is incomprehensible to us now, will one day become familiar and comprehensible. All we have to do is to work and do our best to assist those who are looking for truth. Here in Russia only a few people are working so far. The vast majority of the educated people I know, do nothing. They aren't looking for anything. They are quite incapable of doing any work. They call themselves intellectuals, but speak to their servants as inferiors and treat the peasants like animals. They're not particularly keen on their studies, they don't do any serious reading, they are bone idle, they merely talk about science, and they understand very little about art. They are all so solemn, they look so very grave, they talk only of important matters, they philosophize. Yet anyone can see that our workers are abominably fed, sleep on bare boards, thirty and forty to a room—bedbugs everywhere, stench, damp, moral turpitude. It's therefore obvious that all our fine phrases are merely a way of deluding ourselves and others. Tell me, where are all those children's crèches[7] people are talking so much about? Where are the reading rooms? You find them only in novels. Actually, we haven't any. All we have is dirt, vulgarity, brutality. I dislike and I'm frightened of all these solemn countenances, just as I'm frightened of all serious conversations. Why not shut up for once?

LOPAKHIN: Well, I get up at five o'clock in the morning, I work from morning till night, and I've always lots of money on me — mine and other people's — and I can see what the people around me are like. One has only to start doing something to realize how few honest, decent people there are about. Sometimes when I lie awake, I keep thinking: Lord, you've given us vast forests, boundless plains, immense horizons, and living here, we ourselves ought really to be giants ————

MRS. RANEVSKY: You want giants, do you? They're all right only in fairy tales. Elsewhere they frighten me. [YEPIKHODOV *crosses the stage in the background, playing his guitar. Pensively.*] There goes Yepikhodov.

ANYA [*pensively*]: There goes Yepikhodov.

GAYEV: The sun's set, ladies and gentlemen.

TROFIMOV: Yes.

GAYEV [*softly, as though declaiming*]: Oh, nature, glorious nature! Glowing with eternal radiance, beautiful and indifferent, you, whom we call Mother, uniting in yourself both life and death, you — life-giver and destroyer . . .

VARYA [*imploringly*]: Darling Uncle!

ANYA: Uncle, again!

TROFIMOV: You'd far better pot the red in the middle.

GAYEV: Not another word! Not another word!

They all sit deep in thought. Everything is still. The silence is broken only by the subdued muttering of Firs. Suddenly a distant sound is heard. It seems to come from the sky, the sound of a breaking string, slowly dying away, melancholy.

MRS. RANEVSKY: What's that?

LOPAKHIN: I don't know. I expect a bucket must have broken somewhere far away in a coal mine, but somewhere a very long distance away.

GAYEV: Perhaps it was a bird, a heron or something.

TROFIMOV: Or an eagle-owl.

MRS. RANEVSKY [*shudders*]: It makes me feel dreadful for some reason.

Pause.

FIRS: Same thing happened before the misfortune: the owl hooted and the samovar kept hissing.

GAYEV: Before what misfortune?

FIRS: Before they gave us our freedom.

---

[7] children's crèches: Day nurseries.

Pause.

MRS. RANEVSKY: Come, let's go in, my friends. It's getting dark. [*To* ANYA.] There are tears in your eyes. What's the matter, darling? [*Embraces her.*]

ANYA: It's nothing, Mother. Nothing.

TROFIMOV: Someone's coming.

A Hiker appears. He wears a shabby white peaked cap and an overcoat; he is slightly drunk.

HIKER: Excuse me, is this the way to the station?

GAYEV: Yes, follow that road.

HIKER: I'm greatly obliged to you sir. [*Coughs.*] Glorious weather . . . [*Declaiming.*] Brother, my suffering brother, come to the Volga, you whose groans . . . [*To* VARYA.] Mademoiselle, won't you give thirty kopecks to a starving Russian citizen?

Varya, frightened, utters a little scream.

LOPAKHIN [*angrily*]: There's a limit to the most disgraceful behavior.

MRS. RANEVSKY [*at a loss*]: Here, take this. [*Looks for some money in her purse.*] No silver. Never mind, have this gold one.

HIKER: Profoundly grateful to you, ma'am. [*Goes out.*]

Laughter.

VARYA [*frightened*]: I'm going away. I'm going away. Good heavens, Mother dear, there's no food for the servants in the house, and you gave him a gold sovereign!

MRS. RANEVSKY: What's to be done with a fool like me? I'll give you all I have when we get home. You'll lend me some more money, Lopakhin, won't you?

LOPAKHIN: With pleasure.

MRS. RANEVSKY: Let's go in. It's time. By the way, Varya, we've found you a husband here. Congratulations.

VARYA [*through tears*]: This isn't a joking matter, Mother.

LOPAKHIN: Okhmelia, go to a nunnery![8]

GAYEV: Look at my hands. They're shaking. It's a long time since I had a game of billiards.

LOPAKHIN: Okhmelia, O nymph, remember me in your prayers!

MRS. RANEVSKY: Come along, come along, it's almost supper time.

VARYA: That man frightened me. My heart's still pounding.

LOPAKHIN: Let me remind you, ladies and gentlemen: The cherry orchard is up for sale on the twenty-second of August. Think about it! Think!

They all go out except Trofimov and Anya.

ANYA [*laughing*]: I'm so glad the hiker frightened Varya. Now we are alone.

TROFIMOV: Varya's afraid we might fall in love. That's why she follows us around for days on end. With her narrow mind she cannot grasp that we are above love. The whole aim and meaning of our life is to bypass everything that is petty and

---

[8] **Okhmelia, go to a nunnery!:** Lopakhin is quoting lines from Shakespeare's *Hamlet* in which Hamlet taunts Ophelia (Okhmelia).

illusory, that prevents us from being free and happy. Forward! Let us march on irresistibly toward the bright star shining there in the distance! Forward! Don't lag behind, friends!

ANYA [*clapping her hands excitedly*]: You talk so splendidly! [*Pause.*] It's so heavenly here today!

TROFIMOV: Yes, the weather is wonderful.

ANYA: What have you done to me, Peter? Why am I no longer as fond of the cherry orchard as before? I loved it so dearly. I used to think there was no lovelier place on earth than our orchard.

TROFIMOV: The whole of Russia is our orchard. The earth is great and beautiful. There are lots of lovely places on it. [*Pause.*] Think, Anya: your grandfather, your great-grandfather, and all your ancestors owned serfs. They owned living souls. Can't you see human beings looking at you from every cherry tree in your orchard, from every leaf and every tree trunk? Don't you hear their voices? To own living souls—that's what has changed you all so much, you who are living now and those who lived before you. That's why your mother, you yourself, and your uncle no longer realize that you are living on borrowed capital, at other people's expense, at the expense of those whom you don't admit farther than your entrance hall. We are at least two hundred years behind the times. We haven't got anything at all. We have no definite attitude toward our past. We just philosophize, complain of depression, or drink vodka. Isn't it abundantly clear that before we start living in the present, we must atone for our past, make an end of it? And atone for it we can only by suffering, by extraordinary, unceasing labor. Understand that, Anya.

ANYA: The house we live in hasn't really been ours for a long time. I'm going to leave it. I give you my word.

TROFIMOV: If you have the keys of the house, throw them into the well and go away. Be free as the wind.

ANYA [*rapturously*]: How well you said it!

TROFIMOV: Believe me, Anya, believe me! I'm not yet thirty, I'm young, I'm still a student, but I've been through hell more than once. I'm driven from pillar to post. In winter I'm half-starved, I'm ill, worried, poor as a beggar. You can't imagine the terrible places I've been to! And yet, always, every moment of the day and night, my heart was full of ineffable visions of the future. I feel, I'm quite sure, that happiness is coming, Anya. I can see it coming already.

ANYA [*pensively*]: The moon is rising.

Yepikhodov can be heard playing the same sad tune as before on his guitar. The moon rises. Somewhere near the poplars Varya is looking for Anya and calling, "Anya, where are you?"

TROFIMOV: Yes, the moon is rising. [*Pause.*] There it is—happiness! It's coming nearer and nearer. Already I can hear its footsteps, and if we never see it, if we never know it, what does that matter? Others will see it.

VARYA [*offstage*]: Anya, where are you?

TROFIMOV: That Varya again! [*Angrily.*] Disgusting!

ANYA: Never mind, let's go to the river. It's lovely there.

TROFIMOV: Yes, let's.

They go out.

VARYA [*offstage*]: Anya! Anya!

Curtain.

ACT THREE

The drawing room, separated by an archway from the ballroom. A candelabra is alight. The Jewish band can be heard playing in the entrance hall. It is the same band that is mentioned in Act Two. Evening. In the ballroom people are dancing the Grande Ronde. Simeonov-Pishchik's voice can be heard crying out, "Promenade à une paire!" They all come out into the drawing room: Pishchik and Charlotte the first couple, Trofimov and Mrs. Ranevsky the second, Anya and a Post Office Clerk the third, Varya and the Stationmaster the fourth, and so on. Varya is quietly crying and dries her eyes as she dances. The last couple consists of Dunyasha and a partner. They walk across the drawing room. Pishchik shouts, "Grande Ronde balancez!" and "Les cavaliers à genoux et remerciez vos dames!"[9]

Firs, wearing a tailcoat, brings in soda water on a tray. Pishchik and Trofimov come into the drawing room.

PISHCHIK: I've got high blood-pressure. I've had two strokes already, and I find dancing hard work. But, as the saying goes, if you're one of a pack, wag your tail, whether you bark or not. As a matter of fact, I'm as strong as a horse. My father, may he rest in peace, liked his little joke, and speaking about our family pedigree, he used to say that the ancient Simeonov-Pishchiks came from the horse that Caligula had made a senator. [*Sits down.*] But you see, the trouble is that I have no money. A hungry dog believes only in meat. [*Snores, but wakes up again at once.*] I'm just the same. All I can think of is money.

TROFIMOV: There really is something horsy about you.

PISHCHIK: Well, a horse is a good beast. You can sell a horse.

From an adjoining room comes the sound of people playing billiards. Varya appears in the ballroom under the archway.

TROFIMOV [*teasing her*]: Mrs. Lopakhin! Mrs. Lopakhin!

VARYA [*angrily*]: Moth-eaten gentleman!

TROFIMOV: Well, I am a moth-eaten gentleman and proud of it.

VARYA [*brooding bitterly*]: We've hired a band, but how we are going to pay for it, I don't know. [*Goes out.*]

TROFIMOV [*to* PISHCHIK]: If the energy you have wasted throughout your life looking for money to pay the interest on your debts had been spent on something else, you'd most probably have succeeded in turning the world upside down.

---

[9] *"Grande . . . dames!":* The instructions for the French dance are: "Promenade à une paire!" or, walk in pairs; "Grande Ronde, balancez!" or, grand round and swing; and "Les cavaliers à genoux et remerciez vos dames," gentlemen, kneel and thank your ladies.

PISHCHIK: Nietzsche,[10] the famous philosopher—a great man, a man of great intellect—says in his works that there's nothing wrong about forging bank notes.

TROFIMOV: Have you read Nietzsche?

PISHCHIK: Well, actually, Dashenka told me about it. I don't mind telling you, though, that in my present position I might even forge bank notes. The day after tomorrow I've got to pay three hundred and ten rubles. I've already got one hundred and thirty. [*Feels his pockets in alarm.*] My money's gone, I've lost my money! [*Through tears.*] Where is it? [*Happily.*] Ah, here it is, in the lining. Lord, the shock brought me out in a cold sweat!

Enter Mrs. Ranevsky and Charlotte.

MRS. RANEVSKY [*hums a popular Georgian dance tune*]:[11] Why is Leonid so late? What's he doing in town? [*To* DUNYASHA] Offer the band tea, please.

TROFIMOV: I don't suppose the auction has taken place.

MRS. RANEVSKY: What a time to have a band! What a time to give a party! Oh, well, never mind. [*Sits down and hums quietly.*]

CHARLOTTE [*hands* PISHCHIK *a pack of cards*]: Here's a pack of cards. Think of a card.

PISHCHIK: All right.

CHARLOTTE: Now shuffle the pack. That's right. Now give it to me. Now, then, my dear Mr. Pishchik, *eins, zwei, drei!*[12] Look in your breast pocket. Is it there?

PISHCHIK [*takes the card out of his breast pocket*]: The eight of spades! Absolutely right! [*Surprised.*] Good Lord!

CHARLOTTE [*holding a pack of cards on the palm of her hand, to* TROFIMOV]: Tell me, quick, what's the top card?

TROFIMOV: Well, let's say the queen of spades.

CHARLOTTE: Here it is. [*To* PISHCHIK]: What's the top card now?

PISHCHIK: The ace of hearts.

CHARLOTTE: Here you are! [*Claps her hands and the pack of cards disappears.*] What lovely weather we're having today. [*A mysterious female voice, which seems to come from under the floor, answers: "Oh yes, glorious weather, madam!"*] You're my ideal, you're so nice! [*The voice: "I like you very much too, madam."*]

STATIONMASTER [*clapping his hands*]: Bravo, Madam Ventriloquist!

PISHCHIK [*looking surprised*]: Good Lord! Enchanting, Miss Charlotte, I'm simply in love with you.

CHARLOTTE: In love! Are you sure you can love? *Guter Mensch, aber schlecter Musikant.*[13]

TROFIMOV [*claps* PISHCHIK *on the shoulder*]: Good old horse!

---

[10] **Nietzsche:** Friedrich Nietzsche (1844–1900), a German philosopher known for his iconoclastic ideas; see p. 728.

[11] **Georgian dance tune:** The *Lezginka*—music for a courtship dance from the Caucasus mountains.

[12] *eins, zwei, drei!*: German for "one, two, three."

[13] *Guter . . . Musikant:* German for "Good man, but a bad musician."

CHARLOTTE: Attention, please. One more trick. [*She takes a rug from a chair.*] Here's a very good rug. I'd like to sell it. [*Shaking it.*] Who wants to buy it?

PISHCHIK [*surprised*]: Good Lord!

CHARLOTTE: *Eins, zwei, drei!* [*Quickly snatching up the rug, which she had let fall, she reveals* ANYA *standing behind it.* ANYA *curtseys, runs to her mother, embraces her, and runs back to the ballroom, amid general enthusiasm.*]

MRS. RANEVSKY [*applauding*]: Bravo, bravo!

CHARLOTTE: Now, once more. *Eins, zwei, drei!* [*Lifts the rug; behind it stands* VARYA, *who bows.*]

PISHCHIK [*surprised*]: Good Lord!

CHARLOTTE: The end! [*Throws the rug over* PISHCHIK, *curtseys, and runs off to the ballroom.*]

PISHCHIK [*running after her*]: The hussy! What a woman, eh? What a woman! [*Goes out.*]

MRS. RANEVSKY: Still no Leonid. I can't understand what he can be doing in town all this time. It must be over now. Either the estate has been sold or the auction didn't take place. Why keep us in suspense so long?

VARYA [*trying to comfort her*]: I'm certain Uncle must have bought it.

TROFIMOV [*sarcastically*]: Oh, to be sure!

VARYA: Our great-aunt sent him power of attorney to buy the estate in her name and transfer the mortgage to her. She's done it for Anya's sake. God will help us and Uncle will buy it. I'm sure of it.

MRS. RANEVSKY: Your great-aunt sent fifteen thousand to buy the estate in her name. She doesn't trust us — but the money wouldn't even pay the interest. [*She covers her face with her hands.*] My whole future is being decided today, my future. . . .

TROFIMOV [*teasing* VARYA]: Mrs. Lopakhin!

VARYA [*crossly*]: Eternal student! Expelled twice from the university, weren't you?

MRS. RANEVSKY: Why are you so cross, Varya? He's teasing you about Lopakhin. Well, what of it? Marry Lopakhin if you want to. He is a nice, interesting man. If you don't want to, don't marry him. Nobody's forcing you, darling.

VARYA: I regard such a step seriously, Mother dear. I don't mind being frank about it: He is a nice man, and I like him.

MRS. RANEVSKY: Well, marry him. What are you waiting for? That's what I can't understand.

VARYA: But, Mother dear, I can't very well propose to him myself, can I? Everyone's been talking to me about him for the last two years. Everyone! But he either says nothing or makes jokes. I quite understand. He's making money. He has his business to think of, and he hasn't time for me. If I had any money, just a little, a hundred rubles, I'd give up everything and go right away as far as possible. I'd have gone into a convent.

TROFIMOV: Wonderful!

VARYA [*to* TROFIMOV]: A student ought to be intelligent! [*In a gentle voice, through tears.*] How plain you've grown, Peter! How you've aged! [*To* MRS. RANEVSKY, *no longer crying.*] I can't live without having something to do, Mother! I must be doing something all the time.

Enter Yasha.

YASHA [*hardly able to restrain his laughter*]: Yepikhodov's broken a billiard cue! [*Goes out.*]

VARYA: What's Yepikhodov doing here? Who gave him permission to play billiards? Can't understand these people! [*Goes out.*]

MRS. RANEVSKY: Don't tease her, Peter. Don't you see she is unhappy enough already?

TROFIMOV: She's a bit too conscientious. Pokes her nose into other people's affairs. Wouldn't leave me and Anya alone all summer. Afraid we might have an affair. What business is it of hers? Besides, the idea never entered my head. Such vulgarity is beneath me. We are above love.

MRS. RANEVSKY: So, I suppose I must be beneath love. [*In great agitation.*] Why isn't Leonid back? All I want to know is: Has the estate been sold or not? Such a calamity seems so incredible to me that I don't know what to think. I'm completely at a loss. I feel like screaming, like doing something silly. Help me, Peter. Say something. For God's sake, say something!

TROFIMOV: What does it matter whether the estate's been sold today or not? The estate's been finished and done with long ago. There's no turning back. The road to it is closed. Stop worrying, my dear. You mustn't deceive yourself. Look the truth straight in the face for once in your life.

MRS. RANEVSKY: What truth? You can see where truth is and where it isn't, but I seem to have gone blind. I see nothing. You boldly solve all important problems, but tell me, dear boy, isn't it because you're young, isn't it because you haven't had the time to live through the consequences of any of your problems? You look ahead boldly, but isn't it because you neither see nor expect anything terrible to happen to you, because life is still hidden from your young eyes? You're bolder, more honest, you see much deeper than any of us, but think carefully, try to understand our position, be generous even a little, spare me. I was born here, you know. My father and mother lived here, and my grandfather also. I love this house. Life has no meaning for me without the cherry orchard, and if it has to be sold, then let me be sold with it. [*Embraces* TROFIMOV *and kisses him on the forehead.*] Don't you see, my son was drowned here. [*Weeps.*] Have pity on me, my good, kind friend.

TROFIMOV: You know I sympathize with you with all my heart.

MRS. RANEVSKY: You should have put it differently. [*Takes out her handkerchief. A telegram falls on the floor.*] My heart is so heavy today. You can't imagine how heavy. I can't bear this noise. The slightest sound makes me shudder. I'm trembling all over. I'm afraid to go to my room. I'm terrified to be alone. . . . Don't condemn me, Peter. I love you as my own son. I'd gladly let Anya marry you, I swear I would. Only, my dear boy, you must study, you must finish your course at the university. You never do anything. You just drift from one place to another. That's what's so strange. Isn't that so? Isn't it? And you should do something about your beard. Make it grow, somehow. [*Laughs.*] You are funny!

TROFIMOV [*picking up the telegram*]: I have no wish to be handsome.

MRS. RANEVSKY: That telegram's from Paris. I get one every day. Yesterday and today. That wild man is ill again, in trouble again. He asks me to forgive him. He begs me to come back to him, and I really think I ought to be going back to Paris to be near him for a bit. You're looking very stern, Peter. But what's to be done, my dear boy? What am I to do? He's ill. He's lonely. He's unhappy. Who'll look after him there? Who'll stop him from doing something silly? Who'll give him his medicine at the right time? And, why hide it? Why be silent about it? I love him. That's obvious. I love him. I love him. He's a millstone round my neck and he's dragging me down to the bottom with him, but I love the millstone, and I can't live without it. [*Presses* TROFIMOV's *hand.*] Don't think badly of me, Peter. Don't say anything. Don't speak.

TROFIMOV [*through tears*]: For God's sake—forgive my being so frank, but he left you penniless!

MRS. RANEVSKY: No, no, no! You mustn't say that. [*Puts her hands over her ears.*]

TROFIMOV: Why, he's a scoundrel, and you're the only one who doesn't seem to know it. He's a petty scoundrel, a nonentity.

MRS. RANEVSKY [*angry but restraining herself*]: You're twenty-six or twenty-seven, but you're still a schoolboy—a sixth-grade schoolboy!

TROFIMOV: What does that matter?

MRS. RANEVSKY: You ought to be a man. A person of your age ought to understand people who are in love. You ought to be in love yourself. You ought to fall in love. [*Angrily.*] Yes! Yes! And you're not so pure either. You're just a prude, a ridiculous crank, a freak!

TROFIMOV [*horrified*]: What is she saying?

MRS. RANEVSKY: "I'm above love!" You're not above love, you're simply what Firs calls a nincompoop. Not have a mistress at your age!

TROFIMOV [*horrified*]: This is terrible! What is she saying? [*Walks quickly into the ballroom, clutching his head.*] It's dreadful! I can't! I'll go away! [*Goes out but immediately comes back.*] All is at an end between us! [*Goes out into the hall.*]

MRS. RANEVSKY [*shouting after him*]: Peter, wait! You funny boy, I was only joking. Peter!

Someone can be heard running rapidly up the stairs and then suddenly falling downstairs with a crash. Anya and Varya scream, followed immediately by laughter.

MRS. RANEVSKY: What's happened?

ANYA [*laughing, runs in*]: Peter's fallen down the stairs! [*Runs out.*]

MRS. RANEVSKY: What an eccentric! [*The* STATIONMASTER *stands in the middle of the ballroom and recites "The Fallen Woman"*[14] *by Alexey Tolstoy. The others listen. But he has hardly time to recite a few lines when the sound of a waltz comes from the entrance hall, and the recitation breaks off. Everyone dances.* TROFIMOV, ANYA,

---

[14] *"The Fallen Woman":* A sentimental poem by a distant relative of Leo Tolstoy.

VARYA, *and* MRS. RANEVSKY *enter from the hall.*] Well, Peter dear, you pure soul, I'm sorry. . . . Come, let's dance. [*Dances with* TROFIMOV.]

Anya and Varya dance together. Firs comes in and stands his walking stick near the side door. Yasha has also come in from the drawing room and is watching the dancing.

YASHA: Well, Grandpa!

FIRS: I'm not feeling too well. We used to have generals, barons, and admirals at our dances before, but now we send for the post office clerk and the stationmaster. Even they are not too keen to come. Afraid I'm getting weak. The old master, the mistress's grandfather that is, used to give us powdered sealing wax for medicine. It was his prescription for all illnesses. I've been taking sealing wax every day for the last twenty years or more. That's perhaps why I'm still alive.

YASHA: You make me sick, Grandpa. [*Yawns*]. I wish you was dead.

FIRS: Ugh, you nincompoop! [*Mutters.*]

Trofimov and Mrs. Ranevsky dance in the ballroom and then in the drawing room.

MRS. RANEVSKY: *Merci.* I think I'll sit down a bit. [*Sits down.*] I'm tired.

Enter Anya.

ANYA [*agitated*]: A man in the kitchen said just now that the cherry orchard has been sold today.

MRS. RANEVSKY: Sold? Who to?

ANYA: He didn't say. He's gone away now.

Anya dances with Trofimov; both go off to the ballroom.

YASHA: Some old man gossiping, madam. A stranger.

FIRS: Master Leonid isn't here yet. Hasn't returned. Wearing his light autumn overcoat. He might catch cold. Oh, these youngsters!

MRS. RANEVSKY: I shall die! Yasha, go and find out who bought it.

YASHA: But he's gone, the old man has. [*Laughs.*]

MRS. RANEVSKY [*a little annoyed*]: Well, what are you laughing at? What are you so pleased about?

YASHA: Yepikhodov's a real scream. Such a fool. Twenty-two Calamities!

MRS. RANEVSKY: Firs, where will you go if the estate's sold?

FIRS: I'll go wherever you tell me, ma'am.

MRS. RANEVSKY: You look awful! Are you ill? You'd better go to bed.

FIRS: Me to bed, ma'am? [*Ironically.*] If I goes to bed, who's going to do the waiting? Who's going to look after everything? I'm the only one in the whole house.

YASHA [*to* MRS. RANEVSKY]: I'd like to ask you a favor, madam. If you go back to Paris, will you take me with you? It's quite impossible for me to stay here. [*Looking round, in an undertone.*] You know perfectly well yourself what an uncivilized country this is—the common people are so immoral—and besides, it's so boring here, the food in the kitchen is disgusting, and on top of it, there's that old Firs wandering about, muttering all sorts of inappropriate words. Take me with you, madam, please!

Enter Pishchik.

PISHCHIK: May I have the pleasure of a little dance, fair lady? [MRS. RANEVSKY *goes with him.*] I'll have one hundred and eighty rubles off you all the same, my dear, charming lady. . . . I will, indeed. [*They dance.*] One hundred and eighty rubles. . . .

They go into the ballroom.

YASHA [*singing softly*]: "Could you but feel the agitated beating of my heart."

In the ballroom a woman in a gray top hat and check trousers can be seen jumping about and waving her arms. Shouts of "Bravo, Charlotte! Bravo!"

DUNYASHA [*stops to powder her face*]: Miss Anya told me to join the dancers because there are lots of gentlemen and very few ladies. But dancing makes me dizzy and my heart begins beating so fast. I say, Firs, the post office clerk said something to me just now that quite took my breath away.

The music becomes quieter.

FIRS: What did he say to you?

DUNYASHA: "You're like a flower," he said.

YASHA [*yawning*]: What ignorance! [*Goes out.*]

DUNYASHA: Like a flower! I'm ever so delicate, and I love people saying nice things to me!

FIRS: You'll come to a bad end, my girl. Mark my words.

Enter Yepikhodov.

YEPIKHODOV: You seem to avoid me, Dunyasha. Just as if I was some insect. [*Sighs.*] Oh, life!

DUNYASHA: What do you want?

YEPIKHODOV: No doubt you may be right. [*Sighs.*] But, of course, if one looks at things from a certain point of view, then, if I may say so and if you'll forgive my frankness, you have reduced me absolutely to a state of mind. I know what Fate has in store for me. Every day some calamity overtakes me, but I got used to it so long ago that I just look at my Fate and smile. You gave me your word, and though I——

DUNYASHA: Let's talk about it some other time. Leave me alone now. Now, I am dreaming. [*Plays with her fan.*]

YEPIKHODOV: Every day some calamity overtakes me, and I—let me say it quite frankly—why, I just smile, laugh even.

Enter Varya from the ballroom.

VARYA: Are you still here, Simon! What an ill-mannered fellow you are, to be sure! [*To* DUNYASHA.] Be off with you, Dunyasha. [*To* YEPIKHODOV.] First you go and play billiards and break a cue, and now you wander about the drawing room as if you were a guest.

YEPIKHODOV: It's not your place to reprimand me, if you don't mind my saying so.

VARYA: I'm not reprimanding you. I'm telling you. All you do is drift about from one place to another without ever doing a stroke of work. We're employing an office clerk, but goodness knows why.

YEPIKHODOV [*offended*]: Whether I work or drift about, whether I eat or play billiards, is something which only people older than you, people who know what they're talking about, should decide.

VARYA: How dare you talk to me like that? [*Flaring up.*] How dare you? I don't know what I'm talking about, don't I? Get out of here! This instant!

YEPIKHODOV [*cowed*]: Express yourself with more delicacy, please.

VARYA [*beside herself*]: Get out of here this minute! Out! [*He goes toward the door, and she follows him.*] Twenty-two Calamities! Don't let me see you here again! Never set foot here again! [YEPIKHODOV *goes out. He can be heard saying behind the door: "I'll lodge a complaint."*] Oh, so you're coming back, are you? [*Picks up the stick which* FIRS *has left near the door.*] Come on, come on, I'll show you! Coming, are you? Well, take that! [*Swings the stick as* LOPAKHIN *comes in.*]

LOPAKHIN: Thank you very much!

VARYA [*angrily and derisively*]: I'm so sorry!

LOPAKHIN: It's quite all right. Greatly obliged to you for the kind reception.

VARYA: Don't mention it. [*Walks away, then looks round and inquires gently.*] I didn't hurt you, did I?

LOPAKHIN: Oh no, not at all. There's going to be an enormous bump on my head for all that.

Voices in the ballroom: "Lopakhin's arrived. Lopakhin!"

PISHCHIK: Haven't heard from you or seen you for ages, my dear fellow! [*Embraces* LOPAKHIN.] Do I detect a smell of brandy, dear boy? We're doing very well here, too.

Enter Mrs. Ranevsky.

MRS. RANEVSKY: Is it you, Lopakhin? Why have you been so long? Where's Leonid?

LOPAKHIN: He came back with me. He'll be here in a moment.

MRS. RANEVSKY [*agitated*]: Well, what happened? Did the auction take place? Speak, for heaven's sake!

LOPAKHIN [*embarrassed, fearing to betray his joy*]: The auction was over by four o'clock. We missed our train and had to wait till half past nine. [*With a deep sigh.*] Oh dear, I'm afraid I feel a little dizzy.

Enter Gayev. He carries some parcels in his right hand and wipes away his tears with his left.

MRS. RANEVSKY: What's the matter, Leonid? Well! [*Impatiently, with tears.*] Quick, tell me for heaven's sake!

GAYEV [*doesn't answer, only waves his hand resignedly to* FIRS, *weeping*]: Here, take these—anchovies, Kerch herrings . . . I've had nothing to eat all day. I've had a terrible time. [*The door of the billiard room is open; the click of billiard balls can be heard and* YASHA's *voice: "Seven and eighteen!"* GAYEV's *expression changes. He is no longer crying.*] I'm awfully tired. Come and help me change, FIRS.

Gayev goes off through the ballroom to his own room, followed by Firs.

PISHCHIK: Well, what happened at the auction? Come, tell us!

MRS. RANEVSKY: Has the cherry orchard been sold?

LOPAKHIN: It has.

MRS. RANEVSKY: Who bought it?

LOPAKHIN: I bought it. [*Pause.* MRS. RANEVSKY *is crushed; she would have collapsed on the floor if she had not been standing near an armchair.* VARYA *takes the keys from her belt, throws them on the floor in the center of the drawing room, and goes out.*] I bought it! One moment, please, ladies and gentlemen. I feel dazed. I can't talk.... [*Laughs.*] Deriganov was already there when we got to the auction. Gayev had only fifteen thousand, and Deriganov began his bidding at once with thirty thousand over and above the mortgage. I realized the position at once and took up his challenge. I bid forty. He bid forty-five. He kept raising his bid by five thousand and I by adding another ten thousand. Well, it was soon over. I bid ninety thousand on top of the arrears, and the cherry orchard was knocked down to me. Now the cherry orchard is mine! Mine! [*Laughs loudly.*] Merciful heavens, the cherry orchard's mine! Come on, tell me, tell me I'm drunk. Tell me I'm out of my mind. Tell me I'm imagining it all. [*Stamps his feet.*] Don't laugh at me! If my father and my grandfather were to rise from their graves and see what's happened, see how their Yermolay, their beaten and half-literate Yermolay, Yermolay who used to run around barefoot in winter, see how that same Yermolay bought this estate, the most beautiful estate in the world! I've bought the estate where my father and grandfather were slaves, where they weren't even allowed inside the kitchen. I must be dreaming. I must be imagining it all. It can't be true. It's all a figment of your imagination, shrouded in mystery. [*Picks up the keys, smiling affectionately.*] She's thrown down the keys. Wants to show she's no longer the mistress here. [*Jingles the keys.*] Oh well, never mind. [*The band is heard tuning up.*] Hey you, musicians, play something! I want to hear you. Come, all of you! Come and watch Yermolay Lopakhin take an axe to the cherry orchard. Watch the trees come crashing down. We'll cover the place with country cottages, and our grandchildren and great-grandchildren will see a new life springing up here. Strike up the music! [*The band plays.* MRS. RANEVSKY *has sunk into a chair and is weeping bitterly. Reproachfully.*] Why did you not listen to me? You poor dear, you will never get it back now. [*With tears.*] Oh, if only all this could be over soon, if only our unhappy, disjointed life could somehow be changed soon.

PISHCHIK [*takes his arm, in an undertone*]: She's crying. Let's go into the ballroom. Let's leave her alone. Come on. [*Takes his arm and leads him away to the ballroom.*]

LOPAKHIN: What's the matter? You there in the band, play up, play up! Let's hear you properly. Let's have everything as I want it now. [*Ironically.*] Here comes the new landowner, the owner of the cherry orchard! [*Knocks against a small table accidentally and nearly knocks over the candelabra.*] I can pay for everything!

Lopakhin goes out with Pishchik. There is no one left in the ballroom except Mrs. Ranevsky, who remains sitting in a chair, hunched up and crying bitterly. The band plays quietly. Anya and

Trofimov come in quickly. Anya goes up to her mother and kneels in front of her. Trofimov remains standing by the entrance to the ballroom.

ANYA: Mother, Mother, why are you crying? My dear, good, kind Mother, my darling Mother, I love you; God bless you, Mother. The cherry orchard is sold. It's gone. That's true, quite true, but don't cry, Mother. You still have your life ahead of you, and you've still got your kind and pure heart. . . . Come with me, darling. Come. Let's go away from here. We shall plant a new orchard, an orchard more splendid than this one. You will see it, you will understand, and joy, deep, serene joy, will steal into your heart, sink into it like the sun in the evening, and you will smile, Mother! Come, darling! Come!

Curtain.

ACT FOUR

The scene is the same as in the first act. There are no curtains at the windows or pictures on the walls. Only a few pieces of furniture are left. They have been stacked in one corner as if for sale. There is a feeling of emptiness. Near the front door and at the back of the stage, suitcases, traveling bags, etc., are piled up. The door on the left is open and the voices of Varya and Anya can be heard. Lopakhin stands waiting. Yasha is holding a tray with glasses of champagne. In the entrance hall Yepikhodov is tying up a box. There is a constant murmur of voices offstage, the voices of peasants who have come to say good-bye. Gayev's voice is heard: "Thank you, my dear people, thank you."

YASHA: The peasants have come to say good-bye. In my opinion, sir, the peasants are decent enough fellows, but they don't understand a lot.

The murmur of voices dies away. Mrs. Ranevsky and Gayev come in through the entrance hall; she is not crying, but she is pale. Her face is quivering. She cannot speak.

GAYEV: You gave them your purse, Lyuba. You shouldn't. You really shouldn't!

MRS. RANEVSKY: I—I couldn't help it. I just couldn't help it.

Both go out.

LOPAKHIN [*calling through the door after them*]: Please take a glass of champagne. I beg you. One glass each before we leave. I forgot to bring any from town, and I could find only one bottle at the station. Please! [*Pause.*] Why, don't you want any? [*Walks away from the door.*] If I'd known, I wouldn't have bought it. Oh well, I don't think I'll have any, either. [YASHA *puts the tray down carefully on a chair.*] You'd better have some, Yasha.

YASHA: Thank you, sir. To those who're going away! And here's to you, sir, who're staying behind! [*Drinks.*] This isn't real champagne. Take it from me, sir.

LOPAKHIN: Paid eight rubles a bottle. [*Pause.*] Damn cold here.

YASHA: The stoves haven't been lit today. We're leaving, anyway. [*Laughs.*]

LOPAKHIN: What's so funny?

YASHA: Oh, nothing. Just feeling happy.

LOPAKHIN: It's October, but it might just as well be summer: it's so sunny and calm. Good building weather. [*Glances at his watch and calls through the door.*] I say, don't forget the train leaves in forty-seven minutes. In twenty minutes we must start for the station. Hurry up!

Trofimov comes in from outside, wearing an overcoat.

TROFIMOV: I think it's about time we were leaving. The carriages are at the door. Where the blazes could my galoshes have got to? Disappeared without a trace. [*Through the door.*] Anya, I can't find my galoshes! Can't find them!

LOPAKHIN: I've got to go to Kharkov. I'll leave with you on the same train. I'm spending the winter in Kharkov. I've been hanging about here too long. I'm worn out with having nothing to do. I can't live without work. Don't know what to do with my hands. They just flop about as if they belonged to someone else.

TROFIMOV: Well, we'll soon be gone and then you can resume your useful labors.

LOPAKHIN: Come on, have a glass of champagne.

TROFIMOV: No, thank you.

LOPAKHIN: So you're off to Moscow, are you?

TROFIMOV: Yes. I'll see them off to town, and I'm off to Moscow tomorrow.

LOPAKHIN: I see. I suppose the professors have stopped lecturing while you've been away. They're all waiting for you to come back.

TROFIMOV: Mind your own business.

LOPAKHIN: How many years have you been studying at the university?

TROFIMOV: Why don't you think of something new for a change? This is rather old, don't you think? — and stale. [*Looking for his galoshes.*] I don't suppose we shall ever meet again, so let me give you a word of advice as a farewell gift: Don't wave your arms about. Get rid of the habit of throwing your arms about. And another thing: To build country cottages in the hope that in the fullness of time vacationers will become landowners is the same as waving your arms about. Still, I like you in spite of everything. You've got fine sensitive fingers, like an artist's, and you have a fine sensitive soul.

LOPAKHIN [*embraces him*]: My dear fellow, thanks for everything. Won't you let me lend you some money for your journey? You may need it.

TROFIMOV: Need it? Whatever for?

LOPAKHIN: But you haven't any, have you?

TROFIMOV: Oh, but I have. I've just got some money for a translation. Got it here in my pocket. [*Anxiously.*] Where could those galoshes of mine have got to?

VARYA [*from another room*]: Oh, take your filthy things! [*Throws a pair of galoshes onto the stage.*]

TROFIMOV: Why are you so cross, Varya? Good heavens, these are not my galoshes!

LOPAKHIN: I had about three thousand acres of poppy sown last spring. Made a clear profit of forty thousand. When my poppies were in bloom, what a beautiful sight they were! Well, so you see, I made forty thousand and I'd be glad to lend you some of it because I can afford to. So why be so high and mighty? I'm a peasant. . . . I'm offering it to you without ceremony.

TROFIMOV: Your father was a peasant, my father was a pharmacist, all of which proves exactly nothing. [LOPAKHIN *takes out his wallet.*] Put it back! Put it back! If you offered me two hundred thousand, I wouldn't accept it. I'm a free man.

Everything you prize so highly, everything that means so much to all of you, rich or poor, has no more power over me than a bit of fluff blown about in the air. I can manage without you. I can pass you by. I'm strong and proud. Mankind is marching toward a higher truth, toward the greatest happiness possible on earth, and I'm in the front ranks!

LOPAKHIN: Will you get there?

TROFIMOV: I will. [*Pause.*] I will get there or show others the way to get there.

The sound of an axe striking a tree can be heard in the distance.

LOPAKHIN: Well, good-bye, my dear fellow. Time to go. You and I are trying to impress one another, but life goes on regardless. When I work hard for hours on end, I can think more clearly, and then I can't help feeling that I, too, know what I live for. Have you any idea how many people in Russia exist goodness only knows why? However, no matter. It isn't they who make the world go round. I'm told Gayev has taken a job at the bank at six thousand a year. He'll never stick to it. Too damn lazy.

ANYA [*in the doorway*]: Mother asks you not to begin cutting the orchard down till she's gone.

TROFIMOV: Really, haven't you any tact at all? [*Goes out through the hall.*]

LOPAKHIN: Sorry, I'll see to it at once, at once! The damned idiots! [*Goes out after* TROFIMOV.]

ANYA: Has Firs been taken to the hospital?

YASHA: I told them to this morning. They must have taken him, I should think.

ANYA [*to* YEPIKHODOV, *who is crossing the ballroom*]: Please find out if Firs has been taken to the hospital.

YASHA [*offended*]: I told Yegor this morning. I haven't got to tell him a dozen times, have I?

YEPIKHODOV: Old man Firs, if you want my final opinion, is beyond repair, and it's high time he was gathered to his fathers. So far as I'm concerned, I can only envy him. [*Puts a suitcase on a hatbox and squashes it.*] There, you see! I knew it. [*Goes out.*]

YASHA [*sneeringly*]: Twenty-two Calamities!

VARYA [*from behind the door*]: Has Firs been taken to the hospital?

ANYA: He has.

VARYA: Why didn't they take the letter for the doctor?

ANYA: We'd better send it on after him. [*Goes out.*]

VARYA [*from the next room*]: Where's Yasha? Tell him his mother's here. She wants to say good-bye to him.

YASHA [*waves his hand impatiently*]: Oh, that's too much!

All this time Dunyasha has been busy with the luggage. Now that Yasha is alone, she goes up to him.

DUNYASHA: You haven't even looked at me once, Yasha. You're going away, leaving me behind. [*Bursts out crying and throws her arms around his neck.*]

YASHA: Must you cry? [*Drinks champagne.*] I'll be back in Paris in a week. Tomorrow we catch the express and off we go! That's the last you'll see of us. I can hardly believe it, somehow. *Vive la France!* I hate it here. It doesn't suit me at all. It's not the kind of life I like. I'm afraid it can't be helped. I've had enough of all this ignorance. More than enough. [*Drinks champagne.*] So what's the use of crying? Behave yourself and you won't end up crying.

DUNYASHA [*powdering her face, looking in a hand mirror*]: Write to me from Paris, please. I did love you, Yasha, after all. I loved you so much. I'm such an affectionate creature, Yasha.

YASHA: They're coming here. [*Busies himself around the suitcases, humming quietly.*]

Enter Mrs. Ranevsky, Gayev, Anya, and Charlotte.

GAYEV: We ought to be going. There isn't much time left. [*Looking at* YASHA.] Who's smelling of pickled herrings here?

MRS. RANEVSKY: In another ten minutes we ought to be getting into the carriages. [*Looks round the room.*] Good-bye, dear house, good-bye, old grandfather house! Winter will pass, spring will come, and you won't be here any more. They'll have pulled you down. The things these walls have seen! [*Kisses her daughter affectionately.*] My precious one, you look radiant. Your eyes are sparkling like diamonds. Happy? Very happy?

ANYA: Oh yes, very! A new life is beginning, Mother!

GAYEV [*gaily*]: It is, indeed. Everything's all right now. We were all so worried and upset before the cherry orchard was sold, but now, when everything has been finally and irrevocably settled, we have all calmed down and even cheered up. I'm a bank official now, a financier. Pot the red in the middle. As for you, Lyuba, say what you like, but you too are looking a lot better. There's no doubt about it.

MRS. RANEVSKY: Yes, my nerves are better, that's true. [*Someone helps her on with her hat and coat.*] I sleep well. Take my things out, Yasha. It's time. [*To* ANYA.] We'll soon be seeing each other again, darling. I'm going to Paris. I'll live there on the money your great-aunt sent from Yaroslavl to buy the estate—three cheers for Auntie!—but the money won't last long, I'm afraid.

ANYA: You'll come home soon, Mother, very soon. I'm going to study, pass my school exams, and then I'll work and help you. We shall read all sorts of books together, won't we, Mother? [*Kisses her mother's hands.*] We shall read during the autumn evenings. We'll read lots and lots of books, and a new, wonderful world will open up to us. [*Dreamily.*] Oh, do come back, Mother!

MRS. RANEVSKY: I'll come back, my precious. [*Embraces her daughter.*]

Enter Lopakhin. Charlotte quietly hums a tune.

GAYEV: Happy Charlotte! She's singing!

CHARLOTTE [*picks up a bundle that looks like a baby in swaddling clothes*]: My darling baby, go to sleep, my baby. [*A sound of a baby crying is heard.*] Hush, my sweet, my darling boy. [*The cry is heard again.*] Poor little darling, I'm so sorry for you! [*Throws the bundle down.*] So you will find me another job, won't you? I can't go on like this.

LOPAKHIN: We'll find you one, don't you worry.

GAYEV: Everybody's leaving us. Varya's going away. All of a sudden, we're no longer wanted.

CHARLOTTE: I haven't anywhere to live in town. I must go away. [*Sings quietly.*] It's all the same to me....

Enter Pishchik.

LOPAKHIN: The nine days' wonder!

PISHCHIK [*out of breath*]: Oh dear, let me get my breath back! I'm all in. Dear friends ... a drink of water, please.

GAYEV: Came to borrow some money, I'll be bound. Not from me this time. Better make myself scarce. [*Goes out.*]

PISHCHIK: Haven't seen you for ages, dearest lady. [*To* LOPAKHIN.] You here too? Glad to see you ... man of immense intellect.... Here, that's for you, take it. [*Gives* LOPAKHIN *money.*] Four hundred rubles. That leaves eight hundred and forty I still owe you.

LOPAKHIN [*puzzled, shrugging his shoulders*]: I must be dreaming. Where did you get it?

PISHCHIK: One moment ... Terribly hot ... Most extraordinary thing happened. Some Englishmen came to see me. They found some kind of white clay on my land. [*To* MRS. RANEVSKY.] Here's four hundred for you too, beautiful ravishing lady. [*Gives her the money.*] The rest later. [*Drinks some water.*] Young fellow in the train just now was telling me that some—er—great philosopher advises people to jump off roofs. "Jump!" he says, and that'll solve all your problems. [*With surprise.*] Good Lord! More water, please.

LOPAKHIN: Who were these Englishmen?

PISHCHIK: I let them a plot of land with the clay on a twenty-four years' lease. And now you must excuse me, my friends. I'm in a hurry. Must be rushing off somewhere else. To Znoykov's, to Kardamonov's ... Owe them all money. [*Drinks.*] Good-bye. I'll look in on Thursday.

MRS. RANEVSKY: We're just leaving for town. I'm going abroad tomorrow.

PISHCHIK: What? [*In a worried voice.*] Why are you going to town? Oh! I see! The furniture, the suitcases ... Well, no matter. [*Through tears.*] No matter. Men of immense intellect, these Englishmen.... No matter.... No matter. I wish you all the best. May God help you.... No matter. Everything in this world comes to an end. [*Kisses* MRS. RANEVSKY's *hand.*] When you hear that my end has come, remember the—er—old horse and say: Once there lived a man called Simeonov-Pishchik; may he rest in peace. Remarkable weather we've been having.... Yes. [*Goes out in great embarrassment, but immediately comes back and says, standing in the doorway.*] My Dashenka sends her regards. [*Goes out.*]

MRS. RANEVSKY: Well, we can go now. I'm leaving with two worries on my mind. One concerns Firs. He's ill. [*With a glance at her watch.*] We still have about five minutes.

ANYA: Firs has been taken to the hospital, Mother. Yasha sent him off this morning.

MRS. RANEVSKY: My other worry concerns Varya. She's used to getting up early and working. Now that she has nothing to do, she's like a fish out of water. She's grown thin and pale, and she's always crying, poor thing. [*Pause.*] You must have noticed it, Lopakhin. As you very well know, I'd always hoped to see her married to you. Indeed, everything seemed to indicate that you two would get married. [*She whispers to* ANYA, *who nods to* CHARLOTTE, *and they both go out.*] She loves you, you like her, and I simply don't know why you two always seem to avoid each other. I don't understand it.

LOPAKHIN: To tell you the truth, neither do I. The whole thing's odd somehow. If there's still time, I'm ready even now. . . . Let's settle it at once and get it over. I don't feel I'll ever propose to her without you here.

MRS. RANEVSKY: Excellent! Why, it shouldn't take more than a minute. I'll call her at once.

LOPAKHIN: And there's champagne here too. Appropriate to the occasion. [*Looks at the glasses.*] They're empty. Someone must have drunk it. [YASHA *coughs.*] Lapped it up, I call it.

MRS. RANEVSKY [*excitedly*]: Fine! We'll go out. Yasha, *allez!*[15] I'll call her. [*Through the door.*] Varya, leave what you're doing and come here for a moment. Come on.

Mrs. Ranevsky goes out with Yasha.

LOPAKHIN [*glancing at his watch*]: Aye. . . .

Pause. Behind the door suppressed laughter and whispering can be heard. Enter Varya.

VARYA [*spends a long time examining the luggage*]: Funny, can't find it.

LOPAKHIN: What are you looking for?

VARYA: Packed it myself, and can't remember.

Pause.

LOPAKHIN: Where are you going now, Varya?

VARYA: Me? To the Ragulins'. I've agreed to look after their house—to be their housekeeper, I suppose.

LOPAKHIN: In Yashnevo, isn't it? About fifty miles from here. [*Pause.*] Aye. . . . So life's come to an end in this house.

VARYA [*examining the luggage*]: Where can it be? Must have put it in the trunk. Yes, life's come to an end in this house. It will never come back.

LOPAKHIN: I'm off to Kharkov by the same train. Lots to see to there. I'm leaving Yepikhodov here to keep an eye on things. I've given him the job.

VARYA: Have you?

LOPAKHIN: This time last year it was already snowing, you remember. Now it's calm and sunny. A bit cold, though. Three degrees of frost.

VARYA: I haven't looked. [*Pause.*] Anyway, our thermometer's broken.

Pause. A voice from outside, through the door: "Mr. Lopakhin!"

LOPAKHIN [*as though he had long been expecting this call*]: Coming! [*Goes out quickly.*]

Varya sits down on the floor, lays her head on a bundle of clothes, and sobs quietly. The door opens and Mrs. Ranevsky comes in cautiously.

---

[15] *allez!:* French for "go!"

MRS. RANEVSKY: Well? [*Pause.*] We must go.

VARYA [*no longer crying, dries her eyes*]: Yes, it's time, Mother dear. I'd like to get to the Ragulins' today, I only hope we don't miss the train.

MRS. RANEVSKY [*calling through the door*]: Anya, put your things on!

Enter Anya, followed by Gayev and Charlotte. Gayev wears a warm overcoat with a hood. Servants and Coachmen come in. Yepikhodov is busy with the luggage.

MRS. RANEVSKY: Now we can be on our way.

ANYA [*joyfully*]: On our way. Oh, yes!

GAYEV: My friends, my dear, dear friends, leaving this house for good, how can I remain silent, how can I, before parting from you, refrain from expressing the feelings which now pervade my whole being——

ANYA [*imploringly*]: Uncle!

VARYA: Uncle dear, please don't.

GAYEV [*dejectedly*]: Double the red into the middle. . . . Not another word!

Enter Trofimov, followed by Lopakhin.

TROFIMOV: Well, ladies and gentlemen, it's time to go.

LOPAKHIN: Yepikhodov, my coat!

MRS. RANEVSKY: Let me sit down a minute. I feel as though I've never seen the walls and ceilings of this house before. I look at them now with such eagerness, with such tender emotion. . . .

GAYEV: I remember when I was six years old sitting on this window sill on Trinity Sunday and watching Father going to church.

MRS. RANEVSKY: Have all the things been taken out?

LOPAKHIN: I think so. [*To* YEPIKHODOV *as he puts on his coat.*] Mind, everything's all right here, Yepikhodov.

YEPIKHODOV [*in a hoarse voice*]: Don't you worry, sir.

LOPAKHIN: What's the matter with your voice?

YEPIKHODOV: I've just had a drink of water and I must have swallowed something.

YASHA [*contemptuously*]: What ignorance!

MRS. RANEVSKY: There won't be a soul left in this place when we've gone.

LOPAKHIN: Not till next spring.

Varya pulls an umbrella out of a bundle of clothes with such force that it looks as if she were going to hit someone with it; Lopakhin pretends to be frightened.

VARYA: Good heavens, you didn't really think that——

TROFIMOV: Come on, let's get into the carriages! It's time. The train will be in soon.

VARYA: There are your galoshes, Peter. By that suitcase. [*Tearfully.*] Oh, how dirty they are, how old. . . .

TROFIMOV [*putting on his galoshes*]: Come along, ladies and gentlemen.

Pause.

GAYEV [*greatly put out, afraid of bursting into tears*]: Train . . . station . . . in off into the middle pocket . . . double the white into the corner.

MRS. RANEVSKY: Come along!

LOPAKHIN: Is everyone here? No one left behind? [*Locks the side door on the left.*] There are some things in there. I'd better keep it locked. Come on!

ANYA: Good-bye, old house! Good-bye, old life!

TROFIMOV: Welcome new life!

Trofimov goes out with Anya. Varya casts a last look round the room and goes out unhurriedly. Yasha and Charlotte, carrying her lap dog, go out.

LOPAKHIN: So, it's till next spring. Come along, ladies and gentlemen. Till we meet again. [*Goes out.*]

Mrs. Ranevsky and Gayev are left alone. They seem to have been waiting for this moment. They fling their arms around each other, sobbing quietly, restraining themselves, as though afraid of being overheard.

GAYEV [*in despair*]: My sister! My sister!

MRS. RANEVSKY: Oh, my dear, my sweet, my beautiful orchard! My life, my youth, my happiness, good-bye! . . .

ANYA [*offstage, happily, appealingly*]: Mo-ther!

TROFIMOV [*offstage, happily, excited*]: Where are you?

MRS. RANEVSKY: One last look at the walls and the windows. Mother loved to walk in this room.

GAYEV: My sister, my sister!

ANYA [*offstage*]: Mo-ther!

TROFIMOV [*offstage*]: Where are you?

MRS. RANEVSKY: We're coming.

They go out. The stage is empty. The sound of all the doors being locked is heard, then of carriages driving off. It grows quiet. The silence is broken by the muffled noise of an axe striking a tree, sounding forlorn and sad. Footsteps can be heard. Firs appears from the door on the right. He is dressed, as always, in a jacket and white waistcoat. He is wearing slippers. He looks ill.

FIRS [*walks up to the door and tries the handle*]: Locked! They've gone. [*Sits down on the sofa.*] Forgot all about me. Never mind. Let me sit down here for a bit. Forgotten to put on his fur coat, the young master has. Sure of it. Gone off in his light overcoat. [*Sighs anxiously.*] I should have seen to it. . . . Oh, these youngsters! [*Mutters something which cannot be understood.*] My life's gone just as if I'd never lived. . . . [*Lies down.*] I'll lie down a bit. No strength left. Nothing's left. Nothing. Ugh, you—nincompoop! [*Lies motionless.*]

A distant sound is heard, which seems to come from the sky, the sound of a breaking string, slowly dying away, melancholy. It is followed by silence, broken only by the sound of an axe striking a tree far away in the orchard.

Curtain.

RABINDRANATH TAGORE
B. INDIA, 1861–1941

rub-in-druh-NAHTH
tuh-GORE

**Rabindranath
Tagore, 1917**
*Tagore's iconic long,
white beard helps
make his visage one of
the most recognized
in India. (Library of
Congress)*

Rabindranath Tagore, the leading figure of the Bengali renaissance of the late nineteenth and early twentieth century, was truly a Renaissance man—a poet, novelist, dramatist, essayist, philosopher, journalist, editor, teacher, painter, and musician. The first Asian writer to win the Nobel Prize, Tagore bridged the gulf between East and West; beginning with traditional forms and moving into modernism, he also linked the nineteenth and twentieth centuries. More than any figure other than Gandhi,[1] Tagore has come to represent India. Appropriately, the national anthems of both India and Bangladesh are taken from poems by Tagore.

A Migratory Bird Having Two Homes. Born in 1861, the fourteenth child in a prominent Brahmin family of writers and thinkers, Tagore inherited the divided consciousness of colonial India. He described "Western imperialism" as "the greatest trial in [India's] history." The British had instituted an "impersonal empire, where the rulers were over us but not among us," Tagore wrote, and the colonial experience had "so disintegrated and demoralized . . . our people that many wondered if India could ever rise again by the genius of her own people." Nevertheless, Tagore did not reject all things British. He compared himself to "a migratory bird having two homes," Bengal and Britain. His education, partly in Calcutta and partly in England, introduced him to literatures in **SANSKRIT, BENGALI,** and English, and all three became part of his personal cultural heritage. So his project to regenerate his people and bring them back to "such a thing as our own mind" was based on a program of synthesizing the best from East and West into a new global culture that he called "the Universal human spirit."

Tagore's universalism, a lifelong commitment that would inform his writing and his social and political activities, was inherited from his father and grandfather, both prominent members of the **HINDU** reform movement, Brahma Samaj. Founded in 1828 by Ram Mohun Roy (1772–1833), the movement sought to rid Hinduism of polytheism, idol worship, and the caste system and to reground its doctrines in reason and intuition. It also accepted some Christian and Islamic doctrines, encouraging a more tolerant and universal religion.

www For links to
more information
about Tagore, see
bedfordstmartins
.com/worldlit
compact.

The Bengali Renaissance. While India was called "the jewel in the crown" of British imperialism at the time of Tagore's birth in 1861, by the 1880s the movement for Indian nationalism and independence, the Congress Movement, had begun to challenge British authority on the subcontinent. The **BENGALI LITERARY RENAISSANCE** was part of this emerging

---

[1] **Gandhi:** Mahatma Gandhi (1869–1948), leader of the Indian independence movement and advocate of nonviolent resistance to colonial rule, a commitment shared by Tagore.

nationalistic consciousness, for it sought to establish a literature and culture that would represent "our reaction against the culture of Europe and its ideals, [and] a newborn sense of self-respect." The new literature was written in Bengali, the everyday language of the people of northeast India, as opposed to Sanskrit, the traditional "literary" language of the region, or English, the language of the oppressor. It also departed from traditional poetic forms and mythological subject matter. Instead, in such modern literary forms as the novel and short story, it realistically described the lives of common people, often drawing on folktales and songs for its models and inspiration.

Rediscovering India.   Tagore's literary career was ignited by his contact with rural India upon his return from school in England. His father sent him to oversee some family estates in the Ganges River valley, and there Tagore rediscovered his native land. He heard the language of the peasants, learned their songs, and absorbed the unchanging life of rural India. The stories and poems that he wrote in the 1890s and in the first decade of the twentieth century reveal the influence of his time in the country. The works' language is realistic and vernacular, and their literary models are not traditional Sanskrit poems but the songs and stories of peasants. In the countryside the cosmopolitan Tagore found the enduring themes of India.

Tagore's short stories, many written in the 1890s, present the differences between city and country as some of the defining divisions of colonial India. Typically in these stories, a city dweller, anglicized by his Western education and contact with the British, is reminded of his Indian roots by an unsettling experience in the countryside. Tagore's poems, many of them songs based on traditional Indian folk songs, caught the attention of Western poets and writers with the publication of his collection, *Gitanjali* (Song Offerings), in 1912, which Tagore himself translated from Bengali into English. **William Butler Yeats**, who was similarly exploring his heritage through Irish folktale and myth, found a soul-brother in Tagore. Yeats was so moved by Tagore's work, he exclaimed, "We have found the new Greece!" Largely on the basis of the English *Gitanjali,* Tagore was awarded the Nobel Prize for literature in 1913.

Tagore and Gandhi.   Tagore's novels—the best-known are *Gora* (1910) and *The Home and the World* (*Ghare-baire,* 1916)—are more political than his stories and poems. They present India as desiring independence but saddled with the mentality of a subject nation. Tagore never viewed independence as an end in itself but as part of a process of regaining national self-respect. He believed India needed to value and integrate the best of its Indian and British heritages, rejecting both superstition and colonial subservience. He proudly accepted a knighthood from the British king in 1915, but in 1919 he rebuked the honor in protest of the Amritsar Massacre, in which British troops killed several hundred Indians at a political demonstration. Although Tagore questioned the economic isolationism in Gandhi's program for Indian independence, he saw Gandhi as a figure who synthesized East and West as he himself was trying to do.

A whole people, a whole civilization, immeasurably strange to us, seems to have been taken up into this imagination; and yet we are not moved because of its strangeness but because we have met our own image, . . . or heard, perhaps for the first time in literature, our voice as in a dream.

– William Butler Yeats, 1912

gee-TAHN-juh-lee

p. 1341

Tagore sang Bengal into a nation.

– Ezra Pound

Gandhi, Tagore wrote, had taken the message of Christianity—the doctrine "that God became man in order to save humanity by taking the burden of its sin and suffering on himself"—and turned it into a principle of nonviolent struggle. In doing so, Gandhi became an expression of "the genius of India [which] has taken from her aggressors the most spiritually significant principle of their culture and fashioned of it a new message of hope for mankind."

The Universal Educator.   Besides writing, Tagore devoted himself to social causes, to the restoration of rural village life in India, and especially to the school he founded in 1901 at Santiniketan, his family estate north of Calcutta. The progressive school, which taught in the Bengali rather than the English language and encouraged students to follow their own interests, was based on the traditional "forest schools" of India in which nature was made the teacher. By 1921, the school had grown to become Visva Bharati, Tagore's conception of a world university that sought to reconcile East and West, country and city, and scientific and spiritual knowledge. He described the university as an institution "for the study of the different cultures and religions of the world and to create that mutual sympathy, understanding, and tolerance on which alone can the unity of mankind rest." Internationally known, Tagore was a world traveler who often lectured at universities in Europe and America in his later years. He died in Calcutta in 1941.

Broken Ties.   A short **BILDUNGSROMAN**, a novel describing a young person's education in life, *Broken Ties* was first published in 1916. It links the self-realization of its narrator, Srivilas, with his growing awareness of his cultural identity as a divided man within a divided land. By the end of the story, the disparities between Eastern mysticism and Western empiricism have been transcended, and Srivilas has managed to reconcile the opposing impulses within himself. Tagore borrowed the form of the novella from the West, but this work's substance is profoundly Indian. Like Tagore's other early stories, the English translation that appeared in 1925 did not specify a translator. Tagore himself probably had a significant role in the translation.

■ FURTHER RESEARCH

Biography
Dutta, Krishna. *Rabindranath Tagore: the Myriad-minded Man.* 2000.
Kripalani, Krishna. *Rabindranath Tagore: A Biography.* 1980.

Criticism
Chatterjee, Bhabatosh. *Rabindranath Tagore and the Modern Sensibility.* 1996.
Lago, Mary. "Modes of Questioning in Tagore's Short Stories," *Studies in Short Fiction* 5 (Fall 1967), 24–36.
——. *Rabindranath Tagore.* 1976.
Srinivaslyengar, K. R. *Rabindranath Tagore: A Critical Introduction.* 1985.

■ PRONUNCIATION

bulbuls: BOOL-boolz
Cahaprasi: chuh-huh-PRUH-see
Dharma: DAR-muh (DHAR-muh)
ghi: GEE
Gitanjali: gee-TAHN-juh-lee
Harimohan: huh-ree-MOH-hun
Jagamohan: juh-guh-MOH-hun
Junagarh Lilandanda: joo-NAH-gar li-lahn-DAHN-duh
Mahatma Gandhi: muh-HAHT-muh GAHN-dee
Magh: MUG, MAHG
moghlai: MOH-gligh, MOO-gligh
nahabat: NAH-baht
narghileh: nar-GEE-leh
Nonibala: noh-ni-BAH-lah
Purandar: poo-rahn-DAR
Rabindranath Tagore: rub-in-druh-NAHTH tuh-GORE
sahebs: SAH-eebz
Sannyasin: sun-YAH-seen
sareng: SAH-reng
Shivatosh: Shi-vuh-TOHSH
Srijut: sree-JOOT, shree-JOOT

∾ Broken Ties

Chapter I
Uncle

1

When I first met Satish he appeared to me like a constellation of stars, his eyes shining, his tapering fingers like flames of fire, his face glowing with a youthful radiance. I was surprised to find that most of his fellow-students hated him, for no other fault than that he resembled himself more than he resembled others. Because with men, as well as with some insects, taking the colour of the surroundings is often the best means of self-protection.

The students in the hostel where I lived could easily guess my reverence for Satish. This caused them discomfort, and they never missed an opportunity of reviling him in my hearing. If you have a speck of grit in your eye it is best not to rub it. And when words smart it is best to leave them unanswered.

But one day the calumny against Satish was so gross that I could not remain silent.

Yet the trouble was that I hardly knew anything about Satish. We never had even a word between us, while some of the other students were his close neighbours, and some his distant relatives. These affirmed, with assurance, that what they said was true; and I affirmed, with even greater assurance, that it was incredible. Then all the residents of the hostel bared their arms, and cried: "What impertinence!"

That night I was vexed to tears. Next day, in an interval between lectures, when Satish was reading a book lying at full length on the grass in College Square, I went up to him without any introduction, and spoke to him in a confused manner, scarcely knowing what I said. Satish shut his book, and looked in my face. Those who have not seen his eyes will not know what that look was like.

Satish said to me: "Those who libel me do so, not because they love to know the truth, but because they love to believe evil of me. Therefore it is useless to try to prove to them that the calumny is untrue."

"But," I said, "the liars must be———"

"They are not liars," interrupted Satish.

"I have a neighbour," he went on, "who has epileptic fits. Last winter I gave him a blanket. My servant came to me in a furious temper, and told me that the boy only feigned the disease. These students who malign me are like that servant of mine. They believe what they say. Possibly my fate has awarded me an extra blanket which they think would have suited them better."

I asked him a question: "Is it true what they say, that you are an atheist?"

He said: "Yes."

I bent my head to the ground. I had been arguing with my fellow-students that Satish could not possibly be an atheist.

I had received two severe blows at the outset of my short acquaintance with Satish. I had imagined that he was a Brahman, but I had come to know that Satish belonged to a Bania[1] family, and I in whose veins flowed a bluer blood was bound duly to despise all Banias. Secondly, I had a rooted belief that atheists were worse than murderers, nay, worse even than beef-eaters.

Nobody could have imagined, even in a dream, that I would ever sit down and take my meals with a Bania student, or that my fanatical zeal in the creed of atheism would surpass even that of my instructor. Yet both these things came to pass.

Wilkins was our professor in the College. His learning was on a level with his contempt for his pupils. He felt that it was a menial occupation to teach literature to Bengali students. Therefore, in our Shakespeare class, he would give us the synonym for "cat" as "a quadruped of the feline species." But Satish was excused from taking notes. The Professor told him: "I will make good to you the hours wasted in this class when you come to my room."

The other less favoured students used to ascribe this indulgent treatment of Satish to his fair complexion and to his profession of atheism. Some of the more worldly-wise among them went to Wilkins's study with a great show of enthusiasm to borrow from him some book on Positivism. But he refused, saying that it would be too hard for them. That they should be held unfit even to cultivate atheism made their minds all the more bitter against Satish.

---

[1] Bania: The Hindu caste of tradesmen.

2

Jagamohan was Satish's uncle. He was a notorious atheist of that time. It would be inadequate to say that he did not believe in God. One ought rather to say that he vehemently believed in no God. As the business of a captain in the navy is rather to sink ships than to steer, so it was Jagamohan's business to sink the creed of theism, wherever it put its head above the water.

The order of his arguments ran like this:

(1) If there be a God, then we must owe our intelligence to Him.

(2) But our intelligence clearly tells us that there is no God.

(3) Therefore God Himself tells us that there is no God.

"Yet you Hindus," he would continue, "have the effrontery to say that God exists. For this sin thirty-three million gods and goddesses exact penalties from you people, pulling your ears hard for your disobedience."

Jagamohan was married when he was a mere boy. Before his wife died he had read Malthus.[2] He never married again.

His younger brother, Harimohan, was the father of Satish. Harimohan's nature was so exactly the opposite of his elder brother's that people might suspect me of fabricating it for the purpose of writing a story. But only stories have to be always on their guard to sustain their reader's confidence. Facts have no such responsibility, and laugh at our incredulity. So, in this world, there are abundant instances of two brothers, the exact opposites of one another, like morning and evening.

Harimohan, in his infancy, had been a weakly child. His parents had tried to keep him safe from the attacks of all maladies by barricading him behind amulets and charms, dust taken from holy shrines, and blessings bought from innumerable Brahmans at enormous expense. When Harimohan grew up, he was physically quite robust, yet the tradition of his poor health lingered on in the family. So nobody claimed from him anything more arduous than that he should continue to live. He fulfilled his part, and did hold on to his life. Yet he never allowed his family to forget for a moment that life in his case was more fragile than in most other mortals. Thus he managed to divert towards himself the undivided attention of all his aunts and his mother, and had specially prepared meals served to him. He had less work and more rest than other members of the family. He was never allowed to forget that he was under the special protection, not only of his aforesaid mother and aunts, but also of the countless gods and goddesses presiding in the three regions of earth, heaven, and air. He thus acquired an attitude of prayerful dependence towards all the powers of the world, both seen and unseen — sub-inspectors, wealthy neighbours, highly placed officials, let alone sacred cows and Brahmans.

Jagamohan's anxieties went altogether in an opposite direction. He would give a wide berth to men of power, lest the slightest suspicion of snobbishness should cling to him. It was this same sentiment which had greatly to do with his defiance of the

---

[2] **Malthus:** Thomas Malthus (1766–1834), English economist whose *Essay on Population* (1798) argued that population growth would inevitably outpace the growth of the food supply.

gods. His knees were too stiff to bend before those from whom favour could be expected.

Harimohan got himself married at the proper time, that is to say, long before the time. After three sisters and three brothers, Satish was born. Everybody was struck by his resemblance to his uncle, and Jagamohan took possession of him, as if he were his own son.

At first Harimohan was glad of this, having regard to the educational advantage of the arrangement; for Jagamohan had the reputation of being the most eminent scholar of that period.

He seemed to live within the shell of his English books. It was easy to find the rooms he occupied in the house by the rows of books about the walls, just as it is easy to find out the bed of a stream by its lines of pebbles.

Harimohan petted and spoilt his eldest son, Purandar, to his heart's content. He had an impression that Purandar was too delicate to survive the shock of being denied anything he wanted. His education was neglected. No time was lost in getting him married, and yet nobody could keep him within the connubial limits. If Hari-mohan's daughter-in-law expressed any disapprobation of his vagaries in that direc-tion, Harimohan would get angry with her and ascribe his son's conduct to her want of tact and charm.

Jagamohan entirely took charge of Satish to save him from similar paternal solicitude. Satish acquired a mastery of the English language while he was still a child, and the inflammatory doctrines of Mill and Bentham[3] set his brain on fire, till he began to burn like a living torch of atheism.

Jagamohan treated Satish, not as his junior, but as his boon companion. He held the opinion that veneration in human nature was a superstition, specially designed to make men into slaves. Some son-in-law of the family wrote to him a letter, with the usual formal beginning:

"To the gracious feet of———"

Jagamohan wrote an answer, arguing with him as follows:

> MY DEAR NOREN—Neither you nor I know what special significance it gives to the feet to call them "gracious." Therefore the epithet is worse than useless, and had better be dropped. And then it is apt to give one a nervous shock when you address your letter only to the feet, completely ignoring their owner. But you should understand, that so long as my feet are attached to my body, you should never dissociate them from their context.
>
> Next, you should bear in mind that human feet have not the advantage of pre-hensibility, and it is sheer madness to offer anything to them, confounding their natural function.
>
> Lastly, your use of the plural inflection to the word "feet," instead of the dual, may denote special reverence on your part (because there are animals with four feet

---

[3] **Mill and Bentham:** James Mill (1773–1836) and Jeremy Bentham (1748–1832), English utilitarian philosophers, economic theorists, and political scientists. Utilitarians argued that the purpose of government was to create the greatest happiness for the greatest number.

which have your particular veneration) but I consider it my duty to disabuse your mind of all errors concerning my own zoological identity. — Yours,   Jagamohan.

Jagamohan used to discuss with Satish subjects which are usually kept out of sight in conversation. If people objected to this plainness of speech with one so young, he would say that you can only drive away hornets by breaking in their nest. So you can only drive away the shamefulness of certain subjects by piercing through the shame itself.

When Satish had completed his College course, Harimohan tried his best to extricate him from his uncle's sphere of influence. But when once the noose is fixed round the neck, it only grows tighter by pulling at it. Harimohan became more and more annoyed at his brother, the more Satish proved recalcitrant. If this atheism of his son and elder brother had been merely a matter of private opinion, Harimohan could have tolerated lt. He was quite ready to pass off dishes of fowl as "kid curry."[4] But matters had now become so desperate that even lies became powerless to white-wash the culprits. What brought things to a head was this:

The positive side of Jagamohan's atheistic creed consisted in doing good to others. He felt a special pride in it, because doing good, for an atheist, was a matter of unmitigated loss. It had no allurements of merit and no deterrents of punishment in the hereafter. If he was asked what concern he had in bringing about "the greatest happiness of the greatest number," he used to answer that his best incentive was that he could expect nothing in return. He would say to Satish:

"Baba,[5] we are atheists. And therefore the very pride of it should keep us absolutely stainless. Because we have no respect for any being higher than ourselves, therefore we must respect ourselves."

There were some leather shops in the neighbourhood kept by Muhammadans. The uncle and nephew bestirred themselves with great zeal in doing good to these Muhammadans and their untouchable leather workers.[6] This made Harimohan beside himself with indignation. Since he knew that any appeal to Scriptures, or to tradition, would have no effect upon these two renegades, he complained to his brother concerning the wasting of his patrimony.

"When my expenditure," his brother answered, "comes up to the amount you have spent upon your full-fed Brahman priests, we shall be quits."

One day Harimohan's people were surprised to find that a preparation was going on in Jagamohan's quarters for a grand feast. The cooks and waiters were all Mussulmans. Harimohan called for his son, and said to him angrily:

"I hear that you are going to give a feast to all your reverend friends, the leather workers."

Satish replied that he was far too poor to think of it. His uncle had invited them.

---

[4] **"kid curry":** In Bengal kid curry is often eaten without blame. But fowl curry would come within the prohibitions. [Translator.]

[5] **"Baba":** A term of endearment, literally "father." [Translator.]

[6] **untouchable . . . workers:** As leather is made from the hides of dead animals, those who work in leather are regarded as unclean by orthodox Hindus. Only the very lowest castes are tanners. [Translator.]

Purandar, Satish's elder brother, was equally indignant. He threatened to drive all the unclean guests away. When Harimohan expressed his protest to his brother, he answered:

"I never make any objection to your offering food to your idols. You should make no objection to my offering food to my gods."

"Your gods!" exclaimed Harimohan.

"Yes, my gods," his brother answered.

"Have you become a theist all of a sudden?" sneered Harimohan.

"No!" his brother replied. "Theists worship the God who is invisible. You idolaters worship gods who are visible, but dumb and deaf. The gods I worship are both visible and audible, and it is impossible not to believe in them."

"Do you really mean to say," cried Harimohan, "that these leather workers and Mussulmans are your gods?"

"Indeed, they are," said Jagamohan; "you shall see their miraculous power when I put food before them. They will actually swallow it, which I defy your gods to do. It delights my heart to see my gods perform such divine wonders. If you are not morally blind, it will delight your heart also."

Purandar came to his uncle, and told him in a high-pitched voice that he was prepared to take desperate measures to stop the proceedings. Jagamohan laughed at him, and said:

"You monkey! If you ever try to lay hands on my gods, you will instantly discover how powerful they are, and I shall not have to do anything to defend them."

Purandar was even a greater coward than his father. He was a tyrant only where he was sure of receiving submission. In this case he did not dare to pick a quarrel with his Muhammadan neighbours. So he came to Satish, and reviled him. Satish gazed at him with those wonderful eyes of his, and remained silent.

The feast was a great success.

3

Harimohan could not take this insult passively. He declared war. The property on whose income the whole family subsisted was a temple endowment. Harimohan brought a suit in the law court against his brother, accusing him of such grave breaches of propriety as made him unworthy of remaining the trustee of a religious endowment. Harimohan had as many witnesses as ever he wished. The whole Hindu neighbourhood was ready to support him.

Jagamohan professed in open court that he had no faith in gods or idols of any description whatever; that all eatable food was for him food to be eaten; that he never bothered his head to find out the particular limb of Brahma from which the Muhammadans had issued, and therefore he had not the smallest hesitation in taking food in their company.

The judge ruled Jagamohan to be unfit to hold the temple property. Jagamohan's lawyers assured him that the decision could be upset by an appeal to the higher Court. But Jagamohan refused to appeal. He said he could not cheat even the gods whom he did not believe in. Only those who had the intelligence to believe such things had the conscience to cheat them.

His friends asked him: "How are you going to maintain yourself?"

He answered: "If I have nothing else to eat, I shall be content to gulp down my last breath."

After this, a partition was made of the family house. A wall was raised from the ground floor to the upper storey, dividing the house into two parts.

Harimohan had great faith in the selfish sanity of prudence in human nature. He was certain that the savour of good living would tempt Satish into his golden trap, away from the empty nest of Jagamohan. But Satish gave another proof that he had neither inherited his father's conscience nor his sanity. He remained with his uncle.

Jagamohan was so accustomed to look upon Satish as his own that he was not surprised to find him remaining on his side after the partition.

But Harimohan knew his brother's temperament very well. He went about talking to people, explaining that the reason why Jagamohan did not let go his hold on Satish was that he expected to make a good thing out of Satish's presence, keeping him as a kind of hostage.

Harimohan almost shed tears while he said to his neighbour: "Could my brother ever imagine that I was going to starve him? Since he is cunning enough to concoct this diabolical plot against me, I shall wait and see whether he is cleverer than I am."

Harimohan's talk about Satish reached Jagamohan's ears. Jagamohan was surprised at his own stupidity in not anticipating such a turn of events.

He said: "Good-bye, Satish."

Satish was absolutely certain that nothing could make Jagamohan change his mind, so he had to take his leave, after having spent his eighteen years of life in his uncle's company.

When Satish had put his books and bedding on the top of the carriage, and driven away, Jagamohan shut the door of his room, and flung himself on the floor. When evening came, and the old servant knocked at the door with the lighted lamp, he got no answer.

Alas for the greatest happiness of the greatest number! The estimate in number is not the only measure of human affairs. The man who counts "one" may go beyond all arithmetic when the heart does the sum. When Satish took his departure, he at once became infinite to Jagamohan.

Satish went into a students' lodging to share a room with one of his friends. Harimohan shed tears while meditating on the neglect of filial duties in this godforsaken age. Harimohan had a very tender heart.

After the partition, Purandar dedicated a room in their portion of the house to the family god. It gave him a peculiar pleasure to know that his uncle must be execrating him for the noise raised every morning and every evening by the sacred conches and prayer gongs.

In order to maintain himself, Satish secured a post as a private tutor. Jagamohan obtained an appointment as head master of a high school. And it became a religious duty with Harimohan and Purandar to persuade parents and guardians to take away their boys from the malign influence of the atheist Jagamohan.

4

One day, after a very long interval of absence, Satish came to Jagamohan. These two had given up the usual form of greeting[7] which passes between elder and younger.

Jagamohan embraced Satish, led him to a chair, and asked him for the news.

There was news indeed!

A girl named Nonibala had taken shelter with her widowed mother in the house of the mother's brother. So long as her mother lived, there was no trouble. But a short time ago her mother had died. Her cousins were rascals. One of their friends had taken away this girl. Then, suspecting her of infidelity, after a while he made her life a constant torture. This had happened in the house next to the one where Satish had his tutorship. Satish wanted to save her from this misery, but he had no money or shelter of his own. Therefore he had come to his uncle. The girl was about to give birth to a child.

Jagamohan, when he heard the story, was filled with indignation. He was not the man to calculate coldly the consequence of his deeds, and he at once said to his nephew: "I have the room in which I keep my books. I can put the girl there."

"But what about your books?" Satish asked in surprise. Very few books, however, were now remaining. During the time when he had been unable to secure an appointment, he had been obliged to eke out a living by selling his books.

Jagamohan said: "Bring the girl at once."

"She is waiting downstairs," said Satish. "I have brought her here." Jagamohan ran downstairs, and found the girl crouching in the corner, wrapped in her *sari*, looking like a bundle of clothes.

Jagamohan, in his deep bass voice, said at once: "Come, little Mother, why do you sit in the dust?"

The girl covered her face, and burst into tears. Jagamohan was not a man to give way to emotion, but his eyes were wet as he turned to Satish and said: "The burden that this girl is bearing is ours."

Then he said to the girl: "Mother, don't be shy on my account. My schoolfellows used to call me 'Mad Jagai,' and I am the same madcap even now."

Then, without hesitation, he took the girl by both her hands, and raised her. The veil dropped from off her face.

The girl's face was fresh and young, and there was no line of hardness or vice in it. The inner purity of her heart had not been stained, just as a speck of dust does not soil a flower. Jagamohan took Nonibala to his upper room, and said to her: "Mother, look what a state my room is in! The floor is all unswept. Everything is upside down; and as for myself, I have no fixed hour for my bath or my meals. Now that you have come to my house, everything will be put right, and even this mad Jagai will be made respectable."

Nonibala had never felt before, even when her mother lived, how much one person could be to another; because her mother had looked upon her, not so much as a daughter, but as a young girl who had to be watched.

----

[7] *usual . . . greeting:* This greeting in Bengal is for the younger to touch the feet of the elder. [Translator.]

Jagamohan employed an elderly woman servant to help Nonibala. At first Noni was afraid lest Jagamohan should refuse to take food from her hand because of her impurity. But it turned out that Jagamohan refused to take his meals unless they were cooked and served by Noni.

Jagamohan was aware that a great wave of calumny was about to break over his head. Noni also felt that it was inevitable, and she had no peace of mind. Within a day or two it began.

The servant who waited on her had at first supposed that Noni was Jagamohan's daughter. But she came one day, saying hard things to Noni, and resigned her service in contempt. Noni became pale with fear, thinking of Jagamohan.

Jagamohan said to her: "My little Mother, the full moon is up in the horizon of my life, so the time is ripe for the flood-tide of revilement. But, however muddy the water may become, it will never stain my moonlight."

An aunt of Jagamohan's came to Harimohan's quarters, and said to him: "Jagai, what a disgrace, what a disgrace! Wipe off this stain of sin from your house."

Jagamohan answered: "You are pious people, and this advice is worthy of you. But if I try to drive away all relics of sin, what will become of the sinner?"

Some old grandmother of a woman came to him, and said: "Send this wench away to the hospital. Harimohan is ready to bear all the cost."

Jagamohan said: "But she is my mother. Because some one is ready to pay expenses, should I send my mother to the hospital?"

The grandmother opened her eyes wide with surprise and said: "Who is this you call your mother?"

Jagamohan replied: "She who nourished life within her womb, and risks her life to give birth to children. I cannot call that scoundrel-father of the child 'Father.' He can only cause trouble, keeping himself safely out of it."

Harimohan's whole body shrank with the utter infamy of the thing. That a fallen woman should be sheltered only on the other side of the wall, and in the midst of a household sacred to the memory of generations of mothers and grandmothers! The disgrace was intolerable.

Harimohan at once surmised that Satish was mixed up in this affair, and that his uncle was encouraging him in his shameful conduct. He was so sure of his facts that he went about spreading the news. Jagamohan did not say a single word to contradict him.

"For us atheists," he said, "the only heaven waiting for good deeds is calumny."

The more the rumour of Jagamohan's doings became distorted, the more he seemed to enjoy it, and his laughter rang loud in the sky. Harimohan and respectable people of his class could never imagine that the uncle could go so far as to jest openly on such a subject, and indulge in loud unseemly buffoonery about it with his own nephew.

Though Purandar had been carefully avoiding that part of the house where his uncle lived, he vowed that he would never rest till he had driven the girl away from her shelter.

At the time when Jagamohan had to go to his school he would shut up all access to his quarters, and he would come back the moment he had any leisure to see how Noni was faring.

One day at noon Purandar, with the help of a bamboo ladder, crossed the boundary wall and jumped down into Jagamohan's part of the house. Nonibala had been resting after the morning meal. The door of her room was open. Purandar, when he saw the sleeping figure of Noni, gave a great start, and shouted out in anger: "So *you* are here, are you?"

Noni woke up and saw Purandar before her. She became pale as death, and her limbs shrank under her. She felt powerless to run away or to utter a single word.

Purandar, trembling with rage, shouted out: "Noni!"

Just then Jagamohan entered the room from behind, and cried: "Get out of this room."

Purandar's whole body began to swell up like an angry cat.

Jagamohan said: "If you don't get out at once, I will call in the police."

Purandar darted a terrible glance at Noni, and went out. Noni fainted.

Jagamohan now understood the whole situation. By questioning, he found out that Satish had been aware that Purandar had seduced Noni; but, fearing an angry brawl, he had not informed Jagamohan of the fact.

For days after this incident Noni trembled like a bamboo leaf. Then she gave birth to a dead child.

One midnight Purandar had driven Noni away from her room, kicking her in anger. Since then he had sought her in vain. When he suddenly found her in his uncle's house, he was seized with an uncontrollable passion of jealousy. He was sure that Satish had enticed her away from him, to keep her for his own pleasure, and had then put her in the very next house to his own in order to insult him. This was more than any mortal man could bear.

Harimohan heard all about it. Indeed, Purandar never took any pains to hide these doings from his father, for his father looked upon his son's moral aberrations with a kindly indulgence. But Harimohan thought it contrary to all notions of decency for Satish to snatch away this girl whom his elder brother, Purandar, had looked upon with favour. He devoutly hoped that Purandar would be successful in recovering his spoil.

It was the time of the Christmas holidays. Jagamohan attended Noni night and day. One evening he was translating a novel of Sir Walter Scott's to her, when Purandar burst into the room with another young man.

When Jagamohan was about to call for the police, the young man said: "I am Noni's cousin. I have come to take her away."

Jagamohan caught hold of Purandar by his neck, and shoved him out of the room and down the stairs. He then turned to the other young man and said: "You are a villain and a scoundrel! You assert this cousin's right of yours to wreck her life, not to protect her."

The young man hurried away. But when he had got to a safe distance, he threatened Jagamohan with legal steps in order to rescue his ward.

Noni said within herself: "O Earth, open and swallow me up!"[8]

---

[8] "O Earth, . . . up!": The reference is to Sita in the Ramayana, who uttered this cry when in extreme trouble. [Translator.]

Jagamohan called Satish, and said to him: "Let me leave this place and go to some up-country town with Noni. It will kill her if this is repeated."

Satish urged that his brother was certain to follow her when once he had got the clue.

"Then what do you propose?" said Jagamohan.

"Let me marry Noni," was the answer.

"Marry Noni!"

"Yes, according to the civil marriage rites."

Jagamohan stood up and went to Satish, and pressed him to his heart.

5

Since the partition of the house, Harimohan had not once entered the house to see his elder brother. But that day he came in, dishevelled, and said:

"Dada,[9] what disaster is this you are planning?"

"I am saving everybody from disaster," said Jagamohan.

"Satish is just like a son to you," said Harimohan, "and yet you can have the heart to see him married to that woman of the street!"

"Yes," he replied, "I have brought him up almost as my own son, and I consider that my pains have borne fruit at last."

"Dada," said Harimohan, "I humbly acknowledge my defeat at your hands. I am willing to write away half my property to you, if only you will not take revenge on me like this."

Jagamohan started up from his chair and bellowed out:

"You want to throw me your dirty leavings, as you throw a dog a bone! I am an atheist — remember that! I am not a pious man like you! I neither take revenge, nor beg for favours."

Harimohan hastened round to Satish's lodgings. He cried out to him:

"Satish! What in the world are you going to do? Can you think of no other way of ruining yourself? Are you determined to plunge the whole family into this hideous shame?"

Satish answered: "I have no particular desire to marry. I only do it in order to save my family from hideous shame."

Harimohan shouted: "Have you not got the least spark of conscience left in you? That girl, who is almost like a wife to your brother ————"

Satish caught him up sharply: "What? Like a wife. Not that word, sir, if you please!"

After that, Harimohan became wildly abusive in his language, and Satish remained silent.

What troubled Harimohan most was that Purandar openly advertised his intention to commit suicide if Satish married Noni. Purandar's wife told him that this would solve a difficult problem — if only he would have the courage to do it.

Satish sedulously avoided Noni all these days, but, when the proposed marriage was settled, Jagamohan asked Satish that Noni and he should try to know each other better before they were united in wedlock. Satish consented.

---

[9] **"Dada"**: Elder brother. [Translator.]

Jagamohan fixed a date for their first talk together. He said to Noni:

"My little Mother, you must dress yourself up for this occasion."

Noni bent her eyes to the ground.

"No, no," said he, "don't be shy, Noni. I have a great longing to see you nicely dressed, and you must satisfy my desire."

He had specially selected some Benares silk and a bodice and veil for Noni. He gave these things to her.

Noni prostrated herself at his feet. This made Jagamohan get up hurriedly. He snatched away his feet from her embrace, and said:

"I see, Noni, I have miserably failed in clearing your mind of all this superstitious reverence. I may be your elder in age, but don't you know you are greater than I am, for you are my mother?"

He kissed her on her forehead and said:

"I have had an invitation to go out, and I shall be late back this evening."

Noni clasped his hand and said:

"Baba, I want your blessing to-night."

Jagamohan replied:

"Mother, I see that you are determined to turn me into a theist in my old age. I wouldn't give a brass farthing for a blessing, myself. Yet I cannot help blessing you when I see your face."

Jagamohan put his hand under her chin, and raised her face, and looked into it silently, while tears ran down her cheeks.

6

In the evening a man ran up to the place where Jagamohan was having his dinner, and brought him back to his house.

He found the dead body of Noni, stretched on the bed, dressed in the things he had given her. In her hand was a letter. Satish was standing by her head. Jagamohan opened the letter, and read:

> Baba, forgive me. I could not do what you wanted. I tried my best, but I could never forget him. My thousand salutations to your gracious feet. —NONIBALA, the Sinner.

CHAPTER II
SATISH

1

The last words of Jagamohan, the atheist, to his nephew, Satish, were: "If you have a fancy for funeral ceremony, don't waste it on your uncle,—reserve it for your father."

This is how he came by his death.

When the plague first broke out in Calcutta, the poor citizens were less afraid of the epidemic than of the preventive staff who wore its badge. Satish's father, Harimohan, was sure that their Mussulman neighbours, the untouchable leather-dealers, would be the first to catch it, and thereupon defile him and his kith and kin by dragging them along into a common end. Before he fled from his house, Harimohan went over to offer refuge to his elder brother, saying: "I have taken a house on the river at Kalna, if you————"

"Nonsense!" interrupted Jagamohan. "How can I desert these people?"

"Which people?"

"These leather-dealers of ours."

Harimohan made a grimace and left his brother without further parley. He next proceeded to his son's lodgings, and to him simply said: "Come along."

Satish's refusal was equally laconic. "I have work to do here," he replied.

"As pall-bearer to the leather-dealers, I suppose?"

"Yes, sir; that is, if my services be needed."

"Yes, sir, indeed! You scamp, you scoundrel, you atheist! If need be you're quite ready to consign fourteen generations of your ancestors to perdition, I have no doubt!"

Convinced that the Kali Yuga[10] had touched its lowest depth, Harimohan returned home, despairing of the salvation of his next of kin. In order to protect himself against contamination he covered sheets of foolscap with the name of Kali, the protecting goddess, in his neatest handwriting.

Harimohan left Calcutta. The plague and the preventive officials duly made their appearance in the locality; and for dread of being dragged off to the plague hospital, the wretched victims dared not call in medical aid. After a visit to one of these hospitals, Jagamohan shook his head and remarked: "What if these people are falling ill,—that does not make them criminals."

Jagamohan schemed and contrived till he obtained permission to use his own house as a private plague hospital. Some of us students offered to assist Satish in nursing: There was a qualified doctor among our number.

The first patient in our hospital was a Mussulman. He died. The next was Jagamohan himself. He did not survive either. He said to Satish: "The religion I have all along followed has given me its last reward. There is nothing to complain of."

Satish had never taken the dust[11] of his uncle's feet while living. After Jagamohan's death he made that obeisance for the first and last time.

"Fit death for an atheist!" scoffed Harimohan when he first came across Satish after the cremation.

"That is so, sir!" agreed Satish, proudly.

2

Just as, when the flame is blown out, the light suddenly and completely disappears, so did Satish after his uncle's death. He went out of our ken altogether.

---

[10] **Kali Yuga:** According to the Hindu Shastras the present age, the Kali Yuga, is the Dark Age when Dharma (civilization) will be at its lowest ebb. [Translator.]

[11] **taken the dust:** Touching the feet of a revered elder, and then one's own head, is called taking the dust of the feet. It is the formal way of doing reverence. [Translator.]

We had never been able to fathom how deeply Satish loved his uncle. Jagamohan was alike father and friend to him,—and, it may be said, son as well; for the old man had been so regardless of himself, so unmindful of worldly concerns, that it used to be one of the chief cares of Satish to look after him and keep him safe from disaster. Thus had Satish received from and given to his uncle his all.

What the bleakness of his bereavement meant for Satish, it was impossible for us to conceive. He struggled against the agony of negation, refusing to believe that such absolute blankness could be true: that there could be emptiness so desolate as to be void even of Truth. If that which seemed one vast "No" had not also its aspect of "Yes," would not the whole universe leak away through its yawning gap into nothingness?

For two years Satish wandered from place to place,—we had no contact with him. We threw ourselves with all the greater zeal into our self-appointed tasks. We made it a special point to shock those who professed belief in any kind of religion, and the fields of good work we selected were such that not a good soul had a good word left for us. Satish had been our flower; when he dropped off, we, the thorns, cast off our sheaths and gloried in our sharpness.

3

Two years had passed since we lost sight of Satish. My mind revolted against harbouring the least thing evil against him, nevertheless I could not help suspecting that the high pitch at which he used to be kept strung must have been flattened down by this shock.

Uncle Jagamohan had once said of a *Sannyasin:*[12] "As the money-changer tests the ring of each coin, so does the world test each man by the response he gives to shocks of loss and pain, and the resistance he offers to the craze for cheap salvation. Those who fail to ring true are cast aside as worthless. These wandering ascetics have been so rejected, as being unfit to take part in the world's commerce,—yet the vagabonds swagger about, boasting that it is they who have renounced the world! The worthy are permitted no loophole of escape from duty,—only withered leaves are allowed to fall off the tree."

Had it come to this, that Satish, of all people, had joined the ranks of the withered and the worthless? Was he, then, fated to leave on the black touchstone of bereavement his mark of spuriousness?

While assailed with these misgivings, news suddenly reached us that Satish (our Satish, if you please!) was making the heavens resound with his cymbals in some out-of-the-way village, singing frenzied *kirtans*[13] as a follower of Lilananda Swami, the Vaishnava revivalist!

---

[12] *Sannyasin:* A Brahman ascetic.

[13] *kirtans:* The *kirtan* is a kind of devotional oratorio sung to the accompaniment of drums and cymbals, the libretto ranging over the whole gamut of human emotions, which are made the vehicle for communion with the Divine Lover. As their feelings get worked up, the singers begin to sway their bodies with, and finally dance to, the rhythm. [Translator.]

It had passed my comprehension, when I first began to know Satish, how he could ever have come to be an atheist. I was now equally at a loss to understand how Lilananda Swami could have managed to lead him in such a dance with his *kirtans.*

And how on earth were we to show our faces? What laughter there would be in the camp of the enemy,—whose number, thanks to our folly, was legion! Our band waxed mightily wroth with Satish. Many of them said they had known from the very first that there was no rational substance in him,—he was all frothy idealism. And I now discovered how much I really loved Satish. He had dealt his ardent sect of atheists their death-blow, yet I could not be angry with him.

Off I started to hunt up Lilananda Swami. River after river I crossed, and trudged over endless fields. The nights I spent in grocers' shops. At last in one of the villages I came up against Satish's party.

It was then two o'clock in the afternoon. I had been hoping to catch Satish alone. Impossible! The cottage which was honoured with the Swami's presence was packed all round with crowds of his disciples. There had been *kirtans* all the morning; those who had come from a distance were now waiting to have their meal served.

As soon as Satish caught sight of me, he dashed up and embraced me fervidly. I was staggered. Satish had always been extremely reserved. His outward calm had been the only measure of his depth of feeling. He now appeared as though intoxicated.

The Swami was resting in the front room, with the door ajar. He could see us. At once came the call, in a deep voice: "Satish!"

Satish was back inside, all in a flurry.

"Who is that?" inquired the Swami.

"Srivilas, a great friend of mine," Satish reported.

During these years I had managed to make a name for myself in our little world. A learned Englishman had remarked, on hearing one of my English speeches: "The man has a wonderful———." But let that be. Why add to the number of my enemies? Suffice it to say that, from the students up to the students' grandparents, the reputation had travelled round that I was a rampaging atheist who could bestride the English language and race her over the hurdles at breakneck speed in the most marvellous manner.

I somehow felt that the Swami was pleased to have me here. He sent for me. I merely hinted at the usual salutation as I entered his room,—that is to say, my joined hands were uplifted, but my head was not lowered.

This did not escape the Swami. "Here, Satish!" he ordered. "Fill me that pipe of mine."

Satish set to work. But as he lit the tinder, it was I who was set ablaze within. Moreover, I was getting fidgety, not knowing where to sit. The only seat in the room was a wooden bedstead on which was spread the Swami's carpet. Not that I confessed to any qualms about occupying a corner of the same carpet on which the great man was installed, but somehow my sitting down did not come off. I remained standing near the door.

It appeared that the Swami was aware of my having won the Premchand-Roychand[14] scholarship. "My son," he said to me, "it is good for the pearl diver if he succeeds in reaching the bottom, but he would die if he had to stay there. He must come up for the free breath of life. If you would live, you must now come up to the light, out of the depths of your learning. You have enjoyed the fruits of your scholarship, now try a taste of the joys of its renunciation."

Satish handed his Master the lighted pipe and sat down on the bare floor near his feet. The Swami leant back and stretched his legs out towards Satish, who began gently to massage them. This was more than I could stand. I left the room. I could, of course, see that this ordering about of Satish and making him fetch and carry was deliberately directed at me.

The Swami went on resting. All the guests were duly served by the householder with a meal of kedgeree. From five o'clock the *kirtans* started again and went on till ten in the night.

When I got Satish alone at last, I said to him: "Look here, Satish! You have been brought up in the atmosphere of freedom from infancy. How have you managed to get yourself entangled in this kind of bondage today? Is Uncle Jagamohan, then, so utterly dead?"

Partly because the playfulness of affection prompted it, partly, perhaps, because precision of description required it, Satish used to reverse the first two syllables of my name and call me Visri.[15]

"Visri," he replied, "while Uncle was alive he gave me freedom in life's field of work,—the freedom which the child gets in the playground. After his death it is he, again, who has given me freedom on the high seas of emotion,—the freedom which the child gains when it comes back to its mother's arms. I have enjoyed to the full the freedom of life's day-time; why should I now deprive myself of the freedom of its evening? Be sure that both these are the gift of that same uncle of ours."

"Whatever you may say," I persisted, "Uncle could have nothing to do with this kind of pipe-filling, leg-massaging business. Surely this is no picture of freedom."

"That," argued Satish, "was the freedom on shore. There Uncle gave full liberty of action to our limbs. This is freedom on the ocean. Here the confinement of the ship is necessary for our progress. That is why my Master keeps me bound to his service. This massaging is helping me to cross over."

"It does not sound so bad," I admitted, "the way you put it. But, all the same, I have no patience with a man who can thrust out his legs at you like that."

"He can do it," explained Satish, "because he has no need of such service. Had it been for himself, he might have felt ashamed to ask it. The need is mine."

I realised that the world into which Satish had been transported had no place for me, his particular friend. The person, whom Satish has so effusively embraced, was not Srivilas, but a representative of all humanity,—just an idea. Such ideas are

---

[14] **the Premchand-Roychand:** The highest prize at Calcutta University. [Translator.]

[15] **Visri:** Ungainly, ugly. [Translator.]

like wine. When they get into the head any one can be embraced and wept over—I, only as much as anybody else. But whatever joys may be the portion of the ecstatic one, what can such embrace signify to me, the other party? What satisfaction am I to get, merely to be accounted one of the ripples on a grand, difference-obliterating flood,—I, the individual I?

However, further argument was clearly useless. Nor could I make up my mind to desert Satish. So, as his satellite, I also danced from village to village, carried along the current of *kirtan* singing.

The intoxication of it gradually took hold of me. I also embraced all and sundry, wept without provocation, and tended the feet of the Master. And one day, in a moment of curious exaltation, Satish was revealed to me in a light for which there can be no other name than divine.

4

With the capture of two such egregious, college-educated atheists as we were, the fame of Lilananda Swami spread far and wide. His Calcutta disciples now pressed him to take up his headquarters at the metropolis.

So Swami Lilananda came on to Calcutta.

Shivatosh had been a devoted follower of Lilananda. Whenever the Swami visited Calcutta he had stayed with Shivatosh. And it was the one delight of Shivatosh's life to serve the Master, together with all his disciples, when they thus honoured his house. When he died he bequeathed all his property to the Swami, leaving only a life-interest in the income to his young childless widow. It was his hope that this house of his would become a pilgrim-centre for the sect.

This was the house where we now went into residence.

During our ecstatic progress through the villages I had been in an elated mood, which I now found it difficult to keep up in Calcutta. In the wonderland of emotion, where we had been revelling, the mystic drama of the courting of the Bride within us and the Bridegroom who is everywhere was being played. And a fitting accompaniment to it had been the symphony of the broad grazing greens, the shaded ferry landing-places, the enraptured expanse of the noonday leisure, the deep evening silences vibrant with the tremolo of cicadas. Ours had been a dream progress to which the open skies of the countryside offered no obstacle. But with our arrival at Calcutta we knocked our heads against its hardness, we got jostled by its crowds, and our dream was at an end.

Yet, was not this the same Calcutta where, within the confines of our students' lodgings, we had once put our whole soul into our studies, by day and by night; where we had pondered over and discussed the problems of our country with our fellow-students in the College Square; where we had served as volunteers at the holding of our National Assemblies; where we had responded to the call of Uncle Jagamohan, and taken the vow to free our minds from all slavery imposed by Society or State? Yes, it was in this self-same Calcutta that, in the flood-tide of our youth, we had pursued our course, regardless of the revilement of stranger and kindred alike, proudly breasting all contrary currents like a boat in full sail. Why, then, should we now fail, in this whirlpool of suffering humanity, ridden with pleasure and pain, driven by hunger and thirst, to keep up the exaltation proper to our tear-drenched cult of emotional Communion?

As I manfully made the attempt, I was beset with doubts at every step. Was I then a mere weakling: unfaithful to my ideal: unworthy of strenuous endeavour? When I turned to Satish, to see how he fared, I found on his countenance no sign to show that Calcutta, for him, represented any geographical reality whatsoever. In the mystic world where he dwelt, all this city life meant no more than a mirage.

5

We two friends took up our quarters, with the Master, in Shivatosh's house. We had come to be his chief disciples, and he would have us constantly near his person.

With our Master and our fellow-disciples we were absorbed day and night in discussing emotions in general and the philosophy of spiritual emotion in particular. Into the very thick of the abstruse complexities which thus engaged our attention, the ripple of a woman's laughter would now and again find its way from the inner apartments.[16] Sometimes there would be heard, in a clear, high-toned voice, the call "Bami!"—evidently a maid-servant of that name.

These were doubtless but trivial interruptions for minds soaring, almost to vanishing point, into the empyrean of idea. But to me they came as a grateful shower of rain upon a parched and thirsty soil. When little touches of life, like shed flower petals, were blown across from the unknown world behind the wall, then all in a moment I could understand that the wonderland of our quest was just there,—where the keys jingled, tied to the corner of Bami's sari; where the sound of the broom rose from the swept floor, and the smell of the cooking from the kitchen,—all trifles, but all true. That world, with its mingling of fine and coarse, bitter and sweet,—that itself was the heaven where Emotion truly held sway.

The name of the widow was Damini. We could catch momentary glimpses of her through opening doors and flapping curtains. But the two of us grew to be so much part and parcel of the Master as to share his privilege,[17] and very soon these doors and curtains were no longer barriers in our case.

Damini[18] was the lightning which gleams within the massed clouds of July. Without, the curves of youth enveloped her in their fulness, within flashed fitful fires. Thus runs an entry in Satish's diary:

> In Nonibala I have seen the Universal Woman in one of her aspects,—the woman who takes on herself the whole burden of sin, who gives up life itself for the sinner's sake, and in dying leaves for the world the balm of immortality. In Damini I see another aspect of Universal Woman. This one has nothing to do with death,—she is the Artist of the Art of Life. She blossoms out, in limitless profusion, in form and

---

[16] **inner apartments:** The women's part of the house. [Translator.]

[17] Women do not observe *purdah* with religious ascetics. [Translator.]

[18] **Damini:** Lightning. [Translator.]

scent and movement. She is not for rejection; refuses to entertain the ascetic; and is vowed to resist the least farthing of payment to the tax-gathering Winter Wind.

It is necessary to relate Damini's previous history.

At the time when the coffers of her father, Annada, were overflowing with proceeds of his jute business, Damini was married to Shivatosh. So long, Shivatosh's fortune had consisted only in his pedigree: It could now count a more substantial addition. Annada bestowed on his son-in-law a house in Calcutta and sufficient money to keep him for life. There were also lavish gifts of furniture and ornaments made to his daughter.

Annada, further, made a futile attempt to take Shivatosh into his own business. But the latter had no interest in worldly concerns. An astrologer had once predicted to Shivatosh that, on the happening of a special conjunction of the stars, his soul would gain its emancipation whilst still in the flesh. From that day he lived in this hope alone, and ceased to find charm in riches, or even in objects still more charming. It was while in this frame of mind that he had become a disciple of Lilananda Swami.

In the meantime, with the subsidence of the jute boom, the full force of the adverse wind caught the heavy-laden bark of Annada's fortune and toppled it over. All his property was sold up and he had hardly enough left to make a bare living.

One evening Shivatosh came into the inner apartments and said to his wife: "The Master is here. He has some words of advice for you and bids you attend."

"I cannot go to him now," answered Damini. "I haven't the time."

What? No time! Shivatosh went up nearer and found his wife seated in the gathering dusk, in front of the open safe, with her ornaments spread out before her. "What in the world is keeping you?" inquired he.

"I am arranging my jewels," was the reply.

So that was the reason for her lack of time. Indeed!

The next day, when Damini opened the safe, she found her jewel-box missing. "My jewels?" she exclaimed, turning inquiringly to her husband.

"But you offered them to the Master. Did not his call reach you at the very moment? — for he sees into the minds of men. He has deigned, in his mercy, to save you from the lure of pelf."

Damini's indignation rose to white heat.

"Give me back my ornaments!" she commanded.

"Why, what will you do with them?"

"They were my father's gift to me. I would return them to him."

"They have gone to a better place," said Shivatosh. "Instead of pandering to worldly needs they are dedicated to the service of devotees."

That is how the tyrannical imposition of faith began. And the pious ritual of exorcism, in all its cruelty, continued to be practised in order to rid Damini's mind of its mundane affections and desires.

So, while her father and her little brother were starving by inches, Damini had to prepare daily, with her own hands, meals for the sixty or seventy disciples who thronged the house with the Master. She would sometimes rebelliously leave out the salt, or contrive to get the viands scorched, but that did not avail to gain her any respite from her penance.

At this juncture Shivatosh died: and in departing he awarded his wife the supreme penalty for her want of faith,—he committed his widow, with all her belongings, to the guardianship of the Master.

6

The house was in a constant tumult with rising waves of fervour. Devotees kept streaming in from all quarters to sit at the feet of the Master. And yet Damini, who had gained the Presence without effort of her own, thrust aside her good fortune with contumely.

Did the Master call her for some special mark of his favour she would keep aloof, pleading a headache. If he had occasion to complain of some special omission of personal attention on her part, she would confess to have been away at the theatre. The excuse was lacking in truth, but not in rudeness.

The other women disciples were aghast at Damini's ways. First, her attire was not such as widows[19] should affect. Secondly, she showed no eagerness to drink in the Master's words of wisdom. Lastly, her demeanour had none of the reverential restraint which the Master's presence demanded. "What a shame," exclaimed they. "We have seen many awful women, but not one so outrageous."

The Swami used to smile. "The Lord," said he, "takes a special delight in wrestling with a valiant opponent. When Damini has to own defeat, her surrender will be absolute."

He began to display an exaggerated tolerance for her contumacy. That vexed Damini still more, for she looked on it as a more cunning form of punishment. And one day the Master caught her in a fit of laughter, mimicking to one of her companions the excessive suavity of his manner towards herself. Still he had not a word of rebuke, and repeated simply that the final *dénouement* would be all the more extraordinary, to which end the poor thing was but the instrument of Providence, and so herself not to blame.

This was how we found her when we first came. The *dénouement* was indeed extraordinary. I can hardly bring myself to write on further. Moreover, what happened is so difficult to tell. The network of suffering, which is woven behind the scenes, is not of any pattern set by the Scriptures, nor of our own devising. Hence the frequent discords between the inner and the outer life—discords that hurt, and wail forth in tears.

There came, at length, the dawn when the harsh crust of rebelliousness cracked and fell to pieces, and the flower of self-surrender came through and held up its dew-washed face. Damini's service became so beautiful in its truth that it descended on the devotees like the blessing of the very Divinity of their devotions.

---

[19] Hindu widows in Bengal are supposed to dress in simple white (sometimes plain brown silk), without border, or ornamentation. [Translator.]

And when Damini's lightning flashes had matured into a steady radiance, Satish looked on her and saw that she was beautiful; but I say this, that Satish gazed only on her beauty, failing to see Damini herself.

In Satish's room there hung a portrait of the Swami sitting in meditation, done on a porcelain medallion. One day he found it on the floor, — in fragments. He put it down to his pet cat. But other little mischiefs began to follow, which were clearly beyond the powers of the cat. There was some kind of disturbance in the air, which now and again broke out in unseen electric shocks.

How others felt, I know not, but a growing pain gnawed at my heart. Sometimes I thought that this constant ecstasy of emotion was proving too much for me. I wanted to give it all up and run away. The old work of teaching the leather-dealers' children seemed, in its unalloyed prose, to be now calling me back.

One afternoon when the Master was taking his siesta, and the weary disciples were at rest, Satish for some reason went off into his own room at this unusual hour. His progress was suddenly arrested at the threshold. There was Damini, her thick tresses dishevelled, lying prone on the floor, beating her head on it as she moaned: "Oh, you stone, you stone, have mercy on me, have mercy and kill me outright!"

Satish, trembling from head to foot with a nameless fear, fled from the room.

7

It was a rule with Swami Lilananda to go off once a year to some remote, out-of-the-way place, away from the crowd. With the month of Magh[20] came round the time for his journey. Satish was to attend on him.

I asked to go too. I was worn to the very bone with the incessant emotional excitement of our cult, and felt greatly in need of physical movement as well as of mental quiet.

The Master sent for Damini. "My little mother," he told her, "I am about to leave you for the duration of my travels. Let me arrange for your stay meanwhile with your aunt, as usual."

"I would accompany you," said Damini.

"You could hardly bear it, I am afraid. Our journeying will be troublesome."

"Of course I can bear it," she answered. "Pray have no concern about any trouble of mine."

Lilananda was pleased at this proof of Damini's devotion. In former years, this opportunity had been Damini's holiday time, — the one thing to which she had looked forward through the preceding months. "Miraculous!" thought the Swami. "How wondrously does even stone become as wax in the Lord's melting-pot of emotion."

So Damini had her way, and came along with us.

---

[20] **month of Magh:** January–February. [Translator.]

8

The spot we reached, after hours of tramping in the sun, was a little promontory on the sea-coast, shaded by cocoa-nut palms. Profound was the solitude and the tranquillity which reigned there, as the gentle rustle of the palm tassels merged into the idle plash of the girdling sea. The place looked like a tired hand of the sleepy shore, limply fallen upon the surface of the waters. On this open hand stood a bluish-green hill, and inside the hill was a sculptured cave-temple of bygone days, which, for all its serene beauty, was the cause of much disquiet amongst antiquarians as to the origin, style, and subject-matter of its sculptures.

Our intention had been to return to the village where we had made our halt, after paying a visit to this temple. That was now seen to be impossible. The day was fast declining, and the moon was long past its full. Lilananda Swami at length decided that we should pass the night in the cave.

All four of us sat down to rest on the sandy soil beneath the cocoa-nut groves fringing the sea. The sunset glow bent lower and lower over the western horizon, as though Day was making its parting obeisance to approaching Night.

The Master's voice broke forth in song — one of his own composition:

> *The day has waned, when at last we meet at the turning;*
> *And as I try to see thy face, the last ray of evening fades into the night.*

We had heard the song before, but never with such complete *rapport* between singer, audience, and surroundings. Damini was affected to tears. The Swami went on to the second verse:

> *I shall not grieve that the darkness comes between thee and my sight, —*
> *Only, for a moment, stand before me, that I may kiss thy feet and wipe them*
> *   with my hair.*

When he had come to the end, the placid even-tide, enveloping sky and waters, was filled, like some ripe, golden fruit, with the bursting sweetness of melody.

Damini rose and went up to the Master. As she prostrated herself at his feet, her loose hair slipped off her shoulders and was scattered over the ground on either side. She remained long thus before she raised her head.

9 (From Satish's Diary)

There were several chambers within the temple. In one of these I spread my blanket and laid myself down. The darkness pent up inside the cave seemed alive, like some great black monster, its damp breath bedewing my body. I began to be haunted by the idea that this was the first of all created animals, born in the beginning of time, with no eyes or ears, but just one enormous appetite. Confined within this cavern for endless ages it knew nothing, having no mind; but having sensibility it felt; and wept and wept in silence.

Fatigue overpowered my limbs like a dead weight, but sleep came not. Some bird, or perhaps bat, flitted in from the outside, or out from the inside, — its wings beating the air as it flew from darkness to darkness; when the draught reached my body it sent a shiver through me, making my flesh creep.

I thought I would go and get some sleep outside. But I could not recollect the direction in which the entrance was. As I crawled on my hands and knees along the way which appeared the right one, I knocked against the cave wall. When I tried a different side, I nearly tumbled into a hollow in which the water dripping through the cracks had collected.

I crawled back to my blanket and stretched myself on it again. Again was I possessed with the fancy that I had been taken right into the creature's maw and could not extricate myself; that I was the victim of a blind hunger which was licking me with its slimy saliva, through which I would be sucked and digested noiselessly, little by little.

I felt that only sleep could save me. My living, waking consciousness was evidently unable to bear such close embrace of this horrible, suffocating obscurity—fit only for the dead to suffer. I cannot say how long after it came upon me,—or whether it was really sleep at all,—but a thin veil of oblivion fell at last over my senses. And while in such half-conscious state I actually felt a deep breathing somewhere near my bare feet. Surely it was not that primeval creature of my imagining!

Then something seemed to cling about my feet. Some real wild animal this time,—was my first thought. But there was nothing furry in its touch. What if it was some species of serpent or reptile, of features and body unknown to me, of whose method of absorbing its prey I could form no idea? All the more loathsome seemed the softness of it,—of this terrible, unknown mass of hunger.

What between dread and disgust, I could not even utter a cry. I tried to push it away with ineffectual thrusts with my legs. Its face seemed to be touching my feet, on which its panting breath fell thickly. What kind of a face had it, I wondered. I launched a more vigorous kick as the stupor left me. I had at first supposed there was no fur, but what felt like a mane now brushed across my legs. I struggled up into a sitting posture.

Something stole away in the darkness. There was also a curious kind of sound. Could it have been sobbing?

Chapter III
Damini

1

We are back in our quarters in the village, near a temple, in a two-storeyed house belonging to one of the Swami's disciples, which had been placed at our disposal. Since our return we see but little of Damini, though she is still in charge of our household affairs. She has made friends with the neighbouring women, and spends most of her spare time in going about with them from one house to another.

The Swami is not particularly pleased. Damini's heart, thinks he, does not yet respond to the call of the ethereal heights. All its fondness is still for earthen walls. In her daily work of looking after the devotees,—formerly like an act of worship with her,—a trace of weariness has become noticeable. She makes mistakes. Her service has lost its radiance.

The Master, at heart, begins to be afraid of her again. Between her brows there darkens a gathering frown; her temple is ruffled with fitful breezes; the loosening knot of her hair lowers over her neck; the pressure of her lips, the gleams from the corner of her eye, her sudden wayward gestures presage a rebellious storm.

The Swami turned to his *kirtans* with renewed attention. The wandering bee, he hoped, would be brought to drink deep of the honey, once enticed in by its fragrance. And so the short cool days were filled to the brim with the foaming wine of ecstatic song.

But no, Damini refused to be caught. The exasperated Swami laughed out one day: "The Lord is out hunting: the resolute flight of the deer adds zest to the chase: but succumb she must, in the end."

When we had first come to know Damini, she was not to be found among the band of devotees clustering round the Master. That, however, did not attract our notice then. But now, her empty place had become conspicuous. Her frequent absences smote us tempestuously.

The Swami put this down to her pride, and that hurt his own pride. As for me,—but what does it matter what I thought?

One day the Master mustered up courage to say in his most dulcet tones: "Damini, my little mother, do you think you will have a little time to spare this afternoon? If so———"

"No," said Damini.

"Would you mind telling me why?"

"I have to assist in making sweetmeats at the Nandi's."

"Sweetmeats? What for?"

"They have a wedding on."

"Is your assistance so indispensably———?"

"I promised to be there."

Damini whisked out of the room without waiting for further questioning.

Satish, who was there with us, was dumbfounded. So many men of learning, wealth, and fame had surrendered at the feet of the Master, and this slip of a girl,—what gave her such hardihood of assurance?

Another evening Damini happened to be at home. The Master had addressed himself to some specially important topic. After his discourse had progressed awhile, something in our faces gave him pause. He found our attention wandering. On looking round he discovered that Damini, who had been seated in the room, sewing in hand, was not to be seen. He understood the reason of our distraction. She was not there, not there, not there,—the refrain now kept worrying him too. He began to lose the thread of his discourse, and at last gave it up altogether.

The Swami left the room and went off to Damini's door. "Damini," he called. "Why are you all alone here? Will you not come and join us?"

"I am engaged," said Damini.

The baffled Swami could see, as he passed by the half-open door, a captive kite in a cage. It had somehow struck against the telegraph wires, and had been lying wounded when Damini rescued it from the pestering crows, and she had been tending it since.

The kite was not the only object which engaged Damini's solicitude. There was a mongrel pup, whose looks were on a par with its breeding. It was discord personified.

Whenever it heard our cymbals, it would look up to heaven and voice forth a prolonged complaint. The gods, being fortunate, did not feel bound to give it a hearing. The poor mortals whose ears happened to be within reach were woefully agonised.

One afternoon, when Damini was engaged in practising horticulture in sundry cracked pots on the roof-terrace, Satish came up and asked her point-blank: "Why is it you have given up coming over there altogether?"

"Over where?"

"To the Master."

"Why, what need have you people of me?"

"We have no need, — but surely the need is yours."

"No, no!" flung out Damini. "Not at all, not at all!"

Taken aback by her heat, Satish gazed at her in silence. Then he mused aloud: "Your mind lacks peace. If you would gain peace————"

"Peace from you, — you who are consumed day and night with your excitement, — where have *you* the peace to give? Leave me alone, I beg and pray you. I was at peace. I would be at peace."

"You see but the waves on the surface. If you have the patience to dive deep, you will find all calm there."

Damini wrung her hands as she cried: "I beseech you, for the Lord's sake, don't insist on my diving downwards. If only you will give up all hope of my conversion, I may yet live."

2

My experience has never been large enough to enable me to penetrate the mysteries of woman's mind. Judging from what little I have seen of the surface from the outside, I have come to the belief that women are ever ready to bestow their heart where sorrow cannot but be their lot. They will either string their garland of acceptance[21] for some brute of a man who will trample it under foot and defile it in the mire of his passions, or dedicate it to some idealist, on whose neck it will get no hold, attenuated as he is, like the dream-stuff of his imaginings.

When left to do their own choosing, women invariably reject ordinary men like me, made up of gross and fine, who know woman to be just woman, — that is to say, neither a doll of clay made to serve for our pastime, nor a transcendental melody to be evoked at our master touch. They reject us, because we have neither the forceful delusions of the flesh, nor the roseate illusions of fancy: we can neither break them on the wheel of our desire, nor melt them in the glow of our fervour to be cast in the mould of our ideal.

Because we know them only for what they are, they may be friendly, but cannot love us. We are their true refuge, for they can rely on our devotion; but our self-dedication comes so easy that they forget it has a price. So the only reward we get is to be used for their purposes; perchance to win their respect. But I am afraid my

---

[21] **garland of acceptance:** In the old days, when a girl had to choose between several suitors, she signified her choice by putting a garland round the neck of the accepted one. [Translator.]

excursions into the region of psychology are merely due to personal grievances, which have my own experience behind them. The fact probably is, what we thus lose is really our gain,—anyway, that is how we may console ourselves.

Damini avoids the Master because she cannot bear him. She fights shy of Satish because for him her feelings are of the opposite description. I am the only person, near at hand, with whom there is no question either of love or hate. So whenever I am with her, Damini talks away to me of unimportant matters concerning the old days, the present times, or the daily happenings at the neighbours' houses. These talks usually take place on the shaded part of the roof-terrace, which serves as a passage between our several rooms on the second storey, where Damini sits slicing betel-nuts.

What I could not understand was, how these trifling talks should have attracted the notice of Satish's emotion-clouded vision. Even suppose the circumstance was not so trifling, had I not often been told that, in the world where Satish dwelt, there were no such disturbing things as circumstances at all? The Mystic Union, in which personified cosmic forces were assisting, was an eternal drama, not an historical episode. Those who are rapt with the undying flute strains, borne along by the ceaseless zephyrs which play on the banks of the ever-flowing Jamuna[22] of that mystic paradise, have no eyes or ears left for the ephemeral doings immediately around them. This much at least is certain, that before our return from the cave, Satish used to be much denser in his perception of worldly events.

For this difference I may have been partly responsible. I also had begun to absent myself from our *kirtans* and discourses, perhaps with a frequency which could not elude even Satish. One day he came round on inquiry, and found me running after Damini's mongoose,—a recent acquisition,—trying to lure it into bondage with a pot of milk, which I had procured from the local milkman. This occupation, viewed as an excuse, was simply hopeless. It could easily have waited till the end of our sitting. For the matter of that, the best thing clearly would have been to leave the mongoose to its own devices, thus at one stroke demonstrating my adherence to the two principal tenets of our cult,—Compassion for all creatures, and Passion for the Lord.

That is why, when Satish came up, I had to feel ashamed. I put down the pot, then and there, and tried to edge away along the path which led back to self-respect.

But Damini's behaviour took me by surprise. She was not in the least abashed as she asked: "Where are you off to, Srivilas Babu?"

I scratched my head, as I mumbled: "I was thinking of joining the———"

"They must have finished by this time. Do sit down."

This coming from Damini, in the presence of Satish, made my ears burn.

Damini turned to Satish. "I am in awful trouble with the mongoose," she said. "Last night it stole a chicken from the Mussulman quarters over there. I dare not leave it loose any longer. Srivilas Babu has promised to look out for a nice big hamper to keep it in."

---

[22] **Jamuna:** A major river in Bengal that flows into the Ganges.

It seemed to me that it was my devotion to her which Damini was using the mongoose to show off. I was reminded how the Swami had given orders to Satish so as to impress me. The two were the same thing.

Satish made no reply, and his departure was somewhat abrupt. I gazed on Damini and could see her eyes flash out as they followed his disappearing figure; while on her lips there set a hard, enigmatic smile.

What conclusion Damini had come to she herself knew best; the only result apparent to me was that she began to send for me on all kinds of flimsy pretexts. Sometimes she would make sweetmeats, which she pressed on me. One day I could not help suggesting: "Let's offer some to Satish as well."

"That would only annoy him," said Damini.

And it happened that Satish, passing that way, caught me in the act of being thus regaled.

In the drama which was being played, the hero and the heroine spoke their parts "aside." I was the one character who, being of no consequence, had to speak out. This sometimes made me curse my lot; none the less, I could not withstand the temptation of the petty cash with which I was paid off, from day to day, for taking up the rôle of middleman.

3

For some days Satish clanged his cymbals and danced his *kirtans* with added vigour. Then one day he came to me and said: "We cannot keep Damini with us any longer."

"Why?" I asked.

"We must free ourselves altogether from the influence of women."

"If that be a necessity," said I, "there must be something radically wrong with our system."

Satish stared at me in amazement.

"Woman is a natural phenomenon," I continued, undaunted, "who will have her place in the world, however much we may try to get rid of her. If your spiritual welfare depends on ignoring her existence, then its pursuit will be like the chasing of a phantom, and will so put you to shame, when the illusion is gone, that you will not know where to hide yourself."

"Oh, stop your philosophising!" exclaimed Satish. "I was talking practical politics. It is only too evident that women are emissaries of Maya,[23] and at Maya's behest ply on us their blandishments,—for they cannot fulfil the design of their Mistress unless they overpower our reason. So we must steer clear of them if we would keep our intellect free."

I was about to make my reply, when Satish stopped me with a gesture, and went on: "Visri, old fellow! let me tell you plainly: if the hand of Maya is not visible to you, that is because you have allowed yourself to be caught in her net. The vision of beauty with which she has ensnared you to-day will vanish, and with the beauty will disappear the spectacles of desire, through which you now see it as greater than all

---

[23] **Maya:** Or Mahamaya, the Hindu goddess who produces illusions of sensory experience.

RABINDRANATH TAGORE

the world. Where the noose of Maya is so glaringly obvious, why be foolhardy enough to take risks?"

"I admit all that," I rejoined. "But, my dear fellow, the all-pervading net of Maya was not cast by my hands, nor do I know the way to escape through it. Since we have not the power to evade Maya, our spiritual striving should help us, while acknowledging her, to rise above her. Because it does not take such a course, we have to flounder about in vain attempts to cut away the half of Truth."

"Well, well, let's have your idea a little more clearly," said Satish.

"We must sail the boat of our life," I proceeded, "along the current of nature, in order to reach beyond it. Our problem is, not how to get rid of this current, but how to keep the boat afloat in its channel until it is through. For that, a rudder is necessary."

"You people who have ceased to be loyal to the Master,— how can I make you understand that in *him* we have just this rudder? You would regulate your spiritual life according to your own whims. That way death lies!" Satish went to the Master's chamber, and fell to tending his feet with fervour.

The same evening, when Satish lit the Master's pipe, he also put forward his plaint against Maya and her emissaries. The smoking of one pipe, however, did not suffice for its adjudication. Evening after evening, pipe after pipe was exhausted, yet the Master was unable to make up his mind.

From the very beginning Damini had given the Swami no end of trouble. Now the girl had managed to set up this eddy in the midst of the smooth course of the devotees' progress. But Shivatosh had thrown her and her belongings so absolutely on the Master's hands that he knew not how or where to cast her off. What made it more difficult still was that he harboured a secret fear of his ward.

And Satish, in spite of all the doubled and quadrupled enthusiasm which he put into his *kirtans,* in spite of all the pipe-filling and massaging in which he tried to rest his heart, was not allowed to forget for a moment that Maya had taken up her position right across the line of his spiritual advance.

One day some *kirtan* singers of repute had arrived, and were to sing in the evening at the temple next door. The *kirtan* would last far into the night. I managed to slip away after the preliminary overture, having no doubt that, in so thick a crowd, no one would notice my absence.

Damini that evening had completely thrown off her reserve. Things which are difficult to speak of, which refuse to leave one's choking throat, flowed from her lips so simply, so sweetly. It was as if she had suddenly come upon some secret recess in her heart, so long hidden away in darkness,—as if, by some strange chance, she had gained the opportunity to stand before her own self, face to face.

Just at this time Satish came up from behind and stood there hesitating, without our being aware of it at the moment. Not that Damini was saying anything very particular, but there were tears in her eyes,— all her words, in fact, were then welling up from some tear-flooded depth. When Satish arrived, the *kirtan* could not have been anywhere near its end. I divined that he must have been goaded with repeated inward urgings to have left the temple then.

As Satish came round into our view, Damini rose with a start, wiped her eyes, and made off towards her room. Satish, with a tremor in his voice, said: "Damini, will you listen to me? I would have a word with you."

Damini slowly retraced her steps, and came and sat down again. I made as though to take myself off, but an imploring glance from her restrained me from stirring. Satish, who seemed to have made some kind of effort meanwhile, came straight to the point.

"The need," said he to Damini, "which brought the rest of us to the Master, was not yours when you came to him."

"No," avowed Damini expectantly.

"Why, then, do you stay amongst his devotees?"

Damini's eyes flamed up as she cried: "Why do I stay? Because I did not come of my own accord! I was a helpless creature, and everyone knew my lack of faith. Yet I was bound hand and foot by your devotees in this dungeon of devotion. What avenue of escape have you left me?"

"We have now decided," stated Satish, "that if you would go to stay with some relative all your expenses will be found."

"You have decided, have you?"

"Yes."

"Well, then,—I have not!"

"Why, how will that inconvenience you?"

"Am I a pawn in your game, that you devotees should play me, now this way, now the other?"

Satish was struck dumb.

"I did not come," continued Damini, "wanting to please your devotees. And I am not going away at the bidding of the lot of you, merely because I don't happen to please you!"

Damini covered her face with her hands and burst out sobbing as she ran into her room and slammed the door.

Satish did not return to the *kirtan* singing. He sank down in a corner of the adjoining roof-terrace and brooded there in silence.

The sound of the breakers on the distant seashore came, wafted along the south breeze, like despairing sighs, rising up to the watching star clusters, from the very heart of the Earth.

I spent the night wandering round and round along the dark, deserted village lanes.

4

The World of Reality has made a determined onslaught on the Mystic Paradise, within the confines of which the Master sought to keep Satish and myself content by repeatedly filling for us the cup of symbolism with the nectar of idea. Now the clash of the actual with the symbolic bids fair to overturn the latter and spill its emotional contents in the dust. The Master is not blind to this danger.

Satish is no longer himself. Like a paper kite, with its regulating knot gone, he is still high in the skies, but may at any moment begin to gyrate groundwards. There is no falling off as yet in the outward rigour of his devotional and disciplinary exercises, but a closer scrutiny reveals the totter of weakening.

As for my condition, Damini has left nothing so vague in it as to require any guess-work. The more she notices the fear in the Master's face, and the pain in Satish's, the oftener she makes me dance attendance on her.

At last it came to this, that when we were engaged in talk with the Master, Damini would sometimes appear in the doorway and interrupt us with: "Srivilas Babu, would you mind coming over this way?" without even condescending to add what I was wanted for.

The Swami would glance up at me; Satish would glance up at me; I would hesitate for a moment between them and her; then I would glance up at the door,—and in a trice I was off the fence and out of the room. An effort would be made, after my exit, to go on with the talk, but the effort would soon get the better of the talk, whereupon the latter would stop.

Everything seemed to be falling to pieces around us. The old compactness was gone.

We two had come to be the pillars of the sect. The Master could not give up either of us without a struggle. So he ventured once more to make an overture to Damini. "My little mother," said he, "the time is coming for us to proceed to the more arduous part of our journey. You had better return from here."

"Return where?"

"Home, to your aunt."

"That cannot be."

"Why?" asked the Swami.

"First of all," said Damini, "she is not my own aunt at all. Why should she bear my burden?"

"All your expenses shall be borne by us."

"Expenses are not the only burden. It is no part of her duty to be saddled with looking after me."

"But, Damini," urged the Swami in his desperation, "can I keep you with me for ever?"

"Is that a question for me to answer?"

"But where will you go when I am dead?"

"I was never allowed," returned Damini icily, "to have the responsibility of thinking that out. I have been made to realise too well that in this world I have neither home nor property; nothing at all to call my own. That is what makes my burden so heavy to bear. It pleased you to take it up. You shall not now cast it on another!"

Damini went off.

"Lord, have mercy!" sighed the Swami.

Damini had laid on me the command to procure for her some good Bengali books. I need hardly say that by "good" Damini did not mean spiritual, of the quality affected by our sect. Nor need I pause to make it clear that Damini had no compunction in asking anything from me. It has not taken her long to find out that making demands on me was the easiest way of making me amends. Some kinds of trees are all the better for being pruned: that was the kind of person I seemed to be where Damini was concerned.

Well, the books I ordered were unmitigatedly modern. The author was distinctly less influenced by Manu[24] than by Man himself. The packet was delivered by the postman to the Swami. He raised his eyebrows, as he opened it, and asked: "Hullo, Srivilas, what are these for?"

I remained silent.

The Master gingerly turned over some of the pages, as he remarked for my benefit that he had never thought much of the author, having failed to find in his writings the correct spiritual flavour.

"If you read them carefully, sir," I suddenly blurted out, "you will find his writings not to be lacking in the flavour of Truth." The fact is, rebellion had been long brewing within me. I was feeling done to death with mystic emotion. I was nauseated with shedding tears over abstract human feelings, to the neglect of living human creatures.

The Master blinked at me curiously before he replied: "Very well, my son, carefully read them I will." He tucked the books away under the bolster on which he reclined. I could perceive that his idea was not to surrender them to me.

Damini, from behind the door, must have got wind of this, for at once she stepped in and asked: "Haven't the books you ordered for me arrived yet?"

I remained silent.

"My little mother!" said the Swami. "These books are not fit for you to read."

"How should you know that?"

The Master frowned. "How, at least, could you know better?"

"I have read the author: you, perhaps, have not."

"Why, then, need you read him over again?"

"When *you* have any need," Damini flared up, "nothing is allowed to stand in *your* way. It is only I who am to have no needs!"

"You forget yourself, Damini. I am a *sannyasin*. I have no worldly desires."

"You forget that I am not a *sannyasin*. I have a desire to read these books. Will you kindly let me have them?"

The Swami drew out the books from under his bolster and tossed them across to me. I handed them over to Damini.

In the end, the books that Damini would have read alone by herself, she now began to send for me to read out to her. It was in that same shaded veranda along our rooms that these readings took place. Satish passed and repassed, longing to join in, but could not, unasked.

One day we had come upon a humorous passage, and Damini was rocking with laughter. There was a festival on at the temple and we had supposed that Satish

---

[24] **Manu:** The Hindu law-giver. [Translator.]

would be there. But we heard a door open behind, through which Satish unexpectedly appeared and came and sat down beside us.

Damini's laughter was at once cut short. I also felt awkward. I wanted badly to say something to Satish, but no words would come, and I went on silently turning over page after page of my book. He rose, and left as abruptly as he had come. Our reading made no further progress that day.

Satish may very likely have understood that while he envied the absence of reserve between Damini and me, its presence was just what I envied in his case. That same day he petitioned the Master to be allowed to go off on a solitary excursion along the sea-coast, promising to be back within a week. "The very thing, my son!" acquiesced the Swami, with enthusiasm.

Satish departed. Damini did not send for me to read to her any more, nor had she anything else to ask of me. Neither did I see her going to her friends, the women of the neighbourhood. She kept her room, with closed doors.

Some days passed thus. One afternoon, when the Master was deep in his siesta, and I was writing a letter seated out on our veranda, Satish suddenly turned up. Without so much as a glance at me, he walked straight up to Damini's door, knocking as he called: "Damini, Damini."

Damini came out at once. A strangely altered Satish met her inquiring gaze. Like a storm-battered ship, with torn rigging and tattered sails, was his condition, — eyes wild, hair dishevelled, features drawn, garments dusty.

"Damini," said Satish, "I asked you to leave us. That was wrong of me. I beg your forgiveness."

"Oh, don't say that," cried the distressed Damini, clasping her hands.

"You must forgive me," he repeated. "I will never again allow that pride to overcome me, which led me to think I could take you or leave you, according to my own spiritual requirements. Such sin will never cross my mind again, I promise you. Do you also promise me one thing?"

"Command me!" said Damini, making humble obeisance.

"You must join us, and not keep aloof like this."

"I will join you," said Damini. "I will sin no more." Then, as she bowed low again to take the dust of his feet, she repeated, "I will sin no more."

5

The stone was melted again. Damini's bewildering radiance remained undimmed, but it lost its heat. In worship and ritual and service her beauty blossomed out anew. She was never absent from the *kirtan* singing, nor when the Master gave his readings and discourses. There was a change in her raiment also. She reverted to the golden brown of plain tussore,[25] and whenever we saw her she seemed fresh from her toilet.

---

[25] **plain tussore:** The tussore silk-worm is a wild variety, and its cocoon has to be used after the moth has cut its way out and flown away, thus not being killed in the process of unwinding the silk. Hence tussore silk is deemed specially suitable for wear on occasions of divine worship. [Translator.]

The severest test came in her intercourse with the Master. When she made her salutation to him, I could catch the glint of severely repressed temper through her half-closed eyelids. I knew very well that she could not bear to take orders from the Master; nevertheless, so complete was her self-suppression, that the Swami was able to screw up the courage to repeat his condemnation of the obnoxious tone of that outrageously modern Bengali writer. The next day there was a heap of flowers near his seat, and under them were the torn pages of the books of the objectionable author.

I had always noticed that the attendance on the Master by Satish was specially intolerable to Damini. Even now, when the Master asked him for some personal service, Damini would try to hustle past Satish and forestall him. This, however, was not possible in every case; and while Satish kept blowing on the tinder to get it into a blaze for the Master's pipe, Damini would have much ado to keep herself in hand by grimly repeating under her breath, "I will sin no more. I will sin no more."

But what Satish had tried for did not come off. On the last occasion of Damini's self-surrender, he had seen the beauty of the surrender only, not of the self behind it. This time Damini herself had become so true for him that she eclipsed all strains of music, and all thoughts of philosophy. Her reality had become so dominant that Satish could no longer lose himself in his visions, nor think of her merely as an aspect of Universal Woman. It was not she who, as before, set off for him the melodies which filled his mind; rather, these melodies had now become part of the halo which encircled her person.

I should not, perhaps, leave out the minor detail that Damini had no longer any use for me. Her demands on me had suddenly ceased altogether. Of my colleagues, who used to assist in beguiling her leisure, the kite was dead, the mongoose had escaped, and as for the mongrel puppy, its manners having offended the Master's susceptibilities, it had been given away. Thus, bereft both of occupation and companionship, I returned to my old place in the assembly surrounding the Master, though the talking and singing and doing that went on there had all alike become horribly distasteful to me.

6

The laboratory of Satish's mind was not amenable to any outside laws. One day, as he was compounding therein, for my special benefit, a weird mixture of ancient philosophy and modern science, with reason as well as emotion promiscuously thrown in, Damini burst in upon us, panting:

"Oh, do come, both of you, come quick!"

"Whatever is the matter?" I cried, as I leapt up.

"Nabin's wife has taken poison, I think," she said.

Nabin was a neighbour, one of our regular *kirtan* singers—an ardent disciple. We hurried after Damini, but when we arrived his wife was dead.

We pieced together her story. Nabin's wife had brought her motherless younger sister to live with them. She was a very pretty girl, and when Nabin's brother had last been home, he was so taken with her that their marriage was speedily arranged. This greatly relieved her elder sister, for, high caste as they were, a suitable bridegroom was not easy to find. The wedding-day had been fixed some months later, when Nabin's brother would have completed his college course. Meanwhile Nabin's wife lit upon the discovery that her husband had seduced her sister. She forthwith insisted on his marrying the unfortunate girl, — for which, as it happened, he did not require much persuasion. The wedding ceremony had just been put through, whereupon the elder sister had made away with herself by taking poison.

There was nothing to be done. The three of us slowly wended our way back, to find the usual throng round the Master. They sang a *kirtan* to him, and he waxed ecstatic in his usual manner, and began to dance with them.

That evening the moon was near its full. One corner of our terrace was over-hung by the branch of a *chalta* tree. At the edge of the shadow, under its thick foliage, sat Damini lost in silent thought. Satish was softly pacing up and down our veranda behind her. I had a hobby for diary-writing, in which I was indulging, alone in my room, with the door wide open.

That evening the *koil*[26] could not sleep; stirred by the south breeze the leaves too were speaking out, and the moonlight, shimmering on them, smiled in response. Something must also have stirred within Satish, for he suddenly turned his steps towards the terrace and went and stood near Damini.

Damini looked round with a start, adjusted her *sari*[27] over the back of her head, and rose as if to leave. Satish called, "Damini!"

She stopped at once, and turning to him appealingly with folded hands she said, "My Master, may I ask you a question?"

Satish looked at her inquiringly, but made no reply.

Damini went on: "Tell me truly, of what use to the world is this thing with which your sect is occupied day and night? Whom have you been able to save?"

I came out from my room and stood on the veranda.

Damini continued: "This passion, passion, passion on which you harp, — did you not see it in its true colours to-day? It has neither religion nor duty; it regards neither wife nor brother, nor the sanctuary of home; it knows neither pity nor trust, nor modesty, nor shame. What way have you discovered to save men from the hell of this cruel, shameless, soul-killing passion?"

I could not contain myself, but cried out: "Oh yes, we have hit upon the wonder-ful device of banishing Woman right away from our territory, so as to make our pur-suit of passion quite safe!"

Without paying any heed to my words, Damini spoke on to Satish: "I have learnt nothing at all from your Master. He has never given me one moment's peace of mind. Fire cannot quench fire. The road along which he is taking his devotees leads neither to courage, nor restraint, nor peace. That poor woman who is dead, — her heart's blood was sucked dry by this Fury, Passion, who killed her. Did you not see the hideous countenance of the murderess? For God's sake, my Master, I

---

[26] *koil:* A bird with a hooting call.

[27] **adjusted her *sari*:** A formal recognition of the presence of an elder. [Translator.]

implore you, do not sacrifice me to that Fury. Oh, save me, for if anybody can save me, it is you!"

For a space all three of us kept silent. So poignant became the silence all around, it seemed to me that the vibrating drone of the *cicadas* was but a swoon-thrill of the pallid sky.

Satish was the first to speak. "Tell me," said he to Damini, "what is it you would have me do for you?"

"Be my *guru*! I would follow none else. Give me some creed—higher than all this—which can save me. Do not let me be destroyed, together with the Divinity which is in me."

Satish drew himself up straight, as he responded: "So be it."

Damini prostrated herself at his feet, her forehead touching the ground, and remained long thus, in reverential adoration, murmuring: "Oh, my Master, my Master, save me, save me, save me from all sin."

7

Once more there was a mighty sensation in our world, and a storm of vituperation in the newspapers—for Satish had again turned renegade.

At first he had defiantly proclaimed active disbelief in all religion and social convention. Next, with equal vehemence, he had displayed active belief in gods and goddesses, rites and ceremonies, not excluding the least of them. Now, lastly, he had thrown to the winds all the rubbish-heaps both of religious and irreligious cults, and had retired into such simple peacefulness that no one could even guess what he believed, or what he did not. True, he took up good works as of old; but there was nothing aggressive about it this time.

There was another event over which the newspapers exhausted all their resources of sarcasm and virulence. That was the announcement of Damini's marriage with me. The mystery of this marriage none will perhaps fathom,—but why need they?

Chapter IV
Srivilas

1

There was once an indigo factory on this spot. All that now remains of it are some tumble-down rooms belonging to the old house, the rest having crumbled into dust. When returning homewards, after performing Damini's last rites, the place, as we passed by it, somehow appealed to me, and I stayed on alone.

The road leading from the river-side to the factory gate is flanked by an avenue of *sissoo* trees. Two broken pillars still mark the site of the gateway, and portions of the garden wall are standing here and there. The only other memento of the past is the brick-built mound over the grave of some Mussulman servant of the factory. Through its cracks, wild flowering shrubs have sprung up. Covered with blossoms, they sway to the breeze and mock at death, like merry maidens shaking with laughter while they chaff the bridegroom on his wedding-day. The banks of the garden pool have caved in and let the water trickle away, leaving the bottom to serve as a bed for a coriander patch. As I sit out on the roadside, under the shade of the avenue, the scent of the coriander, in flower, goes through and through my brain.

I sit and muse. The factory, of which these remnants are left, like the skeleton of some dead animal by the wayside, was once alive. From it flowed waves of pleasure and pain in a stormy succession, which then seemed to be endless. Its terribly efficient English proprietor, who made the very blood of his sweating cultivators run indigo-blue, — how tremendous was he compared to puny me! Nevertheless, Mother Earth girded up her green mantle, undismayed, and set to work so thoroughly to plaster over the disfigurement wrought by him and his activities, that the few remaining traces require but a touch or two more to vanish for ever.

This scarcely novel reflection, however, was not what my mind ruminated over. "No, no!" it protested. "One dawn does not succeed another merely to smear fresh plaster[28] over the floor. True, the Englishman of the factory, together with the rest of its abominations, are all swept away into oblivion like a handful of dust, — but my Damini!"

Many will not agree with me, I know. Shankaracharya's[29] philosophy spares no one. All the world is *maya*, a trembling dewdrop on the lotus leaf. But Shankaracharya was a *sannyasin*. "Who is your wife, who your son?" were questions he asked, without understanding their meaning. Not being a *sannyasin* myself, I know full well that Damini is not a vanishing dewdrop on the lotus leaf.

But, I am told, there are householders also, who say the same thing. That may be. They are mere householders, who have lost only the mistress of their house. Their home is doubtless *maya*, and so likewise is its mistress. These are their own handiwork, and when done with any broom is good enough for sweeping their fragments clean away.

I did not keep house long enough to settle down as a householder, nor is mine the temperament of a *sannyasin*, — that saved me. So the Damini whom I gained became neither housewife nor *maya*. She ever remained true to herself, — my Damini. Who dares to call her a shadow?

Had I known Damini only as mistress of my house, much of this would never have been written. It is because I knew her in a greater, truer relation, that I have no hesitation in putting down the whole truth, recking nothing of what others may say.

Had it been my lot to live with Damini, as others do in the everyday world, the household routine of toilet and food and repose would have sufficed for me as for them. And after Damini's death, I could have heaved a sigh and exclaimed with Shankaracharya: "Variegated is the world of *maya!*" before hastening to honour the suggestion of some aunt, or other well-meaning elder, by another attempt to sample its variety by marrying again. But I had not adjusted myself to the domestic world,

---

[28] **smear fresh plaster:** The wattle-and-daub cottages of a Bengal village are cleaned and renovated every morning by a moist clay mixture being smeared by the housewife over the plinth and floors. [Translator.]

[29] **Shankaracharya:** Or Shankara, an eighth-century Hindu theologian, sometimes said to be the founder of the principal sects of Hinduism.

like a foot in a comfortable old shoe. From the very outset I had given up hope of happiness,—no, no, that is saying too much; I was not so non-human as that. Happiness I certainly hoped for, but I did not arrogate to myself the right to claim it.

Why? Because it was I who persuaded Damini to give her consent to our marriage. Not for us was the first auspicious vision[30] in the rosy glow of festive lamps, to the rapturous strains of wedding pipes. We married in the broad light of day, with eyes wide open.

2

When we went away from Lilananda Swami, the time came to think of ways and means, as well as of a sheltering roof. We had all along been more in danger of surfeit than of starvation, with the hospitality which the devotees of the Master pressed on us, wherever we went with him. We had almost come to forget that to be a householder involves the acquiring, or building, or at least the renting of a house, so accustomed had we become to cast the burden of its supply upon another, and to look on a house as demanding from us only the duty of making ourselves thoroughly comfortable in it.

At length we recollected that Uncle Jagamohan had bequeathed his share of the house to Satish. Had the will been left in Satish's custody, it would by this time have been wrecked, like a paper boat, on the waves of his emotion. It happened, however, to be with me; for I was the executor. There were three conditions attached to the bequest which I was responsible for carrying out. No religious worship was to be performed in the house. The ground floor was to be used as a school for the leather-dealers' children. And after Satish's death, the whole property was to be applied for the benefit of that community. Piety was the one thing Uncle Jagamohan could not tolerate. He looked on it as more defiling even than worldliness; and probably these provisions, which he facetiously referred to in English as "sanitary precautions," were intended as a safeguard against the excessive piety which prevailed in the adjoining half of the house.

"Come along," I said to Satish. "Let's go to your Calcutta house."

"I am not quite ready for that yet," Satish replied.

I did not understand him.

"There was a day," he explained, "when I relied wholly on reason, only to find at last that reason could not support the whole of life's burden. There was another day, when I placed my reliance on emotion, only to discover it to be a bottomless abyss. The reason and the emotion, you see, were alike mine. Man cannot rely on himself alone. I dare not return to town until I have found my support."

"What then do you suggest?" I asked.

"You two go on to the Calcutta house. I would wander alone for a time. I seem to see glimpses of the shore. If I allow it out of my sight now, I may lose it for ever."

---

[30] **auspicious vision:** At one stage of the wedding ceremony a red screen is placed round the Bride and Bridegroom, and they are asked to look at each other. This is the Auspicious Vision. [Translator.]

As soon as we were by ourselves, Damini said to me: "That will never do! If he wanders about alone, who is to look after him? Don't you remember in what plight he came back when he last went wandering? The very idea of it fills me with fear."

Shall I tell the truth? This anxiety of Damini's stung me like a hornet, leaving behind the smart of anger. Had not Satish wandered about for two whole years after Uncle Jagamohan's death, — had that killed him? My question did not remain unuttered. Rather, some of the smart of the sting got expressed with it.

"I know, Srivilas Babu," Damini replied. "It takes a great deal to kill a man. But why should he be allowed to suffer at all, so long as the two of us are here to prevent it?"

The two of us! Half of that meant this wretched creature, Srivilas! It is of course a law of the world, that in order to save some people from suffering others shall suffer. All the inhabitants of the earth may be divided into two such classes. Damini had found out to which I belonged. It was compensation, indeed, that she included herself in the same class.

I went and said to Satish: "All right, then, let us postpone our departure to town. We can stay for a time in that dilapidated house on the river-side. They say it is subject to ghostly visitations. This will serve to keep off human visitors."

"And you two?" inquired Satish.

"Like the ghosts, we shall keep in hiding as far as possible."

Satish threw a nervous glance at Damini, — there may have been a suggestion of dread in it.

Damini clasped her hands as she said imploringly: "I have accepted you as my *guru*. Whatever my sins may have been, let them not deprive me of the right to serve you."

3

I must confess that this frenzied pertinacity of Satish's quest is beyond my understanding. There was a time when I would have laughed to scorn the very idea. Now I had ceased to laugh. What Satish was pursuing was fire indeed, no will-o'-the-wisp. When I realised how its heat was consuming him, the old arguments of Uncle Jagamohan's school refused to pass my lips. Of what avail would it be to find, with Herbert Spencer, that the mystic sense might have originated in some ghostly superstition, or that its message could be reduced to some logical absurdity? Did we not see how Satish was burning, — his whole being aglow?

Satish was perhaps better off when his days were passing in one round of excitement, — singing, dancing, serving the Master, — the whole of his spiritual effort exhausting itself in the output of the moment. Since he has lapsed into outward quiet, his spirit refuses to be controlled any longer. There is now no question of seeking emotional satisfaction. The inward struggle for realisation is so tremendous within him, that we are afraid to look on his face.

I could remain silent no longer. "Satish," I suggested, "don't you think it would be better to go to some *guru* who could show you the way and make your spiritual progress easier?"

This only served to annoy him. "Oh, do be quiet, Visri," he broke out irritably. "For goodness' sake keep quiet! What does one want to make it easier for? Delusion alone is easy. Truth is always difficult."

"But would it not be better," I tried again, "if some *guru* were to guide you along the path of Truth?"

Satish was almost beside himself. "Will you never understand," he groaned, "that I am not running after any geographical truth? The Dweller within can only come to me along my own true path. The path of the *guru* can only lead to the *guru's* door."

What a number of opposite principles have I heard enunciated by this same mouth of Satish! I, Srivilas, once the favourite disciple of Uncle Jagamohan,—who would have threatened me with a big stick if I had called him Master,—had actually been made by Satish to massage the legs of Lilananda Swami. And now not even a week has passed but he needs must preach to me in this strain! However, as I dared not smile, I maintained a solemn silence.

"I have now understood," Satish went on, "why our Scriptures say that it is better to die in one's own *dharma*[31] rather than court the terrible fate of taking the *dharma* of another. All else may be accepted as gifts, but if one's *dharma* is not one's own, it does not save, but kills. I cannot gain my God as alms from anybody else. If I get Him at all, it shall be I who win Him. If I do not, even death is better."

I am argumentative by nature, and could not give in so easily. "A poet," said I, "may get a poem from within himself. But he who is not a poet needs must take it from another."

"I am a poet," said Satish, without blenching.

That finished the matter. I came away.

Satish had no regular hours for meals or sleep. There was no knowing where he was to be found next. His body began to take on the unsubstantial keenness of an over-sharpened knife. One felt this could not go on much longer. Yet I could not muster up courage to interfere. Damini, however, was utterly unable to bear it. She was grievously incensed at God's ways. With those who ignored Him, God was powerless,—was it fair thus to take it out of one who was helplessly prostrate at His feet? When Damini used to wax wroth with Lilananda Swami, she knew how to bring it home to him. Alas, she knew not how to bring her feelings home to God!

Anyhow, she spared no pains in trying to get Satish to be regular in satisfying his physical needs. Numberless and ingenious were her contrivances to get this misfit creature to conform to domestic regulations. For a considerable space Satish made no overt objection to her endeavours. But one morning he waded across the shallow river to the broad sand-bed along the opposite bank, and there disappeared from sight.

The sun rose to the meridian; it gradually bent over to the west; but there was no sign of Satish. Damini waited for him, fasting, till she could contain herself no longer.

---

[31] *dharma:* A key concept in Hinduism with many meanings. In this passage, it refers to the essential quality of one's nature.

She put some food on a salver, and with it toiled through the knee-deep water, and at last found herself on the sand-bank.

It was a vast expanse on which not a living creature of any kind was to be seen. The sun was cruel. Still more so were the glowing billows of sand, one succeeding the other, like ranks of crouching sentinels guarding the emptiness. As she stood on the edge of this spreading pallor, where all limits seemed to have been lost, where no call could meet with any response, no question with any answer, Damini's heart sank within her. It was as if her world had been wiped away and reduced to the dull blank of original colourlessness. One vast "No" seemed to be stretched at her feet. No sound, no movement, no red of blood, no green of vegetation, no blue of sky, — but only the drab of sand. It looked like the lipless grin of some giant skull, the tongue-less cavern of its jaws gaping with an eternal petition of thirst to the unrelenting fiery skies above.

While she was wondering in what direction to proceed, the faint track of foot-steps caught Damini's eye. These she pursued, and went on and on, over the undu-lating surface, till they stopped at a pool on the farther side of a sand-drift. Along the moist edge of the water could be seen the delicate tracery of the claw-marks of innu-merable water-fowl. Under the shade of the sand-drift sat Satish.

The water was the deepest of deep blue. The fussy snipe were poking about on its margin, bobbing their tails and fluttering their black-and-white wings. At some distance were a flock of wild duck quacking vigorously, and seeming never to get the preening of their feathers done to their own satisfaction. When Damini reached the top of the mound, which formed one bank of the pool, the ducks took themselves off in a body, with a great clamour and beating of wings.

Satish looked round and saw Damini. "Why are you here?" he cried.

"I have brought you something to eat," said Damini.

"I want nothing," said Satish.

"It is very late———" ventured Damini.

"Nothing at all," repeated Satish.

"Let me then wait a little," suggested Damini. "Perhaps later on———?"

"Oh, why will you———" burst out Satish, but as his glance fell on Damini's face he stopped short.

Damini said nothing further. Tray in hand she retraced her steps through the sand, which glared round her like the eye of a tiger in the dark.

Tears had always been rarer in Damini's eyes than lightning flashes. But when I saw her that evening, — seated on the floor, her feet stretched out before her, — she was weeping. When she saw me her tears seemed to burst through some obstruction and showered forth in torrents. I cannot tell what it felt like within my breast. I came near and sat down on one side.

When she had calmed herself a little I inquired: "Why does Satish's health make you so anxious?"

"What else have I to be anxious about?" she asked simply. "All the rest he has to think out for himself. There I can neither understand nor help."

"But consider, Damini," I said. "When man's mind puts forth all its energy into one particular channel, his bodily needs become reduced correspondingly. That is why, in the presence of great joy or great sorrow, man does not hunger or thirst. Satish's state of mind is now such that it will do him no harm even if you do not look after his body."

"I am a woman," replied Damini. "The building up of the body with our own body, with our life itself, is our *dharma*. It is woman's own creation. So when we women see the body suffer, our spirit refuses to be comforted."

"That is why," I retorted, "those who are busy with things of the spirit seem to have no eyes for you, the guardians of mere bodies!"

"Haven't they!" Damini flared up. "So wonderful, rather, is the vision of their eyes, it turns everything topsy-turvy."

"Ah, woman," said I to myself. "That is what fascinates you. Srivilas, my boy, next time you take birth, take good care to be born in the world of topsy-turvydom."

4

The wound which Satish inflicted on Damini that day on the sands had this result, that he could not remove from his mind the agony he had seen in her eyes. During the succeeding days he had to go through the purgatory of showing her special consideration. It was long since he had freely conversed with us. Now he would send for Damini and talk to her. The experiences and struggles through which he was passing were the subject of these talks.

Damini had never been so exercised by his indifference as she now was by his solicitude. She felt sure this could not last, because the cost was too much to pay. Some day or other Satish's attention would be drawn to the state of the account, and he would discover how high the price was; then would come the crash. The more regular Satish became in his meals and rest, as a good householder should, the more anxious became Damini, the more she felt ashamed of herself. It was almost as if she would be relieved to find Satish becoming rebellious. She seemed to be saying: "You were quite right to hold aloof. Your concern for me is only punishing yourself. That I cannot bear!—I must," she appeared to conclude, "make friends with the neighbours again, and see if I cannot contrive to keep away from the house."

One night we were roused by a sudden shout: "Srivilas! Damini!" It must have been past midnight, but Satish could not have taken count of the hour. How he passed his nights we knew not, but the way he went on seemed to have cowed the very ghosts into flight.

We shook off our slumbers, and came out of our respective rooms to find Satish on the flagged pavement in front of the house, standing alone in the darkness. "I have understood!" he exclaimed as he saw us. "I have no more doubts."

Damini softly went up and sat down on the pavement. Satish absently followed her example and sat down too. I also followed suit.

"If I keep going," said Satish, "in the same direction along which He comes to me, then I shall only be going further and further away from Him. If I proceed in the opposite direction, then only can we meet."

I silently gazed at his flaming eyes. As a geometrical truth what he said was right enough. But what in the world was it all about?

"He loves form," Satish went on, "so He is continually descending towards form. We cannot live by form alone, so we must ascend towards His formlessness. He is free, so His play is within bonds. We are bound, so we find our joy in freedom. All our sorrow is because we cannot understand this."

We kept as silent as the stars.

"Do you not understand, Damini?" pursued Satish. "He who sings proceeds from his joy to the tune; he who hears, from the tune to joy. One comes from freedom into bondage, the other goes from bondage into freedom; only thus can they have their communion. He sings and we hear. He ties the bonds as He sings to us, we untie them as we hear Him."

I cannot say whether Damini understood Satish's words, but she understood Satish. With her hands folded on her lap she kept quite still.

"I was hearing His song through the night," Satish went on, "till in a flash the whole thing became clear to me. Then I could not keep it to myself, and called out to you. All this time I had been trying to fashion Him to suit myself, and so was deprived. — O Desolator! Breaker of ties! Let me be shattered to pieces within you, again and again, for ever and ever. Bonds are not for me, that is why I cannot hold on to bonds for long. Bonds are yours, and so are you kept eternally bound to creation. Play on, then, with our forms and let me take my flight into your formlessness. — O Eternal, you are mine, mine, mine!" — Satish departed into the night towards the river.

After that night, Satish lapsed back into his old ways, forgetful of all claims of rest or nourishment. As to when his mind would rise into the light of ecstasy, or lapse into the depths of gloom, we could make no guess. May God help her who has taken on herself the burden of keeping such a creature within the wholesomeness of worldly habit. . . .

5

It had been stiflingly oppressive the whole day. In the night a great storm burst on us. We had our several rooms along a veranda, in which a light used to be kept burning all night. That was now blown out. The river was lashed into foaming waves, and a flood of rain burst forth from the clouds. The splashing of the waves down below, and the dashing of the torrents from above, played the cymbals in this chaotic revel of the gods. Nothing could be seen of the deafening movements which resounded within the depths of the darkness, and made the sky, like a blind child, break into shivers of fright. Out of the bamboo thickets pierced a scream as of some bereaved giantess. From the mango groves burst the cracking and crashing of breaking timber. The river-side echoed with the deep thuds of falling masses from the crumbling banks. Through the bare ribs of our dilapidated house the keen blasts howled and howled like infuriated beasts.

On such a night the fastenings of the human mind are shaken loose. The storm gains entry and plays havoc within, scattering into disorder its well-arranged furniture of convention, tossing about its curtains of decorous restraint in disturbing revealment. I could not sleep. But what can I write of the thoughts which assailed my sleepless brain? They do not concern this story.

"Who is that?" I heard Satish cry out all of a sudden in the darkness.

"It is I, — Damini," came the reply. "Your windows are open, and the rain is streaming in. I have come to close them."

As she was doing this, she found Satish had got out of his bed. He seemed to stand and hesitate, just for a moment, and then he went out of the room.

Damini went back to her own room and sat long on the threshold. No one returned. The fury of the wind went on increasing in violence.

Damini could sit quiet no longer. She also left the house. It was hardly possible to keep on one's feet in the storm. The sentinels of the revelling gods seemed to be scolding Damini and repeatedly thrusting her back. The rain made desperate attempts to pervade every nook and cranny of the sky.

A flash rent the sky from end to end with terrific tearing thunder. It revealed Satish standing on the river brink. With a supreme effort Damini reached him in one tempestuous rush, outvying the wind. She fell prone at his feet. The shriek of the storm was overcome by her cry: "At your feet, I swear I had no thought of sin against your God! Why punish me thus?"

Satish stood silent.

"Thrust me into the river with your feet, if you would be rid of me. But return you must!"

Satish came back. As he re-entered the house he said: "My need for Him whom I seek is immense, — so absolutely, that I have no need for anything else at all. Damini, have pity on me and leave me to Him."

After a space of silence Damini said: "I will."

6

I knew nothing of this at the time, but heard it all from Damini afterwards. So when I saw through my open door the two returning figures pass along the veranda to their rooms, the desolation of my lot fell heavy on my heart and took me by the throat. I struggled up from my bed. Further sleep was impossible that night.

Next morning, what a changed Damini met my eyes! The demon dance of last night's storm seemed to have left all its ravages on this one forlorn girl. Though I knew nothing of what had happened, I felt bitterly angry with Satish.

"Srivilas Babu," said Damini, "will you take me on to Calcutta?"

I could guess all that these words meant for her; so I asked no question. But, in the midst of the torture within me, I felt the balm of consolation. It was well that Damini should take herself away from here. Repeated buffeting against the rock could only end in the vessel being broken up.

At parting, Damini made her obeisance to Satish, saying: "I have grievously sinned at your feet. May I hope for pardon?"

Satish, with his eyes fixed on the ground, replied: "I also have sinned. Let me first purge my sin away, and then will I claim forgiveness."

It became clear to me, on our way to Calcutta, what a devastating fire had all along been raging within Damini. I was so scorched by its heat that I could not restrain myself from breaking out in revilement of Satish.

Damini stopped me frenziedly. "Don't you dare talk so in my presence!" she exclaimed. "Little do you know what he saved me from! You can only see my sorrow. Had you no eyes for the sorrow he has been through, in order to save me? The hideous tried once to destroy the beautiful, and got well kicked for its pains. — Serve it right! — Serve it right!" — Damini began to beat her breast violently with her clenched hands. I had to hold them back by main force.

When we arrived in the evening, I left Damini at her aunt's and went over to a lodging-house, where I used to be well known. My old acquaintances started at sight of me. "Have you been ill?" they cried.

By next morning's post I got a letter from Damini. "Take me away," she wrote. "There is no room for me here."

It appeared that her aunt would not have her. Scandal about us was all over the town. The Pooja numbers of the weekly newspapers had come out shortly after we had given up Lilananda Swami. All the instruments for our execution had been kept sharpened. The carnage turned out to be worthy of the occasion. In our *shastras*[32] the sacrifice of she-animals is prohibited. But, in the case of modern human sacrifice, a woman victim seems to add to the zest of the performers. The mention of Damini's name was skilfully avoided. But no less was the skill which did away with all doubt as to the intention. Anyhow, it had resulted in this shrinkage of room in the house of Damini's distant aunt.

Damini had lost her parents. But I had an idea that her brother was living. I asked Damini for his address, but she shook her head, saying they were too poor. The fact was, Damini did not care to place her brother in an awkward position. What if he also came to say there was no room?

"Where will you stay, then?" I had to inquire.

"I will go back to Lilananda Swami."

I could not trust myself to speak for a time, — I was so overcome. Was this, then, the last cruel trick which Fate had held in reserve?

"Will the Swami take you back?" I asked at length.

"Gladly!"

Damini understood men. Sect-mongers rejoice more in capturing adherents than in comprehending truths. Damini was quite right. There would be no dearth of room for her at Lilananda's, but ————

"Damini," I said, just at this juncture. "There is another way. If you promise not to be angry, I will mention it."

"Tell me," said Damini.

"If it is at all possible for you to think of marrying a creature, such as I am————"

"What are you saying, Srivilas Babu?" interrupted Damini. "Are you mad?"

---

[32] *shastras:* Hindu scriptures.

"Suppose I am," said I. "One can sometimes solve insoluble problems by becoming mad. Madness is like the wishing carpet of the *Arabian Nights*. It can waft one over the thousand petty considerations which obstruct the everyday world."

"What do you call petty considerations?"

"Such as: What will people think? — What will happen in the future? — and so on, and so forth."

"And what about the vital considerations?"

"What do you call vital?" I asked in my turn.

"Such as, for instance: What will be your fate if you marry a creature like me?" said Damini.

"If that be a vital consideration, I am reassured. For I cannot possibly be in a worse plight than now. Any movement of my prostrate fortune, even though it be a turning over to the other side, cannot but be a sign of improvement."

Of course I could not believe that some telepathic news of my state of mind had never reached Damini. Such news, however, had not, so far, come under the head of "Important" — at least it had not called for any notice to be taken. Now action was definitely demanded of her.

Damini was lost in silent thought.

"Damini," I said, "I am only one of the very ordinary sort of men, — even less, for I am of no account in the world. To marry me, or not to marry me, cannot make enough difference to be worth all this thought."

Tears glistened in Damini's eyes. "Had you been an ordinary man, it would not have cost me a moment's hesitation," she said.

After another long silence, Damini murmured: "You know what I am."

"You also know what I am," I rejoined.

Thus was the proposal mooted, relying more on things unspoken than on what was said.

7

Those who, in the old days, had been under the spell of my English speeches had mostly shaken off their fascination during my absence; except only Naren, who still looked on me as one of the rarest products of the age. A house belonging to him was temporarily vacant. In this we took shelter.

It seemed at first that my proposal would never be rescued from the ditch of silence, into which it had lumbered at the very start; or at all events that it would require any amount of discussion and repair work before it could be hauled back on the high road of "yes" or "no."

But man's mind was evidently created to raise a laugh against mental science, with its sudden practical jokes. In the spring, which now came upon us, the Creator's joyous laughter rang through and through this hired dwelling of ours.

All this while Damini never had the time to notice that I was anybody at all; or it may be that the dazzling light from a different quarter had kept her blinded. Now that her world had shrunk around her, it was reduced to me alone. So she had no help but to look on me with seeing eyes. Perhaps it was the kindness of my fate which contrived that this should be her first sight of me.

By river and hill and seashore have I wandered along with Damini, as one of Lilananda's *kirtan* party, setting the atmosphere on fire with passionate song, to the beat of drum and cymbal. Great sparks of emotion were set free as we rang the changes on the text of the Vaishanava poet: *The noose of love hath bound my heart to thy feet.* Yet the curtain which hid me from Damini was not burnt away.

But what was it that happened in this Calcutta lane? The dingy houses, crowding upon one another, blossomed out like flowers of paradise. Verily God vouchsafed to us a miracle. Out of this brick and mortar He fashioned a harp-string to voice forth His melody. And with His wand He touched me, the least of men, and made me, all in a moment, wonderful.

When the curtain is there, the separation is infinite; when it is lifted, the distance can be crossed in the twinkling of an eye. So it took no time at all. "I was in a dream," said Damini. "It wanted this shock to wake me. Between that 'you' of mine and this 'you' of mine, there was a veil of stupor. I salute my Master again and again, for it is he who dispelled it."

"Damini," I said, "do not keep your gaze on me like that. Before, when you made the discovery that this creation of God is not beautiful, I was able to bear it; but it will be difficult to do so now."

"I am making the discovery," she replied, "that this creation of God has its beauty."

"Your name will go down in history!" I exclaimed. "The planting of the explorer's flag on the South Pole heights was child's play to this discovery of yours. 'Difficult' is not the word for it. You will have achieved the impossible!"

I had never realised before how short our spring month of Phalgun[33] is. It has only thirty days, and each of the days is not a minute more than twenty-four hours. With the infinite time which God has at His disposal, such parsimony I failed to understand!

"This mad freak that you are bent on," said Damini; "what will your people have to say to it?"

"My people are my best friends. So they are sure to turn me out of their house."

"What next?"

"Next it will be for you and me to build up a home, fresh from the very foundations, that will be our own special creation."

"You must also fashion afresh the mistress of your house, from the very beginning. May she also be your creation, with no trace left of her old battered condition!"

We fixed a day in the following month for the wedding. Damini insisted that Satish should be brought over.

"What for?" I asked.

"He must give me away."

Where the madcap was wandering I was not sure. I had written several letters, but with no reply. He could hardly have given up that old haunted house, otherwise

---

[33] **Phalgun:** Spring.

my letters would have been returned as undelivered. The chances were that he had not the time to be opening and reading letters.

"Damini," said I, "you must come with me and invite him personally. This is not a case for sending a formal invitation letter. I could have gone by myself, but my courage is not equal to it. For all we know, he may be on the other side of the river, superintending the preening of ducks' feathers. To follow him there is a desperate venture of which you alone are capable!"

Damini smiled. "Did I not swear I would never pursue him there again?"

"You swore you would not go to him with food any more. That does not cover your going over to invite him to a repast!"

8

This time everything passed off smoothly. We each took Satish by one hand and brought him along with us back to Calcutta. He was as pleased as a child receiving a pair of new dolls!

Our idea had been to have a quiet wedding. But Satish would have none of that. Moreover, there were the Mussulman friends of Uncle Jagamohan. When they heard the news, they were so extravagantly jubilant that the neighbours must have thought it was for the Amir of Kabul or the Nizam of Hyderabad, at the very least. But the height of revelry was reached by the newspapers in a very orgy of calumny. Our hearts, however, were too full to harbour any resentment. We were quite willing to allow the blood-thirstiness of the readers to be satisfied, and the pockets of the proprietors to be filled, — along with our blessings to boot.

"Come and occupy my house, Visri, old fellow," said Satish.

"Come with us, too," I added. "Let us set to work together over again."

"No, thank you," said Satish. "My work is elsewhere."

"You won't be allowed to go till you have assisted at our house-warming," insisted Damini.

This function was not going to be a crowded affair, Satish being the only guest. But it was all very well for him to say: "Come and occupy my house." That had already been done by his father, Harimohan, — not directly, but through a tenant. Harimohan would have entered into possession himself, but his worldly and other-worldly advisers warned him that it was best not to risk it, — a Mussulman having died there of the plague. Of course the tenant to whom it was offered ran the same spiritual and physical risks, but then why need he be told?

How we got the house out of Harimohan's clutches is a long story. The Mussulman leather-dealers were our chief allies. When they got to know the contents of the will, we found further legal steps to be superfluous.

The allowance which I had all along been getting from home was now stopped. It was all the more of a joy to us to undertake together the toil of setting up house without outside assistance. With the seal of Premchand-Roychand it was not difficult for me to secure a professorship. I was able to supplement my income by publishing notes on the prescribed text-books, which were eagerly availed of as patent nostrums for passing examinations. I need not have done so much, for our own wants were few. But Damini insisted that Satish should not have to worry about his own living while we were here to prevent it.

There was another thing about which Damini did not say a word. I had to attend to it secretly. That was the education of her brother's son and the marriage of his daughter. Both of these matters were beyond the means of her brother himself. His house was barred to us, but pecuniary assistance has no caste to stand in the way of its acceptance. Moreover, acceptance did not necessarily involve acknowledgment. So I had to add the sub-editorship of a newspaper to my other occupations.

Without consulting Damini, I engaged a cook and two servants. Without consulting me, Damini sent them packing the very next day. When I objected, she made me conscious how ill-judged was my attempted consideration for her. "If I am not allowed," she said, "to do my share of work while you are slaving away, where am I to hide my shame?"

My work outside and Damini's work at home flowed on together like the confluent Ganges and Jumna. Damini also began to teach sewing to the leather-dealers' little girls. She was determined not to take defeat at my hands. I am not enough of a poet to sing how this Calcutta house of ours became Brindaban[34] itself, our labours the flute strains which kept it enraptured. All I can say is that our days did not drag, neither did they merely pass by,—they positively danced along.

One more springtime came and went; but never another.

Ever since her return from the cave-temple Damini had suffered from a pain in her breast, of which, however, she then told no one. This suddenly took a turn for the worse, and when I asked her about it she said: "This is my secret wealth, my touchstone. With it, as dower, I was able to come to you. Otherwise I would not have been worthy."

The doctors, each of them, had a different name for the malady. Neither did they agree in their prescriptions. When my little hoard of gold was blown away between the cross-fire of the doctors' fees and the chemist's bills, the chapter of medicament came to an end, and change of air was advised. As a matter of fact, hardly anything of changeable value was left to us except air.

"Take me to the place from which I brought the pain," said Damini. "It has no dearth of air."

When the month of Magh ended with its full moon and Phalgun began, while the sea heaved and sobbed with the wail of its lonely eternity, Damini, taking the dust of my feet, bade farewell to me with the words:

"I have not had enough of you. May you be mine again in our next birth."

---

[34] **Brindaban:** A center for Hindu pilgrimage in north central India.

WILLIAM BUTLER YEATS
B. IRELAND, 1865–1939

Spanning the dizzying changes in aesthetics and politics between 1890 and 1939, the work of William Butler Yeats epitomizes the contradictory impulses of early modernist society and culture—its recognition of a world consumed by violent conflict, emptied of value and tradition, and yet struggling to find some idea, some system, some myth to hold itself together. As Yeats wrote in a prophetic poem, "Things fall apart; the centre cannot hold; / . . . and everywhere / The ceremony of innocence is drowned." As a leading figure of the IRISH LITERARY RENAISSANCE, a poet, statesman, critic, and visionary, Yeats strove in his research of the occult, in his revitalization of Irish myth and legend, and in his poetry to bring meaning and purpose to his contemporaries. Often considered to be the greatest poet writing in English in the early modernist period, Yeats spoke not only to Ireland and to his generation, but, as Chinua Achebe's *Things Fall Apart* attests, to people of all countries and to the generation of writers that followed him.

William Butler Yeats, 1908
(Hulton/Archive)

p. 1604

Sligo and Dublin. William Butler Yeats was born in Sandymount, a suburb of Dublin, Ireland, on June 13, 1865. Through his father, the lawyer-turned-painter John Butler Yeats, William was linked to a line of clergymen; and through his mother, Susan Pollexfen, to a line of seafarers who captured the imagination of the young boy. When William was three years old, he accompanied his family to London where his father took up the study of painting. William attended the Godolphin School and cultivated a strong sense of nostalgia for Ireland. Fortunately, his family on both sides had connections to county Sligo, on the west coast of Ireland, where the young boy visited his grandfather in the shadow of his revered Ben Bulben, the chief peak of the Sligo Mountains. Here, on summer vacations and holidays in later years, Yeats would ramble in the countryside and listen to tales about fairies and Irish folk heroes. In 1880, the family returned to Ireland, eventually taking a house overlooking Howth harbor just north of Dublin. Yeats's father, who had maintained a caring but stern supervision over his son's education, placed William in Erasmus High School where he began writing poetry. After leaving high school, Yeats attended art school at the Metropolitan School of Art where his father taught. There he met George Russell (1867–1935), or A. E., an artist, poet, and mystic in whom the young Yeats found a kindred spirit.

The Making of a Poet. Another significant meeting came in 1885, when Yeats met the Irish Fenian leader John O'Leary (1830–1907), whom Yeats later described as the embodiment of "Romantic Ireland." The Fenian Society was a secret organization of Irish nationalists founded in 1858 that promoted Irish independence from England by means of violent revolution. Through O'Leary, Yeats associated with some of the

www For more information about Yeats and the 21st-century relevance of his work, see bedfordstmartins .com/worldlit compact.

soon-to-be leaders of the Irish nationalist movement. In the next year, Yeats gave up his studies in art and returned to London, where he devoted his energies to writing and joined in quasi-philosophical and occult discussions with Madame Blavatsky (1831–1891) and her Theosophical Society, which promoted the reconciliation of Eastern religious doctrines with Western mysticism. These two often contradictory elements of Yeats's character, the political and the spiritual, lent to his life and poetry their characteristic tension and ambiguity. Both his life and work were marked by a struggle to attain a pure vision of art out of an exacting confrontation with the cold imperfections of human life. Those imperfections were compounded by the political strife of early twentieth-century Ireland and by the advent of World War I.

Yeats's embrace of Theosophy inspired a mind already well stocked in the legends and folklore of Ireland. In 1889, with the help of O'Leary, the young poet published his first book, *The Wanderings of Oisin and Other Poems.* This collection of early lyrics and ballads accompanying the long title poem, an allegorical story of a journey into the land of the fairies based on Irish legend, shows an influence of the PRE-RAPHAELITES in its sensuous imagery and dreamy medievalism and an influence of Theosophy in its Indian subjects.

During the next few years Yeats edited several collections of Irish folktales, fairy tales, and ballads, and even collaborated on an edition of the works of the Romantic poet William Blake (1757–1827), whose mythmaking and visionary spirituality Yeats found congenial to his literary sensibility. In the early 1890s, Yeats also helped to found the Rhymers' Club, the National Literary Society in Dublin, and the London-Irish Literary Society. In this same period he wrote *The Countess Cathleen* (1892), a play inspired by Maud Gonne, with whom Yeats had fallen in love two years earlier. An uncompromising Irish nationalist determined to free Ireland from English rule, Gonne did not return the love Yeats so passionately offered her. Although Yeats accompanied her on some of her many travels between Dublin, London, and Paris to support the Irish cause, she would not consent to marry him when he asked for her hand in 1891. This was only the first of many refusals from Gonne that would haunt the poet's life and work to the very end.

The Irish Poet.   In 1892 a second publication, *The Countess Cathleen and Various Legends and Lyrics,* was published, and a few of Yeats's lyrics appeared in *The Yellow Book,* a notorious periodical associated with Aubrey Beardsley (1872–1898), Max Beerbohm (1872–1956), and Ernest Dowson (1867–1900), key figures of the aesthete movement in FIN-DE-SIÈCLE London, which held that the pursuit of beauty was the sole purpose of art. Yeats's London circle also included the poets and critics Lionel Johnson (1867–1902), George Moore (1852–1933), and Arthur Symons (1865–1945), who shared Yeats's interest in Blake and the FRENCH SYMBOLISTS. The year 1893 saw the publication of *The Rose,* a collection of poems on Irish themes that includes "The Lake Isle of Innisfree." In 1896, Yeats met Lady Augusta Gregory (1852–1932), a writer, Irish patriot, and wealthy patron of Irish literature, and the following he spent the first of many summers at her country house at Coole Park, Galway, in the west of Ireland. Here Yeats, Lady Gregory, and playwrights Edward Martyn (1859–1923) and J. M. Synge (1871–1909) planned the Irish National Theatre, which they founded in 1899. That year marks the beginning of the Irish Literary Renaissance; it was also the year that *The Wind Among the Reeds* was published, a collection that brought Yeats's synthesis of Irish legend, private reverie, and esoteric symbolism to perfection.

As a founder of the Irish National Theatre, which found a home in the Abbey Theatre, Dublin, in 1904, Yeats had to deal with its practical problems, not the least of which was protecting it from the narrow-minded provincialism, petty morality, and rank hypocrisy of the Irish middle classes. Bitter and out of patience with protests over the production of J. M. Synge's *The Playboy of the Western World* (1907) and with the Dublin Corporation's refusal to provide a gallery for the collection of French paintings offered it by Sir Hugh Lane, Yeats roundly condemned the shopkeeper mentality of Dubliners in "September 1913" and other poems published in *Responsibilities* (1914), which first appeared in 1913 as *Poems Written in Discouragement.* Up to that time, Yeats had published two important collections of poems, *In the Seven Woods* (1904) and *The Green Helmet and Other Poems* (1910), and he had produced some of his plays, including *Cathleen ni Houlihan* (1902) and *On Baile's Strand* (1904), which opened the Abbey Theatre. The American poet Ezra Pound (1885–1972), whom Yeats met in 1909, encouraged the Irishman to study Japanese *Nō* plays,[1] and in the year of one of Ireland's greatest political crises, 1916, Yeats produced *At the Hawk's Well,* a play for masked dancers based on his study of Japanese theater.

In 1916, Yeats's attention was caught by the "terrible beauty" of the Easter Rebellion in Dublin. Because he had spent much of his time since 1907 in England, the rising of the Irish nationalists who seized the Dublin post office in a bold but failed attempt to throw off English rule took Yeats by surprise. His qualified praise in "Easter 1916" for the leaders of the Easter Rebellion, many of whom were executed, marked a sort of reconciliation with Ireland, to which he returned. Yeats married Georgie Hyde-Lees (but not before he'd proposed to Iseult Gonne, Maud's daughter), took up residence at Ballylee, in Galway, and eventually became a senator of the newly established Irish Free State in 1922. Through the medium of Hyde-Lees, who professed to have psychic powers, Yeats wrote *A Vision* (1925), a prophetic work that sets out the esoteric system of symbols and the complex theory of cyclical history that informs his greatest collections of poetry, *The Tower* (1928) and *The Winding Stair* (1933). He was awarded the Nobel Prize in Literature in 1923 "for his always inspired poetry; which in a highly artistic form gives expression to the spirit of a whole nation."

After contracting a lung disease, Yeats retired from the senate in 1928 and in the following year left Ballylee to travel in Italy and southern

---

[1]**Japanese *Nō* plays:** The highly elaborate and ritualistic classical theater of Japan known for its minimalist approach to plot, scenery, and stage effects and the stately performance and Zen-like mastery of its actors; *Nō* means "talent" or "accomplishment."

The Abbey Theatre, Dublin, c. 1930
The Abbey Theatre was home to the Irish National Theatre, cofounded and directed by Yeats and Lady Gregory, which helped further the cause of Irish independence and cultural revival through its productions of nationalistic and political plays, some of which were written by Yeats himself. (Hulton/Archive)

France. The nearly seventy-year-old poet continued writing poetry and plays and in his last years produced a stunning series of poems that cut to the brute realities of life, old age, and the body, what Yeats called his return to the "foul rag-and-bone shop of the heart." Yeats died in 1939 in the south of France, "in the dead of winter," to quote from W. H. Auden's (1907–1973) poetic tribute to Yeats, but his "gift survived it all."

That gift was great and varied, and in following the course of Yeats's poetry from the Pre-Raphaelite dreaminess of *The Wanderings of Oisin,* to the spare colloquialism and symbolic density of *The Tower* and *The Winding Stair,* to the tightly wrought, concrete realism of *Last Poems,* one can track some of the important transformations of early-twentieth-century poetry. Yeats's distinctive signature, however—the deeply felt tension between his spiritual, aesthetic ideals and his unflinching grasp of the contradictions and disturbing complexities of mortal life—insistently qualifies any attempt to see Yeats's work as merely representative of a given movement. With its mellifluous tone and natural simplicity, "The Lake Isle of Innisfree" captures some of the Pre-Raphaelite qualities of Yeats's poetry of the 1890s. This poem typifies the otherworldliness of Yeats's early work, before he made the radical turn in the late 1890s to face the world head-on and to become the poet-legislator of Ireland and its culture.

"Easter 1916."   This poem was first published in a privately printed, limited edition of only twenty-five copies entitled *Easter, 1916,* and later in *New Statesman,* on October 23, 1920; it was again published in the collection

TIME AND PLACE

Twentieth-Century Ireland: Irish Independence

On April 24, 1916, while England was engaged in war on the continent of Europe, Irish nationalists staged the Easter Rising in an attempt to overthrow British rule. The fighting was chaotic and fierce, but short-lived. When it subsided five days after it began, 450 were dead, more than 2,500 injured, and many parts of Dublin destroyed. In May the British executed fifteen of the rebels after a series of public court-martials. The rebellion was memorialized by the great Irish literary figures of the day who, like William Butler Yeats (1865–1939), a committed nationalist and one-time member of the Irish Republican Brotherhood, shared the fighters' patriotic sentiment. (See "Easter 1916," p. 1348, for Yeats's poetic memorial to the uprising.) Yeats wrote of Patrick Henry Pearse (1879–1916), the leader who was also a poet and an educator who championed education for Irish children in Gaelic. Pearse had become the first president of the newly declared 1916 Irish republic before the British executed him in May for his part in the rebellion. James Connolly (1868–1916), the leader of the Irish Citizen Army, which participated in the rebellion, also lost his life.

Michael Collins (1890–1922), imprisoned for his actions in the Rising, went on to reorganize the Irish Republican Army (IRA) and launch full-scale guerrilla war against British government forces in Ireland, which resulted in 1921 in a treaty partitioning Ireland into Ulster (Northern Ireland) and the Irish Republic in the south. Collins was killed in an ambush in the civil war in 1922. Writers such as Yeats, Sean O'Casey, Samuel Beckett, Brendan Behan, James Joyce, and George Bernard Shaw were inspired by, if sometimes critical of, those who fought for Irish independence.

Derailment of Train by Guerrillas, Belfast, 1923. A violent struggle between the Irish and the British arose from the Irish independence movement, which often employed guerrilla tactics, as in this Belfast scene where Irish guerrillas derail a train. Many Irish writers, like Yeats, were conflicted by the physical-force wing of Irish nationalism. *(The Art Archive/Dagli Orti)*

Michael Robartes and the Dancer in 1921. Composed in September 1916, when Yeats was staying with Maud Gonne MacBride, the poem records Yeats's deeply felt response to the failed Easter Rising in Dublin, which began on Easter Monday, April 24, 1916. During the rebellion, members of the Irish Volunteers, the Irish Republican Brotherhood, and the Irish

Citizen Army occupied several important buildings, including the General Post Office in Dublin, and read a Proclamation of the Provisional Government, declaring independent nationhood for Ireland. The rebellion was effectively quashed by the British five days later; fifteen of its leaders were executed. Troubled by the event and "despondent about the future," Yeats wrote to Lady Gregory that he was "trying to write a poem on the men executed — 'terrible beauty has been born again.'"

The Poetry of Vision.   Yeats's verse of the twenties and thirties is partly contingent on the symbolic system of *A Vision* (1925), which Yeats received in part from his wife's automatic writing and in part from a complex synthesis of his studies of esoteric and occult thinkers ranging from Greek philosopher Empedocles (c. 495–c. 435 B.C.E.) to William Blake. This complex system involves a web of correspondences, derived from twenty-eight phases of the moon, between cosmic, national, and personal history. Most important for the poems included here, *A Vision* describes history as the movement of two intersecting cones or spinning "gyres." These gyres, which symbolize the opposites of subjectivity and objectivity, beauty and truth, and value and fact, expand and contract at regular intervals of two thousand years. Thus, every two thousand years a new system of values gains ascendancy. An avatar — Helen of Troy, Christ, the unnameable "beast" of "The Second Coming" — marks the beginning of each new age. Yeats saw the beginning of the twentieth century as the beginning of an objective cycle, which would mean a period hostile to art, spiritual vision, and individuality. This system underlies the symbolism of poems such as "Leda and the Swan" and "The Second Coming," both of which inaugurate ages of brutality and objective values before and after the subjective age of Christ, which reached its height in the flourishing of art and humanism in the Renaissance. Yeats's celebration of a world of pure art in "Sailing to Byzantium" pays tribute to the Byzantine period when, according to Yeats's view, art appeared to transcend the fleshly frailties of human experience. For Yeats, in early Byzantium "the painter, the mosaic worker, the worker in gold and silver, the illuminator of sacred books, were almost impersonal, almost perhaps without the consciousness of individual design, absorbed in their subject-matter and that the vision of a whole people."

Stubborn Mortality.   Yeats was never able to reconcile his passionate search for a systematic pattern behind human events with his insistence that we "Cast a cold eye / On life, on death." The poetry of his late period embodies a struggle between the quiet permanence of art and the mortality of life, the joy of spiritual desire and the grief of human love. "Among School Children," for example, weighs the burdens of physical aging and mortality against the vitality of sexual generation and the hopes of youth. In the final stanzas, Yeats suggests that the images people project for themselves and for their children potentially set them up for disappointment or lead to life-sapping projects that deprive one of the fullness or immediacy of a life lived truly in the moment. Rather than project images or set one's sights upon some plan, it is better to fuse the image with the lived experience so that the dancer and the dance merge as one indistinct being.

■ **FURTHER RESEARCH**

Editions
Albright, Daniel, ed. *W. B. Yeats: The Poems.* 1990.
Allt, Peter, and Russell K. Alspach, eds. *The Variorum Edition of the Poems of W. B. Yeats.* 1957.
Finneran, Richard J., ed. *Yeats, The Poems: A New Edition.* 1983.

Biography
Brown, Terence. *The Life of W. B. Yeats: A Critical Biography.* 1999.
Ellman, Richard. *Yeats: The Man and the Masks.* Revised ed. 1978.
Jeffares, Norman A. *W. B. Yeats: A New Biography.* 1988.

Criticism
Bloom, Harold, ed. *William Butler Yeats.* 1986.
Cullingford, Elizabeth. *Gender and History in Yeats's Love Poetry.* 1993.
Ellman, Richard. *The Identity of Yeats.* 1964.
Finneran, Richard J., ed. *Critical Essays on W. B. Yeats.* 1986.
Fleming, Deborah, ed. *Learning the Trade: Essays on W. B. Yeats and Contemporary Poetry.* 1993.
Jeffares, Norman A. *A New Commentary on the Collected Poems of W. B. Yeats.* 1983.
Malins, Edward. *A Preface to Yeats.* 1977.
O'Donnell, William H. *The Poetry of William Butler Yeats: An Introduction.* 1986.
Rosenthal, M. L. *Running to Paradise: Yeats's Poetic Art.* 1994.

Spoken Word
"William Butler Yeats." Caedmon Records.

℘ The Lake Isle of Innisfree[1]

I will arise and go now, and go to Innisfree,
And a small cabin build there, of clay and wattles made:
Nine bean-rows will I have there, a hive for the honeybee,
And live alone in the bee-loud glade.

And I shall have some peace there, for peace comes dropping slow,
Dropping from the veils of the morning to where the cricket sings;
There midnight's all a glimmer, and noon a purple glow,
And evening full of the linnet's wings.

I will arise and go now, for always night and day
I hear lake water lapping with low sounds by the shore;
While I stand on the roadway, or on the pavements grey,
I hear it in the deep heart's core.

10

---

[1] **Innisfree:** An island in Lough Gill, county Sligo, in northwestern Ireland.

Easter 1916

I have met them at close of day
Coming with vivid faces
From counter or desk among grey
Eighteenth-century houses.
I have passed with a nod of the head
Or polite meaningless words,
Or have lingered awhile and said
Polite meaningless words,
And thought before I had done
Of a mocking tale or a gibe
To please a companion
Around the fire at the club,
Being certain that they and I
But lived where motley is worn:
All changed, changed utterly:
A terrible beauty is born.

That woman's[1] days were spent
In ignorant good-will,
Her nights in argument
Until her voice grew shrill.
What voice more sweet than hers
When, young and beautiful,
She rode to harriers?[2]
This man[3] had kept a school
And rode our wingèd horse;
This other[4] his helper and friend
Was coming into his force;
He might have won fame in the end,
So sensitive his nature seemed,
So daring and sweet his thought.
This other man[5] I had dreamed
A drunken, vainglorious lout.

---

[1] **That woman:** Constance Gore-Booth, an Irish nationalist from county Sligo.

[2] **harriers:** Dogs resembling small foxhounds used in packs for hunting rabbits.

[3] **This man:** Patrick Pearse, a schoolmaster and Gaelic poet; the winged horse is Pegasus, horse of the Muses.

[4] **This other:** Thomas MacDonagh, a poet and playwright.

[5] **This other man:** Major John MacBride, who had married then separated from Maud Gonne, Yeats's lifelong love.

He had done most bitter wrong
To some who are near my heart,
Yet I number him in the song;
He, too, has resigned his part
In the casual comedy;
He, too, has been changed in his turn,
Transformed utterly:
40   A terrible beauty is born.

Hearts with one purpose alone
Through summer and winter seem
Enchanted to a stone
To trouble the living stream.
The horse that comes from the road,
The rider, the birds that range
From cloud to tumbling cloud,
Minute by minute they change;
A shadow of cloud on the stream
50   Changes minute by minute;
A horse-hoof slides on the brim,
And a horse plashes within it;
The long-legged moor-hens dive,
And hens to moor-cocks call;
Minute by minute they live:
The stone's in the midst of all.

Too long a sacrifice
Can make a stone of the heart.
O when may it suffice?
60   That is Heaven's part, our part
To murmur name upon name,
As a mother names her child
When sleep at last has come
On limbs that had run wild.
What is it but nightfall?
No, no, not night but death;
Was it needless death after all?
For England may keep faith
For all that is done and said.
70   We know their dream; enough
To know they dreamed and are dead;
And what if excess of love
Bewildered them till they died?
I write it out in a verse —
MacDonagh and MacBride

And Connolly[6] and Pearse
Now and in time to be,
Wherever green is worn,
Are changed, changed utterly:
80   A terrible beauty is born.

---

[6] **Connolly:** James Connolly, the chief leader of the Easter Rebellion.

∾ The Second Coming

Turning and turning in the widening gyre[1]
The falcon cannot hear the falconer;
Things fall apart; the centre cannot hold;
Mere anarchy is loosed upon the world,
The blood-dimmed tide is loosed, and everywhere
The ceremony of innocence is drowned;
The best lack all conviction, while the worst
Are full of passionate intensity.

Surely some revelation is at hand;
10   Surely the Second Coming is at hand.
The Second Coming! Hardly are those words out
When a vast image out of *Spiritus Mundi*[2]
Troubles my sight: somewhere in sands of the desert
A shape with lion body and the head of a man,
A gaze blank and pitiless as the sun,
Is moving its slow thighs, while all about it
Reel shadows of the indignant desert birds.
The darkness drops again; but now I know
That twenty centuries of stony sleep
20   Were vexed to nightmare by a rocking cradle,
And what rough beast, its hour come round at last,
Slouches towards Bethlehem to be born?

---

[1] **the widening gyre:** The gyre refers to Yeats's theory of historical cycles developed in *A Vision*. Yeats imagines history as a dynamic set of interlocking cone-shaped spirals. At the end of each two-thousand-year cycle, a new spirit governs human consciousness and the affairs of the world. This poem, which envisions an age dominated by indifference and authoritarianism, ironically announces itself as the second coming, which refers to the second coming of Christ and the end of the world.

[2] *Spiritus Mundi:* Spirit of the World; in Yeats's scheme a sort of collective consciousness or "Great Memory" that links the human race by a shared set of archetypes and symbols.

❧ Sailing to Byzantium

1

That is no country for old men. The young
In one another's arms, birds in the trees
—Those dying generations—at their song,
The salmon-falls, the mackerel-crowded seas,
Fish, flesh, or fowl, commend all summer long
Whatever is begotten, born, and dies.
Caught in that sensual music all neglect
Monuments of unageing intellect.

2

An aged man is but a paltry thing,
A tattered coat upon a stick, unless
Soul clap its hands and sing, and louder sing
For every tatter in its mortal dress,
Nor is there singing school but studying
Monuments of its own magnificence;
And therefore I have sailed the seas and come
To the holy city of Byzantium.

3

O sages standing in God's holy fire
As in the gold mosaic of a wall,
Come from the holy fire, perne in a gyre,[1]
And be the singing-masters of my soul.
Consume my heart away; sick with desire
And fastened to a dying animal
It knows not what it is; and gather me
Into the artifice of eternity.

4

Once out of nature I shall never take
My bodily form from any natural thing,
But such a form as Grecian goldsmiths make
Of hammered gold and gold enamelling

---

[1] **perne in a gyre:** To spin in a cone-shaped spiral; see "The Second Coming," note 1.

To keep a drowsy Emperor awake;
30   Or set upon a golden bough to sing
To lords and ladies of Byzantium
Of what is past, or passing, or to come.

Leda and the Swan

A sudden blow: the great wings beating still
Above the staggering girl, her thighs caressed
By the dark webs, her nape caught in his bill,
He holds her helpless breast upon his breast.

How can those terrified vague fingers push
The feathered glory from her loosening thighs?
And how can body, laid in that white rush,
But feel the strange heart beating where it lies?

A shudder in the loins engenders there
10   The broken wall, the burning roof and tower
And Agamemnon[1] dead.
                              Being so caught up,
So mastered by the brute blood of the air,
Did she put on his knowledge with his power
Before the indifferent beak could let her drop?

---

[1] **Agamemnon:** King of Mycenae and leader of the Greek forces against Troy; because he sacrificed his daughter Iphigenia to gain favorable winds to reach Troy, Agamemnon was murdered by his wife, Clytemnestra, on his return home from the war.

Among School Children

1

I walk through the long schoolroom questioning;
A kind old nun in a white hood replies;
The children learn to cipher and to sing,
To study reading-books and history,
To cut and sew, be neat in everything
In the best modern way — the children's eyes

In momentary wonder stare upon
A sixty-year-old smiling public man.[1]

2

I dream of a Ledaean body,[2] bent
Above a sinking fire, a tale that she
Told of a harsh reproof, or trivial event
That changed some childish day to tragedy—
Told, and it seemed that our two natures blent
Into a sphere from youthful sympathy,
Or else, to alter Plato's parable,
Into the yolk and white of the one shell.[3]

3

And thinking of that fit of grief or rage
I look upon one child or t'other there
And wonder if she stood so at that age—
For even daughters of the swan can share
Something of every paddler's heritage—
And had that colour upon cheek or hair,
And thereupon my heart is driven wild:
She stands before me as a living child.

4

Her present image floats into the mind—
Did Quattrocento finger[4] fashion it
Hollow of cheek as though it drank the wind
And took a mess of shadows for its meat?
And I though never of Ledaean kind
Had pretty plumage once—enough of that,
Better to smile on all that smile, and show
There is a comfortable kind of old scarecrow.

---

[1] **public man:** In 1922, Yeats was elected senator of the Irish Free State.

[2] **Ledaean body:** As beautiful as Leda, mother of Helen of Troy (see "Leda and the Swan," note 1).

[3] **Plato's . . . shell:** Plato's *Symposium* explains that true lovers are the two halves of a once complete being; when torn asunder by the gods, the two halves continually seek reunion with each other.

[4] **Quattrocento finger:** The hand of a fifteenth-century Italian painter or artist, such as Masaccio (1401–1428), Leonardo da Vinci (1452–1519), or Sandro Botticelli (1444–1510).

5

What youthful mother, a shape upon her lap
Honey of generation had betrayed,
And that must sleep, shriek, struggle to escape
As recollection or the drug decide,
Would think her son, did she but see that shape
With sixty or more winters on its head,
A compensation for the pang of his birth,
40 Or the uncertainty of his setting forth?

6

Plato thought nature but a spume that plays
Upon a ghostly paradigm of things;
Solider Aristotle played the taws
Upon the bottom of a king of kings;
World-famous golden-thighed Pythagoras[5]
Fingered upon a fiddle-stick or strings
What a star sang and careless Muses heard:
Old clothes upon old sticks to scare a bird.

7

Both nuns and mothers worship images,
50 But those the candles light are not as those
That animate a mother's reveries,
But keep a marble or a bronze repose.
And yet they too break hearts—O Presences
That passion, piety or affection knows,
And that all heavenly glory symbolise—
O self-born mockers of man's enterprise;

8

Labour is blossoming or dancing where
The body is not bruised to pleasure soul,
Nor beauty born out of its own despair,
60 Nor blear-eyed wisdom out of midnight oil.

---

[5] **Plato . . . Pythagoras:** Plato (427–347 B.C.E.) believed that things in nature were mere shadows of a perfect ideal form beyond the reach of ordinary sensibility; Aristotle (384–322 B.C.E.), who studied the natural world more closely than Plato, was Alexander the Great's tutor and so perhaps "played the taws," that is, spanked his young pupil; Pythagoras (582–507 B.C.E.) studied mathematics and music and was said to have a golden thighbone.

O chestnut-tree, great-rooted blossomer,
Are you the leaf, the blossom or the bole?
O body swayed to music, O brightening glance,
How can we know the dancer from the dance?

∾ LU XUN
B. CHINA, 1881–1936

Lu Xun, the pen name of Zhou Shuren, was born into comfortable circumstances and expected to become an educated member of the professional classes. He first challenged those expectations when he turned his
back on a career in the civil service and left China to study medicine in
Japan. Once trained as a surgeon, however, he realized that what he
wished to cure most was the backward condition of the Chinese people,
not merely their bodily illnesses. "The most important thing," he wrote,
"was to change their spirit, and since at that time I felt that literature was
the best means to that end, I decided to promote a literary movement."
Creating a new school of writing called CRITICAL REALISM[1] that examined
social tendencies through the actions of realistic characters, Lu Xun's
writing was marked by a tough-mindedness that exposed those within
China who prevented social progress. Lu Xun was a fierce opponent of
the conventional Chinese morality that was handed down to each new
generation through the doctrines of CONFUCIANISM, which stresses obedience, reverence for the past, and constricting rules of acceptable behavior. Confucianism, he said, had "cannibalized" China. Although he died
before Mao Zedong and the Chinese Communist Party[2] seized control of
the country after World War II, Lu Xun was recognized by the Communist leader as the spiritual father of the Chinese Revolution.

A Revolutionary Life.   While a medical student in Japan, Lu Xun came
across a photograph from the Russo-Japanese War of 1904–05. The picture showed a Chinese prisoner about to be beheaded by the Japanese
surrounded by a group of Chinese who appeared indifferent to the fate of
their countryman. Lu Xun decided to challenge the apathy of the Chinese

loo-SHWEN

My themes were
usually the unfortu-
nates of this abnor-
mal society. My aim
was to expose the
disease and draw
attention to it so that
it might be cured.
        – LU XUN

---

[1] **critical realism:** The idea of critical realism became increasingly connected to Lu Xun's notion of revolution.
In an address to the League of Left-Wing Writers (1930), a group he had helped to form, Lu Xun stated: "Revolution is a bitter thing, mixed with filth and blood, not as lovely or perfect as poets think. Of course there is
destruction in a revolution, but construction is even more necessary to it; and while destruction is straightforward, construction is troublesome."

[2] **Mao . . . Party:** Mao Zedong (1893–1976) was a founding member of the Chinese Communist Party (1921).
After breaking with the Kuomintang nationalists in 1927, Mao Zedong consolidated his authority against both
the invading Japanese and the Kuomintang and ousted the Chinese nationalists in 1949.

Portrait of Lu Xun,
c. 1900

*The writer Lu Xun
was revered by
Mao Zedong and
the Communists.
(© Bettmann/
CORBIS)*

by returning home and creating a movement to win the youth of China to the cause of social change, starting the literary journal *New Youth* and working as a teacher. His first short story, "A Madman's Diary" (1918), is a scathing attack on what Lu Xun saw as a cannibalistic society that was devouring itself. Considered the first work of modern Chinese literature, it was written in vernacular and colloquial Chinese rather than in the usual literary language. The "madman" who narrates the story is obsessed by the growing paranoia that he lives in a society of cannibals.

From 1920 to 1926 Lu Xun worked in the anti-imperialist movement in Beijing (Peking), and in 1927 he moved to Canton, then a seat of revolutionary activity. After the coup d'état of Chiang Kai-shek and his Kuomintang army[3] later that year, Lu Xun retreated to Shanghai, where he lived his last ten years fighting the Japanese imperialists on the one hand and Chiang Kai-shek's rightist government on the other. He organized the League of Left-Wing Writers and wrote more than six hundred essays under many pen names while dodging political repression. Though encouraged by the successes of the Chinese Communists, he never joined the Communist Party. He died of tuberculosis in Shanghai in 1936.

Political Fiction.   Lu Xun wrote many political essays, commentaries, literary sketches, and reminiscences, but his literary reputation is based on the twenty-six short stories that were published between 1918 and 1935 and gathered in three collections: *Call to Arms* (1922), *Wandering* (1925), and *Old Tales Retold* (1935). The recurrent theme in nearly all of the stories is the oppressive hold of the past on the present. Influenced by the work of European Realists, especially the Russian writers Nikolai Gogol (1809–1852) and Maxim Gorky (1868–1936), Lu Xun described his subject as "the unfortunates of this abnormal society. My aim was to expose the disease and draw attention to it so that it might be cured." In "The New Year's Sacrifice," for example, he shows how the feudal family system in China "murders" a woman who is treated as property and sold into two wretched marriages and who finally dies as an outcast beggar on New Year's day. The story's irony and bleak satire are characteristic of Lu Xun's work. In "Regret for the Past," he writes of two lovers who defy social rules by living together and rejecting established gender roles. The social rejection and financial hardship they suffer as a result of their defiance, however, destroys their love, drives them apart, and presages their deaths. Lu Xun's stories always lead to the conclusion that so destructive a culture has to be changed.

Regarded as a
national hero and
canonized by the
Chinese Communist
Party, Lu Xun has
been revered as the
intellectual source of
the Chinese Revolu-
tion who prepared
the ideological
ground for Mao
Zedong.

— DANIEL S. BURT,
critic, 2001

"A Madman's Diary."   This story, first published in *New Youth* magazine in 1918 and reprinted in the collection *Call to Arms* (1922), purports to be the diary of a man who believes everyone around him, including

---

[3] **Chiang . . . army:** Chiang Kai-shek (1887–1975) originally supported the separatist Chinese government of Sun Yat-sen in 1918, occupied the capital of Beijing in 1928, then lost ground to the Communist Party and was finally forced to withdraw with his army to the island of Taiwan in 1949.

members of his own family, are cannibals who want to eat him. Lu Xun may have had Gogol in mind as he wrote, for Gogol, whose work Lu Xun had translated into Chinese, had written a story by the same title about an office worker who believes he is the king of Spain. The comic tone of Gogol's story, however, is quite different from the dark cynicism of Lu Xun's tale, which is closer to Jonathan Swift's satire "A Modest Proposal" (1729), which used cannibalism as a savage way to satirize the British oppression of the Irish people. Lu Xun is attacking the influence of Confucianism, the centuries-old doctrine that guided Chinese society well into the twentieth century, suppressing individualism, nonconformity, and social progress. Its virtues of benevolence, righteousness, and morality only thinly disguised the dog-eat-dog voraciousness underneath, a truth that only the madman seems able to see.

■ FURTHER RESEARCH

Translations
Lyell, William A., trans. *Diary of a Madman and Other Stories.* 1990.
Yang, Xianyi, and Gladys Yang, trans. *The Complete Stories of Lu Xun.* 1981.

Criticism
Lee, Leo Ou-fan. *Voices from the Iron House: A Study of Lu Xun.* 1987.
Lyell, William A. *Lu Hsun's Vision of Reality.* 1976.

■ PRONUNCIATION

Ah Gui: ah-GWAY
Bao Si: bow-SUH
Chen Duxiu: chun-doo-SHYOO
Chiang Kai-shek: jahng-kigh-SHEK
Chong Zhen: chohng-JUN
Da Ji: dah-JEE
Diao Chan: dyow-CHAHN
Dong Zhuo: dohng-JWOH
Fu Xi: foo-SHEE
Kuomintang: gwoh-min-DAHNG, kwoh-min-TAHNG
Lu Xun: loo-SHWEN
Mao Zedong: mow-dzuh-DOHNG
Qian: chee-EN
Qing: CHING
Shaoxing: show-SHING
Tianshui: tyen-SHWAY
Xuan De, Xuan Tong: shwen-DUH, shwen-TOHNG
Weizhuang: way-JWAHNG
Zhang: JAHNG
Zhao, Zhao Baiyan, Zhao Sichen: JOW, jow-bah-YAN, jow-suh-CHUN
Zhou: JOH
Zi You Dang: dzuh-yoh-DAHNG
Zou: DZOH
Zuo Zhuan: dzwoh-JWEN

Lu Xun was the major leader in the Chinese cultural revolution. He was not only a great writer but a great thinker and a great revolutionist. . . . Lu Xun breached and stormed the enemy citadel; on the cultural front he was the bravest and most correct, the firmest, the most loyal, and the most ardent national hero, a hero without parallel in our history.

– MAO ZEDONG

WWW For more information about Lu Xun and the culture and context of twentieth-century China, see bedfordstmartins .com/worldlit compact.

A Madman's Diary

Translated by Yang Xianyi and Gladys Yang

Two brothers, whose names I need not mention here, were both good friends of mine in high school; but after a separation of many years we gradually lost touch. Some time ago I happened to hear that one of them was seriously ill, and since I was going back to my old home I broke my journey to call on them. I saw only one, however, who told me that the invalid was his younger brother.

"I appreciate your coming such a long way to see us," he said, "but my brother recovered some time ago and has gone elsewhere to take up an official post." Then, laughing, he produced two volumes of his brother's diary, saying that from these the nature of his past illness could be seen, and that there was no harm in showing them to an old friend. I took the diary away, read it through, and found that he had suffered from a form of persecution complex. The writing was most confused and incoherent, and he had made many wild statements; moreover he had omitted to give any dates, so that only by the colour of the ink and the differences in the writing could one tell that it was not written at one time. Certain sections, however, were not altogether disconnected, and I have copied out a part to serve as a subject for medical research. I have not altered a single illogicality in the diary and have changed only the names, even though the people referred to are all country folk, unknown to the world and of no consequence. As for the title, it was chosen by the diarist himself after his recovery, and I did not change it.

I

Tonight the moon is very bright.

I have not seen it for over thirty years, so today when I saw it I felt in unusually high spirits. I begin to realize that during the past thirty-odd years I have been in the dark; but now I must be extremely careful. Otherwise why should that dog at the Chao house have looked at me twice?

I have reason for my fear.

II

Tonight there is no moon at all, I know that this bodes ill. This morning when I went out cautiously, Mr. Chao had a strange look in his eyes, as if he were afraid of me, as if he wanted to murder me. There were seven or eight others, who discussed me in a whisper. And they were afraid of my seeing them. All the people I passed were like that. The fiercest among them grinned at me; whereupon I shivered from head to foot, knowing that their preparations were complete.

I was not afraid, however, but continued on my way. A group of children in front were also discussing me, and the look in their eyes was just like that in Mr. Chao's while their faces too were ghastly pale. I wondered what grudge these children could have against me to make them behave like this. I could not help calling out: "Tell me!" But then they ran away.

I wonder what grudge Mr. Chao can have against me, what grudge the people on the road can have against me. I can think of nothing except that twenty years ago I trod on Mr. Ku Chiu's[1] accounts sheets for many years past, and Mr. Ku was very displeased. Although Mr. Chao does not know him, he must have heard talk of this and decided to avenge him, so he is conspiring against me with the people on the road. But then what of the children? At that time they were not yet born, so why should they eye me so strangely today, as if they were afraid of me, as if they wanted to murder me? This really frightens me, it is so bewildering and upsetting.

I know. They must have learned this from their parents!

III

I can't sleep at night. Everything requires careful consideration if one is to understand it.

Those people, some of whom have been pilloried by the magistrate, slapped in the face by the local gentry, had their wives taken away by bailiffs, or their parents driven to suicide by creditors, never looked as frightened and as fierce then as they did yesterday.

The most extraordinary thing was that woman on the street yesterday who spanked her son and said, "Little devil! I'd like to bite several mouthfuls out of you to work off my feelings!" Yet all the time she looked at me. I gave a start, unable to control myself; then all those green-faced, long-toothed people began to laugh derisively. Old Chen hurried forward and dragged me home.

He dragged me home. The folk at home all pretended not to know me; they had the same look in their eyes as all the others. When I went into the study, they locked the door outside as if cooping up a chicken or a duck. This incident left me even more bewildered.

A few days ago a tenant of ours from Wolf Cub Village came to report the failure of the crops, and told my elder brother that a notorious character in their village had been beaten to death; then some people had taken out his heart and liver, fried them in oil and eaten them, as a means of increasing their courage. When I interrupted, the tenant and my brother both stared at me. Only today have I realized that they had exactly the same look in their eyes as those people outside.

Just to think of it sets me shivering from the crown of my head to the soles of my feet.

They eat human beings, so they may eat me.

I see that woman's "bite several mouthfuls out of you," the laughter of those green-faced, long-toothed people and the tenant's story the other day are obviously secret signs. I realize all the poison in their speech, all the daggers in their laughter. Their teeth are white and glistening: they are all man-eaters.

---

[1] **Ku Chiu:** The name literally means Mr. Ancient Times. Lu Xun uses him to represent Confucianism and its long history of oppression.

It seems to me, although I am not a bad man, ever since I trod on Mr. Ku's accounts it has been touch-and-go. They seem to have secrets which I cannot guess, and once they are angry they will call anyone a bad character. I remember when my elder brother taught me to write compositions, no matter how good a man was, if I produced arguments to the contrary he would mark that passage to show his approval; while if I excused evil-doers, he would say: "Good for you, that shows originality." How can I possibly guess their secret thoughts—especially when they are ready to eat people?

Everything requires careful consideration if one is to understand it. In ancient times, as I recollect, people often ate human beings, but I am rather hazy about it. I tried to look this up, but my history has no chronology, and scrawled all over each page are the words: "Virtue and Morality." Since I could not sleep anyway, I read intently half the night, until I began to see words between the lines, the whole book being filled with the two words—"Eat people."

All these words written in the book, all the words spoken by our tenant, gaze at me strangely with an enigmatic smile.

I too am a man, and they want to eat me!

IV

In the morning I sat quietly for some time. Old Chen brought lunch in: one bowl of vegetables, one bowl of steamed fish. The eyes of the fish were white and hard, and its mouth was open just like those people who want to eat human beings. After a few mouthfuls I could not tell whether the slippery morsels were fish or human flesh, so I brought it all up.

I said, "Old Chen, tell my brother that I feel quite suffocated, and want to have a stroll in the garden?' Old Chen said nothing but went out, and presently he came back and opened the gate.

I did not move, but watched to see how they would treat me, feeling certain that they would not let me go. Sure enough! My elder brother came slowly out, leading an old man. There was a murderous gleam in his eyes, and fearing that I would see it he lowered his head, stealing glances at me from the side of his spectacles.

"You seem to be very well today," said my brother.

"Yes," said I.

"I have invited Mr. Ho here today," said my brother, "to examine you."

"All right," said I. Actually I knew quite well that this old man was the executioner in disguise! He simply used the pretext of feeling my pulse to see how fat I was; for by so doing he would receive a share of my flesh. Still I was not afraid. Although I do not eat men, my courage is greater than theirs. I held out my two fists, to see what he would do. The old man sat down, closed his eyes, fumbled for some time and remained still for some time; then he opened his shifty eyes and said, "Don't let your imagination run away with you. Rest quietly for a few days, and you will be all right."

Don't let your imagination run away with you! Rest quietly for a few days! When I have grown fat, naturally they will have more to eat; but what good will it do me, or how can it be "all right"? All these people wanting to eat human flesh and at the same time stealthily trying to keep up appearances, not daring to act promptly, really made me nearly die of laughter. I could not help roaring with laughter, I was so amused. I knew that in this laughter were courage and integrity. Both the old man and my brother turned pale, awed by my courage and integrity.

But just because I am brave they are the more eager to eat me, in order to acquire some of my courage. The old man went out of the gate, but before he had gone far he said to my brother in a low voice, "To be eaten at once!" And my brother nodded. So you are in it too! This stupendous discovery, although it came as a shock, is yet no more than I had expected: the accomplice in eating me is my elder brother!

The eater of human flesh is my elder brother!

I am the younger brother of an eater of human flesh!

I myself will be eaten by others, but none the less I am the younger brother of an eater of human flesh!

V

These few days I have been thinking again: suppose that old man were not an executioner in disguise, but a real doctor; he would be none the less an eater of human flesh. In that book on herbs, written by his predecessor Li Shih-chen,[2] it is clearly stated that men's flesh can be boiled and eaten; so can he still say that he does not eat men?

As for my elder brother, I have also good reason to suspect him. When he was teaching me, he said with his own lips, "People exchange their sons to eat." And once in discussing a bad man, he said that not only did he deserve to be killed, he should "have his flesh eaten and his hide slept on."[3] I was still young then, and my heart beat faster for some time, he was not at all surprised by the story that our tenant from Wolf Cub Village told us the other day about eating a man's heart and liver, but kept nodding his head. He is evidently just as cruel as before. Since it is possible to "exchange sons to eat," then anything can be exchanged, anyone can be eaten. In the past I simply listened to his explanations, and let it go at that; now I know that when he explained it to me, not only was there human fat at the corner of his lips, but his whole heart was set on eating men.

VI

Pitch dark. I don't know whether it is day or night. The Chao family dog has started barking again.

The fierceness of a lion, the timidity of a rabbit, the craftiness of a fox. . . .

---

[2] **Shih-chen:** A pharmacologist (1518–1595); his *Taxonomy of Medicinal Herbs* was the standard work on the subject in China.

[3] These quotations are from the classic *Zuozhuan* (third century B.C.E.).

VII

I know their way; they are not willing to kill anyone outright, nor do they dare, for fear of the consequences. Instead they have banded together and set traps everywhere, to force me to kill myself. The behaviour of the men and women in the street a few days ago, and my elder brother's attitude these last few days, make it quite obvious. What they like best is for a man to take off his belt, and hang himself from a beam; for then they can enjoy their heart's desire without being blamed for murder. Naturally that sets them roaring with delighted laughter. On the other hand, if a man is frightened or worried to death, although that makes him rather thin, they still nod in approval.

They only eat dead flesh! I remember reading somewhere of a hideous beast, with an ugly look in its eye, called "hyena" which often eats dead flesh. Even the largest bones it grinds into fragments and swallows: the mere thought of this is enough to terrify one. Hyenas are related to wolves, and wolves belong to the canine species. The other day the dog in the Chao house looked at me several times; obviously it is in the plot too and has become their accomplice. The old man's eyes were cast down, but that did not deceive me!

The most deplorable is my elder brother. He is also a man, so why is he not afraid, why is he plotting with others to eat me? Is it that when one is used to it he no longer thinks it a crime? Or is it that he has hardened his heart to do something he knows is wrong?

In cursing man-eaters, I shall start with my brother, and in dissuading man-eaters, I shall start with him too.

VIII

Actually, such arguments should have convinced them long ago. . . .

Suddenly someone came in. He was only about twenty years old and I did not see his features very clearly. His face was wreathed in smiles, but when he nodded to me his smile did not seem genuine. I asked him: "Is it right to eat human beings?"

Still smiling, he replied, "When there is no famine how can one eat human beings?"

I realized at once, he was one of them; but still I summoned up courage to repeat my question:

"Is it right?"

"What makes you ask such a thing? You really are . . . fond of a joke. . . . It is very fine today."

"It is fine, and the moon is very bright. But I want to ask you: Is it right?"

He looked disconcerted, and muttered: "No. . . ."

"No? Then why do they still do it?"

"What are you talking about?"

"What am I talking about? They are eating men now in Wolf Cub Village, and you can see it written all over the books, in fresh red ink."

His expression changed, and he grew ghastly pale. "It may be so," he said, staring at me. "It has always been like that. . . ."

"Is it right because it has always been like that?"

"I refuse to discuss these things with you. Anyway, you shouldn't talk about it. Whoever talks about it is in the wrong!"

I leaped up and opened my eyes wide, but the man had vanished. I was soaked with perspiration. He was much younger than my elder brother, but even so he was in it. He must have been taught by his parents. And I am afraid he has already taught his son: that is why even the children look at me so fiercely.

IX

Wanting to eat men, at the same time afraid of being eaten themselves, they all look at each other with the deepest suspicion. . . .

How comfortable life would be for them if they could rid themselves of such obsessions and go to work, walk, eat and sleep at ease. They have only this one step to take. Yet fathers and sons, husbands and wives, brothers, friends, teachers and students, sworn enemies and even strangers, have all joined in this conspiracy, discouraging and preventing each other from taking this step.

X

Early this morning I went to look for my elder brother. He was standing outside the hall door looking at the sky, when I walked up behind him, stood between him and the door, and with exceptional poise and politeness said to him:

"Brother, I have something to say to you."

"Well, what is it?" he asked, quickly turning towards me and nodding.

"It is very little, but I find it difficult to say. Brother, probably all primitive people ate a little human flesh to begin with. Later, because their outlook changed, some of them stopped, and because they tried to be good they changed into men, changed into real men. But some are still eating—just like reptiles. Some have changed into fish, birds, monkeys and finally men; but some do not try to be good and remain reptiles still. When those who eat men compare themselves with those who do not, how ashamed they must be. Probably much more ashamed than the reptiles are before monkeys.

"In ancient times Yi Ya boiled his son for Chieh and Chou to eat; that is the old story.[4] But actually since the creation of heaven and earth by Pan Ku men have been eating each other, from the time of Yi Ya's son to the time of Hsu Hsi-lin,[5] and from the time of Hsu Hsi-lin down to the man caught in Wolf Cub Village. Last year they executed a criminal in the city, and a consumptive soaked a piece of bread in his blood and sucked it.

---

[4] **Yi Ya . . . story:** According to an ancient text, *Guan Zi*, Yi Ya cooked his son and presented him to Duke Huan of Chi, who reigned from 685 to 643 B.C.E., because the Duke had never tasted the flesh of children. Chieh and Chou were tyrants from an earlier period. The madman has made a historical mistake here.

[5] **Hsu Hsi-lin:** A revolutionary who assassinated a high official of the Ching dynasty in 1907. After he was executed for the crime, his heart and liver were eaten.

"They want to eat me, and of course you can do nothing about it single-handed; but why should you join them? As man-eaters they are capable of anything. If they eat me, they can eat you as well; members of the same group can still eat each other. But if you will just change your ways immediately, then everyone will have peace. Although this has been going on since time immemorial, today we could make a special effort to be good, and say this is not to be done! I'm sure you can say so, brother. The other day when the tenant wanted the rent reduced, you said it couldn't be done."

At first he only smiled cynically, then a murderous gleam came into his eyes, and when I spoke of their secret his face turned pale. Outside the gate stood a group of people, including Mr. Chao and his dog, all craning their necks to peer in. I could not see all their faces, for they seemed to be masked in cloths; some of them looked pale and ghastly still, concealing their laughter. I knew they were one band, all eaters of human flesh. But I also knew that they did not all think alike by any means. Some of them thought that since it had always been so, men should be eaten. Some of them knew that they should not eat men, but still wanted to; and they were afraid people might discover their secret; thus when they heard me they became angry, but they still smiled their cynical, tight-lipped smile.

Suddenly my brother looked furious, and shouted in a loud voice:

"Get out of here, all of you! What is the point of looking at a madman?"

Then I realized part of their cunning. They would never be willing to change their stand, and their plans were all laid; they had stigmatized me as a madman. In future when I was eaten, not only would there be no trouble, but people would probably be grateful to them. When our tenant spoke of the villagers eating a bad character, it was exactly the same device. This is their old trick.

Old Chen came in too, in a great temper, but they could not stop my mouth, I had to speak to those people:

"You should change, change from the bottom of your hearts!" I said. "You must know that in the future there will be no place for man-eaters in the world.

"If you don't change, you may all be eaten by each other. Although so many are born, they will be wiped out by the real men, just like wolves killed by hunters. Just like reptiles!"

Old Chen drove everybody away. My brother had disappeared. Old Chen advised me to go back to my room. The room was pitch dark. The beams and rafters shook above my head. After shaking for some time they grew larger. They piled on top of me.

The weight was so great, I could not move. They meant that I should die. I knew that the weight was false, so I struggled out, covered in perspiration. But I had to say:

"You should change at once, change from the bottom of your hearts! You must know that in the future there will be no place for man-eaters in the world. . . ."

XI

The sun does not shine, the door is not opened, every day two meals.

I took up my chopsticks, then thought of my elder brother; I know now how my little sister died: it was all through him. My sister was only five at the time. I can still remember how lovable and pathetic she looked. Mother cried and cried, but he begged her not to cry, probably because he had eaten her himself, and so her crying made him feel ashamed. If he had any sense of shame. . . .

My sister was eaten by my brother, but I don't know whether mother realized it or not.

I think mother must have known, but when she cried she did not say so outright, probably because she thought it proper too. I remember when I was four or five years old, sitting in the cool of the hall, my brother told me that if a man's parents were ill, he should cut off a piece of his flesh and boil it for them if he wanted to be considered a good son;[6] and mother did not contradict him. If one piece could be eaten, obviously so could the whole. And yet just to think of the mourning then still makes my heart bleed; that is the extraordinary thing about it!

XII

I can't bear to think of it.

I have only just realized that I have been living all these years in a place where for four thousand years they have been eating human flesh. My brother had just taken over the charge of the house when our sister died, and he may well have used her flesh in our rice and dishes, making us eat it unwittingly.

It is possible that I ate several pieces of my sister's flesh unwittingly, and now it is my turn. . . .

How can a man like myself, after four thousand years of man-eating history — even though I knew nothing about it at first — ever hope to face real men?

XIII

Perhaps there are still children who have not eaten men? Save the children. . . .

---

[6]**if a man's . . . good son:** An example of the kind of doctrines taught in traditional Confucian literature to illustrate filial piety, one of the primary Confucian virtues.

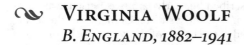

VIRGINIA WOOLF
B. ENGLAND, 1882–1941

Virginia Woolf's novels break away from early-twentieth-century literary conventions to reflect women's thought patterns, viewpoints, and sense of time. Although in her private life Woolf avoided Freudian analysis,[1] in her fiction she advanced the MODERNIST narrative techniques of

---

[1] **Freudian analysis:** Sigmund Freud (1856–1939) is the father of psychoanalysis.

Virginia Woolf, 1929
Woolf at age forty-seven. (Hulton / Archive)

STREAM OF CONSCIOUSNESS and SYMBOLISM that drew heavily on Freud's theories, and she and her husband, Leonard Woolf, made Freud's works widely available in English translation through their Hogarth Press. Though wary like many of her female contemporaries of being labeled a "feminist," Woolf wrote two volumes of pioneering feminist essays exploring women's creativity and the factors that might inhibit it.

Virginia Woolf is too often remembered not for her accomplishments but for the intermittent mental illness that ultimately led to her suicide during the dark days of early World War II. Woolf was much more than her illness and her death: a woman with a genius for friendship; in her own, soft-spoken manner, a feminist; a devoted wife and partner; and above all, a brilliant, innovative writer who was by turns playful, philosophical, lyrical, analytical, sensuous, affectionate, perceptive, and fiercely life-affirming.

A Stimulating Childhood.

Adeline Virginia Stephen was born in London on January 25, 1882, the third child and second daughter of Leslie and Julia Princep Stephen. Woolf and her older sister, Vanessa, were close companions all their lives, and Virginia adored her older brother, Thoby. A younger brother, Adrian, was born in 1883. Both parents had been previously married and widowed, and Woolf had half siblings on both sides of the family. The children of her mother's first marriage—Stella, George, and Gerald Duckworth—were to figure importantly in Woolf's early life.

Woolf's father was the epitome of the eminent VICTORIAN. Not wealthy but sufficiently well-off, he was a literary man—a critic, scholar, magazine editor, and biographer. Woolf's mother, Julia Stephen, was celebrated for her lively charm and her perfect profile, and Virginia was the uneasy heir of her mother's beauty. The Duckworth and Stephen children grew up in the heady intellectual atmosphere of a household that regularly entertained such luminaries of late Victorian culture as the writers Alfred, Lord Tennyson; Henry James; and George Meredith;[2] the painters Holman Hunt and Edward Burne-Jones; and the actress Ellen Terry.[3] Woolf's great-aunt on her mother's side was the pioneering photographer Julia Cameron.

There were pleasures and injuries in this upbringing, especially during the summers spent in the family's country house on the Cornwall coast, and, overall, Woolf described her early family experience as "tangled and matted with emotion." The most sinister element was the sexual abuse she and Vanessa suffered at the hands of their two Duckworth half brothers in childhood and adolescence. As an adult Woolf wrote of the abuse, but like many victims she seems never to have connected the past

www   For links to more information about Woolf, quizzes on her work, and information about the culture and context of twentieth-century Europe, see bedfordstmartins .com/worldlit compact.

---

[2] Tennyson . . . Meredith: Alfred, Lord Tennyson (1809–1892) was poet laureate of England. Henry James (1843–1916) was an American novelist. George Meredith (1828–1909) was an English novelist and poet.

[3] Hunt . . . Terry: Holman Hunt (1827–1910) was an English painter. Edward Burne-Jones (1833–1898) was an English painter and designer. Ellen Terry (1848–1928) was a renowned English actress.

abuse with her problems in adulthood, namely her sexual frigidity and her mental illness. Instead, she concluded that she was born naturally deficient in sensuality and mental health.

Like most girls of their social class, Woolf and her sister were tutored at home by their mother and a series of governesses. Formal education was reserved for boys, but Leslie Stephen was wise enough to discern his daughter Virginia's gifts. When she asked to learn ancient Greek, he was happy to hire a tutor. He allowed her to read any book in his library and enjoyed discussing literature with her. Her mother imparted a different sort of influence, imbued as she was with the Victorian ideal that women fulfilled their highest natures by serving others cheerfully. When grown, Woolf would characterize that ideal as "The Angel in the House" and identify it as the dangerous spirit that keeps women from expressing themselves, making them intent on pleasing men rather than being true to their own natures and talents.

Death and Depression.   More traumatic events marred Woolf's adolescence, beginning with the sudden death of her mother when Virginia was thirteen. Her much-beloved half sister, Stella Duckworth, became the maternal figure for her stepfamily, but a scant two years later, while honeymooning with her new husband, she too died, of a sudden acute infection. Virginia's father grew more and more depressed and withdrawn, and Virginia and Vanessa had to run the household until his death in 1904. Although Virginia's grief for him was enough to precipitate a second breakdown — the first occurred after her mother's death — his death eventually freed her. She began teaching at a night school for working-class people, joined the suffrage movement, and wrote book reviews.

By 1905, Thoby, Vanessa, Virginia, and Adrian Stephen had moved together into a flat in the Bloomsbury section of London and began keeping lively company with Thoby's friends, a household arrangement that lasted until Thoby's death of typhoid fever the following year. Many of the brilliant men who came to the Stephen children's home were members of a society at Cambridge called the Apostles. Most were on their way to becoming the intellectual lights of their generation. Many were bisexual or gay, and their uninhibited discussions often centered on sexuality as well as art and politics. Eventually their circle, called "Bloomsbury" by social historians, included historian Lytton Strachey; economic theorist John Maynard Keynes; novelist E. M. Forster; art critic Roger Fry; artist and art critic Clive Bell,[4] whom Vanessa would marry in 1907; and civil administrator Leonard Woolf, later a policy developer for the Labour Party who became Virginia's husband in 1912.

---

[4] **Strachey . . . Bell:** Bloomsbury began as a social group, but through its members' writings developed into a cultural force that broke free from Victorian restrictions. Lytton Strachey (1880–1932) wrote biographies. John Maynard Keynes (1883–1946) became known for Keynesian economics, which involves government control of interest and tax rates. E. M. Forster (1879–1970) wrote very important novels about the English middle class, including *A Passage to India* (1924). Roger Fry (1866–1934) was an art critic who championed Cézanne and other French painters. Clive Bell (1881–1964) was an art critic whose books include *Landmarks in Nineteenth-Century Painting* (1927).

Something, she meant, is immune from change, and shines out (she glanced at the window with its ripple of reflected lights) in the face of the flowing, the fleeting, the spectral, like a ruby; so that again tonight she had the feeling she had had once today, already, of peace, of rest. Of such moments, she thought, the thing is made that endures.

– VIRGINIA WOOLF, *To the Lighthouse*, 1927

Creating a Space for Writing.   For Virginia Stephen, Leonard Woolf proved the wisest choice she could have made. Always held as something of an outsider because he was Jewish, Leonard provided for Virginia a slight distancing from the intense, intellectual involvements of Bloomsbury. For the rest of his life, his real occupation would be to care tenderly for his wife, nursing her through her terrifying bouts of illness, arranging her life, protecting and supporting her, and keeping her as well and productive as possible. Leonard Woolf's presence enabled his wife to write; it was only after their marriage that she managed to complete her first novel, *The Voyage Out* (1915), which she had begun in 1907. With *Jacob's Room* (1922), Woolf began to experiment with subject and narrative form. In her next novel, *Mrs. Dalloway* (1925), Woolf centered on a single day in the lives of a London society woman and a shell-shocked veteran of World War I.

Until she was forty-four and had written *To the Lighthouse* (1927), whose main character, Mrs. Ramsey, is based on her mother, Woolf was literally haunted by the apparition and voice of Julia Stephen. The ebullient tour de force, *Orlando* (1928), was inspired by Woolf's delight in her adventurous cross-dressing friend, Vita Sackville-West. *Orlando*'s protagonist begins as a male adolescent in Elizabethan England, undergoes a mysterious sex change around the time of the Restoration, and while still in her thirties and a woman, ends up as a successful female writer in contemporary London. In 1928, Woolf delivered the lectures on women and creativity at Newnham College, Cambridge, that would become *A Room of One's Own* (1929), excerpts of which are presented here. With her next book, *The Waves* (1931), Woolf's work began to grow less exuberant, reflecting her difficulty in the last decade of her life of maintaining the mental health necessary to write.

One offshoot of Woolf's long quest for health was the establishment of Hogarth Press, originally conceived as a project that would engage Virginia in simple therapeutic tasks such as typesetting and bookbinding. The press, however, became a commercial and artistic success, publishing authors such as Katherine Mansfield[5] and T. S. Eliot[6] as well as the Woolfs' own work. Leonard Woolf's greatest literary achievement would prove to be the sensitive, detailed memoirs and diaries in which he chronicled his and Virginia's years together. Despite at least one significant affair between Virginia and another woman—the flamboyant Sackville-West—the Woolfs remained a devoted couple from the time of their marriage until Virginia's death twenty-nine years later. Together she and Leonard wrote and ran Hogarth Press when she was well; and together they contrived to get her through the major breakdowns that came regularly with the completion of each book.

---

[5] **Katherine Mansfield** (1888–1923): A short-story writer born in New Zealand.

[6] **T. S. Eliot** (1888–1965): An American-born poet who moved to England; he gave expression to the destruction of World War I with his startling poem *The Waste Land* (1922). See page 1450.

Virginia's Suicide.   In March 1941, anguished by the death of a favorite nephew in the Spanish civil war and by the Nazi bombings that destroyed both her and Leonard's London house and the building that housed Hogarth Press, Virginia feared that she was about to undergo a permanent breakdown that would leave her a burden to her husband. On March 28, she weighted her pockets with heavy stones and waded into the River Ouse below their country house in Sussex. After her body was recovered, Leonard buried Virginia's ashes beneath one of the great elms there and chose for her epitaph a sentence from *The Waves* (1931): "Against you I will fling myself, unvanquished and unyielding, O Death!"

New Directions for the Novel.   Both *The Voyage Out* and Woolf's second novel, *Night and Day* (1919), are relatively conventional novels about young women not unlike herself exploring questions of marriage and art. *Jacob's Room*, which is about a young man who resembles Virginia's brother, Thoby, represents a stylistic departure; it does not present the major incidents in the protagonist's life either chronologically or directly—we learn of Jacob's death only by way of his mother's cleaning out his room and wondering how to dispose of his personal effects. The main theme seems to be the impossibility of truly knowing the inner workings of Jacob or any other person. *Mrs. Dalloway* furthers the experimentation with the stream-of-consciousness technique. Woolf moves the narrative point of view back and forth between Mrs. Dalloway and the person who is in some sense her alter ego, one a sane and the other an insane character, gradually revealing the deep similarities between them, although they never meet. In the lyrical, semiautobiographical *To the Lighthouse* (1927), the novel that was to exorcise her mother's presence, Woolf explores the theme of women's roles while continuing to advance the stream-of-consciousness narrative technique by using an impressionistic sense of time rather than the hours of a day.

Thought by many to be her masterpiece, *The Waves* is Woolf's most experimental novel, with six different characters' stream-of-consciousness monologues all meditating on the death of a friend they hold in common, a character again modeled on Thoby. *The Years* (1937) brought Woolf her first wide popularity, setting forth the history of an upper-class English family, from the late Victorian age to the present. As political events in Europe darkened, she wrote *I Take Three Guineas* (1938), a brilliant feminist and pacifist work in which she explores the connections between Fascism and the patriarchy in which she had been raised. Not surprisingly, the book received many negative reviews as a tract for what E. M. Forster called "extreme feminism." *Between the Acts* (1941), the book Woolf finished drafting just before her death, is a complex narrative: Neighboring families in the country anticipate and then attend a village pageant. The work considers issues of time, history, loss, and the question of what endures despite and beyond them.

A Room of One's Own.   Published in 1929, *A Room of One's Own* is concerned with the second-class role of women in modern society. From its

> Life is not a series of gig lamps symmetrically arranged; but a luminous halo, a semitransparent envelope surrounding us from the beginning of consciousness to the end. Is it not the task of the novelist to convey this varying, this unknown and uncircumscribed spirit, whatever aberration or complexity it may display, with as little mixture of the alien and external as possible?
>
> – VIRGINIA WOOLF, 1925

title has come the now-popular idea that a woman writer needs "a room of her own" to pursue her calling. In the chapter reprinted here, Woolf returns frustrated from the British Museum library, where she has been unable to find any text to help her understand why women have not achieved equality with men. She is desperate to account for the disparity, but none of the books helps. Glancing through her own copy of Trevelyan's *History of England,* the narrator sees that women are all but excised from history, save for the most cursory and condescending references, and she understands that she will need to fashion for herself a model of what life might have been like for an Elizabethan woman with Shakespeare's gifts. The sensuous detail with which Woolf fleshes out this sadly predictable story and the beautifully controlled tone in which she tells it are essayist and feminist Virginia Woolf at her best.

"Three Pictures" and "The Fascination of the Pool."   The second piece, "Three Pictures," was written in 1929 but not published until 1942 in *The Death of the Moth,* after Woolf's death. In it Woolf imaginatively discusses three pictures, creating a thin line between essay and fiction. By using the metaphor of pictures and how "we must needs be pictures to each other," Woolf illustrates the layers of reality that lie beneath surface impressions, the difference between appearance and reality, and how difficult it is to penetrate beneath the "picture" and really know another person and his or her situation.

In "The Fascination of the Pool," Woolf uses the metaphor of a pool to explore the meanderings of memory, the ways that thoughts become layered in the mind and shift from one story to another; as Woolf says, beneath the surface of the water "went on some profound under-water life like the brooding, the ruminating of a mind." The mind contains bits of experiences that in their disembodied state float freely through the "water" of consciousness. When these pieces join together, individuals emerge with their kernels of history and intersecting stories. In the third paragraph, time itself becomes layered with meaning. We long to get to the bottom of the pool, to finally understand all the voices, and at times it seems as if we actually approach this possibility, only to have the moment slip away.

■ FURTHER RESEARCH

Biography
Bell, Quentin. *Virginia Woolf.* 1972.
Reid, Panthea. *Art and Affection: A Life of Virginia Woolf.* 1996.
Rose, Phyllis. *Woman of Letters: A Life of Virginia Woolf.* 1978.

Bibliography
Dick, Susan. *The Complete Shorter Fiction of Virginia Woolf.* 1989.
Kirkpatrick, B. J. *A Bibliography of Virginia Woolf.* 1997.

History and Culture
Bell, Quentin. *Bloomsbury.* 1968.
Laurence, Patricia Ondek. *The Reading of Silence: Virginia Woolf in the English Tradition.* 1991.
Todd, Pamela. *Bloomsbury at Home.* 1999.

Criticism

Bowlby, Rachel. *Feminist Destinations and Further Essays on Virginia Woolf.* 1997.
Clements, Patricia, and Isobel Grundy, eds. *Virginia Woolf: New Critical Essays.* 1983.
Homans, Margaret, ed. *Virginia Woolf: A Collection of Critical Essays.* 1993.
Marcus, Jane. *Virginia Woolf and the Language of Patriarchy.* 1987.
Nalbantian, Suzanne. *Aesthetic Autobiography: From Life to Art in Marcel Proust, James Joyce, Virginia Woolf, and Anaïs Nin.* 1994.

FROM

ꙮ A Room of One's Own

CHAPTER 3 [SHAKESPEARE'S SISTER][1]

It was disappointing not to have brought back in the evening some important statement, some authentic fact. Women are poorer than men because—this or that. Perhaps now it would be better to give up seeking for the truth, and receiving on one's head an avalanche of opinion hot as lava, discoloured as dish-water. It would be better to draw the curtains; to shut out distractions; to light the lamp; to narrow the enquiry and to ask the historian, who records not opinions but facts, to describe under what conditions women lived, not throughout the ages, but in England, say in the time of Elizabeth.

For it is a perennial puzzle why no woman wrote a word of that extraordinary literature when every other man, it seemed, was capable of song or sonnet. What were the conditions in which women lived, I asked myself; for fiction, imaginative work that is, is not dropped like a pebble upon the ground, as science may be; fiction is like a spider's web, attached ever so lightly perhaps, but still attached to life at all four corners. Often the attachment is scarcely perceptible; Shakespeare's plays, for instance, seem to hang there complete by themselves. But when the web is pulled askew, hooked up at the edge, torn in the middle, one remembers that these webs are not spun in mid-air by incorporeal creatures, but are the work of suffering human beings, and are attached to grossly material things, like health and money and the houses we live in.

I went, therefore, to the shelf where the histories stand and took down one of the latest, Professor Trevelyan's *History of England.*[2] Once more I looked up Women, found "position of," and turned to the pages indicated. "Wife-beating," I read, "was a recognised right of man, and was practised without shame by high as well as low. . . . Similarly," the historian goes on, "the daughter who refused to marry the gentleman

---

[1] Woolf has just returned from the library of the British Museum, where she has had no success in finding books that might help her understand why women seem to have achieved so much less than men throughout history.

[2] *History of England:* G. M. Trevelyan's *History of England* (1926) was, in Woolf's day, the most popular short history of the nation.

of her parents' choice was liable to be locked up, beaten and flung about the room, without any shock being inflicted on public opinion. Marriage was not an affair of personal affection, but of family avarice, particularly in the 'chivalrous' upper classes. . . . Betrothal often took place while one or both of the parties was in the cradle, and marriage when they were scarcely out of the nurses' charge." That was about 1470, soon after Chaucer's time. The next reference to the position of women is some two hundred years later, in the time of the Stuarts. "It was still the exception for women of the upper and middle class to choose their own husbands, and when the husband had been assigned, he was lord and master, so far at least as law and custom could make him. Yet even so," Professor Trevelyan concludes, "neither Shakespeare's women nor those of authentic seventeenth-century memoirs, like the Verneys and the Hutchinsons,[3] seem wanting in personality and character." Certainly, if we consider it, Cleopatra must have had a way with her; Lady Macbeth, one would suppose, had a will of her own; Rosalind, one might conclude, was an attractive girl.[4] Professor Trevelyan is speaking no more than the truth when he remarks that Shakespeare's women do not seem wanting in personality and character. Not being a historian, one might go even further and say that women have burnt like beacons in all the works of all the poets from the beginning of time—Clytemnestra, Antigone, Cleopatra, Lady Macbeth, Phèdre, Cressida, Rosalind, Desdemona, the Duchess of Malfi, among the dramatists; then among the prose writers: Millamant, Clarissa, Becky Sharp, Anna Karenina, Emma Bovary, Madame de Guermantes[5]—the names flock to mind, nor do they recall women "lacking in personality and character." Indeed, if woman had no existence save in the fiction written by men, one would imagine her a person of the utmost importance; very various; heroic and mean; splendid and sordid; infinitely beautiful and hideous in the extreme; as great as a man, some think even greater.[6] But this is woman in fiction. In fact, as Professor Trevelyan points out, she was locked up, beaten and flung about the room.

---

[3] **Verneys . . . Hutchinsons:** Authors of family memoirs of seventeenth-century England.

[4] **Cleopatra . . . girl:** Shakespeare's heroines from the plays *Antony and Cleopatra, Macbeth*, and *As You Like It*, respectively. Woolf is using the irony of understatement here.

[5] **Clytemnestra . . . Guermantes:** All are famous women characters from drama and fiction. In order, they are from Aeschylus's *Agamemnon;* Sophocles' *Antigone;* Shakespeare's *Antony and Cleopatra* and *Macbeth;* Racine's *Phèdre;* Shakespeare's *Troilus and Cressida, As You Like It,* and *Othello;* Webster's *The Duchess of Malfi;* Congreve's *The Way of the World;* Richardson's *Clarissa;* Thackeray's *Vanity Fair;* Tolstoy's *Anna Karenina;* Flaubert's *Madame Bovary;* and Proust's *Remembrance of Things Past.*

[6] **a person of . . . even greater:** "It remains a strange and almost inexplicable fact that in Athena's city, where women were kept in almost Oriental suppression as odalisques or drudges, the stage should yet have produced figures like Clytemnestra and Cassandra, Atossa and Antigone, Phèdre and Medea, and all the other heroines who dominate play after play of the 'misogynist' Euripides. But the paradox of this world where in real life a respectable woman could hardly show her face alone in the street, and yet on the stage woman equals or surpasses man, has never been satisfactorily explained. In modern tragedy the same predominance exists. At all events, a very cursory survey of Shakespeare's work (similarly with Webster, though not with Marlowe or Jonson) suffices to reveal how this dominance, this initiative of women, persists from Rosalind to Lady Macbeth. So too in Racine; six of his tragedies bear their heroines' names; and what male characters of his shall we set against Hermione and Andromaque, Bérénice and Roxane, Phèdre and Athalie? So again with Ibsen; what men shall we match with Solveig and Nora, Hedda and Hilda Wangel and Rebecca West?"—F. L. LUCAS, *Tragedy,* pp. 114–15. [Woolf's note.]

A very queer, composite being thus emerges. Imaginatively she is of the highest importance; practically she is completely insignificant. She pervades poetry from cover to cover; she is all but absent from history. She dominates the lives of kings and conquerors in fiction; in fact she was the slave of any boy whose parents forced a ring upon her finger. Some of the most inspired words, some of the most profound thoughts in literature fall from her lips; in real life she could hardly read, could scarcely spell, and was the property of her husband.

It was certainly an odd monster that one made up by reading the historians first and the poets afterwards—a worm winged like an eagle; the spirit of life and beauty in a kitchen chopping up suet. But these monsters, however amusing to the imagination, have no existence in fact. What one must do to bring her to life was to think poetically and prosaically at one and the same moment, thus keeping in touch with fact—that she is Mrs. Martin, aged thirty-six, dressed in blue, wearing a black hat and brown shoes; but not losing sight of fiction either—that she is a vessel in which all sorts of spirits and forces are coursing and flashing perpetually. The moment, however, that one tries this method with the Elizabethan woman, one branch of illumination fails; one is held up by the scarcity of facts. One knows nothing detailed, nothing perfectly true and substantial about her. History scarcely mentions her. And I turned to Professor Trevelyan again to see what history meant to him. I found by looking at his chapter headings that it meant—

"The Manor Court and the Methods of Open-field Agriculture . . . The Cistercians and Sheep-farming . . . The Crusades . . . The University . . . The House of Commons . . . The Hundred Years' War . . . The Wars of the Roses . . . The Renaissance Scholars . . . The Dissolution of the Monasteries . . . Agrarian and Religious Strife . . . The Origin of English Sea-power . . . The Armada . . ." and so on. Occasionally an individual woman is mentioned, an Elizabeth, or a Mary; a queen or a great lady. But by no possible means could middle-class women with nothing but brains and character at their command have taken part in any one of the great movements which, brought together, constitute the historian's view of the past. Nor shall we find her in any collection of anecdotes. Aubrey[7] hardly mentions her. She never writes her own life and scarcely keeps a diary; there are only a handful of her letters in existence. She left no plays or poems by which we can judge her. What one wants, I thought—and why does not some brilliant student at Newnham or Girton[8] supply it?—is a mass of information; at what age did she marry; how many children had she as a rule; what was her house like; had she a room to herself; did she do the cooking; would she be likely to have a servant? All these facts lie somewhere, presumably, in parish registers and account books; the life of the average Elizabethan woman must be scattered about somewhere, could one collect it and make a book of it. It would be ambitious beyond my daring, I thought, looking about the shelves for books that were not there, to suggest to the students of those famous colleges that they should rewrite history, though I own that it often seems a little queer as it is, unreal, lopsided; but why should they not add a supplement to history? calling it, of

---

[7] **Aubrey:** John Aubrey (1626–1697) was a British diarist.

[8] **Newnham or Girton:** Women's colleges of Cambridge University.

course, by some inconspicuous name so that women might figure there without impropriety? For one often catches a glimpse of them in the lives of the great, whisking away into the background, concealing, I sometimes think, a wink, a laugh, perhaps a tear. And, after all, we have lives enough of Jane Austen; it scarcely seems necessary to consider again the influence of the tragedies of Joanna Baillie upon the poetry of Edgar Allan Poe;[9] as for myself, I should not mind if the homes and haunts of Mary Russell Mitford[10] were closed to the public for a century at least. But what I find deplorable, I continued, looking about the bookshelves again, is that nothing is known about women before the eighteenth century. I have no model in my mind to turn about this way and that. Here am I asking why women did not write poetry in the Elizabethan age, and I am not sure how they were educated; whether they were taught to write; whether they had sitting-rooms to themselves; how many women had children before they were twenty-one; what, in short, they did from eight in the morning till eight at night. They had no money evidently; according to Professor Trevelyan they were married whether they liked it or not before they were out of the nursery, at fifteen or sixteen very likely. It would have been extremely odd, even upon this showing, had one of them suddenly written the plays of Shakespeare, I concluded, and I thought of that old gentleman, who is dead now, but was a bishop, I think, who declared that it was impossible for any woman, past, present, or to come, to have the genius of Shakespeare. He wrote to the papers about it. He also told a lady who applied to him for information that cats do not as a matter of fact go to heaven, though they have, he added, souls of a sort. How much thinking those old gentlemen used to save one! How the borders of ignorance shrank back at their approach! Cats do not go to heaven. Women cannot write the plays of Shakespeare.

Be that as it may, I could not help thinking, as I looked at the works of Shakespeare on the shelf, that the bishop was right at least in this; it would have been impossible, completely and entirely, for any woman to have written the plays of Shakespeare in the age of Shakespeare. Let me imagine, since facts are so hard to come by, what would have happened had Shakespeare had a wonderfully gifted sister, called Judith, let us say. Shakespeare himself went, very probably—his mother was an heiress—to the grammar school, where he may have learnt Latin—Ovid, Virgil, and Horace[11]—and the elements of grammar and logic. He was, it is well known, a wild boy who poached rabbits, perhaps shot a deer, and had, rather sooner than he should have done, to marry a woman in the neighbourhood, who bore him a child rather quicker than was right. That escapade sent him to seek his fortune in London. He had, it seemed, a taste for the theatre; he began by holding horses at the stage door. Very soon he got work in the theatre, became a successful actor, and lived at the hub of the universe, meeting everybody, knowing everybody, practising his art on the boards, exercising his wits in the streets, and even getting access to the palace

---

[9] **Baillie . . . Poe:** Baillie was an English dramatist (1762–1851); Edgar Allan Poe (1809–1849) was an American poet and fiction writer.

[10] **Mitford:** Mary Russell Mitford (1787–1855) wrote accounts of life in the English countryside.

[11] **Ovid . . . Horace:** Great Roman poets of the Augustan Age, standard fare for any schoolboy learning Latin.

of the queen. Meanwhile his extraordinarily gifted sister, let us suppose, remained at home. She was as adventurous, as imaginative, as agog to see the world as he was. But she was not sent to school. She had no chance of learning grammar and logic, let alone of reading Horace and Virgil. She picked up a book now and then, one of her brother's perhaps, and read a few pages. But then her parents came in and told her to mend the stockings or mind the stew and not moon about with books and papers. They would have spoken sharply but kindly, for they were substantial people who knew the conditions of life for a woman and loved their daughter—indeed, more likely than not she was the apple of her father's eye. Perhaps she scribbled some pages up in an apple loft on the sly, but was careful to hide them or set fire to them. Soon, however, before she was out of her teens, she was to be betrothed to the son of a neighbouring wool-stapler.[12] She cried out that marriage was hateful to her, and for that she was severely beaten by her father. Then he ceased to scold her. He begged her instead not to hurt him, not to shame him in this matter of her marriage. He would give her a chain of beads or a fine petticoat, he said; and there were tears in his eyes. How could she disobey him? How could she break his heart? The force of her own gift alone drove her to it. She made up a small parcel of her belongings, let herself down by a rope one summer's night and took the road to London. She was not seventeen. The birds that sang in the hedge were not more musical than she was. She had the quickest fancy, a gift like her brother's, for the tune of words. Like him, she had a taste for the theatre. She stood at the stage door; she wanted to act, she said. Men laughed in her face. The manager—a fat, loose-lipped man—guffawed. He bellowed something about poodles dancing and women acting—no woman, he said, could possibly be an actress. He hinted—you can imagine what. She could get no training in her craft. Could she even seek her dinner in a tavern or roam the streets at midnight? Yet her genius was for fiction and lusted to feed abundantly upon the lives of men and women and the study of their ways. At last—for she was very young, oddly like Shakespeare the poet in her face, with the same grey eyes and rounded brows—at last Nick Greene the actor-manager took pity on her; she found herself with child by that gentleman and so—who shall measure the heat and violence of the poet's heart when caught and tangled in a woman's body?—killed herself one winter's night and lies buried at some crossroads where the omnibuses now stop outside the Elephant and Castle.[13]

That, more or less, is how the story would run, I think, if a woman in Shakespeare's day had had Shakespeare's genius. But for my part, I agree with the deceased bishop, if such he was—it is unthinkable that any woman in Shakespeare's day should have had Shakespeare's genius. For genius like Shakespeare's is not born among labouring, uneducated, servile people. It was not born in England among the Saxons and the Britons. It is not born today among the working classes. How, then, could it have been born among women whose work began, according to Professor

---

[12] **wool-stapler:** Wool-dealer.

[13] **Elephant and Castle:** A pub. As a suicide, Judith could not be buried in consecrated ground. Burial at a crossroads was thought to keep the restless spirits of suicides safely in their graves.

Trevelyan, almost before they were out of the nursery, who were forced to it by their parents and held to it by all the power of law and custom? Yet genius of a sort must have existed among women as it must have existed among the working classes. Now and again an Emily Brontë or a Robert Burns[14] blazes out and proves its presence. But certainly it never got itself on to paper. When, however, one reads of a witch being ducked, of a woman possessed by devils, of a wise woman selling herbs, or even of a very remarkable man who had a mother, then I think we are on the track of a lost novelist, a suppressed poet, of some mute and inglorious Jane Austen, some Emily Brontë who dashed her brains out on the moor or mopped and mowed about the highways crazed with the torture that her gift had put her to. Indeed, I would venture to guess that Anon, who wrote so many poems without signing them, was often a woman. It was a woman Edward Fitzgerald,[15] I think, suggested who made the ballads and the folk-songs, crooning them to her children, beguiling her spinning with them, or the length of the winter's night.

This may be true or it may be false — who can say? — but what is true in it, so it seemed to me, reviewing the story of Shakespeare's sister as I had made it, is that any woman born with a great gift in the sixteenth century would certainly have gone crazed, shot herself, or ended her days in some lonely cottage outside the village, half witch, half wizard, feared and mocked at. For it needs little skill in psychology to be sure that a highly gifted girl who had tried to use her gift for poetry would have been so thwarted and hindered by other people, so tortured and pulled asunder by her own contrary instincts, that she must have lost her health and sanity to a certainty. No girl could have walked to London and stood at a stage door and forced her way into the presence of actor-managers without doing herself a violence and suffering an anguish which may have been irrational — for chastity may be a fetish invented by certain societies for unknown reasons — but were none the less inevitable. Chastity had then, it has even now, a religious importance in a woman's life, and has so wrapped itself round with nerves and instincts that to cut it free and bring it to the light of day demands courage of the rarest. To have lived a free life in London in the sixteenth century would have meant for a woman who was poet and playwright a nervous stress and dilemma which might well have killed her. Had she survived, whatever she had written would have been twisted and deformed, issuing from a strained and morbid imagination. And undoubtedly, I thought, looking at the shelf where there are no plays by women, her work would have gone unsigned. That refuge she would have sought certainly. It was the relic of the sense of chastity that dictated anonymity to women even so late as the nineteenth century. Currer Bell, George Eliot, George Sand,[16] all the victims of inner strife as their writings prove, sought ineffectively to veil themselves by using the name of a man. Thus they did homage to the convention, which if not implanted by the other sex was liberally

---

[14] Brontë . . . Burns: The Scots poet Robert Burns (1759–1796) came from the working class; the novelist Emily Brontë (1818–1848) had been raised as the sheltered and isolated daughter of a country curate.

[15] Edward Fitzgerald (1809–1883): A popular poet and translator.

[16] Currer Bell . . . Sand: The male pen names of the writers Charlotte Brontë, Marian Evans, and Aurore Dupin.

encouraged by them (the chief glory of a woman is not to be talked of, said Pericles,[17] himself a much-talked-of man), that publicity in women is detestable. Anonymity runs in their blood. The desire to be veiled still possesses them. They are not even now as concerned about the health of their fame as men are, and, speaking generally, will pass a tombstone or a signpost without feeling an irresistible desire to cut their names on it, as Alf, Bert, or Chas. must do in obedience to their instinct, which murmurs if it sees a fine woman go by, or even a dog, Ce chien est à moi.[18] And, of course, it may not be a dog, I thought, remembering Parliament Square, the Sièges Allée[19] and other avenues; it may be a piece of land or a man with curly black hair. It is one of the great advantages of being a woman that one can pass even a very fine negress without wishing to make an Englishwoman of her.

That woman, then, who was born with a gift of poetry in the sixteenth century, was an unhappy woman, a woman at strife against herself. All the conditions of her life, all her own instincts, were hostile to the state of mind which is needed to set free whatever is in the brain. But what is the state of mind that is most propitious to the act of creation, I asked. Can one come by any notion of the state that furthers and makes possible that strange activity? Here I opened the volume containing the Tragedies of Shakespeare. What was Shakespeare's state of mind, for instance, when he wrote *Lear* and *Antony and Cleopatra*? It was certainly the state of mind most favourable to poetry that there has ever existed. But Shakespeare himself said nothing about it. We only know casually and by chance that he "never blotted a line."[20] Nothing indeed was ever said by the artist himself about his state of mind until the eighteenth century perhaps. Rousseau perhaps began it. At any rate, by the nineteenth century self-consciousness had developed so far that it was the habit for men of letters to describe their minds in confessions and autobiographies. Their lives also were written, and their letters were printed after their deaths. Thus, though we do not know what Shakespeare went through when he wrote *Lear,* we do know what Carlyle went through when he wrote the *French Revolution;* what Flaubert went through when he wrote *Madame Bovary;* what Keats[21] was going through when he tried to write poetry against the coming of death and the indifference of the world.

And one gathers from this enormous modern literature of confession and self-analysis that to write a work of genius is almost always a feat of prodigious difficulty. Everything is against the likelihood that it will come from the writer's mind whole and entire. Generally material circumstances are against it. Dogs will bark; people will interrupt; money must be made; health will break down. Further, accentuating

---

[17] **Pericles** (c. 500–429 B.C.E.): A powerful Athenian statesman.

[18] **Ce chien . . . moi:** "That dog is mine" (French).

[19] **Parliament . . . Allée:** The seats of power of England and France; Woolf sees the root of colonialism in the male desire to possess.

[20] **"never . . . line":** Ben Jonson claimed this in *Timber, or Discoveries* (1691).

[21] **Carlyle . . . Keats:** All these authors encountered adversity. The first draft of Thomas Carlyle's *The French Revolution* (1837) was accidentally burned; Gustave Flaubert was charged with obscenity for writing *Madame Bovary* (1857); Keats wrote his great odes knowing he was soon to die of tuberculosis.

all these difficulties and making them harder to bear is the world's notorious indifference. It does not ask people to write poems and novels and histories; it does not need them. It does not care whether Flaubert finds the right word or whether Carlyle scrupulously verifies this or that fact. Naturally, it will not pay for what it does not want. And so the writer, Keats, Flaubert, Carlyle, suffers, especially in the creative years of youth, every form of distraction and discouragement. A curse, a cry of agony, rises from those books of analysis and confession. "Mighty poets in their misery dead"[22] — that is the burden of their song. If anything comes through in spite of all this, it is a miracle, and probably no book is born entire and uncrippled as it was conceived.

But for women, I thought, looking at the empty shelves, these difficulties were infinitely more formidable. In the first place, to have a room of her own, let alone a quiet room or a sound-proof room, was out of the question, unless her parents were exceptionally rich or very noble, even up to the beginning of the nineteenth century. Since her pin money, which depended on the good will of her father, was only enough to keep her clothed, she was debarred from such alleviations as came even to Keats or Tennyson or Carlyle, all poor men, from a walking tour, a little journey to France, from the separate lodging which, even if it were miserable enough, sheltered them from the claims and tyrannies of their families. Such material difficulties were formidable; but much worse were the immaterial. The indifference of the world which Keats and Flaubert and other men of genius have found so hard to bear was in her case not indifference but hostility. The world did not say to her as it said to them, Write if you choose; it makes no difference to me. The world said with a guffaw, Write? What's the good of your writing? Here the psychologists of Newnham and Girton might come to our help, I thought, looking again at the blank spaces on the shelves. For surely it is time that the effect of discouragement upon the mind of the artist should be measured, as I have seen a dairy company measure the effect of ordinary milk and Grade A milk upon the body of the rat. They set two rats in cages side by side, and of the two one was furtive, timid, and small, and the other was glossy, bold, and big. Now what food do we feed women as artists upon? I asked, remembering, I suppose, that dinner of prunes and custard.[23] To answer that question I had only to open the evening paper and to read that Lord Birkenhead[24] is of opinion — but really I am not going to trouble to copy out Lord Birkenhead's opinion upon the writing of women. What Dean Inge[25] says I will leave in peace. The Harley Street[26] specialist may be allowed to rouse the echoes of Harley Street with his vociferations without raising a hair on my head. I will quote, however, Mr. Oscar Browning,[27]

---

[22] **"Mighty . . . dead":** A line from William Wordsworth's poem "Resolution and Independence."

[23] **dinner . . . custard:** Earlier, Woolf describes eating such a meal at a women's college while male students dine heartily.

[24] **Lord Birkenhead:** The Earl of Birkenhead, lord chancellor of England from 1919 to 1922, reportedly said women's achievements amounted to nothing.

[25] **Dean Inge:** William Ralph Inge, dean of St. Paul's Cathedral, 1911–1934.

[26] **Harley Street:** Location of fashionable London doctors' offices.

[27] **Oscar Browning** (1837–1923): Lecturer in history at Cambridge.

because Mr. Oscar Browning was a great figure in Cambridge at one time, and used to examine the students at Girton and Newnham. Mr. Oscar Browning was wont to declare "that the impression left on his mind, after looking over any set of examination papers, was that, irrespective of the marks he might give, the best woman was intellectually the inferior of the worst man." After saying that Mr. Browning went back to his rooms—and it is this sequel that endears him and makes him a human figure of some bulk and majesty—he went back to his rooms and found a stable-boy lying on the sofa—"a mere skeleton, his cheeks were cavernous and sallow, his teeth were black, and he did not appear to have the full use of his limbs. . . . 'That's Arthur' [said Mr. Browning]. 'He's a dear boy really and most high-minded.'" The two pictures always seem to me to complete each other. And happily in this age of biography the two pictures often do complete each other, so that we are able to interpret the opinions of great men not only by what they say, but by what they do.

But though this is possible now, such opinions coming from the lips of important people must have been formidable enough even fifty years ago. Let us suppose that a father from the highest motives did not wish his daughter to leave home and become writer, painter, or scholar. "See what Mr. Oscar Browning says," he would say; and there was not only Mr. Oscar Browning; there was the *Saturday Review*; there was Mr. Greg[28]—the "essentials of a woman's being," said Mr. Greg emphatically, "are that *they are supported by, and they minister to, men*"—there was an enormous body of masculine opinion to the effect that nothing could be expected of women intellectually. Even if her father did not read out loud these opinions, any girl could read them for herself; and the reading, even in the nineteenth century, must have lowered her vitality, and told profoundly upon her work. There would always have been that assertion—you cannot do this, you are incapable of doing that—to protest against, to overcome. Probably for a novelist this germ is no longer of much effect; for there have been women novelists of merit. But for painters it must still have some sting in it; and for musicians, I imagine, is even now active and poisonous in the extreme. The woman composer stands where the actress stood in the time of Shakespeare. Nick Greene, I thought, remembering the story I had made about Shakespeare's sister, said that a woman acting put him in mind of a dog dancing. Johnson repeated the phrase two hundred years later of women preaching. And here, I said, opening a book about music, we have the very words used again in this year of grace, 1928, of women who try to write music. "Of Mlle. Germaine Tailleferre one can only repeat Dr. Johnson's dictum concerning a woman preacher, transposed into terms of music. 'Sir, a woman's composing is like a dog's walking on his hind legs. It is not done well, but you are surprised to find it done at all.'"[29] So accurately does history repeat itself.

Thus, I concluded, shutting Mr. Oscar Browning's life and pushing away the rest, it is fairly evident that even in the nineteenth century a woman was not encouraged to

---

[28] **Mr. Greg:** W. W. Greg (1875–1959), editor, librarian, and reviewer.

[29] **"Of Mlle. . . . 'at all'":** *A Survey of Contemporary Music* [1924], Cecil Gray, p. 246. [Woolf's note.] Germaine Tailleferre (1892–1983) was a French composer, a disciple of Erik Satie.

be an artist. On the contrary, she was snubbed, slapped, lectured, and exhorted. Her mind must have been strained and her vitality lowered by the need of opposing this, of disproving that. For here again we come within range of that very interesting and obscure masculine complex which has had so much influence upon the woman's movement; that deep-seated desire, not so much that *she* shall be inferior as that *he* shall be superior, which plants him wherever one looks, not only in front of the arts, but barring the way to politics too, even when the risk to himself seems infinitesimal and the suppliant humble and devoted. Even Lady Bessborough, I remembered, with all her passion for politics, must humbly bow herself and write to Lord Granville Leveson-Gower: ". . . notwithstanding all my violence in politics and talking so much on that subject, I perfectly agree with you that no woman has any business to meddle with that or any other serious business, farther than giving her opinion (if she is ask'd)."[30] And so she goes on to spend her enthusiasm where it meets with no obstacle whatsoever upon that immensely important subject, Lord Granville's maiden speech in the House of Commons. The spectacle is certainly a strange one, I thought. The history of men's opposition to women's emancipation is more interesting perhaps than the story of that emancipation itself. An amusing book might be made of it if some young student at Girton or Newnham would collect examples and deduce a theory—but she would need thick gloves on her hands, and bars to protect her of solid gold.

But what is amusing now, I recollected, shutting Lady Bessborough, had to be taken in desperate earnest once. Opinions that one now pastes in a book labelled cock-a-doodle-dum and keeps for reading to select audiences on summer nights once drew tears, I can assure you. Among your grandmothers and great-grandmothers there were many that wept their eyes out. Florence Nightingale shrieked aloud in her agony.[31] Moreover, it is all very well for you, who have got yourselves to college and enjoy sitting-rooms—or is it only bed-sitting-rooms?—of your own to say that genius should disregard such opinions; that genius should be above caring what is said of it. Unfortunately, it is precisely the men or women of genius who mind most what is said of them. Remember Keats. Remember the words he had cut on his tombstone.[32] Think of Tennyson; think—but I need hardly multiply instances of the undeniable, if very unfortunate, fact that it is the nature of the artist to mind excessively what is said about him. Literature is strewn with the wreckage of men who have minded beyond reason the opinions of others.

And this susceptibility of theirs is doubly unfortunate, I thought, returning again to my original enquiry into what state of mind is most propitious for creative work, because the mind of an artist, in order to achieve the prodigious effort of freeing whole and entire the work that is in him, must be incandescent, like

---

[30] ". . . notwithstanding . . . (ask'd)": Henrietta Spencer's correspondence with Lord Granville, foreign secretary under William Gladstone, was well known.

[31] Florence . . . agony: See *Cassandra,* by Florence Nightingale, printed in *The Cause,* by R. Strachey. [Woolf's note.] Ray Strachey's 1928 book was a history of British feminism with an appendix by Nightingale.

[32] words . . . tombstone: "Here lies one whose name was writ in water."

Shakespeare's mind, I conjectured, looking at the book which lay open at *Antony and Cleopatra*. There must be no obstacle in it, no foreign matter unconsumed.

For though we say that we know nothing about Shakespeare's state of mind, even as we say that, we are saying something about Shakespeare's state of mind. The reason perhaps why we know so little of Shakespeare—compared with Donne or Ben Jonson or Milton—is that his grudges and spites and antipathies are hidden from us. We are not held up by some "revelation" which reminds us of the writer. All desire to protest, to preach, to proclaim an injury, to pay off a score, to make the world the witness of some hardship or grievance was fired out of him and consumed. Therefore his poetry flows from him free and unimpeded. If ever a human being got his work expressed completely, it was Shakespeare. If ever a mind was incandescent, unimpeded, I thought, turning again to the bookcase, it was Shakespeare's mind.

༖ Three Pictures

THE FIRST PICTURE

It is impossible that one should not see pictures; because if my father was a blacksmith and yours was a peer of the realm, we must needs be pictures to each other. We cannot possibly break out of the frame of the picture by speaking natural words. You see me leaning against the door of the smithy with a horseshoe in my hand and you think as you go by: "How picturesque!" I, seeing you sitting so much at your ease in the car, almost as if you were going to bow to the populace, think what a picture of old luxurious aristocratical England! We both are quite wrong in our judgments no doubt, but that is inevitable.

So now at the turn of the road I saw one of these pictures. It might have been called "The Sailor's Homecoming" or some such title. A fine young sailor carrying a bundle; a girl with her hand on his arm; neighbours gathering round; a cottage garden ablaze with flowers; as one passed one read at the bottom of that picture that the sailor was back from China, and there was a fine spread waiting for him in the parlor; and he had a present for his young wife in his bundle; and she was soon going to bear him their first child. Everything was right and good and as it should be, one felt about that picture. There was something wholesome and satisfactory in the sight of such happiness; life seemed sweeter and more enviable than before.

So thinking I passed them, filling in the picture as fully, as completely as I could, noticing the colour of her dress, of his eyes, seeing the sandy cat slinking round the cottage door.

For some time the picture floated in my eyes, making most things appear much brighter, warmer, and simpler than usual; and making some things appear foolish; and some things wrong and some things right, and more full of meaning than before. At odd moments during that day and the next the picture returned to one's mind, and one thought with envy, but with kindness, of the happy sailor and his wife; one wondered what they were doing, what they were saying now. The imagination supplied other pictures springing from that first one, a picture of the sailor cutting firewood, drawing water; and they talked about China; and the girl set his present on the chimneypiece where everyone who came could see it; and she sewed at her baby clothes, and all the doors and windows were open into the garden so that the birds were flittering and the bees humming, and Rogers—that was his name—could not say how much to his liking all this was after the China seas. As he smoked his pipe, with his foot in the garden.

THE SECOND PICTURE

In the middle of the night a loud cry rang through the village. Then there was a sound of something scuffling; and then dead silence. All that could be seen out of the window was the branch of lilac tree hanging motionless and ponderous across the road. It was a hot still night. There was no moon. The cry made everything seem ominous. Who had cried? Why had she cried? It was a woman's voice, made by some extremity of feeling almost sexless, almost expressionless. It was as if human nature had cried out against some iniquity, some inexpressible horror. There was dead silence. The stars shone perfectly steadily. The fields lay still. The trees were motionless. Yet all seemed guilty, convicted, ominous. One felt that something ought to be done. Some light ought to appear tossing, moving agitatedly. Someone ought to come running down the road. There should be lights in the cottage windows. And then perhaps another cry, but less sexless, less wordless, comforted, appeased. But no light came. No feet were heard. There was no second cry. The first had been swallowed up, and there was dead silence.

One lay in the dark listening intently. It had been merely a voice. There was nothing to connect it with. No picture of any sort came to interpret it, to make it intelligible to the mind. But as the dark arose at last all one saw was an obscure human form, almost without shape, raising a gigantic arm in vain against some overwhelming iniquity.

THE THIRD PICTURE

The fine weather remained unbroken. Had it not been for that single cry in the night one would have felt that the earth had put into harbour; that life had ceased to drive before the wind; that it had reached some quiet cove and there lay anchored, hardly moving, on the quiet waters. But the sound persisted. Wherever one went, it might be for a long walk up into the hills, something seemed to turn uneasily beneath the surface, making the peace, the stability all round one seem a little unreal. There were the sheep clustered on the side of the hill; the valley broke in long tapering waves like the fall of smooth waters. One came on solitary farmhouses. The puppy rolled in the yard. The butterflies gambolled over the gorse. All was as quiet, as safe [as] could be. Yet, one kept thinking, a cry had rent it; all this beauty had been an accomplice that night; had consented to remain calm, to be still beautiful; at any moment it might be sundered again. This goodness, this safety were only on the surface.

And then to cheer oneself out of this apprehensive mood one turned to the picture of the sailor's homecoming. One saw it all over again producing various little details—the blue colour of her dress, the shadow that fell from the yellow flowering tree—that one had not used before. So they had stood at the cottage door, he with his bundle on his back, she just lightly touching his sleeve with her hand. And a sandy cat had slunk round the door. Thus gradually going over the picture in every detail, one persuaded oneself by degrees that it was far more likely that this calm and content and goodwill lay beneath the surface than anything treacherous, sinister. The sheep grazing, the waves of the valley, the farmhouse, the puppy, the dancing butterflies were in fact like that all through. And so one turned back home, with one's mind fixed on the sailor and his wife, making up picture after picture of them so that one picture after another of happiness and satisfaction might be laid over that unrest, that hideous cry, until it was crushed and silenced by their pressure out of existence.

Here at last was the village, and the churchyard through which one must pass; and the usual thought came, as one entered it, of the peacefulness of the place, with its shady yews, its rubbed tombstones, its nameless graves. Death is cheerful here, one felt. Indeed, look at that picture! A man was digging a grave, and children were picnicking at the side of it while he worked. As the shovels of yellow earth were thrown up, the children were sprawling about eating bread and jam and drinking milk out of large mugs. The gravedigger's wife, a fat fair woman, had propped herself against a tombstone and spread her apron on the grass by the open grave to serve as a tea-table. Some lumps of clay had fallen among the tea things. Who was going to be buried, I asked. Had old Mr Dodson died at last? "Oh! no. It's for young Rogers, the sailor," the woman answered, staring at me. "He died two nights ago, of some foreign fever. Didn't you hear his wife? She rushed into the road and cried out . . . Here, Tommy, you're all covered with earth!"

What a picture it made!

∽ The Fascination of the Pool[1]

It may have been very deep—certainly one could not see to the bottom of it. Round the edge was so thick a fringe of rushes that their reflections made a darkness like the darkness of very deep water. However in the middle was something white. The big farm a mile off was to be sold and some zealous person, or it may have been a joke on

---

[1] "The Fascination of the Pool." This piece comes from a typescript with holograph revisions, dated May 29, 1929. Leonard Woolf relates that when Virginia had an idea for a short story, she would quickly sketch out the theme and then put the notes in a desk drawer; the sketch might or might not be retrieved later for revision. In fact, the only book of short stories that appeared in Virginia Woolf's lifetime was *Monday or Tuesday* (1921). "The Fascination of the Pool" lay in manuscript form until it was collected in *The Complete Shorter Fiction of Virginia Woolf* (1985).

All footnotes come from the Susan Dick edition of the work.

the part of a boy, had stuck one of the posters advertising the sale, with farm horses, agricultural implements, and young heifers, on a tree stump by the side of the pool. The centre of the water reflected the white placard and when the wind blew the centre of the pool seemed to flow and ripple like a piece of washing. One could trace the big red letters in which Romford Mill was printed in the water. A tinge of red was in the green that rippled from bank to bank.

But if one sat down among the rushes and watched the pool—pools have some curious fascination, one knows not what—the red and black letters and the white paper seemed to lie very thinly on the surface, while beneath went on some profound underwater life like the brooding, the ruminating of a mind. Many, many people must have come there alone, from time to time, from age to age, dropping their thoughts into the water, asking it some question, as one did oneself this summer evening. Perhaps that was the reason of its fascination—that it held in its waters all kinds of fancies, complaints, confidences, not printed or spoken aloud, but in a liquid state, floating one on top of another, almost disembodied. A fish would swim through them, be cut in two by the blade of a reed; or the moon would annihilate them with its great white plate. The charm of the pool was that thoughts had been left there by people who had gone away and without their bodies their thoughts wandered in and out freely, friendly and communicative, in the common pool.

Among all these liquid thoughts some seemed to stick together and to form recognisable people—just for a moment. And one saw a whiskered red face formed in the pool leaning low over it, drinking it. I came here in 1851 after the heat of the Great Exhibition.[2] I saw the Queen open it. And the voice chuckled liquidly, easily, as if he had thrown off his elastic side boots and put his top hat on the edge of the pool. Lord, how hot it was! and now all gone, all crumbled, of course, the thoughts seemed to say, swaying among the reeds. But I was a lover, another thought began, sliding over the other silently and orderly as fish not impeding each other. A girl; we used to come down from the farm (the placard of its sale was reflected on the top of the water) that summer, 1662. The soldiers never saw us from the road. It was very hot. We lay here. She was lying hidden in the rushes with her lover, laughing into the pool and slipping into it, thoughts of eternal love, of fiery kisses and despair. And I was very happy, said another thought glancing briskly over the girl's despair (for she had drowned herself). I used to fish here. We never caught the giant carp but we saw him once—the day Nelson fought at Trafalgar.[3] We saw him under the willow—my word! what a great brute he was! They say he was never caught. Alas, alas sighed a voice, slipping over the boy's voice. So sad a voice must come from the very bottom of the pool. It raised itself under the others as a spoon lifts all the things in a bowl of water. This was the voice we all wished to listen to. All the voices slipped gently away to the side of the pool to listen to the voice[4] which so sad it seemed—it must surely know the reason of all this. For they all wished to know.

---

[2] the Great Exhibition: Held in the Crystal Palace in Hyde Park and opened by Queen Victoria on May 1, 1851.

[3] Nelson . . . Trafalgar: Lord Nelson was killed while defeating Napoleon's fleet in a battle off Cape Trafalgar on October 21, 1805.

[4] the voice: VW has cancelled "of the great seer" here.

One drew closer to the pool and parted the reeds so that one could see deeper, through the reflections, through the faces, through the voices to the bottom. But there under the man who had been to the Exhibition; and the girl who had drowned herself and the boy who had seen the fish; and the voice which cried alas alas! yet there was always something else. There was always another face, another voice. One thought came and covered another. For though there are moments when a spoon seems about to lift all of us, and our thoughts and longings and questions and confessions and disillusions into the light of day, somehow the spoon always slips beneath and we flow back again over the edge into the pool. And once more the whole of its centre is covered over with the reflection of the placard which advertises the sale of Romford Mill Farm. That perhaps is why one loves to sit and look into pools.

TEXT IN CONTEXT

❧ FRANZ KAFKA
B. PRAGUE, 1883–1924

Franz Kafka, c. 1910
*Kafka at around the
age of twenty-seven.
(Hulton/Archive)*

The writings of Franz Kafka courageously explore the fears and
frustrations of life in the modern age, how it feels to be manipulated
by large institutions and betrayed by family and friends. The Industrial Revolution of the nineteenth century had undoubtedly produced
immense wealth and a new middle class, but the centers of power in the
expanding cities were large bureaucracies in which individuals were lost
and dehumanized. Much of Kafka's writing deals with the intimidation
of the individual by governments and courts of law. Kafka also wrote of
faceless, heartless, modern corporations in which individuals become
nonentities caught up in legalistic, administrative maneuvers. Often
these governmental or corporate systems are too complex and elusive
for people to understand and, finally, survive.

Kafka did not officially belong to the French school of SURREALISM,[1]
but his blend of precise detail, ordinary reality, and nightmare is surreal
in nature. Making use of Freud's revelations about the subconscious,
Kafka accepts the dominance of dream realities and portrays the everyday
as something that can turn in an instant into a nightmare in which lives
are distorted. Kafka's work embodies a disturbing loss of faith in the fundamental institutions of Western civilization—universities, churches,
courts, and governments—and implicitly argues that if God still exists
in the post–World War I era—and many doubted He did—then He has
retreated into the vast recesses of the cosmos, out of touch and out of

---

[1] **French . . . surrealism:** Founded by André Breton (1896–1966), who believed that Freud's discoveries about
the world of dreams should be incorporated into literature. Breton defined *surrealism* as the attempt to blend
ordinary reality with dream realities in order to better reflect the movements and profundities of modern
consciousness.

hearing. Given the absence of both rational control in the world and a model of the universe that included God, Kafka was brilliantly prophetic about the rise of TOTALITARIANISM in the twentieth century and the horrifying effect that Fascist and Communist regimes would have on millions—as well as about the alienating influence of international corporations. It is no wonder that at this seemingly hopeless time European intellectuals turned to some variety of EXISTENTIALISM.

An Early Conflict: Work and Writing.

Franz Kafka was born in Prague (then part of the Austro-Hungarian empire) in 1883 to Julie Löwy, a kindly woman from a family of rabbis, and Hermann Kafka, a self-made man who had worked his way from village butcher to city entrepreneur. The aggressive and domineering Hermann pressured his son into becoming a businessman; Franz was well-educated, earning a doctor of law degree from German University in Prague. Despite an early passion for writing, he took a job in the semigovernmental Workers' Accident Insurance Institute, where he had ample opportunity to observe the laborious machinations of a bureaucracy in the Austro-Hungarian empire.

www For links to more information about Kafka, a quiz on *The Metamorphosis*, and information on the 21st-century relevance of Kafka, see bedfordstmartins .com/worldlit compact.

The Workers' Accident Insurance Institute
This postcard depicts the insurance company where Kafka was employed. He became a respected executive despite feeling torn between his passion for writing and his career. (Art Resource)

Kafka felt caught between his continued passion for writing and his desire to do well in his career, as he remarks in this journal entry:

> Now these two vocations (writing and working in an office) cannot be compatible and have a fortunate outcome in common. The smallest success in the one field becomes a great disaster in the other . . . At the office I fulfill my obligations outwardly, but not my inner ones, and every unfulfilled inner obligation turns into a misfortune which does not find its way out of me.

Somehow he managed to succeed at both endeavors, becoming a respected executive handling claims and litigation as well as a successful writer.

An Overwhelming Father.   Exacerbating the pain he felt in his relationship with his father, Kafka lived at home for most of his life. In the essay, "A Letter to My Father," he writes of his feelings of inferiority and humiliation, feelings that not surprisingly pervade the consciousness of his fictional characters:

> I was, after all, depressed even by your mere physical presence. I remember for instance how often we undressed together in the same bathing-hut. There was I, skinny, weakly, slight, you strong, tall, broad. Even inside the hut I felt myself a miserable specimen, and what's more not only in your eyes but in the eyes of the whole world, for you were for me the measure of all things.

Kafka was twice engaged to Felice Bauer but didn't marry, and the failure of this relationship became an additional burden. Although his stories were praised by his friends, he was insecure about his writing and resisted publishing his work; only a few of his short stories and two novellas, *The Metamorphosis* (*Die Verwandlung*, 1915) and *The Penal Colony* (*Die Strafkolonie*, 1919) were published during his lifetime.

Tuberculosis.   In 1917 Kafka was found to have tuberculosis, and he eventually suffered from tuberculosis of the larynx, a particularly hateful illness for someone who spent his life struggling to communicate. After living in various sanatoriums in Prague, Kafka moved to Berlin in 1922, where his relationship with Dora Dymant brought him some happiness before he died on June 3, 1924. Before dying he asked his friend and executor, Max Brod, to burn his unpublished papers, which included three unfinished novels. Brod disregarded his friend's request and published a number of short stories and sketches as well as the incomplete novels *The Trial* (*Der Prozess*, 1925), *The Castle* (*Das Schloss*, 1926), and *Amerika* (1927), all of which deal with the effects of totalitarianism on individuals.

I was, after all, depressed even by your mere physical presence. I remember for instance how often we undressed together in the same bathing-hut. There was I, skinny, weakly, slight, you strong, tall, broad. Even inside the hut I felt myself a miserable specimen, and what's more not only in your eyes but in the eyes of the whole world, for you were for me the measure of all things.

– KAFKA to his father, 1919

Cracking the Frozen Sea Within.   Kafka wrote, "The books we need are the kind that act upon us like a nightmare, that make us suffer like the death of someone we love more than ourselves . . . a book should serve as the ax for the frozen sea within us" — and he proceeded to write such books. Kafka typically takes the point of view of a victim, someone who is confused about a particular system of power, the people in control, and how to gain access. In *The Trial,* the accused actually has an opportunity to speak to his accusers, but he knows neither the nature of his crime nor why he has been found guilty. In *The Castle,* contact with decision makers is not possible. There might be a telephone line into the interior of a power structure, but it is uncertain who might pick up the phone on the other end and what transaction might take place. Social power, like God, has receded into anonymity, not unlike the contemporary frustration of trying to reach an actual person at a phone company, but instead having to deal with recorded messages and an automated system.

Kafka is a master of the short sketch that ends with a twist; he actually revived the biblical form of the PARABLE[2] for a modern audience. A short parable called "Before the Law," an ALLEGORY[3] of modern life, encapsulates Kafka's persistent themes. A man approaches the gateway of the Law, but a gatekeeper prevents him from entering. Finally, after years in front of the gate and endless discussions with the gatekeeper, the man asks one final question before dying: "Everyone strives to reach the Law, so how does it happen that for all these many years no one but myself has ever begged for admittance?" The gatekeeper answers, "No one else could ever be admitted here, since this gate was made only for you. I am now going to shut it." For Kafka, this gateway stands for all the institutional, doctrinal, and religious barriers that individuals confront over a lifetime.

Metamorphosis into an Insect.   The demeaning, dehumanizing distance in *The Metamorphosis* is found within the home and the family, where parents and adult children live together without caring for one another, where people talk without communicating. *The Metamorphosis* is typical of a number of Kafka's works in that it places an everyday, ordinary world side by side with extraordinary phenomena. The story

Metamorphosis . . . certainly represents the horrible imagery of an ethic of lucidity. But it is also the product of that incalculable amazement man feels at being conscious of the beast he becomes effortlessly. In this fundamental ambiguity lies Kafka's secret. These perpetual oscillations between the natural and the extraordinary, the individual and the universal, the tragic and the everyday, the absurd and the logical, are found throughout his work. . . .

– ALBERT CAMUS, 1955

---

[2] **parable:** A short narrative designed to present a lesson about life; parables were popular during biblical times.

[3] **allegory:** An allegory explains a concept or theory by turning the parts of the theory into characters in a narration.

The books we need are the kind that act upon us like a nightmare, that make us suffer like the death of someone we love more than ourselves . . . a book should serve as the ax for the frozen sea within us.

– KAFKA

begins with Gregory Samsa's discovery that in his physical form he has been turned into an insect. Gregory's condition corresponds to the psychological state of an individual who awakens to the full dimensions of being trapped in a sense of helplessness and alienation in his or her everyday life. Gregory's family, to whom he has dedicated his working life, is unsympathetic to his plight. Even though the unfortunate, pitiable change in him is completely out of his control, his parents and, eventually, even his sister feel he has let them down. One of the most dehumanizing scenes in the story occurs when Mr. Samsa reasserts his authority as the head of the household and drives his son back into his room, throwing fruit at him. One of the apples that lodges in Gregory's back rots and festers until Gregory dies without understanding what has happened to him. Gregory's misfortune ironically forces his family out of their passive dependence; as they detach themselves from his suffering, they appear to take charge of their own lives and make plans for the future.

The heartless bureaucracy was not unknown to the nineteenth century; after all, Tolstoy's Ivan Ilych[4] became a cog in Russia's legal system. But Franz Kafka's haunting version of the modern world, which makes the line between the ruling elite and the rest of society impossibly vague and suffocating, has been immensely influential in the twentieth century. Although Kafka's writings had very little impact during his lifetime, audiences after World War II have found his portrayal of modern bureaucratic alienation and the paralyzing insecurities that individuals suffer in their private lives both prescient and profound. He continues to strike a deep chord in Western consciousness.

■ FURTHER RESEARCH

Biography
Brod, Max. *Franz Kafka: A Biography.* 1960.
Hayman, Ronald. *Kafka: A Biography.* 1982.
Pawel, Ernest. *The Nightmare of Reason, A Life of Franz Kafka.* 1984.

Criticism
Bloom, Harold, ed. *Franz Kafka's* The Metamorphosis. 1988.
Fickert, Kurt. *End of a Mission: Kafka's Search for Truth in His Last Stories.* 1993.
Gray, Ronald, ed. *Kafka: A Collection of Critical Essays.* 1962.

---

[4] **Ivan Ilych:** Tolstoy's *The Death of Ivan Ilych* deals with a man who spends his life working to attain a middle-class, comfortable existence and ends up depressed and alone on his deathbed. (See p. 989.)

∾ The Metamorphosis

Translated by J. A. Underwood

I

Gregory Samsa woke from uneasy dreams one morning to find himself changed into a giant bug. He was lying on his back, which was of a shell-like hardness, and when he lifted his head a little he could see his dome-shaped brown belly, banded with what looked like reinforcing arches, on top of which his quilt, while threatening to slip off completely at any moment, still maintained a precarious hold. His many legs, pitifully thin in relation to the rest of him, threshed ineffectually before his eyes.

"What's happened to me?" he thought. This was no dream. His room, a normal human room except that it was rather too small, lay peacefully between the four familiar walls. Above the table, which was littered with a collection of drapery samples — Samsa was a traveller — hung the picture that he had recently cut out of a magazine and mounted in an attractive gilt frame. It showed a lady in a fur hat and boa, sitting up straight and holding out an enormous fur muff that entirely concealed her forearms.

Gregory's gaze shifted to the window, and the murky weather — raindrops beat audibly on the zinc windowsill — made him feel quite melancholy. "Why don't I go back to sleep for a bit and forget all the fooling about?" he thought, but this was impossible: he liked to sleep on his right side, and in his present state he was unable to assume that position. Try as he might to throw himself over to the right, he always rocked back into his previous position. He must have made a hundred attempts; he shut his eyes to keep out the sight of all those toiling legs; and he gave up only when he became aware of a faint, dull ache in his side of a kind he had never felt before.

"God," he thought, "what a gruelling job I chose! On the go day in and day out. The business side of it is much more hectic than in the office itself, and on top of that there's the wretched travelling, the worry about train connections, the awful meals eaten at all hours, and the constant chopping and changing as far as human relationships are concerned, never knowing anyone for long, never making friends. Oh, to hell with the whole thing!" He felt a slight itch high up on his belly; pushed himself, on his back, slowly closer to the bedpost, the better to lift his head; located the itchy place, which was covered with a lot of tiny white spots he did not know what to make of; and tried to touch the place with a leg, withdrawing it immediately, however, because the contact sent cold shivers through him.

He slid back into his original position. "These early mornings," he thought, "are enough to drive one round the bend. A man needs his sleep. Other travellers live like kept women. I mean, when I go back to the hotel during the morning to write up my orders, some fellows are just sitting down to their breakfast. If I tried that on with my boss I'd be out on my ear immediately. Might not be a bad thing for me, at that. If it weren't for my parents I'd have handed in my notice long ago; I'd have gone to see the boss and given him a piece of my mind. Why, he'd have fallen off his desk! Funny habit, that, his sitting on the desk and talking down to his employees from a great height, especially since you have to step right up close because of his deafness. Ah well, there's still hope; once I've got the money together to pay off my parents' debt to him — that might take another five or six years — I'll definitely do it. I'll take the plunge. Meanwhile, though, I'd better get up; my train leaves at five."

And he looked across at the alarm clock that stood ticking on the wardrobe. "Heavens above!" he thought. It was half past six, and the hands were moving steadily onwards; in fact it was after half past, it was almost a quarter to. Had the alarm not rung? He could see from the bed that it had been set correctly for four o'clock; it must have rung. Yes, but — how could he have slept calmly through a ring so loud it shook the furniture? Well, not calmly, he hadn't slept calmly, but probably all the more soundly for that. What was he to do now, though? The next train left at seven; to catch that would have meant a frantic rush, and there were the samples to be packed, and he was not feeling particularly spry to start with, far from it. And even if he did catch the train he was in for a rocket from the boss because the office boy would have been at the station at five and would have reported his absence long ago, the office boy being a tool of the boss and a spineless, mindless creature. What if he were to report sick? No, that would be highly embarrassing as well as suspicious, Gregory not having had a day's illness in his five years with the firm. The boss would be sure to bring the health-insurance company's doctor round and blame his parents for having an idle son, cutting short all their protests by quoting the doctor's view that people were invariably in perfect health, just work-shy. And would he in fact be so wrong in this case? Aside from a certain drowsiness, quite superfluous after his long sleep, Gregory really felt very fit and was even aware of having an unusually robust appetite.

As he was rapidly considering all this, though without managing to make up his mind to get out of bed — the alarm clock was just striking a quarter to seven — there came a cautious knock on the door at the head of his bed. "Gregory," — it was his mother speaking — "it's a quarter to seven. Weren't you going off this morning?" That gentle voice! Gregory gave a start when he heard his own voice in reply; it was unmistakably his, but blended with it, as if welling up irrepressibly from below, was a distressing squeak that allowed the words to retain their clarity only for a moment, afterwards distorting their resonance to the point where one wondered whether one had heard correctly. Gregory had wanted to answer at length and explain everything, but in the circumstances he confined himself to saying, "Yes, yes — thank you, mother, I'm just getting up." Because of the wooden door the alteration in Gregory's voice was presumably not noticeable outside, for his mother, reassured by his words, went shuffling off. Their brief exchange, however, had alerted the other members of the family to the fact that Gregory, unexpectedly, was still at home, and soon his father was knocking at the door on one side, not hard, but with his fist. "Gregory, Gregory," he called, "what is it?" And after a little while he repeated his admonishment in a deeper voice: "Gregory! Gregory!" At the door on the other side his sister was quietly plaintive: "Gregory? Are you all right? Can I get you anything?" "Just coming," Gregory replied to them both, trying by means of the most careful enunciation and by leaving long pauses between the words to remove any conspicuous quality from his voice. His father did indeed go back to his breakfast, but his sister whispered, "Gregory, open the door, *please.*" Nothing was further from Gregory's mind, however; in fact he was congratulating himself on his cautious habit, adopted from his travels, of locking all the doors of his room at night even when he was at home.

He first wanted to get up in peace and quiet, dress, and above all have breakfast, and only then contemplate the future, because as he knew full well he would never think things through to a sensible conclusion as long as he remained in bed. He recalled having quite often felt some slight pain in bed, possibly as a result of having lain awkwardly, which had turned out to be purely imaginary once he was up, and he was curious to see how this morning's imaginings would gradually evaporate. Not for a moment did he doubt that the alteration in his voice was merely an early symptom of that occupational affliction of commercial travellers, the streaming cold.

Getting rid of the quilt was quite simple; all he needed to do was to puff himself up a little and it fell to the floor. After that, however, things became difficult, particularly since he was so extraordinarily broad. He would have needed arms and hands to lift himself up, but instead he had only a large number of legs that were in continuous, multifarious motion and in any case quite beyond his control. Whenever he tried to bend one it promptly stretched out straight; and if he did eventually manage to make the leg execute the desired movement all the others, left as it were to their own devices, went on working away in a state of the most acute and painful excitement. "Right — that's enough dawdling in bed!" Gregory told himself.

First he tried to get the lower part of his body out of bed, but this lower part, which incidentally he had not yet seen and of which he could form no very clear idea, proved too unwieldy; progress was so slow; and when finally, in a kind of rage, he summoned all his strength and recklessly thrust himself forward he had mistaken the direction, striking the lower bedpost a violent blow, and the sharp pain he felt informed him that it was this lower part of his body that was perhaps the most sensitive at the moment.

So he tried to get his upper body out of bed first, carefully twisting his head round towards the edge of the mattress. He managed this without difficulty, and despite its width and great weight his body did eventually begin to follow the movement of his head. But when at length he had his head out beyond the edge of the bed in mid air he suddenly thought better of continuing, afraid that if in the end he let himself fall like that it would take a miracle to prevent his sustaining a head injury. And the last thing he wanted to do just then was to lose consciousness; he would rather stay in bed.

But when after a similar struggle he lay back with a sigh in his first position and again saw his legs locked in what seemed if anything even fiercer combat than before, powerless to bring any kind of order into their chaos, he again told himself that he could not possibly stay where he was and that the only sensible thing was to risk all for even the faintest hope of somehow freeing himself from his bed. At the same time he was careful to remind himself at intervals that desperate decisions were no substitute for cool, calm thought. At such moments he focused as sharply as his eyes would allow on the window; unfortunately the sight of the morning mist, which even shrouded the other side of the narrow street, had little to offer in the way of brisk reassurance. "Seven o'clock already," he said to himself as the alarm clock struck again, "seven o'clock and still such a mist." And for a while he lay quiet, hardly breathing, hoping perhaps that total silence might bring about a return to normal, everyday reality.

But then he said to himself, "Before a quarter past seven strikes I simply must be out of bed — right out. Anyway, someone will be here from the office by then to ask about me, because the office opens before seven o'clock." And he set about rocking the whole length of his body evenly out of bed. If he allowed himself to fall out in this way his head, which he intended to lift smartly as he fell, would presumably remain unhurt. His back appeared to be hard; probably falling onto the carpet would do no damage to that. What worried him most was the thought of the loud crash that would inevitably accompany his fall and in all likelihood occasion if not alarm, at least concern beyond the various doors. But he would have to take that risk.

When Gregory was already leaning half out of bed — the new method was not so much work as play, since all he had to do was to keep rocking to and fro — it occurred to him how simple everything would be if someone were to come to his assistance. Two strong people — he had in mind his father and the maid — would have been quite sufficient; they need only have slid their arms under his arched back, eased him out of bed, bent down with him, and simply waited with patient vigilance until he had swung himself over onto the floor, where his legs would then, he hoped, acquire some purpose. So, quite apart from the fact that the doors were locked, should he really have called for help? In spite of his predicament he was unable to suppress a smile at the thought.

He had reached the stage where, if he rocked a little harder, he almost lost his balance, and he was very soon going to have to make up his mind once and for all because in five minutes it would be a quarter past seven — when the doorbell rang. "That'll be someone from the office," he said to himself and almost froze, except that his legs started dancing about all the more frantically. There was a moment's silence. "They're not letting him in," Gregory said to himself, caught up in some absurd hope. But then of course, as always, the maid strode purposefully to the door and opened it. The visitor's first word of greeting sufficed to tell Gregory who it was — the chief clerk himself. Why was Gregory of all people fated to work for a firm where the least little omission promptly aroused the greatest suspicion? Were all employees without exception knaves; was there not one single loyal and devoted person among them who, having failed to turn a mere couple of hours one morning to the firm's advantage, was driven so distracted by qualms of conscience as to become incapable of getting out of bed? Would it not have been enough to send an apprentice round to inquire, assuming this whole inquisition to be necessary in the first place? Did the chief clerk really have to come in person, so demonstrating to the entire, innocent family that the investigation of this suspicious affair could be entrusted only to a person of his discernment. And it was more in consequence of the state of agitation into which Gregory was thrown by these reflections than as a result of a genuine decision that he now swung himself out of bed with all his might. There was a loud thump, though not in fact a crash. To some extent his fall had been softened by the carpet, and also his back was more resilient than Gregory had thought — hence the muffled and really quite unremarkable sound. But he had not been careful enough about his head and had banged it; he twisted it round and rubbed it on the carpet in anger and pain.

"Something just fell down in there," said the chief clerk in the room on the left. Gregory tried to imagine whether something similar might not happen to the chief clerk one day as had happened to him this morning. One had to admit it was possible. But as if in brusque reply to this question the chief clerk, in the next room, now took several resolute steps that made his patent-leather boots creak. From the room on the right Gregory's sister informed him in a whisper, "Gregory, the chief clerk's here." "I know," Gregory said under his breath, not daring to raise his voice to the point where his sister could have heard his reply.

"Gregory," came his father's voice from the room on the left, "the chief clerk has come round to ask why you didn't leave on the early train. We don't know what to tell him. In any case he'd like a word with you personally. So please will you open the door. He'll have the goodness, I'm sure, to overlook the mess in your room." Meanwhile the chief clerk put in a friendly, "Good morning, Mr Samsa." "He's not well," Gregory's mother told the chief clerk as his father was still talking through the door. "He's not well, sir, you can take it from me. What else would make Gregory miss his train? Why, the boy thinks of nothing but his work! It makes me quite cross that he never goes out in the evening; now he's just had a whole week in town, but every evening he spent at home. He sits there with us at the table and quietly reads the paper or pores over timetables. His only amusement is when he does his fretwork. He made a little picture frame, for instance, which took him two or three evenings; you'll be surprised how pretty it is; it's hanging up in his room; you'll see it in a moment, when Gregory opens the door. I'm glad you're here, sir, by the way; we'd never have got Gregory to unlock the door by ourselves, he's so stubborn; and I'm sure he's unwell, although he said he wasn't this morning." "Won't be a moment," Gregory said slowly and deliberately, keeping quite still in order not to miss a word of this exchange. "I likewise, madam, can think of no other explanation," said the chief clerk. "Let us hope it's nothing serious. On the other hand I am bound to say that those of us who are in business are—unfortunately or if you like fortunately—very often obliged simply to shrug off minor indispositions for business reasons." "Can the chief clerk come in, then?" asked his father impatiently, knocking on the door again. "No," said Gregory. In the room on the left an embarrassed silence fell; in the room on the right his sister began to sob.

Why did his sister not go round and join the others? Probably she had only just got out of bed and had not even begun dressing yet. And whyever was she crying? Was it because he did not get up and let the chief clerk in, because he was in danger of losing his job and because the boss would then start pestering his parents again about those old debts? Worries of that kind were surely quite superfluous for the present. Gregory was still around and had not the slightest intention of abandoning his family. Just at the moment he happened to be lying on the carpet, and no one who was aware of his condition would seriously have expected him to let the chief clerk into the room. But this minor discourtesy, for which a suitable excuse could easily be found at a later stage, hardly constituted grounds for firing Gregory on the spot. And to Gregory's way of thinking it would have been far more sensible to leave him in peace now instead of plaguing him with tears and exhortations. But of course it was the uncertainty that was upsetting the others and that accounted for their behaviour.

"Mr Samsa," the chief clerk now called out in a louder voice, "what is going on? You barricade yourself in your room, answer in monosyllables, are causing your parents grave and unnecessary concern, and are in addition — this merely by the by — neglecting your professional duties in a quite outrageous manner. On behalf of your parents and your superior I ask you most earnestly for an immediate and unequivocal explanation. I am astonished, I really am. I knew and believed you to be a calm and reasonable person, and suddenly you seem bent on manifesting these freakish whims. Your superior in fact intimated to me this morning a possible explanation for your absences — it had to do with the cash-up recently entrusted to you — but I assure you I gave him virtually my word of honour that that could not possibly be the true explanation. Now, however, having witnessed your incredible obstinacy, I find myself losing all inclination to plead your cause in any way whatsoever. I would add that your position is very far from assured. It was my original intention to tell you all this in private but, since you choose to make me waste my time here in this fruitless fashion, I see no reason why your good parents should not hear it too. Your figures recently have been most unsatisfactory; this is not of course the season for doing a lot of business, we recognize that; but a season for doing no business at all does not exist and cannot, Mr Samsa, be allowed to exist."

"But, sir," cried Gregory, most upset and forgetting everything else in his excitement, "I'm just going to open the door, this very moment. A slight indisposition, a dizzy spell, prevented me from getting up. I'm still in bed. But I already feel perfectly fit again. I'm getting out of bed now. Just be patient for a moment. Things aren't going quite as well as I expected. I'm all right, though. Funny how something like that can hit you. Yesterday evening I was fine, my parents will tell you, or rather, I already had a sort of feeling then that something might be wrong. You'd think it would have shown on my face. Whyever didn't I send word to the office! One always thinks, doesn't one, that one can get over these things without staying at home. Sir, spare my parents this ordeal, please! All these reproaches you've levelled against me are quite unfounded; no one's ever said a word to me about any of this. You may not have seen the latest batch of orders I sent in. Incidentally I'll be on my way by the eight o'clock train; the few hours' rest has done me good. Don't let me keep you, sir; I'll be in the office myself directly; would you be so kind as to tell the boss so with my compliments?"

And while Gregory was blurting all this out, barely aware of what he was saying, he had managed to reach the wardrobe without difficulty, no doubt as a result of the practice already acquired in bed, and was now trying to use it to pull himself upright. He really did intend to open the door; he intended to let himself be seen and have a word with the chief clerk; he was eager to find out what the others, wanting him as they now did, would say when they saw him. If they panicked, Gregory would be absolved of responsibility and could relax. If on the other hand they reacted calmly, then he too would have no call to get excited and could indeed, if he hurried, be at the station by eight. At first he kept slipping on the wardrobe's smooth surface, but in the end, after one final heave, he was standing erect; he had completely forgotten about the pains in his lower region, acute though they were. Next he let himself fall against the back of a nearby chair, gripping it around the edge with his legs. Having got himself under control in this way, he stopped talking; now he could listen to what the chief clerk had to say.

"Did you understand a word of that?" the chief clerk was asking Gregory's parents. "I suppose he's not trying to make complete fools of us?" "Heavens," cried his mother, already in tears, "he may be seriously ill and here we are, tormenting him. Meg!" she shouted then, "Meg!" "Yes, Mother?" cried his sister from the other side. They were communicating through Gregory's room. "You must go round to the doctor this minute. Gregory's ill. Quickly, now—fetch the doctor. Did you hear Gregory talking just then?" "That sounded like an animal," said the chief clerk in a quiet voice that contrasted sharply with the mother's yelling. "Anna! Anna!" his father shouted down the hall in the direction of the kitchen, clapping his hands as he did so, "fetch a locksmith immediately!" In a moment the two girls were running down the hall with a rustle of skirts—how had his sister got dressed so quickly?—and pulling open the door. There was no sound of it being slammed shut behind them; probably they had left it open, as so often happens in homes visited by a major calamity.

Gregory, however, felt much calmer. So they could no longer understand what he said, although his words had seemed to him quite clear, clearer than before; perhaps his ear had made the necessary adjustment. Still, they were now convinced that all was not well with him, and they were prepared to help. The confidence and assurance with which the first instructions had been issued had done him good. He felt involved once more in the body of mankind and expected both men, the doctor and the locksmith, without in fact distinguishing in any precise way between them, to achieve great and surprising things. In order to make his voice as clear as possible for the coming decisive discussion he gave a little cough, though taking great care to muffle it lest this sound too should turn out different from human coughing, which was an issue he no longer felt competent to judge. Meanwhile silence had fallen in the adjoining room. Possibly his parents were sitting around the table with the chief clerk and whispering; possibly they were all leaning against the door, listening.

Using the chair, Gregory slowly pushed himself towards the door, let go of it when he got there, threw himself against the door, used this to support himself in an upright position—the balls of his feet had a small amount of adhesive on them—and there took a moment's rest from his labours. Then he set about trying to use his mouth to turn the key in the lock. Unfortunately it seemed he had no proper teeth—how was he to grip the key?—although admittedly his jaws were very strong; and indeed with their help he actually managed to move the key, ignoring the fact that in doing so he was clearly damaging himself in some way since a brown fluid began to pour from his mouth, run down over the key, and drip onto the floor. "Listen," the chief clerk said in the adjoining room, "he's turning the key." This was an enormous encouragement to Gregory; but they should all have called out to him, including his father and mother: "Go to it, Gregory," they should have called, "go on—turn that key!" And in the belief that they were all following his efforts in great excitement he bit down blindly on the key with all the strength he could muster. As the key gradually rotated in the lock he shuffled round in an arc; he was now supporting himself with his mouth alone, either hanging from the key or, if pressing was in order, pressing down on it once more with the whole weight of his body. The sharper sound as the bolt finally snapped back was literally a tonic to Gregory. With a sigh of relief he said to himself, "I didn't need the locksmith, then." And he laid his head on the door handle to finish opening the door.

His having to open the door in this way meant that he himself could still not be seen when the door was already open quite wide. He first had to work himself slowly round his leaf of the door, and he had to do it very carefully if he did not want to fall flat on his back before entering the other room. He was engaged in this difficult manoeuvre, too busy to notice anything else, when he heard the chief clerk suddenly utter a loud "Oh!"—it sounded like a gust of wind—and then he saw too, because the chief clerk had been nearest to the door, how he pressed a hand to his gaping mouth and started slowly giving ground as if an invisible force had been driving him steadily backwards. His mother, who despite the presence of the chief clerk was standing there with her hair all undone and still tousled from the night, looked first with clasped hands at his father, then took two steps towards Gregory and sank down, her skirts billowing in circles around her, her face lowered to her bosom and quite invisible. His father looked hostile and clenched a fist as if to force Gregory back into his room; then, with a diffident glance round the living-room, he shaded his eyes with his hands and wept until his great chest shook.

Gregory did not in fact enter the room now but leant against the inside of the other, still bolted leaf of the door in such a way that only half his body could be seen, and above it his head, tilted to one side, peering out at them. It had grown much lighter meanwhile; clearly visible across the street was a section of the endless, grey-black building opposite—it was a hospital—with its hard, regular windows punched in the façade; rain was still falling, but only in huge, individually visible drops that were also being hurled to earth literally one by one. A superabundance of breakfast things littered the table, because for Gregory's father breakfast was the main meal of the day, which he used to sit over for hours, reading a variety of newspapers. Hanging on the wall opposite was a photograph of Gregory taken when he was in the army, showing him as a lieutenant: one hand on his sword, a carefree smile on his lips, his whole bearing and uniform commanding respect. The door to the hall was open, and since the front door stood open too one could see out onto the landing and the top of the stairs.

"Right," said Gregory, well aware that he was the only one to have retained his composure, "I shall now get dressed, pack my samples, and be off. You will let me go, won't you? You see, sir, I am not a stubborn person and I like my work; it's a wearisome business, travelling, but I couldn't live without it. Where are you off to, sir? Back to the office? Are you? Will you make a faithful report of all this? One may find oneself temporarily incapacitated as far as work is concerned, but that is precisely the time to look back on one's previous achievements and bear in mind that afterwards, once the hindrance has been overcome, one will undoubtedly work all the harder and with even greater application. I'm so deeply beholden to the boss, as you well know. On the other hand I have my responsibility towards my parents and my sister. I'm in a tight spot, but I shall work my way out of it. Only don't make it more difficult for me than it is already. Stick up for me in the office! We travellers are not liked, I know. People think we earn a mint of money and have a great life into the bargain. That is their preconception, and they have no particular occasion to review it. But you, sir, have a better grasp of the circumstances than the rest of the staff — indeed, between you and me, a better grasp than the boss himself, who in his capacity as employer readily allows his judgement to err to an employee's disadvantage. You also appreciate how easily the traveller, who spends almost the entire year away from the office, can fall victim to gossip, ill luck, and unjustified complaints — with not the slightest chance of defending himself, since he usually hears nothing whatever about them and it is only when he returns exhausted from a trip that he reaps the appalling consequences, the root causes of which can by then no longer be unravelled. Sir, before you go, just give me some indication that you agree with at least a small part of what I have said!"

But the chief clerk had turned away with a shrug at Gregory's first words, although he continued to look back at Gregory over his shoulder with pursed lips. And during the whole of Gregory's speech he was not still for a moment but kept moving, without taking his eyes off Gregory, towards the door — very slowly, though, inch by inch, as if there existed some secret injunction against leaving the room. He had reached the hall already, and from the sharp movement with which he withdrew his foot from the living-room for the last time one might have thought he had just scorched his sole. Once in the hall, he stretched his right hand out in front of him towards the stairs as if some almost supernatural deliverance awaited him there.

Gregory realized that he could under no circumstances allow the chief clerk to leave in this frame of mind if he did not want his position with the firm to be very seriously jeopardized. His parents did not understand these things too well; they had formed the conviction over the years that with this job Gregory was taken care of for life; moreover they were now so preoccupied with their immediate worries as to have quite lost the faculty of foresight. Gregory, however, had not. The chief clerk must be detained, mollified, persuaded, and ultimately won over; Gregory's future and that of his family depended on it! If only his sister had been there! She was clever; she had already been in tears when Gregory was still lying quietly on his back. Undoubtedly the chief clerk, who was quite a lady's man, would have allowed himself to be swayed by her; she would have closed the front door and talked him out of his panic in the hall. But his sister was not there, and Gregory must do something himself. So, forgetting that he was still quite unfamiliar with his present capabilities as far as moving about was concerned, forgetting too that his last speech had possibly if not probably been understood as little as the previous one, he let go of the door; thrust himself through the doorway; tried to go to the chief clerk, who was already — absurdly — clutching the landing banister with both hands; but promptly fell, giving a little cry as he groped for a hold, onto his many legs. No sooner had this happened than, for the first time that morning, he experienced a feeling of physical well-being; his legs, with firm ground under them, responded perfectly, as he discovered to his delight; indeed they strove impatiently to carry him where he wanted to go; and he was immediately convinced that an end to all the agony was at hand. But even as he lay there, swaying with pent-up movement, on the floor not far from his mother, just opposite where she knelt in a state of seemingly total self-absorption, she suddenly sprang up, arms outstretched, fingers splayed, cried, "Help, for the love of God, help!"; craned her head forward as if trying to see Gregory better while on the contrary she was taking frenzied steps backwards; forgot the breakfast table behind her and, when she reached it, hopped distractedly up on it and sat on the edge; and seemed quite unaware of the fact that the overturned coffee pot beside her was emptying itself copiously onto the carpet.

"Mother, mother," said Gregory softly, looking up at her. He had forgotten all about the chief clerk for the moment, though at the sight of the coffee pouring out he could not stop himself snapping at the air several times with his jaws. At this his mother let out another yell, fell off the table, and fled into the arms of his father as he hurried towards her. But Gregory had no time for his parents now; the chief clerk, already on the stairs, had laid his chin on the banister for one last look back. Gregory took a run to make doubly sure of catching him; the chief clerk must have suspected something then because he leapt down several steps at once and disappeared, his parting cry of "Shoo!" echoing back up the stairwell. Unfortunately Gregory's father, who until now had been relatively composed, appeared to find the chief clerk's flight thoroughly unsettling, because instead of going after the man himself or at least not obstructing Gregory in his pursuit he seized the chief clerk's stick, which the latter had left behind on a chair together with his hat and coat, took a large newspaper from the table in his other hand, and with much stamping of his feet and brandishing of the stick and newspaper started to drive Gregory back into his room. None of Gregory's pleas availed, none were even understood; bend his head as meekly as he might, his father only stamped the louder. Across the room his mother, despite the cold weather, had thrown open a window and was leaning out, a long way out, pressing her face into her hands. This caused a powerful draught between street and stairwell that made the curtains billow, the newspapers rustle on the table, and one or two sheets even go floating across the floor. His father kept up the relentless pressure, hissing like a madman. Gregory, however, had had no practice at walking backwards and really could not go very fast. If only he could have turned round he would have been back in his room in an instant, but he was afraid of taxing his father's patience by so time-consuming a manoeuvre, with the stick in his father's hand threatening at any moment to deliver a mortal blow to his back or head. In the end, though, Gregory had no alternative, for he found to his dismay that he could not even control his direction in reverse; so with repeated anxious glances at his father he began to turn himself round as quickly as possible, which in the event was very slowly indeed. His father, perhaps realizing that he meant well, did not hinder him in this but even, from a distance, directed the rotation process intermittently with the end of his stick. If only it had not been for that unbearable hissing from his father! It threw Gregory into utter confusion. He was already nearly half-way round when, through continually listening for the hiss, he made a mistake and started turning the other way. But when, happily, he was facing the doorway at last, it became clear that his body was too wide to pass through just like that. His father, of course, given his state of mind at that moment, did not even begin to think of, for example, opening the other leaf of the door to provide Gregory with sufficient width of passage. His one and only idea was that Gregory must be got back into his room as quickly as possible. Nor would he ever have permitted the elaborate preparations Gregory would have had to make in order to assume an upright position and possibly get through the door that way. Instead he acted as if there had been no obstacle, urging Gregory on even more noisily than before; it no longer sounded like the voice of just one father behind him; things were really in earnest now, and Gregory thrust himself at the opening, come what might. One side of his body lifted up, he lay at an angle in the doorway, his flank was rubbed quite raw, some nasty-looking stains appeared on the white door, soon he was stuck fast and couldn't have moved another inch unaided, his legs on one side hanging quivering in mid air while those on the other were squashed painfully against the floor — at which point his father gave him a truly liberating shove from behind and he went flying right into his room, bleeding profusely. The door was banged to with the stick, and at last there was silence.

II

Not until dusk did Gregory wake from a sleep so deep it had been like a coma. He would undoubtedly have woken before long even without being disturbed, because he felt quite rested and no longer sleepy, but his impression was that he had been roused by a quick footstep and by the door to the hall being carefully shut. The light of the electric street lamps shone wanly on the ceiling in places and on the upper parts of the various pieces of furniture, but down below, where Gregory lay, it was dark. Probing still rather awkwardly with his feelers, which he was only now beginning to appreciate, he pushed himself slowly over to the door to see what had happened there. His left side seemed to be one long scar; it pulled unpleasantly, and he was reduced to limping on his twin rows of legs. Moreover one leg had suffered severe damage during the course of the morning's events — it was almost a miracle that only the one had been damaged — and trailed lifelessly behind.

Not until he had reached the door did he notice what had in fact drawn him in that direction, namely the smell of something to eat. For there stood a bowl of sweetened milk with little slices of white bread floating in it. He could have laughed for joy, because he felt even hungrier than he had in the morning, and he promptly plunged almost his whole head into the milk. But he soon drew it out again in disappointment; it was not only that eating was difficult for him on account of his tender left side — and he could only eat if his whole body panted systematically — but also that he did not at all like the taste, although ordinarily milk was his favourite drink, which would have been why his sister had brought it for him; indeed it was with a feeling almost of disgust that he turned aside from the bowl and crawled back into the middle of the room.

In the living-room the gas had been lit, as Gregory could see through the gap between the doors, but whereas usually at this time Gregory's father liked to read the afternoon paper aloud to his mother and sometimes to his sister, too, now there was not a sound to be heard. Well, perhaps the reading aloud, which his sister was always telling him about in her letters, had dropped out of use in recent weeks. But the whole flat was so quiet, though it was surely not empty. "What a peaceful life the family was leading!" Gregory said to himself, and as he stared fixedly into the darkness he felt enormously proud of having been able to provide his parents and his sister with such a life in so pleasant a flat. But what if all this peace, all this prosperity, all this satisfied contentment were to end in terror? Rather than risk losing himself in such thoughts Gregory preferred to move about, and he began crawling back and forth across the room.

Once during the long evening the door on one side and once the door on the other were opened a crack and then quickly closed again; someone had presumably felt the urge to come in but had had too many misgivings. Gregory stationed himself right by the door to the living-room, determined to get his diffident visitor into the room somehow or other or at least find out who it was; but from then on the door was not opened again, and Gregory waited in vain. In the morning, with the doors locked, everyone had wanted to come in; now that he had opened one door and the others had clearly been opened during the day no one came any more, and the keys had even been taken and put back in the locks from outside.

It was late into the night before the living-room light went out, and then it quickly became clear that his parents and his sister had in fact stayed up all that time, because the three of them could quite distinctly be heard tiptoeing away. Now no one would be coming into Gregory's room until morning, surely, so he had a long while in which to consider in peace and quiet how best to reorganize his life. But the tall, spacious room, in which he was obliged to lie flat on the floor, frightened him without his being able to discover why, because after all it was his room and he had been living in it for five years—and with a half-unconscious change of direction, and not without a slight feeling of shame, he went scuttling under the couch, where despite the fact that his back was a little squeezed and he could no longer lift his head he immediately felt very much at home, his only regret being that his body was too wide to be accommodated under the couch in its entirety.

There he spent the whole night, some of it in a doze from which his stomach kept waking him with a start, but some of it a prey to worries and obscure hopes, all of which, however, led him to the conclusion that for the time being he must keep calm and try, by being patient and exercising great consideration, to make it easier for his family to bear the inconvenience to which he was in his present state quite frankly obliged to put them.

Early the next morning, almost before it was light, Gregory had an opportunity to test the firmness of his new resolutions when his sister, almost fully dressed, opened the door from the living-room and nervously peered in. She did not spot Gregory straight away, but when she noticed him under the couch—God, he must be somewhere, he couldn't just have flown away—she got such a fright that she involuntarily slammed the door shut again. But as if thinking better of her action she opened it again immediately and tiptoed into the room, rather as if she were in the presence of a chronic invalid or even a stranger. Gregory, his head pushed forward to the edge of the couch, watched her. Would she notice that he had left the milk — though not because he had no appetite, far from it — and would she bring some other food that suited him better? If she did not do so of her own accord he would rather starve than tell her, despite what was really a terrible urge to dart out from under the couch, hurl himself at his sister's feet, and beg her to bring him something good to eat. His sister, however, noticing immediately and with some surprise that the bowl was still full, with only a little milk spilt around it, picked it up — not, admittedly, with her bare hands but with a rag — and carried it out. Gregory was extremely curious to know what she would bring in its stead, and he devoted a great deal of thought to it. But never could he have guessed what his sister, in the goodness of her heart, actually did. She brought him a whole selection of things, all laid out on an old newspaper, to see what he liked. There were some old, half-rotten vegetables; the bones from supper, covered with congealed white sauce; some raisins and almonds; a piece of cheese that Gregory had pronounced inedible two days previously; a slice of dry bread, another spread with butter, and another spread with butter and salted. As well as all this she brought back the bowl, which it had probably been decided once and for all should be Gregory's, this time with water in it. Very tactfully, knowing that Gregory would not eat in her presence, she then withdrew and even turned the key in the lock to let Gregory know that he could set to as he pleased. Gregory's legs whirred as he crossed to where the food was. His wounds must incidentally have healed up completely by now, for he felt no further impediment; he was astonished at this and remembered how he had nicked his finger with a knife more than a month ago and how the wound had still been quite painful the day before yesterday. "Have I perhaps become less sensitive?" he thought, sucking greedily at the piece of cheese, to which of all the things available he had been most immediately and emphatically drawn. With tears of contentment in his eyes, he demolished in quick succession the cheese, the vegetables, and the sauce. The fresh food did not appeal to him; in fact, finding even the smell of it intolerable, he went so far as to drag the things he wanted to eat a little way off. He had long finished all the food and was simply lazing about when, as a sign that he should withdraw, his sister began slowly turning the key. This roused him immediately, although he had been more than half asleep, and he hurried back beneath the couch. But it required enormous strength of mind for him to stay under the couch even for the short time his sister spent in the room, because as a result of his copious meal his body had swollen slightly and in that narrow space he could hardly breathe. Between bouts of near-suffocation he watched with somewhat protruding eyes as his unsuspecting sister swept together with a broom not only the scraps but even the food Gregory had left untouched, as if realizing that it too was no longer needed, and hurriedly threw everything into a pail that she covered with a wooden lid before carrying it out. Hardly was her back turned before Gregory emerged from beneath the couch to stretch and distend himself.

This was how Gregory now received his food each day, once in the morning when his parents and the maid were still asleep, and a second time after the family's lunch, because then his parents had another little sleep and the maid was sent off on some errand or other by his sister. Doubtless they no more wished Gregory to starve than she did, but perhaps it would have been too much for them to learn about his eating habits other than by hearsay, perhaps his sister was concerned to spare them even what might have been only a minor sorrow, for in all conscience they could be said to be suffering enough.

What excuses had been used on that first morning to get the doctor and the locksmith out of the flat again Gregory was never able to discover, because since there was no understanding him it did not occur to anyone, not even to his sister, that he might be able to understand other people, so that when his sister was in his room he had to content himself with her intermittent sighs and invocations of the saints. It was only later, when she had grown accustomed to things to a certain extent—there could never of course be any question of her becoming fully accustomed—Gregory occasionally caught a remark that was meant well enough or could be so interpreted. "He enjoyed his food today," she would comment if Gregory had scoffed the lot, whereas if the opposite was the case, and by degrees it came more and more often to be so, she would say almost sadly, "Oh, he's left everything again."

But while Gregory was unable to learn any news directly he did pick up a certain amount from the adjoining rooms, and as soon as he heard voices he would run to the door concerned and press his whole body up against it. Particularly in the early days there was no conversation that did not in some way, if only obliquely, have to do with him. For two days there were discussions at every meal as to how they should now conduct themselves, but between mealtimes, too, the same subject kept coming up, because there were always at least two members of the family at home; presumably no one wanted to stay at home on his or her own, and there could be no question of leaving the flat completely deserted. Also the maid had come to his mother on the very first day—it was not clear how much she knew of what had happened—and asked on bended knee to be discharged immediately, and when a quarter of an hour later she came back to say goodbye she expressed thanks for her discharge with tears in her eyes, as if it had been the greatest blessing ever bestowed on her in that house, and spontaneously delivered herself of a fearful oath to the effect that she would never breathe a word to anyone.

This meant that Gregory's sister, together with his mother, now had to do the cooking as well, although there was not much work involved as they were hardly eating anything. Again and again Gregory heard one of them vainly exhorting the others to eat, only to receive the inevitable reply, "No, thank you, I've had enough," or words to that effect. No drinking went on either. His sister was always asking his father if he wanted a beer, generously offering to go out for it herself, and when he said nothing she suggested, with a view to removing any misgivings he might have, that she could even send the janitor, but eventually Gregory's father told her firmly, "No," and the subject was not mentioned again.

In the course of the very first day his father gave both his mother and his sister a comprehensive account of the family's financial circumstances and prospects. Every now and then he got up from the table and went over to the small patent safe that he had retrieved from the collapse of his business five years before to fetch a receipt or a notebook or whatever it might be. He could be heard unlocking it—a complicated process—and, having removed what he wanted, locking it again. In part these elucidations of his father's were the first gratifying communications to have reached

Gregory's ears since his captivity began. He had always assumed that his father had been left with nothing whatsoever from that business; at least, his father had never said anything to him to the contrary, nor as a matter of fact had Gregory ever asked him about it. The catastrophe had plunged them all into utter despair, and Gregory's sole concern at that time had been to do everything to erase it from the family's memory as swiftly as possible. That was when he had begun to work with quite exceptional enthusiasm and from being a minor clerk had become a traveller virtually overnight, as such of course enjoying an entirely different earning potential since his results, if he was successful, were immediately convertible, in terms of commission, into cash that could be taken home and laid on the table before the astonished and delighted eyes of the family. Those had been marvellous times, and they had never recurred since, at least not with the same splendour, although subsequently Gregory was earning so much money that he was in a position to meet the expenses of the entire family and indeed did so. They had simply started taking it for granted, not just the family but Gregory himself; they accepted the money gratefully, Gregory provided it willingly, but no special warmth seemed to be engendered any more. Only his sister had remained close to Gregory in spite of everything, and since unlike himself she was very fond of music and could play the violin most movingly it was his secret ambition, regardless of the expense that would inevitably be involved—he'd manage to cover that in some other way—to send her to the Conservatory in the following year. During his brief stays in the city the Conservatory often cropped up in conversation with his sister, but never as anything more than a beautiful dream that could not possibly come true, and even those innocent references were unwelcome to their parents' ears; Gregory, however, had quite definite ideas on the subject and meant to make his announcement with some solemnity on Christmas Eve.

Such were the thoughts—quite futile in his present condition—that passed through his head as he stood glued to the door, listening. Once or twice, too tired to take in any more, he inadvertently let his head droop and knock against the door, but he lifted it again immediately because even the tiny sound it made had been heard in the next room, and they had all stopped talking. "What's he up to now?" his father said after a while, obviously looking towards the door, and only then was the interrupted conversation gradually resumed.

Gregory now became thoroughly acquainted—for his father tended to be very repetitive, partly because he had not concerned himself with these matters for some time, partly too because Gregory's mother did not always grasp everything on first hearing—with the fact that, the catastrophe notwithstanding, an admittedly very small amount of capital still survived from the old days, now of course slightly swollen by the interest that had been allowed to accumulate in the mean time. Furthermore the money that Gregory had brought home each month—he had kept only the loose change for himself—had not all been used up and had itself accumulated to form a modest capital. Behind his door Gregory nodded enthusiastically, delighted to hear of this unexpected prudence and thrift. He could in fact have used the money to clear some more of his father's debt to the boss, and the day when he could write that item off completely would have been very much nearer, but as things were his father's arrangement was undoubtedly the better one.

The fact remained that the sum was nowhere near enough for the family to be able, for example, to live off the interest; it might be enough to support them for one or at most two years, but that was all. In other words it was money that ought not in fact to be touched at all but ought to be put aside for an emergency; the money for day-to-day expenses had to be earned. Now Gregory's father, though in good health, was an old man who had not worked for the past five years and in any case could not take on very much; during those five years, which had been the first holiday of his arduous yet unsuccessful life, he had put on a great deal of weight and become very clumsy in his movements as a result. And was Gregory's old mother to start going out to work when, crippled as she was by asthma, she found it an effort to walk round the flat and spent every other day lying on the sofa with the window open, gasping for breath? And was his sister to go out to work, a child of only seventeen whose life until then surely no one would have begrudged her, consisting as it had of dressing prettily, sleeping long hours, lending a hand with the housework, indulging in a few modest pleasures, and above all playing the violin? Whenever the talk turned to this necessity for earning money Gregory let go of the door and threw himself down on the cool leather sofa beside it, burning with shame and grief.

Often he lay there right through the night, not sleeping a wink but simply scratching at the leather for hours on end. Or he embarked on the laborious task of pushing a chair over to the window and crawling up the wall to the sill in order to brace himself in the chair and lean against the glass, obviously in response to some memory of the feeling of freedom it had once given him to look out of the window. Because the fact of the matter was that, as the days went by, even things that were quite close he saw less and less clearly; the hospital opposite, the all-too-frequent sight of which he had formerly cursed, he could not see at all now, and had he not known full well that he lived in the quiet but entirely urban Charlotte Street he might have thought his window overlooked a wilderness in which the grey sky and the grey earth merged indistinguishably. His thoughtful sister needed to see the chair standing there on only two occasions before she began, each time she had tidied up his room, pushing it carefully back beneath the window and even, from then on, leaving the inner casement open.

If only Gregory had been able to speak to his sister and thank her for everything she was having to do for him he could have borne her attentions more easily; as it was they pained him. Admittedly she tried to cover up the awkwardness of the situation as much as possible, and of course as time went by she became better and better at doing so, but in time, too, Gregory acquired a keener perception of things. Even her entrance was terrible for him. As soon as she had stepped over the threshold, and without even pausing to shut the door, for all her usual concern to spare everyone the sight of Gregory's room, she ran straight to the window, tore it open with fumbling hands as if she were on the point of suffocating, and stood by it for a while, no matter how cold the weather, taking deep breaths. She terrified Gregory twice daily with this running and banging; he spent the whole time trembling under the couch, yet he was perfectly sure she would have spared him the experience had she anyhow found it in her power to remain in a room occupied by Gregory with the window closed.

Once—this must have been a month after Gregory's metamorphosis, by which time his sister no longer had any particular reason to be astonished at his appearance—she came a little earlier than usual and found Gregory, motionless and at his most terrifying, still looking out of the window. Gregory would not have been surprised had she not come in, because his position made it impossible for her to open the window immediately, but not only did she not come in, she even withdrew smartly and shut the door; a stranger might almost have thought Gregory had been lying in wait for her with the intention of biting her. Gregory, of course, hid under the couch immediately, but he had to wait until noon before his sister returned, and when she did she seemed much more agitated than usual. He realized from this that she still found the sight of him unbearable and would inevitably go on finding it unbearable, and that it probably cost her a great effort of self-control not to run at the sight of even the small portion of his body that stuck out from beneath the couch. To spare her even this sight he one day, took his sheet, carried it over to the couch on his back—the job took him four hours—and there arranged it in such a way as to cover him completely, so that his sister could not see him even when she bent down. Had she considered the sheet unnecessary she could after all have removed it, because surely it was obvious that it could not be Gregory's idea of fun to cut himself off so utterly and completely, yet she left the sheet as it was, and Gregory even thought he detected a look of gratitude when at one point, to see how his sister was taking the new arrangement, he carefully lifted the sheet a little with his head.

For the first fortnight his parents could not bring themselves to enter his room, and he often heard them expressing unqualified approval of his sister's present efforts, whereas before they had thought her a fairly ineffectual sort of girl and had frequently lost patience with her. Now, however, both his father and his mother often waited outside Gregory's room while his sister cleaned it out, and no sooner had she emerged than she had to give them a detailed account of the state of the room, what Gregory had eaten, how he had behaved this time, and whether perhaps some slight improvement were noticeable. His mother in fact wanted to visit Gregory relatively early on, but his father and sister restrained her, initially using arguments based on common sense to which Gregory listened attentively and in full agreement. Subsequently they had to restrain her by force, and when she then cried out, "Let me go to Gregory, my poor, unfortunate son! Don't you see that I must go to him?" Gregory thought it might not be a bad idea if his mother did come in, not every day of course but perhaps once a week; she understood things so much better than his sister, who for all her pluck was still a mere child and, when all was said and done, had perhaps only taken on so hard a task in a fit of childish exuberance.

Gregory's wish to see his mother was soon fulfilled. He did not like to show himself at the window during the day, if only for his parents' sake; he could not move about much in the few square metres of floor space; lying still he found difficult enough at night; eating no longer gave him the slightest pleasure; so to amuse himself he adopted the habit of crawling all over the walls and ceiling. He was particularly partial to hanging from the ceiling; this was quite different from lying on the floor; one could breathe more freely; gentle vibrations went coursing through the body; and in the almost blissful state of abstraction that Gregory found himself in up there it sometimes happened that, much to his own astonishment, he let go and went crashing to the floor. But of course he now had his body under much better control than before, and even a fall like that did not harm him. Gregory's sister noticed his new pastime straight away—he left traces of adhesive behind when he crawled—and took it into her head to give Gregory as much crawling-space as possible by removing such items of furniture, chiefly the wardrobe and the desk, as precluded it. She could not, however, do this on her own; she dared not ask her father to help; the maid would certainly not have lent a hand because, although for her sixteen or so years of age she had stuck it out bravely since the departure of the previous cook, she had asked as a special dispensation to be allowed to keep the kitchen permanently locked and to be obliged to open it only on receipt of a specific signal; so his sister had no alternative but to take advantage of one of the father's absences to fetch Gregory's mother. And along his mother promptly came, uttering cries of pleasure and excitement, though she fell silent at the door of Gregory's room. First, of course, his sister checked whether everything was all right in the room, only then letting the mother enter. Gregory had very hastily pulled the sheet down even lower and made more folds, and the whole arrangement really did look as if a sheet had simply been thrown over the couch at random. Gregory also refrained from stealing a glance under the sheet this time; he was prepared to forgo seeing his mother on this occasion, content with the fact that she had come at last. "Come on, you can't see him," said his sister, obviously leading his mother by the hand. Gregory listened as the two frail women started to shift the old, rather heavy wardrobe; he could tell that his sister was deliberately doing most of the work herself the whole time, ignoring the anxious warnings of the mother, who was afraid she was going to strain herself. It took a very long time. After they had been at it for perhaps a quarter of an hour his mother said they should leave the wardrobe where it was: for one thing it was too heavy, they would not be finished before father came back, and with the wardrobe in the middle of the room they would be blocking Gregory's every move; for another thing it was by no means certain that in removing his furniture they were doing Gregory a favour. It seemed to her that the opposite was the case; she found the sight of the bare walls downright depressing; and who was to say that Gregory's reaction would not be the same, since he had had the furniture for ages, was used to it, and would feel lonely in the empty room. "And isn't it," his mother concluded in a low voice—in fact she had been virtually whispering the whole time as if to make sure that Gregory, of whose exact whereabouts she was unaware, should not even hear the sound of her voice, since she was already convinced he would not understand the words—"isn't it as if by removing the furniture we were showing that we had given up all hope of improvement and were callously leaving him to his own devices? I believe the best thing would be to try to keep the room exactly as it was, then when Gregory returns to us he will find everything the same and it will be that much easier for him to forget the time between."

Hearing his mother's words, "Gregory realized that the fact that no one had addressed him directly in the past two months, coupled with the monotony of life in the bosom of the family, must have considerably muddled his wits; this was the only explanation he could find of his seriously having wanted his room cleared. Did he really wish to have his warm, friendly room, cosily furnished as it was with family heirlooms, transformed into a cave in which he would admittedly be able to crawl all over the place unimpeded but at the price of rapidly and completely forgetting his human past? Why, he was on the verge of forgetting already, and he had been rallied only by hearing his mother's voice again after all this time. Nothing was to be removed; it must all stay; the positive influence that the furniture had on his condition was something he could not do without; and if the furniture prevented him from indulging in his stupid crawling, that was no disadvantage but a very good thing.

Unfortunately his sister thought otherwise; in discussions of Gregory's affairs she had taken to presenting herself, not without some justification, as something of an expert compared with her parents, so that on this occasion too the mother's advice was sufficient reason as far as the daughter was concerned for insisting on the removal not only of the wardrobe and the desk, which was all she had had in mind originally, but of every piece of furniture in the room, the indispensable couch excepted. It was of course more than mere childish defiance and the self-confidence she had so unexpectedly and laboriously acquired in recent weeks that impelled her to make this demand; she had also observed with her own eyes how Gregory required a great deal of space for crawling, whereas he did not, so far as one could see, have the slightest use for the furniture. But perhaps another contributory factor was the highly romantic nature of girls of that age, which, seeking gratification at every turn, had in the present instance led Meg into the temptation of trying to make Gregory's plight even more horrific, thereby putting herself in a position to render him even greater services. Because in a room in which Gregory patrolled empty walls probably no one but Meg would ever dare to set foot.

And so it was that she would not allow her resolve to be shaken by her mother, who even with the room as it was appeared to be nervous and unsure of herself, soon falling silent and giving the sister what help she could to move the wardrobe out. Well, Gregory could manage without the wardrobe at a pinch, but the desk must stay. And no sooner had the women left the room with the wardrobe, groaning as they flattened themselves against it, than Gregory poked his head out from under the couch to see how he might prudently and as far as possible tactfully intervene. As luck would have it, however, his mother came back first, leaving Meg in the other room with her arms around the wardrobe, rocking it to and fro without of course moving it an inch. Now his mother was not used to the sight of him; it might make her ill; so Gregory scurried backwards in some alarm until he was right at the far end of the couch, though he was too late to prevent the sheet at the front from swaying slightly, just enough to catch his mother's eye. She stopped short, stood quite still for a moment, then went back to Meg.

Although Gregory kept telling himself that nothing out of the ordinary was happening, it was only a few bits of furniture being moved about, he was soon forced to admit that the women's to-ing and fro-ing, their muttered cries, and the scraping of the furniture on the floor were affecting him like a great turmoil that was being fuelled from all sides, and however firmly he drew in his head and legs and pressed his body to the floor the conclusion was inescapable that he was not going to be able to put up with it for long. They were clearing his room out, taking away everything that was dear to him; the wardrobe, which contained his fret-saw and the other tools, was already gone; now they were freeing his desk from the holes it had dug in the floor, the desk at which as a student of commerce and before that as a schoolboy, in fact ever since his junior-school days, he had sat and laboured over his essays — no, he simply hadn't time to scrutinize the good intentions of the two women, whose existence he had in any case almost forgotten since they were now toiling in exhausted silence, and all that could be heard was the heavy tramp of their feet.

The upshot was that he darted from his hiding-place — the women happened to be leaning against the desk in the next room, getting their breath back — changed direction four times, quite unable to decide what to salvage first, then, spotting the picture of the lady all in furs where it hung conspicuously on the otherwise bare wall, quickly crawled up to it and pressed himself against the glass, which offered a firm purchase and did his hot belly good. This picture at least, which Gregory was now completely covering, surely no one would take away from him. He twisted his head round towards the living-room door to observe the women's return.

They had not given themselves much of a rest and were already coming back; Meg had her arm around her mother and was virtually carrying her. "All right, what shall we take next?" she said, looking about her. Then her eyes met Gregory's up on the wall. Probably only because her mother was there she retained her composure, bent her head closer to her mother to prevent her from looking about her, and said, if with somewhat tremulous haste, "Come, let's go back in the living-room for a moment, shall we?" It was dear to Gregory what Meg was up to: she meant to get her mother out of harm's way and then chase him down from the wall. Well, just let her try! He was sitting on his picture and was not going to part with it. He'd leap off in Meg's face first.

But Meg's words had served only to increase the mother's agitation; she now stepped to one side, saw the huge brown blotch on the flowered wallpaper, cried out, before she had really registered the fact that it was Gregory she was looking at, in a shrill, strident voice, "Oh God, oh God!" and with arms outstretched as if giving up altogether fell back on the couch and lay still. "Gregory!" cried his sister, shaking her fist and glaring at him. It was the first time she had addressed him directly since the metamorphosis. She ran into the next room for some sort of essence that might revive her unconscious mother; Gregory wanted to help — time enough later to save the picture — but he was stuck fast to the glass and had to tear himself free; then he too ran into the next room as if there were some advice he could give his sister, like in the old days, but had to stand behind her doing nothing while she rummaged among various bottles, and gave her a fright when she turned round; one bottle fell to the floor and broke; a sliver of glass flew in Gregory's face, wounding him, and some pungent medicament swirled round him; Meg wasted no more time but gathered up as many bottles as she could and ran with them back to her mother, slamming the door behind her with her foot. Gregory was now cut off from his mother, who — and it was his fault — might be on the point of death; he could not open the door without frightening away his sister, and she must stay with their mother; there was nothing he could do except wait; and in an agony of anxiety and self-reproach he began to crawl about, all over everything, walls, furniture, ceiling, until eventually, in his despair, with the whole room starting to spin round him, he fell right in the middle of the big table.

For a while Gregory lay there weakly; around him all was silence; possibly that was a good sign. Then there came a ring at the door. The maid was of course locked in her kitchen, so Meg had to go. It was Gregory's father. "What's happened?" was the first thing he said; presumably Meg's appearance had given the game away. Meg answered in a muffled voice, obviously with her face buried against her father's chest, "Mother fainted but she's all right now. Gregory's got out." "I knew it," said the father, "I kept telling you it would happen, but you women never listen." It was clear to Gregory that his father had misinterpreted Meg's all-too-brief report and assumed that he had been responsible for some act of violence. He must now attempt to placate his father, having neither the time nor the means to put him right. Accordingly he made a run for the door of his room and pressed himself against it in order that his father should see as soon as he entered the living-room that his intentions were of the best, that he was prepared to go back into his room immediately, and that it was not necessary to drive him there but only to open the door, when he would promptly disappear.

His father, however, was in no mood to spot such niceties; "Ah!" he cried on entering, and his tone of voice suggested simultaneous rage and delight. Gregory pulled his head back from the door and swung it round towards his father. The man who stood there bore no resemblance to the mental image Gregory had had of him; admittedly he had neglected of late, through his new-found interest in crawling, to concern himself to the same extent as previously with events in the rest of the flat, and he ought in fact to have been quite prepared to find that things had changed. Yes, but, even so, could this really be his father? The same man as had lain wearily in bed, buried in his pillows, when Gregory left on a business trip; had greeted him from an armchair in his dressing-gown when Gregory returned home in the evening; had even found it beyond him to rise to his feet, merely raising his arms to indicate that he was pleased; and had, on the rare occasions when they went for a walk together, on a couple of Sundays a year and on the principal public holidays, shuffled along between Gregory and his mother, managing, though they were pretty slow walkers themselves, to go a little more slowly still, wrapped in his old overcoat, always placing his walking-stick with great care, and, when he wanted to say something had almost invariably come to a complete halt and gathered his escort about him? Now, however, he was drawn up to his full height; dressed in a severe blue uniform with gilt buttons of the kind worn by bank commissionaires; the high, stiff collar of his jacket was topped by a powerful double chin; beneath the bushy eyebrows his piercing dark eyes had a fresh, alert look; the usually dishevelled white hair had been meticulously combed down, parted, and brilliantined. Tossing his cap, which bore a gold monogram, probably that of a bank, in an arc that took it right across the room onto the couch and pushing back the long flaps of his uniform jacket to thrust his hands into his trouser pockets, he bore down on Gregory with a look of grim determination on his face. Probably he did not know himself what he meant to do; nevertheless he raised his feet to an unusual height, and Gregory was amazed at the enormous size of the soles of his boots. Not that he dwelt on his amazement, remembering as he did from the very first day of his new life that his father believed the only way to treat him was with the utmost severity; no, he fled from his father's advance, stopping whenever his father came to a halt and hurrying on again the moment his father moved. They made several circuits of the room like this without anything decisive happening, indeed without the whole performance, so slowly was it enacted, even having the appearance of a chase. For this reason Gregory also kept to the floor for the time being, especially since he was afraid his father might look upon a retreat to the walls or ceiling as evidence of conspicuous ill will. But he had to admit to himself that he would not be able to keep up even this kind of running for long, because where his father took one step he had to make a whole host of movements. He was beginning to experience difficulty in breathing, and it was a fact that even in his previous life his lungs had never been wholly reliable. As he staggered on, barely keeping his eyes open in order to save all his strength for his legs, not even, in his lethargy, considering any other escape than by running, having already almost forgotten that the walls were at his disposal, though in this room they were cluttered with elaborately carved furniture, all notches and protruberances—something was lobbed gently over his shoulder, struck the floor just in front of him, and rolled away. It was an apple; another went flying after it; Gregory came to a terrified halt, further running being pointless now that his father had decided to bombard him. He had filled his pockets from the fruit bowl on the sideboard and was throwing one apple after another without even taking aim first. The small, red apples rolled around the floor as if electrified, bumping into one another. One feebly tossed apple struck Gregory a glancing blow on the back, doing no damage. But another that came flying after it hit him on the back and sank right in; Gregory tried to drag himself forward as though the shocking, unbelievable pain might go away if he moved; but it was like being pinned to the ground, and he stretched himself out, all his senses a complete blur. The last thing he saw was the door of his room being wrenched open and his mother rushing out past his shrieking sister, in her chemise because his sister had started undressing her to ease her breathing while she was unconscious, rushing up to his father with her tucked-up skirts spilling to the floor one by one as she ran, stumbling over the skirts as she fell upon his father and, with her arms around him, in absolute union with him—but Gregory's sight was already failing at this point— her hands cupping the back of his father's head, begged him to spare Gregory's life.

III

The severity of Gregory's wound, from which he suffered for more than a month— no one daring to remove the apple, it remained lodged in his flesh as a visible reminder—seemed to have brought home even to his father that, for all his present deplorable and repugnant appearance, Gregory was a member of the family and was therefore not to be treated as an enemy; on the contrary, family duty required them to swallow their loathing and simply grin and bear it.

And if in all likelihood Gregory had now, as a result of his injury, permanently lost some of his mobility and for the present resembled an elderly invalid in that it took him endless minutes to cross from one side of his room to the other—crawling on the walls and ceiling being out of the question—he felt fully compensated for this deterioration in his condition by the fact that every evening the door to the living-room, which he was in the habit of keeping a sharp eye on for as much as an hour or two beforehand, was thrown open and he was allowed to lie in the darkness of his room, invisible from next door, and observe the whole family around the brightly-lit table and listen to their conversation — all this as it were by general consent, in other words under very different circumstances from before.

Gone, of course, were the lively exchanges of earlier days, which Gregory had always recalled with a certain nostalgia in those tiny hotel rooms as he threw his weary body down on yet another damp bed. Now it was mostly a very peaceful time. His father fell asleep in his chair soon after supper; his mother and sister kept reminding each other to be quiet; his mother, leaning forward into the light, sewed lingerie for a fashion shop; his sister, who had taken a job as a shop assistant, spent her evenings learning shorthand and French with a view, possibly, to securing a better position later on. Occasionally his father would wake up, and as if unaware that he had been asleep he would say to the mother, "You're doing a lot of sewing again today!" and go straight back to sleep, while mother and sister exchanged tired smiles.

With an almost mulish obstinacy Gregory's father refused to take off his commissionaire's uniform even in the house; and while his dressing-gown hung idle on the peg he slept fully dressed in his place at table as if permanently ready for duty, all ears, even here, for the dictates of his superior. As a result the uniform, which had not been new to start with, defied all Gregory's mother's and sister's efforts to keep it clean, and Gregory often spent whole evenings gazing at the appallingly stained garment, bright with its ever-polished buttons, in which the old man slept in great discomfort and yet at his ease.

As soon as the clock struck ten Gregory's mother tried by quietly talking to his father to wake him up and coax him into going to bed, because it was not proper sleep that he was getting where he was and sleep was something that, having to report for duty at six o'clock, he needed very badly. But with the wilfulness that had characterized him since he had taken this humble job he invariably insisted on staying up longer, although he regularly dozed off and afterwards it was only with the greatest difficulty that he could be persuaded to exchange chair for bed. No matter how much Gregory's mother and sister urged him with mild reproaches, for a quarter of an hour he went on slowly shaking his head with his eyes firmly closed, refusing to stand up. Gregory's mother plucked at his sleeve, whispering blandishments in his ear, and his sister left her work to go to her mother's aid, but the effect on Gregory's father was nil. He only slumped deeper into his chair. Not until the women grasped him under the armpits did he open his eyes, look from mother to sister, and say, "What a life! So much for a quiet old age!" Then, leaning on the two women, he would rise awkwardly to his feet as if he were an enormous burden even to himself, allow the women to escort him to the door, and there wave them away to continue on his own, while Gregory's mother quickly put down her sewing and his sister her pen in order to run after him and offer further assistance.

Who in this overworked and exhausted family had time to give Gregory any more attention than was absolutely necessary? The housekeeping budget was progressively curtailed; the maid was dismissed after all; a big, rawboned cleaning-woman with wispy white hair came in mornings and evenings to do the heaviest work; everything else Gregory's mother took care of, on top of all her sewing. It even reached the point where various pieces of family jewellery, formerly worn with great delight by Gregory's mother and sister on evenings out and other festive occasions, were sold, as Gregory learnt the same evening when the family discussed the prices fetched. But the main complaint was always that, while the flat was far too big for their present circumstances, they could not leave it because of the insoluble problem of how to move Gregory. Gregory, however, fully appreciated that he was not the only consideration in the way of a move, since it would have been a simple matter to transport him in a suitable crate fitted with a few air-holes; no, what chiefly held the family back from finding a new flat was their feeling of utter despair and the idea that they had been struck by a misfortune exceeding anything ever experienced within their entire circle of friends and relations. What the world requires of poor people they were fulfilling to the last degree; the father fetched breakfast for minor bank officials; the mother sacrificed herself for the underwear of total strangers; the sister ran back and forth behind the counter at her customers' beck and call; to do any more was beyond the family's power. And the wound in Gregory's back began to hurt all over again when his mother and sister, having put his father to bed, came back, left their work where they had dropped it, moved their chairs closer together until they were sitting cheek to cheek; and when his mother, indicating Gregory's room, said, "Shut the door now, Meg," and he was in darkness again, while in the other room the women wept together or possibly sat dry-eyed, staring at the table-top.

Gregory's nights and days passed almost entirely without sleep. He thought intermittently of taking the affairs of the family in hand again just as before, the very next time the door opened; after a long interval the boss and the chief clerk reappeared in his thoughts together with the other clerks and the apprentices, the dim-witted errand boy, two or three friends from other firms, a provincial hotel chamber-maid of brief, fond memory, a cashier in a hat shop whom he had courted in earnest but rather too slowly — they all appeared, interspersed with strangers or people he had forgotten, but instead of helping him and his family they were without exception unapproachable and he was glad to see them go. Afterwards, however, he was again in no mood to bother about his family; he was merely angry at the appalling service, and although he could think of nothing he might have felt like eating he began to plan ways of gaining access to the larder, there to help himself to what, even if he was not hungry, was after all no more than his due. With no thought any longer of how she might particularly please Gregory, his sister now hurriedly shoved any old thing into his room with her foot before leaving for work in the morning and again after lunch, and in the evening, regardless of whether the food had perhaps merely been picked at or — as was usually the case — left completely untouched, she swept it out again with a whisk of her broom. The cleaning, which she now always did in the evenings, could not have taken less time. The walls of Gregory's room were streaked with dirt, and balls of dust and little heaps of excrement dotted the floor. At the beginning Gregory used to position himself, when his sister arrived, in corners that were particularly bad in this respect, intending his action as a sort of reproach to her. But he could have stayed there for weeks without his sister mending her ways; the fact was, she could see the dirt as clearly as he could, only she had made up her mind to leave it. At the same time she watched with, for her, a quite novel sensitivity—it had come over the whole family, in fact—that the cleaning of Gregory's room should remain her prerogative. On one occasion Gregory's mother had subjected his room to a major spring-clean, which, had taken several buckets of water to complete successfully—all the humidity upsetting Gregory too, of course, so that he flopped down on the couch in a sulk and lay still—but she did not go unpunished. As soon as Gregory's sister saw the change in his room that evening she ran into the living-room, deeply hurt, and despite her mother's imploringly upraised hands burst into a paroxysm of tears of which her parents—the father had of course started up out of his chair in alarm—were at first astonished and helpless witnesses; until they too began to get excited; father upbraiding mother to his right for not leaving the cleaning of the room to Gregory's sister; and to his left yelling at the sister that she would never be allowed to clean Gregory's room again; while Gregory's mother tried to drag his father, who was beside himself with rage, into the bedroom; his sister, shaking with sobs, pounded the table with her little fists; and Gregory himself hissed aloud in his fury at the fact that no one thought of shutting the door and sparing him this noisy scene.

But even if his sister, exhausted from her day's work, had had enough of looking after Gregory as she had once done, there was still no need for Gregory's mother to have taken her place and still no reason why Gregory should be neglected. For now the cleaning-woman was there. This elderly widow, whose powerful build had presumably helped her to weather the worst in the course of her long life, had no particular horror of Gregory. Without as it were being nosy she had once inadvertently opened the door of Gregory's room, and at the sight of Gregory, who was taken completely by surprise and began running to and fro although no one was chasing him, she had stood there in amazement with her hands clasped before her. Since then she had not let a day go by without, morning and evening, opening the door a crack and peeping in at Gregory. The first few times she had also called him to her, using words she probably regarded as affable, such as "Come on, you old dung beetle, come over here!" or "Look at the old dung beetle!" Addressed in this fashion, Gregory had made no reply but stayed where he was without moving as though the door had never been opened. If only, instead of letting the woman plague him to no purpose as the mood took her, they had told her to clean his room out every day! One early morning—heavy rain, possibly in token of the coming of spring, was beating at the window-panes—Gregory felt so bitter when the cleaning-woman started using those words again that he turned, though very slowly and rather decrepitly, as if to attack her. Instead of taking fright, however, the cleaning-woman merely picked up a nearby chair and raised it high in the air, and from the way in which she stood there with her mouth wide open it was clear that she would shut her mouth only when the chair in her hand had come crashing down on Gregory's back. "You keep your distance, all right?" she asked as Gregory turned away again; then she calmly put the chair back in the corner.

Gregory was now eating almost nothing. Only when he happened to walk past the food put down for him did he aimlessly take a bite, which he kept in his mouth for hours and then usually spat out again. At first he thought it was sadness at the state of his room that had spoilt his appetite, but in fact the changes in his room were something to which he became reconciled very quickly. They had got into the habit of putting in with him things that could not be accommodated elsewhere, and there were now a great many such things because they had let one room of the flat to three lodgers. These earnest gentlemen—all three wore full beards, as Gregory discovered on one occasion through a crack in the door—were sticklers for order, not only in their room but also, now that they were installed as lodgers, as far as the whole household was concerned, which meant particularly the kitchen. They had no time for useless junk and even less if it was dirty. Moreover they had brought most of their furniture with them. As a result, many things had become superfluous for which there was no market but which on the other hand no one wanted to throw away. All of them found their way into Gregory's room, as did the ash bucket and the rubbish bin from the kitchen. Everything that was temporarily out of use the cleaning-woman, who was always in a great hurry, simply flung into Gregory's room; Gregory was usually lucky enough to see only the object in question and the hand holding it. The cleaning-woman may have meant to fetch the things again when she had a moment or throw them all out at one go; in fact they stayed where they had landed, except when Gregory forced a path through the stuff and shifted it, at first because he had to, there being no other space for crawling, but subsequently with ever-increasing pleasure, although the aftermath of such expeditions was that he relapsed, dead-tired and in a mood of deep gloom, into hours of lying without moving.

As the lodgers sometimes had supper at home as well, eating in the communal living-room, there were evenings when the living-room door stayed shut, but Gregory found it quite easy to forgo the opening of the door; there had already been evenings when, with the door open, he had not taken advantage of the fact but had lain motionless in the darkest corner of his room, unnoticed by the family. On one occasion, however, the cleaning-woman having left the door to the living-room ajar, it stayed that way and was still ajar when the lodgers came home in the evening and the lamp was lit. They sat down at the head of the table, where Gregory's father and mother and Gregory himself had formerly eaten, unfolded their napkins, and picked up their knives and forks. Promptly Gregory's mother appeared in the doorway with a dish of meat and right behind her his sister with another dish piled high with potatoes. Steam rose thickly from both. The lodgers bent over the dishes as they were placed in front of them; it was as if they wanted to inspect the food before eating it, and indeed the one in the middle, evidently an authority in the eyes of the other two, actually cut through a piece of meat while it was still on the dish, clearly in order to establish whether it was done or whether it should perhaps be sent back to the kitchen. He was satisfied, and Gregory's mother and sister, who had been watching apprehensively, broke into relieved smiles.

The family ate in the kitchen. Gregory's father, however, before going to the kitchen, came into the living-room and with a bow, cap in hand, made a tour of the table. The lodgers rose as one man and mumbled something into their beards. Afterwards, when they were alone, they ate in almost complete silence. It struck Gregory as odd that, of all the multifarious sounds of eating, the one that stood out most persistently was the champing of their teeth; it was as if they meant to show him that one needed teeth to eat and that even the finest of toothless jaws were good for nothing. "I do feel like eating," Gregory said worriedly to himself, "but not these things. The way these lodgers stuff themselves — and I'm starving!"

That same evening — and Gregory could not remember hearing it once during the whole time — the sound of the violin came from the kitchen. The lodgers had finished their supper, the middle one had produced a newspaper and given the other two a page each, and they were now leaning back in their chairs, reading and smoking. When the violin began to play they looked up, got to their feet, and tiptoed to the hall doorway, where they stood huddled together. Their movements must have been audible in the kitchen because Gregory's father called out, "Would the gentlemen perhaps rather not have the violin played? It can be stopped immediately." "On the contrary," said the middle lodger, "would the young lady not like to come in here and play in the living-room where it's much cosier and more relaxed?" "Why, certainly!" cried Gregory's father as if he had been the violinist. The lodgers came back into the room and waited. Soon Gregory's father entered with the music stand, his mother with the music, and his sister with the violin. His sister calmly got everything ready to play; his parents, who had never let rooms before and consequently overdid the politeness towards their lodgers, dared not even sit in their own chairs; Gregory's father leant against the door, his right hand inserted between two buttons of his livery jacket; his mother, however, offered a chair by one of the lodgers, sat down where the gentleman had happened to put it, which was tucked away in a corner.

Gregory's sister began to play, while his father and mother, one on each side of her, followed the movements of her hands with close attention. Drawn by her playing, Gregory ventured forward a little way until his head was inside the living-room. He gave scarcely a thought to the fact that he had been showing so little regard for others recently, whereas before he had prided himself on his altruism. And now there was even more reason for his staying out of sight because, as a result of the dust that lay everywhere in his room and blew about at the slightest disturbance, he too was covered in dust; he dragged lengths of thread, hairs, and scraps of left-over food around with him on his back and flanks; he was far too apathetic altogether to do as he had previously done several times a day, which was to lie on his back and rub himself on the carpet. Yet in spite of it all he had no inhibitions about edging forward onto the spotless floor of the living-room.

Not that anyone paid any attention to him. The family was completely absorbed in the violin-playing; the lodgers, however, having begun by stationing themselves, hands in pockets, much too close behind his sister's music stand where they could all see the score, which must surely have bothered his sister, soon retired muttering to the window and stood there with heads lowered, watched anxiously by Gregory's father. It now looked very much as if, disappointed in their expectation of hearing some beautiful or entertaining violin-playing, they were fed up with the whole performance and were allowing their peace to be disturbed further only out of politeness. Particularly the way in which they all blew their cigar smoke into the air out of nose and mouth together suggested a high degree of irritation. Yet his sister was playing so beautifully. Her face was tilted to one side; her eyes had a sad, searching look as they followed the lines of the score. Gregory crawled a little farther into the room and pressed his head to the floor in the hope of perhaps meeting her gaze. Could he really be an animal, if music affected him so deeply? He felt as if he were being shown the way to that food he so longed for without knowing what it was. He was determined to reach his sister and suggest by tugging at her skirt that she should bring her violin and come into his room, because no one here was rewarding her playing as he wished to reward it. He wanted to keep her in his room and not let her go, at least not while he lived; for the first time his nightmarish appearance would serve some useful purpose; he meant to be at all the doors of his room simultaneously and spit in his attackers' faces; his sister, though, must not be coerced but must stay with him of her own free will; she should sit beside him on the couch and lower her ear to his mouth, and he would then confide to her that it had been his firm intention to send her to the Conservatory and that if this mishap had not intervened he would have told everyone so at Christmas—presumably Christmas had already passed—and would have turned a deaf ear to any objections. Following this declaration his sister would burst into tears of emotion and Gregory would lift himself up to the level of her shoulder and kiss her bare neck, for since she had been going out to work she had worn neither neckband nor collars.

"Mr Samsa!" the middle lodger cried, addressing Gregory's father and pointing, without another word, at the slowly advancing Gregory. The music stopped; the middle lodger looked at his friends with a smile and a shake of the head before turning back to Gregory. Gregory's father seemed to feel that getting rid of Gregory was less urgent for the moment than reassuring the lodgers, although the lodgers, far from being upset, appeared to be deriving more amusement from Gregory than they had from the violin-playing. He hurried over to them and tried by spreading his arms to drive them into their room, at the same time using his body in an attempt to block their view of Gregory. At this they did in fact turn a little nasty, though there was no knowing whether it was because of the father's behaviour or because of the realization now dawning on them that they had unwittingly had such a creature as Gregory for a next-door neighbour. They demanded explanations of Gregory's father, their own arms flew up, they plucked nervously at their beards and only slowly gave ground in the retreat to their room. Meanwhile his sister had recovered from the forlorn mood into which she had lapsed following the abrupt interruption of her playing; after dangling violin and bow loosely in her hands for a while and continuing to gaze at the score as if she were still playing, she had suddenly pulled herself together, laid the instrument in her mother's lap where she sat fighting for breath with labouring lungs, and run into the next room, which the lodgers, driven on by Gregory's father, were now approaching more rapidly. Quilts and pillows could be seen flying into the air and falling back into place, guided by his sister's practised hands. Before the lodgers even reached the room she had finished making the beds and slipped out again. Gregory's father appeared to have fallen a prey to his own obstinacy once more, this time to the point of forgetting completely the respect that, after all, he owed his paying guests. He kept driving them on and driving them on until, right in the doorway of the room, the middle lodger stamped his foot with a sound like thunder and stopped Gregory's father in his tracks. "I hereby give notice," he said with upraised hand, looking round to include Gregory's mother and sister as well, "that in view of the disgusting circumstances obtaining in this flat and in this family"—here he suddenly decided to spit on the floor—"I intend to quit my room immediately. I shall not of course pay a thing for the days I have already spent in residence here; on the contrary, I shall be considering whether to lodge a—believe me—very easily justifiable claim against you for damages." He stopped talking and looked straight ahead of him as if waiting for something. And indeed his two friends chimed in promptly with the words, "We too give notice as of now." At that he seized the door handle and slammed the door.

Gregory's father groped his way to his chair and slumped into it; he might have been stretching out for his customary evening nap, except that the violent nodding of his head, almost as though it had come loose, showed that he was anything but asleep. All this time Gregory had been lying motionless where the lodgers had first spotted him. Disappointment at the failure of his plan but perhaps also the weakness brought on by prolonged starvation had robbed him of all possibility of movement. Dreading with a kind of certainty that a general state of collapse was about to break over him at any moment, he waited. Not even the violin alarmed him when, having slipped from his mother's trembling fingers, it fell from her lap and hit the floor with a loud, ringing sound.

"My dear parents," said Gregory's sister, banging her hand down on the table by way of an introduction, "we can't go on like this. I see that even if you perhaps don't. I refuse to utter my brother's name in front of this creature, so all I say is: we must try to get rid of it. We've tried our level best to look after it and put up with it, and I believe no one can reproach us in the slightest."

"She's right, by God," Gregory's father said to himself. His mother, who had still not managed to get her breath back, now put a hand to her mouth and with a crazed look in her eyes began coughing hollowly.

His sister hurried over to her and put a hand on her forehead. His father appeared to have been set thinking along more specific lines by the girl's words; he had sat up in his chair and was playing with his cap among the plates that still lay on the table from the lodgers' supper, casting occasional glances at the motionless Gregory.

"We must somehow get rid of it," said Gregory's sister, now addressing only his father because the mother could hear nothing above her coughing, "or it will be the death of you both, I can see it coming. When people have to work as hard as we do they cannot take this everlasting worry at home as well. I can't either." And she burst into such floods of tears that they splahed down onto her mother's face, from which she wiped them with perfunctory movements of her hands.

"But, my child," said her father pityingly and with evident understanding, "what are we to do?"

Gregory's sister merely shrugged her shoulders in token of the perplexity that had come over her with her tears, contrasting with her earlier assurance.

"If he understood what we said," Gregory's father began half wonderingly, but his sister, still weeping, waved a hand violently to show that it was out of the question.

"If he understood what we said," Gregory's father repeated as, by closing his eyes, he took in the girl's conviction that this was impossible, "we might perhaps be able to come to an arrangement with him. But as things are…"

"It has to go," his sister cried. "It's the only way, Father. You must just try to get out of the habit of thinking it's Gregory. That's been our undoing, in fact, that we've believed it for so long. But how can it be Gregory? If it were he would long ago have seen the impossibility of people living in the same house as such an animal and would have gone away of his own accord. In which case we would have no brother but could at least go on living and could honour his memory. As it is, the brute persecutes us, drives away the lodgers, and clearly means to take over the whole flat and have us sleeping out on the street. Look, Father," she screamed suddenly, "there he goes again!" And in a state of panic that Gregory found quite incomprehensible she even left her mother's side, actually using the back of the chair to push herself off as though she would rather sacrifice her mother than remain in Gregory's vicinity, and dashed behind her father, who then, prompted purely by her reaction, also stood up and half raised his arms in front of the girl as though to protect her.

But of course nothing was further from Gregory's mind than to try to inspire fear in anyone, let alone his sister. He had simply begun to turn himself round in order to make his way back to his room, only it looked rather spectacular because in his ailing condition he had to help this difficult process along with his head by repeatedly lifting it in the air and bringing it down on the floor with a bang. He stopped and looked round. Apparently they had recognized that he meant well; the alarm had been only a momentary one. Now they were looking at him in sad-eyed silence. His mother was lying in her chair with her legs outstretched and pressed together, so exhausted that she could barely keep her eyes open; his father and sister were sitting together, she with one arm draped round his father's neck.

"I suppose it's all right to turn round now," thought Gregory, and he went back to work. He could not help panting with the effort, and every now and then he had to pause for a rest. Not that anyone put him under pressure: it was all left to him. As soon as he had completed his turn he set off in a straight line. He was amazed at the enormous distance separating him from his room and could not understand how in his enfeebled state he had made the same journey almost without realizing it a short while before. Concentrating entirely on crawling fast, he hardly noticed the fact that not a word, not a cry from any member of his family disturbed his progress. Not until he had reached the doorway did he turn his head, and then not completely because he could feel his neck becoming stiff; nevertheless he saw that behind him nothing had changed except that his sister had risen to her feet. His last glimpse was of his mother, now fast asleep.

Almost before he was inside his room the door was hurriedly pushed to, bolted, and locked. The sudden noise behind him frightened Gregory so much that his legs gave way. It was his sister who had been in such a hurry. She had been on her feet, already, waiting; she had then sprung forward nimbly—Gregory had not even heard her coming—and, with a cry of "At last!" for her parents' benefit, she had turned the key in the lock.

"Now what?" Gregory asked himself as he looked about him in the darkness. He quite soon discovered that he could no longer move at all. He was not surprised; in fact what struck him as unnatural was that he had actually been able to get about until then on such thin legs. Otherwise he felt comparatively comfortable. Admittedly he hurt all over, but he had the impression that the pains were gradually becoming fainter and fainter and would eventually go away together. The rotten apple in his back and the inflamed area around it, now completely covered with a soft dust, were almost forgotten. He recalled his family with sympathy and love. His own belief that he must go was if possible even firmer than his sister's. He remained in this state of vacant and peaceable reflection until the church clock struck three in the morning. He lived to see the first signs of the general brightening outside the window. Then, independently of his will, his head sank to the floor and his last breath streamed feebly from his nostrils.

When the cleaning-woman arrived in the early morning—out of sheer, bustling energy she slammed all the doors, no matter how often she had been asked not to, so hard that throughout the flat, from the moment of her arrival onwards, peaceful sleep was an impossibility—she noticed nothing out of the ordinary about Gregory at first on her customary brief visit. She thought he was deliberately lying so still, playing the injured party; she credited him with boundless intelligence. Happening to have the long-handled broom in her hand, she tried to tickle Gregory with it from the door. When even this was unsuccessful she lost patience and gave Gregory a little prod, and it was only when she had shifted him from his place without encountering any resistance that her attention was aroused. She was quick to grasp the true state of affairs, reacting with a look of surprise and a low whistle; then, without wasting any more time, she tore open the bedroom door and bellowed into the darkness within, "Take a look at this—the thing's snuffed it! It's lying here dead as a doornail!"

The Samsas were sitting up in the matrimonial bed and had first to overcome their alarm at the cleaning-woman's irruption before there was any question of registering her announcement. Then, however, Mr and Mrs Samsa got quickly out of bed, one on each side, Mr Samsa throwing the quilt round his shoulders, Mrs Samsa wearing only her nightdress; thus attired, they entered Gregory's room. Meanwhile the door to the living-room, where Meg had been sleeping since the lodgers moved in, had also opened; Meg was fully dressed as though she had not even been to bed, an impression her pale face seemed to confirm. "Dead?" said Mrs Samsa, looking inquiringly up at the cleaning-woman although she could verify everything herself and even see for herself without verification. "I reckon so," said the cleaning-woman, and to prove it she gave Gregory's corpse another great sideways shove with the broom. Mrs Samsa made as if to put a restraining hand on the broom but did not do so. "Well," said Mr Samsa, "thanks be to God." He crossed himself, and the three women followed his example. Meg, her eyes fixed on the corpse, said, "See how thin he was. Well, he hadn't eaten anything for ages, had he? The food used to come out exactly as it had gone in." Gregory's body was indeed completely flat and dried out, as could be seen only now that it was no longer raised on its legs and there was nothing else about it to distract the eye.

"Meg, come into our room for a moment," said Mrs Samsa, smiling wistfully, and Meg, not without a backward glance at the corpse, followed her parents into their bedroom. The cleaning-woman closed the door and opened the window wide. Despite the earliness of the hour the fresh air already held a trace of mildness, for by this time it was the end of March.

The three lodgers emerged from their room and stared about them in astonishment, looking for their breakfast; they had been forgotten. "Where's our breakfast?" the middle lodger gruffly demanded of the cleaning-woman. But she put a finger to her lips and in silence gestured quickly to the lodgers to come into Gregory's room. They came, and in the already quite bright room, with their hands in the pockets of their somewhat threadbare jackets, they stood around Gregory's corpse.

Then the bedroom door opened and Mr Samsa appeared in his livery, his wife on one arm and his daughter on the other. They were all slightly red-eyed from crying, Meg occasionally pressing her face against her father's arm.

"Get out of my flat this instant," said Mr Samsa, pointing to the door without letting go of the women. "How do you mean?" said the middle lodger, stunned but managing a honeyed smile. The other two had their hands behind their backs and were rubbing them together as if in delighted anticipation of a major row that, moreover, promised to turn out in their favour. "I mean precisely what I say," replied Mr Samsa, and with his two escorts he began to walk straight towards the middle lodger. The latter made no move at first but stood looking at the floor as if things were falling into a fresh pattern in his mind. "All right, we'll go," he concluded, looking up at Mr Samsa as though, in a sudden access of humility, he were even seeking fresh approval for this decision. Mr Samsa merely nodded curtly several times, glaring at him. Sure enough, the lodger promptly turned and strode out into the hall. His two friends, who had stopped rubbing their hands and started listening intently some time ago, now went literally scurrying after him as if afraid that Mr Samsa might reach the hall before them and cut them off from their leader. Out in the hall all three of them took their hats from the hat stand, drew their sticks from the stick rack, bowed silently, and left the flat. Prompted by what turned out to be a quite unfounded distrust, Mr Samsa stepped out onto the landing with the two women; there they leant on the banister and watched the three gentlemen slowly but surely descending the long stairwell, disappearing at a particular turn of the staircase between each floor and reemerging a moment or two later; the lower they went, the more the Samsa family lost interest in them, and as a butcher's man passed them coming up and then climbed high above them, proudly bearing his tray on his head, Mr Samsa soon left the landing with the women, and they went back into their flat as though relieved.

They decided to spend the day resting and going for a walk. They had not only earned this break from work; they needed it, and needed it badly. So they sat down at the table and wrote three letters of apology, Mr Samsa to his superiors, Mrs Samsa to the man who sent her needlework, and Meg to the proprietor of the shop she served in. While they were writing, the cleaning-woman came in to say that she was going since her morning work was done. The three letter-writers merely nodded at first without looking up; only when the cleaning-woman continued to show no sign of leaving did they look up in some irritation. "Well?" Mr Samsa asked. The cleaning-woman stood smiling in the doorway as though she had some excellent news to announce to the family but would surrender it only on being quizzed at length. The little ostrich feather that stood up almost vertically from her hat and had been a source of irritation to Mr Samsa throughout her period of service bobbed and dipped in all directions. "What was it you wanted?" asked Mrs Samsa, who was the person for whom the cleaning-woman still had most respect. "Yes, well," the cleaning-woman replied before a peal of amiable laughter prevented her from continuing for a moment, "if you were worrying about how to get rid of that rubbish next door, you needn't. It's already dealt with." Mrs Samsa and Meg bent over their letters as if to go on writing; Mr Samsa, realizing that the cleaning-woman now intended to launch into a full description, countered with a resolutely outstretched hand. Prevented from telling her story, she recalled the great hurry she was in, and with a clearly offended "Bye, all," she whirled round and left the flat amid a fearful banging of doors.

"She'll be getting her notice this evening," said Mr Samsa, but neither his wife nor his daughter offered any response, the cleaning-woman having apparently shattered their so recently acquired peace of mind once more. They got up, crossed to the window, and stood with their arms around each other. Mr Samsa turned in his chair to face them and watched them in silence for a while. Then he called out, "Look, come over here. Forget about the past, can't you? And have a bit of consideration for me." The women obeyed him immediately, hurrying over to him, caressing him, and quickly finishing their letters.

Afterwards the three of them left the flat together, which was something they had not done for months, and took the tram out into the country. They had the carriage to themselves, and it was full of warmth and sunlight. Leaning back comfortably in their seats, they discussed their prospects, which closer examination revealed to be not at all bad, because all three employments—and they had never really questioned one another about this before—were most advantageous and, particularly as far as the future was concerned, very promising indeed. The chief immediate improvement in their situation could of course be expected from a simple change of accommodation; they now wanted to take a smaller, less expensive flat that was at the same time better located and altogether more practical than their present one, which Gregory had found. As they discussed these things Mr and Mrs Samsa, watching their daughter become increasingly animated, were struck almost simultaneously by the realization that in recent months, despite all the troubles that had drained the colour from her cheeks, she had blossomed into a beautiful, full-bosomed girl. Speaking more quietly now, and communicating almost unconsciously through glances, they thought about how the time was also coming when they must start looking round for a nice husband for her. And they saw it as a sort of confirmation of their newfound dreams and good intentions when, at the end of the journey, their daughter was the first to stand up, stretching her young body.

Modernism

p. 1386

Nearly all the characteristics of modernist literature that we associate with the works of writers such as **Franz Kafka** can be found in the literature of the nineteenth century. The Romantics portrayed the artist as a lonely figure alienated from the rest of mankind. Flaubert hid the writer behind the objectivity of his text. Nietzsche declared that God had died, and Dostoevsky explored the implications of the funeral. The symbolist poets abandoned Victorian didacticism and adopted a formal aestheticism. And in the final decades of the century novelists turned away from the social panoramas explored by the great novelists of the nineteenth century to focus on the inner worlds of their characters. So literary historians have variously asserted that modernism began with the Romantic rejection of classicism, with Flaubert defining the canons of realism, with the disillusionment following the publication of Darwin's *Origin of Species* (1859) or with the turn in the novel away from Victorian conventions.

The term *modernism*, however, is used most often to describe the work of writers who emerged at about the time of World War I whose work brings together many of these characteristics. The horror and devastation of the war shattered belief in a stable, meaningful, and ordered existence and seemed to confirm the disillusioning perspectives of Darwin, Marx and Nietzsche. Many writers and artists were convinced that Western culture was in decline and that a new era was about to begin. New theories in the fields of psychology, science, and philosophy fostered a growing uncertainty about the nature of reality, and writers experimented with new ways to reflect this suddenly unfamiliar world. **Virginia Woolf**, for example, claimed in

p. 1365

Twentieth-Century America: The Armory Show

Modernism in the visual arts entered the United States in the Armory Show in New York in 1913, perhaps the most notorious art exhibition in American history. Although the show included about thirteen hundred works, most of them by established and conventional artists, the furor was caused by the European modernists, painters like Pablo Picasso, Henri Matisse, Paul Gauguin, and Wassily Kandinsky. Their works shocked the American public who were used to conventional realism. The primitivism of Gauguin; the "childish, crude, and amateurish" work, as one critic put it, by Matisse; and the fragmented images of the cubists offended viewers who described these paintings as "nasty, lewd, immoral, and indecent." Even ex-President Theodore Roosevelt became an art critic, commenting, "There is no reason why people should not call themselves Cubists, or Octogonists, Parallelopipedonists, or Knights of the Isosceles Triangle, or Brothers of the Cosine, if they so desire; as expressing anything serious and permanent, one term is fatuous as another."

The painting in the show that proved most offensive was Marcel Duchamp's cubist classic *Nude Descending a Staircase,* depicting several fragmented figures superimposed sequentially to give the sense of motion. Picasso said that cubism depicted "not what you see, but what you know is there," giving the painter's own inner vision primacy as the subject of a painting. Like the modernist writers who retreated from the panoramic

Wassily Kandinsky, Composition 4, *1911   This example of Kandinsky's work was painted only two years before the famous Armory Show of 1913. His later works became even more abstract and expressionistic. (The Art Archive)*

realism of the great social novels of the nineteenth century—works like Thackeray's *Vanity Fair* (1848) or Tolstoy's *War and Peace* (1865–69)—the painters turned away from the popular literary and historical subjects to portray the painter's inner vision. The works of the cubists fragmented their subjects into discontinuous images, like the images in a dream, but the cubist abstractions were not the most revolutionary works in the show. A painting by the Russian Wassily Kandinsky, *Improvisation No. 27*, took modernism a logical step further by depicting brightly colored images that had no referent in the real world at all. Kandinsky said the images came from his unconscious mind and the painting was perhaps the first example of what later would come to be called abstract expressionism.

her 1924 essay "Character in Fiction" that "the Edwardian tools are the wrong ones for us to use." Breaking away from what she deemed the "materialist" conventions of her predecessors, Woolf insisted that fiction must focus not on the external world and its trappings of setting and plot but on the interior reality of characters' thoughts, perceptions, and emotions. In "Modern Fiction," she asserted the central tenet of modernism:

> Look within. . . . Examine for a moment an ordinary mind on an ordinary day. The mind receives a myriad impressions — trivial, fantastic, evanescent, or engraved with the sharpness of steel. From all sides they come, an incessant show of innumerable atoms; and as they fall, as they shape themselves into the life of Monday or Tuesday, the accent falls differently from of old. . . . Life is not a series of gig lamps symmetrically arranged; but a luminous halo, a semi-transparent envelope surrounding us from the beginning of consciousness to the end.

To capture that "luminous halo," Woolf developed a stream-of-consciousness technique that presented the inner life of her characters.

Other writers experimented in different ways. T. S. Eliot's **"The Love Song of J. Alfred Prufrock"** exhibits what would become Eliot's stylistic trademarks: disconnected lines, ironic side comments, colloquialisms mixed with fragments of past masters, like Shakespeare, and animal or fish imagery. Prufrock's world, if not as radical as Kafka's, in which a man can awaken one morning as a pitiable beetle, is nevertheless modern, decadent, despairing, and sad.

p. 1434

DREAM THEORY

p. 1429

The avatar and catalyst for modernism's inward turn was **Sigmund Freud** (1856–1937), the Viennese physician who applied scientific procedures to describe the hidden and unobserved dimensions of the human psyche. Freud was particularly interested in phenomena that were previously unexplained or ignored — bizarre events, dreams, jokes, and slips of the tongue, for example. From his observations and clinical practice treating hysteria, he mapped the realm of the unconscious and its connections to the conscious, rational side of human nature. Freud himself was an important writer and many of his essays have become literary classics. His most

Marc Chagall, *I and the Village,* 1911
Marc Chagall (1887–1985) was a celebrated painter of the modernist era whose work is often difficult to categorize. The overlapping dreamlike images in this painting typify surrealism while the geometry suggests cubism. (© Digital Image © The Museum of Modern Art/Licensed by SCALA /Art Resource. © 2007 Artist Rights Society [ARS], New York/ADAGP, Paris)

influential scientific work was probably *The Interpretation of Dreams* (1899); many of his more speculative and philosophic later essays, like *Totem and Tabu* (1913), *Beyond the Pleasure Principle* (1920), *Civilization and Its Discontents* (1930), and *Moses and Monotheism* (1939), have a more literary cast. Freud's work also influenced nearly all of the writers of his time. His discovery of the importance of sexuality in the development of the individual led novelists like D. H. Lawrence (1885–1930) and James Joyce (1882–1941) to openly treat human sexuality. More broadly, he suggested new ways to understand symbols, narrative point of view, plot, and discontinuity in narrative. His influence on twentieth-century literature was pervasive, often unrecognized by the writers who were indebted to his pioneering work for the inward turn in theirs.

More than anything else, perhaps, it was Freud's interest in dreams, developed in *The Interpretation of Dreams,* that influenced his contemporaries. Writers sought to represent the symbolic content and discontinuous narrative of dreams and to explain their characters through their dream life. The selection from ***Origin and Development of Psycho-Analysis*** summarizes Freud's dream theory and explains the importance of dreams in his psychology.

p. 1430

Kafka shares with Freud an interest in the bizarre, the absurdities, and the discontinuities of dream. Although Kafka considered psychoanalysis "a helpless error," many critics have found Freudian ideas very helpful in understanding his stories. Kafka himself, speaking of *The Metamorphosis,* said that "the terror of art is that the dream reveals the reality." His comment would seem to support readings of the story that take the beetle as Gregor's nightmare self-projection, even though Kafka's matter-of-fact narrative style resists symbolic interpretation.

p. 1442

Japanese novelist and playwright Abe Kobo has often been compared to Kafka, for his stories also involve bizarre twists, black humor, and nightmare situations narrated in a matter-of-fact realistic style. "**The Red Cocoon**" presents a metamorphosis in which a man is transformed into a hollow cocoon. Narrated by the cocoon himself, the symbolic implications of this change are left unexplained as the story ends with black humor, the narrator noting that he has been tossed into a child's toy box.

SURREALISM

Other writers were quick to assimilate Freudian dream theory. The surrealists, who sought a "super reality" that transcended the limitations of the rational and realistic, found in dreams expressions of the unconscious that offered the key to such mystical transcendence. André Breton (p. 1438), in *The Surrealist Manifesto* (1924), extends Freud's dream work to a spiritual dimension, finding in the spontaneity and "realities" of dreams the keys not simply to understanding the waking life but to go beyond it. Although surrealism was short-lived as a literary movement, it has influenced many writers who include dreams, dream images, and discontinuous symbolism in their work. Examples in this anthology include Federico García Lorca, Pablo Neruda, Léopold Sédar Senghor, and Aimé Césaire.

MAGICAL REALISM

Influenced by European modernism, the writers of the magical realist movement in Latin America used realistic techniques to narrate stories that link mundane with miraculous or supernatural events. Gabriel García Márquez's story of an angel who appears in a rural village encapsulates his realistic technique in the title of the story that reduces the miraculous angel to "**A Very Old Man with**

The tone that I eventually used in *One Hundred Years of Solitude* was based on the way my grandmother used to tell stories. She told things that sounded supernatural and fantastic, but she told them with complete naturalness. . . . What was most important was the expression she had on her face. She did not change her expression at all when telling her stories and everyone was surprised. In previous attempts to write, I tried to tell the story without believing in it. I discovered that what I had to do was believe in them myself and write them with the same expression with which my grandmother told them: with a brick face.

– GABRIEL GARCÍA
MÁRQUEZ

Cover of *Minotaure*,
1934
*André Breton was
involved in the
publication of several
journals including
Minotaure, which
ran from 1933 to 1939.
A lavish publication
in its time, the
journal featured
original works by
artists such as Pablo
Picasso and Salvador
Dalí. (The Art
Archive)*

Enormous Wings." The story itself objectively describes the ways
in which the villagers deal with and finally turn their backs on the
dreamlike situation of a supernatural visitation.

p. 1445

∾ SIGMUND FREUD
B. AUSTRIA, 1856–1939

Sigmund Freud, the father of psychoanalysis, did not discover the unconscious mind, nor did he discover sex, but his writings made the unconscious and sex central to the twentieth century's understanding of human
nature. He shocked the world with his theories of infant sexuality, repression, sublimation, and the Oedipus complex. He made the journey into
the self, into the hidden and repressed corridors and closets of childhood,
a paradigm of the modern spiritual journey. He was a major influence on
Carl Jung, who took Freudianism in a somewhat different direction,
rediscovering the importance of mythology and comparative religion for
subsequent generations. Certain aspects of Freud's legacy are now a part
of daily life: the importance of taking charge of one's own life, the value
of the inward journey, the necessity for healing the traumas of one's past
life with counseling, support groups, and storytelling.

Born of Jewish parents on May 6, 1856, at Freiburg in Moravia
(a region today in the Czech Republic), Freud spent most of his life in

**Portrait of
Sigmund Freud**
*The father of psycho-
analysis, Freud made
contributions to
psychology and
culture that still
resonate today.
(The Art Archive/
Museum der Stadt
Wien/Dagli
Orti [A])*

Vienna. Given the importance Freud later placed on childhood, it is ironic that very little is known about his. In fact, he destroyed large numbers of documents in order to frustrate inquisitive biographers. He began his university studies in 1873, gravitating toward medicine. After studying medicine, with a specialty in neurology, he went to Paris in 1885 to study hysteria under the neurologist Jean Charcot. A Viennese physician, Josef Breuer, gave Freud the key for therapeutic healing. He told Freud about curing the symptoms of hysteria by "getting the patient to recollect in hypnosis the circumstances of their origin and to express the emotions accompanying them." Freud tried out the method, and together they published a book on what they called the "cathartic method"; *Studien über Hysterie* (1895) was the starting point of psychoanalysis. Freud discovered that hypnosis was not a satisfactory tool for treating hysteria, so he developed free association and dream analysis as ways to explore the unconscious. Freud's *The Interpretation of Dreams,* published in 1899, revolutionized our understanding of the mind and quickly became a classic of scientific literature. After 1923 Freud applied his psychoanalytic theories to culture, making significant contributions to anthropology, education, sociology, art, and literature. Recently Freud's theories have come under a great deal of criticism, especially in the area of women's psychology, but his pioneering efforts in the area of the unconscious are invaluable.

In lay terms, Freud rediscovered the importance of childhood and emphasized that childhood experiences continue to influence individuals in their adult lives. His psychoanalytic method proposed that neurosis could be healed when traumatic experiences that have been repressed or denied are recovered as an individual reconstructs his or her personal history. In literary terms, Freud validated the importance of storytelling by maintaining that the painful effects of early abuse can be alleviated when an individual learns how to tell his or her story. He also changed the way stories were told, as the process of discontinuous recall replaced the chronological narratives of the nineteenth century.

FROM

✎ Origin and Development of Psycho-Analysis

Translated by Harry W. Chase

THIRD LECTURE

Interpretation of dreams is in fact the *via regia*[1] to the interpretation of the unconscious, the surest ground of psycho-analysis and a field in which every worker must win his convictions and gain his education. If I were asked how one could become a psycho-analyst, I should answer, through the study of his own dreams. With great tact all opponents of the psycho-analytic theory have so far either evaded

---

[1] *via regia:* The proper way.

any criticism of *The Interpretation of Dreams*[2] or have attempted to pass over it with the most superficial objections. If, on the contrary, you will undertake the solution of the problems of dream life, the novelties which psycho-analysis present to your thoughts will no longer be difficulties.

You must remember that our nightly dream productions show the greatest outer similarity and inner relationship to the creations of the insane, but on the other hand are compatible with full health during waking life. It does not sound at all absurd to say that whoever regards these normal sense illusions, these delusions and alterations of character as matter for amazement instead of understanding, has not the least prospect of understanding the abnormal creations of diseased mental states in any other than the lay sense. You may with confidence place in this lay group all the psychiatrists of today. Follow me now on a brief excursion through the field of dream problems.

In our waking state we usually treat dreams with as little consideration as the patient treats the irruptive ideas which the psycho-analyst demands from him. It is evident that we reject them, for we forget them quickly and completely. The slight valuation which we place on them is based, with those dreams that are not confused and nonsensical, on the feeling that they are foreign to our personality, and, with other dreams, on their evident absurdity and senselessness. Our rejection derives support from the unrestrained shamelessness and the immoral longings which are obvious in many dreams. Antiquity, as we know, did not share this light valuation of dreams. The lower classes of our people today stick close to the value which they set on dreams; they, however, expect from them, as did the ancients, the revelation of the future. I confess that I see no need to adopt mystical hypotheses to fill out the gaps in our present knowledge, and so I have never been able to find anything that supported the hypothesis of the prophetic nature of dreams. Many other things, which are wonderful enough, can be said about them.

And first, not all dreams are so foreign to the character of the dreamer, are incomprehensible and confused. If you will undertake to consider the dreams of young children from the age of a year and a half on, you will find them quite simple and easy to interpret. The young child always dreams of the fulfilment of wishes which were aroused in him the day before and were not satisfied. You need no art of interpretation to discover this simple solution, you only need to inquire into the experiences of the child on the day before (the "dream day"). Now it would certainly be a most satisfactory solution of the dream-riddle, if the dreams of adults, too, were the same as those of children, fulfilments of wishes which had been aroused in them during the dream day. This is actually the fact; the difficulties which stand in the way of this solution can be removed step by step by a thorough analysis of the dream.

There is first of all, the most weighty objection that the dreams of adults generally have an incomprehensible content, which shows wish-fulfilment least of anything. The answer is this: these dreams have undergone a process of disguise, the

---

[2] *The Interpretation of Dreams:* (1899) Freud's important work presenting his dream theory and method of interpreting dreams.

psychic content which underlies them was originally meant for quite different verbal expression. You must differentiate between the *manifest dream-content,* which we remember in the morning only confusedly, and with difficulty clothe in words which seem arbitrary, and the *latent dream-thoughts,* whose presence in the unconscious we must assume. This distortion of the dream (*Traumentstellung*) is the same process which has been revealed to you in the investigations of the creations (*symptoms*) of hysterical subjects; it points to the fact that the same opposition of psychic forces has its share in the creation of dreams as in the creation of symptoms.

The manifest dream-content is the disguised surrogate for the unconscious dream-thoughts, and this disguising is the work of the defensive forces of the ego, of the resistances. These prevent the repressed wishes from entering consciousness during the waking life, and even in the relaxation of sleep they are still strong enough to force them to hide themselves by a sort of masquerading. The dreamer, then, knows just as little the sense of his dream as the hysterical knows the relation and significance of his symptoms. That there are latent dream-thoughts and that between them and the manifest dream-content there exists the relation just described — of this you may convince yourselves by the analysis of dreams, a procedure the technique of which is exactly that of psycho-analysis. You must abstract entirely from the apparent connection of the elements in the manifest dream and seek for the irruptive ideas which arise through free association, according to the psycho-analytic laws, from each separate dream element. From this material the latent dream-thoughts may be discovered, exactly as one divines the concealed complexes of the patient from the fancies connected with his symptoms and memories. From the latent dream-thoughts which you will find in this way, you will see at once how thoroughly justified one is in interpreting the dreams of adults by the same rubrics as those of children. What is now substituted for the manifest dream-content is the real sense of the dream, is always clearly comprehensible, associated with the impressions of the day before, and appears as the fulfilling of an unsatisfied wish. The manifest dream, which we remember after waking, may then be described as a *disguised* fulfilment of *repressed* wishes.

It is also possible by a sort of synthesis to get some insight into the process which has brought about the disguise of the unconscious dream-thoughts as the manifest dream-content. We call this process *dream-work* (*Traumarbeit*). This deserves our fullest theoretical interest, since here as nowhere else we can study the unsuspected psychic processes which are existent in the unconscious, or, to express it more exactly, *between* two such separate systems as the conscious and the unconscious. Among these newly discovered psychic processes, two, condensation (*Verdichtung*), and displacement or transvaluation, change of psychic accent (*Verschiebung*), stand out most prominently. Dream-work is a special case of the reaction of different mental groupings on each other, and as such is the consequence of psychic fission. In all essential points it seems identical with the work of disguise, which changes the repressed complex in the case of failing repression into symptoms.

You will furthermore discover by the analysis of dreams, most convincingly your own, the unsuspected importance of the rôle which impressions and experiences from early childhood exert on the development of men. In the dream life, the child, as it were, continues his existence in the man, with a retention of all his traits and wishes, including those which he was obliged to allow to fall into disuse in his later years. With irresistible might it will be impressed on you by what processes of development, of repression, sublimation, and reaction there arises out of the child, with its peculiar gifts and tendencies, the so-called normal man, the bearer and partly the victim of our painfully acquired civilization. I will also direct your attention to the fact that we have discovered from the analysis of dreams that the unconscious makes use of a sort of symbolism, especially in the presentation of sexual complexes. This symbolism in part varies with the individual, but in part is of a typical nature, and seems to be identical with the symbolism which we suppose to lie behind our myths and legends. It is not impossible that these latter creations of the people may find their explanation from the study of dreams.

Finally, I must remind you that you must not be led astray by the objection that the occurrence of anxiety-dreams *(Angsttraüme),* contradicts our idea of the dream as a wish-fulfilment. Apart from the consideration that anxiety dreams also require interpretation before judgment can be passed on them, one can say quite generally that the anxiety does not depend in such a simple way on the dream content as one might suppose without more knowledge of the facts and more attention to the conditions of neurotic anxiety. Anxiety is one of the ways in which the ego relieves itself of repressed wishes which have become too strong, and so is easy to explain in the dream, if the dream has gone too far towards the fulfilling of the objectionable wish.

You see that the investigation of dreams was justified by the conclusions which it has given us concerning things otherwise hard to understand. But we came to it in connection with the psycho-analytic treatment of neurotics. From what has been said, you can easily understand how the interpretation of dreams, if it is not made too difficult by the resistance of the patient, can lead to a knowledge of the patient's concealed and repressed wishes and the complexes which he is nourishing.

T. S. ELIOT
B. UNITED STATES, 1888–1965

Eliot's dramatic monologue, "The Love Song of J. Alfred Prufrock," a masterful portrait of the spirit of ennui, of weariness and boredom, first appeared in the Chicago literary magazine *Poetry* in June 1915 and was included in Eliot's first book of poems, *Prufrock and Other Observations,* published in 1917. Prufrock appears to embody the debilitating self-consciousness of the modern middle class and its inability to create meaningful human relationships. Trapped within social manners and unable to get beyond decorousness, Prufrock is separated from passion and sexuality.

For more on T. S. Eliot, see page 1450.

❧ The Love Song of J. Alfred Prufrock

S'io credesse che mia risposta fosse
A persona che mai tornasse al mondo,
Questa fiamma staria senza piu scosse.
Ma perciocche giammai di questo fondo
Non torno vivo alcun, s'i'odo il vero,
Senza tema d'infamia ti rispondo.[1]

Let us go then, you and I,
When the evening is spread out against the sky
Like a patient etherized upon a table;
Let us go, through certain half-deserted streets,
The muttering retreats
Of restless nights in one-night cheap hotels
And sawdust restaurants with oyster shells:
Streets that follow like a tedious argument
Of insidious intent
To lead you to an overwhelming question . . .
Oh, do not ask, "What is it?"
Let us go and make our visit.

In the room the women come and go
Talking of Michelangelo.[2]

The yellow fog that rubs its back upon the windowpanes,
The yellow smoke that rubs its muzzle on the windowpanes
Licked its tongue into the corners of the evening,
Lingered upon the pools that stand in drains,
Let fall upon its back the soot that falls from chimneys,
Slipped by the terrace, made a sudden leap,
And seeing that it was a soft October night,
Curled once about the house, and fell asleep.

And indeed there will be time
For the yellow smoke that slides along the street,
Rubbing its back upon the windowpanes;

---

[1] *S'io credesse . . . rispondo:* The epigraph is from Dante's *Inferno* (27.61–66); Guido da Montefeltro, whose punishment for fraud is being wrapped in a flame, agrees to identify himself: "If I thought that I was speaking to someone who would ever return to the world, this flame would shake no more, but since no one has ever returned alive from this place, if what I hear is true, I answer you without fear of infamy." Thus, the implication is that Prufrock, the narrator in Eliot's poem, can speak honestly.

[2] In the room . . . Michelangelo: It appears that Prufrock is going to this room to visit a woman friend; women speak of Michelangelo (1475–1564), the famous Italian painter and sculptor.

There will be time, there will be time
To prepare a face to meet the faces that you meet;
There will be time to murder and create,
And time for all the works and days of hands[3]
30   That lift and drop a question on your plate;
Time for you and time for me,
And time yet for a hundred indecisions,
And for a hundred visions and revisions,
Before the taking of a toast and tea.

  In the room the women come and go
Talking of Michelangelo.

  And indeed there will be time
To wonder, "Do I dare?" and, "Do I dare?"
Time to turn back and descend the stair,
40   With a bald spot in the middle of my hair—
(They will say: "How his hair is growing thin!")
My morning coat, my collar mounting firmly to the chin,
My necktie rich and modest, but asserted by a simple pin—
(They will say: "But how his arms and legs are thin!")
Do I dare
Disturb the universe?
In a minute there is time
For decisions and revisions which a minute will reverse.

  For I have known them all already, known them all—
50   Have known the evenings, mornings, afternoons,
I have measured out my life with coffee spoons;
I know the voices dying with a dying fall
Beneath the music from a farther room.
  So how should I presume?

  And I have known the eyes already, known them all—
The eyes that fix you in a formulated phrase,
And when I am formulated, sprawling on a pin,
When I am pinned and wriggling on the wall,
Then how should I begin
60   To spit out all the butt-ends of my days and ways?
  And how should I presume?

---

[3]**works . . . hands:** The ancient Greek poet Hesiod (eighth century B.C.E.) wrote a long poem, *Works and Days,* about farm work; Eliot is contrasting meaningful work to empty social gestures.

And I have known the arms already, known them all—
Arms that are braceleted and white and bare
(But in the lamplight, downed with light brown hair!)
Is it perfume from a dress
That makes me so digress?
Arms that lie along a table, or wrap about a shawl.
    And should I then presume?
    And how should I begin?

70   Shall I say, I have gone at dusk through narrow streets
And watched the smoke that rises from the pipes
Of lonely men in shirt-sleeves, leaning out of windows? . . .

    I should have been a pair of ragged claws
Scuttling across the floors of silent seas.

    And the afternoon, the evening, sleeps so peacefully!
Smoothed by long fingers,
Asleep . . . tired . . . or it malingers,
Stretched on the floor, here beside you and me.
Should I, after tea and cakes and ices,
80 Have the strength to force the moment to its crisis?
But though I have wept and fasted, wept and prayed,
Though I have seen my head (grown slightly bald) brought in upon a platter,[4]
I am no prophet—and here's no great matter;
I have seen the moment of my greatness flicker,
And I have seen the eternal Footman hold my coat, and snicker,
And in short, I was afraid.

    And would it have been worth it, after all,
After the cups, the marmalade, the tea,
Among the porcelain, among some talk of you and me,
90 Would it have been worth while,
To have bitten off the matter with a smile,
To have squeezed the universe into a ball
To roll it toward some overwhelming question,
To say: "I am Lazarus,[5] come from the dead,
Come back to tell you all, I shall tell you all"—
If one, settling a pillow by her head,

---

[4] **Though I . . . platter:** John the Baptist was beheaded by King Herod; his head was brought to Queen Herodias on a silver platter (Matthew 14:3–11).

[5] **Lazarus:** Raised from the dead by Jesus (John 11:1–44).

Should say: "That is not what I meant at all.
That is not it, at all."

And would it have been worth it, after all,
100 Would it have been worth while,
After the sunsets and the dooryards and the sprinkled streets,
After the novels, after the teacups, after the skirts that trail along the floor—
And this, and so much more?—
It is impossible to say just what I mean!
But as if a magic lantern threw the nerves in patterns on a screen:
Would it have been worth while
If one, settling a pillow or throwing off a shawl,
And turning toward the window, should say:
          "That is not it at all,
110   That is not what I meant, at all."

          No! I am not Prince Hamlet,[6] nor was meant to be;
Am an attendant lord, one that will do
To swell a progress,[7] start a scene or two,
Advise the prince; no doubt, an easy tool,
Deferential, glad to be of use,
Politic, cautious, and meticulous;
Full of high sentence,° but a bit obtuse;   opinions
At times, indeed, almost ridiculous—
Almost, at times, the Fool.

120   I grow old . . . I grow old . . .
I shall wear the bottoms of my trousers rolled.

          Shall I part my hair behind? Do I dare to eat a peach?
I shall wear white flannel trousers, and walk upon the beach.
I have heard the mermaids singing, each to each.
I do not think that they will sing to me.

I have seen them riding seaward on the waves
Combing the white hair of the waves blown back
When the wind blows the water white and black.

We have lingered in the chambers of the sea
130 By sea-girls wreathed with seaweed red and brown
Till human voices wake us, and we drown.

---

[6] **Prince Hamlet:** Shakespeare's Hamlet (c. 1602) is known for his indecision.

[7] **progress:** A journey made by members of the royal court.

ANDRÉ BRETON
B. FRANCE, 1896–1966

One of the founders of the French surrealist movement, André Breton is known as the "Pope of Surrealism" for his defining role in the movement and his continuing commitment to its principles. Although he studied medicine and neuropsychology, Breton turned to poetry and the arts as part of the Dada movement in the early nineteen hundreds and later as the founder of surrealism. The surrealists sought to go beyond ordinary reality by liberating the truths of the unconscious mind. To do so, they tried to tap the world of dreams, using automatic writing and spontaneous creation to short-circuit the conscious interference of the rational mind. Breton's debt to Freud is apparent in this program and in the passage from *The Surrealist Manifesto,* the first of three such documents (1924, 1930, 1934) that he drafted. Although he wrote many poems and essays and edited several literary magazines and collections of literary works, he is remembered for these manifestoes that defined the surrealist movement.

FROM

The Surrealist Manifesto

Translated by Patrick Waldberg

We are still living under the reign of logic, but the logical processes of our time apply only to the solution of problems of secondary interest. The absolute rationalism which remains in fashion allows for the consideration of only those facts narrowly relevant to our experience. Logical conclusions, on the other hand, escape us. Needless to say, boundaries have been assigned even to experience. It revolves in a cage from which release is becoming increasingly difficult. It too depends upon immediate utility and is guarded by common sense. In the guise of civilization, under the pretext of progress, we have succeeded in dismissing from our minds anything that, rightly or wrongly, could be regarded as superstition or myth; and we have proscribed every way of seeking the truth which does not conform to convention. It would appear that it is by sheer chance that an aspect of intellectual life — and by far the most important in my opinion — about which no one was supposed to be concerned any longer has, recently, been brought back to light. Credit for this must go to Freud. On the evidence of his discoveries a current of opinion is at last developing which will enable the explorer of the human mind to extend his investigations, since he will be empowered to deal with more than merely summary realities. Perhaps the imagination is on the verge of recovering its rights. If the depths of our minds conceal strange forces capable of augmenting or conquering those on the surface, it is in our greatest interest to capture them; first to capture them and later to submit them, should the occasion arise, to the control of reason. The analysts themselves can only gain by this. But it is important to note that there is no method fixed a priori for the execution of this enterprise, that until the new order it can be considered the province of poets as well as scholars, and that its success does not depend upon the more or less capricious routes which will be followed.

It was only fitting that Freud should appear with his critique on the dream. In fact, it is incredible that this important part of psychic activity has still attracted so little attention. (For, at least from man's birth to his death, thought presents no solution of continuity; the sum of dreaming moments—even taking into consideration pure dream alone, that of sleep—is from the point of view of time no less than the sum of moments of reality, which we shall confine to waking moments.) I have always been astounded by the extreme disproportion in the importance and seriousness assigned to events of the waking moments and to those of sleep by the ordinary observer. Man, when he ceases to sleep, is above all at the mercy of his memory, and the memory normally delights in feebly retracing the circumstance of the dream for him, depriving it of all actual consequence and obliterating the only *determinant* from the point at which he thinks he abandoned this constant hope, this anxiety, a few hours earlier. He has the illusion of continuing something worthwhile. The dream finds itself relegated to a parenthesis, like the night. And in general it gives no more counsel than the night. This singular state of affairs seems to invite a few reflections:

1. **Within the limits** to which its performance is restricted (or what passes for performance), *the dream,* according to all outward appearances, is continuous and bears traces of organization. Only memory claims the right to edit it, to suppress transitions and present us with a series of dreams rather than the dream. Similarly, at no given instant do we have more than a distinct representation of realities whose co-ordination is a matter of will. It is important to note that nothing leads to a greater dissipation of the constituent elements of the dream. I regret discussing this according to a formula which in principle excludes the dream. For how long, sleeping logicians, philosophers? I would like to sleep in order to enable myself to surrender to sleepers, as I surrender to those who read me with their eyes open, in order to stop the conscious rhythm of my thought from prevailing over this material. Perhaps my dream of last night was a continuation of the preceding night's, and will be continued tonight with an admirable precision. It could be, as they say. And as it is in no way proven that, in such a case, the "reality" with which I am concerned even exists in the dream state, or that it does not sink into the immemorial, then why should I not concede to the dream what I sometimes refuse to reality—that weight of self-assurance which by its own terms is not exposed to my denial? Why should I not expect more of the dream sign than I do of a daily increasing degree of consciousness? Could not the dreams as well be applied to the solution of life's fundamental problems? Are these problems the same in one case as in the other, and do they already exist in the dream? Is the dream less oppressed by sanctions than the rest? I am growing old and, perhaps more than this reality to which I believe myself confined, it is the dream, and the detachment that I owe to it, which is ageing me.

2. **I return to the waking state.** I am obliged to retain it as a phenomenon of interference. Not only does the mind show a strange tendency to disorientation under these conditions (this is the clue to slips of the tongue and lapses of all kinds whose secret is just beginning to be surrendered to us), but when functioning normally the mind still seems to obey none other than those suggestions which rise from that deep night I am commending. Sound as it may be, its equilibrium is relative. The mind hardly dares express itself and, when it does, is limited to stating that this idea or that woman has an effect on it. What effect it cannot say; thus it gives the measure of its subjectivism and nothing more. The idea, the woman, disturbs it, disposes it to less severity. Their role is to isolate one second of its disappearance and remove it to the sky in that glorious acceleration that it can be, that it is. Then, as a last resort, the mind invokes chance—a more obscure divinity than the others—to whom it attributes all its aberrations. Who says that the angle from which that idea is presented which affects the mind, as well as what the mind loves in that woman's eye, is not precisely the same thing that attracts the mind to its dream and reunites it with data lost through its own error? And if things were otherwise, of what might the mind not be capable? I should like to present it with the key to that passage.

3. **The mind of the dreaming man** is fully satisfied with whatever happens to it. The agonizing question of possibility does not arise. Kill, plunder more quickly, love as much as you wish. And if you die, are you not sure of being roused from the dead? Let yourself be led. Events will not tolerate deferment. You have no name. Everything is inestimably easy.

What power, I wonder, what power so much more generous than others confers this natural aspect upon the dream and makes me welcome unreservedly a throng of episodes whose strangeness would overwhelm me if they were happening as I write this? And yet I can believe it with my own eyes, my own ears. That great day has come, that beast has spoken.

If man's awakening is harsher, if he breaks the spell too well, it is because he has been led to form a poor idea of expiation.

4. **When the time comes** when we can submit the dream to a methodical examination, when by methods yet to be determined we succeed in realizing the dream in its entirety (and that implies a memory discipline measurable in generations, but we can still begin by recording salient facts), when the dream's curve is developed with an unequalled breadth and regularity, then we can hope that mysteries which are not really mysteries will give way to the great Mystery. I believe in the future resolution of these two states—outwardly so contradictory—which are dream and reality, into a sort of absolute reality, a surreality, so to speak, I am aiming for its conquest, certain that I myself shall not attain it, but too indifferent to my death not to calculate the joys of such possession.

ABÉ KOBO
B. JAPAN, 1924–1993

Abé Kobo, best known outside of Japan for the novel *The Woman in the Dunes* (1962), is one of Japan's most acclaimed writers. Dealing with themes of alienation and displacement like many of his European, African, and Latin American peers, Abé views human existence in the modern world of mass production and consumption as a condition of absurdity. While Abé's settings and characters are Japanese, the circumstances they face and the struggle they undertake to find meaning and to discover identity extend beyond national boundaries and speak to readers everywhere.

Abé Kimifusa, who later changed his name to Abé Kobo, was born in Tokyo in 1924. Abé grew up in Mukden (now Shanyeng), Manchuria, where his father was a doctor. Although Abé also studied medicine, he never practiced, choosing instead a literary career.

The Woman in the Dunes (1962), perhaps the most widely known of Abé's works, won the Yomiuri Prize for literature and brought Abé's work worldwide recognition. The novel recounts the story of a schoolteacher and amateur entomologist, Jumpei Niki, who is taken prisoner in a remote village while on vacation collecting insects for his hobby. Jumpei takes refuge with a young widow who lives in a house continuously buried by collapsing sand dunes. Accepting his Sisyphean task of survival under these conditions, Jumpei helps the woman in her never-ending struggle to survive by shoveling sand. When he finally has the chance to escape, he chooses in an act of existential good faith to stay.

Throughout his work Abé transformed into surreal and sometimes nightmarish metaphors the alienation and absurdity he found in the modern industrializing world of postwar Japan. With "The Red Cocoon" (1950), Abé began a series of stories about metamorphoses that includes *The Wall* and "The Stick" (1955). Comparable to Kafka's *The Metamorphosis*, though written in a more self-consciously surrealistic style, "The Red Cocoon" has as its theme the precariousness of identity and the devaluation of individuality in a postwar world that has witnessed genocide, massive civilian casualties in war, and the use of devastating weapons, including the atomic bomb.

> . . . Abé's early surrealist stories, which are a mixture of science fiction, humor, and the motif of homelessness, are . . . appealing precisely because they mute the pain of alienation through their formal facetiousness, and because they introduce but do not probe the ramifications of the modern dilemma of loss.
> – VAN C. GESSEL, critic, 1989

❧ The Red Cocoon

Translated by Lane Dunlop

The sun is starting to set. It's the time when people hurry home to their roosts, but I don't have a roost to go back to. I go on walking slowly down the narrow cleft between the houses. Although there are so many houses lined up along the streets, why is there not one house which is mine? I think, repeating the same question for the hundredth time.

When I take a piss against a telephone pole, sometimes there's a scrap of rope hanging down, and I want to hang myself. The rope, looking at my neck out of the corner of its eye, says: "Let's rest, brother." And I want to rest, too. But I can't rest. I'm not the rope's brother, and besides, I still can't understand why I don't have a house.

Every day, night comes. When night comes, you have to rest. Houses are to rest in. If that's so, it's not that I don't have a house, is it?

Suddenly, I get an idea. Maybe I've been making a serious mistake in my thinking. Maybe it's not that I don't have a house, but that I've forgotten it. That's right, it could be. For example, I stop in front of this house I happen to be passing. Might not this be my house? Of course, compared to other houses, it has no special feature that particularly breathes out that possibility, but one could say the same of any house. That cannot be a proof canceling the fact that this may be my house. I'm feeling brave. OK, let's knock on the door.

I'm in luck. The smiling face of a woman looks out of a half-opened window. She seems kind. The wind of hope blows through the neighborhood of my heart. My heart becomes a flag that spreads out flat and flutters in the wind. I smile, too. Like a real gentleman, I say:

"Excuse me, but this isn't my house by any chance?"

The woman's face abruptly hardens. "What? Who are you?"

About to explain, all of a sudden I can't. I don't know what I should explain. How can I make her understand that it's not a question now of who I am? Getting a little desperate, I say:

"Well, if you think this isn't my house, will you please prove it to me?"

"My god . . ." The woman's face is frightened. That gets me angry.

"If you have no proof, it's all right for me to think it's mine."

"But this is my house."

"What does that matter? Just because you say it's yours doesn't mean it's not mine. That's so."

Instead of answering, the woman turns her face into a wall and shuts the window. That's the true form of a woman's smiling face. It's always this transformation that gives away the incomprehensible logic by which, because something belongs to someone, it does not belong to me.

But, why . . . why does everything belong to someone else and not to me? Even if it isn't mine, can't there be just one thing that doesn't belong to anyone?

Sometimes, I have delusions. That the concrete pipes on construction sites or in storage yards are my house. But they're already on the way to belonging to somebody.

Because they become someone else's, they disappear without any reference to my wishes or interest in them. Or they turn into something that is clearly not my house.

Well then, how about park benches? They'd be fine, of course. If they were really my house, and if only he didn't come and chase me off them with his stick . . . Certainly they belong to everybody, not to anybody. But he says:

"Hey, you, get up. This bench belongs to everybody. It doesn't belong to anybody, least of all you. Come on, start moving. If you don't like it, you can spend the night in the basement lockup at the precinct house. If you stop anyplace else, no matter where, you'll be breaking the law."

The Wandering Jew — is that who I am?

The sun is setting. I keep walking.

A house . . . houses that don't disappear, turn into something else, that stand on the ground and don't move. Between them, the cleft that keeps changing, that doesn't have any one face that stays the same . . . the street. On rainy days, it's like a paint-loaded brush, on snowy days it becomes just the width of the tire ruts, on windy days it flows like a conveyor belt. I keep walking. I can't understand why I don't have a house, and so I can't even hang myself.

Hey, who's holding me around the ankle? If it's the rope for hanging, don't get so excited, don't be in such a hurry. But that's not what it is. It's a sticky silk thread. When I grab it and pull it, the end's in a split between the upper and sole of my shoe. It keeps getting longer and longer, slippery-like. This is weird. My curiosity makes me keep pulling it in. Then something even weirder happens. I'm slowly leaning over. I can't stand up at a right angle to the ground. Has the earth's axis tilted or the gravitational force changed direction?

A thud. My shoe drops off and hits the ground. I see what's happening. The earth's axis hasn't tilted, one of my legs has gotten shorter. As I pull at the thread, my leg rapidly gets shorter and shorter. Like the elbow of a frayed jacket unraveling, my leg's unwinding. The thread, like the fiber of a snake gourd, is my disintegrating leg.

I can't take one more step. I don't know what to do. I keep on standing. In my hand that doesn't know what to do either, my leg that has turned into a silk thread starts to move by itself. It crawls out smoothly. The tip, without any help from my hand, unwinds itself and like a snake starts wrapping itself around me. When my left leg's all unwound, the thread switches as natural as you please to my right leg. In a little while, the thread has wrapped my whole body in a bag. Even then, it doesn't stop but unwinds me from the hips to the chest, from the chest to the shoulders, and as it unwinds it strengthens the bag from inside. In the end, I'm gone.

Afterward, there remained a big empty cocoon.

Ah, now at last I can rest. The evening sun dyes the cocoon red. This, at least, is my house for sure, which nobody can keep me out of. The only trouble is now that I have a house, there's no "I" to return to it.

Inside the cocoon, time stopped. Outside, it was dark, but inside the cocoon it was always evening. Illumined from within, it glowed red with the colors of sunset. This outstanding peculiarity was bound to catch his sharp policeman's eye. He spotted me, the cocoon, lying between the rails of the crossing. At first he was angry, but soon changing his mind about this unusual find, he put me into his pocket. After tumbling around in there for a while, I was transferred to his son's toy box.

GABRIEL GARCÍA MÁRQUEZ

B. COLOMBIA, 1927

Ben Martin, *Gabriel García Márquez*, 1984 *García Márquez in his home library in Colombia. (Ben Martin/Timepix)*

The fictional village of Macondo, where Gabriel García Márquez sets many of his novels and stories, is based on the obscure village of Aracataca in northeastern Colombia where the author spent his early childhood. Although he left the village when he was eight, he guaranteed its literary survival by naming it "Macondo" in his work and making it one of modern literature's mythic places of the imagination. Though he has lived and worked internationally, García Márquez's writings almost always go back to Macondo, whose history and mythology distill his experience and embody his view of the human condition.

García Márquez was inspired to write fiction by reading the MODERNIST writers of the early twentieth century. Reading Kafka's *The Metamorphosis* (Borges's Spanish translation) was a watershed for García Márquez: "I thought to myself that I didn't know anyone was allowed to write things like that. If I had known, I would have started writing much earlier." But the most important influence on the author's writing, it turned out, was his grandmother and her way of telling stories.

One Hundred Years of Solitude (1967), his best-known work, is the saga of the founding of Macondo and its rise and fall over a century. It combines realistic detail with folk legends and myths; hyperbolic, archetypal characters; and fantastic, dreamlike events. It chronicles seven generations of the family of the founder, José Arcadio Buendía. The town and its history become an imaginative microcosm of the Latin American experience and, indeed, the human experience, for its mythic dimensions reach from the Garden of Eden to the Flood to the Apocalypse. Its mixture of realism, myth, and the miraculous has been called "MAGICAL REALISM."

"A Very Old Man with Enormous Wings" This short story, written shortly after *One Hundred Years of Solitude* and included in a collection of García Márquez's stories in 1972, recounts in deadpan, realistic narration a series of bizarre and miraculous events—a voice characteristic of the author's magical realism. The angel of the story's title does not have the appearance of a supernatural being but rather that of an unkempt and disheveled old man. As each of the villagers seeks to "explain" the angel and deny or ignore his supernatural nature, García Márquez reveals their superstition and self-interest and satirizes institutions such as the church. The ending may surprise readers as it does the villagers; it also raises questions about the presence of the miraculous in the midst of the mundane.

✑ A Very Old Man with Enormous Wings

Translated by Gregory Rabassa

On the third day of rain they had killed so many crabs inside the house that Pelayo had to cross his drenched courtyard and throw them into the sea, because the newborn child had a temperature all night and they thought it was due to the stench. The world had been sad since Tuesday. Sea and sky were a single ash-gray thing and the sands of the beach, which on March nights glimmered like powdered light, had become a stew of mud and rotten shellfish. The light was so weak at noon that when Pelayo was coming back to the house after throwing away the crabs, it was hard for him to see what it was that was moving and groaning in the rear of the courtyard. He had to go very close to see that it was an old man, a very old man, lying face down in the mud, who, in spite of his tremendous efforts, couldn't get up, impeded by his enormous wings.

Frightened by that nightmare, Pelayo ran to get Elisenda, his wife, who was putting compresses on the sick child, and he took her to the rear of the courtyard. They both looked at the fallen body with mute stupor. He was dressed like a ragpicker. There were only a few faded hairs left on his bald skull and very few teeth in his mouth, and his pitiful condition of a drenched great-grandfather had taken away any sense of grandeur he might have had. His huge buzzard wings, dirty and half-plucked, were forever entangled in the mud. They looked at him so long and so closely that Pelayo and Elisenda very soon overcame their surprise and in the end found him familiar. Then they dared speak to him, and he answered in an incomprehensible dialect with a strong sailor's voice. That was how they skipped over the inconvenience of the wings and quite intelligently concluded that he was a lonely castaway from some foreign ship wrecked by the storm. And yet, they called in a neighbor woman who knew everything about life and death to see him, and all she needed was one look to show them their mistake.

"He's an angel," she told them. "He must have been coming for the child, but the poor fellow is so old that the rain knocked him down."

On the following day everyone knew that a flesh-and-blood angel was held captive in Pelayo's house. Against the judgment of the wise neighbor woman, for whom angels in those times were the fugitive survivors of a celestial conspiracy, they did not have the heart to club him to death. Pelayo watched over him all afternoon from the kitchen, armed with his bailiff's club, and before going to bed he dragged him out of the mud and locked him up with the hens in the wire chicken coop. In the middle of the night, when the rain stopped, Pelayo and Elisenda were still killing crabs. A short time afterward the child woke up without a fever and with a desire to eat. Then they felt magnanimous and decided to put the angel on a raft with fresh water and provisions for three days and leave him to his fate on the high seas. But when they went out into the courtyard with the first light of dawn, they found the whole neighborhood in front of the chicken coop having fun with the angel, without the slightest reverence, tossing him things to eat through the openings in the wire as if he weren't a supernatural creature but a circus animal.

Father Gonzaga arrived before seven o'clock, alarmed at the strange news. By that time onlookers less frivolous than those at dawn had already arrived and they were making all kinds of conjectures concerning the captive's future. The simplest among them thought that he should be named mayor of the world. Others of sterner mind felt that he should be promoted to the rank of five-star general in order to win all wars. Some visionaries hoped that he could be put to stud in order to implant on earth a race of winged wise men who could take charge of the universe. But Father Gonzaga, before becoming a priest, had been a robust woodcutter. Standing by the wire, he reviewed his catechism in an instant and asked them to open the door so that he could take a close look at that pitiful man who looked more like a huge decrepit hen among the fascinated chickens. He was lying in a corner drying his open wings in the sunlight among the fruit peels and breakfast leftovers that the early risers had thrown him. Alien to the impertinences of the world, he only lifted his antiquarian eyes and murmured something in his dialect when Father Gonzaga went into the chicken coop and said good morning to him in Latin. The parish priest had his first suspicion of an impostor when he saw that he did not understand the language of God or know how to greet His ministers. Then he noticed that seen close up he was much too human: He had an unbearable smell of the outdoors, the back side of his wings was strewn with parasites and his main feathers had been mistreated by terrestrial winds, and nothing about him measured up to the proud dignity of angels. Then he came out of the chicken coop and in a brief sermon warned the curious against the risks of being ingenuous. He reminded them that the devil had the bad habit of making use of carnival tricks in order to confuse the unwary. He argued that if wings were not the essential element in determining the difference between a hawk and an airplane, they were even less so in the recognition of angels. Nevertheless, he promised to write a letter to his bishop so that the latter would write to his primate so that the latter would write to the Supreme Pontiff in order to get the final verdict from the highest courts.

His prudence fell on sterile hearts. The news of the captive angel spread with such rapidity that after a few hours the courtyard had the bustle of a marketplace and they had to call in troops with fixed bayonets to disperse the mob that was about to knock the house down. Elisenda, her spine all twisted from sweeping up so much marketplace trash, then got the idea of fencing in the yard and charging five cents admission to see the angel.

The curious came from far away. A traveling carnival arrived with a flying acrobat who buzzed over the crowd several times, but no one paid any attention to him because his wings were not those of an angel but, rather, those of a sidereal bat. The most unfortunate invalids on earth came in search of health: a poor woman who since childhood had been counting her heartbeats and had run out of numbers; a Portuguese man who couldn't sleep because the noise of the stars disturbed him; a sleepwalker who got up at night to undo the things he had done while awake; and many others with less serious ailments. In the midst of that shipwreck disorder that made the earth tremble, Pelayo and Elisenda were happy with fatigue, for in less than a week they had crammed their rooms with money and the line of pilgrims waiting their turn to enter still reached beyond the horizon.

The angel was the only one who took no part in his own act. He spent his time trying to get comfortable in his borrowed nest, befuddled by the hellish heat of the oil lamps and sacramental candles that had been placed along the wire. At first they tried to make him eat some mothballs, which, according to the wisdom of the wise neighbor woman, were the food prescribed for angels. But he turned them down, just as he turned down the papal lunches that the penitents brought him, and they never found out whether it was because he was an angel or because he was an old man that in the end he ate nothing but eggplant mush. His only supernatural virtue seemed to be patience. Especially during the first days, when the hens pecked at him, searching for the stellar parasites that proliferated in his wings, and the cripples pulled out feathers to touch their defective parts with, and even the most merciful threw stones at him, trying to get him to rise so they could see him standing. The only time they succeeded in arousing him was when they burned his side with an iron for branding steers, for he had been motionless for so many hours that they thought he was dead. He awoke with a start, ranting in his hermetic language and with tears in his eyes, and he flapped his wings a couple of times, which brought on a whirlwind of chicken dung and lunar dust and a gale of panic that did not seem to be of this world. Although many thought that his reaction had been one not of rage but of pain, from then on they were careful not to annoy him, because the majority understood that his passivity was not that of a hero taking his ease but that of a cataclysm in repose.

Father Gonzaga held back the crowd's frivolity with formulas of maidservant inspiration while awaiting the arrival of a final judgment on the nature of the captive. But the mail from Rome showed no sense of urgency. They spent their time finding out if the prisoner had a navel, if his dialect had any connection with Aramaic, how many times he could fit on the head of a pin, or whether he wasn't just a Norwegian with wings. Those meager letters might have come and gone until the end of time if a providential event had not put an end to the priest's tribulations.

It so happened that during those days, among so many other carnival attractions, there arrived in town the traveling show of the woman who had been changed into a spider for having disobeyed her parents. The admission to see her was not only less than the admission to see the angel, but people were permitted to ask her all manner of questions about her absurd state and to examine her up and down so that no one would ever doubt the truth of her horror. She was a frightful tarantula the size of a ram and with the head of a sad maiden. What was most heartrending, however, was not her outlandish shape but the sincere affliction with which she recounted the details of her misfortune. While still practically a child she had sneaked out of her parents' house to go to a dance, and while she was coming back through the woods after having danced all night without permission, a fearful thunderclap rent the sky in two and through the crack came the lightning bolt of brimstone that changed her into a spider. Her only nourishment came from the meatballs that charitable souls chose to toss into her mouth. A spectacle like that, full of so much human truth and with such a fearful lesson, was bound to defeat without even trying that of a haughty angel who scarcely deigned to look at mortals. Besides, the few miracles attributed to the angel showed a certain mental disorder, like the blind man who didn't recover his sight but grew three new teeth, or the paralytic who didn't get to walk but almost won the lottery, and the leper whose sores sprouted sunflowers. Those consolation miracles, which were more like mocking fun, had already ruined the angel's reputation when the woman who had been changed into a spider finally crushed him completely. That was how Father Gonzaga was cured forever of his insomnia and Pelayo's courtyard went back to being as empty as during the time it had rained for three days and crabs walked through the bedrooms.

The owners of the house had no reason to lament. With the money they saved they built a two-story mansion with balconies and gardens and high netting so that crabs wouldn't get in during the winter, and with iron bars on the windows so that angels wouldn't get in. Pelayo also set up a rabbit warren close to town and gave up his job as bailiff for good, and Elisenda bought some satin pumps with high heels and many dresses of iridescent silk, the kind worn on Sunday by the most desirable women in those times. The chicken coop was the only thing that didn't receive any attention. If they washed it down with creolin and burned tears of myrrh inside it every so often, it was not in homage to the angel but to drive away the dungheap stench that still hung everywhere like a ghost and was turning the new house into an old one. At first, when the child learned to walk, they were careful that he not get too close to the chicken coop. But then they began to lose their fears and got used to the smell, and before the child got his second teeth he'd gone inside the chicken coop to play, where the wires were falling apart. The angel was no less standoffish with him than with other mortals, but he tolerated the most ingenious infamies with the patience of a dog who had no illusions. They both came down with chicken pox at the same time. The doctor who took care of the child couldn't resist the temptation to listen to the angel's heart, and he found so much whistling in the heart and so many sounds in his kidneys that it seemed impossible for him to be alive. What surprised him most, however, was the logic of his wings. They seemed so natural on that completely human organism that he couldn't understand why other men didn't have them too.

When the child began school it had been some time since the sun and rain had caused the collapse of the chicken coop. The angel went dragging himself about here and there like a stray dying man. They would drive him out of the bedroom with a broom and a moment later find him in the kitchen. He seemed to be in so many places at the same time that they grew to think that he'd been duplicated, that he was reproducing himself all through the house, and the exasperated and unhinged Elisenda shouted that it was awful living in that hell full of angels. He could scarcely eat and his antiquarian eyes had also become so foggy that he went about bumping into posts. All he had left were the bare cannulae of his last feathers. Pelayo threw a blanket over him and extended him the charity of letting him sleep in the shed, and only then did they notice that he had a temperature at night, and was delirious with the tongue twisters of an old Norwegian. That was one of the few times they became alarmed, for they thought he was going to die and not even the wise neighbor woman had been able to tell them what to do with dead angels.

And yet he not only survived his worst winter, but seemed improved with the first sunny days. He remained motionless for several days in the farthest corner of the courtyard, where no one would see him, and at the beginning of December some large, stiff feathers began to grow on his wings, the feathers of a scarecrow, which looked more like another misfortune of decrepitude. But he must have known the reason for those changes, for he was quite careful that no one should notice them, that no one should hear the sea chanteys that he sometimes sang under the stars. One morning Elisenda was cutting some bunches of onions for lunch when a wind that seemed to come from the high seas blew into the kitchen. Then she went to the window and caught the angel in his first attempts at flight. They were so clumsy that his fingernails opened a furrow in the vegetable patch and he was on the point of knocking the shed down with the ungainly flapping that slipped on the light and couldn't get a grip on the air. But he did manage to gain altitude. Elisenda let out a sigh of relief, for herself and for him, when she saw him pass over the last houses, holding himself up in some way with the risky flapping of a senile vulture. She kept watching him even when she was through cutting the onions and she kept on watching until it was no longer possible for her to see him, because then he was no longer an annoyance in her life but an imaginary dot on the horizon of the sea.

TEXT IN CONTEXT

ꙮ T. S. ELIOT
B. UNITED STATES, 1888–1965

T. S. Eliot, 1948
*Eliot in his office at
the Institute for
Advanced Study.
(Hulton/Archive)*

T. S. Eliot's poem *The Waste Land,* the most notable twentieth-century poem in English, appeared in the November 1922 issue of the literary magazine *The Dial. The Waste Land* depicts the modern world as a devastated place whose land has lost its regenerative capacity, whose cities are sites of pollution and despair, and whose human relationships are empty and sterile, without moral or spiritual value. More than any other single work, it also reflects the disillusionment of American intellectuals, some of them European expatriates, with Western society at the end of World War I. Nonlinear in structure, fragmented in organization, and obscure in its references, the poem seemed destined for a limited audience; but after being augmented by notes by the author and supported by interpretive reviews and essays, it went on to establish itself as a monument of its age.

It is now common to identify the postwar period in Europe and America as the "wasteland," the spiritual and intellectual condition that promoted the spread of EXISTENTIALISM in the 1930s, '40s, and '50s. In 1948, twenty-six years after the poem's publication, Eliot was awarded the Nobel Prize in literature, and as Elizabeth Drew recounts, a symposium held to pay tribute to his influence "contained contributions from forty-seven writers from more than a dozen different countries, and hailed the poet-critic-dramatist as perhaps the most powerful literary influence in the civilized world of today." Eliot was like an entire literary movement in himself: a poet, an enormously popular lecturer on both sides of the Atlantic, a leading critic, a publisher of an influential literary magazine, and a director of a prominent publishing house in London.

Eliot came to symbolize the traditional and the conservative in religion, politics, and literature, but his poems are marvelously innovative and experimental. He was heavily influenced by the FRENCH SYMBOLISTS,[1] who had broken with traditional subject matter and polite, poetic language. He was attracted to STREAM-OF-CONSCIOUSNESS writing, which could pull together experiences and images from disparate periods and locales. Above all, he was well read and in favor of drawing from the broad reaches of European and world literature. He once described the challenge for the twentieth-century writer: "Our civilization comprehends great variety and complexity, and this variety and complexity, playing upon a refined sensibility, must produce various and complex results. The poet must become more and more comprehensive, more allusive, more indirect, in order to force, to dislocate if necessary, language into meaning."

Eliot and *The Waste Land* had their detractors, especially among American poets. It was believed that the poem turned the attention of American writers away from the tradition of **Walt Whitman**— optimistic, democratic, and nationalistic—to a more pessimistic, elitist, and cosmopolitan aesthetic that virtually silenced homegrown literature for a decade and made the recovery of a native literature difficult even in the Depression years of the 1930s, when new struggles produced new literary impulses. American poet William Carlos Williams (1883–1963) commented in retrospect that *The Waste Land* "wiped out our world as if an atomic bomb had been dropped on it."

From St. Louis to Harvard.   Thomas Stearns Eliot was born September 26, 1888, in St. Louis, Missouri, the youngest son of seven children. His family, which was highly intellectual and literary, had come from Massachusetts and maintained strong connections to New England. Eliot's grandfather William Greenleaf Eliot, a graduate of Harvard Divinity School, moved to St. Louis in 1834 where he founded the first Unitarian church; he also founded Washington University in 1859. Eliot's mother, Charlotte Champe Stearns, was a writer of biographies and religious verse. Eliot spent his summers in New England, eventually attending Milton Academy in Massachusetts, and in 1906 he entered Harvard University and came under the influence of Irving Babbit, the classical, anti-Romantic author of *Rousseau*

www For links to more information about Eliot, quizzes on his poetry, and information on Eliot's 21st-century relevance, see bedford stmartins.com/ worldlitcompact.

p. 845

---

[1]**French Symbolists:** Nineteenth-century French Symbolists Charles Baudelaire (1821–1867), Stéphane Mallarmé (1842–1898), and Paul Verlaine (1844–1896) made use of symbols as a means of evoking the inner world of consciousness.

and Romanticism. Three years later he began graduate work in philosophy, again at Harvard. He completed a master's degree in one year and went to Paris to study at the Sorbonne; he then returned to Harvard and began a doctoral dissertation on F. H. Bradley.[2] Around this time he wrote "**The Love Song of J. Alfred Prufrock,**" a poem that captures the frustration and disillusionment of the age.

p. 1434

Critical Years of Transition.   The years 1914 and 1915 figure prominently in Eliot's life as a writer. World War I broke out while he was studying in Germany on a traveling fellowship from Harvard, pushing him to England, where he settled down and lived for the rest of his life. He did not return to Harvard to finish his doctorate, and he turned from philosophy to poetry. In 1915 he married Vivien Haigh-Wood and in London met Ezra Pound, a transplanted American poet from the Midwest who loved to shepherd new talent into the public eye. Pound persuaded Harriet Monroe, the editor of the Chicago-based *Poetry,* to publish "The Love Song of J. Alfred Prufrock" (June 1915) and introduced Eliot to the director of Egoist Press, Harriet Weaver. Weaver published Eliot's first book of poems, *Prufrock and Other Observations,* in 1917, the same year the poet took a job as a clerk in a bank, Lloyd's of London. Eliot became a forerunner of the "Lost Generation," the international set of American writers who declared their disaffection with European politics and society after the slaughter of so many young soldiers in World War I.

Our civilization comprehends great variety and complexity, and this variety and complexity, playing upon a refined sensibility, must produce various and complex results. The poet must become more and more comprehensive, more allusive, more indirect, in order to force, to dislocate if necessary, language into meaning.

– T. S. ELIOT, 1921

The Waste Land.   Clearly Eliot was in crisis in 1921 and 1922 when he wrote *The Waste Land,* as his security and happiness were being challenged on several fronts. For some time he had struggled to overcome the puritanical element in his family history; poems such as "Prufrock" treated the theme of sexual repression, whereas other early poems were surprisingly bawdy and crude, often self-consciously primitive in their depiction of characters and situations. His wife, Vivien, who was mentally unstable, was suffering from bouts of neuralgia and insomnia. Meanwhile, Eliot's family had withdrawn their financial support, thinking that Eliot was wasting his life in literature; then his father died in 1919. When Eliot had a breakdown, a neurologist suggested he take a leave from his work at the bank, and Eliot found

[2] **F. H. Bradley** (1846–1924): English philosopher who emphasized the private nature of individual experience in *Appearance and Reality* (1893); he influenced Eliot's private imagery.

Europe in 1914

In the summer of 1914, most of Europe was divided into two camps: the Triple Alliance of Germany, Austria-Hungary, and Italy and the Triple Entente—Great Britain, France, and Russia. This division was intensified by the nationalist aspirations of ethnic groups within the European empires, especially in the Balkans. There Serbian nationalists were inflamed by Austria's annexation in 1908 of Bosnia-Herzegovina, which they coveted as part of a "greater Serbia." On June 28, 1914, Archduke Francis Ferdinand, the heir to the Austro-Hungarian throne, was assassinated in the Bosnian capital Sarajevo by a Serbian. This event triggered military mobilizations by the rival alliances, plunging Europe into World War I.

psychiatric help in Lausanne, Switzerland, in the winter of 1921, the time of the writing of *The Waste Land*. Again Pound came to his aid: He collected money for Eliot's support and helped edit the poem in manuscript, seeing it through to publication in 1922. *The Waste Land* first appeared in England in the first issue of *Criterion* (October 1922)

Although Eliot deferred to Yeats as "the greatest poet" of his time, he was himself the most famous. A man of keen intellect, capable of developing a philosophical position as well as a new rhythm and intonation, trained in classics, fluent in French and German, Eliot was better equipped than any other poet to bring verse fully into the twentieth century. As James Joyce remarked of him in a notebook, he abolished the idea of poetry for ladies.

— RICHARD ELLMANN, critic, 1973

and in America in *The Dial* (November 1922). Eliot's original poem, before it was edited and drastically reduced by Ezra Pound, and unpublished drafts of the poem were made available to scholars in 1968 from the manuscript collections of John Quinn, a New York patron of the arts. A facsimile edition of the poem with original drafts was edited by Valerie Eliot, his second wife, and published in 1971.

A number of letters written by Eliot during the creation of *The Waste Land* corroborate his vulnerable and sometimes desperate emotional and financial circumstances. One close friend, the American critic Edmund Wilson, called the poem "nothing more or less than a most distressingly moving account of Eliot's own agonized state of mind," and Eliot himself said of the poem in 1947 that he had written it "simply to relieve" his feelings. Nevertheless the work elevated Eliot into the top tier of modern poetry; no one in the twentieth century had painted such an inclusive portrait of the world as it was after World War I while making use of the diverse conventions of Western literature.

Christianity and Conservatism.   In 1922, Eliot resigned from the editorial board of *The Dial* and started a heavily influential cultural magazine, *The Criterion,* the critical focus of which was a conservative assessment of the relationship between culture and society. From this point on, Eliot's life and work turned toward literary and religious orthodoxy and political conservatism. He became a British subject in 1927, and in the same year he took communion in the Anglican Church. He committed his first wife to a mental institution and was able to overcome his own emotional distress. In 1930, he published *Ash Wednesday,* a poem of religious conversion, and later in the decade wrote the first section of a long Christian poem, *Four Quartets,* which he completed in 1943. When Eliot turned to writing drama, most of it too held a religious message. Two of his major plays, the early historical drama *Murder in the Cathedral* (1935) and the later contemporary work *The Cocktail Party* (1949), both concern Christian martyrdom, an unusual topic for the twentieth century. In later life Eliot worked as a senior editor for Faber and Faber, a leading British publisher, rarely traveling to the United States. He eventually remarried—happily this time—and died peacefully in 1965.

The Complexities of *The Waste Land*.   Two characteristics of *The Waste Land* (1922) are immediately challenging. The first is its composition: It moves from one image to another and from situation to situation without any explanation or transition. David Daiches explains: "Eliot's real novelty—and the cause of much bewilderment when his poems first appeared—was his deliberate elimination of all merely connective and transitional passages, his building up of the total pattern of meaning through the immediate juxtaposition of images. . . ." In fact, it was American poet Ezra Pound who in editing the poem cut away much of that connective tissue, making the work both startling and hard to follow. The second challenge of *The Waste Land* are the many literary excerpts quoted in their original languages: Greek and Latin classics, medieval Romance, Elizabethan drama, German opera, French Symbolist poetry, and religious writings, from Christian to Buddhist sources to the Indian Upanishads.[3]

Eliot introduced his notes for the publication of *The Waste Land* in book form with a comment about his influences:

> Not only the title, but the plan and a good deal of the incidental symbolism of the poem were suggested by Miss Jessie L. Weston's book on the Grail legend: From *Ritual to Romance* (Cambridge). . . . To another work of anthropology I am indebted in general, one which has influenced our generation profoundly; I mean The Golden Bough; I have used especially the two volumes Adonis, Attis, Osiris. Anyone who is acquainted with these works will immediately recognize in the poem certain references to vegetation ceremonies.

Mythological Themes.   In the European Middle Ages a Christian myth developed around the Grail, which according to legend was the cup or platter used by Jesus at the Last Supper and then used by Joseph of Arimathea to collect Jesus' blood at the Crucifixion. The Grail became the possession of a series of Grail kings in an uncertain location. In the stories that were told of it, a brave knight from King Arthur's court—usually Perceval—endures a perilous journey in order to find the Grail, which is hidden away in the castle of the sexually wounded Fisher King. By asking the right questions, the knight can heal the king and reinvigorate the land. Jessie Weston in her book connects the Grail stories to older fertility rituals involved with the annual plant cycle of birth, death, and rebirth. Elizabeth Drew explains:

---

[3] **Upanishads:** A series of writings containing the ancient wisdom of India; written between c. the ninth and the first centuries B.C.E.

Miss Weston found the Grail legends to be Christianized versions, via the "mystery" religions,[4] of the ancient fertility cults. She believed the knight's "quest" to be a version of older initiation rites into religious mysteries concerned with the union of the physical with the source of spiritual being. These faiths, she thinks, were spread into western Europe by Syrian merchants and later transformed into the stories of the Grail.

James George Frazer's *The Golden Bough* (1890) is a brilliant work of comparative mythology about early fertility myths and rituals in the ancient Near East and Mediterranean region, with a focus on the dying-and-rising god-hero-king whose life and sacrificial death were annually reenacted in imitation of the seasonal cycle of plants. Eliot translates the Grail quest into the modern search for meaning.

The underlying theme of *The Waste Land* concerns time: The present time can be appreciated and understood only in the context of the past. Only within the context and continuity of past wisdom can a pattern be found that will comprehend the fragmentation of modern society. The death images of rock, dust, bones, and polluted water are paradoxically also the potential of new life. The blind Tiresias, who becomes an amalgam of modern men in the poem, needs a new vision, a new set of eyes by which he can be healed and the modern city transformed.

Eliot's tendency to combine emotional, historical, mythical, and literary references is complicated enough; the footnotes he provided in later editions of the work attest to the obscurity of some of his sources and the compression of his ideas and images.

Reactions to *The Waste Land*.   *The Waste Land*'s first generation of critics were kept busy trying to explain the poem to a somewhat baffled literary audience. Edmund Wilson led the way in a long essay in *The Dial* in December 1922, illuminating a number of references based on his reading of Eliot's own notes, which were soon being published with the poem. Critic Kathleen Raine, however, not only understood the work but thought *it* had understood everything:

> Eliot wants to suggest in the rhythms of his verse the movement of thought in a living mind, and thus to communicate the exact pattern of his meaning not so much by logical structure as by emotional suggestion.
>
> – F. O. Matthiessen, 1947

---

[4] **"mystery" religions:** Mystery cults were very popular in ancient Greece and Rome for at least one thousand years, beginning c. 1000 B.C.E. The details of their inner workings were kept secret, but all shared a rigorous rite of initiation, a concern about death, and a hope for immortality centered on a deity who had personal knowledge of the afterlife. The most popular Greek versions were the Orphic and Eleusinian mysteries. The mysteries of Isis and Mithra were favored in the Roman world.

For my generation T. S. Eliot's early poetry, more than the work of any other poet, has enabled us to know our world imaginatively. All those who have lived in the Waste Land of London, can, I suppose, remember the particular occasion on which, reading T. S. Eliot's poems for the first time, an experience of the contemporary world that had been nameless and formless, suddenly received its apotheosis.

And American critic Malcolm Cowley feels he and other young writers understood the poem well but that it didn't speak for them:

> The idea was a simple one. Beneath the rich symbolism of *The Waste Land,* the wide learning expressed in seven languages, the actions conducted on three planes, the musical episodes, the geometrical structure—beneath and by means of all this, we felt the poet was saying that the present is inferior to the past. The past was dignified; the present is barren of emotion. The past was a landscape nourished by living fountains; now the fountains of spiritual grace are dry. . . . It happened that we were excited by the adventure of living in the present. The famous "postwar mood of aristocratic disillusionment" was a mood we had never really shared. It happened that Eliot's subjective truth was not our own.

E. E. Cummings, an American poet, asked why Eliot could not write his own lines instead of borrowing from dead poets. And modern American novelist Ernest Hemingway wrote in *Transatlantic Review:* "If I knew that by grinding Mr. Eliot into a fine dry powder and sprinkling that powder over Mr. Conrad's grave Mr. Conrad would shortly appear, looking very annoyed at the forced return, and commence writing, I would leave for London early tomorrow with a sausage grinder."

■ **FURTHER RESEARCH**

Biography
Ackroyd, Peter. *T. S. Eliot: A Life.* 1984.
Bush, Ronald. *T. S. Eliot: A Study in Character and Style.* 1984.
Childs, Donald J. *T. S. Eliot: Mystic, Son and Lover.* 1997.
Gordon, Lyndall. *T. S. Eliot: An Imperfect Life.* 1988.

Criticism
Albright, Daniel. *Quantum Poetics.* 1997.
Bush, Ronald, ed. *T. S. Eliot: The Modernist in History.* 1991.
Cattaui, Georges. *T. S. Eliot.* 1966.
Julius, Anthony. *T. S. Eliot: Anti-Semitism and Literary Form.* 1995.
Knoll, Robert E., ed. *Storm over* The Waste Land. 1964.
Moody, David A., ed. *The Cambridge Companion to T. S. Eliot.* 1994.
Palmer, Marja. *Men and Women in T. S. Eliot's Early Poetry.* 1996.
Smith, Grover. *The Waste Land.* 1983.

∾ The Waste Land[1]

*"Nam Sibyllam quidem Cumis ego ipse oculis meis vidi in ampulla pendere, et cum
illi pueri dicerent: Σίβυλλα τί θέλεις; respondebat illa: ἀποθανεῖν θέλω."*[2]

For Ezra Pound
il miglior fabbro.[3]

I. THE BURIAL OF THE DEAD[4]

April is the cruellest month, breeding
Lilacs out of the dead land, mixing
Memory and desire, stirring
Dull roots with spring rain.
Winter kept us warm, covering
Earth in forgetful snow, feeding
A little life with dried tubers.
Summer surprised us, coming over the Starnbergersee
With a shower of rain; we stopped in the colonnade,
10   And went on in sunlight, into the Hofgarten,
And drank coffee, and talked for an hour.
Bin gar keine Russin, stamm' aus Litauen, echt deutsch.[5]
And when we were children, staying at the archduke's,
My cousin's, he took me out on a sled,
And I was frightened. He said, Marie,
Marie, hold on tight. And down we went.
In the mountains, there you feel free.
I read, much of the night, and go south in the winter.

What are the roots that clutch, what branches grow
20   Out of this stony rubbish? Son of man,[6]

---

[1] Eliot added some notes for the publication of *The Waste Land* in book form by Boni and Liveright, New York, December 1922. These are identified by (E). We have omitted or departed from these notes as has seemed fitting, while adding additional notes for clarification.

[2] "For I saw with my own eyes the Sibyl from Cumae hanging in a bottle, and when the boys asked her, 'Sibyl, what do you want?' she would reply, 'I want to die.'"—Petronius, *Satyricon,* 48. According to legend, the prophetess had been granted a long life but not perpetual youth, and so she was hideously shriveled with age. Compare Madame Sosostris and Tiresias, fortune-tellers later to appear in *The Waste Land.*

[3] *il miglior fabbro:* "The better maker [poet]." Eliot compliments his friend Ezra Pound, who edited the poem into its final form during the period of Eliot's hospitalization. The Italian original is Dante's praise of the poet Arnaut Daniel, from the *Purgatorio,* 26, 117.

[4] **The Burial of the Dead:** Title of the funeral service in *The Book of Common Prayer.*

[5] **Bin . . . deutsch:** "I'm not Russian at all; I come from Lithuania, pure German." The remark is ironical; little is "pure" in the poem. The scene is from the vicinity of Munich, in south Germany.

[6] **Son of man:** God's address to the prophet Ezekiel (Ezekiel 2:1).

You cannot say, or guess, for you know only
A heap of broken images, where the sun beats,
And the dead tree gives no shelter, the cricket no relief,[7]
And the dry stone no sound of water. Only
There is shadow under this red rock,
(Come in under the shadow of this red rock),
And I will show you something different from either
Your shadow at morning striding behind you
Or your shadow at evening rising to meet you;
30 I will show you fear in a handful of dust.[8]
        Frisch weht der Wind
        Der Heimat zu
        Mein Irisch Kind,
        Wo weilest du?[9]
"You gave me hyacinths first a year ago;
"They called me the hyacinth girl."
— Yet when we came back, late, from the Hyacinth garden,
Your arms full, and your hair wet, I could not
Speak, and my eyes failed, I was neither
40 Living nor dead, and I knew nothing,
Looking into the heart of light, the silence.
Oed' und leer das Meer.[10]

      Madame Sosostris,[11] famous clairvoyante,
Had a bad cold, nevertheless
Is known to be the wisest woman in Europe,
With a wicked pack of cards.[12] Here, said she,
Is your card, the drowned Phoenician Sailor,
(Those are pearls that were his eyes.[13] Look!)
Here is Belladonna,[14] the Lady of the Rocks,

---

[7] **the cricket no relief:** Compare Ecclesiastes 12:5.

[8] **handful of dust:** Compare "Ashes to ashes, dust to dust" in the funeral service.

[9] **Frisch . . . du?:** The lyric in German is from Wagner's opera version of *Tristan and Isolde*: "Fresh blows the wind / toward the homeland. / My Irish girl / where do you abide?"

[10] **Oed' . . . Meer:** From *Tristan and Isolde*: "Waste and empty the sea." The dying Tristan looks out to sea and finds no sign of Isolde's ship.

[11] **Madame Sosostris:** A fortune-teller; her name is close to that of the Egyptian pharaoh Seostris.

[12] **wicked . . . cards:** Tarot cards, thought to have originated in ancient Egypt for the purposes of divination.

[13] **Those . . . eyes:** Shakespeare, *The Tempest*, I, ii, 399–402. Consolation of Ariel to Ferdinand over his father, who is feared drowned:
    Those are pearls that were his eyes;
    Nothing of him that doth fade,
    But doth suffer a sea-change
    Into something rich and strange.

[14] **Belladonna:** Italian for "lovely lady," but also a poison.

50   The lady of situations.
Here is the man with three staves, and here the Wheel,[15]
And here is the one-eyed merchant, and this card,
Which is blank, is something he carries on his back,
Which I am forbidden to see. I do not find
The Hanged Man.[16] Fear death by water.
I see crowds of people, walking round in a ring.
Thank you. If you see dear Mrs. Equitone,
Tell her I bring the horoscope myself:
One must be so careful these days.

60   Unreal City,
Under the brown fog of a winter dawn,[17]
A crowd flowed over London Bridge, so many,
I had not thought death had undone so many.[18]
Sighs, short and infrequent, were exhaled,
And each man fixed his eyes before his feet.
Flowed up the hill and down King William Street,
To where Saint Mary Woolnoth kept the hours
With a dead sound on the final stroke of nine.[19]
There I saw one I knew, and stopped him, crying: "Stetson!
70   "You who were with me in the ships at Mylae![20]
"That corpse you planted last year in your garden,
"Has it begun to sprout? Will it bloom this year?
"Or has the sudden frost disturbed its bed?
"Oh keep the Dog far hence, that's friend to men,
"Or with his nails he'll dig it up again![21]
"You! hypocrite lecteur! — mon semblable, — mon frère!"[22]

---

[15] **the man . . . the Wheel:** Eliot says that he associates, "quite arbitrarily," the "man with three staves" with the Fisher King, who appears later. The Wheel could be the wheel of fortune.

[16] **Hanged Man:** Eliot himself confesses that he has "departed to suit my own convenience" from the symbolism of the Tarot pack (E).

[17] **Unreal . . . dawn:** Echoes Baudelaire's "Swarming city, city full of dreams, / where the specter in broad daylight accosts the passerby," from *The Flowers of Evil.*

[18] **I . . . many:** Dante's comment in the *Inferno,* seeing the citizens of Hell: "Such a long procession / of people, I had not thought / death had undone so many" (*Inferno,* 3, 55–57).

[19] **Sighs . . . nine:** Eliot supplies commonplace scenes from London: St. Mary Woolnoth, a church in the business district, and the dead sound in the tower clock, "a phenomenon which I have often noticed" (E).

[20] **"Stetson . . . Mylae!":** Stetson is the name of the average businessman, perhaps connected to the American hat manufacturer; Mylae is the site of a victorious Roman sea battle against Carthage in 260 B.C.E., a pointless war fought over commercial interests and thereby comparable to World War I.

[21] **"Oh keep . . . up again!":** Compare the nearly identical passage in John Webster, *The White Devil* (1612), V, iv, 97–98, where the dog is called "foe to man."

[22] **"You! . . . frère!":** Baudelaire, preface to *Flowers of Evil;* French for "Hypocrite reader! My double, my brother!"

II. A GAME OF CHESS[23]

The Chair she sat in, like a burnished throne,[24]
Glowed on the marble, where the glass
Held up by standards wrought with fruited vines
80 From which a golden Cupidon peeped out
(Another hid his eyes behind his wing)
Doubled the flames of sevenbranched candelabra
Reflecting light upon the table as
The glitter of her jewels rose to meet it,
From satin cases poured in rich profusion;
In vials of ivory and coloured glass
Unstoppered, lurked her strange synthetic perfumes,
Unguent, powdered, or liquid — troubled, confused
And drowned the sense in odours; stirred by the air
90 That freshened from the window, these ascended
In fattening the prolonged candle-flames,
Flung their smoke into the laquearia,[25]
Stirring the pattern on the coffered ceiling.
Huge sea-wood fed with copper
Burned green and orange, framed by the coloured stone,
In which sad light a carvèd dolphin swam.
Above the antique mantel was displayed
As though a window gave upon the sylvan scene[26]
The change of Philomel, by the barbarous king
100 So rudely forced;[27] yet there the nightingale
Filled all the desert with inviolable voice
And still she cried, and still the world pursues,
"Jug Jug" to dirty ears.
And other withered stumps of time
Were told upon the walls; staring forms
Leaned out, leaning, hushing the room enclosed.

---

[23] A GAME OF CHESS: Eliot appears to be recalling two plays by Thomas Middleton: for the title, *A Game of Chess* (1624), and for the plot, *Women Beware Women* (1657), in which a woman is seduced while her mother-in-law is engrossed in a chess game.

[24] The Chair . . . throne: Note the description of Cleopatra in Shakespeare, *Antony and Cleopatra*, II, ii, 190: "The barge she sat in, like a burnished throne. . . ."

[25] laquearia: A panelled ceiling; Eliot here refers to a banquet scene in Virgil's *Aeneid* prepared by Dido for Aeneas: "Lighted lamps hung from the coffered ceiling / Rich with gold leaf, and torches with high flames / Prevailed over the night." (Robert Fizgerald, trans.)

[26] sylvan scene: Eliot notes Milton's use of "Sylvan scene" in a description of Eden in *Paradise Lost,* 4, 140.

[27] The change . . . forced: "Ovid, *Metamorphoses*, VI, Philomela" (E). Philomela is raped by her brother-in-law, who cuts out her tongue; the gods, taking pity on her, transform her into a nightingale.

Footsteps shuffled on the stair.
Under the firelight, under the brush, her hair
Spread out in fiery points
110   Glowed into words, then would be savagely still.

      "My nerves are bad to-night. Yes, bad. Stay with me.
"Speak to me. Why do you never speak. Speak.
      "What are you thinking of? What thinking? What?
"I never know what you are thinking. Think."[28]

      I think we are in rats' alley
Where the dead men lost their bones.

      "What is that noise?"
                    The wind under the door.
"What is that noise now? What is the wind doing?"
120   Nothing again nothing.
                                    "Do
"You know nothing? Do you see nothing? Do you remember
"Nothing?"
      I remember
Those are pearls that were his eyes.
"Are you alive, or not? Is there nothing in your head?"
                                    But

O O O O that Shakespeherian Rag—
It's so elegant
130   So intelligent[29]
"What shall I do now? What shall I do?"
"I shall rush out as I am, and walk the street
"With my hair down, so. What shall we do to-morrow?
"What shall we ever do?"
                    The hot water at ten.
And if it rains, a closed car at four.
And we shall play a game of chess,
Pressing lidless eyes and waiting for a knock upon the door.

      When Lil's husband got demobbed,[30] I said—
140   I didn't mince my words, I said to her myself,

---

[28] **"My nerves . . . Think"**: Commonly thought to reflect Eliot's own marital experience with his first wife, Vivien.

[29] **O . . . intelligent**: Adapted from "The Shakespearean Rag," a popular dance song (1912).

[30] **demobbed**: Demobilized from military service.

HURRY UP PLEASE ITS TIME[31]
Now Albert's coming back, make yourself a bit smart.
He'll want to know what you done with that money he gave you
To get yourself some teeth. He did, I was there.
You have them all out, Lil, and get a nice set,
He said, I swear, I can't bear to look at you.
And no more can't I, I said, and think of poor Albert,
He's been in the army four years, he wants a good time,
And if you don't give it him, there's others will, I said.

150   Oh is there, she said. Something o' that, I said.
Then I'll know who to thank, she said, and give me a straight look.
HURRY UP PLEASE ITS TIME
If you don't like it you can get on with it, I said.
Others can pick and choose if you can't.
But if Albert makes off, it won't be for lack of telling.
You ought to be ashamed, I said, to look so antique.
(And her only thirty-one.)
I can't help it, she said, pulling a long face,
It's them pills I took, to bring it off, she said.

160   (She's had five already, and nearly died of young George.)
The chemist[32] said it would be all right, but I've never been the same.
You are a proper fool, I said.
Well, if Albert won't leave you alone, there it is, I said,
What you get married for if you don't want children?
HURRY UP PLEASE ITS TIME
Well, that Sunday Albert was home, they had a hot gammon,[33]
And they asked me in to dinner, to get the beauty of it hot—
HURRY UP PLEASE ITS TIME
HURRY UP PLEASE ITS TIME

170   Goonight Bill. Goonight Lou. Goonight May. Goonight.
Ta ta. Goonight. Goonight.
Good night, ladies, good night, sweet ladies, good night, good night.[34]

III. THE FIRE SERMON[35]

The river's tent is broken: the last fingers of leaf
Clutch and sink into the wet bank. The wind
Crosses the brown land, unheard. The nymphs are departed.

---

[31] HURRY . . . TIME: Announcement of closing time in a London pub.

[32] chemist: Druggist.

[33] gammon: Ham.

[34] Good . . . night: Ophelia's mad song from Shakespeare, *Hamlet*, IV, v, 69–70.

[35] THE FIRE SERMON: A sermon by Buddha against the fires of the senses, against the flames of passion and desire.

Sweet Thames, run softly, till I end my song.[36]
The river bears no empty bottles, sandwich papers,
Silk handkerchiefs, cardboard boxes, cigarette ends
Or other testimony of summer nights. The nymphs are departed.
180   And their friends, the loitering heirs of city directors;
Departed, have left no addresses.
By the waters of Leman I sat down and wept . . .[37]
Sweet Thames, run softly till I end my song,
Sweet Thames, run softly, for I speak not loud or long.
But at my back in a cold blast I hear
The rattle of the bones, and chuckle spread from ear to ear.[38]
A rat crept softly through the vegetation
Dragging its slimy belly on the bank
While I was fishing in the dull canal
190   On a winter evening round behind the gashouse
Musing upon the king my brother's wreck
And on the king my father's death before him.[39]
White bodies naked on the low damp ground
And bones cast in a little low dry garret,
Rattled by the rat's foot only, year to year.
But at my back from time to time I hear
The sound of horns and motors, which shall bring
Sweeney to Mrs. Porter in the spring.
O the moon shone bright on Mrs. Porter
200   And on her daughter
They wash their feet in soda water[40]
Et O ces voix d'enfants, chantant dans la coupole![41]

---

[36] **my song:** From "Prothalamion," a marriage song by Edmund Spenser (1596).

[37] **By . . . wept . . . :** Compare Psalm 137:1: "By the rivers of Babylon, there we sat down, yea, we wept, when we remembered Zion." Leman is the French name of Lake Geneva in Switzerland, where Eliot was hospitalized while completing *The Waste Land.* The word also means "lover" in early English.

[38] **But at . . . ear:** Compare "But at my back I always hear / Time's wingèd chariot hurrying near," Andrew Marvell, "To His Coy Mistress," 21–22. (E)

[39] **Musing . . . before him:** Recalls Ferdinand's presumed loss of his father in Shakespeare, *The Tempest,* I, ii, 389–91 (E):

> . . . Sitting on a bank,
> Weeping against the king my father's wreck,
> This music crept by me on the waters.

This reference also recalls the story of the Fisher King from anthropological sources.

[40] **O the moon . . . soda water:** Eliot says, "I do not know the origin of the ballad from which these lines are taken: It was reported to me from Sydney, Australia" (E). The ballad was a soldier's song from World War I; in the song Mrs. Porter and her daughter are prostitutes, and the soda water is a douche, not a foot wash. In other contexts, however, washing the feet is a ritual of purification.

[41] *Et . . . coupole!:* "And Oh, those voices of children, singing in the cupola!" The final line of Paul Verlaine's sonnet "Parsifal."

Twit twit twit
Jug jug jug jug jug jug
So rudely forc'd.
Tereu[42]

Unreal City
Under the brown fog of a winter noon
Mr. Eugenides, the Smyrna merchant
210 Unshaven, with a pocket full of currants
C.i.f. London: documents at sight,
Asked me in demotic French
To luncheon at the Cannon Street Hotel
Followed by a weekend at the Metropole.[43]

At the violet hour, when the eyes and back
Turn upward from the desk, when the human engine waits
Like a taxi throbbing waiting,
I Tiresias, though blind, throbbing between two lives,
Old man with wrinkled female breasts,[44] can see
220 At the violet hour, the evening hour that strives
Homeward, and brings the sailor home from sea,
The typist home at teatime, clears her breakfast, lights
Her stove, and lays out food in tins.
Out of the window perilously spread
Her drying combinations touched by the sun's last rays,
On the divan are piled (at night her bed)
Stockings, slippers, camisoles, and stays.
I Tiresias, old man with wrinkled dugs
Perceived the scene, and foretold the rest—
230 I too awaited the expected guest.
He, the young man carbuncular,[45] arrives,
A small house agent's clerk, with one bold stare,
One of the low on whom assurance sits

---

[42] **Twit . . . Tereu:** Recalls the rape of Philomela and the song of the nightingale, II, 98–103.

[43] **Mr. Eugenides . . . Metropole:** A Greek merchant from a Turkish port city with a pocketful of currants shipped duty-free to London invites the narrator in vulgar French to lunch in a businessman's hotel in London followed by an illicit weekend in an expensive tourist hotel in Brighton.

[44] **I . . . breasts:** The speaker is Tiresias, who because of spells cast by the gods has been both a man and a woman. When asked who has the greater sexual pleasure, he answers that a woman does; in anger, the goddess Juno strikes him blind, but her husband Jupiter gives him the gift of prophecy (Ovid, *Metamorphoses*, 3, 320–38). "Tiresias, although a mere spectator and not indeed a 'character,' is yet the most important personage in the poem, uniting all the rest" (E).

[45] **carbuncular:** Suffering from acne.

As a silk hat on a Bradford[46] millionaire.
The time is now propitious, as he guesses,
The meal is ended, she is bored and tired,
Endeavours to engage her in caresses
Which still are unreproved, if undesired.
Flushed and decided, he assaults at once;
240 Exploring hands encounter no defence;
His vanity requires no response,
And makes a welcome of indifference.
(And I Tiresias have foresuffered all
Enacted on this same divan or bed;
I who have sat by Thebes below the wall
And walked among the lowest of the dead.)
Bestows one final patronising kiss,
And gropes his way, finding the stairs unlit . . .
        She turns and looks a moment in the glass,
250 Hardly aware of her departed lover;
Her brain allows one half-formed thought to pass:
"Well now that's done: and I'm glad it's over."
When lovely woman stoops to folly[47] and
Paces about her room again, alone,
She smoothes her hair with automatic hand,
And puts a record on the gramophone.

        "This music crept by me upon the waters"
And along the Strand, up Queen Victoria Street.
O City city, I can sometimes hear
260 Beside a public bar in Lower Thames Street,
The pleasant whining of a mandoline
And a clatter and a chatter from within
Where fishmen lounge at noon: where the walls
Of Magnus Martyr[48] hold
Inexplicable splendour of Ionian white and gold.

---

[46] **Bradford:** A town in the north of England where fortunes were made off profiteering during World War I.

[47] **When . . . folly:** First line of a song by Olivia in *The Vicar of Wakefield,* a novel by Oliver Goldsmith (1766):
    When lovely woman stoops to folly
    And finds too late that men betray
    What harm can soothe her melancholy,
    What art can wash the guilt away?

[48] **Magnus Martyr:** London church with a beautiful interior praised by Eliot in his notes; built by Sir Christopher Wren at the end of the seventeenth century.

The river sweats
Oil and tar
The barges drift
With the turning tide
270 Red sails
Wide
To leeward, swing on the heavy spar.
The barges wash
Drifting logs
Down Greenwich reach
Past the Isle of Dogs.
　　　　Weialala leia
　　　　Wallala leialala[49]

Elizabeth and Leicester
280 Beating oars[50]
The stern was formed
A gilded shell
Red and gold
The brisk swell
Rippled both shores
Southwest wind
Carried down stream
The peal of bells
White towers
290 　　　　Weialala leia
　　　　Wallala leialala

"Trams and dusty trees.
Highbury bore me. Richmond and Kew
Undid me. By Richmond I raised my knees
Supine on the floor of a narrow canoe."

"My feet are at Moorgate, and my heart
Under my feet. After the event
He wept. He promised 'a new start.'
I made no comment. What should I resent?"

---

[49] Weialala . . . leialala: "The Song of the (three) Thames-daughters begins here" (E). These creations of the poet's, parodies of Wagner's Rhine Maidens from the opera *Twilight of the Gods,* sing their refrain in lines 277–78 and 290–91 and speak separately in lines 292–306, each identifying a place along the Thames where she was debauched.

[50] Elizabeth . . . oars: The story of the dalliance of Queen Elizabeth and Robert Dudley, Earl of Leicester, while cruising in a barge down the Thames. Eliot took the story from James A. Froude's biography *Elizabeth,* vol. I, ch. 4.

300   "On Margate Sands.
        I can connect
        Nothing with nothing.
        The broken fingernails of dirty hands.
        My people humble people who expect
        Nothing."
                    la la

        To Carthage then I came[51]
        Burning burning burning burning[52]
        O Lord Thou pluckest me out
310   O Lord Thou pluckest[53]

        burning

IV. DEATH BY WATER[54]

Phlebas the Phoenician, a fortnight dead,
Forgot the cry of gulls, and the deep sea swell
And the profit and loss.
                    A current under sea
Picked his bones in whispers. As he rose and fell
He passed the stages of his age and youth
Entering the whirlpool.
                    Gentile or Jew
320 O you who turn the wheel and look to windward,
Consider Phlebas, who was once handsome and tall as you.

V. WHAT THE THUNDER SAID[55]

After the torchlight red on sweaty faces
After the frosty silence in the gardens
After the agony in stony places
The shouting and the crying

---

[51] To Carthage . . . came: St. Augustine, *The Confessions*, III, 1.

[52] Burning . . . burning: Refrain from Buddha's "Fire Sermon," which argues against the fires of passion (E).

[53] O Lord . . . pluckest: "From St. Augustine's *Confessions* again. The collocation of these two representatives of Eastern and Western asceticism, as the culmination of this part of the poem, is not an accident" (E).

[54] DEATH BY WATER: Phlebas is a poetic creation, perhaps an ancestor of Mr. Eugenides, who in drowning is purified by being stripped of his worldly attributes. The reader is left to decide whether Phlebas's death is a sacrificial act leading to rebirth or a pointless waste.

[55] WHAT THE THUNDER SAID: Eliot comments: "In the first part of Part V three themes are employed: the journey to Emmaus, the approach to the Chapel Perilous . . . and the present decay of eastern Europe" (E). The opening lines of the section refer to the story of the betrayal and Crucifixion of Christ.

Prison and palace and reverberation
Of thunder of spring over distant mountains
He who was living is now dead[56]
We who were living are now dying
330   With a little patience

      Here is no water but only rock
Rock and no water and the sandy road
The road winding above among the mountains
Which are mountains of rock without water
If there were water we should stop and drink
Amongst the rock one cannot stop or think
Sweat is dry and feet are in the sand
If there were only water amongst the rock
Dead mountain mouth of carious[57] teeth that cannot spit
340   Here one can neither stand nor lie nor sit
There is not even silence in the mountains
But dry sterile thunder without rain
There is not even solitude in the mountains
But red sullen faces sneer and snarl
From doors of mudcracked houses
                  If there were water

     And no rock
     If there were rock
     And also water
350   And water
     A spring
     A pool among the rock
     If there were the sound of water only
     Not the cicada
     And dry grass singing
     But sound of water over a rock
     Where the hermit-thrush sings in the pine trees
     Drip drop drip drop drop drop drop
     But there is no water

360   Who is the third who walks always beside you?[58]
When I count, there are only you and I together

---

[56] **Of thunder of spring . . . dead:** The Passion of Christ in the Garden of Gethsemane is merged here with the vegetation cycle.

[57] **carious:** From carrion: decaying (flesh).

[58] **the third . . . beside you?:** Eliot refers to an Antarctic expedition in which a party of explorers "had the constant delusion that there was *one more member* than could actually be counted" (E). Also, in the story of the journey to Emmaus (Luke 24:13–34), a third person appears to join the two disciples: Jesus.

But when I look ahead up the white road
There is always another one walking beside you
Gliding wrapt in a brown mantle, hooded
I do not know whether a man or a woman[59]
—— But who is that on the other side of you?

What is that sound high in the air[60]
Murmur of maternal lamentation
Who are those hooded hordes swarming
370 Over endless plains, stumbling in cracked earth
Ringed by the flat horizon only
What is the city over the mountains
Cracks and reforms and bursts in the violet air
Falling towers
Jerusalem Athens Alexandria
Vienna London
Unreal

A woman drew her long black hair out tight
And fiddled whisper music on those strings
380 And bats with baby faces in the violet light
Whistled, and beat their wings
And crawled head downward down a blackened wall
And upside down in air were towers
Tolling reminiscent bells, that kept the hours
And voices singing out of empty cisterns and exhausted wells.

In this decayed hole among the mountains
In the faint moonlight, the grass is singing
Over the tumbled graves, about the chapel
There is the empty chapel, only the wind's home.[61]
390 It has no windows, and the door swings,
Dry bones can harm no one.
Only a cock stood on the rooftree
Co co rico co co rico[62]
In a flash of lightning. Then a damp gust
Bringing rain

---

[59] **a man or a woman:** May refer to the prophet Tiresias.

[60] **that sound . . . air:** Eliot cites a comment by Hermann Hesse that "already half of Europe . . . is on the way to chaos, going drunk in holy madness along the edge of the abyss, and sings, sings drunkenly and hymnlike as Dmitri Karamazov sang." (Hesse, *Look into Chaos* [*Blick ins Chaos*], 1920.)

[61] **the chapel . . . home:** The Chapel Perilous of the Grail legend, cited in Jessie Weston's *From Ritual to Romance.*

[62] **Co co . . . rico:** The cock's crow suggests the breaking of a spell.

    Ganga[63] was sunken, and the limp leaves
Waited for rain, while the black clouds
Gathered far distant, over Himavant.[64]
The jungle crouched, humped in silence.
400 Then spoke the thunder
D<small>A</small>
Datta:[65] what have we given?
My friend, blood shaking my heart
The awful daring of a moment's surrender
Which an age of prudence can never retract
By this, and this only, we have existed
Which is not to be found in our obituaries
Or in memories draped by the beneficent spider[66]
Or under seals broken by the lean solicitor
410 In our empty rooms
D<small>A</small>
Dayadhvam: I have heard the key
Turn in the door once and turn once only[67]
We think of the key, each in his prison
Thinking of the key, each confirms a prison
Only at nightfall, aethereal rumours
Revive for a moment a broken Coriolanus[68]
D<small>A</small>
Damyata: The boat responded
420 Gaily, to the hand expert with sail and oar
The sea was calm, your heart would have responded
Gaily, when invited, beating obedient
To controlling hands

                I sat upon the shore
Fishing,[69] with the arid plain behind me

---

[63] Ganga: The Ganges River in India.

[64] Himavant: The Himalaya Mountains.

[65] *Datta . . . Damyata:* The words *datta* (give), l. 402; *dayadhvam* (sympathize), l. 412; and *damyata* (control), l. 419. According to the Brihadaranyaka Upanishads (c. 900–800 B.C.E.), the thunder god Prajapati commands that humans practice charity, sympathy, and self-control as a spiritual exercise. Apparently Eliot saw this as a redemptive or cleansing activity.

[66] memories . . . spider: Compare Webster, *The White Devil,* V, vi: "They'll remarry / . . . ere the spider / Make a thin curtain for your epitaphs."

[67] I have . . . once only: Compare Dante, *The Inferno,* 33, 46–47: "And I heard them below locking the door / Of the horrible tower," from Count Ugolino's story of being locked in a tower to starve, along with his children.

[68] Coriolanus: That is, a tyrant, possibly a betrayer.

[69] Fishing: The Fisher King of the Grail legend, in whose voice the poem ends.

Shall I at last set my lands in order?[70]
London Bridge is falling down falling down falling down
Poi s'ascose nel foco che gli affina[71]
Quando fiam uti chelidon—O swallow swallow[72]
460   *Le Prince d'Aquitaine à la tour abolie*[73]
These fragments I have shored against my ruins
Why then Ile fit you. Hieronymo's mad againe.[74]
Datta. Dayadhvam. Damyata.

       Shantih   shantih   shantih[75]

---

[70] set . . . order?: Isaiah 38:1, "Set thine house in order, for thou shalt die and not live."

[71] *Poi . . . affina: The Purgatorio,* 26, 48, "Then he hid himself in the purifying fire." The poet Arnaut Daniel leaves Dante, imploring him to remember his suffering.

[72] O . . . swallow: "When will I be like the swallow?" Eliot cites "The Vigil of Venus," a late Latin poem in which Philomela is turned into a swallow, and also the story of Philomela in parts II and III of *The Waste Land.*

[73] *Le Prince . . . abolie:* "The prince of Aquitaine at the ruined tower," from a sonnet by the symbolist poet Gerard de Nerval, "El Desdichado" (1854). The disinherited prince is expressing "the black sun of melancholy."

[74] Ile fit . . . againe: See Thomas Kyd, *The Spanish Tragedy* (1594). Hieronymo "fits" (serves) his enemies by writing a play for them that exposes their crimes, then revenging himself upon them.

[75] shantih: Repeated as here, a formal ending to an Upanishad. "The Peace which passeth understanding" is our equivalent to this word (E).

War, Conflict, and Resistance

The twentieth century will be remembered as one of the bloodiest in the history of mankind. Among other disasters, two great "world" wars swept through Europe and parts of Asia and Africa and drew the United States into the fighting, ultimately threatening European influence around the globe. The First World War is said to have killed off an entire generation of European men and the Second World War, in some ways a continuation of the first, decimated civilian populations with aerial bombing and culminated in the nuclear destruction of two Japanese cities, Hiroshima and Nagasaki, at the hands of the United States. Moreover, the century was rife with civil war, revolution, wars against colonial domination, and ethnic and religious conflicts. From the bloody revolutions in Mexico (1910–1920) and Russia (1918–1920) to civil war in Spain to the fighting between Hindu India and Muslim Pakistan and between Israel and Palestine, the century was marked with violent confrontation. That so much writing of the twentieth century is, like **The Waste Land,** about war or the devastation caused by war is one testimony to the pervasiveness of the era's conflict and violence.

p. 1458

THE WORLD WARS

World War I (1914–18) was fought on two fronts: the eastern front, where scores of casualties were exacted from the Balkan states and from Russia, and the western front, where bitter trench warfare led to the slaughter of millions of soldiers from France, England, Germany, Italy, the United States, and other countries. Civilian

Mercedes Vallejo, Free Drawing, 1938
Mercedes Vallejo was just fourteen when he was wounded during the Spanish civil war. He drew this recollection of the capture of Teruel while he was being treated in the hospital. (Mandeveille Special Collections, UC San Diego)

"The blood-dimmed tide is loosed, and everywhere / The ceremony of innocence is drowned" — With these words, Yeats, in 1921, announced the dominant theme of the twentieth century's consciousness and much of its serious literature.

– DANIEL STERN,
New York Times

populations also came under attack from artillery bombardment and armies of occupation.

The Second World War (1939–45) originated in Germany and was brought about in part by the harsh surrender terms imposed on that country at the end of the First World War and in part by the racist and expansionist ambitions of German leader Adolf Hitler. Tens of millions of lives in Russia, Germany, and throughout Europe were lost. At the same time, Japan, allied with Germany, conquered China, the rest of Southeast Asia, and Burma. The United States and its allies fought Japan on the islands and at sea, in the Pacific. Aerial bombing, as in the First World War, accounted for enormous civilian casualties, this time throughout Europe, the British Isles, and Japan. Perhaps the most horrifying aspect of this war was the attempt by Nazi Germany to bring about the "Final Solution of the Jewish Question" — the planned extermination of an entire people. Some seven million Jews were murdered, most of them in Nazi concentration camps, during the course of the war.

Scene during the Siege of Teruel,
Spain. April 1, 1938
*The Spanish civil war (1936–39)
was a battle between the leftist
Republicans and Francisco
Franco's Fascists. Franco, who
was backed by Hitler and
Mussolini, ultimately won,
ruling until his death in 1975.
(Library of Congress, LC-USZ62
112445)*

THE LOST GENERATION

The two world wars marked a turning point in the consciousness of
Western Europe. At issue was the concept of Western civilization by
which Europe had justified its political and economic domination
of non-Western peoples.

The American émigré poet Ezra Pound, commenting on the
decimation of Europe as the First World War raged on, spoke of the
decline of the West:

> There died a myriad,
> And of the best, among them,
> For an old bitch gone in the teeth,
> For a botched civilization. . . .

The sense of loss and dissolution that followed the First World
War eventually grew beyond that of a generation or even Western
civilization as a whole. As T. S. Eliot asked between the wars, "After
such knowledge, what forgiveness?" And after the terror of the
Second World War, language itself seemed to falter. The ability of
authors to represent the common concerns of humanity was called
into question, as confidence in political and moral authority declined
in the West. Some writers turned from modernity to embrace one of
the world religions. Others sought relief in rebuilding their languages
and cultures from the fragments of the devastated societies of Europe
and the Far East.

Twentieth-Century Europe: Guernica

On the afternoon of April 26, 1937, twenty-five or more German bomber planes attacked the Basque town of Guernica in northeastern Spain. For three hours the planes dropped high explosive and incendiary bombs on the town. Citizens who tried to flee from the carnage were strafed from above with machine gunfire. After burning for three days, the town, the cultural capital of the Basque region of Spain, was 70 percent destroyed and sixteen hundred of its citizens (one-third of its population) were killed or wounded.

This incident, which outraged international opinion at the time, may be the most remembered episode of the Spanish civil war. The war began as a *coup d'etat* by a group of military officers led by General Francisco Franco, who sought to replace the republican government with a military dictatorship. Although the Second Spanish Republic had been established only three years earlier, the republican forces proved much stronger and more determined than the generals expected. The republican coalition of liberal democrats, socialists, trade unionists, communists, and Basque and Catalan nationalists held out for three years against Franco's fascist forces. Both sides received support from outside of Spain. The republican cause drew idealistic young men and leftists from many countries into international brigades—among them Ernest Hemingway, whose novel *For Whom the Bell Tolls* (1940) was based on his experiences there. The fascists had the support of Spanish monarchists and the Catholic Church and military aid from Hitler and Mussolini. The war in Spain gave the German Luftwaffe an opportunity to test the effectiveness of their new bombing planes and their strategy of demoralizing the enemy through intense aerial bombardment. Guernica was, in a sense, a test for the tactic of aerial bombardment that would be so important in World War II.

Guernica is remembered today, however, because of Pablo Picasso's painting *Guernica*—probably the most well-known painting of the twentieth century. When the bombing raid occurred, Picasso, then working in Paris, had already been hired to paint a mural for the Spanish pavilion at the Paris World's Fair of 1937, but he had not yet found a suitable subject. On the day that he learned of the attack, Picasso began the painting. The huge canvas—26 feet wide and 11 feet tall—was completed by mid-June, a complex composition of fragmented and tangled bodies done in stark black, white, and gray. Although its symbolism puzzled many who attended the exposition, the painting became an icon of the republican cause in Spain. Picasso refused to explain the symbolism of his painting, but he did say: "My whole life as an artist has been nothing but a continuous struggle against reaction and the death of art. In the picture I am painting—which I shall call *Guernica*—I am expressing my horror of the military which is now plundering Spain into an ocean of misery and death."

After Franco won the civil war in March 1939, Picasso declared that the painting would not go to its intended home in Spain until the fascist government was replaced with a republican one. In the meantime, the painting had a temporary home in the Museum of Modern Art in New York City, where it was housed until 1981 when, after the reestablishment of democracy in Spain, it took up residence in its native land for the first time.

Pablo Picasso, *Guernica*, 1937. *Picasso's iconic mural is housed in the permanent collection of the Museo Reina Sophia, Spain's national museum of art. (The Art Archive)*

THEMES AND PERSPECTIVES

The First World War saw the rise of the machine, an increased use of artillery, and the failed strategy of trench warfare, in addition to the utter dehumanization of the soldiers who were injured and killed by these "advances" in the art of war. The idealism of those sent to fight, many of them college trained and well read in the classics, was shattered along the nearly stationary western front that ran from Belgium to Switzerland, where their comrades didn't simply fall to the ground and die but were sent flying through the air or were exploded where they stood. Many poets, like young p. 1485 Englishman **Wilfred Owen,** died in battle, leaving behind a poetic legacy of disillusionment and despair. Using the biblical story of Abraham and Isaac, Owen attacked his father's generation who sacrificed their sons, "half the seed of Europe," in the war. Similarly disillusioned by the Russo-Japanese War (1904–05), Japanese writer p. 1484 **Yosano Akiko** begs her brother not to fight. A whole generation of antiwar writers emerged from the disillusioning conflicts at the beginning of the century.

In the period "between the two wars," as a French phrase puts it, writers warned in vain of what was still to come, trying to rouse an already battered humanity to confront evil where it first appeared.

British Soldiers with Gas Masks
This image from World War I illustrates one of the terrors of the new warfare. (© Hulton-Deutsch Collection/ CORBIS)

German novelist **Erich Maria Remarque** recalled the horror of
trench warfare in *All Quiet on the Western Front* (1929), and Bertolt
Brecht, a German socialist poet and playwright, warned his countrymen of the coming of "the house painter," his contemptuous term for
the future dictator Adolf Hitler. Those and other premonitions went
unheeded or were heard too late.

EH-rik muh-REE-uh
ruh-MARK

WAR ACROSS THE WORLD

The formerly mostly exclusive role of the writer changed somewhat
in the Second World War. Although some were soldiers who still
wrote of battles, World War II spared precious few of its experience;
often it was the ordinary citizen who wrote of the destruction of
cities or of being in hiding or of surviving the Holocaust. Those
closest to the suffering remembered it in later years in their poems,
sometimes living only long enough to finish the work of recording
the horror of Nazi extermination. **Nellie Sachs,** a survivor of both
world wars, struggled to write down her memories of the death
camps of World War II. **Paul Celan,** whose parents died in the death

p. 1497

p. 1498

Franciszek Jazwieki,
Portrait of an
Unknown Prisoner,
1942–43. Pencil and
Crayon on
Cardboard
*Jazwieki, a prisoner
in Auschwitz, the
horrendous
concentration camp
in Poland, completed
over one hundred
portraits of his fellow
prisoners between
1942 and 1945. Note
the prisoner number
visible in this portrait.
(Courtesy of the
Auschwitz-Birkenau
State Museum)*

Holocaust Survivors at Buchenwald *This photograph was taken at the Buchenwald concentration camp upon its liberation by U.S. troops. The Nobel Prize–winning author Elie Wiesel can be seen on the right of the center bunk. (© Bettmann/ CORBIS)*

camps, finished writing of his experiences at the hands of the Nazis only to commit suicide when his work was done. With terrible irony the war had democratized suffering and death, bringing it home to the people of more than half the world.

People lost a fundamental trust in the outcome of human action. The enormity of the Holocaust and the nightmarish destruction wrought by nuclear weapons dwarfed the human perspective even further. The poetry that was written at this time struggled to recover its grounding in language. **Tamura Ryuichi,** a leading poet of Japan and a foe of Japanese militarism, borrowed the idea from T. S. Eliot that the modern world was a wasteland consisting of fragments among the ruins. For Polish Nobelist **Wislawa Szymborska,** the postwar world was one in which terrorists blew up pubs on a Saturday evening and in which the scale of things had become inverted. Russian poet **Andrei Voznesensky,** celebrating the victory of the Soviet Union over the German invaders, becomes a latter-day Goya, the Spanish artist whose etchings "Disasters of War" shocked sensibilities in the early nineteenth century.

tah-MOO-rah
ree-oo-EE-chee

vis-WAH-vah
shim-BORE-skah

VUZ-nih-SYEN-skee

VIETNAM

For Americans the world wars were triumphs. The United States entered the First World War late enough to escape much of the dev-astation that decimated the armies of Europe; the victories of the Second World War, though attained through great sacrifice, had brought down the evil Nazi regime and saved at least some of the world for democracy. The Vietnam War, however, brought home to Americans the disillusionment experienced by Europeans in the earlier conflicts. An undeclared war without clear objectives, the fighting in Vietnam divided the United States and ended with retreat rather than victory. Tim O'Brien, a veteran of the war and the American writer who has proved most able to express the mixed feelings prompted by it, describes the reaction of an American recruit to having killed for the first time in the short story **"The Man I Killed."** Like a moving passage from Remarque's *All Quiet on the Western Front,* in which a German soldier recognizes his common humanity with the Frenchman he has slain, O'Brien's soldier imagines the life of the young Vietnamese man whose corpse lay before him.

p. 1506

PALESTINE AND ISRAEL

In the wake of the Holocaust, Western powers took the lead in responding to demands for a Jewish state. A United Nations

American Troops Wading across River, Ben Khe, South Vietnam, 1965
American troops in Vietnam were fighting in terrain previously unknown to them. In addition to challenging topographical elements and weather conditions, Americans were fighting an enemy they couldn't actually see most of the time and for reasons that became increasingly unclear. (© Bettmann/CORBIS)

commission in 1948, which overruled the objections of the Palestinians and neighboring Arab states, divided Palestine into two parts, a Jewish region and a Palestinian one. The turmoil that has ensued led to the first of several wars between the new state of Israel and its Arab neighbors. A war in 1948 left Palestine with even less land than the partition had proposed and left many Palestinians refugees living in crowded camps in surrounding countries or in exile elsewhere in the world. Several wars between Israel and Middle Eastern Arab countries have erupted since, each ending in Palestinian defeat and deepened resentment.

fah-DWAH too-KAHN;
p. 1510

For dispossessed Palestinians, loss of their land is a great hardship, as is seen in the poems of **Fadwa Tuqan.** In "**Song of Becoming**" Tuqan writes of schoolboys who once played games and flew kites in the wind but who grew up and became angry and, finally, gave their

p. 1512

lives to martyrdom. **Mahmoud Darwish,** a Palestinian of a later generation than Tuqan, may be one of those boys. His response to the situation is resistance rather than despair. In his eyes, the land is sodden with the blood of forty-nine villagers slain by Israeli troops, and he issues the warning, "Beware of my anger," after he catalogs the humiliations inflicted on the colonized Palestinians as they

yeh-HOO-duh
ah-mee-CHIGH

pass through Israeli checkpoints. **Yehuda Amichai,** Israel's most prominent poet, also writes about schoolchildren. Acknowledging

**Israeli Soldiers by the
Dome of the Rock,
1967**
*Israeli soldiers
celebrate the capture
of Old Jerusalem from
the Jordanians in the
Six Day War. They
cheer in front of the
Dome of the Rock,
a mosque sacred
to all Muslims.
(© Bettmann/
CORBIS)*

the human toll on both sides of the warfare, Amichai laments kindergartners who will grow up in a world without pity.

TIANANMEN SQUARE

In 1989, when the People's Army crushed the student movement that was demonstrating for democratic reforms in Tiananmen Square, in Beijing, hundreds of students were killed and many more imprisoned or driven into exile. On the banners carried by protesters in the square were passages from the poetry of **Bei Dao,** a leading writer in the democracy movement who had earlier gone into exile in the West. In poems like "**Declaration,**" Bei Dao gives expression to the hopes and later the disillusionment of those in the People's Republic of China who sought democratic reform.

bay DOW

p. 1517

■ **FURTHER RESEARCH**

Anthologies

Eberhart, Richard, and Selden Rodman, eds. *War and the Poet.* 1945.
Forché, Carolyn, ed. *Against Forgetting: Twentieth-Century Poetry of Witness.* 1993.
Silkin, Jon, ed. *The Penguin Book of First World War Poetry.* 1981.
Stallworthy, Jon. *The Oxford Book of War Poetry.* 1984.

Criticism and Comment

Cohen, J. M. *Poets of This Age: 1908–1965.* 1966.
Fussell, Paul. *The Great War and Modern Memory.* 1975.
Hamburger, Michael. *The Truth of Poetry.* 1982.

■ **PRONUNCIATION**

Yehuda Amichai: yeh-HOO-duh ah-mee-CHIGH
Bei Dao: bay DOW
Erich Maria Remarque: EH-rik muh-REE-uh ruh-MARK
Wislawa Szymborska: vis-WAH-vah shim-BORE-skah
Tamura Ryuichi: tah-MOO-rah ree-oo-EE-chee
Fadwa Tuqan: fah-DWAH too-KAHN
Voznesensky: vuz-nih-SYEN-skee

YOSANO AKIKO
B. JAPAN, 1878–1942

Feminist poet, critic, translator, and teacher, Yosano Akiko shocked audiences at the beginning of the twentieth century with her frankly sensual poetry, published in her first collection *Tangled Hair* (1901). The wife of poet and literary editor Yosano Tekkan and the mother of eleven children, she published several more volumes of poetry, social commentaries, and an autobiographical novel, *Akarumi e* (*To the Light*). "I Beg You, Brother: Do Not Die," published in 1904 during the Russo-Japanese War, is the best-known Japanese antiwar poem of the twentieth century. Addressed to her brother Chūzaburō, a soldier in the Japanese army, the poem angered many of her contemporaries who considered it unpatriotic.

I Beg You, Brother: Do Not Die

Translated by Jay Rubin

Oh my little brother, I weep for you
And beg you: do not die —
You, last-born and most beloved.
Did our parents
Put a blade into your hand
And teach you to kill men?
"Kill men and die in battle," did they say
And raise you so 'til twenty-four?

It is you who are to carry on the name
You who are to be master of
This proud, old merchant house.
I beg you: do not die.
What concern is it of yours
If the Russian fortress[1] falls or stands?
Of this, the merchant household code
Says nothing.

I beg you: do not die.
His Imperial Majesty — he himself —

10

---
[1] Russian fortress: Port Arthur, a Russian naval base in China.

20 Enters not the field of battle.
So vast and deep his sacred heart:
He cannot wish for you to spill
Your own blood and another's,
To die the death of beasts,
To think such death is glory!

Oh my little brother
I beg you: do not die in battle.
To add to mother's grief
When she lost father this autumn past,
They took her son
30 And left her to protect the house.
I hear of "peace" in this great Emperor's reign,
And yet our mother's hair grows ever whiter.

Your pliant, young bride crouches weeping
In the shadows of the shop curtains.
Do you think of her, or have you forgotten?
Imagine the heart of this sweet girl—
Not ten months were you together!
Who else has she in all the world
To care for her but you?
40 I beg you, brother: do not die.

❧ WILFRED OWEN
B. ENGLAND, 1893–1918

The English poet Wilfred Owen is generally regarded as the great national poet of his generation. Owen's life was tragically cut short on the battlefield. He saw World War I from a soldier's point of view and related it in matter-of-fact, public language to his countrymen. He rejected the idealism of upper-class British schoolboys who had studied war from Latin authors. Thus he calls the prescription of Horace, "Dulce et decorum est pro patria mori," the "old Lie."

∾ Dulce et Decorum Est[1]

Bent double, like old beggars under sacks,
Knock-kneed, coughing like hags, we cursed through sludge,
Till on the haunting flares we turned our backs
And towards our distant rest began to trudge.
Men marched asleep. Many had lost their boots
But limped on, blood-shod. All went lame; all blind;
Drunk with fatigue; deaf even to the hoots
Of tired, outstripped Five-Nines[2] that dropped behind.

Gas! Gas![3] Quick, boys! — An ecstasy of fumbling,
Fitting the clumsy helmets just in time;
But someone still was yelling out and stumbling,
And flound'ring like a man in fire or lime . . .
Dim, through the misty panes[4] and thick green light,
As under a green sea, I saw him drowning.

In all my dreams, before my helpless sight,
He plunges at me, guttering, choking, drowning.

If in some smothering dreams you too could pace
Behind the wagon that we flung him in,
And watch the white eyes writhing in his face,
His hanging face, like a devil's sick of sin;
If you could hear, at every jolt, the blood
Come gargling from the froth-corrupted lungs,
Obscene as cancer, bitter as the cud
Of vile, incurable sores on innocent tongues, —
My friend, you would not tell with such high zest
To children ardent for some desperate glory,
The old Lie: Dulce et decorum est
Pro patria mori.

---

[1] Dulce et Decorum Est: The beginning of a line from Horace, which in full means "Sweet and fitting it is to die for your country."

[2] Five-Nines: 5.9 inch–caliber shells.

[3] Gas! Gas!: Poison gas, usually mustard gas, was commonly used in trench warfare in World War I.

[4] the misty panes: The cloudy eye lenses on the gas mask.

∾ The Parable of the Old Man and the Young[1]

So Abram rose, and clave the wood, and went,
And took the fire with him, and a knife.
And as they sojourned both of them together,
Isaac the first-born spake and said, My Father,
Behold the preparations, fire and iron,
But where the lamb for this burnt-offering?
Then Abram bound the youth with belts and straps,
And builded parapets and trenches there,
And stretchèd forth the knife to slay his son.
When lo! an angel called him out of heaven,
Saying, Lay not thy hand upon the lad,
Neither do anything to him. Behold,
A ram, caught in a thicket by its horns;
Offer the Ram of Pride instead of him.
But the old man would not so, but slew his son,
And half the seed of Europe, one by one.

10

---

[1] Based on the biblical story of Abraham and Isaac, Genesis 22.

∾ ANNA AKHMATOVA
B. RUSSIA, 1889–1966

Increasingly recognized as one of the greatest poets of the twentieth century, Anna **Akhmatova** was one of the leading figures in a group of Russian poets known as the ACMEISTS that included her first husband, Nikolai Gumilev (1886–1921) and Osip Mandelstam (1891–1938). They rejected what they saw as the mystifications of SYMBOLISM in favor of a poetry of linguistic clarity and precision. While other writers were killed during Stalin's regime, Akhmatova survived the postrevolutionary repression; her work is a testament to the generation of Russians whose lives span the period from just before the Russian Revolution to the post-Stalinist fifties and sixties.

ahk-MAH-tuh-vuh

Anna Akhmatova was born Anya Gorenko on June 23, 1889, in Odessa, Russia; she was the daughter of Inna Stogova and Andrei Gorenko, a well-to-do officer in the Russian merchant marine. Her father, oddly, despised the idea of having a poet in the family, so much so that, when she was seventeen, Anya took the Tatar name of her great-grandmother, Anna Akhmatova, to avoid bringing disgrace to the Gorenko name.

www For links to more information about Akhmatova, see bedford stmartins.com/ worldlitcompact.

Nathan Altman, *Portrait of Anna Akhmatova,* 1914
Akhmatova's striking physical appearance led many artists and photographers to produce her portrait. (Scala/Art Resource, NY)

> A poet is someone to whom it is impossible to give anything and from whom it is impossible to take anything away.
>
> — ANNA AKHMATOVA

Before the revolution Akhmatova published three volumes of elegiac love poetry, which were enthusiastically received, but *Anno Domini MCMXXI* (1921), published after the revolution, often strikes a foreboding tone as Akhmatova attests to the devastation of the civil war and the deterioration of politics and human rights.

From 1922 to 1940 the government effectively banned Akhmatova's poetry. In May 1934, Akhmatova witnessed the arrest of fellow poet Osip Mandelstam in Moscow; in the next year Akhmatova's third husband,

N. N. Punin (1888–1953) and her only child, Lev Gumilev (1912–1992), were arrested in the first wave of purges following the assassination of Josef Stalin's deputy, Sergei Kirov. Akhmatova petitioned Stalin successfully to have her husband and son released, but both were arrested again in 1949. Punin died in a Siberian prison camp in 1953; Akhmatova's son did not leave prison again until 1956.

With the death of Stalin in 1953, Akhmatova was restored to her rightful place as a publicly honored poet. In her last years she was again able to publish her work with a minimal degree of censorship, and she was elected to the presidium of the Writer's Union.

Requiem (1963) is a cycle of poems reflecting on the grave suffering of the Russian people during Josef Stalin's Great Terror of the late 1930s. A modern epic comparable to T. S. Eliot's *The Waste Land,* the poem is a series of short lyric and narrative verses written in a variety of forms that record Akhmatova's stages of grieving for the loss of her husband and son framed by a Dedication, Prologue, and two Epilogues. Invoking classical and religious myth, *Requiem* transcends the personal and serves as a testimony of all who lost family members to exile, imprisonment, or execution during Stalin's regime, which lasted from the late 1920s until his death in 1953. In Part 10, Crucifixion, a grieving mother, who stands for all the women waiting in line for a glimpse of their loved ones through the prison windows, identifies with Mary witnessing the death of Jesus. Similarly Epilogue II alludes to the myth of Niobe, who turned into a weeping statue on Mount Sipylus after her children are slain by Apollo and Artemis. Through these figures, the poem becomes transhistorical, pointing to the tragedy that is human history.

> Akhmatova's poetry ranks with the best of world poetry: Her works concluded the classical period of nineteenth-century Russian literature and served as a foundation and one of the main components of the new art. Her life gave to her contemporaries a model of dignity, loyalty, courage, and strength which people can discover within themselves during times of hardship. Her existence proved that a fragile, lonely person — who could have led a life burdened by vulnerability and helplessness — can achieve heroic stature.
>
> – ANATOLY NAIMAN, critic, 1992

❧ Requiem

Translated by Judith Hemschemeyer

No, not under the vault of alien skies,[1]
And not under the shelter of alien wings—
I was with my people then,
There, where my people, unfortunately, were.

---

[1] **vault . . . skies:** An allusion to Alexander Pushkin's "Message to Siberia."

INSTEAD OF A PREFACE

In the terrible years of the Yezhov terror,[2] I spent seventeen months in the prison lines of Leningrad.[3] Once, someone "recognized" me. Then a woman with bluish lips standing behind me, who, of course, had never heard me called by name before, woke up from the stupor to which everyone had succumbed and whispered in my ear (everyone spoke in whispers there):

"Can you describe this?"

And I answered: "Yes, I can."

Then something that looked like a smile passed over what had once been her face.

DEDICATION

Mountains bow down to this grief,
Mighty rivers cease to flow,
But the prison gates hold firm,
And behind them are the "prisoners' burrows"
And mortal woe.
For someone a fresh breeze blows,
For someone the sunset luxuriates—
We wouldn't know, we are those who everywhere
Hear only the rasp of the hateful key
And the soldiers' heavy tread.
We rose as if for an early service,
Trudged through the savaged capital
And met there, more lifeless than the dead;
The sun is lower and the Neva[4] mistier,
But hope keeps singing from afar.
The verdict . . . And her tears gush forth,
Already she is cut off from the rest,
As if they painfully wrenched life from her heart,
As if they brutally knocked her flat,
But she goes on . . . Staggering . . . Alone . . .
Where now are my chance friends
Of those two diabolical years?
What do they imagine is in Siberia's storms,

---

[2] **Yezhov terror:** Nikolai Yezhov (1895–1939) was chief of Stalin's secret police from 1936 to 1938, during the Purge, or Terror.

[3] **I spent . . . Leningrad:** Akhmatova's son, Lev Gumilev, had been imprisoned in Leningrad.

[4] **Neva:** The river that flows through Leningrad.

What appears to them dimly in the circle of the moon?
I am sending my farewell greeting to them.

PROLOGUE

40

That was when the ones who smiled
Were the dead, glad to be at rest.
And like a useless appendage, Leningrad
Swung from its prisons.
And when, senseless from torment,
Regiments of convicts marched,
And the short songs of farewell
Were sung by locomotive whistles.
The stars of death stood above us
And innocent Russia writhed

50

Under bloody boots
And under the tires of the Black Marias.[5]

1

They led you[6] away at dawn,
I followed you, like a mourner,
In the dark front room the children were crying,
By the icon shelf the candle was dying.
On your lips was the icon's chill.
The deathly sweat on your brow . . . Unforgettable! —
I will be like the wives of the Streltsy,[7]
Howling under the Kremlin towers.

2

60

Quietly flows the quiet Don,[8]
Yellow moon slips into a home.

He slips in with cap askew,
He sees a shadow, yellow moon.

---

[5] **Black Marias:** Cars used to conduct convicts to prison.

[6] **you:** Nikolai Punin, Akhmatova's third husband, who was arrested in 1935.

[7] **the Streltsy:** An elite troop who mutinied against Peter the Great in 1698; their wives pleaded in vain under the "Kremlin towers" as nearly 2,500 of the men were executed.

[8] **Don:** One of the major rivers of Russia; it flows south into the Sea of Azov.

This woman is ill,
This woman is alone,

Husband in the grave,[9] son in prison,
Say a prayer for me.

3

No, it is not I, it is somebody else who is suffering.
I would not have been able to bear what happened,
70   Let them shroud it in black,
And let them carry off the lanterns . . .
                                        Night.

4

You should have been shown, you mocker,
Minion of all your friends,
Gay little sinner of Tsarskoe Selo,
What would happen in your life —
How three-hundredth in line, with a parcel,
You would stand by the Kresty prison,[10]
Your fiery tears
80   Burning through the New Year's ice.
Over there the prison poplar bends,
And there's no sound — and over there how many
Innocent lives are ending now . . .

5

For seventeen months I've been crying out,
Calling you home.
I flung myself at the hangman's feet,
You are my son and my horror.
Everything is confused forever,
And it's not clear to me
90   Who is a beast now, who is a man,
And how long before the execution.
And there are only dusty flowers,
And the chinking of the censer, and tracks
From somewhere to nowhere.

---

[9] Husband . . . grave: Her first husband, Nikolai Gumilev, who was executed in 1921.

[10] Kresty prison: The Leningrad prison where her son was held.

And staring me straight in the eyes,
And threatening impending death,
Is an enormous star.[11]

6

The light weeks will take flight,
I won't comprehend what happened.
100 Just as the white nights[12]
Stared at you, dear son, in prison,
So they are staring again,
With the burning eyes of a hawk,
Talking about your lofty cross,
And about death.

7. THE SENTENCE[13]

And the stone word fell
On my still-living breast.
Never mind, I was ready.
I will manage somehow.

110 Today I have so much to do:
I must kill memory once and for all,
I must turn my soul to stone,
I must learn to live again—

Unless . . . Summer's ardent rustling
Is like a festival outside my window.
For a long time I've foreseen this
Brilliant day, deserted house.

8. TO DEATH

You will come in any case—so why not now?
I am waiting for you—I can't stand much more.
120 I've put out the light and opened the door
For you, so simple and miraculous.
So come in any form you please,
Burst in as a gas shell

---

[11] **Who is a beast . . . star:** The apocalyptic imagery here derives in part from Revelation 8:10–12 and 9:7–11.

[12] **white nights:** Leningrad is far enough north that in the summer it never becomes completely dark.

[13] **The Sentence:** This section is dated on the day of her son's sentencing to labor camp, June 22, 1939.

Or, like a gangster, steal in with a length of pipe,
Or poison me with typhus fumes.
Or be that fairy tale you've dreamed up.
So sickeningly familiar to everyone—
In which I glimpse the top of a pale blue cap
And the house attendant white with fear.
130   Now it doesn't matter anymore. The Yenisey[14] swirls,
The North Star shines.
And the final horror dims
The blue luster of beloved eyes.

9

Now madness half shadows
My soul with its wing,
And makes it drunk with fiery wine
And beckons toward the black ravine.

And I've finally realized
That I must give in,
140   Overhearing myself
Raving as if it were somebody else.

And it does not allow me to take
Anything of mine with me
(No matter how I plead with it,
No matter how I supplicate):

Not the terrible eyes of my son—
Suffering turned to stone,
Not the day of the terror,
Not the hour I met with him in prison,

150   Not the sweet coolness of his hands,
Not the trembling shadow of the lindens,
Not the far-off, fragile sound—
Of the final words of consolation.

10. CRUCIFIXION

*"Do not weep for Me, Mother,
I am in the grave."*[15]

---

[14] The Yenisey: A river in Siberia, along which were located many concentration camps.

[15] *"Do not . . . grave"*: A refrain from a Russian Orthodox prayer sung during the Easter or Holy Week service.

1

A choir of angels sang the praises of that momentous hour,
And the heavens dissolved in fire.
To his Father He said: "Why hast Thou forsaken me!"[16]
And to his Mother: "Oh, do not weep for Me . . ."

2

Mary Magdalene beat her breast and sobbed,
The beloved disciple turned to stone,
But where the silent Mother stood, there
No one glanced and no one would have dared.

160

EPILOGUE I

I learned how faces fall,
How terror darts from under eyelids,
How suffering traces lines
Of stiff cuneiform on cheeks,
How locks of ashen-blonde or black
Turn silver suddenly,
Smiles fade on submissive lips
And fear trembles in a dry laugh.
And I pray not for myself alone,
But for all those who stood there with me
In cruel cold, and in July's heat,
At that blind, red wall.

170

EPILOGUE II

Once more the day of remembrance[17] draws near.
I see, I hear, I feel you:

The one they almost had to drag at the end,
And the one who tramps her native land no more,

And the one who, tossing her beautiful head,
Said: "Coming here's like coming home."

I'd like to name them all by name,
But the list has been confiscated and is nowhere to be found.

180

---

[16] **"Why . . . me!"**: Jesus' last words according to Matthew 27:46.

[17] **day of remembrance**: Literally translated, this line refers to Remembrance Day, a memorial service of
Russian Orthodox Church held one year after a person's death.

I have woven a wide mantle for them
From their meager, overheard words.

I will remember them always and everywhere,
I will never forget them no matter what comes.

And if they gag my exhausted mouth
Through which a hundred million scream,

Then may the people remember me
On the eve of my remembrance day.

190 And if ever in this country
They decide to erect a monument to me,

I consent to that honor
Under these conditions — that it stand

Neither by the sea, where I was born:
My last tie with the sea is broken,

Nor in the tsar's garden near the cherished pine stump,[18]
Where an inconsolable shade looks for me,

But here, where I stood for three hundred hours,
And where they never unbolted the doors for me

200 This, lest in blissful death
I forget the rumbling of the Black Marias,

Forget how that detested door slammed shut
And an old woman howled like a wounded animal.

And may the melting snow stream like tears
From my motionless lids of bronze,[19]

And a prison dove coo in the distance,
And the ships of the Neva sail calmly on.

---

[18] **Nor . . . pine stump:** Alluding to her childhood, when she had taken walks around Tsarkoe Selo, the site of some of her fondest memories, including those of her first husband.

[19] **motionless lids of bronze:** The children of Niobe, the daughter of Tantalus, were slain by Artemis and Apollo after Niobe had offended their mother, Leto. Niobe turned into a weeping statue that has become a classic symbol of maternal grief.

❧ NELLIE SACHS
B. GERMANY, 1891–1970

Nellie Sachs, a German Jew, survived Nazi persecution and emigrated to
Sweden in the late 1930s. Her first book of poems had been published
before the Nazi takeover; she spent her later life as a translator while
writing about the Holocaust and won the Nobel Prize in literature in 1966.
"O the Chimneys" remembers the ovens in the extermination camps.

❧ O the Chimneys

Translated by Michael Roloff

And though after my skin worms destroy this body, yet in my flesh shall I see God.
— JOB 19:26

O the chimneys
On the ingeniously devised habitations of death
When Israel's body drifted as smoke
Through the air —
Was welcomed by a star, a chimney sweep,
A star that turned black
Or was it a ray of sun?

O the chimneys!
Freedomway for Jeremiah and Job's dust —
Who devised you and laid stone upon stone
The road for refugees of smoke

O the habitations of death,
Invitingly appointed
For the host who used to be a guest —
O you fingers
Laying the threshold
Like a knife between life and death —

O you chimneys,
O you fingers
And Israel's body as smoke through the air!

PAUL CELAN

B. ROMANIA, 1920–1970

Paul Celan was born Paul Antschel in Romania in 1920, the son of German-speaking Jews. After medical studies in France, he returned to Romania in 1939 where he taught Romance languages. In 1940, when political control of the area passed from the Russians to the Nazis and the Romanian Fascists, Celan's mother and father were arrested and placed in a Nazi concentration camp where they both died; Paul himself was freed from a forced labor camp in 1944. After 1948, Celan lived in Paris until he drowned himself in the Seine when he was fifty. He wrote his poetry—most of it about the trauma he, his countrymen, and other Jews had experienced in World War II—in a broken, nearly hysterical language reminiscent of the work of German expressionist poet August Stramm. Celan was chief among those who raised the question of whether German could again be a literary language after the war. "Death Fugue," with its repetition of unrelated lines and phrases, is a haunting evocation of the state of postwar European society. Translator John Felstiner calls the haunting image that opens the poem, the "Black milk of daybreak," the best-known lines in Celan's poetry since they evoke the bleakness of the Holocaust turning light to darkness. In his version of the poem, Felstiner enhances the traumatic repetitions by leaving some of them, especially at the end, in the original German, suggesting that one can never forget so painful a past.

Death Fugue

Translated by John Felstiner

Black milk of daybreak we drink it at evening
we drink it at midday and morning we drink it at night
we drink and we drink
we shovel a grave in the air there you won't lie too cramped
A man lives in the house he plays with his vipers he writes
he writes when it grows dark to Deutschland° your golden hair   Germany
    Marguerite[1]
he writes it and steps out of doors and the stars are all sparkling
      he whistles his hounds to come close

---

[1] **golden hair Marguerite:** Allusions to the heroine of Goethe's *Faust* and Heinrich Heine's golden-haired Lorelei, two familiar symbols of the feminine in classic German literature.

he whistles his Jews into rows has them shovel a grave in the ground
he orders us strike up and play for the dance

Black milk of daybreak we drink you at night
we drink you at morning and midday we drink you at evening
we drink and we drink
A man lives in the house he plays with his vipers he writes
he writes when it grows dark to Deutschland your golden hair Marguerite
your ashen hair Shulamith[2] we shovel a grave in the air
                          there you won't lie too cramped
He shouts jab this earth deeper you lot there you others sing up and play
he grabs for the rod in his belt he swings it his eyes are blue

jab your spades deeper you lot there you others play on for the dancing

Black milk of daybreak we drink you at night
we drink you at midday and morning we drink you at evening
we drink and we drink
a man lives in the house your goldenes Haar Marguerite
your aschenes Haar Shulamith he plays with his vipers
He shouts play death more sweetly Death is a master from Deutschland
he shouts scrape your strings darker you'll rise then in smoke to the sky
you'll have a grave then in the clouds there you won't lie too cramped

Black milk of daybreak we drink you at night

we drink you at midday Death is a master aus Deutschland
we drink you at evening and morning we drink and we drink
this Death is ein Meister aus Deutschland his eye it is blue
he shoots you with shot made of lead shoots you level and true
a man lives in the house your goldenes Haar Margarete
he looses his hounds on us grants us a grave in the air
he plays with his vipers and daydreams
                     der Tod ist ein Meister aus Deutschland
dein goldenes Haar Margarete
dein aschenes Haar Shulamith

---

[2] **ashen hair Shulamith:** The "black and comely" princess in the Song of Songs in the Hebrew Scriptures, often seen as a symbol of the Jewish people.

TAMURA RYUICHI

B. JAPAN, 1923–1998

Tamura Ryuichi was first exposed to English and American literary culture while attending high school in Tokyo, just before the outbreak of World War II. He attempted to avoid the draft by entering university but was conscripted in 1943. When he returned to Tokyo, a city devastated by aerial bombing, he found work as an editor and helped establish a literary group named "The Waste Land" after the poem by T. S. Eliot. Tamura's war experience informs part of a highly ambitious body of work that has won him world recognition. "A Vertical Coffin" addresses, much in the spirit of Eliot and Ezra Pound, civilization as a whole.

A Vertical Coffin

Translated by Samuel Grolmes and Tsumura Yumiko

I

Do not touch my corpse with your hands
Your hands
cannot touch "death"
As for my corpse
mix it in the crowd
let the rain fall on it

    We do not have hands
    We do not have hands that should touch death

I know the windows of the city
10   I know the windows where there is no one
No matter what city I go to
you have never been inside the room
Marriage and work
passion and sleep   and even death too
are chased out of your rooms
and become unemployed like you are

    We do not have a profession
    We do not have a profession that should touch death

I know the rain in the city
20   I know that crowd of umbrellas

No matter what city I go to
you have never been under the roof
Value and belief
revolution and hope   and even life
were kicked out from under your roof
and became unemployed like you are

    We do not have a profession
    We do not have a profession that should touch life

II

Do not let my corpse sleep on the ground
30 Your death
cannot rest on the ground
As for my corpse
put it in a vertical coffin
and let it stand up

    There is no grave on the earth for us
    There is no grave on the earth to put our corpses in
I know death on the earth
I know the meaning of death on the earth
No matter what country I go to
40 your death has never been put into a grave
The young girls' corpses go floating down the river
The blood of a small bird that was shot to death   and man voices that
      were slaughtered
have been chased out of your earth
and will become an exile like you are

    There is no country on the earth for us
    There is no country on the earth worth our deaths

I know the value of this earth
I know the lost value of the earth
No matter what country I go to
50 your life has never been fulfilled with great things
The wheat that was mowed as far as into the future
the trapped beasts   also little sisters
are chased out of your lives
become exiles like you are

    There is no country on the earth for us
    There is no country on the earth worth our lives

III

Do not burn my corpse in the fire
Your deaths
cannot be burned with fire
60   As for my corpse
hang it inside civilization
Let it rot

        We do not have fire
        We do not have a fire which should burn a corpse

I know your civilization
I know your civilization that has neither love nor death
No matter which house I go to
you have never been with a family
A father's single tear
70   the painful joy of a mother delivering a baby   and even the matter
            of heart
was chased out of your houses
became sick people like you are

        We do not have love
        We have nothing but the love of a sick person

I know your hospital rooms
I know your dreams that continue from bed to bed
No matter what hospital room I go to
you have never been really asleep
Drooping hands from the bed
80   eyes that were opened by great things   also thirsty hearts
are chased out of your hospital rooms
become sick people like you are

        We do not have poison
        We do not have a poison to heal us

WISLAWA SZYMBORSKA
B. POLAND, 1923

Wislawa Szymborska, a self-described private person, has spent her whole life in western Poland, where she was born, attended school, and has worked for nearly thirty years as a columnist and poetry editor for the literary magazine *Zycie Literacia.* In spite of her differences with the Communist regime in Poland and her disillusionment with its aims, she was able to publish sixteen volumes of poetry and several volumes of essays during the Communist era. Accepting the Nobel Prize in 1996, she remarked, "inspiration is not the exclusive privilege of poets or artists generally. There is, has been, and will always be a certain group of people whom inspiration visits. It's made up of all who've consciously chosen their calling and do their job with love and imagination." The humility in this statement is also apparent in Szymborska's poems, which treat big events with modest matter-of-factness and quiet irony.

The Terrorist, He Watches

Translated by Robert A. Maguire and Magnus Jan Krynski

The bomb will go off in the bar at one twenty p.m.
Now it's only one sixteen p.m.
Some will still have time to get in,
some to get out.

The terrorist has already crossed to the other side of the street.
The distance protects him from any danger,
and what a sight for sore eyes:

A woman in a yellow jacket, she goes in.
A man in dark glasses, he comes out.
Guys in jeans, they are talking.
One seventeen and four seconds.
That shorter guy's really got it made, and gets on a scooter,
and that taller one, he goes in.

One seventeen and forty seconds.
That girl there, she's got a green ribbon in her hair.
Too bad that bus just cut her off.
One eighteen p.m.
The girl's not there any more.

10

Was she dumb enough to go in, or wasn't she?
20   That we'll see when they carry them out.

One nineteen p.m.
No one seems to be going in.
Instead a fat baldy's coming out.
Like he's looking for something in his pockets and
at one nineteen and fifty seconds
he goes back for those lousy gloves of his.

It's one twenty p.m.
The time, how it drags.
Should be any moment now.
30   Not yet.
Yes, this is it.
The bomb, it goes off.

﹏ ANDREI VOZNESENSKY
B. RUSSIA, 1933

Andrei Voznesensky was first published in the Soviet *Literaturnaya Gazeta* in 1958, during the "thaw" in the cold war that lasted until 1961 under Premier Nikita Khrushchev. Voznesensky's trips to the United States with poet Yevgeni Yevtushenko and their friendship with American poets Lawrence Ferlinghetti and Allen Ginsberg helped renew cultural relations between the two countries. Voznesensky disclaimed politics as a motivating force in his work, advocating a "pure poetry" that looks "deep into the human mind, right inside the brain" and arguing that "our poetry's future lies in association, metaphors reflecting the interdependence of phenomena, their mutual transformation." Ironically, his best-known poem is patriotic. "I Am Goya" celebrates the Russian victory over the Nazis in the German invasion of the Soviet Union in August 1944 and recalls Spanish painter Francisco de Goya (1746–1828), whose images of slaughter and resistance dignified the situation of the peasantry in the Napoleonic Wars at the beginning of the nineteenth century.

❧ I Am Goya

Translated by Stanley Kunitz

I am Goya[1]
of the bare field, by the enemy's beak gouged
till the craters of my eyes gape
I am grief

I am the tongue
of war, the embers of cities
on the snows of the year 1941
I am hunger

I am the gullet
10   of a woman hanged whose body like a bell
tolled over a blank square
I am Goya

O grapes of wrath!
I have hurled westward
                         the ashes of the uninvited guest!
and hammered stars into the unforgetting sky — like nails
I am Goya

---

[1] **Goya:** Francisco de Goya (1746–1828), Spanish artist whose etchings late in life of the horrors of war have endured in the collective European memory. [Editors' note.]

❧ TIM O'BRIEN
B. UNITED STATES, 1946

Born and raised in rural Minnesota, Tim O'Brien was drafted into the infantry in 1968 after graduating from Macalester College. Opposed to the Vietnam War, he served for two years as a foot soldier in Vietnam and was awarded the Purple Heart. After leaving the military he did graduate work at Harvard School of Government, worked as a reporter at the *Washington Post,* and has written numerous books, several of which are based on his experience in Vietnam, including the novel *Going After Cacciato* (1978), the memoir *If I Die in a Combat Zone, Box Me Up and Ship Me Home* (1973), and the volume of short stories *The Things They Carried* (1990). "The Man I Killed" comes from that collection of stories.

❧ The Man I Killed

His jaw was in his throat, his upper lip and teeth were gone, his one eye was shut, his other eye was a star-shaped hole, his eyebrows were thin and arched like a woman's, his nose was undamaged, there was a slight tear at the lobe of one ear, his clean black hair was swept upward into a cowlick at the rear of the skull, his forehead was lightly freckled, his fingernails were clean, the skin at his left cheek was peeled back in three ragged strips, his right cheek was smooth and hairless, there was a butterfly on his chin, his neck was open to the spinal cord and the blood there was thick and shiny and it was this wound that had killed him. He lay face-up in the center of the trail, a slim, dead, almost dainty young man. He had bony legs, a narrow waist, long shapely fingers. His chest was sunken and poorly muscled—a scholar, maybe. His wrists were the wrists of a child. He wore a black shirt, black pajama pants, a gray ammunition belt, a gold ring on the third finger of his right hand. His rubber sandals had been blown off. One lay beside him, the other a few meters up the trail. He had been born, maybe, in 1946 in the village of My Khe near the central coastline of Quang Ngai Province, where his parents farmed, and where his family had lived for several centuries, and where, during the time of the French, his father and two uncles and many neighbors had joined in the struggle for independence. He was not a Communist. He was a citizen and a soldier. In the village of My Khe, as in all of Quang Ngai, patriotic resistance had the force of tradition, which was partly the force of legend, and from his earliest boyhood the man I killed would have listened to stories about the heroic Trung sisters and Tran Hung Dao's famous rout of the Mongols and Le Loi's final victory against the Chinese at Tot Dong. He would have been taught that to defend the land was a man's highest duty and highest privilege. He had accepted this. It was never open to question. Secretly, though, it also frightened him. He was not a fighter. His health was poor, his body small and frail. He liked books. He wanted someday to be a teacher of mathematics. At night, lying on his mat, he could not picture himself doing the brave things his father had done, or his uncles, or the heroes of the stories. He hoped in his heart that he would never be tested. He hoped the Americans would go away. Soon, he hoped. He kept hoping and hoping, always, even when he was asleep.

"Oh, man, you fuckin' trashed the fucker," Azar said. "You scrambled his sorry self, look at that, you *did,* you laid him out like Shredded fuckin' Wheat."

"Go away," Kiowa said.

"I'm just saying the truth. Like oatmeal."

"Go," Kiowa said.

"Okay, then, I take it back," Azar said. He started to move away, then stopped and said, "Rice Krispies, you know? On the dead test, this particular individual gets A-plus."

Smiling at this, he shrugged and walked up the trail toward the village behind the trees.

Kiowa kneeled down.

"Just forget that crud," he said. He opened up his canteen and held it out for a while and then sighed and pulled it away. "No sweat, man. What else could you do?"

Later, Kiowa said, "I'm serious. Nothing *anybody* could do. Come on, stop staring."

The trail junction was shaded by a row of trees and tall brush. The slim young man lay with his legs in the shade. His jaw was in his throat. His one eye was shut and the other was a star-shaped hole.

Kiowa glanced at the body.

"All right, let me ask a question," he said. "You want to trade places with him? Turn it all upside down — you *want* that? I mean, be honest."

The star-shaped hole was red and yellow. The yellow part seemed to be getting wider, spreading out at the center of the star. The upper lip and gum and teeth were gone. The man's head was cocked at a wrong angle, as if loose at the neck, and the neck was wet with blood.

"Think it over," Kiowa said.

Then later he said, "Tim, it's a *war*. The guy wasn't Heidi — he had a weapon, right? It's a tough thing, for sure, but you got to cut out that staring."

Then he said, "Maybe you better lie down a minute."

Then after a long empty time he said, "Take it slow. Just go wherever the spirit takes you."

The butterfly was making its way along the young man's forehead, which was spotted with small dark freckles. The nose was undamaged. The skin on the right cheek was smooth and fine-grained and hairless. Frail-looking, delicately boned, the young man would not have wanted to be a soldier and in his heart would have feared performing badly in battle. Even as a boy growing up in the village of My Khe, he had often worried about this. He imagined covering his head and lying in a deep hole and closing his eyes and not moving until the war was over. He had no stomach for violence. He loved mathematics. His eyebrows were thin and arched like a woman's, and at school the boys sometimes teased him about how pretty he was, the arched eyebrows and long shapely fingers, and on the playground they mimicked a woman's walk and made fun of his smooth skin and his love for mathematics. The young man could not make himself fight them. He often wanted to, but he was afraid, and this increased his shame. If he could not fight little boys, he thought, how could he ever become a soldier and fight the Americans with their airplanes and helicopters and bombs? It did not seem possible. In the presence of his father and uncles, he pretended to look forward to doing his patriotic duty, which was also a privilege, but at night he prayed with his mother that the war might end soon. Beyond anything else, he was afraid of disgracing himself, and therefore his family and village. But all he could do, he thought, was wait and pray and try not to grow up too fast.

"Listen to me," Kiowa said. "You feel terrible, I know that."

Then he said, "Okay, maybe I *don't* know."

Along the trail there were small blue flowers shaped like bells. The young man's head was wrenched sideways, not quite facing the flowers, and even in the shade a single blade of sunlight sparkled against the buckle of his ammunition belt. The left cheek was peeled back in three ragged strips. The wounds at his neck had not yet clotted, which made him seem animate even in death, the blood still spreading out across his shirt.

Kiowa shook his head.

There was some silence before he said, "Stop *staring.*"

The young man's fingernails were clean. There was a slight tear at the lobe of one ear, a sprinkling of blood on the forearm. He wore a gold ring on the third finger of his right hand. His chest was sunken and poorly muscled — a scholar, maybe. His life was now a constellation of possibilities. So, yes, maybe a scholar. And for years, despite his family's poverty, the man I killed would have been determined to continue his education in mathematics. The means for this were arranged, perhaps, through the village liberation cadres, and in 1964 the young man began attending classes at the university in Saigon, where he avoided politics and paid attention to the problems of calculus. He devoted himself to his studies. He spent his nights alone, wrote romantic poems in his journal, took pleasure in the grace and beauty of differential equations. The war, he knew, would finally take him, but for the time being he would not let himself think about it. He had stopped praying; instead, now, he waited. And as he waited, in his final year at the university, he fell in love with a classmate, a girl of seventeen, who one day told him that his wrists were like the wrists of a child, so small and delicate, and who admired his narrow waist and the cowlick that rose up like a bird's tail at the back of his head. She liked his quiet manner; she laughed at his freckles and bony legs. One evening, perhaps, they exchanged gold rings.

Now one eye was a star.

"You okay?" Kiowa said.

The body lay almost entirely in shade. There were gnats at the mouth, little flecks of pollen drifting above the nose. The butterfly was gone. The bleeding had stopped except for the neck wounds.

Kiowa picked up the rubber sandals, clapping off the dirt, then bent down to search the body. He found a pouch of rice, a comb, a fingernail clipper, a few soiled piasters, a snapshot of a young woman standing in front of a parked motorcycle. Kiowa placed these items in his rucksack along with the gray ammunition belt and rubber sandals.

Then he squatted down.

"I'll tell you the straight truth," he said. "The guy was dead the second he stepped on the trail. Understand me? We all had him zeroed. A good kill — weapon, ammunition, everything." Tiny beads of sweat glistened at Kiowa's forehead. His eyes moved from the sky to the dead man's body to the knuckles of his own hands. "So listen, you best pull your shit together. Can't just sit here all day."

Later he said, "Understand?"

Then he said, "Five minutes, Tim. Five more minutes and we're moving out."

The one eye did a funny twinkling trick, red to yellow. His head was wrenched sideways, as if loose at the neck, and the dead young man seemed to be staring at some distant object beyond the bell-shaped flowers along the trail. The blood at the neck had gone to a deep purplish black. Clean fingernails, clean hair — he had been a soldier for only a single day. After his years at the university, the man I killed returned with his new wife to the village of My Khe, where he enlisted as a common rifleman with the 48th Vietcong Battalion. He knew he would die quickly. He knew he would see a flash of light. He knew he would fall dead and wake up in the stories of his village and people.

Kiowa covered the body with a poncho.

"Hey, you're looking better," he said. "No doubt about it. All you needed was time — some mental R&R."

Then he said, "Man, I'm sorry."

Then later he said, "Why not talk about it?"

Then he said, "Come on, man, talk."

He was a slim, dead, almost dainty young man of about twenty. He lay with one leg bent beneath him, his jaw in his throat, his face neither expressive nor inexpressive. One eye was shut. The other was a star-shaped hole.

"Talk," Kiowa said.

❧ FADWA TUQAN
B. *PALESTINE, 1917–2003*

One of Palestine's most important poets, Fadwa Tuqan was born in the West Bank town of Nablus in 1917. Raised in a conservative, middle-class Islamic household, she describes in her early poetry what it was like growing up under strict rules that limited her freedom of expression and movement. Nonetheless, in part due to the assistance of her brother, the celebrated poet Ibrahim Tuqan (1905–1941), Fadwa read widely in Islamic literature and moved to Jerusalem in 1939, a city that she describes as having lifted the veil separating the two sexes. After her brother's death, she returned to Nablus, which remained her primary place of residence throughout her life. Her early *divan,* or collections of poetry, including *I Found It* (1957), were celebrated for their candid portrayal of a woman's love and feelings. After the Israeli occupation of the West Bank and Gaza that followed the Six-Day War of 1967, Fadwa turned to more political themes in her writing, calling for justice for the Palestinians and recognition of Palestine as a nation. Her poetic works include *In Front of the Closed Door* (1967), *Horsemen of the Night* (1969), *Alone on the Summit of the World* (1973), and *Daily Nightmares* (1988). Her important autobiography, *Mountainous Journey* (1985), describes her life up to the 1967 war.

∽ Song of Becoming

Translated by Naomi Shihab Nye

They're only boys
who used to frolic and play
releasing in the western wind
their blue red green kites
the colour of the rainbow
jumping, whistling, exchanging spontaneous jokes
and laughter
fencing with branches, assuming the roles
of great heroes in history.

10 They've grown suddenly now
grown more than the years of a lifetime
grown, merged with a secret word of love
carried its letters like a Bible, or a Quran
read in whispers

They've grown more than the years of a lifetime
become the trees plunging deep into the earth
and soaring high towards the sun
They're now the voice that rejects
they're the dialectics of destruction and building anew
20 the anger burning on the fringes of a blocked horizon
invading classroom, streets, city quarters
centering on the squares
and facing sullen tanks with a stream of stones.

With plain rejection they now shake the gallows of the dawn
assailing the night and its deluge
They've grown, grown more than the years of a lifetime
become the worshipped and the worshipper
When their torn limbs merged with the stuff of our earth,
they became a legend
30 They grew, and became the bridge
they grew, grew and became
larger than all poetry.

◌ YEHUDA AMICHAI
B. GERMANY, 1924–2000

Israel's most renowned contemporary poet, Yehuda Amichai was born in Würzburg in 1924. Seeking refuge from the Nazis, his family emigrated to what was at the time Palestine and took up residence in Jerusalem, where Yehuda attended school and studied Hebrew. During World War II Amichai served in the British army, and in the war of independence and the wars of 1956 and 1973 he was a commando in the Israeli army. Between the wars Amichai enrolled at Hebrew University, where he studied Hebrew literature and wrote poetry. His first book of poems, *Now and in Other Days,* appeared in 1955. After graduating, Amichai worked as a teacher in secondary schools and continued to write verse. With his second volume, *Two Hopes Away* (1958), he fully realized the poetic power of the colloquial language of the emerging state of Israel—a modernized form of Hebrew—and received international recognition. In the 1970s and '80s, Amichai held visiting professorships at several American higher-learning institutions, including the University of California, Berkeley, and New York University. When Shimon Peres, Yitzhak Rabin, and Yasir Arafat shared the Nobel Peace Prize in 1994, Amichai's poems were read at the ceremony. By his death in September 2000, Amichai had published two novels, several short stories, and eleven collections of poetry. His memories of war drive the imagery and themes of many of his poems, and his firsthand experience of brutal killings inspired the longing for peace that permeates his work.

◌ God Has Pity on Kindergarten Children

Translated by Assia Gutmann

God has pity on children in kindergartens,
He pities school children—less.
But adults he pities not at all.

He abandons them,
Sometimes they have to crawl on all fours
In the roasting sand
To reach the dressing station,
And they are streaming with blood.

But perhaps
He will have pity on those who love truly
And take care of them

10

And shade them,
Like a tree over the sleeper on the public bench.

Perhaps even we will spend on them
Our last pennies of kindness
Inherited from mother,

So that their own happiness will protect us
Now and on other days.

ॐ Mahmoud Darwish
B. PALESTINE, 1941–2008

The foremost Palestinian poet of the conflict between Israel and Palestine, Mahmoud Darwish was about seven years old in 1948 when the Israelis occupied his native village of Al-Birwah, near Akka (Acre). For a year his family took refuge in Lebanon, after which they returned to Galilee and Mahmoud began writing poetry as an elementary-school student. He published his first volume of poems, *Birds without Wings*, in 1960 and followed with three more collections by 1967. In 1969 he was awarded the Lotus Prize at the Fourth Afro-Asian Writers Conference.

As his reputation as a writer grew, Darwish became increasingly active in the pro-Arab branch of the Israeli Communist Party, *Rakah*, and served for a while as editor of its newspaper, *Al-Ittihad* (*Unity*), published biweekly in Haifa. While working as a journalist and editor, Darwish was continually under surveillance by the Israelis and several times was placed under house arrest. In 1971 he announced his exile from Israel and settled for a year in Cairo, where he contributed to the newspaper *al-Ahram*. In the next year he published *I Love You, I Love You Not* and moved to Beirut, where he lived for the next ten years, writing poetry, directing the Palestinian Center for Research, and editing *Shu'un Falastiniyya* (*Palestinian Affairs* magazine). Later Darwish moved to Damascus, Syria, working again as an editor and journalist. He eventually became president of the Union of Arab Poets, and he served as a member of the Executive Committee of the Palestine Liberation Organization until 1993. After residing for some time in Paris and serving as editor of the Palestinian literary review, *Al-Karmel*, in 1996 Darwish returned for the first time to Israel and was greeted by crowds of celebrating Palestinians. After that visit he said, "As long as my soul is alive no one can smother my feeling of nostalgia to a country which I still consider as Palestine."

As a poet living outside of his homeland, Darwish communicates an exile's powerful sense of loss and desire for his land in his work. He also celebrates the human dignity of the Palestinians and dramatically describes the fear and suffering of his people. He has published more than thirty books of poetry and prose; two of his most recent books are *Memory for Forgetfulness: August, Beirut, 1982* (1995) and *Bed of a Stranger* (1998). The poem "Identity Card," one of the most celebrated of all his poems among Palestinians, stems from an incident when an Israeli censor changed the word "Palestine" in one of his poems to "Eretz Israel," or land of Israel.

❧ Victim Number 18[1]

Translated by Denys Johnson-Davies

Once the olive grove was green.
It was, and the sky
A grove of blue. It was, my love.
What changed it that evening?

At the bend in the track they stopped the lorry of workers.
So calm they were.
They turned us round towards the east. So calm they were.

Once my heart was a blue bird, O nest of my beloved.
The handkerchiefs I had of yours were all white. They were, my love.
10   What stained them that evening?
I do not understand at all, my love.

At the bend in the track they stopped the lorry of workers.
So calm they were.
They turned us round towards the east. So calm they were.

From me you'll have everything,
Yours the shade and yours the light,
A wedding-ring and all you want,
And an orchard of trees, of olive and fig.
And as on every night I'll come to you.
20   In the dream I'll enter by the window and throw you jasmine.
Blame me not if I'm a little late:
They stopped me.

---

[1] **Victim Number 18:** This title refers to the massacre at Kafr Qassem in 1956, in which Israeli troops killed forty-nine unarmed villagers, an incident leading to the 1956 war.

∽ Identity Card

Translated by Denys Johnson-Davies

Put it on record.
    I am an Arab
And the number of my card is fifty thousand
I have eight children
And the ninth is due after summer.
What's there to be angry about?

Put it on record.
    I am an Arab
Working with comrades of toil in a quarry.
10 I have eight children
For them I wrest the loaf of bread,
The clothes and exercise books
From the rocks
And beg for no alms at your door,
    Lower not myself at your doorstep.
    What's there to be angry about?

Put it on record.
    I am an Arab.
I am a name without a title,[1]
20 Patient in a country where everything
Lives in a whirlpool of anger.
    My roots
    Took hold before the birth of time
    Before the burgeoning of the ages,
    Before cypress and olive trees,
    Before the proliferation of weeds.
My father is from the family of the plough
    Not from highborn nobles.
And my grandfather was a peasant
30   Without line or genealogy.
My house is a watchman's hut
    Made of sticks and reeds.
Does my status satisfy you?
    I am a name without a surname.

---

[1] **without a title:** Arabs often use titles, such as "Bey" or "Pasha"; to lack a title is an indication of his lack of official acknowledgment of his identity.

Put it on record.
　　I am an Arab.
Colour of hair: jet black.
Colour of eyes: brown.
My distinguishing features:
40　　On my head the *'iqal* cords over a *keffiyeh*[2]
　　Scratching him who touches it.
My address:
　　I'm from a village, remote, forgotten,
　　Its streets without name
　　And all its men in the fields and quarry.

　　What's there to be angry about?

Put it on record.
　　I am an Arab.
You stole my forefathers' vineyards
50　　And land I used to till,
　　I and all my children,
　　And you left us and all my grandchildren
　　Nothing but these rocks.
　　Will your government be taking them too
　　As is being said?

So!
　　Put it on record at the top of page one:
　　I don't hate people,
　　I trespass on no one's property.
60　And yet, if I were to become hungry
　　I shall eat the flesh of my usurper.
　　Beware, beware of my hunger
　　And of my anger!

---

[2] *'iqal . . . keffiyeh*: A *keffiyeh* is a head scarf worn by Arab men, which is held in place by a black cord known as an *'iqal*.

Bei Dao, which literally means North Island, is the pen name of Zhao Zhenkai, one of China's most important and widely acclaimed contemporary poets. Born in Beijing in 1949, Bei Dao was educated at the prestigious Fourth Middle School. In 1966, as a young member of the Red Guard, he took part in the Cultural Revolution, a movement that from 1966 to 1976 sent thousands of city dwellers into exile in the country as part of an effort to unify the nation by making urban intellectuals, writers, and academics share the life and work of peasants. After three years, his hopes for a meaningful transformation of culture disappointed, he turned to construction work and began writing poetry. He participated in the demonstrations at Tiananmen Square in 1976, protesting the policies of Chairman Mao Zedong and the so-called Gang of Four. His most famous poem, "The Answer," which was read at the demonstrations, established his as an important voice of the democratic movement in China.

After the death of Mao Zedong that same year, party restrictions on literary and cultural production were loosened, and in 1979 Bei Dao started a groundbreaking literary magazine, *Jintian* (*Today*). Already known as a writer of subversive verse that expressed the hopes of those looking for democratic reforms from the new leader, Deng Xiaoping, Bei Dao became the leader of the Misty school of poets, so named for its experiments with form and syntax and often obscure and surrealistic imagery. The difficult works of Misty poets challenged both official party ideology and the outworn, orthodox conventions of Socialist Realism.

Bei Dao's work has helped to create a new poetic idiom for contemporary Chinese poets, and he has also been a leader in transforming contemporary Chinese literature by experimenting with and publishing new narrative and poetic forms. *Today* was banned in 1980, and as the promise of Deng Xiaoping's government dimmed and Bei Dao faced official censure for his work, his poetry began to reflect the bitter disappointment of his generation.

In the mid-1980s Bei Dao left China to travel throughout the United States and Europe. He returned to China in 1988 and in the following year helped to launch a petition for the release of Wei Jingsheng and others imprisoned for taking part in the democracy movement. This drive eventually exploded in the massacre at Tiananmen Square on June 4, 1989. This time Bei Dao was in Europe during the demonstration, but the student protesters had printed lines of his poetry on their banners. Forced into exile, Bei Dao spent several years teaching in Europe and the United States, holding positions at the University of Michigan and Beloit College in Wisconsin, among others. In 2006 he was granted permission to return to China.

∽ **Declaration**

for Yu Luoke[1]

Translated by Bonnie S. McDougall

Perhaps the final hour is come
I have left no testament
Only a pen, for my mother
I am no hero
In an age without heroes
I just want to be a man

The still horizon
Divides the ranks of the living and the dead
I can only choose the sky
10   I will not kneel on the ground
Allowing the executioners to look tall
The better to obstruct the wind of freedom

From star-like bullet holes shall flow
A blood-red dawn

---

[1] *for Yu Luoke:* The first draft of this poem was written in 1975. Some good friends of mine fought side by side with Yu Luoke, and two of them were thrown into prison where they languished for three years. This poem records our tragic and indignant protest in that tragic and indignant period. [Author's note.]

❧ FEDERICO GARCÍA LORCA
B. SPAIN, 1898–1936

www For links to more information about Lorca and a quiz on his poetry, see bedford stmartins.com/ worldlitcompact.

At dawn on August 19, 1936, a month after the beginning of the Spanish civil war, the internationally celebrated poet Federico García Lorca was shot by a firing squad near an ancient Moorish spring outside the city of Granada and buried in an unmarked grave. He was thirty-eight years old. The month before, he had told his friend Damaso Alonso, "I will never be political. I am a revolutionary because there are no true poets who are not revolutionaries. But political I will never, never be!" But Lorca, who also made a habit of saying "I am on the side of the poor," whose homosexuality was apparent in several of his most accessible works, and who had publicly stated that the fall of Moorish Granada in 1492 was a "disastrous event," was evidently political enough to merit assassination in the eyes of the "black squads"—Fascist gunmen who roamed the major cities of Spain in those terrible days. After his martyrdom, Lorca became the world's poet and playwright. Today his works survive in all the languages of Europe.

Lorca's early reputation rested on collections of lyrics—especially *Gypsy Ballads*—that were heavily influenced by his roots in Andalusia and possessed a primal, almost mythic, energy associated with gypsies and flamenco. His residence in New York City in 1929 and 1930 led to a more surrealistic stage in his poetry; in *Poet in New York,* the city, on the edge of the Great Depression, becomes a symbol of the blackness and inhumanity that threaten Spain and has been seen as a premonition of Lorca's own death. In the second half of his brief writing career Lorca emerged as one of the great Spanish dramatists, perhaps the greatest since the Golden Age of Spanish drama in the sixteenth and seventeenth centuries, when Lope de Vega (1562–1635) and Pedro Calderón de la Barca (1600–1681) lived. In highly poetic language and imaginative settings, Lorca's plays deal with the dark, earthy forces of sexuality, fertility, and the moon. His technical experimentation has been compared to that of Pirandello and Brecht.[1] His fiery, emotional, often surrealistic writing— poetry and drama alike—is unique in tone and impact, and brings together a variety of materials ranging from Spanish nursery rhymes and children's songs to the "deep songs" of the Andalusian provinces, folk songs, and ballads of Moorish and Gypsy influence. Though dark-complexioned, Lorca claimed no Moorish or Gypsy blood. His sympathy for these peoples (as well as for Native and African Americans), however, is a marked component of his work.

---

[1] **Pirandello and Brecht:** Luigi Pirandello (1867–1936), an Italian playwright, uses a play within a play in order to challenge the line between art and reality in his most famous drama, *Six Characters in Search of an Author* (1921). Bertolt Brecht (1898–1956), a German playwright known for *The Threepenny Opera* (1928) and *Mother Courage* (1939), employs unusual stage effects and lighting to comment on society's problems.

The Young Writer.   The first child of a well-to-do family, Lorca was born in 1898 in the rural town of Fuente Vaqueros in the province of Granada; his family moved to the city in 1909. Educated in private schools, Federico showed an affinity for music, but his father, a practical man who distrusted the arts, insisted that he study law. (A revealing anecdote has his father telling the family servant, "Give him an omelette of chrysanthemums! of violets! of twilight!" when the teenage Lorca came in late to dinner because he had been gazing too long at the twilight.) Although Lorca was indifferent toward his studies at the University of Madrid, he did immerse himself in the classical writers of Spain. He traveled to central Spain in 1916 and 1917, where he studied folk music and storytelling. His first book, *Impressions and Landscapes* (*Impressiones y Paiajes,* 1918), financed by his father once he was convinced of its artistic merit, is a record of these early explorations.

Fortunate to have both artistic connections and family support—whatever his father's misgivings—Lorca was able to join the Students' Residence in Madrid, a renowned center for young artists, scholars, and writers, in 1919. He lived there for nine years, gaining celebrity as a musician and poet. Other resident artists there included filmmaker Luis Buñuel and painter Salvador Dalí.[2] Dalí was important to Lorca in two respects: He helped introduce the young poet to the doctrines of surrealism, a leading art movement of the twenties, and for years he was the object of Lorca's romantic passion. The relationship lasted from 1922 to 1928, when Lorca left the Residence.

By 1922, Lorca had organized folk festivals of "deep song," the passionate lyrics of the province of Andalusia. His own volume of poetic imitations of this music was published in 1931. Meanwhile, still at the Residence, Lorca had published small editions of his poetry, organized puppet shows based on folk stories, written and directed a play (a critical disaster in its single stage appearance), presented an exhibit of his drawings, and participated in a 1927 literary conference organized by the highly cultivated bullfighter Ignacio Sanchez Mejías, whom Lorca was to eulogize seven years later in his most famous poem.

Lorca's first real collections of poetry, *Book of Poems* (*Libro de Poemas,* 1921) and *Songs* (*Canciones,* 1921–1924), showed his promise as a young writer, but *Gypsy Ballads* (*Romancero Gitano,* 1928) brought him fame throughout his country. The later volume shows Lorca's attraction to colorful landscapes, the earthy sensuality of rural life, and the theme of death.

Maturity and Early Death.   In 1928, the year *Gypsy Ballads* was published, Lorca was to undergo the deepest emotional crisis of his life, probably attributable to his inner conflicts over his homosexuality and the

. . . there has been no more beautiful mind than Lorca's.
– STARK YOUNG, critic, 1948

If it was not given to [Lorca] to explore the full scope of tragic art, as it was given to Shakespeare and the Greeks to do, he remains at least the chief lyric dramatist of the first half of the century.
– JOHN GASSNER, critic, 1967

[2] Buñuel . . . Dalí: Luis Buñuel (1900–1983) was a filmmaker who collaborated with Salvador Dalí in surreal, poetic films and also made films of social criticism such as *Los olvidados* (1949). Salvador Dalí (1904–1989) became a surrealist painter in the 1920s; his famous painting *The Persistence of Memory* (1931) is an otherworldly landscape filled with limp watches.

merciless exposure occasioned by his sudden fame. He accepted the offer of a former professor, Fernando de los Ríos, to visit New York City in June 1929. Although he studied at Columbia University through the fall semester, he learned very little English, and the poetry he wrote is replete with images of cultural and emotional alienation. Most of the volume *Poet in New York* (*Poeta en Nueva York*) was written during this stay in New York; it was published posthumously in 1940. Its poems, many of which challenge the reader's imagination with their unique and surreal images, are filled with pictures and sounds of the desolation Lorca discovered through his numerous walks in the city at this difficult time in America. He was particularly troubled by the plight of the blacks in Harlem — a short distance from Columbia University. In the poem "Ode to Walt Whitman" — included here — Lorca laments what he sees as the corruption of the healthy sexuality envisioned by Whitman.

Lorca returned to Spain at the time of the establishment of the Second Republic, celebrating with his countrymen the fragile victory of a broadly based democratic movement (1931–36). He initiated an arts project called "The Hut," literally a house on wheels that transported classical theater to small towns and villages. Traveling with the company, Lorca edited classical drama to conform to ordinary people's tastes and thus developed a strong rapport with the popular audience. This experience prepared him to write his own drama. Lorca's earlier plays, like *The Shoemaker's Marvelous Wife* (*La zapatera prodigosa*), were influenced by the folk elements of puppet theater and the tradition of sixteenth-century Italian *commedia dell'arte*. (*Commedia* was a type of comedy that used stock characters like the silly old man, the clever servant, and the lover to weave a play around an elaborate, absurd plot.) Lorca became renowned, however, primarily for three later plays dealing with elemental passions that challenge the limitations of social mores and result in death. His first great tragedy, *Blood Wedding* (*Bodas de sangre*), originally performed in 1933, is about a fatal attraction between a married man and a woman who run away on the day of her wedding. *Blood Wedding* is called a poetic drama, which in this play means realistic drama with lyrical interludes. Although based on a newspaper story of a bride who ran off with her lover on the night of her wedding, Lorca elevates the journalistic account to tragedy by surrounding the actions of the characters with the larger forces of fate. Since the end of the drama is known or at least suspected by the first act, the real focus of the play is the characters and what drives them, as if the play were a primitive wedding ritual involving primal emotions. Themes of love and death and marriage and funerals pervade Lorca's poetry as well as his plays. The Spanish title, *Bodas de sangre* (*Blood Weddings*), is plural; several "weddings" take place during the play.

Yerma, performed in 1934, is about a woman who yearns for motherhood, but her husband is sterile. The traveling performances of "The Hut" ceased production in the face of growing political tension in April 1936. Lorca finished his last great play about women in the spring of 1936, just before the beginning of the Spanish civil war and Lorca's death that

It should not be overlooked that, from the first childlike and ingratiating lyrics of his youth, there is a bitter root *(raíz amarga)*. At its most revealing level, we find in Lorca a spirit obsessed with primitive passion, with earthy emotion and, above all, with a vision of death — his great and all-embracing theme.

– ÁNGEL DEL RÍO, *Poet in New York*, 1955

summer. *The House of Bernarda Alba* (*La casa de Bernarda Alba*) is about a mother whose tyranny over her daughters leads to a tragic suicide. It was not performed until 1945.

"Lament for Ignacio Sanchez Mejías."   Lorca's last great poetic work, "Llanto por Ignácio Sánchez Mejías" (1935), was inspired by the death of his friend, the bullfighter Ignacio Sanchez Mejías (1891–1934). Mejías, a cultivated, handsome son of a doctor, was an avant-garde playwright and a patron of the arts as well as a bullfighter. He competed as a matador between 1920 and 1922 and again between 1924 and 1927. He came out of his second retirement in 1934 and agreed to fight one additional time, stepping in for his injured rival, Domingo Ortega. On August 11 he was gored by the bull Granadino and died two days later from a gangrene infection after a twelve-hour ambulance ride to Madrid. The poem, organized in four movements, is recognized as a classic of Spanish literature. Preceding Lorca's execution by less than two years, the "Lament" is often regarded as Lorca's anticipation of his own death.

The poem uses a variety of forms and themes. The repeated phrase "five in the afternoon" in the work's first section draws on the repetition of the *cante jondo,* or "deep song," to create a haunting chorus of sadness and a sense of inevitability. This chorus is a good example of the difficulty of translating Lorca. The first two lines of "Lament" are quite simple and yet difficult to duplicate in English:

> *A las cinco de la tarde.*
> *Eran las cinco en punto de la tarde.*
>
> At five in the afternoon.
> It was exactly five in the afternoon.

The first line in Spanish is made up of two anapests—two unstressed syllables followed by a stressed syllable. The second line immediately interrupts that pattern by beginning with a stressed syllable, thereby urgently qualifying the time frame for the reader. The second line of the translation, dissimilarly, begins with three unstressed syllables, which diminishes the insistence on the exact time. *En punto* means "exactly," but with an extra precision and sharpness, since *punto* also carries the sense of "dot, point, sharp, precision"—a distant echo of the sharp point of a bull's horn or a matador's sword.

The poem's second section, "The Spilled Blood," surrounds the bullfighter's death with tactile images of a bleeding body. In the last two sections of "Lament," "The Laid Out Body" and "Absent Soul," Lorca explores the consequences and injustice of Mejías's death. The Catholic consolation of heaven does not appease the profound sorrow of his passing. In fact, Lorca thinks the beautiful, remarkable man will soon be forgotten, "like all the dead of the Earth, / like all the dead who are forgotten / in a heap of lifeless dogs." Of course, quite the reverse is true—Lorca's "Lament" immortalizes Ignacio Sanchez Mejías along with its creator.

■ **FURTHER RESEARCH**

Biography
Gibson, Ian. *Federico García Lorca: A Life.* 1989.
Londre, Felicia Hardinson. *Federico García Lorca.* 1984.
MacCurdy, G. Grant. *Federico García Lorca: Life, Work, and Criticism.* 1986.

Criticism
Adams, Mildred. *García Lorca: Playwright and Poet.* 1984.
Anderson, Andrew. *Lorca's Late Poetry.* 1990.
Morris, C. Brian. *Son of Andalusia: The Lyrical Landscapes of Federico García Lorca.* 1997.
Nandorfy, Martha. *The Poetics of Apocalypse: Federico García Lorca's "Poet in New York."* 2003.
Newton, Candelas. *Understanding Federico García Lorca.* 1995.
Pollin, Alice, and Philip H. Smith. *Concordance to the Plays and Poems of Federico García Lorca.* 1975.
Predmore, Richard L. *Lorca's New York Poetry.* 1980.
Stainton, Leslie. *Lorca: A Dream of Life.* 1999.

ᔧ Ode to Walt Whitman[1]

Translated by Stephen Spender and J. L. Gili

Along the East River and the Bronx
the boys were singing showing their waists,
with the wheel, the oil, the leather and the hammer.
Ninety thousand miners extracted silver from rocks
and children drew stairs and perspectives.

But none would sleep,
none wanted to be a river,
none loved the great leaves,
none, the blue tongue of the beach.

10   Along the East River and the Queensborough
the boys were fighting with Industry,
and the Jews were selling to the faun of the river
the rose of the Circumcision,[2]
and the sky rushed through bridges and roofs
herds of bison pushed by the wind.

---

[1] For a discussion of Walt Whitman and his poetry, see pp. 845–861.

[2] **Circumcision:** The Spanish version does not capitalize *circuncisión*, which is used as a sign of the covenant between Yahweh, the God of Israel, and Jewish men.

But none would pause,
none wanted to be a cloud,
none searched for the ferns
nor the yellow wheel of the tambourine.

20   When the moon rises,
the pulleys will turn to disturb the sky:
a boundary of needles will fence in the memory
and the coffins will carry away those who do not work.

New York of slime,
New York of wires and death:
What angel do you carry hidden in your cheek?
What perfect voice will tell the truths of the wheat?
Who, the terrible dream of your stained anemones?

Not for one moment, beautiful aged Walt Whitman,
30   have I failed to see your beard full of butterflies,
nor your shoulders of corduroy worn out by the moon,
nor your thighs of virginal Apollo,
nor your voice like a pillar of ashes:
ancient and beautiful as the mist,
you moaned like a bird
with the sex transfixed by a needle,
enemy of the satyr,
enemy of the vine,
and lover of bodies under the rough cloth.
40   Not for one moment; virile beauty,
who in mountains of coal, posters and railways,
dreamed of being a river and sleeping like a river
with that comrade who would place in your breast
the small pain of an ignorant leopard.

Not for one moment, Adam of blood, male,
lone man in the sea, beautiful aged Walt Whitman,
because through the terraces,
clustered around the bars,
pouring out of sewers in bunches,
50   trembling between the legs of chauffeurs
or revolving on the platforms of absinthe,
the pansies,[3] Walt Whitman, dreamed of you.

---

[3] **pansies:** Lorca uses the Spanish *maricas,* which is the feminine version of *maricón,* both of which are negative names for effeminate gay men — in the same category as "pansy," "fairy," and "sissy." Interestingly, Lorca uses the masculine article with a feminine noun: *los maricas.*

This one also! This one! And they fall
on your chaste and luminous beard,
Northern blonds, Negroes of the sands,
multitudes of shrieks and gestures,
like cats or like snakes,
the pansies, Walt Whitman, the pansies,
muddy with tears, flesh for the whip,
60   boot or bite of subduers.

This one also! This one! Tainted fingers
appear on the shore of your dreams
when the friend eats your apple
with a faint taste of petrol
and the sun sings along the navels
of boys that play under bridges.

But you did not search for the scratched eyes,
or the very dark swamp where children are submerged,
or the frozen saliva,
70   or the wounded curves resembling toad's bellies
which the pansies carry in cars and terraces
while the moon strikes at them along the corners of fear.

You searched for a nude who was like a river.
Bull and dream that would join the wheel with the seaweed,
father of your agony, camellia of your death,
and would moan in the flames of your hidden Equator.

Because it is just that man does not search for his delight
in the jungle of blood of the following morning.
The sky has shores where to avoid life,
80   and certain bodies must not repeat themselves in the dawn.

Agony, agony, dream, ferment and dream.
This is the world, my friend, agony, agony.
The corpses decompose under the clock of the cities.
War passes weeping with a million grey rats,
the rich give to their mistresses
small illuminated moribunds,
and Life is not noble, nor good, nor sacred.

Man can, if he wishes, lead his desire
through vein of coral or celestial nude:
90   tomorrow love will be rocks, and Time
a breeze which comes sleeping through the branches.

That is why I do not raise my voice, aged Walt Whitman,
against the little boy who writes
a girl's name on his pillow,
nor the boy who dresses himself in the bride's trousseau
in the darkness of the wardrobe,
nor the solitary men in clubs
who drink the water of prostitution with nausea,
nor the men with a green stare
100   who love man and burn their lips in silence.
But against you, yes, pansies of the cities,
of tumescent flesh and unclean mind,
mud of drains, harpies, unsleeping enemies
of Love which distributes crowns of joy.

Against you always, you who give boys
drops of soiled death with bitter poison.
Against you always,
Fairies of North America,
Pájaros of Havana,
110   *Jotos* of Mexico,
Sarasas of Cadiz,
Apios of Seville,
Cancos of Madrid,
Floras of Alicante,
Adelaidas of Portugal.[4]

Pansies of the world, murderers of doves!
Women's slaves, bitches of their boudoirs,
opened with the fever of fans in public squares
or ambushed in frigid landscapes of hemlock.

120   Let there be no quarter! Death
flows from your eyes
and clusters grey flowers on the shores.
Let there be no quarter! Take heed!
Let the perplexed, the pure,
the classicists, the noted, the supplicants,
close the gates of the Bacchanalia.

And you, beautiful Walt Whitman, sleep on the Hudson's banks,
with your beard toward the Pole and your hands open.

---

[4] ***Pájaros, Jotos, Sarasas, Apios, Cancos, Floras, Adelaidas:*** Colloquial versions of *maricas,* but with different connotations. For example, *pájaros* means "birds" and *floras* means "flowers." See note 3.

130
Bland clay or snow, your tongue is calling for
comrades that keep watch on your gazelle without a body.
Sleep; nothing remains.
A dance of walls agitates the meadows
and America drowns itself in machines and lament.
I want the strong air of the most profound night
to remove flowers and words from the arch where you sleep,
and a black boy to announce to the gold-minded whites
the arrival of the reign of the ear of corn.

Lament for Ignacio Sanchez Mejías

Translated by Stephen Spender and J. L. Gili

1. Cogida[1] and Death

At five in the afternoon.[2]
It was exactly five in the afternoon.
A boy brought the white sheet
at five in the afternoon.
A frail of lime[3] ready prepared
at five in the afternoon.
The rest was death, and death alone
at five in the afternoon.

10
The wind carried away the cottonwool
at five in the afternoon.
And the oxide scattered crystal and nickel[4]
at five in the afternoon.
Now the dove and the leopard[5] wrestle
at five in the afternoon.

---

[1] cogida: Goring by a bull; also means "harvesting."

[2] At five . . . afternoon: The body of Sanchez Mejías, removed from a mortuary in Madrid at five in the after-noon on August 14, 1934, was carried through the streets, then transported by train to Seville for burial.

[3] frail of lime: A basket of lime used to disinfect a dead body.

[4] cottonwool . . . nickel: Cottonwool suggests cotton surgical dressing; oxide (rust) suggests the color of blood; crystal suggests the doctors' glass beakers; nickel suggests medical instruments. This stanza rather surre-alistically describes the actual goring and attempts at treatment.

[5] dove . . . leopard: Symbols of peace and violence, respectively. The inscription on the cover of the printed edition of the poem reads "a dove . . . gathered him up."

And a thigh with a desolate horn
at five in the afternoon.
The bass-string struck up
at five in the afternoon.
Arsenic bells and smoke
at five in the afternoon.
Groups of silence in the corners
at five in the afternoon.
And the bull alone with a high heart!
At five in the afternoon.
When the sweat of snow was coming
at five in the afternoon,
when the bull ring was covered in iodine
at five in the afternoon,
death laid eggs in the wound
at five in the afternoon.
At five in the afternoon.
Exactly at five o'clock in the afternoon.

A coffin on wheels is his bed
at five in the afternoon.
Bones and flutes resound in his ears
at five in the afternoon.
Now the bull was bellowing through his forehead
at five in the afternoon.
The room was iridescent with agony
at five in the afternoon.
In the distance the gangrene now comes
at five in the afternoon.

Horn of the lily through green groins
at five in the afternoon.
The wounds were burning like suns
at five in the afternoon,
and the crowd was breaking the windows[6]
at five in the afternoon.
At five in the afternoon.
Ah, that fatal five in the afternoon!
It was five by all the clocks!
It was five in the shade of the afternoon!

---

[6] the crowd . . . windows: Suggests a crowd of followers clamoring to see Sanchez Mejías on his deathbed. No such incident is known to have occurred.

2. THE SPILLED BLOOD

I will not see it!

Tell the moon to come[7]
for I do not want to see the blood
of Ignacio on the sand.

I will not see it!

The moon wide open.
Horse of still clouds,
60   and the grey bull ring of dreams
with willows in the barreras.
I will not see it!

Let my memory kindle!
Warn the jasmines
of such minute whiteness!

I will not see it!

The cow of the ancient world
passed her sad tongue
over a snout of blood
70   spilled on the sand,
and the bulls of Guisando,[8]
partly death and partly stone,
bellowed like two centuries
sated with treading the earth.
No.
I do not want to see it!
I will not see it!

Ignacio goes up the tiers[9]
with all his death on his shoulders.
80   He sought for the dawn
but the dawn was no more.
He seeks for his confident profile

---

[7] **Tell . . . come:** According to tradition, the moon comes to suck up the blood of the world before turning red in a lunar eclipse.

[8] **bulls of Guisando:** Weathered, ancient stone statuary depicting bulls, in Madrid.

[9] **Ignacio . . . tiers:** Lorca imagines a scene in which the bullfighter goes up the tiers of the arena.

and the dream bewilders him.
He sought for his beautiful body
and encountered his opened blood.
I will not see it!
I do not want to hear it spurt
each time with less strength:
that spurt that illuminates
90 the tiers of seats, and spills
over the corduroy and the leather
of a thirsty multitude.
Who shouts that I should come near!
Do not ask me to see it!

His eyes did not close
when he saw the horns near,
but the terrible mothers[10]
lifted their heads.
And across the ranches,
100 an air of secret voices rose,
shouting to celestial bulls,
herdsmen of pale mist.
There was no prince in Seville
who could compare with him,
nor sword like his sword
nor heart so true.
Like a river of lions
was his marvellous strength,
and like a marble torso
110 his firm drawn moderation.
The air of Andalusian Rome°   Seville
gilded his head
where his smile was a spikenard[11]
of wit and intelligence.
What a great torero in the ring!
What a good peasant in the sierra!
How gentle with the sheaves!
How hard with the spurs!
How tender with the dew!
120 How dazzling in the fiesta!

---

[10] **terrible mothers:** Lorca envisioned these awesome presences as the Three Fates who announce the hour of death.

[11] **spikenard:** A white flower common to Andalusia; suggests his teeth.

How tremendous with the final
banderillas of darkness![12]

But now he sleeps without end.
Now the moss and the grass
open with sure fingers
the flower of his skull.
And now his blood comes out singing;
singing along marshes and meadows,
sliding on frozen horns,
faltering soulless in the mist,
stumbling over a thousand hoofs
like a long, dark, sad tongue,
to form a pool of agony
close to the starry Guadalquivir.[13]
Oh, white wall of Spain!
Oh, black bull of sorrow!
Oh, hard blood of Ignacio!
Oh, nightingale of his veins!
No.
I will not see it!
No chalice can contain it,
no swallows can drink it,
no frost of light can cool it,
nor song nor deluge of white lilies,
no glass can cover it with silver.
No.
I will not see it!

3. The Laid Out Body

Stone is a forehead where dreams grieve
without curving waters and frozen cypresses.
Stone is a shoulder on which to bear Time
with trees formed of tears and ribbons and planets.

I have seen grey showers move towards the waves
raising their tender riddled arms,
to avoid being caught by the lying stone
which loosens their limbs without soaking the blood.

---

[12] ***banderillas* of darkness:** Colorful, barbed darts stuck into the shoulders of the bull to aggravate him.

[13] **Guadalquivir:** River in Andalusia associated with the bullfighter's blood.

For stone gathers seed and clouds,
skeleton larks and wolves of penumbra:[14]
but yields not sounds nor crystals nor fire,
only bull rings and bull rings and more bull rings without walls.

160   Now, Ignacio the well born lies on the stone.
All is finished. What is happening? Contemplate his face:
death has covered him with pale sulphur
and has placed on him the head of a dark minotaur.[15]

All is finished. The rain penetrates his mouth.
The air, as if mad, leaves his sunken chest,
and Love, soaked through with tears of snow,
warms itself on the peak of the herd.

What are they saying? A stenching silence settles down.
We are here with a body laid out which fades away,
170   with a pure shape which had nightingales
and we see it being filled with depthless holes.

Who creases the shroud? What he says is not true![16]
Nobody sings here, nobody weeps in the corner,
nobody pricks the spurs, nor terrifies the serpent.
Here I want nothing else but the round eyes
to see this body without a chance of rest.

Here I want to see those men of hard voice.
Those that break horses and dominate rivers;
those men of sonorous skeleton who sing
180   with a mouth full of sun and flint.

Here I want to see them. Before the stone.
Before this body with broken reins.
I want to know from them the way out
for this captain strapped down by death.

I want them to show me a lament like a river
which will have sweet mists and deep shores,
to take the body of Ignacio where it loses itself
without hearing the double panting of the bulls.

---

[14] **penumbra:** A shadowy, borderline area.

[15] **minotaur:** The bullfighter is compared to a mythical sacrificial creature, half bull and half man.

[16] **not true!:** Lorca does not want to be distracted from the reality of the dead body by conventional pieties.

190 Loses itself in the round bull ring of the moon
which feigns in its youth a sad quiet bull:
loses itself in the night without song of fishes
and in the white thicket of frozen smoke.

I don't want them to cover his face with handkerchiefs
that he may get used to the death he carries.
Go, Ignacio; feel not the hot bellowing.
Sleep, fly, rest: even the sea dies!

4. ABSENT SOUL

The bull does not know you, nor the fig tree,
nor the horses, nor the ants in your own house.
The child and the afternoon do not know you
200 because you have died for ever.

The back of the stone does not know you,
nor the black satin in which you crumble.
Your silent memory does not know you
because you have died for ever.

The autumn will come[17] with small white snails,
misty grapes and with clustered hills,
but no one will look into your eyes
because you have died for ever.

Because you have died for ever,
210 like all the dead of the Earth,
like all the dead who are forgotten
in a heap of lifeless dogs.

Nobody knows you. No. But I sing of you.
For posterity I sing of your profile and grace.
Of the signal maturity of your understanding.
Of your appetite for death and the taste of its mouth.
Of the sadness of your once valiant gaiety.

It will be a long time, if ever, before there is born
an Andalusian so true, so rich in adventure.
220 I sing of his elegance with words that groan,
and I remember a sad breeze through the olive trees.

---

[17] **The autumn will come:** Autumn is the season following Sanchez Mejías's death.

JORGE LUIS BORGES
B. ARGENTINA, 1899–1986

Jorge Luis Borges created his own version of the short story in which he expresses the modern dissolution of conventional reality by blurring the traditional line between fiction and historical scholarship. In the aftermath of World War I, many writers felt that traditional, understandable models of reality were shattered and that reality was at best fragmented. As a native of Argentina, Borges set the stage for other experimental Latin American writers to follow, like Gabriel García Márquez (p. 1444), Julio Cortázar, and Carlos Fuentes,[1] by exploring the psychological boundaries between interior and exterior reality, playing with multiple identities, and intersecting different times and places.

Borges has been compared to Franz Kafka (p. 1386), whom he translated. Indeed, both were devoted to the exploration of consciousness, but while Kafka's stories deal with the dreamlike landscapes of the emotions, Borges's are very intellectual, drawing from the storehouse of world literature. Borges draws on esoteric literature and the wisdom traditions of world cultures to create subtle connections and unusual synchronicity in his stories. An international writer, Borges moves easily from one language to another in his work, just as his characters cross national boundaries with ease, pursuing their livelihoods abroad. Nowhere, of course, does Borges provide a magic key that unlocks a comprehensive, previously hidden plan for the cosmos, but he tantalizes us with the possibility that such a key exists, and that reality—for the artist at least—is an act of the imagination.

Crossing Cultures. Born on August 24, 1899, in Buenos Aires, Argentina, **Jorge Luis Borges** was raised in a home where languages and books were important. Jorge's mother, Lenore Acevedo Suarez, was a translator, and his father, Jorge Guillermos Borges, was a teacher, lawyer, and writer. Since his paternal grandmother was English and lived with the family, Borges grew up speaking both English and Spanish. When asked about the central event of his childhood, he answered, "I should say my father's library." In that library filled with English as well as Spanish books, the young Borges read a large number of classics. His father expected him to be a writer, and he was not disappointed. Borges began early, writing his first story at age seven and publishing a Spanish translation of Irish writer Oscar Wilde's "The Happy Prince" in a Buenos Aires newspaper at age nine.

In 1914 World War I broke out and the Borges family, then traveling in Europe, was stranded in Geneva, Switzerland, where Borges completed

Jorge Luis Borges
Although popular in Argentina, Borges's work did not find an international audience until later in the writer's life, and then he was showered with praise. (Charles H. Phillips/Timepix)

HOR-hay loo-EES
BOR-hays

---

[1] **Cortázar . . . Fuentes:** Julio Cortázar (1914–1984), a writer from Argentina, gained notoriety for his experimental novel *Hopscotch* in 1965. Carlos Fuentes's (b. 1928) many novels deal with Mexico's history and its social struggles; he is Mexico's most famous living writer.

www For links to more information about Borges, a quiz on "The Garden of Forking Paths," and information about Borges's relevance in the 21st century, see bedford stmartins.com/ worldlitcompact.

secondary school at the Collège de Genève. He became proficient in Latin and French in school and taught himself German and German philosophy at home. In Spain, after the war, Borges became acquainted with a group of young writers called the ULTRAISTS who rejected middle-class materialism and sought refuge in the artifice of poetry, in exotic images and metaphor. Returning to Buenos Aires in 1921, Borges became very active in the literary scene of that city, where from 1920 to 1930 he published four books of essays and three books of poetry. He founded three literary magazines and contributed to numerous others, including *Sur* (*South*), the most famous literary review of South America, and published three collections of unusual short stories: *The Garden of Forking Paths* (*El jardin de los senderos que se bifurcan*) in 1941, *Fictions* (*Ficciones*) in 1944, and *El Aleph* (1949).

Borges worked in a library in Buenos Aires from 1938 to 1946, but his opposition to the dictatorship of Juan Perón, who came to power in 1946, led to his dismissal from the job. The Perónistas offered him work as a chicken inspector in the city market, but he found a teaching job instead. After the fall of Perón in 1955, Borges was made director of the National Library, a position emblematic of his love for literature and vast learning. Unfortunately, his eyesight gradually failed in the mid 1950s; concerning his appointment and his eyesight, he said, "I speak of God's splendid irony in granting me at once 800,000 books and darkness." He was forced to dictate his writing. In 1961 he won the International Publishers' Prize, which he shared with Samuel Beckett (p. 1557). He published a final collection of stories in 1970, *Doctor Brodie's Report* (*El informe de Brodie*). Besides traveling to various parts of the world, he spent his final years lecturing and teaching in universities, including the University of Texas and Michigan State. For most of Borges's life his mother lived with him, but late in life he married twice. His first marriage was to Elsa Astela Millán in 1967, the second to his longtime secretary, María Kodama, in 1986, shortly before he died of liver cancer in Geneva, Switzerland, where he is buried.

Philosophy, comparative philologies, archaeology, everything has been evolving, progressing, breaking new ground. But we know little as ever about why we are born again each morning. Despite the comings and goings of the collective unconscious, we know equally little about the meanings of our very symbols. Borges restates, in a few allegorical pages, the circular, ceremonial direction of our curious, groping, thrilling, and atrocious ignorance.

– ANTHONY KERRIGAN, critic, 1962

The Many Facets of Borges's Mind.   Early on Borges was interested in writing poetry and essays. From 1936 to 1939 he wrote a weekly column for the newspaper *El Hogar* in which he covered a broad range of literatures and was interested in connecting Argentinean literature to the traditions of Europe and America. His first real fame, however, came with the publication of short stories in the collections *Ficciones* and *El Aleph*. Borges was influenced by the IDEALISTIC belief that reality is essentially a network of ideas rather than a collection of material sensations; thus many of the stories in these collections read like essays, with frequent references to books, authors, and translations — some real, some imaginary. The short stories take their themes from mythology, ancient religions, Gnosticism,[2]

---

[2] **Gnosticism:** An ancient sect in the Middle East whose adherents believed that hidden knowledge held the key to the universe. Throughout history Gnostics have formed secret societies with secret scriptures and have believed they understood the workings of the cosmos.

Jewish mysticism,[3] and various esoteric authors. Often a story's plot involves a puzzle and a search for an answer that is intricately intertwined with obscure details and that has an unexpected twist—a kind of mind game. In "Death and the Compass," for example, the detective Erik Lönnrot discovers the identity of a murderer by using the lore surrounding the Tetragrammaton,[4] the mystical name of God, but becomes trapped in the labyrinth of his own knowledge. In Borges's writings, the library is a symbol of the world's knowledge; somewhere there is an answer, but it is buried under thousands, if not millions, of layers.

"The Garden of Forking Paths."   Borges's detective story "The Garden of Forking Paths" was originally published in a collection of the same name in 1941 and eventually republished in *Labyrinths* (1962), an appropriate title for Borges's writings, since he is a master at creating tantalizing mazes that can be navigated only by picking up on the nearly invisible thread of clues Borges weaves into his narration. One dimension of the story consists of Yu Tsun's communicating the location of a British bombing target to his chief in Berlin, but another aspect entirely is the labyrinth discovered in a text by Yu Tsun's ancestor called *The Garden of Forking Paths,* which in its very structure models a universe comprising multiple planes of time in which individuals play several diverse roles. Even though the detective story is resolved in the final paragraph, Borges leaves the reader with the unmistakable impression that he or she is part of a larger network of relationships that transcend everyday understanding.

At times Borges's concerns with multiple planes of consciousness and esoteric learning are a game wherein he plays with the frontiers of the mind; at other times he seems to be reaching for a SYNCRETISTIC mythology—one that would blend ancient wisdom with modern psychology. He challenges a modern society that has lost contact with the meaningful symbols of its own traditions and lacks the vision for unifying whatever cultural fragments remain. After his extensive meanderings through archaeology, philology, philosophy, comparative religion, and world literature, Borges offers this final epigraph from the German mystic Angelus Silesius (seventeenth century), which concludes *Other Inquisitions* 1937–1952, a collection of essays.

> *Freund, es ist auch genug. Im Fall du mehr willst lesen,*
> *So geh und werde selbst die Schrift und selbst das Wesen.*

> Friend, this is enough. If finally you want to read more,
> Go and be yourself the letter and yourself the spirit.

> When one thinks of Borges, one thinks more of a literature than of a writer. Borges's stories and poems are aimed at the universe, unlike the writer with clearly defined scopes and goals. . . . Throughout his vast oeuvre, one keeps discovering the man of refined intellect, the philosopher, the "writer for writers" as he was considered some twenty years ago. . . ."
>
> – MAURICIO BETANCOURT, 2001

---

[3] **Jewish mysticism:** Like all forms of mysticism, Jewish mysticism focuses on learning and practices that lead to unity with the creator. Its teachings are called the Cabala or Kabala. Cabala strives to discover hidden meanings in every letter, number, and word of the Hebrew Scriptures.

[4] **Tetragrammaton:** The four letters in the Hebrew alphabet said to make up god's unspeakable name, YHWH; this name and its uses are believed to contain special powers.

■ FURTHER RESEARCH

Biography
McMurray, George R. *Jorge Luis Borges.* 1980.
Monegal, Emir Rodriquez. *Jorge Luis Borges.* 1978.
Woodall, James. *Borges: A Life.* 1996.

Criticism
Alazraki, Jaime, ed. *Critical Essays on Jorge Luis Borges.* 1987.
Bell-Villada, Gene H. *Borges and His Fiction: A Guide to His Mind and Art.* 1999.
DiGiovanni, Norman Thomas. *Lesson of the Master: Borges and His Work.* 2003.
Dunham, Lowell, and Ivar Ivask, eds. *The Cardinal Points of Borges.* 1971.
Fishburn, Evelyn, and Psiche Hughes. *A Dictionary of Borges.* 1990.
Isbister, Rob, and Peter Standish. *A Concordance to the Works of Jorge Luis Borges,*
    1899–1986. 1992.

■ PRONUNCIATION
Jorge Luis Borges: HOR-hay loo-EES BOR-hays

∿ The Garden of Forking Paths

Translated by Donald A. Yates

On page 22 of Liddell Hart's *History of World War I* you will read that an attack against the Serre-Montauban line by thirteen British divisions (supported by 1,400 artillery pieces), planned for the 24th of July, 1916, had to be postponed until the morning of the 29th. The torrential rains, Captain Liddell Hart comments, caused this delay, an insignificant one, to be sure.

The following statement, dictated, reread, and signed by Dr. Yu Tsun, former professor of English at the *Hochschule*[1] at Tsingtao, throws an unsuspected light over the whole affair. The first two pages of the document are missing.

". . . and I hung up the receiver. Immediately afterwards, I recognized the voice that had answered in German. It was that of Captain Richard Madden. Madden's presence in Viktor Runeberg's apartment meant the end of our anxieties and— but this seemed, *or should have seemed,* very secondary to me—also the end of our lives. It meant that Runeberg had been arrested or murdered.[2] Before the sun set on that day, I would encounter the same fate. Madden was implacable. Or rather, he was obliged to be so. An Irishman at the service of England, a man accused of laxity and perhaps of treason, how could he fail to seize and be thankful for such a miraculous

---

[1] *Hochschule:* University (German).

[2] **Runeberg . . . murdered:** A hypothesis both hateful and odd. The Prussian spy Hans Rabener, alias Viktor Runeberg, attacked with drawn automatic the bearer of the warrant for his arrest, Captain Richard Madden. The latter, in self-defense, inflicted the wound which brought about Runeberg's death. (Editor's note.) [Borges provided this "Editor's note" as part of the story.]

opportunity: the discovery, capture, maybe even the death of two agents of the German Reich? I went up to my room; absurdly I locked the door and threw myself on my back on the narrow iron cot. Through the window I saw the familiar roofs and the cloud-shaded six o'clock sun. It seemed incredible to me that that day without premonitions or symbols should be the one of my inexorable death. In spite of my dead father, in spite of having been a child in a symmetrical garden of Hai Feng, was I—now—going to die? Then I reflected that everything happens to a man precisely, precisely *now*. Centuries of centuries and only in the present do things happen; countless men in the air, on the face of the earth and the sea, and all that really is happening is happening to me ... The almost intolerable recollection of Madden's horselike face banished these wanderings. In the midst of my hatred and terror (it means nothing to me now to speak of terror, now that I have mocked Richard Madden, now that my throat yearns for the noose) it occurred to me that that tumultuous and doubtless happy warrior did not suspect that I possessed the Secret. The name of the exact location of the new British artillery park on the River Ancre. A bird streaked across the gray sky and blindly I translated it into an airplane and that airplane into many (against the French sky) annihilating the artillery station with vertical bombs. If only my mouth, before a bullet shattered it, could cry out that secret name so it could be heard in Germany ... My human voice was very weak. How might I make it carry to the ear of the Chief? To the ear of that sick and hateful man who knew nothing of Runeberg and me save that we were in Staffordshire and who was waiting in vain for our report in his arid office in Berlin, endlessly examining newspapers ... I said out loud: *I must flee.* I sat up noiselessly, in a useless perfection of silence, as if Madden were already lying in wait for me. Something—perhaps the mere vain ostentation of proving my resources were nil—made me look through my pockets. I found what I knew I would find. The American watch, the nickel chain and the square coin, the key ring with the incriminating useless keys to Runeberg's apartment, the notebook, a letter which I resolved to destroy immediately (and which I did not destroy), a crown, two shillings and a few pence, the red and blue pencil, the handkerchief, the revolver with one bullet. Absurdly, I took it in my hand and weighed it in order to inspire courage within myself. Vaguely I thought that a pistol report can be heard at a great distance. In ten minutes my plan was perfected. The telephone book listed the name of the only person capable of transmitting the message; he lived in a suburb of Fenton, less than a half hour's train ride away.

I am a cowardly man. I say it now, now that I have carried to its end a plan whose perilous nature no one can deny. I know its execution was terrible. I didn't do it for Germany, no. I care nothing for a barbarous country which imposed upon me the abjection of being a spy. Besides, I know of a man from England—a modest man—who for me is no less great than Goethe.[3] I talked with him for scarcely an hour, but during that hour he was Goethe ... I did it because I sensed that the Chief somehow feared people of my race—for the innumerable ancestors who merge

---

[3] **Goethe:** Johann Wolfgang von Goethe (1749–1832), a German writer. (See p. 553.)

within me. I wanted to prove to him that a yellow man could save his armies. Besides, I had to flee from Captain Madden. His hands and his voice could call at my door at any moment. I dressed silently, bade farewell to myself in the mirror, went downstairs, scrutinized the peaceful street and went out. The station was not far from my home, but I judged it wise to take a cab. I argued that in this way I ran less risk of being recognized; the fact is that in the deserted street I felt myself visible and vulnerable, infinitely so. I remember that I told the cab driver to stop a short distance before the main entrance. I got out with voluntary, almost painful slowness; I was going to the village of Ashgrove but I bought a ticket for a more distant station. The train left within a very few minutes, at eight-fifty. I hurried; the next one would leave at nine-thirty. There was hardly a soul on the platform. I went through the coaches; I remember a few farmers, a woman dressed in mourning, a young boy who was reading with fervor the *Annals* of Tacitus,[4] a wounded and happy soldier. The coaches jerked forward at last. A man whom I recognized ran in vain to the end of the platform. It was Captain Richard Madden. Shattered, trembling, I shrank into the far corner of the seat, away from the dreaded window.

From this broken state I passed into an almost abject felicity. I told myself that the duel had already begun and that I had won the first encounter by frustrating, even if for forty minutes, even if by a stroke of fate, the attack of my adversary. I argued that this slightest of victories foreshadowed a total victory. I argued (no less fallaciously) that my cowardly felicity proved that I was a man capable of carrying out the adventure successfully. From this weakness I took strength that did not abandon me. I foresee that man will resign himself each day to more atrocious undertakings; soon there will be no one but warriors and brigands; I give them this counsel: *The author of an atrocious undertaking ought to imagine that he has already accomplished it, ought to impose upon himself a future as irrevocable as the past.* Thus I proceeded as my eyes of a man already dead registered the elapsing of that day, which was perhaps the last, and the diffusion of the night. The train ran gently along, amid ash trees. It stopped, almost in the middle of the fields. No one announced the name of the station. "Ashgrove?" I asked a few lads on the platform. "Ashgrove," they replied. I got off.

A lamp enlightened the platform but the faces of the boys were in shadow. One questioned me, "Are you going to Dr. Stephen Albert's house?" Without waiting for my answer, another said, "The house is a long way from here, but you won't get lost if you take this road to the left and at every crossroads turn again to your left." I tossed them a coin (my last), descended a few stone steps and started down the solitary road. It went downhill, slowly. It was of elemental earth; overhead the branches were tangled; the low, full moon seemed to accompany me.

For an instant, I thought that Richard Madden in some way had penetrated my desperate plan. Very quickly, I understood that that was impossible. The instructions to turn always to the left reminded me that such was the common procedure

---

[4]**Tacitus:** Roman historian (55–117 C.E.).

for discovering the central point of certain labyrinths. I have some understanding of labyrinths: Not for nothing am I the great grandson of that Ts'ui Pên who was governor of Yunnan and who renounced worldly power in order to write a novel that might be even more populous than the *Hung Lu Meng*[5] and to construct a labyrinth in which all men would become lost. Thirteen years he dedicated to these heterogeneous tasks, but the hand of a stranger murdered him—and his novel was incoherent and no one found the labyrinth. Beneath English trees I meditated on that lost maze: I imagined it inviolate and perfect at the secret crest of a mountain; I imagined it erased by rice fields or beneath the water; I imagined it infinite, no longer composed of octagonal kiosks and returning paths, but of rivers and provinces and kingdoms . . . I thought of a labyrinth of labyrinths, of one sinuous spreading labyrinth that would encompass the past and the future and in some way involve the stars. Absorbed in these illusory images, I forgot my destiny of one pursued. I felt myself to be, for an unknown period of time, an abstract perceiver of the world. The vague, living countryside, the moon, the remains of the day worked on me, as well as the slope of the road which eliminated any possibility of weariness. The afternoon was intimate, infinite. The road descended and forked among the now confused meadows. A high-pitched, almost syllabic music approached and receded in the shifting of the wind, dimmed by leaves and distance. I thought that a man can be an enemy of other men, of the moments of other men, but not of a country: not of fireflies, words, gardens, streams of water, sunsets. Thus I arrived before a tall, rusty gate. Between the iron bars I made out a poplar grove and a pavilion. I understood suddenly two things, the first trivial, the second almost unbelievable: The music came from the pavilion, and the music was Chinese. For precisely that reason I had openly accepted it without paying it any heed. I do not remember whether there was a bell or whether I knocked with my hand. The sparkling of the music continued.

From the rear of the house within a lantern approached: a lantern that the trees sometimes striped and sometimes eclipsed, a paper lantern that had the form of a drum and the color of the moon. A tall man bore it. I didn't see his face, for the light blinded me. He opened the door and said slowly, in my own language: "I see that the pious Hsi P'êng persists in correcting my solitude. You no doubt wish to see the garden?"

I recognized the name of one of our consuls and I replied, disconcerted, "The garden?"

"The garden of forking paths."

Something stirred in my memory and I uttered with incomprehensible certainty, "The garden of my ancestor Ts'ui Pên."

"Your ancestor? Your illustrious ancestor? Come in."

The damp path zigzagged like those of my childhood. We came to a library of Eastern and Western books. I recognized bound in yellow silk several volumes of

---

[5] *Hung Lu Meng: The Dream of the Red Chamber*, also called *The Story of the Stone* (1791), a long, very famous Chinese novel.

the Lost Encyclopedia, edited by the Third Emperor of the Luminous Dynasty[6] but never printed. The record on the phonograph revolved next to a bronze phoenix. I also recall a *famille rose*[7] vase and another, many centuries older, of that shade of blue which our craftsmen copied from the potters of Persia . . .

Stephen Albert observed me with a smile. He was, as I have said, very tall, sharp-featured, with gray eyes and a gray beard. He told me that he had been a missionary in Tientsin "before aspiring to become a Sinologist."

We sat down—I on a long, low divan, he with his back to the window and a tall circular clock. I calculated that my pursuer, Richard Madden, could not arrive for at least an hour. My irrevocable determination could wait.

"An astounding fate, that of Ts'ui Pên," Stephen Albert said. "Governor of his native province, learned in astronomy, in astrology, and in the tireless interpretation of the canonical books, chess player, famous poet and calligrapher—he abandoned all this in order to compose a book and a maze. He renounced the pleasures of both tyranny and justice, of his populous couch, of his banquets and even of erudition—all to close himself up for thirteen years in the Pavilion of the Limpid Solitude. When he died, his heirs found nothing save chaotic manuscripts. His family, as you may be aware, wished to condemn them to the fire; but his executor—a Taoist or Buddhist monk—insisted on their publication."

"We descendants of Ts'ui Pên," I replied, "continue to curse that monk. Their publication was senseless. The book is an indeterminate heap of contradictory drafts. I examined it once: In the third chapter the hero dies, in the fourth he is alive. As for the other undertaking of Ts'ui Pên, his labyrinth . . ."

"Here is Ts'ui Pên's labyrinth," he said, indicating a tall lacquered desk.

"An ivory labyrinth!" I exclaimed. "A minimum labyrinth."

"A labyrinth of symbols," he corrected. "An invisible labyrinth of time. To me, a barbarous Englishman, has been entrusted the revelation of this diaphanous mystery. After more than a hundred years, the details are irretrievable; but it is not hard to conjecture what happened. Ts'ui Pên must have said once: *I am withdrawing to write a book.* And another time: *I am withdrawing to construct a labyrinth.* Everyone imagined two works; to no one did it occur that the book and the maze were one and the same thing. The Pavilion of the Limpid Solitude stood in the center of a garden that was perhaps intricate; that circumstance could have suggested to the heirs a physical labyrinth. Ts'ui Pên died; no one in the vast territories that were his came upon the labyrinth; the confusion of the novel suggested to me that *it* was the maze. Two circumstances gave me the correct solution of the problem. One: the curious legend that Ts'ui Pên had planned to create a labyrinth which would be strictly infinite. The other: a fragment of a letter I discovered."

---

[6] **Third . . . Dynasty:** The Yung-lo emperor of the Ming dynasty who commissioned an extensive encyclopedia in the fifteenth century.

[7] *famille rose:* Pink family (French), referring to Chinese enamelware.

Albert rose. He turned his back on me for a moment; he opened a drawer of the black and gold desk. He faced me and in his hands he held a sheet of paper that had once been crimson, but was now pink and tenuous and cross-sectioned. The fame of Ts'ui Pên as a calligrapher had been justly won. I read, uncomprehendingly and with fervor, these words written with a minute brush by a man of my blood: *I leave to the various futures (not to all) my garden of forking paths.* Wordlessly, I returned the sheet. Albert continued:

"Before unearthing this letter, I had questioned myself about the ways in which a book can be infinite. I could think of nothing other than a cyclic volume, a circular one. A book whose last page was identical with the first, a book which had the possibility of continuing indefinitely. I remembered too that night which is at the middle of the Thousand and One Nights when Scheherezade (through a magical oversight of the copyist) begins to relate word for word the story of the Thousand and One Nights, establishing the risk of coming once again to the night when she must repeat it, and thus on to infinity. I imagined as well a Platonic, hereditary work, transmitted from father to son, in which each new individual adds a chapter or corrects with pious care the pages of his elders. These conjectures diverted me; but none seemed to correspond, not even remotely, to the contradictory chapters of Ts'ui Pên. In the midst of this perplexity, I received from Oxford the manuscript you have examined. I lingered, naturally, on the sentence: *I leave to the various futures (not to all) my garden of forking paths.* Almost instantly, I understood: 'the garden of forking paths' was the chaotic novel; the phrase 'the various futures (not to all)' suggested to me the forking in time, not in space. A broad rereading of the work confirmed the theory. In all fictional works, each time a man is confronted with several alternatives, he chooses one and eliminates the others; in the fiction of Ts'ui Pên, he chooses — simultaneously — all of them. *He creates,* in this way, diverse futures, diverse times which themselves also proliferate and fork. Here, then, is the explanation of the novel's contradictions. Fang, let us say, has a secret; a stranger calls at his door; Fang resolves to kill him. Naturally, there are several possible outcomes: Fang can kill the intruder, the intruder can kill Fang, they both can escape, they both can die, and so forth. In the work of Ts'ui Pên, all possible outcomes occur; each one is the point of departure for other forkings. Sometimes, the paths of this labyrinth converge: For example, you arrive at this house, but in one of the possible pasts you are my enemy, in another, my friend. If you will resign yourself to my incurable pronunciation, we shall read a few pages."

His face, within the vivid circle of the lamplight, was unquestionably that of an old man, but with something unalterable about it, even immortal. He read with slow precision two versions of the same epic chapter. In the first, an army marches to a battle across a lonely mountain; the horror of the rocks and shadows makes the men undervalue their lives and they gain an easy victory. In the second, the same army traverses a palace where a great festival is taking place; the resplendent battle seems to them a continuation of the celebration and they win the victory. I listened with proper veneration to these ancient narratives, perhaps less admirable in themselves than the fact that they had been created by my blood and were being restored to me by a man of a remote empire, in the course of a desperate adventure, on a Western isle. I remember the last words, repeated in each version like a secret commandment: *Thus fought the heroes, tranquil their admirable hearts, violent their swords, resigned to kill and to die.*

From that moment on, I felt about me and within my dark body an invisible, intangible swarming. Not the swarming of the divergent, parallel, and finally coalescent armies, but a more inaccessible, more intimate agitation that they in some manner prefigured. Stephen Albert continued:

"I don't believe that your illustrious ancestor played idly with these variations. I don't consider it credible that he would sacrifice thirteen years to the infinite execution of a rhetorical experiment. In your country, the novel is a subsidiary form of literature; in Ts'ui Pên's time it was a despicable form. Ts'ui Pên was a brilliant novelist, but he was also a man of letters who doubtless did not consider himself a mere novelist. The testimony of his contemporaries proclaims—and his life fully confirms—his metaphysical and mystical interests. Philosophic controversy usurps a good part of the novel. I know that of all problems, none disturbed him so greatly nor worked upon him so much as the abysmal problem of time. Now then, the latter is the only problem that does not figure in the pages of the *Garden.* He does not even use the word that signifies *time.* How do you explain this voluntary omission?"

I proposed several solutions—all unsatisfactory. We discussed them. Finally, Stephen Albert said to me:

"In a riddle whose answer is chess, what is the only prohibited word?"

I thought a moment and replied, "The word *chess.*"

"Precisely," said Albert. "*The Garden of Forking Paths* is an enormous riddle, or parable, whose theme is time; this recondite cause prohibits its mention. To omit a word always, to resort to inept metaphors and obvious periphrases, is perhaps the most emphatic way of stressing it. That is the tortuous method preferred, in each of the meanderings of his indefatigable novel, by the oblique Ts'ui Pên. I have compared hundreds of manuscripts, I have corrected the errors that the negligence of the copyists has introduced, I have guessed the plan of this chaos, I have reestablished—I believe I have reestablished—the primordial organization, I have translated the entire work: It is clear to me that not once does he employ the word 'time.' The explanation is obvious: *The Garden of Forking Paths* is an incomplete, but not false, image of the universe as Ts'ui Pên conceived it. In contrast to Newton and Schopenhauer,[8] your ancestor did not believe in a uniform, absolute time. He believed in an infinite series of times, in a growing, dizzying net of divergent, convergent, and parallel times. This network of times which approached one another, forked, broke off, or were unaware of one another for centuries, embraces *all* possibilities of time. We do not exist in the majority of these times; in some you exist, and not I; in others I, and not you; in others, both of us. In the present one, which a favorable fate has granted me, you have arrived at my house; in another,

---

[8] **Newton and Schopenhauer:** Isaac Newton (1642–1727), an English mathematician; Arthur Schopenhauer (1788–1860), a German philosopher.

while crossing the garden, you found me dead; in still another, I utter these same words, but I am a mistake, a ghost."

"In every one," I pronounced, not without a tremble to my voice, "I am grateful to you and revere you for your re-creation of the garden of Ts'ui Pên."

"Not in all," he murmured with a smile. "Time forks perpetually toward innumerable futures. In one of them I am your enemy."

Once again I felt the swarming sensation of which I have spoken. It seemed to me that the humid garden that surrounded the house was infinitely saturated with invisible persons. Those persons were Albert and I, secret, busy, and multiform in other dimensions of time. I raised my eyes and the tenuous nightmare dissolved. In the yellow and black garden there was only one man; but this man was as strong as a statue . . . this man was approaching along the path and he was Captain Richard Madden.

"The future already exists," I replied, "but I am your friend. Could I see the letter again?"

Albert rose. Standing tall, he opened the drawer of the tall desk; for the moment his back was to me. I had readied the revolver. I fired with extreme caution. Albert fell uncomplainingly, immediately. I swear his death was instantaneous—a lightning stroke.

The rest is unreal, insignificant. Madden broke in, arrested me. I have been condemned to the gallows. I have won out abominably; I have communicated to Berlin the secret name of the city they must attack. They bombed it yesterday; I read it in the same papers that offered to England the mystery of the learned Sinologist Stephen Albert who was murdered by a stranger, one Yu Tsun. The Chief had deciphered this mystery. He knew my problem was to indicate (through the uproar of the war) the city called Albert, and that I had found no other means to do so than to kill a man of that name. He does not know (no one can know) my innumerable contrition and weariness.

✒ PABLO NERUDA
B. CHILE, 1904–1973

Not only is Pablo Neruda one of the greatest poets to have written in Spanish, he is also one of the finest poets of the twentieth century to have written in any language. Like William Blake, Walt Whitman, and William Butler Yeats, Neruda created poems in which history, politics, and personal experience coalesce into language. Neruda's unabashed devotion to his native Chile is reminiscent of Walt Whitman's passionate love for the people and places of the United States. Neruda's poems are intimately tied to the soil and sea of Chile, and, like Whitman, he delighted in the common things around him, objects of simple grace like spoons, salt,

www For links to more information about Neruda, see bedfordstmartins .com/worldlit compact.

and socks. He also incorporated history into his poems, especially the conquest and exploitation of Latin America by Europe and the United States. His large body of work helped bring to the people of Chile and all of Latin America a sense of pride and an identity separate from that of their conquerors.

Although he won a number of international peace awards and literary prizes, including the Nobel Prize in Literature in 1971, Neruda did not become widely known or popular in the United States in his lifetime; his bold mixture of leftist politics and poetry alienated American critics and publishers. In his later years, without relinquishing his Chilean roots, Neruda searched for bonds that would reach across national boundaries and draw men and women together in a joint human enterprise.

Exposure to World Culture.   Pablo Neruda was born Ricardo Eliezer Neftali Reyes y Basoalto on July 12, 1904, in the southern Chilean town of Parral. His father, Jose del Carmen Reyes, was a railroad worker. His mother, Rosa de Basoalto, died when Pablo was three or four years old; his father's second wife, Trinidad Candia, was described by Neruda as "the tutelary angel of my childhood." They moved south of Parral to the small town of Temuco, where Pablo spent his childhood in a lush environment of dense forest, sultry rains, and pungent odors—the sensorium of experience at the center of Neruda's poems. As a child he announced, "I'm going out to hunt poems," and he was enormously successful: From childhood on he seemed to see his life in terms of language, of fitting words to the occasion. To that end Neruda was blessed with a mentor early on, the poet Gabriela Mistral, a headmistress in Temuco and the first Latin American writer to receive the Nobel Prize in Literature (1945). Mistral took Neruda under her wing and exposed him to European literature. In 1920 at the age of sixteen, he published poems and articles under his new name, Pablo Neruda, after a nineteenth-century Czech writer, Jan Neruda. He adopted the pseudonym out of fear of ridicule from his family. Mistral recommended him for a scholarship when he was seventeen to study French literature at the Instituto Pedagogica in Santiago, the cultural and political capital of Chile. Leading a bohemian lifestyle in the capital city, Neruda read poets like the FRENCH SYMBOLISTS Arthur Rimbaud (1854–1891) and **Charles Baudelaire.** Between 1923 and 1926 he wrote five books of poetry, but it was the second, *Twenty Love Poems and a Song of Despair* (*Veinte poemas de amor y una cancion desesperada*, 1924), that brought him praise and national recognition at the age of twenty.

p. 929

Like other Latin American countries, Chile rewards its writers with diplomatic posts, and for more than fifteen years Neruda was a Chilean consul in various countries. At the young age of twenty-three he was sent to Southeast Asia; he lived in Rangoon, Colombo, Singapore, and Batavia between 1927 and 1932, bearing witness to a troubled period when countries were struggling for their independence from Europe. Neruda's poems of this time, which show the influence of SURREALISM, were collected in *Residence on Earth* (*Residencia en la tierra*). In 1933 he returned to Chile and was then assigned to Buenos Aires, then to Madrid, where *Residence on Earth,* Parts I and II, were published in 1935 to much acclaim

and the admiration of Spanish poets. When the SPANISH CIVIL WAR broke
out in 1936 and Neruda's friend the brilliant poet **Federico García Lorca**
was executed by the Civil Guard, Neruda, whose poems had become
angry and sad, became outspokenly anti-Fascist. In an interview he spoke
of those years: "The most intense memories . . . are those of my life
in Spain — that great brotherhood of poets. It was terrible to see that
republic of friends destroyed by the civil war. My friends were scattered:
Some were exterminated right there — like García Lorca and Miguel
Hernández;[1] others went into exile."

p. 1518

Into Politics.   Neruda was recalled from Madrid by the Chilean government in 1937, then reassigned to Spain and France to aid Republican
Spanish refugees. Then from 1939 to 1943 he acted as Chilean consul to
Mexico before returning to Santiago, where he became a member of the
central committee of the Chilean Communist Party and was elected to
the senate. In a series of letters beginning in 1947, Neruda accused Chile's
president, Gonzalez Videla, of betraying Chile in dealings with the United
States. When he lost his case against Videla before Chile's Supreme Court
and Communism was declared illegal by Chile's Congress, Neruda was
forced into exile; he traveled to Mexico, France, Italy, the Soviet Union,
and China.

Chile had been unique in Latin America in that it democratically
elected presidents, a tradition that ended with the military dictatorship of
Pinochet in 1974. But even within its democracies, there had been an
ongoing power struggle in Chile in the modern period between the conservative upper classes and the working classes — not unlike other Latin
American countries, in which the distribution of wealth was radically
disproportionate. Chilean labor unions had clamored for recognition
and peasants had demanded land reform. Neruda's evident sympathies
with the downtrodden began to appear in his poetry.

A major collection of Neruda's poems, *General Song* (*Canto general,*
1950) — 340 poems grouped into fifteen sections — caught the world's
attention with its depiction of Latin American history, geography, and
the politics of its dictators. Neruda raised the hackles of U.S. government
officials with his depiction of the exploitation of Latin American people
and resources by huge corporations like the United Fruit Company. The
poet himself celebrated the people of the United States even while he criticized U.S. corporations and politicos; a few years earlier he had paid
tribute to American writers, the American frontier, and Abraham Lincoln
in "Let the Rail Splitter Awake" (1948), expressing the belief that the
United States shared in the destiny of all the Americas.

World Fame.   Neruda was translated and honored all over the world,
especially in socialist countries, in the 1950s and '60s. Settling into his
famous house, Isla Negra, on the Pacific coast in Chile, Neruda carried on

On the one hand is
the soil of the conti-
nent itself, before
names were devised
for it, with its natural
riches, its fertility,
and its prototypal
people augmented in
the course of time by
men of all races who
felt . . . a flame of
freedom and charity
in their hearts, from
fray Bartolomé de las
Casas or Alonso de
Ercilla, to San
Martín, Lincoln, and
Martí to the striker
jailed in Iquique or
an *ejidatario* from
Sonora: all Ameri-
cans. On the other
hand, there are rapa-
cious and covetous
men, from Columbus
to Cortés, to Rosas
and García Moreno,
to a Somoza or a Tru-
jillo and the masters
of Anaconda Copper
and United Fruit.
— LUIS MONGUIÓ, 1961,
    on the theme of
    General Song

---

[1]**Miguel Hernández** (1910–1942): Spanish poet whose work dealt with social injustice.

a love affair with the Chilean people while cultivating a fellowship with a wide circle of poets both at home and abroad. His poetic voice mellowed and his attitude toward life was celebratory in more than a dozen new collections, including *The Stones of Chile* (*Las piedras de Chile*, 1969), *Isla Negra: A Notebook* (*Memorial de Isla Negra*, 1964), and *World's End* (*Fin de mundo*, 1969).

Neruda was appointed the Chilean ambassador to France when Salvador Allende was elected president of Chile in 1970, the first duly elected socialist in the Americas, and Chile declared a national holiday when the poet was awarded the Nobel Prize in 1971. Neruda returned to Chile in 1973 in poor health and died in a Santiago clinic on September 23, heartbroken by the military coup that had led to the assassination of Allende just days before, on September 11, and led to the brutally repressive dictatorship of General Augusto Pinochet. Neruda's *Memoirs* (*Confiso que he vivido: Memorias*) was published in 1974; an English translation appeared in 1977. Nine additional volumes of his poetry were published posthumously.

A Sampling of Poems. Despite his active commitment to politics, Neruda's poetic output was enormous; a 1962 edition of his poems, set in small print, ran to 1,832 pages. The genius of his poetry lies in its earthy imagery, in his use of all the senses to create a strong and vigorous language. Neruda was instrumental in helping to free Latin American writers from artificial restraints and cerebral quaintness. The poems on the following pages are a sampling from the different periods of his long writing career. The first two, "Ode with a Lament" and "Sexual Water," are from *Residence on Earth*, which presents Neruda's version of the post–World War I "wasteland," a disheveled world unhinged from destiny and purpose. There is an underlying sadness in these poems even as Neruda looks to surreal images in the hope of discovering a deeper pattern of connections through dreamlike associations. "Ode with a Lament" immediately links a conventional image with the startling phrase, "O pressure of doves." A dazzling combination of traditional poetic images juxtaposed with exotic metaphors follow as the poem develops the themes of death, sorrow, and broken things.

"Sexual Water" is an extended treatment of sexual energy or libido. Like Walt Whitman, Neruda was devoted to the world of real objects and he loved to make lists and to shade them with potential danger. An ongoing theme of these poems seems to be that if there is any way to reassemble the world, it must begin with the physical world and not with some abstract, metaphysical system.

General Song (1950), the large collection of Neruda's poems, represents a change in the poet's writing style and purpose. His earlier surreal poems, which were keyed to the natural world, had developed a personal, even private lexicon of meaning. In *General Song*, Neruda connects with the history of the Americas, with the intent to communicate the ongoing struggle for its heart and soul. "Hymn and Return," collected in Part VII

Now let us use the good word "Americanism." Neruda constantly reminds us of Whitman, much more for his deep breath and that ease of the American man, who knows neither hindrances nor obstacles, than for his verse of huge proportions. His Americanism is present in his works in the form of a vigorous freedom, in a blessed audacity, and in a bitter fertility.

– GABRIELA MISTRAL

of *General Song,* points to the new direction of the whole volume: Neruda's love affair with Chile will spread throughout the Americas. In a visionary sequence of poems early in *General Song, The Heights of Macchu Picchu,* inspired by a pilgrimage to the ancient Inca stronghold in the Peruvian Andes, the poet arrives at Macchu Picchu and connects with an ancient civilization. It is as if he finds a source of hope in the airy vastness of the Andean stronghold. The succeeding sections deal with the greed, power, wealth, suffering, and hope in the social and political struggles of the colonial history of the Americas. The prosaic language of "The United Fruit Co." borders on simple propaganda in poetic form. Its declarative statements are direct indictments of various dictators—listed by name—and ruthless corporations that exploited various Latin American countries for cheap labor and natural resources. The concluding stanza about the suffering of Indians is similar to a number of other Latin American works that convey the evils of European colonialism through the plight of the Indian in the Americas.

In *Elementary Odes* (*Odas elementales,* 1954 and 1956) Neruda uses a simple voice as a means of reaching Latin American working classes and produces a charming series of poems about simple objects like socks, tomatoes, and lemons. "Poet's Obligation," published in *Full Powers* (*Plenos poderes,* 1962), echoes Walt Whitman's empathy for other and diverse human beings and his desire to give voice to the silent. The poet, according to Neruda, has an obligation to free those people who live in prisons—whether they be prison cells, factories, or offices.

■ **FURTHER RESEARCH**

Biography
Teitelboim, Volodia. *Neruda: An Intimate Biography.* 1991.

Editions
Neruda, Pablo. *Neruda's Garden: An Anthology of Odes.* Maria Jacketti, trans. 1995.
——. *Odes to Common Things.* Ken Krabbenhoft, trans. 1994.

History and Culture
Rodman, Selden. "Pablo Neruda's Chile." In *South America of the Poets.* 1970.

Criticism
Costa, Rene de. *The Poetry of Pablo Neruda.* 1979.
Duran, Manuel, and Margery Safir. *Earth Tones: The Poetry of Pablo Neruda.* 1981.
Riess, Frank. *The World and the Stone: Language and Imagery in Neruda's* Canto General. 1972.
Santi, Enrico Mario. *Pablo Neruda, The Poetics of Prophecy.* 1982.

Ode with a Lament

Translated by H. R. Hays

O girl among the roses, O pressure of doves,
O citadel of fishes and rosebushes,
Your souis a bottle full of dry salt
And your skin is a bell full of grapes.

Unfortunately I have nothing to give you except fingernails
Or eyelashes, or melted pianos,
Or dreams which pour from my heart in torrents,
Dusty dreams that race like black riders,
Dreams full of speed and affliction.

10   I can only love you with kisses and poppies,
With garlands wet by the rain,
Gazing at yellow dogs and horses red as ashes.

I can only love you with waves behind me,
Between wandering gusts of sulphur and pensive waters,
Swimming toward cemeteries that flow in certain rivers
With wet pasturage growing above sad tombs of plaster,
Swimming through submerged hearts
And pale catalogues of unburied children.
There is much death, many funereal events
20   In my forsaken passions and desolate kisses,
There is a water that falls on my head,
While my hair grows,
A water like time, a black torrential water,
With a nocturnal voice, with a cry
Of a bird in the rain, like an interminable
Shadow of a wet wing sheltering my bones,
While I dress myself, while
Interminably I look at myself in mirrors and windows,
I hear someone calling me, calling me with sobs,
30   With a sad voice rotted by time.
You are on foot, on the earth, full
Of fangs and lightings.
You generate kisses and you kill ants.
You weep with health, with onions, with bees,
With burning alphabet.
You are like a blue and green sword
And you ripple when touched like a river.

Come to my soul dressed in white, like a branch
Of bleeding roses and cups of ashes,
40   Come with an apple and a horse,
Because there is a dark room there and a broken candelabra,
Some twisted chairs that wait for winter,
And a dead dove with a number.

✑ Sexual Water

Translated by H. R. Hays

Running in single drops,
In drops like teeth,
In thick drops of marmalade and blood,
Running in drops,
The water falls,
Like a sword of drops
Like a rending river of glass,
It falls biting,
Striking the axis of symmetry, hitting on the
10   Ribs of the soul,
Breaking castoff things, soaking the darkness.

It is only a gust, damper than tears,
A liquid, a sweat, a nameless oil,
A sharp movement,
Creating itself, thickening itself,
The water falls,
In slow drops,
Toward the sea, toward its dry ocean,
Toward its wave without water.

20   I see a long summer and a death rattle coming out of a granary,
Cellars, cicadas,
Towns, stimuli,
Habitations, girl children
Sleeping with hands on their hearts,
Dreaming with pirates, with fire,
I see ships,
I see trees of spinal cord
Bristling like furious cats,
I see blood, daggers, and women's stockings,

30   I see men's hair,
I see beds, I see corridors where a virgin screams,
I see blankets and organs and hotels.

I see stealthy dreams,
I accept the preceding days,
And also origins and also memories,
Like an eyelid dreadfully raised by force
I am watching.

And then there is this sound:
A red noise of bones,
40   An adhering of flesh,
And legs yellow as grain stalks joining together.
I am listening among explosions of kisses,
I am listening, shaken among breathing and sobs.

I am watching, hearing
With half my soul on sea and half my soul on land,
And with both halves of my soul I look at the world.

And though I close my eyes and cover my heart
Completely,
I see a deaf water falling
50   In deaf drops.

It is like a hurricane of gelatin,
Like a cataract of sperm and medusas.
I see a muddy rainbow flowing.
I see its waters passing through my bones.

Hymn and Return

Translated by Robert Bly

Country, my country, I turn my blood in your direction.
But I am begging you the way a child begs its mother,
with tears:
          take this blind guitar
and these lost features.
I left to find sons for you over the earth,

I left to comfort those fallen with your name made of snow,
I left to build a house with your pure timber,
I left to carry your star to the wounded heroes.

10   Now I want to fall asleep in your substance.
Give me your clear night of piercing strings,
your night like a ship, your altitude covered with stars.

My country: I want to change my shadow.
My country: I want to have another rose.
I want to put my arm around your narrow waist
and sit down on your stones whitened by the sea
and hold the wheat back and look deep into it.
I am going to pick the thin flower of nitrate,[1]
I am going to feel the icy wool of the field,
20   and staring at your famous and lonesome sea-foam
I'll weave with them a wreath on the shore for your beauty.

Country, my country,
entirely surrounded by aggressive water
and fighting snow,
the eagle and the sulphur come together in you,
and a drop of pure human light
burns in your antarctic hand of ermine and sapphire,
lighting up the hostile sky.

My country, take care of your light! Hold up
30   your stiff straw of hope
into the blind and frightening air.
All of this difficult light has fallen on your isolated land,
this future of the race,
that makes you defend a mysterious flower
alone, in the hugeness of an America that lies asleep.

---

[1] **nitrate:** Nitrates are an important part of the economy in Chile; they can be very dangerous to the workmen who mine them. [Editors' note.]

The United Fruit Co.

Translated by Robert Bly

When the trumpet sounded, it was
all prepared on the earth,
and Jehovah parceled out the earth
to Coca-Cola, Inc., Anaconda,
Ford Motors, and other entities:
The Fruit Company, Inc.
reserved for itself the most succulent,
the central coast of my own land,
the delicate waist of America.
It rechristened its territories
as the "Banana Republics"
and over the sleeping dead,
over the restless heroes
who brought about the greatness,
the liberty and the flags,
it established the comic opera:
abolished the independencies,
presented crowns of Caesar,
unsheathed envy, attracted
the dictatorship of the flies,
Trujillo flies, Tacho flies,
Carias flies, Martinez flies,
Ubico flies,[1] damp flies
of modest blood and marmalade,
drunken flies who zoom
over the ordinary graves,
circus flies, wise flies
well trained in tyranny.

Among the bloodthirsty flies
the Fruit Company lands its ships,
taking off the coffee and the fruit;
the treasure of our submerged
territories flows as though
on plates into the ships.

---

[1] **Trujillo flies . . . Ubico flies:** Dictators in Central America: Rafael Leonidas Trujillo Molina in the Dominican Republic, 1930–38 and 1942–52; Maximiliano Hernández Martínez in El Salvador, 1931–44; Tiburcio Carías Andino in Honduras, 1933–49; Jorge Ubico in Guatemala, 1931–44. [Editors' note.]

Meanwhile Indians are falling
into the sugared chasms
of the harbors, wrapped
for burial in the mist of the dawn:
a body rolls, a thing
40   that has no name, a fallen cipher,
a cluster of dead fruit
thrown down on the dump.

The Heights of Macchu Picchu

Translated by Jack Schmitt

VI

And so I scaled the ladder of the earth
amid the atrocious maze of lost jungles
up to you, Macchu Picchu.
High citadel of terraced stones,
at long last the dwelling of him whom the earth
did not conceal in its slumbering vestments.
In you, as in two parallel lines,
the cradle of lightning and man
was rocked in a wind of thorns.

10   Mother of stone, sea spray of the condors.

Towering reef of the human dawn.

Spade lost in the primal sand.

This was the dwelling, this is the site:
here the full kernels of corn rose
and fell again like red hailstones.

Here the golden fiber emerged from the vicuña[1]
to clothe love, tombs, mothers,
the king, prayers, warriors.

---

[1] **vicuña**: An animal that was found wild in the Andes; it is related to the llama and well known for its soft, shaggy wool.

Here man's feet rested at night
20 beside the eagle's feet, in the high gory
retreats, and at dawn
they trod the rarefied mist with feet of thunder
and touched lands and stones
until they recognized them in the night or in death.

I behold vestments and hands,
the vestige of water in the sonorous void,
the wall tempered by the touch of a face
that beheld with my eyes the earthen lamps,
that oiled with my hands the vanished
30 wood: because everything — clothing, skin, vessels,
words, wine, bread —
is gone, fallen to earth.

And the air flowed with orange-blossom
fingers over all the sleeping:
a thousand years of air, months, weeks of air,
of blue wind, of iron cordillera,[2]
like gentle hurricanes of footsteps
polishing the solitary precinct of stone.

---

[2] **cordillera:** A mountain range.

∾ Ode to Salt

Translated by Robert Bly

I saw the salt
in this shaker
in the salt flats.
I know
you
will never believe me,
but
it sings,
the salt sings, the hide
10 of the salt plains,
it sings
through a mouth smothered
by earth.
I shuddered in those deep

solitudes
when I heard
the voice
of
the salt
20   in the desert.
Near Antofagasta°   a city in northern Chile
the entire
salt plain
speaks:
it is a
broken
voice,
a song full
of grief.
30   Then in its own mines
rock salt, a mountain
of buried light,
a cathedral through which light passes,
crystal of the sea, abandoned
by the waves.

And then on every table
on this earth,
salt,
your nimble
40   body
pouring out
the vigorous light
over
our foods.
Preserver
of the stores
of the ancient ships,
you were
an explorer
50   in the ocean,
substance
going first
over the unknown, barely open
routes of the sea-foam.
Dust of the sea, the tongue
receives a kiss
of the night sea from you:
taste recognizes
the ocean in each salted morsel,

60   and therefore the smallest,
the tiniest
wave of the shaker
brings home to us
not only your domestic whiteness
but the inward flavor of the infinite.

❧ Poet's Obligation

Translated by Alastair Reid

To whoever is not listening to the sea
this Friday morning, to whoever is cooped up
in house or office, factory or woman
or street or mine or harsh prison cell:
to him I come, and, without speaking or looking,
I arrive and open the door of his prison,
and a vibration starts up, vague and insistent,
a great fragment of thunder sets in motion
the rumble of the planet and the foam,
10   the raucous rivers of the ocean flood,
the star vibrates swiftly in its corona,
and the sea is beating, dying and continuing.

So, drawn on by my destiny,
I ceaselessly must listen to and keep
the sea's lamenting in my awareness,
I must feel the crash of the hard water
and gather it up in a perpetual cup
so that, wherever those in prison may be,
wherever they suffer the autumn's castigation,
20   I may be there with an errant wave,
I may move, passing through windows,
and hearing me, eyes will glance upward
saying "How can I reach the sea?"
And I shall broadcast, saying nothing,
the starry echoes of the wave,
a breaking up of foam and of quicksand,
a rustling of salt withdrawing,
the grey cry of sea-birds on the coast.

So, through me, freedom and the sea
30   will make their answer to the shuttered heart.

❧ SAMUEL BECKETT
B. IRELAND, 1906–1989

Samuel Beckett, Irish-born playwright, novelist, story writer, poet, and translator, emigrated to Paris where he created a substantial body of work in which many memorable characters search for meaning in a confusing and enigmatic world. In his mature work Beckett is guided by a sense of comedy that nevertheless rarely dilutes his bleak view of life. While he is comparable to a variety of literary figures—including his mentor, the Irish word wizard James Joyce—his spiritual kinship extends to an even more diverse lot, including Italian playwright Luigi Pirandello, Dutch artist Bram van Velde,[1] and comedic film actors such as Buster Keaton.[2]

Samuel Beckett
Beckett in middle age. (© Topham/The Image Works)

Like many writers of his time, Beckett contributed to the broad literary and artistic movement that today is called MODERNISM. Influenced by the psychoanalytic theories of Sigmund Freud (p. 1429; 1856–1939), which sought the cure to neurosis in the individual's buried past, and by Carl Jung (1875–1961), who found in world myths and symbols evidence of a collective unconscious, modernist writers and artists endeavored to express the hidden inner life of the individual. A member of the French Underground during the Nazi occupation of France in the Second World War, Beckett emerged from the experience as one of the most profound voices of the European generation that sought to understand the human predicament—"L'ABSURD," as the French called it. Although he shared the interests of many of his peers, Beckett, characteristically, worked alone. While Jean-Paul Sartre, Albert Camus (p. 1580), and other French writers created a literary movement based on *l'absurd,* Beckett wrote largely without recognition in the Paris that they, too, inhabited.

Beckett's play *Waiting for Godot* (1952) will probably number among the great works of literature of all time. His early writings in English, influenced by Joyce, and his adept translations of poetry and fiction from several European languages quickly established his reputation as a master stylist. But he separated himself from such prose masters as Joyce later in his career, making his own mark with dramatic dialogues written with poetic brevity. Time and again Beckett's characters drive home a point, often painfully, by saying the unsayable in simple language. Beckett so strove after simplicity that he switched from writing in English to writing in French because, he said, he was less tempted by the subtleties of his adopted tongue.

---

[1] **Bram van Velde** (1895–1981): A close friend of Beckett's and the principal subject of an article he wrote on the state of painting in modern Europe. Beckett frequently appears to be describing his own position when writing of van Velde: He speaks of modern art being "in mourning for the object" and of the artist's "fidelity to failure," so that, being "obliged to act, he makes an expressive act, even if only of itself, of its impossibility, of its obligation."

[2] **Buster Keaton** (1895–1966): One of the early generation of film comedians that included Charlie Chaplin and Harold Lloyd. Beckett was a great admirer of the art of slapstick comedy and was pleased when Buster Keaton was engaged to play in *Film,* Beckett's only work for the cinema, a short film produced in 1964.

www For links to more information about Beckett, see bedfordstmartins .com/worldlit compact.

Early Life. Samuel Beckett was born on the outskirts of Dublin on April 13, 1906. Driven to apply himself while still very young by a domineering Protestant mother who recognized his extraordinary intellectual abilities, he was later educated at Trinity College, Dublin, receiving his bachelor's degree in 1928. Although he joined the Trinity College faculty, he resigned his post at the end of 1931, disappointing friends and supporters. Beckett lived miserably for a time in London, traveled in Germany, and finally settled in Paris in 1936. He wrote his two earliest novels, *Murphy* (1938) and *Watt* (written between 1942 and 1944), in English but was already writing in French at the start of World War II.

Although Beckett, a habitual loner except for infrequent forays into society, would probably have preferred to shun the world and devote himself solely to his writing, the times would not allow it. Despite his professed desire to remain neutral in politics, Beckett joined the French resistance against the German occupation in 1941, following the German invasion of France and the fall of Paris in 1940. At first, the resistance did little more than remind the French people that the war against Germany was ongoing outside France. But soon Beckett's apartment in Paris became a "drop" for microfilm photographs destined for Britain of German installations. Matters heated up in 1942, when some of Beckett's friends were arrested, and many Parisians, primarily Jews, were either shot or sent to concentration camps. Beckett moved south to Roussillon, then a free city but later occupied by the Germans as they, too, moved south. Beckett stayed a step ahead of the German Gestapo, or secret police, until the war ended. He was awarded the croix de guerre, the French medal for bravery, in 1945.

The Siege in the Room. Restored to Paris in 1946, Beckett began to conduct what he called "the siege in the room." Biographer Anthony Cronin describes this as "a reduction to bare necessities, being driven back on oneself, being stripped of all resources save the ultimate ones of desperation and self-reliance." Writing in French, Beckett produced many of his major works in these years: the two novels *Molloy* (1951) and *Malone Dies* (1951), *Waiting for Godot* (1952), and the novel *The Unnameable* (1953). He followed these with a number of other plays and short pieces originally intended for radio, including *Krapp's Last Tape* (1958).

By now Beckett lived in some degree of comfort. His reputation had been established and his small circle of friends proved impressively loyal. Even so, he suffered from a number of minor illnesses: cysts, rashes, insomnia, dizzy spells, stomach pains, bad teeth, panic attacks, and hypochondria. He had been the victim of a stabbing on a Paris street in 1938, possibly the result of an argument with a pimp, which resulted in lung damage that lasted for the rest of his life. But as he approached old age his complaints lessened. The grimness of his work did not. He referred to *Texts for Nothing*, thirteen short pieces written after *The Unnameable*, as "nothing more than the grisly afterbirth" of that novel.

In 1969, largely as a result of the success of *Waiting for Godot*, Beckett was awarded the Nobel Prize in Literature. The citation for the prize remarked that it was for "a body of work that, in new forms of fiction and the theatre, has transmuted the destitution of modern man into his exaltation." Beckett himself remained somewhat aloof from the award, commenting that he was "lacking in Nobel fiber" and worrying aloud whether he would even try to write again after all the commotion. He asked his publisher, Jerome Lindon, to accept the award in his place. In fact, though he lived twenty years longer, he wrote little new work after receiving the honor, devoting himself instead to the staging of his existing dramas. He died in December 1989.

The Beckett Man.   All Beckett's works present in one form or another what one of his biographers has called the "Beckett man"—a seriocomic character who rejects the central Western European beliefs in the life of reason, progress, and liberal optimism. Typically unemployed and without ambition in the ordinary sense, the Beckett man reels from his memory of education, society's attempt to instill in him such traditional values as honor, dignity, and courage. His experience of love is limited, though he dimly recalls the influence of his mother when he was a child. He regards physical distress, including paralysis, as ordinary and even vaguely pleasurable. The only virtue he appears to possess is a capacity to endure. Beckett's characters become increasingly enfeebled, even paralyzed, in later works until in *The Unnameable* the main character is reduced to a creature who hangs in a bottle and has only the power of reflection.

After the war, Beckett began to question the stance of his earlier characters like Murphy and Watt who had cleverly tried to deny or demolish their relationship to what they called "the big world." Perhaps moved by his participation in and knowledge of the real dangers of the French resistance, Beckett detected a certain arrogance in his early work. Instead of infusing new characters with his own learning and cleverness, he left them alone in the world, which they saw as an ominous and unknowable place. The more vulnerable Beckett made them to outside forces, the more their stature tended to grow in the eyes of the audience. Of the novel *Molloy* (written between 1947 and 1949), Beckett said, "I conceived *Molloy* and what followed the day I realized my own stupidity."

Waiting for Godot.   *Waiting for Godot* (written between 1947 and 1949, and published in French in 1952) followed *Molloy.* In *Godot,* the characters Vladimir and Estragon assemble to meet a mysterious character named Godot. Both complain of small maladies, both occasionally rise to the expectation that Godot will arrive, but both ultimately give up again. The theme of the play is repeated throughout in one way or another: "Nothing to be done." The actors, as a critic has noted, are imprisoned by their own dialogue, which always comes back to the same place. Not that nothing ever happens; someone comes, but it is not Godot. It is Pozzo, whom Estragon and Vladimir first mistakenly identify as Godot only to disavow their hasty error. Eventually, Pozzo leaves for the fair, where he

What is the essence of the experience of being? asks Beckett. And so he begins to strip away the inessentials.

– Martin Esslin, critic, 1961

has determined to sell his slave, Lucky. But in the second act of the play, Pozzo and Lucky return through the same door through which they had left. Both are enfeebled: Pozzo is blind and Lucky is unable to speak. At the end of each of the two acts there appears a boy who announces that Godot will not come today, "but surely tomorrow." But Godot does not arrive the next day either. Vladimir summarizes the action of the play in a speech during the second act:

> Tomorrow, when I wake, or think I do, what shall I say of today? That with Estragon my friend, at this place, until the fall of night, I waited for Godot? That Pozzo passed, with his carrier, and that he spoke to us? Probably. But in all that what truth will there be?

Waiting for Godot is a work that has been interpreted as operating on many levels: as slapstick comedy; as a play about the death of God (*God-ot* could be heard as a pun in English); as an EXISTENTIALIST drama in which man is left alone to act in the world but can find no basis for action; as a play about time and its destruction of possibility. But no matter how one sees it, in the end the theatergoer is caught up in the spare beauty of the play's dialogue, the amount of interest it creates in the midst of apparent hopelessness, the surprising degree to which one identifies with the characters, however weak they are. A play about despair, *Waiting for Godot* maintains an atmosphere of faint, unreasonable hope that carries both the audience and the actors, however reluctantly, through to the drama's conclusion.

Krapp's Last Tape.   Beckett saw his writings of the late 1940s as the height of his creativity, disparaging subsequent works for their lack of development. In 1956 he commented, "For some authors writing gets easier the more they write. For me it gets more and more difficult. For me the area of possibilities gets smaller and smaller." Beckett made an effort to escape this narrowing field of possibilities in a radio play called *All that Fall,* broadcast in 1956. The piece recounts memories of Beckett's youth in the Irish landscape, a theme more accessible to the listening audience than was his other work at the time. But while *All that Fall* was scripted in a public voice, *Krapp's Last Tape* (1958), Beckett's next major play, returned fiercely to inner reflection. Beckett, who had not so much as seen a tape recorder when he wrote this play, imagined a reclusive, ineffectual drunkard on his sixty-ninth birthday listening to tapes he had recorded on his twenty-eighth and thirty-ninth birthdays. (To account for the earlier use of the tape recorder, invented only around 1950, the play is set on "a late evening in the future.") The unsettling bleakness of the play emerges from the conflicts and disharmonies between the three persons that constitute Krapp at twenty-eight, thirty-nine, and sixty-nine.

■ **FURTHER RESEARCH**

Biographies
Bair, Deidre. *Samuel Beckett: A Biography.* 1978.
Cronin, Anthony. *Samuel Beckett: The Last Modernist.* 1999.

Criticism

Esslin, Martin, ed. *Samuel Beckett: A Collection of Critical Essays.* 1965.

Fletcher, John, and John Spurling. *Beckett the Playwright.* 1985.

Harvey, Lawrence. *Samuel Beckett: Poet and Critic.* 1970.

Kenner, Hugh. *Samuel Beckett: A Critical Study.* 1965.

——, ed. *A Reader's Guide to Samuel Beckett.* 1973.

Mercier, Vivien. *Beckett/Beckett.* 1977.

Pattie, David. *The Complete Critical Guide to Samuel Beckett.* 2001.

❧ Krapp's Last Tape

A late evening in the future.

Krapp's den.

Front center a small table, the two drawers of which open towards audience.

Sitting at the table, facing front, i.e., across from the drawers, a wearish[1] old man: Krapp.

Rusty black narrow trousers too short for him. Rusty black sleeveless waistcoat, four capacious pockets. Heavy silver watch and chain. Grimy white shirt open at neck, no collar. Surprising pair of dirty white boots, size ten at least, very narrow and pointed.

White face. Purple nose. Disordered grey hair. Unshaven.

Very nearsighted (but unspectacled). Hard of hearing.

Cracked voice. Distinctive intonation.

Laborious walk.

On the table a tape recorder with microphone and a number of cardboard boxes containing reels of recorded tapes.

Table and immediately adjacent area in strong white light. Rest of stage in darkness.

Krapp remains a moment motionless, heaves a great sigh, looks at his watch, fumbles in his pockets, takes out an envelope, puts it back, fumbles, takes out a small bunch of keys, raises it to his eyes, chooses a key, gets up and moves to front of table. He stoops, unlocks first drawer, peers into it, feels about inside it, takes out a reel of tape, peers at it, puts it back, locks drawer, unlocks second drawer, peers into it, feels about inside it, takes out a large banana, peers at it, locks drawer, puts keys back in his pocket. He turns, advances to edge of stage, halts, strokes banana, peels it, drops skin at his feet, puts end of banana in his mouth and remains motionless, staring vacuously before him. Finally he bites off the end, turns aside and begins pacing to and fro at edge of stage, in the light, i.e. not more than four or five paces either way, meditatively eating banana.

---

[1] *wearish:* Lean, wizened.

He treads on skin, slips, nearly falls, recovers himself, stoops and peers at skin and finally pushes it, still stooping, with his foot over the edge of stage into pit. He resumes his pacing, finishes banana, returns to table, sits down, remains a moment motionless, heaves a great sigh, takes keys from his pockets, raises them to his eyes, chooses key, gets up and moves to front of table, unlocks second drawer, takes out a second large banana, peers at it, locks drawer, puts back keys in his pocket, turns, advances to edge of stage, halts, strokes banana, peels it, tosses skin into pit, puts end of banana in his mouth and remains motionless, staring vacuously before him. Finally he has an idea, puts banana in his waistcoat pocket, the end emerging, and goes with all the speed he can muster backstage into darkness. Ten seconds. Loud pop of cork. Fifteen seconds. He comes back into light carrying an old ledger and sits down at table. He lays ledger on table, wipes his mouth, wipes his hands on the front of his waistcoat, brings them smartly together and rubs them.

KRAPP *(briskly)*: Ah! *(He bends over ledger, turns the pages, finds the entry he wants, reads.)* Box . . . thrree . . . spool . . . five. *(He raises his head and stares front. With relish.)* Spool! *(Pause.)* Spooool! *(Happy smile. Pause. He bends over table, starts peering and poking at the boxes.)* Box . . . thrree . . . thrree . . . four . . . two . . . *(with surprise)* nine! good God! . . . seven . . . ah! the little rascal! *(He takes up box, peers at it.)* Box thrree. *(He lays it on table, opens it, and peers at spools inside.)* Spool . . . *(he peers at ledger)* . . . five . . . *(he peers at spools)* . . . five . . . five . . . ah! the little scoundrel! *(He takes out a spool, peers at it.)* Spool five. *(He lays it on table, closes box three, puts it back with the others, takes up the spool.)* Box thrree, spool five. *(He bends over the machine, looks up. With relish.)* Spooool! *(Happy smile. He bends, loads spool on machine, rubs his hands.)* Ah! *(He peers at ledger, reads entry at foot of page.)* Mother at rest at last . . . Hm . . . The black ball . . . *(He raises his head, stares blankly front. Puzzled.)* Black ball? . . . *(He peers again at ledger, reads.)* The dark nurse . . . *(He raises his head, broods, peers again at ledger, reads.)* Slight improvement in bowel condition . . . Hm . . . Memorable . . . what? *(He peers closer.)* Equinox, memorable equinox. *(He raises his head, stares blankly front. Puzzled.)* Memorable equinox? . . . *(Pause. He shrugs his shoulders, peers again at ledger, reads.)* Farewell to—*(he turns the page)*—love.

He raises his head, broods, bends over machine, switches on and assumes listening posture, i.e. leaning forward, elbows on table, hand cupping ear towards machine, face front.

TAPE *(strong voice, rather pompous, clearly Krapp's at a much earlier time)*: Thirty-nine today, sound as a—*(Settling himself more comfortably he knocks one of the boxes off the table, curses, switches off, sweeps boxes and ledger violently to the ground, winds tape back to beginning, switches on, resumes posture.)* Thirty-nine today, sound as a bell, apart from my old weakness, and intellectually I have now every reason to suspect at the . . . *(hesitates)* . . . crest of the wave—or thereabouts. Celebrated the awful occasion, as in recent years, quietly at the Winehouse. Not a soul. Sat before the fire with closed eyes, separating the grain from the husks. Jotted down a few notes, on the back of an envelope. Good to be back in my den, in my old rags. Have just eaten I regret to say three bananas and only with difficulty refrained from a fourth. Fatal things for a man with my condition. *(Vehemently.)* Cut 'em out! *(Pause.)* The new light above my table is a great improvement. With all this darkness round me I feel less alone. *(Pause.)* In a way. *(Pause.)* I love to get up and move about in it, then back here to . . . *(hesitates)* . . . me. *(Pause.)* Krapp.

Pause.

The grain, now what I wonder do I mean by that, I mean . . . *(hesitates)* . . . I suppose I mean those things worth having when all the dust has—when all *my* dust has settled. I close my eyes and try and imagine them.

Pause. Krapp closes his eyes briefly.

Extraordinary silence this evening, I strain my ears and do not hear a sound. Old Miss McGlome always sings at this hour. But not tonight. Songs of her girlhood, she says. Hard to think of her as a girl. Wonderful woman though. Connaught,[2] I fancy. *(Pause.)* Shall I sing when I am her age, if I ever am? No. *(Pause.)* Did I sing as a boy? No. *(Pause.)* Did I ever sing? No.

Pause.

Just been listening to an old year, passages at random. I did not check in the book, but it must be at least ten or twelve years ago. At that time I think I was still living on and off with Bianca in Kedar Street. Well out of that, Jesus yes! Hopeless business. *(Pause.)* Not much about her, apart from a tribute to her eyes. Very warm. I suddenly saw them again. *(Pause.)* Incomparable! *(Pause.)* Ah well . . . *(Pause.)* These old P.M.s[3] are gruesome, but I often find them—*(Krapp switches off, broods, switches on)*—a help before embarking on a new . . . *(hesitates)* . . . retrospect. Hard to believe I was ever that young whelp. The voice! Jesus! And the aspirations! *(Brief laugh in which Krapp joins.)* And the resolutions! *(Brief laugh in which Krapp joins.)* To drink less, in particular. *(Brief laugh of Krapp alone.)* Statistics. Seventeen hundred hours, out of the preceding eight thousand odd, consumed on licensed premises[4] alone. More than 20%, say 40% of his waking life. *(Pause.)* Plans for a less . . . *(hesitates)* . . . engrossing sexual life. Last illness of his father. Flagging pursuit of happiness. Unattainable laxation. Sneers at what he calls his youth and thanks to God that it's over. *(Pause.)* False ring there. *(Pause.)* Shadows of the opus . . . magnum.[5] Closing with a—*(brief laugh)*—yelp to Providence. *(Prolonged laugh in which Krapp joins.)* What remains of all that misery? A girl in a shabby green coat, on a railway-station platform? No?

Pause.
When I look—

Krapp switches off, broods, looks at his watch, gets up, goes backstage into darkness. Ten seconds. Pop of cork. Ten seconds. Second cork. Ten seconds. Third cork. Ten seconds. Brief burst of quavering song.

---

[2] **Connaught:** Northwestern county of Ireland. [3] **P.M.s:** Postmortems. [4] **licensed premises:** A pub or liquor store. [5] **opus . . . magnum:** *Magnum opus,* Latin for "great work."

KRAPP *(sings)*:   Now the day is over,
                Night is drawing nigh-igh,
                Shadows—

Fit of coughing. He comes back into light, sits down, wipes his mouth, switches on, resumes his listening posture.

TAPE:—back on the year that is gone, with what I hope is perhaps a glint of the old eye to come, there is of course the house on the canal where mother lay a-dying, in the late autumn, after her long viduity *(Krapp gives a start)*, and the—*(Krapp switches off, winds back tape a little, bends his ear closer to machine, switches on)*—a-dying, after her long viduity, and the—

Krapp switches off, raises his head, stares blankly before him. His lips move in the syllables of "viduity." No sound. He gets up, goes backstage into darkness, comes back with an enormous dictionary, lays it on table, sits down, and looks up the word.

KRAPP *(reading from dictionary)*: State—or condition of being—or remaining—a widow—or widower. *(Looks up. Puzzled.)* Being—or remaining? . . . *(Pause. He peers again at dictionary. Reading.)* "Deep weeds of viduity" . . . Also of an animal, especially a bird . . . the vidua or weaver-bird . . . Black plumage of male . . . *(He looks up. With relish.)* The vidua-bird!

Pause. He closes dictionary, switches on, resumes listening posture.

TAPE:—bench by the weir[6] from where I could see her window. There I sat, in the biting wind, wishing she were gone. *(Pause.)* Hardly a soul, just a few regulars, nursemaids, infants, old men, dogs. I got to know them quite well—oh by appearance of course I mean! One dark young beauty I recollect particularly, all white and starch, incomparable bosom, with a big black hooded perambulator, most funereal thing. Whenever I looked in her direction she had her eyes on me. And yet when I was bold enough to speak to her—not having been introduced—she threatened to call a policeman. As if I had designs on her virtue! *(Laugh. Pause.)* The face she had! The eyes! Like . . . *(hesitates)* . . . chrysolite![7] *(Pause.)* Ah well . . . *(Pause.)* I was there when—*(Krapp switches off, broods, switches on again)*—the blind went down, one of those dirty brown roller affairs, throwing a ball for a little white dog, as chance would have it. I happened to look up and there it was. All over and done with, at last. I sat on for a few moments with the ball in my hand and the dog yelping and pawing at me. *(Pause.)* Moments. Her moments, my moments. *(Pause.)* The dog's moments. *(Pause.)* In the end I held it out to him and he took it in his mouth, gently, gently. A small, old, black, hard, solid rubber ball. *(Pause.)* I shall feel it, in my hand, until my dying day. *(Pause.)* I might have kept it. *(Pause.)* But I gave it to the dog.

---

[6] **weir:** Millpond.   [7] **chrysolite:** A pale green semiprecious stone.

Pause.
Ah well . . .

Pause.
Spiritually a year of profound gloom and indigence until that memorable night in March, at the end of the jetty, in the howling wind, never to be forgotten, when suddenly I saw the whole thing. The vision, at last. This I fancy is what I have chiefly to record this evening, against the day when my work will be done and perhaps no place left in my memory, warm or cold, for the miracle that . . . *(hesitates)* . . . for the fire that set it alight. What I suddenly saw then was this, that the belief I had been going on all my life, namely — *(Krapp switches off impatiently, winds tape forward, switches on again)* — great granite rocks the foam flying up in the light of the lighthouse and the wind-gauge spinning like a propellor, clear to me at last that the dark I have always struggled to keep under is in reality my most — *(Krapp curses, switches off, winds tape forward, switches on again)* — unshatterable association until my dissolution of storm and night with the light of the understanding and the fire — *(Krapp curses louder, switches off, winds tape forward, switches on again)* — my face in her breasts and my hand on her. We lay there without moving. But under us all moved, and moved us, gently, up and down, and from side to side.

Pause.
Past midnight. Never knew such silence. The earth might be uninhabited.

Pause.
Here I end —

Krapp switches off, winds tape back, switches on again.
— upper lake, with the punt, bathed off the bank, then pushed out into the stream and drifted. She lay stretched out on the floorboards with her hands under her head and her eyes closed. Sun blazing down, bit of a breeze, water nice and lively. I noticed a scratch on her thigh and asked her how she came by it. Picking gooseberries, she said. I said again I thought it was hopeless and no good going on, and she agreed, without opening her eyes. *(Pause.)* I asked her to look at me and after a few moments — *(pause)* — after a few moments she did, but the eyes just slits, because of the glare. I bent over her to get them in the shadow and they opened. *(Pause. Low.)* Let me in. *(Pause.)* We drifted in among the flags and stuck. The way they went down, sighing, before the stem! *(Pause.)* I lay down across her with my face in her breasts and my hand on her. We lay there without moving. But under us all moved, and moved us, gently, up and down, and from side to side.

Pause.
Past midnight. Never knew —

Krapp switches off, broods. Finally he fumbles in his pockets, encounters the banana, takes it out, peers at it, puts it back, fumbles, brings out the envelope, fumbles, puts back envelope, looks at his watch, gets up, and goes backstage into darkness. Ten seconds. Sound of bottle against glass, then brief siphon. Ten seconds. Bottle against glass alone. Ten seconds. He comes back a little unsteadily into light, goes to front of table, takes out keys, raises them to his eyes, chooses key, unlocks first drawer, peers into it, feels about inside, takes out reel, peers at it, locks drawer, puts keys back in his pocket, goes and sits down, takes reel off machine, lays it on dictionary, loads virgin reel on machine, takes envelope from his pocket, consults back of it, lays it on table, switches on, clears his throat, and begins to record.

KRAPP: Just been listening to that stupid bastard I took myself for thirty years ago, hard to believe I was ever as bad as that. Thank God that's all done with anyway. *(Pause.)* The eyes she had! *(Broods, realizes he is recording silence, switches off, broods. Finally.)* Everything there, everything, all the — *(Realizes this is not being recorded, switches on.)* Everything there, everything on this old muckball, all the light and dark and famine and feasting of . . . *(hesitates)* . . . the ages! *(In a shout.)* Yes! *(Pause.)* Let that go! Jesus! Take his mind off his homework! Jesus! *(Pause. Weary.)* Ah well, maybe he was right. *(Pause.)* Maybe he was right. *(Broods. Realizes. Switches off. Consults envelope.)* Pah! *(Crumples it and throws it away. Broods. Switches on.)* Nothing to say, not a squeak. What's a year now? The sour cud and the iron stool. *(Pause.)* Revelled in the word spool. *(With relish.)* Spooool! Happiest moment of the past half million. *(Pause.)* Seventeen copies sold, of which eleven at trade price to free circulating libraries beyond the seas. Getting known. *(Pause.)* One pound six and something, eight I have little doubt. *(Pause.)* Crawled out once or twice, before the summer was cold. Sat shivering in the park, drowned in dreams and burning to be gone. Not a soul. *(Pause.)* Last fancies. *(Vehemently.)* Keep 'em under! *(Pause.)* Scalded the eyes out of me reading *Effie*[8] again, a page a day, with tears again. Effie . . . *(Pause.)* Could have been happy with her, up there on the Baltic, and the pines, and the dunes. *(Pause.)* Could I? *(Pause.)* And she? *(Pause.)* Pah! *(Pause.)* Fanny came in a couple of times. Bony old ghost of a whore. Couldn't do much, but I suppose better than a kick in the crutch. The last time wasn't so bad. How do you manage it, she said, at your age? I told her I'd been saving up for her all my life. *(Pause.)* Went to Vespers once, like when I was in short trousers. *(Pause. Sings.)*

> Now the day is over,
> Night is drawing nigh-igh,
> Shadows — *(coughing, then almost inaudible)* — of the evening
> Steal across the sky.

(Gasping.) Went to sleep and fell off the pew. *(Pause.)* Sometimes wondered in the night if a last effort mightn't — *(Pause.)* Ah finish your booze now and get to your bed. Go on with this drivel in the morning. Or leave it at that. *(Pause.)* Leave it at that. *(Pause.)* Lie propped up in the dark — and wander. Be again in the dingle[9] on a Christmas Eve, gathering holly, the red-berried. *(Pause.)* Be again on Croghan on a Sunday morning, in the haze, with the bitch, stop and listen to the bells. *(Pause.)* And so on. *(Pause.)* Be again, be again. *(Pause.)* All that old misery. *(Pause.)* Once wasn't enough for you. *(Pause.)* Lie down across her.

---

[8] *Effie: Effi Briest* (1895), a novel by Theodor Fontane.   [9] **dingle**: Wooded hollow.

Long pause. He suddenly bends over machine, switches off, wrenches off tape, throws it away, puts on the other, winds it forward to the passage he wants, switches on, listens staring front.

TAPE:—gooseberries, she said. I said again I thought it was hopeless and no good going on, and she agreed, without opening her eyes. *(Pause.)* I asked her to look at me and after a few moments—*(pause)*—after a few moments she did, but the eyes just slits, because of the glare. I bent over her to get them in the shadow and they opened. *(Pause. Low.)* Let me in. *(Pause.)* We drifted in among the flags and stuck. The way they went down, sighing, before the stem! *(Pause.)* I lay down across her with my face in her breasts and my hand on her. We lay there without moving. But under us all moved, and moved us, gently, up and down, and from side to side.

Pause. Krapp's lips move. No sound.

Past midnight. Never knew such silence. The earth might be uninhabited.

Pause.

Here I end this reel. Box—*(pause)*—three, spool—*(pause)*—five. *(Pause.)* Perhaps my best years are gone. When there was a chance of happiness. But I wouldn't want them back. Not with the fire in me now. No, I wouldn't want them back.

Krapp motionless staring before him. The tape runs on in silence.

CURTAIN

∾ NAGUIB MAHFOUZ
B. EGYPT, 1911–2006

When Naguib Mahfouz received the Nobel Prize in 1988, he was the first Arabic writer to be so recognized. Although he was Egypt's premier novelist and deserving of such a distinction for his work, the prize was widely regarded in the Arab world as recognition for Arabic literature generally. Mahfouz and fellow Egyptian writer Tawfiq al-Hakim had been pioneers in creating modern Arabic literature, al-Hakim largely in drama, Mahfouz in fiction. Both writers had managed to create, indeed invent, a new Arabic literary idiom, one that was free of the formality and remoteness of classical literary Arabic but that also had a refinement and a versatility that contemporary colloquial Arabic lacked. The prize was seen as an acknowledgment of both men's achievement in remaking the language and establishing a literature comparable to those of Europe, America, and Asia.

Naguib Mahfouz
Mahfouz was the first Egyptian to win the Nobel Prize in literature.
(© Topham/The Image Works)

Creating a Modern Arabic Literature.   After its golden age in the ninth, tenth, and eleventh centuries, Arabic literature went into decline. When

www   For links to
more information
about Mahfouz
and a quiz on
"Zaabalawi," see
bedfordstmartins
.com/worldlit
compact.

nuh-GEEB mah-FOOZ

the Ottoman empire established Turkish as the language of commerce
and government in the early modern period, Arabic literature virtually
disappeared. As the Ottomans lost power in the nineteenth and early
twentieth centuries, however, Arabic was revived, but the hiatus in its use
as a literary language meant that there were no models for such modern
literary forms as the novel. Traditional Arabic literature was almost
exclusively poetry. Those who hoped to revive Arabic literature and make
it modern had to discover or create a literary and accessible language and
adapt modern literary forms to the Islamic culture.

A Career in Government Service.   Born in 1911 in the Gamaliya district
of Cairo, the seventh child in a middle-class family of modest means,
Naguib Mahfouz spent his earliest years in the crowded districts of the
old city. He attended government schools and graduated with a degree in
philosophy from the University of Cairo in 1934. After graduation he
decided to become a professional writer and worked for a few years
as a journalist before entering the Egyptian civil service in 1939, where
he worked for the next thirty-two years. There he adapted novels for
the movies and television before going on to become the director of the
national Cinema Organization, the governmental agency that manages
the film industry in Egypt. He retired from the civil service in 1971.

A Literary Career.   Mahfouz's first book, *The Whisper of Madness,* a collection of short stories, appeared in 1938. He continued to write during
his years with the civil service and in his retirement, producing more
than forty novels and fourteen volumes of short stories. His writing
career can be divided into four periods. From 1939 to 1944, Mahfouz set
out to write a series of historical novels modeled after the novels of Sir
Walter Scott (1771–1832), the Scottish writer whose Waverley novels, treating the history of Scotland in the seventeenth and eighteenth centuries,
were written as an allegory of Scotland's emergence into nationhood and
national identity. Mahfouz planned to trace the history of Egypt from
ancient times to his own day. He completed only three of the thirty books
he planned to write, all on ancient Egypt, and in them indirectly cri-
tiqued contemporary Egypt. *The Struggle for Thebes* (1944), for example,
was interpreted as an allegory, or a symbolic representation, of the British
occupation and the presence in Egypt of a ruling aristocracy of foreigners. Many of Mahfouz's novels are a fictional representation of the history
and contemporary situation of Egypt, articulating the author's view that
the novelist serves as an "informer that engages in re-creating a collective
memory and thus produces and offers knowledge of a given society and
an alternative articulation of that society's history."

> The novelist serves
> as an "informer
> that engages in
> re-creating a collec-
> tive memory and
> thus produces and
> offers knowledge of a
> given society and an
> alternative articula-
> tion of that society's
> history.
>
> – NAGUIB MAHFOUZ

Social Realism.   With *A New Cairo* (1945), Mahfouz entered a second
stage of his writing career, during which he produced the SOCIAL-REALIST
novels about contemporary Egypt for which he is widely known. *The
Cairo Trilogy,* made up of *Palace Walk, Palace of Desire,* and *Sugar Street,*
written in the early fifties but not published until 1956 and 1957, trace

Cairo, c. 1912

This street scene shows the great Mohammed-el-Worde mosque in the background.
(Library of Congress, LC USZ62 099022)

three generations of a Cairo family from 1918 to 1944. In the tumultuous period between the two world wars, Egypt went through continuous political and social upheaval, much of it involving the place of Britain in Egyptian affairs and the growing movement for Egyptian independence. The repeated attempts to get rid of the British army, to expel foreigners who controlled the Egyptian government and economy, and to replace a corrupt monarchy with a constitutional government boiled over into revolution in 1919 and again in the 1950s. Meanwhile a rapidly growing population exacerbated the social inequities and poverty that plagued the nation. Mahfouz's realistic novels about the suffering and struggles of the middle and lower classes chronicle the human consequences of the government's and the foreign powers' neglect of the people of Egypt. Edward Fox describes politics in Mahfouz's books as "simply another of the evils that afflict humankind, a force whose harm one may be lucky enough to avoid." Mahfouz may have temporarily suspended this persistent cynicism in the early fifties, in hopes that Gamal Abdel Nasser (1918–1970), the Egyptian military officer who led the army coup that deposed the corrupt king Farouk in 1952, would bring positive political change. Nasser, named the first president of the republic of Egypt in 1956, sought to modernize Egypt and to improve the lives of the poor through such measures as land reform. Mahfouz had completed the *Cairo* trilogy before Nasser came to power in 1952 but delayed its publication until 1956, when he lost hope that Nasser would make a difference in the lives of the people. Mahfouz's novels of the sixties openly criticize the Nasser regime.

Existential Modernism and Arabic Traditions.   After the publication of the trilogy, Mahfouz's work changed again. The transitional novel, published in 1959 and translated as *Children of Gebelawi* and *Children of the Alley,* is a history of mankind in which God, Adam, Moses, Jesus, and Muhammad appear as figures in a modern family saga that is also an allegory of mankind's religious history. Unable to secure a publisher in Egypt, Mahfouz published the book in Lebanon. It was subsequently attacked for taking license with sacred history and was banned in nearly every Islamic country, even though its theme could be said to be how greed for material things takes humanity away from God. Mahfouz further developed this theme in his EXISTENTIALIST and MODERNIST novels of the 1960s, works such as *The Thief and the Dogs* (1961) that probe the inner workings of an individual's mind, making use of STREAM-OF-CONSCIOUSNESS and SURREALIST techniques. In the fourth stage of his career, beginning in about the mid seventies, Mahfouz turned from European modernism to the traditions of Arabic literature, drawing on *Arabian Nights* and other Arabic classics and folklore for novels like *Arabian Nights and Days* (1982) and *The Journey of Ibn Fattouma* (1983).

"Zaabalawi."   Written in the early 1960s, Mahfouz's story "Zaabalawi" raises many of the same concerns as the controversial *Children of the Alley.* Like that novel, the story is concerned with the secularization of Egyptian life and the loss of religious traditions. The narrator's search for **Zaabalawi** is a quest for his own spiritual roots, for the truths hidden in the memories of old men living in the older parts of Cairo and for an understanding that transcends the rational and scientific explanations of things.

■ **FURTHER RESEARCH**

Background

Allen, Roger M. A. *The Arabic Novel: An Historical and Critical Introduction*. 1982.

Criticism

El-Enany, Rasheed, ed. *Naguib Mahfouz: The Pursuit of Meaning*. 1993.
Gordon, Hayim. *Naguib Mahfouz's Egypt*. 1990.
Le Gassick, Trevor, ed. *Perspectives on Naguib Mahfouz*. 1991.
Mikhail, Mona. *Studies in the Short Fiction of Mahfouz and Idris*. 1992.
Somekh, Sasson. "'Zaabalawi' — Author, Theme, and Technique," *Journal of Arabic Literature*, I (1970), 24–35.

■ **PRONUNCIATION**

Hassanein: hah-sah-NANE
Naguib Mahfouz: nuh-GEEB mah-FOOZ
Qamar: kah-MAR
Tabakshiyya: tah-bahk-SHEE-yah
Umm al-Ghulam: OOM ahl-goo-LAHM
Wanas al-Damanhouri: wah-NAHS ahl-dah-mahn-HOO-ree
Zaabalawi: zah-bah-LAH-wee

✑ Zaabalawi

Translated by Denys Johnson-Davies

Finally I became convinced that I had to find Sheikh[1] Zaabalawi.
The first time I had heard of his name had been in a song:

Oh what's become of the world, Zaabalawi?
They've turned it upside down and taken away its taste.

It had been a popular song in my childhood, and one day it had occurred to me to demand of my father, in the way children have of asking endless questions:
"Who is Zaabalawi?"

He had looked at me hesitantly as though doubting my ability to understand the answer. However, he had replied, "May his blessing descend upon you, he's a true saint of God, a remover of worries and troubles. Were it not for him I would have died miserably—"

---

[1] **Sheikh:** Title of respect, especially for older, important men.

In the years that followed, I heard my father many a time sing the praises of this good saint and speak of the miracles he performed. The days passed and brought with them many illnesses, for each one of which I was able, without too much trouble and at a cost I could afford, to find a cure, until I became afflicted with that illness for which no one possesses a remedy. When I had tried everything in vain and was overcome by despair, I remembered by chance what I had heard in my childhood: Why, I asked myself, should I not seek out Sheikh Zaabalawi? I recollected my father saying that he had made his acquaintance in Khan Gaafar[2] at the house of Sheikh Qamar, one of those sheikhs who practiced law in the religious courts, and so I took myself off to his house. Wishing to make sure that he was still living there, I made inquiries of a vendor of beans whom I found in the lower part of the house.

"Sheikh Qamar!" he said, looking at me in amazement. "He left the quarter ages ago. They say he's now living in Garden City and has his office in al-Azhar Square."[3]

I looked up the office address in the telephone book and immediately set off to the Chamber of Commerce Building, where it was located. On asking to see Sheikh Qamar, I was ushered into a room just as a beautiful woman with a most intoxicating perfume was leaving it. The man received me with a smile and motioned me toward a fine leather-upholstered chair. Despite the thick soles of my shoes, my feet were conscious of the lushness of the costly carpet. The man wore a lounge suit and was smoking a cigar; his manner of sitting was that of someone well satisfied both with himself and with his worldly possessions. The look of warm welcome he gave me left no doubt in my mind that he thought me a prospective client, and I felt acutely embarrassed at encroaching upon his valuable time.

"Welcome!" he said, prompting me to speak.

"I am the son of your old friend Sheikh Ali al-Tatawi," I answered so as to put an end to my equivocal position.

A certain languor was apparent in the glance he cast at me; the languor was not total in that he had not as yet lost all hope in me.

"God rest his soul," he said. "He was a fine man."

The very pain that had driven me to go there now prevailed upon me to stay.

"He told me," I continued, "of a devout saint named Zaabalawi whom he met at Your Honor's. I am in need of him, sir, if he be still in the land of the living."

The languor became firmly entrenched in his eyes, and it would have come as no surprise if he had shown the door to both me and my father's memory.

"That," he said in the tone of one who has made up his mind to terminate the conversation, "was a very long time ago and I scarcely recall him now."

Rising to my feet so as to put his mind at rest regarding my intention of going, I asked, "Was he really a saint?"

"We used to regard him as a man of miracles."

"And where could I find him today?" I asked, making another move toward the door.

---

[2] **Khan Gaafar:** A shopping district in Cairo.

[3] **al-Azhar Square:** A section of Cairo near a famous mosque and the university.

"To the best of my knowledge he was living in the Birgawi Residence in al-Azhar," and he applied himself to some papers on his desk with a resolute movement that indicated he would not open his mouth again. I bowed my head in thanks, apologized several times for disturbing him, and left the office, my head so buzzing with embarrassment that I was oblivious to all sounds around me.

I went to the Birgawi Residence, which was situated in a thickly populated quarter. I found that time had so eaten at the building that nothing was left of it save an antiquated façade and a courtyard that, despite being supposedly in the charge of a caretaker, was being used as a rubbish dump. A small, insignificant fellow, a mere prologue to a man, was using the covered entrance as a place for the sale of old books on theology and mysticism.

When I asked him about Zaabalawi, he peered at me through narrow, inflamed eyes and said in amazement, "Zaabalawi! Good heavens, what a time ago that was! Certainly he used to live in this house when it was habitable. Many were the times he would sit with me talking of bygone days, and I would be blessed by his holy presence. Where, though, is Zaabalawi today?"

He shrugged his shoulders sorrowfully and soon left me, to attend to an approaching customer. I proceeded to make inquiries of many shopkeepers in the district. While I found that a large number of them had never even heard of Zaabalawi, some, though recalling nostalgically the pleasant times they had spent with him, were ignorant of his present whereabouts, while others openly made fun of him, labeled him a charlatan, and advised me to put myself in the hands of a doctor — as though I had not already done so. I therefore had no alternative but to return disconsolately home.

With the passing of days like motes in the air, my pains grew so severe that I was sure I would not be able to hold out much longer. Once again I fell to wondering about Zaabalawi and clutching at the hope his venerable name stirred within me. Then it occurred to me to seek the help of the local sheikh of the district; in fact, I was surprised I had not thought of this to begin with. His office was in the nature of a small shop, except that it contained a desk and a telephone, and I found him sitting at his desk, wearing a jacket over his striped galabeya.[4] As he did not interrupt his conversation with a man sitting beside him, I stood waiting till the man had gone. The sheikh then looked up at me coldly. I told myself that I should win him over by the usual methods, and it was not long before I had him cheerfully inviting me to sit down.

"I'm in need of Sheikh Zaabalawi," I answered his inquiry as to the purpose of my visit.

He gazed at me with the same astonishment as that shown by those I had previously encountered.

"At least," he said, giving me a smile that revealed his gold teeth, "he is still alive. The devil of it is, though, he has no fixed abode. You might well bump into him as you go out of here, on the other hand you might spend days and months in fruitless searching."

---

[4] **galabeya:** Traditional Arab robe.

"Even you can't find him!"

"Even I! He's a baffling man, but I thank the Lord that he's still alive!"

He gazed at me intently, and murmured, "It seems your condition is serious."

"Very."

"May God come to your aid! But why don't you go about it systematically?" He spread out a sheet of paper on the desk and drew on it with unexpected speed and skill until he had made a full plan of the district, showing all the various quarters, lanes, alleyways, and squares. He looked at it admiringly and said, "These are dwelling-houses, here is the Quarter of the Perfumers, here the Quarter of the Coppersmiths, the Mouski,[5] the police and fire stations. The drawing is your best guide. Look carefully in the cafés, the places where the dervishes perform their rites, the mosques and prayer-rooms, and the Green Gate,[6] for he may well be concealed among the beggars and be indistinguishable from them. Actually, I myself haven't seen him for years, having been somewhat preoccupied with the cares of the world, and was only brought back by your inquiry to those most exquisite times of my youth."

I gazed at the map in bewilderment. The telephone rang, and he took up the receiver.

"Take it," he told me, generously. "We're at your service."

Folding up the map, I left and wandered off through the quarter, from square to street to alleyway, making inquiries of everyone I felt was familiar with the place. At last the owner of a small establishment for ironing clothes told me, "Go to the calligrapher Hassanein in Umm al-Ghulam — they were friends."

I went to Umm al-Ghulam,[7] where I found old Hassanein working in a deep, narrow shop full of signboards and jars of color. A strange smell, a mixture of glue and perfume, permeated its every corner. Old Hassanein was squatting on a sheepskin rug in front of a board propped against the wall; in the middle of it he had inscribed the word "Allah"[8] in silver lettering. He was engrossed in embellishing the letters with prodigious care. I stood behind him, fearful of disturbing him or breaking the inspiration that flowed to his masterly hand. When my concern at not interrupting him had lasted some time, he suddenly inquired with unaffected gentleness, "Yes?"

Realizing that he was aware of my presence, I introduced myself. "I've been told that Sheikh Zaabalawi is your friend; I'm looking for him," I said.

His hand came to a stop. He scrutinized me in astonishment. "Zaabalawi! God be praised!" he said with a sigh.

"He *is* a friend of yours, isn't he?" I asked eagerly.

---

[5] the Mouski: A central market bazaar.

[6] the Green Gate: Medieval gate in Cairo.

[7] Umm al-Ghulam: Street in Cairo.

[8] "Allah": "God" in Arabic.

"He was, once upon a time. A real man of mystery: He'd visit you so often that people would imagine he was your nearest and dearest, then would disappear as though he'd never existed. Yet saints are not to be blamed."

The spark of hope went out with the suddenness of a lamp snuffed by a power-cut.

"He was so constantly with me," said the man, "that I felt him to be a part of everything I drew. But where is he today?"

"Perhaps he is still alive?"

"He's alive, without a doubt. . . . He had impeccable taste, and it was due to him that I made my most beautiful drawings."

"God knows," I said, in a voice almost stifled by the dead ashes of hope, "how dire my need for him is, and no one knows better than you of the ailments in respect of which he is sought."

"Yes, yes. May God restore you to health. He is, in truth, as is said of him, a man, and more. . . ."

Smiling broadly, he added, "And his face possesses an unforgettable beauty. But where is he?"

Reluctantly I rose to my feet, shook hands, and left. I continued wandering eastward and westward through the quarter, inquiring about Zaabalawi from everyone who, by reason of age or experience, I felt might be likely to help me. Eventually I was informed by a vendor of lupine[9] that he had met him a short while ago at the house of Sheikh Gad, the well-known composer. I went to the musician's house in Tabakshiyya,[10] where I found him in a room tastefully furnished in the old style, its walls redolent with history. He was seated on a divan, his famous lute beside him, concealing within itself the most beautiful melodies of our age, while somewhere from within the house came the sound of pestle and mortar and the clamor of children. I immediately greeted him and introduced myself, and was put at my ease by the unaffected way in which he received me. He did not ask, either in words or gesture, what had brought me, and I did not feel that he even harbored any such curiosity. Amazed at his understanding and kindness, which boded well, I said, "O Sheikh Gad, I am an admirer of yours, having long been enchanted by the renderings of your songs."

"Thank you," he said with a smile.

"Please excuse my disturbing you," I continued timidly, "but I was told that Zaabalawi was your friend, and I am in urgent need of him."

"Zaabalawi!" he said, frowning in concentration. "You need him? God be with you, for who knows, O Zaabalawi, where you are."

"Doesn't he visit you?" I asked eagerly.

"He visited me some time ago. He might well come right now; on the other hand I mightn't see him till death!"

I gave an audible sigh and asked, "What made him like that?"

---

[9] **lupine:** Beans.   [10] **Tabakshiyya:** District in Cairo named for the straw trays that are made and sold there.

The musician took up his lute. "Such are saints or they would not be saints," he said, laughing.

"Do those who need him suffer as I do?"

"Such suffering is part of the cure!"

He took up the plectrum and began plucking soft strains from the strings. Lost in thought, I followed his movements. Then, as though addressing myself, I said, "So my visit has been in vain."

He smiled, laying his cheek against the side of the lute. "God forgive you," he said, "for saying such a thing of a visit that has caused me to know you and you me!"

I was much embarrassed and said apologetically, "Please forgive me; my feelings of defeat made me forget my manners."

"Do not give in to defeat. This extraordinary man brings fatigue to all who seek him. It was easy enough with him in the old days when his place of abode was known. Today, though, the world has changed, and after having enjoyed a position attained only by potentates, he is now pursued by the police on a charge of false pretenses. It is therefore no longer an easy matter to reach him, but have patience and be sure that you will do so."

He raised his head from the lute and skillfully fingered the opening bars of a melody. Then he sang:

I make lavish mention, even though I blame myself, of those I love,
For the stories of the beloved are my wine.[11]

With a heart that was weary and listless, I followed the beauty of the melody and the singing.

"I composed the music to this poem in a single night," he told me when he had finished. "I remember that it was the eve of the Lesser Bairam.[12] Zaabalawi was my guest for the whole of that night, and the poem was of his choosing. He would sit for a while just where you are, then would get up and play with my children as though he were one of them. Whenever I was overcome by weariness or my inspiration failed me, he would punch me playfully in the chest and joke with me, and I would bubble over with melodies, and thus I continued working till I finished the most beautiful piece I have ever composed."

"Does he know anything about music?"

"He is the epitome of things musical. He has an extremely beautiful speaking voice, and you have only to hear him to want to burst into song and to be inspired to creativity. . . ."

"How was it that he cured those diseases before which men are powerless?"

"That is his secret. Maybe you will learn it when you meet him."

But when would that meeting occur? We relapsed into silence, and the hubbub of children once more filled the room.

---

[11] "I make . . . wine": Lines from a poem by the medieval mystic Ibn al-Farid.

[12] Lesser Bairam: Holiday celebrated at the end of the month of Ramadan.

Again the sheikh began to sing. He went on repeating the words "and I have a memory of her" in different and beautiful variations until the very walls danced in ecstasy. I expressed my wholehearted admiration, and he gave me a smile of thanks. I then got up and asked permission to leave, and he accompanied me to the front door. As I shook him by the hand, he said, "I hear that nowadays he frequents the house of Hagg Wanas al-Damanhouri. Do you know him?"

I shook my head, though a modicum of renewed hope crept into my heart.

"He is a man of private means," the sheikh told me, "who from time to time visits Cairo, putting up at some hotel or other. Every evening, though, he spends at the Negma Bar in Alfi Street."

I waited for nightfall and went to the Negma Bar. I asked a waiter about Hagg Wanas, and he pointed to a corner that was semisecluded because of its position behind a large pillar with mirrors on all four sides. There I saw a man seated alone at a table with two bottles in front of him, one empty, the other two-thirds empty. There were no snacks or food to be seen, and I was sure that I was in the presence of a hardened drinker. He was wearing a loosely flowing silk galabeya and a carefully wound turban; his legs were stretched out toward the base of the pillar, and as he gazed into the mirror in rapt contentment, the sides of his face, rounded and handsome despite the fact that he was approaching old age, were flushed with wine. I approached quietly till I stood but a few feet away from him. He did not turn toward me or give any indication that he was aware of my presence.

"Good evening, Mr. Wanas," I greeted him cordially.

He turned toward me abruptly, as though my voice had roused him from slumber, and glared at me in disapproval. I was about to explain what had brought me to him when he interrupted in an almost imperative tone of voice that was none the less not devoid of an extraordinary gentleness. "First, please sit down, and, second, please get drunk!"

I opened my mouth to make my excuses but, stopping up his ears with his fingers, he said, "Not a word till you do what I say."

I realized I was in the presence of a capricious drunkard and told myself that I should at least humor him a bit. "Would you permit me to ask one question?" I said with a smile, sitting down.

Without removing his hands from his ears he indicated the bottle. "When engaged in a drinking bout like this, I do not allow any conversation between myself and another unless, like me, he is drunk, otherwise all propriety is lost and mutual comprehension is rendered impossible."

I made a sign indicating that I did not drink.

"That's your lookout," he said offhandedly. "And that's my condition!"

He filled me a glass, which I meekly took and drank. No sooner had the wine settled in my stomach than it seemed to ignite. I waited patiently till I had grown used to its ferocity, and said, "It's very strong, and I think the time has come for me to ask you about—"

Once again, however, he put his fingers in his ears. "I shan't listen to you until you're drunk!"

He filled up my glass for the second time. I glanced at it in trepidation; then, overcoming my inherent objection, I drank it down at a gulp. No sooner had the wine come to rest inside me than I lost all willpower. With the third glass, I lost my memory, and with the fourth the future vanished. The world turned round about me and I forgot why I had gone there. The man leaned toward me attentively, but I saw him—saw everything—as a mere meaningless series of colored planes. I don't know how long it was before my head sank down onto the arm of the chair and I plunged into deep sleep. During it, I had a beautiful dream the like of which I had never experienced. I dreamed that I was in an immense garden surrounded on all sides by luxuriant trees, and the sky was nothing but stars seen between the entwined branches, all enfolded in an atmosphere like that of sunset or a sky overcast with cloud. I was lying on a small hummock of jasmine petals, more of which fell upon me like rain, while the lucent spray of a fountain unceasingly sprinkled the crown of my head and my temples. I was in a state of deep contentedness, of ecstatic serenity. An orchestra of warbling and cooing played in my ear. There was an extraordinary sense of harmony between me and my inner self, and between the two of us and the world, everything being in its rightful place, without discord or distortion. In the whole world there was no single reason for speech or movement, for the universe moved in a rapture of ecstasy. This lasted but a short while. When I opened my eyes, consciousness struck at me like a policeman's fist and I saw Wanas al-Damanhouri regarding me with concern. Only a few drowsy customers were left in the bar.

"You have slept deeply," said my companion. "You were obviously hungry for sleep."

I rested my heavy head in the palms of my hands. When I took them away in astonishment and looked down at them, I found that they glistened with drops of water.

"My head's wet," I protested.

"Yes, my friend tried to rouse you," he answered quietly.

"Somebody saw me in this state?"

"Don't worry, he is a good man. Have you not heard of Sheikh Zaabalawi?"

"Zaabalawi!" I exclaimed, jumping to my feet.

"Yes," he answered in surprise. "What's wrong?"

"Where is he?"

"I don't know where he is now. He was here and then he left."

I was about to run off in pursuit but found I was more exhausted than I had imagined. Collapsed over the table, I cried out in despair, "My sole reason for coming to you was to meet him! Help me to catch up with him or send someone after him."

The man called a vendor of prawns and asked him to seek out the sheikh and bring him back. Then he turned to me. "I didn't realize you were afflicted. I'm very sorry. . . ."

"You wouldn't let me speak," I said irritably.

"What a pity! He was sitting on this chair beside you the whole time. He was playing with a string of jasmine petals he had around his neck, a gift from one of his admirers, then, taking pity on you, he began to sprinkle some water on your head to bring you around."

"Does he meet you here every night?" I asked, my eyes not leaving the doorway through which the vendor of prawns had left.

"He was with me tonight, last night, and the night before that, but before that I hadn't seen him for a month."

"Perhaps he will come tomorrow," I answered with a sigh.

"Perhaps."

"I am willing to give him any money he wants."

Wanas answered sympathetically, "The strange thing is that he is not open to such temptations, yet he will cure you if you meet him."

"Without charge?"

"Merely on sensing that you love him."

The vendor of prawns returned, having failed in his mission.

I recovered some of my energy and left the bar, albeit unsteadily. At every street corner I called out "Zaabalawi!" in the vague hope that I would be rewarded with an answering shout. The street boys turned contemptuous eyes on me till I sought refuge in the first available taxi.

The following evening I stayed up with Wanas al-Damanhouri till dawn, but the sheikh did not put in an appearance. Wanas informed me that he would be going away to the country and would not be returning to Cairo until he had sold the cotton crop.

I must wait, I told myself; I must train myself to be patient. Let me content myself with having made certain of the existence of Zaabalawi, and even of his affection for me, which encourages me to think that he will be prepared to cure me if a meeting takes place between us.

Sometimes, however, the long delay wearied me. I would become beset by despair and would try to persuade myself to dismiss him from my mind completely. How many weary people in this life know him not or regard him as a mere myth! Why, then, should I torture myself about him in this way?

No sooner, however, did my pains force themselves upon me than I would again begin to think about him, asking myself when I would be fortunate enough to meet him. The fact that I ceased to have any news of Wanas and was told he had gone to live abroad did not deflect me from my purpose; the truth of the matter was that I had become fully convinced that I had to find Zaabalawi.

Yes, I have to find Zaabalawi.

Albert Camus, c. 1945
*Algerian-born
Camus, photographed
here at about age
thirty-two, died in a
car accident in 1960
at the age of forty-
seven. (Hulton /
Archive)*

ahl-BARE kah-MOO

Albert Camus is usually associated with EXISTENTIALISM, the popular philosophical and literary movement of the mid twentieth century exemplified in the writings of Jean-Paul Sartre. In a secular world that seemed to run according to natural law rather than God's will and that resonated with Kafka's nightmares and T. S. Eliot's "wasteland," existentialism focused on the freedom that humans must exercise when making choices, when deciding who they are and how they will act. In Camus's early writings, such as *The Stranger* (1942) and *The Myth of Sisyphus and Other Essays* (1942), the author depicts a world that offers no purpose and little meaning to its inhabitants. Camus, calling this secular reality ABSURD, was quickly identified as the philosopher of the absurd, the outsider, and the gentle hedonist.

The two great wars of the first half of the twentieth century, with their massive destruction of human life and social ideals, left many wondering whether there was anything or anyone in which to believe. Camus looked at the postwar era with courage, honesty, and sensitivity. He became the quintessential rebel, starting a peoples' theater, joining and then rejecting the Communist Party, writing social polemics for newspapers, fighting in the French Underground against the Nazis, and refusing to side with either the French or the Algerians in the Algerian struggle for independence in the 1950s. He denounced tyranny, terrorism, and FASCISM, whether they occurred on the extreme right or the extreme left. And he searched for the basis of meaning and social commitment in a world disillusioned with traditional beliefs, movements, and institutions.

Since his death in 1960, Camus's popularity has periodically waxed and waned, but his writings have consistently encouraged a serious discussion of social issues and invited readers to commit themselves to bettering the human condition.

Beginning Life in Poverty. **Albert Camus** was born on November 7, 1913, in Mondovi, Algeria, in what was then French North Africa. His father, a transplanted Frenchman, was an illiterate farmer who was killed at the first Battle of Marne in World War I. His mother, who was originally from Spain, moved her family—Albert and his brother, uncle, and grandmother—to a two-room apartment in Belcourt, a working-class suburb of Algiers, where she worked as a charwoman. Raised by his maternal grandmother who used a whip to discipline him, Camus was permanently affected by the silence in his relationship with his illiterate, deaf mother who rarely spoke.

Ordinarily, he would have worked after completing elementary school, but a teacher, Louis Germain, to whom Camus would later dedicate his Nobel Prize speech, recognized his intellectual gifts and arranged for a scholarship to the lycée in the European section of Algiers (now Lycée Albert Camus). As a scholarship student from a poor, working-class neighborhood, the young Camus met with the prejudice and arrogance of his schoolmates, sons of wealth and privilege whose first allegiance was to Europe rather than to North Africa. These experiences influenced the youthful writings of Camus in 1932 when he took the side of the oppressed, seeking to give voice to the sufferings of those who like his mother were largely silent. His sympathy for the plight of the working class guided his moral and political struggles for the rest of his life. Winning honors both as a young scholar of philosophy and as a passionate goalie for the soccer team at the University of Algiers, Camus's world collapsed at age seventeen when he was diagnosed with tuberculosis; a year's convalescence was prescribed. Undoubtedly, his brush with death and subsequent unreliable health had a profound effect on the young man.

www For links to more information about Camus, see bedfordstmartins .com/worldlit compact.

Left-Wing Politics.   Camus married Simone Hie in 1933. Influenced by the liberal writings of such French writers as **André Gide** and **André Malraux**[1] and the apparent sympathy Communists showed toward the plight of the Arabs, Camus joined the Algerian Communist Party in 1934 and founded The Labor Theater (*Le Théâtre du Travail*). While working at various jobs, Camus directed, wrote, and adapted plays for this peoples' theater, which performed on the docks in Algiers. Camus broke with the Communist Party in 1937 because of its growing hostility toward the Arab cause. His first collection of essays, *The Wrong and the Right Side* (*L'Envers et l'endroit,* 1937) reveals his passionate attachment to the people and landscapes of North Africa. As an **AGNOSTIC**, he characterizes the twin poles of his secular religion in these essays as Yes and No: a passionate Yes to "life with its face of tears and sun, life in the salt sea and on warm stones," but a resounding No to injustice and oppression. In "Return to Tipasa" he writes, "Yes, there is beauty and there are the humiliated. Whatever may be the difficulties of the undertaking, I should like never to be unfaithful either to one or to the others." In 1938 he joined the staff of a left-wing newspaper, *Alger-Républicain,* for which he wrote book reviews and a series of articles critical of the government's treatment of the Kabyles, a mountain people south of Algiers. He was eventually forced out of Algeria because of his politics. Living in Paris, he worked for *Paris-Soir* and continued to write.

ahn-DRAY ZHEED;
ahn-DRAY mahl-ROH

Pursuing the Absurd.   It was at this time that Camus devised an ambitious plan that reflected his extraordinary gifts as a writer and thinker: He would write a philosophical essay, a novel, and a play around one particular theme and if possible publish all three works together. For his first theme he chose the absurd. *The Myth of Sisyphus* (*Le Mythe de Sisyphe,* 1942), a collection of essays, explains how absurdity arises

---

[1] **Gide . . . Malraux:** André Gide (1869–1951) wrote poems, plays, and novels that focused on the importance of self-examination and the life of the senses. André Malraux (1901–1976), like Camus, was a French intellectual who combined writing with political action; his most famous novel, *Man's Fate* (1934), is about the Shanghai uprising and the Communist encroachment in China.

mur-SOH

from one's longing for clear answers about the nature of reality in an irrational, incomprehensible world—absurdity exists in the gulf between human need and the "unreasonable silence of the world." *The Stranger* (*L'Étranger,* 1942), Camus's most famous—and disturbing—novel, presents an absurd hero, **Meursault**, who refuses to adopt the social and religious conventions of his day and is therefore a stranger to his society. The play *Caligula* (1945) takes the idea of liberty to destructive extremes and completes the triumvirate on the absurd.

World War II interfered with Camus's plans for developing a second theme. He joined the French resistance movement in 1942, and in 1943, after another attack of tuberculosis, became a publisher's reader and a member of the administrative staff at Gallimard, a position he held until he died. The next year he became editor of the underground newspaper *Combat,* writing editorials and articles. In most of his writing of this period, and as a consequence of his associations with French existentialism and Jean-Paul Sartre, Camus examines the grounds for moral responsibility in a world in which God and religious institutions no longer provide a comprehensive vision and an imperative for ethical action. In a secular world, what connects us to the plight of our neighbors and thrusts us into the social arena? Several of Camus's plays depict life in a world in which restraints have been lifted and anything is possible: *The Misunderstanding* (*Le Malentendu,* 1944), *The State of Siege* (*L'État de siège,* 1948), and *The Just Assassins* (*Les Justes,* 1948).

. . . there is a *passion* of the absurd. The absurd man will not commit suicide; he wants to live, without relinquishing any of his certainty, without a future, without hope, without illusion, and without resignation either. He stares at death with passionate attention and this fascination liberates him. He experiences the "divine irresponsibility" of the condemned man.

– JEAN-PAUL SARTRE,
1955

Revolution and Morality.   In 1947 Camus published *The Plague* (*La Peste*), a novel that sets up a situation in which he can test his ideas: He gradually reveals the ethical motivations and psychological needs of the book's characters in a North African city besieged and isolated by the plague. *The Rebel* (*L'Homme révolté,* 1951), written as a complement to *The Plague,* discusses the nature of revolution and the relation of means and ends in political movements. Camus asks if the sacrifices demanded by the new secular prophets like Marx and Lenin[2] will lead ultimately to better societies. These works were attacked by Sartre and others. In 1952, Camus broke with Sartre over a fundamental issue: The latter accepted the evils of Stalinism[3] as a means to an end—a more humane society. Camus refused to exchange present sufferings for abstract promises of a better future, regardless of whether those promises were made by a socialist philosopher or a religious prophet.

Camus's final novel, *The Fall* (*La Chute,* 1956), is a strange, ironic monologue about personal responsibility and the darkness surrounding human motivation. His last volume of short stories, *Exile and the Kingdom* (*L'Exil et le royaume,* 1957), captures the poignant loneliness of being caught between two cultures: of being born in North Africa and yet

---

[2] **Marx and Lenin:** Karl Marx (1818–1883) was a social philosopher and founder of modern socialism. Nikolai Lenin (1870–1924) led the Communist Revolution of 1917 in Russia.

[3] **Stalinism:** A form of Marxism associated with Josef Stalin (1879–1953), the Communist dictator of the Soviet Union from 1922 to 1953. Stalin harshly repressed all dissent and upheld the absolute central authority of his government. Millions died under his brutal orchestration of the USSR's industrialization.

feeling like a colonial and an exile, all the while searching for a home, a "kingdom." This colonial dilemma was repeated for Europeans throughout Africa, India, and Southeast Asia, but for Camus it represented a universal condition: To have been born anywhere with full consciousness was to be an exile, estranged in one's own country or kingdom.

Albert Camus received the Nobel Prize in Literature in 1957, one of the youngest persons to be awarded that honor. Tragically, he died in a car crash en route to Paris on January 4, 1960 — a rather absurd conclusion to a tremendously productive and worthwhile life.

"The Guest."   The Algerian struggle for independence from France in the 1950s amply illustrated the complexity of revolutionary situations. Recognizing the deep loyalties that both the Algerian-born French and Arab Algerians had toward their homeland, Camus risked the criticism of leftists and sought a reconciliation between the French government and the Algerian rebels, the FLN. This struggle, which polarized attitudes and forced an unwanted partisanship on both the Algerian Arabs and the Algerian French, serves as the volatile setting for Camus's "The Guest," taken from his collection *Exile and the Kingdom*. In this story, colonialism has reached into the Algerian backcountry, but Camus creates a situation in which the ideal of individual freedom takes precedence over political ideology and local politics. Even though French domination is symbolized in the local schoolteacher Daru, who distributes food to his drought-stricken region and teaches French geography to his pupils, the remote desert setting of the story provides an open arena for individual choices — Daru is free to act.

Real class differences are first introduced by showing Balducci, the gendarme, riding on his horse while the Arab prisoner, with hands bound, is walking. When Daru is given custody of the prisoner, he seeks ways to give the Arab his freedom. Through small signs of decency, Daru affirms the prisoner's common humanity and at the same time preserves his own set of values. Although there is little real, verbal communication between them, Daru acknowledges the minimal bond of their shared meals and lodgings. Daru resents both the legal system that interposed itself in the Arab's family quarrel and the subjugated Arab who failed to avoid capture. Even when presented with his freedom, the Arab ironically is incapable of escaping. Furthermore, Daru returns to the schoolhouse to find that his efforts on behalf of the Arab are totally misunderstood by other Arabs. Like Camus himself, Daru feels the loneliness of one who is neither an exile nor at home in the kingdom, a situation reflected in the collection title *Exile and the Kingdom*.

"The Myth of Sisyphus."   In this short philosophical essay, Camus takes the Greek myth of the condemned Sisyphus and reinterprets it through the lens of existentialism. Sisyphus was sentenced by the gods to spend eternity in Hades attempting to roll a stone up a hill, only to fail each time. Traditionally understood as the legend of man condemned to a fate worse than death, the legend of Sisyphus is viewed by Camus as a metaphor for the condition of the human being on earth. Living in a world where there are no universal rules, no boundaries validated by

Some time ago I summed up *The Stranger* by a statement which I recognize is highly paradoxical: "In our society, any man who does not weep at the funeral of his mother risks being sentenced to death." I only wished to say that the hero of the book was sentenced because he did not play the game . . . he refuses to lie. To lie is not only to say what is not. It is also, it is above all, to say more than what is, and, in matters of the human heart, to say more than what one feels. This is what we do, all of us, every day, to simplify life. . . . One would not be greatly mistaken in reading in *The Stranger* the account of a man who, without any heroic posturing, consents to die for the truth.

– ALBERT CAMUS, preface to the 1955 edition of *L'Étranger*

transcendent rewards and punishments, Camus uses the word *absurd* to describe the gap between what humans yearn for and actual reality. We yearn for clarity, for example, but see that the world science has created is incomprehensible. We would like to belong to the world, to feel at home on the earth, and yet, with all our learning, we feel estranged. The unbelievably beautiful cosmos that stretches beyond our vision in the night sky remains cool and indifferent; nothing in nature reaches out to us, nothing takes us in its arms. In this kind of world Camus creates a hero who attends to the business of pushing a rock up a hill without any hope of ultimate redemption. Sisyphus's heroism in the underworld is exhibited by his courageous attentiveness to his eternal task. There is no god to pat Sisyphus on the back and tell him his struggle was worth it, that it all fit into an eternal plan.

■ **FURTHER RESEARCH**

Biography
Bronner, St. E. *Albert Camus, the Thinker, the Artist, the Man.* 1996.
Lottman, Herbert. *Albert Camus: A Biography.* 1980.

History and Culture
Brée, Germaine. *Albert Camus.* 1961.
McBride, Joseph. *Albert Camus, Philosopher and Litterateur.* 1992.

Criticism
Bosman, Catherine S. *Albert Camus.* 2001.
Brée, Germaine. *Camus: A Collection of Critical Essays.* 1961.
Douglas, Kenneth, ed. *Yale French Studies: Albert Camus.* 1960.
Eastman, Jennifer. *Albert Camus: The Mythic and the Real.* 2001.
Ellison, David R. *Understanding Albert Camus.* 1990.
Rizzuto, Anthony. *Camus: Love and Sexuality.* 1998.
Thody, Philip. *Albert Camus: A Study of His Work.* 1957.

■ **PRONUNCIATION**

Albert Camus: ahl-BARE kah-MOO
André Gide: ahn-DRAY ZHEED
André Malraux: ahn-DRAY mahl-ROH
Meursault: mur-SOH

∿ The Guest

Translated by Justin O'Brien

The schoolmaster was watching the two men climb toward him. One was on horseback, the other on foot. They had not yet tackled the abrupt rise leading to the schoolhouse built on the hillside. They were toiling onward, making slow progress in the snow, among the stones, on the vast expanse of the high, deserted plateau. From time to time the horse stumbled. Without hearing anything yet, he could see the breath issuing from the horse's nostrils. One of the men, at least, knew the region.

They were following the trail although it had disappeared days ago under a layer of dirty white snow. The schoolmaster calculated that it would take them half an hour to get onto the hill. It was cold; he went back into the school to get a sweater.

He crossed the empty, frigid classroom. On the blackboard the four rivers of France,[1] drawn with four different colored chalks, had been flowing toward their estuaries for the past three days. Snow had suddenly fallen in mid-October after eight months of drought without the transition of rain, and the twenty pupils, more or less, who lived in the villages scattered over the plateau had stopped coming. With fair weather they would return. Daru now heated only the single room that was his lodging, adjoining the classroom and giving also onto the plateau to the east. Like the class windows, his window looked to the south too. On that side the school was a few kilometers from the point where the plateau began to slope toward the south. In clear weather could be seen the purple mass of the mountain range where the gap opened onto the desert.

Somewhat warmed, Daru returned to the window from which he had first seen the two men. They were no longer visible. Hence they must have tackled the rise. The sky was not so dark, for the snow had stopped falling during the night. The morning had opened with a dirty light which had scarcely become brighter as the ceiling of clouds lifted. At two in the afternoon it seemed as if the day were merely beginning. But still this was better than those three days when the thick snow was falling amidst unbroken darkness with little gusts of wind that rattled the double door of the classroom. Then Daru had spent long hours in his room, leaving it only to go to the shed and feed the chickens or get some coal. Fortunately the delivery truck from Tadjid, the nearest village to the north, had brought his supplies two days before the blizzard. It would return in forty-eight hours.

Besides, he had enough to resist a siege, for the little room was cluttered with bags of wheat that the administration left as a stock to distribute to those of his pupils whose families had suffered from the drought. Actually they had all been victims because they were all poor. Every day Daru would distribute a ration to the children. They had missed it, he knew, during these bad days. Possibly one of the fathers or big brothers would come this afternoon and he could supply them with grain. It was just a matter of carrying them over to the next harvest. Now shiploads of wheat were arriving from France and the worst was over. But it would be hard to forget that poverty, that army of ragged ghosts wandering in the sunlight, the plateaus burned to a cinder month after month, the earth shriveled up little by little, literally scorched, every stone bursting into dust under one's foot. The sheep had died then by thousands and even a few men, here and there, sometimes without anyone's knowing.

In contrast with such poverty, he who lived almost like a monk in his remote schoolhouse, nonetheless satisfied with the little he had and with the rough life, had felt like a lord with his whitewashed walls, his narrow couch, his unpainted shelves, his well, and his weekly provision of water and food. And suddenly this snow,

---

[1] **four rivers of France:** The Seine, Loire, Rhône, and Gironde rivers; French geography is being taught rather than Algerian.

without warning, without the foretaste of rain. This is the way the region was, cruel to live in, even without men—who didn't help matters either. But Daru had been born here. Everywhere else, he felt exiled.

He stepped out onto the terrace in front of the schoolhouse. The two men were now halfway up the slope. He recognized the horseman as Balducci, the old gendarme he had known for a long time. Balducci was holding on the end of a rope an Arab who was walking behind him with hands bound and head lowered. The gendarme waved a greeting to which Daru did not reply, lost as he was in contemplation of the Arab dressed in a faded blue jellaba,[2] his feet in sandals but covered with socks of heavy raw wool, his head surmounted by a narrow, short chèche.[3] They were approaching. Balducci was holding back his horse in order not to hurt the Arab, and the group was advancing slowly.

Within earshot, Balducci shouted: "One hour to do the three kilometers from El Ameur!" Daru did not answer. Short and square in his thick sweater, he watched them climb. Not once had the Arab raised his head. "Hello," said Daru when they got up onto the terrace. "Come in and warm up." Balducci painfully got down from his horse without letting go the rope. From under his bristling mustache he smiled at the schoolmaster. His little dark eyes, deep-set under a tanned forehead, and his mouth surrounded with wrinkles made him look attentive and studious. Daru took the bridle, led the horse to the shed, and came back to the two men, who were now waiting for him in the school. He led them into his room. "I am going to heat up the classroom," he said. "We'll be more comfortable there." When he entered the room again, Balducci was on the couch. He had undone the rope tying him to the Arab, who had squatted near the stove. His hands still bound, the chèche pushed back on his head, he was looking toward the window. At first Daru noticed only his huge lips, fat, smooth, almost Negroid; yet his nose was straight, his eyes were dark and full of fever. The chèche revealed an obstinate forehead and, under the weathered skin now rather discolored by the cold, the whole face had a restless and rebellious look that struck Daru when the Arab, turning his face toward him, looked him straight in the eyes. "Go into the other room," said the schoolmaster, "and I'll make you some mint tea." "Thanks," Balducci said. "What a chore! How I long for retirement." And addressing his prisoner in Arabic: "Come on, you." The Arab got up and, slowly, holding his bound wrists in front of him, went into the classroom.

With the tea, Daru brought a chair. But Balducci was already enthroned on the nearest pupil's desk and the Arab had squatted against the teacher's platform facing the stove, which stood between the desk and the window. When he held out the glass of tea to the prisoner, Daru hesitated at the sight of his bound hands. "He might perhaps be untied." "Sure," said Balducci. "That was for the trip." He started to get to his feet. But Daru, setting the glass on the floor, had knelt beside the Arab. Without

[2]jellaba: "Djellaba": a long, loose robe worn by men and women in some Arab countries.
[3]chèche: A head scarf or turban.

saying anything, the Arab watched him with his feverish eyes. Once his hands were free, he rubbed his swollen wrists against each other, took the glass of tea, and sucked up the burning liquid in swift little sips.

"Good," said Daru. "And where are you headed?"

Balducci withdrew his mustache from the tea. "Here, son."

"Odd pupils! And you're spending the night?"

"No. I'm going back to El Ameur. And you will deliver this fellow to Tinguit. He is expected at police headquarters."

Balducci was looking at Daru with a friendly little smile.

"What's this story?" asked the schoolmaster. "Are you pulling my leg?"

"No, son. Those are the orders."

"The orders? I'm not . . ." Daru hesitated, not wanting to hurt the old Corsican. "I mean, that's not my job."

"What! What's the meaning of that? In wartime people do all kinds of jobs."

"Then I'll wait for the declaration of war!"

Balducci nodded.

"O.K. But the orders exist and they concern you too. Things are brewing, it appears. There is talk of a forthcoming revolt. We are mobilized, in a way."

Daru still had his obstinate look.

"Listen, son," Balducci said. "I like you and you must understand. There's only a dozen of us at El Ameur to patrol throughout the whole territory of a small department[4] and I must get back in a hurry. I was told to hand this guy over to you and return without delay. He couldn't be kept there. His village was beginning to stir; they wanted to take him back. You must take him to Tinguit tomorrow before the day is over. Twenty kilometers shouldn't faze a husky fellow like you. After that, all will be over. You'll come back to your pupils and your comfortable life."

Behind the wall the horse could be heard snorting and pawing the earth. Daru was looking out the window. Decidedly, the weather was clearing and the light was increasing over the snowy plateau. When all the snow was melted, the sun would take over again and once more would burn the fields of stone. For days, still, the unchanging sky would shed its dry light on the solitary expanse where nothing had any connection with man.

"After all," he said, turning around toward Balducci, "what did he do?" And, before the gendarme had opened his mouth, he asked: "Does he speak French?"

"No, not a word. We had been looking for him for a month, but they were hiding him. He killed his cousin."

"Is he against us?"

"I don't think so. But you can never be sure."

"Why did he kill?"

"A family squabble, I think. One owed the other grain, it seems. It's not at all clear. In short, he killed his cousin with a billhook. You know, like a sheep, *kreezk!*"

---

[4] **department:** A territorial unit.

Balducci made the gesture of drawing a blade across his throat and the Arab, his attention attracted, watched him with a sort of anxiety. Daru felt a sudden wrath against the man, against all men with their rotten spite, their tireless hates, their blood lust.

But the kettle was singing on the stove. He served Balducci more tea, hesitated, then served the Arab again, who, a second time, drank avidly. His raised arms made the jellaba fall open and the schoolmaster saw his thin, muscular chest.

"Thanks, kid," Balducci said. "And now, I'm off."

He got up and went toward the Arab, taking a small rope from his pocket.

"What are you doing?" Daru asked dryly.

Balducci, disconcerted, showed him the rope.

"Don't bother."

The old gendarme hesitated. "It's up to you. Of course, you are armed?"

"I have my shotgun."

"Where?"

"In the trunk."

"You ought to have it near your bed."

"Why? I have nothing to fear."

"You're crazy, son. If there's an uprising, no one is safe, we're all in the same boat."

"I'll defend myself. I'll have time to see them coming."

Balducci began to laugh, then suddenly the mustache covered the white teeth.

"You'll have time? O.K. That's just what I was saying. You have always been a little cracked. That's why I like you, my son was like that."

At the same time he took out his revolver and put it on the desk.

"Keep it; I don't need two weapons from here to El Ameur."

The revolver shone against the black paint of the table. When the gendarme turned toward him, the schoolmaster caught the smell of leather and horseflesh.

"Listen, Balducci," Daru said suddenly, "every bit of this disgusts me, and first of all your fellow here. But I won't hand him over. Fight, yes, if I have to. But not that."

The old gendarme stood in front of him and looked at him severely.

"You're being a fool," he said slowly. "I don't like it either. You don't get used to putting a rope on a man even after years of it, and you're even ashamed—yes, ashamed. But you can't let them have their way."

"I won't hand him over," Daru said again.

"It's an order, son, and I repeat it."

"That's right. Repeat to them what I've said to you: I won't hand him over."

Balducci made a visible effort to reflect. He looked at the Arab and at Daru. At last he decided.

"No, I won't tell them anything. If you want to drop us, go ahead; I'll not denounce you. I have an order to deliver the prisoner and I'm doing so. And now you'll just sign this paper for me."

"There's no need. I'll not deny that you left him with me."

"Don't be mean with me. I know you'll tell the truth. You're from hereabouts and you are a man. But you must sign, that's the rule."

Daru opened his drawer, took out a little square bottle of purple ink, the red wooden penholder with the "sergeant-major" pen he used for making models of penmanship, and signed. The gendarme carefully folded the paper and put it into his wallet. Then he moved toward the door.

"I'll see you off," Daru said.

"No," said Balducci. "There's no use being polite. You insulted me."

He looked at the Arab, motionless in the same spot, sniffed peevishly, and turned away toward the door. "Good-by, son," he said. The door shut behind him. Balducci appeared suddenly outside the window and then disappeared. His footsteps were muffled by the snow. The horse stirred on the other side of the wall and several chickens fluttered in fright. A moment later Balducci reappeared outside the window leading the horse by the bridle. He walked toward the little rise without turning around and disappeared from sight with the horse following him. A big stone could be heard bouncing down. Daru walked back toward the prisoner, who, without stirring, never took his eyes off him. "Wait," the schoolmaster said in Arabic and went toward the bedroom. As he was going through the door, he had a second thought, went to the desk, took the revolver, and stuck it in his pocket. Then, without looking back, he went into his room.

For some time he lay on his couch watching the sky gradually close over, listening to the silence. It was this silence that had seemed painful to him during the first days here, after the war. He had requested a post in the little town at the base of the foothills separating the upper plateaus from the desert. There, rocky walls, green and black to the north, pink and lavender to the south, marked the frontier of eternal summer. He had been named to a post farther north, on the plateau itself. In the beginning, the solitude and the silence had been hard for him on these wastelands peopled only by stones. Occasionally, furrows suggested cultivation, but they had been dug to uncover a certain kind of stone good for building. The only plowing here was to harvest rocks. Elsewhere a thin layer of soil accumulated in the hollows would be scraped out to enrich paltry village gardens. This is the way it was: Bare rock covered three quarters of the region. Towns sprang up, flourished, then disappeared; men came by, loved one another or fought bitterly, then died. No one in this desert, neither he nor his guest, mattered. And yet, outside this desert neither of them, Daru knew, could have really lived.

When he got up, no noise came from the classroom. He was amazed at the unmixed joy he derived from the mere thought that the Arab might have fled and that he would be alone with no decision to make. But the prisoner was there. He had merely stretched out between the stove and the desk. With eyes open, he was staring at the ceiling. In that position, his thick lips were particularly noticeable, giving him a pouting look. "Come," said Daru. The Arab got up and followed him. In the bedroom, the schoolmaster pointed to a chair near the table under the window. The Arab sat down without taking his eyes off Daru.

"Are you hungry?"

"Yes," the prisoner said.

Daru set the table for two. He took flour and oil, shaped a cake in a frying-pan, and lighted the little stove that functioned on bottled gas. While the cake was cooking, he went out to the shed to get cheese, eggs, dates, and condensed milk. When the cake was done he set it on the window sill to cool, heated some condensed milk diluted with water, and beat up the eggs into an omelette. In one of his motions he knocked against the revolver stuck in his right pocket. He set the bowl down, went into the classroom, and put the revolver in his desk drawer. When he came back to the room, night was falling. He put on the light and served the Arab. "Eat," he said. The Arab took a piece of the cake, lifted it eagerly to his mouth, and stopped short.

"And you?" he asked.

"After you. I'll eat too."

The thick lips opened slightly. The Arab hesitated, then bit into the cake determinedly.

The meal over, the Arab looked at the schoolmaster. "Are you the judge?"

"No, I'm simply keeping you until tomorrow."

"Why do you eat with me?"

"I'm hungry."

The Arab fell silent. Daru got up and went out. He brought back a folding bed from the shed, set it up between the table and the stove, perpendicular to his own bed. From a large suitcase which, upright in a corner, served as a shelf for papers, he took two blankets and arranged them on the camp bed. Then he stopped, felt useless, and sat down on his bed. There was nothing more to do or to get ready. He had to look at this man. He looked at him, therefore, trying to imagine his face bursting with rage. He couldn't do so. He could see nothing but the dark yet shining eyes and the animal mouth.

"Why did you kill him?" he asked in a voice whose hostile tone surprised him.

The Arab looked away.

"He ran away. I ran after him."

He raised his eyes to Daru again and they were full of a sort of woeful interrogation. "Now what will they do to me?"

"Are you afraid?"

He stiffened, turning his eyes away.

"Are you sorry?"

The Arab stared at him openmouthed. Obviously he did not understand. Daru's annoyance was growing. At the same time he felt awkward and self-conscious with his big body wedged between the two beds.

"Lie down there," he said impatiently. "That's your bed."

The Arab didn't move. He called to Daru:

"Tell me!"

The schoolmaster looked at him.

"Is the gendarme coming back tomorrow?"

"I don't know."

"Are you coming with us?"

"I don't know. Why?"

The prisoner got up and stretched out on top of the blankets, his feet toward the window. The light from the electric bulb shone straight into his eyes and he closed them at once.

"Why?" Daru repeated, standing beside the bed.

The Arab opened his eyes under the blinding light and looked at him, trying not to blink.

"Come with us," he said.

In the middle of the night, Daru was still not asleep. He had gone to bed after undressing completely; he generally slept naked. But when he suddenly realized that he had nothing on, he hesitated. He felt vulnerable and the temptation came to him to put his clothes back on. Then he shrugged his shoulders; after all, he wasn't a child and, if need be, he could break his adversary in two. From his bed he could observe him, lying on his back, still motionless with his eyes closed under the harsh light. When Daru turned out the light, the darkness seemed to coagulate all of a sudden. Little by little, the night came back to life in the window where the starless sky was stirring gently. The schoolmaster soon made out the body lying at his feet. The Arab still did not move, but his eyes seemed open. A faint wind was prowling around the schoolhouse. Perhaps it would drive away the clouds and the sun would reappear.

During the night the wind increased. The hens fluttered a little and then were silent. The Arab turned over on his side with his back to Daru, who thought he heard him moan. Then he listened for his guest's breathing, become heavier and more regular. He listened to that breath so close to him and mused without being able to go to sleep. In this room where he had been sleeping alone for a year, this presence bothered him. But it bothered him also by imposing on him a sort of brotherhood he knew well but refused to accept in the present circumstances. Men who share the same rooms, soldiers or prisoners, develop a strange alliance as if, having cast off their armor with their clothing, they fraternized every evening, over and above their differences, in the ancient community of dream and fatigue. But Daru shook himself; he didn't like such musings, and it was essential to sleep.

A little later, however, when the Arab stirred slightly, the schoolmaster was still not asleep. When the prisoner made a second move, he stiffened, on the alert. The Arab was lifting himself slowly on his arms with almost the motion of a sleepwalker. Seated upright in bed, he waited motionless without turning his head toward Daru, as if he were listening attentively. Daru did not stir; it had just occurred to him that the revolver was still in the drawer of his desk. It was better to act at once. Yet he continued to observe the prisoner, who, with the same slithery motion, put his feet on the ground, waited again, then began to stand up slowly. Daru was about to call out to him when the Arab began to walk, in a quite natural but extraordinarily silent way. He was heading toward the door at the end of the room that opened into the shed. He lifted the latch with precaution and went out, pushing the door behind him but without shutting it. Daru had not stirred. "He is running away," he merely thought. "Good riddance!" Yet he listened attentively. The hens were not fluttering; the guest must be on the plateau. A faint sound of water reached him, and he didn't know what it was until the Arab again stood framed in the doorway, closed the door carefully, and came back to bed without a sound. Then Daru turned his back on him and fell asleep. Still later he seemed, from the depths of his sleep, to hear furtive steps around the schoolhouse. "I'm dreaming! I'm dreaming!" he repeated to himself. And he went on sleeping.

When he awoke, the sky was clear; the loose window let in a cold, pure air. The Arab was asleep, hunched up under the blankets now, his mouth open, utterly relaxed. But when Daru shook him, he started dreadfully, staring at Daru with wild eyes as if he had never seen him and such a frightened expression that the schoolmaster stepped back. "Don't be afraid. It's me. You must eat." The Arab nodded his head and said yes. Calm had returned to his face, but his expression was vacant and listless.

The coffee was ready. They drank it seated together on the folding bed as they munched their pieces of the cake. Then Daru led the Arab under the shed and showed him the faucet where he washed. He went back into the room, folded the blankets and the bed, made his own bed, and put the room in order. Then he went through the classroom and out onto the terrace. The sun was already rising in the blue sky; a soft, bright light was bathing the deserted plateau. On the ridge the snow was melting in spots. The stones were about to reappear. Crouched on the edge of the plateau, the schoolmaster looked at the deserted expanse. He thought of Balducci. He had hurt him, for he had sent him off in a way as if he didn't want to be associated with him. He could still hear the gendarme's farewell and, without knowing why, he felt strangely empty and vulnerable. At that moment, from the other side of the schoolhouse, the prisoner coughed. Daru listened to him almost despite himself and then, furious, threw a pebble that whistled through the air before sinking into the snow. That man's stupid crime revolted him, but to hand him over was contrary to honor. Merely thinking of it made him smart with humiliation. And he cursed at one and the same time his own people who had sent him this Arab and the Arab too who had dared to kill and not managed to get away. Daru got up, walked in a circle on the terrace, waited motionless, then went back into the schoolhouse.

The Arab, leaning over the cement floor of the shed, was washing his teeth with two fingers. Daru looked at him and said: "Come." He went back into the room ahead of the prisoner. He slipped a hunting-jacket on over his sweater and put on walking-shoes. Standing, he waited until the Arab had put on his *chèche* and sandals. They went into the classroom and the schoolmaster pointed to the exit, saying: "Go ahead." The fellow didn't budge. "I'm coming," said Daru. The Arab went out. Daru went back into the room and made a package of pieces of rusk, dates, and sugar. In the classroom, before going out, he hesitated a second in front of his desk, then crossed the threshold and locked the door. "That's the way," he said. He started toward the east, followed by the prisoner. But, a short distance from the schoolhouse, he thought he heard a slight sound behind them. He retraced his steps and examined the surroundings of the house, there was no one there. The Arab watched him without seeming to understand. "Come on," said Daru.

They walked for an hour and rested beside a sharp peak of limestone. The snow was melting faster and faster and the sun was drinking up the puddles at once, rapidly cleaning the plateau, which gradually dried and vibrated like the air itself. When they resumed walking, the ground rang under their feet. From time to time a bird rent the space in front of them with a joyful cry. Daru breathed in deeply the fresh morning light. He felt a sort of rapture before the vast familiar expanse, now almost entirely yellow under its dome of blue sky. They walked an hour more, descending toward the south. They reached a level height made up of crumbly rocks. From there on, the plateau sloped down, eastward, toward a low plain where there were a few spindly trees and, to the south, toward outcroppings of rock that gave the landscape a chaotic look.

Daru surveyed the two directions. There was nothing but the sky on the horizon. Not a man could be seen. He turned toward the Arab, who was looking at him blankly. Daru held out the package to him. "Take it," he said. "There are dates, bread, and sugar. You can hold out for two days. Here are a thousand francs too." The Arab took the package and the money but kept his full hands at chest level as if he didn't know what to do with what was being given him. "Now look," the schoolmaster said as he pointed in the direction of the east, "there's the way to Tinguit. You have a two-hour walk. At Tinguit you'll find the administration and the police. They are expecting you." The Arab looked toward the east, still holding the package and the money against his chest. Daru took his elbow and turned him rather roughly toward the south. At the foot of the height on which they stood could be seen a faint path. "That's the trail across the plateau. In a day's walk from here you'll find pasturelands and the first nomads. They'll take you in and shelter you according to their law." The Arab had now turned toward Daru and a sort of panic was visible in his expression. "Listen," he said. Daru shook his head: "No, be quiet. Now I'm leaving you." He turned his back on him, took two long steps in the direction of the school, looked hesitantly at the motionless Arab, and started off again. For a few minutes he heard nothing but his own step resounding on the cold ground and did not turn his head. A moment later, however, he turned around. The Arab was still there on the edge of the hill, his arms hanging now, and he was looking at the schoolmaster. Daru felt something rise in his throat. But he swore with impatience, waved vaguely, and started off again. He had already gone some distance when he again stopped and looked. There was no longer anyone on the hill.

Daru hesitated. The sun was now rather high in the sky and was beginning to beat down on his head. The schoolmaster retraced his steps, at first somewhat uncertainly, then with decision. When he reached the little hill, he was bathed in sweat. He climbed it as fast as he could and stopped, out of breath, at the top. The rock-fields to the south stood out sharply against the blue sky, but on the plain to the east a steamy heat was already rising. And in that slight haze, Daru, with heavy heart, made out the Arab walking slowly on the road to prison.

A little later, standing before the window of the classroom, the schoolmaster was watching the clear light bathing the whole surface of the plateau, but he hardly saw it. Behind him on the blackboard, among the winding French rivers, sprawled the clumsily chalked-up words he had just read: "You handed over our brother. You will pay for this." Daru looked at the sky, the plateau, and, beyond, the invisible lands stretching all the way to the sea. In this vast landscape he had loved so much, he was alone.

∽ The Myth of Sisyphus

Translated by Justin O'Brien

The gods had condemned Sisyphus[1] to ceaselessly rolling a rock to the top of a mountain, whence the stone would fall back of its own weight. They had thought with some reason that there is no more dreadful punishment than futile and hopeless labor.

If one believes Homer, Sisyphus was the wisest and most prudent of mortals. According to another tradition, however, he was disposed to practice the profession of highwayman. I see no contradiction in this. Opinions differ as to the reasons why he became the futile laborer of the underworld. To begin with, he is accused of a certain levity in regard to the gods. He stole their secrets. Ægina, the daughter of Æsopus, was carried off by Jupiter. The father was shocked by that disappearance and complained to Sisyphus. He, who knew of the abduction, offered to tell about it on condition that Æsopus would give water to the citadel of Corinth. To the celestial thunderbolts he preferred the benediction of water. He was punished for this in the underworld. Homer tells us also that Sisyphus had put Death in chains. Pluto could not endure the sight of his deserted, silent empire. He dispatched the god of war, who liberated Death from the hands of her conqueror.

It is said also that Sisyphus, being near to death, rashly wanted to test his wife's love. He ordered her to cast his unburied body into the middle of the public square. Sisyphus woke up in the underworld. And there, annoyed by an obedience so contrary to human love, he obtained from Pluto permission to return to earth in order to chastise his wife. But when he had seen again the face of this world, enjoyed water and sun, warm stones and the sea, he no longer wanted to go back to the infernal darkness. Recalls, signs of anger, warnings were of no avail. Many years more he lived facing the curve of the gulf, the sparkling sea, and the smiles of earth. A decree of the gods was necessary. Mercury came and seized the impudent man by the collar and, snatching him from his joys, led him forcibly back to the underworld, where his rock was ready for him.

You have already grasped that Sisyphus is the absurd hero. He *is*, as much through his passions as through his torture. His scorn of the gods, his hatred of death, and his passion for life won him that unspeakable penalty in which the whole being is exerted toward accomplishing nothing. This is the price that must be paid for the passions of this earth. Nothing is told us about Sisyphus in the underworld. Myths are made for the imagination to breathe life into them. As for this myth, one sees merely the whole effort of a body straining to raise the huge stone, to roll it and push it up a slope a hundred times over; one sees the face screwed up, the cheek tight

---

[1] **Sisyphus:** In order to spite his brother Salmoneus, Sisyphus seduced Salmoneus's daughter Tyro and had two children with her; she killed them when she learned the reason for his love. Sisyphus then committed an impious act for which he was condemned to Hades where for eternity he had to push an enormous boulder to the top of a hill. Near the top, the stone was fated to roll down again.

against the stone, the shoulder bracing the clay-covered mass, the foot wedging it, the fresh start with arms outstretched, the wholly human security of two earth-clotted hands. At the very end of his long effort measured by skyless space and time without depth, the purpose is achieved. Then Sisyphus watches the stone rush down in a few moments toward that lower world whence he will have to push it up again toward the summit. He goes back down to the plain.

It is during that return, that pause, that Sisyphus interests me. A face that toils so close to stones is already stone itself! I see that man going back down with a heavy yet measured step toward the torment of which he will never know the end. That hour like a breathing-space which returns as surely as his suffering, that is the hour of consciousness. At each of those moments when he leaves the heights and gradually sinks toward the lairs of the gods, he is superior to his fate. He is stronger than his rock.

If this myth is tragic, that is because its hero is conscious. Where would his torture be, indeed, if at every step the hope of succeeding upheld him? The workman of today works every day in his life at the same tasks, and this fate is no less absurd. But it is tragic only at the rare moments when it becomes conscious. Sisyphus, proletarian of the gods, powerless and rebellious, knows the whole extent of his wretched condition: It is what he thinks of during his descent. The lucidity that was to constitute his torture at the same time crowns his victory. There is no fate that cannot be surmounted by scorn.

If the descent is thus sometimes performed in sorrow, it can also take place in joy. This word is not too much. Again I fancy Sisyphus returning toward his rock, and the sorrow was in the beginning. When the images of earth cling too tightly to memory, when the call of happiness becomes too insistent, it happens that melancholy rises in man's heart: This is the rock's victory, this is the rock itself. The boundless grief is too heavy to bear. These are our nights of Gethsemane. But crushing truths perish from being acknowledged. Thus, Œdipus at the outset obeys fate without knowing it. But from the moment he knows, his tragedy begins. Yet at the same moment, blind and desperate, he realizes that the only bond linking him to the world is the cool hand of a girl. Then a tremendous remark rings out: "Despite so many ordeals, my advanced age and the nobility of my soul make me conclude that all is well." Sophocles' Œdipus, like Dostoevsky's Kirilov,[2] thus gives the recipe for the absurd victory. Ancient wisdom confirms modern heroism.

One does not discover the absurd without being tempted to write a manual of happiness. "What! by such narrow ways—?" There is but one world, however. Happiness and the absurd are two sons of the same earth. They are inseparable. It would be a mistake to say that happiness necessarily springs from the absurd discovery. It happens as well that the feeling of the absurd springs from happiness. "I conclude that all is well," says Œdipus, and that remark is sacred. It echoes in the wild and limited universe of man. It teaches that all is not, has not been, exhausted. It drives out

---

[2] **Kirilov:** A character in Dostoevsky's novel *The Possessed* (1872) who believed that men would become gods by overcoming their fear of death

of this world a god who had come into it with dissatisfaction and a preference for futile sufferings. It makes of fate a human matter, which must be settled among men.

All Sisyphus's silent joy is contained therein. His fate belongs to him. His rock is his thing. Likewise, the absurd man, when he contemplates his torment, silences all the idols. In the universe suddenly restored to its silence, the myriad wondering little voices of the earth rise up. Unconscious, secret calls, invitations from all the faces, they are the necessary reverse and price of victory. There is no sun without shadow, and it is essential to know the night. The absurd man says yes and his effort will henceforth be unceasing. If there is a personal fate, there is no higher destiny, or at least there is but one which he concludes is inevitable and despicable. For the rest, he knows himself to be the master of his days. At that subtle moment when man glances backward over his life, Sisyphus returning toward his rock, in that slight pivoting he contemplates that series of unrelated actions which becomes his fate, created by him, combined under his memory's eye and soon sealed by his death. Thus, convinced of the wholly human origin of all that is human, a blind man eager to see who knows that the night has no end, he is still on the go. The rock is still rolling.

I leave Sisyphus at the foot of the mountain! One always finds one's burden again. But Sisyphus teaches the higher fidelity that negates the gods and raises rocks. He too concludes that all is well. This universe henceforth without a master seems to him neither sterile nor futile. Each atom of that stone, each mineral flake of that night-filled mountain, in itself forms a world. The struggle itself toward the heights is enough to fill a man's heart. One must imagine Sisyphus happy.

TEXT IN CONTEXT

∾ CHINUA ACHEBE
B. NIGERIA, 1930

A novelist, poet, short-story writer, writer of children's literature, essayist, editor, and teacher, **Chinua Achebe** is one of the most influential West African writers of the twentieth century. Achebe has also worked as a radio producer, writer, and director, and he has served on diplomatic missions for Biafra during the Nigerian civil war and was deputy president of the People's Redemption Party in 1983. With subtlety and complexity, Achebe's novels portray from an insider's point of view traditional African society and culture, especially as it clashes with the forces of colonialism and the vestiges of its ghost in postcolonial Nigeria. Like fellow African writers Wole Soyinka (b. 1934) from Nigeria and **Ngugi Wa Thiong'o** (b. 1938) from Kenya, Achebe has articulated in his work a sustaining moral vision for African consciousness and identity, engaging directly the difficult problems Africa faces in the postcolonial era and recovering a sense of the African spirit as it emerges from traditional folktales, stories, and customs. Though Achebe writes in English, his novels capture the rich imagery and rhythms of his native country's proverbs and tales.

CHIN-wah
ah-CHAY-bay

en-GOO-gee wah
thee-ONG-oh

Chinua Achebe
(© Ralph Orlowski/
Reuters/CORBIS)

English and Ibo Education.   Chinua Achebe was born November 16, 1930, in Ogidi, Nigeria, the fifth child of Isaiah Okafor Achebe and Janet Iloegbunam, Ibo missionary teachers who raised him in a Christian household. Although he received his education in English at the British missionary schools in Ogidi, he developed an attachment to traditional Ibo stories through his mother and sister. In his teens he studied at the Government College in Umuahia and then attended

p. 1154

University College in Ibadan from 1948 to 1953, receiving a bachelor's degree. He had entered college on a scholarship to study medicine, but after his first year he switched to the liberal arts, including English literature. His reading in European, especially British, literature brought home to Achebe the often condescending and false image of Africa presented by European writers such as Joyce Cary (1888–1957) and **Joseph Conrad**. Achebe began writing his first novel, *Things Fall Apart* (1958), as a direct repudiation of the image of Nigeria presented in Cary's *Mister Johnson* (1939).

Civil War and Independence.   Upon graduation from the university at Ibadan, Achebe worked as a producer and director for the Nigerian Broadcasting Service until civil war erupted in 1967. Nigeria had gained its independence from Britain in 1960, the year before Achebe's marriage to Christie Chinwe Okoli. In the vacuum created by the withdrawal of British colonial authority, three tribal groups— the **Ibo** (or Igbo), Hausa-Fulani, and Yoruba—competed against one another for power. The civil war, which lasted until 1970, did little to resolve those rivalries, and since the time of the war Nigeria has been ruled by a succession of dictators, some posing as supporters of democracy. During the war, Biafra, a state of Ibo speakers in eastern Nigeria, seceded from the rest of the country. Achebe supported the Biafran independence movement, working for the Biafran Ministry of Information. That experience served him well, especially in *A Man of the People* (1966) and *Anthills of the Savannah* (1987), in which he focuses on the corruption, power-mongering, and hope for democratic freedoms that characterize Nigerian politics even today. A collection of poetry, *Christmas in Biafra,* winner of the Commonwealth Poetry Prize, and a collection of short stories, *Girls at War,* were written during the civil war.

EE-boh

International Acclaim.   In the early 1970s Achebe accepted visiting professorships at the University of Massachusetts, Amherst, where he again taught from 1987 to 1988, and the University of Connecticut at Storrs. During this time he taught literature and founded and edited *Okike,* a journal of African literature and criticism. In addition, he founded the Heinemann African Writers Series, which has established African literature written in English as a major force in contemporary world literature. In 1976 Achebe returned to Nigeria as a teacher and senior research fellow at the University of Nigeria, Nsukka. He has continued to be involved in Nigerian political life, primarily as a commentator, and in 1983 he published *The Trouble with Nigeria,* a nonfiction critique of the political corruption of his country.

www For links to more information about Chinua Achebe, a quiz on *Things Fall Apart,* and information about Achebe's twenty-first-century relevance, see bedfordstmartins .com/worldlit compact.

Representing Africa.   Achebe describes himself as a "political writer" whose work is "concerned with universal human communication across racial and cultural boundaries as a means of fostering respect for all people." He set out to correct the distorted representation of Africa that European writers had delivered to European audiences and to show the adverse impact that colonization had had upon indigenous cultures. His first three novels, which make up a kind of trilogy, directly accomplish those objectives. *Things Fall Apart* (1958), chosen here to represent Achebe, shows Nigeria at the advent of British colonization. It takes place in the Ibo villages of **Umuofia** in the late 1880s, a time when English missionaries and administrators first began to appear. The Europeans were interested in the Niger delta region for its palm oil, and in 1879 Englishman George Goldie formed the United Africa Company to drive out the French, who had conquered most of western Africa in the previous decade. Eventually becoming the Royal Niger Company and granted a royal charter, Goldie's company established a monopoly in the region by about 1884. By 1893, Nigeria was declared a British colony, and cocoa, timber, rubber, coconuts, and palm oil began to flow out of the country on British ships. The novel focuses on the psychological and cultural consequences of that history as it affects the leader Okonkwo, who struggles to preserve his and his people's integrity and sovereignty in the face of the changes in law and religion that the colonizers have brought.

oo-MWOH-fee-ah

No Longer at Ease.   Achebe's next two novels, *No Longer at Ease* (1960) and *Arrow of God* (1964), continue the story of Umuofia in the two generations after Okonkwo's. Although *Arrow of God* is the third novel in the series, it tells the story of the second generation in Umuofia in the 1920s. Ezeulu, a spiritual leader, also must grapple with the gap between European and African ways. Another flawed hero, Ezeulu plans to use his son to spy on Western schools. The scheme fails when the son, Oduche, is converted and turns against his father and his father's god. Ezeulu manages to get arrested, is imprisoned by the British, and finally embitters his own people by carrying out a heavy penalty on them; the entire village turns against him. *No Longer at Ease* takes readers into the 1950s, when a grandson of Okonkwo, the English-educated Obi Okonkwo, fails to integrate Ibo tradition with European ideals. The would-be hero represents the educated elite, whose aspirations have more often than not failed to materialize in Nigeria. Obi returns to his country a kind of stranger, turns against his people, and falls into the political corruption he'd hoped to eradicate.

The Igbo have always
lived in a world of
continual struggle,
motion, and
change — a feature
conspicuous in the
tautness, overreach,
and torsion of their
art; it is like a
tightrope walk, a
hairbreadth brush
with the boundaries
of anarchy.

– CHINUA ACHEBE

p. 1350

p. 1159

Anthills of the Savannah.   Achebe's next three novels focus primarily
on political corruption in the post-1960 period — after Nigerian independence. *A Man of the People* (1966) condemns the abuse of power
and corruption, as does *Anthills of the Savannah* (1988). The latter
novel, one of the most highly acclaimed of Achebe's works, follows a
set of friends — Ikem, Sam, and Chris — whose friendship falls apart
as Sam, who has become a military dictator of the imaginary West
African country of Kangan, loses the support and confidence of Ikem,
an editor, and Chris, the Minister of Information. To preserve his
power, Sam resorts to propaganda, repression, and finally, the extermination of opponents and critics. As in the case of *A Man of the
People,* which seemed to anticipate much of the corruption of the
1970s, *Anthills of the Savannah* appears to have prophesied the duplicity and arbitrary wielding of power of the present regime in Nigeria.
Anthills ends with cautious optimism, noting the important role of
women in the movement for reform. With his latest novel pointing
to the uncertain future, Achebe's work so far constitutes a history,
in fiction, of colonialism and independence in Nigeria from the
nineteenth century to the present.

Things Fall Apart.   *Things Fall Apart,* one of the first and finest novels
of postindependence African literature in English, launched Achebe on
the project of tracing Nigeria's history in his fiction. The title comes
from William Butler Yeats's **"The Second Coming,"** a visionary poem
announcing the birth of a "rough beast . . . slouching toward Bethlehem." That beast here appears to be the erosion of Ibo society, portrayed in unsurpassed detail, sensitivity, and understanding, after its
devastating encounter with European colonialism. Set in roughly the
same period as Conrad's **Heart of Darkness** (1902), the novel presents
the early encounter with European missionaries from the African —
specifically, the Ibo — point of view. Some of the incidents of this
encounter, such as the raid on Abame mentioned in Chapter 15, are
based on actual historical incidents — in this case, a British attack on
the town of Ahiara, which took place in 1905, to avenge the killing of
a missionary. Achebe's critique of British colonialism, however, comes
less through the documentation of such incidents and more through
the celebration of Ibo culture. To counteract the portrayal of the
African as a shadowy figure in novels such as Joyce Cary's *Mister
Johnson* (1939) and Conrad's *Heart of Darkness,* Achebe in this novel
and others honors, without resorting to sentimentality, the humanity and dignity of the African people. In *Things Fall Apart,* Achebe

**Yoruba sculpture,
1881**

*This carved wood
statue from the
Yoruba culture of
Nigeria depicts a
European missionary
nun with five
African children.
(© Bildarchiv
Preussischer
Kulturbesitz/Art
Resource)*

presents that humanity in part through the character of the village
leader, Okonkwo, whose actions involve him in almost every aspect
of the complex culture and religious life of the Ibo in Umuofia.

Okonkwo is a complex and tragic hero who is as noble and flawed
as an Achilles or a Creon.[1] While Okonkwo embodies many of the
virtues of his society—courage, industry, and material success—he
also demonstrates a dangerous stubbornness and self-satisfaction. His
killing of **Ikemefuna** and his rejection of his son Nwoye are presented
unsympathetically; indeed, like Creon's in *Antigone,* Okonkwo's rigidity
and heavy-handedness eventually lead to his downfall. As in later novels, and like his compatriot writer Wole Soyinka, Achebe, in *Things Fall
Apart,* recognizes the need for the preservation of tradition but also
affirms a cautious and controlled acceptance of those European ideas
and practices that can enhance African culture and make it stronger.

ee-kay-may-FOO-nah

---

[1] **Creon:** The king of Thebes; represented in Sophocles' (496–406 B.C.E.) play *Antigone* as a man who refuses to
bend the rules of the state.

Nigerian servants transporting a British official, 1910
British administrators ruled indirectly in Nigeria, appointing native leaders to
collect taxes and carry out other duties on behalf of the government. The various
native societies and traditions in Nigeria had mixed reactions to this system, and
the appointed leaders were often met with resistance. (The Art Archive/John Meck)

The English missionaries and administration officials exacerbate
the misfortunes visited upon Okonkwo. The white missionary at
Mbanta articulates the uninformed prejudice against native religion
and culture, which the novel has just elaborated in fine detail. Achebe
introduces the missionary comically; the villagers mock his interpreter's
use of their language as he mistakes the word meaning "my buttocks"
for "myself." Many of the Mbanta men are astounded at the missionaries' pronouncements that their gods are dead and have no power; they
laugh with incredulity at a missionary's claims that his is the only living
and powerful god. *Things Fall Apart* ends tragically, with Okonkwo

humiliated by the beating he received in the white man's jail and with his deep disappointment that the men of Umuofia would not stand up, as he had, to the encroachment of the English. Okonkwo's death is symbolic, in many ways, of the death of Ibo society itself; the novel questions whether that death was necessary and gives its African readers reason to believe in the importance of preserving what is best in their traditions.

■ **FURTHER RESEARCH**

Gikandi, Simon. *Reading Chinua Achebe: Language and Ideology in Fiction*. 1991.
Innes, C. L. *Chinua Achebe*. 1990.
———, and Bernth Lindfors, eds. *Critical Perspectives on Chinua Achebe*. 1978.
Iyasere, Solomon Ognede, ed. *Understanding* Things Fall Apart: *Selected Essays and Criticism*. 1998.
Killam, G. D. *The Writings of Chinua Achebe*. 1977.
Oqede, Ode. *Achebe and the Politics of Representation: Form Against Itself from Colonial Conquest and Occupation to Post-Independence Disillusionment*. 2001.
Turkington, Kate. *Chinua Achebe:* Things Fall Apart. 1977.
Wren, Robert M. *Achebe's World: The Historical and Cultural Context of the Novels of Chinua Achebe*. 1980.

■ **PRONUNCIATION**

Chinua Achebe: CHIN-wah ah-CHAY-bay
Chielo: chee-AY-loh
egwugwu: ay-GWOO-gwoo
Erulu: ay-ROO-loo
Ezeani: ay-zay-AH-nee
Ezeugo: ay-zay-OO-goh
Ibo: EE-boh
Idemili: ee-DAY-mee-lee
Ikemefuna: ee-kay-may-FOO-nah
Mbari: em-BAH-ree
Ndulue: en-doo-loo-AY
Ngugi Wa Thiong'o: en-GOO-gee wah thee-ONG-oh
Nwakibie: nwah-kee-BEE-ay
Nwayieke: nwah-yee-AY-kay
Umuofia: oo-MWOH-fee-ah

[Achebe's characters] have a vital relationship with the social and economic landscape. We can see, and feel, how his characters, their worldview, their very aspirations, have been shaped by a particular environment in a particular historical place. They live in history . . . because they are the makers of history.

– NGUGI WA THIONG'O, novelist and critic, 1972

❧ Things Fall Apart

Part I

1

Okonkwo was well known throughout the nine villages and even beyond. His fame rested on solid personal achievements. As a young man of eighteen he had brought honor to his village by throwing Amalinze the Cat. Amalinze was the great wrestler who for seven years was unbeaten, from Umuofia to Mbaino. He was called the Cat because his back would never touch the earth. It was this man that Okonkwo threw in a fight which the old men agreed was one of the fiercest since the founder of their town engaged a spirit of the wild for seven days and seven nights.

The drums beat and the flutes sang and the spectators held their breath. Amalinze was a wily craftsman, but Okonkwo was as slippery as a fish in water. Every nerve and every muscle stood out on their arms, on their backs and their thighs, and one almost heard them stretching to breaking point. In the end Okonkwo threw the Cat.

That was many years ago, twenty years or more, and during this time Okonkwo's fame had grown like a bush-fire in the harmattan. He was tall and huge, and his bushy eyebrows and wide nose gave him a very severe look. He breathed heavily, and it was said that, when he slept, his wives and children in their houses could hear him breathe. When he walked, his heels hardly touched the ground and he seemed to walk on springs, as if he was going to pounce on somebody. And he did pounce on people quite often. He had a slight stammer and whenever he was angry and could not get his words out quickly enough, he would use his fists. He had no patience with unsuccessful men. He had had no patience with his father.

Unoka, for that was his father's name, had died ten years ago. In his day he was lazy and improvident and was quite incapable of thinking about tomorrow. If any money came his way, and it seldom did, he immediately bought gourds of palm-wine, called round his neighbors and made merry. He always said that whenever he saw a dead man's mouth he saw the folly of not eating what one had in one's lifetime. Unoka was, of course, a debtor, and he owed every neighbor some money, from a few cowries[1] to quite substantial amounts.

He was tall but very thin and had a slight stoop. He wore a haggard and mournful look except when he was drinking or playing on his flute. He was very good on his flute, and his happiest moments were the two or three moons after the harvest when the village musicians brought down their instruments, hung above the fireplace. Unoka would play with them, his face beaming with blessedness and peace. Sometimes another village would ask Unoka's band and their dancing *egwugwu*[2] to

---

[1] **cowries:** A sixty-pound bag of cowries—mollusk shells used as currency—was worth about one pound sterling.

[2] *egwugwu:* Dancers who masquerade as spirits of the village ancestors.

come and stay with them and teach them their tunes. They would go to such hosts for as long as three or four markets,[3] making music and feasting. Unoka loved the good fare and the good fellowship, and he loved this season of the year, when the rains had stopped and the sun rose every morning with dazzling beauty. And it was not too hot either, because the cold and dry harmattan wind was blowing down from the north. Some years the harmattan was very severe and a dense haze hung on the atmosphere. Old men and children would then sit round log fires, warming their bodies. Unoka loved it all, and he loved the first kites that returned with the dry season, and the children who sang songs of welcome to them. He would remember his own childhood, how he had often wandered around looking for a kite sailing leisurely against the blue sky. As soon as he found one he would sing with his whole being, welcoming it back from its long, long journey, and asking it if it had brought home any lengths of cloth.

That was years ago, when he was young. Unoka, the grown-up, was a failure. He was poor and his wife and children had barely enough to eat. People laughed at him because he was a loafer, and they swore never to lend him any more money because he never paid back. But Unoka was such a man that he always succeeded in borrowing more, and piling up his debts.

One day a neighbor called Okoye came in to see him. He was reclining on a mud bed in his hut playing on the flute. He immediately rose and shook hands with Okoye, who then unrolled the goatskin which he carried under his arm, and sat down. Unoka went into an inner room and soon returned with a small wooden disc containing a kola nut, some alligator pepper, and a lump of white chalk.[4]

"I have kola," he announced when he sat down, and passed the disc over to his guest.

"Thank you. He who brings kola brings life. But I think you ought to break it," replied Okoye, passing back the disc.

"No, it is for you, I think," and they argued like this for a few moments before Unoka accepted the honor of breaking the kola. Okoye, meanwhile, took the lump of chalk, drew some lines on the floor, and then painted his big toe.

As he broke the kola, Unoka prayed to their ancestors for life and health, and for protection against their enemies. When they had eaten they talked about many things: about the heavy rains which were drowning the yams, about the next ancestral feast and about the impending war with the village of Mbaino. Unoka was never happy when it came to wars. He was in fact a coward and could not bear the sight of blood. And so he changed the subject and talked about music, and his face beamed. He could hear in his mind's ear the blood-stirring and intricate rhythms of the *ekwe*

---

[3] **three or four markets:** One-and-a-half to two weeks; the Ibo week has four days—Eke, the market day; Afo, a half-working day; and Oye and Nkwo, full working days.

[4] **kola . . . chalk:** All items used in hospitality ceremonies. Kola nuts, like coffee, contain caffeine and so offer a mild stimulant; alligator pepper is a black pepper reserved especially for kola; and the chalk is used for visitors to draw their personal mark.

and the *udu* and the *ogene,*[5] and he could hear his own flute weaving in and out of them, decorating them with a colorful and plaintive tune. The total effect was gay and brisk, but if one picked out the flute as it went up and down and then broke up into short snatches, one saw that there was sorrow and grief there.

Okoye was also a musician. He played on the *ogene.* But he was not a failure like Unoka. He had a large barn full of yams and he had three wives. And now he was going to take the Idemili[6] title, the third highest in the land. It was a very expensive ceremony and he was gathering all his resources together. That was in fact the reason why he had come to see Unoka. He cleared his throat and began:

"Thank you for the kola. You may have heard of the title I intend to take shortly."

Having spoken plainly so far, Okoye said the next half a dozen sentences in proverbs. Among the Ibo the art of conversation is regarded very highly, and proverbs are the palm-oil with which words are eaten. Okoye was a great talker and he spoke for a long time, skirting round the subject and then hitting it finally. In short, he was asking Unoka to return the two hundred cowries he had borrowed from him more than two years before. As soon as Unoka understood what his friend was driving at, he burst out laughing. He laughed loud and long and his voice rang out clear as the *ogene,* and tears stood in his eyes. His visitor was amazed, and sat speechless. At the end, Unoka was able to give an answer between fresh outbursts of mirth.

"Look at that wall," he said, pointing at the far wall of his hut, which was rubbed with red earth so that it shone. "Look at those lines of chalk"; and Okoye saw groups of short perpendicular lines drawn in chalk. There were five groups, and the smallest group had ten lines. Unoka had a sense of the dramatic and so he allowed a pause, in which he took a pinch of snuff and sneezed noisily, and then he continued: "Each group there represents a debt to someone, and each stroke is one hundred cowries. You see, I owe that man a thousand cowries. But he has not come to wake me up in the morning for it. I shall pay you, but not today. Our elders say that the sun will shine on those who stand before it shines on those who kneel under them. I shall pay my big debts first." And he took another pinch of snuff, as if that was paying the big debts first. Okoye rolled his goatskin and departed.

When Unoka died he had taken no title at all and he was heavily in debt. Any wonder then that his son Okonkwo was ashamed of him? Fortunately, among these people a man was judged according to his worth and not according to the worth of his father. Okonkwo was clearly cut out for great things. He was still young but he had won fame as the greatest wrestler in the nine villages. He was a wealthy farmer and had two barns full of yams, and had just married his third wife. To crown it all he had taken two titles and had shown incredible prowess in two inter-tribal wars. And so although Okonkwo was still young, he was already one of the greatest men of his time. Age was respected among his people, but achievement was revered. As the

---

[5] *ekwe . . . ogene:* A wooden drum, clay drum, and iron gong, respectively.

[6] **Idemili:** A river god, associated with the sacred python.

elders said, if a child washed his hands he could eat with kings. Okonkwo had clearly washed his hands and so he ate with kings and elders. And that was how he came to look after the doomed lad who was sacrificed to the village of Umuofia by their neighbors to avoid war and bloodshed. The ill-fated lad was called Ikemefuna.

2

Okonkwo had just blown out the palm-oil lamp and stretched himself on his bamboo bed when he heard the *ogene* of the town crier piercing the still night air. *Gome, gome, gome, gome,* boomed the hollow metal. Then the crier gave his message, and at the end of it beat his instrument again. And this was the message. Every man of Umuofia was asked to gather at the market place tomorrow morning. Okonkwo wondered what was amiss, for he knew certainly that something was amiss. He had discerned a clear overtone of tragedy in the crier's voice, and even now he could still hear it as it grew dimmer and dimmer in the distance.

The night was very quiet. It was always quiet except on moonlight nights. Darkness held a vague terror for these people, even the bravest among them. Children were warned not to whistle at night for fear of evil spirits. Dangerous animals became even more sinister and uncanny in the dark. A snake was never called by its name at night, because it would hear. It was called a string. And so on this particular night as the crier's voice was gradually swallowed up in the distance, silence returned to the world, a vibrant silence made more intense by the universal trill of a million million forest insects.

On a moonlight night it would be different. The happy voices of children playing in open fields would then be heard. And perhaps those not so young would be playing in pairs in less open places, and old men and women would remember their youth. As the Ibo say: "When the moon is shining the cripple becomes hungry for a walk."

But this particular night was dark and silent. And in all the nine villages of Umuofia a town crier with his *ogene* asked every man to be present tomorrow morning. Okonkwo on his bamboo bed tried to figure out the nature of the emergency—war with a neighboring clan? That seemed the most likely reason, and he was not afraid of war. He was a man of action, a man of war. Unlike his father he could stand the look of blood. In Umuofia's latest war he was the first to bring home a human head. That was his fifth head; and he was not an old man yet. On great occasions such as the funeral of a village celebrity he drank his palm-wine from his first human head.

In the morning the market place was full. There must have been about ten thousand men there, all talking in low voices. At last Ogbuefi Ezeugo stood up in the midst of them and bellowed four times, *"Umuofia kwenu,"*[7] and on each occasion he faced a different direction and seemed to push the air with a clenched fist. And ten

---

[7] *"Umuofia kwenu"*: "Umuofia united."

thousand men answered *"Yaa!"* each time. Then there was perfect silence. Ogbuefi Ezeugo was a powerful orator and was always chosen to speak on such occasions. He moved his hand over his white head and stroked his white beard. He then adjusted his cloth, which was passed under his right armpit and tied above his left shoulder.

"Umuofia kwenu," he bellowed a fifth time, and the crowd yelled in answer. And then suddenly like one possessed he shot out his left hand and pointed in the direction of Mbaino, and said through gleaming white teeth firmly clenched: "Those sons of wild animals have dared to murder a daughter of Umuofia." He threw his head down and gnashed his teeth, and allowed a murmur of suppressed anger to sweep the crowd. When he began again, the anger on his face was gone and in its place a sort of smile hovered, more terrible and more sinister than the anger. And in a clear unemotional voice he told Umuofia how their daughter had gone to market at Mbaino and had been killed. That woman, said Ezeugo, was the wife of Ogbuefi Udo, and he pointed to a man who sat near him with a bowed head. The crowd then shouted with anger and thirst for blood.

Many others spoke, and at the end it was decided to follow the normal course of action. An ultimatum was immediately dispatched to Mbaino asking them to choose between war on the one hand, and on the other the offer of a young man and a virgin as compensation.

Umuofia was feared by all its neighbors. It was powerful in war and in magic, and its priests and medicine men were feared in all the surrounding country. Its most potent war-medicine was as old as the clan itself. Nobody knew how old. But on one point there was general agreement—the active principle in that medicine had been an old woman with one leg. In fact, the medicine itself was called *agadi-nwayi,* or old woman. It had its shrine in the centre of Umuofia, in a cleared spot. And if anybody was so foolhardy as to pass by the shrine after dusk he was sure to see the old woman hopping about.

And so the neighboring clans who naturally knew of these things feared Umuofia, and would not go to war against it without first trying a peaceful settlement. And in fairness to Umuofia it should be recorded that it never went to war unless its case was clear and just and was accepted as such by its Oracle—the Oracle of the Hills and the Caves. And there were indeed occasions when the Oracle had forbidden Umuofia to wage a war. If the clan had disobeyed the Oracle they would surely have been beaten, because their dreaded *agadi-nwayi* would never fight what the Ibo call a *fight of blame.*

But the war that now threatened was a just war. Even the enemy clan knew that. And so when Okonkwo of Umuofia arrived at Mbaino as the proud and imperious emissary of war, he was treated with great honor and respect, and two days later he returned home with a lad of fifteen and a young virgin. The lad's name was Ikemefuna, whose sad story is still told in Umuofia unto this day.

The elders, or *ndichie,* met to hear a report of Okonkwo's mission. At the end they decided, as everybody knew they would, that the girl should go to Ogbuefi Udo to replace his murdered wife. As for the boy, he belonged to the clan as a whole, and there was no hurry to decide his fate. Okonkwo was, therefore, asked on behalf of the clan to look after him in the interim. And so for three years Ikemefuna lived in Okonkwo's household.

Okonkwo ruled his household with a heavy hand. His wives, especially the youngest, lived in perpetual fear of his fiery temper, and so did his little children. Perhaps down in his heart Okonkwo was not a cruel man. But his whole life was dominated by fear, the fear of failure and of weakness. It was deeper and more intimate than the fear of evil and capricious gods and of magic, the fear of the forest, and of the forces of nature, malevolent, red in tooth and claw. Okonkwo's fear was greater than these. It was not external but lay deep within himself. It was the fear of himself, lest he should be found to resemble his father. Even as a little boy he had resented his father's failure and weakness, and even now he still remembered how he had suffered when a playmate had told him that his father was *agbala.* That was how Okonkwo first came to know that *agbala* was not only another name for a woman, it could also mean a man who had taken no title. And so Okonkwo was ruled by one passion — to hate everything that his father Unoka had loved. One of those things was gentleness and another was idleness.

During the planting season Okonkwo worked daily on his farms from cock-crow until the chickens went to roost. He was a very strong man and rarely felt fatigue. But his wives and young children were not as strong, and so they suffered. But they dared not complain openly. Okonkwo's first son, Nwoye, was then twelve years old but was already causing his father great anxiety for his incipient laziness. At any rate, that was how it looked to his father, and he sought to correct him by constant nagging and beating. And so Nwoye was developing into a sad-faced youth.

Okonkwo's prosperity was visible in his household. He had a large compound enclosed by a thick wall of red earth. His own hut, or *obi,* stood immediately behind the only gate in the red walls. Each of his three wives had her own hut, which together formed a half moon behind the *obi.* The barn was built against one end of the red walls, and long stacks of yam stood out prosperously in it. At the opposite end of the compound was a shed for the goats, and each wife built a small attachment to her hut for the hens. Near the barn was a small house, the "medicine house" or shrine where Okonkwo kept the wooden symbols of his personal god and of his ancestral spirits. He worshipped them with sacrifices of kola nut, food, and palm-wine, and offered prayers to them on behalf of himself, his three wives and eight children. So when the daughter of Umuofia was killed in Mbaino, Ikemefuna came into Okonkwo's household. When Okonkwo brought him home that day he called his most senior wife and handed him over to her.

"He belongs to the clan," he told her. "So look after him."

"Is he staying long with us?" she asked.

"Do what you are told, woman," Okonkwo thundered, and stammered. "When did you become one of the *ndichie* of Umuofia?"

And so Nwoye's mother took Ikemefuna to her hut and asked no more questions.

As for the boy himself, he was terribly afraid. He could not understand what was happening to him or what he had done. How could he know that his father had taken a hand in killing a daughter of Umuofia? All he knew was that a few men had arrived at their house, conversing with his father in low tones, and at the end he had been taken out and handed over to a stranger. His mother had wept bitterly, but he had been too surprised to weep. And so the stranger had brought him, and a girl, a long, long way from home, through lonely forest paths. He did not know who the girl was, and he never saw her again.

3

Okonkwo did not have the start in life which many young men usually had. He did not inherit a barn from his father. There was no barn to inherit. The story was told in Umuofia, of how his father, Unoka, had gone to consult the Oracle of the Hills and the Caves to find out why he always had a miserable harvest.

The Oracle was called Agbala, and people came from far and near to consult it. They came when misfortune dogged their steps or when they had a dispute with their neighbors. They came to discover what the future held for them or to consult the spirits of their departed fathers.

The way into the shrine was a round hole at the side of a hill, just a little bigger than the round opening into a henhouse. Worshippers and those who came to seek knowledge from the god crawled on their belly through the hole and found themselves in a dark, endless space in the presence of Agbala. No one had ever beheld Agbala, except his priestess. But no one who had ever crawled into his awful shrine had come out without the fear of his power. His priestess stood by the sacred fire which she built in the heart of the cave and proclaimed the will of the god. The fire did not burn with a flame. The glowing logs only served to light up vaguely the dark figure of the priestess.

Sometimes a man came to consult the spirit of his dead father or relative. It was said that when such a spirit appeared, the man saw it vaguely in the darkness, but never heard its voice. Some people even said that they had heard the spirits flying and flapping their wings against the roof of the cave.

Many years ago when Okonkwo was still a boy his father, Unoka, had gone to consult Agbala. The priestess in those days was a woman called Chika. She was full of the power of her god, and she was greatly feared. Unoka stood before her and began his story.

"Every year," he said sadly, "before I put any crop in the earth, I sacrifice a cock to Ani, the owner of all land. It is the law of our fathers. I also kill a cock at the shrine of Ifejioku, the god of yams. I clear the bush and set fire to it when it is dry. I sow the yams when the first rain has fallen, and stake them when the young tendrils appear. I weed—"

"Hold your peace!" screamed the priestess, her voice terrible as it echoed through the dark void. "You have offended neither the gods nor your fathers. And when a man is at peace with his gods and his ancestors, his harvest will be good or bad according to the strength of his arm. You, Unoka, are known in all the clan for the weakness of your machete and your hoe. When your neighbors go out with their ax to cut down virgin forests, you sow your yams on exhausted farms that take no labor to clear. They cross seven rivers to make their farms; you stay at home and offer sacrifices to a reluctant soil. Go home and work like a man."

Unoka was an ill-fated man. He had a bad *chi*[8] or personal god, and evil fortune followed him to the grave, or rather to his death, for he had no grave. He died of the swelling which was an abomination to the earth goddess. When a man was afflicted with swelling in the stomach and the limbs he was not allowed to die in the house. He was carried to the Evil Forest and left there to die. There was the story of a very stubborn man who staggered back to his house and had to be carried again to the forest and tied to a tree. The sickness was an abomination to the earth, and so the victim could not be buried in her bowels. He died and rotted away above the earth, and was not given the first or the second burial. Such was Unoka's fate. When they carried him away, he took with him his flute.

With a father like Unoka, Okonkwo did not have the start in life which many young men had. He neither inherited a barn nor a title, nor even a young wife. But in spite of these disadvantages, he had begun even in his father's lifetime to lay the foundations of a prosperous future. It was slow and painful. But he threw himself into it like one possessed. And indeed he was possessed by the fear of his father's contemptible life and shameful death.

There was a wealthy man in Okonkwo's village who had three huge barns, nine wives and thirty children. His name was Nwakibie and he had taken the highest but one title which a man could take in the clan. It was for this man that Okonkwo worked to earn his first seed yams.

He took a pot of palm-wine and a cock to Nwakibie. Two elderly neighbors were sent for, and Nwakibie's two grown-up sons were also present in his *obi*. He presented a kola nut and an alligator pepper, which were passed round for all to see and then returned to him. He broke the nut saying: "We shall all live. We pray for life, children, a good harvest, and happiness. You will have what is good for you and I will have what is good for me. Let the kite perch and let the eagle perch too. If one says no to the other, let his wing break."

After the kola nut had been eaten Okonkwo brought his palm-wine from the corner of the hut where it had been placed and stood it in the center of the group. He addressed Nwakibie, calling him "Our father."

"*Nna ayi*,"[9] he said. "I have brought you this little kola. As our people say, a man who pays respect to the great paves the way for his own greatness. I have come to pay you my respects and also to ask a favor. But let us drink the wine first."

Everybody thanked Okonkwo and the neighbors brought out their drinking horns from the goatskin bags they carried. Nwakibie brought down his own horn, which was fastened to the rafters. The younger of his sons, who was also the youngest man in the group, moved to the center, raised the pot on his left knee and

---

[8] *chi:* Literally, one's personal god; the *chi* may be thought of as the spiritual double of the person existing in the world, which acts as a guide to the fulfillment of one's destiny. To act against the *chi* is to act against one's own best interests, as Okonkwo will do later when he kills Ikemefuna.

[9] *"Nna ayi":* "Our father."

began to pour out the wine. The first cup went to Okonkwo, who must taste his wine before anyone else. Then the group drank, beginning with the eldest man. When everyone had drunk two or three horns, Nwakibie sent for his wives. Some of them were not at home and only four came in.

"Is Anasi not in?" he asked them. They said she was coming. Anasi was the first wife and the others could not drink before her, and so they stood waiting.

Anasi was a middle-aged woman, tall and strongly built. There was authority in her bearing and she looked every inch the ruler of the womenfolk in a large and prosperous family. She wore the anklet of her husband's titles, which the first wife alone could wear.

She walked up to her husband and accepted the horn from him. She then went down on one knee, drank a little, and handed back the horn. She rose, called him by his name and went back to her hut. The other wives drank in the same way, in their proper order, and went away.

The men then continued their drinking and talking. Ogbuefi Idigo was talking about the palm-wine tapper, Obiako, who suddenly gave up his trade.

"There must be something behind it," he said, wiping the foam of wine from his mustache with the back of his left hand. "There must be a reason for it. A toad does not run in the daytime for nothing."

"Some people say the Oracle warned him that he would fall off a palm tree and kill himself," said Akukalia.

"Obiako has always been a strange one," said Nwakibie. "I have heard that many years ago, when his father had not been dead very long, he had gone to consult the Oracle. The Oracle said to him, 'Your dead father wants you to sacrifice a goat to him.' Do you know what he told the Oracle? He said, 'Ask my dead father if he ever had a fowl when he was alive.'" Everybody laughed heartily except Okonkwo, who laughed uneasily because, as the saying goes, an old woman is always uneasy when dry bones are mentioned in a proverb. Okonkwo remembered his own father.

At last the young man who was pouring out the wine held up half a horn of the thick, white dregs and said, "What we are eating is finished." "We have seen it," the others replied. "Who will drink the dregs?" he asked. "Whoever has a job in hand," said Idigo, looking at Nwakibie's elder son Igwelo with a malicious twinkle in his eye.

Everybody agreed that Igwelo should drink the dregs. He accepted the half-full horn from his brother and drank it. As Idigo had said, Igwelo had a job in hand because he had married his first wife a month or two before. The thick dregs of palm-wine were supposed to be good for men who were going in to their wives.

After the wine had been drunk Okonkwo laid his difficulties before Nwakibie.

"I have come to you for help," he said. "Perhaps you can already guess what it is. I have cleared a farm but have no yams to sow. I know what it is to ask a man to trust another with his yams, especially these days when young men are afraid of hard work. I am not afraid of work. The lizard that jumped from the high iroko tree to the ground said he would praise himself if no one else did. I began to fend for myself at an age when most people still suck at their mothers' breasts. If you give me some yam seeds I shall not fail you."

Nwakibie cleared his throat. "It pleases me to see a young man like you these days when our youth has gone so soft. Many young men have come to me to ask for yams but I have refused because I knew they would just dump them in the earth and leave them to be choked by weeds. When I say no to them they think I am hard hearted. But it is not so. Eneke the bird says that since men have learned to shoot without missing, he has learned to fly without perching. I have learned to be stingy with my yams. But I can trust you. I know it as I look at you. As our fathers said, you can tell a ripe corn by its look. I shall give you twice four hundred yams. Go ahead and prepare your farm."

Okonkwo thanked him again and again and went home feeling happy. He knew that Nwakibie would not refuse him, but he had not expected he would be so generous. He had not hoped to get more than four hundred seeds. He would now have to make a bigger farm. He hoped to get another four hundred yams from one of his father's friends at Isiuzo.

Share-cropping was a very slow way of building up a barn of one's own. After all the toil one only got a third of the harvest. But for a young man whose father had no yams, there was no other way. And what made it worse in Okonkwo's case was that he had to support his mother and two sisters from his meagre harvest. And supporting his mother also meant supporting his father. She could not be expected to cook and eat while her husband starved. And so at a very early age when he was striving desperately to build a barn through share-cropping Okonkwo was also fending for his father's house. It was like pouring grains of corn into a bag full of holes. His mother and sisters worked hard enough, but they grew women's crops, like coco-yams, beans, and cassava. Yam, the king of crops, was a man's crop.

The year that Okonkwo took eight hundred seed-yams from Nwakibie was the worst year in living memory. Nothing happened at its proper time; it was either too early or too late. It seemed as if the world had gone mad. The first rains were late, and, when they came, lasted only a brief moment. The blazing sun returned, more fierce than it had ever been known, and scorched all the green that had appeared with the rains. The earth burned like hot coals and roasted all the yams that had been sown. Like all good farmers, Okonkwo had begun to sow with the first rains. He had sown four hundred seeds when the rains dried up and the heat returned. He watched the sky all day for signs of rain clouds and lay awake all night. In the morning he went back to his farm and saw the withering tendrils. He had tried to protect them from the smoldering earth by making rings of thick sisal leaves around them. But by the end of the day the sisal rings were burned dry and gray. He changed them every day, and prayed that the rain might fall in the night. But the drought continued for eight market weeks and the yams were killed.

Some farmers had not planted their yams yet. They were the lazy easy-going ones who always put off clearing their farms as long as they could. This year they were the wise ones. They sympathized with their neighbors with much shaking of the head, but inwardly they were happy for what they took to be their own foresight.

Okonkwo planted what was left of his seed-yams when the rains finally returned. He had one consolation. The yams he had sown before the drought were his own, the harvest of the previous year. He still had the eight hundred from Nwakibie and the four hundred from his father's friend. So he would make a fresh start.

But the year had gone mad. Rain fell as it had never fallen before. For days and nights together it poured down in violent torrents, and washed away the yam heaps. Trees were uprooted and deep gorges appeared everywhere. Then the rain became less violent. But it went from day to day without a pause. The spell of sunshine which always came in the middle of the wet season did not appear. The yams put on luxuriant green leaves, but every farmer knew that without sunshine the tubers would not grow.

That year the harvest was sad, like a funeral, and many farmers wept as they dug up the miserable and rotting yams. One man tied his cloth to a tree branch and hanged himself.

Okonkwo remembered that tragic year with a cold shiver throughout the rest of his life. It always surprised him when he thought of it later that he did not sink under the load of despair. He knew that he was a fierce fighter, but that year had been enough to break the heart of a lion.

"Since I survived that year," he always said, "I shall survive anything." He put it down to his inflexible will.

His father, Unoka, who was then an ailing man, had said to him during that terrible harvest month: "Do not despair. I know you will not despair. You have a manly and a proud heart. A proud heart can survive a general failure because such a failure does not prick its pride. It is more difficult and more bitter when a man fails *alone*."

Unoka was like that in his last days. His love of talk had grown with age and sickness. It tried Okonkwo's patience beyond words.

4

"Looking at a king's mouth," said an old man, "one would think he never sucked at his mother's breast." He was talking about Okonkwo, who had risen so suddenly from great poverty and misfortune to be one of the lords of the clan. The old man bore no ill will towards Okonkwo. Indeed he respected him for his industry and success. But he was struck, as most people were, by Okonkwo's brusqueness in dealing with less successful men. Only a week ago a man had contradicted him at a kindred meeting which they held to discuss the next ancestral feast. Without looking at the man Okonkwo had said: "This meeting is for men." The man who had contradicted him had no titles. That was why he had called him a woman. Okonkwo knew how to kill a man's spirit.

Everybody at the kindred meeting took sides with Osugo when Okonkwo called him a woman. The oldest man present said sternly that those whose palm-kernels were cracked for them by a benevolent spirit should not forget to be humble. Okonkwo said he was sorry for what he had said, and the meeting continued.

But it was really not true that Okonkwo's palm-kernels had been cracked for him by a benevolent spirit. He had cracked them himself. Anyone who knew his grim struggle against poverty and misfortune could not say he had been lucky. If ever a man deserved his success, that man was Okonkwo. At an early age he had achieved fame as the greatest wrestler in all the land. That was not luck. At the most one could say that his *chi* or personal god was good. But the Ibo people have a proverb that when a man says yes his *chi* says yes also. Okonkwo said yes very strongly; so his *chi* agreed. And not only his *chi* but his clan too, because it judged a man by the work of his hands. That was why Okonkwo had been chosen by the nine villages to carry a message of war to their enemies unless they agreed to give up a young man and a virgin to atone for the murder of Udo's wife. And such was the deep fear that their enemies had for Umuofia that they treated Okonkwo like a king and brought him a virgin who was given to Udo as wife, and the lad Ikemefuna.

The elders of the clan had decided that Ikemefuna should be in Okonkwo's care for a while. But no one thought it would be as long as three years. They seemed to forget all about him as soon as they had taken the decision.

At first Ikemefuna was very much afraid. Once or twice he tried to run away, but he did not know where to begin. He thought of his mother and his three-year-old sister and wept bitterly. Nwoye's mother was very kind to him and treated him as one of her own children. But all he said was: "When shall I go home?" When Okonkwo heard that he would not eat any food he came into the hut with a big stick in his hand and stood over him while he swallowed his yams, trembling. A few moments later he went behind the hut and began to vomit painfully. Nwoye's mother went to him and placed her hands on his chest and on his back. He was ill for three market weeks, and when he recovered he seemed to have overcome his great fear and sadness.

He was by nature a very lively boy and he gradually became popular in Okonkwo's household, especially with the children. Okonkwo's son, Nwoye, who was two years younger, became quite inseparable from him because he seemed to know everything. He could fashion out flutes from bamboo stems and even from the elephant grass. He knew the names of all the birds and could set clever traps for the little bush rodents. And he knew which trees made the strongest bows.

Even Okonkwo himself became very fond of the boy—inwardly of course. Okonkwo never showed any emotion openly, unless it be the emotion of anger. To show affection was a sign of weakness; the only thing worth demonstrating was strength. He therefore treated Ikemefuna as he treated everybody else—with a heavy hand. But there was no doubt that he liked the boy. Sometimes when he went to big village meetings or communal ancestral feasts he allowed Ikemefuna to accompany him, like a son, carrying his stool and his goatskin bag. And, indeed, Ikemefuna called him father.

Ikemefuna came to Umuofia at the end of the carefree season between harvest and planting. In fact he recovered from his illness only a few days before the Week of Peace began. And that was also the year Okonkwo broke the peace, and was punished, as was the custom, by Ezeani, the priest of the earth goddess.

Okonkwo was provoked to justifiable anger by his youngest wife, who went to plait her hair at her friend's house and did not return early enough to cook the afternoon meal. Okonkwo did not know at first that she was not at home. After waiting in vain for her dish he went to her hut to see what she was doing. There was nobody in the hut and the fireplace was cold.

"Where is Ojiugo?" he asked his second wife, who came out of her hut to draw water from a gigantic pot in the shade of a small tree in the middle of the compound.

"She has gone to plait her hair."

Okonkwo bit his lips as anger welled up within him.

"Where are her children? Did she take them?" he asked with unusual coolness and restraint.

"They are here," answered his first wife, Nwoye's mother. Okonkwo bent down and looked into her hut. Ojiugo's children were eating with the children of his first wife.

"Did she ask you to feed them before she went?"

"Yes," lied Nwoye's mother, trying to minimize Ojiugo's thoughtlessness.

Okonkwo knew she was not speaking the truth. He walked back to his *obi* to await Ojiugo's return. And when she returned he beat her very heavily. In his anger he had forgotten that it was the Week of Peace. His first two wives ran out in great alarm pleading with him that it was the sacred week. But Okonkwo was not the man to stop beating somebody half-way through, not even for fear of a goddess.

Okonkwo's neighbors heard his wife crying and sent their voices over the compound walls to ask what was the matter. Some of them came over to see for themselves. It was unheard of to beat somebody during the sacred week.

Before it was dusk Ezeani, who was the priest of the earth goddess, Ani, called on Okonkwo in his *obi*. Okonkwo brought out kola nut and placed it before the priest.

"Take away your kola nut. I shall not eat in the house of a man who has no respect for our gods and ancestors."

Okonkwo tried to explain to him what his wife had done, but Ezeani seemed to pay no attention. He held a short staff in his hand which he brought down on the floor to emphasize his points.

"Listen to me," he said when Okonkwo had spoken. "You are not a stranger in Umuofia. You know as well as I do that our forefathers ordained that before we plant any crops in the earth we should observe a week in which a man does not say a harsh word to his neighbor. We live in peace with our fellows to honor our great goddess of the earth without whose blessing our crops will not grow. You have committed a great evil." He brought down his staff heavily on the floor. "Your wife was at fault, but even if you came into your *obi* and found her lover on top of her, you would still have committed a great evil to beat her." His staff came down again. "The evil you have done can ruin the whole clan. The earth goddess whom you have insulted may refuse to give us her increase, and we shall all perish." His tone now changed from anger to command. "You will bring to the shrine of Ani tomorrow one she-goat, one hen, a length of cloth, and a hundred cowries." He rose and left the hut.

Okonkwo did as the priest said. He also took with him a pot of palm-wine. Inwardly, he was repentant. But he was not the man to go about telling his neighbors that he was in error. And so people said he had no respect for the gods of the clan. His enemies said his good fortune had gone to his head. They called him the little bird *nza* who so far forgot himself after a heavy meal that he challenged his *chi*.

No work was done during the Week of Peace. People called on their neighbors and drank palm-wine. This year they talked of nothing else but the *nso-ani*[10] which Okonkwo had committed. It was the first time for many years that a man had broken the sacred peace. Even the oldest men could only remember one or two other occasions somewhere in the dim past.

Ogbuefi Ezeudu, who was the oldest man in the village, was telling two other men who came to visit him that the punishment for breaking the Peace of Ani had become very mild in their clan.

"It has not always been so," he said. "My father told me that he had been told that in the past a man who broke the peace was dragged on the ground through the village until he died. But after a while this custom was stopped because it spoiled the peace which it was meant to preserve."

"Somebody told me yesterday," said one of the younger men, "that in some clans it is an abomination for a man to die during the Week of Peace."

"It is indeed true," said Ogbuefi Ezeudu. "They have that custom in Obodoani. If a man dies at this time he is not buried but cast into the Evil Forest. It is a bad custom which these people observe because they lack understanding. They throw away large numbers of men and women without burial. And what is the result? Their clan is full of the evil spirits of these unburied dead, hungry to do harm to the living."

After the Week of Peace every man and his family began to clear the bush to make new farms. The cut bush was left to dry and fire was then set to it. As the smoke rose into the sky kites appeared from different directions and hovered over the burning field in silent valediction. The rainy season was approaching when they would go away until the dry season returned.

Okonkwo spent the next few days preparing his seed-yams. He looked at each yam carefully to see whether it was good for sowing. Sometimes he decided that a yam was too big to be sown as one seed and he split it deftly along its length with his sharp knife. His eldest son, Nwoye, and Ikemefuna helped him by fetching the yams in long baskets from the barn and in counting the prepared seeds in groups of four hundred. Sometimes Okonkwo gave them a few yams each to prepare. But he always found fault with their effort, and he said so with much threatening.

"Do you think you are cutting up yams for cooking?" he asked Nwoye. "If you split another yam of this size, I shall break your jaw. You think you are still a child. I began to own a farm at your age. And you," he said to Ikemefuna, "do you not grow yams where you come from?"

Inwardly Okonkwo knew that the boys were still too young to understand fully the difficult art of preparing seed-yams. But he thought that one could not begin too early. Yam stood for manliness, and he who could feed his family on yams from one harvest to another was a very great man indeed. Okonkwo wanted his son to be a great farmer and a great man. He would stamp out the disquieting signs of laziness which he thought he already saw in him.

---

[10] *nso-ani:* "Earth's taboo," a serious offense against the earth goddess Ani.

"I will not have a son who cannot hold up his head in the gathering of the clan. I would sooner strangle him with my own hands. And if you stand staring at me like that," he swore, "Amadiora[11] will break your head for you!"

Some days later, when the land had been moistened by two or three heavy rains, Okonkwo and his family went to the farm with baskets of seed-yams, their hoes and machetes, and the planting began. They made single mounds of earth in straight lines all over the field and sowed the yams in them.

Yam, the king of crops, was a very exacting king. For three or four moons it demanded hard work and constant attention from cock-crow till the chickens went back to roost. The young tendrils were protected from earth-heat with rings of sisal leaves. As the rains became heavier the women planted maize, melons, and beans between the yam mounds. The yams were then staked, first with little sticks and later with tall and big tree branches. The women weeded the farm three times at definite periods in the life of the yams, neither early nor late.

And now the rains had really come, so heavy and persistent that even the village rain-maker no longer claimed to be able to intervene. He could not stop the rain now, just as he would not attempt to start it in the heart of the dry season, without serious danger to his own health. The personal dynamism required to counter the forces of these extremes of weather would be far too great for the human frame.

And so nature was not interfered with in the middle of the rainy season. Sometimes it poured down in such thick sheets of water that earth and sky seemed merged in one gray wetness. It was then uncertain whether the low rumbling of Amadiora's thunder came from above or below. At such times, in each of the countless thatched huts of Umuofia, children sat around their mother's cooking fire telling stories, or with their father in his *obi* warming themselves from a log fire, roasting and eating maize. It was a brief resting period between the exacting and arduous planting season and the equally exacting but light-hearted month of harvests.

Ikemefuna had begun to feel like a member of Okonkwo's family. He still thought about his mother and his three-year-old sister, and he had moments of sadness and depression. But he and Nwoye had become so deeply attached to each other that such moments became less frequent and less poignant. Ikemefuna had an endless stock of folk tales. Even those which Nwoye knew already were told with a new freshness and the local flavor of a different clan. Nwoye remembered this period very vividly till the end of his life. He even remembered how he had laughed when Ikemefuna told him that the proper name for a corn cob with only a few scattered grains was *eze-agadi-nwayi,* or the teeth of an old woman. Nwoye's mind had gone immediately to Nwayieke, who lived near the udala tree. She had about three teeth and was always smoking her pipe.

---

[11] **Amadiora:** The god of thunder and lightning.

Gradually the rains became lighter and less frequent, and earth and sky once again became separate. The rain fell in thin, slanting showers through sunshine and quiet breeze. Children no longer stayed indoors but ran about singing:

> *"The rain is falling, the sun is shining,*
> *Alone Nnadi is cooking and eating."*

Nwoye always wondered who Nnadi was and why he should live all by himself, cooking and eating. In the end he decided that Nnadi must live in that land of Ikemefuna's favorite story where the ant holds his court in splendor and the sands dance forever.

5

The Feast of the New Yam was approaching and Umuofia was in a festival mood. It was an occasion for giving thanks to Ani, the earth goddess and the source of all fertility. Ani played a greater part in the life of the people than any other deity. She was the ultimate judge of morality and conduct. And what was more, she was in close communion with the departed fathers of the clan whose bodies had been committed to earth.

The Feast of the New Yam was held every year before the harvest began, to honor the earth goddess and the ancestral spirits of the clan. New yams could not be eaten until some had first been offered to these powers. Men and women, young and old, looked forward to the New Yam Festival because it began the season of plenty— the new year. On the last night before the festival, yams of the old year were all disposed of by those who still had them. The new year must begin with tasty, fresh yams and not the shriveled and fibrous crop of the previous year. All cooking pots, calabashes, and wooden bowls were thoroughly washed, especially the wooden mortar in which yam was pounded. Yam foo-foo and vegetable soup was the chief food in the celebration. So much of it was cooked that, no matter how heavily the family ate or how many friends and relatives they invited from neighboring villages, there was always a large quantity of food left over at the end of the day. The story was always told of a wealthy man who set before his guests a mound of foo-foo so high that those who sat on one side could not see what was happening on the other, and it was not until late in the evening that one of them saw for the first time his in-law who had arrived during the course of the meal and had fallen to on the opposite side. It was only then that they exchanged greetings and shook hands over what was left of the food.

The New Yam Festival was thus an occasion for joy throughout Umuofia. And every man whose arm was strong, as the Ibo people say, was expected to invite large numbers of guests from far and wide. Okonkwo always asked his wives' relations, and since he now had three wives his guests would make a fairly big crowd.

But somehow Okonkwo could never become as enthusiastic over feasts as most people. He was a good eater and he could drink one or two fairly big gourds of palm-wine. But he was always uncomfortable sitting around for days waiting for a feast or getting over it. He would be very much happier working on his farm.

The festival was now only three days away. Okonkwo's wives had scrubbed the walls and the huts with red earth until they reflected light. They had then drawn patterns on them in white, yellow, and dark green. They then set about painting themselves with cam wood and drawing beautiful black patterns on their stomachs and on their backs. The children were also decorated, especially their hair, which was shaved in beautiful patterns. The three women talked excitedly about the relations who had been invited, and the children reveled in the thought of being spoiled by these visitors from the motherland. Ikemefuna was equally excited. The New Yam Festival seemed to him to be a much bigger event here than in his own village, a place which was already becoming remote and vague in his imagination.

And then the storm burst. Okonkwo, who had been walking about aimlessly in his compound in suppressed anger, suddenly found an outlet.

"Who killed this banana tree?" he asked.

A hush fell on the compound immediately.

"Who killed this tree? Or are you all deaf and dumb?"

As a matter of fact the tree was very much alive. Okonkwo's second wife had merely cut a few leaves off it to wrap some food, and she said so. Without further argument Okonkwo gave her a sound beating and left her and her only daughter weeping. Neither of the other wives dared to interfere beyond an occasional and tentative, "It is enough, Okonkwo," pleaded from a reasonable distance.

His anger thus satisfied, Okonkwo decided to go out hunting. He had an old rusty gun made by a clever blacksmith who had come to live in Umuofia long ago. But although Okonkwo was a great man whose prowess was universally acknowledged, he was not a hunter. In fact he had not killed a rat with his gun. And so when he called Ikemefuna to fetch his gun, the wife who had just been beaten murmured something about guns that never shot. Unfortunately for her, Okonkwo heard it and ran madly into his room for the loaded gun, ran out again and aimed at her as she clambered over the dwarf wall of the barn. He pressed the trigger and there was a loud report accompanied by the wail of his wives and children. He threw down the gun and jumped into the barn, and there lay the woman, very much shaken and frightened but quite unhurt. He heaved a heavy sigh and went away with the gun.

In spite of this incident the New Yam Festival was celebrated with great joy in Okonkwo's household. Early that morning as he offered a sacrifice of new yam and palm-oil to his ancestors he asked them to protect him, his children, and their mothers in the new year.

As the day wore on his in-laws arrived from three surrounding villages, and each party brought with them a huge pot of palm-wine. And there was eating and drinking till night, when Okonkwo's in-laws began to leave for their homes.

The second day of the new year was the day of the great wrestling match between Okonkwo's village and their neighbors. It was difficult to say which the people enjoyed more—the feasting and fellowship of the first day or the wrestling contest of the second. But there was one woman who had no doubt whatever in her mind. She was Okonkwo's second wife, Ekwefi, whom he nearly shot. There was no festival in all the seasons of the year which gave her as much pleasure as the wrestling match. Many years ago when she was the village beauty Okonkwo had won her heart by throwing the Cat in the greatest contest within living memory. She did not marry him then because he was too poor to pay her bride-price. But a few years later she ran away from her husband and came to live with Okonkwo. All this happened many years ago. Now Ekwefi was a woman of forty-five who had suffered a great deal in her time. But her love of wrestling contests was still as strong as it was thirty years ago.

It was not yet noon on the second day of the New Yam Festival. Ekwefi and her only daughter, Ezinma, sat near the fireplace waiting for the water in the pot to boil. The fowl Ekwefi had just killed was in the wooden mortar. The water began to boil, and in one deft movement she lifted the pot from the fire and poured the boiling water over the fowl. She put back the empty pot on the circular pad in the corner, and looked at her palms, which were black with soot. Ezinma was always surprised that her mother could lift a pot from the fire with her bare hands.

"Ekwefi," she said, "is it true that when people are grown up, fire does not burn them?" Ezinma, unlike most children, called her mother by her name.

"Yes," replied Ekwefi, too busy to argue. Her daughter was only ten years old but she was wiser than her years.

"But Nwoye's mother dropped her pot of hot soup the other day and it broke on the floor."

Ekwefi turned the hen over in the mortar and began to pluck the feathers.

"Ekwefi," said Ezinma, who had joined in plucking the feathers, "my eyelid is twitching."

"It means you are going to cry," said her mother.

"No," Ezinma said, "it is this eyelid, the top one."

"That means you will see something."

"What will I see?" she asked.

"How can I know?" Ekwefi wanted her to work it out herself.

"Oho," said Ezinma at last. "I know what it is — the wrestling match."

At last the hen was plucked clean. Ekwefi tried to pull out the horny beak but it was too hard. She turned round on her low stool and put the beak in the fire for a few moments. She pulled again and it came off.

"Ekwefi!" a voice called from one of the other huts. It was Nwoye's mother, Okonkwo's first wife.

"Is that me?" Ekwefi called back. That was the way people answered calls from outside. They never answered yes for fear it might be an evil spirit calling.

"Will you give Ezinma some fire to bring to me?" Her own children and Ikemefuna had gone to the stream.

Ekwefi put a few live coals into a piece of broken pot and Ezinma carried it across the clean swept compound to Nwoye's mother.

"Thank you, Nma," she said. She was peeling new yams, and in a basket beside her were green vegetables and beans.

"Let me make the fire for you," Ezinma offered.

"Thank you, Ezigbo," she said. She often called her Ezigbo, which means "the good one."

Ezinma went outside and brought some sticks from a huge bundle of firewood. She broke them into little pieces across the sole of her foot and began to build a fire, blowing it with her breath.

"You will blow your eyes out," said Nwoye's mother, looking up from the yams she was peeling. "Use the fan." She stood up and pulled out the fan which was fastened into one of the rafters. As soon as she got up, the troublesome nanny-goat, which had been dutifully eating yam peelings, dug her teeth into the real thing, scooped out two mouthfuls and fled from the hut to chew the cud in the goats' shed. Nwoye's mother swore at her and settled down again to her peeling. Ezinma's fire was now sending up thick clouds of smoke. She went on fanning it until it burst into flames. Nwoye's mother thanked her and she went back to her mother's hut.

Just then the distant beating of drums began to reach them. It came from the direction of the *ilo,* the village playground. Every village had its own *ilo* which was as old as the village itself and where all the great ceremonies and dances took place. The drums beat the unmistakable wrestling dance—quick, light, and gay, and it came floating on the wind.

Okonkwo cleared his throat and moved his feet to the beat of the drums. It filled him with fire as it had always done from his youth. He trembled with the desire to conquer and subdue. It was like the desire for woman.

"We shall be late for the wrestling," said Ezinma to her mother.

"They will not begin until the sun goes down."

"But they are beating the drums."

"Yes. The drums begin at noon but the wrestling waits until the sun begins to sink. Go and see if your father has brought out yams for the afternoon."

"He has. Nwoye's mother is already cooking."

"Go and bring our own, then. We must cook quickly or we shall be late for the wrestling."

Ezinma ran in the direction of the barn and brought back two yams from the dwarf wall.

Ekwefi peeled the yams quickly. The troublesome nanny-goat sniffed about, eating the peelings. She cut the yams into small pieces and began to prepare a pottage, using some of the chicken.

At that moment they heard someone crying just outside their compound. It was very much like Obiageli, Nwoye's sister.

"Is that not Obiageli weeping?" Ekwefi called across the yard to Nwoye's mother.

"Yes," she replied. "She must have broken her water-pot."

The weeping was now quite close and soon the children filed in, carrying on their heads various sizes of pots suitable to their years. Ikemefuna came first with the biggest pot, closely followed by Nwoye and his two younger brothers. Obiageli brought up the rear, her face streaming with tears. In her hand was the cloth pad on which the pot should have rested on her head.

"What happened?" her mother asked, and Obiageli told her mournful story. Her mother consoled her and promised to buy her another pot.

Nwoye's younger brothers were about to tell their mother the true story of the accident when Ikemefuna looked at them sternly and they held their peace. The fact was that Obiageli had been making *inyanga*[12] with her pot. She had balanced it on

---

[12] *inyanga:* Bragging or showing off.

her head, folded her arms in front of her, and began to sway her waist like a grown-up young lady. When the pot fell down and broke she burst out laughing. She only began to weep when they got near the iroko tree outside their compound.

The drums were still beating, persistent and unchanging. Their sound was no longer a separate thing from the living village. It was like the pulsation of its heart. It throbbed in the air, in the sunshine, and even in the trees, and filled the village with excitement.

Ekwefi ladled her husband's share of the pottage into a bowl and covered it. Ezinma took it to him in his *obi*.

Okonkwo was sitting on a goatskin already eating his first wife's meal. Obiageli, who had brought it from her mother's hut, sat on the floor waiting for him to finish. Ezinma placed her mother's dish before him and sat with Obiageli.

"Sit like a woman!" Okonkwo shouted at her. Ezinma brought her two legs together and stretched them in front of her.

"Father, will you go to see the wrestling?" Ezinma asked after a suitable interval.

"Yes," he answered. "Will you go?"

"Yes." And after a pause she said: "Can I bring your chair for you?"

"No, that is a boy's job." Okonkwo was specially fond of Ezinma. She looked very much like her mother, who was once the village beauty. But his fondness only showed on very rare occasions.

"Obiageli broke her pot today," Ezinma said.

"Yes, she has told me about it," Okonkwo said between mouthfuls.

"Father," said Obiageli, "people should not talk when they are eating or pepper may go down the wrong way."

"That is very true. Do you hear that, Ezinma? You are older than Obiageli but she has more sense."

He uncovered his second wife's dish and began to eat from it. Obiageli took the first dish and returned to her mother's hut. And then Nkechi came in, bringing the third dish. Nkechi was the daughter of Okonkwo's third wife.

In the distance the drums continued to beat.

6

The whole village turned out on the *ilo*, men, women, and children. They stood round in a huge circle leaving the center of the playground free. The elders and grandees of the village sat on their own stools brought there by their young sons or slaves. Okonkwo was among them. All others stood except those who came early enough to secure places on the few stands which had been built by placing smooth logs on forked pillars.

The wrestlers were not there yet and the drummers held the field. They too sat just in front of the huge circle of spectators, facing the elders. Behind them was the big and ancient silk-cotton tree which was sacred. Spirits of good children lived in that tree waiting to be born. On ordinary days young women who desired children came to sit under its shade.

There were seven drums and they were arranged according to their sizes in a long wooden basket. Three men beat them with sticks, working feverishly from one drum to another. They were possessed by the spirit of the drums.

The young men who kept order on these occasions dashed about, consulting among themselves and with the leaders of the two wrestling teams, who were still outside the circle, behind the crowd. Once in a while two young men carrying palm fronds ran round the circle and kept the crowd back by beating the ground in front of them or, if they were stubborn, their legs and feet.

At last the two teams danced into the circle and the crowd roared and clapped. The drums rose to a frenzy. The people surged forward. The young men who kept order flew around, waving their palm fronds. Old men nodded to the beat of the drums and remembered the days when they wrestled to its intoxicating rhythm.

The contest began with boys of fifteen or sixteen. There were only three such boys in each team. They were not the real wrestlers; they merely set the scene. Within a short time the first two bouts were over. But the third created a big sensation even among the elders who did not usually show their excitement so openly. It was as quick as the other two, perhaps even quicker. But very few people had ever seen that kind of wrestling before. As soon as the two boys closed in, one of them did something which no one could describe because it had been as quick as a flash. And the other boy was flat on his back. The crowd roared and clapped and for a while drowned the frenzied drums. Okonkwo sprang to his feet and quickly sat down again. Three young men from the victorious boy's team ran forward, carried him shoulder high, and danced through the cheering crowd. Everybody soon knew who the boy was. His name was Maduka, the son of Obierika.

The drummers stopped for a brief rest before the real matches. Their bodies shone with sweat, and they took up fans and began to fan themselves. They also drank water from small pots and ate kola nuts. They became ordinary human beings again, talking and laughing among themselves and with others who stood near them. The air, which had been stretched taut with excitement, relaxed again. It was as if water had been poured on the tightened skin of a drum. Many people looked around, perhaps for the first time, and saw those who stood or sat next to them.

"I did not know it was you," Ekwefi said to the woman who had stood shoulder to shoulder with her since the beginning of the matches.

"I do not blame you," said the woman. "I have never seen such a large crowd of people. Is it true that Okonkwo nearly killed you with his gun?"

"It is true indeed, my dear friend. I cannot yet find a mouth with which to tell the story."

"Your *chi* is very much awake, my friend. And how is my daughter, Ezinma?"

"She has been very well for some time now. Perhaps she has come to stay."

"I think she has. How old is she now?"

"She is about ten years old."

"I think she will stay. They usually stay if they do not die before the age of six."

"I pray she stays," said Ekwefi with a heavy sigh.

The woman with whom she talked was called Chielo. She was the priestess of Agbala, the Oracle of the Hills and the Caves. In ordinary life Chielo was a widow with two children. She was very friendly with Ekwefi and they shared a common shed in the market. She was particularly fond of Ekwefi's only daughter, Ezinma, whom she called "my daughter." Quite often she bought beancakes and gave Ekwefi some to take home to Ezinma. Anyone seeing Chielo in ordinary life would hardly believe she was the same person who prophesied when the spirit of Agbala was upon her.

The drummers took up their sticks and the air shivered and grew tense like a tightened bow.

The two teams were ranged facing each other across the clear space. A young man from one team danced across the center to the other side and pointed at whomever he wanted to fight. They danced back to the center together and then closed in.

There were twelve men on each side and the challenge went from one side to the other. Two judges walked around the wrestlers and when they thought they were equally matched, stopped them. Five matches ended in this way. But the really exciting moments were when a man was thrown. The huge voice of the crowd then rose to the sky and in every direction. It was even heard in the surrounding villages.

The last match was between the leaders of the teams. They were among the best wrestlers in all the nine villages. The crowd wondered who would throw the other this year. Some said Okafo was the better man; others said he was not the equal of Ikezue. Last year neither of them had thrown the other even though the judges had allowed the contest to go on longer than was the custom. They had the same style and one saw the other's plans beforehand. It might happen again this year.

Dusk was already approaching when their contest began. The drums went mad and the crowds also. They surged forward as the two young men danced into the circle. The palm fronds were helpless in keeping them back.

Ikezue held out his right hand. Okafo seized it, and they closed in. It was a fierce contest. Ikezue strove to dig in his right heel behind Okafo so as to pitch him backwards in the clever *ege* style. But the one knew what the other was thinking. The crowd had surrounded and swallowed up the drummers, whose frantic rhythm was no longer a mere disembodied sound but the very heartbeat of the people.

The wrestlers were now almost still in each other's grip. The muscles on their arms and their thighs and on their backs stood out and twitched. It looked like an equal match. The two judges were already moving forward to separate them when Ikezue, now desperate, went down quickly on one knee in an attempt to fling his man backwards over his head. It was a sad miscalculation. Quick as the lightning of Amadiora, Okafo raised his right leg and swung it over his rival's head. The crowd burst into a thunderous roar. Okafo was swept off his feet by his supporters and carried home shoulder high. They sang his praise and the young women clapped their hands:

> *"Who will wrestle for our village?*
> *   Okafo will wrestle for our village.*
> *Has he thrown a hundred men?*
> *   He has thrown four hundred men.*
> *Has he thrown a hundred Cats?*
> *   He has thrown four hundred Cats.*
> *Then send him word to fight for us."*

7

For three years Ikemefuna lived in Okonkwo's household and the elders of Umuofia seemed to have forgotten about him. He grew rapidly like a yam tendril in the rainy season, and was full of the sap of life. He had become wholly absorbed into his new family. He was like an elder brother to Nwoye, and from the very first seemed to have kindled a new fire in the younger boy. He made him feel grown-up; and they no longer spent the evenings in mother's hut while she cooked, but now sat with Okonkwo in his *obi,* or watched him as he tapped his palm tree for the evening wine. Nothing pleased Nwoye now more than to be sent for by his mother or another of his father's wives to do one of those difficult and masculine tasks in the home, like splitting wood, or pounding food. On receiving such a message through a younger brother or sister, Nwoye would feign annoyance and grumble aloud about women and their troubles.

Okonkwo was inwardly pleased at his son's development, and he knew it was due to Ikemefuna. He wanted Nwoye to grow into a tough young man capable of ruling his father's household when he was dead and gone to join the ancestors. He wanted him to be a prosperous man, having enough in his barn to feed the ancestors with regular sacrifices. And so he was always happy when he heard him grumbling about women. That showed that in time he would be able to control his women-folk. No matter how prosperous a man was, if he was unable to rule his women and his children (and especially his women) he was not really a man. He was like the man in the song who had ten and one wives and not enough soup for his foo-foo.

So Okonkwo encouraged the boys to sit with him in his *obi,* and he told them stories of the land—masculine stories of violence and bloodshed. Nwoye knew that it was right to be masculine and to be violent, but somehow he still preferred the stories that his mother used to tell, and which she no doubt still told to her younger children—stories of the tortoise and his wily ways, and of the bird *eneke-nti-oba*[13] who challenged the whole world to a wrestling contest and was finally thrown by the cat. He remembered the story she often told of the quarrel between Earth and Sky long ago, and how Sky withheld rain for seven years, until crops withered and the dead could not be buried because the hoes broke on the stony Earth. At last Vulture was sent to plead with Sky, and to soften his heart with a song of the suffering of the sons of men. Whenever Nwoye's mother sang this song he felt carried away to the distant scene in the sky where Vulture, Earth's emissary, sang for mercy. At last Sky was moved to pity, and he gave to Vulture rain wrapped in leaves of coco-yam. But as he flew home his long talon pierced the leaves and the rain fell as it had never fallen before. And so heavily did it rain on Vulture that he did not return to deliver his message but flew to a distant land, from where he had espied a fire. And when he got there he found it was a man making a sacrifice. He warmed himself in the fire and ate the entrails.

---

[13] *eneke-nti-oba:* "Swallow with the ear of a crocodile," a kind of bird that appears in many fables and proverbs.

That was the kind of story that Nwoye loved. But he now knew that they were for foolish women and children, and he knew that his father wanted him to be a man. And so he feigned that he no longer cared for women's stories. And when he did this he saw that his father was pleased, and no longer rebuked him or beat him. So Nwoye and Ikemefuna would listen to Okonkwo's stories about tribal wars, or how, years ago, he had stalked his victim, overpowered him, and obtained his first human head. And as he told them of the past they sat in darkness or the dim glow of logs, waiting for the women to finish their cooking. When they finished, each brought her bowl of foo-foo and bowl of soup to her husband. An oil lamp was lit and Okonkwo tasted from each bowl, and then passed two shares to Nwoye and Ikemefuna.

In this way the moons and the seasons passed. And then the locusts came. It had not happened for many a long year. The elders said locusts came once in a generation, reappeared every year for seven years, and then disappeared for another lifetime. They went back to their caves in a distant land, where they were guarded by a race of stunted men. And then after another lifetime these men opened the caves again and the locusts came to Umuofia.

They came in the cold harmattan season after the harvests had been gathered, and ate up all the wild grass in the fields.

Okonkwo and the two boys were working on the red outer walls of the compound. This was one of the lighter tasks of the after-harvest season. A new cover of thick palm branches and palm leaves was set on the walls to protect them from the next rainy season. Okonkwo worked on the outside of the wall and the boys worked from within. There were little holes from one side to the other in the upper levels of the wall, and through these Okonkwo passed the rope, or *tie-tie*, to the boys and they passed it round the wooden stays and then back to him; and in this way the cover was strengthened on the wall.

The women had gone to the bush to collect firewood, and the little children to visit their playmates in the neighboring compounds. The harmattan was in the air and seemed to distill a hazy feeling of sleep on the world. Okonkwo and the boys worked in complete silence, which was only broken when a new palm frond was lifted on to the wall or when a busy hen moved dry leaves about in her ceaseless search for food.

And then quite suddenly a shadow fell on the world, and the sun seemed hidden behind a thick cloud. Okonkwo looked up from his work and wondered if it was going to rain at such an unlikely time of the year. But almost immediately a shout of joy broke out in all directions, and Umuofia, which had dozed in the noon-day haze, broke into life and activity.

"Locusts are descending," was joyfully chanted everywhere, and men, women, and children left their work or their play and ran into the open to see the unfamiliar sight. The locusts had not come for many, many years, and only the old people had seen them before.

At first, a fairly small swarm came. They were the harbingers sent to survey the land. And then appeared on the horizon a slowly moving mass like a boundless sheet of black cloud drifting towards Umuofia. Soon it covered half the sky, and the solid mass was now broken by tiny eyes of light like shining star dust. It was a tremendous sight, full of power and beauty.

Everyone was now about, talking excitedly and praying that the locusts should camp in Umuofia for the night. For although locusts had not visited Umuofia for many years, everybody knew by instinct that they were very good to eat. And at last the locusts did descend. They settled on every tree and on every blade of grass; they settled on the roofs and covered the bare ground. Mighty tree branches broke away under them, and the whole country became the brown-earth color of the vast, hungry swarm.

Many people went out with baskets trying to catch them, but the elders counseled patience till nightfall. And they were right. The locusts settled in the bushes for the night and their wings became wet with dew. Then all Umuofia turned out in spite of the cold harmattan, and everyone filled his bags and pots with locusts. The next morning they were roasted in clay pots and then spread in the sun until they became dry and brittle. And for many days this rare food was eaten with solid palm-oil.

Okonkwo sat in his *obi* crunching happily with Ikemefuna and Nwoye, and drinking palm-wine copiously, when Ogbuefi Ezeudu came in. Ezeudu was the oldest man in this quarter of Umuofia. He had been a great and fearless warrior in his time, and was now accorded great respect in all the clan. He refused to join in the meal, and asked Okonkwo to have a word with him outside. And so they walked out together, the old man supporting himself with his stick. When they were out of earshot, he said to Okonkwo:

"That boy calls you father. Do not bear a hand in his death." Okonkwo was surprised, and was about to say something when the old man continued:

"Yes, Umuofia has decided to kill him. The Oracle of the Hills and the Caves has pronounced it. They will take him outside Umuofia as is the custom, and kill him there. But I want you to have nothing to do with it. He calls you his father."

The next day a group of elders from all the nine villages of Umuofia came to Okonkwo's house early in the morning, and before they began to speak in low tones Nwoye and Ikemefuna were sent out. They did not stay very long, but when they went away Okonkwo sat still for a very long time supporting his chin in his palms. Later in the day he called Ikemefuna and told him that he was to be taken home the next day. Nwoye overheard it and burst into tears, whereupon his father beat him heavily. As for Ikemefuna, he was at a loss. His own home had gradually become very faint and distant. He still missed his mother and his sister and would be very glad to see them. But somehow he knew he was not going to see them. He remembered once when men had talked in low tones with his father; and it seemed now as if it was happening all over again.

Later, Nwoye went to his mother's hut and told her that Ikemefuna was going home. She immediately dropped her pestle with which she was grinding pepper, folded her arms across her breast and sighed, "Poor child."

The next day, the men returned with a pot of wine. They were all fully dressed as if they were going to a big clan meeting or to pay a visit to a neighboring village.

They passed their cloths under the right armpit, and hung their goatskin bags and sheathed machetes over their left shoulders. Okonkwo got ready quickly and the party set out with Ikemefuna carrying the pot of wine. A deathly silence descended on Okonkwo's compound. Even the very little children seemed to know. Throughout that day Nwoye sat in his mother's hut and tears stood in his eyes.

At the beginning of their journey the men of Umuofia talked and laughed about the locusts, about their women, and about some effeminate men who had refused to come with them. But as they drew near to the outskirts of Umuofia silence fell upon them too.

The sun rose slowly to the center of the sky, and the dry, sandy footway began to throw up the heat that lay buried in it. Some birds chirruped in the forests around. The men trod dry leaves on the sand. All else was silent. Then from the distance came the faint beating of the *ekwe*. It rose and faded with the wind—a peaceful dance from a distant clan.

"It is an *ozo*[14] dance," the men said among themselves. But no one was sure where it was coming from. Some said Ezimili, others Abame or Aninta. They argued for a short while and fell into silence again, and the elusive dance rose and fell with the wind. Somewhere a man was taking one of the titles of his clan, with music and dancing and a great feast.

The footway had now become a narrow line in the heart of the forest. The short trees and sparse undergrowth which surrounded the men's village began to give way to giant trees and climbers which perhaps had stood from the beginning of things, untouched by the ax and the bush-fire. The sun breaking through their leaves and branches threw a pattern of light and shade on the sandy footway.

Ikemefuna heard a whisper close behind him and turned round sharply. The man who had whispered now called out aloud, urging the others to hurry up.

"We still have a long way to go," he said. Then he and another man went before Ikemefuna and set a faster pace.

Thus the men of Umuofia pursued their way, armed with sheathed machetes, and Ikemefuna, carrying a pot of palm-wine on his head, walked in their midst. Although he had felt uneasy at first, he was not afraid now. Okonkwo walked behind him. He could hardly imagine that Okonkwo was not his real father. He had never been fond of his real father, and at the end of three years he had become very distant indeed. But his mother and his three-year-old sister . . . of course she would not be three now, but six. Would he recognize her now? She must have grown quite big. How his mother would weep for joy, and thank Okonkwo for having looked after him so well and for bringing him back. She would want to hear everything that had happened to him in all these years. Could he remember them all? He would tell her about Nwoye and his mother, and about the locusts. . . . Then quite suddenly a thought came upon him. His mother might be dead. He tried in vain to force the

---

[14] *ozo:* One of the four titles or ranks in the Ibo society; they are Ozo, Idemili, Omalo, and Erulu.

thought out of his mind. Then he tried to settle the matter the way he used to settle such matters when he was a little boy. He still remembered the song:

> *Eze elina, elina!*
> > *Sala*
>
> *Eze ilikwa ya*
> *Ikwaba akwa oligholi*
> *Ebe Danda nechi eze*
> *Ebe Uzuzu nete egwu*
> > *Sala*[15]

He sang it in his mind, and walked to its beat. If the song ended on his right foot, his mother was alive. If it ended on his left, she was dead. No, not dead, but ill. It ended on the right. She was alive and well. He sang the song again, and it ended on the left. But the second time did not count. The first voice gets to Chukwu, or God's house. That was a favorite saying of children. Ikemefuna felt like a child once more. It must be the thought of going home to his mother.

One of the men behind him cleared his throat. Ikemefuna looked back, and the man growled at him to go on and not stand looking back. The way he said it sent cold fear down Ikemefuna's back. His hands trembled vaguely on the black pot he carried. Why had Okonkwo withdrawn to the rear? Ikemefuna felt his legs melting under him. And he was afraid to look back.

As the man who had cleared his throat drew up and raised his machete, Okonkwo looked away. He heard the blow. The pot fell and broke in the sand. He heard Ikemefuna cry, "My father, they have killed me!" as he ran towards him. Dazed with fear, Okonkwo drew his machete and cut him down. He was afraid of being thought weak.

As soon as his father walked in, that night, Nwoye knew that Ikemefuna had been killed, and something seemed to give way inside him, like the snapping of a tightened bow. He did not cry. He just hung limp. He had had the same kind of feeling not long ago, during the last harvest season. Every child loved the harvest season. Those who were big enough to carry even a few yams in a tiny basket went with grownups to the farm. And if they could not help in digging up the yams, they could gather firewood together for roasting the ones that would be eaten there on the farm. This roasted yam soaked in red palm-oil and eaten in the open farm was sweeter than any meal at home. It was after such a day at the farm during the last harvest that Nwoye had felt for the first time a snapping inside him like the one he now felt. They were returning home with baskets of yams from a distant farm across the stream when they heard the voice of an infant crying in the thick forest. A sudden hush had fallen on the women, who had been talking, and they had quickened their steps. Nwoye had heard that twins were put in earthenware pots and thrown away in the forest, but he had never yet come across them. A vague chill had

---

[15] *Eze elina, . . . Sala:* "King don't eat, don't eat! / Sala / King if you eat it / You will weep for the abomination / Where Danda installs a king / Where Uzuzu dances / Sala." *Danda* means "ant"; *Uzuzu,* "sand"; and *Sala,* which has no meaning, is a refrain.

descended on him and his head had seemed to swell, like a solitary walker at night who passes an evil spirit on the way. Then something had given way inside him. It descended on him again, this feeling, when his father walked in, that night after killing Ikemefuna.

8

Okonkwo did not taste any food for two days after the death of Ikemefuna. He drank palm-wine from morning till night, and his eyes were red and fierce like the eyes of a rat when it was caught by the tail and dashed against the floor. He called his son, Nwoye, to sit with him in his *obi*. But the boy was afraid of him and slipped out of the hut as soon as he noticed him dozing.

He did not sleep at night. He tried not to think about Ikemefuna, but the more he tried the more he thought about him. Once he got up from bed and walked about his compound. But he was so weak that his legs could hardly carry him. He felt like a drunken giant walking with the limbs of a mosquito. Now and then a cold shiver descended on his head and spread down his body.

On the third day he asked his second wife, Ekwefi, to roast plantains for him. She prepared it the way he liked — with slices of oil-bean and fish.

"You have not eaten for two days," said his daughter Ezinma when she brought the food to him. "So you must finish this." She sat down and stretched her legs in front of her. Okonkwo ate the food absent-mindedly. "She should have been a boy," he thought as he looked at his ten-year-old daughter. He passed her a piece of fish.

"Go and bring me some cold water," he said. Ezinma rushed out of the hut, chewing the fish, and soon returned with a bowl of cool water from the earthen pot in her mother's hut.

Okonkwo took the bowl from her and gulped the water down. He ate a few more pieces of plantain and pushed the dish aside.

"Bring me my bag," he asked, and Ezinma brought his goatskin bag from the far end of the hut. He searched in it for his snuff-bottle. It was a deep bag and took almost the whole length of his arm. It contained other things apart from his snuff-bottle. There was a drinking horn in it, and also a drinking gourd, and they knocked against each other as he searched. When he brought out the snuff-bottle he tapped it a few times against his kneecap before taking out some snuff on the palm of his left hand. Then he remembered that he had not taken out his snuff-spoon. He searched his bag again and brought out a small, flat, ivory spoon, with which he carried the brown snuff to his nostrils.

Ezinma took the dish in one hand and the empty water bowl in the other and went back to her mother's hut. "She should have been a boy," Okonkwo said to himself again. His mind went back to Ikemefuna and he shivered. If only he could find some work to do he would be able to forget. But it was the season of rest between the harvest and the next planting season. The only work that men did at this time was covering the walls of their compound with new palm fronds. And Okonkwo had already done that. He had finished it on the very day the locusts came, when he had worked on one side of the wall and Ikemefuna and Nwoye on the other.

"When did you become a shivering old woman," Okonkwo asked himself, "you, who are known in all the nine villages for your valor in war? How can a man who has killed five men in battle fall to pieces because he has added a boy to their number? Okonkwo, you have become a woman indeed."

He sprang to his feet, hung his goatskin bag on his shoulder and went to visit his friend, Obierika.

Obierika was sitting outside under the shade of an orange tree making thatches from leaves of the raffia-palm. He exchanged greetings with Okonkwo and led the way into his *obi*.

"I was coming over to see you as soon as I finished that thatch," he said, rubbing off the grains of sand that clung to his thighs.

"Is it well?" Okonkwo asked.

"Yes," replied Obierika. "My daughter's suitor is coming today and I hope we will clinch the matter of the bride-price. I want you to be there."

Just then Obierika's son, Maduka, came into the *obi* from outside, greeted Okonkwo and turned towards the compound.

"Come and shake hands with me," Okonkwo said to the lad. "Your wrestling the other day gave me much happiness." The boy smiled, shook hands with Okonkwo and went into the compound.

"He will do great things," Okonkwo said. "If I had a son like him I should be happy. I am worried about Nwoye. A bowl of pounded yams can throw him in a wrestling match. His two younger brothers are more promising. But I can tell you, Obierika, that my children do not resemble me. Where are the young suckers that will grow when the old banana tree dies? If Ezinma had been a boy I would have been happier. She has the right spirit."

"You worry yourself for nothing," said Obierika. "The children are still very young."

"Nwoye is old enough to impregnate a woman. At his age I was already fending for myself. No, my friend, he is not too young. A chick that will grow into a cock can be spotted the very day it hatches. I have done my best to make Nwoye grow into a man, but there is too much of his mother in him."

"Too much of his grandfather," Obierika thought, but he did not say it. The same thought also came to Okonkwo's mind. But he had long learned how to lay that ghost. Whenever the thought of his father's weakness and failure troubled him he expelled it by thinking about his own strength and success. And so he did now. His mind went to his latest show of manliness.

"I cannot understand why you refused to come with us to kill that boy," he asked Obierika.

"Because I did not want to," Obierika replied sharply. "I had something better to do."

"You sound as if you question the authority and the decision of the Oracle, who said he should die."

"I do not. Why should I? But the Oracle did not ask me to carry out its decision."

"But someone had to do it. If we were all afraid of blood, it would not be done. And what do you think the Oracle would do then?"

"You know very well, Okonkwo, that I am not afraid of blood; and if anyone tells you that I am, he is telling a lie. And let me tell you one thing, my friend. If I were you I would have stayed at home. What you have done will not please the Earth. It is the kind of action for which the goddess wipes out whole families."

"The Earth cannot punish me for obeying her messenger," Okonkwo said. "A child's fingers are not scalded by a piece of hot yam which its mother puts into its palm."

"That is true," Obierika agreed. "But if the Oracle said that my son should be killed I would neither dispute it nor be the one to do it."

They would have gone on arguing had Ofoedu not come in just then. It was clear from his twinkling eyes that he had important news. But it would be impolite to rush him. Obierika offered him a lobe of the kola nut he had broken with Okonkwo. Ofoedu ate slowly and talked about the locusts. When he finished his kola nut he said:

"The things that happen these days are very strange."

"What has happened?" asked Okonkwo.

"Do you know Ogbuefi Ndulue?" Ofoedu asked.

"Ogbuefi Ndulue of Ire village," Okonkwo and Obierika said together.

"He died this morning," said Ofoedu.

"That is not strange. He was the oldest man in Ire," said Obierika.

"You are right," Ofoedu agreed. "But you ought to ask why the drum has not beaten to tell Umuofia of his death."

"Why?" asked Obierika and Okonkwo together.

"That is the strange part of it. You know his first wife who walks with a stick?"

"Yes. She is called Ozoemena."

"That is so," said Ofoedu. "Ozoemena was, as you know, too old to attend Ndulue during his illness. His younger wives did that. When he died this morning, one of these women went to Ozoemena's hut and told her. She rose from her mat, took her stick and walked over to the *obi*. She knelt on her knees and hands at the threshold and called her husband, who was laid on a mat. 'Ogbuefi Ndulue,' she called, three times, and went back to her hut. When the youngest wife went to call her again to be present at the washing of the body, she found her lying on the mat, dead."

"That is very strange, indeed," said Okonkwo. "They will put off Ndulue's funeral until his wife has been buried."[16]

"That is why the drum has not been beaten to tell Umuofia."

"It was always said that Ndulue and Ozoemena had one mind," said Obierika. "I remember when I was a young boy there was a song about them. He could not do anything without telling her."

"I did not know that," said Okonkwo. "I thought he was a strong man in his youth."

"He was indeed," said Ofoedu.

---

[16] **"That is . . . buried"**: A wife who died soon after her husband might be blamed for his death, therefore the concern here.

Okonkwo shook his head doubtfully.

"He led Umuofia to war in those days," said Obierika.

Okonkwo was beginning to feel like his old self again. All that he required was something to occupy his mind. If he had killed Ikemefuna during the busy planting season or harvesting it would not have been so bad; his mind would have been centered on his work. Okonkwo was not a man of thought but of action. But in absence of work, talking was the next best.

Soon after Ofoedu left, Okonkwo took up his goatskin bag to go.

"I must go home to tap my palm trees for the afternoon," he said.

"Who taps your tall trees for you?" asked Obierika.

"Umezulike," replied Okonkwo.

"Sometimes I wish I had not taken the *ozo* title," said Obierika. "It wounds my heart to see these young men killing palm trees in the name of tapping."

"It is so indeed," Okonkwo agreed. "But the law of the land must be obeyed."

"I don't know how we got that law," said Obierika. "In many other clans a man of title is not forbidden to climb the palm tree. Here we say he cannot climb the tall tree but he can tap the short ones standing on the ground. It is like Dimaragana, who would not lend his knife for cutting up dog-meat because the dog was taboo to him, but offered to use his teeth."

"I think it is good that our clan holds the *ozo* title in high esteem," said Okonkwo. "In those other clans you speak of, *ozo* is so low that every beggar takes it."

"I was only speaking in jest," said Obierika. "In Abame and Aninta the title is worth less than two cowries. Every man wears the thread of title on his ankle, and does not lose it even if he steals."

"They have indeed soiled the name of *ozo*," said Okonkwo as he rose to go.

"It will not be very long now before my in-laws come," said Obierika.

"I shall return very soon," said Okonkwo, looking at the position of the sun.

There were seven men in Obierika's hut when Okonkwo returned. The suitor was a young man of about twenty-five, and with him were his father and uncle. On Obierika's side were his two elder brothers and Maduka, his sixteen-year-old son.

"Ask Akueke's mother to send us some kola nuts," said Obierika to his son. Maduka vanished into the compound like lightning. The conversation at once centered on him, and everybody agreed that he was as sharp as a razor.

"I sometimes think he is too sharp," said Obierika, somewhat indulgently. "He hardly ever walks. He is always in a hurry. If you are sending him on an errand he flies away before he has heard half of the message."

"You were very much like that yourself," said his eldest brother. "As our people say, 'When mother-cow is chewing grass its young ones watch its mouth.' Maduka has been watching your mouth."

As he was speaking the boy returned, followed by Akueke, his half-sister, carrying a wooden dish with three kola nuts and alligator pepper. She gave the dish to her father's eldest brother and then shook hands, very shyly, with her suitor and his relatives. She was about sixteen and just ripe for marriage. Her suitor and his relatives surveyed her young body with expert eyes as if to assure themselves that she was beautiful and ripe.

She wore a coiffure which was done up into a crest in the middle of the head. Cam wood was rubbed lightly into her skin, and all over her body were black patterns drawn with *uli*.[17] She wore a black necklace which hung down in three coils just above her full, succulent breasts. On her arms were red and yellow bangles, and on her waist four or five rows of *jigida,* or waist beads.

When she had shaken hands, or rather held out her hand to be shaken, she returned to her mother's hut to help with the cooking.

"Remove your *jigida* first," her mother warned as she moved near the fireplace to bring the pestle resting against the wall. "Every day I tell you that *jigida* and fire are not friends. But you will never hear. You grew your ears for decoration, not for hearing. One of these days your *jigida* will catch fire on your waist, and then you will know."

Akueke moved to the other end of the hut and began to remove the waist-beads. It had to be done slowly and carefully, taking each string separately, else it would break and the thousand tiny rings would have to be strung together again. She rubbed each string downwards with her palms until it passed the buttocks and slipped down to the floor around her feet.

The men in the *obi* had already begun to drink the palm-wine which Akueke's suitor had brought. It was a very good wine and powerful, for in spite of the palm fruit hung across the mouth of the pot to restrain the lively liquor, white foam rose and spilled over.

"That wine is the work of a good tapper," said Okonkwo.

The young suitor, whose name was Ibe, smiled broadly and said to his father: "Do you hear that?" He then said to the others: "He will never admit that I am a good tapper."

"He tapped three of my best palm trees to death," said his father, Ukegbu.

"That was about five years ago," said Ibe, who had begun to pour out the wine, "before I learned how to tap." He filled the first horn and gave to his father. Then he poured out for the others. Okonkwo brought out his big horn from the goatskin bag, blew into it to remove any dust that might be there, and gave it to Ibe to fill.

As the men drank, they talked about everything except the thing for which they had gathered. It was only after the pot had been emptied that the suitor's father cleared his voice and announced the object of their visit.

Obierika then presented to him a small bundle of short broomsticks. Ukegbu counted them.

"They are thirty?" he asked.

Obierika nodded in agreement.

"We are at last getting somewhere," Ukegbu said, and then turning to his brother and his son he said: "Let us go out and whisper together." The three rose and went outside. When they returned Ukegbu handed the bundle of sticks back to Obierika.

---

[17] *uli*: A black dye used to decorate the body.

He counted them; instead of thirty there were now only fifteen. He passed them over to his eldest brother, Machi, who also counted them and said:

"We had not thought to go below thirty. But as the dog said, 'If I fall down for you and you fall down for me, it is play.' Marriage should be a play and not a fight; so we are falling down again." He then added ten sticks to the fifteen and gave the bundle to Ukegbu.

In this way Akueke's bride-price was finally settled at twenty bags of cowries. It was already dusk when the two parties came to this agreement.

"Go and tell Akueke's mother that we have finished," Obierika said to his son, Maduka. Almost immediately the women came in with a big bowl of foo-foo. Obierika's second wife followed with a pot of soup, and Maduka brought in a pot of palm-wine.

As the men ate and drank palm-wine they talked about the customs of their neighbors.

"It was only this morning," said Obierika, "that Okonkwo and I were talking about Abame and Aninta, where titled men climb trees and pound foo-foo for their wives."

"All their customs are upside-down. They do not decide bride-price as we do, with sticks. They haggle and bargain as if they were buying a goat or a cow in the market."

"That is very bad," said Obierika's eldest brother. "But what is good in one place is bad in another place. In Umunso they do not bargain at all, not even with broomsticks. The suitor just goes on bringing bags of cowries until his in-laws tell him to stop. It is a bad custom because it always leads to a quarrel."

"The world is large," said Okonkwo. "I have even heard that in some tribes a man's children belong to his wife and her family."

"That cannot be," said Machi. "You might as well say that the woman lies on top of the man when they are making the children."

"It is like the story of white men who, they say, are white like this piece of chalk," said Obierika. He held up a piece of chalk, which every man kept in his *obi* and with which his guests drew lines on the floor before they ate kola nuts. "And these white men, they say, have no toes."

"And have you never seen them?" asked Machi.

"Have you?" asked Obierika.

"One of them passes here frequently," said Machi. "His name is Amadi."

Those who knew Amadi laughed. He was a leper, and the polite name for leprosy was "the white skin."

9

For the first time in three nights, Okonkwo slept. He woke up once in the middle of the night and his mind went back to the past three days without making him feel uneasy. He began to wonder why he had felt uneasy at all. It was like a man wondering in broad daylight why a dream had appeared so terrible to him at night. He stretched himself and scratched his thigh where a mosquito had bitten him as he slept. Another one was wailing near his right ear. He slapped the ear and hoped he had killed it. Why do they always go for one's ears? When he was a child his mother had told him a story about it. But it was as silly as all women's stories. Mosquito, she had said, had asked Ear to marry him, whereupon Ear fell on the floor in uncontrollable laughter. "How much longer do you think you will live?" she asked. "You are already a skeleton." Mosquito went away humiliated, and any time he passed her way he told Ear that he was still alive.

Okonkwo turned on his side and went back to sleep. He was roused in the morning by someone banging on his door.

"Who is that?" he growled. He knew it must be Ekwefi. Of his three wives Ekwefi was the only one who would have the audacity to bang on his door.

"Ezinma is dying," came her voice, and all the tragedy and sorrow of her life were packed in those words.

Okonkwo sprang from his bed, pushed back the bolt on his door and ran into Ekwefi's hut.

Ezinma lay shivering on a mat beside a huge fire that her mother had kept burning all night.

"It is *iba*,"[18] said Okonkwo as he took his machete and went into the bush to collect the leaves and grasses and barks of trees that went into making the medicine for *iba*.

Ekwefi knelt beside the sick child, occasionally feeling with her palm the wet, burning forehead.

Ezinma was an only child and the center of her mother's world. Very often it was Ezinma who decided what food her mother should prepare. Ekwefi even gave her such delicacies as eggs, which children were rarely allowed to eat because such food tempted them to steal. One day as Ezinma was eating an egg Okonkwo had come in unexpectedly from his hut. He was greatly shocked and swore to beat Ekwefi if she dared to give the child eggs again. But it was impossible to refuse Ezinma anything. After her father's rebuke she developed an even keener appetite for eggs. And she enjoyed above all the secrecy in which she now ate them. Her mother always took her into their bedroom and shut the door.

Ezinma did not call her mother *Nne* like all children. She called her by her name, Ekwefi, as her father and other grown-up people did. The relationship between them was not only that of mother and child. There was something in it like the companionship of equals, which was strengthened by such little conspiracies as eating eggs in the bedroom.

Ekwefi had suffered a good deal in her life. She had borne ten children and nine of them had died in infancy, usually before the age of three. As she buried one child after another her sorrow gave way to despair and then to grim resignation. The birth of her children, which should be a woman's crowning glory, became for Ekwefi mere physical agony devoid of promise. The naming ceremony after seven market weeks

---

[18] *iba*: Fever.

became an empty ritual. Her deepening despair found expression in the names she gave her children. One of them was a pathetic cry, Onwumbiko — "Death, I implore you." But Death took no notice; Onwumbiko died in his fifteenth month. The next child was a girl, Ozoemena — "May it not happen again." She died in her eleventh month, and two others after her. Ekwefi then became defiant and called her next child Onwuma — "Death may please himself." And he did.

After the death of Ekwefi's second child, Okonkwo had gone to a medicine man, who was also a diviner of the Afa Oracle, to inquire what was amiss. This man told him that the child was an *ogbanje*,[19] one of those wicked children who, when they died, entered their mothers' wombs to be born again.

"When your wife becomes pregnant again," he said, "let her not sleep in her hut. Let her go and stay with her people. In that way she will elude her wicked tormentor and break its evil cycle of birth and death."

Ekwefi did as she was asked. As soon as she became pregnant she went to live with her old mother in another village. It was there that her third child was born and circumcised on the eighth day. She did not return to Okonkwo's compound until three days before the naming ceremony. The child was called Onwumbiko.

Onwumbiko was not given proper burial when he died. Okonkwo had called in another medicine man who was famous in the clan for his great knowledge about *ogbanje* children. His name was Okagbue Uyanwa. Okagbue was a very striking figure, tall, with a full beard and a bald head. He was light in complexion and his eyes were red and fiery. He always gnashed his teeth as he listened to those who came to consult him. He asked Okonkwo a few questions about the dead child. All the neighbors and relations who had come to mourn gathered round them.

"On what market-day was it born?" he asked.

"*Oye*," replied Okonkwo.

"And it died this morning?"

Okonkwo said yes, and only then realized for the first time that the child had died on the same market-day as it had been born. The neighbors and relations also saw the coincidence and said among themselves that it was very significant.

"Where do you sleep with your wife, in your *obi* or in her own hut?" asked the medicine man.

"In her hut."

"In future call her into your *obi*."

The medicine man then ordered that there should be no mourning for the dead child. He brought out a sharp razor from the goatskin bag slung from his left shoulder and began to mutilate the child. Then he took it away to bury in the Evil Forest, holding it by the ankle and dragging it on the ground behind him. After such treatment it would think twice before coming again, unless it was one of the stubborn ones who returned, carrying the stamp of their mutilation — a missing finger or perhaps a dark line where the medicine man's razor had cut them.

---

[19] **child . . . *ogbanje*:** The *ogbanje* is locked into a pattern of early death and cyclic rebirth unless its *iyi-uwa*, a stone that links it to the spirit world, is found and destroyed so that the child can live.

By the time Onwumbiko died Ekwefi had become a very bitter woman. Her husband's first wife had already had three sons, all strong and healthy. When she had borne her third son in succession, Okonkwo had gathered a goat for her, as was the custom. Ekwefi had nothing but good wishes for her. But she had grown so bitter about her own *chi* that she could not rejoice with others over their good fortune. And so, on the day that Nwoye's mother celebrated the birth of her three sons with feasting and music, Ekwefi was the only person in the happy company who went about with a cloud on her brow. Her husband's wife took this for malevolence, as husbands' wives were wont to. How could she know that Ekwefi's bitterness did not flow outwards to others but inwards into her own soul; that she did not blame others for their good fortune but her own evil *chi* who denied her any?

At last Ezinma was born, and although ailing she seemed determined to live. At first Ekwefi accepted her, as she had accepted others — with listless resignation. But when she lived on to her fourth, fifth, and sixth years, love returned once more to her mother, and, with love, anxiety. She determined to nurse her child to health, and she put all her being into it. She was rewarded by occasional spells of health during which Ezinma bubbled with energy like fresh palm-wine. At such times she seemed beyond danger. But all of a sudden she would go down again. Everybody knew she was an *ogbanje.* These sudden bouts of sickness and health were typical of her kind. But she had lived so long that perhaps she had decided to stay. Some of them did become tired of their evil rounds of birth and death, or took pity on their mothers, and stayed. Ekwefi believed deep inside her that Ezinma had come to stay. She believed because it was that faith alone that gave her own life any kind of meaning. And this faith had been strengthened when a year or so ago a medicine man had dug up Ezinma's *iyi-uwa.* Everyone knew then that she would live because her bond with the world of *ogbanje* had been broken. Ekwefi was reassured. But such was her anxiety for her daughter that she could not rid herself completely of her fear. And although she believed that the *iyi-uwa* which had been dug up was genuine, she could not ignore the fact that some really evil children sometimes misled people into digging up a specious one.

But Ezinma's *iyi-uwa* had looked real enough. It was a smooth pebble wrapped in a dirty rag. The man who dug it up was the same Okagbue who was famous in all the clan for his knowledge in these matters. Ezinma had not wanted to cooperate with him at first. But that was only to be expected. No *ogbanje* would yield her secrets easily, and most of them never did because they died too young — before they could be asked questions.

"Where did you bury your *iyi-uwa?*" Okagbue had asked Ezinma. She was nine then and was just recovering from a serious illness.

"What is *iyi-uwa?*" she asked in return.

"You know what it is. You buried it in the ground somewhere so that you can die and return again to torment your mother."

Ezinma looked at her mother, whose eyes, sad and pleading, were fixed on her.

"Answer the question at once," roared Okonkwo, who stood beside her. All the family were there and some of the neighbors too.

"Leave her to me," the medicine man told Okonkwo in a cool, confident voice. He turned again to Ezinma. "Where did you bury your *iyi-uwa?*"

"Where they bury children," she replied, and the quiet spectators murmured to themselves.

"Come along then and show me the spot," said the medicine man.

The crowd set out with Ezinma leading the way and Okagbue following closely behind her. Okonkwo came next and Ekwefi followed him. When she came to the main road, Ezinma turned left as if she was going to the stream.

"But you said it was where they bury children?" asked the medicine man.

"No," said Ezinma, whose feeling of importance was manifest in her sprightly walk. She sometimes broke into a run and stopped again suddenly. The crowd followed her silently. Women and children returning from the stream with pots of water on their heads wondered what was happening until they saw Okagbue and guessed that it must be something to do with *ogbanje.* And they all knew Ekwefi and her daughter very well.

When she got to the big udala tree Ezinma turned left into the bush, and the crowd followed her. Because of her size she made her way through trees and creepers more quickly than her followers. The bush was alive with the tread of feet on dry leaves and sticks and the moving aside of tree branches. Ezinma went deeper and deeper and the crowd went with her. Then she suddenly turned round and began to walk back to the road. Everybody stood to let her pass and then filed after her.

"If you bring us all this way for nothing I shall beat sense into you," Okonkwo threatened.

"I have told you to let her alone. I know how to deal with them," said Okagbue.

Ezinma led the way back to the road, looked left and right and turned right. And so they arrived home again.

"Where did you bury your *iyi-uwa?*" asked Okagbue when Ezinma finally stopped outside her father's *obi*. Okagbue's voice was unchanged. It was quiet and confident.

"It is near that orange tree," Ezinma said.

"And why did you not say so, you wicked daughter of Akalogoli?" Okonkwo swore furiously. The medicine man ignored him.

"Come and show me the exact spot," he said quietly to Ezinma.

"It is here," she said when they got to the tree.

"Point at the spot with your finger," said Okagbue.

"It is here," said Ezinma touching the ground with her finger. Okonkwo stood by, rumbling like thunder in the rainy season.

"Bring me a hoe," said Okagbue.

When Ekwefi brought the hoe, he had already put aside his goatskin bag and his big cloth and was in his underwear, a long and thin strip of cloth wound round the waist like a belt and then passed between the legs to be fastened to the belt behind. He immediately set to work digging a pit where Ezinma had indicated. The neighbors sat around watching the pit becoming deeper and deeper. The dark top soil soon gave way to the bright red earth with which women scrubbed the floors and walls of huts. Okagbue worked tirelessly and in silence, his back shining with perspiration. Okonkwo stood by the pit. He asked Okagbue to come up and rest while he took a hand. But Okagbue said he was not tired yet.

Ekwefi went into her hut to cook yams. Her husband had brought out more yams than usual because the medicine man had to be fed. Ezinma went with her and helped in preparing the vegetables.

"There is too much green vegetable," she said.

"Don't you see the pot is full of yams?" Ekwefi asked. "And you know how leaves become smaller after cooking."

"Yes," said Ezinma, "that was why the snake-lizard killed his mother."

"Very true," said Ekwefi.

"He gave his mother seven baskets of vegetables to cook and in the end there were only three. And so he killed her," said Ezinma.

"That is not the end of the story."

"Oho," said Ezinma. "I remember now. He brought another seven baskets and cooked them himself. And there were again only three. So he killed himself too."

Outside the *obi* Okagbue and Okonkwo were digging the pit to find where Ezinma had buried her *iyi-uwa*. Neighbors sat around, watching. The pit was now so deep that they no longer saw the digger. They only saw the red earth he threw up mounting higher and higher. Okonkwo's son, Nwoye, stood near the edge of the pit because he wanted to take in all that happened.

Okagbue had again taken over the digging from Okonkwo. He worked, as usual, in silence. The neighbors and Okonkwo's wives were now talking. The children had lost interest and were playing.

Suddenly Okagbue sprang to the surface with the agility of a leopard.

"It is very near now," he said. "I have felt it."

There was immediate excitement and those who were sitting jumped to their feet.

"Call your wife and child," he said to Okonkwo. But Ekwefi and Ezinma had heard the noise and run out to see what it was.

Okagbue went back into the pit, which was now surrounded by spectators. After a few more hoe-fuls of earth he struck the *iyi-uwa*. He raised it carefully with the hoe and threw it to the surface. Some women ran away in fear when it was thrown. But they soon returned and everyone was gazing at the rag from a reasonable distance. Okagbue emerged and without saying a word or even looking at the spectators he went to his goatskin bag, took out two leaves and began to chew them. When he had swallowed them, he took up the rag with his left hand and began to untie it. And then the smooth, shiny pebble fell out. He picked it up.

"Is this yours?" he asked Ezinma.

"Yes," she replied. All the women shouted with joy because Ekwefi's troubles were at last ended.

All this had happened more than a year ago and Ezinma had not been ill since. And then suddenly she had begun to shiver in the night. Ekwefi brought her to the fireplace, spread her mat on the floor and built a fire. But she had got worse and worse. As she knelt by her, feeling with her palm the wet, burning forehead, she prayed a thousand times. Although her husband's wives were saying that it was nothing more than *iba,* she did not hear them.

· · ·

Okonkwo returned from the bush carrying on his left shoulder a large bundle of grasses and leaves, roots and barks of medicinal trees and shrubs. He went into Ekwefi's hut, put down his load and sat down.

"Get me a pot," he said, "and leave the child alone."

Ekwefi went to bring the pot and Okonkwo selected the best from his bundle, in their due proportions, and cut them up. He put them in the pot and Ekwefi poured in some water.

"Is that enough?" she asked when she had poured in about half of the water in the bowl.

"A little more . . . I said *a little*. Are you deaf?" Okonkwo roared at her.

She set the pot on the fire and Okonkwo took up his machete to return to his *obi*.

"You must watch the pot carefully," he said as he went, "and don't allow it to boil over. If it does its power will be gone." He went away to his hut and Ekwefi began to tend the medicine pot almost as if it was itself a sick child. Her eyes went constantly from Ezinma to the boiling pot and back to Ezinma.

Okonkwo returned when he felt the medicine had cooked long enough. He looked it over and said it was done.

"Bring me a low stool for Ezinma," he said, "and a thick mat."

He took down the pot from the fire and placed it in front of the stool. He then roused Ezinma and placed her on the stool, astride the steaming pot. The thick mat was thrown over both. Ezinma struggled to escape from the choking and overpowering steam, but she was held down. She started to cry.

When the mat was at last removed she was drenched in perspiration. Ekwefi mopped her with a piece of cloth and she lay down on a dry mat and was soon asleep.

10

Large crowds began to gather on the village *ilo* as soon as the edge had worn off the sun's heat and it was no longer painful on the body. Most communal ceremonies took place at that time of the day, so that even when it was said that a ceremony would begin "after the midday meal" everyone understood that it would begin a long time later, when the sun's heat had softened.

It was clear from the way the crowd stood or sat that the ceremony was for men. There were many women, but they looked on from the fringe like outsiders. The titled men and elders sat on their stools waiting for the trials to begin. In front of them was a row of stools on which nobody sat. There were nine of them. Two little groups of people stood at a respectable distance beyond the stools. They faced the elders. There were three men in one group and three men and one woman in the other. The woman was Mgbafo and the three men with her were her brothers. In the other group were her husband, Uzowulu, and his relatives. Mgbafo and her brothers were as still as statues into whose faces the artist has molded defiance. Uzowulu and his relative, on the other hand, were whispering together. It looked like whispering, but they were really talking at the top of their voices. Everybody in the crowd was talking. It was like the market. From a distance the noise was a deep rumble carried by the wind.

An iron gong sounded, setting up a wave of expectation in the crowd. Everyone looked in the direction of the *egwugwu* house. *Gome, gome, gome, gome* went the gong, and a powerful flute blew a high-pitched blast. Then came the voices of the *egwugwu,* guttural and awesome. The wave struck the women and children and there was a backward stampede. But it was momentary. They were already far enough where they stood and there was room for running away if any of the *egwugwu* should go towards them.

The drum sounded again and the flute blew. The *egwugwu* house was now a pandemonium of quavering voices: *Aru oyim de de de dei!*[20] filled the air as the spirits of the ancestors, just emerged from the earth, greeted themselves in their esoteric language. The *egwugwu* house into which they emerged faced the forest, away from the crowd, who saw only its back with the many-colored patterns and drawings done by specially chosen women at regular intervals. These women never saw the inside of the hut. No woman ever did. They scrubbed and painted the outside walls under the supervision of men. If they imagined what was inside, they kept their imagination to themselves. No woman ever asked questions about the most powerful and the most secret cult in the clan.

Aru oyim de de de dei! flew around the dark, closed hut like tongues of fire. The ancestral spirits of the clan were abroad. The metal gong beat continuously now and the flute, shrill and powerful, floated on the chaos.

And then the *egwugwu* appeared. The women and children sent up a great shout and took to their heels. It was instinctive. A woman fled as soon as an *egwugwu* came in sight. And when, as on that day, nine of the greatest masked spirits in the clan came out together it was a terrifying spectacle. Even Mgbafo took to her heels and had to be restrained by her brothers.

Each of the nine *egwugwu* represented a village of the clan. Their leader was called Evil Forest. Smoke poured out of his head.

The nine villages of Umuofia had grown out of the nine sons of the first father of the clan. Evil Forest represented the village of Umueru, or the children of Eru, who was the eldest of the nine sons.

"*Umuofia kwenu!*" shouted the leading *egwugwu,* pushing the air with his raffia arms. The elders of the clan replied, "*Yaa!*"

"*Umuofia kwenu!*"

"*Yaa!*"

"*Umuofia kwenu!*"

"*Yaa!*"

Evil Forest then thrust the pointed end of his rattling staff into the earth. And it began to shake and rattle, like something agitating with a metallic life. He took the first of the empty stools and the eight other *egwugwu* began to sit in order of seniority after him.

---

[20] *Aru . . . dei!:* "Body of my friend, greetings."

Okonkwo's wives, and perhaps other women as well, might have noticed that the second *egwugwu* had the springy walk of Okonkwo. And they might also have noticed that Okonkwo was not among the titled men and elders who sat behind the row of *egwugwu*. But if they thought these things they kept them within themselves. The *egwugwu* with the springy walk was one of the dead fathers of the clan. He looked terrible with the smoked raffia body, a huge wooden face painted white except for the round hollow eyes and the charred teeth that were as big as a man's fingers. On his head were two powerful horns.

When all the *egwugwu* had sat down and the sound of the many tiny bells and rattles on their bodies had subsided, Evil Forest addressed the two groups of people facing them.

"Uzowulu's body, I salute you," he said. Spirits always addressed humans as "bodies." Uzowulu bent down and touched the earth with his right hand as a sign of submission.

"Our father, my hand has touched the ground," he said.

"Uzowulu's body, do you know me?" asked the spirit.

"How can I know you, father? You are beyond our knowledge."

Evil Forest then turned to the other group and addressed the eldest of the three brothers.

"The body of Odukwe, I greet you," he said, and Odukwe bent down and touched the earth. The hearing then began.

Uzowulu stepped forward and presented his case.

"That woman standing there is my wife, Mgbafo. I married her with my money and my yams. I do not owe my in-laws anything. I owe them no yams. I owe them no coco-yams. One morning three of them came to my house, beat me up, and took my wife and children away. This happened in the rainy season. I have waited in vain for my wife to return. At last I went to my in-laws and said to them, 'You have taken back your sister. I did not send her away. You yourselves took her. The law of the clan is that you should return her bride-price.' But my wife's brothers said they had nothing to tell me. So I have brought the matter to the fathers of the clan. My case is finished. I salute you."

"Your words are good," said the leader of the *egwugwu*. "Let us hear Odukwe. His words may also be good."

Odukwe was short and thickset. He stepped forward, saluted the spirits, and began his story.

"My in-law has told you that we went to his house, beat him up, and took our sister and her children away. All that is true. He told you that he came to take back her bride-price and we refused to give it him. That also is true. My in-law, Uzowulu, is a beast. My sister lived with him for nine years. During those years no single day passed in the sky without his beating the woman. We have tried to settle their quarrels time without number and on each occasion Uzowulu was guilty—"

"It is a lie!" Uzowulu shouted.

"Two years ago," continued Odukwe, "when she was pregnant, he beat her until she miscarried."

"It is a lie. She miscarried after she had gone to sleep with her lover."

"Uzowulu's body, I salute you," said Evil Forest, silencing him. "What kind of lover sleeps with a pregnant woman?" There was a loud murmur of approbation from the crowd. Odukwe continued:

"Last year when my sister was recovering from an illness, he beat her again so that if the neighbors had not gone in to save her she would have been killed. We heard of it, and did as you have been told. The law of Umuofia is that if a woman runs away from her husband her bride-price is returned. But in this case she ran away to save her life. Her two children belong to Uzowulu. We do not dispute it, but they are too young to leave their mother. If, in the other hand, Uzowulu should recover from his madness and come in the proper way to beg his wife to return she will do so on the understanding that if he ever beats her again we shall cut off his genitals for him."

The crowd roared with laughter. Evil Forest rose to his feet and order was immediately restored. A steady cloud of smoke rose from his head. He sat down again and called two witnesses. They were both Uzowulu's neighbors, and they agreed about the beating. Evil Forest then stood up, pulled out his staff and thrust it into the earth again. He ran a few steps in the direction of the women; they all fled in terror, only to return to their places almost immediately. The nine *egwugwu* then went away to consult together in their house. They were silent for a long time. Then the metal gong sounded and the flute was blown. The *egwugwu* had emerged once again from their underground home. They saluted one another and then reappeared on the *ilo*.

"*Umuofia kwenu!*" roared Evil Forest, facing the elders and grandees of the clan.

"*Yaa!*" replied the thunderous crowd; then silence descended from the sky and swallowed the noise.

Evil Forest began to speak and all the while he spoke everyone was silent. The eight other *egwugwu* were as still as statues.

"We have heard both sides of the case," said Evil Forest. "Our duty is not to blame this man or to praise that, but to settle the dispute." He turned to Uzowulu's group and allowed a short pause.

"Uzowulu's body, I salute you," he said.

"Our father, my hand has touched the ground," replied Uzowulu, touching the earth.

"Uzowulu's body, do you know me?"

"How can I know you, father? You are beyond our knowledge," Uzowulu replied.

"I am Evil Forest. I kill a man on the day that his life is sweetest to him."

"That is true," replied Uzowulu.

"Go to your in-laws with a pot of wine and beg your wife to return to you. It is not bravery when a man fights with a woman." He turned to Odukwe, and allowed a brief pause.

"Odukwe's body, I greet you," he said.

"My hand is on the ground," replied Odukwe.

"Do you know me?"

"No man can know you," replied Odukwe.

"I am Evil Forest, I am Dry-meat-that-fills-the-mouth, I am Fire-that-burns-without-faggots. If your in-law brings wine to you, let your sister go with him. I salute you." He pulled his staff from the hard earth and thrust it back.

"*Umuofia kwenu!*" he roared, and the crowd answered.

"I don't know why such a trifle should come before the *egwugwu*," said one elder to another.

"Don't you know what kind of man Uzowulu is? He will not listen to any other decision," replied the other.

As they spoke two other groups of people had replaced the first before the *egwugwu*, and a great land case began.

11

The night was impenetrably dark. The moon had been rising later and later every night until now it was seen only at dawn. And whenever the moon forsook evening and rose at cock-crow the nights were as black as charcoal.

Ezinma and her mother sat on a mat on the floor after their supper of yam foo-foo and bitter-leaf soup. A palm-oil lamp gave out yellowish light. Without it, it would have been impossible to eat; one could not have known where one's mouth was in the darkness of that night. There was an oil lamp in all the four huts on Okonkwo's compound, and each hut seen from the others looked like a soft eye of yellow half-light set in the solid massiveness of night.

The world was silent except for the shrill cry of insects, which was part of the night, and the sound of wooden mortar and pestle as Nwayieke pounded her foo-foo. Nwayieke lived four compounds away, and she was notorious for her late cooking. Every woman in the neighborhood knew the sound of Nwayieke's mortar and pestle. It was also part of the night.

Okonkwo had eaten from his wives' dishes and was now reclining with his back against the wall. He searched his bag and brought out his snuff-bottle. He turned it on to his left palm, but nothing came out. He hit the bottle against his knee to shake up the tobacco. That was always the trouble with Okeke's snuff. It very quickly went damp, and there was too much saltpeter in it. Okonkwo had not bought snuff from him for a long time. Idigo was the man who knew how to grind good snuff. But he had recently fallen ill.

Low voices, broken now and again by singing, reached Okonkwo from his wives' huts as each woman and her children told folk stories. Ekwefi and her daughter, Ezinma, sat on a mat on the floor. It was Ekwefi's turn to tell a story.

"Once upon a time," she began, "all the birds were invited to a feast in the sky. They were very happy and began to prepare themselves for the great day. They painted their bodies with red cam wood and drew beautiful patterns on them with *uli*.

"Tortoise saw all these preparations and soon discovered what it all meant. Nothing that happened in the world of the animals ever escaped his notice; he was full of cunning. As soon as he heard of the great feast in the sky his throat began to itch at the very thought. There was a famine in those days and Tortoise had not eaten a good meal for two moons. His body rattled like a piece of dry stick in his empty shell. So he began to plan how he would go to the sky."

"But he had no wings," said Ezinma.

"Be patient," replied her mother. "That is the story. Tortoise had no wings, but he went to the birds and asked to be allowed to go with them.

"'We know you too well,' said the birds when they had heard him. 'You are full of cunning and you are ungrateful. If we allow you to come with us you will soon begin your mischief.'

"'You do not know me,' said Tortoise. 'I am a changed man. I have learned that a man who makes trouble for others is also making it for himself.'

"Tortoise had a sweet tongue, and within a short time all the birds agreed that he was a changed man, and they each gave him a feather, with which he made two wings.

"At last the great day came and Tortoise was the first to arrive at the meeting place. When all the birds had gathered together, they set off in a body. Tortoise was very happy and voluble as he flew among the birds, and he was soon chosen as the man to speak for the party because he was a great orator.

"'There is one important thing which we must not forget,' he said as they flew on their way. 'When people are invited to a great feast like this, they take new names for the occasion. Our hosts in the sky will expect us to honor this age-old custom.'

"None of the birds had heard of this custom but they knew that Tortoise, in spite of his failings in other directions, was a widely traveled man who knew the customs of different peoples. And so they each took a new name. When they had all taken, Tortoise also took one. He was to be called *All of you*.

"At last the party arrived in the sky and their hosts were very happy to see them. Tortoise stood up in his many-colored plumage and thanked them for their invitation. His speech was so eloquent that all the birds were glad they had brought him, and nodded their heads in approval of all he said. Their hosts took him as the king of the birds, especially as he looked somewhat different from the others.

"After kola nuts had been presented and eaten, the people of the sky set before their guests the most delectable dishes Tortoise had ever seen or dreamed of. The soup was brought out hot from the fire and in the very pot in which it had been cooked. It was full of meat and fish. Tortoise began to sniff aloud. There was pounded yam and also yam pottage cooked with palm-oil and fresh fish. There were also pots of palm-wine. When everything had been set before the guests, one of the people of the sky came forward and tasted a little from each pot. He then invited the birds to eat. But Tortoise jumped to his feet and asked: 'For whom have you prepared this feast?'

"'For all of you,' replied the man.

"Tortoise turned to the birds and said: 'You remember that my name is *All of you*. The custom here is to serve the spokesman first and the others later. They will serve you when I have eaten.'

"He began to eat and the birds grumbled angrily. The people of the sky thought it must be their custom to leave all the food for their king. And so Tortoise ate the best part of the food and then drank two pots of palm-wine, so that he was full of food and drink and his body filled out in his shell.

"The birds gathered round to eat what was left and to peck at the bones he had thrown all about the floor. Some of them were too angry to eat. They chose to fly home on an empty stomach. But before they left each took back the feather he had lent to Tortoise. And there he stood in his hard shell full of food and wine but without any wings to fly home. He asked the birds to take a message for his wife, but they all refused. In the end Parrot, who had felt more angry than the others, suddenly changed his mind and agreed to take the message.

"'Tell my wife,' said Tortoise, 'to bring out all the soft things in my house and cover the compound with them so that I can jump down from the sky without very great danger.'

"Parrot promised to deliver the message, and then flew away. But when he reached Tortoise's house he told his wife to bring out all the hard things in the house. And so she brought out her husband's hoes, machetes, spears, guns, and even his cannon. Tortoise looked down from the sky and saw his wife bringing things out, but it was too far to see what they were. When all seemed ready he let himself go. He fell and fell and fell until he began to fear that he would never stop falling. And then like the sound of his cannon he crashed on the compound."

"Did he die?" asked Ezinma.

"No," replied Ekwefi. "His shell broke into pieces. But there was a great medicine man in the neighborhood. Tortoise's wife sent for him and he gathered all the bits of shell and stuck them together. That is why Tortoise's shell is not smooth."

"There is no song in the story," Ezinma pointed out.

"No," said Ekwefi. "I shall think of another one with a song. But it is your turn now."

"Once upon a time," Ezinma began, "Tortoise and Cat went to wrestle against Yams—no, that is not the beginning. Once upon a time there was a great famine in the land of animals. Everybody was lean except Cat, who was fat and whose body shone as if oil was rubbed on it . . ."

She broke off because at that very moment a loud and high-pitched voice broke the outer silence of the night. It was Chielo, the priestess of Agbala, prophesying. There was nothing new in that. Once in a while Chielo was possessed by the spirit of her god and she began to prophesy. But tonight she was addressing her prophecy and greetings to Okonkwo, and so everyone in his family listened. The folk stories stopped.

"*Agbala do-o-o-o! Agbala ekeneo-o-o-o,*" came the voice like a sharp knife cutting through the night. "*Okonkwo! Agbala ekene gio-o-o-o! Agbala cholu ifu ada ya Ezinmao-o-o-o!*"[21]

At the mention of Ezinma's name Ekwefi jerked her head sharply like an animal that had sniffed death in the air. Her heart jumped painfully within her.

---

[21] *"Agbala do-o-o-o! . . . Ezinmao-o-o-o!":* "Agbala wants something! Agbala greets," . . . "Okonkwo! Agbala greets you! Agbala wants to see his daughter Ezinma!"

The priestess had now reached Okonkwo's compound and was talking with him outside his hut. She was saying again and again that Agbala wanted to see his daughter, Ezinma. Okonkwo pleaded with her to come back in the morning because Ezinma was now asleep. But Chielo ignored what he was trying to say and went on shouting that Agbala wanted to see his daughter. Her voice was as clear as metal, and Okonkwo's women and children heard from their huts all that she said. Okonkwo was still pleading that the girl had been ill of late and was asleep. Ekwefi quickly took her to their bedroom and placed her on their high bamboo bed.

The priestess screamed. "Beware, Okonkwo!" she warned. "Beware of exchanging words with Agbala. Does a man speak when a god speaks? Beware!"

She walked through Okonkwo's hut into the circular compound and went straight toward Ekwefi's hut. Okonkwo came after her.

"Ekwefi," she called, "Agbala greets you. Where is my daughter, Ezinma? Agbala wants to see her."

Ekwefi came out from her hut carrying her oil lamp in her left hand. There was a light wind blowing, so she cupped her right hand to shelter the flame. Nwoye's mother, also carrying an oil lamp, emerged from her hut. The children stood in the darkness outside their hut watching the strange event. Okonkwo's youngest wife also came out and joined the others.

"Where does Agbala want to see her?" Ekwefi asked.

"Where else but in his house in the hills and the caves?" replied the priestess.

"I will come with you, too," Ekwefi said firmly.

"*Tufia-a!*"[22] the priestess cursed, her voice cracking like the angry bark of thunder in the dry season. "How dare you, woman, to go before the mighty Agbala of your own accord? Beware, woman, lest he strike you in his anger. Bring me my daughter."

Ekwefi went into her hut and came out again with Ezinma.

"Come, my daughter," said the priestess. "I shall carry you on my back. A baby on its mother's back does not know that the way is long."

Ezinma began to cry. She was used to Chielo calling her "my daughter." But it was a different Chielo she now saw in the yellow half-light.

"Don't cry, my daughter," said the priestess, "lest Agbala be angry with you."

"Don't cry," said Ekwefi, "she will bring you back very soon. I shall give you some fish to eat." She went into the hut again and brought down the smoke-black basket in which she kept her dried fish and other ingredients for cooking soup. She broke a piece in two and gave it to Ezinma, who clung to her.

"Don't be afraid," said Ekwefi, stroking her head, which was shaved in places, leaving a regular pattern of hair. They went outside again. The priestess bent down on one knee and Ezinma climbed on her back, her left palm closed on her fish and her eyes gleaming with tears.

"*Agbala do-o-o-o! Agbala ekeneo-o-o-o!* . . ." Chielo began once again to chant greetings to her god. She turned round sharply and walked through Okonkwo's hut,

---

[22] *"Tufia-a!":* An oath; literally, "spitting out."

bending very low at the eaves. Ezinma was crying loudly now, calling on her mother. The two voices disappeared into the thick darkness.

A strange and sudden weakness descended on Ekwefi as she stood gazing in the direction of the voices like a hen whose only chick has been carried away by a kite. Ezinma's voice soon faded away and only Chielo was heard moving farther and farther into the distance.

"Why do you stand there as though she had been kidnapped?" asked Okonkwo as he went back to his hut.

"She will bring her back soon," Nwoye's mother said.

But Ekwefi did not hear these consolations. She stood for a while, and then, all of a sudden, made up her mind. She hurried through Okonkwo's hut and went outside. "Where are you going?" he asked.

"I am following Chielo," she replied and disappeared in the darkness. Okonkwo cleared his throat, and brought out his snuff-bottle from the goatskin bag by his side.

The priestess's voice was already growing faint in the distance. Ekwefi hurried to the main footpath and turned left in the direction of the voice. Her eyes were useless to her in the darkness. But she picked her way easily on the sandy footpath hedged on either side by branches and damp leaves. She began to run, holding her breasts with her hands to stop them flapping noisily against her body. She hit her left foot against an outcropped root, and terror seized her. It was an ill omen. She ran faster. But Chielo's voice was still a long way away. Had she been running too? How could she go so fast with Ezinma on her back? Although the night was cool, Ekwefi was beginning to feel hot from her running. She continually ran into the luxuriant weeds and creepers that walled in the path. Once she tripped up and fell. Only then did she realize, with a start, that Chielo had stopped her chanting. Her heart beat violently and she stood still. Then Chielo's renewed outburst came from only a few paces ahead. But Ekwefi could not see her. She shut her eyes for a while and opened them again in an effort to see. But it was useless. She could not see beyond her nose.

There were no stars in the sky because there was a rain-cloud. Fireflies went about with their tiny green lamps, which only made the darkness more profound. Between Chielo's outbursts the night was alive with the shrill tremor of forest insects woven into the darkness.

"*Agbala do-o-o-o!* . . . *Agbala ekeneo-o-o-o!* . . ." Ekwefi trudged behind, neither getting too near nor keeping too far back. She thought they must be going towards the sacred cave. Now that she walked slowly she had time to think. What would she do when they got to the cave? She would not dare to enter. She would wait at the mouth, all alone in that fearful place. She thought of all the terrors of the night. She remembered that night, long ago, when she had seen *Ogbu-agali-odu*, one of those evil essences loosed upon the world by the potent "medicines" which the tribe had made in the distant past against its enemies but had now forgotten how to control. Ekwefi had been returning from the stream with her mother on a dark night like this when they saw its glow as it flew in their direction. They had thrown down their water-pots and lain by the roadside expecting the sinister light to descend on them and kill them. That was the only time Ekwefi ever saw *Ogbu-agali-odu*.

But although it had happened so long ago, her blood still ran cold whenever she remembered that night.

The priestess's voice came at longer intervals now, but its vigor was undiminished. The air was cool and damp with dew. Ezinma sneezed. Ekwefi muttered, "Life to you." At the same time the priestess also said, "Life to you, my daughter." Ezinma's voice from the darkness warmed her mother's heart. She trudged slowly along.

And then the priestess screamed. "Somebody is walking behind me!" she said. "Whether you are spirit or man, may Agbala shave your head with a blunt razor! May he twist your neck until you see your heels!"

Ekwefi stood rooted to the spot. One mind said to her: "Woman, go home before Agbala does you harm." But she could not. She stood until Chielo had increased the distance between them and she began to follow again. She had already walked so long that she began to feel a slight numbness in the limbs and in the head. Then it occurred to her that they could not have been heading for the cave. They must have by-passed it long ago; they must be going towards Umuachi, the farthest village in the clan. Chielo's voice now came after long intervals.

It seemed to Ekwefi that the night had become a little lighter. The cloud had lifted and a few stars were out. The moon must be preparing to rise, its sullenness over. When the moon rose late in the night, people said it was refusing food, as a sullen husband refuses his wife's food when they have quarrelled.

"*Agbala do-o-o-o! Umuachi! Agbala ekene unuo-o-o!*" It was just as Ekwefi had thought. The priestess was now saluting the village of Umuachi. It was unbelievable, the distance they had covered. As they emerged into the open village from the narrow forest track the darkness was softened and it became possible to see the vague shape of trees. Ekwefi screwed her eyes up in an effort to see her daughter and the priestess, but whenever she thought she saw their shape it immediately dissolved like a melting lump of darkness. She walked numbly along.

Chielo's voice was now rising continuously, as when she first set out. Ekwefi had a feeling of spacious openness, and she guessed they must be on the village *ilo*, or playground. And she realized too with something like a jerk that Chielo was no longer moving forward. She was, in fact, returning. Ekwefi quickly moved away from her line of retreat. Chielo passed by, and they began to go back the way they had come.

It was a long and weary journey and Ekwefi felt like a sleepwalker most of the way. The moon was definitely rising, and although it had not yet appeared on the sky its light had already melted down the darkness. Ekwefi could now discern the figure of the priestess and her burden. She slowed down her pace so as to increase the distance between them. She was afraid of what might happen if Chielo suddenly turned round and saw her.

She had prayed for the moon to rise. But now she found the half-light of the incipient moon more terrifying than darkness. The world was now peopled with vague, fantastic figures that dissolved under her steady gaze and then formed again in new shapes. At one stage Ekwefi was so afraid that she nearly called out to Chielo for companionship and human sympathy. What she had seen was the shape of a man climbing a palm tree, his head pointing to the earth and his legs skywards. But at that very moment Chielo's voice rose again in her possessed chanting, and Ekwefi recoiled, because there was no humanity there. It was not the same Chielo who sat with her in the market and sometimes bought beancakes for Ezinma, whom she called her daughter. It was a different woman—the priestess of Agbala, the Oracle of the Hills and Caves. Ekwefi trudged along between two fears. The sound of her benumbed steps seemed to come from some other person walking behind her. Her arms were folded across her bare breasts. Dew fell heavily and the air was cold. She could no longer think, not even about the terrors of night. She just jogged along in a half-sleep, only waking to full life when Chielo sang.

At last they took a turning and began to head for the caves. From then on, Chielo never ceased in her chanting. She greeted her god in a multitude of names—the owner of the future, the messenger of earth, the god who cut a man down when his life was sweetest to him. Ekwefi was also awakened and her benumbed fears revived.

The moon was now up and she could see Chielo and Ezinma clearly. How a woman could carry a child of that size so easily and for so long was a miracle. But Ekwefi was not thinking about that. Chielo was not a woman that night.

"Agbala do-o-o-o! Agbala ekeneo-o-o-o! Chi negbu madu ubosi ndu ya nato ya uto daluo-o-o!"[23]

Ekwefi could already see the hills looming in the moonlight. They formed a circular ring with a break at one point through which the foot-track led to the center of the circle.

As soon as the priestess stepped into this ring of hills her voice was not only doubled in strength but was thrown back on all sides. It was indeed the shrine of a great god. Ekwefi picked her way carefully and quietly. She was already beginning to doubt the wisdom of her coming. Nothing would happen to Ezinma, she thought. And if anything happened to her could she stop it? She would not dare to enter the underground caves. Her coming was quite useless, she thought.

As these things went through her mind she did not realize how close they were to the cave mouth. And so when the priestess with Ezinma on her back disappeared through a hole hardly big enough to pass a hen, Ekwefi broke into a run as though to stop them. As she stood gazing at the circular darkness which had swallowed them, tears gushed from her eyes, and she swore within her that if she heard Ezinma cry she would rush into the cave to defend her against all the gods in the world. She would die with her.

Having sworn that oath, she sat down on a stony ledge and waited. Her fear had vanished. She could hear the priestess's voice, all its metal taken out of it by the vast emptiness of the cave. She buried her face in her lap and waited.

She did not know how long she waited. It must have been a very long time. Her back was turned on the footpath that led out of the hills. She must have heard a noise behind her and turned round sharply. A man stood there with a machete in his hand. Ekwefi uttered a scream and sprang to her feet.

---

[23] *"Agbala . . . daluo-o-o!"*: "Agbala wants something! Agbala greets . . . *Chi* who kills a man on the day his life is so pleasant he gives thanks!"

"Don't be foolish," said Okonkwo's voice. "I thought you were going into the shrine with Chielo," he mocked.

Ekwefi did not answer. Tears of gratitude filled her eyes. She knew her daughter was safe.

"Go home and sleep," said Okonkwo. "I shall wait here."

"I shall wait too. It is almost dawn. The first cock has crowed."

As they stood there together, Ekwefi's mind went back to the days when they were young. She had married Anene because Okonkwo was too poor then to marry. Two years after her marriage to Anene she could bear it no longer and she ran away to Okonkwo. It had been early in the morning. The moon was shining. She was going to the stream to fetch water. Okonkwo's house was on the way to the stream. She went in and knocked at his door and he came out. Even in those days he was not a man of many words. He just carried her into his bed and in the darkness began to feel around her waist for the loose end of her cloth.

12

On the following morning the entire neighborhood wore a festive air because Okonkwo's friend, Obierika, was celebrating his daughter's *uri*. It was the day on which her suitor (having already paid the greater part of her bride-price) would bring palm-wine not only to her parents and immediate relatives but to the wide and extensive group of kinsmen called *umunna*. Everybody had been invited — men, women, and children. But it was really a woman's ceremony and the central figures were the bride and her mother.

As soon as day broke, breakfast was hastily eaten and women and children began to gather at Obierika's compound to help the bride's mother in her difficult but happy task of cooking for a whole village.

Okonkwo's family was astir like any other family in the neighborhood. Nwoye's mother and Okonkwo's youngest wife were ready to set out for Obierika's compound with all their children. Nwoye's mother carried a basket of coco-yams, a cake of salt, and smoked fish which she would present to Obierika's wife. Okonkwo's youngest wife, Ojiugo, also had a basket of plantains and coco-yams and a small pot of palm-oil. Their children carried pots of water.

Ekwefi was tired and sleepy from the exhausting experiences of the previous night. It was not very long since they had returned. The priestess, with Ezinma sleeping on her back, had crawled out of the shrine on her belly like a snake. She had not as much as looked at Okonkwo and Ekwefi or shown any surprise at finding them at the mouth of the cave. She looked straight ahead of her and walked back to the village. Okonkwo and his wife followed at a respectful distance. They thought the priestess might be going to her house, but she went to Okonkwo's compound, passed through his *obi* and into Ekwefi's hut and walked into her bedroom. She placed Ezinma carefully on the bed and went away without saying a word to anybody.

Ezinma was still sleeping when everyone else was astir, and Ekwefi asked Nwoye's mother and Ojiugo to explain to Obierika's wife that she would be late. She had got ready her basket of coco-yams and fish, but she must wait for Ezinma to wake.

"You need some sleep yourself," said Nwoye's mother. "You look very tired."

As they spoke Ezinma emerged from the hut, rubbing her eyes and stretching her spare frame. She saw the other children with their water-pots and remembered that they were going to fetch water for Obierika's wife. She went back to the hut and brought her pot.

"Have you slept enough?" asked her mother.

"Yes," she replied. "Let us go."

"Not before you have had your breakfast," said Ekwefi. And she went into her hut to warm the vegetable soup she had cooked last night.

"We shall be going," said Nwoye's mother. "I will tell Obierika's wife that you are coming later." And so they all went to help Obierika's wife — Nwoye's mother with her four children and Ojiugo with her two.

As they trooped through Okonkwo's *obi* he asked: "Who will prepare my afternoon meal?"

"I shall return to do it," said Ojiugo.

Okonkwo was also feeling tired, and sleepy, for although nobody else knew it, he had not slept at all last night. He had felt very anxious but did not show it. When Ekwefi had followed the priestess, he had allowed what he regarded as a reasonable and manly interval to pass and then gone with his machete to the shrine, where he thought they must be. It was only when he had got there that it had occurred to him that the priestess might have chosen to go round the villages first. Okonkwo had returned home and sat waiting. When he thought he had waited long enough he again returned to the shrine. But the Hills and the Caves were as silent as death. It was only on his fourth trip that he had found Ekwefi, and by then he had become gravely worried.

Obierika's compound was as busy as an anthill. Temporary cooking tripods were erected on every available space by bringing together three blocks of sun-dried earth and making a fire in their midst. Cooking pots went up and down the tripods, and foo-foo was pounded in a hundred wooden mortars. Some of the women cooked the yams and the cassava, and others prepared vegetable soup. Young men pounded the foo-foo or split firewood. The children made endless trips to the stream.

Three young men helped Obierika to slaughter the two goats with which the soup was made. They were very fat goats, but the fattest of all was tethered to a peg near the wall of the compound. It was as big as a small cow. Obierika had sent one of his relatives all the way to Umuike to buy that goat. It was the one he would present alive to his in-laws.

"The market of Umuike is a wonderful place," said the young man who had been sent by Obierika to buy the giant goat. "There are so many people on it that if you threw up a grain of sand it would not find a way to fall to earth again."

"It is the result of a great medicine," said Obierika. "The people of Umuike wanted their market to grow and swallow up the markets of their neighbors. So they made a powerful medicine. Every market day, before the first cock-crow, this medicine stands on the market ground in the shape of an old woman with a fan. With this magic fan she beckons to the market all the neighboring clans. She beckons in front of her and behind her, to her right and to her left."

"And so everybody comes," said another man, "honest men and thieves. They can steal your cloth from off your waist in that market."

"Yes," said Obierika. "I warned Nwankwo to keep a sharp eye and a sharp ear. There was once a man who went to sell a goat. He led it on a thick rope which he tied round his wrist. But as he walked through the market he realized that people were pointing at him as they do to a madman. He could not understand it until he looked back and saw that what he led at the end of the tether was not a goat but a heavy log of wood."

"Do you think a thief can do that kind of thing single-handed?" asked Nwankwo.

"No," said Obierika. "They use medicine."

When they had cut the goats' throats and collected the blood in a bowl, they held them over an open fire to burn off the hair, and the smell of burning hair blended with the smell of cooking. Then they washed them and cut them up for the women who prepared the soup.

All this anthill activity was going smoothly when a sudden interruption came. It was a cry in the distance: *Oji odu achu ijiji-o-o! (The one that uses its tail to drive flies away!)* Every woman immediately abandoned whatever she was doing and rushed out in the direction of the cry.

"We cannot all rush out like that, leaving what we are cooking to burn in the fire," shouted Chielo, the priestess. "Three or four of us should stay behind."

"It is true," said another woman. "We will allow three or four women to stay behind."

Five women stayed behind to look after the cooking-pots, and all the rest rushed away to see the cow that had been let loose. When they saw it they drove it back to its owner, who at once paid the heavy fine which the village imposed on anyone whose cow was let loose on his neighbors' crops. When the women had exacted the penalty they checked among themselves to see if any woman had failed to come out when the cry had been raised.

"Where is Mgbogo?" asked one of them.

"She is ill in bed," said Mgbogo's next-door neighbor. "She has *iba*."

"The only other person is Udenkwo," said another woman, "and her child is not twenty-eight days yet."

Those women whom Obierika's wife had not asked to help her with the cooking returned to their homes, and the rest went back, in a body, to Obierika's compound.

"Whose cow was it?" asked the women who had been allowed to stay behind.

"It was my husband's," said Ezelagbo. "One of the young children had opened the gate of the cow-shed."

Early in the afternoon the first two pots of palm-wine arrived from Obierika's in-laws. They were duly presented to the women, who drank a cup or two each, to help them in their cooking. Some of it also went to the bride and her attendant maidens, who were putting the last delicate touches of razor to her coiffure and cam wood on her smooth skin.

When the heat of the sun began to soften, Obierika's son, Maduka, took a long broom and swept the ground in front of his father's *obi*. And as if they had been waiting for that, Obierika's relatives and friends began to arrive, every man with his goatskin bag hung on one shoulder and a rolled goatskin mat under his arm. Some of them were accompanied by their sons bearing carved wooden stools. Okonkwo was one of them. They sat in a half-circle and began to talk of many things. It would not be long before the suitors came.

Okonkwo brought out his snuff-bottle and offered it to Ogbuefi Ezenwa, who sat next to him. Ezenwa took it, tapped it on his kneecap, rubbed his left palm on his body to dry it before tipping a little snuff into it. His actions were deliberate, and he spoke as he performed them:

"I hope our in-laws will bring many pots of wine. Although they come from a village that is known for being closefisted, they ought to know that Akueke is the bride for a king."

"They dare not bring fewer than thirty pots," said Okonkwo. "I shall tell them my mind if they do."

At that moment Obierika's son, Maduka, led out the giant goat from the inner compound, for his father's relatives to see. They all admired it and said that that was the way things should be done. The goat was then led back to the inner compound.

Very soon after, the in-laws began to arrive. Young men and boys in single file, each carrying a pot of wine, came first. Obierika's relatives counted the pots as they came. Twenty, twenty-five. There was a long break, and the hosts looked at each other as if to say, "I told you." Then more pots came. Thirty, thirty-five, forty, forty-five. The hosts nodded in approval and seemed to say, "Now they are behaving like men." Altogether there were fifty pots of wine. After the pot-bearers came Ibe, the suitor, and the elders of his family. They sat in a half-moon, thus completing a circle with their hosts. The pots of wine stood in their midst. Then the bride, her mother, and a half a dozen other women and girls emerged from the inner compound, and went round the circle shaking hands with all. The bride's mother led the way, followed by the bride and the other women. The married women wore their best cloths and the girls wore red and black waist-beads and anklets of brass.

When the women retired, Obierika presented kola nuts to his in-laws. His eldest brother broke the first one. "Life to all of us," he said as he broke it. "And let there be friendship between your family and ours."

The crowd answered: *"Ee-e-e!"*

"We are giving you our daughter today. She will be a good wife to you. She will bear you nine sons like the mother of our town."

"Ee-e-e!"

The oldest man in the camp of the visitors replied: "It will be good for you and it will be good for us."

"Ee-e-e!"

"This is not the first time my people have come to marry your daughter. My mother was one of you."

"Ee-e-e!"

"And this will not be the last, because you understand us and we understand you. You are a great family."

"*Ee-e-e!*"

"Prosperous men and great warriors." He looked in the direction of Okonkwo. "Your daughter will bear us sons like you."

"*Ee-e-e!*"

The kola was eaten and the drinking of palm-wine began. Groups of four or five men sat round with a pot in their midst. As the evening wore on, food was presented to the guests. There were huge bowls of foo-foo and steaming pots of soup. There were also pots of yam pottage. It was a great feast.

As night fell, burning torches were set on wooden tripods and the young men raised a song. The elders sat in a big circle and the singers went round singing each man's praise as they came before him. They had something to say for every man. Some were great farmers, some were orators who spoke for the clan; Okonkwo was the greatest wrestler and warrior alive. When they had gone round the circle they settled down in the center, and girls came from the inner compound to dance. At first the bride was not among them. But when she finally appeared holding a cock in her right hand, a loud cheer rose from the crowd. All the other dancers made way for her. She presented the cock to the musicians and began to dance. Her brass anklets rattled as she danced and her body gleamed with cam wood in the soft yellow light. The musicians with their wood, clay, and metal instruments went from song to song. And they were all gay. They sang the latest song in the village:

> "*If I hold her hand*
>   *She says, 'Don't touch!'*
> *If I hold her foot*
>   *She says, 'Don't touch!'*
> *But when I hold her waist-beads*
>   *She pretends not to know.*"

The night was already far spent when the guests rose to go, taking their bride home to spend seven market weeks with her suitor's family. They sang songs as they went, and on their way they paid short courtesy visits to prominent men like Okonkwo, before they finally left for their village. Okonkwo made a present of two cocks to them.

13

Go-di-di-go-go-di-go. Di-go-go-di-go. It was the *ekwe* talking to the clan. One of the things every man learned was the language of the hollowed-out wooden instrument. Diim! Diim! Diim! boomed the cannon at intervals.

The first cock had not crowed, and Umuofia was still swallowed up in sleep and silence when the *ekwe* began to talk, and the cannon shattered the silence. Men stirred on their bamboo beds and listened anxiously. Somebody was dead. The cannon seemed to rend the sky. Di-go-go-di-go-di-di-go-go floated in the message-laden night air. The faint and distant wailing of women settled like a sediment of sorrow on the earth. Now and again a full-chested lamentation rose above the wailing whenever a man came into the place of death. He raised his voice once or twice in manly sorrow and then sat down with the other men listening to the endless wailing of the women and the esoteric language of the *ekwe.* Now and again the cannon boomed. The wailing of the women would not be heard beyond the village, but the *ekwe* carried the news to all the nine villages and even beyond. It began by naming the clan: *Umuofia obodo dike,* "the land of the brave." *Umuofia obodo dike! Umuofia obodo dike!* It said this over and over again, and as it dwelt on it, anxiety mounted in every heart that heaved on a bamboo bed that night. Then it went nearer and named the village: *"Iguedo of the yellow grinding-stone!"* It was Okonkwo's village. Again and again Iguedo was called and men waited breathlessly in all the nine villages. At last the man was named and people sighed "E-u-u, Ezeudu is dead." A cold shiver ran down Okonkwo's back as he remembered the last time the old man had visited him. "That boy calls you father," he had said. "Bear no hand in his death."

Ezeudu was a great man, and so all the clan was at his funeral. The ancient drums of death beat, guns and cannon were fired, and men dashed about in frenzy, cutting down every tree or animal they saw, jumping over walls and dancing on the roof. It was a warrior's funeral, and from morning till night warriors came and went in their age groups. They all wore smoked raffia skirts and their bodies were painted with chalk and charcoal. Now and again an ancestral spirit or *egwugwu* appeared from the underworld, speaking in a tremulous, unearthly voice and completely covered in raffia. Some of them were very violent, and there had been a mad rush for shelter earlier in the day when one appeared with a sharp machete and was only prevented from doing serious harm by two men who restrained him with the help of a strong rope tied round his waist. Sometimes he turned round and chased those men, and they ran for their lives. But they always returned to the long rope he trailed behind. He sang, in a terrifying voice, that Ekwensu, or Evil Spirit, had entered his eye.

But the most dreaded of all was yet to come. He was always alone and was shaped like a coffin. A sickly odor hung in the air wherever he went, and flies went with him. Even the greatest medicine men took shelter when he was near. Many years ago another *egwugwu* had dared to stand his ground before him and had been transfixed to the spot for two days. This one had only one hand and it carried a basket full of water.

But some of the *egwugwu* were quite harmless. One of them was so old and infirm that he leaned heavily on a stick. He walked unsteadily to the place where the corpse was laid, gazed at it a while, and went away again — to the underworld.

The land of the living was not far removed from the domain of the ancestors. There was coming and going between them, especially at festivals and also when an old man died, because an old man was very close to the ancestors. A man's life from birth to death was a series of transition rites which brought him nearer and nearer to his ancestors.

Ezeudu had been the oldest man in his village, and at his death there were only three men in the whole clan who were older, and four or five others in his own age group. Whenever one of these ancient men appeared in the crowd to dance unsteadily the funeral steps of the tribe, younger men gave way and the tumult subsided.

It was a great funeral, such as befitted a noble warrior. As the evening drew near, the shouting and the firing of guns, the beating of drums, and the brandishing and clanging of machetes increased.

Ezeudu had taken three titles in his life. It was a rare achievement. There were only four titles in the clan, and only one or two men in any generation ever achieved the fourth and highest. When they did, they became the lords of the land. Because he had taken titles, Ezeudu was to be buried after dark with only a glowing brand to light the sacred ceremony.

But before this quiet and final rite, the tumult increased tenfold. Drums beat violently and men leaped up and down in frenzy. Guns were fired on all sides and sparks flew out as machetes clanged together in warriors' salutes. The air was full of dust and the smell of gunpowder. It was then that the one-handed spirit came, carrying a basket full of water. People made way for him on all sides and the noise subsided. Even the smell of gunpowder was swallowed in the sickly smell that now filled the air. He danced a few steps to the funeral drums and then went to see the corpse.

"Ezeudu!" he called in his guttural voice. "If you had been poor in your last life I would have asked you to be rich when you come again. But you were rich. If you had been a coward, I would have asked you to bring courage. But you were a fearless warrior. If you had died young, I would have asked you to get life. But you lived long. So I shall ask you to come again the way you came before. If your death was the death of nature, go in peace. But if a man caused it, do not allow him a moment's rest." He danced a few more steps and went away.

The drums and the dancing began again and reached fever-heat. Darkness was around the corner, and the burial was near. Guns fired the last salute and the cannon rent the sky. And then from the center of the delirious fury came a cry of agony and shouts of horror. It was as if a spell had been cast. All was silent. In the center of the crowd a boy lay in a pool of blood. It was the dead man's sixteen-year-old son, who with his brothers and half-brothers had been dancing the traditional farewell to their father. Okonkwo's gun had exploded and a piece of iron had pierced the boy's heart.

The confusion that followed was without parallel in the tradition of Umuofia. Violent deaths were frequent, but nothing like this had ever happened.

The only course open to Okonkwo was to flee from the clan. It was a crime against the earth goddess to kill a clansman, and a man who committed it must flee from the land. The crime was of two kinds, male and female. Okonkwo had committed the female, because it had been inadvertent. He could return to the clan after seven years.

That night he collected his most valuable belongings into head-loads. His wives wept bitterly and their children wept with them without knowing why. Obierika and half a dozen other friends came to help and to console him. They each made nine or ten trips carrying Okonkwo's yams to store in Obierika's barn. And before the cock crowed Okonkwo and his family were fleeing to his motherland. It was a little village called Mbanta, just beyond the borders of Mbaino.

As soon as the day broke, a large crowd of men from Ezeudu's quarter stormed Okonkwo's compound, dressed in garbs of war. They set fire to his houses, demolished his red walls, killed his animals, and destroyed his barn. It was the justice of the earth goddess, and they were merely her messengers. They had no hatred in their hearts against Okonkwo. His greatest friend, Obierika, was among them. They were merely cleansing the land which Okonkwo had polluted with the blood of a clansman.

Obierika was a man who thought about things. When the will of the goddess had been done, he sat down in his *obi* and mourned his friend's calamity. Why should a man suffer so grievously for an offense he had committed inadvertently? But although he thought for a long time he found no answer. He was merely led into greater complexities. He remembered his wife's twin children, whom he had thrown away. What crime had they committed? The Earth had decreed that they were an offense on the land and must be destroyed. And if the clan did not exact punishment for an offense against the great goddess, her wrath was loosed on all the land and not just on the offender. As the elders said, if one finger brought oil it soiled the others.

PART II

14

Okonkwo was well received by his mother's kinsmen in Mbanta. The old man who received him was his mother's younger brother, who was now the eldest surviving member of that family. His name was Uchendu, and it was he who had received Okonkwo's mother twenty and ten years before when she had been brought home from Umuofia to be buried with her people. Okonkwo was only a boy then and Uchendu still remembered him crying the traditional farewell: "Mother, mother, mother is going."

That was many years ago. Today Okonkwo was not bringing his mother home to be buried with her people. He was taking his family of three wives and their children to seek refuge in his motherland. As soon as Uchendu saw him with his sad and weary company he guessed what had happened, and asked no questions. It was not until the following day that Okonkwo told him the full story. The old man listened silently to the end and then said with some relief: "It is a female *ochu*."[24] And he arranged the requisite rites and sacrifices.

Okonkwo was given a plot of ground on which to build his compound, and two or three pieces of land on which to farm during the coming planting season. With the help of his mother's kinsmen he built himself an *obi* and three huts for his wives. He then installed his personal god and the symbols of his departed fathers. Each of Uchendu's five sons contributed three hundred seed-yams to enable their cousin to plant a farm, for as soon as the first rain came farming would begin.

At last the rain came. It was sudden and tremendous. For two or three moons the sun had been gathering strength till it seemed to breathe a breath of fire on the

---

[24] *ochu:* Manslaughter; because the killing was unintentional, it is a "female" crime.

earth. All the grass had long been scorched brown, and the sands felt like live coals to the feet. Evergreen trees wore a dusty coat of brown. The birds were silenced in the forests, and the world lay panting under the live, vibrating heat. And then came the clap of thunder. It was an angry, metallic, and thirsty clap, unlike the deep and liquid rumbling of the rainy season. A mighty wind arose and filled the air with dust. Palm trees swayed as the wind combed their leaves into flying crests like strange and fantastic coiffure.

When the rain finally came, it was in large, solid drops of frozen water which the people called "the nuts of the water of heaven." They were hard and painful on the body as they fell, yet young people ran about happily picking up the cold nuts and throwing them into their mouths to melt.

The earth quickly came to life and the birds in the forests fluttered around and chirped merrily. A vague scent of life and green vegetation was diffused in the air. As the rain began to fall more soberly and in smaller liquid drops, children sought for shelter, and all were happy, refreshed, and thankful.

Okonkwo and his family worked very hard to plant a new farm. But it was like beginning life anew without the vigor and enthusiasm of youth, like learning to become left-handed in old age. Work no longer had for him the pleasure it used to have, and when there was no work to do he sat in a silent half-sleep.

His life had been ruled by a great passion—to become one of the lords of the clan. That had been his life-spring. And he had all but achieved it. Then everything had been broken. He had been cast out of his clan like a fish onto a dry, sandy beach, panting. Clearly his personal god or *chi* was not made for great things. A man could not rise beyond the destiny of his *chi*. The saying of the elders was not true—that if a man said yea his *chi* also affirmed. Here was a man whose *chi* said nay despite his own affirmation.

The old man, Uchendu, saw clearly that Okonkwo had yielded to despair and he was greatly troubled. He would speak to him after the *isa-ifi*[25] ceremony.

The youngest of Uchendu's five sons, Amikwu, was marrying a new wife. The bride-price had been paid and all but the last ceremony had been performed. Amikwu and his people had taken palm-wine to the bride's kinsmen about two moons before Okonkwo's arrival in Mbanta. And so it was time for the final ceremony of confession.

The daughters of the family were all there, some of them having come a long way from their homes in distant villages. Uchendu's eldest daughter had come from Obodo, nearly half a day's journey away. The daughters of Uchendu's brothers were also there. It was a full gathering of *umuada*,[26] in the same way as they would meet if a death occurred in the family. There were twenty-two of them.

They sat in a big circle on the ground and the bride sat in the center with a hen in her right hand. Uchendu sat by her, holding the ancestral staff of the family. All

---

[25] *isa-ifi:* A ceremony held to determine the fidelity of a wife who has been separated from her husband for a long period of time.

[26] *umuada:* A celebration of the female members of a clan upon their return home.

the other men stood outside the circle, watching. Their wives watched also. It was evening and the sun was setting.

Uchendu's eldest daughter, Njide, asked the questions.

"Remember that if you do not answer truthfully you will suffer or even die at childbirth," she began. "How many men have lain with you since my brother first expressed the desire to marry you?"

"None," she answered simply.

"Answer truthfully," urged the other women.

"None?" asked Njide.

"None," she answered.

"Swear on this staff of my fathers," said Uchendu.

"I swear," said the bride.

Uchendu took the hen from her, slit its throat with a sharp knife, and allowed some of the blood to fall on his ancestral staff.

From that day Amikwu took the young bride to his hut and she became his wife. The daughters of the family did not return to their homes immediately but spent two or three days with their kinsmen.

On the second day Uchendu called together his sons and daughters and his nephew, Okonkwo. The men brought their goatskin mats, with which they sat on the floor, and the women sat on a sisal mat spread on a raised bank of earth. Uchendu pulled gently at his gray beard and gnashed his teeth. Then he began to speak, quietly and deliberately, picking his words with great care:

"It is Okonkwo that I primarily wish to speak to," he began. "But I want all of you to note what I am going to say. I am an old man and you are all children. I know more about the world than any of you. If there is any one among you who thinks he knows more let him speak up." He paused, but no one spoke.

"Why is Okonkwo with us today? This is not his clan. We are only his mother's kinsmen. He does not belong here. He is an exile, condemned for seven years to live in a strange land. And so he is bowed with grief. But there is just one question I would like to ask him. Can you tell me, Okonkwo, why it is that one of the commonest names we give our children is Nneka, or 'Mother is Supreme'? We all know that a man is the head of the family and his wives do his bidding. A child belongs to its father and his family and not to its mother and her family. A man belongs to his fatherland and not to his motherland. And yet we say Nneka—'Mother is Supreme.' Why is that?"

There was silence. "I want Okonkwo to answer me," said Uchendu.

"I do not know the answer," Okonkwo replied.

"You do not know the answer? So you see that you are a child. You have many wives and many children—more children than I have. You are a great man in your clan. But you are still a child, *my* child. Listen to me and I shall tell you. But there is one more question I shall ask you. Why is it that when a woman dies she is taken home to be buried with her own kinsmen? She is not buried with her husband's kinsmen. Why is that? Your mother was brought home to me and buried with my people. Why was that?"

Okonkwo shook his head.

"He does not know that either," said Uchendu, "and yet he is full of sorrow because he has come to live in his motherland for a few years." He laughed a mirthless laughter, and turned to his sons and daughters. "What about you? Can you answer my question?"

They all shook their heads.

"Then listen to me," he said and cleared his throat. "It's true that a child belongs to its father. But when a father beats his child, it seeks sympathy in its mother's hut. A man belongs to his fatherland when things are good and life is sweet. But when there is sorrow and bitterness he finds refuge in his motherland. Your mother is there to protect you. She is buried there. And that is why we say that mother is supreme. Is it right that you, Okonkwo, should bring to your mother a heavy face and refuse to be comforted? Be careful or you may displease the dead. Your duty is to comfort your wives and children and take them back to your fatherland after seven years. But if you allow sorrow to weigh you down and kill you, they will all die in exile." He paused for a long while. "These are now your kinsmen." He waved at his sons and daughters. "You think you are the greatest sufferer in the world? Do you know that men are sometimes banished for life? Do you know that men sometimes lose all their yams and even their children? I had six wives once. I have none now except that young girl who knows not her right from her left. Do you know how many children I have buried—children I begot in my youth and strength? Twenty-two. I did not hang myself, and I am still alive. If you think you are the greatest sufferer in the world ask my daughter, Akueni, how many twins she has borne and thrown away. Have you not heard the song they sing when a woman dies?

"'*For whom is it well, for whom is it well?*
There is no one for whom it is well.'

"I have no more to say to you."

15

It was in the second year of Okonkwo's exile that his friend, Obierika, came to visit him. He brought with him two young men, each of them carrying a heavy bag on his head. Okonkwo helped them put down their loads. It was clear that the bags were full of cowries.

Okonkwo was very happy to receive his friend. His wives and children were very happy too, and so were his cousins and their wives when he sent for them and told them who his guest was.

"You must take him to salute our father," said one of the cousins.

"Yes," replied Okonkwo. "We are going directly." But before they went he whispered something to his first wife. She nodded, and soon the children were chasing one of their cocks.

Uchendu had been told by one of his grandchildren that three strangers had come to Okonkwo's house. He was therefore waiting to receive them. He held out his hands to them when they came into his *obi*, and after they had shaken hands he asked Okonkwo who they were.

"This is Obierika, my great friend. I have already spoken to you about him."

"Yes," said the old man, turning to Obierika. "My son has told me about you, and I am happy you have come to see us. I knew your father, Iweka. He was a great man. He had many friends here and came to see them quite often. Those were good days when a man had friends in distant clans. Your generation does not know that. You stay at home, afraid of your next-door neighbor. Even a man's motherland is strange to him nowadays." He looked at Okonkwo. "I am an old man and I like to talk. That is all I am good for now." He got up painfully, went into an inner room, and came back with a kola nut.

"Who are the young men with you?" he asked as he sat down again on his goatskin. Okonkwo told him.

"Ah," he said. "Welcome, my sons." He presented the kola nut to them, and when they had seen it and thanked him, he broke it and they ate.

"Go into that room," he said to Okonkwo, pointing with his finger. "You will find a pot of wine there."

Okonkwo brought the wine and they began to drink. It was a day old, and very strong.

"Yes," said Uchendu after a long silence. "People traveled more in those days. There is not a single clan in these parts that I do not know very well. Aninta, Umuazu, Ikeocha, Elumelu, Abame — I know them all."

"Have you heard," asked Obierika, "that Abame is no more?"

"How is that?" asked Uchendu and Okonkwo together.

"Abame has been wiped out," said Obierika. "It is a strange and terrible story. If I had not seen the few survivors with my own eyes and heard their story with my own ears, I would not have believed. Was it not on an Eke day that they fled into Umuofia?" he asked his two companions, and they nodded their heads.

"Three moons ago," said Obierika, "on an Eke market day a little band of fugitives came into our town. Most of them were sons of our land whose mothers had been buried with us. But there were some too who came because they had friends in our town, and others who could think of nowhere else open to escape. And so they fled into Umuofia with a woeful story." He drank his palm-wine, and Okonkwo filled his horn again. He continued:

"During the last planting season a white man had appeared in their clan."

"An albino," suggested Okonkwo.

"He was not an albino. He was quite different." He sipped his wine. "And he was riding an iron horse. The first people who saw him ran away, but he stood beckoning to them. In the end the fearless ones went near and even touched him. The elders consulted their Oracle and it told them that the strange man would break their clan and spread destruction among them." Obierika again drank a little of his wine. "And so they killed the white man and tied his iron horse to their sacred tree because it looked as if it would run away to call the man's friends. I forgot to tell you another thing which the Oracle said. It said that other white men were on their way. They were locusts, it said, and that first man was their harbinger sent to explore the terrain. And so they killed him."

"What did the white man say before they killed him?" asked Uchendu.

"He said nothing," answered one of Obierika's companions.

"He said something, only they did not understand him," said Obierika. "He seemed to speak through his nose."

"One of the men told me," said Obierika's other companion, "that he repeated over and over again a word that resembled Mbaino. Perhaps he had been going to Mbaino and had lost his way."

"Anyway," resumed Obierika, "they killed him and tied up his iron horse. This was before the planting season began. For a long time nothing happened. The rains had come and yams had been sown. The iron horse was still tied to the sacred silk-cotton tree. And then one morning three white men led by a band of ordinary men like us came to the clan. They saw the iron horse and went away again. Most of the men and women of Abame had gone to their farms. Only a few of them saw these white men and their followers. For many market weeks nothing else happened. They have a big market in Abame on every other Afo day and, as you know, the whole clan gathers there. That was the day it happened. The three white men and a very large number of other men surrounded the market. They must have used a powerful medicine to make themselves invisible until the market was full. And they began to shoot. Everybody was killed, except the old and the sick who were at home and a handful of men and women whose *chi* were wide awake and brought them out of that market." He paused.

"Their clan is now completely empty. Even the sacred fish in their mysterious lake have fled and the lake has turned the color of blood. A great evil has come upon their land as the Oracle had warned."

There was a long silence. Uchendu ground his teeth together audibly. Then he burst out:

"Never kill a man who says nothing. Those men of Abame were fools. What did they know about the man?" He ground his teeth again and told a story to illustrate his point. "Mother Kite once sent her daughter to bring food. She went, and brought back a duckling. 'You have done very well,' said Mother Kite to her daughter, 'but tell me, what did the mother of this duckling say when you swooped and carried its child away?' 'It said nothing,' replied the young kite. 'It just walked away.' 'You must return the duckling,' said Mother Kite. 'There is something ominous behind the silence.' And so Daughter Kite returned the duckling and took a chick instead. 'What did the mother of this chick do?' asked the old kite. 'It cried and raved and cursed me,' said the young kite. 'Then we can eat the chick,' said her mother. 'There is nothing to fear from someone who shouts.' Those men of Abame were fools."

"They were fools," said Okonkwo after a pause. "They had been warned that danger was ahead. They should have armed themselves with their guns and their machetes even when they went to market."

"They have paid for their foolishness," said Obierika. "But I am greatly afraid. We have heard stories about white men who made the powerful guns and the strong drinks and took slaves away across the seas, but no one thought the stories were true."

"There is no story that is not true," said Uchendu. "The world has no end, and what is good among one people is an abomination with others. We have albinos among us. Do you not think that they came to our clan by mistake, that they have strayed from their way to a land where everybody is like them?"

Okonkwo's first wife soon finished her cooking and set before their guests a big meal of pounded yams and bitter-leaf soup. Okonkwo's son, Nwoye, brought in a pot of sweet wine tapped from the raffia palm.

"You are a big man now," Obierika said to Nwoye. "Your friend Anene asked me to greet you."

"Is he well?" asked Nwoye.

"We are all well," said Obierika.

Ezinma brought them a bowl of water with which to wash their hands. After that they began to eat and to drink the wine.

"When did you set out from home?" asked Okonkwo.

"We had meant to set out from my house before cock-crow," said Obierika. "But Nweke did not appear until it was quite light. Never make an early morning appointment with a man who has just married a new wife." They all laughed.

"Has Nweke married a wife?" asked Okonkwo.

"He has married Okadigbo's second daughter," said Obierika.

"That is very good," said Okonkwo. "I do not blame you for not hearing the cock crow."

When they had eaten, Obierika pointed at the two heavy bags.

"That is the money from your yams," he said. "I sold the big ones as soon as you left. Later on I sold some of the seed-yams and gave out others to sharecroppers. I shall do that every year until you return. But I thought you would need the money now and so I brought it. Who knows what may happen tomorrow? Perhaps green men will come to our clan and shoot us."

"God will not permit it," said Okonkwo. "I do not know how to thank you."

"I can tell you," said Obierika. "Kill one of your sons for me."

"That will not be enough," said Okonkwo.

"Then kill yourself," said Obierika.

"Forgive me," said Okonkwo, smiling. "I shall not talk about thanking you any more."

16

When nearly two years later Obierika paid another visit to his friend in exile the circumstances were less happy. The missionaries had come to Umuofia. They had built their church there, won a handful of converts, and were already sending evangelists to the surrounding towns and villages. That was a source of great sorrow to the leaders of the clan; but many of them believed that the strange faith and the white man's god would not last. None of his converts was a man whose word was heeded in the assembly of the people. None of them was a man of title. They were mostly the kind of people that were called *efulefu*, worthless, empty men. The imagery of an *efulefu* in the language of the clan was a man who sold his machete and wore the sheath to battle. Chielo, the priestess of Agbala, called the converts the excrement of the clan, and the new faith was a mad dog that had come to eat it up.

What moved Obierika to visit Okonkwo was the sudden appearance of the latter's son, Nwoye, among the missionaries in Umuofia.

"What are you doing here?" Obierika had asked when after many difficulties the missionaries had allowed him to speak to the boy.

"I am one of them," replied Nwoye.

"How is your father?" Obierika asked, not knowing what else to say.

"I don't know. He is not my father," said Nwoye, unhappily.

And so Obierika went to Mbanta to see his friend. And he found that Okonkwo did not wish to speak about Nwoye. It was only from Nwoye's mother that he heard scraps of the story.

The arrival of the missionaries had caused a considerable stir in the village of Mbanta. There were six of them and one was a white man. Every man and woman came out to see the white man. Stories about these strange men had grown since one of them had been killed in Abame and his iron horse tied to the sacred silk-cotton tree. And so everybody came to see the white man. It was the time of the year when everybody was at home. The harvest was over.

When they had all gathered, the white man began to speak to them. He spoke through an interpreter who was an Ibo man, though his dialect was different and harsh to the ears of Mbanta. Many people laughed at his dialect and the way he used words strangely. Instead of saying "myself" he always said "my buttocks." But he was a man of commanding presence and the clansmen listened to him. He said he was one of them, as they could see from his color and his language. The other four black men were also their brothers, although one of them did not speak Ibo. The white man was also their brother because they were all sons of God. And he told them about this new God, the Creator of all the world and all the men and women. He told them that they worshipped false gods, gods of wood and stone. A deep murmur went through the crowd when he said this. He told them that the true God lived on high and that all men when they died went before Him for judgment. Evil men and all the heathen who in their blindness bowed to wood and stone were thrown into a fire that burned like palm-oil. But good men who worshipped the true God lived forever in His happy kingdom. "We have been sent by this great God to ask you to leave your wicked ways and false gods and turn to Him so that you may be saved when you die," he said.

"Your buttocks understand our language," said someone light-heartedly and the crowd laughed.

"What did he say?" the white man asked his interpreter. But before he could answer, another man asked a question: "Where is the white man's horse?" he asked. The Ibo evangelists consulted among themselves and decided that the man probably meant bicycle. They told the white man and he smiled benevolently.

"Tell them," he said, "that I shall bring many iron horses when we have settled down among them. Some of them will even ride the iron horse themselves." This was interpreted to them but very few of them heard. They were talking excitedly among themselves because the white man had said he was going to live among them. They had not thought about that.

At this point an old man said he had a question. "Which is this god of yours," he asked, "the goddess of the earth, the god of the sky, Amadiora or the thunderbolt, or what?"

The interpreter spoke to the white man and he immediately gave his answer. "All the gods you have named are not gods at all. They are gods of deceit who tell you to kill your fellows and destroy innocent children. There is only one true God and He has the earth, the sky, you and me and all of us."

"If we leave our gods and follow your god," asked another man, "who will protect us from the anger of our neglected gods and ancestors?"

"Your gods are not alive and cannot do you any harm," replied the white man. "They are pieces of wood and stone."

When this was interpreted to the men of Mbanta they broke into derisive laughter. These men must be mad, they said to themselves. How else could they say that Ani and Amadiora were harmless? And Idemili and Ogwugwu too? And some of them began to go away.

Then the missionaries burst into song. It was one of those gay and rollicking tunes of evangelism which had the power of plucking at silent and dusty chords in the heart of an Ibo man. The interpreter explained each verse to the audience, some of whom now stood enthralled. It was a story of brothers who lived in darkness and in fear, ignorant of the love of God. It told of one sheep out on the hills, away from the gates of God and from the tender shepherd's care.

After the singing the interpreter spoke about the Son of God whose name was Jesu Kristi. Okonkwo, who only stayed in the hope that it might come to chasing the men out of the village or whipping them, now said:

"You told us with your own mouth that there was only one god. Now you talk about his son. He must have a wife, then." The crowd agreed.

"I did not say He had a wife," said the interpreter, somewhat lamely.

"Your buttocks said he had a son," said the joker. "So he must have a wife and all of them must have buttocks."

The missionary ignored him and went on to talk about the Holy Trinity. At the end of it Okonkwo was fully convinced that the man was mad. He shrugged his shoulders and went away to tap his afternoon palm-wine.

But there was a young lad who had been captivated. His name was Nwoye, Okonkwo's first son. It was not the mad logic of the Trinity that captivated him. He did not understand it. It was the poetry of the new religion, something felt in the marrow. The hymn about brothers who sat in darkness and in fear seemed to answer a vague and persistent question that haunted his young soul—the question of the twins crying in the bush and the question of Ikemefuna who was killed. He felt a relief within as the hymn poured into his parched soul. The words of the hymn were like the drops of frozen rain melting on the dry palate of the panting earth. Nwoye's callow mind was greatly puzzled.

17

The missionaries spent their first four or five nights in the marketplace, and went into the village in the morning to preach the gospel. They asked who the king of the village was, but the villagers told them that there was no king. "We have men of high title and the chief priests and the elders," they said.

It was not very easy getting the men of high title and the elders together after the excitement of the first day. But the missionaries persevered, and in the end they were received by the rulers of Mbanta. They asked for a plot of land to build their church.

Every clan and village had its "evil forest." In it were buried all those who died of the really evil diseases, like leprosy and smallpox. It was also the dumping ground for the potent fetishes of great medicine men when they died. An "evil forest" was, therefore, alive with sinister forces and powers of darkness. It was such a forest that the rulers of Mbanta gave to the missionaries. They did not really want them in their clan, and so they made them that offer which nobody in his right senses would accept.

"They want a piece of land to build their shrine," said Uchendu to his peers when they consulted among themselves. "We shall give them a piece of land." He paused, and there was a murmur of surprise and disagreement. "Let us give them a portion of the Evil Forest. They boast about victory over death. Let us give them a real battlefield in which to show their victory." They laughed and agreed, and sent for the missionaries, whom they had asked to leave them for a while so that they might "whisper together." They offered them as much of the Evil Forest as they cared to take. And to their greatest amazement the missionaries thanked them and burst into song.

"They do not understand," said some of the elders. "But they will understand when they go to their plot of land tomorrow morning." And they dispersed.

The next morning the crazy men actually began to clear a part of the forest and to build their house. The inhabitants of Mbanta expected them all to be dead within four days. The first day passed and the second and third and fourth, and none of them died. Everyone was puzzled. And then it became known that the white man's fetish had unbelievable power. It was said that he wore glasses on his eyes so that he could see and talk to evil spirits. Not long after, he won his first three converts.

Although Nwoye had been attracted to the new faith from the very first day, he kept it secret. He dared not go too near the missionaries for fear of his father. But whenever they came to preach in the open marketplace or the village playground, Nwoye was there. And he was already beginning to know some of the simple stories they told.

"We have now built a church," said Mr. Kiaga, the interpreter, who was now in charge of the infant congregation. The white man had gone back to Umuofia, where he built his headquarters and from where he paid regular visits to Mr. Kiaga's congregation at Mbanta.

"We have now built a church," said Mr. Kiaga, "and we want you all to come in every seventh day to worship the true God."

On the following Sunday, Nwoye passed and re-passed the little red-earth and thatch building without summoning enough courage to enter. He heard the voice of singing and although it came from a handful of men it was loud and confident. Their church stood on a circular clearing that looked like the open mouth of the Evil Forest. Was it waiting to snap its teeth together? After passing and re-passing by the church, Nwoye returned home.

It was well known among the people of Mbanta that their gods and ancestors were sometimes long-suffering and would deliberately allow a man to go on defying them. But even in such cases they set their limit at seven market weeks or twenty-eight days. Beyond that limit no man was suffered to go. And so excitement mounted in the village as the seventh week approached since the impudent missionaries built their church in the Evil Forest. The villagers were so certain about the doom that awaited these men that one or two converts thought it wise to suspend their allegiance to the new faith.

At last the day came by which all the missionaries should have died. But they were still alive, building a new red-earth and thatch house for their teacher, Mr. Kiaga. That week they won a handful more converts. And for the first time they had a woman. Her name was Nneka, the wife of Amadi, who was a prosperous farmer. She was very heavy with child.

Nneka had had four previous pregnancies and childbirths. But each time she had borne twins, and they had been immediately thrown away. Her husband and his family were already becoming highly critical of such a woman and were not unduly perturbed when they found she had fled to join the Christians. It was a good riddance.

One morning Okonkwo's cousin, Amikwu, was passing by the church on his way from the neighboring village, when he saw Nwoye among the Christians. He was greatly surprised, and when he got home he went straight to Okonkwo's hut and told him what he had seen. The women began to talk excitedly, but Okonkwo sat unmoved.

It was late afternoon before Nwoye returned. He went into the *obi* and saluted his father, but he did not answer. Nwoye turned round to walk into the inner compound when his father, suddenly overcome with fury, sprang to his feet and gripped him by the neck.

"Where have you been?" he stammered.

Nwoye struggled to free himself from the choking grip.

"Answer me," roared Okonkwo, "before I kill you!" He seized a heavy stick that lay on the dwarf wall and hit him two or three savage blows.

"Answer me!" he roared again. Nwoye stood looking at him and did not say a word. The women were screaming outside, afraid to go in.

"Leave that boy at once!" said a voice in the outer compound. It was Okonkwo's uncle, Uchendu. "Are you mad?"

Okonkwo did not answer. But he left hold of Nwoye, who walked away and never returned.

He went back to the church and told Mr. Kiaga that he had decided to go to Umuofia where the white missionary had set up a school to teach young Christians to read and write.

Mr. Kiaga's joy was very great. "Blessed is he who forsakes his father and his mother for my sake," he intoned. "Those that hear my words are my father and my mother."

Nwoye did not fully understand. But he was happy to leave his father. He would return later to his mother and his brothers and sisters and convert them to the new faith.

As Okonkwo sat in his hut that night, gazing into a log fire, he thought over the matter. A sudden fury rose within him and he felt a strong desire to take up his machete, go to the church, and wipe out the entire vile and miscreant gang. But on further thought he told himself that Nwoye was not worth fighting for. Why, he cried in his heart, should he, Okonkwo, of all people, be cursed with such a son? He saw clearly in it the finger of his personal god or *chi*. For how else could he explain his great misfortune and exile and now his despicable son's behavior? Now that he had time to think of it, his son's crime stood out in its stark enormity. To abandon the gods of one's father and go about with a lot of effeminate men clucking like old hens was the very depth of abomination. Suppose when he died all his male children decided to follow Nwoye's steps and abandon their ancestors? Okonkwo felt a cold shudder run through him at the terrible prospects, like the prospect of annihilation. He saw himself and his fathers crowding round their ancestral shrine waiting in vain for worship and sacrifice and finding nothing but ashes of bygone days, and his children the while praying to the white man's god. If such a thing were ever to happen, he, Okonkwo, would wipe them off the face of the earth.

Okonkwo was popularly called the "Roaring Flame." As he looked into the log fire he recalled the name. He was a flaming fire. How then could he have begotten a son like Nwoye, degenerate and effeminate? Perhaps he was not his son. No! he could not be. His wife had played him false. He would teach her! But Nwoye resembled his grandfather, Unoka, who was Okonkwo's father. He pushed the thought out of his mind. He, Okonkwo, was called a flaming fire. How could he have begotten a woman for a son? At Nwoye's age Okonkwo had already become famous throughout Umuofia for his wrestling and his fearlessness.

He sighed heavily, and as if in sympathy the smoldering log also sighed. And immediately Okonkwo's eyes were opened and he saw the whole matter clearly. Living fire begets cold, impotent ash. He sighed again, deeply.

18

The young church in Mbanta had a few crises early in its life. At first the clan had assumed that it would not survive. But it had gone on living and gradually becoming stronger. The clan was worried, but not overmuch. If a gang of *efulefu* decided to live in the Evil Forest it was their own affair. When one came to think of it, the Evil Forest was a fit home for such undesirable people. It was true they were rescuing twins from the bush, but they never brought them into the village. As far as the villagers were concerned, the twins still remained where they had been thrown away. Surely the earth goddess would not visit the sins of the missionaries on the innocent villagers?

But on one occasion the missionaries had tried to overstep the bounds. Three converts had gone into the village and boasted openly that all the gods were dead and impotent and that they were prepared to defy them by burning all their shrines.

"Go and burn your mothers' genitals," said one of the priests. The men were seized and beaten until they streamed with blood. After that nothing happened for a long time between the church and the clan.

But stories were already gaining ground that the white man had not only brought a religion but also a government. It was said that they had built a place of judgment in Umuofia to protect the followers of their religion. It was even said that they had hanged one man who killed a missionary.

Although such stories were now often told they looked like fairy-tales in Mbanta and did not as yet affect the relationship between the new church and the clan. There was no question of killing a missionary here, for Mr. Kiaga, despite his madness, was quite harmless. As for his converts, no one could kill them without having to flee from the clan, for in spite of their worthlessness they still belonged to the clan. And so nobody gave serious thought to the stories about the white man's government or the consequences of killing the Christians. If they became more troublesome than they already were they would simply be driven out of the clan.

And the little church was at that moment too deeply absorbed in its own troubles to annoy the clan. It all began over the question of admitting outcasts.

These outcasts, or *osu*, seeing that the new religion welcomed twins and such abominations, thought that it was possible that they would also be received. And so one Sunday two of them went into the church. There was an immediate stir; but so great was the work the new religion had done among the converts that they did not immediately leave the church when the outcasts came in. Those who found themselves nearest to them merely moved to another seat. It was a miracle. But it only lasted till the end of the service. The whole church raised a protest and was about to drive these people out, when Mr. Kiaga stopped them and began to explain.

"Before God," he said, "there is no slave or free. We are all children of God and we must receive these our brothers."

"You do not understand," said one of the converts. "What will the heathen say of us when they hear that we receive *osu* into our midst? They will laugh."

"Let them laugh," said Mr. Kiaga. "God will laugh at them on the judgment day. Why do the nations rage and the peoples imagine a vain thing? He that sitteth in the heavens shall laugh. The Lord shall have them in derision."

"You do not understand," the convert maintained. "You are our teacher, and you can teach us the things of the new faith. But this is a matter which we know." And he told him what an *osu* was.

He was a person dedicated to a god, a thing set apart — a taboo forever, and his children after him. He could neither marry nor be married by the free-born. He was in fact an outcast, living in a special area of the village, close to the Great Shrine. Wherever he went he carried with him the mark of his forbidden caste — long, tangled, and dirty hair. A razor was taboo to him. An *osu* could not attend an assembly of the free-born, and they, in turn, could not shelter under his roof. He could not take any of the four titles of the clan, and when he died he was buried by his kind in the Evil Forest. How could such a man be a follower of Christ?

"He needs Christ more than you and I," said Mr. Kiaga.

"Then I shall go back to the clan," said the convert. And he went. Mr. Kiaga stood firm, and it was his firmness that saved the young church. The wavering converts drew inspiration and confidence from his unshakable faith. He ordered the outcasts to shave off their long, tangled hair. At first they were afraid they might die.

"Unless you shave off the mark of your heathen belief I will not admit you into the church," said Mr. Kiaga. "You fear that you will die. Why should that be? How are you different from other men who shave their hair? The same God created you and them. But they have cast you out like lepers. It is against the will of God, who has promised everlasting life to all who believe in His holy name. The heathen say you will die if you do this or that, and you are afraid. They also said I would die if I built my church on this ground. Am I dead? They said I would die if I took care of twins. I am still alive. The heathen speak nothing but falsehood. Only the word of our God is true."

The two outcasts shaved off their hair, and soon they were the strongest adherents of the new faith. And what was more, nearly all the *osu* in Mbanta followed their example. It was in fact one of them who in his zeal brought the church into serious conflict with the clan a year later by killing the sacred python, the emanation of the god of water.

The royal python was the most revered animal in Mbanta and all the surrounding clans. It was addressed as "Our Father," and was allowed to go wherever it chose, even into people's beds. It ate rats in the house and sometimes swallowed hens' eggs. If a clansman killed a royal python accidentally, he made sacrifices of atonement and performed an expensive burial ceremony such as was done for a great man. No punishment was prescribed for a man who killed the python knowingly. Nobody thought that such a thing could ever happen.

Perhaps it never did happen. That was the way the clan at first looked at it. No one had actually seen the man do it. The story had arisen among the Christians themselves.

But, all the same, the rulers and elders of Mbanta assembled to decide on their action. Many of them spoke at great length and in fury. The spirit of wars was upon them. Okonkwo, who had begun to play a part in the affairs of his motherland, said that until the abominable gang was chased out of the village with whips there would be no peace.

But there were many others who saw the situation differently, and it was their counsel that prevailed in the end.

"It is not our custom to fight for our gods," said one of them. "Let us not presume to do so now. If a man kills the sacred python in the secrecy of his hut, the matter lies between him and the god. We did not see it. If we put ourselves between the god and his victim we may receive blows intended for the offender. When a man blasphemes, what do we do? Do we go and stop his mouth? No. We put our fingers into our ears to stop us hearing. That is a wise action."

"Let us not reason like cowards," said Okonkwo. "If a man comes into my hut and defecates on the floor, what do I do? Do I shut my eyes? No! I take a stick and break his head. That is what a man does. These people are daily pouring filth over us, and Okeke says we should pretend not to see." Okonkwo made a sound full of disgust. This was a womanly clan, he thought. Such a thing could never happen in his fatherland, Umuofia.

"Okonkwo has spoken the truth," said another man. "We should do something. But let us ostracize these men. We would then not be held accountable for their abominations."

Everybody in the assembly spoke, and in the end it was decided to ostracize the Christians. Okonkwo ground his teeth in disgust.

That night a bell-man went through the length and breadth of Mbanta proclaiming that the adherents of the new faith were thenceforth excluded from the life and privileges of the clan.

The Christians had grown in number and were now a small community of men, women, and children, self-assured and confident. Mr. Brown, the white missionary, paid regular visits to them. "When I think that it is only eighteen months since the Seed was first sown among you," he said, "I marvel at what the Lord hath wrought."

It was Wednesday in Holy Week and Mr. Kiaga had asked the women to bring red earth and white chalk and water to scrub the church for Easter; and the women had formed themselves into three groups for this purpose. They set out early that morning, some of them with their water-pots to the stream, another group with hoes and baskets to the village red-earth pit, and the others to the chalk quarry.

Mr. Kiaga was praying in the church when he heard the women talking excitedly. He rounded off his prayer and went to see what it was all about. The women had come to the church with empty water-pots. They said that some young men had chased them away from the stream with whips. Soon after, the women who had gone for red earth returned with empty baskets. Some of them had been heavily whipped. The chalk women also returned to tell a similar story.

"What does it all mean?" asked Mr. Kiaga, who was greatly perplexed.

"The village has outlawed us," said one of the women. "The bell-man announced it last night. But it is not our custom to debar anyone from the stream or the quarry."

Another woman said, "They want to ruin us. They will not allow us into the markets. They have said so."

Mr. Kiaga was going to send into the village for his men-converts when he saw them coming on their own. Of course they had all heard the bell-man, but they had never in all their lives heard of women being debarred from the stream.

"Come along," they said to the women. "We will go with you to meet those cowards." Some of them had big sticks and some even machetes.

But Mr. Kiaga restrained them. He wanted first to know why they had been outlawed.

"They say that Okoli killed the sacred python," said one man.

"It is false," said another. "Okoli told me himself that it was false."

Okoli was not there to answer. He had fallen ill on the previous night. Before the day was over he was dead. His death showed that the gods were still able to fight their own battles. The clan saw no reason then for molesting the Christians.

19

The last big rains of the year were falling. It was the time for treading red earth with which to build walls. It was not done earlier because the rains were too heavy and would have washed away the heap of trodden earth; and it could not be done later because harvesting would soon set in, and after that the dry season.

It was going to be Okonkwo's last harvest in Mbanta. The seven wasted and weary years were at last dragging to a close. Although he had prospered in his motherland Okonkwo knew that he would have prospered even more in Umuofia, in the land of his fathers where men were bold and warlike. In these seven years he would have climbed to the utmost heights. And so he regretted every day of his exile. His mother's kinsmen had been very kind to him, and he was grateful. But that did not alter the facts. He had called the first child born to him in exile Nneka — "Mother is Supreme" — out of politeness to his mother's kinsmen. But two years later when a son was born he called him Nwofia — "Begotten in the Wilderness."

As soon as he entered his last year in exile Okonkwo sent money to Obierika to build him two huts in his old compound where he and his family would live until he built more huts and the outside wall of his compound. He could not ask another man to build his own *obi* for him, nor the walls of his compound. Those things a man built for himself or inherited from his father.

As the last heavy rains of the year began to fall, Obierika sent word that the two huts had been built and Okonkwo began to prepare for his return, after the rains. He would have liked to return earlier and build his compound that year before the rains stopped, but in doing so he would have taken something from the full penalty of seven years. And that could not be. So he waited impatiently for the dry season to come.

It came slowly. The rain became lighter and lighter until it fell in slanting showers. Sometimes the sun shone through the rain and a light breeze blew. It was a gay and airy kind of rain. The rainbow began to appear, and sometimes two rainbows, like a mother and her daughter, the one young and beautiful, and the other an old and faint shadow. The rainbow was called the python of the sky.

Okonkwo called his three wives and told them to get things together for a great feast. "I must thank my mother's kinsmen before I go," he said.

Ekwefi still had some cassava left on her farm from the previous year. Neither of the other wives had. It was not that they had been lazy, but that they had many children to feed. It was therefore understood that Ekwefi would provide cassava for the feast. Nwoye's mother and Ojiugo would provide the other things like smoked fish, palm-oil, and pepper for the soup. Okonkwo would take care of meat and yams.

Ekwefi rose early on the following morning and went to her farm with her daughter, Ezinma, and Ojiugo's daughter, Obiageli, to harvest cassava tubers. Each of them carried a long cane basket, a machete for cutting down the soft cassava stem, and a little hoe for digging out the tuber. Fortunately, a light rain had fallen during the night and the soil would not be very hard.

"It will not take us long to harvest as much as we like," said Ekwefi.

"But the leaves will be wet," said Ezinma. Her basket was balanced on her head, and her arms folded across her breasts. She felt cold. "I dislike cold water dropping on my back. We should have waited for the sun to rise and dry the leaves."

Obiageli called her "Salt" because she said that she disliked water. "Are you afraid you may dissolve?"

The harvesting was easy, as Ekwefi had said. Ezinma shook every tree violently with a long stick before she bent down to cut the stem and dig out the tuber. Sometimes it was not necessary to dig. They just pulled the stump, and earth rose, roots snapped below, and the tuber was pulled out.

When they had harvested a sizable heap they carried it down in two trips to the stream, where every woman had a shallow well for fermenting her cassava.

"It should be ready in four days or even three," said Obiageli. "They are young tubers."

"They are not all that young," said Ekwefi. "I planted the farm nearly two years ago. It is a poor soil and that is why the tubers are so small."

Okonkwo never did things by halves. When his wife Ekwefi protested that two goats were sufficient for the feast he told her that it was not her affair.

"I am calling a feast because I have the wherewithal. I cannot live on the bank of a river and wash my hands with spittle. My mother's people have been good to me and I must show my gratitude."

And so three goats were slaughtered and a number of fowls. It was like a wedding feast. There was foo-foo and yam pottage, egusi soup and bitter-leaf soup and pots and pots of palm-wine.

All the *umunna*[27] were invited to the feast, all the descendants of Okolo, who had lived about two hundred years before. The oldest member of this extensive family was Okonkwo's uncle, Uchendu. The kola nut was given him to break, and he prayed to the ancestors. He asked them for health and children. "We do not ask for wealth because he that has health and children will also have wealth. We do not pray to have more money but to have more kinsmen. We are better than animals because we have kinsmen. An animal rubs its itching flank against a tree, a man asks his kinsman to scratch him." He prayed especially for Okonkwo and his family. He then broke the kola nut and threw one of the lobes on the ground for the ancestors.

As the broken kola nuts were passed round, Okonkwo's wives and children and those who came to help them with the cooking began to bring out the food. His sons brought out the pots of palm-wine. There was so much food and drink that many kinsmen whistled in surprise. When all was laid out, Okonkwo rose to speak.

"I beg you to accept this little kola," he said. "It is not to pay you back for all you did for me in these seven years. A child cannot pay for its mother's milk. I have only called you together because it is good for kinsmen to meet."

Yam pottage was served first because it was lighter than foo-foo and because yam always came first. Then the foo-foo was served. Some kinsmen ate it with egusi soup and others with bitter-leaf soup. The meat was then shared so that every member of the *umunna* had a portion. Every man rose in order of years and took a share.

---

[27] *umunna:* The male members of the clan.

Even the few kinsmen who had not been able to come had their shares taken out for them in due term.

As the palm-wine was drunk one of the oldest members of the *umunna* rose to thank Okonkwo:

"If I say that we did not expect such a big feast I will be suggesting that we did not know how open-handed our son, Okonkwo, is. We all know him, and we expected a big feast. But it turned out to be even bigger than we expected. Thank you. May all you took out return again tenfold. It is good in these days when the younger generation consider themselves wiser than their sires to see a man doing things in the grand, old way. A man who calls his kinsmen to a feast does not do so to save them from starving. They all have food in their own homes. When we gather together in the moonlit village ground it is not because of the moon. Every man can see it in his own compound. We come together because it is good for kinsmen to do so. You may ask why I am saying all this. I say it because I fear for the younger generation, for you people." He waved his arm where most of the young men sat. "As for me, I have only a short while to live, and so have Uchendu and Unachukwu and Emefo. But I fear for you young people because you do not understand how strong is the bond of kinship. You do not know what it is to speak with one voice. And what is the result? An abominable religion has settled among you. A man can now leave his father and his brothers. He can curse the gods of his fathers and his ancestors, like a hunter's dog that suddenly goes mad and turns on his master. I fear for you; I fear for the clan." He turned again to Okonkwo and said, "Thank you for calling us together."

PART III

20

Seven years was a long time to be away from one's clan. A man's place was not always there, waiting for him. As soon as he left, someone else rose and filled it. The clan was like a lizard; if it lost its tail it soon grew another.

Okonkwo knew these things. He knew that he had lost his place among the nine masked spirits who administered justice in the clan. He had lost the chance to lead his warlike clan against the new religion, which, he was told, had gained ground. He had lost the years in which he might have taken the highest titles in the clan. But some of these losses were not irreparable. He was determined that his return should be marked by his people. He would return with a flourish, and regain the seven wasted years.

Even in his first year in exile he had begun to plan for his return. The first thing he would do would be to rebuild his compound on a more magnificent scale. He would build a bigger barn than he had had before and he would build huts for two new wives. Then he would show his wealth by initiating his sons into the *ozo* society. Only the really great men in the clan were able to do this. Okonkwo saw clearly the high esteem in which he would be held, and he saw himself taking the highest title in the land.

As the years of exile passed one by one it seemed to him that his *chi* might now be making amends for the past disaster. His yams grew abundantly, not only in his motherland but also in Umuofia, where his friend gave them out year by year to sharecroppers.

Then the tragedy of his first son had occurred. At first it appeared as if it might prove too great for his spirit. But it was a resilient spirit, and in the end Okonkwo overcame his sorrow. He had five other sons and he would bring them up in the way of the clan.

He sent for the five sons and they came and sat in his *obi*. The youngest of them was four years old.

"You have all seen the great abomination of your brother. Now he is no longer my son or your brother. I will only have a son who is a man, who will hold his head up among my people. If any one of you prefers to be a woman, let him follow Nwoye now while I am alive so that I can curse him. If you turn against me when I am dead I will visit you and break your neck."

Okonkwo was very lucky in his daughters. He never stopped regretting that Ezinma was a girl. Of all his children she alone understood his every mood. A bond of sympathy had grown between them as the years had passed.

Ezinma grew up in her father's exile and became one of the most beautiful girls in Mbanta. She was called Crystal of Beauty, as her mother had been called in her youth. The young ailing girl who had caused her mother so much heartache had been transformed, almost overnight, into a healthy, buoyant maiden. She had, it was true, her moments of depression when she would snap at everybody like an angry dog. These moods descended on her suddenly and for no apparent reason. But they were very rare and short-lived. As long as they lasted, she could bear no other person but her father.

Many young men and prosperous middle-aged men of Mbanta came to marry her. But she refused them all, because her father had called her one evening and said to her: "There are many good and prosperous people here, but I shall be happy if you marry in Umuofia when we return home."

That was all he had said. But Ezinma had seen clearly all the thought and hidden meaning behind the few words. And she had agreed.

"Your half-sister, Obiageli, will not understand me," Okonkwo said. "But you can explain to her."

Although they were almost the same age, Ezinma wielded a strong influence over her half-sister. She explained to her why they should not marry yet, and she agreed also. And so the two of them refused every offer of marriage in Mbanta.

"I wish she were a boy," Okonkwo thought within himself. She understood things so perfectly. Who else among his children could have read his thoughts so well? With two beautiful grown-up daughters his return to Umuofia would attract considerable attention. His future sons-in-law would be men of authority in the clan. The poor and unknown would not dare to come forth.

Umuofia had indeed changed during the seven years Okonkwo had been in exile. The church had come and led many astray. Not only the low-born and the outcast but sometimes a worthy man had joined it. Such a man was Ogbuefi Ugonna, who had taken two titles, and who like a madman had cut the anklet of his titles and cast it away to join the Christians. The white missionary was very proud of him and he was one of the first men in Umuofia to receive the sacrament of Holy Communion, or Holy Feast as it was called in Ibo. Ogbuefi Ugonna had thought of the Feast in terms of eating and drinking, only more holy than the village variety. He had therefore put his drinking-horn into his goatskin bag for the occasion.

But apart from the church, the white men had also brought a government. They had built a court where the District Commissioner judged cases in ignorance. He had court messengers who brought men to him for trial. Many of these messengers came from Umuru on the bank of the Great River, where the white men first came many years before and where they had built the center of their religion and trade and government. These court messengers were greatly hated in Umuofia because they were foreigners and also arrogant and high-handed. They were called *kotma,* and because of their ash-colored shorts they earned the additional name of Ashy-Buttocks. They guarded the prison, which was full of men who had offended against the white man's law. Some of these prisoners had thrown away their twins and some had molested the Christians. They were beaten in the prison by the *kotma* and made to work every morning clearing the government compound and fetching wood for the white Commissioner and the court messengers. Some of these prisoners were men of title who should be above such mean occupation. They were grieved by the indignity and mourned for their neglected farms. As they cut grass in the morning the younger men sang in time with the strokes of their machetes:

> Kotma *of the ash buttocks,*
> *He is fit to be a slave.*
> *The white man has no sense,*
> *He is fit to be a slave.*

The court messengers did not like to be called Ashy-Buttocks, and they beat the men. But the song spread in Umuofia.

Okonkwo's head was bowed in sadness as Obierika told him these things.

"Perhaps I have been away too long," Okonkwo said, almost to himself. "But I cannot understand these things you tell me. What is it that has happened to our people? Why have they lost the power to fight?"

"Have you not heard how the white man wiped out Abame?" asked Obierika.

"I have heard," said Okonkwo. "But I have also heard that Abame people were weak and foolish. Why did they not fight back? Had they no guns and machetes? We would be cowards to compare ourselves with the men of Abame. Their fathers had never dared to stand before our ancestors. We must fight these men and drive them from the land."

"It is already too late," said Obierika sadly. "Our own men and our sons have joined the ranks of the stranger. They have joined his religion and they help to uphold his government. If we should try to drive out the white men in Umuofia we should find it easy. There are only two of them. But what of our own people who are following their way and have been given power? They would go to Umuru and bring the soldiers, and we would be like Abame." He paused for a long time and then said: "I told you on my last visit to Mbanta how they hanged Aneto."

"What has happened to that piece of land in dispute?" asked Okonkwo.

"The white man's court has decided that it should belong to Nnama's family, who had given much money to the white man's messengers and interpreter."

"Does the white man understand our custom about land?"

"How can he when he does not even speak our tongue? But he says that our customs are bad; and our own brothers who have taken up his religion also say that our customs are bad. How do you think we can fight when our own brothers have turned against us? The white man is very clever. He came quietly and peaceably with his religion. We were amused at his foolishness and allowed him to stay. Now he has won our brothers, and our clan can no longer act like one. He has put a knife on the things that held us together and we have fallen apart."

"How did they get hold of Aneto to hang him?" asked Okonkwo.

"When he killed Oduche in the fight over the land, he fled to Aninta to escape the wrath of the earth. This was about eight days after the fight, because Oduche had not died immediately from his wounds. It was on the seventh day that he died. But everybody knew that he was going to die and Aneto got his belongings together in readiness to flee. But the Christians had told the white man about the accident, and he sent his *kotma* to catch Aneto. He was imprisoned with all the leaders of his family. In the end Oduche died and Aneto was taken to Umuru and hanged. The other people were released, but even now they have not found the mouth with which to tell of their suffering."

The two men sat in silence for a long while afterwards.

21

There were many men and women in Umuofia who did not feel as strongly as Okonkwo about the new dispensation. The white man had indeed brought a lunatic religion, but he had also built a trading store and for the first time palm-oil and kernel became things of great price, and much money flowed into Umuofia.

And even in the matter of religion there was a growing feeling that there might be something in it after all, something vaguely akin to method in the overwhelming madness.

This growing feeling was due to Mr. Brown, the white missionary, who was very firm in restraining his flock from provoking the wrath of the clan. One member in particular was very difficult to restrain. His name was Enoch and his father was the priest of the snake cult. The story went around that Enoch had killed and eaten the sacred python, and that his father had cursed him.

Mr. Brown preached against such excess of zeal. Everything was possible, he told his energetic flock, but everything was not expedient. And so Mr. Brown came to be respected even by the clan, because he trod softly on its faith. He made friends with some of the great men of the clan and on one of his frequent visits to the neighboring villages he had been presented with a carved elephant tusk, which was a sign of dignity and rank. One of the great men in that village was called Akunna and he had given one of his sons to be taught the white man's knowledge in Mr. Brown's school.

Whenever Mr. Brown went to that village he spent long hours with Akunna in his *obi* talking through an interpreter about religion. Neither of them succeeded in converting the other but they learned more about their different beliefs.

"You say that there is one supreme God who made heaven and earth," said Akunna on one of Mr. Brown's visits. "We also believe in Him and call Him Chukwu. He made all the world and the other gods."

"There are no other gods," said Mr. Brown. "Chukwu is the only God and all others are false. You carve a piece of wood—like that one" (he pointed at the rafters from which Akunna's carved *Ikenga*[28] hung), "and you call it a god. But it is still a piece of wood."

"Yes," said Akunna. "It is indeed a piece of wood. The tree from which it came was made by Chukwu, as indeed all minor gods were. But He made them for His messengers so that we could approach Him through them. It is like yourself. You are the head of your church."

"No," protested Mr. Brown. "The head of my church is God Himself."

"I know," said Akunna, "but there must be a head in this world among men. Somebody like yourself must be the head here."

"The head of my church in that sense is in England."

"That is exactly what I am saying. The head of your church is in your country. He has sent you here as his messenger. And you have also appointed your own messengers and servants. Or let me take another example, the District Commissioner. He is sent by your king."

"They have a queen," said the interpreter on his own account.

"Your queen sends her messenger, the District Commissioner. He finds that he cannot do the work alone and so he appoints *kotma* to help him. It is the same with God, or Chukwu. He appoints the smaller gods to help Him because His work is too great for one person."

"You should not think of Him as a person," said Mr. Brown. "It is because you do so that you imagine He must need helpers. And the worst thing about it is that you give all the worship to the false gods you have created."

"That is not so. We make sacrifices to the little gods, but when they fail and there is no one else to turn to we go to Chukwu. It is right to do so. We approach a great man through his servants. But when his servants fail to help us, then we go to the last source of hope. We appear to pay greater attention to the little gods but that is not so. We worry them more because we are afraid to worry their Master. Our fathers knew that Chukwu was the Overlord and that is why many of them gave their children the name Chukwuka — 'Chukwu is Supreme.'"

---

[28] *Ikenga:* A carved figure symbolizing a man's strength, made from wood and the horns of a ram.

"You said one interesting thing," said Mr. Brown. "You are afraid of Chukwu. In my religion Chukwu is a loving Father and need not be feared by those who do His will."

"But we must fear Him when we are not doing His will," said Akunna. "And who is to tell His will? It is too great to be known."

In this way Mr. Brown learned a good deal about the religion of the clan and he came to the conclusion that a frontal attack on it would not succeed. And so he built a school and a little hospital in Umuofia. He went from family to family begging people to send their children to his school. But at first they only sent their slaves or sometimes their lazy children. Mr. Brown begged and argued and prophesied. He said that the leaders of the land in the future would be men and women who had learned to read and write. If Umuofia failed to send her children to the school, strangers would come from other places to rule them. They could already see that happening in the Native Court, where the D.C. was surrounded by strangers who spoke his tongue. Most of these strangers came from the distant town of Umuru on the bank of the Great River where the white man first went.

In the end Mr. Brown's arguments began to have an effect. More people came to learn in his school, and he encouraged them with gifts of singlets and towels. They were not all young, these people who came to learn. Some of them were thirty years old or more. They worked on their farms in the morning and went to school in the afternoon. And it was not long before the people began to say that the white man's medicine was quick in working. Mr. Brown's school produced quick results. A few months in it were enough to make one a court messenger or even a court clerk. Those who stayed longer became teachers; and from Umuofia laborers went forth into the Lord's vineyard. New churches were established in the surrounding villages and a few schools with them. From the very beginning religion and education went hand in hand.

Mr. Brown's mission grew from strength to strength, and because of its link with the new administration it earned a new social prestige. But Mr. Brown himself was breaking down in health. At first he ignored the warning signs. But in the end he had to leave his flock, sad and broken.

It was in the first rainy season after Okonkwo's return to Umuofia that Mr. Brown left for home. As soon as he had learned of Okonkwo's return five months earlier, the missionary had immediately paid him a visit. He had just sent Okonkwo's son, Nwoye, who was now called Isaac, to the new training college for teachers in Umuru. And he had hoped that Okonkwo would be happy to hear of it. But Okonkwo had driven him away with the threat that if he came into his compound again, he would be carried out of it.

Okonkwo's return to his native land was not as memorable as he had wished. It was true his two beautiful daughters aroused great interest among suitors and marriage negotiations were soon in progress, but, beyond that, Umuofia did not appear to have taken any special notice of the warrior's return. The clan had undergone such profound change during his exile that it was barely recognizable. The new religion and government and the trading stores were very much in the people's eyes and minds. There were still many who saw these new institutions as evil, but even they talked and thought about little else, and certainly not about Okonkwo's return.

And it was the wrong year too. If Okonkwo had immediately initiated his two sons into the *ozo* society as he had planned he would have caused a stir. But the initiation rite was performed once in three years in Umuofia, and he had to wait for nearly two years for the next round of ceremonies.

Okonkwo was deeply grieved. And it was not just a personal grief. He mourned for the clan, which he saw breaking up and falling apart, and he mourned for the warlike men of Umuofia, who had so unaccountably become soft like women.

22

Mr. Brown's successor was the Reverend James Smith, and he was a different kind of man. He condemned openly Mr. Brown's policy of compromise and accommodation. He saw things as black and white. And black was evil. He saw the world as a battlefield in which the children of light were locked in mortal conflict with the sons of darkness. He spoke in his sermons about sheep and goats and about wheat and tares. He believed in slaying the prophets of Baal.

Mr. Smith was greatly distressed by the ignorance which many of his flock showed even in such things as the Trinity and the Sacraments. It only showed that they were seeds sown on a rocky soil. Mr. Brown had thought of nothing but numbers. He should have known that the kingdom of God did not depend on large crowds. Our Lord Himself stressed the importance of fewness. Narrow is the way and few the number. To fill the Lord's holy temple with an idolatrous crowd clamoring for signs was a folly of everlasting consequence. Our Lord used the whip only once in His life — to drive the crowd away from His church.

Within a few weeks of his arrival in Umuofia Mr. Smith suspended a young woman from the church for pouring new wine into old bottles. This woman had allowed her heathen husband to mutilate her dead child. The child had been declared an *ogbanje,* plaguing its mother by dying and entering her womb to be born again. Four times this child had run its evil round. And so it was mutilated to discourage it from returning.

Mr. Smith was filled with wrath when he heard of this. He disbelieved the story which even some of the most faithful confirmed, the story of really evil children who were not deterred by mutilation, but came back with all the scars. He replied that such stories were spread in the world by the Devil to lead men astray. Those who believed such stories were unworthy of the Lord's table.

There was a saying in Umuofia that as a man danced so the drums were beaten for him. Mr. Smith danced a furious step and so the drums went mad. The overzealous converts who had smarted under Mr. Brown's restraining hand now flourished in full favor. One of them was Enoch, the son of the snake-priest who was believed to have killed and eaten the sacred python. Enoch's devotion to the new faith had seemed so much greater than Mr. Brown's that the villagers called him the outsider who wept louder than the bereaved.

Enoch was short and slight of build, and always seemed in great haste. His feet were short and broad, and when he stood or walked his heels came together and his feet opened outwards as if they had quarreled and meant to go in different directions. Such was the excessive energy bottled up in Enoch's small body that it was always erupting in quarrels and fights. On Sundays he always imagined that the sermon was preached for the benefit of his enemies. And if he happened to sit near one of them he would occasionally turn to give him a meaningful look, as if to say, "I told you so." It was Enoch who touched off the great conflict between church and clan in Umuofia which had been gathering since Mr. Brown left.

It happened during the annual ceremony which was held in honor of the earth deity. At such times the ancestors of the clan who had been committed to Mother Earth at their death emerged again as *egwugwu* through tiny ant-holes.

One of the greatest crimes a man could commit was to unmask an *egwugwu* in public, or to say or do anything which might reduce its immortal prestige in the eyes of the uninitiated. And this was what Enoch did.

The annual worship of the earth goddess fell on a Sunday, and the masked spirits were abroad. The Christian women who had been to church could not therefore go home. Some of their men had gone out to beg the *egwugwu* to retire for a short while for the women to pass. They agreed and were already retiring, when Enoch boasted aloud that they would not dare to touch a Christian. Whereupon they all came back and one of them gave Enoch a good stroke of the cane, which was always carried. Enoch fell on him and tore off his mask. The other *egwugwu* immediately surrounded their desecrated companion, to shield him from the profane gaze of women and children, and led him away. Enoch had killed an ancestral spirit, and Umuofia was thrown into confusion.

That night the Mother of the Spirits walked the length and breadth of the clan, weeping for her murdered son. It was a terrible night. Not even the oldest man in Umuofia had ever heard such a strange and fearful sound, and it was never to be heard again. It seemed as if the very soul of the tribe wept for a great evil that was coming—its own death.

On the next day all the masked *egwugwu* of Umuofia assembled in the marketplace. They came from all the quarters of the clan and even from the neighboring villages. The dreaded Otakagu came from Imo, and Ekwensu, dangling a white cock, arrived from Uli. It was a terrible gathering. The eerie voices of countless spirits, the bells that clattered behind some of them, and the clash of machetes as they ran forwards and backwards and saluted one another, sent tremors of fear into every heart. For the first time in living memory the sacred bull-roarer was heard in broad daylight.

From the marketplace the furious band made for Enoch's compound. Some of the elders of the clan went with them, wearing heavy protections of charms and amulets. These were men whose arms were strong in *ogwu*, or medicine. As for the ordinary men and women, they listened from the safety of their huts.

The leaders of the Christians had met together at Mr. Smith's parsonage on the previous night. As they deliberated they could hear the Mother of Spirits wailing for her son. The chilling sound affected Mr. Smith, and for the first time he seemed to be afraid.

"What are they planning to do?" he asked. No one knew, because such a thing had never happened before. Mr. Smith would have sent for the District Commissioner and his court messengers, but they had gone on tour on the previous day.

"One thing is clear," said Mr. Smith. "We cannot offer physical resistance to them. Our strength lies in the Lord." They knelt down together and prayed to God for delivery.

"O Lord, save Thy people," cried Mr. Smith.

"And bless Thine inheritance," replied the men.

They decided that Enoch should be hidden in the parsonage for a day or two. Enoch himself was greatly disappointed when he heard this, for he had hoped that a holy war was imminent; and there were a few other Christians who thought like him. But wisdom prevailed in the camp of the faithful and many lives were thus saved.

The band of *egwugwu* moved like a furious whirlwind to Enoch's compound and with machete and fire reduced it to a desolate heap. And from there they made for the church, intoxicated with destruction.

Mr. Smith was in his church when he heard the masked spirits coming. He walked quietly to the door which commanded the approach to the church compound, and stood there. But when the first three or four *egwugwu* appeared on the church compound he nearly bolted. He overcame this impulse and instead of running away he went down the two steps that led up to the church and walked towards the approaching spirits.

They surged forward, and a long stretch of the bamboo fence with which the church compound was surrounded gave way before them. Discordant bells clanged, machetes clashed and the air was full of dust and weird sounds. Mr. Smith heard a sound of footsteps behind him. He turned round and saw Okeke, his interpreter. Okeke had not been on the best of terms with his master since he had strongly condemned Enoch's behavior at the meeting of the leaders of the church during the night. Okeke had gone as far as to say that Enoch should not be hidden in the parsonage, because he would only draw the wrath of the clan on the pastor. Mr. Smith had rebuked him in very strong language, and had not sought his advice that morning. But now, as he came up and stood by him confronting the angry spirits, Mr. Smith looked at him and smiled. It was a wan smile, but there was deep gratitude there.

For a brief moment the onrush of the *egwugwu* was checked by the unexpected composure of the two men. But it was only a momentary check, like the tense silence between blasts of thunder. The second onrush was greater than the first. It swallowed up the two men. Then an unmistakable voice rose above the tumult and there was immediate silence. Space was made around the two men, and Ajofia began to speak.

Ajofia was the leading *egwugwu* of Umuofia. He was the head and spokesman of the nine ancestors who administered justice in the clan. His voice was unmistakable and so he was able to bring immediate peace to the agitated spirits. He then addressed Mr. Smith, and as he spoke clouds of smoke rose from his head.

"The body of the white man, I salute you," he said, using the language in which immortals spoke to men.

"The body of the white man, do you know me?" he asked.

Mr. Smith looked at his interpreter, but Okeke, who was a native of distant Umuru, was also at a loss.

Ajofia laughed in his guttural voice. It was like the laugh of rusty metal. "They are strangers," he said, "and they are ignorant. But let that pass." He turned round to his comrades and saluted them, calling them the fathers of Umuofia. He dug his rattling spear into the ground and it shook with metallic life. Then he turned once more to the missionary and his interpreter.

"Tell the white man that we will not do him any harm," he said to the interpreter. "Tell him to go back to his house and leave us alone. We liked his brother who was with us before. He was foolish, but we liked him, and for his sake we shall not harm his brother. But this shrine which he built must be destroyed. We shall no longer allow it in our midst. It has bred untold abominations and we have come to put an end to it." He turned to his comrades. "Fathers of Umuofia, I salute you"; and they replied with one guttural voice. He turned again to the missionary. "You can stay with us if you like our ways. You can worship your own god. It is good that a man should worship the gods and the spirits of his fathers. Go back to your house so that you may not be hurt. Our anger is great but we have held it down so that we can talk to you."

Mr. Smith said to his interpreter: "Tell them to go away from here. This is the house of God and I will not live to see it desecrated."

Okeke interpreted wisely to the spirits and leaders of Umuofia: "The white man says he is happy you have come to him with your grievances, like friends. He will be happy if you leave the matter in his hands."

"We cannot leave the matter in his hands because he does not understand our customs, just as we do not understand his. We say he is foolish because he does not know our ways, and perhaps he says we are foolish because we do not know his. Let him go away."

Mr. Smith stood his ground. But he could not save his church. When the *egwugwu* went away the red-earth church which Mr. Brown had built was a pile of earth and ashes. And for the moment the spirit of the clan was pacified.

23

For the first time in many years Okonkwo had a feeling that was akin to happiness. The times which had altered so unaccountably during his exile seemed to be coming round again. The clan which had turned false on him appeared to be making amends.

He had spoken violently to his clansmen when they had met in the marketplace to decide on their action. And they had listened to him with respect. It was like the good old days again, when a warrior was a warrior. Although they had not agreed to kill the missionary or drive away the Christians, they had agreed to do something substantial. And they had done it. Okonkwo was almost happy again.

For two days after the destruction of the church, nothing happened. Every man in Umuofia went about armed with a gun or a machete. They would not be caught unawares, like the men of Abame.

Then the District Commissioner returned from his tour. Mr. Smith went immediately to him and they had a long discussion. The men of Umuofia did not take any notice of this, and if they did, they thought it was not important. The missionary often went to see his brother white man. There was nothing strange in that.

Three days later the District Commissioner sent his sweet-tongued messenger to the leaders of Umuofia asking them to meet him in his headquarters. That also was not strange. He often asked them to hold such palavers, as he called them. Okonkwo was among the six leaders he invited.

Okonkwo warned the others to be fully armed. "An Umuofia man does not refuse a call," he said. "He may refuse to do what he is asked; he does not refuse to be asked. But the times have changed, and we must be fully prepared."

And so the six men went to see the District Commissioner, armed with their machetes. They did not carry guns, for that would be unseemly. They were led into the courthouse where the District Commissioner sat. He received them politely. They unslung their goatskin bags and their sheathed machetes, put them on the floor, and sat down.

"I have asked you to come," began the Commissioner, "because of what happened during my absence. I have been told a few things but I cannot believe them until I have heard your own side. Let us talk about it like friends and find a way of ensuring that it does not happen again."

Ogbuefi Ekwueme rose to his feet and began to tell the story.

"Wait a minute," said the Commissioner. "I want to bring in my men so that they too can hear your grievances and take warning. Many of them come from distant places and although they speak your tongue they are ignorant of your customs. James! Go and bring in the men." His interpreter left the courtroom and soon returned with twelve men. They sat together with the men of Umuofia, and Ogbuefi Ekwueme began to tell the story of how Enoch murdered an *egwugwu*.

It happened so quickly that the six men did not see it coming. There was only a brief scuffle, too brief even to allow the drawing of a sheathed machete. The six men were handcuffed and led into the guardroom.

"We shall not do you any harm," said the District Commissioner to them later, "if only you agree to cooperate with us. We have brought a peaceful administration to you and your people so that you may be happy. If any man ill-treats you we shall come to your rescue. But we will not allow you to ill-treat others. We have a court of law where we judge cases and administer justice just as it is done in my own country under a great queen. I have brought you here because you joined together to molest others, to burn people's houses and their place of worship. That must not happen in the dominion of our queen, the most powerful ruler in the world. I have decided that you will pay a fine of two hundred bags of cowries. You will be released as soon as you agree to this and undertake to collect that fine from your people. What do you say to that?"

The six men remained sullen and silent and the Commissioner left them for a while. He told the court messengers, when he left the guardroom, to treat the men with respect because they were the leaders of Umuofia. They said, "Yes, sir," and saluted.

As soon as the District Commissioner left, the head messenger, who was also the prisoners' barber, took down his razor and shaved off all the hair on the men's heads. They were still handcuffed, and they just sat and moped.

"Who is the chief among you?" the court messengers asked in jest. "We see that every pauper wears the anklet of title in Umuofia. Does it cost as much as ten cowries?"

The six men ate nothing throughout that day and the next. They were not even given any water to drink, and they could not go out to urinate or go into the bush when they were pressed. At night the messengers came in to taunt them and to knock their shaven heads together.

Even when the men were left alone they found no words to speak to one another. It was only on the third day, when they could no longer bear the hunger and the insults, that they began to talk about giving in.

"We should have killed the white man if you had listened to me," Okonkwo snarled.

"We could have been in Umuru now waiting to be hanged," someone said to him.

"Who wants to kill the white man?" asked a messenger who had just rushed in. Nobody spoke.

"You are not satisfied with your crime, but you must kill the white man on top of it." He carried a strong stick, and he hit each man a few blows on the head and back. Okonkwo was choked with hate.

As soon as the six men were locked up, court messengers went into Umuofia to tell the people that their leaders would not be released unless they paid a fine of two hundred and fifty bags of cowries.

"Unless you pay the fine immediately," said their head-man, "we will take your leaders to Umuru before the big white man, and hang them."

This story spread quickly through the villages, and was added to as it went. Some said that the men had already been taken to Umuru and would be hanged on the following day. Some said that their families would also be hanged. Others said that soldiers were already on their way to shoot the people of Umuofia as they had done in Abame.

It was the time of the full moon. But that night the voice of children was not heard. The village *ilo* where they always gathered for a moon-play was empty. The women of Iguedo did not meet in their secret enclosure to learn a new dance to be displayed later to the village. Young men who were always abroad in the moonlight kept their huts that night. Their manly voices were not heard on the village paths as they went to visit their friends and lovers. Umuofia was like a startled animal with ears erect, sniffing the silent, ominous air and not knowing which way to run.

The silence was broken by the village crier beating his sonorous *ogene*. He called every man in Umuofia, from the Akakanma age group upwards, to a meeting in the marketplace after the morning meal. He went from one end of the village to the other and walked all its breadth. He did not leave out any of the main footpaths.

Okonkwo's compound was like a deserted homestead. It was as if cold water had been poured on it. His family was all there, but everyone spoke in whispers. His daughter Ezinma had broken her twenty-eight day visit to the family of her future husband, and returned home when she heard that her father had been imprisoned, and was going to be hanged. As soon as she got home she went to Obierika to ask what the men of Umuofia were going to do about it. But Obierika had not been home since morning. His wives thought he had gone to a secret meeting. Ezinma was satisfied that something was being done.

On the morning after the village crier's appeal the men of Umuofia met in the marketplace and decided to collect without delay two hundred and fifty bags of cowries to appease the white man. They did not know that fifty bags would go to the court messengers, who had increased the fine for that purpose.

24

Okonkwo and his fellow prisoners were set free as soon as the fine was paid. The District Commissioner spoke to them again about the great queen, and about peace and good government. But the men did not listen. They just sat and looked at him and at his interpreter. In the end they were given back their bags and sheathed machetes and told to go home. They rose and left the courthouse. They neither spoke to anyone nor among themselves.

The courthouse, like the church, was built a little way outside the village. The footpath that linked them was a very busy one because it also led to the stream, beyond the court. It was open and sandy. Footpaths were open and sandy in the dry season. But when the rains came the bush grew thick on either side and closed in on the path. It was now dry season.

As they made their way to the village the six men met women and children going to the stream with their water-pots. But the men wore such heavy and fearsome looks that the women and children did not say *"nno"* or "welcome" to them, but edged out of the way to let them pass. In the village little groups of men joined them until they became a sizable company. They walked silently. As each of the six men got to his compound, he turned in, taking some of the crowd with him. The village was astir in a silent, suppressed way.

Ezinma had prepared some food for her father as soon as news spread that the six men would be released. She took it to him in his *obi.* He ate absent-mindedly. He had no appetite; he only ate to please her. His male relations and friends had gathered in his *obi,* and Obierika was urging him to eat. Nobody else spoke, but they noticed the long stripes on Okonkwo's back where the warder's whip had cut into his flesh.

The village crier was abroad again in the night. He beat his iron gong and announced that another meeting would be held in the morning. Everyone knew that Umuofia was at last going to speak its mind about the things that were happening.

Okonkwo slept very little that night. The bitterness in his heart was now mixed with a kind of childlike excitement. Before he had gone to bed he had brought down his war dress, which he had not touched since his return from exile. He had shaken out his smoked raffia skirt and examined his tall feather head-gear and his shield. They were all satisfactory, he had thought.

As he lay on his bamboo bed he thought about the treatment he had received in the white man's court, and he swore vengeance. If Umuofia decided on war, all would be well. But if they chose to be cowards he would go out and avenge himself. He thought about wars in the past. The noblest, he thought, was the war against Isike. In those days Okudo was still alive. Okudo sang a war song in a way that no other man could. He was not a fighter, but his voice turned every man into a lion.

"Worthy men are no more," Okonkwo sighed as he remembered those days. "Isike will never forget how we slaughtered them in that war. We killed twelve of their men and they killed only two of ours. Before the end of the fourth market week they were suing for peace. Those were days when men were men."

As he thought of these things he heard the sound of the iron gong in the distance. He listened carefully, and could just hear the crier's voice. But it was very faint. He turned on his bed and his back hurt him. He ground his teeth. The crier was drawing nearer and nearer until he passed by Okonkwo's compound.

"The greatest obstacle in Umuofia," Okonkwo thought bitterly, "is that coward, Egonwanne. His sweet tongue can change fire into cold ash. When he speaks he moves our men to impotence. If they had ignored his womanish wisdom five years ago, we would not have come to this." He ground his teeth. "Tomorrow he will tell them that our fathers never fought a 'war of blame.' If they listen to him I shall leave them and plan my own revenge."

The crier's voice had once more become faint, and the distance had taken the harsh edge off his iron gong. Okonkwo turned from one side to the other and derived a kind of pleasure from the pain his back gave him. "Let Egonwanne talk about a 'war of blame' tomorrow and I shall show him my back and head." He ground his teeth.

The marketplace began to fill as soon as the sun rose. Obierika was waiting in his *obi* when Okonkwo came along and called him. He hung his goatskin bag and his sheathed machete on his shoulder and went out to join him. Obierika's hut was close to the road and he saw every man who passed to the marketplace. He had exchanged greetings with many who had already passed that morning.

When Okonkwo and Obierika got to the meeting place there were already so many people that if one threw up a grain of sand it would not find its way to the earth again. And many more people were coming from every quarter of the nine villages. It warmed Okonkwo's heart to see such strength of numbers. But he was looking for one man in particular, the man whose tongue he dreaded and despised so much.

"Can you see him?" he asked Obierika.

"Who?"

"Egonwanne," he said, his eyes roving from one corner of the huge marketplace to the other. Most of the men sat on wooden stools they had brought with them.

"No," said Obierika, casting his eyes over the crowd. "Yes, there he is, under the silk-cotton tree. Are you afraid he would convince us not to fight?"

"Afraid? I do not care what he does to *you*. I despise him and those who listen to him. I shall fight alone if I choose."

They spoke at the top of their voices because everybody was talking, and it was like the sound of a great market.

"I shall wait till he has spoken," Okonkwo thought. "Then I shall speak."

"But how do you know he will speak against war?" Obierika asked after a while.

"Because I know he is a coward," said Okonkwo. Obierika did not hear the rest of what he said because at that moment somebody touched his shoulder from behind and he turned round to shake hands and exchange greetings with five or six friends. Okonkwo did not turn round even though he knew the voices. He was in no mood to exchange greetings. But one of the men touched him and asked about the people of his compound.

"They are well," he replied without interest.

The first man to speak to Umuofia that morning was Okika, one of the six who had been imprisoned. Okika was a great man and an orator. But he did not have the booming voice which a first speaker must use to establish silence in the assembly of the clan. Onyeka had such a voice; and so he was asked to salute Umuofia before Okika began to speak.

"*Umuofia kwenu!*" he bellowed, raising his left arm and pushing the air with his open hand.

"*Yaa!*" roared Umuofia.

"*Umuofia kwenu!*" he bellowed again, and again and again, facing a new direction each time. And the crowd answered, "*Yaa!*"

There was immediate silence as though cold water had been poured on a roaring flame.

Okika sprang to his feet and also saluted his clansmen four times. Then he began to speak:

"You all know why we are here, when we ought to be building our barns or mending our huts, when we should be putting our compounds in order. My father used to say to me: 'Whenever you see a toad jumping in broad daylight, then know that something is after its life.' When I saw you all pouring into this meeting from all the quarters of our clan so early in the morning, I knew that something was after our life." He paused for a brief moment and then began again:

"All our gods are weeping. Idemili is weeping, Ogwugwu is weeping, Agbala is weeping, and all the others. Our dead fathers are weeping because of the shameful sacrilege they are suffering and the abomination we have all seen with our eyes." He stopped again to steady his trembling voice.

"This is a great gathering. No clan can boast of greater numbers or greater valor. But are we all here? I ask you: Are all the sons of Umuofia with us here?" A deep murmur swept through the crowd.

"They are not," he said. "They have broken the clan and gone their several ways. We who are here this morning have remained true to our fathers, but our brothers have deserted us and joined a stranger to soil their fatherland. If we fight the stranger we shall hit our brothers and perhaps shed the blood of a clansman. But we must do it. Our fathers never dreamed of such a thing, they never killed their brothers. But a white man never came to them. So we must do what our fathers would never have done. Eneke the bird was asked why he was always on the wing and he replied: 'Men have learned to shoot without missing their mark and I have learned to fly without perching on a twig.' We must root out this evil. And if our brothers take the side of evil we must root them out too. And we must do it *now*. We must bail this water now that it is only ankle deep. . . ."

At this point there was a sudden stir in the crowd and every eye was turned in one direction. There was a sharp bend in the road that led from the marketplace to the white man's court, and to the stream beyond it. And so no one had seen the approach of the five court messengers until they had come round the bend, a few paces from the edge of the crowd. Okonkwo was sitting at the edge.

He sprang to his feet as soon as he saw who it was. He confronted the head messenger, trembling with hate, unable to utter a word. The man was fearless and stood his ground, his four men lined up behind him.

In that brief moment the world seemed to stand still, waiting. There was utter silence. The men of Umuofia were merged into the mute backcloth of trees and giant creepers, waiting.

The spell was broken by the head messenger. "Let me pass!" he ordered.

"What do you want here?"

"The white man whose power you know too well has ordered this meeting to stop."

In a flash Okonkwo drew his machete. The messenger crouched to avoid the blow. It was useless. Okonkwo's machete descended twice and the man's head lay beside his uniformed body.

The waiting backcloth jumped into tumultuous life and the meeting was stopped. Okonkwo stood looking at the dead man. He knew that Umuofia would not go to war. He knew because they had let the other messengers escape. They had broken into tumult instead of action. He discerned fright in that tumult. He heard voices asking: "Why did he do it?"

He wiped his machete on the sand and went away.

25

When the District Commissioner arrived at Okonkwo's compound at the head of an armed band of soldiers and court messengers he found a small crowd of men sitting wearily in the *obi*. He commanded them to come outside, and they obeyed without a murmur.

"Which among you is called Okonkwo?" he asked through his interpreter.

"He is not here," replied Obierika.

"Where is he?"

"He is not here!"

The Commissioner became angry and red in the face. He warned the men that unless they produced Okonkwo forthwith he would lock them all up. The men murmured among themselves, and Obierika spoke again.

"We can take you where he is, and perhaps your men will help us."

The Commissioner did not understand what Obierika meant when he said, "Perhaps your men will help us." One of the most infuriating habits of these people was their love of superfluous words, he thought.

Obierika with five or six others led the way. The Commissioner and his men followed, their firearms held at the ready. He had warned Obierika that if he and his men played any monkey tricks they would be shot. And so they went.

There was a small bush behind Okonkwo's compound. The only opening into this bush from the compound was a little round hole in the red-earth wall through which fowls went in and out in their endless search for food. The hole would not let a man through. It was to this bush that Obierika led the Commissioner and his men. They skirted round the compound, keeping close to the wall. The only sound they made was with their feet as they crushed dry leaves.

Then they came to the tree from which Okonkwo's body was dangling, and they stopped dead.

"Perhaps your men can help us bring him down and bury him," said Obierika. "We have sent for strangers from another village to do it for us, but they may be a long time coming."

The District Commissioner changed instantaneously. The resolute administrator in him gave way to the student of primitive customs.

"Why can't you take him down yourselves?" he asked.

"It is against our custom," said one of the men. "It is an abomination for a man to take his own life. It is an offense against the Earth, and a man who commits it will not be buried by his clansmen. His body is evil, and only strangers may touch it. That is why we ask your people to bring him down, because you are strangers."

"Will you bury him like any other man?" asked the Commissioner.

"We cannot bury him. Only strangers can. We shall pay your men to do it. When he has been buried we will then do our duty by him. We shall make sacrifices to cleanse the desecrated land."

Obierika, who had been gazing steadily at his friend's dangling body, turned suddenly to the District Commissioner and said ferociously: "That man was one of the greatest men in Umuofia. You drove him to kill himself; and now he will be buried like a dog. . . ." He could not say any more. His voice trembled and choked his words.

"Shut up!" shouted one of the messengers, quite unnecessarily.

"Take down the body," the Commissioner ordered his chief messenger, "and bring it and all these people to the court."

"Yes, sah," the messenger said, saluting.

The Commissioner went away, taking three or four of the soldiers with him. In the many years in which he had toiled to bring civilization to different parts of Africa he had learned a number of things. One of them was that a District Commissioner must never attend to such undignified details as cutting a hanged man from the tree. Such attention would give the natives a poor opinion of him. In the book which he planned to write he would stress that point. As he walked back to the court he thought about that book. Every day brought him some new material. The story of this man who had killed a messenger and hanged himself would make interesting reading. One could almost write a whole chapter on him. Perhaps not a whole chapter but a reasonable paragraph, at any rate. There was so much else to include, and one must be firm in cutting out details. He had already chosen the title of the book, after much thought: *The Pacification of the Primitive Tribes of the Lower Niger.*

Images of Africa

p. 1722

p. 1604

p. 1159
Chinua Achebe suggests in his essay "**An Image of Africa**" that he wrote the novel *Things Fall Apart* as a response to Joseph Conrad's *Heart of Darkness* and its white European perspective on Africa. Even though Conrad's novel may offer a more sympathetic treatment of Africa than that found in the Tarzan stories of Edgar Rice Burroughs (1875–1950), written at about the same time, *Heart of Darkness* is nonetheless, as Achebe contends, a distorted, one-sided view, an imperial perspective that constructs Africa as a savage continent in need of civilizing and Christianizing. It is black to Europe's white; dark instead of light. It is violent, wild, Other. Africa, identified by modern anthropologists as the site of *Homo sapiens*' first emergence, was not thought of at the turn of the century as a homeland. The West traced its origins to Greece and Rome, not to Cairo and Timbuktu. Many colonized blacks and those of the DIASPORA living in Europe and America absorbed this Eurocentric point of view, and as they denigrated Africa, they denied their heritage and themselves. **W. E. B. Du Bois**

doo-BOYZ

p. 1703
describes this phenomenon in *The Souls of Black Folk* as the African American "double-consciousness," a state in which the African is in conflict with the American. Along with many other black writers of the twentieth century, Du Bois sought to heal this racial self-alienation by changing the Western image of Africa, challenging the colonial oppression that supported it, and celebrating a positive account of African heritage.

Cover of *The
Missionary News*,
March 15, 1866
*Nineteenth-century
missionary societies
published periodicals
to generate support
and to report on their
progress in the field.
The illustrated
publications were a
source of cultural
images for audiences
in colonizing nations.
This cover depicts a
European view of an
African town on the
Congo river. (The Art
Archive)*

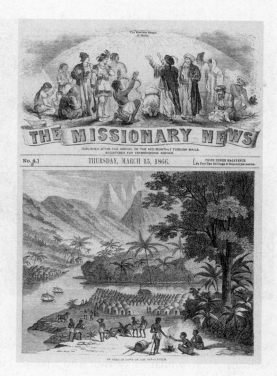

PAN-AFRICANISM

By affirming his own African heritage and encouraging other blacks
to do the same, Du Bois allied himself with a movement later called
Pan-Africanism that was based on the idea that blacks everywhere
shared a common heritage and a common destiny. Historians trace
the roots of the movement back to the late eighteenth century, when
Sierra Leone was established in 1787 as a refuge in west Africa for
freed and runaway slaves. American abolitionists facilitated the
founding of a similar state, Liberia, in the 1820s. By the mid nineteenth century some historians had begun to develop a perspective
on Africa that highlighted the greatness in the African past, including the achievements of the ancient Egyptians. Yet even apologists
for "the dark continent," such as Liberian author Edward Blyden
(1832–1912), considered late-nineteenth-century Africa to be in a
"state of barbarism." Blyden accepted a Western progressivist view of
Africa and seems to echo Conrad's Marlow when he asserts: "There

Aaron Douglas, *Into Bondage*, 1936. Oil on canvas *Douglas, an artist of the Harlem Renaissance, painted murals on public buildings and founded the art department at Fisk University in Nashville, Tennessee. (In the Collection of The Corcoran Gallery of Art, Museum Purchase and partial gift from Thurlow Evans Tibbs Jr., The Evans Tibbs Collection)*

is not a single mental or moral deficiency now existing among Africans, . . . to which we cannot find a parallel in the past history of Europe." Blyden and his contemporaries thought that blacks who returned to Africa would bring with them the civilizing influences of the West and that these would help to transform the continent.

Du Bois, who coined the term *Pan-Negroism* to characterize his ideas, was part of a philosophical tradition that can be traced to the Romantic nationalism of German philosopher Johann Gottfried Herder (1744–1803). Herder, who influenced European nationalism in such countries as Italy and Germany, described world history as the development of groups of people bound together by language, culture, mythology, and traditions. Du Bois sought to reconnect blacks in the diaspora with their African heritage. He saw African Americans as the "advance guard of the Negro people," for they had the education and the experience of the modern world that would enable them to lead the movement, which Du Bois considered part of the international struggle for social justice. He organized a Pan-African Congress in Paris in 1919 to coincide with the Versailles peace conference that ended World War I, hoping to convince world leaders that the Wilsonian principle of self-determination should be

One ever feels his two-ness, — an American, a Negro; two souls, two thoughts, two unreconciled strivings; two warring ideals in one dark body, whose dogged strength alone keeps it from being torn asunder.

– W. E. B. Du Bois

applied to Africans as well as Europeans, giving Africans the power to decide their future.

Du Bois saw the Pan-African movement as part of the larger fight against European colonialism; his contemporary at the beginning of the century, Marcus Garvey (1887–1940), a Jamaican who had emigrated to New York City, emphasized another dimension of the movement — the desire of American blacks to return to the African homeland. Known as the "Black Moses," Garvey preached "Back to Africa" and "Africa for the Africans," leading thousands in a march through the streets of Harlem. Few of his followers actually returned to Africa, however, and Garvey's crusade fell apart in the mid twenties when he was imprisoned for mail fraud.

Du Bois, however, maintained the Pan-African dream throughout his long life. He convened several Pan-African congresses in the period between the wars, finally passing the mantle of leadership to a younger generation, in particular to **Kwame Nkrumah** (1909–1972) of Ghana at the fifth Pan-African Congress held in Manchester, England, in 1945. Just after World War II, when colonies throughout Africa were seeking independence, Nkrumah, who would become the first prime minister of the newly independent nation of Ghana in 1957, was the first African to lead the Pan-African movement. He envisioned a United States of Africa, which would unite the continent and welcome back Africans from the diaspora. Although his dream soon gave way to the more powerful forces of tribalism and nationalism in Africa, it had in a small way a symbolic realization when in 1961 Du Bois emigrated to Ghana.

KWAH-may
en-KROO-mah

THE HARLEM RENAISSANCE

Although Garvey's movement failed to populate Africa with black Americans, its energy, broad appeal, and positive view of Africa contributed to a cultural awakening in the States that in the arts became known as the Harlem Renaissance. Led by writers, artists, and musicians, many from the Caribbean and the American South, this movement that began in the 1920s was characterized by an affirmation of blackness, a celebration of African culture and traditions, and a search for an African heritage. Like the Romantic nationalists of nineteenth-century Europe, the writers of the Harlem Renaissance collected their people's folklore and celebrated their own culture.

For I was born, far from my native clime, / Under the white man's menace, out of time.

– CLAUDE MCKAY, "Outcast"

pp. 1705, 1706

pp. 1708, 1707

Du Bois wrote about the sorrow songs — the songs of the slaves — in *The Souls of Black Folk,* and James Weldon Johnson put together what is now the standard collection of Negro spirituals, songs that in his poem "O Black and Unknown Bards" Johnson traces to Africa. Claude McKay, a Jamaican emigrant to Harlem, turned conventional connotations of "black" and "white" on their heads and celebrated blackness in such poems as "**To the White Fiends**" and "**Outcast.**" Countee Cullen's "**Heritage**" and Langston Hughes's "**The Negro Speaks of Rivers**" imagine a romantic Africa. Inspired in part by the writers of the IRISH LITERARY RENAISSANCE, these poets implicitly compared their situation to that of the Irish, and like the mythic Ireland celebrated by Yeats and his fellow Irish poets, similarly looked to the past, to a time before slavery and the ravages of colonial oppression. Although none of the Harlem writers of the twenties and thirties except Du Bois actually emigrated to Africa, they made it into an "imaginary homeland" as well as a destination for the many artists, writers, and civil rights activists who traveled to Africa or settled there in the later years of the century.

NÉGRITUDE

In the influential novel *Banjo* (1929), Claude McKay's hero advises a skeptical black student to read the writers of the Irish Renaissance: "If you were sincere in your feelings about racial advancement," he says, "you would turn for example to whites of a different type. You would study the Irish cultural and social movement." The Irish writers had turned to Celtic mythology and Irish history as sources of ethnic identity and used their writing to promote Irish independence from British colonialism. The Harlem artists were also devoted to the cause of liberation. When blacks from the French colonies looked for writers to emulate, they discovered the Parisian avantgarde, particularly the SURREALISTS, and the writers of the Harlem Renaissance, most notably Claude McKay. The founders of the NÉGRITUDE movement in Paris in the early thirties, three students from French colonies in Africa and the Caribbean — **Léopold Sédar Senghor** (p. 1711) from Senegal, **Aimé Césaire** (p. 1714) from Martinique, and Léon Damas from French Guiana — set out with aims similar to those of the Harlem group. Senghor characterized McKay as their spiritual mentor, "the true inventor of Négritude," he wrote.

lay-oh-POHLD say-DAR sawng-GORE; eh-MAY seh-ZAR

"I speak not of the word, but of the values of Négritude. . . . Far from seeing in one's blackness an inferiority, one accepts it, one lays claim to it with pride, one cultivates it, lovingly." Senghor expressed this acceptance in poems like "**Black Woman,**" which metaphorically celebrates Africa, and "**Prayer to the Masks,**" an evocation of Senghor's African heritage. In *Notebook of a Return to the Native Land,* one of the most important works of French SURREALISM, Césaire returns to Martinique to confront its poverty, suffering, and history of slavery; by the end of the poem, in the sections presented below, he has come to accept his homeland in all its pain and suffering.

p. 1712

p. 1713

p. 1715

Describing Négritude poetry as "in our time, the only great revolutionary poetry," French existentialist philosopher Jean-Paul Sartre (1905–1980), in the influential essay "Black Orpheus," catalogs the themes of the poems as "exile, slavery, the Africa-Europe couple and the great . . . division of the world into black and white." He describes the map of the world imagined by the Négritude poets as composed of three circles whose centers overlap:

> . . . in the foreground—forming the first of three concentric circles—extends the land of exile, colorless Europe; then comes the dazzling circle of the Islands and of childhood; . . . the last circle is Africa, burnt, oily like a snake's skin, flickering like a flame, between being and nothingness, more *real* than the "eternal boulevards with cops" but absent, beyond attainment, disintegrating Europe with its black but invisible rays: Africa, an *imaginary* continent.

Sartre saw self-conscious absorption in blackness as a stage in a dialectical process—a process of change involving a thing and its opposite—that would eventually bring about a society that transcends racial categories. Although Senghor described Négritude as an evolutionary dynamic, his categories seem fixed. He characterizes, for example, the African personality type as emotional, intuitive, physical, and creative, and the European as rational, mechanical, and mental. "Emotion is black," he asserted, "as Reason is Hellenic." For such delineations he has been criticized as an "essentialist," one who adopts the categories of nineteenth-century European racism while rejecting their valuation. Césaire, who coined the term *Négritude,* seems to have the more evolutionary notion: "My Négritude has a ground," he wrote. "It is a fact that there is a black culture: It is historical, there is nothing biological about it." By recognizing Négritude

What would you expect to find, when the muzzle that has silenced the voices of black men is removed? That they would thunder your praise? . . . For the white man has enjoyed for three thousand years the privilege of seeing without being seen. It was a seeing pure and uncomplicated; the light of his eyes drew all things from their primeval darkness . . . . Today these black men have fixed their gaze upon us and our gaze is thrown back in our eyes. . . . black torches, in their turn, light the world.

– JEAN-PAUL SARTRE

Since our past has
been vilified by impe-
rialism, and since an
imperialist education
has tried to equip us
with all manner of
absurd views and
reactions to our past,
we need to reclaim
and rehabilitate our
genuine past, to
repossess our true
and entire history in
order to acquire a
secure launching pad
into our future.

– CHINWEIZU ET AL.

as part of a historical process and not an essential category, Césaire can choose to change history; in the existential moment of his return to Martinique, he can choose to transform suffering into celebration.

POSTCOLONIAL AFRICA

As African nations achieved political independence after World War II, there was great ambivalence regarding how much of the colonial past had to be given up in order to reach a collective psychic independence. Many Africans hoped to retain the benefits of Western culture while others argued that all traces of European influence had to be eradicated. For writers, that could mean rejecting the language in which they were educated and the language in which they wrote. Many Africans have found fault with the Pan-African and Négritude movements. Since both were led by blacks in the diaspora, they appeared to some as a black imperialism that would simply replace white imperialism and continue to direct the course of Africa from outside the continent. Furthermore, in the postwar struggles for independence, many former colonies in Africa were more concerned with their national identity than with their "pan-African" connections to other nations. Négritude was criticized for its unrealistic romanticism, its failure to acknowledge the inequities and injustices within many African societies.

During the second half of the twentieth century, many African American writers made pilgrimages to decolonized Africa and continued to celebrate the dream of return, albeit with a more realistic view of the continent's difficulties. James Baldwin was prompted to skepticism, however. Already a resident of North Africa for some time, he attended the Conference of Black Writers held in Paris in 1956 at which Senghor called for black authors worldwide to celebrate their common culture. Baldwin asked what, beyond suffering, all blacks had in common and doubted that the African elements in his own heritage were more important than the American ones. Although some African American writers—Alice Walker, for example, in *The Color Purple* (1982)—continued to see a return to Africa as a utopian project, others recognized its difficulties and believed the real journey called for looking within. **Gwendolyn Brooks**, after visiting Africa, acknowledged that the "Afrika" she sought was herself and that the continent she visited had much "work . . . to be done."

p. 1720

Twentieth-Century Europe: The Congress of Black Writers

After World War II, the movements to secure independence from their European colonizers spread throughout the colonial countries of Asia and Africa. At an important conference held in 1955 in Bandung, Indonesia, several newly independent nations of Africa and, especially, southeast Asia met to establish economic and cultural ties and to oppose the colonialism of both sides in the cold war—the West and the Soviet Union. This group of nonaligned nations, including Egypt, Indonesia, India, and Pakistan, condemned "colonialism in all its manifestations" and came to be known as the "Third World."

A year later, at the Sorbonne in Paris on September 19, 1956, a meeting inspired by the Asian-dominated Bandung Conference, convened to address the situation of black writers and artists—most of them from still-colonized countries in Africa and the Caribbean. The organizer of the conference, Senegalese writer and publisher Alioune Diop, editor of the influential journal of black writing *Présence Africaine,* brought together artists, writers, and intellectuals from many countries, particularly from the French colonies in Africa and the Caribbean. Those who attended included Léopold Sédar Senghor, Aimé Césaire, and Frantz Fanon from the Francophone culture. The most prominent English-speaking writers who attended were George Lamming, the Barbadian novelist who had published *In the Castle of My Skin* (1953), and American novelist Richard Wright, author of *Native Son* (1940) and *Black Boy* (1945), who had taken up residence in France after the war. Pablo Picasso contributed a drawing for the poster announcing the event.

Opening ceremony of the Congress of Black Writers and Artists, 1956   Included on the panel are Richard Wright (second from left), Alioune Diop (standing), and Aimé Césaire (third from right). (© Roger-Viollet/ The Image Works)

The American delegation to the conference, composed of academics and intellectuals, was marginalized by its noncolonial, English-speaking status, and by the absence of W. E. B. Du Bois, who in the wake of McCarthyism and the cold war, was denied a passport by the U.S. State Department. In a letter to the conference, Du Bois explained his absence: "Any Negro-American who travels abroad today must either not discuss race conditions in the United States or say the sort of thing which our State Department wishes the world to believe. . . . It would be a fatal mistake if new Africa becomes the tool and cat's paw of the colonial powers and allows the vast power of the United States to mislead it into investment and exploitation of labor. I trust the black

Twentieth-Century Europe: The Congress of Black Writers continued

writers of the world will understand this and will set themselves to lead Africa toward the light and not backward toward a new colonialism where hand in hand with Britain, France, and the United States, black capital enslaves black labor again." Du Bois's condemnation of colonialism was echoed in much harsher terms by many participants at the conference. Aimé Césaire moved the meeting to several spontaneous acclamations with his assertion that Europeans ruthlessly destroyed the languages, customs, tribes, and lives of the Africans and replaced them with nothing, intending to keep them in a state of subject barbarism.

American writer James Baldwin, covering the conference as a journalist, reflected the ambivalence of many American blacks who considered their culture more American than African. To Baldwin, the central issue of the meeting seemed to be whether there was a single black culture that linked African Americans with blacks from the colonies in Africa and elsewhere. "What, beyond the fact that all black men at one time or another left Africa, or have remained there," he asked, "do they really have in common?" He challenged Senghor's appropriation of Richard Wright's autobiography as an example of African literature. "*Black Boy* is

the study of the growing up of a Negro boy in the Deep South," he asserted, "and is one of the major American autobiographies." For African American writers this issue — whether there is a single black culture — has remained a troubling concern, described early in the century by Du Bois as reconciling the "two warring ideals within one dark body": the American and the Negro.

On September 19, 2006, a conference at the Sorbonne, organized by UNESCO and the W. E. B. Du Bois Institute for African and African American Research at Harvard, commemorated the fiftieth anniversary of the "important moment of history" in 1956. In his speech to the meeting, Nigerian playwright Wole Soyinka celebrated the goal of the earlier conference, which sought "to demolish the doctrines on which the mission of colonialism was raised, and challenge the scripture — both religious and philosophical — on whose authority the inhuman commerce in black flesh — Arab and European — had been justified." But, he went on to point out, those goals had not been achieved, for the genocide in Darfur, propagated with the collusion of the nations of the Western and the Islamic worlds, revealed just how much was left to be done.

■ **PRONUNCIATION**
Aimé Césaire: eh-MAY seh-ZAR
W. E. B. Du Bois: doo-BOYZ
Kwame Nkrumah: KWAH-may en-KROO-mah
Léopold Sédar Senghor: lay-oh-POHLD say-DAR sawng-GORE

W. E. B. Du Bois

b. United States, 1868–1963

William Edward Burghardt Du Bois was born in Great Barrington, Massachusetts, where he was brought up to love liberty and democracy and was not subjected to racial discrimination. In 1885 he traveled to Fisk University, a black college in Nashville, where he encountered a world sharply divided between black and white. Returning to New England for graduate studies at Harvard University, he majored in philosophy and history and wrote a celebrated dissertation, "The Suppression of the Slave Trade in the United States of America," in 1896. He became, in the words of African American studies professor Cornel West, the greatest "American intellectual of African descent . . . produced in this country." Du Bois taught at several universities, including Wilberforce and the University of Pennsylvania, and he served for many years as the Director of Publicity and Research for the National Association for the Advancement of Colored People (NAACP), an organization he helped to found. Among his many important books are *The Philadelphia Negro* (1899), *The Souls of Black Folk* (1903), *John Brown* (1909), *Black Reconstruction* (1935), and *Dusk of Dawn: An Essay Toward an Autobiography of a Race Concept* (1940). In 1961 he moved to Ghana and became a citizen two years later, the year he died.

In the following selection from *The Souls of Black Folk,* Du Bois analyzes the African American's "double-consciousness"—the apparently irreconcilable duality of being both American and black in which many African Americans are compelled to live.

W. E. B. Du Bois
(Photographs and Prints Division, Schomburg Center for Research in Black Culture, The New York Public Library, Astor, Lenox, and Tilden Foundations)

The Souls of Black Folk

FROM CHAPTER 1
OF OUR SPIRITUAL STRIVINGS

After the Egyptian and Indian, the Greek and Roman, the Teuton and Mongolian, the Negro is a sort of seventh son, born with a veil, and gifted with second-sight in this American world,—a world which yields him no true self-consciousness, but only lets him see himself through the revelation of the other world. It is a peculiar sensation, this double-consciousness, this sense of always looking at one's self through the eyes of others, of measuring one's soul by the tape of a world that looks on in amused contempt and pity. One ever feels his two-ness,—an American, a Negro; two souls, two thoughts, two unreconciled strivings; two warring ideals in one dark body, whose dogged strength alone keeps it from being torn asunder.

The history of the American Negro is the history of this strife, — this longing to attain self-conscious manhood, to merge his double self into a better and truer self. In this merging he wishes neither of the older selves to be lost. He would not Africanize America, for America has too much to teach the world and Africa. He would not bleach his Negro soul in a flood of white Americanism, for he knows that Negro blood has a message for the world. He simply wishes to make it possible for a man to be both a Negro and an American, without being cursed and spit upon by his fellows, without having the doors of Opportunity closed roughly in his face.

This, then, is the end of his striving: to be a co-worker in the kingdom of culture, to escape both death and isolation, to husband and use his best powers and his latent genius. These powers of body and mind have in the past been strangely wasted, dispersed, or forgotten. The shadow of a mighty Negro past flits through the tale of Ethiopia the Shadowy and of Egypt the Sphinx. Throughout history, the powers of single black men flash here and there like falling stars, and die sometimes before the world has rightly gauged their brightness. Here in America, in the few days since Emancipation, the black man's turning hither and thither in hesitant and doubtful striving has often made his very strength to lose effectiveness, to seem like absence of power, like weakness. And yet it is not weakness, — it is the contradiction of double aims. The double-aimed struggle of the black artisan — on the one hand to escape white contempt for a nation of mere hewers of wood and drawers of water, and on the other hand to plough and nail and dig for a poverty-stricken horde — could only result in making him a poor craftsman, for he had but half a heart in either cause. By the poverty and ignorance of his people, the Negro minister or doctor was tempted toward quackery and demagogy; and by the criticism of the other world, toward ideals that made him ashamed of his lowly tasks. The would-be black *savant* was confronted by the paradox that the knowledge his people needed was a twice-told tale to his white neighbors, while the knowledge which would teach the white world was Greek to his own flesh and blood. The innate love of harmony and beauty that set the ruder souls of his people a-dancing and a-singing raised but confusion and doubt in the soul of the black artist; for the beauty revealed to him was the soul-beauty of a race which his larger audience despised, and he could not articulate the message of another people. This waste of double aims, this seeking to satisfy two unreconciled ideals, has wrought sad havoc with the courage and faith and deeds of ten thousand thousand people, — has sent them often wooing false gods and invoking false means of salvation, and at times has even seemed about to make them ashamed of themselves. . . .

CLAUDE McKAY
B. JAMAICA, 1889–1948

Claude McKay began writing poems in Caribbean dialect while still a child. Recognized by the Jamaican Institute of Arts and Sciences for two volumes of poetry he published in 1912, McKay was awarded a scholarship to study in the United States. After two years of studying agriculture at Tuskegee Institute and Kansas State University, McKay went to New York, where he became a writer and editor for radical journals. His most important collection of poems, *Harlem Shadows* (1922), was published at the beginning of the Harlem Renaissance. His short and very intense lyric poetry is technically conservative, following English literary forms, but politically radical: McKay was the most militant writer of the Harlem Renaissance.

McKay left New York in 1923, living abroad in France, Britain, and North Africa, where he published several novels including *Home to Harlem* (1928) and *Banjo* (1929). In identifying McKay as the spiritual founder of the Négritude movement, Léopold Senghor said,

> Claude McKay can rightfully be considered the true inventor of Négritude. I speak not of the word, but of the values of Négritude. . . . Far from seeing in one's blackness an inferiority, one accepts it, one lays claim to it with pride, one cultivates it lovingly.

McKay's novel *Banjo* was particularly influential for the Négritude writers, who responded to its frank and affirmative treatment of blackness.

James L. Allen,
Claude McKay
McKay wrote novels and short stories as well as poetry. (Photographs and Print Division, Schomburg Center for Research in Black Culture, The New York Public Library, Astor, Lenox, and Tilden Foundations)

To the White Fiends

Think you I am not fiend and savage too?
Think you I could not arm me with a gun
And shoot down ten of you for every one
Of my black brothers murdered, burnt by you?
Be not deceived, for every deed you do
I could match—out-match: am I not Afric's son,
Black of that black land where black deeds are done?
But the Almighty from the darkness drew
My soul and said: Even thou shalt be a light
Awhile to burn on the benighted earth,
Thy dusky face I set among the white
For thee to prove thyself of higher worth;
Before the world is swallowed up in night,
To show thy little lamp: go forth, go forth!

10

∾ Outcast

For the dim regions whence my fathers came
My spirit, bondaged by the body, longs.
Words felt, but never heard, my lips would frame;
My soul would sing forgotten jungle songs.
I would go back to darkness and to peace,
But the great western world holds me in fee,
And I may never hope for full release
While to its alien gods I bend my knee.
Something in me is lost, forever lost,
Some vital thing has gone out of my heart,
And I must walk the way of life a ghost
Among the sons of earth, a thing apart.

For I was born, far from my native clime,
Under the white man's menace, out of time.

∾ LANGSTON HUGHES
B. UNITED STATES, 1902–1967

Langston Hughes was born and raised in the Midwest, influenced by such writers as Paul Lawrence Dunbar and Carl Sandburg. After attending Columbia University briefly in 1922, he left school and worked his way across the Atlantic to Europe and Africa on a freighter. His first book of poems, *The Weary Blues* (1925), reveals his fascination with jazz and the blues as well as the spirituals of his youth. Besides twelve volumes of poetry, Hughes wrote novels, plays, essays, and historical works. He is perhaps best known for his short stories, many of which are included in a late collection, *I Wonder as I Wander* (1956). Known for his generosity and his support of many younger writers, Hughes defended the right of young black authors "to express our dark-skinned selves without fear or shame." An early star of the Harlem Renaissance, Hughes dedicated "The Negro Speaks of Rivers" to W. E. B. Du Bois. In that poem Hughes traces his heritage by associating the Mississippi, the river near his childhood home in St. Louis, with rivers in Africa and the Middle East.

William H. Johnson,
*Jitterbugs, 1940–45.
Oil on plywood
Johnson, a painter
during the Harlem
Renaissance, was
known for his
renderings of black
New York nightlife.
Jazz figured greatly
in his work, as it
did in the poetry
of his friend
Langston Hughes.
(Smithsonian
American Art
Museum,
Washington, DC /
Art Resource, NY)*

∽ The Negro Speaks of Rivers

I've known rivers:
I've known rivers ancient as the world and older than the flow of human
    blood in human veins.

My soul has grown deep like the rivers.

I bathed in the Euphrates when dawns were young.
I built my hut near the Congo and it lulled me to sleep.
I looked upon the Nile[1] and raised the pyramids above it.

I heard the singing of the Mississippi when Abe Lincoln went down to New
    Orleans, and I've seen its muddy bosom turn all golden in the sunset.

I've known rivers:
Ancient, dusky rivers.

10   My soul has grown deep like the rivers.

---

[1] **Euphrates . . . Nile:** The Euphrates River flows through the ancient kingdom of Babylon, from present-day
Turkey through Syria and Iraq; the Congo flows through the Republic of Congo in central Africa into the
Atlantic Ocean; the Nile runs through Egypt into the Mediterranean Sea. [Editors' note.]

COUNTEE CULLEN
B. UNITED STATES, 1903–1946

Yet do I marvel at this curious thing: / To make a poet black, and bid him sing!

– COUNTEE CULLEN

Countee Cullen, the adopted son of a Methodist minister living in New York, earned a B.A. at New York University and an M.A. at Harvard before returning to teach school in New York City. As with many writers of the Harlem Renaissance, Cullen's first collection of poems, reflecting the energies of the group, was his strongest. After *Color* was published in 1925, Cullen served as the editor of the important black magazine *Opportunity,* and his poems appeared in many periodicals. Like the work of Claude McKay, Cullen's verse is formally traditional but at the same time intense and political.

Heritage

For Harold Jackman

What is Africa to me:
Copper sun or scarlet sea,
Jungle star or jungle track,
Strong bronzed men, or regal black
Women from whose loins I sprang
When the birds of Eden sang?
One three centuries removed
From the scenes his fathers loved,
Spicy grove, cinnamon tree,
10 *What is Africa to me?*

So I lie, who all day long
Want no sound except the song
Sung by wild barbaric birds
Goading massive jungle herds,
Juggernauts of flesh that pass
Trampling tall defiant grass
Where young forest lovers lie,
Plighting troth beneath the sky.
So I lie, who always hear,
20 Though I cram against my ear
Both my thumbs, and keep them there,
Great drums throbbing through the air.
So I lie, whose fount of pride,

Dear distress, and joy allied.
Is my somber flesh and skin,
With the dark blood dammed within
Like great pulsing tides of wine
That, I fear, must burst the fine
Channels of the chafing net
30   Where they surge and foam and fret.
Africa? A book one thumbs
Listlessly, till slumber comes.
Unremembered are her bats
Circling through the night, her cats
Crouching in the river reeds,
Stalking gentle flesh that feeds
By the river brink; no more
Does the bugle-throated roar
Cry that monarch claws have leapt
40   From the scabbards where they slept.
Silver snakes that once a year
Doff the lovely coats you wear,
Seek no covert in your fear
Lest a mortal eye should see;
What's your nakedness to me?
Here no leprous flowers rear
Fierce corollas in the air;
Here no bodies sleek and wet,
Dripping mingled rain and sweat,
50   Tread the savage measures of
Jungle boys and girls in love.
What is last year's snow to me,
Last year's anything? The tree
Budding yearly must forget
How its past arose or set —
Bough and blossom, flower, fruit,
Even what shy bird with mute
Wonder at her travail there,
Meekly labored in its hair.
60   *One three centuries removed*
From the scenes his fathers loved,
Spicy grove, cinnamon tree,
What is Africa to me?

So I lie, who find no peace
Night or day, no slight release
From the unremittant beat
Made by cruel padded feet

Walking through my body's street.
Up and down they go, and back,
70   Treading out a jungle track.
So I lie, who never quite
Safely sleep from rain at night—
I can never rest at all
When the rain begins to fall;
Like a soul gone mad with pain
I must match its weird refrain;
Ever must I twist and squirm,
Writhing like a baited worm,
While its primal measures drip
80   Through my body, crying, "Strip!
Doff this new exuberance.
Come and dance the Lover's Dance!"
In an old remembered way
Rain works on me night and day.

Quaint, outlandish heathen gods
Black men fashion out of rods,
Clay, and brittle bits of stone,
In a likeness like their own,
My conversion came high-priced;
90   I belong to Jesus Christ,
Preacher of humility,
Heathen gods are naught to me.

Father, Son, and Holy Ghost,
So I make an idle boast;
Jesus of the twice-turned cheek,
Lamb of God, although I speak
With my mouth thus, in my heart
Do I play a double part.
Ever at Thy glowing altar
100   Must my heart grow sick and falter,
Wishing He I served were black,
Thinking then it would not lack
Precedent of pain to guide it,
Let who would or might deride it;
Surely then this flesh would know
Yours had borne a kindred woe.
Lord, I fashion dark gods, too,
Daring even to give You
Dark despairing features where,
110   Crowned with dark rebellious hair,

Patience wavers just so much as
Mortal grief compels, while touches
Quick and hot, of anger, rise
To smitten cheek and weary eyes.
Lord, forgive me if my need
Sometimes shapes a human creed.
All day long and all night through,
One thing only must I do:
Quench my pride and cool my blood,
Lest I perish in the flood,
Lest a hidden ember set
Timber that I thought was wet
Burning like the dryest flax,
Melting like the merest wax,
Lest the grave restore its dead.
Not yet has my heart or head
In the least way realized
They and I are civilized.

120

∾ LÉOPOLD SÉDAR SENGHOR
B. SENEGAL, 1906–2001

Léopold Sédar Senghor, the son of a wealthy Catholic merchant, was
born in 1906 in Joal, a predominantly Muslim port town in Senegal. As a
child, Senghor received a traditional African education as well as a formal
introduction to European culture. Eventually, he completed his education, first at the Lycée Louis le Grand and later at the Sorbonne. In Paris
Senghor joined with other French-speaking African and Caribbean
writers, including Aimé Césaire (b. 1913) from Martinique, to lay the
foundations of what would become known as the Négritude movement.
Together Senghor, Césaire, and Léon Damas founded *Black Student*
(*L'Éudiant noir*), a journal exploring questions of race and celebrating
African culture. After obtaining the equivalent of a master's degree from
the Sorbonne in 1932 with a thesis on Baudelaire, Senghor went on to
become the first African to receive the prestigious *agrégation,* a fellowship
for advanced study in France, for which he had to become a French
citizen.

Senghor's teaching career was interrupted by World War II; he
fought on the northern front and was captured by the Germans in 1940.
While in the prison camps, Senghor wrote many of the poems that would
later appear in *Shadow Songs* (*Chants d'ombre,* 1945) and *Black Hosts*
(*Hosties noires,* 1948). Released in 1942, Senghor returned to teaching

Quite simply, *négri-
tude* is the *sum total of
the values of the civi-
lization of the African
world.*
– LÉOPOLD SÉDAR
SENGHOR, *Pierre
Teilhard de Chardin et
la Politique Africaine,*
1962

and in 1944 became the Professor of African Languages at the École Nationale de la France d'Outre Mer (National School of the Overseas French Territories). After the war Senghor entered a new phase of his career, publishing *Chants d'ombre* and being elected to the French Constituent Assembly as a deputy for Senegal.

Starting in his student years, Senghor wrote for and organized the then-burgeoning Négritude movement. In addition to founding the short-lived journal *L'Étudiant noir,* Senghor helped to found two other journals, *The Human Condition* (*Condition humaine*) and *African Presence* (*Présence Africaine*). Throughout his career, Senghor's writings celebrated Africa's cultural heritage and attempted to promote a new view of African culture and society.

In 1948, the year he published his second collection of poetry, *Hosties noires,* Senghor also published *Anthology of the New Black and Madagascan Poetry* (*Anthologie de la nouvelle poésie nègre et malgache*) with a preface by Jean-Paul Sartre. Sartre's introduction to the groundbreaking work that brought together works of French-speaking black writers articulated for the first time the constituent features of Négritude and its historical and cultural importance. *Songs for Naett* (*Chants pour Naëtt*), Senghor's third volume of poetry, appeared in 1949; his next book of poems, *Ethiopiques,* would not appear until 1960, as he devoted much time and energy to politics. In the forties and fifties, Senghor founded several political parties and sat on various political committees. Representing the interests of Senegal in particular and French Africa in general, Senghor attempted to reshape the relationship between France and its colonies into one of an equal balance of power. After Senegal finally won its independence in 1960, Senghor was elected president of that nation, holding the position until 1981 when he retired.

∾ Black Woman

Translated by Melvin Dixon

Naked woman, black woman
Dressed in your color[1] that is life, in your form that is beauty!
I grew up in your shadow. The softness of your hands
Shielded my eyes, and now at the height of Summer and Noon,
From the crest of a charred hilltop I discover you, Promised Land[2]
And your beauty strikes my heart like an eagle's lightning flash.

---

[1] **your color:** Both the green of the African landscape and the black of the woman's skin.

[2] **Promised Land:** An allusion to the land promised to the exiled Israelites in the Book of Exodus.

Naked woman, dark woman
Ripe fruit with firm flesh, dark raptures of black wine,
Mouth that gives music to my mouth
10 Savanna of clear horizons, savanna quivering to the fervent caress
Of the the East Wind,[3] sculptured tom-tom, stretched drumskin
Moaning under the hands of the conqueror
Your deep contralto voice is the spiritual song of the Beloved.

Naked woman, dark woman
Oil no breeze can ripple, oil soothing the thighs
Of athletes and the thighs of the princes of Mali[4]
Gazelle with celestial limbs, pearls are stars
Upon the night of your skin. Delight of the mind's riddles,
The reflections of red gold from your shimmering skin
20 In the shade of your hair, my despair
Lightens in the close suns of your eyes.

Naked woman, black woman
I sing your passing beauty and fix it for all Eternity
before jealous Fate reduces you to ashes to nourish the roots of life.

---

[3] **East Wind:** The Hamattan, a wind that blows across Senegal between November and April from the Sahara Desert to the northeast.

[4] **Mali:** African nation east of Senegal that has roots in the ancient African kingdom of Mali.

❧ Prayer to the Masks

Translated by Melvin Dixon

Masks![1] O Masks!
Black mask, red mask, you white-and-black masks
Masks of the four cardinal points where the Spirit blows
I greet you in silence!
And you, not the least of all, Ancestor with the lion head.[2]
You keep this place safe from women's laughter
And any wry, profane smiles
You exude the immortal air where I inhale

---

[1] **Masks!:** African ancestral masks, kept in a sacred place and believed to contain the spirits of ancestors who provide protection for the living.

[2] **Ancestor with the lion head:** The lion is the totem animal, the symbolic emblem, of the Senghor family.

The breath of my Fathers.
10 Masks with faces without masks, stripped of every dimple
And every wrinkle
You created this portrait, my face leaning
On an altar of blank paper
And in your image, listen to me!
The Africa of empires is dying—it is the agony
Of a sorrowful princess
And Europe, too, tied to us at the navel.
Fix your steady eyes on your oppressed children
Who give their lives like the poor man his last garment.
20 Let us answer "present" at the rebirth of the World
As white flour cannot rise without the leaven.
Who else will teach rhythm to the world
Deadened by machines and cannons?
Who will sound the shout of joy at daybreak to wake orphans and the dead?
Tell me, who will bring back the memory of life
To the man of gutted hopes?
They call us men of cotton, coffee, and oil
They call us men of death.
But we are men of dance, whose feet get stronger
30 As we pound upon firm ground.

❧ AIMÉ CÉSAIRE
B. MARTINIQUE, 1913–2008

I say right on! The old negritude / progressively cadavers itself / the horizon breaks, recoils and expands / and through the shredding of clouds the flashing of a sign / the slave ship cracks everywhere . . .

– AIMÉ CÉSAIRE,
Notebook of a Return to the Native Land

Poet, playwright, and politician from the island of Martinique in the French Caribbean, Césaire brings a MODERNIST perspective to bear on the themes of decolonization, Western racism, and négritude. Educated in France in the 1930s, Césaire was influenced by the French modernists, particularly André Breton and the SURREALISTS. In Paris he also met Léopold Sédar Senghor from Senegal and Léon Gotran Damas from Guiana; together they founded the NÉGRITUDE movement, which sought to counter European racism with positive meanings for blackness. After World War II Césaire was elected mayor of Fort-de-France, the capital of Martinique, and deputy to the French Assembly, in which role he fought for anticolonialist causes until he retired from politics in 1993. Césaire's long poem *Notebook of a Return to the Native Land* (*Cahier d'un retour au pays natal*, 1939; English translation, 1947) became the manifesto and masterwork of the Négritude movement. It is also one of the most important works of French surrealism. The selection presented here is taken from the end of the poem where Césaire accepts and celebrates his race, his heritage, and his identity. Earlier in the poem, he has cataloged the poverty and misery of his native land, the cruelty and brutality of slavery, and the debased sense of self that he and his countrymen have adopted.

All notes are the editors' unless otherwise marked.

FROM

∾ Notebook of a Return to the Native Land

Translated by Clayton Eshleman and Annette Smith

And my special geography too; the world map made for my own use, not tinted with the arbitrary colors of scholars, but with the geometry of my spilled blood, I accept both the determination of my biology, not a prisoner to a facial angle, to a type of hair, to a well-flattened nose, to a clearly Melanian coloring, and negritude, no longer a cephalic index, or plasma, or soma, but measured by the compass of
    suffering
and the Negro every day more base, more cowardly, more sterile, less profound, more spilled out of himself, more separated from himself, more wily with himself, less immediate to himself,

I accept, I accept it all

and far from the palatial sea that foams beneath the suppurating syzygy[1] of blisters, miraculously lying in the despair of my arms the body of my country, its bones shocked and, in its veins, the blood hesitating like a drop of vegetal milk at the injured point of the bulb . . .

Suddenly now strength and life assail me like a bull and the water of life overwhelms the papilla[2] of the morne, now all the veins and veinlets are bustling with new blood and the enormous breathing lung of cyclones and the fire hoarded in volcanoes and the gigantic seismic pulse which now beats the measure of a living body in my firm conflagration.

And we are standing now, my country and I, hair in the wind, my hand puny in its enormous fist and now the strength is not in us but above us, in a voice that drills the night and the hearing like the penetrance of an apocalyptic wasp.[3] And the voice

---

[1] **suppurating syzygy:** The festering tides.

[2] **papilla:** Nipple.

[3] **apocalyptic wasp:** Like the plagues suffered by the Israelites in Egypt. See Exodus, Ch. 5–11.

proclaims that for centuries Europe has force-fed us with lies and bloated us with
pestilence,
for it is not true that the work of man is done
that we have no business being on earth
that we parasite the world
that it is enough for us to heel to the world
where the work has only begun
and man still must overcome all the interdictions wedged in the recesses of his
fervor and no race has a monopoly on beauty, on intelligence, on strength

and there is room for everyone at the convocation of conquest and we know now
that the sun turns around our earth lighting the parcel designated by our will alone
and that every star falls from sky to earth at our omnipotent command.

I now see the meaning of this trial by the sword: my country is the "lance of night"
of my Bambara[4] ancestors. It shrivels and its point desperately retreats toward the
haft when it is sprinkled with chicken blood and it says that its nature requires the
blood of man, his fat, his liver, his heart, not chicken blood.

    And I seek for my country not date hearts, but men's hearts which, in order to
enter the silver cities through the great trapezoidal gate, beat with warrior blood,
and as my eyes sweep my kilometers of paternal earth I number its sores almost
joyfully and I pile one on top of the other like rare species, and my total is ever
lengthened by unexpected mintings of baseness.

And there are those who will never get over not being made in the likeness of God
but of the devil, those who believe that being a nigger is like being a second-class
clerk; waiting for a better deal and upward mobility; those who beat the drum of
compromise in front of themselves, those who live in their own dungeon pit; those
who drape themselves in proud pseudomorphosis;[5] those who say to Europe: "You
see, I *can* bow and scrape, like you I pay my respects, in short, I am no different
from you; pay no attention to my black skin: the sun did it."

And there is the nigger pimp, the nigger askari,[6] and all the zebras shaking themselves
in various ways to get rid of their stripes in a dew of fresh milk. And in the midst of
all that I say right on! my grandfather dies, I say right on! the old negritude
progressively cadavers itself.

---

[4] **Bambara**: An ethnic group in Mali. The ritual referred to is one in which human blood is sprinkled on spears
to make them effective.

[5] **pseudomorphosis**: A false personality.

[6] **askari**: The Swahili term in East Africa for African colonial soldiers.

No question about it: he was a good nigger. The Whites say he was a good nigger, a really good nigger, massa's good ole darky. I say right on!

He was a good nigger, indeed,
poverty had wounded his chest and back and they had stuffed into his poor brain
that a fatality impossible to trap weighed on him; that he had no control over his
own fate; that an evil Lord had for all eternity inscribed Thou Shall Not in his pelvic
constitution; that he must be a good nigger; must sincerely believe in his
worthlessness, without any perverse curiosity to check out the fatidic hieroglyphs.

He was a very good nigger

and it never occurred to him that he could hoe, burrow, cut anything, anything else
really than insipid cane

He was a very good nigger.

And they threw stones at him, bits of scrap iron, broken bottles, but neither these
stones, nor this scrap iron, nor these bottles . . . O peaceful years of God on this
terraqueous clod!

and the whip argued with the bombilation[7] of the flies over the sugary dew of our
sores.

I say right on! The old negritude
progressively cadavers itself
the horizon breaks, recoils and expands
and through the shredding of clouds the flashing of a sign
the slave ship cracks everywhere . . . Its belly convulses and resounds . . . The
ghastly tapeworm of its cargo gnaws the fetid guts of the strange suckling of the sea!

And neither the joy of sails filled like a pocket stuffed with doubloons, nor the tricks
played on the dangerous stupidity of the frigates of order[8] prevent it from hearing
the threat of its intestinal rumblings

In vain to ignore them the captain hangs the biggest loudmouth nigger from the
main yard or throws him into the sea, or feeds him to his mastiffs

Reeking of fried onions the nigger scum rediscovers the bitter taste of freedom in its
spilled blood

---

[7] **bombilation:** Swarming.

[8] **frigates of order:** Ships sent out from England to enforce Britain's abolition of slavery.

And the nigger scum is on its feet

the seated nigger scum
unexpectedly standing
standing in the hold
standing in the cabins
standing on deck
standing in the wind
standing under the sun
standing in the blood
    standing
        and
            free
standing and no longer a poor madwoman in her maritime freedom and
destitution gyrating in perfect drift[9]
and there she is:
most unexpectedly standing
standing in the rigging
standing at the tiller
standing at the compass
standing at the map
standing under the stars
    standing
        and
            free
and the lustral[10] ship fearlessly advances on the crumbling water.

And now our ignominious plops are rotting away!
by the clanking noon sea
by the burgeoning midnight sun
listen sparrow hawk who holds the keys to the orient
by the disarmed day
by the stony spurt of the rain

listen dogfish that watches over the occident

listen white dog of the north, black serpent of the south that cinches the sky girdle
There still remains one sea to cross
oh still one sea to cross
that I may invent my lungs

---

[9] **drift:** An allusion to the Ship of Fools on which the insane were put out to sea and set adrift. Here the slave
ship is adrift after the slaves have taken it over.

[10] **lustral:** Purifying. By revolting the slaves are purified.

that the prince may hold his tongue
that the queen may lay me
still one old man to murder
one madman to deliver
that my soul may shine bark shine
bark bark bark
and the owl[11] my beautiful inquisitive angel may hoot.
The master of laughter?
The master of ominous silence?
The master of hope and despair?
The master of laziness? Master of the dance?
    It is I!
and for this reason, Lord,
the frail-necked men
receive and perceive deadly triangular calm[12]

Rally to my side my dances
you bad nigger dances
the carcan-cracker dance[13]
the prison-break dance
the it-is-beautiful-good-and-legitimate-to-be-a-nigger-dance
Rally to my side my dances and let the sun bounce on the racket of my hands

but no the unequal sun is not enough for me
coil, wind, around my new growth
light on my cadenced fingers
to you I surrender my conscience and its fleshy rhythm
to you I surrender the fire in which my weakness smolders
to you I surrender the "chain-gang"
to you the swamps
to you the nontourist of the triangular circuit
devour wind
to you I surrender my abrupt words
devour and encoil yourself
and self-encoiling embrace me with a more ample shudder
embrace me unto furious us
embrace, embrace US
but after having drawn from us blood
drawn by our own blood!

---

[11] the owl: Césaire's guardian angel.

[12] triangular calm: Césaire associates the triangular slave trade—operating between Europe, Africa, and America—with the Christian Holy Trinity, traditionally represented by a triangle.

[13] carcan-cracker dance: The carcan was an iron collar fixed around the necks of slaves, and this dance was a dance of freedom.

embrace, my purity mingles only with yours
so then embrace
like a field of even filagos[14]
at dusk
our multicolored purities
and bind, bind me without remorse
bind me with your vast arms to the luminous clay
bind my black vibration to the very navel of the world
bind, bind me, bitter brotherhood
then, strangling me with your lasso of stars
rise,
Dove[15]
rise
rise
rise
I follow you who are imprinted on my ancestral white cornea.
rise sky licker
and the great black hole where a moon ago I wanted to drown it is there I will now
fish the malevolent tongue of the night in its motionless veerition![16]

---

[14] filagos: Casuarina trees.

[15] Dove: The Christian symbol of the Pentecost.

[16] veerition: Coined from the Latin verb *verri,* meaning "to sweep," "to scrape a surface," and ultimately "to scan." (Translators' note.)

✍ GWENDOLYN BROOKS
B. UNITED STATES, 1917–2000

> You did not know the
> Black continent /
> that had to be
> reached / was you.
>
> – GWENDOLYN
> BROOKS, "To the
> Diaspora"

Gwendolyn Brooks was born in Kansas but is identified with Chicago, the city where she grew up and whose Negro ghetto, Bronzeville, is the subject of many of her poems. She began writing early and was a regular contributor to the black Chicago newspaper *The Defender* by the time she was sixteen. Brooks was inspired by the work of Langston Hughes, whom she met at church and who became a friend and mentor. Her work mixes the language of black preachers with street talk and draws on the rhythms of jazz and the blues to describe the everyday life of blacks. Many of her finest early poems are verbal portraits of the inhabitants of "Bronzeville." After attending the Second Black Writers' Conference at Fisk University in 1967, Brooks adopted a more activist voice and, addressing her poems to a black audience, wrote about the issues raised by the civil rights movement and the Black Nationalists. She traveled to Africa in 1971 and 1974. Among her many books of poetry are *A Street in Bronzeville* (1945), *Bronzeville Boys and Girls* (1956), and *Blacks* (1987).

To the Diaspora[1]

you did not know you were Afrika

When you set out for Afrika
you did not know you were going.
Because
you did not know you were Afrika.
You did not know the Black continent
that had to be reached
was you.

I could not have told you then that some sun
would come,
10   somewhere over the road,
would come evoking the diamonds
of you, the Black continent—
somewhere over the road.
You would not have believed my mouth.

When I told you, meeting you somewhere close
to the heat and youth of the road,
liking my loyalty, liking belief,
you smiled and you thanked me but very little believed me.

Here is some sun. Some.
20   Now off into the places rough to reach.
Though dry, though drowsy, all unwillingly a-wobble,
into the dissonant and dangerous crescendo.
Your work, that was done, to be done to be done to be done.

---

[1] **Diaspora:** A dispersion of people from their native land; here, specifically, Africans living outside of Africa.
[Editors' note.]

CHINUA ACHEBE
B. NIGERIA, 1930

In the following transcript of a lecture delivered at the University of Massachusetts in February 1975, Nigerian novelist Chinua Achebe challenges the status of *Heart of Darkness* (p. 1159) as one of the great books of Western literature. Conrad's novel, Achebe argues, does not treat its African characters as fully human. Achebe's own novel *Things Fall Apart* can be read as a response to Conrad's story. (For more on Chinua Achebe and the text of *Things Fall Apart*, see p. 1597.)

All notes are the editors' unless otherwise indicated.

An Image of Africa

It was a fine autumn morning at the beginning of this academic year such as encouraged friendliness to passing strangers. Brisk youngsters were hurrying in all directions, many of them obviously freshmen in their first flush of enthusiasm. An older man, going the same way as I, turned and remarked to me how very young they came these days. I agreed. Then he asked me if I was a student too. I said no, I was a teacher. What did I teach? African literature. Now that was funny, he said, because he never had thought of Africa as having that kind of stuff, you know. By this time I was walking much faster. "Oh well," I heard him say finally, behind me, "I guess I have to take your course to find out."

A few weeks later I received two very touching letters from high-school children in Yonkers, New York, who — bless their teacher — had just read *Things Fall Apart*. One of them was particularly happy to learn about the customs and superstitions of an African tribe.

I propose to draw from these rather trivial encounters rather heavy conclusions which at first sight might seem somewhat out of proportion to them: But only at first sight.

The young fellow from Yonkers, perhaps partly on account of his age but I believe also for much deeper and more serious reasons, is obviously unaware that the life of his own tribesmen in Yonkers, New York, is full of odd customs and superstitions and, like everybody else in his culture, imagines that he needs a trip to Africa to encounter those things.

The other person being fully my own age could not be excused on the grounds of his years. Ignorance might be a more likely reason; but here again I believe that something more willful than a mere lack of information was at work. For did not that erudite British historian and Regius Professor at Oxford, Hugh Trevor Roper, pronounce a few years ago that African history did not exist?

If there is something in these utterances more than youthful experience, more than a lack of factual knowledge, what is it? Quite simply it is the desire — one might indeed say the need — in Western psychology to set up Africa as a foil to Europe, a place of negations at once remote and vaguely familiar in comparison with which Europe's own state of spiritual grace will be manifest.

This need is not new: which should relieve us of considerable responsibility and perhaps make us even willing to look at this phenomenon dispassionately. I have neither the desire nor, indeed, the competence to do so with the tools of the social and biological sciences. But, I can respond, as a novelist, to one famous book of European fiction, Joseph Conrad's *Heart of Darkness,* which better than any other work I know displays that Western desire and need which I have just spoken about. Of course, there are whole libraries of books devoted to the same purpose, but most of them are so obvious and so crude that few people worry about them today. Conrad, on the other hand, is undoubtedly one of the great stylists of modern fiction and a good storyteller into the bargain. His contribution therefore falls automatically into a different class — permanent literature — read and taught and constantly evaluated by serious academics. *Heart of Darkness* is indeed so secure today that a leading Conrad scholar has numbered it "among the half-dozen greatest short novels in the English language."[1] I will return to this critical opinion in due course because it may seriously modify my earlier suppositions about who may or may not be guilty in the things of which I will now speak.

Heart of Darkness projects the image of Africa as "the other world," the antithesis of Europe and therefore of civilization, a place where a man's vaunted intelligence and refinement are finally mocked by triumphant bestiality. The book opens on the River Thames, tranquil, resting peacefully "at the decline of day after ages of good service done to the race that peopled its banks." But the actual story takes place on the River Congo, the very antithesis of the Thames. The River Congo is quite decidedly not a River Emeritus. It has rendered no service and enjoys no old-age pension. We are told that "going up that river was like travelling back to the earliest beginning of the world."

Is Conrad saying then that these two rivers are very different, one good, the other bad? Yes, but that is not the real point. What actually worries Conrad is the lurking hint of kinship, of common ancestry. For the Thames, too, "has been one of the dark places of the earth." It conquered its darkness, of course, and is now at peace. But if it were to visit its primordial relative, the Congo, it would run the terrible risk of hearing grotesque, suggestive echoes of its own forgotten darkness, and of falling victim to an avenging recrudescence of the mindless frenzy of the first beginnings.

I am not going to waste your time with examples of Conrad's famed evocation of the African atmosphere. In the final consideration it amounts to no more than a

---

[1] **"among . . . language"**: Albert J. Guerard, Introduction to *Heart of Darkness* (New York: New American Library, 1950), p. 9.

steady, ponderous, fake-ritualistic repetition of two sentences, one about silence and the other about frenzy. An example of the former is "It was the stillness of an implacable force brooding over an inscrutable intention" and of the latter, "The steamer toiled along slowly on the edge of a black and incomprehensible frenzy." Of course, there is a judicious change of adjective from time to time so that instead of "inscrutable," for example, you might have "unspeakable," etc., etc.

The eagle-eyed English critic, F. R. Leavis, drew attention nearly thirty years ago to Conrad's "adjectival insistence upon inexpressible and incomprehensible mystery." That insistence must not be dismissed lightly, as many Conrad critics have tended to do, as a mere stylistic flaw. For it raises serious questions of artistic good faith. When a writer, while pretending to record scenes, incidents and their impact, is in reality engaged in inducing hypnotic stupor in his readers through a bombardment of emotive words and other forms of trickery, much more has to be at stake than stylistic felicity. Generally, normal readers are well armed to detect and resist such underhand activity. But Conrad chose his subject well—one which was guaranteed not to put him in conflict with the psychological predisposition of his readers or raise the need for him to contend with their resistance. He chose the role of purveyor of comforting myths.

The most interesting and revealing passages in *Heart of Darkness* are, however, about people. I must quote a long passage from the middle of the story in which representatives of Europe in a steamer going down the Congo encounter the denizens of Africa:

> We were wanderers on a prehistoric earth, on an earth that wore the aspect of an unknown planet. We could have fancied ourselves the first of men taking possession of an accursed inheritance, to be subdued at the cost of profound anguish and of excessive toil. But suddenly, as we struggled round a bend, there would be a glimpse of rush walls, of peaked grass-roofs, a burst of yells, a whirl of black limbs, a mass of hands clapping, of feet stamping, of bodies swaying, of eyes rolling, under the droop of heavy and motionless foliage. The steamer toiled along slowly on the edge of a black and incomprehensible frenzy. The prehistoric man was cursing us, praying to us, welcoming us—who could tell? We were cut off from the comprehension of our surroundings; we glided past like phantoms, wondering and secretly appalled, as sane men would be before an enthusiastic outbreak in a madhouse. We could not remember because we were travelling in the night of first ages, of those ages that are gone, leaving hardly a sign—and no memories.
>
> The earth seemed unearthly. We are accustomed to look upon the shackled form of a conquered monster, but there—there you could look at a thing monstrous and free. It was unearthly, and the men were—No, they were not inhuman. Well, you know, that was the worst of it—this suspicion of their not being inhuman. It would come slowly to one. They howled and leaped, and spun, and made horrid faces; but what thrilled you was just the thought of your remote kinship with this wild and passionate uproar. Ugly. Yes, it was ugly enough; but if you were man enough you would admit to yourself that there was in you just the faintest trace of a response to the terrible frankness of that noise, a dim suspicion of there being a meaning in it which you—you so remote from the night of first ages—could comprehend.

Herein lies the meaning of *Heart of Darkness* and the fascination it holds over the Western mind: "What thrilled you was just the thought of their humanity — like yours. . . . Ugly."

Having shown us Africa in the mass, Conrad then zeros in on a specific example, giving us one of his rare descriptions of an African who is not just limbs or rolling eyes:

> And between whiles I had to look after the savage who was fireman. He was an improved specimen; he could fire up a vertical boiler. He was there below me, and, upon my word, to look at him was as edifying as seeing a dog in a parody of breeches and a feather hat, walking on his hind legs. A few months of training had done for that really fine chap. He squinted at the steam gauge and at the water gauge with an evident effort of intrepidity — and he had filed his teeth, too, the poor devil, and the wool of his pate shaved into queer patterns, and three ornamental scars on each of his cheeks. He ought to have been clapping his hands and stamping his feet on the bank, instead of which he was hard at work, a thrall to strange witchcraft, full of improving knowledge.

As everybody knows, Conrad is a romantic on the side. He might not exactly admire savages clapping their hands and stamping their feet but they have at least the merit of being in their place, unlike this dog in a parody of breeches. For Conrad, things (and persons) being in their place is of the utmost importance.

Towards the end of the story, Conrad lavishes great attention quite unexpectedly on an African woman who has obviously been some kind of mistress to Mr. Kurtz and now presides (if I may be permitted a little imitation of Conrad) like a formidable mystery over the inexorable imminence of his departure:

> She was savage and superb, wild-eyed and magnificent . . . She stood looking at us without a stir and like the wilderness itself, with an air of brooding over an inscrutable purpose.

This Amazon is drawn in considerable detail, albeit of a predictable nature, for two reasons. First, she is in her place and so can win Conrad's special brand of approval; and second, she fulfills a structural requirement of the story; she is a savage counterpart to the refined, European woman with whom the story will end:

> She came forward, all in black with a pale head, floating towards me in the dusk. She was in mourning. . . . She took both my hands in hers and murmured, "I had heard you were coming" . . . She had a mature capacity for fidelity, for belief, for suffering.

The difference in the attitude of the novelist to these two women is conveyed in too many direct and subtle ways to need elaboration. But perhaps the most significant difference is the one implied in the author's bestowal of human expression to the one and the withholding of it from the other. It is clearly not part of Conrad's purpose to confer language on the "rudimentary souls" of Africa. They only "exchanged short grunting phrases" even among themselves but mostly they were too busy with their frenzy. There are two occasions in the book, however, when

Conrad departs somewhat from his practice and confers speech, even English speech, on the savages. The first occurs when cannibalism gets the better of them:

> "Catch 'im," he snapped, with a bloodshot widening of his eyes and a flash of sharp white teeth — "catch 'im. Give 'im to us." "To you, eh?" I asked; "what would you do with them?" "Eat 'im!" he said curtly . . .

The other occasion is the famous announcement:

> Mistah Kurtz — he dead.

At first sight, these instances might be mistaken for unexpected acts of generosity from Conrad. In reality, they constitute some of his best assaults. In the case of the cannibals, the incomprehensible grunts that had thus far served them for speech suddenly proved inadequate for Conrad's purpose of letting the European glimpse the unspeakable craving in their hearts. Weighing the necessity for consistency in the portrayal of the dumb brutes against the sensational advantages of securing their conviction by clear, unambiguous evidence issuing out of their own mouth, Conrad chose the latter. As for the announcement of Mr. Kurtz's death by the "insolent black head in the doorway," what better or more appropriate *finis* could be written to the horror story of that wayward child of civilization who willfully had given his soul to the powers of darkness and "taken a high seat amongst the devils of the land" than the proclamation of his physical death by the forces he had joined?

It might be contended, of course, that the attitude to the African in *Heart of Darkness* is not Conrad's but that of his fictional narrator, Marlow, and that far from endorsing it Conrad might indeed be holding it up to irony and criticism. Certainly, Conrad appears to go to considerable pains to set up layers of insulation between himself and the moral universe of his story. He has, for example, a narrator behind a narrator. The primary narrator is Marlow but his account is given to us through the filter of a second, shadowy person. But if Conrad's intention is to draw a *cordon san-itaire*[2] between himself and the moral and psychological malaise of his narrator, his care seems to me totally wasted because he neglects to hint however subtly or tenta-tively at an alternative frame of reference by which we may judge the actions and opinions of his characters. It would not have been beyond Conrad's power to make that provision if he had thought it necessary. Marlow seems to me to enjoy Conrad's complete confidence — a feeling reinforced by the close similarities between their careers.

Marlow comes through to us not only as a witness of truth, but one holding those advanced and humane views appropriate to the English liberal tradition which required all Englishmen of decency to be deeply shocked by atrocities in Bulgaria or the Congo of King Leopold of the Belgians or wherever. Thus Marlow is able to toss out such bleeding-heart sentiments as these:

> They were all dying slowly — it was very clear. They were not enemies, they were not criminals, they were nothing earthly now — nothing but black shadows of disease

---

[2] *cordon sanitaire:* A buffer.

and starvation, lying confusedly in the greenish gloom. Brought from all the recesses of the coast in all the legality of time contracts, lost in uncongenial surroundings, fed on unfamiliar food, they sickened, became inefficient, and were then allowed to crawl away and rest.

The kind of liberalism espoused here by Marlow/Conrad touched all the best minds of the age in England, Europe, and America. It took different forms in the minds of different people but almost always managed to sidestep the ultimate question of equality between white people and black people. That extraordinary missionary, Albert Schweitzer,[3] who sacrificed brilliant careers in music and theology in Europe for a life of service to Africans in much the same area as Conrad writes about, epitomizes the ambivalence. In a comment which I have often quoted but must quote one last time Schweitzer says: "The African is indeed my brother but my junior brother." And so he proceeded to build a hospital appropriate to the needs of junior brothers with standards of hygiene reminiscent of medical practice in the days before the germ theory of disease came into being. Naturally, he became a sensation in Europe and America. Pilgrims flocked, and I believe still flock even after he has passed on, to witness the prodigious miracle in Lamberene, on the edge of the primeval forest.

Conrad's liberalism would not take him quite as far as Schweitzer's, though. He would not use the word "brother" however qualified; the farthest he would go was "kinship." When Marlow's African helmsman falls down with a spear in his heart he gives his white master one final disquieting look.

> And the intimate profundity of that look he gave me when he received his hurt remains to this day in my memory—like a claim of distant kinship affirmed in a supreme moment.

It is important to note that Conrad, careful as ever with his words, is not talking so much about *distant kinship* as about someone *laying a claim* on it. The black man lays a claim on the white man which is well-nigh intolerable. It is the laying of this claim which frightens and at the same time fascinates Conrad, ". . . the thought of their humanity—like yours . . . Ugly."

The point of my observations should be quite clear by now, namely, that Conrad was a bloody racist. That this simple truth is glossed over in criticism of his work is due to the fact that white racism against Africa is such a normal way of thinking that its manifestations go completely undetected. Students of *Heart of Darkness* will often tell you that Conrad is concerned not so much with Africa as with the deterioration of one European mind caused by solitude and sickness. They will point out to you that Conrad is, if anything, less charitable to the Europeans in the story than he is to the natives. A Conrad student told me in Scotland last year that Africa is merely a setting for the disintegration of the mind of Mr. Kurtz.

Which is partly the point: Africa as setting and backdrop which eliminates the African as human factor. Africa as a metaphysical battlefield devoid of all recognizable

---

[3] **Albert Schweitzer** (1875–1965): Alsatian philosopher, theologian, musician, writer, physicist, and missionary; he gave his life to a medical mission and hospital at Lamberene, in Gabon, West Africa.

humanity, into which the wandering European enters at his peril. Of course, there is a preposterous and perverse kind of arrogance in thus reducing Africa to the role of props for the breakup of one petty European mind. But that is not even the point. The real question is the dehumanization of Africa and Africans which this age-long attitude has fostered and continues to foster in the world. And the question is whether a novel which celebrates this dehumanization, which depersonalizes a portion of the human race, can be called a great work of art. My answer is: No, it cannot. I would not call that man an artist, for example, who composes an eloquent instigation to one people to fall upon another and destroy them. No matter how striking his imagery or how beautifully his cadences fall, such a man is no more a great artist than another may be called a priest who reads the mass backwards or a physician who poisons his patients. All those men in Nazi Germany who lent their talent to the service of virulent racism whether in science, philosophy, or the arts have generally and rightly been condemned for their perversions. The time is long overdue for taking a hard look at the work of creative artists who apply their talents, alas often considerable as in the case of Conrad, to set people against people. This, I take it, is what Yevtushenko[4] is after when he tells us that a poet cannot be a slave trader at the same time, and gives the striking example of Arthur Rimbaud,[5] who was fortunately honest enough to give up any pretenses to poetry when he opted for slave trading. For poetry surely can only be on the side of man's deliverance and not his enslavement; for the brotherhood and unity of all mankind and against the doctrines of Hitler's master races or Conrad's "rudimentary souls."

Last year was the fiftieth anniversary of Conrad's death. He was born in 1857, the very year in which the first Anglican missionaries were arriving among my own people in Nigeria. It was certainly not his fault that he lived his life at a time when the reputation of the black man was at a particularly low level. But even after due allowances have been made for all the influences of contemporary prejudice on his sensibility, there remains still in Conrad's attitude a residue of antipathy to black people which his peculiar psychology alone can explain. His own account of his first encounter with a black man is very revealing:

> A certain enormous buck nigger encountered in Haiti fixed my conception of blind, furious, unreasoning rage, as manifested in the human animal to the end of my days. Of the nigger I used to dream for years afterwards.

Certainly, Conrad had a problem with niggers. His inordinate love of that word itself should be of interest to psychoanalysts. Sometimes his fixation on blackness is equally interesting as when he gives us this brief description:

> A black figure stood up, strode on long black legs, waving long black arms.

---

[4]**Yevtushenko:** Yevgeny Yevtushenko (b. 1933), Russian poet known in the West in particular for his poems criticizing Stalinism.

[5]**Arthur Rimbaud** (1854–1891): French Symbolist poet who abandoned poetry for a life of adventure; among his later occupations were slave trading and gunrunning.

as though we might expect a black figure striding along on black legs to wave *white* arms! But so unrelenting is Conrad's obsession.

As a matter of interest Conrad gives us in *A Personal Record* what amounts to a companion piece to the buck nigger of Haiti. At the age of sixteen Conrad encountered his first Englishman in Europe. He calls him "my unforgettable Englishman" and describes him in the following manner:

> [his] calves exposed to the public gaze . . . dazzled the beholder by the splendor of their marble-like condition and their rich tone of young ivory . . . The light of a headlong, exalted satisfaction with the world of men . . . illumined his face . . . and triumphant eyes. In passing he cast a glance of kindly curiosity and a friendly gleam of big, sound, shiny teeth . . . his white calves twinkled sturdily.

Irrational love and irrational hate jostling together in the heart of that tormented man. But whereas irrational love may at worst engender foolish acts of indiscretion, irrational hate can endanger the life of the community. Naturally, Conrad is a dream for psychoanalytic critics. Perhaps the most detailed study of him in this direction is by Bernard C. Meyer, M.D. In this lengthy book, Dr. Meyer follows every conceivable lead (and sometimes inconceivable ones) to explain Conrad. As an example, he gives us long disquisitions on the significance of hair and hair-cutting in Conrad. And yet not even one word is spared for his attitude to black people. Not even the discussion of Conrad's anti-Semitism was enough to spark off in Dr. Meyer's mind those other dark and explosive thoughts. Which only leads one to surmise that Western psychoanalysts must regard the kind of racism displayed by Conrad as absolutely normal despite the profoundly important work done by Frantz Fanon[6] in the psychiatric hospitals of French Algeria.

Whatever Conrad's problems were, you might say he is now safely dead. Quite true. Unfortunately, his heart of darkness plagues us still. Which is why an offensive and totally deplorable book can be described by a serious scholar as "among the half dozen greatest short novels in the English language," and why it is today perhaps the most commonly prescribed novel in the twentieth-century literature courses in our own English Department here. Indeed the time is long overdue for a hard look at things.

There are two probable grounds on which what I have said so far may be contested. The first is that it is no concern of fiction to please people about whom it is written. I will go along with that. But I am not talking about pleasing people. I am talking about a book which parades in the most vulgar fashion prejudices and insults from which a section of mankind has suffered untold agonies and atrocities in the past and continues to do so in many ways and many places today. I am talking about a story in which the very humanity of black people is called in question. It seems to me totally inconceivable that great art or even good art could possibly reside in such unwholesome surroundings.

---

[6] Frantz Fanon (1925–1961): Psychiatrist and theorist of the colonial mind from Martinique; author of *Black Skin, White Masks* (1952) and *The Wretched of the Earth* (1961).

Secondly, I may be challenged on the grounds of actuality. Conrad, after all, sailed down the Congo in 1890 when my own father was still a babe in arms, and recorded what he saw. How could I stand up in 1975, fifty years after his death and purport to contradict him? My answer is that as a sensible man I will not accept just any traveller's tales solely on the grounds that I have not made the journey myself. I will not trust the evidence even of a man's very eyes when I suspect them to be as jaundiced as Conrad's. And we also happen to know that Conrad was, in the words of his biographer, Bernard C. Meyer, "notoriously inaccurate in the rendering of his own history."[7]

But more important by far is the abundant testimony about Conrad's savages which we could gather if we were so inclined from other sources and which might lead us to think that these people must have had other occupations besides merging into the evil forest or materializing out of it simply to plague Marlow and his dispirited band. For as it happened, soon after Conrad had written his book an event of far greater consequence was taking place in the art world of Europe. This is how Frank Willett, a British art historian, describes it:

> Gauguin had gone to Tahiti, the most extravagant individual act of turning to a non-European culture in the decades immediately before and after 1900, when European artists were avid for new artistic experiences, but it was only about 1904–5 that African art began to make its distinctive impact. One piece is still identifiable; it is a mask that had been given to Maurice Vlaminck in 1905. He records that Derain was "speechless" and "stunned" when he saw it, bought it from Vlaminck and in turn showed it to Picasso and Matisse, who were also greatly affected by it. Ambroise Vollard then borrowed it and had it cast in bronze . . . The revolution of twentieth century art was under way![8]

The mask in question was made by other savages living just north of Conrad's River Congo. They have a name, the Fang people, and are without a doubt among the world's greatest masters of the sculptured form. As you might have guessed, the event to which Frank Willett refers marked the beginning of cubism and the infusion of new life into European art that had run completely out of strength.

The point of all this is to suggest that Conrad's picture of the people of the Congo seems grossly inadequate even at the height of their subjection to the ravages of King Leopold's International Association for the Civilization of Central Africa. Travellers with closed minds can tell us little except about themselves. But even those not blinkered, like Conrad, with xenophobia, can be astonishingly blind.

Let me digress a little here. One of the greatest and most intrepid travellers of all time, Marco Polo, journeyed to the Far East from the Mediterranean in the thirteenth century and spent twenty years in the court of Kublai Khan in China. On his return to Venice he set down in his book entitled *Description of the World* his impressions of the peoples and places and customs he had seen. There are at least two

---

[7] "notoriously . . . history": Meyer, p. 30.

[8] Gaugin . . . under way: Frank Willett, *African Art* (New York: Praeger, 1971), pp. 35–36.

extraordinary omissions in his account. He says nothing about the art of printing unknown as yet in Europe but in full flower in China. He either did not notice it at all or if he did, failed to see what use Europe could possibly have for it. Whatever reason, Europe had to wait another hundred years for Gutenberg. But even more spectacular was Marco Polo's omission of any reference to the Great Wall of China nearly four thousand miles long and already more than one thousand years old at the time of his visit. Again, he may not have seen it; but the Great Wall of China is the only structure built by man which is visible from the moon![9] Indeed, travellers can be blind.

As I said earlier, Conrad did not originate the image of Africa which we find in his book. It was and is the dominant image of Africa in the Western imagination and Conrad merely brought the peculiar gifts of his own mind to bear on it. For reasons which can certainly use close psychological inquiry, the West seems to suffer deep anxieties about the precariousness of its civilization and to have a need for constant reassurance by comparing itself to Africa. If Europe, advancing in civilization, could cast a backward glance periodically at Africa trapped in primordial barbarity, it could say with faith and feeling: There, but for the grace of God, go I. Africa is to Europe as the picture is to Dorian Gray[10]—a carrier onto whom the master unloads his physical and moral deformities so that he may go forward, erect and immaculate. Consequently, Africa is something to be avoided just as the picture has to be hidden away to safeguard the man's jeopardous integrity. Keep away from Africa, or else! Mr. Kurtz of *Heart of Darkness* should have heeded that warning and the prowling horror in his heart would have kept its place, chained to its lair. But he foolishly exposed himself to the wild irresistible allure of the jungle and lo! the darkness found him out.

In my original conception of this talk I had thought to conclude it nicely on an appropriately positive note in which I would suggest from my privileged position in African and Western culture some advantages the West might derive from Africa once it rid its mind of old prejudices and began to look at Africa not through a haze of distortions and cheap mystification but quite simply as a continent of people— not angels, but not rudimentary souls either—just people, often highly gifted people and often strikingly successful in their enterprise with life and society. But as I thought more about the stereotype image, about its grip and pervasiveness, about the willful tenacity with which the West holds it to its heart; when I thought of your television and the cinema and newspapers, about books read in schools and out of school, of churches preaching to empty pews about the need to send help to the heathen in Africa, I realized that no easy optimism was possible. And there is something totally wrong in offering bribes to the West in return for its good opinion of Africa. Ultimately, the abandonment of unwholesome thoughts must be its own and only

---

[9] About the omission of the Great Wall of China, I am indebted to *The Journey of Marco Polo* as recreated by artist Michael Foreman, published by *Pegasus Magazine,* 1974. [Achebe's note.]

[10] **Africa is . . . Dorian Gray:** In Oscar Wilde's novel *The Picture of Dorian Gray* (1891), a portrait of the protagonist bears all his marks of age and guilt while he himself remains young.

reward. Although I have used the word *willful* a few times in this talk to characterize the West's view of Africa it may well be that what is happening at this stage is more akin to reflex action than calculated malice. Which does not make the situation more, but less, hopeful. Let me give you one last and really minor example of what I mean.

Last November the *Christian Science Monitor* carried an interesting article written by its education editor on the serious psychological and learning problems faced by little children who speak one language at home and then go to school where something else is spoken. It was a wide-ranging article taking in Spanish-speaking children in this country, the children of migrant Italian workers in Germany, the quadrilingual phenomenon in Malaysia, and so on. And all this while the article speaks unequivocally about *language.* But then out of the blue sky comes this:

> In London there is an enormous immigration of children who speak Indian or Nigerian dialects, or some other native language.[11]

I believe that the introduction of *dialects,* which is technically erroneous in the context, is almost a reflex action caused by an instinctive desire of the writer to downgrade the discussion to the level of Africa and India. And this is quite comparable to Conrad's withholding of language from his rudimentary souls. Language is too grand for these chaps; let's give them dialects. In all this business a lot of violence is inevitably done to words and their meaning. Look at the phrase "native language" in the above excerpt. Surely the only native language possible in London is Cockney English. But our writer obviously means something else—something Indians and Africans speak.

Perhaps a change will come. Perhaps this is the time when it can begin, when the high optimism engendered by the breathtaking achievements of Western science and industry is giving way to doubt and even confusion. There is just the possibility that Western man may begin to look seriously at the achievements of other people. I read in the papers the other day a suggestion that what America needs at this time is somehow to bring back the extended family. And I saw in my mind's eye future African Peace Corps Volunteers coming to help you set up the system.

Seriously, although the work which needs to be done may appear too daunting, I believe that it is not one day too soon to begin. And where better than at a University?

---

[11] In London . . . language: *Christian Science Monitor,* Nov. 15, 1974, p. 11.

❧ DEREK WALCOTT
B. ST. LUCIA, 1930

Growing up on the Caribbean island of St. Lucia, Derek Walcott was exposed at an early age to a wide range of peoples and customs whose roots extended to Africa, Asia, and Europe. The history of the region also included indigenous peoples who had been largely exterminated by Spanish explorers in the sixteenth century. Walcott's substantial body of work—poetry and plays—addresses the social and political realities of a diverse and turbulent history. Like other West Indian writers and artists, Walcott is interested in the search for identity within such a cultural collage.

After the decimation of the original West Indians through slavery and disease, some five million Africans were brought in to work as slaves on the islands' plantations in the seventeenth and eighteenth centuries. After the abolition of slavery in the nineteenth century, East Indian, Chinese, Portuguese, and Irish immigrants were recruited to work the fields of sugar cane. An early pattern of an elite white ruling class dominating a peasant working class comprising various ethnic groups prevailed into the twentieth century. Thus, the most basic question of identity concerning the West Indies has to do with the name of these islands and their residents. The current name, "West Indies," perpetuates the misnomer coined by Columbus in 1492 when he called the native peoples of the Americas "Indians" and used "West" to distinguish them from the "East Indians" of India. The terms *Greater* and *Lesser Antilles* have also been used for the region, but *Antilles* was the name of a legendary island located between Europe and Japan on medieval maps; after Columbus's "discovery," the Spanish called the islands *Antillas*. Residents of the West Indies have a complicated relationship not only with their personal identity but with that of their land as well.

Walcott's writings are a personal odyssey, a search for a mosaic that would harmonize the diversity of his native region, a vision complicated by the multiplicity of languages spoken there—English, Spanish, French, and Dutch—not to mention a variety of CREOLE dialects and island PATOIS (a regional form of a language). Walcott, himself a combination of different ethnic groups, sympathizes with the various social classes and mores on the islands. His writings appeal to many who see themselves as ethnic and cultural MESTIZOS[1]—peoples of mixed origins. The experience of native peoples under European colonizers is one of the fundamental stories of the Americas and of central importance to such modern writers as Pablo Neruda of Chile, Carlos Fuentes of Mexico, and Leslie Marmon Silko of the southwestern United States.

Rune Hellestad, *Derek Walcott, 1992 The Nobel Prize–winning poet and playwright. (© Rune Hellestad/CORBIS)*

www

www For links to more information about Derek Walcott and a quiz on his poetry, see bedford stmartins.com/ worldlitcompact.

---

[1] *mestizos: Mestizo,* a Spanish word meaning "mixed," was first used in Latin American countries to refer to children of a mixed couple, a Spanish or a Portuguese with an indigenous person; with the intermarrying of various immigrant groups since, *mestizo* has come to have a broader application.

No poet rivals Mr.
Walcott in humor,
emotional depth,
lavish inventiveness
in language or in the
ability to express the
thoughts of his char-
acters. . . ."

    – *The New York Times
       Book Review*

Walcott's Mixed Heritage.

Derek Walcott was born of racially mixed parentage on January 23, 1930, in Castries, the capital of St. Lucia. His mother was white and his father black, an official and artist who died shortly after Derek's birth. His mother then became headmistress at a Methodist elementary school. Derek, who was Protestant and middle class in a largely black, Roman Catholic, working-class society, experienced the tension between contrasting cultures at an early age. Moreover, his first language was English in a society that spoke French creole (a blend of French and the language originally spoken on the islands).

Early in his secondary education at St. Mary's College, in Castries, Walcott discovered his calling as a poet, his responsibility to protect his island's heritage, and his sympathy for the poor. His first two volumes of poetry, *25 Poems* (1948) and *Epitaph for the Young* (1949), are about his childhood on St. Lucia. In 1950, along with Maurice Mason, Walcott founded the St. Lucian Arts Guild, where he produced *Henri Christophe* (1950), a historical play about the Haitian revolution. Derek's twin brother, Roddy, ran this influential theater when Derek left to attend the University of the West Indies in Kingston, Jamaica, on a scholarship. After receiving a B.A., Walcott taught school in Kingston, later working as a feature writer for *The Sunday Guardian,* out of Port-of-Spain, Trinidad.

Education in the United States and the Search for Roots in the West Indies.

A Rockefeller Fellowship in theater brought Walcott to New York University in 1957. The civil rights movement in the United States during the late 1950s and the 1960s opened Walcott's eyes to the complexities of race issues. Returning to Port-of-Spain in 1959, Walcott founded Trinidad Theatre Workshop (known originally as Little Carib Theatre Workshop), which occupied him for close to two decades, until 1976. In his first important collection of poems, *In a Green Night: Poems 1948–1962* (1962), work that extended his reputation beyond the Caribbean, Walcott explored his heritage as a West Indian. During this time he also wrote one of his most impressive plays, *Dream on Monkey Mountain* (1967), in which the dreams of the hero, Makak, give voice to the history of colonial oppression and a peoples' ties to Africa. *The Castaway* (1969) uses the figure of Robinson Crusoe to embody the solitary search for identity. *Another Life* (1973) is a series of autobiographical poems that invoke the spirit of the ancient Greek traveler Odysseus and the meaning of the search for home.

In his next two collections of poetry, *Sea Grapes* (1976) and *Star Apple Kingdom* (1977), Walcott wrote about the role of the poet as well as the legacy of slavery, "the MIDDLE PASSAGE," and colonial domination. The plays *Ti-Jean and His Brothers* (1958) and *Pantomime* (1978) also deal with the consequences and the legacy of slavery. *The Joker of Seville* (1974) retells Tirso de Molina's sixteenth-century story of Don Juan in a West Indian setting. *O Babylon!* was published with *The Joker* and involves a RASTAFARIAN[2] cult in Jamaica.

To begin with, we are
poor. That gives us a
privilege. . . . The
stripped and naked
man, however
abused, however dis-
abused of old beliefs,
instinctually, even
desperately begins
again as a craftsman.

    – DEREK WALCOTT,
              1974

---

[2] Rastafarian: Having to do with a religious cult in Jamaica that regards the late Haile Selassie of Ethiopia as the messiah; reggae music and the late Bob Marley are associated with Rastafarianism.

In 1979, Walcott was named an honorary member of the American Academy of Arts and Letters. His travels between the United States and the Caribbean stimulated the poems in *The Fortunate Traveler* (1981), in which he recognizes the stark contrast of the powerful, wealthy United States with the impoverished Caribbean. Walcott's *Collected Poems* was published in 1986, followed by *The Arkansas Testament* (1987), a collection of poems about St. Lucia. In *Omeros* (1990), an epic poem loosely related to Homer's epics and to Dante's *Divine Comedy*,[3] Walcott weaves together many of the themes of his previous writing while celebrating the rich folk traditions of African descendants in the West Indies. In 1992, he was awarded the Nobel Prize in Literature.

Selected Poems.   The poems selected here touch on themes central to Walcott's writings. Like a number of writers sympathetic to the impact of colonization on indigenous peoples, Walcott was carried by his work into the very culture that symbolizes domination and oppression — that of white America. The poem "A Latin Primer" deals with the influence of Walcott's education on the process of his becoming a poet, the tension between the educational opportunities provided by the privileged elite and the richness of the folk traditions preserved by the oppressed majority. "White Magic" further explores the cultural conflict between white secularism and the folk traditions of the islands. The United States provides Walcott with the opportunity to publish and work at universities, but his involvement with its culture has the potential to estrange him from the Caribbean culture of his childhood. His poetry, in fact, voices the yearning of an outsider for the rich textures of island life. In the two poems that follow, Walcott writes tightly, compactly, employing end rhyme with a light touch.

"The Light of the World" reveals the anatomy of estrangement through the symbol of a beautiful island woman. Though a looser rhythm prevails here, the poem's images are characteristically dense and thoughtful. In "For Pablo Neruda," Walcott pays tribute to a fellow American poet — a Chilean — whose broad sympathies embraced the ethnic and historical extremes of North and South America. Walcott's poetic style has affinities with Neruda's: Both make use of rich, complex metaphors as a means of yoking the disparate suffering caused by European conquest and the potential contradictions of living in a multicultural society.

> The Caribbean has remained a green place, even if, as Derek Walcott has written, "the golden apples of this sun are shot with acid." Between the nightmare of the slave barracoons [barracks], and the vision of Adamic islands, have emerged the imagined worlds. . . .
> – LOUIS JAMES, critic, 1999

■ **FURTHER RESEARCH**

Historical and Cultural Background
Brathwaite, Kamau. *Roots.* 1993.
Hulme, Peter, and Neil L. Whitehead, eds. *Wild Majesty: Encounters with Caribs from Columbus to the Present Day.* 1992.
James, Louis. *Caribbean Literature in English.* 1999.

---

[3] **Homer's . . . Comedy:** Homer (eighth century B.C.E.) wrote the *Iliad* and the *Odyssey*; Dante (1265–1321) wrote the *Divine Comedy*, a trilogy about a spiritual pilgrimage to the underworld and then to purgatory and heaven.

Critical Works on Derek Walcott

Erada, Rei. *Derek Walcott's Poetry: American Mimicry.* 1992.

Goldstraw, Irma. *Derek Walcott: An Annotated Bibliography of His Writings,* 1944–1984. 1984.

Hamner, Robert D. *Derek Walcott.* 1994.

———, ed. *Critical Perspectives on Derek Walcott.* 1993.

King, Bruce L. *The Theatre of Derek Walcott.* 1996.

Thieme, John. *Derek Walcott.* 1999.

∽ A Latin Primer

(In Memoriam: H. D. Boxill)

I had nothing against which
to notch the growth of my work
but the horizon, no language
but the shallows in my long walk

home, so I shook all the help
my young right hand could use
from the sand-crusted kelp
of distant literatures.

The frigate bird[1] my phoenix,[2]
I was high on iodine,
one drop from the sun's murex
stained the foam's fabric wine;

ploughing white fields of surf
with a boy's shins, I kept
staggering as the shelf
of sand under me slipped,

then found my deepest wish
in the swaying words of the sea,
and the skeletal fish
of that boy is ribbed in me;

---

[1] **frigate bird:** A large, tropical seabird with V-shaped wings and tail; the *Fregata magnificens.*

[2] **phoenix:** A mythical bird from ancient Egypt; said to renew itself by rising out of its own ashes, it symbolizes immortality.

but I saw how the bronze
dusk of imperial palms
curled their fronds into questions
over Latin exams.

I hated signs of scansion.
Those strokes across the line
drizzled on the horizon
and darkened discipline.

They were like Mathematics
that made delight Design,
arranging the thrown sticks
of stars to sine and cosine.[3]

Raging, I'd skip a pebble
across the sea's page; it still
scanned its own syllable:
trochee, anapest, dactyl.[4]

Miles,[5] foot soldier. *Fossa,*
a trench or a grave. My hand
hefts a last sand bomb to toss
at slowly fading sand.

I failed Matriculation
in Maths; passed it; after that,
I taught Love's basic Latin:
Amo, amas, amat.[6]

In tweed jacket and tie
a master at my college
I watched the old words dry
like seaweed on the page.

I'd muse from the roofed harbour
back to my desk, the boys'

---

[3] **sine and cosine:** Technical terms in trigonometry.

[4] **trochee . . . dactyl:** Common patterns of accented and unaccented syllables of words in a line of verse.

[5] *Miles:* Latin for "soldier"; also refers to Nelson Appleton Miles (1839–1925), a U.S. soldier who worked his way up from foot soldier to general. After the Civil War, Miles led troops against Native Americans in the West and fought in the Caribbean during the Spanish-American War (1895–1898).

[6] *Amo, amas, amat:* The first conjugation of the Latin *amare,* "to love."

heads plunged in paper
softly as porpoises.

The discipline I preached
made me a hypocrite;
their lithe black bodies, beached,
would die in dialect;

I spun the globe's meridian,
showed its sealed hemispheres,
but where were those brows heading
60   when neither world was theirs?

Silence clogged my ears
with cotton, a cloud's noise;
I climbed white tiered arenas
trying to find my voice,

and I remember: it was on a
Saturday near noon, at Vigie,[7]
that my heart, rounding the corner
of Half-Moon Battery,[8]

stopped to watch the foundry
70   of midday cast in bronze
the trunk of a gommier tree
on a sea without seasons,

while ochre Rat Island
was nibbling the sea's lace,
that a frigate bird came sailing
through a tree's net, to raise

its emblem in the cirrus,
named with the common sense
of fishermen: sea scissors,
80   *Fregata magnificens,*

---

[7] **Vigie:** The Vigie peninsula forms the northern side of the Castries Harbor of St. Lucia, an island in the Caribbean.

[8] **Half-Moon Battery:** Remnant of a fortification from the three hundred years of fighting between England and France over ownership of St. Lucia.

ciseau-la-mer,[9] the patois[10]
for its cloud-cutting course;
and that native metaphor
made by the strokes of oars,

with one wing beat for scansion,
that slowly levelling V
made one with my horizon
as it sailed steadily

beyond the sheep-nibbled columns
90   of fallen marble trees,
or the roofless pillars once
sacred to Hercules.[11]

---

[9] *ciseau-la-mer:* French for "sea scissors," or "scissors of the sea."

[10] **patois:** A local dialect that is a variation of an area's standard language.

[11] **Hercules:** Roman name of the Greek hero and god Heracles; the ancient Pillars of Hercules flanked the Strait of Gibraltar between Gibraltar, in Europe, and Mt. Acha, in Africa.

℘ White Magic

(For Leo St. Helene)

The *gens-gagée*[1] kicks off her wrinkled skin.
Clap her soul in a jar! The half-man wolf
can trot with bending elbows, rise, and grin
in lockjawed lycanthropia.[2] Censers dissolve
the ground fog with its whistling, wandering souls,
the unbaptized, unfinished, and uncursed
by holy fiat. The island's griots[3] love
our mushroom elves, the devil's parasols
who creep like grubs from a trunk's rotten holes,
10   their mouths a sewn seam, their clubfeet reversed.

---

[1] *gens-gagée:* Island patois for "spirit being."

[2] **lycanthropia:** From the Greek *lykoi* (wolf) and *anthropos* (man); lycanthropy is the belief that one has become a wolf.

[3] **griots:** Members of a hereditary caste among the peoples of western Africa whose function is to keep an oral history of the tribe or village and to tell the stories, songs, and poems of the people.

Exorcism cannot anachronize
those signs we hear past midnight in a wood
where a pale woman like a blind owl flies
to her forked branch, with scarlet moons for eyes
bubbling with doubt. You heard a silver splash?
It's nothing. If it slid from mossed rocks
dismiss it as a tired crab, a fish,
unless our water-mother with dank locks
is sliding under this page below your pen,
20   only a simple people think they happen.
Dryads and hamadryads[4] were engrained
in the wood's bark, in papyrus, and this paper;
but when our dry leaves crackle to the deer-
footed, hobbling hunter, Papa Bois,[5]
he's just Pan's[6] clone, one more translated satyr.
The crone who steps from her jute sugar sack
(though you line moonlit lintels with white flour),
the *beau l'homme*[7] creeping towards you, front to back,
the ferny footed, faceless, mouse-eared elves,
30   these fables of the backward and the poor
marbled by moonlight, will grow white and richer.
Our myths are ignorance, theirs are literature.

---

[4] **Dryads and hamadryads:** Deities or nymphs of the woods; hamadryads are spirits of particular trees.

[5] **Papa Bois:** Refers to a notorious pirate, Jambe de Bois (French for "wooden leg"), who had a hideout on Pigeon Island, off the west coast of St. Lucia.

[6] **Pan:** Greek god of pastures, flocks, and shepherds; symbolic of the sexual energy of nature, which took the form of a goatlike creature, the satyr. This figure was "translated" by medieval Christians into Satan.

[7] *beau l'homme:* French for "handsome man."

⌘ The Light of the World

Kaya now, got to have kaya now,
Got to have kaya now,
For the rain is falling.
   — BOB MARLEY[1]

Marley was rocking on the transport's stereo
and the beauty was humming the choruses quietly.
I could see where the lights on the planes of her cheek
streaked and defined them; if this were a portrait

---

[1] **Bob Marley** (1945–1981): Jamaican-born reggae singer committed to nonviolence and the Rastafarian religion.

you'd leave the highlights for last, these lights
silkened her black skin; I'd have put in an earring,
something simple, in good gold, for contrast, but she
wore no jewelry. I imagined a powerful and sweet
odour coming from her, as from a still panther,
and the head was nothing else but heraldic.
When she looked at me, then away from me politely
because any staring at strangers is impolite,
it was like a statue, like a black Delacroix's[2]
Liberty Leading the People, the gently bulging
whites of her eyes, the carved ebony mouth,
the heft of the torso solid, and a woman's,
but gradually even that was going in the dusk,
except the line of her profile, and the highlit cheek,
and I thought, O Beauty, you are the light of the world!

It was not the only time I would think of that phrase
in the sixteen-seater transport that hummed between
Gros-Islet[3] and the Market, with its grit of charcoal
and the litter of vegetables after Saturday's sales,
and the roaring rum shops, outside whose bright doors
you saw drunk women on pavements, the saddest of all things,
winding up their week, winding down their week.
The Market, as it closed on this Saturday night,
remembered a childhood of wandering gas lanterns
hung on poles at street corners, and the old roar
of vendors and traffic, when the lamplighter climbed,
hooked the lantern on its pole and moved on to another,
and the children turned their faces to its moth, their
eyes white as their nighties; the Market
itself was closed in its involved darkness
and the shadows quarrelled for bread in the shops,
or quarrelled for the formal custom of quarrelling
in the electric rum shops. I remember the shadows.

The van was slowly filling in the darkening depot.
I sat in the front seat, I had no need for time.
I looked at two girls, one in a yellow bodice
and yellow shorts, with a flower in her hair,
and lusted in peace, the other less interesting.

---

[2]**Delacroix:** Eugène Delacroix (1798–1863), French Romantic painter whose visit to Morocco in 1832 inspired an interest in "exotic" subjects.

[3]**Gros-Islet:** Fishing village on the northwest coast of St. Lucia known for its weekly carnivals.

That evening I had walked the streets of the town
where I was born and grew up, thinking of my mother
with her white hair tinted by the dyeing dusk,
and the tilting box houses that seemed perverse
in their cramp; I had peered into parlours
with half-closed jalousies, at the dim furniture,
Morris chairs,[4] a centre table with wax flowers,
50   and the lithograph of *Christ of the Sacred Heart*,[5]
vendors still selling to the empty streets—
sweets, nuts, sodden chocolates, nut cakes, mints.

An old woman with a straw hat over her headkerchief
hobbled towards us with a basket; somewhere,
some distance off, was a heavier basket
that she couldn't carry. She was in a panic.
She said to the driver: *"Pas quittez moi à terre,"*
which is, in her patois: "Don't leave me stranded,"
which is, in her history and that of her people:
60   "Don't leave me on earth," or, by a shift of stress:
"Don't leave me the earth" [for an inheritance];
"Pas quittez moi à terre, Heavenly transport,
Don't leave me on earth, I've had enough of it."
The bus filled in the dark with heavy shadows
that would not be left on earth; no, that would be left
on the earth, and would have to make out.
Abandonment was something they had grown used to.

And I had abandoned them, I knew that there
sitting in the transport, in the sea-quiet dusk,
70   with men hunched in canoes, and the orange lights
from the Vigie[6] headland, black boats on the water;
I, who could never solidify my shadow
to be one of their shadows, had left them their earth,
their white rum quarrels, and their coal bags,
their hatred of corporals, of all authority.
I was deeply in love with the woman by the window.
I wanted to be going home with her this evening.

---

[4] **Morris chairs:** Large armchairs with adjustable backs and removable cushions, named after the English artist and poet William Morris (1834–1896).

[5] *Christ of the Sacred Heart:* Image depicting the exposed heart of Jesus encircled by either flames or thorns. Partly because of St. Margaret Mary Alacoque's visions in the seventeenth century, the Roman Catholic Church approved the "enthronement" of this image in the home, symbolizing the sovereignty of Christ over the family.

[6] **Vigie:** See note 7 for "A Latin Primer."

I wanted her to have the key to our small house
by the beach at Gros-Islet; I wanted her to change
80   into a smooth white nightie that would pour like water
over the black rocks of her breasts, to lie
simply beside her by the ring of a brass lamp
with a kerosene wick, and tell her in silence
that her hair was like a hill forest at night,
that a trickle of rivers was in her armpits,
that I would buy her Benin[7] if she wanted it,
and never leave her on earth. But the others, too.

Because I felt a great love that could bring me to tears,
and a pity that prickled my eyes like a nettle,
90   I was afraid I might suddenly start sobbing
on the public transport with the Marley going,
and a small boy peering over the shoulders
of the driver and me at the lights coming,
at the rush of the road in the country darkness,
with lamps in the houses on the small hills,
and thickets of stars; I had abandoned them,
I had left them on earth, I left them to sing
Marley's songs of a sadness as real as the smell
of rain on dry earth, or the smell of damp sand,
100   and the bus felt warm with their neighbourliness,
their consideration, and the polite partings

in the light of its headlamps. In the blare,
in the thud-sobbing music, the claiming scent
that came from their bodies. I wanted the transport
to continue forever, for no one to descend
and say a good night in the beams of the lamps
and take the crooked path up to the lit door,
guided by fireflies; I wanted her beauty
to come into the warmth of considerate wood,
110   to the relieved rattling of enamel plates
in the kitchen, and the tree in the yard,
but I came to my stop. Outside the Halcyon Hotel.
The lounge would be full of transients like myself.
Then I would walk with the surf up the beach.
I got off the van without saying good night.
Good night would be full of inexpressible love.
They went on in their transport, they left me on earth.

---

[7] **Benin:** West African nation on the Gulf of Guinea; also a city in southern Nigeria known for its art.

Then, a few yards ahead, the van stopped. A man
shouted my name from the transport window.
120   I walked up towards him. He held out something.
A pack of cigarettes had dropped from my pocket.
He gave it to me. I turned, hiding my tears.
There was nothing they wanted, nothing I could give them
but this thing I have called "The Light of the World."

∽ For Pablo Neruda[1]

I am not walking on sand,
but I feel I am walking on sand,
this poem is accompanying me on sand.
Fungus lacing the rock,
on the ribs, mould. Moss
feathering the mute roar
of the staved-in throat
of the wreck, the crab gripping.

Why this loop of correspondences,
10   as your voice grows hoarser
than the chafed Pacific? Your voice
falling soundless as snow on
the petrified Andes, the snow
like feathers from the tilting
rudderless condors,[2]
emissary in a black suit, who
walks among eagles, hand, whose
five-knuckled peninsula
bars the heartbreaking ocean?

20   Hear the ambassador of velvet
open the felt-hinged door,
the black flag flaps toothless

---

[1] **Pablo Neruda** (1904–1973): Chilean poet who wrote about the effects of colonialism on the Americas; a number of his poems depict the oppression of the Indians. (See p. 1543.)

[2] **condors:** In a famous line in *The Heights of Macchu Picchu,* a collection of poems about the ancient Inca city of the title located high in the Andes, Neruda mentions condors, a bird with a wingspread of 12 feet common to the Andes.

over Isla Negra.[3] You said
when others like me despaired:
climb the moss-throated stairs
to the crest of Macchu Picchu,[4]
break your teeth like a pick on
the obdurate, mottled terraces,
wear the wind, soaked with rain
30   like a cloak, above absences,

and for us, in the New World,
our older world, you became
a benign, rigorous uncle,
and through you we fanned open
to others, to the sand-rasped
mutter of César Vallejo,[5] to
the radiant, self-circling
sunstone of Octavio,[6] men
who, unlike the Saxons,[7] I am tempted
40   to call by their Christian names;

we were all netted to one rock
by vines of iron, our livers
picked by corbeaux and condors
in the New World, in a new word,
brotherhood, word which arrests
the crests of the snowblowing ocean
in its flash to a sea of sierras,
the round fish mouths of our children,
the word *cantan*.[8] All this
50   you have done for me. Gracias.

---

[3] **Isla Negra:** Pablo Neruda had a house in Isla Negra, on the Pacific coast in Chile. When he was in residence there, he flew a flag.

[4] **Macchu Picchu:** See note 2.

[5] **César Vallejo** (1892–1938): Peruvian poet particularly interested in social change.

[6] **Octavio:** Octavio Paz (1914–1998), a Nobel Prize winner from Mexico who often wrote about the Mexican search for identity in its Indian past; Paz's long poem "Sunstone" is a critique of Mexican apathy. *Sunstone* can also refer to gold.

[7] **Saxons:** Originally, a Germanic tribe, some of whom conquered England in the fifth and sixth centuries; the term *Anglo-Saxon* usually refers to England and the English.

[8] ***cantan:*** Spanish for "You (plural) sing" or "They sing."

ALIFA RIFAAT

B. EGYPT, 1930

www For links to more information about Alifa Rifaat and a quiz on "My World of the Unknown," see bedfordstmartins .com/worldlit compact.

AH-lee-fah ree-FAHT

Contrary to the stereotype of submissive, veiled, and voiceless victims of a male-dominated society, Arab women have been amassing a considerable body of work in Arabic literature. Some of this writing takes a vigorous feminist stand on issues of women's rights and women's sexuality. One of the first feminist writers in Arabic literature was the poet Aisha al-Taymuriyya (1840–1902), a member of the Turkish aristocracy in Egypt. Between 1892 and 1920 several journals focusing on and produced by women came out of Egypt and circulated throughout the Arabic world. In 1995, at the first Arab Women Book Fair, held in Cairo, more than 150 women writers participated from throughout the Arab world and more than 1,500 titles were on display by publishers. Among the principal Arabic feminists writing today are Hanan al-Shaykh (b. Lebanon, 1945); Ghada al-Samman (b. Syria, 1942); Fadia Faqir (b. Jordan, 1956); Alia Mamdouh (b. Iraq, 1944); Liana Badr (b. Palestine, 1952); and Nawal el-Saadawi (b. 1931) and **Alifa Rifaat** from Egypt. Through translations, al-Shaykh, el-Saadawi, and Rifaat in particular have received widespread attention and acclaim throughout the East and West, and the reception of their work has generated interest in and controversy over the role of women in the Arab world as well as the politics of literary reception in a global culture. The award-winning Rifaat has been recognized abroad and in Egypt as a gifted stylist and a controversial pioneer in writing about social conditions and sexual politics concerning Egyptian women.

Education and Marriage. Fatma Abdulla Rifaat was born on June 5, 1930, in Cairo, into the family of a well-to-do architect, Abdulla, and his wife, Zakia. Raised in the countryside where her family owned property, Fatma was a precocious child who demonstrated early her gift for writing. At the age of nine, she wrote a short story describing "despair in our village," for which she was punished. After receiving her primary school diploma, Rifaat attended the British Institute in Cairo from 1946 to 1949. Though she wanted to enroll in the College of Fine Arts at Cairo and go on to the university, her father, who believed that arts and literature would interfere with her duties as a wife and mother, refused her wishes and forced her to marry. Of that situation, Rifaat explains: "All decisions in our family are made by the menfolk; we are proud of our Arab origin and hold on to certain Arab customs, among which is the belief that the marriage of girls and their education remains the business of the man. The men taught us to be ladies in society and mistresses of the home only. As for the arts and literature, they were a waste of time and even forbidden." After an eight-month unconsummated marriage with a mining engineer, in July 1952 Fatma married a cousin with the same surname, Hussein Rifaat, a police officer with whom she had a daughter and two sons. Because Hussein's work took him to several posts at a number of towns and villages, Rifaat, like the wife in "My World of the Unknown," had the opportunity to observe Egyptian life in all its diversity.

Reclaiming the Writer. Having experimented with oil painting and music, Rifaat returned to writing short stories, "a thing," she explains, "that clashed with my marriage." When her first story was published in 1955, her husband "created a storm," even though she had published her work under a pseudonym, Alifa Rifaat. She nevertheless continued to publish until 1960, when her husband demanded that she stop writing altogether. For more than a decade Rifaat complied, during which time she avidly studied literature and read on Sufism, science, astronomy, and history. In about 1973, after she had suffered a long bout of illness, her husband conceded that she might resume her writing. During that time of reclaiming her voice, Rifaat wrote "My World of the Unknown," a story that immediately garnered her both praise and blame for its treatment of the protagonist's sexuality. Beginning in 1974, Rifaat published many short stories in the literary journal *al-Thaqafa al-usbu'iya,* followed by the collection of short stories *Eve Returns with Adam to Paradise* (1975) and the novel *The Jewel of Pharo* (1978). After her husband's death in 1979 Rifaat met the British translator Denys Johnson-Davies, who, Rifaat explains, encouraged her to abandon some of the Romantic elements of her early work and to use colloquial language for dialogue. Several collections of her stories were published in the early 1980s, including *Who Can This Man Be?* (1981), *The Prayer of Love* (1983), *A House in the Land of the Dead* (1984), and *Love Conspired on Me* (1985). In 1983, *Distant View of a Minaret,* a collection of stories selected and translated by Denys Johnson-Davies, among them "My World of the Unknown," was published in English before appearing in Arabic two years later. In 1984 Rifaat won the Excellence Award from the Modern Literature Assembly. She has contributed nearly one hundred short stories to Arabic and English magazines, and her work has been produced for British, Egyptian, and German radio and television. Her novel *Girls of Baurdin* was published in 1995.

Awakening. Unlike some of her contemporaries, such as el-Saadawi and al-Shaykh, Rifaat draws primarily on Arab tradition in her fiction. A devout Muslim well read in the Islamic holy book, the QUR'AN, and in the collected laws and traditions of Islam, the HADITH, she seeks to reconcile Islamic teachings, which she believes have been misinterpreted with regard to women, with current practices. However, as recently as 1999, *Distant View of a Minaret* was pulled from the shelves of the bookstore at the American University in Cairo for offending public morality and injuring good taste. Critics oppose Rifaat's frank exploration of female sexuality. "Most of my stories," Rifaat has observed, "revolve around a woman's right to a fully effective and complete sexual life in marriage; that and the sexual and emotional problems encountered by women in marriages are the most important themes of my stories." Her own marriage was initially unfulfilling because she had been told nothing

More convincingly than any other woman writing in Arabic today, Alifa Rifaat . . . lifts the veil on what it means to be a woman living within a traditional Muslim society.

– DENYS JOHNSON-
DAVIES, translator,
1983

JIN

about the act of making love. She adds, however, that Western models of sexual education and sexual liberation are inappropriate for Arab peoples, who have a strong commitment to Muslim religion and Arabic culture. "Our society," she explains, "does not allow us to experience sex freely as Western women may. We have our traditions and our religion in which we believe." In this story, Rifaat indeed does not express Western notions of libido but accounts for the narrator's sexual awakening by way of Islamic myth and Arabic folk belief.

"My World of the Unknown."   In Rifaat's "My World of the Unknown," the known world the narrator inhabits is that of middle-class, somewhat Westernized Egyptian women whose menfolk are thoroughly absorbed in the gray workaday world of urban bureaucracy and whose children are off at school, leaving them to occupy their days with supervising households. Though she says little about her life prior to the action of the story, it is apparent that the narrator's wifely existence has left her feeling dry and depleted in body and soul. When her preoccupied husband is transferred to a post in the countryside, her subconscious stirs and directs her toward the mysterious house where the deeper needs of her imagination, her sexuality, and her spirit may be met. In the house on the canal, she feels alive and open to the natural world, and her whole being is refreshed and quickened when she enters into a magical love affair with a beautiful female snake. The snake is apparently a **djinn** — one of a host of corporeal beings Allah created from smokeless fire who are said to live in a parallel universe to ours. Arab folklore abounds with tales of comings and goings between these worlds, and such encounters may be for good or for ill, since the djinn, like human beings, may be evil or helpful. In any case, to glimpse their world of the unknown alters a human being forever; such an experience seems to have driven Aneesa, the house's previous occupant, into madness, and by the end of the story, when the husband clumsily destroys his wife's idyll by killing one of the snake's own kind, the narrator may be mad as well, for her whole life is focused on the slim hope that she will be reunited with her snake lover. Like the supernatural world, human sexuality is at once a territory of great beauty and joy and, equally, of great risk. By daring to explore her own desires and by reaching out sexually and spiritually toward a very different — and female — being, the narrator invites danger and sorrow, but to have drawn back from the adventure would have meant continuing to live out a mechanical, meaningless existence.

■ **FURTHER RESEARCH**

Ahmed, Leila. "Arab Culture and Writing Women's Bodies." *Feminist Issues* 12 (2): 41–55.

al-Ali, Nadje Sadig. *Gender Writing/Writing Gender: The Representation of Women in a Selection of Modern Egyptian Literature.* 1994.

Elkhadem, Saad. "The Representation of Women in Early Egyptian Fiction: A Survey." *The International Fiction Review* 23 (1996): 76–90.

Olive, Barbara A. "Writing Women's Bodies: A Study of Alifa Rifaat's Short
    Fiction." *The International Fiction Review* 23 (1996): 44–50.
Salti, Ramzi. "Feminism and Religion in Alifa Rifaat's Short Stories." *The Interna-
    tional Fiction Review* 18.2 (1991): 108–12.

■ PRONUNCIATION

djinn: JIN
Alifa Rifaat: AH-lee-fah ree-FAHT
souk: SOOK

∾ My World of the Unknown

Translated by Denys Johnson-Davies

There are many mysteries in life, unseen powers in the universe, worlds other
than our own, hidden links and radiations that draw creatures together and whose
effect is interacting. They may merge or be incompatible, and perhaps the day will
come when science will find a method for connecting up these worlds in the same
way as it has made it possible to voyage to other planets. Who knows?

Yet one of these other worlds I have explored; I have lived in it and been linked
with its creatures through the bond of love. I used to pass with amazing speed
between this tangible world of ours and another invisible earth, mixing in the two
worlds on one and the same day, as though living it twice over.

When entering into the world of my love, and being summoned and yielding to
its call, no one around me would be aware of what was happening to me. All that
occurred was that I would be overcome by something resembling a state of languor
and would go off into a semi-sleep. Nothing about me would change except that I
would become very silent and withdrawn, though I am normally a person who is
talkative and eager to go out into the world of people. I would yearn to be on my
own, would long for the moment of surrender as I prepared myself for answering
the call.

Love had its beginning when an order came through for my husband to be
transferred to a quiet country town and, being too busy with his work, delegated to
me the task of going to this town to choose suitable accommodation prior to his taking up the new appointment. He cabled one of his subordinates named Kamil and
asked him to meet me at the station and to assist me.

I took the early morning train. The images of a dream I had had that night came
to me as I looked out at the vast fields and gauged the distances between the towns
through which the train passed and reckoned how far it was between the new town
in which we were fated to live and beloved Cairo.

The images of the dream kept reappearing to me, forcing themselves upon my
mind: images of a small white house surrounded by a garden with bushes bearing

yellow flowers, a house lying on the edge of a broad canal in which were swans and tall sailing boats. I kept on wondering at my dream and trying to analyse it. Perhaps it was some secret wish I had had, or maybe the echo of some image that my unconscious had stored up and was chewing over.

As the train arrived at its destination, I awoke from my thoughts. I found Kamil awaiting me. We set out in his car, passing through the local *souk*.[1] I gazed at the mounds of fruit with delight, chatting away happily with Kamil. When we emerged from the *souk* we found ourselves on the bank of the Mansoura canal, a canal on which swans swam and sailing boats moved to and fro. I kept staring at them with uneasy longing. Kamil directed the driver to the residential buildings the governorate had put up for housing government employees. While gazing at the opposite bank a large boat with a great fluttering sail glided past. Behind it could be seen a white house that had a garden with trees with yellow flowers and that lay on its own amidst vast fields. I shouted out in confusion, overcome by the feeling that I had been here before.

"Go to that house," I called to the driver. Kamil leapt up, objecting vehemently: "No, no,— no one lives in that house. The best thing is to go to the employees' buildings."

I shouted insistently, like someone hypnotized: "I must have a look at that house." "All right," he said. "You won't like it, though — it's old and needs repairing." Giving in to my wish, he ordered the driver to make his way there.

At the garden door we found a young woman, spare and of fair complexion. A fat child with ragged clothes encircled her neck with his burly legs. In a strange silence, she stood as though nailed to the ground, barring the door with her hands and looking at us with doltish enquiry.

I took a sweet from my bag and handed it to the boy. He snatched it eagerly, tightening his grip on her neck with his podgy, mud-bespattered feet so that her face became flushed from his high-spirited embrace. A half-smile showed on her tightly closed lips. Taking courage, I addressed her in a friendly tone: "I'd like to see over this house." She braced her hands resolutely against the door. "No," she said quite simply. I turned helplessly to Kamil, who went up to her and pushed her violently in the chest so that she staggered back. "Don't you realize," he shouted at her, "that this is the director's wife? Off with you!"

Lowering her head so that the child all but slipped from her, she walked off dejectedly to the canal bank where she lay down on the ground, put the child on her lap, and rested her head in her hands in silent submission.

Moved by pity, I remonstrated: "There's no reason to be so rough, Mr. Kamil. Who is the woman?" "Some mad woman," he said with a shrug of his shoulders, "who's a stranger to the town. Out of kindness the owner of this house put her in charge of it until someone should come along to live in it."

---

[1] *souk:* An outdoor market or bazaar.

With increased interest I said: "Will he be asking a high rent for it?" "Not at all," he said with an enigmatic smile. "He'd welcome anyone taking it over. There are no restrictions and the rent is modest — no more than four pounds."

I was beside myself with joy. Who in these days can find somewhere to live for such an amount? I rushed through the door into the house with Kamil behind me and went over the rooms: five spacious rooms with wooden floors, with a pleasant hall, modern lavatory, and a beautifully roomy kitchen with a large verandah over-looking vast pistachio-green fields of generously watered rice. A breeze, limpid and cool, blew, playing with the tips of the crop and making the delicate leaves move in continuous dancing waves.

I went back to the first room with its spacious balcony overlooking the road and revealing the other bank of the canal where, along its strand, extended the houses of the town. Kamil pointed out to me a building facing the house on the other side. "That's where we work," he said, "and behind it is where the children's schools are."

"Thanks be to God," I said joyfully. "It means that everything is within easy reach of this house — and the *souk*'s nearby too." "Yes," he said, "and the fishermen will knock at your door to show you the fresh fish they've caught in their nets. But the house needs painting and re-doing, also there are all sorts of rumours about it — the people around here believe in djinn[2] and spirits."

"This house is going to be my home," I said with determination. "Its low rent will make up for whatever we may have to spend on re-doing it. You'll see what this house will look like when I get the garden arranged. As for the story about djinn and spirits, just leave them to us — we're more spirited than them."

We laughed at my joke as we left the house. On my way to the station we agreed about the repairs that needed doing to the house. Directly I reached Cairo I cabled my husband to send the furniture from the town we had been living in, specifying a suitable date to fit in with the completion of the repairs and the house being ready for occupation.

On the date fixed I once again set off and found that all my wishes had been car-ried out and that the house was pleasantly spruce with its rooms painted a cheerful orange tinge, the floors well polished and the garden tidied up and made into small flowerbeds.

I took possession of the keys and Kamil went off to attend to his business, hav-ing put a chair on the front balcony for me to sit on while I awaited the arrival of the furniture van. I stretched out contentedly in the chair and gazed at the two banks with their towering trees like two rows of guards between which passed the boats with their lofty sails, while around them glided a male swan heading a flotilla of females. Halfway across the canal he turned and flirted with them, one after the other, like a sultan amidst his harem.

---

[2] djinn: The djinn are intelligent corporeal beings created by Allah out of smokeless fire. They inhabit a sort of parallel universe to ours, although Arabic folklore recounts comings and goings between the two worlds. They may appear to human beings in the guise of an animal or in human form; the narrator's lover in this story does both. One whole sura of the Qur'an is devoted to the djinn. The English word *genie* is derived from *djinn*.

Relaxed, I closed my eyes. I projected myself into the future and pictured to myself the enjoyment I would have in this house after it had been put in order and the garden fixed up. I awoke to the touch of clammy fingers shaking me by the shoulders.

I started and found myself staring at the fair-complexioned woman with her child squatting on her shoulders as she stood erect in front of me staring at me in silence. "What do you want?" I said to her sharply. "How did you get in?" "I got in with this," she said simply, revealing a key between her fingers.

I snatched the key from her hand as I loudly rebuked her: "Give it here. We have rented the house and you have no right to come into it like this." "I have a lot of other keys," she answered briefly. "And what," I said to her, "do you want of this house?" "I want to stay on in it and for you to go," she said. I laughed in amazement at her words as I asked myself: Is she really mad? Finally I said impatiently: "Listen here, I'm not leaving here and you're not entering this house unless I wish it. My husband is coming with the children, and the furniture is on the way. He'll be arriving in a little while and we'll be living here for such period of time as my husband is required to work in this town."

She looked at me in a daze. For a long time she was silent, then she said: "All right, your husband will stay with me and you can go." Despite my utter astonishment I felt pity for her. "I'll allow you to stay on with us for the little boy's sake," I said to her gently, "until you find yourself another place. If you'd like to help me with the housework I'll pay you what you ask."

Shaking her head, she said with strange emphasis: "I'm not a servant. I'm Aneesa." "You're not staying here," I said to her coldly, rising to my feet. Collecting all my courage and emulating Kamil's determination when he rebuked her, I began pushing her in the chest as I caught hold of the young boy's hand. "Get out of here and don't come near this house," I shouted at her. "Let me have all the keys. I'll not let go of your child till you've given them all to me."

With a set face that did not flicker she put her hand to her bosom and took out a ring on which were several keys, which she dropped into my hand. I released my grip on the young boy. Supporting him on her shoulders, she started to leave. Regretting my harshness, I took out several piastres from my bag and placed them in the boy's hand. With the same silence and stiffness she wrested the piastres from the boy's hand and gave them back to me. Then she went straight out. Bolting the door this time, I sat down, tense and upset, to wait.

My husband arrived, then the furniture, and for several days I occupied myself with putting the house in order. My husband was busy with his work and the children occupied themselves with making new friends and I completely forgot about Aneesa, that is until my husband returned one night wringing his hands with fury: "This woman Aneesa, can you imagine that since we came to live in this house she's been hanging around it every night. Tonight she was so crazy she blocked my way and suggested I should send you off so that she might live with me. The woman's gone completely off her head about this house and I'm afraid she might do something to the children or assault you."

Joking with him and masking the jealousy that raged within me, I said: "And what is there for you to get angry about? She's a fair and attractive enough woman — a blessing brought to your very doorstep!" With a sneer he took up the telephone, muttering: "May God look after her!"

He contacted the police and asked them to come and take her away. When I heard the sound of the police van coming I ran to the window and saw them taking her off. The poor woman did not resist, did not object, but submitted with a gentle sadness that as usual with her aroused one's pity. Yet, when she saw me standing in tears and watching her, she turned to me and, pointing to the wall of the house, called out: "I'll leave her to you." "Who?" I shouted. "Who, Aneesa?" Once again pointing at the bottom of the house, she said: "Her."

The van took her off and I spent a sleepless night. No sooner did day come than I hurried to the garden to examine my plants and to walk round the house and carefully inspect its walls. All I found were some cracks, the house being old, and I laughed at the frivolous thought that came to me: Could, for example, there be jewels buried here, as told in fairy tales?

Who could "she" be? What was the secret of this house? Who was Aneesa and was she really mad? Where were she and her son living? So great did my concern for Aneesa become that I began pressing my husband with questions until he brought me news of her. The police had learnt that she was the wife of a well-to-do teacher living in a nearby town. One night he had caught her in an act of infidelity, and in fear she had fled with her son and had settled here, no one knowing why she had betaken herself to this particular house. However, the owner of the house had been good enough to allow her to put up in it until someone should come to live in it, while some kind person had intervened on her behalf to have her name included among those receiving monthly allowances from the Ministry of Social Affairs. There were many rumours that cast doubt upon her conduct: People passing by her house at night would hear her conversing with unknown persons. Her madness took the form of a predilection for silence and isolation from people during the daytime as she wandered about in a dream world. After the police had persuaded them to take her in to safeguard the good repute of her family, she was returned to her relatives.

The days passed and the story of Aneesa was lost in oblivion. Winter came and with it heavy downpours of rain. The vegetation in my garden flourished though the castor-oil plants withered and their yellow flowers fell. I came to find pleasure in sitting out on the kitchen balcony looking at my flowers and vegetables and enjoying the belts of sunbeams that lay between the clouds and lavished my balcony with warmth and light.

One sunny morning my attention was drawn to the limb of a nearby tree whose branches curved up gracefully despite its having dried up and its dark bark being cracked. My gaze was attracted by something twisting and turning along the tip of a branch: Bands of yellow and others of red, intermingled with bands of black, were creeping forward. It was a long, smooth tube, at its end a small striped head with two bright, wary eyes.

The snake curled round on itself in spiral rings, then tautened its body and moved forward. The sight gripped me; I felt terror turning my blood cold and freezing my limbs.

My senses were numbed, my soul intoxicated with a strange elation at the exciting beauty of the snake. I was rooted to the spot, wavering between two thoughts that contended in my mind at one and the same time: Should I snatch up some implement from the kitchen and kill the snake, or should I enjoy the rare moment of beauty that had been afforded me?

As though the snake had read what was passing through my mind, it raised its head, tilting it to right and left in thrilling coquetry. Then, by means of two tiny fangs like pearls, and a golden tongue like a twig of *arak* wood, it smiled at me and fastened its eyes on mine in one fleeting, commanding glance. The thought of killing left me. I felt a current, a radiation from its eyes that penetrated to my heart ordering me to stay where I was. A warning against continuing to sit out there in front of it surged inside me, but my attraction to it paralysed my limbs and I did not move. I kept on watching it, utterly entranced and captivated. Like a bashful virgin being lavished with compliments, it tried to conceal its pride in its beauty, and, having made certain of captivating its lover, the snake coyly twisted round and gently, gracefully glided away until swallowed up by a crack in the wall. Could the snake be the "she" that Aneesa had referred to on the day of her departure?

At last I rose from my place, overwhelmed by the feeling that I was on the brink of a new world, a new destiny, or rather, if you wish, the threshold of a new love. I threw myself onto the bed in a dreamlike state, unaware of the passage of time. No sooner, though, did I hear my husband's voice and the children with their clatter as they returned at noon than I regained my sense of being a human being, wary and frightened about itself, determined about the existence and continuance of its species. Without intending to I called out: "A snake — there's a snake in the house."

My husband took up the telephone and some men came and searched the house. I pointed out to them the crack into which the snake had disappeared, though racked with a feeling of remorse at being guilty of betrayal. For here I was denouncing the beloved, inviting people against it after it had felt safe with me.

The men found no trace of the snake. They burned some wormwood and fumigated the hole but without result. Then my husband summoned Sheikh Farid, Sheikh of the Rifa'iyya[3] order in the town, who went on chanting verses from the Qur'an as he tapped the ground with his stick. He then asked to speak to me alone and said:

"Madam, the sovereign of the house has sought you out and what you saw is no snake, rather it is one of the monarchs of the earth — may God make your words pleasant to them — who has appeared to you in the form of a snake. Here in this house there are many holes of snakes, but they are of the non-poisonous kind. They inhabit houses and go and come as they please. What you saw, though, is something else."

---

[3] **Sheikh of the Rifa'iyya:** The sheikh is the local head of a conservative Islamic order.

"I don't believe a word of it," I said, stupefied. "This is nonsense. I know that the djinn are creatures that actually exist, but they are not in touch with our world, there is no contact between them and the world of humans."

With an enigmatic smile he said: "My child, the Prophet[4] went out to them and read the Qur'an to them in their country. Some of them are virtuous and some of them are Muslims, and how do you know there is no contact between us and them? Let your prayer be 'O Lord, increase me in knowledge' and do not be nervous. Your purity of spirit, your translucence of soul have opened to you doors that will take you to other worlds known only to their Creator. Do not be afraid. Even if you should find her one night sleeping in your bed, do not be alarmed but talk to her with all politeness and friendliness."

"That's enough of all that, Sheikh Farid. Thank you," I said, alarmed, and he left us.

We went on discussing the matter. "Let's be practical," suggested my husband, "and stop all the cracks at the bottom of the outside walls and put wire-mesh over the windows, also paint wormwood all round the garden fence."

We set about putting into effect what we had agreed. I, though, no longer dared to go out onto the balconies. I neglected my garden and stopped wandering about in it. Generally I would spend my free time in bed. I changed to being someone who liked to sit around lazily and was disinclined to mix with people; those diversions and recreations that previously used to tempt me no longer gave me any pleasure. All I wanted was to stretch myself out and drowse. In bewilderment I asked myself: Could it be that I was in love? But how could I love a snake? Or could she really be one of the daughters of the monarchs of the djinn? I would awake from my musings to find that I had been wandering in my thoughts and recalling to mind how magnificent she was. And what is the secret of her beauty? I would ask myself. Was it that I was fascinated by her multi-coloured, supple body? Or was it that I had been dazzled by that intelligent, commanding way she had of looking at me? Or could it be the sleek way she had of gliding along, so excitingly dangerous, that had captivated me?

Excitingly dangerous! No doubt it was this excitement that had stirred my feelings and awakened my love, for did they not make films to excite and frighten? There was no doubt but that the secret of my passion for her, my preoccupation with her, was due to the excitement that had aroused, through intense fear, desire within myself; an excitement that was sufficiently strong to drive the blood hotly through my veins whenever the memory of her came to me, thrusting the blood in bursts that made my heart beat wildly, my limbs limp. And so, throwing myself down in a pleasurable state of torpor, my craving for her would be awakened and I would wish for her coil-like touch, her graceful gliding motion.

And yet I fell to wondering how union could come about, how craving be quenched, the delights of the body be realized, between a woman and a snake. And did she, I wondered, love me and want me as I loved her? An idea would obtrude

---

[4] **the Prophet:** Muhammad (c. 570–632 C.E.), the founder of Islam.

itself upon me sometimes: Did Cleopatra, the very legend of love, have sexual intercourse with her serpent after having given up sleeping with men, having wearied of
amorous adventures with them so that her sated instincts were no longer moved
other than by the excitement of fear, her senses no longer aroused other than by bites
from a snake? And the last of her lovers had been a viper that had destroyed her.

I came to live in a state of continuous torment, for a strange feeling of longing
scorched my body and rent my senses, while my circumstances obliged me to carry
out the duties and responsibilities that had been placed on me as the wife of a man
who occupied an important position in the small town, he and his family being
objects of attention and his house a Kaaba[5] for those seeking favours; also as a
mother who must look after her children and concern herself with every detail of
their lives so as to exercise control over them; there was also the house and its chores,
this house that was inhabited by the mysterious lover who lived in a world other
than mine. How, I wondered, was union between us to be achieved? Was wishing for
this love a sin or was there nothing to reproach myself about?

And as my self-questioning increased so did my yearning, my curiosity, my
desire. Was the snake from the world of reptiles or from the djinn? When would the
meeting be? Was she, I wondered, aware of me and would she return out of pity for
my consuming passion?

One stormy morning with the rain pouring down so hard that I could hear the
drops rattling on the window pane, I lit the stove and lay down in bed between the
covers seeking refuge from an agonizing trembling that racked my yearning body
which, ablaze with unquenchable desire, called out for relief.

I heard a faint rustling sound coming from the corner of the wall right beside
my bed. I looked down and kept my eyes fixed on one of the holes in the wall, which
I found was slowly, very slowly, expanding. Closing my eyes, my heart raced with
joy and my body throbbed with mounting desire as there dawned in me the hope
of an encounter. I lay back in submission to what was to be. No longer did I care
whether love was coming from the world of reptiles or from that of the djinn, sovereigns of the world. Even were this love to mean my destruction, my desire for it was
greater.

I heard a hissing noise that drew nearer, then it changed to a gentle whispering
in my ear, calling to me: "I am love, O enchantress. I showed you my home in your
sleep; I called you to my kingdom when your soul was dozing on the horizon of
dreams, so come, my sweet beloved, come and let us explore the depths of the azure
sea of pleasure. There, in the chamber of coral, amidst cool, shady rocks where
reigns deep, restful silence lies our bed, lined with soft, bright green damask, inlaid
with pearls newly wrenched from their shells. Come, let me sleep with you as I have
slept with beautiful women and have given them bliss. Come, let me prise out your

---

[5] **Kaaba:** Metaphorically, the house is a pilgrimage site; the Kaaba is the small cubical building within the Great
Mosque at Mecca that houses the Black Stone, the holiest relic in Islam. Muslims worldwide face toward the
Kaaba when they pray.

pearl from its shell that I may polish it and bring forth its splendour. Come to where no one will find us, where no one will see us, for the eyes of swimming creatures are innocent and will not heed what we do nor understand what we say. Down there lies repose, lies a cure for all your yearnings and ills. Come, without fear or dread, for no creature will reach us in our hidden world, and only the eye of God alone will see us; He alone will know what we are about and He will watch over us."

I began to be intoxicated by the soft musical whisperings. I felt her cool and soft and smooth, her coldness producing a painful convulsion in my body and hurting me to the point of terror. I felt her as she slipped between the covers, then her two tiny fangs, like two pearls, began to caress my body; arriving at my thighs, the golden tongue, like an *arak* twig, inserted its pronged tip between them and began sipping and exhaling; sipping the poisons of my desire and exhaling the nectar of my ecstasy, till my whole body tingled and started to shake in sharp, painful, rapturous spasms—and all the while the tenderest of words were whispered to me as I confided to her all my longings.

At last the cool touch withdrew, leaving me exhausted. I went into a deep slumber to awake at noon full of energy, all of me a joyful burgeoning to life. Curiosity and a desire to know who it was seized me again. I looked at the corner of the wall and found that the hole was wide open. Once again I was overcome by fear. I pointed out the crack to my husband, unable to utter, although terror had once again awakened in me passionate desire. My husband filled up the crack with cement and went to sleep.

Morning came and everyone went out. I finished my housework and began roaming around the rooms in boredom, battling against the desire to surrender myself to sleep. I sat in the hallway and suddenly she appeared before me, gentle as an angel, white as day, softly undulating and flexing herself, calling to me in her bewitching whisper: "Bride of mine, I called you and brought you to my home. I have wedded you, so there is no sin in our love, nothing to reproach yourself about. I am the guardian of the house, and I hold sway over the snakes and vipers that inhabit it, so come and I shall show you where they live. Have no fear so long as we are together. You and I are in accord. Bring a container with water and I shall place my fingers over your hand and we shall recite together some verses from the Qur'an, then we shall sprinkle it in the places from which they emerge and shall thus close the doors on them, and it shall be a pact between us that your hands will not do harm to them."

"Then you are one of the monarchs of the djinn?" I asked eagerly. "Why do you not bring me treasures and riches as we hear about in fables when a human takes as sister her companion among the djinn?"

She laughed at my words, shaking her golden hair that was like dazzling threads of light. She whispered to me, coquettishly: "How greedy is mankind! Are not the pleasures of the body enough? Were I to come to you with wealth we would both die consumed by fire."

"No, no," I called out in alarm. "God forbid that I should ask for unlawful wealth. I merely asked it of you as a test, that it might be positive proof that I am not imagining things and living in dreams."

She said: "And do intelligent humans have to have something tangible as evidence? By God, do you not believe in His ability to create worlds and living beings? Do you not know that you have an existence in worlds other than that of matter and the transitory? Fine, since you ask for proof, come close to me and my caresses will put vitality back into your limbs. You will retain your youth. I shall give you abiding youth and the delights of love—and they are more precious than wealth in the world of man. How many fortunes have women spent in quest of them? As for me I shall feed from the poisons of your desire, the exhalations of your burning passion, for that is my nourishment and through it I live."

"I thought that your union with me was for love, not for nourishment and the perpetuation of youth and vigour," I said in amazement.

"And is sex anything but food for the body and an interaction in union and love?" she said. "Is it not this that makes human beings happy and is the secret of feeling joy and elation?"

She stretched out her radiant hand to my body, passing over it like the sun's rays and discharging into it warmth and a sensation of languor.

"I am ill," I said. "I am ill. I am ill," I kept on repeating. When he heard me my husband brought the doctor, who said: "High blood pressure, heart trouble, nervous depression." Having prescribed various medicaments he left. The stupidity of doctors! My doctor did not know that he was describing the symptoms of love, did not even know it was from love I was suffering. Yet I knew my illness and the secret of my cure. I showed my husband the enlarged hole in the wall and once again he stopped it up. We then carried the bed to another corner.

After some days had passed I found another hole alongside my bed. My beloved came and whispered to me: "Why are you so coy and flee from me, my bride? Is it fear of your being rebuffed or is it from aversion? Are you not happy with our being together? Why do you want for us to be apart?"

"I am in agony," I whispered back. "Your love is so intense and the desire to enjoy you so consuming. I am frightened I shall feel that I am tumbling down into a bottomless pit and being destroyed."

"My beloved," she said. "I shall only appear to you in beauty's most immaculate form."

"But it is natural for you to be a man," I said in a precipitate outburst, "seeing that you are so determined to have a love affair with me."

"Perfect beauty is to be found only in woman," she said, "so yield to me and I shall let you taste undreamed of happiness; I shall guide you to worlds possessed of such beauty as you have never imagined."

She stretched out her fingers to caress me, while her delicate mouth sucked in the poisons of my desire and exhaled the nectar of my ecstasy, carrying me off into a trance of delicious happiness.

After that we began the most pleasurable of love affairs, wandering together in worlds and living on horizons of dazzling beauty, a world fashioned of jewels, a world whose every moment was radiant with light and formed a thousand shapes, a thousand colours.

As for the opening in the wall, I no longer took any notice. I no longer complained of feeling ill, in fact there burned within me abounding vitality. Sometimes I would bring a handful of wormwood and, by way of jest, would stop up the crack, just as the beloved teases her lover and closes the window in his face that, ablaze with desire for her, he may hasten to the door. After that I would sit for a long time and enjoy watching the wormwood powder being scattered in spiral rings by unseen puffs of wind. Then I would throw myself down on the bed and wait.

For months I immersed myself in my world, no longer calculating time or counting the days, until one morning my husband went out on the balcony lying behind our favoured wall alongside the bed. After a while I heard him utter a cry of alarm. We all hurried out to find him holding a stick, with a black, ugly snake almost two metres long, lying at his feet.

I cried out with a sorrow whose claws clutched at my heart so that it began to beat wildly. With crazed fury I shouted at my husband: "Why have you broken the pact and killed it? What harm has it done?" How cruel is man! He lets no creature live in peace.

I spent the night sorrowful and apprehensive. My lover came to me and embraced me more passionately than ever. I whispered to her imploringly: "Be kind, beloved. Are you angry with me or sad because of me?"

"It is farewell," she said. "You have broken the pact and have betrayed one of my subjects, so you must both depart from this house, for only love lives in it."

In the morning I packed up so that we might move to one of the employees' buildings, leaving the house in which I had learnt of love and enjoyed incomparable pleasures.

I still live in memory and in hope. I crave for the house and miss my secret love. Who knows, perhaps one day my beloved will call me. Who really knows?

ᴄᴡ SALMAN RUSHDIE
B. INDIA, 1947

After Ayatollah Khomeini of Iran urged zealous Muslims to assassinate him, **Salman Rushdie**, a Muslim born in India who has since become a British citizen, became a story on the evening news. His crime, according to the ayatollah, was demonizing the Prophet Muhammad in his novel *The Satanic Verses* (1989). For Rushdie, the conflict with Islamic fundamentalism was probably inevitable, for his varied cultural heritage and multicultural identity made of him what he calls a "translated man." A product of Indian and Islamic roots, a British education, and total self-immersion in Western popular culture, Rushdie is seen by Muslim fundamentalists as someone who has been corrupted by the secular

SAL-mun RUSH-dee

Phil Wilkinson,
Salman Rushdie, 1998
Since the Iranian
threat on his life was
lifted in 1999, Rushdie
has lived in full view
of the public. (© Star
Images/Topham/The
Image Works)

www   For links to
more information
about Salman
Rushdie and a quiz
on "The Courter,"
see bedford
stmartins.com/
worldlitcompact.

materialism of the West. From another perspective, Rushdie can be seen as a successor to such Indian writers as Ram Mohun Roy (1772–1833), Syed Ahmed Khan (1817–1898), and Rabindranath Tagore (1861–1941), who sought to integrate East and West. From still another viewpoint, Rushdie becomes an avatar of POSTMODERNISM, a citizen of many cultures who speaks for an emerging global consciousness. "The Courter," which follows, is an autobiographical story that explores some of the gains and losses of such a cultural translation.

Almost One of "Midnight's Children."   Born in Bombay in 1947, the year that India gained its independence from Britain, Salman Rushdie, though not one of "Midnight's Children"—children born in the first hour of Indian independence—was a postcolonial child. His father, a Cambridge-educated Muslim businessman who would move his family to Pakistan when his son was seventeen, kept the family in the cosmopolitan and predominantly Hindu Bombay during the years of Salman's childhood. There the boy received a British education, read the Hindu classics, and watched the films produced by Bollywood, India's prolific film industry. At fourteen, Salman was sent to Rugby, a famous English public school near London where he was considered an outsider, treated as an inferior, and excluded from many social activities. After three years in England, Rushdie rejoined his family, who had moved to Pakistan while he was away, but he was equally uncomfortable in Pakistan, where his English accent marked him as different. At his father's urging to accept a scholarship to attend Cambridge University, Rushdie reluctantly returned to England in 1965, a choice he has characterized as "one of the most disorienting moments of my life."

But Cambridge proved to be friendlier than Rugby, and Rushdie thrived there as a student. After completing a degree in history in 1968, he returned to Pakistan and worked for a television station in Karachi. His stay didn't last long. Displaced from the intellectual and cosmopolitan life he had known in England and frustrated by the censorship of media in Pakistan, he returned to London in 1970 to work as an actor and advertising copywriter while setting out on a writing career. His first work, *Grimus: A Novel* (1975), a science-fiction version of the classical Sufi poem, *Conference of the Birds,* received mixed reviews and generated little interest. His breakthrough as an author came with his second novel, *Midnight's Children* (1981), the story of his childhood and youth in Bombay between 1947 and 1977 and the lives of his parents and grandparents in the three decades before his birth. The novel doubles as a national ALLEGORY,[1] telling the story of the emergence of India as an independent country. With complex plotting and extravagant invention, Rushdie brings nearly every major event in the sixty years of Indian history that the novel spans into the lives of his two central characters. The novel received the most prestigious British literary award, the Booker Prize, in 1981.

---

[1] **national allegory:** A story in which the characters represent forces or figures in the history of a nation, often a nation in the process of asserting its independence or establishing its national identity.

Confronting Islam.   In *Shame* (1983), Rushdie wrote a similarly extravagant but less successful tale of the modern history of Pakistan. Its fictional versions of the vagaries and brutalities in Pakistani politics offended some Muslim readers, but Rushdie escaped direct censure and censorship by not identifying the setting as Pakistan. He was less cautious in his next novel. *The Satanic Verses* (1988) takes Islamic history as its subject matter, working legends about Muhammad into a contemporary story of movie actors and popular culture. Rushdie's license with Muhammad and the Qur'an so offended many orthodox Muslims that Iran's ayatollah Khomeini issued a *fatwa*, a decree calling on "all zealous Muslims to execute [those responsible for the novel] quickly, wherever they may find them, so that no one will dare to insult the Islamic sanctions. Whoever is killed on this path will be regarded as a martyr, God willing." Rushdie went into hiding; the Norwegian publisher of *The Satanic Verses* was shot and wounded; an Italian translator stabbed; a Japanese translator killed. In Islamic countries several deaths reportedly occurred as a result of the

Having been borne across the ocean, we are translated men. It is normally supposed that something always gets lost in translation; I cling, obstinately, to the notion that something can also be gained.

– SALMAN RUSHDIE, "Imaginary Homelands," 1991

"We Are Ready to Kill Rushdy," 1989
At a pro-Iranian rally, a girl in Beirut, Lebanon, calls for the death of Salman Rushdie. Behind her is a portrait of Ayatollah Khomeini, who declared a fatwa, *or death sentence, on Rushdie after he allegedly blasphemed Islam in his novel* The Satanic Verses. *(© Reuters/CORBIS)*

decree. While Western writers defended Rushdie's novel and his right to speak, many moderate Muslims in the West considered the novel an "unprecedented assault on Islam" and, like the president of the Massachusetts Institute of Technology (M.I.T.) Islamic Society, considered "the reaction of the vast majority of Muslims . . . remarkably mild." Even Naguib Mahfouz (p. 1567), the Egyptian novelist whose *Children of the Alley* (1959) had been attacked by Islamic fundamentalists and banned in nearly every Islamic country, criticized Rushdie—and Khomeini: "I believe that the wrong done by Khomeini towards Islam and the Muslims," he wrote, "is no less than that done by the author himself."

Rushdie's Response.   Forced into seclusion, Rushdie wrote a "children's book," *Haroun and the Sea of Stories* (1990), that made the tradition of the *Arabian Nights* into an allegory of the author's predicament. Haroun, son of the storyteller Rashid Khalifa, sets out on a journey to restore his father's voice and to cleanse the sea of stories that has been poisoned by the tyrant Khattam-Shud, who claims that "stories make trouble." Haroun asserts that "stories are fun," but Khattam-Shud counters, "The world, however, is not for fun. . . . The world is for Controlling." Even in seclusion Rushdie was not to be silenced; his children's book was a tribute to the imagination, which tyranny would suppress. Rushdie once said, "If somebody's trying to shut you up, sing louder and louder and if possible, better. My experience just made me all the more determined to write the very best books I could find it in myself to write."

Rushdie's novels and stories are filled with extravagant inventions, bizarre plot twists, and a melange of allusions to songs, movies, and other elements of popular culture. Rushdie has been compared to Swift and Sterne[2] as a satirist, to Kafka and Günter Grass[3] as an allegorist, and to Gabriel García Márquez and the MAGICAL REALISTS as an inventor of bizarre and surreal worlds. Since the *fatwa* was lifted in 1999, Rushdie has come out of hiding and moved from London to New York City. He has recently published *The Ground beneath Her Feet* (1999), a rock-and-roll retelling of the myth of Orpheus and Eurydice, *Fury* (2001), about a doll-obsessed professor who moves from London to New York, and *Shalimar the Clown* (2005), a novel about the dispute between India and Pakistan over Kashmir. In 2007 Queen Elizabeth of Great Britain awarded a knighthood to Rushdie for his services to literature, a decision that prompted violent protests in Pakistan and other Muslim countries.

[2] **Sterne:** Laurence Sterne (1713–1768) in *Tristram Shandy* employed a digressive and allusive, stream-of-consciousness style of writing for comic and satiric purposes. Rushdie has acknowledged his indebtedness to Sterne as well as to James Joyce (1882–1941), the Irish stream-of-consciousness writer who reveled in wordplay and allusions.

[3] **Günter Grass** (b. 1927): German novelist who authored *The Tin Drum* (1959), an allegory of German history in the twentieth century much like Rushdie's treatment of Indian and Pakistani history.

"**The Courter.**"   The volume of short stories in which "The Courter" originally appeared, *East, West* (1994), illustrates in its organization Rushdie's hybrid self. Of the nine stories in the collection, three are about the East, three are about the West, and three concern the meeting of East and West. "The Courter" comes from the book's final section. Set in an apartment building in London inhabited by a colony of displaced Indians, the story contrasts the connection of the Indian maid Certainly-Mary to her homeland with that of the narrator, an adolescent schoolboy at the time of the action, to his. The story explores the difficulties of moving between cultures and the differences between the responses of the older generation and the youth in adapting to a strange way of life.

> If Rushdie's persecutors have made the experience of rootless nomadism all too literal for him, he's still teaching the rest of us why we can't go home again.
> – HENRY LOUIS GATES JR., writer and critic, 1995

■ **FURTHER RESEARCH**

Booker, M. Keith, ed. *Critical Essays on Salman Rushdie.* 1999.
Cundy, Catherine. *Salman Rushdie.* 1996.
Goonetilleke, D. C. R. A. *Salman Rushdie.* 1998.
Israel, Nico. *Outlandish, Writing between Exile and Diaspora.* 2000.

■ **PRONUNCIATION**

Chhoti: CHOH-tee
Dasashwamedh-ghat: duh-suh-shwah-MADE GAHT
Salman Rushdie: SAL-mun RUSH-dee
Varanasi: vuh-RAH-nuh-see
Zbigniew: ZBIG-nyef

◐ The Courter

1

Certainly-Mary was the smallest woman Mixed-Up the hall porter had come across, dwarfs excepted, a tiny sixty-year-old Indian lady with her greying hair tied behind her head in a neat bun, hitching up her red-hemmed white sari in the front and negotiating the apartment block's front steps as if they were Alps. "No," he said aloud, furrowing his brow. What would be the right peaks. Ah, good, that was the name. "Ghats,"[1] he said proudly. Word from a schoolboy atlas long ago, when India felt as far away as Paradise. (Nowadays Paradise seemed even further away but India, and Hell, had come a good bit closer.) "Western Ghats, Eastern Ghats, and now Kensington Ghats," he said, giggling. "Mountains."

   She stopped in front of him in the oak-panelled lobby. "But ghats in India are also stairs," she said. "Yes yes certainly. For instance in Hindu holy city of Varanasi,

---

[1] "**Ghats**": Hindi word for a mountain range and also for a flight of steps leading down to a river. Two particular ranges in India are the Eastern Ghats, along the Bay of Bengal, and the Western Ghats, along the Arabian Sea.

where the Brahmins sit taking the filgrims' money is called Dasashwamedh-ghat. Broad-broad staircase down to River Ganga.[2] O, most certainly! Also Manikarnika-ghat.[3] They buy fire from a house with a tiger leaping from the roof — yes certainly, a statue tiger, coloured by Technicolor, what are you thinking? — and they bring it in a box to set fire to their loved ones' bodies. Funeral fires are of sandal. Photographs not allowed; no, certainly not."

He began thinking of her as Certainly-Mary because she never said plain yes or no; always this O-yes-certainly or no-certainly-not. In the confused circumstances that had prevailed ever since his brain, his one sure thing, had let him down, he could hardly be certain of anything any more; so he was stunned by her sureness, first into nostalgia, then envy, then attraction. And attraction was a thing so long forgotten that when the churning started he thought for a long time it must be the Chinese dumplings he had brought home from the High Street carry-out.

English was hard for Certainly-Mary, and this was a part of what drew damaged old Mixed-Up towards her. The letter p was a particular problem, often turning into an f or a c; when she proceeded through the lobby with a wheeled wicker shopping basket, she would say, "Going shocking," and when, on her return, he offered to help lift the basket up the front ghats, she would answer, "Yes, fleas." As the elevator lifted her away, she called through the grille: "Oé, courter! Thank you, courter. O, yes, certainly." (In Hindi and Konkani,[4] however, her p's knew their place.)

So: thanks to her unexpected, somehow stomach-churning magic, he was no longer porter, but courter. "Courter," he repeated to the mirror when she had gone. His breath made a little dwindling picture of the word on the glass. "Courter courter caught." Okay. People called him many things, he did not mind. But this name, this courter, this he would try to be.

2

For years now I've been meaning to write down the story of Certainly-Mary, our ayah,[5] the woman who did as much as my mother to raise my sisters and me, and her great adventure with her "courter" in London, where we all lived for a time in the early sixties in a block called Waverley House; but what with one thing and another I never got round to it.

Then recently I heard from Certainly-Mary after a longish silence. She wrote to say that she was ninety-one, had had a serious operation, and would I kindly send

---

[2] **Varanasi . . . Ganga:** Varanasi, formerly Benares, a sacred city on the River Ganga (Ganges) — the sacred Hindu river running through the heart of Bengal — where Hindu pilgrims come to bathe in the river and to cremate their dead. The Dasashwamedh-ghat is a series of steps leading down to the river, the most popular ghat for pilgrims who come to bathe.

[3] **Manikarnika-ghat:** The "burning ghat" is a set of stairs where bodies are brought to be cremated.

[4] **Konkani:** The language of an ethnic group living mainly along the west coast of India.

[5] **ayah:** Maid or nursemaid.

her some money, because she was embarrassed that her niece, with whom she was now living in the Kurla district of Bombay, was so badly out of pocket.

I sent the money, and soon afterwards received a pleasant letter from the niece, Stella, written in the same hand as the letter from "Aya" — as we had always called Mary, palindromically dropping the "h." Aya had been so touched, the niece wrote, that I remembered her after all these years. "I have been hearing the stories about you folks all my life," the letter went on, "and I think of you a little bit as family. Maybe you recall my mother, Mary's sister. She unfortunately passed on. Now it is I who write Mary's letters for her. We all wish you the best."

This message from an intimate stranger reached out to me in my enforced exile from the beloved country of my birth and moved me, stirring things that had been buried very deep. Of course it also made me feel guilty about having done so little for Mary over the years. For whatever reason, it has become more important than ever to set down the story I've been carrying around unwritten for so long, the story of Aya and the gentle man whom she renamed — with unintentional but prophetic overtones of romance — "the courter." I see now that it is not just their story, but ours, mine, as well.

3

His real name was Mecir: You were supposed to say Mishirsh because it had invisible accents on it in some Iron Curtain language in which the accents had to be invisible, my sister Durré said solemnly, in case somebody spied on them or rubbed them out or something. His first name also began with an m but it was so full of what we called Communist consonants, all those z's and c's and w's walled up together without vowels to give them breathing space, that I never even tried to learn it.

At first we thought of nicknaming him after a mischievous little comic-book character, Mr. Mxyztplk from the Fifth Dimension, who looked a bit like Elmer Fudd and used to make Superman's life hell until ole Supe could trick him into saying his name backwards, Klptzyxm, whereupon he disappeared back into the Fifth Dimension; but because we weren't too sure how to say Mxyztplk (not to mention Klptzyxm) we dropped that idea. "We'll just call you Mixed-Up," I told him in the end, to simplify life. "Mishter Mikshed-Up Mishirsh." I was fifteen then and bursting with unemployed cock and it meant I could say things like that right into people's faces, even people less accommodating than Mr. Mecir with his stroke.

What I remember most vividly are his pink rubber washing-up gloves, which he seemed never to remove, at least not until he came calling for Certainly-Mary . . . At any rate, when I insulted him, with my sisters Durré and Muneeza cackling in the lift, Mecir just grinned an empty good-natured grin, nodded, "You call me what you like, okay," and went back to buffing and polishing the brasswork. There was no point teasing him if he was going to be like that, so I got into the lift and all the way to the fourth floor we sang *I Can't Stop Loving You* at the top of our best Ray Charles voices, which were pretty awful. But we were wearing our dark glasses, so it didn't matter.

4

It was the summer of 1962, and school was out. My baby sister Scheherazade was just one year old. Durré was a beehived fourteen; Muneeza was ten, and already quite a handful. The three of us—or rather Durré and me, with Muneeza trying desperately and unsuccessfully to be included in our gang—would stand over Scheherazade's cot and sing to her. "No nursery rhymes," Durré had decreed, and so there were none, for though she was a year my junior she was a natural leader. The infant Scheherazade's lullabies were our cover versions of recent hits by Chubby Checker, Neil Sedaka, Elvis, and Pat Boone.

"Why don't you come home, Speedy Gonzales?" we bellowed in sweet disharmony: But most of all, and with actions, we would jump down, turn around, and pick a bale of cotton. We would have jumped down, turned around, and picked those bales all day except that the Maharaja of B—— in the flat below complained, and Aya Mary came in to plead with us to be quiet.

"Look, see, it's Jumble-Aya who's fallen for Mixed-Up," Durré shouted, and Mary blushed a truly immense blush. So naturally we segued right into a quick me-oh-my-oh; son of a gun, we had big fun. But then the baby began to yell, my father came in with his head down bull-fashion and steaming from both ears, and we needed all the good-luck charms we could find.

I had been at boarding school in England for a year or so when Abba took the decision to bring the family over. Like all his decisions, it was neither explained to nor discussed with anyone, not even my mother. When they first arrived he rented two adjacent flats in a seedy Bayswater mansion block called Graham Court, which lurked furtively in a nothing street that crawled along the side of the ABC Queensway cinema towards the Porchester Baths. He commandeered one of these flats for himself and put my mother, three sisters, and Aya in the other; also, on school holidays, me. England, where liquor was freely available, did little for my father's *bonhomie,* so in a way it was a relief to have a flat to ourselves.

Most nights he emptied a bottle of Johnnie Walker Red Label and a soda-siphon. My mother did not dare to go across to "his place" in the evenings. She said: "He makes faces at me."

Aya Mary took Abba his dinner and answered all his calls (if he wanted anything, he would phone us up and ask for it). I am not sure why Mary was spared his drunken rages. She said it was because she was nine years his senior, so she could tell him to show due respect.

After a few months, however, my father leased a three-bedroom fourth-floor apartment with a fancy address. This was Waverley House in Kensington Court, W8. Among its other residents were not one but two Indian Maharajas, the sporting Prince P—— as well as the old B—— who has already been mentioned. Now we were jammed in together, my parents and Baby Scare-zade (as her siblings had affectionately begun to call her) in the master bedroom, the three of us in a much smaller room, and Mary, I regret to admit, on a straw mat laid on the fitted carpet in the hall. The third bedroom became my father's office, where he made phone calls and kept his *Encyclopaedia Britannica,* his *Reader's Digests,* and (under lock and key) the television cabinet. We entered it at our peril. It was the Minotaur's[6] lair.

One morning he was persuaded to drop in at the corner pharmacy and pick up some supplies for the baby. When he returned there was a hurt, schoolboyish look on his face that I had never seen before, and he was pressing his hand against his cheek.

"She hit me," he said plaintively.

"Hai! Allah-tobah![7] Darling!" cried my mother, fussing. "Who hit you? Are you injured? Show me, let me see."

"I did nothing," he said, standing there in the hall with the pharmacy bag in his other hand and a face as pink as Mecir's rubber gloves. "I just went in with your list. The girl seemed very helpful. I asked for baby compound, Johnson's powder, teething jelly, and she brought them out. Then I asked did she have any nipples, and she slapped my face."

My mother was appalled. "Just for that?" And Certainly-Mary backed her up. "What is this nonsense?" she wanted to know. "I have been in that chemist's shock, and they have flenty nickels, different sizes, all on view."

Durré and Muneeza could not contain themselves. They were rolling round on the floor, laughing and kicking their legs in the air.

"You both shut your face at once," my mother ordered. "A madwoman has hit your father. Where is the comedy?"

"I don't believe it," Durré gasped. "You just went up to that girl and said," and here she fell apart again, stamping her feet and holding her stomach, "*'have you got any nipples?'*"

My father grew thunderous, empurpled. Durré controlled herself. "But Abba," she said, at length, "here they call them teats."

Now my mother's and Mary's hands flew to their mouths, and even my father looked shocked. "But how shameless!" my mother said. "The same word as for what's on your bosoms?" She coloured, and stuck out her tongue for shame.

"These English," sighed Certainly-Mary. "But aren't they the limit? Certainly-yes; they are."

I remember this story with delight, because it was the only time I ever saw my father so discomfited, and the incident became legendary and the girl in the pharmacy was installed as the object of our great veneration. (Durré and I went in there just to take a look at her—she was a plain, short girl of about seventeen, with large, unavoidable breasts—but she caught us whispering and glared so fiercely that we fled.) And also because in the general hilarity I was able to conceal the shaming truth that I, who had been in England for so long, would have made the same mistake as Abba did.

---

[6] **Minotaur:** In Greek mythology, the threatening creature, half bull and half man, at the center of the labyrinth in Crete who is slain by Theseus.

[7] **Allah-tobah!:** Oh my God!

It wasn't just Certainly-Mary and my parents who had trouble with the English language. My schoolfellows tittered when in my Bombay way I said "brought-up" for upbringing (as in "where was your brought-up?") and "thrice" for three times and "quarter-plate" for side-plate and "macaroni" for pasta in general. As for learning the difference between nipples and teats, I really hadn't had any opportunities to increase my word power in that area at all.

5

So I was a little jealous of Certainly-Mary when Mixed-Up came to call. He rang our bell, his body quivering with deference in an old suit grown too loose, the trousers tightly gathered by a belt; he had taken off his rubber gloves and there were roses in his hand. My father opened the door and gave him a withering look. Being a snob, Abba was not pleased that the flat lacked a separate service entrance, so that even a porter had to be treated as a member of the same universe as himself.

"Mary," Mixed-Up managed, licking his lips and pushing back his floppy white hair. "I, to see Miss Mary, come, am."

"Wait on," Abba said, and shut the door in his face.

Certainly-Mary spent all her afternoons off with old Mixed-Up from then on, even though that first date was not a complete success. He took her "up West" to show her the visitors' London she had never seen, but at the top of an up escalator at Piccadilly Circus, while Mecir was painfully enunciating the words on the posters she couldn't read — *Unzip a banana,* and *Idris when I's dri* — she got her sari stuck in the jaws of the machine, and as the escalator pulled at the garment it began to unwind. She was forced to spin round and round like a top, and screamed at the top of her voice, "O BAAP! BAAPU-RÉ! BAAP-RÉ-BAAP-RÉ-BAAP!"[8] It was Mixed-Up who saved her by pushing the emergency stop button before the sari was completely unwound and she was exposed in her petticoat for all the world to see.

"O, courter!" she wept on his shoulder. "O, no more escaleater, courter, nevermore, surely not!"

My own amorous longings were aimed at Durré's best friend, a Polish girl called Rozalia, who had a holiday job at Faiman's shoe shop on Oxford Street. I pursued her pathetically throughout the holidays and, on and off, for the next two years. She would let me have lunch with her sometimes and buy her a Coke and a sandwich, and once she came with me to stand on the terraces at White Hart Lane[9] to watch Jimmy Greaves's first game for the Spurs. "Come on you whoi-oites," we both shouted dutifully. "Come on you *Lily-whoites.*" After that she even invited me into the back room at Faiman's, where she kissed me twice and let me touch her breast, but that was as far as I got.

---

[8] "O BAAP! . . . BAAP!": An expression of embarrassment; "Oh God!"

[9] White Hart Lane: The home stadium in London of the professional soccer team the Tottenham Hot Spurs. Jimmy Greaves was one of the Spurs' star players.

And then there was my sort-of-cousin Chandni, whose mother's sister had married my mother's brother, though they had since split up. Chandni was eighteen months older than me, and so sexy it made you sick. She was training to be an Indian classical dancer, Odissi as well as Natyam,[10] but in the meantime she dressed in tight black jeans and a clinging black polo-neck jumper and took me, now and then, to hang out at Bunjie's, where she knew most of the folk-music crowd that frequented the place, and where she answered to the name of Moonlight, which is what *chandni* means. I chain-smoked with the folkies and then went to the toilet to throw up.

Chandni was the stuff of obsessions. She was a teenage dream, the Moon River come to Earth like the Goddess Ganga,[11] dolled up in slinky black. But for her I was just the young greenhorn cousin to whom she was being nice because he hadn't learned his way around.

She-E-rry, won't you come out tonight? yodelled the Four Seasons. I knew exactly how they felt. *Come, come, come out toni-yi-yight.* And while you're at it, love me do.

6

They went for walks in Kensington Gardens. "Pan," Mixed-Up said, pointing at a statue. "Los' boy. Nev' grew up."[12] They went to Barkers and Pontings and Derry & Toms[13] and picked out furniture and curtains for imaginary homes. They cruised supermarkets and chose little delicacies to eat. In Mecir's cramped lounge they sipped what he called "chimpanzee tea"[14] and toasted crumpets in front of an electric bar fire.

Thanks to Mixed-Up, Mary was at last able to watch television. She liked children's programmes best, especially *The Flintstones*. Once, giggling at her daring, Mary confided to Mixed-Up that Fred and Wilma reminded her of her Sahib and Begum Sahiba upstairs; at which the courter, matching her audaciousness, pointed first at Certainly-Mary and then at himself, grinned a wide gappy smile and said, "Rubble."

Later, on the news, a vulpine Englishman with a thin moustache and mad eyes declaimed a warning about immigrants, and Certainly-Mary flapped her hand at the set: "Khali-pili bom marta," she objected, and then, for her host's benefit translated: "For nothing he is shouting shouting. Bad life! Switch it off."

They were often interrupted by the Maharajas of and B—— and P——, who came downstairs to escape their wives and ring other women from the call-box in the porter's room.

---

[10] **Odissi . . . Natyam:** Odissi is the traditional dance of Orissa, a state on the east coast of India. Natyam is one of the oldest dance forms in southern India.

[11] **Goddess Ganga:** The Hindu goddess of the sacred Ganga River.

[12] **"Pan . . . grew up":** A statue of Peter Pan in Kensington Gardens celebrates James Barrie's tale of the lost boy who never grew up, *Peter Pan*.

[13] **Barkers . . . Toms:** Fashionable London stores.

[14] **"chimpanzee tea":** The television advertisements for a popular brand of English tea featured chimpanzees dressed as humans.

"Oh, baby, forget that guy," said sporty Prince P——, who seemed to spend all his days in tennis whites, and whose plump gold Rolex was almost lost in the thick hair on his arm. "I'll show you a better time than him, baby; step into my world."

The Maharaja of B—— was older, uglier, more matter-of-fact. "Yes, bring all appliances. Room is booked in name of Mr. Douglas Home. Six forty-five to seven fifteen. You have printed rate card? Please. Also a two-foot ruler, must be wooden. Frilly apron, plus."

This is what has lasted in my memory of Waverley House, this seething mass of bad marriages, booze, philanderers, and unfulfilled young lusts; of the Maharaja of P—— roaring away towards London's casinoland every night, in a red sports car with fitted blondes, and of the Maharaja of B—— skulking off to Kensington High Street wearing dark glasses in the dark, and a coat with the collar turned up even though it was high summer; and at the heart of our little universe were Certainly-Mary and her courter, drinking chimpanzee tea and singing along with the national anthem of Bedrock.

But they were not really like Barney and Betty Rubble at all. They were formal, polite. They were . . . courtly. He courted her, and, like a coy, ringleted ingénue with a fan, she inclined her head, and entertained his suit.

7

I spent one half-term weekend in 1963 at the home in Beccles, Suffolk of Field Marshal Sir Charles Lutwidge-Dodgson, an old India hand and a family friend who was supporting my application for British citizenship. "The Dodo,"[15] as he was known, invited me down by myself, saying he wanted to get to know me better.

He was a huge man whose skin had started hanging too loosely on his face, a giant living in a tiny thatched cottage and forever bumping his head. No wonder he was irascible at times; he was in Hell, a Gulliver trapped in that rose-garden Lilliput[16] of croquet hoops, church bells, sepia photographs, and old battle-trumpets.

The weekend was fitful and awkward until the Dodo asked if I played chess. Slightly awestruck at the prospect of playing a Field Marshal, I nodded; and ninety minutes later, to my amazement, won the game.

I went into the kitchen, strutting somewhat, planning to boast a little to the old soldier's long-time housekeeper, Mrs. Liddell. But as soon as I entered she said: "Don't tell me. You never went and won?"

"Yes," I said, affecting nonchalance. "As a matter of fact, yes, I did."

---

[15]**Dodgson . . . "The Dodo":** Charles Lutwidge Dodgson was the given name of Lewis Carroll (1832–1898), author of *Alice in Wonderland,* a novel he based on a story he told to Alice Liddell and her sisters. The Dodo, a character in the story, is said to be Carroll's projection of himself. The author could not pronounce his given name without stuttering.

[16]**Gulliver . . . Lilliput:** On the first of his voyages in Jonathan Swift's *Gulliver's Travels* (1726), Gulliver visits Lilliput, a land whose inhabitants are tiny human beings.

"Gawd," said Mrs. Liddell. "Now there'll be hell to pay. You go back in there and ask him for another game, and this time make sure you lose."

I did as I was told, but was never invited to Beccles again.

Still, the defeat of the Dodo gave me new confidence at the chessboard, so when I returned to Waverley House after finishing my O levels,[17] and was at once invited to play a game by Mixed-Up (Mary had told him about my victory in the Battle of Beccles with great pride and some hyperbole), I said: "Sure, I don't mind." How long could it take to thrash the old duffer, after all?

There followed a massacre royal. Mixed-Up did not just beat me; he had me for breakfast, over easy. I couldn't believe it—the canny opening, the fluency of his combination play, the force of his attacks, my own impossibly cramped, strangled positions—and asked for a second game. This time he tucked into me even more heartily. I sat broken in my chair at the end, close to tears. *Big girls don't cry*, I reminded myself, but the song went on playing in my head: *That's just an alibi.*

"Who are you?" I demanded, humiliation weighing down every syllable. "The devil in disguise?"

Mixed-Up gave his big, silly grin. "Grand Master," he said. "Long time. Before head."

"You're a Grand Master," I repeated, still in a daze. Then in a moment of horror I remembered that I had seen the name Mecir in books of classic games. "Nimzo-Indian," I said aloud. He beamed and nodded furiously.

"That Mecir?" I asked wonderingly.

"That," he said. There was saliva dribbling out of a corner of his sloppy old mouth. This ruined old man was in the books. He was in the books. And even with his mind turned to rubble he could still wipe the floor with me.

"Now play lady," he grinned. I didn't get it. "Mary lady," he said. "Yes yes certainly."

She was pouring tea, waiting for my answer. "Aya, you can't play," I said, bewildered.

"Learning, baba," she said. "What is it, na? Only a game."

And then she, too, beat me senseless, and with the black pieces, at that. It was not the greatest day of my life.

8

From *100 Most Instructive Chess Games* by Robert Reshevsky, 1961:

> *M. Mecir—M. Najdorf*
> *Dallas 1950, Nimzo-Indian Defense*
> The attack of a tactician can be troublesome to meet—that of a strategist even more so. Whereas the tactician's threats may be unmistakable, the strategist confuses the issue by keeping things in abeyance. He threatens to threaten!

---

[17] **O levels:** Exams given at the end of an "ordinary-level" secondary education to establish eligibility for a diploma.

Take this game for instance: Mecir posts a Knight at Q6 to get a grip on the center. Then he establishes a passed Pawn on one wing to occupy his opponent on the Queen side. Finally he stirs up the position on the King-side. What does the poor bewildered opponent do? How can he defend everything at once? Where will the blow fall?

Watch Mecir keep Najdorf on the run, as he shifts the attack from side to side!

Chess had become their private language. Old Mixed-Up, lost as he was for words, retained, on the chessboard, much of the articulacy and subtlety which had vanished from his speech. As Certainly-Mary gained in skill—and she had learned with astonishing speed, I thought bitterly, for someone who couldn't read or write or pronounce the letter p—she was better able to understand, and respond to, the wit of the reduced maestro with whom she had so unexpectedly forged a bond.

He taught her with great patience, showing-not-telling, repeating openings and combinations and endgame techniques over and over until she began to see the meaning in the patterns. When they played, he handicapped himself, he told her her best moves and demonstrated their consequences, drawing her, step by step, into the infinite possibilities of the game.

Such was their courtship. "It is like an adventure, baba," Mary once tried to explain to me. "It is like going with him to his country, you know? What a place, baap-ré! Beautiful and dangerous and funny and full of fuzzles. For me it is a big-big discovery. What to tell you? I go for the game. It is a wonder."

I understood, then, how far things had gone between them. Certainly-Mary had never married, and had made it clear to old Mixed-Up that it was too late to start any of that monkey business at her age. The courter was a widower, and had grown-up children somewhere, lost long ago behind the ever-higher walls of Eastern Europe. But in the game of chess they had found a form of flirtation, an endless renewal that precluded the possibility of boredom, a courtly wonderland of the aging heart.

What would the Dodo have made of it all? No doubt it would have scandalised him to see chess, chess of all games, the great formalisation of war, transformed into an art of love.

As for me: My defeats by Certainly-Mary and her courter ushered in further humiliations. Durré and Muneeza went down with the mumps, and so, finally, in spite of my mother's efforts to segregate us, did I. I lay terrified in bed while the doctor warned me not to stand up and move around if I could possibly help it. "If you do," he said, "your parents won't need to punish you. You will have punished yourself quite enough."

I spent the following few weeks tormented day and night by visions of grotesquely swollen testicles and a subsequent life of limp impotence—finished before I'd even started, it wasn't fair!—which were made much worse by my sisters' quick recovery and incessant gibes. But in the end I was lucky; the illness didn't spread to the deep South. "Think how happy your hundred and one girlfriends will be, bhai,"[18] sneered

---

[18] **bhai:** Brother.

Durré, who knew all about my continued failures in the Rozalia and Chandni departments.

On the radio, people were always singing about the joys of being sixteen years old. I wondered where they were, all those boys and girls of my age having the time of their lives. Were they driving around America in Studebaker convertibles? They certainly weren't in my neighbourhood. London, W8 was Sam Cooke country that summer. *Another Saturday night . . .* There might be a mop-top love-song stuck at number one, but I was down with lonely Sam in the lower depths of the charts, how-I-wishing I had someone, etc., and generally feeling in a pretty goddamn dreadful way.

<h1 style="text-align:center">9</h1>

"Baba, come quick."

It was late at night when Aya Mary shook me awake. After many urgent hisses, she managed to drag me out of sleep and pull me, pajama'ed and yawning, down the hall. On the landing outside our flat was Mixed-Up the courter, huddled up against a wall, weeping. He had a black eye and there was dried blood on his mouth.

"What happened?" I asked Mary, shocked.

"Men," wailed Mixed-Up. "Threaten. Beat."

He had been in his lounge earlier that evening when the sporting Maharaja of P—— burst in to say, "If anybody comes looking for me, okay, any tough-guy type guys, okay, I am out, okay? Oh you tea. Don't let them go upstairs, okay? Big tip, okay?"

A short time later, the old Maharaja of B—— also arrived in Mecir's lounge, looking distressed.

"Suno, listen on," said the Maharaja of B——. "You don't know where I am, samajh liya?[19] Understood? Some low persons may inquire. You don't know. I am abroad, achha?[20] On extended travels abroad. Do your job, porter. Handsome recompense."

Late at night two tough-guy types did indeed turn up. It seemed the hairy Prince P—— had gambling debts. "Out," Mixed-Up grinned in his sweetest way. The tough-guy types nodded, slowly. They had long hair and thick lips like Mick Jagger's. "He's a busy gent. We should of made an appointment," said the first type to the second. "Didn't I tell you we should of called?"

"You did," agreed the second type. "Got to do these things right, you said, he's royalty. And you was right, my son, I put my hand up, I was dead wrong. I put my hand up to that."

"Let's leave our card," said the first type. "Then he'll know to expect us."

"Ideal," said the second type, and smashed his fist into old Mixed-Up's mouth. "You tell him," the second type said, and struck the old man in the eye. "When he's in. You mention it."

---

[19] samajh liya?: Do you understand?   [20] achha?: Yeah?

He had locked the front door after that; but much later, well after midnight, there was a hammering. Mixed-Up called out, "Who?"

"We are close friends of the Maharaja of B——" said a voice. "No, I tell a lie. Acquaintances."

"He calls upon a lady of our acquaintance," said a second voice. "To be precise."

"It is in that connection that we crave audience," said the first voice.

"Gone," said Mecir. "Jet plane. Gone."

There was a silence. Then the second voice said, "Can't be in the jet set if you never jump on a jet, eh? Biarritz, Monte, all of that."

"Be sure and let His Highness know," said the first voice, "that we eagerly await his return."

"With regard to our mutual friend," said the second voice. "Eagerly."

What does the poor bewildered opponent do? The words from the chess book popped unbidden into my head. *How can he defend everything at once? Where will the blow fall? Watch Mecir keep Najdorf on the run, as he shifts the attack from side to side!*

Mixed-Up returned to his lounge and on this occasion, even though there had been no use of force, he began to weep. After a time he took the elevator up to the fourth floor and whispered through our letter-box to Certainly-Mary sleeping on her mat.

"I didn't want to wake Sahib," Mary said. "You know his trouble, na? And Begum Sahiba is so tired at end of the day. So now you tell, baba, what to do?"

What did she expect me to come up with? I was sixteen years old. "Mixed-Up must call the police," I unoriginally offered.

"No, no, baba," said Certainly-Mary emphatically. "If the courter makes a scandal for Maharaja-log, then in the end it is the courter only who will be out on his ear."

I had no other ideas. I stood before them feeling like a fool, while they both turned upon me their frightened, supplicant eyes.

"Go to sleep," I said. "We'll think about it in the morning." *The first pair of thugs were tacticians,* I was thinking. *They were troublesome to meet. But the second pair were scarier; they were strategists. They threatened to threaten.*

Nothing happened in the morning, and the sky was clear. It was almost impossible to believe in fists, and menacing voices at the door. During the course of the day both Maharajas visited the porter's lounge and stuck five-pound notes in Mixed-Up's waistcoat pocket. "Held the fort, good man," said Prince P——, and the Maharaja of B—— echoed those sentiments: "Spot on. All handled now, achha? Problem over."

The three of us—Aya Mary, her courter, and me—held a council of war that afternoon and decided that no further action was necessary. The hall porter was the front line in any such situation, I argued, and the front line had held. And now the risks were past. Assurances had been given. End of story.

"End of story," repeated Certainly-Mary doubtfully, but then, seeking to reassure Mecir, she brightened. "Correct," she said. "Most certainly! All-done, finis."

She slapped her hands against each other for emphasis. She asked Mixed-Up if he wanted a game of chess; but for once the courter didn't want to play.

10

After that I was distracted, for a time, from the story of Mixed-Up and Certainly-Mary by violence nearer home.

My middle sister Muneeza, now eleven, was entering her delinquent phase a little early. She was the true inheritor of my father's black rage, and when she lost control it was terrible to behold. That summer she seemed to pick fights with my father on purpose; seemed prepared, at her young age, to test her strength against his. (I intervened in her rows with Abba only once, in the kitchen. She grabbed the kitchen scissors and flung them at me. They cut me on the thigh. After that I kept my distance.)

As I witnessed their wars I felt myself coming unstuck from the idea of family itself. I looked at my screaming sister and thought how brilliantly self-destructive she was, how triumphantly she was ruining her relations with the people she needed most.

And I looked at my choleric, face-pulling father and thought about British citizenship. My existing Indian passport permitted me to travel only to a very few countries, which were carefully listed on the second right-hand page. But I might soon have a British passport and then, by hook or by crook, I would get away from him. I would not have this face-pulling in my life.

At sixteen, you still think you can escape from your father. You aren't listening to his voice speaking through your mouth, you don't see how your gestures already mirror his; you don't see him in the way you hold your body, in the way you sign your name. You don't hear his whisper in your blood.

On the day I have to tell you about, my two-year-old sister Chhoti Scheherazade, Little Scare-zade, started crying as she often did during one of our family rows. Amma and Aya Mary loaded her into her push-chair and made a rapid getaway. They pushed her to Kensington Square and then sat on the grass, turned Scheherazade loose and made philosophical remarks while she tired herself out. Finally, she fell asleep, and they made their way home in the fading light of the evening. Outside Waverley House they were approached by two well-turned-out young men with Beatle haircuts and the buttoned-up, collarless jackets made popular by the band. The first of these young men asked my mother, very politely, if she might be the Maharani of B——.

"No," my mother answered, flattered.

"Oh, but you are, madam," said the second Beatle, equally politely. "For you are heading for Waverley House and that is the Maharaja's place of residence."

"No, no," my mother said, still blushing with pleasure. "We are a different Indian family."

"Quite so," the first Beatle nodded understandingly, and then, to my mother's great surprise, placed a finger alongside his nose, and winked. "Incognito, eh. Mum's the word."

"Now excuse us," my mother said, losing patience. "We are not the ladies you seek."

The second Beatle tapped a foot lightly against a wheel of the push-chair. "Your husband seeks ladies, madam, were you aware of that fact? Yes, he does. Most assiduously, may I add."

"Too assiduously," said the first Beatle, his face darkening.

"I tell you I am not the Maharani Begum," my mother said, growing suddenly alarmed. "Her business is not my business. Kindly let me pass."

The second Beatle stepped closer to her. She could feel his breath, which was minty. "One of the ladies he sought out was our ward, as you might say," he explained. "That would be the term. Under our protection, you follow. Us, therefore, being responsible for her welfare."

"Your husband," said the first Beatle, showing his teeth in a frightening way, and raising his voice one notch, "damaged the goods. Do you hear me, Queenie? He damaged the fucking goods."

"Mistaken identity, fleas," said Certainly-Mary. "Many Indian residents in Waverley House. We are decent ladies; *fleas.*"

The second Beatle had taken out something from an inside pocket. A blade caught the light. "Fucking wogs," he said. "You fucking come over here, you don't fucking know how to fucking behave. Why don't you fucking fuck off to fucking Wogistan? Fuck your fucking wog arses. Now then," he added in a quiet voice, holding up the knife, "unbutton your blouses."

Just then a loud noise emanated from the doorway of Waverley House. The two women and the two men turned to look, and out came Mixed-Up, yelling at the top of his voice and windmilling his arms like a mad old loon.

"Hullo," said the Beatle with the knife, looking amused. "Who's this, then? Oh oh fucking seven?"

Mixed-Up was trying to speak, he was in a mighty agony of effort, but all that was coming out of his mouth was raw, unshaped noise. Scheherazade woke up and joined in. The two Beatles looked displeased. But then something happened inside old Mixed-Up; something popped, and in a great rush he gabbled, "Sirs sirs no sirs these not B—— women sirs B—— women upstairs on floor three sirs Maharaja of B—— also sirs God's truth mother's grave swear."

It was the longest sentence he had spoken since the stroke that had broken his tongue long ago.

And what with his torrent and Scheherazade's squalls there were suddenly heads poking out from doorways, attention was being paid, and the two Beatles nodded gravely. "Honest mistake," the first of them said apologetically to my mother, and actually bowed from the waist. "Could happen to anyone," the knife-man added, ruefully. They turned and began to walk quickly away. As they passed Mecir, however, they paused. "I know you, though," said the knife-man. "*Jet plane. Gone.*" He made a short movement of the arm, and then Mixed-Up the courter was lying on the pavement with blood leaking from a wound in his stomach. "All okay now," he gasped, and passed out.

11

He was on the road to recovery by Christmas; my mother's letter to the landlords, in which she called him a "knight in shining armour," ensured that he was well looked after, and his job was kept open for him. He continued to live in his little ground-floor cubbyhole, while the hall porter's duties were carried out by shift-duty staff. "Nothing but the best for our very own hero," the landlords assured my mother in their reply.

The two Maharajas and their retinues had moved out before I came home for the Christmas holidays, so we had no further visits from the Beatles or the Rolling Stones. Certainly-Mary spent as much time as she could with Mecir; but it was the look of my old Aya that worried me more than poor Mixed-Up. She looked older, and powdery, as if she might crumble away at any moment into dust.

"We didn't want to worry you at school," my mother said. "She has been having heart trouble. Palpitations. Not all the time, but."

Mary's health problems had sobered up the whole family. Muneeza's tantrums had stopped, and even my father was making an effort. They had put up a Christmas tree in the sitting-room and decorated it with all sorts of baubles. It was so odd to see a Christmas tree at our place that I realised things must be fairly serious.

On Christmas Eve my mother suggested that Mary might like it if we all sang some carols. Amma had made song-sheets, six copies, by hand. When we did *O come, all ye faithful* I showed off by singing from memory in Latin. Everybody behaved perfectly. When Muneeza suggested that we should try *Swinging on a Star* or *I Wanna Hold Your Hand* instead of this boring stuff, she wasn't really being serious. So this is family life, I thought. This is it.

But we were only playacting.

A few weeks earlier, at school, I'd come across an American boy, the star of the school's Rugby football team, crying in the Chapel cloisters. I asked him what the matter was and he told me that President Kennedy had been assassinated. "I don't believe you," I said, but I could see that it was true. The football star sobbed and sobbed. I took his hand.

"When the President dies, the nation is orphaned," he eventually said, brokenheartedly parroting a piece of cracker-barrel wisdom he'd probably heard on Voice of America.

"I know how you feel," I lied. "My father just died, too."

Mary's heart trouble turned out to be a mystery; unpredictably, it came and went. She was subjected to all sorts of tests during the next six months, but each time the doctors ended up by shaking their heads: They couldn't find anything wrong with her. Physically, she was right as rain; except that there were these periods when her heart kicked and bucked in her chest like the wild horses in *The Misfits*,[21] the ones whose roping and tying made Marilyn Monroe so mad.

---

[21] *The Misfits:* A western film (1960) written by Arthur Miller and starring Marilyn Monroe, Clark Gable, and Montgomery Clift about a roundup of wild horses.

Mecir went back to work in the spring, but his experience had knocked the stuffing out of him. He was slower to smile, duller of eye, more inward. Mary, too, had turned in upon herself. They still met for tea, crumpets, and *The Flintstones*, but something was no longer quite right.

At the beginning of the summer Mary made an announcement.

"I know what is wrong with me," she told my parents, out of the blue. "I need to go home."

"But, Aya," my mother argued, "homesickness is not a real disease."

"God knows for what-all we came over to this country," Mary said. "But I can no longer stay. No. Certainly not." Her determination was absolute.

So it was England that was breaking her heart, breaking it by not being India. London was killing her, by not being Bombay. And Mixed-Up? I wondered. Was the courter killing her, too, because he was no longer himself? Or was it that her heart, roped by two different loves, was being pulled both East and West, whinnying and rearing, like those movie horses being yanked this way by Clark Gable and that way by Montgomery Clift, and she knew that to live she would have to choose?

"I must go," said Certainly-Mary. "Yes, certainly. *Bas.* Enough."

That summer, the summer of '64, I turned seventeen. Chandni went back to India. Durré's Polish friend Rozalia informed me over a sandwich in Oxford Street that she was getting engaged to a "real man," so I could forget about seeing her again, because this Zbigniew was the jealous type. Roy Orbison sang *It's Over* in my ears as I walked away to the Tube, but the truth was that nothing had really begun.

Certainly-Mary left us in mid-July. My father bought her a one-way ticket to Bombay, and that last morning was heavy with the pain of ending. When we took her bags down to the car, Mecir the hall porter was nowhere to be seen. Mary did not knock on the door of his lounge, but walked straight out through the freshly polished oak-panelled lobby, whose mirrors and brasses were sparkling brightly; she climbed into the back seat of our Ford Zodiac and sat there stiffly with her carry-on grip on her lap, staring straight ahead. I had known and loved her all my life. *Never mind your damned courter,* I wanted to shout at her, *what about me?*

As it happened, she was right about the homesickness. After her return to Bombay, she never had a day's heart trouble again; and, as the letter from her niece Stella confirmed, at ninety-one she was still going strong.

Soon after she left, my father told us he had decided to "shift location" to Pakistan. As usual, there were no discussions, no explanations, just the simple fiat. He gave up the lease on the flat in Waverley House at the end of the summer holidays, and they all went off to Karachi, while I went back to school.

I became a British citizen that year. I was one of the lucky ones, I guess, because in spite of that chess game I had the Dodo on my side. And the passport did, in many ways, set me free. It allowed me to come and go, to make choices that were not the ones my father would have wished. But I, too, have ropes around my neck, I have them to this day, pulling me this way and that, East and West, the nooses tightening, commanding, *choose, choose.*

I buck, I snort, I whinny, I rear, I kick. Ropes, I do not choose between you. Lassoes, lariats, I choose neither of you, and both. Do you hear? I refuse to choose.

A year or so after we moved out I was in the area and dropped in at Waverley House to see how the old courter was doing. Maybe, I thought, we could have a game of chess, and he could beat me to a pulp. The lobby was empty, so I knocked on the door of his little lounge. A stranger answered.

"Where's Mixed-Up?" I cried, taken by surprise. I apologised at once, embarrassed. "Mr. Mecir, I meant, the porter."

"I'm the porter, sir," the man said. "I don't know anything about any mix-up."

↷ EDWIDGE DANTICAT
B. HAITI, 1969

Although she is still a young woman, Edwidge Danticat is probably the most important Haitian American author writing today. Her novels and short stories present not only the immigrant experience but also the troubled history of her homeland.

From Haiti to New York.   Born in Haiti in 1969, Danticat was raised by an aunt after her parents emigrated to New York without her. During her childhood she was deeply influenced by Haitian oral storytelling, an influence she acknowledged in the title to her collection of short stories *Krik? Krak!* (1995), derived from the Haitian tradition of a storyteller calling out "Krik?" and willing listeners gathering around and responding "Krak!" She especially remembers listening to her grandmother telling stories about her grandfather who had resisted the U.S. occupation of Haiti between the two world wars. Commenting on the importance of such stories, she told an interviewer for the British newspaper *The Guardian,* "These things are not written anywhere. Sitting with an older person tells you another side."

When she was twelve Danticat joined her parents in New York. As a child she had spoken Creole and learned French in school. She learned English only after moving to New York and recalls that there was a time when, as a child, she was "completely between languages," able to express herself orally in Creole but unable to write in any language. After graduating from Clara Barton High School in Brooklyn, she earned degrees in French literature from Barnard College and in creative writing from Brown University.

Novels of the Haitian experience.   Her master's thesis became her first published novel, *Breath, Eyes, Memory* (1994). Narrated by Sophie, whose personal history in Haiti and New York resembles Danticat's, the novel

"[Edwidge Danticat is] doing for Haiti's history of violence and vengeance what Toni Morrison did for the US in tackling the horrors of slavery and its aftermath."

– ROBERT ANTONI, West Indian novelist

tells the lives of four generations of women of the Caro family. Viewed as a feminist novel, which Danticat dedicated to "the brave women of Haiti, grandmothers, mothers, aunts, sisters, cousins, daughters, and friends, on this shore and other shores," the novel disturbed some Haitian readers for betraying community "secrets" with its account of the Haitian practice of "testing" to confirm a daughter's virginity.

Danticat's second novel, *The Farming of Bones* (1998), tells the story of a Haitian maid working in the Dominican Republic at the time of the Haitian massacre in 1937, when Dominican dictator Raphael Trujillo's troops murdered thousands of Haitians who were working in the Dominican sugar cane fields, farming bones. The book's title carries multiple meanings, referring both to the gathering of cane and to the massacre, and so invokes the events of 1937 as well as the economic history that created them. Danticat's account of the events is based in part on oral stories that she heard from older Haitians who had survived the massacre. Her most recent novel, *The Dew Breaker* (2004) also deals with Haiti's violent history in its story of a Haitian American who learns that her father was a torturer for the Tonton Macoutes, the secret police under dictators Papa Doc Duvalier and his son Baby Doc.

Danticat has maintained ties with her homeland and has made films about Haiti and its history. She lives in the large Haitian community in Miami and teaches creative writing at New York University and the University of Miami.

"Children of the Sea."   Using alternating diary entries by two Haitian young people, a radical activist who has escaped Haiti on a boat headed for Florida and his girlfriend left behind, Danticat dramatizes in "Children of the Sea" the horrors that prompt Haitians to risk their lives to reach the United States. Set in 1991–92 after the military coup that overthrew the first Aristide government, the story was nearly contemporary with its periodical publication in 1993 under the title "From the Ocean Floor." It was included in Danticat's 1995 collection of short stories *Krik? Krak!*. When the book was nominated for the National Book Award, Danticat told an NPR interviewer, "I wanted to raise the voice of a lot of the people that I knew growing up, for the most part, . . . poor people who had extraordinary dreams but also very amazing obstacles." The story assumes at least some familiarity with Haitian politics and history and an awareness of the different treatment that Haitian boat people have received in the United States from that accorded to Cubans. These political issues, however, remain in the background. In the foreground, in a style that British novelist Fay Weldon says "delicately tiptoes through bougainvillea and butterflies into minefields of rape, mayhem, insanity, suicide, terror," Danticat focuses on the stories of the two young people, their immediate personal relationships, and their hopes and fears.

■ **FURTHER RESEARCH**

Newson, Adele S., and Linda Strong-Leek, eds. *Winds of Change: The Transforming Voices of Caribbean Women Writers and Scholars.* 1998.

❧ Children of the Sea

They say behind the mountains are more mountains. Now I know it's true. I also know there are timeless waters, endless seas, and lots of people in this world whose names don't matter to anyone but themselves. I look up at the sky and I see you there. I see you crying like a crushed snail, the way you cried when I helped you pull out your first loose tooth. Yes, I did love you then. Somehow when I looked at you, I thought of fiery red ants. I wanted you to dig your fingernails into my skin and drain out all my blood.

I don't know how long we'll be at sea. There are thirty-six other deserting souls on this little boat with me. White sheets with bright red spots float as our sail.

When I got on board I thought I could still smell the semen and the innocence lost to those sheets. I look up there and I think of you and all those times you resisted. Sometimes I felt like you wanted to, but I knew you wanted me to respect you. You thought I was testing your will, but all I wanted was to be near you. Maybe it's like you've always said. I imagine too much. I am afraid I am going to start having nightmares once we get deep at sea. I really hate having the sun in my face all day long. If you see me again, I'll be so dark.

Your father will probably marry you off now, since I am gone. Whatever you do, please don't marry a soldier. They're almost not human.

haiti est comme tu l'as laissé. yes, just the way you left it. bullets day and night. same hole. same everything. i'm tired of the whole mess. i get so cross and irritable. i pass the time by chasing roaches around the house. i pound my heel on their heads. they make me so mad. everything makes me mad. i am cramped inside all day. they've closed the schools since the army took over. no one is mentioning the old president's[1] name. papa burnt all his campaign posters and old buttons. manman buried her buttons in a hole behind the house. she thinks he might come back. she says she will unearth them when he does. no one comes out of their house. not a single person. papa wants me to throw out those tapes of your radio shows. i destroyed some music tapes, but i still have your voice. i thank god you got out when you did. all the other youth federation members have disappeared. no one has heard from them. i think they might all be in prison. maybe they're all dead. papa worries a little about you. he doesn't hate you as much as you think. the other day i heard him asking manman, do you think the boy is dead? manman said she didn't know. i think he regrets being so mean to you. i don't sketch my butterflies anymore because i don't even like seeing the sun. besides, manman says that butterflies can bring news. the bright ones bring happy news and the black ones warn us of deaths. we have our whole lives ahead of us. you used to say that, remember? but then again things were so very different then.

---

[1] **the old president:** Jean-Bertrand Aristide (b. 1953), democratically elected president of Haiti in 1990, held office for seven months in 1991 and again from 1994 to 1996.

There is a pregnant girl on board. She looks like she might be our age. Nineteen or twenty. Her face is covered with scars that look like razor marks. She is short and speaks in a singsong that reminds me of the villagers in the north. Most of the other people on the boat are much older than I am. I have heard that a lot of these boats have young children on board. I am glad this one does not. I think it would break my heart watching some little boy or girl every single day on this sea, looking into their empty faces to remind me of the hopelessness of the future in our country. It's hard enough with the adults. It's hard enough with me.

I used to read a lot about America before I had to study so much for the university exams. I am trying to think, to see if I read anything more about Miami. It is sunny. It doesn't snow there like it does in other parts of America. I can't tell exactly how far we are from there. We might be barely out of our own shores. There are no borderlines on the sea. The whole thing looks like one. I cannot even tell if we are about to drop off the face of the earth. Maybe the world is flat and we are going to find out, like the navigators of old. As you know, I am not very religious. Still I pray every night that we won't hit a storm. When I do manage to sleep, I dream that we are caught in one hurricane after another. I dream that the winds come of the sky and claim us for the sea. We go under and no one hears from us again.

I am more comfortable now with the idea of dying. Not that I have completely accepted it, but I know that it might happen. Don't be mistaken. I really do not want to be a martyr. I know I am no good to anybody dead, but if that is what's coming, I know I cannot just scream at it and tell it to go away.

I hope another group of young people can do the radio show. For a long time that radio show was my whole life. It was nice to have radio like that for a while, where we could talk about what we wanted from government, what we wanted for the future of our country.

There are a lot of Protestants on this boat. A lot of them see themselves as Job or the Children of Israel. I think some of them are hoping something will plunge down from the sky and part the sea for us. They say the Lord gives and the Lord takes away. I have never been given very much. What was there to take away?

if only I could kill. if i knew some good *wanga* magic,[2] i would wipe them off the face of the earth. a group of students got shot in front of fort dimanche prison today. they were demonstrating for the bodies of the radio six. that is what they are calling you all. the radio six. you have a name. you have a reputation. a lot of people think you are dead like the others. they want the bodies turned over to the families. this afternoon, the army finally did give some bodies back. they told the families to go

---

[2] *wanga* magic: *Wanga*, or magic charms in the *vodou* religion of Haiti, are fetishes that concentrate spiritual power in order to protect oneself from or to attack one's enemies, but not to the extent of death. This religion is a syncretization, or intermixing, of African Benin and Christian faiths whose intricate and complex set of practices do not much resemble those of Western religions. At its foundation is a belief in spirits, or *lwa*, that mediate between the human and the natural and supernatural worlds. Together, the *lwa* form a pantheon much like a family or ensemble, each *lwa* having a particular realm over which it rules. They are not gods, but mediators between a monotheistic god and humans; each *lwa* has been associated with a Catholic saint.

collect them at the rooms for indigents at the morgue. our neighbor madan roger came home with her son's head and not much else. honest to god, it was just his head. at the morgue, they say a car ran over him and took the head off his body. when madan roger went to the morgue, they gave her the head. by the time we saw her, she had been carrying the head all over port-au-prince.[3] just to show what's been done to her son. the macoutes[4] by the house were laughing at her. they asked her if that was her dinner. it took ten people to hold her back from jumping on them. they would have killed her, the dogs. i will never go outside again. not even in the yard to breathe the air. they are always watching you, like vultures. at night i can't sleep. i count the bullets in the dark. i keep wondering if it is true. did you really get out? i wish there was some way i could be sure that you really went away. yes, i will. i will keep writing like we promised to do. i hate it, but i will keep writing. you keep writing too, okay? and when we see each other again, it will seem like we lost no time.

Today was our first real day at sea. Everyone was vomiting with each small rocking of the boat. The faces around me are showing their first charcoal layer of sunburn. "Now we will never be mistaken for Cubans,"[5] one man said. Even though some of the Cubans are black too. The man said he was once on a boat with a group of Cubans. His boat had stopped to pick up the Cubans on an island off the Bahamas. When the Coast Guard came for them, they took the Cubans to Miami and sent him back to Haiti. Now he was back on the boat with some papers and documents to show that the police in Haiti were after him. He had a broken leg too, in case there was any doubt.

One old lady fainted from sunstroke. I helped revive her by rubbing some of the salt water on her lips. During the day it can be so hot. At night, it is so cold. Since there are no mirrors, we look at each others faces to see just how frail and sick we are starting to look.

Some of the women sing and tell stories to each other to appease the vomiting. Still, I watch the sea. At night, the sky and the sea are one. The stars look so huge and so close. They make for very bright reflections in the sea. At times I feel like I can just reach out and pull a star down from the sky as though it is a breadfruit or a calabash or something that could be of use to us on this journey.

When we sing, *Beloved Haiti, there is no place like you. I had to leave you before I could understand you,* some of the women start crying. At times, I just want to stop in the middle of the song and cry myself. To hide my tears, I pretend like I am getting another attack of nausea, from the sea smell. I no longer join in the singing.

---

[3] **port-au-prince:** Port-au-Prince, the capital of Haiti and its largest city.

[4] **the macoutes:** The *tonton macoutes,* the infamously brutal paramilitary troops who pursued and executed the opponents of "Papa Doc" Duvalier (1907–1971), the president of Haiti. Duvalier was elected president in 1957, and in 1964 he declared himself president for life. His rule of Haiti was a cruel dictatorship. The *tonton macoutes* are still a potent military force in the country.

[5] **". . . mistaken for Cubans":** Many Cuban people leave their home for the United States in the same manner as the Haitian boat people described in this story.

You probably do not know much about this, because you have always been so closely watched by your father in that well-guarded house with your genteel mother. No, I am not making fun of you for this. If anything, I am jealous. If I was a girl, maybe I would have been at home and not out politicking and getting myself into something like this. Once you have been at sea for a couple of days, it smells like every fish you have ever eaten, every crab you have ever caught, every jellyfish that has ever bitten your leg. I am so tired of the smell. I am also tired of the way the people on this boat are starting to stink. The pregnant girl, Célianne, I don't know how she takes it. She stares into space all the time and rubs her stomach.

I have never seen her eat. Sometimes the other women offer her a piece of bread and she takes it, but she has no food of her own. I cannot help feeling like she will have this child as soon as she gets hungry enough.

She woke up screaming the other night. I thought she had a stomach ache. Some water started coming into the boat in the spot where she was sleeping. There is a crack at the bottom of the boat that looks as though, if it gets any bigger, it will split the boat in two. The captain cleared us aside and used some tar to clog up the hole. Everyone started asking him if it was okay, if they were going to be okay. He said he hoped the Coast Guard would find us soon.

You can't really go to sleep after that. So we all stared at the tar by the moonlight. We did this until dawn. I cannot help but wonder how long this tar will hold out.

papa found your tapes. he started yelling at me, asking if I was crazy keeping them. he is just waiting for the gasoline ban to be lifted so we can get out of the city. he is always pestering me these days because he cannot go out driving his van. all the american factories are closed.[6] he kept yelling at me about the tapes. he called me selfish, and he asked if i hadn't seen or heard what was happening to man-crazy whores like me. i shouted that i wasn't a whore. he had no business calling me that. he pushed me against the wall for disrespecting him. he spat in my face. i wish those macoutes would kill him. i wish he would catch a bullet so we could see how scared he really is. he said to me, i didn't send your stupid trouble maker away. i started yelling at him. yes, you did. yes, you did. yes, you did, you pig peasant. i don't know why i said that. he slapped me and kept slapping me really hard until manman came and grabbed me away from him. i wish one of those bullets would hit me.

The tar is holding up so far. Two days and no more leaks. Yes, I am finally an African. I am even darker than your father. I wanted to buy a straw hat from one of the ladies, but she would not sell it to me for the last two gourdes[7] I have left in change. Do you think your money is worth anything to me here? she asked me. Sometimes, I forget where I am. If I keep daydreaming like I have been doing, I will walk off the boat to go for a stroll.

---

[6] all . . . closed: Many North American companies, attracted to Haiti because of the low labor costs, pulled out during the political uncertainties of the 1990s.

[7] gourdes: Official currency of Haiti.

The other night I dreamt that I died and went to heaven. This heaven was nothing like I expected. It was at the bottom of the sea. There were starfishes and mermaids all around me. The mermaids were dancing and singing in Latin like the priests do at the cathedral during Mass. You were there with me too, at the bottom of the sea. You were with your family, off to the side. Your father was acting like he was better than everyone else and he was standing in front of a sea cave blocking you from my view. I tried to talk to you, but every time I opened my mouth, water bubbles came out. No sounds.

they have this thing now that they do. if they come into a house and there is a son and mother there, they hold a gun to their heads. they make the son sleep with his mother. if it is a daughter and father, they do the same thing. some nights papa sleeps at his brother's, uncle pressoir's house. uncle pressoir sleeps at our house, just in case they come. that way papa will never be forced to lie down in bed with me. instead, uncle pressoir would be forced to, but that would not be so bad. we know a girl who had a child by her father that way. that is what papa does not want to happen, even if he is killed. there is still no gasoline to buy. otherwise we would be in ville rose already. papa has a friend who is going to get him some gasoline from a soldier. as soon as we get the gasoline, we are going to drive quick and fast until we find civilization. that's how papa puts it, civilization. he says things are not as bad in the provinces. i am still not talking to him. i don't think i ever will. manman says it is not his fault. he is trying to protect us. he cannot protect us. only god can protect us. the soldiers can come and do with us what they want. that makes papa feel weak, she says. he gets angry when he feels weak. why should he be angry with me? i am not one of the pigs with the machine guns. she asked me what really happened to you. she said she saw your parents before they left for the provinces. they did not want to tell her anything. i told her you took a boat after they raided the radio station. you escaped and took a boat to heaven knows where. she said, he was going to make a good man, that boy. sharp, like a needle point, that boy, he took the university exams a year before everyone else in this area. manman has respect for people with ambitions. she said papa did not want you for me because it did not seem as though you were going to do any better for me than he and manman could. he wants me to find a man who will do me some good. someone who will make sure that i have more than i have now. it is not enough for a girl to be just pretty anymore. we are not that well connected in society. the kind of man that papa wants for me would never have anything to do with me. all anyone can hope for is just a tiny bit of love, manman says, like a drop in a cup if you can get it, or a waterfall, a flood, if you can get that too. we do not have all that many high-up connections, she says, but you are an educated girl. what she counts for educated is not much to anyone but us anyway. they should be announcing the university exams on the radio next week. then i will know if you passed. i will listen for your name.

We spent most of yesterday telling stories. Someone says, Krik? You answer, Krak! And they say, I have many stories I could tell you, and then they go on and tell these stories to you, but mostly to themselves. Sometimes it feels like we have been at sea longer than the many years that I have been on this earth. The sun comes up and goes down. That is how you know it has been a whole day. I feel like we are sailing for Africa. Maybe we will go to Guinin,[8] to live with the spirits, to be with everyone who has come and has died before us. They would probably turn us away from there too. Someone has a transistor and sometimes we listen to radio from the Bahamas. They treat Haitians like dogs in the Bahamas, a woman says. To them, we are not human. Even though their music sounds like ours. Their people look like ours. Even though we had the same African fathers who probably crossed these same seas together.

Do you want to know how people go to the bathroom on the boat? Probably the same way they did on those slaves ships years ago. They set aside a little corner for that. When I have to pee, I just pull it, lean over the rail, and do it very quickly. When I have to do the other thing, I rip a piece of something, squat down and do it, and throw the waste in the sea. I am always embarrassed by the smell. It is so demeaning having to squat in front of so many people. People turn away, but not always. At times I wonder if there is really land on the other side of the sea. Maybe the sea is endless. Like my love for you.

last night they came to madan roger's house. papa hurried inside as soon as madan roger's screaming started. the soldiers were looking for her son. madan roger was screaming, you killed him already. we buried his head. you can't kill him twice. they were shouting at her, do you belong to the youth federation with those vagabonds who were on the radio? she was yelling, do i look like a youth to you? can you identify your son's other associates? they asked her. papa had us tiptoe from the house into the latrine out back. we could hear it all from there. i thought i was going to choke on the smell of rotting poupou. they kept shouting at madan roger, did your son belong to the youth federation? wasn't he on the radio talking about the police? did he say, down with tonton macoutes? did he say, down with the army? he said that the military had to go; didn't he write slogans? he had meetings, didn't he? he demonstrated on the streets. you should have advised him better. she cursed on their mothers' graves. she just came out and shouted it, i hope your mothers will never rest in their cursed graves! she was just shouting it out, you killed him once already! you want to kill me too? go ahead. i don't care anymore. i'm dead already. you have already done the worst to me that you can do. you have killed my soul. they kept at it, asking her questions at the top of their voices: was your son a traitor? tell me all the names of his friends who were traitors just like him. madan roger finally shouts, yes, he was one! he belonged to that group. he was on the radio. he was on the streets at these demonstrations. he hated you like i hate you criminals. you killed him. they start to pound at her. you can hear it. you can hear the guns coming down on her head. it sounds like they are cracking all the bones in her body. manman whispers to papa, you can't just let them kill her. go and give them some money like you gave them for your daughter. papa says, the only money i have left is to get us out of here tomorrow. manman whispers, we cannot just stay here and let them kill her.

---

[8] **Guinin:** Guinea, in Africa, where the *vodou* faithful believe the *lwa*, or spirits, originated. It is a region considered irretrievably lost and purely mythical.

manman starts moving like she is going out the door. papa grabs her neck and pins her to the latrine wall. tomorrow we are going to ville rose, he says. you will not spoil that for the family. you will not put us in that situation. you will not get us killed. going out there will be like trying to raise the dead. she is not dead yet, manman says, maybe we can help her. i will make you stay if i have to, he says to her. my mother buries her face in the latrine wall. she starts to cry. you can hear madan roger screaming. they are beating her, pounding on her until you don't hear anything else. manman tells papa, you cannot let them kill somebody just because you are afraid. papa says, oh yes, you *can* let them kill somebody because you are afraid. they are the law. it is their right. we are just being good citizens, following the law of the land. it has happened before all over this country and tonight it will happen again and there is nothing we can do.

Célianne spent the night groaning. She looks like she has been ready for a while, but maybe the child is being stubborn. She just screamed that she is bleeding. There is an older woman here who looks like she has had a lot of children herself. She says Célianne is not bleeding at all. Her water sack has broken.

The only babies I have ever seen right after birth are baby mice. Their skin looks veil thin. You can see all the blood vessels and all their organs. I have always wanted to poke them to see if my finger would go all the way through the skin.

I have moved to the other side of the boat so I will not have to look *inside* Célianne. People are just watching. The captain asks the midwife to keep Célianne steady so she will not rock any more holes into the boat. Now we have three cracks covered with tar. I am scared to think of what would happen if we had to choose among ourselves who would stay on the boat and who should die. Given the choice to make a decision like that, we would all act like vultures, including me.

The sun will set soon. Someone says that this child will be just another pair of hungry lips. At least it will have its mother's breasts, says an old man. Everyone will eat their last scraps of food today.

there is a rumor that the old president is coming back. there is a whole bunch of people going to the airport to meet him. papa says we are not going to stay in port-au-prince to find out if this is true or if it is a lie. they are selling gasoline at the market again. the carnival groups[9] have taken to the streets. we are heading the other way, to ville rose. maybe there i will be able to sleep at night. it is not going to turn out well with the old president coming back, manman now says. people are just too hopeful, and sometimes hope is the biggest weapon of all to use against us. people will believe anything. they will claim to see the christ return and march on the cross backwards if there is enough hope. manman told papa that you took the boat. papa told me before we left this morning that he thought himself a bad father for everything that happened. he says a father should be able to speak to his children like a

---

[9] **carnival groups:** Traditionally, groups of people form to sing and dance in procession throughout the Haitian countryside, starting at Mardi Gras and continuing each weekend during Lent.

civilized man. all the craziness here has made him feel like he cannot do that any-more. all he wants to do is live. he and manman have not said a word to one another since we left the latrine. i know that papa does not hate us, not in the way that i hate those soldiers, those macoutes, and all those people here who shoot guns. on our way to ville rose, we saw dogs licking two dead faces. one of them was a little boy who was lying on the side of the road with the sun in his dead open eyes. we saw a soldier shoving a woman out of a hut, calling her a witch. he was shaving the woman's head, but of course we never stopped. papa didn't want to go in madan roger's house and check on her before we left. he thought the soldiers might still be there. papa was driving the van real fast. i thought he was going to kill us. we stopped at an open market on the way. manman got some black cloth for herself and for me. she cut the cloth in two pieces and we wrapped them around our heads to mourn madan roger. when i am used to ville rose, maybe i will sketch you some butterflies, depending on the news that they bring me.

Célianne had a girl baby. The woman acting as a midwife is holding the baby to the moon and whispering prayers. . . . *God, this child You bring into the world, please guide her as You please through all her days on this earth.* The baby has not cried.

We had to throw our extra things in the sea because the water is beginning to creep in slowly. The boat needs to be lighter. My two gourdes in change had to be thrown overboard as an offering to Agwé,[10] the spirit of the water. I heard the captain whisper to someone yesterday that they might have to *do something* with some of the people who never recovered from seasickness. I am afraid that soon they may ask me to throw out this notebook. We might all have to strip down to the way we were born, to keep ourselves from drowning.

Célianne's child is a beautiful child. They are calling her Swiss, because the word *Swiss* was written on the small knife they used to cut her umbilical cord. If she was my daughter, I would call her soleil, sun, moon, or star, after the elements. She still hasn't cried. There is gossip circulating about how Célianne became pregnant. Some people are saying that she had an affair with a married man and her parents threw her out. Gossip spreads here like everywhere else.

Do you remember our silly dreams? Passing the university exams and then studying hard to go until the end, the farthest of all that we can go in school. I know your father might never approve of me. I was going to try to win him over. He would have to cut out my heart to keep me from loving you. I hope you are writing like you promised. Jésus, Marie, Joseph! Everyone smells so bad. They get into arguments and they say to one another, "It is only my misfortune that would lump me together with an indigent like you." Think of it. They are fighting about being superior when we all might drown like straw.

---

[10] **Agwé:** One of the *lwa,* he is captain and protector of ships on the sea and ruler of fishing. His consort, Lasiren, is a *lwa* in the form of a mermaid. She brings luck and money from the ocean's depths, where she makes her own unearthly music.

There is an old toothless man leaning over to see what I am writing. He is sucking on the end of an old wooden pipe that has not seen any fire for a very long time now. He looks like a painting. Seeing things simply, you could fill a museum with the sights you have here. I still feel like such a coward for running away. Have you heard anything about my parents? Last time I saw them on the beach, my mother had a *kriz.*[11] She just fainted on the sand. I saw her coming to as we started sailing away. But of course I don't know if she is doing all right.

The water is really piling into the boat. We take turns pouring bowls of it out. I don't know what is keeping the boat from splitting in two. Swiss isn't crying. They keep slapping her behind, but she is not crying.

of course the old president didn't come. they arrested a lot of people at the airport, shot a whole bunch of them down. i heard it on the radio. while we were eating tonight, i told papa that i love you. i don't know if it will make a difference. i just want him to know that i have loved somebody in my life. in case something happens to one of us, i think he should know this about me, that i have loved someone besides only my mother and father in my life. i know you would understand. you are the one for large noble gestures. i just wanted him to know that i was capable of loving somebody. he looked me straight in the eye and said nothing to me. i love you until my hair shivers at the thought of anything happening to you. papa just turned his face away like he was rejecting my very birth. i am writing you from under the banyan tree in the yard in our new house. there are only two rooms and a tin roof that makes music when it rains, especially when there is hail, which falls like angry tears from heaven. there is a stream down the hill from the house, a stream that is too shallow for me to drown myself. manman and i spend a lot of time talking under the banyan tree. she told me today that sometimes you have to choose between your father and the man you love. her whole family did not want her to marry papa because he was a gardener from ville rose and her family was from the city and some of them had even gone to university. she whispered everything under the banyan tree in the yard so as not to hurt his feelings. i saw him looking at us hard from the house. i heard him clearing his throat like he heard us anyway, like we hurt him very deeply somehow just by being together.

Célianne is lying with her head against the side of the boat. The baby still will not cry. They both look very peaceful in all this chaos. Célianne is holding her baby tight against her chest. She just cannot seem to let herself throw it in the ocean. I asked her about the baby's father. She keeps repeating the story now with her eyes closed, her lips barely moving.

She was home one night with her mother and brother Lionel when some ten or twelve soldiers burst into the house. The soldiers held a gun to Lionel's head and ordered him to lie down and become intimate with his mother. Lionel refused. Their mother told him to go ahead and obey the soldiers because she was afraid that they

---

[11] *kriz:* Probably "crisis"—meaning "fit"—in *kreyol,* the Haitian language.

would kill Lionel on the spot if he put up more of a fight. Lionel did as his mother told him, crying as the soldiers laughed at him, pressing the gun barrels farther and farther into his neck.

Afterwards, the soldiers tied up Lionel and their mother, then they each took turns raping Célianne. When they were done, they arrested Lionel, accusing him of moral crimes. After that night, Célianne never heard from Lionel again.

The same night, Célianne cut her face with a razor so that no one would know who she was. Then as facial scars were healing, she started throwing up and getting rashes. Next thing she knew, she was getting big. She found out about the boat and got on. She is fifteen.

manman told me the whole story today under the banyan tree. the bastards were coming to get me. they were going to arrest me. they were going to peg me as a member of the youth federation and then take me away. papa heard about it. he went to the post and paid them money, all the money he had. our house in port-au-prince and all the land his father had left him, he gave it all away to save my life. this is why he was so mad. tonight manman told me this under the banyan tree. i have no words to thank him for this. i don't know how. you must love him for this, manman says, you must. it is something you can never forget, the sacrifice he has made. i cannot bring myself to say thank you. now he is more than my father. he is a man who gave everything he had to save my life. on the radio tonight, they read the list of names of people who passed the university exams. you passed.

We got some relief from the seawater coming in. The captain used the last of his tar, and most of the water is staying out for a while. Many people have volunteered to throw Célianne's baby overboard for her. She will not let them. They are waiting for her to go to sleep so they can do it, but she will not sleep. I never knew before that dead children looked purple. The lips are the most purple because the baby is so dark. Purple like the sea after the sun has set.

Célianne is slowly drifting off to sleep. She is very tired from the labor. I do not want to touch the child. If anybody is going to throw it in the ocean, I think it should be her. I keep thinking, they have thrown every piece of flesh that followed the child out of her body into the water. They are going to throw the dead baby in the water. Won't these things attract sharks?

Célianne's fingernails are buried deep in the child's naked back. The old man with the pipe just asked, "Kompè, what are you writing?" I told him, "My will."

i am getting used to ville rose. there are butterflies here, tons of butterflies. so far none has landed on my hand, which means they have no news for me. i cannot always bathe in the stream near the house because the water is freezing cold. the only time it feels just right is at noon, and then there are a dozen eyes who might see me bathing. i solved that by getting a bucket of water in the morning and leaving it in the sun and then bathing myself once it is night under the banyan tree. the banyan now is my most trusted friend. they say banyans can last hundreds of years. even the branches that lean down from them become like trees themselves. a banyan could become a forest, manman says, if it were given a chance. from the spot where i stand under the banyan, i see the mountains, and behind those are more mountains still. so many mountains that are bare like rocks. i feel like all those mountains are pushing me farther and farther away from you.

She threw it overboard. I watched her face knot up like a thread, and then she let go. It fell in a splash, floated for a while, and then sank. And quickly after that she jumped in too. And just as the baby's head sank, so did hers. They went together like two bottles beneath a waterfall. The shock lasts only so long. There was no time to even try and save her. There was no question of it. The sea in that spot is like the sharks that live there. It has no mercy.

They say I have to throw my notebook out. The old man has to throw out his hat and his pipe. The water is rising again and they are scooping it out. I asked for a few seconds to write this last page and then promised that I would let it go. I know you will probably never see this, but it was nice imagining that I had you here to talk to.

I hope my parents are alive. I asked the old man to tell them what happened to me, if he makes it anywhere. He asked me to write his name in "my book." I asked him for his full name. It is Justin Moïse André Nozius Joseph Frank Osnac Maximilien. He says it all with such an air that you would think him a king. The old man says, "I know a Coast Guard ship is coming. It came to me in my dream." He points to a spot far into the distance. I look where he is pointing. I see nothing. From here, ships must be like a mirage in the desert.

I must throw my book out now. It goes down to them, Célianne and her daughter and all those children of the sea who might soon be claiming me.

I go to them now as though it was always meant to be, as though the very day that my mother birthed me, she had chosen me to live life eternal, among the children of the deep blue sea, those who have escaped the chains of slavery to form a world beneath the heavens and the blood-drenched earth where you live.

Perhaps I was chosen from the beginning of time to live there with Agwé at the bottom of the sea. Maybe this is why I dreamed of the starfish and the mermaids having the Catholic Mass under the sea. Maybe this was my invitation to go. In any case, I know that my memory of you will live even there as I too become a child of the sea.

today i said thank you. i said thank you, papa, because you saved my life. he groaned and just touched my shoulder, moving his hand quickly away like a butterfly. and then there it was, the black butterfly floating around us. i began to run and run so it wouldn't land on me, but it had already carried its news. i know what must have happened. tonight i listened to manman's transistor under the banyan tree. all i hear from the radio is more killing in port-au-prince. the pigs are refusing to let up. i don't know what's going to happen, but i cannot see staying here forever. i am writing to you from the bottom of the banyan tree. manman says that banyan trees are holy and sometimes if we call the gods from beneath them, they will hear our voices clearer. now there are always butterflies around me, black ones that i refuse to let find my hand. i throw big rocks at them, but they are always too fast. last night on the radio, i heard that another boat sank off the coast of the bahamas. i can't think about you being in there in the waves. my hair shivers. from here, i cannot even see the sea. behind these mountains are more mountains and more black butterflies still and a sea that is endless like my love for you.

GLOSSARY OF LITERARY AND CRITICAL TERMS

Absurd Literary movement that evolved in France in the 1950s. The Absurdists saw the universe as irrational and meaningless. They rejected conventional PLOT and DIALOGUE in their work, emphasizing the incoherence of the world.

Accent The emphasis, or stress, given to a syllable or word in pronunciation. Accents can be used to emphasize a particular word in a sentence: *Is* she con*tent* with the *con*tents of the *yel*low *pack*age?

Acmeists A group of twentieth-century Russian poets, most notably Anna Akhmatova (1889–1966), who rejected Symbolism in favor of linguistic clarity.

Acropolis The most fortified part of a Greek city, located on a hill; the most famous acropolis is in Athens and is the site of the Parthenon.

Act A major division in the action of a play. In many full-length plays, acts are further divided into SCENES, which often mark a point in the action when the location changes or when a new character arrives.

Age of Pericles The golden age of Athens in the fifth century B.C.E. when Pericles (c. 495–429 B.C.E.) was the head of the Athenian government. During this period, Athenian democracy reached its height; the Parthenon was constructed and drama and music flourished.

Agnosticism The belief that the existence of God or anything beyond material phenomena can be neither proved nor disproved. The French ENLIGHTENMENT philosopher François Voltaire (1694–1778) is considered by many to be the father of agnosticism. The term *agnostic*, however, was first used by the English biologist Thomas Huxley (1825–1895) in 1869.

Ahasuerus, the Wandering Jew A legendary figure during ancient times who was said to have mocked Jesus en route to the crucifixion and was therefore doomed to wander the earth in penance until Judgment Day.

Allegory A narrative in which the characters, settings, and episodes stand for something else. Traditionally, most allegories come in the form of stories that correlate to spiritual concepts; examples of these can be found in Dante's *Divine Comedy* (1321). Some later allegories allude to political, historical, and sociological ideas.

Alliteration The repetition of the same consonant sound or sounds in a sequence of words, usually at the beginning of a word or stressed syllable: "*descending dew drops*"; "*luscious lemons.*" The repetition is based on the sounds of the letters, not the spelling of the words; for example, "*keen*" and "*car*" alliterate, but "*car*" and "*cite*" do not, even though both begin with *c*. Used sparingly, alliteration can intensify ideas by emphasizing key words.

Allusion A brief reference to a person, place, thing, event, or idea in history or literature. These references can be to a scene from one of Shakespeare's plays, a historic figure, a war, a great love story, a biblical authority, or anything else that might enrich an author's work. Allusions imply that the writer and the reader share similar knowledge and function as a kind of shorthand.

Ambiguity Allows for two or more simultaneous interpretations of a word, phrase, action, or situation, all of whose meanings are supported by the work. Deliberate ambiguity can contribute to the effectiveness and richness of a piece of writing; unintentional ambiguity obscures meaning and may confuse readers.

Anagram A word or phrase made up of the same letters as another word or phrase; *heart* is an anagram of *earth*. Often considered merely an exercise of one's ingenuity, anagrams are sometimes used by writers to conceal proper names, veil messages, or suggest important connections between words, such as between *hated* and *death*.

Antagonist The character, force, or collection of forces in fiction or drama that opposes the PROTAGONIST and gives rise to the conflict in the story; an opponent of the protagonist, such as Caliban in Shakespeare's play *The Tempest*.

Antihero A PROTAGONIST who has the opposite of most of the traditional attributes of a hero. He or she may be bewildered, ineffectual, deluded, or merely pathetic. Often what antiheroes learn, if they learn anything at all, is that they are isolated in an existence devoid of God or any absolute value.

Apartheid The South African system of official racial segregation, which was established in 1948 and lasted until the early 1990s. The term *apartheid* means "state of being separate." Apartheid divided people into racial categories—colored, or Indian, as well as black and white—and severely limited the movements and activities of the colored and black groups, giving particular privilege to people of European heritage. After intense international pressure, the resistance movement leader, Nelson Mandela (b. 1918), was released

from prison in 1990. One year later he became the country's first black president.

Apostrophe A statement or address made either to an implied interlocutor, sometimes a nonhuman figure or PERSONIFICATION. Apostrophes often provide a speaker with the opportunity to reveal his or her internal thoughts.

Archetype A universal symbol that evokes deep and sometimes unconscious responses in a reader. In literature, characters, images, and themes that symbolize universal meanings and basic human experiences are considered archetypes. Common literary archetypes include quests, initiations, scapegoats, descents to the underworld, and ascents to heaven.

Aryans A people who settled in Iran (Persia) and northern India in prehistoric times. Their language was also called Aryan, and it gave rise to the Indo-European languages of South Asia. Linguists now use the term *Aryan* to refer to Indo-Aryan languages. In the nineteenth and twentieth century the term was appropriated (most infamously by Adolf Hitler and the Nazi government) to define a "pure" race of people responsible for the progress of the modern world and superior to non-Aryans.

Aside In drama, a speech directed to the audience that supposedly is not audible to the other characters onstage.

Associationism A British eighteenth- and nineteenth-century school of philosophy that derived its ideas from, among others, philosophers John Locke (1632–1704) and David Hume (1711–1776). Associationists believed that one's view of reality is formed from bits and pieces of sensations that join together through patterns of association.

Assonance The repetition of vowel sounds in nearby words, as in "asl*ee*p under a tr*ee*" or "*ea*ch *e*vening." When the words also share similar endings, as in "asl*ee*p in the d*ee*p," rhyme occurs. Assonance is an effective means of emphasizing important words.

Atheism The belief that God does not exist and that the Earth evolved naturally.

Avant-garde Writers, artists, filmmakers, and musicians whose work is innovative, experimental, or unconventional.

Bataan Death March The forced march of 10,000 American and 65,000 Filipino soldiers who were captured in 1942 by the Japanese on the Bataan Peninsula of the Philippines during World War II; the prisoners of war, many of whom were suffering from exhaustion, malaria, and other ailments, were compelled to march 55 miles from Marivales to San Fernando. They were then packed into railroad cars and taken to Capas, where they were made to march another 8 miles to a prison camp. Up to 650 Americans and some 10,000 Filipinos died before reaching the camp, where still many others died.

Ballad An uncomplicated verse originally meant to be sung; it generally tells a dramatic tale or simple story. Ballads are associated with the oral traditions or folklore of common people. The folk ballad stanza usually consists of four lines of alternating tetrameter (four accented syllables) and trimeter (three accented syllables) following a rhyme scheme of *abab* or *abcb*.

Ballad stanza A four-line stanza, known as a QUATRAIN, consisting of alternating eight- and six-syllable lines. Usually, only the second and fourth lines rhyme (an *abcb* pattern). Samuel Taylor Coleridge adapted the ballad stanza in *The Rime of the Ancient Mariner* (1798).

Battle of Dresden A battle in 1813 outside the capital of Saxony, where Napoleon defeated an allied army of 400,000 men. It was Napoleon's last great victory before his final defeat one year later.

Battle of Plassey Plassey was the village in West Bengal, India, where the British defeated the Bengal army in 1757, which led to Britain's domination of northeast India.

Bengali Traditional language of Bengal in eastern India, now the national language of Bangladesh and the official language of the West Bengal region of India; also, someone who comes from Bangladesh or West Bengal.

Bengali literary renaissance A movement in the second half of the nineteenth century to develop literature in the Bengali language that would describe the everyday life of contemporary Bengal. Rabindranath Tagore, Madhusudan Dutta, and Bankim Chandra Chatterjee were important writers of the movement.

Bhagavad Gita An ancient text of Hindu wisdom from the first century B.C.E. or first century C.E. inserted into the epic poem *The Mahabharata.*

Bible-based calendar Calendar based on Scripture that dates the creation of the earth at 4004 B.C.E. Archbishop James Ussher constructed it in the mid seventeenth century.

Bildungsroman A novel that traces the PROTAGONIST's development, generally from birth or childhood into maturity. An early prototype is Goethe's *Wilhelm Meister's Apprenticeship* (1795–96). The form has flourished in the ensuing two centuries and includes such modern masterpieces as James Joyce's *Portrait of the Artist as a Young Man* (1916).

Bill of Rights A document that spells out the rights of a citizen in either England or the United States of America. The American Bill of Rights, the first ten amendments to the Constitution, was ratified in 1791 and guarantees freedom of religion, press, assembly, and petition; the right to bear arms; protection under the law; and the right to a speedy trial. See also ENGLISH BILL OF RIGHTS.

Biographical criticism An approach to literature that maintains that knowledge of an author's life experiences can aid in the understanding of his or her work. Although biographical information can sometimes complicate one's interpretation of a work and some FORMALIST CRITICS, such as the NEW CRITICS, disparage the use of an author's biography as a tool for textual interpretation, learning about the life of an author can often enrich a reader's appreciation for that author's work.

Blank verse Unrhymed IAMBIC PENTAMETER. Blank verse is the form closest to the natural rhythms of English speech and is therefore the most common pattern found in traditional English narrative and dramatic poetry, from Shakespeare to the writers of the early twentieth century.

Bolshevik Revolution The revolution in Russia in 1917 in which the government of the hereditary tsar was overthrown and replaced by a Communist regime under the leadership of Vladimir Lenin. After the Bolshevik Revolution, the Russian empire became the Union of Soviet Socialist Republics, or USSR.

Bourgeoisie Prosperous urban middle class that emerged in the wake of the INDUSTRIAL REVOLUTION and gained wealth and power in the nineteenth century. In MARXIST theory, the bourgeoisie is identified as the owners and operators of industry, as opposed to the PROLETARIAT, who live by the sale of their labor.

Brahman In the UPANISHADS—sacred Hindu texts—Brahman is the ultimate reality that transcends all names and descriptions and is the single unifying essence of the universe. A brahman, or brahmin, is also a Hindu priest and thus of the highest caste in the traditional Hindu caste system.

Brahmanism A religion that recognizes the creator, Brahma, and the priestly class of brahmans who administer Hindu rituals.

Buddhism A religion founded in India in the sixth century B.C.E. by Siddhartha Gautama, the Buddha. While Buddhism has taken different forms in the many areas of the world to which it has spread, its central tenet is that life is suffering caused by desire. In order to obtain salvation, or nirvana, one must transcend desire through following an eightfold path that includes the practice of right action and right mindfulness.

Bunraku New name for JORURI, traditional Japanese puppet theater.

Bushido The code of honor and conduct of the Japanese SAMURAI class. *Bushido* emphasizes self-discipline and bravery.

Byronic hero A character based on the heroes in the poems of Lord Byron (1788–1824), such as Childe Harold, Manfred, and Cain. The Byronic hero is an outsider, even an outlaw—proud, defiant, and moody—who seems burdened by an undefined sense of guilt or misery.

Cacophony In literature, language that is discordant and difficult to pronounce, such as the line "never my numb plunker fumbles" from John Updike's "Player Piano." Cacophony (from the Greek for "bad sound") may be unintentional, or it may be used for deliberate dramatic effect; also refers to the combination of loud, jarring sounds.

Caesura A pause within a line of poetry that contributes to the line's RHYTHM. A caesura can occur anywhere within a line and need not be indicated by punctuation. In SCANSION, caesuras are indicated by a double vertical line.

Canon The works generally considered by scholars, critics, and teachers to be the most important to read and study and that collectively constitute the masterpieces of literature. Since the 1960s, the traditional English and American literary canons, consisting mostly of works by white male writers, have been expanding to include many female writers and writers of varying ethnic backgrounds.

Captivity narratives Autobiographical accounts detailing American colonists' experiences as prisoners of Native Americans; extremely popular from the late seventeenth century through the nineteenth century. Often written to illustrate spiritual or moral growth through trials, these narratives typically describe a dramatic capture and lengthy travels and ordeals, culminating in escape or release. Much was made of the divide between "savage" and "civilized" society, of fear of assimilation into an alien culture, and of the promise of salvation for the chosen few.

Carpe diem Latin phrase meaning "seize the day." This is a common literary theme, especially in lyric poetry, conveying that life is short, time is fleeting, and one should make the most of present pleasures. Andrew Marvell's poem "To His Coy Mistress" is a good example.

Catharsis Meaning "purgation," or the release of the emotions of pity and fear by the audience at the end of a tragedy. In *Poetics*, Aristotle discusses the importance of catharsis. The audience faces the misfortunes of the PROTAGONIST, which elicit pity and compassion. Simultaneously, the audience confronts the protagonist's failure, thus receiving a frightening reminder of human limitations and frailties.

Character, characterization A character is a person presented in a dramatic or narrative work; characterization is the process by which a writer makes a character seem real to the reader.

Chivalric romances Idealized stories from the medieval period that espoused the values of a sophisticated courtly society. These tales centered around the lives of knights who were faithful to God, king, and country and willing to sacrifice themselves for these causes and for the love and protection of women. Chivalric romances were highly moral and fanciful, often pitting knights against dark or supernatural forces.

Chorus In Greek tragedies, a group of people who serve mainly as commentators on the play's characters and events, adding to the audience's understanding of a play by expressing traditional moral, religious, and social attitudes. The role of the chorus is occasionally used by modern playwrights.

Cliché An idea or expression that has become tired and trite from overuse. Clichés often anesthetize readers and are usually signs of weak writing.

Closet drama A play that is to be read rather than performed onstage. In closet dramas, literary art outweighs all other considerations.

Colloquial Informal diction that reflects casual, conversational language and often includes slang expressions.

Comedy A work intended to interest, involve, and amuse readers or an audience, in which no terrible disaster occurs and which ends happily for the main characters.

Comic epic One of the earliest English novelists, Henry Fielding (1707–1754) characterized the kind of literature he was creating in his novel *Joseph Andrews* (1742) as "a comic epic in prose," thus distinguishing it from serious or tragic epic poems that treated noble characters and elevated subjects. His novel was about common people and everyday events.

Comic relief A humorous scene or incident that alleviates tension in an otherwise serious work. Often these moments enhance the thematic significance of a story in addition to providing humor.

Communist A supporter of the political system in which all property and wealth is owned collectively by and shared equally among all members of society. Communism derived largely from the theories of Karl Marx and Friedrich Engels, as presented in *The Communist Manifesto* (1848).

Conflict In a literary work, the struggle within the PLOT between opposing forces. The PROTAGONIST is engaged in a conflict with the ANTAGONIST.

Confucianism A religion / philosophy that has influenced Chinese and East Asian spirituality and culture for over two thousand years. Based on the writings of Confucius (Kongfuzi; 551–479 B.C.E.), Confucianism asserts that humans can improve and even perfect themselves through education and moral reform. In its various manifestations, Confucianism has affected the social and political evolution of China and East Asia while providing a spiritual and moral template.

Connotation Implications going beyond the literal meaning of a word that derive from how the word has been commonly used and from ideas or things associated with it. For example, the word *eagle* in the United States connotes ideas of liberty and freedom that have little to do with the term's literal meaning.

Consonance A common type of near-rhyme or half rhyme that consists of identical consonant sounds preceded by different vowel sounds: *home, same; worth, breath.*

Continental Congress Assembly of delegates representing the thirteen British colonies in North America. The First Continental Congress convened in 1774 and drafted a petition to King George III; the Second

Continental Congress met in 1775, organized an army under the leadership of George Washington, and adopted the Declaration of Independence on July 4, 1776.

Convention A characteristic of a literary GENRE that is understood and accepted by readers and audiences because it has become familiar. For example, the division of a play into acts and scenes is a dramatic convention, as are SOLILOQUIES and ASIDES.

Cosmogony A theory that explains the origins of the universe.

Couplet A two-line, rhymed stanza. Pope is the master of the HEROIC COUPLET, a two-line, rhymed, iambic-pentameter stanza that completes its thought within the closed two-line form.

Creole The culture and language of some of the Spanish and French settlers of South and North America. Many Creoles speak a mixed form of French, Spanish, and English.

Crimean War (1853–1856) A war fought on the Crimean peninsula in the Black Sea between the Russians and the allied forces of the British, the French, and the Ottoman Turks. The war arose from religious conflicts in the Middle East. When Austria threatened to enter the war, Russia agreed to peace terms resulting in the Treaty of Paris (1856), but the shift in power had long-lasting effects, notably the unification of Germany and Italy.

Crisis The moment in a work of drama or fiction where the elements of the conflict reach the point of maximum tension. The crisis is part of the work's structure but is not necessarily the emotional crescendo, or climax.

Critical realism Politically driven, early-twentieth-century school of Chinese literature pioneered by Lu Xun (1881–1936); examines societal tendencies through the actions of realistic characters.

Cubism An early-twentieth-century movement centered in France, primarily in painting and collage, that attempted to show objects from several perspectives at once; proponents included the artists Pablo Picasso (1881–1973) and Georges Braque (1882–1963).

Cultural criticism An approach to literature that focuses on the historical as well as the social, political, and economic contexts of a work. Popular culture — mass-produced and mass-consumed cultural artifacts ranging from advertising to popular fiction to television to rock music — is seen on equal footing with "high culture." Cultural critics use widely eclectic strategies, such as NEW HISTORICISM, psychology, gender studies, and DECONSTRUCTION, to analyze not only literary texts but everything from radio talk shows to comic strips, calendar art, commercials, travel guides, and baseball cards.

Dadaism An early-twentieth-century AVANT-GARDE movement inaugurated by French poets Tristan Tzara (1896–1963) and Hans Arp (1887–1966) and German poet Hugo Ball (1886–1927), all living in Zurich during World War I. Stressing irrationality and the absurdity of life in an era of mechanized mass-destruction, dadaism is often seen as nihilistic; in its emphasis on free association and instinctive composition, it can be viewed as a precursor to surrealism. The French painter Marcel Duchamp (1887–1968) may be dadaism's most renowned practitioner.

Daoism (Taoism) A religion / philosophy based on the *Dao De Jing* of Laozi (Lao-tzu) that emphasizes individual freedom, spontaneity, mystical experience, and self-transformation, and is the antithesis of CONFUCIANISM. In pursuit of the *dao,* or the Way — the eternal creative reality that is the essence of all things — practitioners embrace simplicity and reject learned wisdom. The Daoist tradition has flourished in China and East Asia for two thousand years.

Decembrist Revolt After the death of Tsar Alexander I (r. 1801–25), a group of liberal officers, many of whom had served in the Napoleonic Wars, attempted in December 1825 to depose his heir, Nicholas I (r. 1825–55), in the hope of bringing to power a ruler who would guarantee them a constitutional monarchy. The officers were crushed by Nicholas, who punished them severely to discourage other reform-minded Russians.

Deconstructionism An approach to literature that suggests that literary works do not yield single fixed meanings because language can never say exactly what one intends it to mean. Deconstructionism seeks to destabilize meaning by examining the gaps in and ambiguities of a text's language. Deconstructionists pay close attention to language in order to discover and describe how a variety of close readings can be generated.

Deism An unorthodox religious philosophy prominent in the seventeenth and eighteenth centuries in northern Europe and America. Deists believe that religious knowledge can be arrived at through reason rather than through revelation or formal religious instruction. Deism constructs God as a rational architect of an orderly world; the deist God creates the world and sets it in motion but does not become directly involved in human affairs.

Denouement French term meaning "unraveling" or "unknotting" used to describe the resolution of a PLOT following the climax.

Dialect A type of informal DICTION. Dialects are spoken by definable groups of people from a particular geographic region, economic group, or social class. Writers use dialect to express and contrast the education, class, and social and regional backgrounds of their characters.

Dialogue Verbal exchange between CHARACTERS. Dialogue reveals firsthand characters' thoughts, responses, and emotional states, and thus makes the characters real to readers or the audience.

Diaspora The wide dispersion of a people or a culture that was formerly located in one place. Two historical diasporas of note are the diaspora of the Jews from Palestine following the Roman destruction of the Second Temple in 70 C.E. and the African diaspora caused by the slave trade. Both the Jews and the Africans were dispersed across many continents.

Diction A writer's choice of words, phrases, sentence structure, and figurative language, which combine to help create meaning.

Didactic poetry Poetry designed to teach an ethical, moral, or religious lesson.

Dionysus The god of wine in Greek mythology, whose cult originated in Thrace and Phrygia — north and east of the Greek peninsula. Dionysus was often blamed for people's irrational behavior and for chaotic situations. However, many Greeks also believed that Dionysus taught them good farming skills, especially those related to wine production. Greek tragedy evolved from a ceremony that honored Dionysus, and the theater in Athens was dedicated to him.

Doggerel A derogatory term for poetry whose subject is trite and whose rhythm and sounds are monotonously heavy-handed.

Drama Derived from the Greek word *dram*, meaning "to do" or "to perform," the term *drama* may refer to a single play, a group of plays, or to plays in general. Drama is designed to be performed in a theater: Actors take on the roles of its characters, perform indicated actions, and deliver the script's DIALOGUE.

Dramatic monologue A type of lyric or narrative poem in which a speaker addresses an imagined and distinct but silent audience in such a way as to reveal a dramatic situation and, often unintentionally, some aspect of the speaker's temperament or personality.

Dualistic tradition Religious and philosophical doctrine dating from ancient times in which the antagonistic forces of good and evil determine the course of events.

Early Modern era Period extending from about 1500 to 1800, marked by the advent of colonialism and capitalism.

Edenic New World Early European immigrants to the New World often described it as a new Eden, a Garden of Paradise.

Edo The ancient name for Tokyo. During the TOKUGAWA period (1600–1868), Edo became the imperial capital of Japan.

Eight-legged essay The *ba-gu wen*, an essay of eight parts written on a Confucian theme and developed during the MING DYNASTY in China (1368–1644) as a requirement for the civil service examinations.

Electra complex The female version of the Oedipus complex as theorized by Sigmund

Freud to describe a daughter's unconscious rivalry with her mother for her father's attention. The name comes from the Greek legend of Electra, who avenged the death of her father by plotting the death of her mother.

Elegiac couplets The conventional strophic form of Latin elegiac love poetry, consisting of one dactylic hexameter line followed by one dactylic pentameter line. A dactylic hexameter line is composed of six feet, each foot comprising one long, or accented, and two short, or unaccented, syllables; the sixth foot may be shortened by one or two syllables; the pentameter line consists of five such feet. The elegiac couplet is also known as a "distich."

Elegy A mournful, contemplative lyric poem often ending in consolation, written to commemorate someone who has died. *Elegy* may also refer to a serious, meditative poem that expresses the speaker's melancholy thoughts.

Elysian land In Greek mythology, some fortunate mortals spend their afterlife in the bliss of the Elysian Fields, or Islands of the Blest, rather than in Hades, the underworld.

End-stopped line A line in a poem after which a pause occurs. End-stopped lines reflect normal speech patterns and are often marked by punctuation.

English Bill of Rights Formally known as "An Act declaring the Rights and Liberties of the Subject, and settling the Succession of the Crown," the English Bill of Rights was passed in December 1689. It conferred the crown upon William and Mary, who succeeded the ousted James II; it stated that no Catholic would ever be king or queen of England, extended civil rights and liberties to the people of England, and confirmed Parliament's power in a constitutional government. See also BILL OF RIGHTS.

Enjambment In poetry, a line continuing without a pause into the next line for its meaning; also called a run-on line.

Enlightenment Refers to a period of time in Europe from the late seventeenth through the eighteenth century, also called the Age of Reason, in which reason, human progress, and order were venerated. The Enlightenment intensified the process of secularization that had begun during the Renaissance and favored the use of empirical science to resolve social problems. Enlightenment philosophers questioned the existing forms of education and politics and fought tyranny and social injustice. Enlightenment ideas led to the American and French Revolutions in the late 1700s. Leading philosophers also questioned the Bible and gave rise to a new movement of freethinkers—people who rejected the church's dogma and encouraged rational inquiry and speculation.

Ennui French for boredom or lack of interest; the term is associated with a widespread discontent with the pleasures of the modern world.

Eos The Greek goddess of the dawn who loved the young men Cleitus, Cephalus, and Orion, the hunter.

Epic A long narrative poem told in a formal, elevated style that focuses on a serious subject and chronicles heroic deeds and events important to a culture or nation.

Epigram A brief, pointed, and witty poem that usually makes a satiric or humorous point. Epigrams are most often written in couplets but can be written in any form.

Epiphany In fiction, when a character suddenly experiences a deep realization about himself or herself; a truth which is grasped in an ordinary rather than a melodramatic moment.

Eros The Greek god of love, associated with both passion and fertility. Freud used the term *Eros* in modern times to signify the human life-drive (desire) at war with THANATOS, the death-drive.

Euphony From the Greek for "good sound"; refers to language that is smooth and musically pleasant to the ear.

Existentialism A school of modern philosophy associated with Jean-Paul Sartre (1905–1980) and Albert Camus (1913–1960) that dominated European thought in the years following World War II. Existentialists are interested in the nature of consciousness and emphasize the role of individual will in shaping existence.

Existentialism holds that discrete, willful acts of choice create the only meaning that exists in an otherwise meaningless universe.

Exposition A narrative device often used at the beginning of a work that provides necessary background information about characters and their circumstances. Exposition explains such matters as what has gone on before, the relationships between characters, theme, and conflict.

Expressionism An artistic and literary movement that originated in Germany in the early twentieth century. Expressionism departs from the conventions of realism to focus on the inner impressions or moods of a character or of the artist. Influenced by the increased mechanization of the modern world and by MARXISM, expressionism often reveals the alienation of the individual.

Fabliau Although the *fabliau* originated in France as a comic or satiric tale in verse, by the time of Giovanni Boccaccio (1313–1375) and Geoffrey Chaucer (1340–1400) the term also stood for bawdy and ribald prose tales like "The Miller's Tale" in Chaucer's *Canterbury Tales* or Boccaccio's "Rustico and Alibech."

Farce A form of humor based on exaggerated, improbable incongruities. Farce involves rapid shifts in action and emotion as well as slapstick comedy and extravagant dialogue.

Fascism An ideology that combines dictatorial government, militarism, control of the personal freedom of a people, extreme nationalism, and government control of business. Fascism peaked between the 1920s and '40s, when Adolf Hitler, Benito Mussolini, and Francisco Franco gained power in Germany, Italy, and Spain respectively.

Feminism A school of thought that examines the oppression, subjugation, or inequality of women. Feminism has flourished since the middle of the twentieth century and has taken different forms, focusing variously on language, the meaning of power, and the institutions that perpetuate sexism.

Feminist criticism An approach to literature that seeks to correct or supplement a predominantly male-dominated critical perspective with a feminist consciousness. Feminist criticism places literature in a social context and uses a broad range of disciplines, including history, sociology, psychology, and linguistics, to provide interpretations that are sensitive to feminist issues.

Fenian Society A secret organization of Irish nationalists founded in 1858 promoting Irish independence from England by means of violent revolution. The organization was named after the Fenians, professional soldiers who served Irish kings in third-century Ireland. With support from cells among Irish emigrants in America, South Africa, and Australia, the Fenian Society, led by James Stephens, launched a rebellion in 1867 that, although it failed, helped to galvanize political opposition to English rule and call attention to the problems in Ireland.

Feudal aristocracy A system of government that existed in Europe in the Middle Ages. The feudal system refers to a mode of agricultural production in which peasants worked for landowners, or lords, in return for debt forgiveness, food, and governmental responsibilities such as military protection. The lords or landowners constitute the upper class, or aristocracy, but at the top of the hierarchy was the monarch who controlled the government and the granting of fiefs, or tracts of land.

Figures of speech Ways of using language that deviate from the literal, denotative meanings of words in order to suggest additional meanings or effects. Figures of speech say one thing in terms of something else, such as when an eager funeral director is described as a vulture.

Fin de siècle French for "end of the century"; generally refers to the final years of the nineteenth century, a time characterized by decadence and ENNUI. Artists of this era romanticized drug addiction and prostitution; open sexuality, including homosexuality, also marked the period. In Paris and Vienna, the Art Nouveau movement in the fine arts flourished and was informed by the blossoming of radical ideas in the wake of the Paris Commune of 1871. Notable fin-de-siècle figures include artists such as Aubrey Beardsley and writers such as Oscar Wilde.

Fixed form A poem characterized by a fixed pattern of lines, syllables, or meter. A SONNET is a fixed form of poetry because it must have fourteen lines.

Flashback A literary or dramatic device that allows a past occurrence to be inserted into the chronological order of a narrative.

Floating World (*ukiyo-e*) A Japanese artistic movement that flourished in the seventeenth, eighteenth, and nineteenth centuries in Tokyo. Ukiyo-e depicts the floating or sorrowful world; its most frequent media are woodblock prints, books, and drawings. Originally considered a popular rather than a high art, ukiyo-e treated literary, classic, and historical themes within a contemporary context, and it was particularly appealing to the emerging merchant classes.

Flying Dutchman The legend of a ghostly ship doomed to sail for eternity. If a vision of it appears to sailors, it signals imminent disaster. Most versions of the story have the captain of the ship playing dice or gambling with the Devil.

Foil A character in a literary work or drama whose behavior or values contrast with those of another character, typically the PROTAGONIST.

Foot A poetic foot is a poem's unit of measurement and decides the rhythm. In English, the iambic, or ascending, foot is the most common.

Foreshadowing Providing hints of what is to happen next in order to build suspense.

Formalist A type of criticism dominant in the early twentieth century that emphasizes the form of an artwork. Two of its prominent schools are Russian formalism, which favors the form of an artwork over its content and argues for the necessity of literature to defamiliarize the ordinary objects of the world, and American NEW CRITICISM, which treats a work of art as an object and seeks to understand it through close, careful analysis.

Formula literature Literature that fulfills a reader's expectations. In detective novels, for instance, the plot may vary among different works, but in the end the detective solves the case in all of them. Science fiction, romance, and Westerns are other examples of formula literature.

Found poem An ordinary collection of words that can be understood differently when arranged or labeled as a poem. A found poem could be something as banal as a "to do" list or personal advertisement, but the poet who "finds" it argues that it has special, unintentional value when presented as a poem.

Founding myth A story that explains how a particular nation or culture came to be, such as Virgil's *Aeneid,* which describes the founding of Rome. Many epic poems, sometimes called national epics, are founding myths.

Four classes In Hindu tradition, humans are created as one of four classes, or *varna:* in descending order, the BRAHMANS (priests), the *Ksatriya* (warriors), the *Vaisya* (merchants and farmers), and the *Sudra* (laborers and servants).

Framed narration Also called *framed tale.* A story within a story. In Chaucer's *Canterbury Tales,* each pilgrim's story is framed by the story of the pilgrimage itself. This device, used by writers from ancient times to the present, enjoyed particular popularity during the thirteenth, fourteenth, and fifteenth centuries and was most fully developed in *The Arabian Nights,* a work in which the framing is multilayered.

Free association A Freudian exercise wherein a patient relates to an analyst anything that comes to his or her mind, no matter how illogical or apparently trivial, without any attempt to censor, shape, or otherwise organize the material. In literature, the term refers to a free flow of the mind's thoughts; it is an important element of stream-of-consciousness writing.

Free verse Highly irregular poetry; typically, free verse does not rhyme.

French Revolution The first of four major revolutions in France in the late eighteenth and nineteenth centuries; it began with the storming of the Bastille in 1789 and ended in the coup of the Eighteenth Brumaire, on November 9–10, 1799, when Napoleon overthrew the revolutionary government. The original goal of the revolution had been to establish a constitutional monarchy that would transfer power from the nobility, headed by King Louis XVI, and the clergy to the middle classes. That aim was abandoned, however, when the king and queen were beheaded in 1793 and a republic was created.

French Symbolists Symbolism was an AVANT-GARDE movement in France in the late nineteenth century that arose from revolutionary experiments with language, verse form, and the use of symbols in the poetry of Stéphane Mallarmé (1842–1898) and Paul Verlaine (1844–1896); according to the Symbolists, poetic language should not delineate ideas but rather evoke feeling and moods, insinuate impressions and connections. French Symbolism, which often is extended to include the poetry of Charles Baudelaire (1821–1867) and Arthur Rimbaud (1854–1891), who anticipated some of its principles, exerted a profound influence on modernist poetry in Russia as well as throughout Europe and the United States.

Freudian criticism A method of literary criticism associated with Freud's theories of psychoanalysis. Early Freudian critics sought to illustrate how literature is shaped by the unconscious desires of the author, but the term has developed and become more broadly defined to encompass many schools of thought that link psychoanalysis to the interpretation of literature.

Gay and lesbian criticism School of literary criticism that focuses on the representation of homosexuality in literature; also interested in how homosexuals read literature and to what extent sexuality and gender is culturally constructed.

Gender criticism Literary school that analyzes how an author's or a reader's sex affects the writing and reading experiences.

Genre A category of artistic works or literary compositions that have a distinctive style or content. Poetry, fiction, and drama are genres. Different genres have dominated at various times and places: In eighteenth-century Europe, the dramatic comedy was the preferred form of theater; in the nineteenth century, the novel was the dominant genre.

Genroku period (1688–1703) A Japanese cultural period during the EDO era when a growing number of affluent *chonin,* or townsmen, sought diversion in the FLOATING WORLD, or *ukiyo-e* — city districts where courtesans, along with theater, dance, song, and the arts, flourished.

German Romanticism A German form of nineteenth-century Romanticism. In addition to German Romantic poets like Friedrich Holderlin (1770–1843), Novalis (1772–1801), and Heinrich Heine (1797–1856), Germany produced the Romantic theorists Friedrich Schlegel (1772–1829), F. W. J. Schelling (1775–1854), and August Wilhelm Schlegel (1767–1845), who believed that the Christian myth needed to be replaced with a modern one.

Ghazal A form of lyric poetry composed of three to seven couplets, called *sh'ir,* that follow the strict rhyme scheme of *aa ba ca da,* and so on, known as the *qafiyah.* Strict adherence to the form requires the use of the *radif,* a word that is repeated in a pattern dictated by the first couplet, throughout the poem. Literally meaning "dialogue with the beloved," the *ghazal,* as practiced in Arabia, Persia, Turkey, and India beginning around 1200, became the predominant form for love poetry.

Giri Japanese term for social duty and responsibility.

Glorious Revolution of 1688 The forced abdication of the Catholic king James II of England, whose attempts to exercise royal authority over Parliament galvanized the largely Protestant

English nation against him. Although largely a bloodless revolution, some fighting between Catholics and Protestants took place in Ireland and Scotland.

Gnostics Members of an ancient sect in the Middle East who believed that hidden knowledge held the key to the universe. Throughout history there have been Gnostics who have formed secret societies with secret scriptures and who have believed they understood the workings of the cosmos.

Gokan A book combining pictures and text; often adapted from classic Chinese or Japanese stories.

Gothic A style of literature (especially novels) in the late eighteenth and early nineteenth centuries that reacted against the mannered decorum of earlier literature. Gothic novels explore the darker side of human experience; they are often set in the past and in foreign countries, and they employ elements of horror, mystery, and the supernatural.

Gothic novel A subgenre of the novel whose works concentrate on mystery, magic, and horror. Especially popular during the late eighteenth and early nineteenth centuries, gothic novels are often set in castles or mansions whose dungeons or secret rooms contribute to the atmosphere of mystery.

Greater Dionysia In ancient Greece, dramas were performed at festivals that honored the god Dionysus: the Lenaea during January and February and the Greater Dionysia in March and April. The best tragedies and comedies were awarded prizes by an Athenian jury.

Hadith Islamic source of religious law and moral guidance. According to tradition, the Hadith were passed down orally to the prophet Muhammad, and today they are critical to the study of the early development of Islam.

Haikai A form of Japanese linked verse that flourished from the sixteenth through the nineteenth centuries, *haikai* is a sequence of alternating stanzas usually composed by two or more writers. The sequence opens with a *hokku*, a three-line stanza of seventeen

syllables that alternate 5, 7, 5; the hokku is followed by alternating three- and two-line stanzas of seventeen and fourteen syllables, respectively. Bashō, the greatest of the haikai masters, preferred a sequence of thirty-six stanzas. Haikai is distinguished from RENGA, an earlier form of Japanese linked verse, primarily by diction and tone; whereas renga, with its origins in court poetry, uses elevated diction and reflects a cultivated seriousness, haikai introduces more colloquial diction, is more lighthearted, and treats common aspects of human experience. The hokku eventually became a separate form, now known as *HAIKU*.

Haiku Unrhymed Japanese poetic form that consists of seventeen syllables arranged in three lines. Although its origins can be traced to the seventeenth century, it is the most popular poetic form in Japan today. See HAIKAI.

Hamartia Error or flaw. In ancient Greek tragedies, the hero falls through his own *hamartia*.

Hellene Greek.

Heroic couplet A rhymed, iambic-pentameter stanza of two lines that completes its thought within the two-line form. Alexander Pope (1688–1744), the most accomplished practitioner of the form in English, included this couplet in his *Essay on Criticism:* "True wit is nature to advantage dressed, / What oft was thought, but ne'er so well expressed."

Hexameter couplets The conventional strophic form of Greek and Latin epic poetry consisting of two dactylic hexameter lines; each line is composed of six feet and each foot comprises one long (accented) and two short (unaccented) syllables. The final foot is known as a catalectic foot, for it is generally shortened by one or two syllables.

Hieros gamos Literally, "sacred marriage"; a fertility ritual in which the god-king or priest-king is united with the goddess or priestess-queen in order to provide a model for the kingdom and establish the king's right to rule.

Hinduism The major religion of India, based upon the ancient doctrines found in the

Sᴀɴꜱᴋʀɪᴛ texts known as the Vᴇᴅᴀꜱ and the Uᴘᴀɴɪꜱʜᴀᴅꜱ, dating from 1000 ʙ.ᴄ.ᴇ.

Historical criticism An approach to literature that uses history as a means of understanding a literary work. Such criticism moves beyond both the facts of an author's life and the text itself to examine the social and intellectual contexts in which the author composed the work.

Homeric Hymns At one time attributed to Homer, the *Homeric Hymns* (seventh–sixth centuries ʙ.ᴄ.ᴇ.) are now believed to have been created by poets from a Homeric school or simply in the style of Homer. Five of the longer hymns contain important stories about gods such as Demeter, Dɪᴏɴʏꜱᴜꜱ, Apollo, Aphrodite, and Hermes.

Hubris Exaggerated pride or arrogance; in Greek tragedies, hubris always causes fatal errors.

Huguenots French Protestant members of the Reformed Church established in France by John Calvin in about 1555. Due to religious persecution, many fled to other countries in the sixteenth and seventeenth centuries.

Hyperbole An exaggerated figure of speech; for example, "I nearly died laughing."

Iambic pentameter A poetic line made up of five feet, or iambs, or a ten-syllable line.

Ibsenism After the plays of Norwegian dramatist Henrik Ibsen (1828–1906): a concern in drama with social problems treated realistically rather than romantically.

Idealism Philosophical Idealism in its various forms holds that objects of perception are in reality mental constructs and not the material objects themselves.

Image The two types of images are literal and figurative. Literal images are very detailed, almost photographic; figurative images are more abstract and often use symbols, such as this image of the night in T. S. Eliot's "The Love Song of J. Alfred Prufrock" (1917):

> Let us go then, you and I,
> When the evening is spread out
>   against the sky
> Like a patient etherized upon a table

Industrial Revolution Advancements in mechanization beginning in the mid eighteenth century that transformed manufacturing, transportation, and agriculture over the next century and a half. Most historians regard the Industrial Revolution as the phenomenon that has had the largest impact on the present, changing the Western world from a rural to an urban society and moving the workplace from the fields to the factories. Because of it, the economy changed rapidly, and the production of goods increased exponentially, raising the West's standard of living. The new working class, however, lived in horrible conditions in the cities.

Industrialization The process of building factories and mass producing goods; typically, also part of urbanization.

Inquisition A medieval institution set up by the Roman Catholic pope to judge and convict anyone who might constitute a threat to papal power. The threats took various forms, including heresy, witchcraft, alchemy, and sorcery. The Inquisition held a great amount of power in medieval Europe, especially in southern European countries. The most powerful was the Spanish Inquisition, authorized in 1478, which executed thousands of victims, among them Jews, Muslims, and heretics, through public burning.

Irish Literary Renaissance A movement of the late nineteenth century of Irish writers, including William Butler Yeats (1865–1939), Lady Gregory (1852–1932), and J. M. Synge (1871–1909), who aimed to revitalize Irish literature and to renew interest in and revaluate Irish myth, legend, folklore, history, and literature. The literary renaissance was part of a broader cultural effervescence in Ireland in the late 1890s that included the founding of the Gaelic League, which promoted the use of the Irish language, and the startup of the Gaelic Athletic Association, which restored Irish sports.

Irony A device used in writing and speech to deliberately express ideas so they can be understood in two ways. In drama, irony occurs when a character does not know something that the other characters or the audience knows.

Jainism A religion founded in India in the sixth century B.C.E. by Vardhaman, who is known as Mahavira, or the "great hero." Formed in direct opposition to the rigid ritualism and hierarchical structure of traditional Hinduism, Jainism espoused asceticism, renunciation of the world, nonviolence, and the sanctity of all living beings.

Jewish mysticism Like all forms of mysticism, Jewish mysticism focuses on learning and practices that lead to unity with the creator; its teachings are referred to as the Cabala, or Kabala.

Joruri The form of puppet theater that developed in Japan in the seventeenth and eighteenth centuries in which expert puppeteers manipulate lifelike dolls while a master chanter, accompanied by the SAMISEN, sings and chants the story, speaks for the characters, and describes the scenes. The term derives from *ningyo,* meaning puppet or doll, and *joruri,* which alludes to the often-told story of Lady Joruri, the main character of a popular story dating back to the fifteenth century who was the subject of the first puppet play. Today joruri is known as BUNRAKU, after the great puppeteer Bunraku-ken Uemura (d. 1810), and Bunraku-ken Uemura II (1813–1873), who established a puppet theater in Osaka in 1842 after interest in joruri declined.

Judgment of Paris In Greek legend, Paris (Alexandros) was selected by the god Zeus to judge which of three goddesses was the most beautiful. He chose Aphrodite, who bribed him by agreeing to help him seduce Helen, the most beautiful woman alive. His stealing of Helen and refusal to return her was the cause of the Trojan War.

Julian calendar Calendar used from the time of Julius Caesar, c. 46 B.C.E., until 1582, when it was generally replaced by the Gregorian calendar, which is still in wide use today.

Kabuki A popular form of Japanese theater primarily about and aimed at the middle classes and that uses only male actors; Kabuki developed in the sixteenth and seventeenth centuries, parallel to JORURI, or puppet theater, which often shares the same plots and stories and even the same plays.

Kibyoshi Literally, "yellow back"; a simple illustrated book usually concerned with life in the licensed quarters.

Laissez-faire A French phrase meaning "let them do"; a doctrine in classical economics that asserts the economy should operate on its own, without interference from the government.

Leitmotifs Themes, brief passages, or single words repeated within a work.

Liberalism An ideology that rejects authoritarian government and defends freedom of speech, association, and religion as well as the right to own property. Liberalism evolved during the ENLIGHTENMENT and became the dominant political idea of the nineteenth century. Both the American and French Revolutions were based on liberal thought.

Limerick A humorous, sometimes nonsensical poem of five lines, with a strict scheme of meter and rhyme.

Line A sequence of words. In poetry, lines are typically measured by the number of feet they contain.

Literary epic A literary epic—as distinguished from folk epics such as the *Mahabharata* or *The Iliad*—that are made up of somewhat loosely linked episodes and closely follow oral conventions—is written with self-conscious artistry, has a tightly knit organic unity, and is stylistically rooted in a written, literate culture. In actuality, great epics often blur the distinction between the oral or folk epic and the literary epic.

Local-color tales Stories that seek to portray the people and way of life of a particular region by describing the speech, dress, and customs of its inhabitants.

Lyric A brief poem that reflects the imagination and emotion of the speaker. With its etymology in the word *lyre,* a lyric poem was originally meant to be sung to the accompaniment of a lyre, a medieval stringed instrument that is associated with poetic inspiration. Although modern lyric poetry is not necessarily meant to be sung, it does retain its melodic quality. Lyric poetry is highly subjective and informed by the speaker's imagination; it has flourished throughout literary history.

Magical realism A movement in fiction in which REALIST technique is used to narrate stories that combine mundane and miraculous events, everyday realities and the supernatural. The term is most often used to describe the work of Colombian novelist Gabriel García Márquez (b. 1928), Mexican author Carlos Fuentes (b. 1928), Peruvian novelist Mario Vargas Llosa (b. 1936), and Argentine author Julio Cortázar (1914–1984).

Manchu Also known as the Jurchen, a people who lived northeast of the Great Wall of China, in the area now known as Manchuria; when civil disturbances weakened the authority of the Ming emperor, the Manchu, with the assistance of some from inside China, took control of Beijing and founded a new empire. Their dynasty, known as the QING or Manchu dynasty, lasted from 1644 to 1911.

Manifest Destiny Term coined in 1845 for the American belief that the United States was not only destined but obligated to expand its territory westward to the Pacific Ocean.

Marxism A school of thought based on the writings of German Socialist thinker Karl Marx. Among its main tenets are the ideas that class struggle is the central element of Western culture, that a capitalist class thrives by exploiting the labor of a working class, and that workers must struggle to overcome their capitalist exploiters through revolution and thereafter establish a socialist society in which private property does not exist and all people have collective control of the means of production and distribution.

Marxist criticism Literary criticism that evolved from Karl Marx's political and economic theories. Marxist critics believe that texts must be understood in terms of the social class and the economic and political positions of their characters and plot.

Masque Developed in the Renaissance, masques are highly stylized and structured performances with an often mythological or allegorical plot, combining drama, music, song, and dance in an elaborate display.

Materialism A worldview that explains the nature of reality in terms of physical matter and material conditions rather than by way of ideas, emotions, or the supernatural.

Meiji Restoration After years of feudal reign in Japan, the emperor was restored to his position in 1868. He adopted *Meiji*, meaning "enlightened rule," as the name of his era. In this period, massive INDUSTRIALIZATION took place in Japan, which became a significant competitor for world power. The military was also strengthened to combat European and American imperialism.

Melodrama A dramatic genre characterized by suspense, romance, and sensation. Melodramas typically have a happy ending.

Mestizos Peoples in the Americas of mixed ethnic or cultural heritage, usually a combination of Spanish and Native American.

Metaphor A comparison of two things that does not use the words *like* or *as*. For example, "love is a rose."

Meter The rhythm of a poem based on the number of syllables in each line and which syllables are accented. See also FOOT.

Michiyuki A conventional form in Japanese drama (and also in fiction) wherein a character's thoughts and feelings are evoked through the places he or she visits on a journey; often, by means of symbolism and allusion, the journey suggests a spiritual transformation.

Middle Passage The transatlantic journey from West Africa to the Caribbean or the Americas of slave ships transporting their human cargo during the time of the slave trade (sixteenth–nineteenth centuries).

Millenarianism A utopian belief that the end of time is imminent, after which there will be a thousand-year era of perfect peace on earth.

Ming dynasty (1368–1644) Founded by Zhu Yuan-zhang, who restored native Chinese rule from the Mongols who had ruled China during the previous Yuan dynasty (1271–1368) established by Kubla Khan. The Ming dynasty saw a flourishing of Chinese culture, the restoration of Confucianism, and the rise of the arts, including porcelain, architecture, drama, and the novel.

Mock epic A form that parodies the EPIC by treating a trivial subject in the elevated style of the epic, employing such conventions as an invocation to the muse, an extended simile, and a heroic epithet that burlesques its subject.

Modernism In its broadest sense, this term refers to European writing and art from approximately 1914, the beginning of World War I, to about 1945, the end of World War II. Although many writers of this time continued to work with the forms of fiction and poetry that had been in place since the nineteenth century, others such as James Joyce (1882–1941), Virginia Woolf (1882–1941), William Faulkner (1897–1962), Rainer Maria Rilke (1875–1926), and Thomas Mann (1875–1955) broke with the past, introducing experimentation and innovation in structure, style, and language. *Modernism* can also refer to a spirit of innovation and experimentation, or the break with nineteenth-century aesthetic and literary thinking and forms, or the exploration of psychological states of mind, alienation, and social rupture that characterized the era between the two world wars.

Monologue A speech of significant length delivered by one person; in drama, a CHARACTER talks to himself or reveals personal secrets without addressing another character.

Mythological criticism A type of literary criticism that focuses on the archetypal stories common to all cultures. Initiated by Carl Jung in the early twentieth century, mythological criticism seeks to reveal how the structures lodged deep in the human consciousness take the form of archetypal stories and are the basis for literature. Jung identified four principal ARCHETYPES that together constitute the Self: Shadow (rejected evil), Anima (feminine side of male self), Animus (masculine side of female self), and Spirit (wise old man or woman).

Narrative poem A poem with only one basic rule: It must tell a story. Ballads, epics, and romances are typically narrative poems.

Narrator The voice that in fiction describes the PLOT or action of a story. The narrator can speak in the first or the third person and, depending on the effect the author wishes to create, can be very visible or almost invisible (an explicit or an implicit narrator); he or she can be involved in the plot or be more distant. See also POINT OF VIEW and SPEAKER.

Naturalism A late-nineteenth-century literary school that sought to apply scientific objectivity to the novel. Led by Émile Zola (1840–1902) and influenced by Darwinism, Naturalists created characters who were ordinary people, whose lives were shaped by the forces of heredity and the environment.

Nawab The title given to a local Muslim ruler in India during the Mughal empire (1526–1857).

Négritude A literary movement founded in the early 1930s by three Black Francophone writers in Paris: Léopold Sédar Senghor (1906–2001), Aimé Césaire (b. 1913), and Léon Damas (1912–1978). In their work, these Négritude writers protested French colonial rule and the European assumption of superiority. They wanted their writings, which honored the traditions and special qualities of the African and Caribbean peoples, to inspire independence movements in the colonies.

Neoclassicism A style of art and architecture that was characterized by the simple, symmetrical forms of classical Greek and Roman art. It originated as a reaction to the Rococo and Baroque styles and was the result of a revival of classical thought in Europe and America. Neoclassical writing characterized the Augustan Age, a period comprising roughly the first half of the eighteenth century. Its name suggests an analogy to the reign of Emperor Augustus in the Roman Empire (63 B.C.E.–14 C.E.), when many of the great Latin poets, especially Virgil, were writing.

Neo-Confucianism Refers generally to the philosophical tradition in China and Japan based on the thought of Confucius (551–479 B.C.E.) and his commentators, particularly Mencius (370–290 B.C.E.) and Zhu Xi (1130–1200). Neo-Confucianism, which arose during the Sung dynasty (960–1279), asserts that the understanding of things must be based on an understanding of their underlying principles; in moral and political philosophy, it emphasizes the study of history, loyalty to family and nation, and order.

Neo-Sensualism Also known as the New Sensibilities or New Perceptionist school, this approach was founded by Kawabata Yasunari and other AVANT-GARDE writers, including Yokomitsu Riichi (1898–1947), and headquartered at the University of Tokyo in the 1920s. In 1924 these writers founded a magazine called *The Literary Age*. Influenced by European writers as well as by Japanese poetic traditions and Nō drama, neo-Sensualists sought to break with the confessional style of REALIST and NATURALIST writers and aimed for a more purely aesthetic, nonlinear style of fiction writing.

Neo-Shintoism *Shinto* is a term given to indigenous Japanese beliefs as distinguished from Buddhism, which was introduced to Japan in the sixth century C.E. In the seventeenth century, Shinto and Confucianist ideals came into contact with one another and produced an ideology that emphasized political philosophy and valued the virtues of wisdom, benevolence, and courage.

New Criticism A type of formalist literary criticism that completely disregards historical and biographical information to focus on the actual text. The New Critics perform a close reading of a work and give special attention to technical devices such as symbols and images and, in poetry, rhythm.

New Historicism A literary school developed as a reaction to NEW CRITICISM in the 1980s; presently, it is one of the leading schools of literary criticism. Like the nineteenth-century historicists, the New Historicists argue that historical and other external contexts must be part of textual analysis.

Nigerian-Biafran War Nigerian civil war that started when the Igbo people declared the eastern region of Nigeria an independent state named the Republic of Biafra. Recognized by only three countries, Biafra was almost immediately attacked by Nigerian troops. After a bloody fight resulting in close to three million casualties, the Biafran government surrendered in January 1970.

Ninjo Japanese term that denotes human feelings or passion, drives that often come into conflict with GIRI, or social duty and responsibility.

Nō The highly elaborate and ritualistic classical theater of Japan, known for its minimalist approach to plot, scenery, and stage effects and the stately performance and Zen-like mastery of its actors; *nō* means "talent" or "accomplishment." The great master and theorist of *Nō* drama is Zeami Motokiyo (1363–1443), who wrote several of the most famous *Nō* plays, including *Atsumori* and *The Lady Aoi*.

Novel An extended work of fictional prose narrative. The novel is a modern outgrowth of earlier genres such as the romance. There is considerable debate as to the origins of the novel; some critics trace it to Cervantes's *Don Quixote* in 1605. In England, the novel came into being in the beginning of the eighteenth century and has since developed far beyond its original realistic and moralistic aims, making it one of the most flexible of literary genres.

Octave A STANZA of eight lines in poetry.

Ode An elevated form of LYRIC generally written on a single theme, using varied metric and rhyme patterns. With the ode, poets working within classical schemes can introduce considerable innovation. There are three major types of odes in English: the Pindaric, or Regular; the Horatian; and the Irregular. The Pindaric ode is structured by three-strophe divisions, modulating between the strophe, antistrophe, and epode, which vary in tone. The Horatian ode uses only one STANZA type with variation introduced within each stanza. The Irregular ode, sometimes called the English ode, allows wide variety among stanza forms, rhyme schemes, and metrical patterns.

Oedipus complex A term from Freudian psychoanalysis that refers to the unconscious male desire to kill one's own father and to sleep with one's own mother. The term derives from the Greek myth of Oedipus, who unknowingly murdered his father and married his mother; his self-inflicted punishment was to blind himself. FREUDIAN CRITICS do not take the complex or the story literally, but frequently use it to examine in literature the guilt associated with sexual desire and competition with or hostility toward one's father.

Onomatopoeia A word that sounds like the thing it refers to: for example, the *buzz* of bees.

Open form Also known as FREE VERSE. A type of poetry that does not follow established conventions of METER, RHYME, and STANZA.

Organic form The concept that the structure of a literary work develops according to an internal logic. The literary work grows and becomes an organic whole that follows the principles of nature, not mechanics. The created work of art is akin to a growing plant that relies on all of its parts working together.

Orientalism The academic study and knowledge of the Middle East and Asia that developed during the imperialism of the nineteenth century. Orientalism is a Western approach to understanding the cultures, languages, and religions of the East. Especially in the early studies, the Orient was seen as exotic and romantic, but its inhabitants were regarded as uncivilized and inferior. Although by now these views have been challenged and changed, they are arguably still prevalent.

Oxymoron A rhetorical figure of speech in which contradictory terms are combined, such as "jumbo shrimp" and "deafening silence."

Parable A short narrative designed to teach a lesson about life in which the moral isn't directly stated; a form popular during biblical times.

Paradox An argument or opinion that is contradictory but true. For instance, "You have to be cruel to be kind."

Paraphrase To rewrite or say the same thing using different words.

Parody A humorous imitation of another, usually serious, work. Parody can be a form of literary criticism that exposes defects in a work, or it can function as an acknowledgement of a work's cultural and literary importance.

Patois A regional dialect of a language.

Persona Literally, a persona is a mask. In literature, a persona is a speaker created by a writer to tell a story or to speak in a poem. A persona is not a character in a story or narrative, nor does a persona necessarily directly reflect the author's personal voice. A persona is a separate self, created by and distinct from the author, through which he or she speaks.

Personification A figure of speech in which abstractions or inanimate objects are given human qualities or form.

Picaresque Term used to describe a novel that is loosely structured around a succession of episodes that focus on a rather thinly drawn *picaro*, or hero. The hero's adventures generally provide a sweeping and detailed view of a society and its customs, which are often satirized by the writer. Examples include Cervantes's *Don Quixote* and Voltaire's *Candide*.

Picture poem A poem whose lines form the image of the object it describes.

Plot The pattern of events or the story told in a narrative or drama.

Point of view The perspective from which the author, SPEAKER, or NARRATOR presents a story. A point of view might be localized within a CHARACTER, in which case the story is told from a first-person point of view. There is a range of possibilities between first-person point of view and omniscience, wherein the story is told from a perspective unlimited by time, place, or character.

Postcolonial criticism Literary analysis of works produced in countries such as India, Africa, and the Caribbean that were once under the control of a colonial power. In some cases the term refers to the analysis of works about the colony written by authors who have been heavily influenced by the colonizing culture.

Postcolonialism The social, political, cultural, and economic practices that arose in response and resistance to colonialism and imperialism. This term also refers to the historical period following the colonial era, corresponding roughly to the second half of the twentieth century.

Postmodernism A literary and artistic movement that flourished in the late twentieth century as both a departure from and a development of MODERNISM. Postmodernism is frequently characterized by self-consciousness and self-reflexiveness: Postmodern literature is aware of the way it operates in a long literary tradition and responds to this awareness by revealing or referring to itself. Postmodern literature differs from modern literature in its emphasis on surface rather than depth, humor rather than psychological anguish, and space rather than time.

Pragmatism A philosophical approach that explains meaning and truth in terms of the application of ideas and beliefs to practical action.

Pre-Raphaelites A group of artists and writers, including John Everett Millais (1829–1896), Dante Gabriel Rossetti (1828–1882), and William Holman Hunt (1827–1910), who rebelled against convention in poetry and painting by means of a strict adherence to details of nature; they aimed to capture what they perceived to be the truth, simplicity, and clarity of medieval painting—its pure colors, spiritual or mystical ambience, and sensuousness.

Problem play A drama in which the conflict arises from contemporary social problems. Bernard Shaw's *Mrs. Warren's Profession* (1893) and Shakespeare's *All's Well That Ends Well* (1602–04) are problem plays.

Proletariat The modern industrial working class, which, as defined by Karl Marx, lives solely by the sale of its labor. See also BOURGEOISIE.

Prologue Text that typically is placed prior to an introduction or that replaces a traditional introduction; often discusses events of importance for the general understanding of the narrative.

Prose poem A poem printed as prose without attention to line breaks. The prose poem argues for the flexibility of poetry by eschewing strict attention to METER and even RHYTHM, yet the language of a prose poem is frequently figurative and characterized by other poetic conventions such as ALLITERATION or internal rhyme.

Protagonist A leading figure or the main character in a drama or other literary work.

Protestant work ethic German sociologist Max Weber (1864–1920) first linked Protestantism to the habits of diligence and hard work that contributed to the rise of capitalism. The Puritans, whose form of Protestantism influenced early American life, interpreted prosperity resulting from work as a sign of God's favor.

Psychological criticism An approach to literature that draws on psychoanalytic theories, especially those of Sigmund Freud (1856–1939) and Jacques Lacan (1901–1981), to understand more fully the text, the writer, and the reader.

Pun A play on words that relies on a word's having more than one meaning or sounding like another word.

Purdah Practice adopted by some Muslims and Hindus that obscures women from public sight by mandating that they wear concealing clothing, especially veils. The custom originated in the seventh century C.E. and is still common in Islamic countries, though it has largely disappeared in Hinduism.

Qing dynasty (1644–1911) Also known as the Manchu dynasty, named after the MANCHU, a people from the north of China who took over China in 1644 with the help of rebel Chinese; the last dynasty in Chinese history, the Qing saw an increase in the influence of foreign interests and trade.

Quatrain A stanza of four lines in a poem.

Qur'an Or Koran; the sacred scriptures of Islam.

Rastafarianism An African-influenced religion that originated in the Caribbean in the twentieth century; venerates the former emperor of Ethiopia, Haile Selassie, forbids the cutting of hair, and embraces black culture and identity.

Rationalist Utilitarianism Revolutionary way of thinking established by, among others, Leon Trotsky (1879–1940). The Rationalist Utilitarians adopted the ethical theory proposed by John Stuart Mill (1806–1873) that all political actions should be directed toward achieving the greatest good for the greatest number of people. Mill, however, believed that decisions based on direct observation should determine action, while the Rationalist Utilitarians held that logical reasoning should play that role.

Reader-response criticism A critical approach to literature in which the primary focus falls on the reader, or the process of reading, not on the author. Reader-response critics believe that a literary work does not possess a fixed idea or meaning; meaning is a function of the perspective of the reader.

Realism Most broadly defined, realism is the attempt to represent the world accurately in literature. As a literary movement, Realism flourished in Russia, France, England, and America in the latter half of the nineteenth century. It emphasized not only accurate representation but the "truth," usually expressed as the consequence of a moral choice. Realist writers deemphasized the shaping power of the imagination and concerned themselves with the experiences of ordinary, middle-class subjects and the dilemmas they faced.

Recognition Based on the Greek concept of tragedy, recognition, or *anagnorisis,* is the point in a story when the PROTAGONIST discovers the truth about his or her situation. Usually this results in a drastic change in the course of the plot.

Reformation Also known as the Protestant Reformation, this sixteenth-century challenge to the authority of the Catholic Church caused a permanent rift in the Christian world, with those loyal to the pope remaining Catholic and those rejecting papal authority forming new Protestant faiths such as the Anglican, Lutheran, Calvinist, Anabaptist, and Presbyterian. The Reformation originated — and was most successful — in Northern Europe, especially Germany; its notable leaders include Martin Luther and John Calvin.

Renaissance man A term used to describe someone accomplished in many disciplines, especially in both science and the arts, like Leonardo da Vinci and other figures from the European Renaissance who were talented in many fields.

Renaissance sonneteers Poets of the European Renaissance who wrote fourteen-line love poems, often addressed to lovers who resisted or ignored their entreaties. Two types of Renaissance sonnets are commonly identified, the Italian and the English. These are alternatively known as the Petrarchan, after the Italian poet Petrarch who originated the form, and the Shakespearean, after the form's preeminent English practitioner. The major difference between the two types is that the Italian usually has five rhymes and the English seven.

Renga A form of traditional Japanese court poetry that uses elevated diction and links a number of haiku-like poems. Usually written by two or more poets who alternate verses, the traditional *renga* is a succession of three- and two-line compositions that evokes a particular season in each verse.

Resolution The point in the plot of a narrative work or drama that occurs after the climax and generally establishes a new understanding; also known as *falling action.*

Reversal The point in the plot of a story or drama when the fortunes of the PROTAGONIST change unexpectedly; also known as the *peripiteia.*

Revolution of 1830 In July 1830, the opponents of King Charles X (r. 1818–24) took to the streets of Paris to protest his corruption and the undermining of liberal reforms. Charles abdicated the throne, and bankers and industrialists brought in King Louis-Philippe (r. 1830–48), who promised to uphold the reforms Charles had tried to dissolve.

Revolution of 1848 Often called the February Revolution, when French king Louis-Philippe (r. 1830–48) was overthrown and the Second Republic was established. This revolution inspired uprisings in many European countries.

Rhyme The repetition of identical or similar-sounding words or syllables, usually accented, in lines of poetry. Rhymes may be at the end of lines or internal to the lines.

Rhythm The pattern of stressed and unstressed syllables in prose and especially in poetry that can lend emphasis, reinforce a sound association, or suggest regularity or recurrence. The rhythm of a literary work can affect the emotional response of the reader or listener.

Romantic hero The PROTAGONIST of a romance, novel, or poem who is shaped by experiences that frequently take the form of combat, love, or adventure. The romantic hero is judged by his actions more than his thoughts, and he is often on a journey that will affect his moral development.

Romanticism A literary and artistic movement that swept through Europe in the early nineteenth century; its defiance of neoclassical principles and rationalism roughly parallels the political upheaval of the French Revolution, with which it is often associated. Romanticism in its simplest form exalts nature, the innocence of children and rustics, private emotion and experience, and the pursuit of political freedom and spiritual transcendence.

Rosetta stone A slab of basalt inscribed with texts in hieroglyphic, demotic, and Greek. Found by Napoleon's troops in Northern Egypt in 1799, it enabled Egyptologist J.-F. Champollion (1790–1832) to decipher Egyptian hieroglyphics for the first time (1821).

Russo-Japanese War (1904–1905) Russia's aggressive Far-Eastern policy following the SINO-JAPANESE WAR (1894–95) and the Russian construction of a railway across Manchuria resulted in increasing animosity between the two nations. Russia twice violated the treaty with China and lost the year-long war with Japan, destabilizing Russian power in the region.

Samsara A HINDU term for the cycle of birth, life, death, and rebirth; many Hindu practices aimed at obtaining release, *moksa,* from the otherwise endless repetition of life and death.

Samurai Japanese feudal aristocrat and member of the hereditary warrior class. Denied recognition in the MEIJI RESTORATION (1867).

Sanskrit The classical language of ancient India, in which many of the major HINDU religious and literary texts were written.

Satire A literary or dramatic genre whose works, such as Jonathan Swift's (1667–1745) *Gulliver's Travels,* attack and ridicule human behavior.

Scansion A system of poetic analysis that involves dividing lines into feet and examining patterns of stressed and unstressed syllables. Scansion is a mechanical way of breaking down verse in order to understand the regularities and irregularities of its METER.

Scene In drama, a subdivision of an ACT.

Script The written version or text of a play or movie that is used by the actors.

Sentimentality Extravagant emotion; T. S. Eliot defined this as "emotion in excess of the facts."

Sepoy The name given to Indians serving in the British army.

Sepoy Mutiny A rebellion in southern India in 1857 started by local Sepoys in reaction to regulations that violated their religion. The rebellion ended in 1858 after the British army intervened.

Sestet A STANZA of six lines; the last stanza of a Petrarchan SONNET is a sestet.

Setting The time, place, and social environment that frame the characters in a story.

Shinju play A play culminating in suicide; one of three major types of *joruri* plays. The others are the *jidaimono,* or history play, and the *sewamono,* a play about contemporary domestic life. Some critics see the *shinju* play as a type of *sewamono.*

Shogun A military ruler of feudal Japan between 1192 and 1867. The shogunate was an inherited position in the military that operated under the nominal control of the emperor.

Simile A figure of speech, introduced by *like* or *as,* in which two things are compared as equals.

Sino-Japanese War (1894–1895) A conflict between Japan and China that revealed the weakness of the declining Chinese empire and the emerging strength of Japan. The war, which developed from a conflict over the control of Korea, culminated in Japan's victory: China recognized the independence of Korea, ceded Taiwan, and lifted trade restrictions with Japan.

Slave narrative Autobiographical narrative by a former slave describing his or her life and mistreatment under slavery, attempts to escape, and ultimate liberation. The narratives, which employed many devices from popular fiction, were accompanied by testimonials to their authenticity.

Slavophile Literally, someone who admires Slavs, a people of Eastern Europe. In nineteenth-century Russia, the term referred to someone who believed in the national traditions of Russia, who felt that Russia had the true religion, and who believed he or she was destined to export Russian teachings and establish the kingdom of God on earth.

Social Realism A type of realism that concentrates on the unpleasant realities of the modern world and attempts to expose injustice and to encourage political reaction.

Socialist Realism A standard for art and literature developed in the Soviet Union in the 1930s; it demanded that art depict the life of the people realistically and celebrate the ideals of the revolution. Mao Zedong (1893–1976) enforced similar standards in China after the People's Republic was established in 1949.

Sociological criticism School of literary criticism that seeks to place a work of art in its social context and define the relationship between the two. Like Marxist critics, sociological critics are oriented toward social class, political ideology, gender roles, and economic conditions in their analyses.

Soliloquy A literary or dramatic discourse in which a character speaks without addressing a listener.

Sonnet A fourteen-line LYRIC poem. The first basic sonnet form is the Italian or Petrarchan sonnet, which is divided into an eight-line octet and a six-line SESTET, each with a specific but varied rhyme pattern. The English or Shakespearean sonnet is divided into three four-line QUATRAINS followed by a two-line COUPLET; the quatrains are rhymed *abab cdcd efef* and the couplet is also end rhymed, *gg.*

Sophists Literally, wise men. Greek teachers who provided instruction in logic and rhetoric to pupils who could afford their expensive fees. Rhetoric was a new discipline whose study was observed to provide an advantage in politics and in the courts. Soon *Sophist* came to mean one who used methods of argumentation that undermined traditional beliefs and manipulated reality. When Socrates (c. 470–399 B.C.E.) challenged the authority of the Sophists, he was brought to trial and executed.

Spanish civil war (1936–39) War between the Falange Fascist Party led by General Francisco Franco and liberal republican loyalist forces; often seen as the staging ground for World War II. The war ended with republican defeat and the establishment of a right-wing dictatorship.

Speaker The person or PERSONA who speaks in a poem—often a created identity who cannot be equated with the poet.

Spiritual autobiography An autobiography that gives special importance to self-examination, interpretation of Scripture, and belief in predestination. St. Augustine's *Confessions* (c. 400), detailing a life of sin, conversion, and spiritual rebirth, is generally regarded as the archetypal spiritual autobiography.

Stage directions Written directions explaining how actors are to move onstage. See also SCRIPT.

Stanza A poetic verse of two or more lines, sometimes characterized by a common pattern of RHYME and METER.

Stock responses Predictable responses to language and symbols. See also CLICHÉ.

Stream of consciousness A term first used by the American philosopher and psychologist William James (1842–1910) to denote the often disjointed and even incoherent flow of ideas, sensations, thoughts, and images running through the conscious mind at any given moment. In literature, "stream of consciousness" generally refers to novels or short stories that attempt to achieve psychological realism by depicting the raw, unedited contents of a character's mind. Such depictions may involve "interior monologues" wherein an author presents a character's thoughts either with (indirect) or without (direct) any commentary, ordering, or editing. This device, associated with high modernism, reached its height in the work of James Joyce.

Stress A syllable receiving emphasis in accordance with a metrical pattern.

Sturm und Drang Literally, "storm and stress." Refers to a period of intense literary activity in the late eighteenth century associated with Idealism and the revolt against stale convention. The movement was named after a play about the American Revolution, and its leading participants included Goethe (1749–1832) and Schiller (1759–1805).

Style The distinctive manner in which an author writes and thus makes his or her work unique. A style provides a kind of literary signature for the writer.

Subplot A PLOT subordinate to the main plot of a literary work or drama.

Superman Also called "overman," or *Übermensch* in German. A term introduced by the German philosopher Friedrich Nietzsche (1844–1900) to denote a superior man who would exercise creative power and live at a level of experience beyond the standards of good and evil and thus represent the goal of human evolution.

Surrealism An aesthetic movement centered in twentieth-century France that extolled the direct and free expression of the unconscious as understood by Freudian psychology; proponents of surrealism include the writer André Breton (1896–1966), who wrote *Manifesto of Surrealism* in 1924; the filmmaker Jean Cocteau (1889–1963); and the painters Salvador Dalí (1904–1989) from France and Joan Miró (1893–1983) from Spain. A combination of precise, realistic detail and dreamlike fantasy characterizes surrealism.

Suspense The anxious emotion of the audience or reader anticipating the outcome of a story or drama, typically having to do with the fate of the PROTAGONIST or another character with whom a sympathetic attachment has been formed.

Symbol A representative of something by association. Though a symbol is often confused with a metaphor, a metaphor compares two dissimilar things while a symbol associates two things. For example, the *word* "tree" is a symbol for an *actual* tree. Some symbols have values that are accepted by most people. A flag, for instance, is for many a symbol of national pride, just as a cross is widely seen as a symbol of Christianity. Knowledge of a symbol's cultural context is sometimes necessary to understand its meaning; an apple pie is an American symbol of innocence that a Japanese person, for example, would not necessarily recognize.

Symbolism As the French writer Paul Valéry (1871–1945) notes in *The Existence of Symbolism* (1939), Symbolism "was not a school. On the contrary, it included many schools of the most divergent types." Symbolism generally refers to a movement among poets in France anticipated in the work of Charles Baudelaire (1821–1867) and Arthur Rimbaud (1854–1891) but practiced as a self-conscious movement by Stéphane Mallarmé (1842–1898), Paul Verlaine (1844–1896), and Jules Laforgue (1860–1887). Symbolists sought to convey the fluidity and evocative harmony of music in their work, and to capture tones, fragrances, sensations, and intuitions rather than concrete images or rational ideas.

Syncretism The attempt to combine differing beliefs, such as philosophy and religion, or two religious systems, such as Christianity and a native African tradition.

Syntax The way parts of speech are arranged in a sentence.

Tantrism A minor HINDU tradition written down in scriptures called Tantras. Tantrism holds the supreme deity to be feminine and teaches that spiritual liberation can be won through erotic practices.

Terza rima A verse form composed of iambic three-line STANZAS. The triplets have ten- or eleven-syllable lines. Terza rima is used to perhaps its most brilliant end in Dante's (1265–1321) *Divine Comedy*.

Tetragrammaton The four consonants of the Hebrew alphabet YHWH used to approximate God's secret name; this name and its utterances are believed to contain special powers.

Thanatos "Death" in Greek. According to Sigmund Freud, our two primary drives are EROS (love) and Thanatos (death).

Theater of the absurd A school of modernist, non-realistic drama especially influential from the 1950s to the '70s. Italian playwright Eugene Ionesco described its subject matter as "man…lost in the world, [so] all his actions become senseless, absurd, useless."

Theme A topic of discussion or a point of view embodied in a work of art.

Theosophical Society Founded in 1875 in London by Helena Petrovna Blavatsky in order to promote the reconciliation of Eastern religious doctrines with Western mysticism. Blavatsky, who wrote *Isis Unveiled* (1877) and faced charges of charlatanism, believed in the spiritual nature of things, the reincarnation of the soul, and the power of grasping one's spiritual essence, particularly by means of mystical experience.

Thesis The presentation of a purpose or hypothetical proposition, or a dissertation with an original point based on research.

Tokugawa era (1600–1868) Period of Japanese history named after Tokugawa Ieyasu (1542–1616), who was named shogun in 1603; also known as the EDO era because Tokugawa made Edo (now Tokyo) the capital. The early Tokugawa was a period of international isolation, political stability, nation building, and prosperity for the middle classes; it was also a time of great literary and cultural growth, particularly in the popular cultural forms such as KABUKI and *JORURI* (puppet) theater, the popular novel, and colored woodblock art, all aimed at the flourishing middle classes. The Tokugawa era ended in 1867 when a group of disaffected SAMURAI restored imperial rule under the teenage emperor Meiji (r. 1867–1912) in the MEIJI RESTORATION and opened Japan's doors to Western trade and cultural exchange.

Tone A manner of expression in writing that indicates a certain attitude toward the subject or the implied audience.

Totalitarianism A system of centralized government in which a single unopposed party exerts total and repressive control over a country's political, social, economic, and cultural life.

Tragedy A dramatic or literary form originating in Greece that deals with serious human actions and issues. The actions must create feelings of fear and compassion in the spectator that are later released (CATHARSIS). Typically, the main character is of a high stature or rank, so his or her fall is substantial. Even though tragedies are sad, they seem both just and believable. The tragedy raises serious moral and philosophical questions about the meaning of life and fate.

Tragicomedy A drama that combines tragedy and comedy and in which moral values are particularly questioned or ridiculed.

Transcendentalism A philosophy derived from ROMANTICISM that flourished in the United States in the early nineteenth century. American writers Ralph Waldo Emerson and Henry David Thoreau championed and articulated the philosophy, which contends that the individual mind has the capability to transcend the human institutions that seek to fetter it. The transcendentalists believed that the most valuable pursuit was to experience, reflect upon, and study nature and its relation to the individual.

Travel narratives A form of narrative that recounts the incidents that occur and the people and things that the narrator meets and sees while visiting a place with which she or he is typically unfamiliar. Prose and poetic accounts about exploration and adventure in unfamiliar lands and places as well as in more or less familiar locations are considered travel narratives. Such narratives typically are told episodically and chronologically, engage in elaborate strategies to validate their authenticity, and raise important and complex questions about the representation of the "other" — that is, the ability of the traveler to depict accurately the people, places, and cultures he or she is describing.

Triplet In poetry, a group of three lines of verse.

Ukiyo-e A school of Japanese woodblock printing arising in the Edo period that captured images of everyday life in the FLOATING WORLD (*ukiyo*). The greatest *ukiyo-e* artists include Moronobu (c. 1618–c. 1694), Harunobu (1725–1770), and Hiroshige (1797–1858).

Ukiyo-zoshi "Stories of the FLOATING WORLD" or "tales of the floating world"; a Japanese style of fiction associated with the hundred-year period from about 1683 to 1783 that took as its subject matter the everyday lives of *chonin,* or townspeople, and was written in colloquial language. Ihara Saikaku is said to be the originator of *ukiyo-zoshi;* many authors in this tradition not only imitated his style but plagiarized his works.

Ultraists A group of Spanish writers who influenced Jorge Luis Borges. The Ultraists rejected middle-class materialism and sought refuge in the artifice of poetry and in exotic images and metaphors.

Understatement A figure of speech that says less than what is intended.

Upanishads A body of sacred texts dating from the seventh century B.C.E. that provide a mystical development of and commentary on earlier Vedic texts.

Urdu An Indo-European language closely related to Hindi. Urdu is the official language of Pakistan and is also spoken in India and Bangladesh.

Utilitarianism An ethical tradition dating from the late eighteenth century that assumes an action is right if it promotes happiness of both the agent and those affected by the act. Judgments of right and wrong depend upon the consequence of an action rather than strictly on motives.

Vedas The earliest Indian sacred texts, written in SANSKRIT, dating from sometime between 1000 and 500 B.C.E.; they contain hymns and ritual lore considered to be revelation, or *sruti.*

Verisimo Italian school of literary Realism influenced by Gustave Flaubert and Émile Zola.

Vernacular fiction Fiction that attempts to capture accurately the typical speech, mannerisms, or dialect of region. *The Satyricon* of the Roman author Petronius is often considered the first work of vernacular fiction.

Verse Poetic writing arranged according to a metrical pattern and composed of a varied number of lines.

Victorian In English history, *Victorian* refers to the age of Queen Victoria (1837–1901) and the values of respectability, social conservatism, and sexual repression characteristic of that time.

Villanelle Originally a complicated French verse form that appeared in English in the 1800s. The villanelle is a nineteen-line poem of five tercets (three-line STANZAS) and a final two-rhyme QUATRAIN. The first and third line of the first tercet repeat alternately, closing the succeeding stanzas.

Well-made play The plays of Augustin Eugène Scribe (1791–1861) and those of his followers, whose popular comedies were especially in vogue during the second half of the nineteenth century, established the rules for the "well-made play." The well-made play was carefully constructed around a single situation that built scene by scene to a climactic revelation. The situation usually involved a misunderstanding, a secret, or a suppressed document that, when discovered, prompted a REVERSAL and a DENOUEMENT. The dialogue was colloquial and realistic, and the subject matter commonplace and trivial. The well-made play was intended to amuse, not instruct.

Weltliteratur Term coined by Goethe for works of literature that transcend local and national concerns to treat universal human themes.

Yin and yang A pair of opposites derived from a dualistic system of ancient Chinese philosophy; symbolically representing the sun and the moon, *yang* is positive, active, and strong, while *yin* is negative, passive, and weak. All things in the universe are formed from the dynamic interaction of these forces.

Yomihon A serious, often didactic "reading book," as opposed to a picture book. This GENRE, popular in the early nineteenth century, often presented historical romances influenced by classic Chinese fiction.

Zen A prominent school of Buddhism that seeks to reveal the essence of the enlightened mind. Zen teaches that everyone has the potential to attain enlightenment but that most are unaware of this potential because they are ignorant. The way to attain enlightenment is through transcending the boundaries of common thought, and the method of study is most frequently the intense, personal instruction of a student by a Zen master.

Acknowledgements Continued from p. iv

Chinua Achebe, "An Image of Africa: Racism in Conrad's *Heart of Darkness*" from *The Massachusetts Review* 18, no. 4 (Winter 1977), pp. 782–794. Copyright © 1978 by The Massachusetts Review, Inc. Reprinted with permission. "Things Fall Apart." Copyright © 1958 by Chinua Achebe. First published by William Heinemann, Ltd., 1958. Reprinted with the permission of Reed Consumer Books, London.

Anna Akhmatova, "Requiem" from *The Complete Poems of Anna Akhmatova,* Second Edition, translated by Judith Hemschemeyer, edited by Roberta Reeder. Copyright © 1989, 1992 by Judith Hemschemeyer. Reprinted with the permission of Zephyr Press, www.zephyrpress.org.

Yehuda Amichai, "God Has Pity on Kindergarten Children," translated by Assia Gutmann, from *Poems.* Copyright © 1968 by Yehuda Amichai. English translation copyright © 1968, 1969 by Assia Gutmann. Reprinted with the permission of HarperCollins Publishers.

Baien Miura, excerpt from "Reply to Taga Bokkei" from *Deep Words: Miura Baien's System of Natural Philosophy,* translated by Rosemary Mercer. Reprinted with the permission of E. J. Brill Publishers, Leiden, The Netherlands.

Matsuo Bashō, "Narrow Road through the Backcountry." Translation and notes have been specially adapted for this anthology from *Backcountry Trails: A Poet's Journey* by Richard Bodner, © 2007 Dragon Mountain Translation Society, 1313 Sixth Street, Las Vegas, NM 87701, rbodner@post.harvard.edu.

Charles Baudelaire, "The Albatross" and "Correspondences," translated by Richard Wilbur, "Hymn to Beauty," translated by Dorothy Martin, from *Flowers of Evil,* Revised Edition, edited by Martheil and Jackson Mathews. Copyright © 1955, 1962, 1989 by New Directions Publishing Corporation. Reprinted with the permission of the publishers. "Carrion," translated by Richard Howard, from *Les Fleurs du Mal.* Copyright © 1982 by Richard Howard. Reprinted with the permission of the translator. "To the Reader," translated by Stanley Kunitz, from *The Collected Poems.* Copyright © 2000 by Stanley Kunitz. Used by permission of W. W. Norton & Company, Inc.

Samuel Beckett, *Krapp's Last Tape.* Copyright © 1958 by Samuel Beckett. Reprinted with the permission of Grove/Atlantic, Inc.

Bei Dao, "Declaration," translated by Bonnie S. McDougall from *The August Sleepwalker.* Copyright © 1988 by Bei Dao. Translation copyright © 1988, 1990 by Bonnie S. McDougall. Reprinted with the permission of New Directions Publishing Corp.

Jorge Luis Borges, "The Garden of Forking Paths" from *Labyrinths: Selected Stories and Other Writings,* translated by Donald A. Yates. Copyright © 1962, 1964 by New Directions Publishing Corporation. Reprinted with the permission of the publisher.

André Breton, excerpt from "The Surrealist Manifesto," translated by Patrick Waldberg, from *Surrealism* (New York: Thames & Hudson, 1997). Reprinted by permission.

Gwendolyn Brooks, "To the Diaspora" from *Blacks.* Copyright © 1987 by Gwendolyn Brooks Blakely. Reprinted by Consent of Brooks Permissions.

Albert Camus, "The Myth of Sisyphus" from *The Myth of Sisyphus and Other Essays,* translated by Justin O'Brien. Copyright © 1955 by Alfred A. Knopf, Inc. "The Guest" from *Exile and the Kingdom,* translated by Justin O'Brien. Copyright © 1957, 1958 by Alfred A. Knopf, Inc. Both used by permission of the Alfred A. Knopf, a division of Random House, Inc.

Rosalia de Castro, "A Glowworm Scatters Flashes through the Moss" and "The Ailing Woman Felt Her Forces Ebb," translated by S. Griswold Morley, from *Beside the River Sar: Selected Poems from En Las Orillas Del Sar.* Copyright 1937 by the Regents of the University of California. Reprinted with the permission of the University of California Press. "It Is Said Plants Cannot Speak" and "I Tend a Beautiful Plant," translated by Lou Charnon-Deutsch, from *Water Lilies: An Anthology of Spanish Women Writers from the Fifteenth through the Nineteenth Century,* edited by Amy Katz Kaminsky. Copyright © 1996 by the Regents of the University of Minnesota. Reprinted with the permission of the University of Minnesota Press.

Evliya Çelebi, ["The Court of Abdal Khan, Governor of Bitlis"] from *The Book of Travels,* translated by Robert Dankoff. Reprinted with the permission of E. J. Brill Publishers, Leiden, The Netherlands.

Paul Celan, "Deathfugue," translated by John Felstiner, from *Selected Poems and Prose of Paul Celan.* Copyright © 2001 by John Felstiner. Used by permission of W. W. Norton & Company, Inc.

Aimé Césaire, excerpt from "Notebook of a Return to the Native Land" from *Aimé Césaire: The Collected Poetry,* translated by Clayton Eshleman and Annette Smith. Copyright © 1983 by The Regents of the University of California. Reprinted with the permission of the University of California Press.

Anton Chekhov, *The Cherry Orchard* from *Four Plays,* translated by David Magarshack. Copyright © 1969 by David Magarshack. Reprinted with the permission of Hill and Wang, a division of Farrar, Straus & Giroux, LLC.

Countee Cullen, "Heritage" from *Color.* Copyright 1925 by Harper & Brothers, renewed 1952 by Ida M. Cullen. Copyrights held by Amistad Research Center, Tulane University. Administered by Thompson and Thompson, Brooklyn, NY.

Edwidge Danticat, "Children of the Sea" from *Krik? Krak!* Copyright © 1995 by Edwidge Danticat. Reprinted with the permission of Soho Press.

Mahmoud Darwish, "Identity Card" and "Victim Number 18," translated by Denys Johnson-Davies from *The Music of Human Flesh* (Washington, D.C.: Three Continents Press, 1980). Copyright © 1980 by Denys Johnson-Davies. Reprinted with the permission of the translator.

René Descartes, excerpt from "Discourse on Method" from *The Philosophical Works of Descartes, Volume 1,* translated by Elizabeth Haldane and G. R. T. Ross. Reprinted with the permission of Cambridge University Press.

Rassundari Devi, "The Third Composition," "The Fourth Composition," and "The Fifth Composition" from *Amar Jiban (My Life),* translated by Tanika Sarkar, from Susie Tharu and K. Lalita, *Women Writing in India: 650 B.C. to Early Twentieth Century* (New York: The Feminist Press, 1991). Reprinted with the permission of the translator.

Emily Dickinson, poems from *The Poems of Emily Dickinson,* edited by Thomas H. Johnson. Copyright by the President and Fellows of Harvard College. Copyright 1951, © 1955, 1979, 1983 by the President and Fellows of Harvard College. Reprinted with the permission of The Belknap Press of Harvard University Press.

Annette von Droste-Hülshoff, "In the Grass," translated by James Edward Tobin, from *An Anthology of German Poetry From Hölderlin to Rilke in English Translation With German Originals* (New York: Anchor Books, 1960). Copyright © 1960 and renewed 1988 by Angel Flores. Reprinted with the permission of the Estate of Angel Flores. "On the Tower," translated by Ruth Klüger, from *The Defiant Muse: German Feminist Poems from the Middle Ages to the Present, a Bilingual Anthology,* edited by Susan L. Cocalis. Reprinted with the permission of the translator.

W. E. B. Du Bois, excerpt from *The Souls of Black Folk: Essays and Sketches.* Reprinted with the permission of the David Graham Du Bois Trust.

T. S. Eliot, "The Waste Land" and "The Love Song of J. Alfred Prufrock" from *Collected Poems, 1909–1962.* Reprinted with the permission of Faber and Faber Limited.

"Follow the Drinkin' Gourd." Words and music by Ronnie Gilbert, Lee Hays, Fred Hellerman, and Pete Seeger. TRO Copyright 1951 and renewed © 1979

Folkways Music Publishers, Inc., New York, NY. Used by permission.

Federico García Lorca, "Lament for Ignacio Sanchez Mejias," "The Faithless Wife," and "Ode to Walt Whitman," translated by Stephen Spender and J. L. Gili, from *The Selected Poems of Federico García Lorca,* edited by Francisco García Lorca and Donald M. Allen. Copyright © 1955 by New Directions Publishing Corporation. Reprinted with the permission of the publisher.

Gabriel García Márquez, "A Very Old Man With Enormous Wings," translated by Gregory Rabassa, from *Leaf Storm and Other Stories.* Copyright © 1971 by Gabriel García Márquez. Reprinted with the permission of HarperCollins Publishers.

Ghalib (Mirza Asadullah Beg Khan), "Don't Skimp with Me Today" and "A Lamp in a Strong Wind" from *The Lightning Should Have Fallen on Ghalib: Selected Poems of Ghalib,* translated by Robert Bly and Sunil Dutta (Hopewell, New Jersey: The Ecco Press, 1999). Reprinted with the permission of Robert Bly. Ghazal V ["The drop dies in the river"], translated by W. S. Merwin, from *East Window: The Asian Translations.* Copyright © 1998 by W. S. Merwin. Reprinted with the permission of The Wylie Agency, Inc. Ghazals XXVI ["It is a long time since my love stayed with me here"] and XXXVII ["There are a thousand desires like this, each needing a lifetime"], translated by W. S. Merwin. Copyright © by W. S. Merwin. Reprinted with the permission of the Wylie Agency, Inc. Ghazals X ["Why didn't I shrink in the blaze of that face?"] and XX ["Is it you, O God, whose coming begins to amaze me?"], translated by Adrienne Rich with Aijaz Ahmad, from *Ghazals of Ghalib* (New York: Columbia University Press, 1971). Reprinted with the permission of the author and Frances Goldin Literary Agent.

Heinrich Heine, "The Asra" from *Heinrich Heine: Lyric Poems and Ballads,* translated by Ernst Feise. Copyright © 1961, 1989 by University of Pittsburgh Press. Reprinted with the permission of University of Pittsburgh Press. "The Minnesingers," translated by Louis Untermeyer, and "The Silesian Weavers," translated by Aaron Kramer from *The Poetry of Heinrich Heine,* edited by Frederic Ewen. Copyright © 1969 by Citadel Press, Inc. All rights reserved. Reprinted with the permission of Citadel Press/Kensington Publishing Corporation, www.kensingtonbooks.com. "A Spruce is Standing Lonely," translated by Gary Harrison. Reprinted by permission of the translator.

Higuchi Ichiyo, "The Thirteenth Night" from *In the Shade of Spring Leaves: The Life and Writings of Higuchi Ichiyo, A Woman of Letters in Meiji Japan,* translated by Robert Lyons Danly. Copyright © 1981 by Robert Lyons Danly. Used by permission of W. W. Norton & Company, Inc.

Friedrich Hölderlin, "The Half of Life" and "Hyperion's Song of Fate," translated by Christopher Middleton, from *Friedrich Hölderlin/Eduard Morike: Selected Poems*. Copyright © 1972 by the University of Chicago. Reprinted with the permission of the University of Chicago Press.

Langston Hughes, "The Negro Speaks of Rivers" from *The Collected Poems of Langston Hughes,* edited by Arnold Rampersad and David Roessel. Copyright © 1994 by The Estate of Langston Hughes. Used by permission of Alfred A. Knopf, a division of Random House, Inc.

Franz Kafka, "The Metamorphosis" translated by J. A. Underwood, from *Franz Kafka: Stories, 1904–1924* (London: MacDonald & Co., 1981). Copyright © 1981 by J. A. Underwood. Reprinted with the permission of the translator.

Immanuel Kant, "What Is Enlightenment?," translated by Mary J. Gregor, from *Practical Philosophy*. Copyright © 1996 by Cambridge University Press. Reprinted with the permission of Cambridge University Press.

Alphonse de Lamartine, "The Lake," translated by Andrea Moorhead. Reprinted with the permission of the translator.

Giacomo Leopardi, "The Infinite" and "To Sylvia" from *A Leopardi Reader,* edited and translated by Ottavio Mark Casale (Champaign: University of Illinois Press, 1981). Copyright © 1981 by the Board of Trustees of the University of Illinois Press. Reprinted with the permission of Linda L. Casale. "The Solitary Thrush" from *Leopardi: Selected Poems,* translated by Eamon Grennan. Copyright © 1997 by Princeton University Press. Reprinted with the permission of Princeton University Press.

Lu Xun, "A Madman's Diary," translated by Yang Xianyi and Gladys Yang from *The Complete Stories of Lu Hsun.* Copyright © 1981 by Foreign Languages Press, Beijing, China. Reprinted with the permission of the publisher.

Naguib Mahfouz, "Zaabalawi" from *Modern Arabic Short Stories,* translated by Denys Johnson-Davies (London: Oxford University Press, 1967). Reprinted with the permission of the translator.

Alessandro Manzoni, "The Fifth of May," translated by Joseph Tusiani, from *From Marino to Marinetti* (New York: Baroque Press, 1974). Copyright © 1974 by Joseph Tusiani. Reprinted with the permission of the translator.

Guy de Maupassant, "Regret," translated by Roger Colet, from *Selected Short Stories.* Copyright © 1971 by Roger Colet. Reprinted with the permission of Penguin Group (UK) Ltd.

Jean-Baptiste Poquelin Molière, *Tartuffe by Molière,* translated by Richard Wilbur. Copyright © 1961, 1962, 1963 and renewed 1989, 1990, 1991 by Richard Wilbur. Reprinted with the permission of Harcourt, Inc. CAUTION: Professionals and amateurs are hereby warned that this translation, being fully protected under the laws of the United States of America, the British Commonwealth, including the Dominion of Canada, and all other countries which are signatories to the Universal Copyright Convention and the International Copyright Union, is subject to royalty. All rights, including professional, amateur, motion picture, recitation, lecturing, public reading, radio broadcasting, and television, are strictly reserved. Particular emphasis is laid on the question of readings, permission for which must be secured from the author's agent in writing. Inquiries on professional rights (except for amateur rights) should be addresses to Curtis Brown, Ltd., 10 Astor Place, New York, NY 10003; inquiries on translation rights should be addressed to Harcourt Inc., Permissions Department, Orlando, FL 32887. The amateur acting rights of *Tartuffe* are controlled exclusively by the Dramatists Play Service, Inc., 440 Park Avenue South, New York, NY 10016. No amateur performance of the play may be given without obtaining in advance the written permission of the Dramatists Play Service Inc. and paying the requisite fee.

Jawaharlal Nehru, "Speech on the Granting of Indian Independence" (August 14, 1947). Reprinted with the permission of Mrs. Priyanks Gandhi Vadra, c/o the Jawaharlal Nehru Memorial Fund.

Pablo Neruda, "Hymn and Return," "Ode to Salt," and "The United Fruit Co.," translated by Robert Bly from *Neruda and Vallejo: Selected Poems,* edited by Robert Bly (Boston: Beacon Press, 1971). Copyright © 1971 by Robert Bly. Reprinted with the permission of the translator. "Ode with a Lament" and "Sexual Water" from *Twelve Spanish Poets: An Anthology,* translated by H. R. Hays (Boston: Beacon Press, 1972). Reprinted with the permission of GRM Associates, Inc., Agents for the Ann Elmo Agency. "Poet's Obligation," translated by Alastair Reid, from *Neruda: Selected Poems.* Copyright © 1970 by Alastair Reid. Reprinted with the permission of the translator. Section VI from "The Heights of Macchu Picchu," translated by Jack Schmitt, from *Canto General.* Copyright © 1991 by Fundacion Pablo Neruda and the Regents of the University of California. Reprinted with the permission of the University of California Press.

Friedrich Nietzsche, excerpts from *The Gay Science* and I,3 from *Thus Spoke Zarathustra* from *The Portable Nietzsche,* translated by Walter Kauffmann. Copyright 1954 by The Viking Press, renewed © 1982 by Viking Penguin Inc. Reprinted with the permission of Viking Penguin, a division of Penguin Group (USA) Inc.

Tim O'Brien, "The Man I Killed" from *The Things They Carried*. Copyright © 1989 by Tim O'Brien. Reprinted with the permission of Houghton Mifflin Company. All rights reserved.

Emilia Pardo Bazán, "The Revolver," translated by Angel Flores, from *Spanish Stories*, edited by Angel Flores (New York: Bantam, 1960). Reprinted with the permission of the Estate of Angel Flores.

Pu Song-Ling, "The Mural," translated by Denis C. Mair and Victor H. Mair, from *The Columbia Anthology of Traditional Chinese Literature*, edited by Victor H. Mair. Copyright © 1994 by Columbia University Press. Reprinted with the permission of the publisher.

Alexander Pushkin, "The Bronze Horseman" from *Selected Poems of Alexander Pushkin*, translated by D. M. Thomas (New York: Viking, 1982). Copyright © 1982 by D. M. Thomas. Reprinted with the permission of John Johnson, Ltd. Authors' Agent, London.

Raja Rao, "Foreword" from *Kantahapura*. Copyright © 1963 by New Directions Publishing Corporation. Reprinted with the permission of the publishers.

Alifa Rifaat, "My World of the Unknown" from *Distant View of a Minaret and Other Stories*, translated by Denys Johnson-Davies. Reprinted with the permission Quartet Books, Ltd., London.

Salman Rushdie, "The Courter" from *East, West*. Copyright © 1994 by Salman Rushdie. Used by permission of Pantheon Books, a division of Random House, Inc.

Nelly Sachs, "O the Chimneys," translated by Michael Roloff, from *O the Chimneys*. Copyright © 1967 and renewed 1995 by Farrar, Straus & Giroux, Inc. Reprinted with the permission of Farrar, Straus & Giroux, LLC.

Ramprasad Sen, selections from *Grace and Mercy in Her Wild Hair: Selected Poems to the Mother Goddess*, translated by Leonard Nathan and Clinton Seely. Reprinted with the permission of Hohn Press.

Léopold Sédar Senghor, "Black Woman" and "Prayer to the Masks," translated by Melvin Dixon, from *The Collected Poetry*. Copyright © 1991 by the Rectors and Visitors of the University of Virginia. Reprinted with the permission of the University of Virginia Press.

Wislawa Szymborska, "The Terrorist, He Watches," translated by Robert A. McGuire and Magnus Jan Krynski, from *Sounds, Feelings, Thoughts: Seventy Poems by Wislawa Szymborska*. Copyright © 1981 by Princeton University Press. Reprinted with the permission of Princeton University Press.

Tamura Ryuichi, "A Vertical Coffin," translated by Samuel Grolmes and Yumiko Tsumura, from *Tamura Ryuichi: Poems, 1946–1998*. Copyright © 1998 by Samuel Grolmes and Yumiko Tsumura. Reprinted with the permission of CCC Books.

Fadwa Tuqan, "Song of Becoming," translated by Naomi Shihab Nye, from *Anthology of Modern Palestinian Literature*, edited and introduced by Salma Khadra Jayyusi (New York: Columbia University Press, 1992). Reprinted with the permission of the translator.

François-Marie Arouet de Voltaire, *Candide, or Optimism*, translated by Daniel Gordon. Copyright © 1998 by St. Martin's Press. Reprinted with the permission of Bedford/St. Martin's.

Andrei Voznesensky, "I Am Goya," translated by Stanley Kunitz, from *Antiworlds and the Fifth Ace*, edited by Patricia Blake and Max Hayward. Copyright © 1966, 1967 by Basic Books, Inc., © 1963 by Encounter, Ltd. Copyright renewed. Reprinted with the permission of Basic Books, a member of Perseus Books Group.

Derek Walcott, "A Latin Primer," "White Magic," and "The Light of the World" from *The Arkansas Testament*. Copyright © 1987 by Derek Walcott. "For Pablo Neruda" from *Sea Grapes*. Copyright © 1976 by Derek Walcott. All reprinted with the permission of Farrar, Straus & Giroux, LLC.

Virginia Woolf, "Shakespeare's Sister" from *A Room of One's Own*. Copyright 1929 by Harcourt Brace & World, Inc., renewed © 1957 by Leonard Woolf. "Three Pictures" from *The Death of the Moth and Other Essays*. Copyright 1942 by Harcourt, Inc., renewed © 1970 by Marjorie T. Parsons, Executrix. "The Fascination of the Pool" from *The Complete Shorter Fiction of Virginia Woolf*, edited by Susan Dick. Copyright © 1985 by Quentin Bell and Anglica Garnett. All reprinted with the permission of Harcourt, Inc.

William Butler Yeats, "Sailing to Byzantium," "Leda and the Swan," and "Among School Children" from *The Poems of W. B. Yeats: A New Edition*, edited by Richard J. Finneran. Copyright © 1940 by Georgie Yeats, renewed © 1968 by Bertha Georgie Yeats, Michael Butler Yeats, and Anne Yeats. Reprinted with the permission of Scribner, a division of the Simon & Schuster Adult Publishing Group.

Yosano Akiko, "I Beg You Brother, Do Not Die" from *Injurious to Public Morals: Writers and the Meiji State*, edited and translated by Jay Rubin. Copyright © 1984 by University of Washington. Reprinted with the permission of the University of Washington Press.

Émile Zola, excerpt from "Preface to the Second Edition" from *Thérèse Raquin*, translated by Leonard Tancock. Copyright © 1962 by Leonard Tancock. Reprinted with the permission of Penguin Group (UK) Ltd.

INDEX